# The
# Vital Birth Records
# of
# Nashua, New Hampshire

# 1887–1935

by
*Gerald Q. Nash*
*Sandra J. Martinson*
*Roland A. Marchand*

HERITAGE BOOKS
2015

# HERITAGE BOOKS
## *AN IMPRINT OF HERITAGE BOOKS, INC.*

**Books, CDs, and more—Worldwide**

For our listing of thousands of titles see our website
at
www.HeritageBooks.com

Published 2015 by
HERITAGE BOOKS, INC.
Publishing Division
5810 Ruatan Street
Berwyn Heights, Md. 20740

International Standard Book Numbers
Paperbound: 978-0-7884-2014-6
Clothbound: 978-0-7884-6154-5

# DEDICATION

We wish to dedicate this book to all Genealogists wherever they may be and further to the American-Canadian Genealogical Society of 4 Elm Street, Manchester New Hampshire, which has been designated to receive all royalties from the publication of this book.

Gerald Q. Nash
Sandra J. Martinson
Roland A. Marchand

# TABLE OF CONTENTS

# INTRODUCTION

This book contains the transcript of the births of Nashua, New Hampshire for 49 years from 1887 to 1935. This information was taken from the published City of Nashua, New Hampshire Annual Reports. There were many births at home during this period that were not registered in the year of birth but were later reported to the City Clerk. These late recordings were never recorded in subsequent annual reports. To find out about these births one would have to make a request to The Nashua City Clerk at Nashua, New Hampshire City Hall, 229 Main Street, Nashua, NH.

The data contained here was transcribed verbatim, except for a few obvious errors, which were corrected.

The births are recorded as follows:

1. Last name of child.
2. First name of child.
3. Date of birth of child.
4. Sex of child designated by M or F.
5. Birth number of child in family.
6. Father's name and place of birth.
7. Mother's name and place of birth.
8. Those of color are designated at end of line as Colored.
9. Those who were stillborn are designated at end of line by Stillborn.

Not all of the births had all of the above information listed. The listing continues as above minus the missing information.

# A History of Nashua, New Hampshire

Nashua, New Hampshire was originally part of Massachusetts, and the first charter for the city was granted by a general assembly in Massachusetts, naming this area "Dunstable". This was granted on October 26, 1673.

Following the formation of the province of New Hampshire, this section of "Dunstable" was incorporated into New Hampshire on April 4, 1764. The name of "Dunstable" persisted until June 23, 1842, when the township then became known as "Nashua"...named for the tribe of Nashua Indians who resided here originally. However, on that same date, Nashua divided in half, with one section being known as "Nashville". On June 28, 1853, Nashville reunited with Nashua, and received a city charter.

Nashua proudly boasts a truly historical background, going back approximately three centuries. The first public meeting house is reputed to have been erected as early as 1678. For a period of about 50 years, the residents of the little settlement were continually harassed by the Indians. At one time, in 1702, during King Philip's War, the town was completely abandoned. Villagers returning to their homes after this were continually beset by wars and ambushes, in which many of the men were killed. However, in 1725, with the death of the warring Indian chief, Paugus, peace was made with the Indians, and the township started a continual steady growth, which still persists today, 237 years later.

Nashua, or "Dunstable" at the time, sent more men to the Continental Army than any other community in the State of New Hampshire. The first post office was erected in 1803, at that time, there were a number of stores, businesses, hotels, and a church. At about that same time, "The Nashua", a canal boat was launched, and the use of this type of boat persisted up until the early 1900's.

Following the adoption and granting of a city charter in 1853, Nashua began a rapid expansion of manufacturing. Schools were built...a police court made, and ward elections were started. A city council was established in 1856. Since that time, Nashua has added more and more schools, churches, and recreational facilities to serve the people of Nashua in a well-rounded program.

(UNKNOWN), Minnie Emma, Apr 12 1902 Sex:F Child# Edward F (Unknown) Hudson, NH & Jane Lambert Canada
ABARE, Henry, Aug 8 1928 Sex:M Child# 1 Henry Abare Troy, NY & Edna Pelletier Cohoes, NY
ABBOT, Marjorie, Apr 23 1929 Sex:F Child# 2 Charles Abbot Wilton, NH & Jennie Knight Washington, NH
ABBOT, Nancy, Feb 20 1931 Sex:F Child# 2 Howard S Abbot Wilton, NH & Edith Downer Winchester, MA
ABBOTT, Donald Gordon, Jul 16 1931 Sex:M Child# 2 Gordon Abbott St Johnsbury, VT & Beatrice Davis Lyndon, VT
ABBOTT, George Herman, Nov 14 1933 Sex:M Child# 1 Roland W Abbott Hudson, NH & Hazel Packard Wakefield, MA
ABBOTT, John Henry, Dec 3 1934 Sex:M Child# 4 Gorden Abbott St Johnsbury, VT & Beatrice Davis Lyndonville, VT
ABBOTT, Nancy Jean, Jan 4 1935 Sex:F Child# 1 Kenneth T Abbott Hudson, NH & Hilda English Baring, ME
ABBOTT, Unknown, Nov 26 1889 Sex:F Child# 1 Cary F Abbott Neville, OH & Jennie Tilton Ashland, MA
ABBOTT, William Everett, Dec 29 1934 Sex:M Child# 2 Roland W Abbott Hudson, NH & Hazel A Packard Wakefield, MA
ABOOD, Leonard Albert, Jun 6 1928 Sex:M Child# 1 Albert E Abood Plattsburg, NY & Yvonne Marois Canada
ABOOD, Mary, Dec 3 1931 Sex:F Child# 2 Albert Abood New York & Yvonne Marois Nashua, NH
ABURTON, Unknown, Jan 2 1888 Sex:M Child# 2 Moses Aburton Vermont & Maggie Aburton Ireland
ABUSEWICZ, Benjamin, May 14 1915 Sex:M Child# 1 Walter Abusewicz Russia & Josephine Sakawicz Russia
ACCSLOWICZ, Joseph, Jul 11 1914 Sex:M Child# 1 Brancha Accslowicz Russia & Apolina Woolen Russia
ACKENON, Ella L, Mar 3 1908 Sex:F Child# 3 Horace Ackenon Nashua, NH & Flavia Papineau Marlboro, MA
ACKERLEY, Philip Warren, Mar 4 1915 Sex:M Child# 6 Fred R Ackerley Cutler, ME & Lilla Dennison Cutler, ME
ACKERMAN, Andrew William, Jun 24 1929 Sex:M Child# 4 Raymond Ackerman Newark, NJ & Mary Diggins Nashua, NH
ACKERMAN, Jean Helen, Mar 24 1932 Sex:F Child# 5 Ray Ackerman Newark, NJ & Mary Diggins Nashua, NH
ACKERMAN, Robert Raymond, Jun 2 1923 Sex:M Child# 1 Raymond Ackerman Newark, NJ & Mary Diggins Nashua, NH
ACKERMAN, Theresa Ruby, Sep 1 1927 Sex:F Child# 3 R Ackerman Newark, NJ & Mary Diggins Nashua, NH
ACKERMAN, Thomas Albert, Apr 8 1925 Sex:M Child# 2 R Ackerman Newark, NJ & Mary Diggins Nashua, NH
ACKERMAN, Unknown, Jan 15 1895 Sex:F Child# 1 George H Ackerman Nashua, NH & Agnes E Gage Springfield
ACKERMAN, Unknown, May 13 1917 Sex:F Child# 1 Charles Ackerman Patterson, NJ & Grace Davis Dracut, MA  Stillborn
ACKERMAN, Unknown, Jun 24 1920 Sex:M Child# 2 Charles Ackerman Patterson, NJ & Grace L Davis Dracut, MA
ACKLEY, Eugene, Feb 7 1922 Sex:M Child# 1 Eugene R Ackley Cutler, ME & Anna Coggins New Haven, CT
ACKLEY, Frederick, Aug 28 1930 Sex:M Child# 4 Eugene Ackley Cutler, ME & Annie Coggins New Haven, CT
ACKLEY, Harry Fred, Nov 19 1910 Sex:M Child# 5 Fred R Ackley Cutler, ME & Lela Dennison Cutler, ME
ACKLEY, John, Jul 29 1926 Sex:M Child# 3 Eugene Ackley Cutler, ME & Annie Coggins New Haven, CT
ACKLEY, William James, Jul 7 1924 Sex:M Child# 2 Eugene Ackley Cutler, ME & Annie Cogins New Haven, CT
ACKSTIN, Joseph, Dec 18 1910 Sex:M Child# 1 Casimir Ackstin Russia & Mickalina Kadkanuti Russia
ACKSTINAS, Bernta, Feb 28 1919 Sex:F Child# 2 Paul Ackstinas Lithuania Russia & Stepanisan Avirginta Lithuania
ACTON, Lucille, Oct 4 1916 Sex:F Child# 1 Frank Acton Canada & Wil Malenfant Canada
ACTON, Wallace, Oct 22 1903 Sex:M Child# 1 Harry U Acton Ohio & Emma Todd New London
ADAM, Martha, Nov 5 1920 Sex:F Child# 3 Mike Adam Greece & Ida Archambault Nashua, NH
ADAM, Mary, Sep 23 1918 Sex:F Child# 2 William Adam Greece & Mary Adam Greece
ADAM, Theodora, Feb 8 1925 Sex:F Child# 4 Antonia Adam Greece & Yoer'zka Frashue Greece
ADAMAWICZ, Joseph, Oct 20 1914 Sex:M Child# 4 Peter Adamawicz Russia & Aga Stangis Russia
ADAMEKITZ, Ellen, Jan 22 1916 Sex:F Child# 2 Peter Adamekitz Russia & Barbara Damilitz Russia
ADAMITIS, Peter, Apr 5 1920 Sex:M Child# 4 Peter Adamitis Lithuania Russia & Berboras Adamantis Lithuania Russia
ADAMONIS, Andrew, Jun 25 1908 Sex:M Child# 1 Andrew Adamonis Russia & Jennie Russia
ADAMOVITCH, Charles, Oct 26 1917 Sex:M Child# 1 Charles Adamovitch Russia & Rosalie Dudul Russia
ADAMOWICZ, Frank, Mar 20 1912 Sex:M Child# 2 Peter Adamowicz Russia & Agae Stangia Russia
ADAMOWICZ, Joseph, Mar 13 1916 Sex:M Child# 5 Peter Adamowicz Russia & Azpy Stangio Russia
ADAMS, Alexandra, Jun 24 1909 Sex:F Child# 1 John Adams Greece & Marie Neven Canada
ADAMS, Constance May, Mar 10 1894 Sex:F Child# 2 James M Adams Nashua, NH & Maria Dame Lynn, MA
ADAMS, Daniel Theophelus, Jun 18 1905 Sex:M Child# 2 Edward L Adams Nashua, NH & Katie M Spence Nashua, NH
ADAMS, David, Jan 15 1927 Sex:M Child# 1 David Adams Nashua, NH & Mary Benley Nashua, NH
ADAMS, Edna May, Oct 16 1908 Sex:F Child# 2 Leory Adams Nashua, NH & Mary G Wells Nashua, NH
ADAMS, Eliott Douglas, Feb 6 1925 Sex:M Child# 2 George Adams Brookdale, NY & Mary Matson Cambridge, MA
ADAMS, Elmer Frank, Mar 11 1896 Sex:M Child# 5 Clinton Adams Bedford, NH & Marth Jane Adams Merrimack, NH
ADAMS, George Edward, Jun 27 1902 Sex:M Child# 1 Edward L Adams Nashua, NH & Katie M Spence Nashua, NH
ADAMS, George Edward, Nov 19 1907 Sex:M Child# 1 Leroy Adams Nashua, NH & Grace Wells Nashua, NH
ADAMS, George Henry, Aug 31 1913 Sex:M Child# 1 John H Adams Boston, MA & Ethel M Hatfield Nashua, NH
ADAMS, Geraldine, Sep 22 1923 Sex:F Child# 2 George Adams Manchester, NH & May A Littlefield Kennebunk, ME
ADAMS, Grace Marion, Sep 10 1914 Sex:F Child# 2 John H Adams Boston, MA & Ethel M Hatfield Nashua, NH
ADAMS, Harry, Jul 20 1894 Sex:M Child# 2 George F Adams Plymouth, NH & Alice E Mignault Saranac, NY
ADAMS, Howard Albert, Dec 16 1916 Sex:M Child# 2 Albert N Adams Epping, NH & Jessie Holt Nashua, NH
ADAMS, James Greenleaf, Mar 24 1892 Sex:M Child# 1 James M Adams Nashua, NH & Marie Dame Lynn, MA
ADAMS, Joan Catherine, Mar 10 1935 Sex:F Child# 2 Joseph Adams Nashua, NH & Catherine Taylor Amherst, NH
ADAMS, Katherine Mitchell, Dec 25 1895 Sex:F Child# 3 James M Adams Nashua, NH & Maria Dame Lynn, MA
ADAMS, Leon Mitchell, May 16 1898 Sex:M Child# 4 James M Adams Nashua, NH & Maria Dame Lynn, MA
ADAMS, Lincoln Dame, May 16 1898 Sex:M Child# 5 James M Adams Nashua, NH & Maria Dame Lynn, MA
ADAMS, Marguerite, May 27 1895 Sex:F Child# 3 Frank W Adams Maine & Ida M Holt Peterboro, NH
ADAMS, Mary Ellen, Dec 10 1932 Sex:F Child# 1 Charles F Adams Norwood, MA & Kath O'Conner Worcester, MA
ADAMS, Nicholas, Jun 21 1916 Sex:M Child# 1 Mike Adams Greece & Alida Archambault Nashua, NH
ADAMS, Phyllys, Dec 30 1910 Sex:F Child# 1 Leland A Adams Norwood, NY & Mabel Herbert Lowell, MA
ADAMS, Raymond Tracy, May 1 1906 Sex:M Child# 1 Tracy A Adams Amherst, NH & Eva D Grave Florence, MA
ADAMS, Robert Chandler, Aug 1 1911 Sex:M Child# 1 Albert N Adams Epping, NH & Jessie Holt Nashua, NH Stillborn
ADAMS, Robert Spence, Apr 6 1919 Sex:M Child# 4 Edward Adams Nashua, NH & Catherine Spence Nashua, NH
ADAMS, Unknown, Apr 19 1888 Sex:F Child# 2 Frank Adams Wilton, ME & Ida Holt Peterborough
ADAMS, Unknown, Sep 15 1889 Sex:M Child# 5 David S Adams Haverhill, MA & Susie E Clemens Nashua, NH
ADAMS, Unknown, Apr 17 1892 Sex:M Child# 1 George F Adams Plymouth & Alice E Mignault Saranac, NY

1

ADAMS, Unknown, Sep 9 1892 Sex:M Child# 1 Henry O Adams Champagne, IL & Mabel Naomi Nashua, NH
ADAMS, Unknown, Mar 31 1893 Sex:F Child# 6 David L Adams Haverhill, MA & Susie E Clemons Nashua, NH
ADAMS, Unknown, Dec 4 1894 Sex:F Child# 2 Henry O Adams Champagne, IL & Mabel N Pond Nashua, NH
ADAMS, Unknown, Oct 19 1923 Sex:M Child# 1 George Adams Greece & Margaret Kasigret Egypt
ADAMS, Unknown, Feb 23 1933 Sex:F Child# 1 Joseph Adams Nashua, NH & Kathrine Taylor Nashua, NH  Stillborn
ADAMS, Wallace Everett, Jan 11 1898 Sex:M Child# 6 Clinton Adams NH & Martha J Shedd NH
ADAMS, Walter Perry, Dec 9 1896 Sex:M Child# 7 David L Adams Haverhill, MA & Susie E Clemons Nashua, NH
ADAMS, Zephirina, Jan 27 1911 Sex:F Child# 2 John Adams Greece & Marie Neveu Canada
ADANNITIS, Annie, Jul 17 1914 Sex:F Child# 1 Peter Adannitis Russia & Barbara Damelitis Russia
ADANNOPOULON, Vashilo, Aug 28 1916 Sex:F Child# 2 Anas Adannopoulon Greece & Ovaranea Staathas Greece
ADEMITIS, Bernice, Feb 25 1922 Sex:F Child# 4 Peter Ademitis Russia & Barbara Divetitis Russia
ADEMOYNIS, Peter, Jan 28 1911 Sex:M Child# 1 Peter Ademoynis Russia & Agae Stangis Russia
ADLER, Charlotte Helen, May 23 1933 Sex:F Child# 2 Theo H Adler Germany & Christine Jasper Germany
ADMOUICZ, Helena, Nov 19 1913 Sex:F Child# 3 Peter Admouicz Russia & Agai Stugis Russia
ADNREWS, Unknown, Jan 6 1918 Sex:F Child# 1 Joseph Andrews Russia & Eva Riscemonick Russia  Stillborn
ADOMAITIS, Petronia, Jun 18 1919 Sex:F Child# 3 Peter Adomaitis Russia & Barbara Danolaitis Russia
ADOMAITIS, Teddy, Feb 15 1911 Sex:M Child# 2 John Adomaitis Russia & Anna Moinkewic Russia
ADOMAITZ, Peter, Feb 23 1907 Sex:M Child# 1 Johan Adomaitz Russia & Anna Mankewcait Russia
ADSHADE, Catherine Lucille, Jul 21 1924 Sex:F Child# 8 John Adshade Nova Scotia & Barbara Lydon Ireland
AESETTE, Joseph E, Mar 24 1887 Sex:M Child# 3 Paul Aesette P Q & Rosanna Lariva P Q
AESETTE, Marie B B, Aug 11 1889 Sex:F Child# 4 Paul Aesette Canada & Rosanna Larive Canada
AESETTE, Marie B E A, Sep 20 1891 Sex:F Child# 5 Paul Aesette Canada & Rosanna Larive Canada
AFGOUN, Alphonse, Jul 10 1915 Sex:M Child# 2 Charley Afgoun Russia & Alexandra Pranjawicz Russia
AFGOUN, Stanislaw, Nov 17 1913 Sex:M Child# 1 Kasimir Afgoun Russia & Alexandra Premawich Russia
AGALEZ, Alta, Nov 24 1902 Sex:F Child# 3 Marle Agalez Armenia & Hosanna Lazarouf Armenia
AGULEY, Florence, Sep 11 1904 Sex:F Child# 5 Mark Aguley Armenia & Rosanna Iskiyan Armenia
AGULEY, Miranosh, Nov 22 1907 Sex:F Child# 4 Mark Aguley Armenia & Ovsanna Isklyan Armenia
AGULEY, Seranosh, Nov 22 1907 Sex:F Child# 3 Mark Aguley Armenia & Ovsanna Isklyan Armenia
AHARONIN, Caranilos, Feb 26 1904 Sex:F Child# 2 Oscar Aharonin Armenia & Lizzie Johnson Armenia
AHERN, John Daniel, Feb 25 1906 Sex:M Child# 3 John J Ahern Fitchburg, MA & Margaret McCarthy Ireland
AIDONA, J Coula, Apr 6 1911 Sex:F Child# 8 John Aidona Greece & Pensikny Dameonon Greece
AIKEN, Martin Carl, Nov 22 1928 Sex:M Child# 2 Frank A Aiken Goffstown, NH & Edna Champion Somerville, MA
AIKEN, Shirley Frances, Mar 25 1925 Sex:F Child# 1 Joseph Aiken Greenfield, NH & Lillian Perham Lowell, MA
AIKIN, Eleanor Case, Jun 26 1920 Sex:F Child# 1 Roy Aikin Nova Scotia & Inez Helena Green Nova Scotia
AINSCO, Unknown, Jul 5 1892 Sex:M Child# 1 Joseph Ainsco Manchester,England & Anna Stanfield Todmorden, England
AINSCOW, Jane Eaton, Feb 26 1923 Sex:F Child# 1 Harry Ainscow Nashua, NH & Marjorie Eaton Nashua, NH
AINSCOW, Robert Stansfield, May 25 1931 Sex:M Child# 2 Harry Ainscow Nashua, NH & Marjorie Eaton Nashua, NH
AKSCINAS, John, Mar 18 1908 Sex:M Child# 1 John Akscinas Russia & Ludoisia Glkcaviazu Russia
AKSEIN, Kastante, May 31 1911 Sex:F Child# 2 John Aksein Russia & Louise Yhkanictu Russia
AKSEYN, Anieka, Sep 17 1905 Sex:F Child# 1 Anthony Akseyn Russia & Roze Griguitis Russia
AKSILOWICZ, Sheila Alice, Aug 19 1935 Sex:F Child# 1 John Aksilowicz Nashua, NH & Patricia Stead England
AKSTIN, Mary, Apr 13 1907 Sex:F Child# 7 Joseph Akstin Russia & Eva Knilonerotie Russia
AKSTIN, Michael, Dec 28 1904 Sex:M Child# 4 Michael Akstin Russia & Katerina Kruxute Russia
AKSTINAS, Franciskus, Feb 2 1917 Sex:M Child# 2 Kaz Akstinas Russia Lithuania & Michalina Karlonas Russia Lithuania
AKSTULIEWICZ, Eileen Dorothy, Jun 3 1931 Sex:F Child# 4 Stanley Akstuliewicz Poland & Josephine Palys Manchester,
AKXTIN, Julia Justing, Oct 31 1916 Sex:F Child# 4 John Akxtin Russia & Loise Yikevic Russia
AKZELOWICK, Valerie, Oct 10 1915 Sex:F Child# 2 Bronislaw Akzelowick Russia & Apolinia Valosonvick Russia
ALASKAS, Anthony, Apr 20 1917 Sex:M Child# 1 Anthony Alaskas Russia & Eva Tamalavich Russia
ALBRO, Robert C, Jr, Jan 2 1913 Sex:M Child# 1 Robert C Albro Springfield, MA & Jeanne Oliphant Jackson, MI
ALDEN, Carol Lynn, Aug 28 1924 Sex:F Child# 1 L J Alden Vermont & Ruby Reed Wilton, NH
ALDONIS, John, Apr 25 1909 Sex:M Child# 1 John Aldonis Russia & Eva Lebednik Russia
ALDONIS, Joseph, Mar 10 1910 Sex:M Child# 1 Frank Aldonis Russia & Alice Ardukenutie Russia
ALDONIS, Joseph, Jul 26 1913 Sex:M Child# 3 John Aldonis Russia & Eva Zabenic Russia
ALDONIS, Michael, Jul 21 1915 Sex:M Child# 4 John Aldonis Russia & Eva Lefednik Russia
ALDONIS, William, Apr 22 1912 Sex:M Child# 4 John Aldonis Russia & Eva Lebednek Russia
ALDRICH, Earl Ralph, Oct 20 1935 Sex:M Child# 2 R A Aldrich Lyme, NH & Marg DesRochers Canada
ALDRICH, Marjorie Beatrice, Jan 23 1916 Sex:F Child# 1 Ralph A Aldrich Lyme, NH & Mabel H Duplissie Nashua, NH
ALDRICH, Richard Clarence, Aug 11 1931 Sex:M Child# 1 Ralph A Aldrich Lyme, NH & Margaret DesRochers Cookshire
ALDRICH, Unknown, Dec 5 1896 Sex:F Child# 1 Eddie M Aldrich E Haven, VT & Mary M Upton Moore's, NY
ALDRICH, Unknown, Nov 21 1917 Sex: Child# 1 William E Aldrich New Ipswich, NH & Mabel Nelson Newbury, MA Stillborn
ALDRICH, Verne Harrison, Jul 20 1931 Sex:M Child# 1 Verne H Aldrich Canaan, NH & Ethel G Lyons Bridgeport, CT
ALECKONIS, Mary, Jun 28 1924 Sex:F Child# 3 Walter Aleckonis Russia & Annie Tartaries Russia  Stillborn
ALESCANITZH, William, Jan 29 1906 Sex:M Child# 2 William Alescanitzh Russia & Eva Ploascess Russia
ALESKEVICIA, Stanie, Nov 3 1904 Sex:F Child# 1 William Aleskevicia Russia & Eva Plosceni Russia
ALEXANDER, Irving Carroll, Dec 19 1929 Sex:M Child# 5 Earl J Alexander Greenfield, NH & Lena Hill Nashua, NH
ALEXANDER, Ivonne, Jul 27 1901 Sex:F Child# 1 Philippe Alexander Canada & Zoe Levesque Canada
ALEXANDER, Joseph Arthur, Feb 19 1905 Sex:M Child# 4 Philippe Alexander Canada & Zoe Levesque Canada
ALEXANDER, Leonard Earle, Jun 6 1934 Sex:M Child# 6 Earl J Alexander Greenfield, NH & Lena Hill Nashua, NH
ALEXANDER, Unknown, Apr 9 1905 Sex:F Child# 1 Herbert T Alexander India & Emma Rice Mass
ALEXANDRE, Lizzie Bell, Sep 29 1889 Sex:F Child# 5 George W Alexandre Plainfield & Assale J Ford Hudson, NH
ALEXANDRE, Marie Dolores, Apr 27 1903 Sex:F Child# 3 Colin Alexandre Canada & Ursule Sirois Canada
ALEXANDRE, Marie Evelina Z, Mar 16 1903 Sex:F Child# 2 Philippe Alexandre Canada & Zoe Levesque Canada
ALEXANDRE, Unknown, Feb 17 1904 Sex:M Child# 3 Philippe Alexandre Canada & Josephine Levesque Canada Stillborn

ALFREN, Charles, Apr 4 1889 Sex:M Child# 1 Christian Alfren Norway & Bridget Lynch Ireland
ALFSAU, John, Jan 1 1893 Sex:M Child# 4 Christian Alfsau Sweden & Delia Lynch Ireland
ALFSEN, Dorothy Naomi, Jun 13 1923 Sex:F Child# 1 Christian Alfsen Nashua, NH & Gladys Hoyt Nashua, NH
ALIE, Jeanne Liliane, Aug 18 1910 Sex:F Child# 3 Joseph Alie Canada & Maria St Onge Canada
ALIE, Louis Lionel, Feb 28 1914 Sex:M Child# 4 Joseph Alie Canada & Maria St Onge Canada
ALIX, Elmer C A, Apr 8 1906 Sex:M Child# 1 Ernest Alix Canada & Rose A Langlois Canada
ALLAIRE, Edouard George, May 21 1928 Sex:M Child# 3 Eddy Allaire Canada & Alice Labrie Manchester, NH
ALLARD, Adaline P, May 20 1895 Sex:F Child# 2 Frederick Allard Boston, MA & Esther Highton Malden, MA
ALLARD, Irene, Apr 23 1913 Sex:F Child# 5 William Allard Canada & Alice Courtemanche Hudson, MA
ALLARD, Jacqueline, May 15 1910 Sex:F Child# 6 F X Allard Canada & Lucienne Simard Canada
ALLARD, Jacques, May 15 1910 Sex:M Child# 7 F X Allard Canada & Lucienne Simard Canada
ALLARD, Joseph Albert R, Nov 6 1907 Sex:M Child# 2 William Allard Canada & Alice Courtemanche Hudson, MA
ALLARD, Lucille Gladys, Jun 6 1909 Sex:F Child# 3 William Allard Canada & Alice Courtemanche Hudson, MA
ALLARD, Marguerite Lucia, Feb 2 1911 Sex:F Child# 4 William Allard Canada & Alice Courtemanche Hudson, MA
ALLARD, Marie Louise L G, May 22 1901 Sex:F Child# 1 William Allard Canada & Alice Courtemanche Ireland
ALLARD, Marie Therese Nancy, Oct 24 1912 Sex:F Child# 8 Xavier Allard Canada & Lucienne Simard Canada
ALLARD, Unknown, Jul 12 1894 Sex:F Child# 1 W Allard Canada & Emma Courtermarche Canada  Stillborn
ALLEMAND, Marie Angeline, Feb 12 1900 Sex:F Child# 10 Charles L Allemand Canada & Sophie Leclerc Canada
ALLEN, Adolphe Alphonse, Mar 9 1914 Sex:M Child# 6 Joseph Allen Canada & Julia St Pierre Canada
ALLEN, Beatrice May, May 3 1922 Sex:F Child# 1 Hallie E Allen Vermont & Beatrice Sweet Canada
ALLEN, Belle Florette C, Oct 9 1918 Sex:F Child# 9 Joseph Allen Canada & Julia St Pierre Canada
ALLEN, Beverly Beatrice, Sep 26 1930 Sex:F Child# 2 Leo L Allen Athol, MA & Olive M Moore Orange, MA
ALLEN, Brenda, Oct 31 1931 Sex:F Child# 1 Horton S Allen Quincy, MA & Nellie Abrahamson Lowell, MA
ALLEN, Camil Alex Romeo, Nov 24 1916 Sex:M Child# 8 Joseph Allen Canada & Julia St Pierre Canada
ALLEN, Carroll Fremont, Mar 7 1919 Sex:M Child# 1 Lynn Allen Fairfield, VT & Linnie Fox Hudson, NH
ALLEN, Cora Belle, Dec 17 1893 Sex:F Child# 4 Oliver C Allen Alabama & Delia W Grass Ft Fairfield, ME
ALLEN, Dania, Feb 25 1917 Sex:F Child# 1 Mike Allen Russia & Marie Russia
ALLEN, James William, May 20 1931 Sex:M Child# 2 William Allen E Pepperell, MA & Ella Pillsbury Pepperell, MA
ALLEN, John, Dec 27 1929 Sex:M Child# 3 Joseph Allen W Fitchburg, MA & Margaret O'Brien E Pepperell, MA
ALLEN, Jos Maurice Leon, Mar 25 1932 Sex:M Child# 2 Rosario Allen St Henri, PQ & Yvonne Desrosiers Nashua, NH
ALLEN, Joseph G Archie, Oct 18 1933 Sex:M Child# 3 Rosario Allen Canada & Y Desrosiers Nashua, NH
ALLEN, Joseph Ovila Roger, Oct 11 1915 Sex:M Child# 7 Joseph Allen Canada & Julia St Pierre Canada
ALLEN, Julie Rosealda I, Jul 16 1911 Sex:F Child# 4 Joseph L Allen Canada & Julia St Pierre Canada
ALLEN, June Pauline, Oct 22 1934 Sex:F Child# 5 Howard Marsh Allen Fairfax, VT & June Marie Neill Calais, ME
ALLEN, Leora Katherine, Nov 20 1903 Sex:F Child# 2 William A Allen Pepperell, MA & Katherine Gilhooly Ireland
ALLEN, Louise May, Feb 11 1933 Sex:F Child# 2 Leo Allen Maine & Hilda Nason Bloomfield, VT
ALLEN, Margaret, Feb 27 1909 Sex:F Child# 5 William Allen Pepperell, MA & Katherine Gilhooley Ireland
ALLEN, Marie Phyllis Oriett, Jul 29 1929 Sex:F Child# 1 Rosario Allen Canada & Yvonne Desrosiers Nashua, NH
ALLEN, Marjorie Augusta, Aug 30 1924 Sex:F Child# 1 Howard M Allen Fairfax, VT & June M Neill Calais, ME
ALLEN, Paul Joseph, Aug 20 1934 Sex:M Child# 3 William Allen E Pepperell, MA & Ella Allen E Pepperell, MA
ALLEN, Richard Moore, Apr 11 1932 Sex:M Child# 3 Leo F Allen Athol, MA & Olive M Moore Orange, MA
ALLEN, Robert Dolor, Dec 19 1935 Sex:M Child# 4 Rosario Allen Canada & Eva Desrosiers Nashua, NH
ALLEN, Robert James, Sep 20 1923 Sex:M Child# 2 Hallie Allen Fairfax, VT & Beatrice Sweet Canada
ALLEN, Unknown, Jul 31 1890 Sex:M Child# 3 Edgar A Allen Nashua, NH & Alice M Marshall Nashua, NH
ALLEN, Unknown, Aug 11 1892 Sex:M Child# 4 Edgar Allen Nashua, NH & Alice M Marshall Hudson, NH
ALLEN, Unknown, Oct 14 1894 Sex:M Child# 2 Myron Allen Vermont & Addie Cote Vermont
ALLEN, Unknown, Jun 14 1928 Sex:M Child# 2 Howard M Allen Fairfax, VT & June Neill Calais, ME  Stillborn
ALLEN, Virginia Phyllis, Aug 13 1929 Sex:F Child# 1 Melancthon Allen Merrimac, MA & Glenys Bates Winslow, ME
ALLEN, Walter Leonard, Jan 25 1931 Sex:M Child# 1 Theodore Allen Gaspe, PQ & Rose Alma St Pierre St Paul Lacro
ALLEN, William, Jan 14 1902 Sex:M Child# 1 William Allen Pepperell, MA & Katherine Gilhooly Ireland
ALLEN, William, Mar 2 1929 Sex:M Child# 1 William Allen E Pepperell, MA & Ella Agnes Pillsbury E Pepperell, MA
ALLESON, Barbara Eva, Oct 19 1930 Sex:F Child# 1 Joseph A Alleson Nashua, NH & Sophie Sabanski Manchester, NH
ALLIE, Blanche Georgette, Feb 22 1917 Sex:F Child# 5 Joseph Allie Canada & Marie St Onge Canada
ALLIE, Marie Julia F, Jun 18 1907 Sex:F Child# 1 Joseph Allie Canada & Maria St Onge Canada
ALLIE, Marie Rose A, Apr 13 1909 Sex:F Child# 2 Joseph Allie Canada & Marie St Onge Canada
ALLISON, Thelma Emma, Jul 26 1908 Sex:F Child# 2 Henry W Allison Concord, NH & Jennie Favor Lawrence, MA
ALLORE, Mary, Jun 29 1887 Sex:F Child# 1 Benjamin Allore NY & Lizzie Waterbury, CT
ALLTON, Robert Adams, Mar 9 1892 Sex:M Child# 1 Norris J Allton Waterford, ME & Della Heywood
ALTMAN, Ben, Jul 31 1901 Sex:M Child# 1 Mose Altman Turkey & Ida Borrison Russia
ALTMAN, Gertie, May 7 1911 Sex:F Child# 3 Max Altman Russia & Ida Borenson Russia
ALTMAN, Unknown, Dec 28 1902 Sex:M Child# 2 Max Altman London & Ida Bonison Russia
ALTOONIAN, Deran, Oct 13 1914 Sex:M Child# 2 Edward Altoonian Turkey & Elmon Melconia Turkey
ALTOONIAN, Herhunt, Jan 21 1913 Sex:M Child# 1 Edward Altoonian Turkey & Elma Mulkonian Turkey
ALUKANIS, John, Sep 15 1914 Sex:M Child# 3 Stevens Alukanis Russia & Michalina Petkovska Russia
ALUKANIS, Kazimierzer, Nov 13 1896 Sex:M Child# 1 K Alukanis Poland & Christie Dolcouvna Poland
ALUKONAS, Wladio, Oct 12 1916 Sex:M Child# 2 Lowdas Alukonas Russia & Annie Fertisilia Russia
ALUKONES, Mary, Mar 23 1910 Sex:F Child# 1 Stiprus Alukones Russia & Michalena Patchkovsk Russia
ALUKONIS, Annie, Mar 14 1921 Sex:F Child# 2 William Alukonis Russia & Eusila Steinamakas Russia
ALUKONIS, Emilia, May 26 1922 Sex:F Child# 3 William A Alukonis Lithuania & Emilia Stilamakas Lithuania
ALUKONIS, John, Jan 6 1925 Sex:M Child# 4 William Alukonis Lithuania & Emily Stelanakas Lithuania
ALUKONIS, Nancy, Jul 7 1931 Sex:F Child# 5 Stephen Alukonis Lithuania & M Putchkowskas Lithuania
ALUKONIS, Stepus, Oct 12 1911 Sex:M Child# 2 Stepius Alukonis Russia & Mich Patckovska Russia
ALUKONIS, Victor, Mar 22 1924 Sex:M Child#  Mike Alukonis Russia & Mary Kasker Russia

AMAZEEN, Unknown, Dec 31 1896 Sex:M Child# 1 Charles W Amazeen Newcastle & Annie H Smith Nashua, NH
AMAZEEN, Unknown, Aug 17 1898 Sex:F Child# 2 Charles W Amazeen New Castle & Annie H Smith Nashua, NH
AMBROSE, Howard Blake, Nov 4 1913 Sex:M Child# 4 Thomas B Ambrose Boston, MA & Marion A Woodbury Natick, MA
AMBROSE, Marion Augusta, Jan 5 1909 Sex:F Child# 3 Thomas B Ambrose Boston, MA & Marion Woodbury Natick, MA
AMBROSE, Thomas Howard, Apr 24 1907 Sex:M Child# 2 Thomas B Ambrose Roxbury, MA & Marion Woodbury Natick, MA
AMEEN, Fred Elias, May 20 1922 Sex:M Child# 6 Massoud Ameen Syria & Mary John Syria
AMES, Kenneth Dodge, May 27 1928 Sex:M Child# 2 Ernest G Ames Milford, NH & Edna Sargent Milford, NH
AMES, Richard Earl, Jan 20 1932 Sex:M Child# 3 Ernest G Ames Milford, NH & Edna Sargent Milford, NH
AMES, Roger Sargent, Aug 1 1926 Sex:M Child# 1 Ernest G Ames Milford, NH & Edna Sargent Milford, NH
AMES, Unknown, Jan 30 1900 Sex:M Child# 2 James E Ames Maine & May G Ford Maine
AMES, Unknown, Feb 14 1900 Sex:F Child# 1 Harry W Ames Mass & Lula Winchenbach Maine
AMES, Unknown, Apr 19 1901 Sex:F Child# 3 Fessenden Ames Fairfield, ME & Eldora Osborn Fairfield, ME
AMETTE, Laura, Feb 2 1890 Sex:F Child# 2 Onesime Amette Canada & Oxelia Mongeace Canada
AMRSTRONG, Mary, Mar 24 1909 Sex:F Child# 1 Fred Armstrong Nashua, NH & Rosanna Leazotte Nashua, NH
ANAGNISTOPOULOS, Unknown, Aug 17 1927 Sex:M Child# 7 A Anagnistopoulos Greece & S Haralamnopoulos Greece
ANAGNOSOPOULOS, Angelike, Oct 13 1919 Sex:F Child# 1 Nich Anagnosopoulos Greece & Alex Karalampopoulous Greece
ANAGNOST, Christos, Feb 16 1926 Sex:M Child# 2 William Anagnost Greece & Stella Zafirion Greece
ANAGNOSTOPOIDOR, Unknown, Jun 20 1931 Sex:M Child# 9 Nich Anagnostopoidor Greece & A Haralampropoulous Greece
ANAGNOSTOPOLOS, Demetrius A, Jul 1 1924 Sex:M Child# 5 N Anagnostopolos Greece & A Haralampopos Greece
ANAGNOSTOPOULOS, Demetrula, Jan 22 1922 Sex:F Child# 3 N Anagnostopoulos Greece & Alndra Haralatopolos Greece
ANAGNOSTOPOULOS, Marie N, Sep 7 1925 Sex:F Child# 6 N Anagnostopoulos Greece & A Haralampopoulos Greece
ANAGNOSTOPOULOS, Vasilios N, Jan 27 1929 Sex:M Child# 8 N Anagnostopoulos Greece & A Haralampopoulos Greece
ANASTASOPOULOS, Unknown, Sep 5 1918 Sex:M Child# 1 A Anastasopoulos Greece & Yiano Pianegopolou Greece
ANASTHAS, Unknown, Mar 8 1933 Sex: Child# P Anasthas Greece & Alice Vaniotes Lowell, MA
ANCTIL, Albert, Jul 20 1912 Sex:M Child# 3 Irenee Anctil Canada & Emelia Dube Canada
ANCTIL, Albert Raymond, Aug 5 1917 Sex:M Child# 1 Albert A Anctil Nashua, NH & Ardelia M Rood Swanton, VT
ANCTIL, Albini Sylvio, Feb 15 1921 Sex:M Child# 11 Gerard Anctil Canada & Florida Deschamp Canada
ANCTIL, Alphonse Roland, Apr 5 1918 Sex:M Child# 2 Wilfrid Anctil Canada & Florilla Pelletier Canada
ANCTIL, Andrew Roger, Oct 21 1929 Sex:M Child# 9 Wilfrid Anctil Canada & Florida Pelletier Canada
ANCTIL, Annette, Feb 13 1928 Sex:F Child# 1 Jos W Anctil Nashua, NH & Clara Guimond Lowell, MA  Stillborn
ANCTIL, Catherine Lilliane, Nov 25 1909 Sex:F Child# 1 Elzebert Anctil Canada & Catherine Anctil Canada
ANCTIL, Conrad, Aug 13 1926 Sex:M Child# 7 Wilfrid Anctil Canada & Florida Pelletier Canada
ANCTIL, David Euclide, Aug 19 1934 Sex:M Child# 4 David Anctil Canada & Jeanne Berube Canada
ANCTIL, Donald Paul, Feb 21 1933 Sex:M Child# 1 Lucien Anctil Nashua, NH & L Jackiborska Nashua, NH
ANCTIL, Edmond B, Jan 12 1903 Sex:M Child# 1 Edmond Anctil Canada & Marie Lemery Fall River, MA
ANCTIL, Ernest Philippe, Apr 23 1909 Sex:M Child# 2 Gerard Anctil Canada & Clarida Deschamps Canada
ANCTIL, Florette A, Apr 12 1909 Sex:F Child# 7 Edmond Anctil Canada & Marie Lemery Fall River, MA
ANCTIL, Francois N A, Mar 31 1901 Sex:M Child# 5 Edmond Anctil Canada & Marie Lemay Fall River, MA
ANCTIL, Francois Orel Armand, May 6 1913 Sex:M Child# 3 Elzabert Anctil Canada & Catherine Anctil Canada
ANCTIL, George, Sep 9 1916 Sex:M Child# 11 Edmond Anctil Canada & Mary Lemery Fall River, MA
ANCTIL, Gerard, Jun 24 1921 Sex:M Child# 4 Wilfrid Anctil Canada & Florida Pelletier Canada
ANCTIL, Germaine Claudette, Feb 15 1914 Sex:F Child# 4 Irene Anctil Canada & Emilie Dube Canada
ANCTIL, J Ernest Theodore, Aug 21 1914 Sex:M Child# 1 Ernest Anctil Canada & Clodia Lafrance Canada
ANCTIL, J Stanislaus Paul A, Jun 13 1911 Sex:M Child# 2 Elzibert Anctil Canada & Catherine Anctil Canada
ANCTIL, James Armand Henri, Dec 2 1918 Sex:M Child# 10 Gerard Anctil Canada & Alamilda Deschamps Canada
ANCTIL, Joseph, Jul 25 1909 Sex:M Child# 1 Irene Anctil Canada & Emelie Dube Canada  Stillborn
ANCTIL, Joseph Aime Gerard, Apr 17 1914 Sex:M Child# 9 Gerard Anctil Canada & Clorilda Deschamps Canada
ANCTIL, Joseph Albert, Jan 3 1913 Sex:M Child# 6 Girard Anctil Canada & Clorilda Deschamps NH
ANCTIL, Joseph Albert Roland, Sep 3 1935 Sex:M Child# 2 Joseph Anctil Canada & Yvonne Pelletier Canada
ANCTIL, Joseph E R, Dec 27 1905 Sex:M Child# 2 Joseph Anctil Canada & Ernestine Nadeau Canada
ANCTIL, Joseph Emile F, Feb 9 1908 Sex:M Child# 1 Gerard Anctil Canada & Claudia Deschamps Canada
ANCTIL, Joseph Paul, Nov 24 1923 Sex:M Child# 3 Arsene Anctil NH & Mathilda Pelletier Conn
ANCTIL, Joseph Wilfred P, Aug 26 1904 Sex:M Child# 1 Joseph Anctil Canada & Ernestine Nadeau Canada
ANCTIL, Joseph Wilfrid, Mar 19 1916 Sex:M Child# 5 Irene Anctil Canada & Emilie Dube Canada  Stillborn
ANCTIL, Jules Ferdinand, Jun 1 1902 Sex:M Child# 9 Jules Anctil Canada & Emelie Deschenes Canada
ANCTIL, Leo Valmore, Oct 12 1918 Sex:M Child# 2 Archie Anctil Nashua, NH & Aurore Prince Nashua, NH
ANCTIL, Lorette, Jan 24 1911 Sex:F Child# 2 Irence Anctil Canada & Emilie Dube Canada
ANCTIL, Lucien F, Sep 14 1904 Sex:M Child# 7 Edmond Anctil Canada & Mary Lemery Fall River, MA
ANCTIL, M Beatrice Annette, Jun 20 1913 Sex:F Child# 3 Joseph Anctil Canada & Ernestine Nadeau Canada
ANCTIL, M Lucille Antoinette, Nov 14 1922 Sex:F Child# 12 Gerard Anctil Canada & Clarilda Deschamp Canada
ANCTIL, M Rose Antoinette, Sep 27 1911 Sex:F Child# 5 Girard Anctil Canada & Clorilda Deschamps Canada
ANCTIL, Marie, Apr 30 1910 Sex:F Child# 4 Gerard Anctil Canada & Clarilda Deschamps Canada
ANCTIL, Marie, Aug 28 1926 Sex:F Child# 7 Irenee Anctil Canada & Emelie Dube Canada
ANCTIL, Marie A Rose, Sep 15 1902 Sex:F Child# 1 Ernest Anctil Canada & Marie Anctil Canada
ANCTIL, Marie Alice Berna, Sep 17 1922 Sex:F Child# 2 Arsene Anctil NH & Mathilda Pelletier Conn
ANCTIL, Marie Ange Rita, Oct 13 1921 Sex:F Child# 1 Arsene Anctil NH & Mathilda Pelletier Conn
ANCTIL, Marie Anne, Apr 30 1910 Sex:F Child# 3 Gerard Anctil Canada & Clarilda Deschamps Canada
ANCTIL, Marie Blanche A, Nov 21 1924 Sex:F Child# 4 Arsene Anctil NH & Mathilda Pelletier Conn
ANCTIL, Marie Delia Rita, Sep 12 1918 Sex:F Child# 4 Elzebert Anctil Maine & Catherine Anctil Canada
ANCTIL, Marie Edith, Oct 5 1903 Sex:F Child# 10 Arsene Anctil Canada & Emelie Deschenes Canada
ANCTIL, Marie Jeanne d'Arc, May 5 1930 Sex:F Child# 1 David Anctil Canada & Jeanne Berube Canada
ANCTIL, Marie Olivette, Jun 21 1913 Sex:F Child# 3 Luc Anctil Canada & Marie A Desjardins Canada
ANCTIL, Marie Solange T, Sep 27 1925 Sex:F Child# 1 Ovid Anctil Canada & Bernadette Blais Canada

4

ANCTIL, Marie Yvonne A, Jul 8 1930 Sex:F Child# 5 Arsene Anctil Nashua, NH & Mathilda Pelletier Waterbury, CT
ANCTIL, Marie Yvonne Anita, Sep 23 1926 Sex:F Child# 1 Ovid Anctil Canada & M Yvonne Plourde Canada
ANCTIL, Maurice, Feb 27 1933 Sex:M Child# 3 David Anctil Canada & Jeanne Berube Canada
ANCTIL, Maurice Romeo, May 4 1924 Sex:M Child# 6 Wilfrid Anctil Canada & Florida Pelletier Canada
ANCTIL, Paul Gerard, Feb 16 1918 Sex:M Child# 6 Irenie Anctil Canada & Emelia Dube Canada
ANCTIL, Paul Roland, Aug 11 1912 Sex:M Child# 10 Edmond Anctil Canada & Mary Lemery Fall River, MA
ANCTIL, Pauline Rita L, Nov 15 1930 Sex:F Child# 1 Edmond K Anctil Nashua, NH & Elizabeth Levesque Sciota, NY
ANCTIL, Pearl Emily, Dec 30 1922 Sex:F Child# 3 Albert Joseph Anctil Nashua, NH & Ardelia Rood Swanton, VT
ANCTIL, Priscilla Jeanne, Mar 6 1932 Sex:F Child# 2 Edmond Anctil Nashua, NH & Eliz Neverett N Adams, MA
ANCTIL, Robert, Sep 10 1931 Sex:M Child# 4 Albert Anctil Nashua, NH & Ardella Rood Vermont  Stillborn
ANCTIL, Roger Leon, Jan 4 1919 Sex:M Child# 2 Albert Joseph Anctil Nashua, NH & Ardelia M Rood Swanton, VT
ANCTIL, Roger Oscar, Jul 4 1931 Sex:M Child# 2 David Anctil Canada & Alice Berube Canada
ANCTIL, Roland, Mar 6 1917 Sex:M Child# 1 Archibald Anctil Nashua, NH & Aurore Prince Nashua, NH
ANCTIL, Romeo, Oct 4 1890 Sex:M Child# 2 Joseph P Anctil Canada & Emilie Desjardins Canada
ANCTIL, Unknown, Sep 14 1927 Sex:F Child# 1 Emile Anctil Nashua, NH & A Marchand
ANCTIL, Victor Leo, Aug 26 1922 Sex:M Child# 5 Wilfrid Anctil Canada & Florida Pelletier Canada
ANCTIL, Wilfrid Joseph, Dec 22 1916 Sex:M Child# 1 Wilfrid Anctil Canada & Florilda Pelletier Canada
ANDEARES, Dracou, Jun 6 1908 Sex:M Child# 5 Nicholas Andeares Greece & Panageota Vlaheisa Greece
ANDEARIS, Unknown, Nov 12 1904 Sex:M Child# 2 Nicholas Andearis Greece & Mary Vlhwace Greece
ANDEARIS, Unknown, Jan 16 1906 Sex:F Child# 3 Nicholas Andearis Greece & Mary Pappas Greece
ANDEORES, Stathasia, May 14 1907 Sex:M Child# 3 Nicholas Andeores Greece & Panagesta Vlahatsa Greece
ANDERSON, Alva Clayton, Nov 16 1923 Sex:M Child# 2 Alva Anderson Bloomington, IN & Henriette Blosy Adelaide
ANDERSON, Annie A, Mar 18 1894 Sex:F Child# 2 Carl E Anderson Sweden & Lucine A Strombard Sweden
ANDERSON, Annie Theresa, Apr 14 1889 Sex:F Child# 4 James Anderson Ireland & Anne Lee Ireland
ANDERSON, Augustus B, Dec 15 1897 Sex:M Child# 8 James Anderson Ireland & Ann Lee Ireland
ANDERSON, Blanche Loraine, Jun 20 1900 Sex:F Child# 2 John Anderson Cambridge, MA & M A Chamberlain NY
ANDERSON, Cora Elizabeth, Nov 7 1921 Sex:F Child# 3 And S Anderson Manchester, NH & Bernice E Marden Manchester,
ANDERSON, Dallas, Jr, Nov 27 1925 Sex:M Child# 3 Dallas Anderson Bloomfield, IN & Blanche Blasy Adelard, PA
ANDERSON, David Downie, Nov 11 1935 Sex:M Child# 2 Nicholas Anderson Manchester, NH & Mary Myshrall Vanceboro,
ANDERSON, Dyke Ellis, Jul 14 1921 Sex:M Child# 1 Robert J Anderson Clinton, MA & Marjorie D Dyke Brattleboro, VT
ANDERSON, Edward Joseph, Dec 2 1933 Sex:M Child# 4 F W Anderson Nashua, NH & Helen Burgess Scotland
ANDERSON, Eleanor, Feb 19 1906 Sex:F Child# 1 William H Anderson Londonderry, NH & Florence S Holmes Portsmouth, NH
ANDERSON, Emma Elizabeth, Apr 6 1922 Sex:F Child# 5 Elmer Anderson Nashua, NH & Regina Desmanche Nashua, NH
ANDERSON, Gertrude Florence, Mar 28 1895 Sex:F Child# 2 Martin B Anderson Sweden & Augusta Sweden
ANDERSON, Harry Marten, Oct 9 1892 Sex:M Child# 1 Martin Anderson Sweden & Augusta Sweden
ANDERSON, Helena, Jul 17 1889 Sex:F Child# 1 John Anderson Lewiston & Hannah Lawson Portland
ANDERSON, Jane Colman, Dec 9 1891 Sex:F Child# 3 John Anderson Scotland & Jane Colman Scotland
ANDERSON, Jessica, Mar 1 1911 Sex:F Child# 1 Harold E Anderson Worcester, MA & Mary Andrews Clinton, MA
ANDERSON, John Robert, Dec 9 1930 Sex:M Child# 2 Francis W Anderson Nashua, NH & Helen Burgess Scotland
ANDERSON, Joseph, Jun 30 1907 Sex:M Child# 3 Willie Anderson Russia & Eva Pluckutis Russia
ANDERSON, Josephine, Jan 6 1895 Sex:F Child# 7 James Anderson Ireland & Annie Lee Ireland
ANDERSON, Leon Edmond, Jul 14 1912 Sex:M Child# 5 Gustave Anderson Sweden & Anita Morin Canada
ANDERSON, Liliane Camille, Nov 7 1908 Sex:F Child# 3 Gustave Anderson Sweden & Anita Morin Canada
ANDERSON, Marie A O, Oct 15 1909 Sex:F Child# 4 Gustave Anderson Sweden & Anita Morin Canada
ANDERSON, Mary Minnie, Jun 12 1915 Sex:F Child# 2 John Anderson Russia & Petra Matronick Russia
ANDERSON, Minnie L, Feb 10 1891 Sex:F Child# 1 Henry M Anderson NH & Blanche E Lawrence NH
ANDERSON, Paulena, Aug 23 1918 Sex:F Child# 3 John Anderson Russia & Patricia Thomson Russia
ANDERSON, Peggy Anne, Apr 7 1932 Sex:F Child# 3 F W Anderson Nashua, NH & Helen Burgess Scotland
ANDERSON, Raymond, Dec 20 1907 Sex:M Child# 2 Gustave Anderson Sweden & Anita Morin Canada
ANDERSON, Robert, Dec 4 1906 Sex:M Child# 1 Gustav Anderson Waltham, MA & Anita Morin Canada
ANDERSON, Samuel Howard, Mar 30 1926 Sex:M Child# 3 Alva Anderson Bloomfield, IN & Henriette Blasey Adelaide,
ANDERSON, Unknown, Oct 29 1889 Sex:M Child# 8 Nathaniel C Anderson Portland & Ella Hall Nashua, NH
ANDERSON, Unknown, Oct 30 1891 Sex:M Child# 4 James Anderson Ireland & Annie Lee Ireland
ANDERSON, Unknown, Jul 25 1893 Sex:F Child# 2 John A Anderson England & Min A Chamberlain Altoona, NY
ANDERSON, Unknown, Sep 13 1911 Sex:M Child# 2 Arthur C Anderson Londonderry, NH & Viola Preston W Acton, MA
ANDERSON, Unknown, Jan 2 1930 Sex:M Child#  Francis W Anderson Nashua, NH & Helen Burgess Scotland
ANDERSON, Wilbur Francis, Jul 14 1907 Sex:M Child# 1 Joseph Anderson Lawrence, MA & Minnie Barr S Lyndeboro, N
ANDERSON, William H, Feb 10 1907 Sex:M Child# 2 William H Anderson Derry, NH & Florence S Holmes Portsmouth, N
ANDONACOPLOS, Christos A, Apr 3 1917 Sex:M Child# 2 Ang Andonacoplos Macedonia & Gozani Stanatila
ANDREAPOULOS, Helene, Sep 19 1915 Sex:F Child# 3 Nicholas Andreapoulo Greece & Anastasia Mankloias Greece
ANDREVSKEWICH, Anthony Tom, Nov 9 1920 Sex:M Child# 2 Jos Andrevskewich Russia & Eva Arasimovich Russia
ANDREW, Alice, May 19 1892 Sex:F Child# 4 John Andrew Chazy, NY & Lizzie Jackson Sciota, NY
ANDREW, Doris Violet, Jan 17 1927 Sex:F Child# 1 Robert A Andrew Hudson, NH & Violette Doherty Nashua, NH
ANDREW, Robert Allen, Apr 28 1934 Sex:M Child# 2 Robert Allen Andrew Hudson, NH & Violetta Doherty Nashua, NH
ANDREWS, Alice M, May 30 1896 Sex:F Child# 2 Charles A Andrews Kingsford, NY & G M Lewis Salem, MA
ANDREWS, Charles Elmer, Sep 1 1916 Sex:M Child# 1 Forrest O Andrews Pepperell, MA & Eva Maud Blodgett Groton,
ANDREWS, Donald, Dec 15 1934 Sex:M Child# 1 Anthony Andrews Chelsea, MA & Beatrice Malette Nashua, NH
ANDREWS, Elizabeth Alvira, Feb 17 1891 Sex:F Child# 2 William A Andrews Hudson, NH & Etta Annis Londonderry, NH
ANDREWS, Frederick Britton, Jan 1 1922 Sex:M Child# 3 Chester A Andrews Hudson, NH & Ada Louise Britton Holli
ANDREWS, Gregory, Oct 3 1920 Sex:M Child# 8 John Andrews Poland Russia & Lena Byko Poland Russia  Stillborn
ANDREWS, Harold, Dec 18 1888 Sex:M Child# 1 Frank A Andrews Nashua, NH & Catherine Baldwin Nashua, NH
ANDREWS, Katherine, May 29 1894 Sex:F Child# 2 Frank A Andrews Nashua, NH & Katherine B Baldwin Nashua, NH
ANDREWS, Peter, Mar 2 1917 Sex:M Child# 1 Peter Andrews Russia & Dorothy Russia

5

ANDREWS, Raymond Gregg, May 6 1896 Sex:M Child# 1 Ed Andrews Nashua, NH & Carrie Gregg Lynn, MA
ANDREWS, Robert Allen, Dec 11 1917 Sex:M Child# 1 Chester H Andrews Hudson, NH & Ada Britton Hollis, NH
ANDREWS, Ruth Henrietta, Dec 27 1918 Sex:F Child# 2 Chester A Andrews Hudson, NH & Ada Britton Hollis, NH
ANDREWS, Unknown, Jul 15 1892 Sex:M Child# 1 Frank A Andrews Nashua, NH & Matilda McVity Bradford, England
ANDREWS, Unknown, May 20 1894 Sex:M Child# 2 Frank A Andrews Nashua, NH & Matilda McVity Bradford, England
ANDREWS, Unknown, Jan 25 1898 Sex:M Child# 2 Charles A Andrews NY & Gertrude May Lewis Salem, MA
ANDREY, Unknown, Aug 20 1911 Sex:F Child# 2 Christos Andrey Greece & Eftihis Bourtalas Greece
ANDRIAPOULON, Etasnia, May 1 1912 Sex:F Child# 1 Christos Andriapoulo Russia & Efthia Bourdala Russia
ANDRUOSKIANCIUS, Joseph, Jan 14 1919 Sex:M Child# 2 Jos Andruoskiancius Russia & Eva Askenokcinte Russia
ANDRUSKEVICH, Alphonse John, May 15 1922 Sex:M Child# 3 Jos Andruskevich Russia & Eva Arasimovich Russia
ANELTEL, Noe Eugene, May 4 1889 Sex:M Child# 7 Mared Aneltel Serola, NY & Mary Marrat NY
ANGEFEDES, Eugene, Sep 9 1926 Sex:M Child# 3 S Angefedes Greece & Elsa Ostenkamp Cincinnati, OH
ANGELILO, Filomena Anna, Jun 15 1935 Sex:F Child# 1 Joseph Angelilo Italy & Mary Pitaro Italy
ANGELL, Marcea Janet, Jul 4 1925 Sex:F Child# 1 Frank C Angell Gloucester, RI & Ida M Coffin Wiscasset, ME
ANGERS, Eugene, Feb 15 1930 Sex:M Child# 2 Roneldo Angers Nashua, NH & Albina Blais Nashua, NH
ANGERS, Maurice, Aug 31 1925 Sex:M Child# 1 Donalda Angers Nashua, NH & Albina Blais Nashua, NH
ANGERS, Romeo, Jul 2 1903 Sex:M Child# 5 Joseph Angers Canada & Albina Fontaine Canada
ANGERS, Ronald Lucien, Nov 20 1905 Sex:M Child# 6 Joseph Angers Canada & Albina Fournier Canada
ANGEW, Veronica, Dec 28 1914 Sex:F Child# 2 Sylvester Angew Russia & Elizabeth Maukiroic Russia
ANGOUNAS, Joseph, May 13 1920 Sex:M Child# 4 Charles Angounas Lithuania Russia & Alexandra Praniawicz Lithuania
ANGUN, Helena, Dec 5 1919 Sex:F Child# 2 Wladislaw Angun Russia & Mary Noreko Russia
ANGUNAS, John, Apr 3 1920 Sex:M Child# 1 Joseph Angunas Russia & Ursula Grygas Russia
ANGUS, David William, Sep 5 1925 Sex:M Child# 1 David Angus Aberdeen, Scotland & Carolyn Luce Woodsville, NH
ANGUS, Irenee Roland, Apr 20 1924 Sex:M Child# 1 Romeo Angus Nashua, NH & Dora Rivard Canada
ANNIS, Alice Louisa, Jul 29 1888 Sex:F Child# 3 Mark Annis Vermont & Mary Brown Ireland
ANNIS, Catherine May, Mar 28 1912 Sex:F Child# 6 Everett P Annis Hudson, NH & Katie McArthur St John, NB  Stillborn
ANNIS, Edna Marice, Sep 21 1932 Sex:F Child# 1 James Annis Wilton, NH & M Johnson Manchester, NH
ANNIS, Gerald Rodman, Dec 19 1925 Sex:M Child# 1 Russell Annis Peru, NY & Frances Goodspeed Plattsburg, NY
ANNIS, Harold Jackson, Jan 13 1922 Sex:M Child# 2 Andrew J Annis Plattsburg, NY & Marion Moody Ogunquit, ME
ANNIS, Leolyn, Jan 15 1928 Sex:F Child# 2 Bernard Annis Hillsborough, NH & Hazel Hill Vermont
ANNIS, Lucille Eloise, Jan 17 1929 Sex:F Child# 3 Bernard E Annis Hillsboro, NH & Hazel Hill Thetford, VT
ANNIS, Meretta Gertrude, Aug 1 1908 Sex:F Child# 4 Everett P Annis Hudson, NH & Kate MacArthur St John, NB
ANNIS, Richard Hamilton, Aug 14 1922 Sex:M Child# 1 Bernard E Annis Hillsboro, NH & Hazel Marion Hill Thetford, VT
ANNIS, Ruth, Apr 22 1917 Sex:F Child# 1 Frederick Annis Maine & Agnes Doyle Nashua, NH
ANOCKLE, Unknown, Nov 20 1888 Sex:M Child# 1 John Anockle N Y & Julia H Canada  Stillborn
ANOSTOPOLON, Unknown, Jun 8 1921 Sex:F Child# 3 Costas Anostopolon Greece & Louise DeAmotote Greece
ANTAGO, Hector, Jan 10 1888 Sex:M Child# 3 Narcise Antago Canada & Ayelee Bollard Nashua, NH
ANTAYA, Anastasie, Jun 20 1899 Sex:F Child# 7 Louis Antaya Canada & Louise St Michel Canada
ANTAYA, Antaya, Dec 10 1890 Sex:M Child# 1 Louis Antaya Canada & Louise St Michel Canada
ANTAYA, Cecile, Oct 5 1894 Sex:F Child# 4 Louis Antaya Canada & Louise St Michel Canada
ANTAYA, Eva Rose, Oct 25 1891 Sex:F Child# 5 Narcisse Antaya Canada & Arzelie Belland Canada
ANTAYA, Leo George N, Dec 1 1909 Sex:M Child# 1 Hector Antaya Nashua, NH & Bernadette April Canada
ANTAYA, Maria Victoria, Oct 23 1901 Sex:F Child# 7 Narcisse Antaya Canada & Arzelle Beland Nashua, NH
ANTAYA, Marie L H, Dec 3 1891 Sex:F Child# 2 Louis Antaya Canada & Louise St Michel Canada
ANTAYA, Unknown, Sep 13 1893 Sex:F Child# 3 Louis Antaya Canada & Louise St Michel Nashua, NH  Stillborn
ANTAYA, Unknown, Dec 11 1900 Sex:M Child# 8 Louis Antaya Canada & Louise St Michel Canada  Stillborn
ANTAYER, Marie Louise, Dec 8 1889 Sex:F Child# 4 Narcisse Antayer Canada & Arzelle Belland Canada
ANTCIL, Unknown, Feb 12 1918 Sex:F Child# 4 Frank Michael Antcil Russia & Adna Czenon Russia  Stillborn
ANTHIL, Sylvia, Jun 13 1889 Sex:F Child# 1 J P Anthil Canada & Emilia Desjardins Canada
ANTIL, Loraine 1, Dec 20 1906 Sex:F Child# 8 Edmond Antil Canada & May Lemery Three Rivers, MA
ANTILLE, Joseph Emebert, Jul 22 1897 Sex:M Child# 7 Arsene Antille Canada & Emelie Deschenes Canada
ANTILLE, M Ange Lucille, May 25 1917 Sex:F Child# 8 Girard Antille Canada & Clairida Deschamps Canada
ANTILLE, Marie Emelie, Nov 16 1899 Sex:F Child# 8 Arsene Antille Canada & Emelie Deschenes Canada
ANTILLE, Marie Rose Cecile, May 25 1917 Sex:F Child# 9 Girard Antille Canada & Clairida Deschamps Canada
ANTONOPOULOS, Unknown, Jul 1 1924 Sex:M Child# 4 C Antonopoulos Greece & O Canelapapolos Greece
ANTOWVRICH, Sylvester, Oct 8 1914 Sex:M Child# 1 Peter Antowvrich Russia & Anna Gulbewicz Russia
ANTROPIK, Chestawa, Jul 20 1915 Sex:F Child# 2 John Antropik Russia & Mary Leonowicz Russia
ANTROPIK, Stanislaus, Apr 7 1914 Sex:M Child# 1 John Antropik Russia & Mary Lenoniwicz Russia
APONIVITCH, Unknown, Jul 25 1919 Sex:F Child# 7 Frank Aponivitch Russia & Antonia Galinierska Russia
APONMOVITCH, Louis Charles, Oct 14 1914 Sex:M Child# 1 Louis C Aponmovitch Russia & Lina Shuticz Russia
APONOVITCH, Joseph, Jan 3 1911 Sex:M Child# 2 Mike Aponovitch Russia & Antoinette Hollem Russia
APONOWICH, Mary, Aug 10 1913 Sex:F Child# 3 Frank Aponowich Russia & Antonia Galanipith Russia
APONOWICZ, Jennie, Jun 24 1919 Sex:F Child# 1 Stephen Aponowicz Russia & Rose Petchakatie Russia
APONRICH, Unknown, Jan 12 1912 Sex:M Child# 3 Frank Aponrich Russia & Antonette Hellens Russia
APONWITCH, Stanley, Nov 5 1914 Sex:M Child# 5 Frank Aponwitch Russia & Antonina Galenski Russia
APOROWICH, Annie, Nov 9 1918 Sex:F Child# 2 Louis Aporowich Russia & Helena Showic Russia
APOSTOLOPOULOS, Orania, Mar 31 1916 Sex:F Child# 1 C Apostolopoulos Greece & Vasiliki Scafida Greece
APOSTOLOPULOS, William, Feb 16 1917 Sex:M Child# 2 George Apostolopulos Greece & Genulia Laruska Greece
APOSTOLOS, Unknown, Aug 29 1921 Sex:F Child# 1 Daniel Apostolos Greece & Galata Coule Greece
APPICI, Francois, Apr 11 1900 Sex:M Child# 3 Ferdinand Appici Italy & Santad Blondi Italy
APPLETON, Edith Louise, Sep 24 1932 Sex:F Child# 1 Scott Appleton Franklin, NH & Ruth E Holt Nashua, NH
APPLETON, Sylvia Ruth, Aug 9 1934 Sex:F Child# 2 Scott S Appleton Franklin, NH & Ruth E Holt Nashua, NH
APRIL, Arthur Leo, Sep 24 1902 Sex:M Child# 8 Joseph April Canada & Rosanna Paquette Canada

APRIL, Charles Hector, Jun 16 1898 Sex:M Child# 5 Treffle April Canada & Aimee Dufour Canada
APRIL, Florence Juliette, Apr 22 1911 Sex:F Child# 14 Alfred April Canada & Marie Bernier Canada
APRIL, Joseph Alphee A, Apr 18 1904 Sex:M Child# 9 Treffle April Canada & Aimee Dufour Canada
APRIL, Joseph Arthur, Apr 26 1901 Sex:M Child# 5 Philias April Canada & Alexina Pelletier Canada
APRIL, Joseph George Leger, Aug 21 1899 Sex:M Child# 6 Treffle April Canada & Aimee Dufour Canada
APRIL, Joseph Philias A, Jan 24 1906 Sex:M Child# 5 Philias April Canada & Alexina Peltier Canada
APRIL, Joseph Thomas, Apr 1 1908 Sex:M Child# 10 Philias April Canada & Alexina Pelletier Canada
APRIL, Joseph Venitien A, Mar 2 1907 Sex:M Child# 9 Philias April Canada & Alexina Pelletier Canada
APRIL, Marie, Aug 26 1901 Sex:F Child# 7 Joseph April Canada & Rose Anna Paquette Canada
APRIL, Marie Adele, Apr 27 1895 Sex:F Child# 3 Joseph April Canada & Rosanna Paquet Canada
APRIL, Marie Agnes E, Nov 22 1902 Sex:F Child# 6 Philias April Canada & Alexina Peltier Canada
APRIL, Marie Aimee C, Mar 14 1910 Sex:F Child# 11 Moise April Canada & Amanda Pelletier Canada
APRIL, Marie Alice I, Mar 20 1900 Sex:F Child# 4 Philias April Canada & Alexina Peltier Canada
APRIL, Marie B A, Mar 12 1897 Sex:F Child# 4 Joseph April Canada & Rosanna Paquet Canada
APRIL, Marie Cecile Therese, Apr 4 1932 Sex:F Child# 1 (No Parents Listed)
APRIL, Marie D, Nov 7 1898 Sex:F Child# 2 Joseph April Canada & Rose Paquette Canada
APRIL, Marie Edith E, Sep 24 1905 Sex:F Child# 10 Treffle April Canada & Aimee Dufour Canada
APRIL, Marie Jeanne d'Arc, Jan 6 1922 Sex:F Child# 6 Ernest April Nashua, NH & Emma Landry Canada
APRIL, Marie Lea, Nov 3 1901 Sex:F Child# 8 Treffle April Canada & Aimee Dufour Canada
APRIL, Marie Lumina D, Feb 22 1904 Sex:F Child# 7 Philias April Canada & Alexina Peltier Canada
APRIL, Marie Mabel, Sep 1 1900 Sex:F Child# 7 Treffle April Canada & Aimee Dufour Canada
APRIL, Marie Theresa, May 20 1925 Sex:F Child# 1 Euside April Nashua, NH & Lena Leclerc Nashua, NH
APRIL, Maurice Emile, Mar 6 1930 Sex:M Child# 2 Emile April Nashua, NH & Lena Leclerc Nashua, NH
APRIL, Norman Raoul, Jul 11 1926 Sex:M Child# 3 Raoul April Nashua, NH & Lillian Gendron Nashua, NH
APRIL, Paul Gerard, May 26 1920 Sex:M Child# 1 Raoul T April Nashua, NH & Lillian Gendron Nashua, NH
APRIL, Pauline Mabel, Jan 29 1923 Sex:F Child# 2 Raoul April Nashua, NH & Lillian Gendron Nashua, NH
APRIL, Raymond Roger, Jul 29 1928 Sex:M Child# 8 Ernest April Nashua, NH & Emma Landry Canada
APRIL, Unknown, Feb 24 1911 Sex:M Child# 10 Moise April Canada & Amanda Pelletier Canada Stillborn
APRIL, Vital Magela, Aug 4 1924 Sex:M Child# 7 Ernest April Nashua, NH & Emma Landry Canada
APRIL, Vivian Margaret, Jul 31 1934 Sex:F Child# 4 Raoul April Nashua, NH & Lillian Gendron Nashua, NH
APRILE, Blanche Yvonne, May 26 1897 Sex:F Child# 4 Treffle Aprile Canada & Aimee Dufour Canada
APRILE, Camille Leon, Aug 31 1902 Sex:M Child# 10 Alfred Aprile Canada & Marie Bernier Canada
APRILE, Emelia, Oct 28 1897 Sex:F Child# 6 Alfred Aprile Canada & Marie Bernier Canada
APRILE, Emelia Irene, Jul 8 1904 Sex:F Child# 12 Alfred Aprile Canada & Marie Bernier Canada
APRILE, Emile Rene, Jul 8 1904 Sex:M Child# 11 Alfred Aprile Canada & Marie Bernier Canada
APRILE, Eva, Mar 9 1891 Sex:F Child# 2 Moise Aprile Canada & Amanda Peltier Canada
APRILE, Jean Baptiste, May 19 1901 Sex:M Child# 9 Alfred Aprile Canada & Marie Bernier Canada
APRILE, Joseph, Jul 31 1893 Sex:M Child# 5 Alfred Aprile Canada & Marie Bernier Canada
APRILE, Joseph Adelard, Oct 1 1892 Sex:M Child# 1 Joseph Aprile Canada & Rosanna Paquet Canada
APRILE, Joseph Adelard, Oct 20 1893 Sex:M Child# 1 Phileas Aprile Canada & Alexina Peltier Canada
APRILE, Joseph Henri A, Nov 6 1898 Sex:M Child# 5 Philias Aprile Canada & Alexina Peltier Canada
APRILE, Joseph L George, Jan 31 1896 Sex:M Child# 3 Triffe Aprile Canada & Aimee Dufour Canada
APRILE, Joseph L Philippe, Mar 28 1894 Sex:M Child# 2 Joseph Aprile Canada & Rosanna Paquette Canada
APRILE, Joseph Treffle R, Jun 12 1894 Sex:M Child# 2 Treffle Aprile Canada & Aimie Dufour Canada
APRILE, Lea Aurore, Mar 13 1897 Sex:F Child# 2 Philias Aprile Canada & Alexina Peltier Canada
APRILE, Nicholas, Jul 12 1895 Sex:M Child# 6 Alfred Aprile Canada & Marie Bernier Canada
APRILE, Unknown, Jan 20 1892 Sex:M Child# 4 Arthur Aprile Canada & Marie Bernier Canada Stillborn
APRILE, Unknown, Feb 11 1893 Sex:F Child# 1 Treffle Aprile Canada & Aimee Dufour Canada Stillborn
APRILLE, David, Aug 11 1899 Sex:M Child# 8 Alfred Aprille Canada & Marie Bernier Canada
APRILLE, Ernest, Jan 14 1890 Sex:M Child# 1 Moise Aprille Canada & Amanda Peltier Canada
APRILLE, Georgianna, Nov 23 1888 Sex:F Child# 2 Alfred Aprille Canada & Maria Bernier Canada
APRILLE, Joseph Alphe, Jun 9 1890 Sex:M Child# 3 Albert Aprille Canada & Marie Bernier Canada
APRILLE, Louis Alfred, Jun 10 1887 Sex:M Child# Alfred Aprille P Q & Marie Bernier PQ
ARBANN, Joseph Bruno, Oct 6 1898 Sex:M Child# 7 Will Arbann Canada & Delima Leberge Canada
ARBORN, Omer Leo, Mar 23 1931 Sex:M Child# 6 William Arborn Nashua, NH & Yvonne Belanger Canada
ARBOUR, Angelina, May 22 1906 Sex:F Child# 11 Will Arbour Canada & Delima Theberge Canada
ARBOUR, Conrad Andrew, Nov 10 1922 Sex:M Child# 1 William Arbour Canada & Yvonne Belanger Canada
ARBOUR, Delina, Oct 3 1891 Sex:F Child# William Arbour Canada & Delina Lebarge Canada
ARBOUR, J B Edmond, Jun 23 1928 Sex:M Child# 5 William Arbour Canada & Yvonne Belanger Canada
ARBOUR, Joseph, Aug 23 1926 Sex:M Child# 4 William Arbour Canada & Yvonne Belanger Canada  Stillborn
ARBOUR, Lillian, Apr 22 1913 Sex:F Child# 1 William Arbour Canada & Liliane Beaucher Lowell, MA
ARBOUR, Marie Louise, Jan 27 1904 Sex:F Child# 10 William Arbour Canada & Delima Theberge Canada
ARBOUR, Maurice Arthur, May 7 1924 Sex:M Child# 2 William Arbour Canada & Yvonne Belanger Canada
ARBOUR, Odile, Oct 7 1902 Sex:F Child# 9 Will Arbour Canada & Delima Theberge Canada
ARBOUR, Victor Roland, Oct 13 1925 Sex:M Child# 3 William Arbour Canada & Yvonne Belanger Canada
ARCHAMBAULT, Adolphe Albert, Aug 15 1909 Sex:M Child# 1 Albert Archambault US & Albina Guenette US
ARCHAMBAULT, Alexandrine, Oct 13 1888 Sex:F Child# 2 M Archambault Canada & Alexandrine Desmarais Canada
ARCHAMBAULT, Alfred, Jul 30 1910 Sex:M Child# 1 John Archambault Nashua, NH & Amanda Roy Canada
ARCHAMBAULT, Alfred Misael, Feb 12 1907 Sex:M Child# 2 F A Archambault Nashua, NH & Corinne Maynard St Albans, VT
ARCHAMBAULT, Alphonse, Jr, Aug 19 1924 Sex:M Child# 1 A Archambault Nashua, NH & Catherine Coffey Nashua, NH
ARCHAMBAULT, Emma, Mar 25 1892 Sex:F Child# 1 Arthur Archambault Canada & Virginie Marcotte NY
ARCHAMBAULT, Fernand Marcel, Dec 23 1923 Sex:M Child# 2 D Archambault Canada & Marie A Tanguay Canada
ARCHAMBAULT, Flora, Apr 12 1894 Sex:F Child# 3 Joseph Archambault Canada & Emma Benoit Melrose, MA

ARCHAMBAULT, Gerard Edward, Aug 22 1935 Sex:M Child# 3 L E Archambault Pepperell, MA & Rosalie Paradis Lawrence, MA
ARCHAMBAULT, Gloria Doris, Apr 17 1930 Sex:F Child# 1 Leo Archambault Pepperell, MA & Rosalie Paradis Lawrence, MA
ARCHAMBAULT, John Arthur, Jun 7 1918 Sex:M Child# 3 Pierre R Archambault Wilton, NH & Eugenie Rainville Nashua, NH
ARCHAMBAULT, Joseph, Feb 19 1903 Sex:M Child# 1 Med Archambault Canada & Mary Marquis Nashua, NH
ARCHAMBAULT, Joseph Alphonse, Nov 25 1893 Sex:M Child# 8 Francis Archambault Canada & Jennie Germain Canada
ARCHAMBAULT, Joseph G, Jan 16 1892 Sex:M Child# 18 Henri Archambault Canada & Julie St Germain Canada
ARCHAMBAULT, Joseph Leon E, Jun 11 1903 Sex:M Child# 1 Ulddric Archambault Canada & Anna Marotte New York
ARCHAMBAULT, Joseph Lewis, Mar 20 1928 Sex:M Child# 1 J E Archambault Concord, NH & Carrie Labombard Nashua, NH
ARCHAMBAULT, Joseph Louis C, Aug 16 1901 Sex:M Child# 11 Charles Archambault Canada & Adele Beauleau Canada
ARCHAMBAULT, Lilian May, Nov 25 1904 Sex:F Child# 2 Mederic Archambault Canada & Anna Marotte Canada
ARCHAMBAULT, Lillienne Beatrice, May 25 1906 Sex:F Child# 3 Mederic Archambault Canada & Annie Marotte New York
ARCHAMBAULT, Lucienna, Feb 14 1900 Sex:F Child# 5 A Archambault Canada & Jennie Marotte New York
ARCHAMBAULT, Marie Blanche, Jul 22 1904 Sex:F Child# 1 Alfrd Archambault Nashua, NH & Corinne Maynard St Albans, VT
ARCHAMBAULT, Marie Delina, Nov 21 1889 Sex:F Child# 6 F Archambault Canada & Jeanne Jermaine Canada
ARCHAMBAULT, Marie Eva, Sep 29 1897 Sex:F Child# 4 Arthur Archambault Canada & Jeanne Marotte NY
ARCHAMBAULT, Marie Rose Eva, Mar 6 1917 Sex:F Child# 2 Pierre Archambault NH & Eugenie Rainville NH
ARCHAMBAULT, Neil David, Aug 12 1935 Sex:M Child# 3 L E Archambault Sterling, MA & Olive Morin Graniteville, MA
ARCHAMBAULT, Rita Irene, Apr 5 1925 Sex:F Child# 3 D Archambault Canada & Maria Tanguay Canada
ARCHAMBAULT, Roland Leo, Apr 1 1932 Sex:M Child# 2 L Archambault Pepperell, MA & Rosalie Paradis Lawrence, MA
ARCHAMBAULT, Rose Delima, Dec 5 1895 Sex:F Child# 3 Arthur Archambault Canada & Jeanne Marotte Canada
ARCHAMBAULT, Sarah Gratia, Nov 30 1901 Sex:F Child# 7 David Archambault Canada & Mary Landry Canada
ARCHAMBAULT, Unknown, Feb 24 1902 Sex:M Child# 6 A Archambault Canada & Eugenie Marotte New York
ARCHAMBAULT, Unknown, Jul 8 1927 Sex:F Child# 2 L Archambault Wilton, NH & Jeannie Ratte Canada
ARCHAMBAULT, Valmare, Dec 16 1889 Sex:M Child# 8 I Archambault Canada & Celina Lalibert Canada  Stillborn
ARCHAMBAULT, William Edward, Nov 1 1931 Sex:M Child# 1 Edward Archambault Pepperell, MA & Flor Vadeboncoeur
ARCHAMBEAU, Alfred Conrad, Jul 2 1894 Sex:M Child# 5 L Archambeau Canada & Mary E Landry Canada
ARCHAMBEAU, Alfred Leon, May 18 1891 Sex:M Child# 7 Frank Archambeau Canada & Jane Germain Canada
ARCHAMBEAU, Alida, Mar 13 1889 Sex:F Child# 5 A Archambeau Canada & Philomene Guertin Canada
ARCHAMBEAU, Amable, Oct 6 1891 Sex:M Child# 6 A Archambeau Canada & Philomene Guertin Canada
ARCHAMBEAU, Anne, Apr 24 1888 Sex:F Child# 5 Frrancis Archambeau Canada & Jane Germain Canada
ARCHAMBEAU, Arsene, Feb 13 1891 Sex:M Child# 5 L Archambeau Canada & Mary E Landry Canada
ARCHAMBEAU, Arthur, Mar 19 1887 Sex:M Child#  F Archambeau P Q & Jennie Germain P Q
ARCHAMBEAU, Henri, Oct 28 1895 Sex:M Child# 9 Frank Archambeau Canada & Jeanne Germain Canada
ARCHAMBEAU, Juliette, May 21 1889 Sex:F Child# 4 L Archambeau Canada & Mederiso Landry Canada
ARCHAMBEAU, Vergine, Apr 25 1888 Sex:F Child# 10 J B Archambeau Canada & Maria Lampro Canada
ARCHAMBEAULT, Adolph E, Sep 4 1887 Sex:M Child# 4 A Archambeault Canada & Philomene Canada
ARCHAMBEAULT, Agnes, Jul 28 1892 Sex:F Child# 2 Joseph Archambeault Canada & Emma Benoit Mass
ARCHAMBEAULT, Joseph Louis Caliste, Nov 7 1924 Sex:M Child# 1 Joseph Archambeault Pepperell, MA & Adrienne Brodeur
ARCHAMBEAULT, Joseph M A, Feb 23 1887 Sex:M Child# 1 M Archambeault P Q & A Desmarais P Q
ARCHAMBEAULT, Lucien Edouard, Dec 4 1926 Sex:M Child# 2 J N Archambeault Pepperell, MA & A Y Brodeur Nashua, NH
ARCHAMBEAULT, Marie Jeannie G, May 28 1929 Sex:F Child# 3 Jos N Archambeault Pepperell, MA & Adrienne Brodeur
ARCHEMBEAU, Jean Baptiste L, Oct 13 1890 Sex:M Child# 1 Joseph Archembeau Canada & Ena Benoit Stoneham, MA
ARCHER, Alice Frances, Jun 8 1918 Sex:F Child# 3 George T Archer Lowell, MA & Nora V Downing Cambridge, MA
ARCHER, Dorothy, Jul 6 1927 Sex:F Child# 2 Charles Archer Nashua, NH & Ethel Sandluld Nashua, NH
ARCHER, George Thomas, Jun 12 1909 Sex:M Child# 1 George T Archer Lowell, MA & Nora Downey Cambridge, MA
ARCHER, Margaret, Jul 11 1913 Sex:F Child# 2 George T Archer Lowell, MA & Lora B Darling Cambridge, MA
ARCHER, Mary Elizabeth, Mar 9 1923 Sex:F Child# 1 Charles Archer Nashua, NH & Ethel Sandlund Nashua, NH
ARCHER, Unknown, Apr 13 1890 Sex:M Child# 6 George Archer Ballardvale, MA & Myra Park Searsport, ME
ARCHIBALD, Ruberta Joyce, Aug 25 1934 Sex:F Child# 2 Arthur Archibald N Berwick, ME & Dorothy Miner Rutland, VT
ARCHIBALD, Unknown, Nov 7 1932 Sex:F Child# 1 A W Archibald N Berwick, ME & Dorothy Miner Rutland, VT
ARECE, John, Apr 17 1896 Sex:M Child# 4 John Arece Russia & Russia
AREL, Henry, Oct 6 1917 Sex:M Child# 1 Henry Arel Canada & Lillian Dumas
AREL, J Albert Alfred, Sep 1 1921 Sex:M Child# 7 Donat Arel Canada & Clara Levesque Canada
AREL, Jos Donah Eugene, May 19 1919 Sex:M Child# 5 Donah Arel Canada & Clara Levesque Canada
AREL, Jos Germain Eugene, Oct 30 1928 Sex:M Child# 9 Donat Arel Canada & Clara Levesque Canada
AREL, Joseph Alfred Emile, Oct 10 1916 Sex:M Child# 3 Donat Arel Nashua, NH & Clara Levesque Canada
AREL, Joseph Robert, Jul 25 1920 Sex:M Child# 6 Dorah Arel Canada & Clara Levesque Canada
AREL, M Blanche Lucienne, Jun 27 1915 Sex:F Child# 2 Donat Arel Canada & Clara Levesque Canada
AREL, Marie Gabriel May, May 30 1925 Sex:F Child# 1 Jacob Arel Canada & Laura Gabriel Canada
AREL, Marie Jeanne, May 11 1914 Sex:F Child# 1 Donat Arel Canada & Clara Levesque Canada
AREL, Marie Laura Yvette, Jun 19 1923 Sex:F Child# 8 Donah Arel Canada & Clara Levesque Canada
AREL, Marie Louise Cecil, Mar 26 1918 Sex:F Child# 4 Donat Arel Canada & Clara Levesque Canada
AREL, Marie Pauline, Jan 13 1929 Sex:F Child# 2 Jacob Arel Canada & Laura Gabriel Canada
AREL, Maurice, Mar 21 1933 Sex:M Child# 10 Donat Arel Canada & Clara Levesque Canada
AREL, Raymond Albert, Oct 26 1922 Sex:M Child# 1 Leon Arel Nashua, NH & Eleanor Lavoie Canada
AREL, Therese, Sep 2 1924 Sex:F Child# 2 Leon Arel Canada & Laura Lavoie Canada
ARLANSKAS, Stanley Mitchell, May 23 1922 Sex:M Child# 5 J P Arlanskas Lithuania & Mary Standick Lithuania
ARLIOUS, Louise Alma, Jan 18 1890 Sex:F Child# 4 William Arlious Canada & Delima Feberge Canada
ARLOUSKAS, Nellie, Sep 5 1919 Sex:F Child# 3 John P Arlouskas Russia & Mary Staushik Russia
ARLOVSKY, Joseph, Aug 31 1910 Sex:M Child# 2 John Arlovsky Russia & Mary Stanchik Russia
ARMERSON, Stanley, Jan 11 1901 Sex:M Child# 3 Frank J Armerson England & Jessie Emman Prince Edw Island
ARMINGTON, Unknown, May 10 1889 Sex:F Child# 7 Harlan Armington Ludlow, VT & Esther Wheaton New York, NY
ARMOLICH, Minnie, Jul 30 1913 Sex:F Child# 2 Joseph Armolich Russia & Eva Slatunis Russia

ARMOLOWICZ, Antony, May 30 1915 Sex:M Child# 3 Joseph Armolowicz Russia & Eva Schletwonnos Russia
ARMSTEAD, Austin Herrick, Dec 30 1924 Sex:M Child# 1 J M Armstead Lowell, MA & Olive Sullivan Springfield, VT
ARMSTRONG, Claire, Sep 9 1921 Sex:F Child# 1 Thomas Armstrong US & Diana Leblanc US
ARMSTRONG, Earl C, Nov 8 1890 Sex:M Child# 2 Walter H Armstrong New York & Stella M Churchill New York
ARMSTRONG, Frances Eileine, Aug 28 1918 Sex:F Child# 2 Frank Armstrong Salem, MA & Daisy Simmons Salem, MA
ARMSTRONG, Thomas Henry Paul, Dec 2 1927 Sex:M Child# 2 T Armstrong Fitchburg, MA & Diana Leblanc Nashua, NH
ARMSTRONG, Unknown, Dec 3 1888 Sex:F Child# 4 J Z Armstrong P Q & H M Armstrong Michigan
ARMSTRONG, Unknown, May 30 1889 Sex:M Child# 1 W H Armstrong New York &  New York  Stillborn
ARNOLD, Agnes Mary, Jul 30 1898 Sex:F Child# 9 David B Arnold Haverhill, MA & Annie Peters Greenville, NH
ARNOLD, David Howard, Jan 7 1925 Sex:M Child# 4 A Frank Arnold NH & Beatrice Rochelle Providence, RI
ARNOLD, Dexter F, May 25 1916 Sex:M Child# 1 A Frank Arnold Greenville, NH & Beatrice Rochelle Providence, RI
ARNOLD, Edward Elkins, Sep 27 1926 Sex:M Child# 2 Edward R Arnold US & Bertha Parker US
ARNOLD, George Elliott, Jr, Dec 16 1934 Sex:M Child# 2 George E Arnold Lincoln, RI & Florence Poole England
ARNOLD, Gerald Francis, Jul 29 1933 Sex:M Child# 4 Edward Arnold Manchester, NH & Bertha Pecker Nashua, NH
ARNOLD, Norma Caroline, Feb 19 1923 Sex:F Child# 3 A Frank Arnold Greenville, NH & Beatrice Rochelle Providence, RI
ARNOLD, Patricia, Apr 20 1925 Sex:F Child# 2 Ralph Arnold Somerville, MA & Mildred Howe Ipswich, MA
ARNOLD, Ralph C, Oct 27 1923 Sex:M Child# 1 Ralph C Arnold Somerville, MA & Mildred Howe Ipswich, MA
ARNOLD, Richard George, Sep 3 1923 Sex:M Child# 1 Edward Arnold Manchester, NH & Bertha E Pecker Nashua, NH
ARNOLD, Ruth Elaine, May 5 1919 Sex:F Child# 2 A Frank Arnold Greenville, NH & Beatrice Rochelle Providence, RI
ARNOLD, Unknown, May 8 1887 Sex:M Child# 2 Leory Arnold Conn & Emma A Millbury, CT
ARNOLD, Unknown, May 27 1893 Sex:M Child# 7 David B Arnold Haverhill & Annie Peters Mason, NH
ARNOLD, Unknown, May 9 1895 Sex:M Child# 8 David Arnold NH & Annie Peters Mason, NH
ARNOLD, Unknown, Oct 16 1900 Sex:M Child# 10 D B Arnold NH & Annie Peters Mason, NH
ARNOLD, Unknown, Dec 7 1902 Sex:F Child# 11 David B Arnold Derry, NH & Annie Peters Greenville, NH
ARNOLD, Unknown, Jan 8 1905 Sex:M Child# 12 David Arnold Greenville & Annie Peters Greenville, NH
ARONOW, Rita, Jul 19 1934 Sex:F Child# 2 Morris Aronow Poland, Russia & Rose Arnold Cirinski Poland, Russia
AROZIAN, Ovne, Aug 10 1908 Sex:F Child# 2 George A Arozian Armenia & Grace Berberian Armenia
ARPIN, Joseph Raymond, Jul 11 1915 Sex:M Child# 4 Pierre Arpin Burlington, VT & Georgianna Provencal Concord, NH
ARPIN, Lawrence, Feb 18 1923 Sex:M Child# 1 Arthur Arpin Willimantic, CT & Dorothy Martin Manchester, NH
ARSENAU, Unknown, Aug 12 1893 Sex:F Child# 4 Joseph Arsenau Canada & Reine Allard Canada  Stillborn
ARSENAULT, Arthur George, Oct 23 1917 Sex:M Child# 3 Fred J Arsenault New Brunswick & Annie Archambault Nashua, NH
ARSENAULT, Arthur Thomas Julien, Jul 3 1913 Sex:M Child# 1 Alf T Arsenault Canada & Annie Archambault Nashua, NH
ARSENAULT, Azilie, Jun 8 1896 Sex:F Child# 2 Pierre Arsenault Canada & Emelie Alain Canada
ARSENAULT, Claudette, Apr 8 1935 Sex:M Child# 3 Alex Arsenault Canada & Marie A Marotte Nashua, NH
ARSENAULT, Irene Isabelle, Nov 28 1932 Sex:F Child# 2 Alex Arsenault Canada & Marie A Marotte Nashua, NH
ARSENAULT, Joseph Omer, Jan 17 1892 Sex:M Child# 1 Francis Arsenault Canada & Marie A Mercier Canada
ARSENAULT, Joseph Robert, Aug 25 1930 Sex:M Child# 1 Alexandre Arsenault Canada & Marie A Marotte Canada
ARSENAULT, Joseph Uldige, May 16 1893 Sex:M Child# 2 Frank Arsenault Canada & Mary A Mercier Canada
ARSENAULT, Mariella, Aug 1 1894 Sex:F Child# 1 Pierre Arsenault Canada & Emelie Allain Canada
ARSENAULT, Unknown, Feb 28 1892 Sex:x Child# 2 Joseph Arsenault Canada & Reine Allard Canada  Stillborn
ARSENAULT, Unknown, Feb 11 1915 Sex:M Child# 2 Fred J Arsenault Canada & Anna Archambeault Nashua, NH
ARSENEAU, Unknown, Feb 2 1893 Sex:M Child# 3 Joseph Arseneau Canada & Irene Allard Canada
ARSENEAU, Unknown, Mar 23 1894 Sex:M Child# 5 Joseph Arseneau Canada & Rene Allard Canada
ARSENEAU, Zoe Regina, Mar 15 1895 Sex:F Child# 6 Joseph Arseneau Canada & Rene Allard Canada
ARSMAN, Ipun, Oct 10 1912 Sex:M Child# 1 William Arsman Russia & Maggie Volouches Russia
ARTON, Marie Aime Carmen, Mar 18 1919 Sex:F Child# 2 Frank Arton Canada & Willimine Malenfant Canada
ARVALIS, Unknown, Aug 1 1924 Sex:M Child# 4 Vaselias G Arvalis Greece & Helen Adams Greece
ASCIN, William, Aug 19 1909 Sex:M Child# 3 Anthony Ascin Russia & Rosa Grigintie Russia
ASHE, Mary Elizabeth, Mar 5 1923 Sex:F Child# 1 Frank Ashe Spencer, MA & Alice Rock Nashua, NH
ASHE, Miriam Gertrude, Apr 3 1902 Sex:F Child# 6 Thomas J Ashe Holyoke, MA & Bridget Flynn Brookfield, MA
ASHE, Thomas Leo, Aug 30 1896 Sex:M Child# 5 Thomas J Ashe Holyoke, MA & Bridget E Flynn W Brookfield, MA
ASHLEY, Hope, Mar 7 1913 Sex:F Child# 1 Walter T Ashley Willimantic, CT & Isabelle Kennedy Somerville, MA Stillborn
ASHLEY, Thelma Elizabeth, Aug 28 1903 Sex:F Child# 3 Charles H Ashley NY & Mary Griswold Loraine, OH
ASHLEY, Thomas, Aug 29 1896 Sex:M Child# 3 George R H Ashley Lincolnshire, Eng & Annie Bowles Yorkshire, England
ASIMAKOPOULOS, Unknown, Jul 11 1929 Sex:M Child# 3 Rodis Asimakopoulos Greece & Zoitsa Tsakonas Greece
ASIMAKOPOULOS, Unknown, Jun 29 1931 Sex:M Child# 4 Rodis Asimakopoulos Greece & Zoetsa Tsacona Greece
ASIMAKOPULOS, Nik, Jan 26 1923 Sex:M Child# 1 Rodis Asimakopulos Greece & Zoitsa Tsakonas Greece
ASKHAM, Frances Amy, Jun 3 1914 Sex:F Child# 4 William Askham Eli Yorkshire, Eng & Florence L Middleton England
ASKHAM, Frank, Apr 9 1917 Sex:M Child# 5 William Askham Sheffield, England & Florence L Middleton Sheffield, Eng
ASPINALL, Marilyn Rae, Sep 3 1922 Sex:F Child# 5 Edward Aspinall Southington, CT & Emma Livingston Southington
ASPYG, Vaspar, Jun 8 1919 Sex:F Child# 1 Costas Aspyg Greece & Evangeli Styko Greece
ASSELIN, Camille Auralia, Oct 20 1895 Sex:F Child# 2 Henri V Asselin Canada & Mary L A Bougard E Douglas, MA
ASSELIN, Camille Henri, Oct 20 1895 Sex:M Child# 1 Henri V Asselin Canada & Mary L A Bougard E Douglas, MA
ASSELIN, Delima, Dec 19 1901 Sex:F Child# 8 Mathias Asselin Canada & Elodie Bathalon Canada
ASSELIN, Edith Lucille, Oct 5 1916 Sex:F Child# 5 Arthur Asselin Canada & Demerise Lachance Canada
ASSELIN, Germaine Irene, Sep 25 1922 Sex:F Child# 2 Emile Asselin Canada & Rose Nadeau Canada
ASSELIN, Jean Bap Louis, Jan 27 1914 Sex:M Child# 4 Arthur Asselin Canada & Demerise Lafrance Canada
ASSELIN, Jos Ernest Roger, May 4 1929 Sex:M Child# 7 Emile Asselin Canada & Rose Nadeau Canada
ASSELIN, Joseph Adrien, Nov 21 1908 Sex:M Child# 2 Arthur Asselin Canada & Demerise Lachance Canada
ASSELIN, Joseph Albert, Nov 14 1913 Sex:M Child# 1 Matthias Asselin Canada & Corona Robidoux Canada
ASSELIN, Joseph Henry, Jul 10 1912 Sex:M Child# 12 Joseph Asselin Canada & Antoinette Faubert Canada
ASSELIN, Leona Rachelle, May 19 1928 Sex:F Child# 6 Emile Asselin Canada & Rose Nadeau Canada
ASSELIN, Marguerite A A, Jun 19 1897 Sex:F Child# 3 Henry V Asselin Canada & Mary E Bougard E Douglass, MA

ASSELIN, Marie Aldea D, Mar 1 1905 Sex:F Child# 7 Joseph Asselin Canada & Antoinette Faubert Canada
ASSELIN, Rita Lydia, Aug 18 1921 Sex:F Child# 1 Emile Asselin Canada & Rose Nadeau Canada
ASSELIN, Marie Rose L, Oct 18 1906 Sex:F Child# 8 Joseph Asselin Canada & Antoinette Faubert Canada
ASSELIN, Mary Gertrude, Jun 27 1911 Sex:F Child# 11 Joseph Asselin Canada & Antoinette Faubert Canada
ASSELIN, Mary R Beatrice, Dec 18 1898 Sex:F Child# 4 Henry V Asselin Canada & Mary A Bougard E Douglas, MA
ASSELIN, Mary Rose A L, Nov 19 1908 Sex:F Child# 9 Joseph Asselin Canada & Antoinette Faubert Canada
ASSELIN, Raymond R, Feb 14 1925 Sex:M Child# 4 Emile Asselin Canada & Rose Nadeau Canada
ASSELIN, Rosario Ovide, Feb 28 1924 Sex:M Child# 3 Emile Asselin Canada & Rose Nadeau Canada
ASSELIN, Rose Eva, Oct 20 1910 Sex:F Child# 3 Arthur Asselin Canada & Demerise Lachance Canada
ASSELIN, Stuart Henry, Apr 13 1906 Sex:M Child# 1 Henry V Asselin Canada & Ella M Nagle London, England
ASSELIN, Theresa Lucille, Dec 5 1926 Sex:F Child# 5 Emile Asselin Canada & Rose Nadeau Canada
ASTENAS, Demetrula, May 11 1918 Sex:F Child# 4 George Astenas Greece & Trigora Demetrios Greece
ASTERION, Rose, Apr 7 1917 Sex:F Child# 3 George Asterion Greece & Trigona Argelon Greece
ATHANASCOYOPOLO, Spiros, Jun 27 1916 Sex:M Child# 3 A Athanascoyopolo Greece & Doria Ghirico Greece
ATHERTON, Deborah, May 9 1933 Sex:F Child# 3 Blaylock Atherton Nashua, NH & K Bremner Boston, MA
ATHERTON, Ives, Feb 25 1903 Sex:M Child# 2 Henry B Atherton Cavendish, VT & Ella Blaylock England
ATHERTON, Janet, Jul 12 1930 Sex:F Child# 2 Blaylock Atherton Nashua, NH & Katherine E Bremner Roxbury, MA
ATHERTON, Joan, Jul 1 1934 Sex:F Child# 1 Harlan E Atherton Wilton, NH & Dorothy Goodrich Benson, VT
ATHERTON, Nancy Jean, Sep 12 1925 Sex:F Child# 1 Blaylock Atherton Nashua, NH & Kath Bremner Roxbury, MA
ATHERTON, Selwyn Ives, Dec 11 1929 Sex:M Child# 1 Ives Atherton Nashua, NH & Doris White W Medford, MA
ATKINSON, Stephen Edward, Sep 3 1933 Sex:M Child# 1 C B Atkinson Nova Scotia & Minnie French Wells, ME
ATKINSON, Unknown, Jul 27 1905 Sex:M Child# 2 William E Atkinson England & Helen Wilson Natick, MA  Stillborn
ATTRIDGE, Elizabeth Eislene, Feb 9 1918 Sex:F Child# 2 Joseph Attridge E Pepperell, MA & Elizabeth B Kennedy
ATTRIDGE, Jane, Oct 9 1921 Sex:F Child# 3 Joseph F Attridge Pepperell, MA & Elizabeth B Kennedy Boston, MA
ATWELL, Jasper Morgan, Jun 19 1927 Sex:M Child# 1 Warren Atwell Nova Scotia & Elizabeth Morgan Scotland
ATWOOD, Allene Glee, Feb 3 1907 Sex:F Child# 1 Frank S Atwood Dexter, MI & May Ethel Dustin Lee, NH
ATWOOD, Paul Caldwell, Apr 12 1910 Sex:M Child# 1 Fred B Atwood Dexter, Michigan & Blanche Caldwell Concord, NH
ATWOOD, Ruth Elizabeth, Jun 16 1911 Sex:F Child# 2 Fred B Atwood Dexter, MI & Blanche Caldwell Concord, NH
ATWOOD, Virginia Victoria, Sep 25 1910 Sex:F Child# 1 Clarence Atwood Nashua, NH & Ada Fudge St Johns, NB
AUBBUT, Joseph Victor R, Oct 4 1905 Sex:M Child# 1 Remi Aubbut Canada & Anna Roy Canada
AUBERT, Joseph Wilfrid, Oct 6 1905 Sex:M Child# 3 Napoleon Aubert Canada & Marie Vion Canada
AUBERTINE, Claude Ernest, Jun 18 1896 Sex:M Child# 1 Charles Aubertine Canada & Edith Metott New York
AUBERTINE, George, Aug 26 1906 Sex:M Child# 2 William Aubertine Nashua, NH & Mary McCarthy Pepperell, MA
AUBERTINE, Unknown, Mar 3 1891 Sex:F Child# 3 Moses P Aubertine Vermont & Margaret Whalen Ireland
AUBERTINE, William, Aug 26 1906 Sex:M Child# 1 William Aubertine Nashua, NH & Mary McCarthy Pepperell, MA
AUBIN, Edouard John, Jul 22 1918 Sex:M Child# 5 Edouard Aubin New York & Georgianna Marquis Nashua, NH
AUBIN, Joseph Alfred A, Nov 12 1905 Sex:M Child# 4 Augustin Aubin New York & Rose D Paradis Canada
AUBIN, Joseph Augustin S A, Jun 14 1901 Sex:M Child# 3 Augustin Aubin New York & Delvina Paradis Canada
AUBIN, Joseph Henri A, Nov 18 1908 Sex:M Child# 1 Joseph Aubin New York & Marie Gendron Canada
AUBIN, Marie Cecile Eva, Mar 8 1899 Sex:F Child# 2 Augustin Aubin Plattsburg, NY & Rose Delima Paradis Canada
AUBIN, Marie R Delima, Feb 13 1898 Sex:F Child# 1 Augustin Aubin Plattsburg, NY & Rose Delima Paradis Canada
AUBIN, Robert Ernest, Mar 6 1917 Sex:M Child# 3 Joseph Aubin Nashua, NH & Marie Gendron Canada
AUBIN, William Raymond, Mar 27 1910 Sex:M Child# 1 Eddie Aubin Plattsburg, NY & Georgianna Marquis Canada
AUBUT, Adrien Albert, Jan 12 1912 Sex:M Child# 6 Remie Aubut Canada & Anna Roy Canada
AUBUT, Albert, Sep 28 1916 Sex:M Child# 6 Remi Aubut Nashua, NH & Anna Roy Canada
AUBUT, George, Aug 10 1895 Sex:F Child# 1 Joseph Aubut Canada & Philomene Marquis Canada
AUBUT, Joseph Arthur, Aug 18 1904 Sex:M Child# 2 Napoleon Aubut Canada & Desanges Vion Canada
AUBUT, Joseph N, Apr 18 1903 Sex:M Child#  Napoleon Aubut Canada & Desanges Vion Canada
AUBUT, Joseph R V O, May 7 1908 Sex:M Child# 1 Victor Aubut Canada & Corinne Piche Canada
AUBUT, Joseph Thomas T, Mar 19 1909 Sex:M Child# 3 Remi Aubut Canada & Anna Roy Canada
AUBUT, Julia Isabelle, Oct 14 1921 Sex:F Child# 7 Remie Aubut Canada & Anna Roy Canada
AUBUT, Laura, Aug 2 1896 Sex:F Child# 2 James Aubut Canada & Alphonsine Marquis Canada
AUBUT, M Eugenie Ivon, Sep 21 1913 Sex:F Child# 7 Napoleon Aubut Canada & Desanges Vion Canada
AUBUT, M L Adelaide, Feb 21 1907 Sex:F Child# 2 Remi Aubut Canada & Anna Roy Canada
AUBUT, Marie Bernadette, Sep 11 1910 Sex:F Child# 4 Remi Aubut Canada & Anna Roy Canada
AUBUT, Marie Claire, Mar 10 1934 Sex:F Child# 1 Adelard Aubut US & Irene Girouard US
AUBUT, Marie J Victoria, Feb 1 1919 Sex:F Child# 8 Remi Aubut Canada & Anna Roy Canada
AUBUT, Marie L Elaine, Jun 16 1931 Sex:F Child# 1 Arthur Aubut Nashua, NH & Ina Isabelle Nashua, NH
AUBUT, Marie Louise, Jun 13 1909 Sex:F Child# 5 Napoleon Aubut Canada & Malvina Dion Canada
AUBUT, Marie Rose, May 1 1907 Sex:F Child# 4 Napoleon Aubut Canada & Desanges Vion Canada
AUBUT, Marie Rose, May 26 1914 Sex:F Child# 6 Remi Aubut Canada & Anna Roy Canada
AUBUT, Raymond, Dec 26 1922 Sex:M Child# 12 Rene Aubut Canada & Anna Roy Canada
AUBUT, Romeo Lionel, Oct 14 1921 Sex:M Child# 8 Remie Aubut Canada & Anna Roy Canada
AUBUT, Sylvio Romeo, Apr 6 1920 Sex:M Child# 7 Remi Aubut Canada & Anna Roy Canada
AUBUT, Theodore Victor, Oct 24 1934 Sex:M Child# 1 Theodore Aubut Nashua, NH & Lea Cloutier Nashua, NH
AUBUT, Unknown, Jan 19 1924 Sex:F Child# 13 Rene Aubut Canada & Anna Roy Canada  Stillborn
AUCCANT, Blanche, Apr 19 1906 Sex:F Child# 2 Antoine Auccant Canada & Albertine Paulus Canada
AUCLAIR, Aimee Jacques, Jul 14 1932 Sex:M Child# 4 Aimee Auclair Nashua, NH & Laura Kerouac Nashua, NH
AUCLAIR, Armand, Aug 26 1912 Sex:M Child# 14 Dennis Auclair Canada & Clara Roy Canada
AUCLAIR, Aurore Jacqueline, Jul 14 1932 Sex:F Child# 3 Aimee Auclair Nashua, NH & Laura Kerouac Nashua, NH
AUCLAIR, Cecile, Oct 20 1897 Sex:F Child# 8 Antime Auclair Canada & Malvina Messier Canada
AUCLAIR, Charles Edward, May 2 1918 Sex:M Child# 2 William J Auclair Turner Falls, MA & Elizabeth McCarron Jogg
AUCLAIR, Corinne Laurette, Jun 19 1911 Sex:F Child# 13 Dennis Auclair Canada & Clara Roy Canada

AUCLAIR, Donald Albert, Dec 12 1934 Sex:M Child# 5 Aime Auclair Nashua, NH & Laura Kerouac Nashua, NH
AUCLAIR, Elizabeth Eveline, Jan 19 1915 Sex:F Child# 1 W J Auclair Turners Falls, MA & Elizabeth McCarron Jogg
AUCLAIR, Honorine Alice, Aug 4 1906 Sex:F Child# 10 Denis Auclair Canada & Clara Roy Canada
AUCLAIR, John Gilmary, Sep 20 1908 Sex:M Child# 1 Joseph E Auclair Canada & Nellie A Shea Nashua, NH
AUCLAIR, Joseph, Jun 18 1928 Sex:M Child# 1 Aime R Auclair Nashua, NH & Laura Kerouac Nashua, NH  Stillborn
AUCLAIR, Joseph Henri F, Mar 5 1893 Sex:M Child# 6 Antrine Auclair Canada & Malvina Messier Canada
AUCLAIR, Joseph Jean B, Jul 27 1909 Sex:M Child# 12 Denis Auclair Canada & Clara Roy Canada
AUCLAIR, Joseph Romeo A, Jun 26 1905 Sex:M Child# 9 Denis Auclair Canada & Clara Roy Canada
AUCLAIR, Laura Alice Zepherin, Aug 27 1929 Sex:F Child# 2 Aime Auclair Nashua, NH & Laura Kerouac Nashua, NH
AUCLAIR, Leon Lucien, Dec 17 1913 Sex:M Child# 15 Denis Auclair Canada & Clara Roy Canada
AUCLAIR, Robert, Jan 3 1911 Sex:M Child# 3 Peter Auclair Canada & Nellie Shea Nashua, NH
AUCLAIR, William J, Jr, Oct 26 1916 Sex:M Child# 2 William Auclair Turners Falls, MA & Elizabeth McCarron Jogg
AUCTIL, Georgina, Feb 23 1894 Sex:F Child# Arsene Auctil Canada & Caroline Ouelette Canada
AUCTIL, Joseph, Jun 18 1894 Sex:M Child# 2 T Auctil Canada & Emeline St Onge Canada
AUCTIL, Joseph, Jun 2 1895 Sex:M Child# 1 Edmond Auctil Canada & Marie L'emmeril Fall River, MA
AUCTIL, Joseph Arthur, Jun 9 1899 Sex:M Child# 7 Baptiste S J Auctil Canada & Zelie Belanger Canada
AUCTIL, Lilian Leonie, May 2 1899 Sex:F Child# 4 Edmond Auctil Canada & Marie Lemeris Fall River, MA
AUCTIL, Rheaume P, Nov 30 1897 Sex:M Child# 3 Edmond Auctil Canada & Marie Lemeris Nashua, NH
AUDAIS, Hermidas A, Oct 5 1887 Sex:M Child# 2 Hermidas Audais Canada & Helene Patiente Canada
AUDETTE, Charles Martin, Sep 1 1929 Sex:M Child# 1 Charles A Audette Fall River, MA & Edna O Kerouac Nashua, NH
AUDETTE, Mary Marcelina, May 26 1922 Sex:F Child# 2 Ernest Audette Canada & Eva Catineau Canada
AUDETTE, Romeo, Oct 25 1925 Sex:M Child# 4 Romeo Audette Canada & Edna Desautel Vermont
AUDETTE, Wilfred Joseph, May 1 1926 Sex:M Child# 1 Wilfred Audette E Douglas, MA & Estelle Matati Nashua, NH
AUFGIN, Bernard, Nov 25 1910 Sex:M Child# 3 Watson Aufgin Russia & Stanilaus Vincey Russia
AUFGIN, Charles, Jan 21 1910 Sex:M Child# 3 Frank Aufgin Russia & Tofiela Bauslage Russia
AUFGIN, Helen, Oct 4 1911 Sex:F Child# 4 Frank Aufgin Russia & Tophelia Advert Russia
AUGANAS, Anna, Jun 19 1918 Sex:F Child# 1 Andrew Auganas Russia & Zophia Obar Russia
AUGERS, Rose Alberta, Jun 22 1901 Sex:F Child# 4 Joseph Augers Canada & Albina Fontaine Canada
AUGUM, Vaclaw, Nov 21 1915 Sex:M Child# 1 Vladislaw Augum Russia & Mary Naijko Russia
AUGUN, John, Jun 15 1917 Sex:M Child# 3 Charles Augun Russia & Alexandria Prunawich Russia
AUGUN, Joseph, Jan 17 1914 Sex:M Child# 1 Sylvester Augun Russia & Elizabeth Mekenic Russia
AUGUNAS, Vigina, Sep 6 1923 Sex:F Child# 5 Joseph Augunas Russia & Ursula Giggas Russia  Stillborn
AUGUS, Unknown, Dec 31 1911 Sex:M Child# 1 Canada & Angeline Augus Canada  Stillborn
AUGUSTIN, Phyllis Mae, Jun 1 1921 Sex:F Child# 1 Ralph Augustin Wilton, NH & Rachel Barker Antrim, NH
AULD, Douglass William, Dec 26 1919 Sex:M Child# 2 Gilbert S Auld Scotland & Ethel Corrine Black Vinalhaven, MA
AUSAINT, Joseph Jean, May 9 1898 Sex:M Child# 1 Alexandre Ausaint Canada & Delima Bibeau Canada
AUSAINT, Joseph Paul E, Mar 16 1900 Sex:M Child# 2 Alexandre Ausaint Canada & Delima Bibeau Canada
AUSAINT, Marie Eva Irene, Apr 9 1904 Sex:F Child# 5 Alex Ausaint Canada & Delima Bibeau Canada
AUSAINT, Marie L Alma, Aug 31 1901 Sex:F Child# 3 Alexandre Ausaint Canada & Delima Bibeau Canada
AUSAINT, Marie Laura, Dec 21 1902 Sex:F Child# 4 Alexandre Ausaint Canada & Delima Bibeau Canada
AUSTIN, Albert Henry, Feb 4 1907 Sex:M Child# 2 Charles H Austin Hollis, NH & Catherine Shanahan Nashua, NH
AUSTIN, Austin, Jul 12 1889 Sex:F Child# 2 Charles Austin Charlestown, MA & Ella Wilson Nashua, NH
AUSTIN, Austin, May 18 1890 Sex:M Child# 2 Arthur C Austin San Francisco, CA & Emma Freeman Duxbury, MA
AUSTIN, Charles F, May 12 1874 Sex:M Child# 2 Mark J Austin Hollis & Agnes J Nashua, NH
AUSTIN, Charles, Jr, Sep 4 1923 Sex:M Child# 1 Charles Austin Maine & Annie L Lulia Mass  Stillborn
AUSTIN, George Albert, Nov 28 1910 Sex:M Child# 1 Arthur L Austin
AUSTIN, Gertrude Millicent, Dec 20 1922 Sex:F Child# 2 Franklin R Austin Canada & Marion Doris Cady Canada
AUSTIN, Grace Lillian, Jul 29 1892 Sex:F Child# 2 Charles H Austin Manchester, NH & Amanda Smith Londonderry, NH
AUSTIN, Hattie C, Dec 11 1871 Sex:F Child# 1 Mark J Austin Hollis & Agnes J Nashua, NH
AUSTIN, Jewel Ann, Nov 16 1933 Sex:F Child# 1 F R Austin Iron Hill, PQ & Hazel M Jewell Hudson, NH
AUSTIN, Kenneth LeRoy, Apr 14 1896 Sex:M Child# 1 A A Austin NH & Mary A Moulton Canada
AUSTIN, Laura, Apr 21 1898 Sex:F Child# 2 A A Austin NH & Mary A Moulton Canada
AUSTIN, Mabel Ruth, Aug 7 1905 Sex:F Child# 1 Charles H Austin Hollis, NH & Catherine Shannahan Nashua, NH
AUSTIN, Margaret Louise, Nov 29 1926 Sex:F Child# 2 George Austin Linden, VT & Irene Young Lisbon, NH
AUSTIN, Phyllis Eva, Jun 4 1924 Sex:F Child# 1 George Austin Lyndonville, VT & Irene Young Lisbon, NH
AUSTIN, Ralph, Jan 23 1921 Sex:M Child# 2 Arthur Austin
AUSTIN, Robert, Jan 23 1921 Sex:M Child# 1 Arthur Austin
AUSTIN, Ruth, Nov 30 1920 Sex:F Child# 1 Frank Austin Canada & Marion Cady Canada
AUSTIN, Unknown, Apr 26 1887 Sex:M Child# 1 Arthur C Austin San Francisco & E A Freeman Danbury, MA
AUTAYA, Louis A, Aug 12 1897 Sex:M Child# 6 Louis Autaya Canada & Louise St Michel Canada
AUTAYA, Marie Alice, May 1 1897 Sex:F Child# 6 Narcisse Autaya Canada & Arzelie Beland Nashua, NH
AUTAYA, Uldege, May 8 1896 Sex:M Child# 5 Louis Autaya Canada & Louise St Michel Canada
AUTIL, Marie A E, May 27 1896 Sex:F Child# 2 Edmond Autil Canada & Mary Lemery Fall River, MA
AVARD, Arthur Hervey, Sep 11 1909 Sex:M Child# 3 Philias Avard US & Nellie Gervais US
AVARD, Blanche May, Dec 17 1901 Sex:F Child# Ezra Avard Nashua, NH & Mathilda McMartin New York
AVARD, Dana, Jul 22 1920 Sex:M Child# 6 Philip Avard Nashua, NH & Nellie Jarvais Malone, NY  Stillborn
AVARD, Edouard Amedee, Mar 27 1904 Sex:M Child# 2 Elzear Avard Nashua, NH & Mathilda McMartin Sciota, NY
AVARD, Irene Isabelle, Apr 21 1904 Sex:F Child# 1 Amedie Avard Nashua, NH & Minnie Peltier Canada
AVARD, Joanne Valerie, Jan 11 1935 Sex:F Child# 3 Walter Avard Nashua, NH & Yvonne Dumaine Nashua, NH
AVARD, Joseph Adelard, Apr 24 1899 Sex:M Child# 4 Charles Avard RI & Beatrice Jalbert Canada
AVARD, Joseph Maurice, May 28 1908 Sex:M Child# 2 Philias Avard NH & Nellie Gervais NY
AVARD, Joseph Raymond, May 6 1920 Sex:M Child# 1 Albert N Avard Nashua, NH & Alice Dube Nashua, NH
AVARD, Lucille T Marie, Apr 27 1931 Sex:F Child# 2 Albert Avard Nashua, NH & Alice Dube Nashua, NH

AVARD, Marie, Jun 10 1900 Sex:F Child# 5 Charles Avard Nashua, NH & Beatrice Julbert Canada
AVARD, Marie Jeannette, Jan 31 1911 Sex:F Child# 4 Philias Avard NH & Nellie Gervais New York
AVARD, Marie Rosanna, Jan 11 1901 Sex:F Child# 1 Alfred Avard Woonsocket, RI & Clerina Emond St Albans, VT
AVARD, Noel Albert, Dec 25 1899 Sex:M Child# 1 Albert Avard Nashua, NH & Marie Dery Lowell, MA
AVARD, Olivette Mary, Sep 21 1912 Sex:F Child# 5 Philip I Avard Nashua, NH & Nellie Jarvis Malone, NY
AVARD, Teresa, Feb 23 1922 Sex:F Child# 7 Philip Avard Nashua, NH & Nellie Gervais Malone, NY
AVARD, Walter Philias, Feb 1 1907 Sex:M Child# 1 Philias Avard US & Elizabeth Gervais US
AVERILL, Catherine, Aug 25 1917 Sex:F Child# 2 Howard Averill Nashua, NH & Lillian Murphy Mass
AVERILL, Theresa Ilene, Jun 20 1915 Sex:F Child# 1 Howard F Averill Williamstown, VT & Lillian Murphy Somerville,MA
AVERY, Arnold Bruce, Apr 20 1934 Sex:M Child# 2 Frederick C Avery Sunapee, NH & Lina Sanborn Sunapee, NH
AVERY, Emma Alice, Nov 14 1915 Sex:F Child# 4 Sherwood Avery NH & Jennie Hickey Somerville, MA
AVERY, Eva, Nov 4 1934 Sex:F Child# 1 Albert Avery Nashua, NH & Eva Donah Nashua, NH
AVERY, Joseph, Mar 22 1914 Sex:M Child# 1 George Avery Nashua, NH & Angeline Vallee Nashua, NH  Stillborn
AVERY, Mandena Augusta, Aug 15 1917 Sex:F Child# 6 Sherwood F Avery Wilton, NH & Jennie May Hickey Somerville, MA
AVERY, Marie Rose L, Feb 4 1912 Sex:F Child# 1 George C Avery Nashua, NH & Angelina Valley Nashua, NH
AVERY, Sherwood Morrill, May 20 1914 Sex:M Child# 2 Sherwood F Avery Wilton, NH & Jennie Hickey Somerville, MA
AVERY, Unknown, Apr 12 1887 Sex:M Child# 2 Charles H Avery Weare & Ida L Hussey Nashua, NH
AVERY, Unknown, Oct 20 1894 Sex:M Child# 3 Charles H Avery Weare & Ida L Hussey Nashua, NH Stillborn
AVERY, Unknown, Jan 9 1907 Sex:F Child# 1 Sherwood F Avery Wilton, NH & Lilla H Jones Nashua, NH
AVERY, Unknown, May 29 1910 Sex:F Child# 2 Sherwood F Avery Wilton, NH & Lilla A Jones Nashua, NH
AWEGELOTOS, Unknown, May 1 1916 Sex:M Child# 2 Polech Awegelotos Greece & Polexene Granopoulos Greece
AWGON, Valeria, Jul 7 1906 Sex:F Child# 1 Frank Awgon Russia & Theophilo Edwart Russia
AWILIN, Basilio, Jul 7 1917 Sex:F Child# 1 William Awilin Greece & Alice Adams Greece
AXTON, Joseph Julius, Mar 18 1914 Sex:M Child# 3 John Axton Russia & Louise Glosiona Russia
AXTON, Julia, Jul 1 1916 Sex:F Child# 1 Paul Axton Russia & Sophia Arventach Russia
AXTON, Wytotius, Apr 8 1922 Sex:M Child# 3 Paul Axton Lithuania & Stephnie Aregurus Lithuania
AYER, Edson, Aug 12 1920 Sex:M Child# 2 Willis E Ayer Claremont, NH & Myrtie Sawyer Thetford, VT
AYER, Hazel Louise, Feb 15 1896 Sex:F Child# 1 Fernando P Ayer Claremont, NH & Sarah L Colby Sutton, NH
AYOTTE, Alfeda, Dec 24 1900 Sex:F Child# 6 Onesime Ayotte Canada & Ansulia Mongeau Canada
AYOTTE, Alfred, Jul 4 1894 Sex:M Child# 2 Inesime Ayotte Canada & Exilia Mongeau Canada
AYOTTE, Alfred Omer, Jan 15 1889 Sex:M Child# 1 A Ayotte Canada & Celia Mongeau Canada
AYOTTE, Armand, Mar 6 1897 Sex:M Child# 5 Onesime Ayotte Canada & Exilia Monjeau Canada
AYOTTE, Armand Roland, Nov 30 1916 Sex:M Child# 1 Omer Ayotte Nashua, NH & Alma Harbour Nashua, NH
AYOTTE, Elaine, Mar 22 1922 Sex:F Child# 3 Omer Ayotte Nashua, NH & Alma Harbour Nashua, NH
AYOTTE, Georges, Nov 17 1895 Sex:M Child# 3 Adelard Ayotte Canada & Adelina Bouchard US
AYOTTE, Lionel, Dec 10 1924 Sex:M Child# 4 Homer Ayotte Nashua, NH & Alma Harbour Nashua, NH
AYOTTE, M Louise R, Aug 3 1892 Sex:F Child# 3 Onesime Ayotte Canada & Ovilla Mongeau Canada
AYOTTE, Paul Robert, May 28 1919 Sex:M Child# 2 Omer Ayotte Nashua, NH & Alma Arbour Nashua, NH
AYOTTE, Rachael, Jun 22 1926 Sex:F Child# 6 Omer Ayotte Nashua, NH & Alma Harbour Nashua, NH
AYOTTE, Raymond Leo, Jun 29 1905 Sex:M Child# 7 Onesime Ayotte Canada & Exilia Mongeau Canada
AYOTTE, Rita, Jun 22 1926 Sex:F Child# 5 Omer Ayotte Nashua, NH & Alma Harbour Nashua, NH
AYOTTE, Theresa, Dec 2 1928 Sex:F Child# 7 Omer Ayotte Nashua, NH & Alma Arbour Nashua, NH
AZAKIAN, Mary A, Nov 3 1902 Sex:F Child# 5 Avatis Azakian Armenia & Rosanna Sarkatian Armenia
AZET, Alice, Dec 24 1896 Sex:F Child# 8 John Azet Canada & Liza Caron Canada
AZET, M R Therese, Feb 12 1894 Sex:F Child# 6 Paul Azet Canada & Rosanna Larivee Canada  Stillborn
BABBITT, Carol Millis, Jun 27 1924 Sex:F Child# 2 C H Babbitt Stoddard, NH & Mat Williamson Freeland, PA
BABBITT, Ethel Jean, Dec 15 1922 Sex:F Child# 1 Charles H Babbitt Stoddard, NH & Ethel Bernier Pennsylvania
BABIN, Lorraine, Nov 29 1896 Sex:F Child# 8 Alfred Babin Canada & Celia Dubrenil Canada
BABORIS, Annie, Jan 7 1922 Sex:F Child# 8 Barney Baboris Russia & Marcella Warculonis Russia
BACHE, Arthur Georges, Jan 9 1896 Sex:M Child# 2 Jules Bache France & Clara Goulet E Douglas, MA
BACHE, Theophile, Oct 7 1894 Sex:M Child# 1 Jules Bache France & Clara Gaulin E Douglass, MA
BACKANOSKI, Vitold, Jan 31 1911 Sex:M Child# 1 Peter Backanoski Russia & Elizabeth Volkavitch Russia
BACKER, Alphonse, Dec 1 1914 Sex:M Child# 7 Thomas Backer Russia & Walerka Lepescka Russia
BACKER, Julia, Jun 27 1915 Sex:F Child# 3 Julius Backer Russia & Aga Volontokawicz Russia
BACKER, Mary, Feb 9 1911 Sex:F Child# 2 Julius Backer Russia & Agae Valentukachutie Russia Stillborn
BACKER, Olga Pauline, Sep 29 1922 Sex:F Child# 8 Thomas Backer Lithuania & Vilma Lepeska Lithuania
BACKER, Stanislaus, Jul 11 1915 Sex:M Child# 6 William Backer Russia & Patronia Bartis Russia
BACKER, Thomas, Oct 19 1910 Sex:M Child# 5 Thomas Backer Russia & Valeria Lepeszkiute Russia
BACKER, Usta, May 16 1908 Sex:F Child# 4 Thomas Backer Russia & Valerica Lapiszkuta Russia
BACON, Electra Lucille, Nov 10 1917 Sex:F Child# 4 Euclid Bacon Salonica, Greece & Eva Leazotte Nashua, NH
BACON, Euclid Charles, May 3 1919 Sex:M Child# 5 Euclid Bacon Salonia, Greece & Eva Leazotte Nashua, NH
BACON, Lawrence, Sep 29 1916 Sex:M Child# 3 Euclid Bacon Salonica, Greece & Eva Leazotte Nashua, NH
BACON, Unknown, Mar 31 1915 Sex:F Child# 2 Euclid C Bacon Greece & Eva Leazotte Nashua, NH
BADA, Wanda, Aug 7 1910 Sex:F Child# 3 Alexander Bada Russia & Elizabeth Kocmna Russia
BADAIAN, Barbara Anne, Dec 14 1930 Sex:F Child# 5 Peter Badaian Armenia & Rose Markarian Nashua, NH
BADARYES, Nellie, May 7 1924 Sex:F Child# 4 Barney Badaryes Lithuania & Mar Walcomes Lithuania
BADEAU, Fabien Omer, Apr 24 1929 Sex:M Child# 10 Alphonse Badeau Concord, NH & Marie Lydia Tellier Canada
BADEAU, Jos Orphee Roger, Jul 7 1932 Sex:M Child# 11 A Badeau Concord, NH & M J Tellier Canada
BADEAU, Joseph Edgar, May 12 1922 Sex:M Child# 7 Alphonse Badeau NH & Marie Lydia Tellier Canada
BADEAU, Joseph Louis Julien, Nov 15 1919 Sex:M Child# 5 Alphonse Badeau Concord, NH & Maria Tellier Canada
BADEAU, Joseph Wilfrid, May 12 1922 Sex:M Child# 8 Alphonse Badeau NH & Marie Lydia Tellier Canada
BADEAU, Joseph Wilfrid Edgar, Mar 9 1927 Sex:M Child# 10 Alphonse Badeau NH & Marie L Tellier Canada
BADEAU, M Florida Lina, Feb 25 1921 Sex:F Child# 6 Alphonse Badeau Concord, NH & Maria Tellier Canada

BADEAU, Marie Anna Jacque, Sep 14 1923 Sex:F Child# 9 Alphonse Badeau NH & Maria Tellier Canada
BADEAU, Marie Clare Maybelle, May 5 1925 Sex:F Child# 10 Alphonse Badeau NH & Marie L Tellier Canada
BADEAU, Marie Juliette Justi, Sep 30 1918 Sex:F Child# 4 Alphonse Badeau NH & Marie Tellier Canada
BADEAU, Marie Rita Susienne, Nov 20 1916 Sex:F Child# 3 Alphonse Badeau Concord, NH & Marie Tellier Canada
BADGER, C Ernest John, Sep 2 1903 Sex:M Child# 2 George E Badger Manchester, NH & Nellie Coyne England
BADGER, James Bradford, Mar 5 1908 Sex:M Child# 3 George E Badger Manchester, NH & Nellie Coyne England
BADGER, Unknown, Sep 28 1887 Sex:F Child# 2 Henry E Badger Warner & Ann E Campbell Keeseville, NY
BADYS, Mary Anna, Jun 14 1915 Sex:F Child# 4 Barry Badys Russia & Marcelle Warcute Russia
BAEKER, Lydia, Jan 16 1927 Sex:F Child# 2 Adolph Baeker Lithuania & Eva Toula Lithuania
BAGDNOWICH, John, Jun 3 1904 Sex:M Child# 2 John Bagdnowich Russia & Agata Slanaoedis Russia
BAGDONIEUS, Rita, Feb 10 1925 Sex:F Child# 5 John Bagdonieus Lithuania & Levasia Berieuski Lithuania
BAGDONOWICZ, Agata, Sep 23 1908 Sex:f Child# 3 John Bagdonowicz Russia & Agata Douglass Russia
BAGLEY, Annie Udelia, Mar 27 1899 Sex:F Child# 1 George E Bagley Sunapee & Minnie F Wheeler Nashua, NH
BAGLEY, Charlotte Elaine, Apr 14 1926 Sex:F Child# 3 Gerald Bagley Lincoln, VT & C Robinson Hudson, NH
BAGLEY, Donald Robinson, Mar 4 1922 Sex:M Child# 2 Gerald Bagley Nashua, NH & Larueat Poulin Canada
BAGLEY, Elizabeth, Sep 12 1920 Sex:F Child# 1 Everett M Bagley Warner, NH & Lillian M Miller Londonderry, NH
BAGLEY, Ralph E, Jul 31 1895 Sex:M Child# 4 Elno Bagley NH & Sadie Sargent NH
BAGLEY, Rexford Earle, Aug 17 1902 Sex:M Child# 2 Elno Bagley Groton & Sadie E Sargent Milbrook
BAGLEY, Thelma B, Oct 15 1919 Sex:F Child# 1 Gerald W Bagley Lincoln, VT & Char E Robinson Hudson, NH
BAGLEY, Warren Thomas, Mar 30 1923 Sex:M Child# 2 Everett M Bagley Warner, NH & Lillian M Miller Londonderry, NH
BAGVADOSKI, Tadeus, May 9 1905 Sex:M Child# 2 Victor Bagvadoski Russia & Orzula Kostaska Russia
BAILEY, Albert Charles, Apr 3 1929 Sex:M Child# 1 Prescott Bailey Nashua, NH & Eva Rainville Nashua, NH
BAILEY, Albert James, Aug 2 1903 Sex:M Child# 2 Frank Bailey New York & Marie Bouchard Canada
BAILEY, Arleen, Feb 22 1913 Sex:F Child# 6 Frank H Bailey Nashua, NH & Georgie May Collins Lyon Mt, NY
BAILEY, Barbara Eleanor, Aug 27 1913 Sex:F Child# 2 Albert E Bailey Nashua, NH & Dora Conlon Boston, MA
BAILEY, Bertha May, May 25 1897 Sex:F Child# 3 Mason C Bailey Bradford, MA & Emma Porter NY
BAILEY, Blanche, Mar 22 1901 Sex:F Child# 1 Frank Bailey New York & Marie Bouchard Canada
BAILEY, Charles, Nov 20 1888 Sex:M Child# 1 S C Bailey Canada & Lillia Lewis Canada
BAILEY, Duane Allan, Jul 27 1929 Sex:M Child# 1 Merton Bailey Nashua, NH & Charlena Underhill Milford, NH
BAILEY, Edna P, Aug 29 1887 Sex:F Child# 3 Frank P Bailey Fisherville & Mary L Vincent Newport, VT
BAILEY, Ethel, Sep 9 1894 Sex:F Child# 4 Fred W Bailey Mass & Mary Emery NH
BAILEY, Everett Morgan, May 28 1935 Sex:M Child# 1 Winston H Bailey W Springfield, NH & Elizabeth Morgan Nashua, NH
BAILEY, Florence Edith, Dec 17 1899 Sex:F Child# 1 Frank P Bailey Nashua, NH & Susie S Bowers Nashua, NH
BAILEY, Fo Winston, May 1 1917 Sex:M Child# 4 Ethan L Bailey Milford, NH & Minnie Snyder Boston, MA
BAILEY, Grace Edna, Nov 21 1902 Sex:F Child# 3 Frank H Bailey Nashua, NH & Georgia M Collins NY
BAILEY, Helen Louise, Dec 6 1918 Sex:F Child# 3 Arthur Bailey Danver, VT & Mattie Salman St Johnsbury, VT
BAILEY, Herbert Alfred, Dec 19 1892 Sex:M Child# 2 Mason T Bailey Boscawen, NH & Emma J Parker Chazy, NY
BAILEY, Howard Henry, Jul 7 1909 Sex:M Child# 2 John W Bailey NH & Ethel Messer Mass
BAILEY, Ida, Mar 22 1888 Sex:F Child# 3 Charles P Bailey Nashua, NH & Anna Albeer Canada
BAILEY, James W, Jan 10 1911 Sex:M Child# 1 James W Bailey Nova Scotia & Florence Johnson Woburn, MA
BAILEY, Janice Emily, Apr 26 1924 Sex:F Child# 2 Herbert Bailey Nashua, NH & Rose Hunter Nashua, NH
BAILEY, Jos Clifford Normand, Apr 11 1932 Sex:M Child# 1 Clifford S Bailey Milford, NH & L E Marquis Nashua, NH
BAILEY, Louise Evelyn, Apr 24 1897 Sex:F Child# 4 Charles A Bailey Louisville, NY & Millicent A Bailey Potsdam
BAILEY, Mabel, Nov 21 1887 Sex:F Child# 3 Fred W Bailey Fitchburg & Mary I Peterboro
BAILEY, Mabel Messer, Mar 15 1907 Sex:F Child# 1 John W Bailey Dorchester, MA & Ethel Messer Lynn, MA
BAILEY, Malcolm Erwin, Feb 27 1933 Sex:M Child# 3 M C Bailey Nashua, NH & C Underhill Milford, NH
BAILEY, Marilyn Charlene, Oct 15 1931 Sex:F Child# 2 Merton Bailey Nashua, NH & Charlena Underhill Milford, NH
BAILEY, Mason, Jan 11 1921 Sex:M Child# 1 Herbert Bailey Nashua, NH & Rose Hunter Nashua, NH
BAILEY, Merton C, Mar 23 1901 Sex:M Child# 2 Frank H Bailey Nashua, NH & Georgie M Collins New York
BAILEY, Nancy Eleanor, Feb 3 1935 Sex:F Child# 2 Ralph H Bailey Nashua, NH & Doris Wilcox Nashua, NH
BAILEY, Nellie F, Jul 18 1904 Sex:F Child# 4 Frank H Bailey Canada & Georgia M Collins New York
BAILEY, Oliver Putney, Dec 8 1920 Sex:M Child# 5 Ethan L Bailey Canada & Rose Ducharme Pelham, NH
BAILEY, Prescott Albert, Dec 28 1909 Sex:M Child# 1 Albert E Bailey Nashua, NH & Dora G Conlon Boston, MA
BAILEY, Ralph H, May 20 1906 Sex:M Child# 5 Frank H Bailey Nashua, NH & Georgia M Collins New York
BAILEY, Roland Victor, Dec 11 1894 Sex:M Child# 3 Charles A Bailey Louisville, NY & Millicent Potsdam, NY
BAILEY, Unknown, Feb 9 1891 Sex:F Child# 1 Albert H Bailey Nashua, NH & Mabel A Fletcher Nashua, NH
BAILEY, Virginia Gilman, Aug 5 1911 Sex:F Child# 2 Albert H Bailey Nashua, NH & Mabel A Fletcher Nashua, NH
BAILEY, Wilmar, Jun 25 1909 Sex:M Child# 2 Wilmar Bailey
BAILEY, Winnifred M, Nov 1 1899 Sex:F Child# 1 F H Bailey Nashua, NH & Georgie N Collins NY
BAILLARGEON, Cecile Gratia, Sep 24 1910 Sex:F Child# 4 Thomas Baillargeon Canada & Mathilda Lavoie New York
BAILLARGEON, Joseph, Jun 8 1915 Sex:M Child#  Thomas Baillargeon Canada & Mathilde Lavoie Malone, NY
BAILLARGEON, Louis A, Aug 17 1899 Sex:M Child# 2 Pierre Baillargeon Canada & Exina Desmarais Canada
BAILLARGEON, Theresa Eugenie M L, Jun 9 1928 Sex:F Child# 6 Philias Baillargeon New Ipswich, NH & V Dancouse
BAILLARGEON, Wilfrid Albert, Mar 16 1914 Sex:M Child# 6 Thomas Baillargeon Canada & Mathilda Lavoie Malone, NY
BAILLIE, Dorothy L, Oct 14 1913 Sex:F Child# 2 Frank A Baillie Trear, Iowa & Ethelyn M Davis Nashua, NH
BAILLIE, Isabel May, Aug 4 1912 Sex:F Child# 1 Frank A Baillie Iowa & Ethel M Bailey Nashua, NH
BAIT, Corinne, Apr 25 1890 Sex:F Child# 1 Pierre Jean Bait Nashua, NH & Elonore Vadnais Canada
BAJOTTE, Marie Rosia, Aug 17 1898 Sex:F Child# 2 Felix Bajotte Canada & Epilda Bergeron Canada
BAKANAUSKAS, John, May 22 1912 Sex:M Child# 4 Julius Bakanauskas Russia & Agnes Vanlautukitie Russia
BAKANOSKI, Mary, Mar 12 1910 Sex:F Child# 2 William Bakanoski Russia & Mary Oliakavitch Russia
BAKANOSKI, William W, Feb 12 1913 Sex:F Child# 3 William W Bakanoski Russia & Mary Anleskawich Russia
BAKANOUCKAS, Kastantie, Aug 17 1903 Sex:F Child# 1 Thomas Bakanouckas Russia & Wal Lieperzkintie Russia
BAKANOUSKI, Nellie, Nov 10 1916 Sex:F Child# 4 William Bakanouski Russia & Mary Olescavitch Russia

BAKANOWSKAS, Hyacintha, Sep 17 1908 Sex:F Child# 1 Julius Bakanowskas Russia & Agate Valentukieut Russia
BAKANOWSKI, Julia, Oct 7 1913 Sex:F Child# 6 Thomas Bakanowski Russia & Waliska Lapiski Russia
BAKANOWSKI, Sophia, Aug 26 1907 Sex:F Child# 1 Wm Bakanowski Russia & Mary Aleskavitch Russia
BAKAUSKI, Joseph, Mar 15 1914 Sex:M Child# 4 Julius Bakauski Russia & Azea Valentukschute Russia
BAKER, Alden W, Apr 19 1895 Sex:M Child# 2 Arthur P Baker Colchester, CT & Abbie L Kimball Boston, MA
BAKER, Alfred, Sep 6 1901 Sex:M Child# 5 Alfred Baker New York & Mary Lane Ireland
BAKER, Alfred W, Apr 17 1893 Sex:M Child# 1 Arthur P Baker Colchester, CT & Abbie L Kimball Boston, MA
BAKER, Allan Elwin, Oct 2 1932 Sex:M Child# 4 Meyer Baker London, England & Eliz Fagerson Nashua, NH
BAKER, Arthur Theodore, Apr 8 1930 Sex:M Child# 3 Arthur T Baker Nashua, NH & Lorraine Dube Nashua, NH
BAKER, Baker, Jun 11 1889 Sex:M Child# 2 Wallace Baker Lowell, MA & Grace S Baker Webster, NH
BAKER, Barbara Ann, Jan 7 1929 Sex:F Child# 1 William Baker Nashua, NH & Mildred Kelley Sandown, NH
BAKER, Barbara Frances, Jun 22 1934 Sex:F Child# 4 Meyer Baker London, England & Elizabeth Fagerson Nashua, NH
BAKER, Beatrice Cecile, Aug 26 1918 Sex:F Child# 1 Andre A Baker Mooers, NY & Rosalie Dowling Nashua, NH
BAKER, Clair Loraine, Mar 12 1923 Sex:F Child# 2 Arthur Baker Nashua, NH & Loraine Dube Nashua, NH
BAKER, Diane Carol, May 22 1934 Sex:F Child# 1 Reuben J Baker Hudson, NH & Frances Maloney Schenectady, NY
BAKER, Dorothy Florette, Apr 14 1922 Sex:F Child# 3 Andrew Baker New York & Rosalie Dowling Nashua, NH
BAKER, Earle Frank, May 6 1896 Sex:M Child# 3 Frank H Baker Montgomery, VT & Ella Shedd Merrimack, NH
BAKER, Ellen Harriet, Dec 1 1893 Sex:F Child# 2 Alfred Baker NY & Mary Lane Ireland
BAKER, Etta M, Nov 21 1892 Sex:F Child# 1 W E P Baker Medford, MA & Abby M Cambridge, MA
BAKER, Evelyn, Mar 26 1913 Sex:F Child# 1 Frank Baker New York & Laura Rolo Nashua, NH
BAKER, Everett Ellsworth, Nov 10 1917 Sex:M Child# 3 Frank Baker New York & Laura Rolo Nashua, NH
BAKER, George Henri Vincent, Jan 22 1919 Sex:M Child# 1 Arthur T Baker Nashua, NH & Loraine Dube Nashua, NH
BAKER, Harold Abbot, Apr 7 1928 Sex:M Child# 2 Myer Baker London, England & Elizabeth Fargerson Nashua, NH
BAKER, Henry, Jan 31 1903 Sex:M Child# 4 H B Baker Worcester, MA & Nellie Burns Nashua, NH
BAKER, Henry Carl, Jr, Apr 22 1932 Sex:M Child# 1 Carl Baker Nashua, NH & L Bathalon Nashua, NH
BAKER, Jean Frances, Jun 2 1930 Sex:F Child# 2 Sidney Francis Baker Hudson, NH & Frances Slavin Nashua, NH
BAKER, Joan, Dec 8 1934 Sex:F Child# 1 Edgar Baker Pepperell, MA & Elizabeth Fisher Los Angeles, CA
BAKER, John Earl, Feb 25 1901 Sex:M Child# 1 William W Baker Hudson, NH & Sarah Oldhall Canada
BAKER, John Robert, Jan 21 1929 Sex:M Child# 1 Sidney F Baker Hudson, NH & Frances M Slavin Nashua, NH
BAKER, Joseph, Jul 15 1898 Sex:M Child# 1 Joseph Baker Canada & Elbertine Lachance Canada
BAKER, Joseph Burns, Apr 29 1898 Sex:M Child# Burnham Baker
BAKER, Katherine, Aug 14 1904 Sex:F Child# 5 Henry W Baker Worcester, MA & Nellie Burns Nashua, NH
BAKER, Laura, Sep 6 1901 Sex:F Child# 6 Alfred Baker New York & Mary Lane Ireland
BAKER, Leona M, Nov 16 1892 Sex:F Child# Walter A Baker Lowell, MA & L Grace Page NH
BAKER, Leonard Ronald, Feb 24 1934 Sex:M Child# 6 Andre Baker New York & Rosalie Dowling Nashua, NH
BAKER, Marion, May 11 1906 Sex:F Child# 6 Henry W Baker Worcester, MA & Nellie Burns Nashua, NH
BAKER, Marion Hills, Sep 20 1911 Sex:F Child# 4 Phoenix C Baker Chazy, NY & Luetta E Hills Hollis, NH
BAKER, Mary, Feb 20 1934 Sex:F Child# 1 William S Baker Scotland & Elizabeth Johnston Scotland Stillborn
BAKER, Mary Catherine, Jun 6 1892 Sex:F Child# 1 Albert Baker NY & Mary Lane Ireland
BAKER, Ralf Thornton, Jul 19 1897 Sex:M Child# 1 Henry W Baker Worcester, MA & Nellie May Burns Nashua, NH
BAKER, Raymond Andre, May 18 1920 Sex:M Child# 2 Andre A Baker Mooers Parks, NY & Roslie Dowling Nashua, NH
BAKER, Richard Donald, May 25 1931 Sex:M Child# 5 Andre Baker New York & Rosalie Dowling Nashua, NH
BAKER, Richard Donald, Dec 21 1935 Sex:M Child# 2 William S Baker Louisville, KY & Elizabeth Mooney Lowell, MA
BAKER, Rita Jeannette, Aug 26 1932 Sex:F Child# 2 Willard Baker Chazy Lake, NY & Irene Prince Southbridge, MA
BAKER, Robert Irving, Feb 26 1928 Sex:M Child# 4 Andrew Baker New York & Rosalie Downing Nashua, NH
BAKER, Roberta Lee, Sep 28 1934 Sex:F Child# 1 Robert Baker Manchester, NH & Dorothea Kimball Fitchburg, MA
BAKER, Shirley Ann, Oct 2 1929 Sex:F Child# 1 Wallace G Baker Hudson, NH & Helen Beatrice Worcester, MA
BAKER, Sumner Henry, Jun 27 1926 Sex:M Child# 2 Myer Baker London, England & Elizabeth Fagerson Nashua, NH
BAKER, Unknown, Mar 8 1888 Sex: Child# 2 Frank H Baker Montgomery, VT & Ella Shedd Merrimack, NH
BAKER, Unknown, Jun 9 1888 Sex:M Child# 1 Charles H Baker, Jr Saco, ME & Agnes Smith Nashua, NH
BAKER, Unknown, Sep 10 1888 Sex:F Child# 1 Fred W Baker Montgomery, Vt & Carlottie Griffith Winchendon, MA
BAKER, Unknown, Oct 27 1891 Sex:F Child# 1 P C Baker New York & Clara G Martin New York
BAKER, Unknown, Aug 14 1893 Sex:M Child# 8 Oscar Baker Whalen, NY & Phene Mignault Chazy, NY
BAKER, Unknown, Jul 14 1899 Sex:M Child# 2 Henry W Baker Worcester, MA & Nellie M Burns Nashua, NH
BAKER, Unknown, Jan 24 1902 Sex:M Child# 3 Henry W Baker Worcester, MA & Nettie Burns Nashua, NH
BAKER, Unknown, Apr 9 1914 Sex:M Child# 1 Adolph Baker Russia & Eva Trainontch Russia
BAKER, Unknown, Jun 26 1926 Sex:M Child# 1 Myer Baker London, England & Elizabeth Fagerson Nashua, NH
BAKER, Viola May, Dec 5 1914 Sex:F Child# 2 Frank Baker New York & Laura Rolo Nashua, NH
BAKER, William, Dec 26 1925 Sex:M Child# 1 Roy E Baker Pekin, IL & Elizabeth Nault Shirley, MA
BAKER, William Henry, Aug 4 1897 Sex:M Child# 4 Alfred Baker NY & Mary Lane Ireland
BAKER, William Wallace, Aug 31 1933 Sex:M Child# 2 Wallace Baker Hudson, NH & Beatrice Smith Worcester, MA
BAKIAN, Simpart, Apr 11 1903 Sex:M Child# 2 Michael Bakian Turkey & Rosa Josephson Turkey
BALAM, Peter, Jun 3 1934 Sex:M Child# 5 Vangel Balam Greece & Alexandria Callioras Greece
BALASKAS, Unknown, Nov 24 1919 Sex:M Child# 1 George Balaskas Greece & Zoe Desmakis Greece
BALASKY, Geraldine, Jul 3 1922 Sex:F Child# 1 William Balasky Russia & Lucy Ptralis Nashua, NH
BALASKY, Unknown, Aug 20 1927 Sex:F Child# 2 William Balasky Russia & Rosie Petrain Nashua, NH
BALASKY, William John, Jun 25 1929 Sex:M Child# 3 William Balasky Russia & Lucy Petralis Nashua, NH
BALCHIVITZ, Brown, Feb 5 1915 Sex:M Child# 3 Mike Blachivitz Russia & Austria
BALCOM, Evelyn Arlene, Feb 23 1907 Sex:F Child# 3 Fred Balcom Groton, MA & Emma Hills Hudson, NH
BALCOM, George Everett, Apr 27 1923 Sex:M Child# 1 Everett Balcom Nashua, NH & Ethel Willette Bay City, MI
BALCOM, Herbert Franklin, Nov 15 1893 Sex:M Child# 2 Fred M Balcom Mass & Emma F Hill Hudson, NH
BALCOM, Lillian Mabel, Apr 18 1921 Sex:F Child# 5 William E Balcom Groton, MA & Alice L Shattuck Nashua, NH
BALCOM, Louis F, Mar 26 1903 Sex:M Child# 11 Walter S Balcom Nashua, NH & Ella M Richardson Pembrook

BALCOM, Unknown, Dec 6 1891 Sex:F Child# 1 Fred M Balcom Groton, MA & Emma Hill Hudson, NH
BALCOM, Unknown, Sep 18 1893 Sex:M Child# 8 Scott Balcom Nashua, NH & E M Hurd Pembroke  Stillborn
BALCOM, Unknown, Sep 5 1894 Sex: Child# 2 Walter S Balcom Nashua, NH & Ella M Hurd Pembroke, NH  Stillborn
BALCOM, Unknown, Dec 31 1921 Sex:F Child# 2 David J Balcom Wilton, NH & Leah Pelletier Wilton, NH
BALDUC, Marie A, Mar 13 1891 Sex:F Child# 3 Louis Balduc Canada & Elmire Cote Canada
BALDWIN, Harold Jesse, Jan 17 1911 Sex:M Child# 1 Jesse B Baldwin Greenfield, NH & Edna T Savage Greenfield, NH
BALDWIN, Harold S, Aug 2 1905 Sex:M Child# 5 Harry Baldwin Nashua, NH & Lillian Spidell Nova Scotia
BALDWIN, Leslie H, Apr 3 1894 Sex:M Child#  Harry G Baldwin Nashua, NH & Lillian Spidell Nova Scotia
BALDWIN, Lida May, Nov 13 1896 Sex:F Child# 2 Harry S Baldwin Nashua, NH & Lillian Spidell Nova Scotia
BALDWIN, Lorraine E, Dec 4 1891 Sex:F Child# 1 Charles H Baldwin Nashua, NH & Minnie H Greeley Nashua, NH
BALDWIN, Raymond C, Mar 24 1902 Sex:M Child# 5 Harry S Baldwin Nashua, NH & L E Spidall Nova Scotia
BALDWIN, Ruth Eileen, Feb 2 1925 Sex:F Child# 1 Harold Baldwin Nashua, NH & Charlotte Crocket Medford, MA
BALDWIN, Unknown, Jan 15 1888 Sex:F Child# 4 Charles H Baldwin Nashua, NH & Amelia Brennan Chazy, NY
BALDWIN, Vera Lillian, Jul 19 1899 Sex:F  H S Baldwin Nashua, NH & L E Goodspeed Nashua, NH
BALEVICA, John, Dec 4 1908 Sex:M Child# 3 John Balevica Russia & Justina Ackstin Russia
BALEVICA, Julia, Sep 21 1906 Sex:F Child# 1 John Balevica Russia & Justina Akstin Russia
BALEVICA, Justina, Dec 4 1908 Sex:F Child# 2 John Balevica Russia & Justina Ackstin Russia
BALEVITCH, Joseph, Dec 14 1909 Sex:M Child# 4 John Balevitch Russia & Justina Ackstin Russia
BALL, Unknown, Oct 6 1899 Sex:M Child# 1 Warren Ball NY & Laura E Fitts NH
BALLAS, Unknown, Jun 3 1925 Sex:M Child# 4 George Ballas Greece & Zoitsa Greece
BALLOU, Conrad Victor, Apr 18 1926 Sex:M Child# 2 Theodore Ballou Romania & Eva Ekstrom Nashua, NH
BALLOU, Frank, Apr 18 1926 Sex:M Child# 1 Theodore Ballou Romania & Eva Ekstrom Nashua, NH
BALOAS, Unknown, Aug 24 1921 Sex:M Child#  Hartsios Baloas Greece & Abrakome Emanuel Greece
BALSAWICH, Alberta, Apr 16 1912 Sex:F Child# 1 Mike Balsawich Russia & Veronica Patkufka Russia
BALTCH, Mark M, Jul 22 1892 Sex:M Child# 3 Frederick Baltch Lowell, MA & Zenith Tewksbury, MA
BALUKONIS, Mary, Dec 23 1914 Sex:F Child# 3 Joseph Balukonis Russia & Ursula Cravlovich Russia
BALUKWICH, Eva, Aug 24 1918 Sex:F Child# 7 William Balukwich Russia & Eva Butchcoual Russia
BAMVILLE, Eva, Aug 6 1903 Sex:F Child# 4 John Bamville Vermont & Marie Blanchette Canada
BANARZKEWICZ, Melvina, Dec 20 1913 Sex:F Child# 2 Peter Banarzkewicz Russia & Melvina Alexza Russia
BANAS, John, Jan 21 1913 Sex:M Child# 1 Isidore Banas Austria & Apolina Agazebeck Austria
BANCROFT, Kenneth Albert, Aug 26 1916 Sex:M Child# 4 Fred L Bancroft Nashua, NH & Ida May Fitzgerald Nashua, NH
BANCROFT, Lloyd Englewood, Jan 10 1933 Sex:M Child# 1 L E Bancroft Hollis, NH & Catherine Straitiff Anita, PA
BANCROFT, Unknown, Jul 9 1894 Sex:M Child# 1 Fred S Bancroft Mass & Lulu G Gilson US
BANCROFT, Unknown, Dec 22 1908 Sex:M Child# 1 Frank W Bancroft Nashua, NH & Martha M Longlois Alburg, VT
BANDONIS, Annie, Mar 20 1915 Sex:F Child# 1 Adam Bandonis Russia & Helena Shirka Russia
BANFILL, Unknown, Aug 28 1904 Sex:M Child# 4 Willie S L Banfill Ossipee, NH & Rosa A Lafarge Richmond, CA
BANKAWSKI, Vladyslaw, Jul 6 1919 Sex:M Child# 5 Vladyslaw Bankawski Russia & Helena Kulavich Russia
BANKOFSKI, Stanley, Sep 11 1914 Sex:M Child# 3 Walter Bankofski Russia & Helena Holavich Russia
BANKOWSKI, Helen, Feb 5 1916 Sex:F Child# 4 Walter Bankowski Russia & Helen Kolalwac Russia
BANKS, Marie Laura, Mar 30 1930 Sex:F Child# 2 Joseph Banks Indiana & Victoria Labrecque Nashua, NH
BANUSKOWICUS, Joseph, Feb 2 1916 Sex:M Child# 4 Andrew Banuskowicus Russia & Mar Sclamoskotye Russia
BANVILLE, Blanche Cecile, Oct 3 1914 Sex:F Child# 5 Jean Banville Canada & Alphonsine Lebrun Canada
BANVILLE, Marie E, Dec 23 1900 Sex:F Child# 2 Achille Banville Canada & Elise Landry Canada
BANVILLE, Napoleon Adrien, Mar 24 1904 Sex:M Child# 1 Jean Banville Canada & Alphonsine Lebrun Canada
BANVILLE, Rose Aldea L, Jun 5 1907 Sex:F Child# 3 Jean Banville Canada & Alphonsine Lebrun Canada
BARABBE, Henri, Aug 23 1896 Sex:M Child# 9 Georges Barabbe US & Melanie Hebert Canada
BARABE, Albertine, Aug 31 1901 Sex:F Child# 6 Georges Barabe Canada & Anna Lacroix Canada
BARABE, Dora, Feb 23 1903 Sex:F Child# 14 George Barabe Canada & Melanie Hebert Canada
BARABE, Helene, May 9 1903 Sex:F Child# 7 George Barabe Canada & Anna Lacroix Canada
BARABY, Alfred Orlando, Apr 1 1919 Sex:M Child# 2 Alfred Baraby Canada & Minnie Oakman Nashua, NH
BARABY, Arthur, Jun 7 1899 Sex:M Child# 12 Georges Baraby Canada & Melanie Hebert Canada
BARABY, Edward, Mar 1 1920 Sex:M Child# 1 John Baraby Nashua, NH & Fanny Axton Lawrence, MA
BARABY, Evelina, Sep 25 1905 Sex:F Child# 15 George Baraby Canada & Melanise Hebert Canada
BARABY, Jean Jacob, Feb 27 1898 Sex:M Child# 11 Georges Baraby Canada & Melanie Hebert Canada
BARABY, Phyllis Catharine, Dec 19 1921 Sex:F Child# 3 Fred Baraby Canada & Minnie Oakman Nashua, NH
BARANAUZKUTIE, Anelka, Jul 10 1907 Sex:F Child# 2 J B Baranauzkutie Russia & Mary Sklutuz Russia
BARANAWSK, Urlina, Jan 14 1911 Sex:M Child# 4 Jonas Baranawsk Russia & Marie Sklinesiutil Russia
BARANAWSKAS, Julius, Nov 2 1913 Sex:M Child# 5 John Baranawskas Russia & Mare Sklinesiute Russia
BARANK, Mary, Sep 22 1918 Sex:F Child# 2 Peter Barank Russia & Adele Gervais Russia
BARANK, Stepana, May 31 1917 Sex:F Child# 1 Peter Barank Russia & Adele Gervis Russia
BARANOUSKAS, Antanas, Nov 8 1904 Sex:M Child# 1 John Baranouskas Russia & Marie Sklinscintie Russia
BARANOUSKY, Marcelia, Oct 25 1904 Sex:F Child# 2 Michael Baranousky Russia & Marcelia Kibirxute Russia
BARANOUSKY, Michael, Oct 25 1904 Sex:M Child# 1 Michael Baranousky Russia & Marcelia Kibirxute Russia
BARANUSKIE, Beverly Alice, Dec 10 1933 Sex:F Child# 2 A Baranuskie Nashua, NH & Bessie Eddy Nashua, NH
BARANUSKIE, Rita Elizabeth, Dec 22 1929 Sex:M Child# 1 Anthony Baranuskie Nashua, NH & Elizabeth Eddy Malone, NY
BARBEAU, Lorraine Ida, Oct 24 1924 Sex:F Child# 1 Albert Barbeau Lowell, MA & Aurore Gendron Pelham, NH
BARBER, Alfred, Jan 18 1909 Sex:M Child# 2 Clinton E Barber Saranac, NY & Lillian Belanger Three Rivers, MA
BARBER, Clarence Howard, Apr 22 1919 Sex:M Child# 2 Laurence L Barber Manchester, CT & Laura Bidwell Manchester
BARBER, Esther Childs, Jan 28 1892 Sex:F Child# 2 Frank H Barber Croydon, NH & Jennie Childs Concord, VT
BARBER, Louis Alfred, Jun 22 1920 Sex:M Child# 1 Louis O Barber Nashua, NH & Pearl C McDermott Brooklyn, NY
BARBER, Louis O, Jan 24 1900 Sex:M Child#  Alfred H Barber New York & A Dubray New York
BARBER, Lucille, Nov 13 1904 Sex:F Child# 10 Alfred H Barber NY & Celia Dubreauil NY
BARCIS, Autanas, Jan 15 1918 Sex:M Child# 1 Autanas Barcis Russia & Lucie Pukiezcinte Russia

BARCIS, Ogruna, Nov 2 1919 Sex:F Child# 2 Antonas Barcis Poland Russia & Lucia Pukiescuite Poland Russia
BARCIS, Peter, Jan 9 1907 Sex:M Child# 5 Nicholas Barcis Russia & Alava Sklukute Russia
BARCLAY, Robert McKinley, Mar 23 1906 Sex:M Child# 1 Harry J Barclay Lowell, MA & Florence M McKinley Nova Scotia
BARDAKAS, Unknown, Jun 27 1928 Sex:F Child# 1 H Bardakas Greece & Freta Podapalos Greece Stillborn
BARDAKOS, Helen, Sep 12 1929 Sex:F Child# 2 Harry Bardakos Greece & Freda Papadopoulos New York, NY
BARDAKOS, Unknown, May 20 1931 Sex:F Child# 3 Harry Bardakos Greece & Aphro Papadopoulos New York, NY
BARETTE, Alfred, Feb 5 1897 Sex:M Child# 1 Alfred Barette Canada & Edwidge Boutin Canada
BARIAULT, Alva Felix, Dec 14 1913 Sex:M Child# 4 Eugene Bariault Canada & Jeanne Deschenes Canada
BARIAULT, Germaine Amelia, Jan 21 1917 Sex:F Child# 5 Eugene Bariault Canada & Jeanne Deschenes Canada
BARIAULT, Helene Agnes, Jan 26 1923 Sex:F Child# 8 Eugene Bariault Canada & Jeanne Deschenes Canada
BARIAULT, Joseph, Aug 14 1919 Sex:M Child# 6 Eugene Bariault Canada & Jeanne Deschesnes Canada
BARIAULT, Joseph Leopold, Oct 5 1895 Sex:M Child# 9 Pierre Bariault Canada & Philomene Ouellette Canada
BARIAULT, Nora Lucille, Sep 11 1910 Sex:F Child# 3 Eugene Bariault Canada & Jeanne Deschenes Canada
BARIAULT, Robert, Sep 2 1909 Sex:M Child# 2 Eugene Bariault Canada & Jeanne Deschenes Canada
BARIE, Rose, Dec 5 1888 Sex:F Child# 1 Kenna Barie Canada & Arzilla Guertin Canada
BARIL, Albina, Sep 8 1889 Sex:F Child# 2 J B Baril Canada & Arthemise Ratte Canada
BARIL, Jean Bte, Oct 13 1887 Sex:M Child# Jean Bte Baril Canada & Arthemise Ratte Canada
BARIL, Joseph H Ovela, Aug 20 1896 Sex:M Child# 5 Jean Baptiste Baril Canada & Arthemise Rate Canada
BARIL, Marie Antoinette, Oct 25 1901 Sex:F Child# 10 Joseph Baril Canada & Radegoude Lavoie Canada
BARITEAU, Aime Joseph, Oct 31 1932 Sex:M Child# 3 Aime Bariteau Nashua, NH & H Starkweather Hancock, NH
BARITEAU, Caleb Nicholas, Mar 27 1934 Sex:M Child# 4 Aime Bariteau Nashua, NH & Harriet Starkweather Hancock, NH
BARITEAU, Dorothy Gertrude, Sep 24 1923 Sex:F Child# 3 Aim Bariteau Nashua, NH & Marion Morris E Boston, MA
BARITEAU, Francoise Leroy, Feb 14 1920 Sex:F Child# 1 Amie J Bariteau Nashua, NH & Mariane J Maurice E Boston, MA
BARITEAU, Joseph Morris, Apr 17 1921 Sex:M Child# 2 Aime J Bariteau Nashua, NH & Marion Morris S Boston, MA
BARITEAU, Marie D E, Sep 3 1896 Sex:F Child# 11 Antoine Bariteau Canada & Cordelia Roy Canada
BARKER, Allan Marsh, May 1 1923 Sex:M Child# 3 Walter L Barker Nashua, NH & Edith Marsh Winchester, MA
BARKER, Allen Francis, Sep 11 1907 Sex:M Child# 7 Allen F Barker Antrim, NH & Emma Duncklee Nashua, NH
BARKER, David Abbott, Jan 29 1923 Sex:M Child# 1 Herman Barker Nashua, NH & Helen Abbott Derry, NH
BARKER, Donald, Mar 5 1915 Sex:M Child# 1 Walter L Barker Nashua, NH & Edith Marsh Winchester, MA Stillborn
BARKER, Edith May, Oct 31 1900 Sex:F Child# 3 E L Barker NH & Jennie M Ellis NH
BARKER, Harold R, Jan 6 1893 Sex:M Child# 1 Frank A Barker Stotsburg, NY & Dora Wright Hennepin, IL
BARKER, Herman Eugene, Jul 5 1897 Sex:M Child# 5 Allan F Barker Antrim, NH & Emma J Duncklee Nashua, NH
BARKER, James A, Jul 30 1888 Sex:M Child# 2 James H Barker Windham, NH & Mary E Pratt Manchester, NH
BARKER, Lawrence Alvin, Feb 2 1910 Sex:M Child# 8 Allen F Barker Antrim, NH & Emma J Duncklee Nashua, NH
BARKER, Mary Elizabeth, May 21 1924 Sex:F Child# 2 Herman Barker Nashua, NH & Helen Abbott Derry, NH
BARKER, Philip Nathan, Jun 27 1900 Sex:M Child# 1 Allen Barker NH & Carrie B Richardson NH
BARKER, Unknown, Jan 15 1888 Sex:F Child# 1 Allen F Barker Antrim & Emma J Duncklee Nashua, NH
BARKER, Unknown, Apr 12 1891 Sex:M Child# 2 Allan F Barker Antrim, NH & Emma J Duncklee Nashua, NH
BARKER, Unknown, Aug 17 1891 Sex:M Child# 3 James H Barker Windham, NH & Mary E Pratt Manchester, NH
BARKER, Unknown, Feb 19 1893 Sex:F Child# 3 Allan F Barker Antrim, NH & Emma J Duncklee Nashua, NH
BARKER, Unknown, Mar 19 1893 Sex:M Child# 1 Eugene F Barker Antrim, NH & Jennie M Ellis Nashua, NH
BARKER, Unknown, Sep 14 1895 Sex:M Child# 4 Allen F Barker Antrim, NH & Emma J Duncklee Nashua, NH
BARKER, Unknown, Oct 16 1895 Sex:M Child# 2 Eugene F Barker Antrim, NH & Jennie M Ellis Nashua, NH
BARKER, Unknown, Feb 12 1902 Sex:M Child# 6 Allan F Barker Antrim, NH & Emma Duncklee Nashua, NH
BARKHOUSE, Ernest Melvin, Jul 20 1934 Sex:M Child# 2 Emory H Barkhouse Nova Scotia & Catherine Burton England
BARKHOUSE, Nancy June, Jun 28 1926 Sex:F Child# 7 Ralph Barkhouse Nova Scotia & Gretchen Vroom Canada
BARKODIS, Unknown, Oct 1 1907 Sex:F Child# 3 Stanis Barkodis Russia & Katalini Keiris Russia
BARKOWSKI, Mary, Oct 26 1912 Sex:F Child# 6 Frank Barkowski Russia & Mary Wilkowska Russia
BARKSWSKI, Adela, Jul 7 1907 Sex:F Child# 3 Frank Barkswski Russia & Mary Uteroske Russia
BARKUS, Bronislada, Oct 1 1910 Sex:F Child# 1 Antonas Barkus Russia & Antonina Kazlaw Russia
BARLOW, James Edward, May 29 1916 Sex:M Child# 2 Joseph Barlow NH & Margaret Cushing NH
BARLOW, William Howard, Sep 5 1918 Sex:M Child# 3 Joseph Barlow Exeter, NH & Margaret Cushing Concord, NH
BARNABY, Irene Elizabeth, Jan 18 1928 Sex:F Child# 2 Roy Barnaby Nova Scotia & Carrie Keay Winthrop, ME
BARNABY, Nelson Steven, Sep 1 1929 Sex:M Child# 2 Chester Barnaby Brookline, NH & Anna Ouillette Brookline, NH
BARNABY, Stephen Martin, Nov 10 1926 Sex:M Child# 1 Stephen Barnaby Worcester, MA & Helena Bergeron Franklin,
BARNARD, Arthur Joseph, Dec 13 1915 Sex:M Child# 1 Arthur Barnard Canada & Bertha Bailey Nashua, NH
BARNARD, Ethel Beatrice, Jan 18 1902 Sex:F Child# 1 Walter Barnard Cleveland, OH & Mable Larkin Nova Scotia
BARNARD, Nelson Everett, Feb 23 1906 Sex:M Child# 2 John S Barnard Dunbarton, NH & Mabel Swan Amherst, NH
BARNARD, Richard Irving, Oct 22 1920 Sex:M Child# 1 Irving M Barnard Fitchburg, MA & Simonne Wattre Beauvais
BARNARD, Robert Emile, Oct 27 1923 Sex:M Child# 2 Irving M Barnard Fitchburg, MA & Simonne Wattre Beauvais
BARNATOUS, Frank, Sep 27 1926 Sex:M Child# 3 Joseph Barnatous Lithuania & Mary Peleski Lithuania
BARNECHE, Marie Nellie Eva, Feb 23 1903 Sex:F Child# 4 Amedee Barneche Mass & Lucie Boutin Canada
BARNES, Beatrice Isabel, Apr 19 1902 Sex:F Child# 1 Royal S Barnes Nashua, NH & Bertha Pudvat Chateauguay, NY
BARNES, Cecil Dexter, Mar 28 1914 Sex:M Child# 2 Alfred D Barnes Nashua, NH & Bertha E Ames Munsonville, NH
BARNES, James A, Apr 15 1887 Sex:M Child# 2 Claude Barnes Milford & Kate Ireland
BARNES, Kate Viola, Feb 10 1895 Sex:F Child# 6 Orlando F Barnes Milford, NH & Kate Hannon Limerick, Ireland
BARNES, Kenneth, May 14 1934 Sex:M Child# 3 Kenneth Barnes Ithaca, NY & Althea Berdette Ithaca, NY
BARNES, Marion Jewell, Dec 28 1905 Sex:F Child# 1 Warren S Barnes Nashua, NH & Ethel M Carter Marlboro, MA
BARNES, Marion K, Feb 8 1893 Sex:F Child# William F Barnes Nashua, NH & Lizzie F Handy New Bedford, MA
BARNES, Unknown, Mar 27 1887 Sex:M Child# 1 Charles A Barnes Nashua, NH & Mary Canada
BARNES, Wade Ellison, Sep 6 1925 Sex:M Child# 1 Leon Barnes Brushton, NY & Barbara White Wilton, NH
BARNES, William F, Apr 3 1892 Sex:M Child# 5 Orlando F Barnes Milford & Kate Hannon Ireland
BARNES, William Frederick, Apr 8 1918 Sex:M Child# 1 Walter N Barnes Nashua, NH & Doris M Bruce Nashua, NH

BARNEY, Alice Ruth, Mar 25 1908 Sex:F Child# 3 F Carlton Barney Nashua, NH & F Ermyntrude Dane Nashua, NH
BARNEY, Francis P, Jun 12 1902 Sex:M Child# 1 Francis C Barney Nashua, NH & E Dane Nashua, NH
BARNEY, Unknown, Nov 12 1904 Sex:F Child# 2 Frank C Barney Nashua, NH & Emyntrude Dane Nashua, NH Stillborn
BARNHART, Unknown, Jun 4 1887 Sex:F Child# 4 C E Barnhart Canada & Louise Wilson NY
BARNORUS, John, Sep 3 1918 Sex:M Child# 4 Joseph Barnorus Russia & Eva Grinkowich Russia
BARNOUSKY, Joseph, Sep 7 1917 Sex:M Child# 8 Michael Barnousky Russia & Marrilla Kabershky Russia
BARNS, Dorothy, Mar 23 1902 Sex:F Child# 2 Charles E Barns Nova Scotia & Irene Hindman Halifax, NS
BARON, Cecile Marie, Apr 30 1935 Sex:F Child# 7 Louis Baron Canada & Exilia Marois Nashua, NH
BARON, Jos Louis Normand, Sep 23 1923 Sex:M Child# 1 (No Parents Listed)
BARON, Joseph Leo Robert, Jun 4 1926 Sex:M Child# 2 Arthur J Baron Biddeford, ME & Olivine Maynard Canada
BARON, Leo Wilfrid, Apr 25 1927 Sex:M Child# 4 Louis Baron Maine & Exilia Marois Nashua, NH
BARON, Lionel Alfred, Sep 3 1922 Sex:M Child# 1 Louis Baron Canada & Azilda Marrott Nashua, NH
BARON, Louis, Jan 23 1931 Sex:M Child# 7 Louis Baron Maine & Exilia Marois Nashua, NH
BARON, Lucille Rena, Feb 26 1929 Sex:F Child# 5 Louis Baron Mass & Exilia Marois Nashua, NH
BARON, Marie A Rita, Jan 3 1923 Sex:F Child# 2 Arthur Baron Biddeford, ME & Olivine Maynard Canada
BARONOSKI, Jean, Mar 25 1917 Sex:M Child# 6 John Baronoski Russia & Mary Scklutiz Russia
BAROONIAN, Rose, Oct 2 1912 Sex:F Child# 1 Tom Baroonian Turkey & H A Tamian Turkey
BAROSKI, Patricia, May 31 1918 Sex:F Child# 2 Sylvester Baroski Russia & Worsula Mefanwich Russia
BAROWKO, Stanislava, Jun 5 1925 Sex:F Child# 3 Julian Barowka Poland & Anna Mentel Poland
BARR, Barbara Helen, Nov 30 1933 Sex:F Child# 1 Bernard C Barr Nova Scotia & Evelyn Gallagher Everett, MA
BARR, Lawrence Wallace, May 7 1922 Sex:M Child# 9 Otis W Barr Weymouth, NS & Clara Alride Weymouth, NS
BARR, Robert, Feb 3 1889 Sex:M Child# 3 Frank Barr Nashua, NH & Alice J Cooper Nashua, NH
BARR, Shirley Elizabeth, Feb 23 1932 Sex:F Child# 1 Bernard C Barr Nova Scotia & Evelyn Gallagher Everett, MA
BARR, Unknown, Mar 10 1889 Sex:M Child# 2 John H Barr Nashua, NH & Belle Barr Milford, NH
BARRABE, Joseph R Romeo, Sep 12 1899 Sex:M Child# 5 George Barrabe Canada & Anna Lacroix Canada
BARRETEAU, Antoine Anne, Oct 17 1898 Sex:M Child# 12 Antoine Barreteau Canada & Cordelia Roy Canada
BARRETT, Agnes M M, Mar 7 1898 Sex:F Child# 1 William Barrett Ireland & Margaret O'Brien Ireland
BARRETT, Alfreda Marguerite, Feb 22 1925 Sex:F Child# 2 Alfred Barrett Nashua, NH & Helen Moriarty Nashua, NH
BARRETT, Ann Mary, Sep 4 1903 Sex:F Child# 5 William J Barrett Ireland & Margaret J O'Brien Ireland
BARRETT, Arthur Lamkin, Jr, Mar 21 1932 Sex:M Child# 3 Arthur L Barrett Lisbon, NH & Isabelle E Smith Waterford
BARRETT, Bettenia, Mar 16 1925 Sex:F Child# 5 Leonard Barrett Nashua, NH & Carril Rankin Lebanon, NH
BARRETT, Beverly Ann, Feb 5 1934 Sex:F Child# 3 Howard L Barrett Lisbon, NH & Dorothy Ellen Smith Ashland, NH
BARRETT, Edward William, May 1 1897 Sex:M Child# 5 William C Barrett Amherst, NH & Mary McGrath Nashua, NH
BARRETT, Enid Estella, Oct 31 1919 Sex:F Child# 4 Leonard Barrett Nashua, NH & Carrie Raukin S Lebanon, ME
BARRETT, Janice Helen, Nov 20 1928 Sex:F Child# 2 Arthur L Barrett Lisbon, NH & Isabelle Smith Waterford, VT
BARRETT, John Arthur, Feb 11 1888 Sex:M Child# 1 John Barrett Newmarket & Nellie Williams St Johnsbury, VT
BARRETT, John Leo, Apr 17 1899 Sex:M Child# 2 William Barrett Ireland & Margaret O'Brien Ireland
BARRETT, John W, Mar 28 1900 Sex:M Child# 6 William C Barrett NH & Mary E McGrath Nashua, NH
BARRETT, Katherine G, Jan 12 1905 Sex:F Child# 6 William J Barrett Ireland & Margaret J O'Brien Ireland
BARRETT, Kenneth Robert, Sep 1 1910 Sex:M Child# 2 Leonard V Barrett S Nashua, NH & Carrie Rankin Lebanon, ME
BARRETT, Leonard Franklin, Apr 25 1915 Sex:M Child# 3 Leonard V Barrett Nashua, NH & Carrie Rankin S Lebanon, ME
BARRETT, Lillian Francis, Feb 8 1902 Sex:F Child# 4 William Barrett Ireland & M O'Brien Ireland
BARRETT, Mary Angela, Sep 13 1900 Sex:F Child# 3 William Barrett Ireland & Margaret O'Brien Ireland
BARRETT, Raymond Adelard, Apr 29 1931 Sex:M Child# 3 Alfred Barrett Nashua, NH & Helen Moriarty Nashua, NH
BARRETT, Robert Tucker, Jul 22 1917 Sex:M Child# 1 Fred Cyrus Barrett Peterborough, NH & Bessie JohnsonTucker
BARRETT, Unknown, Feb 10 1893 Sex:M Child# 4 William C Barrett Amherst & Mary E Grant Nashua, NH
BARRETT, William Patrick, Jan 15 1906 Sex:M Child# 7 William J Barrett Ireland & Margaret J O'Brien Ireland
BARRETTE, Dora Eva, Oct 26 1900 Sex:F Child# 3 Alfred Barrette Canada & Edwidge Boutin Canada
BARRETTE, Joseph Archille C, Jan 16 1906 Sex:M Child# 7 Alfred Barrette Canada & Edwidge Boutin Canada
BARRETTE, Joseph Oscar, Nov 27 1902 Sex:M Child# 4 Alfred Barrette Canada & Edwidge Boutin Canada
BARRETTE, Marie E Flossie, Mar 4 1899 Sex:F Child# 2 Alfred Barrette Canada & Edwidge Boutin Canada
BARRETTE, William Edward, Jan 3 1904 Sex:M Child# 5 Alfred Barrette Canada & Edwidge Boutin Canada
BARRIAULT, David, Mar 23 1908 Sex:M Child# 1 Eugene Barriault Canada & Jeanne Deschesnes Canada
BARRIAULT, Leo Robert, Mar 31 1925 Sex:M Child# 9 Eugene Barriault Canada & Jeanne Deschenes Canada
BARRIAULT, Lorraine Juliette, Oct 8 1927 Sex:F Child# 10 Eugene Barriault Canada & Jeanne Deschenes Canada
BARRIAULT, Robert Joseph, Apr 15 1935 Sex:M Child# 1 Robert Barriault Nashua, NH & Lena Rancourt N Conway, NH
BARRIE, Raymond Leroy, Jan 29 1898 Sex:M Child# 2 Fredrick S Barrie Quebec & Ida A Stebbins Newbury, VT
BARRON, Cleophas Normand, Nov 9 1923 Sex:M Child# 2 Louis Barron Canada & Exilia Marois Nashua, NH
BARRON, Donald Harding, Jul 26 1919 Sex:M Child# 4 John S Barron Merrimack, NH & Julia Emily Thayer Newport, VT
BARRON, John Lawrence, Mar 28 1918 Sex:M Child# 3 John S Barron Merrimack, NH & Julia Emily Thayer Newport, VT
BARRON, Philip Sheridan, Nov 26 1926 Sex:M Child# 5 John Barron Merrimack, NH & Julia Thayer Newport, VT
BARRON, Raymond, Aug 14 1921 Sex:M Child# 1 Arthur Barron Biddeford, ME & Oliverine Maynard Canada
BARRON, Unknown, May 17 1895 Sex:M Child# 1 Joseph Barron Canada & Emma Collette New York Stillborn
BARROW, Ralph Roland, Nov 20 1920 Sex:M Child# 6 Frederick W Barrow Middleboro, MA & Ethel Smith Middleboro, MA
BARROWS, Earl Clifford, Mar 20 1922 Sex:M Child# 5 Fred W Barrows Middleboro, MA & Ethyl Smith Middleboro, MA
BARRY, Agnes Annette, Oct 5 1905 Sex:F Child# 1 Frank Barry US & Olivine Lavoie US
BARRY, Arline Margaret, Dec 31 1928 Sex:F Child# 1 William Barry Leominster, MA & Margaret Wheeler Marlow, NH
BARRY, Barbara Ann, Jul 15 1932 Sex:F Child# 3 Daniel Barry Wilton, NH & K O'Connell Troy, NY
BARRY, Catherine, May 13 1920 Sex:F Child# 2 Raymond Barry Blackstone, MA & Celestine Coffey Nashua, NH
BARRY, Charles Edward, May 1 1915 Sex:M Child# 8 Frank Barry Nashua, NH & Delvina Lavoie Nashua, NH
BARRY, Dorothy Joan, May 8 1931 Sex:F Child# 7 William H Barry Nashua, NH & Dora Ann McLaughlin Maynard, MA
BARRY, Eleanor Frances, May 14 1923 Sex:F Child# 3 Raymond Leo Barry Blackstone, MA & Celestine Coffey Nashua, NH
BARRY, Elizabeth Rita, Jul 17 1926 Sex:F Child# 13 Frank Barry NH & Lavina Lavoie NH

BARRY, Ernest James, Dec 10 1923 Sex:M Child# 12 Frank Barry NH & Laviea Lavoie NH
BARRY, Francis C Leonard, Jun 9 1919 Sex:M Child# 11 Frank Barry Nashua, NH & Olivine Lavoie Nashua, NH
BARRY, Irene, Apr 2 1909 Sex:F Child# 4 William Barry Nashua, NH & L Lavoie Nashua, NH
BARRY, James, Nov 20 1923 Sex:M Child# 3 William Barry Nashua, NH & Dora McLaughlin Maynard, MA
BARRY, Jane Mary, Dec 31 1931 Sex:F Child# 3 William H Barry Nashua, NH & Mabel S Monica Egg Harbor, WI
BARRY, Jeannette, Jan 6 1914 Sex:F Child# 7 Frank Barry US & Olivine Lavoie US
BARRY, John, Jun 17 1925 Sex:M Child# 4 William Barry Nashua, NH & Dora McLaughlin Maynard, MA
BARRY, John Charles, Nov 21 1907 Sex:M Child# 3 Frank Barry Nashua, NH & Vina Lavoie Nashua, NH
BARRY, John Edward, Sep 19 1916 Sex:M Child# 1 Raymond L Barry Blackstone, MA & Celestine K Coffey Nashua, NH
BARRY, John Francis, Jul 6 1893 Sex:M Child# 4 James Barry Nashua, NH & Mary Ireland
BARRY, Joseph, Jul 28 1929 Sex:M Child# 14 Frank Barry Nashua, NH & Lavina Lavoie Nashua, NH Stillborn
BARRY, Lillian Alice, Jan 6 1892 Sex:F Child# 3 James F Barry Milford, NH & Mary A Gleason Ireland
BARRY, Lucille Helene, Oct 22 1921 Sex:F Child# 11 Frank Barry NH & Lavina Lavoie NH
BARRY, Mary Katherine, May 17 1899 Sex:F Child# 6 James Barry Nashua, NH & Mary Gleason Ireland
BARRY, May Ruth, Apr 15 1912 Sex:F Child# 6 Frank M Barry US & Olivine Lavoie US
BARRY, Mildred Pearl, Aug 13 1917 Sex:F Child# 10 Frank Barry Nashua, NH & Lavina Lavoie Nashua, NH
BARRY, Richard Alfred, Aug 13 1910 Sex:M Child# 5 Frank Barry US & Olivine Lavoie US
BARRY, Richard Lawrence, Mar 23 1929 Sex:M Child# 2 Walter Barry Goffs Falls, NH & Sarah McMahon Nashua, NH
BARRY, Theresa Florence, Jan 11 1927 Sex:F Child# 5 William H Barry Nashua, NH & Dora McLaughlin Maynard, MA
BARRY, Unknown, Oct 19 1927 Sex:M Child# 1 Walter Barry Goffs Falls, NH & Sarah McMahon Nashua, NH
BARRY, Walter John, May 9 1917 Sex:M Child# 2 William H Barry Nashua, NH & Dora McLaughlin Maynard, MA
BARRY, William E, Jun 14 1914 Sex:M Child# 1 William H Barry Nashua, NH & Dora McLaughlin Maynard, MA
BARRY, William Henry, Jun 5 1889 Sex:M Child# 2 James Barry Milford, NH & Mary Gleason Ireland
BARRY, William Henry, Feb 3 1930 Sex:M Child# 2 William H Barry Nashua, NH & Mabel Monica Egg Harbor, WI
BARSANTI, Alice Lucia, Dec 13 1930 Sex:F Child# 1 Renaldo Barsanti Italy & Josephine Italy
BARSANTI, Doris, Apr 3 1934 Sex:F Child# 2 Rudolph Barsanti Italy & Josephine Lippi Italy
BARSELON, Aglae, Jun 24 1915 Sex:F Child# 2 Duhaime Barselon Canada & Laura Martineau Berlin, NH
BARSLOW, Alice M, Aug 11 1908 Sex:F Child# 2 G F Barslow New York & Catherine Redicain Lowell, MA
BARSLOW, Winnifred D, Mar 29 1907 Sex:F Child# 1 Alfred G Barslow Bedford, NY & Katherine Redigan Lowell, MA
BARSTOW, Edward Harvey, Mar 25 1913 Sex:M Child# 3 Fred G Barstow Bedford, NY & Katherine Redican Lowell, MA
BARSTOW, Unknown, Dec 12 1909 Sex:F Child# 3 Fred C Barstow New York & Kathaline Ridigan Lowell, MA
BARSTOW, Unknown, Feb 8 1911 Sex:M Child# 4 Fred G Barstow New York & Katherine Redigan Lowell, MA
BART, Adolphe, Apr 17 1898 Sex:F Child# 4 Pierre Jean Bart Canada & Elenore Vadvais Canada
BART, Albert, Mar 31 1891 Sex:M Child# 2 Pierre Jean Bart Canada & Eleonore Vadnais Canada
BART, Laetitia, Nov 27 1889 Sex:F Child# 6 Francois J Bart Canada & Caroline Duchesneau Canada
BART, Ralph Antonio, Jun 9 1903 Sex:M Child# 6 Pierre Jean Bart Nashua, NH & Eleonore Vadnais Canada
BARTACHAWI, John Joseph, Mar 9 1921 Sex:M Child# 5 Wadislas Bartachawi Poland & Christine Bartsachaw Poland
BARTASWICZ, Veronica, Nov 3 1923 Sex:F Child# 1 John Bartaswicz Lithuania & Veronica Velkofski Lithuania
BARTES, Malvina, Aug 30 1914 Sex:F Child# 9 Michael Bartes Russia & Lina Schkívet Russia
BARTHOLLOMOU, Hermano Alamo, Sep 9 1921 Sex:M Child# 1 Her A Barthollomou N Antonio, TX & Natalie True Waban, MA
BARTIS, Robert Charles, May 14 1931 Sex:M Child# 2 John Bartis Nashua, NH & Hazel Lovejoy Hollis, NH
BARTIS, Stanislaus, Jul 22 1911 Sex:M Child# 8 Mikelas Bartis Russia & Helona Skluciute Russia
BARTIS, Widoret, Mar 20 1918 Sex:m Child# 8 Michael Bartis Russia & Alena Bartis Russia
BARTKUS, Charles Robert, Dec 19 1925 Sex:M Child# 2 Anth J Bartkus Lithuania & A Kazlauskas Lithuania
BARTLER, Mary Olivine, Feb 9 1914 Sex:F Child# 1 Maurice Bartler Randolph, ME & M L Gagne Nashua, NH
BARTLETT, John Thomas, Oct 25 1927 Sex:M Child# 3 Harry Bartlett Keene, NH & Mildred Hannon Sterling, MA
BARTLETT, Laurence Sawyer, Nov 8 1923 Sex:M Child# 1 Alfred Bartlett Ponemah, NH & Winifred Sawyer Hillsboro, NH
BARTLETT, Marion Fuller, Mar 12 1895 Sex:F Child# 1 David N Bartlett Cornish & Emma L Fuller Keene
BARTLETT, Olive, Aug 30 1905 Sex:F Child# 1 Langley S Bartlett New Brunswick & Lorinda Simpson Maine
BARTLETT, Unknown, Nov 17 1888 Sex:M Child# 2 James Bartlett Brookline, MA & Bessie F Horne Boston, MA
BARTLETT, Unknown, Jun 30 1927 Sex:F Child# 1 (No Parents Listed)
BARTLSOLES, Walerije, Aug 4 1915 Sex:F Child# 1 Jerry Bartlsoles Russia & Walerje Lakaski Russia
BARTOCHAWICZ, John, Aug 10 1915 Sex:M Child# 1 Alex Bartochawicz Russia & Aerta Virsotska Russia
BARTOGEWICZ, Antony, Jun 29 1912 Sex:M Child# 1 Vladislaw Bartogewic Russia & Chritina Stepanowicz Russia
BARTON, Alfred William, Jul 23 1906 Sex:M Child# 1 George V Barton Tarrytown, NY & Lillian Collette Nashua, NH
BARTON, Arthur Robert, Dec 17 1924 Sex:M Child# 3 Louis Barton Canada & Exelia Marois Nashua, NH
BARTON, Carrie Vernice C, Jun 22 1909 Sex:F Child# 3 George V Barton Tarrytown, NY & Lillian Collette Nashua, NH
BARTON, Hormidas Albert, Oct 21 1907 Sex:M Child# 2 George V Barton New York & Lillian Collette Nashua, NH
BARTOSAWICZ, John, Jan 6 1925 Sex:M Child# 2 John Bartosawicz Lithuania & Veronica Velkofski Lithuania
BARTOSIEWICZ, Helen Eva, Sep 1 1928 Sex:F Child# 3 Wm Bartosiewicz Lithuania & J Bartosiewicz Lithuania
BARTOSIEWICZ, Joseph Ray, Feb 8 1925 Sex:M Child# 1 William Bartosiewicz Lithuania & Jose Bartosiewicz Lithuania
BARTOSOVICZ, Helena Mary, Jun 9 1915 Sex:F Child# 3 Vadislof Bartosovicz Russia & Christiana Martin Russia
BARTOSWICZ, Edmund, Jun 4 1918 Sex:M Child# 4 Vladys'w Bartoswicz Poland &  Poland
BARTRAND, Ernestine, Dec 18 1919 Sex:F Child# 3 Fran X Bartrand Nashua, NH & Anna Bergeron Pepperell, MA Stillborn
BARUNSWSKAS, William, Jul 11 1921 Sex:M Child# 9 Mich Barunswskas Russia & Marcella Kibertzes Russia
BARYSIS, Josephine, Sep 23 1919 Sex:F Child# 6 George Barysis Russia & Eva Bladis
BASCOMB, Wallace Chase, Sep 8 1897 Sex:M Child#  Samuel Bascomb Vermont & Carrie Holden Hollis, NH
BASIL, Joseph, Nov 14 1892 Sex:M Child#  J B Basil Canada & Arthemise Ratte Canada
BASIL, Pierre William, Aug 4 1894 Sex:M Child# 4 J B Basil Canada & Artheniese Ratte Canada
BASIL, Remi Pierre, Jul 3 1890 Sex:M Child# 2 Remi Basil Canada & Arzelie Guerton Canada
BASLER, Unknown, Jul 22 1914 Sex:F Child# 2 George Basler Clinton, MA & Euphenia McFadyen Prince Edward Island
BASLER, William, Jun 8 1913 Sex:M Child# 1 George Basler Plymouth, MA & Euphemia McFudgen Canada
BASSETT, Arnold R, Jr, Nov 19 1928 Sex:M Child# 2 A R Bassett Penacook, NH & Vivian McCann Pelham, NH

BASSETT, Edith Inez, Apr 28 1920 Sex:F Child# 6 John Bassett Malone, NY & Edith Ware Gibson Nashua, NH
BASSETT, Jeannette Bernice, Oct 1 1910 Sex:F Child# 3 John Bassett Malone, NY & Edith M Gibson Nashua, NH
BASSETT, John Jeremiah, Apr 20 1917 Sex:M Child# 5 John Bassett Malone, NY & Edith Gibson Nashua, NH
BASSETT, Mina Emma May, Jul 24 1908 Sex:F Child# 2 John Bassett Malone, NY & Edith M Gibson Nashua, NH
BASSETT, Pearl Evelyn, Sep 14 1925 Sex:F Child# 2 Hermie Bassett Constable, NY & Laura E Skinner Nashua, NH
BASSETT, Ruth Nellie, Mar 26 1906 Sex:F Child# 1 John Bassett NY & Edith M Gibson Nashua, NH
BASSORAS, Unknown, Jan 8 1925 Sex:F Child# 4 Massona Bassoras Syria & Maria Massano Syria
BASTIB, Marilda, Sep 30 1890 Sex:F Child# 2 Germain Bastib Canada & Marie Gagnon Canada
BASTIL, Marie A, Apr 1 1889 Sex:F Child# 1 Germain Bastil Canada & Marie Gagnon Canada
BASTIL, Marie A, Apr 29 1892 Sex:F Child# 3 Germain Bastil Canada & Marie Gagnon Canada
BASTILE, Cecile Blanche Rita, Jul 4 1922 Sex:F Child# 10 Achile Bastile Canada & Emma Bourgoin Canada
BASTILE, Roger Henri, Dec 7 1920 Sex:m Child# 9 Archie Bastile NH & Marguerite Downey Mass
BASTILLE, Jacqueline Delia, Jun 5 1929 Sex:F Child# 1 Adelard Bastille Canada & Jeannette Desmarais Nashua, NH
BASTILLE, Joseph Alfred, Aug 4 1892 Sex:M Child# 6 Alfred Bastille Canada & Georgianna St Pierre Canada
BASTILLE, Joseph Arthur, Feb 1 1891 Sex:M Child# 5 Alfred Bastille Canada & Georgianna St Pierre Canada
BASTILLE, Joseph Victor Rob, Apr 30 1919 Sex:M Child# 8 A G Bastille Canada & Emma Bourgeoin Canada
BASTILLE, Marie Angelina, Aug 7 1915 Sex:F Child# 6 Archille Bastille Canada & Emma Bourgoin Canada
BASTILLE, Nap Albert Roland, Nov 17 1917 Sex:M Child# 7 Achille Bastille Canada & Emma Bourgoin Canada
BASTILLE, Renee Therese, Sep 3 1930 Sex:F Child# 2 Adelard Bastille Canada & Juliette Demarais Nashua, NH
BASTOW, Elizabeth Beatrice, Sep 21 1920 Sex:F Child# 1 Stephen W Bastow Central Falls, RI & Katherine Boesch L
BATCHELDER, Barbara Alice, Apr 4 1929 Sex:F Child# 1 Walter Batchelder Brookline, NH & Alemeda Frost Brookline, NH
BATCHELDER, Kenneth Atherton, Jul 12 1927 Sex:M Child# 4 C J Batchelder Wilton, NH & Nellie Bugbee Wilton, NH
BATCHELDER, Laura Alice, Apr 15 1898 Sex:F Child# Cyrus Batchelder Navant, ME & Ellen Jessemen Newport, Canada
BATCHELDER, Robert Edson, Nov 16 1917 Sex:M Child# 1 Clarence Batchelder Concord, NH & Nora Ormsbe Concord, NH
BATCHELDER, William C, Aug 24 1896 Sex:M Child# 4 Cyrus Batchelder Levant, ME & Ellen Jasseman Newport, Canada
BATHALON, Albert Leo, Sep 6 1933 Sex:M Child# 2 L Bathalon Nashua, NH & G Lavigne Nashua, NH
BATHALON, Alice Beatrice L, Apr 2 1910 Sex:F Child# 9 Dieudonne Bathalon Canada & Adeline Gauthier Canada
BATHALON, Dieudonne Roger, Aug 20 1930 Sex:M Child# 1 Joseph Bathalon Nashua, NH & Lucienne Boutin Canada
BATHALON, Gloria, Jul 11 1924 Sex:F Child# 1 Rene Bathalon Canada & Jeanne Morrissette Nashua, NH
BATHALON, Jos Jean B L A, Apr 19 1907 Sex:M Child# 8 Dieudonne Bathalon Canada & Clara Gauthier Canada
BATHALON, Jos Richard Conrad, Nov 13 1932 Sex:M Child# 2 Joseph Bathalon Nashua, NH & Lucienne Boutin Canada
BATHALON, Joseph Henry F, Jun 9 1895 Sex:M Child# 4 Dieudonne Bathalon Canada & Arthemise Gauthier Canada
BATHALON, Marianne Madeline, Sep 16 1932 Sex:F Child# 1 Leo Bathalon Nashua, NH & M Lavigne Nashua, NH
BATHALON, Marie Adele, Jan 13 1901 Sex:F Child# 6 Dieudonne Bathalon Canada & Clara Gauthier Canada
BATHALON, Marie R E, May 31 1898 Sex:F Child# 5 Dieudonnie Bathalon Canada & Adeline Gauthier Canada
BATHALON, Robert Joseph, Jul 13 1934 Sex:M Child# 3 Joseph Bathalon Nashua, NH & Lucienne Boutin Canada
BATHALON, Unknown, Mar 23 1906 Sex: Child# 7 Dieudonne Bathalon Canada & Adeline Gauthier Canada Stillborn
BATKIEWICZ, Stephanie, Jun 1 1928 Sex:F Child# 8 Jos Batkiewicz Poland & Helena Varsotika Poland
BATLAY, Anna, Jul 1 1903 Sex:F Child# 2 Frank Batlay Austria & Nora Kiveck Austria
BATURA, Anna, Jul 13 1915 Sex:F Child# 2 Bolaslaw Batura Russia & Catherine Sankowska Russia
BATURA, John, May 17 1917 Sex:M Child# 3 Boleslaw Batura Poland Russia & Kate Poland Russia
BATURON, Stanislas, Jun 11 1914 Sex:M Child# 1 Boleslow Baturon Russia & Kate Baturan Russia
BAUDET, Abeline, Apr 17 1889 Sex:F Child# 10 Joseph Baudet Canada & Flore Lusignan Canada
BAUDRY, Napoleon, Sep 30 1891 Sex:M Child# 8 Napoleon Baudry Nashua, NH & Mathilde Beauregard Nashua, NH
BAUER, Arlene Elsie, Mar 11 1926 Sex:F Child# 3 Paul Bauer Lawrence, MA & Helen Kirsch Germany
BAUER, Roland, May 20 1929 Sex:M Child# 4 Paul Bauer Lawrence, MA & Helen Kirsch Germany
BAULMETIS, Soterios, Aug 19 1915 Sex:M Child# 2 John Baulmetis Greece & Evazelia Zaime Greece
BAUMZEUWICH, Staube, Aug 25 1911 Sex:F Child# 2 W Baumzeuwich Russia & T Bennsorah Vilno
BAUSH, Vladislas, Jul 16 1909 Sex:M Child# 1 William Baush Russia & Getrousa Miskavitch Russia
BAUVAIS, Myrtle Harriette, Jun 3 1917 Sex:F Child# 1 George Bauvais Bristol, NH & Georgiana Ouellette Fall River
BAUVIL, Maria, May 26 1902 Sex:F Child# 3 Archibald Bauvil Canada & Elise Landry Canada
BAXTER, Unknown, Feb 27 1900 Sex:F Child# 6 Albert F Baxter Rhode Island & Ida A Young NH
BAZIN, Pauline Lucille, Jul 30 1930 Sex:F Child# 2 Romeo Bazin Lawrence, MA & Josephine Belcourt Candia, NH
BAZIN, Romeo Robert, Oct 25 1927 Sex:M Child# 1 Romeo Bazin Lawrence, MA & J Belcourt E Candia, NH
BAZINET, Marguerite, Nov 2 1925 Sex:F Child# 4 Wilfred J Bazinet Canada & Marie Paquette Canada
BAZINET, Wilfrid, Jun 21 1922 Sex:M Child# 2 Wilfrid J Bazinet Canada & Mary Paquette Canada
BEACH, Mona Joan Marie, Mar 20 1932 Sex:F Child# 1 Robert Beach Berlin, NH & Evelyn Asselin Manchester, NH
BEACH, Roberta Pauline M, Jun 20 1935 Sex:F Child# 1 Robert Beach Berlin, NH & Evelyn Asselin Barton, VT
BEACHER, Mary Delima Eleanor, Feb 19 1933 Sex:F Child# 2 Ed J Beacher St Jean, Canada & Melina Duprey Nashua, NH
BEADOIN, Normand Raymond, May 18 1928 Sex:M Child# 1 Odilon Beadoin Canada & Dianna Lavoie Canada
BEAL, Roger Frank, Nov 13 1928 Sex:M Child# 2 Jarvis Beal Newton Ctr, MA & Florence Nott Norwich, VT
BEALAND, Nancy May, Jun 16 1934 Sex:F Child# 1 George Bealand Reeds Ferry, NH & Alice Singleton Westfield, MA
BEALAND, Richard Lee, Mar 5 1935 Sex:M Child# 2 Leo Bealand Reeds Ferry, NH & Isabelle Pelletier Nashua, NH
BEALAND, Roberta, Jan 23 1933 Sex:F Child# 1 Leo A Bealand NH & Shirley Brennan Nashua, NH
BEALS, Elizabeth Helen, Feb 13 1908 Sex:F Child# 4 William H Beals Epping, NH & Helen Johnson Canada
BEAN, Daisy Emma, Mar 30 1913 Sex:F Child# 1 Charles E Bean US & Emma Chase US
BEAN, Donald Edward, Oct 25 1909 Sex:M Child# 1 Harry E Bean Henniker, NH & Alice M Goodwin Londonderry, NH
BEAN, Forrest Babkirk, Oct 18 1926 Sex:M Child# 2 Francis W Bean Merrimack, NH & Augusta Babkirk New Brunswick
BEAN, Frank Warren, Mar 17 1917 Sex:M Child# 3 W A Bean Nashua, NH & Alice E Pound Nashua, NH
BEAN, Harry, Apr 2 1912 Sex:M Child# 1 (No Parents Listed)
BEAN, Ida M, Mar 24 1888 Sex:F Child# 7 Peter Bean Canada & Lizzie Dimmaris Canada
BEAN, Martha Edna, May 12 1914 Sex:F Child# 3 W A Bean Nashua, NH & Alice Pound Nashua, NH
BEAN, Mildred Edith, Feb 10 1897 Sex:F Child# 6 Frank A Bean Manchester, NH & Addie Kenyon Pomfret, VT

BEAN, Myrtie, Oct 1 1896 Sex:F Child# 3 Fred P Bean Bristol & Sena Johnson Sweden
BEAN, Ralph, Nov 27 1894 Sex:M Child#  Fred P Bean NH & Cena Johnson US
BEAN, Unknown, Mar 8 1898 Sex:M Child# 5 A Bean Canada & Cassie Cahill Mass
BEAN, Unknown, Jun 6 1900 Sex:F Child# 1 Frank R Bean NH & Rilla P Wilson NB
BEAN, Walter H, Feb 29 1912 Sex:M Child# 2 Walter A Bean Nashua, NH & Alice Pound Nashua, NH Stillborn
BEAN, Willie A, Jan 18 1887 Sex:M Child# 4 Frank A Bean Manchester & Addie S Hartford, VT
BEARD, Clarence Asa, Jul 16 1903 Sex:M Child# 2 William A Beard Hillsborough & Minnie E Kennedy Lowell, MA
BEARD, Elizabeth Caroline, Nov 23 1922 Sex:F Child# 1 John Beard E Boston, MA & Priscilla Warner Cambridge, MA
BEARD, Elmer Francis, Jan 14 1905 Sex:M Child# 3 William A Beard Hillsboro & Minnie Kennedy Lowell, MA
BEARD, Leslie Katherine, Jan 8 1906 Sex:F Child# 4 William A Beard New Boston, NH & Minne E Kennedy Lowell, MA
BEARD, Theresa, Oct 28 1904 Sex:F Child# 1 Eugene B Beard New Ipswich, NH & Abbie A Wilson New Ipswich, NH
BEARD, Unknown, Sep 1 1898 Sex:M Child# 4 Neuman Beard Poland & Lena Ullendorff Berlin, Germany
BEARD, William James, Jan 22 1901 Sex:M Child# 1 William H Beard New Boston, NH & Minnie Kennedy Lowell, MA
BEARSE, Barbara, Jul 30 1924 Sex:F Child# 1 Norman Bearse Laconia, NH & Frances Arnold Somerville, MA
BEARSE, Beverly, Aug 11 1928 Sex:F Child# 2 Norman Bearse Laconia, NH & Frances Arnold Somerville, MA
BEASON, Emily Agnes, Aug 8 1909 Sex:F Child# 1 Charles J Beason Ireland & Mary Bohan Ireland
BEATON, Fred Ernest, Feb 26 1903 Sex:M Child# 2 William E Beaton Canada & Annie Potry New York
BEATON, Pauline Dorothy, May 30 1925 Sex:F Child# 2 Frederick Beaton Nashua, NH & Lydia Waluke Toledo, OH
BEATTON, Ellsworth W, Oct 15 1897 Sex:M Child#  William E Beatton Canada & Annie Potrie NY
BEAUBIEN, Claria, May 28 1888 Sex:F Child# 2 Alphonse Beaubien Canada & Clemence Millette Canada
BEAUBIEN, Lois Eleanor, Apr 27 1933 Sex:F Child# 1 O J Beaubien Sandown, NH & Doris Watson Amherst, MA
BEAUCHAMP, Agnes, Oct 25 1895 Sex:F Child# 9 Ulric Beauchamp Canada & Delina Montpetel Canada
BEAUCHAMP, Evelyn Rosa, Apr 1 1927 Sex:F Child# 1 Jean Beauchamp Canada & Mary Lefebvre Pepperell, MA
BEAUCHAMP, Jeannette Ann, Apr 11 1930 Sex:F Child# 2 Origina Beauchamp Canada & Marie L Lefebvre Pepperell, MA
BEAUCHAMPS, J B Robert, Aug 30 1905 Sex:M Child# 2 Joseph Beauchamps Canada & Evanalline Tardy Canada
BEAUCHAMPS, Laurette Irene, Jan 20 1907 Sex:F Child# 3 Joseph Beauchamps Canada & Evangeline Tardy Canada
BEAUCHAMPS, Lucien Leo, Mar 27 1904 Sex:M Child# 1 Joseph Beauchamps Canada & Evangeline Tardif Canada
BEAUCHEMIN, Joseph Pierre, Jan 27 1892 Sex:M Child# 4 Philias Beauchemin Canada & Rosanna Canada
BEAUCHEMIN, Viviane Henriette, Sep 18 1930 Sex:F Child# 1 Frederic Beauchemin New York, NY & Estelle Pelletier
BEAUCHER, Edgar Louis, Oct 25 1926 Sex:M Child# 3 Ludger Beaucher Canada & Blanche Dube Nashua, NH
BEAUCHER, Ludger Roger, Oct 13 1921 Sex:M Child# 2 Ludger Beaucher Canada & Blanche Dube Nashua, NH
BEAUCHER, Normand Edgar, Mar 3 1920 Sex:M Child# 1 Ludger Beaucher Canada & Blanche Dube Nashua, NH
BEAUCHESNE, Joseph, Dec 6 1923 Sex:M Child# 3 Emile Beauchesne Canada & Delia Turcotte Rhode Island Stillborn
BEAUCHESNE, Joseph Henri, Jun 3 1914 Sex:M Child# 2 Alfred Beauchesne Lewiston, ME & Clara Desmarais Nashua, NH
BEAUCHESNE, M Rose Jeanne Anna, Mar 26 1913 Sex:F Child# 1 Emery Beauchesne Canada & Delia Turcotte Canada
BEAUCHINE, Joseph Robert, Feb 27 1919 Sex:M Child# 2 Emery Beauchine Canada & Delia Turcotte Providence, RI
BEAUDET, Armand Albert, Jul 26 1930 Sex:M Child# 4 Albert Beaudet Manchester, NH & Marie Fortin Amesbury, MA
BEAUDET, Jacqueline Jeannette, May 5 1935 Sex:F Child# 4 Arthur Beaudet Manchester, NH & Dolores Delorme Nashua, NH
BEAUDET, Joseph Arthur Donald, Feb 7 1917 Sex:M Child# 1 Arthur Beaudet Canada & Amanda Laflamme Littleton, NH
BEAUDET, Robert Lucien, May 24 1928 Sex:M Child# 3 Albert W Beaudet Manchester, NH & Marie Fortin NH
BEAUDETTE, Barbara Anne, Nov 16 1935 Sex:F Child# 1 Rod Beaudette Nashua, NH & Lillian Lafontaine Nashua, NH
BEAUDETTE, Beverly Anne, Nov 16 1935 Sex:F Child# 2 Rod Beaudette Nashua, NH & Lillian Lafontaine Nashua, NH
BEAUDETTE, Lucille Beatrice E, Aug 31 1908 Sex:F Child# 5 Joseph Beaudette Canada & Marie L Gelinas Canada
BEAUDETTE, Marie Antoinette, Jun 26 1904 Sex:F Child# 1 Wilfred Beaudette Canada & Rose Paquette Canada
BEAUDETTE, Marie Blanche Noella, Jan 28 1918 Sex:F Child# 8 Joseph Beaudette Canada & Marie Louise Gelines Canada
BEAUDETTE, Rodrique F X, Nov 30 1905 Sex:M Child# 4 Joseph Beaudette Canada & M L Gelinas Canada
BEAUDETTE, Sylvio Roland, May 25 1910 Sex:M Child# 5 Edouard Beaudette Canada & Marie Granbois Canada
BEAUDETTE, Therese Leona, Apr 8 1910 Sex:F Child# 6 Joseph Beaudette Canada & Marie L Gelinas Canada
BEAUDIN, Agnes Bernatte, Mar 13 1919 Sex:F Child# 8 Simeon Beaudin Suncook, NH & Mary Pecor Montpelier, VT
BEAUDIN, Antoinnette Lillian, Apr 7 1917 Sex:F Child# 7 Simeon Beaudin Suncook, NH & Mary Recor Montpelier, VT
BEAUDIN, Florance Elise, Jan 1 1921 Sex:F Child# 9 Simeon Beaudin Suncook, NH & Mary Elise Pecor Montpelier, VT
BEAUDIN, Gerard Joseph W, Sep 5 1930 Sex:M Child# 7 Ovila Beaudin Canada & Diana Lavoie Canada
BEAUDIN, Henry Albert, Oct 24 1922 Sex:M Child# 10 Sim E Beaudin Suncook, NH & Mary Elise Pecor Montpelier, VT
BEAUDIN, Wilfred William, Mar 25 1915 Sex:M Child# 6 Simeon Beaudin US & Marie E Picard US
BEAUDOIN, Adelard, Feb 26 1900 Sex:M Child# 4 Napoleon Beaudoin Canada & Georgiana Laflamme Canada
BEAUDOIN, Arthur Oscar, Apr 15 1913 Sex:M Child# 5 Simeon E Beaudoin Canada & Marie Elise Picard Canada
BEAUDOIN, Aurore, Jun 20 1901 Sex:F Child# 5 Napoleon Beaudoin Canada & Georgina Laflamme Canada
BEAUDOIN, Christiana, Oct 2 1922 Sex:F Child# 1 Henry Beaudoin Canada & Eugenie Grevet France
BEAUDOIN, Jos David Valmore, Apr 3 1916 Sex:M Child# 2 Arthur Beaudoin Canada & Cordelia Gelinas Canada
BEAUDOIN, Marie Jeanne L, Dec 3 1910 Sex:F Child# 12 Joseph Beaudoin Canada & Celina Berube Canada
BEAUDOIN, Sybil Arlene, Aug 18 1922 Sex:F Child# 1 Spencer Beaudoin Nashua, NH & Irene Stone Nashua, NH
BEAUDOIN, Victoria Jeannette, Dec 27 1909 Sex:F Child# 1 Arthur Beaudoin Canada & Cordelia Gelinas Canada
BEAUDRY, Unknown, Jan 20 1899 Sex:M Child# 4 Ray F Beaudry Middlebury, VT & Mary Alice Wilder Whitingham, VT
BEAULIER, Marie A, Jun 27 1890 Sex:F Child# 2 Charles Beaulier Canada & Georgianna Dumais Canada
BEAULIEU, Alfred, Jul 30 1899 Sex:M Child# 9 Alphonse Beaulieu Canada & Pomela Antille Canada
BEAULIEU, Alfred, Mar 10 1903 Sex:M Child# 13 Joseph Beaulieu Canada & Celina Soucy Canada
BEAULIEU, Alphonse Gerard, Aug 9 1925 Sex:M Child# 3 Napoleon Beaulieu Canada & Marie E Caron Canada
BEAULIEU, Amelia, Jan 7 1896 Sex:F Child# 13 William Beaulieu Canada & Zelie Belanger Canada
BEAULIEU, Arthur, Jul 29 1920 Sex:M Child# 1 Napoleon Beaulieu Canada & Marie S Caron Nashua, NH
BEAULIEU, Aurasie, Nov 1 1897 Sex:F Child# 9 Charles Beaulieu Canada & Georgiana Dumais Canada
BEAULIEU, Charles Eugene O, Apr 16 1892 Sex:M Child# 6 Charles Beaulieu Canada & Georgianna Dumais Canada
BEAULIEU, Eleanor Mae, Jun 21 1927 Sex:F Child# 2 Joseph Beaulieu Canada & J Wilkaites Russia
BEAULIEU, Emile Dorilas, Apr 2 1931 Sex:M Child# 1 Emile Beaulieu Canada & Albina Claveau Canada

BEAULIEU, Frank Willie, Apr 27 1890 Sex:M Child# 3 Alphonse Beaulieu Canada & Pamela Antille Canada
BEAULIEU, Gertrude Jacqueline, Jan 7 1926 Sex:F Child# 1 Napoleon Beaulieu Canada & Rose A Boudreau Rhode Island
BEAULIEU, Helene Doris, Sep 12 1926 Sex:F Child# 6 Adelard Beaulieu Canada & Mary Bosse Canada
BEAULIEU, Herve Gerard, Feb 2 1921 Sex:M Child# 1 Herve Beaulieu Canada & Jeanne Deschenes Canada
BEAULIEU, Ida Annette, Feb 10 1931 Sex:F Child# 1 Paul Beaulieu Canada & Anne M Belanger Canada
BEAULIEU, Irene Louise, Apr 16 1920 Sex:F Child# 3 Adelard Beaulieu Canada & Mary Boni Canada
BEAULIEU, J Fran Gon Elie, Feb 8 1919 Sex:M Child# 1 Elie Beaulieu Canada & Delima Levesque Canada
BEAULIEU, J N Raymond, Jul 28 1922 Sex:M Child# 3 Elie Beaulieu Canada & Delima Levesque Canada
BEAULIEU, Jacqueline, Oct 16 1935 Sex:F Child# 4 Walter Beaulieu Brookline, NH & Doro Fessenden Brookline, NH
BEAULIEU, Joseph, Dec 9 1907 Sex:M Child# 15 Charles Beaulieu Canada & Georgianna Dumais Canada
BEAULIEU, Joseph, Apr 17 1926 Sex:M Child# 1 Joseph Beaulieu Canada & J Wilkiates Russia
BEAULIEU, Joseph A, May 20 1899 Sex:M Child# 10 Charles Beaulieu Canada & Georgianna Dumais Canada
BEAULIEU, Joseph A E, Jun 19 1898 Sex:M Child# 10 Joseph Beaulieu Canada & Celina Foucy Canada
BEAULIEU, Joseph A Victor, May 23 1931 Sex:M Child# 4 Alphonse Beaulieu Canada & Eva Rose Lavoie Nashua, NH
BEAULIEU, Joseph Albert, Jul 18 1928 Sex:M Child# 3 Alph Beaulieu Canada & Eva Lavoie Nashua, NH
BEAULIEU, Joseph C M, Sep 2 1893 Sex:M Child# 6 Charles Beaulieu Canada & Georgianna Dumais Canada
BEAULIEU, Joseph E, Jun 4 1904 Sex:M Child# 14 Joseph Beaulieu Canada & Celina Soucy Canada
BEAULIEU, Joseph Everett, Oct 18 1889 Sex:M Child# 11 William Beaulieu Canada & E Belanger Canada
BEAULIEU, Joseph George Gerard, Nov 4 1934 Sex:M Child# 4 Paul Beaulieu Canada & A Marie Belanger Canada
BEAULIEU, Joseph Guillaume, May 6 1906 Sex:M Child# 14 Charles Beaulieu Canada & Georgiana Dumais Canada
BEAULIEU, Joseph Leo Armand, Feb 23 1925 Sex:M Child# 1 Alphonse Beaulieu Canada & Eva Rose Lavoie Nashua, NH
BEAULIEU, Joseph Leo P, Oct 5 1904 Sex:M Child# 13 Charles Beaulieu Canada & Georgiana Dumais Canada
BEAULIEU, Joseph Normand, Jun 2 1922 Sex:M Child# 2 Henry Beaulieu Nashua, NH & Jeanne Deschenes Canada
BEAULIEU, Joseph O, Jan 25 1895 Sex:M Child# 7 Charles Beaulieu Canada & Georgianna Dumais Canada
BEAULIEU, Joseph P E Norman, Dec 21 1935 Sex:M Child# 2 Paul Beaulieu Mt Carmel, Canada & Mary Belanger Quebec
BEAULIEU, Joseph Robert Lionel, Aug 14 1926 Sex:M Child# 2 Lionel Beaulieu Canada & Alice Young Nashua, NH
BEAULIEU, Joseph Robert Lucien, Mar 14 1933 Sex:M Child# 3 Paul Beaulieu Canada & Anne M Belanger Canada
BEAULIEU, Joseph Roland Etienn, Jun 11 1924 Sex:M Child# 2 Joseph E Beaulieu Canada & Alida H Riendeau Nashua, NH
BEAULIEU, Joseph Roland Lionel, Apr 25 1918 Sex:M Child# 1 Joseph Beaulieu Canada & Yvonne Caron Canada
BEAULIEU, Joseph T G, Dec 21 1899 Sex:M Child# 2 Joseph Beaulieu Canada & Celina Soucy Canada
BEAULIEU, Joseph William Rober, Jan 25 1934 Sex:M Child# 2 Armand Beaulieu Canada & Marion Labranche Nashua, NH
BEAULIEU, Laura Annette, Jul 9 1928 Sex:F Child# 7 Thos Beaulieu Canada & Georgianna Lavoie Canada
BEAULIEU, Lawrence Amos, Feb 21 1927 Sex:M Child# 1 Louis L Beaulieu Oldtown, ME & Bertha A Currier Nashua, NH
BEAULIEU, Lea Jeannette, Jul 9 1928 Sex:F Child# 8 Thos Beaulieu Canada & Georgianna Lavoie Canada
BEAULIEU, Leonard, Feb 4 1933 Sex:M Child# 2 Emile Beaulieu Canada & Albina Claveau Canada
BEAULIEU, Lillian Aurore, Sep 1 1923 Sex:F Child# 5 Adelard Beaulieu Canada & Mary Bosse Canada
BEAULIEU, Lionel Herve, Dec 10 1933 Sex:M Child# 8 Herve Beaulieu Nashua, NH & Jeanne Deschenes Canada
BEAULIEU, Lorraine Cecile, Dec 5 1928 Sex:F Child# 3 L Beaulieu Canada & Alice Young Nashua, NH
BEAULIEU, Louisette Mary, May 17 1932 Sex:F Child# 7 Hervey Beaulieu Nashua, NH & Jane Deschenes Canada
BEAULIEU, M Gabrielle Olivette, Aug 26 1920 Sex:F Child# 2 Elie Beaulieu Canada & Delima Levesque Canada
BEAULIEU, Madeline Rita, Apr 27 1927 Sex:F Child# 2 Napoleon Beaulieu Canada & Rose A Boudreau Rhode Island
BEAULIEU, Marg Florence, Nov 23 1915 Sex:F Child# 1 Adelard Beaulieu Canada & Marie Anne Bosse Canada
BEAULIEU, Marie, Jul 29 1888 Sex:F Child# 6 Joseph Beaulieu Canada & Celina Louice Canada
BEAULIEU, Marie A, Dec 2 1890 Sex:F Child# 7 Joseph Beaulieu Canada & Celina Souci Canada
BEAULIEU, Marie Alice, Jul 28 1918 Sex:F Child# 1 Napoleon Beaulieu Canada & Agnes Bouchard Canada
BEAULIEU, Marie Alice Simone, Oct 26 1912 Sex:F Child# 1 Octave Beaulieu Canada & Alice Boucher Canada
BEAULIEU, Marie Ann Lucille, Sep 10 1929 Sex:F Child# 7 Adelard Beaulieu Canada & Mary Bosse Canada
BEAULIEU, Marie Anne, May 1 1899 Sex:F Child# 14 William Beaulieu Canada & Agelie Belanger Canada
BEAULIEU, Marie B I, Mar 13 1900 Sex:F Child# 7 Cleophas Beaulieu Canada & Elise Raymond Canada
BEAULIEU, Marie Beatrice, Oct 24 1925 Sex:F Child# 4 Herve Beaulieu Nashua, NH & Jeanne Deschenes Canada
BEAULIEU, Marie Cecile, Nov 14 1926 Sex:F Child# 4 Napoleon Beaulieu Canada & Estella Caron Canada
BEAULIEU, Marie Clara Bertha, Jul 25 1924 Sex:F Child# 4 Thomas Beaulieu Canada & Georgianna Lavoie Canada
BEAULIEU, Marie E, Apr 8 1889 Sex:F Child# 2 Charles Beaulieu Canada & Georgianna Dumais Canada
BEAULIEU, Marie G, Jun 17 1887 Sex:F Child# 1 Charles Beaulieu P Q & Marie G Dumais P Q
BEAULIEU, Marie Gertrude, Oct 18 1921 Sex:F Child# 2 Napoleon Beaulieu Canada & Marie Caron Canada
BEAULIEU, Marie Ida, Nov 17 1899 Sex:F Child# 4 Delphin Beaulieu Canada & Melvina Michaud Canada
BEAULIEU, Marie Jeanne Rita, Oct 23 1926 Sex:F Child# 2 Alphonse Beaulieu Canada & Eva Rose Lavoie Nashua, NH
BEAULIEU, Marie L E, Oct 17 1900 Sex:F Child# 11 Charles Beaulieu Canada & Georgianna Dumais Canada
BEAULIEU, Marie L Jean Pauline, May 16 1935 Sex:F Child# 1 Omer Beaulieu Canada & Armande Cote Manchester, NH
BEAULIEU, Marie Laura Alida, May 13 1921 Sex:F Child# 1 Etienne J Beaulieu Canada & Alida H Riendeau Nashua, NH
BEAULIEU, Marie Louise A, Dec 20 1905 Sex:F Child# 15 Joseph Beaulieu Canada & Celina Soucy Canada
BEAULIEU, Martial Philip Henry, Mar 25 1925 Sex:M Child# 1 Lionel Beaulieu Canada & Alice Young NH
BEAULIEU, Mary Delia, Dec 14 1891 Sex:F Child# 12 William Beaulieu Canada & Zelie Belanger Canada
BEAULIEU, Maurice Fernand, Aug 19 1927 Sex:F Child# 1 Emile Beaulieu Canada & Leda Marquis Canada
BEAULIEU, Maxime A, Sep 20 1896 Sex:M Child# 9 Joseph Beaulieu Canada & Celina Soucy Canada
BEAULIEU, Maxime Pierre, Apr 16 1892 Sex:M Child# 5 Charles Beaulieu Canada & Georgianna Dumais Canada
BEAULIEU, Norman August, Apr 30 1935 Sex:M Child# 4 Leon Beaulieu Canada & Alice Young Nashua, NH
BEAULIEU, Obeline, Oct 2 1892 Sex:F Child# 8 Joseph Beaulieu Canada & Celina Souce Canada
BEAULIEU, Olida Adelaide, Jan 14 1903 Sex:F Child# 4 Charles Beaulieu Canada & Georgiana Dumais Canada
BEAULIEU, Paul A, May 4 1901 Sex:M Child# 12 Joseph Beaulieu Canada & Celina Soucy Canada
BEAULIEU, Rachel, Oct 26 1932 Sex:F Child# 1 A Beaulieu Canada & Anna Labranche Nashua, NH
BEAULIEU, Raoul, May 20 1910 Sex:M Child# 2 Hilaire Beaulieu Canada & A Pomerleau Canada
BEAULIEU, Raymond, Jun 12 1927 Sex:M Child# 5 Henry Beaulieu Canada & Jeanne Deschenes Canada

BEAULIEU, Raymond, May 14 1930 Sex:M Child# 1 Leopold Beaulieu Canada & Lillian Paradis Nashua, NH
BEAULIEU, Raymond Amedee, Jan 17 1930 Sex:M Child# 3 Louis L Beaulieu Maine & Bertha Currier Nashua, NH
BEAULIEU, Robert Maurice, Aug 16 1922 Sex:M Child# 4 Adelard Beaulieu Canada & Marie Bosse Canada
BEAULIEU, Roger Arthur, Jun 25 1934 Sex:M Child# 2 Charles A Beaulieu Canada & Jeanne Alice Kerouac Canada
BEAULIEU, Therese, Jul 20 1930 Sex:F Child# 6 Herve Beaulieu Nashua, NH & Antoinette Deschenes Canada
BEAULIEU, Thomas, Nov 26 1892 Sex:M Child# 9 Elvi Beaulieu Canada & Marie Ouellette Canada
BEAULIEU, Thomas A, Oct 5 1896 Sex:M Child# 8 Charles Beaulieu Canada & Georgina Dumais Canada
BEAULIEU, Thomas Armand, Nov 16 1923 Sex:M Child# 1 Thomas Beaulieu Canada & Delvina Desjardins Canada
BEAULIEU, Unknown, Jul 12 1894 Sex:F Child# 7 Alphonse Beaulieu Canada & Pamela Auctil Canada Stillborn
BEAULIEU, Unknown, Nov 28 1894 Sex:F Child# 1 George E Beaulieu Coopersville, NY & Lucina Faucher Coaticook, PQ
BEAULIEU, Yvette, Jan 27 1924 Sex:F Child# 3 Henri Beaulieu Nashua, NH & Jeanne Deschenes Canada
BEAULIEU, Yvonne, Jan 26 1899 Sex:F Child# 10 Eloie Beaulieu Canada & Marie Ouellette Canada
BEAULIEU, Yvonne Blanche T, Nov 26 1928 Sex:F Child# 2 Louis Beaulieu Maine & Bertha Currier Nashua, NH
BEAUPRE, Annette, Mar 11 1930 Sex:F Child# 1 Phydime Beaupre Nashua, NH & Melina Lavoie Nashua, NH Stillborn
BEAUPRE, Elise Stella, Sep 15 1904 Sex:F Child# 1 Joseph Beaupre Canada & Elise Dufour Canada
BEAUPRE, Fiding, Oct 13 1893 Sex:M Child# 3 Auguste Beaupre Canada & Cimida Ouellette Canada
BEAUPRE, Jeanne Olivette, Sep 21 1916 Sex:F Child# 8 Alvary Beaupre Canada & Georgi Beauregard Canada
BEAUPRE, Joseph Edouard, Feb 6 1917 Sex:M Child# 1 Joseph Beaupre Salmon Falls, NH & Wilda Forest Canada
BEAUPRE, Laurent Dolor, May 16 1915 Sex:M Child# 6 Alvarez Beaupre Canada & Georgiana Beauregard Canada
BEAUPRE, Louis Raymond, Apr 7 1917 Sex:M Child# 1 Joseph Beaupre Canada & Lea Rioux Nashua, NH
BEAUPRE, Lucienne Estelle, Jun 20 1911 Sex:F Child# 1 Frederic H Beaupre Canada & Anna Boisseau Canada
BEAUPRE, M Lucile Madeline, Jan 31 1913 Sex:F Child# 6 Alvarez Beaupre Canada & George Beauregard Canada
BEAUPRE, Marie, Apr 24 1918 Sex:F Child# 9 Alvarez Beaupre Canada & Grgianna Beauregard Canada Stillborn
BEAUPRE, Marie Albina Wilda, Mar 20 1920 Sex:F Child# 2 Joseph Beaupre Salmon Falls, NH & Wilda Forest Canada
BEAUPRE, Mary, May 21 1918 Sex:F Child# 3 Arthur Beaupre Derby Line, VT & Edith Martin W Derby, VT
BEAUPRE, Mary Ann, Nov 4 1914 Sex:F Child# 1 Frank Beaupre Canada & Mary Willette Canada
BEAUPRE, Robert, Nov 26 1921 Sex:M Child# 3 Joseph Beaupre NH & A Forest
BEAUPRE, William Henry, May 15 1917 Sex:M Child# 2 Arthur Beaupre Vermont & Edith Martin Vermont
BEAUREGARD, Alice, Jan 9 1901 Sex:F Child# 5 Edmond Beauregard Canada & Ida Benoit Canada
BEAUREGARD, Anita Theresa, Dec 12 1929 Sex:F Child# 2 Ernest Beauregard Nashua, NH & Isabelle Bouchard Nashua, NH
BEAUREGARD, Aurora, May 22 1892 Sex:F Child# 1 Moise Beauregard Canada & Aglaie Plante Maine
BEAUREGARD, Ernest, Apr 16 1905 Sex:M Child# 7 Pierre Beauregard Canada & Rose Delima Aubert Canada
BEAUREGARD, Eva, Jun 3 1896 Sex:F Child# 1 H Beauregard Canada & Georgianna Messier Canada
BEAUREGARD, Henry, Apr 13 1892 Sex:M Child# 3 Andre Beauregard Canada & Exilda Cote Canada
BEAUREGARD, Jeannie Alice, Oct 22 1889 Sex:F Child# 7 Louis Beauregard Canada & Jennie Verbonlone Vermont
BEAUREGARD, Jerry, Jan 6 1892 Sex:M Child# Andre Beauregard Canada & Desange Berube Canada
BEAUREGARD, Joseph Arthur, Jan 25 1909 Sex:M Child# 9 Pierre Beauregard Canada & Ozina Aubut Canada
BEAUREGARD, Joseph Jean, Jan 20 1897 Sex:M Child# 3 Pierre Beauregard Canada & Oselina Aubut Canada
BEAUREGARD, Lilian Florette, Mar 24 1912 Sex:F Child# 10 Pierre Beauregard Canada & Rosanna Aubut Canada
BEAUREGARD, Lucien Romeo, Jan 13 1918 Sex:M Child# 12 Pierre Beauregard Canada & Rosalina Auburt Canada
BEAUREGARD, Ludger Leon, Oct 21 1890 Sex:M Child# 1 Joseph Beauregard Canada & Caroline Bourre Canada
BEAUREGARD, M Juliette, Jul 18 1895 Sex:F Child# 1 Pierre Beauregard Canada & Rose Aubut Canada
BEAUREGARD, Marianne Eva R, Mar 16 1907 Sex:F Child# 8 Pierre Beauregard Canada & Oselina Aubut Canada
BEAUREGARD, Marie Alice, May 9 1898 Sex:F Child# 4 Pierre Beauregard Canada & Rosa Aubu Canada
BEAUREGARD, Marie Anna, Jan 20 1897 Sex:F Child# 2 Pierre Beauregard Canada & Oselina Aubut Canada
BEAUREGARD, Marie L Z B D, Sep 23 1887 Sex:F Child# 1 N Beauregard P Q & Blanche P Q
BEAUREGARD, Rita Isabelle, Jul 17 1924 Sex:F Child# 1 Ernest Beauregard Nashua, NH & Isabelle Bouchard Nashua, NH
BEAUREGARD, Unknown, Dec 8 1887 Sex:M Child# 2 Clement Beauregard P Q & Exilda Cote Newport, VT Stillborn
BEAUREGARD, Unknown, Jan 1 1889 Sex:M Child# 4 Joe Beauregard Canada & Zenai Belland Canada Stillborn
BEAUREGARD, Unknown, Jul 2 1889 Sex:M Child# 5 Joseph Beauregard Canada & Zenalde Belland Canada Stillborn
BEAUREGARD, Unknown, Jun 8 1903 Sex: Child# 5 Pierre Beauregard Calais & Rosilda Aubut Canada
BEAUREGARD, Victor, Apr 9 1933 Sex:M Child# 1 Vic Beauregard Nashua, NH & A Laukosh Nashua, NH
BEAUREGARD, Victor Robert, May 26 1914 Sex:M Child# 11 Pierre Beauregard Canada & Rose Aubut Canada
BEAUREGARD, Wilfrid, Dec 20 1901 Sex:M Child# 5 Pierre Beauregard Canada & Roselina Aubu Canada
BEAUREGARD, Winifred Millicent, Jan 8 1924 Sex:F Child# 1 W Beauregard Nashua, NH & Mildred Pelky Sciota, NY
BEAUSOLEIL, Alina Cecile, Sep 5 1919 Sex:F Child# 2 Louis Beausoleil Canada & Alexina Anctil Canada
BEAUSOLEIL, Estelle Jeanne d'Arc, Jan 25 1929 Sex:F Child# 6 Honore Beausoleil Nashua, NH & Cecile Cote Nashua, NH
BEAUSOLEIL, Gloria Julienne, Jun 30 1924 Sex:F Child# 2 William Beausoleil Nashua, NH & Cecile Cote Nashua, NH
BEAUSOLEIL, Joseph Henry, Aug 6 1901 Sex:M Child# 3 Joseph Beausoleil Canada & Delia Kenney New York Stillborn
BEAUSOLEIL, Loraine, Jul 12 1931 Sex:F Child# 5 Honore Beausoliel Nashua, NH & Cecile Cote Nashua, NH
BEAUSOLEIL, Marcel J Hector, Oct 5 1921 Sex:M Child# 2 Joseph Beausoleil New Ipswich, NH & Lullia Boisvert
BEAUSOLEIL, Marie C H, Sep 10 1899 Sex:F Child# 1 Alfred M Beausoleil NY & A Malenfant Canada
BEAUSOLEIL, Maurice, Mar 24 1934 Sex:M Child# 6 Honore Beausoleil Nashua, NH & Cecile Cote
BEAUSOLEIL, Raymond C Henry, Nov 18 1922 Sex:M Child# 1 Honore Beausoleil Nashua, NH & Cecile Cote Lowell, MA
BEAUSOLEIL, Rita Carmel, Nov 18 1926 Sex:F Child# 3 Honore Beausoleil Nashua, NH & Cecile Cote Lowell, MA
BEAUSOLEIL, William Honore, Oct 15 1901 Sex:M Child# 2 Melvie Beausoleil NY & Alphonsine Malenfant Canada
BEAUVAIS, Mrytle Harriette, Dec 21 1918 Sex:F Child# 2 George Beauvais Canada & Gertrude Ouellette US
BEBARD, Joseph Armand, Jun 6 1896 Sex:M Child# 3 Stanislas Bebard Canada & Marie Laforest Nashua, NH
BECHARD, Amede Lucien, Nov 15 1926 Sex:M Child# 4 Rosario Bechard Canada & Laura Desmarais Manchester, NH
BECHARD, Annette Cecile, Sep 15 1913 Sex:F Child# 3 Auguste Bechard Canada & Marie Anne Jean Canada
BECHARD, Arthur, Oct 28 1922 Sex:M Child# 5 Joseph Bechard Canada & Laura Gilbert Barre, VT
BECHARD, Charles Arthur, Dec 10 1918 Sex:M Child# 3 Joseph Bechard Canada & Laura Gilbert Graniteville, VT
BECHARD, Dolores Mona, Mar 27 1931 Sex:F Child# 15 Auguste Bechard St Pascal, PQ & Marie Anne Jean Mont Carmel

BECHARD, Dora Isabelle, Mar 24 1926 Sex:F Child# 11 Auguste Bechard Canada & Marie Anne Jean Canada
BECHARD, Emma Rita, May 9 1926 Sex:F Child# 16 Joseph Bechard Canada & Eva Bouchard Canada
BECHARD, Eva Rita, May 25 1926 Sex:F Child# 7 Joseph J Bechard Canada & Laura Gilbert Barre, VT
BECHARD, Florentine, Mar 14 1901 Sex:F Child# 7 Thomas Bechard Canada & Elise Migneau Canada
BECHARD, Irene B, Aug 13 1924 Sex:F Child# 6 Joseph Bechard Canada & Laura Gilbert Graniteville, VT
BECHARD, J Auguste Rene, Nov 4 1921 Sex:M Child# 8 Auguste Bechard Canada & Marie Anne Jean Canada
BECHARD, J Lionel Raymond, Dec 14 1914 Sex:M Child# 1 Auguste Bechard Canada & Marie Anne Jean Canada
BECHARD, Jos Adolphe Maurice, Dec 14 1917 Sex:M Child# 6 Auguste Bechard Canada & Marie Anna Jean Canada
BECHARD, Joseph A A, Oct 26 1898 Sex:M Child# 6 Thomas Bechard Canada & Elise Mignault Canada
BECHARD, Joseph Albert, May 12 1916 Sex:M Child# 1 Joseph Bechard Canada & Laura Gilbert Graniteville, VT
BECHARD, Joseph H N, May 19 1911 Sex:M Child# 1 Charles Bechard Canada & Ida Masson Canada
BECHARD, Joseph Jean Leo, Aug 27 1916 Sex:M Child# 5 Auguste Bechard Canada & Marie Anne Jean Canada
BECHARD, Joseph Lucien, Jul 2 1928 Sex:M Child# 16 Jos Bechard Canada & Eva Bouchard Canada
BECHARD, Joseph R T, Jul 10 1912 Sex:M Child# 2 Charles T Bechard Canada & Alida Masson Canada
BECHARD, Joseph Robert, Dec 1 1920 Sex:M Child# 4 Joseph Bechard Nashua, NH & Marie Bourgeois Manchester, VT
BECHARD, Joseph Roger, May 25 1928 Sex:M Child# 8 Joseph T Bechard Canada & Laura Gilbert Barre, VT
BECHARD, Marie Ange J, Apr 21 1911 Sex:F Child# 1 Auguste Bechard Canada & Marie Anne Jean Canada
BECHARD, Marie Anne Therese, Aug 1 1919 Sex:F Child# 7 Auguste Bechard Canada & M A Jean Canada
BECHARD, Marie Claire Simonne, Mar 17 1923 Sex:F Child# 9 Auguste Bechard Canada & Marie Anne Jean Canada
BECHARD, Marie Jacqueline Flo, May 20 1928 Sex:F Child# 12 August Bechard Canada & Marie Anne Jean Canada
BECHARD, Marie Lea Rachel, Feb 29 1932 Sex:F Child# 11 Jos T Bechard Canada & Laura Gilbert Vermont
BECHARD, Marie Liliane Olivet, Jul 7 1912 Sex:F Child# 2 Auguste Bechard Canada & Marie Anne Jean Canada
BECHARD, Marie Louise Carmel, Aug 25 1924 Sex:F Child# 10 Auguste Bechard Canada & Marie Anne Jean Canada
BECHARD, Mary, May 25 1928 Sex:F Child# 9 Joseph T Bechard Canada & Laura Gilbert Barre, VT
BECHARD, Mary A L, Apr 12 1917 Sex:F Child# 2 Joseph Bechard Canada & Laura Gilbert Graniteville, VT
BECHARD, Mary A T, Jun 10 1929 Sex:F Child# 10 Joseph Bechard Canada & Laura Gilbert Graniteville, VT
BECHARD, Mary Jane, Jun 26 1915 Sex:F Child# 3 Charles L Bechard Canada & Alida Mason Canada
BECK, Adeline Josephine, Oct 15 1933 Sex:F Child# 3 Joseph B Beck N Brookfield, MA & J A Pickens Ashburnham, MA
BECK, Dorothy Ludlow, Jun 16 1918 Sex:F Child# 2 Ernest W Beck Birmingham, England & Elizabeth E Ludlow Waltham, MA
BECK, Elizabeth V, Jun 11 1916 Sex:F Child# 1 Ernest W Beck Bermingham, England & Elizabeth E Ludlow Waltham, MA
BEDAKAS, Unknown, Nov 26 1926 Sex:F Child# 1 James Bedakas Greece & C Poulakida Greece
BEDARD, Albert Earl, Jun 18 1927 Sex:M Child# 1 William Bedard Canada & Clotilda Ledoux Vermont
BEDARD, Antonio, Nov 3 1899 Sex:M Child# 4 Stanislas Bedard Canada & Marie L Laforest Canada
BEDARD, Blanche, Aug 7 1894 Sex:F Child# 2 Stanislas Bedard Canada & M Louise Laforest Nashua, NH
BEDARD, Charles Emile, May 14 1929 Sex:M Child# 2 Emile Bedard Lawrence, MA & Lucienne Dupont Nashua, NH
BEDARD, Donald Alfred, Jun 21 1927 Sex:M Child# 2 Cyrille Bedard Canada & Rose Ducharme Pelham, NH
BEDARD, Edouard, Mar 24 1893 Sex:M Child# 1 Stanislas Bedard Canada & M Louise Laforest Nashua, NH
BEDARD, Edward, Jan 1 1894 Sex:M Child# 11 Joseph Bedard Canada & Marianne Paul Canada
BEDARD, Emma Jane, Feb 2 1893 Sex:F Child# 2 Narcisse Bedard Canada & Emma Richard Canada
BEDARD, Gertrude Edith, Jan 7 1925 Sex:F Child# 1 Alphie Bedard Nashua, NH & Laura Labree Altona, NY
BEDARD, Gilberte, Jan 24 1922 Sex:F Child# 4 Rodolphe Bedard Nashua, NH & Yvonne Auclair Canada
BEDARD, Helen Frances, Dec 8 1920 Sex:F Child# 1 Cyrille Bedard Michigan & Elise Marquis Canada
BEDARD, Hortense, Oct 31 1925 Sex:F Child# 5 Rodolphe Bedard Nashua, NH & Yvonne Auclair Canada
BEDARD, Jos Emile Lionel, Dec 21 1925 Sex:M Child# 2 Edward Bedard Nashua, NH & Camille Migneault Nashua, NH
BEDARD, Joseph, Feb 16 1895 Sex:M Child# 12 Joseph Bedard Canada & Marie A Paul Canada
BEDARD, Joseph Richards, Sep 2 1908 Sex:M Child# 5 Nelson Bedard Canada & Emma Richard Canada
BEDARD, Juliet Lucile, Jun 25 1917 Sex:F Child# 2 Randolph Bedard Nashua, NH & Yvonne LeClair Montreal, Quebec
BEDARD, Luc Romeo, Mar 23 1894 Sex:M Child# 3 Narcisse Bedard Canada & Emma Richard Canada
BEDARD, Lydia Florence, Sep 24 1930 Sex:F Child# 2 William Bedard Canada & Clothilda Ledoux St Albans, VT
BEDARD, Marie, Jan 12 1891 Sex:F Child# 9 Joseph Bedard Canada & Marie Paul Canada
BEDARD, Marie Louise, Mar 15 1887 Sex:F Child# 1 Jean Bte Bedard P Q & Rosalie Larive P Q
BEDARD, Marie Louise, Jul 2 1892 Sex:F Child# 10 Joseph Bedard Canada & Marie Paul Canada
BEDARD, Narcisse Edgar Romeo, Oct 25 1915 Sex:M Child# 1 Rudolphe Bedard Nashua, NH & Yvonne Auclair Canada
BEDARD, Paul Roger, Aug 18 1918 Sex:M Child# 3 Rudolph Bedard Nashua, NH & Yvonne Auclaire Nashua, NH
BEDARD, Pauline Claire, Sep 19 1933 Sex:F Child# 3 Emile Bedard US & Rhea Perreault US
BEDARD, Rodolphe Narcisse, Apr 10 1890 Sex:M Child# 1 Narcisse Bedard Canada & Emma Richard Canada
BEDARD, Rosiana, May 8 1903 Sex:F Child# 1 Xavier Bedard Canada & Rebecca Lampron Canada
BEDARD, Wilfrid Alphee, Sep 7 1895 Sex:M Child# 4 Narcisse Bedard Canada & Emma J Richard Canada
BEDARD, Yvonne Estelle, Jul 30 1927 Sex:F Child# 6 Rodolphe Bedard Nashua, NH & Yvonne Auclaire Canada
BEDELL, Georgine, Mar 14 1922 Sex:F Child# 1 George Bedell Vermont & Ivy Clegg Canada
BEDELL, Marilyn Rita, Mar 10 1930 Sex:F Child# 2 Earl Bedell
BEDELL, Ralph Winfield, May 3 1894 Sex:M Child# 1 Winfield G Bedell Madison & Gertie M Walker Biddeford, ME
BEGIN, Alice, Apr 30 1925 Sex:F Child# 5 Napoleon Begin Canada & Angelina Boairet Michigan
BEGIN, Benjamin, Sep 17 1919 Sex:M Child# 2 Napoleon Begin Canada & Angelina Bourre Linden, MI
BEGIN, Cecile, May 12 1921 Sex:F Child# 3 Napoleon Begin Canada & Angelina Boure Michigan
BEGIN, Irene, May 6 1923 Sex:F Child# 4 Napoleon Begin Canada & Angelina Boury Canada
BEGNACHE, Joseph Edgar D, May 24 1920 Sex:M Child# 7 Napoleon Begnache Canada & Alida Doucet Canada
BEGNACHE, Joseph Maurice G, Apr 23 1924 Sex:M Child# 9 Napoleon Begnache Canada & Alide Doucet Canada
BEGNACHE, Lianne Marie Rose, Feb 27 1917 Sex:F Child# 5 Napoleon Begnache Canada & Alida Doucette Canada
BEGNACHE, Marie Elodie B, Mar 26 1909 Sex:F Child# 1 Paul Begnache Canada & Alide Doucette Canada
BEGNACHE, Marie Gertrude, Apr 24 1918 Sex:F Child# 6 Napoleon Begnache Canada & Alida Doucet Canada
BEGNACHE, Marie Violette, Aug 26 1910 Sex:F Child# 2 Paul Begnache Canada & Olida Doucette Canada
BEGNACHE, Raymond, Mar 8 1922 Sex:M Child# 8 Napoleon Begnache Canada & Ida Doucet Canada

BEGNOCHE, Henri Francois, Mar 28 1914 Sex:M Child# 4 Napoleon Begnoche Canada & Ida Doucet Canada
BEIGERON, Marie N A, Feb 5 1888 Sex:F Child# 1 Homer Beigeron P Q & Albina Lefebvre P Q
BEINWICH, Weidzlewie, Jun 20 1914 Sex:F Child# 1 Jasper Beinwich Russia & Greslyle Reidsewc Russia
BEISEBOIS, Alexander Frederick, Apr 6 1890 Sex:M Child# Alexandre Beisebois Canada & Cordelia Richard Nashua, NH
BELAIR, Alfred Bernard, Jul 8 1929 Sex:M Child# 2 Alfred Belair Canada & Angeline Bernard Nashua, NH
BELAIR, Laura Estelle, Nov 17 1932 Sex:F Child# 4 Alfred Belair Canada & Angeline Bernard Nashua, NH
BELAIR, Muriel Claire, Sep 7 1931 Sex:F Child# 2 Alfred Belair Canada & Angeline Benard Nashua, NH
BELAIRE, Unknown, Jul 29 1892 Sex:M Child# 4 Philippe Belaire Canada & Marie Rosignol Canada
BELAIS, Blanche Lorraine, Jun 28 1928 Sex:F Child# 1 Alfred F Belais Canada & Angelina Bernard Nashua, NH
BELAND, Alberta Lorette, May 28 1922 Sex:F Child# 2 Godefroi Beland Canada & Alberta Angus Nashua, NH
BELAND, Alice Mabel, Jan 6 1911 Sex:F Child# 1 Hector Beland NH & Pearl Page NH
BELAND, Amanda, May 23 1907 Sex:F Child# 1 Alfred Beland Nashua, NH & Alexandrine Hudon Canada
BELAND, Gloria Madelaine, Oct 6 1932 Sex:F Child# 6 Rosario Beland Nashua, NH & Evangeline Anctil Nashua, NH
BELAND, Joseph H, Nov 9 1898 Sex:M Child# 7 Ephrem Beland Canada & Emma Beland Canada
BELAND, Joseph Leon, Jun 1 1903 Sex:M Child# 9 Ephrem Beland Canada & Emma Boutin Canada
BELAND, Joseph Romeo, May 10 1906 Sex:M Child# 10 Ephraim Beland Canada & Emma Boutin Canada
BELAND, Marie, Aug 5 1894 Sex:F Child# 5 Dolphis Beland Nashua, NH & Aldina Desmarais Canada
BELAND, Maurice Edmond, Apr 30 1924 Sex:M Child# 5 Rosario Beland Nashua, NH & Evan Anctil Nashua, NH
BELAND, Paul Raymond, Apr 11 1917 Sex:M Child# 1 Rosario Beland Nashua, NH & Evangeline Anctil Nashua, NH
BELAND, Roger Phillip, Oct 17 1935 Sex:M Child# 7 Rosario Beland Nashua, NH & Evangeline Anctil Nashua, NH
BELAND, Rosario, Apr 16 1895 Sex:M Child# 5 Ephrem Beland Canada & Emma Boutin Canada
BELAND, Wilfrid, Aug 26 1901 Sex:M Child# 8 Ephrem Beland Canada & Emma Boutin Canada
BELANGER, Albert Ernest, Feb 1 1929 Sex:M Child# 3 Wilfrid Belanger Nashua, NH & Eva Manseau Canada
BELANGER, Alfred Daniel, Jul 6 1935 Sex:M Child# 2 Alfred Belanger Canada & Florence Smit Poland
BELANGER, Alfred Henry, Jul 29 1929 Sex:M Child# 3 Alfred Belanger Nashua, NH & Laurine Fecteau Nashua, NH
BELANGER, Alice, Feb 18 1889 Sex:F Child# 1 Ialonian Belanger Canada & Sianna Levesque Canada
BELANGER, Alphonse Gerard, Oct 13 1923 Sex:M Child# 6 Adelard Belanger Canada & R A Boucher Canada
BELANGER, Alphonse Sylvio, Apr 20 1926 Sex:M Child# 3 Alphonse Belanger Canada & Alida Leveille Nashua, NH
BELANGER, Andrew Jos Patrick, Jun 22 1923 Sex:M Child# 2 Andrew J P Belanger Nashua, NH & Caroline Bumford CO
BELANGER, Armand, Apr 8 1887 Sex:M Child# Auguste Belanger P Q & Arthemise Dube P Q
BELANGER, Audre, Mar 17 1895 Sex:M Child# 5 Solomon Belanger Canada & Diana Leveque Canada
BELANGER, Beatrice Cecile, Mar 30 1925 Sex:F Child# 2 Alph Belanger Canada & Aleda Leveille Nashua, NH
BELANGER, Bertha Lorette, Oct 13 1930 Sex:F Child# 4 Wilfred Belanger Nashua, NH & Eva Manseau Canada
BELANGER, Bertrand, Feb 4 1923 Sex:M Child# 1 Charles E Belanger Canada & Blanche Beaupre Canada
BELANGER, Carlton, Feb 7 1932 Sex:M Child# 10 George Belanger Nashua, NH & Eva Gauvin Sutton, MA
BELANGER, Carmen Marguerite, Aug 15 1928 Sex:F Child# 8 George Belanger Canada & Edith Marquis Nashua, NH
BELANGER, Constance Marie Anne, Apr 21 1927 Sex:F Child# 2 Wilfrid Belanger Nashua, NH & Eva Manceau Canada
BELANGER, Daniel Aldege, Jan 12 1918 Sex:M Child# 11 Charles Belanger NH & Rose Normand Canada
BELANGER, Dorilda, Sep 6 1893 Sex:F Child# 4 Solomon Belanger Canada & A Levesque Canada
BELANGER, Edgar Wilfrid, Jun 27 1914 Sex:M Child# 2 Emile Belanger Canada & Adele Bernier Canada
BELANGER, Edna Louise, Sep 28 1925 Sex:F Child# 2 Albert Belanger Canada & Blanche Levesque Nashua, NH
BELANGER, Emile, Aug 7 1922 Sex:M Child# 5 Adelard Belanger Canada & Rosanna Boucher Canada Stillborn
BELANGER, Emile Adrien, May 27 1913 Sex:M Child# 15 George Belanger Canada & Ida Pelletier Canada
BELANGER, Emma Yvonne, Apr 16 1905 Sex:F Child# 1 Bruno Belanger Canada & Rose Anna Marotte Canada
BELANGER, George Adrien, Feb 27 1917 Sex:M Child# 2 Adelard Belanger Canada & Rosanna Boucher Canada
BELANGER, George Henri, Nov 10 1911 Sex:M Child# 3 Bruno Belanger Canada & Exian Marotte New York
BELANGER, Georges, Mar 30 1896 Sex:M Child# 2 Charles Belanger US & Rose Nonuaud Canada
BELANGER, Gerald Normand, Oct 20 1925 Sex:M Child# 3 Charles Belanger Canada & Marie Canada
BELANGER, Gerald Solomon, Jul 28 1927 Sex:M Child# 4 Andrew Belanger Nashua, NH & Caroline Bumford Colebrook
BELANGER, Germaine Amanda, Sep 13 1912 Sex:F Child# 2 Felix Belanger Canada & Amanda Lavoie Canada
BELANGER, Hector Elzebert, Aug 17 1901 Sex:M Child# 7 Philippe Belanger Canada & Phenie Desrosiers Canada
BELANGER, Helena Irene, Feb 17 1933 Sex:F Child# 11 George Belanger Nashua, NH & Eva Gauvin Sutton, MA
BELANGER, Irene Jeannette, May 26 1931 Sex:F Child# 4 Alfred Belanger Nashua, NH & Lauriane Fecteau Nashua, NH
BELANGER, J Alfred Donat, Jun 27 1915 Sex:M Child# 2 Joseph Belanger Canada & Exina Masse Canada
BELANGER, J Henri Omer, Apr 11 1913 Sex:M Child# 12 Clovis Belanger Canada & Virginie Roy Canada
BELANGER, J Jean Baptiste O, Aug 29 1911 Sex:M Child# 11 George Belanger Canada & Ida Pelletier Canada
BELANGER, Jean Baptiste, May 21 1905 Sex:M Child# 12 Solomon Belanger Canada & Diana Levesque Canada
BELANGER, Jean Maurice, May 17 1930 Sex:M Child# 9 George E Belanger Canada & Edith Marquis Nashua, NH
BELANGER, Joan Rolande, Sep 17 1929 Sex:F Child# 2 Thomas Belanger Nashua, NH & Regina Girouard Nashua, NH
BELANGER, Jos Alphonse Oscar, Nov 22 1916 Sex:M Child# 5 Alphonse Belanger Canada & Arma Dionne Canada
BELANGER, Jos Frederick Paul, Jun 29 1928 Sex:M Child# 1 Thos Belanger Nashua, NH & Regina Girouard Nashua, NH
BELANGER, Jos George Robert, Feb 8 1920 Sex:M Child# 1 George A Belanger Nashua, NH & Marie J Bourgoin Canada
BELANGER, Jos Raymond Alfred, Dec 24 1923 Sex:M Child# 2 George A Belanger Nashua, NH & Marie Jeane Bourgois
BELANGER, Jos Robert William, Jul 9 1935 Sex:M Child# 2 William Belanger Nashua, NH & Irene Fecteau Nashua, NH
BELANGER, Joseph, Apr 30 1909 Sex:M Child# 13 Phillippe Belanger Canada & Euphemie Desrosiers Canada
BELANGER, Joseph, Aug 2 1919 Sex:M Child# 2 A Belanger Canada & Alice Caron Canada
BELANGER, Joseph, May 22 1920 Sex:M Child# 3 Teranius Belanger Canada & Alice Carron Canada
BELANGER, Joseph A R, Mar 30 1909 Sex:M Child# 9 Charles Belanger NH & Rose Normand Canada
BELANGER, Joseph A Solomon, Sep 28 1896 Sex:M Child# 5 Solomon Belanger Canada & Diana Leveque Canada
BELANGER, Joseph Aguestin, Aug 20 1888 Sex:M Child# 19 Augusta Belanger Canada & Arthimisse Dubi Nashua, NH
BELANGER, Joseph Albert G, May 8 1924 Sex:M Child# 1 Albert Belanger Canada & Blanche Levesque Nashua, NH
BELANGER, Joseph Alfred, Jul 2 1896 Sex:M Child# 4 Joseph Belanger Canada & Alice Ouellette Canada
BELANGER, Joseph Alfred, Dec 6 1897 Sex:M Child# 4 Philippe Belanger Canada & Euphemis Desrosiers Canada

BELANGER, Joseph Armand J, Jul 13 1910 Sex:M Child# 11 Clovis Belanger Canada & Virginie Roy Canada
BELANGER, Joseph Arthur, Jan 22 1894 Sex:M Child# 2 Joseph Belanger Canada & Alice Ouelette Canada
BELANGER, Joseph Edmond, Jul 2 1913 Sex:M Child# 9 Napoleon Belanger Canada & Georgianna Godbout Canada
BELANGER, Joseph Emile, Sep 1895 Sex:M Child# 2 Philippe Belanger Canada & Phemie Desrosiers Canada
BELANGER, Joseph Emile S, Sep 7 1902 Sex:M Child# 2 Sylvio Belanger Canada & Adele Ross Canada
BELANGER, Joseph Ernest, Sep 9 1896 Sex:M Child# 4 Clovis Belanger Canada & Virginie Roy Canada
BELANGER, Joseph G, Apr 10 1922 Sex:M Child# 1 Andrew Belanger Nashua, NH & Caroline Bumford Colebrook, NH
BELANGER, Joseph Hector, Aug 6 1907 Sex:M Child# 2 Bruno Belanger Canada & Rose Anna Marotte New York
BELANGER, Joseph J B, Oct 8 1899 Sex:M Child# 1 Ernest Belanger Canada & Marguerite Brisebois Canada
BELANGER, Joseph Leo Wilfred, Apr 24 1900 Sex:M Child# 6 Philippe Belanger Canada & Eupher'ie Desrosiers Canada
BELANGER, Joseph Leon A, Oct 17 1904 Sex:M Child# 9 Philippe Belanger Canada & Euphemie Desrosiers Canada
BELANGER, Joseph Lorenzo, Jul 30 1893 Sex:M Child# 1 Ernest Belanger Canada & Marguerite Brisebois Canada
BELANGER, Joseph Maurice, Jan 28 1915 Sex:M Child# 10 Charles Belanger NH & Rose Normand Canada
BELANGER, Joseph Moise, Jun 13 1909 Sex:M Child# 1 Moise Belanger Canada & Edith Pelletier Canada
BELANGER, Joseph Napoleon, May 28 1892 Sex:M Child# 1 Joseph Belanger Canada & Alice Ouellette Canada
BELANGER, Joseph Philippe, Jan 30 1899 Sex:M Child# 5 Philippe Belanger Canada & Euphenire Desrosiers Canada
BELANGER, Joseph Ray Camille, Jan 18 1935 Sex:M Child# 5 Alphonse Belanger Canada & Alide Leveille Nashua, NH
BELANGER, Joseph Raymond, Aug 31 1932 Sex:M Child# 1 Joseph Belanger Canada & Cecile Belanger Salem, MA
BELANGER, Joseph Robert Henry, Jul 16 1927 Sex:M Child# 1 H J P Belanger Nashua, NH & Mary J Nadeau Nashua, NH
BELANGER, Joseph Roland Edgar, Jun 14 1916 Sex:M Child# 4 Moise Belanger Canada & Edith Pelletier Canada
BELANGER, Joseph Theodore, Mar 14 1918 Sex:M Child# 5 Moise Eug Belanger Canada & Edith Pelletier Canada
BELANGER, Joseph Wilfred, May 15 1901 Sex:M Child# 7 Clodis Belanger Canada & Virginie Roy Canada
BELANGER, Joseph Wilfred, Mar 7 1911 Sex:M Child# 2 Moise Belanger Canada & Edith Pelletier Canada
BELANGER, Joseph William, Dec 11 1905 Sex:M Child# 10 Philippe Belanger Canada & Euphemie Desrosiers Canada
BELANGER, Joseph Xavier, Oct 12 1930 Sex:M Child# 4 Odillon Belanger Canada & Ida Deagon Canada
BELANGER, Josephine Ernestine, Oct 9 1896 Sex:F Child# 3 Philippe Belanger Canada & Euphemie Desrosiers Canada
BELANGER, Julien, Jul 5 1924 Sex:M Child# 1 Odilion Belanger Canada & Ida D'Anjou Canada
BELANGER, Julien Emile, Nov 4 1912 Sex:M Child# 1 Emile Belanger Canada & Adele Bernier Canada
BELANGER, Juliette Marie Rose, Jul 15 1912 Sex:F Child# 1 Joseph Belanger Canada & Exina Masse Canada
BELANGER, Lawrence Rochel, Mar 21 1925 Sex:F Child# 1 Alfred Belanger Nashua, NH & Lauriane Fecteau Nashua, NH
BELANGER, Lilia Estelle, Mar 13 1921 Sex:F Child# 3 George Belanger Canada & Edith Marquis Nashua, NH
BELANGER, Louise, Mar 30 1901 Sex:F Child# Ernest Belanger Canada & Maggie Brisebois NH
BELANGER, Lucien Wilfrid, May 29 1927 Sex:M Child# 7 G Belanger, Jr Canada & Edith Marquis Nashua, NH
BELANGER, Lucille Catherine, Aug 28 1927 Sex: Child# Alfred Belanger Canada & Florence Soscist Poland
BELANGER, M Germaine Isabelle, Aug 29 1915 Sex:F Child# 13 Clovis Belanger Canada & Virginie Roy Canada
BELANGER, M Louise, Sep 28 1898 Sex:F Child# 4 Charles Belanger Canada & Rose Norman Canada
BELANGER, M Lucille Carmelle, Jun 6 1915 Sex:F Child# 4 Alphonse Belanger Canada & Anna Dionne Canada
BELANGER, M Lucille Rita, Jul 19 1914 Sex:F Child# 2 Adelard Belanger Canada & Irene Anctil Canada
BELANGER, Marguerite, Jul 9 1924 Sex:F Child# 2 C E Belanger Canada & Blanche Beaupre Canada
BELANGER, Marie, May 20 1900 Sex:F Child# 6 Louis Belanger Canada & Anna Levesque Canada
BELANGER, Marie, Mar 30 1901 Sex:F Child# Ernest Belanger Canada & Maggie Brisebois NH
BELANGER, Marie A Jeanne D'Arc, Jul 19 1934 Sex:F Child# 10 George Belanger St Antonet, PQ & Edith Marquis Nashua
BELANGER, Marie Alphonsine, Aug 22 1894 Sex:F Child# 2 Ernest Belanger Canada & Marguerite Brisbois Canada
BELANGER, Marie Annette Jeanne, Jan 12 1929 Sex:F Child# 2 Joseph H Belanger Nashua, NH & Marie J Nadeau Nashua, NH
BELANGER, Marie Annette Theres, Feb 27 1923 Sex:F Child# 7 Alphonse Belanger Canada & Anna Dionne Canada
BELANGER, Marie B A, Apr 17 1903 Sex:F Child# 8 Clovis Belanger Canada & Virginie Roy Canada
BELANGER, Marie Bertha Estelle, Feb 10 1927 Sex:F Child# 8 Alphonse Belanger Canada & Anna Dionne Canada
BELANGER, Marie Blanche A, Jul 23 1903 Sex:F Child# 10 Solomon Belanger Canada & Diana Levesque Canada
BELANGER, Marie Blanche L, Oct 24 1900 Sex:F Child# 1 Sylvio Belanger Canada & Adele Ross Canada
BELANGER, Marie Carmel Gertrud, Apr 12 1918 Sex:F Child# 1 Teranius Belanger Canada & Alice Caron Nashua, NH
BELANGER, Marie Claudia B, Jul 5 1905 Sex:F Child# 9 Clovis Belanger Canada & Virginie Roy Canada
BELANGER, Marie Delia Eva, Jan 11 1899 Sex:F Child# 1 Arsene Belanger Canada & Angelina Ross Canada
BELANGER, Marie E Anna, May 14 1899 Sex:F Child# 1 Joseph Belanger Canada & Eugenie Bernier Canada
BELANGER, Marie Edith, Oct 10 1912 Sex:F Child# 3 Moise Belanger Canada & Edith Pelletier Canada
BELANGER, Marie Elaise, Sep 2 1889 Sex:F Child# 20 A Belanger Canada & Arthemise Dube Canada
BELANGER, Marie Elise B Y, Apr 13 1907 Sex:F Child# 1 Felix Belanger Canada & Helene Lavoie Canada
BELANGER, Marie Eva Alice, Mar 20 1907 Sex:F Child# 11 Philippe Belanger Canada & Euphemie Desrosiers Canada
BELANGER, Marie Eva Y, Jun 2 1901 Sex:F Child# 9 Solomon Belanger Canada & Diana Levesque Canada
BELANGER, Marie Ida Annette, Apr 22 1934 Sex:F Child# 8 Adelard Belanger Canada & Rose Boucher Canada
BELANGER, Marie Irene Lucille, Apr 28 1919 Sex:F Child# 6 Alphonse Belanger Canada & Anna Dionne Canada
BELANGER, Marie Jacqueline, Jun 22 1934 Sex:F Child# 2 Joseph Belanger St Anthony, Quebec & Cecile Belanger
BELANGER, Marie Jeanne, Sep 28 1912 Sex:F Child# 3 Alphonse Belanger Canada & Amanda Dionne Canada
BELANGER, Marie Jeanne A, Mar 30 1907 Sex:F Child# 10 Clovis Belanger Canada & Virginie Roy Canada
BELANGER, Marie L Albina, Feb 16 1899 Sex:F Child# 8 Solomon Belanger Canada & Diana Levesque Canada
BELANGER, Marie L Delia, Dec 19 1897 Sex:F Child# 5 Clovis Belanger Canada & Virginie Roy Canada
BELANGER, Marie Laura A, May 30 1911 Sex:F Child# 2 Alphonse Belanger Canada & Annette Dionne Canada
BELANGER, Marie Liliane E, May 4 1908 Sex:F Child# 12 Philippe Belanger Canada & Euphemie Desrosiers Canada
BELANGER, Marie Mathilda, Jun 28 1896 Sex:F Child# 3 Ernest Belanger Canada & Marguerite Brisbois Canada
BELANGER, Marie R D, Nov 28 1897 Sex:F Child# 7 Solomon Belanger Canada & Diana Levesque Canada
BELANGER, Marie R Yvonne, Sep 13 1903 Sex:F Child# 8 Philip Belanger Canada & Euphemie Desrosiers Canada
BELANGER, Marie Rose, Sep 18 1894 Sex:F Child# 1 Philippe Belanger Canada & Euphemie Desrosiers Canada
BELANGER, Marie Rose, Jun 9 1897 Sex:F Child# 3 Charles Belanger Canada & Rose Normand Canada
BELANGER, Marie Theresa, Mar 20 1927 Sex:F Child# 3 Alphonse Belanger Canada & Bertha Girard Canada

BELANGER, Mary Flose, Dec 28 1890 Sex:F Child# 21 Auguste Belanger Canada & Artemise Dube Canada
BELANGER, Mary Margaret Dana, Jul 28 1927 Sex:F Child# 5 Andrew Belanger Nashua, NH & Caroline Bumford Colebrook,NH
BELANGER, Mary Rita Louise, Apr 1 1924 Sex:F Child# 1 Alphonse Belanger Canada & Ida Leveille Nashua, NH
BELANGER, Normande Georgette, Aug 31 1929 Sex:F Child# 7 George Belanger Nashua, NH & Eva Gauvin Wilkinsonville
BELANGER, Omer Francois, Dec 3 1933 Sex:M Child# 6 Wilfrid Belanger Nashua, NH & Eva Manseau Canada
BELANGER, Paul, May 3 1915 Sex:M Child# 1 Adelard Belanger Canada & Rose Anna Boucher Canada
BELANGER, Paul Alfred, Sep 8 1924 Sex:M Child# 3 Andre Belanger Nashua, NH & Caroline Bumford Colebrook, NH
BELANGER, Pauline, Nov 27 1932 Sex:F Child# 5 Wilfred Belanger Nashua, NH & Eva Manseau Canada
BELANGER, Philippe Armand, Aug 23 1919 Sex:M Child# 2 George Belanger, Jr Canada & Edith Marquis Nashua, NH
BELANGER, Pierre Henri, Oct 8 1903 Sex:M Child# 2 Joseph Belanger Canada & Albertine Prevost Canada
BELANGER, Rachael Adrienne, Aug 27 1924 Sex:F Child# 5 George Belanger Canada & Edith Marquis Nashua, NH
BELANGER, Raoul Conrad F, Nov 19 1924 Sex:M Child# 7 Adelard Belanger Canada & Rose A Boucher Canada
BELANGER, Raymond, Feb 23 1935 Sex:M Child# 1 Hector Belanger Nashua, NH & Yvonne Gagnon Canada
BELANGER, Raymond Roger, Jan 24 1914 Sex:M Child# 4 Bruno Belanger Canada & Exina Marotte New York
BELANGER, Rita Gertrude, Nov 15 1922 Sex:F Child# 4 George Belanger, Jr Canada & Edith Marquis Nashua, NH
BELANGER, Robert Emile, Sep 25 1933 Sex:M Child# 1 Emile Belanger Canada & Anna Theriault Nashua, NH
BELANGER, Robert Normand, Nov 12 1925 Sex:M Child# 6 George Belanger, Jr Canada & Edith Marquis Nashua, NH
BELANGER, Roland Alfred, May 26 1925 Sex:M Child# 4 Joseph Belanger Nashua, NH & Antoinette Fortin Canada
BELANGER, Roland Noel, Dec 21 1918 Sex:M Child# 3 Adelard Belanger Canada & Rosanna Boucher Canada
BELANGER, Solomon, Dec 26 1899 Sex:M Child# 9 Solomon Belanger Canada & Diana Levesque Canada Stillborn
BELANGER, Sylvio, Jul 7 1908 Sex:M Child# 1 Adelard Belanger Canada & Marie Demange Canada
BELANGER, Theodore, Feb 10 1928 Sex:M Child# 1 Theo O Belanger New York & Alx'dra Alexopolos Nashua, NH
BELANGER, Theresa Claire, Apr 25 1927 Sex:F Child# 3 Odilion Belanger Canada & Ida Deragon Canada
BELANGER, Theresa Jeanne d'Arc, Aug 24 1926 Sex:F Child# 2 Alfred Belanger Nashua, NH & Laurian Fecteau Canada
BELANGER, Theresa Lorraine, Sep 24 1929 Sex:F Child# 3 Albert Belanger Canada & Blanche Levesque Nashua, NH
BELANGER, Thomas, Aug 1 1890 Sex:M Child# 2 Solomon Belanger Canada & Dianna Lenique Canada
BELANGER, Unknown, Jul 16 1893 Sex:M Child# 1 Edmond Belanger Canada & Clara Lebel Canada Stillborn
BELANGER, Unknown, Jul 15 1902 Sex:M Child# Ernest Belanger Canada & Maggie Brisebois NH
BELANGER, Unknown, Feb 24 1911 Sex:M Child# 14 Philippe Belanger Canada & Euphemie Desrosiers Canada Stillborn
BELANGER, Unknown, Jul 26 1919 Sex:M Child# 4 Ernest Belanger
BELANGER, Unknown, Sep 10 1919 Sex:M Child# 5 Moise Belanger Canada & A Pelletier Canada Stillborn
BELANGER, Victor Raymond, Dec 31 1926 Sex:M Child# 7 Adelard Belanger Canada & R A Boucher Canada
BELANGER, Victor Roland, Apr 8 1918 Sex:M Child# 1 George G Belanger Canada & Edith Marquis Nashua, NH
BELANGER, Vivian Loretta, Jan 24 1934 Sex:F Child# 1 William Belanger Nashua, NH & Irene Fecteau Nashua, NH
BELANGER, Wilfred Oliver, Aug 30 1925 Sex:M Child# 1 Wilfred Belanger Nashua, NH & Eva Manceau Canada
BELASKY, Donald Thomas, Aug 26 1933 Sex:M Child# 4 William Belasky Lithuania & Lucy Petralis Nashua, NH
BELAVANCE, Bernadette, Feb 15 1896 Sex:F Child# 10 Thomas Belavance Canada & Adile Peltier Canada
BELAVANCE, Leopold, Nov 28 1898 Sex:M Child# 1 Alfred Belavance Canada & Leda Michaud Canada
BELAVANCE, Marie Bernadette, Nov 28 1889 Sex:F Child# 2 Paul Belavance Canada & Sophie Martin Canada
BELAWANCY, Unknown, Nov 17 1909 Sex:F Child# Watslif Belawancy Russia & Russia
BELAWSKI, Adam S, Oct 27 1921 Sex:M Child# 5 Adam J Belawski Russia & Josie Zylonis Russia
BELAWSKI, Julia B, Oct 27 1921 Sex:F Child# 4 Adam J Belawski Russia & Josie Zylonis Russia
BELCK, Joseph, Feb 8 1915 Sex:M Child# 4 Anton Belck Russia & Tafillia Trusewick Russia
BELCOURT, Eseline, Nov 15 1899 Sex:F Child# 1 Evariste Belcourt Canada & Emelia Chicoine Canada
BELCOURT, J Jean Roland, Jun 2 1911 Sex:M Child# 5 Napoleon Belcourt Canada & Pomela Descoteaux Canada
BELCOURT, Jacqueline Gertrude, May 17 1926 Sex:F Child# 1 Fernando Belcourt Canada & Pearl Edwards Hudson, NH
BELCOURT, Josephine, Apr 4 1914 Sex:F Child# 1 John Belcourt Manchester, NH & Louisa Lemere Hooksett, NH Still
BELCOURT, M Eugenie Lorette, Mar 11 1915 Sex:F Child# 6 Napoleon Belcourt Canada & Parmela Descoteaux Canada
BELCOURT, Unknown, May 18 1927 Sex:F Child# 11 Donat Belcourt Canada & Elzire Stglais Canada Stillborn
BELDING, Cherry, Jul 10 1887 Sex:F Child# 2 Rufus P Belding Westford, CT & Imogene Reynolds Cummingsville, CT
BELDONIS, Mary, Sep 8 1920 Sex:F Child# 3 Adam Beldonis Lithuania & Lena Skirkatis Lithuania
BELENSKI, Annie Julia, Apr 17 1915 Sex:F Child# 2 Rejnny Belenski Russia & Elizab Markofsky Austria
BELESTE, Marie, May 15 1887 Sex:F Child# Magloire Beleste Quebec & Devise Caron Quebec
BELETIZ, Alexander, May 9 1914 Sex:M Child# 1 Alexander Beletiz Russia & Michela Patascenti Russia
BELFLEUR, Edouard, Jun 30 1904 Sex:M Child# 6 Maxime Belfleur Canada & Clara Malenfant Salmon Falls, NH
BELFLEUR, Emelia Maria, Oct 21 1898 Sex:F Child# 3 Maxime Belfleur Canada & Clara Malenfaut Salmon Falls, NH
BELFLEUR, Joseph Maxime, Jun 17 1897 Sex:M Child# 2 Maxime Belfleur Canada & Clarinda Malenfaut Salmon Falls, NH
BELFLEUR, Jules Alvah, Nov 26 1900 Sex:M Child# 4 Max Belfleur Canada & Clara Malenfant
BELFLEUR, Rose Valida, Feb 1 1902 Sex:F Child# 5 Maxime Belfleur Canada & Clarina Malenfant Salmon Falls, NH
BELHUMEUR, Irene Yolande, Jun 5 1930 Sex:F Child# 2 Euclide Belhumeur Canada & Laurensa Cardinal Canada
BELHUMEUR, Joseph Albert, Sep 11 1930 Sex:M Child# 1 J M Belhumeur Canada & Therese Deschenes Canada
BELHUMEUR, Paul, Oct 4 1933 Sex:M Child# 2 Jean Belhumeur Canada & T Deschesne Nashua, NH
BELINSKI, Rene, Aug 11 1913 Sex:M Child# 1 Rene Belinski Russia & Elizabeth Markofska Austria
BELISLE, George Ernest, Jan 13 1900 Sex:M Child# 2 Rosario Belisle Canada & Henriette Lucier Canada
BELISLE, Joseph Aurel A F, Mar 14 1904 Sex:M Child# 6 Oscar Belisle Canada & Albina Chabot Canada
BELISLE, Joseph Oscar, Apr 25 1896 Sex:M Child# 2 Oscar Belisle Canada & Albina Chabot Canada
BELISLE, Laura Beatrice, Nov 8 1902 Sex:F Child# 3 Rosario Belisle Canada & Henriette Lussier Canada
BELISLE, M B Eva, Nov 10 1894 Sex:F Child# 1 Oscar Belisle Canada & Albina Chabot Canada
BELISLE, Marie Andree A, Jul 11 1899 Sex:F Child# 4 Oscar Belisle Canada & Albina Chabot Canada
BELISLE, Marie Hermina G, Aug 14 1905 Sex:F Child# 7 Joseph Oscar Belisle Canada & Albina Chabot Canada
BELISLE, Marie L Agnes, Feb 8 1898 Sex:F Child# 3 Oscor Belisle Canada & Albina Chabot Canada
BELISLE, Roland Henri, Aug 10 1901 Sex:M Child# 5 J Oscar Belisle Canada & Albina Chabot Canada
BELL, Charles Frank, May 31 1896 Sex:M Child# 2 George F Bell Hollis, NH & Mary L Wright Pepperell, MA

BELL, David Malcolm, Nov 2 1928 Sex:M Child# 1 Donald Bell Canada & Florence Walker Melrose, MA
BELL, Helen M, Mar 26 1888 Sex:F Child# 6 Henry J Bell England & Eliza England
BELL, John Eastman, Nov 4 1928 Sex:M Child# 1 L Eastman Bell Hollis, NH & M B McAuliffe Boston, MA
BELL, Lillian May, Nov 25 1904 Sex:F Child# 2 Eugene Bell W Chazy, NY & Bertha Hewson W Chazy, NY
BELL, Lorrain, May 7 1895 Sex:F Child# 1 George F Bell Hollis, NH & Mary L Wright Pepperell, MA
BELL, Martha Worcester, Aug 17 1931 Sex:F Child# 2 Harry Bell Hollis, NH & Helen Worcester Hollis, NH
BELL, Richard Wright, Aug 28 1933 Sex:M Child# 2 John E Bell Hollis, NH & M B McAuliffe Boston, MA
BELL, S Livingston, Aug 15 1891 Sex:M Child#  Henry J Bell Brighton, England & W Stanley Liverpool, England
BELLABAN, Louis, Jan 19 1918 Sex:M Child# 5 Charley Bellaban Russia & Josei Christopswicz Russia
BELLAND, Claudia, Aug 17 1891 Sex:F Child# 3 Ephrem Belland Canada & Emma Goulet Canada
BELLAND, Emile, Mar 10 1893 Sex:M Child# 4 Ephrem Belland Canada & Emma Boutin Canada
BELLAND, Gaudias, Dec 11 1896 Sex:M Child# 6 Ephrem Belland Canada & Emma Boutin Canada
BELLAND, Joseph H, Sep 5 1889 Sex:M Child# 4 Delphis Belland Nashua, NH & Alecina Desmarais Canada
BELLAND, Theophile, Nov 8 1889 Sex:M Child# 2 Ephrem Belland Canada & Emma Boutin Canada
BELLARANCE, Alfred, Nov 10 1892 Sex:M Child# 5 Ferdinand Bellarance Canada & Sophie Martin Canada
BELLARANCE, Ernest, Nov 10 1892 Sex:M Child# 4 Ferdinand Bellarance Canada & Sophie Martin Canada
BELLARD, Alfred, Apr 12 1888 Sex:M Child# 1 Ephraim Bellard Canada & Emma Bontin Canada
BELLARD, Rossana, Jan 6 1888 Sex:F Child# 3 Dolpheus Bellard Nashua, NH & Edna Dimmaris St Marie, PQ
BELLAVANCE, Adelard, Nov 4 1893 Sex:M Child# 9 Thomas Bellavance Canada & Adele Peltier Canada
BELLAVANCE, Albert, Jul 17 1932 Sex:M Child# 6 A Bellavance Canada & Imelda Desbien Canada
BELLAVANCE, Alberta, Aug 12 1897 Sex:F Child# 2 Paul Bellavance Canada & Anna Dube Canada
BELLAVANCE, Alvine, Aug 8 1900 Sex:F Child# 3 Joseph Bellavance Canada & Rosanna Lapierre Nashua, NH
BELLAVANCE, Angelina Emilda, May 27 1907 Sex:F Child# 6 J A Bellavance Canada & Rosanna Lapierre US
BELLAVANCE, Armand, Jul 7 1932 Sex:M Child# 3 A Bellavance Nashua, NH & Gladys Burns Milford, NH
BELLAVANCE, Armand Roger, Sep 19 1927 Sex:M Child# 2 C Bellavance Nashua, NH & Rose Caron Canada
BELLAVANCE, Arthur, Jul 3 1901 Sex:M Child# 3 Alfred Bellavance Canada & Leda Michaud Canada
BELLAVANCE, Arthur Ferdinand, Sep 7 1908 Sex:M Child# 7 J A Bellavance US & Rosanna Lapierre US
BELLAVANCE, Blanche Adele, Oct 26 1889 Sex:F Child# 11 Antoine Bellavance Canada & Virginie Dionne Canada
BELLAVANCE, Blanche Ivonne, Jan 14 1892 Sex:F Child# 4 Ferdinand Bellavance Canada & Sophie Martin Canada
BELLAVANCE, Donald Ronald, Apr 26 1929 Sex:M Child# 3 Conrad Bellavance Nashua, NH & Rose Caron Canada
BELLAVANCE, Emile, Oct 21 1893 Sex:M Child# 7 Ferdinand Bellavance Canada & Sophie Martin Canada
BELLAVANCE, Estelle, Jun 17 1932 Sex:F Child# 6 C Bellavance Nashua, NH & Rose Caron Canada
BELLAVANCE, Eugene, May 7 1896 Sex:M Child# 9 Ferd Bellavance Canada & Sophie Martin Canada
BELLAVANCE, Horace Conrad, May 6 1906 Sex:M Child# 6 Alfred Bellavance Canada & Leda Michaud Canada
BELLAVANCE, Jean Baptiste, Mar 24 1895 Sex:M Child# 11 Nazaire Bellavance Canada & Marie Theriault Canada
BELLAVANCE, Jean Lorraine, Feb 3 1931 Sex:F Child# 4 Conrad Bellavance Nashua, NH & Rose Caron Canada
BELLAVANCE, Jeannette Elaine, Feb 3 1931 Sex:F Child# 5 Conrad Bellavance Nashua, NH & Rose Caron Canada
BELLAVANCE, Joan, Nov 17 1928 Sex:F Child# 1 A Bellavance Nashua, NH & Gladys Burns Milford, NH
BELLAVANCE, Joseph Arthur, Feb 14 1901 Sex:M Child# 12 Ferdinand Bellavance Canada & Sophie Martin Canada
BELLAVANCE, Joseph Ernest, Jan 21 1903 Sex:M Child# 13 Nazaire Bellavance Canada & Marie F Theriault Canada
BELLAVANCE, Joseph Jean B, Jul 11 1898 Sex:M Child# 1 Joseph Bellavance Canada & Marie Thibault Canada
BELLAVANCE, Joseph Jude, Oct 8 1934 Sex:M Child# 5 Armand Bellavance Nashua, NH & Gladys Burns Milford, NH
BELLAVANCE, Joseph Leopold, Sep 21 1896 Sex:M Child# 2 Joseph Bellavance Canada & Rosanna Lapierre Nashua, NH
BELLAVANCE, Joseph S A, May 31 1903 Sex:M Child# 4 Alfred Bellavance Canada & Leda Michaud Canada
BELLAVANCE, Kathline, Feb 2 1913 Sex:F Child# 9 J A Bellavance Canada & Rosa Lapierre US Stillborn
BELLAVANCE, Leo, Mar 24 1896 Sex:M Child# 1 Paul Bellavance Canada & Anna Dube Canada
BELLAVANCE, Leonida A, Feb 9 1900 Sex:F Child# 1 Jean Bellavance Canada & Eva Dube Canada
BELLAVANCE, Louis Donat, Jun 12 1898 Sex:M Child# 10 Ferdinand Bellavance Canada & Sophie Marten Canada
BELLAVANCE, Marie Anna G, Mar 1 1899 Sex:F Child#  Napoleon Bellavance Canada & Anna Dube Canada
BELLAVANCE, Marie Elmire, Jul 2 1897 Sex:F Child# 12 Nazaire Bellavance Canada & Marie Theriault Canada
BELLAVANCE, Marie Theresa Hermin, Oct 4 1927 Sex:F Child# 4 Albert Bellavance Canada & Emelda Desbiens Canada
BELLAVANCE, Mary Rasidma, Dec 21 1890 Sex:F Child# 3 Ferdinand Bellavance Canada & Sophie Martin Canada
BELLAVANCE, Nancy Marie, Jan 21 1930 Sex:F Child# 2 Armand Bellavance Nashua, NH & Gladys Burns Milford, NH
BELLAVANCE, Robert, Jul 17 1932 Sex:M Child# 7 A Bellavance Canada & Imelda Desbien Canada
BELLAVANCE, Rose June, Aug 18 1933 Sex:F Child# 7 Conrad Bellavance Nashua, NH & Rose Caron Canada
BELLAVANCE, Samuel Jean, Aug 21 1902 Sex:M Child# 4 Joseph Bellavance Canada & Rosanna Lapierre Nashua, NH
BELLAVANCE, Shirley Yolande, Aug 11 1934 Sex:F Child# 8 Conrad Bellavance Nashua, NH & Rose Caron Canada
BELLAVANCE, Sylvia Patricia, Apr 26 1926 Sex:F Child# 1 Conrad Bellavance Nashua, NH & Rose Caron Canada
BELLAVANCE, Theodore Henri, Nov 18 1910 Sex:M Child# 8 J A Bellavance US & Rosanna Lapierre US
BELLAVANCE, Thomas, Mar 23 1895 Sex:M Child# 8 Ferd Bellavance Canada & Sophie Martin Canada
BELLAVANCE, Unknown, Jan 6 1893 Sex:M Child# 1 Wilfrid Bellavance Canada & Luce Peltier Canada
BELLAVANCE, Unknown, Jul 13 1894 Sex:M Child# 2 Wilfred Bellavance Canada & Luce Peltier Canada Stillborn
BELLAVANCE, Unknown, Jun 10 1895 Sex: Child# 2 Wilfred Bellavance Canada & Lucie Peltier Canada Stillborn
BELLAVANCE, Wilfrid V, Jul 31 1899 Sex:M Child# 11 Ferdinand Bellavance Canada & Sophia Martin Canada
BELLAVEN, Marianne, Aug 10 1916 Sex:F Child# 4 Charley Bellaven Russia & Geor Christopolowicz Russia
BELLE, Liliane Hedorilda, Nov 10 1906 Sex:F Child# 7 Philias Belle Canada & Marie Touchette Canada
BELLE, M Aimee, Aug 15 1911 Sex:F Child# 14 Philias Belle Canada & Marie Touchette Canada
BELLE, Nellie, Mar 5 1909 Sex:F Child# 9 Philias Belle Canada & Marie Touchette Canada
BELLE, Norman Claud, Nov 11 1906 Sex:M Child# 1 Edward H Belle Worcester, MA & Maud Goodwin
BELLE, Olivier Arthur, May 8 1910 Sex:M Child# 10 Phileas Belle Canada & Marie Touchette Canada
BELLE, Roland Raymond, Nov 18 1907 Sex:M Child# 8 Philias Belle Canada & Marie Touchette Canada
BELLEAU, Albina, Mar 15 1896 Sex:F Child# 1 Philippe Belleau Bay City, MI & Claudia Morin Canada
BELLEFLEUR, Joseph L, Jun 11 1896 Sex:M Child# 1 Maxime Bellefleur NB, PQ & Clarina Malenfaut Salmon Falls, NH

BELLEFLEUR, Juliette, Feb 11 1924 Sex:F Child# 1 Herves Bellefleur Nashua, NH & Celia Trudeau Nashua, NH
BELLEFLEUR, Marie Cecile, Jun 19 1926 Sex:F Child# 2 Henry Bellefleur Nashua, NH & Cecile Trudeau Nashua, NH
BELLEFLEUR, Nancy Rita, Jun 19 1933 Sex:F Child# 1 William Bellefleur Portsmouth, NH & Irene Cummings Nashua, NH
BELLEMOUR, Jos Euclide Clement, Sep 17 1925 Sex:M Child# 1 Euclide Bellemour Canada & L Cardinal Canada
BELLEN, Lilian, Mar 27 1912 Sex:F Child# 2 Victor Bellen US & Pearl Page US
BELLERANCE, Joseph, Feb 15 1894 Sex:M Child# 10 Nazaire Bellerance Canada & Marie Theriault Canada
BELLEROSE, Adelard, Aug 31 1914 Sex:M Child# 6 Adelard Bellerose US & Marguerite Duvarney Scotland
BELLEROSE, Cecile T, Nov 19 1891 Sex:F Child# 2 Paul Bellerose Canada & Zenaide Gaudet Canada
BELLEROSE, Edouard Paul, Jan 29 1910 Sex:M Child# 3 Adelard Bellerose Nashua, NH & Marguerite Duvernay Scotland
BELLEROSE, Eleanor Madeline, Jul 28 1931 Sex:F Child# 3 Louis Bellerose Quincy, MA & Rose Curtis Fitchburg, MA
BELLEROSE, Eleanor Madeline, Jul 28 1932 Sex:F Child# 4 Louis Bellerose Quincy, MA & Rose Curtis Fitchburg, MA
BELLEROSE, Leopold, May 8 1889 Sex:M Child# 1 Paul Bellerose Canada & Zenalde Gaudet Canada
BELLEROSE, Marguerite Josephine, Sep 7 1908 Sex:F Child# 2 Adelard Bellerose Nashua, NH & Maggie Duvernay Scotland
BELLEROSE, Mildred, Jun 16 1913 Sex:F Child# 5 Adelard Bellerose Nashua, NH & Marguerite Devine Scotland
BELLEROSE, Paul Edward, Jan 25 1930 Sex:M Child# 2 Louis Bellerose Quincy, MA & Rose Curtis Fitchburg, MA
BELLEROSE, Pauline Frances, Mar 20 1911 Sex:F Child# 4 Adelard Bellerose Nashua, NH & Margaret Devany Scotland
BELLEROSE, Stella, Aug 10 1893 Sex:F Child# 3 Louis Bellerose Canada & Aglae Dionne Canada
BELLEROSE, Unknown, Apr 14 1890 Sex:F Child# 2 Louis Bellerose Canada & Aglace Dionne Canada Stillborn
BELLEROSE, Unknown, Mar 22 1897 Sex:F Child# 1 Paul Bellerose Canada & Clara Cimon Canada Stillborn
BELLEVANCE, Exilda Bertha L, Sep 4 1904 Sex:F Child# 5 Joseph Bellevance Canada & Rosanna Lapierre Nashua, NH
BELLEVANCE, Joseph Henry Roland, Jan 24 1925 Sex:M Child# 1 Albert Bellevance Canada & Emelda Desbiens Canada
BELLEVANCE, Joseph Louis Maurice, Jan 24 1925 Sex:M Child# 2 Albert Bellevance Canada & Emelda Desbiens Canada
BELLEVANCE, Marie Adeline, Sep 23 1898 Sex:F Child# 2 Joseph Bellevance Canada & Rosanna Lapierre Nashua, NH
BELLEVANCE, Marie Blanche Agnes, Apr 1 1926 Sex:F Child# 3 Albert Bellevance Canada & Emilda Desbiens Canada
BELLEVANCE, Marie Eugenie L, Jul 6 1904 Sex:F Child# 1 Paul Bellevance Canada & Eugenie Michaud Canada
BELLEVANCE, Unknown, May 14 1933 Sex:F Child# 1 Theo Bellevance Nashua, NH & Evelyn S Bagley Meredith, NH
BELLEVANCE, Wilfrid Edouard, Nov 20 1928 Sex:M Child# 5 A Bellevance Canada & Imelda Desbiens Canada
BELLEVANCE, Yvonne, May 2 1904 Sex:F Child# 5 Alfred Bellevance Canada & Leda Michaud Canada
BELLEVIEW, Albert J, Nov 28 1888 Sex:M Child# 1 Ferdinand Belleview Canada & Sophia Guartine Canada
BELLEW, Rita Elizabeth, May 5 1926 Sex:F Child# 2 Everett Bellew Dorchester, MA & Katherine Casey Milford, NH
BELLIVEAU, Joseph, Mar 9 1933 Sex:M Child# 3 Emile Belliveau Canada & Kusienne Roy Canada
BELLIVEAU, Mary Yvonne Priscilla, Sep 6 1928 Sex:F Child# 2 E Belliveau Canada & Lucienne Roy Canada
BELLMMEUR, Joseph, Nov 16 1931 Sex:M Child# 2 J M Bellmmeur Canada & Therese Deschenes Canada Stillborn
BELLMORE, Gloria Winifred, Oct 19 1916 Sex:F Child# 2 Leonard Bellmore Michigan & Venitia Martin New York
BELOUSKY, Annie, Jul 30 1912 Sex:F Child# 1 Adam Belousky Poland & Josephine Zelonis Poland
BELOWSKI, Weslaw John, Sep 23 1913 Sex:M Child# 2 Adam J Belowski Russia & Josie Zilonis Russia
BELROSE, Louis Michael, Oct 8 1928 Sex:M Child# 1 Louis Belrose Quincy, MA & Mary Rose Curtis Fitchburg, MA
BELSKI, Unknown, Mar 4 1895 Sex:M Child# 2 Zigmont Belski Poland & Christina Poplanska Poland Stillborn
BELSKI, Zose, Dec 22 1891 Sex:F Child# 1 Zeigman Belski Russia & Christine Palska Russia
BELSUS, Mary, Sep 21 1919 Sex:F Child# 2 Alexander Belsus Russia & Michelena Pataznati Russia
BELTIS, John, Sep 3 1922 Sex:M Child# 3 Alex Beltis Lithuania & Michaelina Transuk Lithuania
BELTRUCWICZ, Stacia, Mar 31 1917 Sex:F Child# 2 Alex Beltrucwicz Russia & Agatha Versotz Russia
BELVILLE, Unknown, Apr 13 1891 Sex:M Child# 1 (No Parents Listed)
BELZIL, Andre Roger, Feb 4 1921 Sex:M Child# 1 Ernest Belzil Canada & Delvina Beaulieu Canada
BELZIL, Auguste Albert, Feb 7 1920 Sex:M Child# 2 Auguste Belzil Canada & Flora Paul Nashua, NH
BELZIL, Gertrude Jeannette, Oct 24 1930 Sex:F Child# 5 Ernest Belzil Canada & Delima Beaulieu Canada
BELZIL, Gladys Sylvia, Sep 24 1926 Sex:F Child# 2 Ernest Belzil Poland & Sarah Chiring Germany
BELZIL, Marie Cecile Josphn, Feb 7 1923 Sex:F Child# 3 Auguste Belzil Canada & Julia Paul Nashua, NH
BELZIL, Normand Ernest, Oct 4 1923 Sex:M Child# 2 Ernest Belzil Canada & Dalvina Beaulieu Canada
BELZIL, Romona Lucille Pearl, Oct 4 1918 Sex:F Child# 1 August Belzil Th Portals, Canada & Julia Paul Nashua, NH
BEMIS, Charles Edward, Apr 8 1935 Sex:M Child# 1 Homer Bemis Pepperell, MA & Esther Phelps Nashua, NH
BEN, Frank, Apr 16 1911 Sex:M Child# 1 Joseph Ben Russia & Ludwika Kucie Russia
BENARD, Joseph, May 2 1912 Sex:M Child# 1 Joseph Benard Russia & Enga Controzy Russia
BENESAVOTZ, Unknown, Jun 2 1921 Sex:F Child# 5 Joseph Benesavotz Poland & Edwiga Contsavatz Poland
BENHAM, Meredith Ellen, Sep 3 1934 Sex:F Child# 1 Milo H Benham Brockton, MA & Maruerite L Rogers Nashua, NH
BENJAMIN, Alva Muriel, Aug 7 1924 Sex:F Child# 1 G L Benjamin Nashua, NH & Pearl Barnes Somerville, MA
BENJAMIN, Annie Margaret, Jan 1 1910 Sex:F Child# 9 Gideon H Benjamin Nova Scotia & Christina McGilvery NS
BENJAMIN, Arthur Brean, Dec 26 1935 Sex:M Child# 1 Art B Benjamin Nashua, NH & Gladys Swift Nashua, NH
BENJAMIN, Arthur Breeman, Sep 3 1905 Sex:m Child# 7 Gideon U Benjamin Nova Scotia & Christina McGilvary NS
BENJAMIN, Chester Everett, Feb 15 1913 Sex:M Child# 3 Delbert Benjamin Nova Scotia & Lillian Bernie Nashua, NH
BENJAMIN, Curtis Eugene, Jul 27 1927 Sex:M Child# 2 James Benjamin Nova Scotia & Lena Stene Manchester, NH
BENJAMIN, Finley Eugene, Aug 23 1923 Sex:M Child# 2 Finley Benjamin Nova Scotia & Anna McCutcheon Canada
BENJAMIN, John Leander, Oct 4 1902 Sex:M Child# Gideon Benjamin Nova Scotia & C McGilvery Nova Scotia
BENJAMIN, Kenneth Eugene, Aug 8 1907 Sex:M Child# 8 Gideon Benjamin Nova Scotia & Christine McGlory Nova Scotia
BENJAMIN, Lillian Bernice, Aug 6 1911 Sex:F Child# 2 Delbert H Benjamin Nova Scotia & Annie Leaor Nashua, NH
BENJAMIN, Mary Arietta H, Sep 14 1911 Sex:F Child# 10 Gideon H Benjamin Nova Scotia & Christina McGilvey NS
BENJAMIN, Mavis Irene, Apr 6 1928 Sex:F Child# 2 Geo L Benjamin Nashua, NH & Pearl Barnes Somerville, MA
BENJAMIN, Muriel May, May 18 1904 Sex:F Child# 1 Emery M Benjamin Nova Scotia & Clara M Earley Nova Scotia
BENJAMIN, Norma Lena, Dec 1 1921 Sex:F Child# 1 Finley L Benjamin Nova Scotia & Anna McCutcheon Canada
BENJAMIN, William Hardin, May 25 1910 Sex:M Child# 1 Delbert H Benjamin Nova Scotia & Annie Leaor Nashua, NH
BENNETT, Alice May, May 16 1917 Sex:F Child# 3 Fred A Bennett Canada & Anna G Shannon Lawrence, MA
BENNETT, Antony, Oct 30 1913 Sex:M Child# 3 John Bennett Russia & Edwiga Kutsawich Russia
BENNETT, Joseph, Jun 6 1904 Sex:M Child# 1 William Bennett Russia & Eva Nortavijutia Russia

28

BENNETT, Josie, May 30 1915 Sex:F Child# 3 Joseph Bennett Russia & Ardvega Koctsorich Russia
BENNETT, Kenneth Robert, May 21 1916 Sex:M Child# 4 Norman Bennett Nova Scotia & Bessie Fielding Nova Scotia
BENNETT, Ladwiga, Apr 14 1908 Sex:F Child# 2 William Bennett Russia & Eva Menartowicz Russia
BENNETT, Lucille, Jun 22 1923 Sex:F Child# 1 Ernest Bennett Canada & Marie Levie Canada
BENNETTE, Henry Leon, Jun 15 1925 Sex:M Child# 5 Raoul G Bennette Canada & Anne M Danjou Rhode Island
BENOIT, Albert Hector, Sep 7 1892 Sex:M Child# 7 Napoleon Benoit Manchester & Delima Bosse Canada
BENOIT, Arthur Willie, Sep 11 1896 Sex:M Child# 6 Pierre Benoit Canada & Mary Belmore Canada
BENOIT, Cecile Olivette, Nov 13 1919 Sex:F Child# 3 Edouard Benoit Nashua, NH & Claudia Pitt Canada
BENOIT, Conrad Leo, Aug 14 1904 Sex:M Child# 4 William Benoit Canada & Mary L Fournier Canada
BENOIT, Edouard, Dec 4 1894 Sex:M Child# 8 Napoleon Benoit Canada & Delima Bosse Canada
BENOIT, Eugene, Sep 13 1902 Sex:M Child# 3 William Benoit Canada & M L Fournier Canada
BENOIT, Florence Yvonne, Feb 19 1913 Sex:F Child# 14 Pierre Benoit Canada & Emma Pelletier Canada
BENOIT, Joseph Hubert, Dec 22 1893 Sex:M Child# 6 Saul Benoit Canada & Cordelia Beauregard Canada
BENOIT, Joseph Leon, May 16 1894 Sex:M Child# 2 Leon Benoit Nashua, NH & Angelina Belanger E Concord, NH
BENOIT, Josephat Philibert, Jun 10 1927 Sex:M Child# 1 Joseph Benoit Nashua, NH & Alice Roy Nashua, NH
BENOIT, Lucille Jeanne, Jun 4 1932 Sex:F Child# 7 A O Benoit Central Falls, RI & Delia Brouillette Central Falls
BENOIT, Marguerite Catherine, Oct 11 1917 Sex:F Child# 2 Edouard Benoit Nashua, NH & Claudia Pitt Canada
BENOIT, Marie Dina, Jan 9 1889 Sex:F Child# 6 Napoleon Benoit Canada & Delina Bosse Canada
BENOIT, Marie G, Jul 14 1892 Sex:F Child# 4 Pierre Benoit Nashua, NH & Evelina Brodeur Canada
BENOIT, Paul Felix, Nov 20 1930 Sex:M Child# 6 Albert Benoit Central Falls, RI & Ida Brouillette Central Falls, RI
BENOIT, Raymond, May 20 1916 Sex:M Child# 1 Edouard Benoit Nashua, NH & Claudia Pitt Canada
BENOIT, Raymond Robert, Aug 24 1919 Sex:M Child# 1 Ronald Benoit Nashua, NH & Beulah Genn Orrs Island, ME
BENOIT, Renald, May 29 1900 Sex:M Child# 2 William Benoit Canada & M Louise Fournier Canada
BENOIT, Rosa Alberta A, Dec 11 1897 Sex:F Child# 1 William J Benoit Canada & Marie L Fournier Canada
BENOIT, Theresa Adeline, Aug 21 1929 Sex:F Child# 1 Willie Benoit Canada & Juliette Ducasse Canada
BENOITT, Joseph, Dec 6 1889 Sex:M Child# 1 Edmund Benoitt Canada & Clara Rock Canada
BENSON, Charles James, Oct 23 1916 Sex:M Child# 4 Charles Benson Ireland & Mary Bowen Ireland
BENSON, Evelyn Beatrice, Nov 4 1918 Sex:F Child# 5 Charles Benson Ireland & Mary K Bowen Ireland
BENSON, Francis Edward, Apr 20 1910 Sex:M Child# 2 Patrick E Benson Ireland & Catherine McGrath Ireland
BENSON, Francis Joseph, Apr 6 1912 Sex:M Child# 2 Charles J Benson Ireland & Mary Bohen Ireland
BENSON, Helen Frances, Apr 11 1908 Sex:F Child# 1 Patrick E Benson Ireland & Katherine A McGrath Ireland
BENSON, Mary Elizabeth, Apr 23 1914 Sex:F Child# 3 Charles J Benson Ireland & Mary K Bohan Ireland
BENSON, Mary Josephine, Mar 18 1915 Sex:F Child# 3 Patrick E Benson Ireland & Catherine McGrath Ireland
BENSON, Unknown, Jun 1 1918 Sex:M Child# 3 William Benson New York & Blanche Pearsons Wilton, NH Stillborn
BENT, Arthur Devine, Mar 18 1934 Sex:M Child# 1 Arthur Bent Lowell, MA & Eva Devine Nashua, NH
BENTLEY, Richard Arnold, Apr 18 1927 Sex:M Child# 1 Arnold Bentley England & Yvonne Soucy Nashua, NH
BERARD, Donald Arthur, May 27 1924 Sex:M Child# 1 Leon Berard Auburn, MA & Clarice Marquis Nashua, NH
BERARD, Frances Pearl, Dec 19 1911 Sex:F Child# 4 Louis Berard US & Daisy Johnson US
BERARD, Gladys, Feb 2 1929 Sex:F Child# 3 Leon Berard Oxford, MA & Clarice Marquis Nashua, NH
BERARD, Hector George, Dec 18 1926 Sex:M Child# 3 Leon Berard Auburn, MA & Clarisse Marquis Nashua, NH
BERARD, Marie Gloria Edna, Jun 20 1925 Sex:F Child# 2 Leon Berard Auburn, MA & Clarisse Marquis Nashua, NH
BERARD, Pauline Elaine, Nov 19 1935 Sex:F Child# 1 Edgar Berard Auburn, MA & Lorette Theriault Nashua, NH
BERASARD, Henri Arthur, Feb 6 1889 Sex:M Child# 2 Jean B Berasard Canada & Roseanna Gadbois Canada
BERG, Leon Woodrow, Jun 22 1913 Sex:M Child# 1 Hans Anton Berg Ossing, NH & Ina Pero Nashua, NH
BERGER, Alfred, May 29 1900 Sex:M Child# 4 E A Berger Canada & Albina Cusson Canada
BERGER, Jos Albert Robert, Nov 16 1932 Sex:M Child# 2 Arsene Berger Canada & Alice Dube Nashua, NH
BERGER, Joseph Louis Roland, Sep 16 1927 Sex:M Child# 1 Arsene Berger Canada & Alice Dube Nashua, NH
BERGER, Lorraine Joan, Nov 20 1933 Sex:F Child# 10 Arthur Berger Nashua, NH & B Bellavance Nashua, NH
BERGERON, Albert, May 19 1926 Sex:M Child# 1 Arthur Bergeron Amesbury, MA & Frances Jarvis Malone, NY
BERGERON, Albina Eva, Jun 4 1909 Sex:F Child# 3 Thomas Bergeron Canada & Mathilde Lavoie US
BERGERON, Alvine Blanche O, Jun 25 1911 Sex:F Child# 1 Arthur O Bergeron US & Blanche Bellavance US
BERGERON, Andre Samuel, Sep 28 1897 Sex:M Child# 6 Omer Bergeron Canada & Albina Lefebvre Canada
BERGERON, Anita Viviane, Jul 6 1919 Sex:F Child# 4 Arthur Bergeron Nashua, NH & Blanche Belavance Nashua, NH
BERGERON, Arthur theodore, Jun 30 1929 Sex:M Child# 8 Arthur Bergeron Nashua, NH & Blanche Bellavance Nashua, NH
BERGERON, Eleanor May, Apr 6 1935 Sex:F Child# 1 Wilfred Bergeron Lowell, MA & Mary Rogers Nashua, NH
BERGERON, Elizabeth Anna, Aug 6 1922 Sex:F Child# 5 Arthur Bergeron US & Blanche Bellavance US
BERGERON, Emma B E, Apr 13 1892 Sex:F Child# 3 Omer Bergeron Canada & Albina Lefebvre Canada
BERGERON, Ferdinand Edgar, Nov 22 1915 Sex:M Child# 3 Arthur Bergeron US & Blanche Bellavance US
BERGERON, Georges O L, Oct 6 1893 Sex:M Child# 4 Omer Bergeron Canada & Albina Lefebvre Canada
BERGERON, Irene Dorothe, Aug 7 1931 Sex:F Child# 9 Arthur Bergeron Nashua, NH & Blanche Bellavance Nashua, NH
BERGERON, Janet Grace, Apr 13 1932 Sex:F Child# 2 Ray Bergeron Winooski, VT & Grace Monette Derry, NH
BERGERON, Jos Clement Laurent, Apr 22 1927 Sex:M Child# 1 Cleomine Bergeron Canada & Marie Thibodeau Canada
BERGERON, Jos Israel Normand, Jun 29 1934 Sex:M Child# 3 Clement Bergeron Canada & Marie C Thibodeau Stillborn
BERGERON, Jos Raoul Normand, May 15 1927 Sex:M Child# 1 Hughes Bergeron Canada & Alice Gauthier Canada
BERGERON, Joseph, Jan 18 1928 Sex:M Child# 3 Oscar Bergeron Canada & Phyllis Chatel Nashua, NH Stillborn
BERGERON, Joseph Meo, Jun 30 1905 Sex:M Child# 4 Archie Bergeron Canada & Selvina Betty Canada
BERGERON, Joseph Paul Sylvio, Jan 11 1929 Sex:M Child# 2 Clement Bergeron Canada & Marie C Thibodeau Canada
BERGERON, Joseph Raymond, Feb 28 1922 Sex:M Child# 2 William Bergeron Canada & Clara Ricard Nashua, NH
BERGERON, Joseph Romeo, Nov 5 1926 Sex:M Child# 2 Oscar Bergeron Canada & Phyllis Chatel Nashua, NH
BERGERON, Leo Laurent Arthur, Dec 24 1913 Sex:M Child# 2 Arthur Bergeron US & Blanche Bellavance US
BERGERON, Louis Robt Chas A, Jun 19 1925 Sex:M Child# 1 Romuald Bergeron Canada & Pearl Gaudette Nashua, NH
BERGERON, Louis T H, Sep 7 1899 Sex:M Child# 8 Omer Bergeron Canada & Albina Lefebvre Canada
BERGERON, Lucien Gregoire, May 6 1933 Sex:M Child# 2 Antony Bergeron Canada & Irene Trudel Nashua, NH

BERGERON, Marie Irene Cesani, Jan 31 1921 Sex:F Child# 1 William Bergeron Canada & Clara Ricard Nashua, NH
BERGERON, Marie L F, Apr 20 1895 Sex:F Child# 6 Omer Bergeron Canada & Albina Lefebore Canada
BERGERON, Natalie May, Oct 26 1933 Sex:F Child# 3 R C Bergeron Winooski, VT & Grace Monette Derry, NH
BERGERON, Omer Arthur, Aug 27 1889 Sex:M Child# 1 Philias Bergeron Canada & Eliza Chamberlain Canada
BERGERON, Oscar Pierre Prosper, Oct 9 1925 Sex:M Child# 1 Oscar Bergeron Canada & Phyllis Chattel Manchester, NH
BERGERON, Philias Julien F, Jan 27 1924 Sex:M Child# 6 Arthur Bergeron Nashua, NH & B Bellavance Nashua, NH
BERGERON, Raymond Charles, Jan 23 1935 Sex:M Child# 4 Raymond Bergeron Winooski, VT & Grace Monette Derry, NH
BERGERON, Robert, Feb 19 1935 Sex:M Child# 3 Antony Bergeron Canada & Irene Trudel Nashua, NH
BERGERON, Robert Antoine, Dec 21 1925 Sex:M Child# 7 Arthur Bergeron Nashua, NH & Blanche Bellavance Nashua, NH
BERGERON, Virginia Ann, Jul 29 1930 Sex:F Child# 1 Raymond Bergeron Winooski, VT & Grace Monette Derry, NH
BERGERON, Wilfrid, Jun 22 1894 Sex:M Child# 2 Philias Bergeron Canada & Eliza Chamberlan Canada
BERGERON, Yvette, Jan 3 1929 Sex:F Child# 2 Hugh Bergeron Canada & Alice Gauthier Canada
BERGERSON, Marie Victoria, Dec 14 1893 Sex:F Child# 6 Louis Bergerson Canada & Malvina Salvail Canada
BERGEVIN, Joan Marie, Nov 26 1935 Sex:F Child# 1 Laurence Bergevin Nashua, NH & Anna Kudalis Nashua, NH
BERGEVIN, Louise Germaine, Mar 7 1915 Sex:F Child# 3 Wilfrid Bergevin Plattsburg, NY & Olivine Roy Nashua, NH
BERGEVIN, Norman Xavier, May 1 1935 Sex:M Child# 1 Leon Bergevin Fitchburg, MA & Jeanne Brousseau Nashua, NH
BERGEVIN, Robert, Aug 18 1916 Sex:M Child# 4 Wilfrid Bergevin Allenburg, NH & Olivine Roy Nashua, NH
BERIAN, Josephine, Jan 4 1891 Sex:F Child# 3 Damase Berian Canada & Marie Frenette Canada
BERIAULT, Raymond Theophile, Aug 28 1920 Sex:M Child# 6 Eugene Beriault Canada & Jeanne Deschenes Canada
BERIEAU, Marie D, Oct 14 1889 Sex:F Child# 1 Damase Berieau Canada & Marie Frenette Canada
BERKOVSKY, Joseph, Aug 11 1910 Sex:M Child# 5 Frank Berkovsky Russia & Mary Vilkorsky Russia
BERNARD, Adrianna R, Jul 9 1895 Sex:F Child# 5 J B Bernard Canada & Rosanna Gadbois Canada
BERNARD, Agnes Angeline, Jun 4 1896 Sex:F Child# 3 Elie Bernard Canada & Philomene Boisvert Canada
BERNARD, Angelina Beatrice, Jan 26 1911 Sex:F Child# 4 Frank Bernard Mass & May Bleau Nashua, NH
BERNARD, Armenia M J, Oct 17 1890 Sex:F Child# 3 J B Bernard Canada & Rosanna Gadbois Canada
BERNARD, Barbara, Mar 20 1923 Sex:F Child# 3 Edwin R Bernard Nashua, NH & Evelyn M Sullivan Nashua, NH
BERNARD, Beatrice, Sep 6 1908 Sex:F Child# 2 Frank Bernard Shirley, MA & Marie A Bleau Nashua, NH
BERNARD, Blanche, Jun 25 1893 Sex:F Child# 2 Elie Bernard Canada & Philomene Boisvert Canada
BERNARD, Clayton Earle, Nov 20 1916 Sex:M Child# 2 Arthur Bernard Canada & Bertha Bailey Nashua, NH
BERNARD, Delia, Jan 16 1900 Sex:F Child# 7 J B Bernard Canada & Rosanna Gadbois Canada
BERNARD, Docite, Apr 13 1895 Sex:M Child# 1 Alex Bernard Fitchburg, MA & Marie Levesque Canada
BERNARD, Donat, Sep 26 1897 Sex:M Child# 6 J B Bernard Canada & Rosanna Gadbois Canada
BERNARD, Edwin Richard, Sep 10 1921 Sex:M Child# 2 Edwin Bernard Nashua, NH & Evelyn Sullivan Nashua, NH
BERNARD, Emma Anna, Mar 1 1893 Sex:F Child# 3 Joseph Bernard Canada & Maria Deschenes Canada
BERNARD, Emma Mary, Apr 8 1922 Sex:F Child# 4 Arthur Bernard Canada & Bertha Bailey Nashua, NH
BERNARD, Ernest, May 13 1921 Sex:M Child# 1 Ernest Bernard Nashua, NH & Helen McDonald Nashua, NH
BERNARD, Ernest Alphonse, Mar 21 1920 Sex:M Child# 2 Dosithe Bernard Nashua, NH & Regina Desmarais Graniteville, MA
BERNARD, Ernest Edward, Dec 6 1917 Sex:M Child# 3 Arthur Ed Bernard St Hyacinthe, PQ & Bertha Bailey Nashua, NH
BERNARD, Frederick William, Aug 12 1900 Sex:M Child# 1 Wilfred Bernard Nashua, NH & Margaret Shaunahan Nashua, NH
BERNARD, George Albert, Dec 22 1923 Sex:M Child# 3 Dosithe Bernard Nashua, NH & Regina Desmarais Graniteville, MA
BERNARD, George Raymond, Jun 7 1923 Sex:M Child# 3 Adelard Bernard Canada & Mathilda Faubert Canada
BERNARD, Henry Willie, Sep 17 1899 Sex:M Child# 3 Etienne Bernard Canada & Virginie Dubreuil Canada
BERNARD, Hermine I, Mar 12 1898 Sex:F Child# 3 Alexandre Bernard Fitchburg, MA & Marie Levesque Canada
BERNARD, Irene Agnes, Jun 15 1933 Sex:F Child# 8 Dosite Bernard Nashua, NH & B Desmarais Graniteville, MA
BERNARD, Jean, Feb 17 1925 Sex:M Child# 4 Adelard Bernard Fitchburg, MA & Mathilda Faubert Nashua, NH
BERNARD, John Benedict, Dec 13 1929 Sex:M Child# 4 Edwin Bernard Nashua, NH & Evelyn Sullivan Nashua, NH
BERNARD, Jos Ernest Andrew, Nov 30 1928 Sex:M Child# 2 Ernest Bernard Canada & Martha Lebrun Canada
BERNARD, Jos Lucien Michael, Feb 19 1933 Sex:M Child# 4 Ernest Bernard St Gervais, PQ & Martha Lebrun Canada
BERNARD, Joseph Henry, Jul 26 1889 Sex:M Child# 2 John B Bernard Canada & M Chartier Canada
BERNARD, Joseph L A, Sep 16 1890 Sex:M Child# 11 Narcisse Bernard Canada & Marie Leblanc Canada
BERNARD, Joseph L Roger, Jan 10 1929 Sex:M Child# 1 Philip Bernard Canada & Rose Roy Lawrence, MA
BERNARD, Joseph Leo Roland, Jun 6 1924 Sex:M Child# 1 Elzear Bernard Canada & Aurore Belanger NH
BERNARD, Julia Evelina, Apr 1 1893 Sex:F Child# 4 Jean B Bernard Canada & Rosanna Gadbois Canada
BERNARD, Juliette Irene, Jun 6 1907 Sex:F Child# 1 Francois Bernard Shirley Village, MA & Anna Bleau Nashua, NH
BERNARD, Leo Normand, Jul 7 1931 Sex:M Child# 5 Louis A Bernard Fitchburg, MA & Mathilda Faubert Canada
BERNARD, Louis, Feb 9 1922 Sex:M Child# 3 Dosithe Bernard Nashua, NH & Regina Desmarais Graniteville, MA
BERNARD, Louis Paul, Aug 10 1920 Sex:M Child# 1 L Ad Bernard US & Mathilda Faubert Canada
BERNARD, Lucille Yvonne, Nov 25 1925 Sex:F Child# 5 Dosite Bernard Nashua, NH & Regina Desmarais Graniteville, MA
BERNARD, Marie, Jun 29 1912 Sex:F Child# 4 Frank Bernard Nashua, NH & Marie Bleau Nashua, NH
BERNARD, Marie Alma, May 22 1893 Sex:F Child# 3 Joseph Bernard Canada & Octavie Proulx Canada
BERNARD, Marie C R, Mar 18 1930 Sex:F Child# 3 Ernest Jos Bernard Canada & Marthe Lebrun Canada
BERNARD, Marie E Anna, Sep 9 1899 Sex:F Child# 1 Omer Bernard Canada & Emma Lampron Canada
BERNARD, Marie E C, May 7 1900 Sex:F Child# 4 Alexander Bernard Mass & Marie Levesque Canada
BERNARD, Marie Hermine, Sep 9 1909 Sex:F Child# 3 Frank Bernard Shirley Village, MA & Marie Bleau Nashua, NH
BERNARD, Marie Jeannette, May 25 1905 Sex:F Child# 5 Alexandre Bernard Canada & Marie Levesque Canada
BERNARD, Marie V, Oct 17 1896 Sex:F Child# 2 Alexandre Bernard Fitchburg, MA & Marie Levesque Canada
BERNARD, Mary Madeline, Aug 17 1927 Sex:F Child# 1 Ernest Bernard Canada & Martha Lebrun Canada
BERNARD, Napoleon, Jun 30 1893 Sex:M Child# 12 Narcisse Bernard Canada & Marie Leblanc Canada
BERNARD, Roland Edouard, Sep 11 1931 Sex:M Child# 7 Dosithe Bernard Nashua, NH & Regina Desmarais Graniteville, MA
BERNARD, Shirley, Mar 27 1920 Sex:F Child# 1 Edwin Bernard Nashua, NH & Evelyn Sullivan Nashua, NH
BERNARD, Theresa Marguerite, Aug 29 1927 Sex:F Child# 6 Dosithe Bernard Nashua, NH & Regina Desmarais Nashua, NH
BERNARD, Therese Agnes, Jan 17 1922 Sex:F Child# 2 Adelard Bernard Fitchburg, MA & Mathilda Faubert Canada
BERNASKAWICZ, Peter Alphonse, Feb 9 1922 Sex:M Child# 2 P Bernaskawicz Lithuania & Antosia Irmalawicz Lithuania

BERNECHE, Marie Olina, Jun 7 1905 Sex:F Child# 5 Amedee Berneche Mass & Lucie Boutin Canada
BERNECHE, Unknown, Sep 14 1898 Sex:M Child# 1 Amedee Berneche Springfield, MA & Lucie Boutin Canada
BERNICE, Rose Anna, Jun 15 1890 Sex:F Child# 4 Odilon Bernice Canada & Philmene Gramont Canada
BERNIER, Achilles, Jul 18 1891 Sex:M Child# 2 Joseph Bernier Canada & Lucienne Gagne Canada
BERNIER, Adrienne, Jan 20 1910 Sex:F Child# 2 Odilon Bernier Canada & Eugenie Bernier Canada
BERNIER, Alberta, Mar 21 1897 Sex:F Child# 9 Guillaume Bernier Canada & D Bellavance Canada
BERNIER, Alberta, Apr 30 1906 Sex:F Child# 3 George Bernier Canada & Ezelia Guimond Canada
BERNIER, Alice, Mar 9 1907 Sex:F Child# 5 Pierre Bernier Canada & Lucia Sirois Canada
BERNIER, Alphonse, Oct 2 1892 Sex:M Child# 3 Joseph Bernier Canada & Lucienne Tagne Canada
BERNIER, Andre W, Feb 21 1895 Sex:M Child# 6 J B Bernier Canada & Helene Belavance Canada
BERNIER, Andrea, Jan 24 1893 Sex:F Child# 4 Edmond Bernier Canada & Clara Rock Canada
BERNIER, Armand Maurice, Jan 5 1922 Sex:M Child# 2 Andre Bernier Nashua, NH & Aline Charron Adams, MA
BERNIER, Arthur Sylvis, Mar 17 1904 Sex:M Child# 4 Pierre Bernier Canada & Lucia Sirois Canada
BERNIER, Camille, Jun 26 1923 Sex:F Child# 2 Edmond Bernier Nashua, NH & Beatrice Moisson Nashua, NH
BERNIER, Camille, Dec 12 1924 Sex:F Child# 1 J E Bernier Canada & Delina Vallie Nashua, NH
BERNIER, Carmel, Oct 29 1932 Sex:F Child# 2 Jos Bernier Canada & Yvonne Boucher Canada
BERNIER, Claire Marguerite, Feb 4 1910 Sex:F Child# 1 Joseph Bernier Canada & Regina Bellavance Canada
BERNIER, Delhia, Sep 21 1888 Sex:F Child# 4 Adelon Bernier Canada & Philomene Ialarnau Canada
BERNIER, Doria Napoleon, Jan 13 1897 Sex:M Child# 6 Edmond Bernier Canada & Clara Rock Canada
BERNIER, Doris Laurette Clair, Jan 8 1927 Sex:F Child# 5 Hector Bernier Canada & Fredeline Bourdon New Bedford, MA
BERNIER, Edgar Rogers, Mar 6 1932 Sex:M Child# 3 Andrew Bernier Nashua, NH & Aline Charron N Adams, MA
BERNIER, Edmond, Aug 7 1900 Sex:m Child# 8 J B Bernier Canada & Helene Bellavance Canada
BERNIER, Eledia, Oct 3 1887 Sex:F Child#  Fidinic Bernier Canada & Marie Clouthier Canada
BERNIER, Elise Jeanne, Jan 22 1901 Sex:F Child# 1 Odilon Bernier Canada & Elize Cote Canada
BERNIER, Elizabeth, Apr 29 1893 Sex:F Child# 6 Guillaume Bernier Canada & Denige Bellavance Canada
BERNIER, Ernest Joseph, Oct 23 1890 Sex:M Child# 1 Edmond Bernier Canada & Clara Rock Nashua, NH
BERNIER, Etiennette, Sep 21 1918 Sex:F Child# 5 Joseph Bernier Canada & Regina Bellavance Canada
BERNIER, Eugenie Rita, Jun 23 1924 Sex:F Child# 1 Joseph Bernier Canada & Laura Nadeau Nashua, NH
BERNIER, Florette Andrea, Oct 8 1920 Sex:F Child# 1 Andrew Bernier Nashua, NH & Aline Charron N Adams, MA
BERNIER, Florilda, Sep 25 1896 Sex:F Child# 7 Jean Bpte Bernier Canada & Helene Bellavance Canada
BERNIER, Germain Donalda, Jan 2 1926 Sex:F Child# 5 Hector Bernier Canada & Fredeline Bourdon New Bedford, MA
BERNIER, Henri Ferdinand, Mar 15 1907 Sex:M Child# 2 Joseph Bernier Canada & Rosanna Levesque Canada
BERNIER, Irene Doris, Oct 19 1933 Sex:F Child# 4 Lucien Bernier Canada & G Desmarais Biddeford, ME
BERNIER, J B Alfred, Dec 23 1891 Sex:M Child# 3 Edmond Bernier Canada & Clara Rock Canada
BERNIER, J Odilon Florien, Jun 6 1914 Sex:M Child# 3 Odilon Bernier Canada & Eugenie Ouellette Canada
BERNIER, Jean Baptiste, Dec 3 1889 Sex:M Child# 5 Jean B Bernier Canada & Milaire Belavance Canada
BERNIER, Jean Baptiste, Apr 1 1894 Sex:M Child# 8 William Bernier Canada & Denige Bellavance Canada
BERNIER, Jean Baptiste, May 10 1904 Sex:M Child# 1 (No Parents Listed)
BERNIER, John Bte, Oct 18 1893 Sex:M Child# 4 Fidime Bernier Canada & Marie Clotier Canada
BERNIER, Jos Alfred Ulderic, Nov 23 1904 Sex:M Child# 6 Joseph Bernier Canada & Emma Caron Canada
BERNIER, Jos Wilbrode H R, Dec 23 1904 Sex:M Child# 4 Odilon Bernier Canada & Marie Rousseau Canada
BERNIER, Joseph, Feb 19 1905 Sex:M Child# 1 Arthur Bernier Canada & Palmarina Cote Canada Stillborn
BERNIER, Joseph, Sep 17 1906 Sex:M Child# 7 Joseph Bernier Canada & Emma Caron Canada
BERNIER, Joseph, May 13 1908 Sex:M Child# 1 Odilon Bernier Canada & Eugenie Ouellette Canada Stillborn
BERNIER, Joseph Amable, Feb 13 1902 Sex:M Child# 4 Joseph Bernier Canada & Emma Caron Canada
BERNIER, Joseph Arthur, Apr 17 1901 Sex:M Child# 2 Felix Bernier Canada & Adelaide Lord Canada
BERNIER, Joseph Audibert, May 1 1898 Sex:M Child# 2 Pierre Bernier Canada & Lucia Sirois Canada Stillborn
BERNIER, Joseph Edward, Aug 14 1894 Sex:M Child# 4 Edmond Bernier Canada & Clara Rock Canada
BERNIER, Joseph H, Jun 15 1896 Sex:M Child# 1 Pierre Bernier Canada & Lucia Sirois Canada
BERNIER, Joseph Leo, Jun 21 1903 Sex:M Child# 5 Joseph Bernier Canada & Emma Caron Canada
BERNIER, Joseph Louis N, Mar 3 1892 Sex:M Child# 4 Phedime Bernier Canada & Marie Cloutier Canada
BERNIER, Joseph Louis P, May 23 1908 Sex:M Child# 8 Joseph Bernier Canada & Emma Caron Canada
BERNIER, Joseph Maurice, Nov 23 1931 Sex:M Child# 2 Hormidos Bernier Nashua, NH & Alma Sirois Lawrence, MA Stillborn
BERNIER, Joseph Normand, Feb 19 1931 Sex:M Child# 1 Joseph Bernier Canada & Yvonne Boucher Canada
BERNIER, Joseph William, Sep 19 1897 Sex:M Child# 6 Fedime Bernier Canada & Marie Cloutier Canada
BERNIER, Laurent Marcel, Dec 7 1912 Sex:M Child# 3 Joseph Bernier Canada & Regina Bellavance Canada
BERNIER, Lauretta Andrea, Jan 19 1903 Sex:F Child# 6 Guillaume Bernier Canada & D Bellavance Canada
BERNIER, Leda Annette, Jan 12 1911 Sex:F Child# 1 Pierre Bernier Canada & Georgina Boutin Canada
BERNIER, Leo, Mar 31 1906 Sex:M Child# 3 Arthur Bernier Canada & Marina Cote Canada
BERNIER, Leo Robert, Dec 10 1919 Sex:M Child# 4 Ernest Bernier Canada & Aline Briand Canada
BERNIER, Leonard Ernest, Mar 22 1933 Sex:M Child# 1 Roland Bernier Canada & Irene Dean Pepperell, MA
BERNIER, Louis Arthur, Mar 15 1907 Sex:M Child# 1 Joseph Bernier Canada & Rosanna Levesque Canada
BERNIER, Louis Maurice, Jan 21 1916 Sex:M Child# 4 Joseph Bernier Canada & Regina Bellavance Canada
BERNIER, Luc Doria, Aug 14 1899 Sex:M Child# 2 Joseph Bernier Canada & Emma Caron Canada
BERNIER, Lucille Regina, Mar 15 1928 Sex:F Child# 3 Joseph Bernier Canada & Regina Lebrun Canada
BERNIER, M E Georgianna, Feb 9 1898 Sex:F Child# 1 Domase Bernier Canada & Victoria St Pierre Canada
BERNIER, M Eugenie Lina, Apr 10 1908 Sex:F Child# 2 George Bernier Canada & Exilda Morin Canada
BERNIER, M Rasalda, Jul 21 1894 Sex:F Child# 1 Odelon Bernier Canada & Marie Rosseau Canada
BERNIER, Marie, Jul 29 1901 Sex:F Child# 1 Phedime Bernier Canada & Agnes Deschesnes Canada
BERNIER, Marie A A, Jul 25 1896 Sex:F Child# 2 Odilon Bernier Canada & Marie Russeau Canada
BERNIER, Marie Ange E, Dec 26 1910 Sex:F Child# 10 Joseph Bernier Canada & Emma Caron Canada
BERNIER, Marie Anita, Dec 20 1899 Sex:F Child# 3 Pierre Bernier Canada & Lucia Sirois Canada
BERNIER, Marie Eug J Bea, Feb 24 1916 Sex:F Child# 4 Odilon Bernier Canada & Eugenie Ouellette Canada

BERNIER, Marie Exilda J, Nov 9 1905 Sex:F Child# 1 George Bernier Canada & Exilda Morin Canada
BERNIER, Marie Leona, Mar 4 1899 Sex:F Child# 3 Odilon Bernier Canada & Marie Russeau Canada
BERNIER, Marie Rita Lucille, Sep 21 1923 Sex:F Child# 1 Hormidas Bernier NH & Alma Sirois Mass
BERNIER, Marie Rose Eva, May 6 1909 Sex:F Child# 9 Joseph Bernier Canada & Emma Caron Canada
BERNIER, Maurice, May 17 1934 Sex:M Child# 4 Joseph A Bernier Canada & Laura E Nadeau Nashua, NH
BERNIER, Narcisse Guillaume, May 11 1911 Sex:M Child# 2 Joseph Bernier Canada & Regina Bellavance Canada
BERNIER, Nolla Georgette, Jun 26 1924 Sex:F Child# 4 Hector Bernier Canada & Fredeline Bourdou New Bedford, MA
BERNIER, Paul Emile, Dec 11 1931 Sex:M Child# 2 Lucien Bernier Canada & Germaine Desmarais US
BERNIER, Pauline, Jul 9 1935 Sex:F Child# 4 Lucien Bernier Canada & Germ Desmarais Canada
BERNIER, Philippe, Jul 15 1887 Sex:M Child# H Bernier P Q & Marceline Duval P Q
BERNIER, Prudent Felix Joseph, Jan 7 1900 Sex:M Child# 1 Felix Bernier Canada & Adelaide Laure Canada
BERNIER, Rachael, Feb 23 1917 Sex:F Child# 5 Arthur Bernier Canada & Palmarina Cote Canada
BERNIER, Rachel Jeannine, Jun 30 1933 Sex:F Child# 3 Albert Bernier Canada & Anna Berube Nashua, NH
BERNIER, Rita Madeleine, Apr 14 1928 Sex:F Child# 7 Hector Bernier Canada & Frede Bourdon New Bedford, MA
BERNIER, Robert Arsene, Nov 22 1919 Sex:M Child# 6 Arthur Bernier Canada & Palmarina Cote Canada
BERNIER, Robert Raymond, Oct 21 1924 Sex:M Child# 1 Albert Bernier Canada & Clara Berube Nashua, NH
BERNIER, Roger Rosaire, Jan 2 1921 Sex:M Child# 13 Thomas Bernier Canada & Marie Lambert Canada
BERNIER, Roland, Feb 13 1911 Sex:M Child# 3 Arthur Bernier Canada & Palmarina Cote Canada
BERNIER, Roland Richard, Jan 30 1935 Sex:M Child# 1 Roland Bernier Canada & Yvonne Labrie Nashua, NH
BERNIER, Sophrenie, Oct 13 1900 Sex:F Child# 3 Joseph Bernier Canada & Emma Caron Canada
BERNIER, Sylvio Raymond, Aug 30 1926 Sex:M Child# 2 Josalphe Bernier Canada & Laura Nadeau Nashua, NH
BERNIER, Theresa Jeannette, Dec 5 1926 Sex:F Child# 2 Alfred Bernier Canada & Anna Berube Nashua, NH
BERNIER, Theresa Pearl, Jun 27 1928 Sex:F Child# 3 Joseph Bernier Canada & Laura Nadeau Nashua, NH
BERNIER, Unknown, Mar 30 1922 Sex:M Child# 1 Edmond Bernier Nashua, NH & Beatrice Moisant Nashua, NH Stillborn
BERNIER, Wilfrid, Aug 14 1899 Sex:M Child# 1 Joseph Bernier Canada & Emma Caron Canada Stillborn
BERNIKOWICZ, Mecjlow, Dec 18 1915 Sex:M Child# 2 Zidorjs Bernikowicz Russia & Gracilia Radiawicz Russia
BERRUBY, Joseph, Mar 2 1893 Sex:M Child# 1 George Berruby Canada & Anna Lacroix Canada
BERRY, Barbara Elizabeth, Apr 5 1912 Sex:F Child# 1 Millard H Berry E Waterville & Hazel L Goodspeed Nashua, NH
BERRY, Grace Louise, Oct 18 1906 Sex:F Child# 2 Frank Berry US & Levanie Lavoie US
BERRY, Jeanne, Feb 7 1929 Sex:F Child# 3 Millard Berry E Waterbury, ME & Hazel Goodspeed Nashua, NH
BERRY, Millard H, Jr, Jan 1 1922 Sex:M Child# 2 Millard H Berry E Waterville, ME & Hazel E Goodspeed Nashua, NH
BERTHEAUME, Marie Irene Gertrude, May 13 1934 Sex:F Child# 3 Wilfrid Bertheaume Canada & Angeline Niquette Canada
BERTHIAMON, Roland Lionel, Jun 15 1924 Sex:M Child# 2 W Berthiamon Canada & Ang Niquette
BERTHIAUME, Beatrice Estelle, Jun 21 1929 Sex:F Child# 4 Arthur Berthiaume Canada & Leocadie Masse Northbridge
BERTHIAUME, Jos Paul Norman, Jul 10 1935 Sex:M Child# 5 Arthur Berthiaume Canada & Leocadie Masse Northbridge
BERTHIAUME, Joseph Raymond, Sep 5 1930 Sex:M Child# 1 Adelard Berthiaume Taftsville, CT & Irene Gagnon Canada
BERTHIAUME, Laurette, Feb 25 1923 Sex:F Child# 1 Wilfred Berthiaume Canada & Angelina Niquette Canada
BERTHIAUME, Marion, Apr 19 1935 Sex:F Child# 4 W Berthiaume Canada & Angelina Niquette Canada
BERTIS, Unknown, Feb 21 1924 Sex:F Child# 3 Serapin Bertis Greece & V Papademetrou Greece
BERTONIS, Josephine, Aug 12 1918 Sex:F Child# 2 Jerry Bertonis Russia & Valaria Zoconisky Russia
BERTOSIWICZ, Stanley, Mar 27 1926 Sex:M Child# 2 W Bertosiwicz Poland & J Bartosiewicz Poland
BERTRAM, Paul Edward, Nov 14 1918 Sex:M Child# 2 Harry A Bertram Nashua, NH & Mary A Farrell Lowell, MA
BERTRAM, Pauline Dorothy, Jan 4 1929 Sex:F Child# 1 William Bertram Chelmsford Ctr, MA & Mabel Speare Wakefield,MA
BERTRAND, Adelbert, Apr 4 1898 Sex:M Child# 5 Albert Bertrand Canada & Alexandr'n Ouellette Canada
BERTRAND, Albert Clement, Apr 26 1893 Sex:M Child# 2 Albert Bertrand Canada & Alexandrine Ouellett Canada
BERTRAND, Albert Richard, Jan 15 1917 Sex:M Child# 1 Harry Bertrand Nashua, NH & Mary Farrell Lowell, MA
BERTRAND, Blanche C, Aug 5 1902 Sex:F Child# 7 Albert Bertrand Canada & A Ouellette Canada
BERTRAND, Donald Ernest, Aug 9 1926 Sex:M Child# 5 Francis Bertrand Nashua, NH & Anna Bergeron Pepperell, MA
BERTRAND, Francois X, Dec 24 1891 Sex:M Child# 1 Albert Bertrand Canada & Alexandrine Ouellett Canada
BERTRAND, Hector, Feb 22 1905 Sex:M Child# 8 Albert Bertrand Canada & Alexandrine Ouellett Canada
BERTRAND, Joseph Armand, Aug 12 1894 Sex:M Child# 3 Albert Bertrand Canada & Alexandrina Oullette Canada
BERTRAND, Joseph Edmond, Aug 12 1896 Sex:M Child# 4 Alfred Bertrand Canada & Alexandrine Oullette Canada
BERTRAND, Joseph Leo, Dec 10 1899 Sex:M Child# 6 Albert Bertrand Canada & Alexandrine Ouellett Canada
BERTRAND, Louise Irene, Jul 18 1906 Sex:F Child# 9 Albert Bertrand Canada & Alexandrine Ouellett Canada
BERTRAND, Maria Elizabeth, Jun 29 1889 Sex:F Child# 1 George Bertrand Canada & Mary Girard Canada
BERTRAND, Marie, Aug 27 1908 Sex:F Child# 10 Albert Bertrand Canada & Alexandrine Ouellet Canada Stillborn
BERTRAND, Marion Jean, Sep 16 1928 Sex:F Child# 2 Jos Leo Bertrand Nashua, NH & Elizabeth Burch Virginia
BERTRAND, Robert Paul, Aug 25 1917 Sex:M Child# 2 Francois Bertrand Nashua, NH & Anna Bergeron Pepperell, MA
BERTRAND, Unknown, Sep 1 1892 Sex:F Child# 5 Norbert Bertrand Canada & Dinas Charron Canada
BERTZANSKIS, Kleanpus, Nov 2 1915 Sex:F Child# 1 Frank Berzanskis Russia & Jonuskaite Vensenta Russia
BERUBE, Adrien Ernest, Apr 29 1911 Sex:M Child# 3 Thomas Berube Canada & Delina Levesque Canada
BERUBE, Adrienne, Jun 4 1897 Sex:f Child# 15 Etienne Berube Canada & Philomene Cote Canada
BERUBE, Albert Euclide, Dec 19 1930 Sex:M Child# 1 Euclide Berube Canada & Alice Gagnon Nashua, NH
BERUBE, Alexina, Oct 21 1901 Sex:F Child# 13 Georges Berube Canada & Melanie Hebert Canada Stillborn
BERUBE, Alice, Aug 15 1904 Sex:F Child# 4 Edouard Berube Canada & Adele April Canada
BERUBE, Alice Gloria Sonia, Mar 13 1929 Sex:F Child# 5 Alfred Berube Canada & Alice Belanger Canada
BERUBE, Alice Jeanne d'Arc, Jun 4 1919 Sex:F Child# 3 Alfred Berube Canada & Alice Belanger Canada
BERUBE, Alphee, Apr 23 1908 Sex:F Child# 10 Jean Berube Canada & Marie Belanger Canada
BERUBE, Andrea, Feb 25 1908 Sex:F Child# 6 Edouard Berube Canada & Adele April Canada
BERUBE, Anita, Dec 2 1923 Sex:F Child# 3 Joseph Berube Canada & Laura Plourde Canada
BERUBE, Annette, Apr 4 1910 Sex:F Child# 7 Edouard Berube Canada & Adele April Canada
BERUBE, Antonio, Jun 20 1900 Sex:M Child# 13 Charles Berube Canada & Esther Gregoire Canada
BERUBE, Arthur, Dec 13 1903 Sex:M Child# 2 Desire Berube Canada & Parmelie Valcour Canada

BERUBE, Athol May, Mar 21 1897 Sex:F Child# 10 Francis H Berube Bangor, ME & Katie Leazotte Altona, NY
BERUBE, Beatrice Olivette, Sep 22 1920 Sex:F Child# 1 Joseph Berube Canada & Laura Ploude Canada
BERUBE, Beatrice Rachel, Apr 4 1926 Sex:F Child# 7 Arthur Berube Canada & Diana Dube Nashua, NH
BERUBE, Bertha, Apr 28 1903 Sex:F Child# 8 Jean Berube Canada & Marie Belanger Canada
BERUBE, Blanche Eva, Sep 7 1902 Sex:F Child# 3 Edouard Berube Canada & Adele Aprile Canada
BERUBE, Cecile, Dec 3 1904 Sex:F Child# 3 Desire Berube Canada & Parmelie Valcour Canada
BERUBE, Cecile Estelle, Jan 5 1917 Sex:F Child# 2 Arthur Berube Canada & Diana Dube Nashua, NH
BERUBE, Celina Aimee I, Feb 9 1905 Sex:F Child# 14 Pierre Berube Canada & Arthemise Roussel Canada
BERUBE, Charles Eugene, Jun 10 1898 Sex:M Child# 3 Isidore Berube Canada & Elsie Dube Canada
BERUBE, Charles Eugene, Dec 20 1913 Sex:M Child# 1 Jean Bte Berube Canada & Delvina Desrosiers Canada
BERUBE, Claire Louise, Sep 11 1931 Sex:F Child# 7 Pierre Berube Canada & Marie L Dionne Nashua, NH
BERUBE, Claire Yvonne, Aug 2 1928 Sex:F Child# 7 Pierre Berube Canada & M L Dionne Nashua, NH
BERUBE, Conrad, Jan 31 1924 Sex:M Child# 6 Arthur Berube Canada & Diana Dube Nashua, NH
BERUBE, Conrad Wilbert, Oct 8 1934 Sex:M Child# 6 Joseph Berube Canada & Laura Plourde Canada
BERUBE, Dorilda, Nov 1 1893 Sex:F Child# 1 J B Berube Canada & Hermine Canada
BERUBE, Dorothy Thelma, Mar 25 1923 Sex:F Child# 1 Eugene Berube Nashua, NH & Edna Hartshorn Canada
BERUBE, Edouard Albert, Jan 9 1901 Sex:M Child# 2 Edouard Berube Canada & Adele April Canada
BERUBE, Elphege Donat, Feb  1915 Sex:M Child# 3 Donat Berube Canada & Florida Lebrun Canada
BERUBE, Emile, Mar 7 1902 Sex:M Child# 1 J B Berube Canada & Aurore Lavoie Canada
BERUBE, Emile Normand, Jun 25 1922 Sex:M Child# 1 Eugene Berube Canada & Y Belanger Canada
BERUBE, Ernest Denis, Oct 27 1926 Sex:M Child# 1 Alfred Berube Canada & Alice Belanger Canada
BERUBE, Ernestine Clare Rita, Jul 5 1929 Sex:F Child# 3 F P Berube Nashua, NH & Pauline Lafrance Canada
BERUBE, Eugene George, Jun 11 1902 Sex:M Child# 3 Desire Berube Canada & Parmelie Valcour Canada
BERUBE, Eva Alice, May 10 1900 Sex:F Child# 4 Philippe Berube Canada & Maria Larocque Canada
BERUBE, Eva Lorraine, Nov 23 1927 Sex:F Child# 2 Arthur Berube Nashua, NH & Eva Dion Nashua, NH
BERUBE, Evelyn, Aug 22 1929 Sex:F Child# 1 Alfred Berube Canada & Mary Lynch Pepperell, MA
BERUBE, Evelyn Carmen, Aug 9 1932 Sex:F Child# 4 Charles E Berube Canada & Laurette Jette Nashua, NH
BERUBE, Fernande Dora Pauline, Jan 5 1924 Sex:F Child# 2 A X Berube Nashua, NH & Pauline Lafrance Canada
BERUBE, Florette Alexandra, Sep 2 1904 Sex:F Child# 3 Elie Berube Canada & Josephine Racine Canada
BERUBE, Francis Girard Paul, May 18 1919 Sex:M Child# 1 Frank X Berube Nashua, NH & Pauline LaFrance Canada
BERUBE, Francois Xavier, Jan 19 1897 Sex:M Child# 10 Pierre Berube Canada & Artemise Roussel Canada
BERUBE, Frederick Benjamin, Aug 4 1913 Sex:M Child# 1 Joseph Berube Fitchburg, MA & Annie Sawyer Rouses Pt, NY
BERUBE, Georgette Louisette, Mar 25 1930 Sex:F Child# 1 Oscar Berube Canada & Rachel Bilodeau Canada
BERUBE, Gerard, Jan 29 1916 Sex:M Child# 1 Arthur Berube Canada & Diana Dube Nashua, NH
BERUBE, Hector Louis G, Jul 10 1904 Sex:M Child# 3 George Berube Canada & Aurea Landry Canada
BERUBE, Henri Etienne, Oct 22 1920 Sex:M Child# 4 Ludger Berube Canada & Delvina Levesque Canada
BERUBE, Homer Henri, Jr, Dec 10 1930 Sex:M Child# 2 Homer Berube Nashua, NH & Lilliane Trudel Nashua, NH
BERUBE, J B Charles, Jan 8 1918 Sex:M Child# 3 Arthur Berube Canada & Diana Dube Nashua, NH
BERUBE, J B Laurent, Dec 30 1917 Sex:M Child# 10 Edouard Berube Canada & Adele April Canada
BERUBE, Jean Baptiste A, May 10 1896 Sex:M Child# 2 Isidor Berube Canada & Elise Dube Canada
BERUBE, Jean Bpatiste B, Jun 5 1907 Sex:M Child# 8 Isidore Berube Canada & Elise Dube Canada
BERUBE, Jean M, Oct 11 1895 Sex:M Child# 4 Jean Berube Canada & Marie Belanger Canada
BERUBE, Jeanette Laurette, Mar 31 1925 Sex:F Child# 2 Charles Berube Canada & Laurette Jette Nashua, NH
BERUBE, Jos Alf Sylvia Henri, Feb 6 1918 Sex:M Child# 1 Pierre Berube Canada & Marie Louise Dionne Nashua, NH
BERUBE, Jos Ludger Camille, Nov 12 1916 Sex:M Child# 2 Jean B Berube Canada & Delvina Desrosiers Canada
BERUBE, Jos Paul Robert, Apr 29 1926 Sex:M Child# 1 Napoleon Berube Canada & Theresa Dube Nashua, NH
BERUBE, Joseph A E, Jan 6 1899 Sex:M Child# 6 Jean Berube Canada & Marie Belanger Canada
BERUBE, Joseph Albert, Jul 5 1903 Sex:M Child# 2 Philippe Berube Canada & Rose Anna Levesque Canada
BERUBE, Joseph Albert E, Jan 29 1908 Sex:M Child# 6 Philippe Berube Canada & Rose Anna Levesque Canada
BERUBE, Joseph Albert R, May 19 1906 Sex:M Child# 2 Donat Berube Canada & Flavie Lebrun Canada
BERUBE, Joseph Arthur, Jul 28 1925 Sex:M Child# 1 Arthur Berube Nashua, NH & Yvonne Dion Nashua, NH
BERUBE, Joseph D T, Aug 4 1896 Sex:M Child# 2 Philippe Berube Canada & Marie Laroque Canada
BERUBE, Joseph Fred, Nov 6 1895 Sex:M Child# 3 Henri Berube Canada & Marie Michaud Canada
BERUBE, Joseph Harvey, Aug 2 1897 Sex:M Child# 5 Jean Berube Canada & Marie Belanger Canada
BERUBE, Joseph Honore, Mar 16 1891 Sex:M Child# 12 Etienne Berube Canada & Philomene Cote Canada
BERUBE, Joseph Isidore, Oct 23 1899 Sex:M Child# 4 Isidore Berube Canada & Elise Dube Canada
BERUBE, Joseph L D, Jul 13 1898 Sex:M Child# 4 Albini Berube Canada & Mathilda Bastille Canada
BERUBE, Joseph Leo Edgar, Oct 1 1918 Sex:M Child#  Philippe Berube Canada & Rose Anna Levesque Canada
BERUBE, Joseph Omer H, Jan 31 1905 Sex:M Child# 4 Henri Berube Canada & Marie Michaud Canada
BERUBE, Joseph Paul Henri, Jul 17 1916 Sex:M Child# 8 Philippe Berube Canada & Rose Anna Levesque Canada
BERUBE, Joseph Philomen, Sep 22 1918 Sex:M Child# 2 J B Berube Canada & Delvina Desrosiers Canada
BERUBE, Joseph Richard C, Oct 5 1930 Sex:M Child# 1 Antonio Berube Nashua, NH & Rose Morissette Nashua, NH
BERUBE, Joseph Victor, May 29 1905 Sex:M Child# 7 Isidore Berube Canada & Elise Dube Canada
BERUBE, Laura Anna, May 5 1906 Sex:F Child# 5 Edouard Berube Canada & Adele April Canada
BERUBE, Leonard Rodolphe, Sep 27 1933 Sex:M Child# 2 Antonio Berube Nashua, NH & Rose Morissette Nashua, NH
BERUBE, Lionel, Apr 30 1927 Sex:M Child# 4 Joseph Berube Canada & Laura Plourde Canada
BERUBE, Lorraine Rita, Oct 21 1935 Sex:F Child# 3 Antonio Berube Nashua, NH & Rose Morrissette Nashua, NH
BERUBE, Louis Joseph, Jul 30 1894 Sex:M Child# 2 Henri Berube Canada & Marie Michaud Canada
BERUBE, Louise E Mary, Apr 5 1930 Sex:F Child# 3 Charles Berube Canada & Laurette Jette Nashua, NH
BERUBE, Lucien David, Jun 8 1914 Sex:M Child# 9 Edouard Berube Canada & Adele April Canada
BERUBE, Ludger Adrien, Mar 4 1908 Sex:M Child# 3 Donat Berube Canada & Flavie Lebrun Canada
BERUBE, M Alice Delia, Mar 9 1893 Sex:F Child# 2 Jean Berube Canada & Marie Belanger Canada
BERUBE, M Anna Albina, Oct 8 1891 Sex:F Child#  Jean Berube Canada & Marie Belanger Canada

BERUBE, M Anne Albina, Oct 29 1913 Sex:F Child# 11 Jean Berube Canada & Marie Belanger Canada
BERUBE, M Cecile A, May 17 1902 Sex:F Child# 5 Auguste Berube Canada & Marie Dumont Canada
BERUBE, M Lillian Lucille, Nov 17 1917 Sex:F Child# 2 Joseph Berube Canada & Anna L Sawyer Coopersville, NY
BERUBE, Maria Diana, Aug 4 1905 Sex:F Child# 1 Andre Berube Canada & Annie Cote Canada
BERUBE, Marie, Feb 27 1924 Sex:F Child# 1 (No Parents Listed)
BERUBE, Marie A D I, Nov 7 1902 Sex:F Child# 1 Joseph Berube Canada & Dolores Berube Canada
BERUBE, Marie Albina Y, Feb 8 1903 Sex:F Child# 13 Pierre Berube Canada & Arthimise Roussel Canada
BERUBE, Marie Alice, Jan 20 1897 Sex:F Child# 3 Albany Berube Canada & Mathilda Bastille Canada
BERUBE, Marie Alice L, Mar 10 1905 Sex:F Child# 4 Philippe Berube Canada & Rose Anna Levesque Canada
BERUBE, Marie Andrea, Sep 10 1899 Sex:F Child# 1 Edouard Berube Canada & Adele April Canada
BERUBE, Marie Anna, Feb 11 1902 Sex:F Child# 1 Philippe Berube Canada & Rose Anna Levesque Canada
BERUBE, Marie Aurore D, Sep 11 1900 Sex:F Child# 12 Pierre Berube Canada & Arthemise Roussell Canada
BERUBE, Marie Bernadette P, Jan 12 1930 Sex:F Child# 5 Jean Baptiste Berube Canada & Delvina Desrosier Canada
BERUBE, Marie Delia, Sep 24 1903 Sex:F Child# 6 Isidore Berube Canada & Elise Dube Canada
BERUBE, Marie Derilda, Sep 20 1894 Sex:F Child# 3 Jean Berube Canada & Marie Belanger Canada
BERUBE, Marie E E, Jan 15 1899 Sex:F Child# 11 Pierre Berube Canada & Arthemise Roussel Canada
BERUBE, Marie E Eva, Dec 22 1904 Sex:F Child# 1 Donat Berube Canada & Flavie Lebrun Canada
BERUBE, Marie Elaine Harriet, Feb 26 1924 Sex:F Child# 1 Charles Berube Canada & Laurette Jette Nashua, NH
BERUBE, Marie Florida, Mar 26 1901 Sex:F Child# 1 George Berube Canada & Armea Landry Canada
BERUBE, Marie Gabrielle P L, Mar 24 1925 Sex:F Child# 5 Peter Berube Canada & Mary L Dion Nashua, NH
BERUBE, Marie Germaine R, Mar 28 1906 Sex:F Child# 2 Ludger Berube Canada & Marie Levesque Canada
BERUBE, Marie Ida Yvonne, Mar 25 1906 Sex:F Child# 5 Philippe Berube Canada & Rose A Levesque Canada
BERUBE, Marie Irene, Feb 11 1902 Sex:F Child# 5 Isidore Berube Canada & Elise Dube Canada
BERUBE, Marie Irene J, Aug 1 1910 Sex:F Child# 7 Philippe Berube Canada & Rose A Levesque Canada
BERUBE, Marie Jeanne Rita, Mar 29 1920 Sex:F Child# 4 Jean Baptiste Berube Canada & Delvina Derosier Canada
BERUBE, Marie Lena, Aug 18 1912 Sex:F Child# 1 Alfred Berube Canada & Alice Belanger Canada
BERUBE, Marie Odille A, Jul 5 1903 Sex:F Child# 3 Philippe Berube Canada & Rose Anna Levesque Canada
BERUBE, Marie R de Lima, May 3 1902 Sex:F Child# 2 George Berube Canada & Anna Landry Canada
BERUBE, Marie Regina, Jul 29 1890 Sex:F Child# 1 Henri Berube Canada & Marie Michaud Canada
BERUBE, Marie Therese, Apr 16 1921 Sex:F Child# 2 Peter Berube Canada & Mary L Dion Nashua, NH
BERUBE, Marie Y Loraine, Apr 22 1931 Sex:F Child# 4 Charles Berube Canada & Yvonne Bouchard Ft Kent, ME
BERUBE, Marie Yvonne Agnes, May 14 1913 Sex:F Child# 2 Napoleon Berube Canada & Victoria Olena Chazy, NY
BERUBE, Mariel Valeria, Sep 20 1924 Sex:F Child# 1 Joseph Berube Canada & Dora Provencher Nashua, NH
BERUBE, Mary Beatrice, Aug 6 1922 Sex:F Child# 3 Peter Berube Canada & Mary Louise Dion Nashua, NH
BERUBE, Mary Jeannette C, Nov 10 1923 Sex:F Child# 4 Peter Berube Canada & Mary L Dion Nashua, NH
BERUBE, Mary Rose, Feb 14 1911 Sex:F Child# 1 Napoleon Berube Canada & Victoria O'Lena New York
BERUBE, Mathilde, Jan 21 1895 Sex:F Child# 2 Albani Berube Canada & Mathilde Bastille Canada
BERUBE, Maurice Alphee, Sep 26 1930 Sex:M Child# 1 Alphee Berube Nashua, NH & Josephine Lacombe Canada
BERUBE, Napoleon Willis, May 11 1914 Sex:M Child# 3 Napoleon Berube Canada & Victoria Olena Sciota, NY
BERUBE, Norman, Apr 6 1933 Sex:m Child# 1 (No Parents Listed)
BERUBE, Ovide Adrien, Sep 6 1920 Sex:M Child# 4 Arthur Berube Canada & Diane Dube Nashua, NH
BERUBE, Patricia Rachel, Aug 21 1927 Sex:F Child# 1 O H Berube Nashua, NH & Lillian Trudel Nashua, NH
BERUBE, Pauline Lucille, Jul 16 1922 Sex:F Child# 5 Arthur Berube Canada & Diana Dube Nashua, NH
BERUBE, Pierre Sylvio U, Jan 24 1903 Sex:M Child# 7 Ignace Berube Canada & Emelie Plourde Canada
BERUBE, Robert Girard, Feb 13 1921 Sex:M Child# 11 Edouard Berube Canada & Adele April Canada
BERUBE, Robert Theophidus, Feb 17 1904 Sex:M Child# 1 Ludger Berube Canada & Delima Levesque Canada
BERUBE, Robert Toussaint, Oct 31 1921 Sex:M Child# 2 Joseph Berube Canada & Laura Plourde Canada
BERUBE, Rodrigue Lucien, Sep 3 1906 Sex:M Child# 4 Desire Berube Canada & Parmelie Valcour Canada
BERUBE, Roger, Sep 14 1925 Sex:M Child# 1 Louis P Berube Canada & Corinne Duclos Nashua, NH
BERUBE, Roland, Apr 8 1927 Sex:M Child# 1 Joseph Berube Canada & Marie Luasseur Canada
BERUBE, Romeo, Jul 18 1912 Sex:M Child# 8 Edouard Berube Canada & Adele April Canada
BERUBE, Romeo Arthur, May 9 1903 Sex:M Child# 2 Isidore Berube Canada & Josephine Racine Canada
BERUBE, Theophile, Feb 27 1892 Sex:M Child# 1 Albani Berube Canada & Mathilda Bastile Canada
BERUBE, Ulric, Dec 29 1904 Sex:M Child# 9 Jean Berube Canada & Marie Belanger Canada
BERUBE, Unknown, Mar 5 1890 Sex:M Child# 4 Frank Berube Maine & Kate Gizott NY Stillborn
BERUBE, Unknown, Jan 26 1892 Sex:M Child# 6 Frank Berube NY & Kate Leazotte NY Stillborn
BERUBE, Unknown, Aug 4 1895 Sex:M Child# 3 Arthur Berube Canada & Philomene Sirois Canada Stillborn
BERUBE, Unknown, Jan 28 1896 Sex:M Child#   Georges Berube Canada & Emma Langlais Canada Stillborn
BERUBE, Unknown, Mar 21 1897 Sex:F Child# 9 Francis H Berube Bangor, ME & Katie Leazotte, NY Stillborn
BERUBE, Unknown, Feb 17 1899 Sex:M Child# 3 Philippe Berube Canada & Maria Larocque Canada Stillborn
BERUBE, Unknown, Jun 13 1926 Sex:M Child# 5 Irenee Berube Canada & Marie L Dionne Nashua, NH Stillborn
BERUBE, Yvette Germaine, Dec 18 1914 Sex:F Child# 2 Alfred Berube Canada & Alice Belanger Canada
BERUBE, Yvonne Lina, Jan 31 1904 Sex:F Child# 2 Joseph Berube Canada & Dolores Berube Canada
BERUNLIE, Marie, Oct 13 1888 Sex:F Child# 1 Pierre Berunlie Canada & Euphenie Gagnon Canada
BERZICH, Jacob, Jun 7 1894 Sex:M Child# 3 Jacob Berzich Russia & Lizie Rasnich Russia
BERZITES, Fannie, May 27 1902 Sex:F Child# 4 Samuel Berzites Russia & Lizzie Beynites Russia
BERZTS, Betsa, Mar 15 1896 Sex:F Child# 3 Sam Berzts Russia & Liza Rasinkovitz Russia
BESLIN, Unknown, Nov 29 1890 Sex:F Child# 13 John Beslin Ireland & Rose Muran Nashua, NH Stillborn
BESSE, Ruth Lillian, Mar 26 1927 Sex:F Child# 2 Cecil E Besse Rochester, MA & Grace L Austin Nashua, NH
BESSE, Thelma Elizabeth, May 19 1924 Sex:F Child# 1 Cecil E Besse Rochester, MA & Grace Austin Nashua, NH
BESSETTE, Marie G, Aug 28 1891 Sex:F Child# 2 Israel Bessette Canada & Victorine Lapointe Canada
BESSETTE, Marie Marguerite E, Jun 7 1911 Sex:F Child# 5 Adelard Bessette Canada & Adele Sabourin Canada
BESSEY, Ellen Kathleen, Jun 29 1920 Sex:F Child# 1 Oscar Y Bessey Bingham, ME & Amy Dill Edgerly Princeton, ME

BESSONETTE, Pierre O, Jun 23 1889 Sex:M Child# 1 P Bessonette Canada & Regina Houde Canada
BESSONNETTE, Marie Rosanna, Jun 8 1891 Sex:F Child# 2 Arthur Bessonnette Canada & Mary Laneville Canada
BESTON, Frederick, Nov 24 1894 Sex:M Child# 13 John Beston Ireland & Rose Moran Nashua, NH
BESTON, Sylvio Frederick, Jan 17 1907 Sex:M Child# 1 William E Beston Nashua, NH & Celina Courtemanche Nashua, NH
BETTER, Unknown, Jul 7 1898 Sex:F Child# 5 Peter Better Mooers Forks, NY & Katherine Hoy Hudson, NH
BETTERS, Ann, Nov 23 1927 Sex:F Child# 1 Homer H Betters Mooers, NY & Grace McAlpine Nashua, NH
BETTERS, Beverly Ann, Oct 13 1928 Sex:F Child# 1 L P Betters Rouses Point, NY & Sylvia Fontaine Nashua, NH
BETTERS, Kathleen, Jan 14 1892 Sex:F Child# 3 Peter Betters Moore's Forks, NY & Katie Hoey Hudson, NH
BETTERS, Unknown, Jan 21 1887 Sex:M Child# 3 Peter Betters NY & Kate Hoy Hudson, NY
BETTERS, Unknown, Aug 29 1895 Sex:F Child# 4 Peter Betters Mooers Forks, NY & Kate Hoy Hudson, NY
BETTERS, Unknown, Mar 31 1902 Sex:F Child# 6 Peter Betters Moores Falls, NY & Catherine F Hoy Hudson, NY
BETTS, Madge, Jul 10 1916 Sex:F Child# 1 Clifford S Betts Brewer, ME & Madge Dorr Cherryfield, ME
BETTS, Merle Emma, Mar 6 1918 Sex:F Child# 2 Clifford S Betts S Berwick, ME & Madge Dorr Cherryfield, ME
BETTY, William Ewart, Nov 29 1928 Sex:M Child# 1 William Betty Scotland & Jeanette Nixon Ayer, MA
BEUKOWSKI, Albert Gerard, Nov 9 1926 Sex:M Child# 2 William Beukowski Poland & Helen Kolarist Poland
BEZA, Sterie Theodore, May 20 1929 Sex:M Child# 1 Sotirios Beza Greece & Vasila Paleoseliti Greece
BEZA, Unknown, Apr 7 1935 Sex:M Child# 2 Sam Beza Greece & Vasila Paleoselite Greece
BEZIL, Ernest Robert, Apr 30 1925 Sex:M Child# 3 Ernest Bezil Canada & Delvina Beaulieu Canada
BIALASKI, Nicla, Jan 23 1911 Sex:F Child# 1 George Bialaski Russia & Christo Yasokavitch Russia
BIANCHI, Barbara Anne, Jun 1 1934 Sex:F Child# 4 Egidio Jos Bianchi Quincy, MA & Irene Bennett Laconia, NH
BIANCHI, Laura Louise, Jul 19 1932 Sex:F Child# 1 T David Bianchi Milford, NH & Rena Vanette France
BIARTHROW, Agnes Mary, May 5 1907 Sex:F Child# 2 Arthur E Biarthrow Vermont & Agnes Dowling Nashua, NH
BIATHROW, Blanch Cecile, Nov 27 1917 Sex:F Child# 8 Arthur Biathrow Vermont & Mary Dowling Nashua, NH
BIATHROW, Dora Isabel, Jun 1 1913 Sex:F Child# 6 Arthur Biathrow Morrisville, VT & Mary A Dowling Nashua, NH
BIATHROW, Helen, Apr 27 1908 Sex:F Child# 3 Arthur E Biathrow Vermont & Mary Agnes Dowling Nashua, NH
BIATHROW, Jennie Rebecca, Jul 21 1909 Sex:F Child# 4 Arthur E Biathrow Morrisville, VT & Agnes Dowling Nashua, NH
BIATHROW, Leon Arthur, Aug 27 1920 Sex:M Child# 9 Arthur E Biathrow Morrisville, VT & Mary A Dowling Nashua, NH
BIATHROW, Raymond Eugene, Apr 22 1924 Sex:M Child# 10 Arthur E Biathrow Morrisville, VT & Mary A Dowling Nashua, NH
BIATHROW, Unknown, Nov 20 1915 Sex:F Child# 7 Arthur Biathrow
BIBEAU, Alfred E, May 6 1903 Sex:M Child# 5 Aime Bibeau Canada & Marie Louise Salvail Canada
BIBEAU, Alphonse George A, Jan 29 1900 Sex:M Child# 3 Annie Bibeau Canada & M L Salvail New Hampshire
BIBEAU, Ant Irene Violette, Aug 27 1916 Sex:F Child# 11 Aime Bibeau Canada & Marie Louise Salvail NH
BIBEAU, Diana Solange, Mar 9 1928 Sex:F Child# 5 Hector Bibeau Mass & Alida Lapaorte Canada
BIBEAU, Donald Nelson, Oct 17 1931 Sex:M Child# 1 Hector Bibeau St Germaine, Canada & Blanche Morton Nashua, NH
BIBEAU, Edgar Edward, Oct 10 1930 Sex:M Child# 3 Edward Bibeau Nashua, NH & Anna Soucy Nashua, NH
BIBEAU, Enrest Roland, Mar 19 1912 Sex:M Child# 1 Armand Bibeau Canada & Georgianna Desrosier Canada
BIBEAU, J Alfred Gerard, Jul 21 1913 Sex:M Child# 2 Emile Bibeau Canada & Edwidge Soucy Canada
BIBEAU, Jeanne D'Arc Frances, Dec 19 1927 Sex:F Child# 3 Henry Bibeau Fisherville, MA & Albertine Brunelle Canada
BIBEAU, Jos Fernand Aime, Apr 20 1926 Sex:M Child# 1 Edouard Bibeau Nashua, NH & Anna Soucy Nashua, NH
BIBEAU, Joseph Aime Armand, Jul 11 1924 Sex:M Child# 3 Edgar Bibeau NH & Blanche Mondor Maine
BIBEAU, Joseph Corade A, Jul 9 1908 Sex:M Child# 1 Emile Bibeau Canada & Edwidge Soucy Canada
BIBEAU, Joseph Ernest, Mar 12 1919 Sex:M Child# 3 Armand Bibeau Canada & Georgina Desrosiers Canada
BIBEAU, Joseph Hector Roger, Aug 24 1924 Sex:M Child# 5 Armand Bibeau Canada & Georgiana Desrosiers Canada
BIBEAU, Joseph Lionel, Nov 19 1917 Sex:M Child# 2 Armand Bibeau Canada & Georgiana Desrosiers Canada
BIBEAU, Marie, Feb 1 1921 Sex:F Child# 1 Edgar Bibeau NH & Blanche Aurore Monda Maine Stillborn
BIBEAU, Marie, Aug 26 1922 Sex:F Child# 2 Edgar Bibeau NH & Blanche Mondor Maine Stillborn
BIBEAU, Marie A A, May 18 1895 Sex:F Child# 1 Paul Bibeau Canada & Marie A Cardin Canada
BIBEAU, Marie A C A, Sep 26 1901 Sex:F Child# 2 Paul Bibeau Canada & Marie A Cardin Canada
BIBEAU, Marie Florida, Nov 21 1901 Sex:F Child# 4 Aime Bibeau Canada & Marie L Salvail NH
BIBEAU, Marie L Alice, Nov 21 1899 Sex:F Child# 1 Pierre Bibeau Canada & Marie L Lefebvre Canada
BIBEAU, Marie Louise Clare, Oct 25 1928 Sex:F Child# 2 Edward Bibeau Nashua, NH & Anna Soucy Nashua, NH
BIBEAU, Marie Louise Yvette, Dec 8 1926 Sex:F Child# 5 Edgar Bibeau Nashua, NH & Blanche Mondar Biddeford, ME
BIBEAU, Marie Rita, Dec 22 1919 Sex:F Child# 1 (No Parents Listed)
BIBEAU, Mary Anita, Jun 5 1921 Sex:F Child# 4 Armand Bibeau Canada & Georgianna Desrosier Canada
BIBEAU, Rene Armand Joseph, Mar 4 1924 Sex:M Child# 3 Hector Bibeau Fisherville, MA & Alida Laporte Farnum, PQ
BIBEAU, Simonne Georgette, Feb 16 1925 Sex:F Child# 4 Hector Bibeau Mass & Alida Laport Canada
BIBEAU, Unknown, Nov 28 1894 Sex:M Child# 1 Aimee Bibeau Canada & M Louise Salvail Nashua, NH Stillborn
BIBEAU, Unknown, Jul 23 1931 Sex:M Child# 6 Hector Bibeau Fisherville, MA & Alida Laporte Canada Stillborn
BICKFORD, Frank Arlen, Oct 31 1934 Sex:M Child# 2 Hollis Bickford Hodgdon, ME & Violet Shannon Houlton, ME
BICKFORD, Horace John, Sep 5 1917 Sex:M Child# 2 Paul Pearl Bickford Madison, NH & A Moore Madison, NH
BICKFORD, Howard Leslie, Mar 21 1924 Sex:M Child# 1 J T Bickford Nashua, NH & Ger W Rideout Lynn, MA
BICKFORD, James Sargent, May 27 1916 Sex:M Child# 1 James L Bickford Nashua, NH & Alice Sargent Hollis, NH
BICKFORD, Jason Tolles, Nov 3 1898 Sex:M Child# 1 James L Bickford Nashua, NH & Marion E Tolles Nashua, NH
BICKFORD, Mary, Jan 5 1911 Sex:F Child# 3 James Bickford Nashua, NH & Marion E Tolles Nashua, NH Stillborn
BICKFORD, Philip Rideout, Dec 26 1925 Sex:M Child# 2 Jason F Bickford Nashua, NH & Geraldine Rideout Lynn, MA
BICKFORD, Robert, Jun 10 1927 Sex:M Child# 2 Jason F Bickford Somerville, MA & Blanche Nutting Dorchester, MA
BICKFORD, Robert Nutting, Sep 28 1929 Sex:M Child# 4 Jason F Bickford Somerville, MA & Blanche Nutting Dorchester
BICKFORD, Sylvia, Sep 28 1929 Sex:F Child# 3 Jason F Bickford Somerville, MA & Blanche Nutting Dorchester, MA
BICKFORD, Unknown, Dec 1 1902 Sex:F Child# 2 James L Bickford Nashua, NH & Marion E Tolles Nashua, NH
BICKFORD, William Edwin, Nov 20 1924 Sex:M Child# 1 Jason T Bickford Somerville, MA & Blanche Nutting Dorchester,MA
BIDEAU, Jos R Noel Etienne, Dec 25 1917 Sex:M Child# 7 Oliver Bideau Canada & Mary Derosier Canada
BIDLACK, Mary Louise, Apr 22 1906 Sex:F Child# 1 Theron Bidlack New York & Mary Salvis Nashua, NH
BIDWELL, Richard Frances, Feb 8 1927 Sex:M Child# 1 Francis Bidwell Norwich, CT & Helene E Newell Wilmington

BIELENSKY, Annie, May 5 1917 Sex:F Child# 2 Stanley Bielensky Lithuania Russia & Eva Mashinuta Lithuania Russia
BIELOSKI, Joseph William, Apr 19 1935 Sex:M Child# 1 Jos Bieloski Cambridge, MA & Mary Burak Lorraine, OH
BIENOVICH, Josie, Dec 10 1916 Sex:F Child# 3 Vladislav Bienovich Russia & Theo Kosakowska Russia
BIENUCHAWICZ, Frank, Jul 11 1919 Sex:M Child# 5 Jos Bienuchawicz Poland Russia & Edwiga Kutzawicz Poland Russia
BIENVENUE, Angelina B, Mar 14 1898 Sex:F Child# 5 H Bienvenue Canada & Angelina Beaupre Canada
BIENVENUE, Flora, Jun 13 1896 Sex:F Child# 1 Frank Bienvenue Canada & Alice Emond Canada
BIENVENUE, Joseph Gedeon, Aug 5 1912 Sex:M Child# 1 Frank Bienvenue Canada & Exilia Bouchard Canada
BIENVENUE, Udgere, Jul 25 1887 Sex:M Child# 10 Theo Bienvenue Canada & Eliza Nadeau Canada
BIENVENUE, Unknown, Jan 11 1906 Sex:M Child# 6 Frank Bienvenue Canada & Alice Armand Canada Stillborn
BIETHROW, Alice Emma, Jul 1 1905 Sex:F Child# 1 Arthur E Biethrow Vermont & Agnes Dowling NH
BIEUVENUE, Dora Bertha, Jan 9 1896 Sex:F Child# 4 Hormidas Bieuvenue Canada & Angelina Beaupre Canada
BIEUVENUE, George T, Feb 16 1892 Sex:M Child# 2 Homidas Bieuvenue Canada & Angelina Beaupre Canada
BIEUVENUE, Hormidas V, Jul 12 1894 Sex:M Child# 3 Hormidas Bieuvenue Canada & Angelina Beaupre Canada
BIGOLDE, Marie Cecile Pearl, Nov 19 1917 Sex:F Child# 4 William Bigolde Canada & Alma Arsenault Canada
BIGOOD, Joseph Isidore A, Feb 12 1908 Sex:M Child# 1 Auguste Bigood Canada & Rose Levesque Canada
BIGWOOD, James George, Jan 17 1919 Sex:M Child# 1 Edward G Bigwood Nashua, NH & Ethel Lorraine Nashua, NH
BIGWOOD, Lauretta, Jul 19 1903 Sex:F Child# 4 James Edw Bigwood New York & Matilda Delorme New York
BIGWOOD, Marjorie Gertrude, Apr 8 1922 Sex:F Child# 3 George E Bigwood Nashua, NH & Ethel Lorraine Nashua, NH
BIGWOOD, Roland Lionel, May 25 1920 Sex:M Child# 2 Ed George Bigwood Nashua, NH & Ethel M Lorraine Nashua, NH
BIGWOOD, Stanley, Dec 19 1925 Sex:M Child# 4 George Bigwood Nashua, NH & Ethel Lorraine Nashua, NH
BIJOLD, Joseph Isidore, Jul 8 1914 Sex:M Child# 2 William Bijold Canada & Alma Arsenault Canada
BIJOLD, Noela Ethel, Dec 25 1921 Sex:F Child# 6 William Bijold Canada & Alma Arsenault Canada
BILEWICZ, Faustyna, Nov 5 1911 Sex:M Child# 2 Vicla Bilewicz Russia & Kune Smietana Austria
BILLEDEAU, Louis, Sep 22 1897 Sex:M Child# 5 John Billedeau Canada & Victoria Gagnon Canada
BILLING, Leslie Harold, Aug 15 1931 Sex:M Child# 1 Leslie H Billing US & Florence Carter NH
BILLINGS, Gary, Oct 12 1934 Sex:M Child# 2 Leslie H Billings Nashua, NH & Florence Carter Nashua, NH
BILLINGS, Jerome Roosevelt, Jul 25 1906 Sex:M Child# 3 Freeman L Billings Maine & Grace W Hope Canada
BILLINGS, Kenneth Wallace, May 16 1908 Sex:M Child# 4 Freeman L Billings Maine & Grace W Hope Canada
BILLINGS, Norma Mae, May 26 1924 Sex:F Child# 6 Joel Earl Billings Princeton, ME & Nellie Hope Canada
BILLINGS, Unknown, Apr 16 1896 Sex:M Child# 1 Everett W Billings NH & Edith O Nichols NH Stillborn
BILLODEAU, Joseph Emile, Apr 24 1907 Sex:M Child# 11 Cyrille Billodeau Canada & Marie Grenier Canada
BILLS, Clayton Hartwell, Feb 7 1904 Sex:M Child# 5 Charles A Bills Nashua, NH & Lizzie E Peacock Greenville, NH
BILLS, Gertrude May, Jan 27 1922 Sex:F Child# 1 Wallace A Bills Nashua, NH & Mabel I Bullard Nashua, NH
BILLS, Leon William, Jan 10 1918 Sex:M Child# 2 Leon William Bills Milford, NH & Edith Gerome Boston, MA
BILLS, Unknown, Jan 6 1926 Sex:F Child# 2 Wallace A Bills Nashua, NH & Mabel L Bullard Nashua, NH
BILLS, Wallace A, Dec 3 1900 Sex:M Child# 4 Charles S Bills Nashua, NH & Lizzie Brookline, NH
BILLSON, Virginia Jane, Oct 2 1924 Sex:F Child# 1 H C Billson Chelmsford, MA & Elizabeth Heminway Milford, NH
BILODEAU, Albert Sylvio, Jul 22 1917 Sex:M Child# 14 Achille Bilodeau Canada & Olivine Ouellette Canada
BILODEAU, Ambrois Girard, Mar 18 1919 Sex:M Child# 2 Joseph Bilodeau Canada & Amanda Couture Canada
BILODEAU, Anna, Mar 7 1902 Sex:F Child# 6 John Bilodeau Canada & Victoria Bilodeau Canada
BILODEAU, Barbara Loraine, Sep 10 1927 Sex:F Child# 1 Alfred Bilodeau Canada & Louiebelle Wallace Nashua, NH
BILODEAU, Eliza, Feb 25 1896 Sex:F Child# 4 Johnny Bilodeau Canada & Victoria Canada
BILODEAU, Eugene, Jan 17 1892 Sex:M Child# 3 Ovide Bilodeau Canada & Eliza Morin Canada
BILODEAU, Eva, Apr 19 1900 Sex:F Child# 8 Arthur Bilodeau Canada & Eugenie Pelletier Canada
BILODEAU, Francis Albert, Oct 1 1929 Sex:M Child# 1 Albert Bilodeau Nashua, NH & Florence Peno Hollis, NH
BILODEAU, George Conrad, Apr 20 1904 Sex:M Child# 11 Arthur Bilodeau Canada & Eugenie Peltier Canada
BILODEAU, Helene, Jul 1 1924 Sex:F Child# 3 Oscar Bilodeau Nashua, NH & Mildred Hunter Marlboro, NH
BILODEAU, Henry Francis, May 6 1921 Sex:M Child# 1 Francis Bilodeau Canada & Exilia Desautels Nashua, NH
BILODEAU, J Ovide Aurel, Mar 28 1915 Sex:M Child# 1 Ovide Bilodeau Canada & Adelina Rossignol Canada
BILODEAU, Joseph, May 11 1906 Sex:M Child# 1 Joseph Bilodeau Canada & Amanda Couture Canada
BILODEAU, Joseph, Dec 28 1917 Sex:M Child# 1 Joseph Bilodeau Canada & Anna Briand Canada Stillborn
BILODEAU, Joseph Adelard, May 10 1914 Sex:M Child# 11 Achille Bilodeau Canada & Olivine Goulet Canada
BILODEAU, Joseph Amedee, Sep 8 1903 Sex:M Child# 8 John Bilodeau Canada & Victoria Gagnon Canada
BILODEAU, Joseph Eugene, Feb 25 1892 Sex:M Child# 1 Arthur Bilodeau Canada & Eugenie Peltier Canada
BILODEAU, Joseph Leo, Jan 15 1909 Sex:M Child# 1 Alfred Bilodeau Canada & Albina Goudreau Nashua, NH
BILODEAU, Joseph Leo, Dec 3 1915 Sex:M Child# 2 Adelard Bilodeau Maine & Rose E Leblanc Mass
BILODEAU, Joseph Louis A, Jun 16 1890 Sex:M Child# 2 Louis Bilodeau Canada & Adele Rioux Canada
BILODEAU, Joseph Noel, Dec 25 1898 Sex:M Child# 7 Arthur Bilodeau Canada & Eugenie Pelletier Canada
BILODEAU, Joseph Ovid Alphee, Sep 29 1916 Sex:M Child# 2 Ovid Bilodeau Canada & Adelina Rossignol Canada
BILODEAU, Joseph Pierre, May 18 1894 Sex:M Child# 4 Arthur Bilodeau Canada & Eugenie Pelletier Canada
BILODEAU, Joseph Robert Leo, Jan 11 1934 Sex:M Child# 2 Augenard Bilodeau Canada & Lena Boucher Nashua, NH
BILODEAU, Joseph Simothe, Mar 29 1894 Sex:M Child# 3 John Bilodeau Canada & Victoria Gagnon Canada
BILODEAU, Louis, Nov 6 1902 Sex:M Child# 10 Arthur Bilodeau Canada & Eugenie Pelletier Canada
BILODEAU, Louis, Sep 25 1907 Sex:M Child# 12 Arthur Bilodeau Canada & Eugenie Pelletier Canada
BILODEAU, Maria, Aug 2 1905 Sex:F Child# 9 John Bilodeau Canada & Victoria Gagnon Canada
BILODEAU, Marie, Jan 11 1914 Sex:F Child# 1 Pierre Bilodeau
BILODEAU, Marie Delina, Oct 5 1895 Sex:F Child# 5 Arthur Bilodeau Canada & Eugenie Pelletier Canada
BILODEAU, Marie E D, Apr 5 1897 Sex:F Child# 6 Arthur Bilodeau Canada & Eugenie Pelletier Canada
BILODEAU, Marie E I, Nov 12 1890 Sex:F Child# 2 Arthur Bilodeau Canada & Eugenie Pettin Canada
BILOLDEAU, Marie Eugenie, Jul 10 1901 Sex:F Child# 9 Arthur Bilodeau Canada & Eugenie Pelletier Canada
BILODEAU, Marie Rose, Nov 9 1933 Sex:F Child# 1 Harry Bilodeau Methuen, MA & Rose Chouinard Canada
BILODEAU, Marie Virginie, Apr 30 1908 Sex:F Child# 10 John Bilodeau Canada & Victoria Gagnon Canada
BILODEAU, Marjorie Elaine, Sep 10 1927 Sex:F Child# 2 Alfred Bilodeau Canada & Louiebelle Wallace Nashua, NH

BILODEAU, Raymond Louis, Feb 2 1923 Sex:M Child# 1 Louis Bilodeau Nashua, NH & Rosilda Dionne Somersworth, NH
BILODEAU, Roland Angenard, Mar 29 1929 Sex:M Child# 1 Angenard Bilodeau Canada & Lina Boucher Nashua, NH
BILODEAU, Theresa Anita, Mar 11 1931 Sex:F Child# 1 John Bte Bilodeau Nashua, NH & Eva Richard Nashua, NH
BILODEAU, Unknown, Sep 16 1924 Sex:F Child# 1 Amedee Bilodeau Canada & Virginie Lambert Nashua, NH Stillborn
BINDRALL, Unknown, Jul 17 1892 Sex:F Child# 1 James Bindrall England & Kate Muldoon England
BINGHAM, Bilding Emerson, Jul 20 1909 Sex:M Child# 1 Herbert B Bingham Nashua, NH & Susie J Ellison Nashua, NH
BINGHAM, Christina, Sep 5 1895 Sex:F Child# 1 Samuel Bingham Lawrence, MA & Mary Glynn Nashua, NH
BINGHAM, David, Sep 18 1912 Sex:M Child# 6 Samuel Bingham Lawrence, MA & Mary Glynn Nashua, NH
BINGHAM, David Thomas, Dec 29 1934 Sex:M Child# 2 Paul Bingham Nashua, NH & Mary Peabody Rowley, MA
BINGHAM, Lois Elizabeth, Nov 12 1911 Sex:F Child# 2 Herbert B Bingham Nashua, NH & Susan J Ellison Nashua, NH
BINGHAM, Samuel, Jan 3 1902 Sex:M Child# 3 Samuel Bingham Lawrence, MA & Mary Glynn Nashua, NH
BINGHAM, Thomas Isaac, Feb 16 1911 Sex:M Child# 5 Samuel Bingham Lawrence, MA & Mary Glynn Nashua, NH
BINKAWICZ, Bronislaw, Apr 6 1915 Sex:F Child# 2 Adolphe Binkawicz Russia & Julia Shliva Austria
BINNET, Joseph, Apr 10 1912 Sex:M Child# 2 Joseph Binnet Russia & Edwiga Kousavitch Russia
BINSCOFSKI, John, Dec 7 1912 Sex:M Child# 4 Walter Binscofski Russia & Helen Colevedge Russia
BIOUSSEAU, Alfred P, May 29 1889 Sex:M Child# 4 Geoffroi Biousseau Canada & Julie Beaneage Canada
BIRCH, Gwendolyn Lillian, Sep 17 1921 Sex:F Child# 3 Henry Will Birch Kansas & Lillian Halquist Illinois
BIRCH, Jeanne Michelle, Sep 29 1915 Sex:F Child# 2 Louis Birch Canada & Anneth Thibodeau Canada
BIRCHALL, Donald Leslie, Nov 25 1921 Sex:M Child# 2 Thomas E Birchall Nashua, NH & Marguerite L Oban W Lebanon, NH
BIRCHALL, Elizabeth, Sep 4 1896 Sex:F Child# 2 James Birchall England & Ellen Degnan Ireland
BIRCHALL, Ellen Frances, Apr 1 1920 Sex:F Child# 1 Hugh F Birchall England & Irene F McDermott Brooklyn, NY
BIRCHALL, Erwin Ned, Mar 7 1914 Sex:M Child# 1 Thomas E Birchall Nashua, NH & Marguerite L Oben W Lebanon, NH
BIRCHALL, James A, Nov 8 1905 Sex:M Child# 6 James A Birchall England & Catherine Muldoon England
BIRCHALL, Lillian Florence, Sep 16 1900 Sex:F Child# 6 Thomas Birchall England & Jane Crompton England
BIRCHALL, Loretta V, Sep 5 1902 Sex:F Child# 5 James A Birchall England & K Muldoon England
BIRCHALL, Margaret Rosanne, Sep 16 1900 Sex:F Child# 7 Thomas Birchall England & Jane Crompton England
BIRCHALL, Mary Agnes, Aug 17 1913 Sex:F Child# 2 Thomas Birchall Nashua, NH & Lillian Barry Nashua, NH
BIRCHALL, Thelma Louise, Jun 4 1923 Sex:F Child# 1 Edward Birchall Nashua, NH & Margaret Oban W Lebanon, NH
BIRCHALL, Thomas, Mar 30 1891 Sex:M Child# 4 Thomas Birchall England & Jane Clampton England
BIRCHALL, Thomas Stevens, Dec 25 1892 Sex:M Child# 7 John Birchall Ireland & Mary O'Brien England
BIRCHALL, Unknown, Oct 26 1889 Sex:F Child# 2 Hugh Birchall Liverpool, England & Winifred Ferrick Liverpool, Eng
BIRCHALL, Unknown, Sep 8 1900 Sex:M Child# 3 James Birchall England & Ellen Degnan Ireland
BIRCHEL, Robert, Aug 23 1914 Sex:M Child# 3 Thomas Birchel Nashua, NH & Lillian Barry Nashua, NH
BIRCHELL, John F, Oct 2 1893 Sex:M Child# 2 James A Birchell England & Kate Muldoon England
BIRCHELL, John Francis, Jul 5 1911 Sex:M Child# 1 Thomas Birchell Nashua, NH & Lillian Barry Nashua, NH
BIRCHELL, Thomas J, Dec 31 1893 Sex:M Child# 1 James F Birchell England & Ella Degnan Ireland
BIRD, Elsie Eleanor, May 28 1922 Sex:F Child# 5 Arthur E Bird New York & Viola Charest Canada
BIRD, Russell Roger, Mar 3 1926 Sex:M Child# 1 Albert Bird Manchester, NH & Frances Morton Nashua, NH
BIRON, Anna, Jan 24 1892 Sex:F Child# 11 Joseph Biron Canada & Lumina Trudel Canada
BIRON, Gabrielle Marie, Jun 1 1920 Sex:F Child# 2 Armand J Biron Canada & Emma Deschamps Haverhill, MA
BIRON, J Albert Antonio, Mar 19 1922 Sex:M Child# 3 Philip Biron Canada & Therese Dionne Canada
BIRON, Jos Arthur Leonard, May 10 1923 Sex:M Child# 4 Philip Biron Canada & Therese Dionne Canada
BIRON, Joseph, Apr 11 1919 Sex:M Child# 2 Philippe Biron Canada & Marie Dionne Canada
BIRON, Louis Albert Marie, Dec 12 1911 Sex:M Child# 1 Louis Biron Canada & Marie Thibaudeau Canada
BIRON, Marie Irene Alice, Jun 28 1924 Sex:F Child# 5 Philipe Biron Canada & Therese Dionne Canada
BIRON, Marie Martha, Sep 10 1919 Sex:F Child# 3 Louis Biron Canada & Eugenie Thibodeau Canada
BIRON, Oliver Jos Armand, Dec 5 1917 Sex:M Child# 1 Ar Jos R Biron Canada & Emma Deschamps Haverhill, MA
BIRON, Robert Leon, Nov 24 1934 Sex:M Child# 1 Leon Biron Canada & Loretta Landry Nashua, NH
BISCAS, Anastasia, Jun 18 1919 Sex:F Child# 7 Costas Biscas Greece & Agoron Gikas Greece
BISHOP, Ada Louise, Aug 7 1924 Sex:F Child# 2 W H Bishop Fremont, NH & Delia Pearson Bedford, NH
BISHOP, Annie Isabelle, Jul 22 1933 Sex:F Child# 1 Walter Bishop Merrimack, NH & Eva Ouellette Manchester, NH
BISHOP, Arthur Otis, Jun 18 1909 Sex:M Child# 5 Oscar N Bishop Fremont, NH & Lizzie Haines New Brunswick
BISHOP, Audrey, Sep 9 1901 Sex:F Child# 1 Cyril Bishop Canada & May Winters NY
BISHOP, Carolyn Mae, Jan 25 1933 Sex:F Child# 5 W H Bishop Fremont, NH & Delia Parson Bedford, NH
BISHOP, Charlotte May, May 22 1928 Sex:F Child# 1 Carl Bishop S Lyndeboro, NH & Lottie Pettengill S Lyndeboro, NH
BISHOP, Donald Pearson, Apr 9 1928 Sex:M Child# 4 William H Bishop Fremont, NH & Delia Pearson Bedford, NH
BISHOP, Dorothy May, May 31 1913 Sex:F Child# 3 William J Bishop Newfoundland & Edith Peacock Hollis, NH
BISHOP, Dorothy May, Feb 29 1924 Sex:F Child# 3 Bernard Bishop Milford, NH & Harriet Farrell Wilton, NH
BISHOP, Elizabeth May, Feb 3 1915 Sex:F Child# 7 Oscar N Bishop Fremont, NH & Elizabeth Haines NB
BISHOP, Eva Louise, Jun 15 1907 Sex:F Child# 5 Harry E Bishop W Epping, NH & Anna Newhall Lynn, MA
BISHOP, Florence, Feb 20 1924 Sex:F Child# 2 George Bishop Freemont, NH & Nellie Askan England
BISHOP, Harold Oscar, Jul 2 1921 Sex:M Child# 1 Oscar N Bishop Fremont, NH & Nellie Askham Sheffield, England
BISHOP, John Loyd, May 4 1908 Sex:M Child# 2 Cyril J Bishop Canada & May Winters New York
BISHOP, Laura Nettie, Sep 27 1906 Sex:F Child# 4 Oscar N Bishop Fremont, NH & Lizzie Haines New Brunswick
BISHOP, Leroy Chester, May 22 1928 Sex:M Child# 2 Carl Bishop S Lyndeboro, NH & Lottie Pettengill S Lyndeboro, NH
BISHOP, Lillian Mahala, Jan 25 1908 Sex:F Child# 3 Fred H Bishop W Epping, NH & Jeanie Shillinglaw Keswick, NB
BISHOP, Lucy Isabell, Dec 27 1911 Sex:F Child# 6 Oscar N Bishop Fremont, NH & Lizzie Haines New Brunswick
BISHOP, Mada Arline, Sep 17 1911 Sex:F Child# 2 William J Bishop Newfoundland & Edith L Peacock Hollis, NH
BISHOP, Nellie Helene, Aug 31 1917 Sex:F Child# 8 Oscar Newell Bishop Fremont, NH & Elizabeth Haines Fredericton
BISHOP, Paul Harold, Jul 19 1909 Sex:M Child# 2 Alfred O Bishop Fremont, NH & Ina H Smith Nashua, NH
BISHOP, Robert Herman, Jun 28 1922 Sex:M Child# 1 William H Bishop Fremont, NH & Delia M Pearson Bedford, NH
BISHOP, Rocksy Annabelle, Aug 18 1904 Sex:F Child# 3 Oscar N Bishop Fremont, NH & Lizzie Haines New Brunswick
BISHOP, Roland Arthur, Mar 11 1928 Sex:M Child# 5 George Bishop Fremont, NH & Nellie Askham England

BISHOP, Wallace Putnam, Dec 8 1910 Sex:M Child# 1 Fred C Bishop Londonderry, NH & Dora A Putnam Nashua, NH
BISHOP, Wesley Burton, Feb 15 1930 Sex:M Child# 6 George Bishop Fremont, NH & Nellie Askham England
BISKADUROS, Unknown, Jun 5 1930 Sex:F Child# 2 Nicholas Biskaduros Greece & Katherine Polipinn New York
BISSETTE, Doris Jeannette, Oct 19 1926 Sex:F Child# 2 Ernest Bissette Canada & Marie A Lavoie Canada
BISSON, Joseph Arthur, Jun 19 1901 Sex:M Child# 2 Charles Bisson Canada & Elzida Doiron Canada
BISSONET, Joseph, May 16 1889 Sex:M Child# 1 Arthur Bissonet Canada & Mary Leneville Canada
BISSONETTE, Damase, Oct 25 1893 Sex:M Child# 7 Theodule Bissonette Canada & Leontine Gauthier Canada
BISSONETTE, Eva Irene M, Oct 31 1902 Sex:F Child# 3 Louis Bissonette Canada & Rosanna Lemay Canada
BISSONETTE, Marie Rose Eva, Mar 10 1901 Sex:F Child# 6 Arthur Bissonette Canada & Marie Laneville Canada
BISSONETTE, Theodule Joseph, Oct 30 1890 Sex:M Child# 5 Theodule Bissonette Canada & Leontine Gauthier Canada
BISSONNETTE, Albert O E, Aug 10 1899 Sex:M Child# 1 Louis Bissonnette Canada & Roseanna Lemay Canada
BISSONNETTE, Arthur, Jan 1 1904 Sex:M Child# 7 Pierre Bissonnette Canada & Regine Houde Canada
BISSONNETTE, Arthur Joseph, Jul 5 1898 Sex:M Child# 5 Arthur Bissonnette Canada & Marie Linneville Canada
BISSONNETTE, Beatrice Laurette, Jan 8 1928 Sex:F Child# 4 Wilfred Bissonnette Canada & Mary Paquette Canada
BISSONNETTE, Caroline, Dec 7 1895 Sex:F Child# 5 Arther Bissonnette Canada & Marie Lauville Canada
BISSONNETTE, Cecile Eveline, Feb 3 1908 Sex:F Child# 3 Joseph E Bissonnette Canada & Marie Parent Canada
BISSONNETTE, Claire Claudia, May 11 1922 Sex:F Child# 3 Oscar Bissonnette Nashua, NH & Emma Messier Newburyport, MA
BISSONNETTE, Everest Oscar, Oct 23 1917 Sex:M Child# 1 Oscar Bissonnette Nashua, NH & Emma Messier Newburyport, MA
BISSONNETTE, J B Alfred, Jun 15 1893 Sex:M Child# 3 Pierre Bissonnette Canada & Regina Houde Canada
BISSONNETTE, James Arthur, Apr 8 1933 Sex:M Child# 1 A Bissonnette Nashua, NH & Anne McAlpine Nashua, NH
BISSONNETTE, Joseph, Jun 20 1894 Sex:M Child# 3 Arthur Bissonnette Canada & Marie Leneville Canada
BISSONNETTE, Joseph, Oct 24 1916 Sex:M Child# 1 Joseph Bissonnette NH & Odelie Roy Canada Stillborn
BISSONNETTE, Joseph Ovila, Jun 30 1891 Sex:M Child# 2 Pierre Bissonnette Canada & Regina Houde Canada
BISSONNETTE, Joseph Roland G, Jan 12 1930 Sex:M Child# 1 Onesime Bissonnette Nashua, NH & Mary Boury Nashua, NH
BISSONNETTE, M Lucienne Anita, Nov 6 1917 Sex:F Child# 2 Joseph Bissonnette NH & Odelie Roy Canada
BISSONNETTE, Marie, Feb 9 1909 Sex:F Child# 1 (No Parents Listed)
BISSONNETTE, Marie Eva, Oct 27 1897 Sex:F Child# 5 Pierre Bissonnette Canada & Georgianna Houde Canada
BISSONNETTE, Marie Louise, May 12 1903 Sex:F Child# 7 Arthur Bissonnette Canada & Marie Leneville Canada
BISSONNETTE, Marie Regina, Apr 24 1909 Sex:F Child# 10 Pierre Bissonnette Canada & Regina Houde Canada
BISSONNETTE, Marie Stella, Aug 20 1908 Sex:F Child# 8 Arthur Bissonnette Canada & Marie Laneville Canada
BISSONNETTE, Paul Edward, Dec 19 1918 Sex:M Child# 3 Oscar Bissonnette Nashua, NH & Emma B Messier Newburyport, MA
BISSONNETTE, Pearl Germaine, Aug 25 1920 Sex:F Child# 1 David Bissonnette Fond du Lac, WI & Clara Delauriers Canada
BISSONNETTE, Pierre Amedie, Aug 2 1900 Sex:M Child# 6 Pierre Bissonnette Canada & Regina Houde Canada
BISSONNETTE, Raymond Ovila, Jul 16 1926 Sex:M Child# 4 Oscar Bissonnette Nashua, NH & Emma Messier Mass
BISSONNETTE, Regina Deliska, Jun 25 1895 Sex:F Child# 4 Pierre Bissonnette Canada & Regina Houde Canada
BISSONNETTE, Rodrigue E O, Jan 2 1903 Sex:M Child# 1 Joseph Bissonnette Canada & Josephine Jauron Canada
BISSONNETTE, Rodrigue Louis, Jun 11 1901 Sex:M Child# 2 Louis Bissonnette Canada & Rosanna Lemay Canada
BISSONNETTE, Unknown, Oct 17 1924 Sex:M Child# 1 Ovila Bissonnette Nashua, NH & Helen Healey Nashua, NH
BISSONNETTE, Unknown, Dec 3 1930 Sex:M Child# 1 Arthur Bissonnette Nashua, NH & Anne McAlpine Nashua, NH Stillborn
BISSOUETTE, Theohile, Oct 3 1888 Sex:M Child# 4 Theodile Bissouette Canada & Leontrue Gauther Canada
BISSOUNETTE, Marie Leopoldine, Feb 21 1892 Sex:F Child# 6 Theodule Bissounette Canada & Leontine Gauthier Canada
BITEMOS, Eva, Jun 11 1918 Sex:F Child# 1 James Bitemos Greece & Mary Pavios Greece
BITERNAS, Unknown, Jan 20 1921 Sex:F Child# 2 James Biternas Greece & Mary Padios Greece
BIXBY, Barbara, Jun 25 1918 Sex:F Child# 4 Clifford E Bixby W Groton, MA & Mary E Clark Newton, MA
BIXBY, Ethelyn, Aug 16 1901 Sex:F Child# 1 Albert B Bixby Burlington, VT & Minnie Blodgett Nashua, NH
BIXBY, Harold John, Dec 29 1893 Sex:M Child# 1 Albert Bixby Essex, VT & Annie Hefrew Chautauquay, NY
BIXBY, Hazel Maude, Nov 20 1894 Sex:F Child# 5 Charles C Bixby Plymouth & Mary E Christie Glasgow, Scotland
BIXBY, Henry W, Sep 26 1896 Sex:M Child# 2 Benjamin F Bixby Warren & Hattie G Taylor Townsend, MA Stillborn
BIXBY, Robert Kenneth, Jun 29 1929 Sex:M Child# 2 (No Parents Listed)
BIXBY, Unknown, Jun 7 1891 Sex:M Child# 1 Benjamin F Bixby Warren & Hattie G Taylor Townsend, MA
BIXBY, Vera Clara, Jun 23 1909 Sex:F Child# 4 Benjamin F Bixby Warren, NH & Versa Brown Canada
BIXBY, Vernon Harlan, Jun 23 1909 Sex:M Child# 3 Benjamin F Bixby Warren, NH & Versa Brown Canada
BIXBY, Wingate, Nov 4 1900 Sex:M Child# 2 John F Bixby Nashua, NH & Jennie E Woodcox NY
BIZIS, Julia, Mar 24 1917 Sex:F Child# 1 Michael Bizis Russia & Julia Akstin Russia
BLACK, Harvey Kingston, Aug 22 1920 Sex:M Child# 1 L Kingston Black Reading, MA & Jessie M Butterfield Antrim, NH
BLACK, Marion Elizabeth, Jul 16 1910 Sex:F Child# 1 James S Black Maine & Susan Sexton Nashua, NH
BLACK, Unknown, Nov 20 1903 Sex:M Child# 1 Fred L Black Rockland, ME & Elgie Idella Woburn, MA
BLACK, Unknown, Feb 9 1934 Sex:F Child#  Bernard Black New York, NY & Frieda Stillman Newburyport, MA
BLACK, William Parker, Feb 14 1925 Sex:M Child# 1 John E Black Bath, ME & Gladys Parker Somerville, MA
BLACK, Winona May, Aug 2 1930 Sex:F Child# 4 Nelson Black New Brunswick & Gertrude Schneider Merrimack, NH
BLACKBURN, Bernice Caroline, Feb 13 1905 Sex:F Child# 1 George Blackburn Boston, MA & Edith R Clark Northampton
BLACKE, Lillian Ruth, Sep 1 1919 Sex:F Child# 6 Charles R Blacke Nashua, NH & Lillian A Rowell Nashua, NH
BLACKENBERG, Ida, Oct 20 1895 Sex:F Child# 9 E Blackenberg Russia & Ida Russia
BLACKMAR, Warren Harris, Mar 28 1895 Sex:M Child# 2 Warren H Blackmar Woodstock, CT & Emeline L Raby Nashua, NH
BLACKMER, Unknown, May 17 1890 Sex:F Child# 1 Warren Blackmer Woodstock, CT & Emma S Raby Nashua, NH
BLACKMIM, Rena Mae, Sep 3 1916 Sex:F Child# 3 Rueal A Blackmim Mooers Forks, NY & Blanch Menter Nashua, NH
BLACO, Margaret M, Sep 29 1915 Sex:F Child# 2 John Blaco Cincinnati, OH & Julia Breen Ireland
BLAIN, Albert I E, Apr 30 1893 Sex:M Child# 3 Jules Blain Canada & Georgina Dufault Canada
BLAIN, Dora Liliane, Apr 11 1909 Sex:F Child# 2 Oliver Blain Sciota, NY & Exilda Laprise
BLAIN, Edward, May 20 1888 Sex:M Child# 2 Augustine Blain Canada & Euginie Lemisuse Canada
BLAIN, Jean Baptiste N, Dec 24 1897 Sex:M Child# 6 Jules Blain Canada & Georgianna Dufault Canada
BLAIN, Louis D, Aug 2 1894 Sex:M Child# 4 Jules Blain Canada & Georgina Dufault Canada
BLAIN, Marie C I, Sep 13 1891 Sex:F Child# 2 Jules Blain Canada & Georgina Dufault Canada

BLAIN, Marie G A, Jul 23 1900 Sex:F Child# 7 Jules Blain Canada & Georgianna Dufault Canada
BLAIN, Marie G R, Mar 21 1890 Sex:F Child# 1 Jules Blain Canada & Georgina Dufault Canada
BLAIN, Marie H, Aug 24 1895 Sex:F Child# 5 Jules Blain Canada & Georgina Dufault Canada
BLAIN, Oscar Emile, Aug 30 1910 Sex:M Child# 3 Olivier Blain Sciota, NY & Exilda Laprise Ashuelot, NH
BLAIN, Rachel Juliette, Feb 6 1908 Sex:F Child# 1 Olivier Blain Sciota, NY & Exilda Laprise Canada
BLAIN, Robert Doria, Mar 31 1913 Sex:M Child# 5 Olivier Blain Canada & Exilda Laprise Canada
BLAINE, Elizabeth Alice, Jul 14 1925 Sex:F Child# 1 Norman J Blaine Williamstown, VT & Alice E Fisher Chazy, NY
BLAIR, Edward Clifford, Oct 31 1929 Sex:M Child# 2 Arthur T Blair Nashua, NH & Beatrice Dansereau Thorntons Ferry
BLAIR, Joseph Henri, May 5 1895 Sex:M Child# 5 Edward Blair Canada & Loua Caron Canada
BLAIR, Leon Edmund, Oct 6 1927 Sex:M Child# 2 Joseph Blair Canada & Lizzie York Fremont, NH
BLAIS, Angela, Apr 17 1928 Sex:F Child# 4 Joseph Blais Nashua, NH & Anais Plourde Canada
BLAIS, Armand Theodore, Sep 9 1926 Sex:M Child# 3 Joseph Blais Rhode Island & Annie Plourde Canada
BLAIS, Arthur Tousaint, Nov 1 1896 Sex:M Child# 10 Edmond Blais Canada & Leontine Caron Canada
BLAIS, Auguse Xavier, Nov 17 1910 Sex:M Child# 9 Ferdinand Blais Canada & Adeline Simard Canada
BLAIS, Auguste, Dec 31 1908 Sex:M Child# 8 Fortunat Blais Canada & Adeline Simard Canada
BLAIS, Elmire Bernadette, Jun 8 1915 Sex:F Child# 1 Ludger Blais Canada & Albina Plante Canada
BLAIS, Eugenie Albina, Dec 3 1906 Sex:F Child# 1 Onesime Blais Canada & Eugenie Duchesneau Canada
BLAIS, Eva, Dec 4 1907 Sex:F Child# 2 Moise Blais Sciota, NY & Rose Comtois Canada
BLAIS, J B Wilfred, Jul 11 1920 Sex:M Child# 5 Philippe Blais Canada & Phidelise Paradis W Wilton, NH
BLAIS, J Eugene Roland, Apr 18 1921 Sex:M Child# 1 Eugene Blais Canada & Alma Gendron Canada
BLAIS, J Louis Julien, Feb 24 1914 Sex:M Child# 13 Telesphore Blais Canada & Marie Plante Canada
BLAIS, J Normand Edmond, Sep 2 1921 Sex:M Child# 4 Adelard Blais Canada & Grazielda Prunier Holyoke, MA
BLAIS, Jos Philippe Oliver, Mar 14 1918 Sex:M Child# 3 Philippe Blais Canada & Phidelise Paradis Wilton, NH
BLAIS, Joseph, Nov 6 1911 Sex:M Child# 10 Ferdinand Blais Canada & Adeline Simard Canada Stillborn
BLAIS, Joseph Louis, May 24 1919 Sex:M Child# 4 Philippe Blais Canada & Phidelise Paradis Wilton, NH
BLAIS, Joseph Wilfrid, Feb 26 1901 Sex:M Child# 10 Michael Blais Canada & Malvina Fortier Canada
BLAIS, Joseph Wilfrid, Oct 22 1910 Sex:M Child# 3 Onesime Blais Canada & Blanche Duchesneau Canada Stillborn
BLAIS, M Amanda Olivette, Oct 15 1914 Sex:F Child# 2 Adelard Blais Canada & Grace Prunier Holyoke, MA
BLAIS, Marie Cecile S, Sep 20 1911 Sex:F Child# 12 Telesphore Blais Canada & Marie Plante Canada
BLAIS, Marie Elise, Jun 26 1905 Sex:F Child# 1 Moise Blais New York & Rose Anna Comtois Canada
BLAIS, Marie Theresa Rita, Nov 8 1926 Sex:F Child# 1 Willis Blais Canada & Aleda St Pierre Canada
BLAIS, Mildred, Mar 14 1920 Sex:F Child# 1 Joseph Blais Canada & Elizabeth York Fremont, NH
BLAIS, Rachel Adrienne, Mar 9 1912 Sex:F Child# 4 Olivier Blais Canada & Casilda Laprise Canada
BLAIS, Robert Roger, Sep 8 1928 Sex:M Child# 2 Willie Blais Canada & Alide St Pierre Canada
BLAIS, Rosanna, Aug 2 1907 Sex:F Child# 7 Ferdinand Blais Canada & Adeline Simard Canada
BLAIS, Solange Doria, Oct 6 1924 Sex:F Child# 2 Joseph Blais Canada & S Plourde Canada
BLAKAITIS, John, Jul 17 1907 Sex:M Child# 1 Adam Blakaitis Russia & Maria Alexa Russia
BLAKAITIS, Nithold, Feb 1 1914 Sex:M Child# 4 Adam Blakaitis Russia &  Russia
BLAKE, Andrea Elizabeth, Nov 19 1921 Sex:F Child# 7 Charles R Blake Nashua, NH & Lillian Rowell Nashua, NH
BLAKE, Beverly Frances, May 5 1920 Sex:F Child# 5 Rodman R Blake Pepperell, MA & Marion Lunt Pepperell, MA
BLAKE, Charles Lewis, May 11 1906 Sex:M Child# 1 Charles R Blake Nashua, NH & Lillian A Rowell Nashua, NH
BLAKE, Dorothy Mae, Jan 15 1916 Sex:F Child# 5 Charles R Blake Nashua, NH & Lillian Rowell Nashua, NH
BLAKE, Ethel May, Oct 28 1893 Sex:F Child# 1 George N Blake NH & Mary H Mayo Vermont
BLAKE, Gene Arnold, Jan 5 1934 Sex:M Child# 2 Arnold Edgar Blake Eddington, ME & Amanda Jensen Wakefield, MA
BLAKE, George Clyde, Aug 30 1924 Sex:M Child# 3 Harold Blake Harrisville, NH & Ada Traver Nashua, NH
BLAKE, Gloria May, Jul 21 1931 Sex:F Child# 1 Arnold Blake Edington, ME & Amanda Jensen Wakefield, MA
BLAKE, Harold Leroy, Jr, Jan 7 1923 Sex:M Child# 2 Harold Leroy Blake Harrisville, NH & Ada Traver Nashua, NH
BLAKE, Helen Laurence, Nov 7 1923 Sex:F Child#  Albion C Blake Maine & Gertrude Laurence Nashua, NH
BLAKE, June Arlene, Jun 8 1920 Sex:F Child# 1 Harold L Blake Harrisville, NH & Ada P Traver Nashua, NH
BLAKE, Leonard, Dec 2 1925 Sex:M Child# 8 Rodman Blake N Conway, NH & Marion Lunt Haverhill, MA
BLAKE, Marion Frances, May 22 1910 Sex:F Child# 3 Charles R Blake Nashua, NH & Lillian Rowell Nashua, NH
BLAKE, Martha Tucker, Dec 9 1928 Sex:F Child# 9 Rodman R Blake Pepperell, MA & Marion Lunt Pepperell, MA
BLAKE, Mildred Annette, Feb 18 1924 Sex:F Child# 7 Rodman Blake Pepperell, MA & Marion Lund Pepperell, MA
BLAKE, Mildred Mary, Nov 24 1922 Sex:F Child# 1 James H Blake Pepperell, MA & Brgd Agnes Cassidy Ireland
BLAKE, Natalie, Nov 25 1908 Sex:F Child# 1 Rodman R Blake E Pepperell, MA & Marion I Lunt E Pepperell, MA
BLAKE, Richard Shattuck, Aug 21 1921 Sex:M Child# 6 Rodman R Blake Pepperell, MA & Marion Lunt Pepperell, MA
BLAKE, Theodore Whitney, Oct 12 1910 Sex:M Child# 2 Rodman R Blake Pepperell, MA & Marion C Lunt Pepperell, MA
BLAKE, Unknown, Mar 27 1887 Sex:M Child# 3 Charles H Blake Nashua, NH & Emma A Manchester
BLAKE, Unknown, Jan 6 1914 Sex:M Child# 3 Rodman R Blake Pepperell, MA & Marion Lunt Pepperell, MA
BLAKE, Virginia Lillian, Jun 26 1914 Sex:F Child# 4 Charles H Blake Nashua, NH & Lillian A Bowell Nashua, NH
BLAKE, Winston Lewis, Feb 16 1918 Sex:M Child# 4 Rodman Blake Pepperell, MA & Marion Lunt Pepperell, MA
BLAKEY, Wallace, Oct 11 1908 Sex:M Child# 1 John M Blakey England & Lula Z Wallace Nashua, NH
BLAKISE, Unknown, May 23 1915 Sex:M Child# 1 John Blakise Russia & Mickalina Skiluta Russia
BLAKITIS, John Robert, Jul 14 1929 Sex:M Child# 1 John Blakitis Nashua, NH & Beryl Nelson Nashua, NH
BLAKITIS, Mocai, Nov 11 1912 Sex:M Child# 3 Adam Blakitis Russia & Mary Alexa Russia
BLAKMUN, Unknown, Apr 5 1913 Sex:M Child# 1 Reuel Blakmun Mooers Forks, NY & Blanche Menter Nashua, NH Stillborn
BLANCHARD, Alice Agnes, Nov 30 1932 Sex:F Child# 3 H J Blanchard Readsboro, VT & Ethel Smith Hamilton, OH
BLANCHARD, Armand Ernest R, Apr 5 1906 Sex:M Child# 10 Ulric Blanchard Canada & Delvina Beaupre Canada
BLANCHARD, Evelyn May, Jul 14 1913 Sex:F Child# 1 Albert W Blanchard Lynn, MA & Eva Estey Hudson Ctr, NH
BLANCHARD, Florence Gladys, Feb 23 1898 Sex:F Child# 6 Charles H Blanchard Nashua, NH & Lilla Dill Nashua, NH
BLANCHARD, Frank Elmer, Aug 8 1894 Sex:M Child# 2 Charles E Blanchard Nashua, NH & Lizzie E Barnes Milford, NH
BLANCHARD, G Wilhelmina, Mar 22 1894 Sex:F Child# 1 Fred M Blanchard Nickleville, NY & Emma M Windrich Manchester
BLANCHARD, Georges Henri R, Apr 28 1901 Sex:M Child# 8 Ulric Blanchard Canada & Delphina Beaupre Canada

BLANCHARD, John Bowers, Dec 7 1925 Sex:M Child# 1 Rich T Blanchard Penacook, NH & Lucy Kate Bowers Nashua, NH
BLANCHARD, Joseph Reginald, Jun 22 1915 Sex:M Child# 4 Jean Bte Blanchard Canada & Stella Tremblay Nashua, NH
BLANCHARD, Luville, Jul 28 1911 Sex:M Child# 1 Fay L Blanchard Manchester, NH & Minnie R Berkeley Brockton, MA
BLANCHARD, Margarita, Apr 22 1899 Sex:F Child# 1 Purl Blanchard New York & Jennie Berube Canada
BLANCHARD, Marie Bertha, Dec 19 1897 Sex:F Child# 1 Robert Blanchard Thorntons Ferry, NH & Armelie Aubin Plattsburg
BLANCHARD, Marie Rose, Dec 2 1903 Sex:F Child# 1 John Blanchard Canada & Stella Trombley NH
BLANCHARD, Mary Julia, Oct 23 1927 Sex:F Child# 1 George H Blanchard Nashua, NH & Ann Lucier Nashua, NH
BLANCHARD, Nancy Lucia, Jan 18 1931 Sex:F Child# 3 George H Blanchard Nashua, NH & Ann Lucier Nashua, NH
BLANCHARD, Olive M, Dec 15 1898 Sex:F Child# 4 Charles E Blanchard Nashua, NH & Lizzie B Barnes Milford, NH
BLANCHARD, Pauline Louise, Oct 1 1895 Sex:F Child# 6 Joseph Blanchard New York & Delia Smith New York
BLANCHARD, Peter Tucker, Dec 7 1925 Sex:M Child# 2 Rich T Blanchard Penacook, NH & Lucy Kate Bowers Nashua, NH
BLANCHARD, Reed, Aug 18 1923 Sex:M Child# 1 Frank E Blanchard Nashua, NH & Mildred Morrill Nashua, NH Stillborn
BLANCHARD, Rudolph Willis, Feb 27 1925 Sex:M Child# 1 Rudolph Blanchard Swampscott, MA & Irene Perrault Nashua, NH
BLANCHARD, Sarah Mattie, Jun 2 1889 Sex:F Child# 1 C E Blanchard Nashua, NH & Lizzie B Barnes Milford, NH
BLANCHARD, Stella Jeannette, May 10 1905 Sex:F Child# 9 Ulric Blanchard Canada & Delphina Beaupre Canada
BLANCHARD, Unknown, Jul 27 1890 Sex:F Child# 1 Willis H Blanchard Nashua, NH & Jessie M Powers Vermont
BLANCHARD, Unknown, Nov 21 1896 Sex:M Child# 2 W H Blanchard Nashua, NH & Jessie M Powers Burke, VT
BLANCHARD, Unknown, Dec 29 1898 Sex:M Child# 7 Charles H Blanchard Brookline, NH & Lillian D Rolleau Nashua, NH
BLANCHET, Albert, Sep 23 1902 Sex:M Child# 1 Waldo A Blanchet Canada & Victoria Gagne Oakdale, MA
BLANCHETTE, Alice, Apr 15 1900 Sex:F Child# 13 Paul Blanchette Canada & Frebrenie Parent Canada
BLANCHETTE, Armance, Jul 4 1905 Sex:F Child# 1 Auguste Blanchette Canada & Armance Dube Canada
BLANCHETTE, Armand Raoul, May 8 1911 Sex:M Child# 3 Auguste Blanchette Canada & Armance Dube Canada
BLANCHETTE, Auguste Irence, Sep 25 1907 Sex:M Child# 2 Auguste Blanchette Canada & Armance Dube Canada
BLANCHETTE, Joseph Leo F, Jun 30 1908 Sex:M Child# 1 J B Blanchette Canada & Marie Girard Canada
BLANCHETTE, Marie Adele G, Sep 7 1910 Sex:F Child# 7 Norbert Blanchette Canada & Dina Parent Canada
BLANCHETTE, Marie Agnes A, Dec 12 1893 Sex:F Child# 5 Arsilde Blanchette Canada & Malvina Gregoire Canada
BLANCHETTE, Marie Anna A, Jun 27 1906 Sex:F Child# 5 Norbert Blanchette Canada & Diana Parent Canada
BLANCHETTE, Marie Blanche, Jun 20 1901 Sex:F Child# Octave Blanchette Canada & Alphonsine Tanguay Canada
BLANCHETTE, Marie Germaine C A, Oct 19 1908 Sex:F Child# 6 Norbert Blanchette Canada & Dina Parent Canada
BLANCHETTE, Marie Lucille Lorain, Oct 20 1916 Sex:F Child# 4 Jean B Blanchette Canada & Marie Girard Canada
BLANCHETTE, Marie Obeline F, Mar 21 1911 Sex:F Child# 2 J B Blanchette Canada & Marie Girard Canada
BLANCHETTE, Mary Agnes Pauline, Jan 4 1931 Sex:F Child# 1 Leo Blanchette Nashua, NH & Lucille Morse Nashua, NH
BLANCHETTE, Mary Alida, Apr 30 1896 Sex:F Child# 6 Arcilde Blanchette Canada & Malvina Gregoire Canada
BLANCHETTE, Norbert Raymond, Jun 2 1914 Sex:M Child# 8 Norbert Blanchette Canada & Dina Parent Canada
BLANCHETTE, Robert Emile, May 15 1931 Sex:M Child# 1 Wilfrid Blanchette Canada & Marie A Archambault Canada
BLANCHETTE, Roger Donald, Sep 22 1934 Sex:M Child# 2 Leo Blanchette Nashua, NH & Lucille Morse Nashua, NH
BLANEY, Agnes, Apr 3 1897 Sex:F Child# 6 Daniel H Blaney Boston, MA & Lizzie Galvan Nashua, NH
BLANEY, Daniel H, Nov 16 1893 Sex:M Child# 5 Daniel H Blaney Boston, MA & Elizabeth Galvan Nashua, NH
BLANEY, Lillian Mary, Sep 23 1898 Sex:F Child# 8 Daniel H Blaney Boston, MA & Elizabeth Galvin Nashua, NH
BLANEY, Rose Helena, Sep 23 1898 Sex:F Child# 7 Daniel H Blaney Boston, MA & Elizabeth Galvin Nashua, NH
BLANK, William Berger, Nov 30 1926 Sex:M Child# 1 Walter J Blank Reed City, MI & Minnie Berger Reed City, MI
BLANKENBERG, Eunice, Sep 23 1912 Sex:F Child# 5 Max Blankenberg Russia & Jeanne R Borofski Lynn, MA
BLANKENBERG, Evelyn C, Dec 24 1909 Sex:F Child# 3 Max Blankenberg Russia & Jennie Borfski Lynn, MA
BLANKENBERG, Unknown, Aug 7 1898 Sex:M Child# 10 Isaac Blankenberg Russia & Ada Mozolovis Russia
BLANKENBORY, Harvey, Oct 10 1893 Sex:M Child# 8 E Blankenbory Russia & Ida Russia
BLANKENBURG, Barbara Velma, Oct 18 1911 Sex:F Child# 4 Max Blankenburg Russia & Jennie Borofski Russia
BLANKENBURG, Unknown, Jun 2 1907 Sex:F Child# 1 Max Blankenburg Russia & Jennie Borofski Lynn, MA
BLAUCHET, Joseph Arthur R, Nov 25 1909 Sex:M Child# 2 J B Blauchet Canada & Marie Girard Canada
BLAY, Paul Conrad, Sep 22 1918 Sex:M Child# 1 Paul L Blay Montreal & Agnes Lumbard Milford, NH
BLAY, Unknown, Oct 29 1888 Sex: Child# 1 Charles W Blay Strafford & Ida W Concord Stillborn
BLEAN, Agnes Beatrice, Mar 23 1911 Sex:F Child# 7 William H Blean New York & Elizabeth Boyer New York
BLEAU, Alfred, Aug 14 1906 Sex:M Child# 5 William H Bleau New York & Elizabeth Boyer New York
BLEAU, Alfred Gerard, Jul 31 1923 Sex:M Child# 2 Alfred Bleau Sciota, NY & Eulalia Gaudreau Nashua, NH
BLEAU, Beatrice, Jul 30 1905 Sex:F Child# 9 Francis Bleau New York & Hermine Chalifoux Canada
BLEAU, Cecile Marianne, Apr 10 1922 Sex:F Child# 1 Alfred Bleau New York & Eulalia Goudreau Nashua, NH
BLEAU, Clorraine Regina, Feb 21 1926 Sex:F Child# 4 Oscar Bleau Nashua, NH & Sadie Carpenter Nashua, NH
BLEAU, Dora, Feb 25 1890 Sex:F Child# 1 Francis Bleau NS & Almina Chalifour Canada
BLEAU, Doris, Feb 3 1933 Sex:F Child# 3 Leo Bleau Altona, NY & Marianne Cote Pepperell, MA
BLEAU, Dorothe, Dec 20 1931 Sex:F Child# 5 Fred Bleau New York & Eululie Goudreau Nashua, NH
BLEAU, Elmer, Jul 19 1892 Sex:M Child# 3 Napoleon Bleau NY & Mary Jalpeau Moors, NY
BLEAU, Eva, Aug 11 1895 Sex:F Child# 4 Francis Bleau US & Hermine Chalifoux US
BLEAU, Jeanne Rachel, Jan 30 1930 Sex:F Child# 6 Fred Bleau New York & Eulalie Gaudreau Nashua, NH
BLEAU, Joseph, Nov 24 1897 Sex:M Child# 5 Napoleon Bleau US & Mary Chalifoux US
BLEAU, Joseph, Aug 31 1928 Sex:M Child# 2 Leo Bleau Altona, NY & M A Cote Pepperell, MA
BLEAU, Joseph Arthur F, Oct 30 1903 Sex:M Child# 8 Francis Bleau New York & Hermina Chalifoux New York
BLEAU, Joseph Hector, Nov 10 1908 Sex:M Child# 6 William H Bleau New York & Lillienne Boyer New York
BLEAU, Joseph Roger, Sep 4 1922 Sex:M Child# 1 George Bleau, Jr New York & Marie Eva Rousseau Canada
BLEAU, Joseph Romeo, Jan 30 1898 Sex:M Child# 4 Francis Bleau US & Elmina Chalifoux Canada
BLEAU, Leo Archie, Apr 4 1904 Sex:M Child# 5 William H Bleau Altoona, NY & Elizabeth Boyer Plattsburg, NY
BLEAU, Louis Ernest, Jan 29 1900 Sex:M Child# 2 William H Bleau New York & Elizabeth Boyer New York
BLEAU, Marie Albina, Dec 8 1899 Sex:F Child# 6 Francois Bleau NY & Hermina Chalifoux Canada
BLEAU, Marie Leona, Sep 17 1905 Sex:F Child# 13 George Bleau New York & Azilda Dube Canada
BLEAU, Mildred Louise, Dec 3 1901 Sex:F Child# 3 William Bleau Plattsburg, NY & Lillian Boyer Plattsburg, NY

BLEAU, Omer, Sep 5 1895 Sex:M Child# 4 Napoleon Bleau US & Mary Chailfone US
BLEAU, Philippe O, Oct 18 1891 Sex:M Child# 1 Francis Bleau New York & Armine Chalifoux New York
BLEAU, Rita, Aug 8 1921 Sex:F Child# 3 John Bleau New York & Wilhelmine Chamard Canada
BLEAU, Roland Hector, Jul 14 1923 Sex:M Child# 3 Oscar Bleau Nashua, NH & Sadie Carpenter Nashua, NH
BLEAU, Simone Theresa, Jun 5 1927 Sex:F Child# 1 Leo Bleau Sciota, NY & Marianne Cote Pepperell, MA
BLEAU, Therese Gabrielle, Dec 26 1924 Sex:F Child# 3 Frederick Bleau Sciota, NY & Eulalie Gaudreau Nashua, NH
BLEKAITIS, Vincenta, Mar 1 1915 Sex:F Child# 3 Adam Blekaitis Russia & Ella Vetchkinta Russia
BLEKAYTYS, Alexandra, Apr 2 1909 Sex:F Child# 1 Adam Blekaytys Russia & Helene Wiczkinte Russia
BLEKYTIS, Joseph, Apr 6 1911 Sex:M Child# 2 Adam Blekytis Russia & Helena Vegikuta Russia
BLENDONIS, Alexander, Jun 4 1917 Sex:M Child# 2 Adam Blendonis Russia & Lena Seilkutas Russia
BLIER, Marie Angelina, May 18 1903 Sex:F Child# 12 Pascal Blier Canada & Eugenie Desjardins Canada
BLIER, Marie Blandine, Aug 22 1907 Sex:F Child# 1 Cyprien Blier Canada & Josephine Charest Canada
BLIER, Marie Laura R, Jul 30 1904 Sex:F Child# 13 Pascal Blier Canada & Eugenie Desjardinis Canada
BLISS, Blanch Ethel, Sep 26 1896 Sex:F Child# 2 Joseph J Bliss Nashua, NH & Ida B Williams Nashua, NH
BLISS, Robert Leslie, Nov 5 1918 Sex:M Child# 1 Roland Bliss Manchester, NH & Margaret Young Hudson, NH
BLISS, Unknown, Feb 8 1894 Sex:M Child# 1 E T Bliss Essex, VT & Ruth Coredine Glasgow, Scotland
BLISS, Unknown, Apr 21 1894 Sex:M Child# 1 Joseph Bliss Nashua, NH & Ida M Williams Nashua, NH
BLITTERS, Beatrice Ina, Jul 23 1902 Sex:F Child# 1 George W Blitters Concord, NH & Ada F Huckins Fitchburg, MA
BLKLECLB, Unknown, Mar 18 1911 Sex:F Child# 3 William Blkleclb Russia & Eva Bodecach Russia
BLODGETT, Caroline Greenleaf, May 3 1922 Sex:F Child# 2 Henry F Blodgett W Concord, NH & Abigail Smith Nashua, NH
BLODGETT, Elizabeth Mary, Dec 25 1917 Sex:F Child# 1 Henry F Blodgett W Concord, NH & Abagail G Smith Nashua, NH
BLODGETT, Loretta Nina, Jun 2 1919 Sex:F Child# 3 Henry C Blodgett Chelsea, MA & Loretta Gray Fall River, MA
BLODGETT, Norma L, Feb 10 1902 Sex:F Child# 2 Fred Blodgett Hudson, NH & Lizzie Fuller Hudson, NH
BLODGETT, Unknown, Jul 10 1887 Sex:M Child# 1 Frank P Blodgett Nashua, NH & Nellie Varney Rochester, NH
BLODGETT, William Albert, Mar 27 1932 Sex:M Child# 1 W E Blodgett Forge Village, MA & C D MacFarlane Malden, MA
BLOIS, Frederick Adelard, Oct 9 1918 Sex:M Child# 3 Adelard Blois Canada & Grace Prunier Holyoke, MA
BLOMBARD, Unknown, Nov 8 1890 Sex:F Child#  Edward Blombard Sweden & Delia Goivan Ireland
BLOMBERG, Edward C, Oct 1 1893 Sex:F Child# 4 Edw N Blomberg Sweden & Delia Galvin Ireland
BLOMBERG, Unknown, Jul 8 1887 Sex:F Child# 2 Edward Blomberg Sweden & Delia Galvin Ireland
BLOOD, Alice May, Sep 28 1907 Sex:F Child# 1 Arthur V Blood Londonderry, NH & Cora E Cilley Nottingham, NH
BLOOD, Arthur Vernon, May 31 1922 Sex:M Child# 3 Arthur V Blood Londonderry, NH & Ethel Chaplice Bartlett, NH
BLOOD, Beverly May, Aug 7 1931 Sex:F Child# 3 William Arthur Blood Pepperell, MA & Lillian Lawrence E Pepperell, MA
BLOOD, Carl C, Jul 14 1896 Sex:M Child#  Harry Blood NH & Bertha Cameron NH
BLOOD, Carol Joyce, Aug 1 1935 Sex:F Child# 4 Willian N Blood Pepperell, MA & Mildred Holt Nashua, NH
BLOOD, Clarence Allen, Jun 15 1907 Sex:M Child# 1 Frederick C Blood Hollis, NH & Louise E Wyman Henniker, NH
BLOOD, Donald Martin, Oct 30 1935 Sex:M Child# 1 Donald Blood Pepperell, MA & Aldie Elliot Nova Scotia
BLOOD, Florence Priscilla, Dec 18 1915 Sex:F Child# 3 George L Blood Nashua, NH & Florence M Tyler Worcester, MA
BLOOD, George, Aug 8 1888 Sex:M Child# 4 Frank Blood Goshen & Susan Sherwin Edington, GA
BLOOD, Hiawatha Ethelbert, Oct 17 1919 Sex:M Child# 2 Arthur V Blood Londonderry, NH & Ethel Chaplin Bartlett, NH
BLOOD, Homer Tyler, Jan 22 1913 Sex:M Child# 1 George L Blood Nashua, NH & Florence M Tyler Worcester, MA
BLOOD, Howard F, Sep 17 1894 Sex:M Child# 2 George F Blood Lyndeboro, NH & Dora P Day Essex, VT
BLOOD, Howard Russell, Apr 9 1929 Sex:M Child# 1 William Blood Pepperell, MA & Lillian Laurence Pepperell, MA
BLOOD, Lester Anson, Sep 20 1896 Sex:M Child# 3 George F Blood Lyndeborough, NH & Dora P Day Essex, VT
BLOOD, Marjorie Loraine, Feb 25 1930 Sex:F Child# 2 William A Blood Pepperell, MA & Lillian Lawrence Pepperell, MA
BLOOD, Natalie Allison, Apr 23 1928 Sex:F Child# 1 Charles A Blood Pepperell, MA & Lucy Holt Nashua, NH
BLOOD, Nathalie M, Mar 8 1914 Sex:F Child# 2 George L Blood Nashua, NH & Florence M Tyler Worcester, MA
BLOOD, Philip Edmund, May 24 1929 Sex:M Child# 2 Andrew Bolld Pepperell, MA & Lucy Holt Nashua, NH
BLOOD, Priscilla Rossman, Feb 7 1909 Sex:F Child# 2 Fred Blood Hollis, NH & Louise E Wyman Henniker, NH
BLOOD, Randolph James, Oct 13 1920 Sex:M Child# 5 George L Blood Nashua, NH & Florence Tyler Worcester, MA
BLOOD, Ruth Evelyn, Sep 24 1907 Sex:F Child#  Ralph M Blood Nashua, NH & H Gertrude Robbins Nashua, NH
BLOOD, Thomas Sherwin, Jul 16 1917 Sex:M Child# 4 George Blood Nashua, NH & Florence Tyler Worcester, MA
BLOOD, Unknown, Oct 8 1888 Sex:M Child# 1 George F Blood Lyndeborough & Dora V Day Essex, VT
BLOOD, Unknown, Mar 12 1915 Sex:F Child# 2 Arthur V Blood Londonderry, NH & Nellie E Kirkwood Nottingham, NH
BLOOD, William Newton, Jan 22 1929 Sex:M Child# 1 William Blood Pepperell, MA & Mildred Holt Pepperell, MA
BLOTT, Margaret Louise, Jan 4 1932 Sex:F Child# 1 Goerge T Blott Bradford, England & Cora Bradley Nashua, NH
BLOW, Doris Jeannette, May 21 1919 Sex:F Child# 2 (No Parents Listed)
BLOW, George, May 7 1921 Sex:M Child# 1 George Blow Canada & Celia Aryell Nashua, NH
BLOW, George Roland, Jun 2 1927 Sex:M Child# 4 Fred Blow Sciota, NY & Eulalia Gaudreau Nashua, NH
BLOW, John, Oct 23 1909 Sex:M Child# 1 George Blow NY & Rose Dube NY
BLOW, Joseph, Jul 3 1926 Sex:M Child# 3 George Blow New York & Eva Rousseau Canada
BLOW, Joseph, Nov 8 1927 Sex:M Child# 4 George Blow New York & Eva Rousseau Canada
BLOW, Marie Eva Annette, Sep 25 1925 Sex:F Child# 2 George Blow New York & Eva Rousseau Canada
BLOW, Mary Lena, Apr 14 1913 Sex:F Child# 2 George Blow Sciota, NY & Rose Dube Sciota, NY
BLOW, Paul, Jun 11 1934 Sex:M Child# 6 Fred Blow Nashua, NH & Eulalie Goudreau Nashua, NH
BLOW, Pearl, Dec 23 1917 Sex:F Child# 2 John Blow Nashua, NH & Wilhem Chamore Canada
BLOW, Robert Joseph, Apr 12 1913 Sex:M Child# 1 John Blow Nashua, NH & Wilhelmina Chamard Canada
BLOW, Robert Walter, Apr 10 1931 Sex:M Child# 1 Robert Walter Blow Nashua, NH & Mabel McGraw Sheridan, ME
BLOW, Roberta Mae, Dec 7 1933 Sex:F Child# 2 Robert W Blow Nashua, NH & Mabel McGraw Forrage Lake, ME
BLOW, Unknown, Feb 28 1929 Sex:F Child# 4 Fred Blow US & Rose Gaudreau Nashua, NH Stillborn
BLOW, William H, Jr, Jan 13 1897 Sex:M Child# 1 William H Blow NY & Lizzie Boyea NY
BLOWE, John, Apr 7 1888 Sex:M Child# 2 Napoleon Blowe Sciota, NY & Mary Challifaux Sciota, NY
BLUE, Edith Dorothy, Aug 17 1922 Sex:F Child# 2 Gilbert A Blue New Brunswick & Blanche M Whittaker Malden, MA
BLUE, Unknown, Jun 26 1924 Sex:M Child# 3 Gilbert A Blue New Brunswick & Blanche Whittaker Malden, MA

BLUE, William Gilbert, Jul 24 1920 Sex:M Child# 1 Gilbert A Blue New Brunswick & Blanche M Whittaker Malden, MA
BLUESTEIN, Phillip Irving, Aug 23 1932 Sex:M Child# 1 Harry Bluestein Russia & R Kleigerman Lawrence, MA
BLUNT, Rene Lucette, Feb 20 1913 Sex:F Child# 1 Harry H Blunt Nashua, NH & Irene M Bradbury Quincy, MA
BLY, Eugene, May 28 1899 Sex:M Child# 1 Waldo H Bly Manchester, NH & Jennie L Nutt Nashua, NH
BOBBIS, Nellie, Jun 18 1915 Sex:F Child# 1 James Bobbis Russia & Agnes Lapiskuta Russia
BOBICK, John Francis, Jul 3 1916 Sex:M Child# 1 John F Bobick Worcester, MA & Marion E Reilly Nashua, NH
BOBICK, Mary Margaret, Nov 23 1917 Sex:F Child# 2 J Francis Bobick Worcester, MA & Marion E Riley Nashua, NH
BOBLEST, Edward, Aug 11 1929 Sex:M Child# 3 James Boblest Lithuania & Agnes Lapaskute Lithuania
BOCTER, Unknown, Nov 21 1912 Sex:M Child# 3 Benjamin Bocter Russia & Marcella Onesoonitie Russia
BODAR, Lobestan, Nov 19 1904 Sex:M Child# 1 Alec Bodar Russia & Kosenan Ebzecto Russia
BODER, Sophie, Feb 8 1912 Sex:F Child# 3 Alexander Boder Russia & Elizabeth Rosman Russia
BODWELL, Victor, Apr 26 1907 Sex:M Child# 1 Charles Bodwell Russia & Mary Sharke Russia
BOGALIA, John, Aug 21 1912 Sex:M Child# 2 John Bogalia Russia & Mary Parnin Russia
BOGDAN, Bolaslov, Sep 3 1920 Sex:M Child# 4 Stanley Bogdan Poland Russia & Sophie Stephanowicz Poland Russia
BOGDEN, Adam, Aug 30 1910 Sex:M Child# 1 John Bogden Russia & Laworaki Borlinen Russia Stillborn
BOGDEN, John, Jun 15 1912 Sex:M Child# 1 Stanley Bogden Russia & Sophie Stepanowicz Russia
BOGDEN, Mary, Aug 6 1916 Sex:F Child# 2 John Bogden Russia & Mary Kedalis Russia
BOGDEN, Murray, Jul 12 1914 Sex:M Child# 2 Stanislaw Bogden Russia & Sophia Stepanowicz Russia
BOGDEN, Stanislava, Dec 1 1910 Sex:F Child# 1 John Bogden Russia & Mary Kondaritz Russia
BOGDONIS, John, Nov 27 1912 Sex:M Child# 2 John Bogdonis Russia & Lawrouska Berlinska Russia
BOGDONIS, Zabella, May 17 1918 Sex:F Child# 3 John Bogdonis Russia & Lanora Berkuski Russia
BOGDZIEWICK, Unknown, Dec 20 1926 Sex:F Child# 2 M Bogdziewick Lithuania & Annie Grenovich Lithuania
BOGDZIEWICK, Unknown, Dec 20 1926 Sex:F Child# 3 M Bogdziewick Lithuania & Annie Grenovich Lithuania
BOGDZLEWIZ, Helen, Jan 6 1924 Sex:F Child# 1 M Bogdzlewiz Russia & Anna Tenoviente Russia
BOGGESS, Edouard, Dec 22 1891 Sex:M Child# 3 David Boggess Canada & Exilda Veuillet Canada
BOGGIS, Alice Mae, Aug 14 1930 Sex:F Child# 5 Edward Boggis Nashua, NH & Doris Nichols Webster, NH
BOGGIS, Donald Earl, Mar 7 1932 Sex:M Child# 6 Edward Boggis Nashua, NH & Doris Nichols New York
BOGGIS, Doris Virginia, Feb 22 1924 Sex:F Child# 2 Edward Boggis Nashua, NH & Doris Nichols Webster, NH
BOGGIS, Earl Fitzray, Feb 14 1926 Sex:M Child# 3 Edward Boggis Nashua, NH & Doris Nichols Webster, NH
BOGGIS, Edward Joseph, Jan 20 1923 Sex:M Child# 1 Edward Boggis Nashua, NH & Doris Nichols Webster, NH
BOGGIS, Elizabeth, Sep 8 1923 Sex:F Child# 1 Henry J Boggis Nashua, NH & Irene Collins Nashua, NH
BOGGIS, Helen Lillian, Jul 9 1934 Sex:F Child# 8 Edward Jos Boggis Nashua, NH & Doris Nichols Webster, NH
BOGGIS, Jeanne Marguerite, Sep 20 1900 Sex:F Child# 3 George Boggis Nashua, NH & Amerilda Theriault Canada
BOGGIS, Joseph Henri, Jul 18 1898 Sex:M Child# 2 George R Boggis Nashua, NH & Amarilda Theriault Canada
BOGGIS, Joseph J M, Jul 28 1896 Sex:M Child# 1 G A Boggis Nashua, NH & Amarilda Theriault Canada
BOGGIS, Joseph Paul A, Jan 27 1910 Sex:M Child# 6 George Boggis Canada & Emerida Theriault Canada
BOGGIS, Marie Irene Ida, Feb 25 1906 Sex:F Child# 5 George Boggis Nashua, NH & Amerilda Theriault Canada
BOGGIS, Marie Velina, Mar 29 1894 Sex:F Child# 4 Louis H Boggis Canada & Exilda Veillett Canada
BOGGIS, Marion Beverly, May 15 1933 Sex:F Child# 7 Edward J Boggis Nashua, NH & Doris Nichols Webster, NH
BOGGIS, Polycarpe, Mar 3 1903 Sex:M Child# 4 George E Boggis Nashua, NH & Amarilda Theriault Canada
BOGGIS, Robert Kenneth, Jul 20 1927 Sex:M Child# 4 Edward Boggis Nashua, NH & Doris Nichols Webster, NH
BOGHIGIAN, Kobar, Sep 28 1914 Sex:F Child# 1 George G Boghigian Turkey & Rose Barcomian Turkey
BOGHIGIN, Charlie, Mar 10 1917 Sex:M Child# 2 George C Boghigin Turkey & Rosie Beauaman Turkey
BOGHIGIN, Nelson G, Apr 27 1918 Sex:M Child# 3 George C Boghigin Turkey & Rosie Baraniein Turkey
BOGISS, David, Jan 14 1890 Sex:M Child# 2 David Bogiss Nashua, NH & Osilda Veillet Canada
BOGOSIAN, Mary, Nov 21 1922 Sex:F Child# 7 Nashan Bogosian Armenia & Lucia Garasian Armenia
BOGOSIAN, Siroop, Jun 25 1924 Sex:M Child# 8 Neshan Bogosian Armenia & Mary Jaranician Armenia
BOHIGIAN, Samuel Paramay, Jan 6 1923 Sex:M Child# 4 George Bohigian Armenia & Rose Barsamian Armenia
BOHIGIAN, Zeroseyea, Aug 26 1925 Sex:F Child# 5 George Bohigian Armenia & Rose L Gartbedian Armenia
BOHONON, Unknown, Jan 22 1901 Sex:F Child# 5 Fred Bohonon Brookline, NH & Mary Martin Prince Edw Island
BOIEA, Emma, May 24 1899 Sex:F Child# 5 Albert Boiea NY & Ellen Canada
BOILAND, Gerald, Jul 23 1933 Sex:M Child# 3 Oswald Boiland Nashua, NH & Adrienne Marquis Nashua, NH
BOILARD, Adelard, Oct 15 1892 Sex:M Child# 10 Joseph Boilard Canada & Marie Charette Canada
BOILARD, Alice Lucile, May 6 1914 Sex:F Child# 1 Theophile Boilard Canada & Ludwina Gravel Nashua, NH
BOILARD, Annette, May 15 1914 Sex:F Child# 1 Sylvio Boilard Nashua, NH & Exilda Grandmaison Nashua, NH
BOILARD, Armand, May 28 1889 Sex:M Child# 9 Joseph Boilard Canada & Marie Charnette Canada
BOILARD, Carmelia, Mar 29 1899 Sex:F Child# 11 Prudent Boilard Canada & Louise Girard Canada
BOILARD, Constance Rita, May 4 1931 Sex:F Child# 1 Oswald Boilard Nashua, NH & Adrienne Marquis Nashua, NH
BOILARD, Dorras, Aug 17 1888 Sex:M Child# 7 Prudent Boilard Canada & Louise Girard Canada
BOILARD, Emile Alphonse, Jul 3 1896 Sex:M Child# 12 Prudent Boilard Canada & M Louise Gerard Canada
BOILARD, Ernest, Mar 2 1895 Sex:M Child# 11 Prudent Boilard Canada & Louise Girard Canada
BOILARD, Ernest Earl, Feb 2 1915 Sex:M Child# 1 Adelard Boilard Nashua, NH & Gertrude Willette Nashua, NH
BOILARD, Estelle, Jun 28 1916 Sex:F Child# 1 William Boilard Nashua, NH & Rose Dumont Nashua, NH
BOILARD, Francis Civio, Aug 8 1891 Sex:M Child# Prudent Boilard Canada & Marie L Girard Canada
BOILARD, Graciella, Sep 11 1901 Sex:F Child# 17 Prudent Boilard Canada & Louise Girard Canada
BOILARD, Joseph Alphonse F, Aug 4 1905 Sex:M Child# 1 Frank Boilard NH & Clara Poirier Canada
BOILARD, Louis Alphege Armand, Nov 2 1914 Sex:M Child# 4 Henry Boilard Nashua, NH & Marie Riendeau Nashua, NH
BOILARD, Marie C, Aug 17 1888 Sex:F Child# 7 Prudent Boilard Canada & Louise Girard Canada
BOILARD, Marie Irene Gloria, Apr 27 1931 Sex:F Child# 7 Sylvio Boilard Nashua, NH & Zelida Grandmaison Nashua, NH
BOILARD, Marie Louise, Dec 29 1897 Sex:F Child# 13 Prudent Boilard Canada & Louise Girard Canada
BOILARD, Marie Rachel, Jul 19 1907 Sex:F Child# 1 Henry Boilard Nashua, NH & Marie Riendeau Nashua, NH
BOILARD, Mary Yivet Alida, May 29 1912 Sex:F Child# 2 Frank Boilard Nashua, NH & Clara Poirier Canada
BOILARD, Oscar, Jan 13 1896 Sex:M Child# 12 Joseph Boilard Canada & Marie Charest Canada

BOILARD, Oscar T J, May 10 1916 Sex:M Child# 2 Sylvio Boilard Nashua, NH & Ida Grandmaison Nashua, NH
BOILARD, Oswald, Jr, Jun 12 1932 Sex:M Child# 2 Oswald Boilard Nashua, NH & A Marquis Nashua, NH
BOILARD, Ovila, Mar 12 1894 Sex:M Child# 12 Joseph Boilard Canada & Maria Charette Canada
BOILARD, Parmelia, Mar 29 1899 Sex:F Child# 12 Prudent Boilard Canada & Louise Girard Canada
BOILARD, Raymond, Aug 17 1916 Sex:M Child# 2 Adelard Boilard NH & Gertrude Ouellette NH
BOILARD, Ronald Clarence, Jul 11 1923 Sex:M Child# 2 Alphonse E Boilard Nashua, NH & Blanche Delude Nashua, NH
BOILARD, Unknown, Jun 26 1900 Sex:M Child# 16 Prudent Boilard Canada & Louise Girard Canada
BOILARD, Unknown, Jan 22 1901 Sex:M Child# 1 Peter Boilard Nashua, NH & Jennie Menter Nashua, NH
BOILARD, Virginie, Mar 5 1912 Sex:F Child# 1 Joseph Boilard US & Catherine Brousseau Canada
BOILARD, Wilfred Robert, Apr 11 1924 Sex:M Child# 6 Sylvio Boilard Nashua, NH & Ida Grandmaison Nashua, NH
BOILARD, Wilfrid, May 4 1893 Sex:M Child# 10 Prudent Boilard Canada & Louise Girard Canada
BOIRE, Amanda Melina, Nov 9 1911 Sex:F Child# 10 Arthur Boire Canada & Amanda Bernier Canada
BOIRE, George Fran Charles, Nov 3 1913 Sex:M Child# 1 George F Boire Mooers, NY & Angelina Lapierre Nashua, NH
BOIRE, Paul Aime, Jan 16 1921 Sex:M Child# 3 George F Boire Mooers, NY & Angelina Lapierre Nashua, NH
BOIRE, Unknown, Jun 2 1916 Sex:M Child# 2 George Boire Mooers, NY & Angeline LaPierre Nashua, NH Stillborn
BOIS, Arthur Robert, Jun 9 1920 Sex:M Child# 3 Arthur A Bois Greenville, NH & Marie B Carle Canada
BOIS, Cecile Therese, Nov 25 1920 Sex:F Child# 1 Joseph Bois Greenville, NH & Emelda Demers Canada
BOIS, Doris, Aug 26 1935 Sex:F Child# 7 Alfred Bois Greenville, NH & Lena Ledoux Woonsocket, RI
BOIS, Florence, Dec 31 1927 Sex:F Child# 4 Alfred O Bois Greenville, NH & Lena Ledoux Rhode Island
BOIS, Homer Leo, Dec 2 1933 Sex:M Child# 1 Leo W Bois Nashua, NH & M Rousseau Nashua, NH
BOIS, Jean Roger, Jan 26 1926 Sex:M Child# 4 Joseph Bois Greenville, NH & Imelda Demers Canada
BOIS, Joseph Albert Rene, Dec 3 1924 Sex:M Child# 2 Alfred Bois Greenville, NH & Lena Ledoux Woonsocket, RI
BOIS, Joseph Oliver Arthur, Aug 24 1924 Sex:M Child# 3 Joseph Bois Greenville, NH & Imelda Demers Canada
BOIS, Leo Normand, Jul 17 1923 Sex:M Child# 2 Joseph Bois Greenville, NH & Imelda Demers Canada
BOIS, Leo Raymond, Nov 10 1918 Sex:M Child# 2 Arthur A Bois Greenville, NH & M Blanche Carl Canada
BOIS, M Blanche Annette, May 22 1917 Sex:F Child# 1 Arthur A Bois Greenville, NH & Marie Blanche Carle Canada
BOIS, Marie Blanche Irene, May 11 1926 Sex:F Child# 3 Alfred Bois NH & Lena Ledoux Rhode Island
BOIS, Marie Juliette Gertr, Jul 10 1923 Sex:F Child# 1 Alfred G Boix Greenville, NH & Lina Ledoux Woonsocket,
BOIS, Marie Lena Lucille, Jan 20 1929 Sex:F Child# 5 Alfred Bois Greenville, NH & Lena Ledoux Woonsocket, RI
BOIS, Mary Rose Sylvia, Nov 16 1918 Sex:F Child# 3 George Bois Mooers, NY & Angelina Lapierre Nashua, NH
BOIS, Rachel Pauline, Sep 4 1931 Sex:F Child# 6 Alfrd Bois Greenville, NH & Lena Ledoux Woonsocket, RI
BOIS, Wilfrid Louis, Dec 4 1927 Sex:M Child# 5 Joseph Bois Greenville, NH & Imelda Demers Canada
BOISCLAIR, Jos N Arthur E, Aug 24 1919 Sex:M Child# 4 Ulderic Boisclair Canada & Eugenie Turcotte Canada
BOISCLAIR, Marie, Aug 2 1915 Sex:F Child# 2 Ulderic Boisclair Canada & Eugenie Turcotte Canada
BOISCLAIRE, J Jean Bte Andre, Apr 5 1914 Sex:M Child# 1 Eulderic Boisclaire Canada & Eugenie Turcotte Canada
BOISCLAIRE, Joseph Girard, Feb 27 1917 Sex:M Child# 3 Ulderic Boisclaire Canada & Eugenie Turcotte Canada
BOISENAULT, Marie Cecile, Jun 4 1934 Sex:F Child# 13 Luc Boisenault Canada & Ernestine Lafrance Canada
BOISSEAU, Evangeliste, May 7 1890 Sex:M Child# 8 Jules Boisseau Canada & Vitaline Robichand Canada
BOISSEAU, Joseph Odias, Jun 10 1892 Sex:M Child# 9 Jules Boisseau Canada & Vitaline Robicland Canada
BOISSEAU, Olivine L, Dec 31 1893 Sex:M Child# 4 Philias Boisseau Canada & Cordelia Avard Canada
BOISSEAU, Philias George, May 26 1890 Sex:M Child# 3 Philias Boisseau Canada & Cordelia Havard Canada
BOISSEL, Joseph Eugene H, Jul 11 1895 Sex:M Child# 6 Charles Boissel Canada & Athenaise Lemay Canada
BOISSELLE, Joseph Edouard, Jan 31 1893 Sex:M Child# 4 Charles Boisselle Canada & Atanais Lemay Canada
BOISSELLE, Marie Jeanne, Apr 25 1894 Sex:F Child# 5 Charles Boisselle Canada & Arthenaise Lemay Canada
BOISSONEAULT, Marie Rose, Feb 16 1914 Sex:F Child# 4 Luc Boissoneault Canada & Ernestine Lafrance Canada
BOISSONNAULT, Jos Normand F, Apr 22 1918 Sex:M Child# 3 Louis Boissonnault Canada & Mary Ange Lafleur Canada
BOISSONNAULT, Yvonne, Apr 1 1917 Sex:F Child# 2 Louis Boissonnault Canada & Marie Ange Lafleur Canada
BOISSONNEAU, Leonard Alfred, Oct 27 1931 Sex:M Child# 12 Luc Boissonneau Canada & Enrestine Lafrance Canada
BOISSONNEAU, Marie Lena Elise, Jun 11 1928 Sex:F Child# 9 L Boissonneau Canada & E Lafrance Canada
BOISSONNEAULT, Marie Anna, Sep 6 1911 Sex:F Child# 3 Luc Boissonneault Canada & Ernestine Lafrance Canada
BOISVERT, Adelard N O, Mar 29 1897 Sex:M Child# 6 Willibald Boisvert Canada & Alphonsine Roy Canada
BOISVERT, Annette Jeanine, Mar 1 1933 Sex:F Child# 3 Leo Boisvert Canada & Juliette Berube Manchester, NH
BOISVERT, Antoinette Adelaide, Oct 27 1919 Sex:F Child# 9 Ernest Boisvert Canada & Emma Chartrain Canada
BOISVERT, Armand J, Oct 11 1891 Sex:M Child# 2 Joseph Boisvert Canada & Philena Lefevre Canada
BOISVERT, Arthur, Sep 22 1891 Sex:M Child# 1 Alphonse Boisvert Canada & Marie Reincourt Canada
BOISVERT, Blanche A, Aug 20 1897 Sex:F Child# 2 Eugene Boisvert Canada & Rosanna Richer Manchester, NH
BOISVERT, Claudia A, Dec 28 1903 Sex:F Child# 6 Eugene Boisvert Canada & Rosanna Richer Manchester, NH
BOISVERT, Constance, Apr 24 1932 Sex:F Child# 1 Normand Boisvert Nashua, NH & Lena Girouard Nashua, NH
BOISVERT, Elmande Elizabeth, Oct 27 1914 Sex:F Child# 8 Eugene Boisvert Canada & Rose Anna Richer Manchester, NH
BOISVERT, Emile Roland, Feb 28 1916 Sex:M Child# 3 Alphonse Boisvert Canada & Josephine Rivard Canada
BOISVERT, Ernest Raymond, Dec 31 1919 Sex:M Child# 3 William A Boisvert US & Aurore Roy US
BOISVERT, Irene A, Apr 6 1899 Sex:F Child# 3 Eugene Boisvert Canada & Rosanna Richer Manchester, NH
BOISVERT, Jeannette Olivette, Feb 1 1917 Sex:F Child# 2 William Boisvert US & Aurore Roy US
BOISVERT, Joan Geneva, Nov 25 1934 Sex:F Child# 2 Normand Boisvert Nashua, NH & Lena Girouard Nashua, NH
BOISVERT, Joseph, Oct 27 1925 Sex:M Child# 7 Alphe Boisvert US & Josephine Rivard Canada
BOISVERT, Joseph Alphonse, Jan 10 1895 Sex:M Child# 8 Mederic Boisvert Canada & Delima Lebrun Canada
BOISVERT, Joseph Lucier, Jul 4 1894 Sex:M Child# 3 Alphonse Boisvert Canada & Marie Rancourt Canada
BOISVERT, Lena, Nov 27 1925 Sex:F Child# 6 Henry Boisvert Canada & Lucia Perron Canada
BOISVERT, Lilian A, Aug 30 1896 Sex:F Child# 1 Eugene Boisvert Canada & Rosanna Richer Manchester, NH
BOISVERT, Lilian Irene, Oct 22 1914 Sex:F Child# 1 William A Boisvert US & Aurore Roy US
BOISVERT, Louis, Apr 5 1893 Sex:M Child# 2 Alphonse Boisvert Canada & Marie Rincourt Canada
BOISVERT, Louis Arthur, Aug 17 1926 Sex:M Child# 1 Louis A Boisvert Nashua, NH & Hilma G Tirrell N Abington, MA
BOISVERT, Louis Edgar, Aug 29 1902 Sex:M Child# 5 Eugene Boisvert Canada & Rosanna Richer Manchester, NH

BOISVERT, Marcel Roger, May 16 1921 Sex:M Child# 4 Alphonse Boisvert Nashua, NH & Josephine Rivard Canada
BOISVERT, Marie Aurore, Feb 22 1896 Sex:F Child# 4 Alphonse Boisvert Canada & Marie Rancourt Canada
BOISVERT, Marie Zilda, Jul 3 1890 Sex:F Child# 1 Joseph Boisvert Nashua, NH & Philana Lefebvre Canada
BOISVERT, Mary M A, May 16 1889 Sex:F Child# 11 A Boisvert Canada & Exilda Rodier Canada
BOISVERT, Maurice Leo, Sep 20 1930 Sex:M Child# 1 Leo Boisvert Canada & Juliette Berube Manchester, NH
BOISVERT, Maurice Normand, Jul 31 1922 Sex:M Child# 4 William A Boisvert US & Aurore Roy US
BOISVERT, Norman Paul, Nov 8 1934 Sex:M Child# 4 Leo Boisvert Canada & Juliette Berube Manchester, NH
BOISVERT, Normand W O, Nov 23 1909 Sex:M Child# 2 Alphonse Boisvert US & Josephine Rivard Canada
BOISVERT, Ralph G, Apr 10 1901 Sex:M Child# 4 Eugene Boisvert Canada & Rosanna Richer Manchester, NH
BOISVERT, Raymond O, Apr 25 1907 Sex:M Child# 7 Eugene Boisvert Canada & Rosanna Richer Manchester, NH
BOISVERT, Rita Louise Eva, Mar 29 1930 Sex:F Child# 3 Louis Boisvert Nashua, NH & Hilma Tirrell Mass
BOISVERT, Robert Girard, Dec 10 1931 Sex:M Child# 2 Leo Boisvert Canada & Juliette Berube Manchester, NH
BOISVERT, Unknown, Apr 26 1893 Sex:M Child# 3 Joseph Boisvert Nashua, NH & Philomene Lefebvre Canada
BOISVERT, Unknown, Sep 22 1928 Sex:M Child# 2 Louis Boisvert Nashua, NH & Hilda Tirrell N Arlington, MA
BOISVERT, Yvonne Laura, Aug 10 1906 Sex:F Child# 1 Alphonse Boisvert Nashua, NH & Josephine Rivard Canada
BOJARSKI, Wadleslaw, Mar 29 1914 Sex:M Child# 2 Antoin Bojarski Austria & Josepha Slivemkar Austria
BOJISS, Mary, Dec 31 1888 Sex:F Child# 7 David Bojiss England & Elizabeth Croteau Canada
BOLASKA, Brons, Sep 9 1915 Sex:F Child# 4 Michael Bolaska Russia & Agnes Brutadonis Russia
BOLASKI, Domimik, Aug 4 1910 Sex:F Child# 3 Michael Bolaski Russia & Agae Bolkadonis Russia
BOLCUN, Veronica, Feb 17 1904 Sex:F Child# 1 Jan Bolcun Russia & Franie Clampoziski Russia
BOLDINI, Guy, Jun 17 1926 Sex:M Child# 1 Guy Boldini Italy & Yvonne Gagnon Nashua, NH
BOLDINI, Pauline Marguerite, May 26 1927 Sex:F Child# 2 Guy Boldini Italy & Yvonne Gagnon Nashua, NH
BOLDRIC, Rosana, Jan 25 1889 Sex:F Child# 2 Louis Boldric Canada & Elmire Cote Canada
BOLDUC, Geraldine Mary, Aug 7 1935 Sex:F Child# 1 Gerald Bolduc Canada & Mary Walsh Manchester, NH
BOLDUC, J Paul Albert, Oct 1 1913 Sex:M Child# 2 Frank Bolduc Canada & Corinne Croteau Maine
BOLDUC, Jean Marcel R, Oct 6 1924 Sex:M Child# 1 Joseph Bolduc Salem, MA & Lillian Levesque Nashua, NH
BOLDUC, Marie Adeline, Mar 4 1895 Sex:F Child# 1 Albert Bolduc Canada & Emma St Onge Canada
BOLDUC, Marie Ange P C, Oct 29 1924 Sex:F Child# 18 Philbert Bolduc Canada & Florilda Poulin Canada
BOLDUC, Marie Beatrice, Jul 30 1900 Sex:F Child# 4 Louis Bolduc Canada & Tarsille Senical Canada
BOLDUC, Rita Olivine, Jun 12 1926 Sex:F Child# 2 Wilfrid Bolduc Augusta, ME & Gertrude Lajoie Nashua, NH
BOLES, Donald Richard, Dec 31 1922 Sex:M Child# 2 Weslie E Boles Nashua, NH & Ruth Augusta Evans Londonderry, NH
BOLES, Russell Alan, Apr 9 1924 Sex:M Child# 3 Wesley Boles Nashua, NH & Ruth Evans Londonderry, NH
BOLES, Wesley Eugene, Sep 27 1899 Sex:M Child# 3 G E Boles Mass & Lizzie J Estey NH
BOLES, Wesley Eugene, Oct 7 1921 Sex:M Child# 1 Wesley Eugene Boles Nashua, NH & Ruth Evans Londonderry, NH
BOLIESLAW, Mary, Feb 20 1921 Sex:F Child# 5 Bosko Bolieslaw Russia & Polly Potkiewich Russia
BOLIS, Henry A, Mar 29 1892 Sex:M Child# 1 Alvin Bolis Plattsburg, NY & Etta Round Huntington, VT
BOLLOSSKI, Unknown, Aug 8 1912 Sex:F Child# 4 Mike Bollosski Russia & Agnes Boltudonis Russia
BOLOSKI, Mary, Feb 1 1917 Sex:F Child# 6 Mike Boloski Russia & Agnes Boloskis Russia
BOLOVATICH, Nellie, Jul 25 1918 Sex:F Child# 1 Felix Bolovatich Russia & Petronella Escuti Russia
BOLSOWICH, Mary, Oct 11 1913 Sex:F Child# 2 Mike Bolsowich Russia & Veronica Bolkofka Austria
BOLSTER, William Henry, Jul 26 1914 Sex:M Child# 1 Arthur L Bolster S Weymouth, MA & Gertrude Pierie Nashua, NH
BOMHEL, Amelia, Oct 4 1925 Sex:F Child# 2 Alexander Bomhel Poland & Mary Goi Poland
BOMRANTCH, Leo, Aug 24 1925 Sex:M Child# 9 Stanley Bomrantch Europe & Nellie Stanvich Europe
BONANFANT, Esther, May 13 1905 Sex:F Child# 1 Joseph Bonanfant Canada & Lea Labonte US
BONASWITCH, Stanley, Sep 14 1917 Sex:M Child# 5 Joseph Bonaswitch Poland & Ludwiga Cousavitch Poland
BONBILLE, Eva Lucille O, Mar 1 1911 Sex:F Child# 1 Luc S Bonbille Canada & Marie L E Bourassa Canada
BONDREAU, Bernadette, Feb 1 1902 Sex:F Child# 6 Isaac Bondreau Canada & Evelina Lussier Canada Stillborn
BONDREAU, Eugenie Beatrice, Feb 1 1902 Sex:F Child# 5 Isaac Bondreau Canada & Evelina Lussier Canada
BONEFANT, William, Aug 12 1888 Sex:M Child# 7 Joseph Bonefant Canada & Fedrance Valancourt Canada
BONENFAIT, Eva, Sep 7 1888 Sex:F Child# 2 Pierre Bonenfait Canada & Delphine Blanchette Canada
BONENFANT, Albert Armand Paul, Sep 3 1935 Sex:M Child# 1 Albert Bonenfant NH & Jeannette Paul Nashua, NH
BONENFANT, Edmond Sylvio, Oct 4 1907 Sex:M Child# 4 Onesime Bonenfant Canada & Elizabeth Pelletier Canada
BONENFANT, Edouard Alferi, Jul 30 1911 Sex:M Child# 5 George Bonenfant Canada & Rosanna Bernier Canada
BONENFANT, George Henri, Feb 19 1907 Sex:M Child# 2 George Bonenfant Canada & Rosanna Bernier Canada
BONENFANT, Germaine, Sep 4 1911 Sex:F Child# 7 Onesime Bonenfant Canada & Elizabeth Pelletier Canada
BONENFANT, Irene Lilian, Jun 14 1908 Sex:F Child# 3 George Bonenfant Canada & Rosanna Bernier Canada
BONENFANT, Isidore Leo, Jan 3 1910 Sex:M Child# 6 Onesime Bonenfant Canada & Elisabeth Pelletier Canada
BONENFANT, Jos Alb Sylvio, Aug 3 1935 Sex:M Child# 1 Sylvio Bonenfant Nashua, NH & Jean Therriault Nashua, NH
BONENFANT, Jos Robert Leo, Jun 28 1935 Sex:M Child# 1 Leo Bonenfant Nashua, NH & Irene Meunier Nashua, NH
BONENFANT, Joseph, Jan 11 1909 Sex:M Child# 5 Onesime Bonenfant Canada & Elizabeth Pelletier Canada Stillborn
BONENFANT, Joseph A, Jun 26 1889 Sex:M Child# 5 Alexis Bonenfant Canada & Adele Grandmaison Canada
BONENFANT, Joseph B, May 8 1921 Sex:M Child# 10 George Bonenfant Canada & Rosanna Bernier Canada Stillborn
BONENFANT, Joseph Edouard A, Aug 14 1903 Sex:M Child# 1 Onesime Bonenfant Canada & Elizabeth Peltier Canada
BONENFANT, Joseph George H, Jun 5 1906 Sex:M Child# 3 Onesime Bonenfant Canada & Elizabeth Peltier Canada
BONENFANT, Joseph Hosanna, Jan 16 1899 Sex:M Child# 17 Francois Bonenfant Canada & Delima Prevost Canada
BONENFANT, M Annette Lucille, May 25 1915 Sex:F Child# 6 George Bonenfant Canada & Rose Anna Bernier Canada
BONENFANT, M Rachelle Alice, Mar 3 1919 Sex:F Child# 8 George Bonenfant Canada & Rosanna Bernier Canada
BONENFANT, Marguerite Eva, Nov 2 1912 Sex:F Child# 6 George Bonenfant Canada & Rosanna Bernier Canada
BONENFANT, Marie Albina Priscil, Jun 16 1926 Sex:F Child# 2 Aug Bonenfant Canada & Eva Leblanc Nashua, NH
BONENFANT, Maurice, Dec 14 1935 Sex:M Child# 2 Hector Bonenfant Nashua, NH & Carmelia Leblanc Canada
BONENFANT, Norman, Jul 7 1933 Sex:M Child# 1 Hector Bonenfant Nashua, NH & Carmela Leblanc Canada
BONENFANT, Olivine Albina, Dec 26 1909 Sex:F Child# 4 George Bonenfant Canada & Rosanna Bernier Canada
BONENFANT, Rose Delima, Mar 13 1910 Sex:F Child# 2 Pierre Bonenfant Canada & Lea Labonte US

BONENFANT, Rose Eva, Feb 22 1906 Sex:F Child# 1 George Bonenfant Canada & Rose Anna Bernier Canada
BONENFANT, Unknown, Aug 28 1913 Sex:M Child# 7 George Bonenfant Canada & Rosanna Bernier Canada Stillborn
BONENFAUT, Delia, Nov 12 1894 Sex:F Child# 6 Pierre Bonenfaut Canada & Delphine Beaushette Canada
BONENFAUT, Joseph D, Mar 21 1893 Sex:M Child# 7 Alexis Bonenfaut Canada & Adele Grandmaison Canada
BONENFAUT, Joseph Onesime H, Nov 20 1904 Sex:M Child# 2 Onesime Bonenfaut Canada & Elizabeth Peltier Canada
BONENFAUT, Laura, Jun 21 1892 Sex:F Child# 4 Pierre Bonenfaut Canada & Delphine Blanchette Canada
BONENFAUT, Marie A, Sep 11 1891 Sex:F Child# 6 Alexis Bonenfaut Canada & Adele Grandmaison Canada
BONENFAUT, Marie B, Nov 29 1892 Sex:F Child# 9 Joseph Bonenfaut Canada & Febranie Vallancourt Canada
BONENFAUT, Marie W, Dec 25 1890 Sex:F Child# 8 Joseph Bonenfaut Canada & Febranie Vaillancour Canada
BONENFAUT, Victor, Sep 30 1893 Sex:M Child# 5 Pierre Bonenfaut Canada & Delphine Canada
BONETTE, Marie Anne, Jul 10 1896 Sex:F Child# 8 Euzebe Bonette Canada & Odinas Russeau Canada
BONETTE, Philip Harmudas, Sep 4 1926 Sex:M Child# 8 Frank Bonette NH & Delia M Jacque Lowell, MA
BONEUFAUT, Joseph B, Aug 29 1894 Sex:M Child# 10 Joseph Boneufaut Canada & Fab'nie Vaillancourt Canada
BONEY, Anna, Jun 2 1907 Sex:F Child# 2 Francis Boney Russia & Taglie Christian Russia
BONIN, Amanda, Jan 7 1894 Sex:F Child# 7 Napoleon Bonin Canada & Melie Pelletier US
BONIN, Emma, Aug 11 1895 Sex:F Child# 8 Napoleon Bonin US & Melie Pelletier US
BONIN, Eva, Nov 27 1895 Sex:F Child# 3 Eugene Bonin Canada & Alma Grenier Canada
BONIN, Irene Beatrice, Jul 28 1910 Sex:F Child# 1 Joseph Bonin Mass & Maude Bonin Nashua, NH
BONIN, Marie E, Jun 25 1901 Sex:F Child# 1 Louis Bonin W Boylston, MA & Irena Lagasse Nashua, NH
BONNEAU, Andrea, Mar 17 1902 Sex:F Child# 3 Thomas Bonneau Canada & Phoebe Bibeau Canada
BONNEAU, Freddie Oscar, Nov 25 1899 Sex:M Child# 2 Thomas Bonneau Canada & Phebee Bibeau Canada
BONNEAU, Joseph, Nov 30 1892 Sex:M Child# 12 Eusebe Bonneau Canada & Desanges Chamberland Canada
BONNEAU, Joseph Elzear, Sep 23 1897 Sex:M Child# 3 Pierre Bonneau Canada & Amelie Morin Canada
BONNEAU, Joseph Hormidas, Dec 16 1898 Sex:M Child# 1 Thomas Bonneau Canada & Phebe Bibeau Canada
BONNEAU, Marie A F, Apr 5 1897 Sex:F Child# 2 Joseph Bonneau Canada & Josephine Lesieur Canada
BONNEAU, Marie Eva, Oct 31 1898 Sex:F Child# 4 Pierre Bonneau Canada & Aurelie Morin Canada
BONNEAU, Unknown, Mar 19 1900 Sex:F Child# 5 Pierre Bonneau Canada & Aurelie Morin Canada Stillborn
BONNENFAUT, Marie Florilda, Oct 20 1896 Sex:F Child# 16 Francois Bonnenfaut Canada & Delima Provost Canada
BONNETT, Blanche, Jun 6 1925 Sex:F Child# Frank Bonnett Marlboro, NH & Delia Jacques Lowell, MA
BONNETT, Helene Elizabeth, Oct 15 1921 Sex:F Child# 2 Charles Bonnett Whitefield, NH & May Howard Worcester, M
BONNETT, Norma Katherine, Oct 31 1923 Sex:F Child# 3 Charles Bonnett Whitefield, NH & May Howard Worcester, MA
BONNETT, Norma Mae, Jul 20 1920 Sex:F Child# 1 Charles E Bonnett Littleton, NH & Mary Howard Worcester, MA
BONNETT, Rita, Aug 17 1923 Sex:F Child# 6 Frank Bonnett Hancock, NH & Delia Jacques Lowell, MA
BONNETT, Theresa, Aug 11 1930 Sex:F Child# 9 Frank Bonnett Marlboro, NH & Delia Jacques Lowell, MA
BONNETT, Unknown, Feb 28 1899 Sex:F Child# 2 Charles E Bonnett Littleton & Christina C Stewart Woodbury, NS
BONNETT, Unknown, May 4 1907 Sex:F Child# 3 Charles E Bonnett Littleton, NH & Tena Crista Woodbury, NS
BONNETTE, Albert, Dec 5 1921 Sex:M Child# 2 Raoul Bonnette Canada & Ann Marie Danjou Arctic Center, RI
BONNETTE, Alice, Jan 2 1903 Sex:F Child# 11 Asa Bonnette Canada & Mary Rousseau Canada
BONNETTE, Alvin Richard, Dec 30 1926 Sex:M Child# 2 David Bonnette Canada & Andrea Cote Canada
BONNETTE, Edward, Dec 10 1920 Sex:M Child# 1 Raoul A Bonnette US & Adeline Cote US
BONNETTE, Gerard, Oct 28 1920 Sex:M Child# 1 Raoul Bonnette Canada & Anne M D'Anjou Arctic Cent, RI
BONNETTE, Gertrude H J, Aug 25 1914 Sex:F Child# 2 Frank E Bonnette NH & Delia Jacques Lowell, MA
BONNETTE, Jeanne d'Arc Rita, May 22 1924 Sex:F Child# 4 Raoul Bonnette Canada & Anne M D'Anjou R I
BONNETTE, Joseph, May 28 1913 Sex:M Child# 12 Frank Bonnette Canada & Rose Archambault Canada
BONNETTE, Joseph Eugene, Nov 29 1903 Sex:M Child# 1 Alfred Bonnette Canada & Elisa Poirier Canada
BONNETTE, Laura Josephine, Sep 21 1932 Sex:F Child# 7 R G Bonnette Canada & Marie Danjour US
BONNETTE, Leo Roger, Apr 30 1922 Sex:M Child# 1 David Bonnette Canada & Andrea Cote Canada
BONNETTE, Leona Emma, Aug 25 1899 Sex:F Child# 10 Euzebe Bonnette Canada & Marie Bousseau Canada
BONNETTE, Lorette Irene, Oct 30 1912 Sex:F Child# 10 Francis Bonnette Canada & Rose Archambault
BONNETTE, Marie, Aug 30 1905 Sex:F Child# 6 Francis E Bonnette Canada & Rose A Archambault Canada
BONNETTE, Olivette, Mar 24 1915 Sex:F Child# 13 Francois Bonnette Canada & Rose Archambault Canada
BONNETTE, Olivette Lucille, Mar 23 1923 Sex:F Child# 3 Raoul Bonnette Canada & Anne M D'Aujou Arctic Ctr, RI
BONNETTE, Shirley Elaine, Nov 25 1935 Sex:F Child# 5 David Bonnette Canada & Andrea V Cote Canada
BONROULOIR, Blanche Irene, Jul 29 1892 Sex:F Child# 11 Timothe Bonrouloir Canada & Victoria Lamontague Canada
BONSAINS, Marie Lilianne, Jan 23 1922 Sex:F Child# 5 Philippe Bonsains Canada & Albina Bouchard Nashua, NH
BONSANG, Albert Victor, Mar 6 1898 Sex:M Child# 2 Joseph Bonsang Canada & Marie Caron Canada
BONSANT, Leo, Apr 19 1905 Sex:M Child# 4 Cyprien Bonsant Canada & Clarina St Pierre Canada
BONSANT, Wilfred, May 10 1903 Sex:M Child# 3 Cyprien Bonsant Canada & Josephine St Pierre Canada
BONSENS, Alfred, Jun 13 1911 Sex:M Child# 2 Philippe Bonsens Canada & Albina Bouchard Canada
BONSENS, Joseph Wilfred, May 19 1910 Sex:M Child# 1 Philippe Bonsens Canada & Albina Bouchard Canada
BONSENS, M Albina Emilia, May 8 1914 Sex:F Child# 3 Philippe Bonsens Canada & Albina Bouchard Canada
BONSENS, Marie Athee Irene, Jun 25 1915 Sex:F Child# 4 Philippe Bonsens Canada & Albina Bouchard Nashua, NH
BONSENS, Marie Ivonne, May 26 1900 Sex:F Child# 1 Cyprien Bonsens Canada & Josephine St Pierre Canada
BONSENT, Joseph, Apr 3 1901 Sex:M Child#   Joseph Bonsent Canada & Marie Caron Canada
BONTIN, Antonia, Feb 9 1894 Sex:F Child# 1 Frederic Bontin Canada & Philomene Pelchah Canada
BONVILLE, M Jeannette Delvina, Mar 29 1932 Sex:F Child# 1 Jean B Bonville Canada & Lucienne Poliquin Nashua, NH
BONVOULOIR, Joseph Medric, Oct 2 1893 Sex:M Child# 12 Thymothe Bonvouloir Canada & Victoria Lamontague Canada
BOOTH, Eleanor Margaret, Jan 29 1934 Sex:F Child# 3 James K Booth New Bedford, MA & Esther Conroy Manchester, NH
BOOTH, Ethelyne May, Jun 30 1897 Sex:F Child# 1 Henry E Booth Shefford, PQ & Eliza J Brown Sheldon, VT
BOOTH, Helen Dorothy, Sep 6 1911 Sex:F Child# 1 Merritt D Booth Nashua, NH & Julia Etta Benedict Winsor, NS
BOOTH, Unknown, Aug 12 1898 Sex:F Child# 2 Henry E Booth Canada & Eliza Brown Sheldon, VT
BORAK, Alphonse, Apr 14 1924 Sex:M Child# 2 Walter Borak Poland & Mary Bonostan Poland
BORAK, Antonia, Feb 19 1923 Sex:F Child# 1 Walter Borak Poland & Mary Bonasta Lithuania

BORAKECK, Joseph, May 15 1902 Sex:M Child# 2 Michael Borakeck Russia & Lena Wslint Russia
BORCAICK, Apolonie, Feb 9 1912 Sex:F Child# 7 Michael Borcaick Russia & Tofiallia Tenba Russia
BORCIAK, Edward, Sep 20 1910 Sex:M Child# 6 Macy Borciak Russia & Teophilia Zenba Austria
BORCIAK, Janice Elizabeth, Jun 17 1935 Sex:F Child# 1 Edward Borciak Nashua, NH & Alice Badar Nashua, NH
BORCIAK, John, Mar 26 1900 Sex:M Child# 1 Mick Borciak Russia & T Zenia Russia
BORCIAK, Stoney, Apr 30 1908 Sex:M Child# 2 Mike Borciak Russia & Teofilia Zinbo Austria
BORDEAU, Edward Earl, Oct 21 1925 Sex:M Child# 3 Edward Bordeau Plattsburg, NY & Eunice Clifford Hollis, NH
BORDEAU, Kathlyn Virginia, Mar 15 1932 Sex:F Child# 4 E A Bordeau Plattsburg, NY & Eunice A Clifford Nashua, NH
BORDEAU, Kenneth Vernon, Mar 29 1923 Sex:M Child# 2 Edward Q Bordeau New York & Eunice Dixon Hollis, NH
BORDEAU, Wallace Wendell, Sep 23 1934 Sex:M Child# 5 Edw Alfred Bordeau Plattsburg, NY & Eunice Alva Clifford
BORDELEAU, Claire Rita Gertrude, Apr 11 1922 Sex:F Child# 5 Rodolphe Bordeleau Gardner, MA & Rosa Lafontaine Lowell
BORDELEAU, George Albert, Apr 23 1917 Sex:M Child# 4 Rodolph Bordeleau W Gardner, MA & Rosa Lafontaine Lowell, MA
BORDELEAU, Jeffrey Arthur, Aug 18 1898 Sex:M Child# 8 Henri Bordeleau Canada & Emelie Thiffault Canada
BORDELEAU, Ludger, Mar 20 1917 Sex:M Child# 3 Conrad Bordeleau W Gardner, MA & Eva Legros Canada
BORDELEAU, M Louise Oneda, Mar 31 1892 Sex:F Child# 5 Henry Bordeleau Canada & Emelie Thifault Canada
BORDELEAU, Prinne, Feb 1 1899 Sex:M Child# 5 Ludger Bordeleau Canada & Mederise Lafleur Fitchburg, MA
BORDELEAU, Sylvio, Sep 1 1895 Sex:M Child# 7 Henri Bordeleau Canada & Emelie Ciffand Canada
BORDEN, Louis, Jan 21 1888 Sex:M Child# 5 Caluesta Borden Canada & Euchauste Lachazelle Canada
BORDEN, Unknown, Jun 8 1930 Sex:M Child# 5 George L Borden Mass & Eva Gagnon Nashua, NH
BORDER, Amelia, Jan 8 1911 Sex:F Child# 2 Barney Border Russia & Marcelle Vorginmute Russia
BORDNAS, Joseph Armand, Dec 22 1907 Sex:M Child# 6 Origen Bordnas Canada & Rose Magnan Canada
BORDUAS, Joseph Henri Gerard, Oct 21 1909 Sex:M Child# 7 H O Borduas Canada & Rose Magnan Canada
BORDUAS, Medore Irigene, Nov 16 1906 Sex:M Child# 5 Origene H Borduas Canada & Rose Magnan Canada
BOREAK, John, Oct 5 1905 Sex:M Child# 4 Michael Boreak Russia & Lina Sklut Russia
BORES, William, Jun 12 1918 Sex:M Child# 5 George Bores Russia & Eva Blynta Russia
BORGAGIAN, Unknown, Apr 13 1902 Sex:M Child# 2 John Borgagian Armenia & Marney Calpasian Armenia
BORGATTI, Hugo, Aug 18 1909 Sex:M Child# 1 Premo Borgatti Italy & Julia Carbone Nashua, NH
BORGELIA, Jeanine, May 7 1931 Sex:F Child# 1 Wilfred Borgelia Nashua, NH & Doris Bernatchey Canada
BORGHI, Leonard Anthony, Jul 14 1925 Sex:M Child# 6 Alfeo Borghi Italy & Gert Leonardi Italy
BORGHI, Norman Caeser, Feb 24 1920 Sex:M Child# 4 Alfeo Borghi Italy & Gertrude Leonardi Italy
BORGHI, Raymond Alfeo, Apr 21 1918 Sex:M Child# 3 Alfeo Borghi Italy & Gertrude Leonardi Italy
BORGHI, Richard Morris, Oct 13 1923 Sex:M Child# 5 Alfeo Borghi Italy & Gertrude Leonardi Italy
BORILEY, Edwin Harry, Mar 20 1910 Sex:M Child# 6 Aimey Boriley Nashua, NH & Felinda Dion Vermont
BORIS, Annie, Aug 28 1911 Sex:F Child# 1 George Boris Russia & Eva Blejuta Russia
BORIS, Joseph, Jan 7 1914 Sex:M Child# 3 George Boris Russia & Eva Blcjute Russia
BORIS, Malvinka, Oct 26 1912 Sex:F Child# 2 George Boris Russia & Eva Boleguita Russia
BORIS, Tolm, Oct 5 1915 Sex:M Child# 3 George Boris Russia & Eva Blynta Russia
BORISON, Deena May, Oct 19 1906 Sex:F Child# 1 Simeon A Borison Russia & Sadie N Karp Austria
BORKAVITCH, Kate, Mar 13 1910 Sex:F Child# 4 Kaiata Borkavitch Russia & Theophila Ignstovitc Russia
BORKAVITCH, Sophia, Mar 13 1910 Sex:F Child# 5 Kaiata Borkavitch Russia & Theophila Ignatovitc Russia
BORNEMAN, Evelyn Hilda, Oct 11 1930 Sex:F Child# 1 Ellsworth E Borneman Townsend, MA & Eva Lavoie Nashua, NH
BORNEMAN, James Willis, Aug 3 1933 Sex:M Child# 2 E Borneman Townsend, MA & Eva G Lavoie Nashua, NH
BOROWSKI, Louis, Jun 14 1925 Sex:M Child# 3 Sylvester Borowski Lithuania & U Melenawicz Lithuania
BORTIS, Aga, Mar 9 1910 Sex:F Child# 7 Nicholas Bortis Russia & Helena Sklucute Russia
BORTIS, Mikolas, Oct 8 1908 Sex:M Child# 6 Mikolas Bortis Russia & Alana Sclucute Russia
BOSKA, Brouca, Jul 6 1923 Sex:F Child# 5 Bola Boska Russia & Palone Kaikewicz Russia
BOSKIS, Jedevije, Nov 13 1916 Sex:F Child# 2 Boleslar Boskis Russia & Poloni Kakesm Russia
BOSLEY, Unknown, Apr 23 1923 Sex:M Child# 1 Herbert Bosley Ashland, NH & Blanche Keyser Bradford, NH Stillborn
BOSLEY, Unknown, Apr 12 1925 Sex:M Child# 2 Herbert Bosley Ashland, NH & Blanche Keyser Bradford, NH Stillborn
BOSLEY, Unknown, May 22 1926 Sex:F Child# 3 Herbert Bosley Ashland, NH & Blanche Keyser Bradford, NH Stillborn
BOSSE, Alcide Robert, Mar 14 1916 Sex:M Child# 3 Albert Bosse Nashua, NH & Lily Jackson Nashua, NH
BOSSE, Charmaine Geneva, May 9 1931 Sex:F Child# 2 Roland S Bosse Manchester, NH & Laura B Boisvert Nashua, NH
BOSSE, Constance Loraine, Oct 3 1932 Sex:F Child# 1 Gaston Bosse Manchester, NH & Noella Ducharme Pelham, NH
BOSSE, Cora Jeannette, Apr 20 1918 Sex:F Child# 1 Joseph Bosse Canada & Valeda Gendron Canada
BOSSE, Edmond, Aug 5 1921 Sex:M Child# 5 Albert Bosse Nashua, NH & Lillian Jackson Nashua, NH
BOSSE, Elphege Raymond, Aug 27 1918 Sex:M Child# 1 Hector Bosse Nashua, NH & Julia Jackson Nashua, NH
BOSSE, Emile, Jul 29 1921 Sex:M Child# 2 Hector Bosse Nashua, NH & Julia Jackson Nashua, NH
BOSSE, Joseph, May 12 1927 Sex:M Child# 6 Joseph Bosse Canada & Octavie Poitras Canada
BOSSE, Joseph A D, Sep 7 1891 Sex:M Child# 7 Francois Bosse Canada & Hermenie Ferland Canada
BOSSE, Joseph Edmond, Nov 10 1919 Sex:M Child# 3 Joseph A Bosse Canada & Marie Octavie Poitra Canada Stillborn
BOSSE, Joseph Louis Armand, Feb 22 1918 Sex:M Child# 2 Joseph Bosse Acton Vale, PQ & Marie Octvie Poitras Montreal
BOSSE, Joseph Roland Roger, Feb 5 1925 Sex:M Child# 3 Joseph P Bosse Canada & Valeda Gendron Canada
BOSSE, Leo Paul Germain, Aug 23 1918 Sex:M Child# 4 Albert Bosse NH & Lillian Jackson NH
BOSSE, Lucille Germaine, May 22 1912 Sex:F Child# 2 Rosario Bosse Canada & Evelina Vadnais Canada
BOSSE, Marie Florida, Feb 26 1893 Sex:F Child# 1 Arthur Bosse Canada & Marie Pleau Vermont
BOSSE, Marie Reine Claire, Sep 6 1916 Sex:F Child# 1 Joseph Bosse Canada & Octavie Poitras Canada
BOSSE, Marie Theresa, May 12 1927 Sex:F Child# 5 Joseph Bosse Canada & Octavie Poitras Canada
BOSSE, Mary Theresa, Feb 7 1930 Sex:F Child# 7 Edward Bosse Woonsocket, RI & Maria O'Brien Nashua, NH
BOSSE, Maurice Claude, Jan 21 1932 Sex:M Child# 4 Hector Bosse Nashua, NH & Julia Jackson Nashua, NH
BOSSE, Rachel Carmille, Dec 23 1920 Sex:F Child# 2 Victor Bosse Canada & Emma St Germaine Greenville, NH
BOSSE, Rav Victor Soloman, Mar 9 1919 Sex:M Child# 1 Victor Bosse Canada & Emma St Germaine Greenville, NH
BOSSE, Roland Albert, Mar 16 1911 Sex:M Child# 1 Albert J Bosse US & Lily Jackson US
BOSSE, Ronald Sylvio, Jul 14 1929 Sex:M Child# 1 Roland Sylvia Bosse Manchester, NH & Laura Boisvert Nashua, NH

BOSSE, Wilfred Lucien, Jun 18 1912 Sex:M Child# 2 Albert J Bosse Nashua, NH & Lily Jackson Nashua, NH
BOSSE, Yvette Gertrude, Sep 8 1919 Sex:F Child# 2 Joseph Bosse Canada & Valeda Gendron Canada
BOSSELAIT, Lucille Leona, Jun 19 1925 Sex:F Child# 1 Leo Bosselait NH & Laura Pelletier Canada
BOSSELAIT, Marie Leona Yvonne, Aug 14 1926 Sex:F Child# 2 Leo Bosselait Greenville, NH & Laura Pelletier Canada
BOSSELAIT, Marie Theresa, Nov 12 1928 Sex:F Child# 4 Leo Bosselait NH & Laura Pelletier Canada
BOSSIE, Jacqueline Therese, Jul 28 1935 Sex:F Child# 2 Roland Bossie Nashua, NH & Norma Caron Canada
BOSSIE, Wilfred Ronald, Dec 17 1935 Sex:M Child# 1 Wilfred Bossie Nashua, NH & Bernice Rockus Nashua, NH
BOSTWICK, Augustus, Nov 6 1906 Sex:M Child# 9 Herbert Bostwick England & Helena Stevenson England
BOSTWICK, Beatrice Helene, May 5 1897 Sex:F Child# 6 Herbert Bostwick England & Helena Stevenson England
BOSTWICK, Edward, Feb 5 1902 Sex:M Child# 8 Herbert Bostwick England & Helena Stevenson England
BOSTWICK, Everett, Aug 18 1892 Sex:M Child# 3 Herbert Bostwick Barnsly, England & Lena Stevenson England
BOSTWICK, Frederick, Jul 25 1891 Sex:M Child# 2 Herbert Bostwick England & Helena Stevenson England
BOSTWICK, George E, Sep 7 1893 Sex:M Child# 4 Herbert Bostwick England & Lena Stephenson England
BOSTWICK, George Edward, Jul 4 1901 Sex:M Child# 7 George Bostwick England & Hannah Aspanell England
BOSTWICK, Hilda, Oct 17 1898 Sex:F Child# 7 Herbert Bostwick England & Helena Stevenson England
BOSTWICK, Ira, Jan 2 1896 Sex:M Child# 5 Herbert Bostwick England & Lena Stevenson England
BOSTWICK, Raymond, Nov 15 1920 Sex:M Child# 2 Herbert Bostwick Lowell, MA & Josephine Sullivan Nashua, NH
BOSWICK, Joseph Horace, Sep 29 1902 Sex:M Child# 8 George Boswick England & Anna Aspinwall England
BOSZKA, Charles, Mar 4 1918 Sex:M Child# 3 Boleska Boszka Russia & Polonia Potkiewich Russia
BOTOPOULOS, John, Jul 13 1919 Sex:M Child# 1 James Botopoulos Greece & Callope Margelon Greece
BOUCHARD, Albina, Feb 5 1889 Sex:F Child# Pierre Bouchard Canada & Olimpe Caron Canada
BOUCHARD, Alphonsine, Jan 8 1901 Sex:F Child# 6 Arthur Bouchard Canada & Marie Charest Canada
BOUCHARD, Annie M Olina, Mar 28 1902 Sex:F Child# 7 Arthur Bouchard Canada & Marie Charest Canada
BOUCHARD, Arthur, Apr 29 1891 Sex:M Child# 1 Arthur Bouchard Canada & Marie Charest Canada
BOUCHARD, Clovis, Jun 22 1907 Sex:M Child# 1 Clovis Bouchard Canada & Josephine Devlin Canada
BOUCHARD, Constance J, Nov 27 1931 Sex:F Child# 1 Albert J Bouchard Canada & Florianne Levesque Nashua, NH
BOUCHARD, Edouard Alfred, Dec 11 1901 Sex:M Child# 6 Joseph Bouchard Canada & Caroline Caron Canada
BOUCHARD, Eva, Sep 21 1895 Sex:F Child# 2 Joseph Bouchard Canada & Caroline Caron Canada
BOUCHARD, Eva, May 26 1899 Sex:F Child# 5 Arthur Bouchard Canada & Marie Charest Canada
BOUCHARD, Eva Eleanore, Jun 2 1928 Sex:F Child# 3 Eleanor Bouchard S Berwick, ME & Anita Bouchard Canada
BOUCHARD, Frank Henry, Aug 22 1900 Sex:M Child# 5 Joseph Bouchard Canada & Caroline Caron Canada
BOUCHARD, George Victor, Feb 22 1932 Sex:M Child# 4 A E Bouchard Nashua, NH & Emelia Durocher Canada
BOUCHARD, Henri, Jul 9 1892 Sex:M Child# 7 Pierre Bouchard Canada & Catherine Pinette Canada
BOUCHARD, Henry, May 1 1934 Sex:M Child# 5 Alfred Bouchard Nashua, NH & Emelia Desroscher Canada
BOUCHARD, Ida, Jul 6 1898 Sex:F Child# 4 Jsoeph Bouchard Canada & Caroline Caron Canada
BOUCHARD, Irene, Oct 16 1909 Sex:F Child# 2 Clovis Bouchard Canada & Josephine Devlin Canada
BOUCHARD, Jos Arthur Edward, May 24 1904 Sex:M Child# 8 Arthur Bouchard Canada & Marie Charest Canada
BOUCHARD, Jos Janelle Bertrand, May 17 1928 Sex:M Child# 1 Alfred Bouchard Nashua, NH & Emelia Desrocher Canada
BOUCHARD, Jos Maurice Leo, Oct 4 1923 Sex:M Child# 10 Julien Bouchard Canada & Marie Lafrance Canada
BOUCHARD, Jos Roland Alfred, Dec 31 1920 Sex:M Child# 11 Julien Bouchard Canada & Marie Lafrance Canada
BOUCHARD, Joseph Arthur Martin, Feb 17 1924 Sex:M Child# 3 Joseph Bouchard Nashua, NH & Grace Bellrose Nashua, NH
BOUCHARD, Joseph Edmund, Aug 6 1927 Sex:M Child# 2 Edmund Bouchard Canada & A Martineault Lowell, MA
BOUCHARD, Joseph Edouard H, Oct 29 1910 Sex:M Child# 12 Arthur Bouchard Canada & Marie Charest Canada
BOUCHARD, Joseph Hormidas, Dec 27 1908 Sex:M Child# 11 Arthur Bouchard Canada & Marie Charest Canada
BOUCHARD, Joseph Julien, Oct 25 1917 Sex:M Child# 7 Julien Bouchard Canada & Marie Lafrance Canada
BOUCHARD, Joseph Maurice Louis, Nov 22 1919 Sex:M Child# 2 Joseph A Bouchard Nashua, NH & Grace Bellrose Nashua, NH
BOUCHARD, Joseph Paul Edgar, Feb 17 1918 Sex:M Child# 1 Joseph Bouchard Nashua, NH & Grace Belrose Nashua, NH
BOUCHARD, Leo, Apr 15 1909 Sex:M Child# 3 Alfred Bouchard Nashua, NH & Lucia Houle Canada Stillborn
BOUCHARD, Louis, Apr 12 1887 Sex:M Child# Pierre Bouchard P Q & Catherine Pinette P Q
BOUCHARD, Louis Samuel, Feb 12 1893 Sex:M Child# 2 Arthur Bouchard Canada & Marie Charest Canada
BOUCHARD, M Therese Annette, Apr 12 1919 Sex:F Child# 8 Julien Bouchard Canada & Marie Lafrance Canada
BOUCHARD, Marguerite Rita, Nov 2 1920 Sex:F Child# 1 Eleonore Bouchard S Berwick, ME & Liticia Bouchard Canada
BOUCHARD, Marie Albina, Jul 16 1909 Sex:F Child# 2 Ernest Bouchard Nashua, NH & Louise Deschenes Michigan
BOUCHARD, Marie Irene, Jul 22 1906 Sex:F Child# 7 Joseph Bouchard Canada & Caroline Caron Canada
BOUCHARD, Marie Irene Cecile, Apr 30 1927 Sex:F Child# 11 Julien J Bouchard Canada & Agnes Lavallee Hooksett, NH
BOUCHARD, Marie Lucille J, Sep 25 1929 Sex:F Child# 2 Alfred Bouchard Nashua, NH & Emelia DuRocher Canada
BOUCHARD, Marie Rosa, Nov 24 1896 Sex:F Child# 3 Joseph Bouchard Canada & Caroline Caron Canada
BOUCHARD, Marie Rosa Anna, Apr 6 1898 Sex:F Child# 4 Arthur Bouchard Canada & Marie Chorest Canada
BOUCHARD, Marie Rose Anna Y, May 6 1907 Sex:F Child# 10 Arthur Bouchard Canada & Marie Charest Canada
BOUCHARD, Marie Stella I, Oct 27 1905 Sex:F Child# 9 Arthur Bouchard Canada & Marie Charest Canada
BOUCHARD, Muriel Marguerite, Feb 4 1930 Sex:F Child# 1 Louis Bouchard Nashua, NH & Juliette Beauregard Nashua, NH
BOUCHARD, Napoleon T, Feb 15 1897 Sex:M Child# 8 Pierre Bouchard Canada & Olympe Caron Canada
BOUCHARD, Omer Arthur, Apr 5 1930 Sex:M Child# 12 Julien Bouchard Canada & Marie Lafrance Canada
BOUCHARD, Robert Norman, Aug 9 1933 Sex:M Child# 2 A J Bouchard Canada & F Levesque Nashua, NH
BOUCHARD, Robert Normand, Nov 18 1931 Sex:M Child# 2 Louis Bouchard Nashua, NH & Juliette Beauregard Nashua, NH
BOUCHARD, Rodolphe, Jun 2 1922 Sex:M Child# 2 Eleonor Bouchard S Berwick, ME & Letitia Bouchard Canada
BOUCHARD, Rose D, Mar 11 1895 Sex:F Child# 3 Arthur Bouchard Canada & Marie Charest Canada
BOUCHARD, Simonne, Feb 1 1915 Sex:F Child# 3 Alfred Bouchard Canada & Lucia Houle Canada
BOUCHARD, Unknown, Nov 11 1890 Sex:M Child# 5 Alphonse Bouchard Canada & Esther Couture Canada Stillborn
BOUCHARD, Unknown, Sep 14 1891 Sex:M Child# 2 J Bouchard Canada & Dora Morin Nashua, NH Stillborn
BOUCHARD, Unknown, May 7 1907 Sex:F Child# 1 Alfred Bouchard Nashua, NH & Lucius Houle Canada Stillborn
BOUCHARD, Unknown, Apr 22 1908 Sex:M Child# 2 Alfred Bouchard Canada & Luciase Houle Canada Stillborn
BOUCHARD, Victoria, Aug 30 1888 Sex:F Child# 3 Alphonse Bouchard Canada & Marie Coutuse Canada

BOUCHARD, Victorien, May 31 1894 Sex:F Child# 1 Joseph Bouchard Canada & Caroline Caron Canada
BOUCHARD, Vivianne, Dec 12 1930 Sex:F Child# 3 Alfred Bouchard Nashua, NH & Emilia Durocher Canada
BOUCHEA, Pauline Rita, Jun 20 1935 Sex:F Child# 1 (No Parents Listed)
BOUCHER, Adelina, May 31 1905 Sex:F Child# 1 Alfred Boucher Canada & Alfreda Berthiaume Canada
BOUCHER, Adrien, Aug 3 1910 Sex:M Child# 2 Sylvain Boucher Canada & Arzenia Lachance Canada
BOUCHER, Agnes Alma, Nov 6 1897 Sex:F Child# 4 Edouard Boucher Canada & Emma Houle Canada
BOUCHER, Albert Normand, Mar 5 1934 Sex:M Child# 3 Normand Boucher Freemont, NH & Laura Dube Nashua, NH
BOUCHER, Alfred, Jun 16 1907 Sex:M Child# 5 Francois Boucher Canada & Anna Gagnon Canada
BOUCHER, Alfred Joseph Arthur, Apr 18 1916 Sex:M Child# 6 Antoin Boucher Canada & Alexandria Leclair Mass
BOUCHER, Alice, Jun 4 1892 Sex:F Child# 4 Joseph Boucher Canada & Salome Bouffard Canada
BOUCHER, Alice, Aug 13 1906 Sex:F Child# 1 Joseph Boucher Canada & Edith Blais Nashua, NH
BOUCHER, Alice Cecilia, Oct 27 1928 Sex:F Child# 1 Ed Boucher Nashua, NH & Madeline Carter Nashua, NH
BOUCHER, Alice Gabrielle, Oct 3 1913 Sex:F Child# 1 Charles Boucher Canada & Oliva Paul Nashua, NH
BOUCHER, Alma, May 10 1896 Sex:F Child# 4 Jean Boucher Canada & Alphonsine Malhoit Canada
BOUCHER, Alphonse Maurier, Oct 21 1918 Sex:M Child# 2 Charles Boucher Canada & Oliva Paul Nashua, NH
BOUCHER, Alphonse Raoul, Sep 19 1923 Sex:M Child# 6 Ernest Boucher Canada & Bertha Cormier Canada
BOUCHER, Alphonse Simeon, Sep 20 1892 Sex:M Child# 10 George Boucher Canada & Felicite Bonenfaut Canada
BOUCHER, Ambroise, Aug 24 1889 Sex:M Child# 2 Joseph Boucher Canada & Salornie Bouffard Canada
BOUCHER, Amedee Joseph, Nov 26 1902 Sex:M Child# 1 Amedee Boucher NH & Delvina Chenette Maine
BOUCHER, Amedee Paul, Apr 17 1925 Sex:F Child# 5 Charles Boucher Canada & Olina Paul Nashua, NH
BOUCHER, Andrew Maurice, Jul 13 1929 Sex:M Child# 10 Ernest Boucher Canada & Bertha Cormier Canada
BOUCHER, Anna, Mar 7 1898 Sex:F Child# 5 Jean Boucher Canada & Alphonsine Malhoit Canada
BOUCHER, Anne Virginia, Jan 13 1932 Sex:F Child# 1 Theodore Boucher Nashua, NH & Rose Dwyer Nashua, NH
BOUCHER, Ant Lorraine Camille, Aug 4 1922 Sex:F Child# 13 Alphonse Boucher Spencer, MA & Mary Levesque Canada
BOUCHER, Arnold Eugene, Jul 27 1915 Sex:M Child# 1 Joseph N Boucher Canada & Elizabeth Millette NH
BOUCHER, Arthur Francis, Aug 15 1934 Sex:M Child# 2 Arthur Geo Boucher Nashua, NH & Frances Frink Chelmsford, MA
BOUCHER, Arthur George, Jul 2 1919 Sex:M Child# 3 Adelard Boucher Canada & Pearl Gadbois Nashua, NH
BOUCHER, Arthur Gerard, Feb 21 1922 Sex:M Child# 5 Ernest Boucher Canada & Bertha Cormier Canada
BOUCHER, Arthur Roger, Feb 16 1922 Sex:M Child# 5 Simeon Boucher Nashua, NH & Lea Nadeau Nashua, NH
BOUCHER, Aurore, Dec 22 1908 Sex:F Child# 8 Leon Boucher Nashua, NH & Lydia Ricard Shirley, MA
BOUCHER, Aurore, Jan 10 1910 Sex:F Child# 10 Joseph Boucher Canada & Lydia Ricard Canada
BOUCHER, Barbara Joan, Dec 26 1930 Sex:F Child# 5 Theodore Boucher Canada & Ruth Lagrand N Adams, MA
BOUCHER, Beatrice, Dec 28 1928 Sex:F Child# 7 Simeon Boucher Nashua, NH & Leona Nadeau Nashua, NH
BOUCHER, Blanche Irene, Jul 6 1900 Sex:F Child# 1 Pasifique Boucher Canada & Emma Boisvert Canada
BOUCHER, Cecile Yaetev, Aug 4 1916 Sex:F Child# 2 Arsene Boucher Canada & Anna Dube Canada
BOUCHER, Celian Bertha, Jun 22 1925 Sex:F Child# 8 Alphonse Boucher Canada & E Grandmaison Canada
BOUCHER, David Gerald, Aug 16 1926 Sex:M Child# 4 Theodore Boucher Canada & Ruth LaGrand N Adams, MA Stillborn
BOUCHER, Diana Jeannine, Mar 28 1935 Sex:F Child# 1 Lucien Boucher Canada & Cecile Letendre Nashua, NH
BOUCHER, Donald Adelard, Aug 29 1934 Sex:M Child# 6 Adelard Boucher Canada & Pearl Gadbois Nashua, NH
BOUCHER, Donald Neil, Mar 15 1935 Sex:M Child# 2 Nelson Boucher Nashua, NH & Mary St Jacques Nashua, NH
BOUCHER, Donat, Jan 31 1931 Sex:M Child# 3 Henri Boucher Nashua, NH & Aurore Mignault Nashua, NH
BOUCHER, Edgar Elzear, Oct 11 1910 Sex:M Child# 7 Alphonse Boucher Nashua, NH & Marie Levesque Canada
BOUCHER, Edmond Alp Albert, Feb 12 1933 Sex:M Child# 1 E J Boucher Nashua, NH & Velma Salvail Manchester, NH
BOUCHER, Edouard Jean, Nov 20 1917 Sex:M Child# 2 Adelard Boucher Canada & Pearl Gadbois NH
BOUCHER, Edouard Raymond, May 13 1915 Sex:M Child# 2 Simeon Boucher Nashua, NH & Lea Nadeau Nashua, NH
BOUCHER, Elwin Louis, Mar 5 1912 Sex:M Child# 5 Louis H Boucher Canada & Agnes Miner Cherebusco, NY
BOUCHER, Emile Euclide, Mar 16 1924 Sex:M Child# 1 Emile Boucher Milford, NH & Juliette Paul Nashua, NH
BOUCHER, Emma, Sep 3 1889 Sex:F Child# 9 Joseph Boucher Canada & Sarah Gagnon Canada
BOUCHER, Estelle Andrea, Feb 16 1922 Sex:F Child# 6 Simeon Boucher Nashua, NH & Lea Nadeau Nashua, NH
BOUCHER, Eugenie Annette, Feb 15 1909 Sex:F Child# 6 Francois Boucher Canada & Anna Gagnon Canada
BOUCHER, Eva, Dec 1 1896 Sex:F Child# 7 Noe Boucher Canada & Virginie Beaudry Canada
BOUCHER, Eva, Mar 21 1904 Sex:F Child# 4 Leon Boucher Canada & Didia Ricard Worcester, MA
BOUCHER, Eva Cecile, Sep 26 1909 Sex:F Child# 3 Joseph Boucher Nashua, NH & Ida Blais St Albans, VT
BOUCHER, Exilda, Nov 9 1898 Sex:F Child# 8 Joseph Boucher Canada & Exilda Havard Canada Stillborn
BOUCHER, Felix, Sep 23 1915 Sex:M Child# 1 Ernest Boucher Canada & Bertha Gagne Canada
BOUCHER, Florence Gabrielle, Jul 17 1926 Sex:F Child# 8 Ernest Boucher Canada & Bertha Cormier Canada
BOUCHER, Florence Lucille, Mar 8 1907 Sex:F Child# 7 Edouard Boucher Canada & Emma Houle Canada
BOUCHER, Francis Geo Sylveste, Feb 3 1925 Sex:M Child# 7 Ernest Boucher Canada & Bertha Cormier Canada
BOUCHEA, Frankie, Jun 1 1906 Sex:M Child# 2 Joseph Boucher, Jr Manchester, NH & Alice Gahagan Cohoes, NY Stillborn
BOUCHER, George Albert, Apr 4 1910 Sex:M Child# 8 Edouard Boucher Canada & Emma Houle Canada
BOUCHER, George Honore, Nov 18 1900 Sex:M Child# 9 Noe Boucher Canada & Virginie Beaudry Canada
BOUCHER, George Jean David, Sep 10 1926 Sex:M Child# 5 Arthur Boucher Canada & Eva Tremblay Nashua, NH
BOUCHER, Georgiana A, Jan 3 1896 Sex:F Child# 3 Edward Boucher Canada & Emma Houle Canada
BOUCHER, Georgina, Oct 31 1887 Sex:F Child#  Joseph A Boucher P Q & Sara Belzelle P Q
BOUCHER, Gerard Arthur, Apr 29 1922 Sex:M Child# 3 Arthur Boucher Canada & Eva Tremblay Nashua, NH
BOUCHER, Gloria Louise, Jan 5 1932 Sex:F Child# 1 Edw J Boucher Canada & Melina R Duprey Nashua, NH
BOUCHER, Gratia, Mar 22 1902 Sex:F Child# 10 Noe Boucher Canada & Virginie Beaudry Canada
BOUCHER, Henri, Sep 19 1892 Sex:M Child# 7 Pierre Boucher Canada & Catherine Pinette Canada
BOUCHER, Henrietta Cecile, Jul 18 1923 Sex:F Child# 2 Adelard Boucher Canada & Evangeline Faucher E Pepperell, MA
BOUCHER, Henry Arestide, Jan 27 1921 Sex:M Child# 1 Henry A Boucher Fall River, MA & Helen L Cameron Hyde Park, MA
BOUCHER, Henry Ernest, Dec 15 1929 Sex:M Child# 5 Samuel E Boucher Canada & Elmire Belanger Canada
BOUCHER, Henry Omer, Jan 30 1891 Sex:M Child# 3 Joseph Boucher Canada & Salomie Bouffard Canada
BOUCHER, Henry Robert, May 10 1909 Sex:M Child# 2 Alfred Boucher Canada & Victoria Gaudette Nashua, NH

BOUCHER, Honore J George, Apr 27 1931 Sex:M Child# 1 Honore J G Boucher Nashua, NH & Domecelia Vitkus Shirley, MA
BOUCHER, Honore Jos George, Mar 26 1932 Sex:M Child# 2 H J G Boucher Nashua, NH & Domecelia Vitkus Shirley, MA
BOUCHER, Hormisdas O I, Jan 29 1899 Sex:M Child# 5 Edouard Boucher Canada & Emma Houle Canada
BOUCHER, Irene, Dec 21 1906 Sex:F Child# 2 Alfred Boucher Canada & Alfrida Berthiaume Canada
BOUCHER, Irene Blanche, Dec 16 1932 Sex:F Child# 8 Simeon Boucher Canada & Lea Nadeau Canada
BOUCHER, Irene Olivette, Feb 4 1917 Sex:F Child# 2 Ernest Boucher Canada & Bertha Cormier Canada
BOUCHER, J Alfred, Jun 28 1897 Sex:M Child# 5 Alphonse Boucher Canada & Adeline Aprile Canada
BOUCHER, J Polydore Lionel, Jun 4 1914 Sex:M Child# 14 Joseph Boucher Canada & Marie Levesque Nashua, NH
BOUCHER, Jane Cecelia, Jan 10 1923 Sex:F Child# 8 Joseph G Boucher Manchester, NH & Alice Gahagan Cohoes, NY
BOUCHER, Jean B, Oct 7 1930 Sex:M Child# 11 Ernest Boucher Canada & Bertha Cormier Canada Stillborn
BOUCHER, Jean George A, May 14 1903 Sex:M Child# 7 Jean Bte Boucher Canada & Delima Meunier Canada
BOUCHER, Jeanne Camille, Aug 20 1929 Sex:F Child# 2 Jos E A Boucher Nashua, NH & Alice Michaud Canada
BOUCHER, Jeanne Isabelle, Feb 16 1919 Sex:F Child# 12 Alphonse Boucher Spencer, MA & Marie Levesque Canada
BOUCHER, Jeannette Eva, Jul 9 1926 Sex:F Child# 5 Adelard Boucher Canada & Pearl Gadbois Nashua, NH
BOUCHER, Joan Madeline, Apr 29 1934 Sex:F Child# 1 Nelson Boucher Nashua, NH & Mary St Jacques Nashua, NH
BOUCHER, John Alfred, Mar 25 1918 Sex:M Child# 7 Joseph Boucher Manchester, NH & Alice Gahagan Cohoes, NY
BOUCHER, Jos Alphonse Armand, May 15 1923 Sex:M Child# 6 Alphonse Boucher Canada & Laura Levesque Canada
BOUCHER, Jos Benoit Reginald, Mar 10 1935 Sex:M Child# 7 Remi Boucher Rhode Island & Anna Bernier Canada
BOUCHER, Jos Geo Albert, Sep 4 1930 Sex:M Child# 1 George J Boucher Milford, NH & Albertine Landry Nashua, NH
BOUCHER, Jos George Edouard, Sep 24 1932 Sex:M Child# 4 J E A Boucher Nashua, NH & M A Michaud Canada
BOUCHER, Jos George Ernest, Dec 21 1925 Sex:M Child# 6 Simon Boucher Nashua, NH & Leonie Nadeau Nashua, NH
BOUCHER, Jos Henry George, Jan 14 1935 Sex:M Child# 3 Adelard Boucher Canada & Evangel Faucher Pepperell, MA
BOUCHER, Jos Paul Emile, Dec 20 1928 Sex:M Child# 4 Remi Boucher Rhode Island & Anna Bernier Canada
BOUCHER, Jos Raymond Roger, Aug 14 1925 Sex:M Child# 2 Remi Boucher Rhode Island & Anna Bernier Canada
BOUCHER, Joseph Adelard, Feb 13 1901 Sex:M Child# 2 Leon Boucher Canada & Lydia Richard Worcester, MA
BOUCHER, Joseph Adelard R, Jun 21 1903 Sex:M Child# 2 Alphonse Boucher Mass & Marie Levesque Canada
BOUCHER, Joseph Albert, Jun 25 1911 Sex:M Child# 1 Simeon Boucher Canada & Lea Nadeau Canada
BOUCHER, Joseph Alphonse C, Apr 28 1924 Sex:M Child# 14 Alphonse Boucher Spencer, MA & Marie Levesque Canada
BOUCHER, Joseph Armand, Jul 26 1906 Sex:M Child# 6 Leon Boucher Canada & Lydia Ricard Canada
BOUCHER, Joseph Charles, Apr 22 1908 Sex:M Child# 2 Charles Boucher Canada & Desinase Marchand Canada
BOUCHER, Joseph Charles E, Sep 28 1914 Sex:M Child# 4 Charles Boucher Canada & Desina Marchand Canada
BOUCHER, Joseph E, Jul 3 1887 Sex:M Child#   Joseph Boucher P Q & Alphonsine Berube P Q
BOUCHER, Joseph Ed Olivier, Aug 22 1902 Sex:M Child# 3 Leon Boucher Canada & Lydia Ricard Canada
BOUCHER, Joseph Edmond, Nov 14 1909 Sex:M Child# 6 Alphonse Boucher Spencer, MA & Marie Levesque Canada
BOUCHER, Joseph Edouard, May 23 1908 Sex:M Child# 2 Joseph Boucher Canada & Edith Blais NY
BOUCHER, Joseph Edouard R, Mar 25 1911 Sex:M Child# 3 Charles Boucher Canada & Desinase Marchand Canada
BOUCHER, Joseph Eusebe, May 14 1901 Sex:M Child# 1 Alphonse Boucher Mass & Marie Levesque Canada
BOUCHER, Joseph Francois G, Apr 3 1901 Sex:M Child# 2 Francois Boucher Canada & Anna Bellzile Canada
BOUCHER, Joseph George Ernest, Aug 29 1932 Sex:M Child# 2 Geo J Boucher Milford, NH & Albertine Landry Nashua, NH
BOUCHER, Joseph Girard, Aug 16 1911 Sex:M Child# 4 Antoine Boucher Canada & Alexandrina Leclerc Mass
BOUCHER, Joseph Henry, May 29 1890 Sex:M Child# 4 Joseph E Boucher Canada & Alphonsine Berube Canada
BOUCHER, Joseph Jean, Jun 19 1923 Sex:M Child# 7 Albert Boucher Canada & Josephine Boucher Canada
BOUCHER, Joseph Jean Bte, May 9 1894 Sex:M Child# 5 J E Boucher Canada & Alphonsine Berube Canada
BOUCHER, Joseph Leon George, Mar 18 1900 Sex:M Child# 1 Leon Boucher Canada & Ledia Richard Mass
BOUCHER, Joseph Manuel, May 17 1900 Sex:M Child# 3 Francois Boucher Canada & Delima Deslandes Canada
BOUCHER, Joseph Maurice, Nov 19 1926 Sex:M Child# 9 Alphonse Boucher Canada & Laura Levesque Canada
BOUCHER, Joseph Paul Arthur, Jan 6 1929 Sex:M Child# 3 Emile Boucher Milford, NH & Julia Paul Nashua, NH
BOUCHER, Joseph Philippe, May 17 1900 Sex:M Child# 2 Francois Boucher Canada & Delima Deslandes Canada
BOUCHER, Joseph Pierre, Jun 24 1898 Sex:M Child# 6 Joseph E Boucher Canada & Alphonsine Berube Canada
BOUCHER, Joseph Pierre Arthur, Jan 10 1910 Sex:M Child# 5 Adelard Boucher Mass & Lucie Dusseault Canada
BOUCHER, Joseph Roger, Mar 26 1922 Sex:M Child# 1 Adelard Boucher Canada & Evangeline Faucher Pepperell, MA
BOUCHER, Joseph Roger Maurice, Jan 10 1927 Sex:M Child# 2 Armand Boucher Canada & Marie A Charest Canada
BOUCHER, Joseph Romeo A, Oct 25 1907 Sex:M Child# 4 Adelard Boucher Mass & Lucie Dussault Canada
BOUCHER, Joseph Romeo Daniel, Jan 8 1934 Sex:M Child# 6 Remi Boucher Nashua, NH & Anna Bernier Canada
BOUCHER, Joseph Wilfrid, May 16 1900 Sex:M Child# 7 Achille Boucher Canada & Aglae Sirois Canada
BOUCHER, June May, Sep 30 1930 Sex:F Child# 2 Edward Boucher Nashua, NH & Madeleine Carter Nashua, NH
BOUCHER, Laurent Urban, Feb 3 1916 Sex:M Child# 10 Alphonse Boucher Nashua, NH & Marie Levesque Canada
BOUCHER, Leda Antoinette, Apr 2 1924 Sex:F Child# 4 Charles Boucher Canada & Olivia Paul Nashua, NH
BOUCHER, Leo, Apr 25 1901 Sex:M Child# 4 Luc Boucher Canada & Eugenie Pelletier Canada
BOUCHER, Leo Raymond, Dec 17 1921 Sex:M Child# 2 Amedee Boucher Canada & Vinnie Charette Maine
BOUCHER, Leonard, Jun 1 1912 Sex:M Child# 8 Alphonse Boucher Nashua, NH & Marie Levesque Canada
BOUCHER, Leonard Joseph, Jun 9 1933 Sex:M Child# 6 Samuel Boucher Canada & E Belanger Canada
BOUCHER, Liliane Irene, Sep 24 1906 Sex:F Child# 1 Alfred Boucher Canada & Victoria Gaudette Nashua, NH
BOUCHER, Liliane Lucienne, Jan 5 1908 Sex:F Child# 1 Joseph Boucher Canada & Marie Lizotte Canada
BOUCHER, Louis Howard, Dec 1 1903 Sex:M Child# 4 Louis H Boucher Canada & Agnes Miner Churubusco, NY
BOUCHER, Louisa, May 1 1888 Sex:F Child# 1 Joseph Boucher Canada & Salomill Bouffard Canada
BOUCHER, Lucille Irene, Feb 11 1918 Sex:F Child# 1 Arthur Boucher Canada & Eva Tremblay Nashua, NH
BOUCHER, Lumina, Apr 28 1889 Sex:F Child# 4 Joseph Boucher Canada & Alphonsine Berube Canada
BOUCHER, M A Albina, Jul 22 1895 Sex:F Child# 1 Louis A Boucher Quebec & Agnes Miner New York
BOUCHER, M Blanche H, Oct 2 1902 Sex:F Child# 3 Francois Boucher Canada & Anne Belleville Canada
BOUCHER, M Celestine, Oct 24 1894 Sex:F Child# 1 Joseph Boucher Canada & Amanda Deschamps Canada
BOUCHER, M Jeanne Germaine, Oct 10 1913 Sex:F Child# 8 Francois Boucher Canada & Marie Anne Gagnon Canada
BOUCHER, M Louise, Sep 11 1894 Sex:F Child# 2 Edouard Boucher Canada & Emma Houle Nashua, NH

BOUCHER, M Louise Pauline, Sep 23 1915 Sex:F Child# 1 Adelard Boucher Canada & Pearl Gadbois Nashua, NH
BOUCHER, Madeline, Jun 25 1915 Sex:F Child# 6 Joseph Boucher Manchester, NH & Alice Gahagan Cohoes, NY
BOUCHER, Marie A Alice, Nov 4 1899 Sex:F Child# 1 Francois Boucher Canada & Anna Belzil Canada
BOUCHER, Marie Alice, Mar 19 1913 Sex:F Child# 3 George Boucher Canada & Berne Gauthier Canada
BOUCHER, Marie Alice Gloria, Nov 9 1926 Sex:F Child# 2 Samuel Boucher Canada & Elmire Belanger Canada
BOUCHER, Marie Alma O, Mar 12 1911 Sex:F Child# 8 George E Boucher Canada & Leah Meunier Canada
BOUCHER, Marie Alma Theresa, Jul 26 1925 Sex:F Child# 1 Armand Boucher Canada & Marie A Charest Canada
BOUCHER, Marie Anna Madeleine, Jun 17 1927 Sex:F Child# 1 J E A Boucher Nashua, NH & M Alice Michaud Canada
BOUCHER, Marie Anne, Feb 1 1901 Sex:F Child# 7 Joseph E Boucher Canada & Alphonsine Berube Canada
BOUCHER, Marie B Emelia, Jul 18 1901 Sex:F Child# 2 Adelard Boucher Mass & Lucie Dussault Canada
BOUCHER, Marie Cecelia, Oct 15 1917 Sex:F Child# 11 Alphonse Boucher Spencer, MA & Marie Levesque Canada
BOUCHER, Marie Cecile, Dec 16 1925 Sex:F Child# 1 Samuel Boucher Canada & Elmie Belanger Canada
BOUCHER, Marie Clara, Jun 28 1905 Sex:F Child# 4 Leon Boucher Canada & Letitia Ricard Canada
BOUCHER, Marie Delia, May 30 1890 Sex:F Child# 5 Joseph Boucher G Fourchette, NY & Exilda Avard Acton Vale
BOUCHER, Marie Delvina C, Mar 24 1899 Sex:F Child# 1 Adelard Boucher Spencer, MA & Lucie Dussault Canada
BOUCHER, Marie Demerise, May 24 1915 Sex:F Child# 6 Adelard Boucher Mass & Lucie Dussault Canada
BOUCHER, Marie Dora, Nov 1 1904 Sex:F Child# 3 Alphonse Boucher Mass & Marie Levesque Canada
BOUCHER, Marie E Xelia, Nov 4 1896 Sex:F Child# 2 Joseph Boucher Canada & Amanda Deschamps Canada
BOUCHER, Marie Eva Rose, Mar 24 1899 Sex:F Child# 12 Prudent Boucher Canada & Marie Dube Canada
BOUCHER, Marie Germain, Apr 12 1917 Sex:F Child# 9 Francois Boucher Canada & Anna Gagnon Canada
BOUCHER, Marie Jeanne, Aug 16 1935 Sex:F Child# 8 Samuel Boucher Canada & Elmire Belanger Canada
BOUCHER, Marie Laura J, Mar 24 1907 Sex:F Child# 5 Alphonse Boucher MA & Marie Levesque Canada
BOUCHER, Marie Louise A, Jan 20 1905 Sex:F Child# 3 Adelard Boucher Mass & Lucie Dusault Canada
BOUCHER, Marie Lucille Rita, May 23 1931 Sex:F Child# 3 J E A Boucher Nashua, NH & Marie A Michaud Canada
BOUCHER, Marie M, Oct 1 1918 Sex:F Child# 4 Alfred Boucher Canada & Victoria Gaudette US
BOUCHER, Marie Malvina, Apr 30 1909 Sex:F Child# 1 Joseph Boucher Canada & Malvina Dion Canada
BOUCHER, Marie Marcelle G, May 11 1924 Sex:F Child# 7 Alphonse Boucher Canada & Laura Levesque Canada
BOUCHER, Marie Ozelie Flora, Feb 6 1906 Sex:F Child# 4 Alphonse Boucher Mass & Marie Levesque Canada
BOUCHER, Marie R Adeline, Mar 12 1899 Sex:F Child# 3 Joseph Boucher Canada & Amanda Deschamps Canada
BOUCHER, Marie R F, May 26 1905 Sex:F Child# 1 Charles Boucher Canada & Desinase Marchand Canada
BOUCHER, Marie Rachille Rita, Jun 5 1927 Sex:F Child# 3 Remi Boucher Rhode Island & Anna Bernier Canada
BOUCHER, Marie Rita Ida, Jul 21 1934 Sex:F Child# 5 Henri Boucher Nashua, NH & Aurore Migneault Nashua, NH
BOUCHER, Marie Rose Clare, Oct 22 1927 Sex:F Child# 3 Samuel Boucher Canada & Elmire Belanger Canada
BOUCHER, Marie Simone Theresa, Dec 29 1928 Sex:F Child# 1 N F Boucher Fremont, NH & Laura O Dube Nashua, NH
BOUCHER, Mary, Sep 7 1934 Sex:F Child# 5 Joseph Boucher Nashua, NH & Alice Michaud Mt Carmel, Quebec Stillborn
BOUCHER, Mary Bertha, Aug 16 1934 Sex:F Child# 3 George Boucher Milford, NH & Albertine Landry Nashua, NH
BOUCHER, Mary Florence Rita, Jun 7 1920 Sex:F Child# 1 Oliver Boucher Nashua, NH & Yvonne Pelletier Nashua, NH
BOUCHER, Mary Frances, Jul 18 1925 Sex:F Child# 3 Theodore Boucher Canada & Ruth Sanborn N Adams, MA
BOUCHER, Mary Gabrielle O, May 31 1924 Sex:F Child# 1 Remi Boucher Rhode Island & Anna Bernier Canada
BOUCHER, Mary Juliette, Aug 11 1912 Sex:F Child# 9 George F Boucher Canada & Lea Meunier Canada
BOUCHER, Mary Rose Levina, Mar 27 1912 Sex:F Child# 11 Leon Boucher Canada & Lydia Record Worcester, MA
BOUCHER, Narcisse, Dec 26 1907 Sex:M Child# 7 Leon Boucher Canada & Lydia Ricard Nashua, NH
BOUCHER, Norman Richard, Dec 26 1933 Sex:M Child# 6 Arthur Boucher Canada & Eva Trombly Nashua, NH
BOUCHER, Normand, Jan 29 1934 Sex:M Child# 1 Wilfred Boucher Nashua, NH & Yvonne Levesque Canada
BOUCHER, Normand Raymond, May 10 1925 Sex:M Child# 2 Emile Boucher Milford, NH & Juliette Paul Nashua, NH
BOUCHER, Normand, Jr, Sep 13 1930 Sex:M Child# 2 Normand Boucher Fremont, NH & Laura O Dube Nashua, NH
BOUCHER, Olivette Jacqueline, Apr 5 1924 Sex:F Child# 3 Oliver Boucher Nashua, NH & Yvonne Pelletier Nashua, NH
BOUCHER, Omer Paul, Dec 22 1932 Sex:M Child# 4 Alfred Boucher Nashua, NH & Aurore Mignault Nashua, NH
BOUCHER, Oscar, Nov 21 1897 Sex:M Child# 1 Francois Boucher Canada & Delima Delande Canada
BOUCHER, Paul Edmond, Dec 20 1928 Sex:M Child# 4 Samuel Boucher Canada & Elmire Belanger Canada
BOUCHER, Philippe Cyrus, Oct 1 1911 Sex:M Child# 9 Francois Boucher Canada & Anna Gagnon Canada
BOUCHER, Priscilly, May 14 1899 Sex:F Child# 8 Noe Boucher Canada & Virginie Boudry Canada
BOUCHER, Rachel Annette, Jun 25 1928 Sex:F Child# 5 Arthur Boucher Canada & Eva Tremblay Nashua, NH
BOUCHER, Raoul Armand, Nov 9 1919 Sex:M Child# 3 Simeon Boucher Nashua, NH & Lea Nadeau Nashua, NH
BOUCHER, Regina, Mar 3 1914 Sex:F Child# 5 Antrium Boucher Canada & Alexandra Leclair Mass
BOUCHER, Rena, Sep 11 1935 Sex:F Child# 1 Albert Boucher Nashua, NH & Emily Johnson Jackson, NH
BOUCHER, Rial, Dec 3 1923 Sex:M Child# 12 Alfred Boucher Canada & Alfreda Berthiaume Canada
BOUCHER, Rita Marjory, May 14 1921 Sex:F Child# 1 Theodore Boucher Canada & Ruth Legrande Mass
BOUCHER, Rita Pearl, Mar 30 1918 Sex:F Child# 3 Ernest Boucher Canada & Bertha Cormier Canada
BOUCHER, Robert, Aug 5 1916 Sex:M Child# 5 Elie Boucher Canada & Rosanna Ouellette Lawrence, MA
BOUCHER, Roger Henry, Dec 12 1926 Sex:M Child# 1 Henry Boucher Nashua, NH & Aurore Migneault Nashua, NH
BOUCHER, Roland Paul, Oct 4 1924 Sex:M Child# 4 Arthur Boucher Canada & Eva Tremblay Nashua, NH
BOUCHER, Rosalie, May 30 1890 Sex:F Child# 6 Joseph Boucher G Fourchette, NY & Exilda Avard Acton Vale, Canada
BOUCHER, Rouvill Henri, Aug 27 1914 Sex:M Child# 9 Alphonse Boucher Spencer & Marie Levesque Canada
BOUCHER, Theodore, May 27 1906 Sex:M Child# 11 Noe Boucher Canada & Virginie Beaudry Canada
BOUCHER, Theodore, Nov 15 1922 Sex:M Child# 4 Adelard Boucher Canada & Pearl Gadbois Nashua, NH
BOUCHER, Theodore Normand, Jr, Jun 9 1924 Sex:M Child# 2 Theodore Boucher Canada & Ruth Sanborn Mass
BOUCHER, Theresa C, Oct 9 1913 Sex:F Child# 4 Joseph Boucher Manchester, NH & Alice C Gahagan Cohoes, NY
BOUCHER, Theresa Doris, Nov 22 1927 Sex:F Child# 9 Ernest Boucher Canada & Bertha Cormier Canada
BOUCHER, Unknown, Dec 9 1887 Sex:M Child# 1 Edward Boucher Plattsburg, NY & Frances Hoyt Malone, NY
BOUCHER, Unknown, Jul 2 1893 Sex: Child# 1 Edouard Boucher Canada & Emma Houle Nashua, NH Stillborn
BOUCHER, Unknown, Dec 18 1907 Sex:M Child# 3 Joseph G Boucher Manchester, NH & Alice Gahagan NY
BOUCHER, Unknown, Jul 15 1925 Sex:M Child# 5 Joseph Boucher Canada & Edith Blais Sciota, NY

BOUCHER, Unknown, Jul 15 1925 Sex:M Child# 5 Joseph Boucher Canada & Edith Blais Sciota, NY
BOUCHER, Unknown, Nov 28 1931 Sex:M Child# 1 Richard A Boucher Fremont, NH & Claudia Parker Hudson, NH
BOUCHER, Victor, May 25 1900 Sex:M Child# 9 Joseph Boucher Canada & Desilda Harvard Canada
BOUCHER, Victor Robert, Feb 2 1933 Sex:M Child# 12 Ernest Boucher Canada & Bertha Cormier Canada
BOUCHER, Vital, Dec 3 1923 Sex:M Child# 11 Alfred Boucher Canada & Alfreda Berthiaume Canada
BOUCHER, Wilfred, Dec 25 1921 Sex:M Child# 2 Oliver Boucher Nashua, NH & Yvonne Pelletier Nashua, NH
BOUCHER, Wilfrid R Andre, Sep 27 1931 Sex:M Child# 6 Samuel Boucher Canada & Elmira Belanger Canada
BOUCHER, Yvonne, Dec 13 1907 Sex:F Child# 10 Alphonse Boucher Canada & Adeline April Canada
BOUCHER, Yvonne Carmelia, Feb 2 1900 Sex:F Child# 6 Edouard Boucher Canada & Emma Houle Canada
BOUCHER, Zelina Carmelle, Apr 20 1922 Sex:F Child# 3 Charles Boucher Canada & Olina Paul Nashua, NH
BOUCKI, Stanislaw, May 23 1912 Sex:M Child# 1 Bolaslov Boucki Russia & Kate Prunawicz Austria
BOUDRAU, Louis Edouard, Mar 12 1900 Sex:M Child# 3 Isaie Boudrau Canada & Obelina Lucier Canada
BOUDREAU, Alfred Ernest, Jun 18 1897 Sex:M Child# 4 Pierre Boudreau Plattsburgh, NY & Agnes Lavallee Canada
BOUDREAU, Ernest Armand, Aug 17 1898 Sex:M Child# 2 Joseph Boudreau Canada & Olbina Lussier Canada
BOUDREAU, Evelina, Feb 4 1897 Sex:F Child# 1 Isaie Boudreau Canada & Eveline Lussier Canada
BOUDREAU, Joseph Henri, Jan 8 1899 Sex:M Child# 5 Pierre Boudreau W Chazy, NY & Agnes Lavallee Canada
BOUDREAU, Lena, Nov 20 1892 Sex:F Child# 1 Pierre Boudreau NY & Agnes Lavalle Canada
BOUDREAU, Leo Roland, Nov 10 1925 Sex:M Child# 1 Oscar Boudreau Suncook, NH & Blanche Michaud Nashua, NH
BOUDREAU, M Aurore, Jul 29 1895 Sex:F Child# 1 Pierre Boudreau New York & Agnes Lavalle Canada
BOUDREAU, Marie Blanche, Dec 27 1903 Sex:F Child# 6 Isaac Boudreau Canada & Oveline Lussier Canada
BOUDREAU, Mary Joan, Dec 2 1932 Sex:F Child# 1 (No Parents Listed)
BOUDREAU, Unknown, Apr 19 1922 Sex:M Child# 1 Wilfred Boudreau Auburn, MA & Ruth Hawkins Milford, NH
BOUFFARD, Ambrosia, Oct 5 1888 Sex:M Child# 1 Ouide Bouffard Canada & Marie Boucher Canada
BOUFFARD, Angelina, Oct 15 1891 Sex:F Child# 2 Ovide Bouffard Canada & Marie Boucher Canada
BOUFFARD, Claude Francis, Aug 9 1923 Sex:M Child# 3 Ledger Jos Bouffard Canada & Margaret Brown Boston, MA
BOUFFARD, Helen Marion, Jul 28 1920 Sex:F Child# 1 Ludger J Bouffard Quebec & Marguerite Boklemon Boston, MA
BOUFFARD, Jos Wilfred Andrian, Sep 7 1925 Sex:M Child# 1 Wilfred Bouffard Canada & Eva Cote Canada
BOUFFARD, Joseph Paul, Apr 16 1933 Sex:M Child# 1 Elph Bouffard Canada & Alice Boucher Nashua, NH
BOUFFARD, Ledger Joseph, Feb 7 1922 Sex:M Child# 2 Ledger J Bouffard Canada & Greta D Brown Boston, MA
BOUFFARD, Marie Adrienne, Nov 27 1926 Sex:F Child# 2 Wilfred Bouffard Canada & Eva Cote Canada
BOUFFARD, Marie Louiseanne M, Mar 26 1929 Sex:F Child# 3 Wilfred Bouffard Canada & Eva Cote Canada
BOUFFORD, Joseph Pierre H, May 13 1930 Sex:M Child# 1 Pierre Boufford Canada & Ernestine Cote Canada
BOUGUILA, John, Jan 4 1900 Sex:M Child# 2 Theophile J Bouguila Russia & Johanna Stulpin Russia
BOUILLARD, Marie, Sep 4 1888 Sex:F Child# 9 Edonard Bouillard P Q & Peilomene Ploude Canada
BOUIN, Marguerite, Jul 24 1897 Sex:F Child# 8 Napoleon Bouin US & Melie Pelletier US
BOUIN, Owen Martin, Oct 2 1899 Sex:M Child# 10 Napoleon Bouin NY & Emelie Pelletier NY
BOULANGER, Edith R Rachel, Apr 1 1920 Sex:F Child# 4 Adelard Boulanger Canada & Irene Anctil Canada
BOULANGER, George Henry, Dec 5 1919 Sex:M Child# 2 Joseph Boulanger Canada & Antoinette Fortin Canada
BOULANGER, George Roland, Dec 1 1916 Sex:M Child# 1 Joseph Boulanger Canada & Antonnette Fortier Canada
BOULANGER, Gerald Irence, Jun 23 1922 Sex:M Child# 5 Adelard Boulanger Canada & Irene Anctil Canada
BOULANGER, Jos Robert Maurice, Nov 15 1917 Sex:M Child# 3 Adelard Boulanger Canada & Irene Anctil Canada
BOULANGER, Joseph Alexandre W, Dec 7 1908 Sex:M Child# 5 Joseph Boulanger Canada & Leona Cote Canada
BOULANGER, Joseph Roland, Jul 13 1932 Sex:M Child# 1 Jos Boulanger Salem, MA & Mildred Parker Nottingham, NH
BOULANGER, Joseph William, Feb 27 1911 Sex:M Child# 6 Philibert Boulanger Canada & Victoria Bolduc Canada
BOULANGER, Laurien Louis, Apr 29 1930 Sex:M Child# 2 Louis Boulanger Canada & Yvonne Latendresse Mass
BOULANGER, Leona Cote, Jan 29 1899 Sex:F Child# 1 Joseph Boulanger Canada & Leona Cote Canada Stillborn
BOULANGER, Liette Albertine, Dec 17 1929 Sex:F Child# 6 Joseph Boulanger Canada & Antoinette Fortin Canada
BOULANGER, M Antoinette Corinne, Jun 23 1913 Sex:F Child# 1 Adelard Boulanger Canada & Irene Anctil Canada
BOULANGER, Marie Alma I, Nov 15 1901 Sex:F Child# 2 Joseph Boulanger Canada & Leona Cote Canada
BOULANGER, Marie Rose Y, Feb 27 1903 Sex:F Child# 2 Joseph Boulanger Canada & Leona Cote Canada
BOULANGER, Muriel Fleurange, Jun 23 1922 Sex:F Child# 6 Adelard Boulanger Canada & Irene Anctil Canada
BOULANGER, Richard, Apr 28 1928 Sex:M Child# 1 Louis Boulanger Canada & Yvon Latendresse Lowell, MA
BOULANGER, Roger Conrad, Jun 22 1921 Sex:M Child# 3 Joseph Boulanger Canada & Antoinette Fortin Canada
BOULASKI, John, Mar 22 1914 Sex:M Child# 4 Mike Boulaski Russia & Agnes Battedonis Russia
BOULAY, Eddie Willie, Apr 2 1894 Sex:M Child# 2 Nicholas Boulay Hudson, MA & Exina Delude Canada
BOULAY, Heniretta Ludivina, Aug 17 1898 Sex:F Child# 1 Levis Boulay Mass & Lila Juen Nova Scotia
BOULAY, Wilfrid, Sep 15 1917 Sex:M Child# 9 Aime Boulay US & Phelonise Dion US
BOULE, Alfred, Apr 8 1892 Sex:M Child# 7 Victor Boule Canada & Exerile Lemery Canada
BOULE, Alphonse E, Jan 6 1894 Sex:M Child# 8 Victor Boule Canada & Exerile Lemery Canada
BOULE, Arthur, Jun 28 1887 Sex:M Child# 5 Victor Boule P Q & E Lemery P Q
BOULE, Blanche Irene, Sep 21 1889 Sex:F Child# 1 G Boule Canada & Alsine Martin Canada
BOULE, Emile, Aug 29 1895 Sex:M Child# 9 Victor Boule Canada & Exerile Lemery Canada
BOULE, Emile Armand, Jan 12 1910 Sex:M Child# 2 Ovide Boule Nashua, NH & Eva Ricard Nashua, NH
BOULE, Eugene, Apr 14 1894 Sex:M Child# 5 Fred Boule Canada & Exilda Martelle Canada
BOULE, Hector, May 15 1887 Sex:M Child# 3 Alfred Boule P Q & Azilda Martel P Q
BOULE, Joseph A, Jun 21 1897 Sex:M Child# 10 Victor Boule Canada & Exerile Lemery Canada
BOULE, Joseph A P, Feb 14 1896 Sex:M Child# 7 Alexander Boule Canada & Nancy Martel Canada
BOULE, Joseph Armand, Aug 30 1901 Sex:M Child# 2 Aime Boule NH & Phelenise Dion Vermont
BOULE, Joseph H, May 15 1894 Sex:M Child# 6 Alex Boule Canada & Nancy Martel Canada
BOULE, Joseph Herman R, Dec 6 1908 Sex:M Child# 1 Ovide Boule Nashua, NH & Eva Ricard Worcester, MA
BOULE, Marie C, Apr 13 1889 Sex:F Child# 6 Victor Boule Canada & Exeulda Lemery Canada
BOULE, Marie Clina, Jan 14 1890 Sex:F Child# 4 Alfred Boule Canada & Exilda Martel Canada
BOULE, Marie E, Jul 1 1891 Sex:F Child# 9 Misael Boule Canada & Vitaline Loranger Canada

BOULE, Marie E Irene, Apr 16 1899 Sex:F Child# 6 Alfred Boule Canada & Exilda Martel Canada
BOULE, Mary Ann, Jun 10 1888 Sex:F Child# 4 Alexandrie Boule Canada & Nancy Martelle Manchester, NH
BOULE, Reginald James, Apr 17 1894 Sex:M Child# 1 Alphonse Boule Canada & Mary Winkley Groton, MA
BOULE, Unknown, May 31 1899 Sex:F Child# 2 Elzear Boule Nashua, NH & Ismeria Ledoux Canada Stillborn
BOULE, Unknown, Jul 23 1919 Sex:F Child# 10 Aime Boule NH & Philonise Dion Vermont
BOULE, Wilfrid H, Feb 4 1901 Sex:M Child# 11 Victor Boule Canada & Emelie Lemery Canada
BOULEY, Alfred Raymond, Jul 23 1921 Sex:M Child# 8 Ovid R Bouley Nashua, NH & Eva Ricard Worcester, MA
BOULEY, Archy Clovis, Jun 3 1906 Sex:M Child# 4 Aimey Bouley Nashua, NH & Malinda Dion W Albery, VT
BOULEY, Charles Octave, Jan 4 1896 Sex:M Child# 3 Ulric Bouley Canada & Lizzie A Lyons Nashua, NH
BOULEY, Clovis, Mar 7 1902 Sex:M Child# 6 Fred Bouley Canada & Exilda Martel Canada
BOULEY, Dolores Colette, Nov 13 1932 Sex:F Child# 7 Claude Bouley Nashua, NH & Alice Delorme Nashua, NH
BOULEY, Edward Robert, Oct 21 1928 Sex:M Child# 2 Arthur Bouley Nashua, NH & Louise LaPlante Concord, NH
BOULEY, Eleonore, Nov 15 1913 Sex:F Child# 5 Ovide Bouley Nashua, NH & Eva Ricard Worcester, MA
BOULEY, Emile Robert, Jan 20 1924 Sex:M Child# 1 Wilfred Bouley Nashua, NH & Lillian Cote Lawrence, MA
BOULEY, Eugene Arthur, Jun 21 1915 Sex:M Child# 8 Aime Bouley US & Philomene Dionne US
BOULEY, Eva Alice, Jul 6 1918 Sex:F Child# 7 Ovide R Bouley Nashua, NH & Eva Record Worcester, MA
BOULEY, Eva Oranie, Aug 21 1892 Sex:F Child# 1 Nicholas Bouley Canada & Exina Dulude Canada
BOULEY, Florence Clare, Nov 11 1916 Sex:F Child# 6 Ovid Bouley Nashua, NH & Eva Record Mass
BOULEY, Francis Lyons, Apr 6 1893 Sex:M Child# 1 Ulric Bouley Canada & Lizzie A Lyons Nashua, NH
BOULEY, Gilbert Dale, Jun 1 1925 Sex:M Child# 5 Claude Bouley Nashua, NH & Alice Delorme Nashua, NH
BOULEY, Henry Joseph, Aug 2 1927 Sex:M Child# 2 Henry Bouley Nashua, NH & Yvonne Bernard Nashua, NH
BOULEY, Henry Raymond, Jul 28 1894 Sex:M Child# 2 Ulric Bouley Canada & Lizzie A Lyons Nashua, NH
BOULEY, Irene Elenor, May 8 1911 Sex:F Child# 3 Ovid Bouley Nashua, NH & Eva Record Worcester, MA
BOULEY, Jeannette Cecile, Aug 6 1926 Sex:F Child# 1 Henry Bouley Nashua, NH & Yvonne Bernard Nashua, NH
BOULEY, Joan Alice, Sep 29 1933 Sex:F Child# 2 Archie Bouley Nashua, NH & Alice Boucher Nashua, NH
BOULEY, John Lyons, Apr 28 1905 Sex:M Child# 7 Ulric Bouley Canada & Elizabeth A Lyons Nashua, NH
BOULEY, Joseph Arthur Leo, Jan 27 1927 Sex:M Child# 2 Wilfred Bouley Lewiston, ME & Lillian Cote Lawrence, MA
BOULEY, Joseph Claude, Dec 27 1921 Sex:M Child# 2 Claude Bouley Nashua, NH & Alice Delorme Nashua, NH
BOULEY, Joseph Paul Roger, May 13 1920 Sex:M Child# 1 Claude Bouley Nashua, NH & Alice Delorme Nashua, NH
BOULEY, June Isabelle, Aug 10 1931 Sex:F Child# 1 Harry Bouley Nashua, NH & Molly Martin Mass
BOULEY, Leo Andre, Apr 26 1932 Sex:M Child# 5 Henry Bouley Nashua, NH & Yvonne Bernard Nashua, NH
BOULEY, Leo Napoleon, Jan 6 1897 Sex:M Child#  N P Bouley Mass & Exina Dulude Canada
BOULEY, Louise Sadie, Jul 30 1912 Sex:F Child# 4 Ovid Bouley Nashua, NH & Eva Record Worcester, MA
BOULEY, Mary Dolores, May 2 1903 Sex:F Child# 2 Ulric Bouley Canada & Lizzie A Lyons Nashua, NH
BOULEY, Mary Helena, May 3 1897 Sex:F Child# 4 Ulric Bouley Canada & Lizzie A Lyons Nashua, NH
BOULEY, Mildred E, Jun 14 1901 Sex:F Child# 5 Ulric Bouley Canada & Elizabeth A Lyons Nashua, NH
BOULEY, Mildred Gladys, May 26 1904 Sex:F Child# 3 Aime Bouley Nashua, NH & Felinda Dion W Albert, VT
BOULEY, Nicholas Levi, Feb 13 1904 Sex:M Child# 2 Levi A Bouley Hudson, MA & Leda Glun Nova Scotia
BOULEY, Norman James, Sep 14 1926 Sex:M Child# 13 Aimey Bouley Nashua, NH & Philenda Dion Alburg, VT Stillborn
BOULEY, Paul Arthur, Jun 16 1924 Sex:M Child# 1 Arthur Bouley Nashua, NH & Louise Laplante Concord, NH
BOULEY, Paul Edward, Nov 5 1925 Sex:M Child# 1 Nicholas Bouley Nashua, NH & Evelyn Gingras Canada
BOULEY, Philip, Aug 17 1923 Sex:M Child# 12 Aime Bouley Nashua, NH & Philmida Dion Alburg, VT
BOULEY, Raymond Paul, May 3 1930 Sex:M Child# 3 Henry Bouley Nashua, NH & Yvonne Bernard Nashua, NH
BOULEY, Raymond Ralph, Aug 12 1908 Sex:M Child# 5 Aimey Bouley Nashua, NH & Felinda Dion Vermont
BOULEY, Rebecca, Jun 23 1891 Sex:F Child# 2 William Bouley Canada & Olivine Martin Canada
BOULEY, Richard, Apr 16 1923 Sex:M Child# 3 Claude Bouley Nashua, NH & A Delorme Nashua, NH
BOULEY, Richard, Feb 21 1928 Sex:M Child# 2 Nicholas Bouley Nashua, NH & Evelyn Gingras Canada
BOULEY, Richard Charles, Oct 23 1931 Sex:M Child# 1 Raymond Bouley Nashua, NH & Mary Veneins Nashua, NH
BOULEY, Robert Eugene, May 20 1931 Sex:M Child# 4 Henry Bouley Nashua, NH & Yvonne Bernard Nashua, NH
BOULEY, Rose Eveline, Sep 3 1898 Sex:F Child# 2 Alphonse A Bouley St Hyancinthe, PQ & Mary A Winkley W Groton, MA
BOULEY, Sylvia Edith, Apr 7 1928 Sex:F Child# 1 Archie Bouley Nashua, NH & Alice Boucher Nashua, NH
BOULEY, Unknown, Apr 29 1928 Sex:F Child# 5 Claude Bouley Nashua, NH & Alice Delorme Nashua, NH Stillborn
BOULEY, Victor, Oct 23 1921 Sex:M Child# 11 Aime V Bouley Nashua, NH & Philinde Dion W Albert, VT
BOULEY, Virginia Alice, Apr 23 1912 Sex:F Child# 7 Aime Bouley Nashua, NH & Felina Dionne Albany, VT
BOULEY, Vivienne Andrea, Jul 5 1924 Sex:F Child# 4 Claude Bouley Nashua, NH & Alice Delorme Nashua, NH
BOULIA, Kenneth Clayton, Oct 3 1928 Sex:M Child# 1 K C Boulia Pepperell, MA & Hattie Raby Nashua, NH
BOULIE, Marie L E, Nov 30 1889 Sex:F Child# 5 Alexandre Boulie Canada & Nancy Martel Manchester, NH
BOULLARD, Unknown, Feb 15 1912 Sex:F Child# 3 Pierre Boullard Canada & Eudase Houle Canada Stillborn
BOULLIER, Alice Constance, Mar 26 1905 Sex:F Child# 2 Jules Boullier France & Constance Carre France
BOULLIER, Emile Jules J, Feb 9 1903 Sex:M Child# 1 Jules Boullier France & Constance Carre France
BOULOMETIS, Christos, Oct 12 1913 Sex:M Child# 1 John Boulometis Greece & Evangelia Zaine Greece
BOULTON, Marcia, May 3 1935 Sex:F Child# 1 Arthur H Boulton Southbridge, MA & Irene Farley Hollis, NH
BOUNEAU, Marie C, Oct 26 1895 Sex:F Child# 2 Pierre Bouneau Canada & Amelie Morin Canada
BOUNETTE, Eva, Apr 1 1895 Sex:F Child#  Eusebe Bounette Canada & Odina Rousseau Canada
BOUNETTE, Joseph Francois, Jan 29 1898 Sex:M Child# 2 Francois Bounette Canada & Rose D Archambault Canada
BOUNIER, Marie Anne A, Aug 17 1890 Sex:F Child# 2 Eugene Bounier Canada & Alma Grenier Canada
BOUNIN, Alma, Apr 9 1888 Sex:F Child# 1 Eugene Bounin Canada & Alma Grenier Canada
BOUNIR, Mary, Dec 24 1890 Sex:F Child# 5 Napoleon Bounir NY & Milia Peltier NY
BOURASSA, Constance Juliette, Aug 13 1930 Sex:F Child# 2 Emery Bourassa Nashua, NH & Germaine Breault Manchester,NH
BOURASSA, Dolores Lucille, Nov 3 1931 Sex:F Child# 3 Emery Bourassa Nashua, NH & Germaine Breault Manchester, NH
BOURASSA, Emery Oliver, Aug 21 1929 Sex:M Child# 1 Emery Bourassa Nashua, NH & Germaine Breault Manchester, NH
BOURASSA, Ephrem, Sep 30 1890 Sex:M Child# 13 Napoleon Bourassa Canada & Josephine Langlois Canada
BOURASSA, Gedeon, Oct 19 1895 Sex:M Child# 3 Gedeon Bourassa Canada & Felicite Thibeau Canada

BOURASSA, Joseph Ernest, May 9 1905 Sex:M Child# 2 Henri Bourassa Canada & Alphonsine Perreault Canada
BOURASSA, Joseph Romeo E, Feb 10 1907 Sex:M Child# 3 Henri Bourassa Canada & Alphonsine Bourassa Canada
BOURASSA, Joseph Wilfrid, Oct 13 1901 Sex:M Child# 6 Gedeon Bourassa Canada & Felecite Thibault New York
BOURASSA, Josephine, Apr 7 1894 Sex:F Child# 2 Gedeon Bourassa Canada & Felicite Thibault US
BOURASSA, Lauretta Beatrice, Jul 6 1914 Sex:F Child# 1 L B Bourassa Hooksett, NH & Marie Richer Nashua, NH
BOURASSA, Lucille Louise A, Jul 4 1910 Sex:F Child# 4 Henri H Bourassa Canada & Alphonsine Perreault Canada
BOURASSA, Marie Aldina, May 19 1897 Sex:F Child# 4 Gedeon Bourassa Canada & Felecite Thibault Clinton Mills, NH
BOURASSA, Marie Claire, May 6 1933 Sex:F Child# 4 E R Bourassa Nashua, NH & G Breourt Manchester, NH
BOURASSA, Marie Rose, Sep 4 1909 Sex:F Child# 2 Noe Bourassa Canada & Laura Lapierre Suncook, NH Stillborn
BOURASSA, Napoleon Cyrille, Mar 19 1893 Sex:M Child# 1 Gedeon Bourasssa Canada & Felicite Thibeau Canada
BOURASSA, Unknown, Feb 24 1899 Sex:M Child# 2 Gideon Bourassa Canada & Felesite Thibeault NY
BOURASSA, Unknown, Jul 18 1928 Sex:F Child# 2 Emile Bourassa Canada & Rose A Levesque Canada
BOURBAULT, Joseph Florant, Aug 14 1924 Sex:M Child# 3 Wilfrid Bourbault Canada & Laura Nadeau Canada
BOURBEAU, Alice Yvonne, Jun 19 1905 Sex:F Child# 10 Norbert Bourbeau Canada & Philomene Cantara Canada
BOURBEAU, J Wilfrid Robert, Oct 31 1921 Sex:M Child# 1 Wilfrid Bourbeau Canada & Laura Nadeau Canada
BOURBEAU, Joseph Armand, May 10 1903 Sex:M Child# 9 Norbert Bourbeau Canada & Philomene Cantara Canada
BOURBEAU, Louis Oscar, Jan 15 1923 Sex:M Child# 2 Wilfred Bourbeau Canada & Laura Nadeau Canada
BOURDEAU, Celia, Nov 25 1888 Sex:F Child# 3 Narcisse Bourdeau Canada & Caroline Aubin Canada
BOURDEAU, Joseph, Sep 15 1892 Sex:M Child# 15 Narcisse Bourdeau Canada & Caroline Aubin Canada
BOURDEAU, Unknown, Jul 7 1891 Sex:M Child# 8 Ambroise Bourdeau Canada & Marie Basil Canada Stillborn
BOURDON, Charles A, Jan 22 1891 Sex:M Child# 1 Charles Bourdon Canada & Zenaide Couture Canada
BOURDON, Gilbert W, Sep 24 1895 Sex:M Child# 1 Theophile Bourdon Canada & Delphine Lapointe Canada
BOURDON, Marie, Dec 21 1898 Sex:F Child# 2 Theophile Bourdon Canada & Julienne Lapoint Sciota, NY
BOURDON, Marie L E, Jun 17 1892 Sex:F Child# 2 Charles Bourdon Canada & Zenaide Couture Canada
BOURDON, Mary Rose Dorothy, Sep 18 1917 Sex:F Child# 1 Charles Bourdon Mass & Rose Gagnon Nashua, NH
BOUREY, Ebdner John, Nov 12 1901 Sex:M Child# 1 John Bourey New York & Jane Woods England
BOUREY, Mary Alice, Jun 17 1907 Sex:F Child# 2 John W Bourey Sciota, NY & Jane J Wood England
BOURGAULT, Jos Wilfred Normand, Jun 22 1923 Sex:M Child# 3 Luke Bourgault Canada & Celina Bois Greenville, NH
BOURGAULT, Joseph Leo Roger, Jul 13 1925 Sex:M Child# 1 Luck Bourgault Canada & Celina Bois Greenville, NH
BOURGEA, Leo E, Sep 13 1933 Sex:M Child# 2 H Bourgea Canada & Marie A Hebert Canada
BOURGEA, Ronald James, Sep 9 1927 Sex:M Child# 1 H Bourgea Canada & Marion Hebert Canada
BOURGEAS, Jacqueline, Jan 22 1935 Sex:F Child# 3 Wilfred Bourgeas Nashua, NH & Dora Bernatches Canada
BOURGEAULT, M Therese Camille, Mar 7 1921 Sex:F Child# 2 Luc Bourgeault Canada & Celina Bois Greenville, NH
BOURGEAULT, Marie Rita Cecile, Jul 20 1919 Sex:F Child# 1 Luc Bourgeault Canada & Celina Bois Greenville, NH
BOURGELAIS, Roger, Mar 21 1933 Sex:M Child# 2 W Bourgelais Nashua, NH & Doria Bernatchez Canada
BOURGELAIS, Unknown, Oct 29 1902 Sex:F Child# 7 Joseph Bourgelais Canada & Delima Theriault Canada
BOURGELAT, Unknown, Apr 13 1900 Sex:M Child# 5 Joseph Bourgelat Canada & Delima Theriault Canada Stillborn
BOURGELET, Joseph Pierre, Aug 7 1901 Sex:M Child# 6 Joseph Bourgelet Canada & Delima Theriault Canada
BOURGELET, Wilfred, Sep 2 1904 Sex:M Child# 8 Joseph Bourgelet Canada & Delima Theriault Canada
BOURGEOIS, Jos Adelard Alfred, Apr 30 1916 Sex:M Child# 12 Pierre Bourgeois Canada & Adelina Cloutier NH
BOURGEOIS, Joseph Desire, May 21 1913 Sex:M Child# 10 Pierre Bourgeois Canada & Adelina Cloutier NH
BOURGEOIS, Joseph Gerard, Jan 27 1934 Sex:M Child# 1 Samuel Bourgeois Nashua, NH & Florence Cassista Nashua, NH
BOURGEOIS, Joseph Samuel, Apr 28 1910 Sex:M Child# 9 Pierre Bourgeois Canada & Adelina Cloutier NH
BOURGEOIS, Marie Jeanne, Apr 19 1922 Sex:F Child# 1 (No Parents Listed)
BOURGEOIS, Mary Jeannette, Jun 28 1924 Sex:F Child# 2 Arthur Bourgeois NH & Maude E Hanson NH
BOURGEOIS, Robert Paul, Apr 27 1934 Sex:M Child# 3 Joseph N Bourgeois Hooksett, NH & Viola Salvail Barton, VT
BOURGEOIS, Therese J, Mar 11 1931 Sex:F Child# 1 Joseph N Bourgeois Hooksett, NH & Viola Salvail Barton, VT
BOURGET, Elizabeth Rose, Dec 28 1932 Sex:F Child# 2 H J Bourget Fitchburg, MA & Rosina McClellan Fitchburg, MA
BOURGET, Rita Anne, Mar 16 1934 Sex:F Child# 2 Henry Bourget Fitchburg, MA & Rosine McLellon Fitchburg, MA
BOURGIE, Marie Lucille Gloria, Dec 16 1926 Sex:F Child# 2 Albert Bourgie Canada & Obeline Viger Canada
BOURGLAS, Wilfred Joseph, Jul 8 1924 Sex:M Child# 1 P J Bourglas Nashua, NH & Cora Alice Hoyt Nashua, NH
BOURGOIN, Lillian Dora, Oct 8 1916 Sex:F Child# 1 Henri Bourgoin Canada & Amie Dube Canada
BOURGOIN, Marie Irene Rosanna, May 1 1916 Sex:F Child# 1 Walter Bourgoin Canada & Rosanna Burelle Nashua, NH
BOURGOIN, Roger, Nov 25 1922 Sex:M Child# 2 Alyre Bourgoin New Brunswick & Elizabeth Beausoleil Canada
BOURGOIS, Louise Olive, Oct 9 1930 Sex:F Child# 1 Camile S Bourgois,Jr Greenville, NH & Martha Petit Lawrence, MA
BOURGOIS, Rachel Florence, Aug 7 1932 Sex:F Child# 2 Jos Bourgois NH & Viola Salvail Vermont
BOURGOUIN, Joseph J, May 30 1895 Sex:M Child# 1 Arthur Bourgouin Canada & Philomene Blanchelle Canada
BOURGOUIN, Joseph Raphael, Mar 19 1892 Sex:M Child# 1 Joseph Bourgouin Canada & Julie Bosse Canada
BOURGOUIN, Julie, May 6 1894 Sex:F Child# 3 Joseph Bourgouin Canada & Julie Bosse Canada
BOURGOUIN, Pierre, Apr 20 1893 Sex:M Child# Joseph Bourgouin Canada & Julie Bosse Canada
BOURLEAU, Marie Delima, Sep 10 1896 Sex:F Child# Gregoire Bourleau Canada & Delima Theriault Canada
BOURNE, Jacqueline Morse, Feb 23 1933 Sex:F Child# 2 H G Bourne Cambridge, MA & Helen A Paul N Windham, ME
BOURQUE, Leopold Ferdinand, Oct 15 1924 Sex:M Child# 1 Albert Bourque Canada & Obeline Voyer Canada
BOURRASSA, Exeas, Nov 21 1903 Sex:M Child# 1 Adam Bourrassa Canada & Delia Houle Canada
BOURY, Esther E, Aug 16 1899 Sex:F Child# 2 Joseph Boury NY & S A Downs NH
BOURY, Mary Rose, Jan 4 1904 Sex:F Child# 3 (No Parents Listed)
BOUSANG, Paul A, Feb 15 1891 Sex:M Child# 6 Amable Bousang Canada & Eugenie Bonenfaut Canada
BOUSANT, Victor, Jun 26 1908 Sex:M Child# 6 Joseph C Bousant Canada & Josephine St Pierre Canada
BOUSENS, Treffle, Aug 17 1901 Sex:M Child# 2 Cyprien Bousens Canada & Josephine St Pierre Canada
BOUSQUET, Isabelle, Jun 1 1917 Sex:F Child# 5 Leon Bousquet Lancaster, NH & Jeanne D'Anjou Canada
BOUSQUET, Joseph Paul Henry, Jul 15 1929 Sex:M Child# 1 Edward Bousquet Canada & Marie Bibeau Fisherville, MA
BOUSQUET, Landa Alfred, May 30 1891 Sex:M Child# 5 Alfred Bousquet Canada & Claire Pinette Canada
BOUSQUET, Lucille, Aug 4 1934 Sex:F Child# 1 Emile Bousquet Canada & Angeline Ouellette Canada

BOUSQUIN, M Alphada G, Mar 16 1919 Sex:F Child# 6 Leon W Bousquin Lancaster, NH & Jennie D'Anjou Canada
BOUTELLE, Charles Francis, Apr 23 1918 Sex:M Child# 1 Francis L Boutelle Gloucester, MA & Edna Moulton Waltham, MA
BOUTELLE, John F, Dec 25 1888 Sex:M Child# 3 John G Boutelle Amherst & Estella M Hildreth Amherst
BOUTHILLIER, J Roger Fernand, Sep 11 1915 Sex:M Child# 14 N Fredrc Bouthillier Canada & Marie L Rocheleau Canada
BOUTHILLIER, M Antoinette A L, Mar 11 1907 Sex:F Child# 10 N F Bouthillier Canada & Marie L Rochelean Canada
BOUTHILLIER, M Berthe Cecile, May 10 1913 Sex:F Child# 13 Nazaire F Bouthillie Canada & Marie L Rocheleau Canada
BOUTHILLIER, M Pierrette Pauln R, Jun 29 1911 Sex:F Child# 12 Frederick Bouthillie Canada & Marie L Rocheleau Canad
BOUTHILLIER, Marie Jeanne J, Jan 18 1909 Sex:F Child# 11 Frederic Bouthillier Canada & Marie L Rocheleau Canada
BOUTHILLIER, Pauline Claire, Oct 17 1932 Sex:F Child# 1 Paul Bouthillier Canada & Clara Dion Manchester, NH
BOUTHILLIER, Unknown, Nov 6 1909 Sex:F Child# 2 Enoch M Bouthillier Halifax, NS & Hattie Lindner Smiths, MA
BOUTHUTTE, Vivian Violet Anita, Sep 27 1917 Sex:F Child# 1 Adelard Bouthutte Canada & Mary Paris Manchester, NH
BOUTILIER, James E, Sep 20 1888 Sex:M Child# 1 Alfred R Boutilier N S & Ella McDonald Canada
BOUTILLIER, Unknown, Aug 31 1907 Sex:M Child# 1 Enoch M Boutillier Halifax, NS & Hattie Lindner Smith, MA
BOUTIN, Joseph, Jul 26 1903 Sex:M Child# 1 Joseph Boutin Canada & Sara Bisson Canada
BOUTIN, Joseph Albert, Apr 11 1907 Sex:M Child# 4 Joseph Boutin Canada & Sara Bisson Canada
BOUTIN, Joseph Philibert, Nov 29 1907 Sex:M Child# 2 Philibert Boutin Canada & Virginie Lamontagne Canada
BOUTIN, Joseph Robert, Feb 19 1916 Sex:M Child# 2 Alfred Boutin Nashua, NH & Anne Paradis Mt Carmel, Canada
BOUTIN, Marie Rose, Feb 23 1906 Sex:F Child# 3 Josephte Boutin Canada & Sara Bisson Canada
BOUTOT, Joseph Oseas, Apr 1 1902 Sex:M Child# 2 Achille Boutot Canada & Diana Ouellette Canada
BOUTOT, Marie Alexina E, Jan 28 1904 Sex:F Child# 4 Achille Boutot Canada & Diana Ouellette Canada
BOUTOTT, Joseph Achille D A, Mar 29 1900 Sex:M Child# 2 Achille Boutott Canada & Dianna Ouellette Canada
BOUTWELL, Alice Lorraine, Dec 25 1919 Sex:F Child# 1 George E Boutwell Pepperell, MA & Ruth Anderson Pepperell, MA
BOUTWELL, Beverly, Jul 14 1921 Sex:F Child# 2 George Boutwell Pepperell, MA & Ruth Anderson Pepperell, MA
BOUTWELL, Dorothy Arleen, Mar 20 1927 Sex:F Child# 4 George Boutwell Pepperell, MA & Ruth Anderson Pepperell, MA
BOUTWELL, Emma, Apr 25 1896 Sex:F Child# Ermon E Boutwell Brookline, NH & Jennie M Frye Wilton, NH
BOUTWELL, Leroy Grant, May 31 1924 Sex:M Child# 3 George Boutwell Pepperell, MA & Ruth Anderson Pepperell, MA
BOUVIER, Miny Bessie, Jan 19 1893 Sex:F Child# 1 Henry Bouvier NY & Cordelia Barrett NY
BOWDEN, Donald Francis, Dec 2 1910 Sex:M Child# 3 John R Bowden Little Rock, AR & Mildred H Hope Canada
BOWDEN, Doris Lillian, Jan 6 1929 Sex:F Child# 6 Robert Bowden Lowell, MA & Ruth Smith Nashua, NH
BOWDEN, Guy Wesley, Mar 1 1919 Sex:M Child# 4 John R Bowden Little Rock, Ark & Mildred Hope Canada
BOWDEN, Marjorie Elaine, Jun 22 1930 Sex:F Child# 3 Robert C Bowden Lowell, MA & Ruth L Smith Nashua, NH
BOWDEN, Mildred Ruth Mary, Mar 31 1927 Sex:F Child# 1 Robert C Bowden Lowell, MA & Ruth L Smith Nashua, NH
BOWEN, Allen Frederick, Mar 21 1891 Sex:M Child# 1 Wilfred S Bowen Lowell, MA & Etta J Duffy Nashua, NH
BOWEN, James Anthony, Jun 13 1926 Sex:M Child# 2 John Bowen Ireland & Catherine Dineen New York, NY
BOWEN, John, Nov 15 1923 Sex:M Child# 1 John Bowen Ireland & Catherine Dineen New York, NY
BOWEN, Warren Porter, Jul 7 1903 Sex:M Child# 2 Frank H Bowen New York & Barbara McDonald Nova Scotia
BOWEN, Willis Herbert, Nov 15 1901 Sex:M Child# 1 Frank H Bowen Saranac, NY & Barbara McDonald Picton, NC
BOWERS, Ella Jane, Feb 13 1891 Sex:F Child# 7 Joseph C Bowers Boston, MA & Ella F Wright Nashua, NH
BOWERS, James Eastman, Aug 15 1889 Sex:M Child# 1 James E Bowers Merrimack, NH & Kate W O'Neil Nashua, NH
BOWERS, Josephine Ella, Nov 29 1910 Sex:F Child# 3 Joseph Bowers Nashua, NH & Catherine Conoly Ireland
BOWERS, Lucy Katherine, Jun 27 1900 Sex:F Child# 1 P F Bowers NH & J E Thayer San Francisco, CA
BOWERS, Perley Foster, Jun 27 1900 Sex:M Child# 2 P F Bowers NH & J E Thayer San Francisco, CA
BOWERS, Rosavel, Aug 16 1901 Sex:F Child# 12 Jonas C Bowers Dracut, MA & Elle F Bowers Nashua, NH
BOWERS, Walter Clarence, Aug 28 1897 Sex:M Child# 1 Willard A Bowers Bolton, MA & Cora B Holland Salem, MA
BOWMAN, Davis, Jul 12 1895 Sex:M Child# 2 Himan Bowman Russia & Yatta Tobinski Russia
BOWMAN, Esther, Sep 30 1893 Sex:F Child# 1 Herman Bowman Russia & Dobensky Russia
BOWMAN, Louis, Mar 5 1902 Sex:M Child# 5 Herian Bowman Russia & Yoti Dolinsky Russia
BOWMAN, Molly, Nov 20 1899 Sex:F Child# 5 H Bowman Russia & Etta Dohisky Russia
BOWMAN, Tobia, Apr 9 1897 Sex:F Child# 3 Haman Bowman Poland & Jata Dubinski Russia
BOYAGIAN, Aramis, Apr 29 1909 Sex:M Child# 1 Garabed Boyagian Armenia & Karan Moorradian Armenia
BOYAJIAN, Ardarast, Oct 25 1898 Sex:M Child# 2 Mardiros Boyajian Armenia & Gohan Harbid Armenia
BOYAJIAN, Carmig, Aug 18 1914 Sex:M Child# 3 Charles Boyajian Turkey & Kainy Mooradian Turkey
BOYAJIAN, Markar, Nov 28 1911 Sex:M Child# 2 Charles Boysjian Turkey & Karan Mooradian Turkey
BOYCE, Dorilda Esther, Mar 18 1924 Sex:F Child# 6 William Boyce NH & Anna Mycue NH
BOYCE, Edith Irene, Aug 2 1919 Sex:F Child# 4 William G Boyce Canterbury, NH & Anna Mycue Danbury, NH
BOYCE, Madeline Clara, Jan 29 1916 Sex:F Child# 2 William J Boyce Canterbury, NH & Anna M Myene Danbury, NH
BOYCE, Zemmer Harriet, Oct 7 1917 Sex:F Child# 3 William G Boyce Canterbury, NH & Anna M Micere Danbury, NH
BOYD, Donald Norbert, Apr 3 1932 Sex:M Child# 1 John H Boyd Penn & Ruth Corlis Lisbon, NH
BOYD, George Fiske W, Oct 4 1909 Sex:M Child# 3 Walter F Boyd Londonderry, NH & Viola Prescott Old Orchard, ME
BOYD, Joan, Oct 14 1928 Sex:F Child# 1 Charles P Boyd Nashua, NH & Violet Lord Nashua, NH
BOYD, Patricia Ann, Apr 30 1935 Sex:F Child# 2 John Boyd Emporium, PA & Ruth Corliss Lyman, NH
BOYD, Unknown, Oct 4 1901 Sex:M Child# 1 Walter I Boyd Londonderry, NH & Viola M Prescott Old Orchard, ME
BOYD, Unknown, May 2 1905 Sex:F Child# 2 Walter T Boyd Londonderry, NH & Viola M Prescott Old Orchard, ME
BOYD, Walter Thomas, Jr, May 23 1913 Sex:M Child# 4 Walter T Boyd Londonderry, NH & Viola Prescott Old Orchard, ME
BOYDIN, Stanley, Dec 16 1918 Sex:M Child# 3 Stanley Boydin Russia & Soph Stanofmovitch Russia
BOYER, Antoinette Germaine, Dec 23 1924 Sex:F Child# 2 Leo Boyer Nashua, NH & Lucette Doucet Rochester, NH
BOYER, Beverly Bernice, Jan 18 1935 Sex:F Child# 5 Edgar Boyer Nashua, NH & Mildred Nutting Waterboro, ME
BOYER, Donald, Feb 10 1935 Sex:M Child# 7 Leo Boyer Nashua, NH & Lucille Doucette Rochester, NH
BOYER, Donald, Oct 15 1935 Sex:M Child# 3 Alfred Boyer Nashua, NH & Andrea Guimond Nashua, NH
BOYER, Donald Roland, Jan 22 1932 Sex:M Child# 1 Frank P Boyer Nashua, NH & Bernice Trembly Nashua, NH
BOYER, Doris Cecille, Nov 27 1930 Sex:F Child# 6 Joseph Leo Boyer Nashua, NH & Lillian L Doucette Rochester, NH
BOYER, Earline Joy, Aug 18 1932 Sex:F Child# 4 Edgar Boyer Nashua, NH & Mildred Nutting Maine
BOYER, Edgar, Nov 12 1901 Sex:M Child# 7 Charles Boyer Plattsburg, NY & Veline Couture Canada

BOYER, Edward Theodore, Jun 1 1928 Sex:M Child# 2 Edgar Boyer Nashua, NH & Blanche Nutting NH
BOYER, Francis X, Jan 18 1893 Sex:M Child# 1 Charles E Boyer Canada & Helene Coutourier Canada
BOYER, Helene Ernestine, Apr 6 1930 Sex:F Child# 3 Edgar Boyer Nashua, NH & Mildred Nutting Maine
BOYER, Irene Eva, Sep 8 1917 Sex:F Child# 8 Victor Boyer Plattsburg, NY & Celina Fournier Canada
BOYER, Janet, Jan 16 1932 Sex:F Child# 1 Ernest Boyer Merrimack, NH & Jeannette Cyr Manchester, NH
BOYER, Jos George Raymond, Nov 13 1912 Sex:M Child# 4 Alfred Boyer New York & Amelia Boilard New Haven, CT
BOYER, Joseph, Feb 12 1895 Sex:M Child# 2 Victor Boyer New York & Celina Fournier Canada
BOYER, Joseph Albert, Jan 8 1896 Sex:M Child# 4 Charles Boyer Canada & Helene Couturier Canada
BOYER, Joseph Arthur, Jan 12 1895 Sex:M Child# 2 Frank Boyer Canada & Helene Dionne NH
BOYER, Joseph Felix, Mar 22 1898 Sex:M Child# 4 Victor Boyer Plattsburg, NY & Celina Fournier Canada
BOYER, Joseph Francis H, Jun 17 1905 Sex:M Child# 1 Francois Boyer New York & Marie Louise Gagnon Mass
BOYER, Joseph Francois, Jun 9 1899 Sex:M Child# 1 Frank Boyer Plattsburgh, NY & Rose A Burette Canada
BOYER, Joseph L A, Jun 23 1896 Sex:M Child# 3 Victor Boyer New York & Celina Fournier Canada
BOYER, Joseph Oscar, Feb 10 1917 Sex:M Child# 1 (No Parents Listed)
BOYER, Leo, Oct 16 1901 Sex:M Child# 6 Victor Boyer Plattsburg, NY & Marie Fournier Canada
BOYER, Lillian Loraine, Sep 29 1926 Sex:F Child# 3 Leo Boyer Nashua, NH & Lucy Doucette Rochester, NH
BOYER, Loraine Yvonne, Dec 8 1932 Sex:F Child# 1 Alfred Boyer US & A Guimont Newport, VT
BOYER, Louisiana, Jan 12 1895 Sex:F Child# 3 Charles Boyer NY & Helene Coutourier Canada
BOYER, Lucille, Jan 14 1924 Sex:F Child# 1 Leo Boyer Nashua, NH & Lucille Doucet Rochester, NH
BOYER, Marie A Josephine, Aug 11 1902 Sex:F Child# 3 Frank Boyer NY & Prosile Barrette Canada
BOYER, Marie Anna, Sep 27 1910 Sex:F Child# 4 Francois Boyer New York & Marie A P Barette Canada
BOYER, Marie Beatrice, Feb 25 1909 Sex:F Child# 3 Francois Boyer New York & Marie L Gagnon Mass
BOYER, Marie Blanche A, Nov 12 1906 Sex:F Child# 3 Alfred Boyer New York & Emelia Boilard NH
BOYER, Marie Celina, Oct 12 1899 Sex:F Child# 5 Victor Boyer NY & Celina Fournier Canada
BOYER, Marie Eva, Dec 11 1906 Sex:F Child# 10 Charles A Boyer New York & Helene Couturier Canada
BOYER, Marie Jeanne, Apr 10 1929 Sex:F Child# 5 Leo Boyer Nashua, NH & Lucille Doucette Rochester, NH
BOYER, Marie Yvonne, Aug 27 1904 Sex:F Child# 2 Alfred Boyer New York & Amelia Boilard NH
BOYER, Marie Yvonne, Jun 8 1906 Sex:F Child# 2 Frank Boyer New York & Marie L Gagnon Mass
BOYER, Pauline, Dec 19 1933 Sex:F Child# 2 Ernest Boyer Nashua, NH & Jeannette Cyr Nashua, NH
BOYER, Raymond, May 14 1935 Sex:M Child# 1 Armand Boyer Nashua, NH & Rose A Chauvin Oxford, MA
BOYER, Robert Reginald, Nov 29 1933 Sex:M Child# 2 Alfred Boyer Nashua, NH & Andrea Guimont Nashua, NH
BOYER, Unknown, Sep 10 1893 Sex:M Child# 1 Charles A Boyer Canada & Helene Coutourier Canada
BOYER, Unknown, Dec 31 1927 Sex:M Child# 4 Leo Boyer Nashua, NH & Lucille Doucete Rochester, NH
BOYER, Victor, Jul 18 1893 Sex:M Child# 1 Victor Boyer Canada & Celina Fournier Canada
BOYINGTON, Clarence, Feb 7 1905 Sex:M Child# 1 James Boyington New Brunswick & Annie Fernandez Nova Scotia
BOYLE, Arthur, Dec 31 1900 Sex:M Child# 6 Joseph Boyle Canada & Julia A Gateley England
BOYNTON, Kenneth Ivan, Aug 15 1896 Sex:M Child# 1 John F Boynton Weare, NH & Flora A Ellor N Richmond, NH
BOYNTON, Viola Elizabeth, Jan 29 1897 Sex:F Child# 8 Frank E Boynton Amherst & Mary Ledoux New York
BRACKETT, Lawrence Joseph, Jul 4 1935 Sex:M Child# 1 Jos W Brackett Dover, NH & Barbara Scruton Strafford, NH
BRADDLEY, Ralph Louis, Aug 21 1916 Sex:M Child# 1 Ralph J Braddley Nashua, NH & Grace Rock Nashua, NH
BRADLEY, Alma Anita, Aug 22 1897 Sex:F Child# 7 William J Bradley Newport Center, VT & Cora B Reed Nashua, NH
BRADLEY, Bridget, Mar 4 1895 Sex:F Child# 5 Cornelius Bradley Ireland & Annie McHugh Ireland
BRADLEY, Cora Lettetia, Nov 18 1909 Sex:F Child# 16 William J Bradley Newport Center, VT & Cora B Reed Nashua, NH
BRADLEY, Elizabeth, Jan 5 1919 Sex:F Child# 1 Frederick A Bradley Nashua, NH & Elizabeth Sullivan Nashua, NH
BRADLEY, Evelyn M, Aug 18 1914 Sex:F Child# 1 Chester W Bradley Nashua, NH & Elva Richards Le Havre, NS
BRADLEY, Frederick William, Apr 18 1917 Sex:M Child# 2 Richard L Bradley Nashua, NH & Tressor A Dean Groton, VT
BRADLEY, Gladys Elaine, Jul 16 1935 Sex:F Child# 3 Maurice Bradley Nashua, NH & Dora McLellan Fitchburg, MA
BRADLEY, Grace Anita, Nov 4 1918 Sex:F Child# 2 Ralph Bradley Nashua, NH & Grace Esther Rock Nashua, NH
BRADLEY, Hannah Agnes, Nov 20 1892 Sex:F Child# 4 Cornelius Bradley Ireland & Annie Hughes Ireland
BRADLEY, Hazel D, Apr 21 1892 Sex:F Child# 1 Allan F Bradley NY & Clara E Denison Maine
BRADLEY, Helen, Sep 11 1899 Sex:F Child# Allen F Bradley NY & Clara E Dewmerson Maine
BRADLEY, Henry Francis, Aug 7 1910 Sex:M Child# 2 Frank Bradley Virginia & Mary Haley Mass
BRADLEY, Jessie, Oct 21 1893 Sex:F Child# 4 William Bradley Newport, VT & Cora B Reed Nashua, NH
BRADLEY, Laura Emma, Jul 31 1897 Sex:F Child# 4 Allen Bradley
BRADLEY, Muriel Eunice, Mar 30 1923 Sex:F Child# 3 Christy S Bradley Nashua, NH & Elva Mae Richards Nova Scotia
BRADLEY, Richard L, Sep 5 1915 Sex:M Child# 1 Richard L Bradley Nashua, NH & Lessar Dean Groton, VT
BRADLEY, Ruth Anna, Aug 3 1903 Sex:F Child# 7 Cornelius Bradley Ireland & Anna McCue Ireland
BRADLEY, Ruth Marion, May 13 1906 Sex:F Child# 13 William J Bradley Newport Centre, VT & Cora B Reed Nashua, NH
BRADLEY, Theresa, Jun 10 1897 Sex:F Child# 5 Cornelius Bradley Ireland & Hannorah McKeon Ireland
BRADLEY, Unknown, May 20 1887 Sex:F Child# 1 Cornelius Bradley Ireland & Hannah Ireland
BRADLEY, Unknown, Dec 8 1888 Sex:F Child# 3 W C Bradley Lowell & Alice B Bradley Worcester, MA
BRADLEY, Unknown, Oct 27 1889 Sex:M Child# 1 William Bradley Newport, VT & Cora B Reed Nashua, NH
BRADLEY, Unknown, Nov 7 1890 Sex:M Child# 2 W J Bradley VT & C B Reed Nashua, NH
BRADLEY, Unknown, Feb 4 1895 Sex:M Child# 5 William J Bradley Newport, VT & Cora B Reed Nashua, NH
BRADLEY, Unknown, Jul 13 1895 Sex:M Child# 3 A H Bradley New York & Clara E Dennison Cutler, ME
BRADLEY, Unknown, Jul 10 1899 Sex:M Child# 8 William J Bradley Vermont & Cora B Reed Nashua, NH
BRADLEY, Unknown, Feb 4 1901 Sex:F Child# 9 William J Bradley Newport Ctr, VT & Cora B Reed Nashua, NH
BRADLEY, Unknown, Apr 11 1905 Sex:M Child# 13 William J Bradley Newport Ctr, VT & Cora B Reid Nashua, NH
BRADLEY, William J Jr, Aug 22 1897 Sex:M Child# 6 William J Bradley Newport Center, VT & Cora B Reed Nashua, NH
BRADLEY, William James, May 19 1934 Sex:M Child# 2 Maurice A Bradley Nashua, NH & Dora McLellan Fitchburg, MA
BRADY, Albert Shirley, Jr, Sep 29 1930 Sex:M Child# 1 Albert S Brady Lynn, MA & Theresa M O'Neil Taunton, MA
BRADY, Anna May, Apr 29 1912 Sex:F Child# 1 Thomas F Brady Nashua, NH & Ellen Shea Nashua, NH
BRADY, Catherine, Nov 11 1895 Sex:F Child# 5 John Brady Fall River, MA & Bridget Mulligan Ireland

BRADY, Janet Theresa, Jun 17 1932 Sex:F Child# 2 Albert S Brady Lynn, MA & Theresa O'Neil Taunton, MA
BRADY, John, Dec 8 1898 Sex:M Child# 6 John Brady Fall River, MA & Bridget Mulligan Ireland
BRADY, Mary Ellen, Feb 3 1892 Sex:F Child# 4 John Brady Fall River, MA & Bridget Mulligan Ireland
BRADY, Unknown, Jul 11 1895 Sex:F Child# 1 Michael Brady Ireland & Sarah McManus Nashua, NH
BRADY, William, Aug 16 1889 Sex:M Child# 3 John Brady Fall River, MA & Bridget Williams Ireland
BRAHANEY, John Edward, Nov 26 1926 Sex:M Child#  J H Brahaney Nashua, NH & Mary A Cadorette Nashua, NH
BRAHANEY, Leonard Harvey, Jun 9 1931 Sex:M Child# 2 James Brahaney Milford, NH & Alma Cote Nashua, NH
BRANDENBERG, Herman August, Dec 20 1926 Sex:M Child# 1 I Brandenberg Hartford, CT & Lillian Moir New York, NY
BRANDLEY, Elinor Winifred, Jun 5 1913 Sex:F Child# 18 William J Brandley Newport Centre, VT & Cora Reed Nashua, NH
BRANIGAN, John, Jr, Dec 13 1935 Sex:M Child# 1 John Branigan US & Lucienne Deneault Nashua, NH
BRANN, Florence Mary, Aug 26 1914 Sex:F Child# 1 Charles P Brann Galveston, TX & Eva M Brooks Newport, England
BRANSTROM, Shirley, Aug 22 1911 Sex:F Child# 1 Gustav Branstrom Sweden & Augusta Johnson Sweden
BRATHROW, Unknown, Feb 13 1912 Sex:M Child# 5 Arthue E Brathrow Vermont & Mary Agnes Dowling Nashua, NH
BRAULT, Achille Robert, Oct 21 1923 Sex:M Child# 5 Paul Brault Canada & Bernadette Ouillette Canada
BRAULT, Donald Edwin, Nov 17 1927 Sex:M Child# 2 Arthur Brault Quincy, MA & Anna Louiselle Newport, NH
BRAULT, Donald Joseph, Apr 7 1932 Sex:M Child# 6 Hector Brault Stanbridge, PQ & Blanche Boucher St Hyacinthe, PQ
BRAULT, Irene, Oct 26 1919 Sex:F Child# 1 George Brault Nashua, NH & Angeline Bernard Canada
BRAULT, Joseph Henry Hector, Jun 17 1924 Sex:M Child# 3 Hector Brault Canada & Blanche Boucher Canada
BRAULT, Joseph L Georges, Jan 7 1895 Sex:M Child# 1 Silas Brault Plattsburg, NY & Zenobie Cadaret Nashua, NH
BRAULT, Marie A A, Dec 17 1896 Sex:F Child# 2 Xilas Brault Plattsburg, NY & Zenobie Cadoret Nashua, NH
BRAULT, Marie T Marguerite, Nov 29 1926 Sex:F Child# 4 Hector Brault Canada & Blanche Boucher Canada
BRAULT, Marie Theresa G, Dec 13 1928 Sex:F Child# 5 Hector Brault Canada & Blanche Boucher Canada
BRAULT, Peter, Jun 5 1892 Sex:M Child# 1 Peter Brault Canada & Phoebe Canada
BRAWIN, Celina Mary, Feb 16 1889 Sex:F Child# 5 James Brawin Underhill, VT & Annie Temple Ireland
BRAWN, Dorothy Lucile, Apr 9 1916 Sex:F Child# 2 Charls P Brawn Galveston, TX & Eva M Brooks England
BRAZAS, Jadwiga, May 8 1911 Sex:M Child# 7 Casimir Brazas Russia & Helen Teusate Russia
BREAUD, Adele, Oct 15 1888 Sex:F Child# 2 Charles Pont Breaud Nashua, NH & Josephine Phaneuf Champlain, NY
BREAULT, Claire Constance, Aug 6 1933 Sex:F Child# 7 Hector Breault Canada & Blanche Boucher Canada
BREAULT, Clorina, Jun 11 1890 Sex:F Child# 2 Joseph Breault Canada & Clara Garnanlt Canada
BREAULT, Marie A M, Aug 6 1902 Sex:F Child# 5 Celas Breault Plattsburg, NY & Zembee Cadorette Nashua, NH
BREAULT, Marie C L, Feb 16 1899 Sex:F Child# 3 Cilas Breault Plattsburgh, NY & Zenolie Cadoret Nashua, NH
BREAULT, Mary R, Jul 7 1887 Sex:F Child# 1 Charles Breault Canada & Mary A Butler Ireland
BREDEAU, Kenneth Earle, Jun 4 1924 Sex:M Child# 1 Eli Bredeau Canada & Gertrude Guill Worcester, MA
BREDEAU, Robert Paul, Jun 28 1926 Sex:M Child# 2 Eli Bredeau Canada & Gertrude Guill Worcester, MA
BREDIS, Albinas, Dec 30 1919 Sex:M Child# 1 William Bredis Russia & Barbara Monius Russia
BREDIS, Ersulia, Apr 4 1921 Sex:F Child# 2 William Bredis Russia & Barbara Morris Russia
BREEN, Agnes May, Jan 29 1892 Sex:F Child# 8 Daniel Breen Ireland & Margaret Nash Ireland
BREEN, Evelyn Agnes, Aug 26 1897 Sex:F Child# 2 Jeremiah Breen Ireland & Bridget Nash Ireland
BREEN, Evelyn Agnes, Jan 4 1922 Sex:F Child# 1 John Michael Breen Nashua, NH & Lillian Trufant Hudson, NH
BREEN, Irene, Mar 3 1897 Sex:F Child# 10 Daniel Breen Ireland & Margaret Nash Ireland
BREEN, John Michael, May 8 1899 Sex:M Child# 3 Andrew Breen Ireland & Bridget Nash Ireland
BREEN, John Michael, Sep 13 1926 Sex:M Child# 2 John M Breen Nashua, NH & Lillian Trufant Hudson, NH
BREEN, Michael, Nov 24 1893 Sex:M Child# 9 Daniel D Breen Ireland & Margaret Nash Ireland
BREEN, Nellie, Jul 6 1890 Sex:F Child# 9 Daniel D Breen Ireland & Margaret Nash Ireland
BRELINSKI, Stevens, Aug 9 1915 Sex:M Child# 1 Stan Brelinski Russia & Eva Marskinuta Russia
BREMNER, Frederic M, Dec 25 1931 Sex:M Child# 1 Frederic M Bremner Boston, MA & Grace M Branchaud Manchester, NH
BRENNAN, Abbie, Aug 6 1893 Sex:F Child# 3 John Brennan Ireland & Kate Nash Ireland
BRENNAN, David Allan, May 31 1930 Sex:M Child# 10 Michael F Brennan Ireland & Annie Currier Burlington, VT
BRENNAN, Donald Robert, Dec 23 1925 Sex:M Child# 8 Michael Brennan Ireland & Annie Currier Ireland
BRENNAN, Elizabeth Jane, Jun 7 1923 Sex:F Child# 6 Michael F Brennan Ireland & Annie Currier Burlington, VT
BRENNAN, Ellen, Aug 6 1893 Sex:F Child# 2 John Brennan Ireland & Kate Nash Ireland
BRENNAN, Mary O S, Mar 30 1910 Sex:F Child# 1 Michael Brennan Ireland & Annie Currier Burlington, VT
BRENNAN, Michael, Aug 17 1888 Sex:M Child# 5 Michael Brennan Ireland & Elizabeth Clifford Ireland
BRENNAN, Paul C, Mar 21 1911 Sex:M Child# 2 Michael F Brennan Ireland & Annie M Currier Burlington, VT
BRENNAN, Ralph, Feb 4 1921 Sex:M Child# 6 Michael Brennan Ireland & Annie Carrier Fremont, NH
BRENNAN, Raymond, Aug 23 1916 Sex:M Child# 4 Michael F Brennan Nashua, NH & Annie Currier Burlington, VT
BRENNAN, Richard John, Oct 14 1927 Sex:M Child# 9 Michael Brennan Ireland & Annie Currier Burlington, VT
BRENNAN, Unknown, Jul 26 1913 Sex:M Child# 3 Michael F Brennan Ireland & Annie Currier Burlington, VT Stillborn
BRENNEN, Dorothy, Dec 1 1918 Sex:F Child# 4 Michael F Brennen Ireland & Annie Currier Burlington, VT
BRESHNENAN, Thomas Ryan, Dec 8 1889 Sex:M Child# 4 T Breshnenan Ireland & Mary Smith Ireland
BRESNAHAN, Annie May, Jul 13 1892 Sex:F Child# 2 George M Bresnahan Manchester & Rose Bignall Nashua, NH
BRESNAHAN, Barbara Anne, Mar 18 1934 Sex:F Child# 1 Edard C Bresnahan Goffstown, NH & Viola Schofield Nashua, NH
BRESNAHAN, Dolores Dorothy, Oct 10 1930 Sex:F Child# 2 John Bresnahan N Adams, MA & Josephine Zedalis Nashua, NH
BRESNAHAN, Patrick E, Nov 6 1912 Sex:M Child# 1 Patrick J Bresnahan Texas & Abeline Poulin Nashua, NH
BRESNAHAN, Sylvia Muriel, Oct 19 1935 Sex:F Child# 2 Edw C Bresnahan Grasmere, NH & Viola L Schofield Nashua, NH
BRESNAHAN, Unknown, Sep 12 1889 Sex:M Child# 1 George M Bresnahan Manchester, NH & Rose E Bignal Nashua, NH
BRESNAHAN, Unknown, Aug 17 1905 Sex:M Child# 3 George M Bresnahan Manchester, NH & Rose E Bresnahan Nashua, NH
BRESNAN, Rose Vera, Aug 17 1915 Sex:F Child# 3 Patrick J Bresnan Dallas, TX & Obeline Poulin Nashua, NH
BRESSETTE, Mabel Irene, Aug 13 1909 Sex:F Child# 2 Perley E Bressette Plattsburgh, NY & Wilhelmina Barber NY
BREW, Jacqueline Claire, Apr 27 1932 Sex:F Child# 1 Winslow Brew Pepperell, MA & Dorothy Parker Pepperell, MA
BREW, Richard Joseph, Dec 28 1932 Sex:M Child# 1 B Brew Hollis, NH & Doris Butterfield Derry, NH
BREWEN, James Philip, Jun 9 1919 Sex:M Child# 1 Peter Brewen Ireland & Ellen V Winn Nashua, NH
BREWER, Albert James, Jul 20 1894 Sex:M Child# 3 Albert H Brewer England & Celia E Swift

BREWER, Celia A, Feb 14 1903 Sex:F Child#  Albert H Brewer England & Delia Swift Buffalo, NY
BREWER, Dorothy Ellen, Oct 11 1921 Sex:F Child# 1 Albert J Brewer Nashua, NH & Mary Rose Morris Nashua, NH
BREWER, Edwin Maurice, Feb 17 1928 Sex:M Child# 4 Albert J Brewer Nashua, NH & Rose Moran Nashua, NH
BREWER, Harold Albert, Apr 6 1914 Sex:M Child# 1 Charles H Brewer Nashua, NH & Georgiana Laflamme Canada
BREWER, Joseph Albert, Sep 1 1922 Sex:M Child# 2 Albert J Brewer Nashua, NH & Mary Rose Morris Nashua, NH
BREWER, Joseph Arthur, Mar 1 1897 Sex:M Child# 5 Albert H Brewer England & Celia E Moriarty Buffalo, NY
BREWER, Mary E, May 11 1892 Sex:F Child# 3 Albert H Brewer England & Celia E Moriarty Buffalo, NY
BREWER, Robert Alfred, Mar 26 1924 Sex:M Child# 3 Albert Brewer Nashua, NH & Rose Morris Nashua, NH
BREWER, Unknown, Jun 8 1888 Sex:M Child# 2 Albert H Brewer England & Salina Morraity Buffalo, NY
BRIAND, Anna, Jul 20 1931 Sex:F Child# 4 Victor Briand Nashua, NH & Delia Nault Nashua, NH
BRIAND, Auguste Louis, Feb 20 1929 Sex:M Child# 8 Auguste Briand Canada & Leonie Pelletier Canada
BRIAND, Eddy Thomas, Oct 19 1932 Sex:M Child# 5 Victor Briand Nashua, NH & Delia Nault Nashua, NH
BRIAND, Ernest Roland, Jul 6 1935 Sex:M Child# 6 Victor Briand Nashua, NH & Delia Nault Nashua, NH
BRIAND, George, May 25 1890 Sex:M Child# 1 Simeon Cout Briand Canada & Mary Jolin Canada
BRIAND, George, Jan 2 1927 Sex:M Child# 1 Victor Briand Nashua, NH & Delia Nault Nashua, NH
BRIAND, Jeannette, Aug 22 1918 Sex:F Child# 2 Auguste Briand Canada & Leonie Pelletier Canada
BRIAND, Leo Edouard, Nov 20 1932 Sex:M Child# 9 Auguste Briand Canada & Leonie Pelletier Canada
BRIAND, Luc Romeo, Jan 13 1920 Sex:M Child# 1 Luc Briand Canada & Marie A Levesque Canada
BRIAND, Marie Irene Doris, Oct 29 1927 Sex:F Child# 6 Etienne Briand Canada & L Savoie Canada
BRIAND, Napoleon Edmond, Oct 11 1923 Sex:M Child# 2 Luck Briand Canada & Marie Anna Levesque Canada
BRIAND, Paul Emile, Sep 30 1930 Sex:M Child# 3 Luc Briand Canada & Marie A Levesque Canada
BRIAND, Rita Fernande, Oct 11 1919 Sex:F Child# 2 Auguste Briand Canada & Leonie Pelletier Canada
BRIAND, Rita Naomi, Jul 15 1928 Sex:F Child# 2 Victor Briand Nashua, NH & Delia Nault Nashua, NH
BRIAND, Ursula, Mar 6 1927 Sex:F Child# 8 Auguste Briand Canada & Leonie Pelletier Canada
BRIAND, Victor, Nov 27 1908 Sex:M Child# 6 George Briand Canada & Clara Chamberlain Canada
BRIANT, Alphonse Leo, Aug 3 1919 Sex:M Child# 3 Etienne Briant Canada & Lodowiska Savoie Canada
BRICAULT, Jean Bte A H, Apr 11 1891 Sex:M Child# 4 Jean Bte Bricault Canada & Rosa Brin Canada
BRICKEY, Doria Viola, Nov 29 1914 Sex:F Child# 2 Leonard E Brickey New York & Ethel A Menter Nashua, NH
BRICKEY, Harold Frank, Oct 9 1916 Sex:M Child# 3 Leonard E Brickey Nashua, NH & Ethel May Mentor Nashua, NH
BRICKEY, Leonard E, Mar 30 1913 Sex:M Child# 1 Leonard E Brickey Plattsburg, NY & Ethel Menter Nashua, NH
BRICKEY, Merton Raymond, Mar 14 1919 Sex:M Child# 4 Leonard C Brickey Ellenburg, NY & Ethel Menter Nashua, NH
BRICKEY, Mildred Evelyn, Aug 3 1925 Sex:F Child# 7 Leonard Brickey Ellenburg, NY & Ethel Menter Nashua, NH
BRICKEY, Norma Loraine, Apr 5 1923 Sex:F Child# 6 Leonard E Brickey Ellenburg, NY & Ethel M Menter Nashua, NH
BRICKEY, Richard Leo, Nov 3 1927 Sex:M Child# 8 Leonard Brickey Ellenburg, NY & Ethel Menter Nashua, NH
BRICKEY, Robert Henry, Jun 24 1921 Sex:M Child# 5 Leonard Brickey Ellenburg, NY & Ethel Menter Nashua, NH
BRICOULT, Marie Theresa, Jan 30 1929 Sex:F Child# 1 Francis Bricoult Manchester, NH & Adelle Archambault Canada
BRIE, Marie Jeanette, May 29 1920 Sex:F Child# 2 Joseph A Brie Nashua, NH & Anna Levesque Nashua, NH
BRIE, Mary Vivian Alma, Dec 20 1918 Sex:F Child# 1 Joseph Arthur Brie Nashua, NH & Anna M Levesque Nashua, NH
BRIEAULT, Marion F Estelle, Jun 8 1931 Sex:F Child# 2 Francis Brieault Manchester, NH & Adele Champeaux Canada
BRIEN, Annie Louise, Jul 20 1912 Sex:F Child# 7 George Brien Canada & Clara Chamberlain Canada
BRIEN, Arthur A, Oct 16 1898 Sex:M Child# 5 Emile Brien Canada & Armida Chagnon Canada
BRIEN, Athaline, Jan 22 1900 Sex:F Child# 2 Edw L Brien Mass & Delia F Whittle NH
BRIEN, Celina Rosanna, May 17 1908 Sex:F Child# 3 Ernest Brien Canada & Marie Parent Canada
BRIEN, Frank G, Aug 4 1900 Sex:M Child#  G G Brien
BRIEN, George, Dec 10 1904 Sex:M Child# 4 Georges Brien Canada & Clara Chamberlain Canada
BRIEN, George Edward, Apr 28 1905 Sex:F Child# 3 Edward L Brien Dalton, MA & Delia F Whittle Nashua, NH
BRIEN, Helene Irene, Jan 11 1911 Sex:F Child# 5 Ernest Brien Canada & Marie Parent Canada
BRIEN, Horace, Apr 29 1905 Sex:M Child# 1 Ernest Brien Canada & Marie Parent Canada
BRIEN, Joseph A, Feb 26 1892 Sex:M Child# 1 Emile Brien Canada & Harmida Chagnon Canada
BRIEN, Leon, Dec 16 1906 Sex:M Child# 5 George Brien Canada & Clara Chamberland Canada
BRIEN, Lucile Blanche, Feb 6 1897 Sex:F Child# 1 Edward L Brien Dalton, MA & Della F Whittle Nashua, NH
BRIEN, Marie Alice, Feb 2 1897 Sex:F Child# 2 Joseph Brien Canada & Mary Cousin Canada
BRIEN, Marie B M, Oct 26 1895 Sex:F Child# 3 Emile Brien Canada & Armida Chagnon Canada
BRIEN, Marie I I, May 28 1894 Sex:F Child# 2 Emile Brien Canada & Armidas Chagnon Canada
BRIEN, Marie R, Mar 4 1897 Sex:F Child# 4 Emile Brien Canada & Armida Chagnon Canada
BRIEN, Marie Yvonne M, Mar 24 1904 Sex:F Child# 10 Alexis Brien Canada & Marie J Bernier Canada
BRIEN, Unknown, Jun 27 1896 Sex:F Child# 1 Andrew J Brien Ireland & Bridget Nash Ireland Stillborn
BRIER, Pierre, Apr 1 1890 Sex:M Child# 1 Pierre Brier Canada & Celina Bouchard Canada
BRIERE, Alfred, Feb 18 1893 Sex:M Child# 8 Joseph Briere Canada & Lucie Hebert Canada
BRIERE, Joseph, Jul 18 1895 Sex:M Child# 9 Joseph Briere Canada & Lucie Hebert Canada
BRIERE, Joseph, Dec 26 1913 Sex:M Child# 6 Philias Briere Canada & Rosanna Willette Canada
BRIERE, Joseph Leo Paul, Sep 2 1928 Sex:M Child# 5 Archile Briere Canada & Eva Robert Lowell, MA
BRIERE, Marie Blanche Theresa, Mar 22 1934 Sex:F Child# 6 (No Parents Listed)
BRIERE, Marie Catherine, Jun 18 1901 Sex:F Child# 13 Joseph Briere NY & Lucie Hebert Canada
BRIGANDI, Jennie, Apr 18 1897 Sex:F Child# 2 John Brigandi Italy & Gaetana Reitane Italy
BRIGGS, Birley, Jr, Dec 19 1935 Sex:M Child# 4 Birley Briggs Carthage, AR & Delilah Esque Rockport, IL Colored
BRIGGS, Edward Burton, May 14 1935 Sex:m Child# 1 Nor E Briggs Reading, MA & Ruth L Parks Geneva, NY
BRIGGS, Mary Bamford, Dec 6 1919 Sex:F Child# 4 James Briggs Springvale, ME & Isabella Wilson Philadelphia, PA
BRIGGS, Vera, May 14 1930 Sex:F Child# 1 Berley Briggs Arkansas & Delilah Esque Illinois Colored
BRIGGS, Vergean, Jan 11 1934 Sex:F Child# 3 Birley Briggs Arkansas & Delilah B M Esque Illinois Colored
BRIGGS, Vivian, May 29 1932 Sex:F Child# 2 Birley Briggs Arkansas & Delilah Esque Brookport, Del Colored
BRIGHAM, George Winfield, Jun 10 1922 Sex:M Child# 6 Louis Brigham New Ipswich, NH & Lydia A Andrews Georgetown
BRIGHAM, Harry Bartelemy, Oct 8 1919 Sex:M Child# 5 Joseph L Brigham New Ipswich & Lydia A Andrews Georgetown

BRIGHAM, Lewis Lazare, Aug 12 1924 Sex:M Child# 6 Louis B Brigham New Ipswich, NH & Lillian Andrews Rowley, MA
BRIGHAM, Mary, May 28 1898 Sex:F Child# 2 Samuel Brigham Lawrence, MA & Mary Glynn Nashua, NH
BRIGHAM, Mary Elizabeth, Jan 8 1898 Sex:F Child# 5 George H Brigham Nashua, NH & Sarah M Medford, MA
BRIGHAM, Unknown, Mar 14 1887 Sex:F Child# 3 George H Brigham Nashua, NH & Sarah M Peasley Milford, MA
BRIGHAM, Unknown, Jul 31 1895 Sex:F Child# 5 George H Brigham Nashua, NH & Sarah M Medford, MA
BRIN, Claire Gloria, Jun 19 1934 Sex:F Child# 1 Leo Brin Lowell, MA & Albina Fortin Nashua, NH
BRIN, Joseph, Feb 19 1889 Sex:M Child# 3 Antoine Brin Canada & Matilda Sieur Canada
BRIN, Joseph F Henri, Sep 22 1899 Sex:M Child# 5 Anselme Brin Canada & Elmina Brisebois Canada
BRIS, Antoine, Jan 28 1891 Sex:M Child# 5 Antoine Bris Canada & Matilda Lesieur Canada
BRIS, Joseph Arthur, Jan 10 1891 Sex:M Child# 1 Arthur Bris Canada & Candalie Gauthier Canada
BRISBOIS, Arthur, Sep 30 1894 Sex:M Child# 3 Alex Brisbois Canada & Cordelia Ricard Canada
BRISEBOIS, Adrien, Oct 10 1898 Sex:m Child# 5 Alexandre Brisebois Canada & Cordelia Ricard Canada
BRISEBOIS, Alphege Armand, May 1 1903 Sex:M Child# 1 Alfred Brisebois Canada & Armida Duclos Canada
BRISEBOIS, Alphonse D, Sep 11 1905 Sex:M Child# 2 Alfred Brisebois Canada & Almida Duclos Canada
BRISEBOIS, Coelia, Sep 24 1891 Sex:f Child# 2 Alex Brisebois Canada & Cordelia Ricard Canada
BRISEBOIS, Elphege, Mar 17 1908 Sex:M Child# 3 Alfred Brisebois Canada & Armeda Duclos Canada
BRISEBOIS, J Paul Rene, Aug 2 1913 Sex:M Child# 4 Frederick Brisebois NH & Rosalie Rioux Canada
BRISEBOIS, Joseph Henri T, Apr 27 1904 Sex:M Child# 1 Joseph Brisebois Canada & Marie E Hudon Canada
BRISEBOIS, Lucille Jane, Nov 2 1934 Sex:F Child# 1 Paul Brisebois Nashua, NH & Irene Courtemanche Nashua, NH
BRISEBOIS, Marie Lea, Sep 21 1916 Sex:F Child# 5 Frederic Brisebois NH & Rosalie Rioux Canada
BRISEBOIS, Pauline Juliette, Oct 1 1935 Sex:F Child# 2 Paul Brisebois Nashua, NH & L Courtemanche Nashua, NH
BRISEBOIS, Raoul L, Jul 12 1896 Sex:M Child# 4 Alexander Brisebois Canada & Cordelia Ricard Nashua, NH
BRISSON, Delphis, Dec 11 1899 Sex:M Child# 5 Alexis Brisson Canada & Marie Lacombe Canada
BRISSON, Joseph, Sep 30 1898 Sex:M Child# 4 Alexis Brisson Canada & Marie Lacombe Canada
BRISSON, Joseph E, Sep 14 1896 Sex:M Child# 2 Alexis Brisson Canada & Marie Lacombe Canada
BRISSON, Marie A, Oct 24 1894 Sex:F Child# 1 Alexis Brisson Canada & Marie Lacombe Canada
BRISSON, Marie A C, Feb 10 1902 Sex:F Child# 6 Alexis Brisson Canada & Marie Lacombe Canada
BRISSON, Marie R, Sep 16 1897 Sex:F Child# 3 Alexis Brisson Canada & Marie Lacombe Canada
BRISSON, Norma Elizabeth, Dec 11 1923 Sex:F Child# 2 Joseph Brisson Nashua, NH & Elizabeth Hopkins Lowell, MA
BRISSON, Paul Raymond, Aug 16 1922 Sex:M Child# 1 Joseph Brisson Nashua, NH & Elizabeth Hopkins Lowell, MA
BRISSON, Roland Francis, Mar 1 1927 Sex:M Child# 3 Francis Brisson Haverhill, MA & Helen McPartland Nashua, NH
BRISSON, Roy, Nov 30 1926 Sex:M Child# 2 Joseph Brisson Nashua, NH & Elizabeth Hopkins Lowell, MA
BRISSON, Unknown, Jun 7 1924 Sex:F Child# 1 Frank Brisson Haverhill, MA & Helen McPartland Nashua, NH Stillborn
BRISSON, Unknown, Oct 10 1925 Sex:M Child# 2 Frank Brisson Haverhill & Helen McPartland Nashua, NH
BRISSON, Virginia Mary, May 31 1931 Sex:F Child# 4 Francis N Brisson Haverhill, MA & Helen McPartlan Nashua, NH
BRISSONNEAULT, J Ernest Gerard, Sep 2 1921 Sex:M Child# 8 Luc Brissonneault Canada & Ernestine Lafrance Canada
BRITON, Mildred Caroline, Feb 20 1909 Sex:F Child# 1 Joseph A Briton Hollis, NH & Augusta Campbell Riverside
BRITTON, Rose Jeanette, Mar 22 1895 Sex:F Child# 2 William H Britton Ireland & Ella Watkins Reeds Ferry, NH
BROADBRIDGE, Lester Leonard, May 1 1911 Sex:M Child# 2 William Broadbridge Canada & Lena Lapham Vermont
BROADBRIDGE, Marie Blanche, Mar 4 1908 Sex:F Child# 1 William Broadbridge Canada & Len Lapan Vermont
BROCHU, Joseph, Jul 26 1935 Sex:M Child# 6 Ovila Brochu Canada & Simone Bergeron Canada
BROCK, Jane Alberte, Aug 4 1889 Sex:F Child# 7 Martin J Brock Germany & G Kellerman Philadelphia, PA
BROCK, Unknown, Jun 19 1896 Sex:F Child# 1 Karl O Brock Lynn, MA & Lillian Pinkham Farmington Stillborn
BROCKI, Wladystaw, Jul 28 1897 Sex:M Child# 3 Joseph Brocki Russia & Iva Plocharczk Russia
BRODERICK, Edward F, May 14 1910 Sex:M Child# 6 Thomas F Broderick Amherst, NH & Flora A Sinclair Lancaster, MA
BRODERICK, John William, Jan 1 1900 Sex:M Child# 2 John W Broderick Nashua, NH & Sadie McBride Nashua, NH
BRODERICK, John William, Apr 22 1923 Sex:M Child# 1 J W Broderick, Jr Nashua, NH & Alice J Fitzpatrick Waltham, MA
BRODERICK, Katherine, Jul 13 1906 Sex:F Child# 4 John W Broderick Nashua, NH & Sadie A McBride Nashua, NH
BRODERICK, Lucile, Nov 12 1912 Sex:F Child# 6 John W Broderick Nashua, NH & Sarah McBride Nashua, NH
BRODERICK, Margaret, Jan 8 1895 Sex:F Child# 1 John J Broderick Ireland & Mary Wilmot Ireland
BRODERICK, Margaret, Aug 20 1909 Sex:F Child# 5 John W Broderick Nashua, NH & Sarah McBride Nashua, NH
BRODERICK, Marjorie Elizabeth, Mar 7 1923 Sex:F Child# 3 Frank M Broderick Mass & Elizabeth Aryell New York
BRODERICK, Unknown, Apr 14 1898 Sex:F Child#   John W Broderick Nashua, NH & Sadie A McBride Nashua, NH
BRODEUR, Adelard Robert, Apr 17 1925 Sex:M Child# 2 Albert Brodeur Nashua, NH & Florida Tremblay Nashua, NH
BRODEUR, Albert Leonard, Mar 28 1927 Sex:M Child# 2 Lionel Brodeur Canada & Marie Gaudreau Nashua, NH
BRODEUR, Alfred, May 27 1889 Sex:M Child# 6 Caliste Brodeur Canada & Clarisse Lachapelle Canada
BRODEUR, Alfred, May 31 1923 Sex:M Child# 4 Alfred Brodeur Canada & Grace Garety Nashua, NH
BRODEUR, Alice Henrietta, Oct 21 1900 Sex:F Child# 12 Calixte Brodeur Canada & E Lachapel Canada
BRODEUR, Annette, Sep 3 1934 Sex:F Child# 3 Hormidas Brodeur Canada & Bertha Duval Nashua, NH
BRODEUR, Armand Joseph, Mar 8 1927 Sex:M Child# 1 Hubert Brodeur Canada & Lillian Jean Nashua, NH
BRODEUR, Bertha Gabrielle, Jun 2 1929 Sex:F Child# 3 Arthur Brodeur Nashua, NH & Isabelle Martel Nashua, NH
BRODEUR, Berthe Lucienne, Feb 14 1904 Sex:F Child# 13 Calixte Brodeur Canada & E Lachapelle Canada
BRODEUR, Charles Mathias, Jan 14 1899 Sex:M Child# 3 Charles Brodeur Canada & Marie Louise Poulin Canada
BRODEUR, Claire Alma, Jun 7 1933 Sex:F Child# 5 Albert Brodeur Nashua, NH & Florida Tremblay Nashua, NH
BRODEUR, Clare Louise, Jul 14 1927 Sex:F Child# 3 Hormidas Brodeur Canada & Bertha Duval Milford, NH
BRODEUR, Cyrille Henri, Oct 23 1902 Sex:M Child# 3 Cyrille Brodeur Canada & Emma Poulin Canada
BRODEUR, Delvina O L, Apr 13 1910 Sex:F Child# 4 Theophile Brodeur,Jr Canada & Clarinda Lagasse Canada
BRODEUR, E Camille Irene, Dec 17 1917 Sex:F Child# 3 Emery A Brodeur Canada & Euc M Duchesneau Canada
BRODEUR, Elizabeth Flora, Feb 20 1924 Sex:F Child# 1 Albert Brodeur Nashua, NH & Florida Tremblay Nashua, NH
BRODEUR, Emma, Dec 14 1896 Sex:F Child# 3 Hubert Brodeur Canada & Rosina Hebert Canada
BRODEUR, Euchariste G, Jan 14 1901 Sex:F Child# 6 Hubert Brodeur Canada & Rosena Hebert Canada
BRODEUR, Eva Agnes, Sep 19 1892 Sex:F Child# 8 Caliste Brodeur Canada & Euch'este Lachapelle Canada
BRODEUR, Georgette, Aug 3 1924 Sex:F Child# 5 Alfred Brodeur Nashua, NH & Grace Garicky Nashua, NH

BRODEUR, Gerard Alfred Louis, Jun 22 1915 Sex:M Child# 1 Alfred Brodeur Nashua, NH & Gracieuse Gariepy Nashua, NH
BRODEUR, Gerard Roger, Feb 9 1929 Sex:M Child# 2 Hubert Brodeur Canada & Lillian Jean Nashua, NH
BRODEUR, Gloria Constance, Mar 26 1926 Sex:F Child# 1 Henry Brodeur Nashua, NH & Rebecca Ravenelle Nashua, NH
BRODEUR, Gloria Noreen, Feb 9 1930 Sex:F Child# 4 Hormidas Brodeur Canada & Bertha Duval NH
BRODEUR, Helene B, Aug 4 1897 Sex:F Child# 3 Henri Brodeur Canada & Elizabeth Bariteau Nashua, NH
BRODEUR, Henri Alfred, Jan 12 1901 Sex:M Child# 4 Charles Brodeur Canada & Marie Louise Poulin Canada
BRODEUR, Henriette Giselle, Feb 19 1924 Sex:F Child# 1 Arthur Brodeur Nashua, NH & Isabelle Martel Nashua, NH
BRODEUR, Henriette Yvonne, Mar 9 1929 Sex:F Child# 3 Henry Brodeur Nashua, NH & Rebecca Ravenelle Nashua, NH
BRODEUR, Irene Lillian, Jan 6 1935 Sex:F Child# 6 Albert Brodeur Nashua, NH & Florida Tremblay Nashua, NH
BRODEUR, Jame Eugenie, Mar 26 1894 Sex:F Child# 9 Caliste Brodeur Canada & Euchariste Harpin Canada
BRODEUR, Jean Bte George, Jan 15 1903 Sex:M Child# 12 Hubert Brodeur Canada & Rosina Hebert Canada
BRODEUR, Jean Paul Robert, Apr 27 1923 Sex:M Child# 6 Charles Brodeur Nashua, NH & Bernadette Duchesnea Canada
BRODEUR, Jeanne d'Arc Lucille, Dec 6 1931 Sex:F Child# 4 Lionel Brodeur Canada & Marie Goudreau Canada
BRODEUR, Jeannette Olive, Nov 18 1919 Sex:F Child# 6 C H Brodeur Nashua, NH & Bernadette Duchesnea Canada
BRODEUR, Joseph, Apr 29 1893 Sex:M Child# 1 (No Parents Listed)
BRODEUR, Joseph, Jul 19 1904 Sex:M Child# 8 Herbert Brodeur Canada & Rosina Hebert Canada
BRODEUR, Joseph, May 28 1905 Sex:M Child# 8 Hubert Brodeur Canada & Rosina Hebert Canada Stillborn
BRODEUR, Joseph, Aug 8 1905 Sex:M Child# 14 Calixte Brodeur Canada & E Lachapelle Canada
BRODEUR, Joseph Albert, Feb 24 1912 Sex:M Child# 7 Ladislas Brodeur Canada & Corinne Drainville Canada
BRODEUR, Joseph D A, Jan 5 1895 Sex:M Child# 2 Henri Brodeur Canada & Elizabeth Bariteau Nashua, NH
BRODEUR, Joseph E A H, Sep 27 1896 Sex:M Child# 10 Calixte Brodeur Canada & Euchariste Lachaplle Canada
BRODEUR, Joseph Octave R, Feb 15 1907 Sex:M Child# 3 Theodore Brodeur Canada & Exilia Nadeau Canada
BRODEUR, Joseph Paul, Apr 25 1898 Sex:M Child# 1 Cyrille Brodeur Canada & Emma Poulin Canada
BRODEUR, Laurien Joseph, Sep 24 1921 Sex:M Child# 3 Alfred Brodeur Canada & Grace Garrity Nashua, NH
BRODEUR, Leandre C V, Dec 8 1908 Sex:M Child# 3 Theophile Brodeur,Jr Canada & Clorilda Lagace Canada
BRODEUR, Louis Maurice, Jul 25 1928 Sex:M Child# 3 Lionel Brodeur Canada & Maril Goudreau Nashua, NH
BRODEUR, Louise Adrienne R, Apr 30 1906 Sex:F Child# 1 Theophile Brodeur Canada & Clarinda Gregoire Canada
BRODEUR, Louise Bertha, Jul 8 1896 Sex:F Child# 1 Charles Brodeur Canada & Marie L Poulin Canada
BRODEUR, Louise E, Aug 2 1898 Sex:F Child# 4 Herbert Brodeur Canada & Roseanna Hebert Canada
BRODEUR, Louise Osilda, Dec 1 1899 Sex:F Child# 5 Herbert Brodeur Canada & Rosina Hebert Canada
BRODEUR, Lucille Denise, Feb 19 1930 Sex:F Child# 4 Albert Brodeur Nashua, NH & Florida Tromblay Nashua, NH
BRODEUR, Lucille Irene, Nov 8 1924 Sex:F Child# 2 Hormidas Brodeur Canada & Bertha Duval Milford, NH
BRODEUR, Luke Cyrille, Mar 20 1928 Sex:M Child# 2 Henry Brodeur Nashua, NH & Rebecca Ravenelle Nashua, NH
BRODEUR, M Anne Evangeline, Oct 31 1915 Sex:F Child# 2 Emery Brodeur Canada & Eucharist Duchesneau Canada
BRODEUR, M R Jeanne D'Arc, May 1 1917 Sex:F Child# 4 Charles H Brodeur Nashua, NH & Bernadette Duchesnea Canada
BRODEUR, Marie, May 3 1910 Sex:F Child# 1 Charles H Brodeur US & Bernadette Duchesnea Canada
BRODEUR, Marie Annette, Mar 11 1926 Sex:F Child# 1 Lionel Brodeur Canada & Marie Goudreau Nashua, NH
BRODEUR, Marie Antoinette, Apr 25 1905 Sex:F Child# 1 Theodore Brodeur Canada & Exilia Nadeau Canada
BRODEUR, Marie Cecile, Nov 14 1933 Sex:F Child# 5 Lionel Brodeur Canada & Marie Gaudreau Nashua, NH
BRODEUR, Marie J U, Oct 20 1909 Sex:F Child# 6 Ladisias Brodeur Canada & Corinne Derinville Lowell, MA
BRODEUR, Marie L A, Jun 22 1893 Sex:F Child# 1 Henri Brodeur Canada & Elizabeth Bariteau Nashua, NH
BRODEUR, Marie Louise E, Apr 10 1896 Sex:F Child# 3 Alderic Brodeur
BRODEUR, Marie R E, Sep 6 1897 Sex:F Child# 2 Charles Brodeur Canada & Marie L Poulin Canada
BRODEUR, Marie Yvonne, Mar 20 1910 Sex:F Child# 4 Theodore Brodeur Canada & Exelia Nadeau Canada
BRODEUR, Mary Madeline, Oct 10 1911 Sex:F Child# 2 Charles H Brodeur Nashua, NH & Bernadette Duchesnea Canada
BRODEUR, Mary Teresa, Nov 12 1912 Sex:F Child# 4 Charles Brodeur Nashua, NH & Bernadette Duchesnea Canada
BRODEUR, Muriel, Feb 24 1928 Sex:F Child# 7 Alfred Brodeur Nashua, NH & Grace Garriepy Nashua, NH
BRODEUR, Paul Arthur, Jan 14 1919 Sex:M Child# 3 Alfred Brodeur Canada & Grace Garity Nashua, NH
BRODEUR, Pauline Germaine, Sep 29 1934 Sex:F Child# 1 Leo Brodeur Canada & Gabrielle Laroche Highgate Ctr, VT
BRODEUR, Philip Ernest Jerome, Dec 17 1925 Sex:M Child# 2 Arthur Brodeur London, England & Isabelle Martil Russia
BRODEUR, Richard George, Dec 14 1921 Sex:M Child# 1 Hormidas Brodeur Canada & Bertha Duval Milford, NH
BRODEUR, Robert Henry, Apr 28 1931 Sex:M Child# 4 Henry Brodeur Nashua, NH & Rebecca Ravenelle Nashua, NH
BRODEUR, Roland Albert, Sep 19 1926 Sex:M Child# 3 Albert Brodeur Nashua, NH & Florida Tremblay Nashua, NH
BRODEUR, Rosalie Emma, Aug 6 1899 Sex:F Child# 2 Cyrille Brodeur Canada & Emma Poulin Canada
BRODEUR, Rose Marie, Jul 9 1933 Sex:F Child# 5 Arthur Brodeur Nashua, NH & Isabelle Martel Nashua, NH
BRODEUR, Simonne Therese, Apr 10 1932 Sex:F Child# 1 Louis Brodeur Nashua, NH & Isabelle Chartier Dunstable, MA
BRODEUR, Theophile Louis, Jul 6 1907 Sex:M Child# 2 Theophile Brodeur Canada & Clarinda Lagace Canada
BRODEUR, Unknown, Sep 18 1890 Sex:M Child# 1 Charles Brodeur Canada & Eliza Hebert Canada Stillborn
BRODEUR, Unknown, Jan 3 1927 Sex:F Child# 6 Alfred Brodeur Nashua, NH & Gracia Gariepy Nashua, NH
BRODEUR, Unknown, Nov 4 1932 Sex:M Child# 6 Hormidas Brodeur Canada & Bertha Duval Milford, NH Stillborn
BROGDON, Thomas Richard, Nov 14 1928 Sex:M Child# 1 Thomas Brogdon Fayetteville, GA & Olive Charron Nashua, NH
BROGHI, Raymond, Mar 1 1914 Sex:M Child# 2 Alfrio Broghi Italy & Gertrude J Lemardis Italy
BROILLARD, Joseph, Jun 1 1917 Sex:M Child# 1 Jos Emile Broillard Nashua, NH & Blanche Addie Delude Nashua, NH
BROISVERT, Edouard, Dec 31 1887 Sex:M Child# 10 Abraham Broisvert P Q & Exilda Rodier Canada
BROMLEY, Edwin Leedham, Jul 30 1930 Sex:M Child# 1 Edwin L Bromley Lawrence, MA & Maude Price Boston, MA
BROMLEY, Everett Harold, Dec 5 1896 Sex:M Child# 1 Samuel Bromley Lawrence, MA & Hattie Grover Natick, MA
BRONARD, Frederick, May 28 1918 Sex:M Child# 8 Joseph Bronard New York & Marceline Mer New York
BROOK, Norman, Sep 14 1923 Sex:M Child# 2 Thomas Brook Portland, ME & Anna Nixon Boston, MA
BROOKS, Clarence Arthur, Mar 21 1906 Sex:M Child# 3 Robert T Brooks Rutland, MA & Ella Skinner Waltham, MA
BROOKS, Ernest Willard, May 4 1931 Sex:M Child# 1 Charles Brooks Pittsfield, NH & Marion Chapman Dunstable, MA
BROOKS, Ettie L, Jan 28 1892 Sex:F Child# 1 George F Brooks NH & Eva E Edmunds NH
BROOKS, Everett Ernest, Aug 16 1915 Sex:M Child# 1 Ernest P Brooks Rockland, MA & Marcia F Patch Johnson, VT
BROOKS, Frank Arthur, Feb 25 1895 Sex:M Child# 2 George A Brooks S Lyndeboro, NH & Eva Edmans S Merrimack, NH

BROOKS, George, Jr, Sep 25 1930 Sex:M Child# 1 George Brooks Pittsfield, NH & Irene Trudeau Nashua, NH
BROOKS, Hazel Joyce, Feb 5 1922 Sex:F Child# 4 W J Brooks England & Dorothy May Legge England
BROOKS, Josephine, Jan 24 1897 Sex:F Child# 3 George A Brooks S Merrimack, NH & Eva Edmunds S Lyndeboro, NH
BROOKS, Lillian Lorraine, Feb 3 1933 Sex:F Child# 2 George F Brooks Pittsfield, NH & Irene Trudeau Nashua, NH
BROOKS, Marion Anita, Jun 9 1912 Sex:F Child# 1 Henry Brooks
BROOKS, Paul Frederick, Sep 18 1916 Sex:M Child# 2 Fred G Brooks Greenfield, NH & Lucy Alice Holt Greenfield, NH
BROOKS, Pauline, Apr 20 1932 Sex:F Child# 2 Lewis Brooks Pittsfield, NH & Palmer Campton, NH
BROOKS, Stanley Irving, Apr 12 1920 Sex:M Child# 1 James A Brooks England & Helen L Smith Rhode Island
BROOKS, Unknown, Jul 26 1892 Sex:M Child# 6 William Brooks NH & Hattie Baker Canada
BROOKS, Unknown, May 14 1900 Sex:M Child# 2 A J Brooks Mass & Lilly Perkins Somersworth, NH
BROOKS, Unknown, Jun 24 1916 Sex:M Child# 4 William J Brooks Trent, England & Mary D Legge England Stillborn
BROPHY, John Thomas, Sep 4 1892 Sex:M Child# 2 John Brophy Portland, ME & Mary O Dwyer Ireland
BROPHY, L Henry, Oct 1 1890 Sex:M Child# 1 Peter Brophy Canada & Nellie Doyle Plattsburg, NY
BROPHY, Lillian Mary, Aug 28 1897 Sex:F Child# 4 John Brophy Portland, ME & Mary O'Dwyer Limerick, Ireland
BROPHY, Marion Ethel, Mar 22 1890 Sex:F Child# 2 John L Brophy Maine & Mary Dwyer Ireland
BROPHY, Mary Aline, Dec 18 1896 Sex:F Child# 1 Peter Brophy Portland, ME & Alice McDormott Nashua, NH
BROSAR, Ralph, Jr, Aug 4 1927 Sex:M Child# 2 Ralph Brosar Nashua, NH & Evelyn Charron Manchester, NH
BROSARD, Dorothy May, May 24 1914 Sex:F Child# 6 Joseph Brosard New York & Marceline Nure New York
BROSARD, Flora, Apr 13 1916 Sex:F Child# 7 Joseph Brosard New York & Marceline Merc New York
BROSARD, Joseph Henry, Apr 10 1912 Sex:M Child# 5 Joseph D Brosard Mooers Fks, NY & Marceline Mere Mooers Fks, NY
BROSKYE, Bertha, Jun 18 1921 Sex:F Child# 7 John Broskye Lithuania Russia & Mary Skat Lithuania Russia
BROSOR, Ralph Willard, Feb 20 1897 Sex:M Child# 3 Lewis Brosor New York & Mary Jane Matott Altona, NY
BROSSARD, Harold, Oct 29 1895 Sex:M Child# 2 Louis Brossard US & Mary Methot US
BROSSARD, May Evelyn, Mar 30 1911 Sex:F Child# 4 Joseph Brossard New York & Merceline Myre New York
BROSSEAU, Alice Jane, Dec 15 1894 Sex:F Child# 2 Louis Brosseau US & Mary Methot US
BROUARD, Arthur Reginald, May 21 1931 Sex:M Child# 2 Joseph Brouard Canada & Olivine Gagnon Nashua, NH
BROUARD, Joseph Wm Edw, Jan 7 1930 Sex:M Child# 1 Joseph Brouard Canada & Olivine Gagnon Nashua, NH
BROUARD, Marie Louise, May 9 1933 Sex:F Child# 3 Joseph Brouard Canada & Olivine Gagnon Nashua, NH
BROUILLARD, Eugenia A, May 3 1891 Sex:F Child# 7 Arsene Brouillard Canada & Marie Ouellette Canada
BROUILLARD, Joseph Robert, Jun 27 1929 Sex:M Child# 4 George Brouillard Canada & Eva Milot Canada
BROUILLARD, Leda Yvonne, Mar 6 1909 Sex:F Child# 2 Edouard Brouillard Canada & Melina Neven Canada
BROUILLET, Unknown, Jun 28 1891 Sex: Child# 7 Joseph Brouillet New York & Lucy Avare Canada
BROUILLETT, Charles Emile, Sep 28 1896 Sex:M Child# 2 Louis Brouillett Canada & Alphonsine Larivee Canada
BROUILLETTE, Joseph E Albert, Jun 5 1899 Sex:M Child# 3 Louis Brouillette Mass & Alphonsine Larivee Canada
BROUSSEAU, Annette Victoria, Oct 2 1922 Sex:F Child# 5 Walter Brousseau Canada & Angeline Gaudette NH
BROUSSEAU, Arthur, May 27 1887 Sex:M Child# Geoffrey Brousseau P Q & Julie Borage P Q
BROUSSEAU, Aubeline, Feb 21 1891 Sex:F Child# 4 Henri Brousseau Canada & M Courtemarche Canada
BROUSSEAU, Edouard, Nov 13 1887 Sex:M Child# Henri Brousseau Champlain & M Courtemarche Canada
BROUSSEAU, George, Oct 1 1893 Sex:M Child# 5 Henry Brousseau Canada & Malvina Courtemanche Canada
BROUSSEAU, George Albert, Jul 31 1908 Sex:M Child# 1 Pierre L Brousseau Canada & Anna Lacasse US
BROUSSEAU, Henri Albert, Mar 1 1920 Sex:M Child# 4 Walter Brousseau Canada & Angeline Gaudette NH
BROUSSEAU, Joseph Alphonse, May 22 1898 Sex:M Child# 2 Jeffrey Brousseau Canada & Arselie Pepin Canada
BROUSSEAU, Joseph Amedee, Mar 9 1896 Sex:M Child# 1 Jeffrey Brousseau Canada & Arselie Pepin Canada
BROUSSEAU, Joseph Paul, Oct 9 1927 Sex:M Child# 7 Walter Brousseau Canada & A Gaudette Nashua, NH
BROUSSEAU, Joseph Walter John, Jan 20 1917 Sex:M Child# 2 Walter Brousseau Canada & Angeline Gaudette NH
BROUSSEAU, Marie Beatrice Ange, Aug 17 1918 Sex:F Child# 3 Walter Brousseau Canada & Angelina Gaudette NH
BROUSSEAU, Marie H, May 15 1900 Sex:F Child# 3 Godfroid Brousseau Canada & Arzelie Pepin Canada
BROUSSEAU, Marie Pauline Rita, Oct 9 1927 Sex:F Child# 6 Walter Brousseau Canada & A Gaudette Nashua, NH
BROW, Gordon Marshall, Apr 30 1921 Sex:M Child# 1 Elmer H Brow Brooklyn, NY & Louise M Morrison Lanesville, MA
BROWN, Agnes, Mar 9 1917 Sex:F Child# 1 George Brown Vermont & Ida Lavoie Canada
BROWN, Alice, Sep 19 1892 Sex:F Child# 1 Arthur C Brown New Hampshire & Ellie J Dame New Hampshire
BROWN, Alice May, Mar 31 1911 Sex:F Child# 1 John Brown Worcester, MA & Marion Carleton Springfield, MA
BROWN, Allen, Mar 8 1914 Sex:M Child# 4 Edward O Brown Dedham, MA & Grace M Perry Springfield, MA
BROWN, Arlene Blanche, Feb 16 1907 Sex:F Child# 2 Frederick E Brown Sudbury, MA & Blanche Tessier Nashua, NH
BROWN, Arthur Frederick, Jun 29 1909 Sex:M Child# 3 William M Brown Princeton, MA & Harriet Holbrook Worcester, MA
BROWN, Arthur Frederick, Feb 17 1933 Sex:M Child# 3 A F Brown Nashua, NH & Mildred Smith Nashua, NH
BROWN, Bertha M, Oct 8 1895 Sex:F Child# 1 Fred H Brown Maine & Lulu M Illinois
BROWN, Betty Laverne, Jun 11 1920 Sex:F Child# 1 George E Brown Tenexa, Kansas & Georgia Farrar Axtell, KS
BROWN, Beverly Billson, Nov 26 1924 Sex:F Child# 1 Marcius Brown Athol, MA & Helen Billson Westford, MA
BROWN, Charles Desire, Aug 17 1897 Sex:M Child# 1 Charles Brown Montpelier, VT & Amarilda Lucier Nashua, NH
BROWN, Charles Edward, Sep 18 1896 Sex:M Child# 2 Don F Brown Nashua, NH & Fanny Nichols
BROWN, Charles Henry, Apr 10 1911 Sex:M Child# 1 Everett L Brown Ellsworth, ME & Bernice E Dunham Ellsworth
BROWN, Cynthia Ann, Jun 6 1924 Sex:F Child# 2 Horace C Brown Goffstown, NH & Ora Reed Berlin, NH
BROWN, Dalton Munroe, Jan 13 1900 Sex:M Child# 1 Martin L Brown Mt Vernon, NH & Bertha Lund Pepperell, MA
BROWN, David, Oct 19 1932 Sex:M Child# 1 Perry Brown Nashua, NH & Germaine Goulet Nashua, NH
BROWN, David Lawson, Mar 12 1933 Sex:M Child# 1 John C Brown New Brunswick & Evelyn Wright Newport Ctr, VT
BROWN, David Wilder, Apr 18 1934 Sex:M Child# 2 Harold E Brown Nashua, NH & Lillian Fecteau Richford, VT
BROWN, Donald Livingston, May 8 1933 Sex:M Child# 2 Rosere L Brown Hanover, NH & Florence E Howe Hollis, NH
BROWN, Doris Mae, Aug 20 1924 Sex:F Child# 3 Elmer H Brown Brookline, NH & Louise N Morrison Gloucester, MA
BROWN, Dorothea E, Nov 5 1902 Sex:F Child# 1 Ernest Brown Wilmot & Ella M Blackman Moores, NY
BROWN, Douglas Harold, Sep 3 1930 Sex:M Child# 1 Harold A Brown Nashua, NH & Lillian Fecteau Richford, VT
BROWN, Duane Francis, Oct 8 1935 Sex:M Child# 3 Harold A Brown Nashua, NH & Lillian Fecteau Richford, VT
BROWN, Edward Albert, Mar 1 1914 Sex:M Child# 1 Leroy C Brown Nashua, NH & Lola M Dukeshire Nova Scotia

BROWN, Edward Otis, Jr, Jan 5 1912 Sex:M Child# 3 Edward Otis Brown Dedham, MA & Grace M Perry Springfield, MA
BROWN, Eleese Virginia, Jun 2 1934 Sex:F Child# 1 Harold C Brown Somerville, MA & Eleese Lowe Randolph, NH
BROWN, Elizebeth, Aug 27 1896 Sex:F Child# 7 A A Brown Nashua, NH & Carrie Wheeler Nashua, NH
BROWN, Enola Frances, Feb 13 1904 Sex:F Child# 1 Fletcher S Brown Baltimore, MD & Enola F Hadlock Nashua, NH
BROWN, Esther Lillian, Feb 9 1920 Sex:F Child# 4 Ernest A Brown Standish, ME & Rose I Gray Wollis Pond, VT
BROWN, Ethel, Mar 6 1888 Sex:F Child# 3 Annise A Brown Nashua, NH & Cora L Wheeler Nashua, NH
BROWN, Frances Louise, Jun 21 1910 Sex:F Child# 1 Ed Brown Nova Scotia & Mary Camaron Nova Scotia
BROWN, Frank, Mar 4 1888 Sex:M Child# 7 Frank A Brown Nashua, NH & Clara E Clark Sanbornton, NH
BROWN, Fred William, Jr, Aug 5 1917 Sex:M Child# 1 Fred Brown Bridgewater, MA & Marion M Ripley Bridgewater, MA
BROWN, George Harry, Sep 17 1930 Sex:M Child# 12 Harry Brown Canada & Ellen Mann Scotland
BROWN, Grace Antoinette, Oct 13 1919 Sex:F Child# 6 James A Brown Somerville, MA & Mary E Laflamme Minneapolis, MN
BROWN, Grace Emma, Jun 28 1908 Sex:F Child# 1 Edward O Brown Dedham, MA & Grace Perry Springfield, MA
BROWN, Harold A, Mar 11 1903 Sex:M Child# 3 A W Brown Waterman, VT & Lillian Davis Enosburg, VT
BROWN, Harry William, Oct 16 1907 Sex:M Child# 11 William M Brown Princeton, MA & Harriet Holbrook Worcester, MA
BROWN, Helen Anabelle, Jul 20 1924 Sex:F Child# 8 William Brown Princeton, MA & Harriet Holbrook Worcester, MA
BROWN, Helen Louise, Oct 23 1915 Sex:F Child# 2 Leroy C Brown Nashua, NH & Leta Dukershire Annapolis, NS
BROWN, Henry George, Oct 27 1909 Sex:M Child# 1 Harry Brown England & Emelinne Boucher Canada
BROWN, Hope, Oct 25 1910 Sex:F Child# 1 Thomas Brown Providence, RI & Ida Russel Lowell, MA
BROWN, Howard Andrew, Feb 20 1932 Sex:M Child# 3 Andrew Brown Liverpool, England & Muriel Allen Fairfax, VT
BROWN, Irving Wallace, Jul 23 1917 Sex:M Child# 1 Charles I Brown Nashua, NH & Lillian Dichard Nashua, NH
BROWN, Ivy Ellen, Apr 25 1893 Sex:F Child# 7 Irving J Brown Wilmot & Lorinda E Corliss Hudson, NH
BROWN, Joseph Alphe, Dec 13 1903 Sex:M Child# 8 Joseph Brown Canada & Amanda Cote Canada
BROWN, Kenneth, Sep 30 1918 Sex:M Child# 2 Fred W Brown US & Marion M Bixby US
BROWN, Kenneth Alvin, Oct 7 1906 Sex:M Child# 3 Charles A Brown Littleton, NH & Effie Cutter Nashua, NH
BROWN, Kenneth Clayton, Nov 11 1926 Sex:M Child# 5 Charles H Brown Arlington, MA & Dorothy A Waters Everett, MA
BROWN, Kenneth James, Aug 28 1918 Sex:M Child# 2 Andrew Brown Liverpool, England & Muriel Jennie Allen Fairfax, VT
BROWN, Kenneth Lawrence, Feb 11 1917 Sex:M Child# 6 Arthur E Brown Merrimack, NH & Edith M McManus Polton, Quebec
BROWN, Leon Edgar, Jul 23 1908 Sex:M Child# 3 E Ferderick Brown Sudbury, MA & Blanche Tessier Nashua, NH
BROWN, Lois Mabel, Jul 23 1908 Sex:F Child# 4 E Ferderick Brown Sudbury, MA & Blanche Tessier Nashua, NH
BROWN, Lulu Araline, Oct 22 1889 Sex:F Child# 1 D H Brown Nashua, NH & Fannie Nichols Hopkinton
BROWN, Mabel Gertrude, Feb 18 1917 Sex:F Child# 5 Edward Otis Brown Dedham, MA & Grace M Perry Springfield, MA
BROWN, Marie C, Jul 4 1887 Sex:F Child# 1 Joseph Brown Canada & Rosalie Rousseau Canada
BROWN, Mary, Nov 8 1909 Sex:F Child# 1 John Brown US & Mary Daley Ireland
BROWN, Mary Agnes, Oct 3 1889 Sex:F Child# 4 Joseph Brown Canada & Rosa Houlon Canada
BROWN, Mike, Aug 1 1910 Sex:M Child# 3 Jim Brown Greece & Celina Marquis Canada
BROWN, Mildred, Dec 20 1905 Sex:F Child# 1 Morris S Brown New Canaan, NB & Mabel Steele Bradford, NH
BROWN, Milton Harvey, Mar 18 1933 Sex:M Child# 1 Herbert Brown Keene, NH & Charlene Steele Hudson, NH
BROWN, Perry, Feb 16 1910 Sex:M Child# 2 Edward O Brown Dedham, MA & Grace M Perry Springfield, MA
BROWN, Rachel, May 18 1910 Sex:F Child# 9 Jacob Brown Russia & Annie Whitmins Russia
BROWN, Raymond W, Jul 1 1897 Sex:M Child#  Edward A Brown Bridgewater, MA & Jennie Woodward Bethel, VT
BROWN, Richard Allan, Jan 22 1932 Sex:M Child# 2 Karl Brown Milford, NH & Mary Richardson Cambridge, MA
BROWN, Robert A, Sep 9 1925 Sex:M Child# 1 Robert A Brown Manchester, NH & Bertha Burton Clinton, MA
BROWN, Robert Benfield, Apr 23 1930 Sex:M Child# 1 Elgene R Brown Milford, NH & Frances Benfield Fremont, NH
BROWN, Robert Royal, Apr 14 1930 Sex:M Child# 1 Kenneth A Brown Nashua, NH & Jane Mulliken Manchester, NH
BROWN, Robert William, Feb 17 1929 Sex:M Child# 1 Roy Brown Wilton, NH & Frances Herrick Lyndeboro, NH
BROWN, Rollin Everett, Aug 8 1932 Sex:M Child# 1 R E Brown Hudson, NH & M Shattuck Amesbury, MA
BROWN, Rose Anna, Aug 2 1902 Sex:F Child# 2 Patrick Brown Ireland & Laura Delisle Manchester, NH
BROWN, Russell Frank, Apr 29 1934 Sex:M Child# 1 Nelson Brown Durham, NH & Olive Richardson Milford, NH
BROWN, Ruth Eleanor, Oct 6 1915 Sex:F Child# 1 Andrew Brown England & Muriel J Allen Fairfax, VT
BROWN, Ruth Marion, Jul 22 1912 Sex:F Child# 1 Fred Elmer Brown Woonsocket, RI & Emily M Burlingame Blackstone
BROWN, Samuel, May 18 1909 Sex:M Child# 2 Jimmy Brown Greece & Celina Marquis Canada
BROWN, Samuel B, Nov 7 1894 Sex:M Child# 1 Samuel A Brown Conn & Lucy E Morgan Mass
BROWN, Sarah J, Aug 5 1892 Sex:F Child# 6 Louis J Brown Alton, NH & Elizabeth Bradford, NH
BROWN, Sullivan W, Aug 5 1898 Sex:M Child# 2 A W Brown Waterman, VT & Lillian Davis Enosburg, VT
BROWN, Theodore Quentin, Jun 16 1926 Sex:M Child# 11 James A Brown Somerville, MA & Mary LaFlamme Minneapolis, MN
BROWN, Unknown, Oct 6 1889 Sex:F Child# 2 Henry C Brown Delton, WI & Clara J Bryant Trusbury, VT
BROWN, Unknown, Sep 20 1889 Sex:M Child# 2 J Frank Brown Nashua, NH & Hattie Burnett Concord, NH
BROWN, Unknown, Jul 2 1889 Sex:M Child# 4 Irving J Brown Wilmot, NH & Nellie Collins Hudson, NH
BROWN, Unknown, Jul 2 1889 Sex:M Child# 5 Irving J Brown Wilmot, NH & Nellie Collins Hudson, NH
BROWN, Unknown, Mar 23 1891 Sex:M Child# 10 Frank Brown Nashua, NH & Clara E NH
BROWN, Unknown, Jun 9 1891 Sex:F Child# 3 Michael Brown Ireland & Alice O'Neil Nashua, NH
BROWN, Unknown, Jun 24 1891 Sex:F Child# 3 J Frank Brown Nashua, NH & Hattie Bunnelle Concord
BROWN, Unknown, Aug 15 1891 Sex:F Child# 1 Edward A Brown Bridgewater, MA & Jennie E Woodward Bethel, VT
BROWN, Unknown, Aug 25 1892 Sex:F Child# 2 John H Brown E Boston, MA & Catherine F McGobern E Boston, MA Stillborn
BROWN, Unknown, Sep 14 1892 Sex:F Child# 8 Albion K Brown Dixfield, ME &  Farmington, ME
BROWN, Unknown, Jun 28 1893 Sex:F Child# 5 Ambros A Brown Nashua, NH & Carrie L Wheeler Nashua, NH
BROWN, Unknown, Jul 1 1894 Sex:M Child#  Edward Brown Mass & Jennie E Woodward Vermont
BROWN, Unknown, Nov 1 1895 Sex:F Child# 1 A W Brown Waterman, VT & Lillian Dane Enosburg, VT
BROWN, Unknown, Oct 13 1898 Sex:M Child# 2 Willard A Brown Mass & Cora B Holland
BROWN, Unknown, Feb 9 1902 Sex:M Child# 1 Charles C Brown Boston, MA & L M Lapham Nashua, NH Stillborn
BROWN, Unknown, Sep 5 1903 Sex:M Child# 2 Charles C Brown Boston, MA & Louise M Lapham Nashua, NH Stillborn
BROWN, Unknown, Feb 1 1904 Sex:M Child# 1 Charles A Brown Littleton, NH & Effie Cutter Nashua, NH
BROWN, Unknown, Apr 22 1907 Sex:M Child# 5 Jacob Brown Russia & Annie Dudlemon Russia

BROWN, Unknown, Nov 23 1909 Sex:F Child# 1 Alphonso P Brown N Chelmsford, MA & Edna A Terrell Nashua, NH
BROWN, Veda Lucile, Jun 7 1919 Sex:F Child# 2 Charles D Brown Nashua, NH & Lillian V Dichard Nashua, NH
BROWN, Virginia, Nov 23 1922 Sex:F Child# 4 Charles H Brown Somerville, MA & Dorothy Audrey Brown Everett, MA
BROWN, Waldo Sydney, Dec 15 1923 Sex:M Child# 2 A Sydney Brown Bradford, MA & Grace P Schrultz Stoddard, NH
BROWN, Wendall Waters, Nov 11 1926 Sex:M Child# 6 Charles H Brown Arlington, MA & Dorothy A Waters Everett, MA
BROWN, William Farrar, Feb 7 1924 Sex:M Child# 2 George Brown Tenexa, Kansas & Georgia Farrar Axtell, MA
BROWN, William Howard, Jan 3 1923 Sex:M Child# 2 Elmer H Brown New York & Louise Morrison Lanesville, MA
BROWN, William Walter, Mar 27 1890 Sex:M Child# 1 John Brown Ireland & Maggie Donahue Ireland
BROWNING, Mary, Mar 28 1891 Sex:F Child# 3 John Browning New York & Ellen Conners Ireland
BROWNRIGG, Albert Edward, Mar 5 1903 Sex:M Child# 1 Albert E Brownrigg Nova Scotia & Amelia F Davidson Nova Scotia
BROWNRIGG, Joanne Elizabeth, Apr 18 1934 Sex:F Child# 2 Albert E Brownrigg Nashua, NH & Irene A Nelson Michigan
BRUCE, Alan Kenneth, Aug 24 1927 Sex:M Child# 2 E M Bruce Winchendon, MA & Mae Laurian Nashua, NH
BRUCE, Clinton C, Sep 20 1902 Sex:M Child#  Wesley J Bruce Nova Scotia & Edna M Colburn Nashua, NH
BRUCE, Constance Elaine, May 25 1934 Sex:F Child# 4 Arthur P Bruce Lebanon, ME & Alberta Stevens Middleton, NH
BRUCE, Donald Martin, Dec 21 1935 Sex:M Child# 3 Ernest Marcus Bruce Winchendon, MA & Mae Clement Mauvian Nashua,NH
BRUCE, Edward Arthur, Mar 2 1927 Sex:M Child# 1 Arthur P Bruce Lebanon, ME & Alberta Stevens Middleton, NH
BRUCE, Evelyn Fae, May 12 1930 Sex:F Child# 3 Arthur P Bruce Lebanon, ME & Alberta Stevens Middleton, NH
BRUCE, Mildred Virginia, Nov 10 1931 Sex:F Child# 6 Walter Bruce Hudson, NH & Anna Hassler Nashville, TN
BRUCE, Ralph Wendell, May 3 1930 Sex:M Child# 5 Walter Bruce Hudson, NH & Anna Hasler Nashville, TN
BRUCE, Robert Eugene, May 7 1928 Sex:M Child# 2 Arthur P Bruce Lebanon, NH & Alberta Stevens Middleton, NH
BRUCE, Robert Harold, Aug 7 1920 Sex:M Child# 1 Ernest Bruce Winchendon, MA & May Laurian Nashua, NH Stillborn
BRUCE, Robert Irving, Mar 7 1928 Sex:M Child# 4 Walter Bruce Hudson, NH & Anna Hassler Nashville, TN
BRUCE, Robert Stacker, Dec 11 1926 Sex:M Child# 2 Lyscom Bruce Plymouth, MA & Margaret Luce Nashua, NH
BRUCE, Unknown, Jul 22 1895 Sex:F Child# 1 George H Bruce Berwick, ME & Mattie L Humphrey Nashua, NH
BRUCE, Unknown, Mar 10 1905 Sex:M Child# 2 Wesley J Bruce Greenwood Sq, NS & Edna M Colburn Nashua, NH
BRUCE, Unknown, Nov 20 1924 Sex:F Child# 1 Lyscom Bruce Windsor, VT & Mary Luce Nashua, NH
BRUEN, Peter Ward, Aug 18 1920 Sex:M Child# 2 Peter Bruen Ireland & Ellen Winn Nashua, NH
BRUEN, Richard M, Apr 18 1922 Sex:M Child# 3 Peter Bruen Ireland & Ellen Winn Nashua, NH
BRULE, Marie Rose A, Dec 23 1901 Sex:F Child# 1 Clovis Brule Canada & Marie Levesque Canada
BRUMBY, Janet E, Mar 11 1922 Sex:F Child# 1 William L Brumby Waltham, MA & Lillian Dunton Pepperell, MA
BRUN, Joseph Alcide, May 13 1898 Sex:M Child# 4 Francois Brun Canada & Melanise Gagmer Canada
BRUN, Joseph Alfred Aune, Sep 9 1898 Sex:M Child# 4 Anselme Brun Canada & Albina Brisebois Canada
BRUN, Marie Florida, Aug 9 1900 Sex:F Child# 6 Francois Brun Canada & Melanise Gagne Canada
BRUNEAU, Arthur Charles, Feb 1 1931 Sex:M Child# 3 Goerge A Bruneau Greenville, NH & Jeannette Constant Nashua, NH
BRUNEAU, Christine George, Jan 31 1923 Sex:F Child# 1 Charles Bruneau New Ipswich, NH & Eugenie Courault France
BRUNEAU, Estelle Lorette, Aug 7 1931 Sex:F Child# 3 Raoul Bruneau Greenville, NH & Ida Fraser Nashua, NH
BRUNEAU, Irene Florence, Sep 2 1929 Sex:F Child# 2 George A Bruneau Greenville, NH & Jeannette Constant Nashua, NH
BRUNEAU, Norbert Charles, Jan 25 1932 Sex:M Child# 2 Charles Bruneau Greenville, NH & Eugenie Courault France
BRUNEAU, Paul Maurice, Jul 12 1927 Sex:M Child# 1 George Bruneau Greenville, NH & J Constant Nashua, NH
BRUNEAU, Robert Maurice, Apr 14 1927 Sex:M Child# 1 Raoul Bruneau Greenville, NH & Ida Fraser Nashua, NH
BRUNEAU, Robert Maurice, Mar 15 1930 Sex:M Child# 2 Raoul Bruneau Greenville, NH & Ida Fraser Nashua, NH
BRUNELL, Marie Beatrice, Mar 6 1900 Sex:F Child# 1 Alphonse Brunell Canada & Cordelia Raymond Canada
BRUNELL, Wilmer Leon, Feb 20 1923 Sex:M Child# 1 John Leon Brunell Wilmot, NH & Marjorie Anderson Antrim, NH
BRUNELLE, Andrew Thomas, Jan 16 1934 Sex:M Child# 1 Andrew Brunelle Nashua, NH & Annie Fleming Manchester, NH
BRUNELLE, Edward Maurice, Mar 1 1934 Sex:M Child# 3 Armond Brunelle Canada & Yvonne Dube Nashua, NH
BRUNELLE, Henry, Feb 9 1926 Sex:M Child# 2 Wilfred Brunelle Lowell, MA & Annette St George
BRUNELLE, Joseph J Norman, Mar 24 1931 Sex:M Child# 1 Armand Brunelle Canada & Yvonne Dube Nashua, NH
BRUNELLE, Lois Priscilla, Apr 9 1933 Sex:F Child# 3 F Brunelle Worcester, MA & Olivette Gendron Nashua, NH
BRUNELLE, Malvina, Sep 19 1887 Sex:F Child#  Octave Brunelle Sciota, NY & Adeline Brunelle Sciota, NY
BRUNELLE, Marie Louise, Jan 21 1892 Sex:F Child# 8 Octave Brunelle Canada & Adeline Canada
BRUNELLE, Marie Therese, Feb 21 1933 Sex:F Child# 2 A Brunelle St Theodore, Canada & Yvonne Dube Nashua, NH
BRUNELLE, Maurice Wilford, Jan 8 1925 Sex:M Child# 1 Wilford Brunelle Manchester, NH & Annette St George Lowell, MA
BRUNELLE, Robert Dennis, Jun 15 1935 Sex:M Child# 2 Andrew Brunelle Nashua, NH & Anne Fleming Manchester, NH
BRUNELLE, Wilfred, Feb 16 1927 Sex:M Child# 3 Wilfrid Brunelle Manchester, NH & A St George Lowell, MA
BRUNT, Arthur Raymond, Jun 19 1929 Sex:M Child# 1 Arthur Brunt Boston, MA & Muriel Canfield Nashua, NH
BRUWIN, William, May 2 1887 Sex:M Child# 4 James Bruwin Underhill, VT & Ann Temple Ireland
BRYANT, Davis King, Nov 2 1927 Sex:M Child# 2 Sumner K Bryant Worcester, MA & Mary S Davis S Portland, ME
BRYANT, Dorothy, Mar 5 1935 Sex:F Child# 5 Summer Bryant Worcester, MA & Mary Davis Portland, ME
BRYANT, Elizabeth, May 26 1907 Sex:F Child# 2 Ernest S Bryant Warehill, MA & Jennie King Portland, ME
BRYANT, Hope Merrill, Jan 20 1917 Sex:F Child# 1 Carl R Bryant Paris, ME & Helen N Merrill Auburn, ME
BRYANT, Kenneth Everett, Oct 29 1909 Sex:M Child# 3 S Wilson Bryant S Hadley Falls, MA & Maud E Burnham Sciota, NY
BRYANT, Paul Richard, Oct 9 1905 Sex:M Child# 2 Sumner W Bryant Holyoke, MA & Maud Burnham Sciota, NY
BRYANT, Sumner K, Jr, Jun 14 1925 Sex:M Child# 1 Sumner Bryant Worcester, MA & Mary Davis Portland, ME Stillborn
BRYANT, Sumner S, Jun 19 1902 Sex:M Child# 1 Wilson S Bryant Mass & Maud Burnham NY
BRYANT, Thelma Mabel, Mar 18 1911 Sex:F Child# 4 Wilson S Bryant US & Maud E Burnham US
BRYANT, William Ernest, Jul 23 1931 Sex:M Child# 4 Sumner Bryant Worcester, MA & Mary Davis Portland, ME
BUCHANAN, Lewis Norton, Oct 17 1925 Sex:M Child# 3 D M Buchanan Canada & Helen Graham Ashburnham, MA
BUCHANAN, Norma Isabel, Nov 9 1927 Sex:F Child# 4 D M Buchanan Canada & Helen Graham Ashburnham, MA
BUCHANAN, Roger Ian, Jun 27 1929 Sex:M Child# 5 D Milton Buchanan Canada & Helen Graham Ashburnham, MA
BUCHARD, Unknown, Jun 9 1888 Sex:F Child# 6 Pierre Buchard Canada & Catherine Penette Canada
BUCHZEL, Apollio, Aug 13 1918 Sex:F Child# 2 Christop Buchzel Russia & Julia Kinlurtanchi Nashua, NH
BUCK, Mary, May 21 1923 Sex:F Child# 1 Arthur Buck Searsmont, ME & Margaret Mallon Nashua, NH
BUCK, Robert James, Sep 23 1924 Sex:M Child# 2 Obed Buck Searsmont, ME & Margaret Mallon Nashua, NH

BUCK, William Obed, Jul 23 1926 Sex:M Child# 3 Obed Buck Searsmont, ME & Margaret Mallon Nashua, NH
BUCKANON, Wallace Neal, Mar 16 1924 Sex:M Child# 2 D M Buckanon Canada & Helen Graham Ashburnham, MA
BUCKINGHAM, Barbara, May 17 1924 Sex:F Child# 1 H C Buckingham Plymouth, PA & Dorothy Coates Laurens, NY
BUCKLEY, Carmen Agnes, Sep 14 1902 Sex:F Child# 2 John Buckley Nashua, NH & Beatrice Hallihan Ogdensburg, NY
BUCKLEY, Catharine May, May 14 1921 Sex:F Child# 4 Henry Buckley Nashua, NH & Claire Levesque Canada
BUCKLEY, Catherine Agnes, Sep 6 1933 Sex:F Child# 6 Joseph Buckley Wilton, NH & C Batalitzky Providence, RI
BUCKLEY, Elizabeth Ann, Jan 8 1932 Sex:F Child# 1 Charles L Buckley N Billerica, MA & Mary E Manning Nashua, NH
BUCKLEY, Henry James, Aug 7 1914 Sex:M Child# 1 Henry M Buckley Nashua, NH & Clare Levesque Canada
BUCKLEY, James, Sep 30 1902 Sex:M Child# 5 M Buckley America & Matilda White Ireland
BUCKLEY, James Daniel, Feb 29 1904 Sex:M Child# 3 John J Buckley Nashua, NH & Beatrice Hallahan Ogdensburg, NY
BUCKLEY, Jeremiah Cornelius, Apr 12 1932 Sex:M Child# 5 Joseph Buckley Wilton, NH & C Batelitzky Providence, RI
BUCKLEY, John Francis, Nov 30 1889 Sex:M Child# 1 Michael Buckley Nashua, NH & Matilda F White Ireland
BUCKLEY, John Ogden, Jan 21 1906 Sex:M Child# 4 John Buckley Nashua, NH & Beatrice Hallahan Ogdensburg, NY
BUCKLEY, Lucille Alice, Aug 10 1924 Sex:F Child# 6 Henry M Buckley Nashua, NH & Claire Levesque Canada
BUCKLEY, Lucille Marie, May 25 1901 Sex:F Child# 1 John Buckley Nashua, NH & Beatrice Hallahan Ogdensburg, NY
BUCKLEY, Mary Lillian, Dec 1 1899 Sex:F Child# 4 Michael Buckley Nashua, NH & Matilda T White Ireland
BUCKLEY, Matilda D, Sep 15 1894 Sex:F Child# 3 Michael Buckley Nashua, NH & Matilda T White Ireland
BUCKLEY, Michael H, Jan 29 1891 Sex:M Child# 2 Michael Buckley Nashua, NH & Matilda White Ireland
BUCKLEY, Rita Matilda, Oct 3 1922 Sex:F Child# 5 Henry Buckley Nashua, NH & Claire Levesque Canada
BUCKLEY, Robert Paul, Nov 13 1925 Sex:M Child# 7 Henry Buckley Nashua, NH & Claire Levesque Canada
BUCKLEY, Virginia Clara, Jun 14 1926 Sex:F Child# 1 George Buckley Northfield, NH & Irene Straw Clinton, MA
BUCKLIN, Evelina Beatrice, Apr 19 1905 Sex:F Child# 4 Charles Bucklin Grafton, MA & Clara Larance Manchester, NH
BUCKLIN, Minnie, Oct 27 1895 Sex:F Child#  Charles H Bucklin NH & Clara M Lawrence NH
BUCKLIN, Viola, Oct 27 1895 Sex:F Child#  Charles H Bucklin NH & Clara M Lawrence NH
BUCLOVECI, Julia, Jul 17 1915 Sex:F Child# 1 Joseph Bucloveci Russia & Wicanta Krusute Russia
BUDER, Claire Irene, May 15 1933 Sex:F Child# 1 Ernest E Buder Webster, MA & Palmarina Bois Nashua, NH
BUDER, Joseph Francis Archi, Oct 15 1918 Sex:M Child# 2 Alexender Buder Germany & Corinne Chagnon Nashua, NH
BUDER, Leona Doris, Oct 6 1920 Sex:F Child# 5 Emile Buder Germany & Clara Seifert Germany
BUDREAU, Unknown, Mar 3 1891 Sex:F Child# 5 John Budreau W Chazy, NY & Henrietta Farvall W Chazy, NY
BUDRO, Earl Loren, Jan 17 1934 Sex:M Child# 1 Earl Harold Budro Nashua, NH & Goldie Maria Scott Jacksonville, FL
BUDRO, Harry, Mar 24 1906 Sex:M Child# 6 Peter F Budro NY & Agnes Lavallee Canada
BUDRO, Jos Albert Arthur, Jan 23 1919 Sex:M Child# 4 Louis Budro New York & Clara Poirier Bedford, NH
BUDRO, Jos Louis Harvey, Jan 9 1917 Sex:M Child# 3 Louis Budro New York & Clara Poirier Bedford, NH
BUDRO, Unknown, Sep 27 1891 Sex:F Child# 1 Alexis Budro New York & Lucy Benton, VT
BUDROW, Joseph Elmer Horace, Mar 21 1912 Sex:M Child# 1 Horace Budrow Franklin, NH & Ida Boucher Haverhill, MA
BUFFUM, Gertrude Eleanor, Apr 28 1916 Sex:F Child# 2 Leon G Buffum Antrim, NH & Ida P Miller Lee, MA
BUFFUM, Laura Gertrude, Sep 26 1914 Sex:F Child# 1 Leon G Buffum Antrim, NH & Ida P Miller E Lee, MA
BUFFUM, Unknown, Jun 22 1912 Sex:F Child# 3 Eldridge F Buffum Waterville, ME & Emma E Ward Woburn, MA
BUFOLD, Marie Philo Evelyn, Jun 4 1912 Sex:F Child# 1 William Bufold Canada & Emma Arsenault Canada
BUFOLD, Raoul, Apr 24 1916 Sex:M Child# 3 William Bufold Canada & Emma Arsenault Canada
BUGAILE, John, Mar 13 1908 Sex:M Child# 1 Ignaci Bugaile Russia & Waleri Stoskowski Russia
BUGAILOW, Mary, Apr 23 1911 Sex:F Child# 1 James Bugailow Russia & Eva Motizikia Russia
BUGBEE, Unknown, Jul 6 1890 Sex:F Child# 4 George L Bugbee VT & R J Clark Maine
BUILMAIR, Joseph Eusebe, Jul 8 1891 Sex:M Child# 7 Ephrem Guilmair Canada & Celina Langelier Canada
BUJOLD, Victor, Dec 25 1919 Sex:M Child# 5 William Bujold Canada & Alma Arsenault Canada
BUKER, Jennie, May 23 1893 Sex:F Child# 4 E H Buker Nashua, NH & Mary J Alexander Canada
BULEDOT, Delphine, Feb 27 1900 Sex:F Child# 6 John Buledot Canada & Victoria Gagnon Canada
BULGEORGON, Odessa, Feb 19 1920 Sex:F Child# 6 Nicholas Bulgeorgon Greece & Fortina Alexia Greece
BULL, Ethel May, Jun 22 1894 Sex:F Child# 6 Elias C Bull Vermont & Almeda Ward NY
BULL, Unknown, Dec 4 1898 Sex:M Child# 2 William J Bull NY & Linnie B Kindall Hopkinton Stillborn
BULLARD, Albert Richard, Mar 18 1927 Sex:M Child# 8 Winfield Bullard Amherst, NH & Maude P Corliss Somerville, MA
BULLARD, Arthur Raymond, May 3 1910 Sex:M Child# 5 Harry O Bullard Amherst, NH & Lizzie Carr S Nashua, NH
BULLARD, Elsie May, Aug 18 1914 Sex:F Child# 4 Winfield Bullard Amherst, NH & Maud Corliss Somerville, MA
BULLARD, Evelyn Gertrude, Dec 5 1917 Sex:F Child# 6 Winfield S Bullard Amherst, NH & Maude P Corliss Somerville, MA
BULLARD, Harold, Mar 23 1912 Sex:M Child# 3 Winfield S Bullard Amherst, NH & Maud E Corliss Somerville, MA
BULLARD, Lorraine Antoinette, Jan 9 1934 Sex:F Child# 2 Maurice Bullard Nashua, NH & Antoinette Codorette Nashua,NH
BULLARD, Mabel, Nov 25 1904 Sex:F Child# 3 Harry O Bullard Mt Vernon, NH & Lizzie M Karr Nashua, NH
BULLARD, Margery Belle, Aug 30 1914 Sex:F Child# 6 Harry O Bullard Mt Vernon, NH & Lizzie M Carr Tyngsboro, MA
BULLARD, Marion Frances, Apr 12 1906 Sex:F Child# 1 Arthur H Bullard Keene, NH & Gertrude J Merrill Amesbury, MA
BULLARD, Mildred Hazel, Sep 10 1916 Sex:F Child# 5 Winfield S Bullard Amherst, NH & Maud P Corliss Somerville, MA
BULLARD, Orville, Nov 25 1904 Sex:M Child# 2 Harry O Bullard Mt Vernon, NH & Lizzie M Karr Nashua, NH
BULLARD, Robert Maurice, Nov 8 1930 Sex:M Child# 1 Maurice Bullard Nashua, NH & Antoinette Cadarette Nashua, NH
BULLARD, Unknown, Dec 16 1902 Sex:M Child# 1 Harry O Bullard Mt Vernon, NH & Lizzie M Karr Tyngsboro, MA
BULLARD, Unknown, Oct 10 1909 Sex:F Child# 1 Charles H Bullard Manchester, NH & Louise Trumble Cochituate, MA
BULLARD, Wayne Everett, Sep 18 1932 Sex:M Child# 1 John Bullard Nashua, NH & D MacCann Canada
BULLARD, Winfield Scott, Nov 26 1923 Sex:M Child# 7 Winfield S Bullard Amherst, NH & Maude P Corliss Somerville, MA
BULLIS, Walter R, Nov 3 1889 Sex:M Child# 3 Merritt A Bullis Rouses Pt, NY & Adda L Barnes Nashua, NH
BULTIS, Eris, May 12 1888 Sex:M Child# 1 Merrit A Bultis New York & Ada Z Barnes Nashua, NH
BULUGEOYAS, George, Sep 19 1918 Sex:M Child# 6 Nicholas Bulugeoyas Greece & Futini Alexion Greece
BUMBLIS, Paul, Jul 5 1915 Sex:M Child# 1 Paul Bumblis Russia & Leus Salkauskate Russia
BUMFORD, Elizabeth Ann, Jun 29 1929 Sex:F Child# 2 Augustus Bumford Colebrook, NH & Hellen Fuller Hartford, CT
BUNDY, Elizabeth Jane, Jul 10 1919 Sex:F Child# 3 Benjamin G Bundy Somerville, MA & Margaret D Duff Haverhill, MA
BUNDY, Margaret Ann, Jun 10 1933 Sex:F Child# 7 Robert S Bundy Nashua, NH & Maude H Conner Mt Vernon, NH

BUNDY, Margaret Clark, Jan 15 1911 Sex:F Child# 1 Benjamin A Bundy Somerville, MA & Margaret Duff Haverhill, MA
BUNDY, Nora B, Jul 20 1893 Sex:F Child# 1 Frank L Bundy NH & Dora J Thompson Mass
BUNDY, Robert Hutchinson, Mar 18 1932 Sex:M Child# 1 B Stewart Bundy Nashua, NH & Maude H Conner Portland, ME
BUNDY, Robert Stewart, Jun 30 1912 Sex:M Child# 2 Benjamin Geo Bundy Somerville, Ma & Margaret D Duff Haverhill, MA
BUNES, Jennie, Nov 12 1890 Sex:F Child# 2 John W Bunes Nashua, NH & Lizzie L Nashua, NH
BUNESKI, Mary Rita, Jul 3 1922 Sex:F Child# 4 Vincantos Buneski Russia & Mary Ykasalutia Russia
BUNKER, Helen Jane, Nov 15 1892 Sex:F Child# 1 Arthur S Bunker Durham, NH & Annie H Bills Stoddard, NH
BUNKER, Maude Bernise G, Feb 19 1924 Sex:F Child# 4 Fred L Bunker NH & Maude Richardson Vermont
BURBANK, Unknown, Sep 13 1888 Sex:F Child# 1 Leonard Burbank Brumbridge, IN & Lottie Dell Russa
BURCHELL, Harold Swett, Oct 7 1904 Sex:M Child# 3 William Burchell Manchester, NH & Grace Rush Manchester, NH
BURDICK, George Franklin, Jan 23 1935 Sex:M Child# 1 Ernest Burdick W Wellington, CT & Julia Nichols Nashua, NH
BUREBE, Georges, Jan 20 1894 Sex:M Child# 2 George Burebe Canada & Anna Lacrove Canada
BUREBIE, Celina, Nov 20 1888 Sex:F Child# 2 Francois Burebie Canada & Virginia Levesque Canada
BUREL, Alfred, Jun 16 1887 Sex:M Child# 1 Isidore Burel Nashua, NH & Clara Cadarette Bolton, MA
BUREL, Emma, Apr 12 1892 Sex:F Child# 4 Joseph Burel Canada & Josephine Blois Canada
BUREL, Joseph Amede, Jan 29 1892 Sex:M Child# 1 Joseph Burel, Jr Canada & Josephine Lawrence Canada
BURELL, Unknown, Jul 12 1889 Sex:M Child# 2 Isadore Burell Nashua, NH & Clara Castonet Nashua, NH Stillborn
BURELLE, Albert, Mar 17 1894 Sex:M Child# 12 Treffle Burelle Canada & Lea Dalbec Canada
BURELLE, Albert, May 20 1914 Sex:M Child# 1 Alphonse Burelle Nashua, NH & Leontine Theberge Canada
BURELLE, Alma, Feb 28 1894 Sex:F Child# 6 Joseph Burelle Canada & Josephine Blais Canada
BURELLE, Alphonse, Aug 5 1887 Sex:M Child#  Joseph Burelle P Q & Josephine Blais P Q
BURELLE, Beatrice Corinne, Jul 10 1916 Sex:F Child# 4 A J Burelle Nashua, NH & Amelia Vina Nashua, NH
BURELLE, Diana, Apr 18 1897 Sex:F Child# 7 Joseph Burelle Canada & Josephine Blais Canada
BURELLE, Ernest, Nov 29 1896 Sex:M Child# 2 Joseph Burelle Nashua, NH & Josephine Laurance Canada
BURELLE, Irene, Nov 11 1909 Sex:F Child# 1 Arthur Burelle Nashua, NH & Amelia Nadeau Nashua, NH
BURELLE, Irene Rita, Oct 10 1919 Sex:F Child# 2 Oneas Burelle Nashua, NH & Laura Gagne Canada
BURELLE, Isabelle, Jul 17 1915 Sex:F Child# 2 Alphonse Burelle Nashua, NH & Leontine Thiberge Canada
BURELLE, Jeanette Lucille, Sep 2 1917 Sex:F Child# 3 Arthur Burelle Nashua, NH & Amelia J Nadeau Nashua, NH
BURELLE, Joseph Edward, Jan 26 1889 Sex:M Child# 10 Treffle Burelle Canada & Lea Dalbec Canada
BURELLE, Josephine, Jun 4 1891 Sex:F Child# 11 Treffle Burelle Canada & Lea Dalbec Canada
BURELLE, Laura, Jan 27 1891 Sex:F Child# 4 Joseph Burelle Canada & Josephine Blois Canada
BURELLE, Ludger Edgar, Nov 25 1918 Sex:M Child# 1 Oneas Burelle Nashua, NH & Laura Gagne Canada
BURELLE, Marie Irene C, Sep 19 1900 Sex:F Child# 4 Isidore Burelle NH & Anna Gaulin Canada
BURELLE, Roland, Jan 27 1922 Sex:M Child# 4 Alphonse Burelle NH & Leontine Thiberge Canada
BURELLE, Unknown, Mar 15 1914 Sex:M Child# 2 Arthur J Burelle Nashua, NH & Amelia Nadeau Nashua, NH
BURGDONOWICH, Yethrentha, Jul 27 1913 Sex:F Child# 1 Frank Burgonowich Russia & Michalina Ackstein Russia
BURGER, James, Sep 17 1889 Sex:M Child# 3 James C Burger New York City & Edith M Ginon Staten Island
BURGESS, Beatrice, Jan 15 1929 Sex:F Child# 3 Richard Burgess Nashua, NH & Irene Miller New York
BURGESS, Dorothy Kenyon, Mar 1 1927 Sex:F Child# 3 R N Burgess Nashua, NH & Irene H Millis New York, NY
BURGESS, John Bernard, Dec 11 1931 Sex:M Child# 6 Richard N Burgess Nashua, NH & Irene H Miller New York, NY
BURGESS, John H, Mar 27 1892 Sex:M Child# 1 John W Burgess St Johns, NB & Stella M Kenyon Vermont
BURGESS, Richard Nelson, May 8 1935 Sex:M Child# 7 Richard N Burgess Nashua, NH & Irene Miller New York, NY
BURGESS, Richard Nelson, Jr, Apr 28 1922 Sex:M Child# 1 Richard N Burgess Nashua, NH & Irene H Miller New York, NY
BURGESS, Robert Leo, Jul 8 1920 Sex:M Child# 2 Leo Burgess Nashua, NH & Marie Pineau Nashua, NH
BURGESS, Robert Miller B, Mar 9 1924 Sex:M Child# 2 R N Burgess Nashua, NH & Irene Miller New York, NY
BURGESS, Stella Mae, Oct 8 1930 Sex:F Child# 4 Richard Burgess Nashua, NH & Irene Miller New York, NY
BURGESS, Therna Julia, Sep 2 1909 Sex:F Child# 2 George H Burgess Worcester, MA & Alice M Swallow Nashua, NH
BURGESS, Unknown, Apr 24 1898 Sex:M Child# 2 John H Burgess NB & Stella Kenyon Pomfret, Canada
BURGESS, Walter Alfred, Aug 9 1908 Sex:M Child# 1 George H Burgess Worcester, MA & Alice M Swallow Nashua, NH
BURKE, Arlene Pearl, Apr 1 1926 Sex:F Child# 2 George E Burke New York & Luella Rock New York
BURKE, Beverly Lorraine, Nov 22 1928 Sex:F Child# 1 John Burke Wilton, NH & Nine Thompson Canada
BURKE, Catherine Louise, Jan 8 1920 Sex:F Child# 3 Peter Burke Ireland & Catherine Shields Ireland
BURKE, Clara Frances, Nov 8 1920 Sex:F Child# 1 Harry C Burke Washington, DC & Yvonne Gelinas Nashua, NH
BURKE, Jeanne Adeline, Feb 24 1925 Sex:F Child# 1 George Burke Constable, NY & Luella Rock Burke, NY
BURKE, Marie, Mar 17 1894 Sex:F Child# 3 Adolphe Burke Canada & Marie L St Germain Canada
BURKE, Mary Alice, Aug 14 1933 Sex:F Child# 1 Donald A Burke Hillsboro, NH & Florence Beaubien Sandown, NH
BURKE, Mary Frances, Jan 27 1918 Sex:F Child# 2 Peter Burke Ireland & Katherine Shields Ireland
BURKE, Raymond Daniel, Feb 26 1921 Sex:M Child# 1 James E Burke Wilton, NH & Margaret Harrington Lowell, MA
BURKE, Tena, Dec 25 1889 Sex:F Child# 1 Charles H Burke Milford, NH & Asenath D Spalding Merrimack, NH
BURKE, Unknown, Jun 23 1888 Sex:M Child# 1 Thomas W Burke Rockland, ME & Nellie E Sweaney Concord, NH
BURKE, Unknown, Oct 22 1889 Sex:M Child# 2 Thomas W Burke Rockland, ME & Nellie M Sweeney Concord, NH
BURKE, Unknown, Jan 19 1892 Sex:M Child# 3 Thomas W Burke Rockland, ME & Nellie M Sweeney NH
BURKE, Unknown, Jan 14 1895 Sex:M Child# 4 Thomas W Burke Rockland, ME & Nellie M Sweeney Concord, NH
BURN, Marie Melina P, Jun 21 1900 Sex:F Child# 6 Henry Burn Canada & Parmelia Neveu Canada
BURNACHE, Joseph Wilfrid, Sep 19 1899 Sex:M Child# 2 Amedee Burnache Mass & Lucie Boutin Canada
BURNEKA, Bernice, Apr 19 1921 Sex:F Child# 1 Michael Burneka Russia & Marcelia Baranowsky US
BURNES, Everett Harrison, Sep 8 1889 Sex:M Child# 3 Royal D Burnes Litchfield & Adelia Prescalt Nashua, NH
BURNETT, Cleon F, Oct 16 1905 Sex:M Child# 3 Fred J Burnett Nashua, NH & Georgia Town Nashua, NH
BURNETT, Esther, Oct 26 1902 Sex:F Child# 2 J Fred Burnett Nashua, NH & Georgie Towne Nashua, NH
BURNETT, Lillian Alice, Sep 5 1903 Sex:F Child# 2 William B Burnett Tennessee & Edna M Smith Nashua, NH
BURNETT, Marion A, Oct 16 1891 Sex:F Child# 1 J F Burnett Nashua, NH & Georgie A Town Nashua, NH
BURNHAM, Alta M, May 31 1890 Sex:F Child# 1 Frank E Burnham Rumney, NH & Bertha E Burke Newport, VT
BURNHAM, Barbara, Dec 10 1925 Sex:F Child# 2 John S Burnham Antrim, NH & Mabel Forbes Nashua, NH

BURNHAM, Boyd Frank, May 15 1920 Sex:M Child# 2 Frank Burnham W Chazy, NY & Gertrude Moran Nashua, NH
BURNHAM, Cornelia Eva, Oct 22 1920 Sex:F Child# 4 Arthur Burnham Nashua, NH & Florence J Conant S Lyndeboro, NH
BURNHAM, David Forbes, Sep 6 1934 Sex:M Child#  John S Burnham Antrim, NH & Mabel Forbes Nashua, NH
BURNHAM, David Frank, Mar 23 1917 Sex:M Child# 6 Arthur L Burnham Nashua, NH & Florence J Conant S Lyndeboro, NH
BURNHAM, Edith, Sep 30 1926 Sex:F Child# 1 H W Burnham Nashua, NH & Ruth Nickerson Mass
BURNHAM, Edward Parker, May 4 1908 Sex:M Child# 1 A W D Burnham Gloucester, MA & Cora L Parker Lyndeboro, NH
BURNHAM, Edward Robert, Sep 5 1922 Sex:M Child# 8 A L Burnham US & Florence T Conant US
BURNHAM, Elizabeth, Oct 16 1922 Sex:F Child# 2 Roland S Burnham Nashua, NH & Elizabeth Harris Nova Scotia
BURNHAM, Fletcher Harris, Feb 18 1921 Sex:M Child# 1 Roland Burnham Nashua, NH & Elizabeth Harris Nova Scotia
BURNHAM, Francis Harriman, Jan 2 1927 Sex:F Child# 1 Roy Burnham Nashua, NH & Florence Bobick Worcester, MA
BURNHAM, Frank Andrew, Sep 3 1912 Sex:M Child# 1 Frank H Burnham Lowell, MA & Christine A Coffey Nashua, NH
BURNHAM, Jane, Aug 16 1928 Sex:F Child# 4 R B Burnham Nashua, NH & Elizabeth Harris Nova Scotia
BURNHAM, Kathleen Frances, May 8 1913 Sex:F Child# 3 Frank H Burnham Henniker, NH & Katherine Madden Keene, NH
BURNHAM, Lester, Mar 16 1897 Sex:M Child#  Frank A Burnham Nashua, NH & Mary J Harriman Deering, NH
BURNHAM, Lester H, Jr, Sep 8 1930 Sex:M Child# 2 Lester H Burnham Nashua, NH & Grace Adams Springfield, OH
BURNHAM, Marjorie Ann, May 9 1931 Sex:F Child# 4 John S Burnham Antrim, NH & Mabel M Forbes Nashua, NH
BURNHAM, Martha, Jul 9 1927 Sex:F Child# 3 John S Burnham Antrim, NH & Mabel M Forbes Nashua, NH
BURNHAM, Melba G, Jul 30 1902 Sex:F Child# 4 Frank A Burnham Nashua, NH & Mary J Harriman Deering, NH
BURNHAM, Mildred J, Oct 29 1900 Sex:F Child# 3 F A Burnham Nashua, NH & Mary J Harriman Deering
BURNHAM, Natalie Louise, Oct 9 1923 Sex:F Child# 1 John S Burnham Antrim, NH & Mabel M Forbes Nashua, NH
BURNHAM, Richard Thompson, Aug 16 1930 Sex:M Child# 2 Roy Burnham Nashua, NH & Florence Bobick Worcester, MA
BURNHAM, Richard Webster, Mar 21 1917 Sex:M Child# 3 George Burnham Nashua, NH & Beatrice Kimball Nashua, NH
BURNHAM, Roland Burke, Feb 28 1896 Sex:M Child# 2 Frank E Burnham Rumney, NH & Bertha E Burke Newport, VT
BURNHAM, Roy Francis, Jul 13 1895 Sex:M Child# 1 Frank A Burnham
BURNHAM, Ruth Alleen, May 20 1899 Sex:F Child# 1 Lewis H Burnham Haverhill & Lizzie F Pitts Kennebunkport, ME
BURNHAM, Shirley, Jul 25 1924 Sex:F Child# 3 Roland Burnham Nashua, NH & Elizabeth Harris Nova Scotia
BURNHAM, Shirley Ann, Dec 4 1928 Sex:F Child# 1 L H Burnham Nashua, NH & Grace Adams Springfield, OH
BURNHAM, Unknown, Feb 3 1891 Sex:M Child# 1 Perley Burnham United States &  United States
BURNHAM, Unknown, Aug 20 1914 Sex:F Child# 5 Arthur L Burnham Nashua, NH & Florence Conant S Lyndeborough, NH
BURNHAM, Wesley Tyrrell, Jan 17 1917 Sex:M Child# 1 Frank Burnham W Chazy, NY & Gertrude May Moran Nashua, NH
BURNS, Amelia Agnes, Dec 18 1900 Sex:F Child# 2 John Burns Ireland & Amelia Landry Canada
BURNS, Annie, Mar 4 1894 Sex:F Child# 2 James F Burns Ireland & Annie McKeon Ireland
BURNS, Annie A, Sep 4 1893 Sex:F Child# 1 Thomas F Burns Nashua, NH & Annie Downing Nashua, NH
BURNS, Arthur, Aug 20 1904 Sex:M Child# 1 Benjamin Emery Burns Wilton, NH & Nina Herrick Oswego, NY
BURNS, Cecelia Mary, May 15 1926 Sex:F Child# 3 Charles Burns Nashua, NH & Grace Taylor New York
BURNS, Charles Alphonse Ed, Jul 3 1902 Sex:M Child# 7 Henry Burns Canada & Parmelie Neveu Canada
BURNS, Donald James, Jun 5 1928 Sex:M Child# 4 Charles Burns Nashua, NH & Grace Taylor Ellenburg, NY
BURNS, Donald Kenneth, Aug 6 1929 Sex:M Child# 2 John M Burns Nashua, NH & Angelina Richard Nashua, NH
BURNS, Doris Emmeline, Mar 19 1915 Sex:F Child# 6 Robert B Burns Hollis, NH & Adeline Keith Nashua, NH
BURNS, Edouard Norman, Sep 30 1915 Sex:M Child# 1 George Burns Nashua, NH & Maria Bussiere Pittsfield, NH
BURNS, Etienne Thomas, May 13 1895 Sex:M Child# 2 Thomas Burns Sherbrooke, PQ & Lucie Dubois Altona, NY
BURNS, Eula Cecile, Aug 18 1905 Sex:F Child# 4 John H Burns Ireland & Amelia Landry Canada
BURNS, Florence May, Jan 26 1911 Sex:F Child# 4 Robert B Burns Hollis, NH & Adeline Keith Nashua, NH
BURNS, Frank, Mar 22 1898 Sex:m Child# 3 Thomas Burns Canada & Lucie Dubois New York, NY
BURNS, Helen, Mar 13 1895 Sex:F Child# 1 Michael H Burns Concord & Annie E Moran Nashua, NH
BURNS, Helen Betsey, Aug 26 1909 Sex:F Child# 3 Robert P Burns Hollis, NH & Adeline L Keith Nashua, NH
BURNS, Henry, Jan 27 1895 Sex:M Child# 3 Henry Burns Nashua, NH & Celia L Reynolds Nashua, NH
BURNS, Ida Irene, Sep 9 1905 Sex:F Child# 8 Henry Burns Canada & Parmelie Neven Canada
BURNS, Irma May, Jun 22 1926 Sex:F Child# 1 James Burns Worcester, MA & Doris Trudell Gilbertville, MA
BURNS, James Hugh, Jan 2 1933 Sex:M Child# 3 James F Burns Worcester, MA & Doris Trudell Gilbertville, MA
BURNS, Joan, Aug 27 1924 Sex:F Child# 2 Charles Burns Nashua, NH & Grace Taylor Ellenburg, NY
BURNS, John, Sep 21 1896 Sex:M Child# 2 Michael H Burns Concord, NH & Annie E Moran Nashua, NH
BURNS, John Charles, Jr, Jan 12 1926 Sex:M Child# 10 John C Burns St Paul, Minn & C E Schneider
BURNS, John Joseph, Mar 18 1897 Sex:M Child# 4 Henry M Burns Nashua, NH & Celia L Reynolds Nashua, NH
BURNS, John Richard, Oct 20 1920 Sex:M Child# 1 John M Burns Nashua, NH & Angelina Richard Nashua, NH
BURNS, John William, Apr 17 1918 Sex:M Child# 8 Robert B Burns Hollis, NH & Adeline Keith Nashua, NH
BURNS, Joseph B, Aug 8 1891 Sex:M Child# 2 George E Burns Ireland & Mary M O'Brien Ireland
BURNS, Joseph Edouard, Dec 10 1896 Sex:M Child# 4 Henry Burns Canada & Parmelie Nepven Canada
BURNS, Josiah Robert, Nov 1 1916 Sex:M Child# 7 Robert B Burns Hollis, NH & Adeline Keith Nashua, NH
BURNS, Julia, Sep 7 1931 Sex:F Child# 1 Samuel Patrick Burns Nashua, NH & Julia Helen Lycette Nashua, NH
BURNS, Julia A, Feb 4 1897 Sex:F Child# 3 Thomas F Burns Nashua, NH & Annie Downey Nashua, NH
BURNS, Kenneth, Aug 17 1928 Sex:M Child# 10 R B Burns Hollis, NH & Adeline Keith Nashua, NH Stillborn
BURNS, Lillian Mary, Nov 30 1898 Sex:F Child# 4 Thomas Burns Nashua, NH & Annie Downey Nashua, NH
BURNS, Lisa, Aug 27 1906 Sex:F Child# 4 Edouard Burns Canada & Georgiana Brouillard Canada
BURNS, Lizzie Agnes, Sep 8 1892 Sex:F Child# 3 J W Burns Nashua, NH & Lizzie L NY
BURNS, M Odiana, Sep 14 1895 Sex:F Child# 3 Henry Burns Canada & Pamelia Neveux Canada
BURNS, Marguerite, Mar 26 1896 Sex:F Child# 2 Edw H Burns Nashua, NH & Mary E Foley Nashua, NH
BURNS, Marie, Apr 11 1917 Sex:F Child# 2 Laurent Burns NH & Marie Buissiere NH
BURNS, Marie A I, Mar 6 1887 Sex:F Child# 5 Thomas W Burns P Q & Zalma Larive P Q
BURNS, Marie Elise, Dec 25 1896 Sex:F Child# 2 Edouard Burns Canada & Georgina Bronillard Canada
BURNS, Marie Laurent, Aug 14 1895 Sex:F Child# 1 Edward Burns Canada & Georgina Brouillard Canada
BURNS, Marie Lisa, Mar 28 1899 Sex:F Child# 5 Henri Burns Canada & Parmelie Neven Canada
BURNS, Marjorie, Apr 30 1927 Sex:F Child# 3 John Burns Nashua, NH & Lucy Archambault Nashua, NH

BURNS, Marjorie Phyllis, Jul 12 1915 Sex:F Child# 1 (No Parents Listed)
BURNS, Mary Agnes, Nov 14 1920 Sex:F Child# 2 Warren R Burns Hollis, NH & Beatrice Benson Ireland
BURNS, Mary Albina, Jul 13 1893 Sex:F Child# 1 I W Burns Canada & Lena Dubois NY
BURNS, Mary Euphinnia, Nov 30 1898 Sex:F Child# 3 Michael H Burns Concord, NH & Annie E Moran Nashua, NH
BURNS, Mary Sylvia Rita, Jan 3 1920 Sex:F Child# 1 Edward Burns Nashua, NH & Antoinette Paul Nashua, NH
BURNS, Parmelie, Dec 14 1899 Sex:F Child# 3 Edward Burns Canada & Georgiana Brouillard Canada
BURNS, Paul Emile, Aug 26 1918 Sex:M Child# 1 Henri Burns NH & Laura Anne Fortin Canada
BURNS, Peter F, Jan 9 1893 Sex:M Child# 1 Henry Burns Nashua, NH & Celia Reynolds Nashua, NH
BURNS, Ralph J, Mar 29 1903 Sex:M Child# 3 John H Burns Ireland & Amelia L Landry Canada
BURNS, Raymond, Jul 10 1922 Sex:M Child# 1 John J Burns Nashua, NH & Lucy Archambeau Nashua, NH
BURNS, Richard, Dec 9 1924 Sex:M Child# 2 John Burns NH & A Archambault NH
BURNS, Rita June, Jun 16 1930 Sex:F Child# 2 James Burns Worcester, MA & Doris A Trudell Gilbertville, MA
BURNS, Robert, Mar 1 1896 Sex:M Child# 4 James Burns Ireland & Annie McKean Ireland
BURNS, Robert, Feb 9 1907 Sex:M Child# 5 John H Burns Ireland & Amelia Landry Canada
BURNS, Robert Alexander, Jan 13 1895 Sex:M Child# 1 Edward H Burns Nashua, NH & Mary E Foley Nashua, NH
BURNS, Robert Charles, Aug 30 1920 Sex:M Child# 1 Charles Burns Nashua, NH & Grace Taylor Ellenburg, NY
BURNS, Robert, Jr, Mar 2 1921 Sex:M Child# 9 Robert Burns Hollis, NH & Adeline Keith Nashua, NH
BURNS, Roger Mollison, Jul 16 1908 Sex:M Child# 3 Ben E Burns Wilton, NH & Isabel Herrick Oswego, NY
BURNS, Rosana, Nov 6 1889 Sex:F Child# 1 Henry M Burns Nashua, NH & Celia Reynolds Nashua, NH
BURNS, Ruth Elisabeth, Aug 16 1908 Sex:F Child# 1 Warren R Burns Hollis, NH & Beatrice Benson Ireland
BURNS, Ruth Herrick, Apr 8 1906 Sex:F Child# 2 Ben E Burns Wilton, NH & Nina Herrick Oswego, NY
BURNS, Samuel, Mar 14 1908 Sex:M Child# 6 John H Burns Ireland & Amelia Landry Canada
BURNS, Thomas, Dec 20 1931 Sex:M Child# 5 Charles Burns Nashua, NH & Grace Taylor Ellenburg, NY
BURNS, Unknown, Aug 16 1889 Sex:M Child# 1 John Burns Nashua, NH & Lizzie Burns Ireland
BURNS, Unknown, Sep 15 1891 Sex:F Child# 1 James F Burns Ireland & Annie E McKeon Ireland
BURNS, Unknown, Oct 15 1891 Sex:F Child# 1 Robert Burns Claremont, NH & Lillie Emery Nashua, NH
BURNS, Unknown, Mar 6 1893 Sex:M Child# 2 James F Burns Ireland & Annie L McKeon Ireland
BURNS, Unknown, Sep 17 1894 Sex:F Child# 2 Thomas F Burns Nashua, NH & Annie Downing Nashua, NH
BURNS, Unknown, Nov 26 1899 Sex:F Child# 5 Thomas Burns Nashua, NH & Annie Downing Nashua, NH
BURQUE, Albert Alexandre, Mar 27 1893 Sex:M Child# 9 Alphonse Burque Canada & Louise Dutilly Canada
BURQUE, Amede, Oct 21 1891 Sex:M Child# 8 Alphonse Burque Canada & Louise Dutilly Canada
BURQUE, Arthur Lambert, Jul 26 1912 Sex:M Child# 2 Arthur Burque Nashua, NH & Lily Lambert Troy, NY
BURQUE, Auguste, May 9 1919 Sex:M Child# 4 Auguste Burque Nashua, NH & Josephine Leclaire Nashua, NH
BURQUE, Auguste Robert, Mar 6 1922 Sex:M Child# 5 Auguste Burque Canada & Mary A Berube Canada
BURQUE, Auguste Robert, Mar 6 1922 Sex:M Child# 5 Auguste Burque Nashua, NH & Josephine Leclerc Nashua, NH
BURQUE, Edna Louise, Mar 7 1908 Sex:F Child# 1 Arthur O Burque Nashua, NH & Lillian Lambert Troy, NY
BURQUE, Elaine Mabel, Jan 20 1917 Sex:F Child# 3 Auguste Burque Nashua, NH & Josephine Leclair Nashua, NH
BURQUE, Eloise Jessie, Mar 4 1919 Sex:F Child# 2 Henri A Burque Nashua, NH & Mabel N Budro W Chazy, NY
BURQUE, Jeanette Irene, Mar 13 1920 Sex:F Child# 2 Amedee Burque Nashua, NH & Clarice Lemieux Nashua, NH
BURQUE, Lillian Agnes, Jan 16 1922 Sex:F Child# 3 Amedee Burque Nashua, NH & Clarice Lemieux Nashua, NH
BURQUE, Lorette Alberta, Jul 30 1925 Sex:F Child# 6 August U Burque Nashua, NH & Josephine Leclair Nashua, NH
BURQUE, Lucien Ernest Joseph, Jun 29 1912 Sex:M Child# 5 Alphonse Burque Canada & Rose Landry Mass
BURQUE, Lucille Yvonne, Dec 22 1907 Sex:F Child# 1 Henri Burque Nashua, NH & Mabel Bourdrault W Chazy, NY
BURQUE, Marie, Aug 9 1888 Sex:F Child# 7 Alphonse Burque Canada & Louise Butilly Canada
BURQUE, Marie, Dec 22 1911 Sex:F Child# 1 Auguste Burque Nashua, NH & Josephine Leclair Nashua, NH
BURQUE, Marie, May 11 1913 Sex:F Child# 2 Auguste Burque Nashua, NH & Josephine Leclerc Nashua, NH Stillborn
BURQUE, Marie Louise, Nov 5 1890 Sex:F Child# 2 Adolphe Burque Canada & Marie L St Jermain Canada
BURQUE, Mary Louise Cecile, Nov 22 1916 Sex:F Child# 1 Amedee Burque Nashua, NH & Clarice Lemieux NH
BURQUE, Unknown, Oct 23 1891 Sex:M Child# 3 Adolphe Burque Canada & Marie L St Germain Canada Stillborn
BURRABY, Unknown, Aug 21 1901 Sex:M Child# 1 Francis H Burraby Maine & Kate Lezott NY
BURREBY, Ida May, Jan 17 1900 Sex:F Child# 10 Frank H Burreby Orono, ME & Kate M Leazotte Altona, NY
BURREBY, Julia, Nov 5 1899 Sex:F Child# 4 Andrew C Burreby Bradford, ME & Teresa Comer S Boston, MA
BURREBY, Unknown, Apr 8 1891 Sex:F Child# 1 Andrew C Burreby Bradford, ME & Theresa Cema Ireland
BURREBY, Unknown, Feb 10 1895 Sex:F Child# 3 Andrew C Burreby Meriden, ME & Theresa Comer Ireland
BURRELL, Georges Ernest, Sep 5 1898 Sex:M Child# 3 Isidore Burrell Nashua, NH & Anna Gaulin Canada
BURRELL, Joseph L, Dec 6 1895 Sex:M Child# 2 Isidore Burrell Canada & Anna Gaulin Canada
BURRELL, Maria, Mar 30 1899 Sex:F Child# 8 Joseph Burrell Canada & Josephine Blais Canada
BURRELL, Unknown, Jul 8 1892 Sex:M Child# 1 Joseph Burrell
BURRELLE, Alphonse Henri, Apr 1 1919 Sex:M Child# 3 Alphonse Burrelle Nashua, NH & Leontine Theberge Canada
BURRELLE, Julia Eva, Oct 7 1898 Sex:F Child# 3 Joseph Burrelle Nashua, NH & Josephine Laurence Canada
BURRILL, Donald Foy, Dec 7 1932 Sex:M Child# 2 Lewis E Burrill Claremont, NH & Elizabeth Melendy Bedford, NH
BURTON, Donald Ervin, Feb 21 1919 Sex:M Child# 1 Walter S Burton Pelham, NH & Mabel Mortlock Hudson, NH
BURTON, Earl Clayton, Jan 12 1935 Sex:M Child# 9 Erwin Burton Pelham, NH & Mary Prince Nashua, NH
BURTON, Elizabeth, Jul 20 1888 Sex:F Child# 3 Samuel C Burton Vermont & Mary T Moore Rhode Island
BURTON, Ernest Harry, Sep 26 1931 Sex:M Child# 7 Ervin Burton Pelham, NH & Mary L Prince Nashua, NH
BURTON, Herbert Adelbert, Mar 19 1930 Sex:M Child# 6 Ervin Burton Pelham, NH & Mary Prince Nashua, NH
BURTON, Kenneth Ervin, May 15 1923 Sex:M Child# 1 Ervin Burton Pelham, NH & Mary Prince Nashua, NH
BURTON, Leonard Roland, Mar 9 1933 Sex:M Child# 8 I J Burton Pelham, NH & May L Prince Nashua, NH
BURTON, Paul Frederick, Nov 25 1925 Sex:M Child# 3 Ervine Burton Pelham, NH & Mary Prince Nashua, NH
BURTON, Richard Clarence, Jan 28 1929 Sex:M Child# 5 Erwin J Burton Pelham, NH & Mary L Prince Nashua, NH
BURTON, Robert Arthur, Jul 28 1924 Sex:M Child# 2 Ervin Burton Pelham, NH & Mary Prince Nashua, NH
BURTT, Bryant Fessenden, Aug 5 1916 Sex:M Child# 2 Charles B Burtt Milford, NH & Mildred L Hatch W Somerville, MA
BURTT, Christine, Feb 3 1926 Sex:F Child# 2 Elgin Burtt Milford, NH & Edith Keith Milford, NH

BURTT, Eudora, Jun 11 1923 Sex:F Child# 4 Charles Burtt Milford, NH & Mildred L Hatch Somerville, MA
BURTT, Harold, Jr, Aug 17 1922 Sex:M Child# 1 Harold Burtt Amherst, NH & Verna M Mandigo Nashua, NH
BURTT, Phyllis, Jul 12 1918 Sex:F Child# 3 Chas Bryant Burtt Milford, NH & Mildred L Hatch Somerville, MA
BURTT, Priscilla, Jan 10 1922 Sex:F Child# 1 Elgin F Burtt Milford, NH & Edith F Keith Milford, NH
BURZINSKY, John, Jun 21 1916 Sex:M Child# 1 Adolf Burzinsky Russia & Uszula Woideczka Russia
BURZINSKY, Stanislaus Joseph, Oct 1 1917 Sex:M Child# 2 Adolf Burzinsky Russia & Ursula Vodichki Russia
BUSCHNOSKY, Eva, Nov 18 1923 Sex:F Child# 5 Eva Buschnosky Russia & Mary Ekoula Russia
BUSH, Charles Eldred, Apr 6 1910 Sex:M Child# 10 Forest L Bush Mason, NH & Etta F Norris Mass
BUSH, Doris Elizabeth, Apr 20 1933 Sex:F Child# 1 John Bush Germany & G Choniclovy Germany
BUSH, Gladys Mozella, Apr 3 1907 Sex:F Child# 8 Forest L Bush Mason, NH & Etta F Norris Charlestown, MA
BUSH, Lincoln Raymond, Feb 12 1909 Sex:M Child# 9 Forest L Bush Mason, NH & Etta F Norris Mass
BUSH, Raymond, Aug 31 1914 Sex:M Child# 3 William Bush Russia & Jennie Bush Russia
BUSH, Stanislava, Dec 5 1910 Sex:F Child# 2 William bush Russia & Katrowsa Miskavitch Russia
BUSHEE, Maud Irene, May 14 1898 Sex:F Child# 4 David A Bushee Warren, MA & Annie A McKilopp Canada
BUSHER, Albert, Mar 9 1911 Sex:M Child# 10 Leon Busher Canada & Lydia Record Worcester, MA
BUSHMAN, Grace Albertine, Aug 5 1908 Sex:F Child# 2 Joseph A Bushman Canada & Inez Darling Derry, NH
BUSHNAUKAS, Julia, Aug 29 1917 Sex:F Child# 2 Wm Bushnaukas Lithuania Russia & Mary Ukasaluta Lithuania Russia
BUSHNIASKIOW, Annie, Jul 9 1916 Sex:F Child# 1 Wilhelm Bushniaskiow Russia & Mary Yukasala Russia
BUSHOR, Unknown, Jan 15 1888 Sex:M Child# 1 Fred H Bushor Plattsburg, NY & Fanny J Harris Manchester, NH
BUSI, Joseph Howard, Sep 24 1915 Sex:M Child# 2 Luvigi Busi Italy & Marie Leonardi Italy
BUSLOVICH, Alphonse Joseph, May 29 1920 Sex:M Child# 2 Joseph Buslovich Russia & Vincentoe Krasutic Russia
BUSLOVICH, Julia Mary, Dec 10 1920 Sex:F Child# 2 Felix Buslovich Lithuania Russia & Petroma Oskofsky Lithuania
BUSLOVICH, Stanley Albert, Nov 20 1921 Sex:M Child# 3 Joseph Buslovich Lithuania & Vincenta Krusinte Lithuania
BUSTIN, George Allen, Jan 27 1901 Sex:M Child# 1 George Allen Bustin St Johns, NB & Jennie L Reynolds St Johns, NB
BUSTIN, Roland Reynolds, Nov 10 1905 Sex:M Child# 2 George A Bustin St John, NB & Jennie Reynolds St John, NB
BUSWELL, Barbara Ethel, Sep 3 1908 Sex:F Child# 5 Arthur H Buswell Bangor, ME & Eva L Webster Nashua, NH
BUSWELL, Clayton Wilcox, Oct 17 1923 Sex:M Child# 1 Wilcox Buswell Epping, NH & Grace A Sawyer Cambridge, MA
BUSWELL, Geraldine Elizabeth, Mar 21 1919 Sex:F Child# 7 Arthur H Buswell Bangor, ME & Eva L Webster Nashua, NH
BUSWELL, Guy William, Oct 6 1903 Sex:M Child# 3 Arthur H Buswell Bangor, ME & Eva L Webster Nashua, NH
BUSWELL, Helen Christine, Jun 18 1906 Sex:F Child# 4 Arthur H Buswell Bangor, ME & Eva L Webster Nashua, NH
BUSWELL, Lucelle Webster, Aug 15 1899 Sex:F Child# 1 Arthur H Buswell Bangor, ME & Eva L Webster Nashua, NH
BUSWELL, Martha Anne, May 24 1921 Sex:F Child# 8 Arthur H Buswell Bangor, ME & Eva Webster Nashua, NH
BUSWELL, Melba Alice, Jan 6 1913 Sex:F Child# 6 Arthur H Buswell Bangor, ME & Eva L Webster Nashua, NH
BUSWELL, Myron, Oct 28 1903 Sex:M Child# 1 William H Buswell Bangor, ME & Lizzie Whipple Nashua, NH
BUSWELL, Ross Gibbs, Jan 3 1902 Sex:M Child# 2 Arthur W Buswell Bangor, ME & Eva W Webster Nashua, NH
BUSWELL, Unknown, Apr 19 1905 Sex:M Child# 2 William H Buswell Bangor, ME & Lizzie Whipple Nashua, NH
BUTEAU, Joseph, Oct 5 1892 Sex:M Child# 1 Alphonse Buteau Canada & Philipine Carriere Canada Stillborn
BUTKA, Lodja, Jun 21 1926 Sex:F Child# 2 C Butka Poland & Annia Kotzanoska Poland
BUTLER, Blanche Lorraine, Nov 2 1918 Sex:F Child# 5 Leonard O Butler Woonsocket, RI & Julia Carter New Boston
BUTLER, Catherine Pearl, May 19 1911 Sex:F Child# 3 Bertrude W Butler Hinsdale, NH & Hazel Draper Wilton, NH
BUTLER, Donald Joseph, Mar 20 1922 Sex:M Child# 4 Carl A Butler E Jaffrey, NH & Anna McCabe Fitchburg, MA
BUTLER, Earl Neil, Jan 2 1932 Sex:M Child# 1 Earl E Butler Nashua, NH & Dorothy Forbes Boston, MA
BUTLER, Edmund Earl, Oct 19 1912 Sex:M Child# 3 Leonard Butler Woonsocket, RI & Julia Carter New Boston, NH
BUTLER, James Clifford, Aug 13 1921 Sex:M Child# 8 Leonard Butler Woonsocket, RI & Julia Carter New Boston, NH
BUTLER, John Angell, Aug 4 1912 Sex:M Child# 1 John Butler Philadelphia, PA & Beatrice A Angell Boston, MA
BUTLER, Joseph Emmett, Sep 3 1908 Sex:M Child# 1 P S Butler
BUTLER, Leonard Jeames, Jul 4 1911 Sex:M Child# 2 Leonard Butler Rhode Island & Julia Carter New Boston, NH
BUTLER, Lucille Emma, Nov 2 1916 Sex:F Child# 6 Leonard O Butler Woonsocket, RI & Julia Carter New Boston, NH
BUTLER, Marjorie Pearl, May 19 1915 Sex:F Child# 4 Leonard Butler Woonsocket, RI & Julia Carter New Boston, NH
BUTLER, Mary Florence, Jun 14 1892 Sex:F Child# 1 Joseph Butler Nashua, NH & Mathilde Boulanger E Concord, NH
BUTLER, Unknown, Jul 23 1894 Sex:M Child# 1 William Butler
BUTLER, Unknown, Jul 12 1895 Sex:M Child# 1 Albert S Butler Pelham, NH & Martha E Farnum Hudson, NH
BUTTERFIELD, Gloria Claire, Feb 10 1932 Sex:F Child# 1 Ernest Butterfield Derry, NH & Catherine Picard Derry, NH
BUTTERFIELD, Joan Priscilla, Oct 20 1930 Sex:F Child# 1 Raymond Butterfield Derry, NH & Helen Plocharczok Poland
BUTTERFIELD, Patricia Ann, Jan 22 1932 Sex:F Child# 2 Ray Butterfield Derry, NH & Helen Plocharczyh Poland
BUTTERFIELD, Rosemond Edith, Aug 25 1896 Sex:F Child# 2 Nathan Butterfield Lowell, VT & Ethel L McMannis Madson
BUTTERFIELD, Unknown, Apr 23 1893 Sex:F Child# 1 N E Butterfield Vermont & Ethel McMannis Canada
BUTTERWORTH, Ethel Melva, Jul 10 1910 Sex:F Child# 1 Fredrick Butterworth Lowell, MA & Agnes Smith England
BUTTLER, Howard Leonard, Mar 2 1920 Sex:M Child# 7 Leonard Buttler Woonsocket, RI & Julia Carter New Boston, MA
BUTTON, Unknown, Jun 23 1928 Sex:M Child# 8 Corbitt J Button Newfoundland & Emma H Stak Pepperell, MA Stillborn
BUTTRICK, Clifton Roy, Dec 27 1920 Sex:M Child# 2 Leander C Buttrick Hudson, NH & Cora Roy Canada
BUTTRICK, Maxime Naomie, Sep 20 1919 Sex:F Child# 1 Leander Buttrick Hudson, NH & Cora Joy Brockville, Ont
BUXTON, Lucille, May 7 1924 Sex:F Child# 2 R K Buxton Nashua, NH & D V Spaulding Townsend, MA
BUXTON, Marion J, Dec 8 1890 Sex:F Child# 1 George E Buxton Nashua, NH & Emma Pourin Milford, NH
BUXTON, Mark Kay, Nov 3 1900 Sex:M Child# 1 Fred T Buxton Nashua, NH & Marion Kay Scotland
BUXTON, Olive M, Mar 25 1901 Sex:F  Charles W Buxton Nashua, NH & Ella F Clemons Boston, MA
BUXTON, Paul W, Feb 18 1897 Sex:M Child# 2 Charles W Buxton Nashua, NH & Ella F Clemons Nashua, NH
BUXTON, Phyllis, Aug 29 1922 Sex:F Child# 1 Richard K Buxton Nashua, NH & Dorothy Spaulding Townsend, MA
BUXTON, Richard Kenneth, Feb 11 1899 Sex:M Child# 3 Charles W Buxton Nashua, NH & Ella F Clemons Nashua, NH
BUXTON, Robert Burns, Aug 1 1895 Sex:M Child# 1 C W Buxton Nashua, NH & Ella H Clemons Nashua, NH
BUXTON, Robert Charles, Feb 27 1928 Sex:M Child# 2 Paul W Buxton Nashua, NH & Hazel E Reynolds Nashua, NH
BUXTON, Unknown, Feb 13 1903 Sex:F Child# 2 Fred T Buxton Nashua, NH & Marion Kay Scotland
BUXTON, Unknown, Aug 3 1911 Sex:F Child# 1 Fred T Buxton Nashua, NH & Marion Kay Scotland

BUZNIANSKA, Josephine, Nov 29 1920 Sex:F Child# 3 William Buznianska Canada & Delvina Lizotte Canada
BUZZELL, Ella Cone, Dec 29 1919 Sex:F Child# 5 Clarence A Buzzell Epsom, NH & Grace K Bodge Barrington, NH
BUZZELL, Unknown, Jul 23 1901 Sex:F Child# 1 George L Buzzell New York & Ida B Marshall Hudson, NH
BYRD, Barbara Joan, Aug 21 1934 Sex:F Child# 10 Watson Byrd Amherst, NH & Lena Maxwell Littleton, MA
BYRNE, Janice May, Nov 25 1934 Sex:F Child# 1 John Byrne Cambridge, MA & Mary Darling Dover, NH
BYRNE, Thomas Edward, Dec 13 1927 Sex:M Child# 1 Thomas A Byrne Canada & Margaret Nash Nashua, NH
BYRNE, William Andrew, Sep 12 1930 Sex:M Child# 3 Thomas Byrne Canada & Margaret M Nash Nashua, NH
BYRNES, John Patrick, Jun 11 1929 Sex:M Child# 2 Thomas Byrnes Canada & Margaret M Nash Nashua, NH
CABANA, Louise Joy, Nov 12 1924 Sex:F Child# 10 Joseph Cabana Montreal, PQ & Frances Pierce Farmington Falls
CACCIVIO, James, Dec 22 1934 Sex:M Child# 2 John Caccivio Italy & Emily Parrott Nashua, NH
CACCIVIO, John David, Feb 4 1932 Sex:M Child# 1 John H Caccivio Italy & Emily Parratt Nashua, NH
CACHIONA, George, Feb 25 1918 Sex:M Child# 1 John Cachiona Romania & Lucretsia Fista Romania
CADDY, Hazel, Oct 1 1899 Sex:F Child# 4 C W Caddy Nashua, NH & Josephine Bechard Canada
CADIEU, Marie Josephine, Jun 3 1901 Sex:F Child# 7 Joseph Cadieu Canada & Floreska Durand Canada
CADIEUX, Beverly Ann, Mar 30 1935 Sex:F Child# 1 Albert Cadieux Nashua, NH & Estelle Bordoin Nashua, NH
CADIEUX, Edward Leo, Mar 26 1930 Sex:M Child# 2 Albert Cadieux Manchester, NH & Viola Trudeau Vermont
CADIEUX, Georgianna, Sep 1 1910 Sex:F Child# 1 George Cadieux Canada & Adrienne Pelletier Canada
CADIEUX, Lillian Mae, May 7 1924 Sex:F Child# 1 Albert Cadieux Manchester, NH & Viola Trudo Middlebury, VT
CADIEUX, Marie A E, Oct 23 1902 Sex:F Child# 7 Joseph Cadieux Canada & Florence Durande Canada
CADIEUX, Marie Jeanne Adrienn, May 9 1912 Sex:F Child# 2 George Cadieux Canada & Adrienne Pelletier Canada
CADIEUX, Marie Rose, Sep 5 1907 Sex:F Child# 10 Joseph Cadieux Canada & Floresca Durand Canada
CADIEUX, Mary Blanche, Apr 29 1916 Sex:F Child# 4 George Cadieux Canada & Adrienne Pelletier Canada
CADIEUX, Rita, May 1 1921 Sex:F Child# 6 George Cadieux Canada & Adrienne Pelletier Canada
CADIEUX, Robert Ronald, Jul 1 1932 Sex:M Child# 1 George Cadieux Canada & Lilliane Cote Manchester, NH
CADIEUX, Roland Wilfred, Dec 16 1924 Sex:M Child# 7 George Cadieux Canada & Adrienne Pelletier Canada
CADIEUX, Romeo Lucien, Nov 27 1904 Sex:M Child# 9 Joseph Cadieux Canada & Florisia Durand Canada
CADORET, Marguerite L, Apr 11 1897 Sex:F Child# 1 Noel Cadoret Nashua, NH & Marguerite Briere New York
CADORETTE, Angelina B, Oct 22 1904 Sex:F Child# 6 Jean B Cadorette Canada & Emma Thibodeau Canada
CADORETTE, Beatrice Blanche, Nov 5 1920 Sex:F Child# 3 Rodrigue Cadorette Canada & Blanche Pontbriand Nashua, NH
CADORETTE, Ernest Edward, Nov 3 1930 Sex:M Child# 2 Roland Cadorette Nashua, NH & Blanche Leblanc Nashua, NH
CADORETTE, Eva Lea, Jul 25 1903 Sex:F Child# 5 Jean Bte Cadorette Canada & Emma Thibodeau Canada
CADORETTE, Francois Noel, Jun 13 1901 Sex:M Child# 2 Noel Cadorette Nashua, NH & Margaret Briere Nashua, NH
CADORETTE, Gerard Roderique, Oct 20 1918 Sex:M Child# 2 Rodrique Cadorette Canada & Blanche Pontbriand Nashua, NH
CADORETTE, Jean Arthur, Jul 22 1933 Sex:M Child# 4 Roland Cadorette Nashua, NH & Blanche Leblanc Nashua, NH
CADORETTE, Joseph Alexander R, Nov 1 1906 Sex:M Child# 7 J B Cadorette Canada & Emma Thibodeau Canada
CADORETTE, Louis, Sep 14 1892 Sex:M Child# 1 Joseph Cadorette Canada & Eulahe Felix Canada
CADORETTE, Marguerite A, Jun 27 1909 Sex:F Child#  J B Cadorette Canada & Emme Thibodeau Canada
CADORETTE, Marie A E, May 26 1898 Sex:F Child# 2 Jean B Cadorette Canada & Emma Thibodeau Canada
CADORETTE, Marie A P, Jan 13 1900 Sex:F Child# 3 J B Cadorette Canada & Emma Thibodeau Canada
CADORETTE, Marie R, Mar 18 1897 Sex:F Child# 1 Jean B Cadorette Canada & Emma Thibodeau Canada
CADORETTE, Normand, Apr 2 1924 Sex:M Child# 5 Rodrige Cadorette Canada & B Pontbriand Nashua, NH
CADORETTE, Rachael Albina, Aug 26 1932 Sex:F Child# 3 Roland Cadorette Nashua, NH & Blanche Leblanc Nashua, NH
CADORETTE, Raymond, Nov 30 1919 Sex:M Child# 3 Rodrigue Cadorette Canada & J Pontbriand Nashua, NH
CADORETTE, Roland Alexander, Aug 25 1929 Sex:M Child# 1 Roland Cadorette Nashua, NH & Blanche Leblanc Nashua, NH
CADORETTE, Therese Priscile, Mar 8 1922 Sex:F Child# 4 Rodrigue Cadorette Canada & Blanche Pontbriand Nashua, NH
CADORETTE, Unknown, Sep 12 1887 Sex:M Child#  Flavin Cadorette Canada & Louise Bosquet Canada Stillborn
CADWELL, Andrea Loraine, Nov 13 1898 Sex:F Child# 2 William H Cadwell Nashua, NH & M Loraine Cotton N Chelmsford,MA
CADWELL, Lucele, Aug 3 1900 Sex:F Child# 3 Harry Cadwell Nashua, NH & Loraine Cotton Nashua, NH
CADWELL, William Dexter, Dec 5 1896 Sex:M Child# 1 W H Cadwell Nashua, NH & Martha L Cotton N Chelmsford, MA
CADY, Arthur Huntley, Sep 22 1911 Sex:M Child# 3 Herbert W Cady Sweetsburg, Quebec & Ella Sweet Richford, VT
CADY, Edward Philip, Jul 8 1927 Sex:M Child# 3 George A Cady Canada & Nellie F Baily Nashua, NH
CADY, Ellen Gwendoline, May 22 1912 Sex:F Child# 2 Edwin E Cady St Albans, VT & Elizabeth H Booth Nashua, NH
CADY, Esther Lillian, Mar 23 1915 Sex:F Child# 3 Erwin E Cady Montpelier, VT & Elizabeth E Booth Nashua, NH
CADY, George Arthur, Feb 3 1924 Sex:M Child# 1 George A Cady Canada & Nellie Bailey Nashua, NH
CADY, Gerald Robert, Aug 26 1925 Sex:M Child# 2 George Arthur Cady Canada & Nellie Bailey Nashua, NH
CADY, Gertrude May, Nov 19 1909 Sex:F Child# 2 Herbert W Cady Sweetsburg, PQ & Ella Sweet Richford, VT
CADY, Jean Ann, Aug 15 1934 Sex:F Child# 2 Arthur Cady Nashua, NH & Jennie Powlowsky Nashua, NH
CADY, Leon Frederick, May 31 1913 Sex:M Child# 4 Herbert W Cady Canada & Ella Sweet Richford, VT
CADY, Mildred Grace, Mar 8 1908 Sex:F Child# 1 Herbert W Cady Sweetsburg, Canada & Ella Phillips Richfort, VT
CADY, Thelma, Nov 16 1914 Sex:F Child# 1 George A Cady Canada & Emma Collins New York
CADY, Unknown, Sep 1 1910 Sex:F Child# 1 Ervin E Cady Montpelier, VT & Elizabeth E Booth Nashua, NH
CAFFRAY, William Edmund, Aug 9 1924 Sex:M Child# 1 R E Caffray Nashua, NH & M R Crompton Montreal, Canada
CAFFREY, Raymond Ellory, Apr 22 1900 Sex:M Child# 1 W E Caffrey NY & Lottie Clark NH
CAFFREY, Unknown, Aug 24 1906 Sex:M Child# 2 W E Caffrey Brooklyn, NY & Lottie Clark Peterboro, NH Stillborn
CAGE, Robert Roger, Mar 4 1914 Sex:M Child# 1 John D Cage Warren, NH & Martha A Oliver Everett, MA
CAHELIKA, Albin, Dec 9 1919 Sex:M Child# 3 Andrew Cahelika Russia & Gelena Mikelewicz Russia
CAHOITE, Alphonse, May 6 1899 Sex:M Child# 7 Simon Cahoite Canada & Lucy Laplante Canada
CAHOUETTE, Marie Albina, Feb 6 1896 Sex:F Child# 3 Joseph Cahouette Skowhegan, ME & Rosalie Marquis Beasom, ME
CAHSZULINES, Joseph, Sep 12 1900 Sex:M Child# 2 Joseph Cahszulines Russia & P Berube Canada
CAKISKIE, Amelia, May 4 1921 Sex:F Child# 5 John Cakiskie Russia & Patta Slachuniena Russia
CAKOWCZ, William, May 20 1913 Sex:M Child# 2 William Cakowcz Russia & Antoca Antolawicz Russia
CALAHAN, James William, Mar 22 1914 Sex:M Child# 4 William Calahan NH & Bernice Bresnahan Mass
CALAWA, Andrew Paul, Nov 11 1929 Sex:M Child# 3 Oscar Calawa Nashua, NH & Alice Pontbriand Nashua, NH

CALAWA, Arthur Robert, Oct 16 1928 Sex:M Child# 2 Oscar Calawa Nashua, NH & Alice Pontbriand Nashua, NH
CALAWA, Irene, Jul 22 1905 Sex:F Child# 7 Peter Calawa Vermont & Lizzie Dionne Alberg, VT
CALAWA, Leon Clarence, Jan 6 1910 Sex:M Child# 8 Peter Calawa US & Elizabeth Dion US
CALAWA, Leon Clarence, Feb 16 1929 Sex:M Child# 1 Leon C Calawa Nashua, NH & Dorothy D Dugas Sterling, MA
CALAWA, Marie Dion, Aug 16 1890 Sex:F Child# 1 Joseph Calawa Canada & Marie Dion Vermont
CALAWA, Marie Eda, Jul 25 1890 Sex:F Child# 1 Pierre Calawa Canada & Elizabeth Dion NY
CALAWA, Mary Rita Cecile, Aug 5 1927 Sex:F Child# 1 Elzear Calawa Nashua, NH & Alice Pontbriand Nashua, NH
CALAWA, Unknown, Feb 9 1924 Sex:F Child# 2 Henry Calawa Nashua, NH & Mary M Zeloski Velma, Russia
CALAWAR, Loraine Catharine, Nov 5 1921 Sex:F Child# 1 Henry Calawar US & Mary Zelosky Russia
CALBONA, Oscar, Sep 14 1894 Sex:M Child# 3 Pierre Calbona Canada & Elizabeth Dionne Canada
CALDARARA, Claire, Jun 23 1930 Sex:F Child# 1 Louis Caldarara Italy & Josephine Marzolia Italy
CALDERARA, Anita Louise, Aug 30 1933 Sex:F Child# 2 L Calderara Italy & J Marzoli Italy
CALDERARA, Frank William, Aug 25 1934 Sex:M Child# 1 Emilio Calderara Milford, NH & Nina Wood Wilton, NH
CALDERARA, Georgiana Beatrice, Dec 23 1916 Sex:F Child# 6 George Calderara Italy & Angelina Biauchi Italy
CALDERARA, John, Apr 25 1924 Sex:M Child# 2 John Calderara Italy & Emelia Crocia Italy
CALDERARA, Joseph Ambrose, Oct 31 1922 Sex:M Child# 1 John Calderara Italy & Emilio Croci Italy
CALDERWOOD, Donald Cameron, May 11 1905 Sex:M Child# 1 W A Calderwood Hollis, NH & Catharine A Courtin MA
CALDERWOOD, Walter A Jr, May 27 1910 Sex:M Child# 2 Walter A Calderwood Hollis, NH & Catherine Curtin Winchendon,MA
CALDWELL, Annette, Oct 11 1919 Sex:F Child# 2 Albert H Caldwell Amherst, NH & Lizzie G Burtt Milford, NH
CALDWELL, Richard Francis, Dec 16 1934 Sex:M Child# 1 Francis Jos Caldwell Manchester, NH & Velma M Fiske Nashua,NH
CALHOUA, Henri, Dec 1 1896 Sex:M Child# 4 Pierre Calhoua Canada & Elizabeth Dion Auburn, VT
CALHOUETTE, Alfred, Sep 18 1893 Sex:M Child# 1 Joseph Calhouette Biddeford, ME & Rosalie Marquis Bassin, ME
CALHOUETTE, Louis F, Sep 8 1894 Sex:M Child# 2 Joseph Calhouette Maine & Rosalie Marquis Maine
CALIN, Marie Rose Diana, Jul 12 1906 Sex:F Child# 6 Alexandre Calin Canada & Ursule Sirois Canada
CALKINS, Lilly Alice, Feb 10 1898 Sex:F Child# 5 John Calkins England & Mary Kelley Ireland
CALLAHAN, Catherine Agnes, Aug 4 1912 Sex:F Child# 3 William Callahan Nashua, NH & Bernice Bresnahan Mass
CALLAHAN, Daniel, Jun 11 1923 Sex:M Child# 5 Charles Callahan Lowell, MA & Isabelle Agnew Dover, NH
CALLAHAN, Ellen, Mar 3 1905 Sex:F Child# 2 James Callahan Ireland & Mary Bresnahan Ireland
CALLAHAN, Francis Joseph, Jul 3 1910 Sex:M Child# 1 William Callahan Nashua, NH & Bernice Bresnahan Fitchburg, MA
CALLAHAN, Johanna, Jun 25 1900 Sex:F Child# 1 James Callahan Ireland & Mary Bresnahan Ireland
CALLAHAN, Margaret Lillian, May 5 1918 Sex:F Child# 6 William Callahan Nashua, NH & Bernice Bresnahan Fitchburg, MA
CALLAHAN, Mary Agnes, Mar 18 1910 Sex:F Child# 3 James Callahan Ireland & Mary Bresnahan Ireland
CALLAHAN, Mary Frances, Feb 19 1906 Sex:F Child# 1 Jeremiah C Callahan Ireland & Frances Collins Nashua, NH
CALLAHAN, Mary Helen, Aug 1 1911 Sex:F Child# 2 William Callahan Nashua, NH & Bernice Bresnahan Fitchburg, MA
CALLAHAN, Patricia, Jul 27 1927 Sex:F Child# 9 William Callahan Nashua, NH & B Bresnahan Fitchburg, MA
CALLAHAN, Robert, Sep 5 1920 Sex:M Child# 2 Wm H Callahan Nashua, NH & Bernice Bresnahan Fitchburg, MA
CALLAHAN, Thomas Edward, Sep 24 1924 Sex:M Child# 8 William H Callahan Nashua, NH & Bernice Bresnahan Fitchburg, MA
CALLAHAN, Unknown, Nov 11 1893 Sex:F Child# 1 John Callahan Ireland & Lizzie Avery Leominster, MA
CALLAHAN, Unknown, Sep 14 1906 Sex:M Child# 1 Charles Callahan Lowell, MA & Isabella Agno Dover, NH
CALLAHAN, Unknown, Aug 2 1910 Sex:F Child# 2 William Callahan Lawrence, MA & Katherine McGravey Mahanoy City,
CALLAHAN, William, Jul 18 1889 Sex:M Child# 9 Cornelius Callahan Ireland & Bridget Palmer Ireland
CALLAHAN, William, Nov 4 1907 Sex:M Child# 2 Charles Callahan Nashua, NH & Isabella Agnew Dover, NH
CALLAHAN, William Henry, Dec 17 1916 Sex:M Child# 5 William H Callahan Nashua, NH & Bernice Bresnahan Fitchburg, MA
CALLAS, Diana Janet, May 19 1932 Sex:F Child# 1 Samuel Callas Greece & Stella Sullivan Poland
CALLIHAN, Maggie Tracy, Sep 6 1898 Sex:F Child# 1 Patrick Callihan Ireland & Mary Tracy Ireland
CALLUCCI, Rose, Sep 12 1924 Sex:F Child# 5 Constant Callucci Italy & Jessie Gallo Italy
CALORUSSA, Marie Rita Yvette, Jul 1 1927 Sex:F Child# 2 Carnina Calorussa Italy & Marie C Lepage Canada
CALVETTI, Norma, Aug 14 1934 Sex:F Child# 2 Arthur Calvetti Italy & Theresa Dutton Canada
CALWA, Albina, Dec 26 1898 Sex:F Child# 5 Pierre Calwa Canada & Elizabeth Dion US
CAMERON, Albert Stanley, Feb 18 1925 Sex:M Child# 1 Albert C Cameron Canada & Bernadette Morin Canada
CAMERON, Charlotte, Feb 25 1906 Sex:F Child# 3 Wilbert Cameron Nashua, NH & Charlotte Herbert Londonderry, NH
CAMERON, Frederick John, Jun 26 1931 Sex:M Child# 2 Albert F Cameron Nova Scotia & Bernetta Morris Chatam, NB
CAMERON, Henry H, Aug 28 1892 Sex:M Child# 1 Wilbert Cameron Nashua, NH & Charlotte Herbert Londonderry, NH
CAMERON, Lucille Wilson, Dec 21 1932 Sex:F Child# 1 H A Cameron Nova Scotia & Louise Baldwin Wilton, NH
CAMERON, Marie Alma A, Sep 23 1900 Sex:F Child# 2 Philippe Cameron Vermont & Ansie Ladry Canada
CAMERON, Marie Anne, Jun 8 1899 Sex:F Child# 1 Moise Cameron Rouses Point, NY & Marie Ladry Canada
CAMERON, Marie C A, Nov 25 1900 Sex:F Child# 2 Moise Cameron NY & Marie Ladrie Canada
CAMERON, Mary Louise, Jun 21 1934 Sex:F Child# 1 John Cameron Schenectady, NY & Fransice Annis Wilton, NH
CAMERON, Unknown, Aug 19 1890 Sex:M Child# 1 Philippe Cameron NY & Anesie Ladry Canada Stillborn
CAMERON, Wilbert F, Sep 3 1903 Sex:M Child# 2 Wilbert H Cameron Nashua, NH & Charlotte Herbert Londonderry, NH
CAMMEDY, John Patrick, Sep 28 1889 Sex:M Child# 3 Patrick Cammedy Ireland & Mary Haley Ireland
CAMPBELL, Arnold Crowell, Aug 14 1914 Sex:M Child# 2 Roy H Campbell Litchfield, NH & Bertha E Griffin Manchester,NH
CAMPBELL, Arnold Theodore, Dec 7 1929 Sex:M Child# 4 Ralph C Campbell Bradford, NH & Elsie Hybsek Manchester, NH
CAMPBELL, Barbara Jean, May 22 1931 Sex:F Child# 5 Oscar Campbell Hudson, NH & Louise Jeannette Nashua, NH
CAMPBELL, Doris, Aug 8 1914 Sex:F Child# 2 Robert F Campbell Bangor, ME & Mary E Bonney Hartford, ME
CAMPBELL, Elaine Virginia, Jun 18 1924 Sex:F Child# 2 Vernon Campbell Palermo, ME & Mildred Lyons Nashua, NH
CAMPBELL, Emma Frances, Sep 25 1900 Sex:F Child# 3 Charles Campbell
CAMPBELL, Frances Tibbetts, Aug 18 1917 Sex:F Child# 3 William Campbell Cambridge, MA & Florence Tibbetts Nashua,NH
CAMPBELL, Frank Arthur, Aug 10 1902 Sex:M Child# 3 F A Campbell Braintree, VT & Annie Warner Southwich, MA
CAMPBELL, Fred Cleavland, Dec 23 1915 Sex:M Child# 2 William H Campbell Cambridge, MA & Louise F Tibbetts Nashua,NH
CAMPBELL, Fred Joel, Dec 19 1898 Sex:M Child# 5 George H Campbell Nashua, NH & Florence A Berry Pepperell, MA
CAMPBELL, George Henry, Jul 13 1897 Sex:M Child# 4 George H Campbell Nashua, NH & Florence A Berry Pepperell, MA
CAMPBELL, Gloria Helen, Mar 24 1926 Sex:F Child# 3 Vernon Campbell Palermo, ME & Mildred Lyon Nashua, NH

CAMPBELL, Gloria Rita, Oct 21 1927 Sex:F Child# 3 Oscar Campbell Hudson, NH & Louise Jennette Nashua, NH
CAMPBELL, Hazel Lizzie, Jun 30 1927 Sex:F Child# 1 Percy Campbell New Brunswick & Larou M Parker Boston, MA
CAMPBELL, Irene Florence, Oct 23 1919 Sex:F Child# 1 George H Campbell Nashua, NH & Ledia Capistrano Mass
CAMPBELL, James Hugh, Jan 28 1897 Sex:M Child# 2 James Campbell Ireland & Lizzie Daley Ireland
CAMPBELL, Jane, Jul 20 1928 Sex:F Child# 1 Frank Campbell Salem, MA & B Ackerman Nashua, NH
CAMPBELL, Jean Maria, Apr 14 1935 Sex:F Child# 1 H W Campbell Londonderry, NH & Bertha Gagnon Hudson, NH
CAMPBELL, Joan Ethel, Apr 14 1935 Sex:F Child# 2 H W Campbell Londonderry, NH & Bertha Gagnon Hudson, NH
CAMPBELL, Margaret, Mar 29 1896 Sex:F Child# 6 John J Campbell Ireland & Ellen Downey Scotland
CAMPBELL, Norma Edna, Mar 18 1922 Sex:F Child# 1 Vernon Campbell Balermo, ME & Mildred Lyon Nashua, NH
CAMPBELL, Oscar Joseph, Dec 31 1893 Sex:M Child# 1 Charles E Campbell Bass River, NS & Annie M Knight Hyde Park, MA
CAMPBELL, Ralph Lee, Aug 15 1931 Sex:M Child# 1 William Campbell Berlin, NH & Dorothy Pierce Plymouth, NH
CAMPBELL, Richard Donald, Mar 1 1923 Sex:M Child# 2 George H Campbell Nashua, NH & Lydia Capistrain E Pepperell,MA
CAMPBELL, Sylvia Dorothy, May 1 1926 Sex:F Child# 2 Oscar Campbell Hudson, NH & Louise Jennette Nashua, NH
CAMPBELL, Unknown, Mar 18 1892 Sex:F Child# 2 George H Campbell Nashua, NH & Florence Berry Newton, MA
CAMPBELL, Unknown, Jul 25 1893 Sex:M Child# 3 George H Campbell Nashua, NH & Florence A Berry Newton, MA
CAMPBELL, Unknown, Sep 29 1895 Sex:F Child# 2 Charles E Campbell Nova Scotia & Annie Knight Hyde Park, MA
CAMPBELL, Unknown, Nov 28 1901 Sex:F Child# 4 Charles E Campbell Bass River, NS & Anna Maria Knight Hyde Park, MA
CAMPBELL, Unknown, Jan 25 1906 Sex:M Child# 2 Clarence T Campbell Hudson, NH & Ella B Whitcher Nashua, NH
CAMPBELL, Unknown, Dec 29 1918 Sex:F Child# 5 Ornam S Campbell Hudson, NH & Hattie Mortlock Nova Scotia
CAMPBELL, Vena Arlene, Nov 26 1923 Sex:F Child# 2 Oscar P Campbell Hudson, NH & Louise Jennette Nashua, NH
CAMPBELL, Verna Lois, Feb 1 1935 Sex:F Child# 4 V W Campbell Balermo, ME & Mildred Lyon Nashua, NH
CAMPBELL, William I D, Feb 7 1893 Sex:M Child# 1 Tyre Campbell Amherst & Mannie Dugle Ireland
CAMPEAU, Joseph Maurice, Feb 21 1930 Sex:M Child# 1 Louis Campeau Canada & Rose Cote Canada
CAMPTON, Harry J, Jul 26 1895 Sex:M Child# 2 J H Campton Lawrence, MA & Stella M Sargent Canada
CANAVAN, Agnes Maria, Sep 27 1907 Sex:F Child# 3 James J Canavan Chicopee, MA & Lillian Connelly Binghamton, NY
CANEY, Unknown, Oct 15 1898 Sex:F Child# 1 Charles W Caney Ellenburg, NY & Daisy B Swallow Rye Stillborn
CANFIELD, Barbara Russell, Sep 28 1912 Sex:F Child# 2 Raymond R Canfield Lenox, MA & Ethel M Adams Nashua, NH
CANFIELD, Muriel May, Nov 21 1908 Sex:F Child# 1 Raymond R Canfield Lenox, MA & Ethel M Adams Nashua, NH
CANTARA, Albert Raymond, Jun 2 1932 Sex:M Child# 3 Edw J Cantara Nashua, NH & Mabel F Smith Nashua, NH
CANTARA, Dorothy May, Jun 4 1924 Sex:F Child# 2 Edward Cantara Nashua, NH & Mabel Smith Nashua, NH
CANTARA, Jerome Cleford, Mar 3 1910 Sex:M Child# 3 Horace Cantara Nashua, NH & Stella Ledoux Vermont
CANTARA, John Edmund, Feb 9 1935 Sex:M Child# 1 Jerome Cantara Nashua, NH & Grace Young Everett, MA
CANTARA, Joseph, Feb 18 1909 Sex:M Child# 2 Horace Cantara Nashua, NH & Estella Ledoux Vermont
CANTARA, Rita Rachel, Apr 6 1934 Sex:F Child# 1 Roland Cantara Nashua, NH & Josephine Laquerre Nashua, NH
CANTARIS, Joseph E, Aug 25 1891 Sex:M Child# 8 Daniel Cantaris Canada & Olivine Lemery Canada
CAOUETTE, Albina, Jan 26 1899 Sex:F Child# 1 Gedeon Caouette Skoagin, ME & Albina Gariepy Canada
CAOUETTE, Alphonse, Jan 13 1900 Sex:M Child# 6 Joseph Caouette Maine & Rosalie Marquis Maine
CAOUETTE, Delima Rosalie, May 10 1901 Sex:F Child# 7 Joseph Caouette Canada & Rosalie Marquis Canada
CAOUETTE, Joseph S Wilfrid, Dec 27 1898 Sex:M Child# 5 Joseph Caouette Skowhegan, ME & Rossalie Marquis Canada
CAOUETTE, Margaret, Nov 8 1899 Sex:F Child# 1 Simeon Caouette Canada & Nelly Burke Ireland
CAOUETTE, Marie Helene, Feb 22 1897 Sex:F Child# 4 Joseph Caouette Maine & Rosa Marquis Beasom, ME
CAPP, Unknown, Nov 25 1888 Sex:M Child# 2 Philip M Capp Wakefield, MA & Besse H Wallace Philadelphia, PA
CAPPUCCIO, Natalie Marie, Jan 8 1930 Sex:F Child# 2 Peter Cappuccio Boston,MA & Alice Woodward Nashua, NH
CAPPUCCIO, Shirely Elizabeth, Nov 11 1928 Sex:F Child# 1 P Cappuccio Boston, MA & Alice Woodward Boston, MA
CAPSALIS, Elaine, Apr 5 1918 Sex:F Child# 1 Christos Capsalis Greece & Marigata Zazora Greece
CARAS, Freda Lena, Dec 8 1923 Sex:F Child# 2 Harry Caras Russia & Ida Padini Russia
CARAYIANI, John, Feb 25 1923 Sex:M Child# 2 Athas Carayiani Greece & Bolon Meykon Greece
CARAYIANIS, Poulo, Jun 7 1923 Sex:M Child# 3 Athas Carayianis Greece & Boulo Mengo Greece
CARBONE, Joseph, Nov 25 1889 Sex:M Child# 1 Elias Carbone Italy & Mary Pezzi Italy
CARBONE, Unknown, Jun 25 1891 Sex:F Child# 2 Charles Carbone Genoa, Italy & Mary Petazzi Milan, Italy
CARBONI, Mary Bertha, Nov 16 1896 Sex:F Child# 4 Charles Carboni Italy & Mary Pitazzi Italy
CARBONI, Michael, Feb 21 1893 Sex:M Child# 3 Charles Carboni Italy & Mary Petazzi Italy
CARBONI, Nicolana, Jun 1 1906 Sex:F Child# 5 Charles Carboni Italy & Mary Petazzi Italy
CARDEN, Hector Claude, Dec 4 1893 Sex:M Child# 2 Dorilla Carden Canada & Eugenie Richard Canada
CARDIN, Adolphe Conrad, Mar 14 1908 Sex:M Child# 1 O P C Cardin Nashua, NH & Sylvia Gay Canada
CARDIN, Adrienne Cecile, May 28 1908 Sex:F Child# 3 Joseph A Cardin Nashua, NH & Mathilda Bourassa Hartford, CT
CARDIN, Alexis, May 27 1904 Sex:M Child# 2 Joseph A Cardin Nashua, NH & M Brousseau N Hartford, CT
CARDIN, Alfred, Apr 3 1893 Sex:M Child# 2 Joseph Cardin Canada & Helene Dubuque Canada
CARDIN, Alice Matilda, Nov 1905 Sex:F Child# 3 Joseph A Cardin Nashua, NH & Matilda Brousseau Hartford, CT
CARDIN, Arthur, Jun 24 1888 Sex:M Child# 3 Perrie Cardin Canada & Anna Lero Canada
CARDIN, Beatrice Irene, Nov 25 1896 Sex:F Child# 3 Dorilla Cardin Canada & Eugenie Richard Canada
CARDIN, Beatrice S, Jul 6 1897 Sex:F Child# 5 Joseph Cardin Canada & Elise Dubuc St Albans, VT
CARDIN, Bernadette, Nov 13 1911 Sex:F Child# 9 Joseph Cardin Canada & Helene Dubuc Canada
CARDIN, Bernard Elphege, May 10 1916 Sex:M Child# 6 Eugene Cardin Nashua, NH & Sarah Moran Nashua, NH
CARDIN, Berthe Irene, Sep 28 1910 Sex:F Child# 6 Joseph A Cardin Nashua, NH & Mathilde Brosseau Hartford, CT
CARDIN, Clifford, May 17 1927 Sex:M Child# 4 Frank Cardin Nashua, NH & Millie Sweet Canada
CARDIN, Delphis, Mar 28 1901 Sex:M Child# 3 Delphis Cardin Canada & Rosilda Dodge Canada
CARDIN, Dolphis, Jun 3 1899 Sex:M Child# 1 Dolphis Cardin Canada & Rosilda Dodge Canada
CARDIN, Gracia, Aug 23 1891 Sex:F Child# 2 Joseph Cardin Canada & Helene Dubuc Canada
CARDIN, Helene A, Jul 15 1890 Sex:F Child# 1 Joseph Cardin Canada & Helene Dubuque St Albans, VT
CARDIN, Jean, Nov 27 1895 Sex:M Child# 7 Pierre Cardin Canada & Celina Herault Canada
CARDIN, John Joseph, Aug 7 1918 Sex:M Child# 7 Eugene Cardin Nashua, NH & Sadie Moran Nashua, NH
CARDIN, Jos Toussaint Fernan, Nov 1 1927 Sex:M Child# 7 Joseph Cardin Canada & Julienne Gauthier Canada

CARDIN, Joseph, Oct 2 1894 Sex:M Child# 6 Pierre Cardin Canada & Anige Lerowe Canada
CARDIN, Joseph A M B, Mar 4 1930 Sex:M Child# 8 Joseph Alexis Cardin Canada & Julienne Gauthier Canada
CARDIN, Joseph E, Oct 2 1888 Sex:M Child# 1 Dorilla Cardin Canada & Eugenne Richard Canada
CARDIN, Joseph L Bertrand, Jul 27 1931 Sex:M Child# 9 Joseph A Cardin Canada & Julienne Gauthier Canada
CARDIN, Joseph Nelson, Apr 21 1921 Sex:M Child# 4 Joseph Cardin Canada & Julienne Gauthier Canada
CARDIN, Joseph Rodolphe, Oct 9 1923 Sex:M Child# 5 Joseph Cardin Canada & Julienne Gauthier Canada
CARDIN, Leo, Apr 23 1900 Sex:M Child# 7 Joseph Cardin Canada & Helene Dubuc Canada
CARDIN, Louis, May 22 1888 Sex:M Child# 7 Alexis Cardin Canada & Anna Birard Canada
CARDIN, Lydia, Oct 4 1894 Sex:F Child# 4 Joseph Cardin Canada & Helene Dubuc Canada
CARDIN, M Anne Helene, Mar 24 1899 Sex:F Child# 6 Joseph Cardin Canada & Helene Dubuque Nashua, NH
CARDIN, M Florence, Sep 16 1914 Sex:F Child# 5 Eugene Cardin Nashua, NH & Sadie Moran Nashua, NH
CARDIN, M Germaine Lucille, May 30 1917 Sex:F Child# 2 Joseph Cardin Canada & Julienne Gauthier Canada
CARDIN, Madeline, Aug 28 1908 Sex:F Child# 2 Eugene Cardin Nashua, NH & Sadie Moran Nashua, NH
CARDIN, Mari Florence Bertha, Feb 18 1916 Sex:F Child# 1 Joseph Cardin Canada & Julienne Gauthier Canada
CARDIN, Marie Anna, Sep 27 1910 Sex:F Child# 3 Eugene Cardin Canada & Sadie Moran Nashua, NH
CARDIN, Marie Denise Laura, Dec 17 1926 Sex:F Child# 3 Hector Cardin Nashua, NH & Rose Perrault Franklin, NH
CARDIN, Marie Evelyn Nancy, Jul 31 1933 Sex:F Child# 10 Joseph A Cardin St Nazaire, PQ & Julienne Gauthier St
CARDIN, Marie Gertrude A, Nov 27 1924 Sex:F Child# 6 Joseph Cardin Canada & Julienne Gauthier Canada
CARDIN, Marie Jeanne d'Arc, Jul 24 1919 Sex:F Child# 3 Joseph Cardin Canada & Julienne Gauthier Canada
CARDIN, Marie O F, Aug 27 1908 Sex:F Child# 1 Arthur Cardin Nashua, NH & Regina Peltier Nashua, NH
CARDIN, Mary Allen S, Jun 13 1901 Sex:F Child# 11 Pierre Cardin Canada & Anna Lareau Canada
CARDIN, Pierre E, Jan 21 1887 Sex:M Child# 2 Pierre Cardin Canada & Anna Gereau Canada
CARDIN, Richard Auguste, Nov 9 1925 Sex:M Child# 2 Hector Cardin Nashua, NH & Rose Perrault Franklin, NH
CARDIN, Rosilda, Mar 14 1900 Sex:F Child# 2 Delphis Cardin Canada & Rosilda Dodge Canada
CARDIN, Sylvia Irene, Jul 1 1905 Sex:F Child# 8 Joseph Cardin Canada & Helene Dubuc Canada
CARDIN, Unknown, Nov 15 1892 Sex:M Child# 6 Pierre Cardin Canada & Anna Lereau Canada Stillborn
CARDIN, Unknown, Jan 9 1912 Sex:F Child# 7 Joseph A Cardin Nashua, NH & Mathilda Brousseau Hartford, CT
CARDIN, Unknown, Mar 5 1920 Sex:F Child# 8 Eugene Cardin Nashua, NH & Sadie Moran Nashua, NH
CARDIN, Unknown, Mar 26 1933 Sex:M Child# 2 (No Parents Listed)
CARDIN, Vincent Russell, Dec 12 1922 Sex:M Child# 2 Frank J Cardin Nashua, NH & Millie C Sweet Canada
CARDIN, Virginia Pauline, Jun 20 1921 Sex:F Child# 1 Hector Cardin Nashua, NH & Rose Perrault Franklin, NH
CARDIN, Vivian Evelyn, Nov 19 1912 Sex:F Child# 4 Eugene Cardin Nashua, NH & Sadie Moran Nashua, NH
CAREY, Frederick Wallace, Jan 18 1933 Sex:M Child# 2 (No Parents Listed)
CAREY, Gertrude, Aug 12 1899 Sex:F Child# 5 Martin Carey Lawrence, MA & Mary McLaughlin NY
CAREY, Mary Ellen Lilly, Mar 9 1918 Sex:F Child# 2 John Carey Kentville, Canada & Mary Kelly Nashua, NH
CAREY, Miller, Dec 23 1903 Sex:M Child# 8 Martin Carey Lawrence, MA & Mary McLaughlin NY
CAREY, Unknown, Feb 9 1913 Sex:M Child# 1 James A Carey Milford, NH & Jennie Doucet Nashua, NH Stillborn
CARICK, Martin, Apr 25 1899 Sex:M Child# 8 Martin Carick Concord, NH & Mary Campbell Lowell, MA
CARIGNAN, Marie Delia, Mar 8 1897 Sex:F Child# 10 Moise Carignan Canada & Genevieve Roux Canada
CARIGNAN, Marie Florilda, Apr 26 1898 Sex:F Child# 11 Moise Carignan Canada & Genevieve Roux Canada
CARIGNAN, Marie Rose, Feb 16 1911 Sex:F Child# 1 William Carignan Canada & Celina Gagnon Fairfield, ME
CARISKIE, Joseph, Oct 20 1914 Sex:M Child# 2 John Cariskie Russia & Petrie Shathinsi Russia
CARKIN, Herbert Beasley, Oct 8 1897 Sex:M Child# 1 Leonard L Carkin Wilton, NH & Matie M Beasley Raleigh Co,
CARKISKA, Grenowefa, Sep 30 1918 Sex:F Child# 4 John Carkiska Russia & Patta Slochunena Russia
CARKISKIE, Sophia, Aug 24 1916 Sex:F Child# 3 John Carkiskie Russia & Nellie Shclomitz Russia
CARLE, George Adelard, Sep 10 1924 Sex:M Child# 2 George Carle Canada & Emilie Boucher Nashua, NH
CARLE, Henry Raoul, May 19 1926 Sex:M Child# 3 George W Carle Canada & A M R Boucher Nashua, NH
CARLE, Joseph Elie Leo, Aug 9 1904 Sex:M Child# 5 Edouard Carle Canada & Diana Trembley Canada
CARLE, Joseph Jules E, Mar 23 1901 Sex:M Child# 4 Edouard Carle Canada & Diana Tremblay Canada
CARLE, Joseph L R C, Apr 12 1903 Sex:M Child# 4 Edouard Carle Montreal, Canada & Diana Tremblay Sorel, Canada
CARLE, Leo Edward, Aug 9 1929 Sex:M Child# 1 Leo Carle Nashua, NH & Yvonne Raby Nashua, NH
CARLE, M Florette Isabelle, Oct 23 1917 Sex:F Child# 3 Olivier Carle Canada & Marie Anne Allard Canada
CARLE, Marie Ange Lillian, Jul 17 1914 Sex:F Child# 1 Olivier Carle Canada & Marie Anna Allard Canada
CARLE, Marie Atala, Aug 7 1916 Sex:F Child# 2 Alphonse Carle Canada & Marie Ann Allard Canada
CARLE, Marie Elise D, Oct 14 1905 Sex:F Child# 6 Edouard Carle Canada & Diana Tremblay Canada
CARLE, Paul Victor, Oct 18 1922 Sex:M Child# 1 George Carle Canada & Emilia Boucher Nashua, NH
CARLE, Theresa Louise, Mar 21 1931 Sex:F Child# 2 Leo Carle Nashua, NH & Yvonne Raby Nashua, NH
CARLETON, Frank Oscar, Sep 28 1918 Sex:M Child# 3 Asa A Carleton Pelham, NH & Stella Wyman Pelham, NH
CARLETON, Unknown, Dec 11 1895 Sex:M Child#  Charles G Carleton Mont Vernon, NH & Lillie M Butler Greenfield, NH
CARLEY, Marion, Jan 9 1898 Sex:F Child# 1 Ernest Carley Lowell, MA & Florence M Hills Hudson, NH
CARLIN, Unknown, Jul 22 1893 Sex:F Child# 3 John R Carlin Vermont & Nellie M Lillie Vermont
CARLSON, Unknown, Nov 2 1899 Sex:F Child# 1 C O Carlson Sweden & Amanda Pearson Sweden
CARLTON, Elaine, Sep 21 1935 Sex:F Child#  Albert L Carlton Keene, NH & Agnes A Pike Laconia, NH
CARLTON, Joseph Leon Robert, Mar 6 1925 Sex:M Child# 1 Clarence Carlton Westport, PA & Marion Moulton Nashua, NH
CARLTON, Unknown, Sep 14 1887 Sex:F Child# 1 John M Carlton Francestown & Mary G Methuen, MA
CARMODY, Mary Ann, May 30 1899 Sex:F Child# 7 Patrick Carmody Ireland & Mary Haley Ireland
CARMODY, Patrick, Oct 8 1893 Sex:M Child# 5 Patrick Carmody Ireland & Mary Haley Ireland
CARNES, John D, Jun 28 1925 Sex:M Child# 1 John D Carnes Concord, NH & Laura D Carr Rainbow Lake, NY
CARNEY, Eunice, Apr 8 1925 Sex:F Child# 2 Joseph G Carney Boston, MA & Bessie E Robbins Bangor, ME
CARON, Adelard, May 26 1897 Sex:M Child# 6 Chrisolugue Caron Canada & Marie Larouche Canada
CARON, Adrien, Jul 8 1901 Sex:m Child# 1 Joseph Anthine Caron Canada & Julienne Chartier New Boston, NH
CARON, Adrien J, Jul 26 1892 Sex:M Child# 12 Francois Caron Canada & Aubeline Morin Canada
CARON, Albert Leo, Apr 8 1919 Sex:M Child# 6 Ernest Caron Canada & Rose Anna Nault Fall River, MA

CARON, Aldea Malvina, Nov 21 1910 Sex:F Child# 10 Honore Caron Canada & Josephine Gingras Canada
CARON, Alfred Elzear, Jul 30 1899 Sex:M Child# 7 Joseph Caron Canada & Adele Bonneau Canada
CARON, Alfred Emile, Aug 30 1902 Sex:M Child# 4 Lud Caron Canada & Delia Labelle Canada
CARON, Alfred Leonard, Jun 9 1913 Sex:M Child# 12 Honore Caron Canada & Amanda Gingras Canada
CARON, Alfred Patrick, Oct 9 1915 Sex:M Child# 6 David Caron Canada & Cecile Ouellette Canada
CARON, Alfred Romeo, Dec 5 1894 Sex:M Child# 4 Emery Caron Canada & Malvina Selville Vergennes, VT
CARON, Alma, Oct 30 1892 Sex:F Child# 4 Chrisotogue Caron Canada & Marie Larouche Canada
CARON, Alphe Roland, Jan 28 1928 Sex:M Child# 1 John Caron US & Rose A Marquis US
CARON, Amable, Mar 15 1895 Sex:M Child# 2 Auguste Caron Nashua, NH & Dorilda Morin Nashua, NH
CARON, Amanda, Sep 17 1887 Sex:F Child# Octave Caron Canada & Marie Larouche P Q
CARON, Andre Aime, May 11 1929 Sex:M Child# 3 Patrick Caron Canada & Lauretta McNicoll Canada
CARON, Anita Eva, Sep 19 1908 Sex:F Child# 2 Ernest Caron Canada & Alma Nault Vermont
CARON, Anne Alvina, Nov 27 1892 Sex:F Child# 13 Belonie Caron Canada & Marie Belanger Canada
CARON, Annette Yvonne, Oct 11 1919 Sex:F Child# 3 Ernest Caron Canada & Blanche Archambeau US
CARON, Arthur, Sep 29 1916 Sex:M Child# 5 Ernest Caron Canada & Rosanna Nault Fall River, MA
CARON, Arthur Adelard, Jan 20 1904 Sex:M Child# 3 Ernest Caron Canada & Oberline Peltier Canada
CARON, Berthe Edith, Apr 24 1903 Sex:F Child# 8 Joseph Caron Canada & Adele Bonneau Canada
CARON, Blanche Theresa, Aug 10 1929 Sex:F Child# 14 David Caron Canada & Cecile Ouillette Canada
CARON, Carmille, May 18 1923 Sex:M Child# 10 David Caron Canada & Cecile Ouellette Canada
CARON, Caroline, May 1 1916 Sex:F Child# 3 Elzear Caron Canada & Flora Levesque Canada
CARON, Chrysologue, Dec 27 1888 Sex:M Child# 11 Charles Caron Canada & Delphine Canada
CARON, Clement Maurice, Sep 10 1904 Sex:M Child# 1 Napoleon Caron Canada & Helene Cardin Nashua, NH
CARON, Deiudonne G, Jan 23 1910 Sex:M Child# 1 Narcisse Caron Canada & Aurore Caron Canada
CARON, Dominique, Feb 24 1894 Sex:M Child# 3 Joseph Caron Canada & Adele Bonneau Canada
CARON, Donald, Dec 27 1917 Sex:M Child# 4 Elzear Caron Canada & Flora Levesque Canada
CARON, Dorothy Cora, Mar 25 1921 Sex:F Child# 5 Elzinard J Caron Canada & Flora Levesque Canada
CARON, Edgar Raoul, Jul 1 1914 Sex:M Child# 1 Mendoza Caron Canada & Blanche Marquis Nashua, NH
CARON, Edwilda Marie Ange, Sep 2 1913 Sex:F Child# 6 Joseph Caron Canada & Adele Gagnon Canada
CARON, Elaine Rita, Jun 21 1929 Sex:F Child# 2 Delphis Caron Canada & Madeleine Lawrence Nashua, NH
CARON, Elise Aline, Sep 2 1907 Sex:F Child# 1 Joseph L Caron US & Maria Langlois Canada
CARON, Emile, Jun 27 1906 Sex:M Child# 2 Joseph Caron Canada & Adele Gagnon Canada
CARON, Emile, Mar 26 1916 Sex:M Child# 8 Alphonse Caron Canada & Rose Dusseault Valley Field, Canada
CARON, Emile Rial, Feb 10 1927 Sex:M Child# 1 Emile Caron Canada & Adele Garivin Canada
CARON, Ernest Olivier, Oct 26 1914 Sex:M Child# 4 Ernest Caron Canada & Rose A Nault Vermont
CARON, Ernest Rudolph, Jan 2 1934 Sex:M Child# 5 Joseph Caron Canada & Adele Lavoie Canada
CARON, Eva, Oct 28 1907 Sex:F Child# 5 Ernest Caron Canada & Oberline Peltier Canada
CARON, Eva Cecelia, Oct 10 1925 Sex:F Child# 9 Ernest Caron Canada & Roseanna Nault Vermont
CARON, Evangeline, Mar 25 1909 Sex:F Child# 1 Jean P Caron Canada & Angelina Dube Canada Stillborn
CARON, Florida, Jun 28 1896 Sex:F Child# 2 Ferdinand Caron Canada & Florida Laplante Salmon Falls, NH
CARON, George, Feb 21 1929 Sex:M Child# 2 John Caron Lewiston, ME & Rose Alma US
CARON, Gertrude Loraine, Jul 14 1927 Sex:F Child# 13 David Caron Canada & Cecile Ouillette Canada
CARON, Hector Camille, Jun 3 1921 Sex:M Child# 3 D Caron Canada & Alma Ouellette Canada
CARON, Henri Ferdinand, Mar 4 1918 Sex:M Child# 3 Dominique Caron Canada & Alma Ouellette Canada
CARON, Henry, Feb 20 1900 Sex:M Child# 14 Olivier Caron Canada & Olivine Marquis Canada
CARON, Henry Delphis, Aug 2 1927 Sex:M Child# 1 Delphis Caron Canada & M Lawrence Nashua, NH
CARON, Henry Edward, Jul 7 1924 Sex:M Child# 1 Henry J Caron Canada & Gert M Bigwood Oakdale, MA
CARON, Hubert Victor, Oct 11 1901 Sex:M Child# 12 Louis Caron Canada & Celina Cote Canada
CARON, Irene Florence, Oct 30 1909 Sex:F Child# 9 Honore Caron Canada & Amanda Gingras Canada
CARON, Irene Lucille, Aug 15 1921 Sex:F Child# 9 David Caron Canada & Cecile Ouellette Canada
CARON, Irenee Napoleon, Feb 18 1892 Sex:M Child# 1 Napoleon Caron Canada & Olivine Ploude Canada
CARON, Isabelle Therese, Oct 15 1900 Sex:F Child# 1 Ernest Caron Canada & Marie Gaulin Canada
CARON, J B Raoul, Mar 4 1906 Sex:M Child# 10 Joseph Caron Canada & Adele Bonneau Canada
CARON, J W Paul, May 26 1926 Sex:M Child# 12 David Caron Canada & Cecelia Ouillette Canada
CARON, Jacqueline Estelle, Nov 25 1931 Sex:F Child# 3 Delphis Caron Canada & Madeline Lawrence Nashua, NH
CARON, Jacqueline Theresa, Mar 27 1928 Sex:F Child# 7 Patrick Caron NH & Laura Poulin Canada
CARON, Janine Muriel, Dec 10 1930 Sex:F Child# 1 Adrien Caron Canada & Antonia Dionne Canada
CARON, Jean, May 27 1921 Sex:M Child# 1 Joseph Caron Canada & Adele Lavoie Canada
CARON, Jeanne Adrienne, Jul 7 1924 Sex:F Child# 1 Adelard Caron Nashua, NH & Bertha Cadieux Canada
CARON, Jeanne Rachel, May 6 1911 Sex:F Child# 2 J B Caron Canada & Angelina Dube Canada
CARON, Jeannette Estelle, Jan 6 1930 Sex:F Child# 5 Oscar J B Caron Indian Orchard, MA & Alma B Lambert Dover, NH
CARON, John Robert Albert, Nov 28 1925 Sex:M Child# 1 John Caron Nashua, NH & Alice Cross Pepperell, MA
CARON, Jos Antonia Dolard, Mar 28 1920 Sex:M Child# 4 Dominique J Caron Canada & Alma Ouellette Canada
CARON, Jos Auguste Henri, Jun 6 1920 Sex:M Child# 2 Auguste Caron Canada & Claudia Ouellette Canada
CARON, Jos Dollard Albert, Jun 6 1920 Sex:M Child# 1 Auguste Caron Canada & Claudia Ouellette Canada
CARON, Jos Gabriel Gerard, Mar 6 1935 Sex:M Child# 2 Alfred Caron Greenville, NH & Rose A St Pierre Greenville, NH
CARON, Jos Jean Emile, Feb 4 1919 Sex:M Child# 5 Francois X Caron Canada & Marie Rose Bayard Canada
CARON, Jos Leo Maurice, Nov 20 1917 Sex:M Child# 3 Pierre J Caron Canada & Albertine Anctil Canada
CARON, Jos Paul Emile Mor, Jul 19 1918 Sex:M Child# 4 Jean Baptiste Caron St Andre Kamou & Angelina Dube St An
CARON, Jos Robert Urbain, Oct 31 1917 Sex:M Child# 7 David Caron Canada & Cecile Ouellette Canada
CARON, Joseph, Jan 9 1896 Sex:M Child# 1 Theophile Caron Canada & Delphine Martin Canada
CARON, Joseph, May 27 1921 Sex:M Child# 1 Joseph Caron Canada & Adele Lavoie Canada
CARON, Joseph, Mar 4 1922 Sex:M Child# 4 Patrick Caron Mass & Cecelia Bruen Nashua, NH
CARON, Joseph Albert, Mar 25 1922 Sex:M Child# 7 Ernest Caron Canada & Rose Anna Nault Vermont

CARON, Joseph Albert A, Aug 7 1905 Sex:M Child# 1 Alphonse Caron Canada & Rose Alma Dusseault Canada
CARON, Joseph Alphonse, Jan 26 1915 Sex:M Child# 7 Alphonse Caron Canada & Rose A Dussault Canada
CARON, Joseph Amable E, Feb 7 1901 Sex:M Child# 1 Amable Caron Canada & Palmyre Dancause Canada
CARON, Joseph Armand, Oct 8 1910 Sex:M Child# 3 Ernest Caron Canada & Josephine Neault Canada
CARON, Joseph D, Sep 14 1891 Sex:M Child# 1 Beloni Caron Canada & Marie Belanger Canada
CARON, Joseph Edouard Henri, Dec 30 1919 Sex:M Child# 8 David Caron Canada & Cecile Ouellette Canada
CARON, Joseph Emile Leo, Jul 29 1927 Sex:M Child# 3 Auguste Caron Canada & Caludia Ouillette Canada
CARON, Joseph Ernest, Jul 13 1894 Sex:M Child# 8 Joseph Caron Canada & Eugenie Cote Canada
CARON, Joseph Horace, Sep 11 1903 Sex:M Child# 1 Joseph H Caron Canada & Emme Pellerin Canada
CARON, Joseph Leopold, Jun 14 1904 Sex:M Child# 9 Auguste Caron Canada & Dorilda Morin Canada
CARON, Joseph Louis, Dec 4 1905 Sex:M Child# 11 Auguste Caron Canada & Dorilda Morin Nashua, NH
CARON, Joseph Louis, Jul 28 1907 Sex:M Child# 12 Auguste Caron Nashua, NH & Dorilda Morin Canada
CARON, Joseph Maurice, Mar 2 1925 Sex:M Child# 3 Auguste Caron Canada & Adele Lavoie Canada
CARON, Joseph Octave, Jan 9 1911 Sex:M Child# 1 Joseph Caron US & Marie Beaudet US
CARON, Joseph Oscar, Jun 17 1908 Sex:M Child# 11 Joseph Caron Canada & Adele Bonneau Canada
CARON, Joseph Ovila, May 30 1903 Sex:M Child# 2 (No Parents Listed)
CARON, Joseph Placide, Nov 5 1891 Sex:M Child# 6 Joseph Caron Canada & Eugenie Cote Canada
CARON, Joseph Robert, Mar 30 1930 Sex:M Child# 2 Emile Caron Canada & Adele Gauvin Canada
CARON, Joseph Roland, Mar 15 1924 Sex:M Child# 4 Ernest Caron Ogdensburg & B Archambeault Nashua, NH
CARON, Joseph Theodore, Dec 4 1905 Sex:M Child# 10 Auguste Caron Canada & Dorilda Morin Nashua, NH
CARON, Laurent Fortunat, Mar 31 1928 Sex:M Child# 10 Ernest Caron Canada & Rose A Nault Barton, VT
CARON, Laurette Olivette, Feb 25 1915 Sex:F Child# 13 Jean Bte Caron Canada & Amanda Gingras Canada
CARON, Leon, Dec 7 1904 Sex:M Child# 1 Joseph Caron Canada & Adele Gagnon Canada
CARON, Leonidas Omer, Dec 28 1907 Sex:M Child# 8 Honore Caron Canada & Amanda Gingras Canada
CARON, Liliane Beatrice, May 3 1910 Sex:F Child# 3 David Caron Canada & Cecile Ouellette Canada
CARON, Lillian, Nov 3 1903 Sex:F Child# 1 Narcisse Caron Westfield, VT & Olive Cayer Newport, VT
CARON, Lillian Leonie, Jul 5 1932 Sex:F Child# 5 Alfred J Caron Greenville, NH & Alexina Bouley Greenville, NH
CARON, Louis Edmond, May 21 1913 Sex:M Child# 10 Gilbert Caron Canada & Claudia Thibault Canada
CARON, Louis Philippe, Dec 25 1890 Sex:M Child# 5 Joseph Caron Canada & Rose Delima Phaneuf Canada
CARON, Louis Philippe, Aug 14 1907 Sex:M Child# 3 Joseph Caron Canada & Adele Gagnon Canada
CARON, Lu Anne, Aug 31 1930 Sex:F Child# 1 William Caron Salmon Falls, NH & Irene McLaughlin Burlington, VT
CARON, Lucia Sylviana, Dec 17 1913 Sex:F Child# 5 Joseph Caron Canada & Rose A Dussault Canada
CARON, Lucille Rachel, Jun 1 1908 Sex:F Child# 2 Ernest Caron Canada & Marie Gaulin Canada
CARON, Lucille Rita, Aug 22 1927 Sex:F Child# 2 Patrick Caron Canada & L McNichol Canada
CARON, M Blanche B, Nov 6 1902 Sex:F Child# 8 Auguste Caron Nashua, NH & Dorilda Morin Nashua, NH
CARON, M Blanche Florette, May 24 1917 Sex:F Child# 2 Frank Caron Canada & Marie Rose Bayard Canada
CARON, M Leopoldine, Nov 9 1891 Sex:F Child# 1 Louis Caron Canada & Odilie Labrie Canada
CARON, M Louise Irene, Feb 22 1911 Sex:F Child# 2 J S Caron Canada & Emma Dancause Canada
CARON, M Regina Aline, Jul 17 1913 Sex:F Child# 5 David Caron Canada & Cecile Ouellette Canada
CARON, M Rosanna, Dec 19 1893 Sex:F Child# 1 Auguste Caron Canada & Dorilda Morin Canada
CARON, Majoric Hubert, Jul 21 1924 Sex:M Child# 4 Willie Caron Canada & Jose de Grandmont Canada
CARON, Marguerite Cecile, May 5 1930 Sex:F Child# 5 Willie Caron Canada & Josephine de Gramant Canada
CARON, Marguerite Mathilda, Jan 25 1928 Sex:F Child# 2 Henry Caron Canada & Gert Grandbois Mass
CARON, Maria A Virginie, Dec 1 1898 Sex:F Child# 1 Joseph Caron Canada & Virginia Thiboutot Canada
CARON, Maria Eva, Nov 5 1898 Sex:F Child# 13 Oliver Caron Canada & Olivine Marquis Canada
CARON, Marie, Feb 20 1904 Sex:F Child# 8 Chrysologue Caron Canada & Marie Larouche Canada
CARON, Marie, Dec 18 1928 Sex:F Child# 4 O J B Caron Ind Orchard, MA & Alma Lambert Dover, NH Stillborn
CARON, Marie Adelia E, Apr 26 1900 Sex:F Child# 2 Ernest Caron Canada & Aubeline Peltier Canada
CARON, Marie Alice, Aug 24 1907 Sex:F Child# 6 Deude Caron Canada & Delia Lebel Canada
CARON, Marie Anna, Jan 8 1895 Sex:F Child# 12 Auguste Caron Canada & Clementine Bernier Canada
CARON, Marie Anna R, Jul 27 1907 Sex:F Child# 1 Ernest Caron Canada & Rose Anna Nault Vermont
CARON, Marie Anne Rachael, Nov 15 1929 Sex:F Child# 8 Patrick Caron NH & Laura Poulin Canada
CARON, Marie Claudia, Jun 24 1889 Sex:F Child# 2 O Ase Caron Canada & Marie Larouche Canada
CARON, Marie D, May 25 1891 Sex:F Child# 1 Joseph Caron Canada & Adele Bernard Canada
CARON, Marie E, Feb 11 1891 Sex:F Child# 1 Napoleon Caron Canada & Demise Arseneau Canada
CARON, Marie E, Jul 11 1895 Sex:F Child# 4 Joseph Caron Canada & Adele Bonneau Canada
CARON, Marie Eugenie, Oct 30 1890 Sex:F Child# 4 Joseph Caron Canada & Eugenie Cote Canada
CARON, Marie Eva, Apr 15 1893 Sex:F Child# 7 Joseph Caron Canada & Eugenie Cote Canada
CARON, Marie G Lucienne, Aug 29 1931 Sex:F Child# 10 Dominique Caron Canada & Alma Ouellette Canada
CARON, Marie Gabrielle, Jul 21 1912 Sex:F Child# 18 Napoleon Caron Canada & Arthemise Dube Canada
CARON, Marie Irene, May 9 1931 Sex:F Child# 3 Emile Caron Canada & Adele Gauvin Canada
CARON, Marie Jean Doris, Sep 13 1933 Sex:F Child# 8 William Caron Canada & J de Grammont Canada
CARON, Marie Jeanne, Oct 19 1904 Sex:F Child# 1 Victor Caron Canada & Delima Dube Canada
CARON, Marie Jeannette Lore, Apr 19 1927 Sex:F Child# 8 Dominick Caron Canada & Alma Ouillette Canada
CARON, Marie Julie Ann, Aug 19 1889 Sex:F Child# 3 Joseph Caron Canada & Julie Cote Canada
CARON, Marie Leopoldine E, Feb 10 1903 Sex:F Child# 1 Joseph Caron Canada & Emma Dancause Canada
CARON, Marie Louisa, Sep 25 1896 Sex:F Child# 8 Joseph Caron Canada & Delima Phaneuf Canada
CARON, Marie Louise, Oct 7 1898 Sex:F Child# 4 Auguste Caron Canada & Dorilda Morin Canada
CARON, Marie Louise, Jun 28 1899 Sex:F Child# 14 Pierre Caron Canada & Marie Anne Soucy Canada
CARON, Marie Louise A, Oct 4 1897 Sex:F Child# 13 Pierre Caron Canada & Marie Anne Souci Canada
CARON, Marie Olivette, Dec 5 1911 Sex:F Child# 4 David Caron Canada & Cecile Ouellette Canada
CARON, Marie Palmire, Aug 13 1905 Sex:F Child# 3 Amable Caron Canada & Palmire Dancause Canada
CARON, Marie R, Mar 7 1901 Sex:F Child# 2 Josepha Caron Canada & Rose Bosse Canada

CARON, Marie R Celina, Feb 18 1902 Sex:F Child# 6 John B Caron Canada & Mary Dumond Canada
CARON, Marie R L, Feb 7 1900 Sex:F Child# 7 O C Caron Canada & Marie Larouche Canada
CARON, Marie Rachelle G, Apr 12 1925 Sex:F Child# 7 Dominick Caron Canada & Alma Ouellette Canada
CARON, Marie Rita Simone, Aug 31 1918 Sex:F Child# 2 Charles E Caron Canada & Angelina Auger Canada
CARON, Marie Rose D, Oct 3 1897 Sex:F Child# 3 Ferdina Caron Canada & Florida Laplante NH
CARON, Marie Rose Yvette, Nov 5 1913 Sex:F Child# 2 Pierre Caron Canada & Albertine Anctil Canada
CARON, Marie Theresa, May 3 1926 Sex:F Child# 7 Elzeard Caron Canada & Flora Levesque Canada
CARON, Marie Theresa, Nov 12 1928 Sex:F Child# 2 John Caron Nashua, NH & Alice Cross Groton, MA
CARON, Marie Theresa F, Jun 16 1929 Sex:F Child# 9 Dominic Caron Canada & Alma Ouillette Canada
CARON, Marie Yvonne, Feb 26 1903 Sex:F Child# 2 Amable Caron Canada & Palmire Dancause Canada
CARON, Mart Oswald, Apr 25 1924 Sex:M Child# 1 J Bte O Caron Nashua, NH & Alma Lambert Dover, NH
CARON, Mary Cecile Anges, Sep 29 1935 Sex:F Child# 1 Wilfred Caron Nashua, NH & Edith Trudeau Nashua, NH
CARON, Octave Mederic, Sep 8 1890 Sex:M Child# 3 Octave Caron Canada & Marie Larouch Canada
CARON, Olivine Dora, Aug 19 1910 Sex:F Child# 12 Joseph Caron Canada & Adele Bonneau Canada
CARON, Omeo, Aug 20 1894 Sex:M Child# 14 Belanie Caron Canada & Marie Belanger Canada
CARON, Patrice Eusebe, Mar 17 1895 Sex:M Child#  Chrysologue Caron Canada & Marie Larouche Canada
CARON, Patricia, Apr 27 1924 Sex:F Child# 5 Patrick Caron Nashua, NH & Laurio Poland Canada
CARON, Paul, May 30 1916 Sex:M Child# 7 Napoleon Caron Canada & Josephine Levesque Canada
CARON, Paul Gilbert, Nov 15 1934 Sex:M Child# 5 Oswald Caron Indian Orchard, MA & Alma Lambert Dover, NH
CARON, Pierre Wilfred, Aug 15 1912 Sex:M Child# 1 Pierre Caron Canada & Albertine Anctil Canada
CARON, Raymond Edward, Mar 13 1933 Sex:M Child# 4 Delphis Caron Canada & Madeline Lawrence US
CARON, Raymond George, Oct 20 1917 Sex:M Child# 2 Ernest Caron Canada & Blanche Archambeau US
CARON, Raymond Luc, Mar 16 1924 Sex:M Child# 5 Elzear Caron Canada & Flora Levesque Canada
CARON, Raymond Maurice, Jan 11 1933 Sex:M Child# 1 Maurice C Caron Nashua, NH & Edith G Beaudet W Chazy, NY
CARON, Raymond Robert, Jun 14 1926 Sex:M Child# 2 Oswald Caron Ind Orchard, MA & Alma Lambert Dover, NH
CARON, Robert, Jul 30 1924 Sex:M Child# 8 Ernest Caron Canada & Rose A Nault Barton, VT
CARON, Robert Maurice, Dec 7 1926 Sex:M Child# 5 Willie Caron Canada & J DeGammon Canada
CARON, Robert Nelson, Jul 29 1925 Sex:M Child# 5 Patrick Caron Nashua, NH & Laura Poulin Canada
CARON, Robert Roger, Apr 20 1927 Sex:M Child# 4 Joseph Caron Canada & Adele Lavoie Canada
CARON, Roger Raoul, Dec 3 1924 Sex:M Child# 11 David Caron Canada & Cecil Ouillette Canada
CARON, Roland Henri, Apr 16 1910 Sex:M Child# 5 Joseph Caron Canada & Adele Gagnon Canada
CARON, Roland Wilfrid, Nov 29 1930 Sex:M Child# 1 Aime Caron Canada & Alice Caron Canada
CARON, Romeo, Mar 5 1914 Sex:M Child# 2 Charles E Caron Canada & Angelina Anger Canada
CARON, Ronald Emile, Jul 6 1935 Sex:M Child# 1 Emile Caron Nashua, NH & Louise L Pelletier Canada
CARON, Rosaire Henry, Nov 29 1919 Sex:M Child# 7 Joseph Caron Canada & Adele Gagnon Canada
CARON, Simonne, Dec 29 1925 Sex:F Child# 1 Patrick Caron Canada & Laurette McNichol Canada
CARON, Sylvio Conrad, Oct 22 1927 Sex:M Child# 3 Oswald Caron Indian Orchard, MA & Alma Lambert Dover, NH
CARON, Thomas Ernest, Apr 3 1898 Sex:M Child# 5 Joseph Caron Canada & Adele Bonneau Canada
CARON, Unknown, Mar 26 1891 Sex:F Child# 1 Theophile Caron Canada & Eugenie Martin Canada Stillborn
CARON, Unknown, Aug 26 1896 Sex:M Child# 2 Joseph Caron Canada & Adele Bonneau Canada
CARON, Unknown, Jun 11 1912 Sex:M Child# 11 Jean B H Caron Canada & Amanda Gingras Canada Stillborn
CARON, Unknown, Nov 25 1915 Sex:M Child# 1 Sylvio Caron Canada & Marie Anne Petrin Canada Stillborn
CARON, Unknown, Jul 30 1927 Sex:M Child# 8 Elzear Caron Canada & Flora Levesque Canada Stillborn
CARON, Wilfred Henry, Feb 4 1907 Sex:M Child# 1 David Caron Canada & Cecile Ouellette Canada
CARON, Yolande, Nov 7 1931 Sex:F Child# 6 Oswald Caron Indian Orchard, MA & Alma Lambert Dover, NH Stillborn
CARON, Yvonne Lumina, Jul 11 1902 Sex:F Child# 1 Ludger Caron Canada & Lumina Dancause Canada
CARON, Zenon Roland, Feb 8 1917 Sex:M Child# 2 Gilbert Caron Canada & Anna Thibault Canada
CAROS, Antricas, Aug 24 1915 Sex:F Child# 4 Nicholas Caros Greece & Nangeli Theodoran Greece
CAROS, Nides, Aug 20 1925 Sex:M Child# 5 Nides Caros Greece & Evan Theodorou Greece
CAROS, Zoe, May 29 1917 Sex:F Child# 5 Nicholas Caron Greece & Mamyel Adams Greece
CAROSA, Unknown, Mar 25 1916 Sex:M Child# 1 Julius Carosa Russia & Victoria Stanas Russia
CARPENTER, Anthony Lawrence, Aug 15 1921 Sex:M Child# 2 Joseph P Carpenter Canada & Agnes M Gilbert Proctor, VT
CARPENTER, Joseph Calvin, Oct 5 1921 Sex:M Child# 4 Arthur L Carpenter Charlestown, MA & Sarah T Eastman Jeff
CARPENTER, Leslie E, Jan 22 1891 Sex:M Child# 1 W E Carpenter Concord & L E Pike Marshfield, VT
CARPENTER, Richard Flagg, Oct 2 1933 Sex:M Child# 4 Napoleon Carpenter Harrisville, RI & Rose Stewart Kittery, ME
CARPENTER, Robert Napoleon, May 23 1932 Sex:M Child# 3 Jos N Carpenter Harrisville, RI & Rose Stewart Kittery, ME
CARPENTER, Unknown, May 17 1896 Sex:M Child# 3 Oliver B Carpenter Vermont & Flora Martin Hill Stillborn
CARPENTIER, Adeline, Mar 16 1904 Sex:F Child# 7 Joseph Carpentier Canada & Melina Lemery Canada
CARPENTIER, Doris Leona, Jul 27 1923 Sex:F Child# 3 Philibert I Carpenti Canada & Agnes Gilbert Proctor, VT
CARPENTIER, Joseph, Jun 28 1894 Sex:M Child# 4 Joseph Carpentier Canada & Melina Lemery Canada
CARPENTIER, Marie Anne C, Dec 9 1897 Sex:F Child# 5 Joseph Carpentier Canada & Melina Lemeris Canada
CARPENTIER, Marie B A, Dec 3 1887 Sex:F Child# 1 Joseph Carpentier P Q & Melina P Q
CARPENTIER, Rose Anne, Jul 20 1900 Sex:F Child# 6 Joseph Carpentier Canada & Melina Lemerey Canada
CARR, Anita, Dec 6 1909 Sex:F Child# 3 Ernest F Carr Concord, NH & Eleanor Keyes Bristol, NH
CARR, Bruce Walker, Jul 28 1920 Sex:M Child# 4 Ernest Frank Carr Concord, NH & Sarah Eleanor Keyes Bristol, NH
CARR, Edward G, Sep 3 1893 Sex:M Child# 1 Henry G Carr Nashua, NH & Viola J Graham Nashua, NH
CARR, Francis Holt, Dec 28 1917 Sex:M Child# 1 Francis Stephen Carr Boston, MA & Bertha Holt Peterboro, NH
CARR, Ruth Naylor, Sep 2 1922 Sex:F Child# 4 True Carr Andover, NH & Marion Foot Orford, NH
CARR, Stephen Field, Mar 29 1920 Sex:M Child# 2 Frances S Carr Boston, MA & Bertha M Holt Peterboro, NH
CARR, Unknown, Dec 13 1910 Sex:M Child# 2 James E Carr England & Anna B Gilman Kennebunk, ME
CARRICK, Alice, Apr 22 1895 Sex:F Child# 6 Martin H Carrick Concord, NH & Mary A Campbell Lowell, MA
CARRICK, George Fanning, Dec 19 1927 Sex:M Child# 1 George Carrick Nashua, NH & Mary Fanning Nashua, NH
CARRICK, George H, Apr 24 1897 Sex:M Child# 7 Martin H Carrick Concord, NH & Mary A Campbell Lowell, MA

CARRICK, John Martin, Aug 10 1935 Sex:M Child# 3 George Carrick Nashua, NH & Mary Fanning Nashua, NH
CARRICK, Patricia Ann, Apr 25 1930 Sex:F Child# 2 George Carrick Nashua, NH & Mary Fanning Nashua, NH
CARRICK, William, Mar 28 1893 Sex:M Child#  Martin H Carrick NH & Mary A Campbell Mass
CARRIER, Emile, Nov 16 1907 Sex:M Child# 1 Jean B Carrier Canada & Clara Lafleur Canada
CARRIER, Gloria Phyllis, Mar 30 1930 Sex:F Child# 1 Emile Carrier Nashua, NH & Amerilda Barriault Canada
CARRIER, Jacline Paulette, Mar 26 1929 Sex:F Child# 1 Leonidos Carrier Canada & Marie Dupont Canada
CARRIER, Joseph Albert E, Dec 30 1910 Sex:M Child# 6 Philias Carrier Canada & Alvina Guay Canada
CARRIER, Joseph Hector R, May 31 1910 Sex:M Child# 3 J B Carrier Canada & Clara Lafleur Canada
CARRIER, Joseph P, Jan 29 1894 Sex:M Child# 1 Philippe Carrier Canada & Amanda Ouellette Canada
CARRIER, Joseph Robert, Nov 10 1920 Sex:M Child# 4 Zoil Carrier Canada & Lumina Tanguay Canada
CARRIER, Joseph Wilfrid, Oct 15 1910 Sex:M Child# 3 Zoel Carrier Canada & Lumina Tanguay Canada
CARRIER, Malcolm Irvin, Jun 29 1926 Sex:M Child# 3 Mederic Carrier Littleton, NH & Blanche Jelly Nashua, NH
CARRIER, Marie Anne, Dec 3 1908 Sex:F Child# 2 Jean B Carrier Canada & Clara Lafleur Canada
CARRIER, Marie Rita, Aug 1 1927 Sex:F Child# 7 Zoel Carrier Canada & Lumina Tanguay Canada
CARRIER, May Rose Lena, Apr 26 1909 Sex:F Child# 5 Phineas A Carrier Canada & Alvina Guay Canada
CARRIER, Phyllis Ellen, Jul 18 1923 Sex:F Child# 3 John Bte Carrier Nashua, NH & Grace Lillian Maden Waltham, MA
CARRIER, Priscilla Ann, Nov 26 1933 Sex:F Child# 2 Emile L Carrier Nashua, NH & A Barriault Canada
CARRIER, Virginia Lillian, Jan 28 1925 Sex:F Child# 4 John B Carrier Nashua, NH & Grace Estes Waltham, MA
CARRIERE, Blanche G, Jul 30 1905 Sex:F Child# 3 Philias Carriere Canada & Malvina Gay Canada
CARRIERE, Clara Donalda, Jul 14 1897 Sex:F Child# 4 Edmond Carriere Canada & Amarine Manseau Canada
CARRIERE, J Edouard N, Jul 21 1911 Sex:M Child# 4 J B Carriere Canada & Clara Lafleur Canada
CARRIERE, Joseph G E, May 19 1903 Sex:M Child# 1 Philias Carriere Canada & Albina Guay Canada
CARRIERE, Leon Antoine, Jul 19 1904 Sex:M Child# 2 Philias Carriere Canada & Albina guy Canada
CARRIERE, Marie C A, Jun 21 1896 Sex:F Child# 3 Edmond Carriere Canada & Amarine Manseau Canada
CARRIERE, Unknown, Jan 17 1912 Sex:M Child# 2 Omer Carriere Canada & Estelle Rioux Canada Stillborn
CARRIERE, Wilfred Edouard, Nov 2 1907 Sex:M Child# 4 Philias Carriere Canada & Alvina Guay Canada
CARRIERES, Aimee Elizabeth, Aug 30 1900 Sex:F Child# 3 John Carrieres Canada & Georgiana Bouchard Canada
CARRIERES, Joseph E, Feb 5 1897 Sex:M Child# 3 Philippe Carrieres Canada & Amanda Ouellette Canada
CARRIERES, Joseph E M, Sep 5 1894 Sex:M Child# 2 Edmond Carrieres Canada & Amarine Manseau Canada
CARRIERES, Joseph H E, Feb 15 1893 Sex:M Child# 1 Edmond Carrieres Canada & Amarine Manseau Canada
CARRIGAN, Joseph Marcel, Feb 16 1894 Sex:M Child# 9 Moise Carrigan Canada & Genevieve Rowe Canada
CARRIGAN, Marion Mary, May 9 1924 Sex:F Child# 1 Richard Carrigan Manchester, NH & Marion Delangis Canada
CARRIGAN, Robert Mullen, Jul 16 1918 Sex:M Child# 2 Alfred J Carrigan Burlington, VT & Ethel G Broderick Boston, MA
CARRIGAN, Rose Alma, Feb 3 1893 Sex:F Child# 8 Joseph Carrigan Canada & Genevieve Roux Canada
CARRIGNAN, Napoleon, Aug 23 1909 Sex:M Child# 2 Joseph Carrignan Canada & Rosalie Audette US
CARROLL, Alma Marguerite, Feb 5 1925 Sex:F Child# 3 Thomas Carroll Ireland & Rose Jeanotte Nashua, NH
CARROLL, Anna Marie, Jul 19 1930 Sex:F Child# 4 James Carroll Lowell, MA & Alice Beauporlant Lowell, MA
CARROLL, Douglas Alan, Mar 24 1930 Sex:M Child# 4 Mark D Carroll Peterboro, NH & Esther Peterson Nashua, NH
CARROLL, Ellen Elizabeth, Aug 12 1897 Sex:F Child# 4 James Carroll Ireland & Nellie Bush Nashua, NH
CARROLL, Frank, Jul 14 1916 Sex:M Child# 7 George Carroll
CARROLL, James Edward, Dec 1 1930 Sex:M Child# 4 Edward P Carroll Nashua, NH & Lillian Russell Nashua, NH
CARROLL, James L, Dec 2 1898 Sex:M Child# 5 James Carroll
CARROLL, John Anthony, Jul 26 1902 Sex:M Child# 5 James Carroll Ireland & Nellie Bush Nashua, NH
CARROLL, John Walter, Apr 24 1935 Sex:M Child# 1 Mark D Carroll Litchfield, NH & Elsie Tanarovicz Nashua, NH
CARROLL, Joseph, Oct 11 1896 Sex:M Child# 3 James Carroll Ireland & Nellie Bushe US
CARROLL, Katherine Elizabeth, Feb 14 1895 Sex:F Child# 2 James Carroll Ireland & Nellie Bush Nashua, NH
CARROLL, Kathryn, Oct 13 1916 Sex:F Child# 1 Timothy F Carroll Stoughton, MA & Katherine A Bowe Woburn, MA
CARROLL, Lawrence Duane, Feb 17 1931 Sex:M Child# 5 Mark Carroll Peterboro, NH & Esther Peterson Nashua, NH
CARROLL, Rose Anna, Sep 5 1921 Sex:F Child# 1 Thomas Carroll Ireland & Rose Anna Jeannette Nashua, NH
CARROLL, Stillman Earle, May 18 1929 Sex:M Child# 3 Edward Paul Carroll Nashua, NH & Lillian Russell Nashua, NH
CARROLL, Thomas Joseph, Dec 10 1922 Sex:M Child# 2 Thomas J Carroll Ireland & Rose Ann Jeanotte Nashua, NH
CARROLL, William, Apr 9 1927 Sex:M Child# 2 William C Carroll Milford, NH & Ada Rieley Derbyshire, England
CARROLL, William Francis, Feb 11 1892 Sex:M Child# 1 James Carroll Ireland & Nellie Bush Nashua, NH
CARRON, Jos Rodolphe Andrew, Sep 23 1923 Sex:M Child# 6 Dominick Carron Canada & Alma Ouellette Canada
CARRON, Joseph L, Sep 25 1892 Sex:M Child# 2 Joseph Carron Canada & Adele Bonneau Canada
CARRON, Marie L C, Mar 21 1901 Sex:F Child# 8 Joseph Carron Canada & Adele Bouneau Canada
CARSEWICZ, Adam, Dec 4 1920 Sex:M Child# 1 Kasimir Carsewicz Poland Russia & Amelia Sedelowskans Poland Russia
CARSON, Jackson Burton, Feb 25 1928 Sex:M Child# 1 J Burton Carson Nova Scotia & Beatrice Martin Concord, NH
CARSON, Richard Donald, Apr 22 1935 Sex:M Child# 2 Robert Carson Rochester, NH & Rose LaHare Pepperell, MA
CARSON, Shirley Mae, May 7 1932 Sex:F Child# 1 Robert Carson NH & Rose LaHare Mass
CARSON, Unknown, Sep 7 1892 Sex:M Child# 2 Edwin H Carson Sharon, VT & Lizzie F Hall Wilton, NH
CARTER, Anna, Jul 9 1926 Sex:F Child# 10 Eugene Carter Nashua, NH & Sadie Moran Nashua, NH
CARTER, Anne Gardner, May 10 1926 Sex:F Child# 3 Eliot A Carter W Newton, MA & Edith Gardner Toledo, OH
CARTER, Carlton Lee, Sep 18 1930 Sex:M Child# 4 Charles Carter Penacook, NH & Yvonne Lecuyer Manchester, NH
CARTER, Christine Mae, Nov 22 1926 Sex:F Child# 4 Ralph W Carter Concord, NH & Anna M Bartlett Northwood, NH
CARTER, David Giles, Nov 2 1921 Sex:M Child# 1 Eliot Avery Carter W Newton, MA & Edith Gardner Toledo, OH
CARTER, Donald Alfred, Aug 30 1928 Sex:M Child# 11 Eugene Carter Nashua, NH & Sadie Moran Nashua, NH
CARTER, Dorothy Mildred, Oct 6 1928 Sex:F Child# 4 L J A Carter Lebanon, NH & Marie H Kelley Sandown, NH
CARTER, Eugene Frank, Apr 30 1907 Sex:M Child# 1 Eugene Carter Nashua, NH & Sarah F Moran Nashua, NH
CARTER, Fannie Kate, Aug 30 1889 Sex:F Child# 2 June A Carter Providence, RI & Belle C Merrill Providence, RI
CARTER, Frank Joseph, Nov 1 1913 Sex:M Child# 1 Joseph L Carter Manchester, NH & Catherine R Hennis Clinton, MA
CARTER, Harold, Jun 26 1900 Sex:M Child# 1 Andrew P Carter NY & Helen Moore Portrush
CARTER, Herman, Oct 30 1901 Sex:M Child# 2 Andrew P Carter Altona, NY & Helen Moors New York

CARTER, John Avery, Jun 16 1924 Sex:M Child# 2 Eliot A Carter W Newport, MA & Edith Gardner Toledo, OH
CARTER, Joseph Lee, Jan 22 1930 Sex:M Child# 7 Fred Carter Quincy, MA & Ruth McMahon Ayer, MA
CARTER, Leonard Joseph, Jan 15 1921 Sex:M Child# 1 Leonard J Carter Lebanon, NH & Marie Kelley NH
CARTER, Madeline Eva, Dec 14 1928 Sex:F Child# 3 Charles Carter Nashua, NH & Yvonne Lecuyer Manchester, NH
CARTER, Marjorie, Dec 12 1932 Sex:F Child# 1 Eugene Carter Nashua, NH & Janice Lynn Nashua, NH
CARTER, Marjorie Eloise, Oct 24 1927 Sex:F Child# 1 Herman Carter Nashua, NH & Vera McCann Northampton, MA
CARTER, Mary Anne, Jul 21 1897 Sex:F Child# 8 Peter Carter Canada & Annie Leron Canada
CARTER, Paul Edward, Dec 21 1926 Sex:M Child# 2 Charles H Carter Penacook, NH & Yvonne Lecuyer Manchester, NH
CARTER, Richard Allan, Dec 16 1933 Sex:M Child# 3 Herman Carter Nashua, NH & Jessie V McCann N Hampton, MA
CARTER, Roy Charles, Jun 2 1930 Sex:M Child# 1 Charles Carter Methuen, MA & Ethel Noyes Wentworth, NH
CARTER, Ruth Madeline, Nov 17 1930 Sex:F Child# 5 Leonard Carter Lebanon, NH & Marie Kelly Sandown, NH
CARTER, Shirley Helen, May 25 1935 Sex:F Child# 4 Herman Carter Nashua, NH & Vera McCann N Hampton, MA
CARTER, Unknown, Aug 26 1891 Sex:M Child# 5 Peter Carter Canada & Annie Leddeau Canada  Stillborn
CARTER, Unknown, Oct 22 1898 Sex:F Child# 1 John H Carter Vermont & Minnie M Davis New York
CARTER, Unknown, Feb 20 1901 Sex:F Child# 1 Frank E Carter Manchester, NH & Florrie M Griswold Nashua, NH Stillborn
CARTER, Unknown, Jun 1 1902 Sex:M Child# 2 Frank E Carter Manchester, NH & F M Griswold Nashua, NH Stillborn
CARTER, Unknown, Jun 13 1921 Sex:F Child# 2 Alphonse Carter Canada & Mary Odesse Manchester, NH Stillborn
CARTER, Unknown, Oct 24 1921 Sex:M Child# 2 Leonard Carter Rutland, VT & Mary Kelley Sandown, NH Stillborn
CARTER, Unknown, Nov 8 1921 Sex:F Child# 9 Eugene Carter Nashua, NH & Sadie Moran Nashua, NH
CARTER, Unknown, Aug 18 1922 Sex:F Child# 3 Alphonse Carter Canada & Mary Odesse Manchester, NH Stillborn
CARTER, Unknown, Dec 21 1922 Sex:F Child# 2 Leonard Carter Sandown, NH & Marie Kelley Sandown, NH
CARTER, Unknown, Dec 30 1923 Sex:M Child# 4 Alphonse Carter Canada & Mary Odesse Manchester, NH Stillborn
CARTER, Virginia Mae, May 21 1933 Sex:F Child# 5 Charles H Carter Penacook, NH & Yvonne Lecuyer Manchester, NH
CARTER, Winthrop L, Jr, Jan 6 1921 Sex:M Child# 4 Winthrop L Carter W Newton, MA & Elizabeth C Barton Newton, MA
CARTEY, Florence Mary, Jan 15 1925 Sex:F Child# 3 Leonard J Cartey Lebanon, NH & Marie Kelley Sandown, NH
CASAVANT, Robert Adelard, May 11 1929 Sex:M Child# 1 Alfred Casavant Sciota, NY & Corinne Galipeau Nashua, NH
CASE, Anne, Jan 7 1891 Sex:F Child# 3 W C Case VT & Etta Jackson Nashua, NH
CASE, Georgie Etta, Dec 3 1903 Sex:F Child# 10 Austin S Case Richford, VT & Etta Jackson Kittery, ME
CASE, Gladys Mabel, Mar 14 1928 Sex:F Child# 1 George R Case Hollis, NH & Gladys Robbins Nashua, NH
CASE, Jean Alice, Apr 19 1925 Sex:F Child# 2 Raymond W Case NH & Lyda M Baldwin NH
CASE, Lillian Edith, Aug 27 1917 Sex:F Child# 2 Raymond W Case Nashua, NH & Clara Winslow Nashua, NH
CASE, Lillian Loraine, Sep 27 1922 Sex:F Child# 1 Raymond W Case Nashua, NH & Lyda M Baldwin Nashua, NH
CASE, Lucy May, Feb 26 1907 Sex:F Child# 3 Samuel H Case US & Elizabeth D Marshall US
CASE, Margie Evelyn, Aug 27 1917 Sex:F Child# 1 Raymond W Case Nashua, NH & Clara Winslow Nashua, NH
CASE, Mary Elizabeth, May 30 1927 Sex:F Child# 3 Raymond Case NH & Lydia Baldwin NH
CASE, Roland Forrest, Jan 28 1905 Sex:M Child# 11 Austin S Case Richford, VT & Georgia E Jackman Kittery, ME
CASE, Ruby, Dec 18 1901 Sex:f Child# 9 Austin S Case Vermont & Ellen Jackson Kittery, ME
CASE, Unknown, Mar 28 1887 Sex:M Child# 1 Austin S Case Richford, VT & Etta G Jackson Kittery, ME
CASE, Unknown, Oct 5 1889 Sex:M Child# 3 Austin S Case Richford, VT & Georgie E Jackson Kittery, ME
CASE, Unknown, Sep 2 1892 Sex:M Child#  Austin Case Richford, VT & Etta Jackson Kittery, ME
CASE, Unknown, Sep 16 1893 Sex:M Child# 5 Austin S Case Richford, VT & Etta Jackson Kittery, ME
CASE, Unknown, Jul 15 1895 Sex:F Child# 6 Austin S Case Richford, VT & Etta Jackson Kittery, ME
CASEY, Mary Katherine, Oct 18 1935 Sex:F Child# 1 John Casey Milford, NH & Winifred Watts Enfield, NH
CASEY, Warner Louis, Mar 28 1931 Sex:M Child# 1 (No Parents Listed)
CASHELMINES, Albert, Sep 2 1902 Sex:M Child# 3 Joseph Cashelmines Russia & Philomene Berube Canada
CASHIONA, Lucretia, Sep 15 1920 Sex:F Child# 2 John Cashiona Greece & Lucretia Testa Greece
CASISTA, Alphonse, Nov 13 1891 Sex:M Child# 9 Francois Casista Canada & Marie Claveau Canada
CASISTA, Francois Abel, Nov 8 1894 Sex:M Child# 11 Francois Casista Canada & Marie Claveau Canada
CASISTA, Henri Arthur, Dec 27 1905 Sex:M Child# 4 George Casista Canada & A Deschenes Canada
CASISTA, Joseph, Feb 13 1921 Sex:M Child# 11 Louis Casista Canada & Virginie Plourde Canada Stillborn
CASISTA, Joseph Albert Oscar, Jun 15 1912 Sex:M Child# 8 Louis Casista Canada & Virginie Plourde Canada
CASISTA, Joseph Francois A N, Sep 19 1910 Sex:M Child# 5 George Casista Canada & Alphnsne Deschesnes Canada
CASISTA, Joseph George Octave, May 2 1900 Sex:M Child# 1 George Casista Canada & Alphonsine Deschesne Canada
CASISTA, Joseph Louis O, Aug 15 1905 Sex:M Child# 3 Louis Casista Canada & Virginie Plourde Canada
CASISTA, Louis John, Mar 24 1908 Sex:M Child# 2 William Casista Canada & Venerence Provencher Canada
CASISTA, Lucienne, Jun 4 1926 Sex:F Child# 1 Hector Casista Canada & G Marquis Canada
CASISTA, Marie, Jul 30 1908 Sex:F Child# 2 Jean Casista Canada & Marie Anne Dumais Canada Stillborn
CASISTA, Marie Albertine, Oct 12 1906 Sex:F Child# 4 Louis Casista Canada & Virginie Plourde Canada
CASISTA, Marie Alida Y, Jul 4 1909 Sex:F Child# 6 Louis Casista Canada & Virginie Plourde Canada
CASISTA, Marie Anne, May 27 1893 Sex:F Child# 10 Francois Casista Canada & Marie Claveau Canada
CASISTA, Marie Anne, Jul 13 1909 Sex:F Child# 3 J B Casista Canada & Marianne Dube Canada
CASISTA, Marie Jeanne B, Jun 21 1908 Sex:F Child# 5 Louis Casista Canada & Virginia Plourde Canada
CASISTA, Marie Mathilda, Apr 13 1911 Sex:F Child# 7 Louis Casista Canada & Virginie Plourde Canada
CASISTA, Marie Violette, Feb 9 1909 Sex:F Child# 2 Joseph Casista Canada & Delvina Maynard Canada
CASISTA, Yvonne, Nov 23 1910 Sex:F Child# 4 J B Casista Canada & M Anne Dumais Canada
CASPAR, Felix, Oct 11 1911 Sex:M Child# 5 Martin Caspar Russia & A Labonkiuta Russia
CASPAR, Peter, Oct 19 1912 Sex:M Child# 6 Martin Caspar Russia & Amelia Lebanic Russia
CASS, Edith, Sep 4 1922 Sex:F Child# 11 Burton Cass Vermont & Mary Corell Peterboro, NH
CASS, Edna H, Jan 9 1920 Sex:F Child# 9 Berton O Cass Vermont & Mary Cornel Peterboro, NH
CASS, Elizabeth Beryl, Jun 1 1922 Sex:F Child# 1 Harley M Cass Vermont & Bernice McKay New Brunswick
CASS, Unknown, Jan 24 1921 Sex:F Child# 10 Berton Cass Vermont & Mary Cornell Peterboro, NH
CASSAVAUGH, Paul, Jun 23 1932 Sex:M Child# 2 A Cassavaugh New York & Corinne Galipeau NH
CASSETT, Harriet, Apr 28 1917 Sex:F Child# 1 Myer Cassett Romania & Sadie Ida Kimball Concord, NH

CASSETTE, Marie Albertine, Feb 3 1915 Sex:F Child# 1 Xavier Cassette Canada & Blanche Pelletier Canada
CASSEVACH, Leo A, Aug 13 1903 Sex:M Child#  Fred Cassevach New York & Emma Mayo New York
CASSEVAH, Robart John, Feb 23 1899 Sex:M Child#  Fred G Cassevah NY & Emma N Mayo NY
CASSEVAH, Unknown, Mar 9 1897 Sex:F Child# 1 Fred Cassevah NY & Emma Mayo NY Stillborn
CASSEVANT, Unknown, Dec 16 1900 Sex:F Child# 3 Fred Cassevant New York & Emma Mayo New York
CASSIDY, Aldon Leroy, May 17 1917 Sex:M Child# 4 Clifford V Cassidy Canada & Ethel M Cummings Hudson, NH
CASSISTA, Achille, Feb 1 1903 Sex:M Child# 3 George Cassista Canada & Alphonsine Deschenes Canada
CASSISTA, Bertrand, Oct 17 1928 Sex:M Child# 3 Hector Cassista Canada & Germaine Marquis Canada
CASSISTA, Helen Priscilla, Apr 8 1934 Sex:F Child# 1 Armedee Cassista Nashua, NH & Marcelle Charest Nashua, NH
CASSISTA, J Amedee, Oct 20 1913 Sex:M Child# 9 Louis Cassista Canada & Virginie Plourde Canada
CASSISTA, Leon Ernest, Feb 18 1908 Sex:M Child# 1 Joseph Cassista Canada & Delvina Maynard Nashua, NH
CASSISTA, M Rose Annette, Feb 15 1915 Sex:F Child# 11 Louis Cassista Canada & Virginie Plourde Canada
CASSISTA, Marie Elmire, Feb 21 1902 Sex:F Child# 1 Simeon Cassista Canada & Clara Joyal NY
CASSISTA, Marie Laura M, May 25 1904 Sex:F Child# 2 Louis Cassista Canada & Virginie Plourde Canada
CASSISTA, Marie Rose Y, Apr 25 1903 Sex:F Child# 1 Louis Cassista Canada & Virginie Plourde Canada
CASSISTA, Raymond, Jul 3 1927 Sex:M Child# 2 Hector Cassista Canada & Germaine Marquis Canada
CASSISTA, Rosa, Aug 26 1903 Sex:F Child# 1 Joseph Cassista Canada & Aurore Beaudreau Canada
CASSISTA, Simeon Wilfrid, Aug 25 1901 Sex:M Child# 2 Georges Cassista Canada & Alphonsine Deschesne Canada
CASTANGUAY, Maurice Guy, Dec 12 1934 Sex:M Child# 3 George Castanguay Canada & Albertine Sirois Canada
CASTIGAN, Kenend, Nov 14 1912 Sex:M Child# 5 Paul Castigan Turkey & Mary Zovartin Turkey  Stillborn
CASTONGUAY, Alphonse William, May 7 1922 Sex:M Child# 2 Antoine Castonguay Canada & Germaine Anctil Canada
CASTONGUAY, Gabrielle Gertrude, Jan 2 1921 Sex:F Child# 1 Antonio Castonguay Canada & Germaine Anctil Canada
CASTONGUAY, J B Wilfrid, Apr 11 1923 Sex:M Child# 3 Antonio Castonguay Canada & Germaine Anctil Canada
CASTONGUAY, Jean Baptiste, Oct 26 1890 Sex:M Child# 2 Joseph Castonguay Canada & Adile Carou Canada
CASTONGUAY, Jeanne d'Arc T, Nov 30 1924 Sex:F Child# 4 A Castonguay Canada & Germaine Anctil Canada
CASTONGUAY, Joseph Henry, May 24 1900 Sex:M Child# 2 Omer Castonguay Canada & Marie L Diane Canada
CASTONGUAY, M Jeanne d'Arc Rita, May 27 1921 Sex:F Child# 1 Charles Castonguay Canada & Amanda Cote Canada
CASTONGUAY, Marie, Sep 8 1931 Sex:F Child# 1 Elude Castonguay Canada & Catherine Sirois Canada
CASTONGUAY, Marie Dorothy, May 24 1923 Sex:F Child# 2 Charles Castonguay Canada & Armanda Cote Canada
CASTONGUAY, Marie L Odile, Jan 1 1899 Sex:F Child# 1 Omer Castonguay Canada & Marie Louise Dionne Canada
CASTONGUAY, Robert Elude, Jul 22 1932 Sex:M Child# 2 E Castonguay Canada & Catherine Sirois Canada
CASTOR, Arline Ruth, Jan 15 1912 Sex:F Child# 2 Carl Castor Vermont & Elizabeth Lovejoy NH
CASTORGUAY, Joseph, Apr 21 1889 Sex:M Child# 1 Joseph Castorguay Canada & Adele Caron Canada
CASWELL, Millard Harold, May 5 1931 Sex:M Child# 4 Maynard H Caswell Newport, VT & Dora Regina Roy Canada
CASWELL, Milton Roy, Jan 9 1922 Sex:M Child# 2 Maynard Caswell Newport, VT & Dora Roy Canada
CASWELL, Priscilla Alden, Dec 30 1917 Sex:F Child# 2 George E Caswell Epping, NH & Irene Lessard Canada
CASWELL, Rosamond, Jun 1 1929 Sex:F Child# 3 Maynard H Caswell Newport, VT & Dora Roy Canada
CATE, Unknown, Jun 20 1898 Sex:F Child# 1 Warren J Cate W Deering & Emma B Lewis Dickerman, NS
CATHON, Unknown, Apr 22 1916 Sex:M Child# 1 John Cathon Greece & Anthe Cthyois Greece
CATHRA, Annie, May 3 1917 Sex:F Child# 2 John Cathra Greece & Authe Ctason Greece
CATTABRIGIA, Annie, Feb 12 1908 Sex:F Child# 1 Celso Cattabrigia Italy & Maria Leonardi Italy
CATTABRIGIA, Carlo, May 2 1909 Sex:M Child# 2 Celso Cattabrigia Italy & Mary Leonardi Italy
CAULFIELD, Elizabeth, Nov 18 1922 Sex:F Child# 4 Thos F Caulfield Boston, MA & Mary H Sullivan Manchester, NH
CAULFIELD, Mary Frances, Oct 12 1916 Sex:F Child# 2 Thmas F Caulfield Boston, MA & Mary H Sullivan Manchester, NH
CAULFIELD, Paul Thomas, Nov 25 1919 Sex:M Child# 3 Thomas F Caulfield Boston, MA & Mary H Sullivan Manchester, NH
CAURCIS, Joseph A, Sep 30 1889 Sex:M Child# 2 Joseph Caurcis Canada & Mary Gesard Canada
CAUTARA, Roland Aurel, Feb 25 1908 Sex:M Child# 1 Horace J Cautara Nashua, NH & Stella M Ledoux St Albans, VT
CAUTARAS, Coine R O, Mar 18 1895 Sex:M Child# 9 Daniel Cautaras Canada & Olivine Lemery Canada
CAUTARAS, Roseanne, Apr 28 1889 Sex:F Child# 7 Daniel Cautaras Canada & Olivine Lemery Canada
CAVANAGH, William Francis, Mar 10 1903 Sex:M Child# 6 Dennis J Cavanagh Ireland & Mary Bradley Ireland
CAVANAUGH, Dennis, Jul 7 1897 Sex:M Child# 4 Dennis J Cavanaugh Ireland & Mary Bradley Ireland
CAVANAUGH, John Joseph, Feb 9 1900 Sex:M Child# 5 Dennis Cavanaugh Ireland & Mary Bradley Ireland
CAVANAUGH, Margaret, Jul 25 1895 Sex:F Child# 3 Dennis Cavanaugh Ireland & Mary Bradley Ireland
CAVANAUGH, Unknown, Sep 26 1894 Sex:F Child# 2 D J Cavanaugh Ireland & Minnie Bradley Ireland Stillborn
CAYWARD, John Carlos, Mar 3 1935 Sex:M Child# 2 Claire Cayward Orleans, NY & Della Martin Vermont
CECKA, William, Jun 19 1914 Sex:M Child# 1 Michael Cecka Russia & Annie Klimaczawcka Russia
CEDERHOLM, Bernard Lionel, Mar 25 1913 Sex:M Child# 4 Adolph Cederholm Sweden & Elizabeth Johnson Sweden
CELLUCCI, Antonio, Jun 1 1920 Sex:M Child# 2 Costonzo Cellucci Italy & Cesidia Gallo Italy
CELLUCCI, Thomas, May 2 1926 Sex:M Child# 6 Constazo Cellucci Italy & Jessie Gallo Italy
CELLUCI, Dominica, Jul 8 1923 Sex:F Child# 4 Costanzo Celluci Italy & Cesidia Gallo Italy
CELOSKI, Richard Kenneth, Feb 17 1932 Sex:M Child# 3 (No Parents Listed)
CENTER, Bruce Carl, Dec 3 1929 Sex:M Child# 2 Carroll H Center Wilton, NH & Winona Frye Wilton, NH
CENTER, Kay Agnes, May 29 1931 Sex:F Child# 2 Leon Frank Center Reeds Ferry, NH & Mabel A Beard Weare, NH
CENTER, Leon Frank, Jr, Jul 6 1934 Sex:M Child# 4 Leon Frank Center Reeds Ferry, NH & Mabel Beard Weare, NH
CENTER, Marjorie Ann, May 17 1931 Sex:F Child# 1 Henry Center Medford, MA & Margaret Dorchester, MA
CENTER, Martha Carole, Jan 21 1934 Sex:F Child# 3 Carroll H Center Wilton, NH & Winona E Frye Wilton, NH
CENTER, Mary Louise, May 18 1934 Sex:F Child# 3 Henry Center Medford, MA & Margaret Dolphin Dorchester, MA
CENTOIENTI, Joseph Gerald John, Sep 23 1923 Sex:M Child# 1 John Centoienti Italy & Marie Anna Lucier MA
CEPLIT, Adolt, Apr 2 1913 Sex:M Child# 3 Adolt Ceplit Russia & Antosa Cinkawich Russia
CEREIER, Rosie, Sep 24 1910 Sex:F Child# 2 Joseph Cereier Russia & Sarah Partner Russia
CERHAGIE, Joseph, Oct 17 1915 Sex:M Child# 1 Kostanta Cerhagie Russia & Victoria Valaguvitch Russia
CERIER, Melvin Myron, Apr 1 1930 Sex:M Child# 2 Louis Cerier Russia & Jennie Zetlan Russia
CERIER, Sidney, May 18 1923 Sex:M Child# 1 Samuel Cerier Russia & Esther B Kaplan Russia

CERIER, William Irving, Mar 1 1926 Sex:M Child# 1 Louis Cerier Russia & Jennie Zeithen Russia
CERNATA, Raymond Paul, Nov 29 1930 Sex:M Child# 1 Paul Cernata Czechoslovakia & Mary Fric Czechoslovakia
CERRIEN, Rose Germaine, Mar 14 1917 Sex:F Child# 1 Euclide Cerrien Manchester, NH & Marie A Arpin Canada
CESNULAWICZEOI, Maletus, Jul 20 1905 Sex:M Child# 3 M Cesnulawiczeoi Russia & Annie Kruszute Russia
CHABOT, Claire Lucille, Feb 13 1932 Sex:F Child# 7 Theoph'us Chabot Canada & M L Lemelin Canada
CHABOT, Claude, Mar 28 1934 Sex:M Child# 6 Francois Chabot Canada & Alma Tanguay Canada
CHABOT, Donald Oscar, Feb 4 1934 Sex:M Child# 8 Theophitus Chabot Canada & Laura Lemelin Canada
CHABOT, Jean Raymond, Feb 9 1928 Sex:M Child# 2 Francis Chabot Canada & Alma Tanguay Canada
CHABOT, Jos Francis Fernand, Jun 4 1928 Sex:M Child# 5 Jos T Chabot Canada & M Laura Lemelin Canada
CHABOT, Jos Lionel Robert, Aug 11 1923 Sex:M Child# 3 Theophatus J Chabot Canada & Marie Lemein Canada
CHABOT, Joseph Jean Paul, May 7 1922 Sex:M Child# 2 J Theophitus Chabot Canada & Laura Lemelin Canada
CHABOT, Julien Roland, Jan 28 1927 Sex:M Child# 1 Francis Chabot Canada & Alma Tanguay Canada
CHABOT, Leo Dominique, Aug 4 1925 Sex:M Child# 4 Theo J Chabot Canada & Laura Lemelin Canada
CHABOT, Lionel Antoine, Dec 8 1932 Sex:M Child# 6 Francois Chabot Canada & Alma Tanguay Canada
CHABOT, Marie Dianne, Oct 29 1931 Sex:F Child# 5 Francois Chabot Canada & Alma Tanguay Canada
CHABOT, Marie R Jeanne d'Arc, Dec 11 1920 Sex:F Child# 1 Theophites Chabot Canada & Laura Lamelin Canada
CHABOT, Paul Marcel, Oct 17 1930 Sex:M Child# 4 Francois Chabot Canada & Alma Tanguay Canada
CHABOT, Theresa Rita, May 5 1929 Sex:F Child# 6 Theophetus J Chabot Canada & Laura Lemelin Canada
CHACOS, Cecelia, Jan 20 1925 Sex:F Child# 1 George Chacos England & Olivette Marquis Nashua, NH
CHACOS, Dolores Olivette, Jul 30 1927 Sex:F Child# 3 G T Chacos England & Olivette Marquis Nashua, NH
CHACOS, Unknown, Aug 3 1926 Sex:M Child# 2 George Chacos England & Olivette Marquis Nashua, NH Stillborn
CHACOS, Unknown, Aug 18 1933 Sex:F Child# 7 George Chacos England & Olivette Marquis Canada
CHACOS, Unknown, Sep 14 1935 Sex:F Child# 8 George Chacos England & Olivette Marquis Canada
CHAGNON, Alfred, Mar 29 1907 Sex:M Child# 2 Octave Chagnon Nashua, NH & Mary Cleary Nashua, NH
CHAGNON, Alphonse O R, Mar 3 1906 Sex:M Child# 2 Telesphore Chagnon Nashua, NH & Marie Dube Canada
CHAGNON, Alphonse R G, Apr 19 1909 Sex:M Child# 3 David Chagnon US & Maria Dupont Canada
CHAGNON, Beatrice A, Oct 13 1903 Sex:F Child# 1 Telesphore Chagnon Nashua, NH & Maria Dube Canada
CHAGNON, Bernadette Rejeanne, Jan 29 1926 Sex:F Child# 6 Omer Chagnon
CHAGNON, Carinne, Jan 7 1888 Sex:F Child# 8 Hercules Chagnon Canada & Sophia Ledoux St Albans, VT
CHAGNON, Denise E L, Jul 30 1910 Sex:F Child# 1 Emile Chagnon Nashua, NH & Alice Peloquin Canada
CHAGNON, Emile Alfred, Jr, Jul 4 1928 Sex:M Child# 1 E A Chagnon Nashua, NH & Alice Peloquin Canada
CHAGNON, Ferdinand Roger, Oct 18 1913 Sex:M Child# 2 Emile A Chagnon Nashua, NH & Alice Poliquin Canada
CHAGNON, George Paul, Nov 8 1910 Sex:M Child# 1 George E Chagnon US & Amanda Dufour Canada
CHAGNON, Germaine L, Oct 13 1899 Sex:F Child# 11 Alphonse Chagnon Canada & Adele St Georges Canada
CHAGNON, Ida Simone, Jul 21 1907 Sex:F Child# 2 David Chagnon Canada & Maria Dupont Canada
CHAGNON, Jos Aime Jean Guy, Mar 27 1927 Sex:M Child# 4 Herve Chagnon Canada & Valeria Forcier Canada
CHAGNON, Joseph, Jan 15 1888 Sex:M Child# 5 Alphonse Chagnon Verchines, PQ & Adile St George Vernumes, PQ
CHAGNON, Joseph, Mar 19 1890 Sex:M Child# 9 Hercules Chagnon Canada & Sophie Ledoux Canada
CHAGNON, Joseph Marcel Omer, Feb 16 1927 Sex:M Child# 1 Eugene Chagnon Canada & Bertha Ritchie Canada
CHAGNON, Julienne Olivette, Jan 9 1913 Sex:F Child# 6 Telesphore Chagnon Nashua, NH & Marie Dube Canada
CHAGNON, Kenneth Paul, May 1 1925 Sex:M Child# 2 Archie Chagnon Nashua, NH & Marie Keanan Nashua, NH
CHAGNON, M Lucille Eleanor, Jan 25 1921 Sex:F Child# 1 Archie H Chagnon Nashua, NH & Anna Marie Keenan Nashua, NH
CHAGNON, Marie D, Nov 1 1898 Sex:F Child# 10 Alphonse Chagnon Canada & Adele St George Canada
CHAGNON, Marie L, Oct 4 1889 Sex:F Child# 3 Alphonse Chagnon Canada & Apoline Dube Canada
CHAGNON, Marie Lucienne, Nov 14 1904 Sex:F Child# 1 David Chagnon US & Maria Dupont Canada
CHAGNON, Marie Oliva A D, Dec 22 1908 Sex:F Child# 3 Telesphore Chagnon Canada & Mary Dube Canada
CHAGNON, Mariette Alene, Jan 8 1920 Sex:F Child# 4 Emile Chagnon Nashua, NH & Alice Peloquin Canada
CHAGNON, Olivine E, Mar 1 1893 Sex:F Child# 10 Hercule Chagnon Canada & Sophie Ledoux St Albans, VT
CHAGNON, Paule Emile, Mar 19 1918 Sex:M Child# 3 Emile Chagnon Nashua, NH & Alice Poloquin St Hyancinthe, PQ
CHAGNON, Robert Emmett, Mar 10 1906 Sex:M Child# 1 Hector Chagnon Nashua, NH & Mary B Cleary Nashua, NH
CHAGNON, Roger R Oscar, Oct 24 1924 Sex:M Child# 5 Omer Chagnon Canada & Aurore Jodoin Nashua, NH
CHAGNON, Unknown, Jul 12 1929 Sex:M Child# 7 Omer Chagnon Canada & Ora Jodoin NH Stillborn
CHAGNON, Virginia Louise, Jan 4 1935 Sex:F Child# 1 Geo P Chagnon Nashua, NH & Mary G Davin Dorchester, MA
CHAGRIN, Arthur, Oct 20 1892 Sex:M Child# 1 Oscar S Chagrin Coopersville, NY & Valerie Trow St Hyacinthe, Canada
CHAGRIN, Frederic, Feb 28 1900 Sex:M Child# 2 Oscar Sans Chagrin New York & Valerie Yvon Canada
CHALIFOUX, Clare Joan, Jul 29 1926 Sex:F Child# 3 John B Chalifoux Canada & Mary L Baker Ellenburg, NY
CHAMARD, Antonia, Sep 27 1913 Sex:F Child# 1 Eustache Chamard Canada & Lumina Guillemain Canada
CHAMARD, J Elzear Rene Leon, Aug 2 1915 Sex:M Child# 5 Ludger Chamard Canada & Amanda Gagnon Canada
CHAMARD, Roger Raymond, Feb 12 1924 Sex:M Child# 1 Joseph A Chamard Canada & Rosanna Lafrance Canada
CHAMARD, Yvonne Liliane, May 6 1916 Sex:F Child# 2 Eustache Chamard Canada & Lumina Guillemain Canada
CHAMART, Therese, Apr 10 1919 Sex:F Child# 4 Eustache Chamart Canada & Lumina Guilmain Canada
CHAMBERLAIN, Annie Muriel, Sep 28 1915 Sex:F Child# 3 Geo M Chamberlain Altona, NY & Maude Murdoe St John, NB
CHAMBERLAIN, Carolyn Ann, Jun 3 1934 Sex:F Child# 4 Chas M Chamberlain Nashua, NH & Lillian Dichard Nashua, NH
CHAMBERLAIN, Charles Manford, Jul 22 1903 Sex:M Child# 1 George M Chamberlain Mason, VT & Annie M Munde St John, NB
CHAMBERLAIN, Ella May, Dec 23 1911 Sex:F Child# 1 Clyde Chamberlain Winsor, ME & Myrtle Brown Brunswick, ME
CHAMBERLAIN, Ernest Albert Herve, Jan 19 1914 Sex:M Child# 9 P Chamberlain Canada & Mathilde Canada
CHAMBERLAIN, Esther May, Feb 3 1905 Sex:F Child# 4 Chas E Chamberlain New York & Minnie Lizotte New York
CHAMBERLAIN, George, Nov 12 1890 Sex:M Child# 2 Louis Chamberlain Canada & Elmire Duany Canada
CHAMBERLAIN, George Howard, Nov 2 1908 Sex:M Child# 2 George M Chamberlain New York & Annie M Mundie St John, NB
CHAMBERLAIN, Harold, May 29 1912 Sex:M Child# 1 Hector Chamberlain Nashua, NH & Julia E Grave Florence, MA
CHAMBERLAIN, Ida Bernice, Feb 11 1900 Sex:F Child# 3 Chas E Chamberlain New York & Minnie Leazotte New York
CHAMBERLAIN, Jeannette Lucille, Sep 26 1920 Sex:F Child# 6 George Chamberlain Nashua, NH & Emelia Senecal Nashua, NH
CHAMBERLAIN, John B Hector, Jun 24 1889 Sex:M Child# 2 John B Chamberlain Nashua, NH & Georgia Lawrence N Chelmsfor

CHAMBERLAIN, Jos George Raymond, Mar 24 1918 Sex:M Child# 4 Geo L Chamberlain Nashua, NH & Amelia Senecal Nashua,NH
CHAMBERLAIN, Lora Frances, Dec 24 1898 Sex:F Child# 2 Wm C Chamberlain Altona, NY & Carrie S Miles Mooers, NY
CHAMBERLAIN, Maria, Jun 27 1892 Sex:F Child# 4 John B Chamberlain US & Georgia Lawrence US
CHAMBERLAIN, Normand Louis, Mar 14 1919 Sex:M Child# 4 George Chamberlain Nashua, NH & Emilia Senecal Nashua, NH
CHAMBERLAIN, Stella Adeline, Jan 4 1913 Sex:F Child# 2 George L Chamberlain Nashua, NH & Amelia C Senecal Nashua,NH
CHAMBERLAN, Adeline, Nov 7 1887 Sex:F Child#   Jean Chamberlan Nashua, NH & Georgina Lawrence N Chelmsford, MA
CHAMBERLAN, Amanda, Oct 4 1894 Sex:F Child# 6 John Chamberlan Canada & Georgiana Lawrence N Chelmsford, MA
CHAMBERLAN, Florence Pauline, Apr 2 1891 Sex:F Child# 3 John Chamberlan Nashua, NH & Georgina Lawrence N Chelmsford
CHAMBERLAN, Marie A C, Aug 10 1890 Sex:F Child# 2 Gaspard Chamberlan Canada & Marie Belanger Canada
CHAMBERLAN, Mary Gertrude, Feb 11 1897 Sex:F Child# 8 J B Chamberlan Nashua, NH & Georgianna Laurence N Chelmsford
CHAMBERLAN, Paul Lawrence, Feb 6 1909 Sex:M Child# 9 John Chamberlan US & Georgia Lawrence US
CHAMBERLAND, Armand Arthur, Nov 30 1907 Sex:M Child# 1 Joseph Chamberland Canada & Alexina Garand Canada
CHAMBERLAND, Clarence Eugene, Aug 28 1932 Sex:M Child# 2 Eugene Chamberlan St Pacome, Canada & Viola Maheu Ne
CHAMBERLAND, Joseph, Jul 11 1893 Sex:M Child# 5 Jean B Chamberland Nashua, NH & Georgiana Laurence Tyngsboro, MA
CHAMBERLAND, Joseph A, May 10 1892 Sex:M Child# 3 Gaspard Chamberland Canada & Marie Belanger Canada
CHAMBERLAND, Joseph Alfred, Dec 3 1933 Sex:M Child# 1 O Chamberland Canada & Aurore Dupont Nashua, NH
CHAMBERLAND, Marie, Oct 31 1888 Sex:F Child# 1 Guspard Chamberland Canada & Marie Belanger Canada
CHAMBERLAND, Marie A L, Dec 12 1907 Sex:F Child# 1 Hector Chamberland Nashua, NH & Athala Levesque Canada
CHAMBERLAND, Oscar Leon, Apr 23 1910 Sex:M Child# 1 Oscar Chamberland Canada & Lumina Laflamme Canada
CHAMBERLIN, Antoine, Feb 24 1899 Sex:M Child# 6 Joseph Chamberlin Canada & Desanges Garon Canada
CHAMBERLIN, Frederick Lawrence, Sep 14 1895 Sex:M Child# 7 John B Chamberlin Nashua, NH & Georg'a M Lawrence
CHAMPAGNE, Albert, Jun 21 1925 Sex:M Child# 1 Dens Champagne Canada & Ernestine Roy Canada
CHAMPAGNE, Clara, Jun 18 1895 Sex:F Child# 9 Ephrem Champagne Canada & Delima Simard Canada
CHAMPAGNE, Cordelia I, Aug 18 1899 Sex:F Child# 11 Ephrem Champagne Canada & Delima Simard Canada
CHAMPAGNE, Elodie A, Jun 4 1900 Sex:F Child# 1 George L Champagne Canada & Regina Cadoret Manchester, NH
CHAMPAGNE, Emelia, Oct 17 1904 Sex:F Child# 14 Ephrene Champagne Canada & Delima Simard Canada
CHAMPAGNE, Florina, Sep 29 1891 Sex:F Child# 7 Ephrem Champagne Canada & Delina Simon Canada
CHAMPAGNE, Henry Raymond, Apr 15 1922 Sex:M Child# 2 Albert H Champagne Lowell, MA & Eva Prince Nashua, NH
CHAMPAGNE, Isabelle, Jun 17 1903 Sex:F Child# 13 Ephrem Champagne Canada & Delima Simard Canada
CHAMPAGNE, Jean V, Jan 13 1897 Sex:M Child# 10 Ephrem Champagne Canada & Delima Simard Canada
CHAMPAGNE, Leo Paul, Jul 20 1921 Sex:M Child# 6 Thomas Champagne Canada & Albertine Bond Canada
CHAMPAGNE, Leon, Jul 23 1901 Sex:M Child# 12 Ephrem Champagne Canada & Delima Simard Canada
CHAMPAGNE, Marie, Feb 23 1926 Sex:F Child# 1 A Champagne Canada & C Champagne Nashua, NH
CHAMPAGNE, Marie A C, May 2 1899 Sex:F Child# 1 Joseph Champagne Canada & Amanda Lafreniere Westbrook, ME
CHAMPAGNE, Marie B A, May 29 1902 Sex:F Child# 2 George L Champagne Canada & R Cadorette Nashua, NH
CHAMPAGNE, Marie Jeannette, Jun 10 1912 Sex:F Child# 6 Gedeon Champagne Canada & Albina Gelinas Canada
CHAMPAGNE, Mary Louise, Sep 29 1891 Sex:F Child# 6 Ephrem Champagne Canada & Delina Simon Canada
CHAMPAGNE, Noel Adrien, Dec 25 1928 Sex:M Child# 1 C Champagne Canada & Yvonne Hebert Canada
CHAMPAGNE, Norman Edmund Chas, Nov 3 1934 Sex:M Child# 3 Norman E C Champagne Boston, MA & Beatrice I Rigney
CHAMPAGNE, Olivette Jeanine, Mar 13 1932 Sex:F Child# 2 C Champagne Canada & Yvonne Hebert Canada
CHAMPAGNE, Ovila, Apr 21 1887 Sex:M Child#   E Champagne P Q & Delvinci Simard P Q
CHAMPAGNE, Robert Oscar, Apr 12 1931 Sex:M Child# 2 Albini Champagne Worcester, MA & Excelia LaFlamme Nashua, NH
CHAMPAGNE, Simeon Charles, Nov 9 1889 Sex:M Child# 5 Ephrem Champagne Canada & Delina Simard Canada
CHAMPAGNE, Sylvio, Mar 14 1903 Sex:M Child# 6 Joseph Champagne Canada & Anna Chartier Nashua, NH
CHAMPAGNE, Unknown, Jan 11 1921 Sex:F Child# 1 Albert Champagne Lowell, MA & Yvonne Prince Nashua, NH
CHAMPAGNE, Unknown, Mar 9 1925 Sex:M Child#   Thomas Champagne Canada & Albertine Berube Canada Stillborn
CHAMPAGUE, Amedee, Jan 23 1893 Sex:M Child# 8 Ephrem Champague Canada & Delima Simard Canada
CHAMPIGNY, Gerard, Apr 19 1927 Sex:M Child# 2 E Champigny Canada & Emma Pinard Canada
CHAMPIGNY, Marie Simone Yvette, May 9 1925 Sex:F Child#   Eusebe Champigny Canada & Emma Pinard Canada
CHAMPIGNY, Rosanna, May 12 1892 Sex:F Child# 1 Albert Champigny W Boylston, MA & Rosanna Moussette Worcester, MA
CHAMPLAIN, Felix, Jul 3 1892 Sex:M Child# 1 Amyr Champlain Canada & Melissa Canada
CHANDERS, Elizabeth, Jul 28 1912 Sex:F Child# 2 George Chanders Greece & Vagia Papanicolaon Greece
CHANDERS, Olga, Sep 7 1913 Sex:F Child# 3 George Chanders Greece & Vagia Papanikous Greece
CHANDLER, Aretus Blood, May 24 1893 Sex:M Child# 1 Edson F Chandler Nashua, NH & S Emma Hopkins Nashua, NH
CHANDLER, Doris Louise, Nov 3 1921 Sex:F Child# 1 Frank Chandler Marlboro, NH & Mary G Johnson Hopkinton, NH
CHANDLER, Elizabeth, Dec 31 1919 Sex:F Child# 1 Aretas B Chandler Nashua, NH & Cordelia Girouard Nashua, NH
CHANDLER, Helen Gertrude, Aug 19 1911 Sex:F Child#   (No Parents Listed)
CHANDLER, John Hopkins, Feb 19 1929 Sex:M Child# 3 Aretas Chandler Nashua, NH & Cordelia Girard Nashua, NH
CHANDLER, Kathleen, Aug 28 1925 Sex:F Child# 2 A B Chandler Nashua, NH & Cordelia Girouard Nashua, NH
CHANDLER, Robert Edward, Mar 29 1934 Sex:M Child# 2 Freeman Geo Chandler Ayer, MA & Florence Hall Lowell, MA
CHANDLER, Unknown, Jan 30 1888 Sex:F Child# 1 Carroll A Chandler Nashua, NH & Nettie M Wheeler Nashua, NH
CHANEST, Marie A, Jan 23 1889 Sex:F Child# 3 Charles Chanest Canada & Odilo Gagon Canada
CHANIEWICZ, Bronka, Jun 5 1927 Sex:F Child# 2 C Chaniewicz Poland & Helen Yeremicz Poland
CHANIEWICZ, Helen, Dec 19 1921 Sex:F Child# 1 Charles Chaniewicz Poland & Helen Jerewicz Poland
CHANTAL, Marguerite, Mar 1 1934 Sex:F Child# 8 Joseph Chantal Canada & Mary Francoeur Nashua, NH
CHANTAL, Raymond Normand, Apr 25 1921 Sex:M Child# 1 Joseph Chantal Canada & Marie Francoeur Nashua, NH
CHANTAL, Robert, Aug 23 1923 Sex:M Child# 3 Joseph Chantal Canada & Marie Francoeur Nashua, NH
CHANTAL, Roland Armand, Mar 19 1926 Sex:M Child#   Joseph Chantal Canada & Marie Francoeur Nashua, NH
CHANTAL, Rose Eva, Oct 1 1924 Sex:F Child# 4 Joseph Chantal Canada & Marie Francoeur Canada
CHANTEL, Joseph Leo Roger, Jul 9 1922 Sex:M Child# 2 Joseph Chantel Canada & Marie Francour Nashua, NH
CHANTEL, Rachel, Apr 29 1931 Sex:F Child# 8 Joseph Chantel Canada & Marie Francois Nashua, NH
CHAPAS, Unknown, May 6 1926 Sex:M Child# 3 James Chapas Greece & Sophia Giamisky Greece
CHAPIN, Eleanor Louise, Apr 17 1933 Sex:F Child# 1 M W Chapin Hartford, CT & D Preston Contoocook, NH

CHAPLAIN, Elizabeth, Sep 16 1910 Sex:F Child# 6 Ezra Chaplain Nova Scotia & Hattie McLean Nova Scotia
CHAPLAIN, Margaret Hall, Feb 25 1912 Sex:F Child# 7 Esra Chaplain Nova Scotia & Hattie MacLean Nova Scotia
CHAPLICK, John, Mar 24 1928 Sex:M Child# 5 Andrew Chaplick Poland & Helena Michalewicz Poland
CHAPLIK, Julius, Mar 29 1917 Sex:M Child# 3 Adolphe Chaplik Russia & Antonia Seukavich Russia
CHAPLIN, Charles F, Jun 26 1905 Sex:M Child# 2 Ezra Chaplin Nova Scotia & Hattie McLean Nova Scotia
CHAPLIN, George Raymond, Jul 30 1908 Sex:M Child# 4 Ezra Chaplin Nova Scotia & Hattie McLean Nova Scotia
CHAPLIN, Unknown, Aug 4 1909 Sex:M Child# 5 Ezra Chaplin Nova Scotia & Hattie MacLean Nova Scotia
CHAPLUK, Nellie Delia, Dec 16 1925 Sex:F Child# 4 Adolphe Chapluk Lithuania & Antosia Sikwick Lithuania
CHAPMAN, Adeline E, Sep 18 1892 Sex:F Child# 2 Frank M Chapman Newmarket, NH & Mederise Lefebvre Nashua, NH
CHAPMAN, Beverly Doris, Aug 12 1926 Sex:F Child# 8 J E Chapman Canada & Etta E McIntire Nashua, NH
CHAPMAN, David R McIntire, Feb 27 1929 Sex:M Child# 9 James Chapman Canada & Etta McIntire Nashua, NH
CHAPMAN, Dorothy Ethel, Aug 14 1922 Sex:F Child# 3 Douglas Chapman Flushing, NY & Ellen Morgan Spencer, MA
CHAPMAN, Elaine Clare, Mar 31 1928 Sex:F Child# 1 James Chapman Lowell, MA & Alphonsine Lizotte Canada
CHAPMAN, Frank W, Oct 17 1891 Sex:M Child# 1 Frank Chapman New Market & Mederise Lefevre Nashua, NH
CHAPMAN, Hilda Frances, Dec 26 1927 Sex:F Child# 1 H T Chapman Hudson, NH & Irene Gallagher Nashua, NH
CHAPMAN, Hubert G, Nov 11 1894 Sex:M Child# 3 Frank M Chapman Newmarket, NH & Mederise Lefebvre Nashua, NH
CHAPMAN, Jacqueline Lucille, Jul 12 1934 Sex:F Child# 5 Wm G Chapman Bridgewater, MA & Dorothy L Smith Winchester
CHAPMAN, James Sheldon, Aug 14 1935 Sex:M Child# 6 Jas F Chapman Lowell, MA & Alphonsine Lizotte Canada
CHAPMAN, Jean, Mar 28 1931 Sex:F Child# 4 James Chapman Lowell, MA & Alphonsine Lizotte Canada  Stillborn
CHAPMAN, Jeanette, Mar 28 1931 Sex:F Child# 3 James Chapman Lowell, MA & Alphonsine Lizotte Canada Stillborn
CHAPMAN, Joyce Etta, Mar 27 1934 Sex:F Child# 5 James Chapman Lowell, MA & Alphonsine Lizotte Quebec
CHAPMAN, Judith Anne, Feb 5 1931 Sex:F Child# 3 William G Chapman Bridgewater, MA & Dorothy L Smith Winchester, MA
CHAPMAN, Lester Jewett, Jan 28 1928 Sex:M Child# 1 W G Chapman Bridgewater, MA & Dorothy L Smith Winchester, MA
CHAPMAN, Norman Paul, Apr 5 1932 Sex:M Child# 5 James Chapman Lowell, MA & A Lizotte Canada
CHAPMAN, Phyllis Jane, Nov 23 1935 Sex:F Child# 6 Wm G Chapman Bridgewater, MA & Dorothy Smith Winchester, MA
CHAPMAN, Richard, Oct 23 1934 Sex:M Child# 1 Arthur Chapman
CHAPMAN, Shirley Elaine, May 16 1932 Sex:F Child# 4 Wm G Chapman Bridgewater, MA & Dorothy L Smith Winchester, MA
CHAPMAN, Shirley Lucille, Aug 16 1929 Sex:F Child# 2 James Chapman Lowell, MA & Alphonsine Lizotte Canada
CHAPMAN, William Gordon, Dec 20 1929 Sex:M Child# 2 William Chapman Bridgewater, MA & Dorothy Smith Winchester, MA
CHAPPAS, Annie, Jan 5 1915 Sex:F Child# 1 Eddie Chappas Russia & Annie Wolenchutte Russia
CHAPPAS, Bernice, Feb 24 1920 Sex:F Child# 3 Vladislof Chappas Russia & Annie Wallinchuta Russia
CHAPUT, Andre Muriel, May 15 1905 Sex:M Child# 4 Napoleon Chaput Canada & Anna Bourgouin Canada
CHAPUT, Blanche A I, Feb 7 1902 Sex:F Child# 2 Napoleon Chaput Canada & Anna Bourgouin Canada
CHAPUT, Eugenie Alberta L, Jun 16 1906 Sex:F Child# 5 Napoleon Chaput Canada & Anna Bourgoin Canada
CHAPUT, Gabrielle Anita, Feb 5 1915 Sex:F Child# 7 Napoleon Chaput Canada & Anna Bourgoin Canada
CHAPUT, Jean Baptiste O P, Jun 24 1907 Sex:M Child# 6 Napoleon Chaput Canada & Anna Bourgoin Canada
CHAPUT, Joseph Victor Roger, May 11 1935 Sex:M Child# 1 Victor Chaput Lowell, MA & Annette Leclerc Lowell, MA
CHAPUT, Marie Gladys Ida, Jun 22 1923 Sex:F Child# 1 Ovila Chaput Canada & Florida Daston Canada
CHAPUT, Marie Victoria, Jul 21 1897 Sex:F Child# 13 Napoleon Chaput Canada & Odile Pigeon Canada
CHAPUT, Napoleon A, May 25 1900 Sex:M Child# 1 Napoleon Chaput Canada & Anna Bourgoin Canada
CHAPUT, Napoleon D V, Sep 11 1903 Sex:M Child# 3 Napoleon Chaput Canada & Anna Bourgoin Canada
CHAPUT, Roger U P N, Jan 30 1932 Sex:M Child# 1 Uriel Chaput Nashua, NH & Marie Anne Jean Nashua, NH
CHARAIT, Albert, Apr 18 1920 Sex:M Child# 1 Albert A Charait Pepperell, MA & Genevieve Parker Nashua, NH
CHARBONNEAU, Claire Irene, Jan 22 1935 Sex:F Child# 2 Wilfred Charbonneau Curan, Ont & Regina Bois Greenville, NH
CHARBONNEAU, Clifford Rosevelt, May 12 1904 Sex:M Child# 5 Frank Charbonneau Sciota, NY & Ellen Carter Andover, MA
CHARBONNEAU, Genievre I A, Feb 13 1894 Sex:F Child# 1 Abram Charbonneau Altona, NY & Flora A Lefebvre Nashua, NH
CHARBONNEAU, Jos Wilfrid, Oct 19 1931 Sex:M Child# 1 Wilfrid Charbonneau Curran, Ont & Regina Bois Greenville, NH
CHARBONNEAU, Marguerite F, Mar 13 1902 Sex:F Child# 1 S E Charbonneau Altoona, NY & Ida M Burreby Nashua, NH
CHARBONNEAU, Marie Emma, Dec 26 1903 Sex:F Child# 2 Gedeon Charbonneau Canada & Georgiana Theberge Canada
CHARBONNEAU, Maurice Hormidas, Nov 24 1917 Sex:M Child# 2 Ernest Charbonneau Ottawa, Canada & Victoria Martel
CHARBONNEAU, Paul Arthur, Dec 25 1935 Sex:M Child# 3 Wilfred Charbonneau Ontario & Regina Bois Nashua, NH
CHAREST, Charles Eugene, Aug 29 1903 Sex:M Child# 4 Louis Charest Canada & Glementine Ouellette Canada
CHAREST, Gerard Adelard, Dec 1 1919 Sex:M Child# 7 Etienne Charest Canada & Helene St Laurent Canada
CHAREST, Gertrude Yvonne, Oct 31 1899 Sex:F Child# 9 Charles Charest Canada & Odile Gagnon Canada
CHAREST, Jeanne Clare, Aug 4 1929 Sex:F Child# 3 Donat Charest Canada & Aurore Levesque Canada
CHAREST, Jos Edgar Adrien, Sep 26 1921 Sex:M Child# 8 Joseph Charest Canada & Marie L Pelletier Canada
CHAREST, Joseph Alfred, Jul 27 1911 Sex:M Child# 3 Etienne Charest Canada & Helene St Laurent Canada
CHAREST, Joseph Ernest, Apr 23 1928 Sex:M Child# 1 J Alfred Charest Canada & Gracia Baillargeon Nashua, NH
CHAREST, Joseph Leon, Jul 27 1918 Sex:M Child# 7 Joseph Charest Canada & Marie L Pelletier Canada
CHAREST, Joseph Omer, Feb 13 1916 Sex:M Child# 6 Joseph Charest Canada & M Louise Pelletier Canada
CHAREST, Joseph Raoul, Sep 29 1926 Sex:M Child# 10 Etienne Charest Canada & H St Laurent Canada
CHAREST, Joseph Robert, Nov 4 1923 Sex:M Child# 9 Etienne Charest Canada & Helene St Laurent Canada
CHAREST, Laura Mathilde, Feb 16 1922 Sex:F Child# 8 Etienne Charest Canada & Helene St Laurent Canada
CHAREST, Marcelle Louise, Mar 25 1914 Sex:F Child# 4 Etienne Charest Canada & Helene St Laurent Canada
CHAREST, Marie Blanche H, May 1 1910 Sex:F Child# 2 Etienne Charest Canada & Helene St Laurent Canada
CHAREST, Marie Elise Rachel, Oct 22 1923 Sex:F Child# 9 Joseph Charest Canada & Marie L Pelletier Canada
CHAREST, Marie Emelie L, Mar 6 1902 Sex:F Child# 1 Joseph A Charest Canada & Pearl Phaneuf NH
CHAREST, Marie Euphemie, Sep 22 1892 Sex:F Child# 5 Charles Charest Canada & Adele Gagnon Canada
CHAREST, Marie Helene A, Sep 19 1910 Sex:F Child# 4 Joseph Charest Canada & Marie Pelletier Canada
CHAREST, Marie Lucille Eug, Mar 18 1916 Sex:F Child# 5 Etienne Charest Canada & Helene St Laurent Canada
CHAREST, Marie Martha, Dec 19 1917 Sex:F Child# 6 Etienne Charest Canada & Helene St Laurent Canada
CHAREST, Marie Pearl Y, Dec 10 1910 Sex:F Child# 3 J A Charest Canada & Pearl A Phaneuf NH
CHAREST, Marie Rose L, Jan 17 1907 Sex:F Child# 1 Arthur Charest Canada & Malvina Hebert Rhode Island

CHAREST, Raymond A, Mar 16 1905 Sex:M Child# 2 Joseph A Charest Canada & Anna Pearl Phaneuf NH
CHAREST, Theodore Rolland, Nov 10 1917 Sex:M Child# 1 Joseph Charest NH & Yvonne Dansereau NH
CHAREST, Unknown, May 24 1927 Sex:F Child# 2 Donat Charest Canada & Yvonne Levesque Canada
CHARETTE, Alice Bernadette, Dec 29 1890 Sex:F Child# 4 Charles Charette Canada & Odile Gagnon Canada
CHARETTE, George Hobson, Oct 11 1898 Sex:M Child# 1 Gideon Charette Lowell, MA & K McLaughlin Edenboro, Scotland
CHARETTE, Joseph, Dec 15 1893 Sex:M Child# 1 (No Parents Listed)
CHARETTE, Joseph Cleophas, Nov 18 1893 Sex:M Child# 6 Charles Charette Canada & Odile Gagnon Canada
CHARETTE, Louis Philippe, Sep 30 1905 Sex:M Child# 5 Louis Charette Canada & Clementine Ouellette Canada
CHARETTE, Marie B G, Jun 25 1897 Sex:F Child# 12 Charles Charette Canada & Odile Gagnon Canada
CHARKAS, Unknown, Jun 3 1916 Sex:M Child# 2 Julius Charkas Russia & Agnes Pertuka Russia
CHARLAND, Beatrice Irene, Jul 20 1928 Sex:F Child# 1 Francis Charland Canada & Irene Carter Manchester, NH
CHARLAND, Bernard Irenee, Feb 2 1930 Sex:M Child# 2 Francois Charland Canada & Irene Cartier US
CHARLAND, Joseph Arthur A, Dec 12 1901 Sex:M Child# 4 Charles Charland Canada & Emma Dargia Canada
CHARLAND, Joseph Gerald Robert, Apr 12 1925 Sex:M Child# 1 Emile Charland Canada & Marie Rose Desclos Nashua, NH
CHARLAND, Joseph Pierre, Apr 3 1895 Sex:M Child# 2 Charles Charland Canada & Emma Largie Canada
CHARLAND, Roanna May, Jun 10 1896 Sex:F Child# 1 Walter W Charland Canada & Anna M Stevens Lyndonville, VT
CHARLAND, Rose Marie, Jun 22 1932 Sex:F Child# 2 Emile Charland Canada & Marie R Desclos Nashua, NH
CHARLAND, Unknown, Jul 13 1897 Sex:M Child# 2 Walter W Charland Sutton, PQ & Anna M Stevens Lyndonville, VT
CHARLES, Mehail N, Oct 7 1913 Sex:M Child# 1 Nicholas Charles Greece & Annie Gatos Greece
CHARLES, Unknown, Aug 3 1915 Sex:F Child# 2 Nicholas Charles Greece & Athen George Greece
CHARLSON, Mary, Dec 20 1901 Sex:F Child# 1 Michael Charlson Turkey & Rosa Josepson Turkey
CHARON, Alice, Apr 1 1894 Sex:F Child# 1 George Charon Canada & Alice Sirois Canada
CHARON, Ernest, Jun 1 1898 Sex:M Child# 1 David Charon Nashua, NH & Rose Anna Belland Nashua, NH
CHARON, Jean Paul, Nov 20 1930 Sex:M Child# 2 Auguste F Charon Manchester, NH & Bertha Dionne Canada
CHARON, Joseph George, Aug 22 1898 Sex:M Child# 5 Philippe Charon Canada & Melina Brunelle Canada
CHARON, Marie, Jun 3 1888 Sex:F Child# 1 Joseph Charon Townsend, MA & Anna Canada
CHARON, Ovila, Jul 14 1892 Sex:M Child# 2 Philip Charon Canada & Melina Brunelle Sciota, NY
CHARPENTER, Emma, Jul 9 1887 Sex:F Child# 2 Alph Charpenter Canada & Marie Sirois Canada
CHARPENTER, Marie, May 5 1888 Sex:F Child# 2 Joseph Charpenter P Q & Rosanna Bouvier P Q
CHARPENTIER, Alma Melina, Nov 19 1903 Sex:F Child# 2 Prosper Charpentier Nashua, NH & Clara Decelles Canada
CHARPENTIER, Doris Lucille, Jan 17 1917 Sex:F Child# 2 Melchior Charpentier Canada & Louise Dumas Nashua, NH
CHARPENTIER, Joseph, Nov 19 1889 Sex:M Child# 2 Joseph Charpentier Canada & Melina Lemery Canada
CHARPENTIER, Joseph Albert, May 1 1914 Sex:M Child# 1 Herve Charpentier Connecticut & Rose A Bissonnette NH
CHARPENTIER, Joseph H George, Feb 16 1896 Sex:M Child# 1 Aime Charpentier Nashua, NH & Emma Laforme Canada
CHARPENTIER, Joseph Hector, Apr 17 1921 Sex:M Child# 4 Mathias Charpentier Canada & Marie Louise Dumas NH
CHARPENTIER, Joseph Hector A, Jan 10 1903 Sex:M Child# 3 P Charpentier, Jr NH & Clara Decelle Canada
CHARPENTIER, Joseph Raymond, Jun 19 1915 Sex:M Child# 1 Melchior Charpentier Canada & Louise Dumas Nashua, NH
CHARPENTIER, Joseph Roger, Oct 11 1918 Sex:M Child# 3 Melchroi Charpentier Canada & Louisa Damas Nashua, NH
CHARPENTIER, Leopoldine, Mar 22 1905 Sex:F Child# 3 Prosper Charpentier Nashua, NH & Clara Decelles Canada
CHARPENTIER, Marie E, Jun 30 1891 Sex:F Child# 3 Joseph Charpentier Canada & Melina Lemery Canada
CHARPENTIER, Marie Eva A, Jan 4 1899 Sex:F Child# 2 Aime Charpentier Nashua, NH & Emma Laforme Canada
CHARPENTIER, Marie Rose A, Aug 15 1901 Sex:F Child# 1 Louis Charpentier Nova Scotia & Clara Manseau Canada
CHARPENTIER, Roland Raoul, Dec 23 1926 Sex:M Child# 3 Raoul Charpentier Nashua, NH & Mary Markarian Nashua, NH
CHARPENTIER, Rose Claire, Apr 30 1906 Sex:F Child# 4 Prosper Charpentier Canada & Clara Decelles Canada
CHARPENTIER, Sylvio Raoul, Sep 12 1901 Sex:M Child# 3 Aime Charpentier Nashua, NH & Emma Laforme Canada
CHARPENTIER, Unknown, Sep 16 1892 Sex:M Child# 1 Prosper Charpentier Canada & Maria Blain Canada Stillborn
CHARPENTIER, Yvonne Alice, Jan 1 1908 Sex:F Child# 5 Prosper Charpentier Nashua, NH & Clara Decelles Canada
CHARPENTIN, Louis M, Aug 7 1890 Sex:M Child# 3 Joseph Charpentin Canada & Rosanna Bourier Canada
CHARREST, Marie C, Feb 29 1896 Sex:F Child# 7 Charles Charrest Canada & Odile Gagnon Canada
CHARRETIER, Aurore Rose, Aug 6 1899 Sex:F Child# 5 Auguste Charretier Canada & Philomene Paradis Canada
CHARRETIER, Joseph A A, Jul 15 1896 Sex:M Child# 2 Auguste Charretier Canada & Philomene Paradis Canada
CHARRETIER, Joseph Louis, Dec 26 1897 Sex:M Child# 4 Auguste Charretier Canada & Philomene Paradis Canada
CHARRETIER, Louis, Nov 19 1892 Sex:M Child# 3 Louis Charretier Canada & Celulie Dufour Canada
CHARRETIER, Marie Alice, Dec 26 1897 Sex:F Child# 3 Auguste Charretier Canada & Philomene Paradis Canada
CHARRETTE, Joseph Alphonse, Sep 30 1912 Sex:M Child# 5 Joseph Charrette Canada & Marie Pelletier Canada
CHARRITIER, Louis, Aug 16 1890 Sex:M Child# 1 Louis Charritier Canada & Celulie Dufour Canada
CHARRON, Aime Wilhelmine, Dec 12 1903 Sex:F Child# 6 George Charron Canada & Alice Sirois Canada
CHARRON, Albina, Sep 23 1900 Sex:F Child# 1 Edw Charron Canada & Albina Grandmaison Nashua, NH
CHARRON, Alfred Benjamin, Jul 16 1898 Sex:M Child# 5 Treffle Charron Canada & Regina Maynard Canada
CHARRON, Alice, Dec 15 1903 Sex:F Child# 11 Charles Charron Canada & O'phena Grandmaison Canada
CHARRON, Antoine L, Feb 19 1895 Sex:M Child# 2 Antoine Charron Canada & Anna Lebel Canada
CHARRON, Armeline, Oct 23 1894 Sex:F Child# 3 Henri Charron Nashua, NH & Alexandrine Bernard W Boylston, MA
CHARRON, Arthur, Jun 24 1893 Sex:M Child# 10 Francois Charron Canada & Marie Beaudry Canada
CHARRON, Arthur, Aug 26 1896 Sex:m Child# 3 Antoine Charron US & Anna Labelle Canada
CHARRON, Arthur, Dec 13 1908 Sex:M Child# 8 George Charron Canada & Alice Sirois Canada Stillborn
CHARRON, Arthur, May 1 1910 Sex:M Child# 9 George Charron Canada & Alice Sirois Canada Stillborn
CHARRON, Arthur Roland, Jan 16 1913 Sex:M Child# 10 George Charron Canada & Alice Sirois Canada
CHARRON, Arthur Silvio, Aug 6 1900 Sex:M Child# 6 Treffle Charron Canada & Regenia Maynard Vermont
CHARRON, Arthur Wilfred, Sep 13 1891 Sex:M Child# 5 Joseph Charron Canada & Melina Desmontigny Canada
CHARRON, Bernadette, Feb 2 1895 Sex:F Child# 6 Joseph Charron Canada & Delima De Montigny Canada
CHARRON, Charles Edouard, Mar 18 1901 Sex:M Child# 6 Charles Charron Townsend, MA & Orp'na Grandmaison Canada
CHARRON, Charles Narcisse, Jul 27 1904 Sex:M Child# 8 Treffle Charron Canada & Regina Maynard Canada
CHARRON, Dorilla, Apr 29 1889 Sex:M Child# 5 Joseph Charron Canada & Rosanna Belanger Canada

CHARRON, Edmond, Mar 8 1897 Sex:M Child# 4 Treffle Charron Canada & Regina Menard St Albans, VT
CHARRON, Edmund Joseph, Sep 8 1919 Sex:M Child# 2 Francois X Charron Nashua, NH & Louise M Martel Concord, MA
CHARRON, Edouard Victor, Jul 1 1915 Sex:M Child# 5 Edouard Charron Nashua, NH & Albina Grandmaison Nashua, NH
CHARRON, Ernest, Jun 25 1895 Sex:M Child# 3 Treffle Charron Canada & Regina Menard St Albans, VT
CHARRON, Eugene, Nov 30 1895 Sex:M Child# 11 Francois Charron Canada & Marie Beaudry Canada
CHARRON, Frances Loretta, Mar 4 1923 Sex:F Child# 2 Alfred Charron Nashua, NH & Irene Courchesne Pepperell, MA
CHARRON, Francois X, Mar 31 1893 Sex:M Child# 2 Treffle Charron Canada & Regina Menard St Albans, VT
CHARRON, Francois Xavier, Apr 30 1917 Sex:M Child# 1 Francois Charron Nashua, NH & Louise Martel Concord, MA
CHARRON, Frank, Oct 20 1890 Sex:M Child# 2 Anastase Charron Champlain, NY & Addie Morse Moorestown, NY
CHARRON, Geo Albert Armand, Feb 22 1925 Sex:M Child# 6 Joseph Charron Canada & Amanda Rioux Canada
CHARRON, George Arthur, Jan 18 1925 Sex:M Child# 1 Arthur Charron Nashua, NH & Julia Blais Sciota, NY
CHARRON, George Joseph, Jul 15 1895 Sex:M Child# 2 George Charron Canada & Alice Sirois Canada
CHARRON, Harvey Alphonse, Jan 13 1920 Sex:M Child# 4 Joseph Charron Canada & Amanda Rioux Canada
CHARRON, Hector, Mar 29 1887 Sex:M Child#   Treffle Charron P Q & Celina Rodier P Q
CHARRON, Hector Roger, Apr 23 1916 Sex:M Child# 11 George Charron Canada & Alice Sirois Canada
CHARRON, Henri, Feb 21 1893 Sex:M Child# 1 Antoine Charron Nashua, NH & Anna Lebelle Canada
CHARRON, Hermenegilde, Mar 1 1898 Sex:M Child# 4 Antoine Charron Canada & Anna Lebel Canada
CHARRON, Irene Beatrice, Nov 15 1917 Sex:F Child# 1 Alfred Charron Nashua, NH & Irene Courchaine Pepperell, MA
CHARRON, J Sylvio Armand, Feb 21 1912 Sex:M Child# 2 Henri Charron Nashua, NH & Leda Courberon Canada
CHARRON, Jeanne D'Arc, Jun 14 1933 Sex:F Child# 3 Ernest Charron Canada & Eva Godbout Canada
CHARRON, Jeannette Rita, Feb 19 1930 Sex:F Child# 8 Joseph Charron Canada & Amanda Rioux Canada
CHARRON, Jos Augustine, Mar 22 1929 Sex:M Child# 1 Auguste Charron Manchester, NH & Bertha Dionne Canada
CHARRON, Jos Emile Dorilla, Jan 23 1904 Sex:M Child# 1 Pierre Charron Canada & Elise Caron Canada
CHARRON, Joseph Emile V, Dec 28 1903 Sex:M Child# 1 Pierre Charron Canada & Valentine Caron Canada
CHARRON, Joseph Henri, Jun 15 1910 Sex:M Child# 1 Henri Charron Nashua, NH & Delila Courberon Canada
CHARRON, Joseph Mederic, Aug 18 1889 Sex:M Child# 1 Charles Charron Townsend, MA & O Grandmaison Canada
CHARRON, June Joanne, Jun 30 1935 Sex:F Child# 1 Henry Charron Nashua, NH & Vivian Carter Nashua, NH
CHARRON, Laura Audria, Jan 2 1897 Sex:F Child# 3 George Charron Canada & Alice Sirois Canada
CHARRON, Leo, Jul 31 1904 Sex:M Child# 2 Albert Charron Canada & Delima Girouard Cohoes, NY
CHARRON, Leo Dollard, Apr 27 1922 Sex:M Child# 5 Joseph Charron Canada & Amanda Rioux Canada
CHARRON, Leopold, Dec 16 1901 Sex:M Child# 5 George Charron Canada & Alice Sirois Canada
CHARRON, Lorraine Marianne, Nov 8 1928 Sex:F Child# 1 Wilfrid A Charron Hudson, NH & Flora Porel Sanford, ME
CHARRON, Louis Alfred, Mar 8 1896 Sex:M Child# 4 Henry Charron Nashua, NH & Alexandrine Bernard Clinton, MA
CHARRON, Louisa, Oct 18 1895 Sex:F Child# 10 Ulric Charron Canada & Melina Theoset Canada
CHARRON, Louise Irene, Oct 3 1906 Sex:F Child# 14 Charles A Charron Taunton, MA & Orphana Grandmaison Canada
CHARRON, Ludivine F, Sep 7 1905 Sex:F Child# 7 George Charron Canada & Alice Sirois Canada
CHARRON, Marie, Jan 27 1895 Sex:F Child# 9 Norbert Charron Canada & Delina Lacasse Canada
CHARRON, Marie A, Jun 5 1892 Sex:F Child# 2 Henri Charron Canada & Alexandrine Bernard Canada
CHARRON, Marie Jacqueline, Mar 20 1920 Sex:F Child# 1 George Charron Nashua, NH & A Ouellette Nashua, NH
CHARRON, Marie L Rebecca, Feb 26 1900 Sex:F Child# 8 Philippe Charron Canada & Melina Brunelle Canada
CHARRON, Marie M Y, Oct 5 1901 Sex:F Child# 8 Philippe Charron Canada & Melina Brunelle Canada
CHARRON, Marie Odelie L, Mar 28 1905 Sex:F Child# 2 George Charron Mass & Anna Thibault Canada
CHARRON, Maynard Neil, Feb 17 1927 Sex:M Child# 3 Arthur Charron Nashua, NH & Julia Bleau New York
CHARRON, Octave, Jun 13 1902 Sex:M Child# 7 Treffle Charron Canada & Regina Maynard Vermont
CHARRON, Odette Yvette Lorrai, Sep 20 1935 Sex:F Child# 10 Joseph Charron Canada & Amanda Rioux Canada
CHARRON, Olive Dehlia, Feb 19 1910 Sex:F Child# 16 Charles Charron Townsend, MA & Orphena Grandmaison Canada
CHARRON, Paul Leonard, Mar 24 1927 Sex:M Child# 7 Joseph Charron Canada & Amanda Rioux Canada
CHARRON, Philip Maurice, Aug 14 1918 Sex:M Child# 3 Joseph Charron Canada & Amanda Rioux Canada
CHARRON, Priscilla Fabienne, Feb 26 1926 Sex:F Child# 2 Arthur Charron Nashua, NH & Julia Bleau New York
CHARRON, Raymond Roland, Feb 23 1932 Sex:M Child# 9 Joseph Charron Canada & Amanda Rioux Canada
CHARRON, Robert Raoul, Jan 5 1918 Sex:M Child# 12 George Charron Canada & Alice Sirois Canada
CHARRON, Roland, Sep 7 1907 Sex:M Child# 3 Edouard Charron Nashua, NH & Albina Grandmaison Nashua, NH
CHARRON, Roland, Jul 6 1908 Sex:M Child# 15 Charles Charron Townsend, MA & Orphena Grandmaison Canada
CHARRON, Roland Barthelemi, May 11 1908 Sex:M Child# 2 Pierre Charron Canada & Valentine Caron Canada
CHARRON, Rosanna, Oct 31 1890 Sex:F Child# 3 Francis Charron Nashua, NH & Delhia Benoit Canada
CHARRON, Rose A, Jun 28 1891 Sex:F Child# 6 Joseph Charron Canada & Rosanna Belanger Canada
CHARRON, Sylvio Edward, Sep 15 1902 Sex:M Child# 2 Edward Charron Nashua, NH & Alb Grandmaison Nashua, NH
CHARRON, Theodore, Jul 14 1896 Sex:M Child# 10 Norbert Charron Canada & Delina Larasse Canada
CHARRON, Theodore, Jul 31 1904 Sex:M Child# 1 Albert Charron Canada & Delima Girouard Cohoes, NY
CHARRON, Toussaint Alvez, Nov 1 1900 Sex:M Child# 3 David Charron Nashua, NH & Rosanna Belland Nashua, NH
CHARRON, Toussaint O, Nov 1 1898 Sex:M Child# 7 Joseph Charron Canada & Melina L Montigny Canada
CHARRON, Unknown, Feb 6 1891 Sex:M Child# 1 Joseph Charron Nashua, NH & Arthermise Benoch Canada Stillborn
CHARRON, Virginie, Dec 2 1892 Sex:F Child# 4 Francis Charron Canada & Delia Benoit Canada
CHARRON, Yvonne, Dec 15 1903 Sex:F Child# 12 Charles Charron Canada & O'phena Grandmaison Canada
CHARROU, Olida, Sep 29 1890 Sex:F Child# 2 Joseph Charrou Townsend, MA & Anna Desmarais Canada
CHARROW, Corinne R, Sep 25 1890 Sex:F Child# 1 Treffle Charrow Canada & Regina Minard St Albans, VT
CHARRUS, Unknown, Oct 2 1913 Sex:F Child# 1 James Charrus Greece & Anita Godelistos Greece
CHARTIER, Alice May, Jan 25 1919 Sex:F Child# 1 Joseph Chartier NH & Sarah Nicholson England
CHARTIER, Clovis H, Sep 17 1906 Sex:M Child# 2 Hector Chartier Nashua, NH & Evelina Desmarais Nashua, NH
CHARTIER, Georges H, Dec 29 1894 Sex:M Child# 9 Narcisse Chartier Canada & Amanda Lussier Canada
CHARTIER, Henri Emile, Sep 11 1900 Sex:M Child# 9 Louis Chartier Canada & Julie Roy Canada
CHARTIER, Ida B L, Feb 1 1898 Sex:F Child# 3 Magloire Chartier Canada & Exina Paulin Canada
CHARTIER, Isabelle Evelina, Aug 13 1905 Sex:F Child# 1 Hector Chartier Nashua, NH & Evelina Desmarais Nashua, NH

CHARTIER, J Baptiste A, Jul 1 1893 Sex:M Child# 8 Narcisse Chartier Canada & Amanda Lussier Canada
CHARTIER, Jos Arthur Roger, Nov 12 1917 Sex:M Child# 2 Arthur Chartier Nashua, NH & Lillian Emery Nashua, NH
CHARTIER, Joseph, Jun 22 1899 Sex:M Child# 8 Louis Chartier Canada & Sedulie Dufour Canada
CHARTIER, Joseph Alphonse, May 3 1895 Sex:M Child# 5 Louis Chartier Canada & Cydule Dufour Canada
CHARTIER, Joseph M H, Jun 28 1887 Sex:M Child# 5 Narcisse Chartier P Q & Amande Lussier P Q
CHARTIER, Juliette Camille Gab, Oct 26 1915 Sex:F Child# 1 Arthur Chartier US & Juliette Salvail Nashua, NH
CHARTIER, Katherine Bertha, Feb 4 1915 Sex:F Child# 1 Horace Chartier Nashua, NH & Bessie Duvarney Ireland
CHARTIER, Leonard Raymond, May 11 1932 Sex:M Child# 1 Raymond Chartier Dunstable, MA & Adella Kristofer Malden, MA
CHARTIER, Louis Frederick A, Apr 12 1920 Sex:M Child# 3 Arthur Chartier Nashua, NH & Lilianne Emery Nashua, NH
CHARTIER, Lucienne Marie, Jun 13 1916 Sex:F Child# 1 Arthur Chartier Nashua, NH & Lilianne Emery Nashua, NH
CHARTIER, M L Anne, Oct 9 1894 Sex:F Child# 1 Auguste Chartier Canada & Philomene Paradis Canada
CHARTIER, Maria A L, Jun 13 1893 Sex:F Child# 2 Magloire Chartier Canada & Aldina Parain Canada
CHARTIER, Marie, Mar 19 1891 Sex:F Child# 1 Magloire Chartier Canada & Alexina Poulin Canada
CHARTIER, Marie A B, Aug 26 1891 Sex:F Child# 7 Narcisse Chartier Canada & Amanda Lussier Canada
CHARTIER, Marie Alice, Feb 25 1897 Sex:F Child# 6 Louis Chartier Canada & Cedulie Dufour Canada
CHARTIER, Marie Aline, Sep 16 1891 Sex:F Child# 2 Louis Chartier Canada & Cedulie Dufour Canada
CHARTIER, Marie Alma, Apr 29 1898 Sex:F Child# 7 Louis Chartier Canada & Cedulie Dufour Canada
CHARTIER, Octavie S, Feb 2 1909 Sex:F Child# 3 Hector Chartier Nashua, NH & Eveline Desmarais Nashua, NH
CHARTIER, Sybil Pearl, Oct 24 1906 Sex:F Child# 1 Joseph Chartier Nashua, NH & Hazel Draper Wilton, NH
CHARTIER, Victor W, Nov 24 1889 Sex:M Child# 6 Narcisse Chartier Canada & Amanda Lussier Canada
CHARTIER, Wilfred A, Oct 31 1901 Sex:M Child# 1 Narcisse Chartier Nashua, NH & Georgiana Cote Canada
CHARTRAIN, Hector, Jan 29 1921 Sex:M Child# 5 Arthur Chartrain Canada & Helena Roy Canada
CHARTRAIN, Natalie, Jul 12 1922 Sex:F Child# 7 Arthur W Chartrain Canada & Helena Roy Canada
CHARTRAIN, Norman, Apr 22 1925 Sex:M Child# 8 Arthur Chartrain Canada & Helen Roy Canada
CHARTRAIN, Rea, Jul 12 1922 Sex:F Child# 6 Arthur W Chartrain Canada & Helena Roy Canada
CHASE, Alfred, Sep 22 1901 Sex:M Child# 3 Stephen Chase Nashua, NH & Mary A Smith Londonderry, NH
CHASE, Almena, Jul 29 1898 Sex:F Child# 2 Steven Chase Nashua, NH & N A Smith Londonderry, NH
CHASE, Annie Elizabeth, Aug 22 1920 Sex:F Child# 1 Clarence E Chase Lancaster, NH & Elizabeth Burbank Canada
CHASE, Charles Everett, Jan 12 1902 Sex:M Child# 1 Bert H Chase N Weare, NH & L B Johnson Milford, NH
CHASE, Doris Emma, Jan 3 1910 Sex:F Child# 1 Goerge S Chase Nashua, NH & Jennie Jeanbard Nashua, NH
CHASE, Dorothy Ethelyn, Oct 4 1917 Sex:F Child# 3 Melvin A Chase Mason, NH & Ethel Doane Nova Scotia
CHASE, Emma, Sep 23 1888 Sex:F Child# 3 A K Chase Nashua, NH & Maria Campbell Nashua, NH
CHASE, Frances Hayes, Sep 8 1918 Sex:F Child# 2 Joseph Park Chase Newburyport, MA & Eva M Clark Wells, ME
CHASE, Frank H, Sep 9 1893 Sex:M Child# 5 Addison K Chase Nashua, NH & Maria A Campbell Halifax, NS
CHASE, George S, Jan 30 1887 Sex:M Child#  A K Chase Nashua, NH & Maria Campbell Halifax
CHASE, George Walter, Nov 19 1914 Sex:M Child# 2 Walter B Chase Nashua, NH & Florence M Hutchins Nashua, NH
CHASE, Gladys Sylvio, Sep 22 1909 Sex:F Child# 2 Walter E Chase Lowell, MA & Mable E Clark E Deering, NH
CHASE, Gloria Norma, Jun 9 1912 Sex:F Child# 2 George S Chase Nashua, NH & Jennie Jambard Nashua, NH
CHASE, Harold Oliver, Jun 25 1935 Sex:M Child# 2 Harold Chase Pepperell, MA & Florence Langley Bath, ME
CHASE, Helene, Aug 2 1894 Sex:F Child# 2 DeWitt C Chase Hudson, NH & Mabel A Nutting Nashua, NH
CHASE, Horace A, Feb 9 1911 Sex:M Child# 3 Walter E Chase Lowell, MA & Mabel Clark Derry, NH
CHASE, Howard N, Jul 11 1907 Sex:M Child# 5 Stephen Chase Nashua, NH & N A Smith Londonderry, NH
CHASE, Katie C, Mar 24 1895 Sex:F Child# 3 Freeborn B Chase Vermont & Elvira H Remick Vermont
CHASE, Katie Mabel, Jul 15 1907 Sex:F Child# 1 Walter E Chase
CHASE, Leonard, Aug 15 1929 Sex:M Child# 4 Ralph Chase St Johnsbury, VT & Hilda Mitchell Brentwood, WI
CHASE, Lucretia Chase, Aug 15 1929 Sex:F Child# 3 Ralph Chase St Johnsbury, VT & Hilda Mitchell Brentwood, WI
CHASE, Martha Janet, Jun 22 1926 Sex:F Child# 2 Leroy Chase Newburyport, MA & Myrie Hanley St Albans, VT
CHASE, Mary Marg Nancy, Oct 22 1921 Sex:F Child# 2 Clarence E Chase Lancaster, NH & Elizabeth Burbank Canada
CHASE, Mildred Evelyn, Feb 17 1896 Sex:F Child# 1 Stephen Chase Nashua, NH & Mary Abby Smith Londonderry, NH
CHASE, Paul Elwin, Dec 1 1922 Sex:M Child# 4 Melvin Chase Mason, NH & Ethelyn Doane Nova Scotia
CHASE, Reginald, Jul 7 1901 Sex:M Child# 1 Bertrand F Chase Nashua, NH & Helen E Fletcher Lowell, MA
CHASE, Ruth, Jun 18 1896 Sex:F Child# 4 Edwin S Chase Piermont & Emma Churchill Lyme, NH
CHASE, Samuel Harrison, Jr, Dec 3 1925 Sex:M Child# 8 Samuel A Chase Canada & Eliz Marshall Nashua, NH
CHASE, Stephen, Jan 16 1906 Sex:M Child# 4 Stephen Chase Nashua, NH & N A Smith Londonderry, NH
CHASE, Unknown, Oct 28 1889 Sex:F Child# 4 Addison K Chase Nashua, NH & Marion K Chase Halifax, NS
CHASE, Unknown, Mar 19 1890 Sex:F Child# 1 DeWitt C Chase Hudson, NH & Mabel Nashua, NH
CHASE, Unknown, Nov 29 1892 Sex:M Child# 5 John K Chase Piermont & Nellie L Hall Manchester
CHASE, Walter, Feb 11 1910 Sex:M Child# 2 Fred Chase Mansfield, MA & May Rood Rochester, NH
CHASE, Willard Moore, May 27 1920 Sex:M Child# 1 Hollis Chase Mass & Phyllis Moore Mass
CHASIN, Lena, Aug 4 1913 Sex:F Child# 1 Adam Chasin Russia & Adora Backer Russia
CHASKY, Alice, Jul 16 1897 Sex:F Child# 2 Harry Chasky Russia & Ida Sharp Russia
CHASON, Peter, Nov 1 1914 Sex:M Child# 2 Adam Chason Russia & Adora Backus Russia
CHASSE, Albert Frederic, Jul 16 1911 Sex:M Child# 2 Zephirin Chasse Canada & Marianne Dumais Canada
CHASSE, Albert Lucien, Mar 7 1905 Sex:M Child# 1 Delphis Chasse Canada & Bertha Moussette Canada
CHASSE, Armand Romeo J, Feb 18 1907 Sex:M Child# 1 J Bte Chasse Canada & Marie Bourbeau Canada
CHASSE, Arthur Philippe, Apr 11 1914 Sex:M Child# 6 J B Chasse Canada & Mary Bourbeau Canada
CHASSE, Charles Eugene, Mar 7 1908 Sex:M Child# 3 Delphis Chasse Nashua, NH & Bertha Morissette Dover, NH
CHASSE, Damasse Richard, Sep 21 1924 Sex:M Child# 11 Jean B Chasse Canada & Mary Bourbeau Canada
CHASSE, Delphis, Jun 3 1923 Sex:M Child# 1 Delphis Chasse Nashua, NH & Bertha Morrisette Dover, NH
CHASSE, Dora Lauretta, Sep 17 1912 Sex:F Child# 5 J B Chasse Canada & Mary Bourbeau Canada
CHASSE, Eugene Adelard, Feb 28 1908 Sex:M Child# 2 J B Chasse Canada & Mary Bourbeau Canada
CHASSE, Irene Beatrice, Jun 3 1911 Sex:F Child# 6 Delphis Chasse Nashua, NH & Bertha Morrissette Dover, NH
CHASSE, Jos Lionel Robert, Oct 18 1927 Sex:M Child# 12 Jean B Chasse Canada & Marie Bourbeau Canada

CHASSE, Jos Paul Maurice, Mar 25 1916 Sex:M Child# 7 Jean Baptiste Chasse Canada & Mary Bourbeau Canada
CHASSE, Joseph, Jan 19 1911 Sex:M Child# 7 Olivier Chasse Canada & Eva Bouset Canada Stillborn
CHASSE, Joseph Armand A, Apr 9 1905 Sex:M Child# 2 Olivier Chasse Canada & Eva Bessette Canada
CHASSE, Joseph Clement F, Jan 14 1907 Sex:M Child# 3 Delphis Chasse NH & Bertha Morrissette NH
CHASSE, Leo Roland, Nov 20 1907 Sex:M Child# 1 Zephirin Chasse Canada & Anna Dumais Canada
CHASSE, Lorraine Patricia, Mar 17 1935 Sex:F Child# 1 Romeo Chasse Nashua, NH & Irene Theriault Nashua, NH
CHASSE, Lucienne Eva, Jun 12 1911 Sex:F Child# 4 J B Chasse Canada & Marie Bourbeau Canada
CHASSE, M Amanda Gertrude, Apr 16 1917 Sex:F Child# 9 Delphis Chasse NH & Bertha Morrissette NH
CHASSE, Marie Jennie Lucille, Oct 6 1917 Sex:F Child# 8 Jean B Chasse Canada & Mary Bourdeau Canada
CHASSE, Marie Juliette A, May 27 1910 Sex:F Child# 3 Jean B Chasse Canada & Marie Bourbeau Canada
CHASSE, Marie P Lucille, Oct 17 1931 Sex:F Child# 2 Aurel Chasse Nashua, NH & Jeannette Barriault Nashua, NH
CHASSE, Marie Rita Gabrielle, Dec 15 1920 Sex:F Child# 9 Jean Baptiste Chasse Canada & Marie Bourbeau Canada
CHASSE, Marie Yvonne Albina, Oct 29 1912 Sex:F Child# 7 Delphis Chasse Nashua, NH & Bertha Morrissette Dover, NH
CHASSE, Marie Yvonne Jean, Sep 19 1919 Sex:F Child# 10 Delphis Chasse Nashua, NH & Bertha Morrissette Dover, NH
CHASSE, Marie Yvonne Leona, May 15 1914 Sex:F Child# 8 Delphis Chasse Nashua, NH & Bertha Morrissette Dover, NH
CHASSE, Maurice Eugene, Jul 4 1934 Sex:M Child# 3 Aurele Chasse Nashua, NH & Jeannette Barriault Nashua, NH
CHASSE, Ovila, Feb 12 1910 Sex:M Child# 5 Delphis Chasse Nashua, NH & Bertha Morissette Dover, NH
CHASSE, Paul Alva, Mar 30 1930 Sex:M Child# 1 Aurela Chasse Nashua, NH & Jeannette Beriault Nashua, NH
CHASSE, Walter Aurel, Feb 5 1906 Sex:M Child# 2 Delphis Chasse Nashua, NH & Bertha Morissette Dover, NH
CHASSEUR, Dora, Jul 1 1907 Sex:F Child# 8 Louis Chasseur Canada & Adele St Laurent Canada
CHASSEUR, Marie Beatrice, Nov 6 1904 Sex:F Child# 6 Louis Chasseur Canada & Marie Levesque Canada
CHASSEUR, Marie Irene G, Sep 8 1910 Sex:F Child# 9 Louis Chasseur Canada & Adelia St Laurent Canada
CHASSEUR, Raymond Auguste, Jul 22 1931 Sex:M Child# 1 Auguste Chasseur Canada & Edna Malette Nashua, NH
CHASSEUR, Rita Constance, Sep 22 1935 Sex:F Child# 2 Auguste Chasseur Canada & Edna Mallette Nashua, NH
CHATTEL, Phyllis, Aug 9 1905 Sex:F Child# 2 Prosper Chattel Manchester, NH & Lucy Lapointe Sciota, NY
CHATTEL, Vivienne Lucille, Oct 5 1903 Sex:F Child# 1 Prosper Chattel NH & Lucie Lapointe NY
CHAUMARD, Marie Germaine A, Dec 3 1906 Sex:F Child# 1 Arsene Chaumard Canada & Hermaine Morel Canada
CHAUSSE, Calixte Joseph, Feb 19 1900 Sex:M Child# 2 Carl Chausse Canada & Alphonsine Gendron Canada
CHAUSSE, Diana, Nov 19 1933 Sex:F Child# 1 Leo Chausse Canada & Anne Charbonneau Lowell, MA
CHAUSSE, Joseph Oscar E, Jun 10 1903 Sex:M Child# 3 Calixte Chausse Canada & Alphonsine Gendron Canada
CHAUSSE, Romeo, Feb 11 1912 Sex:M Child# 2 Calixte Chausse Canada & Alphonsine Gendron Canada
CHAUTEL, Rita, Oct 2 1929 Sex:F Child# 6 Joseph Chautel Canada & Marie Francoeur Nashua, NH
CHEBOWICZ, Geneva, Nov 8 1919 Sex:F Child# 1 Anthony Chebowicz Poland Russia & Theresa Narkowicz Poland Russia
CHEBOWICZ, Micheslov, Dec 10 1914 Sex:M Child# 1 Romeo Chebowicz Russia & Stanislava Narkawicz Russia
CHEDEKEL, Deborah Selma, Aug 23 1931 Sex:F Child# 3 Samuel Chedekel Russia & Rebecca Zubick Poland
CHEDNAUSLI, Annie, Dec 1 1914 Sex:F Child# 1 Louis Chednausli Russia & Louis Baranauski Russia
CHEETHAM, Donald Norman, Apr 21 1930 Sex:M Child# 1 Norman Cheetham England & Lucy Bishop NH
CHEEVER, David Ward, Dec 22 1935 Sex:M Child# 2 Silas W Cheever S Lyndeboro, NH & Claire Hulette Gardner, MA
CHEEVER, Frank Alvin, Jr, Jan 15 1912 Sex:M Child# 1 Frank Alvin Cheever Greenfield, NH & Winnie V Corey NS
CHEEVER, Richard Norcross, Aug 30 1934 Sex:M Child# 1 Silas Cheever S Lyndeboro, NH & Claire Hulette Gardner, MA
CHEEVER, Unknown, Sep 14 1916 Sex:F Child# 3 Harold D Cheever Greenfield, NH & Nellie Balmforth England
CHEMARD, Dorothy Rita, Feb 24 1932 Sex:F Child# 1 A W Chemard Michigan & Mabel Holmes Wakefield, MA
CHENARD, Francois, Jun 19 1934 Sex:M Child# 1 Francois Chenard Canada & Gertrude St Laurent Nashua, NH
CHENARD, Germaine Louise, Jul 16 1926 Sex:F Child# 11 Francis Chenard Canada & Anna Dumont Canada
CHENARD, Gertrude, Sep 29 1935 Sex:F Child# 2 Francois Chenard Canada & Gert St Laurent Nashua, NH
CHENARD, Roland Victor, Feb 4 1913 Sex:M Child# 4 Ludger Chenard Canada & Amanda Gagnon Canada
CHENARGOS, James, Aug 30 1919 Sex:M Child# 8 James Chenargos Greece & Annie Moros Greece
CHENETTE, Alfred I, Aug 23 1887 Sex:M Child# 1 Alex Chenette P Q & Aufedie Saindon P Q
CHENETTE, Unknown, Apr 23 1891 Sex:M Child# 6 Louis Chenette Canada & Alvira Monitt Canada Stillborn
CHENEVERT, M Marguerite, Jul 25 1891 Sex:F Child# 5 Valaire Chenevert Canada & Antonia Sylvester Canada
CHENEY, Adelbert Hitchcock, May 29 1932 Sex:M Child# 6 A H Cheney Nashua, NH & Emma Kenney Philadelphia, PA
CHENEY, Florence Clark, Oct 24 1909 Sex:F Child# 1 George W Cheney Nashua, NH & Mabel E Clark Providence, RI
CHENEY, Frank Ellis, Feb 24 1896 Sex:M Child# 4 J M Cheney Wilmot & Adelia S Hitchcock Hattey, PQ
CHENEY, Franklin Clyde, Feb 21 1923 Sex:M Child# 1 William M Cheney Rouses Point, NY & Margaret Clyde Hudson, NH
CHENEY, Jos Walter Dunklee, Aug 19 1934 Sex:M Child# 2 Frank Cheney Nashua, NH & Lucy Dunklee S Lyndeboro, NH
CHENEY, Martha Ann, May 1 1924 Sex:F Child# 2 William M Cheney Ross Point, NY & Margaret Clyde Hudson, NH
CHENEY, Nellie Elizabeth, Oct 25 1935 Sex:F Child# 3 Frank E Cheney Nashua, NH & Lucy Dunklee Lyndeboro, NH
CHENEY, Unknown, Sep 4 1898 Sex:M Child# 5 Joseph W Cheney Wilmot & Sarah A Hitshrock Halty, PQ
CHENEY, Unknown, Oct 14 1910 Sex:M Child# 2 George W Cheney Nashua, NH & Mabel E Clark Providence, RI Stillborn
CHENY, Unknown, Feb 16 1893 Sex:F Child# 3 Joseph M Cheny Wilmot & Adella S Hitchcock Canada
CHERETTO, Emma, Mar 10 1889 Sex:F Child# 5 Louis Cheretto Canada & Delina Morin Canada
CHERKES, Eugene, Jun 9 1914 Sex:M Child# 3 Julius Cherkes Russia & Aggie Petich Russia
CHERKES, John, Jun 9 1914 Sex:M Child# 2 Julius Cherkes Russia & Aggie Petich Russia
CHEROS, Justina, Oct 5 1913 Sex:F Child# 1 Climos Cheros Russia & Rosie Grancomage Russia
CHERREW, Joseph H, Apr 24 1890 Sex:M Child# 1 Henri Cherrew Nashua, NH & Alexandrine Bernard W Boylston, MA
CHERRIER, Regina, May 16 1893 Sex:F Child# 1 Clement Cherrier Canada & Amande Poirier Canada
CHES, Annie, Jul 31 1910 Sex:F Child# 1 Mike Ches Russia & Agnes Swiec Austria
CHESBOROUGH, Unknown, Dec 19 1904 Sex:M Child# 1 Sam F Chesborough NY & Eva M Dion Nashua, NH Stillborn
CHESIEN, Michael, Oct 28 1912 Sex:M Child# 1 Romoldy Chesien Russia & Zofia Bagdanowich Russia
CHESLEY, Irving, May 21 1892 Sex:M Child# 3 George W Chesley Concord & Sarah L W Concord
CHESLEY, Stanley, Sep 2 1910 Sex:M Child# 3 Henniker Chesley Nova Scotia & Maggie Brown Nova Scotia
CHESMOLAWICZ, Julius, Jul 31 1915 Sex:M Child# 1 Waych Chesmolawicz Russia & Julia Gaizuta Russia
CHESNOLAWICZ, Alice, Jan 18 1921 Sex:F Child# 2 Woit Chesnolawicz Russia & Julia Gaeditis Russia

CHESNOLAWICZ, Josie, Sep 22 1912 Sex:F Child# 1 Peter Chesnolawicz Russia & Maria Nadzacuta Russia
CHESNULEVICH, Kenneth John, Aug 16 1928 Sex:M Child# 1 J Chesnulevich Nashua, NH & Vera Owens St John, NB
CHESNULEVICH, Ralph Owen, Jul 10 1931 Sex:M Child# 2 John Chesnulevich Nashua, NH & Vera Owens St John, NB
CHESSEN, John, Oct 27 1916 Sex:M Child# 3 John Chessen Russia & Ursula Koptin Russia
CHESSEN, Stanislaw, May 17 1912 Sex:M Child# 1 John Chessen Russia & Ursula Kupchunis Russia
CHESSON, Frank, Oct 23 1919 Sex:M Child# 4 John Chesson Russia & Ursula Kupshun Russia
CHESTER, Julia, May 22 1910 Sex:F Child# 2 John Chester Russia & Josie Nazaka Russia
CHESTER, Phyllis Edna, Jan 31 1928 Sex:F Child# 3 William Chester Russia & Sarah Zimberg Nashua, NH
CHESTER, Shirley, Nov 18 1923 Sex:F Child# 2 William Chester Russia & Sarah Zimberg Nashua, NH
CHESTMOLOWEZ, Frank, Feb 1 1916 Sex:M Child# 3 Stanley Chestmolowez Russia & Mickola Wolasty Russia
CHESTNER, Bertha, Jun 8 1929 Sex:F Child# 3 Steves Chestner Lithuania & Julia Gartis Lithuania
CHESTNER, Josie, Jul 23 1908 Sex:F Child# 1 John Chestner Russia & Rosa Nadzaika Russia
CHESTNUT, Mary, May 25 1915 Sex:F Child# 3 Martin Chestnut Russia & Antonia Lakawich Russia
CHEVERETTE, Joseph Louis E, May 4 1924 Sex:M Child# 6 Joseph Cheverette Canada & Amanda Desmoris Nashua, NH
CHEVORETTE, Pauline Esther, Nov 14 1925 Sex:F Child# 7 Jos Chevorette Canada & Am Desmarais Nashua, NH
CHEVRETTE, Evelyn Emma J, Jun 24 1919 Sex:F Child# 3 Joseph Chevrette Canada & Amanda Desmarais Nashua, NH
CHEVRETTE, J Louis Lamatien, May 8 1911 Sex:M Child# 2 Alfred Chevrette Canada & Marie Bacon Canada
CHEVRETTE, J Robert Edgar, Oct 31 1911 Sex:M Child# 1 Joseph Chevrette Canada & Amanda Desmarais Nashua, NH
CHEVRETTE, Joseph Robert Gerard, Jun 17 1927 Sex:M Child# 8 Joseph Chevrette Canada & A Desmarais Nashua, NH
CHEVRETTE, M Louise Gertrude, Jan 29 1914 Sex:F Child# 2 Joseph Chevrette Canada & Amanda Desmarais Canada
CHEVRETTE, Marie, Aug 31 1909 Sex:F Child# 1 Alfred Chevrette Canada & Marie Bacon Canada
CHEVRETTE, Paul Alcide, Oct 17 1920 Sex:M Child# 6 Joseph Chevrette Canada & Amanda Desmarais Nashua, NH
CHEVRETTE, Victor Robert, Aug 6 1916 Sex:M Child# 3 Joseph Chevrette Canada & Amanda Desmarais Nashua, NH
CHICK, Esther Mae, Jun 20 1928 Sex:F Child# 2 Walter Chick Kennebunkport, ME & Blanche Corey Nova Scotia
CHICK, Jennie Frances, Jun 17 1927 Sex:F Child# 1 Walter Chick Maine & Blanche Corey Nova Scotia
CHIFLOWITZ, Lillian, Dec 18 1914 Sex:F Child# 1 Jacob Chiflowitz Russia & Devarinsky Russia
CHILDS, Leslie Ferguson, May 5 1893 Sex:M Child# 1 Lester P Childs Brockton, MA & Irene Chester Lynn, MA
CHIMIKLES, Tom George, May 1 1916 Sex:M Child# 4 George Chimikles Greece & Versilika Kures Greece
CHIMIKLES, Unknown, Nov 9 1918 Sex:F Child# 5 George Chimikles Greece & Vereilika Kures Greece
CHIMIKLES, Unknown, Jun 22 1923 Sex:F Child# 7 George Chimikles Greece & Versilika Kures Greece
CHIMIKLIS, Demetia, Dec 27 1914 Sex:F Child# 4 George Chimiklis Greece & Vitsilika Kures Greece
CHIMIKUS, Unknown, Oct 6 1928 Sex:M Child# 9 George Chimikus Greece & Vasiliki Couris Greece
CHIMKLES, Vasilike, Oct 2 1915 Sex:F Child# 1 Peter Chimkles Greece & Elami Mockakos Greece
CHINARD, Mary Cecile J D, May 6 1924 Sex:F Child# 10 Francois Chinard Canada & Anna Dumont Canada
CHIPLOVITZ, Frances Mary, Apr 14 1916 Sex:F Child# 2 Jacob Chiplovitz Russia & Ida Divornisky Russia
CHIROPOLISH, Flovis, Aug 28 1915 Sex:F Child# 3 Frank Chiropolish Austria & Francis Vitruol Austria
CHISHOLM, Mary Gwendolin, Nov 16 1916 Sex:F Child# 1 Colin J Chisholm Nova Scotia & Edna G Levene Three Rivers
CHIST, Frank, Jun 2 1923 Sex:M Child# 5 Mike Chist Russia & Agnes Sivetts Russia
CHIVTINOS, Jermaine Hellen, Jul 4 1927 Sex:F Child# 1 Stergios Chivtinos Greece & Katina Kalaba Greece
CHOENSKI, Vladislof, Jun 5 1916 Sex:M Child# 1 Joe Choenski Russia & Zophie Warovski Russia
CHOINIERE, Irene Louise, Jan 26 1888 Sex:F Child# 7 Edward Choiniere Farnham, PQ & Josephine Aesette P Q
CHOINIERE, Joseph Adolphe, May 11 1899 Sex:M Child# 1 Adolphe Choiniere Canada & Marie Perrault Canada
CHOINIERE, Marie E, Oct 14 1889 Sex:F Child# 8 Edouard Choiniere Canada & Josephine Aesette Canada
CHOINNIERE, Alice E, Feb 19 1887 Sex:F Child# 1 Theo Choinniere Canada & Alice Cote Canada
CHOMARD, Ronald Sylvio, Apr 25 1935 Sex:M Child# 1 (No Parents Listed)
CHOMASTULOS, John, Nov 23 1920 Sex:M Child# 2 Charlie Chomastulos Greece & Evangeline Deasp Greece
CHOMSKI, Andrew, Nov 30 1907 Sex:M Child# 1 John Chomski Russia & Elsbieta Rapszis Russia
CHOPAS, George, Aug 23 1924 Sex:M Child# 2 James Chopas Greece & Sophia Giamisky Greece
CHOPOS, George, Apr 1 1921 Sex:M Child# 1 James Chopos Greece & Sophia Giamasis Greece
CHOTE, Mazaire Romeo, Nov 26 1909 Sex:M Child# 4 Carl Chote
CHOUINARD, Alfred, May 25 1902 Sex:M Child# 3 A Chouinard Canada & Atala Belanger Canada
CHOUINARD, Cecile Rita, Dec 1 1929 Sex:F Child# 1 Joseph Chouinard Canada & Ida Ouillette Nashua, NH
CHOUINARD, Ida Annette, May 26 1931 Sex:F Child# 2 Joseph Chouinard Canada & Ida Ouellette Nashua, NH
CHOUINARD, Marie Aimee, May 15 1899 Sex:F Child# 1 Alfred Chouinard Canada & Attala Belanger Canada
CHOUINARD, Theodore, Jan 21 1933 Sex:M Child# 3 Joseph Chouinard Canada & Ida Ouellette Nashua, NH
CHOUINARD, Victor Joseph, Nov 30 1900 Sex:M Child# 2 Alfred Chouinard Canada & Athala Bellanger Canada
CHOUINARDE, Barbara, May 17 1930 Sex:F Child# 2 Charles Chouinarde Fitchburg, MA & Blanche Early Fall River, MA
CHRAPOWISKI, Unknown, Apr 26 1921 Sex:F Child# 2 M Chrapowiski Russia & Egeperk Oly Russia
CHRETIEN, Joseph, Sep 19 1890 Sex:M Child# 2 Henri Chretien Van Buren, ME & Methaide Violette Van Buren, ME
CHRETIEN, Lucille Doris, Mar 27 1925 Sex:F Child# 2 Napoleon Chretien New Ipswich, NH & Adrienne Carle Canada
CHRETIEN, Vivienne Zema, Feb 17 1917 Sex:F Child# 2 Alphonse Chretien Canada & A Pelletier Canada
CHRISMAN, Marie, Feb 1 1920 Sex:F Child# 1 William J Chrisman Mass & Rose A Petrain Canada
CHRISMAN, Roger William, Jan 18 1929 Sex:M Child# 2 William Chrisman Lowell, MA & Rose Petrin Canada
CHRISTAPOLITZ, Vladislaw, May 3 1911 Sex:M Child# 2 Vldslw Christapolitz Russia & Eva Kodalitz Russia
CHRISTENSEN, Lillian Ella, Jul 18 1915 Sex:F Child# 2 William Christensen Vermont & Lillian Frenette NH
CHRISTIAN, Arthur, Jun 2 1915 Sex:M Child# 7 Friend Christian Saranac, NY & Ida McCune Saranac, NY
CHRISTIAN, Carl Francis, Oct 12 1910 Sex:M Child# 2 Fred Christian Dannemora, NY & Alice Cune Saranac, NY
CHRISTIAN, Gladys Evaline, Aug 16 1906 Sex:F Child# 3 Friend Christian Saranac, NY & Ida McCune Saranac, NY
CHRISTIAN, Helen Clara, Aug 11 1909 Sex:F Child# 5 Friend Christian Saranac, NY & Ida McCune Saranac, NY
CHRISTIAN, Howard Louis, Jan 9 1904 Sex:M Child# 2 Fred Louis Christian Saranac, NY & Ida McKeon Saranac, NY
CHRISTIAN, James Milton, Mar 8 1902 Sex:M Child# 1 T Louis Christian NY & Ida McCune NY
CHRISTIAN, Jeanne Theresa, Oct 9 1934 Sex:F Child# 4 Napoleon Christian New Ipswich, NH & Adrienne Carle Canada
CHRISTIAN, Jos Henry Romeo, Nov 11 1925 Sex:M Child# 2 Francis Christian Montreal, Canada & Odele Moreau Nashua, NH

CHRISTIAN, Josephine Norbert F, Sep 6 1924 Sex:M Child# 1 Francis Christian Canada & Odele Moreau Nashua, NH
CHRISTIAN, Lorraine, Jun 22 1928 Sex:F Child# 4 M Christian Nashua, NH & Minnie Lalmond Nashua, NH Stillborn
CHRISTIAN, Milton James, Sep 19 1925 Sex:M Child# 2 Milton Christian Nashua, NH & Minnie Lalmond Nashua, NH
CHRISTIAN, Nancy Jane, Apr 15 1932 Sex:F Child# 1 Ronald Christian Nashua, NH & Edna Lindquist Nashua, NH
CHRISTIAN, Richard Eugene, Mar 8 1930 Sex:M Child# 1 Eugene Christian Goffstown, NH & Laura Foisie Nashua, NH
CHRISTIAN, Robert, Jul 12 1933 Sex:M Child# 2 Carl F Christian Nashua, NH & Lillian Decelle Nashua, NH
CHRISTIAN, Robert James, Jul 19 1921 Sex:M Child# 4 Fred H Christian Dannemora, NY & Alice A Cuane Saranac, NY
CHRISTIAN, Unknown, Dec 18 1907 Sex:M Child# 4 Friend Christian Saranac, NY & Ida McCune Saranac, NY
CHRISTIAN, Unknown, Apr 24 1911 Sex:F Child# 6 Friend Christian Saranac, NY & Ida McCune Saranac, NY
CHRISTIAN, Unknown, Aug 21 1916 Sex:F Child# 3 Fred H Christian Saranac, NY & Alice McCune Saranac, NY Stillborn
CHRISTIAN, Unknown, Aug 9 1917 Sex:M Child# 8 Friend Christian Saranac, NY & Ida McClure Saranac, NY
CHRISTIAN, Unknown, Apr 30 1924 Sex:F Child# 1 Milton Christian Nashua, NH & Minnie Lalmond Nashua, NH
CHRISTIAN, Unknown, Dec 3 1926 Sex:F Child# 2 Milton Christian NH & Minnie Lalmond NH Stillborn
CHRISTIAN, Unknown, May 1 1928 Sex:M Child# 3 Francis Christian Canada & Odile Moreaux Nashua, NH Stillborn
CHRISTIAN, Unknown, Mar 4 1930 Sex:F Child# 5 Milton Christian Nashua, NH & Minnie Lalmond Nashua, NH Stillborn
CHRISTIANO, Mary Dorothy, Jan 24 1916 Sex:F Child# 9 Eugene Christiano Italy & Clara Vallee NH
CHRISTIANSON, Marlene Andrea, Apr 1 1935 Sex:F Child# 1 Wm Christianson Barre, VT & Elizabeth Monahan Manchester
CHRISTIE, Alice Bernadette, Aug 28 1908 Sex:F Child# 8 James F Christie Mass & Grace Livingstone Nashua, NH
CHRISTIE, Esther, Oct 25 1896 Sex:F Child# 3 James Christie Worcester, MA & Grace Livingston Nashua, NH
CHRISTIE, James, Nov 11 1901 Sex:M Child# 5 James Christie Worcester, MA & Grace Livingston Nashua, NH
CHRISTIE, John Henry, Sep 21 1926 Sex:M Child# 1 Charles Christie Nashua, NH & Alice Martin W Roxbury, MA
CHRISTIE, Pauline Joan, Jan 27 1932 Sex:F Child# 2 James Christie Nashua, NH & Lucille Leclair Nashua, NH
CHRISTIE, Richard, Mar 6 1934 Sex:M Child# 4 Richard Christie Manchester, NH & Clara Beaudette US
CHRISTIE, Theresa Hazel, Jan 24 1906 Sex:F Child# 7 James F Christie Worcester, MA & Grace Livingston Nashua, NH
CHRISTIE, Unknown, Oct 19 1887 Sex:F Child# 7 John C Christie Mass & Kate Mass
CHRISTIE, Unknown, Nov 18 1899 Sex:M Child# 3 James Christie Mass & Grace Livingston Nashua, NH
CHRISTIEN, Marie Claire, Jan 4 1924 Sex:F Child# 1 Napoleon Christien New Ipswich, NH & Adrienne Carle Canada
CHRISTIN, Cecile, Sep 18 1912 Sex:F Child# 7 Eugene Christin Italy & Clara Vallee NH
CHRISTOPOLIDGE, John, Jul 21 1917 Sex:M Child# 3 L Christopolidge Poland Russia & Eva Codalis Poland Russia
CHRISTOPOLIS, Stelania, Apr 26 1917 Sex:F Child# 4 Frank Christopolis Russia & Fannie Mytrova Austria
CHRISTOPOULAS, Agnes, Mar 12 1916 Sex:F Child# 1 Benj Christopoulas Russia & Mary Dubowick Russia
CHRISTY, John, Jan 3 1928 Sex:M Child# 4 Richard J Christy Manchester, NH & Clara Beaudet Canada
CHRITTIEN, Joseph D, Sep 25 1887 Sex:M Child# 6 Bte Chrittien P Q & Philomene P Q
CHSULUR, Peter, Apr 23 1909 Sex:M Child# 2 Stephen Chsulur Russia & Meake Volantokivitch Russia
CHURCH, Carl Edward, Jr, Dec 6 1935 Sex:M Child# 1 Carl E Church Hudson, NH & Isabel Forbes Nashua, NH
CHURCH, Ruth Norma, May 22 1908 Sex:F Child# 2 Hosmer C Church Boston, MA & Jessie M Barnard Peterboro, NH
CHURCH, Virginia, Oct 2 1922 Sex:F Child# 2 Carl Church Bangor, ME & Anna Hutchings England
CHURCHILL, Henry Meldin, Dec 15 1900 Sex:M Child# 2 Charles A Churchill Mass & Lillian Hammond NB
CHURCHILL, Unknown, Apr 25 1887 Sex:M Child# 1 Irving H Churchill Lowell, MA & Ellen Corey Littleton, MA
CHUVIRAGO, Felix, Aug 29 1909 Sex:M Child# 1 Michael Chuvirago Russia & Emelia Mickanovitch Russia
CIESINN, Edward, Oct 13 1908 Sex:M Child# 1 Roma Ciesinn Russia & Zofie Bagdonowicz Russia
CIESLUKIEWICZ, Richard Thomas, Oct 6 1931 Sex:M Child# 1 Thomas Cieslukiewicz Poland & Elise Berube Canada
CIRONE, Unknown, Apr 13 1899 Sex:M Child# 1 Charles R Cirone Italy & Louise M Ingalls Bridgeton, ME
CLAFFIN, Leon Nathan, Jr, Apr 25 1921 Sex:M Child# 3 Leon C Claffin Hancock, VT & Abbie J Eaton Rochester, VT
CLANCEY, Unknown, Feb 8 1887 Sex:F Child# 8 Bernard Clancey Ireland & Bridget Gaffney Ireland
CLANCY, Catherine Mary, May 20 1923 Sex:F Child# 2 Frank B Clancy Nashua, NH & Emma F Delaney Nashua, NH
CLANCY, Charles James, Oct 24 1891 Sex:M Child# 10 Bernard Clancy Ireland & Bridget Gaffney Ireland
CLANCY, Elizabeth, Mar 2 1893 Sex:F Child# 2 Benjamin Clancy Ireland & Bridget Gaffney Ireland
CLANCY, Francis Bernard, Nov 22 1921 Sex:M Child# 1 Frank B Clancy Nashua, NH & Emma F Delaney Nashua, NH
CLANCY, Joseph, Dec 20 1889 Sex:M Child# 8 William Clancy Ireland & Maggie Keenan Ireland
CLANCY, Onesime Omer, Mar 22 1891 Sex:M Child# 9 Louis Clancy Canada & Philomene Schine Canada
CLANCY, Unknown, Dec 11 1888 Sex:F Child# 9 Bernard Clancy Ireland & Bridget Ireland
CLANCY, Unknown, Sep 27 1891 Sex:M Child#  William Clancy Ireland &  Ireland
CLAREY, Celia K, Sep 16 1899 Sex:F Child# 7 James Clarey Ireland & Margaret Winn Ireland
CLAREY, James, Feb 24 1891 Sex:M Child# 3 James Clarey Ireland & Maggie Winn Ireland
CLAREY, John Joseph, Mar 5 1889 Sex:M Child# 2 James Clarey Ireland & Maggie Winn Ireland
CLAREY, Marguerite, Jul 7 1897 Sex:F Child# 6 James Clarey Ireland & Margaret Winn Ireland
CLARK, Beverly Ann, Mar 15 1935 Sex:F Child# 3 William Clark Vermont & Dorothy Woods Nashua, NH
CLARK, Beverly Priscilla, Nov 4 1924 Sex:F Child# 1 Otis Clark Nashua, NH & Lillian Claire Nashua, NH
CLARK, Clark, Apr 15 1889 Sex:M Child# 5 Henry Clark Ireland & Mary Alger Ireland
CLARK, Dorothy Alma, May 18 1921 Sex:F Child# 3 Edward W Clark Syracuse, NY & Signe Ekdahl Brooklyn, NY
CLARK, Douglas Overtown, Oct 3 1918 Sex:M Child# 1 Norman Clark Newcastle, England & Cora A Gilson Nashua, NH
CLARK, Edward, Oct 5 1916 Sex:M Child# 1 Edward J Clark Nashua, NH & Julia Shea Ireland
CLARK, Elizabeth, Aug 8 1893 Sex:F Child# 13 John Clark Ireland & Lisay Darcy Ireland
CLARK, Elizabeth Jane, Mar 14 1919 Sex:F Child# 2 E Everett Clark Pittsfield, NH & Dorothy F Chapman Gillingham
CLARK, Elizabeth Jean, Nov 1 1931 Sex:F Child# 2 Eugene L Clark Lowell, MA & Ruth E McKenney Leominster, MA
CLARK, Ellery, Sep 15 1893 Sex:M Child# 1 Mark M Clark Wilton, NH & Eliza Milford, NH
CLARK, Evangeline C, Mar 14 1889 Sex:F Child# 4 W P Clark New Hampshire & Sarah E Davis New Hampshire
CLARK, Frederick Arthur, Jun 9 1922 Sex:M Child# 1 Victor A Clark Bristol, VT & Florence Smith Pelham, NH
CLARK, George Fred, Mar 17 1900 Sex:M Child# 1 George F Clark ME & Lena M Graham VT
CLARK, George Herbert, Apr 20 1899 Sex:M Child# 1 (No Parents Listed)
CLARK, George Herbert, Jr, Jan 17 1921 Sex:M Child# 1 George Clark Nashua, NH & Mary Hudon Nashua, NH
CLARK, Gordon Alfred, Jun 30 1933 Sex:M Child# 5 James M Clark Manchester, NH & Ethel Thompson Manchester, NH

CLARK, Harriet Isabel, Jul 17 1928 Sex:F Child# 3 H A Clark Kennebunkport, ME & Isabel G Foss Beechmont, MA
CLARK, Herbert S, Jan 31 1901 Sex:M Child# 6 James L Clark Lyndeboro, NH & Lizzie Wallace Nashua, NH
CLARK, James Marr, Jr, Nov 8 1930 Sex:M Child# 4 James M Clark Manchester, NH & Ethel Thompson Manchester, NH
CLARK, Kenneth Gerald, Jun 3 1926 Sex:M Child# 3 George Clark Nashua, NH & Rose Hudon Nashua, NH
CLARK, Louise, Oct 18 1925 Sex:F Child# 5 Horace Clark Lynn, MA & Ethel Wilkins N Clarendon, VT
CLARK, Margret Helen, Sep 28 1932 Sex:F Child# 2 William Clark Newfane, VT & Dorothy Woods Nashua, NH
CLARK, Marian Elizabeth, Jun 24 1912 Sex:F Child# 2 John Dustin Clark Nashua, NH & Marion L Ward Nashua, NH
CLARK, Marion Shirley, Aug 30 1922 Sex:F Child# 2 Harry L Clark Lyndeboro, NH & Carrie R Stark Pepperell, MA
CLARK, Mary Elizabeth, Jan 7 1901 Sex:F Child# 1 John Clark Ireland & Mary Shannahan Nashua, NH
CLARK, Nillie Clark, Aug 2 1890 Sex:F Child# 11 John Clark Ireland & Eliza Dearcy Ireland
CLARK, Norman Edgar, Sep 11 1922 Sex:M Child# 1 John A Clark Gardiner, ME & Etta Stevens Dracut, MA
CLARK, Otis Ray, May 9 1896 Sex:M Child# 2 Daniel Clark Virginia & Angie Rollins Pelham, NH
CLARK, Richard Ayer, Jun 25 1915 Sex:M Child# 1 Fred L Clark Nashua, NH & Mabel C Holt Nashua, NH Stillborn
CLARK, Richard Holt, Jul 26 1919 Sex:M Child# 2 Fred Laureston Clark Nashua, NH & Mable Cassimere Holt Nashua, NH
CLARK, Richard Leonard, Jan 24 1928 Sex:M Child# 1 Ottis Clark Nashua, NH & Lucy Russell Greenfield, NH
CLARK, Robert Wilbur, Nov 12 1922 Sex:M Child# 2 George Clark Nashua, NH & Mary Rose Hudon Nashua, NH
CLARK, Thomas W W, Mar 6 1893 Sex:M Child#  Henry Clark England & Fannie Morin Ireland
CLARK, Unknown, Mar 10 1888 Sex:F Child# 2 James L Clark Lyndeboro, NH & H Lizzie Mallore Merrimack, NH
CLARK, Unknown, Sep 22 1891 Sex:F Child# 2 George R Clark Peterboro & Lula O'Leazotte Champlain, NY
CLARK, Unknown, Feb 5 1892 Sex:F Child# 1 Daniel Clark Virginia & Angie Rollins NH
CLARK, Unknown, Nov 14 1892 Sex:M Child# 1 Edward Clark Ireland & Lizzie Briton Ireland Stillborn
CLARK, Unknown, Apr 1 1899 Sex:F Child# 5 James L Clark Lyndeboro, NH & Elizabeth Wallace Nashua, NH
CLARK, Unknown, Jun 6 1904 Sex:M Child# 3 William H Clark Deering, NH & Mary J Perley Salem, MA
CLARK, Unknown, May 28 1914 Sex:M Child# 1 Edward E Clark Pittsfield, NH & Dorothy Chapman England
CLARK, Unknown, Jun 2 1929 Sex:M Child# 1 Elwood Clark Milford, MA & Rachael Elian Worcester, MA
CLARK, Warren Paul, Jan 1 1934 Sex:M Child# 1 Warren Paul Clark Jamaica, VT & Loretta Pinette Nashua, NH
CLARK, William Arthur, Nov 17 1931 Sex:M Child# 1 William C Clark Newfane, VT & Dorothy Wood Nashua, NH
CLARKE, Josephine Anna, Feb 3 1916 Sex:F Child#  Edward W Clarke Syracuse, NY & Signe E Ekdahl Brooklyn, NY
CLARKSON, Beverly June, May 29 1925 Sex:F Child# 2 Sydney Clarkson Northampton, MA & Viola Lambert Nashua, NH
CLARKSON, Corine Frances, Mar 31 1928 Sex:F Child# 4 Sidney Clarkson North Hampton, NH & Viola Lambert Nashua, NH
CLARKSON, Douglas Frank, Nov 17 1926 Sex:M Child# 3 S W Clarkson N Hampton, MA & Viola C Lambert Nashua, NH
CLARKSON, George S, Oct 19 1891 Sex:M Child# 1 Thomas H Clarkson Nashua, NH & Ellen M Sullivan Nashua, NH
CLARKSON, Signey Wright, Jr, Mar 26 1923 Sex:M Child# 1 Sidney W Clarkson N Hampton, NH & Viola Lambert Nashua, NH
CLARKSON, Thomas Harry, Mar 14 1896 Sex:M Child# 1 Thomas H Clarkson Nashua, NH & Nellie M Sullivan Nashua, NH
CLARRIDGE, Cynthia Delight, Jun 8 1935 Sex:F Child# 2 D H Clarridge Milford, MA & Alice Ramsdell Nashua, NH
CLARRIDGE, Duane Ramsdell, Apr 16 1932 Sex:M Child# 1 Duane Clarridge Milford, MA & Alice Ramsdell Nashua, NH
CLARY, Mary, Aug 9 1887 Sex:F Child# 1 James Clary Ireland & Maggie Winn Ireland
CLASSON, Doris Ethelyn, Oct 29 1909 Sex:F Child# 2 Walter Classon Nashua, NH & Alice H Weston Waterville, MA
CLASSON, Gerald Kendall, May 22 1935 Sex:M Child# 1 Gerald W Classon Nashua, NH & Susie Watson Littleton, NH
CLASSON, Gerald Weston, Apr 2 1908 Sex:M Child# 1 Walter H Classon Nashua, NH & Alice H Weston Waterbury, MA
CLASSON, Lester Wallace, Jul 11 1898 Sex:M Child#  Charles W Classon Leominster, MA & Elima J French Fitchburg, MA
CLASSON, Unknown, Jan 17 1894 Sex:F Child# 5 C W Classon Leominster, MA & Ermina J French Fitchburg, MA
CLAVEAU, Agnes Rita, Jun 14 1919 Sex:F Child# 4 Armase Claveau Canada & Emelia Delude Canada
CLAVEAU, Marie Jeanne, Dec 17 1905 Sex:F Child# 1 Armace Claveau Canada & Amelia Delude Canada
CLAVEAU, Sylvia, Oct 27 1907 Sex:F Child# 2 Armace Claveau Canada & Emelie Delude Canada
CLEANCY, Kate S, Apr 18 1887 Sex:F Child# 7 William Cleancy Ireland & Marg Keenen Ireland
CLEARY, Annie, Apr 20 1893 Sex:F Child# 4 James Cleary Ireland & Margaret Winn Ireland
CLEARY, John Thomas, Dec 15 1930 Sex:M Child# 1 James H Cleary Mass & Marguerite Leary E Pepperell, MA
CLEARY, Philip, Dec 18 1894 Sex:M Child#  James Cleary Ireland & Margaret Winn Ireland
CLEARY, Unknown, Jun 19 1924 Sex: Child# 1 Walter Cleary Groton, MA & Adeline Burns Nashua, NH Stillborn
CLEARY, Unknown, Jul 15 1926 Sex:M Child# 2 Walter H Cleary Groton, MA & Adeline Burns Nashua, NH Stillborn
CLEEKAY, Constance May, May 2 1923 Sex:F Child# 1 James Cleekay Dublin, NH & Hilda Nevera Lancaster, NH
CLEGG, Mary Ellen, Dec 30 1892 Sex:F Child# 3 Joseph Clegg England & Marguerite Chaze Canada
CLEGG, Richard Charles, Apr 12 1901 Sex:M Child# 3 Charles H Clegg Gainsville, VT & Maud Heath Nashua, NH
CLEMAS, Joseph, Sep 21 1910 Sex:M Child# 4 Joseph Clemas Russia & Magdeline Krushus Russia
CLEMENCE, Joseph, Oct 21 1895 Sex:M Child# 1 John Clemence Poland & Alexandrina Jozenes Poland
CLEMENS, Mary, Sep 29 1915 Sex:F Child# 1 Joseph Clemens Russia & Mary Zebrupute Russia
CLEMENS, Roger Douglas, Aug 9 1932 Sex:M Child# 1 (No Parents Listed)
CLEMENT, Charles Austin, Apr 19 1922 Sex:M Child# 1 Charles A Clement Fall River, MA & Effie M Austin Nashua, NH
CLEMENT, Dixie Laura, Jan 5 1907 Sex:F Child# 1 Henry W Clement Nashua, NH & Candace P Hatch Bristol, VT
CLEMENT, Earl Richard, Apr 29 1923 Sex:M Child# 5 Harry E Clement Hudson, NH & Mary E Baskin Waterford, NB
CLEMENT, Earl W, Oct 4 1897 Sex:M Child# 1 George B Clement Nashua, NH & Luella E Piplar Nashua, NH
CLEMENT, Edna Frances, Apr 28 1926 Sex:F Child# 1 Edward Clement Hudson, NH & Ruby Jaquith Boston, MA Stillborn
CLEMENT, Edna Lucille, Jul 22 1912 Sex:F Child# 2 Harry E Clement Hudson, NH & Mary E Buskin Waterford, NB
CLEMENT, Edward, Feb 28 1903 Sex:M Child# 7 Elmer Clement Hudson, NH & Emily Wilcox E Boston, MA
CLEMENT, Esther, Jun 2 1921 Sex:F Child# 4 Harry Clement Hudson, NH & Mary E Baskin Waterford, NB
CLEMENT, Evelyn May, Oct 9 1910 Sex:F Child# 1 Harry E Clement Hudson, NH & Mary E Basken Waterford, NB
CLEMENT, Forest N, Jul 2 1887 Sex:M Child# 2 James A Clement Warren & Emma J Carr Nashua, NH
CLEMENT, Frances Murial, Apr 22 1918 Sex:F Child# 3 Harry E Clement Hudson, NH & Mary E Baskin Waterford, NB
CLEMENT, Gordon Emile, Nov 19 1929 Sex:M Child# 1 David Scott Clement Scotland & Doris Shulze Providence, RI
CLEMENT, Gretchen, Mar 17 1932 Sex:F Child# 2 David S Clement Scotland & Doris Shulze Cambridge, MA
CLEMENT, Ina Rolfe, Jul 9 1896 Sex:F Child# 1 James E Clement Nashua, NH & L Mabel Rolfe Nashua, NH
CLEMENT, James Markland, Mar 27 1909 Sex:M Child# 1 Walter H Clement Nashua, NH & Laura Perry Newark, NJ

CLEMENT, Marion Louise, Aug 7 1927 Sex:F Child# 1 John Clement England & Mabel Lemkey Chicago, IL
CLEMENT, Nancy Janet, Mar 25 1934 Sex:F Child# 9 William W Clement S Boston, MA & Viola Nichols St Johnsbury, VT
CLEMENT, Phyllis Evelyn, Nov 1 1905 Sex:F Child# 3 James E Clement Nashua, NH & L Mabel Rolfe Nashua, NH
CLEMENT, Richard Walter, Apr 13 1916 Sex:M Child# 2 Walter H Clement Nashua, NH & Laura Perry Newark, NJ
CLEMENT, Robert Otis, Dec 1 1917 Sex:M Child# 1 Otis D Clement Hudson, NH & Gladys E Nixon Laconia, NH
CLEMENT, Shirley Elizabeth, Apr 8 1919 Sex:F Child# 2 Otis E Clement Hudson, NH & Gladys E Nixon Laconia, NH
CLEMENT, Unknown, Apr 28 1898 Sex:F Child# 2 James E Clement Nashua, NH & L Mabel Ralfe Nashua, NH
CLEMENT, Unknown, Jul 21 1929 Sex:M Child# 2 Edward Clement Hudson, NH & Ruby Jaquith Boston, MA Stillborn
CLEMENT, William David, Mar 9 1921 Sex:M Child# 3 Otis D Clement Hudson, NH & Gladys E Nixon Laconia, NH
CLEMENT, William Earl, Feb 15 1935 Sex:M Child# 1 (No Parents Listed)
CLEMENTS, Unknown, Apr 6 1917 Sex:M Child# 6 Arthur Clements Allenburg, NY & Lena Leazotte Nashua, NH
CLEMMENS, Anna, Nov 25 1916 Sex:F Child# 2 Joseph Clemmens Russia & Mary Zebrusche Russia
CLEMMONS, George Allison, Apr 19 1896 Sex:M Child# 1 George H Clemmons NH & Edith M Horne NH
CLEMONS, Alfred Russell, Aug 26 1909 Sex:M Child#  Wallace E Clemons New York & Elizabeth A Wells Liverpool, Eng
CLEMONS, Arthur Joseph Wright, May 20 1913 Sex:M Child# 3 Arthur H Clemons New York & Lena Leazotte Nashua, NH
CLEMONS, Daisy Caroline, Apr 1 1907 Sex:F Child# 4 Wallace E Clemons New York & Elizabeth A Wells England
CLEMONS, Dorothy Hazel, Oct 30 1910 Sex:F Child# 1 Arthur H Clemons New York & Lena Leazott Nashua, NH
CLEMONS, Effie Cora, Dec 28 1911 Sex:F Child# 2 Arthur H Clemons New York & Lena Leazotte Nashua, NH
CLEMONS, Harold P, Jun 11 1897 Sex:M Child# 5 Lewis Clemons Harristown, NY & E L Finnigan Beechamtown, NY
CLEMONS, Harold Victor, Apr 29 1911 Sex:F Child# 1 Wallace E Clemons Nashua, NH & Catherine McGrail Mass
CLEMONS, Hazel, Oct 14 1904 Sex:F Child# 5 Wallace Clemons New York & Elizabeth E Wells England
CLEMONS, Helen M, Aug 17 1896 Sex:F Child# 8 Ruben B Clemons Herrotstown, NY & Louisa Brough Clarenceville, PQ
CLEMONS, James William, Feb 8 1916 Sex:M Child# 5 Arthur H Clemons New York & Lena Leazott Nashua, NH
CLEMONS, Ralph Solon, Oct 20 1912 Sex:M Child# 8 Wallacae Clemons Ellenburg, NY & Elizabeth A Wells Liverpool, Eng
CLEMONS, Richard Louis, Jul 24 1914 Sex:M Child# 4 Arthur H Clemons New York & Lena Leazott Nashua, NH
CLEMONS, Solon, Aug 2 1892 Sex:M Child# 6 Reuben Clemons NY & Liza Trow Canada
CLEMONS, Theodore Ray, Sep 20 1908 Sex:M Child# 8 Wallace Clemons New York & Elizabeth Wells England
CLEMONS, Unknown, Oct 19 1894 Sex:F Child# 7 Reuben B Clemons N Elba, NY & Eliza M Brough Clarenceville, Quebec
CLEMONS, Unknown, Jun 29 1899 Sex:M Child# 6 Lewis C Clemons Harriotstown, NY & Emeline L Finnigan Beakmantown, NY
CLEMONS, Unknown, Apr 17 1901 Sex:F Child# 6 Louis Clemons
CLEMONS, Walter Irdale, Jan 5 1906 Sex:M Child# 6 Wallace Clemons New York & Elisabeth A Wells England
CLERMONT, Geraldine, Oct 7 1926 Sex:F Child# 1 Harold Clermont Nashua, NH & Harriet Coffin Waltham, MA
CLERMONT, Joseph, Jul 20 1924 Sex:M Child# 1 Harold Clermont Nashua, NH & Josephine Darling Nashua, NH
CLERMONT, Ruth Helen, Jun 5 1930 Sex:F Child# 2 Harold Clermont Nashua, NH & Harriett Coffin Waltham, MA
CLERMONT, Theo May, Mar 21 1933 Sex:F Child# 3 Harold Clermont Nashua, NH & Harriett Coffin Waltham, MA
CLEVELAND, Cora Frances, Nov 8 1889 Sex:F Child# 2 A L Cleveland Brookline, NH & Laura Wright Nashua, NH
CLEVELAND, Gladys M A E, Aug 5 1895 Sex:F Child# 1 John C Cleveland Vermont & Georgie Mandigo New York
CLEVELAND, Gladys May, Jan 19 1892 Sex:F Child# 3 Addison L Cleveland Townsend, MA & Laura Wright Nashua, NH
CLIFFORD, Alice R, Jun 29 1894 Sex:F Child# 5 Patrick F Clifford Ireland & Hannah M Shea Ireland
CLIFFORD, Annie Elizabeth, Jul 7 1892 Sex:F Child# 4 Patrick F Clifford Ireland & Hannah M Shea Ireland
CLIFFORD, Beth, Oct 28 1894 Sex:F Child# 10 Patrick J Clifford Ireland & Elizabeth A Sullivan Nashua, NH
CLIFFORD, Cornelius, Oct 31 1893 Sex:M Child# 4 Corneilus Clifford Ireland & Margaret Mullen Milford, NH
CLIFFORD, David Alexander, Mar 5 1893 Sex:M Child# 9 Patrick J Clifford Ireland & Elizabeth A Sullivan Nashua, NH
CLIFFORD, Edward, Jun 15 1889 Sex:M Child# 1 Corneilus Clifford Ireland & Margaret Mullen Milford, NH
CLIFFORD, Francis, Mar 20 1928 Sex:M Child# 6 Timothy Clifford Ireland & Marguerite Winn Nashua, NH
CLIFFORD, Grace Evelyn, Jun 13 1896 Sex:F Child# 6 Patrick F Clifford Ireland & Hannah M Shea Ireland
CLIFFORD, Hannah Josie, Sep 5 1889 Sex:F Child# 2 Patrick F Clifford Ireland & Hannah M Shea Ireland
CLIFFORD, Harold Michael, Feb 8 1921 Sex:M Child# 1 Harold W Clifford Nashua, NH & Mary L Murphy New Bedford, MA
CLIFFORD, Horace A, Nov 8 1898 Sex:M Child# 7 Patrick T Clifford Ireland & Hanna M Shea Ireland
CLIFFORD, James, Jan 18 1919 Sex:M Child# 3 Timothy Clifford Ireland & Margaret M Winn Nashua, NH
CLIFFORD, John, Nov 21 1888 Sex:M Child# 1 Patrick Clifford Ireland & Mary Ann Downing Nashua, NH
CLIFFORD, John Augustus, Jul 14 1891 Sex:M Child# 3 Patrick F Clifford Ireland & Hannah M Shea Ireland
CLIFFORD, John Robert, Aug 21 1912 Sex:M Child# 3 John Clifford Ireland & Margaret Sullivan Ireland
CLIFFORD, Katherine, May 17 1909 Sex:F Child# 2 John Clifford Ireland & Margaret M Sullivan Ireland
CLIFFORD, Lucille, Mar 13 1915 Sex:F Child# 2 Timothy Clifford Ireland & Margaret M Winn Nashua, NH
CLIFFORD, Mabel, Jan 10 1896 Sex:F Child# 5 Cornelius Clifford Ireland & Margaret Mullen Milford, NH
CLIFFORD, Margaret, Dec 19 1922 Sex:F Child# 2 Harold M Clifford Nashua, NH & Mary L Murphy New Bedford, MA Stillbo
CLIFFORD, Mary C, Oct 18 1888 Sex:F Child# 7 Patrick Clifford Ireland & Elizabeth A Sullivan Nashua, NH
CLIFFORD, Mary Eileen, Mar 17 1924 Sex:F Child# 3 Harold M Clifford Nashua, NH & Mary Murphy New Bedford, MA
CLIFFORD, Mary Ellen, May 28 1906 Sex:F Child# 1 John Clifford Ireland & Margaret Sullivan Ireland
CLIFFORD, Paulina, Feb 8 1891 Sex:F Child# 8 Patrick J Clifford Ireland & Elizabeth Sullivan Nashua, NH
CLIFFORD, Philip, Jun 8 1892 Sex:M Child# 2 John I Clifford Ireland & Bridget McLaughlin Ireland
CLIFFORD, Robert, Nov 10 1913 Sex:M Child# 1 Timothy Clifford Ireland & Marguerite M Winn Nashua, NH
CLIFFORD, Samuel W, Jun 24 1890 Sex:M Child# 1 Samuel W Clifford Boston, MA & Myra Fiske Columbus, OH
CLIFFORD, Timothy Gerald, May 11 1921 Sex:M Child# 4 Timothy Clifford Ireland & Margaret M Winn Nashua, NH
CLIFFORD, Unknown, Jun 23 1901 Sex:M Child# 7 Patrick Clifford Ireland & Hannah Shea Ireland
CLIFFORD, Walter Clifford, Apr 16 1890 Sex:M Child# 2 Patrick Clifford Ireland & Mary A Downing Nashua, NH
CLIFFORD, Walter John, Jul 19 1923 Sex:M Child# 5 Timothy Clifford Ireland & Margaret Winn Nashua, NH
CLINTON, Millard Wilmot, Apr 24 1915 Sex:M Child# 1 Millard H Clinton Nashua, NH & Ida Chase Lowell, MA
CLINTON, William Edward, Jul 6 1935 Sex:M Child# 1 Charles W Clinton Nova Scotia & Esther Hanton Barton, VT
CLOUGH, Charles William, Jun 21 1912 Sex:M Child# 1 Alfred W Clough
CLOUGH, Constance, Oct 30 1924 Sex:F Child# 2 Joseph P Clough Nashua, NH & Helen G Holt Nashua, NH
CLOUGH, Dennise Estelle, Aug 29 1935 Sex:F Child# 2 Alfred A Clough Lowell, MA & Doris E Goddard Nashua, NH

CLOUGH, Edward G, Mar 25 1914 Sex:M Child# 1 Robert E Clough Nashua, NH & Sadie M Garland Nashua, NH
CLOUGH, Elinor Bradford, May 9 1890 Sex:F Child# 4 Joseph L Clough Nashua, NH & Florence Aldrich Warwick, RI
CLOUGH, Florence Emery, May 27 1896 Sex:F Child# 6 Joseph L Clough Nashua, NH & Florence E Aldrich Warwick, RI
CLOUGH, James Arthur, Oct 5 1915 Sex:M Child# 3 Alfred Clough Greenland, NH & Ruth Plummer Epping, NH
CLOUGH, Joseph Lowell, Mar 13 1926 Sex:M Child# 3 Joseph P Clough Nashua, NH & Helen G Holt Nashua, NH
CLOUGH, Lillian A, Aug 8 1902 Sex:F Child# 7 Joseph L Clough Nashua, NH & Florence Aldrich RI
CLOUGH, Lucien Albert, Sep 23 1893 Sex:M Child# 5 Joseph L Clough Nashua, NH & Florence E Aldrich Warwick, RI
CLOUGH, Marjorie Adams, Feb 29 1912 Sex:F Child# 1 Joseph P Clough Nashua, NH & Cora B Porter Nashua, NH
CLOUGH, Rachael, Jan 15 1918 Sex:F Child# 1 Joseph P Clough Nashua, NH & Helen G Holt Nashua, NH
CLOUGH, Robert A, Nov 2 1887 Sex:M Child# 3 Joseph Clough Nashua, NH & Florence Aldrich Warwick, RI
CLOUGH, Ruth, Jan 26 1914 Sex:F Child# 2 Alfred W Clough Greenland, NH & Ruth Plummer Epping, NH
CLOUTIER, Albert Fernand, Nov 10 1927 Sex:M Child# 8 Emile Cloutier Canada & A Alaire Canada
CLOUTIER, Alice Beatrice, Jun 24 1927 Sex:F Child# 1 Armand Cloutier Nashua, NH & Effie Clemons Nashua, NH
CLOUTIER, Beatrice Florence, Aug 5 1925 Sex:F Child# 7 Emile Cloutier Canada & Alphonsine Alarie Canada
CLOUTIER, Charles Roger, Jul 24 1931 Sex:M Child# 10 Emile Cloutier Canada & Alphonsine Alaire Canada
CLOUTIER, Eugene, Mar 17 1907 Sex:M Child# 4 Olivier Cloutier Canada & Antonia Tardy Canada
CLOUTIER, Flore, Mar 28 1933 Sex:F Child# 5 Henri Cloutier Manchester, NH & Cecile Raymond Manchester, NH
CLOUTIER, Florence, Mar 28 1933 Sex:F Child# 6 Henri Cloutier Manchester, NH & Cecile Raymond Manchester, NH
CLOUTIER, Francis Gile, Aug 5 1928 Sex:M Child# 2 Henry Cloutier Manchester, NH & Cecile Raymond Manchester, NH
CLOUTIER, Henry Raymond, Feb 5 1927 Sex:M Child# 1 Henry A Cloutier Manchester, NH & Cecile Raymond Manchester, NH
CLOUTIER, Irene Violette, Oct 18 1933 Sex:F Child# 4 Alfred J Cloutier Canada & Irene Peloquin Manchester, NH
CLOUTIER, J Bte Rene, Nov 15 1933 Sex:M Child# 11 Emile Cloutier Canada & Alphonsine Alaire Canada
CLOUTIER, Joseph, Nov 20 1902 Sex:M Child# 10 Ernest Cloutier Canada & Emelie Morneau Canada Stillborn
CLOUTIER, Joseph Albert, May 20 1911 Sex:M Child# 5 Olivier Cloutier Canada & Antonia Tardif Canada
CLOUTIER, Joseph Albert, Jun 18 1929 Sex:M Child# 2 Albert Cloutier Nashua, NH & Effie Clemons Nashua, NH
CLOUTIER, Joseph Armand, Apr 15 1907 Sex:M Child# 13 Ernest Cloutier Canada & Emelie Morneau Canada
CLOUTIER, Joseph Henry Robert, Jun 25 1932 Sex:M Child# 1 Joseph Cloutier Canada & Ella Levesque E Barre, VT
CLOUTIER, Laureine Yvette, Oct 18 1933 Sex:F Child# 5 Alfred J Cloutier Canada & Irene Peloquin Manchester, NH
CLOUTIER, Lorraine Beatrice, Oct 24 1933 Sex:F Child# 2 Joseph Cloutier Canada & Ella Levesque Barre, VT
CLOUTIER, M Blanche Juliette, Dec 3 1917 Sex:F Child# 1 Joseph E Cloutier Canada & Alma Messier Canada
CLOUTIER, M Germaine Lillian, Feb 4 1913 Sex:F Child# 14 Ernest Cloutier Canada & Emelie Morneau Canada
CLOUTIER, M Irene Juliette, Mar 1 1915 Sex:F Child# 8 Odilon Cloutier Manchester, NH & Amanda Proulx Canada
CLOUTIER, Marcel Emile, Sep 11 1929 Sex:M Child# 3 Henry A Cloutier Manchester, NH & Cecile Raymond Manchester, NH
CLOUTIER, Maria Loraine, May 27 1929 Sex:F Child# 2 Evariste Cloutier Canada & Alma Mercier Canada
CLOUTIER, Marie Alice, Apr 15 1907 Sex:F Child# 12 Ernest Cloutier Canada & Emelie Morneau Canada
CLOUTIER, Marie Antoinette, Jul 12 1924 Sex:F Child# 6 Emile Cloutier Canada & Alphonsine Alair Canada
CLOUTIER, Marie Diana A, Jun 17 1906 Sex:F Child# 1 Albert Cloutier Canada & Leona Pelletier Rindge, NH
CLOUTIER, Marie Ivonne, Feb 17 1901 Sex:F Child# 2 Edouard Cloutier Canada & Leonline Nolette Canada
CLOUTIER, Marie Jeanne A, Apr 27 1905 Sex:F Child# 3 Olivier Cloutier Canada & Antonia Tardif Canada
CLOUTIER, Marie Regina I, Apr 19 1901 Sex:F Child# 9 Ernest Cloutier Canada & Emelie Morneau Canada
CLOUTIER, Mary Noelle C, Dec 25 1930 Sex:F Child# 4 Henry Cloutier Manchester, NH & Cecile Raymond Manchester, NH
CLOUTIER, Omer George, Feb 6 1921 Sex:M Child# 1 Omer Cloutier Merrimac, MA & Marjorie Ballsdon Winchester, MA
CLOUTIER, Peter, Jan 19 1900 Sex:M Child# 2 Peter Cloutier
CLOUTIER, Richard Maurice, Jul 15 1935 Sex:M Child# 3 Joseph Cloutier Canada & Ella Levesque Barre, VT
CLOUTIER, Robert Joseph, Sep 7 1929 Sex:M Child# 1 Joseph Cloutier Pittsfield, NH & Catherine Rich Nashua, NH
CLOUTIER, Ruth Arlene, Sep 26 1934 Sex:F Child# 3 Armand Jos Cloutier Nashua, NH & Eva Lavoie Nashua, NH
CLOUTIER, Unknown, Jan 17 1905 Sex:F Child# 11 Ernest Cloutier Canada & Emelie Morneau Canada Stillborn
CLOUTIER, Wilfred, Mar 23 1929 Sex:M Child# 9 Emile Cloutier Canada & Alphonsine Alaire Canada
CLOW, Lila May, Aug 28 1895 Sex:F Child#  Josiah A Clow P E Island & Ada Jane Ward Baltimore, VT
CLUKAY, Gertrude Elizabeth, Oct 26 1917 Sex:F Child# 1 Harry Clukay Jaffrey, NH & Gertrude Donovan Peterboro, NH
CLUKEY, Unknown, Jan 12 1919 Sex:M Child# 2 Harry Clukey Jaffrey, NH & Gertrude Peterboro, NH
COATES, Julia, Jan 3 1892 Sex:F Child# 7 James Coates Windsor, VT & Annie McAndrews Ireland
COATS, Margaret Jane, Apr 14 1893 Sex:F Child# 8 James Coats Windsor, VT & Annie McAndrews Ireland
COBB, Louise Staples, Jun 3 1897 Sex:F Child# 1 S R Cobb Wellfleet, MA & Alice May Staples S Boston, MA
COBB, Unknown, Mar 11 1895 Sex:M Child#  (No Parents Listed)
COBB, Unknown, Jan 1 1899 Sex:F Child# 2 Sewell R Cobb Wellfleet, MA & Alice Mary Staples S Boston, MA
COBLEIGH, Donald Carter, Apr 7 1935 Sex:M Child# 3 Gerald F Cobleigh Littleton, NH & Alberta Bernier Nashua, NH
COBLEIGH, Dorothy Jacqueline, Apr 25 1933 Sex:F Child# 3 Neal Cobleigh Lebanon, NH & Dorothy Esson Nashua, NH
COBLEIGH, Geralyn Elizabeth, Mar 30 1933 Sex:F Child# 2 G F Cobleigh Littleton, NH & Alberta Bernier Nashua, NH
COBLEIGH, Joan Alice, Oct 10 1931 Sex:F Child# 1 Gerald Cobleigh Littleton, Nh & Alberta Bernier Nashua, NH
COBLEIGH, Marshall William, Jun 4 1930 Sex:M Child# 1 Neil W Cobleigh Lebanon, NH & Dorothy Esson Nashua, NH
COBLEIGH, Richard Esson, Aug 2 1931 Sex:M Child# 2 Neal W Cobleigh Lebanon, NH & Dorothy Esson Nashua, NH
COBURN, Arthur, Aug 25 1888 Sex:M Child# 2 Forest P Coburn Nashua, NH & Aleseandriac Ayette Canada
COBURN, Franklin E, Nov 9 1907 Sex:M Child# 3 George M Coburn Nashua, NH & Anna F Buker Goshen, NH
COBURN, J Henri Albert, Dec 29 1913 Sex:M Child# 1 Henry Coburn Lowell, MA & Diana Nadeau Nashua, NH
COBURN, M Augustine, Feb 28 1894 Sex:F Child# 5 Forest Coburn Nashua, NH & Alexandrine Azet Canada
COCHRAN, Lorin Francis, Apr 8 1892 Sex:M Child# 3 William H Cochran Maine & Ida L Sanford Greenfield, NH
CODY, Catherine, Mar 7 1924 Sex:F Child# 2 John Michael Cody Peabody, MA & Julia Sullivan Nashua, NH
CODY, Gerald Arthur, Jul 15 1933 Sex:M Child# 1 Arthur H Cody Nashua, NH & J A Poulousky Nashua, NH
CODY, John Daniel, Aug 6 1922 Sex:M Child# 1 John Michael Cody Peabody, MA & Mary Julia Sullivan Nashua, NH
CODY, Theresa, Feb 18 1927 Sex:F Child# 3 John M Cody Peabody, MA & Mary J Sullivan Nashua, NH
COFFEE, Albert G, Feb 17 1893 Sex:M Child# 1 John Coffee Nashua, NH & Katie Gaffney Nashua, NH
COFFEE, Marguerite, Jun 10 1898 Sex:F Child# 6 Daniel Coffee Nashua, NH & Catherine Dillon Vermont

COFFEY, Albert, Apr 26 1922 Sex:M Child# 1 Albert Coffey Nashua, NH & Korleen Henderson Watertown, NY
COFFEY, Albert Lawrence, May 28 1911 Sex:M Child# 3 Michael E Coffey Ashby, MA & Georgietta Nelson Nova Scotia
COFFEY, Annie, Dec 18 1891 Sex:F Child# 1 Daniel J Coffey Nashua, NH & A F Dillon Vermont
COFFEY, Conrad John, Feb 2 1924 Sex:M Child# 2 Albert G Coffey Nashua, NH & Kor Henderson Watertown, NY
COFFEY, Daniel, Mar 19 1888 Sex:M Child# 2 Jerry D Coffey Ireland & Margaret Callahan Ireland
COFFEY, Donald Charles, Dec 15 1926 Sex:M Child# 3 Albert Coffey Nashua, NH & Korleen Henderson Watertown, NY
COFFEY, Joseph, Aug 24 1895 Sex:M Child# 4 Daniel J Coffey Rutland, VT & Catherine Dellin Nashua, NH
COFFEY, Kathleen, Apr 13 1901 Sex:F Child# 8 Daniel Coffey Nashua, NH & Katherine Dillon Rutland, VT
COFFEY, Marion Helena, Dec 10 1923 Sex:F Child# 1 Everett Coffey Nashua, NH & Margaret Casey Milford, NH
COFFEY, Martha A, Feb 22 1917 Sex:F Child# 4 Michael Coffey Ashby, MA & Georgietta Nelson Scotch Vlg, NS
COFFEY, Mary Ilene, Aug 18 1902 Sex:F Child# 4 John W Coffey Nashua, NH & Katherine Gaffney Nashua, NH
COFFEY, Mary Olive, Feb 8 1905 Sex:F Child# 6 Daniel Coffey Nashua, NH & Catherine Dillon Vermont
COFFEY, Paul, Sep 3 1904 Sex:M Child# 5 John W Coffey Nashua, NH & Katherine L Gaffney Nashua, NH
COFFEY, Unknown, Dec 22 1895 Sex:F Child# John W Coffey Nashua, NH & Katherine F Gaffney Nashua, NH
COFFEY, Unknown, Jan 7 1900 Sex:F Child# 7 D J Coffey NH & Catherine Dillon Vermont Stillborn
COFFEY, Unknown, Nov 1 1902 Sex:F Child# 9 Dan J Coffey Nashua, NH & Catherine Dillon Rutland, VT Stillborn
COFFEY, William, Feb 10 1911 Sex:M Child# 1 William Coffey Providence, RI & Lucy Stevens Montreal, Canada
COFFEY, William Bryan, Oct 11 1896 Sex:M Child# 4 Daniel Coffey Nashua, NH & Catherine Dillon Vermont
COFFREY, Daniel, Aug 10 1890 Sex:M Child# 1 Daniel Coffrey Nashua, NH & Catherine Dillon Vermont
COFRAN, Marie M, Apr 1 1906 Sex:F Child# 1 William Cofran Boston, MA & Elizabeth Thibodeau Bethlehem, NH
COGGER, Forrest Henry, Jul 3 1922 Sex:M Child# 2 Henry Cogger Pelham, NH & Gertrude G Sampson St R Falls, NY
COGGER, Gloria Pearl, Aug 21 1928 Sex:F Child# 4 Henry Cogger Pelham, NH & Gertrude Sampson St Regis Falls, NY
COGGER, Mildred Lucille, Aug 11 1923 Sex:F Child# 3 Patrick H Cogger Pelham, NH & Gertrude Sampson St Regis Fls, NY
COGGER, Rosalind Gertrude, Jan 13 1921 Sex:F Child# 1 Patrick H Cogger Pelham, NH & Gertrude Sampson Waverly,
COGGER, William Sampson, Feb 8 1935 Sex:M Child# 5 P Henry Cogger Pelham, NH & Gertrude Sampson St Regis Falls, NY
COGGINS, Celia, Oct 29 1902 Sex:F Child# 7 James Coggins Ireland & Elizabeth Degnan Ireland
COGGINS, John, Jul 27 1889 Sex:M Child# 1 James Coggins Ireland & Lizzie Dedmon Ireland
COGLEY, Vivian Rosetta, Aug 16 1925 Sex:F Child# 1 Clarence E Cogley N Concord, VT & Lucille M James Reading, MA
COHAN, Unknown, Mar 10 1891 Sex:M Child# 3 Simon W Cohan Poland & Jennie Goldstein Poland Stillborn
COHEN, Abraham Samuel, Mar 31 1908 Sex:M Child# 5 Simon Cohen Russia & Annie F Goldberg Russia
COHEN, Bessie, Jul 1 1907 Sex:F Child# 3 Samuel M Cohen Russia & Lillian Goodman Russia
COHEN, Casper, May 28 1924 Sex:M Child# 1 Maurice Cohen Rochester, NH & Eva Gordon Russia
COHEN, Davie, Apr 19 1917 Sex:M Child# 5 Joseph Cohen Russia & Bessie Sklava Russia
COHEN, Dinah, Mar 24 1904 Sex:F Child# 2 Julius Cohen Russia & Pearl Horlink Russia
COHEN, Gertrude, Jan 8 1915 Sex:F Child# 4 Julius Cohen Russia & Pearl Harlink Russia
COHEN, Goldie, Mar 24 1904 Sex:F Child# 1 Julius Cohen Russia & Pearl Horlink Russia
COHEN, goldie, Jan 17 1905 Sex:F Child# 1 Benjamin H Cohen Russia & Sadie Goldberg Russia
COHEN, Goldie, Nov 5 1906 Sex:F Child# 1 Moses H Cohen Germany & Sara J Mirsky Russia
COHEN, Harry, Dec 12 1889 Sex:M Child# 3 Simeon W Cohen Poland & Jennie Goldstern Poland
COHEN, Himan, Sep 8 1903 Sex:M Child# 4 Simon Cohen Russia & Annie F Goldberg Russia
COHEN, Ida F, Apr 14 1906 Sex:F Child# 2 Samuel M Cohen Russia & Lillian Goodman Russia
COHEN, Julia, May 5 1904 Sex:F Child# 1 Samuel Cohen Russia & Lillian Goodman Russia
COHEN, Levina, Aug 4 1912 Sex:F Child# 3 Julius Cohen Russia & Pearl Horlink Russia
COHEN, Lillie, Dec 12 1899 Sex:F Child# 3 Simon Cohen Russia & Annie Goldberg Russia
COHEN, Louis, Jun 13 1907 Sex:M Child# 3 Benjamin H Cohen Russia & Sadie Goldberg Russia
COHEN, Louis A, Dec 4 1895 Sex:M Child# 1 Simon W Cohen Poland & Annie F Goldberg Poland
COHEN, Marion, May 5 1906 Sex:F Child# 2 Benjamin H Cohen Russia & Sadie Goldberg Russia
COHEN, May Rosa, Feb 21 1898 Sex:F Child# 2 Simon Cohen Russia & Anna Goldberg Russia
COHEN, Reuben, May 21 1911 Sex:M Child# 1 Max Cohen Russia &  Russia
COLARD, Unknown, Feb 3 1931 Sex:M Child# 1 Adolph Colard Canada & Rachel Perreault Canada
COLBONA, Delhia, Aug 2 1901 Sex:F Child# 2 Pierre Colbona Canada & Elizabeth Dion Canada
COLBURN, Alice Melia, May 18 1889 Sex:F Child# 1 John L Colburn Newbury, NH & Eva Dion W Boylston, MA
COLBURN, Carl William, May 7 1917 Sex:M Child# 2 Leroy A Colburn Nashua, NH & Mamie Davis Nashua, NH
COLBURN, Eliane Marie, Jan 12 1924 Sex:F Child# 1 Roland Colburn Nashua, NH & Edna Woodwardy York, ME
COLBURN, Evaline Vestina, Jul 23 1891 Sex:F Child# 1 Sydney B Colburn Chelmsford, MA & Mattie A Poff Hudson, NH
COLBURN, G Wesley, Sep 20 1916 Sex:M Child# 1 James W Colburn Nashua, NH & Johanna G Smith Glasgow, Scotland
COLBURN, George, Aug 7 1890 Sex:M Child# 3 Forest Colburn Nashua, NH & Alesandrine Asette Canada
COLBURN, James Wesley, Jul 11 1894 Sex:M Child# 1 James E Colburn Brookline & Mabel E Collins Nashua, NH
COLBURN, Jane, May 15 1926 Sex:F Child# 2 Murray Colburn Nashua, NH & Aorice Fullford Newburyport, MA Stillborn
COLBURN, Janette, May 24 1933 Sex:F Child# 6 Archie R Colburn Hollis, NH & J P Whitten Westport, ME
COLBURN, Louise N, Dec 5 1892 Sex:F Child# 4 Henry Colburn Boston, MA & Annie McKay Concord
COLBURN, Mary, Aug 31 1902 Sex:F Child# 3 Almon E Colburn NH & Ella Bailey NH
COLBURN, Murray O, Mar 3 1924 Sex:M Child# 1 Murray O Colburn Nashua, NH & Florence Fullford Newburyport, MA
COLBURN, Nancy Ruth, Feb 16 1928 Sex:F Child# 3 Murray O Colburn Nashua, NH & Florice Fullford Newburyport, MA
COLBURN, Naomi Helen, Sep 6 1917 Sex:F Child# 1 Wm A Colburn Nashua, NH & Helen R McFarland Everett, MA
COLBURN, Philip Ellis, Jul 4 1931 Sex:M Child# 4 Murray Colburn Nashua, NH & Florice Fullford Newburyport, MA
COLBURN, Taylor, May 3 1892 Sex:M Child# 1 Seth Colburn Francestown, NH & Hazel Manchester, NH
COLBURN, Unknown, Dec 28 1887 Sex:F Child# 1 James E Colburn Brookline & Lizzie J Townsend
COLBURN, Unknown, Jul 29 1889 Sex:M Child# 6 Eugene T Colburn Hollis & Sarah O Colburn Keysville
COLBURN, Unknown, May 23 1891 Sex:M Child# 1 Charles N Colburn Natick, MA & Luella Baker Scarboro, ME
COLBURN, Unknown, Jul 20 1891 Sex:M Child# 1 Frederick R Colburn Nashua, NH & Nellie M Brown Friendship, ME
COLBURN, Unknown, Jul 12 1893 Sex:M Child# 2 Fred R Colburn
COLBURN, William Roy, Jul 28 1898 Sex:M Child# 2 Almon E Colburn Hollis, NH & Ella Simon Bailey Nashua, NH

COLBY, Charles H, Jan 13 1900 Sex:M Child# 6 John Colby Tilton, NH & Mary Carpenter Montreal, PQ
COLBY, Dorothy Isabel, Jun 21 1908 Sex:F Child# 1 Arthur F Colby Nashua, NH & Alta Colby Perkinsville, VT
COLBY, Edward Henry, May 15 1905 Sex:M Child# 3 John Colby Tilton, NH & Ida F Eayers S Merrimack, NH
COLBY, Elizabeth Muriel, Nov 18 1910 Sex:F Child# 2 Arthur F Colby Nashua, NH & Atta Colby Perkinsville, VT
COLBY, Eva May, Apr 29 1906 Sex:F Child# 2 John Colby Tilton, NH & Ida F Eayrs Merrimack, NH
COLBY, Floretta Pearl, Sep 14 1914 Sex:F Child# 9 John Colby Franklin, NH & Ida Eayrs Merrimack, NH
COLBY, Frank Elmer, Feb 3 1909 Sex:M Child# 4 John Colby Tilton, NH & Ida F Eayrs Merrimack, NH
COLBY, George Elmer, Dec 15 1915 Sex:M Child# 10 John Colby Tilton, MA & Ida F Ayers Merrimack, NH
COLBY, Gertrude Irene, Mar 26 1913 Sex:F Child# 8 John Colby Franklin, NH & Ida Eayrs Merrimack, NH
COLBY, Irving J, Jun 27 1893 Sex:M Child# 2 John Colby E Andover & Mary Carpenter Canada
COLBY, John B, Sep 13 1888 Sex:M Child# 1 John B Colby Tilton & Mary Carpenter Canada
COLBY, John Francis, Jun 22 1907 Sex:M Child# 3 John Colby Tilton, NH & Ida F Eayres Merrimack, NH
COLBY, May Esther, May 17 1893 Sex:F Child# 2 Frank H Colby Bidwell, CT & Helen Frye Hopkinton, NH
COLBY, Unknown, Feb 26 1903 Sex:M Child# 2 George C Colby Sutton & Florence Dunbar Warner
COLBY, Unknown, Jun 14 1904 Sex:M Child# 2 John Colby Tilton, NH & Ida F Eayers Merrimack, NH
COLDWELL, Leslie Aubrey, Apr 9 1928 Sex:M Child# 1 L D Coldwell Nova Scotia & Gwen Fluke Nova Scotia
COLDWELL, Shirley Marie, Apr 10 1932 Sex:F Child# 2 Dimock Coldwell Nova Scotia & Gwen Fluke Nova Scotia
COLE, Anna Louise, Jan 7 1923 Sex:F Child# 4 Frank Winslow Cole Salem, MA & Gladys Sanders Hudson, NH
COLE, Charles Davidson, Jul 3 1922 Sex:M Child# 2 George Alden Cole Winchester, MA & Elizabeth McLeod Boston, MA
COLE, Elizabeth, Jul 29 1902 Sex:F Child# 2 Russell Cole Boston, MA & Velma Cummings Nashua, NH
COLE, Ella Mae, Jul 4 1927 Sex:F Child# 6 Guy H Cole Prospect Harbor, ME & Doris I Colwell Steuben, ME
COLE, Floyd Herbert, Feb 7 1904 Sex:M Child# 1 Fred H Cole Ellenburg, NY & Loretta Clegg Lowell, MA
COLE, Harlow Whittier, Mar 31 1918 Sex:M Child# 1 William Cole Liverpool, NS & Nellie Blanche Brown Fremont, NS
COLE, Martha, Jul 12 1899 Sex:F Child# 1 Russell Cole Boston, MA & Velma Cummings Nashua, NH
COLE, Martha Elizabeth, Mar 5 1924 Sex:F Child# 3 George A Cole Winchester, MA & Elizabeth McLeod Boston, MA
COLE, Mary L, Jun 25 1906 Sex:F Child# 3 Russell Cole Boston, MA & Velma Cummings Nashua, NH
COLE, Oscar E, May 19 1924 Sex:M Child# 4 Guy Cole Pros Harbor, ME & Doris Colwell Stuben, ME
COLE, Philip Girard, Jul 22 1929 Sex:M Child# 1 Jasper Cole Exeter, NH & Irene Lebrun Rochester, NH
COLE, Richard Carlton, Nov 18 1926 Sex:M Child# 2 Ray C Cole Manchester, NH & Mary Danjou Randolph, VT
COLE, Russell, Jr, Oct 17 1908 Sex:M Child# 4 Russell Cole Boston, MA & Velma Cummings Nashua, NH
COLE, Unknown, Sep 12 1905 Sex:M Child#  Fred H Cole Ellenburgh, NY & Loretta E Clegg Lowell, MA
COLE, Wenona Laura, Aug 29 1903 Sex:F Child# 5 Frederick Cole Vermont & Kate Glarvin NH
COLEMAN, Frank Richard, Nov 8 1925 Sex:M Child# 2 Frank H Coleman Gardner, MA & Esther Weston Hudson, NH
COLEMAN, Gladys, Jul 26 1926 Sex:F Child# 4 Robert Coleman Woburn, MA & Mary Bowley Lowell, MA
COLEMAN, Helen Besse, Mar 18 1928 Sex:F Child# 1 Charles Coleman Sunapee, NH & Lela Bosse Dover, NH
COLEMAN, Helen June, Jun 1 1918 Sex:F Child# 3 Michael Coleman Ireland & Catherine Maddox Nashua, NH
COLEMAN, Leonard George, Sep 6 1925 Sex:M Child# 2 George W Coleman Woburn, MA & Eva Gaudette Canada
COLEMAN, Lorraine Doris, Feb 21 1935 Sex:F Child# 4 Walter Coleman Nashua, NH & Grace Chateauneuf Lowell, MA
COLEMAN, Marie Lucille, Jul 27 1922 Sex:F Child# 1 George Coleman Mass & Eva Gaudette Canada
COLEMAN, Mildred Theresa, Aug 10 1933 Sex:F Child# 5 Robert Coleman Woburn, MA & Mary D Bouley Lowell, MA
COLEMAN, Richard, Jan 26 1934 Sex:M Child# 3 Walter Coleman Malden, MA & Grace Chateauneuf Lowell, MA
COLEMAN, Robert James, Dec 5 1923 Sex:M Child# 3 Robert F Coleman Woburn, MA & Mary Delena Bouley Lowell, MA
COLEMAN, Roy Albert, Jan 7 1916 Sex:M Child# 2 Robert Coleman Woburn, MA & Mary Delvina Bouley Lowell, MA
COLEMAN, Unknown, Sep 28 1914 Sex:M Child# 1 Dennison J Coleman Boston, MA & Alice M Barker Antrim, NH
COLEMAN, Unknown, Dec 13 1932 Sex:F Child# 1 W F Coleman Malden, MA & G Chateauneuf Lowell, MA Stillborn
COLIN, Honore, Mar 4 1902 Sex:M Child# 4 Alexander Colin Canada & Ursule Sirois Canada
COLIN, Marie Ivonne, Jul 29 1907 Sex:F Child# 7 Alexandre Colin Canada & Ursule Sirois Canada
COLLARD, Alberta Claudia, Jan 29 1913 Sex:F Child# 2 Hormidas Collard Canada & Roselda Roy Canada
COLLARD, Joseph Ernest, May 26 1910 Sex:M Child# 1 Hormidas Collard Canada & Rosilda Roy Canada
COLLET, Stella, Jun 19 1891 Sex:F Child# 3 Joseph Collet Sciota, NY & Jennie Gagne Bangor, NY
COLLETTE, Alfred, Feb 17 1888 Sex:M Child# 2 Alfred Collette Sciotia, NY & Delina Goyette Sciotia, NY
COLLETTE, Ernest, Apr 15 1890 Sex:M Child# 2 John Collette Sciota, NY & Jennie Gagne Brandon, NY
COLLETTE, Eva Gratia, Jun 28 1892 Sex:F Child# 4 A B Collette Sciota, NY & Delima Goyette Sciota, NY
COLLETTE, Honnidass, Dec 31 1890 Sex:M Child# 3 Alfred Collette Moores Jct, NY & Pelima Goyet Moores Jct, NY
COLLETTE, Joseph R V, Feb 9 1889 Sex:M Child# 2 Franciede Collette Canada & Emma Brodeur Canada
COLLETTE, Katherine, May 2 1915 Sex:F Child# 3 Medouse Collette Nashua, NH & Katherine Murphy Nashua, NH
COLLETTE, Lorenzo, Sep 27 1894 Sex:M Child# 5 A B Collette Canada & Delima Goyette Canada
COLLETTE, Lorenzo M, Oct 6 1916 Sex:M Child# 4 Hormidas J Collette Nashua, NH & Katherine L Murphy Nashua, NH
COLLETTE, Robert, Sep 30 1910 Sex:M Child# 1 Medouse I Collette Nashua, NH & Katherine Murphy Nashua, NH
COLLETTE, S Theophile, Apr 24 1891 Sex:M Child# 2 Alphonse Collette Canada & P Des Trois Maisons Canada
COLLETTE, Unknown, Oct 22 1912 Sex:M Child# 2 Hormidas J Collette Nashua, NH & Katherine L Murphy Nashua, NH
COLLEY, Dixon W, Jul 19 1903 Sex:M Child# 1 William H Colley Falmouth, ME & Agnes Dixon Providence, RI
COLLIER, David William, Feb 20 1928 Sex:M Child# 10 James H Collier Saginaw, MI & Ida M Martelle Canada Stillborn
COLLIER, James Leo, Jun 20 1929 Sex:M Child# 1 Nelson A Collier Litchfield, NH & Margaret Lavigne Manchester, NH
COLLIN, Joseph Adelard, Jul 11 1905 Sex:M Child# 5 Alexandre Collin Canada & Ursule Sirois Canada
COLLINS, Alexander, Jun 9 1896 Sex:M Child# 6 Fred Collins Canada & Mary Hibbard Port Henry
COLLINS, Barbara Joan, May 22 1929 Sex:F Child# 1 Francis Collins Nashua, NH & Leona Smith Nashua, NH
COLLINS, Charles Sumner, Dec 11 1901 Sex:M Child# 2 Charles S Collins Bow, NH & Elizabeth E Cary Claremont, NH
COLLINS, Dolores, Jun 22 1904 Sex:F Child# 4 Alex Collins Canada & Ursule Sirois Canada
COLLINS, Eugenia June, Jun 10 1914 Sex:F Child# 5 John F Collins Marlboro, MA & Ruth Mayo Sciota, NY
COLLINS, Florence, Mar 24 1908 Sex:F Child# 4 John F Collins Marlboro, MA & Ruth L Mayo W Chazy, NY
COLLINS, Frances Mae, Jul 23 1903 Sex:F Child# 2 John Collins Marlboro & Ruth Mayo New York
COLLINS, Francis, Oct 2 1890 Sex:F Child# 4 James Collins Ireland & Margaret Dunn New York Stillborn

COLLINS, Francis Anthony, Jr, May 22 1932 Sex:M Child# 2 Francis A Collins Nashua, NH & Leona Smith Nashua, NH
COLLINS, Frederick, Sep 11 1894 Sex:M Child# 3 Michael Collins Ireland & Mary E Mylett England
COLLINS, Gladys Abbie, Jun 1 1895 Sex:F Child# 3 Edward A Collins Concord, NH & Mabel Simpson Pembroke, NH
COLLINS, Harold Martin, Apr 6 1910 Sex:M Child# 1 James Collins N Walpole, NH & Mary Richard Canada
COLLINS, Irene Mabel, Feb 15 1897 Sex:F Child# 4 Edward A Collins Concord, NH & Mabel Simpson Pembroke, NH
COLLINS, James Richard, Jul 24 1911 Sex:M Child# 2 James M Collins Bellows Falls, VT & Mary Richard Canada
COLLINS, John Edward, Jun 10 1916 Sex:M Child# 1 Frederick Collins Pembroke, NH & Marie L Dolan Nashua, NH
COLLINS, John Howard, Jun 25 1906 Sex:M Child# 4 John F Collins Marlboro, MA & Ruth Mayo W Chazy, NY
COLLINS, John Joseph, Jul 29 1935 Sex:M Child# 1 John J Collins Roxbury, MA & Helene O'Brien Ireland
COLLINS, Joseph Edouard, Aug 26 1893 Sex:M Child# 2 Joseph Collins Canada & Philomene Tardy Canada
COLLINS, Lucie Amanda, Aug 4 1891 Sex:F Child# 4 Alphonse Collins Canada & Marie Hebert Canada
COLLINS, Lucy Priscilla, Feb 25 1912 Sex:F Child# 4 John F Collins Marlboro, MA & Ruth Mayo Sciota, NY
COLLINS, Nancy Ruth, Jul 30 1934 Sex:F Child# 3 Francis Collins Nashua, NH & Leona Smith Nashua, NH
COLLINS, Patrick Henry, Apr 30 1926 Sex:M Child# 2 Fred Collins Pembroke, NH & Marie Dolan Nashua, NH
COLLINS, Pearl Adel, Mar 20 1907 Sex:F Child# 1 Raymond G Collins Lyon Mt, NY & Melvina Bathalon Canada
COLLINS, Rita Marie, May 10 1930 Sex:F Child# 3 Fred E A Collins Pembroke, NH & Marie L Dolan Nashua, NH
COLLINS, Russell, Mar 12 1908 Sex:M Child# 3 Charles S Collins Grantham, NH & Ellinor C Carey Claremont, NH
COLLINS, Unknown, May 7 1894 Sex:M Child# 2 Edward A Collins Concord, NH & Mabel O Simpson Pembroke, NH
COLLINS, Unknown, Jun 26 1902 Sex:M Child# 1 John Collins Boston, MA & Ruth Mayo NY
COLLINS, Virginia, Mar 13 1912 Sex:F Child# 5 Edw A Collins Concord, NH & Mabel O Simpson Pembroke, NH
COLLINS, William King, Nov 18 1893 Sex:M Child# 1 Charles S Collins Grafton, NH & Anna L King Nashua, NH
COLLISON, Harriet Elizabeth, Jul 15 1909 Sex:F Child# 3 Henry W Collison Concord, NH & Jennie Favor Lawrence, MA
COLMAN, Charles Kingsbury, May 14 1929 Sex:M Child# 2 Charles D Colman, Jr Farmington, NH & Lela Alberta Besse
COLOMBE, Joseph Arthur, Feb 6 1903 Sex:M Child# 2 Joseph Colombe NY & Helen Arnot NY
COLOMBE, Ovila, Oct 5 1884 Sex:F Child# Joseph Colombe Canada & Elumina Paquette Canada
COLUMB, Arthur Joseph, Jan 28 1924 Sex:M Child# 1 Arthur J Columb Nashua, NH & Rose Caron Nashua, NH Stillborn
COLUMB, Arthur Joseph, May 19 1925 Sex:M Child# 2 Arthur Columb Nashua, NH & Rose Caron Nashua, NH
COLUMB, Eva Marie, Jan 19 1900 Sex:F Child# 1 Joseph Columb New York & Nellie L Amnot New York
COMEAU, Anne Jeanne, Jan 5 1905 Sex:F Child# 3 Albert Comeau Canada & Mary Bergeron Canada
COMEAU, Eugene, Aug 15 1903 Sex:M Child# 2 Albert Comeau Canada & Marie Bergeron Canada
COMEAU, Francois Henri G, Jan 14 1934 Sex:M Child# 2 Benjamin Comeau Haverhill, MA & Marie Chenard Canada
COMEAU, Hector Albert, Jul 18 1907 Sex:M Child# 1 Joseph Comeau Canada & Celina Guillemain Canada
COMEAU, Louise Yvonne, Nov 8 1901 Sex:F Child# 1 Albert Comeau Canada & Marie Bergeron Canada
COMEAU, Mary Therese Aimee, Oct 31 1932 Sex:F Child# 1 Benjamin Comeau Haverhill, MA & Marie A Chenard Canada
COMMERFORD, Theresa Rita, Nov 22 1928 Sex:F Child# 1 Jas Commerford Lowell, MA & Evelyn Richard Lowell, MA
COMOLLI, Arthur Emil, Sep 24 1932 Sex:M Child# 2 A E Comolli Barre, VT & Mar Hallisey Nashua, NH
COMOLLI, Dennis Joseph, Sep 24 1932 Sex:M Child# 1 A E Comolli Barre, VT & Mar Hallisey Nashua, NH
COMOLLI, Edward Randall, Jul 19 1935 Sex:M Child# 2 Edward Comolli W Hoboken, NJ & Mildred Randall Milford, NH
COMOLLI, Ferdinand Marsh, Apr 14 1924 Sex:M Child# 1 Feruccio Comolli Italy & Jennie Caccivio Italy
COMOLLI, Joan, Nov 27 1931 Sex:F Child# 1 Leo A Comolli Barre, VT & Evelyn Wilkins Milford, NH
COMOLLI, Richard David, Aug 13 1926 Sex:M Child# 2 Feraccio Comolli Italy & Jennie Caccivio Italy Stillborn
COMPRISSO, Unknown, Mar 29 1917 Sex:F Child# 1 Martin Comprisso Russia & Melvina Robeck Russia
COMTAUIAN, Mary, Nov 7 1905 Sex:F Child# 6 Harry Comtauian Armenia & Isinoff Kedian Armenia
CONANT, Gordon, Mar 18 1899 Sex:M Child# 2 George H Conant Winooski, VT & Kit Gaines Plattsburgh, NY
CONBINIS, Brunia, Jun 1 1917 Sex:F Child# 4 Andre Conbinis Russia & Mary Koslowski Russia
CONCOMBE, Marie D A, May 3 1892 Sex:F Child# 3 Joseph Concombe Canada & Elumine Paquet Canada
CONE, Charles, Jun 2 1914 Sex:M Child# 3 Benjamin Cone NH & Catherine McGrail Mass
CONE, Frederick McGrail, Jan 10 1910 Sex:M Child# 1 Benjamin F Cone Nashua, NH & Catherine A McGrail Mass
CONE, Joseph, Jul 11 1918 Sex:M Child# 5 Benjamin Cone NH & Katherine McGrail Mass
CONE, Robert Joseph, Jun 18 1915 Sex:M Child# 4 Benjamin Cone Nashua, NH & Katherine McGrail Mass
CONEROY, Mary Isabella, Jan 16 1898 Sex:F Child# 6 Thomas Coneroy Clinton, MA & Sera DeRinsseau Canada
CONERY, Amos Roland, Jan 23 1935 Sex:M Child# 2 Robert A Conery Nashua, NH & Elizabeth R Ford Nashua, NH
CONERY, Constance Jane, Mar 17 1933 Sex:F Child# 1 Robert A Conery Nashua, NH & Elizabeth Ford Nashua, NH
CONERY, Unknown, Oct 12 1910 Sex:M Child# 13 Amos R Conery New York & Jessie E Robinson Halifax, NS
CONEY, Everett H, Jun 6 1898 Sex:M Child# 2 Edwin Coney Nashua, NH & Cora M Gove Portsmouth, NH
CONEY, Margaret Theresa, Jan 3 1930 Sex:F Child# 2 Everett Coney Nashua, NH & Margaret Casey Milford, NH
CONGDON, Allen Ramsdell, Sep 17 1906 Sex:M Child# 2 Charles E Congdon E Greenwich, RI & Ann M Ransdell Nashua, NH
CONGDON, Esther Barbara, Jan 9 1929 Sex:F Child# 1 Bert Congdon Walpole, MA & Mary Haslam Lowell, MA
CONGDON, Robert Dinsmore, Oct 28 1904 Sex:M Child# 1 Charles E Congdon E Greenwich, RI & Ann M Ramsdell Nashua, NH
CONGDON, Robert Gordon, Nov 17 1930 Sex:M Child# 2 Bert W Congdon Walpole, MA & Mary J Haslam Lowell, MA
CONLEY, Dona Leigh, Nov 30 1931 Sex:F Child# 1 Leo Conley Dexter, NY & Alice Moody Roxbury, MA
CONLEY, Doris Gloria, Feb 18 1935 Sex:F Child# 1 Charles Conley Marlboro, MA & Elena Lavoie Nashua, NH
CONLEY, Mary Annette, Jul 2 1926 Sex:F Child# 1 Thomas Conley New York & Mabel Bailey Bennington, NH
CONLEY, Unknown, May 7 1930 Sex:F Child# 4 Thomas Conley Norwood, NY & Mabel Bailey Bennington, NH
CONLIN, Ann Elizabeth, Apr 25 1929 Sex:F Child# 2 John Conlin Windsor, VT & Katherine Riley Nashua, NH
CONLIN, James Edward, Aug 7 1932 Sex:M Child# 3 John S Conlin Windsor, VT & Katherine Riley Nashua, NH
CONLON, Alice Louise, Jan 16 1904 Sex:F Child# 7 James Conlon Ireland & Catherine Morahan Ireland
CONLON, James, May 5 1891 Sex:M Child# 3 Thomas Conlon Ireland & Anna M O'Bairne Ireland
CONLON, John, Apr 22 1892 Sex:M Child# 3 James Conlon Ireland & Katie Morahan Ireland
CONLON, John Henry, Mar 4 1927 Sex:M Child# 1 John Conlon Windsor, VT & Catherine Riley Nashua, NH
CONLON, Josephine, May 8 1889 Sex:F Child# 2 Thomas Conlon Ireland & Maria Conlon Ireland
CONLON, Robert Paul, Mar 10 1926 Sex:M Child# 1 John Conlon Nashua, NH & Dora Laforme Nashua, NH
CONLON, Thomas Frances, May 5 1898 Sex:M Child# 5 James Conlon Ireland & Katherine Morahan Ireland

CONLON, Thomas Harold, Nov 30 1909 Sex:M Child# 1 Thomas J Conlon Boston, MA & Annie Needham Ireland
CONLON, Unknown, Jan 12 1888 Sex:F Child# 1 James Conlon Ireland & Catherine Morhan Ireland
CONLON, Unknown, Apr 30 1888 Sex:M Child# 3 Thomas Conlon Ireland & Mary Conlon Ireland
CONLON, Unknown, Apr 1 1890 Sex:M Child# 2 James Conlon Ireland & Kate Morahan Ireland
CONLON, Walter F, May 25 1901 Sex:M Child# 6 James Conlon Ireland & Katherine Morahan Ireland
CONNELL, Maurice Westley, Sep 21 1921 Sex:M Child# 2 Otis Connell Hudson, NH & Lucy Longard Nova Scotia
CONNELL, Orrin Hardis, Aug 18 1914 Sex:M Child# 1 Orrin H Connell Hudson, NH & Clarabell Hare Burke, NY
CONNELL, Unknown, Jul 9 1888 Sex:M Child# 5 Jeremiah O Connell Ireland & Mary Glynn Lawrence, MA Stillborn
CONNELL, Unknown, Sep 17 1916 Sex:M Child# 2 Orrin Connell Nashua, NH & Clarabelle Hare Burke, NY
CONNELLY, Mary, Jul 11 1925 Sex:F Child# 1 Patrick Connelly Manchester, NH & Margaret Murphy Manchester, NH
CONNELLY, Mary Elizabeth, Apr 18 1926 Sex:F Child# 5 Edward Connelly Waterbury, CT & Sadie Bosworth Naugatuck, CT
CONNER, Marion, Nov 17 1891 Sex:F Child# 2 Sidney Conner Campton & Carrie Leonard Newbury, VT
CONNERTY, Katie May, May 28 1892 Sex:F Child# 1 Joseph Connerty Windsor, VT & Maggie E Moran Nashua, NH
CONNOLLY, Albert Bernard, Jul 26 1916 Sex:M Child# 8 James Connolly N Abington, MA & Mary Keneally Whitman, MA
CONNOLLY, Constance Ida, Apr 8 1934 Sex:F Child# 4 Patrick J Connolly Manchester, NH & Margaret Murphy Manchester
CONNOLLY, Marjorie Ann, Mar 2 1928 Sex:F Child# 3 Patrick Connolly Manchester, NH & Marg Murphy Manchester, NH
CONNOLLY, Robert Francis, Jan 20 1927 Sex:M Child# 2 Patrick Connolly Manchester, NH & Margaret Murphy Manchester
CONNOR, Anna Irea, Feb 28 1898 Sex:F Child# 4 Michael Connor Ireland & Anna Eagan Nashua, NH
CONNOR, Bridget, Jan 25 1906 Sex:F Child# 2 Patrick Connor Ireland & Delia Mulligan Ireland
CONNOR, Connor, May 30 1889 Sex:M Child# 2 James G Connor Woburn, MA & Ida Whipple Nashua, NH
CONNOR, David Joseph, Nov 9 1933 Sex:M Child# 2 Daniel J Connor Nashua, NH & Anna Herlihy Cambridge, MA
CONNOR, Etta, Mar 11 1902 Sex:F Child# 2 James H Connor Mass & Mary E Petterson NY
CONNOR, Euphemia, Mar 28 1906 Sex:F Child# 3 James Connor Winchester & Mary Peterson NY
CONNOR, Frank Walter, Jul 15 1932 Sex:M Child# 3 H P Connor Henniker, NH & M F Sargent Henniker, NH
CONNOR, Gwendolyn Marie, Oct 6 1924 Sex:F Child# 1 John Connor Worcester, MA & Marie Connor Nashua, NH
CONNOR, James Henry, Aug 5 1931 Sex:M Child# 1 Daniel Connor Nashua, NH & Anna Herlihey Cambridge, MA
CONNOR, Leo Francis, Dec 15 1903 Sex:M Child# 7 John Connor Ireland & Mary Maber Ireland
CONNOR, Maria, May 7 1892 Sex:F Child# 2 Michael Connor Ireland & Annie Egan Nashua, NH
CONNOR, Martin, Jan 20 1904 Sex:M Child# 1 Patrick Connor Ireland & Delia Mulligan Ireland
CONNOR, Mary, Feb 18 1907 Sex:F Child# 3 Patrick Connor Ireland & Delia Mulligan Ireland
CONNOR, Michael, May 11 1894 Sex:M Child# 3 Michael Connor Ireland & Annie Eagan Nashua, NH
CONNOR, Richard Kibble, Sep 29 1934 Sex:M Child# 1 William Jos Connor Nashua, NH & Grace E Kibble Milford, NH
CONNOR, Shirley Ann, Jan 8 1935 Sex:F Child# 4 Clarence Connor Manchester, NH & Doris Partridge Manchester, NH
CONNOR, Unknown, Mar 2 1888 Sex: Child# 2 John W Connor Nashua, NH & Alice N Connor Ireland Stillborn
CONNOR, Unknown, Jun 3 1888 Sex:F Child# 2 James E Connor Somerville & Annie Lavan Nashua, NH
CONNOR, Unknown, Jan 14 1890 Sex:F Child#  John Connor Ireland & Rose Ireland
CONNOR, Unknown, Sep 30 1891 Sex:M Child# 3 J G Connor Woburn, MA & Ida Whipple New York
CONNOR, Unknown, Feb 7 1892 Sex:M Child# 7 Matthew Connor Roxbury, MA & Mary Dempsey New Haven, CT
CONNOR, Unknown, Dec 29 1913 Sex:M Child# 2 Charles J Connor Keene, NH & Mabel Miles Cambridge, MA Stillborn
CONNOR, Unknown, Jun 4 1926 Sex:M Child# 2 Harold Connor Henniker, NH & Marion Sargent Henniker, NH
CONNOR, William Joseph, Jan 16 1903 Sex:M Child# 7 Michael Connor Ireland & Ann Eagan Ireland
CONNORS, Agnes, Dec 18 1894 Sex:F Child# 3 John Connors Nashua, NH & Katherine Ward Ireland
CONNORS, Daniel Joseph, Aug 7 1900 Sex:M Child# 1 James H Connors Mass & Mary Peterson Canada
CONNORS, Dennis, Nov 27 1900 Sex:M Child# 14 John J Connors Ireland & Katherine Connors Ireland
CONNORS, George Francis, Jan 8 1891 Sex:M Child# 1 Michael Connors Ireland & Anna Egan Nashua, NH
CONNORS, George Francis, Aug 21 1901 Sex:M Child# 15 Michael Connors Ireland & Ann Eagan Nashua, NH
CONNORS, Henri, Dec 28 1890 Sex:M Child# 1 Frank Connors
CONNORS, Margaret Ann, Aug 15 1935 Sex:F Child# 1 John M Connors Portsmouth, NH & Mary Harrigan Boston, MA
CONREY, Joseph A E, Mar 30 1893 Sex:M Child# 2 John Conrey Canada & Josephine Beaulieu Canada
CONSEGNY, Edmond Jean, Jul 16 1924 Sex:M Child# 3 Jean Consegny Nashua, NH & Agnes E Gaudette Nashua, NH
CONSIDINE, John Francis, Sep 23 1917 Sex:M Child# 1 John F Considine Ireland & Mary Kaurahan Nashua, NH
CONSIGNEY, Robert Harvey, Dec 25 1926 Sex:M Child# 4 Jean B Consigney Nashua, NH & Agnes Gaudette Nashua, NH
CONSIGNY, Marie Alice, Jan 10 1898 Sex:F Child# 1 Joseph Consigny Canada & Theotis Blanchard New Brunswick
CONSTANT, Adrien, Jun 28 1912 Sex:M Child# 10 Calixte Constant Canada & Anna Prince Canada
CONSTANT, Albert Normand, Oct 6 1933 Sex:M Child# 4 Arthur Constant Nashua, NH & Yvonne Ouellette Nashua, NH
CONSTANT, Alfred Roger, Apr 10 1927 Sex:M Child# 1 Alfred Constant Nashua, NH & Yvonne Ouillette Nashua, NH
CONSTANT, Beatrice Loretta, Nov 17 1929 Sex:F Child# 4 Wilfrid Constant Pittsfield, NH & Orise Burns Nashua, NH
CONSTANT, Bertha, Mar 22 1900 Sex:F Child# 3 Calixte Constant Canada & Anna Prince Canada
CONSTANT, Blanche Theresa, Dec 13 1929 Sex:F Child# 2 Arthur Constant Nashua, NH & Yvonne Ouillette Nashua, NH
CONSTANT, Cecile, Jun 28 1912 Sex:F Child# 11 Calixte Constant Canada & Anna Prince Canada
CONSTANT, Elizabeth, Feb 15 1926 Sex:F Child# 2 Wilfrid Constant Pittsfield, NH & Orise Burns Nashua, NH
CONSTANT, Ernest Leo, Oct 18 1910 Sex:M Child# 9 Calixte Constant Canada & Anna Prince Canada
CONSTANT, Eva, Jun 8 1897 Sex:F Child# 1 Calixte Constant Canada & Anna Prince Canada
CONSTANT, Henri Donat, Jun 9 1904 Sex:M Child# 5 Calixte Constant Canada & Anna Prince Canada
CONSTANT, Jeanette Aurore, Jul 29 1905 Sex:F Child# 6 Calixte Constant Canada & Anna Prince Canada
CONSTANT, Jeanne Rita, Jan 10 1931 Sex:F Child# 3 Arthur Constant Nashua, NH & Yvonne Ouellette Nashua, NH
CONSTANT, Joseph Ernest, Mar 27 1894 Sex:M Child# 2 Frank Constant Canada & Marie Girard Canada
CONSTANT, Marie, Dec 21 1915 Sex:F Child# 12 Calixte Constant Canada & Anna Prince Canada Stillborn
CONSTANT, Marie Rose B, May 3 1892 Sex:F Child# 1 Francois Constant Canada & Marie Girard Canada
CONSTANT, Norman Edward, May 10 1931 Sex:M Child# 5 Wilfred N Constant Pittsfield, NH & Orise Burns Nashua, NH
CONSTANT, Raymond George, Feb 18 1928 Sex:M Child# 3 Wilfred Constant Pittsfield, NH & Orise Burns Nashua, NH
CONSTANT, Rita, Apr 13 1908 Sex:F Child# 8 Calixte Constant Canada & Anna Prince Canada
CONSTANT, Robert Henry, May 2 1933 Sex:M Child# 6 Wilfrid Constant NH & Orise Burns Nashua, NH

CONSTANT, Rose Liliane, Nov 21 1906 Sex:F Child# 7 Calixte Constant Canada & Anna Prince Canada
CONSTANT, Yvonne Malvina, Sep 27 1924 Sex:F Child# 1 Wilfred Constant Pittsfield, MA & Orise Burns Nashua, NH
CONSTANTARIS, Julia, Feb 19 1916 Sex:F Child# 5 Stecios Constantaris Greece & Tessia Constantaris Greece
CONSTANTINA, Margherita, Jul 23 1921 Sex:F Child# 5 James Constantina Italy & Maria Saloma Italy
CONSTANTINE, Rose Germaine, Apr 22 1911 Sex:F Child# 1 Charlie Constantine Greece & Rose Dionne US
CONTRAVITCH, Nora Justina, Sep 11 1910 Sex:F Child# 2 Lukas Contravitch Russia & Zophia Klabitza Austria
CONTSONIKAS, Jeremiah, Apr 7 1920 Sex:M Child# 2 Michael Contsonikas Greece & Katherine O'Neil Manchester, NH
CONTSONIKAS, Margaret, Apr 7 1920 Sex:F Child# 3 Michael Contsonikas Greece & Katherine O'Neil Manchester, NH
CONTURE, Rose Delima, Feb 15 1894 Sex:F Child# 3 Antoine Conture Canada & A Archambault Canada
CONVERSE, Howard Wentworth, Nov 30 1916 Sex:M Child# 5 Walter O Converse Amherst, NH & Maude Wentworth Nashua, NH
CONVERSE, Mabel Blanche O, May 14 1909 Sex:F Child# 1 Dolbert Converse Fairfield, VT & Ina Orne Westmore, VT
CONWAY, Paul T, Jun 24 1896 Sex:M Child# 1 Nicholas S Conway Southington, CT & Kittie M Feely Rutland, VT
COOK, Benjamin F, Jan 14 1890 Sex:M Child# 1 Benjamin F Cook Salem, MA & Alice Andover, NH
COOK, Charlotte Virginia, Jul 10 1932 Sex:F Child# 1 Hector Cook Nova Scotia & Marian Dane Hudson, NH
COOK, Janet Moreen, Jan 3 1935 Sex:F Child# 5 L Richard Cook Everett, MI & Florence D Handy Cadillac, MI
COOK, Julia Lynn, Mar 3 1933 Sex:F Child# 1 E T Cook Dorchester, MA & Julia L Pitner Cohutta, GA
COOK, Keith Byron, May 26 1933 Sex:M Child# 4 Richard L Cook Michigan & Florence Hardy Michigan
COOK, Mary Philomene, Feb 3 1927 Sex:F Child# 3 John Cook Lawrence, MA & Mary Morin Canada
COOK, Prudence S, Sep 1 1920 Sex:F Child# 5 George H Cook Fremont, NH & Catherine Wooley Groton, MA
COOK, Unknown, Jan 2 1888 Sex:M Child# 1 Charles N Cook Chataugua, NY & Cora M Nichols Waltham
COOKE, Nancy Ellen, Oct 13 1930 Sex:F Child# 2 Hersey Cooke Nova Scotia & Lucy Burnham Wilton, NH
COOKOSKY, John Thomas, Sep 22 1914 Sex:M Child# 1 Robert Cookosky Russia & Polina Wersoska Russia
COOKSAN, Frank Shattuck, Jr, Jun 24 1921 Sex:M Child# 1 Frank S Cooksan New Sharon, ME & Hyldegarde Major
COOMBS, Kenneth Melzar, Mar 7 1921 Sex:M Child# 2 Everett C Coombs Saugus, MA & Emma B Bastow Lowell, MA
COOMBS, Norma Louise, Oct 4 1926 Sex:F Child# 3 Oscar M Coombs Providence, RI & F B Urguhart Nashua, NH
COOMBS, Ruth Ward, Jan 28 1918 Sex:F Child# 2 Oscar M Coombs Nashua, NH & Florence Urquhart Nashua, NH
COPP, Dewey Sampson, Jun 28 1899 Sex:M Child# 1 B F Copp Augusta, ME & Della Herlburtt NY
COPP, Grace Elizabeth, Feb 9 1897 Sex:F Child# 5 Philip M Copp Wakefield, MA & Bessie H Wallace Philadelphia, PA
COPP, Harold Edward, Mar 13 1892 Sex:M Child# 3 Philip M Copp Wakefield, MA & Bessie H Wallace Philadelphia, PA
COPP, Roger Edward, Aug 28 1919 Sex:M Child# 1 Harold E Copp Nashua, NH & Maude Harley Georgetown, ME
COPP, Unknown, Oct 31 1894 Sex:F Child# 4 Philip M Copp Wakefield, MA & Bessie H Wallace Philadelphia, PA
COPP, Unknown, Feb 25 1895 Sex:F Child# 5 Turtan F Copp Stanstead, PQ & Nellie Peckham Woburn, MA
COPP, Unknown, Jun 20 1898 Sex:M Child# 1 Benjamin F Copp Batavia, NY & Delia A Hurlburt Lion Mt, NY Stillborn
CORADINE, Thomas, Jul 5 1892 Sex:M Child# 1 Thomas Coradine Glasgow & Jennie Burkinshaw Pepperell, MA
CORADINE, Unknown, May 19 1894 Sex:M Child# 2 Thomas Coradine Scotland & Jennie Burkenshaw Mass
CORAS, Unknown, Jan 23 1919 Sex:M Child# 3 James F Coras Greece & Haida Karathanoies Greece
CORBETT, Shirley, Apr 9 1929 Sex:F Child# 1 Harold S Corbett Clarkson, NY & Alice May Wright Nashua, NH
CORBIERE, Bertha A G, Dec 11 1897 Sex:F Child# 2 George Corbiere Canada & Anais Labonville Nashua, NH
CORBIN, Francois Xavier, Dec 19 1896 Sex:M Child# 2 Francois Corbin Canada & Justine Richard Canada
CORBIN, Joseph Henry Albert, Nov 20 1933 Sex:M Child# 5 Francois Corbin Nashua, NH & Loretta Viens Taunton, MA
CORBIN, Leo Ludger, Sep 22 1927 Sex:M Child# 3 F Corbin, Jr Nashua, NH & Lauretta Vien Taunton, MA
CORBIN, Marie Alice, Mar 15 1899 Sex:F Child# Francois Corbin Canada & Justine Richard Canada
CORBIN, Marie Blanche Rita, Sep 19 1923 Sex:F Child# 1 Francis Corbin NH & Laurette Viens Taunton, MA
CORBIN, Marie Lucille Cecile, Dec 9 1925 Sex:F Child# 2 Francis Corbin NH & Lauretta Viens Taunton, MA
CORBIN, Mary Ellen, Oct 4 1892 Sex:F Child# 2 Joseph Corbin Canada & Victoria Beaulieu Canada
CORBIN, Paul, Mar 18 1930 Sex:M Child# 4 Francois Corbin, Jr Nashua, NH & Lorette Vien Taunton, MA
COREY, Alice, Jan 23 1934 Sex:F Child# 2 John Corey Kentville, NS & Aurore Bordeleau Lowell, MA
COREY, Bessie Alline, Sep 29 1896 Sex:F Child# 5 George W Corey Chesterfield & Annie G Fellows S Keene, NH
COREY, Doris Muriel, Sep 21 1924 Sex:F Child# 4 John Corey Nova Scotia & Mary Ellen Kelley Salem, MA
COREY, George Albert, Jun 11 1918 Sex:M Child# 1 Albert Corey New York & Ethel G Chandler Nashua, NH
COREY, Guy Russell, Jan 18 1916 Sex:M Child# 1 John Corey Nova Scotia & Mary J Kelley Salem, MA
COREY, Helen Louise, Jul 12 1928 Sex:F Child# 7 John C Corey Nova Scotia & Mary E Kelley Salem, MA
COREY, John Cecil, Sep 8 1922 Sex:M Child# 4 John C Corey Nova Scotia & Mary E Kelley Salem, MA
COREY, Merilyn, Jan 30 1934 Sex:F Child# 3 Lawrence E Corey Brookline, NH & Virginia Lathe Saugus, MA
COREY, Rita, Aug 3 1926 Sex:F Child# 6 John Corey Nova Scotia & Mary Kelley Salem, MA
COREY, Ruth Elinor, Dec 31 1929 Sex:F Child# 8 John Corey Nova Scotia & Mary E Kelley Salem, MA
COREY, Truman George, Sep 29 1896 Sex:M Child# 6 George W Corey Chesterfield & Annie G Fellows S Keene, NH
COREY, Unknown, Dec 6 1901 Sex:M Child# 3 Charles W Corey Ellenburg, NY & Dalay P Swallow Rye Stillborn
COREY, Unknown, May 6 1920 Sex:M Child# 3 John C Corey Nova Scotia & Mary Kelley Salem, MA
CORKA, Unknown, Jan 17 1915 Sex:M Child# 2 Adam Corka Russia & Mary Tola Russia
CORLISS, Arlene A, May 17 1920 Sex:F Child# 4 Arthur Corliss Somerville, MA & Elizabeth Larouche Bedford, NH
CORLISS, Beatrice, Jun 25 1918 Sex:F Child# 3 Arthur Corliss Boston, MA & Elizabeth Larouche Bedford, NH
CORLISS, Edward B, Oct 16 1893 Sex:M Child# 2 John Corliss Ireland & Agnes Solomon NY
CORLISS, James F, Sep 25 1891 Sex:M Child# 1 John Corliss Ireland & A E Solomon New York
CORMACK, Ellen Esther, Apr 22 1895 Sex:F Child# 5 James Cormack Scotland & Margaret Shaughnessy Milford, MA
CORMACK, Unknown, Feb 10 1891 Sex:M Child# 3 J L K Cormack Scotland & Margaret Scotland
CORMACK, William I, Mar 9 1893 Sex:M Child# 4 James L Cormack Scotland & Marg'e A Shaughealy Milford, MA
CORMIER, Andre Royal, May 10 1930 Sex:M Child# 2 David Cormier Canada & Florence Boucher Nashua, NH
CORMIER, Celina, Apr 12 1889 Sex:F Child# 7 Octavo Cormier Canada & Hermine Gironard Canada
CORMIER, Charles Bruno, Oct 10 1928 Sex:M Child# 1 David Cormier Canada & Florence Boucher Canada
CORMIER, Isidore Edouard, Nov 5 1924 Sex:M Child# 2 William Cormier Vermont & Marie A Boucher Nashua, NH
CORMIER, Joseph Charles, Sep 7 1896 Sex:M Child# 3 Charles Cormier Canada & Amida Landry Canada
CORMIER, Marie, Aug 29 1916 Sex:F Child# 3 Rodolphe Cormier NH & Exilda Messier Mass

CORMIER, Marie Lorette Alice, Feb 17 1914 Sex:F Child# 2 Rodolphe Cormier NH & Exilda Messier Mass
CORMIER, Napoleon Deus A, Oct 26 1905 Sex:M Child# 1 Deus Cormier Canada & Marie Elise Cormier Canada
CORMIER, Paul Bertrand, Jan 13 1920 Sex:M Child# 4 Rodolphe Cormier Manchester, NH & Exilda Messier Newburyport, MA
CORMIER, Richard Eugene, Mar 2 1924 Sex:M Child# 7 Rudolphe Cormier Manchester, NH & Exilda Messier Newburyport, MA
CORMIER, Robert Emile, Mar 2 1924 Sex:M Child# 6 Rudolphe Cormier Manchester, NH & Exilda Messier Newburyport, MA
CORMIER, Vincent Laurent, Mar 14 1918 Sex:M Child# 4 Rodolphe Cormier NH & Exilda Messier Mass
CORMIER, William Louis Ant, Mar 16 1921 Sex:M Child# 1 William Cormier Canada & Marie A Boucher Nashua, NH
CORMOILLIER, Marie, Feb 16 1888 Sex:F Child# 4 Napoleon Cormoillier P Q & Malvina Massi P Q
CORNELLIER, Marjorie Lorraine, Sep 2 1933 Sex:F Child# 1 L Cornellier Lowell, MA & Lorraine Gardner Pepperell, MA
CORON, Wilson Bolko, Dec 3 1917 Sex:M Child# 2 Sigmund A Coron Poland & Tessy Mathuscki Poland
CORONIS, Joseph Sam, Oct 27 1915 Sex:M Child# 2 James Coronis Greece & Lena Bilodeau Nashua, NH
CORONNIS, Stambola, Jul 3 1916 Sex:F Child# 4 Lewis Coronnis Greece & Cnstantina Spiliasis Greece
COROSA, Melvina Barnta, Apr 30 1915 Sex:F Child# 1 Andrew Corosa Russia & Melvina Lepeska Russia
COROSA, Witantas, Nov 4 1921 Sex:M Child# 2 Julius Corosa Russia & Victoria Stanapiedzu Russia
CORRIS, Ann Charlotte, Sep 27 1917 Sex:F Child# 2 Charles S Corris Italy & Margaret Delorey Nashua, NH
CORRIVEAU, Alice Eva, Oct 4 1899 Sex:F Child# 12 Ernest Corriveau Canada & Henriette Guerette Canada
CORRIVEAU, Blanche A, Jun 8 1898 Sex:F Child# 11 Ernest Corriveau Canada & Harriette Guerette Canada
CORRIVEAU, Claire Louise, Nov 15 1923 Sex:F Child# 3 Dona Corriveau Canada & Clara C Pinet Nashua, NH
CORRIVEAU, Emerencienne L, May 28 1930 Sex:F Child# 2 Hector Corriveau Canada & Alice Cloutier Nashua, NH
CORRIVEAU, George, Dec 27 1906 Sex:M Child# 17 Ernest Corriveau Canada & Henriette Guerrette Canada
CORRIVEAU, Irene Lilliane, Jan 30 1934 Sex:F Child# 4 Hector Corriveau Canada & Alice Cloutre Nashua, NH
CORRIVEAU, Isabelle Mariette, Nov 8 1921 Sex:F Child# 2 Donat Corriveau Canada & Clara Pinette Nashua, NH
CORRIVEAU, Jos Hector Robert, Mar 26 1929 Sex:M Child# 2 Hector Corriveau Canada & Alice Cloutier Nashua, NH
CORRIVEAU, Joseph C, Jul 7 1902 Sex:M Child# 15 Ernest Corriveau Canada & Henriette Guerette Canada
CORRIVEAU, Joseph L, Oct 30 1893 Sex:M Child# 8 Ernest Corriveau Canada & Henriette Guerette Canada
CORRIVEAU, Joseph Selvio R, Sep 4 1905 Sex:M Child# 16 Ernest Corriveau Canada & Henriette Guerette Canada
CORRIVEAU, Lea, Nov 2 1896 Sex:F Child# 10 Ernest Corriveau Canada & Henrietta Guerette Canada
CORRIVEAU, Marie Albina, Feb 22 1895 Sex:F Child# 9 Ernest Corriveau St Antoine, PQ & Henriette Guerette Canada
CORRIVEAU, Marie Camille, Dec 28 1918 Sex:F Child# 2 Douet Corriveau Canada & Clare Pinet Nashua, NH
CORRIVEAU, Roland, Aug 11 1903 Sex:M Child# 15 Ernest Corriveau Canada & Henriette Guerette Canada
CORRIVEAU, Rose Henriette, Mar 16 1901 Sex:F Child# 13 Ernest Corriveau Canada & Henriette Guerette Canada
CORRIVEAU, Rose Marie Madeline, Feb 11 1929 Sex:F Child# 4 Donat Corriveau Canada & Clara Pinet Nashua, NH
CORSON, Nancy Jean, Nov 18 1934 Sex:F Child# 1 Carl Edward Corson Rochester, NH & Thelma Watson Cushman, MA
COSGROVE, Winnifred Hazel, May 1 1896 Sex:F Child# 1 N J Cosgrove Winchendon, MA & Mary A Segurson Fitchburg, MA
COSISTA, Gerald Denis, May 9 1930 Sex:M Child# 4 Hector Cosista Canada & Germaine Marquis Canada
COSTARAS, Unknown, Aug 21 1924 Sex:F Child# 2 James Costaras Greece & Aglira Sionou Greece
COSTAS, Eleftheria, Jan 24 1919 Sex:F Child# 2 George Costas Greece & Keratsou Greece
COSTELLO, Andrew J B, Sep 18 1913 Sex:M Child# 2 Joseph Costello Manchester, NH & Mary Barron Winooski, VT
COSTELLO, John Francis, Jr, Jul 9 1932 Sex:M Child# 1 J F Costello England & Eleanor Bradley Nashua, NH
COSTELLO, Joyce, Jan 22 1933 Sex:F Child# 2 Wm B Costello Nashua, NH & Marjorie E Johnson Bedford, NH
COSTELLO, William Barron, Apr 12 1908 Sex:M Child# 1 Robert J Costello Manchester, NH & Mary A Barron Winooski, VT
COSTELLO, William Barron, Jr, Oct 8 1930 Sex:M Child# 1 Wm B Costello Nashua, NH & Marjorie E Johnson Bedford, NH
COSTIGAN, Joseph Peter, Oct 28 1924 Sex:M Child# 2 J P Costigan Waterbury, CT & Blanche Bayer Waterbury, CT
COSTOUIKAS, Unknown, Feb 25 1920 Sex:M Child# 5 James Costouikas Greece & Sophie Kres Greece
COTA, William J Duncan, Feb 9 1898 Sex:M Child# 1 Philip Cota Chebance, IL & Maimie Mcphail Clachan, Canada
COTE, Adeline, Nov 28 1895 Sex:F Child# 1 Gilbert Cote Canada & Angele Brisson Canada
COTE, Albert E N, Feb 22 1895 Sex:M Child# 17 Eusebe Cote Canada & Adeline Gravelle Canada
COTE, Albina, Jul 15 1887 Sex:F Child# Philippe Cote P Q & Evelina Lancley P Q
COTE, Albina, Jul 2 1893 Sex:F Child# 2 Pierre Cote Canada & Alma Trottier St Albans, VT
COTE, Alfred, Oct 18 1892 Sex:M Child# 3 Treffle Cote Canada & Marie Venillery Canada
COTE, Alfred, Jul 31 1899 Sex:M Child# 5 Pierre Cote Canada & Alma Trottier St Albans, VT
COTE, Alfred Norman, Jun 15 1932 Sex:M Child# 5 Alfred Cote Nashua, NH & Annette Chagnon Canada
COTE, Alfred Paul, Oct 12 1933 Sex:M Child# 5 Alberic Cote Canada & Cecile Hebert Nashua, NH
COTE, Alfred, Jr, Jun 17 1932 Sex:M Child# 1 Alfred Cote Nashua, NH & Annette Chagnon Canada
COTE, Alice Blanche Etien, Sep 27 1914 Sex:F Child# 7 Cleophas Cote Canada & Juliana Berube Canada
COTE, Alice Leonie, Sep 8 1931 Sex:F Child# 5 Robert Cote Canada & Celidase Desrochers Sanbornville, NH
COTE, Alphonse Aurelle, Sep 23 1907 Sex:M Child# 5 Ludger Cote Canada & Julie Roy St Albans, VT
COTE, Alphonse Normand, Feb 7 1910 Sex:M Child# 2 Prudent Cote Canada & Aurelie Levesque Canada
COTE, Alvin Norbert, Jan 1 1934 Sex:M Child# 3 Adelard Cote Nashua, NH & Erma Grandmaison Nashua, NH
COTE, Amanda Aglae, Jul 21 1897 Sex:F Child# 8 Eugene Cote Canada & Fidelga Girouard Canada
COTE, Amedee, Jul 9 1910 Sex:M Child# 7 Ludger Cote Canada & Julia Roy St Albans, VT
COTE, Annette Elodie, May 26 1910 Sex:F Child# 2 Wilfrid Cote Canada & Josephine Starrett US
COTE, Annie, May 7 1902 Sex:F Child# 5 Louis Cote Canada & Stephanie Roy St Albans, VT
COTE, Armand, Oct 13 1923 Sex:M Child# 6 Francis X Cote Canada & Denise Blais Canada
COTE, Armand Sylvio, Sep 2 1909 Sex:M Child# 6 Ludger Cote Canada & Julia Roy Montgomery, VT
COTE, Arthur, Jul 22 1893 Sex:M Child# 3 Frederic Cote Canada & Eveline Beauregard Canada
COTE, Arthur Amedee, Mar 14 1889 Sex:M Child# 1 Nazaire Cote Canada & Adele Martin Canada
COTE, Arthur Paul, Jun 18 1929 Sex:M Child# 3 Arthur Cote Canada & Marguerite Manning Canada
COTE, Beatrice, Aug 31 1903 Sex:F Child# 2 Cleophas Cote Canada & Juliana Berube Canada
COTE, Beatrice, Jul 28 1904 Sex:F Child# 6 Joseph Leon Cote Sherbrooke, PQ & Agnes Proulx St Zephirin, Canada
COTE, Blanche Beatrice, Feb 28 1913 Sex:F Child# 13 Victor Cote Canada & Marie Dionne Canada
COTE, Blanche Jeannette, Aug 23 1920 Sex:F Child# 1 Aurele Cote Canada & Blanche Belanger Canada
COTE, Blanche Pauline, Jul 21 1925 Sex:F Child# 3 Albert Cote Canada & Marie A Lambert Canada

COTE, Calixte Ed, Oct 31 1902 Sex:M Child# 1 Edmond E Cote Canada & M L Guenette Canada
COTE, Carmel Clarissa, Feb 11 1929 Sex:F Child# 1 Wilfrid Cote Canada & Marie Demers Canada
COTE, Charles Ross, Aug 14 1925 Sex:M Child# 2 Charles Cote Canada & Diana Ross Nashua, NH
COTE, Claire Eva, Jun 1 1923 Sex:F Child# 1 Leon P Cote Canada & Dora Lampron US
COTE, Claire Loretta, Apr 4 1920 Sex:F Child# 1 Charles Cote Canada & Diana Ross Nashua, NH
COTE, Clare Priscilla, Aug 21 1929 Sex:F Child# 1 Victor Cote Nashua, NH & Annette Desrosiers Nashua, NH
COTE, Claudette Lorraine, Sep 12 1931 Sex:F Child# 2 Adelard Cote Nashua, NH & Erma Grandmaison Nashua, NH
COTE, Clifford Conrad, Jan 19 1924 Sex:M Child# 1 Romeo Cote Canada & Rosalma Ansant Nashua, NH
COTE, Dolores Leda, Nov 18 1926 Sex:F Child# 3 Romeo Cote Canada & Rose A Aussaint Nashua, NH
COTE, Donald Romeo, Nov 12 1930 Sex:M Child# 4 Romeo Cote Canada & Rosalina Ossant Nashua, NH
COTE, Dora Exilda, Mar 11 1907 Sex:F Child# 1 Aime Cote Canada & Clerina Caron Canada
COTE, Dorothy Edris, Aug 6 1924 Sex:F Child# 2 Aurelle Cote Canada & Blanche Belanger Canada
COTE, Edmond, Dec 26 1928 Sex:M Child# 3 Edmund Cote Nashua, NH & Leah Raby Nashua, NH
COTE, Edouard Ludger, Sep 7 1895 Sex:M Child# 2 Charles Cote Canada & Julie Roy Barre, VT
COTE, Edward, May 25 1891 Sex:M Child# 1 Pierre Cote Canada & Alma Desmarais Canada
COTE, Eleanor Theresa, Jan 9 1933 Sex:F Child# 6 Joseph Cote Canada & Anna Hamel Nashua, NH
COTE, Ernest Ferdinand, Feb 3 1906 Sex:M Child# 2 Napoleon Cote Newport, VT & Alma Cusson Canada
COTE, Estelle Henriette, Apr 9 1930 Sex:F Child# 4 Robert Cote Canada & Celedose Desrochers Sanbornville, NH
COTE, Eva, May 5 1894 Sex:F Child# 1 Joseph Cote Canada & Marie Dube Canada
COTE, Fedora Edith Amanda, Mar 28 1912 Sex:F Child# 5 Joseph Cote Canada & Amerilda Mercier Canada
COTE, Ferdinand L, Aug 6 1902 Sex:M Child# 6 Victor Cote Canada & Marie Drouin Canada
COTE, Fernando Emile, Oct 8 1903 Sex:M Child# 1 Alfred Cote Canada & Enesore Morin NH
COTE, Florence Therese, May 12 1931 Sex:F Child# 2 Raoul Cote Nashua, NH & Rose Lamarre Milford, NH
COTE, Frederick Ward, Jan 21 1906 Sex:M Child# 1 Moses Cote Nashua, NH & Lillian Ward Winchester, MA
COTE, Gabrielle Eldora, Jul 11 1918 Sex:F Child# 2 Edouard J Cote US & Emma Dupont Canada
COTE, Gene Patrica, Mar 14 1925 Sex:F Child# 2 Joseph Cote Canada & Anna Hamel Nashua, NH
COTE, George, Apr 13 1890 Sex:M Child# 5 Henri Cote Canada & Matilda Boisvert Canada
COTE, George Leo N, Mar 18 1908 Sex:M Child# 10 Narcisse Cote Canada & Wilhelmine Deschesne Canada
COTE, George Ohilip, Oct 21 1902 Sex:M Child# 4 Ludger Cote Canada & Julie Roy Montgomery, VT
COTE, Georges Edmond, Feb 9 1896 Sex:M Child# 10 Georges Cote Canada & Elizabeth Caye Canada
COTE, Georges Leonard, Jun 3 1904 Sex:M Child# 1 Napoleon Cote Vermont & Alma Cusson Canada
COTE, Germaine M, Apr 9 1905 Sex:F Child# 1 Eugene Cote Canada & Henriette Emond Canada
COTE, Gertrude Alice, May 11 1924 Sex:F Child# 2 Alfred Cote Canada & Ant Descheneau NH
COTE, Helene, Jan 30 1901 Sex:F Child# 4 Louis Cote Canada & Stephanie Roy St Albans, VT
COTE, Helene Dorinda, Jun 14 1894 Sex:F Child# 1 Prudent Cote Canada & Marie Metayer Canada
COTE, Henri, Sep 29 1899 Sex:M Child# 5 Stanislas Cote Canada & Ophedie Deschesne Canada
COTE, Henri Armand, Sep 5 1907 Sex:M Child# 4 Prudent Cote Canada & Aurelia Lavigne Canada
COTE, Henry Edouard, Jun 2 1899 Sex:M Child# 5 Majorie Cote Canada & Mary June Blain W Boylston, MA
COTE, Hormidas, Jun 18 1904 Sex:M Child# 2 Edmond E Cote Nashua, NH & Marie L Guenette Canada
COTE, Hormidas Conrad, Jun 28 1904 Sex:M Child# 6 Louis Cote Canada & Stephanie Roy St Albans, VT
COTE, Irene Germaine, Apr 21 1923 Sex:F Child# 2 Charles E Cote Canada & Bernadette Pinette Canada
COTE, Irene Therese, Jan 28 1924 Sex:F Child# 3 Edmond Cote Nashua, NH & Delina Beaudien Canada
COTE, J E David Roger, Apr 19 1922 Sex:M Child# 1 Sylvio Cote Canada & Leda Labelle NH
COTE, Jacqueline, Nov 14 1923 Sex:F Child# 2 Albert Cote Canada & Marion Lambert Nashua, NH
COTE, James Bosworth, Jun 11 1910 Sex:M Child# 2 James Cote Maine & Mary Rideout Maine
COTE, Jean B, Jun 25 1931 Sex:M Child# 5 Sylvio Cote Canada & Lida Labelle Nashua, NH
COTE, Jean Paul Henry, Dec 29 1925 Sex:M Child# 4 Arthur Cote Canada & Georgia Lambert Central Falls, RI
COTE, Jeanne Florence, May 22 1920 Sex:F Child# 2 Leon Cote Canada & Dora Lampron US
COTE, Jeannette Amand, Aug 20 1924 Sex:F Child# 1 Alfred Cote Nashua, NH & Annette Chagnon Canada
COTE, Joesph Charles Wm, Mar 17 1924 Sex:M Child# 2 William Cote NH & Eveline Cloutier US
COTE, Jos Alfred Altheold, Aug 7 1919 Sex:M Child# 1 Alfred Cote Canada & Antoinette Deschesne NH
COTE, Jos Ronald Leo, Sep 9 1928 Sex:M Child# 1 Adelard Cote Nashua, NH & I Grandmaison Nashua, NH
COTE, Jos Wilfred Roger, May 9 1928 Sex:M Child# 1 Joseph Cote Canada & Antoinette Couture Canada
COTE, Joseph, May 17 1894 Sex:M Child# 6 Henri Cote Canada & Mathilde Boisvert Canada
COTE, Joseph, Apr 26 1907 Sex:M Child# 4 Ferdinand Cote Canada & Emelie Dube Canada Stillborn
COTE, Joseph A E, Nov 15 1904 Sex:M Child# 2 Fernando Cote Canada & Eliza Morin NH
COTE, Joseph A H, May 3 1895 Sex:M Child# 2 Magoriane Cote Canada & Mary J Blain W Boylston, MA
COTE, Joseph Adrien, Oct 10 1901 Sex:M Child# 6 Majorique Cote Canada & Marie Jeanne Blane Mass
COTE, Joseph Albert Paul, Sep 4 1908 Sex:M Child# 1 Francois Cote Canada & Anna Salva Canada
COTE, Joseph Albert Paul, Jun 10 1924 Sex:M Child# 2 Sylvio Cote Canada & Leda Labelle NH
COTE, Joseph Alfred, Dec 9 1890 Sex:M Child# 2 Nazaire Cote Canada & Adele Martin Canada
COTE, Joseph Alfred, Jan 25 1893 Sex:M Child# 2 Narcisse Cote Canada & Wilhelm'e Deschesne Canada
COTE, Joseph Alfred E, Oct 18 1900 Sex:M Child# 11 Antoine Cote Canada & Victoria Gagnon Canada
COTE, Joseph Alphe E G, Dec 6 1910 Sex:M Child# 2 Alphe Cote Canada & Emelia Marquis Canada
COTE, Joseph Alvin, Jul 22 1900 Sex:M Child# 5 Joseph Cote Canada & Marie Dube Canada
COTE, Joseph Auguste Rock, May 7 1904 Sex:M Child# 3 Ferdinand Cote Canada & Emelie Dube Canada
COTE, Joseph Chas Albert, Jun 20 1900 Sex:M Child# 6 Naricsse Cote Canada & Wilhelmine Deschene Canada
COTE, Joseph E, May 30 1897 Sex:M Child# 4 Pierre Cote Canada & Alma Desmarais Canada
COTE, Joseph E E, Mar 7 1897 Sex:M Child# 4 Narcisse Cote Canada & Wilhel'ine Desches'e Canada
COTE, Joseph Edmund, Nov 23 1922 Sex:M Child# 4 Edmund J Cote Nashua, NH & Emma Dupont Canada
COTE, Joseph Emilio, Sep 3 1916 Sex:M Child# 1 Jean Baptiste Cote Canada & Delvina Michaud Canada
COTE, Joseph Ernest Ludger, Mar 18 1912 Sex:M Child# 12 Victor Cote Canada & Marie Dionne Canada
COTE, Joseph Eugene, Sep 27 1896 Sex:M Child# 3 Joseph Cote Canada & Marie Dube Canada

COTE, Joseph George, Sep 23 1904 Sex:M Child# 11 Antoine Cote Canada & Victoria Gagnon Canada
COTE, Joseph George A, Nov 9 1903 Sex:M Child# 1 Ferdinand Cote Vermont & Albina Robillard Canada
COTE, Joseph Girard A, Apr 25 1911 Sex:M Child# 4 Fernando Cote Canada & Enizard Morin NH
COTE, Joseph Henri, Nov 9 1898 Sex:M Child# 4 Joseph Cote Canada & Marie Louise Dube Canada
COTE, Joseph L P A A, Jul 19 1900 Sex:M Child# 6 Victor Cote Canada & Marie Dionne Canada
COTE, Joseph Leo, Dec 2 1903 Sex:M Child# 1 Alfred Cote Canada & Rosa Desjardins Lewiston, ME
COTE, Joseph Lucien, Feb 2 1908 Sex:M Child# 10 Victor Cote Canada & Marie Dionne Canada
COTE, Joseph M Ernest, Nov 21 1901 Sex:M Child# 9 Jean Bte Cote Canada & Ernestine Lebel Canada
COTE, Joseph R J B, Jul 5 1903 Sex:M Child# 8 Narcisse Cote Canada & Wilhelmina Deschenes Canada
COTE, Joseph Richard Henri, Sep 12 1918 Sex:M Child# 4 Wilfred Cote Canada & Josephine Starrett Nashua, NH
COTE, Joseph Robert, Mar 13 1917 Sex:M Child# 4 Edward J Cote Nashua, NH & Emma Dupont Canada Stillborn
COTE, Joseph Robert Bruno, Dec 4 1925 Sex:M Child# 4 Elzear L Cote Nashua, NH & Marie Provencher Nashua, NH
COTE, Joseph Roger, Sep 13 1915 Sex:M Child# 1 Ernest Cote Nashua, NH & Aurore Boudreau Nashua, NH
COTE, Julie Regina A, Jul 5 1897 Sex:F Child# 2 Ludger Cote Canada & Julie Roy Westfield, VT
COTE, Laura, Jan 15 1919 Sex:F Child# 3 Aime Cote Canada & Clare Carron Canada
COTE, Lea Rita, Sep 16 1924 Sex:F Child# 3 Charles E Cote Canada & Bernadette Pinette Canada
COTE, Leon Arthur, Sep 19 1905 Sex:M Child# 2 Jessie Cote US & Regina Lemiuex Canada
COTE, Lillian Olivette, Oct 9 1916 Sex:F Child# 3 Aime Cote Canada & Claudia Caron Canada
COTE, Louis E, Dec 10 1893 Sex:M Child# 16 Eusebe Cote Canada & Adeline Gravel Canada
COTE, Louis George, Aug 1 1927 Sex:M Child# 3 Alberie Cote Canada & Cecile Hebert Nashua, NH
COTE, Louis Philippe, Aug 23 1895 Sex:M Child# 1 Louis Cote Canada & Stephanie Roy St Albans, VT
COTE, Lucien Leo, Mar 28 1924 Sex:M Child# 1 Emile Cote Canada & Diana Lafrance Canada
COTE, Lucille Annette, Jul 13 1928 Sex:F Child# 3 Robert Cote Canada & C Desrochers Sanbornville, NH
COTE, Lucille Gertrude, Jul 30 1920 Sex:F Child# 2 Ernest Cote NH & Julienne Strong NH
COTE, Lucille Isabelle, Dec 16 1920 Sex:F Child# 1 Edmond J Cote US & Delima Beaulieu Canada
COTE, Lucille Rita, Feb 24 1918 Sex:F Child# 1 Theobald Cote Nashua, NH & Catherine Rogers Nashua, NH
COTE, Lucille Rochelle, Jan 18 1914 Sex:F Child# 4 Prudent Cote Canada & Aurelie Levesque Canada
COTE, M A Alice, Apr 20 1894 Sex:F Child# 3 Narcisse Cote Canada & Wilhelmine Deschene Canada
COTE, M A Helene, Mar 22 1895 Sex:F Child# 2 Joseph Cote Canada & Marie Dube Canada
COTE, M Adeline Josephine, Apr 15 1915 Sex:F Child# 3 Wilfred Cote Nashua, NH & Josephine Starrett US
COTE, M Adrienne Alice, Jul 5 1921 Sex:F Child# 1 William Cote NH & Eveline Cloutier Mass
COTE, M Anne, Jan 14 1894 Sex:F Child# 1 Joseph Cote Canada & M Louise Dube Canada
COTE, M Bernadette D, Mar 14 1907 Sex:F Child# 9 Narcisse Cote Canada & Wilhelm Deschenes Canada
COTE, M Georgiana B, Apr 9 1902 Sex:F Child# 7 Narcisse Cote Canada & Wilhelmine Deschenes Canada
COTE, M Jeanne Lina, Aug 17 1908 Sex:F Child# 14 Antoine Cote Canada & Victoria Gagnon Canada
COTE, M Marg Dolores, Mar 13 1922 Sex:F Child# 1 Albert Cote Canada & Marie Aime Lambert Nashua, NH
COTE, Madeline Theresa, Jun 28 1925 Sex:F Child# 2 Romeo Cote Canada & R A Ossaut Canada
COTE, Margaret, Mar 13 1898 Sex:F Child# 1 Alfred E Cote Nashua, NH & Margaret Cote Boston, MA
COTE, Margaret Leona Marie, Jun 14 1925 Sex:F Child# 1 Ephrem Cote Canada & Marie Morin Canada
COTE, Maria, May 5 1897 Sex:F Child# 3 Joseph Cote Canada & Marie Louise Dube Canada
COTE, Marie, Feb 20 1894 Sex:F Child# 4 Nazaire Cote Canada & Adele Martel Canada
COTE, Marie, Sep 23 1895 Sex:F Child# 7 Henri Cote Canada & Methilde Boisvert Canada
COTE, Marie, Jun 16 1904 Sex:F Child# 1 Jesse Cote Canada & Regina Lemieux Canada
COTE, Marie A, Feb 23 1898 Sex:F Child# 4 Magorique Cote Canada & Mary L Blain W Boylston, MA
COTE, Marie Adelaide, Jun 20 1898 Sex:F Child# 8 Henri Cote Canada & Mathilda Boisvert Canada
COTE, Marie Albina, Mar 27 1892 Sex:F Child# 1 Michel Cote Canada & Celina Caron Canada
COTE, Marie Albina Eva, Feb 19 1899 Sex:F Child# 3 Louis Cote Canada & Stephanie Roy St Albans, VT
COTE, Marie Alma C, Apr 9 1898 Sex:F Child# 4 Joseph Cote Canada & Marie Dube Canada
COTE, Marie Anne, Aug 21 1900 Sex:F Child# 5 Joseph Cote Canada & Marie Louise Dube Canada
COTE, Marie Anne B, May 25 1902 Sex:F Child# 2 Ferdinand Cote Canada & Emelie Dube Canada
COTE, Marie Anne Y, Jul 17 1905 Sex:F Child# 4 Gilbert Cote Canada & Angele Brisson Canada
COTE, Marie Bertha L, Feb 19 1892 Sex:F Child# 3 Nazaire Cote Canada & Adele Martin Canada
COTE, Marie H C, Jun 1 1898 Sex:F Child# 5 Narcisse Cote Canada & W Deschenes Canada
COTE, Marie J J J, Mar 18 1897 Sex:F Child# 19 Eusebe Cote Canada & Adeline Gravelle Canada
COTE, Marie L, Apr 1 1895 Sex:F Child# 3 Pierre Cote Canada & Alma Trottier St Albans, VT
COTE, Marie L, Sep 7 1896 Sex:F Child# 3 Magorique Cote Canada & Mary Janne Blain W Boylston, MA
COTE, Marie Louise, Jul 20 1897 Sex:F Child# 4 Stanislas Cote Canada & Ophidie Deschenes Canada
COTE, Marie Pauline Jean, Aug 30 1933 Sex:F Child# 4 Leon Cote Canada & Dora Lampron Nashua, NH
COTE, Marie R Evalienne, Aug 20 1917 Sex:F Child# 2 Jean Baptiste Cote Canada & Delvina Mechaud Canada
COTE, Marie Regina, May 14 1905 Sex:F Child# 3 Cleophas Cote Canada & Delima Berube Canada
COTE, Marie Rose, Jul 7 1909 Sex:F Child# 2 Aime Cote Canada & Clarina Caron Canada
COTE, Marie Rose Rolande, Jun 6 1922 Sex:F Child# 2 Edmond Cote Nashua, NH & Delima Beaulieu Canada
COTE, Marie S L, May 8 1897 Sex:F Child# 2 Louis Cote Canada & Stephanie Roy St Albans, VT
COTE, Marie Sylvia B, Jun 1 1908 Sex:F Child# 3 Fernando Cote Canada & Eliza Morin NH
COTE, Marie Sylvia L, Nov 11 1927 Sex:F Child# 4 Sylvio Cote Canada & Leda Labelle Nashua, NH
COTE, Marie Yvonne, Jul 2 1902 Sex:F Child# 12 Antoine Cote Canada & Victoria Gagnon Canada
COTE, Marie Yvonne, Jan 17 1904 Sex:F Child# 8 Victor Cote Canada & Marie Dionne Canada
COTE, Mariette Constance, Dec 8 1925 Sex:F Child# 3 Sylvio Cote Canada & Leda Labelle Nashua, NH
COTE, Mary Amerlia Gilbert, Mar 30 1912 Sex:F Child# 3 Alpheu Cote Canada & Amelia Marquis Canada
COTE, Mary Arleen Claudett, Mar 29 1935 Sex:F Child# 5 Leon Cote Canada & Dora Lampron Nashua, NH
COTE, Mary C, Dec 12 1889 Sex:F Child# 3 Edward Cote Canada & Mary J Jackson Canada
COTE, Mary C S, Dec 12 1890 Sex:F Child# 3 Emanuel Cote Canada & Mary J C Jackson Canada
COTE, Mary Elizabeth Ella, Sep 3 1923 Sex:F Child# 2 Joseph Cote Canada & Anna Phillips Hamel Nashua, NH

COTE, Mary Rita Claire, Jan 18 1935 Sex:F Child# 7 Robert Cote Canada & Celedase Desrochers Sanbornville, NH
COTE, Maurice Raymond, Feb 16 1928 Sex:M Child# 7 Francis X Cote Canada & Delise Blais Canada
COTE, N Antonio, Dec 14 1891 Sex:M Child# 1 Narcisse Cote Canada & Wilhelmine Cote Canada
COTE, Norman Joseph, Nov 16 1935 Sex:M Child# 2 Alphonse Cote Canada & Marcia Theroux Nashua, NH
COTE, Norman Marc Hilaire, Apr 2 1935 Sex:M Child# 1 Marc Cote Canada & Jeannette Paradis Canada
COTE, Normand Donald, Jul 5 1935 Sex:M Child# 3 Emile Cote Canada & Diane Lafrance Nashua, NH
COTE, Obia, Nov 27 1893 Sex:F Child# 3 Stanislas Cote Canada & Ophidie Deschenes Canada
COTE, Oliva Emile, Sep 10 1900 Sex:M Child# 3 Ludger Cote Canada & Marie Leblanc Canada
COTE, Oliva Emma, Dec 29 1904 Sex:F Child# 1 Albert Cote US & Emma Dodge Canada
COTE, Patricia Beatrice, Dec 11 1928 Sex:F Child# 4 Alfred Cote Nashua, NH & Annette Chagnon Canada
COTE, Paul, Oct 8 1915 Sex:M Child# 10 Louis Cote Canada & Stephanie Roy St Albans, VT
COTE, Pauline Gloria, Jun 17 1935 Sex:F Child# 1 Arthur Cote Quebec & Alberta Gagne Quebec
COTE, Pearl Robert, Sep 9 1912 Sex:M Child# 6 Cleophas Cote Canada & Juliana Berube Canada
COTE, Philippe L E, Mar 26 1894 Sex:M Child# 1 Magloire Cote Canada & Marie I Blain Canada
COTE, Rachel Germaine, Aug 19 1931 Sex:F Child# 4 Alberic Cote Canada & Cecile Hebert Nashua, NH
COTE, Rachel Gertrude, Aug 13 1927 Sex:F Child# 2 Emile Cote Canada & Diana Lafrance Canada
COTE, Raymond B, Aug 23 1910 Sex:M Child# 5 Cleophas Cote Canada & Julianna Berube Canada
COTE, Raymond Gerard, Aug 15 1929 Sex:M Child# 3 Edmund Cote Nashua, NH & Delima Beaulieu Canada
COTE, Raymond Leo, Dec 15 1923 Sex:M Child# 3 Ernest Cote NH & Julienne Strong NH
COTE, Raymond Roland, Mar 8 1927 Sex:M Child# 1 Lorenzo Cote Canada & Eva Desclos Nashua, NH
COTE, Regina, Apr 30 1896 Sex:F Child# 5 Nazaire Cote Canada & Odile Martin Canada
COTE, Regina Gertrude L, Aug 4 1915 Sex:F Child# 14 Victor Cote Canada & Marie Dionne Canada
COTE, Richard Patrick, Nov 10 1928 Sex:M Child# 4 Joseph Cote Canada & Anna Hamel Nashua, NH
COTE, Rita Leona Lea, May 23 1927 Sex:F Child# 1 Edmond Cote Nashua, NH & Lea Raby Nashua, NH
COTE, Robert Charles, Jul 10 1910 Sex:M Child# 2 Francois Cote Canada & Anna Salva Canada
COTE, Robert Joseph Paul, Aug 14 1935 Sex:M Child# 1 Paul Cote Canada & Barbara Warden Nashua, NH
COTE, Robert Leon Andre, Apr 3 1933 Sex:M Child# 6 Robert Cote Canada & Celedas Durocher Sanborn, NH
COTE, Robert Normand, May 22 1929 Sex:M Child# 1 Raoul Cote Nashua, NH & Rose Lamarre Milford, NH
COTE, Roger, Apr 9 1927 Sex:M Child# 3 Edmund Cote Nashua, NH & Delima Beaulieu Canada
COTE, Roger Desire, Jun 2 1932 Sex:M Child# 5 Romeo Cote Canada & Rose A Ausant Nashua, NH
COTE, Roland Jos Etienne, Mar 9 1917 Sex:M Child# 1 Ernest Cote NH & Lillienne Strong NH
COTE, Rose, Sep 15 1934 Sex:F Child# 1 Thomas Cote Nashua, NH & Claire Lavoie Nashua, NH
COTE, Rose Alma, Apr 22 1899 Sex:F Child# 2 Gilbert Cote Canada & Angela Brisson Canada
COTE, Rose Anna, Apr 24 1893 Sex:F Child# 5 Henry Cote Canada & Mathilde Boisvert Canada
COTE, Rose Elizabeth, Mar 3 1910 Sex:F Child# 8 Louis Cote Canada & Stephanie Roy St Albans, VT
COTE, Simeon, Apr 7 1912 Sex:M Child# 9 Louis Cote Canada & Stephanie Roy St Albans, VT
COTE, Simone Adrienne, Mar 28 1907 Sex:F Child# 4 Cleophas Cote Canada & Julie Anna Berube Canada
COTE, Sylvia Antoine, Mar 8 1918 Sex:M Child# 1 Leon Cote Canada & Dora Lampron US
COTE, Sylvia Lauriane, Oct 11 1906 Sex:F Child# 7 Louis Cote Canada & Stephanie Roy St Albans, VT
COTE, Theresa Emma, Nov 4 1925 Sex:F Child# 2 Alberic Cote Canada & Cecile Hebert Nashua, NH
COTE, Therese, Oct 10 1895 Sex:F Child# 2 Joseph Cote Canada & M Louise Dube Canada
COTE, Thomas, Apr 20 1899 Sex:M Child# 3 Joseph Cote Canada & Marie Perrault Canada
COTE, Thomas Romeo, Jan 31 1910 Sex:M Child# 11 Victoire Cote Canada & Marie Dionne Canada
COTE, Unknown, May 7 1893 Sex:F Child#   Joseph S Cote Manchester & Victorine Lovely E Douglas, MA
COTE, Unknown, Oct 8 1894 Sex:M Child# 2 Charles Cote Canada & Rose Pelletier Canada Stillborn
COTE, Unknown, Feb 6 1896 Sex:F Child# 18 Eusebe Cote Canada & Adelaide Gravel Canada Stillborn
COTE, Unknown, Jun 25 1899 Sex:M Child# 11 George Cote Canada & Isabelle Cayer Newport, VT Stillborn
COTE, Unknown, Sep 25 1907 Sex: Child# 1 Alphe Cote Canada & Aurelia Marquis Canada Stillborn
COTE, Unknown, Jul 9 1922 Sex:M Child# 1 Henry Cote Nashua, NH & Alice St Jean Canada Stillborn
COTE, Unknown, Mar 25 1924 Sex:F Child# 4 John Cote Maine & Josephine Bolduc Canada Stillborn
COTE, Unknown, Jul 22 1925 Sex:M Child# 5 Edmond Cote Nashua, NH & Emma Dupont Canada Stillborn
COTE, Unknown, May 26 1926 Sex:F Child# 1 Edmond Cote Nashua, NH & Lea Raby Nashua, NH
COTE, Unknown, Jan 28 1927 Sex:M Child# 6 Edward Cote Nashua, NH & Emma Dupont Canada Stillborn
COTE, Unknown, Aug 15 1932 Sex:M Child# 1 Alphonse Cote Mt Carmelle, PQ & Marcia Theroux Nashua, NH Stillborn
COTE, Unknown, Jan 8 1934 Sex:M Child# 5 Pierre Charles Cote Manchester, NH & Bessie Evelyn Boyer Manchester, NH
COTE, Viatem A Ed, Jul 13 1902 Sex:M Child# 1 Cleophas Cote Canada & Juliana Berube Canada
COTE, Wilfred Samuel, Jul 30 1912 Sex:M Child# 2 Wilfred Cote Nashua, NH & Josephine Storrett US
COTE, Wilfrid Victor, Feb 28 1924 Sex:M Child# 3 Wilfrid V Cote Canada & A Deschesne Nashua, NH
COTE, William, Oct 28 1906 Sex:M Child# 7 Joseph L Cote Canada & Agnes Proulx Canada
COTE, Willie, Mar 3 1906 Sex:M Child# 2 Eugene Cote Canada & Henriette Emond Canada
COTE, Yvette Lucille, Feb 1 1931 Sex:F Child# 2 Joseph Cote Canada & Antoinette Coutu Canada
COTIE, Elie Theobald, Feb 8 1888 Sex:M Child# 4 Edmond Cotie Canada & Victoria Breault Canada
COTIE, Emma, Jan 1 1888 Sex:F Child# 3 Henry Cotie Canada & Metilda Boisvert Canada
COTIE, Rossanna, Nov 25 1888 Sex:F Child# 1 Stainslus Cotie Canada & Oppidie Deschane Canada
COTSONICUS, John Demetrius, Apr 3 1916 Sex:M Child# 1 John Cotsonicus Greece & Rose Anna Charest Canada
COTSONIKAS, Mary, Oct 18 1916 Sex:F Child# 3 James Cotsonikas Greece & Dolphie Krass Greece
COTSONIKAS, Unknown, Oct 13 1921 Sex:F Child# 6 Costas Cotsonikas Greece & Sophia Krenzt Greece
COUBRON, Irene Yvonne, Sep 14 1903 Sex:F Child# 9 David Coubron Canada & Emma Belanger Canada
COUGHLIN, Adeline, Nov 23 1908 Sex:F Child# 6 William Coughlin Cleary, OH & Philomene Bonneville Canada
COUGHLIN, Helen Davenport, Dec 3 1908 Sex:F Child# 1 Benj F D Coughlin Woburn, MA & Admah L Davenport Ayer, MA
COUGHLIN, James Earl Martin, Oct 21 1923 Sex:M Child# 3 Leo A Coughlin Maine & Aurelie Landry NH
COUGHLIN, Leonard Lewis, Mar 27 1921 Sex:M Child# 2 Leo Coughlin Maine & Aurelie Landry NH
COUGHLIN, Marie Alice, Sep 22 1910 Sex:F Child# 7 William Coughlin Ohio & Philomene Bonville Canada

COUGHLIN, Maurice, Jan 18 1897 Sex:M Child# 1 Maurice Coughlin
COUGHLIN, Nellie, Nov 30 1906 Sex:F Child# 5 William Coughlin Olena, OH & Philomene Banville Canada
COUGHLIN, Richard Antoine, May 17 1918 Sex:M Child# 1 Leo A Coughlin Maine & Aurelie Landry NH
COULAHAN, Unknown, Jan 7 1891 Sex:M Child# 1 John H Coulahan VT & Mary A Kearns Manchester, NH
COULKEEN, Edward Henry, Oct 24 1895 Sex:M Child# 4 John Coulkeen Ireland & Mary Kelley Ireland
COULOMBE, Claude Louis, Feb 26 1933 Sex:M Child# 2 Armand Coulombe Canada & Aldea Ray Canada
COULOMBE, Joseph, Apr 4 1930 Sex:M Child# 1 Armand A Coulombe Canada & Adela Roy Canada Stillborn
COULOMBE, Marie L D, Jul 4 1896 Sex:F Child# 4 Joseph Coulombe Canada & Lumina Paquette Canada
COULOMBE, Marie Theresa C, Sep 15 1929 Sex:F Child# 1 Arthur Coulombe Canada & Rose Beaupre Canada
COULOMBE, Pauline, Aug 19 1934 Sex:F Child# 2 Joseph Coulombe Canada & Jeannette Martin Nashua, NH
COULOMBE, Theresa Elsie, Apr 6 1932 Sex:F Child# 1 Joseph Coulombe Canada & Jeanette Martin Manchester, NH
COUNTERMANCHE, Mitchel I, Mar 8 1890 Sex:M Child# 1 Alb't Countermanche Nashua, NH & Kate Mamthaugh Ireland
COUNTERMARCH, Adie, Jan 23 1888 Sex:F Child# 3 Louis Countermarch St Dominque, PQ & Everline Lawrence Manchester,NH
COUNTERMARCHE, Marie, Sep 7 1888 Sex:F Child# 8 Regis Countermarche Canada & Narzette Collette Canada
COURBANT, Maurice Edmund, May 12 1934 Sex:M Child# 7 Wilfrid Courbant NH & Ovise Burns Nashua, NH
COURBERON, Marie Andrea, Jul 21 1898 Sex:F Child# 7 David Courberon Canada & Emma Belanger Canada
COURBRON, Emma Ida, Nov 8 1900 Sex:F Child# 8 David Courbron Canada & Emma Belanger Canada
COURCHAINE, Richard William, Mar 9 1926 Sex:M Child# 1 W Courchaine Westford, MA & Eva Pine Westford, MA
COURCIS, Irene Eleonard, Jul 11 1892 Sex:F Child# 4 Joseph Courcis Canada & Marie Lessard Canada
COURCIS, Joseph, Jan 29 1891 Sex:M Child# 3 Joseph Courcis Canada & Marie Lessard Canada
COURCIS, Marie, Sep 12 1888 Sex:F Child# 1 Joseph Courcis Canada & Marie Gessard Nashua, NH
COURCY, Antoinette, Jul 11 1901 Sex:F Child# 9 Joseph Courcy Canada & Marie Lessard Canada
COURCY, Florida Yvonne, Dec 13 1906 Sex:F Child# 4 Emile Courcy Canada & Flavie Caron Canada
COURCY, John George, Nov 23 1891 Sex:M Child# 1 John Courcy Canada & Josephine Beaulier Canada
COURCY, Joseph, Apr 16 1899 Sex:M Child# 8 Joseph Courcy Canada & Marie Lessard Canada
COURCY, Joseph E Albert, Oct 30 1896 Sex:M Child# 5 Johnny Courcy Canada & Josephine Beaulieu Canada
COURCY, Joseph Jean Emile, Dec 16 1902 Sex:M Child# 1 Emile Courcy Canada & Flavie Caron Canada
COURCY, Leo Archie Emile, May 1 1930 Sex:M Child# 1 Emile Courcy Nashua, NH & Pearl Blow Nashua, NH
COURCY, Lillian Rose Alice, Nov 5 1931 Sex:F Child# 2 Emile Courcy Nashua, NH & Pearl Blow Nashua, NH
COURCY, M Josephine, Dec 21 1895 Sex:F Child#  Joseph Courcy Canada & Marie Lessard Canada
COURCY, Marie, Jan 4 1904 Sex:F Child# 10 Joseph Courcy Canada & Marie Lessard Canada
COURCY, Marie Louise, Oct 3 1897 Sex:F Child# 7 Joseph Courcy Canada & Marie Lessard Canada
COURCY, Marie Rosanna, May 10 1904 Sex:F Child# 2 Emile Courcy Canada & Flavie Caron Canada
COURCY, Marie Rosilda, Dec 31 1893 Sex:F Child# 5 Joseph Courcy Canada & Marie Lessard Canada
COURCY, Misael, Sep 5 1905 Sex:M Child# 3 Emile Courcy Canada & Sophie Caron Canada Stillborn
COURCY, Unknown, Dec 3 1895 Sex:F Child# 4 John Courcy Canada & Josephine Beaulieu Canada
COUREY, Jos Clarence Robert, Feb 11 1934 Sex:M Child# 4 Emile Courey Nashua, NH & Pearl Blow Nashua, NH
COURNOLLIER, Marie E, Sep 7 1890 Sex:F Child# 5 Napoleon Cournollier Canada & Malvina Masse Canada
COURONIS, Samuel, Oct 26 1911 Sex:M Child# 1 Lewis Couronis Greece & Dena Spylios Greece
COURONIS, Xanthipe, Oct 14 1917 Sex:F Child# 5 Louis Couronis Greece & Diana Greece
COURONNIS, James, Nov 20 1913 Sex:M Child# 2 Louis Couronnis Greece & Diana Spylios Greece
COUROUNIS, Mary Lena, Mar 3 1914 Sex:F Child# 1 James Courounis Greece & Lena Bilodeau Nashua, NH
COUROUNIS, Unknown, Nov 23 1921 Sex:M Child# 3 James Courounis Greece & Lena Biladon US
COUROUNIS, Unknown, Nov 24 1932 Sex:M Child# 8 James Courounis Greece & Lena Bilodeau Nashua, NH
COUROUNIS, Unknown, Jul 23 1934 Sex:F Child# 9 James Courounis Greece & Lena Bilodeau Nashua, NH
COURSY, Therese Joan, Jan 30 1933 Sex:F Child# 3 Emile Coursy Nashua, NH & Pearl Bleau Nashua, NH
COURTEAU, Arthur Joseph, Jul 23 1920 Sex:M Child# 2 Joseph Courteau Methuen, MA & Josephine Ouellette Lawrence, MA
COURTEAU, M Loretta Eveline, Nov 30 1922 Sex:F Child# 3 Joseph Courteau Methuen, MA & Josephine Ouellette Lawrence
COURTEMANCHE, Albert, Feb 13 1925 Sex:M Child# 14 Joseph Courtemanche Nashua, NH & Evan Desroleau Canada
COURTEMANCHE, Alfred, Feb 13 1925 Sex:M Child# 13 Joseph Courtemanche Nashua, NH & Evan Desroleau Canada
COURTEMANCHE, Beatrice Cecile, Dec 12 1915 Sex:F Child# 6 Joseph Courtemanche Nashua, NH & Evangeline Dupont Canada
COURTEMANCHE, Blanche Cecile, Jan 11 1923 Sex:F Child# 3 Albert Courtemanche Manchester, NH & Virginia Moquin
COURTEMANCHE, Clarisse Olivette, Feb 3 1901 Sex:F Child# 9 Regis Courtemanche Canada & Arselie Collette Canada
COURTEMANCHE, Emery R, May 24 1901 Sex:M Child# 2 Alfred Courtemanche Canada & Rosalie Guenette Canada
COURTEMANCHE, Eva, Apr 5 1912 Sex:F Child# 5 Joseph Courtemanche US & Evangeline Deroleau Canada
COURTEMANCHE, Evangeline Lillian, Jan 21 1931 Sex:F Child# 1 (No Parents Listed)
COURTEMANCHE, George, Apr 21 1894 Sex:M Child# 3 Euclid Courtemanche Canada & Eva Cote Canada
COURTEMANCHE, Germaine Juliette, Mar 27 1911 Sex:F Child# 4 Joseph Courtemanche US & Evan Desrouleau Canada
COURTEMANCHE, Henri, Dec 22 1907 Sex:M Child# 1 Joseph Courtemanche US & Evangeline Dupont Canada
COURTEMANCHE, Irene, Jun 26 1914 Sex:F Child# 7 Joseph Courtemanche Nashua, NH & Evangelina Duclos Canada
COURTEMANCHE, Joseph, Jun 3 1891 Sex:M Child# 1 Euclid Courtemanche Nashua, NH & Eva Cote Canada
COURTEMANCHE, Joseph, Feb 3 1927 Sex:M Child# 1 (No Parents Listed)
COURTEMANCHE, Leo, Nov 16 1910 Sex:M Child# 2 Adelard Courtemanche Hudson, MA & Ida Lacroix Nashua, NH
COURTEMANCHE, Leon Hector, Jun 19 1909 Sex:M Child# 2 Joseph Courtemanche US & Evangeline Dupont Canada
COURTEMANCHE, Lilian Marguerite, May 26 1913 Sex:F Child# 6 Joseph Courtemanche US & Evangeline Desroleau Canada
COURTEMANCHE, Lillian, Feb 5 1898 Sex:F Child# 2 Alfred Courtemanche Canada & Rosalie Guerette Canada
COURTEMANCHE, Malvina Eva, Sep 25 1892 Sex:F Child# 3 Alfred Courtemanche Canada & Ernestine Brien Canada
COURTEMANCHE, Marie Marguerite R, Jun 8 1927 Sex:F Child# 6 A Courtemanche Manchester, NH & Virginia Moquin Canada
COURTEMANCHE, Marie Theresa Violet, Jun 8 1927 Sex:F Child# 5 A Courtemanche Manchester, NH & Virginia Moquin
COURTEMANCHE, Mary Leola, Jul 15 1907 Sex:F Child# 1 Leo Courtemanche Hudson, MA & Mary Demers Manchester, NH
COURTEMANCHE, Moris Alvin, Oct 18 1920 Sex:M Child# 10 Jos Courtemanche Canada & Evangeline Dupont Canada
COURTEMANCHE, Normand Romeo, Feb 19 1908 Sex:M Child# 1 Adelard Courtemanche Hudson, NH & Ida Lacroix Nashua, NH
COURTEMANCHE, Paul Emile, May 11 1935 Sex:M Child# 1 (No Parents Listed)

COURTEMANCHE, Rachel June, Jun 4 1928 Sex:F Child# 16 Jos Courtemanche Nashua, NH & E Derouleau Canada
COURTEMANCHE, Robert William, Nov 14 1934 Sex:M Child# 1 Henry Courtemanche Nashua, NH & Genevieve Milinkevic
COURTEMANCHE, Ulric, Oct 31 1889 Sex:M Child# 1 Ulric Courtemanche Nashua, NH & Lucy Lyons Nashua, NH
COURTEMARCHE, Adeline, Jul 20 1888 Sex:F Child# 1 Alric Courtemarche Canada & Lucy Lyons Canada
COURTEMARCHE, Exilia, Nov 13 1893 Sex:F Child# 1 Hector Courtemarche Canada & Alphonsine Gendron Canada
COURTEMARCHE, Marie Rosanna, Jun 29 1891 Sex:F Child# 1 Alfred Courtemarche Canada & Ernestine Brien Canada
COURTEMARCHE, Mary Christine, Dec 23 1893 Sex:F Child# 2 Albert Courtemarche Nashua, NH & Kate Murtaugh Ireland
COURTEMARCHE, Philip, Jun 25 1892 Sex:M Child# 2 Euclide Courtemarche Canada & Eva Cote Canada
COURTEMARSH, John Lyons, Jun 10 1891 Sex:M Child# 3 Ulric Courtemarsh Canada & Lucy L Lyons Nashua, NH
COURTEMARSH, Lucy Irene, Mar 11 1895 Sex:F Child# 4 Ulric Courtemarsh Canada & Lucy J Lyons Nashua, NH
COURTEMAUCHE, Catherine, Apr 28 1895 Sex:F Child# 3 Albert Courtemauche Nashua, NH & Catherine Martin Ireland
COURTEMAUCHE, Nelson, Oct 27 1893 Sex:M Child# 1 Fred Courtemauche Canada & Celina Picteau Canada
COURTES, Spiros, Dec 27 1918 Sex:M Child# 3 Andreas Courtes Greece & Greece
COURTMAUCHE, Adjutor, Dec 7 1893 Sex:M Child# 1 Alfred Courtmauche Canada & Rosalie Guenette Canada
COUSIGNEY, J Baptiste, Jun 17 1900 Sex:M Child# 2 Joseph Cousigney Canada & Theotis Blanchard Canada
COUSIGNY, Marie Albina, Feb 8 1903 Sex:F Child# 3 Joseph Cousigny Canada & Theotis Blanchard Nashua, NH
COUSTARAS, Christos, Sep 10 1921 Sex:M Child# 1 Dem Coustaras Greece & Azelaia Siamon Greece
COUTARA, Edward Paul, Jun 1 1920 Sex:M Child# 1 Edward Coutara Nashua, NH & Mabel Smith Nashua, NH
COUTCHARLIS, Unknown, Jul 26 1927 Sex:M Child# 2 George Coutcharlis Greece & Mary Savate Greece
COUTCHAVHS, Melponaene, Apr 17 1926 Sex:F Child# 1 George Coutchavhs Greece & Mary Sarate Greece
COUTEMANCHE, Doris Jeannette, May 16 1923 Sex:F Child# 11 Jos Coutemanche NH & Evelyn Dupont Canada
COUTSOMIKIS, Marie Agnes, May 4 1918 Sex:F Child# 2 John Coutsomikis Greece & Rose Charest Canada
COUTSONICA, Drakula, Mar 18 1908 Sex:F Child# 10 Dimite Coutsonica Greece & Anarstassia Fardele Greece
COUTSONIKAS, Despon, May 11 1918 Sex:F Child# 1 Michael Coutsonikas Greece & Katherine O'Neil Manchester, NH
COUTSONIKAS, Katherine, Mar 24 1922 Sex:F Child# 4 Michael Coutsonikas Greece & Katherine O'Neil Manchester, NH
COUTSONIKAS, Nellie, Mar 10 1918 Sex:F Child# 4 Zise Coutsonikas Greece & Sofia Kryer Greece
COUTSONIKIS, Horace Andre, Mar 16 1920 Sex:M Child# 3 John Coutsonikis Greece & Rose Charest Canada
COUTURE, Alice Lucille, Apr 8 1919 Sex:F Child# 3 George Couture Canada & Agnes Fortin Three Rivers, MA
COUTURE, Annette Olivette, Jul 31 1921 Sex:F Child# 2 Arthur Couture Nashua, NH & Adrienne Girard Canada
COUTURE, Donald Lionel, Feb 24 1931 Sex:M Child# 1 Lionel Couture Gardner, MA & Rose Derosier Canada
COUTURE, Ernest R, Apr 10 1911 Sex:M Child# 8 Fortune Couture Canada & Melanie Paris Canada
COUTURE, Evelyn Jeannette, Dec 8 1923 Sex:F Child# 2 Ancelet Couture Nashua, NH & Blanche Salvi Nashua, NH
COUTURE, Frances Theresa Rita, Aug 13 1925 Sex:F Child# 2 Joseph A Couture NH & Eugenie Dichard NH
COUTURE, Henri, Dec 2 1900 Sex:M Child# 5 Fortnia Couture Canada & Melenie Paris Canada
COUTURE, Ida Florida, Aug 7 1900 Sex:F Child# 1 Arthur Couture Canada & Alice Fournier Canada
COUTURE, Joseph A F, Apr 13 1897 Sex:M Child# 3 Fortuna Couture Canada & Melanie Paris Canada
COUTURE, Joseph Adelard, Mar 10 1899 Sex:M Child# 1 Adelard Couture Nashua, NH & Julie Chretien Canada
COUTURE, Joseph Amedee, Feb 16 1896 Sex:M Child# 4 Antoine Couture Canada & Alphonse Archambault Canada
COUTURE, Joseph Anaclet, Nov 27 1893 Sex:M Child# 1 Fortuna Couture Canada & Melanie Paris Canada
COUTURE, Joseph Edmond, May 19 1898 Sex:M Child# 4 Fortuna Couture Canada & Melanie Paris Canada
COUTURE, Maria, Jun 27 1892 Sex:F Child# 2 Antoine Couture Canada & Alph'ne Archambault Canada
COUTURE, Marie Emma, Aug 17 1897 Sex:F Child# 5 Antoine Couture Canada & A Archambault Canada
COUTURE, Marie Laure, Sep 5 1896 Sex:F Child# 3 Joseph Couture Canada & Mathilde Sinclair Canada
COUTURE, Marie Lea Irene, Aug 18 1913 Sex:F Child# 3 George Couture Canada & Agnes Fortin Canada
COUTURE, Marie Louise, Mar 17 1895 Sex:F Child# 2 Fortuna Couture Canada & Melaine Paris Canada
COUTURE, Marie Lucia, Apr 10 1902 Sex:F Child# 11 Pierre Couture Canada & Virginie Bonneau Canada
COUTURE, Marie O I, Oct 12 1905 Sex:F Child# 7 Fortuna Couture Canada & Melanie Paris Canada
COUTURE, Melvine M L, Nov 10 1901 Sex:F Child# 6 Portuna Couture Canada & Milanie Paris Canada
COUTURE, Napoleon Victor, Jan 2 1891 Sex:M Child# 1 Antoine Couture Canada & A Archambault Canada
COUTURE, Norman Arthur, Jan 10 1926 Sex:M Child# 3 Anaclet Couture Nashua, NH & Blanche Salvail Nashua, NH
COUTURE, Odelie Jeanne, Apr 3 1922 Sex:F Child# 1 Joseph A Couture Milton, NH & Jennie C Dichard Merrimack, NH
COUTURE, Raymond, Jun 16 1919 Sex:M Child# 1 Arthur Couture Nashua, NH & Adrienne Girard Canada
COUTURE, Romeo, Nov 3 1920 Sex:M Child# 1 Anaclet Couture Nashua, NH & Blanch Salvail Nashua, NH
COUTURE, Unknown, Jun 9 1891 Sex:M Child# 2 Antoine Couture Canada & A Archambault Canada Stillborn
COUTURIE, Yvonne Theresa, Mar 20 1927 Sex:F Child# 4 Leo Couturie Canada & Alida Leveillee Nashua, NH
COUTURIER, Antoinette, Feb 22 1904 Sex:F Child# 7 Eugene Couturier Canada & Leontine Gagnon Canada
COUTURIER, Daniel Eugene, May 3 1928 Sex:M Child# 1 Eugene Couturier Canada & Rachel Laurence Nashua, NH
COUTURIER, Delmina G, Jul 16 1902 Sex:F Child# 6 Eugene Couturier Canada & Leontine Gagnon Canada
COUTURIER, Eugene, Oct 22 1900 Sex:M Child# 5 Eugene Couturier Canada & Livitine Gagnon Canada
COUTURIER, Gaston Jos Eugene, Mar 11 1932 Sex:M Child# 6 Leo Couturier Canada & Bertha Girard Canada
COUTURIER, Jacqueline Mary, Feb 28 1935 Sex:F Child# 9 Leo Couturier Canada & Bertha Gerard Canada
COUTURIER, Marie, Mar 11 1892 Sex:F Child# 2 Stanislas Couturier Canada & Melina Mignault Canada
COUTURIER, Marie Giselle, Apr 25 1924 Sex:F Child# 1 Leo Couturier Canada & Bertha Gerard Canada
COUTURIER, Marie Theresa Edna, Jul 2 1926 Sex:F Child# 6 J B Couturier Canada & A Belleville Canada
COUTURIER, Normand, Jul 26 1928 Sex:M Child# 4 Leo Couturier Canada & Bertha Girard Canada
COUTURIER, Paul Emile, Oct 15 1925 Sex:M Child# 2 Leo Couturier Canada & Bertha Girard Canada
COUTURIER, Robert Joseph, Feb 28 1935 Sex:M Child# 8 Leo Couturier Canada & Bertha Gerard Canada
COUTURIER, Robert Normand, Oct 9 1922 Sex:M Child# 3 Doria Couturier Canada & Flora Lozeau Canada
COVEY, Arnold Dean, Oct 20 1910 Sex:M Child# 2 Harry B Covey New York & Marion Dean Scotland
COVEY, Britnell, Aug 26 1911 Sex:M Child# 5 Charles L Covey Vermont & Elizabeth O Tibbetts NH
COVEY, Dorothy Mae, May 1 1921 Sex:F Child# 4 Albert Covey Scranton, PA & Ethel Chandler Nashua, NH
COVEY, Earle Richard, Oct 4 1922 Sex:M Child# 5 Albert Covey Schroom Lake, NY & Ethel Chandler Nashua, NH
COVEY, Edgar Richard, Feb 12 1929 Sex:M Child# 1 Herbert R Covey Nashua, NH & Helen Stickney Nashua, NH

COVEY, Edward Robert, Feb 12 1929 Sex:M Child# 2 Herbert R Covey Nashua, NH & Helen Stickney Nashua, NH
COVEY, Gertrude Elizabeth, May 1 1921 Sex:F Child# 3 Albert Covey Scranton, PA & Ethel Chandler Nashua, NH
COVEY, Gladys Grace, Mar 4 1926 Sex:F Child# 6 Albert Covey Schroon Lake, NY & Ethel Chandler Nashua, NH
COVEY, Harry Raymond, Aug 18 1909 Sex:M Child# 1 Harry B Covey New York & Marion Dean Scotland
COVEY, Herbert R, May 10 1930 Sex:M Child# 3 Herbert R Covey Nashua, NH & Helen Stickney Nashua, NH
COVEY, Hubert R, Oct 1 1905 Sex:M Child# 4 Charles W Covey Ellenburg, NY & Daisy P Swallow Rye, NH
COVEY, Lester Lorenzo, Mar 19 1908 Sex:M Child# 2 William H Covey Schroon Lake, NY & Annis Lamb Chateaugay, NY
COVEY, Lola Ida, Aug 26 1911 Sex:F Child# 6 Charles L Covey Vermont & Elizabeth O Tibbetts NH
COVEY, Paul Emery, Feb 22 1935 Sex:M Child# 2 Harry Covey Nashua, NH & Lucille Bourassa Nashua, NH
COVEY, Reid Lyle, Jun 13 1935 Sex:M Child# 1 Lyle H Covey Ellenburg, NY & Helen Reid Nashua, NH
COVEY, Robert Earl, Jun 26 1920 Sex:M Child# 2 Albert Covey New York, NY & Ethel Chandler Nashua, NH
COVEY, Ronald Harry, Apr 30 1932 Sex:M Child# 1 Harry Covey Nashua, NH & Lucille Bourassa Nashua, NH
COVEY, Unknown, May 21 1900 Sex:M Child# 2 Charles W Covey NY & Daisy P Swallow NH Stillborn
COVEY, Unknown, Dec 9 1903 Sex:M Child# 3 Charles Covey NY & Daisy Swallow NH
COVOHIS, Unknown, Sep 12 1915 Sex:F Child# 1 Evangelos Covohis Greece & Eudoxia Cavamita Greece Stillborn
COWETTE, Margaret Evans, Dec 17 1907 Sex:F Child# 5 Henry J Cowette Newport, VT & Corena Boudin Manchester, NH
COX, Doris Rose, Aug 5 1931 Sex:F Child# 8 Floyd Cox Crossville, TN & Lucy Patterson Knoxville, TN
COX, Lloyd David, Mar 17 1933 Sex:M Child# 1 Floyd Cox Crossville, TN & Lucy Patterson Knoxville, TN
COX, Unknown, Nov 23 1917 Sex:F Child# 1 Frederick W Cox Northampton, England & Dorothy Thurber Nashua, NH
COX, Unknown, Nov 23 1917 Sex:F Child# 2 Frederick W Cox Northampton, England & Dorothy Thurber Nashua, NH
COY, Phyllis Letitia, Sep 30 1916 Sex:F Child# 2 Robert Edward Coy Clinton, MA & Fanny Pero Nashua, NH
COY, Robert Edward, Jr, Sep 20 1921 Sex:M Child# 3 Robert Coy Clinton, MA & Fannie Pero Nashua, NH
COY, Sylvia Louise, Oct 8 1914 Sex:F Child# 1 Robert E Coy Clinton, MA & Fanny S Pero Nashua, NH
COYNE, Bernard Thomas, Sep 7 1910 Sex:M Child# 1 Bernard Coyne New Brunswick & Catherine McNamara Maine
COZLOUSVIS, Jule, Aug 29 1910 Sex:M Child# 3 Jonos Cozlousvis Russia & Benirie Voytratie Russia
CRAFT, Philip Warren, Jun 7 1920 Sex:M Child# 4 Parson Craft Wilmington, VT & Margaret Barry Readsboro, VT
CRAFTS, Unknown, Dec 29 1888 Sex:M Child# 3 George E Crafts Maine & Rose Carter Mass
CRAMER, William A, Sep 25 1893 Sex:M Child# 4 C J Cramer Boston, MA & A M Miller Halifax, NS
CRANE, Unknown, Oct 6 1907 Sex:M Child# 1 Irving H Crane
CRAVELLE, Julian Girouard, Feb 25 1908 Sex:M Child# 1 Charles Cravelle Nashua, NH & Louise Jette Canada
CREAMER, Rachel, May 31 1912 Sex:F Child# 2 Joseph Creamer Milan, Italy & Imelda Magrone Milan, Italy
CREASE, D Caroline Eugenie, Mar 20 1932 Sex:F Child# 2 Lewis Crease New York, NY & Denise Lixon France
CRECCHI, Albert, Dec 21 1908 Sex:M Child# 4 John Crecchi Bologna, Italy & Mary Partushepi Bologna, Italy
CREINOWIEZ, William, Oct 10 1918 Sex:M Child# 1 William Creinowiez Russia & Mary Greginta Russia
CREMA, Joseph, Jul 6 1910 Sex:M Child# 1 Ecdlis Crema Italy & Imelde Magnosia Italy Stillborn
CREPEAU, Joseph, Apr 25 1891 Sex:M Child# 4 Ernest Crepeau Canada & Henriette Guerette Canada
CRESRIN, Stanislas, Aug 28 1911 Sex:M Child# 1 Marcin Cresrin Russia & Antonia Lawkawick Russia
CRESUN, Jadua, Oct 25 1915 Sex:F Child# 1 Julius Cresun Russia & Josie Karpier Russia
CRESZUN, Ann, Nov 23 1914 Sex:F Child# 2 Jan Creszun Russia & Ursula Kuptin Russia
CROCKETT, Lillian Frances, Mar 10 1928 Sex:F Child# 3 Charles Crockett Mass & Emily Silva Mass
CROCKETT, Unknown, Aug 26 1930 Sex:F Child# 1 Malcolm Crockett Chelsea, MA & Mildred Burleigh Boston, MA Stillborn
CROFT, Anna Barbara, Nov 8 1919 Sex:F Child# 5 Harold R Croft E Fairfield, VT & Flora R Graham Springfield, MA
CROFT, Flora June, Jun 17 1913 Sex:F Child# 3 Harold Reed Croft E Fairfield, VT & Flora R Graham Springfield, MA
CROFT, Unknown, Mar 10 1918 Sex:F Child# 4 Harold P Croft Vermont & Flora Graham Mass
CROISETIERE, Colette, Jun 21 1928 Sex:F Child# 1 W Croisetiere Nashua, NH & Rose Lavoie Canada
CROISETIERE, Jacqueline, Mar 31 1934 Sex:F Child# 3 Wilfrid Croisetiere Fall River, MA & Rosilda Lavoie Canada
CROISETIERE, Robert Richard, Jul 4 1930 Sex:M Child# 2 Wilfrid Croisetiere US & Rosilda Lavoie Canada
CROKER, George August, Dec 22 1926 Sex:M Child# 1 William Croker Nashua, NH & Rose Levesque Nashua, NH
CROKIEM, Antosia, Dec 29 1920 Sex:F Child# 2 Anthony Crokiem Lithuania Russia & Helen Ukaniawicz Lithuania Russia
CROMPTON, Dorothy R Stella, Aug 24 1921 Sex:F Child# 1 Harry J Crompton Nashua, NH & Margaret Michiels Hamburg, Ger
CROMPTON, Harriet June, Jun 5 1927 Sex:F Child# 3 H J Crompton Nashua, NH & Margaret Michiels Hamburg, Germany
CROMPTON, Shirley Margaret, May 7 1923 Sex:F Child# 2 Harry J Crompton Nashua, NH & Margaret Michiels Hamburg, Ger
CRONIN, Arthur William, Nov 13 1926 Sex:M Child# 3 Arthur Cronin Portsmouth, NH & Mildred Miner Boscawen, NH
CRONIN, Dennis Francis, Dec 29 1895 Sex:M Child# 3 Jeremiah Cronin Ireland & Ellen Humphreys Ireland
CRONIN, Helen Dorothy, Feb 15 1896 Sex:F Child# 1 George M Cronin Gloucester, MA & Ida A Parsons Gloucester, MA
CRONIN, Jeremiah, Jul 25 1898 Sex:M Child# 4 Jeremiah Cronin Ireland & Ellen Huaphris Ireland
CRONIN, Johannah C, Dec 28 1893 Sex:F Child# 2 Jeremiah D Cronin Ireland & Ellen Humphrey Ireland
CRONIN, John, Oct 10 1891 Sex:M Child# 1 J D Cronin Ireland & Ellen Humphrey Ireland
CRONIN, John F Edward, May 1 1890 Sex:M Child# 1 John H Cronin Ireland & Kate O'Hern Hyannis, MA
CRONIN, Joseph Gerald, Apr 6 1934 Sex:M Child# 3 Stephen Cronin Nashua, NH & Evelyn LaPointe Everett, MA
CRONIN, Stephen Francis, Dec 9 1902 Sex:M Child# 5 Jeremiah Cronin Ireland & Ellen Humphrey Ireland
CRONIN, Unknown, Dec 19 1927 Sex:M Child# 2 Stephen Cronin Nashua, NH & Evelyn Lapointe Derry, NH
CROOKER, Beverly Joan, Jan 27 1934 Sex:F Child# 4 Chester E Crooker Fitchburg, MA & Mildred Cummings Fitchburg, MA
CROOKER, Charles Miles, Dec 27 1900 Sex:M Child# 4 George M Crooker NH & Mary Calahan VT
CROOKER, Chester Eaton, Feb 5 1929 Sex:M Child# 1 Chester E Crooker Fitchburg, MA & Mildred A Cummings Fitchburg
CROOKER, Earl William, Jan 26 1935 Sex:M Child# 2 How B Crooker Amherst, NH & Leona Langille Gulf Shore, NS
CROOKER, Gerald Cummings, Sep 14 1930 Sex:M Child# 2 Chester E Crooker Fitchburg, MA & Mildred Fitchburg, MA
CROOKER, Isabelle Hazel, Sep 8 1935 Sex:F Child# 4 William Crooker Nashua, NH & Rose Levesque Nashua, NH
CROOKER, Jeanne Audrey, Dec 20 1933 Sex:F Child# 1 Ward E Crooker Everett, MA & Helen Hooper Malden, MA
CROOKER, Lillian, Mar 16 1898 Sex:F Child# 2 George M Crooker Fall River, MA & Mary Callahan St Albans, VT
CROOKER, Ruth, Aug 4 1905 Sex:F Child# 1 George M Crooker Amherst, NH & Mary A Cassidy Worcester, MA
CROOKER, Unknown, Jun 3 1887 Sex:F Child# 2 Henry E Crooker Amherst & Fannie L Bennett Canada
CROOKER, Unknown, Nov 18 1909 Sex:M Child# 1 George M Crooker Nashua, NH & Louisa Labounty Greenfield, NH

CROOKER, William A, Feb 3 1903 Sex:M Child# 5 George M Crooker Fall River, MA & Mary A Callahan St Albans, VT
CROOKER, William Edward, Nov 28 1933 Sex:M Child# 3 William Crooker Nashua, NH & Rose Levesque Nashua, NH
CROOMBS, Richard Norton, May 30 1916 Sex:M Child# 1 Os M Croombs, Jr Providence, RI & Florence Urquhart Nashua, NH
CROSBY, Elizabeth, Jun 22 1915 Sex:F Child# 4 William F Crosby Hillsboro, NH & Grace Hart Northfield, MA
CROSBY, Helen, Nov 19 1910 Sex:F Child# 2 William F Crosby Hillsborough, NH & Grace Hart Northfield, MA
CROSBY, Norman Jones, May 16 1917 Sex:M Child# 5 William F Crosby Hillsboro, NH & Grace M Hart Northfield, MA
CROSBY, Ralph William, Apr 26 1908 Sex:M Child# 1 William F Crosby Hillsboro, NH & Grace P Hart Northfield, NH
CROSBY, Richard Freeman, Nov 22 1912 Sex:M Child# 3 William F Crosby Hillsboro, NH & Grace Hart Northfield, MA
CROSBY, Unknown, Mar 28 1934 Sex:M Child# 6 Harry Eugene Crosby Nova Scotia & Mildred Sollows Nova Scotia Stillborn
CROSDALE, Unknown, Sep 17 1906 Sex: Child# 1 P J Crosdale New Brunswick & Mary O Connor New Brunswick Stillbo
CROSS, Elizabeth Anna, Mar 9 1924 Sex:F Child# 1 Merton S Cross Franklin, NH & Florence G Rock Burke, NY
CROSS, Flora Elizabeth, Oct 6 1917 Sex:F Child# 1 Roy H Cross Nashua, NH & Lena M Avery Londonderry, NH
CROSS, Frank Kenneth, Jun 24 1924 Sex:M Child# 2 Frank Cross Franklin, NH & Alice Oak Sydney, NS
CROSS, George Wesley, May 11 1924 Sex:M Child# Wesley Cross Nashua, NH & Harriet George Epping, NH Stillborn
CROSS, Harold Randolph, Oct 18 1915 Sex:M Child# 2 Raymond L Cross Lynn, MA & Lillian E Baskin Essex, NB
CROSS, Harry Oake, Sep 10 1921 Sex:M Child# 1 Frank Cross Franklin, NH & Alice Oake Canada
CROSS, Helen Caroline, Nov 7 1931 Sex:F Child# 1 Nathan E Cross Hudson, NH & Emma J Lane Lempster, NH
CROSS, Irving Noyes, Nov 26 1912 Sex:M Child# 1 Raymond L Cross Waltham, MA & Lillian E Basken Waterford, ME
CROSS, Roy Herbert, May 26 1891 Sex:M Child# 1 Herbert A Cross Hudson, NH & Nellie E Smith Hudson, NH
CROSS, Shirley Helen, Aug 29 1926 Sex:F Child# 4 Raymond Cross Lynn, MA & Lillian E Baskin New Brunswick
CROSS, Virginia Loraine, Oct 10 1924 Sex:F Child# 3 Guy W Cross Franklin, NH & Ethel May Haynes Franklin, NH
CROSS, Walter F, Jul 16 1903 Sex:M Child# 5 C F Cross Iowa & Esther G Williams Conn
CROSSLAND, Barbara Ann, Nov 28 1935 Sex:F Child# 1 Edward Crossland Carlisle, MA & Ada Cutting Lowell, MA
CROTEAU, Alfred, Oct 1 1902 Sex:M Child# 2 Alfred Croteau Nashua, NH & Julie Peltier Canada
CROTEAU, Virginie Flora, Sep 15 1903 Sex:F Child# 2 Wilfrid Croteau Nashua, NH & Julia Peltier Canada
CROUSE, Lillian Esther, Apr 6 1896 Sex:F Child# John Crouse Syracuse, NY & Catherine Moran Nashua, NH
CROWELL, Alice, Jan 12 1909 Sex:F Child# Frank E Crowell Calais, ME & Ann E McCracken Milltown, NB
CROWELL, Almae, Jan 12 1909 Sex:F Child# 3 Frank E Crowell Calais, ME & Ann E McCracken Milltown, NB
CROWELL, Andrew Arthur, Jun 11 1929 Sex:M Child# 2 Arthur Crowell Milford, NH & Beatrice Leclair Boston, MA
CROWELL, Elizabeth, Aug 3 1906 Sex:F Child# 2 Frank E Crowell Calais, ME & Ann McCracken NB
CROWELL, George Edward, Jun 17 1903 Sex:M Child# Frank E Crowell Calais, ME & Ann E McCracken New Brunswick
CROWELL, Judith Griffin, Jul 27 1917 Sex:F Child# 2 Walter A Crowell Manchester, NH & Bertha J Griffin Litchfield
CROWELL, Nancy Parker, Feb 4 1914 Sex:F Child# 1 Walter A Crowell Manchester, NH & Bertha J Griffin Litchfield, NH
CROWELL, Priscilla Beatrice, Feb 18 1928 Sex:F Child# 1 Arthur F Crowell Milford, NH & Beatrice LeClair Boston, MA
CROWELL, Richard Alan, Dec 23 1933 Sex:M Child# 3 Arthur F Crowell Milford, NH & B S LeClair Boston, MA
CROWELL, Walter Andrew, Nov 10 1927 Sex:M Child# 3 Walter Crowell Manchester, NH & Bertha Griffin Litchfield, NH
CROWLEY, Daniel Eugene, Jun 1 1932 Sex:M Child# 2 Walter Crowley Groton, MA & Florence Cotton Pepperell, MA
CROWLEY, Helen Louise, Jan 5 1900 Sex:F Child# 2 James H Crowley Suncook, NH & Mary McAuliffe Nashua, NH
CROWLEY, Joan, Jul 1 1930 Sex:F Child# 1 Walter Crowley Groton, MA & Florence Cotton Pepperell, MA
CROWLEY, Leona Dorothy, Nov 24 1920 Sex:F Child# 1 Timothy L Crowley Groton, MA & Yvonne M Briand Fall River, MA
CROWLEY, Mary Ellis, Jul 21 1898 Sex:F Child# 1 James H Crowley Suncook, NH & Mary McAuliffe Nashua, NH
CROWN, M Hazel, Mar 13 1901 Sex:F Child# 2 John Crown Syracuse, NY & N Moran Nashua, NH
CRUM, Mary Marguerite, Nov 26 1909 Sex:F Child# 2 Charles Crum Ohio & Marguerite Ryan Ireland
CRUMB, Evelyn Frances, Sep 8 1904 Sex:F Child# 1 Charles F Crumb Minneapolis, MN & Margaret F Ryan Ireland
CRUZA, Roland Fern Guest, Mar 31 1923 Sex:M Child# 1 Adolphus Cruza Russia & Alice C Guest Hollis, NH
CRYSZKA, Florence, Feb 28 1918 Sex:F Child# 3 Mike Cryszka Russia & Annie Klemasziswska Russia
CUDHEA, David Woodbury, Jul 8 1931 Sex:M Child# 1 Frederick Cudhea Nova Scotia & Lois Woodbury Nashua, NH
CUDHEA, Lois Eleanor, Nov 6 1916 Sex:F Child# 1 William T Cudhea Nova Scotia & Ruby Saunders Nashua, NH
CUDHEA, Mary Lou, Apr 29 1934 Sex:F Child# 2 Frederick Cudhea Nova Scotia & Lois Woodbury Nashua, NH
CUDHEA, Phyllis Isabelle, Feb 3 1931 Sex:F Child# 1 Thurston Cudhea NS & Isabelle Rooney NS
CUDWORTH, Betty Mae, Jun 20 1933 Sex:F Child# 1 C A Cudworth Nashua, NH & Elvira J Maryell W Bridgewater, MA
CUDWORTH, Clarence Arthur, Aug 18 1901 Sex:M Child# 1 Moses W Cudworth Rindge & Clara L Weston Dunstable, MA
CUDWORTH, Ernestine Mae, Dec 28 1930 Sex:F Child# 2 Arthur I Cudworth Hudson, NH & Maud Sharp W Virginia
CUDWORTH, Jessie Louise, Jun 13 1935 Sex:F Child# 3 Art I Cudworth Hudson, NH & Maude Sharp W Virginia
CUDWORTH, Leon Edward, Mar 22 1904 Sex:M Child# 2 Moses W Cudworth Rindge, NH & Clara L Weston Dunstable, MA
CUDWORTH, Myron Leslie, Jun 25 1907 Sex:M Child# 3 Moses W Cudworth Rindge, NH & Clara L Weston Dunstable, MA
CUDYHEA, Geraldine Eva, Aug 31 1919 Sex:F Child# 2 William C Cudyhea Nova Scotia & Ruby Saunders Nashua, NH
CUIPAK, Mary, Mar 1 1919 Sex:F Child# 10 Albert Cuipak Austria & Margaret Felidski Austria
CULLEN, Annie, Jan 8 1893 Sex:F Child# 2 Michael Cullen Ireland & Mary E Millet England
CULLEN, John W, Sep 30 1891 Sex:M Child# 1 Michael Cullen Ireland & Mary E Menott Ireland
CULLEN, Margaret Louise, Jan 11 1892 Sex:F Child# 6 George Cullen Ireland & Rosanna Keegon Lowell, MA
CULLEN, Maud Belle, Feb 28 1897 Sex:F Child# 1 Warren Cullen Richford, VT & Margaret Lynch Ireland
CULLING, Dorothy Virginia, Aug 8 1932 Sex:F Child# 1 Robert Culling Potsdam, NY & Dorothea Gauthier Waltham, MA
CUMMING, Mildred Avis, Feb 4 1917 Sex:F Child# 1 R LeRoy Cumming Nashua, NH & Edna M Littlefield Pepperell, M
CUMMING, Wilhelmina H, Dec 17 1912 Sex:F Child# 1 George T Cumming Canada & Wilhelmina H Preston Calais, ME
CUMMINGHAM, George Royal, Nov 14 1912 Sex:M Child# 3 George Cunningham St John, NB & Amy Rogers Dartmouth
CUMMINGS, Agnes E, May 18 1916 Sex:F Child# 6 James Cummings Ireland & Margaret Gordon Ireland
CUMMINGS, Althea Louise, Jul 20 1918 Sex:F Child# 2 Leroy Cummings Nashua, NH & Edna Littlefield Pepperell, MA
CUMMINGS, Ann May, Jan 29 1910 Sex:F Child# 5 James Cummings Ireland & Margaret Gordon Ireland
CUMMINGS, Arthur L, Jul 1 1929 Sex:M Child# 4 Richard Cummings Nashua, NH & Edith Virgin Concord, NH
CUMMINGS, Charles Allen, Feb 16 1895 Sex:M Child# 1 Lewis A Cummings Dunstable, MA & Josie Gravelle E Douglas, MA
CUMMINGS, Dorothy May, May 1 1925 Sex:F Child# 1 R Cummings Nashua, NH & Edith Virgin Concord, NH
CUMMINGS, Dorothy Meredith, Oct 13 1932 Sex:F Child# 1 J Cummings Pepperell, MA & Viola Harris Pepperell, MA

CUMMINGS, Elinor V, Dec 13 1927 Sex:F Child# 3 R W Cummings Nashua, NH & Edith Virgin Concord, NH
CUMMINGS, Gladys May, Mar 26 1907 Sex:F Child# 2 Roger B Cummings Nashua, NH & Mabel Cleveland Skowhegan, ME
CUMMINGS, James Goodwin, Apr 10 1903 Sex:M Child# 2 R J Cummings Saco, ME & Ella F Robbins Nashua, NH
CUMMINGS, James Gordon, Jun 8 1908 Sex:M Child# 4 James Cummings Ireland & Margaret Gordon Ireland
CUMMINGS, James Richard, Jul 2 1926 Sex:M Child# 2 R W Cummings Nashua, NH & Edith M Nigin Concord, NH
CUMMINGS, Joan, Jul 27 1930 Sex:F Child# 5 Richard W Cummings Nashua, NH & Edith Virgin Concord, NH
CUMMINGS, John Foster, Nov 5 1934 Sex:M Child# 2 John H Cummings Ipswich, MA & Viola Harris E Pepperell, MA
CUMMINGS, Josephine Alice, Jun 11 1901 Sex:F Child# 1 James Cummings Ireland & Margaret Gordon Ireland
CUMMINGS, Josephine Ruth, Jun 24 1912 Sex:F Child# 3 Roger B Cummings Nashua, NH & Mabel Cleveland Skowhegan, ME
CUMMINGS, Marguerite Etta, Feb 6 1904 Sex:F Child# 2 James Cummings Ireland & Margaret Gordon Ireland
CUMMINGS, Mary, Jan 23 1906 Sex:F Child# 3 James Cummings Ireland & Margaret Gordon Ireland
CUMMINGS, Mavis Edna, Sep 10 1920 Sex:F Child# 3 Leroy Cummings Nashua, NH & Edna Littlefield Pepperell, MA
CUMMINGS, Paul Richard, Jun 17 1927 Sex:M Child# 1 James Cummings Nashua, NH & Evelyn Gilbert Proctor, VT
CUMMINGS, Phyllis May, Sep 18 1926 Sex:F Child# 1 Willard Cummings Nashua, NH & Marguerite Rule Nashua, NH
CUMMINGS, Roger Lee, Nov 27 1928 Sex:M Child# 1 A Cummings
CUMMINGS, Teresa Elizabeth, Apr 3 1902 Sex:F Child# 1 R J Cummings Saco, ME & Ella F Robbins Nashua, NH
CUMMINGS, Thomas Adelard, Aug 26 1928 Sex:M Child# 2 Jas P Cummings Nashua, NH & Evelina Gilbert Vermont
CUMMINGS, Unknown, May 12 1887 Sex:M Child# 1 George W Cummings Hudson, NH & Anna Spaulding Nashua, NH
CUMMINGS, Unknown, May 6 1888 Sex:F Child# 2 Alden E Cummings Hudson & Nellie Nashua, NH
CUMMINGS, Unknown, Nov 25 1889 Sex:F Child# 3 W B Cummings Mass & Emma C Kidder Mass
CUMMINGS, Unknown, Nov 16 1932 Sex:M Child# 2 C Cummings Nashua, NH & Clara Wheeler Keene, NH Stillborn
CUMMINGS, Willard William, Nov 6 1905 Sex:M Child# 1 Roger B Cummings Nashua, NH & Mabel F Cleveland Skowhegan, ME
CUNNIFF, Bernard William, Jan 12 1933 Sex:M Child# 1 B A Cunniff E Pepperell, MA & Beatrice Lynch E Pepperell, MA
CUNNINGHAM, Amy Louise, Dec 19 1916 Sex:F Child# 6 George Cunningham St John, NB & Amy Louise Rogers Strafford, VT
CUNNINGHAM, Dorothy Muriel, Oct 12 1925 Sex:F Child# 2 L P Cunningham Maine & Marie C Dube Canada
CUNNINGHAM, Howard Elmer, Sep 29 1913 Sex:M Child# 3 George Cunningham St Johns, NB & Amy Rogers Strafford, VT
CUNNINGHAM, James Joseph, May 31 1914 Sex:M Child# 2 Alex Cunningham Scotland & Grace Karr Scotland
CUNNINGHAM, Leory Harold, Jul 25 1894 Sex:M Child# 1 E F Cunningham St Johnsbury, VT & Caroline F Rogers Nashua, NH
CUNNINGHAM, M Gladys Lillianne, Oct 10 1919 Sex:F Child# 1 Irving Cunningham Maine & Marie Dube Canada
CUNNINGHAM, Paul Martin, Jr, Oct 19 1922 Sex:M Child# 1 P M Cunningham NH & Doris Prophy Fall River, MA
CUNNINGHAM, Philip Hall, Apr 13 1922 Sex:M Child# 2 W D Cunningham Maine & Essie M Myshrall Maine
CUNNINGHAM, Phyllis, Sep 4 1918 Sex:F Child# 1 Walt D Cunningham Newcastle, ME & Essie M Myshrall Vanceboro, ME
CUNNINGHAM, Reginald Elmer, Nov 15 1899 Sex:M Child# 2 Elmer F Cunningham Vermont & Carrie F Rogers Nashua, NH
CUNNINGHAM, Ruth Elizabeth, Sep 21 1915 Sex:F Child# 5 George Cunningham St John, NB & Amy L Rogers Strafford, VT
CUNNINGHAM, Unknown, Sep 13 1902 Sex:F Child# 3 E F Cunningham Whitefield & Caroline F Rogers Nashua, NH
CURRAN, Frank, Jul 15 1903 Sex:M Child# 1 Frank Curran Nashua, NH & Albina Jordon Lowell, MA
CURRAN, John, Feb 1 1905 Sex:M Child# 2 Frank Curran Nashua, NH & Albina Jordan Lowell, MA
CURRAN, Martha Dorothy, Feb 1 1911 Sex:F Child# 4 Frank Curran Nashua, NH & Albina Jordan Lowell, MA
CURRAN, Reta Katherine, Mar 10 1907 Sex:F Child# 3 Frank Curran Nashua, NH & Albina Jordon Lowell, MA
CURRIE, Duncan, Jul 11 1889 Sex:M Child# 1 Duncan Currie England & Maggie Law Chicago, IL
CURRIE, James, Jan 8 1892 Sex:M Child# 3 James Currie Scotland & Margaret Connor Scotland
CURRIE, William Coulter, Aug 27 1926 Sex:M Child# 6 John Currie Scotland & Elizabeth Coulter Scotland
CURRIER, Abraham, Aug 4 1909 Sex:M Child# 1 Joseph Currier Russia & Sarah Partner Russia
CURRIER, Betram Adams, Oct 4 1897 Sex:M Child# 2 Fred E Currier Hollis, NH & Lizzie Carrie Adams S Merrimack, NH
CURRIER, Dorothy Lucille, Mar 22 1910 Sex:F Child# 1 Arthur A Currier Hopkinton, NH & Mabel Haynes Willobash
CURRIER, Gerald Robbin, Jul 7 1920 Sex:M Child# 2 Medrick Currier Littleton, NH & Blanche Jelly Nashua, NH
CURRIER, Pauline Milton, Jul 20 1918 Sex:F Child# 4 Ralph P Currier Amherst, NH & Mary L Hunt Weymouth, MA
CURRIER, Philip Joseph, Feb 26 1925 Sex:M Child# 6 Ralph Currier Amherst, NH & Mary L Hunt S Weymouth, MA
CURRIER, Robert Hunt, Aug 12 1920 Sex:M Child# 5 Ralph P Currier Amherst, NH & Mary Hunt S Weymouth, MA
CURRIER, Unknown, Dec 20 1887 Sex:M Child# 2 George D Currier Unity & Laura Snow Franklin, ME
CURRIER, Unknown, Aug 14 1890 Sex:F Child# 3 George D Currier Unity, NH & Laura Snow Franklin, ME
CURRIER, Unknown, Jan 19 1891 Sex:F Child# 1 Fred Currier Hollis, NH & Lizzie Adams S Merrimack, NH Stillborn
CURRIER, Unknown, May 18 1919 Sex:F Child# 1 Charles Currier Island Pond, VT & Margaret Fellows Nashua, NH
CURRUL, Barbara Ann, Jul 4 1924 Sex:F Child# 2 William H Currul Halifax, NS & Helen F Hamilton Cambridge, MA
CURRUL, Bertha May, Dec 29 1928 Sex:F Child# 3 Russell A Currul Denver, CO & Ellen Kilburn Henniker, NH
CURRUL, Robert Hamilton, Nov 6 1921 Sex:M Child# 1 William H Currul Halifax, NS & Helen F Hamilton Cambridge, MA
CURRY, James Francis, Jr, Jun 22 1932 Sex:M Child# 1 J F Curry N Chelmsford, MA & Irene Roche Nashua, NH
CURTICE, Doris Maude, Apr 5 1905 Sex:F Child# 1 Clarence E Curtice Nashua, NH & Sadie M Pease Wilton, ME
CURTICE, Raymond Francis, Sep 10 1906 Sex:M Child# 4 Eugene E Curtice Nashua, NH & Hattie J Barber W Medway, MA
CURTICE, Unknown, Jan 13 1887 Sex:M Child# 2 Theodore Curtice Saugus, MA & Carrie H Bryant's Point, ME
CURTIS, Anna, Sep 21 1895 Sex:F Child# 8 Mitchell Curtis Canada & Melina Lafontaine Canada
CURTIS, Clara, Jan 15 1891 Sex:F Child# 6 Michel Curtis Canada & Melvina Fontaine Canada
CURTIS, Clarence Lester, Jul 4 1908 Sex:M Child# 2 Clarence E Curtis Nashua, NH & Bertha May Pease Milton, ME
CURTIS, Edouard, Jan 5 1900 Sex:M Child# 11 Mitchel Curtis Canada & Melina Fontaine Canada
CURTIS, Emile Wilfred, Jr, Nov 19 1931 Sex:M Child# 1 Emile W Curtis Fitchburg, MA & Alice Surette Greenville, NH
CURTIS, Eva M, Dec 9 1889 Sex:F Child# 1 James A Curtis NY & Minnie Eva Nolan NY
CURTIS, Frederick, Feb 8 1933 Sex:M Child# 2 Emile Curtis Fitchburg, MA & Alice Surette Greenville, NH
CURTIS, Joseph, Jul 27 1893 Sex:M Child# 7 Michael Curtis Canada & Emeline Fontaine Canada
CURTIS, Marie Aurore, Oct 12 1898 Sex:F Child# 10 Michael Curtis Canada & Emelia Fontaine Canada
CURTIS, Unknown, Feb 14 1888 Sex:M Child# 3 Theodore Curtis
CURTIS, Unknown, Nov 9 1893 Sex:M Child# 2 Eugene E Curtis Nashua, NH & Hattie I Barber W Medway, MA
CURTIS, Unknown, Feb 16 1895 Sex:F Child# 3 Eugene E Curtis Nashua, NH & Hattie I Barber W Medway, MA
CURTIS, Unknown, Oct 19 1897 Sex:F Child# 9 Michel Curtis Canada & Melina Fontaine Canada Stillborn

CURTIS, Unknown, Jan 18 1931 Sex:M Child# 8 Andrew Curtis Greece & Alpenipe Greece
CUSANA, Frankiska, Nov 11 1918 Sex:F Child# 7 Nicholas Cusana Greece & Stamoula Tigas Greece
CUSHING, Blanche Arline, Oct 7 1926 Sex:F Child# 5 Emery Cushing NH & Alice Lemire Canada
CUSHING, Herbert A, Mar 12 1909 Sex:M Child# 2 Andrew H Cushing Weymouth, MA & Elizabeth Delorey Merland, NS
CUSHING, Mary Ella, Aug 21 1907 Sex:F Child# 6 Edw J Cushing Concord, NH & Mary Morrison Ireland
CUSHING, Shirley Anne, Oct 26 1934 Sex:F Child# 6 Emery Cushing NH & Alice Lemire Canada
CUSHING, William Henry, Sep 8 1895 Sex:M Child# 3 Edward J Cushing Concord & Mary Morrisey Ireland
CUSSON, Eleonore, Apr 25 1891 Sex:F Child# 9 Etienne Cusson Canada & Zoe Vincent Canada
CUSSON, Emma, May 20 1893 Sex:F Child# 2 Omer Cusson Canada & Delvina Miclette Canada
CUSSON, Laura Alma, Apr 19 1904 Sex:F Child# 4 Omer Cusson Canada & Delvina Miclette Canada
CUSSON, Matilda, May 23 1891 Sex:F Child# 1 Omer Cusson Canada & Delvina Miclette Canada
CUTLER, David Sanford, Jr, Oct 17 1920 Sex:M Child# 1 David S Cutler G Barrington, MA & Hazel H Wavle Harford
CUTTER, Barbara Deering, Aug 30 1903 Sex:F Child# 1 George A Cutter Vineyard, KS & Mabelle L Mudie Chicago, IL
CUTTER, Cattie, Jul 21 1888 Sex:F Child# 4 George H Cutter Merrimack & Jessie Manning Nashua, NH
CUTTER, Clifford Wayland, May 22 1908 Sex:M Child# 1 Fred S Cutter Nashua, NH & Gladys S Mandigo Canada
CUTTER, Ernest, Jun 4 1914 Sex:M Child# 4 Phinais Cutter Nashua, NH & Aurore Picher Nashua, NH
CUTTER, Florette Irene, Oct 1 1919 Sex:F Child# 5 Phineas Cutter Nashua, NH & Aurore Richer Canada
CUTTER, Frank Samuel, Jun 16 1912 Sex:M Child# 3 Fred S Cutter Nashua, NH & Gladys Mandigo Canada
CUTTER, Helen Priscilla, Jan 26 1932 Sex:F Child# 8 Charles N Cutter Cambridge, MA & Esther Mitchell Brunswick
CUTTER, Ida Mabel, Nov 27 1908 Sex:F Child# 6 Harry Cutter Nashua, NH & Ruth Bowley Vermont
CUTTER, Janet, Jan 20 1889 Sex:F Child# 1 Henry A Cutter NH & Katherine M NH
CUTTER, Joseph Philias V R, Dec 22 1910 Sex:M Child# 1 Philias Cutter Nashua, NH & Aurore Piche Canada
CUTTER, Madeleine, Dec 6 1892 Sex:F Child# 2 Henry A Cutter Nashua, NH & Katherine M Greeley Nashua, NH
CUTTER, Marie Alla Lucille, Oct 5 1916 Sex:F Child# 4 Phinias Cutter US & Aurore Picher US
CUTTER, Ralph Milo, Dec 20 1895 Sex:M Child# 8 Fred R Cutter Lowell, MA & Ida Dickerman Nashua, NH
CUTTER, Raymond, Jan 4 1935 Sex:M Child# 1 Raymond Cutter Nashua, NH & Violet Drouin Nashua, NH
CUTTER, Robert Charles, Aug 9 1935 Sex:M Child# 1 Rob Chas Cutter Peterboro, NH & Eleanor Gleason Dublin, NH
CUTTER, Rodolphe, Dec 17 1920 Sex:M Child# 6 Phineas Cutter Nashua, NH & Aurore Picher Canada
CUTTER, Ruth Irene, May 12 1910 Sex:F Child# 2 Fred S Cutter Nashua, NH & Gladys Mandigo Canada
CUTTER, Unknown, Oct 14 1888 Sex:M Child# 4 Fred R Cutter Nashua, NH & Ida Dickerman Nashua, NH
CUTTER, Unknown, Aug 24 1890 Sex:M Child# 5 Fred R Cutter Lowell, MA & Ida Dickerman Nashua, NH
CUTTER, Unknown, Dec 21 1890 Sex:M Child# 5 George H Cutter Merrimack, NH & Jessie S Manning Nashua, NH
CUTTER, Unknown, Mar 30 1892 Sex:F Child# 6 Fred R Cutter Lowell, MA & Ida Dickermann Nashua, NH
CUTTER, Unknown, May 30 1892 Sex:F Child# 6 George H Cutter Amherst & Jessie F Manning Nashua, NH
CUTTER, Unknown, Jun 29 1894 Sex:F Child# 7 George H Cutter Merrimack & Jessie F Manning Nashua, NH
CUTTER, Unknown, Jul 23 1894 Sex:F Child# 7 Fred R Cutter Lowell, MA & Ida Dickerman Nashua, NH
CUTTER, Unknown, Jan 20 1895 Sex:M Child# 1 Solomon M Cutter Portland, OR & Annie Freeman Marblehead, MA
CUTTER, Unknown, Apr 25 1913 Sex:F Child# 2 Phinias Cutter Nashua, NH & Aurore Piche Canada Stillborn
CUTTS, Charles, Oct 28 1923 Sex:M Child# 4 Charles A Cutts Newport, NH & Roma Hutchinson Lyndeboro, NH
CUZAS, Julia Mary, Feb 13 1918 Sex:F Child# 2 Vladas Cuzas Russia & Mary Stopls Russia
CWILUIK, Antosia, Dec 16 1916 Sex:F Child# 1 John Cwiluik Russia & Eva Marchinski Russia
CWILUIK, Eva, Dec 16 1918 Sex:F Child# 2 John Cwiluik Russia & Eva Marchinski Russia
CYNE, Benjamin Franklin, Apr 29 1911 Sex:M Child# 2 Benjamin Cyne Ellenburgh, NY & Elizabeth Wells Liverpool,
CYR, George, Jan 17 1920 Sex:M Child# 2 Theodore Cyr Maine & A Hebert Peabody, MA
CYR, John Arthur, Sep 19 1929 Sex:M Child# 1 John Percy Cyr Pembroke, NH & Jane Dowd Nashua, NH
CYR, Nancy Dowd, Jul 27 1934 Sex:F Child# 2 John Percy Cyr Pembroke, NH & Jane Frances Dowd Nashua, NH
CYR, Raymond, Apr 18 1928 Sex:M Child# 2 Theodore Cyr US & Yvonne Gelinas US
CYR, Unknown, Dec 15 1925 Sex:M Child# 1 Theodore Cyr Lawrence, MA & Yvonne Gelinas Nashua, NH
CYUNSKIS, Zophie, Sep 1 1905 Sex:F Child# 1 Stanislaus Cyunskis Russia & Maryona Giedrimate Russia
CZAPLIK, Valerka, May 29 1915 Sex:F Child# 1 Andrew Czaplik Russia & Helen Mikalevicz Russia
CZENGNULENICZ, Helena Maria, Feb 7 1896 Sex:F Child# 4 John Czengnulenicz Poland & Tojila Zenaizinte Poland
CZENGNULENICZ, Maria Monica, Feb 7 1896 Sex:F Child# 4 John Czengnulenicz Poland & Tojila Zenaizinte Poland
CZENKONES, John, Aug 28 1917 Sex:M Child# 2 Toney Czenkones Russia & Celia Alkelevic Russia
CZERNECKI, Unknown, Mar 8 1918 Sex:M Child# 1 Marian Czernecki Austria & Bernice Demska Austria
CZESNULEWICZ, Jennie, Jun 15 1905 Sex:F Child# 1 William Czesnulewicz Russia & Jennie Saliuciutie Russia
CZIESWALEUC, John, Feb 15 1908 Sex:M Child# 1 Mikale Czieswaleuc Russia & Sitpas Walentukuwich Russia
D'AMBOISE, Lorraine, Oct 3 1928 Sex:F Child# 3 Wilfrid D'Amboise Nashua, NH & N Duchesneau Nashua, NH
D'AMBOISE, Marie Elmire, Jan 5 1892 Sex:F Child# 3 Felix D'Amboise Canada & Emma Sirois Canada
D'AMOUR, Joseph Arthur, Mar 21 1918 Sex:M Child# 3 Cyrisse D'Amour Canada & Anna Marie Parent Canada
D'AMOUR, Marie Anita Edna, Jun 4 1916 Sex:F Child# 2 Cyrisse D'Amour Canada & Marie Parent Canada
D'AMOUR, Marie Annette Yvette, Mar 27 1915 Sex:F Child# 1 Cyriss D'Amour Canada & Anne M Parent Canada
D'ANJOU, Alice Emelia, Jan 12 1917 Sex:F Child# 2 Joseph D'Anjou Canada & Emelia Pelerin Amesbury, MA
D'ANJOU, Alphonse Thomas, Dec 21 1920 Sex:M Child# 3 Joseph D'Anjou Canada & Emelia Pelerin Amesbury, MA
D'ANJOU, Beatrice Caroline, May 24 1926 Sex:F Child# 1 Antonia D'Anjou Canada & Lillian Marquis Nashua, NH
D'ANJOU, Jos Roger William, Mar 20 1929 Sex:M Child# 5 Joseph D'Anjou Canada & Emelia Pellerine Mass
D'ARAGON, Marguerite Isabelle, May 13 1923 Sex:F Child# 5 Joseph A D'Aragon Canada & Antoinette Monjean Canada
D'ARGIE, Marie Eva, Aug 23 1894 Sex:F Child# 3 Napoleon D'Argie Canada & Rosanna Richard Canada
D'JOHN, Evangelos A, Mar 29 1918 Sex:M Child# 3 Alex D'John Greece & Evelyn D'John Greece
D'OUVILLE, Marie S Lucia, May 10 1898 Sex:F Child# 6 Edouard D'Ouville Canada & Anna Hamel Canada
DABANIS, Deimitra, Dec 2 1916 Sex:F Child# 1 Kostas Dabanis Greece & Ellen Macronoul Greece
DABIE, Joseph Charles E, Mar 16 1889 Sex:M Child# 1 Charles Dabie Canada & Celina Francour Canada
DABIS, Mary, Aug 8 1900 Sex:F Child# Sam Dabis E Rochester & Lottie Spellman
DACHOS, Joan Efthia, Feb 8 1930 Sex:F Child# 4 Sam Dachos Greece & Mildred Burnham Nashua, NH

DACHOS, Melba Josephine, Jun 5 1923 Sex:F Child# 1 Sam Dachos Greece & Mildred Burnham Nashua, NH
DACHOS, Unknown, Jun 18 1933 Sex:F Child# 5 Sam Dachos Greece & Mildred Burnham Nashua, NH
DAFNIS, Unknown, Nov 17 1931 Sex:M Child# 1 Nicholas Dafnis Greece & Evanthia Antonioo Greece
DAGOPOULOU, Unknown, Aug 17 1922 Sex:M Child# 1 John Dagopoulou Greece & Katrina Gahman Greece
DAHAR, June Wilhaim, Sep 6 1935 Sex:F Child# 3 Saheed W Dahar Syria & Mercedes Sacre Cuba
DAHER, Gloria, Oct 12 1928 Sex:F Child# 1 S W Daher Syria & Mercedes Sacre Syria
DAHOR, Victor William, Jan 5 1930 Sex:M Child# 2 Saheed W Dahor Syria & Mercedes Sacra Havana, Cuba
DAIGLE, Arthur, May 4 1896 Sex:M Child# 5 Adolphe Daigle Canada & Aldea Boulanger Canada
DAIGLE, John Henri Edouard, Jul 30 1918 Sex:M Child# 2 Leonard Daigle Canada & Rosilda Tremblay NH
DAIGLE, Leonard Frederic R, Sep 18 1916 Sex:M Child# 1 Leonard Daigle Canada & Rosilda Tremblay NH
DAIGLE, Lillian Cecelia, Jan 6 1920 Sex:F Child# 3 Leonard A Daigle Canada & Rosilda Trombley Nashua, NH
DAIGLE, Louis Armand, Feb 19 1904 Sex:M Child# 7 Alfred Daigle Canada & Alexandrina Roberge Canada
DAIGLE, Marie L I, May 4 1890 Sex:F Child# 2 Alexandre Daigle Vermont & Marie Riendou Vermont
DAIGLE, Robert Arthur, Aug 30 1921 Sex:M Child# 4 Leonard E Daigle Canada & Roselda Trombley Nashua, NH
DAIGNEAU, Helena Ruth, Jun 15 1924 Sex:F Child# 3 A E Daigneau Montgomery, VT & Nellie E Sargent Franklin, NH
DAIGNEAU, Kenneth Earl, Jun 4 1929 Sex:M Child# 4 Allard E Daigneau NH & Nellie E Sargent NH
DAILEY, John William, Apr 22 1932 Sex:M Child# 1 Francis A Dailey Ludlow, VT & Doris P Webb Ware, MA
DAINE, George Albert, Sep 15 1925 Sex:M Child# 3 Chester H Daine Malden, MA & Helen E Riley Nashua, NH
DAKSARVICH, Nellie, Nov 28 1922 Sex:F Child# 2 Peter Daksarvich Lithuania Russia & Agnes Grigute Lithuania Russia
DALANSKY, Lena, Mar 5 1903 Sex:F Child# 3 Simon Dalansky Russia & Bessie Borsin Russia
DALAS, Unknown, Apr 20 1917 Sex:M Child# 1 Anfleas Dalas Greece & Marie Goulas Greece
DALEY, Eleanor Louise, Jul 20 1924 Sex:F Child# 3 Benjamin T Daley Auburndale, MA & Eunice K Lewis Phippsburg,
DALEY, Francis William, Oct 2 1921 Sex:M Child# 2 Francis W Daley Franklin, KY & Phoebe Hall Nashua, NH
DALEY, Helen Veronica, Sep 17 1909 Sex:F Child# 1 Patrick Daley Ireland & Nora Courtney Ireland, NY
DALEY, Hugh, Aug 28 1907 Sex:M Child# 6 Frank Daley Ireland & Jane Crosby Ireland
DALEY, John H, Jan 4 1887 Sex:M Child# 6 Kazan Daley Ireland & Nellie Peterboro
DALEY, Peter, Jul 17 1921 Sex:M Child# 2 Peter Daley Providence, RI & Elma Mary Demanche Nashua, NH
DALIS, Clenecke, Jul 1 1912 Sex:F Child# 2 Demosthenes Dalis Greece & Alexandra Antopolo Greece
DALKEWICZ, Unknown, Mar 17 1913 Sex:M Child# 2 Peter Dalkewicz Russia & Anna Kaglauchos Russia Stillborn
DALLAS, Unknown, Nov 9 1923 Sex:F Child# 3 George Dallas Greece & Laura Reed Berlin, NH
DALTON, Edward Frank, Sep 1 1935 Sex:M Child# 1 Roland Dalton Nashua, NH & Helen Trumbull Nashua, NH
DALTON, Harvey Franklin, Sep 14 1905 Sex:M Child# 14 James Dalton Dundee, Scotland & Isabell Ireland Dundee, Scot
DALTON, Stanley Hatch, Apr 3 1896 Sex:M Child# 2 Henry F Dalton Amesbury, MA & Lura B Hubbard Nashua, NH
DALY, Catherine Gertrude, Nov 16 1916 Sex:F Child# 4 Patrick Daly Ireland & Nora Courtney Ireland
DALY, Evelyn Irene, Jul 6 1920 Sex:F Child# 1 Frank W Daly Franklin, KY & Phoebe Hall Nashua, NH
DALY, Francis John, Jun 25 1905 Sex:M Child# 5 Francis Daly Ireland & Jeanne Crossy Ireland
DALY, John Edward, Dec 2 1911 Sex:M Child# 2 Patrick Daly Ireland & Nora Courtney Ireland
DALY, Mary Josephine, Oct 6 1913 Sex:F Child# 3 Patrick J Daly Ireland & Nora Courtney Ireland
DALY, Winifred Elizabeth, Jan 7 1911 Sex:F Child# 1 Bernard Daly Ireland & Winifred Bruen Ireland
DAMAPOKES, Parskeve, Mar 14 1921 Sex:F Child# 3 Thomas Damapokes Greece & Hellen Papachristou Greece
DAMASKOW, Unknown, Nov 18 1918 Sex:M Child# 3 John Damaskow Greece & Efrogyne Harris Greece
DAMBOIS, Beatrice Jeanne, Apr 2 1921 Sex:F Child# 1 Wilfrid Dambois Nashua, NH & Naomi Duchesneau Nashua, NH
DAMBOIS, Marie Eva, Jun 30 1890 Sex:F Child# 2 Felix Dambois Canada & Emme Sirois Canada
DAMBOISE, Aurelle, May 24 1904 Sex:F Child# 11 Felix Damboise Canada & Emma Sirois Canada
DAMBOISE, Denise Lemire, Oct 24 1900 Sex:F Child# 4 Achilles Damboise Canada & Armanse Sirois Canada
DAMBOISE, Felix Charles, Apr 13 1899 Sex:M Child# 8 Felix Damboise Canada & Emma Sirois Canada
DAMBOISE, George Achille, Jun 3 1893 Sex:M Child# 4 Felix Damboise Canada & Emma Sirois Canada
DAMBOISE, Helene Alice, Mar 13 1903 Sex:F Child# 10 Felix Damboise Canada & Emma Sirois Canada
DAMBOISE, Henry, Oct 25 1901 Sex:M Child# 9 Felix Damboise Canada & Emma Sirois Canada
DAMBOISE, Joseph Henri, Jan 17 1895 Sex:M Child# 1 Achille Damboise Canada & Armance Sirois Canada
DAMBOISE, Joseph Oliva, Jul 31 1897 Sex:M Child# 2 Achille Damboise Canada & Armance Sirois Canada
DAMBOISE, Joseph Wilfrid, Feb 26 1896 Sex:M Child# 6 Felix Damboise Canada & Emma Sirois Canada
DAMBOISE, Marie Alma, Jul 20 1897 Sex:F Child# 7 Felix Damboise Canada & Emma Sirois Canada
DAMBOISE, Marie Gracia, Aug 20 1898 Sex:F Child# 3 Achille Damboise Canada & Armance Sirois Canada
DAMBOISE, Philippe, Oct 2 1903 Sex:M Child# 5 Achille Damboise Canada & Hermence Sirois Canada
DAMBROIS, Germaine Camille, Nov 10 1919 Sex:F Child# 1 Joseph F Dambrois Nashua, NH & Lydia St Germaine E Jaffrey
DAMBROISE, Gloria Estelle, Apr 18 1935 Sex:F Child# 1 Aurel Dambroise Nashua, NH & Marie A Gendron Canada
DAMBROSKY, Vironica, Jan 17 1918 Sex:F Child# 3 Frank Dambrosky Russia & Sophie Veskofski Russia
DAME, Annie D, Sep 13 1887 Sex:F Child# 1 John Dame Wilton & Bridget Doyle Ireland
DAME, Calvin Wilbur, Nov 1 1933 Sex:M Child# 5 Chester Dame Malden, MA & Helen Riley Nashua, NH Stillborn
DAME, Edward Gerald, Dec 6 1922 Sex:M Child# 2 Chester H Dame Malden, MA & Helen E Riley Nashua, NH
DAME, Patrick, Apr 9 1889 Sex:M Child# 2 Warren Dame Wells, NH & Bridget Doyle Ireland
DAME, Robert Dexter, Jun 1 1921 Sex:M Child# 1 Chester H Dame Malden, MA & Helen Riley Nashua, NH
DAME, Roger Allan, Apr 16 1927 Sex:M Child# 4 Chester H Dame Malden, MA & Helen E Riley Nashua, NH
DAMON, Earl Allen, Jul 20 1922 Sex:M Child# 1 Harold A Damon Nashua, NH & Dorothy Frost Milton, NH
DAMON, Harold Allen, Jan 20 1894 Sex:M Child# 3 E A Damon
DAMON, Harold Lane, Jul 20 1924 Sex:M Child# 2 Harold Damon Nashua, NH & Dorothy Frost Milton, VT
DAMOUN, Woodrow, Jan 18 1918 Sex:M Child# 4 Ludovic Damoun Montreal, Canada & Emma Charbonneau Plattsburg, NY
DANATSKOU, Eheodora, Jun 15 1915 Sex:F Child# 1 John Dantaskou Greece & Euphiosine Hanis Greece
DANCAUSE, Eva Yvonne, Nov 18 1905 Sex:F Child# 2 Joseph Dancause Canada & Marie Richard Canada
DANCAUSE, Eva Yvonne, Feb 19 1913 Sex:F Child# 5 Joseph Dancause Canada & Marie Richard Canada
DANCAUSE, Henri Albert W, Jul 27 1903 Sex:M Child# 1 Joseph Dancause Canada & Marie Richard Canada
DANCAUSE, M Eva Olivine, Nov 8 1910 Sex:F Child# 4 Joseph Dancause Canada & Marie Richard Canada

DANCAUSE, Marie Liliane E, Apr 1 1907 Sex:F Child# 3 Joseph Dancause Canada & Marie Richard Canada
DANDELIN, George Leonard, Oct 2 1894 Sex:M Child# 2 Georges Dandelin Nashua, NH & Angelina Gerouard Nashua, NH
DANDLEY, Grace, Sep 11 1888 Sex:F Child# 9 William H Dandley Nashua, NH & Kate Donnelly Nashua, NH
DANDLEY, Herbert Edward, Jr, Sep 14 1924 Sex:M Child# 2 H E Dandley
DANDLEY, Lucy Catherine, Nov 7 1922 Sex:F Child# 1 Herbert W Dandley Nashua, NH & Josephine O'Neil Nashua, NH
DANDLEY, Noel Clark, Dec 14 1933 Sex:M Child# 4 H E Dandley Nashua, NH & Josephine O'Neil Nashua, NH
DANDLEY, Quentin Karl, May 24 1935 Sex:M Child# 5 Herb E Dandley Nashua, NH & Josephine O'Neil Nashua, NH
DANDON, Helen, Apr 12 1917 Sex:F Child# 4 Bill Dandon Greece & Olga Adonacopoulo Greece
DANDOS, Unknown, Jun 18 1915 Sex:F Child# 6 Basilios Dandos Greece & Olga Harmantas Greece
DANDURANT, Herman John, Sep 9 1915 Sex:M Child# 1 John Dandurant Swanton, VT & Annie Driscoll Ireland
DANE, Andrea, Apr 18 1919 Sex:F Child# 3 Wilbur E Dane Lawrence, MA & Mabel Fletcher Nashua, NH
DANE, Clarence, Mar 27 1902 Sex:M Child# 3 Ellery C Dane Nashua, NH & Amy L Barker Antrim, NH
DANE, Dorothy Louise, Dec 18 1921 Sex:F Child# 1 Richard C Dane Nashua, NH & Madeline V Campbell Nashua, NH
DANE, Eleanor, May 12 1916 Sex:F Child# 2 Wilbur E Dane Lawrence, MA & Mabel L Fletcher Nashua, NH
DANE, Ellery Clarke, Jun 13 1904 Sex:M Child# 4 Ellery C Dane Nashua, NH & Amy L Barker Antrim, NH
DANE, Irene May, May 25 1897 Sex:F Child# 1 (No Parents Listed)
DANE, Rhoda Elizabeth, Dec 18 1909 Sex:F Child# 5 Ellery C Dane Nashua, NH & Amy L Barker Antrim, NH
DANE, Richard Carl, May 7 1899 Sex:M Child# 2 Ellery C Dane Nashua, NH & Amy Barker Antrim, NH
DANE, Unknown, Jul 23 1897 Sex:M Child# Elery C Dane Nashua, NH & Amy Barker Antrim, NH Stillborn
DANE, Unknown, Jan 19 1911 Sex:M Child# 1 Wilbur E Dane Lawrence, MA & Mabel C Fletcher Nashua, NH
DANFORTH, Amy Ella, May 6 1896 Sex:F Child# George C Danforth Lowell, MA & Emma Gerald Bangor, ME
DANFORTH, Doratha, Jan 19 1890 Sex:F Child# 1 George E Danforth Nashua, NH & Anna P March Nashua, NH
DANFORTH, Helen Jane, Apr 17 1893 Sex:F Child# 1 George W Danforth Hudson, MA & Mary Thomas Fisherville
DANFORTH, John Thomas, Jun 26 1894 Sex:M Child# 1 James Danforth Ireland & Mary Ireland
DANFORTH, Mary Josephine, Apr 13 1934 Sex:F Child# 6 William Danforth Wells, ME & Margaret Gardner Dunstable, MA
DANFORTH, Ruth Gardner, Jun 20 1925 Sex:F Child# 3 William Danforth Sandown, NH & Margaret Gardner Dunstable, MA
DANGOT, Valarka, May 1 1912 Sex:F Child# 1 Peter Dangot Russia & Ursula Bargiuskitie Russia
DANIELLA, Bolislaw, Sep 17 1918 Sex:M Child# 4 Anthony Daniella Russia & Julia Metrawicz Russia
DANIELOWICZ, John, May 6 1919 Sex:M Child# 1 Joseph Danielowicz Poland Russia & Mary Helenevska Poland Russia
DANIELS, Albert John, Mar 4 1894 Sex:M Child# 1 Frederick H Daniels London, England & Annie M Wheeler Nashua, NH
DANIELS, Beatrice, Mar 27 1896 Sex:F Child# 2 Frederick H Daniels London, England & Annie M Wheeler Nashua, NH
DANIELS, Jane, Jun 7 1916 Sex:F Child# 1 Edward Perry Daniels Michigan & Helene Peck Schenectady, NY
DANIELS, John Harris, Aug 9 1928 Sex:M Child# 2 Harris Daniels Milford, NH & Emma Bianchi Milford, NH
DANIELS, Leslie Wallace, Oct 10 1909 Sex:M Child# 1 William F Daniels Westwood, MA & Mildred A Thomas Lowell, MA
DANIELS, Unknown, Mar 15 1911 Sex:M Child# 2 William Daniels Westwood, MA & Mildred A Thomas Lowell, MA
DANIELS, Unknown, Jul 26 1911 Sex:M Child# 1 Oliver D Daniels Henniker, NH & Florence Brown Deering, NH
DANILEWICZ, Eva, Jun 18 1921 Sex:F Child# 2 Joseph Danilewicz Russia & mary Galenweka Russia
DANIS, Marie, Jan 22 1924 Sex:F Child# 1 Walter Danis Russia & Emelia Danis Russia Stillborn
DANJOU, Cecile Yvonne, Sep 17 1912 Sex:F Child# 1 Joseph Danjou Canada & Emelia Pelerin Amesbury, MA
DANKAS, Unknown, Mar 8 1924 Sex:F Child# 5 Demetrius Danksa Greece & S B Coulais Greece
DANLEY, Florence, Jun 23 1893 Sex:F Child# 12 William H Danley Nashua, NH & Katie E Donnelly Nashua, NH
DANPHINAIS, Henri Robert, Jul 19 1933 Sex:M Child# 5 O Danphinais Nashua, NH & Irene Bernard Nashua, NH
DANSEREAU, Joseph, Oct 15 1906 Sex:M Child# 8 Joseph Dansereau Canada & Anna Belanger NH Stillborn
DANSEREAU, Marie A A, Jul 2 1898 Sex:F Child# 1 Joseph Dansereau Canada & Anna Belanger Nashua, NH
DANSEREAU, Marie Blanche Y, Sep 23 1899 Sex:F Child# 2 Joseph Dansereau Canada & Anne Belanger NH
DANSEREAU, Marie Dora L, May 11 1901 Sex:F Child# 3 Joseph Dansereau Canada & Anna Belanger NH
DANSEREAU, Paul Jos Henry, Oct 25 1919 Sex:M Child# 1 Henry C Dansereau Nashua, NH & Nathalie Lessard Pepperell, MA
DANTOS, Nicolas, Jul 14 1914 Sex:M Child# 6 William Dantos Greece & Olga Thatus Greece
DANVILLE, Irene, Feb 19 1902 Sex:F Child# 7 Edouard Danville Canada & Angelina Hamel Canada
DANVILLE, Juliette Angelina, Mar 8 1904 Sex:F Child# 7 Edouard Danville Canada & Angelina Hamel Canada
DAONKAS, Unknown, Jul 4 1921 Sex:M Child# 3 Demetrios Daonkas Greece & Stamonia Greece
DARASCKAVEICH, Helena, Sep 13 1917 Sex:F Child# 5 A Darasckaveich Russia & Anne Verbonaite Russia
DARASKIEWICZ, Albina, Nov 10 1923 Sex:F Child# 8 Alex Daraskiewicz Poland & Annie Rebanawich Poland
DARDARIAN, Vartooke, Jun 20 1927 Sex:F Child# 1 Sarkis Dardarian Sevas, Turkey & Marian Chakerian Sevas, Turkey
DARGIE, Joseph Armand, Feb 13 1903 Sex:M Child# 2 Napoleon Dargie Canada & Zephirine Cote Canada
DARGIE, Joseph Arthur, Oct 29 1899 Sex:M Child# 1 Gregoire Dargie Canada & Eliza Charland Canada
DARGIE, M Corona, Aug 8 1895 Sex:F Child# 2 Joseph Dargie Canada & Mathilde St Germain Canada
DARGIE, Unknown, Feb 4 1902 Sex:F Child# 1 Napoleon Dargie Canada & Zephirine Cote Canada
DARGIS, Emma A, Jul 30 1897 Sex:F Child# 6 Napoleon Dargis Canada & Rosianne Richard Canada
DARLING, Anna, Jun 11 1908 Sex:F Child# 7 Anthony Darling Russia & Mary Russia
DARLING, Charles, Sep 8 1912 Sex:M Child# 9 Anthony Darling Russia & Elizabeth Kudzaniuti Russia
DARLING, Eva, Apr 4 1919 Sex:F Child# 12 Anthony Darling Russia & Elizabeth Kodiewiz Russia
DARLING, Helen Nellie, Jan 30 1915 Sex:F Child# 3 Anthony Darling Russia & Elizabeth Kudzewich Russia
DARLING, Jossie, Apr 29 1899 Sex:F Child# 1 Antoine Darling Russia & Mary Mieliemska Russia
DARLING, Julian, Jul 21 1917 Sex:M Child# 11 Anthony Darling Russia & Elizabeth Cochewicz Russia
DARLING, Stanist Owas, Oct 2 1900 Sex: Child# 2 Antony Darling Russia & Mary Meliska Russia
DASES, Christos Esedas, Mar 31 1910 Sex:M Child# 4 Nicholas Dases Greece & Mary Pasbasis Greece
DAUBEISE, Felix, Nov 30 1888 Sex:M Child# 1 Felix Daubeise Canada & Emma Sirois Canada
DAUDLEY, June Priscilla, Sep 22 1929 Sex:F Child# 3 Herbert Daudley Nashua, NH & Josephine O'Neil Nashua, NH
DAUFAULT, Irene B, Feb 14 1888 Sex:F Child# 4 Georges Daufault W Boylston, MA & Philomene Launiere Plattsburg, NY
DAULPHINAIS, Irene, Dec 25 1926 Sex:F Child# 1 W Daulphinais Nashua, NH & Irene Bernard Nashua, NH
DAUPHINA, Elizabeth Juliette, Mar 29 1928 Sex:F Child# 2 Wilmer Dauphina Nashua, NH & Irene Barnard Nashua, NH
DAUPHINAIS, Harry Francis, Jun 2 1932 Sex:M Child# 4 W Dauphinais Nashua, NH & Irene Bernard Nashua, NH

DAUPHINAIS, Wilmore, Jul 25 1900 Sex:M Child# 3 J B Dauphinais Canada & M I Lessard Nashua, NH
DAVARIZ, Joseph, May 14 1902 Sex:M Child# 4 Anthony Davariz Russia & Mary Milarite Russia
DAVENPORT, Charles L, May 1 1887 Sex:M Child# 1 Wood'n Davenport Lewiston, ME & Cynthia E Canada
DAVENPORT, Mabell H, May 23 1890 Sex:F Child# 3 Woodman Davenport Maine & Cynthia Bennett Canada
DAVENPORT, Priscilla, Nov 26 1918 Sex:F Child# 3 Norman Davenport Boston, MA & Ida Pillsbury Croydon, NH
DAVENPORT, Stephen Thomas, Mar 29 1926 Sex:M Child# 7 Norman Davenport Boston, MA & Ida Pillsbury Croydon, NH
DAVENPORT, Unknown, Oct 11 1888 Sex:M Child# 2 W F Davenport Phillips, ME & Cynthia E Bennett Brooklyn, C E
DAVID, Ann Louise, Feb 5 1931 Sex:F Child# 3 Charles David Farmington, NH & Lela Alberta Bessey Dover, NH
DAVID, Blanche Alberta, Jul 31 1898 Sex:F Child# 11 Onesime David Canada & Elise Desautels Canada
DAVID, George Honorius, Jun 20 1902 Sex:M Child# 13 Onesime David Canada & Elise Desautels Canada
DAVID, Joseph Elplege L, Mar 18 1901 Sex:M Child# 12 Onesime David Canada & Elise Desautels Canada
DAVIDSON, Betty Ann, Mar 3 1932 Sex:F Child# 2 Law G Davidson W Virginia & Thelma P Dillin Hendley, Neb
DAVIDSON, Edgar Robert, Oct 16 1928 Sex:M Child# 2 E A Davidson Berlin, NH & Grace Barry Nashua, NH
DAVIDSON, Jane Elizabeth, May 11 1927 Sex:F Child# 1 G A Davidson Berlin, NH & Grace Barry Nashua, NH
DAVIES, Franklin J, Dec 22 1887 Sex:M Child# 2 Samuel Davies England & C L Manchester Rhode Island
DAVIS, Amy Elizabeth, Jun 24 1917 Sex:F Child# 2 Stilman G Davis Nashua, NH & Harriet E Gilbert Chicago, IL
DAVIS, Barbara, Aug 9 1910 Sex:F Child# 1 Warren H Davis Hubbardston, MA & Jennie L Clark Gardiner, MA
DAVIS, Barbara, Mar 6 1921 Sex:F Child# 1 Herman H Davis Woodbury, VT & Tilby Keller Brooklyn, NY
DAVIS, Bennie, Nov 2 1904 Sex:M Child# 3 Samuel Davis Russia & Yetta Perlinan Russia
DAVIS, Bruce, Sep 23 1916 Sex:M Child# 6 James W Davis Enosburg, VT & Ethel M Bruce Lakeport, NH
DAVIS, Carlton Edwin, Sep 8 1907 Sex:M Child# 3 Frank H Davis Vermont & Villa Stevens Woodsville, NH
DAVIS, Carroll, Nov 27 1918 Sex:M Child# 7 James W Davis Enosburg, VT & Ethel Bruce Lakeport, NH
DAVIS, Charles Leon, Oct 6 1889 Sex:M Child# 2 George E Davis Nova Scotia & Tilly M McGilvey Nova Scotia
DAVIS, Clare, Dec 28 1923 Sex:F Child# 5 Thomas J Davis Pepperell, MA & Margaret Lully Pepperell, MA
DAVIS, Dexter William, Sep 5 1890 Sex:M Child# 1 Henry W Davis Monson, ME & Annie E Jackson Canada
DAVIS, Diana Clare, Dec 11 1928 Sex:F Child# 4 Carl F Davis Nashua, NH & Corinne Bisson Manchester, NH
DAVIS, Dorothy, Nov 12 1910 Sex:F Child# 3 Albert A Davis, Jr Tyngsboro, MA & Pearl Marston Plainfield, NH
DAVIS, Dorothy, May 21 1920 Sex:F Child# 3 Stilman G Davis Nashua, NH & Harriet Gilbert Chicago, IL
DAVIS, Earl Francis, Nov 10 1897 Sex:M Child# 5 Henry W Davis Monson, ME & Anna E Jackson Canada
DAVIS, Earl Maurice, Jan 9 1925 Sex:M Child# 3 Earl Francis Davis Nashua, NH & Corenne Basson Manchester, NH
DAVIS, Eleanor Elizabeth, May 21 1924 Sex:F Child# 1 Leon David Davis Hillsboro, NH & Natalie E Wheeler Nashua, NH
DAVIS, Ella Ellen, Oct 31 1934 Sex:F Child# 3 Francis Davis Brooklyn, NY & Eva Mitchell Sidney, ME
DAVIS, Elmer Charles, Aug 24 1906 Sex:M Child# 2 Charles J Davis NH & Catherine A Holland NH
DAVIS, Ethel, Oct 27 1890 Sex:F Child# 3 Frank E Davis Nashua, NH & Amy E Green New York
DAVIS, Eva S, Jul 13 1896 Sex:F Child#  Abraham Davis Russia & Sadie Forman Russia
DAVIS, Evelyn Mary, Sep 20 1923 Sex:F Child# 3 Frank H Davis Pittsburg, NH & Mildred Bennett St Johnsbury, VT
DAVIS, Faith Gardner, Dec 10 1908 Sex:F Child# 1 Charles Davis St John, NB & Julia Sherman Lowell, MA
DAVIS, Forest Kendell, Feb 1 1918 Sex:M Child# 2 Harold M Davis Dorchester, MA & Louise E Foster Burlington, MA
DAVIS, George Albert, May 18 1927 Sex:M Child# 1 George A Davis Lowell, MA & Elsie A Smith Rochester, NH
DAVIS, George Hathaway, Aug 4 1914 Sex:M Child# 2 Warren H Davis Hubberdstown, MA & Jennie S Clark Gardner, MA
DAVIS, Georges, Mar 20 1897 Sex:M Child# 1 Chester E Davis Leominster, MA & Marie Morin Nashua, NH
DAVIS, Gertie, Mar 11 1908 Sex:F Child# 4 Samuel Davis Russia & Yetta Pillman Russia
DAVIS, Harry, Aug 24 1910 Sex:M Child# 5 Samuel Davis Russia & Etta Pelman Russia
DAVIS, Harry Willis, Oct 6 1895 Sex:M Child# 4 Harry W Davis Maine & Annie Jackson Canada
DAVIS, Herbert Armstrong, Aug 23 1899 Sex:M Child# 1 Walter M Davis Mass & Cynthia M Armstrong NY Stillborn
DAVIS, Jacqueline Norma, Oct 28 1930 Sex:F Child# 5 Henry A Davis Hollis, NH & Annie Wright Wilton, NH
DAVIS, Jean Elizabeth, Oct 9 1935 Sex:F Child# 1 Donald Davis Dorchester, MA & Dorothy Johnson Bedford, NH
DAVIS, Jean V, Jun 21 1931 Sex:F Child# 1 Townsend King Davis Trenton, NJ & Helen G Butler New York, NY
DAVIS, Jeremy Hayward, Dec 5 1925 Sex:M Child# 3 Bernard M Davis Canada & Ruth W Towle Canada
DAVIS, Joseph Tully, Aug 2 1926 Sex:M Child# 6 Thomas Davis Pepperell, MA & Margaret Tully Pepperell, MA
DAVIS, Junior, Jul 14 1930 Sex:M Child# 5 Earl Davis Nashua, NH & Corinne Bisson Manchester, NH
DAVIS, Kenneth William, Oct 27 1925 Sex:M Child# 2 John M Davis Hillsboro, NH & Janet M Gillispie Prince Edw Island
DAVIS, Law Montgomery, Mar 8 1917 Sex:M Child# 3 John C Davis Boston, MA & Ella Chellis Loud W Newfield, ME
DAVIS, Leon David, Jr, Jun 13 1927 Sex:M Child# 2 Leon D Davis Hillsboro, NH & Natalie Wheeler Nashua, NH
DAVIS, Marie, Dec 19 1898 Sex:F Child# 5 Auguste Davis Canada & Denise Drolet Canada
DAVIS, Marie Chlotilda, May 17 1892 Sex:F Child# 2 Harry Davis Maine & Anna Jackson Canada
DAVIS, Marion, May 20 1924 Sex:F Child# 4 Stilman G Davis Nashua, NH & Harriet Gilbert Chicago, IL
DAVIS, Norma Etta, Sep 5 1929 Sex:F Child# 2 Charles Davis Nashua, NH & Mildred Fuller Tyngsboro, MA
DAVIS, Olive F, May 17 1893 Sex:F Child# 2 H W Davis Maine & Annie E Jackson Canada
DAVIS, Paul, Nov 16 1919 Sex:M Child# 4 Thomas J Davis Pepperell, MA & Margaret C Tully Pepperell, MA
DAVIS, Priscilla, Jul 12 1920 Sex:F Child# 3 Harold Davis Dorchester, MA & Louise Foster Burlington, VT
DAVIS, Priscilla, Sep 24 1922 Sex:F Child# 4 Harold M Davis Hingham, MA & Evangeline Foster Burlington, VT
DAVIS, Priscilla Madeline, Sep 13 1921 Sex:F Child# 1 Earl Fran Davis Nashua, NH & Corine M Bisson Manchester, NH
DAVIS, Richard F, May 20 1914 Sex:M Child# 5 James W Davis Enosburg, VT & Ethel M Bruce Lakeport, NH
DAVIS, Robert Elkins, Jul 9 1922 Sex:M Child# 2 Earl L Davis Hillsboro, NH & Carrie Bello Elkins Pepperell, MA
DAVIS, Roger Norman, Feb 13 1923 Sex:M Child# 2 Earl F Davis Nashua, NH & Corinne Bisson Manchester, NH
DAVIS, Rose, Jan 9 1902 Sex:F Child# 2 Samuel Davis Russia & Yetta Palnus Russia
DAVIS, Rose Gertrude, May 8 1911 Sex:F Child# 2 John Davis Portland, ME & Bella Merrill England
DAVIS, Ruth Anna, Mar 3 1901 Sex:F Child# 1 Fred A Davis Nashua, NH & Louise Coffey Nashua, NH
DAVIS, Ruth Anne, Jan 17 1935 Sex:F Child# 1 Richard Davis E Pepperell, MA & Ruth H Leach Manchester, NH
DAVIS, Sally Avesta, Jan 21 1936 Sex:F Child# 4 Clayton W Davis Fitchburg, MA & Clara Swallow Nashua, NH
DAVIS, Samuel, Oct 26 1899 Sex:M Child# 2 Abram Davis Russia & Sadie Farman Russia
DAVIS, Stillman, Nov 15 1887 Sex:M Child# 2 Frank E Davis Nashua, NH & Amy E Ellenbury, NY

DAVIS, Stilman George, Jr, May 14 1916 Sex:M Child# 1 Stilman G Davis Nashua, NH & Harriet E Gilbert Chicago, IL
DAVIS, Sumner Paul, Jan 14 1935 Sex:M Child# 3 William Davis Russia & Nettie Kessler Russia
DAVIS, Sybil, Apr 11 1896 Sex:F Child# 2 Arthur H Davis Nashua, NH & Sara Cummings Nashua, NH
DAVIS, Unknown, Sep 15 1891 Sex:F Child# 1 Arthur M Davis Oxford, MA & Nellie P Dodge Sutton, MA
DAVIS, Unknown, Sep 19 1891 Sex:F Child# 2 Fred Davis Oxford, MA & Annie Morrison Canada
DAVIS, Unknown, Aug 8 1893 Sex:M Child# 3 Fred H Davis Oxford, MA & Annie Morrison Winslow, CA
DAVIS, Unknown, Mar 12 1895 Sex:F Child# 4 Fred H Davis Oxford, MA & Annie Morrison Sherbrooke, Canada
DAVIS, Unknown, Mar 12 1895 Sex:F Child# 1 Arthur H Davis Nashua, NH & Sara F Cummings Nashua, NH
DAVIS, Unknown, Sep 23 1898 Sex:M Child# 3 Arthur H Davis Nashua, NH & Sarah Cummings Nashua, NH
DAVIS, Unknown, Sep 7 1899 Sex:M Child# 1 W L Davis NH & Etta Green Mass
DAVIS, Unknown, Oct 24 1901 Sex:M Child# 2 Weslley Davis Lakeport & Etta Green Lowell, MA Stillborn
DAVIS, Unknown, Nov 22 1906 Sex:M Child# 1 Lozier Davis Cushing, ME & Selina Birmingham Galveston, TX
DAVIS, Warren Horace, Jr, May 14 1916 Sex:M Child# 3 Warren H Davis Hubbardston, MA & Jennie L Clark Gardner, MA
DAVISON, Albert L, Apr 21 1895 Sex:M Child# 1 L A Davison Lyme & J A Bennett Canterbury, PQ
DAVISON, Unknown, Jul 4 1893 Sex:F Child# George W Davison Philadelphia, PA & Emma J Kenny Maine
DAWSON, George Vincent, Feb 24 1930 Sex:M Child# 1 George Dawson Canada & Dorothy Hughes Dover, NH
DAWSON, Thomas Harold, Dec 15 1933 Sex:M Child# 2 George V Dawson Canada & Dorothy Hughes Dover, NH
DAY, Frederick Davis, May 21 1891 Sex:M Child# 1 C M Day Boston, MA & Lizzie M Bancroft Montreal, Canada
DAY, Phyllis Winifred, Oct 5 1928 Sex:F Child# 2 Kenneth F Day Wesley, ME & D M Lovejoy Hollis, NH
DAY, Unknown, Mar 25 1927 Sex:M Child# 1 Kenneth F Day Wesley, ME & Doris M Lovejoy Hollis, NH Stillborn
DAYO, Charles Louis, Sep 18 1912 Sex:M Child# 2 Conrad Dayo US & Ruth Raby US
DAYO, Dorothy Marie, Apr 18 1911 Sex:F Child# 1 Conrad Dayo US & Ruth Raby US
DAYO, Robert Earl, Aug 2 1914 Sex:M Child# 3 Conrad Dayo US & Ruth Willett US
DAYOT, Sophia, Mar 23 1914 Sex:F Child# 5 Peter Dayot Russia & Besse Borzinsci Russia
DAZUCK, Horace Vaslour, Feb 13 1917 Sex:M Child# 1 Charley Dazuck Russia Poland & Helena Sereizick Russia Poland
DE FORREST, Mary K, Jan 24 1899 Sex:F Child# 2 Charles De Forrest Lewiston, ME & Lizzie Fournier Canada
de KER'K, Marie Anne, Jun 3 1895 Sex:F Child# 15 J LeBrisse de Ker'k Canada & Clementine Bernier Canada
DE WOLFE, Alberta S, Feb 25 1899 Sex:F Child# 2 A E De Wolfe Nashua, NH & Vedora C Shaw Augusta, ME
DEACON, Alfred James, Apr 14 1900 Sex:M Child# 2 A J Deacon England & Edith Duncan England
DEACON, Annie, Nov 30 1897 Sex:F Child# 1 Alfred Deacon England & Edith Duncan England
DEACON, Charles Henry, Jun 25 1914 Sex:M Child# 8 Alfred J Deacon England & Edith Duncan England
DEACON, Edith Gertrude, Jul 11 1917 Sex:F Child# 9 Alfred J Deacon England & Edith Duncan England
DEACON, John, Oct 10 1911 Sex:M Child# 7 Alfred J Deacon England & Edith Duncan England
DEACON, William Edward, Jul 27 1905 Sex:M Child# 5 Alfred J Deacon England & Edith Duncan England
DEAN, Charles Hobson, Jun 7 1898 Sex:M Child# William Dean Scotland & Mary Campbell Scotland
DEAN, Claude Reynold, Feb 15 1933 Sex:M Child# 1 Vernice Dean Nashua, NH & Dorothy Mayo Nashua, NH
DEAN, Edouard Roger Girard, Dec 14 1918 Sex:M Child# 8 James I Dean Michigan & Lea Beaulieu Canada
DEAN, Elbra M, Dec 8 1895 Sex:F Child# 1 Arthur W Dean Taunton, MA & Anna M Hamblett Milford, NH
DEAN, Gladys Irene, Sep 20 1918 Sex:F Child# 4 Thomas F Dean US & Laura Desrosiers Canada
DEAN, Harwood Samuel, Sep 27 1914 Sex:M Child# 2 Thomas Dean Milton, NH & Celina Desrosiers Canada
DEAN, Helen Irene, Oct 31 1922 Sex:F Child# 1 George Collins Dean Brookline, NH & Frances K McKelvie Littleton, NH
DEAN, Henry P N, Aug 16 1893 Sex:M Child# 1 Pierre Dean Nashua, NH & Rosanna Salvail Greenville, NH
DEAN, J Willfid William, Dec 17 1915 Sex:M Child# 6 James Dean Michigan & Lea Beaulieu Canada
DEAN, Joseph Ernest J, Sep 4 1906 Sex:M Child# 1 James Dean NH & Marie L Pelletier Canada
DEAN, Joseph George A, May 4 1908 Sex:M Child# 1 James Dean Michigan & Lea Beaulieu Canada
DEAN, Joseph Thomas Amedee, Jan 2 1912 Sex:M Child# 3 James Dean Michigan & Lea Beaulieu Canada
DEAN, Juliette Beatrice, Dec 21 1908 Sex:F Child# 3 James Dean NH & Marie Pelletier Canada
DEAN, Louis O, Sep 7 1891 Sex:M Child# 4 James Dean Canada & Amelie Marquis Canada
DEAN, M Lil R A Loretta, May 29 1913 Sex:F Child# 4 James Dean Michigan & Lea Beaulieu Canada
DEAN, Marie Beatrice, May 24 1916 Sex:F Child# 3 F Edward Dean Wilton, NH & Celina Desrosiers Canada
DEAN, Marie Elodie Ida, Jul 14 1914 Sex:F Child# 5 James Dean Michigan & Lea Beaulieu Canada
DEAN, Marie Florence D, Jul 18 1910 Sex:F Child# 6 James L Dean Michigan & Lea Beaulieu Canada
DEAN, Miriam Gertrude, Feb 17 1922 Sex:F Child# 1 Edward Dean NH & Amanda Schofield Nova Scotia
DEAN, Paul Sceva, Dec 9 1935 Sex:M Child# 1 Reynold A Dean Lebanon, NH & Muriel Sanders Nashua, NH
DEAN, Pierre, Apr 20 1890 Sex:M Child# 3 James Dean Michigan & Aurelia Marquis Canada
DEAN, Rita Velma, Apr 14 1927 Sex:F Child# 1 Henry Dean Nashua, NH & Elsie Lambert Vermont
DEAN, Robert, Aug 23 1917 Sex:M Child# 7 James Dean Michigan & Lea Beaulieu Canada
DEAN, Smith, Aug 14 1896 Sex:M Child# 2 Sidney S Dean Nova Scotia & Susan Dean Nova Scotia
DEAN, Unknown, Dec 19 1910 Sex:M Child# 5 Walter E Dean Lebanon, NH & Adell C H Porter Isle Lamotte, VT
DEANE, Darlene Joan, Jul 19 1933 Sex:F Child# 1 John I Deane Derry, NH & F M Burque Keene, NH
DEANE, Ruth May, Sep 14 1934 Sex:F Child# 2 John Irving Deane Derry, NH & Florence M Burke Keene, NH
DEANE, Wilfred Edward, Feb 8 1913 Sex:M Child# 1 Thomas Edward Deane Milton, NH & Celina Desrosiers Canada
DEARBORN, Barbara, Aug 6 1908 Sex:F Child# 1 Sam S Dearborn Milford, NH & May A Chandler Nashua, NH
DEARBORN, Katherine Laton, Jul 7 1896 Sex:F Child# 1 Frank A Dearborn Milford, NH & Clara K Laton Nashua, NH
DEARBORN, Unknown, Aug 28 1894 Sex:F Child# 5 Richard H Dearborn Corinth, VT & Nellie M Whitney Randolph, VT
DEASON, Rose Jeanette, Aug 29 1934 Sex:F Child# 2 William Deason Ft Worth, TX & Beatrice Weightman Barre, VT
DEBELLES, Mary, Apr 1 1912 Sex:F Child# 1 Peter Debelles Greece & Anastasia Apostolis Greece
DEBIEN, Joseph Homer, Feb 16 1922 Sex:M Child# 5 Omer Debien Canada & Adele Lafrance Canada
DEBOISBRAUD, Joseph, Jul 23 1928 Sex:M Child# 1 Leo Deboisbraud
DEBOISBRIAND, Alfred Girard, Sep 9 1928 Sex:M Child# 6 A DeBoisbriand Nashua, NH & Desneiges Dugas Canada
DEBOISBRIAND, Joseph Paul Roger, Apr 24 1932 Sex:M Child# 3 Leo Deboisbriand Nashua, NH & Albina Morin Canada
DEBOISBRIAND, Marie Ida Lorilda, Mar 8 1912 Sex:F Child# 6 Ernest DeBoisbriand Canada & Marie Parent Canada
DEBOISBRIAND, Morris, Aug 5 1914 Sex:M Child# 8 Ernest Desboisbriand Canada & Marie Parent Canada

DEBOISBRIAND, Unknown, May 14 1913 Sex:M Child# 7 Ernest Deboisbriand Canada & Mary Parent Canada
DEBOISBRIANT, Eva Adrienne, Mar 4 1908 Sex:F Child# 1 Horace Deboisbriant Canada & Delia Levesque Canada
DEBOISBRIANT, Marie Rose, Jul 9 1909 Sex:F Child# 2 Horace Deboisbriant Canada & Delia Levesque Canada
DEBOISBRIANT, William, Jul 31 1909 Sex:M Child# 4 Ernest Deboisbriant Canada & Marie Parent Canada
DEBOISBRIEN, Henri L S, Dec 1 1906 Sex:M Child# 3 Napoleon Deboisbrien Canada & Helene Salvail Nashua, NH
DEBOISBRIEN, Joseph O N L, Apr 14 1903 Sex:M Child# 1 N Deboisbrien Canada & Helene Salvail Nashua, NH
DEBOISBRIEN, Marie H O, May 7 1904 Sex:F Child# 2 Napoleon Deboisbrien Canada & Helene Salvail Nashua, NH
DEBOLOUSKA, Ann, Oct 12 1923 Sex:F Child# 3 Anthony Debolouska Lithuania & Amelia Yarks Lithuania
DEBOSBRIAND, Joseph E R, Jan 17 1907 Sex:M Child# 2 Ernest Debosbriand Canada & Marie Parent Canada
DEBOWIEZ, Joseph, Apr 7 1918 Sex:M Child# 1 Joseph Debowiez Russia & Josephine Petkawiez Russia
DECELLE, Esther Adrienne Mary, Jun 19 1926 Sex:F Child# 1 Alexander Decelle Ashland, NH & Adrienne Marquis Nashua
DECELLE, Jean Baptiste, Jul 4 1898 Sex:M Child# 7 J B Decelle Canada & Helene Collins Ireland
DECELLE, Jos Lucien Albert, Feb 8 1933 Sex:M Child# 2 Al P Decelle Nashua, NH & Marie Petrain Natick, RI
DECELLE, Joseph, Jun 10 1894 Sex:M Child# 2 Joseph Decelle Canada & Regina Paquet Canada
DECELLE, Joseph, Mar 5 1915 Sex:M Child# 8 Louis R Decelle Canada & Josephine Tessier Canada Stillborn
DECELLE, Joseph, Jul 28 1918 Sex:M Child# 10 Louis R Decelle St Caesaire, PQ & Josephine Tessier Canada
DECELLE, Lillian, Feb 5 1912 Sex:F Child# 7 Louis R Decelle Canada & Josephine Tessier Canada
DECELLE, Lucille Theresa, Nov 15 1928 Sex:F Child# 1 Albert Decelle Nashua, NH & Marie L Petrin Natick, RI
DECELLE, M Regina J, Jan 26 1902 Sex:F Child# 1 Louis Decelle Canada & Josephine Tessier Canada
DECELLE, Margaret Rita, Jul 1 1920 Sex:F Child# 10 Louis R Decelle Canada & Josephine Tessier Canada
DECELLE, Unknown, Oct 28 1895 Sex:F Child# 5 John B Decelle Canada & Ellen Colliern Limerick, Ireland
DECELLES, Agnes, May 26 1900 Sex:F Child# 3 Joseph Decelles Canada & Regina Paquette Canada
DECELLES, Alfred George, Sep 26 1918 Sex:M Child# 4 William Decelles Nashua, NH & Clara Galipeau Grovenerdale
DECELLES, Antoine, Jan 28 1897 Sex:M Child# 6 J B Decelles Canada & Helen Collier Ireland
DECELLES, Gerard Andre, Jun 6 1920 Sex:M Child# 5 William DeCelles Nashua, NH & Clara Galipeau Grovernerdale
DECELLES, Jean B, Jan 22 1889 Sex:M Child# 1 Jean B Decelles Canada & Ellen Collaers Ireland
DECELLES, Laura Agnes, Dec 29 1908 Sex:F Child# 5 Louis Decelles Canada & Josephine Tessier Canada
DECELLES, Louis, Apr 23 1935 Sex:M Child# 3 Albert Decelles Nashua, NH & Annette Petrain Natick, RI
DECELLES, Louis Alexandre, Nov 9 1903 Sex:M Child# 2 Louis Decelles Canada & Josephine Tessier Canada
DECELLES, Maria Olivette Lina, Jul 10 1912 Sex:F Child# 4 William Decelles Nashua, NH & Clara Galipeau Canada
DECELLES, Marie E A, Feb 21 1907 Sex:F Child# 4 Louis Decelles Canada & Josephine Tessier Canada
DECELLES, Prospere A, Sep 28 1905 Sex:M Child# 3 Louis Decelles Canada & Josephine Tessier Canada
DECELLES, Rosanna, Feb 12 1892 Sex:F Child# 3 John B Decelles Canada & Ellen Coliers Ireland
DECELLES, Rose Anna A, Dec 30 1910 Sex:F Child# 6 Louis Decelles Canada & Josephine Tessier Canada
DECELLES, Unknown, Nov 19 1890 Sex:M Child# 9 Gedeon Decelles Canada & Elmire Lambert Nashua, NH Stillborn
DECELLES, Unknown, Sep 6 1892 Sex:M Child# 12 Gedeon Decelles Canada & Elmire Lambert Nashua, NH Stillborn
DECELLES, Victor Leo, Sep 5 1921 Sex:M Child# 6 William Decelles Nashua, NH & Clara Galipeau N Grovernerdale
DECELLES, William C, Dec 13 1893 Sex:M Child# 4 Jean B Decelles Canada & Ellen Colliers Ireland
DECHARD, Lillian Vera, Jan 21 1902 Sex:F Child#   Joseph C Dechard Canada & Lottie C Annis Londonderry, NH
DECHESNEAU, Joseph Arthur, Jan 14 1892 Sex:M Child# 5 Nazaire Duchesneau Canada & Helene Languay Canada
DECHINES, Joseph Amedee, Aug 25 1896 Sex:M Child# 2 Pierre Dechines Canada & Madeleine Mercier Canada
DECKER, Mildred Frances, Jun 26 1896 Sex:F Child# 1 Wilmot Decker
DECLAIRE, Pauline, Oct 19 1891 Sex:F Child# 2 Joseph Declaire Canada & Louise Frenette Canada
DECLOS, Alfred, Jul 5 1889 Sex:M Child# 1 Oscar Declos Canada & Georgina Gadbois Spencer, MA
DECLOS, Corinne, Dec 24 1894 Sex:F Child#   Ozias Declos Canada & Georgina Gadbois Canada
DECLOS, Ernest Wilfrid, May 4 1898 Sex:M Child# 3 Alphe Declos Canada & Marie Fortin Canada
DECLOS, Francois Ernest, Jul 9 1894 Sex:M Child# 1 Oliver Declos Canada & Louise Monty Canada
DECLOS, Maria B, Sep 27 1893 Sex:F Child# 1 Joseph Declos Canada & Georgianna Charron Nashua, NH
DECLOS, Osias Henry, Aug 12 1891 Sex:M Child# 2 Oscar Declos Canada & Georgina Gadbois Canada
DECLOS, Silvia, Nov 22 1894 Sex:M Child# 2 Joseph Declos Canada & Georgina Charron Nashua, NH
DECOCHER, Irene Agnes, Mar 31 1929 Sex:F Child# 1 Walter DeCocher Lowell, MA & Beatrice Jeannette Nashua, NH
DECOTEAU, Elmer Antoine Joseph, Feb 6 1912 Sex:M Child# 2 Eli Decoteau Canada & Laura Gay Canada
DECOURCY, Henry Edward, Jan 4 1925 Sex:M Child# 1 Henry E Decourcy Whitefield, NH & Catherine Moriarty Nashua, NH
DECOURCY, Shirley Theresa, Feb 27 1927 Sex:F Child# 2 Henry Decourcy Whitefield, NH & Cath Moriarty Nashua, NH
DEDERIAN, Pargushy, Jun 14 1926 Sex:M Child# 3 M D Dederian Armenia & Bergesky Bogarian Armenia
DEDNES, Unknown, Nov 30 1921 Sex:M Child# 7 Peter Dednes Greece & Helen Spiropoulos Greece
DEDUCIS, Unknown, Apr 8 1914 Sex:M Child# 2 Peter Deducis Greece & A Sprivanopoulos Greece
DEDUCIS, Unknown, Dec 27 1918 Sex:F Child# 1 Peter Deducis Greece & Annie Spiroanpouli Greece
DEDUSIS, Spiro P, Feb 13 1917 Sex:M Child# 4 Peter Dedusis Greece & Annie Spiroanopoulos Greece
DEDUSIS, Unknown, Jan 24 1916 Sex:F Child# 3 Peter Dedusis Greece & Annie Spiroanopoulos Greece
DEE, Daphney, Jul 12 1927 Sex:F Child# 1 John Dee Pepperell, MA & Teckla Wells Indiana
DEESCHAMPS, Louis Philippe, Jan 12 1902 Sex:M Child# 6 Joseph Deschamps Canada & Odile Malenfant Canada
DEFOE, Marie Beatrice, Mar 11 1915 Sex:F Child# 1 Edward N Defoe Nashua, NH & Cora Maranda Nashua, NH
DEFOREST, Albert, May 1 1900 Sex:M Child# 3 Charles DeForest Mass & Lizzie Fournier Canada
DEFOREST, Mary Josephine, Sep 21 1897 Sex:F Child# 1 Charles Deforest Lewiston, ME & Elizabeth Foucy Canada
DEFOREST, Unknown, Dec 29 1901 Sex:M Child# 4 Charles DeForest Maine & Mary E Canada
DEFREES, Burton Sill, Feb 21 1926 Sex:M Child# 3 Burton S DeFrees Kansas & Wena R Lawson Lynn, MA
DEFREES, Virginia Kay, Jun 28 1922 Sex:F Child# 2 Burton DeFrees Sterling, KS & Wena Lawson Lynn, MA
DEFRIEST, De Forest, Aug 31 1888 Sex:M Child# 2 Alva H Defriest New York City & Sophia Benjamin Riverhead, NY
DEGAN, Charles, Jun 21 1917 Sex:M Child# 7 Daniel Degan Boston, MA & Catherine Philbin Edinborough,Scotland
DEGAN, Helen, Jan 24 1911 Sex:F Child# 5 Daniel Degan US & Catherine Philbin US
DEGARSIS, Unknown, Jan 1 1916 Sex:M Child# 8 Alexander Degarsis Russia & Victoria Paplakuts Russia
DEGASIS, Amelia, May 22 1909 Sex:F Child# 5 Aleck Degasis Russia & Victoria Papicski Russia

DEGASIS, Ann Victoria, Oct 3 1905 Sex:F Child# 3 Aleck Degasis Russia & Victoria Poploski Russia
DEGASIS, Carole Victoria, Jan 9 1935 Sex:F Child# 1 Bolic Degasis Nashua, NH & Marjorie Clough Nashua, NH
DEGASIS, Diana, Aug 6 1934 Sex:F Child# 1 Danile Degasis Nashua, NH & Rachel Rataf Lithuania
DEGASIS, Florence S, Jan 1 1920 Sex:F Child# 8 Alexander Degasis Russia & Victoria Paploski Russia
DEGASIS, John, Jul 29 1902 Sex:M Child# 1 Alex Degasis Russia & Victoria Poplopka Russia
DEGASIS, Justine, Apr 28 1907 Sex:F Child# 4 Alexander Degasis Russia & Victoria Paploskie Russia
DEGASSES, Daniel A, Mar 3 1911 Sex:M Child# 6 Alexander Degasses Russia & Victoria Paplauski Russia
DEGESIS, Eugenie, Oct 29 1913 Sex:F Child# 6 Alexander Degesis Russia & Victoria Papalowski Russia
DEGNAN, Ann Mary, Oct 5 1917 Sex:F Child# 2 Bart I Degnan Nashua, NH & Anna M Murphy Adams, MA
DEGNAN, Barbara, Sep 3 1908 Sex:F Child# 2 Peter J Degnan Nashua, NH & Leona H Otis Nashua, NH
DEGNAN, Bernard Francis, Oct 18 1893 Sex:M Child# 4 James Degnan Ireland & Sarah McLaughlin Ireland
DEGNAN, Henri Albert, Jan 24 1902 Sex:M Child# 7 William Degnan Canada & Delima Courcy Canada
DEGNAN, James H, Nov 5 1891 Sex:M Child# 3 James Degnan Ireland & Sarah McLaughlin Ireland
DEGNAN, James William, Jr, Jul 1 1921 Sex:M Child# 1 James W Degnan Worcester, MA & Mary C Horman Collinsville
DEGNAN, Mary Ann, Aug 31 1888 Sex:F Child# 1 James Degnan Ireland & Sarah McLaughlin Ireland
DEGNAN, Paul, Jul 10 1919 Sex:M Child# 3 Bart I Degnan Nashua, NH & Anna M Murphy Adams, MA
DEGNAN, Unknown, Nov 21 1914 Sex:F Child# 4 Daniel W Degnan Boston, MA & Catherine Phibbin Scotland
DEGRAMMON, Lucy, Nov 14 1912 Sex:F Child# 6 Winfred DeGrammon Canada & Anna Trepanier Canada
DEGRAMMON, Mary Andrian, May 21 1911 Sex:F Child# 5 Wilfred D DeGrammon Canada & Anna Trepanier Augusta, ME
DEGRENIER, Robert Joseph, Nov 29 1935 Sex:M Child# 1 Jos H Degrenier Shelburne, MA & Minnie Bernard Nashua, NH
DEHETRE, John B, Oct 21 1890 Sex:M Child# 10 Telespose Dehetre Canada & Aurelie Bacot Canada
DEHLORIAN, Dehlman, Sep 19 1888 Sex:F Child# 2 Henry Dehlorian Brooklyn, NY & Maggie Wallace Philadelphia, PA
DEJARLAIS, Elaine, Jun 2 1935 Sex:F Child# 6 Alf P DeJarlais Nashua, NH & Millie C Sweet Sutton, Quebec
DELACOMBE, Joseph A, Jun 4 1889 Sex:M Child# 16 D Delacombe Canada & Marie Pouliot Canada
DELACOMBE, Unknown, Jun 4 1889 Sex:M Child# 15 D Delacombe Canada & Marie Pouliot Canada
DELAFONT, Alice May, Apr 4 1910 Sex:F Child# 2 Charles Delafont Canada & Laura J Robbins Nashua, NH
DELAGE, Joseph Gerard, Jul 20 1934 Sex:M Child# 7 Arthur Delage Lowell, MA & Mabel Villandry Leominster, MA
DELANEY, Arthur Henri, Jun 28 1894 Sex:M Child# 4 William Delaney US & Emelie Jodoin St Albans, VT
DELANEY, Patrick Edward, Dec 1 1918 Sex:M Child# 1 Patrick E Delaney Ireland & Bernice Guttie Nashua, NH Stillborn
DELANSKY, Philip, Feb 16 1910 Sex:M Child# 4 Simon Delansky Russia & Betsy Bonanstein Russia
DELAUNY, Marguerite Ruth, Jul 27 1897 Sex:F Child# 2 Daniel Delauny Nova Scotia & Maggie Kingston St John, NB
DELAUNY, Mary Ann L, Jun 27 1897 Sex:F Child# 6 Willie Delauny Nova Scotia & Emelie Jodoin St Albans, VT
DELAURAY, Mary Lilian, Mar 11 1899 Sex:F Child# 3 Daniel Delauray NS & Marguerite Kingston St John, NB
DELAURY, Charles Augustus, Nov 20 1898 Sex:M Child# 4 Charles Delaury Weymouth, MA & Bertha Thompson Nashua, NH
DELAURY, Daniel Joseph, Oct 17 1895 Sex:M Child# 1 Daniel Delaury Nova Scotia & Maggie Kingston St John, NB
DELAURY, M R Delima, Aug 19 1895 Sex:F Child# 5 Willie Delaury NS & Emelie Jodoin St Albans, VT
DELFEN, Melie, Oct 3 1896 Sex:F Child# 1 Joseph Delfen Italy & Marie Gagnon Canada
DELINSKY, Abraham, Jun 4 1925 Sex:M Child# 3 Simon Delinsky Russia & Eva Feldman Russia
DELINSKY, Mary, Nov 7 1912 Sex:F Child# 5 Simon Delinsky Russia & Bessie Boronstein Russia
DELINSKY, Mildred Pearl, Feb 6 1924 Sex:F Child# 2 Simeon Delinsky Russia & Eva Fieldman Russia
DELISLE, Blanche Yvonne, Mar 18 1908 Sex:F Child# 2 Pierre Delisle Canada & Marie Laporte Canada
DELISLE, Henri, May 31 1906 Sex:M Child# 1 Pierre Delisle Canada & Clara Laporte Canada
DELISLE, Laurette Pauline, May 27 1935 Sex:F Child# 1 Trefle Delisle Canada & M Aurore Pinette US
DELONG, Marjorie Helen, Nov 28 1904 Sex:F Child# 1 Morton A Delong Ellenburg, NY & Ethel M Carey Hillsboro, NH
DELONNE, Zepheren Euclide, Feb 14 1891 Sex:M Child# 2 Eugene Delonne Canada & Rosa Groteau Nashua, NH
DELOREY, Bertha Frances, Mar 28 1897 Sex:F Child# 3 Charles R Delorey Weymouth, MA & Bertha L Thompson Nashua, NH
DELOREY, Daniel J, Apr 27 1894 Sex:M Child# 2 Charles R Delorey N Weymouth, MA & Bertha Thompson Nashua, NH
DELOREY, Francis Grant, Aug 6 1913 Sex:M Child# 8 Charles Delorey Mass & Bertha Thompson Nashua, NH
DELOREY, Lillian G A, Jan 15 1909 Sex:F Child# 7 Charles R Delorey Mass & Bertha L Thompson NH
DELOREY, Martin, Jul 13 1903 Sex:M Child# 6 Charles R Delorey Weymouth, MA & Bertha L Thompson Nashua, NH
DELOREY, William Edward, Apr 24 1901 Sex:M Child# 5 Charles R Delorey Weymouth, MA & Bertha L Thompson Nashua, NH
DELORME, Albertine, Jun 10 1897 Sex:F Child# 2 Esdras Delorme Canada & Josephine Gagnon Canada
DELORME, Alice, Mar 28 1895 Sex:F Child# 1 Esdras Delorme Canada & Josephine Gagnon Canada
DELORME, Alice Florette, Apr 4 1911 Sex:F Child# 9 Esdras Delorme Canada & Josephine Gagnon Canada
DELORME, Armand Albain, Sep 14 1904 Sex:M Child# 6 Esdras Delorme Canada & Josephine Gagnon Canada
DELORME, Emilda Dolores, Mar 13 1909 Sex:F Child# 8 Esdras Delorme Canada & Josephine Gagnon Canada
DELORME, Hormidas Albert, Apr 19 1903 Sex:M Child# 5 Esdras Delorme Canada & Josephine Gagnon Canada
DELORME, Marie Andrea, Feb 5 1899 Sex:F Child# 3 Esdras Delorme Canada & Josephine Gagnon Canada
DELORME, Oberline Eva, Sep 6 1900 Sex:F Child# 4 Esdra Delorme Canada & Josephine Gagnon Canada
DELORME, Wilfred Roland, Sep 27 1906 Sex:M Child# 7 Esdras Delorme Canada & Josephine Gagnon Canada
DELORRIER, Joseph, Mar 19 1887 Sex:M Child# 9 Joseph Delorrier NY & Marguerite Grant NY
DELORY, Edmond Louis, Mar 22 1892 Sex:M Child# 2 William Delory Canada & Melie Jodoin Vermont
DELORY, George Alphonse, Feb 23 1893 Sex:M Child# 3 Willie Delory Nova Scotia & Melie Jodoin Vermont
DELORY, Marguerite Loretta, Feb 27 1893 Sex:F Child# 1 Charles R Delory Weymouth, MA & Bertha Thompson Nashua, NH
DELORY, William Joseph, Nov 28 1890 Sex:M Child# 1 William Delory Canada & Melia Jadoin VT
DELUDE, Emma Germaine, Apr 8 1922 Sex:F Child# 4 Evermond Delude NH & Clorinthe Lafrance Canada
DELUDE, Ernest, Jul 27 1891 Sex:M Child# 2 Joseph Delude Canada & Exina Scott Canada
DELUDE, Florette Rita, Jan 20 1920 Sex:F Child# 2 Albert Delude Nashua, NH & Ida Levesque Canada
DELUDE, George Gerard, Oct 12 1921 Sex:M Child# 4 Alfred Delude Canada & Josephine Lafrance Canada
DELUDE, George Henry, Aug 3 1929 Sex:M Child# 7 Evermont Delude Nashua, NH & Clarinda Lafrance Canada
DELUDE, Hector Arthur Gerard, Dec 12 1920 Sex:M Child# 3 Evemont Delude US & Clariside Lafrance Canada
DELUDE, Irene Rita, Aug 16 1932 Sex:F Child# 8 E Delude Nashua, NH & C Lafrance Canada
DELUDE, Jeanne Beatrice, Sep 1 1920 Sex:F Child# 3 Alfred Delude Canada & Josephine Lafrance Canada

DELUDE, Jos Rolland Jean, Sep 7 1919 Sex:M Child# 2 Joseph Delude NH & Alma Boucher NH
DELUDE, Joseph, Apr 21 1888 Sex:M Child# 12 Joseph Delude Canada & Agnes Beriner Canada
DELUDE, Joseph, Apr 25 1916 Sex:M Child# 1 Evrimond Delude Nashua, NH & Clarenthe Lafrance Canada
DELUDE, Josephine Gertrude, Jan 28 1923 Sex:F Child# 5 Alfred Delude Canada & Josephine Lafrance Canada
DELUDE, Leo, Jan 16 1916 Sex:M Child# 1 Clarence Delude Canada & Marie Lavoie Canada
DELUDE, Lorraine Agnes, Oct 31 1915 Sex:F Child# 1 Ernest Delude Nashua, NH & Delia Levesque Canada
DELUDE, Louis Sylvio Robert, Nov 30 1925 Sex:M Child# 5 Evermont Delude Nashua, NH & Clorinde Lafrance Canada
DELUDE, M Blanche Lorette, Feb 23 1921 Sex:F Child# 3 Joseph Delude NH & Alma Boucher NH
DELUDE, Marie Anne Cecile, Oct 31 1917 Sex:F Child# 2 Alfred Delude Nashua, NH & Josephine Lafrance Canada
DELUDE, Marie Blanche, Mar 6 1900 Sex:F Child# 6 Joseph Delude Canada & Alexina Scott Canada
DELUDE, Maurice Lionel, Sep 8 1931 Sex:M Child# 2 Victor Delude Nashua, NH & Lena Landry Nashua, NH
DELUDE, May Lillian B, Feb 7 1907 Sex:F Child# 3 Polydore Delude Willimantic, CT & Josephine Roy Canada
DELUDE, Norbert Wilfred, Nov 17 1925 Sex:M Child# 3 Albert Delude Nashua, NH & Ida Levesque Canada
DELUDE, Olivette Eva, Jul 26 1920 Sex:F Child# 3 Ernest Delude US & Delia Levesque Canada
DELUDE, Osias Lionel, May 24 1903 Sex:M Child#  Joseph Delude Canada & Alexina Aeott Canada
DELUDE, Paul Delano, Jan 15 1934 Sex:M Child# 5 Ernest Delude Nashua, NH & Delia Levesque Nashua, NH
DELUDE, Raymond Victor, Aug 21 1929 Sex:M Child# 1 Victor Delude Nashua, NH & Lena Landry Nashua, NH
DELUDE, Romeo Normand, Sep 4 1922 Sex:M Child# 4 Ernest Delude US & Delia Levesque Canada
DELUDE, Rose Anna Irene, Jun 9 1905 Sex:F Child# 8 Joseph Delude Canada & Exina Scott Canada
DELUDE, Theresa Eva, May 1 1927 Sex:F Child# 6 Evermont Delude Nashua, NH & Clorinthe Lafrance Canada
DELZOPPO, Dora Nicoleta, Sep 10 1927 Sex:F Child# 4 Camillo Delzoppo Italy & P Salviani Italy
DELZOPPO, Maria Camilla, Jun 14 1925 Sex:F Child# 3 Camillo Delzoppo Italy & Yvonne Roy Italy
DELZOPPO, Tommaso Vincenza, Jul 20 1926 Sex:M Child# 3 C DelZoppo Italy & P Salviani Italy
DEMANCHE, Albert Ernest, Oct 11 1932 Sex:M Child# 8 H Demanche, Jr Nashua, NH & Rose Obin Nashua, NH
DEMANCHE, Alfred Ernest Joseph, Aug 12 1932 Sex:M Child# 1 E Demanche Nashua, NH & M Bonenfant Nashua, NH
DEMANCHE, Arthur, Feb 9 1909 Sex:M Child# 10 Henry Demanche Canada & Liza Parent Canada
DEMANCHE, Edouard Joseph, Feb 17 1903 Sex:M Child# 6 Henri Demanche Canada & Eliza Parent Canada
DEMANCHE, Edward Joseph, May 30 1935 Sex:M Child# 2 H J Demanche Nashua, NH & Elvina Gerow N Conway, NH
DEMANCHE, Eugene, Apr 17 1894 Sex:M Child# 1 Henry Demanche Canada & Elisa Parent Canada
DEMANCHE, Eva Rose, Feb 13 1922 Sex:F Child# 2 Henry Demanche NH & Rose Obin NH
DEMANCHE, Georgianna Irene, Nov 11 1931 Sex:F Child# 4 Joseph Demanche Nashua, NH & Marie Anna Lagace Canada
DEMANCHE, Hector, Jan 28 1907 Sex:M Child# 9 Henry Demanche Canada & Liza Parent Canada
DEMANCHE, Henri Augustus, Nov 6 1920 Sex:M Child# 1 Henri Demanche NH & Rose Obin NH
DEMANCHE, J Louis O'Neil, Oct 6 1911 Sex:M Child# 2 Thomas Demanche Canada & Marianne Gagnon Canada
DEMANCHE, Jennie Gloria, Jul 18 1930 Sex:F Child# 1 Hector Demanche Nashua, NH & Elvina Gerow NH
DEMANCHE, Jos Armand Horace, Sep 10 1934 Sex:M Child# 9 Henry Demanche Nashua, NH & Rose Obin Nashua, NH
DEMANCHE, Jos Arthur Andrew, Aug 4 1923 Sex:M Child# 3 Henry Demanche Nashua, NH & Rose Obin Nashua, NH
DEMANCHE, Jos Maurice Robert, Mar 9 1928 Sex:M Child# 2 Louis Demanche Nashua, NH & Marie L Morin Canada
DEMANCHE, Jos Napoleon R, Oct 8 1929 Sex:M Child# 3 Joseph Demanche Nashua, NH & Marie A Lagace Canada
DEMANCHE, Jos Robert Oliver, Feb 2 1926 Sex:M Child# 2 Joseph Demanche Nashua, NH & Anna Lagasse Nashua, NH
DEMANCHE, Joseph Albert, Dec 19 1933 Sex:M Child# 1 Albert Demanche Nashua, NH & Agnes Paradise Fitchburg, MA
DEMANCHE, Joseph Henri, Dec 16 1898 Sex:M Child# 4 Henri Demanche Canada & Liza Parent Canada
DEMANCHE, Joseph Leo Louis, Jan 10 1931 Sex:M Child# 7 Henri Demanche, Jr Nashua, NH & Rose Aubin Nashua, NH
DEMANCHE, Lorin Joseph George, Aug 21 1914 Sex:M Child# 3 Thomas Demanche Canada & Marie Anne Gagnon Canada
DEMANCHE, Louis Adelard, Jun 7 1895 Sex:M Child# 2 Henry Demanche Canada & Elisa Parent Canada
DEMANCHE, Marie Elise Jeannett, Jul 24 1924 Sex:F Child# 1 Joseph Demanche NH & Marie A Lagasse Canada
DEMANCHE, Maurice Wilfred, Sep 16 1927 Sex:M Child# 5 Henry Demanche Nashua, NH & Rose Obin Nashua, NH
DEMANCHE, Norman William, Aug 13 1925 Sex:M Child# 4 Henry Demanche Nashua, NH & Rosa Obin Nashua, NH
DEMANCHE, Paul Arthur, Nov 15 1928 Sex:M Child# 6 Henry Demanche Nashua, NH & Rose Obin Nashua, NH
DEMANCHE, Rose Anna, Nov 24 1905 Sex:F Child# 8 Henry Demanche Canada & Lizzie Parent Canada
DEMANCHE, Vitaline, Jul 12 1900 Sex:F Child# 3 George Demanche Canada & Emma Cognac Canada
DEMANCHE, Vitaline, Oct 24 1904 Sex:F Child# 7 Henri Demanche Canada & Eliza Parent Canada
DEMAR, Arthur, Sep 28 1888 Sex:M Child# 11 Zephirin Demar Canada & Victoria Gerard Canada
DEMARAIS, Edouard L, Nov 10 1897 Sex:M Child# 1 Leon Demarais St Albans, VT & Delia Grenon Wilton, NH
DEMARAIS, Leo, Apr 4 1906 Sex:M Child# 3 Leon Demarais St Albans, VT & Clara Jean Nashua, NH
DEMARAIS, Marie Jeannette, Jan 31 1901 Sex:F Child# 2 Joseph A Demarais Canada & Elmire Jodoin St Albans, VT
DEMARAIS, Robert Paul, Feb 1 1925 Sex:M Child# 2 Edward Demarais Nashua, NH & Grace Dalton Calais, ME
DEMARCHE, Joseph, Feb 21 1916 Sex:M Child# 4 Thomas Demarche Canada & Marianne Gagnon Canada Stillborn
DEMARIS, Ezra, Dec 16 1888 Sex:M Child# 1 Elzian Demaris Canada & Marie Lavalle Canada
DEMARIS, Rose Dubuque, Aug 8 1890 Sex:F Child# 1 Alexandre Demaris St Albans, VT & Rose Dubuque St Albans, VT
DEMARIUS, Amanda Adile, Dec 4 1889 Sex:F Child# 4 Philius Demarius Canada & Adile C Gray Canada
DEMARS, Joseph A, Apr 6 1893 Sex:M Child# 1 Albert Demars Canada & Annie Gauthier Canada
DEMARSH, Ernest, Apr 21 1911 Sex:M Child# 11 Henry Demarsh Canada & Liza Parent Canada
DEMARSH, Mary Emma, Feb 19 1901 Sex:F Child# 5 Henry Demarsh Canada & Eliza Perrault Canada
DEMAUCHE, Marie Eugenie, Nov 14 1896 Sex:F Child# 3 Henry Demauche Canada & Eliza Parent Canada
DEMERS, Anita Marie, May 4 1921 Sex:F Child# 10 Arthur Demers Canada & Hermine Levesque Canada
DEMERS, Bernadette Yvonne, Mar 1 1911 Sex:F Child# 5 Arthur Demers Canada & Hermine Levesque Canada
DEMERS, Eugene, Apr 3 1894 Sex:M Child# 3 Joseph Demers Canada & Virginia Goulette Canada
DEMERS, George Robert, Aug 27 1919 Sex:M Child# 2 Philomon Demers Canada & Dorilda Belanger Nashua, NH
DEMERS, Henry Emile, Dec 17 1928 Sex:M Child# 15 Arthur Demers Canada & Hermine Levesque Canada
DEMERS, Irene Annette, Feb 7 1915 Sex:F Child# 6 Felix Demers Canada & Laura Vigneux Canada
DEMERS, Jos Robert Normand, Jan 30 1918 Sex:M Child# 1 Philamon Demers Canada & Dorilda Belanger Nashua, NH
DEMERS, Joseph Arthur, Apr 13 1913 Sex:M Child# 6 Arthur Demers Canada & Herminie Levesque Canada

DEMERS, Joseph Louis Lucien, Jun 28 1924 Sex:M Child# 13 Arthur Demers
DEMERS, Joseph N, Jan 23 1887 Sex:M Child# 10 Zephriam Demers Canada & Victoria Girard Canada
DEMERS, Joseph Rolland, Oct 8 1919 Sex:M Child# 10 Arthur Demers Canada & Hermine Levesque Canada
DEMERS, Laurette, Aug 15 1926 Sex:F Child# 14 Arthur Demers Canada & Hermine Levesque Canada
DEMERS, Lorretta, Oct 9 1933 Sex:F Child# 1 (No Parents Listed)
DEMERS, M Lillian Beatrice, Nov 18 1922 Sex:F Child# 12 Arthur Demers Canada & Hermine Levesque Canada
DEMERS, M Therese Rachelle, Sep 16 1922 Sex:F Child# 4 Philomon Demers Canada & Dorilda Belanger Nashua, NH
DEMERS, Marie Lea, Apr 26 1918 Sex:F Child# 8 Arthur Demers Nashua, NH & Herminine Levesque Canada
DEMERS, Marie Olina, Sep 20 1900 Sex:F Child# 1 Alexandre Demers NH & Rose Anna Dichard NH
DEMERS, Marie Rosa, May 16 1895 Sex:F Child# 3 Zepherin Demers Canada & Minnie Mercier New York
DEMERS, Maurice Arthur, Aug 16 1931 Sex:M Child# 1 Theodore Demers Nashua, NH & Laura Parland Canada
DEMERS, Maurice Ernest, Jan 17 1924 Sex:M Child# 5 Philomon Demers P I, Canada & Dorilda Belanger Nashua, NH
DEMERS, Maurice Leonard, Jul 21 1934 Sex:M Child# 1 Maurice L Demers Canada & Sonia Levesque Nashua, NH
DEMERS, Paul Guy Normand, Jan 14 1934 Sex:M Child# 10 Paul Demers Canada & Alma Lesmerises Manchester, NH
DEMERS, Richard, Jun 30 1935 Sex:M Child# 2 Maurice Demers Canada & Sonia Levesque Nashua, NH
DEMERS, Rita Dorothy, Aug 18 1921 Sex:F Child# 3 Philomon Demers Canada & Dorilda Belanger Nashua, NH
DEMERS, Unknown, Jun 13 1896 Sex:M Child# 4 Zephrin Demers Canada & Minie Mercier Canada Stillborn
DEMERS, Unknown, Jan 6 1921 Sex:F Child# 1 Joseph Demers Berwick, ME & Delmarie Ouellette Canada Stillborn
DEMERS, Wilfred Roland, Nov 18 1932 Sex:M Child# 2 Theo Demers US & Laura Ferland US
DEMITANOS, Haido, Aug 4 1919 Sex:F Child# 3 Adam Demitanos Greece & Agaista Tamanikis Greece
DEMONTIGNEY, Willie, Oct 21 1893 Sex:M Child#  Henry de Montigney Canada & Rosalide Belle Canada
DEMONTIGNY, Alice Georgina, Sep 19 1904 Sex:F Child# 4 George DeMontigny Canada & Mary A Delorey Nova Scotia
DEMONTIIGNY, Arthur, Apr 2 1908 Sex:M Child# 8 Arthur DeMontigny Canada & Amelia Boisvert Canada
DEMONTIGNY, Auguste, Sep 6 1901 Sex:M Child# 1 Oseas DeMontigny Putnam, CT & Marie Gauthier Canada
DEMONTIGNY, Elaine Marie, Jun 16 1931 Sex:F Child# 1 Robert DeMontigny Nashua, NH & Loretta Jeanotte Nashua, NH
DEMONTIGNY, Estella Euphemia, Feb 6 1906 Sex:F Child# 5 George DeMontigny Canada & Mary Alice Delorey US
DEMONTIGNY, Gerard Edouard, Oct 31 1910 Sex:M Child# 9 Arthur DeMontigny Canada & Amelia Boisvert Canada
DEMONTIGNY, Helen Gertrude, Feb 2 1908 Sex:F Child# 6 George Demontigny & Mary A Delorey US
DEMONTIGNY, Henry George, Oct 14 1909 Sex:M Child# 7 George Demontigny Canada & Mary Delorey US
DEMONTIGNY, Irene Adelia, Feb 11 1905 Sex:F Child# 6 Arthur DeMontigny Canada & Amelia Boisvert Canada
DEMONTIGNY, Jane Elizabeth, Oct 17 1933 Sex:F Child# 2 Rob DeMontigny Nashua, NH & L Jeannotte Nashua, NH
DEMONTIGNY, Louis Ernest, Jun 24 1906 Sex:M Child# 7 Arthur DeMontigny Canada & Amelia Boisvert Canada
DEMONTIGNY, Robert Arthur, Jul 25 1903 Sex:M Child# 5 Arthur DeMontigny Canada & Amelia Boisvert Canada
DEMONTIQUY, Emile, Jan 27 1892 Sex:M Child# 1 Henry Demontiquy Canada & Rose A Belle Canada
DEMONTY, Unknown, Dec 4 1901 Sex:F Child# 2 George Demonty Canada & Alice Demonty NS
DEMPELIS, Costas, Sep 2 1929 Sex:M Child# 9 Peter J Dempelis Greece & A Apostolopoulos Greece
DEMPSEY, Mary E, Nov 12 1889 Sex:F Child# 1 Timothy B Dempsey Northfield, VT & Annie Early Nashua, NH
DENAULT, Albert, Mar 25 1906 Sex:M Child# 10 Philippe Denault Canada & Philomene Deschamps Canada
DENAULT, Aurore Delia, Sep 7 1914 Sex:F Child# 10 Frank Denault Canada & Mathilda Deschamps Canada
DENAULT, Eugene Adeline, Jan 6 1906 Sex:F Child# 4 Joseph Denault Canada & Mathilda Deschamps Canada
DENAULT, Jos Albert Raymond, Mar 8 1932 Sex:M Child# 3 Francis Denault Nashua, NH & H Desbiens Berlin, NH
DENAULT, Lucille Bertha, May 28 1925 Sex:F Child# l Albert Denault Nashua, NH & Eva Ferryall New York
DENAULT, Ludger Henry, Dec 23 1924 Sex:M Child# 1 Onisfor Denault Nashua, NH & Blanche Voyer Canada
DENAULT, Marie Annie, Aug 31 1903 Sex:F Child# 2 Francois Denault Canada & Mathilda Deschamps Canada
DENAULT, Marie Rose A L, Nov 5 1903 Sex:F Child# 9 Philias Denault Canada & Philomene Deschamps Canada
DENAULT, Mary Eva Theresa Y, May 21 1928 Sex:F Child# 2 Albert Denault Nashua, NH & Eva Ferryall New York
DENAULT, Telesphore, Sep 26 1902 Sex:M Child# 1 Frank Denault Canada & Mathilda Deschamps Canada
DENEAULT, Frank, Aug 15 1904 Sex:M Child# 3 Frank Deneault Canada & Mathilda Deschamps Canada
DENEAULT, Joseph Alfred, Sep 4 1912 Sex:M Child# 9 Frank Deneault Canada & Mathilde Deschamps Canada
DENEAULT, Marie Anne, Mar 3 1926 Sex:F Child# 2 Onicefor Deneault Nashua, NH & Blanche Voyer Canada
DENEAULT, Marie Irene L, Mar 28 1910 Sex:F Child# 7 Frank Deneault Canada & Mathilde Deschamps Canada
DENEAULT, Mathilda Rachel, Dec 27 1928 Sex:F Child# 2 Francis Deneault Nashua, NH & L Desbiens Canada
DENEAULT, Theresa Evangeline, Jun 10 1925 Sex:F Child# 1 Francis Deneault Nashua, NH & Leocade Deshaies Canada
DENEAUX, Joseph A, Nov 22 1888 Sex:M Child# 4 Phillipe Deneaux Canada & Emilie Germain Canada
DENIS, Alfred, Sep 5 1892 Sex:M Child# 2 Alfred Denis Canada & Arinenie Reeves Canada
DENIS, Ernest Albert, Jun 25 1919 Sex:M Child# 2 Louis Denis Canada & Marie L Cote Canada
DENIS, Joseph A Romeo, Apr 9 1931 Sex:M Child# 1 Louis Denis St Francoise, PQ & Marie L Cote St Francois, PQ
DENIS, Jos Cleophas, Mar 26 1935 Sex:M Child# 6 Louis Denis St Francoise, PQ & Marie L Cote St Francoise, PQ
DENIS, Joseph Emile Rene, Apr 8 1921 Sex:M Child# 1 Emile Denis Canada & Anna Turcotte Canada
DENIS, Leo Robert, Apr 18 1924 Sex:M Child# 3 Louis Denis Canada & Marie L Cote Canada
DENIS, Marie Annette F, May 13 1924 Sex:F Child# 5 Emile Denis Canada & Anna Turcotte Canada
DENIS, Marie Claire Louise, Apr 15 1935 Sex:F Child# 7 Emile Denis St Francoise, PQ & Anna Turcotte St Hubert, PQ
DENIS, Marie Eglantine Ida, Aug 30 1927 Sex:F Child# 4 Louis Denis Canada & Marie L Cote Canada
DENIS, Marie Emma, Oct 6 1891 Sex:F Child# 11 Louis Denis Centralville, RI & Elise Thibault Canada
DENIS, Marie Rochelle T, Apr 11 1929 Sex:F Child# 6 Emile Denis Canada & Anna Turcotte Canada
DENIS, Marie Rosalie Aldea, Jan 24 1923 Sex:F Child# 4 Emile Denis Canada & Anna Turcotte Canada
DENIS, Natalie Lucille, Aug 20 1933 Sex:F Child# 6 Louis Denis Canada & Marie Louise Cote Canada
DENISON, Robert Russell, Mar 19 1933 Sex:M Child# 2 Robert R Denison Warren, OH & Muriel Green PA
DENNING, Phyllis Marie, Aug 2 1930 Sex:F Child# 1 John Denning New Brunswick & Margaret McKay Nashua, NH
DENNIS, Doris, Jul 14 1919 Sex:F Child# 3 Floyd Dennis Vermont & Dora Tremblay NH
DENOIT, Mary Ann, Nov 19 1888 Sex:F Child# 8 Perrie Dunoit Canada & Artaimise Cotie Canada
DENTON, Marion Celia, Aug 23 1902 Sex:F Child# 3 Fred H Denton Lewis, NY & J S Cleland Lewis, NY
DEPACHER, Phyllis Gertrude, Apr 19 1933 Sex:F Child# 2 W L DePacher Lowell, MA & B Jeannotte Nashua, NH

DEPONT, Eddy Roland, Sep 18 1927 Sex:M Child# 3 Adelard Depont Canada & B Couture Canada
DEPONT, Germaine Theresa, Oct 9 1926 Sex:F Child# 2 Adelard Depont Canada & Belzemire Couture Canada
DEPONT, Marie Celina G, Jun 7 1930 Sex:F Child# 5 Adelard Depont Canada & Bellezemire Couture Canada
DEPONT, Marie Jeannette M, Dec 10 1928 Sex:F Child# 4 Adelard Depont Canada & Belle Z Couture Canada
DEPONT, Marie Lorraine, Oct 12 1934 Sex:F Child# 1 Arthur Depont Canada & Lillian Desrosiers Nashua, NH
DEPONT, Normand, Dec 18 1934 Sex:M Child# 1 Alphonse Depont Canada & Celina Theriault Nashua, NH
DEPONTBRIAND, Robert Gilbert, Oct 20 1932 Sex:M Child# 1 A de Pontbriand Mass & Anna Baltusar Penn
DEPONTBRIAND, Unknown, Mar 1 1928 Sex:F Child# 4 H Depontbriand Worcester, MA & Vivian Poisan Newport, VT
DERBY, Bernice Ruth, Jun 19 1923 Sex:F Child# 2 Marshall A Derby Keene, NH & Ruth Ashford Antrim, NH
DERBY, Donald Edwin, Sep 11 1921 Sex:M Child# 1 Marshall A Derby Keene, NH & Ruth Ashford Antrim, NH
DERBY, Russell Elvin, May 4 1923 Sex:M Child# 1 Clinton Derby Concord, NH & Mabel Felsh Lowell, MA
DERDARIAN, Karruyre, Apr 19 1915 Sex:F Child# 2 Manasse Derdarian Turkey & Bergiby Derdarian Turkey
DERDERIAN, Mary, Sep 10 1908 Sex:F Child# 1 Harry Derderian Turkey & Haganoush Bedegian Turkey
DERDERIAN, Puzint, May 24 1912 Sex:F Child# 1 Manosi Derderian Turkey & Berguhy Kovuckian Turkey
DERDORIAN, Harry, Jan 8 1913 Sex:M Child# 2 Harry Derdorian Turkey & Higanos Bedigia Turkey
DEREOTEAU, Joseph Henry, Jan 13 1889 Sex:M Child# 3 P Dereoteau Canada & Pamela Morin Canada
DERKEVOCKIAN, Anternik, Sep 21 1906 Sex:M Child# 1 Pen Derkevockian Turkey & Victoria Chakarian Turkey
DERLING, Peter, Jul 11 1909 Sex:M Child# 1 Anthony Derling Russia & Eliz Kodziawichute Russia
DERMANOOGIAN, Anna, Apr 27 1927 Sex:F Child# 2 K Dermanoogian Turkey & Yexa Sahagian Turkey
DERMARAIS, Mary C, Apr 12 1889 Sex:F Child# 6 Joseph Dermarais Canada & Mary Pairier NY
DERNERS, Marie Louise E, Nov 16 1890 Sex:F Child# 2 Napoleon Derners Nashua, NH & Amore Roussel Canada
DEROCHER, James Edward, Jr, Dec 14 1928 Sex:M Child# 1 J E DeRocher Nashua, NH & Hazel E Cronin Groton, MA
DEROCHER, Unknown, Jan 7 1898 Sex:M Child# 1 James D DeRocher Orono, ME & Annie M Waters Nashua, NH
DEROSIER, Edward Gilbert, Feb 1 1922 Sex:M Child# 1 Adelard Derosier Canada & Eva Blais Canada
DERUBBO, Ralph, Jul 19 1925 Sex:M Child# 5 Joseph DeRubbo Italy & Annie Infanti Italy
DERY, Emile Adrien E, Jul 1 1907 Sex:M Child# 3 Cyriac Dery Canada & Maria Provost Canada
DERY, Gracieuse Exilda, Jan 4 1906 Sex:F Child# 2 Ciriac Dery Canada & Maria Prevost Canada
DERY, Uldoric Adelard, Nov 15 1904 Sex:M Child# 1 Cyriac Dery Canada & Maria Provost Canada
DESANTELS, Aurore, Jun 5 1897 Sex:F Child# 2 Henri Desantels Canada & Exilia Fournier Canada
DESANTELS, Marie Essa, Feb 25 1897 Sex:F Child# 7 Alphonse Desantels Canada & Melodie Landry Canada
DESAULT, Unknown, Jul 16 1934 Sex:M Child# 4 Alfred Desault Canada & Elise Raymond Canada Stillborn
DESAULTEL, Joseph, Apr 30 1920 Sex:M Child# 4 (No Parents Listed)
DESAUTEL, Catherine Pearl, Sep 21 1914 Sex:F Child# 2 Frank J Desautel Nashua, NH & Margaret L Diggins Nashua, NH
DESAUTEL, Edmond, Mar 5 1935 Sex:M Child# 1 Edmond Desautel Nashua, NH & Shirley Brennan Nashua, NH
DESAUTEL, Joseph Edm Alphonse, May 6 1912 Sex:M Child# 1 Edmond Desautel Nashua, NH & Fredeline Blais Canada
DESAUTEL, Pearl Rhea, May 21 1935 Sex:F Child# 2 Armand Desautel Nashua, NH & Rhea Caron Nashua, NH
DESAUTELL, Dorothy Agnes, Mar 10 1916 Sex:F Child# 3 Frank J Desautell Nashua, NH & Margaret E Diggins Nashua, NH
DESAUTELLE, Antoine A, Jan 11 1887 Sex:F Child# 2 Alph Desautelle P Q & Melode Landee P Q
DESAUTELS, Albina Anna, Apr 7 1915 Sex:F Child# 3 Alphonse Desautels Nashua, NH & Hermine Fortier Fall River, MA
DESAUTELS, Alice May, May 3 1913 Sex:F Child# 1 Frank J Desautels Nashua, NH & Margaret J Diggins Nashua, NH
DESAUTELS, Arthur, Feb 10 1891 Sex:M Child# 4 Alphonse Desautels Canada & Melodie Landry Canada
DESAUTELS, Cecile Anita, Nov 22 1934 Sex:F Child# 5 Ovila Desautels Nashua, NH & Corinne Guerette Nashua, NH
DESAUTELS, Corinne Andrea, Jan 9 1904 Sex:F Child# 10 Alphonse Desautels Canada & Melodie Landry Canada
DESAUTELS, Donat Philodore, Nov 28 1905 Sex:M Child# 4 J B Desautels Canada & Elise Fournier Canada
DESAUTELS, Exelia, Aug 14 1895 Sex:M Child# 1 Henri Desautels Canada & Exelia Fournier Canada
DESAUTELS, Francis, Feb 17 1891 Sex:M Child# 1 Francis Desautels Canada & Emma St Martin Canada
DESAUTELS, Girard Ludger, Aug 22 1931 Sex:M Child# 4 Ovila H Desautels Nashua, NH & Corinne Guerrette Nashua, NH
DESAUTELS, Henri, Jul 1 1893 Sex:M Child# 5 Alphonse Desautels Canada & Melodie Landry Canada
DESAUTELS, Janvier Victor, Jan 1 1905 Sex:M Child# 4 Francis Desautels Canada & Emma Desmarais Canada
DESAUTELS, Jean Baptiste, Jun 20 1894 Sex:M Child# 2 J B Desautels Canada & Elise Fournier Canada
DESAUTELS, Joseph Aime, Feb 12 1905 Sex:M Child# 5 Henri Desautels Canada & Azilia Fournier Canada
DESAUTELS, Joseph Armand, Nov 28 1905 Sex:M Child# 5 J B Desautels Canada & Elise Fournier Canada
DESAUTELS, Joseph Armand, Jr, Oct 2 1930 Sex:M Child# 1 Joseph A Desautels Nashua, NH & Rhea Caron Nashua, NH
DESAUTELS, M E Elise, Dec 15 1894 Sex:F Child# 6 Alphonse Desautels Canada & Melodie Landry Canada
DESAUTELS, M Lena Yvette, Oct 26 1913 Sex:F Child# 2 Alphonse Desautels Nashua, NH & Mina Fortier Fall River, MA
DESAUTELS, M Rose Bernadette, Sep 23 1914 Sex:F Child# 2 Edmond Desautels Nashua, NH & Fredeline Blais Canada
DESAUTELS, Marie Alvine, Jun 2 1911 Sex:F Child# 6 Henri Desautels Canada & Exilda Fournier Canada
DESAUTELS, Marie E, Sep 23 1892 Sex:F Child# 2 Francis Desautels Canada & Emms St Martin Canada
DESAUTELS, Marie Elise, Aug 24 1892 Sex:F Child# 1 J B Desautels Canada & Elise Fournier Canada
DESAUTELS, Marie Jessie, Apr 30 1899 Sex:F Child# 3 Henri Desautels Canada & Exelia Fournier Canada
DESAUTELS, Marie Rose Delia, Jan 1 1914 Sex:F Child# 2 (No Parents Listed)
DESAUTELS, Ovila, Jul 15 1901 Sex:M Child# 4 Henri Desautels Canada & Exilia Freniere Canada
DESAUTELS, Ovila Paul Henry, Apr 13 1929 Sex:M Child# 3 Ovila Desautels Nashua, NH & Corinne Guerrette Nashua, NH
DESAUTELS, Pearl Rita, May 4 1928 Sex:F Child# 2 Ovila Desautels Nashua, NH & Corrine Guerette Nashua, NH
DESAUTELS, Rudolphe, Mar 17 1899 Sex:M Child# 5 Francis Desautels Canada & Emma St Martin Canada
DESAUTELS, T Antoinette, Jan 24 1901 Sex:F Child# 9 Alphonse Desautels Canada & Eulodia Landry Canada
DESAUTELS, Theresa Evelyn J, Jun 22 1926 Sex:F Child# 1 Ovilia Desautels Nashua, NH & Corinne Guerete Nashua, NH
DESAUTELS, Unknown, Nov 8 1907 Sex:M Child# 7 Francis Desautels Canada & Emma St Martin Canada Stillborn
DESAW, Eva, Jun 6 1919 Sex:F Child# 1 Lemma Desaw E Deckson, NY & Jennie Cappatain France
DESBIEN, Jeanine Maria, Apr 19 1934 Sex:F Child# 2 Gerard Desbien Canada & Alma Lafrance Canada
DESBIEN, Omer Real, Nov 16 1925 Sex:M Child# 6 Omer Desbien Canada & Angela Lafrance Canada
DESBIENS, Gerard Real, Aug 3 1927 Sex:M Child# 1 Gerard Desbiens Canada & Alma Lafrance Canada
DESBOISBRIAND, Cecile, Jun 14 1924 Sex:F Child# 5 Alf Desboisbriand Nashua, NH & Desmiges Dugas Canada

DESBOISBRIAND, Jos Leo Roland, Dec 25 1929 Sex:M Child# 2 Leo Desboisbriand Nashua, NH & Albina Morin Canada
DESBOISBRIAND, Marie Herminda E, Aug 2 1925 Sex:F Child# 5 A Desboisbriand NH & Desneiges Dugas Canada
DESBOISBRIAND, Marie Rose Mariella, Dec 7 1928 Sex:F Child# 1 H Desboisbriand Nashua, NH & Rose Marquis Nashua, NH
DESBOISBRIAND, Ronalda Marella, May 2 1935 Sex:F Child# 2 H Desboisbriand Nashua, NH & Rose A Marquis Nashua, NH
DESBOISBRIAND, Unknown, Dec 14 1922 Sex:F Child# 3 Alfred Desboisbriand Nashua, NH & Desneiges Dugas Canada
DESBOISBRIEN, Louis Ferdinand, Sep 16 1919 Sex:M Child# 1 Alf Desboisbrien Nashua, NH & Desneiges Dugas Canada
DESCELLES, Lorraine Nanette, May 20 1927 Sex:F Child# 2 Alex Descelles Nashua, NH & A Marquis Nashua, NH
DESCHAIN, Lucille, Jul 19 1925 Sex:F Child# 2 Joseph Deschain Canada & Adele Berube Canada
DESCHAMP, Emeline, Oct 3 1892 Sex:F Child# 8 Edmond Deschamp Canada & Albina Olivier Canada
DESCHAMPS, Adeline Rachelle, Jul 3 1903 Sex:F Child# 4 Oseas O Deschamps Nashua, NH & Octavie Lucier Nashua, NH
DESCHAMPS, Alida, Feb 20 1889 Sex:F Child# 11 Louis Deschamps St Hyacinth, PQ & Adeline Desmarais St Simon
DESCHAMPS, Angelique R, Mar 17 1900 Sex:F Child# 2 O O Deschamps Nashua, NH & Octavie Lucier Nashua, NH
DESCHAMPS, Bernadette, Aug 2 1908 Sex:F Child# 7 Osias O Deschamps US & Octavie Lussier US
DESCHAMPS, Edmond, Jun 9 1887 Sex:M Child#  E Deschamps P Q & Albina Olivier P Q
DESCHAMPS, Edouard Ernest, Mar 28 1912 Sex:M Child# 8 Osios O Deschamps US & Octavie Lucier US
DESCHAMPS, Emile, Mar 19 1899 Sex:M Child# 4 Louis Deschamps Canada & Odile Malenfant Canada
DESCHAMPS, Gertrude Sylvia, Jul 19 1907 Sex:F Child# 6 Oslas O Deschamps US & Octavie Lucier US
DESCHAMPS, Helene, Mar 25 1887 Sex:F Child#  Louis Deschamps P Q & Helene Desmaris P Q
DESCHAMPS, Joseph, Aug 1 1900 Sex:M Child#  Joseph Deschamps Canada & Odile Malenfant Canada
DESCHAMPS, Joseph, May 28 1902 Sex:M Child# 1 Joseph Deschamps Canada & Melina Desmarais Nashua, NH
DESCHAMPS, Joseph Damase A, May 7 1911 Sex:M Child# 5 Philias Deschamps Canada & Marie Dion Canada
DESCHAMPS, Joseph Napoleon, Jul 10 1896 Sex:M Child# 2 Joseph Deschamps Canada & Ozelda Malenfant Canada
DESCHAMPS, Joseph Ovide, Sep 15 1897 Sex:M Child# 3 Joseph Deschamps Canada & Odile Malenfant Canada
DESCHAMPS, Joseph Phillippe A, Jan 7 1911 Sex:M Child# 1 Philippe Deschamps Canada & Vitabline Dion Canada
DESCHAMPS, Louis Ludger, Jan 7 1902 Sex:M Child# 2 O O Deschamps Nashua, NH & Octavie Lucier Nashua, NH
DESCHAMPS, Ludger Robert, Feb 1 1899 Sex:M Child# 1 Osias O Deschamps Nashua, NH & Octavie Lucier Nashua, NH
DESCHAMPS, Marguerite Elizabeth, Sep 8 1916 Sex:F Child# 1 Edgar Deschamps Haverhill, MA & Leona Jette Nashua, NH
DESCHAMPS, Marie Adelia, Mar 23 1895 Sex:F Child# 1 Joseph Deschamps Canada & Odile Malenfant Canada
DESCHAMPS, Marie Alberta, Jan 26 1904 Sex:F Child# 7 Joseph Deschamps Canada & Odile Malenfant Canada
DESCHAMPS, Marie Anna Y, Apr 18 1903 Sex:F Child# 3 Philias Deschamps Canada & Marie Dion Canada
DESCHAMPS, Marie Anne I, Jun 14 1896 Sex:F Child# 2 Joseph Deschamps Canada & Virginia Daunais Canada
DESCHAMPS, Marie Therese O, Sep 12 1905 Sex:F Child# 5 Osias O Deschamps US & Octavie Lucier US
DESCHAMPS, Omer Leo, Jun 3 1914 Sex:M Child# 2 Philippe Deschamps Canada & Vitaline Dion Canada
DESCHAMPS, Roger Henry, Jul 18 1924 Sex:M Child# 6 D Deschamps Canada & Marie Dion Canada
DESCHAMPS, Theresa, Mar 8 1928 Sex:F Child# 1 (No Parents Listed)
DESCHARD, Adelard James Ed, Dec 19 1920 Sex:M Child# 1 Adelard Deschard Nashua, NH & Daisy Bush England
DESCHENES, Adrienne, Apr 30 1913 Sex:F Child# 12 Jean Deschenes Canada & Marie Roy Canada
DESCHENES, Agnes Hermine, Mar 6 1924 Sex:F Child# 4 Henri Deschenes Nashua, NH & Clair Stanton Canada
DESCHENES, Alice, Apr 22 1895 Sex:F Child# 1 Pierre Deschenes Canada & Madeleine Mercier Canada
DESCHENES, Amedee, Feb 14 1895 Sex:M Child# 2 Clement Deschenes Canada & Ledia Rioux Canada
DESCHENES, Andre Oscar, Apr 27 1932 Sex:M Child# 1 Antoine Deschenes Canada & Therese Bousquet Canada
DESCHENES, Clement Albert, Apr 5 1918 Sex:M Child# 2 Henrie J Deschenes US & Claire Stanton Canada
DESCHENES, Francois Maurice, Dec 10 1916 Sex:M Child# 1 Francois Deschenes Canada & Marie Maurais Canada
DESCHENES, Gabrielle, Mar 29 1924 Sex:F Child# 1 Joseph Deschenes Canada & Adele Berube Canada
DESCHENES, J Maurice Roland, Aug 19 1922 Sex:M Child# 2 J B Deschenes Canada & Marie Plourde Canada
DESCHENES, Jean Henry, Jan 30 1904 Sex:M Child# 8 Clement Deschenes Canada & Lydia Rioux Canada
DESCHENES, John Bernard, Nov 19 1934 Sex:M Child# 6 John B Deschenes Canada & Mary Plourde Canada
DESCHENES, John Joseph, Feb 22 1920 Sex:M Child# 1 Anatole Deschenes Canada & Ida Vigneault Nashua, NH
DESCHENES, Joseph, Nov 26 1918 Sex:M Child# 2 Auguste Deschenes Canada & Diana Jean Canada Stillborn
DESCHENES, Joseph Humfrold, Jan 21 1900 Sex:M Child# 4 Louis Deschenes Canada & Helene Antille Canada
DESCHENES, Joseph Oliver Roger, Jun 3 1918 Sex:M Child# 2 Francois Deschenes Canada & Marie Maurois Canada
DESCHENES, Ledia, Jan 5 1895 Sex:F Child# 12 Theophile Deschenes Canada & Ophidie Cote Canada
DESCHENES, Louis David H, Aug 20 1897 Sex:M Child# 2 Louis Deschenes Canada & Helene Antille Canada
DESCHENES, Lucille, Mar 3 1921 Sex:F Child# 1 J B Deschenes Canada & Marie Plourde Canada
DESCHENES, Lumina, Dec 28 1897 Sex:F Child# 5 Clement Deschenes Canada & Lydia Rioux Canada
DESCHENES, Lydia, Dec 28 1897 Sex:F Child# 4 Clement Deschenes Canada & Lydia Rioux Canada
DESCHENES, Marie Antoinette, Nov 16 1897 Sex:F Child# 3 Pierre Deschenes Canada & Madelein Mercier Canada
DESCHENES, Marie Clare, Jul 29 1929 Sex:F Child# 3 Joseph Deschenes Canada & Adele Berube Canada
DESCHENES, Marie H Agnes, May 25 1899 Sex:F Child# 6 Clement Deschenes Canada & Lidia Rioux Canada
DESCHENES, Marie Jeanne, Jan 3 1923 Sex:F Child# 2 Anatole Deschenes Canada & Ida Vigneault Nashua, NH
DESCHENES, Marie Margaret, Feb 11 1922 Sex:F Child# 2 Anatole Deschenes Canada & Ida Migneault Nashua, NH
DESCHENES, Mary Virginia, May 16 1929 Sex:F Child# 1 Joseph A Deschenes E Jaffrey, NH & Mary J Jackson Portsmouth
DESCHENES, Raoul Armand, Aug 9 1929 Sex:M Child# 5 J B Deschenes Canada & Marie Plourde Canada
DESCHENES, Roger Armand, Mar 28 1924 Sex:M Child# 3 J B Deschenes Canada & Marie Plourde Canada
DESCHENES, Theresa Muriel, Sep 12 1926 Sex:F Child# 4 T B Deschenes Canada & Marie Plourde Canada
DESCHENES, Unknown, Mar 25 1912 Sex:M Child# 4 Pierre Deschenes Canada & Madeline Mercier Canada Stillborn
DESCHENES, Unknown, Feb 11 1913 Sex:F Child# 1 Auguste Deschenes Canada & Diana Jean Canada Stillborn
DESCHENES, Yolande, Nov 17 1916 Sex:F Child# 1 Herve Deschenes US & Claire Stanton Canada
DESCHESNE, David A, Dec 29 1892 Sex:M Child# 1 Albany Deschesne Canada & Delvina Jean Canada
DESCHESNE, Heliane Calombe, Aug 27 1898 Sex:F Child# 3 Louis Deschesne Canada & Helene Auctil Canada
DESCHESNE, Joseph P W, Aug 1 1896 Sex:M Child# 1 Louis Deschesne Canada & Helene Auctil Canada
DESCHESNE, Leonie, Aug 1 1896 Sex:f Child# 3 Clement Deschesne Canada & Lydia Rioux Canada
DESCHESNES, Julia Yvonne, Jun 12 1901 Sex:F Child# 7 Theophile Deschesnes Canada & Lydia Rioux Canada

DESCHESNES, Marie Gilberte Leoni, Sep 17 1920 Sex:F Child# 3 Harvey Deschesnes Wisconsin & Claire Stanton Canada
DESCLOS, Aimee Adrienne, Jul 11 1913 Sex:F Child# 2 Alphonse Desclos Canada & Eugenie Dube Canada
DESCLOS, Alberic Fernand, Dec 15 1927 Sex:M Child# 2 Ernest Desclos Nashua, NH & Germaine Hebert Canada
DESCLOS, Amanda M A, May 25 1909 Sex:F Child# 7 Maxine Desclos Canada & Eugenia Sirois Canada
DESCLOS, Beatrice, Nov 15 1923 Sex:F Child# 1 Emile Desclos Nashua, NH & Lillian Lavoie Nashua, NH
DESCLOS, Donat, May 8 1926 Sex:M Child# 2 Leo A Desclos Nashua, NH & K M Toohey Lowell, MA
DESCLOS, Elodie O, Apr 19 1897 Sex:F Child# 4 Oscar Desclos Canada & Georgina Gadbois Spencer, MA
DESCLOS, Emile Marcel, Jul 10 1926 Sex:M Child# 1 Ernest Desclos Nashua, NH & Germaine Hebert Canada
DESCLOS, Irene, Jul 20 1906 Sex:F Child# 5 Maxime Desclos Canada & Eugenie Sirois Canada
DESCLOS, J B Ernest Elphege, Jun 24 1921 Sex:M Child# 10 Maxime Desclos Canada & Eugenie Sirois Canada
DESCLOS, Joan Alice, Aug 5 1934 Sex:F Child# 1 Louis Desclos Nashua, NH & Alice Lavoie Nashua, NH
DESCLOS, Joseph Charles L R, Oct 6 1910 Sex:M Child# 7 Alphe Desclos Canada & Mary Fortin Canada
DESCLOS, Joseph R Roland, Aug 4 1931 Sex:M Child# 2 Wilfred J Desclos Newmarket, NH & Lucienne Millard Canada
DESCLOS, Joseph Rodrigue, Jul 28 1907 Sex:M Child# 6 Alphe Desclos Canada & Marie Fortin Canada
DESCLOS, Joseph Thimothee, Nov 13 1911 Sex:M Child# 8 Maxime Desclos Canada & Eugenie Sirois Canada
DESCLOS, Leo A, Jr, May 15 1927 Sex:M Child# 3 Leo A Desclos Nashua, NH & K M Toohey Lowell, MA
DESCLOS, Louis Roger, Sep 20 1930 Sex:M Child# 4 Ernest Desclos Nashua, NH & Germaine Hebert Canada
DESCLOS, M Eugenie Rachel, May 10 1913 Sex:F Child# 9 Maxime Desclos Canada & Eugenie Sirois Canada
DESCLOS, M Louise Andrea, Jul 11 1913 Sex:F Child# 1 Alphonse Desclos Canada & Eugenie Dube Canada
DESCLOS, Marie, Mar 20 1923 Sex:F Child# 1 Louis Desclos NH & Aldea Salvail NH
DESCLOS, Marie Alice, Jan 9 1903 Sex:F Child# 5 Maxime Desclos Canada & Eugenie Sirois Canada
DESCLOS, Marie Anna, Apr 25 1908 Sex:F Child# 6 Maxime Desclos Canada & Eugenie Sirois Canada
DESCLOS, Marie Annette Rita, Apr 6 1929 Sex:F Child# 1 Wilfrid J Desclos Newmarket, NH & Lucienne Millard Canada
DESCLOS, Marie Blanche, Jan 9 1901 Sex:F Child# 4 Alphie Desclos Canada & Marie Fortin Canada
DESCLOS, Marie Claire Lucille, Nov 18 1932 Sex:F Child# 2 W J Desclos Newmarket, NH & Lucienne Millard Canada
DESCLOS, Marie Eva, May 24 1904 Sex:F Child# 4 Maxime Desclos Canada & Eugenie Sirois Canada
DESCLOS, Marie Irene, Jun 14 1899 Sex:F Child# 1 Maxime Desclos Canada & Eugenie Sirois Canada
DESCLOS, Marie Jeanne Agnes, Feb 14 1914 Sex:F Child# 9 Delphe Desclos Canada & Marie Fortin Canada
DESCLOS, Marie Rose, Aug 20 1900 Sex:F Child# 2 Maxim Desclos Canada & Eugenie Sirois Canada
DESCLOS, Normand, Jan 14 1910 Sex:M Child# 8 Olivier Desclos Canada & Louise Monty Canada
DESCLOS, Ozias Henri, Aug 12 1894 Sex:M Child# 1 Delphe Desclos Canada & Marie Forten Canada
DESCLOS, Patrick Joseph, Mar 17 1896 Sex:M Child# 2 Dalphe Desclos Nashua, NH & Marie Fortin Nashua, NH
DESCLOS, Patrick Oseas, Mar 17 1902 Sex:M Child# 5 Olivier Desclos Canada & Louisa Monty Canada
DESCLOS, Paul Roland, Oct 9 1931 Sex:M Child# 5 Ernest Desclos Nashua, NH & Germaine Hebert Canada
DESCLOS, Pauline Catherine, Jul 2 1929 Sex:F Child# 3 Ernest Desclos Nashua, NH & Germaine Hebert Canada
DESCLOS, Robert Roland, Jan 14 1912 Sex:M Child# 8 Delphe Desclos Canada & Marie Fortin Canada
DESCLOS, Therese Emmeline, Aug 29 1915 Sex:F Child# 10 Delphis Desclos Canada & Mary Fortin Canada
DESCLOS, Virginia, Aug 16 1924 Sex:F Child# 1 Leo A Desclos Nashua, NH & Catherine Toohey Lowell, MA
DESCOTEARE, Mederic Henri, Jan 18 1890 Sex:M Child# 1 Napoleon Descoteare Canada & Philomene Morin Canada
DESCOTEAU, Elias Eugene, Jul 27 1913 Sex:M Child# 3 Elias J Descoteau Canada & Laura M Gray Canada
DESCOTEAU, Emelie Mary, Feb 10 1916 Sex:F Child# 5 Elas Descoteau Canada & Laura Gray Canada
DESCOTEAU, John Milton, Jul 31 1914 Sex:M Child# 2 Origene Descoteau Canada & Cilamire Belcourt Canada
DESCOTEAU, Jos James Norman, Dec 28 1916 Sex:M Child# 3 Origine Descoteau Canada & Celanire Belcourt Canada
DESCOTEAU, Joseph Frank, Nov 20 1893 Sex:M Child# 5 Napoleon Descoteau Canada & Anna Doucette Canada
DESCOTEAU, Joseph Henri, Jun 18 1919 Sex:M Child# 7 Helas Descoteau Canada & Laura Gaie Canada
DESCOTEAU, Joseph Louis Henri, May 28 1919 Sex:M Child# 4 Origine Descoteau Canada & Celanire Belcourt Canada
DESCOTEAU, M Laura Priscilla, Jul 27 1922 Sex:F Child# 5 Origene J Descoteau Canada & Celanire F Belcourt Canada
DESCOTEAU, M Lumina, Aug 26 1892 Sex:F Child# 4 Napoleon Descoteau Canada & Annie Doucette Canada
DESCOTEAU, Mary Lorraine G, Aug 31 1929 Sex:F Child# 7 Origine Descoteau Canada & Celanire Belcourt Canada
DESCOTEAU, Mary Lottie Laura, Apr 14 1917 Sex:F Child# 6 Elas Descoteau Canada & Laura Gray Canada
DESCOTEAU, Walter, Sep 3 1914 Sex:M Child# 3 E J Descoteau Canada & D M Gray Canada
DESCOTEAUX, Alphonse Eugene R, Apr 5 1904 Sex:M Child# 5 Michel Descoteaux Vermont & Exilia Morissette Maine
DESCOTEAUX, Arthur, Dec 11 1896 Sex:M Child# 1 Michel Descoteaux White River Jct, VT & Exilia Morissette Maine
DESCOTEAUX, Blanche Emilie, Mar 22 1905 Sex:F Child# 6 Michel Descoteaux White River Jct, VT & Exilia Morrissette
DESCOTEAUX, Edouard, Sep 1 1898 Sex:M Child# 3 Michel Descoteaux White River Jct, VT & Exilia Morissette Maine
DESCOTEAUX, Ernest Fernand, Jun 13 1930 Sex:M Child# 4 Ovilda Descoteaux Canada & Rodophine Gauthier Canada
DESCOTEAUX, Jos M Normand, Dec 12 1929 Sex:M Child# 1 Emery Descoteaux Canada & Florida Levesque Nashua, NH
DESCOTEAUX, Joseph Gideon, Jan 13 1901 Sex:M Child# 4 John Descoteaux Canada & Marie Bergeron Canada
DESCOTEAUX, Joseph P E, Jul 9 1903 Sex:M Child# 10 Philippe Descoteaux Canada & Marie Morin Canada
DESCOTEAUX, Leonie Cecile Angela, Aug 8 1928 Sex:F Child# 3 H Descoteaux Canada & Eva Cote Nashua, NH
DESCOTEAUX, Liliane Florence, Jan 1 1931 Sex:F Child# 4 Henri Descoteaux Canada & Eva Cote Nashua, NH
DESCOTEAUX, Marie A Y, Mar 14 1898 Sex:F Child# 2 Michael Descoteaux White River Jct, VT & Exilia Morissette Maine
DESCOTEAUX, Marie Germaine T, Oct 29 1926 Sex:F Child# 6 O Descoteaux Canada & Celanie Belcourt Canada
DESCOTEAUX, Napoleon, Dec 16 1909 Sex:M Child# 1 Elias Descoteaux Canada & Laura Gay US
DESCOTEAUX, Napoleon Henry, Jul 18 1909 Sex:M Child# 1 Origene Descoteaux Canada & Celanire F Belcourt Canada
DESCOTEAUX, Odias Omer, Dec 1 1921 Sex:M Child# 1 Henry Descoteaux Canada & Eva Cote Nashua, NH
DESCOTEAUX, Rodolph Sylvio, Mar 31 1927 Sex:M Child# 2 Henry Descoteaux Canada & Eva Cote Nashua, NH
DESELLES, Francois X, Aug 2 1887 Sex:M Child# 8 Gedeon Deselles P Q & Elmere Lambert Nashua, NH
DESFORGES, Marie Eva E, Apr 22 1906 Sex:F Child# 1 George Desforges Canada & Eva Menard Canada
DESGROSSEILIERS, Jean Maurice, Oct 9 1916 Sex:M Child# 2 Chas Desgrosseiliers Manchester, NH & M J Deboisbriand
DESGROSSEILLERS, Joseph, Aug 4 1920 Sex:M Child# 5 Chas Desgrosseillers Manchester, NH & M J Desboisbriand
DESGROSSEILLERS, M Janie F, Aug 11 1919 Sex:F Child# 3 Chas Desgrosseillers Manchester, NH & M J Desboisbriand
DESHAMETS, Joseph X, Mar 27 1902 Sex:M Child# 3 Xavier Deshamets Canada & Marie Roy Canada

DESHONG, Hector, Jun 17 1893 Sex:M Child# 1 Phil Deshong Lawrence, MA & Matilda Nashua, NH
DESILETS, Armand, Jan 7 1905 Sex:M Child# 8 Philippe Desilets Berlin & Victoria Cabana Canada
DESILETS, Ernest Alexandre, Apr 8 1906 Sex:M Child# 9 Philippe Desilets Canada & Victoria Cabana Canada
DESJARDIN, Anna Rita, Apr 9 1933 Sex:F Child# 7 P Desjardin Canada & Anna Boucher Nashua, NH
DESJARDIN, Arlene, Apr 16 1926 Sex:F Child# 2 Joseph Desjardin Lowell, MA & Doris Scanlon Boston, MA
DESJARDIN, Marguerite, Jun 19 1930 Sex:F Child# 7 Pierre Desjardin Canada & Anna Boucher Canada
DESJARDIN, Normand, Jan 29 1928 Sex:M Child# 5 Pierre Desjardin Canada & Anna Boucher US
DESJARDIN, Raoul Herve, Feb 26 1925 Sex:M Child# 4 Pierre Desjardin Canada & Aline Boucher Nashua, NH
DESJARDIN, Unknown, Feb 27 1919 Sex:M Child# 1 Adelard Desjardin Bradley, ME & Jenny Dichard Nashua, NH Stillborn
DESJARDIN, Unknown, Dec 11 1934 Sex:F Child# 1 Pierre Desjardin Canada & Claudia Lavoie Canada
DESJARDINS, Arthur Armand Jean, Nov 14 1922 Sex:M Child# 4 Emile Desjardins Canada & Aurore Morrissette Canada
DESJARDINS, Arthur Roger, Sep 20 1926 Sex:M Child# 2 F Desjardins Canada & G B Morin Canada
DESJARDINS, Dora Antoinette, Jul 23 1921 Sex:F Child# 3 Antoine Desjardins Canada & Delvina Ouellette Nashua, NH
DESJARDINS, Euclide Leonard, Aug 25 1926 Sex:M Child# 2 Euclide Desjardins Canada & Rose Plourde Canada
DESJARDINS, Evette Annette, Oct 2 1921 Sex:F Child# 3 Adelard Desjardins Bradley, ME & Eugenie Dichard Nashua, NH
DESJARDINS, Helene C, Sep 26 1900 Sex:F Child# 2 Aug Desjardins Canada & Marie Dufour Canada
DESJARDINS, J Armand Adrien, Oct 21 1913 Sex:M Child# 1 Ferdinand Desjardins Canada & Eugenie Boucher Canada
DESJARDINS, Jos Alb Leo Conrad, Dec 5 1919 Sex:M Child# 3 Emile Desjardins Canada & Aurore Morrissette Canada
DESJARDINS, Jos Pierre Leo, Sep 15 1923 Sex:M Child# 3 Pierre Desjardins Canada & Anna Boucher NH
DESJARDINS, Joseph, Feb 1 1925 Sex:M Child# 5 Joseph Desjardins Canada & Eva Levesque Canada
DESJARDINS, Joseph Albert Roland, Aug 3 1935 Sex:M Child# 1 Jos F Desjardins Canada & Marie O Michaud Canada
DESJARDINS, Joseph Emilion Herve, Aug 20 1916 Sex:M Child# 1 Emile Desjardins Canada & Aurore Morrissette Canada
DESJARDINS, Joseph Francis, May 23 1925 Sex:M Child# 1 Joseph Desjardins Lowell, MA & Doris Sanborn Boston, MA
DESJARDINS, Joseph Gaul, Jul 26 1918 Sex:M Child# 1 Antoine Desjardins Canada & Delvina Ouellette Canada
DESJARDINS, Loraine Leona, Sep 27 1932 Sex:F Child# 7 A Desjardins Canada & D Ouellette Nashua, NH
DESJARDINS, M Augustine, Feb 22 1904 Sex:F Child# 4 Auguste Desjardins Canada & Maria Dufour Canada
DESJARDINS, M Beatrice, Oct 4 1895 Sex:F Child# 13 Achille Desjardins Canada & Arthemise Lavoie Canada
DESJARDINS, M Gabrielle B, Jun 16 1914 Sex:F Child# 1 Louis Desjardins Canada & Virginie Bellavance Canada
DESJARDINS, M Lorraine Olivette, Feb 19 1921 Sex:F Child# 1 Pierre Desjardins Canada & Anna Boucher NH
DESJARDINS, M Rachelle Olivette, Jun 16 1914 Sex:F Child# 2 Louis Desjardins Canada & Virginie Bellavance Canada
DESJARDINS, Maria, Feb 15 1902 Sex:M Child# 3 Aug Desjardins Canada & Maria Dufour Canada
DESJARDINS, Marie Bernadette, Mar 20 1903 Sex:F Child# 2 Auguste Desjardins Canada & Sara Dionne Canada
DESJARDINS, Marie Claire Yve V, Feb 4 1918 Sex:F Child# 2 Emile Desjardins St Louis K, PQ & Aurore Morrissett
DESJARDINS, Maurice Antonio, Feb 22 1923 Sex:M Child# 4 Antoine Desjardins Canada & Dalvina Ouellette Nashua, NH
DESJARDINS, Paul Robert, Sep 9 1931 Sex:M Child# 3 Fortunat Desjardins Canada & Bernadette Morin Canada
DESJARDINS, Raymond Albert, Jan 22 1929 Sex:M Child# 6 Pierre Desjardins Canada & Anna Boucher Nashua, NH
DESJARDINS, Robert, Mar 17 1913 Sex:M Child# 1 Joseph Desjardins Canada & Leontine St Jean Canada
DESJARDINS, Roland Albert, Oct 1 1929 Sex:M Child# 6 Antoine Desjardins Canada & Delvina Ouillette Nashua, NH
DESJARDINS, Theresa Lauretta, Jul 16 1927 Sex:F Child# 5 A Desjardins Canada & Delvina Ouillette Nashua, NH
DESJARDINS, Unknown, Apr 12 1929 Sex:F Child# 1 Joseph Desjardins Oldtown, ME & Eva Soucy Bonner, Montana
DESJARDINS, Yvonne Beatrice, Jul 20 1922 Sex:F Child# 2 Pierre Desjardins Canada & Anna Boucher NH
DESJARLAIS, Albina, Jul 22 1915 Sex:F Child# 1 William Desjarlais Canada & Anna Theriault Nashua, NH
DESJARLAIS, Armand, Feb 28 1920 Sex:M Child# 5 Ferdinand Desjarlais Canada & Eugenie Boucher Canada
DESJARLAIS, George Girard, Mar 12 1927 Sex:M Child# 9 F Desjarlais Canada & Eugenie Boucher Canada
DESJARLAIS, Gerald Raymond, Apr 6 1923 Sex:M Child# 7 Ferdinand Desjarlais Canada & Eugenie Boucher Canada
DESJARLAIS, Jeanne Laurette, Jan 4 1919 Sex:F Child# 4 Ferdinand Desjarlais Canada & Eugenie Boucher Canada
DESJARLAIS, Lucien Robert, Feb 12 1917 Sex:M Child# 3 Ferninand Desjarlais Canada & Eugenie Boucher Canada
DESJARLAIS, Lucille Leona, Jul 8 1915 Sex:F Child# 2 Ferdinand Desjarlais Canada & Eugenie Boucher Canada
DESJARLAIS, Marie Ange Isabelle, Nov 4 1921 Sex:F Child# 6 Ferdinand Desjarlais Canada & Eugenie Boucher Canada
DESJARLAIS, Maurice A Anjalbert, Feb 3 1929 Sex:M Child# 10 Ferdinand Desjarlais Canada & Eugenie Boucher Canada
DESJARLAIS, Paul Harvey, Dec 2 1930 Sex:M Child# 11 Ferdinand Desjarlais Louisville, PQ & Eugenie Boucher Canada
DESJARLAIS, Roger Albert, Nov 21 1924 Sex:M Child# 8 F Desjarlais Canada & Eugenie Boucher Canada
DESJARLETS, Marie Octavie, Mar 1 1905 Sex:F Child# 1 Arthur Desjarlets Canada & Zelma Roy Canada
DESLAURIER, Andrea, Jan 31 1901 Sex:F Child# 4 Hormidas Deslaurier Canada & Delphine Dufault Canada
DESLAURIER, Bernardin, Nov 27 1899 Sex:m Child# 3 Hermisdas Deslaurier Canada & Delphine Dufault Canada
DESLAURIER, Joseph E, Aug 10 1894 Sex:M Child# 1 H Deslaurier Canada & Delphine Dufault Canada
DESLAURIER, Marie Isabelle Pearl, Nov 10 1918 Sex:F Child# 1 Edouard Deslaurier NH & Alma Gervais NH
DESLAURIER, Ovide, Jun 11 1896 Sex:M Child# 2 H Deslaurier Canada & Delphine Dufault Canada
DESLAURIERS, Jean Alfred Eugene, Feb 25 1916 Sex:M Child# 3 Irving J Deslauriers US & Victoria Carpenter US
DESLAURIERS, Joseph Leger, Aug 20 1905 Sex:M Child# 1 Ephraim Deslauriers Canada & Josephine Levesque Canada
DESLAURIERS, Marie Olivette G, Sep 27 1910 Sex:F Child# 6 Hormidas Deslauriers Canada & Delphine Dufault Canada
DESLAURIERS, Roland, Feb 9 1904 Sex:M Child# 5 Hormidas Deslauriers Canada & Delphine Dufault Canada
DESLAURIES, Donald Gerald, Jul 13 1929 Sex:M Child# 1 Luger Deslauries Nashua, NH & Beatrice Lamb Nashua, NH
DESLISLE, Evelyn Anna, Oct 16 1925 Sex:F Child# 1 Alphonse Deslisle
DESMANCHE, Marie Lucille, Oct 30 1922 Sex:F Child# 1 Louis Desmanche Nashua, NH & Marie L Morin Canada
DESMARAIS, Aldea, Mar 30 1907 Sex:M Child# 2 Frank Desmarais Nashua, NH & Regina Grandmaison Nashua, NH
DESMARAIS, Alexandrine, Jan 4 1891 Sex:F Child# 4 Georges Desmarais Canada & Josephine Jeannotte Nashua, NH
DESMARAIS, Alfred, Mar 6 1887 Sex:M Child# 4 Joseph Desmarais Canada & Marie Poirus NY
DESMARAIS, Alfred Christopher, Aug 13 1917 Sex:M Child# 1 Chris Desmarais Nashua, NH & Dorilda Bouchard Nashua, NH
DESMARAIS, Alice, Sep 19 1911 Sex:F Child# Charles F Desmarais St Albans, VT & Mary A Broderick Nashua, NH
DESMARAIS, Alphee Normand, Feb 1 1923 Sex:M Child# 2 Henry G Desmarais Nashua, NH & Alexina Malenfant Canada
DESMARAIS, Antoinette, Feb 15 1894 Sex:F Child# 8 Joseph Desmarais Canada & Marie Poirier Canada
DESMARAIS, Antoinette, Nov 5 1894 Sex:F Child# 1 Antoine Desmarais Canada & Phelanise Laporte NY

DESMARAIS, Armand Emery, May 10 1902 Sex:M Child# 1 Leon Desmarais St Albans, VT & Clara Jean Canada
DESMARAIS, Arsene Alexandre, Feb 5 1906 Sex:M Child# 5 Leon Desmarais St Albans, VT & Delia Grenon Canada
DESMARAIS, Arthur A, Jan 16 1902 Sex:M Child# 11 F X Desmarais Canada & A Jeannotte Canada
DESMARAIS, Auguste Henri, Oct 14 1907 Sex:M Child# 6 Leon Desmarais St Albans, VT & Delia Grenon Wilton, NH
DESMARAIS, Aurore Elmire, Sep 22 1904 Sex:M Child# 4 Leon Desmarais St Albans, VT & Delia Grenon Wilton, NH
DESMARAIS, Beatrice Lorette, Dec 18 1925 Sex:F Child# 1 L Desmarais Nashua, NH & Eugenie Marquis Nashua, NH
DESMARAIS, Cecilia Angelina, Aug 27 1908 Sex:F Child# 6 Joseph Desmarais St Albans, VT & Elmire Jodoin St Albans
DESMARAIS, Charles Broderick, Jun 25 1908 Sex:M Child# 1 Charles F Desmarais St Albans, VT & Mary H Broderick
DESMARAIS, Claudette, Sep 12 1931 Sex:F Child# 2 William Desmarais Nashua, NH & Eva St George Lowell, MA
DESMARAIS, David Robert, Mar 13 1912 Sex:M Child# 8 Leon Desmarais St Albans, VT & Delia Grenon Wilton, NH
DESMARAIS, Edmond Romeo, Sep 30 1899 Sex:M Child# 1 Joseph Desmarais Canada & Elmire Jodoin St Albans, VT
DESMARAIS, Edward James, Sep 17 1923 Sex:M Child# 1 Edward Desmarais Nashua, NH & Grace Isabell Dalton Calais, ME
DESMARAIS, Eli, Jul 31 1901 Sex:M Child# 5 Antoine Desmarais Canada & Philomene Laporte Canada
DESMARAIS, Elizabeth, Apr 27 1888 Sex:F Child# 4 Francis X Desmarais P Q & Alexandrine Jeanotte P Q
DESMARAIS, Ernest Robert, Mar 10 1926 Sex:M Child# 3 Henry Desmarais Nashua, NH & Alexina Malenfant Canada
DESMARAIS, Eva, Jan 21 1905 Sex:F Child# 6 Antoine Desmarais Canada & Phelanise Laporte Canada
DESMARAIS, Florida Alvine, Apr 23 1904 Sex:F Child# 1 Louis Desmarais Nashua, NH & Celina Caron Canada
DESMARAIS, Frank Edouard, Oct 16 1900 Sex:M Child# 1 Frank Desmarais Nashua, NH & Oida Brickey NY
DESMARAIS, George Albert, Mar 25 1907 Sex:M Child# 1 Hubert Desmarais NH & Hermine Gauthier NH
DESMARAIS, Georges, Apr 29 1889 Sex:M Child# 3 Georges Desmarais Canada & Josephine Jeannotte Nashua, NH
DESMARAIS, Gerard Eli, Aug 21 1924 Sex:M Child# 3 Joseph Desmarais Nashua, NH & Carina Lagasse Nashua, NH
DESMARAIS, Gloria Rachel, Mar 26 1921 Sex:F Child# 2 Joseph A Desmarais Nashua, NH & Corina Lagasse Nashua, NH
DESMARAIS, Hector X, Jul 17 1890 Sex:M Child# 5 Francis N Desmarais Canada & Alexandrine Jeannott Canada
DESMARAIS, Helen, Sep 3 1923 Sex:F Child# 5 Charles F Desmarais St Albans, VT & Mary Broderick Nashua, NH
DESMARAIS, Henri, Jul 27 1906 Sex:M Child# 6 Charles Desmarais Canada & Mathilda Delacombe Canada
DESMARAIS, Henry, May 8 1893 Sex:M Child# 5 Herbert Desmarais Canada & Julie Facto Canada
DESMARAIS, Henry, Jul 8 1924 Sex:M Child# 2 Eugene Desmarais Canada & Delia E Belanger Nashua, NH
DESMARAIS, J Henri Ernest, Nov 25 1913 Sex:M Child# 6 Leon Desmarais St Albans, VT & Clara Jean Canada
DESMARAIS, Jacqueline, Dec 1 1927 Sex:F Child# 1 William Desmarais Westford, MA & Eva St George Lowell, MA
DESMARAIS, Jeannette Anita, Apr 28 1918 Sex:F Child# 1 Anselus C Desmarais Nashua, NH & Bertha I Lemire Nashua, NH
DESMARAIS, Jos Henry Edouard, May 27 1928 Sex:M Child# 4 Henr Desmarais Nashua, NH & Alexina Malenfant Canada
DESMARAIS, Joseph, Apr 10 1889 Sex:M Child# 1 Antoine Desmarais St Simon, PQ & Zoe Lepage St Elot, PQ
DESMARAIS, Joseph, Jul 29 1890 Sex:M Child# 1 Charles Desmarais St Albans, VT & Mathilde Lacombe Canada
DESMARAIS, Joseph Antoine, Feb 2 1896 Sex:M Child# 2 Antoine Desmarais Canada & Philanise Laporte Mooers, NY
DESMARAIS, Joseph C, Mar 26 1897 Sex:M Child# 9 Francis X Desmarais Canada & Alex'drine Jeannotte Canada
DESMARAIS, Joseph C A, Sep 9 1890 Sex:M Child# 16 Alexande Desmarais Canada & Hermine Penet Canada
DESMARAIS, Joseph Edward, May 29 1919 Sex:M Child# 2 Christ Desmarais Westford, MA & Dorilida Bouchard Nashua, NH
DESMARAIS, Joseph Honore, Jun 4 1907 Sex:M Child# 7 Antoine Desmarais Canada & Phelonise Laporte Canada
DESMARAIS, Joseph N, Mar 15 1891 Sex:M Child# 7 Joseph Desmarais Canada & Marie Porier Ellensburg, NY
DESMARAIS, Joseph N, Aug 2 1898 Sex:M Child# 1 George Desmarais St Albans, VT & Josephine Lucas Canada
DESMARAIS, Joseph Thomas Arthur, Jan 14 1900 Sex:M Child# 4 Antoine Desmarais Canada & Philamise Laporte NY
DESMARAIS, Juliette, Nov 2 1909 Sex:F Child# 5 Leon Desmarais St Albans, VT & Clara Jean Canada
DESMARAIS, Juliette Delia, Mar 14 1902 Sex:F Child# 3 Leon Desmarais St Albans, VT & Delia Grenon Wilton, NH
DESMARAIS, Laura Angela, Nov 20 1925 Sex:F Child# 1 Roland Desmarais Manchester, NH & Victoria Lussier Canada
DESMARAIS, Lawrence, Jr, Feb 15 1931 Sex:M Child# 2 Lawrence Desmarais Nashua, NH & Eugenie Marquis Canada
DESMARAIS, Lena Dorothy, Oct 8 1929 Sex:F Child# 3 Emery Desmarais Nashua, NH & Della Rioux Nashua, NH
DESMARAIS, Leo, Oct 8 1921 Sex:M Child# 1 Eugene Desmarais Canada & Delia Belanger Nashua, NH
DESMARAIS, Leon, Jun 2 1910 Sex:M Child# 8 George Desmarais Canada & Mary Allard Vermont
DESMARAIS, Leon, Nov 2 1918 Sex:M Child# 5 Leon Desmarais St Albans, VT & Clara Jean Canada
DESMARAIS, Lillian Theresa, Feb 8 1928 Sex:F Child# 2 Emery Desmarais Nashua, NH & Delia Rioux Nashua, NH
DESMARAIS, Louis Joseph Leo, Apr 15 1931 Sex:M Child# 5 Henry Desmarais Nashua, NH & Elexina Malenfant Canada
DESMARAIS, Louis Leon, Apr 23 1930 Sex:M Child# 1 Aurelee U Desmarais Nashua, NH & Lena Lorraine Nashua, NH
DESMARAIS, M Emelie, Dec 31 1895 Sex:F Child# 2 Charles Desmarais Nashua, NH & Mathilda Lacombe Canada
DESMARAIS, M Eva M, Feb 9 1902 Sex:F Child# 4 Charles Desmarais St Albans, VT & Mathilda Lacombe Canada
DESMARAIS, M Lucille Rochelle, Jan 28 1917 Sex:F Child# 4 Frank Desmarais Nashua, NH & Regina Grandmaison Nashua
DESMARAIS, M Rose Liliane, Nov 21 1908 Sex:F Child# 8 Antoine Desmarais Canada & Phelanise Laporte Canada
DESMARAIS, Marie, Feb 25 1903 Sex:F Child# 9 George Desmarais Canada & Josephine Jeannotte Nashua, NH
DESMARAIS, Marie A A, Jul 26 1892 Sex:F Child# 6 Francis X Desmarais Canada & Alexand'ne Jeannotte Canada
DESMARAIS, Marie Antoinette, Feb 14 1913 Sex:F Child# 1 Joseph Desmarais NH & Rose Simard Canada
DESMARAIS, Marie C B, Apr 7 1895 Sex:F Child# 6 Georges Desmarais Canada & Josephine Jeannotte Nashua, NH
DESMARAIS, Marie Jeanne Estelle, Oct 25 1929 Sex:F Child# 3 Napoleon Desmarais Nashua, NH & Marie L Pelletier
DESMARAIS, Marie O, Jul 26 1887 Sex:F Child# 2 Georges Desmarais P Q & Josephine Jeannotte Nashua, NH
DESMARAIS, Marie O, Mar 11 1893 Sex:F Child# 2 Charles Desmarais St Albans, VT & Mathilde Lacombe Canada
DESMARAIS, Marie O I, Jul 17 1892 Sex:F Child# 5 George Desmarais Canada & Josehnine Jeannotte Nashua, NH
DESMARAIS, Marie Rita, Feb 15 1925 Sex:F Child# 4 Chris Desmarais Mass & Donelde Bouchard Nashua, NH
DESMARAIS, Marie T F, Nov 16 1899 Sex:F Child# 10 Francois X Desmarais Canada & Alexandrine Jeann'te Canada
DESMARAIS, Mary Elizabeth, Jun 21 1932 Sex:F Child# 5 Edw Desmarais Nashua, NH & Grace Dalton Calais, ME
DESMARAIS, Normand, Jul 11 1925 Sex:M Child# 1 Napoleon Desmarais Nashua, NH & Marie L Pelletier Canada
DESMARAIS, Olivette, Aug 18 1920 Sex:F Child# 2 Anslem Desmarais Nashua, NH & Bertha Lemire Nashua, NH
DESMARAIS, Paul Henry Philias, Jun 22 1921 Sex:M Child# 1 Henry Desmarais Nashua, NH & M Malenfant Canada
DESMARAIS, Pierre, Oct 8 1912 Sex:M Child# 3 Frank Desmarais Nashua, NH & Regina Grandmaison Nashua, NH
DESMARAIS, Ralph Henry, Oct 18 1934 Sex:M Child# 6 Edward Desmarais Nashua, NH & Grace Dalton Calais, ME
DESMARAIS, Raoul Alfred, May 17 1904 Sex:M Child# 4 Joseph Desmarais Canada & Elmira Jodoin St Albans, VT

117

DESMARAIS, Raymond, Dec 13 1920 Sex:M Child# 3 Christpher Desmarais Nashua, NH & Dorilda Bouchard Nashua, NH
DESMARAIS, Raymond, Aug 17 1925 Sex:M Child# 3 Eugene Desmarais Canada & Delia Belanger Nashua, NH
DESMARAIS, Raymond Leonard, Oct 23 1919 Sex:M Child# 8 Leon Desmarais St Albans, VT & Clara Jean Canada
DESMARAIS, Raymond Lucien, Oct 13 1928 Sex:M Child# 4 Ed Desmarais Nashua, NH & Grace Dalton Maine
DESMARAIS, Regina, Mar 15 1898 Sex:F Child# 3 Antoine Desmarais Canada & Phelanise Laporte US
DESMARAIS, Richard Leon, Jul 23 1927 Sex:M Child# 3 Edward Desmarais Nashua, NH & Grace Dalton Maine
DESMARAIS, Rita Muriel, May 18 1919 Sex:F Child# 1 Joseph Desmarais Nashua, NH & Corinne Lagasse Nashua, NH
DESMARAIS, Robert Arthur, Apr 14 1930 Sex:M Child# 5 Christpher Desmarais Mass & Dorilda Bouchard NH
DESMARAIS, Robert Emery, Jr, Sep 16 1932 Sex:M Child# 3 Robert Desmarais Nashua, NH & Della Rioux Canada
DESMARAIS, Robert Paul, Apr 17 1918 Sex:M Child# 4 Charles F Desmarais St Albans, VT & Mary A Broderick Nashua, NH
DESMARAIS, Roger, Aug 21 1933 Sex:M Child# 2 Albert Desmarais Nashua, NH & Lucille Theriault Nashua, NH
DESMARAIS, Roland Robert L, Jan 1 1903 Sex:M Child# 3 Joseph Desmarais Canada & Elmire Jodoin St Albans, VT
DESMARAIS, Rolande Anita, Jun 2 1929 Sex:F Child# 2 Roland Desmarais Manchester, NH & Victoria Lussier Canada
DESMARAIS, Romeo, Apr 14 1908 Sex:M Child# 4 Leon Desmarais St Albans, VT & Clara Jean Canada
DESMARAIS, Ruth, Nov 14 1916 Sex:F Child# 3 Charles F Desmarais St Albans, VT & Mary A Broderick Nashua, NH
DESMARAIS, Sylvia, Apr 30 1905 Sex:F Child# 1 Frank Desmarais Nashua, NH & Regina Grandmaison Nashua, NH
DESMARAIS, Sylvio Edward, Aug 16 1933 Sex:M Child# 4 E Desmarais Canada & Delia Belanger Nashua, NH
DESMARAIS, Sylvio Maurice, Jan 29 1923 Sex:M Child# 1 Edouard Desmarais Nashua, NH & Imdela Dumont Canada
DESMARAIS, Sylvio Raymond, Jul 30 1927 Sex:M Child# 2 Edward Desmarais Canada & Imelda Desmarais Canada
DESMARAIS, Therese Olivine, Jan 14 1910 Sex:F Child# 7 Leon Desmarais St Albans, VT & Delia Garneau Wilton, NH
DESMARAIS, Ulric Aurelle, Dec 20 1903 Sex:M Child# 2 Leon Desmarais St Albans, VT & Clara Jean Canada
DESMARAIS, Unknown, Jun 9 1899 Sex:F Child# 2 Leon Desmarais Vermont & Delia Grinon NH
DESMARAIS, Unknown, Aug 16 1901 Sex:M Child# 8 George Desmarais Canada & Josephine Jeannotte Nashua, NH Stillborn
DESMARAIS, Yolande Annette, Apr 14 1927 Sex:F Child# 2 N Desmarais Nashua, NH & Marie L Pelletier Canada
DESMARAISE, Normand Robert, Dec 13 1926 Sex:M Child# 1 Emery Desmaraise Nashua, NH & Della Rioux Nashua, NH
DESMARCHEE, Joseph, Apr 10 1888 Sex:M Child# 1 Joseph Desmarchee Canada & Emma Peltier Canada
DESMARIS, Leonard, Nov 10 1934 Sex:M Child# 2 Raymond Desmaris Lowell, MA & Marion Cote Isle Verte, Canada
DESMONLIN, Maria D, Sep 12 1899 Sex:F Child# 3 Francois Desmonlin Vermont & Josephine Gregoire Great Falls
DESMONT, Marie Adele, Mar 11 1891 Sex:F Child# 3 Joseph Desmont Canada & Laure Gamache Canada
DESMOULIN, Joseph Louis, Oct 21 1901 Sex:M Child# 4 Francois Desmoulin Williamstown, VT & Josephine Gregoire
DESMOULINS, Alcide Raoul, Jan 3 1903 Sex:M Child# 5 Francois Desmoulins White River Jct, VT & Josephine Gregoire
DESMUND, Marie L F, Aug 12 1889 Sex:F Child# 4 Herbert Desmund Canada & Julie Facto Canada
DESPINS, Joseph, Aug 7 1918 Sex:M Child# 1 Archille Despins Nashua, NH & Ernestine Belanger Nashua, NH Stillborn
DESPONTBRIAND, Muriel Orra, Jul 23 1926 Sex:F Child# 3 H DesPontbriand Mass & Vivian Moisseau Vermont
DESPRE, Joseph, Jun 18 1901 Sex:M Child# 5 Henri Despre Canada & Angelina Drouin Canada
DESPRES, Alice, Dec 11 1911 Sex:F Child# 3 Gilbert Despres Canada & Mathilda Levesque Canada
DESPRES, Cecile Adrienne, Dec 14 1918 Sex:F Child# 5 Jean B Despres Canada & Philomene Raymond Canada
DESPRES, Edgar Louis Philip, Apr 2 1912 Sex:M Child# 1 Jean B Despres Canada & Marie P Raymond Canada
DESPRES, Fernand, Jun 26 1917 Sex:M Child# 4 J B Despres Canada & Marie Raymond Canada
DESPRES, Gerard, Jun 11 1922 Sex:M Child# 7 J Bte Despres Canada & Marie Raymond Canada
DESPRES, Isabelle, Dec 8 1916 Sex:F Child# 5 Gilbert Despres Canada & Mathilda Levesque Canada
DESPRES, Joseph Alphonse, Jan 30 1909 Sex:M Child# 2 Gilbert Despres Canada & E Levesque Canada
DESPRES, Joseph Normand, Nov 30 1906 Sex:M Child# 1 Gilbert Despres Canada & Mathilda Levesque Canada
DESPRES, M Yvonne Mathilde, Jul 22 1914 Sex:F Child# 4 Gilbert Despres Canada & Mathilde Levesque Canada
DESPRES, Marcella Anesie, Jan 15 1914 Sex:F Child# 2 Jean B Despres Canada & Philomene Raymond Canada
DESPRES, Marie Anna, Oct 6 1899 Sex:F Child# 1 Calixte Despres Canada & Amanda Desjardins Canada
DESPRES, Paul, Nov 8 1919 Sex:M Child# 6 Gilbert Despres Canada & Mathilda Levesque Canada
DESPRES, Paul Henry, Oct 12 1927 Sex:M Child# 8 John B Despres Canada & Marie Raymond Canada
DESPRES, Raymond Norman, Jul 28 1915 Sex:M Child# 3 Jean Bte Despres Canada & Marie Raymond Canada
DESPREZ, Calixte Joseph, Aug 13 1902 Sex:M Child# 2 Calixte Desprez Canada & Amanda Desjardins Canada
DESRAISSEAU, Claire Aurore, Apr 27 1917 Sex:F Child# 3 Oscar DesRaisseau Canada & Julia Gagnon Canada
DESROCHERS, Blanche Olena, Jan 20 1903 Sex:F Child# 3 Francois Desrochers Canada & Exilda Landry Canada
DESROCHERS, Charles Roland, Jul 26 1907 Sex:M Child# 2 Charles Desrochers Canada & Celia Michaud Canada
DESROCHERS, Marie Anna Eva, Feb 7 1901 Sex:F Child# 3 Joseph Desrochers Canada & Maria Dumay Canada
DESROCHERS, Pauline Marie Rose G, Sep 18 1928 Sex:F Child# 2 R G DesRochers Manchester, NH & Beatrice Gervais
DESROCHERS, Wilfred Robert, Oct 29 1908 Sex:M Child# 3 Charles Desrochers Canada & Celia Michaud Nashua, NH
DESROCHES, Alivier A, Oct 23 1892 Sex:M Child# 2 Alfred Desroches Spencer, MA & Marie Dube Canada
DESROCHES, Etna Rachel, Feb 21 1906 Sex:F Child# 1 Charles Desroches Canada & Celia Michaud Nashua, NH
DESROCHES, Joseph Adelard, Mar 17 1896 Sex:M Child# 2 Joseph Desroches Canada & Marie Dumais Canada
DESROSIA, Ineognito, Oct 31 1888 Sex:F Child# 1 Canada & Herminia Desrosia Canada
DESROSIER, Alexina, Jan 22 1892 Sex:F Child# 1 Alexis Desrosier Canada & Arsene Grandmaison Canada
DESROSIER, Donald Norbert, Sep 19 1933 Sex:M Child# 3 Arche Desrosier Nashua, NH & Yvonne Lavoie Nashua, NH
DESROSIER, J Armand Hector, Feb 15 1922 Sex:M Child# 9 Eugene Desrosier Canada & Julienne Bourbeau Canada
DESROSIER, Joseph Adelard, Mar 5 1893 Sex:M Child# 1 Emile Desrosier Canada & Claudia Desbien Canada
DESROSIER, Joseph Auguste M, Apr 15 1916 Sex:M Child# 1 Alderic Desrosier
DESROSIER, Marie Ardelia Dora, Jun 20 1924 Sex:F Child# 10 Eugene Desrosier Canada & Julienne Bourbeau Canada
DESROSIER, Marie Y Camille, Apr 27 1931 Sex:F Child# 11 Eugene Desrosier Canada & Julienne Bourbeau Canada
DESROSIER, Normand Lionel, Oct 16 1932 Sex:M Child# 2 A Desrosier Nashua, NH & Yvonne Lavoie Nashua, NH
DESROSIER, Raymond Maurice, Sep 23 1931 Sex:M Child# 1 Archie Desrosier Nashua, NH & Yvonne Lavoie Nashua, NH
DESROSIERS, Adeline J, Apr 14 1933 Sex:F Child# 7 Jos Desrosiers St Albans, VT & Mary Riley Salem, MA
DESROSIERS, Albert, Oct 16 1924 Sex:M Child# 1 Ludger Desrosiers Canada & Alba Voyer Canada
DESROSIERS, Armand Norbert, Nov 16 1906 Sex:M Child# 2 Oscar Desrosiers Canada & Rosanna Bourbeau Canada
DESROSIERS, Arselia Fabiola, May 25 1905 Sex:F Child# 1 Oscar Desrosiers Canada & Rose Anna Bourbault Canada

DESROSIERS, Blanche Jeannette, Dec 2 1911 Sex:F Child# 4 Eugene Desrosiers Canada & Julienne Bourbeau Canada
DESROSIERS, Claire Yvonne, May 4 1932 Sex:F Child# 3 Ernest Desrosiers Nashua, NH & Philomene Noel Nashua, NH
DESROSIERS, Emma Rosanna, Jun 13 1905 Sex:F Child# 11 Eugene Desrosiers Canada & Valerie Ferland Canada
DESROSIERS, Eugene Leo, Mar 30 1903 Sex:M Child# 3 Eugene Desrosiers Canada & Louisa Dorge Canada
DESROSIERS, Eva, May 18 1898 Sex:F Child# 1 Mederic Desrosiers Canada & Louisa Dodge Canada
DESROSIERS, Eva Rose, Feb 5 1902 Sex:F Child# 4 Alph Desrosiers Canada & Seraphine Carrier Canada
DESROSIERS, Gerald Roger, Sep 29 1925 Sex:M Child# 2 Charles E Desrosiers Nashua, NH & Marie April Canada
DESROSIERS, Irene Lilian, Oct 12 1908 Sex:F Child# 6 Alphonse Desrosiers Canada & Seraphine Carrier Canada
DESROSIERS, James, Jun 7 1929 Sex:M Child# 1 Omer J Desrosiers Greenville, NH & Olive Lizotte Canada
DESROSIERS, Jeanne Cecile, Apr 16 1927 Sex:F Child# 1 Ernest Desrosiers Nashua, NH & Philomene Noel Nashua, NH
DESROSIERS, Jeanne Marie, Sep 21 1927 Sex:F Child# 1 A B Desrosiers Easthampton, MA & Helen Wood Chelsea, MA
DESROSIERS, Joseph, May 24 1887 Sex:M Child#  Joseph Desrosiers P Q & Lumella Peltier P Q
DESROSIERS, Joseph, Dec 19 1895 Sex:M Child# 1 Francois Desrosiers Canada & Delina Emond Canada
DESROSIERS, Joseph A, May 19 1887 Sex:M Child# 6 Ovide Desrosiers P Q & Celina Mathews P Q
DESROSIERS, Joseph Adelard, Sep 13 1910 Sex:M Child# 2 Eugene Desrosiers Canada & Julienne Bourbeau Canada
DESROSIERS, Joseph Albert, Jul 19 1902 Sex:M Child# 8 Remi Desrosiers Canada & Amanda Cloutier Mass
DESROSIERS, Joseph Alexandre, Oct 16 1899 Sex:M Child# 2 Alexandre Desrosiers Canada & Alphonsine Label Canada
DESROSIERS, Joseph Alexandre, Mar 13 1904 Sex:M Child# 4 Alex Desrosiers Canada & Alphonsine Lebel Canada
DESROSIERS, Joseph Alfred Roger, Aug 11 1916 Sex:M Child# 6 Eugene Desrosiers Canada & Julienne Bombeault Canada
DESROSIERS, Joseph Alphonse, Feb 9 1896 Sex:M Child# 2 Alphonse Desrosiers Canada & Seraphine Carriere Canada
DESROSIERS, Joseph Art Robert, Jun 8 1919 Sex:M Child# 8 Eugene Desrosiers Canada & Julienne Bourbeault Canada
DESROSIERS, Joseph Ernest, Jan 8 1894 Sex:M Child# 2 Ernest Desrosiers Canada & Valarie Peltier Canada
DESROSIERS, Joseph Leo, Mar 2 1935 Sex:M Child# 4 Ernest Desrosiers Nashua, NH & Philomene Noel Nashua, NH
DESROSIERS, Joseph M A, Aug 28 1903 Sex:M Child# 10 Eugene Desrosiers Canada & Valere Ferland Canada
DESROSIERS, Laurette Cecile, Jul 16 1915 Sex:F Child# 8 Alphonse Desrosiers Canada & Seraphine Carrier Canada
DESROSIERS, Laurette Olivette, Mar 1 1912 Sex:F Child# 7 Alphonse Desrosiers Canada & Seraphine Carrier
DESROSIERS, Lausias, Apr 24 1905 Sex:M Child# 9 Remi Desrosiers Canada & Amanda Cloutier Canada
DESROSIERS, Lillian G, May 15 1913 Sex:F Child# 1 Philip Desrosiers Canada & Lea Weiner Canada
DESROSIERS, Lorraine Cecile, Jan 20 1935 Sex:F Child# 1 (No Parents Listed)
DESROSIERS, Louis Albert, Sep 12 1900 Sex:M Child# 2 Mederic Desrosiers Canada & Louisa Dodge Canada
DESROSIERS, M Olivette Germaine, Mar 16 1914 Sex:F Child# 7 Mederic Desrosiers Canada & Louisa Dodge US
DESROSIERS, Marie Agnes V, Aug 4 1908 Sex:F Child# 1 Damase Desrosiers Canada & Rose A Mignault Canada
DESROSIERS, Marie Alida, Feb 16 1904 Sex:F Child# 5 Alphonse Desrosiers Canada & Seraphine Carrier Canada
DESROSIERS, Marie Anne, Sep 29 1894 Sex:F Child# 1 Alphonse Desrosiers Canada & Ceraphine Carriers Canada
DESROSIERS, Marie Anne Irene, Sep 28 1918 Sex:F Child# 1 Charles E Desrosiers Nashua, NH & Marie April Canada
DESROSIERS, Marie Cecile Annette, Dec 12 1935 Sex:F Child# 4 Archy Desrosiers Nashua, NH & Yvonne Lavoie Nashua NH
DESROSIERS, Marie Eva, Jun 3 1900 Sex:F Child# 3 Alexis Desrosiers Canada & Arsene Grandmaison Canada
DESROSIERS, Marie G A, Dec 11 1905 Sex:F Child# 1 Hormidas Desrosiers Canada & Rosina Roy Canada
DESROSIERS, Marie Gabrielle L, Jan 25 1918 Sex:F Child# 7 Eugene Desrosiers Canada & Julienne Bourbault Canada
DESROSIERS, Marie Ida, Apr 3 1896 Sex:F Child# 2 Alexis Desrosiers Canada & Arsenne Grandmaison Canada
DESROSIERS, Marie Rose Yvonne, May 25 1930 Sex:F Child# 2 Adelard Desrosiers Canada & Emilienne Voyer Nashua, NH
DESROSIERS, Marie Yvonne, Sep 27 1901 Sex:F Child# 3 Alexandre Desrosiers Canada & Alphonsine Lebel Canada
DESROSIERS, Oscar Archie, Jun 11 1909 Sex:M Child# 2 Eugene Desrosiers,Jr Canada & Julienne Bourbeau Canada
DESROSIERS, Raoul Paul, Aug 20 1924 Sex:M Child# 1 Adelard Desrosiers Canada & Emilienne Voyer New Bedford, MA
DESROSIERS, Raymond Edmond, Jan 21 1908 Sex:M Child# 5 Mederic Desrosiers Canada & Louisa Dodge Canada
DESROSIERS, Remi Alexis, Apr 7 1910 Sex:M Child# 11 Remi Desrosiers Canada & Marie Cloutier Canada
DESROSIERS, Roger Eugene J C, Jul 10 1930 Sex:M Child# 1 Eugene Desrosiers Canada & Adrienne Roy Canada
DESROSIERS, Roland Lucien, Jun 10 1914 Sex:M Child# 5 Eugene Desrosiers Canada & Julienne Bourbeau Canada
DESROSIERS, Romeo, Oct 1 1908 Sex:M Child# 10 Remi Desrosiers Canada & Amanda Cloutier Canada
DESROSIERS, Therese Lorette, Jul 30 1930 Sex:F Child# 2 Ernest Desrosiers Nashua, NH & Philomene Noel Nashua, NH
DESROSIERS, Uldege, Aug 5 1906 Sex:M Child# 12 Eugene Desrosiers Canada & Valerie Ferland Canada
DESROSIERS, William Edouard, Nov 19 1905 Sex:M Child# 4 Mederic Desrosiers Canada & Louis Dodge Canada
DESROSIERS, Yvonne Alma, Jul 5 1907 Sex:F Child# 1 Eugene Desrosiers Canada & Julienne Bourbeau Canada
DESVACELA, Unknown, Jul 4 1918 Sex:F Child# 1 Aristi Desvacela Greece & Vacela Bale Greece
DETH, George Wilford, Dec 24 1900 Sex:M Child# 1 Richard Deth Vermont & M M Thompson New York
DEVALITES, Unknown, Dec 13 1928 Sex:F Child# 3 Costas Devalites Greece & E Kyradgis Greece
DEVEAUX, Alma Eva, Oct 18 1887 Sex:F Child#  Philippe Deveaux Canada & Amelie Germain Canada
DEVEREAUX, Kearn William, Jul 5 1925 Sex:M Child# 1 K J P Devereaux Boston, MA & Jeanette Gravelle Nashua, NH
DEVEREUX, Donald alfred, Nov 1 1934 Sex:M Child# 4 G Donald Devereux Roxbury, MA & Lillian Gravelle Nashua, NH
DEVEREUX, Francis Kearn, Jul 16 1931 Sex:M Child# 1 Kearn Devereux England & Josephine Dunne England
DEVEREUX, Joan Annette, Jan 15 1932 Sex:F Child# 2 Kearn Devereux Boston, MA & Jeanette Gravelle Nashua, NH
DEVEREUX, Joseph Colin, Dec 12 1932 Sex:M Child# 2 Kearn Devereux England & Josephine Dunne England
DEVEREUX, Mary, Aug 26 1931 Sex:F Child# 2 Donald Devereux Mass & Lillian Gravelle Nashua, NH
DEVEREUX, Natalie Lillian, Oct 7 1930 Sex:F Child# 1 Donald Devereux Roxbury, MA & Lillian Gravelle Nashua, NH
DEVINE, Alice Teresa, Oct 22 1895 Sex:F Child#  Michael J Devine Boston, MA & Ellen J Galise Boston, MA
DEVINE, William Joseph, Mar 20 1897 Sex:M Child# 7 Michael J Devine Boston, MA & Ellen J Galice Boston, MA
DEVINNELLS, Donald Arthur, Jun 5 1926 Sex:M Child# 3 Frank Devinnells Hopkinton, NH & G Richardson Peterboro, NH
DEVLIN, Joseph Arthur, Feb 25 1924 Sex:M Child# 1 Joseph A Devlin Canada & Catherine T Brady Nashua, NH
DEVLIN, Patricia, Apr 13 1927 Sex:F Child# 2 Joseph A Devlin Wolftown, Canada & Catherine Brady Nashua, NH
DEVREAUX, Elaine Marie, Aug 17 1928 Sex:F Child# 2 Kearn Devreaux Boston, MA & Jeannette Gravelle Nashua, NH
DEWARE, Basil William, Apr 14 1934 Sex:M Child# 2 Basil Deware Pepperell, MA & Ellen Spofford Townsend, MA
DEWELL, Marjorie Elizabeth, Sep 21 1935 Sex:F Child# 1 Phillip F Dewell New York, NY & Odelia McGraw Portage
DEWEY, Arthur F, Aug 15 1892 Sex:M Child#  Frank B Dewey Mass & Polly Keith Vermont

DEWEY, Reginald, Nov 7 1915 Sex:M Child# 1 (No Parents Listed)
DEWITT, Lyle Brooks, Aug 5 1927 Sex:M Child# 5 Austin L Dewitt New Brunswick & Alice Dickinson New Brunswick
DEWOLFE, Dorothy, Jan 11 1894 Sex:F Child# 1 A E DeWolfe Nashua, NH & Vedora C Shaw Augusta, ME
DEWOLFE, Katherine Mary, Nov 26 1917 Sex:F Child# 2 William Dewolfe Montreal, Canada & Katherine Summers
DEWOLFE, William Patrick, Jun 10 1921 Sex:M Child# 2 William P DeWolfe Montreal, Canada & Katharin Summers
DEWYEA, Unknown, Nov 26 1894 Sex:M Child# 1 Joseph M Dewyea Bremen, ME & Ida M Bancroft Litchfield, NH
DEXTER, Anita Betty, Aug 15 1914 Sex:F Child# 2 Perley R Dexter Oakland, ME & Maud Nichols Nashua, NH
DEXTER, Clara, Aug 22 1899 Sex:F Child# 1 George L Dexter Maine & Mary Sheehy Ireland
DEXTER, Earle Lewis, Jan 12 1906 Sex:M Child# 1 Arthur L Dexter Providence, RI & Susie F Watts Bedford, MA
DEXTER, Unknown, Sep 18 1914 Sex:M Child# 3 Arthur L Dexter Providence, RI & Susie T Watts Bedford, MA
DIAMANTOPOULOS, Atanisios, Feb 19 1912 Sex:M Child# 2 Ang Diamantopoulos Greece & Tesias Tagwalou Greece
DIAMANTOPOULOS, Unknown, Sep 7 1914 Sex:M Child# 4 Ang Diamantopoulos Greece & Anastasia Lanjelos Greece Stillborn
DIAMANTOPOULOS, Unknown, Sep 22 1915 Sex:F Child# 6 A J Diamantopoulos Greece & Anastasia Tangalow Greece
DIAMANTOPOULOS, Unknown, Sep 11 1916 Sex:M Child# 6 A Diamantopoulos Greece & Anastasia Tongalon Greece Stillborn
DICEY, Carl Cote, May 31 1930 Sex:M Child# 1 Jess Dicey Alexander, NH & Jennie Cote Hill, NH
DICHARD, Alberta Beatrice, Mar 2 1931 Sex:F Child# 1 Albert Dichard NH & Beatrice Davis Rhode Island
DICHARD, Donald John, Jan 30 1929 Sex:M Child# 3 Philip Dichard Lawrence, MA & Lillian Green Nashua, NH
DICHARD, Edward Alphonse, Jun 12 1929 Sex:M Child# 1 Edward Dichard Merrimack, NH & Christine Rodgers Nashua, NH
DICHARD, Ernest, Nov 29 1917 Sex:M Child# 1 (No Parents Listed)
DICHARD, Francois Paul, Jun 20 1930 Sex:M Child# 1 Francois W Dichard Thorntons Ferry, NH & Marie A Fortier Canada
DICHARD, Irene Rose, Sep 22 1932 Sex:F Child# 2 Albert Dichard NH & Beatrice Davis NH
DICHARD, Joseph Jean O, Aug 16 1897 Sex:M Child# 1 Alphonse Dichard Nashua, NH & Henriette Lafleur Plattsburg, NY
DICHARD, Joseph Laurence, Nov 14 1916 Sex:M Child# 1 Elzear Dichard Nashua, NH & Minnie Boisvert Nashua, NH
DICHARD, Joseph Pascal L, Jun 18 1900 Sex:M Child# 6 Joseph Dichard Canada & Anastasie Raymond Canada
DICHARD, Kenneth Philip, Aug 21 1927 Sex:M Child# 2 Philip Dichard Lawrence, MA & Lillian Green Nashua, NH
DICHARD, Laura, Dec 4 1898 Sex:F Child# 2 George Dichard Canada & Leda Blanchette Canada
DICHARD, Laura Irene, Mar 7 1905 Sex:F Child# 8 Ludger Dichard Canada & Gracia Deschenes Canada
DICHARD, Leo Maurice, Sep 16 1921 Sex:M Child# 2 Alfred Dichard Merrimack, NH & Lydia Gauthier New York
DICHARD, Lillian Vera, Jan 21 1901 Sex:F Child# 1 Joseph Dichard Nashua, NH & Lottie Annis Londonderry, NH
DICHARD, Lionel George, Mar 8 1933 Sex:M Child# 1 G J Dichard Merrimack, NH & L B Boucher Nashua, NH
DICHARD, M Eva Eudaxie, Oct 2 1892 Sex:F Child# 1 George Dichard Canada & Leda Blanchette Canada
DICHARD, Margaret Jean, Mar 11 1924 Sex:F Child# 2 Adelard Dichard Nashua, NH & Daisy Bush Bristol, England
DICHARD, Maurice, Jan 27 1920 Sex:M Child# 2 Elzear Dichard Nashua, NH & Mamie Boisvert Nashua, NH
DICK, Donald Francis, Feb 26 1930 Sex:M Child# 1 Albert T Dick Everett, MA & Agnes Riney Milford, NH
DICK, Edna Louise, Oct 19 1924 Sex:F Child# 1 Louis Dick Milford, NH & Anna Davidson Temple, NH  Stillborn
DICKERMAN, Kenneth Blood, Oct 5 1921 Sex:M Child# 1 Albert P Dickerman Hollis, NH & Myrth F Abbott Brooklyn, NY
DICKERSON, Unknown, Oct 3 1909 Sex:F Child# 3 Walter W Dickerson New York & Anna Sullivan Ireland
DICKERSON, Unknown, Jan 15 1911 Sex:M Child# 4 Walter W Dickerson Plattsburg, NY & Anna Sullivan Ireland
DICKINSON, Carle, Oct 21 1898 Sex:M Child# 1 Charles H Dickinson Keene, NH & Addie M Campbell Londonderry, NH
DICKINSON, Charles Robert, Aug 17 1932 Sex:M Child# 2 Carl N Dickinson Nashua, NH & V E Hewitt Newburg, NY
DICKSON, Zester Joseph, Jul 16 1906 Sex:M Child# 1 Walter W Dickson New York & Hannah M Sullivan Ireland
DICKSTEIN, Esther, Aug 8 1921 Sex:F Child# 4 Philip Dickstein Russia & Bessie Stappuk Russia
DICKSTEIN, Maurice, Feb 22 1926 Sex:M Child# 6 Philip Dickstein Russia & Bessie Stepack Russia
DIERSCHMIDT, Evelyn Verna, Jul 30 1925 Sex:F Child# 1 Otho Dierschmidt Germany & Mary Gibbons Wilton, NH
DIEUSON, Mary Ellen, Jan 15 1889 Sex:F Child# 3 James Dieusen Ireland & Julia Grechan Ireland
DIGGINS, Albert Francis, Nov 8 1896 Sex:M Child# 5 Thomas Diggins Ireland & Margaret Reardon Ireland
DIGGINS, Albert, Jr, Jan 7 1929 Sex:M Child# 2 Albert Diggins Nashua, NH & Lena Levesque Nashua, NH
DIGGINS, Catherine Gertrude, Jan 31 1893 Sex:F Child# 2 Thomas Diggins Ireland & Margaret Reardon Ireland
DIGGINS, Daniel Herbert, Dec 1 1905 Sex:M Child# 10 Thomas Diggins Ireland & Margaret Reardon Ireland
DIGGINS, Donald Paul, Dec 17 1924 Sex:M Child# 1 Paul Diggins Nashua, NH & Thaila Miller Nashua, NH
DIGGINS, Doris, Oct 24 1935 Sex:F Child# 5 Albert Diggins Nashua, NH & Lena Levesque Nashua, NH
DIGGINS, Dorothy Agnes, Jul 31 1910 Sex:F Child# 11 Thomas Diggins Ireland & Margaret Reardon Ireland
DIGGINS, Edward James, Sep 4 1924 Sex:M Child# 1 John P Diggins Nashua, NH & Sylvia Caron Canada
DIGGINS, Gloria, Oct 1 1931 Sex:F Child# 3 Albert Diggins Nashua, NH & Lena Levesque Nashua, NH
DIGGINS, Helen, Jun 21 1902 Sex:F Child# 8 Thomas Diggins Ireland & Margaret Reardon Ireland
DIGGINS, John P, Mar 2 1894 Sex:M Child# 3 Thomas Diggins Ireland & Margaret Reardon Ireland
DIGGINS, John Patrick, Mar 22 1928 Sex:M Child# 3 John P Diggins Nashua, NH & Sylvia Caron Canada
DIGGINS, Lucille, Jul 8 1927 Sex:F Child# 1 Albert Diggins Nashua, NH & Lena Levesque Nashua, NH
DIGGINS, Margaret Isabella, Nov 23 1891 Sex:F Child# 1 Thomas Diggins Ireland & Margaret Reardon Ireland
DIGGINS, Mary, Aug 18 1900 Sex:F Child# Thomas Diggins Ireland & Margaret Reardon Ireland
DIGGINS, Paul, Sep 8 1898 Sex:M Child# 6 Thomas Diggins Ireland & Margaret Reardon Ireland
DIGGINS, Ruth, Dec 13 1903 Sex:F Child# 9 Thomas Diggins Ireland & Margaret Reardon Ireland
DIGGINS, Ruth Sylvia, Dec 31 1926 Sex:F Child# 2 John P Diggins Nashua, NH & Sylvia Caron Canada
DIGGINS, Thomas Edward, Nov 30 1895 Sex:M Child# 4 Thomas Diggins Ireland & Margaret Reardon Ireland
DIGGINS, Thomas Robert, Jan 3 1934 Sex:M Child# 4 Albert Diggins Nashua, NH & Lena Levesque Nashua, NH
DILLON, Eleanor, Aug 24 1905 Sex:F Child# 1 William Dillon Prince Edward Island & Alice Scanlan Nashua, NH
DILLON, Unknown, Apr 11 1917 Sex:M Child# 1 Francis Dillon Jaffrey, NH & Laura Lafleur E Jaffrey, NH
DIMETRIOS, Andigoni, Oct 24 1918 Sex:F Child# 4 Thomas Dimetrios Greece & Theodota Mikali Greece
DIMINIE, Bessie May, Feb 4 1895 Sex:F Child# 2 Henry Diminie Malone, NY & Adelaide Malette Malone, NY
DINAN, Elizabeth Hope, Nov 18 1922 Sex:F Child# 4 James F Dinan Ashland, MA & Amy G Kitchener England
DINAN, Geraldine, Mar 26 1911 Sex:F Child# 1 James F Dinan Ashland, MA & Amy G Kitchener Medford, England
DINAN, James Francis, Jr, Jul 2 1919 Sex:M Child# 3 James F Dinan Ashland, MA & Amy Kitchener England
DINAN, Robert Joseph, Jun 19 1925 Sex:M Child# 5 James F Dinan Ashland, MA & Amy Kitchener Bedford, England

DINANDO, Louis Oppice, Jul 10 1896 Sex:M Child# 1 Fer Dinando Italy & Santa Ablondi Italy
DINEEN, James, Dec 22 1887 Sex:M Child# 2 James Dineen Ireland & Julia Ireland
DINEEN, Unknown, May 9 1892 Sex: Child# 5 James Dineen Ireland & Julia Ireland
DINELLE, Laura, Mar 30 1909 Sex:F Child# 1 Napoleon Dinelle Canada & Celamire Fortin Three Rivers, MA
DINGLEY, Mary Standish, Oct 4 1931 Sex:F Child# 1 Bret Harte Dingley Maine & Irene Dion Taunton, MA
DIOLISH, Stanley, Mar 26 1916 Sex:M Child# 2 Valerion Diolish Russia & Salomea Torkasg Austria
DION, Albert, May 28 1908 Sex:M Child# 1 Henry Dion Malone, NY & Corinne Desmarais Nashua, NH
DION, Alfred, Aug 5 1907 Sex:M Child# 7 Joseph Dion Canada & Marianne Nadeau Canada
DION, Alma, Dec 2 1903 Sex:F Child# 3 Joseph Dion Canada & Marie Anne Nadeau Canada
DION, Andre Viateur, Feb 11 1909 Sex:M Child# 3 Louis Dion Canada & Marie Louise Soucy Nashua, NH
DION, Anna Irene, Apr 29 1911 Sex:F Child# 2 Joseph Dion Canada & Anna Chenette Canada
DION, Armand Louis, Jul 24 1909 Sex:M Child# 4 J B Dion Winooski, VT & Dora Gauthier Nashua, NH
DION, Arthur Emile, May 20 1915 Sex:M Child# 1 Arthur J Dion Malone, NY & Eva Lussier Nashua, NH
DION, Aurelie Andrea, Sep 21 1910 Sex:F Child# 5 John B Dion Burlington, VT & Dora Gauthier Nashua, NH
DION, Beatrice, Apr 7 1908 Sex:F Child# 15 Alex Dion Malone, NY & Emma Dumas Malone, NY
DION, Beatrice Sylvia, Feb 23 1910 Sex:F Child# 1 Joseph Dion Canada & Ann Chenette Canada
DION, Bernadette, Oct 2 1892 Sex:F Child# 2 Elzeard Dion Canada & Elizabeth Canada
DION, Blanche Sylvia, Jun 22 1907 Sex:F Child# 3 John B Dion Nashua, NH & Dora Gauthier Nashua, NH
DION, Cecile Marie A, Dec 9 1910 Sex:F Child# 1 Francois Dion Canada & Amelia Emond Canada
DION, Edna, Nov 5 1918 Sex:F Child# 2 Arthur Dion Somersworth, MA & Maude Boucher Nashua, NH
DION, Eugene Arthur, Apr 20 1918 Sex:M Child# 3 Arthur Dion Malone, NY & Eva Lussier Nashua, NH
DION, Eugenie Anaise, Sep 10 1908 Sex:F Child# 1 Francois Dion Canada & Eugenie Boucher Canada
DION, Frances Sylvia, Sep 14 1923 Sex:F Child# 5 Henry Dion Malone, NY & Corinne Desmarais Nashua, NH
DION, Frederic, Mar 16 1890 Sex:M Child# 11 Raphael Dion Canada & Adeline Lambert Canada
DION, Gracia, Apr 11 1906 Sex:F Child# 14 Alex Dion Malone, NY & Emma Dumais Malone, NY
DION, Helen Margaret, Jun 26 1905 Sex:F Child# 1 Leon A Dion Nashua, NH & Elizabeth C Spence Nashua, NH
DION, Henry Robert, Jun 11 1909 Sex:M Child# 1 Henry A Dion Nashua, NH & Rose Winn Nashua, NH
DION, Ida Gertrude, May 16 1911 Sex:F Child# 2 Henry Dion New York & Corinne Desmarais Nashua, NH
DION, Jacqueline Elaine, Apr 1 1935 Sex:F Child# 1 Sylvio Dion Nashua, NH & Yvonne Morency Lynn, MA
DION, Jos Andree Norman, Mar 27 1932 Sex:M Child# 4 Edmond Dion Canada & Olivine Roy Canada
DION, Joseph, Jun 19 1893 Sex:M Child# 12 Raphael Dion Canada & Adeline Lambert Canada
DION, Joseph Albert, May 26 1900 Sex:M Child# 1 Joseph Dion Canada & Delvina Mailloux Canada
DION, Joseph Donald, May 24 1925 Sex:M Child# 1 Joseph Dion Westville, NH & Lillian Aryell Nashua, NH
DION, Joseph Leo, Aug 7 1923 Sex:M Child# 3 Leo Dion Newmarket, NH & Delia Noel Nashua, NH
DION, Joseph Leo Pierre, Oct 28 1925 Sex:M Child# 12 Amedee Dion Vermont & D Chamberland Canada
DION, Laura, Jan 22 1898 Sex:F Child# 10 Alex Dion Malone, NY & Emma Dumas Malone, NY
DION, Leon, Oct 3 1899 Sex:M Child# 11 Alex Dion NY & Emma Dumas NY
DION, Leon Royal, Aug 27 1916 Sex:M Child# 2 Arthur Dion Malone, NY & Eva Lussier Nashua, NH
DION, Lillian, Apr 12 1922 Sex:F Child# 2 Lewis Dion Newmarket, NH & Delia Noel Nashua, NH
DION, Loraine Grace, Dec 22 1923 Sex:F Child# 4 Arthur G Dion Malone, NY & Eva Lucier Nashua, NH
DION, Marguerite, Aug 7 1891 Sex:F Child#  Alphonse Dion Canada & Helene Olivier Canada
DION, Marie A, Jul 23 1902 Sex:F Child# 2 Joseph Dion Canada & Marie A Nadeau Canada
DION, Marie A E, Aug 15 1887 Sex:F Child# 10 Raphael Dion Canada & Deline Lembert Canada
DION, Marie Anna Olivette, Aug 26 1924 Sex:F Child# 1 Edmond Dion Canada & Olivinne Roy Canada
DION, Marie Anne, Aug 5 1907 Sex:F Child# 6 Joseph Dion Canada & Marianne Nadeau Canada
DION, Marie Aurelie, Dec 1 1892 Sex:F Child# 12 Alphonse Dion Canada & Helene Olivier Canada
DION, Marie Bertha Lucille, Jul 28 1920 Sex:F Child# 1 William Dion NH & Antoinette Basil NH
DION, Marie Dora, Jul 16 1897 Sex:F Child# 1 Philippe Dion Milton & Exilda Rouleau Nashua, NH
DION, Marie Doris, Sep 6 1928 Sex:F Child# 13 Amedee Dion Vermont & D Chamberland
DION, Marie Rose Anna, Jun 15 1906 Sex:F Child# 5 Louis Dion Canada & Marie Anne Nadeau Canada
DION, Marie Rose Edna, Apr 8 1903 Sex:F Child# 1 John B Dion Winoosky Falls, VT & Dora Gauthier Nashua, NH
DION, Mary Ann S, May 18 1890 Sex:F Child# 1 Elzeard Dion Canada & Mary E Tirnoncy Canada
DION, Mary Corinne L, May 1 1900 Sex:F Child# 2 Joseph Dion Canada & Mary King Canada
DION, Maurice Gerard, Jan 4 1921 Sex:M Child# 4 Henry Dion Malone, NY & Corinne Desmarais Nashua, NH
DION, Normand, Mar 5 1904 Sex:M Child# 13 Alex Dion Malone, NY & Emma Dumas Malone, NY
DION, Normand, Sep 30 1925 Sex:M Child# 1 Horin Dion Rhode Island & Regina Toussant Canada
DION, Olivier Ernest, Jul 12 1894 Sex:M Child# 13 Alphonse Dion Canada & Helene Olivier Canada
DION, Raphael, Apr 16 1910 Sex:M Child# 4 Amedee Dion US & Delia Chamberlain Canada
DION, Raymond, Mar 21 1912 Sex:M Child# 5 Joseph Dion Canada & Anna Chenette Canada
DION, Robert Albert, Sep 27 1932 Sex:M Child# 1 Albert Dion Nashua, NH & Irene Gravelle Nashua, NH
DION, Robert Julien, Apr 29 1929 Sex:M Child# 3 Edmund Dion Canada & Olivine Roy Canada
DION, Robert Roland, Apr 13 1927 Sex:M Child# 2 Edmund Dion Canada & Olivine Lacroix Canada
DION, Roger Roland, Jul 26 1934 Sex:M Child# 2 Albert Dion Nashua, NH & Irene Gravelle Nashua, NH
DION, Romeo, Feb 11 1905 Sex:M Child# 1 Louis Dion Canada & Marie L Soucy Nashua, NH
DION, Sylvio, Apr 7 1906 Sex:M Child# 2 Louis Dion Canada & Marie Louise Soucy Nashua, NH
DION, Sylvio, Jun 4 1917 Sex:M Child# 3 Henri Dion Malone, NY & Corine Desmarais Nashua, NH
DION, Therese Alice, Feb 4 1931 Sex:F Child# 1 Omer Dion Exeter, NH & Delia Rioux Nashua, NH Stillborn
DION, Therese Rita, Feb 27 1931 Sex:F Child# 5 Louis Dion Newmarket, NH & Delia Noel Nashua, NH
DION, Unknown, May 7 1918 Sex:F Child# 1 Louis Dion Nashua, NH & Delia Noel Nashua, NH
DION, Viviane, Feb 6 1908 Sex:F Child# 1 William Dion W Alburg, VT & Elisabeth Ryan Nashua, NH
DION, William, Aug 24 1901 Sex:M Child# 12 Alex Dion Malone, NY & Emma Dumont Malone, NY
DIONE, Claudia B E, Mar 8 1887 Sex:F Child# 9 Alphonse Dione P Q & Vitaline Burt St Albans, VT
DIONE, Lionel Wilfred B, Jan 15 1919 Sex:M Child# 1 Rosario Dione Manchester, NH & Antoinette Beaudon Manchester

DIONE, Marie R, Nov 10 1887 Sex:F Child# 2 Cleophas Dione P Q & Victoria P Q
DIONE, Raymond, Apr 7 1888 Sex:M Child# 10 Alphonse Dione Canada & Helen Oliver Canada
DIONNE, Adile, Feb 29 1888 Sex:F Child# 12 Elzeard Dionne Canada & Marceline Morois Canada
DIONNE, Agnes Dorothy, Mar 17 1925 Sex:F Child# 4 William Dionne US & Georgia Lacombe Nashua, NH
DIONNE, Albert Robert, Jul 4 1924 Sex:M Child# 2 Adelard Dionne Nashua, NH & Stella Leclerc Nashua, NH
DIONNE, Alfred, Jun 20 1931 Sex:M Child# 6 Arthur Dionne Lowell, MA & Grace Lemiere Canada
DIONNE, Alfred D, Mar 29 1892 Sex:M Child# 5 Cleophas Dionne Canada & Victoria Vaillancour Canada
DIONNE, Alfred N, Mar 6 1897 Sex:M Child# 2 Georges Dionne Canada & Julianna Nadeau Canada
DIONNE, Alice Gertrude, Mar 27 1903 Sex:F Child# 9 Thomas Dionne Canada & Marie Boulanger Canada
DIONNE, Alphe Normand, Jun 29 1926 Sex:M Child# 5 William Dionne Lawrence, MA & G Larouche Nashua, NH
DIONNE, Annette, Oct 21 1904 Sex:F Child# 1 Walter Dionne US & Marie Anne Roy US
DIONNE, Annette Lucille, Aug 22 1932 Sex:F Child# 1 Emile Dionne Canada & Elise Marquis Vermont
DIONNE, Annette Pauline, Jun 2 1930 Sex:F Child# 8 William Dionne US & Georgianna Larouche Nashua, NH
DIONNE, Annette Rita, Dec 24 1926 Sex:F Child# 2 Francis Dionne Canada & Juliette D'Amour Canada
DIONNE, Arthur, Jun 24 1921 Sex:M Child# 1 Jos Etienne Dionne Milford, NH & Agnes St Laurent Nashua, NH
DIONNE, Arthur W R, Nov 21 1892 Sex:M Child# 11 Alphonse Dionne Canada & Delia Burth St Albans, VT
DIONNE, Bertha Imelda, Jun 27 1933 Sex:F Child# 10 William Dionne Lawrence, MA & Georgina Larouche Nashua, NH
DIONNE, Cecile, Nov 26 1932 Sex:F Child# 7 Arthur Dionne Lowell, MA & Grace Lemire Canada
DIONNE, Charles Eugene, May 18 1907 Sex:M Child# 2 Eugene Dionne Canada & Clarina Theriault Canada
DIONNE, Claria A, Sep 16 1889 Sex:F Child# 9 Elzear Dionne Canada & Philominie Richard Canada
DIONNE, Constance, Jan 27 1934 Sex:F Child# 1 Andre Dionne Canada & Annette Duval Canada
DIONNE, Dorothe Marguerite, Jan 24 1934 Sex:F Child# 1 Xavier Dionne Canada & Ida Duval Canada
DIONNE, Edmond, Oct 10 1923 Sex:M Child# 2 Alfred N Dionne Nashua, NH & Lydia Deschenes Nashua, NH
DIONNE, Edmond Henri, Nov 2 1915 Sex:M Child# 5 Jean Bte Dionne Canada & Angelina Poirier Canada
DIONNE, Egide, Oct 11 1913 Sex:M Child# 4 Eugene Dionne Canada & Marie Jean Deenison Canada
DIONNE, Elwin Arthur, Sep 6 1920 Sex:M Child# 3 Arthur Dionne Somersworth, NH & Maude Boucher Nashua, NH
DIONNE, Emile Paul, Aug 5 1925 Sex:M Child# 4 Louis Dionne Newmarket, NH & Delia Noel Nashua, NH
DIONNE, Emilinne Beatrice, Sep 4 1917 Sex:F Child# 7 Charles Dionne Canada & Julienna Bonenfant Nashua, NH
DIONNE, Ernest Roger, Jul 20 1926 Sex:M Child# 15 Joseph Dionne Canada & Ida Berube Canada
DIONNE, Eugenie Annette, Apr 24 1900 Sex:F Child# 2 Fereol Dionne Canada & Anna Ledoux NH
DIONNE, Eva Jeannette, Oct 17 1916 Sex:F Child# 6 Eugene Dionne Canada & Mary Dennison Canada
DIONNE, Eveline Irene, Apr 30 1902 Sex:F Child# 3 Joseph A Dionne Canada & Marie Pelletier Canada
DIONNE, Everett Ralph, Sep 6 1920 Sex:M Child# 4 Arthur Dionne Somersworth, NH & Maude Boucher Nashua, NH
DIONNE, Flora Fernande, Dec 24 1904 Sex:F Child# 1 Jean B Dionne Canada & Agneline Poirier Canada
DIONNE, George, Jan 22 1922 Sex:M Child# 1 Alfred Dionne Nashua, NH & Lydia Deschenes Nashua, NH
DIONNE, George Henry, Sep 14 1920 Sex:M Child# 8 Charles Dionne Canada & Julianna Bonenfant Nashua, NH
DIONNE, Gertrude Jeannette, Apr 9 1910 Sex:F Child# 3 Charles Dionne Canada & Julianna Bonenfant Nashua, NH
DIONNE, Gratia, Oct 19 1888 Sex:F Child# 10 Alphonse Dionne Canada & Delia Burth Canada
DIONNE, Henri, Nov 21 1907 Sex:M Child# 3 Joseph Dionne Canada & Ida Berube Canada
DIONNE, Henri Sylvis, Aug 6 1904 Sex:M Child# 2 Israel Dionne Canada & Madeline Rivard Canada
DIONNE, Henry, May 24 1934 Sex:M Child# 1 Henry Dionne Nashua, NH & Yvette Houle Nashua, NH
DIONNE, Holda Adrienne, Apr 23 1929 Sex:F Child# 6 Wilfrid Dionne Nashua, NH & Georgianna Larouche Nashua, NH
DIONNE, Howard Edward, May 19 1906 Sex:M Child# 2 Joseph E Dionne Nashua, NH & Gertrude O McDonald Mt Vernon, NH
DIONNE, Howard William, Apr 2 1899 Sex:M Child# 1 Henry W Dionne Nashua, NH & Delia Miner Churubusco, NY
DIONNE, Ida Eva, Apr 20 1915 Sex:F Child# 5 Eugene Dionne Canada & Mary Jane Dennison Canada
DIONNE, Irence, Dec 20 1911 Sex:M Child# 5 Joseph Dionne Canada & Ida Berube Canada
DIONNE, Irene, Feb 16 1906 Sex:F Child# 2 Joseph Dionne Canada & Ida Berube Canada
DIONNE, Irene Clare, Oct 20 1927 Sex:F Child# 6 William Dionne Mass & G Larouche Nashua, NH
DIONNE, Irene Rita, Oct 31 1922 Sex:F Child# 12 Joseph Dionne Canada & Ida Berube Canada
DIONNE, Isabelle, Jun 9 1905 Sex:F Child# 3 Edward Dionne Nashua, NH & Josephine J Carey Nashua, NH
DIONNE, Isabelle Yvonne, Nov 27 1914 Sex:F Child# 6 Charles Dionne Canada & Julianna Bonenfant Nashua, NH
DIONNE, J B Edgar Romeo, Oct 20 1908 Sex:M Child# 2 Charles Dionne Canada & Juliana Bonenfant Canada
DIONNE, J Celestin Robert, May 19 1914 Sex:M Child# 4 Honore Dionne Canada & Aimee Michaud Canada
DIONNE, J Raymond Theodore, Mar 23 1913 Sex:M Child# 5 Charles Dionne Canada & Rose J Bonenfant Canada
DIONNE, J Roger Ph Armand, Aug 23 1915 Sex:M Child# 5 Honore Dionne Canada & Aimee Michaud Canada
DIONNE, Jean Baptiste, Aug 15 1891 Sex:M Child# 7 Regis Dionne Canada & Philomene Jalbert Canada
DIONNE, Jos Andre Wilfrid, Feb 4 1920 Sex:M Child# 10 Joseph Dionne Canada & Ida Berube Canada
DIONNE, Jos Paul William, Apr 20 1923 Sex:M Child# 2 Joseph Dionne Milford, MA & Agnes St Laurent Nashua, NH
DIONNE, Joseph, Aug 15 1920 Sex:M Child# 1 (No Parents Listed)
DIONNE, Joseph, Mar 14 1921 Sex:M Child# 2 Auguste F Dionne Canada & Marguerite Soucy Canada Stillborn
DIONNE, Joseph, May 21 1921 Sex:M Child# 1 Wilfrid Dionne Lawrence, MA & Georgianna Larouche Nashua, NH
DIONNE, Joseph A, Mar 31 1892 Sex:M Child# 3 Thomas Dionne Canada & Marie Boulanger Canada
DIONNE, Joseph A A, Dec 1 1893 Sex:M Child# 4 Thomas Dionne Canada & Marie Boulanger Canada
DIONNE, Joseph A A, May 1 1896 Sex:M Child# 1 Auguste Dionne Canada & Anna Bonenfaut Canada
DIONNE, Joseph A P, Jul 31 1900 Sex:M Child# 1 Alphonse Dionne Canada & Lumina Valiere Canada
DIONNE, Joseph Achille, Mar 11 1896 Sex:M Child#   Joseph A Dionne Canada & Marie Pelletier Canada
DIONNE, Joseph Albert, Mar 15 1898 Sex:M Child# 6 Thomas Dionne Canada & Mary Boulanger Canada
DIONNE, Joseph Albert N, Oct 2 1930 Sex:M Child# 2 Albert Dionne Nashua, NH & Yvonne Roi Nashua, NH
DIONNE, Joseph Alphonse, Jul 29 1891 Sex:M Child# 2 Jules Dionne Canada & Lea Dionne Canada
DIONNE, Joseph Alphonse, Jul 19 1895 Sex:M Child# 2 Alphonse Dionne Canada & Rosanna Tremblay Canada
DIONNE, Joseph Amable, Aug 30 1895 Sex:M Child# 3 Francois Dionne Canada & Virginie Pellerin Canada
DIONNE, Joseph Edmond A, Nov 12 1930 Sex:M Child# 5 Joseph E Dionne Milford, NH & Agnes St Laurent Nashua, NH
DIONNE, Joseph Eugene A, Feb 15 1909 Sex:M Child# 7 Alphonse Dionne Canada & Lumina Valliere Canada

DIONNE, Joseph G A, Feb 19 1896 Sex:M Child# 1 Georges Dionne Canada & Julianna Nadeau Canada
DIONNE, Joseph G Albert, Jan 5 1902 Sex:M Child# 5 George Dionne Canada & Juliana Nadeau Canada
DIONNE, Joseph G Donat, Feb 12 1903 Sex:M Child# 6 Joseph G Dionne Canada & Juliana Nadeau Canada
DIONNE, Joseph Gaston, May 5 1921 Sex:M Child# 1 (No Parents Listed)
DIONNE, Joseph Henri A, Dec 31 1897 Sex:M Child# 2 Joseph A Dionne Canada & Marie C Pelletier Canada
DIONNE, Joseph Jean B R, Jun 24 1906 Sex:M Child# 1 Honore Dionne Canada & Aimee Michaud Canada
DIONNE, Joseph Leo D, Mar 14 1905 Sex:M Child# 10 Thomas Dionne Canada & Marie Boulanger Canada
DIONNE, Joseph Paul Armand, Jan 17 1918 Sex:M Child# 6 Honore Dionne Canada & Aimie Michaud Canada
DIONNE, Joseph Raymond, Nov 23 1928 Sex:M Child# 16 Joseph Dionne Canada & Ida Berube Canada
DIONNE, Joseph Roger, Nov 2 1931 Sex:M Child# 9 William Dionne Lawrence, MA & Georgiana Larouche Nashua, NH Stillbo
DIONNE, Joseph T, Jan 7 1889 Sex:M Child# 1 Thomas Dionne Riviere du Loup & Marie Boulanger Canada
DIONNE, Joseph T P, Dec 15 1890 Sex:M Child# 2 Thomas Dionne Canada & Marie Boulanger Canada
DIONNE, Joseph Wilfred, Oct 18 1909 Sex:M Child# 3 Honore Dionne Canada & Aimee Michaud Canada
DIONNE, Leda, May 15 1899 Sex:F Child# 8 Jules Dionne Canada & Lea Dionne Canada
DIONNE, Leo, Dec 24 1927 Sex:M Child# 5 Arthur Dionne Lowell, MA & Graziella Lemire Canada
DIONNE, Leo Gerard, Jul 3 1933 Sex:M Child# 2 Pierre Dionne Canada & Lucienne Jean Canada
DIONNE, Leon Everett, Oct 21 1933 Sex:M Child# 4 Donat Dionne Nashua, NH & Sylvia Cote Nashua, NH
DIONNE, Lillian, Dec 25 1906 Sex:F Child# 5 Hermenegilde Dionne Canada & Marie Nadeau Canada
DIONNE, Louis Philip, Sep 11 1925 Sex:M Child# 3 Alfred N Dionne Nashua, NH & Lydia Deschanes Nashua, NH
DIONNE, Louise Alice, Jun 5 1899 Sex:F Child# 1 Fereol Dionne Canada & Anna Ledoux Franklin Falls
DIONNE, M Blanche A, Jan 7 1902 Sex:F Child# 7 Thomas Dionne Canada & Marie Boulanger Canada
DIONNE, M Juliette A H, Jan 17 1908 Sex:F Child# 2 Honore Dionne Canada & Aime Michaud Canada
DIONNE, M Lilianne Olivette, Sep 4 1911 Sex:F Child# 4 Charles Dionne Canada & Rose J Bonenfant Nashua, NH
DIONNE, M Therese Camille, Mar 14 1921 Sex:F Child# 11 Joseph Dionne Canada & Ida Berube Canada
DIONNE, Marguerite Eva, Jun 2 1925 Sex:F Child# 1 Francis Dionne Canada & Juliette D'Amour Canada
DIONNE, Marianne Emma, Mar 9 1903 Sex:F Child# 3 Feriol Dionne Canada & Anna Ledoux Franklin Falls
DIONNE, Marie, Oct 13 1890 Sex:F Child# 4 Cleophas Dionne Canada & Victoria Vaillancour Canada
DIONNE, Marie, Mar 18 1898 Sex:F Child# 13 Charles Dionne Canada & Marie Landry Canada
DIONNE, Marie, Mar 24 1928 Sex:F Child# 1 Donat Dionne Nashua, NH & Sylvia Cote Nashua, NH Stillborn
DIONNE, Marie A A, Nov 26 1898 Sex:F Child# 3 George Dionne Canada & Julie A Nadeau Canada
DIONNE, Marie Adrienne, Aug 28 1907 Sex:F Child# 1 Charles Dionne Canada & Juliana Bonenfant Nashua, NH
DIONNE, Marie Alice Lilliane, Apr 26 1916 Sex:F Child# 8 Joseph Dionne Canada & Ida Berube Canada
DIONNE, Marie Alida, Feb 18 1899 Sex:F Child# 2 Philippe Dionne Milton & Exilda Rouleau Nashua, NH
DIONNE, Marie Andrea S, Jun 19 1905 Sex:F Child# 7 George Dionne Canada & Juliana Nadeau Canada
DIONNE, Marie Anna, Mar 26 1900 Sex:F Child# 7 Thomas Dionne Canada & Marie Boulanger Canada
DIONNE, Marie Anna A, Feb 26 1903 Sex:F Child# 6 Israel Dionne Canada & Adele Rivard Canada
DIONNE, Marie Beatrice, Jun 14 1925 Sex:F Child# 1 Albert Dionne Nashua, NH & Filomina Salviani Nashua, NH
DIONNE, Marie Claire, Jan 22 1905 Sex:F Child# 1 Eugene Dionne Canada & Clarina Theriault Canada Stillborn
DIONNE, Marie Drinette A, Aug 1 1924 Sex:F Child# 3 Alphonse Dionne NH & Elise Vaillancourt Canada
DIONNE, Marie Edith, Mar 18 1897 Sex:F Child# 2 Frank Dionne Canada & Virginie Pellerin Canada
DIONNE, Marie Frances Rita, May 9 1929 Sex:F Child# 2 Donat Dionne Nashua, NH & Sylvia Cote Nashua, NH
DIONNE, Marie Irene, Dec 18 1905 Sex:F Child# 4 Philippe Dionne NH & Exilda Rouleau NH
DIONNE, Marie J A, Jun 16 1900 Sex:F Child# 4 George Dionne Canada & Julien Nadeau Canada
DIONNE, Marie Jeanne Cecile, Aug 2 1918 Sex:F Child# 9 Joseph Dionne St Epephane, PQ & Ida Berube Canada
DIONNE, Marie Lorette Edith, Jan 8 1924 Sex:F Child# 13 Joseph Dionne P I, Canada & Ida Berube P I, Canada
DIONNE, Marie R E, Oct 16 1895 Sex:F Child# 5 Thomas Dionne Canada & Marie Boulanger Canada
DIONNE, Marie Rose, Feb 1 1892 Sex:F Child# 9 Felix Dionne Canada & Caroline Turcotte Canada
DIONNE, Marie Simonne Alma, Feb 24 1925 Sex:F Child# 14 Joseph Dionne Canada & Ida Berube Canada
DIONNE, Marie Yvonne A, Jul 1 1911 Sex:F Child# 3 Eugene Dionne Canada & Mary J Denison Canada
DIONNE, Mary Alice Theresa, May 13 1929 Sex:F Child# 4 Jos Etienne Dionne Milford, NH & Agnes St Lawrence Nashua
DIONNE, Mary Elizabeth, Dec 31 1928 Sex:F Child# 6 Ernest Dionne Nashua, NH & Dora McLaughlin Maynard, MA
DIONNE, Maurice Adrien, Oct 24 1909 Sex:M Child# 4 J B Dionne Canada & Angelina Poirier Canada
DIONNE, Maurice Adrien, Feb 2 1926 Sex:M Child# 1 Adrien Dionne Canada & Fabiola Lavoie Canada
DIONNE, Mercedes, May 15 1917 Sex:F Child# 1 Arthur J Dionne Somersworth, NH & Maude Boucher Nashua, NH
DIONNE, Miriam, Mar 4 1902 Sex:F Child# 2 Edward Dionne Nashua, NH & Josephine Carey Nashua, NH
DIONNE, Olivine Hortense, Apr 17 1906 Sex:F Child# 2 J B Dionne Winooski, VT & Dora Gauthier Nashua, NH
DIONNE, Omer Odila, Dec 1 1925 Sex:M Child# 1 Omer Dionne Pepperell, MA & Yvonne Rioux Pepperell, MA
DIONNE, Ovila Normand, Jun 14 1935 Sex:M Child# 3 Rosaire Dionne Canada & Adele Migneault Canada
DIONNE, Patrice, Mar 17 1910 Sex:M Child# 4 Joseph Dionne Canada & Ida Berube Canada
DIONNE, Paul Alphe, Jul 19 1913 Sex:M Child# 6 Joseph Dionne Canada & Ida Berube Canada
DIONNE, Paul Herve, Jun 18 1930 Sex:M Child# 4 Alfred N Dionne Nashua, NH & Lydia Deschenes Nashua, NH
DIONNE, Philip Roland George, Nov 5 1922 Sex:M Child# 2 William Dionne Lawrence, MA & Georgianna Larouche Nashua
DIONNE, Ralph George, Sep 2 1927 Sex:M Child# 5 Arthur J Dionne Somersworth, NH & Maude Boucher Nashua, NH
DIONNE, Raymond Maurice, Jul 21 1928 Sex:M Child# 3 Francis Dionne Canada & Juliette D'Amour Canada
DIONNE, Raymond, Jr, Feb 9 1930 Sex:M Child# 2 Raymond Dionne Lynn, MA & Elisabeth Krosky Poland
DIONNE, Rebecca, Mar 23 1908 Sex:F Child# 1 Eugene Dionne Canada & Marie Jane Dennison Canada
DIONNE, Rena Janine, Jun 17 1930 Sex:F Child# 1 Albert Dionne Canada & Jeanne Thibault Canada
DIONNE, Rhea, Oct 16 1909 Sex:F Child# 2 Eugene Dionne Canada & Mary J Dennison Canada
DIONNE, Richard Arthur, Jun 29 1933 Sex:M Child# 1 Wilfrid E Dionne Canada & Florence Rousseau Nashua, NH
DIONNE, Richard Daniel, Oct 24 1929 Sex:M Child# 1 Daniel Dionne Nashua, NH & Mabel Richard Athol, MA
DIONNE, Richard Delano, May 10 1933 Sex:M Child# 2 Albert Dionne Canada & J Thibault Canada
DIONNE, Robert Adelard, Nov 2 1930 Sex:M Child# 2 Donat Dionne Nashua, NH & Sylvia Cote Nashua, NH
DIONNE, Robert Joseph, Dec 19 1914 Sex:M Child# 7 Joseph Dionne Canada & Ida Berube Canada

DIONNE, Roger, Jun 4 1931 Sex:M Child# 2 Rosaire Dionne Southbridge, MA & Adele Migneault Canada
DIONNE, Roger Robert, May  1 1934 Sex:M Child# 2 Romeo Dionne Nashua, NH & Berthe Brodeur Nashua, NH
DIONNE, Roland Alfred, Jul 1 1934 Sex:M Child# 3 Albert Dionne Nashua, NH & Yvonne Roy Nashua, NH
DIONNE, Roland Robert, Jul 4 1913 Sex:M Child# 5 J B Dionne Canada & Angelina Poirier Canada
DIONNE, Ruth E, Jul 7 1901 Sex:F Child# 2 Henry W Dionne Nashua, NH & Delia Miner Cherrybusco, NY
DIONNE, Ruth Mary, Oct 23 1900 Sex:F Child# 1 E A A Dionne Nashua, NH & Josephine Carey Nashua, NH
DIONNE, Stella Anita, Oct 24 1934 Sex:F Child# 11 William Dionne Canada & Georgianna Larouche Nashua, NH
DIONNE, Theodore Leo, Mar 4 1925 Sex:M Child# 3 Joseph Dionne Milford, NH & A St Laurent Nashua, NH
DIONNE, Theresa Rita, Dec 9 1929 Sex:F Child# 1 Rosaire Dionne Southbridge, MA & Adele Migneault Canada
DIONNE, Therese Jeanne, Feb 18 1924 Sex:F Child# 3 William Dionne Lawrence, MA & Georgia Larouche Nashua, NH
DIONNE, Unknown, Jul 11 1891 Sex: Child# 9 J B Dionne New York & Marie Bonir New York Stillborn
DIONNE, Unknown, Oct 15 1925 Sex:F Child# 3 Adelard Dionne Nashua, NH & Stella Leclair Nashua, NH
DIONNE, Wilfrid, Jun 8 1908 Sex:M Child# 3 Eugene Dionne Canada & Clarina Berube Canada
DIONNE, Wilifrid Albert, Aug 1 1907 Sex:M Child# 3 J B Dionne Canada & Angelica Poirier Canada
DISANTELS, Joseph Louis, Jan 11 1896 Sex:M Child# 3 Jean B Disantels Canada & Elise Fournier Canada
DISBEAU, Arthur Francis, Jan 26 1892 Sex:M Child# 1 Francis Disbeau Canada & Lillian Hildreth Chelmsford, MA
DITRIZAC, Arthur, Jan 3 1912 Sex:M Child# 3 Ernest Ditrizac Canada & Alice Andrews Nashua, NH
DIXON, Grace Louise, Nov 7 1916 Sex:F Child# 1 John Dixon England & Eunice Clifford Hollis, NH Stillborn
DIXON, Margaret Elizabeth, Apr 29 1922 Sex:F Child# 1 Arthur L Dixon Mason, NH & Margaret Bennett Kentucky
DIXON, Rachel, Mar 31 1906 Sex:F Child# 1 William J Dixon Sherbrooke, Canada & Eldora Hoit Nashua, NH
DIXON, Unknown, Jun 10 1911 Sex:M Child#  Ralph Dixon Concord, NH & Melvina Miner Lakeport, NH
DOANE, Ralph Bernard, Aug 10 1925 Sex:M Child# 3 Roger H Doane New Bedford, MA & Vivian Adams W Derby, VT
DOANE, Ruth Edna, Mar 7 1927 Sex:F Child# 4 Roger H Doane New Bedford, MA & Vivian L Adams Derby Ctr, VT
DOBBENS, Francis, Jul 22 1905 Sex:M Child# 7 William Dobbens Malone, NY & Mary Briere Fort Henry, VT
DOBBENS, Henry, Aug 16 1904 Sex:M Child# 7 William E Dobbens US & Marie Briere US
DOBBENS, Unknown, May 21 1902 Sex:M Child# 4 Henry Dobbens Malone, NY & Margaret Harding Lawrence, MA
DOBBINS, Hannah, Sep 4 1892 Sex:F Child# 1 Prentiss Dobbins Keene, NH & Alma M Kingston, NH
DOBBINS, Henry Ed, Nov 12 1899 Sex:M Child# 3 Henry J Dobbins NY & Margaret Harding Mass
DOBBINS, Nellie, Jan 2 1893 Sex:F Child# 1 Henry J Dobbins Malone, NY & Rose McLoughlin Canada
DOBBINS, Unknown, Apr 1 1887 Sex:F Child# 11 Edmond Dobbins Malone, NY & Julia McCaffrey Malone, NY
DOBENS, Alice, Apr 12 1896 Sex:F Child# 3 W E Dobens Malone, NY & Mary Briere Port Henry
DOBENS, Alice, Apr 8 1901 Sex:F Child# 6 W E Dobens Nashua, NH & Marie Briere NS
DOBENS, Alice Augusta, Apr 2 1898 Sex:F Child# 2 Henry Dobens Malone, NY & Margaret Harding Lawrence, MA
DOBENS, Arthur Chester, Feb 3 1905 Sex:M Child# 5 Henry J Dobens Malone, NY & Margaret Harding Lawrence, MA
DOBENS, Charles, Dec 29 1897 Sex:M Child# 4 W E Dobens Nashua, NH & Mary Briere Rouses Point, NY
DOBENS, Chester Warren, Feb 4 1910 Sex:M Child# 1 Geo Chester Dobens Nashua, NH & Helen Warren Nashua, NH
DOBENS, Daniel, Jan 4 1913 Sex:M Child# 13 William E Dobens Malone, NY & Marie P Briere Port Henry, NY
DOBENS, Donald Edward, Jun 25 1931 Sex:M Child# 2 Arthur C Dobens Nashua, NH & Elizabeth McLeod Alexandria, NH
DOBENS, Doris Joan, Dec 3 1931 Sex:F Child# 1 Frederick J Dobens Nashua, NH & Mary Lavoie Canada
DOBENS, Elizabeth Annie, Dec 23 1930 Sex:F Child# 3 Frederick H Dobens Nashua, NH & Leona LaFontaine Nashua, NH
DOBENS, Frederic, Oct 21 1906 Sex:M Child# 11 W E Dobens Malone, NY & Philomene Briere Port Henry, NY
DOBENS, Frederick Howard, Aug 15 1905 Sex:M Child# 1 Frederick J Dobens Nashua, NH & Annie Sullivan Nashua, NH
DOBENS, Helen, Jun 3 1921 Sex:F Child# 4 George C Dobens Nashua, NH & Helen Warren Nashua, NH
DOBENS, Kenneth Anthony, Mar 29 1930 Sex:M Child# 4 George L Dobens Nashua, NH & Gertrude F Maguire Waltham, MA
DOBENS, Leonard Lawrence, Nov 16 1932 Sex:M Child# 3 A C Dobens Nashua, NH & Elizabeth MacLeod Alexandria, NH
DOBENS, Marion Elizabeth, Feb 9 1918 Sex:F Child# 3 Geo Chester Dobens Nashua, NH & Helen Warren Nashua, NH
DOBENS, Matthew, Jul 23 1914 Sex:M Child# 10 W E Dobens Malone, NY & Philomene Briere Port Henry, NY
DOBENS, Pauline, Apr 28 1934 Sex:F Child# 2 Frederick J Dobens Nashua, NH & Mary Lavoie Canada
DOBENS, Priscilla Dorothy, Jun 28 1924 Sex:F Child# 1 Frederick Dobens Nashua, NH & Leona Lafontaine Nashua, NH
DOBENS, Raymond, Mar 6 1910 Sex:M Child# 11 W E Dobens Malone, NY & M P Bryere Port Henry, NY
DOBENS, Raymond Joseph, Jul 28 1906 Sex:M Child# 2 Frederick J Dobens Nashua, NH & Annie Sullivan Nashua, NH
DOBENS, Richard, Sep 12 1927 Sex:M Child# 3 G L Dobens Nashua, NH & G F Maguire Waltham, MA
DOBENS, Robert Raymond, Dec 10 1928 Sex:M Child# 2 Frederick Dobens Nashua, NH & Leona Fontaine Nashua, NH
DOBENS, Ruth, Sep 9 1908 Sex:F Child# 7 W E Dobens Malone, NY & Mary Briere Fort Henry, NY
DOBENS, Unknown, Oct 27 1894 Sex:F Child# 2 W E Dobens Nashua, NH & Philomene Briere Canada
DOBENS, Unknown, Oct 3 1915 Sex:F Child# 2 George C Dobens Nashua, NH & Helen Warren Nashua, NH
DOBENS, Unknown, Sep 24 1925 Sex:M Child# 5 George C Dobens Nashua, NH & Helen Warren Nashua, NH
DOBENS, Unknown, Dec 11 1928 Sex:F Child# 6 George Dobens Nashua, NH & Helen Warren Nashua, NH
DOBENS, William, Jun 30 1893 Sex:M Child# 1 W E Dobens Malone, NY & Philomene Briere Port Henry, NY
DOBENS, William Henry, Mar 10 1919 Sex:M Child# 2 William H Dobens Nashua, NH & Addie Nadeau Nashua, NH
DOBIOSKI, Anna, Sep 20 1903 Sex:F Child# 1 S Dobioski Poland & Anna Lobenski Poland
DOBROVIESKI, Felix, Oct 12 1926 Sex:M Child# 3 K Dobrovieski Poland & Katie Kopic Poland
DOBROWOLSKI, Charles, Apr 11 1929 Sex:M Child# 4 Constanty Dobrowolsk Poland & Katazina Hopick Hungary
DOBROWOLSKI, Ludwika, Apr 5 1923 Sex:F Child# 2 C Dobrowolski Poland & Katizma Kopich Hungary
DOBROWSKI, Edward, Oct 11 1921 Sex:M Child# 1 Constant Dobrowski Poland & Katherine Kopie Hungary
DOBSON, Agnes Leona, Oct 2 1907 Sex:F Child# 1 Fred Dobson New Brunswick & Daisy M Sumers New Brunswick
DOBSON, Ruth Elnor, Aug 3 1910 Sex:F Child# 2 Fred Dobson New Brunswick & Maud Somers New Brunswick
DOCELLES, Pierre, Aug 16 1890 Sex:M Child# 2 Jean B Docelles Canada & Ellen Colliers Ireland
DODGE, Albert, May 7 1905 Sex:M Child# 2 Emond Dodge Canada & Aurelie Gagnon Canada
DODGE, Albert, Nov 27 1932 Sex:M Child# 2 Albert Dodge
DODGE, Anna Grace, Feb 27 1907 Sex:F Child# 2 Elwin Dodge Merrimack, NH & Eda Anna Blake Groton, MA
DODGE, Carrol, Apr 22 1892 Sex:M Child# 6 (No Parents Listed)
DODGE, Dorothy A, Apr 1 1904 Sex:F Child# 2 W D Dodge Nashua, NH & Vinnie R Clark Nashua, NH

DODGE, Edmond, Dec 7 1903 Sex:M Child# 1 Edmond Dodge Canada & Aurelle Gagnon Canada
DODGE, Francis Willard, Aug 7 1910 Sex:M Child# 2 Isaac W Dodge Nashua, NH & Carrie E Flint Lyme, NH
DODGE, Hazel Veda, Mar 13 1901 Sex:F Child# 1 Elwin H Dodge Thorntons Ferry, NH & Veda A Blake Groton, MA
DODGE, Irene Marie Anne, Jun 26 1897 Sex:F Child# 1 James Dodge Nashua, NH & Lina Lord Manchester, NH
DODGE, James Cassius, Sep 30 1899 Sex:M Child# 2 Fred M Dodge NH & Ella F Dodge Mass
DODGE, Loretta Irene, Nov 5 1908 Sex:F Child# 3 Edmond Dodge Canada & Aurelie Gagnon Canada
DODGE, Lucretia Faxon, May 6 1914 Sex:F Child# 4 Isaac W Dodge Nashua, NH & Carrie Flint Lyme, NH
DODGE, Marguerite, Oct 3 1895 Sex:F Child# 1 W D Dodge Nashua, NH & Vinnie R Hall Nashua, NH
DODGE, Oliver Harris, Jan 26 1912 Sex:M Child# 3 Isaac W Dodge Nashua, NH & Carrie E Flint Lyme, NH
DODGE, Sabra Cordelia, Jan 13 1909 Sex:F Child# 1 Isaac W Dodge Nashua, NH & Carrie E Flint Lyme, NH
DODGE, Unknown, Aug 24 1890 Sex:F Child# 6 George F Dodge Greenfield, NH & Evealine Pate England
DODGE, Vera Ellen, Sep 1 1896 Sex:F Child# 1 F M Dodge Manchester, NH & Ella F Doyle Oakdale, MA
DODOSIS, James, Nov 24 1912 Sex:M Child# 3 Angelus Dodosis Greece & Kienis Spylios Greece
DOE, Louise F, Feb 17 1917 Sex:F Child# 1 John Doe Lakeport, NH & Frances Hodge Lakeport, NH
DOGOPOULOS, Unknown, Jul 16 1924 Sex:M Child# 3 John Dogopoulos Greece & Athena Geogoions Greece
DOHERTY, Alice, Apr 2 1900 Sex:F Child# 9 John Doherty Ireland & Ann Mulligan Ireland
DOHERTY, Anna Mae, Jul 11 1916 Sex:F Child# 5 John Doherty St John, NB & Anna Mae Charon Lowell, MA
DOHERTY, Bernard, Aug 10 1892 Sex:M Child# 6 John Doherty Ireland & Ann Mulligan Ireland
DOHERTY, Clara, Apr 5 1905 Sex:F Child# 3 Fredrick A Doherty St Albans, VT & Sarah Simpson Moore's Jct, NY
DOHERTY, Francis, Aug 8 1909 Sex:M Child# 1 Charles N Doherty St John, NB & Catherine S Cronin Cambridge, MA
DOHERTY, Henry Austin, May 13 1905 Sex:M Child# 2 John D Doherty St Johns, NB & Annie Charron Lowell, MA
DOHERTY, Hiram, Nov 10 1907 Sex:M Child# 3 John H Doherty Nova Scotia & Annie Charron Lowell, MA
DOHERTY, Irene Cecelia, Mar 3 1911 Sex:F Child# 4 John Doherty St Johns, NB & Annie M Sharon Lowell, MA
DOHERTY, James C, Jun 2 1889 Sex:M Child# 4 John Doherty Ireland & Ann Mulligan Ireland
DOHERTY, James Edward, Sep 17 1897 Sex:M Child# 6 Jeremiah Doherty Nashua, NH & Katherine Crowley Ireland
DOHERTY, John Edwards, Feb 18 1919 Sex:M Child# 6 John H Doherty St John, NB & Anna May Charon Lowell, MA
DOHERTY, Joseph Leonard, Aug 11 1911 Sex:M Child# 1 Michael Doherty Ireland & Margaret J Walsh Ireland
DOHERTY, Mary A, Mar 4 1908 Sex:F Child# 1 John Doherty Woonsocket, RI & Mary Duggan Woolich, England
DOHERTY, Mary Muriel, Apr 25 1930 Sex:F Child# 1 Frank Doherty Canada & Hannah Hickey Canada
DOHERTY, Shirley Pearl, May 28 1934 Sex:F Child# 1 Francis Doherty Nashua, NH & Irene Bibeau Canada
DOHERTY, Thomas, Oct 11 1894 Sex:M Child# 7 John Doherty Ireland & Ann Mulligan Ireland
DOHERTY, Unknown, Nov 17 1887 Sex:F Child# 3 John Doherty Ireland & Ann Mulligan Ireland
DOHERTY, Unknown, Aug 27 1931 Sex:M Child#  James H Doherty Pelham, NH & Mary Ellen Cassidy Lowell, MA
DOHERTY, Violetta, Dec 1 1903 Sex:F Child# 1 John H Doherty St Johns, NB & Annie Charron Lowell, MA
DOHERTY, William, Jan 13 1891 Sex:M Child# 5 John Doherty Ireland & Ann Mulligan Ireland
DOKOS, Joseph Andre, Apr 23 1923 Sex:M Child# 1 Sotarios Dokos Greece & Anita Lamarche Manchester, NH
DOLAN, Agnes Lorretta, Apr 10 1899 Sex:F Child# 6 James S Dolan Nashua, NH & Marguerite Gorman Nashua, NH
DOLAN, Alice, Jan 1 1914 Sex:F Child# 1 Fred J Dolan Worcester, MA & Minnie Meehan Ireland
DOLAN, Catherine, Jun 17 1893 Sex:F Child# 3 James Dolan Nashua, NH & Maggie Gorman Nashua, NH
DOLAN, Catherine, Apr 21 1896 Sex:F Child#  James S Dolan Nashua, NH & Margaret Gorman Nashua, NH
DOLAN, Catherine G, Jul 11 1894 Sex:F Child# 4 James S Dolan Nashua, NH & Maggie Gorman Nashua, NH
DOLAN, Edward Francis, Nov 16 1925 Sex:M Child# 1 Edward F Dolan Lowell, MA & Grace Hauer York, PA
DOLAN, Hilda, May 13 1896 Sex:F Child# 4 Patrick H Dolan Nashua, NH & Mary E McMannus Nashua, NH
DOLAN, John William, Jul 17 1889 Sex:M Child# 1 James Dolan Nashua, NH & Margaret Gorman Nashua, NH
DOLAN, Leo, Sep 9 1891 Sex:M Child# 2 Patrick H Dolan Nashua, NH & Mary E McMannus Nashua, NH
DOLAN, Loretta Ann, Mar 28 1925 Sex:F Child# 3 Fred Dolan Worcester, MA & Mamie Meehan Ireland
DOLAN, Mary, Mar 29 1906 Sex:F Child# 3 Thomas Dolan Ireland & Ann Moriarty Ireland
DOLAN, Mary Frances, Jan 18 1891 Sex:F Child# 2 James Dolan Nashua, NH & Margaret Gorman Nashua, NH
DOLAN, Mary Gertrude, Nov 29 1915 Sex:F Child# 2 Fred J Dolan Worcester, MA & Minnie Meehan Ireland
DOLAN, Mary Lauretta, May 12 1889 Sex:F Child# 1 Patrick H Dolan Nashua, NH & Mary McManus Nashua, NH
DOLAN, Patricia Ann, Mar 31 1933 Sex:F Child# 2 Charles E Dolan Worcester, MA & Irene Dufault Worcester, MA
DOLAN, Paul, Dec 31 1893 Sex:M Child# 3 Patrick H Dolan Nashua, NH & Mary E McMannus Nashua, NH
DOLLOF, Janet Helen, Jan 13 1932 Sex:F Child# 1 Herbert Dollof Haverhill, MA & E M Holden Salem, MA
DOLLY, Catherine, Dec 8 1916 Sex:F Child# 2 Edward Dolly Ireland & Annie Moriarty Nashua, NH
DOLLY, Mary, Jul 20 1914 Sex:F Child# 1 Edward Dolly Ireland & Annie Moriarty Nashua, NH
DOMANCHE, Unknown, Jan 29 1894 Sex:M Child# 1 (No Parents Listed)
DOMBOROSKY, Frank, Nov 8 1915 Sex:M Child# 2 Frank Domborosky Russia & Zophia Weokofski Russia
DOMBROWSKI, Charles, Feb 24 1930 Sex:M Child#  Frank Dombrowski Lithuania & Sofia Verkuste Lithuania
DOMBROWSKI, John, Jul 18 1923 Sex:M Child# 4 Frank Dombrowski Lithuania & Zofia Wirkusua Lithuania
DOMOBOLES, Mary, Mar 4 1912 Sex:F Child# 1 Kostos Domoboles Greece & Mary Koliope Greece
DONAHOE, Elizabeth Margaret, Nov 12 1894 Sex:F Child# 1 Thomas J Donahoe Ireland & Julia M Shea Nashua, NH
DONAHOE, Frank, Oct 30 1893 Sex:M Child# 1 Daniel Donahoe Springfield & Katherine Nashua, NH
DONAHUE, Arthur, Dec 1 1890 Sex:M Child# 2 John Donahue Ireland & Bridget Brennan Ireland
DONAHUE, Delia, Sep 21 1889 Sex:F Child# 1 John J Donahue Ireland & Bridget Brennan Ireland
DONAHUE, Eleanor Marie, Aug 9 1922 Sex:F Child# 1 J Joseph Donahue Ayer, MA & Nellie A Attridge E Pepperell, MA
DONAHUE, Elizabeth, Oct 5 1892 Sex:F Child# 3 John J Donahue Ireland & Bridget Brennan Ireland
DONAHUE, John P, Feb 27 1898 Sex:M Child# 3 Thomas J Donahue Ireland & Julia M Shea Nashua, NH
DONAHUE, Marion, Mar 5 1901 Sex:F Child# 4 Thomas Donahue Ireland & Julia M Shea Nashua, NH
DONAHUE, Unknown, Apr 29 1896 Sex:M Child# 2 Daniel Donahue Concord & Ellen Haley Ireland Stillborn
DONAIS, Armand, Dec 24 1925 Sex:M Child# 6 Joseph Donais New York & Eva Asselin New York
DONAIS, Beatrice, Dec 16 1918 Sex:F Child# 3 Wilfred Donais New York & Gracia Girouard New York
DONAIS, Cleophas Philias, Apr 12 1920 Sex:M Child# 4 Wilfrid Donais New York & Grace Girouard New York
DONAIS, Eva Eugenie, Sep 20 1914 Sex:F Child# 3 Joseph Donais New York & Eva Asselin New York

DONAIS, Gloria Ruth, Dec 29 1926 Sex:F Child# 7 Wilfird Donais Plattsburg, NY & Gracia Giroux Plattsburg, NY
DONAIS, Joseph Edgar, Jan 10 1912 Sex:M Child# 1 Joseph Donais New York & Eva Asselin New York
DONAIS, Joseph Harold, May 31 1918 Sex:M Child# 4 Joseph Donais New York & Eva Asselin New York
DONAIS, Joseph Hector, Nov 3 1915 Sex:M Child# 1 Wilfred Donais New York & Grace Giroux New York
DONAIS, Joseph Robert, Mar 16 1917 Sex:M Child# 2 Wilfred Donais New York & Grace Giroux New York
DONAIS, Loraine Rachelle, Jul 23 1923 Sex:F Child# 6 Wilfrid Donais New York & Gracia Girouard New York
DONAIS, M Lorina Anna, Sep 21 1921 Sex:F Child# 5 Joseph Donais New York & Eva Asselina New York
DONAIS, Marie Jeannette, Nov 2 1921 Sex:F Child# 5 Wilfrid Donais New York & Grace Giroux New York
DONAIS, Marie Rhea, Oct 4 1913 Sex:F Child# 2 Joseph Donais New York & Eva Asselin New York
DONKAVITCH, Stephan, Oct 16 1911 Sex:M Child# 3 Peter Donkavitch Russia & Agae Gregiuta Russia
DONLOS, Unknown, Mar 3 1923 Sex:M Child# 1 Philip Donlos Greece & Bessie Andrews Greece
DONNAHUE, Edward John, Aug 11 1894 Sex:M Child# 1 Daniel Donnahue Concord & Ellen Healey Ireland
DONNAHUE, Lillian, Mar 8 1896 Sex:F Child# 2 Thomas J Donnahue Ireland & Julia M Shea Nashua, NH
DONNALLY, Unknown, Mar 30 1902 Sex:M Child# 1 John P Donnally Hudson, NH & Dolly A Carmock Lowell, MA
DONNAN, Sarah, Aug 29 1911 Sex:F Child# 3 Zachary Donnan Russia & Eva Noselewitcz Russia
DONNELLY, Eugene Emmet, Jul 11 1929 Sex:M Child# 5 Eugene E Donnelly Hudson, NH & Lillian M Lambert Nashua, NH
DONNELLY, Marjorie Eleanor, Jun 26 1922 Sex:F Child# 1 Emmet Donnelly Hudson, NH & Lillian M Lambert Nashua, NH
DONNELLY, Norma Elizabeth, Oct 3 1926 Sex:F Child# 4 E E Donnelly Hudson, NH & Lillian Lambert Nashua, NH
DONNELLY, Patricia Ann, Oct 19 1924 Sex:F Child# 3 E E Donnelly Hudson, NH & Lillian M Lambert Nashua, NH
DONOHUE, John Albert, Oct 8 1895 Sex:M Child# 4 John J Donohue Ireland & Bridget Brennan Ireland
DONOVAN, John, Jul 18 1920 Sex:M Child# 1 Timothy H Donovan Pepperell, MA & Celia Woods Lowell, MA
DOOLITTLE, James Hamilton, Nov 3 1931 Sex:M Child# 3 Theodore D Doolittle Springfield, MA & Marjorie A Clough
DOOLITTLE, Richard Porter, Nov 3 1931 Sex:M Child# 2 Theodore D Doolittle Springfield, MA & Marjorie A Clough
DORAN, Helen Elizabeth, Nov 18 1930 Sex:F Child# 2 Thomas Edw Doran Derry, NH & Helen Doherty Pelham, NH
DORAY, Melvin Alphonse, Sep 26 1935 Sex:M Child# 2 Melvin A Doray Winchendon, MA & Jennie Biathrow Nashua, NH
DORAY, Sylvia Mae, Jul 12 1934 Sex:F Child# 1 Melvin A Doray Winchendon, MA & Jennie Biathrow Nashua, NH
DOREY, Phyllis Ruth, Jul 10 1897 Sex:F Child# 4 Stanley G Dorey Halifax, NS*& Arabella J Warner Halifax, NS
DORIS, Alfred Lorenzo, Apr 2 1913 Sex:M Child# 1 Alfred Doris Canada & Claudia Morin Nashua, NH
DORIS, Artee Diateur, Jan 27 1914 Sex:M Child# 2 Alfred Doris Canada & Claudia Morin Nashua, NH
DORIS, Jos Wilburt Winfrid, May 31 1917 Sex:M Child# 4 Alfred Doris Canada & Claudia Morin Nashua, NH
DORIS, Marie Colette, Nov 7 1923 Sex:F Child# 6 Alfred Doris Canada & Claudie Morin Nashua, NH
DORIS, Marie Lea, Jul 4 1891 Sex:F Child# 3 Alphonse Doris Canada & Olivine Royer Canada
DORIS, Marie Pauline, May 24 1915 Sex:F Child# 3 Alfred Doris Canada & Claudia Morin Nashua, NH
DORMAN, Alexander, Jan 14 1913 Sex:M Child# 4 Zachary Dorman Russia & Eva Russia
DORMAN, Louis, May 9 1910 Sex:M Child# 2 Zachary Dorman Russia & Eva Nosekewitz Russia
DORSETT, Carl I, Mar 18 1903 Sex:M Child# 2 Hiram O Dorsett Horicon, NY & Bertha E Wagner George, VT
DORSETT, Dorothy, May 22 1914 Sex:F Child# 1 Elroy Dorsett Nashua, NH & Alice Monroe Nashua, NH
DORSETT, Elroy O, Apr 8 1897 Sex:M Child# 1 Hiram O Dorsett Horicon, NY & Bertha E Wagner George, VT
DORSETT, Karl Gilbert, Jan 17 1928 Sex:M Child# 4 Elroy Dorsett Nashua, NH & Alice Monroe Nashua, NH
DORSETT, Richard Paul, Nov 27 1918 Sex:M Child# 3 Elroy D Dorsett Nashua, NH & Alice Munroe Nashua, NH
DORSETT, Robert Elroy, Dec 24 1916 Sex:M Child# 2 Elroy David Dorsett Nashua, NH & Alice Monroe Nashua, NH
DORVOT, Wana, Mar 14 1916 Sex:F Child# 3 Peter Dorvot Russia & Urzuly Besznoz Russia
DOSDOORIAN, Anna, Mar 7 1906 Sex:F Child# 6 Hagop Dosdoorian Turkey & Agonny Kashmanian Turkey
DOSDOORIAN, Caraken, Sep 14 1904 Sex:M Child# 2 Hagop Dosdoorian Armenia & Agony Kosimainan Armenia
DOSDOORIAN, Nooart, Aug 16 1907 Sex:F Child# 7 Hagop Dosdoorian Armenia & Agaany Kasmanian Armenia
DOTY, Floyd Dearborn, Sep 15 1908 Sex:M Child# 2 Orman Doty Vermontville, NY & Theresa Kenesknecht Westland, NY
DOTY, Unknown, Oct 14 1911 Sex:M Child# 4 Philip Doty Franklin, NY & Rena Hoey Redford, NY
DOUBAS, Unknown, Jan 18 1928 Sex:M Child# 3 Philip Doubas Greece & B Andewpooloo Greece
DOUCET, Alfred, Jun 30 1890 Sex:M Child# 8 Simeon Doucet Canada & Denise Monty Canada
DOUCET, Blanche Albertine, Jan 29 1889 Sex:F Child# Stanislas Doucet Canada & Henriette Chagnon Canada
DOUCET, Jeannette Evelyn, Sep 13 1922 Sex:F Child# 1 Alfred Doucet Nashua, NH & Evelina Morin Nashua, NH
DOUCET, Joseph Arthur, Feb 22 1901 Sex:M Child# 6 John Doucet Canada & Adele Boissonault Canada
DOUCET, Norman Francis, Aug 25 1923 Sex:M Child# 2 Alfred Doucet Nashua, NH & Evelina Morin Nashua, NH
DOUCET, Philip Paul, Dec 1 1924 Sex:M Child# 3 Philip Doucet Newmarket, NH & Louise Martin Nashua, NH
DOUCET, Robert Clarence, May 15 1927 Sex:M Child# 6 Philip Doucet Newmarket, NH & Louisa Martin Nashua, NH
DOUCET, Unknown, Jul 22 1920 Sex:F Child# 1 Philip Doucet Newmarket, NH & Louise Martin Nashua, NH Stillborn
DOUCETTE, Alfred Raymond, Jul 30 1921 Sex:M Child# 2 Philip J Doucette Newmarket, NH & Louise Martin Nashua, NH
DOUCETTE, Althea Louise, Jan 6 1929 Sex:F Child# 6 Philip Doucette Newmarket, NH & Louise Martin Nashua, NH
DOUCETTE, John Francis, May 29 1923 Sex:M Child# 4 Philip H Doucette Newmarket, NH & Louise Martin Nashua, NH
DOUCETTE, Joseph, Feb 1 1892 Sex:M Child# 8 Simeon Doucette Canada & Denise Monty Canada
DOUCETTE, Joseph Louis R, Jul 24 1898 Sex:M Child# 10 Simeon Doucette Canada & Denis Monty Canada
DOUCETTE, Unknown, Aug 6 1892 Sex:M Child# 9 Simeon Doucette Canada & Denise Monty Canada Stillborn
DOUCETTE, Unknown, Aug 9 1896 Sex:M Child# Simeon Doucette Canada & Denise Monty Canada
DOUCHEWICZ, Mamie, Aug 5 1914 Sex:F Child# 4 Peter Douchewicz Russia & Agnes Greginta Russia
DOUELA, Victor, Jul 23 1914 Sex:M Child# 3 Antona Douela Russia & Julia Bitarawitch Russia
DOUGAS, William, Dec 24 1911 Sex:M Child# 5 John Dougas Russia & Mary Grigoutic Russia
DOUGHERTY, Joseph, Oct 14 1896 Sex:M Child# 8 John Dougherty Ireland & Annie Mulligan Ireland
DOUGHTY, Carl Edward, Jan 20 1925 Sex:M Child# 4 Sidney C Doughty Pittsfield, NH & Nettie Truax Canada
DOUGHTY, Donald Sidney, Jul 6 1920 Sex:M Child# 1 Sidney C Doughty Pittsfield, NH & Nettie L Truax Canada
DOUGHTY, George Gilbert, Jul 21 1921 Sex:M Child# 2 Sidney C Doughty Pittsfield, NH & Nettie L Truax Canada
DOUGHTY, Helen Mary, Apr 9 1930 Sex:F Child# 5 Sidney Doughty Pittsfield, NH & Nettie Truax Canada
DOUGLAS, Lloyd Alan, Mar 1 1928 Sex:M Child# 1 Thomas Douglas Scotland & Myrtle Suppers Trenton, NJ
DOUGLAS, Unknown, May 14 1900 Sex:M Child# 5 H S Douglas NB & Lizzie Douglas NB

DOUGLASS, Clarence Edwin, Jul 10 1896 Sex:M Child# 1 James E Douglass Charlestown, PEI & Ella J Dooley Londonderry
DOUGLASS, John Michael, Feb 24 1906 Sex:M Child# 3 John Douglass Russia & Agata Stanpedis Russia
DOULAS, Nicholas, May 27 1925 Sex:M Child# 2 Philip Doulas Greece & E Amndropoulis Greece
DOUVILLE, Constance Claire, Aug 5 1924 Sex:F Child# 2 Edward Douville Nashua, NH & Diana Morin Salem, MA
DOUVILLE, Joseph Ernest, May 8 1897 Sex:M Child# 5 Edouard Douville Canada & Anna Hamel Canada
DOUVILLE, Lucien Wilfrid, Jun 9 1922 Sex:M Child# 1 Edward Douville Nashua, NH & Diana Morin Salem, MA
DOUVILLE, Lucille Dorothy, Mar 25 1911 Sex:F Child# 10 Edward Douville Canada & Annie Hamel Canada
DOVILLE, Edouard Emile, May 17 1895 Sex:M Child# 3 Edouard Doville Canada & Anna Hamel Canada
DOVILLE, Louisa, Jan 24 1894 Sex:F Child# 3 Edouard Doville Canada & Annie Hamel Canada
DOW, Bernice Mae, Jan 27 1935 Sex:F Child# 3 David Dow Newhampton, NH & Gladys McGarry Concord, MA
DOW, Evelyn Elizabeth, Nov 26 1925 Sex:F Child# 1 Frederick W Dow
DOW, Joan Ruth, Jun 14 1932 Sex:F Child# 1 Ernest Dow NH & Maybelle Foster NH
DOW, Marlene Eupheme, Mar 28 1935 Sex:F Child# 2 Earl Dow Wentworth, NH & Margaret Noyes Wentworth, NH
DOW, Unknown, Dec 7 1887 Sex:M Child# 9 Loren S Dow VT & Harriet B Marsh Maine
DOWD, Barbara Louise, Jul 16 1928 Sex:F Child# 3 Thomas J Dowd Nashua, NH & Joanna Murphy Norwood, MA
DOWD, Elizabeth Ann, Nov 18 1931 Sex:F Child# 4 Thomas Dowd Nashua, NH & Johanna Murphy Norwood, MA
DOWD, Jane Frances, Jun 15 1897 Sex:F Child# 6 Thomas J Dowd Ireland & Jennie F Gorman Nashua, NH
DOWD, Jean Eleanor, Apr 13 1927 Sex:F Child# 2 Thomas J Dowd Nashua, NH & Joanna Murphy Norwood, MA
DOWD, Joan Marie, Aug 24 1925 Sex:F Child# 1 Thomas Dowd Nashua, NH & Joanna Murphy Norwood, MA
DOWD, Karl Edmund, May 3 1934 Sex:M Child# 1 Karl Edmund Dowd Nashua, NH & Edna Louise Burque Nashua, NH
DOWD, Karl Edward, May 10 1899 Sex:M Child# 7 Thomas J Dowd Ireland & Jennie Gorman Nashua, NH
DOWD, Leo B, Feb 15 1896 Sex:M Child# 5 Thomas J Dowd Ireland & Jennie Gorman Nashua, NH
DOWD, Leo Benedict, Jr, Aug 8 1926 Sex:M Child# 3 Leo B Dowd Nashua, NH & Mary Kilbane Nashua, NH
DOWD, Lillian A, Oct 1 1891 Sex:F Child# 3 Thomas J Dowd Ireland & Jennie F Gorman Nashua, NH
DOWD, Patricia Mary, Aug 30 1922 Sex:F Child# 1 Leo B Dowd Nashua, NH & Mary E Kilbane Nashua, NH
DOWD, Unknown, Feb 5 1888 Sex:M Child# 1 Thomas J Dowd Ireland & Jennie Groman Nashua, NH
DOWD, Unknown, Feb 4 1890 Sex:F Child# 2 Thomas J Dowd Ireland & Jennie F Nashua, NH
DOWD, Unknown, Jul 14 1893 Sex:F Child# 4 Thomas J Dowd Ireland & Jennie Gorman Nashua, NH
DOWD, Unknown, Dec 2 1894 Sex:F Child# 7 E W Dowd Berlin, CT & Hattie E Butler New Britain, CT Stillborn
DOWD, Virginia Christine, Dec 25 1923 Sex:F Child# 2 Leo B Dowd Nashua, NH & Mary Kilbane Nashua, NH
DOWLING, Alice, Aug 30 1890 Sex:F Child# 1 Joseph Dowling Canada & Mary Sullivan Canada
DOWLING, Celia Rose, Nov 29 1894 Sex:F Child# 4 James Dowling Canada & Emma Langley Canada
DOWLING, Hannah, Jun 21 1888 Sex:F Child# 6 James Dowling Canada & Emma Lougais Canada
DOWLING, Helen C, Dec 5 1897 Sex:F Child# 5 Joseph T Dowling Canada & Mary E Sullivan Ireland
DOWLING, James, Jun 7 1896 Sex:M Child# 8 John Dowling Warwick, PQ & Delia Nash Ireland
DOWLING, John, Apr 9 1889 Sex:M Child# 4 John Dowling Canada & Delia Nash Ireland
DOWLING, Joseph, Nov 25 1895 Sex:M Child# 4 Joseph Dowling Canada & Mary E Sullivan Ireland
DOWLING, Katherine, Jan 14 1891 Sex:F Child# 5 John Dowling Canada & Bridget Nash Ireland
DOWLING, Leo Paul, Mar 29 1925 Sex:M Child# 1 Leo Dowling Lowell, MA & Rose Pelletier Canada
DOWLING, Mary J, May 9 1892 Sex:F Child# 2 Joseph T Dowling Canada & Mary Sullivan Ireland
DOWLING, Michael J, Aug 22 1887 Sex:M Child#  Andrew Dowling Canada & Catherine Karmety Ireland
DOWLING, Raymond Edward, Oct 1 1926 Sex:M Child# 2 Leo J Dowling Lowell, MA & Rose Pelletier Canada
DOWLING, Robert Andrew, Jan 15 1894 Sex:M Child# 3 Joseph F Dowling Canada & Mary E Sullivan Ireland
DOWLING, Unknown, Dec 13 1887 Sex:M Child# 3 John Dowling P Q & Bridget Nash Ireland Stillborn
DOWLING, Unknown, Apr 22 1893 Sex:M Child# 6 John Dowling Warwick, PQ & Bridget Nash Ireland
DOWLING, Unknown, Dec 26 1894 Sex:F Child# 6 John Dowling Canada & Bridget Nash Ireland
DOWNEY, Albert Francis, Nov 12 1924 Sex:M Child# 1 Albert Downey Nashua, NH & Teresa Keating Franklin, NH
DOWNEY, Albert T, Aug 3 1896 Sex:M Child# 6 Thomas Downey Nashua, NH & Mary E McGlynn Nashua, NH
DOWNEY, Donald, Jan 9 1915 Sex:M Child# 5 Michael Downey Cambridge, MA & Elizabeth Reynolds Worcester, MA
DOWNEY, Edward Neil, May 4 1926 Sex:M Child# 2 Albert Downey Nashua, NH & Theresa Keating Franklin, NH
DOWNEY, Emond, Nov 7 1904 Sex:M Child# 10 Thomas Downey Nashua, NH & Mary E McGlynn Nashua, NH
DOWNEY, Frances M, Jul 25 1905 Sex:M Child# 1 Michael J Downey Cambridge, MA & Elizabeth Reynolds Leicester, MA
DOWNEY, Frank, Feb 24 1895 Sex:M Child# 5 Thomas Downey Nashua, NH & Mary E McGlynn Nashua, NH
DOWNEY, Getter D, Mar 30 1915 Sex:F Child# 1 Perley O Downey N Sherburne, VT & Helen Guerin Winchester, MA
DOWNEY, Helen, Apr 13 1907 Sex:F Child# 2 Michael J Downey Cambridge, MA & Elizabeth Reynolds Worcester, MA
DOWNEY, Henry Louis, Feb 11 1909 Sex:M Child# 1 Dennis H Downey Cambridge, MA & Mary A Caten Lawrence, MA
DOWNEY, Jacqueline Theresa, Oct 8 1929 Sex:F Child# 2 John F Downey Nashua, NH & Alice Welch Nashua, NH
DOWNEY, James, Jan 19 1898 Sex:M Child# 7 Thomas Downey Nashua, NH & Mary E McGlynn Nashua, NH
DOWNEY, Kate, Feb 20 1892 Sex:F Child# 4 Patrick Downey Ireland & Hannah Sullivan Nashua, NH
DOWNEY, Katherine, Nov 8 1911 Sex:F Child# 4 Michael Downey Cambridge, MA & Elizabeth Reynolds Worcester, MA
DOWNEY, Mary Ellen, Jul 2 1893 Sex:F Child# 4 Thomas Downey Nashua, NH & Mary E McGlynn Nashua, NH
DOWNEY, Mary Margaret, Apr 7 1927 Sex:F Child# 1 John Downey Nashua, NH & Alice Welch Nashua, NH
DOWNEY, Paul, Apr 28 1915 Sex:M Child# 4 Dennis H Downey Cambridge, MA & Mary A Cated Lawrence, MA
DOWNEY, Robert, Dec 10 1911 Sex:M Child# 3 Dennis A Downey Nashua, NH & Mary A Caten Lawrence, MA
DOWNEY, Robert M, Apr 5 1900 Sex:M Child# 8 Thomas Downey Nashua, NH & Mary E McGlynn Nashua, NH
DOWNEY, Thomas Walter, Jun 1 1918 Sex:M Child# 5 Dennis H Downey Cambridge, MA & Mary A Caten Lawrence, MA
DOWNING, Ann, Feb 2 1928 Sex:F Child# 2 John Downing Nashua, NH & Florence Merrill Salisbury, NH
DOWNING, Cecelia, Nov 3 1910 Sex:F Child# 1 Thomas Downing Nashua, NH & Helen Rock Nashua, NH
DOWNING, Cynthia, Jul 20 1927 Sex:F Child# 2 John Downing Prince Edw Island & Clara Pearson Amherst, NH
DOWNING, Earl B, Jan 12 1895 Sex:M Child# 1 Burtuno Downing Vermont & Ada Mandigo NY
DOWNING, Francis, Mar 12 1910 Sex:M Child# 2 Dennis H Downing Cambridge, MA & Mary A Caten Lawrence, MA
DOWNING, John Edward, May 24 1915 Sex:M Child# 3 Thomas Downing Nashua, NH & Ellen Rock Nashua, NH
DOWNING, Mary Jane, Jan 17 1890 Sex:F Child# 3 Patrick Downing Ireland & Hanna M Sullivan Nashua, NH Stillborn

DOWNING, Priscilla, Jul 20 1927 Sex:F Child# 1 John Downing Prince Edw Island & Clara Pearson Amherst, NH
DOWNING, Thomas, Jun 29 1890 Sex:M Child# 2 Thomas Downing Nashua, NH & Mary E McGlynn Nashua, NH
DOWNING, Thomas, Sep 21 1913 Sex:M Child# 2 Thomas Downing Nashua, NH & Nellie Rock Nashua, NH
DOWNING, Unknown, Apr 22 1891 Sex:M Child# 2 Charles R Downing Norwich, CT & Alice A Bradley Brentwood
DOWNING, Unknown, Nov 20 1891 Sex:F Child# 3 Thomas Downing Nashua, NH & Mary E Nashua, NH
DOWNING, Unknown, Jul 19 1894 Sex:F Child# 4 C E Downing Warwick, MA & Alice Bradley Brentwood
DOWSEWICZ, John, Oct 6 1908 Sex:M Child# 1 Peter Dowsewicz Russia & Agota Griginte Russia
DOYING, Richard Edgar, Oct 17 1919 Sex:M Child# 1 Bidwell C Doying Nashua, NH & Ina M Manning Lowell, MA
DOYING, Unknown, Feb 2 1893 Sex:F Child# 3 Charles E Doying Warwick, PQ & Alice Bradley Brentwood
DOYLE, Agnes, Dec 14 1887 Sex:F Child# 10 John M Doyle Ireland & Bridget Moran Ireland
DOYLE, Albert, Oct 20 1891 Sex:M Child# 4 James H Doyle Nashua, NH & Mary Cordell Massachusetts
DOYLE, Augustus Bryan, Sep 11 1900 Sex:M Child# 2 William E Doyle Mass & Margaret F Sullivan Nashua, NH
DOYLE, Catherine, Apr 30 1888 Sex:F Child# 1 James Doyle Nashua, NH & Mary Cordell Woburn, MA
DOYLE, Catherine, Nov 21 1888 Sex:F Child# 3 John Doyle Ireland & Sarah Doherty Ireland
DOYLE, Daniel Charles, Jan 2 1927 Sex:M Child# 1 Daniel P Doyle Lowell, MA & Bertha Levesque Lowell, MA
DOYLE, Daniel Gralton, Jan 15 1899 Sex:M Child# 1 William E Doyle Oakdale, MA & Margaret F Sullivan Nashua, NH
DOYLE, Elizabeth, Aug 16 1887 Sex:f Child# 1 Jeremiah Doyle New Boston & Luella Lussier Nashua, NH
DOYLE, Ellen Dorothy, May 2 1918 Sex:F Child# 1 John A Doyle Worcester, MA & Louise Lemery Nashua, NH
DOYLE, Evelyn May, Oct 5 1900 Sex:F Child# 1 Michael J Doyle Nashua, NH & Lillian M Hamelin Mooers Fork, NY
DOYLE, James, Jul 4 1887 Sex:M Child#  (No Parents Listed)
DOYLE, James Henry, Mar 4 1893 Sex:M Child# 4 John Doyle Nashua, NH & Lizzie O'Neil Lowell, MA
DOYLE, Jeremiah J, Jun 25 1897 Sex:M Child# 5 Jeremiah J Doyle New Boston, NH & Louise Lucier Nashua, NH
DOYLE, John Edward, Oct 19 1922 Sex:M Child# 1 Edward F Doyle Lowell, MA & Margaret Cushing Concord, NH
DOYLE, Lillian, Aug 7 1890 Sex:F Child# 3 James H Doyle Nashua, NH & Mary E Cordell Woburn, MA
DOYLE, Lizzie, Nov 28 1895 Sex:F Child# 4 Arthur Doyle Ireland & Mary Mitchell Ireland
DOYLE, Madeline, Apr 11 1896 Sex:F Child# 6 John Doyle Nashua, NH & Lizzie O'Neil Lowell, MA
DOYLE, Madeline Elizabeth, Dec 23 1908 Sex:F Child# 2 Michael J Doyle Nashua, NH & Lillian Hamlin Mooer's, NY
DOYLE, Marjorie, Feb 13 1924 Sex:F Child# 3 Daniel Doyle Milford, NH & Therese Cummings Nashua, NH
DOYLE, Mary Ellen, Dec 16 1892 Sex:F Child# 2 Arthur J Doyle Ireland & Mary Mitchell Ireland
DOYLE, Mary Frances, Jun 19 1889 Sex:F Child# 2 James H Doyle Nashua, NH & Mary E Cordell Woburn, MA
DOYLE, Mary Julia, Dec 26 1895 Sex:F Child# 4 J J Doyle New Boston & Louise Lucier Nashua, NH
DOYLE, Patricia Clare, Mar 16 1928 Sex:F Child# 2 Daniel P Doyle Lowell, MA & Bertha Levesque Lowell, MA
DOYLE, Paul Harold, Nov 24 1926 Sex:M Child# 3 Edward F Doyle Lowell, MA & Margaret Cushing Concord, NH
DOYLE, Paul I, Feb 19 1891 Sex:M Child# 2 J J Doyle New Boston & Louella Lucier Nashua, NH
DOYLE, Philip Melvin, May 22 1928 Sex:M Child# 2 Walter J Doyle Milford, NH & Azubah Austin E Jaffrey, NH
DOYLE, Raymond, Nov 25 1905 Sex:M Child# 4 William E Doyle Oakdale, MA & Margaret Sullivan Nashua, NH
DOYLE, Richard, Dec 15 1891 Sex:M Child# 1 Arthur Doyle Ireland & Mary Mitchell Ireland
DOYLE, Richard Gould, May 15 1932 Sex:M Child# 1 Britton H Doyle Franklin, PA & Beatrice Whitney Worcester, MA
DOYLE, Robert J, Mar 11 1894 Sex:M Child# 3 Jeremiah J Doyle New Boston & Louise Lucier Nashua, NH
DOYLE, Samuel Francis, Jan 3 1925 Sex:M Child# 2 Edward F Doyle Lowell, MA & Margaret Cushing Concord, NH
DOYLE, Sarah, Jul 25 1890 Sex:F Child# 4 John Doyle Ireland & Sarah Doherty Ireland
DOYLE, Unknown, Sep 3 1889 Sex:F Child# 1 Charles E Doyle Canada & Alice Bradford, NH
DOYLE, Unknown, Mar 19 1894 Sex:F Child# 2 John W Doyle Jonesport, ME & Ella P Leseur, Minn
DOYLE, William, Apr 7 1902 Sex:M Child# 7 William E Doyle Oakdale, MA & M F Sullivan Nashua, NH
DOYLE, William B, Apr 18 1899 Sex:M Child# 6 Jeremiah J Doyle New Boston & Louella Lucier Nashua, NH
DOYON, Alice Rita, Apr 7 1930 Sex:F Child# 1 Willie Doyon Canada & Aurore Beauchamp Canada
DOYON, Marie Lea Florence, Oct 7 1917 Sex:F Child# 1 Wilfrid Doyon Canada & Florence Poirier Canada
DRABANOVITCH, Sophia, Aug 20 1922 Sex:F Child# 5 Mich Drabanovitch Poland & Mary Lancavitch Poland
DRABENIVICZ, Francis, Mar 7 1924 Sex:M Child# 6 M Drabenivicz Poland & Mary Rendavitch Poland
DRABER, Benjamin, Feb 4 1917 Sex:M Child# 2 Michael Draber Russia & Mary Rankavich Russia
DRABINOWICZ, Charles, Nov 24 1918 Sex:M Child# 3 Michael Drabinowicz Russia & Mary Renkewicz Russia
DRABINSWICZ, Helena, Oct 27 1920 Sex:F Child# 4 Mike Drabinswicz Poland Russia & Mary Renkiewicz Poland Russia
DRAGON, Francis J, Jan 20 1887 Sex:M Child#  Francois Dragon NY & Judie St Jean P Q
DRAGON, Maud May, Sep 4 1895 Sex:F Child# 3 Gilbert Dragon Champlain, NY & Louisa J Nicklieu Sand Lake, NY
DRAGON, Unknown, Jul 13 1891 Sex:M Child# 1 Gilbert Dragon Champlain, NY & Louisa Nicklien Sand Lake, NY
DRAGON, Unknown, Nov 5 1892 Sex:F Child# 2 Gilbert Dragon Champlain, NY & Louisa Nichols Sand Lake, NY
DRAKE, Charles A, Aug 21 1893 Sex:M Child# 3 Charles E Drake Tyngsboro, MA & Susan E Gay Litchfield, NH
DRAMANLOPOL, Unknown, Jul 24 1917 Sex:F Child#  Andre Dramanlopol Greece & Anastasa Greece Stillborn
DRAPEAU, Joseph, Apr 24 1931 Sex:M Child# 3 George Drapeau Somersworth, NH & Leona Lachance Rochester, NH Stillborn
DRAPER, Allen Shattuck, Jul 24 1919 Sex:M Child# 1 Bert S Draper Greenfield, NH & Marion Shattuck Nashua, NH
DRAPER, Lawrence Leland, Jul 8 1921 Sex:M Child# 2 Bert S Draper Greenfield, NH & Marian Shattuck Nashua, NH
DRAPER, Leo Henry, Feb 5 1896 Sex:M Child# 4 Willis H Draper Wilton, NH & Susie M Cramb So Lyndeboro, NH
DRAPER, Russell Sanborn, Feb 22 1928 Sex:M Child# 3 Bert S Draper Greenfield, NH & Marian Shattuck Nashua, NH
DRASDOWSKI, Adam, Oct 20 1911 Sex:M Child# 5 Adam Drasdowski Russia & Mart Erlitsluta Russia
DRASKAVITCH, Eva, Dec 24 1910 Sex:F Child# 1 Alex Draskavitch Russia & Annie Urbanoutch Russia
DRASKAWICH, Rosa, Jun 23 1925 Sex:F Child# 9 Aleck Draskawich Lithuania & A Urbenowich Lithuania
DRASKAWICZ, Annie, Aug 5 1915 Sex:F Child# 4 Alex Draskawicz Russia & Annie Urbanawicz Russia
DRASKAWICZ, Julia, Mar 15 1914 Sex:F Child# 4 Alex Draskawicz Russia & Annie Urbanawicz Russia
DRASKAWICZ, Marguerita, May 15 1912 Sex:F Child# 2 Alex Draskawicz Russia & Annie Urbanawicz Russia
DRASKAWICZ, Minnie, Dec 29 1920 Sex:F Child# 7 Alex Draskawicz Lithuania Russia & Annie Urbanawicz Lithuania Russia
DRASTIS, Unknown, Dec 15 1921 Sex:M Child# 5 Vasil Drastis Greece & Katharine Papas Greece
DRAYTON, Unknown, Sep 20 1919 Sex:F Child# 1 Henry J Drayton England & Maud Broome England Stillborn
DRESHER, George Wilfred, Aug 18 1900 Sex:M Child# 4 George Dresher Germany & Corinne Cote Canada

128

DREW, Mary Ann, Sep 26 1932 Sex:F Child#  Frank W Drew Canada & Alice Ingerson Francestown, NH
DRIES, Arlene Pearl, Apr 24 1918 Sex:F Child# 1 William Dries Plymouth, MA & Delia Bairyaidi Italy
DRIRAN, Elenior, May 5 1916 Sex:F Child# 2 James F Driran Ashland, MA & Amy Kitchener Bedford, England
DRISCHER, Alice, Jun 12 1899 Sex:F Child# 3 Georges Drischer Germany & Corinne Cote Canada
DRISCOLL, Daniel Leo, May 17 1931 Sex:M Child# 2 Daniel Leo Driscoll Pepperell, MA & Madeline Murray Pepperell, MA
DRISCOLL, Elizabeth Jane, May 17 1931 Sex:F Child# 3 Daniel L Driscoll Pepperell, MA & Madeline Murray Pepperell,MA
DRISCOLL, Robert, Feb 20 1930 Sex:M Child# 1 Daniel L Driscoll Pepperell, MA & Madeleine Murray Pepperell, MA
DRISCOLL, Sally Ann, Jun 21 1927 Sex:F Child# 2 John L Driscoll Maine & Clara Peaghet NH
DRISKAVITCH, Agnes, Jul 4 1927 Sex:F Child# 10 Alex Driskavitch Lithuania & Annie Urpenwich Lithuania
DRISKAVITCH, Mary, Jul 4 1927 Sex:F Child# 11 Alex Driskavitch Lithuania & Annie Urpenwich Lithuania
DRIVER, Alice Maud, Nov 7 1910 Sex:F Child# 1 Harry Driver Washington, DC & Minnie Hill Connecticut
DROBYEZ, Marian, Sep 6 1914 Sex:F Child# 1 Valerian Drobyez Russia & Solomeyer Tokash Austria
DRODEW, Arthur O, Aug 27 1890 Sex:M Child# 7 Calevite Drodew Canada & Eucharriste Lachapell Canada
DROHAN, Barbara Ann, Jun 16 1933 Sex:F Child# 4 Walter Drohan Quincy, MA & Irma Hayden Hartford, CT
DROHAN, Joseph William, May 10 1935 Sex:M Child# 2 Thomas Drohan Cambridge, MA & Dorothy McCarthy Lynn, MA
DROHAN, Nancy Jeanne, Jan 26 1932 Sex:F Child# 3 Walter J Drohan Quincy, MA & Irma Hayden Hartford, CT
DROHAN, Thomas Henry, Sep 2 1929 Sex:M Child# 1 Thomas Drohan Cambridge, MA & Dorothy McCarthy Lynn, MA
DROUIN, Arthur Roland Joseph, Jan 16 1923 Sex:M Child# 1 Adelard Drouin Nashua, NH & Stella Leclerc Nashua, NH
DROUIN, J Alfred Romuald, Apr 2 1922 Sex:M Child# 4 Gideon Drouin Canada & Ida Charpentier Canada
DROUIN, Joseph Alfred, Nov 5 1902 Sex:M Child# 3 Joseph Drouin Canada & Georgiana Poulin Canada
DROUIN, Joseph Alphonse A, Jul 28 1900 Sex:M Child# 1 Alphonse Drouin Canada & Olivine Cliche Canada
DROUIN, Joseph Gedeon, Dec 10 1907 Sex:M Child# 5 Joseph Drouin Canada & Georgianna Poulin Canada
DROUIN, M Beatrice Melina, Apr 1 1915 Sex:F Child# 1 Gedeon Drouin Canada & Ida Charpentier Canada
DROUIN, Marie Alice Rachelle, Sep 16 1914 Sex:F Child# 1 (No Parents Listed)
DROUIN, Marie B C, Feb 5 1899 Sex:F Child# 1 Joseph Drouin Canada & Georgina Poulin Canada
DROUIN, Marie Isabelle Rita, Apr 8 1919 Sex:F Child# 3 Gedeon Drouin Canada & Ida Charpentier Canada
DROUIN, Marie Louise V, Mar 16 1910 Sex:F Child# 4 Joseph Drouin Canada & Georgianna Poulin Canada
DROUIN, Marie Rose, Aug 23 1900 Sex:F Child# 2 Joseph Drouin Canada & Georgiana Poulin Canada
DROUIN, Marie Rose A, Jan 9 1901 Sex:F Child# 1 Joseph Drouin Canada & Marie Drouin Canada
DROWNS, William Perley, Jr, Jun 20 1925 Sex:M Child# 4 William Drowns Wells, ME & Agnes Harrington Brunswick, ME
DRUDEAU, Charles, Sep 19 1890 Sex:M Child# 1 Charles Drudeau Montpelier, VT & Victorine Bedard Rutland, VT
DRUM, Unknown, Sep 27 1890 Sex:M Child# 4 James Drum Ireland & Julia Guihan Ireland Stillborn
DRUMM, Anna, Dec 31 1898 Sex:F Child# 4 Andrew H Drumm Townsend, MA & Bessie Downing Nashua, NH
DRUMM, Dennis William, May 20 1903 Sex:M Child# 5 Andrew H Drumm Townsend, MA & Bessie A Downing Nashua, NH
DRUMM, Helen Agnes, Mar 16 1896 Sex:F Child# 3 Andrew H Drumm Townsend, MA & Bessie A Nashua, NH
DRUMM, Lillian Mary, Mar 8 1890 Sex:F Child# 7 A H Drumm Townsend, MA & Bessie A Nashua, NH
DRUMM, Unknown, Jan 7 1892 Sex:M Child# 2 Andrew H Drumm Townsend, MA & Bessie A Nashua, NH
DRUMVILLE, Lillian Katherine, Mar 2 1915 Sex:F Child# 10 John Drumville Ireland & Mary Garlen Ireland
DUBE, Adeline G, Sep 22 1887 Sex:F Child# 15 Honore Dube Canada & G Robichaud Canada
DUBE, Agnes Dolores, Jan 6 1926 Sex:F Child# 3 Alfred Dube Nashua, NH & Alice Larouche Canada
DUBE, Albert, Sep 8 1904 Sex:M Child# 7 Joseph Dube Canada & Marie Corbin Canada
DUBE, Albert, Oct 18 1910 Sex:M Child# 1 Alphonse Dube Canada & Delina Levesque Canada
DUBE, Albina Bibiane, Dec 2 1918 Sex:F Child# 3 Leo P Dube Nashua, NH & Leda Gamanche Berlin, NH
DUBE, Alexander Dosithe, Sep 6 1908 Sex:M Child# 5 J B Dube Canada & Eugenie Plourde Canada
DUBE, Alfred, Mar 14 1892 Sex:M Child# 4 David Dube Canada & Rosanna Plante Nashua, NH
DUBE, Alfred, Mar 10 1909 Sex:M Child# 3 Charles Dube Canada & Rosanna Hamel Canada
DUBE, Alfred, Mar 6 1926 Sex:M Child# 2 Alphe Dube Nashua, NH & Marie Gadbois Canada
DUBE, Alfred Henry, Dec 7 1900 Sex:M Child# 1 Henri Dube Canada & Alina Reynolds NH
DUBE, Alice Albertine, Dec 25 1905 Sex:F Child# 1 Albert Dube Canada & Alice Courcy Canada
DUBE, Alice Rose, Dec 1 1909 Sex:F Child# 2 Joseph Dube Canada & Rosalie Dube Canada
DUBE, Alphonse Theo, Nov 14 1894 Sex:M Child# 4 Auguste Dube Canada & Marie Dumont Canada
DUBE, Andre Bernardin, Dec 2 1918 Sex:M Child# 2 Leo P Dube Nashua, NH & Leda Gamanche Berlin, NH
DUBE, Annette Alice, Feb 19 1933 Sex:F Child# 3 Albert Dube Canada & Lydia Morin Graniteville, VT
DUBE, Arthur, Mar 18 1889 Sex:M Child# 2 David Dube Canada & Rosanna Plaute Canada
DUBE, Arthur, Jun 20 1896 Sex:M Child# 2 Pierre Dube Canada & Elise Rioux Canada
DUBE, Arthur, Aug 25 1899 Sex:M Child# 1 Luc Dube Canada & Rosanna Gauthier Canada
DUBE, Arthur John B, Jun 8 1910 Sex:M Child# 2 Henry Dube New York & Linda Paquette New York
DUBE, Arthur R, Feb 7 1902 Sex:M Child# 2 Elzear Dube Canada & Lucy Hysette Canada
DUBE, Auzaire Laura, Oct 25 1906 Sex:F Child# 8 Ferdinand Dube Canada & Clara St Jean Canada
DUBE, Barbara Mesajo, Aug 5 1929 Sex:F Child# 1 Oscar Dube NH & Jennie Mesago Wilton, NH
DUBE, Barbara Ruth, Jun 25 1922 Sex:F Child# 1 Peter Dube Lawrence, MA & Ruth Bradley Nashua, NH
DUBE, Blanche A L, Sep 2 1893 Sex:F Child# 5 Vincent Dube Canada & Emma Lefebvre Canada
DUBE, Carmen Yolande, Sep 6 1923 Sex:F Child# 1 Elzear Dube Canada & Laura Theriault Canada
DUBE, Catherine Simone, Jun 12 1905 Sex:F Child# 7 Ferdinand Dube Canada & Clara St Jean Canada
DUBE, Cecile Pauline, Aug 1 1931 Sex:F Child# 1 Hervey Dube Nashua, NH & Lillian LaForest Morris, NY
DUBE, Cecille Lorette, Oct 23 1919 Sex:F Child# 2 Joseph Dube Nashua, NH & Demrise Pero Nashua, NH
DUBE, Charles, Jul 21 1888 Sex:M Child# 9 Raphelle Dube Canada & Margaret St Pierre Canada
DUBE, Charles, Feb 5 1896 Sex:M Child# 5 Charles Dube Canada & Celina Francoeur Canada
DUBE, Charles Raymond, Apr 8 1918 Sex:M Child# 2 Napoleon Dube Canada & Delia Renaud Nashua, NH
DUBE, Claire Eugene, Apr 21 1906 Sex:F Child# 5 J B Dube Canada & Eugenie Plourde Canada
DUBE, Cleophas Alfred, May 26 1911 Sex:M Child# 3 Joseph Dube Canada & Rosalie Dube Canada
DUBE, Colombe A, Aug 2 1901 Sex:F Child# 6 Ferdina Dube Canada & Clara St Jean Canada
DUBE, Constance Jeanne, Nov 1 1926 Sex:F Child# 2 Ernest Dube Nashua, NH & Victoria Lord Nashua, NH

DUBE, Daniel Telesphore, Apr 17 1933 Sex:M Child# 2 Simeon Dube Nashua, NH & Jeannette Blais Canada
DUBE, Demetrius Aug, Jan 13 1902 Sex:M Child# 5 Joseph Dube Canada & Marie Corbin Canada
DUBE, Dorilda Denise, Dec 19 1922 Sex:F Child# 9 Joseph Dube Canada & Rosalie Dube Canada
DUBE, Edith Doris, Oct 26 1911 Sex:F Child# 2 Victor Dube US & Eveline Lemire Canada
DUBE, Edouard Louis F, Feb 20 1910 Sex:M Child# 1 J B Dube Canada & Zephrine Lavigne Canada
DUBE, Elzard, Nov 27 1888 Sex:M Child# 12 Elzard Dube Canada & Aglae Michard Canada
DUBE, Elzear Joseph, Jan 4 1895 Sex:M Child# 1 Elzear Dube Canada & Lucie Azette St Albans, VT
DUBE, Ernest Claude, Jul 9 1926 Sex:M Child# 2 Elzear Dube Canada & Laura Therriault Canada
DUBE, Ernest Leo, Jun 13 1913 Sex:M Child# 3 Louis Dube US & Philomene Marquis Canada
DUBE, Frederick Joseph, Jul 31 1928 Sex:M Child# 2 Joseph Dube Nashua, NH & Frances Fredrick Peterborough, NH
DUBE, Geneva Sylvia, Apr 13 1907 Sex:F Child# 3 Honore Dube, Jr Canada & Lena Runnels NH
DUBE, George Florent, Feb 21 1899 Sex:M Child# 7 Charles Dube Canada & Celina Francoeur Canada
DUBE, George Henry Oscar, Jan 12 1931 Sex:M Child# 4 Francois Dube Canada & Yvonne Levesque Canada
DUBE, Georges, Aug 22 1887 Sex:M Child# 2 Michel Dube P Q & Delvina Deschene P Q
DUBE, Gerald, Apr 14 1935 Sex:M Child# 2 Cyprien L Dube Nashua, NH & Helene Osborne Manchester, NH
DUBE, Gerald Camille, Dec 9 1935 Sex:M Child# 1 Theodore Dube
DUBE, Helen Elaine, Dec 17 1927 Sex:F Child# 3 Peter Dube Lawrence, MA & Ruth Bradley Nashua, NH
DUBE, Henri Roland, Nov 22 1917 Sex:M Child# 1 Leo P Dube Nashua, NH & Leda Gamarche Berlin, NH
DUBE, Henry, Aug 14 1903 Sex:M Child# 6 Joseph Dube Canada & Marie Corbin Canada
DUBE, Irene, Dec 14 1893 Sex:F Child# 2 J Bte Dube Canada & Jeanne Lebel Canada
DUBE, Irene Noela, Dec 22 1916 Sex:F Child# 8 Thaddie Dube Canada & Amanda Marquis Canada
DUBE, J Clepha Leo, Nov 10 1914 Sex:M Child# 5 Joseph Dube Canada & Rosalie Dube Canada
DUBE, J George Florin, Oct 7 1914 Sex:M Child# 10 Jean B Dube Canada & Eugenie Plourde Canada
DUBE, J Girard Armand, Nov 25 1913 Sex:M Child# 1 Xavier Dube Canada & Alma Courcy Canada
DUBE, J Honore Gerard, Oct 20 1911 Sex:M Child# 7 J B Dube Canada & Eugenie Plourde Canada
DUBE, J Louis Cyprien, Aug 16 1911 Sex:M Child# 7 Ludger Dube Canada & Marie Levesque Canada
DUBE, J Louis de Gon, Jun 20 1911 Sex:M Child# 4 Pierre Dube Canada & Anesie Despres Canada
DUBE, J Paul Adrien, Jul 21 1913 Sex:M Child# 6 Joseph Dube Canada & Anaise Bechard Canada
DUBE, J William Leo, Sep 23 1921 Sex:M Child# 10 Joseph Dube Canada & Anaise Richard Canada
DUBE, Jean Edouard, Dec 20 1902 Sex:M Child# 1 J B Dube Canada & Eugenie Plourde Canada
DUBE, Jean Maurice, Mar 30 1921 Sex:M Child# 1 Alfred Dube Nashua, NH & Alice Larouche Canada
DUBE, Jeanne Alberta, Jul 30 1920 Sex:F Child# 11 Ludger Dube Canada & Marie Levesque Canada
DUBE, Joachim, Dec 28 1903 Sex:M Child# 2 Jean Bte Dube Canada & Eugenie Plourde Canada
DUBE, John Baptist Noel, Dec 25 1933 Sex:M Child# 1 John B Dube Nashua, NH & Olivette Gallant Nashua, NH
DUBE, Jos Ernest Adrien, Jun 20 1920 Sex:M Child# 9 Joseph Dube Canada & Anaise Bechard Canada
DUBE, Jos G A Albert, Apr 24 1920 Sex:M Child# 3 Arthur Dube NH & Delima Fortier Canada
DUBE, Jos Roland Alfred, Sep 30 1935 Sex:M Child# 1 Alfred Dube Canada & Rose Dube Nashua, NH
DUBE, Jos Thomas Wilfrid, Nov 25 1922 Sex:M Child# 11 Joseph Dube Canada & Aneise Bechard Canada
DUBE, Joseph, Aug 22 1887 Sex:M Child# 1 Michel Dube P Q & Delvina Deschene P Q
DUBE, Joseph, Jul 10 1891 Sex:M Child# 4 Vincent Dube Canada & Emma Lefebvre Canada
DUBE, Joseph, Aug 13 1892 Sex:M Child# 6 Joseph Dube Canada & Marie D Canada
DUBE, Joseph, Oct 10 1901 Sex:M Child# 1 Jean Baptiste Dube Canada & Eugenie Plourde Canada Stillborn
DUBE, Joseph, Jun 12 1904 Sex:M Child# 1 Pierre Dube Canada & Philomene Despres Canada
DUBE, Joseph, Oct 18 1910 Sex:M Child# 2 Alphonse Dube Canada & Delina Levesque Canada
DUBE, Joseph, Nov 23 1929 Sex:M Child# 1 Althiode Dube Nashua, NH & Gracie Fluette Nashua, NH
DUBE, Joseph A Raymond, Nov 11 1931 Sex:M Child# 2 Altheode Dube Nashua, NH & Gracia Fluette Nashua, NH
DUBE, Joseph Albert, Apr 27 1905 Sex:M Child# 3 Ludger Dube Canada & Marie Levesque Canada
DUBE, Joseph Alfred, Dec 11 1899 Sex:M Child# 1 Joseph Dube Canada & Marie Corbin Canada
DUBE, Joseph Alfred, Sep 4 1904 Sex:M Child# 1 Joseph Dube Canada & Rose Chantal Canada
DUBE, Joseph Alfred, Dec 22 1915 Sex:M Child# 6 Joseph Dube Canada & Anaise Bechard Canada
DUBE, Joseph Alphe, Nov 8 1899 Sex:M Child# 1 Thimothe Dube Canada & Clarilda Dumais Canada
DUBE, Joseph Alphonse, Apr 14 1918 Sex:M Child# 1 Aldolphe Dube Canada & Alice Cousigny US
DUBE, Joseph Armand A, Jul 27 1904 Sex:M Child# 1 Joseph Dube Canada & Anaise Bechard Canada
DUBE, Joseph Arthur, Apr 9 1891 Sex:M Child# 1 William Dube Canada & Helene Dionne Canada
DUBE, Joseph Arthur Wm, Jan 21 1908 Sex:M Child# 5 Ludger Dube Canada & Marie Levesque Canada
DUBE, Joseph C, Sep 3 1887 Sex:M Child# David Dube Canada & Rosanna Plante Nashua, NH
DUBE, Joseph Charles R, Feb 28 1909 Sex:M Child# 4 Joseph Dube Canada & Anaise Bechard Canada
DUBE, Joseph Charles Rob, Jun 14 1916 Sex:M Child# 6 Albert Dube Canada & Alice Conrey Canada
DUBE, Joseph D X, Mar 10 1890 Sex:M Child# 2 Dumas Dube Canada & Marie Levesque Canada
DUBE, Joseph Edward, Jun 30 1918 Sex:M Child# 2 Arthur Dube Nashua, NH & Bertha Monier Nashua, NH
DUBE, Joseph Ernest, Dec 1 1908 Sex:M Child# 3 Albert Dube Canada & Alice Courcy Canada
DUBE, Joseph Fabian, Oct 17 1909 Sex:M Child# 6 Ludger Dube Canada & Marie Levesque Canada
DUBE, Joseph Henri, May 6 1894 Sex:M Child# 2 Joseph Dube Canada & Caroline Emond Canada
DUBE, Joseph Henri L, Aug 17 1910 Sex:M Child# 5 Joseph Dube Canada & Rose Chantal Canada
DUBE, Joseph Hermenigilde, May 18 1891 Sex:M Child# 1 Henry Dube Canada & Marie Roussel Canada
DUBE, Joseph Herve, May 11 1908 Sex:M Child# 3 Pierre Dube Canada & Anasie Despres Canada
DUBE, Joseph J B Louis, Apr 29 1910 Sex:M Child# 6 Jean B Dube Canada & Eugenie Plourde Canada
DUBE, Joseph Jean L, May 13 1924 Sex:M Child# 12 Joseph Dube Canada & Anoise Bechard Canada
DUBE, Joseph Leo, Jun 25 1931 Sex:M Child# 2 Arthur Dube Canada & Emiliana Picard Canada Stillborn
DUBE, Joseph Leo Alfred, Mar 4 1904 Sex:M Child# 1 Joseph Dube Canada & Eliza Levesque Canada
DUBE, Joseph Leo Arthur, Feb 8 1898 Sex:M Child# 2 Honore Dube Canada & Eugenie Boucher Canada
DUBE, Joseph Louis E, Jan 25 1909 Sex:M Child# 1 Louis Dube Fall River, MA & Philomene Marquis Canada
DUBE, Joseph N, Mar 3 1893 Sex:M Child# 2 Henri Dube Canada & Marie Roussel Canada

DUBE, Joseph Noel P A, Apr 16 1893 Sex:M Child# 1 Joseph Dube Canada & Caroline Emond Canada
DUBE, Joseph Oscar A, Oct 15 1907 Sex:M Child# 3 Joseph Dube Canada & Anaise Bechard Canada
DUBE, Joseph Paul Emile, Mar 16 1915 Sex:M Child# 12 Timothe Dube Canada & Marie Labrie Canada
DUBE, Joseph Prudent A, Mar 29 1907 Sex:M Child# 2 Arsene Dube Canada & Augustine Levesque Canada
DUBE, Joseph Robert, Feb 23 1919 Sex:M Child# 8 Joseph Dube Canada & Anoise Richard Canada
DUBE, Joseph Roger, Jan 17 1921 Sex:M Child# 3 Thomas Dube Canada & Alice Charest Canada
DUBE, Joseph Roger Lionel, Apr 19 1912 Sex:M Child# 1 Edmond Morin Canada & Exilda Dube Canada
DUBE, Joseph Saul, Nov 4 1893 Sex:M Child# 4 Joseph Dube Canada & Delvina Canada
DUBE, Joseph Stanislaus, Jun 14 1913 Sex:M Child# 9 Jean Bte Dube Canada & Eugenie Plourde Canada
DUBE, Joseph Sylvio, Nov 26 1897 Sex:M Child# 2 Louis Dube Vallet Brook, ME & Marie Theriault Canada
DUBE, Joseph Theodore, Apr 26 1903 Sex:M Child# 20 Honore Dube, Sr Canada & Eugenie Boucher Canada
DUBE, Joseph Theodore, Feb 11 1919 Sex:M Child# 2 Arthur Dube NH & Delima Fortier Canada
DUBE, Joseph, Jr, Oct 8 1918 Sex:M Child# 1 Joseph Dube Nashua, NH & Mary Ann Fen Nashua, NH Stillborn
DUBE, Julienne, Nov 4 1894 Sex:F Child# 3 J B Dube Canada & Jeanne Labelle Canada
DUBE, Lambert Frederick, Oct 14 1921 Sex:M Child# 1 Ernest Dube Nashua, NH & Victoria Lord Nashua, NH
DUBE, Leo, Dec 21 1897 Sex:M Child# 2 Alfred Dube Canada & Marie Alix Danielsonville, CT
DUBE, Leonire, Apr 24 1890 Sex:F Child# 13 Elzeard Dube Canada & Aglae Michaud Canada
DUBE, Leontine, Jul 12 1892 Sex:F Child# Joseph Dube Canada & Leontine Francoeur Canada
DUBE, Lionel Maurice Tel, Mar 31 1914 Sex:M Child# 1 Thomas Dube Canada & Alice Chenette Canada
DUBE, Louis P J, Nov 28 1896 Sex:M Child# 1 Louis Dube Canada & Marie Theriault Canada
DUBE, Louis Philippe, Apr 11 1897 Sex:M Child# 4 Joseph Dube Canada & Caroline Emond Canada
DUBE, Lucia, Jan 14 1892 Sex:F Child# 1 J B Dube Canada & Jeanne Lebelle Canada
DUBE, Ludger Ferdinand, Feb 16 1921 Sex:M Child# 4 Paul Dube Nashua, NH & Delia Renaud Nashua, NH
DUBE, Ludger Francois, Jan 16 1901 Sex:M Child# 2 Ludger Dube Canada & Anna Laplante Canada
DUBE, M A Dora, Dec 12 1894 Sex:F Child# 8 David Dube Canada & Genevieve Ouellette Canada
DUBE, M Alice Cecile, Aug 2 1914 Sex:F Child# 5 Pierre Dube Canada & Anesie Duprey Canada
DUBE, M Jeanne Rochelle, Mar 14 1922 Sex:F Child# 4 Thomas Dube Canada & Alice Charette Canada
DUBE, M Juliette Lucienne, Dec 12 1916 Sex:F Child# 13 Thimothe Dube Canada & Marie Labrie Canada
DUBE, M Laura Georgette, Jan 12 1913 Sex:F Child# 9 Ferdinand Dube Canada & Clara St Jean Canada
DUBE, M Regina, Oct 23 1895 Sex:F Child# 7 Honore Dube Canada & Eugenie Boucher Canada
DUBE, Magloire, Jun 18 1893 Sex:M Child# 5 David Dube Canada & Rosanna Plante Canada
DUBE, Marie, Jun 11 1898 Sex:F Child# 3 Joseph Dube Canada & Marie Corbin Canada
DUBE, Marie, Mar 3 1917 Sex:F Child# 7 Joseph Dube Canada & Rosalie Canada Stillborn
DUBE, Marie, Jul 5 1920 Sex:F Child# 6 Albert Dube Canada & Alice Courcy Canada
DUBE, Marie A A, May 18 1891 Sex:F Child# 9 Jean Dube Canada & Aime Gagnon Canada
DUBE, Marie A A, Oct 12 1898 Sex:F Child# 1 Charles Dube Canada & Anais Levesque Canada
DUBE, Marie Adele A, Apr 25 1901 Sex:F Child# 5 Alfred Dube Canada & Marie Alex Canada
DUBE, Marie Alice, Apr 13 1899 Sex:F Child# 4 Ferdina Dube Canada & Clara St Jean Canada
DUBE, Marie Alice Cecil, Feb 18 1918 Sex:F Child# 1 Arthur Dube NH & Delvina Fortier Canada
DUBE, Marie Alice D, Nov 27 1901 Sex:F Child# 1 Ludger Dube Canada & Marie Levesque Canada
DUBE, Marie Alice L, Dec 24 1910 Sex:F Child# 2 Joseph Dube Canada & Alice Corbin Canada
DUBE, Marie Alma, Jan 9 1889 Sex:F Child# David Dube Canada & Genevieve Ouellette Canada
DUBE, Marie Alma Eva, Jul 5 1903 Sex:F Child# 2 Ludger Dube Canada & Marie Levesque Canada
DUBE, Marie Angeline, Feb 20 1897 Sex:F Child# 4 J B Dube Canada & Jeanne Lebel Canada
DUBE, Marie Anita Dona, Jun 17 1917 Sex:F Child# 1 Arthur Dube Nashua, NH & Bertha Monier Nashua, NH
DUBE, Marie Anna, May 26 1894 Sex:F Child# 1 Pierre Dube Canada & Elise Rioux Canada
DUBE, Marie Anna, Nov 30 1922 Sex:F Child# 2 Francis Dube Canada & Yvonne Levesque Canada
DUBE, Marie Anne, Oct 6 1905 Sex:F Child# 2 Joseph Dube Canada & Rose Chantal Canada
DUBE, Marie Azilda, Mar 12 1905 Sex:F Child# 2 Joseph Dube Canada & Azilda Levesque Canada
DUBE, Marie Blanche, May 1 1890 Sex:F Child# 2 Charles Dube Canada & Celina Franciun Canada
DUBE, Marie Blanche A, Mar 2 1899 Sex:F Child# 3 Honore Dube Canada & Eugenie Boucher Canada
DUBE, Marie Cecile, Oct 1 1918 Sex:F Child# 10 Ludger Dube Canada & Marie Levesque Canada
DUBE, Marie Delina, Jul 14 1891 Sex:F Child# 3 Charles Dube Canada & Celina Francoeur Canada
DUBE, Marie Dora Gertrude, Oct 19 1928 Sex:F Child# 2 Albert Dube Canada & Lydia Morin Vermont
DUBE, Marie Elise Laura, Jun 8 1911 Sex:F Child# 5 Joseph Dube Canada & Anaise Bechard Canada
DUBE, Marie Eva, Dec 21 1897 Sex:F Child# 1 Alfred Dube Canada & Marie Alix Danielsonville, CT
DUBE, Marie Eva, Dec 20 1900 Sex:F Child# 2 Charles Dube Canada & Anaise Levesque Canada
DUBE, Marie Eva Rose, Apr 20 1900 Sex:F Child# 5 Ferdinand Dube Canada & Clara St Jean Canada
DUBE, Marie Eva Rose, Jan 4 1907 Sex:M Child# 3 Joseph Dube Canada & Rose Chantel Canada
DUBE, Marie Irene L, Aug 4 1908 Sex:F Child# 4 Joseph Dube Canada & Rose Chantal Canada
DUBE, Marie Jeanne R, Apr 11 1907 Sex:F Child# 2 Albert Dube Canada & Alice Courcy Canada
DUBE, Marie Laurette Alice, Jul 5 1925 Sex:F Child# 2 Francis Dube Canada & Yvonne Levesque Canada
DUBE, Marie Lea A, Dec 26 1905 Sex:F Child# 2 Joseph Dube Canada & Anaise Bechard Canada
DUBE, Marie Leona, Jan 1 1908 Sex:F Child# 13 Thomas Dube Canada & Athaise Boucher Canada
DUBE, Marie Leontine, Jul 11 1892 Sex:F Child# 7 Joseph Dube Canada & Leontine Leclair Canada
DUBE, Marie Lilian, Mar 17 1910 Sex:F Child# 1 Joseph Dube Canada & Virginie Plourde Nashua, NH
DUBE, Marie Lina Germaine, Apr 8 1911 Sex:F Child# 4 Albert Dube Canada & Alice Courcy Canada
DUBE, Marie Lorette, Dec 8 1934 Sex:F Child# 2 Albert Dube Nashua, NH & Clara Aubut Nashua, NH
DUBE, Marie Louise Annette, Sep 14 1918 Sex:F Child# 6 Joseph Dube Canada & Rosalie Dube Canada
DUBE, Marie Louise Aurore, Oct 16 1912 Sex:F Child# 8 Ludger Dube Canada & Mari Levesque Canada
DUBE, Marie Lucille Annett, Jan 27 1928 Sex:F Child# 14 Joseph Dube Canada & Anaise Bechard Canada
DUBE, Marie Lucille Doris, Dec 5 1925 Sex:F Child# 2 Joseph Dube Hancock, NH & Yvonne Couture Dover, NH
DUBE, Marie Rose Blanche, May 2 1916 Sex:F Child# 11 Jean Baptiste Dube Canada & Eugenie Plourde Canada

DUBE, Marie Rose I L, Dec 20 1909 Sex:F Child# 1 Joseph Dube Canada & Alice Corbin Canada
DUBE, Marie Rose Y, Jan 11 1907 Sex:F Child# 3 Joseph Dube Canada & Exilda Levesque Canada
DUBE, Marie Simone, Aug 29 1915 Sex:F Child# 9 Ludger Dube Canada & Marie Levesque Canada
DUBE, Marie Theresa, Oct 11 1926 Sex:F Child# 1 Arthur Dube Canada & Emeline Picard Canada
DUBE, Marie Theresa Lucille, May 8 1926 Sex:F Child# 13 Joseph Dube Canada & Anaise Richard Canada
DUBE, Marie Therese, Oct 8 1893 Sex:F Child# 4 Charles Dube Canada & Celina Francoeur Canada
DUBE, Marie Yvonne, May 28 1908 Sex:F Child# 5 Leon Dube Canada & Marie Larouche Canada
DUBE, Marie Yvonne Lucia, Mar 29 1913 Sex:F Child# 4 Joseph Dube Canada & Rosalie Dube Canada
DUBE, Marie Yvonne Theresa, Aug 15 1927 Sex:F Child# 1 Albert Dube Canada & Lydia Morin Graniteville, VT
DUBE, Mary, Oct 18 1902 Sex:F Child# 1 Martin Dube Austria & Elizabeth Masreck Austria
DUBE, Mary, Oct 11 1932 Sex:F Child# 15 Joseph Dube St Jean De Dieu & Anaise Bechard St Pascal, PQ Stillborn
DUBE, Mary Constance Nancy, Jun 16 1935 Sex:F Child# 3 Simeon Dube Nashua, NH & Jeanette Blais Canada
DUBE, Mary Eliza, Aug 4 1891 Sex:F Child# 2 Odillon Dube Canada & Gracia Beaulieu Canada
DUBE, Maurice, Dec 23 1925 Sex:M Child# 3 Philip Dube Canada & Jose Bourque Canada
DUBE, Norman Francis, Dec 24 1916 Sex:M Child# 1 Eugene Dube Nashua, NH & Mary Sirois Canada
DUBE, Norman Roland, Feb 12 1930 Sex:M Child# 5 Napoleon Dube Canada & Delia Renaud Nashua, NH
DUBE, Oscar Leande, May 4 1903 Sex:M Child# 2 Honore Dube, Jr Canada & Lena Reynolds Manchester, NH
DUBE, Paul, Mar 9 1912 Sex:M Child# 1 (No Parents Listed)
DUBE, Paul Robert, Sep 2 1919 Sex:M Child# 3 Napoleon Dube Canada & Delia Reno Nashua, NH
DUBE, Pierre Rene, Jr, Oct 14 1932 Sex:M Child# 1 Rene Dube Canada & F Beauregard Nashua, NH
DUBE, Polydoro, Jul 10 1887 Sex:M Child# Jean Dube P Q & Amie Gagnon P Q
DUBE, Raymond Bradley, Jul 21 1925 Sex:M Child# 2 Peter Dube Lawrence, MA & Ruth Bradley Nashua, NH
DUBE, Remi, May 9 1897 Sex:M Child# 6 Charles Dube Canada & Celina Francoeur Canada
DUBE, Renee Elizabeth, Apr 25 1928 Sex:F Child# 1 Rene Dube Nashua, NH & Frances Cross E Pepperell, MA
DUBE, Reta Annette, Feb 12 1924 Sex:F Child# 1 Joseph Dube Maine & Yvonne Couture Nashua, NH
DUBE, Robert Alvin, Nov 7 1933 Sex:M Child# 1 William J Dube Nashua, NH & Florette Anctil Nashua, NH
DUBE, Robert Leo, Aug 5 1935 Sex:M Child# 4 Albert Dube Canada & Lydia Morin Graniteville, VT
DUBE, Robert Paul, Nov 27 1918 Sex:M Child# 2 Thomas Dube Canada & Alice Charest Mass
DUBE, Roger Robert, Dec 26 1934 Sex:M Child# 3 Joseph Dube Methuen, MA & Yvonne Couture Nashua, NH
DUBE, Rose Aimee Aurore, Jun 7 1911 Sex:F Child# 2 Louis Dube Canada & Philomene Marquis Canada
DUBE, Selina, Nov 21 1889 Sex:F Child# 1 Odilon Dube Canada & Atins Beaulieu Canada
DUBE, Stanislaus Rene, Dec 28 1901 Sex:M Child# 4 Honore Dube Canada & Eugenie Boucher Canada
DUBE, Therese Anita, Jul 15 1923 Sex:F Child# 1 Philip Dube Canada & Josephine Bourque Canada
DUBE, Therese Eugenie, Oct 15 1931 Sex:F Child# 1 Simeon Dube Nashua, NH & Jeannette Blais Canada
DUBE, Thomas, Feb 8 1893 Sex:M Child# 3 Odillon Dube Canada & Gracieuse Beaulieu Canada
DUBE, Thomas Henri, Apr 10 1899 Sex:M Child# 3 Alfred Dube Canada & Mari Alyx Canada
DUBE, Timothe Simeon, Apr 7 1905 Sex:M Child# 3 J B Dube Canada & Eugenie Plourde Canada
DUBE, Unknown, Jun 5 1889 Sex:M Child# 5 Joseph Dube Canada & Exina Gagnon Canada Stillborn
DUBE, Unknown, Jan 18 1890 Sex:M Child# 1 Jules Dube Canada & Anna Canada
DUBE, Unknown, Apr 15 1890 Sex:F Child# 11 Raphael Dube Canada & Julienne St Orge Woonsocket, RI
DUBE, Unknown, Jul 22 1895 Sex:M Child# 4 Joseph Dube Canada & Caroline Emond Canada Stillborn
DUBE, Unknown, Jan 21 1908 Sex:M Child# 8 Joseph Dube Canada & Marie Louise Dube Canada Stillborn
DUBE, Unknown, Nov 3 1908 Sex:M Child# 1 Joseph Dube Canada & Rosalie Dube Canada Stillborn
DUBE, Unknown, Sep 3 1913 Sex:F Child# 5 Albert Dube Canada & Alice Courcy Canada Stillborn
DUBE, Victor Paul Emile, Nov 19 1928 Sex:M Child# 3 Elzear Dube Canada & Laura Therriault Canada
DUBE, Victorien, May 9 1898 Sex:M Child# 5 Joseph Dube Canada & Caroline Emond Canada
DUBE, Vital Alphonse, Sep 4 1924 Sex:M Child# 2 Philip Dube Canada & Josephine Bourque Canada
DUBE, Wilfred, Feb 24 1911 Sex:M Child# 11 Alfred Dube Canada & Marie Alix Canada
DUBE, Yvette, Jun 23 1927 Sex:F Child# 1 Alfred Dube Nashua, NH & Alice Larouche Canada
DUBE, Yvonne, May 19 1906 Sex:F Child# 4 Ludger Dube Canada & Marie Levesque Canada
DUBE, Yvonne, Oct 21 1915 Sex:F Child# 4 Louis Dube Canada & Marie Marquis Canada
DUBIE, Houoie, Feb 4 1888 Sex:M Child# 3 Vincent Dubie Canada & Emma Lefebvre Canada
DUBLOW, Anna, Jul 20 1917 Sex:F Child# 3 Antony Dublow Russia & Mary Kilman Russia
DUBLOW, Anthony Jacob, Oct 31 1921 Sex:M Child# 4 Anthony J Dublow Russia & Mary Killman Russia
DUBLOW, Helen, Apr 27 1915 Sex:F Child# 2 Antony Dublow Russia & Mary Kilman Russia
DUBOIS, Adelina B, Mar 27 1894 Sex:F Child# 2 Euclide Dubois
DUBOIS, Albert Victor, Mar 20 1910 Sex:M Child# 1 Victor Dubois Canada & Louise Donduro New Rochelle, NY
DUBOIS, Alfred Arthur, Aug 12 1904 Sex:M Child# 7 Ferdinand Dubois Sherbrooke, PQ & Mary Ann Flynn Canada
DUBOIS, Andre, Oct 23 1891 Sex:M Child# 6 Philias Dubois Altony & Marie L Bellerose Canada
DUBOIS, Anna, Oct 26 1887 Sex:F Child# Joseph Dubois P Q & Anna Moranda P Q
DUBOIS, Arthur Henry, Sep 4 1906 Sex:M Child# 2 Stephen Dubois Nashua, NH & Mary McMahan Malden, MA
DUBOIS, Bertha, Mar 20 1893 Sex:F Child# 2 Euclide Dubois Altoona, NY & Eugenie Mercure Canada
DUBOIS, Bruce Earl, Jul 2 1933 Sex:M Child# 1 Bruce B DuBois Lowell, MA & Myrtle L Welch Boston, MA
DUBOIS, Celina, Dec 4 1888 Sex:F Child# 3 Joseph Dubois Canada & Anna Maranda Canada
DUBOIS, Doris Lucille, Jul 29 1930 Sex:F Child# 2 Leo Dubois Nashua, NH & Amande Roy Canada
DUBOIS, Dorothy, Jun 27 1915 Sex:F Child# 5 Stephen Dubois Nashua, NH & Mary McMahon Malden, MA
DUBOIS, Edmond, Nov 29 1901 Sex:M Child# 5 Ferdina Dubois Canada & Mary M Flynn Canada
DUBOIS, Emile Victor, Dec 17 1912 Sex:M Child# 3 Harvey Dubois Nashua, NH & Grace Wilkins Nashua, NH
DUBOIS, Ernest, Aug 31 1905 Sex:M Child# 1 Stephen Dubois Nashua, NH & Mary McMahan Malden, MA
DUBOIS, Eugene Israel, Sep 9 1895 Sex:M Child# 4 William Dubois New York & Eugenie Mercure Canada
DUBOIS, Florence Irene, Mar 7 1913 Sex:F Child# 2 Charles H Dubois US & Eva Racine Canada
DUBOIS, Gloria Eva, Apr 3 1912 Sex:F Child# 1 Charles J Dubois US & Eva Racine Canada
DUBOIS, Harvey, Apr 9 1889 Sex:M Child# 4 Philias Dubois Altona, NY & Marie L Bellerose Canada

DUBOIS, Henri, Feb 19 1891 Sex:M Child# 10 Olivier Dubois Canada & Octavie Lanciane Canada
DUBOIS, Irene Alice, Feb 4 1910 Sex:F Child# 1 Elidore Dubois Greenville, NH & Emma Lagasse Canada
DUBOIS, Jessie, Dec 8 1891 Sex:F Child# 1 William Dubois Canada & Jennie Mercure Canada
DUBOIS, John Joseph, Feb 9 1912 Sex:M Child# 4 Steven Dubois NH & Mary McMahon Mass
DUBOIS, Joseph, Aug 26 1890 Sex:M Child# 5 Philias Dubois Altona, NY & Marie L Bellerose Canada
DUBOIS, Joseph, Aug 1 1898 Sex:M Child# 9 Peilias Dubois Altona, NY & Marie L Bellerose Canada
DUBOIS, Joseph Aldege, Nov 29 1896 Sex:M Child# 5 Euclide Dubois Altona & Eugenie Mercure Canada
DUBOIS, Joseph Alfred, May 6 1897 Sex:M Child# 2 Elie Dubois Rathford, NY & Odile Dumais Canada
DUBOIS, Joseph F E, Jan 20 1900 Sex:M Child# 10 Philias Dubois New York & Marie L Bellerose Canada
DUBOIS, Joseph Gerald, Oct 5 1935 Sex:M Child# 3 Alphonse Dubois Nashua, NH & Eva R Rheaume Nashua, NH
DUBOIS, Joseph H A, Nov 11 1894 Sex:M Child# 7 Philias Dubois Altona, NY & Marie L Bellerose Canada
DUBOIS, Joseph Leo, May 8 1905 Sex:M Child# 7 Euclide Dubois Altoona, NY & Eugenie Mercure Winooski, VT
DUBOIS, Joseph Pierre, Oct 23 1895 Sex:M Child# 1 Elie Dubois Ratford, NY & Odile Dumais Canada
DUBOIS, Leopold Armand, Jul 31 1932 Sex:M Child# 2 L A Dubois Nashua, NH & Eva Rheaume Nashua, NH
DUBOIS, Louis Alphonse, Dec 8 1890 Sex:M Child# 4 Joseph Dubois Canada & Alma Maranda Canada
DUBOIS, Louise Elizabeth, Aug 29 1918 Sex:F Child# 4 Harvey D Dubois Nashua, NH & Grace D Wilkins Nashua, NH
DUBOIS, Madeline Shirley, Apr 29 1926 Sex:F Child# 5 Harvey Dubois Nashua, NH & Grace D Wilkins Nashua, NH
DUBOIS, Marie Emerilda, Jan 7 1898 Sex:F Child# 6 Euclide Dubois Altona, NY & Eugenie Mercure Canada
DUBOIS, Marie Nettie, Jul 6 1892 Sex:F Child# 9 Louis Dubois France & Marie Presse Canada
DUBOIS, Paul, Apr 23 1928 Sex:M Child# 1 Ludger Dubois Gonic, NH & Rita Leach Haverhill, MA
DUBOIS, Philene Grace, Dec 2 1932 Sex:F Child# 2 Philip Dubois Nashua, NH & Francis Bearor Hudson, NH
DUBOIS, Philip Harvey, Sep 20 1931 Sex:M Child# 1 Philip Dubois Nashua, NH & Frances Bearor Hudson, NH
DUBOIS, Philippe, Jan 8 1904 Sex:M Child# 7 Joseph Dubois Canada & Anna Maranda Canada
DUBOIS, Phillip, Jul 15 1910 Sex:M Child# 2 Harvey Dubois Nashua, NH & Grace Wilkins Nashua, NH
DUBOIS, Raymond Philippe, Mar 21 1910 Sex:M Child# 3 Stephen E Dubois Nashua, NH & Mary McMann Malden, MA
DUBOIS, Robert Honore, Oct 13 1925 Sex:M Child# 2 Honore Dubois Nashua, NH & Eva Boucher Nashua, NH
DUBOIS, Rosaire Therese, Dec 29 1930 Sex:F Child# 1 Alphonse Dubois Nashua, NH & Eva Rheaume Nashua, NH
DUBOIS, Rosanna Julia, Aug 12 1904 Sex:f Child# 6 Ferdinand Dubois Sherbrooke, PQ & Mary Ann Flynn Canada
DUBOIS, Theresa Blanc Pauline, Mar 31 1935 Sex:F Child# 4 Leo Dubois Nashua, NH & Armande Roy Canada
DUBOIS, Unknown, Nov 26 1893 Sex:M Child# 9 Louis Dubois Canada & Marie Presse Canada Stillborn
DUBOIS, Unknown, Jun 21 1897 Sex:F Child# 8 Philippe Dubois Altona, NY & Marie L Bellerose Canada Stillborn
DUBOIS, Virginie Camille, Sep 21 1923 Sex:F Child# 1 Honore Dubois Nashua, NH & Eva Boucher Nashua, NH
DUBOIS, Warren Livingston,Jr, Sep 9 1923 Sex:M Child# 2 Warren L DuBois New Jersey & Ernestine C Kelly Saco, ME
DUBOIS, Wilfrid Robert, Aug 5 1932 Sex:M Child# 3 Leo Dubois Nashua, NH & Amanda Roy Canada
DUBOWIK, John, Aug 15 1923 Sex:M Child# 1 Wladislav Dubowik Poland & Joseph Finkowicz Poland
DUBOWIK, Stanslaw, Dec 4 1926 Sex:M Child# 3 W Dubowik Poland & J Firkouwicz Poland
DUBRAY, Jean Ann, Jan 27 1927 Sex:F Child# 2 Edgar Dubray Nashua, NH & Margaret Young Worcester, MA
DUBRAY, Shirley Mae, Jan 3 1925 Sex:F Child# 1 Edgar E Dubray Nashua, NH & Margaret Young Worcester, MA
DUBREAUIL, Philmore Conrad, Dec 27 1904 Sex:M Child# 2 Ernest J Dubreuil Bedford, NY & Julia J Ledoux Nashua, NH
DUBREIL, Ernest, Jan 22 1902 Sex:M Child# 1 Edgar Debreil New York & Julie Ledoux Nashua, NH
DUBREUIL, Albina Amanda, Jun 14 1906 Sex:F Child# 2 Napoleon Dubreuil Manchester, NH & Georgian Labonte Nashua, NH
DUBREUIL, Dexter J, May 16 1898 Sex:M Child# 1 Philemon Dubreuil Saranac, NY & Mathilda Malhoit Nashua, NH
DUBREUIL, Ernest Ovide, May 5 1899 Sex:M Child# 2 Phil Dubreuil Saranac, NY & Mathilde Mailhoit Nashua, NH
DUBREUIL, Harry George, Jun 20 1902 Sex:M Child# 3 Philmore Dubreuil Saranac, NY & M Malhiot Nashua, NH
DUBREUIL, Joseph Victor A, Aug 21 1909 Sex:M Child# 3 Napoleon Dubreuil NH & Georgina Labonte
DUBREUIL, Marie Lina, Mar 16 1901 Sex:F Child# 1 Napoleon Dubreuil Canada & Georgiana Labonte Canada
DUBREUIL, Philmore, Oct 5 1906 Sex:M Child# 4 Philmore J Dubreuil US & Mathilda Malhoit US
DUBUC, Arthur, Sep 12 1930 Sex:M Child# 2 Roland Dubuc Nashua, NH & Dorothy Thompson US
DUBUC, Estelle Annette, Jan 25 1908 Sex:F Child# 3 A R Dubuc Canada & Emma Harpin Canada
DUBUC, Henri Maurice, Mar 4 1907 Sex:M Child# 2 A R Dubuc Canada & Emma Harpin Canada
DUBUC, Robert Leonard, May 6 1927 Sex:M Child# 1 Charles Dubuc Nashua, NH & Dorothy Thompson Wilton, NH
DUBUQUE, Blanche Irene, Aug 17 1906 Sex:F Child# 1 Napoleon Dubuque St Albans, VT & Blanche Messier Canada
DUBUQUE, Charles Edouard, Sep 4 1904 Sex:M Child# 1 Arthur R Dubuque Canada & Emma Harpin Canada
DUBUQUE, Joseph Henri, Dec 17 1891 Sex:M Child# 1 Joseph Dubuque Maine & Ulalie Faucher Canada
DUBUQUE, Katherine Eva Rose, Nov 26 1908 Sex:F Child# 2 Napoleon Dubuque St Albans, VT & Blanche Messier Canada
DUBUQUE, Wilfred, Jan 5 1920 Sex:M Child# 4 Alfred Dubuque Montpelier, VT & Maud Fremont Bridgeport, CT
DUCAS, Roger Conrad, May 3 1930 Sex:M Child# 2 Henri Ducas Canada & Dolorosa Rochette Canada
DUCASSE, Normand, Sep 14 1927 Sex:M Child# 2 Hervie Ducasse Canada & Rose Rochette Canada
DUCHARME, Beatrice, Oct 15 1922 Sex:F Child# 3 Alfred Ducharme Canada & Marie L Pelletier Canada
DUCHARME, Dorris Reta, Jul 13 1924 Sex:F Child# 2 Raoul Ducharme Canada & Ernestine Lafroniere Canada
DUCHARME, Florence Mary, Jul 28 1924 Sex:F Child# 1 Henry Ducharme Canada & Alph Bouchard Nashua, NH
DUCHARME, J Alfred Corade, Sep 20 1914 Sex:M Child# 2 Alfred Ducharme Canada & M Louise Pelletier Canada
DUCHARME, Joseph, Nov 15 1909 Sex:M Child# 1 Alfred Ducharme Canada & Marie L Pelletier Canada Stillborn
DUCHARME, Joseph Henri W, Jul 2 1930 Sex:M Child# 1 Henri Ducharme Canada & Bertha Ouellette Fall River, MA
DUCHARME, Marie Armande Juliet, Feb 19 1923 Sex:F Child# 1 Raoul Ducharme Canada & Ernestine Lafreniere Canada
DUCHARME, Marie Therese Alvina, Feb 15 1933 Sex:F Child# 2 Henri Ducharme Canada & Alberta Ouellette Fall River, MA
DUCHARME, Richard Edward, Nov 21 1930 Sex:M Child# 3 Walter Ducharme Lowell, MA & Eva Frenette Canada
DUCHENAULT, Florida, Jan 4 1892 Sex:F Child# 9 Cyprien Duchenault Canada & Georgina Laflamme Canada
DUCHENAULT, Marie L B, Mar 8 1889 Sex:F Child# 13 D Duchenault Canada & Milena Curran Canada
DUCHENE, Diana, Sep 19 1889 Sex:F Child# 9 Octave Duchene Canada & Marie Cyr Canada
DUCHENEAU, Amarilda Alexandra, May 26 1899 Sex:F Child# 3 Jean Ducheneau Canada & Delphine Proulx Canada
DUCHENEAU, Amore Alice, Mar 8 1912 Sex:F Child# 10 Nazaire Ducheneau Canada & Helene Tanguay Canada
DUCHENEAU, Angelina, Nov 2 1903 Sex:F Child# 11 Pierre Ducheneau Canada & Ernestine Boulard Canada

DUCHENEAU, Auguste, May 4 1890 Sex:M Child# 14 Didime Ducheneau Canada & Melina Cusson Canada
DUCHENEAU, Henri, Apr 27 1892 Sex:M Child# 15 Fidime Ducheneau Canada & Melina Cusson Canada
DUCHENEAU, Stanislas, Mar 27 1889 Sex:M Child# 3 Nazaire Ducheneau Canada & Helene Tanguay Canada
DUCHESNE, Charles David, Oct 4 1891 Sex:M Child# 10 Octave Duchesne Canada & Marie Cyr Canada
DUCHESNE, Harry, May 22 1905 Sex:M Child# 1 Aime Duchesne Canada & Viola Labonte US
DUCHESNE, Joseph Hormidas, Jan 9 1894 Sex:M Child# 11 Octave Duchesne Canada & Marie Cyr Canada
DUCHESNE, Mildred Viola, Jul 18 1906 Sex:F Child# 2 Aime Duchesne NH & Viola Labonte NH
DUCHESNEAU, Albert, Apr 28 1917 Sex:M Child# 4 Adelard Duchesneau Canada & Emelia Rousseau Nashua, NH
DUCHESNEAU, Antoinette Delia, Oct 22 1897 Sex:F Child# 4 Stanislas Duchesneau Canada & Antoinette Gendron Canada
DUCHESNEAU, Arthur, Nov 14 1896 Sex:M Child# 4 Jean Duchesneau Canada & Delphine Proulx Canada
DUCHESNEAU, Hervey Odias, Jul 9 1923 Sex:M Child# 6 Alfred Duchesneau Canada & Florida Rousseau Nashua, NH
DUCHESNEAU, J George Pierre, Apr 22 1921 Sex:M Child# 4 Stan Duchesneau Canada & Agnes Blais Rhode Island
DUCHESNEAU, Jeannette Fabiola, Nov 26 1919 Sex:F Child# 5 Alfred Duchesneau Canada & Florida Rousseau Nashua, NH
DUCHESNEAU, Joseph, Aug 21 1893 Sex:M Child# 16 Didime Duchesneau Canada & Melina Cusson Canada
DUCHESNEAU, Joseph Albert A, Sep 18 1924 Sex:M Child# 5 S Duchesneau Canada & Agnes Blais Rhode Island
DUCHESNEAU, Joseph Dedime Henri, Mar 21 1916 Sex:M Child# 2 Edmond Duchesneau Canada & Marie Desjardins Canada
DUCHESNEAU, Joseph Leo Adrien, Jun 9 1917 Sex:M Child# 2 Stanislas Duchesneau Canada & Agnes Blais Rhode Island
DUCHESNEAU, Joseph Ovide, Sep 25 1890 Sex:M Child# 4 Nazaire Duchesneau Canada & Ellen Languay Canada
DUCHESNEAU, Joseph Raoul, Jul 2 1895 Sex:M Child# 17 Didime Duchesneau Canada & Melina Cusson Canada
DUCHESNEAU, Joseph Stanislas, Oct 22 1897 Sex:M Child# 3 Stanislas Duchesneau Canada & Antoinette Gendron Canada
DUCHESNEAU, Josephine, Sep 12 1893 Sex:F Child# 2 Jean Duchesneau Canada & Delphine Proulx Canada
DUCHESNEAU, Lea, Apr 27 1900 Sex:F Child# 1 Napoleon Duchesneau Canada & Anna Theberge Canada
DUCHESNEAU, M Bernadette Sol, Feb 8 1919 Sex:F Child# 3 Stan Duchesneau Canada & Agnes Blais Rhode Island
DUCHESNEAU, M Blanche Julienne, Sep 9 1915 Sex:F Child# 1 Stanislas Duchesneau Canada & Agnes Blais Rhode Island
DUCHESNEAU, M Jeanne Louise, Mar 28 1915 Sex:F Child# 1 Edmond Duchesneau Canada & Marie Desjardins Canada
DUCHESNEAU, Marie, Jan 2 1906 Sex:F Child# 4 Napoleon Duchesneau Canada & Anna Theberge Canada
DUCHESNEAU, Marie, Oct 8 1907 Sex:F Child# 15 Nazaire Duchesneau Canada & Helene Tanguay Canada
DUCHESNEAU, Marie B E, Apr 1 1898 Sex:F Child# 18 Didime Duchesneau Canada & Melina Cusson Canada
DUCHESNEAU, Martha Angela, Jul 16 1927 Sex:F Child# 6 S Duchesneau Canada & Agnes Blais Natick, RI
DUCHESNEAU, Morris Royal, Dec 17 1933 Sex:M Child# 1 R Duchesneau Manchester, NH & Clea Ricard Nashua, NH
DUCHESNEAU, Natalie Denise, Sep 3 1926 Sex:F Child# 1 Ralph Duchesneau Nashua, NH & Ernestine Lemery Nashua, NH
DUCHESNEAU, Phyllis Barbara, Sep 23 1925 Sex:F Child# 1 Harry Duchesneau Nashua, NH & Elvira Gordon Salem, MA
DUCHESNEAU, Unknown, Jan 22 1916 Sex:F Child# 4 Adelard Duchesneau Canada & Amelia Rousseau Nashua, NH Stillborn
DUCHESNEAU, Willia Napoleon, Apr 10 1904 Sex:M Child# 3 Napoleon Duchesneau Canada & Anna Theberge Canada
DUCHESNEOU, Emile, Aug 13 1888 Sex:M Child# 2 Jean Duchesneou Canada & Alphona St Dow Canada
DUCKLEE, Flora Gertrude, Aug 29 1902 Sex:F Child# 2 Leroy W Ducklee Nashua, NH & Emma S Adams Nashua, NH
DUCLOS, Amede Rhyian, Jul 28 1925 Sex:M Child# 13 Amede Duclos Canada & Florida Dupont Canada
DUCLOS, Antonio, Mar 12 1889 Sex: Child# 3 Joseph Duclos Canada & Eurelle St Hilaire Canada
DUCLOS, Armand, Aug 31 1896 Sex:M Child# 6 Robert Duclos Canada & Malvina Ouellette Canada
DUCLOS, Edmond S, Jun 25 1900 Sex:M Child# 4 Olivier Duclos Canada & Louise Monty Canada
DUCLOS, Elsie Coraine, Mar 20 1917 Sex:F Child# 2 Alfred Duclos Nashua, NH & Jessie Lambert Montgomery, VT
DUCLOS, Emile Silvio, Aug 16 1898 Sex:M Child# 3 Oliver Duclos Canada & Louisa Monty Canada
DUCLOS, Eva Lydia, May 20 1906 Sex:F Child# 6 Oscar Duclos Canada & Georgiana Gadbois US
DUCLOS, Gabriel, Jan 23 1910 Sex:F Child# 5 Amedee Duclos Canada & Amanda Bourque Canada
DUCLOS, Georges Irene, Sep 4 1901 Sex:M Child# 11 Robert Duclos Canada & Malvina Ouellette Canada
DUCLOS, Geraldine Bertha, Jan 1 1932 Sex:F Child# 1 Henry O Duclos Laconia, NH & M A Garland Nashua, NH
DUCLOS, Henri Philippe, Feb 11 1899 Sex:M Child# 9 Romain Duclos Canada & Malvina Ouellette Canada
DUCLOS, Jos Alexander Ernest, Apr 10 1918 Sex:M Child# 6 Samuel Duclos Canada & Josephine Duclos Canada
DUCLOS, Jos Conrad Normand, Aug 8 1934 Sex:M Child# 3 Julien Duclos Canada & Bella Trudel Woonsocket, RI
DUCLOS, Jos Raymond Ernest, Mar 2 1929 Sex:M Child# 2 Albert Duclos Nashua, NH & Sylvia Desmarais Nashua, NH
DUCLOS, Joseph Adelard A, Nov 27 1924 Sex:M Child# 9 Samuel Duclos Canada & Josephine Charest Canada
DUCLOS, Joseph Albert Armand, Jul 28 1926 Sex:M Child# 2 Albert Duclos Nashua, NH & Sylvia Desmarais Nashua, NH
DUCLOS, Joseph Armand, Jan 31 1916 Sex:M Child# 5 Samuel Duclos Canada & Josephine Charest Canada
DUCLOS, Joseph W N, Aug 15 1897 Sex:M Child# 12 Joseph E N Duclos Canada & Emelie St Hilaire Canada
DUCLOS, Joseph Wilfred, Aug 22 1890 Sex:M Child# 4 R Duclos Canada & Malvina Ouellette Canada
DUCLOS, Leo Arthur, Sep 3 1896 Sex:M Child# 2 Olivier Duclos Canada & Louise Monty Canada
DUCLOS, Louis Arthur, May 12 1901 Sex:M Child# 5 Oscar Duclos Canada & Georgiana Godbois Spencer, MA
DUCLOS, Louis Hector E, Aug 18 1906 Sex:M Child# 7 Olivier Duclos Canada & Louise Monty Canada
DUCLOS, Lucien Roger, May 18 1915 Sex:M Child# 8 Amedee Duclos Canada & Amanda Bourque Canada
DUCLOS, M Lucienne Theresa, Oct 3 1922 Sex:F Child# 10 Amedee Duclos Canada & Florida Dupont Canada
DUCLOS, Margaret, Dec 27 1917 Sex:F Child# 1 Wilfred Duclos Nashua, NH & Sybil O'Neil Nashua, NH
DUCLOS, Marie, Oct 7 1904 Sex:F Child# 13 Robert Duclos Canada & Malvina Ouellette Canada
DUCLOS, Marie Antoinette S, Mar 12 1920 Sex:F Child# 7 Samuel Duclos Canada & Josephine Charest Canada
DUCLOS, Marie Irene Rita, Dec 30 1921 Sex:F Child# 8 Samuel Duclos Canada & Josephine Charest Canada
DUCLOS, Marie Josephine, May 28 1912 Sex:F Child# 3 Samuel Duclos Canada & Josephine Charest Canada
DUCLOS, Marie Lorraine B, Jul 7 1924 Sex:F Child# 12 Amedee Duclos Canada & Florida Dupont Canada
DUCLOS, Marie R Theodile, Aug 17 1896 Sex:M Child# 11 Joseph E N Duclos Canada & Emilie St Hilaire Canada
DUCLOS, Oscar Louis, May 4 1915 Sex:M Child# 1 Alfred Duclos Nashua, NH & Jessie Lambert Montgomery, VT
DUCLOS, Ovila, May 12 1894 Sex:M Child# 7 Romain Duclos Canada & Malvina Ouellette Canada
DUCLOS, Paul Arthur, Jun 27 1903 Sex:M Child# 12 Robert Duclos Canada & Malvina Ouellette Canada
DUCLOS, Paul Ovide, Jun 3 1904 Sex:M Child# 6 Olivier Duclos Canada & Louise Monty Canada
DUCLOS, Real Armand, Sep 8 1911 Sex:M Child# 6 Amedee Duclos Canada & Amanda Bourque Canada
DUCLOS, Roland Ernest, Feb 1 1913 Sex:M Child# 7 Amedee Duclos Canada & Amanda Bourque Canada

DUCLOS, Rosanna, Oct 31 1891 Sex:F Child# 5 Robert Duclos Canada & Malvina Ouellette Canada
DUCLOS, Stella, Oct 7 1904 Sex:F Child# 14 Robert Duclos Canada & Malvina Ouellette Canada
DUCLOS, Unknown, Apr 27 1890 Sex:F Child# 4 Joseph Duclos Canada & Emilie St Helaire Canada Stillborn
DUCLOS, Unknown, May 11 1891 Sex: Child# 6 J E N Duclos Canada & Emilie St Helaire Canada Stillborn
DUCLOS, Unknown, Jan 1 1893 Sex:M Child# 6 N Duclos Canada & Agnes Moreau Canada  Stillborn
DUCLOS, Unknown, Jan 11 1893 Sex:M Child# 6 Robert Duclos Canada & Malvina Ouellette Canada
DUCLOS, Unknown, Apr 10 1894 Sex:M Child# 4 J E N Duclos Canada & Emelie St Hilaire Canada Stillborn
DUCLOS, William, Aug 30 1900 Sex:M Child# 10 Robert Duclos Canada & Malvina Ouellette Canada
DUCLUC, Mary Rose, Nov 2 1890 Sex:F Child# Joseph Ducluc Brattleboro, VT & Louise Funette Ottawa, PQ
DUCLUS, Rose Aimee, Jan 5 1914 Sex:F Child# 4 Samuel Duclus Canada & Josephine Charest Canada
DUDLEY, Boyd III, Jun 3 1913 Sex:M Child# 1 Boyd Dudley Hamilton, ME & Madge Netherton Garden City, KS
DUDLEY, Emily, May 12 1927 Sex:F Child# 2 Albert Dudley Hollis, NH & Marion Sand Hollis, NH
DUDLEY, Lizzie, Apr 17 1899 Sex:F Child# 1 Noah Dudley Canada & Lizzie Burns Hollis, NH
DUDLEY, Lorraine May, Dec 11 1924 Sex:F Child# 1 Albert Dudley Hollis, NH & Marion Sanders Hollis, NH
DUDLEY, Ralph Eugene, Jul 2 1934 Sex:M Child# 1 Earl Dudley Hollis, NH & Jeanette Desrosiers Nashua, NH
DUDLEY, Robert Eugene, Dec 3 1922 Sex:M Child# 2 Clarence G Dudley Concord, VT & Laura Racine Concord, NH
DUERSCHMIDT, Alice May, Sep 8 1921 Sex:F Child# 4 Rud Duerschmidt Germany & Elizabeth McGrath Lynn, MA
DUFAULT, Eleanore Verna, Mar 20 1916 Sex:F Child# 2 Edward N Dufault Nashua, NH & Cora Maranda Nashua, NH
DUFAULT, Joseph Arcade, Jun 25 1902 Sex:M Child# 3 Arcade Dufault Canada & Ida Dupras Canada
DUFAULT, Leo Charles, Apr 10 1901 Sex:M Child# 3 S Edward Dufault Lowell, MA & Elizabeth Gagnon Canada
DUFAULT, Marie Aurore A, Mar 13 1900 Sex:F Child# 2 Arcade Dufault Canada & Ida Duprat Canada
DUFAULT, Nazarie, Feb 11 1896 Sex:M Child# 1 Edward Dufault US & Elise Gagnon Canada
DUFAULX, Joseph E P, Jun 9 1909 Sex:M Child# 5 Arcade Dufaulx Canada & Ida Dupras Canada
DUFAULX, Pearl Lucille, Oct 6 1917 Sex:F Child# 8 Arcade Dufaulx Canada & Ida Dupras Canada
DUFF, Kenneth Edward, Oct 16 1900 Sex:M Child# 1 S B Duff NB & Agnes L Wilson Canada
DUFFENEY, Lela, Oct 7 1909 Sex:F Child# 7 John Duffeney New York & Mary Lessard Nashua, NH
DUFFENEY, Phil Raymond, Jan 28 1907 Sex:M Child# 4 John Duffeney New York & Mary Lessard Nashua, NH
DUFFINA, Clara Eva, May 11 1913 Sex:F Child# 8 John B Duffina Mooers, NY & Elizabeth Lesard Nashua, NH
DUFFINA, George Neal, Jun 7 1935 Sex:M Child# 6 Wilmer Duffina Nashua, NH & Irene Bernard Nashua, NH
DUFFINA, Gerald Paul, Mar 2 1934 Sex:M Child# 3 John Duffina Brockton, MA & Yvonne Belanger Nashua, NH
DUFFINA, Joseph Archille, Apr 23 1928 Sex:M Child# 1 J Baptiste Duffina Mass & Yvonne Belanger Nashua, NH
DUFFINA, Marie Doris T, Jan 24 1930 Sex:F Child# 2 John Duffina Brockton, MA & Yvonne Belanger Nashua, NH
DUFFINA, Wilmer J, May 17 1929 Sex:M Child# 4 Wilmer Duffina Lowell, MA & Irene Bernard Nashua, NH
DUFFY, Alice Irene, Feb 8 1919 Sex:F Child# 5 Thomas Duffy Rhode Island & Angelina Larocque Mass
DUFFY, Florence, May 4 1920 Sex:F Child# 6 Thomas Duffy Warren, RI & Angeline Larocque Mass
DUFFY, James Bernard, Feb 25 1928 Sex:M Child# 2 Luke Robert Duffy Dover, NH & Addie L Brigham Hartford, CT
DUFFY, Marie Louise, Nov 17 1903 Sex:F Child# 1 Terrence J Duffy Nashua, NH & Mary A Larivee Nashua, NH
DUFFY, Paul, Apr 24 1914 Sex:M Child# 3 John A Duffy Manchester, NH & Mary E Golden Plattsburg, NY
DUFFY, Unknown, Mar 17 1903 Sex: Child# 1 John A Duffy Manchester, NH & Nellie E Golden Plattsburg, NY Stillborn
DUFFY, Unknown, Aug 20 1905 Sex:F Child# 2 John A Duffy Manchester, NH & Mary E Golden Plattsburg, NY
DUFOE, Charles Peter, May 22 1931 Sex:M Child# 3 Joseph H Dufoe Marlboro, MA & Irene Robbins Nashua, NH
DUFOE, Joseph Henry, Jr, Apr 30 1926 Sex:M Child# 1 Joseph H Dufoe Marlboro, MA & Irene Robbins Nashua, NH
DUFOE, Norma Flora, Oct 7 1932 Sex:F Child# 4 Jos H Dufoe Marlboro, MA & Irene Robbins Nashua, NH
DUFOE, Robert Earl, Mar 31 1935 Sex:M Child# 5 J H Dufoe Marlboro, MA & Irene Robbins Nashua, NH
DUFORE, Mamie E, Feb 20 1888 Sex:F Child# 6 Napoleon Dufore P Q & Emma Gagnon P Q
DUFOULT, Marie Irene, Mar 25 1898 Sex:F Child# 1 Arcade Dufoult Canada & Ida Duprat Canada
DUFOUR, Anna Celina, Apr 18 1893 Sex:F Child# 1 Telesphore Dufour Canada & Maria Sirois Canada
DUFOUR, Daniel Norman, Jun 28 1933 Sex:M Child# 2 Thomas Dufour Fall River, MA & Eva Gagnon Nashua, NH
DUFOUR, Donald Paul, Feb 10 1929 Sex:M Child# 2 Henry Dufour Marlboro, MA & Irene Robbins Nashua, NH
DUFOUR, Eva, Aug 26 1888 Sex:F Child# 13 Joseph Dufour Canada & Marceline Levesque Canada
DUFOUR, Henry Raymond, Mar 13 1930 Sex:M Child# 3 Henry Dufour Lowell, MA & Amelia Morin New Bedford, MA
DUFOUR, J Albert D L, Apr 6 1911 Sex:M Child# 9 Telesphore Dufour Canada & Maria Sirois Canada
DUFOUR, J Armand Edmond, Jun 8 1914 Sex:M Child# 10 Telesphore Dufour Canada & Marie Sirois Canada
DUFOUR, Jacqueline Jeannine, Oct 6 1930 Sex:F Child# 1 Alfred Dufour Nashua, NH & Germaine Baril Canada
DUFOUR, Jos Chas J Robert, Feb 5 1916 Sex:M Child# 5 David Dufour Canada & M Claire Paquette Canada
DUFOUR, Jos Oscar Alfred, Nov 16 1904 Sex:M Child# 6 Telesphore Dufour Canada & Henriette Sirois Canada
DUFOUR, Jos Roland Philip, Jun 23 1928 Sex:M Child# 1 (No Parents Listed)
DUFOUR, Joseph Alfred A G, Nov 11 1909 Sex:M Child# 8 Telesphore Dufour Canada & Maria Sirois Canada
DUFOUR, Joseph Alfred Donald, Jul 12 1932 Sex:M Child# 2 Alfred Dufour Nashua, NH & Germaine Baril Canada
DUFOUR, Joseph T Raoul, Apr 19 1890 Sex:M Child# 14 Joseph Dufour Canada & Marcelina Levegne Canada
DUFOUR, Leger Adrien S, Jul 1 1905 Sex:M Child# 2 Leger Dufour Canada & Josephine Bouchard Canada
DUFOUR, Marie Dorilda, Oct 3 1902 Sex:F Child# 5 Telesphore Dufour Canada & Maria Sirois Canada
DUFOUR, Marie Eugenie, Apr 9 1895 Sex:F Child# 2 Telesphore Dufour Canada & Marie Sirois Canada
DUFOUR, Marie Eva, Dec 2 1906 Sex:F Child# 1 Charles H Dufour Canada & Eva Desclos Canada
DUFOUR, Marie Germaine H, Jan 31 1918 Sex:F Child# 6 David Dufour Canada & Marie Clara Paquette Canada
DUFOUR, Marie Gertrude, Apr 19 1920 Sex:F Child# 7 David Dufour Canada & Claire Paquette Canada
DUFOUR, Marie Irene B, Feb 3 1908 Sex:F Child# 7 Telesphore Dufour Canada & Maria Sirois Canada
DUFOUR, Marie Ivonne E, Jun 24 1907 Sex:F Child# 3 Leger Dufour Canada & Josephine Bouchard Canada
DUFOUR, Marie Yvonne D, Aug 7 1900 Sex:F Child# 4 Telesphore Dufour Canada & Maria Sigouin Canada
DUFOUR, Mary Jane Doris, Nov 14 1933 Sex:F Child# 3 Clovis Dufour Lowell, MA & Bertha Lessard Lowell, MA
DUFOUR, Olivette Rita, Feb 16 1922 Sex:F Child# 1 Henry Dufour Lowell, MA & Emelia Morin New Bedford, MA
DUFOUR, Patricia, Apr 20 1933 Sex:F Child# 3 Henry Dufour Lowell, MA & Amelia Morin New Bedford, MA
DUFOUR, Roger M Raymond, Jun 16 1931 Sex:M Child# 1 Thomas Dufour Fall River, MA & Eva Gagnon Nashua, NH

DUFOUR, Rose Ida, Jun 8 1902 Sex:F Child# 1 Leger Dufour Canada & Josephine Bouchard Canada
DUFRESNE, Violette, Feb 3 1922 Sex:F Child# 1 Eddie Dufresne
DUGAN, Ellen, Sep 24 1889 Sex:F Child# 2 James Dugan Ireland & Sarah W Laughlin Ireland
DUGAN, Harold, Sep 15 1898 Sex:M Child# 1 Michael Dugan Nashua, NH & Ida Claremont Sciota, NY
DUGAN, James Joseph, Dec 19 1929 Sex:M Child# 3 John Dugan Nashua, NH & Esther Canavan Dorchester, MA
DUGAN, Jose, Jul 13 1907 Sex:F Child# 4 John Dugan Russia & Mary Grigontie Russia
DUGAN, Joseph, May 30 1913 Sex:M Child# 3 Andrew Dugan Russia & Mary Kaslofski Russia
DUGAN, Robert Edward, Oct 19 1925 Sex:M Child# 2 John Dugan Hudson, NH & Esther Canavan Dorchester, MA
DUGAN, Ruth Esther, Apr 9 1922 Sex:F Child# 1 John Daniel Dugan Nashua, NH & Esther Ruth Canavan Dorchester, MA
DUGAS, Eveline Germaine, Aug 17 1915 Sex:F Child# 1 Charles Dugas Canada & Zelia Sirois Canada
DUGAS, John William, May 25 1933 Sex:M Child# 2 John Dugas Worcester, MA & Irene Calawa Nashua, NH
DUGAS, Joseph Edmond, Jun 8 1923 Sex:M Child# 5 Charles Dugas Canada & Exilia Sirois Canada
DUGAS, Marie, Sep 19 1902 Sex:F Child# 3 Joseph Dugas Canada & Olivine Comtois Canada
DUGAS, Marion Katherine, Dec 10 1932 Sex:F Child# 2 William E Dugas Mass & Cecilla Gaskin Oregon
DUGAS, Mary Lorraine, Feb 16 1918 Sex:F Child# 3 Charles H Dugas Canada & Zelia Sirois Canada
DUGAS, Maurice Edgar, Aug 16 1919 Sex:M Child# 4 Charles Dugas Canada & Ezilia Sirois Canada
DUGAS, Normand Paul, May 8 1925 Sex:M Child# 6 Charles Dugas Canada & Zelia Sirois Canada
DUGAS, Robert Roland, Sep 28 1916 Sex:M Child# 2 Charles Dugas Canada & Zelia Sirois Canada
DUGAS, Wilfrid, Aug 29 1905 Sex:M Child# 4 Joseph Dugas Canada & Josephine Comtois Canada
DUGIN, May, Apr 5 1904 Sex:F Child# 7 John Dugin Russia & Mary Kariguta Russia
DUGNAY, Joseph Alexandre, Jun 21 1899 Sex:M Child# 5 William Dugnay Canada & Delima Courcy Canada
DUGNAY, Joseph Olivier, Feb 17 1898 Sex:M Child# 4 William Dugnay Canada & Delima Coursil Canada
DUGNAY, William, Nov 12 1900 Sex:M Child# 6 William Dugnay Canada & Delima Coursy Canada
DUGRE, Alice Yvette, Dec 26 1910 Sex:F Child# 2 George Dugre Canada & Alma Charpentier Canada
DUGRE, Armande, Aug 15 1911 Sex:F Child# 4 Eugene Dugre Canada & Georgianna Houle Canada
DUGRE, Beatrice Lucille, Apr 30 1907 Sex:F Child# 3 Eugene Dugre Canada & Georgianna Houle Canada
DUGRE, Josephine Rose A R, Dec 2 1908 Sex:F Child# 1 George Dugre Canada & Alma Charpentier Canada
DUGRE, Roland George, Jul 13 1905 Sex:M Child# 2 Eugene Dugre Canada & Georgiana Houle Canada
DUGRE, Wilfrid L, Dec 15 1900 Sex:M Child# 1 Eugene Dugre Canada & Georgiana Houle Canada
DUGRES, Marie A, Jun 5 1892 Sex:F Child# 1 Arthur Dugres Canada & Caroline Ouellette Canada
DUGUAY, Helene, Jan 19 1895 Sex:F Child# 2 William Duguay Canada & Delima Courcey Canada
DUGUAY, James William, Mar 12 1896 Sex:M Child# 3 William Duguay Canada & Delima Courcy Canada
DUGUAY, Joseph Adelard, Dec 8 1893 Sex:M Child# 1 William Duguay Canada & Delima Courcy Canada
DUGUAY, Marie Flavie, Mar 20 1896 Sex:F Child# 2 Victor Duguay Canada & Flavie Gagnon Canada
DUGUE, Bernardette, Aug 21 1893 Sex:F Child# 2 Arthur Dugue Canada & Caroline Ouellette Canada
DUHAIME, Jules, Mar 6 1904 Sex:M Child# 1 Zoel Duhaime Canada & Eugenie Moreau Canada
DUHAMEL, Alice Evangeline, Oct 22 1900 Sex:F Child# 8 Charles Duhamel Canada & Jessie Malhoit Nashua, NH
DUHAMEL, Antoinette A, Dec 19 1909 Sex:F Child# 13 Charles Duhamel Canada & Jessie Malhiot US
DUHAMEL, Bernadette Gabrielle, Mar 22 1924 Sex:F Child# 7 Rosario Duhamel Canada & Eugene Walker Nashua, NH
DUHAMEL, Charles Wilfrid, Apr 27 1896 Sex:M Child# 4 Charles Duhamel Canada & Lessie Malhoit Nashua, NH
DUHAMEL, Emile Ernest, Aug 11 1906 Sex:M Child# 11 Charles Duhamel Canada & Jessie Malhoit Nashua, NH
DUHAMEL, Eva, Jun 27 1893 Sex:F Child# 3 Charles Duhamel Canada & Jessie Malhoit Nashua, NH
DUHAMEL, George Robert, Nov 2 1927 Sex:M Child# 6 R M Duhamel Canada & Eugenie Walker Nashua, NH
DUHAMEL, Germaine Olivette, Dec 20 1913 Sex:F Child# 15 Charles Duhamel Canada & Jessie Malhoit US
DUHAMEL, Henri Alfred, Sep 30 1894 Sex:M Child# 4 Charles Duhamel Canada & Jessie Malhiot Nashua, NH
DUHAMEL, Jos Julien Richard, Oct 30 1928 Sex:M Child# 7 R M Duhamel Canada & Eugenie Walker Canada
DUHAMEL, Laurette Rita, Jul 9 1934 Sex:F Child# 4 Charles W Duhamel Nashua, NH & Lilliane Anctil Nashua, NH
DUHAMEL, Laurette Ruth, Nov 19 1921 Sex:F Child# 2 R M Duhamel Canada & Eugenie Walker Nashua, NH
DUHAMEL, Leo, Apr 25 1899 Sex:M Child# 7 Charles Duhamel Canada & Jessie Malhoit Nashua, NH
DUHAMEL, Loraine Camile, Jul 31 1924 Sex:F Child# 1 Wilfred Duhamel Nashua, NH & Lillian Anctil Nashua, NH
DUHAMEL, Louis Alphonse, Nov 3 1897 Sex:M Child# 6 Charles Duhamel Canada & Jessie Malhoit Nashua, NH
DUHAMEL, Lucille, Oct 18 1919 Sex:F Child# 2 Leo Duhamel Nashua, NH & Eva Fouquette Nashua, NH
DUHAMEL, Madeline Jeannette, Jan 27 1931 Sex:F Child# 3 Wilfred Duhamel Nashua, NH & Lillian Anctil Nashua, NH
DUHAMEL, Marie Alida, Nov 24 1908 Sex:F Child# 12 Charles Duhamel Canada & Jessie Malhoit US
DUHAMEL, Marie Jeanne, Sep 24 1904 Sex:F Child# 10 Charles Duhamel Canada & Jessie Malhoit Nashua, NH
DUHAMEL, Philip Maurice, Jun 19 1926 Sex:M Child# 5 Rosario Duhamel Canada & Eugenie Walker Nashua, NH
DUHAMEL, Rosario Paul, Jan 4 1923 Sex:M Child# 3 Rosario Duhamel Canada & Eugenie Walker Nashua, NH
DUHAMEL, Sicille Albina, Sep 17 1902 Sex:F Child# Charles Duhamel Canada & Jessie Malhiot Nashua, NH
DUHAMEL, Theodore Roger, Aug 11 1911 Sex:M Child# 14 Charles Duhamel Canada & Jessie Malhoit US
DUHAMEL, Unknown, Dec 28 1890 Sex:M Child# 1 Charles Duhamel Canada & Jessie Malhoit Nashua, NH
DUHAMEL, Unknown, Oct 20 1926 Sex:F Child# 2 Wilfred Duhamel Nashua, NH & Lillian Anctil Nashua, NH
DUHARNCH, Anna Adilia, May 26 1892 Sex:F Child# 2 Charles Duharnch Canada & Jessie Malhoit Nashua, NH
DUKETT, Norma June, Jun 13 1899 Sex:F Child# Jason M Dukett Peru, NY & Martha Kelsey Chazy, NY
DULUDE, Adrien Wilfrid, Apr 8 1907 Sex:M Child# 9 Joseph Dulude Canada & Alexina Scott Canada
DULUDE, Agnes Andrea, Apr 14 1896 Sex:F Child# 2 J B Dulude Canada & Mary Richard Nashua, NH
DULUDE, Albert, Sep 14 1896 Sex:M Child# 5 Joseph Dulude Canada & Exina Scott Canada
DULUDE, Blanche, Oct 27 1897 Sex:F Child# 3 Jean B Dulude Canada & Marie Richard Nashua, NH
DULUDE, Clara, May 20 1889 Sex:F Child# 13 Joseph Dulude Canada & Agnes Bernier Canada
DULUDE, Eva R, Mar 9 1894 Sex:F Child# 15 Joseph Dulude Canada & Agnes Bernier Canada
DULUDE, Evremond, Mar 27 1893 Sex:M Child# 3 Joseph Dulude Canada & Exina Scott Canada
DULUDE, Georgiana B, Mar 28 1900 Sex:F Child# 3 J B Dulude Canada & Mary Richard Nashua, NH
DULUDE, Jos Pierre Rob Ern, Apr 29 1916 Sex:M Child# 1 Albert Dulude Nashua, NH & Adele Levesque Canada
DULUDE, Joseph Alixis, Jun 7 1892 Sex:M Child# Joseph Dulude Canada & Agnes Bernier Canada

DULUDE, Joseph J B, Apr 28 1895 Sex:M Child# 4 Joseph Dulude Canada & Exina Scott Canada
DULUDE, Joseph Jean Roger, Feb 24 1918 Sex:M Child# 1 Joseph Dulude Nashua, NH & Alma Boucher Canada
DULUDE, M Jeanne R Alice, May 13 1919 Sex:F Child# 2 Ernest Dulude Nashua, NH & Delia Levesque Canada
DULUDE, M Marguerite Jul, May 19 1919 Sex:F Child# 2 Evermont Dulude Nashua, NH & Clarinthe LaFrance Canada
DULUDE, Victor Emery, Jan 4 1909 Sex:M Child# 10 Joseph Dulude Canada & Exina Scott Canada
DUMAINE, Adrienne, Jan 22 1922 Sex:F Child# 1 Henry C Dumaine Nashua, NH & Pauline Murphy Nashua, NH
DUMAINE, Alfred Ernest, Sep 11 1919 Sex:M Child# 1 Ernest Dumaine Nashua, NH & Edith Boucher Canada
DUMAINE, Ernest Aswald, May 9 1896 Sex:M Child# 13 J B Dumaine Canada & Octavie Burque Canada
DUMAINE, Gerard Osias, Aug 6 1920 Sex:M Child# 6 Arthur Dumaine US & Valeria Gauthier Canada
DUMAINE, Helene Gertrude, Apr 6 1908 Sex:F Child# 2 John B Dumaine Canada & Lena Levack Nashua, NH
DUMAINE, Henry, Dec 4 1924 Sex:M Child# 2 Henry C Dumaine Nashua, NH & Pauline Murphy Nashua, NH
DUMAINE, Honorius, Jul 29 1889 Sex:M Child# 9 Jean B Dumaine Canada & Octavie Burque Canada
DUMAINE, Jean Arthur O, Oct 27 1904 Sex:M Child# 2 J Arthur Dumaine US & Valerie Gauthier Canada
DUMAINE, Joseph L E, Jun 28 1891 Sex:M Child# 10 Bt Dumaine Canada & Octavie Burque Canada
DUMAINE, Marie Louise A, Apr 8 1907 Sex:F Child# 3 J Arthur Dumaine US & Valerie Gauthier Canada
DUMAINE, Marie Valerie, Mar 16 1924 Sex:F Child# 7 Arthur Dumaine Nashua, NH & Valerie Gauthier Canada
DUMAINE, Octavie Yvonne, May 24 1903 Sex:F Child# 1 Arthur Dumaine Nashua, NH & Valerie Gauthier Canada
DUMAINE, Ralph, Dec 27 1901 Sex:M Child# 1 Jean B Dumaine Canada & Leona G Levack Nashua, NH
DUMAINE, Roger Eugene, Dec 12 1921 Sex:M Child# 2 Ernest Dumaine Nashua, NH & Edith Boucher Canada
DUMAINE, Unknown, Sep 12 1927 Sex:F Child# 1 Emile Dumaine Nashua, NH & Alice Lavoie Manchester, NH
DUMAINE, Victoria, Sep 13 1894 Sex:F Child# 12 J B Dumaine Canada & Octavie Burque Canada
DUMAINE, William Burque, Sep 26 1898 Sex:M Child# 14 J B Dumaine Canada & Octavie Burque Canada
DUMAINE, Winceslas, Sep 27 1892 Sex:M Child# 11 Jean Bte Dumaine Canada & Octave Burque Canada
DUMAINE, Yvette Alice Delia, Aug 16 1929 Sex:F Child# 2 Emile Dumaine Nashua, NH & Alice Lavoie Manchester, NH
DUMAIS, Alfred Thomas, Oct 20 1894 Sex:M Child# 2 Louis Dumais Canada & Exilda Moreau Canada
DUMAIS, Bertrand, Oct 1 1935 Sex:M Child# 6 Charles Dumais Canada & Rose Levesque Canada
DUMAIS, Charles Roger, Aug 25 1927 Sex:M Child# 4 Charles Dumais Canada & Rose Levesque Canada
DUMAIS, Denis Gerald, Aug 11 1919 Sex:M Child# 4 Jean Bte Dumais Canada & Eugenie Simard Canada
DUMAIS, Earnest Camille, Dec 31 1917 Sex:M Child# 3 Louis A Dumais Nashua, NH & Florina Desmarais Nashua, NH
DUMAIS, Frances Theresa, Jan 16 1927 Sex:F Child# 9 John B Dumais Canada & Eugenie Simard Canada
DUMAIS, George Joseph, Dec 26 1913 Sex:M Child# 2 George Dumais Canada & Annie St Martin Canada
DUMAIS, Gilbert, Jan 11 1932 Sex:M Child# 5 Charles Dumais Canada & Rose Levesque Canada
DUMAIS, J Jean Bte Theodore, Jun 2 1915 Sex:M Child# 1 Jean Bte Dumais Canada & Eugenie Simard Canada
DUMAIS, Jean Paul, Jan 23 1934 Sex:M Child# 12 J Bte Dumais Canada & Eugenie Simard Canada
DUMAIS, Jean Pauline, Jan 10 1926 Sex:F Child# 3 Charles Dumais Canada & Rose Levesque Canada
DUMAIS, Jeannette R S, Apr 29 1920 Sex:F Child# 4 Louis Dumais Nashua, NH & Florilda Desmarais Nashua, NH
DUMAIS, Jos Robert Harve, Jul 20 1916 Sex:M Child# 3 George Dumais Canada & Annie St Martin Canada
DUMAIS, Joseph, Feb 4 1915 Sex:M Child# 4 Louis Dumais Nashua, NH & Florida Desmarais Nashua, NH
DUMAIS, Joseph Achille, Aug 22 1912 Sex:M Child# 1 George Dumais Canada & Annie St Martin Canada
DUMAIS, Joseph Alfred, Jun 9 1893 Sex:M Child# 10 Honore Dumais Canada & Elumina Dionne Canada
DUMAIS, Joseph Florien, Apr 8 1924 Sex:M Child# 7 George Dumais Canada & Annie St Martin Canada
DUMAIS, Joseph Roger Lucien, Jun 9 1918 Sex:M Child# 4 George Dumais Canada & Annie St Martin Canada
DUMAIS, Jules Richard, Mar 21 1931 Sex:M Child# 11 Jean Bte Dumais Canada & Eugenie Simard Canada
DUMAIS, Lorette Camille, May 26 1925 Sex:F Child# 7 J Bte Dumais Canada & Eugenie Simard Canada
DUMAIS, Louis Augustin, May 16 1892 Sex:M Child# 1 Louis Dumais Canada & Exilda Moreau Canada
DUMAIS, Marie Alberta, Jan 3 1897 Sex:F Child# 3 Louis Dumais Canada & Exilda Mareau Canada
DUMAIS, Marie Colette, Dec 18 1920 Sex:F Child# 5 J B Dumais Canada & Eugenie Simard Canada
DUMAIS, Marie E, Dec 7 1889 Sex:F Child# 1 Paul Dumais Canada & Phebee Bergeron Canada
DUMAIS, Marie Irene, Mar 9 1920 Sex:F Child# 5 George Dumais Canada & Annie St Martin Canada
DUMAIS, Marie Olivene, Oct 4 1921 Sex:F Child# 6 George Dumais Canada & Annie St Martin Canada
DUMAIS, Marie Paule, Oct 12 1917 Sex:F Child# 3 J B Dumais Canada & Eugenie Simard Canada
DUMAIS, Marie Rita, May 9 1928 Sex:F Child# 9 George Dumais Canada & Annie St Martin Canada
DUMAIS, Marie Theresa Lucille, Jun 12 1926 Sex:F Child# 8 George Dumais Canada & Annie St Martin Canada
DUMAIS, Noela Odette, Dec 25 1928 Sex:F Child# 10 L B Dumais Canada & A Simard Canada
DUMAIS, Ovide, Jul 25 1891 Sex:M Child# 14 Honore Dumais Canada & Lamina Dionne Canada
DUMAIS, Roger, Mar 7 1935 Sex:M Child# 1 Alphonse Dumais Canada & Irene Paradis Nashua, NH
DUMAIS, Rosanna, Aug 30 1889 Sex:F Child# 13 Honore Dumais Canada & Lumina Dionne Canada
DUMAIS, Unknown, Mar 13 1892 Sex:F Child# 15 Honore Dumais Canada & Lomena Dionne Canada Stillborn
DUMAIS, Victor Daniel, Jun 1 1916 Sex:M Child# 2 Jean Bap Dumais Canada & Eugenie Simard Canada
DUMAIS, Yolande Rose, Aug 31 1924 Sex:F Child# 2 Charles Dumais Canada & Rose D Ouellette Canada
DUMAS, Albert Raymond, Nov 20 1933 Sex:M Child# 4 William Dumas Canada & Rose Goudreau Nashua, NH
DUMAS, Aurele Maurice, Oct 22 1916 Sex:M Child# 2 Louis Dumas Nashua, NH & Houlda Desmarais Nashua, NH
DUMAS, Beatrice Emma, Nov 15 1898 Sex:F Child# 4 Treffle Dumas Canada & Elmire Masse Canada
DUMAS, Claire Rachel, Jan 9 1932 Sex:F Child# 3 William Dumas Canada & Rose A Gaudreau Nashua, NH
DUMAS, Edward, Sep 27 1913 Sex:M Child# 1 Leon Dumas Nashua, NH & Alice Brennan Nashua, NH
DUMAS, Eva, Apr 3 1910 Sex:F Child# 3 Arthur Dumas E Douglass, MA & Delia Derosiers Canada
DUMAS, Francis Theresa, Aug 19 1928 Sex:F Child# 1 William Dumas Canada & R A Goudreau Nashua, NH
DUMAS, Germaine Olivette, Jan 31 1935 Sex:F Child# 5 William Dumas Canada & Rosanna Goudreau Nashua, NH
DUMAS, Jeannie Florence, Aug 21 1929 Sex:F Child# 2 William Dumas Canada & Rosanna Gaudreau Nashua, NH
DUMAS, M Rita Henrietta, Sep 13 1922 Sex:F Child# 6 John B Dumas Canada & Eugenie Simard Canada
DUMAS, Madeleine, Nov 11 1923 Sex:F Child# 7 J B Dumas Canada & Josephine Simard Canada
DUMAS, Marguerite E, Dec 20 1901 Sex:F Child# 10 Napoleon Dumas Canada & Parmela Galipeau Canada
DUMAS, Maria Eliza, Jan 7 1890 Sex:F Child# 3 Napoleon Dumas Douglas, MA & Pamelia Galipeau Montreal, Canada

DUMAS, Marie Annette, May 27 1923 Sex:F Child# 1 Charles Dumas Canada & Rose Levesque Canada
DUMAS, Marie Jeanne Rita, Mar 15 1934 Sex:F Child# 10 George Dumas Canada & Annie St Martin Canada
DUMAS, Marie Rose Aldea, Jan 8 1908 Sex:F Child# 2 Arthur Dumas E Douglass, MA & Aldea Desrosiers Canada
DUMAS, Maurice Arthur, Sep 20 1933 Sex:M Child# 1 Arthur Dumas Canada & Alpheda Lupien Manchester, NH
DUMAS, Napoleon Remi, Sep 1 1906 Sex:M Child# 1 Arthur Dumas E Douglass, MA & Delia Desrosiers Canada
DUMAS, Philomene Leona, Jul 10 1894 Sex:F Child# 6 Napoleon Dumas Mass & Pomela Galipeau Montreal, Canada
DUMAS, Unknown, Mar 18 1928 Sex:M Child# 1 Gilbert Dumas
DUMESNIL, Henri, Nov 1 1896 Sex:M Child# 3 Henri Dumesnil US & Adeline Mallette US
DUMONT, Albert Gerard, Oct 25 1917 Sex:M Child# 13 Gonzague Dumont Canada & Ernestine Pelletier Canada
DUMONT, Albina Laurette, Nov 13 1906 Sex:F Child# 10 Frederic Dumont Canada & Celina Dufour Canada
DUMONT, Alma Cecile, Jun 1 1915 Sex:F Child# 12 Gonzague Dumont Canada & Ernestine Pelletier Canada
DUMONT, Aurelie Dolores, Jun 19 1900 Sex:F Child# 1 Aime Dumont Canada & Aurelia Bissonnette Canada
DUMONT, Bessie Haskins, Mar 12 1924 Sex:F Child# 4 Joseph Dumont Canada & Bessie Haskins Hunt, VT
DUMONT, Blanche Irene, Mar 15 1907 Sex:F Child# 1 Aime Dumont Canada & Imelda Leblanc Canada
DUMONT, Cecile Lorraine, Mar 30 1931 Sex:F Child# 1 Ludger Dumont Canada & Aurore Marquis Canada
DUMONT, Corinne Leontine, May 28 1904 Sex:F Child# 8 Ferdinand Dumont Canada & Celina Dufour Canada
DUMONT, Elgin, Mar 3 1909 Sex:M Child# 2 Aime Dumont Canada & Imelda Leblanc Canada
DUMONT, Ernest, Jun 7 1930 Sex:M Child# 1 Wilfred Dumont Canada & Artillia Laquerre Nashua, NH
DUMONT, Jeannette Irene, Mar 17 1920 Sex:F Child# 1 Alfred Dumont Nashua, NH & Bertha Lefebvre Brandon, NY
DUMONT, Joseph, Aug 2 1920 Sex:M Child# 15 Gonzague Dumont Canada & Ernestine Pelletier Canada
DUMONT, Joseph A Telesphon, Jan 20 1900 Sex:M Child# 6 Ferdina Dumont Canada & Celina Dufour Canada
DUMONT, Joseph Allen, Jan 23 1927 Sex:M Child# 3 Joseph Dumont Canada & Elizabeth Haskins Huntington, VT
DUMONT, Joseph Robert, Oct 9 1933 Sex:M Child# 2 Ferd Dumont Canada & A Charron Manchester, NH
DUMONT, Joseph Robert Omer, Mar 9 1912 Sex:M Child# 11 Ferdinand Dumont Canada & Celina Duford Canada
DUMONT, Leo Albert, Jun 12 1922 Sex:M Child# 1 Joseph F Dumont Canada & Bernadette Bonnette Nashua, NH
DUMONT, Louis, Aug 23 1894 Sex:M Child# 2 Ferdinand Dumont Canada & Celina Dufour Canada
DUMONT, Lucille Emilienne, Mar 8 1924 Sex:F Child# 3 Alfred Dumont Nashua, NH & Bertha LeBoeuf Brandon, NY
DUMONT, Lucille Therese, Jun 2 1925 Sex:F Child# 2 Joseph Dumont Canada & Bessie Haskins Huntington, VT
DUMONT, Maria Irene C, Oct 7 1905 Sex:F Child# 9 Ferdinand Dumont Canada & Celina Dufour Canada
DUMONT, Marie Blanche, Sep 28 1901 Sex:F Child# 7 Ferdina Dumont Canada & Celina Dufour Canada
DUMONT, Marie Claire Therese, Aug 12 1923 Sex:F Child# 2 Joseph Dumont Canada & Bernadette Bonette Nashua, NH
DUMONT, Marie Diana, May 15 1899 Sex:F Child# 4 Joseph Dumont Canada & Aurelie Ouellette Canada
DUMONT, Marie Eva C, Dec 19 1896 Sex:F Child# 7 Antoine Dumont Canada & Priscille Guerette Canada
DUMONT, Marie Lea, Nov 14 1895 Sex:F Child# 3 Ferdina Dumont Canada & Celina Dufour Canada
DUMONT, Marie Lucille, Jun 3 1934 Sex:F Child# 4 Wilfred Dumont Canada & Arthilia Lacquerre Nashua, NH
DUMONT, Marie Phyllis, May 3 1932 Sex:F Child# 1 F Dumont Canada & Angeline Charron Manchester, NH
DUMONT, Mary Rachel Therese, Mar 1 1932 Sex:F Child# 1 (No Parents Listed)
DUMONT, Normand, Feb 11 1935 Sex:M Child# 3 Ferdinand Dumont Canada & Angeline Chagnon Manchester, NH
DUMONT, Omelina Paula, Apr 11 1897 Sex:F Child# 11 Ferdinand Dumont Canada & Pomela St Pierre Canada
DUMONT, Paul, Mar 30 1933 Sex:M Child# 3 Wilfrid Dumont Canada & A Laquerre Nashua, NH
DUMONT, Rene Octave, Aug 16 1935 Sex:M Child# 3 Octave Dumont Lawrence, MA & Obeline Goyett Nashua, NH
DUMONT, Rita Angelina, Jul 22 1934 Sex:F Child# 2 Octave Dumont Lawrence, MA & Oveline Goyette Nashua, NH
DUMONT, Sylvio Alphonse, Jul 22 1912 Sex:M Child# 11 Gonzague Dumont Canada & Ernestine Pelletier Canada
DUMONTE, Wilfrid, Jan 21 1932 Sex:M Child# 2 Wilfrid Dumont Canada & Artillia Laquerre Nashua, NH
DUMONTE, Unknown, Nov 19 1899 Sex:F Child# 1 George Dumonte Canada & Mamie Delorie US
DUMOULIN, Irene Celina, Feb 12 1904 Sex:F Child# 6 Frank Dumoulin Vermont & Josephine Gregoire NH
DUNBAR, Clarence Tolser, Jan 6 1910 Sex:M Child# 2 Alfred F Dunbar Arlington, MA & Lenetta G Tolser Cochituate, MA
DUNBAR, Leonard Alfred, Oct 6 1907 Sex:M Child# 1 Alfred F Dunbar Arlington, MA & Lauretta G Lober Cochituate, MA
DUNBAR, Phyllis Mary, Nov 10 1924 Sex:F Child# 1 (No Parents Listed)
DUNBAR, Ruby Louise, Aug 4 1913 Sex:F Child# 3 Alfred F Dunbar Arlington, MA & Lanetta Loker Cochituate, MA
DUNCAN, Archibald, Oct 8 1907 Sex:M Child# 6 Alfred J Duncan Chatham, England & Edith Duncan Kent, England
DUNCAN, Richard Edward, Feb 6 1930 Sex:M Child# 4 Bertram A Duncan Lynn, MA & Bertha B Emerson Lynn, MA
DUNCKLEE, Charles Franklyn, Nov 5 1930 Sex:M Child# 7 Merton Duncklee Grafton, NH & Clare Harvey Nashua, NH
DUNCKLEE, Frank Harland, Apr 25 1892 Sex:M Child# 4 Eugene P Duncklee Hollis & Tina Snyder Ohio
DUNCKLEE, Irving Leslie, Jan 22 1911 Sex:M Child# 2 Merton L Duncklee Enfield, NH & Clara L Harvey Nashua, NH
DUNCKLEE, Malcolm Chester, Apr 12 1927 Sex:M Child# 3 Ralph Duncklee Brookline, NH & Mildred Boles Greenfield, NH
DUNCKLEE, Marion Beatrice, Oct 15 1905 Sex:F Child# 3 Leroy W Duncklee Nashua, NH & Emma L Adams Nashua, NH
DUNCKLEE, Merton Leslie, Jun 26 1919 Sex:M Child# 4 Merton L Duncklee Grafton, NH & Clara Harvey Nashua, NH
DUNCKLEE, Robert Francis, Jun 14 1899 Sex:M Child# 1 Leroy W Duncklee Nashua, NH & Emma L Adams Nashua, NH
DUNCKLEE, Shirley Maude, May 21 1927 Sex:F Child# 5 Merton Duncklee Grafton, NH & Clara Harvey Nashua, NH
DUNCKLEE, Thelma Elizabeth, Feb 13 1926 Sex:F Child# 2 Ralph Duncklee Brookline, NH & Mildred Boles Greenfield, NH
DUNCKLEE, Unknown, Jul 7 1888 Sex: Child# 3 Eugene R Duncklee Hollis, NH & Christine Snyder Berneen, OH
DUNCKLEE, Unknown, Dec 25 1889 Sex:F Child# 4 Eugene B Duncklee Hollis, NH & Christine Snyder Benecke, OH
DUNCKLEE, Unknown, Dec 10 1894 Sex:F Child# 1 Ozro J Duncklee Brookline, NH & Lena J Jones Milford, NH
DUNCKLEE, Virginia Louise, Sep 24 1929 Sex:F Child# 6 Merton L Duncklee Grafton, NH & Clara Harvey Nashua, NH
DUNCKLEE, William Adams, Sep 10 1910 Sex:M Child# 4 Leroy W Duncklee Nashua, NH & Emma L Adams Nashua, NH
DUNHAM, Barbara Natalie, Nov 12 1927 Sex:F Child# 1 G H Dunham Calais, ME & Daisy LaBounty Canada
DUNHAM, Dorothy Madeline, Dec 20 1908 Sex:F Child# 2 John W Dunham Grand Manan, ME & Essie Scott Tower Hill
DUNKLEE, Herbert Harvey, Aug 31 1918 Sex:M Child# 4 Walter C Dunklee Hollis, NH & Elzbeth A Kenniston Newton
DUNLAP, Ruth Frances, May 19 1913 Sex:F Child# 3 Fred A Dunlap Salisbury, NH & Abbie F Shaw Salisbury, NH
DUNLAP, Unknown, Apr 3 1899 Sex:M Child# 1 Albert Dunlap Nashua, NH & Sarah Sullivan Nashua, NH
DUNLAP, Virginia Holt, Aug 1 1910 Sex:F Child# 2 J Archibald Dunlap Nashua, NH & Olla L Holt Nashua, NH
DUNLAVITCH, Unknown, Nov 21 1923 Sex:F Child# 3 Joseph Dunlavitch Poland & Mary Halnewicz Poland

DUNN, Francis Dennis, May 14 1924 Sex:M Child# 4 Christopher Dunn Ireland & Agnes McMann Ireland
DUNN, Jaclyn Marsh, Dec 27 1919 Sex:F Child# 1 Harold C Dunn Brockton, MA & Ruth E Marsh Nashua, NH
DUNN, Margaret Mary, Apr 26 1920 Sex:F Child# 2 Christ H Dunn Ireland & Agnes Mann Ireland
DUNN, Marie Lena, May 31 1906 Sex:F Child# 2 Alfred Dunn NH & Louisa Halie CT
DUNN, Mary Cushing, Dec 9 1922 Sex:F Child# 2 Harold C Dunn Brockton, MA & Ruth E March Nashua, NH
DUNN, Sadie Christina, Dec 16 1890 Sex:F Child# 2 Bernerd J Dunn Worcester, MA & Lizzie Lowney Ireland
DUNN, Thomas Andrew, May 23 1923 Sex:M Child# 3 Christopher H Dunn Ireland & Agnes Mann Ireland
DUNN, Unknown, Aug 11 1887 Sex:F Child# 1 C E Dunn Maine & Abbie M Littleton
DUNNE, Christopher Henry, Jul 16 1926 Sex:M Child# 5 C H Dunne Ireland & Brigid A Mann Ireland
DUPELL, Frank Augustus, Oct 31 1896 Sex:M Child# 5 John Dupell Redford, NY & Addie Porter Carthage, NY
DUPERE, Joseph Albert O, May 3 1930 Sex:M Child# 1 Edward Dupere Canada & Helene Boucher Nashua, NH
DUPEREZ, Marie A L, Feb 8 1892 Sex:F Child# 2 John Duperez Canada & Emma Jacques Canada
DUPLISSE, Mabel Addie, Jul 3 1917 Sex:F Child# 2 Raymond Duplisse Nashua, NH & Addie Nashua, NH
DUPLISSE, Raymond H, Nov 25 1914 Sex:M Child# 1 Raymond H Duplisse Nashua, NH & Addie Elsen Nashua, NH
DUPLISSE, Richard Earle, Dec 29 1918 Sex:M Child# 3 Raymond Duplisse Nashua, NH & Addie Alfsen Nashua, NH
DUPLISSIE, Ralph Aldrich, Feb 8 1921 Sex:M Child# 4 Raymond Duplissie Nashua, NH & Addie Alfsen Nashua, NH
DUPONT, Adelard Lucien, Aug 5 1925 Sex:M Child# 1 Adelard Dupont Canada & Belzymis Couture Canada
DUPONT, Adolphe D, Dec 8 1895 Sex:M Child# 2 Adolphe Dupont Canada & Cordelia Guenette Canada
DUPONT, Aurore E, Feb 10 1900 Sex:F Child# 5 Adolphe Dupont Canada & Cordelia Guenette Canada
DUPONT, Cordelia, Feb 13 1894 Sex:F Child# 1 Adolphe Dupont Canada & Cordelia Guenette Canada
DUPONT, Eileen Margaret, Mar 31 1931 Sex:F Child# 2 Wilfred Dupont Nashua, NH & Germaine Duval Nashua, NH
DUPONT, Francois Xavier L, Aug 25 1908 Sex:M Child# 6 Francois X Dupont Canada & Corine Salvail Fall River, MA
DUPONT, George Oswald, Jun 25 1897 Sex:M Child# 12 Isaac Dupont Canada & Isilda Biron Canada
DUPONT, Germaine Lucille, Aug 23 1929 Sex:F Child# 1 Wilfrid Dupont Nashua, NH & Germaine Duval Nashua, NH
DUPONT, Henry Gerald, Jun 15 1935 Sex:M Child# 1 Adelard Dupont Nashua, NH & Yvonne Levesque Freemont, NH
DUPONT, Jeanne Lucille, Apr 8 1924 Sex:F Child# 3 Leo Dupont Nashua, NH & Jeanne Laroche Dover, NH
DUPONT, Joseph, May 28 1928 Sex:M Child# 7 Leon Dupont Canada & Alice Bernier Canada
DUPONT, Joseph A, Sep 11 1903 Sex:M Child# 3 Francois X Dupont Canada & Corine Salvail Fall River, MA
DUPONT, Joseph Albani A, Jan 26 1909 Sex:M Child# 9 Joseph Dupont Canada & Rosalie Dumont Canada
DUPONT, Joseph O A, Jan 17 1902 Sex:M Child# 2 F X Dupont Canada & Corinne Salvail Fall River, MA
DUPONT, Joseph P R, Oct 22 1906 Sex:M Child# 5 Francois X Dupont Canada & Corinne Salvail Fall River, MA
DUPONT, Leo, Apr 11 1897 Sex:M Child# 2 Adlophe Dupont Canada & Cordelia Guerrette Canada
DUPONT, Leon, Nov 7 1905 Sex:M Child# 4 Francis C Dupont Canada & Corinne Salvail Fall River, MA
DUPONT, Leonard Ronald, May 22 1926 Sex:M Child# 1 Adrien Dupont Warren, RI & Adrienne Rivieres Nashua, NH
DUPONT, Lionel, Jan 27 1923 Sex:M Child# 3 Joseph Dupont Canada & Martha St Laurent Canada
DUPONT, Lucienne Irene, Feb 25 1904 Sex:F Child# 1 Achille Dupont Canada & E Desroleau Canada
DUPONT, Marie, Dec 29 1920 Sex:F Child# 10 Hector Dupont Manchester, NH & Florida Belanger Canada
DUPONT, Marie Lorraine Corin, Dec 14 1932 Sex:F Child# 3 Wilfrid Dupont Nashua, NH & Germaine Duval Nashua, NH
DUPONT, Marie Phedora, Dec 16 1892 Sex:F Child# 14 Alarie Dupont Canada & Pamelia Belanger Canada
DUPONT, Melendy, May 6 1898 Sex:F Child# 3 Adolphe Dupont Canada & Cordelia Guerette Canada
DUPONT, Normand Elphege, May 9 1927 Sex:M Child# 6 Leon Dupont Canada & Alice Bernier Lowell, MA
DUPONT, Pierre, May 28 1928 Sex:M Child# 8 Leon Dupont Canada & Alice Bernier Canada
DUPONT, Roger Henry Ernest, Jun 2 1928 Sex:M Child# 2 Adrien Dupont Warren, RI & Adrienne Riviere Nashua, NH
DUPONT, Unknown, Sep 23 1917 Sex:F Child# 2 Louis P Dupont Canada & Amelia Murray Redford, NY
DUPONT, Unknown, Aug 4 1920 Sex:F Child# 1 Elie Dupont Manchester, NH & Delia Langelier Canada
DUPONT, Wilfrid Leon, Dec 13 1934 Sex:M Child# 4 Wilfrid Dupont Nashua, NH & Germaine Duval Nashua, NH
DUPRA, Alfred, Sep 15 1892 Sex:M Child# 10 Francois J Dupra Canada & Rosanna Leduc Canada
DUPRAS, Arthur Elie, Nov 12 1909 Sex:M Child# 1 Henry Dupras Lowell, MA & Celina Belanger Canada
DUPRAS, George, Nov 20 1888 Sex:M Child# 12 Gaten Dupras Canada & Rosanna Leduc Canada
DUPRAS, Marie A R, Mar 8 1891 Sex:F Child# 1 Victor Dupras Canada & Alphonsine Gravel Nashua, NH
DUPRAS, Mary Gloria, Dec 23 1914 Sex:F Child# 4 Henry Dupras Mass & Celina Belanger Canada
DUPRE, Andrie, Jul 14 1888 Sex:M Child# 3 Philip Dupre Sciota, NY & Harrie Jeannotte Sciota, NY
DUPRE, Blanche Aurore, Apr 19 1903 Sex:F Child# 2 Ephrem Dupre Canada & Marie L Gauthier Canada
DUPRE, Joseph Arthur, Feb 17 1911 Sex:M Child# 2 Henri Dupre Lowell, MA & Celina Belanger Canada
DUPRE, Joseph Henry, Apr 27 1908 Sex:M Child# 1 Henry Dupre Lowell, MA & Clara Desmarais Nashua, NH
DUPRE, Lester Mervin, Nov 2 1922 Sex:M Child# 2 Edward Dupre Barre, VT & Rose Archambault Nashua, NH
DUPRE, Marie Blanche A, Apr 7 1904 Sex:F Child# 7 Ephrem Dupre Canada & Marie L Gauthier Canada
DUPRE, Melina Irenee, Oct 28 1901 Sex:F Child# 1 Ephrem Dupre Canada & Marie L Gauthier Canada
DUPRE, Unknown, Jun 1 1915 Sex:M Child# 1 Thomas J Dupre Lewiston, ME & Lydia Larocque Nashua, NH Stillborn
DUPRES, Alida Palmena, Jul 22 1890 Sex:F Child# 9 Francois J Dupres Canada & Rosanna Leduc Canada
DUPRES, Arthur, Aug 27 1890 Sex:M Child# 1 Johnny Dupres Canada & Emma Jacques Canada
DUPRES, Jos Albert Roland, Sep 7 1917 Sex:M Child# 1 Albert Dupres Canada & Marianna Caouette Canada
DUPRES, Loraine Yvette, Dec 2 1920 Sex:F Child# 6 Jean Bte Dupres S Alexandria, NH & Bertha J McDonald Concord, NH
DUPRES, Marie, Jan 30 1895 Sex:F Child# 4 Victor Dupres Canada & Alphonsine Gravel Nashua, NH
DUPREY, Anna Marie, Nov 16 1932 Sex:F Child# 4 Thos J Duprey Lewiston, ME & Anna Deroche Salem, MA
DUPREY, Cecile Annette, Jan 23 1928 Sex:F Child# 2 Thomas J Duprey Lewiston, ME & Anna Deroche Salem, MA
DUPREY, Delia Evangeline, Sep 25 1902 Sex:F Child# 1 Frank Duprey Lewiston, ME & Mary Perron New York
DUPREY, Jean Elizabeth, Jun 20 1934 Sex:F Child# 6 Edward Duprey Northfield, VT & Rose Archambault Nashua, NH
DUPREY, Loraine, May 6 1928 Sex:F Child# 3 Edward Duprey Barre, VT & R Archambeault Nashua, NH
DUPREY, Louis, Oct 21 1894 Sex:M Child# 1 Louis J Duprey Manville, RI & Blanche B Stevens Nashua, NH
DUPREY, Pierre Isidore, Jan 27 1930 Sex:M Child# 3 Thomas Duprey Lewiston, ME & Anna Deroche Salem, MA
DUPREY, Rachel Madeline, Dec 29 1920 Sex:F Child# 1 Edward Duprey Barre, VT & Rose Archambault Nashua, NH
DUPREY, Richard Allen, Sep 20 1929 Sex:M Child# 1 Robert Duprey Berlin, VT & Theresa DeMontigny Nashua, NH

DUPREY, Thomas, Jul 2 1926 Sex:M Child# 1 Thomas Duprey Lewiston, ME & Anna Deroche Salem, MA
DUQUET, Adeline, Feb 19 1892 Sex:F Child# 6 Ephreme Duquet Canada & Melvina Lafrance Canada
DUQUETTE, Albert Charles, Jan 1 1924 Sex:M Child# 3 Edmond Duquette US & Merida Lariviere US
DUQUETTE, Claire Florence, Aug 1 1933 Sex:F Child# 5 Edmond Duquette Nashua, NH & Marilda Larivierre St Johns, NB
DUQUETTE, Ephrem, May 2 1893 Sex:M Child# 8 Ephrem Duquette Canada & Malvina Lafrance Canada
DUQUETTE, Evangeline, May 30 1902 Sex:F Child# 17 Ephrem Duquette Canada & Malvina Lafrance Canada
DUQUETTE, Irene Gertrude, Nov 16 1919 Sex:F Child# 3 Daniel Duquette US & Angeline Ouellette Canada
DUQUETTE, Jeanne Anne, Jun 24 1930 Sex:F Child# 1 Ephrem Duquette Nashua, NH & Jeanne Poirier Canada
DUQUETTE, Jos Alfred Henri, Mar 31 1920 Sex:M Child# 5 Valmar Duquette Canada & Marie Louise Marquis Canada
DUQUETTE, Joseph A, Jan 21 1918 Sex:M Child# 2 J Adolph Duquette Canada & Dora Quakenbush Saratoga, NY Stillborn
DUQUETTE, Joseph A Norman, Dec 11 1931 Sex:M Child# 4 Valmor Duquette Canada & Marie Louise Marquis Canada
DUQUETTE, Joseph Albert, Nov 16 1901 Sex:M Child# 8 Eugene Duquette Canada & Agnes Mongeau Canada
DUQUETTE, Joseph Eugene, Aug 21 1900 Sex:M Child# 12 Ephrem Duquette Canada & Malvina Lafrance Canada
DUQUETTE, Joseph Omer, Nov 15 1901 Sex:M Child# 7 Eugene Duquette Canada & Agnes Mongeau Canada
DUQUETTE, Juliette, Jun 17 1895 Sex:F Child# 8 Ephrem Duquette Canada & Malvina Lafrance Canada
DUQUETTE, Juliette, Apr 14 1932 Sex:F Child# 5 Edmond Duquette US & A Lariviere US  Stillborn
DUQUETTE, Juliette Mignonne, Dec 18 1906 Sex:F Child# 5 Joseph Duquette Canada & Marie Champagne Canada
DUQUETTE, Louis Hector, Jul 18 1921 Sex:M Child# 2 Edmond Duquette Nashua, NH & Marilda Lariviere St Johnsbury, VT
DUQUETTE, Marie Helena, Oct 27 1897 Sex:F Child# 13 Ephrem Duquette Canada & Malvina Lafrance Canada
DUQUETTE, Mary Ann Ang Rita, Jun 3 1920 Sex:F Child# 4 Jos Adolph Duquette Canada & Mary D Quackenbush NY
DUQUETTE, Mary Rose Juliet, May 30 1919 Sex:F Child# 2 Adolph Duquette Canada & Dora Quackenbush Crescent, NY
DUQUETTE, Norman H, May 31 1927 Sex:M Child# 4 Edmond Duquette Nashua, NH & Marita Lariviere St Johnsbury Ctr, VT
DUQUETTE, Paul Henri, Feb 17 1919 Sex:M Child# 2 Ferdinand Duquette Canada & Delvina Ouellette Nashua, NH
DUQUETTE, Philippe, Sep 23 1899 Sex:M Child# 6 Eugene Duquette Canada & Agnes Mongeau Canada
DUQUETTE, Prosper, Jun 4 1917 Sex:M Child# 1 Adolphe Duquette Canada & Doris Quackenbush Crescent, NY
DUQUETTE, Raoul, Oct 15 1916 Sex:M Child# 1 Ferdinand Duquette Canada & Delvina Ouellette Nashua, NH
DUQUETTE, Raymond, Jan 1 1918 Sex:M Child# 1 Edmond Duquette Nashua, NH & Marita Lariviere St Johnsbury, VT
DUQUETTE, Robert, Jul 15 1914 Sex:M Child# 1 Daniel Duquette Nashua, NH & Angeline Ouellette Canada
DUQUETTE, Rose Anna, Sep 22 1899 Sex:F Child# 5 Eugene Duquette Canada & Agnes Mongeau Canada
DURAND, Horace Gerard, Apr 24 1920 Sex:M Child# 5 Edouard Durand Mass & Ludivine Rondeau Canada
DURAND, Joseph, Jun 1 1911 Sex:M Child# 2 Joseph Durand Canada & Josephine Bernard Canada Stillborn
DURAND, Joseph Arthur, Jul 25 1904 Sex:M Child# 1 Joseph Durand Canada & Josephine Bernard Nashua, NH
DURAND, Joseph Robert, Sep 6 1917 Sex:M Child# 4 Edouard Durand Mass & Ludivine Rondeau Canada
DURAND, M Germaine Beatrice, Nov 29 1912 Sex:F Child# 1 Edouard Durand Mass & Ludivine Rouleau Canada
DURAND, Marie Lucienne L, Aug 12 1924 Sex:F Child# 7 Edward Durand Ware, MA & Ludwine Rondeau Canada
DURAND, Marie Yolande, Mar 5 1914 Sex:F Child# 2 Edouard Durand Mass & Ludivine Rouleau Canada
DURAND, Normand, Mar 26 1926 Sex:M Child# 4 Philip Durand Marlboro, MA & Josephine Dupres Marlboro, MA
DURAND, Thomas Paul, Nov 29 1932 Sex:M Child# 11 Edward Durand Ware, MA & Ludivine Rondeau Canada
DURAND, Unknown, Nov 8 1923 Sex:M Child# 3 Philip Durand Marlboro, MA & Josephine Dupree Marlboro, MA Stillborn
DURANT, Donald, Nov 23 1917 Sex:M Child# 2 Philippe Durant Marlboro, MA & Josephine Dupries Marlboro, MA
DURANT, Florence Mabel Am, May 3 1916 Sex:F Child# 1 Harold E Durant Pepperell, MA & Flora M Trembell Manchester
DURANT, Forest Leroy, Oct 31 1908 Sex:M Child# 3 Milo A Durant Londonderry, NH & Emma A Stearns Hollis, NH
DURANT, Harry William, Nov 19 1910 Sex:M Child# 1 Louis A Durant Petticodiac, NB & Louise M Dion Nashua, NH
DURANT, Joseph Albert L, Aug 19 1930 Sex:M Child# 10 Edward Durant Ware, MA & Ludivinne Rondeau Canada
DURANT, Joseph Edward, Jul 10 1922 Sex:M Child# 6 Edward Durant Ware, MA & Ludivine Rondeau Canada
DURANT, Joseph Ernest, Jul 19 1928 Sex:M Child# 9 Edward Durant Ware, MA & L Rondeau Canada
DURANT, Marie Ferlande Helen, Jan 16 1927 Sex:F Child# 8 Edward Durant Danbury, NH & K Rondeau Canada
DURANT, Marie Jeanne Annette, Mar 2 1928 Sex:F Child# 1 Jeffrey Durant Canada & Lena Dube Canada
DUREAU, Mary Ellen, Jan 16 1889 Sex:F Child# 3 James Dureau Ireland & Julia Gerhon Ireland
DURIVAGE, Deborah, Jun 3 1931 Sex:F Child# 1 Ellsworth Durivage Hudson, NH & Priscilla Ellis Bath, ME
DUROCHER, Harvey, Jr, Jan 4 1935 Sex:M Child# 1 Harvey Durocher Canada & Marie Pare Canada
DUROCHER, Rita Lucille, Dec 9 1933 Sex:F Child# 2 Theo Durocher Canada & Aurelle Levesque Nashua, NH
DUROCHER, Theresa Leona Janine, May 15 1929 Sex:F Child# 4 Romeo Durocher Canada & Blanche Messier Haverhill, MA
DUROCHER, Unknown, Oct 24 1932 Sex:M Child# 1 Theo Durocher Canada & Aurelle Levesque Nashua, NH Stillborn
DUROCHER, Yvette Helaire, Aug 10 1935 Sex:F Child# 3 Theode Durocher Canada & Aurelle Levesque Nashua, NH
DUROUNSKY, Albina, Feb 16 1912 Sex:F Child# 1 Antony Durounsky Russia & Mary Kellman Russia
DURRELL, Dorothy Ellsworth, Jun 5 1904 Sex:F Child# 1 William Durrell Maine & Lizzie Ellsworth Canada
DURRELL, Frederick Stephen, Jan 5 1923 Sex:M Child# 3 Fred Herbert Durrell S Braintree, MA & Marion S Lourain
DURRELL, Mabel Violet, May 3 1930 Sex:F Child# 1 Laforest W Durrell Lexington, MA & Marjorie L Smith Chelsea, MA
DURST, Unknown, Mar 17 1924 Sex:M Child# 2 Herman Durst Indiana & Gelma Lucier Maine
DUSABLON, Marcia Vitaline, Feb 21 1903 Sex:F Child# 4 Charles Dusablon Canada & Cezarie Peltier Canada
DUSABLON, Unknown, Oct 13 1903 Sex:M Child# 4 Charles Dusablon Canada & Cezarie Peltier Canada Stillborn
DUSAULT, Mary Elise, Jun 7 1935 Sex:F Child# 5 Alfred Dusault Canada & Elise Raymond Canada
DUSCHENEAU, Marie Aurore N, Nov 6 1900 Sex:F Child# 1 Emile Duscheneau Canada & Aurore Theroux Canada
DUSEAULT, Armand Ephrem, Dec 14 1918 Sex:M Child# 2 Emile Duseault Nashua, NH & Lina Duquette Nashua, NH
DUSEAULT, Irene Yvonne, Oct 24 1920 Sex:F Child# 3 Emile Duseault Nashua, NH & Lena Duquette Nashua, NH
DUSEAULT, Rose Lucille, Sep 17 1931 Sex:F Child# 4 Alfred Duseault Canada & Elise Raymond Canada
DUSKZAVITCH, William, Dec 16 1909 Sex:M Child# 2 Peter Duskzavitch Russia & Aga Grigute Russia
DUSSAULT, Emile, Jul 26 1894 Sex:M Child# 8 Joseph Dussault Canada & Elisa Chattelon Canada
DUSSAULT, Jeannette Emerilda, Mar 20 1929 Sex:F Child# 4 Emile Dussault Nashua, NH & Lina Duquette Nashua, NH
DUSSAULT, Jos Alfred Emilien, May 14 1917 Sex:M Child# 1 Joseph E Dussault NH & Marie L Duquette NH
DUSSAULT, Joseph E Gerard, May 26 1920 Sex:M Child# 1 Alfred Dussault Canada & Elise Raymond Canada
DUSSAULT, Lorette Lena, Dec 3 1935 Sex:F Child# 5 Emile Dussault Nashua, NH & Lena Duquette Nashua, NH

DUSSAULT, Marie Juliette Ida, May 25 1924 Sex:F Child# 3 Alfred Dussault Canada & Elsie Raymond Canada
DUSSEAULT, J Cyrisse Adrien, Aug 1 1921 Sex:M Child# 2 Alfred Dusseault Canada & Elise Raymond Canada
DUSTIN, Barbara Ann, Jun 12 1934 Sex:F Child# 3 Lawrence Dustin Nashua, NH & Florence Ouillette Proctor, VT
DUSTIN, Dorothy May, Dec 7 1924 Sex:F Child# 1 Augustin Dustin Salem, MA & Blanche Bonah Nashua, NH
DUSTIN, Earl Wallace, Aug 23 1921 Sex:M Child# 6 Edward O Dustin Nashua, NH & Isabel R Brown Needham, MA
DUSTIN, Erwin F, May 8 1887 Sex:M Child# 1 Timothy W Dustin Nashua, NH & Elsie J Manchester
DUSTIN, Everett L, Mar 6 1913 Sex:M Child# 2 Edward O Dustin Nashua, NH & Roberta I Brown Needham, MA
DUSTIN, Frank Elmer, Jan 13 1919 Sex:M Child# 5 Edward O Dustin Nashua, NH & Isabel Brown Needham, MA
DUSTIN, Frankie L, Oct 20 1897 Sex:M Child# 5 Ira J Dustin Hill & Lily A Brown Wilmot
DUSTIN, Irene, Apr 28 1922 Sex:F Child# 4 Perley R Dustin S Alex, NH & Bertha J MacDonald Concord, NH
DUSTIN, Lawrence, Feb 9 1911 Sex:M Child# 1 Edward Dustin Nashua, NH & Isabel Brown Needham, MA
DUSTIN, Lawrence, Jr, Jul 27 1930 Sex:M Child# 1 Lawrence Dustin Nashua, NH & Florence Ouellette Proctor, VT
DUSTIN, Lily May, Jul 25 1918 Sex:F Child# 2 Perley Dustin S Alexandria & Bertha McDonald Concord, NH
DUSTIN, Marie Jane, Sep 10 1932 Sex:F Child# 3 Walter Dustin Nashua, NH & Mary V Lavoie Methuen, MA
DUSTIN, Marion Leona, Oct 6 1916 Sex:F Child# 4 Edward O Dustin Nashua, NH & Roberta L Brown Needham, MA
DUSTIN, Paul William, Jul 25 1935 Sex:M Child# 4 Lawrence Dustin Nashua, NH & Florence Ouellette Vermont
DUSTIN, Pearl Beatrice, Oct 5 1921 Sex:F Child# 1 Walter E Dustin Nashua, NH & Virginia Lavoie Lawrence, MA
DUSTIN, Richard Lawrence, Feb 22 1932 Sex:M Child# 2 Lawrence Dustin Nashua, NH & Florence Ouellette Nashua, NH
DUSTIN, Robert Herman, Nov 26 1914 Sex:M Child# 3 Edward O Dustin Nashua, NH & Roberta I Brown Needham, MA
DUSTIN, Robert Oscar, Jul 1 1928 Sex:M Child# 2 Oscar Dustin Salem, NH & Blanche Boin Nashua, NH
DUSTIN, Ruth, Dec 3 1920 Sex:F Child# 3 Perley R Dustin Canada & Bernadette Raymond Canada
DUSTIN, Unknown, Feb 4 1888 Sex:M Child# 3 W F Dustin Antrim & Etta Batchelder Hudson
DUSTIN, Unknown, Dec 31 1898 Sex:F Child# 6 Ira J Dustin Hill & Liley Abby Brown Wilmot
DUSTIN, Unknown, Aug 18 1901 Sex:M Child# 7 Ira J Dustin Hill & Lillie A Brown Wilmot
DUSTIN, Viola Mae, Jun 23 1910 Sex:F Child# 1 Walter Dustin Salem, NH & Ellen Delong Nova Scotia
DUSTIN, Zelia, Dec 23 1906 Sex:F Child# 8 Ira Dustin Hill & Lillie A Brown Wilmot
DUTILLY, Alphonse H A, Jan 13 1887 Sex:M Child# 3 Augustin Dutilly P Q & Julie Boule P Q
DUTILLY, Elprege George R, Jun 21 1901 Sex:M Child# 3 Louis Dutilly Canada & Ida Cote Canada
DUTILLY, Eusebe S U, Mar 25 1899 Sex:M Child# 1 Louis Dutilly Canada & Ida Cote Worcester, MA
DUTILLY, Francois X A, Sep 19 1903 Sex:M Child# 4 Louis Dutilly Canada & Ida Cote Worcester, MA
DUTILLY, Jean Philippe, Feb 18 1910 Sex:M Child# 7 Louis Dutilly Canada & Ida Cote Worcester, MA
DUTILLY, Jeanne G B, Oct 10 1905 Sex:F Child# 5 Louis Dutilly Canada & Ida Cote Worcester, MA
DUTILLY, M Olivette Cecile, Dec 3 1908 Sex:F Child# 6 Louis Dutilly Nashua, NH & Ina Cote Canada
DUTILLY, Robert Lionel A, Feb 17 1900 Sex:M Child# 2 Louis Dutilly Canada & Ida Cote Mass
DUTNEY, Dexter Leigh, Oct 31 1922 Sex:M Child# 3 Wallace Dutney Prince Edward Island & Edith R West Lowell, MA
DUTNEY, Unknown, Aug 15 1915 Sex:F Child# 1 Wallace L Dutney Prince Idward Island & Edith West Lowell, MA
DUTNEY, Unknown, Jul 10 1917 Sex:M Child# 2 Wallace L Dutney Murrya R, PEI & Cote Roberts West Lowell, MA
DUTREZAC, George, Aug 12 1899 Sex:M Child# 2 Armase Dutrezac Canada & Eugenie Bonvouloir Canada
DUTRISAC, Eugenie Alice, Dec 13 1908 Sex:F Child# 1 Ernest Dutrisac Canada & Alice Gendron NH
DUTRISAC, Henri, Dec 7 1897 Sex:M Child# 1 Hormas Dutrisac Canada & Eugenie Bonvouloir Canada
DUTRIZAC, William Andrews, Aug 16 1922 Sex:M Child# 5 Ernest Dutrizac Canada & Alice Andrews Nashua, NH
DUTTON, Arthur F, Sep 20 1896 Sex:M Child# 6 George W Dutton S Merrimack, NH & Hattie A Leach Milford, NH
DUTTON, Dora A, Nov 19 1891 Sex:F Child# 1 Charles H Dutton S Merrimack, NH & Dora A Ford Hudson, NH
DUTTON, Elwin Walter, Jul 29 1928 Sex:M Child# 2 Ernest E Dutton Hollis, NH & Florence M Read Merrimack, NH
DUTTON, Ernest Elmer, May 24 1926 Sex:M Child# 1 Ernest E Dutton Hollis, NH & Florence M Reed Merrimack, NH
DUTTON, Ethel Maud, Mar 15 1894 Sex:F Child# 6 George Dutton US & Hattie Leach US
DUTTON, Herbert Charles, Dec 4 1928 Sex:M Child# 1 Charles Dutton Nashua, NH & Carrie Smith Bennington, NH
DUTTON, Lawrence Francis, Oct 30 1933 Sex:M Child# 3 Leon Dutton Deering, NH & Lena Provost Manchester, NH
DUTTON, Mary L, Dec 1 1887 Sex:F Child# 1 George W Dutton Merrimack & Hattie A Leach Milford
DUTTON, Ralph Edward, May 28 1931 Sex:M Child# 3 Ernest Elmer Dutton Hollis, NH & Florence Read Merrimack, NH
DUTTON, Unknown, Mar 13 1887 Sex:F Child# 1 Charles H Dutton Merrimack & Ella M Hall Salem, NH
DUTTON, Unknown, Jul 9 1892 Sex:F Child# 2 William A Dutton Reading, MA & Grace M Alexander Brattleboro, VT
DUTTON, Unknown, Nov 19 1892 Sex: Child# George Dutton
DUTTON, Unknown, Apr 8 1903 Sex:M Child# 9 George W Dutton Merrimack, NH & Hattie A Leach Milford, NH
DUTTON, Unknown, Aug 1 1923 Sex:F Child# 1 Andrew Dutton Milford, NH & Margaret Rossister Milford, NH
DUVAL, Albert William, Jul 23 1930 Sex:M Child# 4 Maurice B Duval Wilton, NH & Elizabeth Donahue Nashua, NH
DUVAL, Alfred Leopold, Aug 16 1928 Sex:M Child# 1 Joseph Duval Canada & Lydia Morin Canada
DUVAL, Andre Roland, Feb 8 1931 Sex:M Child# 5 Omer Duval Nashua, NH & M L Moreau Nashua, NH
DUVAL, Auguste Harvey, Mar 29 1897 Sex:M Child# 2 Arsene Duval Canada & Albina Roch Canada
DUVAL, Auguste Ludger, Dec 5 1900 Sex:M Child# 2 Auguste Duval Canada & Ida Roy Canada
DUVAL, Aurele Armand, Jul 6 1927 Sex:M Child# 1 Aurele Duval Canada & Emma Dion Nashua, NH
DUVAL, Barbara Ann, Mar 22 1928 Sex:F Child# 2 Alfred Duval Milford, NH & Margaret Devlin Canada
DUVAL, Cecile Beatrice, Nov 4 1902 Sex:F Child# 4 Arsene Duval Canada & Albina Rock Canada
DUVAL, Claudette Sylvia, Sep 14 1935 Sex:F Child# 4 Leo Duval Canada & Irene Chamard Nashua, NH
DUVAL, Dolores Gertrude, Nov 28 1925 Sex:F Child# 3 Omer Duval Nashua, NH & Louise Moreau Nashua, NH
DUVAL, Eva Rose Albina, Jan 21 1895 Sex:F Child# 1 Arsene Duval Canada & Albina Rock Canada
DUVAL, George Henry, Nov 9 1925 Sex:M Child# 1 Alfred Duval Milford, NH & Margaret Devlin Canada
DUVAL, Georgiana, Jun 5 1906 Sex:F Child# 3 Alfred W Duval Wilton, NH & Exilda Desrosiers Canada
DUVAL, Gertrude Jeannine, May 15 1934 Sex:F Child# 3 Leo Duval Canada & Irene Chamard Nashua, NH
DUVAL, Jacqueline Irene, Jul 30 1932 Sex:F Child# 2 Leo Duval Canada & Irene Chamard US
DUVAL, John Donahue, Oct 30 1925 Sex:M Child# 3 Maurice DuVal Milton, NH & Elizabeth Donahue Nashua, NH
DUVAL, Joseph Omer, Dec 9 1899 Sex:M Child# 1 Auguste Duval Canada & Ida Roy Canada
DUVAL, Leopold, Oct 7 1930 Sex:M Child# 1 Henri Duval Canada & Fleurange Forcier Manchester, NH

DUVAL, M Antoinette, Aug 24 1895 Sex:F Child# 12 Joseph Duval Canada & Alphonsine Dumais Canada
DUVAL, M Gertrude J, Aug 16 1908 Sex:F Child# 5 Arsene Duval Canada & Albina Rock Canada
DUVAL, Marie, Jan 7 1910 Sex:F Child# 1 Louis Duval NH & Blanche Corriveau Canada
DUVAL, Marie Jeanne O, Jun 11 1910 Sex:F Child# 6 Arsene Duval Canada & Albina Rock Canada
DUVAL, Marie Z Athania, Dec 26 1898 Sex:F Child# 13 Joseph Duval Canada & Alphonsine Dumais Canada
DUVAL, Mary A, Sep 9 1898 Sex:F Child# 3 Arsene Duval Canada & Albina Rocque Canada
DUVAL, Maurice Byron, Jr, Nov 21 1917 Sex:M Child# 1 Maurice B Duval Wilton, NH & Elizabeth Donahue Nashua, NH
DUVAL, Nathalie Carol Ann, Jan 23 1929 Sex:F Child# 1 Peter Duval Canada & Lauretta Richard Nashua, NH
DUVAL, Richard George, Nov 30 1920 Sex:M Child# 2 Maurice B Duval Canada & Jura Gilbert Graniteville, VT
DUVAL, Roger Lorenzo, Sep 22 1922 Sex:M Child# 3 Omer Duval Nashua, NH & M L Moreau Nashua, NH
DUVAL, Therese, Aug 1 1931 Sex:F Child# 1 Leo Duval Canada & Irene Chamard US
DUVAL, Yolande Estelle, Oct 26 1927 Sex:F Child# 4 Omer Duval Nashua, NH & M L Moreau Nashua, NH
DUVARNEY, Dora Anne Marie, Aug 19 1929 Sex:F Child# 2 Victor C Duvarney Nashua, NH & Laura Lefebvre Nashua, NH
DUVARNEY, Edith, Dec 14 1934 Sex:F Child# 5 Victor DuVarney Nashua, NH & Laura Lefebvre Nashua, NH
DUVARNEY, Ernest Adelard, Oct 20 1915 Sex:M Child# 4 Adelard Duvarney Canada & Eugenie Dube Canada
DUVARNEY, Victor Clovis, Oct 17 1926 Sex:M Child# 1 V C DuVarney Nashua, NH & Laura Lefebvre Nashua, NH
DUVERNAY, Edgar Sylvio, Aug 31 1911 Sex:M Child# 2 Adelard Duvernay US & Eugenie Dube Canada
DUVERNAY, Edith Eugenie, Jan 24 1914 Sex:F Child# 3 Adelard Duvernay Canada & Eugenie Dube Canada
DUVERNAY, Marie Louise, Nov 24 1902 Sex:F Child# 3 Hector Duvernay Canada & M L Lizotte Canada
DUVERNAY, Mary Ethel, Jan 27 1897 Sex:F Child# 1 David Duvernay Canada & Elmire Beauregard Gorham
DUVERNAY, Victor Clovis, Jul 10 1902 Sex:M Child# 1 Adelard Duvernay Canada & Eugene Dube Canada
DUVERNAY, Wilfrid Adesdat, Sep 12 1897 Sex:M Child# 2 Hector Duvernay Canada & Marie Louise Lizotte Canada
DUVERNEY, William Hector, Nov 10 1895 Sex:M Child# 1 Hector Duverney Canada & M Louise Lizotte Canada
DVARSTSKA, John, Jan 13 1907 Sex:M Child# 1 Constan Dvarstska Russia & Dorothy Gregurti Russia
DWOREKOS, Frank, Aug 31 1908 Sex:M Child# 2 Kastanta Dworekos Russia & Doro'a Grigitie Russia
DWYEA, Lauretta, Jan 27 1901 Sex:F Child# 1 John Dwyea Nashua, NH & Rose Brennan Ireland
DWYER, Agnes, Jul 22 1899 Sex:F Child# 3 Daniel Dwyer Ireland & Odele Desmarais St Albans, VT
DWYER, Ambrose, Aug 14 1902 Sex:M Child# 12 John O Dwyer Ireland & Mary Harrahan Ireland
DWYER, Augustin, Jul 9 1906 Sex:M Child# 9 Daniel Dwyer Ireland & Odile Desmarais St Albans, VT
DWYER, Augustus, Jr, Mar 21 1933 Sex:M Child# 2 Augustus Dwyer Nashua, NH & Thelma Smith Nashua, NH
DWYER, Beatrice C T, Mar 27 1913 Sex:F Child# 2 Francis T Dwyer Nashua, NH & Beatrice A Gelinas Nashua, NH
DWYER, Charles, Nov 14 1900 Sex:M Child# 4 Daniel Dwyer Ireland & Adile Desmarais Vermont
DWYER, Charles Allison, Jun 19 1915 Sex:M Child# 3 Francis T Dwyer Nashua, NH & Beatrice Gelinas Nashua, NH
DWYER, Daniel, Apr 5 1893 Sex:M Child# 6 John O Dwyer Ireland & Mary Hanrahan Ireland
DWYER, Earl Francis, Oct 2 1910 Sex:M Child# 1 Francis Dwyer Nashua, NH & Beatrice Gelinas Nashua, NH
DWYER, Elizabeth Carmelita, Nov 26 1923 Sex:F Child# 2 Walter Dwyer Nashua, NH & Helen Gerety Nashua, NH
DWYER, Elizabeth Rose, Jan 31 1932 Sex:F Child# 1 Augustus Dwyer Nashua, NH & Thelma Smith Nashua, NH
DWYER, Francis F, Jun 5 1890 Sex:M Child# 5 John Dwyer Ireland & Mary Henahan Ireland
DWYER, Hermene, May 18 1898 Sex:F Child# 2 Daniel Dwyer Ireland & Odile Desmarais St Albans, VT
DWYER, James Alex, Jan 2 1904 Sex:M Child# 7 Daniel Dwyer Ireland & Odile Desmarais St Albans, VT
DWYER, Jane Elizabeth, Aug 1 1928 Sex:F Child# 3 Ambrose Dwyer Nashua, NH & Laura Baker Nashua, NH
DWYER, Joan Gertrude, Aug 1 1928 Sex:F Child# 2 Ambrose Dwyer Nashua, NH & Laura Baker Nashua, NH
DWYER, John, Nov 23 1901 Sex:M Child# 6 Daniel Dwyer Ireland & Odile Desmarais St Albans, VT
DWYER, John, May 3 1934 Sex:M Child# 6 Walter Henry Dwyer Nashua, NH & Helen Gerety Nashua, NH
DWYER, John C, Dec 9 1891 Sex:M Child# 5 John Dwyer Ireland & Mary Heurehan Ireland
DWYER, John Edward, Dec 24 1925 Sex:M Child# 2 John Dwyer Conn & Eliz McLaughlin Nashua, NH
DWYER, John Joseph, Sep 5 1918 Sex:M Child# 1 Daniel J Dwyer Jewet City, CT & Mary McLaughlin Nashua, NH
DWYER, John Richard, Sep 5 1935 Sex:M Child# 1 Francis Dwyer Pepperell, MA & Doris Milan Pepperell, MA
DWYER, Joseph, Feb 16 1889 Sex:M Child# 3 John Dwyer Ireland & Mary Dwyer Ireland
DWYER, Joseph, Mar 27 1923 Sex:M Child# 1 John E Dwyer Versailles, CT & Elizabeth Dwyer Nashua, NH
DWYER, Joseph P, Aug 13 1896 Sex:M Child# 1 Daniel Dwyer Ireland & Odile Desmarais St Albans, VT
DWYER, Judith Valiere, Aug 27 1935 Sex:F Child# 4 Augusta Dwyer Nashua, NH & Thelma Smith Nashua, NH
DWYER, Lucille Catherine, Dec 19 1925 Sex:F Child# 3 Walter Dwyer Nashua, NH & Helen Garity Nashua, NH
DWYER, Marie O, Sep 17 1908 Sex:F Child# 11 Daniel Dwyer Ireland & Odile Demarais St Albans, VT
DWYER, Mary, Dec 26 1919 Sex:F Child# 2 Daniel J Dwyer Jewett City, CT & Mary McLaughlin Nashua, NH
DWYER, Mary Elain, Jun 27 1914 Sex:F Child# 3 John Dwyer Nashua, NH & Rose Brennan Ireland
DWYER, Mary Elizabeth, Aug 2 1916 Sex:F Child# 1 John C Dwyer Nashua, NH & Gertrude M Duval Milford, NH
DWYER, Mary Elizabeth, Jul 8 1926 Sex:F Child# 1 Ambrose Dwyer Nashua, NH & Laura Baker Nashua, NH
DWYER, Mary Thelma, Jul 15 1934 Sex:F Child# 3 Augustus Dwyer Nashua, NH & Thelma Smith Nashua, NH
DWYER, Philip Russell, Dec 15 1931 Sex:M Child# 5 Walter H Dwyer Nashua, NH & Helen Gerety Nashua, NH
DWYER, Raphael, Dec 15 1902 Sex:M Child# 2 John H Dwyer Nashua, NH & Rose Brennan Ireland
DWYER, Richard Paul, Aug 12 1935 Sex:M Child# 7 Walter H Dwyer Nashua, NH & Helen Gerity Nashua, NH
DWYER, Robert Francis, Oct 7 1930 Sex:M Child# 4 Walter H Dwyer Nashua, NH & Helen Gerety Nashua, NH
DWYER, Rosanna Irene, Sep 15 1907 Sex:F Child# 10 Daniel Dwyer Ireland & Odile Desmarais St Albans, VT
DWYER, Ruth Anna, Aug 16 1922 Sex:F Child# 3 Daniel Dwyer Jewett City, CT & Mary McLaughlin Nashua, NH
DWYER, Thomas H, Nov 19 1904 Sex:M Child# 8 Daniel Dwyer Ireland & Odile Desmarais St Albans, VT
DWYER, Violet May, Sep 9 1929 Sex:F Child# 4 Earl Dwyer Merrimack, NH & Doris Lowell Franklin, NH
DWYER, William Francis, May 8 1934 Sex:M Child# 1 William F Dwyer Maynard, MA & Eunice Boyce Penacook, NH
DWYER, Winifred Agnes, Nov 23 1901 Sex:F Child# 2 Daniel Dwyer Ireland & Odile Desmarais St Albans, VT
DYAN, Ruth Murtland P, Oct 5 1906 Sex:F Child# 2 Frank E Dyan Battle Creek, MI & Annie Montrose Sackville, NB
DYER, Philip Marrion, May 31 1922 Sex:M Child# 1 Philip Albert Dyer S Portland, ME & Mary E Ator Jacksonville
DYKE, Cora May, Jan 25 1903 Sex:F Child# 2 Lucius E Dyke Morristown, VT & Mabel L Robinson Hyde Park, VT
DYNET, Horace, Aug 14 1888 Sex:M Child# 4 Ephraim Dynet Canada & Melvina Lefrance Canada

DZISKA, Brunka, Dec 23 1925 Sex:F Child# 4 John Dziska Poland & Albina Klematu Poland
DZISKO, Annie, Feb 25 1919 Sex:F Child# 1 John Dzisko Russia & Albina Klimiata Russia
DZISKO, Stasia, Jul 14 1923 Sex:F Child# 3 John Dzisko Poland & Albina Clemeata Poland
DZMENT, John W, Mar 15 1896 Sex:M Child# 2 Eli Dzment PI & Susan Poole PI
EACON, Unknown, Jun 8 1915 Sex:F Child# 3 Albert Eacon England & Helen Stephens England Stillborn
EAGLETON, Raymond, Sep 24 1913 Sex:M Child# 2 Harry Eagleton Lynn, MA & Marie Emery Leominster, MA Stillborn
EARL, Unknown, Jun 15 1921 Sex:F Child# 3 William Earl Greece & Helen Adams Greece
EARLEY, Albert Leo, Feb 6 1898 Sex:M Child# 5 John Earley Nashua, NH & Ellen F Harrington Manchester, NH
EARLEY, Hazel May, Feb 5 1895 Sex:F Child# 3 John M Earley Nashua, NH & Nellie Harrington Manchester, NH
EARLEY, John W, Nov 24 1891 Sex:M Child# 1 John M Earley Nashua, NH & Nellie Harrington Manchester, NH
EARLEY, Pauline Janice, Jul 23 1922 Sex:F Child# 1 Harley G Earley Nova Scotia & Gertrude Gleave Lawrence, MA
EARLEY, Unknown, Apr 4 1929 Sex:F Child# 1 Charles Earley Nashua, NH & Esther McDonough Dover, NH
EARLY, Charles F, Aug 28 1887 Sex:M Child#  John Early Nashua, NH & Catherine McManis Worcester, MA
EARLY, James, May 30 1893 Sex:M Child#  John Early Nashua, NH & Nellie Harrington Manchester
EARLY, Robert Francis, Jul 3 1896 Sex:M Child# 4 John M Early Nashua, NH & Nellie Harrington Manchester, NH
EASM, Joseph Albert, Nov 26 1934 Sex:M Child# 1 Joseph Easm England & Anna Letour Nashua, NH
EASON, Thomas Albert, Aug 21 1917 Sex:M Child# 2 Albert Eason England & Ellen Stephens England
EASTMAN, Marylin Elise, Jul 1 1922 Sex:F Child# 3 Manasah Eastman Jefferson, NH & Nellie Nevers Lancaster, NH
EASTMAN, Unknown, May 23 1890 Sex:F Child# 1 J H Eastman Weare, NH & J M Colby Henniker, NH
EASTMAN, Unknown, Aug 22 1891 Sex:F Child# 1 Charles E Eastman Nashua, NH & Florence A Judd Nashua, NH
EASTMAN, Unknown, Apr 6 1898 Sex:F Child# 1 Walter C Eastman Henniker, NH & C L Richardson Pembroke, NH
EASTMAN, Unknown, Jun 5 1921 Sex:M Child# 1 Harold Eastman Franklin, MA & Vivian Fletcher Brownington, VT
EATON, Alice Mary, Jun 30 1927 Sex:F Child# 6 Albert Eaton N Reading, MA & Eva R Smith Hudson, NH
EATON, Arthur Edward, May 8 1924 Sex:M Child# 3 Herbert L Eaton Kensington, NH & Mil E Reynolds Hudson, NH
EATON, Clayton Albert, Jr, Feb 4 1924 Sex:M Child# 1 Clayton A Eaton Bradford, MA & Lorraine Lemery Nashua, NH
EATON, Dorothy Lucille, Dec 8 1917 Sex:F Child# 8 Harold W Eaton Nashua, NH & Florence Brousseau Canada
EATON, Ethel Grace, Oct 15 1920 Sex:F Child# 2 Herbert L Eaton NH & Mildred Reynolds NH
EATON, Eugene Howard, Jun 19 1914 Sex:M Child# 1 Harold Eaton Nashua, NH & Florence Brousseau Ontario
EATON, Helen G, Apr 17 1912 Sex:F Child# 1 George G Eaton Nashua, NH & Georgiana Ricard Nashua, NH
EATON, Helen Julia, Feb 21 1925 Sex:F Child# 5 Albert H Eaton N Reading, MA & Eva R Smith Hudson, NH
EATON, James Albert, May 8 1924 Sex:M Child# 4 Herbert L Eaton Kensington, NH & Mil E Reynolds Hudson, NH
EATON, John Herbert, May 2 1922 Sex:M Child# 3 Herbert Eaton NH & Mildred Reynolds Hudson, NH
EATON, Margorie Eva, Apr 23 1896 Sex:F Child# 5 George E Eaton Enfield & Lena Farley Londonderry
EATON, Mildred M, Aug 27 1911 Sex:F Child# 3 Edward G Eaton Nashua, NH & Leona M Greenwood Cambridge, MA
EATON, Paul Conant, Dec 18 1905 Sex:M Child# 1 Ivory C Eaton Nashua, NH & E Edna Conant Nashua, NH
EATON, Richard Gilbert, Jul 17 1926 Sex:M Child# 2 George Eaton Nashua, NH & Georgianna Recard Nashua, NH
EATON, Ruth, Feb 8 1908 Sex:F Child# 2 Ivory C Eaton Nashua, NH & E Edna Conant Nashua, NH
EATON, Stanley Herbert, Oct 30 1931 Sex:M Child# 7 Albert Eaton N Reading, MA & Eva Smith Hudson, NH
EATON, Unknown, Aug 23 1887 Sex:F Child# 3 George E Eaton Enfield & Etta L Farley Londonderry
EATON, Unknown, Nov 8 1889 Sex:F Child# 4 George E Eaton Enfield, NH & Ellen Taylor Londonderry, NH
EATON, Unknown, Nov 3 1892 Sex:M Child# 3 W G Eaton Nashua, NH & Arvilla New York
EATON, Unknown, Feb 24 1899 Sex:M Child# 1 Elmer W Eaton Nashua, NH & Sarah E Thurber Nashua, NH
EATON, William, Nov 14 1888 Sex:M Child# 1 Elmer W Eaton Nashua, NH & Abbie K Spalding Lawrence, MA
EAULETTE, Loria, Feb 8 1884 Sex:F Child# 2 Javerede Eaulette Canada & Emma Brodeur Canada
EBBETT, Doris Grace, Jul 28 1921 Sex:F Child# 3 Raymond Ebbett Fort Fairfield, ME & Maude Ellis Chatham, MA
ECCLESTON, Edith Laura, Jan 15 1900 Sex:F Child# 4 Frank D Eccleston Griswold, CT & Jennie M Kimball Haverhill, MA
ECCLESTON, Unknown, Jan 20 1891 Sex:M Child# 2 Harry O Eccleston Conn & Ida L Nye Nashua, NH
ECONOMOPULOS, Anna, Mar 6 1926 Sex:F Child# 6 J Economopulos Greece & Anna Kostantakis Greece
ECONOMOPULOS, Unknown, Jul 21 1915 Sex:F Child# 1 Sprio Economopulos Greece & Diamante Kufapulo Greece
ECONOMOPULOS, Vion, Apr 7 1918 Sex:M Child# 3 Speir Economopulos Greece & Diamanto Konfopulou Greece
ECONOMOU, Nicholas N, Jun 11 1921 Sex:M Child# 6 Nicholas Economou Greece & Vasilikia Brazicotir Greece
ECONOMOU, Unknown, Aug 25 1919 Sex:M Child# 5 N A Economou Greece & Vasilick J Brijiotes Greece
ECONOMOU, Unknown, Apr 27 1930 Sex:F Child#  William Economou Greece & Kate Kostolakas Greece
ECONOMPOULOS, Unknown, Jul 24 1924 Sex:M Child# 4 G Econompoulos Greece & N Dozopple Greece
ECONOPOULOS, Unknown, Nov 19 1916 Sex:F Child# 2 Spiros Econopoulos Greece & Deman Kupopolous Greece
EDDY, Madeline, Mar 19 1905 Sex:F Child# 1 Floyd Eddy Vermont & Ina Dall Canada
EDDY, Oscar Edward, Jul 8 1904 Sex:M Child# 2 Herbert Eddy Cambridge, MA & Kate Sills W Newbury, MA
EDELSTEIN, Bertha, Oct 31 1912 Sex:F Child# 3 Myers Edelstein Russia & Rebecca Silverman Russia
EDELSTEIN, Edward Seymour, May 20 1908 Sex:M Child# 1 Myer Edelstein Russia & Rebecca Silverman Russia
EDELSTEIN, Harrold G, Oct 23 1909 Sex:M Child# 2 Myer Edelstein Russia & Rebecca Silverman Russia
EDELSTEIN, Pauline, Oct 21 1919 Sex:F Child# 4 Myer Edelstein Russia & Rebecca Silverman Russia
EDMONDS, Clarence Wood Edm, Oct 25 1918 Sex:M Child# 1 Aaron Edmonds Deerfield, NH & Lillian MacKenzie Nova Scotia
EDMONDS, Margaret Jean, May 24 1927 Sex:F Child# 3 A T Edmonds Deerfield, NH & Lillie MacKenzie Nova Scotia
EDMONDS, Norman Wallace, Sep 19 1924 Sex:M Child# 2 A F Edmonds Deerfield, NH & Lillian MacKenzie Nova Scotia
EDSON, Ardella G, Nov 2 1891 Sex:F Child# 1 E A Edson Vermont & Jennie Case Vermont
EDSON, Edson, Mar 4 1889 Sex: Child# 1 Eugene A Edson Seema, NY & Jennie D Case Fletcher, VT Stillborn
EDWARD, Ethel Irene, Feb 24 1908 Sex:F Child# 1 Joseph Edward Nashua, NH & Mary Ethel Carkin Wilton, NH
EDWARD, George David, May 12 1922 Sex:M Child# 1 Benjamin H Edward Waltham, MA & Charlotte M Coutts Marlboro, MA
EDWARDS, Arthur Lowell, Sep 13 1910 Sex:M Child# 6 Arthur B Edwards New Brunswick & Lucy Eayrs Hudson, NH
EDWARDS, Charles Bert, Mar 5 1905 Sex:M Child# 2 Arthur B Edwards L Brighton, NB & Lucy M Eayns Hudson, NH
EDWARDS, John J, Feb 13 1894 Sex:M Child# 1 Henry Edwards Manchester & Mary Moreland Ireland
EDWARDS, Lena Augusta, Jan 28 1907 Sex:F Child# 4 Arthur B Edwards New Brunswick & Lucy Eayrs Hudson, NH
EDWARDS, Thelma Louise, Oct 12 1908 Sex:F Child# 5 Arthur B Edwards New Brunswick & Lucy Eayrs Hudson, NH

EFTHEMION, Unknown, May 27 1927 Sex:M Child# 2 T Efthemion Greece & T Tasios Greece
EFTHIMIOS, Marie C, Jul 3 1927 Sex:F Child# 1 C Efthimios Greece & Isabel Hovanesian Nashua, NH
EGGLESTON, Unknown, Jul 28 1889 Sex: Child# 1 H O Eggleston Conn & Ida L Cook Nashua, NH
EGGLESTON, Unknown, Jan 31 1895 Sex:F Child# 1 Frank B Eggleston Griswold, CT & Jennie M Kimball Haverhill, MA
EGLETON, Unknown, Mar 17 1908 Sex:F Child# 1 Harry Egleton Worcester, MA & Marie Emery Leominster, MA
EKDAHL, Naomi Marguerite, Sep 19 1914 Sex:F Child# 1 Adolph G Ekdahl Chicago, IL & Naomi M Goldwaithe Nashua, NH
EKONOMOU, Panageota, Aug 7 1925 Sex:F Child# 1 William Ekonomou Greece & E Kostoulakos Greece
EKSTROM, Marion, Nov 29 1906 Sex:F Child# 1 Edward Ekstrom Tyngsboro, MA & Ambrye J Metcalf Rindge, NH
EKSTROM, Roland George, Jan 31 1909 Sex:M Child# 1 Edward C Ekstrom Tyngsboro, MA & Ambrie J Metcalf Rindge, NH
EKSTROM, Ruth Gertrude, Nov 24 1911 Sex:F Child# 2 Edward C Ekstrom Tyngsboro, MA & Annie J Metcalf Rindge, NH
EKSTRON, Frank C, Jun 22 1889 Sex:M Child# 4 Charles S Ekstron Sweden & Ida C Blumber Sweden
ELBLING, Phineas, Feb 27 1934 Sex:M Child# 3 Alexander Elbling Russia & Ida Sushelsky Russia
ELDER, Unknown, May 17 1893 Sex:M Child# 1 John Elder Franklin Centre,CA & Martha N Harwood La Patrie, CA
ELDER, Unknown, Jun 6 1895 Sex:F Child# 2 John Elder Franklin, Canada & Martha N Harwood La Patrie, Canada
ELDRIDGE, John William, Aug 22 1921 Sex:M Child# 1 Clarence C Eldridge Orrington, ME & Grace E Hamar Bar Harbor, ME
ELDRIDGE, Lloyd Edmund, Jr, Nov 21 1925 Sex:M Child# 1 Lloyd E Eldridge St Henry, NY & Edna L Dupas Lynn, MA
ELDRIDGE, Unknown, Apr 16 1912 Sex:M Child# 3 Percy A Eldridge Wareham, MA & Elizabeth Sullivan New York
ELF, Loring Taft, Dec 12 1931 Sex:M Child# 2 John Elf Sweden & Elizabeth B Homer Boston, MA
ELFSEN, Addie M, Jul 8 1897 Sex:F Child# 10 Christian Elfsen Sweden & Bridget Lynch Ireland
ELFSEN, Unknown, Jul 8 1897 Sex:F Child# 11 Christian Elfsen Sweden & Bridget Lynch Ireland Stillborn
ELFSON, Joseph, Nov 26 1906 Sex:M Child# 14 Christian Elfson Sweden & Bridget Lynch Ireland
ELFSON, Unknown, Oct 1901 Sex:M Child# 8 Christian Elfson Sweden & Bridget Lynch Ireland
ELKINS, Clinton Howard, Sep 15 1897 Sex:M Child# Harvey Elkins Troy, NY & Hattie Burns Troy, NY
ELKINS, Edmund Solomon, Oct 12 1903 Sex:M Child# 6 Samuel O Elkins N Troy, VT & K A Markham Ayer, MA
ELKINS, Evette, Jun 27 1898 Sex:F Child# 4 Samuel O Elkins W Troy, VT & Katherine A Markham Ayer, MA
ELKINS, Geraldine Ruth, Feb 14 1897 Sex:F Child# 3 Samuel O Elkins Troy, VT & Kate A Markham Ayer Jct, MA
ELKINS, Julia Yvette, Oct 11 1899 Sex:F Child# 5 Samuel O Elkins Vermont & Catherine A Markham Mass
ELKINS, Leora Annie, Nov 27 1895 Sex:F Child# 2 Samuel O Elkins N Troy, VT & Kate A Markham Ayer, MA
ELKINS, Miriam Eileen, Mar 25 1894 Sex:F Child# 1 O Salmon Elkins North Troy, VT & Caroline A Markham Ayer Jct, MA
ELLINGTON, Lois, Aug 15 1932 Sex:F Child# 1 Wm Ellington Annapolis, IN & H M Johnson Metropolis, IL
ELLIOTT, Doris, Jul 14 1913 Sex:F Child# 1 Richard P Elliott Belmont, NS & Grace E Blake E Quogue, LI, NY
ELLIOTT, Emily, Sep 16 1896 Sex:F Child# 2 Ambrose Elliott Mason & Julia E Longphee
ELLIOTT, Lucille Jane, Aug 19 1920 Sex:F Child# 6 Guy M Elliott Hancock, NH & Eva Bonette Nashua, NH
ELLIOTT, William, Aug 7 1898 Sex:M Child# 3 Henry W Elliott Stoddard & Ora M Nash Ludlow, VT
ELLIS, Dorris May, Oct 15 1901 Sex:F Child# 3 James V Ellis Maine & Martha J Ingham New York
ELLIS, Marion Irene, Mar 24 1929 Sex:F Child# 4 John W Ellis Mass & Irene M Henri Saco, ME
ELLIS, Walter Raymond, Oct 5 1926 Sex:M Child# 1 Joseph H Ellis Cambridge, MA & Ellen Smith Northbridge, MA
ELLISON, Annie, Jul 2 1899 Sex:F Child# 6 George C Ellison Vermont & Annie S Leazotte New York
ELLISON, Gage L, Jan 30 1892 Sex:M Child# 11 George C Ellison Vermont & Annie S Leazotte NY
ELLISON, Hazel Alice, May 13 1896 Sex:F Child# 5 George C Ellison Vermont & Annie S Leazotte NY
ELLISON, Unknown, Jun 3 1909 Sex:M Child# 1 Wellington Ellison Pr Edward Island & Delia Tracy Kerry, ME
ELLSWORTH, Clinton Elmer, Jul 21 1922 Sex:M Child# 6 Oscar Ellsworth Gilmanton, NH & Mabel E Durand Derry, NH
ELLSWORTH, Muriel Arline, Jan 9 1926 Sex:F Child# 2 Orville Ellsworth Eden, VT & Annie Firth Shelburne, NS
ELLSWORTH, Ruth Elaine, Apr 27 1922 Sex:F Child# 1 Orville Ellsworth Eden, VT & Annie Eula Firth Shelburne, NS
ELLWOOD, Jerry Hanks, Feb 2 1914 Sex:M Child# 1 Will Ellwood Sheldon, VT & Nettie Smith Londonderry, NH Stillborn
ELOSEN, Christopher, Mar 4 1895 Sex:M Child# 5 Christopher Elosen Sweden & Bridget Lynch Ireland
ELOSEN, Unknown, Jan 2 1894 Sex:M Child# 4 Christopher Elosen Sweden & Bridget Lynch Ireland
ELOSEN, Unknown, Mar 22 1896 Sex:M Child# 7 Christian Elosen Norway & Bridget Lynch Ireland
ELOSEN, Unknown, Mar 22 1896 Sex:M Child# 8 Christian Elosen Norway & Bridget Lynch Ireland
ELOSON, Frederick, Jun 23 1890 Sex:M Child# 2 Christopher Eloson Norway & Delie Lynch Ireland
ELPERT, Abraham, Nov 6 1892 Sex:M Child# 11 Louis Elpert Russia & Lea Russia
EMALAWICZ, Antanias, May 21 1917 Sex:F Child# 3 Joe Emalawicz Russia & Eva Slarcimas Russia
EMANOWICH, Vincent, Jan 28 1917 Sex:M Child# 1 Stanislaw Emanowich Russia & Leocarda Kashan Russia
EMERSON, Howard James, Mar 30 1913 Sex:M Child# 1 John Emerson Nashua, NH & Florence Mockler Nashua, NH
EMERSON, Ileene Julia, Nov 1 1918 Sex:F Child# 2 John A Emerson Nashua, NH & Nora Mockler Nashua, NH
EMERSON, Kennett Nathaniel, Nov 5 1915 Sex:M Child# 2 George Y Emerson Mass & Sadie F Corbett Mass
EMERSON, Mildred Estelle, Jan 2 1913 Sex:F Child# 1 George Y Emerson Stoughton, MA & Sarah F Corbett Stoughton, MA
EMERSON, Muriel, Apr 13 1918 Sex:F Child# 2 Walter Emerson Goffstown, NH & Effie Teakles Norton, NB
EMERSON, Norma Beverly, Sep 24 1930 Sex:F Child# 1 Norm B C Emerson Framingham, MA & Roberta Bourn Templeton, MA
EMERSON, Unknown, Jun 30 1889 Sex:M Child# 3 Fred J Emerson New Hampshire & Emma D Austin New Hampshire
EMERSON, Unknown, Apr 30 1891 Sex:M Child# 4 F J Emerson Hopkinton & E R Austin Claremont
EMERSON, Unknown, May 14 1896 Sex:F Child# 5 Fred J Emerson Hopkinton, NH & Emily Austin Claremont, NH
EMERSON, Unknown, Mar 24 1898 Sex:M Child# 6 Fred J Emerson Hopkinton, NH & Emily V Austin Claremont, NH
EMERY, Alice Lavina, Nov 28 1912 Sex:F Child# 5 Frank D Emery Newfield, ME & Belle Bradshaw Nova Scotia
EMERY, Benjamin, Jun 17 1901 Sex:M Child# 3 Benjamin Emery Maine & Elizabeth McGraw NB
EMERY, Bessie P, Nov 25 1896 Sex:F Child# 1 Verie Emery Canada & Margrett Henderson Canada
EMERY, Camille Anne, Jul 26 1922 Sex:F Child# 1 Arthur G Emery Nashua, NH & Bertha Gariepy Nashua, NH
EMERY, Eugene Alfred, Apr 13 1929 Sex:M Child# 3 Fred Emery Nashua, NH & Helena Bouley Nashua, NH
EMERY, George A F, Aug 25 1893 Sex:M Child# 3 Alfred Emery Nashua, NH & Febranie Dionne Canada
EMERY, Lea Delina, Oct 4 1895 Sex:F Child# 4 Alfred Emery Nashua, NH & Euphemie Dionne Canada
EMERY, Louis E, Sep 14 1890 Sex:M Child# 1 Alfred Emery Nashua, NH & Euphemie Dionne Canada
EMERY, Margaret Louise, Oct 15 1921 Sex:F Child# 2 Clarence F Emery Bar Harbor, ME & Laura M Willand Fall River, MA
EMERY, Marie Bernadette, Sep 3 1894 Sex:F Child# 3 Charles Emery Nashua, NH & Victoria Dionne Canada

EMERY, Marie D, Aug 9 1888 Sex:F Child# 1 Charles Emery Nashua, NH & Victoria Dione Canada
EMERY, Marie R, Mar 3 1892 Sex:F Child# 2 Alfred Emery Canada & Euphemie Dionne Canada
EMERY, Maurice Donald, Feb 23 1931 Sex:M Child# 4 Fred Emery Nashua, NH & Helena Bouley Nashua, NH
EMERY, Noel R, Dec 23 1895 Sex:M Child# 7 Adelard Emery Canada & Thersile Chartrand Ellensburg, NY
EMERY, Russell, May 31 1915 Sex:M Child# 6 Frank B Emery Newfield, ME & Belle Bradshaw Nova Scotia
EMERY, Stanley Frederick, Dec 22 1924 Sex:M Child# 4 Herbert Emery Pelham, NH & Beatrice Gerard Greenfield, NH
EMERY, Unknown, Jan 11 1887 Sex:F Child# 6 Daniel Emery Nashua, NH & Catherine Nashua, NH
EMERY, Unknown, Sep 14 1898 Sex:F Child# 2 Riveras B Emery Hatley, PQ & Maggie Henderson Veness, PQ
EMERY, Unknown, Feb 25 1923 Sex:F Child# 4 Clarence F Emery Bar Harbor, ME & Laura May Willard Fall River, MA
EMERY, William E, Aug 8 1891 Sex:M Child# 2 Charles Emery Nashua, NH & Victoria Dionne Canada
EMERY, Winifred Marietta, Aug 13 1927 Sex:F Child# 2 Fred Emery Nashua, NH & Helena Bouley Nashua, NH
EMMERSON, Dorothy Irene, Oct 11 1916 Sex:F Child# 3 George Y Emmerson Stoughton, MA & Sadie F Corbett Stoughton, MA
EMMONS, Dora Violet, Mar 6 1924 Sex:F Child# 5 Joseph Emmons Nashua, NH & Maude Gelinas Nashua, NH
EMMONS, Joseph Raymond, Jul 31 1924 Sex:M Child# 5 George A Emmons NH & Rosalie Burgess Manchester, NH
EMMONS, Leo Paul, Nov 5 1932 Sex:M Child# 10 Jos Emmons Canada & Amanda Gelinas Nashua, NH
EMOND, Albert Omer, Jul 21 1924 Sex:M Child# 2 Adelard Emond Canada & Elsie Dumais Canada
EMOND, Arthur, Apr 14 1916 Sex:M Child# 1 Joseph Emond Canada & Amanda Gelinas Nashua, NH
EMOND, Cecile Dora, Oct 11 1919 Sex:F Child# 3 Joseph Emond Nashua, NH & Amanda Gelinas Nashua, NH
EMOND, Henri Albert, Dec 1 1920 Sex:M Child# 2 George Emond Deerfield, NH & M Catherine Marston Pr Edw Island
EMOND, Irene, Oct 31 1917 Sex:F Child# 2 Joseph Emond Canada & Amanda Gelinas Nashua, NH
EMOND, Jos Donat Arthur, May 25 1923 Sex:M Child# 5 Aurel Emond Canada & Marie Anne Emound Canada
EMOND, Joseph Aldege Euclid, Aug 29 1924 Sex:M Child# 6 Aurel Emond Canada & Marie A Emond Canada
EMOND, Joseph Arthur, Dec 27 1893 Sex:M Child# 10 Pierre Emond Canada & Marie Plourde Canada
EMOND, Joseph C L, Aug 5 1891 Sex:M Child# 9 Pierre Emond Canada & Marie Plourde Canada
EMOND, Joseph Louis A, Mar 11 1909 Sex:M Child# 10 Phillippe Emond Canada & Anna Levesque Canada
EMOND, Joseph Treffle, Mar 16 1896 Sex:M Child# 12 Pierre Emond Canada & Marie Plourde Canada
EMOND, Louis Arthur, Oct 8 1919 Sex:M Child# 1 George Emond NH & Rosalie Bourgeois NH
EMOND, M Theresa Jacqueline, May 22 1928 Sex:F Child# 7 Joseph Emond Canada & Amanda Gelinas Nashua, NH
EMOND, Marie Odile, Apr 12 1895 Sex:F Child# 9 Alex Emond Canada & Marguerite Lero Canada
EMOND, Narcisse, Mar 8 1898 Sex:M Child# 10 Alexander Emond Canada & Marguerite Lihero Canada
EMOND, Paul Lionel, Aug 26 1934 Sex:M Child# 3 David Emond Greenville, NH & Albina Boulay Greenville, NH
EMOND, Regina, Mar 16 1895 Sex:F Child# 11 Pierre Emond Canada & Marie Plourde Canada
EMOND, Robert Normand, Jul 25 1928 Sex:M Child# 3 Adelard Emond Canada & Elise Dumais Canada
EMOND, Rose Yvonne, Aug 8 1930 Sex:F Child# 8 Joseph Emond Canada & Amanda Gelinas Nashua, NH
EMOND, Unknown, Jul 6 1923 Sex:F Child# 4 George Emond Canada & Rosalie Bourgeois
EMOND, Unknown, Feb 8 1926 Sex:M Child# 6 Joseph Emond Lowell, MA & Amanda Gelinas
EMONT, Isabelle Alice, Jan 13 1926 Sex:F Child# 1 David Emont Greenville, NH & Albina Bouley Greenville, NH
ENFSTATHION, Constantine S, Jul 9 1921 Sex:M Child# 5 Stathis Enfstathion Greece & Ecaterine Aneste Greece
ENFSTATHION, Nicolaos, Jul 9 1921 Sex:M Child# 4 Stathis Enfstathion Greece & Ecaterine Aneste Greece
ENGLISH, Barbara Ann, Dec 28 1930 Sex:F Child# 6 William G English Kentville, NS & Nina Scott Baring, ME
ENGLISH, Donald Leroy, Nov 10 1924 Sex:M Child# 7 Edward English Nova Scotia & Florence Aptt Nova Scotia
ENGLISH, Gerald Arthur, Mar 4 1927 Sex:M Child# 1 William G English Canada & Nina Scott Maine
ENGLISH, Helena May, Oct 17 1920 Sex:F Child# 2 William English Canada & Nancy Scott Maine
ENGLISH, Lawrence Roland, Nov 14 1922 Sex:M Child# 6 Edward English Nova Scotia & Florence Aptt Nova Scotia
ENGLISH, Pearl Lorena, Dec 20 1922 Sex:F Child# 2 William English Canada & Nancy Scott Maine
ENGLISH, Robert Allen, Apr 14 1929 Sex:M Child# 8 Edward English Nova Scotia & Florence Aptte Nova Scotia
ENGLISH, Unknown, Dec 14 1935 Sex:M Child# William G English Kempvill, NS & Nina Mae Scott Baring, ME
ENGLISH, Vivian, Oct 19 1926 Sex:F Child# 8 C W English Kentville, NS & A L Cogswell St John, NB
ENGLISH, Wilfred Hezekiah, May 22 1928 Sex:M Child# 9 Charles W English Nova Scotia & Adeline Cogswell St John, NB
ENGLISH, William Garfield, Sep 22 1925 Sex:M Child# 3 William G English Canada & Nina Scott US
ENRIGHT, Alice Jane, Nov 24 1898 Sex:F Child# 2 John T Enright Ireland & Rosanna Gadbois Nashua, NH
ENRIGHT, Arthur Cornelius, Oct 9 1904 Sex:M Child# 4 John Enright Ireland & Rosanna Gadbois Nashua, NH
ENRIGHT, Edith Anna, Mar 2 1907 Sex:F Child# 1 Edward Enright Ireland & Julia Shea Ireland
ENRIGHT, Edward B, Sep 20 1905 Sex:M Child# 1 John J Enright Ireland & Mary E Shea Ireland
ENRIGHT, Eleanor, Sep 20 1913 Sex:F Child# 5 Edward Enright Ireland & Julia Shea Ireland
ENRIGHT, Elecia May, Dec 19 1906 Sex:F Child# 2 John Enright Ireland & Mary E Shea Ireland
ENRIGHT, Hesther Elizabeth, Jun 4 1908 Sex:F Child# 2 Edward T Enright Ireland & Julia Shea Ireland
ENRIGHT, John W, Oct 3 1911 Sex:M Child# 4 Edward Enright Ireland & Julia Shea Ireland
ENRIGHT, Robert Arthur, May 13 1932 Sex:M Child# 2 Arthur Enright Nashua, NH & Emma Voisin N Hartford, CT
ENSCEMB, Maurice C, Jan 30 1890 Sex:M Child# 1 James T Enscemb Sweden & Sarah B Peterson Maine
ENTWISTLE, Mary, Oct 3 1888 Sex:F Child# 1 Holden Entwistle England & Mary A Whitman England
ENWRIGHT, Edward Allen, May 27 1897 Sex:M Child# 1 John Enwright Ireland & Rosanna Gadbois Canada
ENWRIGHT, Therese Ivonne, May 6 1901 Sex:F Child# 3 John Enwright Ireland & Rosanna Godbois Nashua, NH
ERB, Catherine A, Oct 12 1895 Sex:F Child# 4 Wilfred N Erb New Brunswick & Catherine Coguis Ireland
ERB, Charles F, Mar 7 1893 Sex:M Child# 2 Edward Erb NB & Lotta M Burgess NB
ERB, Frederick Austin, Sep 27 1922 Sex:M Child# 1 Austin Erb Nova Scotia & Maude B Smith Nashua, NH
ERB, Helen Frances, Jun 12 1892 Sex:F Child# 2 Wilfred M Erb New Brunswick & Kate Coggins Ireland
ERB, Leslie Howard, Apr 12 1924 Sex:M Child# 2 Austin W Erb Nova Scotia & Maude B Smith Nashua, NH
ERB, Loretta, Aug 6 1898 Sex:F Child# 5 Wilfred N Erb Sussex, NB & Catherine Goggins Ireland
ERB, Marjorie Elinor, Jan 12 1926 Sex:F Child# 2 James E Erb New Brunswick & Nellie Quirk Ireland
ERB, Mary, Dec 5 1900 Sex:F Child# Howard Erb Canada & H Holmes Canada
ERB, Robert Curtis, Jr, Mar 13 1933 Sex:M Child# 1 Robert Curtis Erb Worcester, MA & Lillian Chaloux Lowell, MA
ERB, Ruth Berry, Nov 14 1926 Sex:F Child# 3 Austin Erb New Brunswick & Maud Smith Nashua, NH

ERB, Sarah Anne, Feb 4 1894 Sex:F Child# 3 Wilford N Erb Essex, NB & Katie Coggins Ireland
ERB, Shirley, Nov 17 1906 Sex:M Child# 1 James E Erb New Brunswick & Nellie Quirk New York
ERB, Unknown, Sep 2 1900 Sex:M Child# 6 Wilford N Erb NB & Katherine Coggins Ireland
ERBB, Eleanor, Sep 25 1919 Sex:F Child# 2 George Erbb Canada & Ruby York Wells, ME
ERICKSON, Beverly May Brown, Feb 17 1932 Sex:F Child# 10 John Erickson
ERICKSON, Carlene, Mar 5 1933 Sex:F Child# 2 E I Erickson Newburyport, MA & Irlene Aikens Newport, NH
ERICKSON, Edla Evangline, Aug 21 1897 Sex:F Child# 4 Frank A Erickson Sweden & Augusta Peterson Sweden
ERICKSON, Eva May, Jan 7 1906 Sex:F Child# 3 Henry Erickson Sweden & Maude Fonance NY
ERICKSON, Gerhard A, Jul 30 1891 Sex:M Child# 1 Frank Erickson Sweden & Augustine Peterson Sweden
ERICKSON, Herbert Henry, Sep 4 1908 Sex:M Child# 7 Henry Erickson Sweden & Maude M Forrance
ERICKSON, Jenny Augusta, Feb 7 1900 Sex:F Child# 5 Frank A Erickson Sweden & Augusta Peterson Sweden
ERICKSON, Judith Matilda, Sep 18 1893 Sex:F Child# 2 Frank A Erickson Sweden & Augusta C Peterson Sweden
ERICKSON, Laura Leola, Aug 18 1898 Sex:F Child# 1 Henry Erickson Sweden & Maud Mellissa Lyon Mt, NY
ERMALA, Florence, May 22 1928 Sex:F Child# 4 Julius Ermala Lithuania & Teophla Cepent Lithuania
ERMALAVITCH, John, Mar 22 1923 Sex:M Child# 10 Joseph Ermalavitch Lithuania & Eva Schleitunis Lithuania
ERMALOVICH, Julian, Mar 24 1928 Sex:M Child# 5 L Ermalovich Poland & Josephine Pitka Poland
ERMALOWICZ, Peter, Apr 23 1916 Sex:M Child# 3 Joe Ermalowicz Russia & Eva Salatumas Russia
ERMELA, Unknown, Jan 17 1922 Sex:F Child# 3 Julius Ermela Russia & Theophile Sepputa Russia
ESILIONIS, Annie, May 17 1924 Sex:F Child# 2 John Esilionis Poland & Cardine Tubinis Poland
ESILIONIS, Mary, May 17 1924 Sex:F Child# 1 John Esilionis Poland & Cardine Tubinis Poland
ESPINOLA, James Robert, Apr 13 1931 Sex:M Child# 4 Gabriel Espinola Portugal & Mary E Cunha Portugal
ESPOZA, Joseph Arthur, Oct 4 1910 Sex:M Child# 1 Charles Espoza Italy & Alice Roy Somersworth, NH
ESSIGMANN, Lester Ralph, Sep 1 1923 Sex:M Child# 4 John M Essigmann Austria & Sybil White Randolph, VT
ESSON, Dorothy Elizabeth, Jul 18 1906 Sex:F Child# 1 William Esson Scotland & Helen Thompson Scotland
ESSON, Jessie Thomson, Feb 15 1918 Sex:F Child# 4 William Esson Scotland & Helen Thomson Scotland
ESSON, Unknown, Sep 9 1911 Sex:M Child# 3 William Esson Scotland & Helen Thompson Scotland
EST, Richard N, Oct 25 1889 Sex:M Child# 1 Edward Est St John, NB & Matilda Burgess St John, NB
ESTES, Hazel Edna, Jan 9 1907 Sex:F Child# 1 Errald V Estes Nashua, NH & Berthana M Horne Nashua, NH
ESTES, June Maden, Jun 21 1919 Sex:F Child#  John Estes Nashua, NH & Grace Maden Waltham, MA
ESTES, Nathan Ant, Jr, Mar 16 1920 Sex:M Child# 1 Nathan A Estes Smithfield, RI & Mary Elizabeth Abbe Springfield
ESTES, Violet Jennie, May 13 1896 Sex:F Child# 1 Nathaniel W Estes Swampscott, MA & Annie R Miller Concord
ESTY, Barbara Ida, Apr 21 1927 Sex:F Child# 3 Ralph Esty Hudson, NH & Vera Bagley Burlington, VT
ESTY, Fred Rupert, Jul 24 1925 Sex:M Child# 2 Ralph Esty Hudson, NH & Vera Bagley Burlington, VT
ESTY, Greta Pauline, Jul 12 1931 Sex:F Child# 5 Ralph Esty Hudson, NH & Vera Bagley Burlington, VT
ESTY, Hobart Bagley, Jun 15 1924 Sex:M Child# 1 Ralph Esty Hudson, NH & Vera Bagley Burlington, VT
ESTY, Norma Elizabeth, Apr 17 1927 Sex:F Child# 1 Ernest Esty Haverhill, MA & Mary Baker Hudson, NH
ESTY, Roy Edward, Jun 20 1928 Sex:M Child# 4 Ralph Esty Hudson, NH & Vera Bugley Burlington, VT
ESTY, Shirley Eleanor, May 6 1931 Sex:F Child# 3 Ernest Esty Haverhill, MA & Mary Baker Hudson, NH
ESTY, Walter George, Jan 15 1929 Sex:M Child# 2 Ernest Esty Haverhill, MA & Mary Baker Hudson, NH
ETHIER, George Richard, Apr 11 1931 Sex:M Child# 1 Joseph Ethier Canada & Rose Bergeron Canada
ETHIER, Liliane Beatrice, May 9 1908 Sex:F Child# 6 Henri Ethier Canada & Edwidge Berthiaume Bay City, MI
EUCLOS, Albert Oscar, May 22 1903 Sex:M Child# 5 Dolphis Euclos Canada & Marie Fortin Canada
EUKOP, Petronele, Feb 1 1911 Sex:M Child# 2 Tony Eukop Russia & Barbara Nokanaite Russia
EUKURBSKAT, Eben, Oct 8 1909 Sex:F Child# 2 John Eukurbskat Poland & Lizzie Adams Russia
EURONOKA, Julius, Oct 18 1914 Sex:M Child# 1 Leo Euronoka Russia & Ouchula Barkawich Russia
EVAN, Carl William, Apr 16 1921 Sex:M Child# 4 Ralph M Evan Nashua, NH & Jeannie A Conners Charlestown, MA
EVANS, Carleton Frank, Nov 6 1925 Sex:M Child# 3 Walter F Evans Gorham, ME & Grace McNayr Hollis, NH
EVANS, Editha Edna, Jul 20 1901 Sex:F Child# 2 Clayson H Evans Milan & Lizzie W Fortier Canada
EVANS, George Henry, Apr 19 1898 Sex:M Child# 3 George Henry Evans England & Catherine Screvan Ireland
EVANS, Grace Muriel, Apr 15 1924 Sex:F Child# 2 Walter F Evans Gorham, ME & Grace McNayer Hollis, NH
EVANS, Howard Augustus, Jan 25 1932 Sex:M Child# 6 Paul Evans Londonderry, NH & Marion Gilson Somerville, MA
EVANS, Irving P, Jul 28 1892 Sex:M Child# 3 Thomas H Evans Chicago, IL & Mehitable Goffstown, NH
EVANS, Lawrence Stanley, Mar 5 1935 Sex:M Child# 7 Paul Evans Londonderry, NH & Marion Gilson Somerville, MA
EVANS, Louise Rogers, Apr 7 1932 Sex:F Child# 3 Russell M Evans Derry, NH & Irma Rogers Derry, NH
EVANS, Marjorie Irma, Dec 20 1929 Sex:F Child# 2 Russell M Evans Derry, NH & Irma Alice Rogers Derry, NH
EVANS, Nelson Loren, Oct 21 1933 Sex:M Child# 1 W A Evans Londonderry, NH & Eveline Nelson Hillsboro, NH
EVANS, Paul Gilson, Apr 28 1922 Sex:M Child# 4 Paul Blodgett Evans Londonderry, NH & Marion Gilson Somerville, MA
EVANS, Pauline Catherine, Apr 25 1916 Sex:F Child# 2 Ralph Morry Evans Nashua, NH & Jennie Connors Boston, MA
EVANS, Priscilla Clara, Dec 24 1930 Sex:F Child# 4 Walter Evans Gorham, ME & Grace D McNayr Nashua, NH
EVANS, Ralph Michael, Oct 18 1918 Sex:M Child# 3 Ralph M Evans Nashua, NH & Jennie Connors Charlestown, MA
EVANS, Robert Lester, Oct 16 1921 Sex:M Child# 1 Walter F Evans Gorham, ME & Grace McNayr Hollis, NH
EVANS, Unknown, Nov 11 1891 Sex:M Child# 2 Henry A Evans Lexington, KY & Edith M Taylor Lynn, MA
EVANS, Unknown, Aug 4 1897 Sex:M Child# 2 William J Evans Wales & Katie Scriven Ireland Stillborn
EVANS, Unknown, Dec 23 1899 Sex:M Child# 3 William G Evans England & Catherine Scriven Ireland Stillborn
EVANS, Unknown, Feb 2 1901 Sex:M Child# 6 William J Evans Swanzy, S Wales & Catherine Scriven Ireland Stillborn
EVANS, Unknown, Aug 12 1903 Sex:M Child# 7 Harry H Evans Madbury & Bertha L Swain Bennington, VT
EVANS, Willie, Feb 27 1897 Sex:M Child# 1 William J Evans Wales & Catherine Scriven Ireland
EVARNO, Andrew, Nov 28 1917 Sex:M Child# 13 Wacile Evarno Russia & Annie Lepassino Russia
EVERETT, Richard Carroll, Sep 29 1916 Sex:M Child# 1 James R Everett Framingham, MA & Elizabeth M Carroll Worcester
EVERETT, Unknown, Aug 7 1889 Sex:M Child# 2 Frank S Everett Chelmsford, MA & Florence B Perkins Acton, MA
EVERETT, Walter L, Apr 9 1895 Sex:M Child# 3 Frank S Everett New London & Florence B Perkins Acton, MA
FABER, Jos Albert Armand, Apr 18 1928 Sex:M Child# 6 Lucien S Faber Canada & Georgianna Hudon Nashua, NH
FABER, Joseph, Mar 24 1908 Sex:M Child# 1 Lucien Faber Canada & Georgianna Beaulieu Nashua, NH

FABER, M Lucienne Simone, Jun 24 1914 Sex:F Child# 3 Lucien M Faber Canada & Georgianna Beaulieu Nashua, NH
FABER, Marianna Yvonne, Jun 22 1912 Sex:F Child# 2 Lucien Faber Canada & Georgianna Hudon Nashua, NH
FABER, Mary Jane Gertrude, Jun 3 1922 Sex:F Child# 5 Lucien Faber Canada & Georgianna Hudon Nashua, NH
FABER, Unknown, Oct 27 1918 Sex:F Child# 4 Lucien Faber Canada & Georgiana Beaulieu
FABER, William Chester, Apr 9 1933 Sex:M Child#  (No Parents Listed)
FAGENSON, Ida, Jul 5 1895 Sex:F Child#  Henry Fagenson Russia & Sarah Russia
FAGENSON, Lizzie, Jun 19 1896 Sex:F Child# 3 Henry Fagenson Russia & Sarah Portrie Russia
FAGERSON, Sylvia, Jan 25 1922 Sex:F Child# 2 William Fagerson Russia & Rose Zelinsky Russia
FAGNENT, Jos Leo Richard, Jun 8 1934 Sex:M Child# 1 Elzear Fagnant Greenville, NH & Imelda Roy Canada
FAHEY, Christina E, Dec 22 1905 Sex:F Child# 7 Martin Fahey Ireland & Bridget Mulqueen Ireland
FAHEY, Lauretta M, Sep 11 1901 Sex:F Child# 1 Martin Fahey Ireland & Bridget Mulqueen Ireland
FAHEY, Mary A, Nov 2 1902 Sex:F Child# 2 Martin Fahey Ireland & Bridget Mulquin Ireland
FAHEY, Mildred Ann, Oct 23 1928 Sex:F Child# 2 Martin J Fahey Alum Bridge, WV & Marie Hallisey Nashua, NH
FAIR, Clarence Goodwin, Dec 4 1915 Sex:M Child# 2 Harry C Fair Nashua, NH & Maude Trombley Nashua, NH
FAIR, Ruth Evelyn, Oct 11 1913 Sex:F Child# 1 Harry C Fair Nashua, NH & Maud Trombley Nashua, NH
FAIRBANKS, Richard Harry, May 25 1935 Sex:M Child# 2 Harry Fairbanks Pelham, NH & Lil Courtemanche Nashua, NH
FAIRBANKS, Unknown, Aug 28 1888 Sex:F Child# 2 C M Fairbanks Hillsborough & Emma B Bartlett Nashua, NH
FAIRBANKS, Unknown, Aug 26 1894 Sex:M Child# 1 Frank G Fairbanks Nashua, NH & Isabelle Cartwright Walsell, Eng
FAIRFIELD, Alfred Joseph, Mar 26 1933 Sex:M Child# 2 Alfred J Fairfield Wilton, NH & Lillian Manning Troy, NH
FAIRFIELD, Beatrice N, Sep 17 1912 Sex:F Child# 6 Benjamin Fairfield New Boston, NH & Etta M Ackerman Bristol, NH
FAIRFIELD, George Benjamin, May 30 1904 Sex:M Child# 2 Benjamin Fairfield New Boston, NH & Etta M Ackerman Bristol
FAIRFIELD, Helen Sabina, Jan 25 1907 Sex:F Child# 3 Benjamin Fairfield New Boston, NH & Etta Mackerman Bristol, NH
FAIRFIELD, Henry Ray, Nov 9 1903 Sex:M Child# 2 George Fairfield
FALCONER, Ruth, Dec 28 1917 Sex:F Child# 1 Alexander Falconer Ayer Jct, MA & Grace Wilson Philadelphia, PA
FALEKOWSKI, Stephanie, Feb 21 1912 Sex:F Child# 2 Stephen Falekowski Russia & Anna Ollander Russia
FALIKOWSKI, Helena, Feb 17 1910 Sex:F Child# 1 Stephan Falikowski Russia & Anna Nolender Russia
FALKOIVSKI, Jadencz Pavail, Feb 1 1914 Sex:M Child# 3 Stefan Falkoivski Russia & Anna Olender Russia
FALLON, Thomas F, Dec 11 1890 Sex:M Child# 7 Patrick Fallon Ireland & Bridget Ireland
FAMULAWICUS, Alice, May 6 1915 Sex:F Child# 1 Peter Famulawicus Russia & Alice Semonite Russia
FANCY, Bradford William, Jun 5 1935 Sex:M Child# 2 Wm A R Fancy Nashua, NH & Thelma Watts Nashua, NH
FANCY, Burpee Albert, Jun 15 1900 Sex:M Child# 1 H A Fancy NS & Ethel M Reid NS
FANCY, Exilla Mary, Feb 17 1906 Sex:F Child# 2 Harold A Fancy Bridgewater, NS & Alice M Benjamin King's Co, NS
FANCY, Frederick Harland, Jul 10 1913 Sex:M Child# 6 Albert H Fancy Bridgewater, NS & Alice Benjamin White Rock, NS
FANCY, Gladys Isabelle, Jul 19 1907 Sex:F Child# 3 Harold Fancy Nova Scotia & Alice Benjamin White Rock, NS
FANCY, Herbert Lestor, Jul 27 1904 Sex:M Child# 1 Albert H Fancy Bridgewater, NS & Alice Benjamin White Rock, NS
FANCY, John, Dec 21 1910 Sex:M Child# 5 Albert H Fancy Nova Scotia & Alice M Benjamin Nova Scotia
FANCY, William A Benjamin, Jan 1 1909 Sex:M Child# 4 Harold Fancy Nova Scotia & Alice Benjamin White Rock, NS
FANOS, Michael G, Jun 19 1925 Sex:M Child# 3 George Fanos Greece & K Sinapoulos Greece
FAONS, Stasulla, Feb 5 1911 Sex:F Child# 9 Mikus Faons Greece & Theodora Spelkopul Greece
FARGANINI, Delias F, Nov 24 1909 Sex:F Child# 1 Elie Farganini Italy & Carolina Baroni Italy
FARGO, Unknown, Feb 28 1898 Sex:F Child# 1 William J Fargo Shelburn Falls, VT & Rossa F Powers Bolton, MA
FARLAND, Alfred John, Feb 26 1935 Sex:M Child# 1 Alfred Farland Malden, MA & Alice Magarian Manchester, NH
FARLAND, Alfred Wilfrid, May 4 1927 Sex:M Child#  Wilfrid Farland Canada & Alice Marquis Nashua, NH
FARLAND, Charles, Mar 11 1892 Sex:M Child# 13 Zepherin Farland Canada & Adele Cournoyer Canada
FARLAND, Joseph C, May 4 1891 Sex:M Child# 12 Zepherin Farland Canada & Adele Cournoyier Canada
FARLAND, Joseph Robert, Aug 10 1923 Sex:M Child# 2 Emile Farland Canada & Maria Boucher Canada
FARLAND, M Elizabeth Aurore, Dec 31 1921 Sex:F Child# 1 Wilfred Farland Canada & Alice Marquis NH
FARLAND, Mary Ella, Mar 10 1919 Sex:F Child# 1 Joseph Farland Canada & Loretta Gokey W Chazy, NY
FARLEY, Earle Dexter, Jan 1 1896 Sex:M Child# 1 Charles J Farley Hollis, NH & Ella P Pierce Hollis, NH
FARLEY, Elizabeth Janice, Apr 30 1922 Sex:F Child# 1 Scott P Farley Hollis, NH & Gladys H Slater Essex Jct, VT
FARLEY, Frank Asa, Aug 2 1922 Sex:M Child# 1 George F Farley Goffstown, NH & Annie Fisher Milford, NH
FARLEY, Louise May, Nov 18 1926 Sex:F Child# 3 George Farley Goffstown, NH & Anna Fisher Milford, NH
FARLEY, Mabel Gertrude, Jul 13 1908 Sex:F Child# 2 George W Farley Gorham, ME & Alberta C Cave England
FARLEY, Marie Evelyn, Jul 2 1933 Sex:F Child# 1 Arthur Farley Manchester, NH & Evelyn Hanscom Lewiston, ME
FARLEY, Marion Ethel, Aug 19 1932 Sex:F Child# 4 George F Farley Goffstown, NH & Amy Fisher Milford, NH
FARLEY, Mildred Eveline, Oct 5 1900 Sex:F Child#  George W Farley Maine & Alberta Cave
FARLEY, Norman George, Feb 25 1924 Sex:M Child# 2 George F Farley Goffstown, NH & Annie L Fisher Milford, NH
FARLEY, Priscilla Margaret, Jul 31 1924 Sex:F Child# 2 Scott P Farley Hollis, NH & Gladys H Slater Essex Jct, VT
FARMER, Elmer Capen, Jan 24 1908 Sex:M Child# 1 Walter H Farmer Conn & Ruth P Capen Somerville, MA
FARMER, Ruth Mildred, Sep 26 1926 Sex:F Child# 5 George A Farmer England & Jennie Smith Canada
FARNALD, Leland Wingate, Feb 19 1919 Sex:M Child# 2 George C Farnald Dover, NH & Goldie Smalley Nashua, NH
FARNHAM, John Marston, Nov 6 1900 Sex:M Child# 1 George W Farnham Nashua, NH & Mary A Marston Canada
FARNSWORTH, Albert H, Jan 29 1891 Sex:M Child# 1 Walter C Farnsworth Wilton, NH & Ida S Graham Wilton, NH
FARNSWORTH, Deborah, Jul 8 1895 Sex:F Child# 5 W O Farnsworth Brookline & Ellen S Corey Dunstable, MA
FARNSWORTH, Unknown, Feb 22 1887 Sex:F Child# 3 James Farnsworth Nashua, NH & Millie Savage Haverhill, MA
FARNSWORTH, Unknown, Apr 26 1887 Sex:M Child# 3 W O Farnsworth Brookline, MA & E S Groton
FARNSWORTH, Unknown, Jun 12 1890 Sex:M Child# 4 Willie O Farnsworth Brookline, NH & Ellen Corey Dunstable, MA
FARNSWORTH, Unknown, Mar 16 1891 Sex:F Child# 1 Harry E Farnsworth Nashua, NH & Grace A Emery Nashua, NH
FARNSWORTH, Unknown, Nov 17 1927 Sex:M Child# 1 W Farnsworth Haverhill, MA & Helen Latulippe Vermont
FARNUM, David Broderick, Oct 12 1931 Sex:M Child# 1 Warren Farnum Nashua, NH & Catherine Broderick Nashua, NH
FARNUM, Warren Salls, Jan 21 1905 Sex:M Child# 2 George W Farnum Nashua, NH & Mary A Marston Stanstead, PQ
FARR, Pearl Ruby, Apr 20 1918 Sex:F Child# 3 Henry Clarence Farr Nashua, NH & Maud Ida Trombley Nashua, NH
FARRAR, Julia, Jul 21 1935 Sex:F Child# 6 Carleton Farrar Lunenberg, MA & Helen G Higgins W Roxbury, MA

FARRAR, Martha, May 22 1934 Sex:F Child# 5 Carleton Farrar Lunenburg, MA & Helen Higgins W Roxbury, MA
FARRELL, Albert, Mar 14 1897 Sex:M Child# 8 Richard Farrell Ireland & Anna Cutter Ireland
FARRELL, Albert, Oct 5 1906 Sex:M Child# 2 John J Farrell Lowell, MA & Catherine McDermott Nashua, NH
FARRELL, Barbara Helen, Oct 19 1929 Sex:F Child# 3 George Farrell Nashua, NH & Loretta DeMontigny Nashua, NH
FARRELL, Cynthia Ethel, Mar 31 1914 Sex:F Child# 1 William H Farrell Nashua, NH & Mabel Davenport Nashua, NH
FARRELL, Francis Charles, Nov 5 1911 Sex:M Child# 2 Frank Farrell Italy & Mary Keenan NH
FARRELL, George Richard, Jun 9 1925 Sex:M Child# 1 George W Farrell Nashua, NH & L DeMontigny Nashua, NH
FARRELL, Harry Francis, Nov 12 1923 Sex:M Child#  Harry G Farrell El Paso, TX & Frances Fay Boston, MA
FARRELL, James, Oct 27 1897 Sex:M Child# 2 Patrick Farrell Ireland & Bridget Connors Ireland
FARRELL, John Kenneth, Mar 19 1908 Sex:M Child# 3 John J Farrell Lowell, MA & Catherine McDermott Nashua, NH
FARRELL, John Nicholas, Sep 22 1909 Sex:M Child# 1 John Farrell Italy & Mary Keegan Nashua, NH
FARRELL, Richard Thomas, Oct 4 1905 Sex:M Child# 1 John J Farrell Lowell, MA & K T McDermott Nashua, NH
FARRELL, Robert Joseph, May 24 1926 Sex:M Child# 4 John J Farrell Lowell, MA & C McDermott Nashua, NH
FARRELL, Stella Mae, Mar 14 1927 Sex:F Child# 2 George W Farrell Nashua, NH & L DeMontigny Nashua, NH
FARRELL, Unknown, Mar 1 1922 Sex:M Child# 3 Frank Farrell Italy & Mary Keegan Nashua, NH Stillborn
FARRIS, Doris May Yvonne, Apr 25 1926 Sex:F Child# 3 Harry M Farris Cutter, ME & M R Levielle Canada
FARRIS, Maynard Raymond, Feb 5 1923 Sex:M Child# 1 Harry M Farris Cutler, ME & Melvina R Leveille Canada
FARROLL, Georges William, Feb 14 1899 Sex:M Child# 9 Richard Farroll Ireland & Anna Cotter Ireland
FARRY, Albert James, Mar 15 1901 Sex:M Child# 2 Michael Farry Nashua, NH & Margaret Cullen Ireland
FARRY, James Edward, Feb 6 1897 Sex:M Child# 1 John Farry Nashua, NH & Katheme Conlon Ireland
FARRY, Margaret M, Jul 26 1903 Sex:F Child# 3 John Farry Nashua, NH & Katherine Conlon Ireland
FARRY, Marion Evelyn, May 13 1899 Sex:F Child# 2 John Farry Nashua, NH & Katherine Conlon Ireland
FARRY, Thomas Bernard, Jan 3 1898 Sex:M Child# 1 Michael Farry Nashua, NH & Margaret A Cullen Ireland
FARWELL, Charles, Aug 30 1888 Sex:M Child# 1 Frank Farwell Hollis & Maggie Harrigan Ireland
FARWELL, Charles Henry, Aug 5 1926 Sex:M Child# 2 Charles H Farwell Nashua, NH & G Charbonneau Nashua, NH
FARWELL, Donald Charles, Nov 13 1924 Sex:M Child#  George Farwell Nashua, NH & Clara Nadeau Nashua, NH
FARWELL, Ethel May, Jan 20 1887 Sex:F Child# 1 E H Farwell Mason & A C Temple
FARWELL, Francis Ellsworth, Dec 30 1917 Sex:M Child# 1 George Farwell Nashua, NH & Clara Nadeau Nashua, NH
FARWELL, George M, Dec 14 1919 Sex:M Child# 2 George Farwell Nashua, NH & Clara Nadeau Nashua, NH
FARWELL, Joseph, Dec 23 1890 Sex:M Child# 2 Frank E Farwell Lawrence, MA & Maggie Harrigan Ireland
FARWELL, Marjorie Mary, Apr 18 1922 Sex:F Child# 1 Charles H Farwell Nashua, NH & Genevieve Charbonneau Nashua, NH
FARWELL, Mildred Lucille, Jun 19 1911 Sex:F Child# 1 Charles H Farwell Nashua, NH & Ella M Johnson Sweden
FARWELL, Ruth, Nov 25 1905 Sex:F Child# 1 George Farwell Harrisville & Lula M Harriman Hillsborough
FARWELL, Theresa Gertrude, Nov 17 1927 Sex:F Child# 4 George Farwell Nashua, NH & Clara Nadeau Nashua, NH
FARWELL, Unknown, Jul 29 1923 Sex:M Child# 1 William Farwell Milford, NH & Una Hutchinson Milford, NH
FARYALL, Carley, May 13 1888 Sex:M Child# 2 John Faryall Sciota, NY & Alice Blois Sciota, NY
FASDICK, Ethel May, Mar 9 1915 Sex:F Child# 3 Charles E Fasdick Peterborough, NH & Ethel M Pratt Nashua, NH
FASSETT, James Adams, Jun 3 1904 Sex:M Child# 1 James H Fasset Nashua, NH & Bertha Smith Mass
FAUBERT, Irene Rosiane, Mar 29 1906 Sex:F Child# 2 Hormidas Faubert Canada & Marianne Bosse Canada
FAUBERT, Jeanne, Jun 21 1908 Sex:F Child# 3 Hormidas Faubert Canada & Marie Bosse Nashua, NH
FAUBERT, Joseph Roville, May 12 1914 Sex:M Child# 1 Rosario Faubert Canada & Delima Levesque Canada
FAUBERT, Joseph Yvan N, Oct 28 1906 Sex:M Child# 1 Elie Faubert Canada & Adwilda St Germain Canada
FAUBERT, Rosalie Beatrice, Feb 14 1904 Sex:F Child# 1 Hormidas Faubert Canada & Marie Anne Bosse Nashua, NH
FAUBERT, Unknown, Apr 21 1897 Sex:F Child# 11 Antoine Faubert Canada & Delima Courtemarche Canada Stillborn
FAUCHER, Florence Edna, Dec 9 1922 Sex:F Child# 1 Louis Faucher Pepperell, MA & Florida Lariviere St Johnsbury, VT
FAUCHER, Joseph Pierre Paul, Dec 18 1916 Sex:M Child# 1 Leo Faucher Michigan & Aurore Bonenfant Canada
FAUCHER, M Claire Yolande, Feb 12 1921 Sex:F Child# 2 Leo Faucher Michigan & Aurore Bonenfant Canada
FAUCHER, M Rose Virginie, Jun 26 1913 Sex:F Child# 1 Henri Faucher Canada & Clarisse Santerre Canada
FAUCHER, Napoleon, Sep 10 1915 Sex:M Child# 2 Louis Faucher Pepperell, MA & Eliza Desautels Nashua, NH
FAUCHER, Unknown, Feb 14 1917 Sex: Child#  Adelard Faucher Canada & Marie L Champagne Canada Stillborn
FAUKAWSKI, Helen, Mar 9 1914 Sex:F Child# 4 Joseph Faukawski Russia & Eva Liniewick Russia
FAURINITE, Annie, Mar 28 1917 Sex:F Child# 2 Charles Faurinite Russia & Mary Carclick Russia
FAUSTINI, John Philip, May 19 1928 Sex:M Child# 1 John Faustini Milford, NH & Josephine Paradis Milford, NH
FAVOR, Pearl E, Mar 28 1899 Sex:F Child# 1 Burt P Favor Weare & M C Clark Auburn
FAVREAU, Julien Albert, Jan 28 1906 Sex:M Child# 3 Harvey Favreau Canada & Alice Morin Canada
FAY, Gloria Therese, Jul 3 1930 Sex:F Child# 6 Joseph Fay NH & Antoinette Bouvin Canada
FAY, Maurice Ovila, Mar 13 1928 Sex:M Child# 5 J O Fay Groveton, NH & Antoin Bouvier Canada
FAY, Pauline Rose, Dec 18 1926 Sex:F Child# 4 Joseph Fay Groveton, NH & Antoinette Bouvier Canada
FEATHERSTONE, Ann, May 28 1899 Sex:F Child# 1 John Featherstone Ireland & Margaret Winn Ireland
FEATHERSTONE, John, Sep 21 1901 Sex:M Child# 2 John Featherstone Ireland & Margaret Winn Ireland
FEATHERSTONE, Robert Everett, Feb 18 1905 Sex:M Child# 3 John J Featherstone Ireland & Margaret Winn Ireland
FECTEAU, Adrien, Feb 24 1905 Sex:M Child# 4 Ferdinand Fecteau Canada & Arthemise Claveau Canada
FECTEAU, Adrienne, Mar 20 1907 Sex:F Child# 6 Ferdinand Fecteau Canada & Arthemise Claveau Canada
FECTEAU, Emile Victor, Feb 14 1906 Sex:M Child# 5 Ferdinand Fecteau Canada & Arthemise Claveau Canada
FECTEAU, Irene Rita, Sep 1 1921 Sex:F Child# 2 Wilfrid Fecteau Canada & Rose Prince Nashua, NH
FECTEAU, M Blanche Laurette, Jul 18 1916 Sex:F Child# 10 Ferdinand Fecteau Canada & Arthemise Claveau Canada
FECTEAU, M Jeanne Alice, Dec 6 1913 Sex:F Child# 9 Ferdinand Fecteau Canada & Arthemise Claveau Canada
FECTEAU, Marie Blanche, Dec 14 1909 Sex:F Child# 7 Ferdinand Fecteau Canada & Arthemise Claveau Canada
FECTEAU, Marie Delia, Feb 24 1899 Sex:F Child# 3 Arthur Fecteau Otter River, MA & Lea Beaulieu Canada
FECTEAU, Marie Irene Adele, Apr 12 1912 Sex:F Child# 8 Ferdinand Fecteau Canada & Artimise Clareau Canada
FEDERAVITCH, John, Oct 14 1927 Sex:M Child# 3 A Federavitch Russia & Laura Kacts Russia
FEDERSAVITCH, Julia, Aug 27 1922 Sex:F Child# 2 Ant Federsavitch Poland & Laura Karchita Lithuania
FEDESOVICH, Unknown, Sep 27 1930 Sex:M Child# 4 Anthony Fedesovich Russia & Lillian Karseta Lithuania

FEDORAK, William, Mar 2 1916 Sex:M Child# 7 Joseph Fedorak Russia & Emelia Krapuska Russia
FEDORITZ, Peter, Mar 12 1912 Sex:M Child# 2 Peter Fedoritz Russia & Louise Belk Russia
FEDORUK, Michael, Jan 23 1918 Sex:M Child# 6 Joseph Fedoruk Poland & Emelia Fedoruk Poland
FEDOURK, Joseph, Dec 31 1919 Sex:M Child# 9 Joseph Fedourk Russia & Amelia Karpousta Russia
FEDSOWICH, Joseph, Oct 29 1933 Sex:M Child# 4 A Fedsowich Russia & Lillian Kasheta Russia
FEENEY, Mary Louise, Mar 15 1910 Sex:F Child# 2 Austin J Feeney Mass & Mary Rogers Vermont
FEIGELSON, Carl, Jun 15 1903 Sex:M Child# 3 Henry Feigelson Russia & Sarah Partner Russia
FEINBERG, Unknown, Sep 9 1895 Sex:M Child  Alex Feinberg Russia & Libbie Alpert Russia
FELCH, Edward, Mar 18 1897 Sex:M Child# 1 Edward Felch Ayer Jct, MA & Carrie L Baker Kemswick, MA
FELCH, Evelyn, Sep 25 1916 Sex:F Child# 1 Elmer T Felch Milford, NH & Mattie L Osgood Milford, NH
FELCH, Philip Preston, Jul 29 1918 Sex:M Child# 2 Elmer S Felch Milford, NH & Mattie L Osgood Milford, NH
FELCH, Richard Elmer, Jan 6 1922 Sex:M Child# 3 Elmer T Felch Milford, NH & Mattie L Osgood Milford, NH
FELCH, Unknown, Oct 20 1916 Sex:F Child# 2 Augustus C Felch Walpole, NH & Meda French Greenfield, NH Stillborn
FELIX, Morris, Nov 21 1934 Sex:M Child# 3 Oscar Felix Suncook, NH & Regina Faucher Manchester, NH
FELIX, Unknown, Sep 27 1932 Sex:F Child# 2 Oscar Felix Hooksett, NH & Regina Faucher Manchester, NH
FELKER, Meldred A, Jan 4 1897 Sex:F Child# 4 A C Felker Barrington & Alice M Foss Strafford
FELKOWSKI, John Antonio, Jun 13 1925 Sex:M Child# 5 Stejhen Felkowski Poland & Anna Poland
FELLOWS, Edna R, Apr 5 1893 Sex:F Child# 1 Oscar Fellows Billerica, MA & Alice O Barker Candia
FELLOWS, Richard Carol, Dec 16 1928 Sex:M Child# 3 E Y Fellows Candia, NH & Mary Ramsey Peterboro, NH
FELTON, Chester Ross, Oct 6 1909 Sex:M Child# 3 William Felton New Jersey & Sarah Young Nova Scotia
FELTON, Chester Ross, Jr, Jan 25 1934 Sex:M Child# 1 Chester Ross Felton Nashua, NH & Lucille Parker Vermont
FELTON, Doris Arlene, Jun 19 1917 Sex:F Child# 3 George Felton S Lyndeborough, NH & Lillian Crocket Merrimac, MA
FELTON, Dorothy Irene, Apr 3 1920 Sex:F Child# 3 George Felton S Lyndeboro, NH & Lillian Crockett Merrimac, MA
FELTON, George Erwin, Dec 19 1918 Sex:M Child# 4 George Felton S Lyndeboro, NH & Lillian Crockett Merrimac, MA
FELTON, Lillian Gertrude, Oct 30 1895 Sex:F Child# 2 George L Felton Ayer Jct, MA & Charlotte Ochlmann Brooklyn
FELTON, Lincoln David, Oct 30 1895 Sex:M Child# 1 George L Felton Ayer Jct, MA & Charlotte Ochlmann Brooklyn,
FELTON, Maurice Garfield, Dec 13 1918 Sex:M Child# 1 James E Felton S Lyndeboro, NH & Marion Munroe Sussex, NS
FELTON, Ruth E, Mar 5 1901 Sex:F Child# 1 James E Felton S Lyndeboro, NH & Alice Woods Nashua, NH
FELTON, Virgie May, Feb 29 1912 Sex:F Child# 1 George W Felton Lyndeborough, NH & Lillian Crockett Merrimac, MA
FELTON, Walter Irwin, Apr 27 1902 Sex:M Child# 2 James E Felton S Lyndeboro, NH & Alice Woods Nashua, NH
FENOVOWIZ, Andrew, Mar 23 1906 Sex:M Child# 1 Andrew Fenovowiz Russia & Alexandra Kopicka Russia
FENSTERMACKER, Marion Charline, Jan 20 1929 Sex:F Child# 1 Russell Fenstermacke Findlay, OH & Grace Snyder Clevelan
FENTON, Loren Irving, Apr 23 1914 Sex:M Child# 3 James Fenton Boston, MA & Isabelle Howe Nashua, NH
FENTON, Unknown, Nov 15 1910 Sex:M Child# 2 James B Fenton Boston, Ma & Isabelle Howe Nashua, NH
FERACENTCH, John, Nov 17 1918 Sex:M Child# 2 John Feracentch Russia & Antoin Melankantch Russia
FERGNANI, William, Mar 30 1914 Sex:M Child# 4 Elio Fergnani Italy & Carolina Borani Italy
FERGUANI, Walter, May 16 1911 Sex:M Child# 2 Elio Ferguani Italy & Catalia Baroni Italy
FERGUSON, Shirley Geraldine, Aug 19 1931 Sex:F Child# 1 Irving Ferguson Alabama & Eva Chandler Acton, ME
FERLAND, Adelard, Jun 7 1897 Sex:M Child# 4 Paul Ferland Canada & Agnes Cardin Canada
FERLAND, Ernest Wilfrid, Nov 26 1907 Sex:M Child# 3 Goerge Ferland Canada & Amanda Havard US
FERLAND, Evangeline, Apr 27 1893 Sex:F Child# 2 Joseph Ferland Canada & Georgiana Gaudreau Canada
FERLAND, Henri Leon, May 10 1902 Sex:M Child# 1 George Ferland Fairfield, ME & Amanda Avard Nashua, NH
FERLAND, Joseph Adelard, Apr 4 1894 Sex:M Child# 3 Joseph Ferland Canada & Georgiana Gandreau Canada
FERLAND, Joseph Euclide, May 27 1897 Sex:M Child# 8 Francois Bosse Canada & Ermine Ferland Canada
FERLAND, Lillian Edna M, May 30 1904 Sex:F Child# 2 George H Ferland Canada & Amanda M Avard Nashua, NH
FERLAND, Olivier S, Feb 12 1887 Sex:M Child  Zepherem Ferland P Q & Adile Comelier P Q
FERLAND, Rose A, Jun 12 1887 Sex:F Child# 4 Joseph Ferland Canada & Angele Paul Canada
FERLAND, Rosilda, Mar 3 1896 Sex:M Child# 4 Paul Ferland Canada & Agnes Cardin Canada
FERLAND, Shirley Diane, Nov 20 1935 Sex:F Child# 6 Alfred Ferland Manchester, NH & Anna Gelinas Canada
FERLANE, J Napoleon Henry, May 16 1921 Sex:M Child# 1 Emile Ferlane Canada & Maria Boucher Canada
FERNALD, Graham Hoyt, Aug 24 1933 Sex:M Child# 1 L H Fernald Tonawanda, NY & Christine Smith Haverhill, MA
FERNANDES, Evangeline Antonia, Mar 24 1935 Sex:F Child# 2 John Fernandes Portugal & Ida Dejesus Mass
FERNANI, William, Jun 1 1912 Sex:M Child# 3 Elio Fernani Italy & Caroline Borani Italy
FERRIN, Luella, Jan 27 1925 Sex:F Child# 1 Fred Ferrin Madison, NH & Ida Hughes Brooklyn, NY
FERRIS, Alfred Albert, Feb 12 1924 Sex:M Child# 2 Harry M Ferris Cutler, ME & Melvina Leveille Canada
FERRY, Raymond, May 17 1922 Sex:M Child# 1 Gilmore Ferry Cutler, ME & M Anne Moreau Nashua, NH
FERRYALL, Mary Lucille, Sep 8 1917 Sex:F Child# 3 Charles A Ferryall Sciota, NY & Bertha May Blow Sciota, NY
FERRYALL, Thelma Pearl, May 20 1910 Sex:F Child# 2 Leo Ferryall Nashua, NH & Olive Bourdeau Burlington, VT
FERRYALL, Zula Orena, Jul 31 1902 Sex:F Child# 2 Fred Ferryall Nashua, NH & Angelina Salvail Greenville, NH
FERTH, Herbert Wentworth, Oct 29 1906 Sex:M Child# 3 Nathaniel Ferth Nova Scotia & Catherine McKay Nova Scotia
FERYALL, John E, Apr 17 1887 Sex:M Child# 1 John Feryall Sciota, NY & Eliza Blais Sciota, NY
FERYALL, Unknown, Sep 11 1899 Sex:M Child# 1 Fred A Feryall Nashua, NH & Agnelina Salvail Greenville, NH Stillborn
FESETTE, Lizzie B, Mar 18 1894 Sex:F Child# 2 Manson Fesette NY & Carrie Pronto NY
FHAIR, Harry C, Jan 2 1888 Sex:M Child# 2 William Fhair Ireland & Lucy Fhair Nashua, NH
FICTAU, Unknown, Dec 8 1895 Sex:F Child# 2 Arthur Fictau Otter River, MA & Leah Boulier NY
FICTEAU, Oziana, Mar 3 1894 Sex:F Child# 1 Arthur Ficteau Otter River, MA & Lea Beaulieu Canada
FIELD, Clesson Mills, Aug 3 1930 Sex:M Child# 3 Clesson Field Milford, NH & Mira Chapman Dunstable, MA
FIELD, Everett, Nov 25 1894 Sex:M Child# 5 Edward Field Manchester & Margaret E Sullivan Nashua, NH
FIELD, Harold, Aug 26 1896 Sex:M Child# 3 William J Field Manchester, NH & Kate E Linnehan Nashua, NH
FIELD, Helen, Nov 25 1890 Sex:f Child# 3 Edward Field Manchester, NH & Maggie E Sullivan Nashua, NH
FIELD, James Francis, Oct 21 1927 Sex:M Child# 2 James F Field Nashua, NH & Marion Classon Nashua, NH
FIELD, Joan Adele, Dec 7 1931 Sex:F Child# 5 Arthur E Field Merrimack, NH & Bertha Roach Concord, NH
FIELD, John Henry, Jr, Jul 23 1889 Sex:M Child# 3 John H Field Manchester, NH & Catherine T Nashua, NH

FIELD, John Linnehan, Sep 14 1893 Sex:M Child# 2 William J Field Manchester & Kate E Linnehan Nashua, NH
FIELD, Kathleen, Apr 8 1899 Sex:F Child# 7 Edward Field Manchester, NH & Margaret Sullivan Nashua, NH
FIELD, Leonard Classon, Dec 6 1924 Sex:M Child# 1 James Field Nashua, NH & Marion Classon Nashua, NH
FIELD, Lucy, Mar 6 1897 Sex:F Child# 6 Edward Field Manchester, NH & Margaret E Sullivan Nashua, NH
FIELD, Manila, May 3 1898 Sex:F Child# 4 William J Field Manchester, NH & Katherine E Linnehan Nashua, NH
FIELD, Margaret, Sep 23 1904 Sex:F Child# 8 Edward Field Manchester, NH & Margaret Sullivan Nashua, NH
FIELD, Marjorie Blanche, May 4 1925 Sex:F Child# 1 Classon Field Milford, NH & Mira Chapman Dunstable, MA
FIELD, Mary, Sep 6 1892 Sex:F Child# 1 William J Field Manchester, NH & Kate E Linchan Nashua, NH
FIELD, May Francis, Oct 17 1892 Sex:F Child# 4 Edward Field Manchester, NH & Margaret E Sullivan Nashua, NH
FIELD, Norma Justine, Apr 19 1896 Sex:F Child# 5 Albert J Field Manchester & Nellie A Field Amherst
FIELD, Ruth Lillian, Feb 7 1927 Sex:F Child# 1 Robert H Field Nashua, NH & Alice Steponovich Nashua, NH
FIELD, Shirley Grace, Oct 18 1926 Sex:F Child# 2 Glesson Field Hollis, NH & Blanche Chapman Dunstable, MA
FIELD, Unknown, May 21 1887 Sex:M Child# 1 Edward Field Manchester & Maggie E Nashua, NH
FIELD, Unknown, May 30 1889 Sex:M Child# 2 Edmund Field New Hampshire & Maggie Field New Hampshire
FIELD, Unknown, Oct 6 1893 Sex:M Child# 3 Albert J Field Manchester & Nellie A Amherst
FIELD, Unknown, Mar 31 1894 Sex:M Child# 4 John H Field Manchester, NH & Kate Sullivan Nashua, NH
FIELD, Unknown, Apr 24 1895 Sex:M Child# 4 Albert J Field Manchester & Mellie A Amherst
FIELD, Unknown, Nov 15 1896 Sex:M Child# 5 John H Field Manchester, NH & Kate Sullivan Nashua, NH
FIELD, Unknown, Jul 30 1902 Sex:M Child# 5 William J Field Manchester, NH & C E Linehan Nashua, NH
FIELD, Wesley Frederick, Oct 12 1919 Sex:M Child# 2 Arthur E Field Merrimack, NH & Bertha Roach Concord, NH
FIELD, William Pratt, Sep 20 1934 Sex:M Child# 1 Francis H Field Amherst, NH & Dorothy Pratt Hudson, NH
FIELDING, Robert Stanley, Aug 24 1924 Sex:M Child# 1 Luther Fielding US & Mary E Bowler Westerly, RI
FIELDMAN, John, Jun 28 1920 Sex:M Child# 1 James A Fieldman Boston, MA & Anne Fieldman Boston, MA Stillborn
FIELDS, Adrian Ruth, Feb 17 1916 Sex:F Child# 3 Warren S Fields Merrimack, NH & Eva Leazott Nashua, NH
FIELDS, Albert F, Mar 25 1888 Sex:M Child# 1 Albert J Fields Amoskeag & Ellen Sullivan Amherst
FIELDS, Olive Doris, Dec 7 1907 Sex:F Child# 1 Warren S Fields Merrimack, NH & Eva Leazotte Nashua, NH
FIELDS, Unknown, Feb 3 1891 Sex:F Child# 2 Albert J Fields Manchester & Nellia A Amherst
FIFIELD, Bernard G, May 6 1905 Sex:M Child# 2 Merton K Fifield New York & Emma Brown Vermont
FIFIELD, Donald Robert, Aug 26 1931 Sex:M Child# 1 Bernard G Fifield Nashua, NH & Reba Foster Bradford, PA
FIFIELD, Dorothy Hattie, Jan 31 1908 Sex:F Child# 1 George E Fifield Chateaugay, NY & Mary A Edson Northfield,
FIFIELD, Edith Elsworth, Jun 3 1908 Sex:F Child# 1 Pliny Fifield New York & Mina Waldron Rye, NH
FIFIELD, Grace, Feb 14 1894 Sex:F Child# 3 Herbert Fifield US & Electa Latrimore US
FIFIELD, Irene, May 10 1903 Sex:F Child# 1 James H Fifield Moores, NY & Charlotte McKay Shelbourne, NS
FIFIELD, Thelma O, Mar 4 1908 Sex:F Child# 3 M K Fifield New York & Emma Brown Cambridge, VT
FIFIELD, Vera Hazel, Jul 17 1899 Sex:F Child# 1 M K Fifield Mooers, NY & Emma Brown Cambridge, VT
FILION, Charles O A, Aug 3 1896 Sex:M Child# 7 J A Filion Canada & Mathilde Laliberte Canada
FILION, Lillian, Feb 4 1904 Sex:F Child# 2 Philippe Filion Canada & Eleonore Paradis Canada
FILION, Lillian Beatrice, Jan 25 1894 Sex:F Child# 5 J A Filion Canada & Mathilde Laliberte Canada
FILION, Marie A Juliette, Aug 17 1898 Sex:F Child# 8 J A Filion Canada & Mathilda Laliberte Canada
FILION, Marie A P, Jan 16 1900 Sex:F Child# 12 Alfred Filion Canada & Philomene Simard Canada
FILION, Marie Alice, Jun 25 1898 Sex:F Child# 11 Alfred Filion Canada & Philomene Simard Canada
FILION, Marie Diana, Sep 29 1902 Sex:F Child# 13 Alfred Filion Canada & Philomene Simard Canada
FILION, Marie J Rachel, Feb 6 1895 Sex:F Child# 6 Joseph A Filion St Damien, PQ & Mathilde Laliberte Canada
FILORAS, Nicholas, Jan 19 1922 Sex:M Child# 4 James Filoras Greece & Ida Karanthanos Greece
FILTON, Edna Louise, Feb 21 1914 Sex:F Child# 2 George W Filton Lyndeborough, NH & Lillian Crockett Merrimac, MA
FILTON, Robert Albert, Sep 4 1935 Sex:M Child# 2 Chester Filton Nashua, NH & Lucille Parker Hartland, VT
FINE, Roy Selig, Aug 14 1922 Sex:M Child# 1 Harry Fine Russia & Esther Feldman Boston, MA
FINELLI, Helen Antonia, May 17 1911 Sex:F Child# 4 John Finelli Italy & Louise Guida Italy
FINERTY, Unknown, Aug 22 1908 Sex:M Child# 7 Francis Finerty Boston, MA & Ellen Murphy Co Cork, Ireland
FINKEL, Bessie Lena, Oct 23 1912 Sex:F Child# 1 Morris Finkel Russia & Esther Springer Russia
FINKEL, Tillie, Mar 5 1919 Sex:F Child# 3 Morris Finkel Russia & Esther Springer Russia
FINN, Albert James, Dec 16 1896 Sex:M Child# 3 Michael Finn Ireland & Annie Kelley Ireland
FINN, Kathleen Burns, Feb 12 1904 Sex:F Child# 2 John W Finn Ireland & Mary E Mulhair Nashua, NH
FINN, Mary A, Jan 28 1894 Sex:F Child# 1 Michael Finn Ireland & Annie M Kelley Ireland
FINN, William, Aug 14 1895 Sex:M Child# 2 Michael Finn Ireland & Annie Kelley Ireland
FINNEGAN, John Bernard, Nov 1 1899 Sex:M Child# 3 John Finnegan Boston, MA & Alice McWeeney Nashua, NH
FINNEGAN, John Brendon, Aug 7 1929 Sex:M Child# 1 Patrick Finnegan Nashua, NH & Margaret Cotter Lowell, MA
FINNEGAN, Leo, Nov 20 1902 Sex:M Child# 5 John A Finnegan Boston, MA & Alice McWeeney Nashua, NH
FINNEGAN, Mary, Dec 15 1900 Sex:F Child# 4 John Finnegan Boston, MA & Alice McWeeney Nashua, NH
FINNEGAN, Sheila Anne, Apr 15 1931 Sex:F Child# 2 Patrick Finnegan Nashua, NH & Margaret Colter Lowell, MA
FINNEGAN, Unknown, May 15 1895 Sex:M Child# 1 John Finnegan Boston, MA & Alice McWeeney Nashua, NH
FINNERTY, Unknown, Nov 2 1905 Sex:M Child# 6 Francis Finnerty Boston, MA & Ellen F Murphy Ireland
FINNIE, Jean Cameron, Jun 5 1925 Sex:M Child# 2 Robert Finnie Dundee, Scotland & Agnes Cameron Lenox, MA
FINNIGAN, Alice, Dec 2 1903 Sex:F Child# 6 John A Finnigan Boston, MA & Alice T McWeeney Nashua, NH
FINNIGAN, Edward Brian, Jun 19 1933 Sex:M Child# 4 Patrick Finnigan Nashua, NH & Margaret Cotter Lowell, MA
FINNIGAN, Martha Rita, Jun 13 1935 Sex:F Child# 5 Patrick Finnigan Nashua, NH & Margaret Cotter Lowell, MA
FINNING, Charles, Sep 6 1901 Sex:M Child# 3 Charles W Finning Nashua, NH & Sabina McWeeney Nashua, NH
FINNING, Francis Joseph, Dec 25 1916 Sex:M Child# 1 Francis J Finning Nashua, NH & Anna F Madden Nashua, NH
FINNING, Mary, Oct 26 1897 Sex:F Child# 2 Charles W Finning Nashua, NH & Sabina McWeeney Nashua, NH
FINNING, Mary Louise, May 9 1891 Sex:F Child# 2 John E Finning Nashua, NH & Kate G Noonan Nashua, NH
FINNING, Robert, Jun 28 1896 Sex:M Child# 1 Charles Finning
FINNING, Unknown, Jul 25 1888 Sex:M Child# 1 John E Finning Nashua, NH & Katie Noonan Nashua, NH
FIRTH, Frank E, Mar 26 1905 Sex:M Child# 2 Nathaniel W Firth Nova Scotia & Catharine McKay Nova Scotia

FISET, Marie I A, Apr 19 1891 Sex:F Child# 1 Charles D Fiset New York & Lumina Gaulin Canada
FISETTE, Elinor Claire, Jan 10 1925 Sex:F Child# 1 George H Fisette Canada & Alice Smith Nashua, NH
FISH, Yvonne Marguerite, Aug 2 1910 Sex:F Child# 1 Raymond D Fish Oriskany, NY & Helen A Flynn Pepperell, MA
FISHER, Barbara French, Jan 24 1932 Sex:F Child# 1 Ralph Fisher Milford, NH & Marion French N Haverhill, NH
FISHER, Carmen Cecile, Dec 30 1933 Sex:F Child# 4 George H Fisher Nashua, NH & Lena Lamoureux Nashua, NH
FISHER, George Anthony, Apr 16 1923 Sex:M Child# 1 Rossiter A Fisher Mass & Anna Rousseau Canada
FISHER, George Harvey, Jan 10 1908 Sex:M Child# 4 George A Fisher Pennsylvania & Agnes Meehan Malone, NY
FISHER, Helen Clara, Jun 29 1917 Sex:F Child# 8 George Fisher Pennsylvania & Agnes Meehan New York
FISHER, James Joseph, Feb 3 1928 Sex:M Child# 2 Rossiter Fisher Mass & Anna Rousseau Canada
FISHER, Jerome Herbert, Jul 23 1910 Sex:M Child# 5 George A Fisher Derby, PA & Agnes Meehan Malone, NY
FISHER, John Raymond, Dec 30 1915 Sex:M Child# 7 George Fisher New York & Agnes Meehan NH
FISHER, Leonard A, Jun 7 1919 Sex:M Child# 9 George Fisher Pennsylvania & Agnes Meehan New York
FISHER, Richard Frederick, Oct 31 1929 Sex:M Child# 2 Oliver A Fisher Charlestown, MA & Ethel A Gould Derry, NH
FISHER, Richard Norton, Feb 5 1911 Sex:M Child# 1 George R Fisher Livermore, ME & Lois W Hunkins Haverhill, MA
FISHER, Robert Edwin, Mar 15 1919 Sex:M Child# 1 John E Fisher Sunapee, NH & Harriet Burtt Milford, NH
FISHER, Unknown, Aug 8 1931 Sex:f Child# 1 Milon J Fisher Nashua, NH & Arlene Blanchard Nashua, NH
FISHER, Wilbert Blanchard, Mar 17 1933 Sex:M Child# 2 Mylon Fisher Chazy, NY & Arlene Blanchard Nashua, NH
FISK, Richard Parker, Jul 14 1935 Sex:M Child# 2 Owen P Fisk Haverhill, MA & Esther Rossiter Manchester, NH
FISK, Theodore C, Sep 23 1904 Sex:M Child# 1 John T Fisk Lexington, MA & Susie Coffin Westcassett, ME
FISKE, Blanche Kathleen, Jan 16 1906 Sex:F Child# 2 John T Fiske Lexington, MA & Susan Coffin Westcassett, ME
FISKE, Harry W, Sep 15 1906 Sex:M Child# 1 Harry Fiske Worcester, MA & Louisa Guertin Nashua, NH
FISKE, Loretta, Apr 9 1908 Sex:F Child# 2 Harry F Fiske Worcester, MA & Louisa Guertin Nashua, NH
FISKE, Theodore Calvin, Mar 16 1935 Sex:M Child# 1 Theodore C Fiske Nashua, NH & Marg McDonald Moncton, NB Stillbor
FISKE, Unknown, Apr 10 1919 Sex:M Child# 4 Harry Fiske Worcester, MA & Louisa Guertin Nashua, NH
FISKE, Velma Mae, Oct 23 1907 Sex:F Child# 3 John T Fiske Lexington, MA & Susan Coffin Wiscasset, ME
FISSETTE, Dorothy Alice, Nov 21 1926 Sex:F Child# 2 George Fissette Canada & Alice Smith Nashua, NH
FISSETTE, Florence Mae, Jun 20 1930 Sex:F Child# 4 George Fissette Canada & Alice Smith Nashua, NH
FISSETTE, Ralph Arthur, Apr 9 1928 Sex:M Child# 3 George Fissette Canada & Alice Smith Nashua, NH
FISSETTE, Robert Warren, Jul 14 1932 Sex:M Child# 5 George Fissette Canada & Alice Smith Nashua, NH
FITCH, Pauline, Jul 16 1892 Sex:F Child# 1 Samuel Fitch Hopkinton, NH & Gertie Marlow, NH
FITZGERALD, Ann, Apr 9 1901 Sex:F Child# 8 William T Fitzgerald Ireland & Ann A Moore Ireland
FITZGERALD, Freddie Raymond, May 7 1893 Sex:M Child# 6 Charles A Fitzgerald Warren & Eva A Hamlet Nashua, NH
FITZGERALD, Irene M, Aug 11 1896 Sex:F Child# 5 William T Fitzgerald Ireland & Annie A Moore Ireland
FITZGERALD, John M, May 27 1899 Sex:M Child# 7 William T Fitzgerald Ireland & Anna Moore Ireland
FITZGERALD, Rufus C, Aug 8 1891 Sex:M Child# 5 C A Fitzgerald Warren & Eva Hamblett Nashua, NH
FITZGERALD, Unknown, Jul 15 1894 Sex:F Child# 4 William T Fitzgerald Ireland & Ann Ireland
FITZGERALD, Unknown, Aug 30 1895 Sex:F Child# 7 Charles A Fitzgerald Warren & Eva A Hamlet Nashua, NH
FITZGERALD, Unknown, Aug 13 1907 Sex:M Child# 4 John P Fitzgerald Brattleboro, VT & Eva Moran Fall River, MA
FITZGERALD, Unknown, Apr 12 1926 Sex:M Child# Fred R Fitzgerald Nashua, NH & Gladys Hayden Chelsea, MA
FITZGERALD, William, Aug 26 1897 Sex:M Child# 6 William T Fitzgerald Ireland & Annie A Moore Ireland
FITZGERALD, William P, Jul 17 1910 Sex:M Child# 1 Gerald E Fitzgerald Winchendon, MA & Florence E Brooks Lawrence
FITZPATRICK, James Leonard, Sep 30 1924 Sex:M Child# 3 Joseph Fitzpatrick Ireland & Annie Lynch Ireland
FITZPATRICK, John Joseph, Sep 11 1922 Sex:M Child# 2 Joseph Fitzpatrick Ireland & Annie Lynch Ireland
FITZPATRICK, Mary Catherine, Dec 26 1918 Sex:F Child# 1 Joseph Fitzpatrick Ireland & Annie Lynch Ireland
FLAGG, Beatrice, May 2 1922 Sex:F Child# 3 Guy E Flagg Woodstock, NB & Beatrice Flather Nashua, NH
FLAGG, Jean, Feb 1 1918 Sex:F Child# 2 Guy E Flagg Woodstock, NB & G Beatrice Flather Nashua, NH
FLAGG, Joan Marilyn, Jul 26 1934 Sex:F Child# 2 Emerson Flagg Townsend, MA & Alice Sullivan Pepperell, MA
FLAGG, Unknown, Jan 29 1916 Sex:F Child# 1 Guy E Flagg Woodstock, NB & Beatrice Flather Nashua, NH Stillborn
FLAHERITY, Unknown, June 2 1890 Sex:M Child# 8 Patrick J Flaherity Ireland & Anna Sullivan Ireland
FLAHERTY, ann, Dec 24 1926 Sex:F Child# 5 Paul Flaherty Nashua, NH & Mary Bermingham Manchester, NH
FLAHERTY, Francis Patrick, Jul 18 1935 Sex:M Child# 2 Henry P Flaherty Nashua, NH & Jane Mullikin Manchester, NH
FLAHERTY, Helen, Apr 1 1923 Sex:F Child# 5 Paul Flaherty Nashua, NH & Mary Birmingham Manchester, NH
FLAHERTY, Paul Robert, Apr 12 1918 Sex:M Child# 3 Paul H Flaherty Nashua, NH & Mary J Birmingtham Manchester, NH
FLAHERTY, Ruth, Aug 31 1920 Sex:F Child# 3 Paul H Flaherty Nashua, NH & Mary J Birmingham Manchester, NH
FLAHERTY, Unknown, Apr 3 1888 Sex:F Child# 7 Patrick J Flaherty Ireland & Annie Sullivan Ireland
FLAHERTY, Unknown, Sep 24 1893 Sex:M Child# 9 Patrick J Flaherty Ireland & Ann Sullivan Ireland
FLAHERTY, Unknown, Aug 20 1914 Sex:F Child# 1 Paul H Flaherty Nashua, NH & Mary Burnigham Manchester, NH
FLAHERTY, Unknown, Nov 7 1915 Sex:F Child# 2 Paul Flaherty Nashua, NH & Mary Birmingham Manchester, NH
FLANAGAN, Barbara Joan, May 17 1928 Sex:F Child# 2 John Flanagan Milford, NH & Margaret Sullivan Nashua, NH
FLANAGAN, Catherine Elizabeth, Oct 30 1926 Sex:F Child# 1 John Flanagan Milford, NH & Margaret Sullivan Nashua, NH
FLANAGAN, James, Oct 15 1930 Sex:M Child# 1 James Flanagan, Jr New York & Lena Kashulines Nashua, NH
FLANAGAN, Leo William, Nov 4 1929 Sex:M Child# 2 Leo Flanagan Milford, NH & Katherine Phelan Cambridge, MA
FLANAGAN, Maurice, Nov 10 1928 Sex:M Child# 1 Leo Flanagan Milford, NH & Katherine Phelan Cambridge, MA
FLANAGAN, Robert Joseph, Jun 3 1932 Sex:M Child# 2 James Flanagan New York & Lena Kashulines Nashua, NH
FLANDERS, Adelaide May, May 27 1901 Sex:F Child# 3 George E Flanders New Boston, NH & Mabel Johnson Goffstown, NH
FLANDERS, Arleen M, Mar 16 1924 Sex:F Child# 4 George H Flanders Nashua, NH & Mary McCormick Salem, MA
FLANDERS, Beatrice, Aug 14 1929 Sex:F Child# 6 George H Flanders Nashua, NH & Mary McCormick Salem, MA
FLANDERS, Benjamin A, Jan 30 1893 Sex:M Child# 2 Edwin D Flanders Alton, NH & Nellie Gordon Nashua, NH
FLANDERS, Edwin D, Aug 23 1890 Sex:M Child# 1 Edwin D Flanders Alton, NH & Nellie Gordon Nashua, NH
FLANDERS, Elmer Lester, Oct 11 1921 Sex:M Child# 3 George H Flanders Nashua, NH & Mary A McCormack Salem, MA
FLANDERS, Elodys Eleanor, Apr 24 1902 Sex:F Child# 1 William A Flanders Alton, NH & Grace Marble Nashua, NH
FLANDERS, Euminnie Louisa, Dec 18 1903 Sex:F Child# 1 Harry C V Flanders Nashua, NH & Elizabeth McGilvary NS
FLANDERS, Francis Ellsworth, Sep 30 1919 Sex:M Child# 2 George H Flanders Nashua, NH & Mary McCormick Salem, MA

FLANDERS, George Henry, Oct 12 1894 Sex:M Child# 1 George E Flanders New Boston, NH & Mabel Johnson Goffstown, NH
FLANDERS, George Warren, Aug 12 1917 Sex:M Child# 1 George H Flanders Nashua, NH & Mary McCormack Salem, MA
FLANDERS, Josephine, Feb 22 1892 Sex:F Child# 1 Ed F Flanders Weare, NH & Mary Rogers Ireland
FLANDERS, Kenneth Raymond, Aug 27 1926 Sex:M Child# 1 R G Flanders Hollis, NH & Alice S Cragin Greenfield, NH
FLANDERS, Lester Burnham, Apr 15 1904 Sex:M Child# 2 William A Flanders Alton, NH & Grace Marble Nashua, NH Stillbo
FLANDERS, Marion Pearl, Dec 5 1912 Sex:F Child# 3 Harry V Flanders Nashua, NH & Elizabeth McGilvray NS
FLANDERS, Mildred Anna, Feb 25 1900 Sex:F Child# 1 E S Flanders New Hampshire & Anna M'Cutchen NB
FLANDERS, Pauline Barbara, Jun 10 1933 Sex:F Child# 7 Frank B Flanders Grantham, NH & Flora A Wise Reeds Ferry, NH
FLANDERS, Ralph Robert, Jul 20 1922 Sex:M Child# 3 Frank R Flanders Grantham, NH & A Flora Wise Merrimack, NH
FLANDERS, Richard Adams, Oct 31 1922 Sex:M Child# 2 Morris W Flanders Sutton, NH & Cora Makepeace Concord, NH
FLANDERS, Ronald Alan, Oct 31 1931 Sex:M Child# 3 Raymond Flanders Hollis, NH & Alice Cragin Greenfield, NH
FLANDERS, Theresa, Feb 20 1931 Sex:F Child# 7 George H Flanders Nashua, NH & Mary A McCormick Salem, MA
FLANDERS, Unknown, Nov 3 1895 Sex:M Child# 2 George E Flanders New Boston & Mabel Johnson Goffstown, NH
FLANDERS, Unknown, Apr 28 1902 Sex:M Child# 2 Ernest L Flanders Hanover & Anna McCutchin NB
FLANDERS, Unknown, Oct 2 1903 Sex:M Child# 3 Ernest S Flanders Hanover, NH & Annie McCutchin NB Stillborn
FLANDERS, Unknown, Nov 11 1925 Sex:F Child# 5 George H Flanders Nashua, NH & Mary McCormack Salem, MA
FLANDERS, William Edward, Sep 25 1916 Sex:M Child# 4 Harry V Flanders Nashua, NH & Elizabeth McGilvary NS
FLANNIGAN, Annie, Mar 1 1898 Sex:F Child# 4 John Flannigan Ireland & Mary Harrigan Ireland
FLANNIGAN, James T, Feb 2 1897 Sex:M Child# 1 John Flannigan Ireland & Mary Harrigan Ireland
FLATHER, Doris, Jan 11 1900 Sex:F Child# 2 Ernest J Flather Nashua, NH & Gertrude A Hooper Nashua, NH
FLATHER, Frances Turner, Jul 19 1910 Sex:F Child# 2 Oscar M Flather Nashua, NH & Gertrude Turner Philadelphia, PA
FLATHER, Herbert H, Jan 14 1902 Sex:M Child# 2 H L Flather Nashua, NH & Mary H Howard Nashua, NH
FLATHER, Herbert Hesselton, Sep 6 1925 Sex:M Child# 1 Herbert H Flather Nashua, NH & Miriam N Warren Nashua, NH
FLATHER, Joseph Howard, Aug 10 1902 Sex:M Child# 1 Herbert L Flather Nashua, NH & Mary H Howard Nashua, NH
FLATHER, Joseph Howard, Jr, Apr 17 1927 Sex:M Child# 2 Joseph H Flather Nashua, NH & Helen Wesson Flint, MI
FLATHER, Mary Lee, Jun 19 1932 Sex:F Child# 3 Herbert Flather Nashua, NH & M N Warren Nashua, NH
FLATHER, Mary Virginia, Nov 10 1903 Sex:F Child# 3 Herbert L Flather Nashua, NH & Mary E Howard Nashua, NH
FLATHER, Ralph Francis, Oct 17 1895 Sex:M Child# 1 Ernest J Flather Nashua, NH & Gertrude A Hooper Nashua, NH
FLATHER, Richard Warren, Jul 19 1930 Sex:M Child# 2 Herbert H Flather Nashua, NH & Miriam Warren Nashua, NH
FLATHER, Unknown, Nov 5 1900 Sex:M Child# 1 Oscar M Flather Nashua, NH & Gertrude P Turner Penn
FLATHER, William H, Jan 5 1908 Sex:M Child# 4 Harry E Flather Nashua, NH & Helen Heath New York, NY
FLEMING, Catherine Loretta, Oct 8 1902 Sex:F Child# 2 Joseph Fleming England & Catherine J Galvin Ireland
FLETCHER, Amos F, Mar 20 1899 Sex:M Child# 10 William C Fletcher Nashua, NH & Mellie Miller Lewiston, ME
FLETCHER, Arline Nattie, May 20 1925 Sex:F Child# 4 George Fletcher Nashua, NH & Alice Powers Lawrence, MA
FLETCHER, Gladys Stanley, Nov 21 1899 Sex:F Child#  Henry O Fletcher Nashua, NH & Mary J Stanley NB
FLETCHER, Hannah, Sep 1 1911 Sex:F Child# 2 Richard D Fletcher England & Lillian R Carroll Mass
FLETCHER, Ida Fay, Apr 23 1894 Sex:F Child# 5 Willie C Fletcher Nashua, NH & Nellie Miller Lewiston, ME
FLETCHER, John Elliott, Feb 9 1909 Sex:M Child# 1 Richard D Fletcher Manchester, England & Lillian R Crowell MA
FLETCHER, Lillian Rebecca, Oct 4 1912 Sex:F Child# 3 Richard D Fletcher England & Lillian R Crowell Mass
FLETCHER, Malcolm Gordon, Jun 22 1919 Sex:M Child# 5 Richard D Fletcher Manchester, England & Lillian R Crowell MA
FLETCHER, Richard Dunston, Sep 9 1917 Sex:M Child# 4 Richard D Fletcher England & Lillian R Crowell Maynard, MA
FLETCHER, Robert Brooks, Dec 16 1924 Sex:M Child# 6 R D Fletcher Manchester, NH & Lillian Crowell Maynard, MA
FLETCHER, Rose Emma, Sep 11 1893 Sex:F Child# 1 Frank E Fletcher MA & Emma M Merrill RI
FLETCHER, Unknown, Sep 18 1890 Sex:F Child# 2 John F Fletcher Nashua, NH & Lizzie Nutting Nashua, NH
FLETCHER, Unknown, Apr 11 1891 Sex:M Child# 4 Will C Fletcher Nashua, NH & Nellie Miller Lewiston, ME
FLEURY, Claude Ronald, Jul 6 1935 Sex:M Child# 1 Conrad Fleury Nashua, NH & Rose Cormier Canada
FLEURY, Eugene Walter, Mar 30 1935 Sex:M Child# 1 Eugene Fleury Suncook, NH & Jeannette Marquis Canada
FLEURY, Irene Olivette, Nov 14 1925 Sex:F Child# 3 Arthur Fleury Canada & Erilia Gendron Canada
FLEURY, J Hormidas Corade, Jun 3 1911 Sex:M Child# 1 Hormidas Fleury Canada & Aurore Ouellette Canada
FLEURY, Louis Ludger, May 20 1906 Sex:M Child# 2 Louis Fleury Canada & Rosanna Blais Canada
FLEURY, M Rita Germaine, Oct 2 1914 Sex:F Child# 2 Hormidas Fleury Canada & Aurore Ouellette Canada
FLEURY, Marie Anita L, Mar 5 1920 Sex:F Child# 1 Arthur Fleury Canada & Exilia Gendron Canada
FLEURY, Marie Rose Alma, Sep 11 1904 Sex:F Child# 1 Louis Fleury Canada & Rose Anna Blais Canada
FLEURY, Roger, Apr 3 1928 Sex:M Child# 6 Willie Fleury Canada & Mina Richard Canada
FLEURY, Unknown, Mar 12 1894 Sex:M Child# 1 H K Fleury Westport, ME & Cora Jackson W Newton, MA
FLEURY, Unknown, Jul 22 1921 Sex:M Child# 2 Arthur Fleury Canada & Ezilia Gendron Canada Stillborn
FLINN, Francis Henry, Jul 14 1892 Sex:M Child# 6 Thomas Flinn Ireland & Mary McGlynn Ireland
FLINN, George, Jun 29 1896 Sex:M Child# 8 Thomas Flinn Ireland & Mary McGlynn Ireland
FLINN, Hugh, Jan 27 1891 Sex:M Child# 5 Thomas Flinn Ireland & Mary McGlynn Ireland
FLINN, James, Aug 15 1887 Sex:M Child# 2 Thomas Flinn Ireland & Mary McGlynn Ireland
FLINN, Thomas, Jul 10 1889 Sex:M Child# 3 Thomas Flinn Ireland & Mary McGlynn Ireland
FLINN, Unknown, Aug 3 1892 Sex:F Child# 2 John J Flinn Medford, MA & Kate Donohue Ireland
FLINT, George H, Aug 22 1890 Sex:M Child# 1 George H Flint Haverhill & Carrie Tenney Milton, NH
FLINT, Joseph G R, Jul 16 1907 Sex:M Child# 2 Leon H Flint Nashua, NH & Rosanna Bonvouloir Canada
FLINT, Unknown, Dec 13 1888 Sex:M Child# 1 Harry D Flint Manchester & Carrie Northboro, MA
FLINT, Unknown, Nov 9 1892 Sex:F Child# 2 Harry D Flint Manchester & Carrie W Fay Waltham, MA
FLINT, Unknown, Mar 14 1908 Sex:F Child# 3 Leon Flint Nashua, NH & Rosei Bonvouloir Canada
FLINTS, Marie Victoria, Jul 4 1906 Sex:F Child# 1 Louis S Flints Nashua, NH & Rosanna Bonvouloir Canada
FLOOD, Genevieve Melda, Sep 22 1892 Sex:F Child# 6 John J Flood Concord, MA & Nellie Rigni Ogdensburg, NY
FLOOD, Lea, Jul 17 1890 Sex:M Child# 4 John J Flood Concord, MA & Mary E Rigeway Malone, NY
FLOOD, Madeline, Nov 30 1902 Sex:F Child# 7 John J Flood Concord, MA & Mary E Rigney Malone, NY
FLOOD, Unknown, Mar 17 1888 Sex:M Child# 4 William Flood Concord, MA & Bridget Flood Ireland
FLOOD, Unknown, Aug 22 1889 Sex:F Child# 4 William F Flood Nashua, NH & Bridget Hacket Ireland Stillborn

FLOOD, Unknown, Oct 26 1893 Sex:M Child# 6 John J Flood Old Concord, MA & Mary E Rigney Malone, NY
FLORAS, Unknown, May 6 1916 Sex:F Child# 1 James Floras Greece & Ida Karantanis Greece
FLORAS, Unknown, Oct 3 1917 Sex:M Child# 2 James Floras Greece & Hazel Karathanon Greece
FLOYD, Beryl Edna, Feb 18 1906 Sex:F Child# 1 Herbert C Floyd Mass & Blanche Merrill Mass
FLOYD, Flavia May, May 28 1904 Sex:F Child# 2 Grovenor L Floyd Bardwell's Fy, MA & Falvia M Papineau Marlboro, MA
FLOYD, Kenneth Herbert, Nov 15 1930 Sex:M Child# 1 Willis Floyd Groton, MA & Florence Therrien Nashua, NH
FLOYD, Maygalia Ettassa, Apr 15 1903 Sex:F Child# 1 Grovenor L Floyd Mass & Flavie Papineau Mass
FLUET, Alphonse Kenneth, Mar 1 1933 Sex:M Child# 2 Amedee Fluet Manchester, NH & Doris Searles Mass
FLUETTE, Blanche Gratia, Dec 5 1903 Sex:F Child# 2 Alphonse Fluette Canada & Marceline Salvail Nova Scotia
FLUETTE, George A, Jul 26 1902 Sex:M Child# 1 Alphonse Fluette Canada & Marceline Salvail Gardner, MA
FLUKE, Beatrice Elaine, Mar 10 1933 Sex:F Child# 5 Guy Russell Fluke Nova Scotia & Georgiana Young Nova Scotia
FLUKE, Donald Austin, Apr 27 1935 Sex:M Child# 2 Austin E Fluke Nova Scotia & Mildred Britton Nashua, NH
FLUKE, Dorothy May, Jan 18 1929 Sex:F Child# 2 Guy Fluke Nova Scotia & Georgiana Young Nova Scotia
FLUKE, Ina Claire, Apr 3 1930 Sex:F Child# 3 Guy Fluke Nova Scotia & Georgiana Young Nova Scotia
FLUKE, Ray Warren, Aug 21 1933 Sex:M Child# 1 Austin Fluke Nova Scotia & Mildred Britton Nashua, NH
FLUKE, Richard Leo, Aug 14 1931 Sex:M Child# 4 Guy Fluke Nova Scotia & Georgina Young Nova Scotia
FLUKE, Robert Roland, Sep 25 1934 Sex:M Child# 6 Guy Russell Fluke Nova Scotia & Georgina Young Nova Scotia
FLYNN, Albert, Aug 22 1900 Sex:M Child# 10 Thomas Flynn Ireland & Mary Glynn Ireland
FLYNN, Alice, Jan 9 1923 Sex:F Child# 5 Michael Flynn Ireland & Mary Lynch Ireland
FLYNN, Alice Beatrice, Sep 21 1912 Sex:F Child# 1 Henry T Flynn Greenfield, NH & Matilda Bonnette Canada
FLYNN, Alice Katherine, Feb 23 1909 Sex:F Child# 11 John Flynn Ireland & Margaret Coffey Ireland
FLYNN, Ann, Jun 4 1900 Sex:F Child# 4 Michael Flynn Ireland & Ann Killkelley Ireland
FLYNN, Ann Mary, Mar 24 1906 Sex:F Child# 3 Thomas J Flynn Lawrence, MA & Celia A Spain Manchester, NH
FLYNN, Bernard Charles, Aug 25 1918 Sex:M Child# 1 Thomas P Flynn Ireland & Rose Clancy Ireland
FLYNN, Charles, Aug 18 1922 Sex:M Child# 1 Martin Flynn Ireland & Delia Kayney Ireland
FLYNN, Elizabeth, Aug 8 1893 Sex:F Child# 4 John J Flynn Ireland & Margaret Coffey Ireland
FLYNN, Ellen Agnes, Jan 24 1898 Sex:F Child# 9 Thomas Flynn Ireland & Mary Glynn Ireland
FLYNN, Francis, Jun 26 1904 Sex:M Child# 4 John Flynn Ireland & Margaret Coffey Ireland
FLYNN, Francis Joseph, May 23 1903 Sex:M Child# 1 Thomas Flynn Lawrence, MA & Celia Splain Manchester, NH
FLYNN, George Alfred, Jun 24 1906 Sex:M Child# 8 John Flynn Ireland & Margaret Coffey Ireland
FLYNN, Henry, Jan 24 1902 Sex:M Child# 8 John Flynn Ireland & Margaret Coffey Ireland
FLYNN, Irene, Jan 9 1923 Sex:F Child# 4 Michael Flynn Ireland & Mary Lynch Ireland
FLYNN, James, Feb 9 1896 Sex:M Child# 5 John L Flynn Ireland & Magerite Coffee Ireland
FLYNN, John Francis, Mar 25 1917 Sex:M Child# 2 John J Flynn Ireland & Delia Benson Ireland
FLYNN, John J, Mar 9 1892 Sex:M Child# 3 John J Flynn Ireland & Margaret Coffee Ireland
FLYNN, Lawrence, Jan 21 1907 Sex:M Child# 2 John W Flynn Nashua, NH & Annie O'Brien Ireland
FLYNN, Margaret, May 22 1898 Sex:F Child# 5 John Flynn Ireland & Margaret Coffey Ireland
FLYNN, Mary Agnes, Aug 30 1889 Sex:F Child# 1 John J Flynn Ireland & Maggie Coffee Ireland
FLYNN, Mary Catherine, Jan 25 1909 Sex:F Child# 1 John J Flynn Ireland & Delia Benson Ireland
FLYNN, Mary Elizabeth, Aug 31 1925 Sex:F Child# 2 Martin Flynn Ireland & Delia Caveney Ireland
FLYNN, Mary Katharine, Nov 23 1917 Sex:F Child# 2 Michael Flynn Ireland & Mary Lynch Ireland
FLYNN, Mary Margaret, Jun 20 1920 Sex:F Child# 2 Thomas P Flynn Ireland & Rose Clancy Ireland
FLYNN, Michael Robert, Jul 17 1910 Sex:M Child# 3 John Flynn Nashua, NH & Annie O'Brien Ireland
FLYNN, Paul Robert, Oct 31 1904 Sex:M Child# 2 Thomas J Flynn Lowell, MA & Celia A Spain Manchester, NH
FLYNN, Robbert Thomas, Oct 20 1912 Sex:M Child# 1 John Flynn New York, NY & Margaret Flynn New York, NY
FLYNN, Rosanna, Nov 29 1890 Sex:F Child# 2 John J Flynn Ireland & Maggie Coffee Ireland
FLYNN, Thomas, Jun 17 1904 Sex:M Child# 1 John Flynn Nashua, NH & Annie O'Brien Ireland
FLYNN, Unknown, Jul 15 1915 Sex:M Child# 1 Michael Flynn Ireland & Mary Lynch Ireland
FOGG, Unknown, Apr 18 1893 Sex:M Child# 1 John J Fogg Onion, ME & Abbie McPeters Greenbush, ME
FOGLIAN, Salvatore, Jul 11 1918 Sex:M Child# 8 Albert Foglian Italy & Teresa Crisca Italy
FOGLIANI, Unknown, Apr 6 1920 Sex:M Child# 10 Alberto Fogliani Italy & Theresa Oresa Italy Stillborn
FOISEE, Alice, Mar 22 1892 Sex:F Child# 4 Philippe Foisee Concord, NH & Aurora Ratte Canada
FOISIE, Amelia Antoinette, Feb 5 1910 Sex:F Child# 2 J B Foisie Amesbury, MA & Olivine Poliquin Canada
FOISIE, Donald Robert, Nov 22 1931 Sex:M Child# 3 (No Parents Listed)
FOISIE, Edouard, Aug 3 1893 Sex:M Child# 5 Philip Foisie Concord & Aurore Ratte Canada
FOISIE, Laura Alice, Jan 28 1912 Sex:F Child# 3 Jean B Foisie US & Olivine Poliquin Canada
FOISIE, Lena Anita, Mar 18 1913 Sex:F Child# 4 John Foisie Amesbury, MA & Olivine Poliquin Canada
FOISIE, Louis Ferdinand, Feb 14 1893 Sex:M Child# 1 Uldige Foisie Canada & Alphonsine L'Oiseau Nashua, NH
FOISIE, Philippe Samuel, Jul 23 1896 Sex:M Child# 6 Philippe Foisie Concord & Aurore Ratte Canada
FOISIE, Unknown, Sep 18 1897 Sex:F Child# 1 Henry Foisie Nashua, NH & Amanda Beaulieu Canada Stillborn
FOISIE, Unknown, Aug 5 1898 Sex:M Child# 2 Henry Foisie Nashua, NH & Amanda Beaulieu Canada Stillborn
FOISY, Catherine L, Jun 16 1897 Sex:F Child# 1 William Foisy Nashua, NH & Stella Beaupre Canada
FOISY, William George, May 27 1898 Sex:M Child# 2 William Foisy Nashua, NH & Stella Beaupre Canada
FOLEY, Alice Catherine, Jan 7 1910 Sex:F Child# 3 Cornelius F Foley Randolph, MA & Ida E Hewins Foxboro, MA
FOLEY, Ann Vivian, Aug 12 1916 Sex:F Child# 1 Charles Foley Mass & Cecelia Brewin Nashua, NH
FOLEY, Arthur Raymond, Aug 21 1920 Sex:M Child# 5 C F Foley Mass & Ida Hewins Mass
FOLEY, Barbara Wilson, Nov 12 1930 Sex:F Child# 1 Charles E Foley Walpole, MA & Ruth Nichols Hawleyville, MA
FOLEY, Catherine Mary, Aug 25 1898 Sex:F Child# 1 Jeremiah Foley Nashua, NH & Mary Fahey Ireland
FOLEY, Elaine V, May 30 1907 Sex:F Child# 1 Joseph F Foley Nashua, NH & Agnes F Hallahan Ogdensburg, NY
FOLEY, Eleanor Hewins, Oct 29 1931 Sex:F Child# 2 Charles Foley Walpole, MA & Ruth Hawley Hawleyville, CT
FOLEY, Florence John, Dec 30 1893 Sex:M Child# 1 James A Foley Nashua, NH & Margaret A Murphy Concord, NH
FOLEY, Helena May, May 14 1917 Sex:F Child# 1 Michael J Foley Manchester, NH & Margaret M Travers St Johns, PQ
FOLEY, James Matthew, Oct 6 1917 Sex:M Child# 2 Charles Foley Mass & Cecilea Brewin Nashua, NH

FOLEY, John Francis, Feb 27 1919 Sex:M Child# 3 Michael J Foley Manchester, NH & Marguerite Travers St John, NB
FOLEY, John Joseph, Mar 4 1922 Sex:M Child# 3 Charles Foley Poland Russia & Mary Schulka Poland Russia
FOLEY, Marie Alice, Aug 18 1898 Sex:F Child# 2 James Foley Canada & Emelie Consigny Canada
FOLEY, Unknown, Apr 28 1912 Sex:M Child# 4 Cornelius F Foley Randolph, MA & Ida Hewins Foxboro, MA
FOLSOM, Blanche, Jan 19 1903 Sex:F Child# 10 Louis Folsom Russia & Bessie Levin Russia
FOLSOM, Henry Albert, Sep 14 1930 Sex:M Child# 1 Henry Folsom Peabody, MA & Beatrice Grover Medford, MA
FONTAINE, Alida, Mar 6 1889 Sex:F Child# 5 J B Fontaine Canada & Melouise Canada
FONTAINE, Dianne, Jul 12 1894 Sex:F Child# 1 Edouard Fontaine Canada & Elzire Jeaubane Nashua, NH
FONTAINE, Edward R, Mar 26 1909 Sex:M Child# 4 Edward Fontaine Canada & Elzire Jambard Nashua, NH
FONTAINE, Elaine Theresa, May 14 1932 Sex:F Child# 1 Victor Fontaine Southbridge, MA & Yvonne Prince Southbridge,MA
FONTAINE, Marie Chronide, Jan 29 1895 Sex:F Child# 4 Joseph Fontaine Canada & Edmire Paquette Canada
FONTAINE, Marie D L, Feb 3 1898 Sex:F Child# 2 Edouard Fontaine Canada & Elzire Jeanbarre Nashua, NH
FONTAINE, Marie L, Jun 12 1887 Sex:F Child# 3 Jean Fontaine Canada & Melanie Miclette Canada
FONTAINE, Sylvia E, Nov 28 1905 Sex:F Child# 3 Edouard Fontaine Canada & Elzire Jeanbarre Nashua, NH
FONTAINE, Unknown, Jan 21 1891 Sex:M Child# 6 Jean Fontaine Canada & Melouise Miclette Canada Stillborn
FONTAINE, Unknown, Sep 6 1910 Sex:M Child# 1 Joseph Fontaine Canada & Mary Dube Canada
FONTAINE, Unknown, Apr 14 1931 Sex:F Child# 1 Emile Fontaine Manchester, NH & Pauline Perrault Nashua, NH
FONTAINE, Yvonne Orine, May 11 1935 Sex:F Child# 2 Victor Fontaine Southbridge, MA & Yvonne Prince Southbridge, MA
FONTAS, John A, Jun 13 1923 Sex:M Child# 2 Apostalos Fontas Greece & Frosina Tsatsa Greece
FOOT, Wells Duncklee, Jr, Sep 19 1920 Sex:M Child# 2 Wells D Foot Peterboro, NH & Gladys E Emery Lyndeboro, NH
FOOTE, Harold, Jr, Jul 23 1924 Sex:M Child# 1 Harold Foote Francestown, NH & Anna Smith Jersey City, NJ
FOOTE, Kenneth A, Nov 11 1900 Sex:M Child# 1 G Manson Foote NC & Margaret L Seavey New York
FOOTE, Lucille Marion, Apr 18 1927 Sex:F Child# 1 Harold C Foote Francestown, NH & Mildred Merrill Smithfield,
FOOTE, Rachel, Jul 5 1903 Sex:F Child# 3 Charles M Foote Colchester & Kate C Joss Lachute, PQ
FOOTE, Ruth, Jun 21 1888 Sex:F Child# 1 Charles F Foote Canada & Katie C George Canada
FORASAVACH, Age, Mar 4 1918 Sex:F Child# 2 Michael Forasavach Russia & Mary Listiz Russia
FORBES, Ann I, Jan 9 1899 Sex:F Child# 2 Charles W Forbes Canada & Francis D Hanscom Maine
FORBES, Catherine Lucy, Nov 3 1913 Sex:F Child# 1 George Robert Forbes Portland, ME & Carrie Mabel Fair Nashua, NH
FORBES, Charles Harold, Mar 15 1906 Sex:M Child# 3 Luther Forbes Canada & Belle Hanscom Maine
FORBES, Edward J, Feb 11 1894 Sex:M Child# 1 John E Forbes Maine & Mary A Morse Maine
FORBES, Ethel May, May 1 1902 Sex:F Child# 3 Charles W Forbes Canada & Frances Hanscomb Maine
FORBES, Louise M, Sep 7 1910 Sex:F Child# 5 C W Forbes Canada & Frances Hanscomb Maine
FORBES, Luther Henry, Jr, Mar 20 1912 Sex:M Child# 5 Luther H Forbes Canada & Belle Hanscom Maine
FORBES, Mabel, Jun 23 1903 Sex:F Child# 4 Charles W Forbes Canada & Frances Hanscomb Maine
FORBES, Marion Isabel, Aug 5 1908 Sex:F Child# 4 Luther H Forbes Canada & Belle Houston Maine
FORBES, Mary Ann, Aug 1 1904 Sex:F Child# 2 Luther H Forbes Canada & Belle Hanscomb Maine
FORBES, Robert Hanscom, Mar 10 1917 Sex:M Child# 7 Luther H Forbes Canada & Bell C Hanscom Maine
FORBES, Roberta Frances, Aug 3 1913 Sex:F Child# 6 Luther H Forbes Canada & Belle C Hanscom Maine
FORBES, Ruth, Jun 1 1902 Sex:F Child# 1 Luther H Forbes Canada & Belle Hanscom Maine
FORBES, Tyler J, Nov 27 1897 Sex:M Child#  Charles W Forbes Pike River, Canada & Francis D Hanscomb Maine
FORCIER, Ernest Orville Arman, Apr 3 1918 Sex:M Child# 2 Alphege Forcier Canada & Louise Vanasse NH
FORCIER, Germaine Antoinette, Oct 23 1912 Sex:F Child# 3 Herman Forcier Canada & Aglae Vanasse Canada
FORCIER, J Raymond Aldege, Nov 8 1914 Sex:M Child# 4 Herman Forcier Canada & Aglaie Vanasse Canada
FORCIER, Jos Napoleon Rene, Nov 1 1917 Sex:M Child# 5 Herman Forcier Canada & Aglaee Vanasse Canada
FORCIER, Joseph Normand A, Sep 1 1910 Sex:M Child# 2 Herman Forcier Canada & Eglace Vanasse Canada
FORCIER, M Rachelle Laura, Apr 2 1916 Sex:F Child# 1 Elphege Forcier Canada & Louise Vanasse NH
FORCIER, Marie Ann L D, Mar 6 1929 Sex:F Child# 3 Napoleon Forcier Canada & Emerantine Corriveau Canada
FORCIER, Marie Louise Margell, Sep 1 1927 Sex:F Child# 2 Napoleon Forcier Canada & E Corriveau Canada
FORCIER, Marie Theresa Ivette, Mar 20 1927 Sex:F Child# 5 Elphege Forcier Canada & Louise Vanasse Nashua, NH
FORCIER, Marie Yvonne, May 13 1908 Sex:F Child# 1 Hermen Forcier Canada & Aglae Vanasse Canada
FORCIER, Robert Maurice, Jun 28 1924 Sex:M Child# 4 Elphege Forcier Canada & Louisa Vanasse Nashua, NH
FORD, Althea Grace, May 31 1920 Sex:F Child# 4 Arthur James Ford Nashua, NH & Emma Glover Amherst, NH
FORD, Arthur Glover, Mar 5 1919 Sex:M Child# 3 Arthur J Ford Nashua, NH & Emma Glover Amherst, NH
FORD, Brenda Mae, Dec 19 1928 Sex:F Child# 3 Joseph Ford Vermont & Pauline Wiley Windsor, VT
FORD, Catharine May, May 12 1921 Sex:F Child# 1 (No Parents Listed)
FORD, Catherine Lucille, Feb 21 1927 Sex:F Child# 8 Arthur Ford Nashua, NH & Emma Glover Amherst, NH
FORD, Charles Marshall, Nov 16 1930 Sex:M Child# 1 David S Ford Lynn, MA & Mary Benjamin Nashua, NH
FORD, Clarence Edward, Aug 4 1906 Sex:M Child# 1 Moses B Ford Hudson, NH & Hattie E Pierce Londonderry, NH
FORD, Dorothy Irene, Jul 22 1926 Sex:F Child# 1 Fred Ford S Merrimack, NH & Irene Lambert Nashua, NH Stillborn
FORD, Dorothy Jane, Feb 10 1922 Sex:F Child# 5 Arthur James Ford Nashua, NH & Emma F Glover Amherst, NH
FORD, Elizabeth Rachel, Oct 3 1913 Sex:F Child# 1 Arthur J Ford Nashua, NH & Emma F Glover Amherst, NH
FORD, Elwin Eugene, Mar 26 1922 Sex:M Child# 2 Bertelle E Ford Merrimack, NH & Helen Marshall Hudson, NH
FORD, Fred H, May 17 1930 Sex:M Child# 2 Fred H Ford Merrimack, NH & Irene E Lambert Nashua, NH
FORD, Gertrude Ethel, Jan 10 1896 Sex:F Child# 6 George E Ford Hudson, MA & Annie Gotham Marblehead, MA
FORD, Herbert, Mar 23 1898 Sex:M Child# 2 John H Ford Tyngsboro, MA & Almira D Macphee Nova Scotia
FORD, James Bancroft, May 22 1930 Sex:M Child# 9 Arthur J Ford Nashua, NH & Emma F Glover Amherst, NH
FORD, Jane A, Mar 9 1887 Sex:F Child#  Arthur C Ford Hudson & Sarah L Tyngsboro
FORD, Jesse Leora, Feb 15 1924 Sex:F Child# 3 Berbelle Ford Merrimack, NH & Helen Marshall Merrimack, NH
FORD, John Henry, Jan 12 1932 Sex:M Child# 2 David Ford Lynn, MA & Mary Benjamin Nashua, NH
FORD, Laura Christine, Jul 10 1925 Sex:F Child# 7 Arthur J Ford Nashua, NH & Emma Glover Amherst, NH
FORD, Leon Christeuson, Nov 11 1923 Sex:M Child# 6 Arthur James Ford Nashua, NH & Emma F Glover Amherst, NH
FORD, Nancy Ann, May 29 1931 Sex:F Child# 1 John Ford Nashua, NH & Evelyn E Hildreth Lowell, MA
FORD, Phyllis, Sep 12 1923 Sex:F Child# 1 John Ford S Merrimack, NH & Pauline Nichols New York

FORD, Ralph Henry, Mar 5 1934 Sex:M Child# 11 Arthur James Ford Nashua, NH & Emma J Glover Amherst, NH
FORD, Ruth Frances, Oct 28 1916 Sex:F Child# 2 Arthur James Ford Nashua, NH & Emma F glover Amherst, NH
FORD, Unknown, Jun 6 1890 Sex:M Child# 2 Bert I Ford Francestown, NH & Anna E Rock Plattsburg, NY
FORD, Unknown, Mar 24 1891 Sex:F Child# 3 Arthur C Ford Hudson, NH & Sarah L Holmes Tyngsboro, MA Stillborn
FORD, Unknown, Oct 11 1909 Sex:M Child# 2 Charles Ford Nashua, NH & Nellie Fuller Hudson, NH
FORD, Winifred F, Oct 14 1888 Sex:F Child# 1 Frank W Ford Maine & Louisa L Webster NH
FORENCE, Pearl Leo, Apr 19 1898 Sex:F Child# 7 John Forence
FORENCE, Tolm Willard, Aug 26 1915 Sex:M Child# 5 George Forence New York & Annie Obin New York
FOREST, Esther, Feb 24 1913 Sex:F Child# 1 (No Parents Listed)
FOREST, Irene Albina, Oct 15 1921 Sex:F Child# 2 Joseph Forest Canada & Anna Morin Canada
FOREST, Joseph Jean G, Jun 18 1910 Sex:M Child# 1 Joseph A Forest Canada & Marie Carrier Canada
FOREST, Joseph Ray Marcel, Jan 4 1916 Sex:M Child# 2 Louis E Forest Canada & Alma Gosselin Canada
FOREST, Oscar Raymond, Jun 5 1918 Sex:M Child# 1 Rosaria Forest Canada & Anna Morin Canada
FOREST, Unknown, Feb 6 1920 Sex:F Child# Louis Forest Canada & Alma Gosselin Canada Stillborn
FORNESS, Norbert Joseph, Mar 9 1933 Sex:M Child# 1 Norbert Forness Allegheny, NY & M Campbell Bingham, NY
FORRANCE, Doris May, Apr 29 1923 Sex:F Child# 3 William A Forrance Lion Mt, NY & Eva Provencal Exeter, NH
FORRENCE, Bradford Pearly, May 9 1896 Sex:M Child# 6 John Forrence Redford, NY & Della Porter Chazy, NY
FORRENCE, Charles Edward, Nov 29 1919 Sex:M Child# 7 George A Forrence Lyon Mt, NY & Anna Obin Plattsburg, NY
FORRENCE, Evelyn Rose, Jul 12 1920 Sex:F Child# 1 William Forrence New York & Eva Provencal Exeter, NH
FORRENCE, Joseph William, Apr 2 1913 Sex:M Child# 4 George Forrence New York & Annie Obin New York
FORRENCE, Marie Mildred, Nov 26 1921 Sex:F Child# 2 William Forrence Newport & Eva Provencal Exeter
FORRENCE, Marjorie Adelaide, Jul 24 1909 Sex:F Child# 2 George A Forrence New York & Anna Obin Plattsburgh, NY
FORRENCE, Mildred Irene, Jul 30 1907 Sex:F Child# 1 George Forrence New York & Annie Aubin New York
FORSAITH, Barbara Harriet, Aug 3 1926 Sex:F Child# 1 Charles Forsaith Nashua, NH & Marguerite Spence Lawrence, MA
FORSAITH, Charles H, Jan 27 1899 Sex:M Child# 4 Charles H Forsaith Nashua, NH & H M Newton Peterborough, NH
FORSAITH, Charles Henry, Jr, Aug 2 1930 Sex:M Child# 2 Charles H Forsaith Nashua, NH & Marguerite Spence Lawrence
FORSAITH, Ralph A, Jun 17 1893 Sex:M Child# 3 Charles H Forsaith Nashua, NH & H M Newton Peterborough, NH
FORSAITH, Unknown, Jun 17 1889 Sex:F Child# 2 Charles Forsaith Nashua, NH & Hattie M Forsaith Peterboro
FORSYTH, James, Feb 28 1934 Sex:M Child# 2 Thomas Forsyth Scotland & Emma Provasoli Milford, NH
FORSYTH, Thomas Jr, Jan 8 1933 Sex:M Child# 1 Thomas Forsyth Scotland & Emma J Proasoli Milford, NH
FORTIER, Elmer Joseph A, May 14 1911 Sex:M Child# 1 Alphonse Fortier Mass & Effie Smith Nashua, NH
FORTIER, Estelle Ruth, Mar 21 1931 Sex:F Child# 7 John Fortier Holoyke, MA & Marion Bedard Canada
FORTIER, Henri Alex, Aug 2 1902 Sex:M Child# 6 Charles Fortier Palmer, MA & Nora Tetrault Fitchburg, MA
FORTIER, Jeannette, Aug 9 1912 Sex:F Child# 1 Alfred Fortier
FORTIER, Jos Maurice Leonard, Mar 3 1935 Sex:M Child# 3 Armand Fortier Nashua, NH & Simone Roussel Canada
FORTIER, Jos Walter Francis, May 14 1927 Sex:M Child# 5 John Fortier Holyoke, MA & Marie A Bedard Canada
FORTIER, Joseph, Mar 11 1916 Sex:M Child# 2 Amedee Fortier Maine & Marie Corbin Canada  Stillborn
FORTIER, Joseph A Sylvio, Sep 19 1931 Sex:M Child# 1 Armand Fortier Nashua, NH & Simonne Rousselle Canada
FORTIER, Joseph Willie, Aug 16 1914 Sex:M Child# 1 Amedee Fortier Maine & Marie Corbin Canada
FORTIER, Louis Arthur, Aug 2 1902 Sex:M Child# 5 Charles Fortier Palmer, MA & Nora Tetrault Fitchburg, MA
FORTIER, Lucille Margaret, Nov 1 1928 Sex:F Child# 6 John J Fortier Holyoke, MA & Marion Bedard Canada
FORTIER, Marie Anne, Aug 11 1924 Sex:F Child# 4 Amedee Fortier Biddeford, ME & Marie Corbin Canada
FORTIER, Marie Irene Felicite, Mar 15 1928 Sex:F Child# 2 Pierre Fortier Canada & Mabel Brault Nashua, NH
FORTIER, Marie Priscilla M, Aug 6 1932 Sex:F Child# 2 Armand Fortier Nashua, NH & Simonne Roussel Canada
FORTIER, Paul, Feb 26 1926 Sex:M Child# 1 Pierre Fortier Canada & Mabel Brault Nashua, NH
FORTIER, Theresa Frances, Aug 11 1934 Sex:F Child# 8 John Fortier Holyoke, MA & Marion Bedard Canada
FORTIER, Unknown, Nov 22 1894 Sex:F Child# 12 Desire Fortier Canada & Demoise Leclair Canada
FORTIER, Yvonne, Jul 14 1919 Sex:F Child# 3 Amedee Fortier Biddeford, ME & Marie Corbin Canada
FORTIN, Almina Bertha W, Aug 6 1905 Sex:F Child# 2 Joseph Fortin Canada & Mary Poney Canada
FORTIN, Cecile Violette, Feb 7 1917 Sex:F Child# 6 Charles Fortin Canada & Diana Dube Canada
FORTIN, Conrad Marcel, Feb 3 1934 Sex:M Child# 3 Roland A Fortin Nashua, NH & Irene Pinsonneault Canada
FORTIN, Corona, Dec 16 1920 Sex:F Child# 7 Charles Fortin Canada & Diana Dube Canada
FORTIN, Donat Eusebe, Jun 28 1905 Sex:M Child# 3 Eusebe Fortin Canada & Alphonsine Gendron Lowell, MA
FORTIN, Eva Anita Cecile, Feb 24 1921 Sex:F Child# 8 Joseph Fortin Canada & Marie Poney Canada
FORTIN, Flora, Jan 26 1907 Sex:F Child# 4 Eusebe Fortin Canada & Flora Goudreau Lowell, MA
FORTIN, Francois Desire, Aug 4 1902 Sex:M Child# 7 Desire Fortin Canada & Anna Masse Canada
FORTIN, Frederick, Feb 16 1909 Sex:M Child# 5 Eusebe Fortin Canada & Flora Goudreau Nashua, NH
FORTIN, George E R, May 7 1902 Sex:M Child# 4 George Fortin Canada & Marie Bonnette Canada
FORTIN, George Irenee, Jul 31 1930 Sex:M Child# 2 Roland Fortin Nashua, NH & Irene Pinsonneault Canada
FORTIN, Georges O, Jan 10 1887 Sex:M Child# Desere Fortin P Q & Demerise Leclers P Q
FORTIN, J Raymond Felix, Jan 8 1914 Sex:M Child# 5 Joseph Fortin Canada & Marie Poney Canada
FORTIN, J Wilfred Napoleon, Nov 19 1911 Sex:M Child# 4 Joseph Fortin Canada & Marie Poney Canada
FORTIN, Jeannette Theresa, Jan 19 1929 Sex:F Child# 1 Roland Fortin Nashua, NH & Irene Pinsonneault Canada
FORTIN, Joseph Albert, Jan 15 1911 Sex:M Child# 2 Charles Fortin Canada & Diana Dube Canada
FORTIN, Joseph Charles, Dec 2 1903 Sex:M Child# 1 Joseph Fortin Canada & Mary Poney Canada
FORTIN, Joseph Charles, Nov 26 1909 Sex:M Child# 1 Charles Fortin Canada & Diana Dube Canada
FORTIN, Joseph D, Jan 10 1887 Sex:M Child# Desere Fortin P Q & Demerise Leclers P Q
FORTIN, Joseph Edward Noel, Dec 22 1918 Sex:M Child# 7 Joseph Fortin Canada & Mary Fortin Canada
FORTIN, Joseph Henry, Jan 30 1897 Sex:M Child# 4 Desire J Fortin Canada & Anna Masse Canada
FORTIN, Joseph J B, Feb 24 1896 Sex:M Child# 8 Thomas Fortin Canada & Pelagie Milliard Canada
FORTIN, Joseph Johnny, Jan 27 1901 Sex:M Child# 7 Desire Fortin Canada & Anna Masse Canada
FORTIN, M Louise Lena, Jun 10 1915 Sex:F Child# 5 Charles Fortin Canada & Diana Dube Canada
FORTIN, M Olivette Jeannette, Nov 20 1915 Sex:F Child# 6 Joseph Fortin Canada & Mary Poney Canada

FORTIN, Marguerite Rita, Jul 15 1927 Sex:F Child# 1 Francis Fortin Nashua, NH & Alice Desclos Nashua, NH
FORTIN, Marie Albina, Feb 6 1895 Sex:F Child# 3 Desire Fortin Canada & Anna Masse Canada
FORTIN, Marie Alice, Mar 5 1894 Sex:F Child# 2 Desire Fortin Canada & Anna Masse Canada
FORTIN, Marie Anne, Mar 22 1913 Sex:F Child# 3 Charles Fortin Canada & Diana Dube Canada
FORTIN, Marie Blanche I, Oct 30 1900 Sex:F Child# 2 Aug Fortin Canada & Celaine Caron Canada
FORTIN, Marie Catherine A, Nov 25 1906 Sex:F Child# 8 Desire Fortin Canada & Anna Masse Canada
FORTIN, Marie Delia, Sep 2 1899 Sex:F Child# 6 Desire Fortin Canada & Anna Masse Canada
FORTIN, Marie Ida, Dec 2 1892 Sex:F Child# 1 Desire Fortin Canada & Anna Masse Canada
FORTIN, Marie Laura, Jul 19 1898 Sex:F Child# 5 Desire Fortin Canada & Anna Masse Canada
FORTIN, Marie Marcella, Jun 5 1904 Sex:F Child# 1 Theophile Fortin Canada & Ernestine Beaulieu Canada
FORTIN, Marie Rose C, Oct 29 1899 Sex:F Child# 1 Aug Fortin Canada & Celanire Caron Canada
FORTIN, Normand, Apr 15 1929 Sex:M Child# 2 Frank Fortin Nashua, NH & Alice Desclos Nashua, NH
FORTIN, Ovila, Apr 14 1914 Sex:M Child# 4 Charles Fortin Canada & Diana Dube Canada
FORTIN, Roger Alfred, Apr 6 1931 Sex:M Child# 3 Frank Fortin Nashua, NH & Alice Desclos Nashua, NH
FORTIN, William Alfred, Sep 23 1903 Sex:M Child# 7 Desire Fortin Canada & Anna Masse Canada
FORTNEY, Rita Lillian, Mar 16 1930 Sex:F Child# 7 Otis Fortney Kentucky & Violet Lucier Maine
FORWARD, Herbert Glenn, Apr 11 1928 Sex:M Child# 3 R Forward New Brunswick & Rachel Johnson NB Stillborn
FOSDICK, Helene Mary, Sep 30 1913 Sex:F Child# 2 Charles E Fosdick Peterboro, NH & Ethel May Pratt Nashua, NH
FOSIE, Mary Louise, Jun 20 1908 Sex:F Child# 1 John Fosie Mass & Olivine Peloquin Canada
FOSS, Aldine D, Jul 15 1911 Sex:F Child# 1 Spencer H Foss Tunbridge, VT & Gertrude Winchester St John, NB
FOSS, Carlene June, May 16 1933 Sex:F Child# 1 Harry P Foss Littleton, NH & V Warburton Hudson, NH
FOSS, Donald George, Mar 8 1922 Sex:M Child# 1 Spencer H Foss N Turnbridge, VT & Helen Haven Toronto, Canada
FOSS, Helena, Aug 30 1925 Sex:F Child# 5 Richard W Foss Jamaica Plains, MA & Mary C O'Brien Ireland
FOSS, Marjorie Helen, Sep 23 1924 Sex:F Child# 2 Spencer H Foss N Tunbridge & Helen Haven Toronto, Canada
FOSSA, Constance Madeline, Aug 15 1924 Sex:F Child# 1 Albert Fossa Beverly, MA & Rose McCutcheon Nashua, NH
FOSSA, Nathalie Frances, Jan 21 1926 Sex:F Child# 1 Francis Fossa Salem, MA & Eva Malette Nashua, NH
FOSTANES, William, Nov 12 1909 Sex:M Child# 1 John Fostanes Greece & Georgina Thomascas Greece
FOSTER, Arthur, Feb 22 1896 Sex:M Child# 3 Arthur P Foster Milford, NH & Julia Scanlan Nashua, NH Stillborn
FOSTER, Carl Ernest, Nov 28 1898 Sex:M Child# 2 Algernon M Foster Brookline & Emma J Woodward Francestown
FOSTER, Donald James, Nov 1 1930 Sex:M Child# 5 Walter Foster Amherst, NH & Grace Floyd Shelbourne, MA
FOSTER, Dorothy Mae, May 1 1929 Sex:F Child# 4 Walter Foster Amherst, NH & Grace Floyd Shelburne, MA
FOSTER, Edgar, Jul 2 1888 Sex:M Child# 1 Jerry Foster N Y & Agnes Bedard N Y
FOSTER, Evelyn, Dec 29 1918 Sex:F Child# 1 Wilbur J Foster Reeds Ferry, NH & Edna Staples Mansfield, MA
FOSTER, Floyd Earl, Nov 17 1927 Sex:M Child# 3 Wallace Foster Amherst, NH & Grace Floyd Mass
FOSTER, George Albert, Aug 30 1896 Sex:M Child# 1 Algernon M Foster Brookline & Emma J Woodward Francestown
FOSTER, June B, Jun 18 1897 Sex:F Child# 1 Fred Foster New York & Myra Dent New York
FOSTER, Laurent Russell, Sep 10 1929 Sex:M Child# 3 George L Foster S Lyndeboro, NH & Lila Currier W Lynn, MA
FOSTER, Leonard Warren, Jan 12 1928 Sex:M Child# 2 George L Foster S Lyndeboro, NH & Lelia D Currier W Lynn, MA
FOSTER, Marion Winnefrid, May 21 1926 Sex:F Child# 1 George L Foster Vermont & Cilia Currier Lynn, MA
FOSTER, Mary Winifred, Nov 19 1890 Sex:F Child# 2 George Foster NY & Agnes Bedard NY
FOSTER, Ralph Normand, Dec 13 1930 Sex:M Child# 4 George L Foster S Lyndeboro, NH & Lilia Currier W Lynn, MA
FOSTER, Raymond Miles, Jun 21 1900 Sex:M Child# 3 Algenon M Foster NH & E J Woodward NH
FOSTER, Shirley Ann, Dec 31 1924 Sex:F Child# 2 Wallace C Foster Amherst, NH & Grace Floyd Shelburne, MA
FOSTER, Unknown, Mar 30 1889 Sex:M Child# 3 William Foster
FOSTER, Unknown, Aug 24 1889 Sex:M Child# 1 Arthur P Foster Milford, NH & Julia Scanlon Nashua, NH
FOSTER, Unknown, Aug 31 1890 Sex:F Child# 2 Arthur P Foster Milford, NH & Julia Scanlon Nashua, NH
FOSTER, Unknown, Jan 25 1891 Sex:M Child# 1 George H Foster Nashua, NH & Carrie A Rye
FOUGERE, Angelina M, Feb 28 1900 Sex:F Child# 4 Charles Fougere Canada & Anna Mousette Nashua, NH
FOUGERE, Marie Elise, Apr 30 1896 Sex:F Child# 2 Charles Fougere Canada & Anna Moussette Nashua, NH
FOUKIS, Eanina, Jan 8 1920 Sex:F Child# 1 Adam Foukis Russia & Adelia Rodzewicz Russia
FOUNDAS, Constantine, Jul 19 1935 Sex:M Child# 1 Constantine Foundas Greece & Euph Panagoulis Nashua, NH
FOUNIER, Joseph, Mar 3 1888 Sex:M Child# 10 Adolph Founier Canada & Delphine Lemard Canada
FOURNETTE, Unknown, Oct 13 1921 Sex:M Child# 8 George Fournette Canada & Laura Roy Mass
FOURNIER, Albert Leger, Sep 10 1904 Sex:M Child# 2 Achilles Fournier Canada & Aglae Dufour Canada
FOURNIER, Camille Hector, Dec 17 1933 Sex:M Child# 1 Gilbert Fournier Greenville, NH & Alice Cloutier Greenville,NH
FOURNIER, Edgar, Mar 16 1926 Sex:M Child# 2 Amede Fournier NH & Eualia Moisant
FOURNIER, Edouard, Apr 1 1897 Sex:M Child# 1 Edouard Fournier Canada & Catherine Duchesneau US
FOURNIER, Felix Eugene, Jun 7 1900 Sex:M Child# 4 Felix Fournier Canada & Sedulie Sirois Canada
FOURNIER, Francois George, Feb 21 1904 Sex:M Child# 1 George Fournier Canada & M Louise Gagnon Canada
FOURNIER, Georges E, Oct 28 1887 Sex:M Child# Louis A Fournier P Q & Julie Cusson P Q
FOURNIER, Gloria Louise, Mar 8 1928 Sex:F Child# 3 Amedee Fournier NH & Eulalia Moisan Vermont
FOURNIER, Hector, Apr 19 1903 Sex:M Child# 1 Achille Fournier Canada & Aglae Dufour Canada
FOURNIER, Jos Edouard Roland, Apr 18 1927 Sex:M Child# 3 Edouard Fournier Nashua, NH & Clara Pelletier Canada
FOURNIER, Joseph Arthur, Jun 12 1895 Sex:M Child# 1 Joseph Fournier Canada & Eugenie Gagne Canada
FOURNIER, Joseph Arthur, Nov 22 1902 Sex:M Child# 6 Felix Fournier Canada & Cedulie Sirois Canada
FOURNIER, Joseph E H, Jun 2 1897 Sex:M Child# 1 F X Fournier Canada & Josephine Vincent Canada
FOURNIER, Joseph F Xavier, Feb 28 1895 Sex:M Child# 4 Xavier Fournier Canada & Josephine Pepin Canada
FOURNIER, Joseph Leon, Aug 14 1901 Sex:M Child# 5 Felix Fournier Canada & Adulie Roy Canada
FOURNIER, Juliette, Mar 2 1895 Sex:F Child# 2 Francois Fournier Canada & Emma Grandmaison Canada
FOURNIER, Loraine Elizabeth, Mar 3 1931 Sex:F Child# 5 Amedee Fournier Greenville, NH & Eulalie Moison Nashua, NH
FOURNIER, Lucille Rita, Sep 4 1924 Sex:F Child# 2 E Fournier Nashua, NH & Clara Pelletier Canada
FOURNIER, M Cecile Eugenie, Nov 10 1914 Sex:F Child# 1 Joachim Fournier Canada & Alphonsine St Pierre Canada
FOURNIER, Marie, Jul 10 1909 Sex:F Child# 2 Joseph Fournier Canada & Angelina Charron Canada

FOURNIER, Marie Alice, Dec 19 1897 Sex:F Child# 2 Felix Fournier Canada & Cedulie Roy Canada
FOURNIER, Marie Anne, Jan 25 1897 Sex:F Child# 1 Felix Fournier Canada & Cedulie Sirois Canada
FOURNIER, Marie Dolores F, Aug 19 1906 Sex:F Child# 1 Joseph Fournier Canada & Angelina Charron Canada
FOURNIER, Marie Irene, Feb 12 1920 Sex:F Child# 1 Edward Fournier Nashua, NH & Clara Pelletier Canada
FOURNIER, Noela Madeline, Dec 25 1932 Sex:F Child# 1 Maurice Fournier NH & M A Dussault Canada
FOURNIER, Paul Normand, May 23 1924 Sex:M Child# 1 Amedee Fournier Greenville, NH & Eulalie Moisau Newport, VT
FOURNIER, Pauline gilberte, Apr 16 1933 Sex:F Child# 2 Edmond Fournier Canada & Irene Berube Nashua, NH
FOURNIER, Pauline Jeannette, Dec 1 1934 Sex:F Child# 2 Maurice Fournier Nashua, NH & Marion Dusseault Canada
FOURNIER, Rachel Claire, Oct 9 1930 Sex:F Child# 1 Edmond Fournier Canada & Irene Berube Nashua, NH
FOURNIER, Roger Andrew, Jul 23 1920 Sex:M Child# 9 Ernest Fournier Canada & Eva Morneau Canada
FOURNIER, Rose Anna, Nov 13 1898 Sex:F Child# 3 Felix Fournier Canada & Sedulie Sirois Canada
FOURNIER, Theresa Melvina, Jan 9 1917 Sex:F Child# 1 Leo A Fournier N Adams, MA & Virginia J Ramsey Lowell, MA
FOURNIER, Unknown, May 18 1892 Sex:M Child# 19 Charles Fournier Canada & Pomela Dion Canada
FOURNIER, Victor Maurice Roger, Jul 10 1914 Sex:M Child# 4 Odilon Fournier Canada & Alida Lagasse Canada
FOURNIER, Wilfrid, Sep 5 1899 Sex:M Child# 2 Edouard Fournier Canada & Catherine Duchesneau NH
FOURNIER, Yolande Theresa, Nov 20 1929 Sex:F Child# 4 Amedee Fournier NH & Eulalia Moisau Vermont
FOURNIER, Yvonne, Jan 26 1915 Sex:F Child# 3 Albert E Fournier Nashua, NH & Elizabeth F Barry Boston, MA
FOWLER, Unknown, Nov 28 1890 Sex:M Child# 1 George W Fowler Pembroke, NH & Etta Bartlett Suncook, NH
FOX, Charles Mylo, Jan 6 1929 Sex:M Child# 6 William C Fox Manchester, NH & Roseanna Arnold Berlin, NH
FOX, Dorothy Ruth, Nov 27 1917 Sex:F Child# 1 Joseph P Fox New York, NY & Ora Stratton Dayton, OH
FOX, Elizabeth Catharine, Aug 7 1921 Sex:F Child# 4 William C Fox Manchester, NH & Rosanna Arnold Berlin, NH
FOX, Evelyn Mary, Aug 17 1924 Sex:F Child# 5 William C Fox Manchester, NH & Rosanna Arnold Berlin, NH
FOX, Faith Ann, Jul 3 1934 Sex:F Child# 7 Archer Fox Lowell, MA & Mabel Fuller Amherst, MA
FOX, Rose Mary, Dec 10 1916 Sex:F Child# 1 William Fox Manchester, NH & Rosanna Arnold Berlin, NH
FOX, Unknown, Aug 16 1920 Sex:M Child# 3 William C Fox Manchester, NH & Rosanna Arnold Berlin, NH Stillborn
FOX, William Child, Jr, Jul 21 1918 Sex:M Child# 2 William Child Fox Manchester, NH & Rosanna Arnold Berlin, NH
FRAISER, Eugene B, Oct 12 1907 Sex:M Child# 11 Pierre Fraiser Canada & Arthemise Brassard Canada
FRAISER, Joseph A, Dec 18 1887 Sex:M Child# 2 Georges Fraiser P Q & Fredeline P Q
FRAISER, Joseph A, Aug 20 1893 Sex:M Child# 5 Pierre Fraiser Canada & Arthemise Brassard Canada
FRAISER, Joseph E, Dec 12 1894 Sex:M Child# 1 Simeon Fraiser Canada & Marie Dube Canada
FRAISER, Joseph E A, Feb 4 1893 Sex:M Child# 4 Georges Fraiser Canada & Freneline Grenier Canada
FRAISER, Joseph H, Dec 13 1898 Sex:M Child# 9 Pierre Fraiser Canada & Arthemise Brassard Canada
FRAISER, Marie A, Sep 4 1894 Sex:F Child# 6 Pierre Fraiser Canada & Arthemise Brassard Canada
FRAISER, Marie A, Dec 13 1897 Sex:F Child# 8 Pierre Fraiser Canada & Arthemise Brassard Canada
FRAISER, Marie B, Oct 19 1898 Sex:F Child# 2 Pierre Fraiser Canada & Marie Lavigne Canada
FRAISER, Marie C, Jul 21 1895 Sex:F Child# 7 Pierre Fraiser Canada & Arthemise Brassard Canada
FRAISER, Marie E, Aug 17 1890 Sex:F Child# 3 Pierre Fraiser Canada & Arthemise Brassard Canada
FRAISER, Marie I, Jan 27 1901 Sex:F Child# 1 Joseph Fraiser Canada & Marie Caron Canada
FRANCIS, Natalie, Dec 9 1904 Sex:F Child# 1 Richard Francis Halifax, NS & Lena Stebbins Newbury, VT
FRANCIS, Richard, Mar 31 1906 Sex:M Child# 2 Richard Francis Halifax, NS & Minnie Stebbins Newbury, VT
FRANCIS, Stanley Joseph F, Aug 27 1908 Sex:M Child# 3 Richard Francis Halifax, NS & Lina Stebbins Newbury, VT
FRANCIS, Unknown, Jul 15 1889 Sex:M Child# 3 Boothby E Francis Jaffrey, ME & Edna French S Midelbly, NH Stillborn
FRANCOEUR, Adrian Philip, Jun 27 1915 Sex:M Child# 2 Albert E Francoeur Canada & Elizabeth Nolan Nashua, NH
FRANCOEUR, Albert, Jan 28 1906 Sex:M Child# 4 Adjutor Francoeur Canada & Delphine Landry Canada
FRANCOEUR, Alfred Donat, May 28 1902 Sex:M Child# 4 Elisee Francoeur Canada & A Levesque Canada
FRANCOEUR, Aug Adrien, Jan 31 1902 Sex:M Child# 1 Adjutor Francoeur Canada & Delphine Landry Canada
FRANCOEUR, Dolores Collombe, Aug 11 1931 Sex:F Child# 1 Napoleon Francoeur Nashua, NH & Bertha Berube Nashua, NH
FRANCOEUR, Dorothy, Jan 7 1918 Sex:F Child# 3 Albert Francoeur Canada & Elizabeth Nolan Boston, MA
FRANCOEUR, Edwin Albert, Sep 29 1913 Sex:M Child# 1 Albert E Francoeur Canada & Elizabeth G Nolan Boston, MA
FRANCOEUR, Elie Wilbrod, Feb 14 1898 Sex:M Child# 4 Elie Francoeur Canada & Aimie Landry Canada
FRANCOEUR, Gabrielle, Apr 28 1935 Sex:F Child# 2 Napoleon Francoeur Nashua, NH & Bertha Berube Nashua, NH
FRANCOEUR, Irene, Mar 18 1894 Sex:F Child# 2 Elie Francoeur Canada & Aimee Landry Canada
FRANCOEUR, Irene Simone, May 9 1914 Sex:F Child# 10 Elise Francoeur Canada & Angelina Levesque Canada
FRANCOEUR, Jeanne A, Mar 2 1902 Sex:F Child# 2 Joseph Francoeur Canada & Celina Hudon Canada
FRANCOEUR, Joseph Arthur U, Dec 12 1903 Sex:M Child# 4 Elize Francoeur Canada & Rosanna Levesque Canada
FRANCOEUR, Joseph Louis, Sep 7 1907 Sex:M Child# 7 Elizee Francoeur Canada & Angelina Levesque Canada
FRANCOEUR, Joseph Roland, Sep 8 1929 Sex:M Child# 4 Alfred Francoeur Nashua, NH & Cecelia Levesque Canada
FRANCOEUR, Joseph Romeo, Oct 29 1930 Sex:M Child# 5 Alfred Francoeur Nashua, NH & Cecelia Levesque Canada
FRANCOEUR, Leo, Apr 9 1896 Sex:M Child# 3 Elie Francoeur Canada & Aimee Landry Canada
FRANCOEUR, Leo, May 14 1903 Sex:M Child# 2 Adjutor Francoeur Canada & Delphine Landry Canada
FRANCOEUR, Loretta Lucille, Apr 12 1928 Sex:F Child# 3 Alf Francoeur Nashua, NH & Cecelia Levesque Canada
FRANCOEUR, Marie Alvine, Nov 6 1905 Sex:F Child# 7 Desire Francoeur Canada & Marie Levesque Canada
FRANCOEUR, Marie Angelina, Aug 13 1900 Sex:F Child# 3 E Francoeur Canada & Angelina Levesque Canada
FRANCOEUR, Marie Celina I, Mar 4 1901 Sex:F Child# 1 Joseph A Francoeur Canada & Celina Hudon Canada
FRANCOEUR, Marie Eva Rose, Oct 11 1911 Sex:F Child# 9 Elise Francoeur Canada & Angelina Levesque Canada
FRANCOEUR, Marie Louise A, Aug 25 1906 Sex:F Child# 12 Philippe Francoeur Canada & Anna Mignault Canada
FRANCOEUR, Marie Rose, Mar 16 1933 Sex:F Child# 6 Alfred Francoeur Nashua, NH & Cecelia Levesque Canada
FRANCOEUR, Marie Yvonne, Jan 2 1909 Sex:F Child# 8 Elize Francoeur Canada & Malvina Levesque Canada
FRANCOEUR, Marjorie Vivienne, Jun 24 1930 Sex:F Child# 3 Horace Francoeur Canada & A Theriault Canada
FRANCOEUR, Mary Amanda, May 1 1892 Sex:F Child# 1 Eli Francoeur Canada & Eme Landry Canada
FRANCOEUR, Normand Conrad, Sep 7 1932 Sex:M Child# 1 L Francoeur Nashua, NH & Alice Berube Suncook, NH
FRANCOEUR, Paul Raymond, Jan 27 1919 Sex:M Child# 1 George Francoeur Canada & Anna Dowling Nashua, NH Stillborn
FRANCOEUR, Phyllis Sara, Apr 10 1930 Sex:F Child# 3 Wilbrod Francoeur Nashua, NH & Esther Levine Keene, NH

FRANCOEUR, Reginald Normand, Nov 15 1924 Sex:M Child# 2 Horace Francoeur Canada & Emelie Therriault Canada
FRANCOEUR, Robert, Jan 25 1925 Sex:M Child# 4 Albert Francoeur Canada & Elizabeth Nolan Boston, MA
FRANCOEUR, Romeo Elie, Sep 18 1904 Sex:M Child# 3 Adjutor Francoeur Canada & Delphine Landry Canada
FRANCOEUR, Romeo Robert, May 10 1926 Sex:M Child# 10 Alfred Francoeur Nashua, NH & Cecile Levesque Canada
FRANCOEUR, Unknown, Aug 3 1922 Sex:M Child# 1 Horace Francoeur Canada & Amelia Therriault Canada
FRANCOEUR, Unknown, Sep 21 1924 Sex:M Child# 1 Alfred Francoeur Nashua, NH & Cecilia Levesque Canada
FRANCOEUR, Victor Joseph, Oct 6 1934 Sex:M Child# 2 Louis Francoeur Nashua, NH & Alice Berube Nashua, NH
FRANCOUR, Cecile, Jul 29 1922 Sex:F Child# 4 Joseph Francour Nashua, NH & Marie Landry Canada
FRANCOUR, Earnest H, Sep 21 1889 Sex:M Child# 2 Maxime Francour Canada & Adelaide Lambert Nashua, NH
FRANK, Catherine Jane, Dec 15 1935 Sex:F Child# 3 Robert Frank Nashua, NH & Beulah Griffin Stafford, CT
FRANK, Constance, Oct 3 1932 Sex:F Child# 1 Robert Frank Nashua, NH & Beulah Griffin Stanford, CT
FRANK, Donald Thomas F, Jul 9 1929 Sex:M Child# 4 Charles Frank Johnstown, NY & Ella Whyte Malone, NY
FRANK, Earl Paul, Aug 19 1932 Sex:M Child# 5 Charles Frank Johnstown, NY & Ella Whyte Malone, NY
FRANK, Robert Kenneth, Oct 4 1933 Sex:M Child# 2 Robert Frank Nashua, NH & Beulah Griffin Stamford, CT
FRANK, Unknown, Sep 21 1907 Sex:F Child# 1 Michael Frank Germany & Mary Jones New Utica, NY
FRANK, Unknown, Aug 3 1910 Sex:F Child# 2 J Fred Frank Canton, OH & Evelyn Lynch Canton, OH
FRANKEWICZ, John, Jun 24 1913 Sex:M Child# 1 Anthony Frankewicz Russia & Paulina Skipos Russia
FRANKEWICZ, Powell, Jan 4 1915 Sex:M Child# 2 Anthony Frankewicz Russia & Paulina Skepor Russia
FRANKLIN, Helen May, Aug 21 1934 Sex:F Child# 1 Guy Franklin Vermont & Carrie Michaud Wilton, NH
FRANZEIM, Norma Reece, Aug 10 1918 Sex:F Child# 3 Norman E Franzeim E Orange, NJ & Emma J Abbe Melrose, CT
FRANZEIM, Norman Achille, Aug 10 1918 Sex:M Child# 2 Norman E Franzeim E Orange, NJ & Emma J Abbe Melrose, CT
FRANZEIN, Frederick Abbe, Nov 7 1916 Sex:M Child# 1 N A Franzein Jersey City, NJ & Emma Isabelle Abbe Enfield, NH
FRASER, Adeline Liliane, Aug 17 1919 Sex:F Child# 3 Adrien Fraser Nashua, NH & Adeline Cote Nashua, NH
FRASER, Adrienne, Nov 6 1917 Sex:F Child# 2 Adrian Fraser US & Adeline Cote US
FRASER, Andrew Robert, Nov 30 1932 Sex:M Child# 2 William Fraser Nashua, NH & Rose Gould Manchester, NH
FRASER, Annette Laura, Jan 8 1928 Sex:F Child# 5 Henry Fraser Nashua, NH & Eva Kerouac Nashua, NH
FRASER, Armande, Jan 16 1907 Sex:F Child# 4 Joseph Fraser Canada & Marie Caron Canada
FRASER, Beatrice, Jun 27 1921 Sex:F Child# 1 Henry Fraser Nashua, NH & Eva Kerouac Nashua, NH
FRASER, Edgar, Sep 30 1928 Sex:M Child# 7 Adrien Fraser Nashua, NH & Adeline Cote Nashua, NH
FRASER, Edouard Adrian, Apr 16 1926 Sex:M Child# 4 Henry Fraser NH & Eva Kerouac Nashua, NH
FRASER, Ernest, Jul 14 1889 Sex:M Child# 2 Pierre Fraser Canada & Arthernise Brassord Canada
FRASER, Eugene Roger, Feb 2 1929 Sex:M Child# 1 Eugene Fraser Canada & Hermenie Girouard Nashua, NH
FRASER, Felicien Armand, Jul 22 1916 Sex:M Child# 1 Adrien Fraser US & Adeline Cote US
FRASER, George Adelard, Apr 6 1894 Sex:M Child# 1 Simon Fraser Canada & Josephine Martin Greenville, NH
FRASER, Gerald Rene, Jun 15 1931 Sex:M Child# 8 Adrien Fraser Nashua, NH & Adeline Cote Nashua, NH
FRASER, Gerald Roland, Dec 10 1920 Sex:M Child# 4 Adrien Fraser US & Adeline Cote US
FRASER, Henry Arthur, Nov 29 1931 Sex:M Child# 6 Henry Fraser Nashua, NH & Eva Kerouac Nashua, NH
FRASER, Irene, Feb 9 1902 Sex:F Child# 2 Joseph Fraser Canada & Marie Caron Canada
FRASER, Irenee, Aug 16 1897 Sex:M Child# 5 Georges Fraser Canada & Fredeline Bastille Canada
FRASER, Jos Paul Simon, Dec 4 1929 Sex:M Child# 1 Eldridge Fraser Nashua, NH & Alice Jean St Regis Falls
FRASER, Joseph, Apr 15 1906 Sex:M Child# 7 George Fraser Canada & Fedeline Grenier Canada
FRASER, Joseph Albert, Jul 3 1896 Sex:M Child# 2 Simon Fraser Canada & Marie Dube Canada
FRASER, Joseph Ernest, Oct 16 1902 Sex:M Child# 7 Simon Fraser Canada & Delima Lechasseur Canada
FRASER, Joseph G Ulric, Oct 4 1896 Sex:M Child# 6 Simon Fraser Canada & Delima Chasseur Canada
FRASER, Joseph Normand, May 8 1930 Sex:M Child# 1 Willie Fraser Nashua, NH & Rose Gould Manchester, NH
FRASER, Joseph William A, Nov 2 1903 Sex:M Child# 3 Joseph Fraser Canada & Marie Caron Canada
FRASER, Leo Walters, May 9 1924 Sex:M Child# 3 Henri Fraser NH & Eva Kerouac NH
FRASER, Liliane, Nov 2 1902 Sex:F Child# 6 George Fraser Canada & Fredeline Grenier Canada
FRASER, Louis Philippe, Jun 17 1895 Sex:M Child# 5 Simon Fraser Canada & Delima Chasseur Canada
FRASER, Lydia Therese, Oct 8 1922 Sex:F Child# 5 Adrien Fraser US & Adeline Cote US
FRASER, Margaret Cecile, Jan 12 1922 Sex:F Child# 1 Irenee Fraser Nashua, NH & Viola Barbber Three Rivers, MA
FRASER, Marguerite, Aug 14 1889 Sex:F Child# 3 Georges Fraser Canada & Fredeline Grenier Canada
FRASER, Marie, May 17 1913 Sex:F Child# 8 Simon Fraser Canada & Delima Chasseur Canada
FRASER, Marie, Jan 8 1934 Sex:F Child# 1 Rene Fraser Nashua, NH & Marie Marquis
FRASER, Marie A Eliane, Dec 23 1899 Sex:F Child# 3 Pierre Fraser Canada & Marie Lavigne Canada
FRASER, Marie Eva, Nov 19 1897 Sex:F Child# 1 Pierre Fraser Canada & Maria Lavigne Canada
FRASER, Marie Louise, Dec 26 1887 Sex:F Child# 1 Pierre Fraser P Q & Arthemise Brassard Canada
FRASER, Norma Jane, Oct 3 1925 Sex:F Child# 1 Adrian Fraser Nashua, NH & N Charbonneau Enfield, NH
FRASER, Royal Arthur, Jan 6 1925 Sex:M Child# 6 Adrien Fraser US & Adeline Cote US
FRASER, Suzanne Doris, Mar 7 1933 Sex:F Child# 1 Ernest J Fraser Nashua, NH & Doris Aubert Dover, NH
FRASIER, Ernestine, Oct 23 1900 Sex:F Child# 10 Pierre Frasier Canada & Artemisie Brassard Canada
FRAYES, Kenneth Asa, Oct 25 1918 Sex:M Child# 1 Asa W Frayes Malden, MA & Margaret Bradley Nashua, NH
FRAZER, Roderick Parkhurst, Feb 12 1911 Sex:M Child# 1 William R Frazer Nova Scotia & Eligia Lydia Wilton, NH
FRAZER, William Alexander, Jan 17 1914 Sex:M Child# 2 William Frazer Nova Scotia & Lydia E Parkhurst Nashua, NH
FRAZIER, Joseph E, Jul 22 1888 Sex:M Child# 1 Simeon Frazier Canada & Delana Chasson Canada
FRECHETTE, Marie Virgina, May 22 1904 Sex:F Child# 6 Napoleon Frechette Canada & Anaise Menard Canada
FREDERIC, Marie Anne, May 1 1894 Sex:F Child# 4 Edmund Frederic Canada & Alphonsine Dansereau Canada
FREDETTE, Alice Adrienne, Dec 22 1898 Sex:F Child# 3 Joseph Fredette Canada & Sophie Lincourt Canada
FREDETTE, Exilda Aldea, Feb 17 1903 Sex:F Child# 4 Joseph Fredette Canada & Sophie Lancour Canada
FREDETTE, Georgianna, Mar 28 1907 Sex:F Child# 7 Napoleon Fredette Canada & Anais Menard Canada
FREDETTE, Joseph Arthur, Jun 12 1902 Sex:M Child# 5 Napoleon Fredette Canada & Anaise Maynard Canada
FREDETTE, Louis Ernest, Nov 26 1893 Sex:M Child# 2 Joseph Fredette Canada & Sophie Lincourt Canada
FREDETTE, Marie Blanche E, Oct 7 1924 Sex:F Child# 7 Joseph Fredette Canada & Blanche Richard Nashua, NH

FREDETTE, Marie Eva Cecile, Mar 2 1923 Sex:F Child# 6 Joseph Fredette Canada & Blanche Richard Nashua, NH
FREDETTE, Marie Fernande Sim, Jun 14 1918 Sex:F Child# 3 Joseph L Fredette Canada & Marie B Richard NH
FREDETTE, Marie Jeanne Camille, May 27 1916 Sex:F Child# 1 Joseph Fredette Canada & M Blanche Richard Canada
FREEMAN, Dorothy Lucille, Jul 23 1917 Sex:F Child# 1 Edward Freeman Manchester, NH & Birdie March Nashua, NH
FREEMAN, Elsa Elizabeth, Jul 8 1917 Sex:F Child# 2 Harold Freeman Charlestown, MA & Pearl Marshall Hancock, NH
FREEMAN, Ethel Pearl, May 30 1915 Sex:F Child# 1 Harold E Freeman Charlestown, MA & Pearl Marshall Hancock, NH
FREEMAN, Irene Syretha, Jul 8 1919 Sex:F Child# 3 Harold E Freeman Charlestown, MA & Pearl Marshall Hancock, NH
FREEMAN, Marion Arlene, Sep 19 1918 Sex:F Child# 2 Edward Freeman Manchester, NH & Birdie March Nashua, NH
FREEMAN, Unknown, May 21 1925 Sex:M Child# 4 Harold Freeman Somerville, MA & Pearl Marshall Hancock, NH Stillborn
FREEMAN, Virginia May, Oct 28 1922 Sex:F Child# 4 Edward Freeman Manchester, NH & Birdie March Nashua, NH
FREEMAN, William Walter, Sep 10 1920 Sex:M Child# 3 Ed A Freeman Manchester, NH & Birdie M March Nashua, NH
FREESE, Francis Trask, Jul 30 1894 Sex:M Child# 4 Henry C Freese Germany & Deidamia W Trask Deerfield, MA
FREESE, George Eugene, Jun 10 1898 Sex:M Child# 6 Henry C Freese Germany & Deidamia W Trash Deerfield, MA
FREESE, Grace Allen, Jul 29 1893 Sex:F Child# Henry C Freese Germany & Deidamia Trask Deerfield, MA
FREESE, Robert William, Sep 17 1892 Sex:M Child# 2 Henry C Freese Germany & Deidamia W Trask Deerfield, MA
FREESE, Unknown, Mar 16 1896 Sex:M Child# 5 Henry C Freese Germany & Derdamia W Trask Deerfield, MA Stillborn
FREEZE, Bertie Christopher, Nov 26 1899 Sex:M Child# 7 Henry C Freeze Germany & D W Trask Mass
FREINIAWICZ, Biruta, Nov 11 1915 Sex:F Child# 2 Andrew Freiniawicz Russia & Vincenta Tomolovicz Russia
FRELIGH, Helen Elizabeth, May 8 1896 Sex:F Child# 1 Claude A Freligh Armada, MI & Mary Helen French Manchester, NH
FRENCH, Alice Geneva, Mar 19 1911 Sex:F Child# 1 J T French Clare Castle, Ire & Frances Freeman Peabody, MA
FRENCH, Beverly Augusta, Feb 1 1926 Sex:F Child# 4 John French Nashua, NH & Winifred E Lund Hudson, NH
FRENCH, Caroline Mae P, Sep 29 1921 Sex:F Child# 1 Carroll French Milford, NH & Gertrude Pirovano Milford, NH
FRENCH, Cornelia Elizabeth, May 3 1895 Sex:F Child# 1 Menzell S French Templeton, MA & Jennie P Stevens Nashua, NH
FRENCH, Earl Winfield, May 11 1907 Sex:M Child# 1 Winfield H French Nashua, NH & Susie F Robbins Nashua, NH
FRENCH, Edward Lambe, Nov 7 1923 Sex:M Child# 3 Lindol French Chelsea, MA & Arlene Pepperell, MA
FRENCH, Fredrick L, Jan 27 1898 Sex:M Child# 4 Fred W French Eaton Corner, PQ & Fannie E Gray Manchester, NH
FRENCH, George Moulton, Jr, Nov 1 1922 Sex:M Child# G Moulton French Nashua, NH & Margaret Whittemore Needham, MA
FRENCH, Gordon Loring, Jun 1 1926 Sex:M Child# 1 Harold G French Hudson, NH & Maude Sargent Leominster, MA Stillbor
FRENCH, Leonard Stevens, Apr 14 1897 Sex:M Child# 2 Menzell S French Templeton, MA & Jennie P Stevens Nashua,
FRENCH, Lindol, Nov 22 1918 Sex:M Child# 1 Lindol French Chelsea, MA & Arleen Deware Pepperell, MA
FRENCH, Manila M, Jan 26 1899 Sex:F Child# 3 Edwin H French Jaffrey, NH & Fannie E Boothby S Waterboro, ME
FRENCH, Marian G, Feb 7 1895 Sex:F Child# 2 Fred W French Canada & Fannie Gray Manchester
FRENCH, Maurice Richard, Mar 28 1921 Sex:M Child# 3 David S French Chester, NH & Esther Dane Nottingham, NH
FRENCH, Patricia Pearl, Nov 5 1932 Sex:F Child# 3 H G French Hudson, NH & Maude Sargent Leominster, MA
FRENCH, Pearl Sylvia, May 10 1908 Sex:F Child# 2 Winfield H French Nashua, NH & Susie Robbins Nashua, NH
FRENCH, Richard Sargent, Aug 27 1929 Sex:M Child# 2 Harold French Hudson, NH & Maude Sargent Leominster, MA
FRENCH, Robert Allen, Oct 28 1921 Sex:M Child# 1 George N French Nashua, NH & Margaret Whittemore Needham, MA
FRENCH, Robert N, Dec 8 1892 Sex:M Child# 1 Walter C French Fitchburg, MA & Jennie T Huston Nashua, NH
FRENCH, Russell Arnold, May 30 1918 Sex:M Child# 3 John H French Nashua, NH & Winnifred E Lund Hudson, NH
FRENCH, Unknown, Oct 12 1887 Sex:F Child# 2 Edwin H French Jaffrey & Fannie Boothby Waterboro, ME
FRENCH, Unknown, May 2 1888 Sex:M Child# 4 George B French Moultonborough & Sarah B Milford
FRENCH, Unknown, Mar 6 1922 Sex:M Child# 2 Lindel French Nashua, NH & Gladys Holt Nashua, NH
FRENCH, Winnifred Clara, Jun 4 1896 Sex:F Child# 2 Fred French Canada & Annie L Gray Manchester, NH
FRENETTE, Mary, Jan 17 1891 Sex:F Child# 2 (No Parents Listed)
FRENETTE, Unknown, Aug 9 1892 Sex:M Child# 3 Henry T Frenette Nashua, NH & Nellie B Wright Nashua, NH
FRENETTE, Unknown, Jun 3 1894 Sex:M Child# 4 Henry T Frenette Nashua, NH & Nellie B Wright Nashua, NH
FRENETTE, Unknown, Apr 15 1899 Sex:M Child# 5 Henry T Frenette Nashua, NH & Nellie B Wright Nashua, NH
FRENETTE, Violette Laurette, Jul 21 1925 Sex:F Child# 9 George Frenette Canada & Laura Roy Lowell, MA
FRESER, Joseph Phillipps, Dec 5 1893 Sex:M Child# 1 Hermengilde Freser Canada & Anna Berube Canada
FRESU, Unknown, Jan 5 1892 Sex:M Child# 1 George A Fresu Grand Isle, VT & Mary Conlin
FREY, Ethelyn Barbara, Feb 20 1924 Sex:F Child# 1 Alfred T Frey Medford, MA & Ethelyn Patch Rockingham, VT
FRIEDBURG, Rosie, Oct 19 1907 Sex:F Child# 6 Joseph Friedburg Germany & Mary Gowitch Russia
FRIEND, Harry Fletcher, Dec 11 1895 Sex:M Child# 1 George E Friend Burke, NY & Ina V Fletcher Nashua, NH
FRISWOLD, Unknown, May 25 1887 Sex:M Child# 1 Henry J Griswold Manchester & Grace M Paris, NY
FROST, Donald Buckman, May 28 1923 Sex:M Child# 4 Harold Frost Milford, MA & Florence Ferguson Lowell, MA
FROST, Lucy, Sep 24 1893 Sex:F Child# 6 Nicholas Frost Gainsville, GA & Cora H Daniels Charlestown, MA
FROST, Unknown, May 3 1887 Sex:M Child# 2 Thomas Frost England & Etta Bradley Granville, NY
FROST, William Joshua, Jul 17 1896 Sex:M Child# 5 William J Frost Eliot, ME & Nellie G Chapman Newmarket, NH
FROSTINI, Rosa, Sep 29 1903 Sex:F Child# 3 Gian Frostini Italy & Maria Dagnoli Italy
FRYE, Barbara Madelyn, Dec 4 1915 Sex:F Child# 6 Orville H Frye Wilton, NH & Francis Delphy Bernardston, MA
FRYE, Charles Franklin, May 4 1895 Sex:M Child# 5 Charles Frye Nashua, NH & Emma Duncklee Greenfield, NH
FRYE, Charles Haven, May 28 1906 Sex:M Child# 4 Charles E Frye Wilton, NH & Bertha M Osborne Palmyra, ME
FRYE, Cora E, Sep 2 1890 Sex:F Child# 3 Charles F Frye Nashua, NH & Emma Duncklee Greenfield, NH
FRYE, Elsworth W, May 9 1897 Sex:M Child# 6 Charles F Frye Nashua, NH & Emma F Dunckley Greenfield, NH
FRYE, Roy Elliot, Apr 12 1900 Sex:M Child# 7 Charles F Frye Nashua, NH & Emma Duncklee NH
FRZECINSKI, Alexandre, Sep 20 1903 Sex:M Child# 1 Joseph Frzecinski Russia & Kataryna Olenda Russia
FRZEWSK, Victorine, Mar 23 1902 Sex:F Child# 1 Emile Frzewsk Russia & Boralia Olender Russia
FUGERE, Marie Alboma, Jun 25 1898 Sex:F Child# 3 Charles Fugere Canada & Anna Moussette Nashua, NH
FUGERE, Marie R A, Jan 14 1894 Sex:F Child# 1 Charles Fugere Canada & Anna Moussette Nashua, NH
FUGERE, Sylvia, Jun 7 1901 Sex:F Child# 5 Charles Fugere Canada & Anna Moussette Canada
FUINARD, Delia, Mar 29 1890 Sex:F Child# 11 Joseph Fuinard Canada & Cesarie Danseureau Canada
FULD, Thelma Irene, Jun 18 1925 Sex:F Child# 3 Arthur E Fuld Merrimack, NH & Bertha Roach Concord, NH
FULLER, Alice Mae, May 4 1910 Sex:F Child# 2 Joseph A Fuller Hudson, NH & Nettie A Mortlock Keene, NH

FULLER, Barbara Eudora, Jan 6 1914 Sex:F Child# 1 Willis L Fuller Hudson, NH & Grace Bills Pepperell, MA
FULLER, Chester Verne, May 8 1919 Sex:M Child# 8 Joseph Fuller Hudson, NH & Nattie Mortlock Keene, NH
FULLER, Chester Walter, Aug 24 1928 Sex:M Child# 1 Chester Fuller Rhode Island & Irene Daly Nashua, NH
FULLER, Enoch Doble, Mar 5 1925 Sex:M Child# 3 Enoch D Fuller Quincy, MA & Abbie Hardy Greenfield, NH
FULLER, Florence Idelia, Jan 6 1897 Sex:F Child# 2 Tilson D Fuller Ellenburgh, NY & Orra I Winslow Ascot, Canada
FULLER, Frederick Leroy, Jul 13 1919 Sex:M Child# 3 Willis L Fuller Hudson, NH & Grace E Bills Pepperell, MA
FULLER, Frederick Ogden, Oct 9 1916 Sex:M Child# 1 Fred O Fuller Waterbury, CT & Katherine Holmes Norwich, CT
FULLER, Geraldine Lois, Aug 22 1917 Sex:F Child# 2 Willis L Fuller Hudson, NH & Grace U Bills Pepperell, MA
FULLER, Kenneth Cassius, Jun 18 1909 Sex:M Child# 1 Dayton D Fuller Hopkinton, NY & Emma H Shonyo Hopkinton, NH
FULLER, Leonard Albert, Jan 11 1932 Sex:M Child# 1 Walter W Fuller Hudson, NH & Annette C LeClair Nashua, NH
FULLER, Lois Clark, Jun 1 1922 Sex:F Child# 3 Warren Clark Fuller Topeka, KS & Marion C Walker Burlington, MA
FULLER, Marion Elizabeth, Oct 8 1921 Sex:F Child# 3 Arthur Fuller New Boston, NH & Elsie M Cady Gilsum, NH
FULLER, Marjorie, Aug 13 1922 Sex:F Child# 2 Enoch D Fuller Quincy, MA & Abbie Hardy Greenfield, NH
FULLER, Virginia, Nov 18 1920 Sex:F Child# 1 Enoch Doble Fuller Quincy, MA & Abbie Hardy Greenfield, NH
FULLER, Walter Willis, Jan 14 1909 Sex:M Child# 1 Joseph A Fuller Hudson, NH & Nettie A Mortlock Keene, NH
FULLER, Wayland Harland, Sep 3 1926 Sex:M Child# 6 Willis L Fuller Nashua, NH & Grace Bills Pepperell, MA
FULLER, William Edward, May 6 1919 Sex:M Child# 2 William E Fuller Manchaug, MA & Ann Kriger Exeter, NH
FULTON, Mary N, Oct 15 1911 Sex:F Child# 4 Edward H Fulton Manchester, NH & Lucy J Hodlin Sciota, NY Stillborn
FULWILER, Madeleine, Aug 11 1921 Sex:F Child# 3 Arthur Fulwiler Dayton, OH & Marguerite Sawtell Nashua, NH
FULWILER, Marguerite, Aug 11 1921 Sex:F Child# 2 Arthur Fulwiler Dayton, OH & Marguerite Sawtell Nashua, NH
FURGERSON, Jean, Feb 23 1931 Sex:F Child# 1 James H Furgerson Nova Scotia & Irene Hawley Canada
FURIFIELD, Henry Martin, Feb 27 1901 Sex:M Child# 1 Benjamin Furifield New Boston & Etta M Ackerman Bristol
GABLETSA, Joanne Cornelia, Dec 4 1930 Sex:F Child# 2 Yanco Gabletsa Romania & Dagmar Swenson New Haven, CT
GABOURY, Geroges, May 14 1889 Sex:M Child# 1 Joseph C Gaboury Burlington, VT & Carrie Lemery Sherburn, VT
GABRIEL, Constance Jeanne, May 6 1931 Sex:F Child# 6 Omer Gabriel US & Alice Meunier Nashua, NH
GABRIEL, Harve Edgar, Aug 17 1920 Sex:M Child# 2 Joseph O Gabriel Canada & Alice Eug Meunier NH
GABRIEL, Isabelle Simonne, Jan 24 1923 Sex:F Child# 3 Joseph O Gabriel Canada & Alice Meunier Nashua, NH
GABRIEL, Joseph Omer, Jr, Jan 19 1919 Sex:M Child# 1 Joseph O Gabriel Canada & Alice Meunier NH
GABRIEL, Joseph Robert Leo, Feb 21 1927 Sex:M Child# 4 Omer Gabriel Canada & Alice Meunier Nashua, NH
GABRIEL, Marie Alice Rita, Aug 26 1928 Sex:F Child# 5 Omer Gabriel Canada & Alice Meunier Nashua, NH
GABRIEL, Paul, Nov 24 1932 Sex:M Child# 1 (No Parents Listed)
GABRIEL, Regina, Jun 26 1917 Sex:F Child# 16 Alexcis Gabriel Canada & Helena Belair Canada
GABRIEL, Unknown, Jul 13 1935 Sex:M Child# 7 Joseph Gabriel US & Alice Meunier US Stillborn
GADBOIS, Fernand Donald, Dec 18 1935 Sex:M Child# 2 Alfred Gadbois Littleton, NH & Eva Dube Nashua, NH
GADBOIS, Julia, Feb 28 1895 Sex:F Child# 4 Edward Gadbois Nashua, NH & Pauline Lampron Nashua, NH
GADBOIS, Julie Emelia, Jul 6 1893 Sex:F Child# 3 Edouard Gadbois Canada & Pauline Lampron Canada
GADBOIS, Julien Godrey J, Aug 29 1924 Sex:M Child# 1 Nashua, NH & Dorilla Gadbois Canada
GADBOIS, Louise Agnes, Jun 19 1890 Sex:F Child# 1 Edward Gadbois
GADBOIS, Marie Pearl, Jul 20 1896 Sex:F Child# 5 Edouard Gadbois Nashua, NH & Pauline Lampron Nashua, NH
GADBOIS, Mary Alice Edna, Aug 13 1931 Sex:F Child# 1 Fred Gadbois Littleton, NH & Eva Dube Nashua, NH
GADBOIS, Rosa Albina, Jul 3 1891 Sex:F Child# 2 Edward Gadbois Nashua, NH & Pauline Lampron Nashua, NH
GADBOIS, Unknown, Aug 5 1902 Sex:M Child# 5 Ed Gadbois NY & M Delorme NY
GADE, Joseph E, May 18 1890 Sex:M Child# 7 Jean Baptiste Gade Canada & Celina Belland Canada
GAFFERRY, Clara, May 15 1889 Sex:F Child# 6 Patrick Gaffery Ireland & Anna Gafferry Ireland
GAFFNEY, Alice, Jan 31 1890 Sex:F Child# 6 James Gaffney Ireland & Mary Ireland
GAFFNEY, Dorothy Elinor, Jun 28 1921 Sex:F Child# 1 Frederick J Gaffney Nashua, NH & Ann I Connor Nashua, NH
GAFFNEY, Edward Joseph, Sep 17 1912 Sex:M Child# 1 Bernard Gaffney Nashua, NH & Helen Moran Nashua, NH
GAFFNEY, Elisee, Aug 22 1889 Sex:F Child# 10 John Gaffney Ireland & Helen Gaffney Ireland
GAFFNEY, Frank, Oct 22 1901 Sex:M Child# 1 Bernard H Gaffney Nashua, NH & Delia Shea Ireland
GAFFNEY, Margaret Belle, Apr 30 1892 Sex:F Child# 7 Patrick Gaffney Ireland & Anna Ireland
GAFFNEY, Regnald Clifton, Mar 23 1900 Sex:M Child# 1 James Gaffney
GAGE, Dorothea, Jan 20 1908 Sex:F Child# 1 Charles C Gage New York & Eva M French NH
GAGE, Edward Everett, Dec 23 1934 Sex:M Child# 1 Edward E Gage Londonderry, NH & Ethel Hagerty Nashua, NH
GAGE, Harry Preston, Sep 29 1922 Sex:M Child# 1 Everett P Gage Bedford, NH & Doris K Miller Nashua, NH
GAGE, John Oliver, Feb 29 1916 Sex:M Child# 2 John D Gage Warren, NH & Martha A Oliver Everett, MA
GAGE, Pauline Freeman, Feb 4 1923 Sex:F Child# 3 John D Gage Waterloo, NH & Martha Oliver Everett, MA
GAGE, Richard Kenneth, May 26 1919 Sex:M Child# 1 Eug Arnold Gage, Jr Hillsboro, NH & Doris Natalie Stearn Ran
GAGE, Unknown, Sep 24 1891 Sex:F Child# 5 Herbert Gage New Boston & Almy J Taylor Waterville, VT
GAGE, Wallace Marsh, Jun 29 1918 Sex:M Child# 1 Edwin S Gage Hudson, NH & Julia F Wallace Nashua, NH
GAGNE, Alice, Dec 28 1899 Sex:F Child# 2 Olivier Gagne Canada & Arthemise Rioux Canada
GAGNE, Alphonse, Mar 1 1901 Sex:M Child# 15 Arthur Gagne Canada & Adeline Simard Canada
GAGNE, Armand Sylvio, Aug 23 1906 Sex:M Child# 6 Hormidas Gagne Canada & Marie Cote Canada
GAGNE, Blanche Lilian, Nov 30 1910 Sex:F Child# 3 Joseph Gagne Nashua, NH & Rose Anna Soucy Canada
GAGNE, Blanche Yvonne, Aug 2 1916 Sex:F Child# 1 Alfred Gagne Canada & Rosanna Arpin Canada
GAGNE, Cecille Ida, Oct 17 1924 Sex:F Child# 3 William Gagne Canada & Josephine Malhoit Nashua, NH
GAGNE, Donald Guy E A, Jun 12 1935 Sex:M Child# 2 Napoleon Gagne Canada & Beatrice Gauthier Nashua, NH
GAGNE, Edgar Alphee, Nov 20 1909 Sex:M Child# Joseph Gagne Canada & Marie Soucy Canada
GAGNE, Edouard, Mar 14 1926 Sex:M Child# 1 Antoine Gagne Canada & Laurette Rivard Nashua, NH
GAGNE, Elphege, Mar 1 1890 Sex:M Child# 1 Felix Gagne Canada & Vitaline Foutaine Canada
GAGNE, Emelia, Jan 11 1887 Sex:F Child# Joseph Gagne P Q & Henriette Berube P Q
GAGNE, Ferdinand, Apr 19 1891 Sex:M Child# 6 Joseph Gagne Canada & Henriette Berube Canada
GAGNE, Florilda, Jul 28 1895 Sex:F Child# 6 Alphonse Gagne Canada & Josephine Bonenfaut Canada
GAGNE, Francis Albe Wilfrid, May 11 1923 Sex:M Child# 1 Ludger Gagne Canada & Eva Rose Dube NH

GAGNE, George, May 11 1905 Sex:M Child# 1 Pierre Gagne Canada & Marie Casista Canada
GAGNE, Georgia Clare, Mar 19 1925 Sex:F Child# 2 Aime Gagne Canada & Evelyn Maynard Nashua, NH
GAGNE, Georgina A, Feb 23 1902 Sex:F Child# 1 Henri Gagne Canada & Elisianne Levesque Canada
GAGNE, I Antoine, Mar 20 1899 Sex:M Child# 13 Arthur Gagne Canada & Adeline Semard Canada
GAGNE, Jos Donat Paul, Sep 21 1929 Sex:M Child# 8 Levi Gagne Canada & Eliene Bouchard Canada
GAGNE, Jos Leo Laurent, Sep 4 1928 Sex:M Child# 3 Ludger Gagne Canada & Eva Rose Dube Nashua, NH
GAGNE, Jos Ovide Raoul, Apr 12 1920 Sex:M Child# 6 Napoleon Gagne Canada & Marie Anna Brien Canada
GAGNE, Joseph Alcide, Dec 3 1913 Sex:M Child# 3 Napoleon Gagne Canada & Marie Anne Brien Canada
GAGNE, Joseph Baptiste O, Feb 19 1906 Sex:M Child# 1 Jean Baptiste Gagne Canada & Exina Desrosiers Canada
GAGNE, Joseph E W, Jun 26 1909 Sex:M Child# 14 Alphonse Gagne Canada & Josephine Bonenfant Canada
GAGNE, Joseph Emile L, Aug 18 1906 Sex:M Child# 2 Pierre Gagne Canada & Marie Casista Canada
GAGNE, Joseph George C, Aug 31 1903 Sex:M Child# 2 Henry Gagne Canada & Elizanne Levesque Canada
GAGNE, Joseph Jules, May 30 1892 Sex:M Child# 7 Joseph Gagne Canada & Henrietta Berube Canada
GAGNE, Joseph Ludger, Mar 10 1889 Sex:M Child# 4 Joseph Gagne Canada & Catherine Berube Canada
GAGNE, Joseph Ludger Robert, Jun 15 1923 Sex:M Child# 8 Napoleon Gagne Canada & Marie Anna Brien Canada
GAGNE, Joseph Narcisse A, Jan 23 1911 Sex:M Child# 4 Jean B Gagne Canada & Alexina Derosiers Canada
GAGNE, Joseph Roland, Nov 11 1935 Sex:M Child# 2 Romeo Gagne Somersworth, NH & Laetitia Lassande Somersworth, NH
GAGNE, Joseph Wilfred R, Jan 22 1930 Sex:M Child# 11 Napoleon Gagne Canada & Marieane Brien Canada
GAGNE, Joseph Zebede R, Oct 26 1924 Sex:M Child# 5 Levis Gagne Canada & Elaine Bouchard Canada
GAGNE, Jules Homere, Mar 18 1909 Sex:M Child# 3 J B Gagne Canada & Alexina Desrosiers Canada
GAGNE, Juliette, Jan 31 1925 Sex:F Child# 4 Alfred Gagne Canada & Rosanna Arpin Canada
GAGNE, Lauretta Theresa, Mar 30 1927 Sex:F Child# 2 Antoine Gagne Canada & Laura Rivard Nashua, NH
GAGNE, Lionel, Jun 4 1912 Sex:M Child# 3 George Gagne Canada & Anna Larose Canada
GAGNE, Louis F P, May 15 1892 Sex:M Child# 2 Francois Gagne Canada & Philomene Paquet Canada
GAGNE, Louis Paul, Jun 21 1928 Sex:M Child# 1 Alphonse Gagne Canada & L Pelletier Nashua, NH
GAGNE, Lucille Rita, May 7 1926 Sex:F Child# 9 George Gagne Canada & Anna Larose Canada
GAGNE, M Albertha Lucille, Mar 25 1917 Sex:F Child# 1 Henry Gagne Nashua, NH & Marie Gagne Canada
GAGNE, M Florilda Simone, Oct 13 1915 Sex:F Child# 4 Napoleon Gagne Canada & Marie Anne Brien Canada
GAGNE, M Jeanne Rita, Dec 14 1921 Sex:F Child# 7 Napoleon Gagne Canada & Marie Anne Briand Canada
GAGNE, M Josephine, Mar 20 1899 Sex:F Child# 14 Arthur Gagne Canada & Adeline Semard Canada
GAGNE, Marcella Gertrude, May 31 1921 Sex:F Child# 1 Amie Gagne Canada & Evelyn Maynard Nashua, NH
GAGNE, Marie Aimee Yolande, Jun 1 1928 Sex:F Child# 7 Levi Gagne Canada & Eleanor Bouchard Canada
GAGNE, Marie Annie Regina, Dec 9 1918 Sex:F Child# 5 Napoleon Gagne Canada & Marie Anne Gagne Canada
GAGNE, Marie Armance, Oct 5 1907 Sex:F Child# 13 Alphonse Gagne Canada & Josephine Bonenfant Canada
GAGNE, Marie Cecile, Jul 7 1890 Sex:F Child# 1 Achille Gagne Canada & Anna Cannelle Canada
GAGNE, Marie Claire Anita, Aug 21 1927 Sex:F Child# 10 Napoleon Gagne Canada & Marie A Brien Canada
GAGNE, Marie Colombe Pearl, Apr 29 1927 Sex:F Child# 2 Ludger Gagne Canada & Eva Rose Dube Nashua, NH
GAGNE, Marie Eva Cecile, Jan 26 1919 Sex:F Child# 5 George Gagne Canada & Anna Larose Canada
GAGNE, Marie Eva Pearl, Dec 2 1917 Sex:F Child# 1 (No Parents Listed)
GAGNE, Marie Irene G, Feb 19 1911 Sex:F Child# 15 Alphonse Gagne Canada & Josephine Bonenfant Canada
GAGNE, Marie Irene G, Oct 23 1911 Sex:F Child# 2 Napoleon Gagne Canada & Marie Anna Brien Canada
GAGNE, Marie Irene Juliette, May 30 1912 Sex:F Child# 16 Alphonse Gagne Canada & Josephine Bonenfant Canada
GAGNE, Marie Martha Fernand, Feb 2 1927 Sex:F Child# 6 Leo Gagne Canada & Elienne Bouchard Canada
GAGNE, Marie Rose A, Jun 12 1896 Sex:F Child# 4 Francois Gagne Canada & Philomene Paquette Canada
GAGNE, Marie Simonne Cecile, Feb 11 1925 Sex:F Child# 9 Napoleon Gagne Canada & Marie A Brien Canada
GAGNE, Marie Yvonne, Oct 31 1907 Sex:F Child# 2 Jean B Gagne Canada & Alexina Desrosiers Canada
GAGNE, Olivine Angelina, Aug 16 1897 Sex:F Child# 5 F X Gagne Canada & Philomene Paquett Canada
GAGNE, Paul Roland, Aug 12 1920 Sex:M Child# 6 George Gagne Canada & Anna Lavoie Canada
GAGNE, Priscilla, Nov 9 1932 Sex:F Child# 2 A Gagne Nashua, NH & Alida Pelletier Nashua, NH
GAGNE, Robert Joseph, Jul 17 1923 Sex:M Child# 2 William Gagne Canada & Zepherine Malhoit Nashua, NH
GAGNE, Roger Conrad, Feb 25 1934 Sex:M Child# 1 Napoleon Gagne Canada & Beatrice Gauthier Nashua, NH
GAGNE, Romeo, Nov 20 1926 Sex:M Child# 5 Alfred Gagne Canada & Rose Arpine Canada
GAGNE, Romeo, Sep 26 1932 Sex:M Child# 7 Ernest Gagne Canada & Rosanna Arpin Canada
GAGNE, Romeo Armand, Jul 13 1917 Sex:F Child# 4 George Gagne Canada & Anna Larose Canada
GAGNE, Rose, Jun 25 1908 Sex:F Child# 1 Joseph Gagne Canada & Rose Alba Soucy Canada
GAGNE, Unknown, Oct 15 1893 Sex:M Child# 3 Archilles Gagne Canada & Anna Camel Canada Stillborn
GAGNIER, Armand Theophile, Jul 18 1918 Sex:M Child# 1 Theophile Gagnier St Bruno, PQ & Ida Dionne St Bruno, PQ
GAGNIER, Joseph, Nov 28 1894 Sex:M Child# 10 Arthur Gagnier Canada & Adeiline Simard Canada
GAGNIER, Joseph Eugenie, Mar 20 1896 Sex:M Child# 1 Arthur Gagnier Canada & Adeline Simard Canada
GAGNIER, Joseph Henri, Sep 28 1897 Sex:M Child# 12 Arthur Gagnier Canada & Adeline Simard Canada
GAGNIER, Joseph Henri, Nov 5 1919 Sex:M Child# 2 Theophile Gagnier Canada & Ida Dionne Canada
GAGNIER, M Jeanne Lucille C, Mar 8 1921 Sex:F Child# 3 Theophile Gagnier Canada & Ida Dionne Canada
GAGNIER, Marie J Jacqueline, Feb 16 1929 Sex:F Child# 1 Evariste Gagnier Canada & Jeanne Tanguay Canada
GAGNON, Achille Wilfred, Jul 15 1905 Sex:M Child# 2 George Gagnon Canada & Adele Casista Canada
GAGNON, Adelard Felix Arthur, Dec 13 1917 Sex:M Child# 2 William Gagnon Canada & Alice Soucy Canada
GAGNON, Adelina, Apr 5 1911 Sex:F Child# 2 Joseph Gagnon US & Lina Bouvier US
GAGNON, Adeline L, Jul 6 1907 Sex:F Child# 2 Magloire Gagnon Canada & Rosanna Tessier Canada
GAGNON, Adrien, Oct 3 1890 Sex:M Child# 3 Hypolite Gagnon Canada & Philomene Dancosse Canada
GAGNON, Adrien Didier, Feb 12 1908 Sex:M Child# 4 Michel Gagnon Canada & R Laboissonniere Canada
GAGNON, Adrien Ferdinand, Jul 9 1910 Sex:M Child# 6 George Gagnon Canada & Adele Cassista Canada
GAGNON, Agnes, Mar 12 1907 Sex:F Child# 14 Arsene Gagnon Canada & Catherine Berube Canada
GAGNON, Albert, Nov 12 1897 Sex:M Child# 6 Thomas Gagnon Canada & Emilie Malhiot Canada
GAGNON, Albert, Apr 20 1924 Sex:M Child# 5 Albert Gagnon Nashua, NH & Anna Gauthier Taunton, MA

GAGNON, Albert Charles, Nov 10 1916 Sex:M Child# 10 Joseph Gagnon Canada & Corinne Bourgeois Wilton, NH
GAGNON, Albert Joseph, May 4 1915 Sex:M Child# 2 George J Gagnon Lebanon, NH & Edith Raymond Amityville, LI, NY
GAGNON, Albert Lucien, Aug 20 1921 Sex:M Child# 5 George Gagnon Canada & Celanise Ricard Canada
GAGNON, Albert Roger, Nov 24 1925 Sex:M Child# 1 Albert Gagnon Canada & Alma Boucher Canada
GAGNON, Albert Roger, Aug 4 1929 Sex:M Child# 2 Albert Gagnon Taunton, MA & Diana Tessier Nashua, NH
GAGNON, Albert Thomas, Mar 2 1921 Sex:M Child# 3 Albert Gagnon Nashua, NH & Anna Gauthier Taunton, MA
GAGNON, Albina Laura, Sep 17 1912 Sex:F Child# 5 Magloire Gagnon Canada & Rosanna Tessier Canada
GAGNON, Alden George, Jun 9 1934 Sex:M Child# 2 Phillip Gagnon Canada & Olivine Ross Canada
GAGNON, Alfred, Feb 17 1893 Sex:M Child# 2 Thomas Gagnon Canada & Melie Malhiot Canada
GAGNON, Alfred, May 25 1896 Sex:M Child# 4 Jean Gagnon Canada & Marie Lavoie Canada
GAGNON, Alfred, Oct 7 1897 Sex:M Child# 8 Arsene Gagnon Canada & Catherine Berube Canada
GAGNON, Alfred, Oct 24 1907 Sex:M Child# 4 George Gagnon Canada & Adele Casista Canada
GAGNON, Alfred Jules, Apr 9 1925 Sex:M Child# 1 Julia Gagnon Nashua, NH & Delina Martin Nashua, NH
GAGNON, Alice, Nov 2 1912 Sex:F Child# 2 Francois Gagnon Canada & Dora Quackembush New York
GAGNON, Alice Germaine, Mar 15 1907 Sex:F Child# 4 Henri Gagnon Nashua, NH & Georgianna Lessard Nashua, NH
GAGNON, Alphonse, Mar 9 1899 Sex:M Child# 11 Will Gagnon Canada & Justine Gagnon Canada
GAGNON, Alphonse Albert, Nov 2 1903 Sex:M Child# 3 Jean Bte Gagnon Canada & Delia Morin Canada
GAGNON, Amarilda Amelia, Jun 2 1903 Sex:F Child# 2 Joseph Gagnon Canada & Corinne Bourgeois Canada
GAGNON, Andre, Feb 23 1915 Sex:M Child# 13 Thomas Gagnon Canada & Emelie Malhoit Canada
GAGNON, Andrea Ivonne O, Jul 22 1897 Sex:F Child# 8 Louis Gagnon Canada & Adele Bernier Canada
GAGNON, Antoine Leonil, Jun 28 1906 Sex:M Child# 3 George Gagnon Canada & Adele Casista Canada
GAGNON, Antoinette, Aug 27 1912 Sex:F Child# 1 Eugene Gagnon Canada & Antoinette Saucier Canada
GAGNON, Armand Emile, Sep 17 1903 Sex:M Child# 3 Victor Gagnon Canada & Loulia Marvis Canada
GAGNON, Armand Hector, Jun 8 1905 Sex:M Child# 4 J B Gagnon Canada & Delima Morin Canada
GAGNON, Armand Raymond, Apr 22 1920 Sex:M Child# 4 Joseph Gagnon Canada & Alexina Marquis Canada
GAGNON, Arthur, Apr 23 1894 Sex:M Child# 1 Michel Gagnon Canada & R Laboissonniere Canada
GAGNON, Arthur, Nov 19 1905 Sex:M Child# 4 Eugene Gagnon Canada & Alice Tardy Canada
GAGNON, Arthur, May 18 1911 Sex:M Child# 16 Arsene Gagnon Canada & Catherine Berube Canada
GAGNON, Arthur Didier, Nov 2 1893 Sex:M Child# 6 Jean Gagnon Canada & Marie Paradis Canada
GAGNON, Beatrice Lorraine, Jul 25 1932 Sex:F Child# 4 Albert J Gagnon Taunton, MA & D L Tessier Nashua, NH
GAGNON, Blanche, Apr 1 1902 Sex:F Child# 6 Jacob Gagnon Canada & Marie Levesque Canada
GAGNON, Camille Amanda, Jul 11 1915 Sex:F Child# 8 Joseph Gagnon Canada & Corine Bourgeois Canada
GAGNON, Carl Davis, Mar 30 1930 Sex:M Child# 2 Victor H Gagnon Nashua, NH & Rosalie E Collins Tewksbury, MA
GAGNON, Catherine Jeanne, Nov 24 1927 Sex:F Child# 3 George Gagnon Nashua, NH & Delia Cousineau Nashua, NH
GAGNON, Cecile Laura, Mar 30 1927 Sex:F Child# 5 Stanislaus Gagnon Canada & Donelda Berube Canada
GAGNON, Cecilia Alice J, Oct 15 1904 Sex:F Child# 3 Joseph Gagnon, Jr Canada & Corinne Bourgeois Canada
GAGNON, Cezarie, Apr 21 1891 Sex:F Child#  Louis Gagnon Canada & Cezarie Cote Canada
GAGNON, Charles, Sep 18 1894 Sex:M Child# 4 Charles Gagnon Canada & Harmelie Gaudreau Canada
GAGNON, Charles Eugene, Dec 4 1900 Sex:M Child# 1 Eugene Gagnon Canada & Alice Tardy Canada
GAGNON, Charles Girard, Jan 30 1924 Sex:M Child# 1 Joseph Gagnon Canada & Rose A Paradis Canada
GAGNON, Claire Germaine, Aug 21 1933 Sex:F Child# 1 Arthur M Gagnon Nashua, NH & Mathilda Brodeur Hooksett, NH
GAGNON, Clara, Mar 2 1898 Sex:F Child# 12 Alfred Gagnon Canada & Solomie Sirois Canada
GAGNON, Clara Celinda, Jun 26 1902 Sex:F Child# 3 Eugene Gagnon Canada & Clara Sirois Canada
GAGNON, Clarina, May 26 1903 Sex:F Child# 11 Lazare Gagnon Canada & Delima Dusseault Canada
GAGNON, Clayton Willoby, Jan 6 1925 Sex:M Child# 1 Victor Gagnon Nashua, NH & Rosalie Collins Tewksbury, MA
GAGNON, Cleo Tel Laurence, Jan 3 1918 Sex:M Child# 3 Joseph Gagnon Canada & Alexina Marquis Canada
GAGNON, Conrad Rolland, May 28 1917 Sex:M Child# 5 Alphonse Gagnon Canada & Maria Gendron Canada
GAGNON, Cora, Mar 12 1909 Sex:F Child# 5 George Gagnon Canada & Adele Casista Canada
GAGNON, David Peter, Jan 4 1935 Sex:M Child# 2 Sylvio Gagnon Nashua, NH & Katherine Ledoux Nashua, NH
GAGNON, Delia Eva, Jan 8 1899 Sex:F Child# 9 Arsene Gagnon Canada & Catherine Berube Canada
GAGNON, Desire Romeo, Sep 12 1910 Sex:M Child# 1 Alphonse Gagnon Canada & Femina Cyr Canada
GAGNON, Dora Lena, Jan 25 1913 Sex:F Child# 10 Eugene Gagnon Canada & Clara Sirois Canada
GAGNON, Doria, Sep 13 1905 Sex:F Child# 13 Arsene Gagnon Canada & Catherine Berube Canada
GAGNON, Doris, Oct 17 1922 Sex:F Child# 3 Alfred Gagnon Berlin, NH & Mary Sullivan Pepperell, MA
GAGNON, Eddy Alvin, Oct 18 1907 Sex:M Child# 13 Thomas Gagnon Canada & Emelie Malhiot Canada
GAGNON, Edouard Henri, May 16 1901 Sex:M Child# 1 John H Gagnon Mass & Grace M Benoit NH
GAGNON, Edward Clarence, Sep 18 1908 Sex:M Child# 2 Albert A Gagnon Salem, MA & Jennie Moquin Windsor, VT
GAGNON, Edward Clarence, Dec 4 1931 Sex:M Child# 1 Edward C Gagnon Nashua, NH & Beatrice Woods Nashua, NH
GAGNON, Ella Rita, Mar 28 1917 Sex:F Child# 2 William Gagnon Fall River, MA & Albina R LaRoche Canada
GAGNON, Elzear, Mar 26 1910 Sex:M Child# 1 George Gagnon Canada & Mariane Bergeron Canada
GAGNON, Emelia, Apr 5 1895 Sex:F Child# 5 Arsene Gagnon Canada & Catherine Berube Canada
GAGNON, Emelia, Jan 7 1901 Sex:F Child# 8 Thomas Gagnon Canada & Emelie Malhoit Canada
GAGNON, Emile Albert, Aug 24 1910 Sex:M Child# 3 George Gagnon Canada & Eugenie Laprise Canada
GAGNON, Emma, Nov 17 1934 Sex:F Child# 5 Albert Gagnon Taunton, MA & Diana Tessier Nashua, NH
GAGNON, Ernest, Apr 1 1889 Sex:M Child# 7 Theophile Gagnon Canada & Henriette Hebert Canada
GAGNON, Ernest Andrew, May 2 1924 Sex:M Child# 7 George Gagnon Canada & Celina Ricard Canada
GAGNON, Ernest Carlton, Jun 2 1911 Sex:M Child# 2 William Gagnon Nashua, NH & Alice Landry Nashua, NH
GAGNON, Ernest Carlton, Aug 18 1934 Sex:M Child# 3 Ernest Gagnon Nashua, NH & Blanche Richards Nashua, NH
GAGNON, Ernest Edmond, Mar 13 1902 Sex:M Child# 1 George Gagnon Canada & Eugenie Laprise Canada
GAGNON, Ernest Eugene, Mar 8 1912 Sex:M Child# 2 Leon Gagnon Nashua, NH & Katherine Diggins Nashua, NH
GAGNON, Ernest Paul, Oct 1 1932 Sex:M Child# 2 Ernest Gagnon Nashua, NH & A Bellavance Moosup, CT
GAGNON, Ernest Roger, Jan 14 1930 Sex:M Child# 13 Alphonse Gagnon Canada & Maria Gendron Canada
GAGNON, Ernestine, Dec 8 1896 Sex:F Child# 11 Alfred Gagnon Canada & Salomee Sirois Canada

GAGNON, Ernestine, Jan 11 1909 Sex:F Child# 6 Euclide Gagnon Canada & Celina Deland Canada
GAGNON, Estelle Therese, Nov 20 1919 Sex:F Child# 4 George Gagnon Canada & Eugenie Laprise Canada
GAGNON, Euclide Armand, Apr 4 1933 Sex:M Child# 3 Wilfrid Gagnon Nashua, NH & Helene Caron Manchester, NH
GAGNON, Eugenie Bernadette, Dec 2 1905 Sex:F Child# 7 Jacob Gagnon Canada & Marie Levesque Canada
GAGNON, Euna, Feb 25 1889 Sex:F Child# 2 Arsene Gagnon Canada & Chatherine Berube Canada
GAGNON, Eva, Sep 18 1895 Sex:F Child# 1 Euclide Gagnon Canada & Celina Deslandes Canada
GAGNON, Eva, Apr 16 1902 Sex:F Child# 9 Thomas Gagnon Canada & Emelie Malhiot Canada
GAGNON, Florence Annabelle, Mar 14 1923 Sex:F Child# 2 Albert Gagnon Nashua, NH & Annabelle Gauthier Taunton, MA
GAGNON, Florence Lucienne, Mar 10 1914 Sex:F Child# 5 George Gagnon Canada & Delia Morin Canada
GAGNON, Florence Lucille, May 10 1932 Sex:F Child# 3 Jos G Gagnon Nashua, NH & Laurette Lefebvre Nashua, NH
GAGNON, Francois, Mar 5 1888 Sex:F Child# 1 Francois Gagnon Canada & Adele Dimmaris Canada
GAGNON, Gabrielle Gilbert, Dec 9 1907 Sex:F Child# 5 Eugene Gagnon Canada & Alice Tardy Canada
GAGNON, George, Feb 9 1887 Sex:M Child#  Celeste Gagnon P Q & Odile Ouellette P Q
GAGNON, George, Dec 19 1900 Sex:M Child# 10 Arsene Gagnon Canada & Catherine Berube Canada
GAGNON, George Adrienne, Apr 8 1929 Sex:M Child# 10 George Gagnon Canada & Celanise Ricard Canada
GAGNON, George Conrad, Jul 27 1908 Sex:M Child# 16 Bonasse Gagnon Canada & Marie Boucher Canada
GAGNON, George Edouard, Dec 30 1902 Sex:M Child# 2 Henry Gagnon Nashua, NH & Geo Lessard Nashua, NH
GAGNON, George Normand, Sep 17 1932 Sex:M Child# 5 George Gagnon Nashua, NH & Delia Cousineau Nashua, NH
GAGNON, George Robert, Nov 29 1916 Sex:M Child# 2 George Gagnon Canada & Celanie Picard Canada
GAGNON, George William, Jul 4 1923 Sex:M Child# 4 William L Gagnon Fall River, MA & Rose Albina LaRoche Canada
GAGNON, Georgianna Rita, Jan 18 1928 Sex:F Child# 2 George Gagnon US & Loretta Lefebvre US
GAGNON, Gerald Edward, Nov 5 1926 Sex:M Child# 2 Edward J Gagnon Hooksett, NH & Rosalie E Nichols St Johnsbury, VT
GAGNON, Gerald Hubert Joseph, Sep 12 1934 Sex:M Child# 1 Wilfrid A J Gagnon Canada & Annette YM Rousselle Nashua,NH
GAGNON, Gloria Adrienne, Apr 19 1930 Sex:F Child# 4 George Gagnon Nashua, NH & Delia Cousineau Nashua, NH
GAGNON, Gloria Geraldine, May 5 1931 Sex:F Child# 1 Napoleon J Gagnon,Jr Canada & Irene A Willette Middle
GAGNON, Gloria Rita, Jul 6 1927 Sex:F Child# 1 Ernest Gagnon Nashua, NH & A Bellevance Conn
GAGNON, Grace Mary, Oct 11 1921 Sex:F Child# 6 Arthur Gagnon Missouri & Eva Ardair Mass
GAGNON, Helen, May 21 1907 Sex:F Child# 1 Albert A Gagnon Salem, MA & Augustine Moquin Windsor, VT
GAGNON, Henri Armand, Aug 1 1915 Sex:M Child# 4 Victor Gagnon Canada & Laudia Marois Canada
GAGNON, Henri C N, Sep 22 1898 Sex:M Child# 8 Antoine Gagnon Canada & Elise Levesque Canada
GAGNON, Henri Emile, Jan 3 1913 Sex:M Child# 1 Emile Gagnon Lowell, MA & Marie Jane Gallant Westbrook, ME
GAGNON, Henry Gerard, Mar 4 1934 Sex:M Child# 1 Albert Gagnon Newmarket, NH & Camille Rodier Nashua, NH
GAGNON, Irene, Nov 13 1916 Sex:F Child# 1 Lewis Gagnon Canada & Irene O'Brien Ireland Stillborn
GAGNON, Irene Eva, Aug 13 1911 Sex:F Child# 1 Louis Gagnon Canada & Lidia Boulanger Canada
GAGNON, Iscar Horace, Sep 4 1898 Sex:M Child# 2 Michel Gagnon Canada & Ros'a Laboissonniere Canada
GAGNON, J Leo Ovila, Sep 22 1915 Sex:M Child# 1 Joseph Gagnon Canada & Elmeria Petrin Canada
GAGNON, J Napoleon Armand, Jan 9 1912 Sex:M Child# 2 Napoleon Gagnon Canada & Georgiana Gagnon Canada
GAGNON, J Walter Roland, Jul 13 1921 Sex:M Child# 2 Honore Gagnon NH & Juliette Bouchard Canada
GAGNON, Jacob Joseph, Nov 10 1894 Sex:M Child# 2 Jacob Gagnon Canada & Marie Levesque Canada
GAGNON, James Emebert, Sep 2 1896 Sex:M Child# 6 Arsine Gagnon Canada & Emelie Dischesne Canada
GAGNON, Jean Baptiste W, Jun 15 1914 Sex:M Child# 6 Eugene Gagnon Canada & Antoinette Saucier Canada
GAGNON, Jean Paul, Mar 14 1933 Sex:M Child# 6 Albert Gagnon Canada & Alice Boucher Canada
GAGNON, Jeanne Alice, Jun 4 1910 Sex:F Child# 7 Gedeon Gagnon Manchester, NH & Antoinette Lacette Canada
GAGNON, Jeanne Lucille, Apr 19 1924 Sex:F Child# 6 Joseph Gagnon Nashua, NH & Marie Fortin Canada
GAGNON, Jeannette, Jun 9 1917 Sex:F Child# 1 Albert Gagnon Canada & Anna Gauthier Taunton, MA
GAGNON, Jeannette, Oct 20 1926 Sex:F Child# 1 George Gagnon US & Loretta Lefebvre US
GAGNON, Jennie Flora, Oct 28 1913 Sex:F Child# 1 Joseph Gagnon Canada & Alexina Mastnon Canada
GAGNON, Jos Armand Girard, Nov 28 1929 Sex:M Child# 1 Armand Gagnon Nashua, NH & Annette Heon Manchester, NH
GAGNON, Jos Emile Edouard, Apr 27 1919 Sex:M Child# 4 Joseph Gagnon Canada & Elmira Petrain Canada
GAGNON, Jos Normand A, Sep 2 1929 Sex:M Child# 11 Joseph Gagnon Canada & Elmira Petrain Canada
GAGNON, Jos Robert Emile, Nov 18 1929 Sex:M Child# 2 Victor O Gagnon Nashua, NH & Laura Duchesneau Canada
GAGNON, Jos Roland Thomas, Oct 17 1935 Sex:M Child# 1 Wilfrid Gagnon Nashua, NH & Lorette Paquette Nashua, NH
GAGNON, Jos Sylvio Augustin, Dec 10 1916 Sex:M Child# 2 Joseph Gagnon Canada & Elmeria Petrain Canada
GAGNON, Jos Wil H Amede, Aug 10 1919 Sex:M Child# 11 Joseph Gagnon Canada & Corine Bourgeois Canada
GAGNON, Jos Wilfrid Samuel, Jun 27 1917 Sex:M Child# 7 Magloire Gagnon Canada & Rose Anna Tessier Canada
GAGNON, Joseph, Dec 14 1893 Sex:M Child# 5 Arsene Gagnon Canada & Catherine Berube Canada
GAGNON, Joseph, Jul 26 1894 Sex:M Child# 11 Louis Gagnon Canada & Cesaire Fournier Canada
GAGNON, Joseph, Aug 6 1908 Sex:M Child# 1 W Gagnon Canada & Alice Soucy Canada
GAGNON, Joseph, Feb 24 1910 Sex:M Child# 1 William Gagnon Nashua, NH & Alice Landry Nashua, NH
GAGNON, Joseph, Aug 22 1911 Sex:M Child# 8 Theodore Gagnon Canada & Aurore Vaillancourt Canada
GAGNON, Joseph, Jul 25 1917 Sex:M Child# 2 George Gagnon Canada & Celanire Ricard Canada
GAGNON, Joseph, Apr 7 1922 Sex:M Child# 1 Alfred Gagnon Canada & Melendy Dupont Nashua, NH
GAGNON, Joseph, Jul 3 1928 Sex:M Child# 1 Arthur Gagnon NH & Rosanna Bernard Rhode Island
GAGNON, Joseph A, Jun 25 1892 Sex:M Child# 5 Jean Gagnon Canada & Marie Paradis Canada
GAGNON, Joseph A H, Oct 19 1908 Sex:M Child# 3 Magloire Gagnon Canada & Rosanna Tessier Canada
GAGNON, Joseph A T, Jul 17 1900 Sex:M Child# 1 Thomas Gagnon Canada & Clara Dionne Canada
GAGNON, Joseph Aime, Nov 12 1910 Sex:M Child# 17 Athanas Gagnon Canada & Marie Ouellette Canada
GAGNON, Joseph Alcide A, Jun 10 1904 Sex:M Child# 2 Theodore Gagnon Canada & Emma Gauthier Canada
GAGNON, Joseph Alexander, Jul 4 1926 Sex:M Child# 3 Joseph Gagnon Nashua, NH & Maria Ross Canada
GAGNON, Joseph Alfred Girald, Jan 28 1932 Sex:M Child# 1 Horace Gagnon Litchfield, NH & Emilanne Fluet Manchester
GAGNON, Joseph Alfred Girard, Apr 13 1923 Sex:M Child# 6 Joseph Gagnon Canada & Elmeria Petrain Canada
GAGNON, Joseph Amedee, Aug 7 1896 Sex:M Child# 2 Victor Gagnon Canada & Eugenie Dube Canada
GAGNON, Joseph Antoine, Feb 15 1900 Sex:M Child# 3 Xavier Gagnon Canada & Elizabeth Lajoie Canada

GAGNON, Joseph Antonio, Jan 30 1911 Sex:M Child# 1 Napoleon Gagnon Canada & Georgianna Gagnon Canada
GAGNON, Joseph Arthur, Dec 4 1889 Sex:M Child# 3 H Gagnon Canada & Alsponse Cusllette Canada
GAGNON, Joseph Arthur, Sep 21 1892 Sex:M Child# 10 Louis Gagnon Canada & Cesarie Fournier Canada
GAGNON, Joseph Arthur, Apr 26 1899 Sex:M Child# 3 Victorien Gagnon Canada & Eugenie Dube Canada
GAGNON, Joseph Chas Eugene, Sep 4 1916 Sex:M Child# 4 Xavier Gagnon Canada & Eugenie Desjardins Canada
GAGNON, Joseph Euclide S, Dec 31 1901 Sex:M Child# 6 Euclide Gagnon Canada & Celina Delorme Canada
GAGNON, Joseph Eugene F, Jun 7 1906 Sex:M Child# 1 Francois Gagnon Canada & Emma Dionne Canada
GAGNON, Joseph George L, Aug 17 1929 Sex:M Child# 4 Albert Gagnon Canada & Alice Boucher Canada
GAGNON, Joseph Gerard, Mar 25 1923 Sex:M Child# 2 Stanislaus Gagnon Canada & Eva Berube Canada
GAGNON, Joseph Girard Robert, Jul 17 1932 Sex:M Child# 1 C E Gagnon Canada & Laura Ricard Greenville, NH
GAGNON, Joseph Harvey, Dec 4 1895 Sex:M Child# 10 Alfred Gagnon Canada & Salomee Sirois Canada
GAGNON, Joseph Hector, Apr 8 1897 Sex:M Child# 7 Amedee Gagnon Canada & Josephine Gagnon Canada
GAGNON, Joseph Hector, Feb 20 1900 Sex:M Child# 9 Antoine Gagnon Canada & Elise Levesque Canada
GAGNON, Joseph Henry Roland, Jun 11 1928 Sex:M Child# 10 Joseph Gagnon Canada & Elmira Petrain Canada
GAGNON, Joseph Isidore A, Sep 11 1906 Sex:M Child# 5 Victorien Gagnon Canada & Eugenie Dube Canada
GAGNON, Joseph J B T, Feb 26 1893 Sex:M Child# 2 Thomas Gagnon Canada & Rosanna Charron Canada
GAGNON, Joseph Leo, May 18 1905 Sex:M Child# 2 Joseph Gagnon Canada & Maria Ross Canada
GAGNON, Joseph Leo Gerard, Nov 6 1932 Sex:M Child# 4 George Gagnon Canada & Anna Emond Canada
GAGNON, Joseph Louis Ernest, Feb 14 1899 Sex:M Child# 5 Louis Gagnon Canada & Adele Bernier Canada
GAGNON, Joseph Octave, Dec 1 1912 Sex:M Child# 8 George Gagnon Canada & Adelle Casista Canada
GAGNON, Joseph Olivier Lione, Sep 8 1912 Sex:M Child# 3 Theophile Gagnon Canada & Aurore Vaillancourt Canada
GAGNON, Joseph Omer Ovide, Apr 15 1900 Sex:M Child# 2 Victor Gagnon Canada & Ledia Marois Canada
GAGNON, Joseph Oscar, May 15 1897 Sex:M Child# 5 Louis Gagnon Canada & Alvina Leblanc Canada
GAGNON, Joseph Philippe S, May 21 1910 Sex:M Child# 7 Victorien Gagnon Canada & Eugenie Dube Canada
GAGNON, Joseph R, Jul 16 1910 Sex:M Child# 5 Joseph Gagnon Canada & Corinne Bourgeois Canada
GAGNON, Joseph R Philippe, Mar 30 1931 Sex:M Child# 1 Philippe Gagnon Canada & Olivinne Ross Canada
GAGNON, Joseph Robert Leo, Jan 4 1930 Sex:M Child# 2 Wilfrid Gagnon Nashua, NH & Helene Caron Manchester, NH
GAGNON, Joseph Thomas, May 25 1899 Sex:M Child# 7 Thomas Gagnon Canada & Emelie Mayotte Canada
GAGNON, Joseph Thomas Henri, Oct 18 1918 Sex:M Child# 1 Henry Gagnon NH & Juliette Bouchard Canada
GAGNON, Joseph V Ovide, Oct 28 1897 Sex:M Child# 1 Victor Gagnon Canada & Claudia Marois Canada
GAGNON, Joseph Victor, Sep 14 1910 Sex:M Child# 1 Jean B Gagnon Canada & M Quackenbury New York
GAGNON, Juliette Florentine, Nov 26 1904 Sex:F Child# 2 George Gagnon Canada & Eugenie Laprise Canada
GAGNON, Juliette Georgette, Jan 9 1915 Sex:F Child# 2 Joseph Gagnon Canada & Alexina Marquis Canada
GAGNON, Juliette Yvette, Oct 27 1919 Sex:F Child# 6 Alphonse Gagnon Canada & Maria Gendron Canada
GAGNON, Laura May, Dec 4 1917 Sex:F Child# 4 Albert A Gagnon Salem, MA & Augustine Moquin Windsor, VT
GAGNON, Leo, Jun 15 1927 Sex:M Child# 11 Alphonse Gagnon Canada & Maria Gendron Canada
GAGNON, Leo Ernest, Nov 8 1904 Sex:M Child# 3 Henri Gagnon Nashua, NH & Georgiana Lessard Nashua, NH
GAGNON, Leo Leonard, Dec 30 1902 Sex:M Child# 2 J H Gagnon Pepperell, MA & Grace Benoit Nashua, NH
GAGNON, Leon Henry, Aug 5 1925 Sex:M Child# 3 Leon H Gagnon Nashua, NH & Cath Diggins Nashua, NH
GAGNON, Leon I I, Jul 25 1891 Sex:M Child# 4 Francis Gagnon Canada & Adele Dumais Canada
GAGNON, Leona, Oct 7 1891 Sex:F Child# 1 Thomas Gagnon Canada & Emilie Malhoit Canada
GAGNON, Leona, Mar 30 1919 Sex:F Child# 2 Albert J Gagnon Nashua, NH & Annabelle Gauthier Taunton, MA
GAGNON, Louis Adelard, Nov 10 1916 Sex:M Child# 9 Joseph Gagnon Canada & Corinne Bourgeois Wilton, NH
GAGNON, Louis Edward, Dec 28 1935 Sex:M Child# 3 Ernest Gagnon Nashua, NH & Albert Bellavance Moosup, CT
GAGNON, Louis Eugene, Dec 28 1899 Sex:M Child# 1 Eugene Gagnon Canada & Clara Sirois Canada
GAGNON, Louis Hector, Jun 12 1914 Sex:M Child# 6 Magloire Gagnon Canada & Rose Anna Tessier Canada
GAGNON, Louis Robert, Dec 6 1934 Sex:M Child# 6 Albert Gagnon Canada & Alice Boucher Canada
GAGNON, Lucien Leopold, Jul 7 1926 Sex:M Child# 2 Louis C Gagnon Canada & Aldea Lacombe Canada
GAGNON, Lucille Antoinette, Jun 4 1933 Sex:F Child# 1 Eugene Gagnon Nashua, NH & Marie J Duhamel Nashua, NH
GAGNON, Lucille Emelda, May 11 1915 Sex:F Child# 1 Georges Gagnon Canada & Celanire Ricard Canada
GAGNON, Ludger, Dec 6 1901 Sex:M Child# 11 Arsene Gagnon Canada & Catherine Berube Canada
GAGNON, Lydia Marie, Sep 24 1889 Sex:F Child# 3 Jean Gagnon Canada & Marie Paradis Canada
GAGNON, M Adele Marguerite, Mar 16 1913 Sex:F Child# 7 Joseph Gagnon Canada & Corinne Bourgeois Canada
GAGNON, M Blanche Yvonne B, Mar 1 1912 Sex:F Child# 3 Joseph Gagnon Canada & Neala Thibault Canada
GAGNON, M Cecile Leona, Aug 15 1913 Sex:F Child# 8 Victorien Gagnon Canada & Eugenie Dube Canada
GAGNON, M Emma Belle W, Jan 2 1920 Sex:F Child# 3 William I Gagnon Fall River, MA & Albina Laroche Canada
GAGNON, M Ivonne, Dec 9 1895 Sex:F Child# 12 Louis Gagnon Canada & Cesarie Fournier Canada
GAGNON, M Judith Rose, Mar 12 1893 Sex:F Child# 3 Charles Gagnon Canada & Armenie Gaudreau Canada
GAGNON, M Lucille Albinna, May 22 1919 Sex:F Child# 3 Napoleon Gagnon Canada & Georgina Gagnon Canada
GAGNON, M Yvonne Jeannette, Jul 17 1913 Sex:F Child# 2 Louis Gagnon Canada & Laetitia Boulanger Canada
GAGNON, M Yvonne L, Oct 25 1908 Sex:F Child# 7 Eugene Gagnon Canada & Clara Sirois Canada
GAGNON, Madeleine, Sep 18 1933 Sex:F Child# 7 George Gagnon US & Delia Cousineau US
GAGNON, Magloire Alexis E, Jan 9 1926 Sex:M Child# 8 Joseph Gagnon Canada & Elmira Petrain Canada
GAGNON, Malvina, Oct 24 1898 Sex:F Child# 3 Euclide Gagnon Canada & Celina Deslangues Canada
GAGNON, Marguerite G, May 7 1908 Sex:F Child# 1 Clement Gagnon Canada & Emma Viens Canada
GAGNON, Maria, Oct 27 1912 Sex:F Child# 5 Joseph Gagnon Canada & Maria Ross Canada
GAGNON, Maria Rita Lucia, Oct 21 1920 Sex:F Child# 5 Joseph Gagnon Canada & Elmina Petrin Canada
GAGNON, Maria wilda Glorise, Jun 25 1924 Sex:F Child# 3 S Gagnon Canada & Eva Berube Canada
GAGNON, Marie, Jan 15 1892 Sex:F Child# 3 Pierre Gagnon Canada & Flavie Bouchard Canada
GAGNON, Marie, Feb 5 1895 Sex:F Child# 9 William Gagnon Canada & Justine Gagnon Canada
GAGNON, Marie, Dec 16 1903 Sex:F Child# 10 Alfred Gagnon Canada & Victoria Gagnon Canada
GAGNON, Marie, Jul 4 1910 Sex:F Child# 4 Joseph Gagnon Canada & Maria Ross Canada
GAGNON, Marie A, Nov 23 1901 Sex:F Child# 1 Henri Gagnon Nashua, NH & Georgiana Lessard Nashua, NH

GAGNON, Marie A L, May 27 1906 Sex:F Child# 1 Joseph Gagnon Canada & Mai E Thibault Canada
GAGNON, Marie Adele E, Mar 15 1895 Sex:F Child# 3 Louis Gagnon Canada & Adele Bernier Canada
GAGNON, Marie Alice, Feb 7 1893 Sex:F Child# 8 William Gagnon Canada & Justine Canada
GAGNON, Marie Alice, Feb 15 1902 Sex:F Child# 2 Eugene Gagnon Canada & Alice Tardif Canada
GAGNON, Marie Alma, Apr 13 1906 Sex:F Child# 12 Thomas Gagnon Canada & Emelie Mailhotte Canada
GAGNON, Marie Ann Janet, Jul 26 1930 Sex:F Child# 3 Albert Gagnon Taunton, MA & Dianne Tessier Nashua, NH
GAGNON, Marie Anne, Jul 12 1890 Sex:F Child# 3 Francois Gagnon Canada & Adele Dumais Canada
GAGNON, Marie Anne A, Aug 1 1897 Sex:F Child# 5 Jean Gagnon Canada & Marie Lavoie Canada
GAGNON, Marie Annette, Jul 6 1921 Sex:F Child# 6 Alphonse Gagnon Canada & Maria Gendron Canada
GAGNON, Marie Annie, Jun 24 1890 Sex:F Child# 1 Louis Gagnon Canada & Adele Bernice Canada
GAGNON, Marie Blanche Rita, May 12 1926 Sex:F Child# 2 George Gagnon Nashua, NH & Delima Cousineau Nashua, NH
GAGNON, Marie Blanche Y, Oct 9 1900 Sex:F Child# 5 Jacob Gagnon Canada & Marie Levesque Canada
GAGNON, Marie Claire, Feb 8 1912 Sex:F Child# 6 Joseph Gagnon Canada & Corinne Bourgeon Canada
GAGNON, Marie Clara, Jun 4 1893 Sex:F Child# 5 Joseph Gagnon Canada & Henriette Berube Canada
GAGNON, Marie Clara, Jun 23 1898 Sex:F Child# 3 Louis Gagnon Canada & Cesarie Gagnon Canada
GAGNON, Marie Clara, Feb 28 1901 Sex:F Child# 2 Eugene Gagnon Canada & Clara Sirois Canada
GAGNON, Marie Doris Pauline, Mar 14 1935 Sex:F Child# 7 George Gagnon Nashua, NH & Delia Nashua, NH
GAGNON, Marie Dorothy, Apr 9 1929 Sex:F Child#  Stanislaus Gagnon Canada & Eva Berube Lowell, MA
GAGNON, Marie E, Jun 16 1896 Sex:F Child# 5 Auguste Gagnon Canada & Marie Beaupre Canada
GAGNON, Marie Emelie, Oct 17 1900 Sex:F Child# 10 Louis Gagnon Canada & Adele Bernier Canada
GAGNON, Marie Eugenie, Feb 9 1897 Sex:F Child# 10 William Gagnon Canada & Justine Gagnon Canada
GAGNON, Marie Eugenie, Oct 4 1911 Sex:F Child# 7 George Gagnon Canada & Adele Cassista Canada
GAGNON, Marie Eva, May 6 1908 Sex:F Child# 15 Arsene Gagnon Canada & Catherine Berube Canada
GAGNON, Marie Germaine, Jan 23 1914 Sex:F Child# 9 Georges Gagnon Canada & Adele Cassista Canada
GAGNON, Marie Germaine, Aug 3 1928 Sex:F Child# 1 Jos A Gagnon Taunton, MA & Diana Tessier Nashua, NH
GAGNON, Marie Gertrude G, Nov 1 1926 Sex:F Child# 2 Albert Gagnon Canada & Alice Boucher Canada
GAGNON, Marie I, Mar 25 1889 Sex:F Child# 2 Francois X Gagnon Canada & Adele Dumais Canada
GAGNON, Marie Jane Lorette, Nov 25 1927 Sex:F Child# 3 Albert Gagnon Canada & Alice Boucher Canada
GAGNON, Marie Juliette, Aug 24 1893 Sex:F Child# 1 Jacob Gagnon Canada & Marie Levesque Canada
GAGNON, Marie Juliette A, Jul 1 1924 Sex:F Child# 7 Joseph Gagnon Canada & Elmeria Petrin Canada
GAGNON, Marie L Yvonne, Jul 8 1901 Sex:F Child# 1 Joseph Gagnon Canada & Corinne Bourgeois Canada
GAGNON, Marie Laura, Dec 18 1896 Sex:F Child# 2 Euclide Gagnon Canada & Celina Deslanger Canada
GAGNON, Marie Lillianne, May 5 1911 Sex:F Child# 9 Eugene Gagnon Canada & Clara Sirois Canada
GAGNON, Marie Lodia, Feb 16 1892 Sex:F Child# 4 Arsene Gagnon Canada & Catherine Berube Canada
GAGNON, Marie Lorette, Apr 9 1923 Sex:F Child# 7 Alphonse Gagnon Canada & Marie Gendron Canada
GAGNON, Marie Louise, Dec 24 1890 Sex:F Child# 3 Arsene Gagnon Canada & Catherine Berube Canada
GAGNON, Marie Louise, Sep 13 1901 Sex:F Child# 1 J B Gagnon Canada & Delia Morin Canada
GAGNON, Marie Louise C, Jun 15 1906 Sex:F Child# 3 Theodore Gagnon Canada & Emma Lanthier Canada
GAGNON, Marie Louise L, Aug 18 1897 Sex:F Child# 2 Arthur Gagnon Canada & Josephine Gagnon Canada
GAGNON, Marie Louise Z, Apr 10 1890 Sex:F Child# 5 Joseph Gagnon Canada & Henrietta Berube Canada
GAGNON, Marie Martha Y, Jun 5 1929 Sex:F Child# 1 George Gagnon Nashua, NH & Margaret Blanchard Canada
GAGNON, Marie Oliva, Oct 23 1892 Sex:F Child# 6 Louis Gagnon Canada & Adele Bernier Canada
GAGNON, Marie Olivinne T, Mar 21 1927 Sex:F Child# 9 Joseph Gagnon Canada & Elmerio Petrain Canada
GAGNON, Marie R A, May 26 1893 Sex:F Child# 5 Francois Gagnon Canada & Adele Dumais Canada
GAGNON, Marie R Adelina, Jan 27 1899 Sex:F Child# 4 Jacob Gagnon Canada & Marie Levesque Canada
GAGNON, Marie R Therese, Aug 3 1931 Sex:F Child# 12 Joseph Gagnon Canada & Elmeria Petrain Canada
GAGNON, Marie Rosanna, Jun 4 1894 Sex:F Child# 1 Pierre Gagnon Canada & Philomene Berube Canada
GAGNON, Marie Rose Theresa, Feb 2 1926 Sex:F Child# 3 Arsene Gagnon Nashua, NH & Alma Pellerine Canada
GAGNON, Marie Therese Juliet, Jun 12 1932 Sex:F Child# 4 L Philip Gagnon St Pacom, Canada & Alden Lacombe Nashua,NH
GAGNON, Marie Victoria D, Sep 4 1901 Sex:F Child# 13 Alfred Gagnon Canada & Victoria Chasse Canada
GAGNON, Marie Victorine, Dec 25 1890 Sex:F Child# 4 Jean Gagnon Canada & Marie Paradis Canada
GAGNON, Marie Virginie A, Feb 2 1908 Sex:F Child# 2 Joseph Gagnon Canada & Mayola Thibault Canada
GAGNON, Marie Yvonne Lucille, Feb 19 1918 Sex:F Child# 3 Joseph Gagnon Canada & Elmina Petrin Canada
GAGNON, Mariette, Nov 14 1933 Sex:F Child# 2 Armand Gagnon Nashua, NH & Harriet Heon Manchester, NH
GAGNON, Mary, Sep 16 1932 Sex:F Child# 2 Ernest Gagnon Nashua, NH & Blanche Richards Nashua, NH
GAGNON, Mary Lydia Doris, Aug 31 1925 Sex:F Child# 1 Victor Gagnon Nashua, NH & Laura Descheneau Canada
GAGNON, Maurice, Jan 9 1934 Sex:M Child# 4 Jos Geo Gagnon Nashua, NH & Laurette Lefebvre Nashua, NH
GAGNON, Maurice Andrew, May 28 1923 Sex:M Child# 6 George Gagnon Canada & Celina Ricard Canada
GAGNON, Mildred Yvonne, Feb 1 1932 Sex:F Child# 7 Stanislas Gagnon Canada & Eva Berube Canada
GAGNON, Mona Cecile, May 1 1920 Sex:F Child# 2 Pierre Gagnon Canada & Caroline Dubois Lawrence, MA
GAGNON, Muriel Rita, Apr 27 1921 Sex:F Child# 5 Joseph Gagnon Canada & Alexina Marquis Canada
GAGNON, Nanette Lucille, Jun 20 1909 Sex:F Child# 2 Clement Gagnon Canada & Emma Gagnon Canada
GAGNON, Norman, Mar 15 1925 Sex:M Child# 7 Arthur Gagnon Canada & Eva Codair Peabody, MA
GAGNON, Oliver, Aug 27 1922 Sex:M Child# 3 William Gagnon Nashua, NH & Alice Landry Nashua, NH
GAGNON, Olivina M, Jan 21 1900 Sex:F Child# 1 Etienne Gagnon Canada & Philomene Pineau Nashua, NH
GAGNON, Olivine Georgiana, Nov 20 1908 Sex:F Child# 4 Joseph Gagnon Canada & Corinne Bourgeois Canada
GAGNON, Paul Albert, Nov 19 1920 Sex:M Child# 5 Albert H Gagnon Salem, NH & Augustine Marquis Windsor, VT
GAGNON, Paul Emile Eli, Sep 14 1921 Sex:M Child# 11 Joseph Gagnon Canada & Rose Anna Ross Canada
GAGNON, Paul Henry Norbert, Jan 29 1926 Sex:M Child# 4 William Gagnon Nashua, NH & Alice Landry Nashua, NH
GAGNON, Paul Leonard, Feb 11 1935 Sex:M Child# 1 Leo Gagnon Nashua, NH & Isabelle Anctil Nashua, NH
GAGNON, Paul Maurice, Jul 4 1924 Sex:M Child# 9 Alphonse Gagnon Canada & Maria Gendron Canada
GAGNON, Pauline Eleanor, Apr 1 1934 Sex:F Child# 2 Achille Gagnon Manchester, NH & Marguerite Smith Manchester, NH
GAGNON, Pelhia, Jan 28 1888 Sex:F Child# 2 Jean Gagnon Canada & Marie Paradis Canada

GAGNON, Philip Joseph, Jun 10 1931 Sex:M Child# 1 Sylvio Gagnon Nashua, NH & Katherine Ledoux Nashua, NH
GAGNON, Philip Louis G, Sep 18 1924 Sex:M Child# 1 Philip Gagnon Mass & Rose A Levesque Rhode Island
GAGNON, Rachel, Feb 13 1935 Sex:F Child# 15 Alphonse Gagnon Canada & Maria Gendron Canada
GAGNON, Raymond, May 17 1925 Sex:M Child# 1 L Philip Gagnon Canada & Aldea Lacombe Canada
GAGNON, Reine Elizabeth, Feb 5 1903 Sex:F Child# 1 Theodore Gagnon Canada & Emma Lanthier Canada
GAGNON, Rita, Aug 16 1921 Sex:F Child# 2 Fred B Gagnon Berlin, NH & Mary T Sullivan E Pepperell, MA
GAGNON, Rita Jean, Feb 25 1929 Sex:f Child# 8 Arthur Gagnon Canada & Eva Codair Peabody, MA
GAGNON, Robert Leon, Jul 4 1931 Sex:M Child# 5 Albert Gagnon Canada & Alice Boucher Canada
GAGNON, Robert Maurice, Jun 7 1928 Sex:M Child# 4 Louis P Gagnon Canada & Aldea Lacombe Nashua, NH
GAGNON, Robert O'Dwyer, May 16 1925 Sex:M Child# 2 Leon Gagnon Nashua, NH & M H O'Dwyer Nashua, NH
GAGNON, Roger, Jun 19 1918 Sex:M Child# 4 Joseph Gagnon Canada & Celanire Ricard Canada
GAGNON, Roger, Feb 9 1926 Sex:M Child# 10 Alphonse Gagnon Canada & Marie Gendron Canada
GAGNON, Rosanna E, Nov 22 1903 Sex:F Child# 1 Magloire Gagnon Canada & Rosanna Tessier Canada
GAGNON, Rosanna Rita, Oct 7 1922 Sex:F Child# 2 Arsene Gagnon Nashua, NH & Alma Pellerin Canada
GAGNON, Rose A Delima, Jul 30 1899 Sex:F Child# 14 Louis Gagnon Canada & Cesarre Fournier Canada
GAGNON, Rose Albina, Mar 14 1915 Sex:F Child# 1 William Gagnon Fall River, MA & Rose A Laroche Canada
GAGNON, Rose Germaine G, Feb 22 1906 Sex:F Child# 3 Michel Gagnon Canada & Rose A Laboissoniere Canada
GAGNON, Stanley Normand, Dec 14 1933 Sex:M Child# 8 Stanislas Gagnon Canada & Eva Berube Lowell, MA
GAGNON, Sylviana Donalda, Dec 28 1921 Sex:F Child# 1 Stanislas Gagnon Canada & Eva Berube Canada
GAGNON, Sylvis, Jun 7 1904 Sex:M Child# 1 George Gagnon Canada & Adele Casista Canada
GAGNON, Therese Jeanine, Feb 21 1932 Sex:F Child# 14 Alphonse Gagnon Canada & Maria Gendron Canada
GAGNON, Thomas, Feb 20 1897 Sex:M Child# 7 Antoine Gagnon Canada & Elise Levesque Canada
GAGNON, Toussaint Louis R, Nov 1 1912 Sex:M Child# 1 Louis Gagnon Canada & Emma Hudon US
GAGNON, Unknown, Feb 21 1889 Sex:F Child# 11 Gilbert Gagnon
GAGNON, Unknown, Aug 17 1892 Sex:M Child# 5 Francois Gagnon Canada &  Canada
GAGNON, Unknown, Dec 25 1893 Sex:F Child# 3 Thomas Gagnon Canada & Melia Malhiot Canada Stillborn
GAGNON, Unknown, Oct 10 1894 Sex:M Child# 4 Thomas Gagnon Canada & Emelie Malhiot Canada Stillborn
GAGNON, Unknown, Feb 5 1896 Sex:M Child#  Thomas Gagnon Canada & Melie Malhoit Canada
GAGNON, Unknown, Jul 23 1899 Sex:F Child# 12 Alfred Gagnon Canada & Victoria Chassee Canada Stillborn
GAGNON, Unknown, Aug 7 1903 Sex: Child# 2 Eugene Gagnon Nashua, NH & Alice Tardif Canada
GAGNON, Unknown, Nov 10 1904 Sex:F Child# 9 Thomas Gagnon Canada & Emelie Mayotte Canada Stillborn
GAGNON, Unknown, Jun 20 1910 Sex:M Child# 1 H Gagnon Nashua, NH & Katherine Diggins Nashua, NH
GAGNON, Unknown, May 12 1924 Sex:F Child#  Henry C Gagnon Nashua, NH & Irene Trombley Haverhill, MA
GAGNON, Unknown, May 11 1927 Sex:M Child# 2 Jules Gagnon Lowell, MA & Delima Martin Canada
GAGNON, Unknown, Jun 2 1929 Sex:F Child# 1 Leo Gagnon Nashua, NH & Marjorie Forrence Nashua, NH Stillborn
GAGNON, Victor Ludger, Feb 10 1925 Sex:M Child#  George Gagnon Nashua, NH & Delia Cousineau Nashua, NH
GAGNON, Victor Roland, May 18 1907 Sex:M Child# 8 Jacob Gagnon Canada & Marie Levesque Canada
GAGNON, Victorien Joseph, Nov 4 1893 Sex:M Child# 1 Victorien Gagnon Canada & Eugenie Dube Canada
GAGNON, Wilfred, Jan 28 1925 Sex:M Child# 9 George Gagnon Canada & Catherine Ricard Canada
GAGNON, Wilfred Edmond, Aug 18 1905 Sex:M Child# 1 Pierre Gagnon Canada & Caroline Dubord Lawrence, MA
GAGNON, Wilfrid, Jul 23 1896 Sex:M Child# 3 Jacob Gagnon Canada & Marie Levesque Canada
GAGNON, Wilfrid, Nov 10 1902 Sex:M Child# 2 J B Gagnon Canada & Delia Morin Canada
GAGNON, Wilfrid, Mar 28 1907 Sex:M Child# 6 Eugene Gagnon Canada & Clara Sirois Canada
GAGNON, Wilfrid Raymond, Apr 14 1928 Sex:M Child# 1 Wilfrid Gagnon Nashua, NH & Helene Caron Manchester, NH
GAGNON, Wm Horace Roland, Jun 11 1913 Sex:M Child# 1 Horace Gagnon Nashua, NH & Laura Dumont Suncook, NH
GAGNON, Yolande Gloria, Dec 7 1928 Sex:F Child# 12 Alph Gagnon Canada & Anna Gendron Canada
GAGNON, Yvonne Cecile, Jul 1 1920 Sex:F Child# 1 Arsene Gagnon Nashua, NH & Alma Pelerin Canada
GAGUE, Lewis, Feb 24 1888 Sex:M Child# 3 Joseph Gague Canada & Hariette Bernve Canada
GAGUE, M L Adelina, May 3 1893 Sex:F Child# 3 Francois Gague Canada & Philomene Paquet Canada
GAIDES, Annie, Dec 14 1923 Sex:F Child# 2 Peter Gaides Lithuania & Agnes Chesnolawitch Lithuania
GAIDES, Rose, Dec 14 1923 Sex:F Child# 3 Peter Gaides Lithuania & Agnes Chesnolawitch Lithuania
GAIDZIS, Wicentas, Jun 5 1907 Sex:M Child# 1 Kazimieras Gaidzis Russia & A Walentuckiewicz Russia
GAILLARDET, Joseph, Nov 7 1891 Sex:M Child# 2 L Gaillardet Canada & Marie Florence Canada
GAITES, Peter, Sep 12 1918 Sex:M Child# 2 Peter Gaites Russia & Rosa Karsakut Russia
GAKIEDIS, Sophia, Oct 2 1907 Sex:F Child# 1 Kostas Gakiedis Greece & Sperina Gakiedis Greece
GALARNEAU, Hermengilde G, Jul 15 1889 Sex:M Child# 1 H Galarneau Canada & Marie Jacques Canada
GALAZAUSKAS, Unknown, Sep 7 1919 Sex:F Child# 5 Kas Galazauskas Russia & Rachael Typkus Russia
GALE, Arthur Reuben, Sep 9 1925 Sex:M Child# 8 Arthur R Gale Saxtons River, VT & Maude Richardson Wolcott, VT
GALE, Donald Chancey, Sep 30 1929 Sex:M Child# 11 Arthur R Gale Saxtons River, VT & Maude Richardson Wolcott, VT
GALE, Shirley Barbara, Feb 18 1927 Sex:F Child# 10 Arthur R Gale Saxtons River, VT & Maude Richardson Wolcott, VT
GALECKI, Stanislaus, Aug 14 1915 Sex:M Child# 2 William Galecki Russia & Mary Cashmen Russia
GALENSKI, Mary, Apr 11 1916 Sex:F Child#  Peter Galenski Russia & Sophia Gazebak Austria
GALGARIAN, Beatrice, Mar 11 1902 Sex:F Child# 2 Takar Galgarian Armenia & Norah Bowen Ireland
GALINAS, Flavie Maria, Feb 19 1896 Sex:F Child# 12 Olesime Galinas Canada & Victoria Houle Canada
GALIPEAU, Alice Beatrice, Jun 18 1907 Sex:F Child# 11 Louis Galipeau Canada & Alma Maranda Canada
GALIPEAU, Alice Gertrude, Oct 8 1934 Sex:F Child# 3 Paul Galipeau Nashua, NH & Mabel Miner Maine
GALIPEAU, Alice Irene, Dec 29 1901 Sex:F Child# 8 Louis Galipeau Canada & Alma Maranda Canada
GALIPEAU, Alma Adrienne, Jul 22 1900 Sex:F Child# 7 Louis Galipeau Canada & Alma Maranda Canada
GALIPEAU, Beatrice, May 24 1933 Sex:F Child# 4 George Galipeau Nashua, NH & Ernestine Lavoie Amque, Canada
GALIPEAU, Blanche Beatrice, Oct 31 1903 Sex:F Child# 9 Louis Galipeau Canada & Alma Maranda Canada
GALIPEAU, Camille Wilfred, Feb 4 1911 Sex:M Child# 12 Louis Galipeau Canada & Alma Maranda Canada
GALIPEAU, Doris Rita, Mar 15 1934 Sex:F Child# 1 Hilaire Galipeau Nashua, NH & Blanche Cassista Nashua, NH
GALIPEAU, Dorothy Gilberta, Apr 20 1923 Sex:F Child# 1 Theodore Galipeau Nashua, NH & Philomene Lavoie Canada

GALIPEAU, Ernestine L, Jul 30 1887 Sex:F Child#  Francois Galipeau P Q & Eliza Plante P Q
GALIPEAU, George Ernest, Aug 1 1931 Sex:M Child# 3 George Galipeau Nashua, NH & Ernestine Lavoie Canada
GALIPEAU, George Joseph, Feb 22 1897 Sex:M Child# 5 Louis Galipeau Montreal, PQ & Alma Maranda St Simon, PQ
GALIPEAU, Joseph Albert Elie, Jan 17 1906 Sex:M Child# 1 Eugene Galipeau Canada & Mattea Maranda Mass
GALIPEAU, Joseph Oscar, May 9 1895 Sex:M Child# 4 Louis Galipeau Montreal, PQ & Alma Maranda St Simon, PQ
GALIPEAU, Lactitia, Mar 12 1890 Sex:F Child# 4 Francis Galipeau Canada & Eliza Plante Canada
GALIPEAU, Leopold Lorenzo, Mar 11 1894 Sex:M Child# 3 Louis Galipeau Canada & Alma Maranda Canada
GALIPEAU, Louis Norbert, Jan 21 1893 Sex:M Child# 2 Louis Galipeau Canada & Alma Maranda Canada
GALIPEAU, Marie, Aug 26 1922 Sex:F Child# 1 George Galipeau Nashua, NH & Ernestine Lavoie Canada
GALIPEAU, Marie Corinne, Jul 18 1905 Sex:F Child# 10 Louis Galipeau Canada & Alma Maranda Canada
GALIPEAU, Marie E A, May 17 1892 Sex:F Child# 5 Francis Galipeau Canada & Elisa Plante Canada
GALIPEAU, Noela, Dec 25 1913 Sex:F Child# 13 Louis Galipeau Canada & Alma Maranda Canada
GALIPEAU, Orpha Adelina, Nov 29 1918 Sex:F Child# 14 Louis Galipeau Canada & Alma Maranda Canada
GALIPEAU, Paul Joseph Ralph, Dec 7 1908 Sex:M Child# 2 Eugene Galipeau Canada & Mattie Lapierre US
GALIPEAU, Paul Richard, Dec 7 1932 Sex:M Child# 2 Paul Galipeau Nashua, NH & Mabel Minor Portland, ME
GALIPEAU, Pearl Jeanne d'Arc, Aug 14 1926 Sex:F Child# 3 Theodore Galipeau Nashua, NH & Philomene Lavoie Canada
GALIPEAU, Robert Eugene, Oct 22 1931 Sex:M Child# 1 Paul Galipeau Nashua, NH & Mabel Miner Portland, ME
GALIPEAU, Theodore, Jan 27 1899 Sex:M Child# 7 Louis Galipeau Canada & Alma Maranda Canada
GALIPEAU, Theodore U, Dec 11 1896 Sex:M Child# 6 Francis Galipeau Canada & Eliza Plante Canada
GALIPEAU, Unknown, Jun 22 1925 Sex:F Child# 2 George Galipeau Nashua, NH & Ernestine Lavoie Canada Stillborn
GALLAGHER, Baley, May 2 1914 Sex:F Child# 7 William C Gallagher Ireland & Tillie Harvey Nashua, NH
GALLAGHER, Christopher, Mar 4 1916 Sex:M Child# 3 Thomas Gallagher Nashua, NH & Abbie York Fremont, NH
GALLAGHER, Cristopher, Jan 30 1890 Sex:M Child# 1 ChristopherGallagher Ireland & Eliza Halpin Ireland
GALLAGHER, Edna May, Jan 26 1914 Sex:F Child# 2 Thomas Gallagher Nashua, NH & Abbie York Fremont, NH
GALLAGHER, James, Sep 30 1895 Sex:M Child# 4 Chrstpher Gallagher Ireland & Eliza Halpin Ireland
GALLAGHER, James, Jan 29 1921 Sex:M Child# 5 Thomas F Gallagher Nashua, NH & Abbie York Fremont, NH
GALLAGHER, John, Aug 1 1898 Sex:M Child# 1 William Gallagher Ireland & Matilda Horvey Nashua, NH
GALLAGHER, Leslie Thomas, Jan 27 1912 Sex:M Child# 1 Thomas J Gallagher Nashua, NH & Abbie A York Freemont, NH
GALLAGHER, Margaret Louise, Jun 1 1919 Sex:F Child# 4 Thomas Gallagher Nashua, NH & Abbie York Freemont, NH
GALLAGHER, Mary Elizabeth, Nov 18 1917 Sex:F Child# 1 Chrstopher Gallagher Nashua, NH & Elizabeth Stevens England
GALLAGHER, Tilly, May 4 1901 Sex:F Child# 3 William Gallagher Ireland & Tilly Harvey Nashua, NH
GALLAND, Unknown, Sep 14 1915 Sex:M Child# 2 Emmanuel Galland Canada & Amanda Richard US
GALLANT, Aime, Nov 5 1915 Sex:M Child# 13 A C Gallant Canada & Leonie Marcoux Canada
GALLANT, Aime Henry, Jan 28 1917 Sex:M Child# 1 Pascal Gallant Maine & Irene Morrissette Nashua, NH
GALLANT, Aurelia Lucille, Jul 15 1919 Sex:F Child# 3 Emanuel Gallant Prince Edward Island & Emanda Richard NH
GALLANT, Donald Benoit, Mar 12 1925 Sex:M Child# 1 Benoit Gallant Canada & Mabel Downey Salem, MA
GALLANT, Doris Josephine, Jun 5 1928 Sex:F Child# 2 J H Gallant Nashua, NH & Amanda Chabot Canada
GALLANT, Francis Andre, Apr 14 1914 Sex:M Child# 1 Manuel Gallant Canada & Amanda Richard US
GALLANT, Gerard, Jul 18 1920 Sex:M Child# 3 Pascal Gallant Westbrook, ME & Irene Morrissette Nashua, NH
GALLANT, Gloria Jacqueline, Apr 7 1933 Sex:F Child# 1 Edward Gallant Nashua, NH & Yvette Lee Nashua, NH
GALLANT, John Henry, Jan 10 1905 Sex:M Child# 7 Aime Gallant Canada & Leonie Marcoux Canada
GALLANT, Joseph Arthur, Jun 30 1935 Sex:M Child# 1 Pascale Gallant Westbrook, ME & Yvonne Francoeur Nashua, NH
GALLANT, Joseph Edward, Apr 15 1913 Sex:M Child# 11 Aime Gallant Canada & Leonie Marcoux Canada
GALLANT, Joseph Henry, Mar 5 1906 Sex:M Child# 8 Aime Gallant Canada & Leonie Marcoux Canada
GALLANT, Joseph Kemis Robert, Aug 11 1914 Sex:M Child# 12 Aime Gallant Canada & Leonie Marcou Canada
GALLANT, Joseph Maurice N, Oct 29 1930 Sex:M Child# 4 Jean Gallant Nashua, NH & Amanda Chabot Canada
GALLANT, Joseph Robert, Dec 15 1927 Sex:M Child# 1 Oscar Gallant Nashua, NH & Cecile Vincent Manchester, NH
GALLANT, Marie Collette D, Jul 26 1929 Sex:F Child# 3 Jean Gallant Nashua, NH & Amanda Chabot Canada
GALLANT, Marie L Jeanne d'Arc, Sep 4 1926 Sex:F Child# 1 Jean H Gallant Nashua, NH & Amanda Chabot Canada
GALLANT, Marie Louise Marguer, May 12 1918 Sex:F Child# 2 Pascal Gallant Maine & Irene Morrissette Nashua, NH
GALLANT, Marie Olivette R, Nov 6 1910 Sex:F Child# 10 Aime Gallant Canada & Leonie Marcoux Canada
GALLANT, Mary Murielle Rita, May 2 1933 Sex:F Child# 5 Jean H Gallant Nashua, NH & Amanda Chabot Canada
GALLIGER, Unknown, Jul 23 1899 Sex:F Child# 2 William Galliger Ireland & Tilly Harvey Nashua, NH
GALLIGHER, Margaret J, Jun 1 1902 Sex:F Child# 4 William Galligher Ireland & Lilly Harvey Nashua, NH
GALLIGHER, Unknown, Jul 12 1905 Sex:M Child# 5 William C Galligher Ireland & Tilly Harvey Nashua, NH
GALLIGHER, Unknown, Aug 18 1910 Sex:F Child# 6 William C Galligher Ireland & Tilly B Harvey Nashua, NH
GALLIPEAU, Raymond Camille, Feb 17 1925 Sex:M Child# 2 Theo Gallipeau Nashua, NH & Philomene Lavoie Canada
GALLUP, Frances Eleanor, Aug 24 1923 Sex:F Child# 7 Harry O Gallup Groton City, NB & Laura Peters St John, NB
GALLUP, Harry Oscar, Dec 23 1919 Sex:M Child# 6 Harry O Gallup Groton Co, NB & Laura Peters St John, NB
GALLUP, Unknown, Mar 14 1916 Sex:F Child# 5 Harry O Gallup Groton Co, NB & Laura Peters St John, NB
GALT, William H, Mar 27 1905 Sex:M Child# 1 George M Galt Ireland & Lida J Batchelder Nashua, NH
GALVIN, Eileene, Jun 8 1905 Sex:F Child# 3 Bartholomew Galvin Ireland & Nellie Wrenn Ireland
GAMACHE, Albert Raymond, Jul 28 1930 Sex:M Child# 5 Albert Gamache Leominster, MA & Margaret Wheeler Marlow, NH
GAMACHE, Aldige Lionel, Aug 25 1929 Sex:M Child# 5 Aldige Gamache Nashua, NH & Laura Cassista Nashua, NH
GAMACHE, Alfred William, Feb 4 1926 Sex:M Child# 5 Leo Gamache NH & Ida Jean NH
GAMACHE, Arthur Ernest, Apr 15 1925 Sex:M Child# 4 Alfred Gamache Canada & Hortmise Poirier Hinsdale, NH
GAMACHE, Arthur Wilfrid, Aug 5 1933 Sex:M Child# 4 Wilfrid Gamache Nashua, NH & Alice Turgeon Nashua, NH
GAMACHE, Arthur, Jr, Apr 14 1921 Sex:M Child# 3 Arthur Gamache Canada & Alice Carr Manchester, NH
GAMACHE, Cecile Bernadette, Feb 27 1933 Sex:F Child# 2 Leo Gamache Nashua, NH & Ida Jean Nashua, NH
GAMACHE, Clarisse Murielle, May 11 1908 Sex:F Child# 3 Clovis Gamache US & Robertine Jodoin Canada
GAMACHE, Clovis George, Jan 7 1910 Sex:M Child# 4 Clovis Gamache US & Robertine Jodoin Canada
GAMACHE, Dora Diana, Mar 25 1928 Sex:F Child# 6 Leo Gamache NH & Ida Jean NH
GAMACHE, Doris Fernande, Mar 26 1925 Sex:F Child# 4 John Gamache NH & Laura Lasalle Canada

GAMACHE, Edouard Aldege, Mar 2 1903 Sex:M Child# 6 Achille Gamache Canada & Alice Ouellette Canada
GAMACHE, Edward Gilbert, Jan 16 1925 Sex:M Child# 4 Leo Gamache NH & Ida Jean NH
GAMACHE, Eugene, Sep 7 1911 Sex:M Child# 6 Clovis Gamache, Jr US & Robertine Jodoin Canada
GAMACHE, Eva Lorette, May 6 1925 Sex:F Child# 2 Aldage Gamache Nashua, NH & Laura Cassista Nashua, NH
GAMACHE, George Lewis, Oct 23 1929 Sex:M Child# 7 Lea A Gamache Nashua, NH & Alida E Jean Nashua, NH
GAMACHE, Geraldine Laura, May 30 1919 Sex:F Child# 1 Wilfred Gamache Berlin, NH & Annabelle Vivian Lyon Mtn, NY
GAMACHE, Girard T, Jan 22 1917 Sex:M Child# 6 Clovis Gamache Nashua, NH & Roberta Jodoin Canada
GAMACHE, Gloria G A, Sep 13 1903 Sex:F Child# 2 Clovis Gamache, Jr Nashua, NH & Robertine Jodoin Canada
GAMACHE, Irene, Jul 27 1928 Sex:F Child# 4 Aldege Gamache Nashua, NH & Laura Casista Nashua, NH
GAMACHE, Jacqueline Theresa, Feb 19 1930 Sex:F Child# 2 Wilfred Gamache Nashua, NH & Alice Turgeon Nashua, NH
GAMACHE, Jos Armand Lionel, May 28 1925 Sex:M Child# 1 Lionel Gamache Nashua, NH & Mary Gingras Canada
GAMACHE, Jos William Alfred, Sep 16 1920 Sex:M Child# 1 Alfred Gamache Canada & Hortense Poirier NH
GAMACHE, Joseph Achille, Mar 18 1894 Sex:M Child# 2 Achille Gamache Canada & Alice Ouellette Canada
GAMACHE, Joseph Clovis Roger, Jan 15 1924 Sex:M Child# 3 John R Gamache Canada & Lousa Lasalle Canada
GAMACHE, Joseph Emilien, Dec 31 1928 Sex:M Child# 1 A Gamache Canada & Melina Daigle Canada
GAMACHE, Joseph F E, Aug 11 1928 Sex:M Child# 3 L Gamache Nashua, NH & Marie Gingras Canada
GAMACHE, Joseph Horace Edgar, Aug 20 1912 Sex:M Child# 2 Horace Gamache Canada & Elmire Fraser Canada
GAMACHE, Joseph Leo Amedee, May 24 1922 Sex:M Child# 2 John Gamache NH & Laura Lasalle Canada
GAMACHE, Joseph Leo Roland, Mar 8 1923 Sex:M Child# 2 Leo Gamache Nashua, NH & Eva Derocher Nashua, NH
GAMACHE, Leo Albert, May 17 1918 Sex:M Child# 1 Leo Alex Gamache Nashua, NH & Ida Evelyn Jean Nashua, NH
GAMACHE, Lionel, Apr 24 1904 Sex:M Child# 7 Achille Gamache Canada & Alice Ouelette Canada
GAMACHE, Louis Joseph R, Aug 20 1901 Sex:M Child# 1 Clovis Gamache Nashua, NH & Robertine Jodoin Canada
GAMACHE, M Lillian Beatrice, Jun 6 1922 Sex:F Child# 2 Alfred Gamache Canada & Hortense Poirier NH
GAMACHE, M Rose Blanche, Dec 8 1908 Sex:F Child# 1 Horace Gamache Canada & Elmire Fraser Canada
GAMACHE, M Wilhelmine Olive, Jul 23 1913 Sex:F Child# 3 Horace Gamache Canada & Elmire Fraser Canada
GAMACHE, Marie, Jan 20 1888 Sex:F Child# 3 J B Gamache Canada & Rose M Brine Canada
GAMACHE, Marie Blanche Floren, May 22 1926 Sex:F Child# 2 Aldege Gamache Nashua, NH & Laura Casista Nashua, NH
GAMACHE, Marie Claire Laurett, Dec 29 1923 Sex:F Child# 3 Alfred Gamache Canada & Hortense Poirier NH
GAMACHE, Marie Irene J, Apr 18 1930 Sex:F Child# 4 Lionel Gamache Nashua, NH & Marie Gingras Canada
GAMACHE, Marie Jeanne d'Arc, Dec 19 1926 Sex:F Child# 5 Alfred Gamache Canada & Hortense Poirier Hinsdale, NH
GAMACHE, Marie Leda, Sep 23 1913 Sex:F Child# 1 Wilfred Gamache Canada & Marie Rioux Canada
GAMACHE, Marie Lucille, Feb 21 1925 Sex:F Child# 3 Leo Gamache Nashua, NH & Eva Deroche Nashua, NH
GAMACHE, Marie M Lorraine, Dec 21 1935 Sex:F Child# 5 Lionel Gamache Nashua, NH & Marie Gingras Canada
GAMACHE, Marie Olivette, Jan 13 1921 Sex:F Child# 1 Leo Gamache Nashua, NH & Eva Derocher Nashua, NH
GAMACHE, Marie Paul Sylvia, Sep 7 1933 Sex:F Child# 6 Lionel Gamache Nashua, NH & Marie Gingras Canada
GAMACHE, Marie Pearl Eva, Jan 4 1927 Sex:F Child# 2 Lionel Gamache Nashua, NH & Marie Gengras Canada
GAMACHE, Marie Rose Eva, Feb 19 1896 Sex:F Child# 3 Achille Gamache Canada & Alice Ouellette Canada
GAMACHE, Marie Sylvia Thelma, Feb 19 1927 Sex:F Child# 5 John Gamache Berlin, NH & Laura LaSalle Canada
GAMACHE, Marie Therese, Jan 30 1923 Sex:F Child# 1 Aldege Gamache Nashua, NH & Laura Cassista Nashua, NH
GAMACHE, Marieanna Anita, Oct 21 1920 Sex:F Child# 1 John R Gamache NH & Laura Lasalle Canada
GAMACHE, Marjorie Rita, Jan 20 1914 Sex:F Child# 5 Clovis Gamache Nashua, NH & Robertine Jodoin Canada
GAMACHE, Mary Florence, Nov 23 1922 Sex:F Child# 3 Leo Gamache NH & Aleda Jean NH
GAMACHE, Mary Therese, Apr 19 1931 Sex:F Child# 1 Jean B Gamache Canada & Yvonne Deschenes Greenville, NH
GAMACHE, Raymond, Jul 9 1923 Sex:M Child# 1 Raymond Gamache Nashua, NH & Rose Anna Tessier Nashua, NH
GAMACHE, Rita Sibyl, Jul 9 1919 Sex:F Child# 2 Leo A Gamache Nashua, NH & Ida Gean Nashua, NH
GAMACHE, Roger Normand P J, May 28 1928 Sex:M Child# 1 Wilfred Gamache Nashua, NH & Alice Turgeon Nashua, NH
GAMACHE, Theresa Germaine, Sep 20 1931 Sex:F Child# 8 Leo Gamache Nashua, NH & Alida Jean Nashua, NH
GAMACHE, Unknown, Mar 13 1923 Sex:F Child# 1 Arthur Gamache Canada & Alice Carr Manchester, NH
GAMACHE, Wilfrid, Feb 19 1931 Sex:M Child# 6 Aldege Gamache Nashua, NH & Laura Casista Nashua, NH
GAMANCHE, Marie Lucille Victor, Nov 17 1918 Sex:F Child# 7 Clovis Gamanche Nashua, NH & Robertine Jodoin Acton, MA
GAMARCHE, Alice, Dec 12 1892 Sex:F Child# 1 Achile Gamarche Canada & Alice Ouellette Canada
GAMARCHE, Arthur Sylvio, Feb 4 1909 Sex:M Child# 10 Achille Gamarche Canada & Alice Ouellette Canada
GAMARCHE, Beatrice Alphonsine, Oct 8 1919 Sex:F Child# 1 Alfred Gamarche Berlin, NH & Desanges Demarais Westford
GAMARCHE, Charles Wilfrid, Mar 10 1900 Sex:M Child# 5 Achille Gamarche Canada & Alice Ouellette Canada
GAMARCHE, Helen Pearl, Aug 2 1921 Sex:F Child# 3 Wilfred Gamarche Brunswick, ME & Annabelle Vivian Lion Mt, NY
GAMARCHE, Jeannette Jeanne, Dec 20 1918 Sex:F Child# 1 Alfred Gamarche Canada & Claudia Lavoie Canada
GAMARCHE, Joseph Leo, Apr 14 1898 Sex:M Child# 4 Achille Gamarche Canada & Alice Ouellette Canada
GAMARCHE, Leontine, Sep 17 1905 Sex:F Child# 8 Achille Gamarche Canada & Alice Ouellette Canada
GAMARCHE, Raymond Elmer, Jul 7 1920 Sex:M Child# 2 Wilfred Gamarche Brunswick, ME & Annabelle Vivian Lion Mt, NY
GAMARCHE, Theodore, Feb 16 1911 Sex:M Child# 11 Achille Gamarche Canada & Alice Ouellette Canada
GAMASH, Carl, Dec 21 1900 Sex:M Child# 4 William Gamash NH & Maud Budro New York
GAMASH, Leon, Nov 11 1895 Sex:M Child# 1 William I Gamash Newport & Maud Budro W Chazy, NY
GAMASH, Lillian, Mar 2 1897 Sex:F Child# 2 William Gamash Newport & Maud Budro W Chazy, NY
GAMASH, William H, Mar 19 1898 Sex:M Child# 3 William Gamash Newport & Maud Budro W Chazy, NY
GAMES, Unknown, Aug 7 1907 Sex:M Child# 4 Peter Games Athens, Greece & Notta Hanjan Athens, Greece
GAMPRON, Unknown, Jun 26 1887 Sex:F Child# 8 Felix Gampron Canada & Elmira Gaouette Canada Stillborn
GANDOTIS, Stanislaw, Jun 28 1908 Sex:M Child# 1 Anton Gandotis Russia & Casimira Stolpiny Russia
GANDREAU, Marie A Eulalie, Oct 16 1897 Sex:F Child# 1 Pascal Gandreau Canada & Elizabeth Levesque Canada
GANDROW, Unknown, May 28 1887 Sex:F Child# 4 Alex Gandrow Plattsburg, NY & Ida Canada
GANDRY, Henry, May 9 1889 Sex:M Child# 1 Exavier Gandry Canada & Felina Brehard Nashua, NH
GANEAU, Bermis M N, Oct 11 1897 Sex:F Child# 7 Abraham Ganeau Bourbonnais, IL & Melina Darche St Anne, IL
GANEAU, Bertha L, Oct 21 1895 Sex:F Child# 6 Abraham Ganeau Kankakee, IL & Melina Darche Kankakee, IL
GANEAU, George F, Jul 29 1891 Sex:M Child# 5 Abraham Ganeau Illinois & Melina Darsh Illinois

GANEAU, Leon R, Mar 10 1889 Sex:M Child# 4 Abraham Ganeau Canada & Molina Darsh Canada
GANEPY, Joseph, Aug 11 1889 Sex:M Child# 2 Charles Ganepy Canada & Marie L St Georges Canada
GANGIOANIS, Constantina, Jun 15 1919 Sex:F Child# 2 Christos Gangioanis Greece & Tasia Lekas Greece
GANGLOIS, Joseph, Apr 27 1888 Sex:M Child# 1 Frank Ganglois Canada & Virginia Nadeau Moors, NY
GANGLOTT, William John, Feb 11 1924 Sex:M Child# 5 William J Ganglott New Jersey & Hazel Wheeler Milford, NH
GANGRAW, Unknown, Jul 10 1895 Sex:F Child# 2 Selden Gangraw New York & Ellyn Morrison Londonderry, NH
GAOUETTE, Joseph Hubert, Aug 30 1891 Sex:M Child# 4 Laurend Gaouette Canada & Soufranie Morin Canada
GAOUETTE, Marie Louise, Oct 26 1892 Sex:F Child#  Thomas Gaouette Canada & Julie Galipean Canada
GAPLINSKI, Unknown, Mar 14 1920 Sex:F Child# 6 Stanley Gaplinski Russia & Helen Zulvost Russia Stillborn
GARACHE, Mary Alice, Nov 19 1889 Sex:F Child# 3 George Garache NY & Matilda Cuollen Nashua, NH
GARAND, Anna Noela, Dec 25 1920 Sex:F Child# 4 Joseph Garand Canada & Adele Dionne Canada
GARAND, Bernadette, Oct 11 1907 Sex:F Child# 2 Louis Garand Canada & Ludivine Laflamme Canada
GARAND, Emile, May 21 1904 Sex:M Child# 11 Theophile Garand Canada & Lucie Fleury Canada
GARAND, Gabrielle, Jul 18 1917 Sex:F Child# 1 Joseph Garand Canada & Adele Dionne Canada
GARAND, Joseph E William, Oct 27 1903 Sex:M Child# 6 Aime Garand Canada & Leonie Marcoux Canada
GARAND, Lea Eugenie, Nov 22 1919 Sex:F Child# 3 Joseph Garand Canada & Adele Dionne Canada
GARAND, M Agnes Elaine, Jul 2 1921 Sex:F Child# 4 Arthur Garand Canada & Clara Salvail NH
GARAND, M Marg Lucille, Jul 13 1916 Sex:F Child# 1 Arthur Garand Canada & Laura Salvail NH
GARAND, Marie Aldea, Feb 19 1910 Sex:F Child# 3 Louis Garand Canada & Ludivine Laflamme Canada
GARAND, Marie Blanche Floret, Apr 14 1918 Sex:F Child# 2 Arthur Garand Canada & Flora Salvail NH
GARAND, Paul Emile, Feb 23 1906 Sex:M Child# 1 Adjutor Garand Canada & Emma Blais Canada
GARAND, Paul Emile, May 9 1923 Sex:M Child# 5 Joseph Garand Canada & Adele Dionne Canada
GARAND, Theophile Edgar, Jan 17 1922 Sex:M Child# 5 Joseph Garand Canada & Adele Dionne Canada
GARAND, Wilfrid Hector, Jun 25 1907 Sex:M Child# 2 Adjutor Garand Canada & Emma Blais Canada
GARANT, Henri, Sep 26 1908 Sex:M Child# 9 Aime Garant Canada & Louise Marcoux Canada
GARANT, Irenee Robert, Sep 23 1918 Sex:M Child# 2 Joseph Garant Canada & Adele Dionne Canada
GARANT, Jos Normand Emile, Aug 9 1922 Sex:M Child# 5 Arthur Garant Canada & Flora Salvail NH
GARANT, Joseph Albert, Nov 17 1932 Sex:M Child# 7 Joseph Garant Canada & Adelle Dion Canada
GARANT, M Beatrice Gertrude, Aug 9 1919 Sex:F Child# 3 Arthur Garant Canada & Clara Salvail NH
GARANT, Marie Rachel Anita, Jan 9 1933 Sex:F Child# 7 Arthur Garant Canada & Flora Salvail Nashua, NH
GARANTE, Ernest Robert, Apr 3 1924 Sex:M Child# 6 Arthur Garante Canada & Flora Salvail Nashua, NH
GARARD, Joseph, Sep 6 1888 Sex:M Child# 1 Alfred Garard Canada & Marie Francocure Canada
GARBARZ, Apolonia, Apr 13 1926 Sex:F Child# 5 Joseph Garbarz Poland & Annie Diecek Poland
GARBARZ, Unknown, Jan 11 1922 Sex:F Child# 5 Joseph Garbarz Poland & Annie Weeck Poland
GARBUS, Paul, Dec 19 1909 Sex:M Child# 1 Valentas Garbus Russia & Edwiga Lepeszka Russia
GARBUS, Peter, Dec 19 1909 Sex:M Child# 2 Valentas Garbus Russia & Edwiga Lepeszka Russia
GARCZEYSKI, John, Oct 28 1905 Sex:M Child# 4 John Garczeyski Russia & Anna Zydecki Russia
GARCZYNSKI, Joseph, Apr 19 1904 Sex:M Child# 3 Joseph Garczynski Russia & Anna Zydecki Russia
GARDIKES, Unknown, Jul 1 1934 Sex:F Child# 3 James Gardikes Greece & Ourania Economou Greece
GARDNER, Betty Ann, Oct 9 1931 Sex:F Child# 4 Richard Gardner Pepperell, MA & Mildred Kemp Groton, MA Stillborn
GARDNER, Beverly Ann, Nov 11 1933 Sex:F Child# 1 Alvin Gardner Oldtown, ME & Esther Giles Nashua, NH
GARDNER, George Alexander, Jun 29 1921 Sex:M Child# 2 George Gardner Haverhill, MA & Margaret White Boston, MA
GARDNER, Gloria Edna, Jun 6 1931 Sex:F Child# 1 Cleon Gardner Old Town, ME & Eva Soucy Missoula, Mont
GARDNER, Pearl, Dec 17 1906 Sex:F Child# 3 Charles Gardner Virginia & Theresa Marr Maine
GARDNER, Raymond Robert, Dec 3 1919 Sex:M Child# 1 Lwslie Gardner Bradley, ME & Olive Lucier Lawrence, MA
GARDNER, Robert Hale, Aug 17 1908 Sex:M Child# 1 George A Gardner Nashua, NH & Myrtle A Hale Rindge, NH
GARDNER, Theresa May, Mar 2 1933 Sex:F Child# 4 William Gardner Somerville, MA & Anna White Newfoundland
GARDNER, Unknown, Feb 19 1888 Sex:M Child# 1 Elmer H Gardner Milford & Mamie Eastman Andover
GARDNER, Unknown, Oct 13 1897 Sex:M Child# 4 E H Gardner Milford, NH & Mary Eastman Andover
GARDNER, Willie, May 24 1888 Sex:M Child# 2 Frank C Gardner Brookline & Hattie Payne Taunton, MA
GARENER, Ruth, Aug 10 1919 Sex:F Child# 1 Arthur W Garener Clinton, MA & Theodora Atwood Ayer, MA
GARETHANE, John, Dec 17 1918 Sex:M Child# 3 John Garethane Greece & Anna Chareo Greece
GARIEPIL, Marie Gracia, Feb 23 1891 Sex:F Child# 1 Victor Gariepil Canada & Delia Bonenfaut Vermont
GARIEPY, Denis Albert, Dec 31 1904 Sex:M Child# 1 Wilfred Gariepy Canada & Graziella Lesage Marlboro, MA
GARIEPY, Edouard, Jun 15 1894 Sex:M Child# 1 Louis Gariepy Canada & Rose Menard St Albans, VT
GARIEPY, Joseph E A Emile, Jan 23 1898 Sex:M Child# 2 Gedeon Gariepy Canada & Victoria Benoit Canada
GARIEPY, M Blanche A R, Dec 27 1895 Sex:F Child# 1 Gedeon Gariepy Canada & Victoria Benoit Canada
GARIEPY, Marie Louise A, Jan 17 1901 Sex:F Child# 1 Wilfrid Gariepy Nashua, NH & Marie Louise Caron Canada
GARIEPY, Mary Anne, Mar 28 1892 Sex:F Child# 2 Victor Gariepy Canada & Marie Bonenfaut Canada
GARLAND, Archie, May 11 1905 Sex:M Child# 1 Arthur H Garland Boston, MA & Bertha M Hill Lowell, MA
GARLAND, Dorothy May, Aug 24 1911 Sex:F Child# 2 George A Garland Nashua, NH & Bertha Hill Lowell, MA
GARLAND, Esther Louise, Jan 21 1898 Sex:F Child# 3 Charles C Garland Portland, ME & Mildred E Garland Portland, ME
GARLAND, Mildred Augusta, Jul 11 1914 Sex:F Child# 3 Arthur H Garland Boston, MA & Bertha M Hill Lowell, MA
GARLAND, Sylvia Grace, May 18 1909 Sex:F Child# 1 Harry M Garland Goffstown, NH & Almira L Wellman Nashua, NH
GARLAND, Unknown, Jun 17 1888 Sex:F Child# 1 Edwin F Garland Nashua, NH & Alice Lucier Canada
GARLAND, Warren William, May 14 1913 Sex:M Child# 2 Harry M Garland Goffstown, NH & Almira L Wellman Nashua, NH
GARLAS, Joseph, Jul 5 1914 Sex:M Child# 1 Velantas Garlas Russia & Zedviga Lepesquaka Russia
GARLON, Unknown, Jan 19 1918 Sex:M Child# 3 John Garlon Russia & Minnie Sarwoski Russia Stillborn
GARON, Donald Lucien, Nov 5 1934 Sex:M Child# 2 Adelard Garon Nashua, NH & Eva Bleau Nashua, NH
GARON, Marguerite Rita, Mar 18 1923 Sex:F Child# 3 Jean B Garon Canada & Mathilda Nashua, NH
GARON, Marie Pauline, Jun 30 1919 Sex:F Child# 1 John Garon Canada & Mathilde Desmarais Nashua, NH
GARON, Norma Jennette, Jul 31 1923 Sex:F Child# 1 Francis Xavier Garon Grand Isle, ME & Annie Genthner
GAROUSKA, Unknown, Aug 16 1897 Sex:F Child#  Paul Garouska

GARREND, Lea, Feb 28 1893 Sex:F Child# 4 Alfred Garrend Canada & Marie Francoeur Canada
GARREND, Rosanna, Jan 30 1891 Sex:F Child# 3 Alfred Garrend Canada & Marie Francoeur Canada
GARREND, Wilfred Joseph A, Jan 12 1890 Sex:M Child# 2 Alfred Garrend Canada & Marie Francoeur Canada Stillborn
GARRETY, Mary, Jun 7 1927 Sex:F Child# 2 Arthur Garrety Milford, NH & M Brahaney Milford, NH
GARRITY, Helen Mary, Mar 14 1920 Sex:F Child# 1 Arthur Garrity Milford, NH & Margaret Brahany Milford, NH
GARRITY, John Thomas, Jan 11 1898 Sex:M Child# 4 James Garrity Ireland & Lucy Burns Nashua, NH
GARRITY, Unknown, Jun 28 1895 Sex:F Child# 3 James Garrity Ireland & Lucy Burns Nashua, NH
GARTCHENSKI, Antonina, Jan 28 1915 Sex:F Child# 1 August Gartchenski Russia & Josie Stanchekuita Russia
GARTIS, Julia, Sep 29 1917 Sex:F Child# 1 Peter Gartis Lithuania Russia & Agnes Chesnolawicz Lithuania Russia
GARWIN, Orville B, Dec 6 1890 Sex:M Child# 1 Arthur O Garwin NH & Anna L Bareins Maine
GASEAU, Marie Louise, Apr 9 1887 Sex:F Child# 3 Abraham Gaseau Montreal & Melina Darsh Ill
GASHY, Peter, May 21 1926 Sex:M Child# 7 Alexander Gashy Austria & Mary Bxlisen Austria
GASKELL, Jason B, Jul 1 1887 Sex:M Child# 3 Leroy L Gaskell Ausable, NY & Ida Owen Wilmington, NY
GASKELL, Unknown, Dec 23 1890 Sex:M Child# 4 Leroy L Gaskell Ausable, NY & Ida Owen Wilmington, NY
GASKILL, Burton B, Aug 27 1914 Sex:M Child# 2 Helsey Gaskill Clintonville, NY & Lulu Hargraves Nashua, NH
GASKILL, Dorothy Elizabeth, Apr 20 1917 Sex:F Child# 3 Halsey Gaskill Clintonville, NY & Lulu Hargraves Nashua, NH
GASKILL, Eleanor Hargraves, Jan 8 1913 Sex:F Child# 1 Halsey B Gaskill Clintonville, NY & Mary L I Hargraves
GASKILL, Elizabeth Helen, Dec 20 1924 Sex:F Child# 2 Raymond Gaskill Nashua, NH & Helen Peters St John, NB
GASKILL, Leroy L, Dec 9 1896 Sex:M Child# 4 Leroy L Gaskill New York & Ida Owen New York Stillborn
GASKILL, Raymond Kenneth, Sep 19 1923 Sex:M Child# 1 Raymond Gaskill Nashua, NH & Helen Peters St John, NB
GASKILL, Raymond Parker, Mar 27 1900 Sex:M Child# 1 Melvin E Gaskill NY & L F Parker Mass
GASKILL, Roger Warren, Sep 10 1924 Sex:M Child# 1 R H Gaskill Clintonville, NY & Rowena P Sawyer Pepperell, MA
GASKILL, Ruth E, Mar 25 1911 Sex:F Child# 1 Burton T Gaskill Clintonville, NY & Mary Kenniston Auburn, NH
GASKILL, Unknown, Mar 21 1900 Sex:M Child# 4 B T Gaskill NY & Mary E Beardsley NY
GASKIN, Robert Arthur, Apr 10 1930 Sex:M Child# 1 Ralph M Gaskin Fairfield, ME & Edith English New Brunswick
GASSELIN, Lewis J Edouard, Mar 18 1890 Sex:M Child# 1 Louis Gasselin Canada & Emma Ouelette Canada
GATAIS, Ida, Nov 2 1918 Sex:F Child# 1 Nicholas Gatais Macedonia & Herkli Girtaire Macedonia
GATCOMB, Carol Jane, Jul 19 1935 Sex:F Child# 1 Richard Gatcomb Nashua, NH & Doris L Smith Nashua, NH
GATCOMB, Earl Milton, Sep 14 1915 Sex:M Child# 8 George Gatcomb Mystic, CT & Fanny Pelkey New York
GATCOMB, Grace Alice, Jan 27 1905 Sex:F Child# 3 George M Gatcomb Mystic, CT & Fannie M Pelkey Ellenburg Dep, NY
GATCOMB, James, Jun 9 1914 Sex:M Child# 7 George Gatcomb Conn & Fanny Pelky New York
GATCOMB, Mildred Louise, Jul 1 1909 Sex:F Child# 5 George M Gatcomb Conn & Fanny Pelky New York
GATCOMB, Ralph Loring, Jun 23 1920 Sex:M Child# 9 George M Gatcomb Mystic, CT & Fanny Pelky New York
GATCOMB, Verne Walton, Dec 22 1911 Sex:M Child# 6 George M Gatcomb Connecticut & Fanny Pelkey New York
GATECKI, Stanislawa, Aug 26 1912 Sex:M Child# 1 Vincente Gatecki Russia & Emilia Merczych Russia
GATES, Charles F, Sep 12 1929 Sex:M Child# 2 Wallace Gates Nashua, NH & Velma Jeannotte Nashua, NH Stillborn
GATES, Charles Martin, Jan 26 1933 Sex:M Child# 2 Joseph E Gates Nashua, NH & L M Haselton Chelmsford, MA
GATES, Edwin Wilder, May 18 1900 Sex:M Child# 2 E L Gates NH & Alice Wilder NS
GATES, Ellen Adeline, Jun 21 1907 Sex:F Child# 1 Frederick J Gates Hollis, NH & Grace Sampson Londonderry, NH
GATES, Howard C Merrill, Mar 26 1920 Sex:M Child# 1 Wallace Gates Hollis, NH & Winnibel Merrill W Buxton, ME
GATES, Joseph Ernest, Jun 17 1905 Sex:M Child# 3 Charles E Gates Hollis, NH & Martena Durant Hollis, NH
GATES, Joseph Ernest, Jr, Jun 24 1930 Sex:M Child# 1 Joseph E Gates Hudson, NH & Lillian Morton Chelmsford, MA
GATES, Kenneth Albert, Jul 16 1922 Sex:M Child# 1 Linsey Gates Springfield, MA & Laura Haines Worcester, MA
GATES, Paul Wallace, Dec 4 1901 Sex:M Child# 3 Edwin L Gates NS & Alice Wildes Gilson NY
GATES, Ruth, Feb 21 1904 Sex:F Child# 1 Edwin Gates Nova Scotia & Alice Gilson NY
GATES, Ruth Geraldine, Nov 4 1930 Sex:F Child# 3 Wallace Gates Nashua, NH & Velma Jeannotte Nashua, NH
GATES, Unknown, Jul 15 1933 Sex:F Child# 4 Wallace Gates Nashua, NH & Velma Jeannotte Nashua, NH
GATES, Wallace E, Apr 21 1903 Sex:M Child# 2 Charles E Gates Hollis, NH & Martena Durant Hollis, NH
GATES, Wallace Emery, Jr, Jul 12 1928 Sex:M Child# 1 W E Gates Nashua, NH & Velma Jeannotte Nashua, NH
GATLO, Frances Mary, Apr 28 1925 Sex:F Child# 1 Antonio Gatlo Italy & Mennie Patti Italy
GATTO, Andrew, Mar 23 1935 Sex:M Child# 1 Andrew Gatto Milford, NH & Dean St Pierre Greenville, NH
GATTO, Anthony Bratolo, May 14 1932 Sex:M Child# 2 Anthony Gatto Italy & Minnie Pattie Italy
GAUDELL, Marie, Jun 2 1888 Sex:F Child# 6 Jean B Gaudell Canada & Celina Belard Canada
GAUDET, Angeline, Oct 3 1889 Sex:F Child# 1 Harice Gaudet Canada & Alexandrie Granel Canada
GAUDET, Divina, Sep 14 1889 Sex:F Child# 1 Moise Gaudet Canada & Melvina Brosseau Canada
GAUDET, Edouard A, May 9 1896 Sex:M Child# 4 Edouard Gaudet Canada & Lea Pateneoude Lowell, MA
GAUDET, Ernest P D, Feb 23 1891 Sex:M Child# 10 Prosper Gaudet Canada & Josephine Lambert Douglass, MA
GAUDET, Exina L, Dec 18 1897 Sex:F Child# 5 Edouard Gaudet Canada & Lea Patenaude Lowell, MA
GAUDET, Henri F, Jul 1 1890 Sex:M Child# 4 Victor Gaudet Canada & Claudia Brien Canada
GAUDET, Joseph E, Jun 30 1889 Sex:M Child# 1 Joseph Gaudet Canada & Emma Cormier Canada
GAUDET, Joseph O, Dec 6 1891 Sex:M Child# 3 Xavier Gaudet Canada & Alexandrine Gravel Nashua, NH
GAUDET, Joseph O, Feb 10 1893 Sex:M Child# 8 Jean B Gaudet Canada & Celina Belland Canada
GAUDET, Marie E, Nov 19 1894 Sex:F Child# 3 Moise Gaudet Canada & Malvina Bourasseau Canada
GAUDET, Marie E R, Jan 27 1893 Sex:F Child# 4 Francois X Gaudet Canada & Alexandrine Gravel Nashua, NH
GAUDET, Marie L, Jun 6 1894 Sex:F Child# 3 Edouard Gaudet Canada & Lea Pateneaude Lowell, MA
GAUDET, Moise, Oct 30 1890 Sex:M Child# 2 Moise Gaudet Canada & Malvina Brousseau Canada
GAUDET, Ruth T, Mar 20 1893 Sex:F Child# 2 Edouard Gaudet Canada & Lea Pateneaude Lowell, MA
GAUDETTE, Agnes Elizabeth, Feb 23 1904 Sex:F Child# 1 Elzear Gaudette Lowell, MA & Grace Harris Nashua, NH
GAUDETTE, Albert, May 21 1893 Sex:M Child# 8 Remi Gaudette Canada & Exilda Havard Canada
GAUDETTE, Alida Lillian, Mar 15 1902 Sex:F Child# 1 Alfred Gaudette Nashua, NH & Eseverine Martel Canada
GAUDETTE, Alma, Mar 4 1896 Sex:F Child# 11 David Gaudette Canada & Celina Renaud Canada
GAUDETTE, Alphonse Emile, Feb 10 1900 Sex:M Child# 3 Napoleon Gaudette Canada & Delphine Morisette Nashua, NH
GAUDETTE, Andre E, Feb 19 1902 Sex:M Child# 8 Edouard Gaudette Canada & Lea Patenaude Lowell, MA

GAUDETTE, Andrea A, Jul 21 1900 Sex:F Child# 6 Moise Gaudette Canada & Alvina Brousseau Canada
GAUDETTE, Annette Melina, Jun 13 1922 Sex:F Child# 1 Hector Gaudette Nashua, NH & Rose A Manseau Canada
GAUDETTE, Arthur, Apr 3 1897 Sex:M Child# 1 Napoleon Gaudette Canada & Delphine Morissette Canada
GAUDETTE, Arthur Emile, Mar 14 1935 Sex:M Child# 1 Arthur Gaudette Nashua, NH & Eva Gerard Nashua, NH
GAUDETTE, Arthur Joseph, Jan 20 1930 Sex:M Child# 7 Delphis H Gaudette Nashua, NH & Elisa Pelletier Montreal, PQ
GAUDETTE, Cecile Rachel A, Jan 2 1906 Sex:F Child# 5 Frank Gaudette Nashua, NH & Virginie Jauron Canada
GAUDETTE, Clarence S, Aug 12 1903 Sex:M Child# 3 Frank Gaudette Nashua, NH & Virginie Jauron Canada
GAUDETTE, David, Mar 6 1888 Sex:M Child# 1 David Gaudette Canada & Celina Ricard Canada
GAUDETTE, Diana Alice, Sep 17 1898 Sex:F Child# 2 Napoleon Gaudette Canada & Delphine Morissette Nashua, NH
GAUDETTE, Dorothy Florette, Feb 18 1926 Sex:F Child# 5 Delphis Gaudette Nashua, NH & Elizabeth Pelletier Canada
GAUDETTE, Edgar Wilfrid, Dec 16 1901 Sex:M Child# 4 Napoleon Gaudette Canada & Delphine Morissette Nashua, NH
GAUDETTE, Emma Gracia, May 20 1891 Sex:F Child# 7 Remi Gaudette Canada & Exilda Havard Canada
GAUDETTE, Ernest Lucien, Dec 9 1903 Sex:M Child# 7 Alphonse Gaudette Canada & Delvina Mireau Canada
GAUDETTE, Eugene, Dec 2 1895 Sex:M Child# 2 Victor Gaudette Canada & Helene Dionne Canada
GAUDETTE, Eugene, Jan 29 1900 Sex:M Child# 2 Hector Gaudette Canada & Emma Lussier Canada
GAUDETTE, Eva Rose, Apr 30 1900 Sex:F Child# 12 David Gaudette Canada & Celina Renaud Canada
GAUDETTE, Evangeline, Apr 23 1887 Sex:F Child#  Remi Gaudette P Q & Exilda Havard P Q
GAUDETTE, Flore Reine, May 19 1889 Sex:F Child# 6 Remi Gaudette Canada & Exilda Navard Canada
GAUDETTE, Florette A, Nov 16 1906 Sex:F Child# 8 Moise Gaudette Canada & Alvina Brousseau Canada
GAUDETTE, Gabriel Xavier, Jun 14 1907 Sex:M Child# 6 Frank Gaudette Nashua, NH & Virginie Jauron Canada
GAUDETTE, Genevieve Sophie, Mar 6 1931 Sex:F Child# 2 Ernest Gaudette Nashua, NH & Violet Kulengoski Nashua,
GAUDETTE, George, Apr 21 1910 Sex:M Child# 8 Alphonse Gaudette Canada & Evelina Mireault Canada
GAUDETTE, Gloria Yvonne, Jul 8 1926 Sex:F Child# 2 Emile Gaudette Nashua, NH & Eva Hudon Nashua, NH
GAUDETTE, Hector, Jun 30 1893 Sex:M Child# 10 David Gaudette Canada & Celina Renaud Canada
GAUDETTE, Hector, Feb 5 1904 Sex:M Child# 2 Hector Gaudette Nashua, NH & Zephirine Martel Canada
GAUDETTE, Hector Conrad, Jul 30 1928 Sex:M Child# 3 Hector Gaudette Nashua, NH & Rose Manseau Canada
GAUDETTE, Henri, Jan 9 1890 Sex:M Child# 8 David Gaudette Canada & Celina Renaud Canada
GAUDETTE, Henri, Jan 3 1898 Sex:M Child# 2 Victor Gaudette Canada & Helene Dionne Canada
GAUDETTE, Henri A, Oct 17 1894 Sex:M Child# 5 F X Gaudette Canada & Alexandrine Gravel Nashua, NH
GAUDETTE, Henri A, Jan 9 1896 Sex:M Child# 4 Moise Gaudette Canada & Alvina Brousseau Canada
GAUDETTE, Henri Edouard, Sep 2 1913 Sex:M Child# 9 Alphonse Gaudette Canada & Eveline Mireault Canada
GAUDETTE, Israel Claude, Aug 8 1895 Sex:M Child# 9 Remi Gaudette Canada & Exilda Havard Canada
GAUDETTE, Joseph, Jun 14 1899 Sex:M Child# 6 Edouard Gaudette Canada & Lea Pateneaude Lowell, MA
GAUDETTE, Joseph, Jul 16 1902 Sex:M Child# 2 Frank Gaudette Nashua, NH & Virginie Jauron Canada
GAUDETTE, Joseph Armand, May 9 1919 Sex:M Child# 3 Eusebe Gaudette Nashua, NH & Leocadie Asselin Canada
GAUDETTE, Joseph Arthur, Apr 20 1903 Sex:M Child# 2 Napoleon Gaudette Canada & Marie Bonvouloir Canada
GAUDETTE, Joseph H Delphis, Mar 21 1899 Sex:M Child# 1 Hector Gaudette Canada & Emma Lucier Canada
GAUDETTE, Joseph Napoleon L, Apr 21 1902 Sex:M Child# 1 Napoleon Gaudette Canada & Marie Bonvouloir Canada
GAUDETTE, Joseph Robert Sylvio, Aug 19 1918 Sex:M Child# 2 Henri Gaudette Nashua, NH & Albina Gervais NH
GAUDETTE, Joseph Victor, May 4 1904 Sex:M Child# 6 Joseph Gaudette Canada & Emma Cormier Canada
GAUDETTE, Leo, Aug 18 1900 Sex:M Child# 1 Frank Gaudette Nashua, NH & Virginie Jauron Canada
GAUDETTE, Leonie I, May 23 1902 Sex:F Child# 7 Moise Gaudette Canada & Alvina Brousseau Canada
GAUDETTE, Lilian Cecile, Sep 5 1910 Sex:F Child# 1 Alfred Gaudette Nashua, NH & Orphana Poney Canada
GAUDETTE, Lina, Dec 27 1900 Sex:F Child# 3 Hector Gaudette Canada & Emma Lucier Canada
GAUDETTE, Loretta Rita, Aug 27 1922 Sex:F Child# 2 Moise Gaudette Nashua, NH & Alice Hysette Nashua, NH
GAUDETTE, Louise R A, Nov 23 1887 Sex:F Child#  Victor Gaudette P Q & Claudia Brien Canada
GAUDETTE, Lucille Andrea, Apr 6 1921 Sex:F Child# 10 Moise Gaudette Nashua, NH & Alice Hysette Nashua, NH
GAUDETTE, Ludgere, Jul 3 1897 Sex:M Child# 5 Moise Gaudette Canada & Alvina Brousseau Canada
GAUDETTE, M Blanche Florette, Jul 1 1914 Sex:F Child# 4 Hector Gaudette Canada & Emma Lussier Canada
GAUDETTE, Marcelle Flora, Feb 26 1924 Sex:F Child# 2 Hector Gaudette Nashua, NH & R Alma Manseau Canada
GAUDETTE, Marie Alma, Jan 14 1917 Sex:F Child# 1 Eusebe Gaudette Nashua, NH & Leocadie Asselin Canada
GAUDETTE, Marie Annette Irene, Jul 9 1922 Sex:F Child# 2 Oliva Gaudette Nashua, NH & Virginia Ricard Canada
GAUDETTE, Marie Beatrice Elise, Jun 22 1920 Sex:F Child# 1 Delphis Gaudette NH & Elise Pelletier Canada
GAUDETTE, Marie Blanche L, Aug 21 1929 Sex:F Child# 5 Eugene A Gaudette Nashua, NH & Blanche E Morin Canada
GAUDETTE, Marie Cecile, May 21 1914 Sex:F Child# 1 Georges Gaudette Nashua, NH & Eugenie Sirois Canada Stillborn
GAUDETTE, Marie Jean Lucille, Nov 21 1920 Sex:F Child# 1 Orvila Gaudette Nashua, NH & M J Virginia Ricard Cana
GAUDETTE, Marie Lil Rose Del, Jan 21 1918 Sex:F Child# 2 Joseph E Gaudette Nashua, NH & Leocadie Asselin Canada
GAUDETTE, Marie Lucille Paulin, May 12 1928 Sex:F Child# 4 E A Gaudette Nashua, NH & Marie B E Morin Canada
GAUDETTE, Maurice Albert, Mar 30 1934 Sex:M Child# 4 Emile Gaudette Nashua, NH & Eva Hudon Nashua, NH
GAUDETTE, Normand Arthur, Jan 1 1930 Sex:M Child# 3 Moise Gaudette Nashua, NH & Alice Hysette Nashua, NH
GAUDETTE, Normand Robert, Oct 14 1934 Sex:M Child# 8 Delphis Gaudette Nashua, NH & Eliza Pelletier Montreal, PQ
GAUDETTE, Ovila Roger, Dec 16 1928 Sex:M Child# 3 Ovila Gaudette Nashua, NH & Virginia Ricard Canada
GAUDETTE, Paul Joseph, Dec 15 1929 Sex:M Child# 1 Ernest Gaudette Nashua, NH & Viola Gaudette Nashua, NH
GAUDETTE, Reinald Emile, Apr 24 1929 Sex:M Child# 8 Emile Gaudette Nashua, NH & Eva Hudon Nashua, NH
GAUDETTE, Robert Leo, Sep 2 1924 Sex:M Child# 1 Leo Gaudette Nashua, NH & Lea Gendron Canada
GAUDETTE, Rochelle Therese, Nov 6 1924 Sex:F Child# 4 Delphis Gaudette Nashua, NH & Elise Pelletier Montreal, PQ
GAUDETTE, Rockford Robert R, Dec 11 1908 Sex:M Child# 7 Frank Gaudette Nashua, NH & Virginie Jauron Canada
GAUDETTE, Roger Lionel, Nov 24 1927 Sex:M Child# 6 Delphis Gaudette Nashua, NH & Elise Pelletier Canada
GAUDETTE, Roland Henri Joseph, Jun 17 1916 Sex:M Child# 1 Henri Gaudette Nashua, NH & Albina Gervais Nashua, NH
GAUDETTE, Roland R Delphis, Jun 16 1921 Sex:M Child# 2 Delphis Gaudette Nashua, NH & Elise Pelletier Canada
GAUDETTE, Sonia Violetta, Dec 12 1904 Sex:F Child# 4 Frank Gaudette Nashua, NH & Virginie Jauron Canada
GAUDETTE, Theresa Gloria, Nov 3 1929 Sex:F Child# 1 Oscar Gaudette Nashua, NH & Alma Santierre Nashua, NH
GAUDETTE, Unknown, Dec 18 1888 Sex:M Child# 3 Victor Gaudette Canada & Claudia Brien Canada

GAUDETTE, Unknown, May 22 1892 Sex:F Child# 9 David Gaudette Canada & Celina Renaud Canada Stillborn
GAUDETTE, Unknown, Jun 16 1899 Sex:M Child# 6 F X Gaudette Canada & Alexandrine Gravel Nashua, NH Stillborn
GAUDETTE, Unknown, Dec 22 1900 Sex:M Child# 7 Ed Gaudette Canada & Lea Patenaude Mass  Stillborn
GAUDETTE, Yolande Alice, Mar 7 1925 Sex:F Child# 1 Emile Gaudette Nashua, NH & Eva Hudon Nashua, NH
GAUDETTE, Yvonne, Sep 3 1900 Sex:F Child# 3 Victor Gaudette Canada & Helene Dionne Canada
GAUDIN, Marie Demerise, Jun 30 1896 Sex:F Child# 5 Charles Gaudin Canada & Olivine Sirois Canada
GAUDREAU, Arthur Howard, Jul 9 1929 Sex:M Child# 5 Napoleon Gaudreau Webster, MA & Margret Houldsworth England
GAUDREAU, Aurore, Jan 22 1904 Sex:F Child# 2 Edward Gaudreau Canada & Flora Boudreau Lowell, MA
GAUDREAU, E M, Aug 17 1899 Sex:F Child# 2 Paschal Gaudreau Canada & Elizabeth Levesque Canada
GAUDREAU, Irene, Mar 7 1921 Sex:F Child# 3 Napoleon Gaudreau Worcester, MA & Margaret Holesworth England
GAUDREAU, John N, May 15 1914 Sex:M Child# 1 Napoleon Gaudreau Webster, MA & Margaret Holesworth England
GAUDREAU, Joseph J A, Nov 2 1887 Sex:M Child# 2 Adelard Gaudreau P Q & Hermine P Q
GAUDREAU, M Angelina Beatrice, Jul 6 1913 Sex:F Child# 1 George Gaudreau Nashua, NH & Adele St Laurent Canada
GAUDREAU, Marie Eva, May 23 1913 Sex:F Child# 11 Ernest Gaudreau Canada & Marie Louise Vacher Canada
GAUDREAU, Marie Lucille Pearl, Mar 28 1918 Sex:F Child# 3 Jos Geo Gaudreau Mass & Adele St Laurant Canada
GAUDREAU, Marie Viola Annette, Jul 20 1923 Sex:F Child# 5 George Gaudreau Mass & Adele St Laurent Canada
GAUDREAU, Napoleon, Mar 21 1899 Sex:M Child# 1 Napoleon Gaudreau Nashua, NH & Olida Lagace Nashua, NH
GAUDREAU, Pauline, Oct 4 1922 Sex:F Child# 4 Napoleon J Gaudreau Webster, MA & Margaret Houldsworth England
GAUKUBOROSKY, Mary, Jun 28 1907 Sex:F Child# 1 John Gaukuborosky Russia & Lizzie Adams Russia
GAUMONT, Joseph Edouard L, Oct 23 1905 Sex:M Child# 10 Edward Gaumont Canada & P Deschamps Canada
GAUMONT, Unknown, Dec 12 1900 Sex:F Child# 1 Napoleon Gaumont Canada & Marie Parent Canada
GAUNON, Edith Frances, Apr 26 1910 Sex:F Child# 1 Frank A Gaunon Mass & Mary E Campbell Nova Scotia
GAUSKI, Peter, Jul 27 1911 Sex:M Child# 1 Benedict O Gauski Russia & Helen Brososki Russia
GAUTHIER, Abraham, Jan 16 1889 Sex:M Child# 3 A Gauthier Nashua, NH & Henriette Gedour Canada
GAUTHIER, Abraham, Jan 11 1894 Sex:M Child# 7 Rene Gauthier Canada & Orise Bergeron Canada
GAUTHIER, Albert Noel, Dec 31 1924 Sex:M Child# 4 Alferie Gauthier Canada & Marie Rose Oliver Canada
GAUTHIER, Albina, Feb 28 1887 Sex:F Child#  Arthur Gauthier P Q & Amanda Martel P Q
GAUTHIER, Alice Marie A L, May 28 1906 Sex:F Child# 1 Joseph Gauthier Canada & Delfica Charbonneau Canada
GAUTHIER, Alphonsine, Apr 3 1889 Sex:F Child# 10 Jean Gauthier Canada & Marie Belanger Canada
GAUTHIER, Auguste, Aug 17 1892 Sex:M Child# 2 Auguste Gauthier Canada & Marie Martin Canada
GAUTHIER, Celina, Jun 30 1893 Sex:M Child# 15 Clement Gauthier Canada & Pauline Labrie Canada
GAUTHIER, Denise Ann, Aug 20 1918 Sex:F Child# 1 George O Gauthier Newport, VT & Marion Davis Nashua, NH
GAUTHIER, Edward Maurice, Mar 3 1901 Sex:M Child# 10 Pierre Gauthier Canada & Oryse Bergeron Canada
GAUTHIER, Ernest, Jul 24 1889 Sex:M Child# 3 Arthur Gauthier Canada & Amanda Martel Canada
GAUTHIER, Eugenie, Sep 22 1892 Sex:F Child# 13 Jean Gauthier Canada & Marie Belanger Canada
GAUTHIER, Gerald Orin, Mar 24 1926 Sex:M Child# 4 George O Gauthier Newport, VT & Marion Davis Nashua, NH
GAUTHIER, Henry, Apr 8 1891 Sex:M Child# 5 Pierre Gauthier Canada & Orise Bergeron Canada
GAUTHIER, Hermine, Aug 12 1895 Sex:F Child# 3 Abraham Gauthier Nashua, NH & Henriette Ledoux Canada
GAUTHIER, Joseph Alphonse, May 28 1893 Sex:M Child# 1 Alphonse Gauthier Canada & Ernestine Dionne Canada
GAUTHIER, Joseph Conrad, Mar 13 1913 Sex:M Child# 3 Pierre Gauthier NH & Fabiola Rousseau NH
GAUTHIER, Joseph Emile, Feb 7 1891 Sex:M Child# 4 Noel Gauthier Canada & Mary Dionne Canada
GAUTHIER, Joseph Leo, Sep 17 1904 Sex:M Child# 3 Jean B Gauthier Canada & Marie Gagne Canada
GAUTHIER, Joseph Paul Leon, Jun 11 1900 Sex:M Child# 1 Noel Gauthier Canada & Alphonsine Levesque Canada
GAUTHIER, Joseph Willie, Jan 20 1911 Sex:M Child# 1 Pierre Gauthier Nashua, NH & Fabiola Rousseau Nashua, NH
GAUTHIER, Laura, Jan 23 1907 Sex:F Child# 1 (No Parents Listed)
GAUTHIER, Lucille Evelyn, Jul 2 1923 Sex:F Child# 3 George O Gauthier Newport, VT & Marion Davis Nashua, NH
GAUTHIER, M A Irene, Jul 17 1891 Sex:F Child# 4 Arthur Gauthier Canada & Amanda Martel Canada
GAUTHIER, M Alice, Dec 7 1895 Sex:F Child# 5 Pierre Gauthier Canada & Marie Perreault Canada
GAUTHIER, M Fabiola Beatrice, Jul 20 1915 Sex:F Child# 5 Peter Gauthier Nashua, NH & Fabiola Rousseau Nashua, NH
GAUTHIER, M Winifred, Aug 17 1895 Sex:F Child# 6 Arthur Gauthier Canada & Amanda Martel Canada
GAUTHIER, Marie, Jul 6 1909 Sex:F Child# 1 Erase Gauthier Canada & Rosanna Pelletier Canada
GAUTHIER, Marie C, Mar 5 1889 Sex:F Child# 2 Noel Gauthier Canada & Marie Dionne Canada
GAUTHIER, Marie E, Apr 1 1887 Sex:F Child#  Noel Gauthier P Q & Marie Dionne P Q
GAUTHIER, Marie E, Jul 31 1891 Sex:F Child# 12 Jean Gauthier Canada & Marie Belanger Canada
GAUTHIER, Marie Elmire, Jun 27 1892 Sex:F Child# 4 Noel Gauthier Canada & Marie Dionne Canada
GAUTHIER, Marie Ernestine, Dec 1 1895 Sex:F Child# 3 Alphonse Gauthier Canada & Ernestine Dionne Canada
GAUTHIER, Marie Theresa, Nov 10 1929 Sex:F Child# 6 Albert Gauthier Canada & Marie Rose Oliver Canada
GAUTHIER, Mary, Mar 21 1917 Sex:F Child# 6 Peter Gauthier Nashua, NH & Fabiola Rousseau Nashua, NH
GAUTHIER, Norbert Paul, Dec 16 1925 Sex:M Child# 2 Raymond Gauthier Newport, VT & Yvon Delacombe Nashua, NH
GAUTHIER, Oscar Horace, May 10 1922 Sex:M Child# 2 Oscar Gauthier Canada & Eva Brodeur Peterboro, NH
GAUTHIER, Paul Arthur, Jan 27 1922 Sex:M Child# 1 Herman J Gauthier US & Cora A Remillard US
GAUTHIER, Pauline Blanchepp, Aug 1 1919 Sex:F Child# 6 Frank D Gauthier Newport, VT & Mary Murray Newport, VT
GAUTHIER, Peter, Jun 4 1914 Sex:M Child# 4 Peter Gauthier Nashua, NH & Fabiola Rousseau Nashua, NH
GAUTHIER, Pierre, Apr 3 1889 Sex:M Child# 11 Jean Gauthier Canada & Marie Belanger Canada
GAUTHIER, Pierre Marie, Jan 27 1912 Sex:F Child# 2 Pierre Gauthier Nashua, NH & Fabiola Rousseau Nashua, NH
GAUTHIER, Raoul, Jun 23 1932 Sex:M Child# 6 A Gauthier Canada & Marie Oliver Canada
GAUTHIER, Raymond Clarence, Sep 9 1924 Sex:M Child# 1 R Gauthier Newport, VT & Yvonne DeLacombe Nashua, NH
GAUTHIER, Rita Louise, Jul 14 1925 Sex:F Child# 1 Eugene Gauthier Maine & May Tibbetts Milford, MA
GAUTHIER, Roland Claude, Nov 6 1934 Sex:M Child# 4 Raymond C Gauthier Newport, VT & Yvonne Lacombe Nashua, NH
GAUTHIER, Romeo Roland, Dec 26 1930 Sex:M Child# 7 Alberic Gauthier Canada & Rose Olivier Canada
GAUTHIER, Russell Eugene, Apr 17 1934 Sex:M Child# 2 Jos Eugene Gauthier Rumford, ME & May Frances Tibbetts Mi
GAUTHIER, Sylvia Elizabeth, Sep 9 1921 Sex:F Child# 2 George O Gauthier Newport, VT & Marion Davis Nashua, NH
GAUTHIER, Theresa Evelyn, Jul 4 1928 Sex:F Child# 3 Ray Gauthier Newport, VT & Yvonne Lecombe Nashua, NH

GAUTHIER, Unknown, Feb 20 1889 Sex:F Child# 5 Alexandre Gauthier Plattsburg, NY & Ida Celicoure Canada
GAUTHIER, Unknown, Jan 20 1928 Sex:F Child# 5 George Gauthier Newport, VT & Marian Davis Nashua, NH Stillborn
GAUTHIER, Virginia Winifred, Dec 16 1929 Sex:F Child# 2 Herman Gauthier US & Cora Riyor US
GAUTHIER, Wilfred, Feb 13 1892 Sex:M Child# 1 (No Parents Listed)
GAUVIN, Alfred Gerard, Dec 6 1925 Sex:M Child# 4 Alfred Gauvin Canada & Bern Raymond Canada
GAUVIN, Arsene, Jul 1 1893 Sex:M Child# 10 Victor Gauvin Canada & Mathilde Riendeau US
GAUVIN, Horace Adrien, Dec 13 1902 Sex:M Child# 3 Alfred Gauvin Canada & Adrianna Pelletier Canada
GAUVIN, Irene Jeanette, Feb 6 1923 Sex:F Child# 2 Alfred Gauvin Canada & Bernadette Raymond Canada
GAUVIN, John B, Jun 24 1890 Sex:M Child# 2 Alphonse Gauvin Canada & Marie Raymond Canada
GAUVIN, Joseph Alfred H, Jun 25 1900 Sex:M Child# 2 Alfred Gauvin Canada & Adelina Pelletier Canada
GAUVIN, Joseph E, Mar 13 1889 Sex:M Child# 9 Victor Gauvin Canada & Matilda Rendeau Middlebury, VT
GAUVIN, Joseph Etienne, Sep 8 1891 Sex:M Child# 10 Victor Gauvin Canada & Mathilde Reindeau Vermont
GAUVIN, Joseph Henri, Jul 8 1897 Sex:M Child# 12 Victor Gauvin Canada & Methilde Riendeau Canada
GAUVIN, M Alice, Jun 14 1895 Sex:F Child# 11 Victor Gauvin Canada & Matilda Riendeau Middlebury, VT
GAUVIN, M Alice Elmire, Dec 5 1920 Sex:F Child# 1 Alfred Gauvin US & Gracia Archambault US
GAUVIN, Reta Irene, May 21 1924 Sex:F Child# 3 Alfred Gauvin Canada & Ber Raymond Canada
GAUVIN, Unknown, Apr 29 1892 Sex:F Child# 3 Alphonse Gauvin Canada & Marie Raymond Canada Stillborn
GAUZIE, M Rose Anna I, Oct 12 1907 Sex:F Child# 1 Wilfred Gauzie Canada & Cleonphine Hudon Canada
GAVALAS, Agelon, Aug 16 1926 Sex:M Child# 3 Harry Gavalas Greece & K Alimerin Greece
GAY, Arthur Evans, Apr 5 1912 Sex:M Child# 1 Henry K Gay Nashua, NH & Bertha A M Evans Exeter, NH
GAY, Elizabeth W, May 20 1914 Sex:F Child# 2 Henry K Gay Nashua, NH & Bertha A Evans Exeter, NH
GAY, Judith Marie, Jan 29 1935 Sex:F Child# 1 Arthur E Gay Nashua, NH & Marguerite Winn Nashua, NH
GAY, Leon Everett, Feb 21 1896 Sex:M Child#  Edward H Gay New York & Grace E Bassett Nashua, NH
GAY, Leonard Billie, Feb 2 1924 Sex:M Child# 1 Leonard R Gay Nashua, NH & Georginia Lasiel Sudbury, MA
GAY, Leroy Bertram, Jan 6 1897 Sex:M Child# 3 Edward H Gay New York & Grace Barrett Nashua, NH
GAY, Robert Allan, Sep 9 1925 Sex:M Child# 2 Leonard Gay Nashua, NH & Georgianna Lassel Sudbury, MA
GAY, Rolando Leonard, Dec 18 1899 Sex:M Child# 3 Elon R Gay Nashua, NH & Maggie Nolan NH
GAY, Unknown, Aug 5 1887 Sex:F Child# 2 Elcon R Gay Nashua, NH & Kate A Boothby S Windham, ME
GAY, Unknown, Aug 5 1891 Sex:M Child# 4 Elon R Gay Nashua, NH & H Katherine Boothby Waterbury, ME
GAY, Unknown, May 5 1894 Sex:F Child#  Edward H Gay NY & Grace Barrett Nashua, NH
GAY, Unknown, Jun 27 1894 Sex:F Child# 3 Elon R Gay Nashua, NH & Katie C Boothby S Waterboro, ME
GAYETTE, Alfred, Feb 5 1890 Sex:M Child# 10 John Gayette Canada & Nancy Cardin Canada
GAYETTE, Marie Laurie, Aug 23 1896 Sex:F Child# 1 Elzear Gayette Canada & Marie Gregoire Canada
GAYNOR, Peter, Feb 13 1915 Sex:M Child# 7 John Gaynor Russia & Mary Aconawicz Russia
GAYON, Joseph, Dec 9 1888 Sex:M Child# 2 Hypolite Gayon Canada & Philomene Darcour Canada
GAZETTE, Eva, Apr 7 1894 Sex:F Child# 2 Alfred Gazette Mass & Mary Calwar Vermont
GAZETTE, Mary, Feb 25 1898 Sex:F Child# 1 Amos Gazette
GAZUKUVICZ, May, May 15 1906 Sex:F Child# 1 John Gazukuvicz Russia & Caroline Grizintie Russia
GEARY, Joseph Clifford, Oct 2 1934 Sex:M Child# 1 Frederic Geary Everett, MA & Violet Dansereau Merrimack, NH
GEAS, Charles Peter, Sep 23 1935 Sex:M Child# 1 Charles F Geas Greece & Esther E Saunders Leominster, MA
GEAUDREAU, Alice May, Apr 1 1917 Sex:F Child# 2 Napoleon Geaudreau Webster, MA & Margaret Houlsworth Lancashire
GEDDES, Bernice May, Jun 25 1914 Sex:F Child# 3 Melbourne D Geddes NB & Mabel Johnson Quincyport, MA
GEDDES, Leonard Harold, Jan 20 1923 Sex:M Child# 3 Harold J Geddes Ellensburgh, NY & Irene Claudia Dow Carlos,
GEDDES, Paul Kenneth, Aug 2 1926 Sex:M Child# 2 Charles E Geddes Glendale, Montana & Jamie Burns Nashua, NH
GEDDES, Thelma Arlene, Jun 16 1915 Sex:F Child# 4 Melbourne D Geddes New Brunswick & Mabel L Johnson Quincyport, MA
GEDDES, William Charles, Dec 13 1923 Sex:M Child# 1 Charles Geddes Montana & Jennie Burns Nashua, NH
GEDIALIS, Stan, Sep 15 1910 Sex:M Child# 1 Stan Gedialis Russia & Amelia Zobridcuta Russia
GEDOWN, Bernadette E, May 20 1889 Sex:F Child# 5 John Gedown St Albans, VT & Clevina Davis Canada
GEDREMOITES, Anna, Jun 23 1916 Sex:F Child# 5 Stenli Gedremoites Russia & Lewanora Kasparaviri Russia
GEDREN, John, Aug 31 1912 Sex:M Child# 3 Stanislaus Gedren Russia & Lewose Kaspowicot Russia
GEDRINES, Stanislaus, Aug 30 1913 Sex:M Child# 3 Alexander Gedrines Russia & Lewonosa Casparalich Russia
GEELRIGM, Frank, Jul 30 1908 Sex:M Child# 1 Stanislas Geelrigm Russia & Fe'ln'a Koepa'awicoi Russia
GEER, Henra George, Sep 23 1910 Sex:M Child# 3 George Geer Mooers, NY & Eva Carter Collinsville, CT
GEER, Hermon Luther, Aug 30 1917 Sex:M Child# 1 George Geer Bakersfield, VT & Ina Morse Pawtucket, RI
GEER, Unknown, Jul 17 1913 Sex:F Child#  George Geer Mooers, NY & Eva Carter Dover, NH  Stillborn
GEGAS, Nickolas, Jan 21 1925 Sex:M Child# 2 Lewis Gegas Greece & Anastasia Rodolo Greece
GEIGER, Bruce Emile, Jun 1 1930 Sex:M Child# 6 Victor Geiger France & Gertrude Nokes E Pepperell, MA
GEIGER, Leon Oliver, Feb 13 1929 Sex:M Child# 5 Victor Geiger France & Gertrude Nokes Pepperell, MA
GEIGER, Ralph Elton, Jul 8 1932 Sex:M Child# 7 Victor Geiger France & Gertrude Nokes E Pepperell, MA
GEINA, Julia, May 5 1917 Sex:F Child# 8 John Geina Lithuania Russia & Mary Akunawich Lithuania Russia Stillborn
GELINA, Marie Amanda, Oct 10 1891 Sex:F Child# 9 Severe Gelina Canada & Remina Labranche Canada
GELINAS, Alfred L G, May 3 1895 Sex:M Child# 3 Alfred J Gelinas Canada & Clara Jackson Canada
GELINAS, Andrea Cecile, Jun 22 1916 Sex:F Child# 4 Alfred Gelinas Canada & Lida Gendron US
GELINAS, Clara Lydia, Nov 8 1892 Sex:F Child# 2 Alfred Gelinas Canada & Clara Jackson Canada
GELINAS, Edwidge Yvette, Oct 13 1919 Sex:F Child# 5 Alfred Gelinas Canada & Lida Gendron US
GELINAS, Eleonore Germaine, Feb 16 1910 Sex:F Child# 2 Alfred Gelinas Canada & Leda Gendron US
GELINAS, Jeanne Agnes, Jun 8 1912 Sex:F Child# 3 Alfred Gelinas Canada & Edwidge L Gendron US
GELINAS, Jeanne Yvonne, Dec 3 1897 Sex:F Child# 4 Alfred J Gelinas Canada & Clara Jackson Canada
GELINAS, Joseph Alphonse, Sep 9 1899 Sex:M Child# 13 Onesime Gelinas Canada & Victoria Houle Canada
GELINAS, Joseph Thomas, May 12 1892 Sex:M Child# 9 Onesime Gelinas Canada & Victoria Houle Canada
GELINAS, Marie Florida, Jul 20 1902 Sex:F Child# 14 Onesime Gelinas Canada & Victoria Houle Canada
GELINAS, Olivier J, Jan 2 1900 Sex:M Child# 5 Alfred J Gelinas Canada & Clara Jackson Canada
GELINAS, Thomas, Oct 29 1893 Sex:M Child# 11 Onesime Gelinas Canada & Victoria Houle Canada

GELMEAU, Alice Beatrice O, Jun 12 1890 Sex:F Child# 1 Fred Gelmeau Canada & Clara E Jackson Canada
GELOZINAS, Franciskus, Dec 15 1906 Sex:M Child# 1 Nickodimae Gelozinas Russia & Annie Patrickut Russia
GEMMEL, Annie W, Apr 9 1891 Sex:F Child# 6 James Gemmel Scotland & Margaret Blake Scotland
GENDION, Marie, Apr 19 1888 Sex:F Child# 1 Napoleon Gendion Canada & Rosanna Avard Canada
GENDREAU, Adelard Maurice, Jun 24 1933 Sex:M Child# 2 Joseph Gendreau Canada & Florida Leblanc Canada
GENDREAU, Marie Luce Dolores, Oct 24 1931 Sex:F Child# 1 Joseph Gendreau Canada & Florida Leblanc Canada
GENDREAU, Paul Henri, Mar 15 1935 Sex:M Child# 3 Joseph Gendreau Canada & Florida Leblanc Canada
GENDRON, Albert, Feb 19 1921 Sex:M Child# 1 Adelard Gendron Canada & Rose St Laurent Canada
GENDRON, Alexandre, Jul 16 1893 Sex:M Child# 5 Alexandre Gendron Canada & Melanise Lemoine Canada
GENDRON, Alexandre, May 14 1897 Sex:M Child# 4 Alexandre Gendron Canada & Melanie Lemoine US
GENDRON, Alfred, Aug 24 1914 Sex:M Child# 1 Ernest Gendron US & Alice Andron US
GENDRON, Alfred Lucien, Mar 2 1918 Sex:M Child# 5 Henri Gendron US & Vitaline Perreault Canada
GENDRON, Alfred Romeo, Jun 18 1893 Sex:M Child# 1 Georges Gendron Canada & Delia Havard Canada
GENDRON, Alfred Wilfred, May 6 1890 Sex:M Child# 2 Napoleon Gendron Canada & Rosa Havard Canada
GENDRON, Alice, Sep 9 1889 Sex:F Child# 2 John Gendron New York & Eliza Jackson New York
GENDRON, Aliva Napoleon, Sep 7 1902 Sex:M Child# 2 Albert Gendron Canada & Emma Buchur Germany
GENDRON, Alphonsine, May 20 1892 Sex:F Child# 2 Alexandre Gendron Canada & Melanise Lemoine Canada
GENDRON, Anna, May 28 1907 Sex:F Child# 11 Prudent Gendron Canada & Malvina Duchesneau Canada
GENDRON, Armand Napoleon, Nov 5 1902 Sex:M Child# 8 E N Gendron Canada & Rose A Avard Canada
GENDRON, Beatrice Juliette, Jun 11 1904 Sex:F Child# 9 Edmond N Gendron Canada & Rosanna Avard Canada
GENDRON, Bernadette, Apr 5 1892 Sex:F Child# 3 Napoleon Gendron Canada & Rosanna Havard Canada
GENDRON, Camille, Jun 19 1915 Sex:F Child# 3 Joseph Gendron Canada & Alma Paul Nashua, NH
GENDRON, Delia, Feb 24 1889 Sex:F Child# 1 A Gendron Canada & Melenise Gemoine E Brookfield, MA
GENDRON, Dolores Yvonne, Sep 19 1896 Sex:F Child# 5 E N Gendron Canada & Rosanna Avard Canada
GENDRON, Dorothy May, Apr 15 1916 Sex:F Child# 1 Wilfrid A Gendron Nashua, NH & Irene B DeGrenier Shelburne, MA
GENDRON, Eliza, Apr 22 1891 Sex:F Child# 2 Alexandre Gendron Canada & Melanise Lemoine Spencer, MA
GENDRON, Esther Helene, Feb 6 1914 Sex:F Child# 3 Henri Gendron US & Victorine Perreault Canada
GENDRON, Exilda V E, Dec 2 1902 Sex:F Child# 1 Arthur Gendron Canada & Luella Gaudette Nashua, NH
GENDRON, Gertrude, Feb 23 1898 Sex:F Child# 3 George Gendron Canada & Delhia Havard Vergennes, VT
GENDRON, Gertrude Simonne, Apr 7 1923 Sex:F Child# 3 Adelard Gendron Canada & Rose St Laurent Canada
GENDRON, Henri Louis Albert, Jan 17 1915 Sex:M Child# 4 Henri Gendron Nashua, NH & Vitaline Perreault Canada
GENDRON, Henry Georges, Sep 29 1896 Sex:M Child# 4 Jean Gendron Chateauguay, NY & Lizzie Jackson Sciota, NY
GENDRON, Isabelle, Mar 24 1917 Sex:F Child# 10 Narcisse Gendron Canada & Anna Belanger Canada
GENDRON, J Louis Armand, Dec 31 1913 Sex:M Child# 17 Prudent Gendron Canada & Marie Duchesneau Canada
GENDRON, J Ludger Narcisse, Aug 22 1914 Sex:M Child# 2 Narcisse Gendron NH & Laura Pelletier Canada
GENDRON, Jos Albert Adrien, Jun 16 1920 Sex:M Child# 2 Auguste Gendron Canada & Alphee Wheeler NH
GENDRON, Jos Rolland Aug, Feb 7 1919 Sex:M Child# 1 Auguste Gendron Canada & Alphee Wheeler NH
GENDRON, Joseph, Sep 5 1894 Sex:M Child# 6 Alex Gendron Canada & Melanise Lemoine Nashua, NH
GENDRON, Joseph, Nov 15 1902 Sex:M Child# 1 Joseph Gendron Canada & Cydemie Morin NH Stillborn
GENDRON, Joseph, Feb 23 1925 Sex:M Child# 2 Auguste Gendron Canada & Effie Wheeler NH
GENDRON, Joseph Adelard, Mar 8 1908 Sex:M Child# 11 Alexandre Gendron Canada & Georgianna Simard Canada
GENDRON, Joseph Albert, Sep 29 1925 Sex:M Child# 6 Joseph Gendron Canada & Alma Paul Nashua, NH
GENDRON, Joseph Albert Romeo, Feb 7 1920 Sex:M Child# 4 Adelard Gendron Canada & Rose Cloutier Mass
GENDRON, Joseph Alfred, Jul 2 1902 Sex:M Child# 4 John Gendron NY & Lizzie Jackson NY
GENDRON, Joseph Amedee, Jun 16 1902 Sex:M Child# 5 Narcisse Gendron Canada & R D Belanger Canada
GENDRON, Joseph Edgar R, Jan 19 1911 Sex:M Child# 2 Henry Gendron Nashua, NH & Vitaline Perrault Canada
GENDRON, Joseph Ernest, Jan 14 1909 Sex:M Child# 8 Narcisse Gendron Canada & Rose Anna Belanger Canada
GENDRON, Joseph Ernest Paul, Apr 6 1922 Sex:M Child# 3 Auguste Gendron Canada & Effie Wheeler NH
GENDRON, Joseph Lionel Robert, Jan 19 1919 Sex:M Child# 3 Adelard Gendron Canada & Rose Cloutier Mass
GENDRON, Joseph Ormand R, Dec 31 1924 Sex:M Child# 7 Alex Gendron Canada & Marie Rodier Canada
GENDRON, Joseph Rene, Jan 9 1927 Sex:M Child# 3 Joseph Gendron Canada & Margaret Owens Canada
GENDRON, Joseph Romeo R, Feb 8 1924 Sex:M Child# 2 Joseph Gendron Canada & Clarisse Lavoie Canada
GENDRON, Joseph Stanislaus L, Apr 27 1912 Sex:M Child# 15 Prudent Gendron Canada & Malvina Duchesneau Canada
GENDRON, Joseph Sylvio, Jan 8 1912 Sex:M Child# 9 Narcisse Gendron Canada & Rose Delima Belanger Canada
GENDRON, Joseph Sylvio, Nov 29 1916 Sex:M Child# 3 Narcisse Gendron Nashua, NH & Laura Pelletier Canada
GENDRON, Joseph William, Sep 21 1913 Sex:M Child# 2 Joseph P Gendron Canada & Alma Paul Nashua, NH
GENDRON, Laurel Mae, Oct 18 1929 Sex:F Child# 5 Auguste Gendron Canada & Effie Wheeler Farmington, NH
GENDRON, Leo, Mar 5 1909 Sex:M Child# 13 Prudent Gendron Canada & Malvina Duchesneau Canada
GENDRON, Leo Paul, Jun 30 1928 Sex:M Child# 7 Jos Gendron Canada & Alma Paul Nashua, NH
GENDRON, Lewis B, May 22 1906 Sex:M Child# 1 Paul S Gendron W Farnham & Florence Wellman Nashua, NH
GENDRON, Lilian Berthe, Feb 1 1894 Sex:F Child# 4 Napoleon Gendron Canada & Rosanna Havard Canada
GENDRON, Louis Lionel, May 20 1915 Sex:M Child# 2 Alexandre Gendron Canada & Wilhemine Robin Canada
GENDRON, M J Germaine Lil, May 15 1916 Sex:F Child# 1 Phil Ad Gendron Canada & Rose Cloutier Mass
GENDRON, M Olivette Cecile, May 4 1917 Sex:F Child# 2 Adelard P Gendron Canada & Marie Rose Cloutier Mass
GENDRON, Marguerite E, Feb 5 1908 Sex:F Child# 2 Paul Gendron Canada & Flossy Wellman Nashua, NH
GENDRON, Marie Anna, Jul 10 1899 Sex:F Child# 8 Alexandre Gendron Canada & Melanise Lemoine Nashua, NH
GENDRON, Marie Aurore, Nov 2 1897 Sex:F Child# 3 Narcisse Gendron Canada & Rose D Belanger Canada
GENDRON, Marie Germaine, Oct 31 1910 Sex:F Child# 13 Joseph Gendron Canada & Marie Simard Canada
GENDRON, Marie Gertrude, Feb 12 1922 Sex:F Child# 2 Adelard Gendron Canada & Rose St Laurent Canada
GENDRON, Marie Jeanette, Jan 27 1905 Sex:F Child# 6 Narcisse Gendron Canada & Anna Belanger Canada
GENDRON, Marie Jennie Alma, Feb 1 1918 Sex:F Child# 4 Joseph Gendron Canada & Alma Paul NH
GENDRON, Marie Lorette, Apr 2 1907 Sex:F Child# 7 Narcisse Gendron Canada & Rose D Belanger Canada
GENDRON, Marie Lorette Simonn, Mar 18 1923 Sex:F Child# 6 Alexander Gendron Canada & Marie Robin Canada

GENDRON, Marie Pearl Muriel, Oct 13 1926 Sex:F Child# 8 Alexander Gendron Canada & Marie Robin Canada
GENDRON, Marie Yvonne, May 24 1910 Sex:F Child# 14 Prudent Gendron Canada & Malvina Duchesneau Canada
GENDRON, Mary Lillian, Jul 15 1903 Sex:F Child# 1 Nelson Gendron NH & Margaret Tafe NH
GENDRON, Mary Theresa Rita, Oct 20 1926 Sex:F Child# 9 Alphonse Gendron Canada & Rosana Ouillette Canada
GENDRON, Napoleon W, Jan 18 1896 Sex:M Child# 2 Georges Gendron Canada & Delia Havard Canada
GENDRON, Narcisse, Dec 24 1892 Sex:M Child# 1 Narcisse Gendron Canada & Rose D Belanger Canada
GENDRON, Olive Olivette, Jul 27 1900 Sex:F Child# 7 E N Gendron Canada & Rosanna Avard Canada
GENDRON, Pauline, Feb 27 1935 Sex:F Child# 1 Honore Gendron Nashua, NH & Lucille Poliquin Nashua, NH
GENDRON, Raymond Alphonse, Jun 14 1934 Sex:M Child# 2 Alphonse J Gendron Canada & Evelyn Nadreau Keene, NH
GENDRON, Raymond Aug, Sep 13 1904 Sex:M Child# 2 Arthur Gendron Canada & Lowella Gaudette Nashua, NH
GENDRON, Robert Paul Ernest, Aug 3 1933 Sex:M Child# 1 Ernest Gendron Nashua, NH & Annette Fagnant Greenville, NH
GENDRON, Roland Wilfrid, Oct 1 1926 Sex:M Child# 1 Alphonse Gendron Canada & J Lampron Nashua, NH
GENDRON, Rosanna, Apr 22 1891 Sex:F Child# 3 Alexandre Gendron Canada & Melanise Lemoine Spencer, MA
GENDRON, Rose Delima, Sep 3 1894 Sex:F Child# 2 Narcisse Gendron Canada & Rose D Belanger Canada
GENDRON, Silvio Arthur, Aug 12 1898 Sex:M Child# 6 Napoleon Gendron Canada & Rosanna Harvard Canada
GENDRON, Unknown, Nov 19 1889 Sex:M Child# 12 Octave Gendron Canada & Eulalie Caouette Canada Stillborn
GENDRON, Unknown, Dec 18 1907 Sex:M Child# 12 Prudent Gendron Canada & Malvina Duchesneau Canada
GENDRON, Unknown, May 31 1908 Sex:M Child# 1 Henry Gendron Nashua, NH & Vitaline Perreault Canada Stillborn
GENDRON, Unknown, Apr 26 1924 Sex:M Child# 4 Adelard Gendron Canada & Rose St Laurent Canada
GENDRON, Unknown, Sep 23 1924 Sex:M Child# 1 Alphonse Gendron Canada & Rose A Ouellette Canada Stillborn
GENDRON, Walter Floyd, Jul 12 1919 Sex:M Child# 2 Wilfred R Gendron Nashua, NH & Irene Degrenier Shelburne, MA
GENDRON, William Edward, Oct 4 1917 Sex:M Child# 2 Egide Gendron Canada & Julia Gadbois Nashua, NH
GENEST, Bertha Loraine Olive, Aug 29 1920 Sex:F Child# 1 Arthur Genest Nashua, NH & Yvonne Levesque Nashua, NH
GENEST, Gerard, Apr 29 1912 Sex:M Child# 2 Joseph Genest Salem, MA & Sarah Benoit Nashua, NH
GENEST, Joseph Romeo Donat, May 18 1918 Sex:M Child# 4 David Genest Pittsfield, NH & Avon Roy Nashua, NH
GENEST, Louis Philippe, Dec 31 1914 Sex:M Child# 1 David Genest Pittsfield, NH & Yvonne Roy Nashua, NH
GENEST, Marie, Jun 4 1899 Sex:F Child# 8 Ernest Genest Canada & Alvina Poisson Canada
GENEST, Mary Florence, Feb 28 1917 Sex:F Child# 3 David Genest NH & Evon Roy NH
GENEST, Paul Emile, Oct 4 1928 Sex:M Child# 2 Arthur Genest Nashua, NH & Y Levesque Nashua, NH
GENEST, Rita Cecille, Jun 12 1919 Sex:F Child# 5 David Genest Pittsfield, NH & Yvonne Roy Nashua, NH
GENGELESKI, Edward, Dec 8 1923 Sex:M Child# 4 Edward Gengeleski Poland & Annie Goletaski Poland
GENKA, Eva, Mar 14 1923 Sex:F Child# 1 Peter Genka Russia & Eva Kudzles Russia
GENKA, Lodig, Jan 15 1924 Sex:M Child# 2 Peter Genka Poland & Eva Kudolis Poland
GENNET, Alfred W, Jun 1 1889 Sex:M Child# 1 William Gennet NY & Agnes Hamilton NY
GENO, Priscilla Phenician, Sep 13 1912 Sex:F Child# 5 Edmund H Geno Pittsford, VT & Ellen Wood Sweden
GENSBURG, Cherry, Mar 8 1891 Sex:F Child# 2 Benjamin Gensburg Russia & Rebecca Lulinski Russia
GENTILLY, Margaret Leona, May 31 1906 Sex:F Child# 1 Edward A Gentilly NH & Agnes McLaughlin Mass
GEORGE, Clark Evans, Feb 13 1933 Sex:M Child# 1 Frank E George Nashua, NH & Jean McDuffee Nashua, NH
GEORGE, Flora E, Sep 19 1893 Sex:F Child# 5 W A George Maine & Myra A Hoagg NH
GEORGE, Henry Carlton, Oct 3 1904 Sex:M Child# 9 William A George Danvers, MA & Maria Hoag Boscawen, NH
GEORGE, Henry L, Mar 11 1891 Sex:M Child# 1 Joseph George England & Helen Sheridan Canada
GEORGE, James L, Nov 1 1898 Sex:M Child# 7 W A George Maine & Myra A Hoagg Nashua, NH
GEORGE, Janice, Sep 11 1927 Sex:F Child# 1 Henry George Nashua, NH & Alice Maker Nashua, NH
GEORGE, Marion Louise, Oct 7 1912 Sex:F Child# 3 Willian N George Fitchburg, MA & Ruby Livingston Nashua, NH
GEORGE, Nellie Livingston, Nov 30 1908 Sex:F Child# 1 William H George Pittsburg, MA & Caroline Livingston Nashua
GEORGE, Robert Harold, Sep 30 1910 Sex:M Child# 2 William H George NH & Ruby C Livingstone Nashua, NH
GEORGE, Unknown, Oct 9 1889 Sex:M Child# 2 Herbert A George Gardner, MA & Annie H George Brighton, MA
GEORGEGEAN, Kostas, Jul 28 1913 Sex:M Child# 2 George Georgegean Greece & Angela Bill Greece
GEORGOPOULOS, George, Feb 12 1933 Sex:M Child# 6 D Georgopoulos Greece & G Kautulas Greece
GEORGOPOULOS, James, Jul 13 1924 Sex:M Child# 1 James Georgopoulos Greece & Gertrude Banajes Greece
GERARD, Georgiana, Mar 9 1920 Sex:F Child# 1 George Gerard Nashua, NH & Delia Rousseau Nashua, NH
GERARD, Ronald, Sep 25 1932 Sex:M Child# 1 (No Parents Listed)
GERETY, Elizabeth Margaret, Jun 15 1892 Sex:F Child# 1 James Gerety Ireland & Lucy E Burns Nashua, NH
GERETY, Philip, Jul 5 1893 Sex:M Child# 2 James Gerety Ireland & Lucy E Burns Nashua, NH
GERICHARD, Elzeard, May 28 1890 Sex:M Child# 3 Joseph Gerichard Canada & Aglae Canada
GERITY, Ann, Jul 7 1922 Sex:F Child# 2 William Gerity Manchester, England & Christina Tyffe Dundee, Scotland
GERITY, William, May 2 1921 Sex:M Child# 1 William Gerity Manchester, England & Christina Tyffe Dundee, Scotland
GERMAIN, Eva, Jun 9 1908 Sex:F Child# 3 Hervey Germain Canada & Philomene Levesque Canada
GERMAIN, Marie Annette, Jul 20 1900 Sex:F Child# 2 Philippe Germain Canada & Aurea Rambault Canada
GERMAIN, Philippe Leo, Mar 13 1907 Sex:M Child# 2 Harvey Germain Canada & Philomene Levesque Canada
GERMAIN, Rose Alice, Aug 1 1898 Sex:F Child# 1 Philias Germain Canada & Rhea Grandbois Canada
GERMINO, Robert Michael, Apr 12 1934 Sex:M Child# 1 Joseph Germino Quincy, MA & Mary Infante Milford, NH
GERNER, Monica, Aug 15 1910 Sex:F Child# 2 John Gerner Russia & Mary Acumin Russia
GERON, Donald Robert, May 24 1931 Sex:M Child# 2 Nelson Geron Vermont & Lena O'Neil Nashua, NH
GERONARD, Marie A, May 17 1891 Sex:F Child# 8 Philias Geronard Canada & Mathilde Bellerose Canada
GEROU, Robert Lyman, Mar 12 1932 Sex:M Child# 1 Bernice Gerou US & Collette LaPlante Canada
GEROUX, Joseph Philips, May 30 1933 Sex:M Child# 2 Bernice Geroux Vermont & Colette Laplante New Britain, CT
GEROUX, Mary Janet, Nov 15 1934 Sex:F Child# 3 Bernice Geroux Vermont & Collette Laplante New Britain, CT
GEROW, Nelson Charles, Feb 28 1927 Sex:M Child# 1 Nelson Gerow Sharon, VT & Lena O'Neil Nashua, NH
GERSOM, Elizabeth, Sep 28 1893 Sex:F Child# 13 Stephen Gersom US & Josephine Vian Canada
GERTRUDE, Silla, Jul 23 1919 Sex:F Child# 4 Lewis Gertrude Canada & Cora W Warren New Boston, NH
GERVAIS, Albina, Feb 23 1896 Sex:F Child# 4 Noe Gervais Canada & Elmire Levesque Canada
GERVAIS, Alma Elmire, Jan 9 1894 Sex:F Child# 3 Noe Gervais Canada & Elmire Levesque Canada

GERVAIS, Denis, Jun 12 1905 Sex:M Child# 7 Denis Gervais Canada & Albina Desmarais Canada
GERVAIS, Edouard Raymond, Apr 25 1921 Sex:M Child# 1 George Gervais Nashua, NH & Rose Anna Morin Canada
GERVAIS, Elmire Irene, Feb 16 1911 Sex:F Child# 12 George Gervais N Adams, MA & Elmire Canada
GERVAIS, Emma, Oct 19 1906 Sex:F Child# 2 Edward Gervais Canada & Malvina Charron Nashua, NH
GERVAIS, George, Feb 25 1892 Sex:M Child# 2 Noe Gervais Canada & Elmire Levesque Canada
GERVAIS, Irene, Mar 14 1901 Sex:F Child# 6 George Gervais Canada & Hermine Levesque Canada
GERVAIS, Joseph, Jul 29 1893 Sex:M Child# 5 Louis Gervais US & Elise Gosselin Canada
GERVAIS, Joseph N, Apr 12 1891 Sex:M Child# 3 Louis N Gervais Glens Falls, NY & Elise Gosselin Canada
GERVAIS, Joseph Wilfred, May 19 1902 Sex:M Child# 7 George N Gervais Canada & Elmire Levesque Canada
GERVAIS, Lilian Beatrice, Oct 20 1907 Sex:F Child# 10 Noe Gervais Canada & Elmire Levesque Canada
GERVAIS, Marie A Ivonne, Aug 21 1897 Sex:F Child# Alphonse Gervais Canada & Marie Russeau Canada
GERVAIS, Marie Elizabeth, Mar 5 1895 Sex:F Child# 6 Louis Gervais New York & Elise Gasselin Canada
GERVAIS, Marie R, Jan 10 1891 Sex:F Child# 9 Onesime Gervais Canada & Georgie Grandmont Canada
GERVAIS, Paul Donald, Aug 16 1930 Sex:M Child# 3 George Gervais Nashua, NH & Rosanna Morin Canada
GERVAIS, Pearl Therese, Oct 15 1923 Sex:F Child# 2 George C Gervais Nashua, NH & R A Morin Canada
GERVAIS, Richard Allen Steven, Apr 6 1926 Sex:M Child# 1 Alexander Gervais
GERVAIS, Rosanna, Aug 12 1889 Sex:F Child# 8 Onestime Gervais Canada & Georgina Moranda Champlain, NY
GERVAIS, Unknown, Aug 20 1906 Sex:M Child# 9 Georges Gervais Canada & Elmire Levesque Canada Stillborn
GERVAIS, Yvonne Lorette, Sep 2 1904 Sex:F Child# 8 Noe Gervais Canada & Elmire Levesque Canada
GERVAISE, Alfred, Aug 26 1890 Sex:M Child# 1 Noe Gervaise Canada & Elmire Levesque Canada
GERVAISE, Joseph Edw E, May 30 1896 Sex:M Child# 8 Joseph Gervaise Canada & Flore Gosselin Canada
GERWARD, Unknown, Jun 21 1889 Sex:F Child# 4 James Gerward Scotland & Maggie Blake Scotland
.GESELAWITCH, Stanley, Mar 18 1917 Sex:M Child# 1 Anthony Geselawitch Lithuania Russia & Antonia Cackla Lithuania
GESIRKAWITCH, John, Dec 31 1916 Sex:M Child# 3 Jos Gesirkawitch Russia & Anthosa Sereizick Russia
GESNKAWICZ, Peter, Sep 18 1916 Sex:M Child# 9 Joseph Gesnkawicz Russia & Agne Kaschetta Russia
GESTER, Norman Roland, Sep 3 1921 Sex:M Child# 2 Henry Gester Belmont, NH & Lea Rioux Nashua, NH
GESUKANVICZ, Annie, Jan 26 1914 Sex:F Child# 1 Joseph Gesukanvicz Russia & Antonina Svreiczik Russia
GESUKAVITCH, Joe, Sep 27 1910 Sex:M Child# 5 John Gesukavitch Russia & Carolina Gregiuta Russia
GESUKAVITCH, John, Aug 26 1910 Sex:M Child# 5 Julius Gesukavitch Russia & Benigna Tamolavitch Russia
GESUKAVITCH, Rosa, Aug 28 1909 Sex:F Child# 4 Julius Gesukavitch Russia & Beuigna Tamalonis Russia
GESUKAWICZ, Josephine, Mar 11 1912 Sex:F Child# 6 John Gesukawicz Russia & Carolina Gregiuta Russia
GETMAN, William H, Mar 22 1901 Sex:M Child# 1 Alfred Getman New York & Sadie H Olena New York
GEURAIN, Unknown, Dec 7 1898 Sex:M Child# 1 John Guerain NY & Alice Ladue Nashua, NH Stillborn
GHEDONE, Bruce Earl, May 2 1934 Sex:M Child# 1 Walter Earl Ghedone Wolfeboro Falls, NH & Charlotte Phelps Nashua
GIBBONS, Barbara, Dec 15 1925 Sex:F Child# 2 J J Gibbons, Jr Milford, NH & Louise Duinmett Liverpool, England
GIBBONS, Margaret Delima, Jul 30 1934 Sex:F Child# 1 Bernard Gibbons Wilton, NH & Gabriel Bergeron Canada
GIBBONS, Norma, Sep 14 1896 Sex:F Child# 6 Charles Gibbons Ireland & Margaret A Fralick Ireland
GIBBONS, Priscilla Anne, Nov 7 1934 Sex:F Child# 1 Lawrence Gibbons Wilton, NH & Mildred Boutwell Wilton, NH
GIBSON, Barbara Jean, Oct 14 1924 Sex:F Child# 1 H E Gibson Windham, NH & Cynthia L Casper Cambridge, MA
GIBSON, Cora Alice, Nov 27 1893 Sex:F Child# 5 E J Gibson St Almonds, PQ & Emma A Willard Littleton
GIBSON, Esther, Mar 28 1894 Sex:F Child# 2 Elmer T Gibson NY & Isabelle Eastman Nashua, NH
GIBSON, Ethel Speare, May 10 1896 Sex:F Child# 1 Henry Gibson Nashua, NH & Sadie Speare Danbury
GIBSON, George Alwis, Jun 27 1895 Sex:M Child# 1 Alwis A Gibson Rindge, NH & Georgiana Card Brunswick, ME
GIBSON, Horace D, Jun 14 1898 Sex:M Child# 1 Aliois A Gibson Rindge, NH & Ada Nolan Webster, MA
GIBSON, John Robert, Jun 23 1911 Sex:M Child# 2 Charles W Gibson Ausable Forks, NY & Grace E Smith Burke, NY
GIBSON, Paul Babcock, Mar 9 1908 Sex:M Child# 1 Charles W Gibson Ausable Forks, NY & Grace E Smith Burke, NY
GIBSON, Paul Babcock, Jan 19 1932 Sex:M Child# 1 Paul B Gibson Nashua, NH & Lora Whitney Worcester, MA
GIBSON, Richard Earl, Nov 2 1925 Sex:M Child# 2 Henry E Gibson Windham, NH & Cynthia Cooper Cambridge, MA
GIBSON, Unknown, Feb 26 1887 Sex:F Child# 5 James W Gibson Richford, VT & Nettie
GIBSON, Unknown, Jun 27 1890 Sex:M Child# 6 Jeremiah Gibson Richford, VT & Nellie Damon Bedford, NH
GIBSON, Unknown, Mar 17 1892 Sex:M Child# 1 E T Gibson NY & Mary E Eastman NH
GIDDESS, Helen Frances, Jan 23 1921 Sex:F Child# 2 Harold Giddess Ellenburg, NY & Irene Dow Minnesota
GIDGE, Lester, Apr 2 1917 Sex:M Child# 1 Harvey Gidge London, England & Blanch Askham Sheffield, England
GIDGE, Natalie, Feb 3 1922 Sex:F Child# 4 Harry Gidge England & Blanche Askham England
GIDGE, Norman, Feb 28 1920 Sex:M Child# 3 Harry Gidge England & Blanche Askham England
GIDGE, Ralph, Oct 19 1925 Sex:M Child# 5 Harry Gidge England & Blanche Askham England
GIDGE, Raymond, Aug 4 1918 Sex:M Child# 2 Harry Gidge Fulham, England & Blanche Askham Sheffield, England
GIDGE, William, Dec 22 1931 Sex:M Child# 7 Harry Gidge England & Blanche Askham England
GIDIE, Julius, Jun 16 1900 Sex:M Child# 1 Peter Gidie Russia & Krisia Jazukenic Russia
GIES, Agnes, Jan 2 1910 Sex:F Child# 1 Peter Gies Russia & Eliza Voluntukavitch Russia
GILBERT, Adelard Arthur Josep, Jan 9 1925 Sex:M Child# 3 Arthur Jos Gilbert Proctor, VT & Mary Galipeau Nashua, NH
GILBERT, Arthur Maurice, Feb 28 1931 Sex:M Child# 5 Albert Gilbert Graniteville, NH & Bernadette Brodeur Nashua, NH
GILBERT, Donald Oliver, Sep 29 1932 Sex:M Child# 4 Frank Gilbert Proctor, VT & Florida Colle Suncook, NH
GILBERT, Dorothy May, Sep 13 1921 Sex:F Child# 2 Louis Gilbert Vermont & Albina Aubertin NH
GILBERT, Edward, Mar 24 1925 Sex:M Child# 2 George Gilbert Proctor, VT & Marcia Bruce Hudson, NH
GILBERT, Edward Paul, Jan 19 1927 Sex:M Child# 2 Wilfred Gilbert Proctor, VT & Obeline Delorme Nashua, NH
GILBERT, Elnora, Feb 2 1911 Sex:F Child# Charles H Gilbert Coventry, VT & Bertha M Dion Vermont
GILBERT, Evaline Mildred, Apr 4 1920 Sex:F Child# 5 Charles H Gilbert Proctor, VT & Bertha Henson Plattsburg, NY
GILBERT, Frank Edward, May 25 1925 Sex:M Child# 2 Frank A Gilbert Proctor, VT & Florida Call Suncook, NH
GILBERT, George Hartshorn, Jul 8 1900 Sex:M Child# 1 Charles H Gilbert VT & Bertha A Dionne VT
GILBERT, Henry Louis, Mar 30 1924 Sex:M Child# 3 Louis I Gilbert Proctor, VT & Albina Aubertin Pittsfield, NH
GILBERT, James Allen, Jul 7 1935 Sex:M Child# 6 Arthur Gilbert Vermont & Adrienne Galipeau Nashua, NH
GILBERT, Janet, Aug 22 1932 Sex:F Child# 5 Albert Gilbert Proctor, VT & A Galipeau Nashua, NH

GILBERT, Laura Lucille, Mar 28 1928 Sex:F Child# 3 Albert Gilbert Graniteville, VT & Bernadette Brodeur Nashua, NH
GILBERT, Leona Elizabeth, May 12 1924 Sex:F Child# 1 Frank O Gilbert Proctor, VT & Florida Colt Suncook, NH
GILBERT, M B Ernestine, Sep 6 1921 Sex:F Child# 2 Arthur J Gilbert Proctor, VT & Adrienne Galipeau Nashua, NH
GILBERT, Mary Hilda Irene, Jan 18 1934 Sex:F Child# 1 Heine Gilbert Woonsocket, RI & Amelia Denault Canada
GILBERT, Richard Louis, May 1 1930 Sex:M Child# 4 Arthur Gilbert Proctor, VT & Adrienne Galipeau Nashua, NH
GILBERT, Robert Albert, Jul 9 1929 Sex:M Child# 4 Albert Gilbert Graniteville, VT & Bernadette Brodeur Nashua, NH
GILBERT, Robert Girard, May 6 1931 Sex:M Child# Wilfred L Gilbert Proctor, VT & Obeline E Delorme Nashua, NH
GILBERT, Roland Adelard, Apr 17 1924 Sex:M Child# 1 Wilfred L Gilbert Proctor, VT & Obeline E Delorme Nashua,
GILBERT, Theresa Lorraine, Oct 15 1926 Sex:F Child# 2 Albert Gilbert Graniteville, VT & B Brodeur Nashua, NH
GILBERT, Unknown, Apr 13 1887 Sex:M Child# 3 Charles Gilbert Maine & Ella Maine
GILBERT, Unknown, Jun 25 1923 Sex:M Child# 1 George E Gilbert Proctor, VT & Marcia H Bruce Hudson, NH Stillborn
GILBERT, Unknown, May 2 1925 Sex:F Child# 1 Albert Gilbert Barre, VT & Berna Brodeur Nashua, NH
GILBERT, William Louis, Sep 11 1919 Sex:M Child# 1 William Gilbert Russia & Agnes Topor Ware, MA
GILBODY, Evelyn Jean, Jul 13 1917 Sex:F Child# 4 William Gilbody Milton, MA & Laura Putney Billerica, MA
GILBODY, Foster Francis, Aug 11 1912 Sex:M Child# 2 William S Gilbody Milton, MA & Laura M Putney Billerica, MA
GILBODY, Roger William, Jun 6 1914 Sex:M Child# 3 William Gilbody Milton, MA & Laura Pritney Billerica, MA
GILE, Tony, Sep 12 1905 Sex:F Child# 1 J H Gile Haverhill & Maggie Clark England
GILES, Charles Henry, Jun 19 1933 Sex:M Child# 4 Charles Giles Ellenburg, NY & Marion Smith Lawrence, MA
GILES, Doris Helen, Feb 14 1928 Sex:F Child# 3 Charles Giles New York & Marion Smith Lawrence, MA
GILES, Dorothy May, Oct 17 1921 Sex:F Child# 6 William G Giles Lion Mt, NY & Bertha Nealy Francestown, NH
GILES, Earl Grant, Apr 15 1911 Sex:M Child# 1 William G Giles Lyon Mt, NY & Bertha Annie Nealey Francestown, NH
GILES, Kenneth, Mar 14 1924 Sex:M Child# 2 Charles Giles Elmburgh, NY & Marion Smith Lawrence, MA
GILES, Lucille Mary, Apr 15 1922 Sex:F Child# 1 Charles Giles New York & Mary Smith Lawrence, MA
GILES, Lucinda, Jul 2 1913 Sex:F Child# 1 James E Giles Ellenburgh, NY & Mary A Mahoney Pepperell, MA
GILES, Marilyn, Jun 4 1935 Sex:F Child# 3 Ralph Giles Lawrence, MA & Alice Hurley Dover, NH
GILES, Mildred Lucille, Jul 19 1913 Sex:F Child# 2 William G Giles Ellenburgh, NY & Bertha Nealey Francestown, NH
GILES, Ralph Regis, Dec 11 1932 Sex:M Child# 2 Ralph J Giles Lawrence, MA & Alice Hurley Dover, NH
GILES, Richard Chamberlain, Jul 28 1922 Sex:M Child# 2 Solon C Giles Ellenburg, NY & Ethel A Anderson Nashua, NH
GILES, Robert Anderson, Jul 4 1921 Sex:M Child# 1 Solon C Giles Ellenburg, NY & Ethel Anderson Nashua, NH
GILES, Unknown, Jan 8 1916 Sex:F Child# 3 James E Giles Ellenburgh, NY & Mary Mahoney Pepperell, MA
GILES, Wilbur Howard, Jun 24 1919 Sex:M Child# 5 William Giles Lion Mt, NY & Bertha Nealey Francestown, NH
GILHOOLEY, Mary, Jan 22 1895 Sex:F Child# 2 Michael Gilhooley Ireland & Bridget Gaffney Ireland
GILHOOLEY, Thomas, Jul 24 1893 Sex:M Child# 1 Michael Gilhooley Ireland & Bridget Gaffney Ireland
GILHOOLY, Thomas James, Sep 10 1901 Sex:M Child# 1 Patrick G Gilhooly Ireland & Katherine McKeon Ireland
GILHOOLY, Unknown, Jan 26 1887 Sex:M Child# 2 Thomas Gilhooly Ireland & Mary Ireland
GILIZOWSKI, Unknown, Oct 4 1916 Sex:F Child# 4 Konstant Gilizowski Russia & Rachael Cippant Russia
GILL, Sophia, Dec 9 1922 Sex:F Child# 2 Julius Gill Poland & Stasia Kilva Poland
GILL, Wadislaw, Aug 31 1924 Sex:M Child# 3 Julius Gill Poland & Stanis Kelawa Poland
GILLERY, Juliette Lillian, Sep 22 1905 Sex:F Child# 1 Arthur Gillery Canada & Delia Ledoux Canada
GILLET, Isabelle I B A, Nov 13 1889 Sex:F Child# 1 Noel E Gillet Canada & Eliza M Lessard Canada
GILLETTE, Robert Vaughan, Apr 26 1920 Sex:M Child# 3 Edwin J Gillette Waterbury, CT & Frances W Anderson Lowell, MA
GILLETTE, Thomas Winthrop, Sep 26 1935 Sex:M Child# 2 Winthrop Gillette Lyme, CT & Mary Murphy Brockton, MA
GILLIS, Unknown, Apr 26 1920 Sex:M Child# 1 Eddy C Gillis Westmoreland, NH & Lucia Humphrey Hartland, VT
GILLOOLY, Edward, Aug 28 1890 Sex:M Child# 4 Tom Gillooly Ireland & Mary McAnnery Ireland
GILMAN, Horace E, Apr 14 1892 Sex:M Child# 2 William V Gilman Albany, NY & Lizzie A Whitney Nashua, NH
GILMAN, James H, Dec 8 1888 Sex:M Child# 2 Alfred Gilman Canada & Regena Demaris Canada
GILMAN, Katherine Anne, Mar 4 1919 Sex:F Child# 1 James Bruce Gilman Lowell, MA & Essa M Starkweather Peru, ME
GILMAN, Lucille Edith, Apr 20 1913 Sex:F Child# 5 George E Gilman Lowell, MA & Eva Burnham Champlain, NY
GILMAN, Nina Maud, Jan 31 1908 Sex:F Child# 3 George E Gilman Three Rivers, Canada & Eva M Burnham Champlain, NY
GILMAN, Robert Emmett, Apr 13 1910 Sex:M Child# 4 George E Gilman Lowell, MA & Eva Burnham Champlain, NY
GILMAN, Theodore Arthur, Dec 18 1914 Sex:M Child# 6 George Gilman Lowell, MA & Eva May Burnham Chazy, NY
GILMAN, Xavier Henri, Dec 19 1890 Sex:M Child# 5 Victor Gilman Canada & Emma Desmarais Canada
GILMARTIN, Richard Edward, Aug 14 1921 Sex:M Child# 2 Edwin Gilmartin Nashua, NH & Abbie Adams Milford, NH
GILMETTE, Joseph Albert, Nov 28 1891 Sex:M Child# 2 Joseph Gilmette Canada & Marie Gilmet Canada
GILMORE, Annie Theresa, Nov 10 1908 Sex:F Child# 2 Patrick Gilmore Ireland & Annie Eagan Ireland
GILMORE, Joan Thomasine, Feb 16 1933 Sex:F Child# 1 J F Gilmore Nashua, NH & Alice Adams Atlantic Ocean
GILMORE, John F, Feb 7 1910 Sex:M Child# 3 Patrick Gilmore Ireland & Annie Eagan Ireland
GILMORE, John Thomas, Apr 25 1903 Sex:M Child# 2 Michael Gilmore Ireland & Mary A F Moran Nashua, NH
GILMORE, Joseph, Oct 3 1924 Sex:M Child# 13 M F Gilmore Ireland & Mary A Moran Nashua, NH
GILMORE, Katherine May, Jul 16 1914 Sex:F Child# 5 Patrick Gilmore Ireland & Annie Egan Ireland
GILMORE, Lillian, Jan 22 1902 Sex:F Child# 1 Michael Gilmore Ireland & Mary F Moran Nashua, NH
GILMORE, Madeline, Oct 1 1916 Sex:F Child# 5 Patrick J Gilmore Ireland & Annie Fagan Ireland
GILMORE, Marguerite, Jul 16 1904 Sex:F Child# 3 Michael J Gilmore Ireland & Mary E Moran Nashua, NH
GILMORE, Mary, Mar 6 1920 Sex:F Child# 10 Michael J Gilmore Ireland & Mary A Moran Nashua, NH
GILMORE, Mathilda May, Jan 13 1908 Sex:F Child# 4 Michael Gilmore Ireland & Mary A Moran Nashua, NH
GILMORE, Michael, Apr 28 1922 Sex:M Child# 11 Michael Gilmore Ireland & Mary A Moran Nashua, NH Stillborn
GILMORE, Michael Francis, Dec 14 1908 Sex:M Child# 5 Michael J Gilmore Ireland & Mary F Moran Nashua, NH
GILMORE, Robert Patrick, Mar 28 1918 Sex:M Child# 6 Patrick Gilmore Ireland & Annie Eagan Ireland
GILMORE, Robert Patrick, Jul 20 1918 Sex:M Child# 6 Michael Gilmore Ireland & Mary F Moran Nashua, NH
GILMORE, Ruth, Feb 5 1917 Sex:F Child# 10 Michael J Gilmore Ireland & Mary P Moran Nashua, NH Stillborn
GILMORE, Thomas Joseph, Jul 23 1912 Sex:M Child# 3 Patrick J Gilmore Ireland & Annie Eagan Ireland
GILMORE, Thomaseine Flora, Jul 3 1935 Sex:F Child# 1 Thomas Gilmore Nashua, NH & Elvera Bernasconi Milford, NH
GILMORE, Unknown, Jul 28 1911 Sex:F Child# 6 Michael J Gilmore Ireland & Mary A F Moran Nashua, NH Stillborn

GILMORE, Unknown, Jul 5 1912 Sex:M Child# 7 Michael J Gilmore Ireland & Mary A Moran Nashua, NH Stillborn
GILMORE, Unknown, Oct 16 1914 Sex:M Child# 9 Michael Gilmore Ireland & Mary A F Moran Nashua, NH Stillborn
GILMORE, Unknown, Sep 24 1915 Sex:F Child# 9 Michael Gilmore Ireland & Mary F Moran Nashua, NH Stillborn
GILMORE, Unknown, Aug 26 1920 Sex:M Child# 8 Patrick Gilmore Ireland & Annie Eagon Ireland Stillborn
GILMORE, Unknown, Aug 18 1923 Sex:M Child# 13 Michael Gilmore Ireland & Mary A Moran Nashua, NH Stillborn
GILMORE, Unknown, Nov 30 1927 Sex:M Child# 13 M F Gilmore Ireland & Mary F Moran Nashua, NH Stillborn
GILMORE, Walter Fred, Jun 11 1920 Sex:M Child# 1 Walter F Gilmore W Acton, MA & Gladys V Lockwood Albany, NY
GILORE, Unknown, Nov 27 1890 Sex:F Child# 2 M J Gilore Nashua, NH & Eliza A Smith Nashua, NH
GILSON, Donald Warren, Mar 4 1932 Sex:M Child# 4 Henry E Gilson Windham, NH & Cynthia L Cooper Cambridge, MA
GILSON, Ella, Jun 29 1891 Sex:F Child# 1 George Gilson England & Alice Garrett Westford, MA
GILSON, Gloria Rita, Dec 3 1928 Sex:F Child# 1 L E Gilson Milford, NH & Mabel Bonin Nashua, NH Stillborn
GILSON, Laura, Aug 7 1888 Sex:F Child# 9 Stephen Gilson Dunstable MA & Josephine Vee Candia
GILSON, Nancy Jean, Aug 19 1933 Sex:F Child# 2 LeRoy E Gilson Milford, NH & Mabel Bonin Nashua, NH
GILSON, Unknown, Jul 23 1892 Sex:F Child# 1 James W Gilson Dunstable, MA & Mary O Clark Clarenceville, CA
GIMOPOULOS, Unknown, Dec 18 1917 Sex:F Child# 1 Thomas Gimopoulos Greece & Helen Papachristos Greece
GINCHARD, Eva, Apr 4 1894 Sex:F Child# 5 Joseph Ginchard Canada & Aglae Canada
GINGAS, William, May 21 1914 Sex:M Child# 6 John Gingas Russia & Peolina Astonute Russia
GINGILISKY, Joseph, Mar 2 1917 Sex:M Child# 1 Edward Gingilisky Poland & Annie Annagilisky Poland
GINGLESKI, Unknown, Mar 23 1924 Sex:M Child# 4 Edward Gingleski Poland & Annie Galetska Poland
GINSBERG, Theodore Elliott, Jun 13 1928 Sex:M Child# 1 Samuel Ginsberg Russia & M R Mitofsky Russia
GIRARD, Carmel Lena, Dec 22 1933 Sex:F Child# 2 Leonard Girard Canada & Delia Levesque Vermont
GIRARD, Charles Henri, Aug 17 1911 Sex:M Child# 1 George Girard Canada & Regina Francoeur Canada
GIRARD, Constance Delia, Jul 19 1935 Sex:F Child# 1 Adrian Girard Canada & Lillian Levesque Vermont
GIRARD, Cordelia, Oct 25 1889 Sex:F Child# 5 Peter Girard Canada & Cordelia Lacois Canada
GIRARD, Florence Edna, May 18 1927 Sex:F Child# 1 Alfred Girard Greenfield, MA & Bertha Hudon Nashua, NH
GIRARD, Frederick Thomas, Mar 7 1930 Sex:M Child# 3 Frederick T Girard Greenfield, NH & Bertha Hudon Nashua, NH
GIRARD, Henri Hector, Jan 27 1908 Sex:M Child# 1 Donat Girard Canada & Georgianna Antaya Nashua, NH
GIRARD, Henri Noe, Jan 15 1890 Sex:M Child# 2 Napoleon Girard Nashua, NH & Celina Laporte Nashua, NH
GIRARD, Henrietta R, Jun 5 1902 Sex:F Child# 3 Cleophas Girard Canada & L Marquis Canada
GIRARD, Jeanne Lucienne, May 23 1932 Sex:F Child# 3 Theophile Girard Nashua, NH & Jos Gagnon Canada
GIRARD, Jeannette Clare, Oct 27 1928 Sex:F Child# 2 F T Girard Greenfield, NH & Bertha Hudon Nashua, NH
GIRARD, Leo Lucien, Nov 11 1927 Sex:M Child# 2 Theophile Girard Nashua, NH & Josephine Gagnon Canada
GIRARD, Lilian Louise, Sep 3 1913 Sex:F Child# 2 Donat Girard Canada & Georgianna Antaya Nashua, NH
GIRARD, Louis E T, Nov 28 1899 Sex:M Child# 2 Theophile Girard Canada & Martine Lavoie Canada
GIRARD, Madeline Jane, May 3 1932 Sex:F Child# 1 Hector Girard Nashua, NH & Lillian Levesque Nashua, NH
GIRARD, Marcel Henry, Dec 6 1927 Sex:M Child# 2 Renee Girard Canada & Adrienne Lussier Canada
GIRARD, Marguertie Camille, Oct 4 1913 Sex:F Child# 2 George Girard Canada & Regina Francoeur Canada
GIRARD, Marie A A, Jul 16 1902 Sex:F Child# 3 Theophile Girard Canada & Martine Lavoie Canada
GIRARD, Marie Doris Florian, Aug 8 1934 Sex:F Child# 2 Albert Girard Canada & Louisiana Noel Nashua, NH
GIRARD, Marie Eva P, Feb 8 1900 Sex:F Child# 10 Francis Girard Canada & Exelie Poulin Canada
GIRARD, Marie Florence, May 27 1902 Sex:F Child# 11 Francis Girard Canada & Zelie Poulin Canada
GIRARD, Marie S, Feb 28 1898 Sex:F Child# 1 Theophile Girard Canada & Martene Lavoie Canada
GIRARD, Mary Claire Lena, Jan 9 1933 Sex:F Child# 1 Albert Girard Canada & Louisiana Noel Nashua, NH
GIRARD, Natalie Louise, Oct 30 1934 Sex:F Child# 4 Fred T Girard Greenfield, NH & Bertha Hudon Nashua, NH
GIRARD, Rita Emma, Feb 20 1935 Sex:F Child# 3 Leonard Girard Canada & Delia Levesque Vermont
GIRARD, Rita Rachel, Oct 6 1916 Sex:F Child# 3 George Girard Canada & A Francoeur Canada
GIRARD, Robert Jos Alphonse, Dec 6 1934 Sex:M Child# 1 Rene Girard Canada & Irene Beland Lowell, MA
GIRARD, Unknown, Feb 21 1897 Sex:M Child# 2 (No Parents Listed)
GIRARD, Victor Adrien, Sep 3 1932 Sex:M Child# 1 Leonard Girard St Liboire, PQ & Delia Levesque Graniteville, PQ
GIRARD, Wilfrid, Oct 7 1924 Sex:M Child# 1 Theophile Girard Nashua, NH & Josephine Gagnon Canada
GIRARD, Yolande C T, Nov 13 1924 Sex:F Child# 5 Henry O Girard Canada & Yvonne Hudon Canada
GIRARD, Yvette Pauline, Dec 3 1933 Sex:F Child# 3 Leo Girard Canada & Yvonne Paradis Canada
GIRENARD, Marguerite A, May 13 1889 Sex:F Child# 6 Pierre Girenard Canada & Melina Pateneaude Canada
GIRONARD, Narcisse W, Jun 4 1889 Sex:M Child# 2 Antoine Gironard NH & Cardelia Bilault St Albans, VT
GIROREARD, Doloris, Apr 18 1890 Sex:F Child# 3 Joseph Giroreard Hudsonville, NH & Mary Couteur Canada
GIROU, Otis Raymond, Mar 5 1919 Sex:M Child# 3 George Girou New York & Helen McDonald Maine
GIROUARD, Albert Laurent, Jul 5 1911 Sex:M Child# 8 Pierre Girouard, Jr Nashua, NH & Clarina Ouellette Maine
GIROUARD, Amede, Jul 30 1889 Sex:M Child# 7 Philias Girouard Canada & Mathilda Bellerose Canada
GIROUARD, Andre, Jun 2 1891 Sex:M Child# 10 Leon Girouard Canada & Mary J Burns Canada
GIROUARD, Anna, Jan 3 1892 Sex:F Child# 3 Antoine Girouard Canada & Cordelia Breault Canada
GIROUARD, Augustin, Mar 5 1892 Sex:M Child# 7 Pierre Girouard Canada & Melina Pateneande Canada
GIROUARD, Augustin, Jul 13 1901 Sex:M Child# 3 Hector Girouard Nashua, NH & Georgina Lamontague Canada
GIROUARD, Augustin A, Aug 12 1887 Sex:M Child# 1 Antoine Girouard N Oxford, NH & Cordelia Breault St Albans, VT
GIROUARD, Beatrice Lucille, Aug 11 1919 Sex:F Child# 1 Eugene Girouard NH & Neddie Therrien NY
GIROUARD, Celestine Rita, Aug 15 1930 Sex:F Child# 2 Henri Girouard Nashua, NH & Regina Dionne Newmarket, NH
GIROUARD, Clara, Mar 1 1899 Sex:F Child# 1 Leon A Girouard Nashua, NH & Delia Hamel Suncook, NH
GIROUARD, Clara Georgiana, Mar 29 1900 Sex:F Child# 2 Victor Girouard Nashua, NH & Georgi Lamontague Canada
GIROUARD, David, Feb 5 1893 Sex:M Child# 5 Joseph Girouard Canada & Arthemise Benoit Canada
GIROUARD, Donald Joseph, Aug 18 1934 Sex:M Child# 2 Leo W Girouard Nashua, NH & Agnes C Trueheart Athol, MA
GIROUARD, Edgar Raymond, Oct 11 1909 Sex:M Child# 2 Alfred Girouard US & Adelaide Dube US
GIROUARD, Emelia, Jan 28 1896 Sex:F Child# 6 Antoine Girouard Canada & Cordelia Breault Canada
GIROUARD, Ernest Arthur, Oct 10 1901 Sex:M Child# 3 Pierre Girouard Nashua, NH & Clarina Ouellette Canada
GIROUARD, Ernest Victor, Nov 12 1919 Sex:M Child# 1 Ernest Girouard NH & Gracia Rancourt NH

GIROUARD, Eugene Henry, Jr, Apr 27 1925 Sex:M Child# 3 E H Girouard Hudson, NH & Nettie Therrien Mooers, NY
GIROUARD, Eva, Jun 18 1892 Sex:F Child# 2 Narcisse Girouard Canada & Adele Levasseur Canada
GIROUARD, Eva, Jun 18 1905 Sex:F Child# 2 Narcisse Girouard Nashua, NH & Clara Lajoie Canada
GIROUARD, George Edward, Jun 11 1921 Sex:M Child# 2 Eugene Girouard Hudson, NH & Nettie Therrien Mooers, NY
GIROUARD, Gracia, Apr 21 1905 Sex:F Child# 8 Antoine Girouard N Sanford, MA & Cordelia Brault Canada
GIROUARD, Henri O, Jan 4 1898 Sex:M Child# 12 Philias Girouard Canada & Mathilde Bellerose Canada
GIROUARD, Irene, May 7 1904 Sex:F Child# 3 Leon Girouard Nashua, NH & Delia Hamel Suncook, NH
GIROUARD, Irene Jeannette, Sep 14 1922 Sex:F Child# 3 Ernest Girouard NH & Gracia Rancourt NH
GIROUARD, J Armand Albert, Aug 17 1915 Sex:M Child# 3 Arthur Girouard NH & Marie J Ducharme Mass
GIROUARD, J Robert Dolard, Jul 6 1913 Sex:M Child# 2 Pierre Girouard, Jr Canada & Pamelia Lavery Canada
GIROUARD, Jos Roland Raymond, Jan 24 1929 Sex:M Child# 4 Joseph Girouard New York & Rosana Gaudreau Canada
GIROUARD, Joseph, Feb 18 1887 Sex:M Child# 4 Joseph Girouard P Q & Hermine Messier P Q
GIROUARD, Joseph, Aug 24 1895 Sex:M Child# 10 Joseph Girouard Canada & Mathilde Bellerose Canada
GIROUARD, Joseph, May 6 1932 Sex:M Child# 1 Ray Girouard Nashua, NH & Valida Bellefleur Nashua, NH Stillborn
GIROUARD, Joseph Alfred, Oct 31 1916 Sex:M Child# 4 Arthur Girouard NH & Marie Ducharme Mass
GIROUARD, Joseph Arthur R, Jan 31 1907 Sex:M Child# 3 Joseph Girouard NH & Dorothy Lapointe New York
GIROUARD, Joseph H H, Aug 9 1899 Sex:M Child# 3 Augustin Girouard Mass & Angeline Desmarais Canada
GIROUARD, Joseph Henri Raoul, Aug 22 1912 Sex:M Child# 5 Narcisse Girouard Canada & Clara Lajoie Canada
GIROUARD, Joseph Luc Bernardin, Jul 4 1912 Sex:M Child# 3 Alfred Girouard Nashua, NH & Adelaide Dube Canada
GIROUARD, Joseph Pierre Lionel, Oct 27 1906 Sex:M Child# 1 Joseph Girouard New York & Rose Anna Gaudreau Canada
GIROUARD, Joseph R Gilbert, Sep 25 1901 Sex:M Child# 1 Joseph Girouard NH & Dorothee Lapointe New York
GIROUARD, Joseph Robert E, Mar 18 1909 Sex:M Child# 7 Pierre Girouard, Jr Nashua, NH & Clarina Ouellette Canada
GIROUARD, Joseph W, Mar 7 1897 Sex:M Child# 7 Joseph Girouard Canada & Herminie Messier Canada
GIROUARD, Laura, Jan 30 1894 Sex:F Child# 9 Philias Girouard Canada & Mathilde Bellerose Canada
GIROUARD, Laura, Mar 8 1905 Sex:F Child# 4 Hector Girouard Nashua, NH & Geo'ana Lamontagne Canada
GIROUARD, Leo Winfred, Apr 22 1925 Sex:M Child# 1 Leo W Girouard Nashua, NH & Mabel Pole Manchester, NH
GIROUARD, Leonida, Oct 13 1903 Sex:F Child# 1 Narcisse Girouard Canada & Clara Lajoie Canada
GIROUARD, Lillian, Jul 14 1916 Sex:F Child# 1 Christopher Girouard Sherbrook, Canada & Elodie Ledoux Nashua, NH
GIROUARD, Lina Adelina, Apr 24 1910 Sex:F Child# 4 Narcisse Girouard Nashua, NH & Flora Girouard Canada
GIROUARD, Louis C A, Feb 14 1898 Sex:M Child# 2 Augustin Girouard Canada & Angeline Desmarais Canada
GIROUARD, Maria Gratia L, Mar 3 1905 Sex:F Child# 4 Pierre Girouard, Jr Nashua, NH & Clarina Ouelette Canada
GIROUARD, Marie Agnes, Sep 2 1897 Sex:F Child# Antoine Girouard N Siford, MA & Cordelia Brault St Albans, VT
GIROUARD, Marie Anne, Jul 6 1890 Sex:F Child# 6 Leon Girouard Canada & Mary J Burns Canada
GIROUARD, Marie Anne, Feb 9 1899 Sex:F Child# 9 Joseph Girouard Nashua, NH & Marie Couture Canada
GIROUARD, Marie C, Jun 6 1895 Sex:F Child# 1 Pierre Girouard Nashua, NH & Clarina Ouellette Canada
GIROUARD, Marie C A, Jun 6 1887 Sex:F Child# 12 Joseph Girouard P Q & Arthemise Benoit P Q
GIROUARD, Marie E L, Jun 7 1892 Sex:F Child# 6 Joseph Girouard Canada & Hermine Messier Canada
GIROUARD, Marie Evelyne, Dec 31 1907 Sex:F Child# 6 Pierre Girouard, Jr Nashua, NH & Clarina Ouellette Canada
GIROUARD, Marie Georgette J, Oct 17 1923 Sex:F Child# 3 Joseph Girouard New York & Rose Goudreau NH
GIROUARD, Marie Isabelle Rita, Oct 21 1920 Sex:F Child# 2 Ernest Girouard NH & Gracia Rancourt NH
GIROUARD, Marie Lucille Germ, Jan 22 1915 Sex:F Child# 2 Joseph Girouard New York & Rose A Goudreau Canada
GIROUARD, Marie Theresa, Jul 9 1929 Sex:F Child# 1 Henry Girouard Nashua, NH & Regina Dionne Newmarket, NH
GIROUARD, Mary, Jun 28 1934 Sex:F Child# 2 Raymond Girouard Nashua, NH & Valide Bellefleur Nashua, NH
GIROUARD, Mary Anne, Oct 29 1892 Sex:F Child# 4 Joseph Girouard Hudsonville, MA & Mary Couture Canada
GIROUARD, Mary Rita, Jun 26 1920 Sex:F Child# 3 Peter Girouard Canada & Pomela Lavery Canada
GIROUARD, Normand Auguste, Jan 4 1933 Sex:M Child# 2 Robert Girouard Nashua, NH & Anna Nadeau Nashua, NH
GIROUARD, Olivette Rita, Sep 23 1921 Sex:F Child# 6 Narcisse Girouard Nashua, NH & Clara Lajoie Canada
GIROUARD, Paul Louis, May 10 1930 Sex:M Child# 1 Claude Girouard Nashua, NH & Blanche Charest Nashua, NH
GIROUARD, Regina, Aug 10 1894 Sex:F Child# 6 Joseph Girouard US & Marie Contourier Canada
GIROUARD, Robert Alfred, Aug 3 1929 Sex:M Child# 1 Robert Girouard Nashua, NH & Anne Nadeau Nashua, NH
GIROUARD, Robert Flavien, Jun 25 1908 Sex:M Child# 1 Alfred Girouard US & Adelaide Dube US
GIROUARD, Rose Delima, Jun 10 1891 Sex:F Child# 4 Joseph Girouard Canada & Marie Couturier Canada
GIROUARD, Therese Olivette, Nov 18 1905 Sex:F Child# 2 Joseph Girouard Nashua, NH & Marie Lapointe Canada
GIROUARD, Unknown, Oct 3 1894 Sex:F Child# 6 Antoine Girouard Canada & Cordelia Brault Canada Stillborn
GIROUARD, Unknown, Feb 15 1900 Sex:F Child# 7 Pierre Girouard Canada & Cordelia Lacasse Canada
GIROUARD, Unknown, Oct 17 1906 Sex:M Child# 5 Pierre Girouard Nashua, NH & Clarina Ouellette Canada Stillborn
GIROUARD, Unknown, May 20 1911 Sex: Child# 1 Wilfred Girouard
GIROUARD, Unknown, Jan 11 1928 Sex:M Child# 2 Leo Girouard Nashua, NH & Mabel Poole Manchester, NH
GIROUARD, Victor Napoleon, Oct 13 1897 Sex:M Child# 1 Hector Girouard Nashua, NH & G Lamontague Canada
GIROUARD, Wilfred N, Jun 30 1897 Sex:M Child# 2 Pierre Girouard Nashua, NH & Clarina Ouellette Canada
GIROUARD, Wilfrid, Apr 6 1902 Sex:M Child# 2 Leon Girouard Nashua, NH & Delia Hamel Suncook, NH
GIROUARD, Yvonne, Feb 11 1896 Sex:F Child# 7 Joseph Girouard US & Ularie Couturiere Canada
GIROUARD, Zepherina, Jun 6 1887 Sex:F Child# 5 Philias Girouard P Q & M Bellerose P Q
GIROUX, Joseph Niliard, May 3 1915 Sex:M Child# 6 William Giroux Maine & Ida Elliott NH
GIROWARD, Joseph, May 16 1888 Sex:M Child# 1 Augustine Giroward Fitchburg, MA & Angeline Desmaris St Hyacinthe
GIROWARD, Mary, Jun 22 1888 Sex:F Child# 6 Phileare Giroward Canada & Matilda Bellerose Canada
GITMAN, Marie Rose, Jun 5 1902 Sex:F Child# 2 Alfred Gitman New York & Sadie Oline New York
GIZOTTE, Isabelle Irene, Dec 3 1891 Sex:F Child# 9 D B Gizotte New York & Melia Gizotte New York
GLAVAN, Mary E, Jan 10 1893 Sex:F Child# 5 John Glavan Ireland & Mary Smith Ireland
GLAVEN, John Francis, Dec 3 1899 Sex:M Child# 7 John Glaven Ireland & Mary Bremahan Ireland
GLAVIN, Unknown, Sep 18 1898 Sex:M Child# John Glavin Ireland & Mary Smith Ireland Stillborn
GLAWSON, Martha Joan, Feb 1 1935 Sex:F Child# 1 George E Glawson Lisbon, NH & Andrea Jefferson N Conway, NH
GLEASON, Alice, Apr 23 1913 Sex:F Child# 4 Luke Gleason Ireland & Mary Roach Ireland

GLEASON, Ann Sophia, Oct 22 1908 Sex:F Child# 2 Luke Gleason Ireland & Mary Roach Ireland
GLEASON, Annie Agnes, Aug 9 1892 Sex:F Child# 1 Luke Gleason Ireland & Annie Murphy Ireland
GLEASON, Dorothy May, Sep 26 1911 Sex:F Child# 3 Luke Gleason Ireland & Mary Roach Ireland
GLEASON, Mary Jane Pontbriand, Feb 14 1927 Sex:F Child# 2 Edmond Gleason Boston, MA & L Pontbriand Shirley, MA
GLEASON, Mary T Pontbriand, Feb 14 1927 Sex:F Child# 1 Edmond Gleason Boston, MA & L Pontbriand Shirley, MA
GLENECK, David John, Nov 7 1933 Sex:M Child# 2 John Gleneck Austria & Adeline Trudel Nashua, NH
GLENWOOD, Robert, Jul 1 1924 Sex:M Child# 2 Robert Glenwood Haverhill, MA & Marie Kittredge Walden, VT
GLIDDEN, Madeline, Jun 25 1923 Sex:F Child# 2 Merton Glidden Bethel, ME & Harriet Hurlburt Weare, NH
GLIDDEN, Marguerite, Jun 5 1920 Sex:F Child# 1 Merton Glidden Bethel, ME & Harriet Hurlbert Weirs, NH
GLINES, Fred L, May 13 1902 Sex:M Child# 2 Dennis B Glines Vermont & Ellen Pettipaw NS
GLINES, Paulina Roseana, Feb 4 1923 Sex:F Child# 1 Francis F Glines Nashua, NH & Laura M Girard Nashua, NH
GLORICKIS, Joseph, Apr 15 1914 Sex:M Child# 1 John Glorickis Russia & Liewa Kireswti Russia
GLOVER, Alice I, Aug 11 1897 Sex:F Child# 2 Charles Glover Warner & Carrie Stanley St John, NB
GLOVER, Herbert I, Jun 19 1900 Sex:M Child# 3 Charles Glover NH & Carrie Stanley NB
GLOVER, Ruth, Oct 4 1925 Sex:F Child# 1 Philip Glover Milford, NH & Irene F Stickney Hollis, NH
GLOVER, Unknown, Dec 8 1895 Sex:M Child# 1 Charles Glover Warner & Carrie Stanley St John, NB
GOBIN, Albert, Jan 1 1926 Sex:M Child# 2 Frank Gobin New York & Jacqueline Smith Salem, MA
GOBIN, George Francis, Nov 8 1923 Sex:M Child# 1 Francis Gobin New York & Jacqueline Smythe Salem, MA
GOBIN, Mary Ann, Nov 24 1928 Sex:F Child# 8 Clayton N Gobin Ellenbury, NY & R Waterman E Hardwick, VT
GODARD, Albert, Mar 12 1900 Sex:M Child# 11 Leon Godard Canada & Delphine Menard Canada
GODARD, Delima, Mar 2 1911 Sex:F Child# 1 Alfred Godard US & Delina Arbour US Stillborn
GODBOUT, Valeur, Feb 5 1907 Sex:M Child# 18 Anselme Godbout Canada & Marilda Boule Canada
GODBOUT, Virginia Margaret, Jul 29 1932 Sex:F Child# 2 F Godbout Haverhill, MA & Thelma Hubbard Haverhill, MA
GODDARD, Carol Ann, Nov 30 1935 Sex:F Child# 2 Rich A Goddard Nashua, NH & Vera Stead Manchester, England
GODDARD, Donald Ray, Feb 18 1915 Sex:M Child# 4 Charles H Goddard Greenfield, NH & Gertrude A Hatch Nashua, NH
GODDARD, Donald Richard, Oct 21 1932 Sex:M Child# 1 R A Goddard Nashua, NH & Vera Stead England
GODDARD, Doris, Nov 19 1909 Sex:F Child# 1 Charles H Goddard Greenfield, NH & Gertrude Hatch Nashua, NH
GODDARD, John, Jr, May 11 1928 Sex:M Child# 2 John Goddard Worcester, MA & Marie Connor Nashua, NH
GODDARD, Richard Ambrose, Jun 21 1911 Sex:M Child# 2 Charles H Goddard Greenfield, NH & Gertrude Hatch Nashua, NH
GODDARD, Robert Wesley, Apr 20 1913 Sex:M Child# 3 Charles H Goddard Greenfield, NH & Gertrude Hatch Nashua, NH
GODEA, Antonina, Oct 18 1912 Sex:F Child# 3 John Godea Russia & Annie Yasolawicz Russia
GODFREY, Unknown, Sep 17 1928 Sex:M Child# 1 Harold Godfrey Ft Payne, AL & Edith Sturgis Standish, ME
GODIN, Alberic Alphonse, Dec 15 1915 Sex:M Child# 6 Alfred Godin Canada & Victorine Miller Canada
GODIN, Charles Edward, Jun 15 1890 Sex:M Child# 3 Charles Godin Canada & Ludivine Sirois Canada
GODIN, Henri Normand, Nov 4 1918 Sex:M Child# 7 Alfred Godin Canada & Victorine Miller Canada
GODIN, Jos Ovila Robert, May 13 1923 Sex:M Child# 9 Alfred Godin Canada & Victorine Muller Canada
GODIN, Joseph Simeon Romeo, Dec 21 1912 Sex:M Child# 3 Romeo Godin Canada & Maud Paquette Canada
GODIN, Marie A, Mar 23 1887 Sex:F Child# 1 Charles Godin P Q & Leodivine Sirois P Q
GODIN, Rosario Roger, May 1 1921 Sex:M Child# 8 Alfred Godin Canada & Victorine Miller Canada
GODIN, Unknown, Mar 4 1892 Sex: Child# 4 Charles Godin Canada & Rosa King Canada
GODIN, Unknown, Apr 7 1892 Sex:F Child# 4 Charles Godin Canada & Rosa King Canada
GODING, Frank, Jul 19 1916 Sex:M Child# 9 Frank C Goding Mass & Carry J Haynes Mass
GODING, Frank Henry, May 13 1915 Sex:M Child# 8 Frank C Goding Sudbury, MA & Josie Haynes Maynard, MA
GODING, Grace Marion, Mar 31 1913 Sex:F Child# 7 Frank C Goding N Sudbury, MA & Josephine Haynes Natick, MA
GODING, Mary, Mar 21 1897 Sex:F Child# 1 Arthur Goding Fitchburg, MA & Mary O'Brien Ireland
GODING, Mary Anna, Nov 10 1902 Sex:F Child# 5 Charles Goding Canada & Mary Sirois Canada
GODING, Ruth Gertrude, Jan 14 1920 Sex:F Child# 10 Frank Goding Mass & Carrie Haines Mass
GODING, Theodoro Alverge, Aug 29 1917 Sex:M Child# 10 Franking Goding Mass & Carrie Haines Mass
GODING, Unknown, Mar 30 1902 Sex:F Child# 2 Frank C Goding Sudbury, MA & Carrie J Haines Maynard, MA
GODING, Unknown, May 17 1904 Sex:M Child# 3 Frank C Goding Sudbury, MA & Carrie J Haynes Maynard, MA
GODING, Unknown, May 17 1904 Sex:M Child# 4 Frank C Goding Sudbury, MA & Carrie J Haynes Maynard, MA
GODING, Unknown, May 5 1906 Sex: Child# 2 Frank C Goding Sudbury, MA & Emma Hawkins Wayland, MA Stillborn
GODITES, Annie, Jul 8 1916 Sex:F Child# 1 John Godites Russia & Pauline Barnatowich Russia
GODREAU, Rosanna Almida, Sep 25 1903 Sex:F Child# 3 Paschal Godreau Canada & Elizabeth Levesque Canada
GOETHA, Anthony, Apr 24 1911 Sex:M Child# 2 John Goetha Russia & Annie Yasolavitch Russia
GOFF, Mary, Mar 19 1896 Sex:F Child# 1 Will Goff
GOFFE, Mary Jane, Mar 2 1924 Sex:F Child# 1 John Goffe Bedford, NH & Edna M Stratton Nashua, NH Stillborn
GOGGIN, Ruth Marion, Jan 31 1891 Sex:F Child# 3 John P Goggin Manchester, NH & Martha P Quinn S Newmarket, NH
GOI, Wanda, Nov 15 1921 Sex:F Child# 3 Joseph Goi Poland & Sophie Diekiewicz Poland
GOING, Dorothy, Dec 17 1922 Sex:F Child# 3 C Wesley Going Townsend, MA & Florence A Twombly S Wilton, NH
GOING, Ruth Elizabeth, Nov 18 1916 Sex:F Child# 2 Leon Priscott Going Westford, MA & Mary Eliz James Groton, MA
GOKEY, Christine Natelie, Jan 30 1912 Sex:F Child# 4 Frank D Gokey Lowell, MA & Mary Murray Vermont
GOKEY, Gorden Edwin, Mar 9 1913 Sex:M Child# 5 Frank B Gokey Vermont & Mary Murray Vermont
GOKEY, Laurence Francis, Jan 22 1911 Sex:M Child# 3 Frank Gokey Vermont & Mary Murray Vermont
GOKEY, Leo Albert Joseph, Jul 19 1902 Sex:M Child# 11 Peter Gokey Canada & Orise Bergeron Canada
GOLD, William Bell, Mar 5 1897 Sex:M Child# 2 Robert H Gold Lexington, VA & Gertrude M Bickford Ripton, VT
GOLDBERG, Louis, Dec 8 1901 Sex:M Child# 6 Benjamin Goldberg Russia & Dora Sutta Russia
GOLDEN, Elisabeth Anne, Mar 27 1933 Sex:F Child# 1 Albert Golden Lowell, MA & Cora Burnham Nashua, NH
GOLDINKOFF, Abe H, Nov 24 1907 Sex:M Child# 9 Lazar Goldinkoff Russia & Rachel B Rabinovitz Russia
GOLDINKOFF, Lena, Oct 14 1905 Sex:F Child# 8 Lazar Goldinkoff Russia & Rachel B Rabinovitz Russia
GOLDMAN, Annie, Feb 1894 Sex:F Child# 6 Manual Goldman Russia & Annie Russia
GOLDMAN, Lizzie, Sep 27 1908 Sex:F Child# 1 Hyman Goldman Russia & Bessie Shapiro US
GOLDMAN, M Ida, Feb 15 1920 Sex:F Child# 2 Simon Goldman England & Fannie Sindeman Russia

GOLDMAN, Philip, Mar 1 1917 Sex:M Child# 2 Samuel Goldman Russia & Sophie Russia
GOLDMAN, Samuel, Mar 12 1920 Sex:M Child# 3 Samuel Goldman Keiv, Russia & Safie Yaffee Keiv, Russia
GOLDMAN, Simeon, Nov 30 1896 Sex:M Child# 6 Manuel Goldman Russia & A Kousnirravich Russia
GOLDMAN, Unknown, Aug 15 1895 Sex:M Child# 7 Manuel Goldman Poland & Anna Poland
GOLDMAN, Unknown, Nov 29 1901 Sex:M Child# 8 Manuel Goldman Poland & Anna Poland
GOLDSTONE, Unknown, Oct 11 1888 Sex:M Child# 1 James Goldstone Poland & Sarah Cohn Poland
GOLDTHWAIT, Eleanor Louise, Jun 4 1918 Sex:F Child# 1 Harold Goldthwait Danvers, MA & Maude Melvin Ipswich, MA
GOLDTHWAIT, Unknown, Nov 1 1893 Sex:F Child# 2 Charles A Goldthwait LaCrosse, WI & Etta F Shedd Salmon Falls, NH
GOLDTHWAITE, Anne Marie, Mar 1 1933 Sex:F Child# 6 R Goldthwaite Danvers, MA & Marjorie Loop Dunstable, MA
GOLDTHWAITE, Barbara Gray, Sep 8 1923 Sex:F Child# 3 Harold Goldthwaite Danvers, MA & Maude Melvin Ipswich, MA
GOLDTHWAITE, Constance A, Aug 12 1910 Sex:F Child# 2 Chas F Goldthwaite Nashua, NH & Alma L Taylor Bridgetown, NJ
GOLDTHWAITE, Cynthia, Jan 25 1925 Sex:F Child# 1 William Goldthwaite Dunstable, MA & Dorothy Nourse Salem, MA
GOLDTHWAITE, Dorothy Melvin, Nov 18 1921 Sex:F Child# 2 Harold Goldthwaite Danvers, MA & Maude Melvin Ipswich, MA
GOLDTHWAITE, Harold, Jr, May 18 1926 Sex:M Child# 4 H Goldthwaite Danvers, MA & Maude Melvin Ipswich, MA
GOLDTHWAITE, Henry Nourse, Jun 13 1927 Sex:M Child# 3 W J Goldthwaite Danvers, MA & Dorothy Nourse Salem, MA
GOLDTHWAITE, Katherine Louise, Aug 3 1908 Sex:F Child# 1 Chas F Goldthwaite Nashua, NH & Alma L Taylor NJ
GOLDTHWAITE, Laurence Winslow, Aug 25 1927 Sex:M Child# 4 Rea Goldthwaite Danvers, MA & Marjorie Loop Dunstable, MA
GOLDTHWAITE, Louise Mae, Oct 7 1922 Sex:F Child# 1 Rea Goldthwaite Danvers, MA & Marjorie Loop Dunstable, MA
GOLDTHWAITE, Rosalie, May 30 1924 Sex:F Child# 2 Rea Goldthwaite Danvers, MA & Marjorie Loop Dunstable, MA
GOLDTHWAITE, Virginia Gray, Jul 22 1926 Sex:F Child# 3 Rea Goldthwaite Danvers, MA & Marjorie M Loop Dunstable, MA
GOLDTHWAITE, Willard Johnson, Jun 13 1927 Sex:M Child# 2 W J Goldthwaite Danvers, MA & Dorothy Nourse Salem, MA
GONDAWICZ, Helena, Jul 7 1912 Sex:F Child# 1 John Gondawicz Russia & Antonia Gregiuta Russia
GONDEWICZ, Joseph, Aug 23 1912 Sex:F Child# 1 Joseph Gondewicz Russia & Leonora Saolinwitka Russia
GONDIC, Edward, Aug 28 1914 Sex:M Child# 1 Stanislaus Gondic Austria & Anna Kourtec Austria
GONDITIS, John B, Jan 18 1918 Sex:M Child# 2 John Gonditis Russia & Petrona Berna Russia
GONDOTIS, Joseph, Nov 10 1911 Sex:M Child# 3 Anton Gondotis Russia & Cas Stoulpiuite Russia
GONDOTIS, Mary, Nov 10 1911 Sex:F Child# 2 Anton Gondotis Russia & Cas Stoulpiuite Russia
GONSQUEBECH, Unknown, Feb 24 1889 Sex:F Child# 4 Paul Gonsquebech Holland & Antoine Switzerland
GONYER, Otta, Jan 23 1910 Sex:F Child# 5 Felix Gonyer New York & Julie Racicot New York
GOODALE, Marjorie Louise, Apr 24 1922 Sex:F Child# 1 Roscoe Goodale Manchester, NH & Muriel Benjamin Nashua, NH
GOODALL, Robert Ernest, Oct 3 1932 Sex:M Child# 2 Ernest Goodall Deering, NH & Olivia Bianchi Milford, NH
GOODHUE, Nancy, Nov 14 1925 Sex:F Child# 2 Samuel S Goodhue Jamestown City, PA & Edith M Cornel Boston, MA
GOODHUE, Raymond, Feb 23 1911 Sex:M Child# 1 Ralph L Goodhue Lawrence, MA & Mary Nichols Troy, NY
GOODHUE, Samuel Harlow, Feb 17 1922 Sex:M Child# 1 Samuel S Goodhue Pennsylvania & Edith Cornell Boston, MA
GOODMAN, Ida, May 26 1901 Sex:F Child# 1 Abraham Goodman Russia & Limnie Buskue Russia
GOODMAN, Irvin Seymour, Apr 13 1919 Sex:M Child# 6 Abraham J Goodman Russia & Lena Taushire Russia
GOODRICH, Adam, Nov 19 1918 Sex:M Child# 4 John Goodrich Russia & Anna Gregas Russia
GOODRICH, John, Apr 19 1916 Sex:M Child# 3 John Goodrich Russia & Antoine Grigas Russia
GOODRIDGE, Herbert Franklin, Nov 14 1924 Sex:M Child# 2 H F Goodridge Fitchburg, MA & Grace R Leeman Walpole, MA
GOODSPEED, Aleda R, Dec 12 1892 Sex:F Child# 4 Clarence E Goodspeed Nashua, NH & Addie M Warren Nashua, NH
GOODSPEED, Donald Humphrey, Jan 20 1925 Sex:M Child# 5 Orlin Goodspeed Plattsburg, NY & Ella Swain Nashua, NH
GOODSPEED, Frederick Eugene, Mar 2 1919 Sex:M Child# 2 Orlin Goodspeed S Plattsburg, NY & Ella Swain Nashua, NH
GOODSPEED, Orlan Eugene, Sep 24 1921 Sex:M Child# 4 Orland Goodspeed Plattsburg, NY & Ella Swain Nashua, NH
GOODSPEED, Unknown, Apr 10 1920 Sex:F Child# 3 Orlin E Goodspeed Plattsburg, NY & Ella C Swain Nashua, NH
GOODSPEED, Velma Louise, Mar 13 1907 Sex:F Child# 1 Willis H Goodspeed Nashua, NH & Mabel D Perkins Boston, MA
GOODSPEED, Willie, Mar 15 1888 Sex:M Child# 2 Clarence E Goodspeed Litchfield & Ada M Warren Nashua, NH
GOODWIN, Beverly Ann, Oct 1 1935 Sex:F Child# 1 Otis G Goodwin Pelham, NH & Sarah Haslim Lowell, MA
GOODWIN, Forest Leonard, Feb 23 1921 Sex:M Child# 1 Wallace Goodwin Nashua, NH & Mabel Davis Dracut, MA
GOODWIN, Gardner, Nov 24 1889 Sex:M Child# 2 Elmer H Goodwin Milford & Mary Eastman Andover
GOODWIN, Harold Edward, Feb 19 1903 Sex:M Child# 2 Walter E Goodwin New York & Julia M Lewis Vermont
GOODWIN, Harold Lloyd, Jul 30 1921 Sex:M Child# 2 Harold L Goodwin Lebanon, NH & Lena Bouley Nashua, NH
GOODWIN, Harold W, Jul 16 1895 Sex:M Child# 1 Amos H Goodwin New Brunswick & Sarah N Wicom Manchester, NH
GOODWIN, Helen Jeannette, Jun 12 1915 Sex:F Child# 1 Daniel H Goodwin Hollis, NH & Anne J Morrison Pepperell, MA
GOODWIN, Joseph, Jun 3 1922 Sex:M Child# 1 Frederick Goodwin Saco, ME & Madeline McCarthy Biddeford, ME
GOODWIN, Lucille Olive, Jun 14 1920 Sex:F Child# 1 Harold L Goodwin Lebanon, NH & Lena Bouley Nashua, NH
GOODWIN, Marion Lucille, Nov 28 1920 Sex:F Child# 3 Ernest Goodwin Kennebunk, ME & Elmire Damboise Nashua, NH
GOODWIN, Marjorie Ruth, Mar 25 1923 Sex:F Child# 3 Harold Goodwin Lebanon, NH & Lena Bouley Nashua, NH
GOODWIN, Thomas Eugene, May 22 1935 Sex:M Child# 2 Ernest Goodwin Plattsburg, NY & Eleanor M Bassett Rutland, VT
GOODWIN, Unknown, Aug 26 1893 Sex:F Child# 2 J E Goodwin Pelham, NH & Mary A McCann Lowell, MA
GOODWIN, Unknown, Apr 26 1898 Sex:F Child# 2 James A Goodwin Middletown, CT & Frances W Brown Hartford, CT
GOODWIN, Unknown, Jun 28 1898 Sex:F Child# 2 Amos H Goodwin Westmoreland, NB & Sarah Wicom Manchester, NH
GOODWIN, Unknown, Aug 22 1898 Sex:M Child# 1 Walter E Goodwin Drewsville & Mae Lewis Wilton, VT
GOODWIN, Unknown, May 15 1922 Sex:M Child# 2 Wallace Goodwin Nashua, NH & Mabel Davis Dracut, MA
GOODWIN, Wallace H, Feb 21 1901 Sex:M Child# 1 W H Goodwin Maine & Grace Urquhart Nashua, NH
GORA, Clarence Edward, Apr 21 1921 Sex:M Child# 3 John G Gora Milwaukee, WI & Andrea Dichard Nashua, NH
GORA, Lucille Yvonne, Nov 11 1923 Sex:F Child# 4 John Gora Milwaukee, WI & Andrea Dichard Nashua, NH
GORA, William Joseph, May 7 1922 Sex:M Child# 4 John George Gora Milwaukee, WI & Andrea Dichard Nashua, NH
GORDON, Arthur Arnold, Nov 29 1925 Sex:M Child# 3 Harry Gordon Russia & Eliz Kligerman Russia
GORDON, Bertha, Jan 27 1924 Sex:F Child# 4 Benjamin Gordon Russia & Ethel Myster Russia
GORDON, Bruce Edward, Nov 6 1931 Sex:M Child# 1 George F Gordon Laconia, NH & Bernice A Howarth Nashua, NH
GORDON, Celia, May 14 1921 Sex:F Child# 2 Harry Gordon Russia & Elizabeth Kligerman Russia
GORDON, David, Nov 10 1893 Sex:M Child# 2 Donald S Gordon Prince Edw Is & Barbara NB
GORDON, Dvoira, Apr 6 1931 Sex:F Child# 4 Harry Gordon Russia & Elizabeth Kligerman Russia

GORDON, Elienor Frances, Apr 13 1922 Sex:F Child# 3 John Gordon Ireland & Mary Wynn Ireland
GORDON, Gerald, Mar 5 1925 Sex:M Child# 2 Hyman Gordon Russia & Bessie Winograd Fall River, MA
GORDON, Jason Donald, Feb 6 1929 Sex:M Child# 3 Hyman Gordon Russia & Bessie Winograd Fall River, MA
GORDON, John Joseph, Jan 31 1925 Sex:M Child# 4 John Joseph Gordon Ireland & Mary Winn Ireland
GORDON, Kent Howorth, Oct 5 1935 Sex:M Child# 2 George F Gordon Laconia, NH & Bernice Howorth Nashua, NH
GORDON, Lionel Irwin, Jul 29 1928 Sex:M Child# 5 Benjamin Gordon Russia & Ethel Meister Russia
GORDON, Mary, Oct 23 1919 Sex:F Child# 1 John J Gordon Ireland & Mary A Winn Ireland Stillborn
GORDON, Mary Emma, Nov 9 1888 Sex:F Child# 2 Charles Gordon Canada & Rosie King Canada
GORDON, Mary Margaret, Mar 24 1921 Sex:F Child# 2 John I Gordon Ireland & Mary Winn Ireland
GORDON, Max, Jun 2 1914 Sex:M Child# 2 Bennie Gordon Russia & Ethel Nuster Russia
GORDON, Phillip, Oct 27 1920 Sex:M Child# 5 Charles Gordon Vina, Russia & Lena Curley Vina, Russia
GORDON, Phyllis Shirley, Jan 16 1921 Sex:F Child# 3 Benjamin Gordon Russia & Ehtel Myster Russia
GORDON, Reuben, Jun 17 1897 Sex:M Child# 1 Benjamin Gordon Russia & Rachel Arnson Russia
GORDON, Robert Andrew, Jul 12 1931 Sex:M Child# 5 John J Gordon Ireland & Mary Winn Ireland
GORDON, Rose, Mar 23 1887 Sex:F Child# 2 Charles Gordon Canada & Rose Canada
GORDON, Unknown, Sep 25 1893 Sex:M Child# 4 Elmer H Gordon Milford & Mary Eastman Andover
GORDON, Unknown, Oct 8 1918 Sex:F Child# 1 Harry Gordon Russia & Elizabeth Silgeman Lawrence, MA Stillborn
GORELLA, Alphonse, Apr 13 1911 Sex:M Child# 1 Adam Gorella Russia & Leron Stistofsky Russia
GORGETTE, Eva, May 9 1894 Sex:F Child# 1 Edmond Gorgette Maine & Alphonsine Gervais Canada
GORGETTE, M Lelia, Nov 4 1895 Sex:F Child# 2 Hermance Gorgette E Douglas, MA & Alphonsine Gervais Canada
GORGETTE, Theophile Alfred, Jan 28 1891 Sex:M Child# 1 Arthur Gorgette E Douglas, MA & Marie Desmarais Brooksville
GORHAM, Dolores Anne, Oct 26 1933 Sex:F Child# 4 James Gorham Bellows Falls, VT & Sarah Griffin Providence, RI
GORHAM, James Joseph, Jul 31 1929 Sex:M Child# 1 James Joseph Gorham Bellows Fls, VT & Sarah Griffin Providence, RI
GORHAM, Joan Elizabeth, Jul 3 1930 Sex:F Child# 2 James J Gorham Vermont & Sarah E Griffin Rhode Island
GORHAM, Paul Maurice, Jun 17 1932 Sex:M Child# 3 James Gorham Maine & Sarah Griffin US
GORHAM, Unknown, Jun 27 1897 Sex:F Child# 1 F W Gorham Westfield, MA & Leora Dickerman Nashua, NH Stillborn
GORMAN, Antoinette Pauline, Feb 7 1913 Sex:F Child# 1 George E Gorman Fishkill Lan, NY & Emma T Cardin Nashua, NH
GORMAN, Esther, Mar 27 1932 Sex:F Child# 5 Walter Gorman Lowell, MA & Gladys Stuart Waverley, NS
GORMAN, Georgia Lorraine, Sep 16 1918 Sex:F Child# 4 George E Gorman Beacon City, NY & Emma Cardin Nashua, NH
GORMAN, Harold Everett, Sep 28 1895 Sex:M Child# 2 Albert J Gorman England & Maud E Brown Nova Scotia
GORMAN, John Richard, Feb 5 1910 Sex:M Child# 4 Frank B Gorman Franklin, NJ & Nellie McGinnis Boston, MA
GORMAN, John Thomas, Jr, May 25 1930 Sex:M Child# 1 John Thomas Gorman Passaic, NJ & Barbara Bean Freeport, ME
GORMAN, Joseph Richard, Apr 5 1929 Sex:M Child# 4 Walter Gorman Lowell, MA & Gladys Stuart Nova Scotia
GORMAN, Leon Arthur, Dec 20 1934 Sex:M Child# 3 John Thos Gorman Passaic, NJ & Barbara Bean Freeport, ME
GORMAN, Lillian, Oct 18 1914 Sex:F Child# 2 George E Gorman E Landing, NY & Emma Cardin Nashua, NH
GORMAN, Lillian Frances, Sep 12 1905 Sex:F Child# 1 Frank E Gorman Gardner, MA & Lillian Powell London, England
GORMAN, M Alice, Jan 29 1917 Sex:F Child# 3 George E Gorman Fishkill Landing, NY & Emma Cardin Nashua, NH
GORMAN, Unknown, May 30 1902 Sex:M Child# 1 John E Gorman Nashua, NH & Alida M Manseau Nashua, NH
GORMAN, Unknown, Mar 16 1916 Sex:F Child# 5 Frank Gorman Franklin, NJ & Nellie McGinis Boston, MA
GORMAN, Walter Fred, Jul 29 1935 Sex:M Child# 6 Walter Gorman Lowell, MA & Gladys Stuart Nova Scotia
GORMAN, William, Jan 29 1907 Sex:M Child# 1 Frank V Gorman Franklin, NJ & Nellie McGinnis Boston, MA
GORMOLOWICK, John, Aug 17 1923 Sex:M Child# 3 Louis Garmolowick Russia & Jose Pitcus Austria
GORSKAS, Cristof, Dec 18 1908 Sex:M Child# 1 Cristof Gorskas Russia & Antonia Bokadie Russia Stillborn
GORSKI, Susan, May 16 1912 Sex:F Child# 3 Kostante Gorski Russia & Mary Patekshiska Austria
GORSKIS, Cecilia, May 19 1914 Sex:F Child# 4 Kostanski Gorskis Russia & Marie Pastikouliska Russia
GOSHDIGION, Mary, Aug 2 1914 Sex:F Child# 6 Paul Goshdigion Russia & Mary Zrakin Russia
GOSHY, Frank, Jan 5 1928 Sex:M Child# 10 Alexander Goshy Poland & Mary Bolisen Poland
GOSS, Bernice Ella, Oct 3 1930 Sex:F Child# 3 Charles E Goss Lowell, MA & Mabel Lund Dunstable, MA
GOSS, Carl Dimick, Mar 24 1916 Sex:M Child# 1 Carl G Goss Vermont & Julia Christin Montreal, Canada
GOSS, Donald Elwin, Sep 7 1933 Sex:M Child# 5 Charles E Goss Lowell, MA & Mabel Lund Dunstable, MA
GOSS, Donald Everett, Mar 16 1924 Sex:M Child# 3 Harold J Goss Milford, NH & Mary E Lund Nashua, NH
GOSS, Dorothy May, Aug 26 1915 Sex:F Child# 1 Harry L Goss Nashua, NH & Eva Mildred Kemp Nashua, NH
GOSS, Harold Winston, Oct 20 1921 Sex:M Child# 2 Harold J Goss Milford, NH & Mary Lund Nashua, NH
GOSS, Laurence, Aug 26 1928 Sex:M Child# 4 Harold John Goss Milford, NH & Mary Lund Nashua, NH
GOSS, Russell Earl, Feb 16 1932 Sex:M Child# 4 Charles E Goss Lowell, MA & Mabel Lund Dunstable, MA
GOSS, Unknown, Jan 12 1890 Sex:M Child# 2 Fred Goss Newbury, VT & Laura Lee Nova Scotia
GOSSELIN, Albert Joseph, Feb 10 1926 Sex:M Child# 3 Albert J Gosselin Berlin, NH & Cora M Langlois Lowell, MA
GOSSELIN, Cora Theresa, Aug 25 1927 Sex:F Child# 4 Albert Gosselin Lowell, MA & Cora Langlois Lowell, MA
GOSSELIN, Donald Alfred, Jun 7 1934 Sex:M Child# 1 Alfred R Gosselin Linwood, MA & Helen Daly Nashua, NH
GOSSELIN, Eugene D, Feb 7 1900 Sex:M Child# 4 Alphonse Gosselin Canada & Philomene Daigneau Canada
GOSSELIN, Grace Odile, Apr 2 1932 Sex:F Child# 5 Albert Gosselin Berlin, NH & Cora Langlois Lowell, MA
GOSSELIN, Jos Robert Marcel, May 29 1929 Sex:M Child# 3 Romeo Gosselin Cambridge, MA & Eva Marcoux Nashua, NH
GOSSELIN, Leo Albert, Dec 5 1935 Sex:M Child# 2 Leo Gosselin Nashua, NH & Thelma Rollins Nashua, NH
GOSSELIN, Leo Alcide, Jan 22 1910 Sex:M Child# 1 Joseph Gosselin Canada & Eugenie Rousseau Canada
GOSSELIN, Ludger Robert, Oct 11 1931 Sex:M Child# 1 Ludger M Gosselin Canada & Phyllis Haskell Nashua, NH
GOSSELIN, Mary Rita, Aug 29 1934 Sex:F Child# 1 Leo Gosselin Nashua, NH & Thelma Lund Nashua, NH
GOSSELIN, Patricia Ann, Sep 18 1933 Sex:F Child# 2 Ludger Gosselin Canada & Phyllis Haskell Nashua, NH
GOTT, Beverly Katherine, Oct 13 1920 Sex:F Child# 5 Victor Gott Lowell, MA & Florence Trudeau Middlebury, VT
GOTT, Charlie Victor, Mar 8 1914 Sex:M Child# 2 Charles V Gott Lowell, MA & Florence Trudeau Middlebury, VT
GOTT, Dorothy Lillian, Mar 3 1913 Sex:F Child# 1 Charles Victor Gott Lowell, MA & Florence M Trudeau Middlebury, VT
GOTT, Richard Edward, Apr 9 1918 Sex:M Child# 4 Charles Victor Gott Lowell, MA & Florence Trudeau Middlebury, VT
GOUDA, Anastasia Milton, Jun 13 1933 Sex:F Child# 1 Milton G Gouda Greece & T Karkovelou Greece
GOUDOURAS, Unknown, Feb 27 1924 Sex:M Child# 4 George Goudouras Greece & Gianoula Liakow Greece

GOUDREAU, Albert Normand, Jul 17 1915 Sex:M Child# 2 Georges Goudreau Nashua, NH & Adele St Laurent Canada
GOUDREAU, Marie, Oct 24 1914 Sex:F Child# 14 Ernest Goudreau Canada & M Louise Vacher Canada Stillborn
GOUDREAU, Richard, Apr 10 1933 Sex:M Child# 1 Alph Goudreau Canada & M L Chouinard
GOUGAS, Constantin, Sep 19 1905 Sex:M Child# 3 John Gougas Russia & Mary Grigoukie Russia
GOUGEOPOULOS, James, Feb 5 1917 Sex:M Child# 3 George Gougeopoulos Nipata, Greece & Vasailon Nipata, Greece
GOUGON, Wilfred, Aug 15 1897 Sex:M Child# 3 Alfred Gougon Canada & Mary Millette NY
GOUIN, Semey, Dec 12 1914 Sex:M Child# 2 Joe Gouin Russia & Bertha Lajovik Russia
GOULD, Earl Monroe, Feb 26 1926 Sex:M Child# 1 Alfred M Gould Windham, NH & Dorothy Greene Swanton, VT
GOULD, Henry W, Jun 25 1889 Sex:M Child# 6 Alonzo Gould Nashua, NH & Minnis S Flanders Nashua, NH
GOULD, James David, Jul 31 1926 Sex:M Child# 1 James Gould Nashua, NH & Gladys Lamonday Nashua, NH
GOULD, Marguerite A, Nov 6 1931 Sex:F Child# 1 Romeo Gould Goffs Falls, NH & Lillian Gilmore Nashua, NH
GOULD, Rodney Dexter, Aug 13 1934 Sex:M Child# 1 James Gould Nashua, NH & Lucille Cadwell Nashua, NH
GOULD, Sara Alta, Nov 17 1924 Sex:F Child# 1 W Doble Gould Milo, ME & Nellie A Tower Hanover, MA
GOULD, Thomas Frederick, Apr 13 1931 Sex:M Child# 1 Warren T Gould Nashua, NH & Mary Wicks Binghamton, NY
GOULD, Unknown, Jul 28 1933 Sex:F Child# 4 Romeo Gould Goffs Falls, NH & Lillian Gilmore Nashua, NH Stillborn
GOULET, Albert Antoine, Apr 21 1911 Sex:M Child# 3 Albert Goulet Canada & Leonie Boutin Canada
GOULET, Arthur Joseph, Jan 9 1921 Sex:M Child# 11 Octave Goulet Mass & Marie Ann Ouellette Canada
GOULET, Beatrice Irene, Nov 28 1907 Sex:F Child# 1 Albert Goulet Canada & Leonie Boutin Canada
GOULET, Charles Henri, Dec 31 1913 Sex:M Child# 6 Octave J Goulet Mass & Marie Anne Ouellette Canada
GOULET, Elmira Rita, May 8 1909 Sex:F Child# 2 Albert Goulet Canada & Leonie Boutin Canada
GOULET, Eugenie Germaine, Jan 26 1915 Sex:F Child# 5 Albert Goulet Canada & Leonie Boutin Canada
GOULET, George Gerald, Feb 21 1922 Sex:M Child# 12 Octave Goulet Mass & M Anne Ouellette Canada
GOULET, Germaine Rachelle, Aug 13 1913 Sex:F Child# 4 Albert Goulet Canada & Leonie Boutin Canada
GOULET, J Octave Julien, Jan 9 1912 Sex:M Child# 5 Octave Goulet E Douglass, MA & Mary A Ouellette Canada
GOULET, Jos Leon Jules, Nov 12 1929 Sex:M Child# 14 Octave Goulet Worcester, MA & Marie Anne Ouellette Canada
GOULET, Joseph Ademard, Mar 7 1916 Sex:M Child# 8 Octave Goulet Mass & Marie Anne Ouellette Canada
GOULET, Joseph Albert, Jan 16 1915 Sex:M Child# 7 Octave Goulet Mass & Marie A Ouellette Canada
GOULET, Joseph Girard, Jul 1 1916 Sex:M Child# 1 Joseph N Goulet Rochester, NH & Marion Legendre Canada
GOULET, Joseph L R, Dec 12 1910 Sex:M Child# 4 Octave J Goulet E Douglass, MA & Mary Anne Ouellette Canada
GOULET, Joseph Oscar L, Dec 10 1909 Sex:M Child# 3 Octave Goulet Mass & Marie A Ouelette Canada
GOULET, Marguerite Therese, Dec 6 1918 Sex:F Child# 10 Octave Goulet Mass & Marie Anne Ouellette Canada
GOULET, Marie Anne Elise, Apr 18 1917 Sex:F Child# 9 Octave Goulet Mass & Marie Anne Ouellette Canada
GOULET, Marie Anne V G, Nov 3 1907 Sex:F Child# 2 Octave Goulet Canada & Marie A Ouellette US
GOULET, Marie Clara H, Aug 20 1924 Sex:F Child# 13 Octave Goulet Mass & Marie A Ouellette Canada
GOULET, Pauline Theresa, Nov 26 1928 Sex:F Child# 8 Francis Goulet Canada & Marie B Gelinas Lowell, MA
GOULET, Raoul Octave, Jul 5 1906 Sex:M Child# 1 Octave Goulet US & Marie Ouellette Canada
GOUMAS, Mary, Apr 8 1935 Sex:F Child# 2 Arthur Goumas Greece & Stravoula Gegas Greece
GOUND, Harold Irving, Jun 10 1921 Sex:M Child# 1 Harold Gound Portland, ME & Hazel M Winters Nova Scotia
GOURZGOS, Stergios, Nov 11 1918 Sex:M Child# 1 Arggrios Gourzgos Greece & Azorore A Gourzgos Greece
GOVE, Joan, Nov 25 1928 Sex:F Child# 2 Lester E Gove Sunapee, NH & Ethel Forbes Nashua, NH
GOVE, Lester Forbes, Nov 11 1926 Sex:M Child# 1 Lester E Gove Sunapee, NH & Ethel May Forbes Nashua, NH
GOVEN, Unknown, May 3 1893 Sex:F Child# 2 Samuel Goven E Fairfield, VT & Elfsie Cherrette Canada
GOVER, Unknown, Nov 18 1891 Sex:F Child# 1 Samuel Gover E Fairfield, VT & Alphonsine Cherett Quebec, PQ
GOY, Anthony, Feb 27 1920 Sex:M Child# 2 Joseph Goy Poland Russia & Sophia Zekiewicz Poland Russia Stillborn
GOY, Anthony Peter, Oct 28 1921 Sex:M Child# 1 Anthony Goy Russia & Agnes Marcus Russia
GOY, Brownie, Nov 6 1918 Sex:M Child# 1 Louis Goy Poland & Eva Walenakawicz Poland
GOY, Charles, Mar 27 1912 Sex:M Child# 1 Raphael Goy Russia & Frances Pouskonges Russia
GOY, Genefa, Feb 27 1927 Sex:F Child# 5 Joseph Goy Poland & Zofia Dikiewicz Poland
GOY, Wanda, Aug 31 1918 Sex:F Child# 1 Joseph Goy Russia & Sophia Dziekewicz Russia Stillborn
GOY, Wanda, Dec 27 1922 Sex:F Child# 2 Ludwick Goy Poland Russia & Eva Valentacantes Poland Russia
GOY, Zofia, Aug 1 1924 Sex:F Child# 4 Joseph Goy Russia & Zofia Lekevicz Russia
GOYAIT, Blanche Viola, Jan 2 1914 Sex:F Child# 6 Henry Goyait Nashua, NH & Laura Morin Canada
GOYAIT, Obeline, Nov 9 1911 Sex:F Child# 5 Henri Goyait Canada & Laura Morin Canada
GOYET, Alfred Gerard, Aug 27 1919 Sex:M Child# 2 Thomas Goyet Chazy, NY & Marie Ouellette Canada
GOYET, Georges, Aug 8 1888 Sex:M Child# 9 John Goyet Vermont & Mary Cardin P Q
GOYET, Unknown, Jan 15 1892 Sex:F Child# 12 John Goyet Canada & Marie A N Cardin Canada Stillborn
GOYET, William Alcide, Aug 10 1897 Sex:M Child# 2 Elzear Goyet Nashua, NH & Mary Gregoire Biddeford, ME
GOYETTE, Albina, Apr 16 1897 Sex:F Child# 17 John Goyette Canada & Nancy Cardin Canada
GOYETTE, Alfred A, Jan 24 1902 Sex:M Child# 5 Amable Goyette Sciota, NY & M A Lafontaine Canada
GOYETTE, Alfred Victor, Sep 12 1901 Sex:M Child# 4 Elzear Goyette Nashua, NH & Marie Arsene Maine
GOYETTE, Amable O, Jan 15 1900 Sex:M Child# 4 Amable Goyette New York & Maria Lafontaine Canada
GOYETTE, Blanche A, Feb 23 1898 Sex:F Child# 3 Amable Goyette Sciota, NY & Marie Lafontaine Canada
GOYETTE, Eddie Henry O, Mar 3 1900 Sex:M Child# 3 Elzear Goyette Nashua, NH & Marie Gregoire Maine
GOYETTE, Edna Zelia, Mar 5 1899 Sex:F Child# 2 Joseph Goyette Nashua, NH & Marguerite Gauthier Canada
GOYETTE, Edward Fred, Sep 19 1912 Sex:M Child# 2 Jos Edward Goyette W Chazy, NY & Phoebe M LeGrande Lowell, MA
GOYETTE, Jean B A E, May 24 1896 Sex:M Child# 2 Amable Goyette New York & Marie Lafountaine Canada
GOYETTE, Joseph, Jul 28 1901 Sex:M Child# 19 John Goyette Canada & Nancy Cardin Canada Stillborn
GOYETTE, Joseph Wallace, Sep 28 1913 Sex:M Child# 3 Joseph E Goyette W Chazy, NY & Phoebe M LaGrande Lowell, MA
GOYETTE, Lorraine Eugenie, Mar 24 1934 Sex:F Child# 1 Leo Goyette Canada & Evelyn Caron Canada
GOYETTE, Louis Paul, Mar 6 1891 Sex:M Child# 11 John Goyette Canada & Nancy Cardin Canada
GOYETTE, Marie A O, Feb 1 1905 Sex:F Child# 6 Amable Goyette Sciota, NY & Marie A Lafontaine Beloeil, PQ
GOYETTE, Marie Delrise J, Aug 2 1897 Sex:F Child# 1 Joseph Goyette Nashua, NH & Marguerite Gauthier Canada
GOYETTE, Marie E E, Oct 10 1906 Sex:F Child# 7 Amable Goyette Sciota, NY & Marie A Lafontaine Canada

GOYETTE, Marie S E, Feb 5 1894 Sex:F Child# 1 Amable Goyette Sciota, NY & Marie Lafontaine Canada
GOYETTE, Robert Oscar, Dec 20 1930 Sex:M Child# 1 Oscar Goyette Nashua, NH & Marguerite McQuane Lowell, MA
GOYETTE, Robert Raymond, Apr 14 1917 Sex:M Child# 1 Thomas Goyette Canada & Marie Ouellette Canada
GOYETTE, Unknown, Nov 9 1892 Sex:F Child# 13 John Goyette Canada & Nancy Cardin Canada  Stillborn
GOYETTE, Unknown, Nov 16 1893 Sex:M Child# 14 John Goyette Canada & Nancy Cardin Canada  Stillborn
GOYETTE, Unknown, Sep 15 1894 Sex:F Child# 15 John Goyette Canada & Nancy Cardin Canada  Stillborn
GOYETTE, Unknown, May 5 1896 Sex:M Child# 10 John Goyette Canada & Nancy Cardin Canada  Stillborn
GOYETTE, Unknown, Mar 22 1898 Sex:F Child# 18 John Goyette Canada & Nancy Cardin Canada
GOZATIS, John, Nov 19 1906 Sex:M Child# 2 Joseph Gozatis Russia & Cecelise Musiel Austria
GOZOTIS, Theresa, Mar 23 1904 Sex:F Child# 1 Joseph Gozotis Poland & Ceze Musel Austria
GRAASKY, Victenta, Dec 6 1915 Sex:M Child# 2 Frank Graasky Russia & Nellie Pitsko Russia
GRADY, Clara, Feb 7 1904 Sex:F Child# 2 James W Grady Lowell, MA & Clara Fisher Germany
GRADY, Harold Victor, Apr 3 1911 Sex:M Child# 3 James W Grady Lowell, MA & Clara C Fischer Germany
GRAHAM, Bradford Charles, Jun 1 1935 Sex:M Child# 1 Edward Graham Windham, NH & Germ Lafontaine Nashua, NH
GRAHAM, Charles Wentworth, Jul 30 1918 Sex:M Child# 7 Charles E Graham S Walpole, MA & Jessie Smith Central Fa
GRAHAM, Flora Mae, Feb 27 1930 Sex:F Child# 1 Arthur G Graham Wenham, MA & Pauline Chamberlain Nashua, NH
GRAHAM, Robert Gage, Oct 18 1931 Sex:M Child# 2 Arthur G Graham Windham, NH & Pauline Chamberlain Nashua, NH
GRAHAM, Shirley Lorraine, Jan 2 1931 Sex:F Child# 2 Arthur M Graham Mansfield, MA & Gladys E Hinds Greenfield
GRAHAM, Unknown, Feb 23 1898 Sex:M Child# 1 Elbridge M Graham Maine & Bertha Savory Mass
GRAHAM, Unknown, Mar 3 1900 Sex:M Child# 3 Elbridge M Graham Maine & Bertha I Savage Mass
GRAHAM, Virginia Pearl, Oct 29 1934 Sex:F Child# 1 Ralph Graham Natick, MA & Beatrice Lund Nashua, NH
GRAKES, Agnes, Jul 8 1915 Sex:F Child# 1 James Grakes Russia & Agnes Parguvis Russia
GRAND, Beverly Virginia, May 5 1917 Sex:F Child# 1 William Grand Nashua, NH & Ida Martin Nashua, NH
GRANDBOIS, Claire Mathilda, Aug 5 1927 Sex:F Child# 1 Oscar Grandbois Nashua, NH & Hilda Mercier Peabody, MA
GRANDBOIS, Edouard, Feb 16 1897 Sex:M Child# 3 Edouard Grandbois Peru, NY & Mathilda Delorme Clayburgh, NY
GRANDBOIS, Frank Roland, May 20 1911 Sex:M Child# 1 Henry Grandbois Canada & Rose Archambault Nashua, NH
GRANDBOIS, Joseph Alfred, Jan 22 1901 Sex:M Child# 7 Jean Grandbois Canada & Delia Frechette Canada
GRANDBOIS, Oscar Bernard, Jul 7 1905 Sex:M Child# 7 James E Grandbois New York & Mathilda Delorme New York
GRANDBOIS, Raymond, Nov 10 1929 Sex:M Child# 2 Oscar Grandbois Nashua, NH & Irene Mercier Peabody, MA
GRANDBOIS, Wilfrid A, Apr 12 1901 Sex:M Child# 4 Edouard Grandbois Clayburg, NY & Mathilde Delorme Clayburg, N
GRANDMAISON, Adolphe, Sep 11 1909 Sex:M Child# 9 Amable Grandmaison Canada & Celina Sirois Canada
GRANDMAISON, Aldea, Dec 7 1898 Sex:F Child# 3 Jules Grandmaison Canada & Marie Dion Canada
GRANDMAISON, Alfred S, Sep 16 1899 Sex:M Child# 2 A P Grandmaison Canada & Octavie Rodier Nashua, NH
GRANDMAISON, Alice Lydia, Sep 3 1891 Sex:F Child# 1 C Grandmaison Canada & Lydia St Laurend Canada
GRANDMAISON, Alma Patricia, Jun 24 1924 Sex:F Child# 2 E Grandmaison Nashua, NH & Mary Hennessey Lowell, MA
GRANDMAISON, Amede, Oct 1 1896 Sex:M Child# 2 Jules Grandmaison Canada & Marie Dion Canada
GRANDMAISON, Anita L, Sep 3 1898 Sex:F Child# 5 Horace Grandmaison Canada & Clara Cote Canada
GRANDMAISON, Arthur Rodolph, Nov 23 1901 Sex:M Child# 3 Al P Grandmaison Canada & Octavie Rodier Nashua, NH
GRANDMAISON, Cecile Reeva, Jan 21 1921 Sex:F Child# 1 Leo Grandmaison NH & Alma Burelle NH
GRANDMAISON, Claire Elizabeth, Jul 4 1933 Sex:F Child# 6 E Grandmaison Nashua, NH & Mary Hennessey Lowell, MA
GRANDMAISON, David, Jul 4 1934 Sex:M Child# 1 Oscar Grandmaison Nashua, NH & Irene Bouchard Nashua, NH  Still
GRANDMAISON, Edouard Sylvio, Oct 6 1903 Sex:M Child# 7 Amable Grandmaison Canada & Celina Sirois Canada
GRANDMAISON, Elma, Mar 8 1901 Sex:F Child# 7 Joseph Grandmaison Canada & Marceline Gagnon Canada
GRANDMAISON, Elzeard, Jan 15 1889 Sex:M Child# 2 J B Grandmaison Canada & Elise Lacombe Canada
GRANDMAISON, Emile Joseph, Jr, Mar 19 1930 Sex:M Child# 5 Emile J Grandmaison Nashua, NH & Mary Hennessey Lowe
GRANDMAISON, Ernest, May 23 1896 Sex:M Child# 4 Joseph Grandmaison Canada & Marceline Gagnon Canada
GRANDMAISON, Francis Raymond, Sep 20 1917 Sex:M Child# 3 Arthur Grandmaison Nashua, NH & Mary Stanton Amesbury
GRANDMAISON, Gloria Alice, May 8 1926 Sex:F Child# 3 E Grandmaison Nashua, NH & Marie Hennessey Lowell, MA
GRANDMAISON, Irma, Feb 1 1904 Sex:F Child# 4 Jules Grandmaison Canada & Marie Dion Canada
GRANDMAISON, Jane, Mar 29 1935 Sex:F Child# 7 E Grandmaison Nashua, NH & Mary Hennessey Lowell, MA
GRANDMAISON, Jeannette Eva, Aug 23 1899 Sex:F Child# 9 Alfred Grandmaison Canada & Louise Ferland Canada
GRANDMAISON, Joseph, Mar 29 1935 Sex:M Child# 8 E Grandmaison Nashua, NH & Mary Hennessey Lowell, MA
GRANDMAISON, Joseph A, Jan 22 1890 Sex:M Child# 6 Alfred Grandmaison Canada & Louise Farland Canada
GRANDMAISON, Joseph Arthur, Aug 3 1896 Sex:M Child# 4 Amable Grandmaison Canada & Celina Sirois Canada
GRANDMAISON, Joseph E C, Oct 21 1893 Sex:M Child# 2 Cyprien Grandmaison Canada & Lydia St Laurent Canada
GRANDMAISON, Joseph Emile, Nov 22 1898 Sex:M Child# 5 Joseph Grandmaison Canada & Marceline Gagnon Canada
GRANDMAISON, Joseph Henry, Jan 29 1898 Sex:M Child# 8 Alfred Grandmaison Canada & Louise Guertin Canada
GRANDMAISON, Joseph L, Nov 29 1894 Sex:M Child# 1 Jules Grandmaison Canada & Marie Dion Canada
GRANDMAISON, Lea Lucille, Sep 20 1909 Sex:F Child# 5 Alfred P Grandmaison Canada & Octavie Rodier Nashua, NH
GRANDMAISON, Lena, Mar 8 1901 Sex:F Child# 6 Joseph Grandmaison Canada & Marceline Gagnon Canada
GRANDMAISON, Leo Gerald, Feb 23 1932 Sex:M Child# 2 Leo Grandmaison Nashua, NH & Alma Burelle Nashua, NH
GRANDMAISON, Louis, Jul 23 1902 Sex:M Child# 3 Alfred Grandmaison Canada & Celina Gingras Hooksett, NH  Stillb
GRANDMAISON, Louis Roland, Nov 14 1910 Sex:M Child# 10 Amable Grandmaison Canada & Celina Sirois Canada
GRANDMAISON, Louise Theresa, Jul 16 1928 Sex:F Child# 4 E Grandmaison Nashua, NH & Mary Jennessey Lowell, MA
GRANDMAISON, M Eva Camille, Apr 28 1922 Sex:F Child# 1 Emile Grandmaison Nashua, NH & Mary Hennessy Lowell, MA
GRANDMAISON, M R Athana, Apr 21 1895 Sex:F Child# 3 Cyprien Grandmaison Canada & Lydia St Laurent Canada
GRANDMAISON, Marie A C, Mar 26 1891 Sex:F Child# 1 Amable Grandmaison Canada & Celina Cirois Canada
GRANDMAISON, Marie A L, Sep 19 1892 Sex:F Child# 2 Amab'e Grandmaison Canada & Celina Sirois Canada
GRANDMAISON, Marie Alma, Sep 15 1904 Sex:F Child# 8 Joseph Grandmaison Canada & Marceline Gagnon Canada
GRANDMAISON, Marie B I, Sep 29 1898 Sex:F Child# 1 Alfred Grandmaison Canada & Octavie Rodier Nashua, NH
GRANDMAISON, Marie Clare Rachelle, Dec 13 1928 Sex:F Child# 2 A Grandmaison Nashua, NH & Emerina Sirois Lawren
GRANDMAISON, Marie E B, Oct 7 1894 Sex:F Child# 3 Amable Grandmaison Canada & Celina Sirois Canada
GRANDMAISON, Marie L Liliane, Dec 8 1898 Sex:F Child# 5 Amable Grandmaison Canada & Celina Sirois Canada

GRANDMAISON, Marie Louise O, Nov 1 1905 Sex:F Child# 4 Alfred Grandmaison Canada & Octavie Rodier Nashua, NH
GRANDMAISON, Mary Agnes, Sep 25 1916 Sex:F Child# 2 Arthur Grandmaison Nashua, NH & Mary A Stanton Mass
GRANDMAISON, Mary Anita, Mar 18 1927 Sex:F Child# 4 H Grandmaison Canada & Odile LePage Canada
GRANDMAISON, Maurice, Feb 20 1925 Sex:M Child# 3 H Grandmaison Canada & Odille LePage Canada
GRANDMAISON, Napoleon Oscar, Aug 24 1907 Sex:M Child# 8 A Grandmaison Canada & Celina Sirois Canada
GRANDMAISON, Paul Roland, Apr 28 1927 Sex:M Child# 1 A Grandmaison Nashua, NH & Emerence Sirois Lawrence, MA
GRANDMAISON, Robert Telesphore, Nov 29 1907 Sex:M Child# 5 Jules Grandmaison Canada & Marie Dion Canada
GRANDMAISON, Robert Victor, May 26 1917 Sex:M Child# 3 Fred Grandmaison Nashua, NH & Agnes Duchesneau Mass
GRANDMAISON, Roland Edward A, May 20 1910 Sex:M Child# 1 Fred Grandmaison Nashua, NH & Agnes Duchesneau Lowell, MA
GRANDMAISON, Sylvia, Apr 23 1913 Sex:F Child# 11 A P Grandmaison Canada & Celina Sirois Canada
GRANDMAISON, Ulric, Jun 14 1904 Sex:M Child# 3 Aime Grandmaison Canada & Eugenie Arseneau Canada
GRANDMAISON, Valmore, Jan 30 1896 Sex:M Child# 4 Horace Grandmaison Canada & Clarisse Cote Canada
GRANDMAISON, Wilfred S, Aug 20 1889 Sex:M Child# 3 H Grandmaison Canada & Clarissa Cote Canada
GRANDMAISON, Wilfrid, Jul 6 1901 Sex:M Child# 6 Amable Grandmaison Canada & Celina Sirois Canada
GRANT, Agnes, Feb 18 1905 Sex:F Child# 5 Willyn Grant Maine & Jane Birchell England
GRANT, Alpin, Jan 21 1888 Sex:F Child# 3 Alpin Grant Nashua, NH & Mary Ann Dorgherty British America
GRANT, Ethel I, Jan 10 1900 Sex:F Child# 1 Charles H Grant Maine & Nettie M Nutting NH
GRANT, Harry Sylvester, Sep 5 1909 Sex:M Child# 1 Michael Grant Newfoundland & Annie Mayou Fitchburg, MA
GRANT, Katherine May, Aug 3 1912 Sex:F Child# 2 John Grant Frazerberry, Scotlnd & Grace Harrington Wilton, NH
GRANT, Mabel G, Dec 19 1894 Sex:F Child# 4 Alpin Grant Nova Scotia & Mary A Doherty England
GRANT, Madeline, Jan 23 1904 Sex:F Child# 4 W R Grant Maine & Jane Birchall Lancashire, England
GRANT, Shirley Ann, Sep 18 1935 Sex:F Child# 5 Edward Grant Clinton, MA & Gladys Raymond Amherst, NH
GRANT, Shirley Ellen, Apr 2 1931 Sex:F Child# 6 George Grant Bridgeport, CT & May Bassett Hartford, CT
GRANT, Unknown, Nov 11 1889 Sex:M Child# 3 Alvin Grant Nova Scotia & Mary Dohorty Ireland
GRANT, Unknown, Oct 6 1890 Sex:M Child# 4 John Grant Aberdeen, Scotland & Mary A Chatmers Aberdeen, Scotland
GRANT, Unknown, Feb 24 1898 Sex:M Child# 5 Alpin Grant Pictou, NS & Mary Doherty Nashua, NH
GRANT, Unknown, Oct 9 1903 Sex:M Child# 5 Alpin Grant Nova Scotia & Mary A Dorothy Nashua, NH
GRANT, Unknown, Jul 2 1911 Sex:F Child# 2 Alpin Grant, Jr Vermont & Dolah F Banks Springvale, ME
GRANT, Unknown, Aug 29 1917 Sex:F Child# 6 Irving Grant NH & Evelyn McIntire Maine Stillborn
GRANT, Wellyn J, Dec 12 1894 Sex:M Child# 1 W R Grant Sweden, ME & Jennie Birshall England
GRASKOWSKI, Chester Joseph, Feb 14 1924 Sex:M Child# 3 Joseph Graskowski Poland & Topilla Mazgolia Poland
GRATCAWICZ, Joseph, Sep 12 1916 Sex:M Child# 1 Adam Gratcawicz Russia & Prania Gruchiaviki Russia
GRAVE, Georges Alfred, Jan 26 1895 Sex:M Child# 9 Nevoll Grave Plattsburg, NY & Alvina Laforce Plattsburg, NY
GRAVEL, Beatrice Edith, Aug 27 1907 Sex:F Child# 2 George Gravel, Jr US & Georgianna Denault Canada
GRAVEL, Clement G, May 29 1887 Sex:M Child# 13 Joseph Gravel P Q & Azilda Benoit P Q
GRAVEL, Eva Blanche, Jul 5 1906 Sex:F Child# 1 George Gravel Nashua, NH & Georgiana Denault Canada
GRAVEL, George Alphonse, Sep 16 1921 Sex:M Child# 2 Horace Gravel Nashua, NH & Nolia Bonenfant Nashua, NH
GRAVEL, Henry, Jan 18 1905 Sex:M Child# 3 Alfred Gravel Nashua, NH & Annette Dumaine Canada Stillborn
GRAVEL, Irene, Jul 5 1911 Sex:F Child# 1 Telesphore Gravel Nashua, NH & Edouardina Desjarlais Canada
GRAVEL, Jeanne Stella, Jul 3 1910 Sex:F Child# 1 Charles Gravel Nashua, NH & M Louise Lebrun Canada
GRAVEL, Jeannette O, Oct 26 1902 Sex:F Child# 1 Alfred Gravel Nashua, NH & Annette Dumaine Canada
GRAVEL, Liliane Alexandrine, Jan 19 1907 Sex:F Child# 3 A F Gravel Nashua, NH & Annette Dumaine Canada
GRAVEL, Telesphore Sylvio, Jun 30 1914 Sex:M Child# 3 Telesphore Gravel Nashua, NH & Edouardina Desjarlais CanaDA
GRAVEL, Yvonne Juliette, Sep 5 1912 Sex:F Child# 2 Telesphore Gravel Canada & Edouardina Desjardin Canada
GRAVELIN, Leo Roger, Jun 15 1930 Sex:M Child# 9 Joseph Gravelin E Templeton, MA & Rose Corriveau Canada
GRAVELLE, Anita Blanche, Oct 20 1919 Sex:F Child# 1 Horace Gravelle Nashua, NH & Nolia Bonenfant Nashua, NH
GRAVELLE, Avila Rodrique, Apr 24 1899 Sex:M Child# 1 Rodrique Gravelle Canada & Lisa Lavallee Canada
GRAVELLE, Evelyn, Jan 1 1916 Sex:F Child# 4 Telesphore Gravelle Nashua, NH & Edouardina Desjarlais Canada
GRAVELLE, J George Euclide, Oct 20 1921 Sex:M Child# 8 Telesphore Gravelle Nashua, NH & Edwardina Desjarlais Canada
GRAVELLE, Jos Stanislas Leo, Sep 10 1917 Sex:M Child# 5 Telesphore Gravelle Nashua, NH & Edwardina Desjarlais
GRAVELLE, Joseph Roland, Oct 26 1920 Sex:M Child# 6 Telesphore Gravelle Nashua, NH & Edouardina Desjarlais Canada
GRAVELLE, Lucile Jeanne d'Arc, Nov 26 1919 Sex:F Child# 6 Telesphore Gravelle Nashua, NH & Edouardina Desjarlais
GRAVELLE, Lucille Olivette, Sep 5 1911 Sex:F Child# 2 Charles Gravelle Nashua, NH & E Lebrun Canada
GRAVELLE, M Gertrude Theresa, Dec 1 1922 Sex:F Child# 3 Horace E Gravelle NH & Nolia Bonenfant
GRAVELLE, Marie Camille Rochel, Feb 16 1923 Sex:F Child# 9 Telesphore Gravelle Nashua, NH & Edwardina Desjarlais
GRAVELLE, Raymond Horace, Jan 6 1925 Sex:M Child# 4 Horace Gravelle NH & Nolia Bonefant NH
GRAVELLE, Roger Roland Richard, Nov 13 1933 Sex:M Child# 5 Horace Gravelle Nashua, NH & Nolio Bonenfant Nashua, NH
GRAVELLE, Roland Gerard, Jan 28 1913 Sex:M Child# 3 Charles Gravelle Nashua, NH & Marie L Lebrun Canada
GRAVELLES, Anita, Feb 15 1912 Sex:F Child# 1 (No Parents Listed)
GRAVES, Bev Valerie Mildred, Jan 8 1917 Sex:F Child# 4 Fred Herb Graves Lynn, MA & Cora Francis Newhall Lynn, MA
GRAVES, Byrle Virginia Mario, Jan 8 1917 Sex:F Child# 5 Fred Herb Graves Lynn, MA & Cora Francis Newhall Lynn, MA
GRAVES, Clara Cecile, Feb 26 1893 Sex:F Child# 12 Charles Graves Canada & ScholastiqueStMichel Canada
GRAVES, Doris, Oct 1 1915 Sex:F Child# 5 John L Graves Prince Edward Island & Mary Eno Lee, NH
GRAVES, Effie, Jan 21 1893 Sex:F Child# 1 Edw A Graves NY & Katie J Mandeville NH
GRAVES, Everett Stewart, Jul 20 1923 Sex:M Child# 2 Reuben S Graves Hudson, NH & Mary Eunice Potter Rutland, VT
GRAVES, Helene Sybil, Feb 5 1921 Sex:F Child# 5 Frederick Graves Lynn, MA & Cora Newhall Lynn, MA
GRAVES, Lillian Agnes, Apr 7 1896 Sex:F Child# 10 Noel Graves Champlain, NY & Alvina Laforce Plattsburg, NY
GRAVES, Ruth Elizabeth, Jan 1 1917 Sex:F Child# 6 John T Graves Prince Edward Island & Mary Eno Lee, NH
GRAVES, Theodore Archy, Jun 4 1891 Sex:M Child# 11 Charles Graves Bedford, NY & S St Michel Bedford, NY
GRAVES, Verne Arthur, Jan 8 1917 Sex:M Child# 6 Fred Herb Graves Lynn, MA & Cora Francis Newhall Lynn, MA
GRAVILLE, Horace, Jul 28 1888 Sex:M Child# 14 Joseph Graville Canada & Azilea Bennoitt Canada
GRAY, Agnes, Oct 11 1905 Sex:F Child# 7 John W Gray Ireland & Bridget Mackie Biddeford, ME
GRAY, Anna, Jul 23 1917 Sex:F Child# 1 John F Gray Nashua, NH & Helen Mary Spellman Nashua, NH

GRAY, Clark Hale, Mar 3 1912 Sex:M Child# 4 Arthur Gray Calais, VT & Grace Maud Cate Laconia, NH
GRAY, David Shattuck, Apr 15 1921 Sex:M Child# 1 Willard E Gray Waltham, MA & Carrie E Shattuck Pepperell, MA
GRAY, Dorothy, May 13 1907 Sex:F Child# 8 John W Gray Ireland & Bridget Mackle Biddeford, ME
GRAY, Edward, May 12 1924 Sex:M Child# 2 Edward Gray Nashua, NH & Katherine O'Neil Nashua, NH
GRAY, Edward Augustus, Dec 28 1892 Sex:M Child# 1 John W Gray Ireland & Bridget Michael Biddeford, ME
GRAY, Fred Everett, Nov 6 1933 Sex:M Child# 2 Vernon H Gray Bradley, ME & Cora Paine Milo, ME
GRAY, George William, Feb 18 1910 Sex:M Child# 9 John W Gray Ireland & Bridget Mackle Biddeford, ME
GRAY, Gertrude M, Oct 14 1899 Sex:F Child# 4 John E Gray Ireland & Bridget Mackel Maine
GRAY, Henry, Jan 29 1904 Sex:M Child# 6 John W Gray Ireland & Bridget E Mackie Ireland
GRAY, John Francis, Mar 30 1896 Sex:M Child# 2 John W Gray Ireland & Bridget Mackle Biddeford, ME
GRAY, Madeline, Mar 16 1912 Sex:F Child# 10 John W Gray Ireland & Bridget Mackle Biddeford, ME
GRAY, Mary, Aug 30 1897 Sex:F Child# 3 John W Gray Ireland & Bridget H Mackle Biddeford, ME
GRAY, Paul, Sep 30 1925 Sex:M Child# 3 Edward Gray Nashua, NH & Catherine O'Neil Nashua, NH
GRAY, Richard Irving, Nov 2 1914 Sex:M Child# 2 Ernest W Gray Nashua, NH & May L Brooks Nashua, NH
GRAY, Robert Brooks, Feb 20 1913 Sex:M Child# 1 Ernest Walter Gray Nashua, NH & May Brooks Nashua, NH
GRAY, Robert Edward, Apr 1 1922 Sex:M Child# 1 Edward Gray Nashua, NH & Katherine O'Neil Nashua, NH
GRAY, Roger Davis, Apr 30 1912 Sex:M Child# 1 George E Gray Somersworth, NH & Abbie S Davis Sebago Lake, ME
GRAY, Ruth, Jan 5 1902 Sex:F Child# 5 John W Gray Ireland & Bridget H Mackie Biddeford, ME
GRAY, Ruth, Oct 18 1923 Sex:F Child# 3 Frank Gray Mass & Louise Spaulding Lowell, MA
GRAY, Ruth Elizabeth, Mar 5 1914 Sex:F Child# 5 Arthur M Gray Calais, VT & Grace M Cate Laconia, NH
GRAY, Unknown, Jan 7 1887 Sex:F Child# 4 George A Gray Stoddard & Nellie Lowell
GRAY, Unknown, Dec 7 1901 Sex:M Child# 9 Mathew J Gray Canada & Mary Lapointe Canada
GREATCH, Peter, Feb 22 1910 Sex:M Child# 1 Dominick Greatch Lithuania & Annie Motuzaite Lithuania
GREAUDINAISON, George, Jul 1 1888 Sex:M Child# 5 Alfred Grreaudinaiso Canada & Louisa Farland Canada
GREDRIMAS, Bronislaw, May 6 1914 Sex:M Child# 4 Stainslaw Gredrimas Russia & Leonora Russia
GREELEY, Gabrielle, Sep 29 1898 Sex:F Child# 1 James T Greeley Nashua, NH & Florence Richardson Keene, NH
GREELEY, James Bonaparte, Jul 11 1902 Sex:M Child# 3 James T Greeley Nashua, NH & Florence Richardson Keene, NH
GREELEY, Margaret Thor'n, Jul 16 1900 Sex:F Child# 2 James T Greeley Nashua, NH & Florence Richardson Keene, NH
GREEN, Agnes Patricia, Aug 13 1915 Sex:F Child# 10 John J Green Ireland & Agnes A Ledoux NH
GREEN, Alice Fletcher, Mar 28 1913 Sex:F Child# 1 Karl Green Lowell, MA & Rachel Fletcher Chelmsford, MA
GREEN, Anna Mary, Jun 18 1902 Sex:F Child# 1 John G Green Ireland & Agnes Ledoux Nashua, NH
GREEN, Annie M, Jun 17 1889 Sex:F Child# 1 Louis Green Ireland & Mary Ryan Ireland
GREEN, Bessie Ada, Jan 3 1909 Sex:F Child# 4 William E Green Tewksbury, MA & Ada E Taylor Nashua, NH
GREEN, Eleanor Lillian, Jan 19 1934 Sex:F Child# 2 Seth Green Nashua, NH & Eva Lucier Nashua, NH
GREEN, Eleonora Winnefred, Jun 19 1910 Sex:F Child# 1 John Green Newfoundland & Inez Wilson New Brunswick
GREEN, Harry Milton, Sep 17 1921 Sex:M Child# 2 Karl Clifford Green Lowell, MA & Lena Talbot Palmer, MA Stillborn
GREEN, Hiram Patterson, Jan 6 1906 Sex:M Child# 4 John G Green Ireland & Agnes Ledoux Nashua, NH
GREEN, Jessie Ida, Jan 3 1909 Sex:F Child# 3 William E Green Tewksbury, MA & Ada E Taylor Nashua, NH
GREEN, John Henry, Aug 6 1903 Sex:M Child# 2 John G Green Ireland & Agnes Ledoux Nashua, NH
GREEN, Joseph, Nov 25 1912 Sex:M Child# 9 John Green Ireland & Agnes May Ireland
GREEN, Julia Gertrude, Oct 25 1918 Sex:F Child# 12 John Green Ireland & Edna Ledoux Nashua, NH
GREEN, Mary Lillian, Oct 17 1904 Sex:F Child# 3 John G Green Ireland & Mary A Ledoux Nashua, NH
GREEN, Nina Ruth, Aug 27 1896 Sex:F Child# 1 George W Green Hollis, NH & Julia E Barrett Lawrence, MA
GREEN, Percey Alonzo, Sep 18 1900 Sex:M Child# 1 H M Green NH & Agnes B Sullivan NY
GREEN, Robert Emmett, Nov 25 1912 Sex:M Child# 8 John Green Ireland & Agnes May Ireland
GREEN, Robert Henry, Oct 4 1921 Sex:M Child# 3 John Green Ireland & Agnes Ledeoux NH
GREEN, Ruth, Oct 24 1913 Sex:F Child# 7 William E Green Tewksbury, MA & Ada E Taylor Nashua, NH Stillborn
GREEN, Virginia Mildred, Jan 18 1917 Sex:F Child# 10 John Green Ireland & Agnes Ledoux Nashua, NH
GREEN, Warren Edward, Jan 27 1921 Sex:M Child# 2 Frank D Green Sterling, MA & Constance Johnston Roxbury, MA
GREENBERG, Minnie Dreyfus, Jul 3 1899 Sex:F Child# 7 Michael Greenberg Russia & Annie Zamuschaesky Russia
GREENE, Alice Catherine, Dec 13 1919 Sex:F Child# 1 George Greene Mass & Lillian More New York
GREENE, Doris Ellena, Apr 25 1911 Sex:F Child# 4 William E Greene Tewksbury, MA & Ada E Taylor Nashua, NH
GREENE, Dorothy Ella, Apr 25 1911 Sex:F Child# 3 William E Greene Tewksbury, MA & Ada E Taylor Nashua, NH
GREENE, Frances Elizabeth, Sep 25 1911 Sex:F Child# 7 John Greene Ireland & Agnes May Nashua, NH
GREENE, George William, Jan 18 1921 Sex:M Child# 4 George L Greene Maine & Lucy Adams Nashua, NH
GREENE, Karl Clifford, May 31 1917 Sex:M Child# 1 Karl C Greene Mass & Lena Talbot Mass
GREENE, Rachel, Apr 17 1914 Sex:F Child# 2 Carl C Greene Lowell, MA & Rachel Fletcher Chelmsford, MA
GREENE, Roselle Mamie, Oct 22 1915 Sex:F Child# 8 William E Greene Tewksbury, MA & Ada E Taylor Nashua, NH
GREENE, Seth, Apr 1 1909 Sex:M Child# 6 John Greene Ireland & Agnes Ledoux Nashua, NH
GREENE, Unknown, Jun 20 1903 Sex:M Child# 1 James A Greene S Merrimack, NH & Maud B Frenette Nashua, NH
GREENLEAF, Beverly June, Jan 30 1934 Sex:F Child# 7 Richard Greenleaf NH & Bernice Miller Maine
GREENLEAF, Clayton Winn, Jul 12 1928 Sex:M Child# 4 H D Greenleaf Merrimack, NH & G W Marshall Hancock, NH
GREENLEAF, George Millett, Jun 12 1919 Sex:M Child# 1 Harry D Greenleaf Merrimack, NH & Grace W Marshall Hancock
GREENLEAF, Harry Dewolf, Jr, Mar 21 1921 Sex:M Child# 2 Harry D Greenleaf Merrimack, NH & Grace W Marshall Hancock
GREENLEAF, Jack Erwin, Jun 18 1932 Sex:M Child# 6 R Greenleaf NH & Bernice Miller Maine
GREENLEAF, John Robert, Dec 6 1930 Sex:M Child# 5 Harry Greenleaf NH & Grace Marshall NH
GREENLEAF, Milton C, May 28 1925 Sex:M Child# 3 Harry Greenleaf Merrimack, NH & Grace Marshall Hancock, NH
GREENLEAF, Norma Francis, Mar 25 1927 Sex:F Child# 3 R J Greenleaf Thorntons Ferry, NH & Bernice Miller Milan, NH
GREENLEAF, Patricia Ann, Jun 14 1928 Sex:F Child# 4 Richard Greenleaf Thorntons Ferry, NH & Bernice Miller Milan
GREENLEAF, Richard Jerome, Oct 15 1924 Sex:M Child# 1 R J Greenleaf Thorntons Ferry, NH & Bernice R Miller Milan
GREENLEAF, Shirley May, Dec 12 1925 Sex:F Child# 2 Richard Greenleaf Thortons Ferry, NH & Bernice Miller Milan
GREENLEAF, William Wayne, Jul 25 1930 Sex:M Child# 5 Richard Greenleaf Thorntons Ferry, NH & Bernice Miller Milan
GREENWOOD, Charles Wallace, Apr 7 1926 Sex:M Child# 2 W Greenwood Pepperell, MA & Dorothy Newton Leominster, MA

GREENWOOD, Norman Alvin, Dec 13 1927 Sex:M Child# 5 W H Greenwood US & Aurore Roy US
GREENWOOD, Roger Wyman, Dec 25 1923 Sex:M Child# 1 William Greenwood Pepperell, MA & Dorothy Newton Leominster, MA
GREENWOOD, Zantine, Aug 17 1932 Sex:M Child# 1 (No Parents Listed)
GREGAS, Alphonse, Aug 15 1917 Sex:M Child# 2 Alphonse Gregas Russia & Mickalena Markie Russia
GREGAS, Andrew, Jan 1 1917 Sex:M Child# 2 James Gregas Russia & Agnes Pangust Russia
GREGAS, Annie, May 16 1908 Sex:F Child# 5 Simon Gregas Lithuania & Annie Sinkavitch Russia
GREGAS, Antoinette, Feb 8 1923 Sex:F Child# 4 Michael Gregas Lithuania & Adele Nomuntawicz Lithuania
GREGAS, Constantin, Jan 21 1915 Sex:M Child# 6 Charles Gregas Russia & Michalina Sinkawicz Russia
GREGAS, Johanna, Jan 28 1927 Sex:F Child# 7 Joseph Gregas Lithuania & Vincenta Yesuka Lithuania
GREGAS, John, Sep 23 1918 Sex:M Child# 2 Michael Gregas Russia & Adele Nanottawicz Russia
GREGAS, Joseph, Nov 27 1918 Sex:M Child# 2 Joseph Gregas Russia & Visanta Yesukovich Russia
GREGAS, Julian Alpens, Jul 1 1928 Sex:M Child# 7 Jos Gregas Lithuania & Vincenta Yasuka Lithuania
GREGAS, Julius, Apr 3 1917 Sex:M Child# 6 Charles Gregas Russia & Mildred Simpavitch Russia
GREGAS, Mamie, Aug 23 1921 Sex:F Child# 3 Joseph Gregas Lithuania & Vincenta Yesnkawicz Lithuania
GREGAS, Michael, Jan 20 1909 Sex:M Child# 1 John Gregas Russia & Mary Alokonuty Russia
GREGAS, Nellie, Aug 23 1921 Sex:F Child# 4 Joseph Gregas Lithuania & Vincenta Yesnkawicz Lithuania
GREGAS, Rita, Dec 15 1918 Sex:F Child# 1 John Gregas Russia & Ann Turlita Russia
GREGAS, Unknown, Jun 11 1921 Sex:F Child# 3 James Gregas Russia & Agnes Paquette Russia
GREGAS, Vithold, Nov 11 1931 Sex:M Child# 9 Joseph Gregas Lithuania & Vincenta Yesukawicz Lithuania
GREGG, Barbara May, Apr 13 1920 Sex:F Child# 1 Guy Gregg NH & Gladys Hadlock NH
GREGG, Helen Elizabeth, Jun 14 1916 Sex:F Child# 1 Donald Gregg Nashua, NH & Antoinette Dion Manchester, NH
GREGG, John Burns, Jun 15 1920 Sex:M Child# 2 Donald B Gregg Nashua, NH & Antoinette Dion Manchester, NH
GREGG, Lucille, Sep 15 1891 Sex:F Child# 4 David A Gregg New Boston & Ella C Fox New Boston
GREGG, Unknown, Mar 6 1888 Sex:F Child# 4 William A Gregg New Boston & Bessie Burns Wilton, NH
GREGG, Unknown, Apr 22 1889 Sex:F Child# 3 David A Gregg New Boston & Ella Fox New Boston
GREGG, Unknown, Apr 1 1890 Sex:F Child# 5 William A Gregg New Boston, NH & Bessie Burns Wilton, NH
GREGOIR, Horace Wilfrid, Apr 3 1898 Sex:M Child# 4 George Gregoir Canada & Amelie Duprez Canada
GREGOIRE, Beatrice, May 31 1895 Sex:F Child# 1 Theobald Gregoire Canada & Wilhelmina Vaill'e't Canada
GREGOIRE, George Deodole, Sep 12 1895 Sex:M Child# 3 George Gregoire Maine & Odelia Duperez Canada
GREGOIRE, Marie H C, Jun 28 1903 Sex:F Child# 4 George Gregoire Canada & Odelie Duperree Canada
GREGOIRE, Marjorie E, Oct 25 1923 Sex:F Child# 1 Horace W Gregoire Nashua, NH & Edith Hamlin Nashua, NH
GREGORY, Unknown, Aug 14 1930 Sex:F Child# 1 George Gregory Lowell, MA & Isabell Maxwell Canada Stillborn
GREGRIA, Jaspar, Mar 4 1902 Sex:M Child# 1 Carlsmer Gregris Russia & Mickalean Trugortch Russia
GREIGAS, August, Apr 3 1928 Sex:M Child# 4 James Greigas Russia & Agnes Paguyette Lithuania
GREIGOR, Mervyn Leigh, Aug 7 1930 Sex:M Child# 1 Michael Greigor Albania & Mary R Geyer Berlin, NH
GRENBURG, Ida, Feb 5 1896 Sex:F Child# 4 Michael Grenburg Russia & Ann Zamachthausky Russia
GRENBURG, Sarah, Feb 5 1896 Sex:F Child# 5 Michael Grenburg Russia & Ann Zamachthausky Russia
GRENIER, Charles Allen, Dec 26 1932 Sex:M Child# 1 Andrew Grenier Carlisle, MA & Elise Levesque Canada
GRENIER, Elie, Apr 24 1894 Sex:M Child# 1 Elie Grenier Canada & Louise Paquin Canada
GRENIER, Henri Rosario, Jun 13 1912 Sex:M Child# 5 Henri Grenier Canada & Marie Louise Fournier Canada
GRENIER, Joseph A U, Aug 6 1905 Sex:M Child# 2 Adelard Grenier Nashua, NH & Marie A Theriault Mass
GRENIER, Joseph Alexander, Nov 12 1907 Sex:M Child# 1 Joseph Grenier Canada & Alexina Gendron Canada
GRENIER, Joseph Arthur L, Sep 3 1903 Sex:M Child# 13 Louis Grenier Canada & Melina Heroux Canada
GRENIER, Leo Armand, Aug 11 1905 Sex:M Child# 13 Louis Grenier Canada & Melina Heroux Canada
GRENIER, Marguerite Isabel, Apr 20 1914 Sex:F Child# 2 Henri Grenier Canada & M Louise Fournier Canada
GRENIER, Marie E, Jul 19 1888 Sex:F Child# 1 Adelard Grenier Canada & Emma Gerward Canada
GRENIER, Marie Philomene, Dec 3 1891 Sex:F Child# 1 Albert Grenier Canada & Amanda Morisette Canada
GRENON, Dorothy Elaine, Nov 13 1935 Sex:F Child# 1 Joseph Grenon Manchester, NH & Albertine Cassett Nashua, NH
GRENON, Ernestine Delia, Nov 17 1903 Sex:F Child# 2 Joseph Grenon Wilton, NH & Ernestine Morin Canada
GRESHEN, Joseph, Jun 3 1912 Sex:M Child# 3 John Greshen Russia & Eva Sunskofski Russia
GRETSKI, Unknown, Aug 2 1901 Sex:M Child# 3 Joseph Gretski Russia & Elizabeth Ruphut Russia Stillborn
GRIBAS, Adamo, Mar 5 1927 Sex:M Child# 1 George Gribas Greece & Efthimea Gugin Greece
GRIBAS, Unknown, Jul 11 1928 Sex:F Child# 2 George Gribas Greece & Eptimia Goden Greece
GRIFFIN, Bernard, Jul 31 1913 Sex:M Child# 6 Stephen Griffin Ireland & Gertrude Moloy NH
GRIFFIN, Francis John, 3rd, Aug 10 1924 Sex:M Child# 1 F J Griffin, Jr Londonderry, NH & Anna L Sullivan Roxbury
GRIFFIN, Frederick J, Jul 1 1926 Sex:M Child# 2 Frank Griffin Londonderry, NH & Anna Sullivan Roxbury, MA
GRIFFIN, Louise Anna, Jan 3 1929 Sex:F Child# 3 Frank Griffin Londonderry, NH & Anna Sullivan Roxbury, MA
GRIFFIN, Margaret, Jan 28 1895 Sex:F Child# 4 Frank Griffin Canada & Margaret Drea Manchester, NH
GRIFFIN, Marjorie Edith, Nov 5 1916 Sex:F Child# 7 Steven Griffin Ireland & Gertrude Molloy Ireland
GRIFFIN, Mary Margaret, Jul 30 1923 Sex:F Child# 2 Patrick Griffin Ireland & Beatrice McGowan Ireland
GRIFFIN, Robert James, Dec 16 1920 Sex:M Child# 1 Patrick Griffin Ireland & Beatrice McGowan Ireland
GRIGAS, Charles, Jan 23 1917 Sex:M Child# 7 John Grigas Russia & Oveline Oscinute Russia
GRIGAS, Frank, Jan 23 1917 Sex:M Child# 8 John Grigas Russia & Oveline Oscinute Russia
GRIGAS, Joseph, Jan 13 1912 Sex:M Child# 5 John Grigas Russia & Paolina Osciuntie Russia
GRIGAS, Julia, Jul 15 1905 Sex:F Child# 3 Charles Grigas Russia & Mikalina Zinbergisti Russia
GRIGAS, Peter, Jun 29 1904 Sex:M Child# 2 John Grigas Russia & P Oxkizenoutha Russia
GRIGAS, Thomas, Dec 29 1902 Sex:M Child# 1 Jan Grigas Russia & Paulina Akxinie Russia
GRIGAS, Unknown, Oct 25 1912 Sex:F Child# 1 George Grigas Macedonia & Stella Dryksos Macedonia Stillborn
GRIGAS, Unknown, Apr 13 1934 Sex:F Child#  Joseph Grigas Lithuania & Vizenta Dominos Lithuania
GRIGAS, Winnie, Dec 6 1914 Sex:F Child# 1 William Grigas Russia & Rose Valaskivitch Russia
GRIGOS, Anna, Jul 27 1909 Sex:F Child# 7 Michael Grigos Russia & Helena Gilbutch Russia
GRIGOS, John, Feb 2 1909 Sex:M Child# 4 John Grigos Russia & Paulina A Kastin Russia
GRIGOS, John, Aug 5 1909 Sex:M Child# 5 Kazimir Grigos Russia & Mikalina Zinkiewiute Russia

GRIMES, Herbert Austin, Apr 16 1930 Sex:M Child# 1 Herbert A Grimes Nantucket, MA & Elizabeth Willett Nashua, NH
GRIMES, John Harvey, Apr 29 1921 Sex:M Child# 1 Warren C Grimes Reading, MA & Doris Rumrill Hillsboro, NH
GRIMOND, Marie Anne, Dec 30 1891 Sex:F Child# Louis Grimond Canada & Victoire Gauthier Canada
GRING, Edward Henry, May 20 1915 Sex:M Child# 1 Leon P Gring Westford, MA & Mary E James Groton, MA
GRIOUARD, Joseph Theophile, Aug 25 1909 Sex:M Child# 4 Joseph Girouard Nashua, NH & Dora Lapointe Sciota, NY
GRIOUARD, Marie Jeannette, Dec 22 1910 Sex:F Child# 1 Pierre Girouard Canada & Pomela Lavery Canada
GRIRES, Zabella, Feb 27 1903 Sex:F Child# 2 Coronier Grires Russia & Michaelina Zinkia Russia
GRISWOLD, Agnes, Jan 12 1893 Sex:F Child# 3 Hiram V Griswold St Johnsbury, VT & Josephine Scribner S Weare, NH
GRISWOLD, Charles G, May 10 1890 Sex:M Child# 1 George M Griswold Manchester, NH & Elsie Rigney Mooers, NY
GRISWOLD, Chauncey, May 27 1893 Sex:M Child# 3 George N Griswold Manchester & Elsie Rigney Mooers, NY
GRISWOLD, Halsey W, Nov 9 1896 Sex:M Child# 5 George N Griswold Manchester, NH & Elsie Rigney Mooers, NY
GRISWOLD, Lester, Oct 8 1891 Sex:M Child# 2 George N Griswold Manchester & Elsie Rigney Mooers, NY
GRISWOLD, Unknown, Jul 11 1888 Sex:M Child# 2 Hiram V Griswold St Johnsbury, VT & Josie W Scribner So Weare, NH
GRISWOLD, Unknown, Jan 11 1895 Sex:M Child# 4 George N Griswold Manchester, NH & Elsie Rigney Mooers, NY
GRISWOLD, Unknown, Sep 10 1896 Sex:F Child# Hiram Griswold Concord, VT & Josephine S Griswold S Weare, NH Stillbor
GRISWOLD, Unknown, Dec 17 1898 Sex:F Child# 6 George N Griswold Manchester, NH & Elsie Rigney Mooers, NY Stillborn
GROBOSKY, Richard, Dec 28 1935 Sex:M Child# 2 George Grobosky Nashua, NH & Julia Lazensky Nashua, NH
GROHOSKY, George, Sep 25 1933 Sex:M Child# 1 George Grohosky Nashua, NH & Julia Lazinsky Nashua, NH
GROKOVSKI, Annie, Aug 16 1917 Sex:F Child# 3 Frank Grokovski Russia & Aniella Pitka Russia
GROKOVSKY, Agnes, Mar 31 1918 Sex:F Child# 1 Joseph Grokovsky Russia & Theophile Masgala Russia
GROKOWSKI, Constantine, Feb 22 1913 Sex:M Child# 1 Frank Grokowski Russia & Aniella Petkin Austria
GRONDIN, James Albert, Dec 13 1934 Sex:M Child# 5 Albert Grondin Salem, MA & Mary Monaghen England
GRONDIN, Joseph Charles, Oct 23 1900 Sex:M Child# 2 Charles Grondin Canada & Rosilda Noel Canada
GRONDIN, Mary Theresa, Jun 12 1933 Sex:F Child# 4 Albert Grondin Mass & Mary Monaghan England
GROOM, Homer Lee, Jun 17 1932 Sex:M Child# 2 H L Groom Tullahoma, TN & Della Berube Nashua, NH
GROOM, Raymond Thomas, Apr 3 1934 Sex:M Child# 3 Homer Groom Tennessee & Delia Berube Nashua, NH
GROOMS, Lucille Lorraine, Feb 2 1931 Sex:F Child# 1 Homer Grooms Tullahoma, TN & Delia Berube Nashua, NH
GROUDIN, Marie Rosilda, Apr 2 1899 Sex:F Child# 1 Charles Groudin Canada & Rosilda Noel Canada
GROVE, Unknown, Jul 22 1895 Sex:M Child# 2 John C Grove Lowell, MA & Maria L Spalding Nashua, NH
GROVER, Charles Irving, Jun 17 1930 Sex:M Child# 2 Irving Grover Nashua, NH & Rachel Hamel Nashua, NH
GROVER, Earl Ware, Jul 6 1900 Sex:M Child# 4 Charles R Grover Mass & Flora Wildes Mass
GROVER, Florence Jeannette, Oct 22 1896 Sex:F Child# 2 Charles R Grover Cambridge, MA & Flora Wildes
GROVER, Floyd M, Mar 22 1896 Sex:M Child# 3 F J Grover Mass & O T Read Vermont
GROVES, John Spaulding, Feb 23 1922 Sex:M Child# 1 Reuben S Groves Hudson, NH & Eunice Potter Rutland, VT
GROVES, Unknown, Jul 28 1893 Sex:M Child# 1 John C Groves Lowell, MA & S Maria Spalding Nashua, NH
GRUBB, Athaleen Grace, Jan 6 1911 Sex:F Child# 3 Franz A Grubb Germany & Caroline Sauer Newton, MA
GRUGAS, Annie, Jun 15 1917 Sex:F Child# 1 Joseph Grugas Lithuania Russia & Vincenta Yesukavicz Lithuania Russia
GRYGIEL, Ernest, Sep 26 1923 Sex:M Child# 4 Alphonse Grygiel Poland & Helena Markiel Poland
GRYGIEL, Ganefa, Sep 17 1919 Sex:F Child# 3 Alphonse Grygiel Russia & Michalena Markian Russia
GRYGIEL, Joseph, Feb 20 1916 Sex:M Child# 1 Alfonsa Grygiel Russia & Meheling Markel Russia
GUAWVICH, Dora, Nov 15 1916 Sex:F Child# 1 Charles Guawvich Greece & Helen Korapese Greece
GUAY, Adalbert, May 28 1898 Sex:M Child# 6 Theophile Guay Canada & Delia Poulin Canada
GUAY, Edouard, Sep 5 1894 Sex:M Child# 4 Theophile Guay Canada & Delia Poulin Canada
GUAY, Irene, May 28 1896 Sex:F Child# 5 Theophile Guay Canada & Delia Poulin Canada
GUAY, Lucille Beatrice, Apr 9 1924 Sex:F Child# 2 Harry Guay NH & Lillian Morin NH
GUAY, Raymond, Jul 5 1926 Sex:M Child# 3 Harry Guay Nashua, NH & Lillian Morin Nashua, NH
GUAY, William, Jan 24 1893 Sex:M Child# 3 Theophil Guay Canada & Delia Poulin Canada
GUBBER, Francis Eugene, Jun 16 1926 Sex:M Child# 1 Adolphus Gubber
GUBIES, Unknown, Nov 3 1932 Sex:F Child# 3 Geo Gubies Greece & Eltimia Gugin Greece
GUDAITIS, Alfred, Jan 1 1920 Sex:M Child# 3 John Gudaitis Russia & Pauline Barnstawich Russia
GUDAITIS, Isidore, Jul 24 1900 Sex:M Child# 1 Isidore Gudaitis Europe & Annie Sechniak Europe
GUDAUTIS, Ruth, Aug 6 1921 Sex:F Child# 4 John Gudautis Russia & Pauline Barnatarish Russia
GUDECKY, Unknown, Dec 17 1917 Sex:F Child# 1 Anthony Gudecky Russia & Mary Sherneskas Russia
GUDREWICZ, Frank, Jul 9 1914 Sex:M Child# 2 John Gudrewicz Russia & Antonia Greginta Russia
GUENETTE, Andrea Regina, Mar 17 1907 Sex:F Child# 1 Emery Guenette Canada & Regina Dupont Canada
GUENETTE, Roger Romeo, Sep 16 1912 Sex:M Child# 2 Emery Guenette Canada & Regina Dupont Canada
GUERARD, Marie Jeanne Aline, Jul 29 1933 Sex:F Child# 1 Ernest Guerard Canada & Berthe Bonin Canada
GUERETTE, Adelard Adrien, Oct 5 1907 Sex:M Child# 2 Auguste Guerette Canada & Emma Chagnon Nashua, NH
GUERETTE, Adolphe, Jun 3 1891 Sex:M Child# 11 Joseph Guerette Canada & Rosalie Cardinal Canada
GUERETTE, Agnes Gertrude, Aug 28 1916 Sex:F Child# 7 Joseph W Guerette Canada & Rose D Decelle Canada
GUERETTE, Albina, Apr 21 1889 Sex:F Child# 10 Joseph Guerette Canada & Rosalie Carchinal Canada
GUERETTE, Anita, Feb 10 1898 Sex:F Child# 2 Joseph Guerette Canada & Amelia Gadbois Worcester, MA
GUERETTE, Anita Andrea Rachell, Jul 11 1913 Sex:F Child# 11 Joseph Guerette Canada & Amelia Gadbois Canada
GUERETTE, Bertha Loraine, Dec 6 1900 Sex:F Child# 4 Joseph Guerette Canada & Amelia Gadbois Mass
GUERETTE, Cecile Rachel, Aug 14 1912 Sex:F Child# 3 Joseph A Guerette Canada & Azilda Lancourt Canada
GUERETTE, Corinne Albertine, Apr 8 1896 Sex:F Child# 1 Joseph Guerette Canada & Emilia Gadbois Worcester, MA
GUERETTE, Cyril Armand Rolland, Jun 5 1914 Sex:M Child# 2 Louis Guerette Canada & Marie Michaud Canada
GUERETTE, Donald Richard, Oct 13 1935 Sex:M Child# 1 Isidore Guerette Canada & Agnes Brodeur Milford, NH
GUERETTE, Donat Albert, Aug 4 1902 Sex:M Child# 5 Joseph Guerette Canada & Amelia Gadbois Worcester, MA
GUERETTE, Doris Anita, Aug 14 1927 Sex:F Child# 4 J A Guerette Canada & Celina Ouillette Bancroft, ME
GUERETTE, Edna Louise, Aug 26 1909 Sex:F Child# 5 Joseph W Guerette Canada & Rose Decelles Canada
GUERETTE, Etienne Raymond, Dec 26 1918 Sex:M Child# 6 Ad Guerette Canada & Azilda Lancourt Putnam, CT
GUERETTE, Etienne Roger, Dec 26 1918 Sex:M Child# 5 Ad Guerette Canada & Azilda Lancourt Putnam, CT

GUERETTE, Helen, Jan 15 1923 Sex:F Child# 2 Joseph A Guerette Canada & Azilda Lancourt Canada
GUERETTE, Irene Regina, Jul 16 1906 Sex:F Child# 3 Joseph Guerette Canada & Rose Delima Decelles Canada
GUERETTE, J A Roger Altheol, Nov 2 1915 Sex:M Child# 3 Louis G Guerette Canada & Marie C Michaud Canada
GUERETTE, J Louis George, Feb 10 1912 Sex:M Child# 1 Louis Geo Guerette Canada & Marie Michaud Canada
GUERETTE, Jean Bte, Sep 15 1887 Sex:M Child# 4 Pierre Guerette P Q & Angele Paradis P Q
GUERETTE, Jeannine Lucienne, Mar 8 1930 Sex:F Child# 1 Lucien Guerette Canada & Rose Desrosiers Canada
GUERETTE, Joan Gloria, Apr 11 1929 Sex:F Child# 5 Joseph A Guerette Canada & Celina Ouillette Bancroft, ME
GUERETTE, Joseph A H, Aug 13 1890 Sex:M Child# 1 Pierre Guerette Canada & Claudia Dionne Canada
GUERETTE, Joseph Alfred A L, Apr 26 1910 Sex:M Child# 4 Auguste Guerette Canada & Emma Chagnon Nashua, NH
GUERETTE, Joseph Auguste A A, Sep 19 1906 Sex:M Child# 1 Auguste Guerette Canada & Emma Chagnon Nashua, NH
GUERETTE, Joseph E, Oct 10 1890 Sex:M Child# 2 Louis Guerette Canada & Eondine Bouchard Canada
GUERETTE, Joseph Gerald A, Sep 11 1911 Sex:M Child# 10 Joseph Guerette Canada & Emilia Gadbois Canada
GUERETTE, Joseph Raymond D A, Feb 21 1909 Sex:M Child# 3 Auguste Guerette Canada & Emma Chagnon Nashua, NH
GUERETTE, Joseph Theodule, Sep 30 1891 Sex:M Child# Pierre Guerette Canada & Claudia Dionne Canada
GUERETTE, Lilian Rose, Sep 29 1899 Sex:F Child# 3 Joseph Guerette Canada & Amelia Gadbois Canada
GUERETTE, Lois Joseph Ray, Aug 3 1935 Sex:M Child# 1 Gerard Guerette Nashua, NH & Isabelle LaForest Nashua, NH
GUERETTE, Loraine Rita, May 5 1926 Sex:F Child# 3 Joseph A Guerette Canada & Celina Ouellette Bancroft, ME
GUERETTE, Louis Leo, Feb 29 1904 Sex:M Child# 1 Joseph N Guerette Canada & Rose D Decelles Canada
GUERETTE, Louis Leo Emile, Aug 16 1905 Sex:M Child# 7 Joseph Guerette Canada & Emilia Gadbois Worcester, MA
GUERETTE, Marie Alberta I, Apr 8 1905 Sex:F Child# 1 Joseph A guerette Canada & Azilda Lancourt Putnam, CT
GUERETTE, Marie Cordelia, Apr 11 1899 Sex:F Child# 1 Etienne Guerette Canada & Hermance Berube Canada
GUERETTE, Marie Emma A I, Feb 11 1907 Sex:F Child# 2 Joseph Adel Guerette Canada & Azilda Lancourt Canada
GUERETTE, Marie Felicite, Jul 5 1893 Sex:F Child# 1 Louis Guerette Canada & Felicite Berube Canada
GUERETTE, Marie Florence, Jun 5 1907 Sex:F Child# 8 Joseph Guerette Canada & Amelia Gadbois Worcester, MA
GUERETTE, Marie Irene Yvonne, Apr 10 1904 Sex:F Child# 6 Joseph Guerette Canada & Amelia Gadbois Canada
GUERETTE, Marie Solange A, Jul 14 1910 Sex:F Child# 9 Joseph Guerette Canada & Emelia Guerette Canada
GUERETTE, Normand, Jun 29 1932 Sex:M Child# 2 Lucien Guerette Canada & Rose Desrosiers Canada
GUERETTE, Philippe Edgar, May 18 1908 Sex:M Child# 3 Joseph Guerette Canada & Rose D Decelles Canada
GUERETTE, Prosper Alfred, Apr 29 1905 Sex:M Child# 2 Joseph Guerette Canada & Rose Delima Decelles Canada
GUERETTE, Theodore Robert, Feb 4 1919 Sex:M Child# 8 Joseph W Guerette Canada & Rose Decelle Canada
GUERETTE, Unknown, Aug 31 1914 Sex:M Child# 12 Joseph Guerette Canada & Amelia Gadbois Mass Stillborn
GUERETTE, Unknown, Feb 17 1916 Sex:F Child# 13 Joseph Guerette Canada & Amelia Gadbois Canada Stillborn
GUERIN, Joseph Philias, Dec 17 1903 Sex:M Child# 1 Joseph Guerin Canada & Philomene Robin Canada
GUERIN, Lawrence Henry, Feb 23 1910 Sex:M Child# 1 Francis Guerin Canada & Rose Bouley Lowell, MA
GUERIN, Unknown, Aug 3 1910 Sex:F Child# 1 Henry Guerin Winchester, MA & Mary Flynn Nashua, NH
GUERNON, Joseph Octave, Aug 17 1902 Sex:M Child# 1 Joseph Guernon Greenville & Ernestine Morin Canada
GUERRETTE, Alphonse Victor, Apr 13 1917 Sex:M Child# 4 J Adelard Guerrette Canada & Azilda Lancourt Canada
GUERRETTE, Annette, Jun 6 1911 Sex:F Child# 6 Joseph Guerette Canada & Rose D Decelles US
GUERRETTE, Elaine Rita, Dec 19 1932 Sex:F Child# 1 Lucien Guerrette Nashua, NH & V Chamberlain Vermont
GUERRETTE, Lionel H E, Mar 7 1917 Sex:M Child# 3 Emery Guerrette Canada & Regina Dupont Canada
GUERRETTE, M Jeanne Lucille, Aug 26 1922 Sex:F Child# 9 Jos W Guerrette Canada & Rose Delima Decelle Canada
GUERRETTE, T Florence Rita, May 5 1922 Sex:F Child# 5 Auguste Guerrette Canada & Emma Rose Chagnon Nashua, NH
GUERRETTE, William Lionel, Oct 17 1924 Sex:M Child# 10 Joseph Guerrette Canada & Rose Decelle Canada
GUERSKIE, Alex, May 29 1913 Sex:M Child# 1 Alex Guerskie Russia & Mary Gauluta Russia
GUERSKIN, Ladirlean, Aug 9 1914 Sex:M Child# 5 Amstophir Guerskin Russia & Ant Roudorskis Russia
GUERTIN, Albert Antoine, Jun 26 1902 Sex:M Child# 3 J B A Guertin Nashua, NH & Angeline Burque Nashua, NH
GUERTIN, Alfred Octave, Dec 3 1905 Sex:M Child# 1 Auguste Guertin Canada & Ludivine Morin Canada
GUERTIN, Alfred V Leo, Dec 2 1899 Sex:M Child# 6 Alphonse Guertin Canada & Clara Simoneau Canada
GUERTIN, Alida, May 5 1889 Sex:F Child# 6 Jean B Guertin Canada & Mary Lesage Canada
GUERTIN, Alphonse Conrad, Oct 12 1918 Sex:M Child# 2 Henri G Guertin Nashua, NH & Josephine Guertin Canada
GUERTIN, Armand Daniel, Nov 15 1910 Sex:M Child# 9 Avila Guertin Canada & Rosalba Fontaine Canada
GUERTIN, Blanche Cordelia, Mar 8 1893 Sex:F Child# 1 Hormidas Guertin Canada & Philomene Comtois Canada
GUERTIN, Daniel, Jan 9 1935 Sex:M Child# 1 (No Parents Listed)
GUERTIN, Eugene, Nov 27 1887 Sex:M Child# Joseph Guertin P Q & Rosanna Roy Canada
GUERTIN, Francis Victor, Aug 17 1900 Sex:M Child# Louis Guertin Canada & Mary Benoit Canada
GUERTIN, George Emile, Dec 11 1900 Sex:M Child# 2 J B A Guertin Nashua, NH & Evangeline Burque Nashua, NH
GUERTIN, Georgette Theresa, Oct 22 1930 Sex:F Child# 1 Antoine Guertin Nashua, NH & Gertrude Vezina Manchester, NH
GUERTIN, Gertrude, Mar 6 1896 Sex:F Child# 4 Alphonse Guertin Canada & Clara Simoneau Canada
GUERTIN, Henri, Sep 29 1916 Sex:M Child# 1 Henri Guertin Nashua, NH & Josephine Gendron Canada
GUERTIN, Henri Octave, Jun 18 1904 Sex:M Child# 4 J B A Guertin Nashua, NH & Angeline Burque Nashua, NH
GUERTIN, Henry, Sep 24 1891 Sex:M Child# 6 L Alfred Guertin Canada & Marie Morin Canada
GUERTIN, Henry John, Apr 25 1894 Sex:M Child# 9 Baptiste Guertin Canada & Mary Lesage Canada
GUERTIN, J Alphonse A, Mar 20 1899 Sex:M Child# 1 J B Almar Guertin Nashua, NH & Angelina Burque Nashua, NH
GUERTIN, John Charles G, Jul 6 1908 Sex:M Child# 6 John B A Guertin Nashua, NH & Angelina Burque Nashua, NH
GUERTIN, Joseph, Apr 13 1888 Sex:M Child# 1 Norbert Guertin Canada & Celina Rousseau Canada
GUERTIN, Joseph Ernest H, Nov 17 1905 Sex:M Child# Avila Guertin Canada & Rose Alba Fontaine Canada
GUERTIN, Joseph Wilfred A, May 31 1892 Sex:M Child# 1 Alfred Guertin Canada & Clara A Simoneau Canada
GUERTIN, Julien R Carod, Jan 27 1898 Sex:M Child# 5 Alphonse Guertin Canada & Clara A Simoneau Canada
GUERTIN, Louis Conrad O, Jul 19 1898 Sex:M Child# 1 Avila Guertin Canada & Rosalba Fontaine Canada
GUERTIN, Louis Paul, Jan 30 1931 Sex:M Child# 2 Victor Guertin Nashua, NH & Marie A Girouard Hudson, NH
GUERTIN, Marie Lorette, Oct 18 1906 Sex:F Child# 6 Avila Guertin Canada & Rose Alba Fontaine Canada
GUERTIN, Marie Therese Y, Jun 15 1908 Sex:F Child# 7 Avila Guertin Canada & Rose Alba Fontaine Canada
GUERTIN, Rachel Rita, May 16 1913 Sex:F Child# 10 Avila Guertin Canada & Rosalba Fontaine Canada

GUERTIN, Raoul Rosario, Jun 19 1900 Sex:M Child# 2 Avela Guertin Canada & Rosalba Fontaine Canada
GUERTIN, Ruth Louise, Aug 18 1933 Sex:F Child# 3 A A Guertin Nashua, NH & Gertrude Vezina Manchester, NH
GUERTIN, Sylvio, Nov 19 1903 Sex:M Child# 4 Avila Guertin Canada & Rose Alba Fontaine Canada
GUERTIN, Unknown, Nov 5 1891 Sex:F Child# 7 J B Guertin Canada & Mary Lesage Canada Stillborn
GUERTIN, Unknown, Feb 19 1893 Sex:F Child# 8 Jean B Guertin Canada & Marie Lesage Canada Stillborn
GUERTIN, Unknown, Mar 11 1894 Sex:M Child# 1 L N T Guertin St Hyacinthe, PQ & Rose N Benoit St Anne, PQ
GUERTIN, Unknown, Mar 21 1898 Sex:M Child# 2 Louis N L Guertin St Hyacinthe, PQ & Mary Rose Benoit Nashua, NH
GUERTIN, Victor Gerard, Apr 8 1906 Sex:M Child# 5 J B A Guertin Nashua, NH & Angeline Burque Nashua, NH
GUERTIN, Victory Telesphore, Jun 5 1929 Sex:M Child# 1 Victor Guertin Nashua, NH & Antoinette Girouard Hudson, NH
GUEST, Dorothy May, Jun 5 1917 Sex:F Child# 1 (No Parents Listed)
GUEST, Ernest Roscoe, Sep 25 1913 Sex:M Child# 12 James B Guest NS & Matilda Selig NS
GUEST, Esther Evelyn, Dec 8 1914 Sex:F Child# 3 William Guest New York & Bertha Nealy NH
GUEST, Frank Phillip, Mar 19 1934 Sex:M Child# 1 Frank Guest Hollis, NH & Bernice McLaughlin Nashua, NH Stillborn
GUEST, Roland Everett, Jan 31 1912 Sex:M Child# 11 Burton Guest Canada & Mathilda Sely Bridgewater, NS
GUESTIRE, Delvina, May 18 1890 Sex:F Child# 3 Joseph Guestire Canada & Rosanna Roy Canada
GUGAN, Peter, Nov 10 1908 Sex:M Child# 5 John Gugan Russia & Mary Grigoutie Russia
GUICHARD, Alfred Wilfred, Dec 6 1924 Sex:M Child# 3 Albert Guichard Canada & Odelie Vien Gonic, NH
GUICHARD, Alice, Mar 13 1900 Sex:F Child# 7 Joseph Guichard Canada & Aglae Guichard Canada
GUICHARD, Angelina, Feb 21 1892 Sex:F Child# 4 Joseph Guichard Canada & Aglai Canada
GUICHARD, Avila, Aug 13 1896 Sex:M Child# 6 Joseph Guichard Canada & Aglae Guichard Canada
GUICHARD, Desneiges Antoinette, Feb 15 1923 Sex:F Child# 2 Albert Guichard Canada & Odelie Vien Gonic, NH
GUICHARD, Irene, Jan 20 1901 Sex:F Child# 6 Ludger Guichard Canada & Gratia Deschesnes Canada
GUICHARD, Jeanne Adelaid, Mar 28 1921 Sex:F Child# 1 Albert Guichard Canada & Odelie Viens Gonic, NH
GUICHARD, Joseph, Mar 4 1902 Sex:M Child# 8 Joseph Guichard Canada & Aglaie Guichard Canada
GUICHARD, Joseph Emile A, Apr 5 1899 Sex:M Child# 5 Joseph Guichard Canada & Anastasie Raymond Canada
GUICHARD, Marie Adele, Sep 6 1893 Sex:F Child# 2 Ludger Guichard Canada & Gracia Deschesne Canada
GUICHARD, Marie Albina L, Nov 10 1903 Sex:F Child# 7 Joseph Guichard Canada & Anastasie Raymond Canada
GUICHARD, Marie Andrea, Jun 1 1899 Sex:F Child# 2 Alphonse Guichard Nashua, NH & Henriette Lafleur Plattsburg, NY
GUICHARD, Maurice Roger, Feb 26 1926 Sex:M Child# 4 Albert Guichard
GUICHARD, Omer, Oct 19 1904 Sex:M Child# 9 Joseph Guichard Canada & Aglas Guichard Canada Stillborn
GUICHARD, Therese, Jan 18 1934 Sex:F Child# 1 Wilfred Guichard Nashua, NH & Caroline Murphy Canada
GUICHARD, Unknown, Jul 13 1893 Sex:M Child# 1 Joseph Guichard Canada & Anasthasia Raymond Canada Stillborn
GUIDIARD, Eugene, Jun 26 1888 Sex:F Child# 2 Joseph Guidiard Canada & Aylve Quichard Canada
GUILBERT, Andria Irene, Mar 7 1920 Sex:F Child# 1 Arthur Guilbert US & Adriane Galipeau US
GUILD, George Herbert, May 4 1919 Sex:M Child# 1 Walter K Guild Methuen, MA & Ruth L Wells
GUILD, Robert William, Oct 31 1922 Sex:M Child# 2 Walter Guild Mass & Ruth Wells NH
GUILL, Charles Francis, Aug 31 1926 Sex:M Child# 1 Charles Guill Worcester, MA & Yvonne Mirault Manchester, NH
GUILL, Marie Lucille, Sep 29 1927 Sex:F Child# 2 Charles Guill Mass & Yvonne Mireault Nashua, NH
GUILL, Nelson Joseph, Jr, Jul 25 1910 Sex:M Child# 4 Nelson J Guill Canada & Sara J Merrick Worcester, MA
GUILL, Ruth Marie, May 10 1906 Sex:F Child# 5 Nelson J Guill Canada & Sarah J Merrick Worcester, MA
GUILLEMAIN, Alfred Remi, Oct 17 1905 Sex:M Child# 3 Ephraim Guillemain Canada & Desneiges April Nashua, NH
GUILLEMAIN, Arthur Leo, Jul 11 1902 Sex:M Child# 1 Ephrem Guillemain Canada & Desneiges April Nashua, NH
GUILLEMAIN, Celia Therese, Dec 12 1915 Sex:F Child# 8 Ephraim Guillemain Canada & Desneiges April Nashua, NH
GUILLEMAIN, David, Dec 5 1903 Sex:M Child# 2 Ephrem Guillemain Canada & Desneiges April Nashua, NH
GUILLEMAIN, Edgar Leo P, Dec 30 1908 Sex:M Child# 1 Alfred Guillemain US & Bernadette Belair US
GUILLEMAIN, Jeanne D'Arc Rol, Aug 11 1919 Sex:F Child# 6 Benedict Guillemain Canada & Marie L Levesque NH
GUILLEMAIN, Omer Roland, Jan 20 1906 Sex:M Child# 5 Alfred Guillemain Canada & Celina Gingras Hooksett, NH
GUILLEMETTE, Alice Andrea, Sep 18 1903 Sex:F Child# 4 Edouard Guillemette Canada & Amanda Canada
GUILLEMETTE, Jos Normand T, Aug 31 1929 Sex:M Child# 3 Adelard Guillemette Canada & Emelia Pelletier Nashua, NH
GUILLEMETTE, Joseph Hector, Aug 16 1923 Sex:M Child# 1 Adelard Guillemette Canada & M Emelia Pelletier NH
GUILLEMETTE, Lucille Dora, Dec 16 1915 Sex:F Child# 6 Edouard Guillemette Canada & Amanda Brisson Canada
GUILLEMETTE, Marie, Sep 25 1896 Sex:F Child# 4 Joseph Guillemette Canada & Adeline Deschenes Canada
GUILLEMETTE, Marie Ange, Apr 27 1912 Sex:F Child# 7 Joseph Guillemette Canada & Adeline Deschenes Canada
GUILLEMETTE, Marie B Eva, Dec 29 1901 Sex:F Child# 3 Edouard Guillemette Canada & Amanda Brisson Canada
GUILLEMETTE, Marie Rita Annette, Jul 4 1925 Sex:F Child# 2 A Guillemette Canada & Emelia Pelletier Nashua, NH
GUILLMETTE, Joseph Arthur, Sep 11 1893 Sex:M Child# 3 Joseph Guillmette Canada & Marie Guillmette Canada
GUILLUNETTE, Joseph Eddie, Jul 2 1900 Sex:M Child# 3 Elzear Guillunette Canada & Albina Michaud Mass
GUILMAIN, Albert Ernest, Jun 10 1914 Sex:M Child# 2 Alfred Guilmain Canada & Alma Levesque Canada
GUILMAIN, Alma Irene, Mar 22 1918 Sex:F Child# 4 Alfred Guilmain Canada & Alma Levesque Canada
GUILMAIN, Armand Lucien, Oct 22 1916 Sex:M Child# 3 Alfred Guilmain Canada & Alma Levesque Canada
GUILMAIN, Berthe Rachel, Feb 23 1913 Sex:F Child# 1 Benedict Guilmain Canada & Marie L Levesque US
GUILMAIN, Conrad Raymond, Apr 9 1908 Sex:M Child# 6 Alfred Guilmain Canada & Nathalie Gingras Canada
GUILMAIN, Edward Daniel G, Jan 26 1924 Sex:M Child# 1 Ed Guilmain Canada & Annie Caron Gilbertville, MA
GUILMAIN, Girard Paul, Jul 16 1931 Sex:M Child# 4 Edouard Guilmain Canada & Anais Caron Gilbertville, MA
GUILMAIN, Hector, Apr 11 1904 Sex:M Child# 11 Victor Guilmain Canada & Emma Desmarais Canada
GUILMAIN, Irenee Raymond, Jan 6 1921 Sex:M Child# 7 R Guilmain Canada & Marie L Levesque US
GUILMAIN, Joseph A, Jul 6 1887 Sex:M Child# 1 Alfred Guilmain Canada & Regina Desmarais Canada
GUILMAIN, Joseph Leo, Jun 3 1913 Sex:M Child# 4 Alfred Guilmain Canada & Alma Levesque Canada
GUILMAIN, Olivette Germaine, Jul 7 1918 Sex:F Child# 5 Benedict Guilmain Canada & Marie L Levesque US
GUILMAIN, Paul Emile Lucien, Feb 20 1921 Sex:M Child# 1 Albert Guilmain Nashua, NH & Claudia Ricard Nashua, NH
GUILMAIN, Pearl, Jul 27 1919 Sex:F Child# 1 Henry Guilmain Canada & Emelie Anctil Nashua, NH
GUILMAIN, Robert Raoul, Oct 21 1914 Sex:M Child# 1 Benedict Guilmain Canada & M L Levesque US
GUILMAIN, Roland, Nov 3 1926 Sex:M Child# 2 Edouard Guilmain Canada & Alice M Deware US

GUILMAIN, Sara Lucille, May 2 1917 Sex:F Child# 3 Benedict Guilmain Canada & Marie Louise Levesque US
GUILMAIN, Unknown, Dec 14 1895 Sex:F Child# Alfred Guilmain Canada & Regina Desmarais Canada Stillborn
GUILMAIN, Vivian Rita, Sep 15 1929 Sex:F Child# 3 Edouard Guilmain Canada & Anaise Caron Gilbertville, MA
GUILMAIN, Yvonne Annette, Jan 27 1916 Sex:F Child# 3 Benedict Guilmain Canada & M Louise Levesque US
GUILMAN, Joseph Albert, Dec 28 1892 Sex:M Child# 8 Ephreme Guilman Canada & Celina Langelier Canada
GUILMAN, Joseph Omer, Dec 31 1892 Sex:M Child# 4 Alfred Guilman Canada & Regina Desmarais Nashua, NH
GUILMAN, Mary Anne, Dec 4 1890 Sex:F Child# 3 Alfred Guilman Canada & Regina Desmarais Canada
GUILMET, Joseph Louis, Apr 7 1898 Sex:M Child# 5 Joseph Guilmet Canada & Adeline Deschenes Canada
GUILMET, M Elizabeth, Sep 21 1894 Sex:F Child# Alfred Guilmet Canada & Georgina Desmarais Nashua, NH
GUILMETTE, Aurore, Jan 12 1894 Sex:F Child# Joseph Guilmette Canada & Adeline Deschenes Canada
GUILMETTE, Edouard Gerard, Sep 4 1913 Sex:M Child# 5 Edouard Guilmette Canada & Amanda Brisson Canada
GUILMETTE, Elpheg, Jan 11 1899 Sex:M Child# 1 Edouard Guilmette Canada & Amanda Brisson Canada
GUILMETTE, Exelia, Jun 15 1895 Sex:F Child# 3 Joseph Guilmette Canada & Deline Deschenes Canada
GUILMETTE, Joseph Achille, Jan 1892 Sex:M Child# 1 Joseph Guilmette Canada & Adeline Deschenes Canada
GUILMETTE, Joseph Elzear, Sep 10 1898 Sex:M Child# 2 Elzear Guilmette Canada & Albina Michaux E Bridgewater, MA
GUILMETTE, Rosanna, Jun 13 1900 Sex:F Child# 2 Edouard Guilmette Canada & Amanda Brisson Canada
GUILMETTE, Rosanna, Sep 29 1906 Sex:F Child# 2 Charles Guilmette Canada & Aurelie Denault Canada
GUILMETTE, Unknown, Dec 24 1913 Sex:F Child# Ovide Guilmette
GUIMOND, Alfred Paul, Nov 14 1907 Sex:M Child# 8 Ulfrin Guimond Canada & Clara Jeanbard Nashua, NH
GUIMOND, Alfred Paul, Aug 17 1935 Sex:M Child# 1 Alfred Guimond Nashua, NH & Arlene Bailey Nashua, NH
GUIMOND, Arthur Roland, Jul 28 1935 Sex:M Child# 1 (No Parents Listed)
GUIMOND, Clara E, May 30 1903 Sex:F Child# 4 Ulfiene Guimond Canada & Clara Jeanbarre Nashua, NH
GUIMOND, Dora Lucille, Sep 7 1917 Sex:F Child# 1 Edouard Guimond Nashua, NH & Adelina Menard Nashua, NH
GUIMOND, Edouard U, Nov 19 1897 Sex:M Child# 1 Ulfrin Guimond Canada & Clara Jeanbarre Nashua, NH
GUIMOND, Ernest Edouard, Aug 2 1918 Sex:M Child# 2 Edouard Guimond Canada & Adelina Menard Canada
GUIMOND, Ernest Leon, Mar 14 1906 Sex:M Child# 2 George Guimond Canada & Eva Burnham Champlain, NY
GUIMOND, Israel H, May 13 1902 Sex:M Child# 3 Ulfin Guimond Canada & Clara Jambard Nashua, NH
GUIMOND, Leo, May 16 1904 Sex:M Child# 1 George E Guimond Canada & Eva Burnham Champlain, NY
GUIMOND, Leo Hector, Nov 11 1906 Sex:M Child# 7 Ulfrin Guimond Canada & Clara Jambard Nashua, NH
GUIMOND, Madeline Joan, Jan 2 1932 Sex:F Child# 1 Edgar Guimond Nashua, NH & Annette Lajoie Nashua, NH
GUIMOND, Marie D G, Aug 6 1904 Sex:F Child# 5 Ulfien Guimond Canada & Clara Jeanbarre Nashua, NH
GUIMOND, Marie I Jeanbarre, Jun 12 1899 Sex:F Child# 2 Ulfrin Guimond Canada & Clara Jeanbarre Nashua, NH
GUIMOND, Marie Olivette Rita, Aug 28 1919 Sex:F Child# 3 Edouard Guimond NH & Adelina Menard NH
GUIMOND, Paul Arthur, Jun 26 1929 Sex:M Child# 1 Edgar Guimond Nashua, NH & Annette Lajoie Nashua, NH
GUIMOND, Robert Leo, Jun 20 1935 Sex:M Child# 4 Edgar Guimond Nashua, NH & Annette Lajoie Nashua, NH
GUIMOND, Romeo A, Sep 19 1905 Sex:M Child# 6 Ulfien Guimond Canada & Clara Jeanbarre Nashua, NH
GUIMOND, William Leo, Dec 21 1935 Sex:M Child# 1 Leo Guimond Nashua, NH & Dolores Gardner Bradley, ME
GUIMONT, Louis, Dec 23 1894 Sex:M Child# 11 Louis Guimont Canada & Victoria Gauthier Canada
GUIMONT, Marie Rose Anna, May 20 1922 Sex:F Child# 3 Aime Guimont Canada & Philomene Lepage Canada
GUIMONT, Rita Delia, Aug 10 1930 Sex:F Child# 2 Edgar Guimont Nashua, NH & Annette Lajoie Nashua, NH
GUIMONT, Unknown, Nov 26 1896 Sex:M Child# 12 Louis Guimont Canada & Victorie Gauthier Canada
GUINETTE, Ruth, Feb 17 1902 Sex:F Child# 1 Joseph Guinette
GUINTHER, Ruth Julia, Jul 6 1923 Sex:F Child# 1 Francis Guinther Clinton, MA & Mamie Fox Clinton, MA
GUKEWICZ, John, Mar 22 1914 Sex:M Child# 2 Maclaw Gukewicz Russia & Lawosa Sawloninuta Russia
GUKIEWICZ, Waclaw, Aug 25 1917 Sex:M Child# 4 Waclaw Gukiewicz Poland Russia & Leonora Laun Poland Russia
GULATEROS, Constantinus, Aug 31 1918 Sex:M Child# 1 George Gulateros Greece & S Pappayonis Greece
GUMB, Barbara Truesdell, Oct 9 1923 Sex:F Child# 1 Wallace R Gumb Lowell, MA & Mary Eliz Gordon Lowell, MA
GUMB, Catherine Ann, Jun 16 1931 Sex:F Child# 3 Wallace R Gumb Lowell, MA & Mary Gordon Lowell, MA
GUMB, Wallace Gordon, Oct 31 1927 Sex:M Child# 2 Wallace R Gumb Lowell, MA & Mary Gordon Lowell, MA
GUPTILL, Albert Jean, Mar 20 1933 Sex:M Child# 1 (No Parents Listed)
GUPTILL, Robert, May 27 1935 Sex:M Child# 2 (No Parents Listed)
GURECKI, Barbara, Mar 29 1903 Sex:F Child# 5 Joseph Gurecki Russia & Elizabeth Rabeck Russia
GURNEY, Blanche Russell, Jun 16 1891 Sex:F Child# 1 C Gurney Maine & F L Jeffs Brookline, NH
GURNEY, Robert Llewyn, Jul 27 1925 Sex:M Child# 1 Arthur Gurney Limestone, ME & Jennie Merrill Old Town, ME
GURNVILLE, Julia G, Nov 2 1888 Sex:F Child# 9 Williame Gurnville Willaston & Mary Alex Canada
GURSKI, Anna, Nov 12 1909 Sex:F Child# 1 Kristof Gurski Russia & Antonio Roudok Russia
GURSKIN, Stanislawa, Nov 8 1910 Sex:M Child# 2 Krisztop Gurskin Russia & Antonina Rudoki Russia
GUSHAIGIAN, Mary, Aug 18 1914 Sex:F Child# 6 Paul Gushaigian Turkey & Mary Zrarkin Turkey
GUSINIZ, Nellie, Nov 13 1914 Sex:F Child# 4 John Gusiniz Russia & Eva Sankowski Russia
GUSTAFSON, Charles Edward, Dec 19 1931 Sex:M Child# 2 Carl E Gustafson Concord, NH & Irene M Dodge Nashua, NH
GUSTAFSON, Jean, Jul 31 1926 Sex:F Child# 1 Carl Gustafson W Concord, NH & Irene Dodge Nashua, NH Stillborn
GUTTERSON, Georgia, Nov 10 1901 Sex:F Child# 1 George P Gutterson Manchester, NH & Lillian B Peavey Exeter, NH
GUY, Joseph, Jul 30 1916 Sex:M Child# 1 Wilfrid Guy Canada & Alice Laverdiere Mass
GUY, Wilfred, Nov 1 1918 Sex:M Child# 2 Wilfred Guy Canada & Alice Laverdiere Mass
GUYAIT, Alice Mabel, Sep 5 1909 Sex:F Child# 4 Albanie Guyait Nashua, NH & Lamie Morin Canada
GUYAIT, Emery, Jul 11 1908 Sex:M Child# 2 Henry Guyait Nashua, NH & Lany Morin Nashua, NH
GUYAIT, Henry, Jul 11 1908 Sex:M Child# 3 Henry Guyait Nashua, NH & Lany Morin Nashua, NH
GUYALT, Joseph Ludger, Aug 18 1907 Sex:M Child# 1 Henry Guyalt Nashua, NH & Dora Morin Canada
GUYNKA, Peter, Oct 17 1916 Sex:M Child# 3 Valery Guynka Russia & Albina Joiveta Russia
GYLE, James Edwin, Mar 26 1925 Sex:M Child# 6 Chas Arthur Gyle Lowell, MA & Mary Lee Pittsburg, PA
GYUKIVICKZ, Jose, Nov 26 1907 Sex:F Child# 2 Julius Gyukivickz Russia & Bahiki Torinlovitz Russia
GZINGLESKE, Mary, Jan 20 1917 Sex:F Child# 1 Tony Gzingleske Russia & Nellie Misiasrek Austria
HABIB, Barbara J, Nov 19 1927 Sex:F Child# 3 John S Habib Syria & Regina Bader Syria

HACKETT, Barbara Ann, May 13 1930 Sex:F Child# 1 Raymond Hackett Pepperell, MA & Anna Moran Nashua, NH
HACKETT, Nancy June, Aug 26 1933 Sex:F Child# 4 Raymond Hackett Pepperell, MA & Anna Moran Nashua, NH
HACKETT, Raymond William, Sep 23 1931 Sex:M Child# 2 Raymond Hackett Pepperell, MA & Anna Moran Nashua, NH
HACKETT, Robert Moran, Sep 3 1932 Sex:M Child# 3 R William Hackett Pepperell, MA & Anna Moran Nashua, NH
HADDOCK, James Carleton, Jun 13 1935 Sex:M Child# 2 James A Haddock Millinockett, ME & Doris Rollins Laconia, NH
HADGIODAMOS, Unknown, Sep 21 1932 Sex:F Child# 8 A Hadgiodamos Greece & E Giaprakas Greece
HADLEY, Edward R, Jun 18 1901 Sex:M Child# 1 (No Parents Listed)
HADLEY, Elizabeth Clara, Jul 21 1935 Sex:F Child# 1 Herman L Hadley Temple, NH & Helen L Blood Elmwood, NH
HADLEY, Hazel Ora, Jun 18 1901 Sex:F Child# 2 (No Parents Listed)
HADLEY, Herbert Davis, Aug 9 1913 Sex:M Child# 1 Lawrence Hadley Sudbury, MA & Helen J Sherbourne Jamaica Plain
HADLEY, Ralph G, Feb 15 1891 Sex:M Child# 4 Dana G Hadley NH & Alice A Gale Nashua, NH
HADLEY, Unknown, Dec 12 1889 Sex:F Child# 3 Dana Hadley NH & Alice A Gale Nashua, NH
HADZMA, William, Mar 30 1914 Sex:M Child# 1 Joseph Hadzma Russia & Petrillis Mikola Russia
HAERENCK, Victor George, Jun 22 1933 Sex:M Child# 4 Camille Haerenck Belgium & Auxilia Dion Canada
HAERINCK, Mary Valerie Delia, Feb 20 1924 Sex:F Child# 1 Camile Haerinck Belgium & Auxilia Dion Canada
HAERINCK, Theophile, Aug 31 1931 Sex:M Child# 3 Camille Haerinck Belgian & Oxilia Dion Canada
HAEVINCK, Marie Ange Carmilla, Jan 24 1928 Sex:F Child# 2 Carmile Haevinck Belgium & Cecelia Dion Canada
HAGARTY, Annie M, Jan 26 1898 Sex:F Child# 7 Patrick Hagarty Ireland & Mary Driscoll Ireland
HAGARTY, John Edward, Jul 23 1892 Sex:M Child# 5 Patrick Hagarty Ireland & Mary Discoll Ireland
HAGARTY, Timothy, Aug 24 1890 Sex:M Child# 5 Daniel C Hagarty Ireland & Catherine Sullivan Ireland
HAGARTY, Wilfrid P, Aug 25 1895 Sex:M Child# 7 Patrick Hagarty Ireland & Mary Driscoll Ireland
HAGEMANN, William Albert, Oct 29 1916 Sex:M Child# 2 William Hagemann New York, NY & Anna Osterhoudt Glascow,
HAGER, Alice Gwendolyn, Mar 10 1904 Sex:F Child# 1 Leslie A Hager Littleton, MA & Cora May Shedd N Walpole, NH
HAGERMAN, Eugene Pilip, Mar 24 1922 Sex:M Child# 3 William A Hagerman New York, NY & Annie Osterhoatt New York
HAGERMAN, Virginia, Jun 23 1915 Sex:F Child# 1 William A Hagerman New York, NY & Anna May Osterhoudt Glascow,
HAGERTY, Anna Angelina, Oct 26 1914 Sex:F Child# 2 Timothy Hagerty Nashua, NH & Anna Foley Conn
HAGERTY, Carole, Jan 29 1935 Sex:F Child# 3 Daniel Hagerty Nashua, NH & Doris Boulia Pepperell, MA
HAGERTY, Catherine, Oct 20 1915 Sex:F Child# 2 Cornelius Hagerty Nashua, NH & Margaret Shea Ireland
HAGERTY, Charles Joseph, Jul 7 1928 Sex:M Child# 5 Joseph Hagerty Nashua, NH & Josephine Dumas Somersworth, NH
HAGERTY, Cornelius John, Jul 4 1925 Sex:M Child# 5 Cornelius Hagerty Nashua, NH & Margaret Shea Ireland
HAGERTY, Dorothy Helen, Feb 22 1914 Sex:F Child# 2 John E Hagerty Nashua, NH & Elizabeth Johnson Hallowell, ME
HAGERTY, Elizabeth, Mar 7 1922 Sex:F Child# 7 John Ed Hagerty Nashua, NH & Elizabeth Johnson Hallowell, ME
HAGERTY, Ethel Mary, Apr 21 1913 Sex:F Child# 1 Timothy Hagerty Nashua, NH & Annie Foley Conn
HAGERTY, Francis Joseph, Dec 16 1916 Sex:M Child# 3 Cornelius Hagerty Nashua, NH & Margaret Shea Ireland
HAGERTY, Frederick, Jan 29 1921 Sex:M Child# 6 John Ed Hagerty Nashua, NH & Elizabeth Johnson Hallowell, ME
HAGERTY, Jeremiah, Feb 4 1890 Sex:M Child# 2 Dennis F Hagerty Ireland & Mary J Ireland
HAGERTY, Johannah, Jan 16 1891 Sex:F Child# 2 Daniel Hagerty Ireland & Julia Dineen Ireland
HAGERTY, John, May 13 1922 Sex:M Child# 5 Timothy P Hagerty Nashua, NH & Katherine McLaughlin Nashua, NH Stilllborn
HAGERTY, John Edward, Mar 15 1919 Sex:M Child# 5 John Ed Hagerty Nashua, NH & Mary Eliz Johnson Hallowell, ME
HAGERTY, John Francis, Sep 3 1892 Sex:M Child# 1 John Hagerty Ireland & Ellen L Garity Nashua, NH
HAGERTY, Kate, Aug 9 1891 Sex:F Child# 3 Dennis F Hagerty Ireland & Mary J Hagerty Ireland
HAGERTY, Lillian, Jun 27 1921 Sex:F Child# 4 Cornelius Hagerty Nashua, NH & Margaret Shea Ireland
HAGERTY, Lucy Ann, Jul 31 1933 Sex:F Child# 2 Daniel Hagerty Nashua, NH & Doris Boulia Pepperell, MA
HAGERTY, Marie, Jul 11 1917 Sex:F Child# 4 John E Hagerty Nashua, NH & Bessie M Johnson Halowell, ME
HAGERTY, Mary Arleen, May 15 1925 Sex:F Child# 1 Wilfred Hagerty Nashua, NH & M L Gaudette Canada
HAGERTY, Mary Barbara, Oct 9 1915 Sex:F Child# 3 John Edw Hagerty Nashua, NH & Elizabeth M Johnson Maine
HAGERTY, Mary Lillian, May 31 1916 Sex:F Child# 3 Timothy Hagerty Nashua, NH & Annie Foley Conn
HAGERTY, Norman Albert, Dec 12 1910 Sex:M Child# 2 Timothy P Hagerty Nashua, NH & Katherine Laughlin Nashua, NH
HAGERTY, Robert, Nov 1 1921 Sex:M Child# 3 Joseph E Hagerty Nashua, NH & Josephine Dumas Somersworth, NH
HAGERTY, Unknown, Feb 9 1913 Sex:M Child# 1 John E Hagerty Nashua, NH & Bessie Johnson Hallowell, ME Stillborn
HAGERTY, William Frances, Oct 31 1917 Sex:M Child# 4 Timothy Hagerty Nashua, NH & Annie Foley Connecticut
HAGGARTY, Helena, Oct 20 1902 Sex:F Child# 14 Patrick Haggarty Ireland & Mary Driscoll Ireland
HAGGERTY, Arthur, Oct 9 1894 Sex:M Child# 1 Arthur Haggerty Sherbrooke, Canada & Laura Stevens Burlington, VT
HAGGERTY, Catherine, Mar 25 1895 Sex:F Child# 8 Daniel C Haggerty Ireland & Catherine Ireland
HAGGERTY, Daniel, Dec 22 1891 Sex:M Child# 6 Daniel Haggerty Ireland & Kate Sullivan Ireland
HAGGERTY, Edward D, Oct 10 1909 Sex:M Child# 1 Timothy P Haggerty Nashua, NH & Kather McLaughlin Nashua, NH
HAGGERTY, George Francis, Oct 5 1895 Sex:M Child# 5 Dennis F Haggerty Ireland & Mary Ireland
HAGGERTY, Hannah, Mar 18 1888 Sex:F Child# Dennis Haggerty Ireland & Mary Haggerty Ireland
HAGGERTY, Jacqueline Ann, Jan 30 1932 Sex:F Child# 2 Wilfred Haggerty Nashua, NH & M L Gaudette St Helene, PQ
HAGGERTY, Joseph, Mar 22 1893 Sex:M Child# 2 Daniel Haggerty Ireland & Julia Dineen Ireland
HAGGERTY, Katherine Winifred, Feb 11 1915 Sex:F Child# 3 Timothy Haggerty Nashua, NH & Cath McLaughlin Nashua, NH
HAGGERTY, Leonard James, Jan 6 1935 Sex:M Child# 6 Jos F Haggerty Nashua, NH & Josephine Dumas Somersworth, NH
HAGGERTY, Margaret, Nov 25 1914 Sex:F Child# 1 Cornelius J Haggerty Nashua, NH & Margaret Shea Ireland
HAGGERTY, Mary, Dec 8 1888 Sex:F Child# 4 Daniel Haggerty Ireland & Kate Ireland
HAGGERTY, Mary A, Nov 18 1889 Sex:F Child# 4 Patrick Haggerty Ireland & Mary Haggerty Ireland
HAGGERTY, Patrick, Nov 15 1887 Sex:M Child# 3 Daniel Haggerty Ireland & Kate Sullivan Ireland
HAGGERTY, Richard, Jan 26 1894 Sex:M Child# 4 Dennis T Haggerty Ireland & Mary J Carey Ireland
HAGGERTY, Thomas Timothy, Mar 5 1918 Sex:M Child# 4 Timothy P Haggerty Nashua, NH & Katherine McLaughlin Nashua,NH
HAGGERTY, Unknown, Jul 16 1900 Sex:F Child# 13 Patrick Haggerty Ireland & Mary Driscoll Ireland
HAGGERTY, Unknown, Feb 15 1916 Sex:F Child# Tim J Haggerty Nashua, NH & Catherine McLaughlin Nashua, NH Stillborn
HAGGERTY, William, Nov 5 1896 Sex:M Child# 2 John Haggerty Ireland & Ellen Garrity Nashua, NH
HAGGERTY, William Jennin, Nov 13 1897 Sex:M Child# 6 Dennis F Haggerty Ireland & Mary Haggerty Ireland
HAGGETT, Martha Cecille, Apr 7 1932 Sex:F Child# 4 Ed B Haggett Gilmanton, NH & I W Borneman Townsend, MA

HAGIANAT, Mary, Oct 3 1921 Sex:F Child# 2 John Hagianat Greece & Alice Chekeris Greece
HAGIDAMOS, Demetrius James, Sep 1 1922 Sex:M Child# 3 Ant Hagidamos Greece & Efrosine Grapakros Greece
HAGIDAMOS, Nicholas, Jul 3 1920 Sex:M Child# 2 Anthony Hagidamos Greece & Efrasing Giaprakos Greece
HAGIGIANAKIS, Charles, Jul 24 1923 Sex:M Child# 3 John Hagigianakis Greece & Elisavet Scansas Greece
HAGNEY, Mary Ellen, May 24 1890 Sex:F Child# 4 Patrick Hagney Ireland & Mary Sheenan Ireland
HAIGHT, Barbara Mary, Nov 30 1928 Sex:F Child# 2 Clar W Haight Medford, WI & Mary E Hopwood Litchfield, NH
HAIGHT, Clarence William, Jan 19 1931 Sex:M Child# 3 Clarence Wm Haight Medford, WI & Mary E Hopwood Litchfield, NH
HAIGHT, Eugene, Jan 5 1925 Sex:M Child# 1 Eugen Haight Litchfield, NH & Cora Louga Manchester, NH
HAIGHT, Marion Ella, Nov 15 1926 Sex:F Child# 1 L W Haight Medford, Wis & Mary E Hapwood Litchfield, NH
HAIGHT, Robert Louis, May 13 1932 Sex:M Child# 4 Eugene Haight Litchfield, NH & Cora M Lougee Manchester, NH
HAINISH, Gloria Elizabeth, Oct 29 1929 Sex:F Child# 2 James Hainish Nova Scotia & Janesta Monroe Nova Scotia
HALATSE, Athanasios, Oct 13 1917 Sex:M Child# 1 (No Parents Listed)
HALDEN, Barbara Evelyn, Feb 3 1924 Sex:F Child# 5 Frank Halden Nashua, NH & Mabel Durant Nashua, NH
HALE, Unknown, May 5 1897 Sex:M Child# 3 Frank Hale Goffstown, NH & Flora B Westcott Hill, NH
HALEY, Alzina J, Apr 26 1887 Sex:F Child# 1 George W Haley S Boston & Isabella H Andover
HALEY, Eva Gertrude, Oct 9 1895 Sex:F Child# 1 Charles E Haley Boston, MA & Ida M Pease Brookdale, NY
HALEY, Herbert Paul, Dec 6 1901 Sex:M Child# 10 Michael Haley Ireland & Ellen Downey Ireland
HALEY, Joseph Albert, Jul 19 1906 Sex:M Child# 1 Joseph Haley Canada & Delia Colette New York
HALEY, Lucille Theresa Mary, Feb 8 1924 Sex:F Child# 2 Herbert Haley NH & Malvina Loraine NH
HALEY, Unknown, Mar 27 1901 Sex:M Child# 2 Edgar C Haley Boston, MA & Alice M Germain Nashua, NH Stillborn
HALFELI, George Parker, Jun 4 1915 Sex:M Child# 1 Martin A Halfeli Switzerland & Mary Bryer Antrim, NH
HALGREN, Barbara, Feb 7 1924 Sex:F Child# 4 Swan Halgren Sweden & Anna Halquist Sweden
HALGREN, Edmund Thomas, Aug 8 1930 Sex:M Child# 2 Emerald Halgren Quincy, MA & Laura Harris Nova Scotia
HALGREN, Robert Swan, May 30 1934 Sex:M Child# 2 Emerald Halgren Quincy, MA & Laura Harris Upperclyde, NS
HALL, Alpha Alphonso, Jul 23 1923 Sex:M Child# 1 Forace Rowe Hall Brookline, NH & Florence C Corliss Middleboro, MA
HALL, Annie Elizabeth, Apr 16 1916 Sex:F Child# 2 Lester M Hall Nashua, NH & Evangelyn M Clark Nashua, NH
HALL, Barbara Alice, Nov 15 1934 Sex:F Child# 1 Earl Norris Hall Nashua, NH & Lillian Sherwin Nashua, NH
HALL, Carolyn Elizabeth, Aug 3 1932 Sex:F Child# 2 James L Hall Nashua, NH & E C Alexander Nashua, NH
HALL, Charles P, Jr, Mar 4 1912 Sex:M Child# 2 Charles P Hall Mooers, NY & Edna A Fortier Woodsville, NH
HALL, Dorothy El Harriett, Jun 14 1913 Sex:F Child# 2 Foster M Hall Mooers, NY & Dorothy M Seaman Nashua, NH
HALL, Earl Norris, May 5 1909 Sex:M Child# 1 James E Hall Nashua, NH & Helen M Reed Nashua, NH
HALL, Edwin Azro, Aug 30 1906 Sex:M Child# 1 Clifford F Hall Walpole, NH & Lydio O Lothrop Coventry, VT
HALL, Ella, Aug 12 1889 Sex:F Child# 10 Richard Hall Ireland & Catherine Curran Ireland
HALL, Ernest Vincent, Sep 11 1920 Sex:M Child# 3 Foster M Hall Mooers, NY & Dorotha M Seaman Nashua, NH
HALL, Eugenia, Mar 17 1893 Sex:F Child# 1 William H Hall Moore's Jct, NY & Eugenia L Blood Nashua, NH
HALL, Evelyn Mary, Oct 9 1927 Sex:F Child# 1 Irving E Hall Nashua, NH & Doris M Hunt Merrimack, NH
HALL, Flossy May, Aug 25 1892 Sex:F Child# 1 Frank A Hall Salem, MA & Mary A Medivier Canada
HALL, Frank Henry, Aug 30 1894 Sex:M Child# 3 Henry A Hall Concord & Jennie Brennan Ireland
HALL, Frank P, May 12 1893 Sex:M Child# 1 Frank P Hall Alfred & Susie Abott Pembroke
HALL, Helen Elizabeth, Sep 14 1915 Sex:F Child# 4 Thomas Hall Glascow, Scotland & Jennie M Russell Manchester, NH
HALL, Henry, Mar 9 1887 Sex:M Child# Henry A Hall Concord & Jennie Brennan Ireland
HALL, Horatio Victor, May 4 1898 Sex:M Child# Horatio J Hall NY & Ida Blood Nashua, NH
HALL, Irene Ella, Jul 10 1896 Sex: Child# 3 William Henry Hall Moores Jct, NY & Eugenia Blood Nashua, NH
HALL, Irving Elliott, Feb 19 1904 Sex:M Child# 1 Webb E Hall Nashua, NH & Hattie E Lawrence Pepperell, MA
HALL, James Lawrence, Sep 16 1905 Sex:M Child# 2 Webb E Hall Nashua, NH & Harriett Lawrence E Pepperell, MA
HALL, Jennie Teresa, Aug 3 1890 Sex:F Child# 2 Henry N Hall Concord, NH & Jennie Brennan Ireland
HALL, Kenneth Walter, Jun 17 1926 Sex:M Child# 2 Walter A Hall Nashua, NH & Leora Elkins Nashua, NH
HALL, Lawrence Arthur, Jr, Sep 27 1934 Sex:M Child# 1 Lawrence Arthur Hall Sanford, ME & Helen R Deans Scotland
HALL, Lucienne Florence, Sep 18 1917 Sex:F Child# 1 Frank Hall Nashua, NH & Madeleine Pelletier Nashua, NH
HALL, Marjorie Lena, Aug 25 1920 Sex:F Child# 1 Walter A Hall Nashua, NH & Leora Elkins Nashua, NH
HALL, Nancy Audrey, Apr 4 1933 Sex:F Child# 1 Nelson Hall Nashua, NH & Theresa Levesque Nashua, NH
HALL, Nelson Delmar, Oct 24 1910 Sex:M Child# 1 Charles P Hall Mooers, NY & Edna A Fortier Woodsville, NH
HALL, Philip Lawrence, Jul 3 1929 Sex:M Child# 1 James Lawrence Hall Nashua, NH & Elizabeth Alexander Nashua, NH
HALL, Phoebe Victoria, Jan 16 1898 Sex:F Child# 1 William H Hall Mooers, NY & Eugenie Blood Nashua, NH
HALL, Priscilla, May 23 1922 Sex:F Child# 1 Henry E Hall Vermont & Avis Trenholm NH
HALL, Richard Irvin, Jun 30 1929 Sex:M Child# 2 Irvin Elliott Hall Nashua, NH & Doris Marion Hunt Merrimack, NH
HALL, Robert A, Aug 22 1916 Sex:M Child# 3 Foster Hall Mooers, NY & Dorothy Seaman Nashua, NH
HALL, Russell, Aug 31 1894 Sex:M Child# 2 William Henry Hall Mooers, NY & Mary J Blood Nashua, NH
HALL, Ruth Annette, Oct 13 1913 Sex:F Child# 3 Thomas Hall England & Jennie May Russell Manchester, NH
HALL, Shirley Ruth, May 13 1933 Sex:F Child# 2 William Hall Chelmsford, MA & Mabel Speare Wakefield, MA
HALL, Unknown, Nov 13 1887 Sex:M Child# 3 John K Hall Mason & Caroline F Nashua, NH
HALL, Unknown, Jun 18 1895 Sex:F Child# 1 George Hall Littleton & Mildred Goodwin Maine
HALL, Unknown, Jul 25 1911 Sex:M Child# 1 Foster Hall Mooers, NY & Dorothy M Seaman Nashua, NH Stillborn
HALL, Unknown, Jun 15 1923 Sex:M Child# 1 Albert Hall Fitchburg, MA & Alice Jeannotte Nashua, NH Stillborn
HALL, Walter Alfred, Aug 8 1893 Sex:M Child# 1 Alfred A Hall Walpole & Carrie Dodge Nashua, NH
HALL, Whitfold Reed, Oct 12 1920 Sex:M Child# 2 J Earlfred Hall Nashua, NH & Helen M Reed Nashua, NH
HALL, William Henry, Jul 23 1914 Sex:M Child# 1 Lester M Hall Nashua, NH & Evangeline M Clark Nashua, NH
HALL, Winston Rowe, Aug 9 1926 Sex:M Child# 2 Foran R Hall Brookline, NH & Florence C Corliss Middleboro, MA
HALL, Winthrop Channing, Mar 7 1926 Sex:M Child# 1 Carl H Hall Milford, NH & Athaleen Brien Nashua, NH
HALL, Woodbury Carroll, Apr 22 1932 Sex:M Child# 3 Woodbury C Hall Farmington, ME & Yvonne Caron Winchendon, MA
HALLESEY, William Richard, Aug 4 1890 Sex:M Child# 2 Michael Hallesey Nashua, NH & Emma Fuller Vermont
HALLISEY, Catherine M, Jan 9 1902 Sex:F Child# 7 J J Hallisey Nashua, NH & Mary J Doyle Nashua, NH
HALLISEY, Dennis Leo, Aug 31 1899 Sex:M Child# 6 J J Hallisey Nashua, NH & Mary J Doyle Nashua, NH

HALLISEY, Dorothy, Feb 12 1905 Sex:F Child# 4 Dennis J Hallisey Nashua, NH & Mary McBride Nashua, NH
HALLISEY, Eileen, Feb 12 1905 Sex:F Child# 3 Dennis J Hallisey Nashua, NH & Mary McBride Nashua, NH
HALLISEY, Emily, Nov 22 1887 Sex:F Child# 1 Michael Hallisey Nashua, NH & Emily Fuller Massachusetts
HALLISEY, Frances Emmeline, Aug 13 1913 Sex:F Child# 1 James B Hallisey Nashua, NH & Sarah Hutchinson Eden, VT
HALLISEY, Harold J, Oct 20 1897 Sex:M Child# 5 Jeremiah J Hallisey Nashua, NH & Mary J Doyle Nashua, NH
HALLISEY, Harold James, Nov 18 1898 Sex:M Child# 1 Dennis Hallisey Nashua, NH & Mary McBride Nashua, NH
HALLISEY, Helen, Nov 14 1893 Sex:F Child# 3 Jeremiah J Hallisey Nashua, NH & Mary J Doyle Nashua, NH
HALLISEY, James, Dec 29 1891 Sex:M Child# 2 J J Hallisey Nashua, NH & Mary J Doyle Nashua, NH
HALLISEY, John, May 5 1893 Sex:M Child# 2 John Hallisey Ireland & Katherine Doyle Nashua, NH
HALLISEY, Madelene M, Jun 28 1898 Sex:F Child# 2 Richard Hallisey Nashua, NH & Mary Albert Houlton, ME
HALLISEY, Margarite, Aug 5 1892 Sex:F Child# 3 Michael Hallisey Nashua, NH & Emma Fuller Vermont
HALLISEY, Maria Albertina, Feb 19 1896 Sex:F Child# 1 Richard Hallisey Nashua, NH & Mamie Albert Holton, ME
HALLISEY, Mary, Oct 19 1895 Sex:F Child# 4 Jeremiah J Hallisey Nashua, NH & Mary J Doyle Nashua, NH
HALLISEY, Mildred Louise, Oct 7 1905 Sex:F Child# 8 Jeremiah J Hallisey Nashua, NH & Mary J Doyle Nashua, NH
HALLISEY, Robert James, Dec 20 1926 Sex:M Child# 2 Harold Hallisey Nashua, NH & Helene Desautels Holyoke, MA
HALLISEY, Unknown, Sep 9 1889 Sex:F Child# 1 Jeremiah Hallisey Nashua, NH & Mary E Doyle Nashua, NH
HALLISEY, Unknown, May 5 1929 Sex:M Child# 1 Daniel Hallisey Lowell, MA & Mary Hughes Somerville, MA
HALLISEY, Unknown, Jan 26 1930 Sex:M Child# 3 Harold Hallisey Nashua, NH & Helen Desautels Holyoke, MA
HALLISEY, Virginia Mary, Feb 4 1925 Sex:F Child# 1 Harold Hallisey Nashua, NH & Helen Desautels Holyoke, MA
HALLISTER, Henry Sprague, Feb 1 1908 Sex:M Child# 4 Clark W Hallister Sherman, TX & G A Hastings NH
HALLISY, William, Feb 23 1889 Sex:M Child# 1 James Hallisy Nashua, NH & Rose Dubuc St Albans, VT
HALLOCK, Edmond, Oct 24 1919 Sex:M Child# 2 Brun Hallock Poland Russia & Edwiga Kourta Poland Russia
HALLOCK, Unknown, Oct 7 1904 Sex:F Child# 1 F Elmer Hallock New York & Marion O Lindsay Lynn, MA Stillborn
HALLQUIST, George M, Feb 23 1892 Sex:M Child# 2 Agalon Hallquist Sweden & Anna Gustaveson Sweden
HALQUIST, Beverly, Aug 22 1920 Sex:F Child# 1 Otto Halquist Nashua, NH & Helen L Hurlburt Laconia, NH Stillborn
HALQUIST, Louise Ellen Chapman, Dec 16 1917 Sex:F Child# 1 Carl Halquist Manchester, NH & Miriam Chapman Manchester
HALZIGOGA, Anastasi Busilios, Feb 21 1916 Sex:M Child# 3 Basilios Halzigoga Greece & Halen Korcovelou Greece
HALZIGOGA, Demetrius B, Jul 3 1924 Sex:M Child# 5 Basil Halzigoga Greece & Ellen Korcovelos Greece
HAM, Unknown, Sep 9 1889 Sex:F Child# 1 Frank D Ham Peabody, MA & Theresa Needham Ashburnham
HAM, Warren Lewis, Nov 4 1926 Sex:M Child# 4 Edward E Ham Leominster, MA & Tokohe Koladrian Pt De Bute, NB
HAMBLETT, Charles Kittredge, Jul 30 1924 Sex:M Child# 1 R Burns Hamblett Nashua, NH & H C Kittredge Nashua, NH
HAMBLETT, Clarence Stuart, Oct 11 1891 Sex:M Child# 4 Fred B Hamblett Nashua, NH & Sarah Sweeney England
HAMBLETT, David Coombs, Jul 9 1927 Sex:M Child# 2 R B Hamblett Nashua, NH & Helen C Kittredge Nashua, NH
HAMBLETT, David Henry, Dec 23 1922 Sex:M Child# 3 Aaron L Hamblett Manchester, NH & Margaret Munroe Nashua, NH
HAMBLETT, Elizabeth May, Dec 18 1921 Sex:F Child# 2 Aaron L Hamblett Manchester, NH & Margaret L Munroe Nashua, NH
HAMBLETT, Macy Stevens, Dec 26 1895 Sex:F Child# 1 Charles J Hamblett Milford, NH & Georgia Stevens Nashua, NH
HAMBLETT, Robert Burns, Dec 23 1898 Sex:M Child# 2 Charles J Hamblett Milford, NH & Georgie Stevens Nashua, NH
HAMBLETT, Ruth Gertrude, Aug 13 1917 Sex:F Child# 1 Auron L Hamblett Manchester, NH & Margaret L Munroe Nashua, NH
HAMBLETT, Stephen, Oct 30 1934 Sex:M Child# 3 Robert Hamblett Nashua, NH & Helen K Kittredge Nashua, NH
HAMBLETT, Unknown, Aug 30 1887 Sex:M Child# 5 Willis L Hamblett Nashua, NH & Hannah Poff Hudson, NH
HAMBLETT, Unknown, Oct 4 1887 Sex:M Child# 1 George A Hamblett Nashua, NH & Emma A Jeffs Marlboro, MA
HAMEL, Albert Emile, Oct 25 1891 Sex:M Child# 3 Moise Hamel Canada & Mary Vaillancourt Canada
HAMEL, Alfred, May 31 1890 Sex:M Child# 2 Moise Hamel Canada & Marie Vallancourt Canada
HAMEL, Augustin, Aug 29 1896 Sex:M Child# 6 Moise Hamel Canada & Leocadie Vaillancour Canada
HAMEL, Carolyn Louise, Jan 28 1934 Sex:F Child# 3 Winfred A Hamel North Troy, VT & Mildred Emery Chelsea, MA
HAMEL, Catherine Eva M, Jan 13 1900 Sex:F Child# 18 J B Hamel Canada & Kate O'Reilly Canada
HAMEL, Charles O, Aug 8 1889 Sex:M Child# 4 Jean B Hamel Canada & Kate O'Reily Canada
HAMEL, Charles Wilfred, Sep 30 1928 Sex:M Child# 3 Charles Hamel Leominster, MA & M C Bent Boston, MA
HAMEL, Doris Mildred, Feb 21 1905 Sex:F Child# 1 Peter H Hamel Lawrence, MA & Ada Belle Smith Hollis, NH
HAMEL, Edward Paul, Jan 18 1920 Sex:M Child# 1 Edward Hamel Newmarket, NH & Hilda Bostwick Nashua, NH
HAMEL, Elizabeth Ann, Feb 2 1929 Sex:F Child# 1 Wilfred A Hamel N Troy, VT & Mildred E Emery Chelsea, MA
HAMEL, Elizabeth Ann, Jun 26 1932 Sex:F Child# 1 Maurice Hamel Manchester, NH & Hazel Moody Lebanon, NH
HAMEL, Elodia, Feb 23 1894 Sex:F Child# 8 John B Hamel Canada & Kate O'Reilly Canada
HAMEL, George Leopold, Jan 7 1892 Sex:M Child# 8 Onesime Hamel Canada & Victoria Laflamme Canada
HAMEL, Grace, May 12 1910 Sex:F Child# 3 Charles Hamel Greenville, NH & Angelina Racine Canada
HAMEL, Henry, Jun 25 1896 Sex:M Child# 9 Onesime Hamel Canada & Victoria Laflamme Canada
HAMEL, Henry Francis, Apr 4 1899 Sex:M Child# 7 Moise Hamel Canada & Marie L Vaillancourt Canada Stillborn
HAMEL, Homer Lewis, Jan 8 1903 Sex:M Child# 3 Joseph S Hamel Vermont & Antonia Aubin Canada
HAMEL, Irene Edna, Jul 14 1926 Sex:F Child# 2 Charles Hamel Leominster, MA & Marguerite Bent Boston, MA
HAMEL, Isabelle Ruth, Jul 31 1895 Sex:F Child# Joseph S Hamel Westfield, VT & Autonia O Aubin St Valentin, PQ
HAMEL, J James Raymond, Aug 17 1922 Sex:M Child# 2 John Hamel Canada & Celestine Gosselin Canada
HAMEL, James Emery, Apr 24 1930 Sex:M Child# 2 Winfrid Hamel Vermont & Mildred Emery Chelsea, MA
HAMEL, Jean Baptiste, Nov 23 1896 Sex:M Child# J B Hamel Canada & Lea Gravel Canada
HAMEL, John Joseph, Apr 16 1921 Sex:M Child# 1 John A Hamel Canada & Clestine Gosselin Canada
HAMEL, Joseph Arthur, Jan 10 1898 Sex:M Child# 11 Onesime Hamel Canada & Victoria Laflamme Canada
HAMEL, Joseph E, Aug 27 1890 Sex:M Child# 5 Jean Baptiste Hamel Canada & Kate O'Reilly Canada
HAMEL, Louis Angeline, Oct 21 1892 Sex:F Child# 4 Moise Hamel Canada & Mary Vaillancourt Canada
HAMEL, Lucienne, Sep 14 1909 Sex:F Child# 3 Ferdinand Hamel Canada & Corinne Champoux Canada
HAMEL, M Louise, Jan 22 1894 Sex:F Child# 5 Moise Hamel Canada & Mary Vaillancourt Canada
HAMEL, Margaret, Oct 22 1924 Sex:F Child# 1 Charles Hamel Leominster, MA & Margaret C But Boston, MA
HAMEL, Marie Margarite, Mar 17 1924 Sex:F Child# 3 John Hamel Canada & Celestine Gosselin Canada
HAMEL, Marion Blanche, Apr 3 1889 Sex:F Child# 1 Morin Hamel Canada & Mary Vallencour Canada
HAMEL, Mary Ellenor, Nov 29 1891 Sex:F Child# 6 J B Hamel Canada & Kate W O'Reilly Canada

HAMEL, Natalie Norma, Jun 6 1919 Sex:F Child# 3 U P Hamel Lawrence, MA & Adabell Smith Hollis, NH
HAMEL, Philippe, Jan 30 1898 Sex:M Child# 17 J Bts Hamel Canada & Kate O'Reilly Canada
HAMEL, Rachelle I, Nov 12 1902 Sex:F Child# 8 Moise Hamel Canada & Leocadie Vaillaincrt Canada
HAMEL, Raymond Uldric, Oct 29 1907 Sex:M Child# 3 Peter U Hamel Lawrence, MA & Ada Belle Smith Hollis, NH
HAMEL, Robert Conrad, Jan 5 1931 Sex:M Child# 3 Edward Hamel Durham, NH & Hilda Bostwick Nashua, NH
HAMEL, Sylvia, Nov 13 1896 Sex:F Child# 10 J Bte Hamel Canada & Kate O'Reilly Canada
HAMEL, Unknown, Nov 15 1892 Sex:M Child# 7 J B Hamel Canada & Katie W O'Reilly Canada Stillborn
HAMEL, Unknown, Jul 26 1894 Sex: Child# 13 J Bte Hamel Canada & Kate O'Reilly Canada Stillborn
HAMEL, Unknown, Dec 14 1921 Sex:M Child# 2 Edward Hamel Newmarket, NH & Hilda Bostwick Nashua, NH
HAMEL, William Hamden, Mar 5 1931 Sex:M Child# 1 Maurice Hamel Manchester, NH & Hazel Moody Lebanon, NH
HAMELIN, Aurore, Aug 13 1891 Sex:F Child# 3 Willard Hamelin Champlain, NY & Louise Gauthier Canada
HAMELIN, Clarence Albert, Oct 2 1896 Sex:M Child# 2 Albert E Hamelin NY & Addie L Fitts N Dunbarton
HAMELIN, Ernest Henry, May 11 1902 Sex:M Child# 4 Felix Hamelin New York & Clara Kerouac Canada
HAMELIN, Joseph Arthur, Jun 9 1900 Sex:M Child# 2 Felix Hamelin Canada & Clara Kerouack Canada
HAMELIN, Joseph Edouard R, Jun 4 1904 Sex:M Child# 5 Felix Hamelin Moore's, NY & Clara Kerouack Varennes, PQ
HAMELIN, Joseph Francois, Jul 25 1901 Sex:M Child# 7 Willard Hamelin New York & Louise Gauthier Canada
HAMELIN, Louis Philippe R, Jul 4 1901 Sex:M Child# 3 Felix Hamelin Moores, NY & Clara Keroak Canada
HAMELIN, Marie Cecelia E, Dec 8 1906 Sex:F Child# 7 Felix Hamelin Moores, NY & Clara Kerouack Canada
HAMELIN, Marie Ida, Mar 16 1896 Sex:F Child# 1 Felix Hamelin Moores Jct, NY & Clara Keroack Varennes, PQ
HAMELIN, Mary, Jun 17 1893 Sex:F Child# 4 Willard Hamelin Canada & Louise Gauthier Canada
HAMELIN, Willie, Dec 15 1896 Sex:M Child# 5 Willard Hamelin US & Louise Gauthier Canada
HAMEWICZ, John, Jun 5 1922 Sex:M Child# 2 Mike Hamewicz Poland & Chaner Smariga Poland
HAMILTON, Charles, Apr 5 1892 Sex:M Child# 1 Louis F Hamilton Fitchburg, MA & Fanny Traver Dover, NH
HAMILTON, Helen, Dec 31 1910 Sex:F Child# 1 Hugh Hamilton Manchester, NH & Mabel Hines Norwich, VT
HAMILTON, Lizzie A, Mar 2 1889 Sex:F Child# 1 Lester A Hamilton Maine & Alla Hall New Hampshire
HAMILTON, Maud, Sep 18 1890 Sex:F Child# 2 R L Hamilton NY & Mertie Ball Easton, NH
HAMILTON, Ralph Alden, Dec 10 1891 Sex:M Child# 2 Leslie A Hamilton Maine & Ella Hall NH
HAMILTON, Unknown, Jul 19 1888 Sex:F Child# 1 B L Hamilton Moores Fall, NY & Nettie M Ball Easton
HAMILTON, Unknown, Jul 30 1892 Sex:F Child# 2 Benjamin C Hamilton Maine & Hattie M NH
HAMILTON, Unknown, Nov 21 1898 Sex:F Child# 2 A J Hamilton Morris Forts, NY & Katie Golden Roxbury, MA
HAMLIN, Agnes Irene, Dec 25 1914 Sex:F Child# 2 Emmet Hamlin Mooers, NY & Josephine A Lyons Milford, NH
HAMLIN, Alvin Hamlin, Jun 25 1899 Sex:M Child# 6 Willard Hamlin NY & Louise Gokey Canada
HAMLIN, Carrie, Jul 21 1888 Sex:F Child# 2 Willard Hamlin Champlain, NY & Louisa Gauthier Canada
HAMLIN, Denese Rita, Mar 29 1924 Sex:F Child# 2 Orlando Hamlin Nashua, NH & H Beausaleille Nashua, NH
HAMLIN, Frank Melvin, Aug 10 1920 Sex:M Child# 1 Orlando D Hamlin Nashua, NH & Helen Beausoleil Nashua, NH
HAMLIN, Helena Lucille, Dec 25 1914 Sex:F Child# 3 Emmet Hamlin Mooers, NY & Josephine A Lyons Milford, NH
HAMLIN, Herbert M, Feb 4 1901 Sex:M Child# 2 Albert Hamlin Dunbarton & Addie Fitts New York, NY
HAMLIN, Leonard Frank, Jul 27 1896 Sex:M Child# 1 Frank Hamlin Middlesex, VT & Anna G Fitts Dunbarton, NH
HAMLIN, Leonard Richard, Jun 18 1932 Sex:M Child# 1 L Hamlin Nashua, NH & Claudia Hamel Canada
HAMLIN, Mary Josephine, Jun 12 1917 Sex:F Child# 4 Emmett Hamlin Mooers, NY & Josephine Lyons Milford, NH
HAMLIN, Mildred Lillian, Jun 27 1911 Sex:F Child# 1 Emmett A Hamlin New York & Josephine Lyons Milford, NH
HAMLIN, Orlando Martin, May 10 1929 Sex:M Child# 3 Orlando Hamlin Nashua, NH & Helen Beausoliel Nashua, NH
HAMLIN, Unknown, Apr 5 1894 Sex:M Child# 1 Albert E Hamlin Mooers, NY & Addie Fitts Dunbarton, NH
HAMLIN, Unknown, Feb 11 1898 Sex:M Child# 2 Frank Hamlin Middlesex, VT & Anna G Fitts Dunbarton, NH
HAMLIN, Unknown, Sep 18 1899 Sex:M Child# 3 Frank Hamlin Middlesex, VT & Anna G Fitts Dunbarton, NH
HAMLIN, Unknown, Nov 11 1931 Sex:M Child# 1 E A Hamlin Mooers, NY & Evelyn Arseneau Canada Stillborn
HAMMAR, Ralph Arthur, Jan 5 1906 Sex:M Child# 1 Arthur L Hammar Milton, MA & Mary M Mortlock Nova Scotia
HAMMAR, Warren Aubrey, Apr 28 1912 Sex:M Child# 4 Arthur Hammar Swampscott, MA & Maud Mortlock Truro, NS
HAMMELIN, Mary V, Feb 22 1887 Sex:F Child# 1 Williard Hammelin Champlain, NY & Louise Gauthier Canada
HAMMER, Morris Clayton, Apr 5 1909 Sex:M Child# 3 Arthur L Hammer Milton, MA & Mary M Mortlock Nova Scotia
HAMMOND, Amy Frances, Dec 8 1912 Sex:F Child# 1 Lewis F Hammond Freeport, ME & Gladys F Blood Whitman, MA
HAMMOND, Doris, Jun 8 1906 Sex:F Child# 1 Harry L Hammond Boston, MA & Ina Martin Hudson, NH
HAMMOND, Edward Ernest, Oct 15 1904 Sex:M Child# 1 Edward E Hammond Worcester, MA & Margaret Morah Plattsburg, NY
HAMMOND, Harry Hathaway, Feb 18 1919 Sex:M Child# 4 Lewis Hammond Freeprot, ME & Gladys Blood Whitman, MA
HAMMOND, Howard William, Jan 10 1926 Sex:M Child# 2 Clar Hammond Rutland, MA & Florence Farnham Gardner, MA
HAMMOND, John Franklin, Nov 17 1924 Sex:M Child# 6 Lewis Hammond Freeport, ME & Gladys Blood Whitman, MA
HAMMOND, John Harland, Aug 20 1912 Sex:M Child# 2 Harry W Hammond Nashua, NH & Nellie Spear Lawrence, MA
HAMMOND, Karl R, Jul 19 1887 Sex:M Child# 3 Charles B Hammond Nashua, NH & Mary L Tracy Nashua, NH
HAMMOND, Lewis Edward, Feb 27 1914 Sex:M Child# 2 Lewis F Hammond Freeport, ME & Gladys Blood Whitman, MA
HAMMOND, Louise Harriet, Feb 21 1921 Sex:F Child# 5 Lewis Hammond Freeport, ME & Gladys Blood Whitman, MA
HAMMOND, Robert Lee, Apr 27 1917 Sex:M Child# 3 Lewis Hammond Freeport, ME & Gladys Blood Whitman, MA
HAMMOND, Roland B, Jul 25 1887 Sex:M Child# 1 Phin A Hammond Nashua, NH & L M Bowman Merrimack
HAMMOND, Unknown, Dec 10 1892 Sex:F Child# 4 Charles B Hammond Nashua, NH & Mary L Tracey Nashua, NH
HANCOCK, Beatrice Vivien, Mar 8 1928 Sex:F Child# 3 Stanton Hancock Nova Scotia & Ora F Stratton Dayton, OH
HANCOCK, David Stratton, Oct 18 1932 Sex:M Child# 5 Stanton Hancock Canada & Ora Stratton Dayton, OH
HANCOCK, Harry Roscoe, Jan 25 1908 Sex:M Child# 1 Charles B Hancock White Rock, NS & Lottie Edna Messim Davenport
HANCOCK, John Albert, Dec 28 1929 Sex:M Child# 4 Stanton Hancock US & Ora Stratton Ohio
HANCOCK, Stanton Alfred, Oct 6 1926 Sex:M Child# 2 S A Hancock Nova Scotia & Ora Straton Dayton, OH
HANDFIELD, Harry Horatio, Sep 26 1907 Sex:M Child# 1 Edward Handfield Albany, NY & Anna E Rushlow Albany Spgs, NY
HANDLEY, Henry W, Sep 22 1893 Sex:M Child# 1 Frank H Handley England & Rose Smith Canada
HANDLIN, James Henry, Nov 10 1920 Sex:M Child# 1 James Henry Handlin Worcester, MA & Alexandrine Charron Nashua, NH
HANDRON, Llewellyn, Nov 11 1921 Sex:M Child# 2 Llewellyn Handron US & Lillian Lajoie US
HANEWIEZE, Mike, Mar 29 1920 Sex:M Child# 1 Mike Hanewieze Russia & Elizabeth Axseno Russia

HANG, Charles Louis, Apr 18 1922 Sex:M Child# 2 Anton J Hang Germany & Charlotte MacDuffie Nashua, NH
HANKS, John William, May 17 1917 Sex:M Child# 3 Frank Hanks Groton, MA & Rose Noel Nashua, NH
HANLIN, Frances Ruth, Oct 19 1921 Sex:F Child# 2 James H Hanlin Worcester, MA & Alexandrine Charron Nashua, NH
HANLON, Dorothy, Apr 14 1921 Sex:F Child# 3 John F Hanlon W Sullivan, ME & Emma Bonnett Meredith, NH
HANRAHAN, Katherine, May 11 1892 Sex:F Child# 2 William Hanrahan Ireland & Nellie Gilhooley Ireland
HANRAHAN, Thomas Joseph, Jan 2 1924 Sex:M Child# 1 Thomas Hanrahan Nashua, NH & Mary Ward Manchester, NH
HANREHAN, John, Jan 16 1905 Sex:M Child# 7 William Hanrehan Ireland & Nellie Gilhooley Ireland
HANSBERRY, Ann Theresa, Aug 13 1929 Sex:F Child# 6 Martin J Hansberry Lowell, MA & Mary K O'Neil Nashua, NH
HANSBERRY, Jane Margaret, Aug 6 1932 Sex:F Child# 7 Martin Hansberry Lowell, MA & Mary O'Neil Nashua, NH
HANSBERRY, Katherine, Sep 15 1919 Sex:F Child# 3 Martin Hansberry Lowell, MA & Catherine O'Neil Nashua, NH
HANSBERRY, Owen Francis, Dec 18 1920 Sex:M Child# 4 Martin Hansberry Lowell, MA & Mary Cath O'Neil Nashua, NH
HANSBERRY, Patricia Ann, Jul 28 1922 Sex:F Child# 5 Martin Hansberry Lowell, MA & Mary K O'Neil Nashua, NH
HANSBERRY, Thomas Stanton, Aug 23 1915 Sex:M Child# 1 Martin J Hansberry Lowell, MA & Mary O'Niel Nashua, NH
HANSCOM, Hubert Harold, Sep 16 1913 Sex:M Child# 2 Thomas H Hanscom Nashua, NH & Neta Colby Perkinsville, VT
HANSCOM, Louis, Jun 2 1906 Sex:M Child# 5 Charles N Hanscom Somersworth & Effie M Smith Albany, NY
HANSCOM, Mary Melba, Nov 12 1910 Sex:F Child# 1 Thomas H Hanscom E Machias, ME & Marion Kennedy Lowell, MA
HANSCOM, Unknown, Sep 12 1895 Sex:M Child# 2 Fred B Hanscom Marlboro, MA & Henriette Putnam Moores, NY
HANSEN, Unknown, Jan 12 1894 Sex: Child# 1 Nathan E Hansen Windham, ME & Harriet C Austin Nashua, NH Stillborn
HANSOM, Charles Sylvester, Mar 8 1922 Sex:M Child# 2 Charles S Hanson Wardsboro, VT & Lillian E Bouley Nashua, NH
HANSON, Arlene Marion, Apr 26 1921 Sex:F Child# 3 Walter H L Hanson Canada & Jessie Hope Canada
HANSON, Audrey Phyllis, Nov 5 1920 Sex:F Child# 1 Charles Hanson Wardsboro, VT & Lillian Boulley Nashua, NH
HANSON, Barbara Hope, Feb 18 1920 Sex:F Child# 2 Walter Hanson Canada & Jessie Hope Canada
HANSON, Carol Elaine, Mar 31 1931 Sex:F Child# 6 Walter H Hanson Canada & Jessie L Hope Canada
HANSON, Clara May, Jan 6 1892 Sex:F Child# 1 Fred S Hanson Marlboro, MA & Etta Putnam Moors, NY
HANSON, Clayton Eugene, May 28 1925 Sex:M Child# 2 Herbert Hanson Hudson, NH & Margaret O'Brien Nashua, NH
HANSON, Earline Winifred, Jun 28 1928 Sex:F Child# 5 W H T Hanson Canada & Jessie Hope Canada Stillborn
HANSON, Elaine Martha, Sep 20 1923 Sex:F Child# 3 Charles S Hanson Wardsboro, VT & Lillian E Bouley Nashua, NH
HANSON, Gerald Stickney, Aug 21 1930 Sex:M Child# 4 Charles Hanson NH & Lillian Bouley Nashua, NH
HANSON, Grace Lillian, Aug 15 1933 Sex:F Child# 7 Walter H Hanson Canada & Jessie Hope Canada
HANSON, Hermon Howard, Sep 2 1918 Sex:M Child# 1 Walter H Hanson Canada & Jessie Hope Canada
HANSON, Lila Hope, Aug 3 1923 Sex:F Child# 4 Walter H Hanson Canada & Jessie Hope Canada
HANSON, Lillian Annabell, Jun 5 1922 Sex:F Child# 1 Roland Hanson Nashua, NH & Roxi Bishop Nashua, NH
HANSON, Marion, Mar 25 1930 Sex:F Child# 4 Roland Hanson Nashua, NH & Roxy Bishop Nashua, NH
HANSON, Raymond George, Aug 30 1924 Sex:M Child# 6 Fred Hanson NH & Minnie Rose NH
HANSON, Richard Robert, Aug 12 1923 Sex:M Child# 1 Richard Hanson Bangor, ME & Yvonne Pageau Littleton, NH
HANSON, Richard Wayne, Jan 19 1935 Sex:M Child# 5 Chas S Hanson S Wardsboro, VT & Esther Bouley Nashua, NH
HAOALAINPOPOULO, Unknown, Dec 30 1932 Sex:M Child# 4 N Haoalainpopoulo Greece & A Philipopoulos Greece
HAPGOOD, William R, Dec 3 1892 Sex:M Child# 2 James Hapgood England & Mary Whittemore Litchfield, NH
HAPWOOD, Unknown, Oct 26 1897 Sex:M Child# 5 James Hapwood England & Mary Whittemore Litchfield, NH
HARDCASTLE, Gertrude, Nov 11 1915 Sex:F Child# 4 John Hardcastle Boston, MA & Marie Murphy Pepperell, MA
HARDWOOD, Madeline Frances, Sep 5 1924 Sex:F Child# 7 William Hardwood Nashua, NH & Catherine McDonald Prince
HARDY, Albert Vernon, Sep 2 1923 Sex:M Child# 2 Albert R Hardy Montgomery, VT & Ethel May Watts Hudson, NH
HARDY, Charles, Oct 5 1934 Sex:M Child# 11 Robert Hardy W Boylston, MA & Bertha Moore Lee, NH
HARDY, Cora Ursula, Oct 1 1914 Sex:F Child# 1 Charles A Hardy Swanzee, NH & Sarah M George Suncook, NH
HARDY, Dudley Davis, Jul 21 1926 Sex:M Child# 1 Roland Hardy Nashua, NH & Bessie Bradley Hudson, NH
HARDY, Eleanor, Jan 2 1928 Sex:F Child# 2 Roland Hardy Nashua, NH & Bessie Bradley Hudson, NH
HARDY, Fath Hazel, Jun 5 1935 Sex:F Child# 1 Eastman Hardy Durham, ME & Hazel Henderson Nashua, NH
HARDY, George Edmond, Nov 21 1897 Sex:M Child# 3 William E Hardy Clinton, MA & Gertrude F Tower Waterville, ME
HARDY, Herald Robert, Aug 29 1902 Sex:M Child# 1 Harlan E Hardy N Londonderry, NH & Ada M Smith Nashua, NH
HARDY, Joan, Apr 18 1932 Sex:F Child# 2 Edwin P Hardy Nashua, NH & Ednah MacDonald Melrose, MA
HARDY, Margaret Louise, Feb 5 1930 Sex:F Child# 10 Robert Hardy W Boylston, MA & Bertha Moore Lee, NH
HARDY, Mary Ann, Jun 3 1916 Sex:F Child# 8 Constant Hardy Canada & Marguerite Stanton Somersworth, NH
HARDY, Russell Munroe, Oct 10 1909 Sex:M Child# 1 Sanford P Hardy W Swanzey, NH & Myrtie Colby Sutton, NH
HARDY, Ruth Edna, Sep 11 1915 Sex:F Child# 2 Sanford P Hardy Swanzey, NH & Myrtie Colby Sutton, NH
HARDY, Unknown, Jan 7 1889 Sex:F Child# 4 Darius Hardy Vermont & Delia CT
HARDY, Unknown, Jan 29 1891 Sex:M Child# 2 Nathaniel Hardy Hollis, NH & Hattie Willoby Hollis, NH
HARDY, Unknown, Apr 24 1891 Sex:F Child# 5 Davis D Hardy Vermont & Lelia CT
HARDY, Unknown, Aug 10 1893 Sex:F Child# 6 Davis D Hardy Vermont & Lelia Conn
HARDY, Unknown, Feb 2 1900 Sex:M Child# 9 Dudley D Hardy Vermont & Lelia Agens Connecticut
HARDY, Unknown, Mar 26 1902 Sex:M Child# 2 M Ed Hardy Canada & Grace Brulkwater Lincolnville, ME
HARDY, Unknown, Dec 5 1903 Sex:M Child# 8 Dudley D Hardy Conn & Lelia M Ayers Vermont
HAREKIS, Unknown, Feb 13 1914 Sex:M Child# 6 Anthony Harekis Russia & Lucia Takolis Russia Stillborn
HAREL, Roland, Aug 4 1909 Sex:M Child# 4 Pierre Harel Canada & Melina Chamberlain Canada
HARGRAVE, Arthur, Apr 7 1888 Sex:M Child# 4 Bartholomew Hargrave England & Eliza Ricard Canada
HARGRAVES, Andrew, Jun 10 1887 Sex:M Child# Theophile Hargraves England & Sarah Laton Amherst
HARGRAVES, Augustus, Feb 3 1904 Sex:M Child# 6 Henry Hargraves England & Delia Devine Conn
HARGRAVES, Benedicte, Feb 14 1907 Sex:M Child# 8 Henry Hargraves England & Delia Devine Conn
HARGRAVES, Catherine Gladis, Sep 13 1899 Sex:F Child# B Hargraves England & Eliza Ricord Canada
HARGRAVES, Frances Joseph, Mar 3 1899 Sex:M Child# 3 Henry Hargraves Ireland & Delia Devine Stamford, CT
HARGRAVES, Francis Henry, Dec 4 1927 Sex:M Child# 1 F J Hargraves Nashua, NH & Delia Henry Nashua, NH
HARGRAVES, James Harold, Sep 25 1905 Sex:M Child# 1 John P Hargraves Nashua, NH & Lucy Donovan Ireland
HARGRAVES, John F, Jan 15 1908 Sex:M Child# 2 John P Hargraves Nashua, NH & Lucy Donovan Ireland
HARGRAVES, John H, Jan 13 1895 Sex:M Child# 1 Henry Hargraves England & Delia Devine

HARGRAVES, John R A, Oct 11 1919 Sex:M Child# 3 John Hargraves Nashua, NH & Chris Courtemanche Nashua, NH
HARGRAVES, Joseph, Feb 7 1897 Sex:M Child# 2 Henry Hargraves England & Delia T Devine Stamford, CT
HARGRAVES, Katherine Arlene, Apr 21 1918 Sex:F Child# 2 John H Hargraves Nashua, NH & M C Courtemanche Nashua, NH
HARGRAVES, Leo, Oct 26 1905 Sex:M Child# 7 Henry Hargraves England & Delia Divine Stamford, CT
HARGRAVES, Margaret, May 16 1908 Sex:F Child# 9 Henry Hargraves England & Delia Devine Conn
HARGRAVES, Mary, Feb 14 1901 Sex:F Child# 4 Henry Hargraves England & Delia Devine Stamford, CT
HARGRAVES, Mary Lula, Feb 22 1891 Sex:F Child# 5 B J Hargraves England & Eliza Recard Canada
HARGRAVES, Mary Theresa, Aug 4 1910 Sex:F Child# 10 Henry Hargraves England & Delia Devine Connecticut
HARGRAVES, Mary Theresa, Dec 10 1928 Sex:F Child# 2 F Hargraves Nashua, NH & Delia Henry Nashua, NH
HARGRAVES, Robert, Aug 24 1913 Sex:M Child# 1 Henry J Hargraves Nashua, NH & Agnes Breen Nashua, NH
HARGRAVES, Rosa Ella, Feb 15 1897 Sex:F Child# 6 B J Hargraves England & Eliza Ricard Canada
HARGRAVES, Unknown, May 25 1902 Sex:M Child# 5 Henry Hargraves England & Delia Quinn Stamford, CT
HARGREAVES, Marilyn Ellen, Jan 20 1935 Sex:F Child# 1 Benedict Hargreaves Nashua, NH & Marguerite Mercier Newport
HARGREAVES, Mary Doris, Jul 14 1923 Sex:F Child# 4 John H Hargreaves Nashua, NH & Mary C Courtemanche Nashua, NH
HARGREAVES, Richard Leo, May 20 1932 Sex:M Child# 3 F J Hargreaves Nashua, NH & Della C Henry Nashua, NH
HARGREAVES, Robert Albert, Apr 4 1925 Sex:M Child# 4 J H Hargreaves Nashua, NH & Chris Courtemach Nashua, NH
HARGREAVES, Robert Paul, May 20 1932 Sex:M Child# 4 F J Hargreaves Nashua, NH & Della C Henry Nashua, NH
HARKAWAY, Martha, Dec 16 1915 Sex:F Child# 1 Joseph Harkaway Russia & Jennie Frank Russia
HARKAWAY, Sylvia Annette, Apr 18 1924 Sex:F Child# 3 Joseph Harkaway Russia & Jennie Frank Russia
HARKAWAY, Unknown, Dec 24 1917 Sex:M Child# 2 Joseph Harkaway Russia & Jennie Frank Russia
HARKAWAY, William Irving, May 7 1928 Sex:M Child# 4 Joseph Harkaway Russia & Jennie Frank Russia
HARKINS, Ronald Albert, Jan 12 1926 Sex:M Child# 6 L H Harkins Nashua, NH & Jennie Tupper Nashua, NH
HARMEY, Mary Florence, Jun 26 1925 Sex:F Child# 4 Francis W Harmey Salem, MA & Florence Austin Sanford, ME
HARMON, Muriel Helen, May 16 1920 Sex:F Child# 3 Harry W Harmon Nashua, NH & Nellie C Spear Lawrence, MA
HARMON, Theo Lucille, Sep 14 1909 Sex:F Child# 1 Harry Harmon Nashua, NH & Nellie Spear Lawrence, MA
HARNEY, Frances, Oct 3 1923 Sex:F Child# 2 Edw Charles Harney Woburn, MA & Dorothy Dennen Pepperell, MA
HARNEY, Unknown, Aug 8 1922 Sex:F Child# 1 Ed Charles Harney Woburn, MA & Dorothy Denneu Pepperell, MA
HARPER, Barbara Mary, May 4 1930 Sex:F Child# 1 Edward Harper Marlboro, NH & Ruth Brahaney Milford, NH
HARPER, Joan Alice, Aug 4 1931 Sex:F Child# 2 Edward Harper Marlboro, NH & Ruth Brahaney Milford, NH
HARPER, Louis E, May 24 1896 Sex:M Child# 2 Joseph F Harper Nashua, NH & Alice B Dolan Nashua, NH
HARPER, Mary Genevieve, Jan 4 1892 Sex:F Child# 1 Joseph Harper Nashua, NH & Alice B Dolan Nashua, NH
HARPIN, J Raoul Edouard, Aug 8 1915 Sex:M Child# 2 Alexis Harpin Douglas, MA & Marie L Levesque Canada
HARPIN, Liliane, Feb 11 1912 Sex:F Child# 2 Pierre Harpin Burlington, VT & Georgianna Provencal Concord, NH
HARPIN, Loretta Margaret, Apr 2 1898 Sex:F Child# 4 Joseph F Harpin Nashua, NH & Alice B Dolan Nashua, NH
HARPIN, Marie Eva, Jan 18 1913 Sex:F Child# 3 Pierre Harpin Burlington, VT & Georgianna Provencal Concord, NH
HARPIN, Marie Jeanne, Oct 4 1905 Sex:F Child# 1 Arthur Harpin Canada & Delima Messier Canada
HARPIN, Pierre, Mar 29 1911 Sex:M Child# 1 Pierre Harpin Burlington, VT & Georgia Provencal Concord, NH Stillborn
HARPIN, Raymond, Dec 9 1904 Sex:M Child# 1 Alexis Harpin E Douglass, MA & Lydia Levesque Canada
HARRIGAN, Ellen, Jan 29 1896 Sex:F Child# 3 James Harrigan Ireland & Kate Calahan Ireland
HARRIGAN, James Christopher, Dec 4 1894 Sex:M Child# 2 James Harrigan Ireland & Kate Callahan Ireland
HARRIGAN, Lillian, Jan 24 1893 Sex:F Child# 1 James Harrigan Ireland & Kate L Callahan Ireland
HARRIMAN, Robert Leroy, Apr 19 1932 Sex:M Child# 9 Asa Harriman Michigan & Laura Hardy Virginia
HARRIMAN, Wallace Burton, Mar 2 1932 Sex:M Child# 3 E W Harriman N Adams, MA & Vivian L Bishop Hollis, NH
HARRIMAN, Walter Roy, Jan 16 1934 Sex:M Child# 1 Walter M Harriman Brockton, MA & Frances Miner Pittsford, VT
HARRIMAN, William Leroy, Nov 19 1934 Sex:M Child# 4 Elliott W Harriman N Arlington, MA & Vivian L Bishop Hollis, NH
HARRINGTON, Frederick, May 17 1892 Sex:M Child# 4 Charles Harrington Lowell, MA & Louise Marlboro, MA
HARRINGTON, Hattie Estelle, Aug 7 1896 Sex:F Child# 1 T J Harrington New York, NY & Mabel L Spencer Lowell, MA
HARRINGTON, James, Jan 16 1888 Sex:M Child# 3 Timothy Harrington Lowell, MA & Mary Ann Welton Lowell, MA
HARRINGTON, Laurice Adeline, Oct 20 1926 Sex:F Child#  L J Harrington Manchester, NH & Alice J Lonergan Cambridge
HARRINGTON, Unknown, Jun 2 1889 Sex:M Child# 4 T Harrington Lowell, MA & Mary A Whelton Lowell, MA Stillborn
HARRINGTON, Unknown, Apr 28 1930 Sex:M Child#  Lawrence Harrington Manchester, NH & Alice J Lonergan Cambridge
HARRIS, Arthur D, Mar 11 1892 Sex:M Child# 2 David J Harris NH & Abbie L Bodwell VT
HARRIS, Barbara Ann, Oct 26 1934 Sex:F Child# 1 Edward Harris Lancaster, MA & Blanche Batchelder Townsend, MA
HARRIS, Carl Bassett, Apr 15 1911 Sex:M Child# 1 Carl P Harris Bradford, NH & Rose Bassett Franklin, NH
HARRIS, Chandler A, Oct 30 1900 Sex:M Child# 4 Edw R Harris England & Maud Allington England
HARRIS, Clifford Earl, Jan 30 1924 Sex:M Child# 2 Fred Harris Littleton, NH & Cora Smith S Royalton, VT
HARRIS, Ernest John, Dec 28 1930 Sex:M Child# 1 John Harris, Jr Gloucester, MA & Florence Barnes Mason, NH
HARRIS, Florence M, Nov 1 1909 Sex:F Child# 1 George Harris Maine & Elizabeth Degory Providence, RI
HARRIS, George, Jul 15 1894 Sex:M Child#  C Harris Russia & F Avey Russia
HARRIS, Grace E, Apr 30 1895 Sex:F Child# 4 James B Harris Litchfield, NH & Martha C Shattuck Andover, MA
HARRIS, Helen Dugget, Sep 20 1908 Sex:F Child# 2 Walter Harris Nashua, NH & Effie Rideout Nashua, NH
HARRIS, Herbert Smith, Sep 20 1908 Sex:M Child# 3 Walter Harris Nashua, NH & Effie Rideout Nashua, NH
HARRIS, Margaret, Jun 27 1890 Sex:F Child# 1 Wilfred R Harris Nashua, NH & Bessie Long Concord, NH
HARRIS, Nettie Marguerite, Aug 10 1897 Sex:F Child# 2 George A Harris Manchester, NH & Pearl Bracy Berwick, ME
HARRIS, Roland K, Jun 20 1893 Sex:M Child#  Charles D Harris Nova Scotia & Louise McKay Nova Scotia
HARRIS, Russell White, Aug 29 1906 Sex:M Child# 1 Walter E Harris Nashua, NH & Effie Rideout Nashua, NH
HARRIS, Shirley Barbara, Dec 25 1926 Sex:F Child# 5 Charles R Harris Berwick, ME & Bertha L Bisbee Wilmington, MA
HARRIS, Shirley Lorraine, Aug 30 1929 Sex:F Child# 1 Edwin Harris S Deerfield, MA & Flora Harris Colraine, MA
HARRIS, Unknown, Dec 6 1889 Sex:F Child# 6 Robert M Harris Nova Scotia & Elizabeth McGill Nova Scotia
HARRIS, Unknown, Apr 29 1892 Sex:M Child# 2 Benjamin Harris NS & Janietta McKay NS
HARRIS, Unknown, Aug 5 1893 Sex:F Child# 8 Robert M Harris Nova Scotia & Elizabeth McKay Nova Scotia
HARRIS, Unknown, Dec 5 1893 Sex:M Child# 3 James B Harris NH & Martha Shattuck Mass
HARRIS, Unknown, Jul 23 1895 Sex:F Child# 10 Robert Harris Nova Scotia & Elizabeth McKay Nova Scotia

HARRIS, Wilbur Edward, Sep 14 1899 Sex:M Child# 3 Edward H Harris England & Maud Arlington England
HARRISON, Isabelle Tressa, Feb 11 1914 Sex:F Child# 2 David Harrison Woodstock, NB & Agnes Snow Northboro, MA
HARRISON, John Albert, Feb 22 1911 Sex:M Child# 1 John A Harrison Ales, VA & Rose B Goodwin Berlin, NH
HARRISON, Mary Genice, May 9 1925 Sex:F Child# 5 David M Harrison Woodstock, NB & Agnes M Snow Northboro, MA
HART, Arthur William, Jr, Aug 14 1930 Sex:M Child# 2 Arthur W Hart Nashua, NH & Louise Fiske Nashua, NH
HART, Barbara Ann, Oct 1 1929 Sex:F Child# 2 Floyd Russell Hart Sunapee, NH & Aril Webster Mars Hill, ME
HART, Blanche Lillian, Apr 27 1934 Sex:F Child# 4 Lloyd Russell Hart Sunapee, NH & Arie Elaine Webster Mars Hill,
HART, Gloria Loretta, Jul 4 1927 Sex:F Child# 1 Arthur W Hart Nashua, NH & Loretta L Fiske Nashua, NH
HART, Katherine May, Feb 14 1920 Sex:F Child# 2 John Hart Plattsburg, NY & May Hammond Rutland, VT
HART, Kenneth Charles, Mar 28 1921 Sex:M Child# 2 Richard Hart Hull, MA & Florence Henderson Nashua, NH
HART, Lloyd Russell, Jr, Oct 20 1925 Sex:M Child# 1 Lloyd Russell Hart Sunapee, NH & Arie E Webster Mars Hill,
HART, Priscilla Elaine, Sep 23 1931 Sex:F Child# 3 Lloyd R Hart Sunapee, NH & Arie E Webster Marshall, ME
HART, Theresa Dorothy, Oct 1 1934 Sex:F Child# 3 Arthur W Hart Nashua, NH & Louise L Fiske Nashua, NH
HART, Unknown, Jan 14 1890 Sex:F Child# 1 Jerry Hart Danvers, MA & Nellie E Flanders Concord, NH
HART, Unknown, Jun 24 1892 Sex:F Child# 2 Jeremiah Hart Danvers, MA & Mary E Flanders Concord, NH
HART, William, Jul 5 1908 Sex:M Child# 2 Arthur Hart
HARTH, Alfred Walter, Jul 24 1905 Sex:M Child# 1 Walter D Harth Georgetown, MA & Lillian M Skidmore Bridgeport, CT
HARTIGAN, Geraldine Clara, Sep 22 1923 Sex:F Child# 1 William Hartigan Claremont, NH & Lydia Champagne Whitefield
HARTIGAN, Leo Thomas, May 11 1908 Sex:M Child# 2 Francis P Hartigan Beverly, MA & Margaret F Welch Peabody, MA
HARTIGAN, William, Aug 15 1916 Sex:M Child# 3 Patrick J Hartigan Ireland & Annie F Gordon Ireland
HARTMAN, Elizabeth Louise, Mar 1 1911 Sex:F Child# 3 Howard E Hartman Mansfield, OH & Lora K Robinson Wakefield, NH
HARTMAN, Florence M, Jun 14 1905 Sex:F Child# 1 Howard E Hartman Mansfield, OH & Ruth L Robinson Maine
HARTMAN, Howard, Oct 12 1909 Sex:M Child# 2 Howard E Hartman Mansfield, OH & Lora K Robinson Wakefield, NH
HARTMAN, Unknown, Oct 31 1917 Sex:F Child# 4 Howard E Hartman Mansfield, OH & Lora Robinson Wakefield, NH Stillborn
HARTSHORN, Unknown, Jun 18 1890 Sex:M Child# 2 John A Hartshorn Townsend, MA & Helen M Searle New Ipswich, NH
HARTWELL, Arthur I O, Jan 22 1902 Sex:M Child# 2 Edward Hartwell Nashua, NH & Emma Lemay Canada
HARTWELL, Blanche, Dec 30 1898 Sex:F Child# 3 Charles B Hartwell Nashua, NH & Telica Trombly NY
HARTWELL, Earl Randolph, Apr 29 1905 Sex:M Child# 1 Irving Hartwell Groton, MA & Eliza Delude Canada
HARTWELL, Ellinoi Liliane, Jun 8 1900 Sex:F Child# 1 Eddie Hartwell Nashua, NH & Emma Lemoy Canada
HARTWELL, Herbert Sumner, Feb 13 1929 Sex:M Child# 1 Herbert S Hartwell Everett, MA & Evelyn Wheeler Nashua, NH
HARTWELL, Irene Mossman, Sep 9 1891 Sex:F Child# 1 C B Hartwell Nashua, NH & F B Trombley Plattsburg, NY
HARTWELL, Marilyn Grace, Feb 6 1931 Sex:F Child# 2 Herbert Hartwell Everett, MA & Evelyn Wheeler Nashua, NH
HARTWELL, Myron Ernest, Aug 10 1926 Sex:M Child# 2 Ernest Hartwell W Groton, MA & Maude Fuller W Groton, MA
HARTWELL, Roy Charles, Aug 23 1897 Sex:M Child# 2 Charles Hartwell Nashua, NH & Felicia Trombly NY
HARTWELL, Unknown, May 18 1887 Sex: Child# 3 Oscar D Hartwell Lisbon, NH & Lizzie Codman Washington, NH
HARVEY, Beatrice Eleanor, Dec 1 1929 Sex:F Child# 1 Harold Davis Harvey Hudson, NH & Phyllis E Clement Nashua, NH
HARVEY, Clara Louise, Sep 20 1888 Sex:F Child# 4 Frank Harvey Freedom & Maud Parmenter Nashua, NH
HARVEY, Clayton Franklin, Oct 25 1926 Sex:M Child# 2 Ralph G Harvey Hudson, NH & Dorilda Larocque Nashua, NH
HARVEY, Ethel, Jun 26 1906 Sex:F Child# 5 Edward J Harvey New York & Maria Flynn Ireland
HARVEY, Eva, Jun 20 1888 Sex:F Child# 3 Charles Harvey Saco, ME & Olive M Fellows Nashua, NH
HARVEY, Joseph Adelard, May 1 1899 Sex:M Child# 6 Joseph Harvey Canada & Fannie Gagnon Canada
HARVEY, Joseph Aime, May 25 1904 Sex:M Child# 9 Joseph Harvey Canada & Euphemie Gagnon Canada
HARVEY, Joseph Etienne L, Feb 4 1893 Sex:M Child# 2 Joseph Harvey Canada & Euphemie Gagnon Canada
HARVEY, Mamie Lena, Dec 2 1899 Sex:F Child# 3 Edward Harvey Canada & Maria Flynn Ireland
HARVEY, Marie Louise, Aug 11 1894 Sex:F Child# 3 Joseph Harvey Canada & Euphemie Gagnon Canada
HARVEY, Marie Merilda, Jun 13 1897 Sex:F Child# 4 Joseph Harvey Canada & Euphemie Gagnon Canada
HARVEY, Marie Olivette B, Nov 22 1906 Sex:F Child# 10 Joseph Harvey Canada & Euphemie Gagnon Canada
HARVEY, Marie R Y, Dec 28 1902 Sex:F Child# 8 Joseph Harvey Canada & Euphemie Gagnon Canada
HARVEY, Phillip, Apr 15 1917 Sex:M Child# 1 Lester Irv Harvey Nashua, NH & Effie Classon Nashua, NH
HARVEY, Ralph Greeley, Oct 30 1899 Sex:M Child# 8 John F Harvey NH & Maud Parmenter Nashua, NH
HARVEY, Raymond, May 11 1922 Sex:M Child# 1 Adelard Harvey Nashua, NH & Leona Ricard Canada
HARVEY, Unknown, Oct 10 1890 Sex:M Child# 5 Frank J Harvey Freedom & Maud Parmenter Nashua, NH
HARVEY, Unknown, Oct 22 1895 Sex:M Child# 4 Joseph Harvey Canada & Phemie Gagnon Canada Stillborn
HARVEY, Unknown, Nov 28 1901 Sex:M Child# 7 Joseph Harvey Canada & Euphemie Gagnon Canada Stillborn
HARVEY, Unknown, Nov 18 1922 Sex:M Child# 1 Ralph G Harvey Hudson, NH & Donilda Larocque Nashua, NH Stillborn
HARWOOD, Agnes Louise, Dec 17 1918 Sex:F Child# 4 William Harwood Nashua, NH & Catherine McDonald PEI
HARWOOD, Catherine Mae, May 4 1920 Sex:F Child# 5 William Harwood Nashua, NH & Catherine McDonald PEI
HARWOOD, Charles William, Sep 14 1900 Sex:M Child# 6 Bert Harwood NH & Kate F Merrill NH
HARWOOD, Forrest Sidney, Sep 8 1924 Sex:M Child# 3 R W Harwood Hudson, NH & Stella M Downing Groveton, NH
HARWOOD, Hazel Elsie, Dec 28 1912 Sex:F Child# 1 Robert Harwood Nashua, NH & Elsie Helena Maloney New York
HARWOOD, John Walter, Sep 10 1924 Sex:M Child# 3 Guy Harwood Nashua, NH & Mary A McDonald PEI
HARWOOD, Joseph Robert, May 29 1923 Sex:M Child# 2 Cornelius G Harwood Nashua, NH & Mary A McDonald PEI
HARWOOD, Lula Louise, Nov 25 1924 Sex:F Child# 1 Robert Harwood Nashua, NH & Helen Maloney New York
HARWOOD, Mary Florentine, Jul 21 1920 Sex:F Child# 1 Guy C Harwood Nashua, NH & Agnes MacDonald PEI
HARWOOD, Monica Mary, Sep 9 1916 Sex:F Child# 3 William H Harwood Nashua, NH & Katherine MacDonald PEI
HARWOOD, Roland Everett, Sep 26 1921 Sex:M Child# 3 Fred C Harwood Nashua, NH & Mary A Stok New Canaan, CT
HARWOOD, Ruth May, May 15 1897 Sex:F Child# 5 Bert Harwood S Lyndeboro, NH & Kate F Merrill Brookline, NH
HARWOOD, Theresa Alice, Jun 5 1931 Sex:F Child# 5 Guy Harwood Nashua, NH & Agnes MacDonald PEI
HARWOOD, Unknown, Aug 19 1890 Sex:M Child# 3 Bert Harwood Lyndeboro, NH & Kate F Merrill Brookline, NH
HARWOOD, Unknown, Oct 12 1892 Sex:M Child# 4 Bert Harwood Lyndeboro, NH & Kate F Merrill Brookline, NH
HARWOOD, Unknown, Nov 9 1909 Sex:M Child# 2 Fred C Harwood Nashua, NH & Marie Tolz New Canaan, CT
HARWOOD, William Henry, May 23 1923 Sex:M Child# 6 William Harwood Nashua, NH & Catherine McDonald PEI
HASALEVRIN, Mary, Apr 12 1914 Sex:F Child# 1 Satareon Hasalevrin Greece & Andonia Kunu Greece

HASALEVRIS, Unknown, Oct 16 1922 Sex:M Child# 5 Lotezios Hasalevris Greece & Antonia Rounoupes Greece
HASALIVUS, Unknown, Jul 12 1917 Sex:F Child# 4 Sam Hasalivus Greece & Antonia Konopy Greece
HASELOPOLOS, Unknown, May 3 1916 Sex:F Child# 2 James Haselopolos Greece & Antonia Apolios Greece
HASELTON, Truman Curtis, Dec 20 1930 Sex:M Child# 1 Truman Haselton Haverhill, MA & Dorothy Mason Winooski, VT
HASILTON, Lawrence Arden, Apr 6 1930 Sex:M Child# 1 William E Hasilton
HASKELL, Cedric Charles, Sep 6 1932 Sex:M Child# 1 Cedric Haskell US & Bertha Asselin US
HASKELL, Frank Leslie, Jr, Apr 24 1911 Sex:M Child# 3 Frank Leslie Haskell Nova Scotia & Mae Baker New York
HASKELL, Leslie Allen, Aug 14 1919 Sex:M Child# 5 Leslie F Haskell Nova Scotia & Mary Adelaide Baker Chataquay, NY
HASKELL, May, Dec 23 1905 Sex:F Child# 3 Leslie Haskell Nova Scotia & Mary A Baker Saranac, NY
HASKELL, May Alice, Mar 31 1917 Sex:F Child# 4 Lesslie F Haskell Nova Scotia & May Baker Savana, NY
HASKELL, Phillis Adelaide, Jan 31 1908 Sex:F Child# 2 F Leslie Haskell Nova Scotia & Adelaide Baker Nashua, NH
HASKELL, Unknown, Jan 11 1928 Sex:M Child# 1 (No Parents Listed)
HASKILL, Rachel Arneita, May 9 1926 Sex:F Child# 7 Leslie F Haskill Nova Scotia & Mae Baker Saranac, NY
HASKIN, Bernice Luella, Nov 14 1916 Sex:F Child# 7 Allen Haskin Vermont & Gladys Honner Vermont
HASKINS, Doris Althea, Nov 19 1920 Sex:F Child# 3 Leonard A Haskins Enfield, NH & Jennie A Tupper Nashua, NH
HASKINS, Doris Irene, Jan 25 1914 Sex:M Child# 5 Allan W Haskins Randolph, VT & Gladys M Haner Hyde Park, VT
HASKINS, June May, Oct 11 1919 Sex:F Child# 2 Leonard A Haskins Enfield, NH & Jennie Tupper Nashua, NH
HASKINS, Leonard, Sep 1 1922 Sex:M Child# 4 Leonard Haskins Enfield, NH & Jennie Tupper Nashua, NH
HASKINS, Lucy May, Jun 7 1892 Sex:F Child# 3 William A Haskins Starksboro, VT & Flora Putnam Starksboro, VT
HASKINS, Merle Fred, Aug 15 1918 Sex:M Child# 8 Allen Haskins Vermont & Gladys Horner Vermont
HASKINS, Olive Jane, Oct 21 1917 Sex:F Child# 1 Leonard A Haskins Lockhaven, NH & Jennie A Tupper Nashua, NH
HASKINS, Richard Earle, Mar 22 1911 Sex:M Child# 4 Allan W Haskins Randolph, VT & Gladys M Horne Hyde Park, VT
HASKINS, Robert Tupper, Jul 20 1924 Sex:M Child# 5 L C Haskins Enfield, NH & Jennie Tupper Nashua, NH
HASKINS, Unknown, May 25 1887 Sex:M Child# 2 William A Haskins Sykesboro, VT & Flora J Putnam Sykesboro, VT
HASKINS, Unknown, Nov 8 1901 Sex:F Child# 4 William A Haskins Starksboro, VT & Flora Putnam Starksboro, VT Stillbo
HASLAM, John William, Oct 19 1933 Sex:M Child# 4 George T Haslam Lowell, MA & Claire Gill England
HASLEFOS, John, Feb 15 1915 Sex:M Child# 2 Sam Haslefos Greece & Antonia Canapulos Greece
HASSLER, Albina Alice Alva, May 3 1922 Sex:F Child# 2 Robert James Hassler Kentucky & Helen May Bassett Warner
HASSLER, Harry Robert, Mar 24 1921 Sex:M Child# 1 Robert J Hassler Kentucky & Helen May Bassett NH
HASSLEY, Elaine Shirley, Sep 1 1923 Sex:F Child# 1 (No Parents Listed)
HASTINGS, Hurdon Ranslow, Jun 14 1933 Sex:M Child# 1 H R Hastings Canada & May E Dale Old Forge, PA
HASTINGS, Unknown, Jul 21 1891 Sex:M Child# 1 Benjamin J Hastings Rochester & Lillian E French Wrentham, MA Stillbo
HASU, Sylvia Elizabeth, May 13 1926 Sex:F Child# 5 Otto Hasu Finland & Lydia Daniels Fitchburg, MA
HATCH, Fred Ames, Nov 30 1926 Sex:M Child# 1 L V Hatch Lebanon, NH & Thelma H Ames Nashua, NH
HATCH, Robert Gaskill, Dec 31 1911 Sex:M Child# 1 Myron J Hatch King City, MO & Lillis Gaskill Nashua, NH
HATCH, Unknown, May 30 1888 Sex:F Child# 9 Chauncy A Hatch Hardwick, VT & Mary S Miller Hyde Park, VT
HATCH, Unknown, Sep 19 1890 Sex:M Child# 1 A P Hatch Hardwick, VT & Mary S Miller Hyde Park, VT
HATCH, Unknown, Jul 11 1899 Sex:F Child# 3 Fred S Hatch Milford, NH & Lula May Crumm Chicago, IL
HATFIELD, Eleanor Cathrine, Jul 6 1931 Sex:F Child# 1 Francis J Hatfield Brookline, MA & Dorothy Birchall Lynn, MA
HATFIELD, Grace F, Jul 28 1892 Sex:F Child# 4 George J Hatfield Sheffield, England & Sarah Newton Sheffield, Eng
HATFIELD, James George, Mar 4 1909 Sex:M Child# 2 George H Hatfield Yorkshire, England & Elizabeth Ryan Milford
HATFIELD, Mary Elisabeth, Mar 18 1908 Sex:F Child# 1 George H Hatfield Yorkshire, England & Elisabeth Ryan Milford
HATFIELD, Mary Francis, Nov 19 1933 Sex:F Child# 2 Francis Hatfield Brookline, MA & Dorothy Birchall Lynn, MA
HATFIELD, Mildred Ball, Jul 24 1920 Sex:F Child# 3 Wm Harold Hatfield Acton, MA & Nettie Alice Stacy New Ipswich
HATFIELD, Unknown, Aug 17 1894 Sex:F Child# 4 George Hatfield Sheffield, England & Sarah Newton Sheffield, Eng
HATFIELD, Willard Frederick, Apr 17 1911 Sex:M Child# 3 George Hatfield, Jr Yorkshire, England & Elizabeth Ryan
HATZDAMAS, Matin, Oct 22 1918 Sex:F Child# 1 Andone Hatzdamas Greece & Efrosine Grapeaka Greece
HATZIGOGA, Efigenia, Nov 3 1914 Sex:F Child# 2 William Hatzigoga Greece & Ellen Corcavelas Greece
HAUG, Anne, Dec 28 1930 Sex:F Child# 6 Anton Haug Germany & Charlotte MacDuffie Nashua, NH
HAUG, Carol Patricia, Oct 1 1928 Sex:F Child# 5 Anton Haug Germany & C MacDuffie Nashua, NH
HAUG, Constance, Feb 18 1924 Sex:F Child# 3 Anton J Haug Germany & Char McDuffy Nashua, NH
HAUG, Elizabeth, Aug 16 1926 Sex:F Child# 4 Anton J Haug Germany & C MacDuffie Nashua, NH
HAUG, Gertrude Barbara, Apr 16 1933 Sex:F Child# 3 Ludwig Haug Germany & G Stassohik Germany
HAUG, Irmagart, Feb 9 1928 Sex:F Child# 2 Ludwig Haug Germany & Gert Staschik Germany
HAUG, Louise Sarah Ann, Aug 26 1934 Sex:F Child# 3 Richard Haug Germany & Madeline Spillane Nashua, NH
HAUG, Marie Josephine, Feb 25 1920 Sex:F Child# 1 Anton J Haug Bevaria Germany & Charlotte MacDuffie Nashua, NH
HAUG, Mary Theresa, Jan 17 1927 Sex:F Child# 1 Richard Haug Germany & Madeline Spillane Nashua, NH
HAUG, Richard Joseph, Mar 9 1930 Sex:M Child# 2 Richard Haug Germany & Madeline Spillane Nashua, NH
HAUGH, Annie Francis, Oct 21 1893 Sex:F Child# 3 James J Haugh Ireland & Mary E Carr Ireland
HAUGH, Mary Catherine, May 17 1895 Sex:F Child# 4 James Haugh Ireland & Mary Carr Ireland
HAUGH, Thomas, Sep 20 1903 Sex:m Child# 8 James Haugh Ireland & Mary Carr
HAUGH, Timothy P, Mar 3 1891 Sex:M Child# 1 James J Haugh Ireland & Mary E Carr Ireland
HAUGH, Unknown, Aug 7 1889 Sex:M Child# 1 Edward Haugh Nashua, NH & Mary A Keenan Nashua, NH
HAUGH, Unknown, Mar 16 1895 Sex:F Child# 3 Edward Haugh Nashua, NH & Mary Keenan Nashua, NH
HAUREHAN, Annie, May 5 1902 Sex:F Child# 6 William Haurehan Ireland & Ellen Gilhooly Ireland
HAVARD, Beatrice, Feb 17 1894 Sex:F Child# 1 Charles Havard Woonsocket, RI & Beatrice Champagne Canada
HAVARD, Joseph Charles, Apr 21 1897 Sex:M Child# 3 Joseph C Havard Canada & Beatrice Jalbert Canada
HAVARD, Mary Rosanna, Apr 13 1895 Sex:F Child# 2 Charles Havard Rhode Island & Beatrice Gilbert Quebec
HAVEN, Arthur Earl, Nov 21 1927 Sex:M Child# 3 Arthur L Haven Washington, NH & Nellie Adel Koch Westville, NY
HAVEN, Walter Arthur, Jul 1 1914 Sex:M Child# 1 Arthur S Haven Washington, NH & Nellie A Rock Westville, NY
HAVEN, William Lester, Oct 8 1916 Sex:M Child# 2 Arthur L Haven Washington, NH & Nellie A Rock Westville, NY
HAVHANNESIAN, Rosa, Nov 14 1906 Sex:F Child# 2 Artin Havhannesian Armenia & Osnif Ateru Armenia
HAWKES, Roland, May 11 1932 Sex:M Child# 3 Jack Hawkes Cambridge, MA & Mary O'Neil Nashua, NH

199

HAWKINS, Walter Jay, Jan 21 1896 Sex:M Child# 4 Charles H Hawkins New London, NY & Nellie Werthy Rome, NY
HAWLEY, Nancy, Jul 30 1906 Sex:F Child# 3 George D Hawley Albany, NY & Elizabeth Scofield Boston, MA
HAWSBURY, Martin, Mar 26 1918 Sex:M Child# 2 Martin J Hawsbury Nashua, NH & Mary K O'Neil Nashua, NH
HAYDEN, Barbara, Sep 9 1924 Sex:F Child# 1 Philip A Hayden Amherst, NH & Ruth W Hadley Brooklyn, NY
HAYDEN, Charles O, Jul 30 1887 Sex:M Child# 1 George A Hayden NH & Alice M California
HAYDEN, Clara Louise, Oct 2 1919 Sex:F Child# 1 Lester J Hayden Hollis, NH & Rose C Felch Sunapee, NH
HAYDEN, Geo Roland L, Sep 25 1929 Sex:M Child# 1 George F Hayden Nashua, NH & Aurore Beaulieu Canada
HAYDEN, Hattie, Aug 3 1888 Sex:F Child# 1 Alfred P Hayden
HAYDEN, Howard LeRoy, Sep 14 1904 Sex:M Child# 1 Fred L Hayden Nashua, NH & Marie L Lebel Nashua, NH
HAYDEN, Unknown, Jul 5 1888 Sex:F Child# 2 Albert Hayden Farmington, ME & Alice Cash San Francisco, CA
HAYDEN, Willard Hadley, Jun 10 1926 Sex:M Child# 2 Philip Hayden Amherst, NH & Ruth Hadley Brooklyn, NY
HAYES, Annie, Mar 27 1890 Sex:F Child# 1 William Hayes Ireland & Catherine Spellman Nashua, NH
HAYES, Gertrude, Jun 9 1914 Sex:F Child# 1 Frederick M Hayes Norwood, MA & Katherine O'Brien Sayersville, NY
HAYES, Harold George, May 31 1930 Sex:M Child# 1 George Hayes Manchester, NH & Florence Bailey Wells River, VT
HAYES, John Thomas, May 23 1891 Sex:M Child# 3 William Hayes Ireland & Katie Spellmel Nashua, NH
HAYNES, Wesley E, Mar 21 1911 Sex:M Child# 1 Charles D Haynes Island Pond, VT & A Eaton Worcester, MA
HAYSETTE, Henry, Jan 21 1916 Sex:M Child# 1 Henry Haysette Nashua, NH & Rose A Parent Nashua, NH
HAYSETTE, Roger, Aug 25 1917 Sex:M Child# 2 Henry Haysette Nashua, NH & Rose A Parent Nashua, NH
HAYWARD, Althea Evelyn, Jul 30 1909 Sex:F Child# 3 Charles W Hayward Merrimack, NH & Lilla A Bohonon Shirley, MA
HAYWARD, Arthur Lewis, Mar 29 1935 Sex:M Child# 3 Stanley Hayward Wilton, NH & Myrtle Hodgman Milford, NH
HAYWARD, Bradford James, Dec 12 1907 Sex:M Child# 2 Charles W Hayward Merrimack, NH & Lilia A Bohanon Shirley, MA
HAYWARD, Caroline Florence, Sep 26 1921 Sex:F Child# 3 Henry Hayward England & Caroline Boucher Canada
HAYWARD, Helen, May 24 1913 Sex:F Child# 1 Henry Hayward England & Caroline Boucher Canada
HAYWARD, Henry Raymond, Dec 4 1922 Sex:M Child# 4 Henry Hayward England & Caroline Boucher Canada
HAYWARD, June, Jun 30 1918 Sex:F Child# 4 Maurice Hayward Hancock, NH & Minnie Pierce Ft Fairfield, ME
HAYWARD, Kathleen Anne, Mar 4 1932 Sex:F Child# 1 H A Hayward Nashua, NH & Alice V Phippard Milford, NH
HAYWARD, Martin Louis, May 14 1910 Sex:M Child# 3 Arthur L Hayward Vermont & Julia De Forest New York
HAYWARD, Morris James, Jr, Nov 16 1910 Sex:M Child# 1 Morris J Hayward Hancock, NH & Mina A Pierce Ft Fairfield, ME
HAYWARD, Robert Henry, Dec 14 1931 Sex:M Child# 1 Leonard M Hayward Amherst, NH & Kathleen T Ryerson Nova Scotia
HAYWARD, Unknown, Sep 11 1926 Sex:F Child# 5 Henry Hayward England & Carolina Boucher Canada
HAYWARD, Walter Eldridge, Jul 12 1904 Sex:M Child# 1 Charles W Hayward Merrimack, NH & Lilla A Bohanan Shirley, MA
HAYWOOD, Clyde Taylor, Sep 21 1914 Sex:M Child# 4 Charles W Haywood Merrimack, NH & Lilla A Bohanan Shirley, MA
HAYWOOD, Dorothy, May 20 1917 Sex:F Child# 2 Henry Haywood England & Caroline Boucher Canada
HAYWOOD, Frances, Dec 8 1916 Sex:F Child# 3 Maurice Haywood Hancock, NH & Minnie Pierce Fort Fairfield, ME
HAYWOOD, Helena Louise, Jul 15 1907 Sex:F Child# 2 Eldridge J Haywood Worcester, MA & Helena Bargener Newport
HAYWOOD, Wenonah, Nov 27 1914 Sex:M Child# 2 Morris J Haywood Hancock, NH & Mina Pierce Fort Fairfield, ME
HAZEN, Alan Martin, May 12 1927 Sex:M Child# 1 Arthur Hazen Mont Vernon, NH & Jessie Dearborn E Mansfield, MA
HAZEN, Unknown, Dec 16 1893 Sex:F Child# 1 Daniel H Hazen Dorchester, MA & Lillian M Walling Torquay, England
HAZEN, Unknown, Oct 19 1895 Sex:F Child# 2 S H Hazen Boston, MA & L M Walling
HEAD, Francis James, Jan 3 1894 Sex:M Child# 5 Thomas Head Ireland & Kate Rafferty Hollis, NH
HEAD, Mary Ellen, Feb 7 1898 Sex:F Child# 6 Thomas Head Ireland & Catherine Head Ireland
HEAD, Mary Frances, Jan 18 1935 Sex:F Child# 1 William Head Watertown, MA & Martha Haddad Berlin, NH
HEAD, Sarah, Dec 4 1889 Sex:F Child#  Thomas Head Ireland & Catherine Naftery Ireland
HEAD, Thomas, Mar 4 1888 Sex:M Child# 3 Thomas Head Ireland & Catherine Rafferty Ireland
HEAGNEY, Patrick, Feb 23 1892 Sex:M Child# 5 Patrick Heagney Ireland & Mary Shenan Ireland
HEALD, Burton K, Jun 4 1916 Sex:M Child# 1 Carl W Heald Milford, NH & Ruth M Keith Pepperell, MA
HEALD, Helen G, Jul 20 1917 Sex:F Child# 1 Phillip C Heald London, England & Helen Spendelow Buffalo, NY
HEALD, James Edward, Jan 21 1931 Sex:M Child# 5 Hermann L Heald Milford, NH & Mary Broughton Wollaston, MA
HEALD, Mary Louise, Aug 27 1926 Sex:F Child# 6 Hermonn Heald Milford, NH & Mary Broughton Wollaston, MA
HEALD, Miriam Ruth, May 24 1929 Sex:F Child# 1 Emory D Heald Milford, NH & Edna E Davis Tilton, NH
HEALD, Richard Broughton, Jun 12 1925 Sex:M Child# 3 Herman L Heald Milford, NH & M A Broughton Wallaston, MA
HEALD, Roger Winston, Jan 20 1921 Sex:M Child# 2 Carl W Heald Milford, NH & Ruta Keith Pepperell, MA
HEALD, Unknown, Jul 27 1892 Sex:F Child# 1 C A Heald Nashua, NH & G L Wallace Nashua, NH
HEALEY, Catherine, Jan 7 1895 Sex:F Child# 5 John A Healey Boston, MA & Katie Barry Nashua, NH
HEALEY, James T, Jul 14 1896 Sex:M Child# 6 John A Healey E Boston, MA & Kate Barry Nashua, NH
HEALEY, John Augustus, Dec 2 1891 Sex:M Child# 4 John A Healey Boston, MA & Katherine Barry Nashua, NH
HEALEY, John Kearns, Apr 11 1920 Sex:M Child# 1 James Healey NH & Agnes Kearns NH
HEALY, Elizabeth Anna, Jun 10 1897 Sex:F Child# 8 Michael Healy Ireland & Ellen Downing Ireland
HEALY, Marjorie Ruth, Apr 17 1925 Sex:F Child# 1 Herbert P Healy Nashua, NH & Marietta Dunham Hopkinton, MA
HEALY, Mary, Mar 19 1891 Sex:F Child# 4 Michael Healy Ireland & Ellen Downey Ireland
HEAPS, Joseph Jr, Aug 14 1934 Sex:M Child# 1 Joseph Heaps, Sr Hopkinton, NH & Rose Marchetti Milford, NH
HEATH, Alvin Emerson, Feb 12 1906 Sex:M Child# 2 Elbridge P Heath Nashua, NH & Bertha L Robinson Nashua, NH
HEATH, Bernice Eleanor, Jul 11 1920 Sex:F Child# 1 George Heath W Springfield, NH & Sadie Gladys Swift Nashua, NH
HEATH, Carol Florence, Jan 11 1896 Sex:F Child# 2 George E Heath Nashua, NH & Cora Annis Hudson, NH
HEATH, Charles Ernest, Feb 18 1927 Sex:M Child# 1 Shearl E Heath
HEATH, Donald William, Sep 30 1929 Sex:M Child# 1 William E Heath Sutton, VT & Bertha F Steger Nashua, NH
HEATH, Fern Prichard, Jul 28 1892 Sex:F Child# 1 George Heath Bow, NH & Cora Annis Tyngsboro, MA
HEATH, Lucille Evelyn, Mar 3 1922 Sex:F Child# 1 George L Heath W Springfield, NH & Sadie Gladys Heath Nashua, NH
HEATH, Mirriam Eleanor, Sep 3 1917 Sex:F Child# 2 Charles H Heath Manchester, NH & Bernice S Hill, NH
HEATH, Unknown, Dec 20 1897 Sex:M Child# 1 Elbridge P Heath Nashua, NH & Bertha A Robinson Nashua, NH
HEATH, Unknown, Dec 30 1902 Sex:F Child# 1 Harry E Heath Harrisville, NH & Mary A Whitcher Landaff
HEATH, Unknown, Apr 21 1916 Sex:M Child# 1 Charles H Heath Manchester, NH & Bernice S Morrell Hill, NH
HEBERT, Amedee, Jul 8 1892 Sex:M Child#  Alphonse Hebert Canada & Rosalie Pion Canada

HEBERT, Berthe R E A, Jun 17 1899 Sex:F Child# 4 John Hebert Canada & Exina Rioux Canada
HEBERT, Blanche Olivette, Nov 20 1911 Sex:F Child# 10 John Hebert Canada & Alexina Rioux Canada
HEBERT, Clarida, Jul 10 1895 Sex:F Child# 9 Thomas Hebert Canada & Celina Gendron Canada
HEBERT, Eva Marie, Apr 29 1898 Sex:F Child# 1 Francis Hebert Canada & Flavie Dion Canada
HEBERT, Fred, Feb 2 1898 Sex:M Child# 2 Fred Hebert Chazy, NY & Anna Good Canada
HEBERT, George Sylvio, Jun 26 1902 Sex:M Child# 6 John Hebert Canada & Exina Roux Canada
HEBERT, Gladys May, Aug 4 1914 Sex:F Child# 3 William Hebert Sciota, NY & Annie Barrett Ireland
HEBERT, John Wilfred, May 20 1931 Sex:M Child# 1 Wilfred Hebert Nashua, NH & Viola Flanders Rockport, MA
HEBERT, Jos George Roland, Feb 19 1916 Sex:M Child# 10 Alfred Hebert Canada & Cleophe Labrecque Canada
HEBERT, Jos Maurice Gerard, Nov 24 1923 Sex:M Child# 3 Leo Hebert NH & Exilia Sylvain Canada
HEBERT, Joseph, Jan 30 1908 Sex:M Child# 8 John Hebert Canada & Alexina Rioux Canada
HEBERT, Joseph, Jan 20 1909 Sex:M Child# 7 Alfred Hebert Canada & Clophee Labrecque Canada
HEBERT, Joseph Alfred, Jan 1 1899 Sex:M Child# 3 Pierre Hebert Canada & Angelina Filion Canada
HEBERT, Joseph Alfred, Feb 24 1905 Sex:M Child# 4 Alfred Hebert Canada & Clophee Labrecque Canada
HEBERT, Joseph Alfred A, Jun 3 1901 Sex:M Child# 2 Alfred Hebert Canada & Clophee Labrecque Canada
HEBERT, Joseph Alonzo L T, Aug 7 1910 Sex:M Child# 8 Alfred Hebert Canada & Clophee Labrecque Canada
HEBERT, Joseph C Theodore, Jun 29 1931 Sex:M Child# 2 Adonia Hebert Nashua, NH & Ethel Daniels Yarmouth, ME
HEBERT, Joseph E, Jun 14 1887 Sex:M Child# 2 Alphonse Hebert Canada & Rosalie Jenpian Canada
HEBERT, Joseph Emile, Sep 18 1903 Sex:M Child# 7 John Hebert Canada & Exiana Rioux Canada
HEBERT, Joseph Henry, Aug 16 1922 Sex:M Child# 1 Adonia Hebert
HEBERT, Joseph Olivier, Nov 27 1891 Sex:M Child# 3 Pierre Hebert Canada & Josephine Lachance Canada
HEBERT, Laurent Armand, Aug 10 1920 Sex:M Child# 2 Albert Hebert Canada & Floriane Girard Canada
HEBERT, Leo, Jan 19 1901 Sex:M Child# 5 John Hebert Canada & Exina Rioux Canada
HEBERT, Leon William, Jun 9 1897 Sex:M Child# 1 Wilfrid Hebert Chazy, NY & Roseanna Labrecque Nashua, NH
HEBERT, M Ange Alice Eug, Apr 23 1913 Sex:F Child# 9 Alfred Hebert Canada & Cleophile Labrecque Canada
HEBERT, M E Antonette, Jun 26 1900 Sex:F Child# 8 Joseph Hebert Canada & Eleonore Brodeur Canada
HEBERT, Marie Ange E, Sep 30 1903 Sex:F Child# 3 Alfred Hebert Canada & Clophee Labrecque Canada
HEBERT, Marie Annie H, May 12 1897 Sex:F Child# 3 John Hebert Canada & Exina Rioux Canada
HEBERT, Marie C D, May 26 1900 Sex:F Child# 1 Alfred Hebert Canada & Cleophia Labrecque Canada
HEBERT, Marie E Anna, Sep 24 1899 Sex:F Child# 9 Napoleon Hebert Canada & Zepherina Rivet Canada
HEBERT, Marie Jeanne Rita, Sep 16 1922 Sex:F Child# 2 Leo Hebert NH & Exilia Sylvain Canada
HEBERT, Marie Jeanne Y, Jul 21 1906 Sex:F Child# 5 Alfred Hebert Canada & Clophee Labrecque Canada
HEBERT, Marie L Cecile, Sep 8 1898 Sex:F Child# 7 Joseph D Hebert Canada & Eleonore Brodeur Canada
HEBERT, Marie Laurette, Jan 17 1907 Sex:F Child# 11 Isidore Hebert Canada & Delina Rousseau Canada
HEBERT, Marie Rose A S, Jan 26 1908 Sex:F Child# 6 Alfred Hebert Canada & Clophee Labrecque Canada
HEBERT, Mildred Anna, Jan 23 1918 Sex:F Child# 4 William Hebert New York & Annie Barrett Ireland
HEBERT, Napoleon Alfred, May 15 1901 Sex:M Child# 10 Charles Hebert Canada & Zepherina Rivet Canada
HEBERT, Ralph Albert, May 31 1912 Sex:M Child# 2 Willie Hebert New York & Annie Barrett Ireland
HEBERT, Ralph Everett, Sep 26 1910 Sex:M Child# 1 William Hebert Chazy, NY & Annie Barrett Ireland
HEGERTY, Dennis, Nov 28 1893 Sex:M Child# 7 Daniel C Hegerty Ireland & Kate Sullivan Ireland
HEINS, Joseph, Dec 8 1923 Sex:M Child# 1 Frank Heins New York & Grace Boucher Nashua, NH Stillborn
HEISBERG, Joseph, Apr 5 1899 Sex:M Child# 3 Louis Heisberg Russia & Ida Rea Russia
HELBERT, Ernest Ray, Dec 5 1916 Sex:M Child# 1 Leon William Helbert Nashua, NH & Sarah Jane Lynn Nashua, NH
HELIE, Joseph L Richard, Mar 10 1931 Sex:M Child# 2 Hermile Helie Quebec, Canada & Marie A Vallieres Manchester, NH
HELIE, Marie Yvonne Gertrude, Feb 15 1933 Sex:F Child# 3 Hermile Helie Canada & Marie A Vallieres Manchester, NH
HELIE, Robert Gerard, Feb 15 1927 Sex:M Child# 2 Emile Helie Canada & M A Valliere Manchester, NH
HELIE, Wilfred Arthur, Aug 30 1934 Sex:M Child# 4 Hermile Helie Canada & Marie A Valiere Manchester, NH
HELLEN, Margaret Josephine, Dec 29 1913 Sex:F Child# 2 Joseph A Hellen Cape Britain & Margaret I Walsh Ireland
HELLISEY, Annie Margaret, Sep 15 1897 Sex:F Child# 1 John Hellisey Nashua, NH & Hattie Scharp Russia
HEMENWAY, Ann, Aug 15 1918 Sex:F Child# 1 Thomas Hemenway Nashua, NH & Oakley St John Yorkville, SC
HEMMENWAY, Unknown, Sep 10 1889 Sex:M Child# 3 C Hemmenway
HENAULT, Marie Donalda, Jun 18 1901 Sex:F Child# 10 Philias Henault Canada & Philomene Deschamps Canada
HENAULT, Marie E, Apr 8 1896 Sex:F Child# 2 Pierre Henault Canada & Rosianne Bellerose Canada
HENAULT, Unknown, May 19 1895 Sex: Child# 1 Pierre Henault Canada & Rose Bellerose Canada
HENDERSON, Arthur Germain, Sep 24 1923 Sex:M Child# 6 Elmer D Henderson NH & Regine Demanche NH
HENDERSON, Dorothy May, Apr 19 1935 Sex:F Child# 11 Elmer Henderson Nashua, NH & Regina Desmanche Nashua, NH
HENDERSON, Elmer D, Dec 16 1891 Sex:M Child# 2 David Henderson NH & Emma Richards NH
HENDERSON, Emily Louise, Mar 6 1902 Sex:F Child# 4 Henry S Henderson Scotland & Carrie Baker Missouri
HENDERSON, Ernest David, Jun 3 1916 Sex:M Child# 2 Elmer D Henderson US & Regina M Desmanche US
HENDERSON, Florence Emma, Aug 17 1898 Sex:F Child# 1 Will A Henderson Antrim, NH & Lizzie Labounty Mooers, NY
HENDERSON, Florence Virginia, May 18 1920 Sex:F Child# 4 Elmer Henderson Nashua, NH & Virginia Desmanche Nashua, NH
HENDERSON, Frank Henry, Apr 24 1918 Sex:M Child# 3 Elmer D Henderson Boston, MA & Regina Demouche Nashua, NH
HENDERSON, Guy Elmer, Sep 8 1900 Sex:M Child# 3 Henry Henderson Scotland & Carrie Baker Missouri
HENDERSON, Hazel Evelyn, Feb 6 1914 Sex:F Child# 1 Elmer D Henderson US & Regina Desmanches US
HENDERSON, Jean Lois, May 26 1931 Sex:F Child# 5 Richard Henderson Dedham, MA & Irene Meuse Wakefield, MA
HENDERSON, John Winfield, Jun 27 1912 Sex:M Child# 4 John W Henderson Scotland & Lucila J Bowles Derry, NH
HENDERSON, June Elizabeth, Apr 26 1933 Sex:F Child# 10 E Henderson Nashua, NH & B Demanche Nashua, NH
HENDERSON, Mildred Viola, Mar 7 1901 Sex:F Child# 2 Will Henderson Amherst & Lizzie Labontee New York
HENDERSON, Norris Raymond, Nov 15 1928 Sex:M Child# 7 E D Henderson Nashua, NH & R DeManche Nashua, NH
HENDERSON, Phyllis Arlene, Oct 4 1925 Sex:F Child# 7 Elmer Henderson Nashua, NH & Regina Demanche Nashua, NH
HENDERSON, Unknown, Dec 9 1898 Sex:M Child# 2 H L N Henderson Merrimack, NH & Carrie L Baker St Louis, MO
HENDERSON, Unknown, Jun 11 1903 Sex: Child# 2 John W Henderson Scotland & Luelle Bowles E Derry, NH
HENDERSON, Unknown, Jun 6 1907 Sex:M Child# 2 John Henderson Scotland & Luella Bowles E Derry, NH

HENDERSON, Unknown, Apr 24 1930 Sex:M Child# 1 Charles Henderson Watertown, NY & Mildred Dunn Taunton, MA
HENDERSON, William, Mar 8 1902 Sex:M Child# 1 John Henderson Scotland & Luella Bolles Derry, NH
HENDERSON, William Louis, Feb 18 1931 Sex:M Child# 9 Elmer Henderson Nashua, NH & Regina Demanche Nashua, NH
HENDRICKS, Marion, Apr 24 1889 Sex:F Child# 1 George W Hendricks Nashua, NH & Nellie Towne Keene, NH
HENDRICKS, Mary, Jun 2 1910 Sex:F Child# 1 Stephen Hendricks Russia & Yzeppa Misckowska Russia Stillborn
HENDRICKSON, Anita Hilda, Aug 21 1925 Sex:F Child# 3 A Hendrickson Rockport & Hilda Sederholm Holbrook, MA
HENDRICKSON, David Joseph, Jul 22 1928 Sex:M Child# 4 A Hendrickson Rockport, MA & Holda Cederholm Holbrook, MA
HENDRICKSON, Elizabeth Anne, Feb 2 1932 Sex:F Child# 5 A Hendrickson Rockport, MA & Hilda Cedarholm Holbrook, MA
HENDRICKSON, Richard Anselm, Apr 3 1923 Sex:M Child# 1 Anselm Hendrickson Rockport, MA & Hilda Cederholm Holbrook
HENDRICKSON, Unknown, Feb 5 1924 Sex:M Child# 2 A Hendrickson Rockport, MA & H Cederholm Holbrook, MA Stillborn
HENNEBERRY, Catherine, Aug 18 1891 Sex:F Child# 1 William Henneberry Ireland & Anna M Lee Pelham, NH
HENNEBERRY, William, Jun 4 1896 Sex:M Child# 3 William Henneberry Ireland & Anna M Lee Pelham, NH
HENNESSEY, Alice Josephine, Jun 12 1930 Sex:F Child# 5 Francis Hennessey Lowell, MA & Edith Bruce Hudson, NH
HENNESSEY, Marguerite Annabel, Feb 19 1933 Sex:F Child# 6 F Hennessey Lowell, MA & Edith Bruce Hudson, NH
HENNESSY, Doris Mae, Jul 13 1920 Sex:F Child# 2 Francis Hennessy Lowell, MA & Edith Bruce Hudson, NH
HENNESSY, Irene Elizabeth, Aug 28 1917 Sex:F Child# 1 Francis Hennessy Lowell, MA & Edith Bruce Hudson, NH
HENNESSY, Mary Ellen, Nov 10 1891 Sex:F Child# 1 John F Hennessy Ireland & Margaret King Ireland
HENNESSY, Richard Paul, Jun 22 1928 Sex:M Child# 4 F T Hennessy Lowell, MA & Edith Bruce Hudson, NH
HENNESSY, Robert Francis, Jul 31 1922 Sex:M Child# 3 Francis P Hennessy Lowell, MA & Edith Bruce Hudson, NH
HENREUX, Ethel Gladys, Dec 22 1919 Sex:F Child# 2 John L Henreux Thompson, CT & Gertrude V Race Walpole, NH
HENRI, Joseph Philias, Sep 6 1903 Sex:M Child# 1 Joseph Henri Canada & Malvina Deschamps Canada
HENRI, Marie G C, Jul 16 1909 Sex:F Child# 7 Ulric Henri Canada & Rosa Forest Canada
HENRI, Mary Agnes, Oct 24 1897 Sex:F Child# 8 Lawrence Henri Ireland & Bridget Nash Ireland
HENRY, Chauncey Sylvester, Sep 24 1924 Sex:M Child# 5 Clarence S Henry Thomaston, ME & Flor L Connelley Roxbury, MA
HENRY, Edward Everett, May 7 1893 Sex:M Child# 2 Edward P Henry Kansas & Ella M George Nashua, NH
HENRY, Ethele Amy May, Jun 21 1897 Sex:F Child# 5 George Henry New York & Josephine Facto New York
HENRY, James, Dec 1 1918 Sex:M Child# 4 Charles Henry Proctor, VT & Bertha Hewson W Chazy, NY
HENRY, John, Dec 2 1890 Sex:M Child# 4 Lawrence Henry Ireland & Bridget Nash Ireland
HENRY, Paul Parker, Sep 23 1927 Sex:M Child# 3 William S Henry Nashua, NH & Marjorie Parker Hartford, VT
HENRY, Robert Payson, Sep 21 1920 Sex:M Child# 2 George Henry Nashua, NH & Marion Hidden Nashua, NH
HENRY, Ruth Athalie, Jun 24 1916 Sex:F Child# 1 George Henry Nashua, NH & Marion Hidden Nashua, NH
HENRY, Unknown, Apr 20 1889 Sex:M Child# 1 Edward T Henry Nashua, NH & Ella George Nashua, NH
HENRY, Warren Edward, Mar 9 1931 Sex:M Child# 3 George P Henry Nashua, NH & Marian Hidden Nashua, NH
HENRY, William II, Sep 9 1887 Sex:M Child# 2 Lawrence Henry Ireland & Bridget Nash Ireland
HENWOOD, Annie Beatrice, Mar 31 1910 Sex:F Child# 3 Arthur Henwood Nova Scotia & Catherine Hyde England
HEON, Francois J M G, Oct 4 1921 Sex:M Child# 1 Maurice Heon Canada & Colombe Dube NH
HEON, J Paul Philippe, Jul 11 1914 Sex:M Child# 10 Ulric Heon Canada & Rosa Forest Canada
HEON, Joseph Paul, Jun 4 1911 Sex:M Child# 8 Ulric Heon Canada & Rosa Forest Canada
HEON, M Stella Francoise, Sep 8 1919 Sex:F Child# 13 Ulric Heon Canada & Rosa Forest Canada
HEON, Marie C, Jan 6 1889 Sex:F Child# 6 Georges Heon Canada PQ & Claris Corriveare Canada
HEON, Marie J Paul Rita, May 31 1922 Sex:F Child# 11 Ulric Heon Canada & Rosa Forest Canada
HEON, Marie Madeline, Feb 2 1918 Sex:F Child# 12 Ulric Heon Canada & Rosa Forest Canada
HEON, Marie Theresa, Nov 7 1916 Sex:F Child# 11 Ulric Heon Canada & Rose Forest Canada
HEON, Marie Yvette G, Jun 4 1911 Sex:F Child# 9 Ulric Heon Canada & Rosa Forest Canada
HEOPS, Donald, Aug 29 1928 Sex:M Child# 1 William Heops Salem, NH & Alice McDermott Harrisville, RI
HERBERT, Albert, Apr 1 1921 Sex:M Child# 1 Leo Herbert Nashua, NH & Exilia Sylvain Canada
HERBERT, Anita, Feb 1 1913 Sex:F Child# 2 Arthur C Herbert Lowell, MA & Jessie E Proctor Hudson, NH
HERBERT, Betty Ann, Jul 31 1933 Sex:F Child# 1 Louis Herbert Pepperell, MA & Irene Barry Nashua, NH
HERBERT, David Greeley, Mar 29 1934 Sex:M Child# 1 William S Herbert Pelham, NH & Georgia Greeley Londonderry, NH
HERBERT, Joseph, Aug 10 1898 Sex:M Child# 2 Willie Herbert Sciota, NY & Rosa Labrecque Nashua, NH
HERBERT, Joseph Henry Albert, Dec 17 1926 Sex:M Child# 1 Henry Herbert Canada & G DeBoisbriand Nashua, NH
HERBERT, Marie Alma, Mar 21 1894 Sex:F Child# 1 John Herbert Canada & Exina Rioux Canada
HERBOT, Stanley, Jul 5 1917 Sex:M Child# 3 John Herbot Russia & Archula Kaskie Russia
HERGET, John Paul, Sep 27 1920 Sex:M Child# 1 Walter L Herget Mass & Catherine Moriarty Nashua, NH
HERLEHY, Daniel Lewis, May 25 1891 Sex:M Child# 3 Patrick H Herlehy Milford, NH & Mary E Sullivan Nashua, NH
HERLEHY, David Henry, Apr 1 1898 Sex:M Child# 5 Patrick H Herlehy Milford, NH & Mary E Sullivan Nashua, NH
HERLEHY, Margaret, Mar 7 1893 Sex:F Child# 4 Patrick H Herlehy Milford, NH & Mary E Sullivan Nashua, NH
HERLEHY, Unknown, Jul 20 1896 Sex:M Child# 5 P H Herlehy Milford, NH & Mary E Sullivan Nashua, NH Stillborn
HERLEY, Unknown, Jan 3 1888 Sex:M Child# 1 Patrick Herley Milford & Mary Sullivan Nashua, NH
HERLIHY, Mary Elizabeth, Jan 9 1901 Sex:F Child# 7 Patrick B Herlihy Milford, NH & Mary E Sullivan Nashua, NH
HEROUX, Anita, Dec 4 1921 Sex:F Child# 2 Alphee Heroux Canada & Eva Gendron Shirley, MA
HEROUX, Lorraine, Jul 2 1924 Sex:F Child# 3 Alphee Heroux Canada & Eva Gendron Shirley, MA
HEROUX, Paul Joseph, May 18 1927 Sex:M Child# 4 Alphee Heroux Canada & Eva Gendron Shirley, MA
HEROUX, Robert, Jun 19 1920 Sex:M Child# 1 Alphee Heroux Canada & Eva Gendron Shirley, MA
HEROUX, Theresa Irene, Apr 19 1929 Sex:F Child# 5 Alphee Heroux Canada & Eva Gendron Shirley, MA
HERRICK, Elizabeth Ann, Oct 10 1932 Sex:F Child# 4 Gilmore Herrick NH & Helen Field Nashua, NH
HERRICK, Elizabeth Reigh, Dec 13 1920 Sex:F Child# 2 Arthur R Herrick Merrimack, NH & Mary E Melvin Derry, NH
HERRICK, Franklin P, Dec 2 1917 Sex:M Child# 1 Arthur H Herrick Merrimack, NH & Mary E Melvin Derry, NH
HERRICK, Herrick, Jun 29 1889 Sex:F Child# 2 Freeman Herrick Londonderry, NH & Ella F Hammond Manchester, NH
HERRICK, Richard Gilmore, Apr 29 1929 Sex:M Child# 3 Gilmore Herrick NH & Helen Field Nashua, NH
HERRICK, Unknown, Jan 1891 Sex:M Child# 3 Freeman L Herrick Londonderry, NH & Ella Hamilton Manchester, NH
HERRICK, Unknown, Aug 1 1924 Sex:F Child# 1 Gilmore Herrick Littleton, NH & Helen Field Nashua, NH Stillborn
HERRICK, Unknown, Apr 21 1927 Sex:F Child# 2 Gilmore Herrick Littleton, NH & Helen Field Nashua, NH

HERRIN, John Hamilton, Jun 2 1929 Sex:M Child# 1 Harold John Herrin Augusta, ME & Ruth Riley Nashua, NH
HERRIN, Richard Harold, Mar 18 1931 Sex:M Child# 2 Harold J Herrin Augusta, ME & Ruth Riley Nashua, NH
HERSEY, Andrea Ethel, May 6 1922 Sex:F Child# 3 Guy S Hersey Mass & Olive Miller Vermont
HERSEY, Edna Jennie, Apr 21 1925 Sex:F Child# 1 Frank Hersey Salisbury, MA & Rena Drew Epsom, NH
HERSEY, Unknown, Sep 13 1928 Sex:F Child# 2 Frank Hersey Mass & Rena Drew Epsom, NH
HESLEY, Ellen, Sep 28 1890 Sex:F Child# 3 John A Hesley Boston, MA & Katharine Barry Nashua, NH
HESSLER, Hazel Lillian, Sep 23 1911 Sex:F Child# 4 Sam Hessler Nova Scotia & Ida Weisburg Kennebunk, ME
HETON, John, Mar 10 1914 Sex:M Child# 1 Navin Heton Greece & Basilici Greece
HEUREHAM, Mary, Feb 3 1891 Sex:F Child# 1 William Heureham Ireland & Nellie Gillooly Ireland
HEVEY, Louise, Mar 15 1930 Sex:F Child#  Michael Hevey Lowell, MA & Catherine Brown England
HEYNIEROIZ, Lucyia, May 7 1898 Sex:F Child# 1 Ontain Heynieroiz Russia & Jozefa Gaturrki Austria
HEYZETT, Marie Eugenie P, Dec 30 1897 Sex:F Child# 3 Leon Heyzett Canada & Eugenie Huot Worcester, MA
HICKEY, George Washington, May 15 1927 Sex:M Child# 1 G W Hickey, Jr Charlestown, MA & Veronica Richard Dorchester
HICKEY, Harrison Daniels, Sep 1 1926 Sex:M Child# 1 Leon P Hickey Nashua, NH & Ruth Rollins Franklin, NH
HICKEY, Jane Isabelle, Oct 24 1902 Sex:F Child# 3 Clarence L Hickey Canada & Julia E Haywood Worcester, MA
HICKEY, John Alvin, Mar 12 1928 Sex:M Child# 1 Arthur Hickey Canada & Brigid Kelley Canada
HICKEY, Leo Paul, Nov 7 1903 Sex:M Child# 5 Henry Hickey Bay City, MI & Ed Berthiaume Canada
HICKEY, Marguerite, Jul 30 1899 Sex:F Child# 2 Clarence Hickey Canada & Julia Haywood Worcester, MA
HICKEY, Marion Moran, Sep 23 1908 Sex:F Child# 4 George W Hickey Manchester, NH & Mary E Moran Nashua, NH
HICKEY, Mary Jane, Aug 15 1931 Sex:F Child# 4 George Hickey Charlestown, MA & Veronica M Richards Boston, MA
HICKEY, Thomas, Jun 9 1903 Sex:M Child# 3 George Hickey Manchester, NH & Mary E Moran Nashua, NH
HICKEY, Unknown, Mar 13 1898 Sex:F Child# 1 Clarence Hickey Aultzville, PQ & Julia Hayward Worcester, MA
HICKEY, Unknown, Aug 7 1915 Sex:M Child# 5 George Hickey Manchester, NH & Mary E Moran Nashua, NH
HICKEY, Veronica Theresa, Sep 15 1928 Sex:F Child# 2 George W Hickey Charlestown, MA & Veronica Richards Boston, MA
HICKEY, William Eldredge, Jul 30 1911 Sex:M Child# 4 Clarence J Hickey Canada & Julia Hayward Nashua, NH Stillborn
HICKEY, William Moran, Jul 5 1930 Sex:M Child# 2 George W Hickey Charlestown, MA & Veronica Richards Boston, MA
HICKS, Harold Edwin, Apr 2 1910 Sex:M Child# 1 Thomas R Hicks Havelock, NB & Mabel L Kinnecome Uxbridge, MA
HIDDEN, Earle W, Sep 24 1903 Sex:M Child# 2 William A Hidden Nashua, NH & Carrie Warren Freedom, ME
HIDDEN, Unknown, Aug 12 1890 Sex:F Child# 1 William A Hidden Nashua, NH & Carrie Warren Freedom, ME
HIGGIMS, Rose Florence, Mar 22 1917 Sex:F Child# 2 Rowe Higgims
HIGGINS, Gena Frances, Sep 1 1912 Sex:F Child# 2 William A Higgins Somerville, MA & Elizabeth A Barnaby Woods
HIGGINS, Martha Beatrice, Jul 17 1918 Sex:F Child# 3 Herman B Higgins Haverhill, MA & Martha Dean Haverhill, MA
HIGGINS, Roy Francis, Apr 8 1924 Sex:M Child# 2 W F Higgins W Milan, NH & Eva Roy Ashland, NH
HIGSON, Sarah Alice, Jul 10 1905 Sex:F Child# 6 William Higson Fall River, MA & Harriet Tomlinson England
HILDRETH, Unknown, May 13 1890 Sex:M Child# 1 Rufus G Hildreth Chelmsford, MA & Alice T Craig Ft Edward, NY
HILDYARD, Beatrice Perle, Apr 25 1898 Sex:F Child# 4 Harry Hildyard England & Maggie Davis Nova Scotia
HILDYARD, Hilda D, May 10 1894 Sex:F Child#  Harry Hildyard England & Maggie Davis Nova Scotia
HILDYARD, Robert Henry B, Jul 15 1900 Sex:M Child# 5 Henry Hildyard England & Maggie Davis NS
HILKAVITCH, Frances, Feb 23 1912 Sex:F Child# 4 Frank Hilkavitch Russia & Rosa Miskanuta Russia
HILKAVITCH, Frank, Nov 17 1908 Sex:M Child# 2 Frank Hilkavitch Russia & Rosa Meskinis Russia
HILKAVITCH, Prania, May 6 1910 Sex:F Child# 3 Frank Hilkavitch Russia & Rosa Michkinuta Russia
HILL, Charles Roswell, May 25 1910 Sex:M Child# 4 Willis G Hill Grandville, VT & Mary E Weaver Manchester, NH
HILL, Dolores Shirley, Nov 13 1935 Sex:F Child# 1 Ralph W Hill Nashua, NH & Madeline Byrne Bellows Falls, VT
HILL, Eva M, Apr 21 1895 Sex:F Child# 2 Charles M Hill Hudson, NH & Gertrude Winters New York
HILL, Everett Byron, Nov 26 1923 Sex:M Child# 2 Henry E Hill Burlington, VT & Avis E Trenholm Nashua, NH
HILL, Frederick Kellum, Oct 5 1893 Sex:M Child# 1 Jarvis B Hill Hudson, NH & Mary L Jameson Nashua, NH
HILL, George James, Dec 10 1927 Sex:M Child# 1 George Hill Pepperell, MA & Anna Messer Pepperell, MA
HILL, George Townsend, Jan 29 1907 Sex:M Child# 4 Harry O Hill Mt Vernon, NH & Annie M Yeoman St Johns, NB
HILL, Harold Judson, Dec 13 1921 Sex:M Child# 2 Edwin Hill Pelham, NH & Clara Wheeler Canada
HILL, Harry Belmont, Jr, Nov 1 1924 Sex:M Child# 1 Harry B Hill Newport News, VA & Jeannette Hill Newburn, NC
HILL, Helen, Nov 1 1898 Sex:F Child# 3 E S Hill Tilton, NH & Frances Stafford Augusta, GA
HILL, Jean Charlotte, Feb 22 1930 Sex:F Child# 3 Edward B Hill Pelham, NH & Clara Wheeler Canada
HILL, Joseph Nathan, Dec 16 1909 Sex:M Child# 1 Nathan Hill New Hampshire & Agnes F Sweet Wells, ME
HILL, Josephine Lulu, Dec 2 1889 Sex:F Child# 1 William Hill Drewsville, MA & Josephine Blanche Canada
HILL, Lena Hazel, Jul 9 1901 Sex:F Child# 1 Frank Hill Hudson, NH & Clara Brown S Merrimack, NH
HILL, Leon Francis, Sep 29 1911 Sex:M Child# 3 Fred W Hill Hollis, NH & Blanche C Waldron Dublin, NH
HILL, Mabel, Feb 10 1895 Sex:F Child#  C W Hill Hudson, NH
HILL, Marion Ann, Jul 7 1929 Sex:F Child# 2 Amos W Hill York, ME & Mabel A Rock Malone, NY
HILL, Marion R, Dec 6 1896 Sex:F Child# 2 Ellon S Hill Tilton, NH & Frances Stafford Augusta, GA
HILL, Marjorie Lucille, May 1 1922 Sex:F Child# 6 Fred Waldo Hill Hollis, NH & Blanche C Waldron Dublin, NH
HILL, Martha Virginia, Sep 27 1921 Sex:F Child# 1 James A Hill England & Carrie McCall Hendersonville, NC
HILL, Ralph Waldo, Jun 30 1913 Sex:M Child# 4 Fred Waldo Hill Hollis, NH & Blanche Waldron Dublin, NH
HILL, Reta May, Jan 9 1924 Sex:F Child# 1 Amos W Hill York, ME & Mabel A Rock Malone, NY Stillborn
HILL, Richard Morris, Jan 28 1918 Sex:M Child# 1 Edwin B Hill Pelham, NH & Clara Wheeler Magog, Quebec
HILL, Rowell, Sep 13 1892 Sex:M Child# 1 L H Hill Amherst & N Jones Maine
HILL, Thomas Gould, Mar 13 1929 Sex:M Child# 2 Roscoe Hill W Groton, MA & Marguerite Chandler Sandown, NH
HILL, Thomas Harry, Mar 19 1925 Sex:M Child# 3 William B Hill Titusville, NJ & Mae Bell Jones Duryea, PA
HILL, Unknown, Sep 6 1888 Sex:F Child# 6 Burton W Hill Dunstable, MA & Sadie A Nourse Littleton, MA
HILL, Unknown, Jul 26 1900 Sex:F Child# 2 Richard H Hill NH & Josephine R Evans NH
HILL, Unknown, Oct 7 1903 Sex:M Child# 5 Ellon S Hill Tilton, NH & Frances Stefford Augusta, ME
HILL, Unknown, Apr 13 1909 Sex:M Child# 1 Fred W Hill Hollis, NH & Blanche C Waldron Dublin, NH
HILL, Unknown, Oct 20 1915 Sex:M Child# 2 William B Hill Titusville, NJ & May B Jones Duryea, PA
HILL, Unknown, Apr 23 1919 Sex:M Child# 5 Fred Waldo Hill Hollis, NH & Blanch Waldron Peterboro, NH

HILL, Warren Rhodes, Apr 17 1895 Sex:M Child# 1 E S Hill Tilton, NH & Frances Stafford Augusta, GA
HILL, William B, Nov 9 1914 Sex:M Child# 1 William B Hill Titusville, NJ & May B Jones Duryen, PA
HILL, William R, Sep 23 1923 Sex:M Child# 1 Lester Hill Lawrence, MA & Aileen Johnson Nashua, NH Stillborn
HILL, William Russell, Sep 2 1924 Sex:M Child# 2 Lester R Hill Lawrence, MA & Aileen Johnson Nashua, NH
HILLS, Donald Terris, Jun 5 1926 Sex:M Child# 1 Robert Hills Oxford, NS & Eva Terris Spring Hill, NS
HILLS, Doris Ann, Sep 2 1928 Sex:F Child# 2 W W Hills Nashua, NH & H M Bailey W Medford, MA
HILLS, Edward Whitney, Jun 17 1915 Sex:M Child# 1 William Hills Nashua, NH & Harriet Ploof Lynn, MA
HILLS, Harold C, Feb 3 1898 Sex:M Child# 3 Calvin W Hills Hudson, NH & Maud B Degroff NY
HILLS, Harriet Virginia, Oct 20 1922 Sex:F Child# 2 Lyman W Hills NH & Mary Cheever NH
HILLS, Lyman Herbert, Nov 30 1921 Sex:M Child# 1 Lyman W Hills Hudson, NH & Mary Niles Cheever S Lyndeboro, NH
HILLS, Rial William, Feb 6 1921 Sex:M Child# 1 William W Hills Nashua, NH & Beatrice Bailey Mass
HILLS, Robert, Nov 6 1918 Sex:M Child# 3 William C Hills Fitchbay, Canada & Hattie Hills Hudson, Wisconsin
HILLS, Unknown, May 25 1891 Sex:M Child# 1 Fred W Hills Merrillville, NY & Sarah E Whitney Chelsea, VT
HILLS, Unknown, Nov 17 1892 Sex:F Child# 2 Calvin W Hills Hudson, NH & Maud Degroff US
HILLS, Wesley Kingston, Jan 20 1920 Sex:M Child# 1 Walter C Hills Antrim, NH & Helene Black Reading, MA
HILLS, Winifred Pearl, Jun 23 1933 Sex:F Child# 1 Eugene Hills Hollis, NH & Marion Messer Hollis, NH
HILMAN, Margaret Nora, Oct 4 1914 Sex:F Child# 1 Fred G Hilman Germany & Vera J Haven Washington, NH
HILTON, Arthur, Aug 13 1913 Sex:M Child# 4 Charles E Hilton Lowell, MA & Ethel M Wragg Mass Stillborn
HILTON, Henry Hoyt, Jun 14 1917 Sex:M Child# 6 Charles E Hilton Lowell, MA & Ethel Hayard Ragg Acton, ME
HILTON, Pauline Georgette, Sep 19 1935 Sex:F Child# 1 George Hilton Lowell, MA & Lucienne Perron Nashua, NH
HILTON, Richard Albert, Jul 12 1920 Sex:M Child# 8 Charles Hilton Lowell, MA & Ethel Wragg Acton, MA
HILTON, Unknown, Feb 4 1916 Sex:M Child# 4 Charles E Hilton Lowell, MA & Ethel M Wragg Maine
HILTON, William Hersom, Aug 8 1918 Sex:M Child# 7 Charles E Hilton Lowell, MA & Ethel H Wragg Acton, MA
HINDS, Albert John, Jr, Apr 24 1925 Sex:M Child# 2 Albert J Hinds, Sr Bellows Falls, VT & Sybel B Day Bellows Falls
HINDS, Juanita B, Aug 7 1923 Sex:F Child# 1 Albert J Hinds Bellows Falls, VT & Sibyl Bernice Day Belllows Falls, VT
HINDS, Ralph A, Apr 24 1903 Sex:M Child# 1 Ralph Hinds Maine & Goldie Sweet Maine
HINGHAM, Unknown, Nov 7 1906 Sex:M Child# 4 Samuel Hingham Lawrence, MA & Mary Glynn Nashua, NH
HINGLEY, Unknown, Jan 19 1911 Sex:F Child#  Harvey Hingley Nova Scotia & Annie Ross Nova Scotia
HIRSCH, Janet Christina, Dec 23 1933 Sex:F Child# 2 Albert E Hirsch Pelham, NH & Gladys McCallum Lowell, MA
HIRSCH, Patricia Gladys, Jul 27 1935 Sex:F Child# 3 Albert E Hirsch Pelham, NH & Gladys McCallum Lowell, MA
HIRSCH, Robert Herbert, Dec 1 1934 Sex:M Child# 2 Carl Hirsch Lowell, MA & Melvina Ross Washington, VT
HIVON, Erline, Dec 21 1897 Sex:F Child#  Samuel Hivon Canada & Ida Collins New Jersey
HOAG, Dorothy, Feb 29 1912 Sex:F Child# 3 George F Hoag Nashua, NH & Loraine McWeeney Nashua, NH
HOAG, Elmer George, Sep 27 1913 Sex:M Child# 3 George F Hoag Nashua, NH & Loraine McWeeney Nashua, NH
HOAG, George Francis, Mar 13 1905 Sex:M Child# 1 George F Hoag Nashua, NH & Loraine McWeeney Nashua, NH
HOAG, Helen, Apr 18 1910 Sex:F Child# 4 David W Hoag Hudson, NH & Nellie M Stillman Belmont, NH
HOAG, Rufus Francis, Jul 10 1909 Sex:M Child# 2 George F Hoag Nashua, NH & Loraine McQueeney Nashua, NH
HOBART, Florence, Oct 20 1916 Sex:F Child# 2 Henry Hobart Nashua, NH & Ida Fortin Nashua, NH
HOBART, Gertrude May, Mar 23 1893 Sex:F Child# 2 Charles M Hobart Concord, NH & Maggie Johnson New York
HOBART, Gladys May, Oct 26 1905 Sex:F Child# 2 Frank A Hobart Nashua, NH & Lizzie A Cutter Nashua, NH
HOBART, Helen May, Mar 2 1899 Sex:F Child# 1 Frank A Hobart Nashua, NH & Lizzie I Cutter Nashua, NH
HOBART, Henri, Sep 20 1892 Sex:M Child# 2 Samuel Hobart Nashua, NH & Marie Burelle Fitchburg, MA
HOBART, Kenneth Augusta, Sep 9 1909 Sex:M Child# 1 Clarence A Hobart Brookline, NH & Addje R Jeanotte Nashua, NH
HOBART, Margaret, Dec 8 1891 Sex:F Child# 4 Alvin E Hobart Nashua, NH & Annie Foley Cambridge, MA
HOBART, Ruth J, Nov 8 1891 Sex:F Child# 1 Charles M Hobart Concord & Maggie L Johnson New York
HOBART, Samuel Desire R, Nov 28 1914 Sex:M Child# 1 Henry Hobart Nashua, NH & Ida Fortin Nashua, NH
HOBART, Unknown, Sep 28 1887 Sex:M Child# 1 William C Hobart
HOBBS, Charles Winthrop, Jr, Nov 20 1926 Sex:M Child# 3 Charles W Hobbs NH & Ruby Build Mass
HOBBS, Harriet Ruth, Jul 7 1928 Sex:F Child# 4 Charles W Hobbs Pelham, NH & Ruby Guild Dracut, MA
HOBERT, Maria, Aug 19 1889 Sex:F Child# 1 Samuel Hobert Nashua, NH & Marie Burelle Ashburnham, MA
HOBSON, Alice, May 11 1888 Sex:F Child# 3 Charles E Hobson Brookline & Jennie M Knight Fisherville
HOBSON, Unknown, Jul 26 1890 Sex:F Child# 4 Charles E Hobson
HODGE, Alfred Herbert, May 20 1923 Sex:M Child# 5 Laurence Hodge Mass & Gertrude Mooney NH
HODGE, Arthur Leonard, Aug 12 1925 Sex:M Child# 6 Lawrence A Hodge Lawrence, MA & Gertrude Mooney Nashua, NH
HODGE, Claude Lester, Jun 14 1921 Sex:M Child# 4 Lawrence Hodge Mass & Gertrude Mooney NH
HODGE, Dorothy, Dec 29 1914 Sex:F Child# 1 Lawrence A Hodge Methuen, MA & Gertrude M Mooney Nashua, NH
HODGE, Ernestine, Nov 26 1920 Sex:F Child# 1 Ernest Hodge Mass & Josephine Thompson Mass
HODGE, Ethel May, Jan 30 1912 Sex:F Child# 1 Theodore S Hodge Vermont & Myra Sullivan Ireland
HODGE, Florence, Jul 2 1918 Sex:F Child# 1 John Hodge Washington, DC & Florence Bruce Hillsborough, NH
HODGE, Florence G, Jun 20 1902 Sex:F Child# 1 Eugene Hodge Lowell, MA & J G Howe Lowell, MA
HODGE, Frederick, Sep 18 1910 Sex:M Child# 9 William Hodge England & Martha Watkinson England
HODGE, John Francis, Feb 22 1923 Sex:M Child# 2 William Hodge Lowell, MA & Madeline Carbone Salem, MA
HODGE, Lawrence Augustus, Oct 2 1927 Sex:M Child# 7 L A Hodge Lawrence, MA & G M Mooney Nashua, NH
HODGE, Loretta Genevieve, Nov 12 1917 Sex:F Child# 2 Lawrence A Hodge Methuen, MA & Gertrude May Mooney Nashua, NH
HODGE, Lorraine Adele, May 19 1924 Sex:F Child# 3 Edw T Hodge Lowell, MA & Adele Jean Nashua, NH
HODGE, Lucile Evelyn, Jun 13 1921 Sex:F Child# 1 Edwin Hodge Mass & Adele Jean NH
HODGE, Martha Jane, May 6 1932 Sex:F Child# 8 Lawrence Hodge Mass & Gertrude Mooney NH
HODGE, Nina Martha, Aug 27 1922 Sex:F Child# 2 Edward Hodge Mass & Adele Jean NH
HODGE, Robert Thompson, Aug 3 1926 Sex:M Child# 2 Ernest Hodge Lowell, MA & Ruth Thompson Athol, MA
HODGE, William Lawrence, Oct 2 1919 Sex:M Child# 3 Lawrence A Hodge Methuen, MA & Gertrude M Mooney Nashua, NH
HODGEMAN, Viola E, Nov 19 1904 Sex:F Child# 2 Charles Hodgeman Lancaster, MA & Edith Caldwell Nashua, NH
HODGEMAN, William F, Sep 17 1903 Sex:M Child# 1 Charles W Hodgeman Lancaster, MA & Edith Caldwell Nashua, NH
HODGES, Marian Arlene, Apr 21 1933 Sex:F Child# 3 Albert Hodges Lynn, MA & L Richardson California

HODGMAN, Angelett, Dec 20 1906 Sex:F Child# 3 Charles Hodgman
HODGMAN, Frederick William, Jun 14 1929 Sex:M Child# 1 Frederick Hodgman Merrimack, NH & Myrtle Lanpher Hanover, NH
HODGMAN, Gerald Edwin, Feb 16 1923 Sex:M Child# 1 Elmer Hodgman Amherst, NH & Frances E Clark Amherst, NH
HODKINSON, Jeanne Dora, Sep 30 1914 Sex:F Child# 2 Harold Hodkinson England & Dora Doyou Canada
HOFFMAN, James Julius, Dec 1 1893 Sex:M Child# 1 Julius M Hoffman Ireland & Mary Keane Ireland
HOFFMAN, Margaret F, Mar 31 1900 Sex:F Child#  Louis Hoffman Manchester, NH & Grace Jones Manchester, NH
HOFFMAN, Unknown, Apr 11 1896 Sex:F Child# 1 Harry Hoffman Bennington, VT & Jessie Watson Troy, NY
HOGAN, Alice Gertrude, Dec 16 1898 Sex:F Child# 2 Austin H Hogan Northfield, VT & Alice M Gillispee Whitneyville
HOGAN, Alice Mary, Mar 20 1934 Sex:F Child# 4 Mark E Hogan Nashua, NH & Beatrice Therrien Springfield, MA
HOGAN, Austin Henry, Jr, Dec 19 1900 Sex:M Child# 3 Austin H Hogan Vermont & Alice M Gillispy Maine
HOGAN, Austin Joseph, Jun 30 1935 Sex:M Child# 3 Austin Hogan Nashua, NH & Andrea Lavoie Nashua, NH
HOGAN, Catherine Elizabeth, Mar 20 1921 Sex:F Child# 2 Mark E Hogan Nashua, NH & Beatrice Therrien Springfield, MA
HOGAN, Daniel Edward, Nov 11 1931 Sex:M Child# 1 Austin Hogan, Jr Nashua, NH & Andrea R Lavoie Nashua, NH
HOGAN, David Robert, Nov 19 1935 Sex:M Child# 5 Mark Hogan Nashua, NH & Beatrice Therrien Springfield, MA
HOGAN, Elizabeth, Aug 23 1892 Sex:F Child# 2 Michael Hogan Ireland & Mary E Hallen Ireland
HOGAN, George Frederick, Jun 24 1922 Sex:M Child# 1 Joseph H Hogan Newmarket, NH & Esther Christie Nashua, NH
HOGAN, Hilda, Jul 28 1899 Sex:F Child# 5 Michael Hogan Ireland & Mary E Hallen Ireland
HOGAN, James Francis, Jun 7 1933 Sex:M Child# 2 Austin Hogan, Jr Nashua, NH & Andrea Lavoie Nashua, NH
HOGAN, John Joseph, Jul 13 1915 Sex:M Child# 8 John J Hogan Canada & Sarah Guimont Canada
HOGAN, John S, May 8 1891 Sex:M Child# 1 Michael Hogan Ireland & Mary E Holden Ireland
HOGAN, Joseph Livingston, May 20 1924 Sex:M Child# 2 Joseph Hogan Newmarket, NH & Esther Christy Nashua, NH
HOGAN, Kenneth Livingston, Sep 8 1925 Sex:M Child# 3 Joseph H Hogan Newmarket, NH & Esther Christie Nashua, NH
HOGAN, Marjorie Lucille, May 23 1925 Sex:F Child# 1 Thos N Hogan Conn & Olive Nash Nashua, NH
HOGAN, Mark Eugene, Apr 25 1897 Sex:M Child# 1 Austin H Hogan Northfield, VT & Alice M Gillespie Whitneyville,
HOGAN, Mark Eugene, Aug 3 1919 Sex:M Child# 1 Mark Eugene Hogan Nashua, NH & Beatrice Therrien Springfield, MA
HOGAN, May Helen, Aug 10 1894 Sex:F Child# 3 Michael Hogan Ireland & Mary E Hallen Ireland
HOGAN, Richard Joseph, Nov 20 1929 Sex:M Child# 3 Mark Hogan Nashua, NH & Beatrice Therrien Springfield, MA
HOGAN, Stephen Thomas, Jan 13 1897 Sex:M Child# 4 Michael Hogan Ireland & Mary E Hallen Ireland
HOGAN, Thomas William, Nov 30 1926 Sex:M Child# 2 Thomas W Hogan Conn & Olive Nash Nashua, NH
HOGAN, Unknown, Jul 21 1901 Sex:F Child# 4 John Hogan New Market & Norah Keliher Ireland
HOGER, William Grant, Jun 20 1918 Sex:M Child# 1 Lewis G Hoger Concord, NH & Esther Drake Concord, NH
HOGG, Unknown, Mar 22 1891 Sex:F Child# 1 Horace A Hogg Sherburne, NS & Lizzie Cloutier Taunton, MA
HOITT, Robert William, Mar 30 1912 Sex:M Child# 1 William B Hoitt Portsmouth, NH & Agnes B Duncklee Nashua, NH
HOITT, Unknown, Apr 28 1889 Sex:M Child# 7 Fred P Hoitt Kittery, ME & Augusta Portsmouth, NH
HOLAK, Jennie, Jan 20 1935 Sex:F Child# 5 Benjamin Holak Poland & Agnes Kurta Poland
HOLBROOK, Doris Elizabeth, Jul 5 1912 Sex:F Child# 3 Ralph Holbrook NH & Eva Brickey New York
HOLBROOK, Earl Lincoln, Feb 12 1906 Sex:M Child# 3 Elmer H Holbrook Penacook, NH & Amelia Oben Plattsburg, NY
HOLBROOK, Eliouese L, Aug 10 1889 Sex:F Child# 1 George P Holbrook Nashua, NH & Jennie L Hildreth Mass
HOLBROOK, Elmer Augustus, Dec 24 1903 Sex:M Child# 3 Elmer H Holbrook Penacook, NH & Minnie Obin Plattsburg, NY
HOLBROOK, Frank William, Feb 5 1900 Sex:M Child# 1 Herbert Holbrook New Hampshire & Florence Baker New York
HOLBROOK, Ida Marion, Jul 16 1925 Sex:F Child# 1 Clarence Holbrook Sharon, MA & Elizabeth Dalcourt Taunton, MA
HOLBROOK, Irene Louise, Mar 20 1905 Sex:F Child# 3 Herbert L Holbrook Great Falls, NH & Florence H Baker Nashua, NH
HOLBROOK, James Wilbur, Dec 15 1904 Sex:M Child# 2 Alphonso R Holbrook Penacook, NH & Mabel Peace England
HOLBROOK, Joseph Robert, Apr 24 1925 Sex:M Child# 2 Elmer Holbrook Nashua, NH & Anabel Girard Canada
HOLBROOK, Lois, Nov 28 1898 Sex:F Child# 2 John Holbrook Nashua, NH & Susie Woodman Manchester, NH
HOLBROOK, Mabel Ruth, Jul 26 1901 Sex:F Child# 2 Herbert L Holbrook Suncook, NH & Florence Faker Suncook, NH
HOLBROOK, Robert James, Oct 26 1932 Sex:M Child# 2 Elmer Holbrook Nashua, NH & Marion Riley Worcester, MA
HOLBROOK, Robert Kenneth, Dec 7 1927 Sex:M Child# 2 R C Holbrook Norfolk, MA & Bessie Smith Woburn, MA
HOLBROOK, Unknown, Nov 30 1894 Sex:M Child# 1 Alphonso Holbrook Nashua, NH & Ella Sauschagun NY Stillborn
HOLBROOK, Unknown, Dec 23 1902 Sex:M Child# 1 Alp Holbrook Henniker, NH & Mabel Peace England
HOLBROOK, Unknown, Jan 23 1905 Sex:F Child# 4 Elmer H Holbrook Penacook, NH & Minnie Obin Plattsburg, NY
HOLBROOK, Viola, Mar 1 1910 Sex:F Child# 2 Ralph Holbrook NH & Eva Brickey New York
HOLDEN, Alfred P, May 22 1898 Sex:M Child#  Andrew P Holden Sweden & Caroline Johnson Sweden
HOLDEN, Blanche, Jul 5 1890 Sex:F Child# 1 Albert E Holden Mass & Sarah A Merrill Mass
HOLDEN, Charles Henry, Oct 24 1903 Sex:M Child# 2 Frank H Holden Nashua, NH & Mabel V Durant Nashua, NH
HOLDEN, Dorothy, Apr 25 1932 Sex:F Child# 1 Gordon A Holden Nashua, NH & Frances Rideout Deblois, ME
HOLDEN, Esther May, Jul 3 1923 Sex:F Child# 2 Fred W Holden Nashua, NH & Gladys Denault Hollis, NH
HOLDEN, Everett Leroy, May 19 1919 Sex:M Child# 2 Fred L Holden Nashua, NH & Lizzie E Holden Hollis, NH
HOLDEN, George Edward, May 19 1919 Sex:M Child# 1 Fred L Holden Nashua, NH & Lizzie E Holden Hollis, NH Stillborn
HOLDEN, George Everett, Nov 9 1933 Sex:M Child# 1 Charles Holden Nashua, NH & Grace Putnam Hudson, NH
HOLDEN, Gordon Amos, Nov 4 1905 Sex:M Child# 2 Fred M Holden Nashua, NH & Celia L Holden Stewartstown, NH
HOLDEN, Hellen May, May 22 1896 Sex:F Child# 9 Andrew P Holden Sweden & Carolina Gonsau Sweden
HOLDEN, Nellie May, Sep 10 1898 Sex:F Child# 3 Frank H Holden Nashua, NH & Marinda Page Hudson, NH
HOLDEN, Ruth Lorraine, May 29 1920 Sex:F Child# 1 Fred W Holden Nashua, NH & Gladys Denault Hollis, NH
HOLDEN, Sally Ann, Nov 21 1934 Sex:F Child# 2 Charles Holden Nashua, NH & Grace Putnam Hudson, NH
HOLDEN, Unknown, Jan 4 1890 Sex:F Child# 6 Andrew P Holden Sweden & Caroline Johnson Sweden
HOLDEN, Unknown, May 19 1892 Sex:M Child# 8 Andrew Holden Sweden & Caroline Johnson Sweden
HOLDEN, Unknown, Sep 1 1892 Sex:F Child#  F M Holden
HOLDEN, Velma Martina, Dec 15 1912 Sex:F Child# 4 Frank Holden Nashua, NH & Mabel Durant Nashua, NH
HOLDEN, Wilfred Leroy, Sep 17 1930 Sex:M Child# 3 Fred L Holden Nashua, NH & Lizzie E Holden Hollis, NH
HOLLACK, Florence, Jul 17 1926 Sex:F Child# 4 Brunislaw Hollack Poland & Edwiga Kurta Poland
HOLLAK, Stanislava, Sep 24 1923 Sex:F Child# 3 Brunislav Hollak Poland & Edwidga Kurta Poland
HOLLAND, Ann Shirley, Jun 17 1931 Sex:F Child# 1 Frank Holland Milford, NH & Margaret Cummings Nashua, NH

HOLLINGS, Jane, Mar 1 1920 Sex:F Child# 1 Charles B Hollings Charlestown, MA & Alice Walker Norwood, MA
HOLLIS, James Henry, Sep 12 1889 Sex:M Child# 5 James Hollis Lancaster, MA & Delia Doyle Lancaster, MA
HOLLOK, Woyeles, Apr 3 1918 Sex:M Child# 1 Bronislau Hollok Russia & Edwiga Kurta Russia
HOLLY, Roland, Apr 23 1909 Sex:M Child# 2 Joseph Holly Canada & Delia Collette New York
HOLLY, Theodore, Feb 21 1911 Sex:M Child# 3 Joseph Holly Canada & Delia Collette New York
HOLLYWOOD, Unknown, Oct 5 1898 Sex:M Child# 1 P Frank Hollywood Bridgewater, MA & Cora Peeler Montague, MA
HOLMAN, Harry, Mar 23 1895 Sex:M Child# 1 Georges Holman New York & Grace Holbrook Nashua, NH
HOLMES, Althea Northrup, Jul 10 1906 Sex:F Child# 2 George R Holmes Gloucester, MA & Evo Pixley S Lee, MA
HOLMES, Charles Sayre, Feb 17 1923 Sex:M Child# 1 Chas Elmer Holmes
HOLMES, Mabel Edna, Aug 29 1905 Sex:F Child# 3 Fred D Holmes Derry, NH & Florence West Fremont, NH
HOLMS, Jeane, Nov 17 1888 Sex:F Child# 2 George G Holms Hudson & Mary Ann Butler Ireland
HOLQUIST, Unknown, Sep 12 1890 Sex:M Child# 1 Egerton Holquist Sweden & Anna Gustavson Sweden
HOLT, Alan Winston, May 4 1933 Sex:M Child# 1 Harold W Holt Milford, NH & Louise Forbes Nashua, NH
HOLT, Arthur Raymond, Sep 20 1898 Sex:M Child#  William F Holt Mass & Mary S Chandler Manchester, NH
HOLT, Barbara Mary, Apr 17 1932 Sex:F Child# 3 Harvey F Holt Nashua, NH & Gladys King Nashua, NH
HOLT, Calvin Harris, Jan 5 1931 Sex:M Child# 1 Richard Duane Holt Nashua, NH & Elizabeth Lee Harris Big Stone
HOLT, David Seymour, Jun 28 1919 Sex:M Child# 3 Duane Holt Weston, VT & Rachael A Seymour Richford, VT
HOLT, Dorothy May, Sep 6 1902 Sex:F Child# 1 Harry F Holt Nashua, NH & Florence A Carkin Wilton, NH
HOLT, Flora May, Apr 21 1889 Sex:F Child# 1 Benjamin F Holt Lyndeboro, NH & Mary G Lucas Winooski, VT
HOLT, George A, Mar 29 1891 Sex:M Child# 2 Burtt J Holt Nashua, NH & Dora Mott New York
HOLT, Gloria Ann, Nov 3 1929 Sex:F Child# 1 Harvey Francis Holt Nashua, NH & Gladys Belle King Nashua, NH
HOLT, Gordon Seymore, Dec 3 1914 Sex:M Child# 1 Duane F Holt Weston, VT & Rachel A Seymore Richford, VT Stillborn
HOLT, Harold Arthur, Dec 11 1935 Sex:M Child# 5 Harvey Holt Nashua, NH & Gladys King Nashua, NH
HOLT, Harold Hazen, Jun 1 1906 Sex:M Child# 2 Enoch C Holt Methuen, MA & Olena Marston Nashua, NH
HOLT, Harry Fremont, Jr, Jun 5 1917 Sex:M Child# 9 Harry F Holt Nashua, NH & Florence Carkin Wilton, NH
HOLT, Irene, Aug 30 1901 Sex:F Child# 1 E Christy Holt Methuen, MA & Olena Marston Nashua, NH
HOLT, Lester Ben, Jan 25 1903 Sex:M Child# 1 William E Holt Nashua, NH & Dorothy F Hanscom Nashua, NH
HOLT, Lucy A, Feb 1 1906 Sex:F Child# 4 Harry F Holt Nashua, NH & Florence A Carkin Wilton, NH
HOLT, Margaret Lucille, Aug 21 1910 Sex:F Child# 3 Fred M Holt Exeter, NH & Albina Robillard Cambridge, MA
HOLT, Marion, Mar 29 1908 Sex:F Child# 3 Enoch C Holt Methuen, MA & Olena Marston Nashua, NH
HOLT, Martin Ellsworth, Jun 2 1919 Sex:M Child# 2 Walter L Holt Nashua, NH & Marion Cushing Woburn, MA
HOLT, Mary Elizabeth, Nov 25 1910 Sex:F Child# 2 J Earlfred Holt Nashua, NH & Helen Reed Nashua, NH
HOLT, Maybell Marguerite, Sep 18 1906 Sex:F Child# 3 Harry F Holt Lyndeboro, NH & Margaret Polk Cambridge, MA
HOLT, Mildred Evelyn, Feb 2 1904 Sex:F Child# 2 Harry F Holt Nashua, NH & Florence Carkin Wilton, NH
HOLT, Natalie Woodard, Aug 12 1924 Sex:F Child# 4 Walter L Holt Nashua, NH & Marion Cushing Woburn, MA
HOLT, Ralph Davis, Oct 29 1906 Sex:M Child# 1 Ralph W Holt Nashua, NH & Gladys E Davis Nashua, NH
HOLT, Ralph Leonardo, Dec 19 1933 Sex:M Child# 4 Harvey Holt Nashua, NH & Gladys King Nashua, NH
HOLT, Ray J, Mar 28 1892 Sex:M Child# 1 R C Holt Nashua, NH & M M Leach New Boston, NH
HOLT, Robert Cushing, Aug 10 1921 Sex:M Child# 3 Walter L Holt Nashua, NH & Marion Cushing Woburn, MA
HOLT, Robert R, Oct 13 1889 Sex:M Child# 1 Bert J Holt Nashua, NH & Dora Mott Nashua, NH
HOLT, Ruth, Apr 21 1908 Sex:F Child# 2 Ralph W Holt Nashua, NH & Galdys Davis Nashua, NH
HOLT, Samuel D, Apr 26 1894 Sex:M Child# 9 Duane F Holt Vermont & Edith F Woodward NH
HOLT, Susie Laura A, Apr 25 1909 Sex:F Child# 6 Harry Holt Nashua, NH & Florence Carkin Nashua, NH
HOLT, Unknown, Aug 23 1887 Sex:F Child# 5 Duane F Holt Weston, VT & Edith Hanover, NH
HOLT, Unknown, Jul 10 1888 Sex:M Child# 9 Hiland A Holt Peterborough & Mary Burns NS
HOLT, Unknown, Jul 20 1891 Sex:M Child# 1 William F Holt Tewksbury, MA & Mary Stetson Manchester, NH
HOLT, Unknown, Dec 30 1891 Sex:F Child# 7 D F Holt Weston, VT & Edith F Woodward Hanover, NH
HOLT, Unknown, Apr 16 1893 Sex:F Child# 8 Duane F Holt Weston, VT & Edith Woodward Hanover, NH
HOLT, Unknown, May 29 1899 Sex:M Child# 11 Duane F Holt Weston, VT & Edith Woodward Hanover, NH
HOLT, Unknown, Sep 15 1912 Sex:F Child# 3 Ralph Holt Nashua, NH & Gladys Davis Nashua, NH
HOLT, Unknown, Nov 25 1912 Sex:M Child# 4 Fred M Holt Exeter, NH & Albina Robilard Cambridge, MA
HOLT, Unknown, Jun 29 1916 Sex:M Child# 2 Duane F Holt Vermont & Rachael A Seymour Richford, VT
HOLT, Unknown, Oct 5 1926 Sex:M Child# 6 Charles W Holt Temple, NH & Nellie Stratton Leominster, MA
HOLT, Vera L, Apr 1 1896 Sex:F Child# 4 Burtt J Holt Nashua, NH & Dora Mott Sandy Hill, NY
HOLT, Vivian Adeline, Mar 3 1905 Sex:F Child# 3 Harry F Holt Nashua, NH & Florence Carkin Wilton, NH
HOLT, Walter L, Jr, Jun 14 1917 Sex:M Child# 1 Walter L Holt Nashua, NH & Marion Cushing Woburn, MA
HOLT, Walter Lowell, Jan 18 1896 Sex:M Child# 10 Duane F Holt Weston, VT & Edith F Woodward Hanover, NH
HOLT, Willard Kingsbury, May 6 1915 Sex:M Child# 1 Charles W Holt Milford, NH & Georgie Ames Ossipee, NH
HOLT, William Francis, Feb 14 1931 Sex:M Child# 2 Harvey Holt Nashua, NH & Gladys King Nashua, NH
HOMOLESKI, Edwin Herbert, Nov 21 1925 Sex:M Child# 2 Alex Homoleski Russia & Ethel Taylor Brookline, NH
HOMOLESKI, Olga Taylor, Nov 13 1923 Sex:F Child# 1 Alexander Homoleski Russia & Ethel Taylor Brookline, NH
HONDROCASTAS, Nicolaos, May 20 1933 Sex:M Child# 2 Jas Hondrocastas Greece & Magdeline Najos Barre, VT
HOOD, Beverly Virginia, Jul 15 1911 Sex:F Child# 1 Robert L Hood Nashua, NH & Gladys A Holt Nashua, NH
HOOD, Charles Hayes, Jr, Jul 30 1919 Sex:M Child# 1 Charles H Hood Nashua, NH & Annie Slate Nashua, NH
HOOD, Glenn Cameron, Mar 5 1920 Sex:M Child# 3 Robert Hood Nashua, NH & Gladys Holt Nashua, NH
HOOD, Jeanne Andrea, Nov 9 1925 Sex:F Child# 11 Charles H Hood Nashua, NH & Annie Slate Nashua, NH
HOOD, Patricia Eudora, Jun 20 1915 Sex:F Child# 2 Robert L Hood Nashua, NH & Gladys Holt Nashua, NH
HOOD, Richard Dean, Aug 1 1933 Sex:M Child# 1 Samuel Hood Nashua, NH & Dianna M Dean Brookline, NH
HOOD, Unknown, Dec 17 1887 Sex:M Child# 1 Euzebe G Hood Nashua, NH & Annie F Cross Nashua, NH
HOOD, Unknown, Mar 26 1887 Sex:M Child# 4 Samuel Hood Ireland & Margarette Ireland
HOOD, Unknown, Mar 11 1889 Sex:M Child# 2 Euzeb G Hood Nashua, NH & Annie F Cross Nashua, NH
HOOD, Unknown, Mar 6 1922 Sex:M Child# 4 Robert L Hood Lincoln, VT & Charlotte Robinson Hudson, VT  Stillborn
HOOHANESIAN, John G, Oct 18 1908 Sex:M Child# 1 Charles Hoohanesian Turkey & Siranoosh Zadoorian Turkey

HOOK, Edmond, May 27 1917 Sex:M Child# 2 James Hook Russia & Victoria Gerden Russia
HOOK, Mary, Jan 26 1917 Sex:F Child# 1 Adam Hook Russia & Mary Schukawane Russia
HOOK, Unknown, Mar 3 1922 Sex:M Child# 2 Adam Hook
HOOKE, Bertha E, Dec 1 1897 Sex:F Child#  Fred G Hooke Brentwood & Eliza A Connor Salem, MA
HOOPEN, Angelo, Jun 21 1905 Sex:M Child# 1 Peter Hoopen Greece & Demetra Gaudreau Greece
HOOPER, Alice Anne, Nov 24 1903 Sex:F Child# 2 Daniel Hooper Nashua, NH & Mary Blanchette Nashua, NH
HOOPER, George Daniel, Jun 6 1902 Sex:M Child# 1 Daniel Hooper New Brunswick & Annie Blanchette Canada
HOOPER, Inez Luella, Feb 23 1894 Sex:F Child# 5 George H Hooper Biddeford, ME & Ella G Hall Strafford, NH
HOOPER, Mardian, Dec 20 1888 Sex:M Child# 3 George W Hooper Biddeford, ME & Ella G Hall Strafford, NH
HOOPER, Ray Hall, Nov 19 1895 Sex:M Child# 6 George W Hooper Biddeford, ME & Etta G Hall Stafford, NH
HOOPER, Wallace Kimball, Dec 23 1925 Sex:M Child# 2 Nat F Hooper Ft Warren, MA & H L Kimball Bethel, VT
HOOPES, Helene, May 27 1911 Sex:F Child# 4 Peter S Hoopes Greece & Demitras Antigianos Greece
HOOPIS, Soteros, Mar 28 1908 Sex:M Child# 3 Peter Hoopis Greece & Themetro Antrew Greece
HOPCHUNIS, Julius, May 1 1912 Sex:M Child# 1 William Hopchunis Russia & Anna Tamolavitch Russia
HOPE, Wesley Parker, Aug 6 1922 Sex:M Child# 1 Charles W Hope Canada & Julia Pratt N Hampton, MA
HOPIS, James, Feb 4 1907 Sex:M Child# 2 Peter Hopis Greece & Demetria Antiari Greece
HOPKINS, David Moody, Dec 26 1921 Sex:M Child# 1 Donald W Hopkins Greenfield, NH & Henriette Moody Turner, ME
HOPKINS, Donna, May 15 1925 Sex:F Child# 2 Donald W Hopkins Greenfield, NH & Henriette Moody Turner, ME
HOPKINS, Elwyn Cleaves, Nov 12 1893 Sex:M Child# 1 Guy Hopkins Nashua, NH & Minnie Cowan Canada
HOPKINS, Ethel A, Oct 31 1891 Sex:F Child# 1 W B Hopkins NH & E J Hall Canada
HOPKINS, Harold Ray, Sep 11 1898 Sex:M Child# 1 Hugh J Hopkins
HOPKINS, Harvey Roy, Jul 6 1904 Sex:M Child# 3 Guy A Hopkins Nashua, NH & Minnie Cowan Linqwick, PQ
HOPKINS, Howard Grovenor, Feb 10 1910 Sex:M Child# 3 Grovenor H Hopkins Nashua, NH & Georgia M Rust Manchester, NH
HOPKINS, Irene Ellen, Aug 11 1906 Sex:F Child# 1 Grosvenor H Hopkins Nashua, NH & Georgia Rust Manchester, NH
HOPKINS, Kenneth B, Sep 17 1913 Sex:M Child# 5 Grovesnor H Hopkins Nashua, NH & Georgia Rust Manchester, NH
HOPKINS, Laverne M, Jan 8 1908 Sex:f Child# 2 Grosvenor H Hopkins Nashua, NH & Georgia Rust Manchester, NH
HOPKINS, Unknown, Dec 27 1900 Sex:M Child#  Guy Hopkins Nashua, NH & Minnie Cowan Canada
HOPPER, Alice Mary, Jan 23 1925 Sex:F Child# 2 Jesse Hopper Birmingham, AL & Alice O'Brien Ireland
HOPPER, Ann Louise, Dec 19 1923 Sex:F Child# 1 Jesse Hopper Birmingham, AL & Alice O'Brien Ireland
HOPPER, Beatrice, Sep 7 1927 Sex:F Child# 4 Jesse Hopper Alabama & Alice O'Brien Ireland
HOPPER, Margaret, Sep 7 1927 Sex:F Child# 3 Jesse Hopper Alabama & Alice O'Brien Ireland
HOPPER, Patricia, Nov 23 1930 Sex:F Child# 5 Jesse Hopper Alabama & Alice O'Brien Ireland
HOPSIK, Joan, Nov 26 1933 Sex:F Child# 6 Valeric Hopsik Poland & Elisabeth Mageika Poland
HOPWOOD, Beulah Mary, Apr 7 1916 Sex:F Child# 2 James W Hopwood Nashua, NH & Ethel M Farley Reeds Ferry, NH
HOPWOOD, Earl J, Apr 1 1896 Sex:M Child# 4 James Hopwood England & Mary Whittemore Litchfield, NH
HOPWOOD, Guy, Sep 17 1894 Sex:M Child# 3 James Hopwood England & Mary Whittemore Litchfield, NH
HOPWOOD, Helen Blanche, Nov 5 1910 Sex:F Child# 2 Charles Hopwood England & Catherine T Clark Lowell, MA
HOPWOOD, James W, Jan 8 1891 Sex:M Child# 1 James Hopwood England & Mary Whittemore Litchfield, NH
HORGAN, Unknown, Oct 28 1887 Sex:F Child# 1 Patrick Horgan Ireland & Hannah Helqeust Sweden
HORN, Unknown, Apr 13 1887 Sex:F Child# 4 Edward O Horn W Lebanon, ME & Bell Nashua, NH Stillborn
HORNE, Laura May, Nov 6 1934 Sex:F Child# 2 Warren B Horne New Glasgow, NS & Elizabeth Cochrane Stellarton, NS
HORNE, Mary Elizabeth, Jul 2 1931 Sex:F Child# 1 Warren B Horne New Glasgow, NS & Elizabeth Cochrane Stellarton,NS
HORNISH, William Hugh C, Dec 9 1924 Sex:M Child# 1 William J Hornish Canada & Genesta Monroe Canada
HORTON, Barbara Shirley, Nov 29 1920 Sex:F Child# 3 George Horton Nashua, NH & Albina Labree Rochester, NH
HORTON, Elizabeth Holden, Aug 15 1927 Sex:F Child# 3 Fred W Horton Nashua, NH & B M Dineault Hollis, NH
HORTON, Fay Elizabeth, Nov 25 1934 Sex:F Child# 2 William Horton Boston, MA & Viola Davis NH
HORTON, Fred, Sep 9 1924 Sex:M Child# 1 Fred Horton Derry, NH & Cora Derosier Richford, VT
HORTON, Geraldine Sadie, Jan 10 1916 Sex:F Child# 1 George F Horton Nashua, NH & Albina S Labrie Rochester, NH
HORTON, Gloria Beverly, Feb 26 1926 Sex:F Child# 4 George Horton Nashua, NH & Albina Labrie Rochester, NH
HORTON, June F, Jun 15 1919 Sex:F Child# 2 George Horton St John, NB & Gertrude Gallagher Milford, MA
HORTON, Lucille Viola, Jan 29 1919 Sex:F Child# 2 George F Horton Nashua, NH & Albina Labrie Rochester, NH
HORTON, Unknown, Feb 10 1888 Sex:M Child# 4 Melvin S Horton Canada & Sadie Cummings Waterville, ME
HORTON, Unknown, Jan 29 1891 Sex:M Child# 2 Lewis A Horton Middletown, CT & Mary Halifax, NS
HORTON, Unknown, Jul 31 1894 Sex:F Child# 5 Melvin D Horton Newport, VT & Sadie S Cummings Maine
HORTON, William Francis, Nov 14 1932 Sex:M Child# 1 William Horton Boston, MA & Viola Davis Lempster, NH
HOTTE, Armand, Apr 30 1925 Sex:M Child# 3 Adelard Hotte Canada & Anna Yvon Canada
HOTTE, Marie Arnande Yvonne, Oct 7 1927 Sex:F Child# 5 Adelard Hotte Canada & Anna Yvon Canada
HOTTE, Rene, Jun 27 1926 Sex:M Child# 4 Adelard Hotte Canada & Anna Yvon Canada
HOUDE, Adeline Irene, Mar 2 1898 Sex:F Child# 3 Joseph Houde Canada & Clara Deschamp Nashua, NH
HOUDE, Alida, Jul 5 1903 Sex:F Child# 5 Joseph Houde Canada & Clara Deschamps Nashua, NH
HOUDE, Armand Osias, Aug 28 1906 Sex:M Child# 8 Joseph Houde Canada & Clara Deschamps Nashua, NH
HOUDE, Beatrice Martha, Jul 25 1918 Sex:F Child# 2 Edmond Houde Canada & Marie Louise Jalbert Canada
HOUDE, Edgar Wilfred, Aug 17 1908 Sex:M Child# 10 Joseph Houde Canada & Clara Deschamps Nashua, NH
HOUDE, Edgar Wilfred, Aug 4 1935 Sex:M Child# 2 Edgar Houde Nashua, NH & Mary Apenovitch Nashua, NH
HOUDE, Joseph Ernest, Oct 2 1893 Sex:M Child# 1 Joseph Houde Canada & Clara Deschamps Nashua, NH
HOUDE, Joseph Felix Paul, Dec 27 1911 Sex:M Child# 1 Alcide Houde Hooksett, NH & Emma Desmarais Canada
HOUDE, Louis Raymond, Jun 6 1905 Sex:M Child# 7 Joseph Houde Canada & Clara Deschamps Nashua, NH
HOUDE, M Lilian, Dec 27 1895 Sex:F Child# 2 Joseph Houde Canada & Clara Deschamps Nashua, NH
HOUDE, Marie Louise A, Nov 8 1901 Sex:F Child# 5 Joseph Houde Canada & Clara Deschamps Nashua, NH
HOUDE, Marie Rose F, May 25 1900 Sex:F Child# 4 Joseph Houde Canada & Clara Deschamps Nashua, NH
HOUDE, Paul Rene, Sep 26 1910 Sex:M Child# 10 Joseph Houde Canada & Clara Deschamps Nashua, NH
HOUDE, Robert Joseph, May 1 1934 Sex:M Child# 1 Edgar Houde Nashua, NH & Mary Aponovitch Nashua, NH
HOUDE, Roger, Sep 18 1919 Sex:M Child# 3 J Edmond Houde Canada & Marie Louise Jalbert Canada

HOUDE, Roger Albert, Apr 16 1916 Sex:M Child# 1 Edmond Houde Canada & M L Emma Galbert Canada
HOUGH, James Joseph, Aug 18 1892 Sex:M Child# 2 James J Hough Ireland & Mary Carr Ireland
HOUGH, John Francis, Sep 30 1901 Sex:M Child# 7 James J Hough Ireland & Mary E Carr Ireland
HOUGH, Josephine T, Mar 4 1897 Sex:F Child#  Jim Hough Ireland & Mary Carr Ireland
HOUGH, Unknown, Oct 5 1891 Sex:F Child# 2 Edward Hough Nashua, NH & Mary A Keenan Nashua, NH
HOUGHTON, Alfred John, May 22 1909 Sex:M Child# 2 Clarence H Houghton N Troy, VT & Anne G Gallagher Worcester, MA
HOUGHTON, Alfred John, Jan 18 1933 Sex:M Child# 1 A J Houghton Nashua, NH & Lulu Signor Brookline, NH
HOUGHTON, Avis Della, Jan 15 1915 Sex:F Child# 1 Chester A Houghton Fall River, MA & Meda A Copeland Fairhaven
HOUGHTON, Patricia May, Feb 7 1934 Sex:F Child# 2 Alfred John Houghton Nashua, NH & Lulu Signor Brookline, NH
HOULDSWORTH, John Holt, Jul 24 1914 Sex:M Child# 1 John B Houldsworth England & Emily Holt England
HOULE, Albert Romeo, Jul 26 1907 Sex:M Child# 4 Evariste Houle Canada & Malvina Paquette Manchester, NH
HOULE, Alice Dunlap, Jan 7 1925 Sex:F Child# 3 Fred E Houle Woonsocket, RI & Grace Whitmore Nova Scotia
HOULE, Amedee Joseph, Mar 26 1935 Sex:M Child# 7 Amedee J Houle Hudson, NH & Florida Bouchard Nashua, NH
HOULE, Annette Rachel, Jul 6 1922 Sex:F Child# 2 Amedee Houle Nashua, NH & Florida Bouchard Nashua, NH
HOULE, Charlotte Priscilla, Mar 10 1929 Sex:F Child# 2 Romeo Houle Manchester, NH & Irene Lucier Nashua, NH
HOULE, Dorothy Sylvia, May 11 1932 Sex:F Child# 2 (No Parents Listed)
HOULE, Elizabeth, Aug 26 1913 Sex:F Child# 1 Philip Houle Nashua, NH & Frances McWha Nashua, NH
HOULE, Elzear E W, Dec 31 1896 Sex:M Child# 5 Francois Houle Canada & Mary Gervais Canada
HOULE, Ethel Josephine, Jun 17 1932 Sex:F Child# 1 Elzear F Houle Dunstable, MA & Beatrice Manchester, NH
HOULE, Eveline Olive, Jun 11 1906 Sex:F Child# 3 Evariste Houle Canada & Malvina Paquette Manchester, NH
HOULE, Francois E, Oct 28 1887 Sex:M Child#  Francis Houle P Q & Marie Gervais P Q
HOULE, Frederick Alton, Nov 26 1915 Sex:M Child# 2 Fred E Houle Woonsocket, RI & Grace Whitmore Nova Scotia
HOULE, George, Dec 5 1891 Sex:M Child# 1 Evariste Houle Canada & Sophie Chagnon St Albans, VT
HOULE, Gerard, May 28 1921 Sex:M Child# 1 Amedee Houle Nashua, NH & Florilda Bouchard Nashua, NH
HOULE, Gloria Lorette, May 20 1926 Sex:F Child# 4 Amedee Houle Hudson, NH & Florida Bouchard Nashua, NH
HOULE, Irene Dorothy C, Jul 17 1921 Sex:F Child# 3 Albert E Houle NH & Laura A Labrie Canada
HOULE, J Louis Rene, Oct 6 1921 Sex:M Child# 1 Louis Houle Canada & Marie Cote Canada
HOULE, J Simon Omer, Dec 8 1915 Sex:M Child# 5 Joseph Houle Canada & Celina Gagne Canada
HOULE, Jos Geo Henri, Jun 14 1930 Sex:M Child# 7 Louis Houle Canada & Marie Cote Canada
HOULE, Jos Maurice Adrien, Dec 26 1928 Sex:M Child# 6 Louis Houle Canada & Marie Cote Canada
HOULE, Joseph, Dec 7 1915 Sex:M Child# 1 Elzear Houle Mass & Elizabella Rood Vermont
HOULE, Joseph Albert Lionel, Jan 29 1917 Sex:M Child# 1 Albert Houle NH & Laura Augusta Labrie Canada
HOULE, Joseph Ed, Aug 18 1923 Sex:M Child# 1 Edmond Houle Mass & Irene Burns NH  Stillborn
HOULE, Joseph Pierre Edgar, Sep 12 1918 Sex:M Child# 6 Joseph Houle Canada & Celina Gagne Canada
HOULE, Joseph Reald Norman, Aug 7 1925 Sex:M Child# 4 Louis Houle Canada & Marie Cote Canada
HOULE, Joseph Sylva H, Mar 30 1911 Sex:M Child# 13 Amedee Houle Canada & Regina Normand Canada
HOULE, Lillian Florence, Jun 20 1931 Sex:F Child# 1 (No Parents Listed)
HOULE, Lucien Roger, Apr 17 1930 Sex:M Child# 1 Leon Houle Canada & Laura Lizotte Canada
HOULE, Lucille, Nov 28 1914 Sex:F Child# 3 Alcide Houle Hooksett, NH & Emma Desmarais Nashua, NH
HOULE, M Leonore, Nov 21 1895 Sex:F Child# 3 Amedee Houle Canada & Regina Normand Canada
HOULE, M Liliane Simone, May 30 1914 Sex:F Child# 4 Joseph Houle Canada & Celina Gagne Canada
HOULE, M Rita Mil Glor, Oct 28 1919 Sex:F Child# 2 Albert E Houle NH & Laura A Labine Canada
HOULE, M Rose Florette, Apr 22 1913 Sex:F Child# 3 Joseph Houle Canada & Celina Gagne Canada
HOULE, Marie Alice Albina, Aug 15 1914 Sex:F Child# 14 Amedee Houle Canada & Regina Normand Canada
HOULE, Marie Ange Beatrice, Aug 16 1927 Sex:F Child# 5 Louis Houle Canada & Marie Cote Canada
HOULE, Marie C, Jun 5 1894 Sex:F Child# 3 Evariste Houle Canada & Sophie Stebens St Albans, VT
HOULE, Marie Cecile, Feb 8 1924 Sex:F Child# 3 Calinete Houle Canada & Rose Niquette Canada
HOULE, Marie Irene Germaine, Apr 9 1923 Sex:F Child# 2 Louis Houle Canada & Marie Cote Canada
HOULE, Marie Jeannette, May 25 1924 Sex:F Child# 3 Louis Houle Canada & Marie Cote Canada
HOULE, Marie Josette Natali, Dec 28 1925 Sex:F Child# 1 Romeo L Houle Manchester, NH & Irene B Lucier Nashua, NH
HOULE, Marie L, Jun 24 1918 Sex:F Child# 4 Elzear J Houle Brookline, NH & Isabelle Rood Swanton, VT
HOULE, Marie Laura H, Apr 15 1910 Sex:F Child# 1 Joseph Houle Canada & Celina Gagne Canada
HOULE, Marie Murielle C, Jul 15 1930 Sex:F Child# 1 Joseph B Houle Canada & Adelia Bernachez Canada
HOULE, Marie O, Jan 23 1893 Sex:F Child# 2 Evariste Houle Canada & Sophie Steben St Albans, VT
HOULE, Marie Rose L, Jan 31 1910 Sex:F Child# 12 Amedee Houle Canada & Regina Normand Canada
HOULE, Marie Theresa Doroth, Apr 11 1926 Sex:F Child# 2 Edmond Houle Westford, MA & Irene Burns Nashua, NH
HOULE, Marie Yvette, Feb 20 1912 Sex:F Child# 2 Joseph Houle Canada & Celina Gagne Canada
HOULE, Mildred, Aug 7 1930 Sex:F Child# 5 Amedee Houle Hudson, NH & Florida Bouchard Nashua, NH
HOULE, Oscar E A, Mar 27 1896 Sex:M Child# 4 Evariste Houle Canada & Sophie Steben St Albans, VT
HOULE, Paul Felix, Nov 5 1913 Sex:M Child# 2 Alcide Houle Hooksett, NH & Emma Desmarais Nashua, NH
HOULE, Raymond, Oct 13 1917 Sex:M Child# 3 Elzear Joseph Houle Brookline, NH & Isabella Rood Swanton, VT Stillborn
HOULE, Richard Clarence, Jun 4 1926 Sex:M Child# 2 Albert Houle New York & Rose Durand New York
HOULE, Rita Amelia, May 25 1932 Sex:F Child# 6 Amede Houle Hudson, NH & Florida Dichard Nashua, NH
HOULE, Rita Beatrice, Jan 30 1925 Sex:F Child# 4 Edmond Houle Canada & Marie L Jalbert Canada
HOULE, Ruth, Jul 31 1919 Sex:F Child# 5 Elzear J Houle Brookline, NH & Isabelle Rood Swanton, VT
HOULE, Theresa Jeanne, Jul 26 1924 Sex:F Child# 3 Amedee Houle Hudson, NH & Florida Richard Nashua, NH
HOULE, Unknown, Nov 20 1892 Sex:M Child# 1 Amedee Houle Canada & Regina Nounand Canada Stillborn
HOULE, Unknown, Mar 17 1894 Sex:M Child# 7 Achille Houle Canada & Exilda Lemire Canada Stillborn
HOULE, Unknown, Sep 26 1920 Sex:F Child# 6 Elzear J Houle Brookline, NH & Isabelle Rood Swanton, VT Stillborn
HOULE, Walter Paul, Jan 5 1916 Sex:M Child# 15 Amedee Houle Canada & Regina Normand Canada
HOULE, William Joseph, Dec 11 1916 Sex:M Child# 2 Elzear Jos Houle Brookline, NH & Isabella Rood Swanton, VT
HOURBALAVEITZ, Marie, Aug 26 1914 Sex:F Child# 1 Peter Hourbalaveitz Russia & Anna Russia Stillborn
HOUSE, Philip Rowe, Sep 14 1933 Sex:M Child# 4 Fred R House Parish, NY & Helen M Wallace Hanover, NH

HOUSE, Unknown, Jun 2 1891 Sex:F Child# 1 Harry H House Troy, VT & Mamie C Hornbeck Westboro, NY
HOUSE, Unknown, Jul 31 1891 Sex:M Child# 4 Millard F House Parish, NY & Allie Rowe Burdette, NY
HOUSNEY, Marguerite, Nov 1 1914 Sex:F Child# 2 Johran Housney Syria & Mary S Saleehy Syria
HOUSTON, Unknown, Dec 11 1919 Sex:M Child# 1 Forrest G Houston Laconia, NH & Mildred H Martin Stoneham, MA
HOVAGIRNIAN, Lactening, Nov 28 1907 Sex:F Child# 2 Misag Hovagirnian Armenia & Keohe Bohosian Armenia
HOVAGROSINIAN, Akovine, Dec 25 1921 Sex:F Child# 2 Urisah Hovagrosinian Armenia & Osaha Hamanejarian Armenia
HOVEY, Unknown, Apr 21 1893 Sex:M Child# 2 William A Hovey St Johnsbury, VT & Sula Silver Nashua, NH
HOWARD, Beatrice E, Mar 16 1890 Sex:F Child# 2 Clarence E Howard Mass & Alice E Harris VT
HOWARD, David Goodale, Jr, Jun 20 1918 Sex:M Child# 1 David G Howard Townsend, MA & Margaret Struthers Mazeppa
HOWARD, Dorothy, Mar 1 1897 Sex:F Child# 1 Edmond T Howard Medway, MA & Delia Annett Kappa, IL
HOWARD, Dorothy May, Apr 27 1909 Sex:F Child# 1 Joseph Howard
HOWARD, Edward P, Jan 25 1891 Sex:M Child# 7 William Howard Grafton, MA & Katie E Degnan Ireland
HOWARD, Elias A, Dec 28 1889 Sex:M Child# 6 William Howard Grafton, MA & Kate E Degnan Ireland
HOWARD, Kate E, Feb 8 1892 Sex:F Child# 8 William Howard Worcester, MA & Kate E Degnan Ireland
HOWARD, Katherine E, Nov 23 1914 Sex:F Child# 2 James H Howard Worcester, MA & Nellie Oben E Pepperell, MA
HOWARD, Lucille Grace, Apr 20 1925 Sex:F Child# 3 William Howard Worcester, MA & Grace McDermott Nashua, NH
HOWARD, Lucy Baldwin, Feb 19 1905 Sex:F Child# 2 Charles W Howard Nashua, NH & Blanche L Baldwin Nashua, NH
HOWARD, Madeline, Jul 19 1916 Sex:F Child# 3 James Howard Mass & Ellen Howard Mass
HOWARD, Paul Francis, Dec 30 1914 Sex:M Child# 1 William F Howard Worcester, MA & Grace E McDermott Nashua, NH
HOWARD, Robert Elwin, Jan 26 1935 Sex:M Child# 2 Jos E Howard Piermont, NH & Ruby Shreves Rochester, MO
HOWARD, Unknown, Feb 8 1892 Sex:F Child# 5 William Howard Nashua, NH & Mary Ireland
HOWARD, Unknown, Nov 16 1901 Sex:M Child# 7 Henry Howard England & Mary Brmean Ireland
HOWARD, Warren Stanton, Aug 29 1919 Sex:M Child# 2 Perlie E Howard Jamaica, VT & Catherine Cronier Cambridge, MA
HOWARD, William Ellsworth, Jul 7 1921 Sex:M Child# 1 Wells R Howard Milford, NH & Eva Isabell Peters Wilton, NH
HOWARD, William Thomas, Dec 18 1917 Sex:M Child# 2 William Howard Nashua, NH & Grace McDermott Nashua, NH
HOWARD, Woodbury, May 10 1902 Sex:M Child# 1 Charles W Howard Nashua, NH & Blanche L Baldwin Nashua, NH
HOWARTH, Anderton, Aug 26 1913 Sex:M Child# 3 Albert Howarth England & Rosie Gallogly Ireland
HOWARTH, Annie, Dec 17 1911 Sex:F Child# 3 John W Howarth England & Elizabeth Wilkinson England
HOWARTH, Gerald Edward, May 12 1919 Sex:M Child# 1 Herbert Howarth England & Lucile W Buswell Nashua, NH
HOWARTH, Harold, Dec 29 1911 Sex:M Child# 4 J William Howarth England & Elizabeth Wilkinson England
HOWE, Alan Francis, Nov 12 1933 Sex:M Child# 1 Elmer F Howe Boston, MA & D Hanscomb Hudson, NH
HOWE, Charles Raymond, Apr 3 1928 Sex:M Child# 1 Raymond Howe Mass & Mary Buckley Nashua, NH Stillborn
HOWE, Evelyn Mae, Mar 20 1930 Sex:F Child# 1 Robert Howe Ipswich, NH & Rose Curtis Lyndeborough, NH
HOWE, Frank Herbert, Mar 16 1926 Sex:M Child# 1 Everett W Howe Ipswich, MA & Margaret Callahan Nashua, NH
HOWE, Harvey, Jun 5 1893 Sex:M Child# 1 Harvey Howe Canada & Catherine Doran Canada
HOWE, Kathryn Louise, Nov 9 1931 Sex:F Child# 2 Robert Henry Howe Ipswich, MA & Rosie Curtis Lyndeboro, NH
HOWE, Leonard John, Jul 15 1921 Sex:M Child# 1 Roy Howe Vermont & Gertrude Gray Nashua, NH
HOWE, Mary Elizabeth, Mar 22 1928 Sex:F Child# 2 Everett W Howe Ipswich, MA & Margaret Callahan Nashua, NH
HOWE, Mary Gertrude, Aug 31 1920 Sex:F Child# 1 Chester L Howe Cambridge, MA & Jessie R Fogg N Hampton, NH
HOWE, Richard Augustus, Oct 22 1929 Sex:M Child# 2 Raymond Howe Ipswich, MA & Mary Buckley Nashua, NH
HOWE, Robert Leonard, May 18 1929 Sex:M Child# 3 Everett W Howe Ipswich, MA & Margaret Callahan Nashua, NH
HOWE, Roberta Rose, May 13 1933 Sex:F Child# 3 Robert H Howe Ipswich, MA & Rose H Curtis Lyndeboro, NH
HOWE, William Robinson, Sep 27 1920 Sex:M Child# 1 Harry R Howe Mansfield, MA & Adonelle L Wilson Cranston, RI
HOWELL, Beverly Anne, Feb 26 1930 Sex:F Child# 1 Clarence Howell St Petersburg, FL & Blanche Lockhard Nashua, NH
HOWLAND, Mary Agnesse, Mar 20 1896 Sex:F Child# 2 A Howland
HOWLETT, Clairemale E, Apr 3 1919 Sex:F Child# 8 Arthur H Howlett Ashford, CT & Edna Wolcott Cavendish, VT
HOWLETT, Eunice Fairbanks, Jun 6 1917 Sex:F Child# 7 A H Howlett Askford, CT & Edna Wolcott Cavendish, VT
HOWLETT, Lillis Emily, Feb 2 1913 Sex:F Child# 4 Arthur Henry Howlett Ashfort, CT & Edna Wolcott Cavendish, VT
HOWLETT, Merle Vinton, Oct 23 1914 Sex:M Child# 5 Arthur H Howlett Ashford, CT & Edna A Wolcott Cavendish, VT
HOWLETT, Unknown, May 5 1916 Sex:M Child# 5 Arthur Howlett Ashford, CT & Edna Wolcott Cavendish, VT
HOWLEY, Henry, Jul 19 1912 Sex:M Child# 1 William T Howley E Weymouth, MA & Lydia V Kelley Brooklyn, NY
HOWORTH, Bernice Alberta, Jul 13 1910 Sex:F Child# 6 Thomas E Howorth England & Jane E Holt England
HOWORTH, Virginia Lucille, Oct 6 1922 Sex:F Child# 2 Herbert Howorth England & Lucille W Buswell Nashua, NH
HOWORTH, Walter, Jul 12 1910 Sex:M Child# 2 John W Howorth England & Elizabeth Wilkinson England
HOYT, Charlotte Eve, Jul 30 1931 Sex:F Child# 1 Reginald Hoyt Epping, NH & Mildred Tamalonis Nashua, NH Stillborn
HOYT, Harold Ernest, Apr 15 1902 Sex:M Child# 2 Ralph E Hoyt Maine & Bertha Wheeler Nashua, NH
HOYT, John Elliott, May 18 1935 Sex:M Child# 2 Reginald W Hoyt W Epping, NH & Lucy Demers Lowell, MA
HOYT, Reginald Paul, Jul 7 1933 Sex:M Child# 1 Reginald Hoyt W Epping, NH & Lucy Demers Lowell, MA
HOYT, Unknown, May 30 1891 Sex:F Child# 8 Fred P Hoyt Kittery, ME & Auguste Portsmouth, NH
HOYT, Yvonne, Aug 6 1906 Sex:F Child# 1 Ernest Hoyt Maine & Aime Chamberlain Canada
HUARD, Agnes Louise, Mar 2 1921 Sex:F Child# 2 Alfred Huard Lewiston, ME & Katherine Young Jefferson, IN
HUARD, George Ray, Jun 20 1900 Sex:M Child# 4 Gustave Huard Canada & Bertha Hart Maine
HUARD, Hazel Olive, Jan 8 1902 Sex:F Child# 6 Gustave A Huard Canada & Bertha G Hart Canada
HUARD, Joseph William, Jan 14 1925 Sex:M Child# 3 Alfred Huard Lewiston, ME & Kath Young Jefferson, IN
HUARD, Patrick, Nov 21 1929 Sex:M Child# 3 Joseph Huard NH & Blanche Martel NH
HUARD, Pauline, Jul 22 1931 Sex:F Child# 4 Joseph Huard NH & Blanche Martel NH
HUARD, Robert Wallace, Mar 19 1931 Sex:M Child# 4 Alfred Huard Lewiston, ME & Catherine Young Jeffersonville, IN
HUARD, Shirley Anne, Nov 10 1935 Sex:F Child# 5 Alfred Huard Maine & Katherine Young Indiana
HUBER, Paul Bickford, Aug 8 1934 Sex:M Child# 2 Richard A Huber Pawtucket, RI & Helen Bickford Nashua, NH
HUBERN, Brony, Aug 10 1910 Sex:F Child# 2 Bennie Hubern Russia & Karos Youkoviski Russia
HUBERT, Denis, May 13 1889 Sex:M Child# 7 Barthelemi Hubert Canada & Eugenie Bibeau Canada
HUBERT, Joseph H A, Nov 9 1896 Sex:M Child# 15 Charles Hubert Canada & Louisa Brodeur Northfield
HUDINE, Agnes C, Oct 15 1892 Sex:F Child# 2 James Hudine Nashua, NH & Mary A Reynolds Nashua, NH

HUDINE, Mary Ann, Sep 20 1891 Sex:F Child# 1 James Hudine Nashua, NH & Mary A Reynolds Nashua, NH
HUDINE, Robert Edward, May 23 1897 Sex:M Child# 3 James Hudine Nashua, NH & Mary Ann Reynolds Nashua, NH
HUDINE, Unknown, Nov 25 1935 Sex:F Child# 1 Howard Hudine Nashua, NH & Kathleen Birchall Nashua, NH Stillborn
HUDON, Annette, Jul 7 1934 Sex:F Child# 3 Philippe Hudon Canada & Leona Bernier Canada
HUDON, Bertrand Ernest Jos, Jun 12 1926 Sex:M Child# 1 Wilbrod Hudon Canada & Marie L Dionne Salem, MA
HUDON, Claire Pauline, Sep 27 1933 Sex:F Child# 1 Antonio Hudon Nashua, NH & Clarina Leblanc Canada
HUDON, Clairmont, Apr 6 1905 Sex:M Child# 9 Thomas Hudon Canada & Celanire Cantin Canada
HUDON, Elaine, Sep 24 1934 Sex:F Child# 2 Alphonse Hudon Canada & Valida Gabriel Canada
HUDON, Emma Jeanne, Jul 10 1909 Sex:F Child# 11 Thomas Hudon Canada & Celanire Cantin Canada
HUDON, Ephrem Albert, Mar 21 1903 Sex:M Child# 8 Thomas Hudon Canada & Celanire Cantin Canada
HUDON, Eva, Mar 4 1900 Sex:F Child# 6 Thomas Hudon Canada & Celanire Quentin Canada
HUDON, Evelyn Gloria, Nov 16 1920 Sex:F Child# 6 Alfred Hudon Canada & Blanche Desmarais Nashua, NH
HUDON, Francis, Feb 28 1918 Sex:F Child# 2 Alfred E Hudon Nashua, NH & Blanche Desmarais Nashua, NH
HUDON, Frank Eugene Victor, Feb 11 1924 Sex:M Child# 3 Theodore Hudon Nashua, NH & Eva St Onge Nashua, NH
HUDON, Genevieve Bets, Jan 3 1898 Sex:F Child# 5 Thomas Hudon Quebec & Celanire Cantin Quebec
HUDON, Gerard, Jul 31 1912 Sex:M Child# 1 Alfred Hudon Berlin, NH & Blanche Desmarais Nashua, NH
HUDON, Homer, Sep 2 1901 Sex:M Child# 7 Thomas Hudon Canada & Celenire Cautin Canada
HUDON, Irene Therese, Apr 6 1922 Sex:F Child# 1 Albert Hudon Canada & Laurence Belanger Canada
HUDON, Jos Norbert Clement, Nov 23 1922 Sex:M Child# 3 Jos Charles Hudon Nashua, NH & Georgianna Morin Canada
HUDON, Joseph, Oct 8 1928 Sex:M Child# 2 Wilfrid Hudon Canada & Leona Bernier Canada
HUDON, Larraine Carmel, Feb 17 1917 Sex:F Child# 2 Alfred E Hudon US & Blanche C Desmarais US
HUDON, Leo, Jr, Jul 3 1927 Sex:M Child# 1 Leo Hudon Nashua, NH & Dorothy Clemons Nashua, NH
HUDON, Louis Edgar E, Oct 13 1911 Sex:M Child# 2 Joseph Hudon Nashua, NH & Georgianna Morin Canada
HUDON, Ludger Maurice, Oct 29 1928 Sex:M Child# 1 Ludger Hudon Nashua, NH & Eva Vien Canada
HUDON, Marie Aurore, Sep 23 1900 Sex:F Child# 5 Alphonse Hudon Canada & Cesarie Poulin Canada
HUDON, Marie Louise A, Jun 13 1933 Sex:F Child# 2 Ludger Hudon Nashua, NH & Eva Viens Canada
HUDON, Marie Theresa Y, Aug 10 1929 Sex:F Child# 2 Maxine Hudon Nashua, NH & Regina Pineault Nashua, NH
HUDON, Mary Simone L, Jul 13 1910 Sex:F Child# 1 Joseph Hudon Nashua, NH & Georgina Morin Canada
HUDON, Ralph Henri, Aug 6 1908 Sex:M Child# 10 Thomas Hudon Canada & Celanire Quentin Canada
HUDON, Ralph Maurice, Apr 20 1928 Sex:M Child# 1 Maxime Hudon Nashua, NH & Regina Peno Nashua, NH
HUDON, Raymond Theodore, Aug 16 1930 Sex:M Child# 6 Theodore Hudon Nashua, NH & Eva St Onge Nashua, NH
HUDON, Raymond Wilbrod, Jan 1 1928 Sex:M Child# 2 Wilbrod Hudon Canada & Louise Dionne Salem, MA
HUDON, Rita Claire, Apr 27 1918 Sex:F Child# 1 Theodore E Hudon Nashua, NH & Eva O St Onge Nashua, NH
HUDON, Roland Addison, Dec 4 1933 Sex:M Child# 3 Maxine Hudon Hudson, NH & Regina Peno Nashua, NH
HUDON, Sylvia Eloise, Oct 17 1928 Sex:F Child# 5 Theodore Hudon Nashua, NH & Eva St Onge Nashua, NH
HUDON, Theodore Eugene, Jan 2 1896 Sex:M Child# 4 Thomas Hudon Canada & Ceneline Cantin Canada
HUDON, Theresa Olena, Aug 24 1921 Sex:F Child# 2 Theodore E Hudon Nashua, NH & Eva O St Onge Nashua, NH
HUDON, Unknown, Sep 16 1904 Sex:F Child# 7 Alphonse Hudon Canada & Cesarie Poulin Canada Stillborn
HUDON, Unknown, Jul 2 1919 Sex:F Child# Alfred E Hudon Berlin, NH & Blanches C Desmarais Nashua, NH
HUDON, Ursula Dolores, Oct 6 1926 Sex:F Child# 4 Theodore Hudon Nashua, NH & Eva St Onge Nashua, NH
HUDON, Yvette Jacqueline, Apr 23 1930 Sex:F Child# 3 Philippe Hudon Canada & Leona Bernier Canada
HUDSON, Charles Prosper, May 22 1891 Sex:M Child# 6 Isaac C Hudson E Haven, VT & Flora Shattuck Milford
HUDSON, Eva O, Apr 18 1895 Sex:F Child# 3 I C Hudson Vermont & Flora Shattuck NH
HUDSON, Marie Geraldine, Mar 27 1931 Sex:F Child# 1 Alphonse Hudson Canada & Valida Gabriel Canada
HUDSON, Valeda Carolyn, Feb 26 1932 Sex:F Child# 1 G E Hudson Sullivan, IL & Lillian Ljungquist Worcester, MA
HUFF, Arthur Schuyler, Mar 29 1905 Sex:M Child# 2 Schuyler Huff Seneca Falls, NY & Hattie Currier Busher Falls
HUFF, Elizabeth Gertrude, Feb 16 1921 Sex:F Child# 1 Roy L Huff Nashua, NH & Lucille B Brien Nashua, NH
HUFF, Howard William, Jun 8 1904 Sex:M Child# 1 Selden Huff Wellington, ME & Ida Dorey Nova Scotia
HUFF, Kenneth Schuyler, Feb 7 1927 Sex:M Child# 3 Roy L Huff Nashua, NH & Lucille B Brian Nashua, NH
HUFF, Leonard Edward, Mar 7 1925 Sex:M Child# 2 Roy L Huff Nashua, NH & Lucille Brien Nashua, NH
HUFF, Robert Arthur, Sep 20 1930 Sex:M Child# 1 Arthur S Huff Nashua, NH & Eunice Blanchard Marlboro, MA
HUFF, Unknown, May 12 1901 Sex:M Child# 1 Schuyler J Huff Seneca Falls, NY & Hattie Currier Bracker Falls, NY
HUGHES, Barnett Lester, Jun 21 1921 Sex:M Child# 2 Elmer C Hughes Ashland, NH & Mae W White Nashua, NH
HUGHES, Lottie, Mar 1 1888 Sex:F Child# 2 Thomas F Hughes Dover & Jennie Williams St Johnsbury, VT
HUGHES, Unknown, Mar 23 1920 Sex:M Child# 1 Elmer Hughes Ashland, NH & Mae White Nashua, NH Stillborn
HUGRON, Gertrude Rose, Jun 25 1922 Sex:F Child# 2 Leon F Hugron Highgate, VT & Beatrice Thibodeau Haverhill, MA
HUGULY, Unknown, Jun 6 1888 Sex:M Child# 3 Patrick Huguly Ireland & Mary Huguly Ireland
HUJSAK, Stanley, Apr 26 1933 Sex:M Child# 11 Stanley Hujsak Poland & Zofia Bednary Poland
HUJSAK, Thomas Paul, Aug 1 1935 Sex:M Child# 12 Stanley Hujsak Poland & Sophie Bednarz Poland
HULL, Unknown, Apr 6 1901 Sex:F Child# 5 Thomas H Hull Canada & Margaret McLean Canada
HUMPHRIES, Richard John, Feb 2 1910 Sex:M Child# 1 Thomas R Humphries Ireland & Agnes E Walsh S Manchester, CT
HUNNEWELL, Muriel, Feb 12 1924 Sex:F Child# 1 Ralph Hunnewell Watertown, MA & Josephine Flanagan Lowell, MA
HUNNEWELL, Ralph Edward, Jr, Apr 1 1925 Sex:M Child# 2 R Hunnewell Watertown, MA & Jose Flanagan Lowell, MA
HUNT, Anna A, Jul 25 1897 Sex:F Child# 1 Fred Hunt Westford, MA & Bertha Smith Nashua, NH
HUNT, Dorothy, Mar 18 1902 Sex:F Child# 5 Albert Hunt Stoddard, NH & Mary Day Essex, VT
HUNT, Dorothy E, Jun 15 1904 Sex:F Child# 1 Arthur W Hunt Randolph, ME & Lillian M Hunt Randolph, ME
HUNT, Edna Day, Jan 26 1896 Sex:F Child# 2 Albert Hunt Stoddard & May Day Vermont
HUNT, Ethel M, Jan 15 1888 Sex:F Child# 3 Albert H Hunt Stoddard & Ida F Hunt Winchester
HUNT, Harland, May 29 1894 Sex:M Child# 2 Albert Hunt NH & Mary A Day Vermont
HUNT, Jane, Mar 28 1916 Sex:F Child# 1 Albert Henry Hunt Winchester, NH & Mabel Clare Hunt Camden, NJ
HUNT, Marion Louise, Sep 29 1924 Sex:F Child# 4 Herman Hunt Windall, MA & Hazel Jackson E Jaffrey, NH
HUNT, Marjorie, May 25 1900 Sex:F Child# 3 Albert Hunt Stoddard, NH & Mary A Day Vermont
HUNT, Ralph, Nov 23 1898 Sex:M Child# Albert Hunt Stoddard, NH & Mary A Day Vermont

HUNT, Ruth, Feb 7 1918 Sex:F Child# 2 Albert Henry Hunt Winchester & Mabel Hunt Camden, NJ
HUNT, Unknown, Mar 17 1900 Sex:M Child# 1 Fred R Hunt ME & Emma L Thorn ME
HUNTER, Walter, Jul 13 1910 Sex:M Child# 1 Carl Hunter Providence, RI & Alice Brittin Marlow, NH
HUNTINGTON, Anna May, Jul 9 1893 Sex:F Child# 3 Charles A Huntington Nashua, NH & Kate I Fuller Maine
HUNTINGTON, Barbara Claire, Aug 3 1924 Sex:F Child# 1 C E Huntington Newburyport, MA & Dorothy Small Nashua, NH
HUNTINGTON, Bessie May, Aug 8 1892 Sex:F Child# 2 Edward P Huntington Nashua, NH & Grace L Flanders Nashua, NH
HUNTINGTON, Charles Alfred, Sep 18 1889 Sex:M Child# 1 E T Huntington Nashua, NH & Grace Flanders Nashua, NH
HUNTINGTON, Helen A, Apr 7 1889 Sex:F Child# 2 C A Huntington Nashua, NH & Kate I Fuller Nashua, NH
HUNTINGTON, Isabella F, Mar 31 1895 Sex:F Child# 1 C A Huntington Nashua, NH & Kate I Fuller Maine
HUNTINGTON, Marion Louise, Jul 25 1920 Sex:F Child# 1 Rodney Huntington Nashua, NH & Hattie Rockwell Hancock, NH
HUNTLEY, Unknown, Oct 22 1908 Sex:M Child# 3 Herman B Huntley Canada & Adelaide L Tasker Lawrence, MA
HUNTOON, Unknown, Sep 11 1889 Sex:M Child# 1 Frank H Huntoon Leominster, NH & Susie M Hoyt Hillsboro Bridge
HUNTOON, Unknown, Mar 18 1891 Sex:F Child# 2 Frank H Huntoon Leominster, MA & Susie M Hoyt Hillsboro Bridge
HURD, Anna May, Feb 17 1918 Sex:F Child# 1 George E Hurd Nashua, NH & Nora McCarvill Prince Edward Island
HURD, Horace Robert, Jul 13 1935 Sex:M Child# 1 Horace Hurd Manchester, NH & Doris Green Nashua, NH
HURD, Jennette Arlene, Aug 25 1919 Sex:F Child# 2 George E Hurd Nashua, NH & Nora McCarvell Prince Edward Island
HURD, June, Aug 22 1925 Sex:F Child# 5 George E Hurd Nashua, NH & Nora McCarville Prince Edw Island
HURD, June Carole, Mar 25 1935 Sex:F Child# 1 Harold Hurd Peterboro, NH & Lillian Hawkins Peterboro, NH
HURD, Marjorie Phyllis, Jun 29 1921 Sex:F Child# 3 George E Hurd Nashua, NH & Nora McCarvill Prince Edward Island
HURD, Ruth Dorothy, Dec 30 1923 Sex:F Child# 4 George E Hurd Nashua, NH & Nora McCarville Prince Edw Island
HURD, Unknown, Jul 6 1887 Sex:F Child# 6 John Hurd Pembroke & Luella Richardson Pembroke Stillborn
HURD, Unknown, Jul 10 1894 Sex:M Child# 1 Nelson Hurd Nashua, NH & Maud E New York, NY
HURLBURT, Edward Donald, Feb 18 1923 Sex:M Child# 1 Irving Hurlburt Warrent, VT & Helen Hagerty Ireland
HURLBURT, Evelyn Lucile, Jul 25 1917 Sex:F Child# 1 Frank E Hurlburt W Gardner, ME & Helen M Hutchins Rumford, ME
HURLBURT, Francis Irving, Mar 26 1924 Sex:M Child# 2 Irving Hurlburt Warren, VT & Helen Haggerty Ireland
HURLEY, Anna Frances, Aug 30 1922 Sex:F Child# 6 Thomas Hurley Milford, NJ & Anna Cooley Wilton, NH
HURLEY, Corinne Frances, Jun 28 1928 Sex:F Child# 4 John T Hurley Wilton, NH & Louise Dunn Boston, MA
HURLEY, Genieve, Sep 20 1889 Sex:F Child# 2 Mike Hurley New York & Mary Dillon Vermont
HURLEY, Jean, Dec 23 1928 Sex:F Child# 1 Joseph E Hurley Wilton, NH & Louise W Dee Caribou, ME
HURLEY, John Edward, Jul 11 1889 Sex:M Child# 2 Patrick Hurley Milford, NH & Mary E Sullivan Nashua, NH
HURLEY, Mary, Aug 1 1887 Sex:F Child# 1 Mike D Hurley NY & Mary Dilon Rutland, VT
HURLEY, Mary Adele, Jan 31 1922 Sex:F Child# 1 William A Hurley Salem, MA & Yvonne Gagnon Nashua, NH
HURLEY, William Edward, Apr 18 1894 Sex:M Child# 4 Michael Hurley NY & Mary Dillon Rutland, VT
HUSE, Charles G, Aug 22 1899 Sex:M Child# 1 Murdock D Huse NH & Katie E Neely NY
HUSE, Donald Earl, Jun 13 1913 Sex:M Child# 3 Sephen S Huse, Jr Amesbury, MA & Helen Thompson Morristown, NJ
HUSKA, Florette Pauline, Oct 5 1929 Sex:F Child# 2 Silverus Huska Austria & Eva Rose Belanger Canada
HUSSEY, Olive Frances, Aug 11 1908 Sex:F Child# 2 Oliver P Hussey Nashua, NH & Anna F Barnes Nashua, NH
HUSSEY, Oliver Webster, Sep 18 1906 Sex:M Child# 1 Oliver P Hussey Nashua, NH & Anna F Barnes Nashua, NH
HUSSEY, Unknown, Sep 7 1890 Sex:M Child# 5 Webster P Hussey Nashua, NH & Ellen Avery Ware, MA
HUSSEY, Unknown, Sep 23 1890 Sex:M Child# 1 Oren P Hussey Nashua, NH & Margie Gregg Wilton, NH
HUSSEY, Webster Merriam, Aug 5 1911 Sex:M Child# 8 Oliver F Hussey Nashua, NH & Anna F Barnes Nashua, NH
HUTCHINS, Francis Byron, Jr, Jan 9 1911 Sex:M Child# 1 Francis B Hutchins Haverhill, MA & Doris E Davidson Nashua
HUTCHINS, Unknown, Sep 14 1888 Sex:F Child# 1 George A Hutchins Methuen, MA & Margaret A Lyons Lawrence, MA
HUTCHINSON, Donald Craig, Oct 18 1934 Sex:M Child# 1 Harold C Hutchinson Wilton, NH & Grace Ramsdell Rumford, ME
HUTCHINSON, Elizabeth Ann, Aug 8 1934 Sex:F Child# 2 Bernard Hutchinson Milford, NH & Mary Paradis Milford, NH
HUTCHINSON, Evelyn, Jan 11 1913 Sex:F Child# 2 Will Hutchinson Milford, NH & Lizzie E Woodward Buckland, MA
HUTCHINSON, Jean Lillian, Oct 28 1934 Sex:F Child# 7 Fred Hutchinson Keene, NH & Kathryn Doyle Amherst, NH
HUTCHINSON, Joan, Jun 10 1925 Sex:F Child# 1 Paul Hutchinson Milford, NH & Doris Stranach Hanover, NH
HUTCHINSON, Marilyn, Jul 18 1925 Sex:F Child# 1 E Hutchinson Milford, NH & Marie Paradis Milford, NH
HUTCHINSON, Paul Fred, Jun 20 1927 Sex:M Child# 2 Paul Hutchinson Milford, NH & Doris Stronach Hanover, NH
HUTCHINSON, Unknown, Nov 13 1888 Sex:M Child# 2 Willis M Hutchinson Wilton & Hattie A Emma Swanzey
HUTCHINSON, Unknown, Mar 14 1891 Sex:F Child# 3 Willis M Hutchinson Wilton & Hattie A Earnes Swansey
HUTTON, Imelda Jacqueline, Jul 22 1924 Sex:F Child# 1 Albert D Hutton Lawrence, MA & Imelda Pellerin Lawrence, MA
HUTTON, Roberta Paula, Mar 11 1928 Sex:F Child# 2 Albert Hutton Lawrence, MA & Imilda Pellerin Lawrence, MA
HYDE, George Millett, Dec 1 1912 Sex:M Child# 2 Edward L Hyde Ayer, MA & Eva J Leclerc Canada
HYDE, Unknown, Mar 24 1917 Sex:M Child# 3 Edward Hyde Ayer Jct, MA & Eva J LeClaire Stanford, Quebec
HYSETTE, Armand Arthur, Nov 4 1920 Sex:M Child# 1 Arthur Hysette Nashua, NH & Aurore Anger Canada
HYSETTE, Charles Eugene, Dec 28 1929 Sex:M Child# 3 Arthur Hysette Nashua, NH & Aurore Angers Canada
HYSETTE, Florence Lorette, Jul 3 1924 Sex:F Child# 2 Arthur Hysette Nashua, NH & Aurore Alger Nashua, NH
IACONE, Mildred Ellen, Sep 6 1932 Sex:F Child# 2 Romeo S Iacone Boston, MA & Mildred MacLean Stoughton, MA
IACONO, Louis, Jr, Oct 3 1931 Sex:M Child# 1 Louis Iacono
IAKUREK, Tolflie, Dec 16 1922 Sex:M Child# 1 Tolflie Iakurek Poland Russia & Rose Ventokay Poland Russia
IEUREKE, Agnes, Jan 12 1920 Sex:F Child# 1 Stanley Ieureke Poland & Mary Falkouska Poland
IGO, Mary Cloe, Sep 8 1897 Sex:F Child# 2 John Igo Scotland & Hattie Bourey NY
IKXEN, Julia, Nov 7 1903 Sex:F Child# 3 Michael Ikxen Russia & Catherina Krusch Russia
ILCAWICH, John, Dec 5 1913 Sex:M Child# 5 Frank Jlcawich Russia & Rosie Merskiuta Russia
IMBO, George, May 13 1890 Sex:M Child# 7 Isaac Imbo Canada & Eulalie Pilor Canada
INGALLS, Francis Winthrop, Oct 2 1908 Sex:M Child# 1 Arthur Ingalls
INGALLS, Homer Sanderson, Mar 14 1931 Sex:M Child# 1 Floyd S Ingalls Heuvelton, NY & Ellen Poland Etna, NH
INGHAM, George Law, Nov 5 1916 Sex:M Child# 1 Harry Ed Ingham Lowell, MA & Mabel Vesta Law Nashua, NH
INGHAM, Unknown, Jul 13 1893 Sex:M Child# 4 Thomas J Ingham Birstall, England & Emma F Butterworth Lawrence, MA
INGHAM, Unknown, Oct 30 1897 Sex:F Child# 1 James R Ingham England & Bertha Fowell Nashua, NH
INGIAN, Aronsyaj Leona, Sep 7 1929 Sex:F Child# 2 Leo Ingian Nashua, NH & Zaraut Tomasian Nashua, NH

INGRAM, Arthur Frederick, Oct 8 1919 Sex:M Child# 1 Arthur F Ingram Montague, MA & Jennie A Lavery Derry, NH
INHAUD, Michand, Mar 10 1888 Sex:M Child# 15 Germain Inhaud Canada & Adlaide Level Canada Stillborn
INJANIAN, Sovan, Jun 3 1902 Sex:M Child# V M Injanian
INJIAN, Shou Shan V, Mar 7 1904 Sex:F Child# 2 Harry Injian Armenia & Arosiag Topalian Armenia
INNESS, Marilyn Elaine, Oct 19 1929 Sex:F Child# 2 Percy Inness Nova Scotia & Vivian Cross Hudson, NH
INNESS, Robert Willoughby, Aug 20 1922 Sex:M Child# 1 Percy W Inness Hantsport, NS & Vivian Cross Hudson, NH
IRAUNDRIAM, Hector, Dec 8 1888 Sex:M Child# 1 Joseph Iraundriam Canada & Marceline Gayon Canada
IRMALAVITCH, Ludwiss, Apr 24 1911 Sex:F Child# 1 Joseph Irmalavitch Russia & Eva Schlesinuta Russia
IRMALAWICZ, Bolislav, Nov 20 1921 Sex:M Child# 2 Louis Irmalawicz Poland & Josie Petka Poland
IRMALAWICZ, Marcella, Jul 29 1922 Sex:F Child# 6 Adam Irmalawicz Poland & Amelia Markiewicz Poland
IRMALAWICZ, William, Aug 27 1921 Sex:M Child# 9 Joseph Irmalawicz Lithuania & Eva Slatonnas Lithuania
IRMALOWICZ, Thadeus, Feb 18 1926 Sex:M Child# 4 Julian Irmalowicz Poland & Josephine Pytka Poland
IRMELA, Alphonse, Jun 20 1918 Sex:M Child# 1 Julius Irmela Russia & Theophila Sepanta Russia
IRMELA, Anastasia, Oct 7 1919 Sex:F Child# 3 Julius Irmela Russia & Theo Sepenta Russia
IRMELA, Lena, Jun 20 1918 Sex:F Child# 2 Julius Irmela Russia & Theophila Sepanta Russia
IRVINE, Barbara Lillian, Jan 31 1925 Sex:F Child# 2 Frank L Irvine Nashua, NH & Rosalyn Birchall Nashua, NH
IRVINE, Frank Lawrence, Aug 29 1934 Sex:M Child# 3 Frank Irvine Nashua, NH & Rosalyn Birchall Nashua, NH
IRVINE, Marjorie Jane, Jul 1 1921 Sex:F Child# 1 Thomas Irvine England & Rose Birchall Nashua, NH
IRVINE, Nellie D, Mar 27 1901 Sex:F Child# 2 Robert J Irvine St Johns, NB & Hermine Belanger Nashua, NH
IRVING, Frank Lawrence, Jan 24 1897 Sex:M Child# 1 Robert G Irving St John & Ermie Belanger Mass
IRWIN, George Alexander, Oct 8 1893 Sex:M Child# 2 John Irwin Ireland & Clara Davis Canada
ISABELL, Lorraine Rolande, Sep 6 1934 Sex:F Child# 1 Roland Isabell Nashua, NH & Lillian Ross Canada
ISABELLE, Aurelie Lucille, Jul 4 1910 Sex:F Child# 4 Simeon Isabelle Canada & Lucie Bousquet Nashua, NH
ISABELLE, Claire, Oct 1 1930 Sex:F Child# 1 Gerard Isabelle Canada & Alda Morin Berlin, NH
ISABELLE, Ina Aldea, Dec 2 1906 Sex:F Child# 3 Simeon Isabelle Canada & Lucie Bousquet Nashua, NH
ISABELLE, Jeanne C, Jul 24 1919 Sex:f Child# 5 Simon Isabelle Canada & Lucie Bousquet Nashua, NH
ISABELLE, Roland Wilfred, Dec 25 1904 Sex:M Child# 2 Simeon Isabelle Canada & Lucie Bousquet Nashua, NH
ISENBECK, Dorothy C A, Jan 29 1897 Sex:F Child# 1 Charles A Isenbeck Wisconsin & Laura W Henderson Boston, MA
ISKIGIAN, Las Edward, May 29 1910 Sex:M Child# 1 Samuel Iskigian Asia & Flora Savortian Asia
ITEN, Laurence Earlemore, Oct 26 1920 Sex:M Child# 1 Edwin E Iten Pepperell, MA & Caroline Harrison Newburyport, MA
ITEN, Ramona Adeline, Apr 14 1931 Sex:F Child# 1 Edwin Edward Iten Pepperell, MA & Charlotte Jensen Everett, MA
IVALES, Unknown, Aug 3 1926 Sex:F Child# 5 William Ivales Greece & Helen Adams Greece
IVALIS, Unknown, Aug 30 1933 Sex:F Child# 7 B G Ivalis Greece & Helen Adams Greece
IVAN, Carol, Dec 18 1935 Sex:F Child# 1 Ray E Ivan Nashua, NH & Jule Kelly New York, NY Stillborn
IVANOSKI, Julius, Jul 27 1917 Sex:M Child# 2 Gabriel Ivanoski Russia & Mathia Dronztute Russia
IVARNOFF, John, Nov 13 1916 Sex:M Child# 5 Varsil Ivarnoff Russia & Annie Lopartin Russia
IVERS, William Johnston, Sep 15 1892 Sex:M Child# 2 James F Ivers Manchester, NH & Helen May Hooksett, NH
IVES, Charles William, Sep 30 1930 Sex:M Child# 6 Merrill Ives Chazy, NY & Bessie Bell Chazy, NY
IVES, Earl Lester, Dec 23 1925 Sex:M Child# 4 Merrill M Ives Mooers, NY & Bessie Bell Chazy, NY
IVES, Howard Franklin, Nov 25 1921 Sex:M Child# 2 Merrill M Ives Mooers, NY & Bessie J Bell Chazy, NY
IVES, Priscilla Mae, May 19 1928 Sex:F Child# 5 Merrill M Ives Chazy, NY & Bessie Bell Chazy, NY
IVES, Ruth Esther, Feb 6 1934 Sex:F Child# 7 Merrill Ives Chazy, NY & Bessie Burnice Chazy, NY
IVIDS, George, Feb 12 1920 Sex:M Child# 2 Vasilias J Ivids Greece & Helene Lookdorm Greece
IVIS, Beatrice Ethel, Sep 24 1920 Sex:F Child# 1 Merril M Ivis New York & Bessie Bell New York
IVON, Adelard Alfred, Jul 28 1897 Sex:M Child# 1 Adelard Ivon Canada & Emma Boucher Canada
IVON, Henri, Feb 14 1896 Sex:M Child# 5 Joseph Ivon Canada & Zepherina Gagnon Canada
IVON, Joseph, Jun 26 1899 Sex:M Child# 2 Adelard Ivon Canada & Aimee Boucher Canada
IVON, Raymond Ernest, Feb 18 1908 Sex:M Child# 3 Samuel Ivon Canada & Ida Collette New York
JACINTHA, Clare Moquin, May 24 1928 Sex:F Child# 1 Joseph Jacintha Middleboro, MA & Annie Moquin Wilton, NH
JACKMAN, Beatrice A Gould, Mar 3 1911 Sex:F Child# 1 (No Parents Listed)
JACKMAN, Thomas, Aug 7 1895 Sex:M Child# 3 James A Jackman Merrimack, NH & Lilla F Mason Peterboro, NH
JACKSON, Armine, Mar 3 1920 Sex:F Child# 2 Elmer Jackson Hamdon, ME & Emma Rousseau Canada
JACKSON, Ester Howard, Oct 7 1900 Sex:F Child# Lester Jackson Mass & Jennie McLane NY
JACKSON, Frank Henry, Jun 25 1934 Sex:M Child# 10 James Jackson Chateaugay, NY & Dorothy P Woodley New York
JACKSON, Helen, Aug 16 1912 Sex:F Child# 1 George F Jackson Nova Scotia & Clara M Smith Nashua, NH
JACKSON, Helene Alice Annette, Jul 29 1928 Sex:F Child# 3 J Wm Jackson Nashua, NH & Marie Chouniere Lowell, MA
JACKSON, John, Mar 1 1890 Sex:M Child# 1 John Jackson NJ & Helene Laramie Canada
JACKSON, John Stonewall, Jul 8 1924 Sex:M Child# 4 John Jackson Nashua, NH & Marie Clouriere Nashua, NH
JACKSON, John William, Mar 19 1900 Sex:M Child# 5 John J Jackson NJ & Helene Laraine Canada
JACKSON, Julia, Sep 17 1892 Sex:F Child# 3 John J Jackson Nashua, NH & Helene Larance Canada
JACKSON, Loraine Julia, Aug 12 1929 Sex:F Child# 4 John W Jackson Nashua, NH & Marie Chouiniere Lowell, MA
JACKSON, M Helene, Sep 12 1895 Sex:F Child# 4 John Jackson New Jersey & Helene Laramee Canada
JACKSON, Marie Lila, Jan 29 1891 Sex:F Child# 2 John Jackson New Jersey & Helene Lawrence Canada
JACKSON, Milton Maurice W, Jun 22 1927 Sex:M Child# 2 J W Jackson Nashua, NH & Marie Chouinere Lowell, MA
JACKSON, Orville Thomas, Jan 24 1920 Sex:M Child# 1 Charles O Jackson Cincinnati, OH & Veronica Callahan St Jo
JACKSON, Richard W, Dec 28 1935 Sex:M Child# 13 James Jackson Chatagua, NY & Dor P Woodley Ogdensburg, NY
JACKSON, Unknown, Oct 25 1890 Sex:F Child# 1 Sears P Jackson Canada & Annie Heal Monson, ME
JACKSON, Unknown, Oct 28 1892 Sex:F Child# 5 John M Jackson Hamden, ME & Maggie A Anthony Kittery, ME
JACKSON, Unknown, Dec 23 1923 Sex:M Child# 9 Elmer E Jackson Kittery, ME & Alma Rousseau Canada Stillborn
JACOBS, Donald, Apr 20 1927 Sex:M Child# 3 Donald S Jacobs Pepperell, MA & M Deware Pepperell, MA
JACOBS, Dorothy, Apr 2 1920 Sex:F Child# 1 Fred M Jacobs W Boylston, MA & Katherine Henry Nashua, NH
JACOBS, Florence, Aug 25 1922 Sex:F Child# 7 Joseph Jacobs Russia & Anna Cross Russia
JACOBS, Joseph, Nov 8 1924 Sex:M Child# 8 Joseph Jacobs Lithuania & Anna Cross Lithuania

JACOBS, Robert Fred, Jul 24 1922 Sex:M Child# 1 Fred N Jacobs W Boylston, MA & Catherine Henry Nashua, NH
JACOBS, Unknown, Jun 22 1923 Sex:F Child# 1 Donald G Jacobs Pepperell, MA & Marguerite M Deware Pepperell, MA
JACOBS, Unknown, Apr 16 1925 Sex:F Child# 2 D G Jacobs Pepperell, MA & Marg Deware Pepperell, MA
JACOBS, Unknown, Dec 5 1931 Sex:M Child# 4 Donald G Jacobs Pepperell, MA & Margarite Deware Pepperell, MA
JACOBS, Unknown, May 14 1933 Sex:M Child# 5 Donald Jacobs Pepperell, MA & M Deware Pepperell, MA
JACQUES, Alfred Alexander, Jul 27 1931 Sex:M Child# 2 Alfred A Jacques Lowell, MA & Yvonne Rodier Nashua, NH
JACQUES, Arthur, Feb 4 1901 Sex:M Child# 7 Moise Jacques Canada & Mrgte Larichaudiere Canada
JACQUES, Barbara Ann Bondonis, Nov 23 1934 Sex:F Child# 1 Phillip Jacques Manchester, NH & Elsie Bondonis Nashua
JACQUES, Denise Jeannette, Jan 15 1928 Sex:F Child# 1 Philip Jacques Nashua, NH & Denise Dambroise Nashua, NH
JACQUES, Giraldine Lorraine, Jul 7 1920 Sex:F Child# 1 Andrew Jacques Manchester, NH & Lorraine Morin Manchester,NH
JACQUES, Louis P A, May 28 1892 Sex:M Child# 1 Louis N Jacques Canada & Alphonsine Dionne Canada
JACQUES, Marie A O, Mar 10 1899 Sex:F Child# 5 Louis N Jacques Canada & Alphonsine Dion Canada
JACQUES, Marie F O, Mar 10 1899 Sex:F Child# 6 Louis N Jacques Canada & Alphonsine Dion Canada
JACQUES, Marie G V, May 6 1897 Sex:F Child# 4 Louis N Jacques Canada & Alphonsine Dion Canada
JACQUES, Paul Ernest, Sep 7 1934 Sex:M Child# 3 Alfred Jacques Lowell, MA & Yvonne Rodier Nashua, NH
JACQUES, Philip Albert, Feb 11 1930 Sex:M Child# 2 Philip Jacques Nashua, NH & Denise Dambroise Nashua, NH
JACQUES, Philippe, Jul 14 1892 Sex:M Child#  Philippe Jacques Canada & Maggie Larichalliere Canada
JACQUES, Unknown, Nov 11 1893 Sex:F Child# 2 N C Jacques Canada & Alphonsine Dion Canada
JACQUES, Unknown, Jun 28 1901 Sex:F Child# 6 Louis N Jacques Canada & Alphonsine Dion Canada Stillborn
JAEDRYGA, Utka, Oct 21 1914 Sex:F Child# 2 Anthony Jaedryga Russia & Ann Kapctun Russia
JAGIELLOVICZ, Dorothy Mary A, Jun 18 1934 Sex:F Child# 1 William Jagiellovicz E Pepperell, MA & Antöinette
JAKENBANSKY, Anna, Feb 26 1907 Sex:F Child# 1 Joseph Jakenbansky Russia & Anna Krigiute Russia
JAKUCIVI, Agatha, Mar 30 1905 Sex:F Child# 1 William Jakucivi Russia & A Sczecurotevicz Russia
JALAIN, Maria Laura, Aug 28 1889 Sex:F Child# 1 Ulriyne Jalain Canada & Valeda Proveanal Canada
JALBERT, Armand Walter, Oct 18 1923 Sex:M Child# 2 Ernest Jalbert Mass & Yvonne Belanger NH
JALBERT, Dolores Jeanne, Apr 7 1933 Sex:F Child# 3 Walter Jalbert Lowell, MA & L Kerouac Nashua, NH
JALBERT, James Edward, Jun 26 1935 Sex:M Child# 2 Joseph Jalbert Canada & Ethel Harvey Nashua, NH
JALBERT, Joseph Eugene R, Apr 29 1930 Sex:M Child# 1 Eugene Jalbert Lowell, MA & Rose Boucher Nashua, NH
JALBERT, Joseph Walter Ludger, Mar 14 1927 Sex:M Child# 2 Walter R Jalbert Lowell, MA & Marie L Kerouac Nashua, NH
JALBERT, Lorette Cecile, Mar 22 1933 Sex:F Child# 4 Aimee Jalbert Canada & Juliette Boivin Canada
JALBERT, Lorraine Therese, Jun 4 1925 Sex:F Child# 1 Walter Jalbert Lowell, MA & Lilianne Kerouac Nashua, NH
JALBERT, Marie Annette Juliet, Mar 2 1925 Sex:F Child# 1 Aime Jalbert Canada & Juliette Boivin Canada
JALBERT, Marie Jeanine Rachel, Aug 28 1935 Sex:F Child# 4 Walter W Jalbert Lowell, MA & Lillianne Kerouac Nashua,NH
JALBERT, Marie Rolande, Jan 20 1932 Sex:F Child# 3 Aime Jalbert Canada & Juliette Potvin Canada
JALBERT, Pauline Noella, Dec 25 1931 Sex:F Child# 2 Victor Jalbert Canada & Claudia Lapierre Canada
JALBERT, Richard Armand, Oct 27 1931 Sex:M Child# 2 Eugene Jalbert Lowell, MA & Rose Boucher Nashua, NH
JALBERT, Roger Fernand, May 16 1929 Sex:M Child# 1 Victor Jalbert Canada & Clarida Luperle Canada
JALBERT, Yvonne, Feb 11 1935 Sex:F Child# 4 Aime Jalbert Canada & Juliette Boivin Vermont
JALINSKI, Anna, Jan 27 1917 Sex:F Child# 4 Stanley Jalinski Russia & Helen Soula Russia
JAMBARD, Aneas, Jul 19 1901 Sex:M Child# 5 Pierre Jambard Nashua, NH & Eleonore Canada
JAMBARD, Cecile Rose de Lima, Jun 24 1912 Sex:F Child# 2 Albert Jambard Nashua, NH & Rose de Lima Lesage Nashua, NH
JAMBARD, Joan Gloria, Apr 16 1933 Sex:F Child# 1 Henry Jambard Nashua, NH & F Levesque Salem, MA
JAMBARD, Joseph, May 13 1929 Sex:M Child# 2 Ralph Jambard Nashua, NH & Eva Lavoie Nashua, NH Stillborn
JAMBARD, Joseph Norman Conrad, Nov 8 1933 Sex:M Child# 3 Ralph Jambard Nashua, NH & Eva Lavoie Nashua, NH
JAMBARD, Lorraine Hazel, Apr 9 1934 Sex:F Child# 2 Theodore Jambard Hollis, NH & Adeline Holt Bennington, NH
JAMBARD, Louis Ernest, May 20 1925 Sex:M Child# 3 Albert H Jambard Nashua, NH & Delina Lesage Nashua, NH
JAMBARD, Marie Rachel Sylvia, Apr 14 1928 Sex:F Child# 1 Ralph Jambard Nashua, NH & Eva Lavoie Nashua, NH
JAMBARD, Noe Henry, Jul 7 1907 Sex:M Child# 1 Albert Jambard Nashua, NH & Delina Lesage Nashua, NH
JAMBARD, Norma Beverley, Jul 18 1932 Sex:F Child# 1 Theo L Jambard Hollis, NH & A Mae Holt Bennington, NH
JAMBARD, Theodore Leo, Aug 7 1906 Sex:M Child# 4 Damas Jambard Nashua, NH & Julie Bouret Rench, NH
JAMES, Edward David, Jan 24 1925 Sex:M Child# 1 Vincent James Groton, MA & Cath Sheehan Roxbury, MA
JAMESON, Horace, Nov 2 1921 Sex:M Child# 4 Edward D Jameson NH & Marion A Knights NH Stillborn
JAMESON, Leona May, Sep 11 1915 Sex:F Child# 1 Edward D Jameson Hooksett, NH & Marion A Knight Merrimack, NH
JANGRAW, Raymond W, Aug 3 1893 Sex:M Child# 1 Selden Jangraw NY & Eliza Morrison NH
JANIOULI, Stavroula, May 1 1919 Sex:F Child# 1 James Janiouli Greece & Mary George Greece
JANKOWSKI, Michael, Sep 16 1920 Sex:M Child# 1 Joseph Jankowski Poland Russia & Eva Jameszewski Poland Russia
JANNOTTE, Theodore George, Jul 5 1928 Sex:M Child# 2 Theo Jannotte Nashua, NH & Beatrice Boilard Nashua, NH
JANOULI, Christos J, Jun 14 1920 Sex:M Child#  James Janouli Greece & Mary Georougos Greece
JANUSZEFSKI, Unknown, Jul 9 1917 Sex:M Child# 11 Kastanty Januszefski Russia & Elizabeth M Popouske Russia
JANUSZEWSKI, Unknown, Oct 4 1900 Sex:F Child#  Charles Januszewski Russia & Mary Zenkicivecz Russia
JAQUES, Marie Rose I, Mar 31 1895 Sex:F Child# 3 Louis N Jaques Canada & Alphonsine Dion Canada
JAQUES, Unknown, Feb 9 1898 Sex:M Child# 5 Moses Jaques Quebec & Maraget Jaques Quebec
JAQUITH, Charles M, Jun 15 1890 Sex:M Child# 2 Clarence E Jaquith NH & Carrie E Barker NH
JAQUITH, Garland, Sep 14 1934 Sex:M Child# 1 Walter F Jaquith Nashua, NH & Sylvia G Garland Nashua, NH
JAQUITH, Harold, May 25 1888 Sex:M Child# 1 Clarence E Jaquith Amherst & Carrie A Barker Candia
JAQUITH, Phillip B, Apr 11 1900 Sex:M Child# 4 Clarence Jaquith NH & Carrie Barker NH
JAQUITH, Ruth A, Jan 23 1910 Sex:F Child# 2 Walter Jaquith Nashua, NH & Alice Lavery Derry, NH
JAQUITH, Unknown, Jul 13 1891 Sex:M Child# 2 Walter E Jaquith Nelson & Mertie J Greenfield
JAQUITH, Walter F, Dec 5 1906 Sex:M Child# 1 Walter S Jaquith Nashua, NH & Alice Levoy Nashua, NH
JAREST, Aime Adelard E, Jan 10 1910 Sex:M Child# 4 Silfrid Jarest Wilton, NH & Aurore Boucher Canada
JAROSZKA, Julia, Sep 30 1932 Sex:F Child# 3 A Jaroszka Lithuania & E Tamulewicz Lithuania
JARRET, Everett O, May 13 1901 Sex:M Child# 1 Charles Jarret Canada & Delia Lampron Canada
JARRETTE, Thomas Francis, Jan 17 1904 Sex:M Child# 4 Jeremie Jarrette NY & Marie Runnell England

JARRON, Unknown, Jan 27 1889 Sex:F Child# 11 Napoleon Jarron Canada & Melina Quintal Canada Stillborn
JARVIS, George Paul, Jr, Dec 28 1926 Sex:M Child# 2 George P Jarvis Peterboro, NH & E J Desrosiers Marlboro, MA
JARVIS, Juliet, Aug 19 1899 Sex:F Child# 5 Noe Jarvis Canada & Elmire Levesque Canada
JARVIS, Pauline Lillian, Jan 8 1919 Sex:F Child# 1 George P Jarvis Peterboro, NH & Estelle Derosier Marlboro, MA
JARVIS, Suomer Sylvia, Aug 19 1921 Sex:F Child# 2 Austin Jarvis Finland & A Cronirons Finland
JASKEVICUTE, Bueite, Aug 8 1920 Sex:F Child# 2 John Jaskevicute Lithuania Russia & Kastave Ovrkys Lithuania Russia
JASOKOWICH, Conagunda, Mar 3 1918 Sex:F Child# 1 Edward Jasokowich Russia & Katie Chapahuhet Russia
JASPER, David, Aug 3 1925 Sex:M Child# 4 Grant Jasper New York & Bernice Fall Lowell, MA
JASPER, Dorothy Grant, May 8 1920 Sex:F Child# 2 Grant Jasper Amsterdam, NY & Bernice L Fall Lowell, MA
JASPER, Forest Whitney, Apr 3 1919 Sex:M Child# 1 Grant Jasper Amsterdam, NY & Bernice Fall Lowell, MA
JASPER, Nancy, Aug 30 1930 Sex:F Child# 5 Grant Jasper Amsterdam, NY & Bernice Fall Lowell, MA
JASULAVICH, Unknown, Sep 24 1927 Sex:F Child# 3 A Jasulavich Russia & A Jesukavich Russia
JATKAWICZ, John, Jun 3 1928 Sex:M Child# 4 Walter Jatkawicz Russia & Stella Jausfzske Russia Poland
JATKWIECZ, Walter, Jr, Oct 6 1920 Sex:M Child# 1 Walter Jatkwiecz Poland Russia & Stella Janusefski Poland Russia
JAUNES, Helen, Jul 10 1924 Sex:F Child# 6 Jacob Jaunes Poland Austria & Mary Less Poland Austria
JAURON, Albina Violet, Nov 15 1911 Sex:F Child# 1 Pio Victor Jauron Nashua, NH & Inez M Wilkins Nashua, NH
JAURON, Elaine Doris, Sep 30 1923 Sex:F Child# 8 Pio Victor Jauron Nashua, NH & Inez Wilkins Nashua, NH
JAURON, Leo Paul, Sep 28 1918 Sex:M Child# 5 Pia Jauron Nashua, NH & Inez Wilkins Nashua, NH
JAURON, Leona Ross, Jan 23 1920 Sex:F Child# 6 Pio Jauron Nashua, NH & Inez Wilkins Nashua, NH
JAURON, Lucile Inez, Aug 31 1913 Sex:F Child# 3 Pio V Jauron Nashua, NH & Inez Wilkins Nashua, NH
JAURON, Madeline Vera, Feb 17 1922 Sex:F Child# 7 Pio V Jauron Nashua, NH & Inez Wilkins Nashua, NH
JAURON, Myrtle Inez, Sep 13 1915 Sex:F Child# 3 Pro Jauron Nashua, NH & Inez Wilkins Nashua, NH
JAURON, Nancy May, Jun 26 1935 Sex:F Child# 12 Pio V Jauron Nashua, NH & Inez Wilkins Nashua, NH Stillborn
JAURON, Patricia Shirley, Mar 18 1927 Sex:F Child# 10 Pio Victor Jauron Nashua, NH & Inez Wilkins Nashua, NH
JAURON, Robert Warren, Jun 24 1925 Sex:M Child# 9 Pio V Jauron Nashua, NH & Inez Wilkins Nashua, NH
JAURON, Roland Victor, Apr 28 1917 Sex:M Child# 4 Pio Jauron Nashua, NH & Inez Wilkins Nashua, NH
JAURON, Unknown, Sep 9 1932 Sex:M Child# 11 Pio Victor Jauron Nashua, NH & Inez Wilkins Nashua, NH Stillborn
JAVIS, Stanley, Feb 11 1914 Sex:M Child# 1 John Javis Austria & Mary Mushus Austria
JAZUKIAVICK, Julius, May 1 1929 Sex:M Child# 2 Edward Jazukiavick Russia & Katie Chaplick Russia
JEAN, Adelard Maurice, Feb 2 1924 Sex:M Child# 4 Henri Jean NH & Marie Laflamme Canada
JEAN, Adele Sicile, Aug 24 1902 Sex:F Child# 7 Stanislas Jean Canada & Eveline Beaulieu Canada
JEAN, Adolphe Amedee, Aug 6 1923 Sex:M Child# 7 Jos N Jean Rockport, MA & Alexander Pelerin Nashua, NH
JEAN, Alfred Thomas, Aug 27 1906 Sex:M Child# 8 Stanislas Jean Canada & Eveline Beaulieu Canada
JEAN, Alice L, Dec 13 1897 Sex:F Child# 1 Frank Jean Canada & Alice Gagnon Canada
JEAN, Amilda Pauline, Apr 2 1929 Sex:F Child# 7 Henry Jean Nashua, NH & Mary Laflamme Canada
JEAN, Antoine Ulderic J, Jan 17 1907 Sex:M Child# 6 Elie Jean Canada & Anastasie Chasse Canada
JEAN, Beatrice Theresa, Apr 27 1926 Sex:F Child# 9 Joseph N Jean Rockport, MA & Alexandra Pelerin Nashua, NH
JEAN, Claire Cecile, Jun 4 1932 Sex:F Child# 12 J N Jean Rockport, MA & Alexandra Pellerin Nashua, NH
JEAN, Claire Marie, Nov 13 1935 Sex:F Child# 3 Zebede Jean NH & Albina Brault NY
JEAN, Claud Rene, Sep 26 1930 Sex:M Child# 7 Thomas Jean Canada & Elise Archambault Canada
JEAN, Claudette Reine, Sep 26 1930 Sex:F Child# 8 Thomas Jean Canada & Elise Archambault Canada
JEAN, Colette Caroline, Jun 11 1923 Sex:F Child# 1 Michael Jean Canada & Irene Cormier Canada
JEAN, Constance, Aug 31 1922 Sex:F Child# 3 Henri Jean Nashua, NH & Azilda Laflamme Canada
JEAN, Ernest, Apr 30 1903 Sex:M Child# 1 Joseph Jean Canada & Marie Ladouceur Canada
JEAN, Eveline Gloria, Jul 3 1929 Sex:F Child# 10 J N Jean Rockport, MA & Alexandra Pellerin Nashua, NH
JEAN, Fenelon Andrew Jos, Nov 18 1929 Sex:M Child# 1 Adelard Jean Canada & Aurore Pelletier Nashua, NH
JEAN, Florence, Jun 14 1894 Sex:F Child# 3 Stanislas Jean Canada & Eveline Beaulieu Canada
JEAN, George, Aug 14 1896 Sex:M Child# 4 Stanislas Jean Canada & Eveline Beaulieu Canada
JEAN, Gerard Noel, Jul 27 1920 Sex:M Child# 1 Thomas N Jean Canada & Elise Archambault Canada
JEAN, Guy Lucien, Feb 4 1930 Sex:M Child# 4 Michel Jean Canada & Irene Cormier Canada
JEAN, Henri, Jun 12 1899 Sex:M Child# 2 Elie Jean Canada & Agnes Chasse Canada
JEAN, Ida Noela, Dec 19 1918 Sex:F Child# 5 Joseph N Jean Rockport, MA & Alexandra Pelerin Nashua, NH
JEAN, Jos Adrien Roland, Apr 7 1928 Sex:M Child# 1 Alphonse Jean Canada & Laura Cote Nashua, NH
JEAN, Jos Maurice Albert, Jul 9 1917 Sex:M Child# 11 Elie Jean Canada & Anastasie Chasse Canada
JEAN, Jos Raymond Irene, Dec 22 1929 Sex:M Child# 2 Alphonse Jean Canada & Laura Cote Manchester, NH
JEAN, Joseph Alfred, Aug 5 1900 Sex:M Child# 6 Stanislas Jean Canada & Eveline Beaulieu Canada
JEAN, Joseph Amedee, Aug 1 1909 Sex:M Child# 9 Stanislas Jean Canada & Eveline Beaulieu Canada
JEAN, Joseph Pierre Z, Sep 30 1900 Sex:M Child# 1 Pierre Jean Canada & Marie Carrignan Canada
JEAN, Joseph W Leo F, Jul 22 1908 Sex:M Child# 7 Elie Jean Canada & Anasthasie Chasse Canada
JEAN, Joseph William, Dec 12 1926 Sex:M Child# 1 William B Jean Canada & Jeanne Venette Lowell, MA
JEAN, Lambert Roland, Jan 3 1920 Sex:M Child# 1 Henri Jean Nashua, NH & Exilda Laflamme Canada
JEAN, Lilian Marie, Sep 6 1904 Sex:F Child# 4 Pierre Jean Canada & Maria Carignan Canada
JEAN, Lorraine, Apr 4 1931 Sex:F Child# 5 Michel Jean Canada & Irene Cormier Canada
JEAN, Louis Henri, Jan 16 1931 Sex:M Child# 11 Joseph N Jean Rockport, MA & Alexandra Pellerin Nashua, NH
JEAN, Louis Lionel, Dec 9 1927 Sex:M Child# 6 Thomas Jean Canada & Elise Archambault Canada
JEAN, Lucien Romeo, Feb 7 1923 Sex:M Child# 3 Thomas Jean Canada & Elise Archambault Canada
JEAN, Lucienne Rita, Feb 7 1923 Sex:F Child# 4 Thomas Jean Canada & Elise Archambault Canada
JEAN, Lucille, Mar 18 1930 Sex:F Child# 2 Zebede Jean Nashua, NH & Albina Breault Plattsburg, NY Stillborn
JEAN, M Anna, Apr 1 1910 Sex:F Child# 5 Pierre Jean Canada & Maria Carignan Canada
JEAN, M C Josephine A, Oct 19 1914 Sex:F Child# 10 Elie Jean Canada & Anasthasie Chasse Canada
JEAN, M Ernestine, Dec 16 1892 Sex:F Child# 7 Joseph Jean Canada & Denoide Reivuack Canada
JEAN, M Irene, Jul 19 1895 Sex:F Child# 9 Joachim Jean Canada & Anaise De Kervack Canada
JEAN, M Louise Florette, Nov 12 1913 Sex:F Child# 6 Pierre Jean Canada & Maria Carignan Canada

JEAN, Marguerite Jeanne, Jul 5 1920 Sex:F Child# 5 Joseph N Jean Rockport, MA & Alexandra Pellerin Nashua, NH
JEAN, Marie Aldea, Apr 2 1904 Sex:F Child# 5 Elie Jean Canada & Anastasie Chasse Canada
JEAN, Marie Anna Jean, Oct 7 1896 Sex:F Child# 1 Ludger Jean Canada & Anna St Jean Canada
JEAN, Marie Anne Juliette, Jul 1 1917 Sex:F Child# 3 Joseph N Jean Mass & Alexandra Pellerin Nashua, NH
JEAN, Marie B M A, Oct 19 1900 Sex:F Child# 3 Elie Jean Canada & Anastasie Chasse Canada
JEAN, Marie Lauretta C, Sep 26 1906 Sex:F Child# 4 Pierre Jean Canada & Maria Carignan Canada
JEAN, Marie Laurette F, Feb 27 1910 Sex:F Child# 8 Elie Jean Canada & Anasthasie Chasse Canada
JEAN, Marie Lucille Ol Rit, Aug 29 1918 Sex:F Child# 10 Pierre Jean Canada & Maria Carrignan Canada
JEAN, Marie Rose E, Jul 14 1902 Sex:F Child# 2 Pierre Jean Canada & Maria Carrignan Canada
JEAN, Marie Rose I, Oct 15 1902 Sex:F Child# 4 Elie Jean Canada & Agnes Chasse Canada
JEAN, Mary Laura, Jan 22 1893 Sex:F Child# 3 Stanislas Jean Canada & Eveline Beaulieu Canada
JEAN, Mary Lucille, Oct 18 1920 Sex:F Child# 1 Joseph Jean Canada & Rosana Demanche Canada
JEAN, Merilda, Nov 18 1897 Sex:F Child# 1 Elie Jean Canada & Anastasie Chasse Canada
JEAN, Merna, Jan 5 1935 Sex:F Child# 3 Walter Jean Nova Scotia & Marie Mayo Haverhill, MA
JEAN, Normand, Aug 15 1924 Sex:M Child# 2 Michael Jean Canada & Irene Cormier Canada
JEAN, Rita Gertrude, May 16 1922 Sex:F Child# 6 Joseph N Jean Rockport, MA & Alexandra Pelerin Nashua, NH
JEAN, Rita Lucienne, Nov 23 1926 Sex:F Child# 1 Lebede Jean Nashua, NH & Albina Breault Plattsburgh, NY
JEAN, Robert, Jul 16 1921 Sex:M Child# 2 Thomas Jean Canada & Elise Archambault Canada
JEAN, Rodolphe Benoit, Oct 22 1925 Sex:M Child# 3 Michael Jean Canada & Irene Cormier Canada
JEAN, Ronald Arthur, Nov 23 1935 Sex:M Child# 1 Ulderic Jean Nashua, NH & Anita St Francois Richford, VT
JEAN, Rose Francis Jac, May 4 1933 Sex:M Child# 8 Henry W Jean Nashua, NH & Mary LaFlamme Canada
JEAN, Sylvio Euclide E, Jun 30 1911 Sex:M Child# 9 Elie Jean Canada & Anasthasie Chasse Canada
JEAN, Sylvio Herve, Nov 27 1926 Sex:M Child# 5 Thomas Jean Canada & Elise Archambault Canada
JEAN, Unknown, Jul 28 1888 Sex:M Child# 3 Joseph Jean Canada & Philomene Gerignes Canada Stillborn
JEAN, Unknown, May 16 1921 Sex:M Child# 2 Henry Jean Nashua, NH & Josephine Laflamme US
JEAN, William Henry, Jun 23 1925 Sex:M Child# 6 Henry Jean Nashua, NH & Marie Laflamme Canada
JEANBANE, Julie A E, Nov 23 1893 Sex:F Child# 1 Damase Jeanbane Nashua, NH & Julie Boune Rindge, NH
JEANBARRE, Ernest A, Aug 5 1897 Sex:M Child# 2 Damase Jeanbarre Nashua, NH & Julie Bourre Rindge, NH
JEANBARRE, Rose D A, Aug 7 1905 Sex:F Child# 3 Damase Jeanbarre Nashua, NH & Julie Bourre Rindge, NH
JEANBART, Arthur, May 21 1895 Sex:M Child# 3 Pierre Jeanbart Canada & Eleonore Canada
JEANBEAU, Marie L I C, Feb 21 1887 Sex:F Child# 6 Louis Jeanbeau P Q & Elzere Gagne P Q
JEANBONE, Marie, May 30 1888 Sex:F Child# 7 Louis Jeanbone Canada & Elzire Gagne Canada
JEANNOTTE, Arthur Alexandre, Nov 3 1905 Sex:M Child# 5 Frederick Jeannotte NH & Alphonse Pepin Canada
JEANNOTTE, Bertha, Oct 12 1892 Sex:F Child# 4 Olivier Jeannotte Canada & Julie Dragon Canada
JEANNOTTE, Emma, Aug 12 1890 Sex:F Child# 3 Olivier Jeannotte New York & Julia Dragan New York
JEANNOTTE, Evelina, Dec 14 1896 Sex:F Child# 5 Olivier Jeannotte US & Julie Dragon US
JEANNOTTE, Francis X N, Jul 31 1905 Sex:M Child# 3 Henri Jeannotte Nashua, NH & Clara Morin Pepperell, MA
JEANNOTTE, Georges T, Oct 13 1895 Sex:M Child# 3 Hector Jeannotte Nashua, NH & Alida Bouin W Boylston, MA
JEANNOTTE, James Howard, Jul 1 1909 Sex:M Child# 1 Howard C Jeannotte Nashua, NH & Marion Farnsworth Nashua, NH
JEANNOTTE, James J, Feb 6 1907 Sex:M Child# 4 Olivier Jeannotte US & Regina Belanger Canada
JEANNOTTE, Jean Baptiste V, Oct 14 1907 Sex:M Child# 6 Frederic Jeannotte NH & Alphonsine Pepin Canada
JEANNOTTE, Jeanne, Jul 30 1923 Sex:F Child#  James A G Jeannotte Nashua, NH & Blanche M Gunter Charlestown, MA
JEANNOTTE, Jennie, Feb 8 1895 Sex:F Child# 6 Olivier Jeannotte US & Julie Dragon US
JEANNOTTE, Joseph Oliver Paul, Mar 24 1926 Sex:M Child# 1 Joseph Jeannotte Nashua, NH & Yvonne Talbot Mass
JEANNOTTE, Joseph Theodore, Dec 21 1902 Sex:M Child# 2 Olivier Jeannotte Canada & Regina Belanger Canada
JEANNOTTE, Josephine, Aug 16 1897 Sex:F Child# 2 Hector Jeannotte Nashua, NH & Gertrude Ward Biddeford, ME
JEANNOTTE, Leo R G, Aug 11 1895 Sex:M Child# 1 Henri Jeannotte Nashua, NH & Clara Morin Pepperell, MA
JEANNOTTE, Lora, Nov 12 1892 Sex:F Child# 3 Alfred M Jeannotte NH & Rebecca Hall NH
JEANNOTTE, Louis Maurice O, Jul 14 1908 Sex:M Child# 3 Arthur A Jeannotte Nashua, NH & Flora Chagnon Canada
JEANNOTTE, Lucille Mary, Jun 13 1917 Sex:F Child# 2 Henry Jeannotte Nashua, NH & Rose A Clark Nashua, NH
JEANNOTTE, Marcella, Mar 27 1927 Sex:F Child# 2 J J Jeannotte Nashua, NH & Yvonne Talbot Lawrence, MA
JEANNOTTE, Marie A, Jul 9 1891 Sex:F Child# 5 Pierre Jeannotte Canada & Pomele Migneault Canada
JEANNOTTE, Marie A A, Apr 29 1893 Sex:F Child# 1 Hector Jeannotte Nashua, NH & Alida Bonin W Boylston, MA
JEANNOTTE, Marie A L, May 9 1902 Sex:F Child# 2 Henri Jeannotte Nashua, NH & Clara Morin Pepperell, MA
JEANNOTTE, Marie B, Jun 12 1894 Sex:F Child# 2 Hector Jeannotte Nashua, NH & Alida Bovin W Boylston, MA
JEANNOTTE, Marie D, Mar 9 1890 Sex:F Child# 4 Pierre Jeannotte Canada & Pomela Migneault Canada
JEANNOTTE, Marie Florence, Oct 15 1898 Sex:F Child# 8 Olivier Jeannotte Sciota, NY & Julie Dragon Sciota, NY
JEANNOTTE, Marie Irene, Jan 25 1901 Sex:F Child# 1 Olivier Jeannotte New York & Regina Belanger Canada
JEANNOTTE, Marie J, Jun 15 1897 Sex:F Child# 4 Hector Jeannotte Nashua, NH & Alida Bonin W Boylston, MA
JEANNOTTE, Marie L R A, Nov 15 1901 Sex:F Child# 2 Frederick Jeannotte NH & Alphonsine Pepin Canada
JEANNOTTE, Marie Louise C, Dec 22 1904 Sex:F Child# 3 Olivier Jeannotte NY & Regina Belanger Canada
JEANNOTTE, Mary Madeline, Aug 16 1920 Sex:F Child# 1 Henry Jeannotte Nashua, NH & Rose Clark Nashua, NH
JEANNOTTE, Mellia, Sep 20 1893 Sex:F Child# 6 Whitford Jeannotte NY & Mellia NY
JEANNOTTE, Ogilvie, Jun 28 1893 Sex:F Child# 1 Pierre Jeannotte Canada & Frances Kitson Canada
JEANNOTTE, Olivette, Oct 19 1905 Sex:F Child# 2 Arthur A Jeannotte Nashua, NH & Flora Chagnon Canada
JEANNOTTE, Patricia Mae, Feb 2 1934 Sex:F Child# 1 Valmore B Jeannotte Nashua, NH & Bernice V Davis Hudson, NH
JEANNOTTE, Pauline Gertie, Feb 2 1896 Sex:F Child# 1 Hector Jeannotte New York & Gertie Ward Maine
JEANNOTTE, Robert Henry, Dec 3 1913 Sex:M Child# 1 Henry Jeannotte Nashua, NH & Rose Clark Nashua, NH
JEANNOTTE, Roland Alvin, May 29 1905 Sex:M Child# 1 Henry J Jeannotte Nashua, NH & Agnes Lefebvre Nashua, NH
JEANNOTTE, Ulderic Ralph G, May 17 1904 Sex:M Child# 1 Arthur A Jeannotte Nashua, NH & Flora Chagnon Canada
JEANNOTTE, Unknown, Jun 18 1890 Sex:F Child# 1 James Jeannotte Swanton Falls, VT & Margaret Ward Wolleston, VT
JEANNOTTE, Unknown, Oct 24 1891 Sex:M Child# 5 Wilfred Jeannotte New York & Julie Hall New York
JEANNOTTE, Unknown, Aug 29 1892 Sex: Child# 2 James F Jeannotte Swanton, VT & Margaret Ward Williston, VT

JEANNOTTE, Unknown, May 29 1910 Sex:F Child# 4 Henri Jeannotte Nashua, NH & Clara Morin Pepperell, MA Stillborn
JEANNOTTE, Unknown, Mar 7 1911 Sex:M Child# 7 Frederic Jeannotte NH & Alphonsine Pepin Canada Stillborn
JEANNOTTE, Unknown, May 30 1918 Sex:M Child# 1 Leo Jeannotte Nashua, NH & Madeline Doyle Nashua, NH Stillborn
JEANNOTTE, William Edouard, Jan 20 1903 Sex:M Child# 4 Frederick Jeannotte NH & Alphonsine Pepin Canada
JEANOTTE, Henriette Louise, Apr 17 1924 Sex:F Child# 1 Theodore Jeanotte Nashua, NH & Beatrice Boilard Nashua, NH
JEANOTTE, Joel M, May 1 1889 Sex:F Child# 8 Cornelius Jeanotte Saxons River, VT & Rosmond Lynn
JEANOTTE, Joseph Frederic A, Aug 11 1900 Sex:M Child# 1 Frederic Jeannotte NH & Alphonsine Pepin Canada
JEANOTTE, Lorraine Anne, Apr 9 1932 Sex:F Child# 1 S A Jeanotte Nashua, NH & Dora Gaudette Hudson, MA
JEANOTTE, Unknown, Nov 5 1889 Sex:M Child# 6 Alfred Jeanotte Nashua, NH & Sophia R Hall Union Village Stillborn
JEBB, Ellen Elizabeth, Sep 1 1933 Sex:F Child# 3 Willard Jebb Milford, NH & Mabel Pearson Bedford, NH
JEBB, Marcia Geneva, Oct 11 1934 Sex:F Child# 1 Thomas Jebb Vermont & Blanche Stillson Portsmouth, NH
JEBB, Richard Pearson, Jan 11 1929 Sex:M Child# 1 Willard Irwin Jebb Milford, NH & Mabel Pearson Bedford, NH
JEBB, Ruth Jane, Jul 10 1930 Sex:F Child# 1 Elbert Jebb Hudson, MA & Ruth Guill Nashua, NH
JEFFERS, John William, Aug 7 1898 Sex:M Child# 2 Thomas T Jeffers Milford, MA & Catherine Buckley Nashua, NH
JEFFERS, Marie Andrea Eliza, Mar 12 1935 Sex:F Child# 1 Elmer Jeffers West Virginia & Blanche Martel Nashua, NH
JEFFERSON, William, Nov 19 1905 Sex:M Child# 2 Arthur R Jefferson North Conway, NH & Jennie H Barker Hillsboro, NH
JEGLINSKI, Wayne Stephen R, Jan 29 1935 Sex:M Child# 1 Stephen Jeglinski Pepperell, MA & Irene Boyce Nashua, NH
JELLEY, Casper R, Dec 8 1889 Sex:M Child# 4 Alfred J Jelley NY & Annie Germain Canada
JELLEY, Charles, Jan 3 1888 Sex:M Child# 1 Charles Jelley New York & Kate McMulquen Ireland
JELLEY, Charles Herbert, Jr, Feb 15 1920 Sex:M Child# 3 Lester W Jelley Hyde Park, MA & Mary Bariteau Montreal
JELLEY, Dale Kenneth, Sep 24 1910 Sex:M Child# 2 Harry L Jelley Nashua, NH & Bertha Bouley Nashua, NH
JELLEY, Gordon D, Jan 17 1908 Sex:M Child# 8 Herbert Jelley Becktown, NY & Dellie Monbleau Detroit, MI
JELLEY, Harvey Hercules, Jun 27 1920 Sex:M Child# 2 Clovis H Jelley Claremont, NH & Ruby Adel Heart Nova Scotia
JELLEY, Henry, Dec 29 1888 Sex:M Child# 3 John Jelley Vermont & Mary Halleran Ireland
JELLEY, Hercules Eugene, Jun 2 1900 Sex:M Child# 3 Henry Jelley NY & Mary Guyett NY
JELLEY, Joseph Zephrin, Mar 23 1928 Sex:F Child# 6 Lester W Jelley Mass & Maria Bariteau Canada
JELLEY, Normand Lester, Sep 7 1923 Sex:M Child# 5 Lester Wm Jelley Hyde Park, MA & Maria Bariteau Montreal, Canada
JELLEY, Pearl, Mar 31 1895 Sex:F Child# 7 Herbert Jelley Plattsburg, NY & Delia Mumbleau Canada
JELLEY, Unknown, Dec 13 1911 Sex:F Child# 3 Harry I Jelley Nashua, NH & Bertha I Bouley Nashua, NH
JELLEY, Unknown, Mar 28 1912 Sex:M Child# 1 Leo E Jelley Nashua, NH & Regina Doris Canada
JELLISON, Addie Emma, Jul 6 1897 Sex:F Child# Edwin F Jellison Hudson, NH & Jane Loubert Canada
JELLISON, Dorothy Claire, Jul 30 1918 Sex:F Child# 1 George F Jellison Nashua, NH & Andrea Bonneau Nashua, NH
JELLISON, George Frank, Jun 6 1898 Sex:M Child# 1 Henry B Jellison Maine & Flora Dougrette Canada
JELLISON, George Henry, May 23 1894 Sex:M Child# 4 William S Jellison Nashua, NH & Mary A Christy Ayer, MA
JELLISON, Hiram P, Mar 10 1896 Sex:M Child# 1 Edwin F Jellison New Hampshire & Jane Loubert Canada
JELLISON, Irene, Aug 20 1898 Sex:F Child# 8 William Jellison Nashua, NH & Mary A Christie Ayer, MA
JELLISON, Marion Henrietta, Jun 21 1896 Sex:F Child# 4 William S Jellison Nashua, NH & Mary A Christie Ayer, MA
JELLISON, Theresa, Feb 17 1888 Sex:F Child# 1 William Jellison Nashua, NH & Mary Ann Christie Ayer Jct, MA
JELLISON, Unknown, Jan 2 1893 Sex:F Child# 3 William S Jellison Nashua, NH & Mary A Christie Ayer Jct, MA
JELLISON, Unknown, Jun 4 1895 Sex:F Child# 4 U S Jellison Nashua, NH & Mary A Christie Ayer, MA
JELLISON, Unknown, Jun 4 1895 Sex:M Child# 5 U S Jellison Nashua, NH & Mary A Christie Ayer, MA
JELLISON, Vinnie, Aug 6 1899 Sex:F Child# 2 Henry Jellison Litchfield, ME & Flora Douyette Canada
JELLY, Charlotte Irene, Oct 9 1917 Sex:F Child# 2 Lester William Jelly Hyde Park, MA & Mary Bearitenu Montreal
JELLY, Jessie Lucille, Aug 20 1921 Sex:F Child# 4 Lester M Jelly Mass & Maria Bariteau Canada
JELLY, Lillian May, Oct 19 1897 Sex:F Child# 1 William B Jelly NY & Alice Bostwick England
JELLY, Malcolm Henry, Apr 26 1918 Sex:M Child# 1 Clovis H Jelly Claremont, NH & Ruby Hearn Bridgetown, NS
JELLY, Paul, Mar 13 1916 Sex:M Child# 1 Lester Jelly Nashua, NH & Maria Bariteau Montreal, PQ
JELLY, Raymond Harry, Mar 8 1907 Sex:M Child# 1 Harry I Jelly Nashua, NH & Bertha Bouley Nashua, NH
JELLY, Ronald Leslie, Aug 4 1934 Sex:M Child# 1 (No Parents Listed)
JELLY, Unknown, Aug 31 1887 Sex:M Child# 2 W John Jelly NY & Mary H Ireland
JEMSEN, Barbara Lillian, Aug 14 1928 Sex:F Child# 1 Axel Jemsen Nashua, NH & Janet Snow Nashua, NH
JENAIS, Joseph Romeo R Ed, Jan 3 1916 Sex:M Child# 2 David Jenais NH & Yvonne Roy NH
JENKINS, Helen Bertha, Jun 19 1921 Sex:F Child# 4 Frank Jenkins Concord, NH & Dorothy Westbrook England
JENKINS, Unknown, Dec 17 1890 Sex:F Child# 4 Edmund H Jenkins Hudson, NH & Alma S Robbins Nashua, NH
JENKINS, Unknown, Apr 4 1894 Sex:M Child# 5 Edward H Jenkins Hudson, NH & Alma L Robbins Nashua, NH
JENKINS, William Earle, Apr 22 1935 Sex:M Child# 1 Cloyce Jenkins Marion, OH & Florence Rock Malone, NY
JENNESS, Eddie, Jan 8 1930 Sex:M Child# 8 Jacob Jenness Poland & Mary Lus Poland
JENNESS, Edward Warren, Mar 31 1911 Sex:M Child# 2 John H Jenness Cambridge, MA & Emma L Gray Belfast, ME
JENNESS, Eleanor Ruth, May 13 1934 Sex:F Child# 5 Daniel W Jenness Ayer, MA & Alice Whitcomb Brookline, NH
JENNESS, Raymond Whitcomb, Apr 29 1922 Sex:M Child# 2 Daniel W Jenness Ayer, MA & Alice B Whitcomb Brookline, NH
JENNESS, Simond, Sep 8 1918 Sex:M Child# 4 Jacob Jenness Austria & Mary Fous Austria
JENNETTE, Unknown, Sep 30 1896 Sex:M Child# 3 Joseph Jennette New York & Lizzie Stuart NB Stillborn
JENNINGS, Herbert M Webster, Jan 2 1921 Sex:M Child# 3 Wilbur S Jennings Hudson, NH & Gladys Snow Boston, MA
JENNINGS, Samuel S, May 22 1895 Sex:M Child# 8 William H Jennings England & Elizabeth Sandins England
JENNINGS, Walter Ernest, Jan 26 1897 Sex:M Child# 8 William H Jennings England & Elizabeth A Sanders England
JENNIRE, Unknown, Sep 25 1910 Sex:M Child# 2 John Jennire NH & Fannie LeCain Mass
JENNISON, Grace Emily, Apr 14 1929 Sex:F Child# 2 Arlon Jennison Keene, NH & Mildred Taylor Manchester, NH
JENSEN, Axel Howard, Feb 21 1905 Sex:M Child# 4 Julius Jensen Denmark & Frederika Hansen Denmark
JENSEN, Dorothy Elizabeth, Aug 16 1926 Sex:F Child# 1 Axton Jensen Keene, NH & Mildred Taylor Manchester, NH
JENSEN, Eleanor Ruth, Feb 22 1930 Sex:F Child# 2 Axel Jensen Nashua, NH & Janet Snow Nashua, NH
JENSEN, Harold J, Jul 23 1911 Sex:M Child# 6 Julius Jensen Denmark & Frederica Hansen Denmark
JENSEN, Janice Edith, Apr 18 1932 Sex:F Child# 3 Axel Jensen Nashua, NH & Janet Snow Nashua, NH
JENSEN, John Chester, Jul 17 1930 Sex:M Child# 1 Chester Jensen Plymouth, MA & Dorothy Phalen Conway, NH

JENSEN, Maude Lillian, Feb 20 1901 Sex:F Child# 2 Julius Jensen Denmark & Fredericka Hansen Denmark
JENSEN, Niles Frederick, Nov 21 1918 Sex:M Child# 7 Julius Jensen Denmark & Fredericka Hansen Denmark
JENSEN, Regnard Edwin, Nov 12 1903 Sex:M Child# 3 Julius Jensen Denmark & Marie C Hansen Denmark
JENSEN, William Julius, Jun 21 1899 Sex:M Child# 1 Julius Jensen Denmark, Sweden & Fredrika Hansen Denmark
JENSEN, Winifred Mary Jane, Jun 23 1924 Sex:F Child# 1 George F Jensen Somerville, MA & Rose Raby Nashua, NH
JENSON, Julianna F, Jul 19 1910 Sex:F Child# 5 Julius Jenson Denmark & Marie K T Hansen Denmark
JEPSON, Frederick Tetlow, Sep 19 1933 Sex:M Child# 1 Frederick Jepson Williamstown, MA & Miriam Smith Newton, MA
JEREMICK, Brazie, May 2 1911 Sex:F Child# 1 Antoni Jeremick Russia & Anna Tamulawitch Russia
JERZEIKIEWICZA, Josephine, Jul 2 1909 Sex:F Child# 3 John Jerzeikiewicza Russia & Carola Gregas Russia
JESKINS, Mary Rose, Jul 14 1913 Sex:F Child# 3 Julius Jeskins Russia & Annie Schraskins Russia
JESUKAVICH, Unknown, Jul 19 1914 Sex:F Child# 7 Thomas Jesukavich Russia & Annie Wercukus Russia Stillborn
JETTE, Adalbert, Oct 8 1898 Sex:M Child# 1 Arthur Jette Canada & Amerilda Gagnon Canada
JETTE, Adria, Aug 24 1901 Sex:F Child# 4 Arthur Jette Canada & Amarilda Gagnon Canada
JETTE, Alfred, Mar 18 1895 Sex:M Child# 12 Desire Jette Canada & Elizabeth Ferland Canada
JETTE, Arthur Valmore, Dec 21 1899 Sex:M Child# 2 Arthur Jette Canada & Amarilda Gagnon Canada
JETTE, Blanche Irene E, Jun 27 1910 Sex:F Child# 1 Albert Jette Canada & Clara Poulin US
JETTE, Blanche Rnalda, Aug 24 1901 Sex:F Child# 3 Arthur Jette Canada & Amarilda Gagnon Canada
JETTE, Cecilia Geraldine, Dec 7 1908 Sex:F Child# 6 Arthur Jette Canada & Amerilda Gagnon Canada
JETTE, Emile Sylvio, Mar 31 1911 Sex:M Child# 7 Arthur Jette Canada & Amerilda Gagnon Canada
JETTE, Irene Laurette, Dec 10 1902 Sex:F Child# 5 Arthur Jette Canada & Amarilda Gagnon Canada
JETTE, Jos Edouard Normand, Jul 31 1925 Sex:M Child# 4 Arthur Jette NH & Delia Deschesneau NH
JETTE, Joseph E L Arthur, May 23 1934 Sex:M Child# 1 Edmund Jette Nashua, NH & Rose Boissoneault Nashua, NH
JETTE, Joseph Ed Ferdinand, Feb 20 1916 Sex:M Child# 9 Arthur Jette Canada & Amarilla Gagnon Canada
JETTE, Joseph Henry, Jun 29 1935 Sex:M Child# 1 Edmont Jette Nashua, NH & R Boissonneault Nashua, NH
JETTE, Louis Edmond, Aug 25 1912 Sex:M Child# 8 Arthur Jette Canada & Amarilda Gagnon Canada
JETTE, M I R Jeanne d'Arc, May 31 1921 Sex:F Child# 1 Adalbert Jette Nashua, NH & Cecile Marquis Manchester, NH
JETTE, M J Oliv Rebecca, Jun 12 1917 Sex:F Child# 11 Arthur Jette Canada & Amerilda Gagnon Canada
JETTE, Marg Antoinette, Jan 15 1922 Sex:F Child# 2 Arthur Jette Nashua, NH & Delia Duchesneau Nashua, NH
JETTE, Marie, May 10 1920 Sex:F Child# 1 Arthur Jette, Jr Nashua, NH & Celia Ducheneault Nashua, NH Stillborn
JETTE, Marie Emerilda  Rita, May 31 1923 Sex:F Child# 3 Arthur Jette, Jr NH & Delia Duchesneau NH
JETTE, Marie G, Oct 8 1887 Sex:F Child# 3 Napoleon Jette P Q & Anna P Q
JETTE, Marie Gertrude T, May 14 1925 Sex:F Child# 4 Adelbert Jette Nashua, NH & Cecile Marquis Manchester, NH
JETTE, Marie Leonard, Nov 21 1892 Sex:F Child# 11 Desire Jette Canada & Elizabeth Farland Canada
JETTE, Marie Rachel Camille, Sep 17 1927 Sex:F Child# 5 Adelbert Jette Nashua, NH & Cecile Marquis Manchester, NH
JETTE, Paul Andre, Mar 30 1914 Sex:M Child# 9 Arthur Jette Canada & Amarilda Gagnon Canada
JETTE, Pauline Ernestine, Nov 1 1911 Sex:F Child# 2 Albert Jette Canada & Clara Poulin US
JEUNES, Adelia Emma, Jan 13 1925 Sex:F Child# 3 D Wallace Jeunes Ayer, MA & A B Whitcombe Brookline, NH
JEWELL, James Lilburn, May 16 1932 Sex:M Child# 1 J L Jewell, Jr Salem, MA & C Homrighouse Herkimer, KS
JEWETT, Jeanne, Jun 28 1932 Sex:F Child# 1 M E Jewett Milford, NH & Louise Roy Bradford, VT
JEWETT, Robert Converse, Nov 6 1919 Sex:M Child# 1 Edwin O Jewett Milford, NH & Agnes Converse Amherst, NH
JEZUKEVICH, Annie, Apr 3 1916 Sex:F Child# 9 John Jezukevich Russia & Caroline Grizas Russia
JEZUKIAVICH, Peter, Jun 6 1917 Sex:M Child# 10 John Jezukiavich Russia & Karolina Grygintie Russia
JEZUKIEWICZ, Josie, May 13 1907 Sex:F Child# 1 John Jezukiewicz Russia & Caroline Grigiutie Russia
JEZUKWICK, Anthony, Aug 22 1921 Sex:M Child# 13 John Jezukwick Russia & Carolina Grigas Russia
JILBERT, Virginia Elizabeth, May 26 1920 Sex:F Child# 1 Louis J Jilbert US & Albina Aubertin US
JISTA, Anna D, Jun 5 1926 Sex:F Child# 4 Demetrius Jista Greece & Efstattus Mente Greece
JKASALA, Julius, Mar 15 1908 Sex:M Child# 1 Joseph Jkasala Russia & Katre Kaziekonis Russia
JLKIAWICZES, Amilker, Sep 27 1907 Sex:F Child# 1 Frank Jlkiawiczes Russia & Rose Mieskinute Russia
JODOIN, Angelina, May 13 1905 Sex:F Child# 3 Joseph Jodoin Canada & Olive Pelletier Canada
JODOIN, Antoinette, Jan 11 1904 Sex:F Child# 2 Georges Jodoin Canada & Ida Girouard Nashua, NH
JODOIN, Clara Gerogiana, May 18 1891 Sex:F Child# 13 Honore Jodoin Canada & Aglae Laforme Canada
JODOIN, Felix, Jun 9 1894 Sex:M Child# 2 Henri Jodoin Canada & Mathilde Lampron Nashua, NH
JODOIN, Gerard Robert, Jun 3 1910 Sex:M Child# 2 Sylvio Jodoin US & Rebecca Mandeville US
JODOIN, Henry, Dec 3 1891 Sex:M Child# 1 Henry Jodoin Canada & Mathilde Lampron Canada
JODOIN, Ida, Jun 30 1900 Sex:F Child# 5 Henri Jodoin Canada & Mathilda Lampron Canada
JODOIN, Joseph A V, Jul 1 1910 Sex:M Child# 5 Joseph Jodoin Canada & Oliva Peltier Canada
JODOIN, Marie C A, Jun 11 1900 Sex:F Child# 1 Joseph Jodoin Canada & Oliva Peltier Canada
JODOIN, Marie L Aurore, Aug 30 1896 Sex:F Child# 3 Henri Jodoin Canada & Methilde Lampron Nashua, NH
JODOIN, Mary Rose, Dec 5 1929 Sex:F Child# 1 Sylvia A Jodoin Burlington, VT & Mary Alice Normand Manchester, NH
JODOIN, Norman Robert, May 23 1935 Sex:M Child# 1 John Jodoin Canada & Gertrude Chamard Leominster, MA
JODOIN, Oscar, Sep 30 1897 Sex:M Child# 3 Honore Jodoin Canada & Mathilde Lampron Canada
JODOIN, Regina A, Sep 22 1906 Sex:F Child# 4 Joseph Jodoin Canada & Oliva Peltier Canada
JOHNSON, Albert, Aug 30 1897 Sex:M Child# 1 C F Johnson Sweden & Mary Anderson Sweden
JOHNSON, Alfred L, Apr 6 1903 Sex:M Child# 9 Alfred Johnson Canada & Mary Young Wilton, NH
JOHNSON, Andrew William, Apr 15 1919 Sex:M Child# 1 John W Johnson Providence, RI & Jessie Lessard Nashua, NH
JOHNSON, Annie Louise, Nov 13 1891 Sex:F Child# 11 Isadore Johnson Canada & Annie Ploude Canada
JOHNSON, Annie Sophie, Aug 15 1901 Sex:F Child# 1 Andrew Johnson Sweden & Sophie Akasson Sweden
JOHNSON, Arthur Wilhelm, Apr 28 1904 Sex:M Child# 2 Andrew Johnson Sweden & Sophia Akasson Sweden
JOHNSON, Barbara Arleen, Mar 3 1929 Sex:F Child# 1 Donald Johnson New Brunswick & Sophie Patrick Nashua, NH
JOHNSON, Beverly Ann, Apr 2 1928 Sex:F Child# 2 Arthur Johnson Merrimack, NH & Mildred Anderson Merrimack, NH
JOHNSON, Charles E, Sep 22 1890 Sex:M Child# 1 Albert Johnson Michigan & Alice NY
JOHNSON, Charles Harold, Oct 7 1935 Sex:M Child# 1 Charles H Johnson Portsmouth, NH & Almeda Bassett Hudson, NH
JOHNSON, Charles W, May 4 1903 Sex:M Child# 2 Charles F Johnson Sweden & Mary Anderson Sweden

JOHNSON, Charles William, Feb 12 1894 Sex:M Child# 1 Arthur Johnson Nashua, NH & Regina Belanger NH
JOHNSON, Charls Bernard, Jul 24 1920 Sex:M Child# 2 Arthur G Johnson Oconco, WI & Eva Jankens Lowell, MA
JOHNSON, Clara, Dec 29 1918 Sex:F Child# 1 Arthur G Johnson Wisconsin & Eva Jenkins Lowell, MA
JOHNSON, David, Aug 21 1901 Sex:M Child# 8 Fred Johnson Canada & Minnie R Young Milton
JOHNSON, Dereise W, May 21 1908 Sex:F Child# 1 Oscar P Johnson Tyngsboro, MA & Evangeline B West Vershire, VT
JOHNSON, Dexter Philip, May 12 1919 Sex:M Child# 2 Oscar P Johnson Tyngsboro, MA & Evangline B West Vershire, VT
JOHNSON, Donald Frederick, Aug 31 1914 Sex:M Child# 3 Travis Johnson Sweden & Mary Maddox Nashua, NH
JOHNSON, Dorothy Charlene, Feb 8 1922 Sex:F Child# 3 Fred L Johnson Nashua, NH & Mildred Gallagher Ellsworth, ME
JOHNSON, Dorothy Mae, Sep 1 1924 Sex:F Child# 6 Travis Johnson Sweden & Mary Maddox Nashua, NH
JOHNSON, Edmund Luke, Dec 30 1932 Sex:M Child# 1 J A Johnson New Brunswick & Edith V Kelly New Brunswick
JOHNSON, Edward R, Apr 26 1904 Sex:M Child# 1 Edward J Johnson Charlestown, MA & Fannie H Weed Oswego, NY
JOHNSON, Elizabeth, Jan 20 1926 Sex:F Child# 2 Maurice Johnson Manchester, NH & Eleanor Pease Nashua, NH
JOHNSON, Elmer Theodore, Jan 6 1905 Sex:M Child# 3 Carl F Johnson Sweden & Mary Anderson Sweden
JOHNSON, Ernest, Nov 3 1896 Sex:M Child# 5 George F Johnson Yarmouth, NS &  Yarmouth, NS
JOHNSON, Eva Mae, Aug 31 1921 Sex:F Child# 3 Arthur G Johnson Oconto, WI & Eva Jenkins Lowell, MA
JOHNSON, Everett Emerson, Oct 13 1890 Sex:M Child# 1 Ernest J Johnson Nova Scotia & L M Bird New Brunswick
JOHNSON, Fanny Weed, May 27 1907 Sex:F Child# 3 Edward J Johnson Charlestown, MA & Fanny Herrick Weed Oswego, NY
JOHNSON, Florence May, Oct 9 1898 Sex:F Child# 6 Fred Johnson Canada & Marie Dionne Milton
JOHNSON, Fred Ledgard, Jul 8 1918 Sex:M Child# 2 Fred L Johnson Nashua, NH & Mildred Gallagher Ellsworth, ME
JOHNSON, George Simeon, Feb 5 1922 Sex:M Child# 1 George S Johnson Highgate, VT & Cora Belle Brown Jamaica, VT
JOHNSON, Gilbert Alfred, Aug 7 1921 Sex:M Child# 3 William Johnson Nashua, NH & Maebelle Taylor Barre, VT
JOHNSON, Grace, Sep 4 1900 Sex:F Child# 1 A Johnson NJ & Agnes Campbell Scotland
JOHNSON, Greta Marie, Sep 8 1933 Sex:F Child# 4 Fred Johnson Sweden & Pauline Carpenter Milford, NH
JOHNSON, Harriet Herrick, Jan 3 1906 Sex:F Child# 2 Edward J Johnson Charlestown, MA & Fannie H Weed Oswego, NY
JOHNSON, Henrietta Elizabeth, Apr 15 1919 Sex:F Child# 1 Wm James Johnson Nashua, NH & Mabelle A Taylor Barre, VT
JOHNSON, J Frederick, Aug 13 1923 Sex:M Child# 4 William Johnson Nashua, NH & Mabel Taylor Barre, VT
JOHNSON, James Edward, Jun 11 1891 Sex:M Child# 2 Frederick Johnson New York & Mary R Young Milton Three R'ds
JOHNSON, Jane, Mar 9 1904 Sex:F Child# 11 Frederic Johnson Canada & Marie Dionne NH Stillborn
JOHNSON, Joseph W, Apr 22 1897 Sex:M Child# 3 C E Johnson Portland, ME & G E Weston Manchester, NH
JOHNSON, Leima Grace, Apr 17 1923 Sex:F Child# 1 Maurice Johnson Manchester, NH & Eleanore Pease Nashua, NH
JOHNSON, Louise Elizabeth, Feb 11 1924 Sex:F Child# 2 Hjalmar Johnson Worcester, MA & Philo Chapman Dunstable, MA
JOHNSON, Lucille Marie, Mar 7 1924 Sex:F Child# 5 Fred Johnson Nashua, NH & Mil Gallagher Ellsworth, ME Stillborn
JOHNSON, M Mabel Pearl, Jun 23 1895 Sex:F Child# 2 Arthur Johnson Manchester, NH & Regina Belanger New Durham, NH
JOHNSON, Marie, Mar 9 1904 Sex:M Child# 10 Frederic Johnson Canada & Marie Dionne NH
JOHNSON, Maris, Jul 30 1904 Sex:M Child# 1 Adaski Johnson Armenia & Ziega Mamagonia Armenia
JOHNSON, Marjorie Elizabeth, Mar 15 1919 Sex:F Child#  Charles S Johnson Halifax, NS & Edna Florence Damon
JOHNSON, Marjorie Marion, Mar 7 1924 Sex:F Child# 4 Fred Johnson Nashua, NH & Mil Gallagher Ellsworth, ME
JOHNSON, May Helen, May 4 1894 Sex:F Child# 9 (No Parents Listed)
JOHNSON, Mildred Augusta, Jan 26 1917 Sex:F Child# 1 Fred Led Johnson Nashua, NH & Mildred Gallagher Ellsworth, ME
JOHNSON, Phyllis Janis, Apr 22 1920 Sex:F Child# 1 Philip R Johnson Gorham, ME & Anna W London Wakefield, MA
JOHNSON, Robert Allen, Feb 24 1932 Sex:M Child# 1 C A Johnson Sweden & Helmi J Johnson Milford, NH
JOHNSON, Robert Waldo, May 5 1931 Sex:M Child# 3 Arthur S Johnson Merrimack, NH & Mildred T Anderson Merrimack, NH
JOHNSON, Ruth Marjorie, Aug 23 1921 Sex:F Child# 5 Fravis Johnson Sweden & Mary Maddox Nashua, NH
JOHNSON, Ruth Virginia, Aug 20 1922 Sex:F Child# 1 Hylmar Johnson Worcester, MA & Philomene Chapman Dunstable, MA
JOHNSON, Shirley Arline, Apr 19 1930 Sex:F Child# 2 Arthur Johnson Nashua, NH & Mabel Holmes Wakefield, MA
JOHNSON, Unknown, Mar 26 1890 Sex:F Child# 1 Fred Johnson Canada & Mary R Young Milton T R, NH Stillborn
JOHNSON, Unknown, Jan 22 1894 Sex:F Child# 4 George F Johnson Nova Scotia & Jessie M Gibson Nova Scotia
JOHNSON, Unknown, Aug 3 1894 Sex:F Child# 2 W M Johnson Nashua, NH & Harriet Ballou New Ipswich, NH
JOHNSON, Unknown, May 27 1900 Sex:F Child# 7 Fred Johnson Canada & Mary Young NH
JOHNSON, Unknown, Sep 13 1910 Sex:F Child# 1 Travis Johnson Sweden & Mary Maddox Nashua, NH
JOHNSON, Unknown, Sep 9 1912 Sex:M Child# 2 Travis Johnson Sweden & Mary Maddox Nashua, NH
JOHNSON, Virginia Louise, Oct 7 1921 Sex:F Child# 1 Leroy Johnson Groton, MA & Claudia McLain Brownsville, ME
JOHNSON, Walton, Jan 3 1915 Sex:M Child# 1 Randolph F Johnson Sweden & Jennie W Nystrum Worcester, MA
JOHNSON, William J, Dec 17 1887 Sex:M Child# 1 Alfred F Johnson Tewksbury & Sarah Keeley England
JOHNSON, William Taylor, Jun 4 1920 Sex:M Child# 2 William J Johnson Nashua, NH & Maebelle Taylor Barre, VT
JOHNSTON, Norman, Oct 22 1901 Sex:M Child# 1 George Johnston St Johns, NB & Fannie Burdett Westboro, MA
JOHNSTON, Unknown, Jun 4 1889 Sex:M Child# 7 Adams Johnston New York & Jennie McMalley New York Stillborn
JOLBERT, Marie Rita Gertrude, Aug 26 1928 Sex:F Child# 2 Aime Jolbert Canada & Juliette Boisvin Canada
JOLI, Joseph, Mar 14 1909 Sex:M Child# 2 George Joli Mass & Eva Trottier Canada
JOLI, Marie Laurienna, Oct 19 1911 Sex:F Child# 9 Louis Joli Canada & Eleonore Caron Canada
JOLICOEUR, Jacqueline, Dec 20 1927 Sex:F Child# 2 Edouard Jolicoeur Fremont, NH & Madeline Revella Brest, France
JOLIE, Harry Chrs, Jul 8 1933 Sex:M Child# 2 Louis Jolie Nashua, NH & Annette Brown Montreal, Canada
JOLIN, Marie Laura, Jan 26 1895 Sex:F Child# 4 Henri Jolin Canada & Valida Provencal Canada
JOLIN, Theophilus, Dec 12 1892 Sex:M Child# 3 Henry Jolin Canada & Taleda Canada
JOLLY, Joseph L, Jun 1 1908 Sex:M Child# 1 George Jolly Ainsdale, MA & Eva Trottier Canada
JONES, Albert William Avery, Jun 15 1912 Sex:M Child# 3 (No Parents Listed)
JONES, Arden William, Oct 24 1935 Sex:M Child# 2 Arden Jones North Troy, VT & Marie Lemay Nashua, NH
JONES, Arthur Joseph, Apr 26 1913 Sex:M Child# 2 William Jones NS & Bessie Hartford NH
JONES, Blanch Alice, Feb 5 1896 Sex:F Child# 5 William Jones Maine & Rachel Brooks Maine
JONES, Carrie Hazel, Dec 19 1896 Sex:F Child# 1 William A Jones New Brunswick & Mattie Sinclair New Brunswick
JONES, Donald R, Nov 27 1896 Sex:M Child# 2 Daniel R Jones New Brunswick & Charlotte M Wilson Quebec
JONES, Elizabeth Lola, Apr 13 1931 Sex:F Child# 2 Albert Jones Amherst, NH & Gladys Greenwood Pepperell, MA
JONES, Francis, Jan 16 1904 Sex:F Child# 6 Patrick Jones Ireland & Nora Connors Ireland

JONES, George P, May 24 1894 Sex:M Child# 1 George A Jones Mass & Clara A Lampron Mass
JONES, Gordon Raymond, Feb 23 1926 Sex:M Child# 1 Gordon Jones Buffalo, NY & Mildred Bouley Nashua, NH
JONES, Harold Putnam, Sep 8 1899 Sex:M Child#  William A Jones NB & Martha J Sivilian NB
JONES, Harold Russell, Apr 27 1915 Sex:M Child# 2 Edward Jones E Candia, NH & Jessie Mandigo Nashua, NH
JONES, James Harold, Jul 10 1896 Sex:M Child# 2 Patrick Jones Ireland & Nora Conners Ireland
JONES, James Milliam, Dec 22 1890 Sex:M Child# 3 Thomas Jones VT & Nellie Quin Ireland
JONES, John Paul, Jul 12 1906 Sex:M Child# 7 Patrick T Jones Ireland & Nora Connors Ireland
JONES, Katherine, Dec 23 1897 Sex:F Child# 3 Patrick Jones Ireland & Norah Connors Ireland
JONES, Leo, Feb 24 1901 Sex:M Child# 4 Patrick Jones Ireland & Sarah Connors Ireland
JONES, Lucille Wilson, Jul 17 1901 Sex:F Child# 3 William A Jones NB & Martha J Sinclair NB
JONES, Maggie Theresa, Jul 3 1889 Sex:F Child# 9 Patrick Jones Ireland & Maggie Nash Ireland
JONES, Marguerite May, Oct 21 1928 Sex:F Child# 1 Albert Jones Amherst, NH & G Greenwood Pepperell, MA
JONES, Marion, Oct 4 1902 Sex:M Child# 5 Patrick Jones Ireland & Norah Connor Ireland
JONES, Mildred Claire, Jan 11 1923 Sex:F Child# 5 Edward Everett Jones Candia, NH & Bessie Mandigo Nashua, NH
JONES, Patrick, Mar 17 1908 Sex:M Child# 8 Patrick Jones Ireland & Norah Connor Ireland
JONES, Pauline, Apr 25 1897 Sex:F Child#  George F Jones Maine & Mary Berry NH
JONES, Robert James, Dec 7 1889 Sex:M Child# 4 Thomas E Jones Northfield, VT & Ellen Quinn Ireland
JONES, Roger, Jan 14 1922 Sex:M Child# 2 William Jones Texas & Fanny Burrell Fall River, MA
JONES, Unknown, Sep 28 1887 Sex:F Child# 2 George T Jones Nashua, NH & A F Matthews Natick, MA
JONES, Unknown, Sep 9 1888 Sex:M Child# 1 Thomas E Jones Ireland & Nellie Ireland
JONES, Unknown, Jun 27 1890 Sex:F Child# 1 George Jones Dexter, ME & Mary Berry Amherst, NH
JONES, Unknown, Sep 7 1892 Sex: Child# 1 William H Jones Lowell, VT & Gertrude E Dudley Lebanon, NH
JONES, Unknown, Nov 27 1893 Sex:M Child# 1 Daniel R Jones NB & Charlotte Wilson Canada
JONES, Unknown, Feb 4 1894 Sex:f Child# 3 George N Jones Maine & Mary Berry NH
JONES, Unknown, Mar 7 1894 Sex:M Child# 2 W H Jones Vermont & Emma G NH
JONES, Unknown, Jun 1 1895 Sex:M Child# 1 Patrick Jones Ireland & Nora Connors Ireland
JONES, Unknown, Sep 23 1895 Sex:M Child# 3 William H Jones Lowell, VT & Emma g Lebanon
JONES, Vivian Octavia, Aug 3 1895 Sex:F Child#  Joshua N Jones NH & Katie A Morrison Canada
JONES, Wilma Charlotte, Apr 30 1905 Sex:F Child# 3 Daniel R Jones New Brunswick & Charlotte M Wilson PQ
JONEZ, Joseph, Sep 24 1916 Sex:M Child# 1 Joseph Jonez Russia & Mary Scrutch Russia
JONIS, John, Oct 2 1923 Sex:M Child# 2 Anthony Jonis Lithuania & Marcella Chesnolavic Lithuania
JORDAN, Edward, Jul 12 1892 Sex:M Child# 1 Daniel P Jordan Concord & Mary A Murphy Nashua, NH
JORDAN, John Joseph, Feb 24 1907 Sex:M Child# 2 Walter Jordan England & Maggie O'Connor England
JORDAN, Lloyd Spurgeon, May 31 1928 Sex:M Child# 2 S C Jordan Nova Scotia & Mary Fluke Nova Scotia
JORDAN, Lorraine Doris, Jan 21 1935 Sex:F Child# 3 Spurgeon Jordan Newtonville, NS & Mary Fluke Lunenburg, NS
JORDAN, Mary Margaret, Sep 7 1902 Sex:F Child# 1 Walter Jordan England & Marugerite O'Connor Ireland
JORDON, Alec, Feb 6 1893 Sex:M Child# 4 Rufus Jordon Livermore Falls, ME & Isabella Patterson, NY
JOSEF, Anne, Sep 28 1934 Sex:F Child# 4 John William Josef Germany & Anna King Nashua, NH
JOSEF, Raymond King, Dec 28 1932 Sex:M Child# 3 John Josef Germany & Anna King Nashua, NH
JOSEF, Richard William, Oct 15 1929 Sex:M Child# 1 John William Josef Germany & Annie May King Nashua, NH
JOSEF, Robert James, Nov 4 1930 Sex:M Child# 2 John Wm Josef Germany & Anna King Nashua, NH
JOSEPH, Eugene Thomas, Aug 18 1923 Sex:M Child# 4 Philip Joseph Nashua, NH & Ida Mary Worcester, MA
JOSEPH, James Albert, Nov 15 1928 Sex:M Child# 8 Michael Joseph Manchester, NH & Y Pichette Manchester, NH
JOSEPH, Patricia Elizabeth, Mar 14 1927 Sex:F Child# 2 Stanislaus Joseph Nashua, NH & Roberta Howes Nashua, NH
JOSITIS, Anthony, Jul 1 1921 Sex:M Child# 6 Alexander Jositis Russia & Nellie Stankavich Russia
JOSLIN, George Clarence, Jul 5 1929 Sex:M Child# 1 Thomas E Joslin Gilford, NH & Constance Latulippe Manchester, NH
JOSLIN, Laurence Frank, Sep 20 1919 Sex:M Child# 2 Wilbur L Joslin Fitchburg, MA & Hazel F Clarkson Northampton, MA
JOSLIN, Richard Francis, May 19 1934 Sex:M Child# 2 Thomas E Joslin Gilford, NH & Constance Latulippe Manchester,NH
JOSLIN, Unknown, Dec 21 1916 Sex:M Child# 1 Wilbur L Joslin Fitchburg, MA & Hazel F Clarkson N Hampton, MA Stillbor
JOSULAUVICH, Unknown, Mar 3 1925 Sex:M Child# 2 A Josulauvich Russia & Anto Josulauvich Russia
JOUBERT, Marie, Feb 4 1888 Sex:F Child# 1 Alphonse Joubert Canada & Delia Geaudet Canada
JOURDOUNAIR, Joseph Harvey, May 4 1892 Sex:M Child# 1 Napoleon Jourdounair Canada & Josephine Tremblay Canada
JOY, Gladys B, Mar 6 1896 Sex:F Child# 1 F L Joy Nashua, NH & Bessie M Blood Nashua, NH
JOY, John Stanley, Apr 26 1925 Sex:M Child# 2 Anthony Joy Poland, Russia & Agnes Markus Lithuania
JOY, Marion Elizabeth, Mar 11 1926 Sex:F Child# 1 Lester A Joy Hudson, NH & Gertrude Tarbell S Lyndeboro, NH
JOYAL, Alice Margo Leonard, Aug 10 1912 Sex:F Child# 2 Henri Joyal Mooers, NY & Victorine Lussier Nashua, NH
JOYAL, Claire Pauline, Jul 31 1930 Sex:F Child# 1 Antonio Joyal Canada & Florence Asselin Burke, Idaho
JOYAL, Cornelia Olivine, Jan 31 1890 Sex:F Child# 2 Cornelius Joyal Plattsburg, NY & Hermine Morin Nashua, NH
JOYAL, Delhia, Apr 26 1892 Sex:F Child# 3 Cornelius Joyal Nashua, NH & Hermine Morin Nashua, NH
JOYAL, Elmire E, Sep 26 1887 Sex:F Child#  Cornelius Joyal Chasey, NY & Hermine Moria Nashua, NH
JOYAL, Florence, Jun 19 1890 Sex:F Child#  Henry Joyal Canada & Marie Goyet Glens Falls, NY
JOYAL, George Henry, Dec 21 1890 Sex:M Child# 4 Hubert Joyal W Chazy, NY & Delina Montbleau Detroit, MI
JOYAL, Gertrude, Apr 5 1887 Sex:F Child#  Hurbert Joyal Plattsburg, NY & D Mont Bleau Canada
JOYAL, Joseph, Jun 4 1899 Sex:M Child# 8 William Joyal Mooers, NY & Odile Dauphinais Mooers, NY
JOYAL, Juliette Marianne, Jan 13 1908 Sex:F Child# 1 Henri Joyal Mooer's, NY & Victorine Lussier Nashua, NH
JOYAL, Maud Elizabeth, Aug 21 1893 Sex:F Child# 6 Hubert Joyal NY &    Mombleau Canada
JOYAL, Paul Robert, Apr 13 1933 Sex:M Child# 3 Antonio Joyal Canada & F Asselin Burke, Idaho
JOYAL, Rene Edmund, Dec 23 1931 Sex:M Child# 2 Antonine Joyal Canada & Florence Asselin Burke, Idaho
JOYAL, Theresa Jeannette, Mar 28 1930 Sex:F Child# 2 Onias Joyal Canada & Eva Gionet Cloversville, NY
JOYCE, Alfred Merrill, Feb 10 1929 Sex:M Child# 3 James H Joyce Wilton, NH & Velma C Quint Haverhill, NH
JOYCE, David James, Jan 25 1930 Sex:M Child# 4 Roland J Joyce Nashua, NH & Mary E Curtin Haverhill, MA
JOYCE, Donald Mason, May 3 1927 Sex:M Child# 3 William A Joyce Nashua, NH & Ethyl Mason Easton, MA
JOYCE, Helen Anne, Feb 21 1926 Sex:F Child# 2 Roland J Joyce Nashua, NH & Mary E Curtin Haverhill, MA

JOYCE, James Carleton, May 30 1930 Sex:M Child# 4 W Anthony Joyce Nashua, NH & Ethyll Mason Easton, MA
JOYCE, Lydianne, Nov 7 1935 Sex:F Child# 8 James H Joyce Tilton, NH & Velma Quirst Haverhill, NH
JOYCE, Margaret Louise, Mar 4 1925 Sex:F Child# 2 Anthony Joyce Nashua, NH & Ethyl Joyce N Easton, MA
JOYCE, Margaret Virginia, May 29 1927 Sex:F Child# 2 James H Joyce Tilton, NH & Velma Quint Haverhill, NH
JOYCE, Patricia Mary, Sep 14 1924 Sex:F Child# 1 Roland Joyce Nashua, NH & Mary E Curtin Haverhill, MA
JOYCE, Richard, Dec 17 1933 Sex:M Child# 6 William A Joyce Nashua, NH & Ethel Mason Easton, MA
JOYCE, Robert Andrew, May 17 1932 Sex:M Child# 5 William A Joyce Nashua, NH & Ethyl Mason Easton, MA
JOYCE, Roland Joseph, Feb 18 1896 Sex:M Child# 1 James P Joyce Nashua, NH & Margaret F O'Brien Swanton, VT
JOYCE, Roland Joseph, Jr, Aug 9 1928 Sex:M Child# 3 Roland J Joyce Nashua, NH & Mary E Curtin Haverhill, MA
JOYCE, William Anthony, Apr 29 1898 Sex:M Child# 2 James P Joyce Nashua, NH & Margaret F O'Brien Swanton, VT
JOYNT, Anastasia Josephine, Jan 29 1932 Sex:F Child# 3 Henry John Joynt Ireland & Mary Crosby Ireland
JOYNT, Sheila Lillian, Sep 19 1934 Sex:F Child# 4 Henry John Joynt Ireland & Mary Crosby Ireland
JOYUL, Unknown, Mar 5 1889 Sex: Child# 3 K Joyul New York & Delia Moulhearn New York
JOZAITIS, Sophia, Jun 5 1916 Sex:F Child# 4 Joseph Jozaitis Russia & Celia Muchal Austria
JOZAITIS, Unknown, Jun 15 1913 Sex:M Child# 2 Alex Jozaitis Russia & Nellie Stemuewicz Russia
JOZARTIS, Minnie, May 14 1911 Sex:F Child# 1 Alexanchia Jozartis Russia & Nellie Stankinvicte Russia
JOZIATIS, Annie, Apr 1 1924 Sex:F Child# 7 Alex Joziatis Lithuania & Nellie Stankevitch Lithuania
JOZIATIS, Mary, Apr 1 1924 Sex:F Child# 8 Alex Joziatis Lithuania & Nellie Stankevitch Lithuania
JOZITIS, George, Jan 25 1917 Sex:M Child# 4 Alexander Jozitis Russia & Nellie Stankavichute Russia
JOZITIS, Michael, Jun 12 1918 Sex:M Child# 5 Alexander Jozitis Russia & Nellie Stankavatukis Russia
JOZOTIS, Unknown, Dec 11 1917 Sex:M Child# 6 Joseph Jozotis Russia & Cecelia Moussel Russia
JOZUKEWI, Mary, Feb 26 1905 Sex:F Child# 1 Julius Jozukewi Russia & Banig Formulew Russia
JSRIEWICZ, Joseph, Jul 4 1906 Sex:M Child# 1 George Jsriewicz Russia & Mary Sinkiewiczuma Russia
JUBERT, Hattie May, Feb 25 1921 Sex:F Child# 2 William Jubert Sciota, NY & Lillian Blow Sciota, NY
JUBERT, Marie Jacqueline, Sep 15 1928 Sex:F Child# 4 William Jubert Chazy, NY & Lillian Blow Sciota, NY
JUBERT, Marie Madeleine, Sep 15 1928 Sex:F Child# 5 William Jubert Chazy, NY & Lillian Blow Sciota, NY
JUBERT, Russell George, Apr 13 1917 Sex:M Child# 1 William Jubert Sciota, NY & Lillian Blow Sciota, NY
JUBERT, Sylvia Jeanette, Nov 20 1925 Sex:F Child# 3 William Jubert Sciota, NY & Lillian Blow Sciota, NY
JUDD, Mary L, Sep 3 1898 Sex:F Child# 1 Charles W Judd Littleton & Annie C Van Tassell Boston, MA
JUDKINS, Unknown, Aug 14 1887 Sex:F Child# 6 Edward G Judkins Sanbornton & Ella M Prescott Waterville, ME
JUEROACK, Unknown, Dec 29 1899 Sex:M Child# 3 Ludger Jueroack Canada & Arthemise Aubue Canada
JUEROACK, Unknown, Dec 29 1899 Sex:F Child# 2 Ludger Jueroack Canada & Arthemise Aubue Canada
JUKNIEWICZ, Jim, Apr 9 1916 Sex:M Child# 1 Frank Jukniewicz Russia & Anna Russia
JUKNIEWICZ, Joseph, Apr 9 1916 Sex:M Child# 2 Frank Jukniewicz Russia & Anna Russia
JUKOSKY, Edward Joseph, Nov 26 1917 Sex:M Child# 2 Ed Jukosky Russia & Jos Korepocokuna Russia
JULEK, Unknown, Dec 4 1921 Sex:M Child# 1 Stanley Julek Poland & Emily Mirozik Poland
JULIAN, Evelyn Ruth, Apr 1 1922 Sex:F Child# 2 Edouard Julian Canada & Irene Jean Nashua, NH
JULIEN, Adrienne Lucille, Mar 25 1923 Sex:F Child# 3 Geo Edward Julien Canada & Irene Jean Nashua, NH
JULIEN, Edwin Robert William, Mar 1 1921 Sex:M Child# 1 Eddie Julien Canada & Irene Jean Nashua, NH
JUNES, Flossie Anne, Apr 14 1890 Sex:F Child# 4 Jacot M Junes Nova Scotia & Emma C Moody Nova Scotia
JUONIS, Julius, Jun 22 1918 Sex:M Child# 2 Joseph Juonis Russia & Mary Eriass Russia
JURACKIS, Alphonse, Aug 13 1925 Sex:M Child# 6 John Jurackis Lithuania & Eva Jurackis Lithuania
JURAGA, Brunislava, Mar 14 1928 Sex:F Child# 1 John Juraga Poland & Nellie A Szerban Poland
JURANIES, Eleanor Ruth, Apr 4 1930 Sex:F Child# 3 Saturny Juranies Russia & Telka Pekula Russia
JURANIS, Leocadis Lena, Aug 7 1918 Sex:F Child# 1 Saturn Juranis Russia & Theela Pakoula Russia
JUREKA, Jamena Juzefa, Feb 22 1933 Sex:F Child# 4 Stanley Jureka Poland & Maria Jureka Poland
JUREKA, Stanislaw, Apr 23 1921 Sex:M Child# 2 Stanislaw Jureka Poland & Maria Falkowska Poland
JUREKA, Wanda, Nov 10 1926 Sex:F Child# 3 Stanislaus Jureka Poland & Mary Falkow Poland
JUREVICZ, Edmund, Feb 14 1915 Sex:M Child# 2 Joseph Jurevicz Russia & Catherine Truxczyn Russia
JUREVICZ, Raymond, Dec 2 1917 Sex:M Child# 4 Juzef Jurewicz Russia & Katarryna Trukzyn Russia
JURIS, Unknown, Nov 24 1928 Sex:M Child# 4 Andrew Juris Greece & Olga Kamveri Greece
JUSTASON, Ernest Lysle, Jul 12 1933 Sex:M Child# 2 Lysle Justason New Brunswick & Simone Hebert Nashua, NH
JUSTASON, Irvin, Sep 28 1931 Sex:M Child# 1 Lysle Justason Canada & Simone Hebert Nashua, NH
JUTRAS, Germaine Aurore, Sep 16 1925 Sex:F Child# 3 Lucien C Jutras Canada & Aurore Rousseau Canada
JUTRAS, Lillian Mary, Mar 18 1935 Sex:F Child# 1 Giles Jutras Quebec & Agnes Gardmore Maine
JUVAISE, Unknown, Nov 19 1890 Sex:F Child# 1 Arthur Juvaise Canada & Metilde Choiners Nashua, NH Stillborn
KABACHINSKI, Jim, Aug 7 1894 Sex:M Child# 1 Poleon Kabachinski Poland & Katie Zalian Poland
KABAZEUSKI, Stania, Nov 28 1905 Sex:M Child# 1 Alex Kabazeuski Russia & Zefiga Alesaka Russia
KACHULINES, Albert, May 13 1905 Sex:M Child# 5 Joseph Kachulines Russia & Philomene Berube Canada
KACHULYNIS, Martin, Sep 15 1903 Sex:M Child# 4 Joseph Kachulynis Russia & Philomene Berube Canada
KADALIS, Anna, Sep 6 1915 Sex:F Child# 2 Anthony Kadalis Russia & Eva Armowicz Russia
KADZIADANNUS, Adolphe, Sep 8 1918 Sex:M Child# 2 Merk Kadziadannus Greece & Slida Archambeau US
KAINERNEOKI, Romeo, Aug 9 1924 Sex:M Child# 9 V Kainerneoki Poland & Annie Dianitrywa Poland
KAIRIS, Michael, Jan 22 1913 Sex:M Child# 1 John Kairis Russia & Mary Narinkawich Russia
KAITOL, Helen, Feb 7 1902 Sex:F Child# 3 Stanislas Kaitol Russia & Parm'la Radomouska Russia
KAKANOUSKI, Antonio, Sep 8 1899 Sex:M Child# 1 Adams Kakanouski Russia & Franke Stwiszewka Russia
KALAKATIONIS, Arthur, Jr, Dec 7 1932 Sex:M Child# 6 A Kalakationis Greece & Dina Demakis Greece
KALAMBSLIKIS, Unknown, Feb 1 1918 Sex:M Child# 3 Athan Kalambslikis Greece & Theodora Exarbron Greece
KALIS, Unknown, May 18 1918 Sex:M Child# 1 James Kalis Greece & Jane Thelip Greece
KALLEAD, Albert John, Feb 7 1924 Sex:M Child# 5 John G Kallead Syria & Massim Koweseley Syria
KALLEAD, Edward, Dec 20 1922 Sex:M Child# 4 John G Kallead Syria & Massion Kowsely Syria
KALLEAD, Emile John George, Jan 7 1925 Sex:M Child# 6 John George Kallead Syria & Marsini Kowcocky Syria
KALLEAD, Genevieve, Jul 29 1928 Sex:F Child# 9 J G Kallead Syria & Massimi Koweslay Syria

KALLEAD, Skakeab, Jan 4 1922 Sex:M Child# 3 John G Kallead Syria & Massini Koweseley Syria
KALLEAD, Vivienne M, Feb 9 1927 Sex:F Child# 8 John G Kallead Syria & M Koweseley Syria
KALONAS, Helina, Jun 9 1917 Sex:F Child# 4 Adolph Kalonas Russia & Mary Barioskute Russia
KALPSH, Helen, Mar 15 1912 Sex:F Child# 1 Frank Kalpsh Russia & Ruth Kasperowitch Russia
KALPSHIR, Frank, Aug 3 1913 Sex:M Child# 2 Frank Kalpshir Russia & Gaudiuta Kasperawich Russia
KALUSTAIN, Margaret, Nov 29 1919 Sex:F Child# 2 Kaspar Kalustain Armenia & Lucy Aronian Armenia
KAMANSKY, Edith, Aug 1 1913 Sex:F Child# 6 Nathan Kamansky Russia & Lizzie Pardner Russia
KAMANSKY, Unknown, Jun 2 1907 Sex:M Child# 4 N Kamansky Russia & Lizzie Partner Russia
KAMENECKY, Stasie, Jan 24 1913 Sex:F Child# 2 Justin Kamenecky Russia & Veronica Sedlaw Russia
KAMENECKY, Wadeslof, Jun 8 1915 Sex:M Child# 4 Victor Kamenecky Russia & Anna Dimetrowa Russia
KAMENITSKI, Annie, Apr 22 1911 Sex:F Child# 1 Ustan Kamenitski Russia & Veronica Sedlevitch Russia
KAMENSKI, Annie, Jun 12 1918 Sex:F Child# 2 Benjamin Kamenski Russia & Fannie Christopowich Russia
KAMENSKI, Bernard Harold, Oct 11 1927 Sex:M Child# 3 N Kamenski Russia & Goldy Russia
KAMENSKI, Dora, May 9 1912 Sex:F Child# 6 Nathan Kamenski Russia & Lizzie Pardner Russia
KAMENSKY, Samuel, Aug 3 1912 Sex:M Child# 1 Joseph Kamensky Russia & Mary Vaisberg Russia
KAMESKIE, Broneslave, Dec 21 1916 Sex:M Child# 1 Carroll Kameskie Russia & Mary Zubreskie Russia
KAMIENCI, George, May 5 1919 Sex:M Child# 6 Victor Kamienci Russia & Ann Dunetrienda Russia
KAMIENICHI, Casimer, Feb 15 1922 Sex:M Child# 8 Victor Kamienichi Poland & Anna Dofinitrova Poland
KAMIENIECKI, Edward, Apr 3 1914 Sex:M Child# 1 Syl Kamieniecki Russia & Edna Galatini Russia
KAMIENIECKI, Josephine, Feb 23 1929 Sex:F Child# 2 Adam Kamieniecki Poland & Malvina Utaruik Poland
KAMIENIECKI, Richard, Nov 17 1934 Sex:M Child# 1 Michael Kamieniecki Siberia & Thelma Usdavin Nashua, NH
KAMIENIECKI, Stefan, Aug 3 1916 Sex:M Child# 5 Victor Kamieniecki Russia & Anna Gemetriava Russia
KAMIENIECKY, Sophie, Mar 28 1922 Sex:F Child# 5 Justin Kamieniecky Russia & Veronika Russia
KAMINIECHY, Genefa, Jun 26 1924 Sex:F Child# 3 C Kaminiechy Poland & Mary Zubrycka Poland
KAMINISKI, Yonina, Jan 25 1917 Sex:F Child# 1 Adam Kaminiski Russia & Malvina Warsich Russia
KAMISKY, Clara, Aug 1 1902 Sex:F Child# Martin Kamisky Russia & Lizzie Portney Russia
KAMURNEHKI, Unknown, Dec 18 1920 Sex:M Child# 7 Victor Kamurnehki Russia & Annie Dimetresian Russia
KANE, Arthur William, Jun 21 1931 Sex:M Child# 1 Arthur William Kane Randolph, MA & Helen J Murphy Quincy, MA
KANE, Mary, Jan 31 1923 Sex:F Child# 1 Joseph Kane Maine & Mary Travers Boston, MA
KANELLOPOLOS, George, Nov 13 1916 Sex:M Child# 3 James Kanellopolos Greece & Ephadit Mankesha Greece
KANOPOLAS, Unknown, Mar 8 1917 Sex:F Child# 2 John Kanopolas Greece & Martha Otto Wisconsin
KANREMECKI, Creslawa, Apr 25 1928 Sex:F Child# 10 Victor Kanremecki Poland & Anna Zimitrow Poland
KANSLAUSKY, Annie, Sep 1 1918 Sex:F Child# 2 Albin Kanslausky Russia & Annie Zapelick Russia
KANTARAWICZ, Julius, Sep 9 1919 Sex:M Child# 3 Louis Kantarawicz Lithuania Russia & Sophia Klebissa Austria
KANTARGIS, Charlotte Elizabeth, Nov 20 1935 Sex:F Child# 1 James Kantargis Manchester, NH & Ruth Gallup Nashua, NH
KANTER, Maurice, Jul 29 1903 Sex:M Child# 4 Henry Kanter Russia & Ada Myrskl Russia
KANTER, William, May 8 1906 Sex:M Child# 6 Henry Kanter Russia & Ida R Mirsky Russia
KAPETANAKIS, Emanuel, Aug 9 1917 Sex:M Child# 4 Markos Kapetanakis Crete & Styliani Marmarcki Crete
KAPISKAS, Vitantas, Mar 21 1927 Sex:M Child# 1 Paul Kapiskas Lithuania & Antonia Saltis Lithuania
KAPLAN, Edward Robert, Mar 9 1935 Sex:M Child# Louis Kaplan Lawrence, MA & Sarah B Fierman Boston, MA
KAPLAND, Saul, Mar 26 1925 Sex:M Child# 2 Max Kapland Russia & Esther Rich Russia
KAPLAND, Zelda, Aug 21 1923 Sex:F Child# 1 Mace Kapland Russia & Esther Rotch Russia
KAPTIN, Anna, Jul 27 1915 Sex:F Child# 2 William Kaptin Russia & Anna Tamulavitch Russia
KAR, Matilda, Sep 8 1889 Sex:F Child# 5 Francis Kar Canada & Mary Brousseau Canada
KARANASH'U, Ermioney, Apr 10 1930 Sex:F Child# 1 Mathew J Karanash'u Greece & Ethel Thomas Greece
KARAUSKI, Alphonse, Dec 25 1925 Sex:M Child# 6 John Karauski Lithuania & Mikatas Karlonas Lithuania
KARAUSKI, Ella Joan, Jun 23 1935 Sex:F Child# 2 Albert Karauski Penn & Olive Charron Nashua, NH
KARAYINIS, Unknown, Nov 24 1920 Sex:M Child# 1 Arthur Karayinis Greece & Bolon Mikyou Greece
KARBONAS, Julius, Jul 27 1914 Sex:M Child# 5 Adolf Karbonas Russia & Mary Barishouskuts Russia
KARCHMER, Dorothy, Sep 2 1910 Sex:F Child# 3 Harry Karchmer Russia & Rebecca Shroder Russia
KARCYEWSKI, John, Oct 12 1931 Sex:M Child# 9 John Karcyewski Poland & Beatrice Slotunas Poland
KARCZENSKI, Richard Donald, Nov 17 1934 Sex:M Child# 10 John Karczenski Lithuania & Beatrice Slarcinas Lithuania
KARCZEWSKA, Doris Nancy, Jun 25 1933 Sex:F Child# 1 (No Parents Listed)
KARCZEWSKI, John, May 24 1923 Sex:M Child# 6 John Karczewski Russia & Petranela Slaiczun Russia
KARKARIAN, Paul, Sep 7 1912 Sex:M Child# 2 Charles Karkarian Armenia & Lizzie Paul Mass
KARKARIAN, Zabal, Jul 21 1907 Sex:M Child# 1 Dor Karkarian Turkey & Actkik Tehakarian Turkey
KARKISKIE, Unknown, Jul 21 1930 Sex:M Child# 8 John Karkiskie Russia & Beatrice Clatinus Russia Stillborn
KARKORIAN, Marguerite, Mar 13 1922 Sex:F Child# 7 Barsam Karkorian Armenia & Elizabeth Paul Lowell, MA
KARLONAS, Adolphe, Jr, Apr 29 1913 Sex:M Child# 1 Adolphe Karlonas Russia & Mary Boreskowski Russia
KARLONAS, Mary, Aug 2 1911 Sex:F Child# 1 Antonas Karlonas Russia & Karata Kuraciute Russia
KARLONAS, Menesia, Aug 1 1920 Sex:F Child# 6 Adolphe Karlonas Lithuania Russia & M Baruchowskuta Lithuania Russia
KARLONES, John Ludwig, Aug 25 1927 Sex:M Child# 8 Adolphus Karlones Lithuania & M Breshowkuti Lithuania
KARLONOS, Eleanor, May 13 1923 Sex:F Child# 7 Adolphus Karlonos Russia & Mary Barisaihute Russia
KARLOWNIZ, Agnes, Dec 24 1915 Sex:F Child# 3 Adolf Karlowniz
KARN, Richard Henry, Dec 19 1934 Sex:M Child# 2 George Karn Nashua, NH & Cecelia Lang Nashua, NH
KARNOW, Julian, Jul 1 1913 Sex:M Child# 3 Charles Karnow Russia & Domitilda Valowicz Russia
KAROSAS, Louis, Aug 19 1918 Sex:M Child# 1 Peter Karosas Russia & Agnes Pekarsky Russia
KARPAS, Melvin, Mar 5 1929 Sex:M Child# 3 Louis L Karpas Russia & Frances Aronson Russia
KARPSTGENE, Olive Violet, Feb 20 1920 Sex:F Child# 3 Osman Karpstgene Germany & Florence Belcher Taunton, MA
KARSAKAS, Helenas, Dec 30 1917 Sex:F Child# 4 Leonard Karsakas Russia & Mikala Kruszas Russia
KARSIK, Michael, Dec 2 1909 Sex:M Child# 2 Leonard Karsik Russia & Mikala Krusuts Russia
KARSON, Adele Albina, Sep 17 1919 Sex:F Child# 1 John Karson Lithuania Russia & Rosa Kroshuta Lithuania Russia
KARSTOCK, Joseph, Jr, Jul 31 1922 Sex:M Child# 1 Joseph Karstock Russia & May Souslough Russia

KARSTOK, Charles, Jan 27 1928 Sex:M Child# 2 Joseph Karstok Russia & Mag Lynn Russia
KARTOSKIE, Bernice, Jan 13 1917 Sex:F Child# 2 Steven Kartoskie Russia & Anna Speckels Russia
KASHERLINE, Odolore, Jan 3 1900 Sex:M Child# 3 Peter Kasherline Russia & Marie Dufresne Canada
KASHPRAINIO, Joseph, Nov 28 1904 Sex:M Child# 1 Martin Kashprainio Russia & Melina Lebecdukute Russia
KASHULENES, Marie Helene, Sep 7 1898 Sex:F Child# 2 Peter Kashulenes Poland & Ernestine Berube Canada
KASHULINAS, Martin Joseph, Apr 24 1929 Sex:M Child# 1 Martin Kashulinas Nashua, NH & Minnie Sunbrabich Lithuania
KASHULINES, Albert, May 6 1904 Sex:M Child# 4 Peter Kashulines Russia & Ernestine Berube Canada
KASHULINES, Albert, Jr, Jul 12 1928 Sex:M Child# 3 A Kashulines Nashua, NH & C Girouard Hudson, NH
KASHULINES, Arena, Apr 15 1908 Sex:F Child# 7 Joseph Kashulines Russia & Philomene Berube Canada
KASHULINES, Arthur Joseph, Jr, Feb 19 1930 Sex:M Child# 1 Arthur J Kashulines Nashua, NH & Ida Cole Nova Scotia
KASHULINES, Clare Arleen, Jul 11 1927 Sex:F Child# 2 A Kashulines Nashua, NH & Celestine Girouard Hudson, NH
KASHULINES, Corona, Jun 30 1913 Sex:F Child# 9 Joseph Kashulines Russia & Philomene Berube Canada
KASHULINES, Helene, Feb 21 1930 Sex:F Child# 5 Albert Kashulines Nashua, NH & Celestine Girouard Nashua, NH
KASHULINES, Joseph, May 15 1927 Sex:M Child# 1 Joseph Kashulines Nashua, NH & Olivine Miro Nashua, NH Stillborn
KASHULINES, Joseph Pierre, Oct 7 1896 Sex:M Child# 1 Joseph P Kashulines Russia & Ernestine Dube Canada
KASHULINES, Leon, Nov 7 1911 Sex:M Child# Joseph Kashulines Russia & Phil Berube Canada
KASHULINES, Louis Anthony, Apr 1 1915 Sex:M Child# 10 Joseph Kashulines Russia & Philomene Berube Canada
KASHULINES, Peter Thomas, Aug 31 1935 Sex:M Child# 7 Albert Kashulines New York & Celestine Girouard Nashua, NH
KASHULINES, Rita Camille, Mar 25 1926 Sex:F Child# 1 Albert Kashulines Nashua, NH & Mae Girard Hudson, NH
KASHULINES, Robert, Jul 12 1928 Sex:M Child# 4 A Kashulines Nashua, NH & C Girouard Hudson, NH
KASHULINIS, Helene, Jan 29 1907 Sex:F Child# 6 Joseph Kashulinis Russia & Philomene Berube Canada
KASIMITCH, Annie, Aug 11 1914 Sex:F Child# 3 John Kasimitch Russia & Antonia Yeremitch Russia
KASKELL, William Earl, Aug 19 1922 Sex:M Child# 6 Leslie Kaskell Nova Scotia & May Baker Saranac, NY
KASMAN, Wanda, Dec 1 1915 Sex:F Child# 1 Gabriel Kasman Russia & Antonia Watazyuska Russia
KASPED, John William, Dec 25 1933 Sex:M Child# 2 John W Kasped Lithuania & Mary Gumbris Lowell, MA
KASPER, Dorothy Catherine, Jul 6 1934 Sex:F Child# 1 Andrew Kasper Lithuania & Anna Banuskevich Lithuania
KASPER, Joseph, Feb 11 1919 Sex:M Child# 1 Kastante Kasper Russia & Josephine Molis Russia
KASPER, Mary, Nov 3 1913 Sex:F Child# 1 Mike Kasper Russia & Agnes Sardis Austria
KASPER, Unknown, Dec 8 1907 Sex:F Child# 4 Martin Kasper Russia & Amelia Labadnikute Russia
KASPERKA, Alphonse, Dec 28 1913 Sex:M Child# 2 Peter Kasperka Russia & Nelmina Norsgrudska Russia
KASYTA, Danice, Apr 19 1901 Sex:F Child# 3 Joseph Kasyta Russia & Anna Czarniaska Russia
KASZETA, John, Nov 14 1909 Sex:M Child# 1 Alek Kaszeta Russia & Marcela Skiaudzecs Russia
KASZULINOS, Marie Delia, Nov 1 1898 Sex:F Child# 1 Joza Kaszulinos Russia & Philomene Berube Canada
KATAVICH, Agnes, Apr 3 1917 Sex:F Child# 6 Boleska Katavich Russia & Tophelia Kiselepas Russia
KATJIGOZ, Mary, May 12 1916 Sex:F Child# 3 George Katjigoz Greece & Anastasopolo Greece
KATOWICH, Anna, Nov 23 1914 Sex:F Child# 3 Julien Katowich Russia & Mary Maszkewich Russia
KATRANIS, Unknown, Mar 29 1921 Sex:M Child# Nicolas Katranis Greece & Zantha Dandas Greece
KATRANIS, Unknown, Dec 21 1929 Sex:F Child# 5 Nicholas Katranis Greece & Xanthi Danton Greece
KATSIAFELES, Unknown, Jul 4 1917 Sex:F Child# 1 George Katsiafeles Greece & A Peeras Greece
KATSIAFICAS, Unknown, Oct 3 1918 Sex:F Child# 1 George Katsiaficas Greece & Atamaise Pereg Greece
KATSIAFICAS, Unknown, Jul 2 1923 Sex:M Child# 4 George Katsiaficas Greece & Athanasia Psira Greece
KATZ, Gertrude Bertha, Jun 29 1918 Sex:F Child# 6 Norris Katz Russia & Fannie Gilbert Russia
KATZ, Harry, Jan 12 1920 Sex:M Child# 7 Morris Katz Russia & Fanny Gilbert Russia
KATZ, Israel, Feb 23 1917 Sex:M Child# 5 Morris Katz Russia & Fannie Gilbert Russia
KATZ, Louis, Sep 24 1921 Sex:M Child# 8 Morris Katz Russia & Fanny Gilbert Russia
KATZ, Mary, Oct 11 1911 Sex:F Child# 4 Louis Katz Russia & Rosie Hatsfeld Russia
KATZ, Michael, Jan 15 1911 Sex:M Child# 2 Morris Katz Russia & Fanny Gilberd Russia
KATZ, Philip, Mar 5 1909 Sex:M Child# 1 Morris Katz Russia & Fannie Gilbert Russia
KATZ, Sarah Frances, Jan 22 1915 Sex:F Child# 4 Morris Katz Russia & Annie Grimm Russia
KAUNELIS, Edward, Jul 3 1927 Sex:M Child# 2 Antanas Kaunelis Lithuania & Emilie Mills Lithuania
KAUSKAUSKAS, Eva, Sep 12 1918 Sex:F Child# 1 Steve Kauskauskas Russia & Kate Danoskowicz Russia
KAWALSKI, Mary, Jul 29 1923 Sex:F Child# 1 (No Parents Listed)
KAWSLAWSKI, Stephanie, Sep 22 1916 Sex:F Child# 1 Albert Kawslawski Russia & Annie Zapalick Russia
KAZANGIAN, Victoria, Apr 20 1910 Sex:F Child# 1 Mearian Kazangian Turkey & Dallitia Kangian Turkey
KAZARIAN, Vache H, Mar 23 1908 Sex:M Child# 3 Harry Kazarian Turkey & Markaid Barsamian Turkey
KAZES, Veronica, May 27 1921 Sex:F Child# 7 Mike Kazes Lithuania & Antonia Stanke Lithuania
KAZLASKAS, Julia Bernice, Mar 14 1931 Sex:F Child# 2 Charles Kazlaskas Nashua, NH & Amelia Elkavich Nashua, NH
KAZLAUSKAS, Charles Frank, May 15 1934 Sex:M Child# 3 Charles Kazlauskas Nashua, NH & Amelia Elkavich Nashua, NH
KAZLAUSKIS, Antonos, Mar 3 1905 Sex:M Child# 1 John Kazlauskis Russia & Biene Moilhuutie Russia
KAZLOUSKIS, Kazimer, Mar 3 1906 Sex:M Child# 2 John Kazlouskis Russia & Benise Waitkewiciait Russia
KEACY, Napoleon, Jr, Oct 14 1920 Sex:M Child# 1 Napoleon Keacy Wilton, NH & Margaret Coffey Nashua, NH
KEAN, Edward Leslie, Nov 15 1904 Sex:M Child# 1 Edward F Kean Ireland & Helen Soule Maine
KEAN, Joanne, Jul 4 1931 Sex:F Child# 1 Walter R Kean Woburn, MA & Ruth Winslow Somerville, MA
KEAN, Warren, Nov 8 1935 Sex:M Child# 2 W Russell Kean Woburn, MA & Ruth Winslow Somerville, MA
KEARNS, Eleanor K, Aug 8 1918 Sex:F Child# 1 Fred Kearns Plattsburg, NY & Bessie Hammond Alburg, VT
KEBORT, Gertrude, Mar 13 1915 Sex:F Child# 1 David Kebort Russia & Petronilla Polhkinsk Russia
KECY, Harriet Elizabeth, Jan 12 1925 Sex:F Child# 4 Napoleon J Kecy Wilton, NH & Marg E Coffey Nashua, NH
KECY, Henry L, Jul 1 1926 Sex:M Child# 5 Napoleon J Kecy Wilton, NH & Margaret Coffey Nashua, NH
KECY, Robert Paul, May 24 1931 Sex:M Child# 6 Napoleon J Kecy Wilton, NH & Margaret Coffey Nashua, NH
KEDALIS, Geneva, Aug 30 1913 Sex:F Child# 1 Anton Kedalis Russia & Eva Yirmalawich Russia
KEDDY, Laura Jessie, Nov 14 1893 Sex:F Child# 1 Charles Keddy Nashua, NH & Josephine Richard Canada
KEDLES, Donat, Oct 14 1909 Sex:M Child# 1 George Kedles Russia & Sala Versn Russia
KEECH, Jane Ann, Jan 30 1935 Sex:F Child# 1 Fred L Keech Vestal, NY & Minnie Carpenter Lowell, MA

KEECY, William Francis, Dec 20 1923 Sex:M Child# 3 Napoleon J Keecy Wilton, NH & Margaret Coffey Nashua, NH
KEEDZWA, Adolphe, Dec 16 1924 Sex:M Child# 2 William Keedzwa Poland Russia & Antoinette Uscovich Poland Russia
KEEGAN, Anna Elizabeth, Sep 19 1893 Sex:F Child# 3 John H Keegan Nashua, NH & Margaret M Costello Chatauqua, NY
KEEGAN, Ellen S, Apr 26 1893 Sex:F Child# 3 Thomas S Keegan Nashua, NH & Elizabeth Sullivan Nashua, NH
KEEGAN, Frances, Nov 6 1891 Sex:F Child# 2 Thomas Keegan Nashua, NH & Elizabeth Sullivan Nashua, NH
KEEGAN, John Henry, Sep 15 1891 Sex:M Child# 2 J H Keegan Nashua, NH & Marguerite Costelle Chatauqua, NY
KEEGAN, May, Apr 1 1888 Sex:F Child# 7 John R Keegan Trenton, NJ & Ellen Sheehan Ireland
KEEGAN, Thomas, Jul 28 1890 Sex:M Child# 1 Thomas F Keegan Nashua, NH & Elizabeth A Sullivan Nashua, NH
KEEGAN, Unknown, May 3 1887 Sex:M Child# 1 John Keegan Nashua, NH & Maggie NY
KEELEY, Arthur Eugene, May 7 1924 Sex:M Child# 3 Arthur Keeley Somerville, MA & Mary Fagan Dover, NH
KEELEY, Catharine, Feb 19 1921 Sex:F Child# 1 Arthur Keeley Somerville, MA & Mary Fagan Dover, NH
KEELEY, Florence, Jul 22 1922 Sex:F Child# 2 Arthur Keeley Dover, NH & Mary Fagan Dover, NH
KEELEY, Unknown, Sep 19 1895 Sex:F Child# 1 Anthony I Keeley England & Nellie M Finning Nashua, NH
KEELY, Charles Anthony, Oct 1 1896 Sex:M Child# 3 Anthony J Keely England & Nellie M Finning Nashua, NH
KEELY, Eleanor Helen, Aug 21 1921 Sex:F Child# 1 Frank W Keely Sandown, NH & Lydia J Parent Nashua, NH
KEELY, Margaret, Oct 1 1896 Sex:F Child# 2 Anthony J Keely England & Nellie M Finning Nashua, NH
KEEN, Delmire, May 12 1910 Sex:F Child# 4 Walter Keen England & Ada Thomas New Brunswick
KEENAN, Anna M, Jun 25 1896 Sex:F Child# 3 John J Keenan Ireland & Ellen McInerny Ireland
KEENAN, Delia, Sep 13 1901 Sex:F Child# 6 John Keenan Ireland & Ellen McInerney Ireland
KEENAN, Ellen May, Feb 24 1900 Sex:F Child# 5 John Keenan Ireland & Ellen McIverney Ireland
KEENAN, Francis Martin, Oct 17 1894 Sex:M Child# 2 John Keenan Ireland & Ellen McKnary Ireland
KEENAN, Frederick, Nov 3 1907 Sex:M Child# 9 John Keenan Ireland & Ellen McInerney Ireland
KEENAN, John J, Oct 10 1893 Sex:M Child# 1 John J Keenan Ireland & Ellen McNarnay Ireland
KEENAN, John Joseph, Apr 28 1922 Sex:M Child# 1 John Keenan Nashua, NH & Mary Ellen Benson Ireland
KEENAN, Louise, Feb 13 1906 Sex:F Child# 8 John Keenan Ireland & Ellen McQuivery Ireland
KEENAN, Margaret, Apr 27 1909 Sex:F Child# 10 John Keenan Ireland & Helen McAneny Ireland
KEENAN, Martin, Jan 12 1893 Sex:M Child# 1 Patrick Keenan Ireland & Norah Harrigan Ireland
KEENAN, Mary Elizabeth, Feb 10 1924 Sex:F Child# 2 John J Keenan Nashua, NH & Mary Benson Ireland
KEENAN, Paul Charles, Dec 14 1926 Sex:M Child# 3 John Keenan Nashua, NH & Mary E Benson Ireland
KEENAN, Thomas, Jun 18 1903 Sex:M Child# 7 John Keenan Ireland & Ellen McInerney Ireland
KEENAN, William Henry, Jan 17 1898 Sex:M Child# 4 John Keenan Ireland & Ellen McInerny Ireland
KEHOE, Andrew, Jun 23 1895 Sex:M Child# 3 Andrew F Kehoe Ireland & Mary Farrar New York
KEHOE, Andrew Francis, Nov 20 1932 Sex:M Child# 2 Andrew Kehoe Nashua, NH & Mary F Keefe Bradford, MA
KEHOE, Ellen, Jan 3 1893 Sex:F Child# 2 Andrew F Kehoe Ireland & Mary Farrell NY
KEHOE, Margaret Therese, Aug 26 1934 Sex:F Child# 3 Andrew Kehoe Nashua, NH & Mary Keefe Bradford, MA
KEHOE, Unknown, Jul 18 1891 Sex:M Child# 1 Andrew F Kehoe Ireland & Mary Farrell New York Stillborn
KEHORIN, Mary Elizabeth, May 30 1914 Sex:F Child# 3 Charles Kehorin Turkey & Lizzie Paul Lowell, MA
KEIKITIS, Vacill Koula, Oct 26 1918 Sex:F Child# 1 George Keikitis Greece & Mary Papadimons Greece
KEIRAS, Mary, Nov 30 1909 Sex:F Child# 1 Anton Keiras Russia & Francesca Alokonis Russia
KEIRSTEAD, Harold William, Feb 22 1929 Sex:M Child# 1 Willard Keirstead New Brunswick & Gladys Tracy Nashua, NH
KEIRSTEAD, Roy Lawson, Mar 17 1930 Sex:M Child# 3 Roy Keirstead New Brunswick & Ethel Gamblin New Brunswick
KEIRYS, Joseph Alphonse, Apr 27 1915 Sex:M Child# 2 John Keirys Russia & Marie Keirys Russia
KEISTEG, Joan Helen, Dec 24 1923 Sex:F Child# 1 Melvin P Keister Lockhaven, PA & Joan Ballou Crab Orchard, KY
KEISTER, Pauline Frances, Nov 24 1928 Sex:F Child# 2 Melvin P Keister Lockhaven, PA & Joanna Ballou Crab Orchard,KY
KEITH, Donald Willard, Dec 12 1923 Sex:M Child# 1 Ralph Keith Hollis, NH & Diana Fontaine Nashua, NH
KEITH, Helen Theresa, Apr 18 1928 Sex:F Child# 4 Charles L Keith Fletcher, VT & Nellie Keenan Wilton, NH
KEITH, James Rouel, Feb 1 1904 Sex:M Child# 1 Morris Henry Keith Vermont & Addie Leclaire NY
KEITH, Robert H, Apr 19 1892 Sex:M Child# 1 G H Keith Vermont & Carrie Bombard New York
KEITH, Unknown, Dec 24 1891 Sex:F Child# Ruel Keith Vermont & A Storm New Brunswick Stillborn
KEITH, Unknown, Jun 29 1893 Sex:F Child# 1 Ruel J Keith Fairfax, VT & Matilda J Storms St Johns, NB
KEITH, Unknown, Aug 15 1895 Sex:F Child# 3 Reuel J Keith Fairfax, VT & Matilda J Stone St Johns, NB
KELLEHER, Willie, Jan 12 1896 Sex:M Child# 6 John Kelleher Ireland & Ellen Hennesy Ireland
KELLEY, Albert James, Apr 25 1898 Sex:M Child# 1 Patrick Kelley Ireland & Bridget Gilhooley Ireland
KELLEY, Alice Flora, Oct 7 1897 Sex:F Child# 2 Henry H Kelley Stratford & Carrie A Griffin Nantasket, MA
KELLEY, Ann Jane, Jan 11 1900 Sex:F Child# 2 Patrick Kelley Ireland & Bridget Gilhooley Ireland
KELLEY, Barbara June, Nov 13 1930 Sex:F Child# 4 Albert Kelley Rochester, NH & Eva Randall Vermont
KELLEY, Charles William, Jr, Jan 15 1923 Sex:M Child# 1 Charles Wm Kelley Farmington, NH & Vieva Fletcher Browning
KELLEY, David Ronald, Jul 27 1928 Sex:M Child# 4 G R Kelley Chelmsford, MA & Dorothy E Wise S Paris, ME
KELLEY, Edward Frank, Jan 17 1924 Sex:M Child# 2 Frank Kelley Sandown, NH & Lydia J Parent Nashua, NH
KELLEY, Ethel May, Dec 22 1893 Sex:F Child# 1 Michael Kelley Boston, MA & Mary E Shea Nashua, NH
KELLEY, Francis W, Feb 10 1908 Sex:M Child# 1 John Kelley Worcester, MA & Alice Buttler Athol, MA
KELLEY, Henry Frank, Oct 7 1897 Sex:M Child# 1 Henry H Kelley Stratford & Carrie A Griffin Nantasket, MA
KELLEY, James Harold, Feb 7 1905 Sex:M Child# 3 John E Kelley Ireland & Sarah T Gaffney Nashua, NH
KELLEY, John, Oct 19 1903 Sex:M Child# 2 John Kelley Ireland & Nellie Gilhooley Ireland
KELLEY, John B, May 25 1902 Sex:M Child# 1 John E Kelley Ireland & Sarah T Gaffney Nashua, NH
KELLEY, Josie Francis, Mar 1 1900 Sex:F Child# 6 P F Kelley Manchester, NH & Mary McMann Scotland
KELLEY, Louise, Jul 8 1915 Sex:F Child# 9 John Kelley Ireland & Sarah Gaffney Nashua, NH
KELLEY, Lucille, Dec 4 1906 Sex:F Child# 4 John E Kelley Ireland & Sarah T Gaffney Nashua, NH
KELLEY, Lucille Rachel, Oct 1 1922 Sex:F Child# 1 Albert J Kelley Rochester, NH & Eva N Randall W Derby, VT
KELLEY, Martha, Oct 19 1906 Sex:F Child# 1 Frank M Kelley Warren, ME & Annie C McKay Nova Scotia
KELLEY, Martha, Jul 8 1915 Sex:F Child# 10 John Kelley Ireland & Sarah Gaffney Nashua, NH
KELLEY, Mary Edith, Mar 25 1903 Sex:F Child# 2 Michael Kelley Boston, MA & Mary B Shea Nashua, NH
KELLEY, Mary Elizabeth, May 9 1903 Sex:F Child# 3 Patrick Kelley Ireland & Bridget Gilhooly Ireland

KELLEY, Mary Eulalia, Nov 27 1903 Sex:F Child# 2 John Kelley Ireland & Sarah Gaffney Nashua, NH
KELLEY, Ruth L, Nov 16 1891 Sex:F Child# 5 William Kelley Woburn, MA & Katie L St Johns, NB
KELLEY, Stella, Aug 2 1900 Sex:F Child# 1 Henry J Kelley Mass & Stella J Reynolds NH
KELLEY, Thomas P, Aug 6 1905 Sex:M Child# Patrick Kelley Ireland & Bridget Gilhooley Ireland
KELLEY, Unknown, May 4 1888 Sex:F Child# 1 Frank M Kelley Warren, ME & Grace M Fletcher Nashua, NH
KELLEY, Unknown, May 4 1888 Sex:F Child# 2 Frank M Kelley Warren, ME & Grace M Fletcher Nashua, NH
KELLEY, Unknown, Jun 9 1888 Sex:M Child# 4 William Kelley Woburn, MA & Kate Livingston N S
KELLEY, Unknown, Nov 5 1890 Sex:M Child# 3 Frank M Kelley Warren, ME & Grace M Fletcher Nashua, NH
KELLEY, Unknown, Dec 17 1898 Sex:M Child# 5 Willard S Kelley Boston, MA & Melissa Wright St Albans, VT
KELLEY, Unknown, Mar 25 1903 Sex:F Child# 3 Michael Kelley Boston, MA & Mary B Shea Nashua, NH
KELLEY, Willis Everett, Nov 16 1924 Sex:M Child# 2 Charles W Kelley Farmington, NH & Bieva E Fletcher Browning
KELLY, Dorothy Lee, Oct 26 1923 Sex:F Child# 2 Albert J Kelly Rochester, NH & Eva M Randall W Derby, VT
KELLY, Durwood Randall, Aug 5 1925 Sex:M Child# 3 Albert J Kelly Rochester, NH & Eva M Randall W Derby, VT
KELLY, Florence, Jul 15 1899 Sex:F Child# 4 James Kelly Clinton, MA & Rose Russell Cohoes, NY
KELLY, Guy Reed, Jul 22 1918 Sex:M Child# 2 Guy Reed Kelly Chelmsford, MA & Dora Wise S Paris, ME
KELLY, Mary, Nov 24 1927 Sex:F Child# 1 Harry J Kelly Canada & M M McCarty Manchester, NH
KELLY, Morrill P, Jul 25 1891 Sex:M Child# 2 Samuel P Kelly Mass & Mary M Morrill Mass
KELLY, Patricia Imelda, Mar 13 1935 Sex:F Child# 1 James Kelly Nashua, NH & Imelda Roy Nashua, NH
KELLY, Ursula, Jul 27 1910 Sex:F Child# 6 John Kelly Ireland & Sarah Gaffney Nashua, NH
KELON, Francisca, May 31 1913 Sex:M Child# 2 Peter Kelon Russia & Annie Meskiuta Russia
KELON, Pranslis, Jun 28 1911 Sex:M Child# 1 Peter Kelon Russia & Annie Maskonis Russia
KELPS, Stephane, Aug 14 1914 Sex:M Child# 3 Frank Kelps Russia & Gertruta Cosparavitc Russia
KELTY, John Hadaway, Aug 16 1929 Sex:M Child# 2 William R R Kelty Roxbury, VT & Maris S Hadaway New York, NY
KEMP, Betty Rose, Sep 1 1931 Sex:F Child# 1 Everett Kemp Canada & Bonna Frink Chelmsford, MA
KEMP, Ella May, Aug 8 1897 Sex:F Child# 1 William H Kemp Canada & Nellie M Dole Claremont, NY
KEMP, John R, Nov 22 1922 Sex:M Child# 1 John E Kemp Leominster, MA & Alice R Dowling Nashua, NH
KEMP, Unknown, Dec 11 1924 Sex:M Child# 1 (No Parents Listed)
KEMP, Violet May, Mar 18 1922 Sex:F Child# 2 Edwin P Kemp Groton, MA & May L Harris Princeton, ME
KENDALL, Abbie, Dec 26 1904 Sex:F Child# 3 Perley A Kendall Londonderry, NH & H Maria Lougee Bedford, NH
KENDALL, Annie, Mar 16 1893 Sex:F Child# 3 Harlan P Kendall Raymond, NH & Lottie Stearns Milford, NH
KENDALL, Barbara, Feb 27 1921 Sex:F Child# 1 Lee S Kimball Milford, NH & Sarah White Unadilla, NY
KENDALL, Forest W, Apr 20 1900 Sex:M Child# 1 H W Kendall NH & Harriet G Law Mass
KENDALL, Germain S, Nov 3 1928 Sex:M Child# 2 Gerald S Kendall Loudon, NH & F A Van Woert Manchester, NH
KENDALL, Helen Lougee, Aug 2 1907 Sex:F Child# 4 Perley A Kendall Londonderry, NH & Henrietta N Lougee Bedford, NH
KENDALL, Phyllis May, Nov 7 1921 Sex:F Child# 1 German S Kendall Loudon, NH & Florence A VanWoert Nashua, NH
KENDALL, Robert Charles, Feb 17 1898 Sex:M Child# 1 Perley H Kendall Londonderry, NH & Maria H Lougee Bedford, NH
KENDALL, Unknown, Sep 9 1888 Sex:M Child# 1 Hergert E Kendall Boston & Leis J Rand New York
KENDALL, Unknown, Feb 16 1891 Sex:M Child# 2 Herbert E Kendall Nashua, NH & Icis J Rand Schuyler Falls, NY
KENDALL, Unknown, Jan 21 1894 Sex:F Child# 3 Herbert E Kendall Boston, MA & Icis J Rand Schuyler Fls, NY Stillborn
KENDALL, Unknown, Oct 22 1899 Sex:F Child# 1 Perley A Kendall NH & Maria Lougee NH
KENDALL, Unknown, Dec 1 1910 Sex:M Child# 1 Albert Kendall Chatham, NB & Isabelle Genest Lake Megantic, PQ
KENDRICK, Barbara Ruth, Oct 2 1923 Sex:F Child# 2 Edgar F Kendrick Amesbury, MA & Emme Zipper Lowell, MA
KENDRICK, Doris Mildred, Dec 19 1926 Sex:F Child# 3 Edgar F Kendrick Amesbury, MA & Emma Zipper Lowell, MA
KENISTON, Mabel, Jan 15 1894 Sex:F Child# 2 O William Keniston NH & Ida Byron Worcester, MA
KENISTON, Myrtle Evelyn, Sep 28 1926 Sex:F Child# 9 C F Keniston Lowell, MA & Mary L Gowing Hudson, NH
KENISTON, Unknown, Nov 19 1920 Sex:F Child# 6 Charles F Keniston Lowell, MA & Mary L Gowing Hudson, NH
KENNEDY, Clarence James, Sep 9 1903 Sex:M Child# 2 Thomas Kennedy Scotland & Lillian Bell Chazy, NY
KENNEDY, Daniel E Jr, May 17 1904 Sex:M Child# 1 Daniel E Kennedy New York, NY & Elizabeth Lord Stoneham, MA
KENNEDY, Edmond Michael, Dec 20 1919 Sex:M Child# 3 Michael E Kennedy Wilton, NH & Catherine T Winn Nashua, NH
KENNEDY, Frances Whiting, Jan 26 1909 Sex:F Child# 2 William H Kennedy Somerville, MA & Jessie A Parker Nashua, NH
KENNEDY, Helen Denise, Aug 10 1917 Sex:F Child# 1 Michael Kennedy Wilton, NH & Catherine T Winn Nashua, NH
KENNEDY, James Bosworth, Jul 12 1909 Sex:M Child# 1 Frank M Kennedy Ireland & Margaret Cannon Ireland
KENNEDY, Margaret Theresa, Feb 13 1931 Sex:F Child# 1 (No Parents Listed)
KENNEDY, Merrian Emma, Aug 5 1905 Sex:F Child# 3 Thomas Kennedy Ohio & Lillian M Bell New York
KENNEDY, Paul, Apr 13 1921 Sex:M Child# 4 Michael Kennedy Wilton, NH & Katharine Winn Nashua, NH
KENNEDY, Robert, Dec 21 1920 Sex:M Child# 1 James W Kennedy Wilton, NH & Catherine E Mullen Ashburnham, MA
KENNEDY, Ruth E, Jan 21 1922 Sex:F Child# 2 James W Kennedy Wilton, NH & Catherine Mullen Ashburnham, MA
KENNEDY, William Parker, Jul 13 1907 Sex:M Child# 1 William H Kennedy Somerville, MA & Jessie A Parker Nashua, NH
KENNEY, Arthur Thomas, Feb 2 1909 Sex:M Child# 1 Thomas E Kenney Canada & Hattie B Russell Enfield, NH
KENNEY, Francis William, Mar 20 1933 Sex:M Child# 2 James F Kenney Concord, NH & Adelaid Austin Pepperell, MA
KENNEY, Harold, Jr, Aug 23 1933 Sex:M Child# 4 Harold Kenney Nova Scotia & F MacDonnell Nova Scotia
KENNEY, Marlene Madge, Sep 21 1935 Sex:F Child# 1 Armand Kenney Nashville, TN & Anna Rivard Nashua, NH
KENNEY, Richard Robert, Feb 22 1935 Sex:M Child# 1 John Kenney Watertown, MA & Janet Gardner Bradley, ME
KENNEY, Unknown, Aug 10 1915 Sex:M Child# 9 John Kenney Canada & Lydia Harding Prince Edward Island Stillborn
KENORKIAN, Uram, Oct 2 1908 Sex:M Child# 2 Kirkor Kenorkian Armenia & Astkik Chakarian Armenia
KENT, Hazel May, Aug 1 1908 Sex:F Child# 2 Gilbert H Kent Vermont & Daisy Dell Vermont
KENYON, George A L, Jul 15 1899 Sex:M Child# 1 James B Kenyon RI & Etta G Kidder Maine
KEOGH, Jennie Agnes, Jul 22 1892 Sex:F Child# 4 William Keogh Dublin, Ireland & Sarah Mullen Milford, NH
KEOUGH, Mary, May 15 1891 Sex:F Child# 3 William J Keough Ireland & Sarha A Mullen Ireland
KEPLUK, Pauline, Jun 28 1914 Sex:F Child# 1 Stephen Kepluk Russia & Katie Paskonigs Russia
KERKORIAN, Charles, Feb 8 1911 Sex:M Child# 1 Charles Kerkorian Armenia & Elizabeth Paul Lowell, MA
KEROAC, Joseph A, Feb 8 1893 Sex:M Child# 14 Jean Bte Keroac Canada & Clementine Bernier Canada
KEROACK, Joseph Emile, Jan 19 1901 Sex:M Child# 2 Joseph Keroack Canada & Emme Levesque Canada

KERORKIAN, Hrachia, Feb 19 1914 Sex:M Child# 1 Baronag Kerorkian Turkey & Parker Turkey
KEROUAC, Cecile Irene, Sep 5 1901 Sex:F Child# 5 Ludger Kerouac Canada & Arthemise Aubut Canada
KEROUAC, Corinne Alida, May 27 1904 Sex:F Child# 4 Joseph Kerouac Canada & Emma Levesque Canada
KEROUAC, Edmond Simeon, Apr 24 1932 Sex:M Child# 2 Arthur Kerouac Canada & Emma Beaudin Manchester, NH
KEROUAC, Eva Marilda, Apr 23 1900 Sex:F Child# 2 Ludger Kerouac Canada & Domrilda Roy Canada
KEROUAC, Hector Robert, Sep 24 1916 Sex:M Child# 9 Ludger Kerouac Canada & Dorilda Roy NH
KEROUAC, Henri Roger, May 29 1932 Sex:M Child# 1 Remi Kerouac Nashua, NH & Juliette Dionne Lowell, MA
KEROUAC, Herve Rodolphe, May 15 1915 Sex:M Child# 5 Joseph Kerouac Canada & Leontine Rouleau Canada
KEROUAC, Irene, Feb 18 1902 Sex:F Child# 3 Ludger Kerouac Canada & Louisa Roy Suncook, NH
KEROUAC, Irene Leontine, Jul 23 1911 Sex:F Child# 3 Joseph Kerouac Canada & Leontine Rouleau Canada
KEROUAC, Jessie Caroline, Jul 1 1930 Sex:F Child# 1 Arthur E Kerouac Canada & Emma Boudin Manchester, NH
KEROUAC, Joan Alva, Jul 8 1935 Sex:F Child# 2 Armand Kerouac Canada & Alva Travers Nashua, NH
KEROUAC, Joseph Luc, Jan 26 1908 Sex:M Child# 6 Joseph H Kerouac Canada & Emma Levesque Canada
KEROUAC, Julienne, Oct 24 1899 Sex:F Child# 1 Joseph Kerouac Canada & Emma Levesque Canada
KEROUAC, Louis Maurice A, Jul 27 1897 Sex:M Child# 1 Ludger Kerouac Canada & Arthemise Aubut Canada
KEROUAC, Marie Beatrice A, Feb 18 1903 Sex:F Child# 1 Joseph Kerouac Canada & Leontine Rouleau Lewiston, ME
KEROUAC, Marie Rose Laura, Aug 6 1906 Sex:F Child# 5 Ludger Kerouac Canada & Dorilda Roy Canada
KEROUAC, Patricia Ann, Nov 3 1933 Sex:F Child# 1 Armand Kerouac Canada & Alva Travers Nashua, NH
KEROUAC, Robert Armand, Feb 26 1914 Sex:M Child# 4 Joseph Kerouac Canada & Leontine Rouleau Canada
KEROUAC, Roland Ernest A, Jun 2 1908 Sex:M Child# 1 Ernest Kerouac Canada & Alice Demontigny Canada
KEROUACK, Edouard, Jun 3 1918 Sex:M Child# 10 Ludger Kerouack Canada & Dorilda Roy US
KEROUACK, Eugene, May 19 1899 Sex:M Child# 1 Ludger Kerouack Canada & Dorilda Roy Suncook, NH
KEROUACK, Lilian, Sep 21 1904 Sex:F Child# 4 Ludger Kerouack Canada & Dorilda Roy Suncook, NH
KEROUACK, Marie Edna O, Feb 4 1907 Sex:F Child# 2 Joseph Kerouack Canada & Leontine Rouleau Lewiston, ME
KERR, Charles King, Jan 6 1928 Sex:M Child# 6 Edmund Kerr NH & Ruth Ripply Mass
KERR, David Cusshing, Mar 16 1917 Sex:M Child# 1 Clough H Kerr Cambridge, MA & Laura G Cusshing Medford, MA
KERR, Ellsworth Richmond, Apr 26 1925 Sex:M Child# 2 Clough Kerr Cambridge, MA & Geraldine Cushing W Medford, MA
KERR, Jane Patricia, Feb 17 1919 Sex:F Child# 3 E B Kerr Warren, NH & R W Ripley Malden, MA
KERR, John Marins, Jul 18 1920 Sex:M Child# 4 E B Kerr Weare, NH & Ruth Ropley Malden, MA
KERR, Robert C, Sep 6 1908 Sex:M Child# 1 Charles W Kerr Ireland & Annie Brennan Ireland
KERR, Robert Parker, Feb 28 1898 Sex:M Child# 1 John Lowry Kerr Farbane, Ireland & Mary Mabel Parker Hudson, NH
KERTIAMIS, Simon, Aug 10 1915 Sex:M Child# 4 Simon Kertiamis Russia & Veronika Szabluwicz Russia
KESALAR, Boluk, Jan 12 1916 Sex:M Child# 1 Austin Kesalar Russia & Isabella Dagus Russia
KESLER, Fannie, Nov 18 1907 Sex:F Child# 3 Sam Kesler Russia & Ida Valsbord Russia
KESSLER, Israel, Oct 20 1915 Sex:M Child# 6 Sam Kessler Russia & Ida Vaisbord Russia
KESSLER, Jennie, Apr 22 1909 Sex:F Child# 4 Samuel Kessler Russia & Ida Vaisbord Russia
KESSLER, Lillian, Dec 2 1916 Sex:F Child# 7 Sam Kessler Russia & Ida Vaisbord Russia
KETAWICZ, Eva, Nov 23 1918 Sex:F Child# 7 Bolislaw Ketawicz Russia & Theophila Kislauta Russia Stillborn
KETTREDGE, Helen Coombs, Nov 10 1898 Sex:F Child# 1 F E Kittredge Concord, NH & Lizzie Mary Coombs Nashua, NH
KEVARACIJUS, Joseph, May 27 1916 Sex:M Child# 3 Vincenta Kevaracijus Russia & Aniciza Stanapedias Russia
KEVOHAN, Angelina, Feb 13 1905 Sex:F Child# 10 Joseph Kevohan Belgium & Athais Pelletier Canada
KEYES, David Atwood, Feb 3 1918 Sex:M Child# 1 Benjamin S Keyes Sterling, MA & Mildred Tooker Harvard, MA
KEYSER, Edward Clifford, Jun 23 1922 Sex:M Child# 1 Charles Keyser Hudson, MA & Vivian Lavelle E Pepperell, MA
KEYSER, Walter, Jun 6 1894 Sex:M Child# 1 William Keyser Nashua, NH & Hattie Bird Marlboro, NY
KEZA, Ionia, May 16 1913 Sex:F Child# 2 Vladislav Keza Russia & Mary Luciawicz Russia
KEZAR, Dominick, May 13 1912 Sex:M Child# 1 Walter Kezar Russia & Mary Ursawich Russia
KEZEWISKI, Julia, Feb 28 1924 Sex:F Child# 8 Leopold Kezewiski Poland & Eva Peske Poland
KEZEWSKI, Marcel, Oct 21 1914 Sex:M Child# 1 Lupold Kezewski Russia & Eva Peska Austria
KHUSHIGIAN, Derouche, Jun 30 1914 Sex:F Child# 1 Aram Khushigian Armenia & Veronica Eskaudrian Armenia
KIAPLUCK, Brunislava, May 10 1917 Sex:F Child# 2 Stephen Kiapluck Russia & Katerina Pouskon Russia
KIBBLE, Olive R, Aug 26 1916 Sex:F Child# 5 Chester R Kibble E Milton, MA & Cora Greenwood Cincinnati, OH
KIBORT, Anthony, Jun 13 1916 Sex:M Child# 2 Daniel Kibort Russia & Petroneli Pelubeuski Russia
KIEPLUCK, Pavol, Mar 11 1917 Sex:M Child# 2 James Kiepluck Poland Russia & Michalina Valeita Poland Russia
KIERSTEAD, David, Aug 10 1928 Sex:M Child# 4 G T Kierstead Canada & Helen Dwyer Nashua, NH
KIERSTEAD, Gerald Thomas, Mar 28 1933 Sex:M Child# 6 G T Kierstead New Brunswick & Helen Dwyer Nashua, NH
KIERSTEAD, Mary Ruth, Jul 27 1934 Sex:F Child# 7 George Kierstead New Brunswick & Helen Dwyer Nashua, NH
KIERSTEAD, Richard, Jan 29 1931 Sex:M Child# 5 G T Kierstead Canada & Helen Dwyer Nashua, NH Stillborn
KIERTIANIS, Jadwiga, Feb 19 1916 Sex:F Child# 3 Stevin Kiertianis Russia & Natalia Janoszewska Russia
KIERTRANIS, Steven, Feb 12 1914 Sex:M Child# 2 Steven Kiertranis Russia & Nettie Jackson Russia
KIEWLIEZ, Wladek, Jun 26 1904 Sex:M Child# 1 Wladek Kiewliez Russia & Sophia Szararkrouska Russia
KILBAN, John Joseph, May 28 1895 Sex:M Child# 2 James Kilban Ireland & Katherine Winn Ireland
KILBAN, Margaret, Feb 28 1894 Sex:F Child# 1 John Kilban Ireland & Katherine Winn Ireland
KILBANE, Ann, Nov 28 1903 Sex:F Child# 6 James Kilbane Ireland & Katherine Winn Ireland
KILBANE, Francis Anthony, Oct 9 1901 Sex:M Child# 5 James Kilbane Ireland & Kate Winn Ireland
KILBANE, James C, Jr, Dec 11 1932 Sex:M Child# 1 James C Kilbane Nashua, NH & N DeFrancesco Italy
KILBANE, James Clement, Oct 8 1908 Sex:M Child# 8 James Kilbane Ireland & Katherine Winn Ireland
KILBANE, Joseph Edmund, Jun 17 1906 Sex:M Child# 7 James Kilbane Ireland & Katherine Winn Ireland
KILBANE, Mary, Sep 6 1899 Sex:F Child# 4 James Kilbane Ireland & Kate Winn Ireland
KILBANE, Philip Joseph, Aug 27 1897 Sex:M Child# 3 James Kilbane Ireland & Kate Winn Ireland
KILBANE, Raymond James, Jan 15 1925 Sex:M Child# 2 Philip J Kilbane Nashua, NH & Laura Dichard Nashua, NH
KILBANE, Robert Philip, Jul 30 1922 Sex:M Child# 1 Philip Kilbane NH & Laura Dichard NH
KILGREW, Winifred, Feb 16 1894 Sex:F Child# 1 Jeremiah Kilgrew Ireland & Kate McCall Ireland
KILGREWE, Lillian May, Dec 26 1896 Sex:F Child# 2 J C Kilgrewe Ireland & Katie McCall Ireland

KILKELLEY, Frank, Aug 27 1906 Sex:M Child# 4 John Kilkelley Ireland & Nellie Gilhooly Ireland
KILKELLEY, James, Jul 19 1900 Sex:M Child# 1 John Kilkelley Ireland & Nellie Gilhooley Ireland
KILKELLEY, John Leonard, Nov 21 1905 Sex:M Child# 2 Thomas G Kilkelley Wilton, NH & Julia T Sullivan Ireland
KILKELLEY, Thomas, Mar 2 1905 Sex:M Child# 3 John Kilkelley Ireland & Nellie Gilhooley Ireland
KILLKELLEY, Robert Paul, Mar 8 1934 Sex:M Child# 1 J Roy Killkelley Wilton, NH & Margaret Proctor Wilton, NH
KILLKELLEY, Thomas, Feb 2 1904 Sex:M Child# 1 Thomas J Killkelley Wilton, NH & Julia T Sullivan Ireland
KILLONS, William, Oct 14 1891 Sex:M Child# 2 William Killons Rutland, VT & Lizzie Fogarthy Lowell, MA
KILMANAS, Eva, Oct 15 1905 Sex:F Child# 1 Julius Kilmanas Russia & Cecilia Waremintie Russia
KILOWICH, Mary, Jul 8 1916 Sex:F Child# 4 Julian Kilowich Russia & Mary Muzkewich Russia
KIMBALL, Ada May, Jul 5 1891 Sex:F Child# 1 William J Kimball Claremont, NH & Louise M Wright Nashua, NH
KIMBALL, Dean Albert, Sep 22 1923 Sex:M Child# 6 Charles V Kimball Canaan, NH & Alice Gamache Sherbrook, Canada
KIMBALL, Doris May, Aug 17 1910 Sex:F Child# 2 Elmer A Kimball Peabody, MA & Grace G Goodridge Peabody, MA
KIMBALL, George, Jun 11 1888 Sex:M Child# 2 O D Kimball Merrimack & Ella Davidson N Y
KIMBALL, James Elton, Mar 25 1907 Sex:M Child# 3 Charles G Kimball Maine & Anastasia Mass
KIMBALL, Jason Stevens, Sep 2 1911 Sex:M Child# 2 John P Kimball Hopkinton, NH & Alice M Tolles Nashua, NH
KIMBALL, Lorenzo Currier, Feb 27 1893 Sex:M Child# 1 Elmer E Kimball Nashua, NH & Carrie Currier Hopkinton, NH
KIMBALL, Lucille Tolles, Mar 9 1909 Sex:F Child# 1 John P Kimball Hopkinton, NH & Alice M Tolles Nashua, NH
KIMBALL, Margery Delora, May 22 1906 Sex:F Child# 1 John F Kimball Nashua, NH & Ethel A Robinson Hudson, NH
KIMBALL, Merilyn, May 8 1935 Sex:F Child# 1 Rupert D Kimball Hopkinton, NH & Helen Reid Litchfield, NH
KIMBALL, Minnie Gertrude, Nov 22 1901 Sex:F Child# 3 Tyre P Kimball Amherst & Minnie E Dougall Ireland
KIMBALL, Roy Earle, Feb 8 1909 Sex:M Child# 1 Elmer H Kimball Peabody, MA & Grace Goodridge Peabody, MA
KIMBALL, Samuel Luther, Jan 11 1899 Sex:M Child# 4 John R Kimball Wilton, NH & Delora Tarbell Wilton, NH
KIMBALL, Stephen Donald, Apr 27 1917 Sex:M Child# 2 Loren Kimball Nashua, NH & Bessie May Sullivan
KIMBALL, Stilman George, Dec 21 1914 Sex:M Child# 2 Samuel M Kimball Boston, MA & Ethel M Davis Nashua, NH
KIMBALL, Unknown, Jun 30 1895 Sex:F Child# 3 John R Kimball Wilton, NH & Delora Tarbell Wilton, NH
KIMBALL, Unknown, Feb 12 1916 Sex:M Child# 4 Charles Kimball Maine & Anna Towhill Mass   Stillborn
KING, Alfred Walter, Mar 26 1925 Sex:M Child# 2 Edward King Enosburg Fls, VT & Lillian Brousseau Manchester, NH
KING, Annie May, Aug 1 1910 Sex:F Child# 1 Isaac J King E Douglass, MA & Georgia L Case Nashua, NH
KING, Charles H, Mar 1 1892 Sex:M Child# 1 Edwin R King Canaan & Elida A Libbey Woburn, MA
KING, Charlotte F, Sep 28 1894 Sex:F Child#  Frank P King NH & Alice Murphy Milford, NH
KING, Corinne Louise, Sep 18 1912 Sex:F Child# 1 Samuel King Chicopee, MA & Dora Green Sutton, VT
KING, Doris Louise, Apr 3 1923 Sex:F Child# 2 Samuel King US & Dora Green US
KING, Edward, Mar 11 1924 Sex:M Child# 1 Edward King Edwinburg, VT & Lillian Boisseau Nashua, NH
KING, Elisabeth Rosalinda, Jan 2 1913 Sex:F Child# 3 Isaac King Nashua, NH & Georgia Lizzie Case Nashua, NH
KING, Elizabeth Ruth, Jul 8 1926 Sex:F Child# 3 Peter King Prince Edw Island & Maude Tellier Nashua, NH
KING, Evelyn Louise, Jan 9 1902 Sex:F Child# 1 C O King Mass & Fannie McVitty England
KING, Gladys Belle, Dec 13 1911 Sex:F Child# 2 Isaac J King E Douglas, MA & Georgia L Case Nashua, NH
KING, Hamlin James, Jan 23 1920 Sex:M Child# 7 Isaac James King E Douglas, MA & Georgia Case Nashua, NH
KING, Irene Madeline, Mar 1 1925 Sex:F Child# 2 Peter King Prince Edw Island & Maude Tellier Nashua, NH
KING, John, Oct 30 1901 Sex:M Child# 2 Willard King Saranac, NY & Annie Morris Canada Stillborn
KING, June Althea, Nov 19 1917 Sex:F Child# 5 Isaac J King E Douglass, MA & Georgia Case Nashua, NH
KING, Melba, Feb 26 1914 Sex:F Child# 4 Isaac J King E Douglas, MA & Georgia Case Nashua, NH
KING, Norman Otis, Feb 19 1904 Sex:M Child# 2 Chandler O King E Douglas, MA & Fannie McVitty England
KING, Pauline Margaret, Mar 20 1923 Sex:F Child# 1 Peter King Prince Edward Island & Maude Tellier Nashua, NH
KING, Ruth Lillian, Aug 22 1921 Sex:F Child# 8 Isaac James King E Douglas, MA & Georgia Lizzie Case Nashua, NH
KING, Sanford Elmer, Jul 20 1922 Sex:M Child# 9 Isaac James King E Douglass, MA & Georgia Case Nashua, NH
KING, Stella May, Dec 17 1896 Sex:F Child# 2 Esara King Saranac, NY & Cora Levingston Eastburn, NY
KING, Unknown, Aug 21 1894 Sex:F Child# 3 Frank E King Saranac, NY & Phebe Annotte Keysville, NY
KINLEY, Unknown, Apr 13 1887 Sex:M Child# 1 Byron Kinley Montreal & Carrie P Q Stillborn
KINSTEAD, Alice Virginia, Oct 13 1925 Sex:F Child# 2 Ray Kinstead Nashua, NH & Ethel Gamblin Nashua, NH
KIRATSOUS, Helen, Nov 1 1929 Sex:F Child# 4 Elias Kiratsous Greece & Kozane Vasilious Greece
KIRBY, James Gilbert, Jul 10 1895 Sex:M Child# 1 Michael Kirby Ireland & Mary E Robinson England
KIRKARIAN, Elizabeth Mae, Feb 14 1935 Sex:F Child# 2 Charles Kirkarian Nashua, NH & Evelyn O'Toole Manchester, NH
KIRKORIAN, Annie Zado, Jan 8 1921 Sex:F Child# 6 Charles Kirkorian Asia & Elizabeth Paul Lowell, MA
KIRKPATRICK, Dorothy Louise, Mar 12 1917 Sex:F Child# 3 Wm R Kirkpatrick Nashua, NH & Jennie Wetmore NB
KIRKPATRICK, John Robertson, Jan 27 1916 Sex:M Child# 2 Wm R Kirkpatrick Nashua, NH & Jennie Wetmore NB
KIRKPATRICK, Marion Elizabeth, Jul 11 1914 Sex:F Child# 1 Wm R Kirkpatrick Nashua, NH & Jennie Wetmore NB
KIRKPATRICK, Philip Wetmore, Jul 10 1921 Sex:M Child# 4 William Kirkpatrick Nashua, NH & Jennie Wetmore Canada
KIRKPATRICK, Ruth Elinor, Jan 8 1925 Sex:F Child# 6 W R Kirkpatrick Nashua, NH & Jennie R Wetmore Nickham, NB
KIRKPATRICK, William Robertson, Feb 10 1923 Sex:M Child# 5 Wm R Kirkpatrick Nashua, NH & Jennie R Wetmore NB
KIRKWOOD, Justine Helene, Oct 12 1919 Sex:F Child# 2 William J Kirkwood Nottingham, NH & Ethel M Ames Wakefield, MA
KIRKWOOD, Robert, Aug 19 1896 Sex:M Child# 5 William M Kirkwood Lubec, ME & Cora E Cilley Nottingham
KIROUAC, Romeo, Feb 10 1911 Sex:M Child# 1 George Kirouac Canada & Eugenie Cote Canada
KIROUACK, Joseph Adelard, Aug 17 1891 Sex:M Child# 2 Jean B Kirouarck Canada & Clementine Bernier Canada
KIRPLUC, Lawakala, Mar 6 1915 Sex:F Child# 1 James Kirpluc Russia & Mikasa Vileta Russia
KIRSTEAD, Harriet Alice, Mar 12 1927 Sex:F Child# 3 G T Kirstead Canada & Helen Dwyer Nashua, NH
KISIEL, Veronica, Aug 11 1925 Sex:F Child# 6 Adolph Kisiel Poland & Tekla Lurgcoryka Lithuania
KISIELEWSKI, John, May 14 1923 Sex:M Child# 5 Adolph Kisielewski Poland & Tell Yuszezynsko Lithuania
KISILUTE, Antosia, Nov 21 1913 Sex:F Child# 1 Dominikos Kisilute Russia & Marijona Kunpiute Russia
KISSEL, Annie, Dec 7 1914 Sex:F Child# 1 Adolphe Kissel Russia & Teskler Lidzwiskwika Russia
KISSEL, Edward Julius, Sep 29 1929 Sex:M Child# 8 Adolph Kissel Poland & Tekla Luzeyska Lithuania
KISSEL, James, Feb 26 1916 Sex:M Child# 2 Adolphe Kissel Russia &  Russia
KISSEL, Vito Joe, Jun 3 1927 Sex:M Child# 7 Adolf Kissel Poland & Fekla Luschinski Lithuania

KISSELL, Mary, Sep 27 1918 Sex:F Child# 3 Adolph Kissell Russia & Tekla Luszyviska Russia
KITAWIC, John, May 3 1913 Sex:M Child# 3 Boleslaw Kitawic Russia & Tofilia Kisel Russia
KITAWIGA, Eva, Apr 13 1912 Sex:F Child# 2 Bolesius Kitawiga Russia & Taspilia Kisilute Russia
KITAWITZ, Alexander, May 6 1915 Sex:M Child# 2 Bayles Kitawitz Russia & Tafila Kislala Russia
KITCHASKI, Lula, Mar 8 1898 Sex:F Child# 1 Euzeb Kitchaski Russia & Eva Jedatzki Russia
KITCHEN, Charlotte C, Feb 10 1922 Sex:F Child# 3 Walter G Kitchen Lowell, MA & Ida Bailey State Center, IA
KITCHENER, Alice May, Feb 16 1910 Sex:F Child# 1 Arthur Kitchener Lowell, MA & Lillian M Weldon Groton, MA
KITCHENER, Arthur A, Sep 17 1921 Sex:M Child# 1 Arthur H Kitchener Lowell, MA & Jennie L Stobel Fitchburg, MA
KITCHENER, Constance Mary, May 8 1927 Sex:F Child# 4 A H Kitchener Lowell, MA & Jennie L Stoebel Fitchburg, MA
KITCHENER, George Henry, Mar 3 1923 Sex:M Child# 2 Arthur H Kitchener Lowell, MA & Jenne L Stoebel Fitchburg, MA
KITCHENER, Lillian Winifred, Jan 31 1912 Sex:F Child# 2 Arthur H Kitchener Annapolis, NS & Lillian G Weldon Ay
KITCHENER, Mary, Jun 16 1924 Sex:F Child# 3 A H Kitchener Lowell, MA & Jennie L Stobel Fitchburg, MA Stillbor
KITOVICZ, Unknown, May 30 1920 Sex:M Child# 8 Bolik Kitovicz Russia & Tophellia Kasalmetia Russia
KITOWICZ, Amelia, Dec 5 1910 Sex:F Child# 1 Bolesine Kitowicz Russia & Talilion Kisiliute Russia
KITOWICZ, Zugia, Apr 22 1914 Sex:F Child# 4 Bolesuis Kitowicz Russia & Tafilia Kisiliute Russia
KITTREDGE, Elaine Thompson, Jun 14 1929 Sex:F Child# 1 Winston Kittredge Milford, NH & Eleanor Coffin Ashmont
KIZALA, William, Jan 14 1905 Sex:M Child# 1 William Kizala Russia & Lavoise Sharametle Russia
KIZALOR, Willie, Sep 26 1918 Sex:M Child# 2 Constant Kizalor Russia & Osabella Degwoves Russia
KIZELA, Antoinette, Jun 12 1915 Sex:F Child# 5 William Kizela Russia & Louisa Sherametia Russia
KIZELA, Joseph, Sep 24 1912 Sex:M Child# 4 Wilhelm Kizela Russia & Lewisa Sheruneta Russia
KIZIRIAN, Aaron, Dec 8 1907 Sex:M Child# 3 Eli Kizirian Armenia & Mary Eawinian Armenia
KLACSENIOKI, Victor, Aug 26 1899 Sex:M Child# 3 F Klacsenioki Poland & V Bronistawa Poland
KLACSYNSKI, Mary, Sep 19 1896 Sex:F Child# 2 F Klacsynski Russia & B Tomonsk Austria
KLACSYNSKI, Wandi, Jan 27 1911 Sex:F Child# 6 Frank Klacsynski Poland & Bonislav Tommauck Austria
KLACYZNSKI, Frank, Jul 21 1901 Sex:M Child# 1 Frank Klacyznski Russia & Bronislaya Tomanski Russia
KLACYZNSKI, John, Jul 21 1901 Sex:M Child# 2 Frank Klacyznski Russia & Bronislaya Tomanski Russia
KLACZYNESKI, Helen, Feb 7 1911 Sex:F Child# 6 Frank Klaczyneski Poland & Bridget Tomanek Austria
KLACZYNSKI, Francis, Jun 7 1908 Sex:M Child# 8 Francis Klaczynski Poland & Bridget Gormanek Austria
KLAMEN, Malvina, Jan 18 1908 Sex:F Child# 2 Anthony Klamen Russia & Rosa Alaskavish Russia
KLAMES, Malvina, Sep 28 1925 Sex:F Child# 5 Joseph Klames Russia & Mary Zabriska Russia
KLEINBERG, Elizabeth Ruby, May 20 1920 Sex:F Child# 1 Louis Kleinberg Romania & Clara Ford Tyngsboro, MA
KLEINBERG, Eva Louise, Sep 7 1928 Sex:F Child# 4 L Kleinberg Romania & Clara Ford Tyngsboro, MA
KLEINBERG, Joseph, Sep 6 1910 Sex:M Child# 2 Abe Kleinberg Russia & Anna Fildman Russia
KLEMAS, Helen Rita, Apr 8 1924 Sex:F Child# 4 Joseph Klemas Russia & Mary Jeborkutz Russia
KLEMENS, Annette, Nov 14 1906 Sex:F Child# 1 Anton Klemens Russia & Rosa Aliskavitch Russia
KLEMENS, Josephine, Mar 19 1918 Sex:F Child# 3 Joseph Klemens Russia & Mary Zabrukutz Russia
KLEMESTA, Julius, Oct 10 1918 Sex:M Child# 1 Valerie Klemesta Russia & Aniella Seriewicz Russia
KLEMONS, Antony, Mar 1 1910 Sex:M Child# 3 Anton Klemons Russia & Rosa Allison Russia
KLEMONS, John, Nov 17 1912 Sex:M Child# 4 Anton Klemons Russia & Rosa Allison Russia
KLEMOS, Alexander, Feb 11 1912 Sex:M Child# 2 Alexander Klemos Russia & Annie Gideliutie Russia
KLERNOZ, Andrew, Dec 4 1917 Sex:M Child# 4 Alexander Klernoz Russia & Anna Zidieliz Russia
KLEZYNSKI, Veronica, Jan 13 1903 Sex:F Child# 1 Frank Klezynski Poland & Thomava Broniska Poland
KLIMANO, Nellie, Mar 7 1920 Sex:F Child# 5 Alexander Klimano Russia & Anne Ziedialute Russia
KLIMAS, Anthony, Apr 20 1915 Sex:M Child# 5 Anthony Klimas Russia & Rose Alkawick Russia
KLIMAS, John, Mar 6 1928 Sex:M Child# 6 Alex Klimas Lithuania & Annie Klimas Lithuania
KLIMAS, Leonard, Feb 1 1935 Sex:M Child# 1 (No Parents Listed)
KLIMATA, Helen, Dec 30 1920 Sex:F Child# 3 Waleryn Klimata Russia & Nellie Kurta Russia
KLIMBERG, Rose Lillian, Apr 10 1921 Sex:F Child# 1 Nathan Klimberg Romania & Minnie Caplan Boston, MA
KLIMOS, Mary, Dec 19 1910 Sex:F Child# 1 Alexander Klimos Russia & Anna Zidichutie Russia
KLODKY, Albert Richard, Mar 16 1922 Sex:M Child# 1 Lewis Klodky Russia & Beaulah Quimby NH
KLZEVISHI, Jadwiga, Dec 15 1915 Sex:M Child# 2 Leophold Klzevishi Russia & Eva Pisha Russia
KNAPP, Donald Maurice, Apr 24 1931 Sex:M Child# 1 Elmer Knapp Byron, ME & Gertrude Lavallee Concord, NH
KNAPP, Martha Colvin, Nov 8 1935 Sex:F Child# 3 Wm T Knapp Watervliet, NY & Florence S Colvin Rutland, VT
KNAPP, Robert Walter, Sep 5 1916 Sex:M Child# 1 Percie R Knapp Arlington, VT & Emma M Clark Wardsboro, VT
KNELL, Norma Phyllis, Dec 7 1928 Sex:F Child# 2 Charles L Knell Marblehead, MA & Janet J Dodger Glasgow, Scotland
KNIGHT, Dorothy Francis, Jan 7 1898 Sex:F Child# 3 Lyman W Knight Charlton, MA & Lottie McKelvie Southbridge, MA
KNIGHT, Dorothy Mildred, Jun 18 1924 Sex:F Child# 1 H W Knight Lawrence, MA & Mildred Flanders Nashua, NH
KNIGHT, Howard William, Jr, Jul 11 1927 Sex:M Child# 3 H W Knight Lawrence, MA & Mildred Flanders Nashua, NH
KNIGHT, Ruth Elva, Apr 23 1926 Sex:F Child# 2 Howard Knight Lawrence, MA & Mildred Flanders Nashua, NH
KNIGHT, Unknown, Nov 1 1889 Sex:M Child# 3 Edward Knight Nashua, NH & A Banners Nashua, NH
KNOTT, Clyde Lyman, Jan 14 1890 Sex:M Child# 4 William G Knott Portsmouth, NH & Mary A Rogers Canada  Stillbor
KNOTT, William G, Feb 13 1887 Sex:M Child# 3 William J Knott Portsmouth & Abbie M P Q
KNOWLTON, Carroll Babbidge, Jr, Oct 11 1926 Sex:M Child# 1 C B Knowlton Maine & Marion Davis New York
KNOWLTON, Robert Davis, Nov 15 1928 Sex:M Child# 2 C B Knowlton Stonington, ME & Marion E Davis Hoosick Falls, ME
KNOX, David, Sep 26 1908 Sex:M Child# 10 Edward Knox Vermont & Victoria Parent Canada
KNOX, Henry E, Sep 22 1897 Sex:M Child# 4 Edmund Knox Vergennes, VT & Victoria Parent Canada
KNOX, Joseph Edward, Mar 15 1895 Sex:M Child# 2 Edward Knox Vergennes, VT & Victoria Parent Canada
KNOX, Joseph W F, Mar 8 1896 Sex:M Child# 2 Henry Knox Vergennes, VT & Anna Demers Canada
KNOX, Joseph Willie, Oct 7 1893 Sex:M Child# 1 Henry Knox US & Annie Demers Canada
KNOX, Robert Thomas, Dec 14 1898 Sex:M Child# 5 Eddie Knox Vergennes, VT & Victoria Parent Canada
KNOX, Rose, Feb 24 1896 Sex:F Child# 3 Edouard Knox Canada & Victoria Parent Canada
KNOX, Unknown, Feb 3 1905 Sex:M Child# 1 William Knox Russia & Susie Stanulionis Russia
KNOX, Unknown, May 28 1911 Sex:F Child# 1 William Knox Nashua, NH & Mary E Smith Nashua, NH

KOBZIK, Wtadystoud, Sep 4 1918 Sex:M Child# 1 Waleri Kobzik Russia & Elizabeth Mosvika Russia
KOCHOKIAN, Rooben, Aug 15 1901 Sex:M Child# 1 Stephen Kochokian Turkey & Bashan Koscian Turkey
KODIALIS, Joseph Anthony, Aug 6 1917 Sex:M Child# 3 Antony Kodialis Russia & Eva Irmalawich Russia
KOERNER, Paul Richard, Sep 27 1932 Sex:M Child# 1 Richard Koerner Lawrence, MA & G Langlois Nashua, NH
KOLINGOFSKY, Unknown, Aug 29 1907 Sex:F Child# 6 V Kolingofsky Russia & A Franzkewitch Russia Stillborn
KOMENECKY, Unknown, Feb 5 1914 Sex:M Child# 3 Justin Komenecky Russia & Veronika Sila Russia
KOMENIATSKY, Brunislav, Nov 12 1920 Sex:F Child# 3 Benny Komeniatsky Poland Russia & Fannie Krvstopowicz Poland
KONDRAT, Gloria, Aug 9 1926 Sex:F Child# 1 Samuel Kondrat Russia & Mary Andrews Russia
KONOTIS, Dionisia, May 22 1916 Sex:F Child# 1 Andrew Konotis Greece & Eglenie Fliganopoulo Greece
KONTEILNISK, Mina, Jan 23 1917 Sex:F Child# 2 Pawol Konteilnisk Russia Poland & Antonia Trosawitch Russia Poland
KONTOCHRISTON, Unknown, Oct 28 1921 Sex:F Child# Zic Kontochriston Greece & Athens Batsos Greece
KONTRAVITCH, Charles, Mar 21 1908 Sex:M Child# 1 Louis Kontravitch Lithuania & Zophia Klabitsza Lithuania
KOPANO, Stephani, Mar 31 1917 Sex:M Child# 3 Vageli Kopano Greece & Dimitro Evagelia Greece
KOPEZICK, Philmena, Sep 12 1920 Sex:F Child# 2 Valera Kopezick Poland Russia & Elizabeth Mazeika Poland Russia
KOPICKO, John T, Oct 28 1914 Sex:M Child# 1 William Kopicko Russia & Mary M Koucka Russia
KOPISKAS, Bertha, Nov 4 1930 Sex:F Child# 2 Paul Kopiskas Lithuania & Antonia Slatley Lithuania
KOPKA, Benjamin, Jul 29 1908 Sex:M Child# 3 John Kopka Russia & Sophia Gacek Russia
KOPKA, Beverly Ann, Oct 29 1935 Sex:F Child# 1 Benjamin Kopka Nashua, NH & Stella Wineski Chelsea, MA
KOPKA, Evelyn Josephine, Oct 16 1928 Sex:F Child# 4 Walter F Kopka Exeter, NH & Irene L Charron Nashua, NH
KOPKA, John, Oct 13 1913 Sex:M Child# 8 John Kopka Russia & Sophia Glacek Austria
KOPKA, Joseph Euzebinsza, Dec 16 1906 Sex:M Child# 2 John Kopka Russia & Sophia Gacek Austria
KOPKA, Joseph John, Jr, May 12 1932 Sex:M Child# 1 Joseph J Kopka Nashua, NH & Alice Williams Manchester, NH
KOPKA, Louise Mary, Sep 11 1933 Sex:F Child# 6 Walter F Kopka Exeter, NH & Irene Charron Nashua, NH
KOPKA, Paul Raymond, Dec 9 1930 Sex:M Child# 5 Walter Kopka Exeter, NH & Irene Charron Nashua, NH
KOPKA, Unknown, Aug 14 1909 Sex:F Child# 5 John Kopka Russia & Sophia Gacek Austria
KOPKA, Unknown, Sep 24 1915 Sex:F Child# 9 John J Kopka Russia & Sophie Gaseik Austria
KOPKA, Unknown, Jul 14 1917 Sex:F Child# 8 John Kopka Russia & Sophie Gadzek Austria
KOPKA, Unknown, Sep 8 1920 Sex:F Child# 11 John Kopka Lithuania & Sophie Gacek Poland
KOPKA, Valeriona, Apr 27 1911 Sex:F Child# 6 John Kopka Russia & Sophia Gacek Russia
KOPKA, Walter, Mar 13 1925 Sex:M Child# 1 Walter Kopka Exeter, NH & Irene Charron Nashua, NH
KOPSICK, Stella, Jun 26 1925 Sex:F Child# 4 Walter Kopsick Poland & Elizabeth Mazeika Poland
KOPSICK, Theophite, Jul 18 1928 Sex:M Child# 5 V Kopsick Poland & E Mazeika Poland
KOPZIK, Sophia, Jun 13 1922 Sex:F Child# 3 Valerie Kopzik Poland & Elizabeth Mazeika Poland
KORB, Anna, Sep 8 1914 Sex:F Child# 5 Woyciech S Korb Russia & Anna Latrois Russia
KORKORIAN, James, Dec 14 1915 Sex:M Child# 4 Charles Korkorian Armenia & Elizabeth Paul Lowell, MA
KORSACK, Julia, Jun 20 1914 Sex:F Child# 3 Leonard Korsack Russia & Mikala Kuruska Russia
KOSIMICH, Antony, Jan 19 1913 Sex:M Child# 2 John Kosimich Russia & Antonina Yalewich Russia
KOSIMITCH, Helen, Apr 8 1922 Sex:F Child# 4 John Kosimitch Poland & Antonina Yeremitch Poland
KOSIMITCH, Joseph, Nov 13 1911 Sex:M Child# 1 John Kosimitch Russia & Antonina Yaremitch Russia
KOSKI, Harold Emil, Oct 23 1932 Sex:M Child# 1 C E Koski Fitchburg, MA & Eva Boucher Tyngsboro, MA
KOSLOWSKI, Lucia, Feb 26 1926 Sex:F Child# 4 A Koslowski Poland & Anna Maker Poland
KOSLOWSKIE, Unknown, Feb 9 1917 Sex:M Child# 1 Albert Koslowskie Russia & Anna Markar Russia
KOSMAN, Gadwiga, Feb 22 1918 Sex:F Child# 2 Gabriel Kosman Russia & Antonie Matyczska Russia
KOSMAN, Stanislaus, Aug 20 1919 Sex:M Child# 3 Gabriel Kosman Russia & Antonia Matczynska Russia
KOSPEROMICZ, Anicia, Sep 3 1903 Sex:F Child# 1 Marcin Kosperomicz Russia & Emelie Lebiednikan Russia
KOTA, Joseph, May 18 1913 Sex:M Child# 1 Adam Kota Russia & Mary Thola Russia
KOURONIS, James, Feb 26 1915 Sex:M Child# 3 Lewis Kouronis Greece & Diana Stylios Greece
KOUROUNIUS, Samuel, Apr 21 1908 Sex:M Child# 1 Demetrius Kourounius Greece & Celanise Marquis Canada
KOURTIS, Peter, Mar 24 1916 Sex:M Child# 1 Andrew Kourtis Greece & Sophia Teka Greece
KOUSEPARN, Unknown, Jan 4 1917 Sex:F Child# 1 Costa Kouseparn Greece & C Lajos Greece
KOUSTANTIN, Crisanthy, Dec 21 1914 Sex:F Child# 3 Stergios Koustantin Greece & Anastasia Ntampavoli Greece
KOUTSATASIAS, Eftinio, Jan 5 1914 Sex:F Child# 2 George Koutsatasias Greece & Eleonore Kanatham Greece
KOUTSONIKAS, Unknown, Mar 25 1921 Sex:M Child# 4 John Koutsonikas Greece & Rose Charest Canada
KOWALSKI, Alexander, Apr 16 1924 Sex:M Child# 1 Alexander Kowalski Poland & Jose Rusitzski Taunton, MA
KOWJEZ, Victor, Jan 3 1918 Sex:M Child# 3 Isydore Berni Kowjez Poland & Gracilia Rodwicz Poland
KOWYNIA, Lygmunt, Mar 3 1918 Sex:M Child# 1 Stanislaw Kowynia Austria & Anna Ciepielon Austria
KOZAKOWSKI, Cady, Jan 30 1916 Sex:F Child# 2 Robert Kozakowski Poland-Russia & Paulina Kazakowski Poland-Russia
KOZIAL, Jenny, Jun 19 1925 Sex:F Child# 2 Alexander Kozial Poland & Magdelena Sak Poland
KOZLOBSKY, Bernice Sophia, Dec 11 1920 Sex:F Child# 1 Stephen Kozlobsky Russia & Sophia Stakielan Nashua, NH
KOZLOUSKY, Joseph, May 24 1926 Sex:M Child# 4 Stephen Koslousky Russia & Sophie Stacklin Nashua, NH
KOZLOWSKA, Regina, Oct 10 1920 Sex:F Child# 3 Aug Kozlowska Russia & Annie Makar Russia
KOZLOWSKI, Robert Philip, Apr 23 1929 Sex:M Child# 5 Stephen Kozlowski Russia & Sophia Stacklin Nashua, NH
KOZLOWSKI, Unknown, Mar 1 1916 Sex:M Child# 1 John Kozlowski Russia & Sophie Holzobce Russia
KOZLOWSKOS, Stanislaus, Mar 26 1923 Sex:M Child# 3 Stephen Kozlowskos Lithuania & Katherine Yunascawit Lithuania
KOZOLKAS, Theodore, Oct 27 1918 Sex:M Child# 1 John Kozolkas Greece & Vasulas Konstans Greece
KOZOURKY, Sabina, Jan 27 1920 Sex:F Child# 3 Albert Kozourky Russia & Annie Capeliki Russia
KRACCIKIN, Unknown, Jan 9 1908 Sex:M Child# 1 Zanon Kraccikin Russia & Mikala Kmenta Russia
KRAMER, Minnie, Oct 11 1915 Sex:F Child# 3 Abraham Kramer Russia & Dora Gilman Russia
KRANCZUN, Mary, Jun 1 1915 Sex:F Child# 1 Jerzy Kranczun Russia & Rose Tunavicz Russia
KRAPONTCKSKI, Unknown, Apr 7 1918 Sex:F Child# 1 Michael Krapontckski Russia & Olga Yazek Russia
KREAM, Harry, Jan 21 1911 Sex:M Child# 5 David Kream Russia & Annie Bernen Russia
KREKORAU, Unknown, Dec 19 1918 Sex:M Child# 5 Charles Krekorau Armenia & Lizzie Paul Lowell, MA
KRETON, Unknown, Mar 4 1913 Sex:F Child# 1 George Kreton Turkey & Dametria Makris Greece

KREZEWSKI, Edmund I, Feb 14 1918 Sex:M Child# 4 Leopold Krezewski Russia & Eva Pysbruew Austria
KREZEWSKI, Walenty, Feb 14 1918 Sex:M Child# 3 Leopold Krezewski Russia & Eva Pysbruew Austria
KRIGEWICK, John, Feb 17 1914 Sex:M Child# 2 John Krigewick Russia & Margaret Petrowick Russia
KRISTOPOWICH, John, Mar 3 1914 Sex:M Child# 2 Fran Kristopowich Russia & Franciska Russia
KRITISOS, Eleftheria, Jan 23 1919 Sex:F Child# 6 Manolis Kritisos Greece & Olymbia Greece
KRITNIS, Owegena, Jan 27 1912 Sex:F Child# 1 Stephen Kritnis Russia & Nettie Jackson Russia
KRIZEWICZE, Constantia, Nov 25 1910 Sex:F Child# 1 Jonas Krizewicze Russia & Magdelena Petruskait Russia
KROMSKY, Victor, Feb 5 1909 Sex:M Child# 1 Joseph Kromsky Russia & Volotka Atzelina Russia
KRUKONIS, Algua Stanley, Jun 25 1915 Sex:M Child# 2 Alexandra Krukonis Russia & Marcellina Aliakwic Russia
KRUKONIS, Amelda Pauline, Jun 21 1923 Sex:F Child# 1 John Krukonis Russia & Amelia Bakanaiskuto Russia
KRUSH, Joseph Michael, Aug 23 1935 Sex:M Child# 1 Joseph Krush Nashua, NH & Antoinette Carloni Milford, NH
KRUSHAS, Joseph, May 3 1910 Sex:M Child# 4 Michael Kurshas Russia & Mikalia Baranauski Russia
KRUSKINS, John, Feb 20 1909 Sex:M Child# 7 Michael Kruskins Russia & Annie Michaelena Russia
KRUSNOWSKA, Eva, Mar 2 1916 Sex:F Child#  Charles Krusnowska Russia & Catherine Swider Austria
KRUSZAS, Michael, Oct 13 1907 Sex:M Child# 6 Michael Kruszas Russia & M Baranaukutie Russia
KRUVATS, Unknown, Mar 6 1917 Sex:M Child# 2 Evangelos Kruvats Greece & Eva Caros Greece
KRYCZTIPVEZ, Unknown, Sep 6 1909 Sex:M Child# 2 John Krycztipvez Russia & Antoinette Cargi Russia
KRYEZTIPREZ, Unknown, Dec 4 1907 Sex:F Child# 1 John Kryeztiprez Russia & Antonette Cargi Russia
KRYNOWSKY, Genievra, May 2 1916 Sex:F Child# 1 Chris Krynowsky Russia & Katherine Swerder Russia
KRYSHTOFONICH, Florence Marion, Jun 2 1918 Sex:F Child# 1 Horian Kryshtofonich Nashua, NH & Annie Smietana Austria
KRYSTAPAWICH, Mary, Nov 27 1909 Sex:F Child# 1 Auskani Krystapawich Russia & Ena Kridictis Russia
KRYSTOPOWICZ, John, Oct 29 1917 Sex:M Child# 2 Bron Krystopowicz Russia & Mary Dubowik Russia
KRZEWSKI, Daniel, Aug 25 1927 Sex:M Child# 8 Leopold Krzewski Poland & Eva Pessi Poland
KRZEWSKI, John, Jan 10 1923 Sex:M Child# 7 Leopold Krzewski Poland & Eva Pyska Poland
KRZEWSKI, Unknown, Jun 15 1904 Sex:F Child#  Emil Krzewski Russia & Rosalia Oleder Russia
KRZEWSKI, Zobia, May 4 1903 Sex:M Child# 2 Emile Krzewski Russia & Rosalia Olender Russia
KUCHINSKI, Steve, Nov 8 1928 Sex:M Child# 8 P Kuchinski Poland & A Tusewicz Poland
KUCZINSKI, Albin, Mar 7 1922 Sex:M Child# 5 Paul Kuczinski Poland & Annette Tursewicz Poland
KUCZNSKI, Donald, Jan 3 1935 Sex:M Child# 10 Paul Kucznski Poland & Antosa Thresevich Poland
KUCZYNSKI, Fabian, Mar 28 1932 Sex:M Child# 9 Paul Kuczynski Poland & A Tursewicz Poland
KUCZYORKSKI, Joseph, Aug 3 1924 Sex:M Child# 6 Paul Kuczyorkski Poland & A Tursewicz Poland
KUDALIS, Julia, Mar 25 1907 Sex:F Child# 1 Karis Kudalis Russia & Didila Werenutz Russia
KUDALIS, Virginia, Sep 10 1928 Sex:F Child# 7 A Kudalis Russia & Eva Ermalovitch Russia
KUDDITIS, Josy, Dec 1 1919 Sex:F Child# 4 Anthony Kudditis Russia & Genny Kudditis Russia
KUDGMA, Jonas, May 16 1907 Sex:m Child# 3 Simonas Kudgma Russia & Petre Skilinciute Russia
KUDIATIS, Fred, Sep 17 1931 Sex:M Child# 8 Anthony Kudiatis Poland & Eva Ermalowicz Lithuania
KUDITIS, John, Jul 19 1926 Sex:M Child# 6 Anthony Kuditis Russia & Eva Kuditis Russia
KUDMA, Inogupas, Mar 3 1912 Sex:M Child# 5 Simon Kudma Russia & Petra Skluite Russia
KUDZMA, Aninka, Jan 22 1910 Sex:F Child# 4 Simona Kudzma Russia & Pitra Skliutas Russia
KUDZMA, Joseph, Oct 31 1909 Sex:M Child# 1 Frank Kudzma Russia & Eleanor Malute Russia
KUDZMA, Thomas George, Jan 1 1935 Sex:M Child# 1 John C Kudzma Nashua, NH & Dora Bouml Lowell, MA
KUDZMA, Waclas, Oct 30 1904 Sex:M Child# 2 Simon Kudzma Russia & Petrunelia Sklut Russia
KUDZNER, Agnes, Aug 6 1920 Sex:F Child# 1 William Kudzner Lithuania Russia & Antonette Uskawich Lithuania Russia
KUEVAL, Mary Ann, Apr 25 1890 Sex:F Child# 1 James Kueval Ireland & Bridge Mulqueen Ireland
KUEZYNSKI, Antonia, Jun 13 1915 Sex:F Child# 1 Paul Kuezynski Russia & Antonia Truscwich Russia
KULAS, Cecilia, Aug 11 1923 Sex:F Child# 10 Joseph Kulas Poland & Elizabeth Sekuska Poland
KULAS, Florence, May 6 1926 Sex:F Child# 11 Joseph Kulas Poland & E Sekulskra Poland
KULAS, Patricia, Nov 24 1930 Sex:F Child# 1 Harry Kulas Lawrence, MA & Helen Hennessey Haverhill, MA
KULIKOWSKI, Leonard, Aug 23 1935 Sex:M Child# 1 Leon Kulikowski Cambridge, MA & M Walentukevich Nashua, NH
KULIMYOWSKAS, Bronislowas, Aug 3 1906 Sex:M Child# 10 Baltrus Kulimyowskas Russia & Ona Franckisiszinte Russia
KULINGAWSKI, Phillip Morris, Mar 29 1935 Sex:M Child# 4 Bern Kulingawski Nashua, NH & Irene Prince Southbridge, MA
KULINGOSKI, Bernard Roland, Sep 6 1933 Sex:M Child# 2 B Kulingoski Nashua, NH & Irene Prince Mass
KULLMAN, Unknown, May 30 1898 Sex:F Child# 3 Lorence J Kullman Germany & Mary Klumbach New York, NY
KULMANN, Charles Frank, Feb 1 1903 Sex:M Child# 4 L J Kulmann Germany & Mary E Klumbach New York, NY
KULMANN, Elizabeth, Jan 15 1905 Sex:F Child# 5 Lawrence J Kulmann Germany & Mary E Klumbach New York, NY
KUMENIECKE, Alfred, Mar 14 1922 Sex:M Child# 2 Karol Kumeniecke Poland & Mary Zubryeha Poland
KUNSENDORP, Helen Gertrude, Jun 1 1922 Sex:F Child# 2 John Kunsendorp Russia & Beatrice Bush Bristol, England
KUNTANIS, Leon, Oct 21 1919 Sex:M Child# 1 Nicolas L Kuntanis Greece & Stavoula Spiliopoulo Greece
KUPCAGUN, John, Aug 27 1913 Sex:M Child# 3 Stanislas Kupcagun Russia & Pauline Ekisala Russia
KUPCHUN, Stanislas, Jun 5 1907 Sex:M Child# 3 Frank Kupchun Russia & Mary Zidalis Russia
KUPCHUN, Susia, Jul 4 1906 Sex:F Child# 2 Frank Kupchun Russia & Mary Zidalis Russia
KUPCHUN, Volum, Jan 7 1909 Sex:M Child# 2 Stanislas Kupchun Russia & Popelina Ykasella Russia
KUPCSUM, Stanislaw, Oct 30 1905 Sex:M Child# 4 Stanislaw Kupscum Russia & Paulina T Kasala Russia
KUPCZUN, Pauline, Jun 1 1924 Sex:F Child# 6 S Kupczun Lithuania & Pauline Exasala Lithuania
KUPCZUNIAS, Frank, Jun 11 1905 Sex:M Child#  Frank Kupczunias Russia & Mary Jidaliute Russia
KUPEVICK, Steven, Jul 14 1916 Sex:M Child# 2 Albert Kupevick Russia & Mary Mackowskic Russia
KUPLOS, Mary, Aug 28 1918 Sex:F Child# 2 James Kuplos Russia & Michalena Valaite Russia
KUPOZUHN, Alphonse, May 10 1920 Sex:M Child# 5 Frank Kupozuhn Russia & Mary Zedalis Russia
KUPRYN, Vladyslaw, Jun 24 1918 Sex:M Child# 2 Marian Kupryn Russia & Malvina Rylodz Russia
KURKLEY, Anita, May 27 1930 Sex:F Child# 1 Joseph Krukley Shirley, MA & Patrona Millina Shirley, MA
KURLANAS, Frank, Aug 5 1914 Sex:M Child# 2 Adolph Kurlanas Russia & Mary Burchkus Russia
KURSAVICH, Edward, Apr 19 1916 Sex:M Child# 1 Benjamin Kursavich Russia & Caroline Kameneski Russia
KURSEWICZ, Gunefa, Oct 29 1918 Sex:F Child# 2 Bronislaw Kursewicz Russia & Karoluna Karnoiskie Russia

KURTA, Bronislawa, Oct 2 1914 Sex:F Child# 1 Bronislaw Kurta Russia & Jos Shimaniska Russia
KURTA, Stanislaus, Nov 3 1926 Sex:F Child# 1 Frank Kurta Poland & Annie Huniawicz Poland
KUSH, John, Jul 6 1913 Sex:M Child# Loyd Kush Russia & Nestor Russia
KUSH, John, Jul 7 1913 Sex:M Child# 2 Ludwig Kush Russia & Nostula Garitska Russia
KUSHYNSKUGA, Chester Joseph, Oct 15 1916 Sex:M Child# 1 Joseph Kushynskuga Russia & Julia Pinowvoski Russia
KUSSON, Mary, Sep 17 1922 Sex:F Child# 3 Nicolas Kusson Greece & Angela Hatzie Greece
KUTAR, Unknown, Feb 18 1920 Sex:M Child# 3 Adolph Kutar Poland & Mary Turla Poland Stillborn
KUWARACIUS, Julius, Sep 26 1913 Sex:M Child# 2 Vincent Kuwaracius Russia & Aniella Stenapajuta Russia
KUZUKAWIZ, Antana, Feb 4 1916 Sex:M Child# 9 Antana Juzukawiz Russia & Ana Kaszecute Russia
KVLOOSTIAN, Unknown, May 12 1914 Sex:M Child# 1 Kaspar Kvloostian Armenia & Lucy Aharonian Armenia
KWARACIUS, Vincenta Leon, Apr 7 1911 Sex:M Child# 1 Vencenta Kwaracius Russia & Anelka Stanapekzute Russia
KYRATZIS, Constantine, Oct 4 1932 Sex:M Child# 2 Geo Kyratzis Greece & Soultana Mouza Greece
KYRATZIS, Unknown, Feb 27 1931 Sex:F Child# 1 George Kyratzis Greece & Soultana Mouza Greece
KYRATZIS, Unknown, Oct 7 1935 Sex:F Child# 3 George Kyratzis Greece & Sultana Mouza Greece
KYRIAZIS, Stavios John, Jun 24 1934 Sex:M Child# 1 John Kyriazis Greece & Anastasia Gramatika Greece
L'HOMME, Anna Eva, Dec 4 1898 Sex:F Child# 3 T L'homme Canada & Zoe Dube Canada
L'HOMME, Louis Philippe, Aug 19 1892 Sex:M Child# 1 Toussaint L'homme Canada & Zoe Dube Canada
LABARE, Marie Isabelle Doris, Jan 20 1926 Sex:F Child# 2 Eugene Labare Nashua, NH & Emelienne Vachon Canada
LABARE, Marie Laura Anita, Jan 20 1926 Sex:F Child# 1 Eugene Labare Nashua, NH & Emelienne Vachon Canada
LABBE, Arthur Albert, Aug 10 1934 Sex:M Child# 7 Arthur Labbe Canada & Blanche Cote Canada
LABBE, Jos Louis Laurent, Nov 5 1935 Sex:M Child# 7 Arthur Labbe Canada & Blanche Cote Canada
LABBE, Marie Alda Lorraine, Nov 5 1935 Sex:F Child# 8 Arthur Labbe Canada & Blanche Cote Canada
LABBY, Norman Jason, Aug 9 1935 Sex:M Child# 2 Hereault A Labby Maine & Hermine Simard Canada
LABEAU, Arthur J N, Oct 20 1890 Sex:M Child# 6 Napoleon LaBeau Canada & Marie Ponteau Canada
LABEL, Marie Regina E, Oct 17 1900 Sex:F Child# 6 Joseph Label Canada & Marie Peltier Canada
LABELLE, Catherine, May 8 1895 Sex:F Child# 7 Joseph Labelle Canada & Josephine Gauthier Canada
LABELLE, Henry David, Aug 5 1927 Sex:M Child# 2 Albert Labelle Nashua, NH & Yvonne Berube Canada
LABELLE, John Albert H, Aug 18 1904 Sex:M Child# 8 Joseph Labelle Sorel, PQ Canada & Marie Peltier Canada
LABELLE, Joseph, May 27 1888 Sex:M Child# 3 Joseph Labelle Canada & Josephine Gauthier Canada
LABELLE, Joseph George Leon, Apr 10 1910 Sex:M Child# 1 Joseph E Labelle Canada & Aglace Ouellet Canada
LABELLE, Joseph Hobart, Jun 13 1928 Sex:M Child# 4 Joseph LaBelle Londonderry, NH & Mildred G Abel Newport Ctr
LABELLE, Joseph Martial, Aug 10 1906 Sex:M Child# 9 Joseph Labelle Canada & Marie Pelletier Canada
LABELLE, Lucille Rita, Jun 13 1923 Sex:F Child# 2 Joseph Labelle Canada & Aglace Ouellette Canada
LABELLE, M Rose Anna, Mar 23 1894 Sex:F Child# 2 Joseph Labelle Canada & Marie Pelletier Canada
LABELLE, Margaret, Jan 3 1911 Sex:F Child# 10 Joseph Labelle Canada & Marie Pelletier Canada
LABELLE, Marie Alphonsine, May 18 1892 Sex:F Child# 13 Achille Labelle Canada & Celanise Laflamme Canada
LABELLE, Marie Leda, Sep 12 1902 Sex:F Child# 7 Joseph Labelle Canada & Marie Peltier Canada
LABELLE, Veronique, Sep 15 1925 Sex:M Child# 1 Albert Labelle Nashua, NH & Yvonne Berube Canada
LABERGE, Joseph Pierre E A, Jun 13 1899 Sex:M Child# 2 Ovide Laberge Canada & Cleophee Baron Canada
LABERGE, Marie E Cleophee, Feb 11 1898 Sex:F Child# 1 Ovide Laberge Canada & Cleophee Baron Canada
LABIER, Normand Edmond, Jan 2 1923 Sex:M Child# 1 Ernest Labier New York & Stella Rainville Altona, NY
LABIER, Reta May, Jan 2 1924 Sex:F Child# 2 Ernest Labier NY & Stella Rainville NY
LABINE, Clara Nathalie, May 20 1920 Sex:F Child# 3 Henri Labine Nashua, NH & Octavie Desmarais Nashua, NH
LABINE, Edmond, Feb 5 1898 Sex:M Child# 14 Joseph Labine Canada & Alphonsine Paquette Canada
LABINE, Edouard, Apr 9 1889 Sex:M Child# 9 Joseph Labine Canada & Alphonsine Paquet Canada
LABINE, Henri E, Nov 28 1887 Sex:M Child# 8 Joseph Labine P Q & Alphonsine P Q
LABINE, Henry, Jr, Dec 1 1933 Sex:M Child# 4 Henry Labine Nashua, NH & O Desmarais Nashua, NH
LABINE, Jeannette, Jun 8 1916 Sex:F Child# 2 Wilfrid Labine Canada & Antonia Pelletier Canada
LABINE, Joseph L A, Jun 30 1906 Sex:M Child# 16 Joseph Labine Canada & Alphonsine Paquette Canada
LABINE, Joseph Maurice Urgel, Aug 6 1912 Sex:M Child# 1 Henri Labine Pepperell, MA & Octavie Desmarais Nashua, NH
LABINE, Joseph U, Dec 7 1896 Sex:M Child# 13 Joseph Labine Canada & Alphonsine Paquette Canada
LABINE, Joseph U, Jun 21 1899 Sex:M Child# 15 Joseph Labine Canada & Alphonsine Paquette Canada
LABINE, Leonard Charles, Feb 16 1920 Sex:M Child# 1 Louis Urgel Labine Nashua, NH & Ila May Lombarde Plainfield
LABINE, Louis N, Jul 16 1894 Sex:M Child# 12 Joseph Labine Canada & Alphonsine Paquet Canada
LABINE, Louis Paul Urgele, Jul 16 1918 Sex:M Child# 2 Henri Labine Nashua, NH & Octavie Desmarais Nashua, NH
LABINE, Marie, May 17 1925 Sex:F Child# 6 Wilfred Labine Canada & Antonia Pelletier Canada
LABINE, Marie B C E, Mar 4 1892 Sex:F Child# 11 Joseph Labine Canada & Alphonsine Paquet Canada
LABINE, Maurice Robert, Aug 4 1919 Sex:M Child# 4 Wilfrid Labine Canada & Antonia Pelletier Canada
LABINE, Unknown, Sep 4 1887 Sex:M Child# 3 Napoleon Labine Canada & Mary Canada
LABINE, V Pauline Alphonsine, Mar 13 1915 Sex:F Child# 1 Edward Labine Nashua, NH & Albina Gadbois Nashua, NH
LABINO, Irenie C B, Nov 5 1890 Sex:F Child# 10 Joseph Labino Canada & Alphonsine Paquet Canada
LABIRE, Joseph Maurice P E, May 4 1924 Sex:M Child# 7 Joseph Labire Mass & Helena Labire Canada
LABLANC, Edmond, Oct 31 1893 Sex:M Child# 7 Jean M Lablanc Canada & Virginnie Pepin Canada
LABOMBARD, Ann, Jun 6 1922 Sex:F Child# 1 William C LaBombard Malone, NY & Edith H Hobart Brookline, NH
LABOMBARD, Bertha, May 18 1892 Sex:F Child# 1 Edouard Labombard NY & Amelie Maynard Canada
LABOMBARD, Carlton Leo, Jul 6 1930 Sex:M Child# 6 Joseph E LaBombard W Chazy, NY & Regina M Morton Nashua, NH
LABOMBARD, Esther Regina, Feb 19 1927 Sex:F Child# 4 J E Labombard New York & Regina M Morton Nashua, NH
LABOMBARDE, Carrie Leda, Feb 26 1909 Sex:F Child# 5 Louis Labombarde Beekmantown, NY & Esther Martin Chazy, NY
LABOMBARDE, Dorothy May, Apr 2 1917 Sex:F Child# 7 Lewis Labombarde Buckmanton, NY & Esther Martin W Chazy, NY
LABOMBARDE, Elie, Oct 7 1922 Sex:M Child# 5 Win E Labombarde Malone, NY & Agens Legendre Canada
LABOMBARDE, Helen May, Sep 1 1931 Sex:F Child# 7 Joseph Labombarde W Chazy, NY & Regina Morton Nashua, NH
LABOMBARDE, Jean, Oct 18 1924 Sex:F Child# 2 William Labombarde Malone, NY & Edith Hobart Brookline, NH
LABOMBARDE, Joseph, Dec 4 1915 Sex:M Child# 1 Winifred Labombarde Malone, NY & Agnes Legendre Canada

LABOMBARDE, Louise Marie, Jan 22 1921 Sex:F Child# 4 Wilfred Labombarde Malone, NY & Agnes E Legendre Canada
LABOMBARDE, M Irma Agnes, Jan 25 1917 Sex:F Child# 2 Wilfred Labombarde Malone, NY & Agnes L Legendre Canada
LABOMBARDE, Marie Rose Alberta, Nov 10 1911 Sex:F Child# 6 Louis Labombarde New York & Esther Martin New York
LABOMBARDE, Theresa Obeline, Nov 7 1925 Sex:F Child# 1 E Labombarde Hollis, NH & Clara Lamontagne Nashua, NH
LABOMBARDE, William Hobart, Nov 30 1926 Sex:M Child# 3 W C Labombarde Malone, NY & Edith Hobart Brookline, NH
LABONT, Marie Emma, Oct 11 1889 Sex:F Child# 2 Joseph Labont Canada & Emma Nadeau NY
LABONTE, Aime Edgar, May 17 1914 Sex:M Child# 1 Joseph Labonte NH & Rose A Theriault NH
LABONTE, Alphonsine A A, Aug 15 1909 Sex:F Child# 5 Thomas C Labonte Vermont & Alphonsine Bonin Canada
LABONTE, Angelina Irene, Oct 31 1906 Sex:F Child# 6 Augustin Labonte Canada & Marie Tetreau Canada
LABONTE, Antoine, May 21 1901 Sex:M Child# 3 Antoine Labonte Franklin, VT & Marie Tetreault Canada
LABONTE, Antonio Rodrigue, Mar 27 1906 Sex:M Child# 5 George Labonte US & Alexina Cyr Canada
LABONTE, Berthe, Jun 30 1905 Sex:F Child# 5 Augustin Labonte Canada & Marie Tetreau Canada
LABONTE, Calixe Charles F J, Jun 7 1908 Sex:M Child# 4 Thomas Labonte Vermont & Alphonsine Benin Canada
LABONTE, Cecile Marie Lea, Sep 28 1927 Sex:F Child# 4 Joseph Labonte Nashua, NH & Emelia Morneau Manchester, NH
LABONTE, George, Jun 16 1903 Sex:M Child# 3 George Labonte NS & Alexina Cyr Canada
LABONTE, Herve Edmond, Aug 11 1907 Sex:M Child# 6 George Labonte Vermont & Alexina Cyr Canada
LABONTE, Jos Arthur Henry, Apr 26 1934 Sex:M Child# 1 Arthur H Labonte Canada & Lida Ricard Nashua, NH
LABONTE, Joseph Charles Rolan, Jul 28 1935 Sex:M Child# 1 Calixte Labonte Nashua, NH & Elize Dube Nashua, NH
LABONTE, Joseph Edgar Francoi, Nov 22 1919 Sex:M Child# 2 Joseph Labonte NH & Emelia Morneau NH
LABONTE, Louise Ruth, Apr 11 1931 Sex:F Child# 2 Arthur Labonte US & Isabelle Champagne Nashua, NH
LABONTE, Lucille Mary Anne, Sep 28 1927 Sex:F Child# 3 Joseph Labonte Nashua, NH & Emelia Morneau Manchester, NH
LABONTE, Maria Alphonsine, Jun 29 1904 Sex:F Child# 4 George L Labonte US & Alexina Alphonsine Canada
LABONTE, Marie A Bertha, Feb 17 1929 Sex:F Child# 1 Arthur H Labonte Canada & Isabelle Champagne Augusta, ME
LABONTE, Marie Rose M A, Jul 25 1906 Sex:F Child# 3 Thomas C Labonte Vermont & Alphonsine Bonin Canada
LABONTE, Marie Rose Yvonne, Feb 20 1926 Sex:F Child# 2 Joseph Labonte Greenfield, NH & Amelia Morneau Manchester
LABONTE, Marthe Anastasie, May 20 1903 Sex:F Child# 4 Augustine Labonte Canada & Marie Tetreau Lawrence, MA
LABONTE, Norman Raymond, Jun 3 1932 Sex:M Child# 2 Alfred Labonte Manchester, NH & Yvonne Bourque New Boston, NH
LABONTE, Thomas Hyacinthe, Mar 18 1905 Sex:M Child# 2 Thomas E Labonte Vermont & Alphonsine Bonin Canada
LABONTE, Thomas R A, Jul 2 1903 Sex:M Child# 1 Damasse Labonte Vermont & Alphonsine Bonin Canada
LABONTY, Loretta, Mar 3 1910 Sex:F Child# 7 George Labonty Newport, VT & Alexina Cyr Canada
LABONVILLE, Angelina Therese, Mar 1 1932 Sex:F Child# 4 Edm Labonville Canada & Emilia Leblanc Canada
LABONVILLE, Joseph Alfred Gerard, Jan 8 1926 Sex:M Child# 1 Edward Labonville Hooksett, NH & Emelia Leblanc Canada
LABONVILLE, Joseph Dolord A, Oct 10 1930 Sex:M Child# 3 Edouard Labonville US & Emilia LeBlanc Canada
LABONVILLE, Marie Alice Girarda, Dec 16 1927 Sex:F Child# 2 E L Labonville Hooksett, NH & Marie Emelia Canada
LABORE, Augustus, Jan 17 1888 Sex:M Child# 3 Eugene Labore Switzerland & Amrasse Gagne Canada
LABOSSIERE, Eugene, Feb 6 1895 Sex:M Child# 1 Clephas Labossiere Canada & Emelie Hudon Canada
LABOUNTY, Doris Marguerite, May 19 1919 Sex:F Child# 2 George R LaBounty Canada & Marguerite M Graves Bradford
LABOUNTY, Eveline Mildred, Oct 28 1905 Sex:F Child# 1 George R Labounty Lacolle, PQ & Edith Chase Nashua, NH
LABOUNTY, George Reginald, Jr, Feb 1 1917 Sex:M Child# 1 George B Labounty La Cove, NY & Margaret M Gravel Re
LABOURY, Arelius, Mar 21 1891 Sex:F Child# Joseph Laboury Burlington, VT & Caroline Leiverise Sherburn, VT
LABRANCHE, Clovis Albert, Nov 9 1914 Sex:M Child# 9 Georges Labranche Canada & Anna Lasalle Canada
LABRANCHE, Eugene George Emile, Mar 19 1913 Sex:M Child# 8 George Labranche Canada & Marie Anna Lasalle Canada
LABRANCHE, Marie Anna, May 10 1910 Sex:F Child# 7 George Labranche Canada & Anna Lasalle Canada
LABRANCHE, Marie Dora, Apr 3 1909 Sex:F Child# 6 George Labranche Canada & Anna Lasalle Canada
LABRANCHE, Rita, Sep 9 1922 Sex:F Child# 1 George Labranche Canada & Elsie Laforest Canada
LABRANCHE, Sylvia Yvette, Sep 21 1907 Sex:F Child# 5 George Labranche Canada & Anna Lassalle Canada
LABRECQUE, Arthur Leon, Jun 23 1899 Sex:M Child# 2 Arthur Labrecque Canada & Delthia Prevost Canada
LABRECQUE, Camille Anna, Jan 11 1915 Sex:F Child# 1 Noe Labrecque Nashua, NH & Anna Dube Nashua, NH
LABRECQUE, Charles Emile, Apr 24 1903 Sex:M Child# 5 Arthur Labrecque Canada & Delthia Prevost Canada
LABRECQUE, Georgianna, Feb 5 1898 Sex:F Child# 1 Joseph Labrecque Nashua, NH & Georgianna Pinette Nashua, NH
LABRECQUE, Jos Rolland Amedee, Oct 6 1917 Sex:M Child# 2 Noe Labrecque NH & Anna Dube NH
LABRECQUE, Joseph Alfred W, May 7 1900 Sex:M Child# 1 Joseph Labrecque Canada & Virginie Grondin Canada
LABRECQUE, Joseph Alphonse, Jul 29 1896 Sex:M Child# 1 Alphonse Labrecque Canada & Marie Bouchard Canada
LABRECQUE, Joseph George Paul, Sep 9 1931 Sex:M Child# 1 Raymond Labrecque Greenville, NH & Olivette Landry Nashua
LABRECQUE, Joseph P, Feb 20 1899 Sex:M Child# 2 Joseph Labrecque Nashua, NH & Georgianna Pinette Nashua, NH
LABRECQUE, Marie Albina, Mar 17 1901 Sex:F Child# 4 Joseph Labrecque NH & Georgianna Pinette NH
LABRECQUE, Marie Victoria, Aug 6 1903 Sex:F Child# 1 Joseph Labrecque Canada & Juliana Peltier Canada
LABRECQUE, Olivine I, May 31 1902 Sex:F Child# 4 Arthur Labrecque Canada & Delthia Prevost Canada
LABRECQUE, Pierre, Sep 2 1905 Sex:M Child# 1 Michel Labrecque Canada & Marie Godbout Canada
LABRECQUE, Unknown, Apr 7 1900 Sex:F Child# 3 Joseph Labrecque NH & Georgianna Pinette NH Stillborn
LABRECQUE, Wilfrid Alfred, Aug 20 1900 Sex:M Child# 3 Arthur Labrecque Canada & Deltia Prevost Canada
LABREE, Camille Arthur, Sep 14 1925 Sex:M Child# 8 Joseph Labree Lowell, MA & Helena Labree Canada
LABREE, Joseph Philip, Nov 29 1925 Sex:M Child# 6 Victor Labree Canada & Alice Labrecque Fall River, MA
LABREQUE, Marie, Mar 25 1887 Sex:F Child# 5 Alp Labreque P Q & Delph Desmarais P Q
LABREQUE, Marie Alvina, May 8 1898 Sex:F Child# 1 Arthur Labreque Canada & Delcia Prevost Canada
LABRESQUE, Francis Noe, Dec 5 1890 Sex:M Child# 1 Francis Labresque Canada & Louise Duclos Canada
LABRIE, Alice Yvonne, Oct 10 1931 Sex:F Child# 10 Victor Labrie Canada & Alice Labrecque Fall River, MA
LABRIE, Alphonsine M, Mar 6 1930 Sex:F Child# 9 Victor Labrie Canada & Alice Labrecque Fall River, MA
LABRIE, Claudette, Jul 23 1934 Sex:F Child# 2 Leo Labrie Canada & Celeste Caron Indian Orchard, MA
LABRIE, Corrine, Oct 8 1931 Sex:F Child# 1 Leo Labrie Canada & Celeste Caron Indian Orchard, MA Stillborn
LABRIE, Geo John Marcel, Dec 3 1929 Sex:M Child# 2 Edward labrie New Bedford, MA & Laura Fortin Canada
LABRIE, Gloria Gabrielle Ire, Oct 6 1934 Sex:F Child# 3 Edward Labrie New Bedford, MA & Laura Fortin Adamsville
LABRIE, Irena, Nov 23 1890 Sex:F Child# 11 George Labrie Canada & Helen Paradis Canada

LABRIE, Leo Lionel, Sep 10 1922 Sex:M Child# 7 Wilfrid Labrie Canada & Antonia Pelletier Canada
LABRIE, Loretta Pauline, Feb 25 1929 Sex:F Child# 8 Victor Labrie Canada & Alice Labrecque Fall River, MA
LABRIE, Lucienne, Feb 1 1915 Sex:F Child# 1 Wilfrid Labrie Canada & Anatole Pelletier Canada
LABRIE, M Juliette Mathilde, Mar 14 1921 Sex:F Child# 5 Joseph Labrie Mass & Helena Labrie Canada
LABRIE, M Madeline Rita, Sep 20 1922 Sex:F Child# 6 Joseph Labrie Mass & Helena Labrie Canada
LABRIE, Marie Albina, Sep 12 1896 Sex:F Child# 3 Narcisse Labrie Canada & Degyple Theriault Canada
LABRIE, Marie Elizabeth, Sep 12 1890 Sex:F Child# 1 David Labrie Canada & Marie E Rioux Canada
LABRIE, Robert Conrad, Jul 6 1931 Sex:M Child# 3 Edouard Labrie New Bedford, MA & Laura Fortin Canada
LABRIE, Theresa Melanie, Apr 2 1927 Sex:F Child# 7 Victor Labrie Canada & Alice Labrecque Fall River, MA
LABRIE, Unknown, Jun 25 1926 Sex:M Child# 6 Wilfrid Labrie Canada & Antonia Pelletier Canada
LABRIE, Unknown, Jan 22 1929 Sex:F Child# 6 Wilfrid Labrie Canada & Antonia Pelletier Canada
LABRIE, Yvonne, May 22 1911 Sex:F Child# 6 Joseph Labrie Canada & Elise Dumont Canada
LABRIQUE, Salomee, Jan 6 1890 Sex:F Child# 2 Louis Labrique Canada & Salomee Charron Canada
LABUCIS, Unknown, Nov 11 1910 Sex:F Child# 1 Jo Lubucis Russia & Elzie Stakos Russia Stillborn
LACAILLADE, Conrad Alfred, Mar 8 1919 Sex:M Child# 1 Alf C Lacaillade Lawrence, MA & Vivian S Labombard Malone
LACASSE, Albert Roger C, Oct 24 1924 Sex:M Child# 4 Ferdinand Lacasse Canada & Adele Viger Canada
LACASSE, Andre, Jan 2 1933 Sex:M Child# 9 Ferd Lacasse Canada & Adelle Viger Canada
LACASSE, Arthur Alfred, Jan 23 1926 Sex:M Child# 5 Ferdinand Lacasse Canada & Idele Viger Canada
LACASSE, Harvey, Jan 1 1933 Sex:M Child# 8 Ferd Lacasse Canada & Adelle Viger Canada
LACASSE, Madeleine Yvette, Jun 17 1927 Sex:F Child# 6 F Lacasse Canada & Adelie Viger Canada
LACASSE, Marie Lorraine, Sep 6 1928 Sex:F Child# 7 Ferd Lacasse Canada & Adele Viger Canada
LACASSE, Rosa Anne May, May 9 1898 Sex:F Child# 5 Joseph Lacasse Canada & Catherine Keeley Canada
LACASSE, William E, Dec 16 1906 Sex:M Child# 1 Joseph Lacasse Canada & Mary Blomberg Nashua, NH
LACHANCE, Adrien Leopold, May 24 1920 Sex:M Child# 5 Joseph Lachance Canada & Marie Bilodeau Canada
LACHANCE, Albina D, May 31 1887 Sex:F Child#  Joseph Lachance P Q & Armina Grenier P Q
LACHANCE, Amanda Adrienne, Sep 23 1915 Sex:F Child# 2 Joseph Lachance Canada & Marie Bilodeau Canada
LACHANCE, Claire Agnes, Jul 17 1931 Sex:F Child# 3 Henri Lachance Nashua, NH & Juliette Fecteau Canada
LACHANCE, Edna Vivian, Aug 17 1911 Sex:F Child# 4 Arthur Lachance Canada & Elize Girouard Nashua, NH
LACHANCE, Ezilia Gertrude, Jun 20 1916 Sex:F Child# 6 Arthur Lachance Canada & Elize Girouard Nashua, NH
LACHANCE, J Henri Philias, Oct 13 1913 Sex:M Child# 1 Joseph Lachance Canada & Marie Bilodeau Canada
LACHANCE, Jean B Pierre, Mar 6 1907 Sex:M Child# 2 Odilon Lachance Canada & Aimee Dube Canada
LACHANCE, Jeanette Alice, Jan 15 1925 Sex:F Child# 9 Joseph Lachance Nashua, NH & Marie Bilodeau Canada
LACHANCE, Joseph, Dec 1 1906 Sex:M Child# 2 Cleophas Lachance Canada & Odile Aubut Canada
LACHANCE, Joseph, Mar 26 1908 Sex:M Child# 6 Moise Lachance Canada & Catherine Paul Canada
LACHANCE, Joseph Henri, Feb 10 1903 Sex:M Child# 2 Arthur Lachance Canada & Elise Girouard Nashua, NH
LACHANCE, Joseph Henri F, Jan 22 1894 Sex:M Child# 5 Joseph Lachance Canada & Armine Grenier Canada
LACHANCE, Joseph Irenee, Jun 20 1931 Sex:M Child# 1 Henri Lachance Canada & Lucille Valiere Canada
LACHANCE, Leo, Feb 4 1909 Sex:M Child# 3 Arthur Lachance Canada & Elise Girouard Nashua, NH
LACHANCE, Leo Henry, Nov 21 1932 Sex:M Child# 1 Leo Lachance Nashua, NH & Lillian Laquerre Nashua, NH
LACHANCE, Lorette, Jul 18 1924 Sex:F Child# 2 Donat Lachance Nashua, NH & Alice Pelletier Nashua, NH
LACHANCE, Lucien, Dec 20 1923 Sex:M Child# 7 Joseph Lachance Wisconsin & Marie Bilodeau Canada
LACHANCE, Lucille Rita, Dec 20 1923 Sex:F Child# 8 Joseph Lachance Wisconsin & Marie Bilodeau Canada
LACHANCE, M A Beatrice J A, Feb 5 1919 Sex:F Child# 4 Joseph Lachance Michigan & Marie Bilodeau Canada
LACHANCE, M Alice Adrienne, Feb 4 1919 Sex:F Child# 3 Alphonse Lachance Maine & Rose Pelletier Canada
LACHANCE, M Aurore Cecile, Jun 29 1913 Sex:F Child# 5 Arthur Lachance Canada & Elise Girouard Nashua, NH
LACHANCE, Maguertte, Feb 9 1935 Sex:F Child# 4 Paul Lachance Canada & Lilliane Duchesneau Canada
LACHANCE, Marie A R, Aug 8 1892 Sex:F Child# 4 Joseph Lachance Canada & Albina Genier Canada
LACHANCE, Marie Ange Rita, Sep 18 1921 Sex:F Child# 3 Alphonse Lachance Biddeford, ME & Rose Pelletier Montreal
LACHANCE, Marie Anne L, Jul 11 1905 Sex:F Child# 1 Odilon Lachance Canada & Aimee Dube Canada
LACHANCE, Marie Jeanne Cecile, Jan 15 1924 Sex:F Child# 1 Paul Lachance Canada & Lil Duchesneau Canada
LACHANCE, Marie Ninette Olivet, Nov 18 1925 Sex:F Child# 2 Paul Lachance Canada & Lillian Duchesneau Canada
LACHANCE, Marie R, Mar 26 1891 Sex:F Child# 3 Joseph Lachance Canada & Almina Grenier Canada
LACHANCE, Marie Rose A, May 24 1901 Sex:F Child# 1 Arthur Lachance Canada & Elise Girouard Nashua, NH
LACHANCE, Philomene Gabrielle, Sep 22 1916 Sex:F Child# 3 Joseph Lachance Canada & Marie Bilodeau Canada
LACHANCE, Pierre Josephat, Jul 14 1896 Sex:M Child# 6 Josephat Lachance Canada & Halmina Grenier Canada
LACHANCE, Raphael, May 27 1890 Sex:M Child# 1 Raphael Lachance Canada & Pamelia Rondeau Canada
LACHANCE, Robert Maurice, Sep 30 1934 Sex:M Child# 2 Henri Lachance Canada & Lucille Valliere Canada
LACHANCE, Roland Gerard, Oct 12 1918 Sex:M Child# 1 Donat Lachance Suncook, NH & Alice Pelletier Nashua, NH
LACHANCE, Theresa Loretta, Aug 11 1928 Sex:F Child# 1 G Lachance Canada & R A Morin Canada
LACHANCE, Unknown, Mar 26 1908 Sex: Child# 6 Moise Lachance Canada & Catherine Paul Canada Stillborn
LACHANCE, Unknown, Jan 5 1930 Sex:F Child# 2 Henri Lachance Nashua, NH & Juliette Fecteau Nashua, NH Stillborn
LACHANCE, Viviane Estelle, Jul 7 1926 Sex:F Child# 1 Henry Lachance Nashua, NH & Juliette Fecteau Canada
LACHAPELLE, Loretta Geraldine, Apr 23 1915 Sex:F Child# 2 Louis Lachapelle Canada & Anna Gaudette Nashua, NH
LACHAPELLE, Louis Roland Camille, Jul 18 1912 Sex:M Child# 1 Louis Lachapelle Canada & Emma Gaudette Nashua, NH
LACHUSKY, Unknown, Jul 29 1915 Sex:M Child# 4 Peter Lachusky Austria & Louise Balsky Russia Stillborn
LACOMBE, Florida Victoria, Dec 22 1905 Sex:F Child# 3 Joseph Lacombe Canada & Maggie Perreault N Adams, MA
LACOMBE, Joseph Cleophas E, Mar 25 1907 Sex:M Child# 4 Joseph Lacombe Canada & Marguerite Perreault Adams, MA
LACOMBE, Joseph Eugene R, Aug 8 1909 Sex:M Child# 1 Joseph Lacombe Canada & Leda Pelletier Canada
LACOMBE, Leo Wilfred, Mar 24 1908 Sex:M Child# 5 Joseph Lacombe Canada & Marguerite Perreault S Adams, MA
LACOMBE, Marie Alice A, Jan 31 1904 Sex:F Child# 2 Joseph Lacombe Canada & M Marg Perreault Adams, MA
LACOMBE, Marie Elise Irene, Jan 19 1905 Sex:F Child# 2 Joseph Lacombe Canada & Marguerite Perreault N Adams, MA
LACOMBE, Marie Emelia, Mar 16 1901 Sex:F Child# 1 Joseph Lacombe Canada & Jos'p'ne Lamontague Canada
LACOMBE, Theresa, May 23 1926 Sex:F Child# 3 Joseph Lacombe Canada & Leda Pelletier Canada

LACOMBE, Unknown, Feb 6 1903 Sex: Child# 1 Joseph Lacombe Canada & Maggie Perrault Adams, MA Stillborn
LACOMBE, Unknown, Sep 19 1924 Sex:M Child# 2 Joseph Lacombe Canada & Leda Pelletier Canada Stillborn
LACOMBE, Unknown, Nov 9 1927 Sex:F Child# 4 Joseph Lacombe Canada & Leda pelletier Canada
LACOMBE, Yvonne, Apr 16 1902 Sex:F Child# 2 Joseph Lacombe Canada & Josephine Lamontagne Canada
LACOURT, Howard Edmund, May 13 1909 Sex:M Child# 1 Peter Lacourt Italy & Emily J Keene Lowell, MA
LACROIX, Gloria Louise, Dec 10 1935 Sex:F Child# 1 Edward Lacroix Nashua, NH & Mary Theriault Nashua, NH
LACROIX, Marie Louise, Aug 26 1887 Sex:F Child# 9 Joseph Lacroix P Q & Julie Lefebvre P Q
LACROSSE, Unknown, Apr 30 1918 Sex:F Child# 4 David LaCrosse Dorchester, MA & Melissa Davis Keene, NH
LACUES, John, Nov 5 1910 Sex:M Child# 2 Adam Lacues Russia & Rosa Bagacanez Russia
LADAUX, Marie Louise, Sep 25 1889 Sex:F Child# 10 Samuel Ladaux Canada & Arilda Laliberte Canada
LADD, Ladd, Aug 2 1889 Sex:M Child# 2 George A Ladd Nashua, NH & Florence Whitcomb Townsend, MA
LADD, Unknown, Jun 12 1889 Sex:M Child# 1 Watson G Ladd Biddeford, ME & Jennie Pettigrew Halifax, NS
LADD, Unknown, Jul 17 1891 Sex:F Child# 3 George A Ladd Nashua, NH & Florence C Whitcomb Townsend, MA
LADOURS, Arthur George, Nov 13 1890 Sex:M Child# 6 James Ladours VT & Emma Canada
LADOUSE, Aderard, May 25 1888 Sex:M Child# 4 Louis Ladouse Fall River, MA & Georganna Hurdle Canada
LADRY, Joseph Adelard, Nov 29 1896 Sex:M Child# 2 Joseph Ladry Canada & Julia Peltier Canada
LAFAYETTE, Archie Frank, May 21 1920 Sex:M Child# 1 Pearly J Lafayette Vermont & Eva Leveille Canada
LAFAYETTE, Clifford, Jul 19 1908 Sex:M Child# 4 Walter A Lafayette Nashua, NH & Nettie M Lamoy E Chazy, NY
LAFAYETTE, Florence, Mar 17 1899 Sex:F Child# 1 James H Lafayette W Chazy, NY & Nellie A Goyait W Chazy, NY Stillbo
LAFAYETTE, Raymond, Jul 22 1921 Sex:M Child# 2 Perley Lafayette Vermont & Eva Leveille Canada
LAFAZANIS, Mary, Mar 11 1916 Sex:F Child# 1 Soutenios Lafazanis Greece & Sofia Sinka Greece
LAFAZONAS, Unknown, Jul 7 1917 Sex:M Child# 2 Sterios Lafazonas Greece & Sofia Greece
LAFLAME, Jeanne, Sep 12 1925 Sex:F Child# 7 Henry N LaFlame Plattsburg, NY & Anna G Carl Keswick, Iowa
LAFLAMME, Albert Arthur, Jan 9 1925 Sex:M Child# 3 George Laflamme Sciota, NY & Rose Lalmond Lowell, MA
LAFLAMME, Albert Wilfred, Jun 3 1912 Sex:M Child# 4 Adolphe Laflamme Canada & Rose Lawrence E Douglass, MA
LAFLAMME, Alice, May 6 1897 Sex:F Child# 1 Barthelemi Laflamme US & Virginie Dodge Canada
LAFLAMME, Alice Blanche, Jan 6 1922 Sex:F Child# 3 Julian Laflamme NH & Lillian Gravel Hudson, NH
LAFLAMME, Andre, Apr 16 1914 Sex:M Child# 1 Philippe Laflamme Sciota, NY & Marie Michaud Canada
LAFLAMME, Arthur Alfred, Mar 21 1934 Sex:M Child# 1 Arthur A LaFlamme Manchester, NH & Mary Dolly Nashua, NH
LAFLAMME, Arthur Maurice, Oct 8 1930 Sex:M Child# 1 Moise Laflamme Canada & Adela Nadeau Canada
LAFLAMME, Atla, Jul 14 1889 Sex:F Child# 1 William Laflamme Canada & Adeline Belanger Canada
LAFLAMME, Barthelmi O, Feb 27 1902 Sex:M Child# 3 Antoine Laflamme Canada & Marie Antil Canada
LAFLAMME, Blanche, Sep 28 1896 Sex:F Child# 3 Julien Laflamme US & Louisa Gaonette US
LAFLAMME, Claire Rochelle, Mar 16 1927 Sex:F Child# 6 A A Laflamme NH & Emma Lapointe NH
LAFLAMME, Donald George, Dec 22 1928 Sex:M Child# 7 George Laflamme Nashua, NH & Emma Forest Nashua, NH
LAFLAMME, Edouard Georges, Aug 22 1898 Sex:M Child# 1 Antoine Laflamme Canada & Marie St Jean Canada
LAFLAMME, Ella, May 27 1887 Sex:F Child# Charles Laflamme Altoona, NY & Jos McMarten Mooers, NY
LAFLAMME, Ernest, Jul 17 1917 Sex:M Child# 1 Julien Laflamme, Jr NH & Lillienne Grave NH
LAFLAMME, Frances, May 7 1935 Sex:F Child# 2 Francis Laflamme Canada & Rose Lavoie Barre, VT
LAFLAMME, Francis, Sep 9 1903 Sex:M Child# 4 Bartholomew Laflamme Sciota, NY & Virginie Dorge Canada
LAFLAMME, Gab Maurice Ernest, Sep 24 1921 Sex:M Child# 2 Louis Do Laflamme Canada & A Archambault Canada
LAFLAMME, George, Apr 19 1890 Sex:M Child# 4 Nelson Laflamme Chazy NY & Rilla Doucet Chazy, NY
LAFLAMME, Helen Dorothy, Jan 12 1926 Sex:F Child# 4 John Laflamme Canada & Mary J Therrien Berlin, NH
LAFLAMME, Henri Louis, Jul 10 1901 Sex:M Child# 3 Barth'lemi Laflamme Plattsburg, NY & Jennie Dodge Canada
LAFLAMME, Jeanne, Mar 28 1921 Sex:F Child# 1 H L LaFlamme Winchendon, MA & Lillian Girouard Nashua, NH
LAFLAMME, Josei D, Sep 27 1891 Sex:F Child# 2 Julius Laflamme Plattsburg, NY & Louise Gowette Plattsburg, NY
LAFLAMME, Joseph Aime Roland, Nov 20 1926 Sex:M Child# 2 Ernest Laflamme Canada & Emma Tanguay Canada
LAFLAMME, Joseph Barthelemy, May 7 1899 Sex:M Child# 5 Julien Laflamme Plattsburg, NY & Louisa Caouette Sciota, NY
LAFLAMME, Joseph Corade, Jun 26 1918 Sex:M Child# 2 George Laflamme NH & Emma Laforest NH
LAFLAMME, Joseph Darius, Sep 27 1920 Sex:M Child# 1 Louis D Laflamme Canada & Alberta Archambault Canada
LAFLAMME, Julien, Oct 26 1894 Sex:M Child# 2 Julien Laflamme US & Louise Caoutte US
LAFLAMME, Laura Olivette, Jun 7 1916 Sex:F Child# 2 Philippe Laflamme Sciota, NY & Leda Michaud Canada
LAFLAMME, Leo Roger, Mar 23 1921 Sex:M Child# 1 Leo Laflamme Nashua, NH & Elise Therrien NH
LAFLAMME, Loraine Lucille, Jan 7 1923 Sex:F Child# 4 George Laflamme Nashua, NH & Emma Laforest Nashua, NH
LAFLAMME, Marie, Mar 16 1912 Sex:F Child# 1 (No Parents Listed)
LAFLAMME, Marie, Nov 9 1917 Sex:F Child# 4 Philibert Laflamme Canada & Olivine Labrecque Canada Stillborn
LAFLAMME, Marie Agnes, Oct 23 1898 Sex:F Child# 2 Bart Laflamme Plattsburg, NY & Jennie Dodge Canada
LAFLAMME, Marie Alvina, Sep 24 1899 Sex:F Child# 2 Antoine Laflamme Canada & Marie Antil Canada
LAFLAMME, Marie Annette, Feb 3 1924 Sex:F Child# 3 Joseph Laflamme Nashua, NH & Andre Rioux Nashua, NH
LAFLAMME, Marie Evelyn, Sep 19 1930 Sex:F Child# 8 Jean Bapt Laflamme Canada & Marie Jane Therrien Berlin, NH
LAFLAMME, Marie Florence Rita, Jan 2 1921 Sex:F Child# 2 Joseph Laflamme Canada & Marie Jeanne Therrien NH
LAFLAMME, Marion, May 7 1935 Sex:F Child# 1 Francis Laflamme Canada & Rose Lavoie Barre, VT
LAFLAMME, Muriel Doris, Jun 12 1932 Sex:F Child# 7 J LaFlamme Canada & Mary J Therrien NH
LAFLAMME, Peter, Sep 13 1910 Sex:M Child# 1 Peter Laflamme Manchester, NH & Bertha Draper Northampton, MA
LAFLAMME, Philip Andrew, Sep 25 1918 Sex:M Child# 2 George Laflamme Sciota, NY & Rose Lalmond Lowell, MA
LAFLAMME, Rachel Phoebe, Feb 29 1928 Sex:F Child# 5 John B LaFlamme Canada & Mary J Therrien Berlin, NH
LAFLAMME, Raymond, Jul 25 1924 Sex:M Child# 5 George Laflamme Nashua, NH & Emma Laforest Nashua, NH
LAFLAMME, Reeni Lionel, Jun 22 1923 Sex:M Child# 3 John Laflamme Canada & Marie Jeanne Therrie NH
LAFLAMME, Rita, Mar 20 1920 Sex:F Child# 3 George Laflamme Nashua, NH & Emma Laforest Nashua, NH
LAFLAMME, Robert Edward, Jan 6 1931 Sex:M Child# 8 George Laflamme Nashua, NH & Emma Laforest Nashua, NH
LAFLAMME, Robert Ernest, Jul 31 1935 Sex:M Child# 8 John LaFlamme Canada & Mary J Therrien Berlin, NH
LAFLAMME, Ruby Joseph, Jul 28 1919 Sex:M Child# 2 Julien Laflamme NH & Lillienne Laforce NH
LAFLAMME, Unknown, Sep 20 1916 Sex:M Child# 1 George Laflamme Sciota, NY & Rose Lalmond Lowell, MA

LAFLAMME, Unknown, Jan 26 1919 Sex:F Child# 1 Jean Bte Laflamme Canada & Marie L Therrien NH
LAFLANTE, Jean Baptiste, May 24 1896 Sex:M Child# 11 David Laflante Canada & Philomene Theriau Canada
LAFLEUR, Alfred, Dec 24 1912 Sex:M Child# 1 Arthur Lafleur Nashua, NH & Elise Forrest Canada
LAFLEUR, Alfred Andrew, Sep 7 1917 Sex:M Child# 2 Arthur Lafleur Nashua, NH & Alice Mary Andrews Nashua, NH
LAFLEUR, Almira, Jan 7 1911 Sex:F Child# 7 Charles F LaFleur Plattsburg, NY & Louise Tessier Sciota, NY Stillborn
LAFLEUR, Arthur, Oct 5 1891 Sex:M Child# 10 Michel Lafleur Canada & Jane Lamoie Canada
LAFLEUR, Dorothy Jeanne, Feb 6 1927 Sex:F Child# 2 Ovila J Lafleur Springfield, MA & Laura Pelletier Nashua, NH
LAFLEUR, Dorothy May, Jan 10 1921 Sex:F Child# 2 William Lafleur Altona, NY & Eva Lafleur Williamstown, VT
LAFLEUR, Joseph, Mar 7 1889 Sex:M Child# 9 Michel Lafleur Altona, NY & Jane Larnoy Altona, NY
LAFLEUR, Joseph, Apr 15 1918 Sex:M Child# 1 William Lafleur New York & Eva Lafleur Vermont
LAFLEUR, Joseph Emilien G, Mar 13 1907 Sex:M Child# 4 Emilien Lafleur Canada & Carolina Caron Canada
LAFLEUR, M Jeanne B, Apr 13 1908 Sex:F Child# 5 Emilien Lafleur Canada & Caroline Caron Canada
LAFLEUR, Marie Clara A, Mar 14 1906 Sex:F Child# 3 Emilien Lafleur Canada & Caroline Caron Canada
LAFLEUR, Marie Doris, Nov 2 1926 Sex:F Child# 4 William Lafleur New York & Eva Lafleur New York
LAFLEUR, Marie Laurette, Jul 13 1932 Sex:F Child# 1 Alfred Lafleur Nashua, NH & L Rousseau Nashua, NH
LAFLEUR, Maurice George, Feb 2 1923 Sex:M Child# 2 Henry Lafleur Canada & Irene Malhout Nashua, NH
LAFLEUR, Raymond, Dec 15 1921 Sex:M Child# 1 Henry Lafleur, Jr Canada & Irene Malhoit Nashua, NH
LAFLEUR, Raymond Harold, Dec 1 1923 Sex:M Child# 1 William Lafleur Vermont & Eva Lafleur Vermont
LAFLEUR, Rosa, Oct 5 1887 Sex:F Child# Michel Lafleur Sciota, NY & Geneive Lauiree Sciota, NY
LAFLEUR, Therese Pearl, Apr 23 1920 Sex:F Child# 16 Henri Lafleur Canada & Emelie Rancour Canada
LAFLEUR, Unknown, Feb 9 1921 Sex:M Child# 1 Roy Lafleur Springfield, MA & Laura Pelletier Nashua, NH
LAFLOOD, Marie Adrienne Jeann, Dec 4 1934 Sex:F Child# 5 Jean LaFlood Canada & Lea Bilodeau Canada
LAFLOTTE, Alcide Ernest, Dec 10 1931 Sex:M Child# 4 Philudor Laflotte Canada & Yvonne Martin Suncook, NH
LAFLOTTE, Cecile, Jul 14 1926 Sex:F Child# 2 Philudor Laflotte Canada & Yvonne Martin Suncook, NH
LAFLOTTE, Eugene Donat, Sep 3 1931 Sex:M Child# 4 Jean Laflotte Canada & Lea Bilodeau Canada
LAFLOTTE, J J Leo, Feb 5 1926 Sex:M Child# 1 Jean Laflotte Canada & Lea Bilodeau Canada
LAFLOTTE, Joseph Anthony Jean, Apr 26 1926 Sex:M Child# Noe LaFlotte Canada & Eva McCue Suncook, NH
LAFLOTTE, Juliette, Jul 11 1930 Sex:F Child# 3 Jean LaFlotte Canada & Leah Bilodeau Canada
LAFLOTTE, Leah Theresa, Mar 29 1929 Sex:F Child# 3 Philudor Laflotte Canada & Yvonne Martin Suncook, NH
LAFLOTTE, Paul Maurice, Oct 29 1928 Sex:M Child# 2 Jean Laflotte Canada & Lea Bilodeau Canada
LAFLOTTE, Romeo, Nov 20 1924 Sex:M Child# 1 Philodar Laflotte Canada & Yvonne Martin Suncook, NH
LAFOND, Robert Wilfred, Sep 23 1897 Sex:M Child# 4 Adelard E Lafond Canada & Marie L Chagnon Canada
LAFONTAIN, Marie Janet, Apr 18 1919 Sex:F Child# 2 Gustave LaFountain Canada & Corana Fortier Canada
LAFONTAINE, Bertha Isabel, Sep 15 1922 Sex:F Child# 4 Edgar Lafontaine Lowell, MA & Velma Rood Swanton, VT
LAFONTAINE, Doris Estelle, Oct 21 1923 Sex:F Child# 5 Edgar Lafontaine Lowell, MA & Velma A Rood Swanton, VT
LAFONTAINE, Evaline H, Feb 8 1897 Sex:F Child# 1 Louis Lafontaine Canada & Henrietta Goyette Moore, NY
LAFONTAINE, Georges, Feb 9 1897 Sex:M Child# 3 Louis Lafontaine Canada & Amanda Girouard Canada
LAFONTAINE, Germaine Adeline, Jul 14 1916 Sex:F Child# 1 Edgar Lafontaine Lowell, MA & Velma A Roode Swanton, VT
LAFONTAINE, Joseph Doria, Jul 27 1890 Sex:M Child# 2 Dosithe Lafontaine Canada & Emma Germain Canada
LAFONTAINE, Joseph Henri E, Jul 28 1892 Sex:M Child# 4 Dosithe Lafontaine Canada & Emma Germain Canada
LAFONTAINE, Joseph Roland, Sep 25 1917 Sex:M Child# 1 Gustave Lafontaine Canada & Corona Forcier Canada
LAFONTAINE, June Esther, Jun 24 1925 Sex:F Child# 6 E LaFontaine Lowell, MA & Velma A Rood Swanton, VT
LAFONTAINE, Leo Albert, Feb 11 1922 Sex:M Child# 2 Amedee Lafontaine Nashua, NH & Liliane Fontaine Nashua, NH
LAFONTAINE, Leo Armand, Feb 17 1904 Sex:M Child# 6 Louis Lafontaine Canada & Amanda Girouard Canada
LAFONTAINE, Louis, Jul 20 1893 Sex:M Child# 1 Louis Lafontaine Canada & Amanda Girouard Canada
LAFONTAINE, Lucille Priscilla, Jan 11 1925 Sex:F Child# 1 Louis Lafontaine Hudson, NH & Florette Jean Nashua, NH
LAFONTAINE, Maria Agnes, May 11 1898 Sex:F Child# 2 Louis Lafontaine Canada & Henriette Goyette Mooers, NY
LAFONTAINE, Marie Amanda L, Nov 11 1909 Sex:F Child# 8 Louis Lafontaine Canada & Amanda Girouard Canada
LAFONTAINE, Marie C Leona, Mar 23 1902 Sex:F Child# 5 Louis Lafontaine Canada & Amanda Girouard Canada
LAFONTAINE, Marie Irene, Sep 21 1906 Sex:F Child# 7 Louis Lafontaine Canada & Amanda Girouard Canada
LAFONTAINE, Paul Heroe, Jul 27 1890 Sex:M Child# 3 Dosithe Lafontaine Canada & Emma Germain Canada
LAFONTAINE, Raymond Amedee, Aug 28 1920 Sex:M Child# 1 Amedee LaFontaine Nashua, NH & Lillian Fontaine Nashua, NH
LAFONTAINE, Rose Agnes, Oct 21 1919 Sex:F Child# 3 Edgar LaFontaine Lowell, MA & Velma Rood Swanton, VT
LAFONTAINE, Sylvia Priscilla, Aug 14 1926 Sex:F Child# 3 A Lafontaine Nashua, NH & Lillian Fontaine Nashua, NH
LAFONTAINE, Velma Viola, Nov 8 1921 Sex:F Child# 3 Edgar Lafontaine Lowell, MA & Velma Rood Swanton, VT
LAFORE, Adeline, Jul 10 1888 Sex:F Child# 2 Jean Baptiste Lafore Canada & Adeline Baud Canada
LAFORE, Napoleon, Mar 26 1888 Sex:M Child# 6 Joseph Lafore Plattsburg, NY & Edmine Lurine Plattsburg, NY
LAFORESH, Florie Emmie, Feb 9 1892 Sex:F Child# 3 Joseph Laforesh Canada & Emma Nadeau NY
LAFOREST, Albert Jean B, May 26 1910 Sex:M Child# 1 Edouard Laforest US & Exilda Roussel Canada
LAFOREST, Albina, Aug 20 1895 Sex:F Child# 6 Pierre Laforest Canada & Marie Bedard Canada
LAFOREST, Alphonse Oscar, Jan 31 1893 Sex:M Child# 5 Pierre Laforest Canada & Marie Bedard Canada
LAFOREST, Ernest Amedee, Nov 21 1911 Sex:M Child# 2 Edouard Laforest US & Exilda Roussel Canada
LAFOREST, Henri Albert, Apr 21 1919 Sex:M Child# 4 Henri Laforest Nashua, NH & Louise Senecal Mooers, NY
LAFOREST, Henry, Aug 7 1888 Sex:M Child# 1 Joseph Laforest Canada & Emma Laforest Sciota, NY
LAFOREST, Irene Agnes, Dec 1 1914 Sex:F Child# 3 Edouard Laforest US & Exilda Roussel US
LAFOREST, Isabelle Eva, Jan 3 1913 Sex:F Child# 3 Edward Laforest US & Exilda Roussel Canada
LAFOREST, Joseph, May 9 1888 Sex:M Child# 2 Pierre Laforest Canada & Maria Bedard Canada
LAFOREST, Joseph, May 27 1917 Sex:M Child# 5 Edouard Laforest Nashua, NH & Exilda Roussel Canada Stillborn
LAFOREST, Joseph Armand Leo, Nov 28 1908 Sex:M Child# 1 Armand Laforest New York & Clemence Bosse Canada
LAFOREST, Joseph Edouard, Jun 2 1895 Sex:M Child# 4 Joseph Laforest NY & Emma Nadeau Canada
LAFOREST, Joseph Girard, Jan 27 1924 Sex:M Child# 6 Edward Laforest Nashua, NH & Exilda Bussell Nashua, NH
LAFOREST, Joseph Oscar, Oct 8 1891 Sex:M Child# 4 Pierre Laforest Canada & Marie Bedard Canada Stillborn
LAFOREST, Joseph Raoul, May 2 1901 Sex:M Child# 8 Pierre Laforest Canada & Marie Bedard Canada

LAFOREST, Marie Lilliene Irene, Oct 26 1912 Sex:F Child# 2 Armand Laforest New York & Clemance Bosse Canada
LAFOREST, Marie Louise, Jan 3 1887 Sex:F Child#  Pierre Laforest P Q & Marie Bedard Canada
LAFOREST, Marie Louise A I, Jan 5 1908 Sex:F Child# 5 Joseph Laforest Canada & Emma Nadeau New York
LAFOREST, Mary, Feb 15 1915 Sex:F Child# 3 Henry Laforest Nashua, NH & Louise Senecal Mooers, NY
LAFOREST, Minnie Doris, Jul 23 1908 Sex:F Child# 1 Ed Laforest
LAFOREST, Peter, Sep 1 1892 Sex:M Child# 2 John Laforest Canada & Excellence Canada
LAFOREST, Theresa, Apr 20 1916 Sex:F Child# 4 Henry Laforest Nashua, NH & Louise Senecal Nashua, NH
LAFOREST, Unknown, Sep 27 1899 Sex:M Child# 7 Pierre Laforest Canada & Mary Bedard Canada Stillborn
LAFOREST, Unknown, Nov 14 1903 Sex:F Child# 2 Frank Laforest New York & Louisa Dube New York Stillborn
LAFOREST, Victor, Apr 2 1914 Sex:M Child# 1 Alfred Laforest US & Albina Cote US
LAFORME, Alice E L, Sep 2 1891 Sex:F Child# 1 Alfred Laforme Canada & Julie Bienvenue Canada
LAFORME, Azarie Alfred A, Oct 25 1901 Sex:M Child# 4 Alfred Laforme Canada & Adwilda Marin Canada
LAFORME, Elise Beatrice, Jul 21 1909 Sex:F Child# 11 Alfred Laforme Canada & Edwilda Morin Canada
LAFORME, Jane Constance, Mar 13 1928 Sex:F Child# 2 Louis Laforme Nashua, NH & Lillian Farland Nashua, NH
LAFORME, Joseph, May 23 1903 Sex:M Child#  Alfred Laforme Canada & Edwidge Marin Canada
LAFORME, Joseph H A, Sep 13 1899 Sex:M Child# 3 Alfred Laforme Canada & Adwilda Morin Canada
LAFORME, Joseph Remeo R, Mar 8 1898 Sex:M Child# 2 Alfred Laforme Canada & Advilda Morin Canada
LAFORME, Joseph Rene, Oct 18 1896 Sex:M Child# 1 Alfred Laforme Canada & Adwilda Marin Canada
LAFORME, Lucienne Sylvia, Nov 28 1899 Sex:F Child# 4 J B Laforme Canada & Hermine Michaude Canada
LAFORME, Marie, Jan 4 1893 Sex:F Child# 2 Philias Laforme Canada & Elise Gaudet Canada
LAFORME, Marie, Jan 29 1912 Sex:F Child# 11 Alfred Laforme Canada & Edwilda Marin Canada Stillborn
LAFORME, Marie B A A, May 14 1896 Sex:F Child# 2 Jean B Laforme Canada & Hermine Michaud Canada
LAFORME, Marie D, Aug 9 1893 Sex:F Child# 1 Alfred Laforme W Boylston, MA & Alphonsine Fontaine Canada
LAFORME, Marie E, May 30 1896 Sex:F Child# 2 Alfred Laforme W Boylston, MA & Alphonsine Fontain Canada
LAFORME, Marie Emma G, Jul 1 1905 Sex:F Child# 6 Alfred Laforme Canada & Edwidge Marin Canada
LAFORME, Marie Imelda O, Apr 18 1907 Sex:F Child# 7 Alfred Laforme Canada & Adwilda Marin Canada
LAFORME, Marie Irene E, Dec 7 1897 Sex:F Child# 3 Jean B Laforme Canada & Herminie Michaud Canada
LAFORME, Mariette Claire Paul, Apr 16 1926 Sex:F Child# 1 Romeo Laforme Nashua, NH & Jeannette Lucier Nashua, NH
LAFORME, Marjorie Yvette, Mar 25 1928 Sex:F Child# 2 Romer Laforme Nashua, NH & Jeanette Lucier Nashua, NH
LAFORME, Philias, Dec 10 1891 Sex:M Child# 1 Philias Laforme Canada & Elise Gaudet Canada
LAFORME, Unknown, May 12 1900 Sex:F Child# 4 Alfred Laforme Canada & Adwilda Morin Canada  Stillborn
LAFORME, Unknown, Apr 25 1904 Sex:F Child# 5 Alfred Laforme Canada & Edwidge Marin Canada
LAFORME, Yolande Germaine, Dec 3 1924 Sex:F Child# 1 Louis Laforme Nashua, NH & Lillian Farland Nashua, NH
LAFORREST, Delia Loretta, Oct 31 1910 Sex:F Child# 2 Henry LaForrest Nashua, NH & Louise Senecal Mooers, NY
LAFOUNTAINE, Edgar Harry, Feb 3 1928 Sex:M Child# 7 E H LaFountaine Lowell, MA & Velma Rood Swanton, VT
LAFRAMBOISE, Joseph, Oct 4 1904 Sex:M Child# 1 Emery Laframboise Canada & Lea Pinette Canada
LAFRANCE, Alfred Noel, Dec 22 1922 Sex:M Child# 2 Henry Lafrance Canada & Albertine Caron Canada
LAFRANCE, Conrad, Sep 29 1925 Sex:M Child# 4 Joseph Lafrance Nashua, NH & Andrea Rioux Nashua, NH
LAFRANCE, Enrest Roland, Dec 6 1919 Sex:M Child# 2 Joseph Lafrance Canada & Alice Baron Lowell, MA
LAFRANCE, Eva Therese, Apr 30 1924 Sex:F Child# 3 Henri Lafrance Canada & Albertine Caron Canada
LAFRANCE, Everett Spencer, Mar 28 1901 Sex:M Child# 1 Fred J LaFrance Canada & Ada Spencer Keene, NH
LAFRANCE, Fernande, Oct 17 1922 Sex:M Child# 2 Joseph Lafrance Nashua, NH & Andrea Rioux Nashua, NH
LAFRANCE, George A, Jul 11 1927 Sex:M Child# 7 J A Lafrance Canada & Alice Baron Lowell, MA
LAFRANCE, Girard, Jul 28 1924 Sex:M Child# 2 Thomas Lafrance Caribou, ME & Lillian Dube Canada
LAFRANCE, Irene Theresa, Mar 22 1929 Sex:F Child# 8 Joseph Lafrance Canada & Alice Rioux Lowell, MA
LAFRANCE, Jos Andre Ronald, Sep 14 1934 Sex:M Child# 9 Joseph Lafrance Nashua, NH & Andrea Rioux Nashua, NH
LAFRANCE, Jos Ernest Arthur, Sep 8 1928 Sex:M Child# 5 Henry Lafrance Canada & Albertine Caron Canada
LAFRANCE, Joseph, Jan 12 1901 Sex:M Child# 2 Joseph Lafrance Canada & Marie P Dube Canada
LAFRANCE, Joseph, May 18 1913 Sex:M Child# 1 Philias Lafrance Canada & Marie Bilodeau Canada
LAFRANCE, Joseph Alphonse C, Mar 9 1908 Sex:M Child# 1 Alphonse Lafrance Canada & Amanda Blais Canada
LAFRANCE, Joseph Arsene, Dec 5 1898 Sex:M Child# 1 Joseph Lafrance Canada & Paula Dube Canada
LAFRANCE, Joseph Bertrand, Aug 17 1920 Sex:M Child# 1 Joseph Lafrance Nashua, NH & Andrea Rioux Nashua, NH
LAFRANCE, Joseph Henri W, Jul 1 1911 Sex:M Child# 2 Esdras Lafrance Canada & Melina Landry Canada
LAFRANCE, Joseph Real Bertrand, Feb 3 1924 Sex:M Child# 3 Zephirin Lafrance Canada & Alivia Jean Canada
LAFRANCE, Joseph Romeo Henry, Jul 15 1925 Sex:M Child# 4 Henry Lafrance Canada & Albertine Caron Canada
LAFRANCE, Joseph Rosaire Gasto, Oct 1 1926 Sex:M Child# 4 Z Lafrance Canada & Oliva Jean Canada
LAFRANCE, Joseph X Leo, Aug 25 1909 Sex:M Child# 1 Esdras Lafrance Canada & Emelina Landry Canada
LAFRANCE, Juliette Cecile, Jan 30 1931 Sex:F Child# 9 Joseph Lafrance Canada & Alice Baron Lowell, MA
LAFRANCE, Leon F, Jan 4 1926 Sex:M Child# 6 Joseph Lafrance Canada & Alice Baron Lowell, MA
LAFRANCE, Lucille Albertine, Apr 5 1921 Sex:F Child# 1 Henri Lafrance Canada & Albertine Caron Canada
LAFRANCE, Marg Jennette L, Jul 10 1921 Sex:F Child# 3 Joseph Lafrance Canada & Alice Mary Baron Lowell, MA
LAFRANCE, Marie, May 8 1889 Sex:F Child# 2 Julian Lafrance Canada & Catherine Lebel Canada
LAFRANCE, Marie Cecile, Jun 8 1927 Sex:F Child# 5 Joseph Lafrance NH & Anria Rioux NH
LAFRANCE, Marie Ernestine, May 21 1889 Sex:F Child# 1 Joseph Lafrance Canada & Arsine Grandmaison Canada
LAFRANCE, Marie Mae C, May 21 1930 Sex:F Child# 5 Zephirim Lafrance Canada & Oliva Jean Canada
LAFRANCE, Marie Yola Constance, Nov 4 1932 Sex:F Child# 8 Jos Lafrance NH & Andrea Rioux NH
LAFRANCE, Marion Alice, May 11 1918 Sex:F Child# 1 Joseph Lafrance Canada & Alice Baron Lowell, MA
LAFRANCE, Mary Blanche, May 28 1910 Sex:F Child# 1 Joseph LaFrance Canada & Mathilde Caron Canada
LAFRANCE, Mary Doris, Nov 8 1933 Sex:F Child# 8 Joseph Lafrance Ile Verte, PQ & Alice Barron Lowell, MA
LAFRANCE, Paul William, Dec 12 1922 Sex:M Child# 4 Joseph E Lafrance Canada & Alice Baron Lowell, MA
LAFRANCE, Rachel Irene, Oct 9 1924 Sex:F Child# 5 Joseph Lafrance Canada & Alice Baron Lowell, MA
LAFRANCE, Robert Leo, May 15 1934 Sex:M Child# 5 Louis Lafrance Canada & Jeannette Rodier Nashua, NH
LAFRANCE, Roland Girard, Jan 17 1931 Sex:M Child# 7 Joseph LaFrance Nashua, NH & Andrea Rioux Nashua, NH

LANDRY, Marie Eunice Theresa, Sep 29 1926 Sex:F Child# 7 Hector Landry Canada & Amanda Rochette Canada
LANDRY, Marie Eva, Nov 1 1899 Sex:F Child# 4 Napoleon Landry Canada & Anaise Anctil Canada
LANDRY, Marie Julia I, Jun 7 1909 Sex:F Child# 9 Charles Landry Canada & Anna Dube Canada
LANDRY, Marie L A, Dec 4 1893 Sex:F Child# 1 Lucien Landry Canada & Malvina Harpin E Douglas, MA
LANDRY, Marie L D, May 17 1887 Sex:F Child# 3 Elise Landry P Q & Vitaline Lapense P Q
LANDRY, Marie Leda, Feb 12 1895 Sex:F Child# 5 Louis Landry Canada & Aurelie Belrose Canada
LANDRY, Marie Lucille L, Jan 8 1922 Sex:F Child# 2 William Landry Canada & Juliette Arel Canada
LANDRY, Marie Rita, Mar 23 1926 Sex:F Child# 1 J B A Landry Canada & Irene Lacombe Nashua, NH
LANDRY, Marie Rosa, Aug 8 1892 Sex:F Child# 1 Louis Landry Mass & Celina Hemond Canada
LANDRY, Mary Cora, Jan 1 1935 Sex:F Child# 9 William Landry Canada & Julia Arel Canada
LANDRY, Mary Jean, Jul 11 1934 Sex:F Child# 1 Homer Landry Nashua, NH & Lillian Girard Nashua, NH
LANDRY, Mary Leocadie, May 9 1931 Sex:F Child# 4 Emile Landry Canada & M L Hamel Nashua, NH
LANDRY, Mathilda, Nov 11 1889 Sex:F Child# 7 Napoleon Landry Nashua, NH & M Beauregard Nashua, NH
LANDRY, May Irene Lucille, Nov 28 1921 Sex:F Child# 2 Antonio Landry Nashua, NH & Alberta Marquis Canada
LANDRY, Napoleon, Dec 30 1895 Sex:M Child# 3 Louis Landry Canada & Celina Emond Canada
LANDRY, Nathanael, Nov 24 1890 Sex:M Child# 4 Nathanael Landry Canada & Georgianna St Peiere Canada
LANDRY, Nellie Liliane, Nov 17 1905 Sex:F Child# 10 Louis Landry Canada & Celina Emond Canada
LANDRY, Norman James, May 20 1925 Sex:M Child# 3 Ernest Landry Nashua, NH & Eva Cote Nashua, NH
LANDRY, Normand, Dec 28 1930 Sex:M Child# 2 George Landry Nashua, NH & Anita Marquis Nashua, NH
LANDRY, Olivette Flora, Jun 11 1921 Sex:F Child# 1 Ernest H Landry Nashua, NH & Rose Dufault Lowell, MA
LANDRY, Olivette S B, Jan 11 1909 Sex:F Child# 3 Elisee Landry Nashua, NH & Helene Morais Canada
LANDRY, Oswald D O, Apr 18 1907 Sex:M Child# 2 Elisee Landry Nashua, NH & Helene Maurais Canada
LANDRY, Ovide Hector, Mar 1 1914 Sex:M Child# 2 Hector Landry Canada & Amanda Rochette Canada
LANDRY, Ovilla, Dec 24 1897 Sex:M Child# 1 Jean B Landry Canada & Marie Beaulieu Canada
LANDRY, Pauline Lucille, Oct 7 1921 Sex:F Child# 2 Sylvis Landry Nashua, NH & Mamie Peno Nashua, NH
LANDRY, Pauline Lucille, Nov 30 1932 Sex:F Child# 3 Honore Landry Nashua, NH & Laura Smith Nashua, NH
LANDRY, Persis May, Jun 21 1906 Sex:F Child# 1 Donat Landry Canada & Dora Golden Hartford, CT
LANDRY, Rachael, Dec 2 1921 Sex:F Child# 3 Emile Landry Nashua, NH & Claudia Boucher Nashua, NH
LANDRY, Raoul, Dec 3 1906 Sex:M Child# 7 John Landry Canada & Marie Beaulieu Canada
LANDRY, Raymond, Mar 29 1927 Sex:M Child# 2 John B Landry Canada & Irene Lacombe Nashua, NH
LANDRY, Rita Marguerite J, Sep 29 1922 Sex:F Child# 1 Noel Landry NH & Marie J St Onge Mass
LANDRY, Robert George, Jul 25 1933 Sex:M Child# 2 Albert Landry Nashua, NH & Eva Lizotte Canada
LANDRY, Roger, Jan 3 1920 Sex:M Child# 2 Emile Landry Nashua, NH & Claudia Boucher Nashua, NH Stillborn
LANDRY, Roland, Jan 2 1902 Sex:M Child# 4 J B Landry Canada & Marie Beaulieu Canada
LANDRY, Romeo Arthur, Apr 27 1909 Sex:M Child# 12 Louis Landry Canada & Celina Emond Canada
LANDRY, Rosaire Sylvio, Jun 10 1910 Sex:M Child# 3 Elizee Landry Nashua, NH & Helene Maurais Canada
LANDRY, Rosalie, Jul 21 1887 Sex:F Child# 4 George Landry Nashua, NH & Rosalie Landry Nashua, NH
LANDRY, Rose Emma, Oct 30 1892 Sex:F Child# 1 Charles Landry Nashua, NH & Emma Bouchard Canada
LANDRY, Roy Bernard, Mar 10 1918 Sex:M Child# 2 Ernest D Landry Nashua, NH & Eva Cote Nashua, NH
LANDRY, Sylvia Irene, May 20 1906 Sex:F Child# 8 Louis Landry Canada & Aurelie Bellerose Canada
LANDRY, Telesphore Fernand, Dec 6 1909 Sex:M Child# 9 John Landry Canada & Marie Beaulieu Canada
LANDRY, Theresa Elizabeth, Mar 31 1929 Sex:F Child# 10 Donat Landry Canada & Dora Golden Hartford, CT
LANDRY, Theresa Mary, Jan 15 1929 Sex:F Child# 4 Asa B Landry Nashua & Catherine M Fox Manchester, NH Stillborn
LANDRY, Thomas Mitchell, Jan 26 1910 Sex:M Child# 3 Donat J Landry Canada & Dora E Golden Hartford, CT
LANDRY, Thomas Mitchell, Mar 6 1935 Sex:M Child# 3 Thomas M Landry Nashua, NH & Irene Livernois Derry, NH
LANDRY, Unknown, Oct 17 1887 Sex:M Child#   Thomas Landry Canada & Louise Moissette Canada Stillborn
LANDRY, Unknown, Apr 17 1892 Sex:M Child# 14 Thomas Landry Canada & Marie L Morisette Canada Stillborn
LANDRY, Unknown, Sep 26 1892 Sex:M Child# 12 Thomas Landry Canada & M Louise Morisette Canada Stillborn
LANDRY, Unknown, Nov 15 1894 Sex:M Child# 2 Lucien Landry Canada & Malvina Harpin E Douglass, MA Stillborn
LANDRY, Unknown, Nov 21 1895 Sex:M Child# 2 Charles Landry Mass & Emma Bouchard Canada Stillborn
LANDRY, Unknown, Nov 21 1895 Sex:M Child# 3 Charles Landry Mass & Emma Bouchard Canada Stillborn
LANDRY, Unknown, May 14 1899 Sex:M Child# 3 Charles Landry Canada & Anna Dube Canada Stillborn
LANDRY, Unknown, Dec 6 1899 Sex:F Child# 2 Bruneau Landry Canada & Marie Pelletier Canada Stillborn
LANDRY, Unknown, Jun 2 1901 Sex:M Child#  Bruneau Landry Canada & Mary Pelky Canada Stillborn
LANDRY, Unknown, Jun 3 1901 Sex:M Child# 7 Bruneau Landry Canada & Mary Pelky Canada Stillborn
LANDRY, Unknown, May 14 1920 Sex:M Child# 1 Antonio Landry Nashua, NH & Bertha Marquis Canada Stillborn
LANDRY, Unknown, Jul 27 1929 Sex:F Child# 2 Ludger Landry Canada & Edna Ellenwood N Pelham, NH Stillborn
LANDRY, Wilfred Donat, Jan 14 1912 Sex:M Child# 4 Donat J Landry Canada & Dora Ellen Golden Hartford, CT
LANDRY, William, Aug 3 1925 Sex:M Child# 1 Frank Landry Canada & Grace Girouard Nashua, NH
LANDRY, William Carroll, Oct 14 1927 Sex:M Child# 1 Leon Landry Nashua, NH & Elise Carroll Canada
LANDY, Joseph, Jul 23 1888 Sex:M Child# 11 Thomas Landy Canada & Louise Moussette Canada
LANE, Gladis R, Jun 12 1897 Sex:F Child# 2 Harry E Lane Maine & Jennie Laflin Maine
LANE, Lillian M, Nov 20 1888 Sex:F Child# 2 Michael Lane N S & Mary Ann Sullivan Nashua, NH
LANE, Louisa Martha, Mar 24 1891 Sex:F Child# 1 Frank H R Lane Maine & Martha I Satchwell Manchester, NH
LANE, Robert, May 29 1892 Sex:M Child# 3 Joseph R Lane Plainfield, NJ & Bertha Rochester, NY
LANGELIER, Eugenie, Jan 30 1903 Sex:F Child# 3 Michael Langelier Canada & Alphonsine Moreau Canada
LANGELIER, Joseph Maurice, Sep 12 1924 Sex:M Child# 3 Charles Langelier Canada & Agnes Proulx Springfield, MA
LANGELIER, Leo Paul, Dec 28 1925 Sex:M Child# 4 Charles Langelier Canada & Agnes Proulx Springfield
LANGELIER, Loretta Aline, Jun 13 1927 Sex:F Child# 4 Albert Langelier Canada & Rose Plourde Canada
LANGELIER, Marie Therese Irene, Apr 27 1922 Sex:F Child# 2 Charles Langelier Canada & Agnes Proulx Mass
LANGELIER, Muriel Edna, Dec 22 1932 Sex:F Child# 5 Albert Langelier Canada & Rose Plourde Canada
LANGELIER, Octave A, Apr 29 1891 Sex:M Child# 9 Coine Langelier Canada & Marie I Chagnon Canada
LANGELIER, Paul Fernard, Dec 26 1925 Sex:M Child# 3 Albert Langelier Canada & Lida Levesque Canada

LANGELIER, Raoul Philip, Mar 9 1929 Sex:M Child# 5 Charles Langelier Canada & Agnes Proulx Springfield, MA
LANGELIER, Rolande Yvonne, Jan 12 1924 Sex:F Child# 2 Albert Langelier St Pascal, Canada & Rose Plourde Canada
LANGELIER, Sylvio Robert, Aug 2 1935 Sex:M Child# 6 Charles Langelier Canada & Agnes Proulx Springfield, MA
LANGELIER, Therese Olivette, Nov 25 1921 Sex:F Child# 1 Albert Langelier Canada & Rose Plourde Canada
LANGERIN, Marie M E, Dec 6 1890 Sex:F Child# 1 Henri Langerin Brookfield, MA & Maderise Desory Canada
LANGES, Unknown, Nov 1915 Sex:F Child# Costas Langes Greece & Olga Poppodopolos Greece Stillborn
LANGESTON, William Charles, Jul 24 1916 Sex:M Child# 1 Ed Frank Langeston Maine & Mildred Reynolds Hudson, NH
LANGILLE, Myrtle Grace, Dec 20 1924 Sex:F Child# 1 Cecile A Langille Nova Scotia & Maude B Terrian Milford, NH
LANGLAIS, Armand J B, Aug 25 1904 Sex:M Child# 2 Jean Langlais Canada & Adele Plourde Canada
LANGLAIS, Eugenie, Feb 26 1903 Sex:M Child# 1 Jean Langlais Canada & Adele Plourde Canada
LANGLAIS, Florence Marie, Jan 19 1896 Sex:F Child# 6 Frank Langlais Canada & Virginie Nadeau NY
LANGLAIS, Hector, Jan 31 1891 Sex:M Child# 3 Frank Langlais Canada & Jennie Madeau New York
LANGLAIS, Joseph Samuel R, Jul 24 1898 Sex:M Child# 1 Alphonse Langlais Canada & Exilda Ledoux Canada
LANGLEY, Unknown, Nov 3 1889 Sex:M Child# 2 William Langley
LANGLIER, Robert Wilfred, Nov 22 1910 Sex:M Child# 1 Claude C Langlier Nashua, NH & Gertrude Lougee Lewiston, ME
LANGLOIR, Francois, Dec 7 1892 Sex:M Child# 2 Francois Langloir Granby, PQ & Virginie Nadeau Moors, NY
LANGLOIS, Adrien, Sep 2 1905 Sex:M Child# 5 J B A Langlois Canada & Azilda Ledoux US
LANGLOIS, Adrienne, Sep 2 1905 Sex:F Child# 6 J B A Langlois Canada & Azilda Ledoux US
LANGLOIS, Alfred Eugene, Aug 3 1923 Sex:M Child# 5 Alfred H Langlois Canada & Victoria M Beaulac Canada
LANGLOIS, Alida Fernande L, Jan 8 1907 Sex:F Child# 3 Arthur Langlois Canada & Regina Archambault Canada
LANGLOIS, Alma Leonide, Apr 5 1900 Sex:F Child# 2 Alphonse Langlois
LANGLOIS, Azilda Adelaide, Jan 17 1907 Sex:F Child# 4 J B A Langlois Canada & Azilda Ledoux Canada
LANGLOIS, Flora, Jun 22 1897 Sex:F Child# Frank Langlois Canada & Virginie Nadeau US
LANGLOIS, Francoise Marguerite, Jul 21 1912 Sex:F Child# 1 Alfred Langlois Canada & Marie Vctria Beaulac Canada
LANGLOIS, Giberta Agnes Her, Sep 23 1917 Sex:F Child# 5 Arthur Langlois Roxton Falls, PQ & Regina Archambeault
LANGLOIS, J Art Rud Louis M, Apr 29 1913 Sex:M Child# 4 Arthur Langlois Canada & Regina Archambeault Canada
LANGLOIS, J Jeanne d'Arc, May 17 1919 Sex:F Child# 6 Arthur Langlois Canada & Regina Archambeault Canada
LANGLOIS, Jean Rene, Oct 30 1918 Sex:M Child# 4 A H Langlois Canada & Victoria Beaulieu Canada
LANGLOIS, Joseph George E, May 25 1907 Sex:M Child# 1 Ernest Langlois Canada & Annie Dumais Canada
LANGLOIS, Louis Isabert, Nov 11 1902 Sex:M Child# 4 Alex Langlois Canada & Alphonsine Levesque Canada
LANGLOIS, Louise C G, Sep 29 1904 Sex:F Child# 1 Arthur Langlois Canada & Regina Archambault Canada
LANGLOIS, Marguerite B R, Oct 2 1905 Sex:F Child# 2 Arthur Langlois Canada & Regina Archambeau Canada
LANGLOIS, Marie Colette, Nov 16 1913 Sex:F Child# 2 Alfred Langlois Canada & M Victoria Beaulac Canada
LANGLOIS, Raymond, Jul 23 1901 Sex:M Child# 3 Alphonse Langlois Canada & Azilda Ledoux Canada
LANGLOIS, Unknown, Jun 1 1899 Sex:M Child# 8 Francois Langlois Canada & Virginie Nadeau Canada Stillborn
LANGLOIS, Victor Beaulac Alfred, Dec 20 1914 Sex:M Child# 3 Alfred Langlois Canada & Victoria Beaulac Canada
LANGLOIS, Virginia, Oct 14 1933 Sex:F Child# 2 (No Parents Listed)
LANGMUIR, Donald, Apr 5 1934 Sex:M Child# 2 John Langmuir Flatbush, NY & Laura Drake Newton, MA
LANGNERUND, Marie J, Jan 2 1889 Sex:F Child# 1 B Langnerund Canada & Olinphe Geryard Canada
LANGUERAND, Joseph Paul, Sep 29 1892 Sex:M Child# 4 Remi Languerand Canada & Olymphe Levesque Canada
LANGWAY, Unknown, Jul 13 1893 Sex:F Child# 1 Philip Langway Claremont, NH & Rosa Cullen Ireland
LANGWAY, Unknown, May 14 1895 Sex:M Child# 2 Philip Langway Claremont & Ireland
LANINSKY, Annie, Jul 26 1915 Sex:F Child# 2 Michael Laninsky Russia & Lud Bugdonowicz Russia
LANNEVILLE, Malvina Lucile, Nov 2 1914 Sex:F Child# 5 Julien Lanneville Canada & Louise Daniel Waterbury, CT
LANNING, Nathaniel K, May 3 1887 Sex:M Child# 2 John G Lanning Trenton, NJ & Sarah E Boston
LANOIE, John Aubray Albert, Oct 31 1931 Sex:M Child# 2 Charlemagne Lanoie Canada & Anna Henry Canada
LANOIE, Mary Gertrude Aline, Feb 21 1934 Sex:F Child# 1 Charles O Lanoie Canada & Germaine Fournier Greenville, NH
LANOIS, Aline Vivian, Jul 7 1925 Sex:F Child# 1 Charles Lanois Canada & Anna Henry Canada
LANSIL, Clifford Lincoln, Sep 5 1929 Sex:M Child# 1 Clifford Lansil Bangor, ME & Charlotte Cotton Pepperell, MA
LANSIL, Melvin Clifford, Aug 12 1925 Sex:M Child# 1 Clyde H Lansil Bradley, ME & Dorothy Soule E Pepperell, MA
LANSOS, Unknown, Aug 10 1916 Sex:M Child# 3 Costas Lansos Greece & Olga Paffa Greece Stillborn
LANTZ, Albert Graden, Sep 26 1927 Sex:M Child# 5 Albert Lantz Nova Scotia & Lena Dresser Northfield, MA
LANTZ, James Earle, Jan 16 1925 Sex:M Child# 4 Albert Lantz Nova Scotia & Lena Dresser Northfield, MA
LANTZAS, John, Dec 5 1920 Sex:M Child# 1 George Lantzas Greece & Anastasia Katsupare Greece
LANTZAS, Unknown, Jan 11 1922 Sex:F Child# George Lantzas Greece & Anastasia Katsupare Greece
LAPAGE, Marcel, Dec 7 1927 Sex:M Child# 7 Octave Lapage Canada & Alice Rousseau Canada
LAPAZA, Mary, Apr 23 1916 Sex:F Child# 2 Clement Lapaza Russia & Anna Hormata Russia
LAPEIRRE, Marie J, Dec 27 1887 Sex:F Child# 4 Pierre Lapeirre Canada & Julia Lussier Canada
LAPELICK, Joseph, Nov 6 1925 Sex:M Child# 4 Andrew Lapelick Poland & H Nichalawicz Poland
LAPEN, Frank, Mar 31 1922 Sex:M Child# 3 Justin Lapen Lithuania & Marcella Antonjec Lithuania
LAPENSE, Francois, Apr 24 1889 Sex:M Child# 4 Vitaline Lapense Canada & Elise Landry Canada
LAPENSKI, Helena, Oct 23 1917 Sex:F Child# 3 Michael Lapenski Russia & Ludorica Bagdanovitc Russia
LAPENSKI, Melvina, Apr 5 1922 Sex:F Child# 4 Michael Lapenski Lithuania & Lucy Bakowitch Lithuania
LAPERCHE, Elianne, Sep 3 1899 Sex:F Child# 8 Elphege Laperche Canada & Alphonsine Bergeron Canada
LAPERCHE, Eveline, Sep 3 1899 Sex:F Child# 9 Elphege Laperche Canada & Alphonsine Bergeron Canada
LAPEZA, Chester, Jun 7 1918 Sex:M Child# 1 William Lapeza Russia & Adale Lukowich Russia
LAPEZO, Henry Theophil, Oct 3 1919 Sex:M Child# 2 William Lapezo Russia & Adella Lewkovicz Russia
LAPHAM, Charles William, Aug 6 1910 Sex:M Child# 3 Charles W Lapham Danamora, NY & Annie L Shea Nashua, NH
LAPHAM, John Richard, Sep 29 1903 Sex:M Child# 1 Charles W Lapham Dannennora, NY & Annie L Shea Nashua, NH
LAPHAM, Joseph, Apr 22 1913 Sex:M Child# 5 Charles W Lapham Danamora, NY & Annie L Shea Nashua, NH
LAPHAM, Kathryn M, Sep 15 1907 Sex:F Child# 2 Charles M Lapham Dannamore, NY & Annie L Shea Nashua, NH
LAPHAM, Mary Alicia, Feb 17 1910 Sex:F Child# 1 Richard Lapham New York & Alicia Connor Nashua, NH
LAPHAM, Maxwell, Apr 22 1913 Sex:M Child# 4 Charles W Lapham Danamora, NY & Annie L Shea Nashua, NH

243

LAPIERRE, Angelina, Jul 22 1890 Sex:F Child# 8 Alfred Lapierre Canada & Exilda Gauthier Canada
LAPIERRE, Antoine Gerard, Apr 28 1922 Sex:M Child# 2 Harry Lapierre Rochester, NH & Alma Valliere Canada
LAPIERRE, Arnold Herbert, Oct 10 1923 Sex:M Child# 1 Herbert Lapierre New York & Laurette Plante NH
LAPIERRE, Beatrice Irene, Jun 10 1904 Sex:F Child# 1 Wilfred Lapierre Canada & Delia Gaudette Nashua, NH
LAPIERRE, Delia Beatrice, Mar 25 1934 Sex:F Child# 1 Wilfred Lapierre Nashua, NH & Beatrice Fortin Canada
LAPIERRE, Donald, Nov 5 1927 Sex:M Child# 2 Herbert Lapierre Sciota, NY & Lena Joubert Sciota, NY
LAPIERRE, Gloria Loretta, Nov 29 1933 Sex:F Child# 2 Herbert Lapierre Nashua, NH & Loretta Plante Nashua, NH
LAPIERRE, Joseph Albert, Mar 4 1914 Sex:M Child# 5 Dominique Lapierre Canada & Amelie Gagnon Canada
LAPIERRE, Joseph Albert M, Aug 5 1905 Sex:M Child# 8 Alfred Lapierre Canada & Agnes Boulette Canada
LAPIERRE, Louis William, Oct 22 1907 Sex:M Child# 2 Wilfred Lapierre Canada & Delia Gaudette Nashua, NH
LAPIERRE, Marie C, Jan 2 1887 Sex:F Child# 1 Pierre Lapierre P Q & Pulcherie Paquet P Q
LAPIERRE, Mary Shirley, Apr 30 1924 Sex:F Child# 1 Herbert Lapierre New York & Laura Jubert New York
LAPIERRE, Mirilda Palmelie, May 3 1916 Sex:F Child# 6 Dominique Lapierre Canada & Aurelie Gagnon Canada
LAPIERRE, Unknown, Mar 29 1894 Sex:M Child# 1 (No Parents Listed)
LAPIN, Broneshave, Jul 10 1917 Sex:M Child# 1 Alexander Lapin Russia & Teofila Narkielon Russia
LAPIN, Melvina, Dec 4 1926 Sex:F Child# 4 Justin Lapin Lithuania & Marcella Antoncik Lithuania
LAPINSKI, Virginia, Jan 7 1929 Sex:F Child# 6 Michael Lapinski Lithuania & Lucy Bagdonowitch Lithuania
LAPLANTE, Alfred I, Feb 19 1900 Sex:M Child# 12 David Laplante Canada & Philomene Therian Canada
LAPLANTE, Arthur, May 6 1887 Sex:M Child# David Laplante P Q & Philomene Theriau P Q
LAPLANTE, Donald Irving, Feb 16 1926 Sex:M Child# 3 David Laplante Canada & Elizabeth Dilling Germany
LAPLANTE, Jos Rodolphe Lucien, Sep 9 1919 Sex:M Child# 7 Joseph Laplante Canada & Adelia Blanchard Canada
LAPLANTE, Joseph Albert, Oct 15 1906 Sex:M Child# 1 Albert Laplante Canada & Rose I Tetrault Canada
LAPLANTE, Joseph Irence, Jan 4 1900 Sex:M Child# 1 David Laplante Canada & Mathilde Brisebois Canada
LAPLANTE, Joseph L, Jul 1 1890 Sex:M Child# 1 Joseph Laplante Canada & Anna Desjardins Canada
LAPLANTE, Joseph Roch M, May 24 1930 Sex:M Child# 1 Alexander Laplante New Britain, CT & Antonette LeMonde Canada
LAPLANTE, Marie Lorett Laura, Jan 13 1916 Sex:F Child# 1 Adolphe Laplante Canada & Alida Masson Canada
LAPLANTE, Marie M Laura, Apr 30 1931 Sex:F Child# 2 Alexandre Laplante New Britain, CT & Antoinette Lemonde Canada
LAPLANTE, Marie Odile, Apr 28 1903 Sex:F Child# 2 Xavier Laplante Canada & Ziliea Desjarlets Canada
LAPLANTE, Paul Joseph Bernard, Jan 12 1932 Sex:M Child# 1 Edward Laplante St Hyacinth, PQ & Juliette Theriault
LAPLANTE, Raymond Francis, Feb 11 1927 Sex:M Child# 4 David Laplante Canada & Elizabeth Dilling Germany
LAPLANTE, Roland, Jul 27 1933 Sex:M Child# 3 Edward LaPlante Canada & Juliet Theriault Nashua, NH
LAPLANTE, Victoria, Apr 24 1901 Sex:F Child# 1 Xavier Laplante Canada & Zelia Desjarlets Canada
LAPLANTE, Wilfrid Ernest, Sep 28 1901 Sex:M Child# 2 David Laplante Canada & Mathilde Brisebois Canada
LAPOINTE, Arthur, Feb 10 1890 Sex:M Child# 14 Jibert Lapointe Canada & Ida Charbonneau NY Stillborn
LAPOINTE, Blanche Irene, Feb 19 1917 Sex:F Child# 9 Joseph Lapointe Canada & Marie Harvey Canada
LAPOINTE, Edmond, Sep 26 1908 Sex:M Child# 7 Joseph Lapointe Canada & Marie Harvey Canada
LAPOINTE, Edouard Francois, May 22 1911 Sex:M Child# 8 Joseph Lapointe Canada & Marie Harvey Canada
LAPOINTE, J Jean Bte Robert, Oct 23 1915 Sex:M Child# 2 Adjutor Lapointe Canada & Marie Plante Canada
LAPOINTE, Joseph, Dec 21 1891 Sex:M Child# 15 Gilbert Lapointe Canada & Ida Charbonneaux New York
LAPOINTE, Joseph Aime, May 29 1905 Sex:M Child# 5 Joseph Lapointe Canada & Marie Harvey Canada
LAPOINTE, Joseph Avila, Mar 15 1904 Sex:M Child# 4 Joseph Lapointe Canada & Mary Harvey Canada
LAPOINTE, Joseph Leo, May 11 1902 Sex:M Child# 3 Joseph Lapointe Canada & Marie Harvey Canada
LAPOINTE, Joseph Leopold R, Jan 12 1907 Sex:M Child# 6 Joseph Lapointe Canada & Marie Harvey Canada
LAPOINTE, Laurent Antonio, Feb 19 1923 Sex:M Child# 6 Adjutor Lapointe Canada & Marie Plante Canada
LAPOINTE, Lucille Elinor, Sep 10 1909 Sex:F Child# 1 Jeremiah Lapointe Canada & Rose A Smith Nashua, NH
LAPOINTE, M Irene Juliette, Oct 1 1921 Sex:F Child# 1 D J Odette Lapointe Lewiston, ME & Albina Consigny Nashua, NH
LAPOINTE, Marie C Aubeline, Mar 23 1899 Sex:F Child# 1 Joseph Lapointe Canada & Marie Harvey Canada
LAPOINTE, Paul Alfred, Sep 9 1925 Sex:M Child# 2 Leo LaPointe Nashua, NH & Stella Jacques Lowell, MA
LAPOINTE, Pauline Rita, Oct 13 1929 Sex:F Child# 1 Ovila Lapointe Nashua, NH & Cora Tardif Manchester, NH
LAPOINTE, Simeon Adjutor, Sep 21 1914 Sex:M Child# 1 Adjutor Lapointe Canada & Marie Plante Canada
LAPOLICE, Joseph Antonio, Mar 17 1922 Sex:M Child# 1 Antonio Lapolice Canada & Lillian Beaudette Manchester, NH
LAPONSIE, Jane, May 11 1933 Sex:F Child# 1 R LaPonsie Wilton, NH & Deborah Wilcox Wilmington, MA
LAPONSIE, Richard, Jun 3 1934 Sex:M Child# 6 Joseph E LaPonsie Canada & Cora Jalbert Lowell, MA
LAPORT, Noell, Dec 24 1888 Sex:M Child# 3 W Raphiel Laport Canada & amanda Michard Canada
LAPORTE, Agnes Rose, Oct 16 1899 Sex:F Child# 2 Aug Laporte Vermont & Marie Tetreau Mass
LAPORTE, Arthur, May 16 1904 Sex:M Child# 4 Alonzo Laporte Nashua, NH & Desneiges Parent Canada
LAPORTE, Blanche E, Nov 2 1894 Sex:F Child# 5 Noe Laporte Canada & Eloemie Bibeault Canada
LAPORTE, Florida, Nov 17 1892 Sex:F Child# 4 Noe Laporte Canada & Noemee Bibeau Canada
LAPORTE, J Alfred, Apr 27 1900 Sex:M Child# 1 Joseph Laporte Canada & Denaige Parent Canada
LAPORTE, Joseph A R, Dec 9 1892 Sex:M Child# 3 Joseph Laporte Canada & Anna Desjardins Canada
LAPORTE, Joseph Edward H, Jul 2 1902 Sex:M Child# 1 Abner Laporte Canada & Evelina Papineau NH
LAPORTE, Joseph T, Sep 19 1895 Sex:M Child# 6 Raphael Laporte Canada & Amanda Michaud Canada
LAPORTE, Laura, Apr 8 1904 Sex:F Child# 1 Albert Laporte New York & Emma Desmarais Canada
LAPORTE, Margaret, Feb 9 1915 Sex:F Child# 5 Alfred Laporte Aetna, NH & Margaret Shanahan Nashua, NH
LAPORTE, Marie, Sep 14 1901 Sex:F Child# 2 Joseph Laporte Canada & Desneige Parent Canada
LAPORTE, Marie D D, May 15 1903 Sex:F Child# 3 Joseph A Laporte Canada & Desneiges Parent Canada
LAPORTE, Marie E, Jan 27 1889 Sex:F Child# 2 Noe Laporte Canada & Noemie Bibeau Canada
LAPORTE, Marie E, Jan 28 1891 Sex:F Child# 3 Noe Laporte Canada & Loemie Bibeau Canada
LAPORTE, Mary, Sep 5 1911 Sex:F Child# 1 Alfred LaPorte Etna, NH & Margaret Shanahan Nashua, NH
LAPORTE, Narcisse, Apr 20 1906 Sex:M Child# 2 Alfred Laporte Moores Jct, NY & Regina Desmarais Canada
LAPORTE, Robert Earl, Mar 16 1920 Sex:M Child# 8 Alonzo Laporte New York & Effie Cutter Nashua, NH
LAPORTE, Wilfred, Oct 22 1892 Sex:M Child# 5 Raphael Laporte Canada & Amanda Michaud Canada
LAPPRE, Cyrille E, Nov 12 1887 Sex:M Child# Henri Lappre Canada & Louise Charron Canada

LAPRE, Emilia Albina, Jun 12 1889 Sex:F Child# 10 Henry Lapre Canada & Louise Charron Canada
LAPRILL, Unknown, Sep 12 1889 Sex:M Child# 10 Joseph Laprill Canada & H Laplante Canada
LAPRISE, Edmond, Apr 21 1908 Sex:M Child# 3 Andre Laprise Canada & M Louise Daigneault US Stillborn
LAPRISE, Joseph Arthur, Dec 16 1895 Sex:M Child# 3 Joseph Laprise Canada & Odile Pelletier Canada
LAPRISE, Louise Georgina, Apr 21 1908 Sex:F Child# 2 Andre Laprise Canada & M Louise Daigneault US
LAQUERRE, Arthur Roper, Feb 5 1928 Sex:m Child# 2 Arthur Laquerre Nashua, NH & Odilie Roy Nashua, NH
LAQUERRE, Blanche Gertrude, Jan 28 1923 Sex:F Child# 2 Jean B Laquerre Nashua, NH & Victoria Ouellette Nashua, NH
LAQUERRE, Blanche Y, Dec 9 1902 Sex:F Child# 5 Joseph Laquerre Canada & Clara Paradis Canada
LAQUERRE, Germaine Colette, Aug 5 1931 Sex:F Child# 5 Alextide Laquerre Nashua, NH & Eva Bouchard Nashua, NH
LAQUERRE, Girard Albert Leo, Oct 21 1932 Sex:M Child# 9 Jean B Laquerre Nashua, NH & Victoria Ouellette Nashua, NH
LAQUERRE, Janet, Sep 17 1935 Sex:F Child# 11 Jean B Laquerre Nashua, NH & Victoria Ouellette Nashua, NH
LAQUERRE, Janice, Sep 17 1935 Sex:F Child# 10 Jean B Laquerre Nashua, NH & Victoria Ouellette Nashua, NH
LAQUERRE, Jean Ernest, Jul 8 1921 Sex:M Child# 12 Jean B Laquerre Canada & Josephine Loraine New York
LAQUERRE, John Baptiste Henry, Nov 7 1934 Sex:M Child# 1 Leo Laquerre Nashua, NH & Isabelle Cote Nashua, NH
LAQUERRE, Jos David Raoul, Sep 9 1923 Sex:M Child# 13 Jean Bte Laquerre Canada & Josephine Loraine New York
LAQUERRE, Joseph Alphonse O, Oct 27 1908 Sex:M Child# 5 Jean Laquerre Canada & Josephine Loraine New York
LAQUERRE, Joseph Cyris H, May 30 1903 Sex:M Child# 1 Cyrisse Laquerre Canada & Arthilia Deziel Canada
LAQUERRE, Joseph Henri, Jul 3 1904 Sex:M Child# 2 Jean Laquerre Canada & Josephine Laraine New York
LAQUERRE, Joseph J B H, Jul 15 1907 Sex:M Child# 4 Jean Laquerre Canada & Josephine Laraine New York
LAQUERRE, Joseph Robert, Feb 3 1931 Sex:M Child# 8 Jean B Laquerre Nashua, NH & Victoria Ouellette Nashua, NH
LAQUERRE, Joseph Wilfrid, Oct 21 1919 Sex:M Child# 11 Jean Laquerre Canada & Josephine Loraine New York
LAQUERRE, Marie Annette, Aug 5 1917 Sex:F Child# 10 Jean Laquerre Canada & Josephine Loraine New York
LAQUERRE, Marie Cesarie, Jun 18 1905 Sex:F Child# 3 Jean Laquerre Canada & Josephine Laraine New York
LAQUERRE, Marie Clara Juliette, Jan 8 1922 Sex:F Child# 1 Jean Bte Laquerre Nashua, NH & Victoria Ouellette Nashua
LAQUERRE, Marie Ida Josephine, May 19 1912 Sex:F Child# 7 Jean Laquerre Canada & Josephine Laraine New York
LAQUERRE, Marie Jeanne Theresa, Jan 19 1927 Sex:F Child# 4 Alextide Laquerre Nashua, NH & Eva Bouchard Nashua, NH
LAQUERRE, Marie Josephine, May 13 1903 Sex:F Child# 1 Jean Laquerre Canada & Josephine Laraine New York
LAQUERRE, Marie Josephine R, Jul 28 1910 Sex:F Child# 6 Jean Laquerre Canada & Josephine Laraine New York
LAQUERRE, Marie Rita, May 23 1915 Sex:F Child# 9 Jean Laquerre Canada & Josephine Lareine New York
LAQUERRE, Marie Rose Irene, Mar 1 1914 Sex:F Child# 8 Jean Laquerre Canada & Josephine Lareine New York
LAQUERRE, Olivette, Oct 19 1917 Sex:F Child# 1 Alextide Laquerre Nashua, NH & Eva Bouchard Nashua, NH
LAQUERRE, Paul Henry, Apr 12 1928 Sex:M Child# 6 Jean B Laquerre Nashua, NH & Victoria Ouellette Nashua, NH
LAQUERRE, Roland Florian, May 12 1922 Sex:M Child# 2 Alexis Laquerre Nashua, NH & Eva Bouchard Nashua, NH
LAQUERRE, Unknown, Nov 26 1929 Sex:M Child# 7 Jean Btst Laquerre Nashua, NH & Victoria Ouellette Nashua, NH Stillbo
LARABEE, Lucille, Jun 2 1925 Sex:F Child# 2 James H Larabee Lowell, MA & Ruth Baker Nashua, NH
LARAINE, Joseph Henri P, Sep 14 1902 Sex:M Child# 4 Joseph Laraine NY & Alphonsine Noel Canada
LARAINE, Joseph Jean B L, Jun 10 1908 Sex:M Child# 4 Louis Laraine New York & Ida Livernois New York
LARAINE, Joseph R G, Feb 1 1909 Sex:M Child# 5 Joseph Laraine New York & Alphonsine Noel Canada
LARAINE, Joseph T E, Dec 27 1905 Sex:M Child# 1 Wilbur Laraine NY & Delima Pinault NH
LARAINE, Louis Samuel A, Jun 28 1911 Sex:M Child# 5 Louis Laraine New York & Adee Livernois New York
LARAINE, M Irene Rachel, Aug 16 1913 Sex:F Child# 4 Louis Laraine New York & Addie Livernois New York
LARAINE, Marie Aveline, Aug 19 1904 Sex:F Child# 2 Louis Laraine New York & Adelaide Livernois New York
LARAINE, Marie Olina, Feb 11 1907 Sex:F Child# 3 Louis Laraine New York & Ida Livermore New York
LARAINE, Mary Mollie, Nov 9 1902 Sex:F Child# 5 George H Laraine Plattsburg, NY & Ethel Caron Canada
LARANATIS, Joseph, Feb 15 1920 Sex:M Child# 4 Charles Laranatis Russia & Mary Caralutis Russia
LARANATIS, Mary, Feb 15 1920 Sex:F Child# 3 Charles Laranatis Russia & Mary Caralutis Russia
LARANCE, Yvonne Irene, Dec 8 1910 Sex:F Child# 1 Narcisse Larance Nashua, NH & Evangeline Caya Canada
LARANGER, Henri, Oct 28 1887 Sex:M Child# 9 Joseph Laranger P Q & Cleophine P Q
LARD, A Wilfrid, Sep 24 1894 Sex:M Child# 7 Auguste Lard Canada & C Fournier Canada
LAREAU, Theresa J, Oct 2 1903 Sex:F Child# 3 J E Lareau Canada & Hermine Bonneau Canada
LAREINE, Mary, Oct 11 1934 Sex:F Child# 1 Raymond Lareine Nashua, NH & Josephine Jakel Nashua, NH
LAREINE, Samuel, Mar 23 1902 Sex:M Child# 1 Louis Laraine NY & Addie Livernois NY
LAREIVE, Josephine, Jan 5 1894 Sex:F Child# 5 George Lareive Canada & Attala Caron Canada
LAREMIE, Joseph Sijefois J B, Jun 24 1906 Sex:M Child# 2 Sijefois Laremie Canada & Marie L Laplante Canada
LARENE, Marie Athala, Mar 24 1898 Sex:F Child# 8 George Larene Plattsburg, NY & Athala Caron Canada
LARENE, Marie Josephine, Sep 15 1896 Sex:F Child# 1 Joseph Larene Plattsburg, NY & Alphonsine Noel Canada
LARENE, Marie R Anna, Aug 26 1898 Sex:F Child# 2 Joseph Larene Plattsburg, NY & Alphonsine Noel Canada
LARENS, Rosanna, Mar 7 1895 Sex:F Child# 5 Georges Larens US & Attala Caron Canada
LAREVE, Olivine A, Oct 30 1892 Sex:F Child# 2 Harmase Lareve St Albans, VT & Albine Dubuc St Albans, VT
LARICHANDIERE, Marie Olenia, Nov 2 1896 Sex:F Child# 2 P Larichandiere Canada & Elise Blanchette Canada
LARICHELIERE, Alfred, Jul 4 1901 Sex:M Child# 3 Alfred Laricheliere Canada & Alice Emond Canada
LARICHELIERRE, Marie Anne, Dec 23 1902 Sex:F Child# 4 Alf Larichelierre Canada & Alice Emond Canada
LARINE, Robert Victor, Nov 17 1918 Sex:M Child# 2 Phillipe T Larine Nashua, NH & Rosanna Larine Canada
LARIVE, Alfred, Aug 31 1917 Sex:M Child# 1 Philippe Larive US & Rosanna Beaulieu Canada Stillborn
LARIVE, George Frederick, Dec 28 1924 Sex:M Child# 3 Alfred Larive Nashua, NH & G Chamberlain Nashua, NH
LARIVE, Irene, Jul 3 1916 Sex:F Child# 1 Harry Larive Nashua, NH & Delia Moriarty Nashua, NH
LARIVE, Joseph, Oct 24 1894 Sex:M Child# 11 Cyrille Larive Canada & Adelaide Guchette Canada
LARIVE, M Eva, Dec 20 1895 Sex:F Child# 12 Cyrille Larive Canada & Adelaide Guenette Canada
LARIVE, Philippe Toussaint, Nov 1 1892 Sex:M Child# 6 Victor Larive Canada & Louise Lesieur Canada
LARIVE, Raymond Arthur, May 4 1920 Sex:M Child# 3 Sam Larive US & Rose Beaulieu Canada
LARIVE, Robert Richard, May 15 1922 Sex:M Child# 2 Alfred Larive Nashua, NH & Gertrude Chamberlain Nashua, NH
LARIVE, Stanislas, Nov 13 1887 Sex:M Child# 4 Leon Larive P Q & Philomene P Q
LARIVE, Unknown, Aug 10 1922 Sex:F Child# 4 Philip S Larive Nashua, NH & Rose Beaulieu Canada Stillborn

LARIVEE, Anaclet, May 17 1891 Sex:M Child# 2 Harmas Larivee St Albans, VT & Albina Dubuque St Albans, VT
LARIVEE, Arthur Edouard, Mar 7 1902 Sex:M Child# 7 Victor Larivee Canada & Louise Lessieur Canada
LARIVEE, Claria Anna, Aug 24 1888 Sex:F Child# 4 Victor Larivee Canada & Louise Lesieur Canada
LARIVEE, Edna Pauline, Nov 15 1927 Sex:F Child# 4 Alfred Larivee Pepperell, MA & G Chamberlain Nashua, NH
LARIVEE, Jerome Roland, Oct 23 1913 Sex:M Child# 1 Daniel Larivee Nashua, NH & Obeline Girard Nashua, NH
LARIVEE, Joseph George, May 15 1898 Sex:M Child# 13 Cyrille Larivee Canada & Adelaide Guerette Canada
LARIVEE, Louis Euzebe, Nov 9 1897 Sex:M Child# 3 Victor Larivee Canada & Ella Kellte Canada
LARIVEE, Marie Evangeline, Nov 27 1897 Sex:F Child# 9 Victor Larivee Canada & Louise Lesieur Canada
LARIVEE, Paul Alfred, Nov 5 1920 Sex:M Child# 1 Alfred Larivee Pepperell, MA & Gertrude Chamberlain Nashua, NH
LARIVEE, Walter, Aug 29 1906 Sex:M Child# 11 Victor Larivee Canada & Louise Lesieur Canada
LARIVER, Henry, Dec 21 1890 Sex:M Child# 5 Victor Lariver Canada & Louise Lesieur Canada
LARIVIE, Harmos, Jan 26 1890 Sex:M Child# 1 Harmos Larivie St Albans, VT & Adina Dubuque St Albans, VT
LARIVIE, Therese Armenie, Oct 14 1894 Sex:F Child# 3 Hormas Larivie St Albans, VT & Albina Dubuc Canada
LAROCHE, Aime Alphonse C, Nov 29 1921 Sex:M Child# 1 Aime Laroche Canada & Antoinette Desautels Nashua, NH
LAROCHE, Alma, Apr 24 1900 Sex:F Child# 3 Frank Laroche Canada & Exilda Landry Canada
LAROCHE, Blanche R A, Dec 10 1904 Sex:F Child# 2 David Laroche Canada & Maria Beaulieu Canada
LAROCHE, David Romeo, May 28 1903 Sex:M Child# 1 David Laroche Canada & Marie Beaudoin Canada
LAROCHE, Ella Parmelia, Nov 28 1907 Sex:F Child# 3 David Laroche Canada & Maria Beaudoin Canada
LAROCHE, Francis, Jan 30 1914 Sex:M Child# 2 Francis Laroche Fall River, MA & Jeanne Gelinas Three Rivers, Que
LAROCHE, Francois Leo, Jan 24 1924 Sex:M Child#  Aimi Laroche Canada & An Desautels Nashua, NH
LAROCHE, Francois Z, Sep 1 1897 Sex:M Child# 1 Francois Laroche Canada & Exildo Landry Canada
LAROCHE, Irene Rose Albina, Sep 5 1911 Sex:F Child# 1 Frank Laroche Canada & Jeanne Gelinas Canada
LAROCHE, J Antoine Amede, Jul 13 1914 Sex:M Child# 10 Francois X Laroche Canada & Exilda Landry Canada
LAROCHE, Juliette Ella, Jun 6 1906 Sex:F Child# 6 Frank Laroche Canada & Exilda Landry Canada
LAROCHE, Marie Ange Theresa, May 20 1928 Sex:F Child# 13 Alfred Laroche Nashua, NH & Emeline Lafrance Canada
LAROCHE, Marie Gertrude G, Jan 5 1910 Sex:F Child# 8 Frank Laroche Canada & Exilda Landry Canada
LAROCHE, Marie Irene L, Dec 12 1910 Sex:F Child# 5 David Laroche Canada & Marie Beaudoin Canada
LAROCHE, Marie Monique A, Aug 25 1908 Sex:F Child# 7 Frank Laroche Canada & Exilda Landry Canada
LAROCHE, Maurice Raymond, Sep 16 1924 Sex:M Child# 11 Alfred Laroche Canada & Ernestine Lafrance Nashua, NH
LAROCHE, Napoleon Wilfrid, Sep 29 1890 Sex:M Child# 2 Napoleon Laroche Canada & Antoinette Grandmais Canada
LAROCHE, Raymond Ovila, Apr 18 1930 Sex:M Child# 1 Romeo Laroche Nashua, NH & Lillian Constant Nashua, NH
LAROCHE, Roman Oswald, Aug 9 1918 Sex:M Child# 7 David Laroche Canada & Marie Beaudoin Canada
LAROCHE, Unknown, Feb 4 1894 Sex:F Child# 1 Henri Laroche US & Sophronie Chalifoux US
LAROCHE, Unknown, Dec 6 1917 Sex:M Child# 1 Francis Laroche Canada & Marie Levesque Canada Stillborn
LAROCQUE, Amedee Edmond, Apr 1 1925 Sex:M Child# 3 Edouard Larocque Nashua, NH & Felicite Fortier Canada
LAROCQUE, Edouard Thomas, Jul 3 1920 Sex:M Child# 2 Edouard Larocque Nashua, NH & Felicite Fortier Canada
LAROCQUE, Gerald Donat, May 20 1913 Sex:M Child# 1 Arthur Larocque Nashua, NH & Herminie Marquis Canada
LAROCQUE, Hector, Aug 27 1909 Sex:M Child# 1 Victor Larocque Nashua, NH & Hattie Richer Lancaster, MA
LAROCQUE, Irene May, Mar 31 1922 Sex:F Child# 3 Oswald Larocque Nashua, NH & Josephine Rogers Elkton, VA
LAROCQUE, Joan Loraine, Jan 13 1934 Sex:F Child# 5 Oswald Larocque Nashua, NH & Josephine Rogers Elkton, VA
LAROCQUE, Jos Philip Adrian, Mar 9 1926 Sex:M Child# 8 Arthur Larocque Nashua, NH & Herminea Roy Canada
LAROCQUE, Jos Robert Ernest, Feb 14 1919 Sex:M Child# 1 Edouard Larocque NH & Felicitee Fortier Canada
LAROCQUE, Joseph Amable, Jun 17 1893 Sex:M Child# 7 Ludger Larocque Canada & Celina Lacombe Canada
LAROCQUE, Leonard Roger, Sep 9 1930 Sex:M Child# 3 Philippe Larocque Nashua, NH & Adrienne Charpentier Nashua, NH
LAROCQUE, Ludger, Oct 3 1890 Sex:M Child# 4 Ludger Larocque Canada & Celina Lacombe Canada
LAROCQUE, M Yvette Lorraine, Apr 14 1919 Sex:F Child# 1 Ernest Larocque NH & Eva Marois Mass
LAROCQUE, Madeline Louise, Jun 2 1922 Sex:F Child# 1 Hector M Larocque Canada & Alma Simard Canada
LAROCQUE, Marc P, Dec 16 1898 Sex:M Child# 6 Marc Larocque Canada & Rosalie Lucier Canada
LAROCQUE, Marc Paul, Jun 1 1920 Sex:M Child# 2 Ernest Larocque Nashua, NH & Eva Marois Cambridge, MA
LAROCQUE, Marguerite Dorilda, Oct 9 1920 Sex:F Child# 2 Oswald Larocque Nashua, NH & Josephine Rogers Elkton, VA
LAROCQUE, Normand Philip, Feb 3 1929 Sex:M Child# 2 Philip Larocque Nashua, NH & Adrienne Charpentier Nashua, NH
LAROCQUE, Paul Normand, Aug 11 1927 Sex:M Child# 2 H M Larocque Nashua, NH & Blanche Lefebvre Nashua, NH
LAROCQUE, Pauline Lydia, Oct 3 1923 Sex:F Child# 4 Oswald P Larocque Nashua, NH & Josephine Rogers Elkton, VA
LAROCQUE, Raymond Frederick, Jul 22 1920 Sex:M Child# 5 Arthur Larocque Nashua, NH & Hermine Roy Canada
LAROCQUE, Raymond J V, Aug 12 1910 Sex:M Child# 2 Victor Larocque Nashua, NH & Hattie Ritchie Lancaster, MA
LAROCQUE, Therese Rita, Nov 6 1924 Sex:F Child# 5 Arthur Larocque Nashua, NH & Hermenia Roy Canada
LAROCQUE, Unknown, Nov 3 1914 Sex:F Child# 3 Victor Larocque Nashua, NH & Hattie Richie Lancaster, MA
LAROCQUE, Unknown, Jan 23 1928 Sex:F Child# 1 Philip Larocque Nashua, NH & A Charpentier Nashua, NH
LAROCQUE, Unknown, Aug 7 1931 Sex:M Child# 5 Oswald Larocque Nashua, NH & Josephine Rogers Elkton, VA
LAROQUE, Devilda, Jan 26 1896 Sex:F Child# 8 Narcisse Laroque Canada & Marie Charron Canada
LAROQUE, Doula, Aug 4 1891 Sex:M Child# 5 Narcesse Laroque Canada & Marie Charron Canada
LAROQUE, Edouard, Dec 8 1894 Sex:M Child# 7 Narcisse Laroque Canada & Marie Charron Canada
LAROQUE, Elidia, Mar 6 1887 Sex:F Child#  Narcisse Laroque P Q & Marie Charon P Q
LAROQUE, Ernest, Dec 2 1895 Sex:M Child# 5 Clare Laroque Canada & Rosalie Lussier Canada
LAROQUE, Exila, May 29 1892 Sex:F Child# 6 Ludger Laroque Canada & Celina Lacombe Canada
LAROQUE, Joseph A, Dec 22 1890 Sex:M Child# 3 M Laroque Canada & Rosalie Lussier Canada
LAROQUE, Louis Vital, Jun 26 1890 Sex:M Child# 3 Louis Laroque Canada & Vitaline Charron Canada
LAROQUE, Marie R A, Jan 30 1892 Sex:F Child# 4 M Laroque Canada & Rosalie Lussier Canada
LAROQUE, Marie R E, Jun 8 1889 Sex:F Child# 2 Mare Laroque Canada & Rosalie Lussier Canada
LAROQUE, Philip Oswald, Apr 26 1893 Sex:M Child# 6 Narcisse Laroque Canada & Marie Charron Canada
LAROQUE, Xavier, Dec 4 1892 Sex:M Child# 4 Louis Laroque Canada & Vitaline Charron Canada
LAROSE, Edward, Apr 30 1926 Sex:M Child# 12 Joseph Larose Canada & Maria Gagnon Nashua, NH
LAROSE, Eugene, Apr 12 1897 Sex:M Child# 3 Archie Larose Canada & Zenaide Cote Canada

LAROSE, Joseph A, Jun 29 1891 Sex:M Child# 1 Alexandre Larose Canada & Adele Farland Canada
LAROSE, Joseph Paul, Jul 17 1928 Sex:M Child# 13 Joseph Larose Canada & Marie Ganon Nashua, NH
LAROUCHE, Adelard, Mar 30 1895 Sex:M Child# 17 Felix Larouche Canada & Caroline Langlois Canada
LAROUCHE, Albert, Jan 13 1910 Sex:M Child# 1 Charles Larouche Canada & Sophie Blanchette Canada
LAROUCHE, Alfred, Sep 11 1914 Sex:M Child# 5 John Larouche Nashua, NH & Exilda Dragon Milford, NH
LAROUCHE, Alfred Alphe, Jul 27 1911 Sex:M Child# 7 George Larouche Canada & Marie Grandmaison Canada
LAROUCHE, Alice Antoinette, Sep 24 1908 Sex:F Child# 3 Joseph Larouche Canada & Melina Ducharme Canada
LAROUCHE, Alphonse, Oct 20 1907 Sex:M Child# 2 John Larouche Canada & Elzilda Dragon Nashua, NH
LAROUCHE, Bernadette, Oct 22 1935 Sex:F Child# 2 Ernest Larouche Nashua, NH & Anita Cloutier Worcester, MA
LAROUCHE, Ernest, Mar 13 1910 Sex:M Child# 2 Alfred Larouche Canada & Ernestine Lachance Canada
LAROUCHE, Eva Yvonne Ida, May 21 1907 Sex:F Child# 5 George Larouche Canada & Marie Grandmaison Canada
LAROUCHE, Henry Raoul, Jun 9 1921 Sex:M Child# 9 Alfred Larouche Canada & Ernestine Lafrance Nashua, NH
LAROUCHE, Henry, Jr, Oct 6 1935 Sex:M Child# 1 Henry Larouche Nashua, NH & Genev Gawarska Wilmington, DE
LAROUCHE, Irene Gertrude, May 26 1915 Sex:F Child# 5 Fred Larouche Canada & Ernestine Lafrance Nashua, NH
LAROUCHE, Joseph A L, Dec 4 1905 Sex:M Child# 1 Joseph Larouche Canada & Exilia Dragon Canada
LAROUCHE, Joseph Adrien, Dec 11 1903 Sex:M Child# 1 Joseph Larouche Canada & Delima Ducharme Canada
LAROUCHE, Joseph Albert G, Dec 24 1911 Sex:M Child# 3 John Larouche Canada & Elzilda Dragon Milford, NH
LAROUCHE, Joseph Clovis, Aug 30 1916 Sex:M Child# 6 Jean B Larouche Canada & Exilda Dragon Milford, NH
LAROUCHE, Joseph Ernest, Apr 14 1913 Sex:M Child# 4 John Larouche Canada & Ezilda Dragon Milford, NH
LAROUCHE, Joseph Robert, Feb 17 1909 Sex:M Child# 1 Alfred Larouche Nashua, NH & Ernestine Lafrance Canada
LAROUCHE, Joseph Robert, Aug 25 1916 Sex:M Child# 6 Alfred Larouche Canada & Ernestine Lafrance Nashua, NH
LAROUCHE, Laure Oliva, Nov 11 1917 Sex:F Child# 7 Alfred Larouche Canada & Ernestine Lafrance Nashua, NH
LAROUCHE, Lionel Real, Aug 18 1929 Sex:M Child# 14 Alfred Larouche Canada & Ernestine Lefrance Nashua, NH
LAROUCHE, Louis Armand, Jan 10 1914 Sex:M Child# 4 Alfred Larouche Canada & Ernestine Lafrance Nashua, NH
LAROUCHE, Louis Fernand, Feb 12 1923 Sex:M Child# 1 Alfred Larouche Canada & Ernestine Lafrance Nashua, NH
LAROUCHE, Marie Adriene, Jun 13 1905 Sex:F Child# 2 Joseph Larouche Canada & Melina Ducharme Canada
LAROUCHE, Marie Ange A, Jan 24 1905 Sex:F Child# 4 George Larouche Canada & Marie Grandmaison Canada
LAROUCHE, Marie E, Nov 11 1890 Sex:F Child# 12 Felis Larouche Canada & Caroline Langlois Canada
LAROUCHE, Marie Eilia, Mar 22 1900 Sex:F Child# 2 George Larouche Canada & S Grandmaison Canada
LAROUCHE, Marie Georgiana, Apr 23 1899 Sex:F Child# 1 George Larouche Canada & Sophrenie Grandmaisn Canada
LAROUCHE, Mary Margaret, Jul 14 1934 Sex:F Child# 1 Ernest Larouche Nashua, NH & Anita Cloutier Worcester, MA
LAROUCHE, Octave Allard, Jun 16 1909 Sex:M Child# 6 George Larouche Canada & Marie Grandmaison Canada
LAROUCHE, Paul Gerard, Dec 2 1926 Sex:M Child# 12 Alfred Larouche Canada & E Lafrance Nashua, NH
LAROUCHE, Rachel Rita, Aug 18 1933 Sex:F Child# 16 Alfred Larouche Canada & E Lafrance US
LAROUCHE, Rosario, Oct 4 1919 Sex:M Child# 8 Alfred Larouche Canada & Ernestine Lafrance Nashua, NH
LAROUCHE, Rose Alba Yvonne, Jun 23 1912 Sex:F Child# 3 Alfred Larouche Canada & Ernestine Lafrance Canada
LAROUCHE, Telesphore Wilfrid, Oct 4 1931 Sex:M Child# 15 Alfred Larouche Nashua, NH & Ernestine Lafrance Nashua
LAROUCHE, Thomas, Dec 6 1891 Sex:M Child# 14 Felice Larouche Canada & Caroline Langlais Canada
LAROUCHE, Thomas, May 3 1893 Sex:M Child# 15 Felix Larouche Canada & Caroline Langlois Canada
LAROUCHE, Yvonne Bertha, Dec 24 1914 Sex:F Child# 6 David Larouche Canada & Maria Beaudoin Canada
LAROUCHE, Yvonne Ida, Jan 10 1913 Sex:F Child# 8 Leo Larouche Canada & Marie Grandmaison Canada
LAROYUE, Louis, Jun 21 1889 Sex:M Child# 4 Narcisse Laroyue Canada & Marie Charron Canada
LARRABEE, Jean, Mar 27 1931 Sex:F Child# 3 James H Larrabee Lowell, MA & Ruth Barker Nashua, NH
LARRABEE, Unknown, May 14 1923 Sex:M Child# 1 James Larrabee Lowell, MA & Ruth Barker Nashua, NH
LARRIVEE, Loraine Louise, Oct 1 1931 Sex:F Child# 1 Arthur Larrivee Nashua, NH & Blanche Blanchard Nashua, NH
LARSEN, Maynard Ludgie, May 29 1911 Sex:M Child# 2 William M Larsen Cambridge, MA & Grace T Marshall Hollis, NH
LARSON, Rudalph Carl, Mar 29 1903 Sex:M Child# 2 Julius Carl Larson Sweden & Anna Berg Sweden
LARVOCHE, Joseph, Dec 8 1888 Sex:M Child# 1 Napoleon Larvoche Canada & A Grandrison Canada
LASAGE, Joseph Amedee, Feb 24 1898 Sex:M Child# 9 Jean Lasage Island Pond, VT & Rose Houle Canada
LASALLE, Joseph, Jan 12 1931 Sex:M Child# Ovila LaSalle Canada & Exilia Guilmette Nashua, NH Stillborn
LASALLE, Joseph Emile, Oct 15 1914 Sex:M Child# 1 Ovila Lasalle Canada & Exilia Guillemette Canada
LASALLE, Joseph Ernest, Dec 30 1916 Sex:M Child# 2 Ovila Lasalle Canada & Exilia Gillemette NH
LASALLE, Marie Antoinette, Jul 3 1918 Sex:F Child# 3 Ovila Lasalle Canada & Exilia Guillemette NH
LASALLE, Marie Beatrice Alice, Oct 14 1923 Sex:F Child# 5 Ovila Lasalle Canada & Exilia Guillemette NH
LASALLE, Marie Rita, Feb 21 1920 Sex:F Child# 4 Ovila Lasalle Canada & Exilia Guillemette NH
LASALLE, Maurice Jean, Jan 29 1927 Sex:M Child# 6 Ovila LaSalle Canada & Exilia Guilmette Nashua, NH
LASALLE, Norbert Jean, Jun 17 1931 Sex:M Child# 2 Edward J LaSalle Nashua, NH & Delia Belanger Nashua, NH
LASKO, Anthony, Nov 11 1917 Sex:M Child# 4 Cypricean Lasko Russia & Sophia Demska Russia
LASTOSKI, Bolestaw, Mar 5 1916 Sex:M Child# 1 Nicholas Lastoski Russia & Amelia Cybulska Russia
LATENEZ, Stanislaus, Feb 28 1920 Sex:M Child# 4 Michael Latenez Russia & Anna Volasenovich Russia
LATEVIS, Malvina, Apr 20 1917 Sex:F Child# 2 Alexander Latevis Russia & Agatha Molut Russia
LATHAN, Unknown, Aug 6 1920 Sex:M Child# 1 Charles Lathan NH & Alice Dupres NH
LATHE, Barbara Ann, Oct 3 1928 Sex:F Child# 3 Elmer C Lathe Lynn, MA & Ethel MacDonald Wakefield, MA
LATHE, Constance Evelyn, Oct 26 1925 Sex:F Child# 2 Elmer Lathe Stoneham, ME & Ethel McDonald Wakefield, MA
LATINES, Agota, Sep 29 1913 Sex:F Child# 2 Alexander Latines Russia & Agota Molute Russia
LATIVESS, Anna, Jun 3 1911 Sex:F Child# 1 Michael Lativess Russia & Anna Valasavitch Russia
LATON, Maria, Dec 16 1891 Sex:F Child# 5 Frank D Laton Nashua, NH & Effie Woods Hillsboro
LATON, Unknown, Jun 14 1889 Sex:F Child# 4 Frank Laton Nashua, NH & Fiffie Woods Stoddard
LATON, Unknown, Sep 16 1895 Sex:F Child# 6 Frank D Laton Nashua, NH & Effie M Wood Stoddard
LATOUE, Norman Arthur, Dec 11 1914 Sex:M Child# 5 Edouard Latoue Nashua, NH & Adae Wilkins Nashua, NH
LATOUR, Alice Hilda, Jun 19 1922 Sex:F Child# 11 Joseph Latour New York & Mary Brow Nova Scotia
LATOUR, Annie Elizabeth, Jan 16 1912 Sex:F Child# 6 Joseph Ed Latour New York & Mary E Brault Nova Scotia
LATOUR, Beatrice Vallerie, Jan 13 1922 Sex:F Child# 8 Edward Latour Nashua, NH & Adne Wilkins Nashua, NH

LATOUR, Celia Elizabeth, Jul 18 1912 Sex:F Child# 4 Edward Latour Nashua, NH & Adrie Wilkins Nashua, NH
LATOUR, Charles, Jan 10 1899 Sex:M Child# 2 Georges D Latour NS & Sarah M Thompson US
LATOUR, Dorothy Marion, Mar 30 1935 Sex:F Child# 1 George Latour Nashua, NH & Marion Leahy W Groton, MA
LATOUR, Edna May, Jan 20 1907 Sex:F Child# 1 Eddie Latour Nashua, NH & Adne F Wilkins Nashua, NH
LATOUR, Francis, Feb 12 1932 Sex:M Child# 1 John Latour Nashua, NH & C Csarnonka Maynard, MA Stillborn
LATOUR, Fred Raymond, Dec 20 1915 Sex:M Child# 8 Joseph Latour New York & Mary E Brow Nova Scotia
LATOUR, George Clement, Oct 6 1908 Sex:M Child# 4 Joseph E Latour Plattsburg, NY & Marie E Brault Harborbush, NS
LATOUR, Irene Agnes, May 15 1910 Sex:F Child# 3 Edward Latour Nashua, NH & Edna Wilkins Nashua, NH
LATOUR, John Henry, May 14 1910 Sex:M Child# 4 J Ed Latour Plattsburg, NY & Marie E Brault Harborbush, NS
LATOUR, Joseph, Feb 2 1905 Sex:M Child# 9 Simon Latour Canada & Valerie Laforest Canada
LATOUR, Joseph Ferdina A, Mar 23 1900 Sex:M Child# 6 Simon Latour Canada & Valerie Laforest Canada
LATOUR, Margaret Lucile, Jan 3 1920 Sex:F Child# 10 Joseph Latour New York & Mary Brow Nova Scotia
LATOUR, Marie Aurore, Jan 9 1899 Sex:F Child# 5 Jean Baptiste Latour Canada & Sophie Cayer Canada
LATOUR, Marie Louise, May 16 1892 Sex:F Child# 6 Octave Latour Canada & Clarissa Maynard Canada
LATOUR, Marie Olivine, Dec 25 1896 Sex:F Child# 5 Simon Latour Canada & Valerie Laforest Canada
LATOUR, Martin, Aug 7 1907 Sex:M Child# 3 J E Latour Plattsburg, NY & Mary Brault Harborbush, NS
LATOUR, Mary Ruth Albina, Apr 17 1919 Sex:F Child# 7 Edward Latour Nashua, NH & Adne Wilkins Nashua, NH
LATOUR, Mildred Anita, Jun 26 1916 Sex:F Child# 6 Edward Latour Nashua, NH & Adne Wilkins Nashua, NH
LATOUR, Paul Richard, Apr 25 1924 Sex:M Child# 12 Joseph Latour Plattsburg, NY & Mary Brow Nova Scotia
LATOUR, Robert Francis, Dec 1 1917 Sex:M Child# 8 Joseph E Latour New York & Mary Brow
LATOUR, Rose Julia, Jan 17 1914 Sex:F Child# 6 Joseph Latour New York & Mary Brown Nova Scotia
LATOUR, Russell Leonard, May 16 1924 Sex:M Child# 1 Edward Latour Nashua, NH & Adne Wilkins Nashua, NH
LATOUR, Stanislas, Feb 18 1902 Sex:M Child# 7 Simon Latour Canada & Valerie Laforest Canada
LATOUR, Unknown, Jul 29 1902 Sex:M Child# 5 George B Latour Dannemora, NY & Sarah Thompson Wilboro, NY Stillborn
LATOUR, Unknown, Mar 1 1906 Sex:F Child# 1 Joseph Latour New York & Mary E Brow Nova Scotia
LATOUR, Unknown, Mar 10 1933 Sex:M Child# 2 William Latour US & Irene Durant US Stillborn
LATOUR, Unknown, Aug 15 1933 Sex:F Child# 2 John Latour Nashua, NH & C Csarnonka Maynard, MA Stillborn
LATOUR, Yvette Valerie, Sep 29 1931 Sex:F Child# 1 William Latour US & Irene Durand US
LATRAVERSE, Henri, Sep 11 1908 Sex:M Child# 1 Henri Latraverse Canada & Dorilda Paris Canada
LATRECH, Mary, Mar 20 1891 Sex:F Child# 3 Louis Latrech Canada & Sloni Charron Canada
LATRON, Unknown, Sep 27 1917 Sex:M Child# 3 Grgyrios A Latron Greece & Marie A Batsda Greece
LATUCH, Adeline Josephine, May 4 1922 Sex:F Child# 5 Henry A Latuch Nashua, NH & Fanny Wright Brookline, NH
LATUCH, Basil Edward, Dec 15 1933 Sex:M Child# 2 Fred Latuch Nashua, NH & Hazel Harwood Nashua, NH Stillborn
LATUCH, Henry, Sep 22 1911 Sex:M Child# 1 Henry Latuch Manchester, NH & Fannie A Wright Brookline, NH
LATUCH, Irene, Oct 16 1916 Sex:F Child# 4 Henry Latuch Nashua, NH & Fannie A Wright Pepperell, MA
LATUCH, Robert Henry, Jan 8 1932 Sex:M Child# 1 Fred W Latuch Nashua, NH & Hazel V Harwood Nashua, NH
LATUCH, Unknown, Feb 11 1935 Sex:M Child# 3 Fred W Latuch Nashua, NH & Hazel Harwood Nashua, NH Stillborn
LATULIPPE, Helen Bernadette, Oct 26 1933 Sex:F Child# 1 Clar Latulippe Vergins, VT & Mary Latulippe Lancaster,
LATULIPPE, Jeanne Mary, Nov 24 1925 Sex:F Child# 9 George J Latulippe S Burlington, VT & Melinda Lavalley Nashua,
LATULIPPE, Mary, Nov 24 1925 Sex:F Child# 10 George J Latulippe S Burlington, VT & Melinda Lavalley Nashua, NH
LATVIS, John, May 1 1922 Sex:M Child# 5 Michael Latvis Lithuania Russia & Anna Vanasinch Lithuania Russia
LATWES, Witontos, Dec 5 1918 Sex:M Child# 4 Alexandre Latwes Russia & Agota Holson Russia
LATWIS, Mary Anna, Apr 30 1909 Sex:F Child# 1 Adam Latwis Russia & Sophy Bogdzewicz Russia
LATWIS, Michael, Jan 24 1918 Sex:M Child# 3 Michael Latwis Russia & Anna Velasmoich Russia
LAUNDRY, Clara, Jan 14 1888 Sex:F Child# 1 Nathaniel Laundry Canada & Georganun St Peter Canada
LAUNSBOY, Louisa Isabel, Oct 22 1905 Sex:F Child# 4 William Launsboy P E Island & Isabella Mallard P E Island
LAURE, Armand, Mar 13 1897 Sex:M Child# 8 Auguste Laure Canada & Severine Fournier Canada
LAURENCE, Alfred Arthur, Oct 2 1922 Sex:M Child# 3 William D Laurence Nashua, NH & Laura Burelle Nashua, NH
LAURENDEAU, Leon, Jul 29 1915 Sex:M Child# 1 Osias Laurendeau Nashua, NH & M L Boucher Nashua, NH Stillborn
LAURENDEAU, Marie, Sep 28 1919 Sex:F Child# 1 Wm L Laurendeau Nashua, NH & Alexandrine Boucher Nashua, NH Stillborn
LAURENDEAU, Marie Ida F, Jun 5 1905 Sex:F Child# 1 Arthur Laurendeau Canada & Ida Lucas Canada
LAURENDEAU, Victor, Mar 16 1922 Sex:M Child# 2 William Laurendeau Canada & Alexandrine Boucher Nashua, NH
LAURETTE, Marie Honoria, Sep 8 1920 Sex:F Child# 2 Philippe Laurette Canada & Roseanna Bellavance Canada
LAURIAN, Doris Hall, Nov 7 1897 Sex:F Child# 3 Charles Laurian NY & Millie Hall NY
LAURIAN, May Clement, Jun 21 1895 Sex:F Child# 1 Arnold A Laurian NY & Nellie E Clement NH
LAVALEE, Rebecca Priscilla, Dec 3 1927 Sex:F Child# 2 Ernest Lavalee Manchester, NH & Eva Boucher Nashua, NH
LAVALLE, Alexandre, Jan 19 1902 Sex:M Child# 10 Alexandre Lavalle Shelburne & B Gandreau Nashua, NH
LAVALLE, Joseph Henri, Sep 28 1903 Sex:M Child# 11 Alexandre Lavalle Suncook & B Grandmond Canada
LAVALLE, Philippe A, Sep 1 1894 Sex:M Child# 5 Alexandre Lavalle Canada & B Grandmoret Canada
LAVALLE, Pierre Amede, Feb 13 1892 Sex:M Child# 13 Daniel Lavalle Canada & Delina Salvail Canada
LAVALLE, Raymond Sylvin, Aug 31 1926 Sex:M Child# 1 Ernest Lavalle Nashua, NH & Eva Boucher Nashua, NH
LAVALLEE, Alfred, Sep 10 1896 Sex:M Child# 6 Alexandre Lavallee NH & Bernadette Grandm't Canada
LAVALLEE, Alice Rose J, Nov 4 1923 Sex:F Child# 1 Raymond LaVallee US & Alice Enright US
LAVALLEE, Belle, May 10 1898 Sex:F Child# 2 Alfred Lavallee Vermont & Martha Belle Drew NH
LAVALLEE, Bernadetta, Oct 1 1898 Sex:F Child# 8 Alex Lavallee Canada & Marie A Geandmont Canada
LAVALLEE, Bertha Mary Louise, Apr 9 1925 Sex:F Child# 1 William Lavallee Epping, NH & Juliet Beaudette Rochester
LAVALLEE, Edward Raymond, Feb 10 1925 Sex:M Child# 2 Raymond Lavallee US & Alice Enwright US
LAVALLEE, Joseph Andre, Oct 6 1897 Sex:M Child# 7 Alexandre Lavallee Canada & R Grandmont Canada
LAVALLEE, Lorette Yvonne, Jan 17 1929 Sex:F Child# 3 William Lavallee Epping, NH & Juliette Beaudette Rochester
LAVALLEE, Lucien Severin, Nov 1 1911 Sex:M Child# 7 Theobalde Lavallee Canada & Rebecca Denison Canada
LAVALLEE, Lucille Juliette, Aug 29 1930 Sex:F Child# 4 William LaVallee Rochester, NH & Juliette Beaudette Rocheste
LAVALLEE, M REb Severina G, Jul 11 1914 Sex:F Child# 8 Theobald Lavallee Canada & Rebecca Denison Canada
LAVALLEE, M Simonne Ernestine, Nov 23 1916 Sex:F Child# 7 Theobalde Lavallee Canada & Rebecca Denison Canada

LAVALLEE, Marie Elizabeth B, May 22 1905 Sex:F Child# 12 Alexandre Lavallee Shelburne, NH & Bernadette Grandmont
LAVALLEE, Marie Severine A, Dec 30 1908 Sex:F Child# 6 Theobalde Lavallee Canada & Rebecca Dennison Canada
LAVALLEE, Rita Lorraine, Mar 21 1929 Sex:F Child# 3 Ernest Lavallee Manchester, NH & Eva Boucher Nashua, NH
LAVALLEE, Theresa Rebecca, Dec 16 1926 Sex:F Child# 2 William Lavallee Epping, NH & Julitte Beaudette Rochester, NH
LAVALLEE, Unknown, Apr 25 1897 Sex:F Child# 1 Alfred Lavallee Vermont & Martha B Drew NH Stillborn
LAVALLEY, Kenneth Arthur, Dec 30 1925 Sex:M Child# 3 R H LaValley Weare, NH & Alice Enright Nashua, NH
LAVALLIE, Edouard, Mar 4 1887 Sex:F Child#  Joseph Lavallie P Q & Marie Labourin P Q
LAVALLIE, Henry Raymond, Jul 22 1924 Sex:M Child# 4 Edmond Lavallie Canada & Alice Laverdiere Mass
LAVALLIE, Pierre, Jan 26 1890 Sex:M Child# 12 Daniel Lavallie Canada & Lina Salvail Canada
LAVALLIE, Rosanna, Feb 12 1887 Sex:F Child#  Daniel Lavallie P Q & Celina Salvail P Q
LAVANCHY, Margaret Louise, Sep 19 1920 Sex:F Child# 1 Charles Lavanchy Switzerland & Ruth Davis Nashua, NH
LAVARNWAY, Ernest Joseph, Aug 28 1920 Sex:M Child# 6 Edward Lavarnway Dannemora, NY & Bernadette Goddeau Saranac
LAVARNWAY, Leo, Aug 30 1922 Sex:M Child# 7 Edward Lavarnway Bickmantown, NY & Bernadette Goddeau Saranac, NY
LAVARNWAY, Leona Beatrice, Oct 3 1924 Sex:F Child# 8 Edw Lavarnway Binghamton, Ny & Bernadette Goddeau Saranac, NY
LAVEILLE, Jos F R Raymond, Dec 8 1920 Sex:M Child# 1 Frank Laveille Milford, NH & Minnie A Snyder Boston, MA
LAVEILLE, M Pearl Gertrude, Dec 6 1921 Sex:F Child# 2 Frank Laveille NH & Yvonne Sylvain Canada
LAVENE, Isaac, May 26 1910 Sex:M Child# 4 Rueben Lavene Russia & Theba Gorden Russia
LAVERDIER, Oscar Maurice, May 2 1923 Sex:M Child# 3 Joseph Laverdier Canada & Malvina Morin Canada
LAVERDIERE, Irene Juliette, Jun 2 1922 Sex:F Child# 2 Joseph Laverdiere Canada & Malvina Morin Canada
LAVERDIERE, Joseph Leopold, Sep 11 1924 Sex:M Child# 4 Joseph Laverdiere Canada & Malvina Morin Canada
LAVERDIERE, Marie, Aug 27 1899 Sex:F Child# 4 Philippe Laverdiere Canada & Cylia Sirois Canada
LAVERDIERE, Normand Gilbert, May 3 1930 Sex:M Child# 1 Elphege Laverdiere Canada & Rose A Desrosiers Canada
LAVERY, Joseph Lionel Roger, Dec 22 1918 Sex:M Child# 1 John Lavery Mass & Cecile Baron Canada
LAVERY, Leo Moss, Nov 30 1913 Sex:M Child# 1 Alfred Lavery Winchendon, NH & Emma Marotte Nashua, NH
LAVERY, Marie C Fernande, Jul 6 1926 Sex:F Child# 4 John B Lavery Mass & Cecile Caron Canada
LAVERY, Marie Rita J, Apr 16 1924 Sex:F Child# 3 John Lavery Mass & Cecile Caron Canada
LAVERY, Marie Therese J, Apr 16 1924 Sex:F Child# 2 John Lavery Mass & Cecile Caron Canada
LAVESQUE, Louis E, Aug 10 1888 Sex:M Child# 1 Louis Lavesque Canada & Salomee Charnon Canada
LAVIGNE, Bernard Edward, Sep 12 1932 Sex:M Child# 1 B Lavigne Nashua, NH & Eva Guilmette Nashua, NH
LAVIGNE, Charles, Jun 4 1905 Sex:M Child# 2 Ephraim Lavigne Canada & Zephirine Simonneau Canada
LAVIGNE, Chas Ephrem Jerome, Jan 14 1933 Sex:M Child# 1 Chas E Lavigne Nashua, NH & Lena Carrier Canada
LAVIGNE, Eustache Gregoire, Sep 20 1906 Sex:M Child# 3 Ephraim Lavigne Canada & Zephirine Simonneau Canada
LAVIGNE, Gerald Roland, Feb 18 1934 Sex:M Child# 3 Gerard Lavigne Nashua, NH & Mildred Moisan Nashua, NH
LAVIGNE, Gerard Roland, Jul 22 1906 Sex:M Child# 2 Adelard Lavigne Canada & Marie A Faubert Canada
LAVIGNE, Jacqueline Roberta, Apr 26 1932 Sex:F Child# 2 Gerard Lavigne Nashua, NH & Mildred Moisan Nashua, NH
LAVIGNE, Jos Conrad Gregory, Aug 21 1934 Sex:M Child# 2 Charles Lavigne Nashua, NH & Lena Darrier Canada
LAVIGNE, Joseph, Mar 8 1907 Sex:M Child# 3 Adelard Lavigne Canada & Marianne Faubert Canada
LAVIGNE, Madeleine G, Jan 23 1910 Sex:F Child# 4 Adelard Lavigne Canada & Marianne Faubert Canada
LAVIGNE, Mary, Aug 19 1930 Sex:F Child# 1 Girouard R Lavigne Nashua, NH & Mildred Moison Nashua, NH
LAVIGNE, Toussaint B, Nov 1 1903 Sex:M Child# 1 Ephrem Lavigne Canada & Zephirine Simoneau Canada
LAVIN, Margaret, Jun 19 1901 Sex:F Child# 3 Joseph C Lavin Manchester, NH & Kate O'Hanlon Ireland
LAVINE, Frances, May 24 1925 Sex:F Child# 5 Julis Lavine Russia & Lena Mentz Russia
LAVOCHE, Precila, May 12 1888 Sex:F Child# 4 Ludger Lavoche Canada & Celina Lacombe Canada
LAVOIE, Adelard, Nov 10 1907 Sex:M Child# 1 Placide Lavoie Canada & Emma Bellerose Canada
LAVOIE, Adelard Ernest, Aug 23 1907 Sex:M Child# 2 Wilbrod Lavoie Canada & Philia Blais Canada
LAVOIE, Albert, Oct 4 1892 Sex:M Child# 11 Hermenegilde Lavoie Canada & Adele Salvail Canada
LAVOIE, Albert, Apr 12 1921 Sex:M Child# 1 Thomas Lavoie Canada & Irene Rossignol Fall River, MA
LAVOIE, Albert Irene, Jun 26 1905 Sex:M Child# 10 Louis Lavoie Canada & Vitaline Lemery Canada
LAVOIE, Albert Roland, Oct 26 1911 Sex:M Child# 4 J B Lavoie Canada & Rosanna Masse Canada
LAVOIE, Albina, Jul 19 1910 Sex:F Child# 6 William Lavoie Canada & Regina Bouley US Stillborn
LAVOIE, Alfred, Sep 6 1895 Sex:M Child# 13 Hermenegilde Lavoie Canada & Adele Salvail Canada
LAVOIE, Alfred, Jun 28 1901 Sex:M Child# 3 Francois Lavoie Canada & Leda Thibault Canada
LAVOIE, Alfred, Nov 13 1909 Sex:M Child# 9 Alphonse Lavoie Canada & Josephine Vezeau Nashua, NH
LAVOIE, Alice, Jul 26 1902 Sex:F Child# 4 Octave Lavoie Canada & Amelia Dube Canada
LAVOIE, Alice Helene, Mar 27 1906 Sex:F Child# 3 William Lavoie Nashua, NH & Wildray Deboisbrien Canada
LAVOIE, Alice Jeannette, Feb 24 1912 Sex:F Child# 3 Olivier Lavoie Malone, NY & Anna Menard Canada
LAVOIE, Alice Josephine, Jan 6 1915 Sex:F Child# 3 Joseph Lavoie Nashua, NH & Emma Decelle Waurigan, CT
LAVOIE, Alida Lillian, Jul 30 1908 Sex:F Child# 6 Francois Lavoie Canada & Leda Thibault Canada
LAVOIE, Alma, Apr 7 1902 Sex:F Child# 5 Amable Lavoie Canada & Philomene Lavoie Canada
LAVOIE, Alma Celina, Mar 7 1903 Sex:F Child# 1 William Lavoie Canada & Wildray Deboisbrien Canada
LAVOIE, Andre Joseph, Aug 24 1901 Sex:M Child# 2 Joseph Lavoie Canada & Hermine Pilon Canada
LAVOIE, Andrea, Sep 18 1907 Sex:F Child# 1 Joseph Lavoie US & Emma Decelles US
LAVOIE, Andrea Lucille, Apr 9 1917 Sex:F Child# 4 Olivier Lavoie Plattsburg, NY & Anna Menard Canada
LAVOIE, Andrew Ludger, Sep 12 1928 Sex:M Child# 3 Ernest Lavoie Nashua, NH & Jeanne Berube Canada
LAVOIE, Antonie, May 19 1935 Sex:M Child# 8 Michel Lavoie Canada & Beatrice Lavoie Canada
LAVOIE, Armand Edmond, Oct 10 1911 Sex:M Child# 6 Joseph Lavoie Canada & Celina Guerette Canada
LAVOIE, Aurore, Oct 25 1904 Sex:F Child# 4 Joseph Lavoie Canada & Hermine Perreault Canada
LAVOIE, Benoit Elphege, Apr 16 1918 Sex:M Child# 8 Joseph Lavoie Canada & Celina Guerette Canada
LAVOIE, Blanche Angelina, Jun 11 1914 Sex:F Child# 7 William Lavoie Canada & Wildray Desboisbrian Canada
LAVOIE, Blanche M Luciana, Aug 22 1917 Sex:F Child# 1 Rosario Lavoie Canada & Anna Boisvert Manchester, NH
LAVOIE, Cecile Anna, Dec 12 1911 Sex:F Child# 6 William Lavoie Canada & W Deboisbriant Canada
LAVOIE, Celina, Oct 5 1901 Sex:F Child# 7 Placide Lavoie Canada & Emma Guichard Canada
LAVOIE, Charles Emile, Jun 24 1908 Sex:M Child# 4 William Lavoie Canada & Wildray Deboisbriant Canada

LAVOIE, Charles Henri, Jul 21 1911 Sex:M Child# 1 Ludger Lavoie Canada & Alma Boucher Canada
LAVOIE, Dominick Leonard, Jun 27 1924 Sex:M Child# 2 Joseph Lavoie Canada & Blanche St Onge Canada
LAVOIE, Donald, Aug 21 1934 Sex:M Child# 4 Auguste Lavoie Canada & Marie J Plourde Canada
LAVOIE, Donald Dudley, Sep 27 1935 Sex:M Child# 2 Harry J Lavoie Leominster, MA & Ruby P Schofield Nashua, NH
LAVOIE, Eddie Isadore, Mar 9 1893 Sex:M Child# 1 Ludger Lavoie Canada & Caroline Robert NH
LAVOIE, Edith Mary, Jun 26 1923 Sex:F Child# 2 Raymond Lavoie Worcester, MA & Edith Bonin Nashua, NH
LAVOIE, Edouard Maurice, May 11 1919 Sex:M Child# 5 Joseph Lavoie Maine & Marie Anne Thibodeau Canada
LAVOIE, Edward Wallace, Jan 6 1929 Sex:M Child# 11 George J Lavoie Nashua, NH & Annie Whitcher Pelham, NH
LAVOIE, Elphege, Dec 3 1904 Sex:F Child# 3 William Lavoie Canada & Regina Loranger Nashua, NH
LAVOIE, Emile, Dec 10 1902 Sex:M Child# 4 Francois Lavoie Canada & Leda Thibault Canada
LAVOIE, Emile Armand, Jul 17 1910 Sex:M Child# 3 Jean B Lavoie Canada & Rosanna Masse Canada
LAVOIE, Ernest Henri, Jan 18 1917 Sex:M Child# 8 William Lavoie Canada & Wildray Deboisbriant Canada
LAVOIE, Eva Gertrude, Jul 17 1915 Sex:F Child# 1 George Lavoie Nashua, NH & Annie Whitcher Pelham, NH
LAVOIE, Eva Rose, Jan 1 1905 Sex:F Child# 1 Alphonse Lavoie Canada & Angelina Gagnon Canada
LAVOIE, Evelyn Theresa, Jul 15 1928 Sex:F Child# 6 Wilfrid Lavoie Canada & E Sirois Nashua, NH
LAVOIE, F Richard Lionel, May 30 1914 Sex:M Child# 1 Wilfrid Lavoie Canada & Ermandine Sirois Canada
LAVOIE, Fernand, Apr 28 1934 Sex:M Child# 7 Michel Lavoie Canada & Beatrice Lavoie Canada
LAVOIE, Florence, Jan 27 1924 Sex:F Child# 2 Joseph Lavoie Canada & Marie A Gagnon Canada
LAVOIE, Florence Edna, Mar 26 1908 Sex:F Child# 1 Olivier Lavoie Malone, NY & Anna Maynard Canada
LAVOIE, Gabriel Marie Ann, Jul 2 1922 Sex:F Child# 5 Wilfred Lavoie Canada & Hermantine Sirois Canada
LAVOIE, Gabrielle, Sep 14 1930 Sex:F Child# 5 Ernest Lavoie Nashua, NH & Jeanne Berube Canada
LAVOIE, George Raymond, Oct 27 1935 Sex:M Child# 6 George R Lavoie New Bedford, MA & Alice L Noonan Nashua, NH
LAVOIE, George Walter, Jan 12 1905 Sex:M Child# 1 George Lavoie NH & Julia Doherty NH
LAVOIE, George Walter, Sep 20 1920 Sex:M Child# 4 George J Lavoie Nashua, NH & Annie E Witcher Pelham, NH
LAVOIE, Georgina, Jun 16 1891 Sex:F Child# 9 H Lavoie Canada & Adele Salvail Canada
LAVOIE, Geraldine, Mar 26 1935 Sex:F Child# 2 Harvey Lavoie Nashua, NH & Alice O'Brien Nashua, NH
LAVOIE, Gerard, Feb 7 1933 Sex:M Child# 3 Auguste Lavoie Canada & Marie J Plourde Canada
LAVOIE, Germaine, Sep 29 1912 Sex:F Child# 2 Ludger Lavoie Canada & Alma Boucher Canada
LAVOIE, Germaine Lucile, Aug 25 1906 Sex:F Child# 5 Joseph Lavoie Canada & Celina Guenette Canada
LAVOIE, Gloria, Sep 9 1930 Sex:F Child# 7 Joseph Lavoie Canada & Olina St Onge Canada
LAVOIE, Gloria Clare, Aug 31 1927 Sex:F Child# 5 Joseph Lavoie Nashua, NH & Emma Lasalle Conn
LAVOIE, Henri, Mar 11 1894 Sex:M Child# 12 John Lavoie Canada & Adele Salvail Canada
LAVOIE, Henri, Mar 18 1899 Sex:M Child# 9 Louis Lavoie Canada & Vitaline Lemery Canada
LAVOIE, Henri Auguste, Aug 10 1932 Sex:M Child# 2 Auguste Lavoie Canada & L Bouchard Nashua, NH
LAVOIE, Henry, Oct 18 1918 Sex:M Child# 9 Achille Lavoie Canada & M L Turcotte Canada
LAVOIE, Henry Arthur, Jan 17 1931 Sex:M Child# 12 George Jos Lavoie Nashua, NH & Annie E Whitcher Pelham, NH
LAVOIE, Hermenezide, Jan 21 1889 Sex:M Child# 8 H Lavoie Canada & A Salvail Canada
LAVOIE, Herve Jean B, Oct 14 1907 Sex:M Child# 1 Jean B Lavoie Canada & Rose Anna Masse Canada
LAVOIE, Hervi, Apr 24 1929 Sex:m Child# 4 Michael Lavoie Canada & Beatrice Lavoie US
LAVOIE, Honore Leo, Jul 22 1918 Sex:M Child# 1 Adelard Lavoie Canada & Josephine Laflamme Canada
LAVOIE, Hormidas, Aug 2 1895 Sex:M Child# 2 Amable Lavoie Canada & Philomene Lavoie Canada
LAVOIE, Hud Aristide, Sep 3 1895 Sex:M Child# Louis Lavoie Canada & Vitaline Lemery Canada
LAVOIE, J A B Raymond, Jun 28 1928 Sex:M Child# 17 Archille Lavoie Canada & Marie L Turcotte Canada
LAVOIE, J Albert Alexandre, Feb 10 1915 Sex:M Child# 6 Charles Lavoie Canada & Eugenie Levesque Canada
LAVOIE, J Alphonse Adrien, Oct 12 1913 Sex:M Child# 6 Wilbrod Lavoie Canada & Filia Blais Canada
LAVOIE, J Amable Leo, May 10 1914 Sex:M Child# 4 Joseph Lavoie Canada & R Anna Levesque Canada
LAVOIE, J B Auguste, Feb 15 1896 Sex:M Child# 1 Auguste Lavoie Canada & Adile Dionne Canada
LAVOIE, J C Roland Harve, Dec 20 1922 Sex:M Child# 5 Ludger Lavoie Canada & Alma Boucher Canada
LAVOIE, J Charles Antonio, Dec 18 1913 Sex:M Child# 6 Achille Lavoie Canada & Marie L Turcotte Canada
LAVOIE, J Charles Eugene, Dec 14 1915 Sex:M Child# 6 Charles Lavoie Canada & Eugenie Levesque Canada
LAVOIE, J Paul Alexander, Dec 27 1912 Sex:M Child# 5 Archille Lavoie Canada & Marie Louise Turcott Canada
LAVOIE, Jean, May 19 1935 Sex:M Child# 9 Michel Lavoie Canada & Beatrice Lavoie Canada
LAVOIE, Jean Irenee, Jan 3 1928 Sex:M Child# 3 Michael Lavoie Canada & Beatrice Lavoie Canada
LAVOIE, Jeanine Lucille, Apr 1 1934 Sex:F Child# 4 Wilfrid Lavoie Nashua, NH & Marie Rose Lavoie Canada
LAVOIE, Jeanne d'Arc Doris, Oct 6 1927 Sex:F Child# 7 Ludger Lavoie Canada & Alma Boucher Canada
LAVOIE, Jeanne Francoise, May 19 1918 Sex:F Child# 2 Joseph Lavoie Canada & Leda Munroe Canada
LAVOIE, Jeannette Isabelle, Oct 10 1916 Sex:F Child# 3 Ludger Lavoie Canada & Alma Boucher Canada
LAVOIE, Jeannette Viola, Dec 14 1915 Sex:F Child# 1 Horace Lavoie Nashua, NH & Eugenie St Cyr Canada
LAVOIE, Joan Beth, Oct 15 1933 Sex:F Child# 3 Harvey Lavoie Nashua, NH & Alice O'Brien Nashua, NH
LAVOIE, Joesph Leo Arthur, Jan 17 1912 Sex:M Child# 5 Wilbrod Lavoie Canada & Filia Blais Canada
LAVOIE, Jos Edmund A, Sep 20 1929 Sex:M Child# 18 Archille Lavoie Canada & Marie L Turcotte Canada
LAVOIE, Jos J B Raoul, Jun 18 1925 Sex:M Child# 1 Raoul Lavoie NH & M M J Deguerre NH
LAVOIE, Jos Maurice Louis, Jul 7 1928 Sex:M Child# 1 Joseph Lavoie Canada & Olena Lavoie Nashua, NH
LAVOIE, Joseph, May 28 1899 Sex:M Child# 1 Octave Lavoie Canada & Melia Dube Canada
LAVOIE, Joseph, Jun 10 1923 Sex:M Child# 1 Joseph Lavoie Canada & Victorine St Onge Canada Stillborn
LAVOIE, Joseph Achille, May 23 1898 Sex:M Child# 3 Samuel Lavoie Canada & Elise Bonsens Canada
LAVOIE, Joseph Albert W, Jan 6 1907 Sex:M Child# 3 Alphonse Lavoie Canada & Angelina Gagnon Canada
LAVOIE, Joseph Alfred, Sep 23 1893 Sex:M Child# 7 Louis Lavoie Canada & Vitaline Lemery Canada
LAVOIE, Joseph Alfred, Dec 4 1897 Sex:M Child# 1 Victorien Lavoie Canada & Anna Paradis Canada
LAVOIE, Joseph Alfred, Jul 12 1929 Sex:M Child# 1 Alfred Lavoie Nashua, NH & Frances O'Meara Nashua, NH
LAVOIE, Joseph Alvey H, Sep 27 1901 Sex:M Child# 2 Victorien Lavoie Canada & Anna Paradis Canada
LAVOIE, Joseph C, Nov 20 1891 Sex:M Child# 2 Louis Lavoie Canada & Adele Desjardins Canada
LAVOIE, Joseph Camille Ferna, Mar 1 1925 Sex:M Child# 5 Joseph A Lavoie NH & Alma Beaulieu Canada

LAVOIE, Joseph Edmond, Feb 18 1910 Sex:M Child# 1 Joseph Lavoie Canada & Maria Bilodeau Canada
LAVOIE, Joseph Edmond, Jun 24 1935 Sex:M Child# 1 Edmond LaVoie Nashua, NH & Amy Hammond Nashua, NH
LAVOIE, Joseph Emile, Aug 23 1898 Sex:M Child# 2 Francois Lavoie Canada & Leda Thibault Canada
LAVOIE, Joseph Emile, May 3 1927 Sex:M Child# 16 Archille Lavoie Canada & Marie L Turcotte Canada
LAVOIE, Joseph G, Jul 30 1887 Sex:M Child# 7 Hermengile Lavoie Canada & Adele Salvail Canada
LAVOIE, Joseph Girard, Apr 10 1917 Sex:M Child# 8 Archille Lavoie Canada & Marie L Turcotte Canada
LAVOIE, Joseph Hector, Apr 10 1921 Sex:M Child# 1 Albert Lavoie Fall River, MA & Armandine Bois Greenville, NH
LAVOIE, Joseph Henry Maurice, Dec 6 1923 Sex:M Child# 1 Ernest Lavoie Lion Mt, NY & Victorine Lovely Nashua, NH
LAVOIE, Joseph Jean B, Feb 5 1932 Sex:M Child# 2 Auguste Lavoie Canada & Jeanne Plourde Canada
LAVOIE, Joseph Laurent, Mar 14 1915 Sex:M Child# 7 Archille Lavoie Canada & Marie L Turcotte Canada
LAVOIE, Joseph Leo Pierre, Apr 10 1918 Sex:M Child# 4 Joseph Lavoie Maine & Marie A Thibodeau Canada
LAVOIE, Joseph Louis E, Jan 16 1908 Sex:M Child# 4 Alphonse Lavoie Canada & Angelina Gagnon Canada
LAVOIE, Joseph Massoice Dori, Mar 22 1924 Sex:M Child# 6 Ludger Lavoie Canada & Alma Boucher Canada
LAVOIE, Joseph Noel, Dec 25 1913 Sex:M Child# 2 Isidore Lavoie Canada & Mathilda St Jean Canada
LAVOIE, Joseph Norman Roger, Aug 12 1932 Sex:M Child# 3 Wilfrid Lavoie Nashua, NH & M Rose Lavoie Canada
LAVOIE, Joseph Normand R, Mar 25 1924 Sex:M Child# 13 Archille Lavoie Canada & Marie L Turcotte Canada
LAVOIE, Joseph Oliver Regina, Jan 14 1934 Sex:M Child# 1 Reginald Lavoie Nashua, NH & Olivette Anderson Nashua, NH
LAVOIE, Joseph P, Sep 3 1893 Sex:M Child# 1 Amable Lavoie Canada & Philomene Lavoie Canada
LAVOIE, Joseph Raoul, Sep 13 1903 Sex:M Child# 1 Alphonse Lavoie Canada & Josephine Vezeau Canada
LAVOIE, Joseph Raoul, Oct 18 1908 Sex:M Child# 3 Wilbrod Lavoie Canada & Philia Blais Canada
LAVOIE, Joseph Robert Paul, May 17 1935 Sex:M Child# 5 Wilfrid Lavoie Nashua, NH & Mary R Lavoie Canada
LAVOIE, Joseph Roland, Jun 7 1924 Sex:M Child# 1 Joseph Louis Lavoie Dunbar, WI & Mathilda Lizotte Butte, MT
LAVOIE, Joseph Roland Ernest, Jan 5 1927 Sex:M Child# 1 Auguste Lavoie Canada & Oliva Bouchard Nashua, NH
LAVOIE, Joseph Wilfred, Feb 18 1900 Sex:M Child# 4 Samuel Lavoie Canada & Elise Boussaint Canada
LAVOIE, Laurel Alice, Jul 4 1922 Sex:F Child# 3 George Lavoie NH & Annie Witcher NH
LAVOIE, Lena Elienne, Dec 27 1904 Sex:F Child# 7 Ludger Lavoie Canada & Caroline Robert NH
LAVOIE, Leo Albert, Jul 6 1932 Sex:M Child# 9 Ludger Lavoie Trois Pistoles, PQ & Alma Boucher St Elois, PQ
LAVOIE, Leo Armand, Mar 18 1906 Sex:M Child# 1 Wilbrod Lavoie Canada & Philia Blais Canada
LAVOIE, Leo Ernest, Oct 29 1906 Sex:M Child# 5 Francois Lavoie Canada & Leda Thibault Canada
LAVOIE, Leo George Joseph, Jan 2 1919 Sex:M Child# 3 Wilfred Lavoie Canada & Ermentine Sirois Canada
LAVOIE, Leo Louis, Jan 25 1925 Sex:M Child# 3 Thomas Lavoie Canada & Irene Rossignol Fall River, MA
LAVOIE, Leo Oscar, Aug 11 1909 Sex:M Child# 2 Joseph Lavoie US & Emma Decelle Canada
LAVOIE, Lilian Josephine, Feb 18 1905 Sex:F Child# 2 William Lavoie Canada & Wildray Deboisbriand Canada
LAVOIE, Loraine Theresa, May 23 1929 Sex:F Child# 2 Raoul Lavoie Nashua, NH & Mable Laquerre Nashua, NH
LAVOIE, Lorraine Angele, Feb 1 1909 Sex:F Child# 1 Joseph Lavoie Canada & Leda Monroe Canada
LAVOIE, Lorraine Colette, Feb 27 1928 Sex:F Child# 2 Dosilva Lavoie Canada & Claire Cormier Canada
LAVOIE, Lottie May, Mar 3 1926 Sex:F Child# 7 George J Lavoie Nashua, NH & Annie E Whitcher Pelham, NH
LAVOIE, Louis Augustus, Aug 18 1934 Sex:M Child# 1 Paul Lavoie Canada & Eva Pederzani Nashua, NH
LAVOIE, Louisa Celia, May 26 1913 Sex:F Child# 4 Olivier Lavoie New York & Anna Maynard Canada
LAVOIE, Louise Janet, Mar 4 1919 Sex:F Child# 3 George J Lavoie Nashua, NH & Annie E Whitcher Pelham, NH
LAVOIE, Lucille Irene, Aug 31 1923 Sex:F Child# 8 George J Lavoie Nashua, NH & Annie Witcher Pelham, NH
LAVOIE, Lucille Lea Madeline, Oct 28 1916 Sex:F Child# 2 Wilfrid Lavoie Canada & Ermentine Sirois Canada
LAVOIE, M Anne F M, Dec 1 1911 Sex:F Child# 4 Charles Lavoie Canada & Eugenie Levesque Canada
LAVOIE, M Florette Jeannette, Dec 21 1921 Sex:F Child# 11 Archille Lavoie Canada & Marie L Turcotte Canada
LAVOIE, M L G Doris, Apr 14 1921 Sex:F Child# 9 Wilbrod Lavoie Canada & Philia Blais Canada
LAVOIE, M Lawrence A Y, Aug 2 1910 Sex:F Child# 5 J B Lavoie Canada & Marie A Lavoie Canada
LAVOIE, M Louise, Nov 17 1895 Sex:F Child# 3 Alfred Lavoie Canada & Eugenie Gagnon Canada
LAVOIE, M Malvina Cecile, Feb 22 1917 Sex:F Child# 3 Joseph Lavoie Maine & Marie Anne Thibodeau Canada
LAVOIE, M Rose Annette, Sep 12 1914 Sex:F Child# 1 Alphonse Lavoie Canada & Rose Dube Canada
LAVOIE, Madeline Aurilie, Apr 17 1918 Sex:F Child# 6 Oliver Lavoie Malone, NY & Anna Menard Canada
LAVOIE, Marguerite, Feb 11 1917 Sex:F Child# 8 Charles Eug Lavoie Canada & Eugenie Levesque Canada
LAVOIE, Marguerite Rachelle, Oct 6 1914 Sex:F Child# 7 Joseph Lavoie Canada & Celina Guerette Canada
LAVOIE, Marie, May 11 1892 Sex:F Child# 9 Samuel Lavoie Canada & Georgianna Sirois Canada
LAVOIE, Marie Alberta, Sep 19 1896 Sex:F Child# 14 Hermenegilde Lavoie Canada & Adele Salvail Canada
LAVOIE, Marie Alma, Nov 17 1894 Sex:F Child# 2 Ludger Lavoie Canada & Caroline Robert Manchester
LAVOIE, Marie Anna, Sep 27 1900 Sex:F Child# 13 Fidime Lavoie Canada & Lumena Paradis Canada
LAVOIE, Marie Anna Irene, Jun 6 1924 Sex:F Child# 2 Thomas Lavoie Nashua, NH & Marie Raymond Canada
LAVOIE, Marie Anne Olive, Sep 18 1916 Sex:F Child# 2 Alphonse Lavoie Canada & Marie Desjardins Canada
LAVOIE, Marie Aurore, May 9 1899 Sex:F Child# 15 Hermenegilde Lavoie Canada & Adele Salvail Canada
LAVOIE, Marie Bertha Cecile, Apr 25 1925 Sex:F Child# 2 Ernest Lavoie Nashua, NH & Jeanne Berube Canada
LAVOIE, Marie Betty, Oct 10 1934 Sex:F Child# 2 Albert Lavoie Nashua, NH & Blanche Blanchet Nashua, NH Stillborn
LAVOIE, Marie Cecile Yvette, May 12 1920 Sex:F Child# 10 Archile Lavoie Canada & Marie L Turcotte Canada
LAVOIE, Marie Claudia A, Jan 10 1909 Sex:F Child# 2 J B Lavoie Canada & Rosanna Masse Canada
LAVOIE, Marie Delia, Mar 17 1903 Sex:F Child# 3 Joseph Lavoie Canada & Hermine Pilon Canada
LAVOIE, Marie Doria, Aug 22 1931 Sex:F Child# 8 Joseph Lavoie Canada & Blanche St Onge Canada
LAVOIE, Marie Doris Lucille, Jul 15 1930 Sex:F Child# 1 Wilfrid Lavoie Nashua, NH & Marie Rose Lavoie Canada
LAVOIE, Marie Elizabeth, Sep 11 1906 Sex:F Child# 1 Henri Lavoie Malone, NY & M Elizabeth O'Brien Beckmantown, NY
LAVOIE, Marie Ferriande A, Sep 8 1924 Sex:F Child# 10 Wilbrod Lavoie Canada & Philia Blais Canada
LAVOIE, Marie Jeanne Adele, Jun 12 1921 Sex:F Child# 1 Thomas Lavoie NH & Marie Raymond Canada
LAVOIE, Marie L, Apr 2 1887 Sex:F Child# 4 Louis Lavoie P Q & Vitaline Lemery P Q
LAVOIE, Marie Laura, Feb 27 1915 Sex:F Child# 1 Alphonse Lavoie Canada & Marie Roy Canada
LAVOIE, Marie Liliane I, Apr 29 1910 Sex:F Child# 4 Wilbrod Lavoie Canada & Philia Blais Canada
LAVOIE, Marie Marguerite H V, Nov 29 1908 Sex:F Child# 2 Charles Lavoie Canada & Eugene Levesque Canada

LAFRANCE, Roland Laurent, Sep 21 1912 Sex:M Child# 2 Joseph Lafrance Canada & Mathilda Caron Canada
LAFRANCE, Unknown, Dec 16 1926 Sex:F Child# 2 Louis Lafrance Canada & Jeannette Rodier Nashua, NH
LAFRENIER, Joseph Norman, Sep 26 1933 Sex:M Child# 2 Joseph Lafrenier Winchendon, MA & Aldea Thibault Canada
LAFRENIERE, Joseph A Wilfrid, Nov 17 1897 Sex:M Child# 1 Wilfrid Lafreniere Canada & Aglace Doucet Canada
LAGACE, Gerard Louis, Nov 11 1931 Sex:M Child# 2 George Lagace Canada & Adrienne Lanoie Nashua, NH
LAGACE, Henri Alfred, Oct 10 1902 Sex:M Child# 4 Henri S Lagace Canada & Louise Fosie Nashua, NH
LAGACE, Henry Albert, Oct 9 1918 Sex:M Child# 2 Henry A Lagace Nashua, NH & Aurea E Gagnon Canada
LAGACE, Joseph Pierre, Feb 28 1917 Sex:M Child# 1 Gaudias Lagace Canada & Georgianna Bilodeau Canada
LAGACE, Lucille Irene, Sep 26 1934 Sex:F Child# 3 George Lagace Canada & Adrienne Lavoie Nashua, NH
LAGACE, Maurice George M, Jul 24 1930 Sex:M Child# 1 George Lagace Canada & Adrienne Lanoie Nashua, NH
LAGACE, Unknown, Feb 23 1899 Sex:M Child# 2 Henri S Lagace Canada & Louisa Foisie Nashua, NH Stillborn
LAGAISKI, Wanda, Jun 19 1916 Sex:F Child# 2 John Lagaiski Austria & Mary Tokasz Austria
LAGANIERE, Irene, May 16 1917 Sex:F Child# 4 Wilfred Laganiere Holyoke, MA & Rose Ouellette Canada
LAGANIERE, Marie Stella Dorilda, Mar 17 1912 Sex:F Child# 2 Wilfred Laganiere Holyoke, MA & Rose Ouellette Canada
LAGANIERE, Wilfrid Norbert, Oct 19 1914 Sex:M Child# 3 Wilfrid Laganiere Holyoke, MA & Rose Ouellette Canada
LAGARNIERE, Marie Rose J S, Nov 18 1909 Sex:F Child# 1 Wilfred Lagarniere Canada & Rose Ouellet Canada
LAGARSKI, Charles, Aug 18 1913 Sex:M Child# 1 John Lagarski Russia & Mary Toksz Russia
LAGAS, Unknown, Apr 8 1916 Sex:F Child# 2 John Lagas Greece & Alexandra Alexipolos Greece
LAGASE, Lucille Armance, Apr 10 1919 Sex:F Child# 4 Dona Lagase Nashua, NH & Rosanna Cote Canada
LAGASSE, Aime F, Aug 31 1887 Sex:M Child# 3 Aime Lagasse P Q & Elizabeth P Q
LAGASSE, Andrienne L, Dec 24 1900 Sex:F Child# 3 H S Lagasse Canada & I L Foisie Nashua, NH
LAGASSE, Camille Alice, Jun 12 1924 Sex:F Child# 3 Victor Lagasse Nashua, NH & Alice Beauregard Nashua, NH
LAGASSE, Claire Juliette Rita, Dec 23 1922 Sex:F Child# 2 Victor Lagasse Nashua, NH & Alice Beauregard Nashua, NH
LAGASSE, Eleopold, Dec 31 1889 Sex:M Child# 6 Leon Lagasse Canada & Adile Riendeau Canada
LAGASSE, Felix Scott, Nov 25 1897 Sex:M Child# 1 Henri S Lagasse Canada & Louise Foisie Nashua, NH
LAGASSE, Hector Irenee, Aug 26 1922 Sex:M Child# 7 Donat Lagasse Nashua, NH & Roseanna Cote Canada
LAGASSE, Henri Edouard, Aug 29 1920 Sex:M Child# 6 Donat Lagasse Canada & Rose Anna Cote Canada
LAGASSE, Irene Jeannette, Feb 1 1924 Sex:F Child# 8 Donat Lagasse Nashua, NH & Rosanna Cote Canada
LAGASSE, Israel Thorndike, Nov 24 1903 Sex:M Child# 5 Henri S Lagasse Canada & Isila L Foisie Nashua, NH
LAGASSE, J Raymond Henry, Aug 6 1922 Sex:M Child# 4 Osias Lagasse Canada & Georgianna Bilodeau Canada
LAGASSE, Jean N, May 17 1887 Sex:M Child# 6 Leon Lagasse P Q & Odile Riendeau P Q
LAGASSE, Jeanne d'Arc Cecile, Jan 30 1921 Sex:F Child# 3 Gaudias Lagasse Canada & Georgianna Bilodeau Canada
LAGASSE, Jos Albert Morris, Dec 17 1932 Sex:M Child# 14 D A Lagasse Nashua, NH & Rosanna Cote St Francoise, PQ
LAGASSE, Jos Robert Herve, Apr 26 1929 Sex:M Child# 12 Donat Lagasse Nashua, NH & Rosanna Cote Canada
LAGASSE, Joseph, May 18 1909 Sex:M Child# 1 William Lagasse Nashua, NH & Rose Gaudette Nashua, NH Stillborn
LAGASSE, Joseph Alfred, Feb 19 1904 Sex:M Child# 8 Odias Lagasse Canada & Luce Dube Canada
LAGASSE, Joseph Alphonse, May 7 1918 Sex:M Child# 2 Gaudios Lagasse Canada & Georgianna Bilodeau Canada
LAGASSE, Joseph Sylvin, Jul 7 1892 Sex:M Child# 5 Amede Lagasse Canada & Sarosine Cote Canada
LAGASSE, Joseph V, Apr 20 1895 Sex:M Child# 9 Leon Lagasse Canada & Odile Riendeau Canada
LAGASSE, Joseph Victor S, Sep 5 1910 Sex:M Child# 2 Wilfrid Lagasse Nashua, NH & Rose A Gaudette Nashua, NH
LAGASSE, Leo Lucien, Aug 24 1921 Sex:M Child# 5 Donat Lagasse Canada & Roseanna Cote Canada
LAGASSE, Marie Blanche Lena, Aug 13 1927 Sex:F Child# 11 Donat Lagasse Nashua, NH & Rosanna Cote Canada
LAGASSE, Marie C, Jan 31 1893 Sex:F Child# 8 Leon Lagasse Canada & Odile Riendeau Canada
LAGASSE, Marie Elise, Aug 16 1905 Sex:F Child# 9 Gaudier Lagasse Canada & Luce Leclaire Canada
LAGASSE, Marie Rose Anna, Feb 13 1917 Sex:F Child# 3 Donat Lagasse Canada & Rose Anna Cote Canada
LAGASSE, Mary Pauline, Apr 29 1935 Sex:F Child# 2 Euclid Lagasse Canada & Malvina Boyer Nashua, NH Stillborn
LAGASSE, Olivette Estelle, Oct 20 1915 Sex:F Child# 4 Wilfred Lagasse Nashua, NH & Rose A Gaudette Nashua, NH
LAGASSE, Pierre Leon Victor, Jun 9 1920 Sex:M Child# 1 Victor Lagasse Nashua, NH & Alice Beauregard Nashua, NH
LAGASSE, Rita Fernande, Apr 2 1925 Sex:F Child# 9 Donat Lagasse Nashua, NH & Roseanna Cote Canada
LAGASSE, Roger Oliver, Jul 30 1926 Sex:M Child# 10 Donat Lagasse Canada & Rose Anna Cote Canada
LAGASSE, Shirley Marie Margar, Feb 11 1935 Sex:F Child# 1 Aime Lagasse Salmon Falls, NH & Theresa Lavoie Canada
LAGASSE, Sylvia Ernestine, Dec 22 1920 Sex:F Child# 3 Henry A Lagasse Nashua, NH & Eva Anna Gagnon Canada
LAGAWSKI, Peter, Mar 25 1914 Sex:M Child# 2 Peter Lagawski Russia & Petroneli Stolypinit Russia
LAGGIS, Unknown, May 23 1930 Sex:F Child# 3 Nick Laggis Greece & Christine Scontsas Greece
LAGGIS, Unknown, Mar 30 1932 Sex:M Child# 4 N P Laggis Greece & Christina Scontsas Greece
LAGLOIS, Albina, Dec 26 1894 Sex:F Child# 5 Frank Laglois Canada & Virginie Nadeau US
LAGOS, Adrienne, Feb 11 1915 Sex:F Child# 1 John Lagos Greece & Alexandra Alexopolo Greece
LAGOS, Unknown, Feb 10 1928 Sex:F Child# 3 John Lagos Greece & Annette Landry Greece
LAGUERRE, Clara, Apr 29 1896 Sex:F Child# 1 Joseph Laguerre Canada & Clara Paradis Canada
LAGUERRE, Joseph G Albert, May 28 1899 Sex:M Child# 3 Joseph Laguerre Canada & Clara Paradis Canada
LAGUERRE, Joseph J B, Sep 25 1900 Sex:M Child# 4 Joseph Laguerre Canada & Clara Paradis Canada
LAGUERRE, Mary Cecil, Jul 9 1924 Sex:F Child# 3 Gene Laguerre Nashua, NH & Victoria Willette Nashua, NH
LAGUERRE, Mary Theresa Alice, Jan 11 1927 Sex:F Child# 5 John B Laguerre Nashua, NH & Victoria Willette Nashua, NH
LAGUERRE, Unknown, Dec 18 1925 Sex:M Child# 2 Alexis Laguerre Marlboro, MA & Eva Bouchard Canada
LAHENNETT, Peter Joseph, Jul 14 1918 Sex:M Child# 1 Peter Lahennett Russia & Regina Blanchette Lowell, MA
LAHEY, Raymond Courtney, Oct 4 1904 Sex:M Child# 2 William C Lahey Hollis, NH & Nellie L Callahan Southboro, MA
LAING, Unknown, Apr 10 1898 Sex:M Child# 1 George C Laing Scotland & Lina Gregerson Norway
LAING, William Martin, Aug 18 1899 Sex:M Child# 2 George C Laing Scotland & Lina Gregarson Norway
LAIPINSKI, Mary, Sep 15 1923 Sex:F Child# 5 Michael Laipinski Lithuania & Ludensa Baganowitch Lithuania
LAIRGUE, Marie, Mar 3 1888 Sex:F Child# 1 Marc Lairgue Canada & Rosalie Lussier Canada
LAITE, Mary Bure, Feb 25 1918 Sex:F Child# 8 Robert E Laite St John, NB & Emily Burkett Dorcester, MA
LAITE, Robert Emerson, Apr 2 1915 Sex:M Child# 7 Robert E Laite Newfoundland & Emily Binkett Dorchester, MA
LAJEUNESSE, Marie Anne, Dec 12 1893 Sex:F Child# 6 Thadse Lajeunesse Canada & Exilda Lacasse Canada

LAJEUNESSE, Sade, Feb 7 1890 Sex:M Child# 4 Sade Lajeunesse Canada & Exilda Gacase Canada
LAJOIE, Alexander R, Aug 8 1899 Sex:M Child# 13 Narcisse Lajoie Canada & Marie Phaneuf Champlain, NY
LAJOIE, Alfred, Sep 30 1927 Sex:M Child# 4 Ernest Lajoie Canada & Alice Bechard Canada
LAJOIE, Amede D, Apr 27 1890 Sex:M Child# 5 Narcisse Lajoie Canada & Marie Phaneuf Champlain, NY
LAJOIE, Auguste Robert, Oct 5 1926 Sex:M Child# 3 Henry Lajoie Canada & Alice Bechard Canada
LAJOIE, Clara Gertrude, Oct 1 1906 Sex:F Child# 15 Darisse Lajoie Canada & Marie Phaneuf Canada
LAJOIE, Doris Olive, Mar 24 1923 Sex:F Child# 1 George L Lajoie Nashua, NH & Ernestine Lapointe US
LAJOIE, Doris Therese, Jul 16 1930 Sex:F Child# 2 Altheal Lajoie Canada & Eva Cote Canada
LAJOIE, Dorothy Rita, Jan 13 1929 Sex:F Child# 5 Ernest Lajoie Canada & Alice Bedard Canada
LAJOIE, Emilienne, Mar 10 1911 Sex:F Child# 2 G H Lajoie Canada & Sidonie Bellerose US
LAJOIE, Estelle Alice, Nov 18 1931 Sex:F Child# 6 Ernest Lajoie Canada & Alice Bechard Canada
LAJOIE, George Albert, Jul 4 1910 Sex:M Child# 1 Albert A Lajoie Nashua, NH & Eva I Getchell Salmon Falls, NH
LAJOIE, Georges, May 30 1893 Sex:M Child# 10 Narcisse Lajoie Canada & Marie Phaneuff Champlain, NY
LAJOIE, Henri, May 23 1888 Sex:M Child# 7 Narcisse Lajoie Canada & Marie Phaneuf Champlain, NY
LAJOIE, Henri Edmond, Oct 27 1896 Sex:M Child# 11 Thomas Lajoie Canada & Josephine Caron Canada
LAJOIE, Honori, May 15 1888 Sex:M Child# 4 Alphonse Lajoie Canada & Amanda Lefebvre Nashua, NH
LAJOIE, Irene, Oct 6 1903 Sex:F Child# 1 Frederic Lajoie Canada & Flora Simard Nashua, NH
LAJOIE, Jos Maurice Roland, Nov 10 1925 Sex:M Child# 1 A Lajoie Canada & Marie Eva Cote Canada
LAJOIE, Joseph Arthur Edgar, Sep 23 1916 Sex:M Child# 5 Ovila Lajoie Canada & Sidonie Bellerose Nashua, NH
LAJOIE, Joseph Raymond O, Sep 23 1916 Sex:M Child# 4 Ovila Lajoie Canada & Sidonie Bellerose Nashua, NH
LAJOIE, Laura, Jun 6 1902 Sex:M Child# 14 N D Lajoie Canada & Marie Phaneuf Canada
LAJOIE, Leo George, Apr 15 1924 Sex:M Child# 2 George Lajoie US & Ernestine Lapointe US
LAJOIE, Leo Gerard, Jan 3 1933 Sex:M Child# 3 George H Lajoie Nashua, NH & Albertine Maynard Canada
LAJOIE, Liliane, Oct 6 1903 Sex:F Child# 2 Frederic Lajoie Canada & Flora Simard Nashua, NH
LAJOIE, Lina, Jun 5 1906 Sex:F Child# 3 Frederic Lajoie Canada & Flore Simard Nashua, NH
LAJOIE, Lucile Alfretta, Apr 25 1915 Sex:F Child# 4 Albert Lajoie Nashua, NH & Eva I Getchell Salmon Falls, NH
LAJOIE, Lucille Irene, Mar 31 1913 Sex:F Child# 3 Ovila Lajoie Canada & Cidonie Bellerose Nashua, NH
LAJOIE, Madeleine, Mar 20 1933 Sex:F Child# 7 Ernest Lajoie Canada & Alice Bechard Canada
LAJOIE, Margaret Sylvia, Oct 2 1926 Sex:F Child# 2 Philip Lajoie Nashua, NH & Emeline Bergeron Pepperell, MA
LAJOIE, Marie, May 9 1908 Sex:F Child# 1 Ovila Lajoie Canada & Celanie Bellerose Canada
LAJOIE, Marie Angela Annette, Jul 13 1923 Sex:F Child# 2 George H Lajoie Nashua, NH & Albertine Maynard Canada
LAJOIE, Marie Claire, Sep 12 1925 Sex:F Child# 1 Philip Lajoie Nashua, NH & Emeline Bergeron E Pepperell, MA
LAJOIE, Maurice Earl, Dec 19 1925 Sex:M Child# 3 George L Lajoie US & Ernestine Lapointe US
LAJOIE, Normand Ernest, Dec 31 1923 Sex:M Child# 2 Ernest Lajoie Canada & Alice Bechard Canada
LAJOIE, Paul Alphonse, May 16 1921 Sex:M Child# 1 George H Lajoie Nashua, NH & Albertine Maynard Canada
LAJOIE, Priscilla Eleanor, Jul 29 1913 Sex:F Child# 3 Albert Lajoie Nashua, NH & Eva I Getchell Salmon Falls, NH
LAJOIE, Robert Cyprien, Sep 5 1903 Sex:M Child# 6 Alphonse Lajoie Canada & Amanda Lefebvre Nashua, NH
LAJOIE, Therese L, Apr 23 1897 Sex:F Child# 12 Narcisse Lajoie Canada & Marie Phaneuf Champlain, NY
LAJOIE, Unknown, Sep 3 1910 Sex:M Child# 1 Henry V Lajoie Nashua, NH & Delia Menard Canada
LAJOIE, Unknown, Jun 23 1912 Sex:M Child# 2 Albert A Lajoie Nashua, NH & Eva I Getchell Salmon Falls, NH
LAJOIE, Vincent A, Mar 27 1887 Sex:M Child# 3 Alp Lajoie P Q & Amanda Lefebvre P Q
LAJOIE, Wilbur, Jun 8 1895 Sex:M Child# 11 Narcisse Lajoie Canada & Marie Phaneuf Champlain, NY
LAJOIE, Wilfred, Jan 19 1892 Sex:M Child# 9 Narcisse Lajoie Canada & Marie Phaneuf NY
LAJOIRE, George H, Jun 12 1890 Sex:M Child# 5 Alphonse Lajoire Canada & Amanda Lefevre Nashua, NH
LAKISTAS, Fanaskas, Jul 10 1915 Sex:M Child# 2 Theodore Lakistas Turkey & Annie Offkis Russia
LALANCETTE, Leo, May 7 1925 Sex:M Child# 2 Pierre Lalancette Canada & Eva Belair Mass
LALANCETTE, Marie Alberta Alma, Nov 3 1932 Sex:F Child# 5 Pierre Lalancette Canada & Eva Belair Mass
LALANCETTE, Marie Beatrice Julie, Feb 11 1927 Sex:F Child# 3 Pierre Lalancette Canada & Eva Belair Mass
LALANCETTE, Wm Hector Alfred, Mar 26 1929 Sex:M Child# 4 Pierre Lalancette Canada & Eva Belair Mass
LALANCHETTE, Mary Evelyn L, Apr 30 1924 Sex:F Child# 1 Pierre Lalanchette Canada & Eva Belair W Warren, MA
LALARE, Ernest Eugene, Oct 23 1910 Sex:M Child# 2 Eugene Lalore Nashua, NH & Lizzie Manotte New York
LALEBERTE, Jean, Jul 30 1888 Sex:M Child# 4 Joseph Laleberte Canada & Josephine Bellerose Canada
LALIBERT, Alma, May 8 1901 Sex:F Child# 1 Georges Lalibert Nashua, NH & Mary A Duchesneau Canada
LALIBERTE, Archie, Apr 8 1902 Sex:M Child# 2 George Laliberte Nashua, NH & M A Ducheneau Canada
LALIBERTE, Armand Rene, Jan 15 1932 Sex:M Child# 8 Raoul Laliberte Canada & Clothilde Roy Canada
LALIBERTE, Bernard, Sep 23 1905 Sex:M Child# 4 George Laliberte Nashua, NH & M A Duchesneau Canada
LALIBERTE, Delta, Apr 26 1903 Sex:F Child# 3 George Laliberte Nashua, NH & Maria Duchaineau Canada
LALIBERTE, Ernest, Feb 5 1926 Sex:M Child# 4 Doria Laliberte Nashua, NH & Zelia Bonenfant Nashua, NH
LALIBERTE, Etienn A, Aug 3 1891 Sex:M Child# 5 Joseph Laleberte Canada & Josephine Bellerose Canada
LALIBERTE, Eunice Adrienne, Jun 26 1923 Sex:F Child# 4 Donat Laliberte Nashua, NH & Eva Larocque Nashua, NH
LALIBERTE, Gabrielle Lorette, May 29 1915 Sex:F Child# 2 Doria Laliberte Nashua, NH & Exilia Bonenfant Nashua, NH
LALIBERTE, Gerard Larocque, Jan 10 1913 Sex:M Child# 1 Doria Laliberte Nashua, NH & Eva Larocque Nashua, NH
LALIBERTE, Gerard Maurice, Feb 3 1934 Sex:M Child# 8 Raoul Laliberte Canada & Clothilde Roy Canada
LALIBERTE, Henri H, Mar 27 1899 Sex:M Child# 8 Joseph Laliberte Canada & Josephine Bellerose Canada
LALIBERTE, Jos Laurent L, Jan 5 1930 Sex:M Child# 7 Raoul Laliberte Canada & Clothilde Roy Canada
LALIBERTE, Joseph A D, Mar 25 1889 Sex:M Child# 8 Augustine Laliberte Canada & Emilie Boisseau Canada
LALIBERTE, Joseph A O, Jul 6 1887 Sex:M Child# 7 Auguste Laliberte P Q & Emelie Boisseau P Q
LALIBERTE, Joseph Lucien E H, Mar 14 1924 Sex:M Child# 3 Raoul Laliberte Canada & Clothide Roy Canada
LALIBERTE, Joseph N D, Oct 5 1887 Sex:M Child# 12 Narcisse Laliberte P Q & Odinase Dulude P Q
LALIBERTE, Joseph Ravul Victor, Aug 20 1898 Sex:M Child# 3 Joseph Laliberte Canada & Leonie Dupre Canada
LALIBERTE, Laliberte, Mar 21 1889 Sex:F Child# 13 Narcisse Laliberte Canada & Dinas Dulude Canada Stillborn
LALIBERTE, Louis Philippe, Apr 1 1901 Sex:M Child# 4 Joseph Laliberte Canada & Leonie Dupre Canada
LALIBERTE, Lucien Dorca, Oct 25 1918 Sex:M Child# 2 Doria Laliberte Nashua, NH & Eva Larocque Nashua, NH

LALIBERTE, Lucille Annette, Nov 4 1912 Sex:F Child# 1 Doria Laliberte Nashua, NH & Zelia Bonenfant Nashua, NH
LALIBERTE, Lucille Rita, Jan 10 1925 Sex:F Child# 1 Emile Laliberte Vermont & Clara Provencher Nashua, NH
LALIBERTE, Madeleine, Oct 8 1935 Sex:F Child# 8 Raoul Laliberte Canada & Clothilda Roy Canada
LALIBERTE, Magloire A E, Mar 6 1906 Sex:M Child# 1 Magloire Laliberte Canada & Honora Lebrun Canada
LALIBERTE, Marie I S, Apr 15 1895 Sex:F Child# 7 Joseph Laliberte Canada & Josephine Bellerose Canada
LALIBERTE, Marie Luisette Julie, Apr 22 1927 Sex:F Child# 5 Raoul Laliberte Canada & Clothilde Roy Canada
LALIBERTE, Marie Raymonde L, Nov 24 1928 Sex:F Child# 6 Raoul Laliberte Canada & Mathilda Roy Canada
LALIBERTE, Marie Theresa Yvonne, Jul 1 1925 Sex:F Child# 4 Raoul Laliberte Canada & Clothilde Roy Canada
LALIBERTE, Maurice Armand Jos, May 6 1918 Sex:M Child# 3 Doria Laliberte Nashua, NH & Zelia Bonenfant Nashua, NH
LALIBERTE, Maurice Edgar, Apr 27 1925 Sex:M Child# 5 Dona Laliberte Nashua, NH & Eva Larocque Nashua, NH
LALIBERTE, Philip Eugene, Apr 25 1921 Sex:M Child# 3 Doria Laliberte Nashua, NH & Eva Larocque Nashua, NH
LALIBERTE, Roger Amedee Joseph, Apr 20 1925 Sex:M Child# 4 Lucien Laliberte Manchester, NH & Diana Letendre
LALIBERTE, Roger Robert, Aug 5 1928 Sex:M Child# 2 Earl Laliberte Vermont & Clara Provencher Nashua, NH
LALIBERTE, Victor I, Oct 30 1893 Sex:M Child# 6 Joseph Laliberte Canada & Josephine Bellerose Canada
LALIBERTE, Yoland J, Feb 11 1919 Sex:F Child# 1 Arthur O Laliberte Nashua, NH & Leonie Lemery Nashua, NH
LALLEMAND, Eugene Lucien, Jul 11 1911 Sex:M Child# 3 Eugene Lallemand Canada & Anna Meland Canada
LALLEMAND, J Armand Lionel, Dec 14 1913 Sex:M Child# 4 Eugene Lallemand Canada & Marie A Michaud Canada
LALLEMAND, Joseph Eugene A, Sep 15 1909 Sex:M Child# 2 Eugene Lallemand Canada & Anna Michaud Canada
LALLEMAND, Louis Walter, Oct 30 1908 Sex:M Child# 14 Charles Lallemand Canada & Sophie Leclerc Canada
LALLEMAND, Marie Rose D, Dec 18 1907 Sex:F Child# 1 Eugene Lallemand Canada & Anna Michaud Canada
LALMAND, Irene Cecilia, Jun 17 1904 Sex:F Child# 13 Charles Lalmand Canada & Sophia Leclaire Canada
LALMAND, Minnie, Mar 31 1903 Sex:F Child# 12 Charles Lalmand Canada & Sophia Leclair Canada
LALMAND, Unknown, Apr 24 1901 Sex:F Child# 11 Charles Lalmand Canada & Sophia Lalmand Canada
LALMAND, Unknown, Sep 3 1907 Sex:M Child# 13 Charls Lalmand Canada & Sophia Leclaire Canada Stillborn
LALMOND, Richard George, Jul 18 1926 Sex:M Child# 2 George Lalmond Lowell, MA & Maude Gabriel Canada
LALUMIERE, Joseph Andrew, Sep 7 1929 Sex:M Child# 2 David Lalumiere Plattsburg, NY & Yvonne Lavalle Manchester, NH
LALUMIERE, Joseph Emile, Jan 12 1934 Sex:M Child# 4 David Lalumiere Plattsburg, NY & Yvonne Lavallee Manchester, NH
LALUMIERE, Marie, Feb 28 1932 Sex:F Child# 3 David Lalumiere NY & Yvonne Lavalle NH
LALUMIERE, Unknown, Jun 30 1927 Sex:M Child# 1 David Lalumiere Plattsburg, NY & Yvonne Lavalle Manchester, NH
LAMANCE, Eva G, Jun 18 1903 Sex:F Child# 2 Narcisse Lamance Manchester, NH & Mary A McGovern Methuen, MA
LAMARCHE, Paul Eaton, Feb 25 1913 Sex:M Child# 2 Alfred J Lamarche Nashua, NH & Lillian M Eaton Nashua, NH
LAMARCHE, Unknown, May 15 1911 Sex:M Child# 1 Alfred J Lamarche Nashua, NH & Lillian M Eaton Nashua, NH
LAMARRE, M Clara Georgianna J, Jan 19 1924 Sex:F Child# 1 Eustache Lamarre Canada & Clara Caron Canada
LAMARSH, Evangelist Josepheus, Dec 10 1918 Sex:M Child# 1 Evangelist Lamarsh Nashua, NH & Mary Morin Canada
LAMB, Arthur Raymond, Jan 14 1910 Sex:M Child# 3 Richard Lamb Chateaugay, NY & Helen Jackman Nashua, NH
LAMB, Barbara Mary, Mar 24 1932 Sex:F Child# 1 Arthur R Lamb Nashua, NH & Mary Bugailow Nashua, NH
LAMB, Edward James, Feb 7 1892 Sex:M Child# 2 James E Lamb Canada & Bridget Driscoll Ireland
LAMB, Geraldine Estelle, Feb 24 1925 Sex:F Child# 2 Horatio Lamb Nashua, NH & Bernice Kirkland Old Town, ME
LAMB, Geraldine Ruth, Feb 24 1925 Sex:F Child# 3 Horatio Lamb Nashua, NH & Bernice Kirkland Old Town, ME
LAMB, James Edward, Oct 5 1932 Sex:M Child# 5 Horatio Lamb Nashua, NH & Bernice Kirkland Oldtown, ME
LAMB, Lloyd, Jr, Dec 9 1934 Sex:M Child# 2 Lloyd Lamb Meredith, NH & Edith Bradford Canada
LAMB, Mary, Jun 18 1912 Sex:F Child# 1 Mike Lamb Russia & Eva Kasea Russia
LAMB, Richard F H, Nov 10 1902 Sex:M Child# 2 James E Lamb Canada & Geo Chalifoux New York
LAMB, Shirley Mae, May 6 1922 Sex:F Child# 1 Horatio Lamb Nashua, NH & Bernice Kirkland Oldtown, ME
LAMB, Thelma Regina, Feb 1 1935 Sex:F Child# 2 Richard Lamb Chateauguay, NY & Ruth Richardson New Boston, NH
LAMB, Unknown, Jan 28 1890 Sex:F Child# 1 James E Lamb Canada & Bridget Driscoll Ireland
LAMB, Unknown, Mar 13 1892 Sex:M Child# 1 Peter Lamb Manchester & Nora Phelan Ireland Stillborn
LAMB, Unknown, Oct 18 1900 Sex:F Child# 1 James E Lamb Canada & Georgiana Chalifoux NY
LAMB, Unknown, Aug 31 1928 Sex:F Child# 4 Horatio Lamb Nashua, NH & Bernice Kerkland Oldtown, ME
LAMBERS, Unknown, Mar 6 1915 Sex:F Child# 3 Nicholas Lambers Greece & Mary Lambrulie Greece
LAMBERT, Albert Lloyd, Jun 5 1929 Sex:M Child# 10 Philip Lambert Canada & Elizabeth Fielding Amesbury, MA
LAMBERT, Cecile Rita, Aug 11 1935 Sex:F Child# 4 Pierre P Lambert Canada & Agnes Pinard Nashua, NH
LAMBERT, Donald Alfred, Dec 1 1930 Sex:M Child# 2 J P Henri Lambert Canada & Agnes Pinard Nashua, NH
LAMBERT, Doris Lorraine, Sep 13 1929 Sex:F Child# 1 Alfred Lambert Vermont & Emma Chauvin Canada
LAMBERT, Edward Cecil, Nov 10 1901 Sex:M Child# 2 Joseph E Lambert Nashua, NH & Lillian Merrill N Charleston
LAMBERT, Edward Philippe, Oct 19 1919 Sex:M Child# 6 Philippe Lambert Canada & Elizabeth Fielding Amesbury, MA
LAMBERT, Ernest Arthur, Mar 17 1922 Sex:M Child# 7 Philip A Lambert Canada & Elizabeth Fielding Amesbury, MA
LAMBERT, Ethel Mae, Sep 26 1916 Sex:F Child# 5 Philip A Lambert Montreal, Canada & Elizabeth Fielding Amesbury, MA
LAMBERT, George Albert, Nov 13 1913 Sex:M Child# 9 Antoine Lambert Canada & Marie L Caron Canada
LAMBERT, Joseph Antoine, Jan 7 1902 Sex:M Child# 3 Antoine Lambert Canada & M L Caron Canada
LAMBERT, Joseph Edouard, Oct 29 1905 Sex:M Child# 1 Joseph Lambert Canada & Victoria Boudreau Canada
LAMBERT, Joseph Henry, Jun 2 1934 Sex:M Child# 3 Pierre P Lambert Canada & Agnes Pinard Nashua, NH
LAMBERT, Joseph Jehovah, Sep 24 1903 Sex:M Child# 7 Joseph Lambert Canada & Marie L Bellerose Canada
LAMBERT, Joseph Romeo, Mar 19 1934 Sex:M Child# 5 Alfred Lambert Canada & Rose Anna Raymond Canada
LAMBERT, Joseph T, Jul 21 1897 Sex:M Child# 1 Antoine Lambert Canada & Marie Louise Caron Canada
LAMBERT, June Elizabeth, Jun 21 1935 Sex:F Child# 1 Walter Lambert Manchester, NH & Julie Chouinard Canada Stillbor
LAMBERT, Lillian May, Jan 16 1904 Sex:F Child# 3 Jos Edw Lambert, Jr Nashua, NH & Lillian E Merrill Charleston
LAMBERT, M Ad Bernadette, Nov 3 1917 Sex:F Child# 11 Hilaire Lambert Canada & Maria Dubois Canada
LAMBERT, M Blanche L, Feb 8 1902 Sex:F Child# 12 Telesphore Lambert Canada & Eugenie Bergeron Canada
LAMBERT, Marie Anne E, Feb 7 1903 Sex:F Child# 1 Hilaire Lambert Canada & Maria Dubois Canada
LAMBERT, Marie Ernestine F, Sep 19 1924 Sex:F Child# 2 Alfred Lambert Canada & Rose A Raymond Canada
LAMBERT, Marie Irene, Oct 30 1911 Sex:F Child# 8 Antoine Lambert Canada & Marie Louise Caron Canada
LAMBERT, Marie Louise, Jan 23 1900 Sex:F Child# 2 Joseph A Lambert Canada & Marie L Caron Canada

LAMBERT, Marie Louise V, Sep 26 1897 Sex:F Child# 1 Francois Lambert Canada & Adelie Jacob Canada
LAMBERT, Marie Lucille, Apr 9 1914 Sex:F Child# 1 Melvin Lambert Canada & J DeGrammont Canada
LAMBERT, Marie Philomene D, Jan 1 1910 Sex:F Child# 7 Antoine Lambert Canada & Marie L Caron Canada
LAMBERT, Marie Victoria N, Nov 26 1906 Sex:F Child# 2 Joseph Lambert Canada & Victoria Beaudrault Canada
LAMBERT, Philip, Mar 13 1923 Sex:M Child# 8 Philip A Lambert Canada & Elizabeth Fielding Amesbury, MA
LAMBERT, Rosalie, Jan 29 1935 Sex:F Child# 6 Alfred Lambert Canada & Rosanna Raymond Canada
LAMBERT, Theodore Fielding, Jun 23 1935 Sex:M Child# 1 Theodore Lambert Manchester, NH & Antoinette Forcier Nashua
LAMBERT, Unknown, Jan 4 1894 Sex: Child# 1 Henry Lambert Canada & Philomene L Hereault Canada Stillborn
LAMBERT, Unknown, Mar 20 1904 Sex:M Child# 3 Henry Lambert Canada & Philomene Herault Canada Stillborn
LAMBERT, Viola Pauline, Jun 18 1900 Sex:F Child# 1 Joseph E Lambert Lowell, MA & Lillian Merrill NH
LAMBERT, William Moore, May 27 1926 Sex:M Child# 9 Philip A Lambert Canada & Elizabeth Fielding Amesbury, MA
LAMBERT, Yolande Pauline, Nov 29 1929 Sex:F Child# 1 J P Henry Lambert Canada & Agnes Pinard Nashua, NH
LAMBSON, Unknown, Sep 30 1925 Sex:M Child# 1 DeWitt C Lambson Southwick & Grace Gold Roanoke, VA Stillborn
LAMLURTZ, Unknown, May 11 1912 Sex:M Child# 5 James Lamlurtz Russia & Lucy Aixton Russia Stillborn
LAMOND, Harold Walter, Jan 12 1924 Sex:M Child# 1 George Lamond Lowell, MA & Maude Gabrielle Canada
LAMONDAY, Edward Donat, Jun 14 1932 Sex:M Child# 1 Ed Lamonday Nashua, NH & Persis Landry Nashua, NH
LAMONE, Constant, Feb 6 1911 Sex:M Child# 1 Joseph Lamone Russia & Annie Ztekuta Russia
LAMONTAGNE, Cecile Sylvia, Jul 15 1925 Sex:F Child# 3 Joseph Lamontagne Canada & Lea Caron Holyoke, MA
LAMONTAGNE, Fernand, Dec 1 1923 Sex:M Child# 1 Albert Lamontagne Canada & L Esperance Canada
LAMONTAGNE, Irene Germaine, Sep 7 1921 Sex:F Child# 2 Arthur Lamontagne Canada & Marie Anna Roy Canada
LAMONTAGNE, Joan May, Feb 2 1929 Sex:F Child# 1 Romeo Lamontagne Manchester, NH & Corinne Gregoire Nashua, NH
LAMONTAGNE, Jos Louis Conrad, Aug 3 1920 Sex:M Child# 9 Pamp Lamontagne Canada & Mary Turner Canada
LAMONTAGNE, Joseph Victor, May 28 1915 Sex:M Child# 7 Pam Lamontagne Canada & Mary Turner Canada
LAMONTAGNE, Leota Lorraine, Dec 17 1924 Sex:F Child# 1 W Lamontagne New Ipswich, NH & Blanche Moreau New Ipswich
LAMONTAGNE, Luella Olivette, Dec 4 1923 Sex:F Child# 3 Arthur Lamontagne Canada & Marie A Roy Canada
LAMONTAGNE, Maria A L, May 14 1901 Sex:F Child# 1 Napoleon Lamontagne Canada & Laura Desmarais Nashua, NH
LAMONTAGNE, Mary Anjou Ardell, Nov 24 1926 Sex:F Child# 4 L Lamontagne Canada & Lea Caron Canada
LAMONTAGNE, Mary Eleanor, Apr 29 1920 Sex:F Child# 1 Joseph Lamontagne Canada & Lea Caron Holyoke, MA
LAMONTAGNE, Noe Laurent, Aug 10 1913 Sex:M Child# 6 Pamphile Lamontagne Canada & Mary Turner Canada
LAMONTAGNE, Paul Armand, Apr 4 1917 Sex:M Child# 8 P Lamontagne Canada & Mary Turner Canada
LAMONTAGNE, Raymond Albert, Jun 16 1930 Sex:M Child# 2 Romeo Lamontagne Manchester, NH & Corinne Gregoire Nashua
LAMONTAGNE, Rita Lucienne, Nov 24 1923 Sex:F Child# 2 Joseph Lamontagne Canada & Lea Caron Canada
LAMONTAGUE, Clara, Jul 20 1898 Sex:F Child# 9 N Lamontague Canada & Aurelie Gagnon Canada
LAMONTAGUE, Flora, Jul 20 1898 Sex:F Child# 10 N Lamontague Canada & Aurelie Gagnon Canada
LAMONY, Annie, May 9 1914 Sex:F Child# 3 Joseph Lamony Russia & Rachael Zepkinta Russia
LAMORE, Marie Alma, Aug 13 1921 Sex:F Child# 1 Lauriel Lamore Canada & Olive Johnson NH
LAMORNEUX, Joseph Albert, May 27 1899 Sex:M Child# 3 Ubald Lamorneux Canada & Marie Rajotte Canada
LAMOTHE, Alfred, Oct 22 1906 Sex:M Child# 1 Henri Lamothe Arctic, RI & Marie Poulin Canada
LAMOTHE, Fernand Girard Josep, Aug 25 1926 Sex:M Child# 5 Josephat Lamothe Canada & Eva Champagne Canada
LAMOTHE, M Olive Noela, Oct 2 1915 Sex:F Child# 1 Theophile Lamothe Conn & Albertine Arnois Canada
LAMOTHE, M Opalma Eva, May 17 1908 Sex:F Child# 2 Henri Lamothe Canada & Marie L Poulin Canada
LAMOTTE, Leo Paul Normand, Sep 24 1930 Sex:M Child# 6 Joseph A Lamotte Canada & Eva Champagne Canada
LAMOUREUX, Marie Lucille Olivet, Oct 9 1912 Sex:F Child# 1 Pierre Lamoureux Canada & Clara Lawrence Canada
LAMOVESKY, Unknown, Sep 23 1910 Sex:M Child# 1 Konstoof Lamovesky Russia & Lena Easukiewich Russia
LAMOY, Philip Thomas, Apr 6 1925 Sex:M Child# 1 Philip Lamoy Hudson, NH & Annie Gembiarich Nashua, NH
LAMOY, Unknown, Apr 25 1891 Sex:F Child# 4 Albert B Lamoy New York & M Boissonneau Canada
LAMPRON, Alphonse Napoleon, Aug 1 1890 Sex:M Child# 8 Joseph Lampron Canada & Elzie Duval Canada
LAMPRON, Arthur Philip, Apr 21 1916 Sex:M Child# 3 Joseph Lampron Nashua, NH & Marie Bernier Canada
LAMPRON, Clement Wilfred, Aug 21 1925 Sex:M Child# 4 S Lampron Canada & Donalda Berube Canada
LAMPRON, David Robert, Feb 8 1935 Sex:M Child# 1 Robert Lampron Nashua, NH & Irene Langley Nashua, NH
LAMPRON, Edouard Robert, Feb 25 1914 Sex:M Child# 2 Joseph Lampron Nashua, NH & Marie Bernier Canada
LAMPRON, Edward John, Aug 23 1909 Sex:M Child# 1 John P Lampron Nashua, NH & Ellen Deschenes Canada
LAMPRON, Geroge Victor, Feb 18 1918 Sex:M Child# 4 Joseph Lampron Nashua, NH & Marie Bernier Canada
LAMPRON, Hermen John, Oct 3 1910 Sex:M Child# 2 John Lampron Nashua, NH & Helen Deschenes Canada
LAMPRON, J Leon Alfred, Aug 19 1915 Sex:M Child# 4 J P Lampron Nashua, NH & Helene Deschenes Canada
LAMPRON, Jessie J Evangeline, Jul 8 1919 Sex:F Child# 5 Joseph Lampron Nashua, NH & Marie Bernier Canada
LAMPRON, Joseph Alphonse, May 7 1895 Sex:M Child# 3 Joseph Lampron Canada & Elvire Duval Canada
LAMPRON, Joseph Felix, Aug 9 1912 Sex:M Child# 1 Joseph A Lampron Nashua, NH & Mary Bernier Canada
LAMPRON, June Hildreth, Oct 22 1929 Sex:F Child# 1 Wilfred E Lampron Nashua, NH & Hildreth A Fisher Hudson, NH
LAMPRON, Loretta Alberta, May 11 1917 Sex:F Child# 1 Ovila L Lampron US & Alberta Lambert US
LAMPRON, Louis Ovila, Feb 8 1897 Sex:M Child# 5 Osias Lampron Canada & Marie Jean Bart Canada
LAMPRON, Lucille Sylvia, Nov 5 1919 Sex:F Child# 2 Ovila Lampron US & Alberta Lambert US
LAMPRON, Marie Eveline, Mar 7 1889 Sex:F Child# 3 Eseeas Lampron Canada & Marie Jean Bart Canada
LAMPRON, Marie Laura Cecile, Feb 9 1913 Sex:F Child# 3 John B Lampron Nashua, NH & Ellen Deschenes Canada
LAMPRON, Marie Louise, Aug 25 1893 Sex:F Child# 16 Joseph Lampron Canada & Alzire Duval Canada
LAMPRON, Unknown, Nov 24 1891 Sex:M Child# 4 Osias Lampron Canada & Marie Jeanvart Canada Stillborn
LAMPRON, Unknown, Aug 25 1905 Sex:M Child# 2 Joseph Lampron Nashua, NH & Jessie Tucker Canada
LAMPRON, Unknown, Aug 25 1905 Sex:M Child# 1 Joseph Lampron Nashua, NH & Jessie Tucker Canada
LAMPRON, Wilfrid Edouard, May 10 1895 Sex:M Child# 4 Osias Lampron Canada & Marie Jeanbart Canada
LAMPROS, Fotrie, May 31 1917 Sex:F Child# 4 Nicholas Lampros Greece & Mary Camproulas Greece
LAMSON, Joseph, May 2 1890 Sex:M Child# 1 Joseph Lamson Windham, NH & Janna Dube Canada
LAMUDGE, Hazel Frances, May 3 1895 Sex:F Child# 1 Charles A Lamudge Ellensburg, NY & Josephine Cheney VT
LANCHEN, Stanley, Apr 7 1914 Sex:M Child# 5 Joseph Lanchen Russia & Jedwega Sarkovach Russia

LANCOURT, Lionel, Jan 27 1927 Sex:M Child# 3 Victor Lancourt Nashua, NH & Delia Labonte Canada
LANCOURT, Romeo, Mar 31 1901 Sex:M Child# 2 Frank Lancourt Fairfield, ME & Emma Lagasse Canada
LANCOURT, Romeo, Jun 17 1919 Sex:M Child# 1 Victor G Lancourt Nashua, NH & Delia Labonte Canada
LANCOURT, Yvette Lucille, Jan 8 1924 Sex:F Child# 2 Victor G Lancourt Nashua, NH & Delia Labonte Canada
LANDERS, Rena, Jul 26 1894 Sex:F Child# 1 Robert H Landers Bridgeport, VT & Bessie Allen Washington, DC
LANDO, Carl Albert Mario, Sep 28 1917 Sex:M Child# 3 Salvator Lando Italy & Erma Pogliani Italy
LANDO, Joseph Mario, May 31 1916 Sex:M Child# 2 Salvatore Lando Italy & Emma Foliano Italy
LANDRY, Adelard, Feb 23 1906 Sex:M Child# 6 Narcisse Landry Canada & Philomene Laprise Canada
LANDRY, Adrien, Feb 28 1908 Sex:M Child# 6 Frank Landry Nashua, NH & Philomene Rheaume Canada
LANDRY, Albert Normand, Mar 5 1926 Sex:M Child# 7 Charles Landry Canada & Clarina Roy Canada
LANDRY, Alberta Gloria, Jun 7 1932 Sex:F Child# 4 Noel Landry Nashua, NH & Marie J St Onge Lowell, MA
LANDRY, Albina, Jul 20 1894 Sex:F Child# 3 J Bte Landry Canada & Elise Labrie Canada
LANDRY, Alfred, Jan 20 1897 Sex:M Child# 4 Louis Landry Canada & Celina Emond Canada
LANDRY, Alphius Allen, Sep 3 1922 Sex:M Child# 2 Ernest Landry Nashua, NH & Rose Dufault Lowell, MA
LANDRY, Alphonse, Feb 22 1895 Sex:M Child# 7 Nathaniel Landry Canada & Georgina St Pierre Canada
LANDRY, Alvin, Nov 11 1898 Sex:M Child# 6 George F Landry Nashua, NH & Melvina Bougor Nashua, NH
LANDRY, Amede A, Nov 19 1897 Sex:M Child# 9 Nathaniel Landry Canada & Georgina St Pierre Canada
LANDRY, Anatole, Jul 13 1891 Sex:F Child# 13 Thomas Landry Canada & Marie L Morisette Canada
LANDRY, Andrew Alphonse, Dec 12 1932 Sex:M Child# 2 Alphonse Landry Canada & R F Ackerman Hawthorne, NJ
LANDRY, Andrew George, May 20 1919 Sex:M Child# 7 Dona J Landry Canada & Dora Golden Hartford, CT
LANDRY, Angeline Annette, Apr 18 1916 Sex:F Child# 6 Dona Landry Canada & Dora Golden Hartford, CT
LANDRY, Anne Marie Priscilla, Jul 27 1935 Sex:F Child# 8 Noel Landry Nashua, NH & M J St Onge Lowell, MA
LANDRY, Armand, Jul 24 1896 Sex:M Child# 2 Charles Landry Canada & Anna Dube Canada
LANDRY, Arthur William, Jul 1 1891 Sex:M Child# 4 George F Landry Nashua, NH & Melvina Boucher Nashua, NH
LANDRY, Arthur William, Jun 13 1924 Sex:M Child# 2 Arthur W Landry Nashua, NH & Eleanor Hamel Nashua, NH
LANDRY, Bertha Ann, Sep 5 1927 Sex:F Child# 1 Ludger Landry Canada & Edna Ellenwood N Pelham, NH
LANDRY, Berthe Lianne, Mar 14 1908 Sex:F Child# 8 John Landry Canada & Marie Beaulieu Canada
LANDRY, Blanche Adrienne, Feb 13 1903 Sex:F Child# 5 John B Landry Canada & Marie Beaulieu Canada
LANDRY, Caroline Irene, Apr 3 1930 Sex:F Child# 1 Thomas M Landry Nashua, NH & Irene Livernois Derry, NH
LANDRY, Cecile Sonia Imelda, Sep 17 1911 Sex:F Child# 5 Lucien Landry Canada & Melvina Harpin Mass
LANDRY, Charles Desire, Apr 25 1901 Sex:M Child# 4 Frank Landry Nashua, NH & Philomene Rheaume Canada
LANDRY, Claire Jacqueline, Aug 5 1932 Sex:F Child# 3 George Landry Nashua, NH & Anita Maynard Nashua, NH
LANDRY, Claire Louise Glorie, Jun 10 1935 Sex:F Child# 3 Nelson Landry Nashua, NH & Lauretta Langlois Nashua, NH
LANDRY, Clare Louise Paulett, May 29 1929 Sex:F Child# 1 Nelson Landry Canada & Loretta Nashua, NH
LANDRY, Constance Gay, Mar 30 1932 Sex:F Child# 2 Thomas Landry Nashua, NH & Irene Livernois Derry, NH
LANDRY, Delores, Mar 25 1899 Sex:F Child# 4 Calvin Landry Canada & Philina Richard Nashua, NH
LANDRY, Dolor, Nov 2 1908 Sex:M Child# 8 Calvin Landry Canada & Ophelina Richard US
LANDRY, Dolores, Apr 5 1892 Sex:F Child# 5 Nathaniel Landry Canada & Georgina St Pierre Canada
LANDRY, Dolores, Oct 14 1934 Sex:F Child# 1 Rosaire Landry Nashua, NH & Dorothy Bacon Nashua, NH
LANDRY, Donald P Rudolph, May 7 1931 Sex:M Child# 2 Nelson Landry Nashua, NH & Loretta Langlois Nashua, NH
LANDRY, Edmond Oscor, Aug 28 1897 Sex:M Child# 3 Napoleon Landry Burlington, VT & Anais Auctil Canada
LANDRY, Eleanor, Oct 19 1922 Sex:F Child# 1 Arthur W Landry Nashua, NH & Eleanor M Hamel Nashua, NH
LANDRY, Elise A, Sep 10 1887 Sex:F Child# Napoleon Landry Nashua, NH & M Beauregard Nashua, NH
LANDRY, Elzeard, Jun 16 1889 Sex:M Child# 5 Hilairo Landry Canada & Angele Levesque Canada
LANDRY, Emelda L Lucille, Jan 29 1919 Sex:F Child# 6 Elisie Landry NH & Helene Maurais Canada
LANDRY, Emile G, Jun 5 1896 Sex:M Child# 8 Nathaniel Landry Canada & Georgina St Pierre Canada
LANDRY, Eugene Philias, May 7 1908 Sex:M Child# 2 Alfred Landry Nashua, NH & Obeline Boisseau Nashua, NH
LANDRY, Eva, Dec 24 1897 Sex:F Child# 5 Louis Landry Canada & Celina Emond Canada
LANDRY, Eva Ruth, Oct 28 1920 Sex:F Child# 1 Alphonse Landry Canada & Ruth Ackerman Hawthorne, NY
LANDRY, Evelina Dora, Jan 16 1905 Sex:F Child# 6 John Landry Canada & Marie Beaulieu Canada
LANDRY, Florette, Jul 7 1895 Sex:F Child# 14 Thomas Landry Canada & M Louise Morisette Canada
LANDRY, George Armand, Apr 16 1930 Sex:M Child# 2 Joseph Landry Nashua, NH & Ida Blow New York
LANDRY, George Frank, Dec 1 1901 Sex:M Child# 7 George F Landry Canada & Malvina Beauregard Canada
LANDRY, George Louis, Nov 13 1906 Sex:M Child# 1 Fred L Landry Nashua, NH & Obeline Boisseau Nashua, NH
LANDRY, George Lucien, May 13 1904 Sex:M Child# 5 Narcisse Landry Canada & Philomene Lapierre Canada
LANDRY, George William, Jun 3 1927 Sex:M Child# 2 Asa B Landry Maine & Catherine Fox Manchester, NH
LANDRY, Georges N R, Apr 29 1906 Sex:M Child# 1 Elise Landry, Jr Nashua, NH & Helene Maurais Canada
LANDRY, Georgianna, Feb 10 1890 Sex:F Child# 12 Thomas Landry Canada & Marie L Mousette Canada
LANDRY, Gerard, Mar 29 1927 Sex:M Child# 3 John B Landry Canada & Irene Lacombe Nashua, NH
LANDRY, Gerard Paul Eugene, Sep 5 1929 Sex:M Child# 5 Noel Landry Nashua, NH & Marie J St Onge Lowell, MA
LANDRY, Gertrude Germaine, Jan 31 1917 Sex:F Child# 4 Hector Landry Canada & Amanda Rochette Canada
LANDRY, Gervaise, Nov 18 1926 Sex:F Child# 4 Emile Landry Nashua, NH & Claudia Boucher Nashua, NH
LANDRY, Girard Robert George, Feb 21 1926 Sex:M Child# 3 Noel Landry NH & Marie J St Onge Mass
LANDRY, Helen Edna, Feb 2 1896 Sex:F Child# 2 George C Landry Nashua, NH & Mary E Labima Nashua, NH
LANDRY, Helene Olivine, Sep 27 1893 Sex:F Child# 6 Nathaniel Landry Canada & Georgianna St Pierre Canada
LANDRY, Heleva, Sep 1 1888 Sex:F Child# 3 George Landry Canada & Malvena Brauregard Canada
LANDRY, Henry N, Apr 21 1899 Sex:M Child# 2 Jean B Landry Canada & Marie Beaulieu Canada
LANDRY, Herminie M, Nov 2 1902 Sex:F Child# 8 Louis Landry E Douglas, MA & Celina Emond Canada
LANDRY, Honore, Nov 11 1894 Sex:M Child# 3 Calvin Landry Canada & Obelina Richard Nashua, NH
LANDRY, Ivonne, Feb 24 1901 Sex:F Child# 5 Calvin Landry Canada & Phelina Richard Nashua, NH
LANDRY, J Ovide Lionel, May 31 1915 Sex:M Child# 3 Hector Landry Canada & Amanda Rochette Canada
LANDRY, Jacqueline Evelyn, Jul 26 1933 Sex:F Child# 1 Ferd Landry Nashua, NH & Cecile Pelletier Cohoes, NY
LANDRY, Jean Bte, Apr 5 1893 Sex:M Child# 4 Louis Landry Canada & Eulalie Bellerose Canada

LANDRY, Jeannette, Apr 10 1907 Sex:F Child# 7 Calvin Landry Canada & Phelina Richard US
LANDRY, Jeannette, Oct 28 1927 Sex:F Child# 6 William Landry Canada & Juliette Arel Canada
LANDRY, Jeannette Irene, Sep 17 1924 Sex:F Child# 2 Sylvio Landry Nashua, NH & Mamie Peno Nashua, NH
LANDRY, Joan Hermance, May 9 1935 Sex:F Child# 1 Alfred Landry Nashua, NH & Isabel Doherty Pelham, NH
LANDRY, John, Sep 13 1894 Sex:M Child# 1 Thomas Landry Scotland & Nora Sweeney Mass
LANDRY, John Henry, Sep 26 1928 Sex:M Child# 1 Joseph Landry Nashua, NH & Ida Blow Scotia, NY
LANDRY, Jos Armond Roger, Jan 29 1933 Sex:M Child# 6 John B Landry Canada & Irene Lacombe US
LANDRY, Jos Leo Normand, Apr 14 1927 Sex:M Child# 4 Noel Landry Nashua, NH & Marie J St Onge Lowell, MA
LANDRY, Jos Raymond Sylv, Nov 14 1920 Sex:M Child# 1 Joseph Landry Canada & Flora Boudreau New Brunswick
LANDRY, Jos Roger Robert, Nov 24 1920 Sex:M Child# 1 William Landry Canada & Juliette Arel Canada
LANDRY, Jos Wm Romeo, Sep 7 1923 Sex:M Child# 3 William Landry Canada & Juliette Arel Canada
LANDRY, Joseph, Nov 22 1892 Sex:M Child# 5 Elise Landry Canada & Vitaline Laperise Canada
LANDRY, Joseph, Dec 24 1896 Sex:M Child# 15 Thomas Landry Canada & Louise Morissette Canada
LANDRY, Joseph, Feb 5 1898 Sex:M Child# 16 Thomas Landry Canada & Louise Morissette Canada
LANDRY, Joseph, Apr 1 1900 Sex:M Child# 6 Elise Landry Canada & Vitaline Lapensie Canada
LANDRY, Joseph, Jan 9 1903 Sex:M Child# 5 Charles Landry Canada & Anna Dube Canada Stillborn
LANDRY, Joseph A Adria, Sep 26 1899 Sex:M Child# 7 J B Landry Canada & Elise Labine Canada
LANDRY, Joseph Aime, Nov 12 1897 Sex:M Child# 6 Napoleon Landry Canada & Marie Menard Canada
LANDRY, Joseph Albert I, Mar 23 1898 Sex:M Child# 6 J B Landry Canada & Elsie Labrie Canada
LANDRY, Joseph Alfred, Nov 6 1923 Sex:M Child# 6 Hector Landry Canada & Amanda Rochette Canada
LANDRY, Joseph Antonio, Jul 21 1898 Sex:M Child# 3 Lucien Landry Canada & Melvina Arpin E Douglas, MA
LANDRY, Joseph Auguste, Oct 24 1906 Sex:M Child# 8 Charles Landry Canada & Anna Dube Canada
LANDRY, Joseph Blair, Apr 30 1924 Sex:M Child# 1 Asa B Landry Hansville, ME & Catherine Fox Manchester, NH
LANDRY, Joseph C Noel, Dec 25 1898 Sex:M Child# 3 Frank Landry Canada & Philomene Rheaume Canada
LANDRY, Joseph Edgar, Sep 11 1903 Sex:M Child# 4 Lucien Landry Canada & Malvina Harpin E Douglass, MA
LANDRY, Joseph Emile, Feb 12 1893 Sex:M Child# 2 J B Landry Canada & Elise Berube Canada
LANDRY, Joseph Francois, Dec 10 1894 Sex:M Child# 1 Frank Landry Canada & Philomene Rheaume Canada
LANDRY, Joseph George, Jan 17 1890 Sex:M Child# 5 George F Landry Nashua, NH & Rosalie Nashua, NH
LANDRY, Joseph George, Nov 29 1900 Sex:M Child# 9 Louis Landry Canada & Aurelie Bellerose Canada
LANDRY, Joseph George A, Nov 6 1898 Sex:M Child# 1 Narcisse Landry Canada & Philomene Laprise Canada
LANDRY, Joseph Honore, Jun 30 1900 Sex:M Child# 3 Narcisse Landry Canada & Philomene Laprise Canada
LANDRY, Joseph Jean B A, Feb 17 1897 Sex:M Child# 5 Jean Baptiste Landry Canada & Elise Labrie Canada
LANDRY, Joseph Napoleon G, Feb 2 1899 Sex:M Child# 6 Louis Landry Canada & Celina Emond Canada
LANDRY, Joseph Omer Albert, Nov 15 1911 Sex:M Child# 4 Elisi Landry Nashua, NH & Helene Morais Canada
LANDRY, Joseph Paul Ovid, Jul 27 1926 Sex:M Child# 5 William Landry Canada & Juliette Arel Canada
LANDRY, Joseph Raymond, Jul 17 1924 Sex:M Child# 2 Noel Landry NH & Marie J St Onge Mass
LANDRY, Joseph W A, Sep 12 1905 Sex:M Child# 7 Charles Landry Canada & Anna Dube Canada
LANDRY, Josephine Dora, Nov 5 1926 Sex:F Child# 8 Dona J Landry Canada & Dora E Golden Hartford, CT
LANDRY, Laura Alice, Oct 12 1901 Sex:F Child# 7 Louis Landry Canada & Celina Emond Canada
LANDRY, Laura Alice, Oct 25 1902 Sex:F Child# 4 Narcisse Landry Canada & P Laprise Canada
LANDRY, Laura Philomene, Aug 23 1896 Sex:F Child# 2 Francois Landry Canada & Philomene Rheaume Canada
LANDRY, Lauren, Feb 26 1918 Sex:M Child# 1 Lawrence Landry Nashua, NH & Claudia Boucher Nashua, NH
LANDRY, Leo, Dec 6 1906 Sex:M Child# 11 Louis Landry E Douglass, MA & Celina Hemond Canada
LANDRY, Leo Almond, Dec 4 1921 Sex:M Child# 8 Dona J Landry Canada & Dora E Golden Hartford, CT
LANDRY, Leon Auguste, Feb 1 1901 Sex:M Child# 10 Nathaniel Landry Canada & Georgina Canada
LANDRY, Leona, Sep 11 1890 Sex:F Child# 2 Calvin Landry Canada & Velina Richard Canada
LANDRY, Leonard Frank, Sep 27 1928 Sex:M Child# 2 Homer Landry Nashua, NH & Laura Smith Nashua, NH
LANDRY, Leopold Roland, May 19 1929 Sex:M Child# 4 J B Landry Canada & Irene Lacombe Nashua, NH
LANDRY, Lillian, Jul 13 1918 Sex:F Child# 5 Charles Landry Canada & Corinne Roy Canada Stillborn
LANDRY, Lillian Dorothy, Apr 2 1931 Sex:F Child# 6 Noel Landry Nashua, NH & Marie J St Onge Lowell, MA
LANDRY, Loraine Lucille, Dec 20 1929 Sex:F Child# 1 George Landry
LANDRY, Loretta, Feb 26 1904 Sex:F Child# 6 Calvin Landry Canada & Phelina Richard Nashua, NH
LANDRY, Louis Albert Paul, Nov 8 1912 Sex:M Child# 1 Hector Landry Canada & Amanda Rochette Canada
LANDRY, Louis Ernest, Mar 13 1915 Sex:M Child# 1 Ernest Landry Nashua, NH & Eva Cote Nashua, NH
LANDRY, Louis Jeremie, Sep 22 1894 Sex:M Child# 2 Louis Landry Canada & Celina Edmond Canada
LANDRY, Louis Joseph, Dec 15 1899 Sex:M Child# 7 Louis Landry Canada & Aurelie Bellerose Canada Stillborn
LANDRY, Louis Leo, Jun 30 1900 Sex:M Child# 3 J B Landry Canada & Marie Beaulieu Canada
LANDRY, Louis Maxime, Sep 22 1903 Sex:M Child# 9 Louis Landry Canada & Celina Emond Canada
LANDRY, Lucille Eldora, Jun 19 1923 Sex:F Child# 8 Charles Landry Canada & Corinne Roy Canada
LANDRY, M A Lucienne, Nov 12 1894 Sex:F Child# 1 Charles Landry Canada & Anna Dube Canada
LANDRY, M Aurore, Aug 9 1895 Sex:M Child# 2 Frank Landry Canada & Anaise Auctil Canada
LANDRY, M Louise A, Sep 22 1892 Sex:F Child# 1 Napoleon Landry Canada & Anaise Anctil Canada
LANDRY, Marie, Sep 26 1899 Sex:F Child# 8 J B Landry Canada & Elise Labine Canada Stillborn
LANDRY, Marie A Clara, May 15 1900 Sex:F Child# 4 Charles Landry Canada & Anna Dube Canada
LANDRY, Marie A P, Sep 26 1897 Sex:F Child# 6 Louis Landry Canada & Eulalie Rivet Canada
LANDRY, Marie Albertime, May 14 1897 Sex:F Child# 1 Narcisse Landry Canada & Philomene Laprise Canada
LANDRY, Marie Alice Y, Jun 10 1904 Sex:F Child# 6 Charles Landry Canada & Anna Dube Canada
LANDRY, Marie Anna, May 16 1889 Sex:F Child# 3 Nathaniel Landry Canada & Georgina St Pierre Canada
LANDRY, Marie Anna G, Feb 24 1920 Sex:F Child# 5 Hector Landry Canada & Amanda Rochette Canada
LANDRY, Marie Anne, Nov 23 1891 Sex:F Child# 1 J B Landry Canada & Elise Labrie Canada
LANDRY, Marie Cora Irene, Aug 12 1933 Sex:F Child# 8 William Landry Canada & Juliet Arel Canada
LANDRY, Marie Doris, Nov 21 1924 Sex:F Child# 4 William Landry Canada & Juliette Arel Canada
LANDRY, Marie Estelle, Apr 13 1929 Sex:F Child# 7 William Landry Canada & Juliette Arel Canada

LAVOIE, Marie Melina, Sep 20 1896 Sex:F Child# 1 Francois Lavoie Canada & Leda Thibault Canada
LAVOIE, Marie Olina, Nov 29 1905 Sex:F Child# 2 Alphonse Lavoie Canada & Angelina Gagnon Nashua, NH
LAVOIE, Marie Oliva B, May 15 1908 Sex:F Child# 3 Alphonse Lavoie Canada & Josephine Veseau NH
LAVOIE, Marie P Josephine, Oct 9 1922 Sex:F Child# 4 Auguste Lavoie Nashua, NH & Alma Beaulieu Canada
LAVOIE, Marie Pearl Theresa, Jan 15 1926 Sex:F Child# 14 Archile Lavoie Canada & Marie L Turcotte Canada
LAVOIE, Marie Rita Anna, Nov 24 1916 Sex:F Child# 8 Wilbrod Lavoie Canada & Philias Blais Canada
LAVOIE, Marie Rose, Jun 12 1900 Sex:F Child# 2 Octave Lavoie Canada & Armelia Dube Canada
LAVOIE, Marie Rose, Jun 16 1903 Sex:F Child# 6 Ludger Lavoie Canada & Caroline Robert NH
LAVOIE, Marie Rose D L, Dec 26 1910 Sex:F Child# 3 Charles Lavoie Canada & Eugenie Levesque Canada
LAVOIE, Marie Rose Eva, Oct 14 1904 Sex:F Child# 6 Octave Lavoie Canada & Amelia Dube Canada
LAVOIE, Marie Rose Jeannette, Mar 21 1911 Sex:F Child# 2 Joseph Lavoie Canada & Marie Bilodeau Canada
LAVOIE, Marie Terese Rita, Jun 3 1933 Sex:F Child# 2 Armand Lavoie Nashua, NH & M R Pelletier Nashua, NH
LAVOIE, Marie Therese Rachel, Dec 9 1912 Sex:F Child# 5 Charles Lavoie Canada & Eugenie Levesque Canada
LAVOIE, Marie Viviane, Apr 26 1908 Sex:F Child# 2 William Lavoie Canada & Regina Boulay Canada
LAVOIE, Marie Yvonne, Apr 2 1907 Sex:F Child# 2 Alphonse Lavoie Canada & Josephine Veseau NH
LAVOIE, Marie Yvonne A, Jul 26 1911 Sex:F Child# 4 Archille Lavoie Canada & Marie L Turcotte Canada
LAVOIE, Marie Yvonne L, Jun 2 1910 Sex:F Child# 3 Archille Lavoie Canada & Marie L Turcotte Canada
LAVOIE, Mary, Dec 27 1907 Sex:F Child# 1 Charles Lavoie Canada & Eugenie Levesque Canada Stillborn
LAVOIE, Mary Louise, Jun 16 1891 Sex:F Child# 10 H Lavoie Canada & Adele Salvail Canada
LAVOIE, Maurice, Aug 16 1928 Sex:M Child# 4 Thomas Lavoie Canada & Irene Rossignol Fall River, MA
LAVOIE, Maurice Gerald, May 27 1931 Sex:M Child# 1 Alcide Lavoie Canada & Annette Cote Lowell, MA
LAVOIE, Michel Real, Jul 2 1926 Sex:M Child# 2 Michel Lavoie Canada & Beatrice Lavoie Canada
LAVOIE, Monique Irene, Mar 17 1930 Sex:F Child# 4 George R Lavoie New Bedford, MA & Alice Noonan Nashua, NH
LAVOIE, Noreen Ann, Oct 15 1932 Sex:F Child# 3 Oscar J Lavoie Lawrence, MA & Blanche Bergeron Burlington, VT
LAVOIE, Normand Alfred, Jan 23 1931 Sex:M Child# 1 Alfred Lavoie Canada & Lillian Gagnon Nashua, NH
LAVOIE, Octave, Aug 28 1901 Sex:F Child# 3 Octave Lavoie Canada & Emelia Dube Canada
LAVOIE, Omer Victor, Feb 28 1930 Sex:M Child# 5 Michael Lavoie Canada & Beatrice Lavoie Canada
LAVOIE, Paul, Apr 17 1922 Sex:M Child# 2 Thomas Lavoie Canada & Irene Rossignol Fall River, MA
LAVOIE, Paul Albert Maurice, Mar 9 1923 Sex:M Child# 12 Achile Lavoie Canada & Marie L Turcotte Canada
LAVOIE, Paul Emile Richard, Sep 11 1915 Sex:M Child# 7 Wilbrod Lavoie Canada & Felia Blais Canada
LAVOIE, Paul Normand, Apr 11 1930 Sex:M Child# 8 Ludger Lavoie Canada & Alma Boucher Canada
LAVOIE, Pauline Jeanne L, Nov 23 1933 Sex:F Child# 2 Alfred Lavoie Canada & Lillian Gagnon Nashua, NH
LAVOIE, Pearl Eva Marie, Jan 2 1921 Sex:F Child# 4 Wilfred Lavoie Canada & Ermentine Sirois
LAVOIE, Pearl Louise, Jan 17 1919 Sex:F Child# 1 George R Lavoie New Bedford, MA & Alice L Noonan Nashua, NH
LAVOIE, Pearl Louise, Aug 12 1922 Sex:F Child# 1 (No Parents Listed)
LAVOIE, Priscilla Jacqueline, Jul 2 1930 Sex:F Child# 5 Thomas Lavoie Canada & Irene Rossignol Fall River, MA
LAVOIE, Raymond Edwin, Aug 15 1920 Sex:M Child# 1 Raymond E Lavoie Worcester, MA & Edith Bonia Nashua, NH
LAVOIE, Raymond Victor, Oct 28 1930 Sex:M Child# 2 Joseph Lavoie Canada & Olena Lavoie Nashua, NH
LAVOIE, Regina Louise, Mar 9 1898 Sex:F Child# 2 Joseph Lavoie Canada & Celina Guenette Canada
LAVOIE, Reginald Theodore, May 30 1910 Sex:M Child# 2 Olivier Lavoie Malone, NY & Anna Menard Canada
LAVOIE, Richard Ernest, Jul 8 1927 Sex:M Child# 10 George J Lavoie Nashua, NH & Annie Whitcher Pelham, NH
LAVOIE, Richard Raymond, Sep 3 1920 Sex:M Child# 2 George R Lavoie New Bedford, MA & Alice Louise Noonan Nashua, NH
LAVOIE, Rita Angela, Feb 28 1914 Sex:F Child# 3 Henry S Lavoie New York & Margaret O'Brien New York
LAVOIE, Robert Adrien, Nov 20 1932 Sex:M Child# 5 George B Lavoie New Bedford, NH & Alice L Noonan Nashua, NH
LAVOIE, Robert Paul, Aug 16 1923 Sex:M Child# 4 Joseph O Lavoie Nashua, NH & Emma Decelle Waukegan, CT
LAVOIE, Rochelle, Sep 14 1930 Sex:F Child# 6 Ernest Lavoie Nashua, NH & Jeanne Berube Canada
LAVOIE, Rodolphe Rene, Sep 12 1925 Sex:M Child# 1 Dozilva Lavoie Canada & Clair Cormier Canada
LAVOIE, Rolande, Nov 9 1934 Sex:F Child# 1 Ernest Lavoie Nashua, NH & Rachel Laquerre Nashua, NH
LAVOIE, Ronald William, Mar 11 1933 Sex:M Child# 1 Harry Jos Lavoie Leominster, MA & Ruby B Schofield Nashua, NH
LAVOIE, Rosanna Beatrice, Dec 27 1909 Sex:F Child# 5 William Lavoie Canada & Wildray Brien Canada
LAVOIE, Rose, Sep 22 1896 Sex:F Child# 3 Amable Lavoie Canada & Philomene Lavoie Canada
LAVOIE, Rose Aimee, Sep 2 1930 Sex:F Child# 1 Armand Lavoie Nashua, NH & Rose Pelletier Nashua, NH
LAVOIE, Rosette, Sep 30 1932 Sex:F Child# 6 Michael Lavoie Canada & Beatrice Lavoie Canada
LAVOIE, Samuel, Jun 23 1896 Sex:M Child# 1 Joseph Lavoie Canada & Celina Guenette Canada
LAVOIE, Simone Lucile, Jun 7 1914 Sex:F Child# 10 Octave Lavoie Canada & Amelia Dube Canada
LAVOIE, Simonne, Apr 13 1925 Sex:F Child# 1 Michael Lavoie Canada & Beatrice Lavoie Canada
LAVOIE, Therese Doris, Feb 24 1933 Sex:F Child# 6 Thomas Lavoie Canada & Irene Rossignoe Fall River, MA
LAVOIE, Therese Olivette, Nov 28 1919 Sex:F Child# 4 Ludger Lavoie Canada & Alma Boucher Canada
LAVOIE, Thomas, Nov 2 1897 Sex:M Child# 2 Auguste Lavoie Canada & Melina Dionne Canada
LAVOIE, Thomas Maurice, Sep 5 1921 Sex:M Child# 3 Auguste Lavoie NH & Alma Beaulieu Canada
LAVOIE, Ulderic, May 4 1900 Sex:M Child# 3 Joseph Lavoie Canada & Celina Guenette Canada
LAVOIE, Ulderic, Jun 18 1904 Sex:M Child# 4 Joseph Lavoie Canada & Celina Guenette Canada
LAVOIE, Unknown, Jun 17 1897 Sex:M Child# 10 Samuel Lavoie Canada & Georgianna Sirois Canada Stillborn
LAVOIE, Unknown, Oct 16 1900 Sex:M Child# 6 Amable Lavoie Canada & Phebe Lavoie Canada Stillborn
LAVOIE, Unknown, Oct 16 1900 Sex:M Child# 5 Amable Lavoie Canada & Phebe Lavoie Canada
LAVOIE, Unknown, Jan 29 1903 Sex:M Child# 1 William Lavoie Nashua, NH & Regina Bouley Nashua, NH Stillborn
LAVOIE, Unknown, Dec 22 1903 Sex:F Child# 2 William Lavoie Springfield, MA & Regina Bouley Nashua, NH Stillborn
LAVOIE, Unknown, Apr 12 1907 Sex: Child# 4 William Lavoie Springfield, MA & Regina Boulay Canada Stillborn
LAVOY, Lillian Florence, Mar 9 1917 Sex:F Child# 4 George Lavoy Nashua, NH & Anne Whitcher Pelham, NH
LAVVIE, Marie E A, Oct 7 1890 Sex:F Child# 8 Samuel Lavvie Canada & Georgiana Sirois Canada
LAW, George Brigham, Feb 15 1919 Sex:M Child# 1 Vernice W Law Nashua, NH & Rosalie Brigham Nashua, NH
LAW, May Ellen, Jul 29 1888 Sex:F Child# 3 John Law Ireland & Ellen Kavanaugh Ireland
LAW, Richard Bean, Oct 26 1922 Sex:M Child# 2 Vernice Law NH & Rosalie Brigham NH

LAW, Shirley Doris, Dec 4 1922 Sex:F Child# 3 William C Law Scotland & Emily Stabler England
LAW, Unknown, Apr 22 1889 Sex:F Child# 7 John B Law Scotland & Maggie Scotland
LAW, Unknown, Oct 23 1893 Sex:M Child# 2 George E Law Springfield, MA & Clara Bean Rutland, VT
LAWENGER, George, Aug 2 1891 Sex:M Child# 3 Anthony Lawenger Canada & Mary Morris Ireland
LAWLER, John, Jun 24 1909 Sex:M Child# 1 Frank Lawler Boston, MA & Mary J O'Neil Boston, MA
LAWRENCE, Addie M, Apr 28 1902 Sex:F Child# 1 Narcisse Lawrence Manchester, NH & M A McGovern Lawrence, MA
LAWRENCE, Alice P, Jul 20 1893 Sex:F Child# 2 Edw W Lawrence Mont Vernon, NH & Mabel L Putnam Wilton, NH
LAWRENCE, Barbara, Apr 3 1933 Sex:F Child# 2 Theo Lawrence Norwood, MA & Frances Kane Caldwell, OH
LAWRENCE, Benjamin, Nov 6 1888 Sex:M Child# 5 Charles Lawrence Manchester & Leonise Carron Canada
LAWRENCE, Ethel Margaret, Feb 18 1908 Sex:F Child# 5 James T Lawrence Cape Breton, NS & Margaret Thompson Ireland
LAWRENCE, Everett George, Mar 2 1892 Sex:M Child# 3 William F Lawrence Townsend, MA & Mary R Hitchings Ayer, MA
LAWRENCE, George, Jun 27 1932 Sex:M Child# 2 A Lawrence Lowell, MA & Cecile Pontbriand Nashua, NH
LAWRENCE, Grace Agnes, Nov 3 1927 Sex:F Child# 4 George Lawrence Westminster, VT & Alice Chamberlain Concord, NH
LAWRENCE, Harry Fletcher, Feb 24 1932 Sex:M Child# 1 H F Lawrence E Pepperell, MA & Ethelyn Watson White River
LAWRENCE, Hector Bt, Jan 20 1891 Sex:M Child# 7 Charles Lawrence Manchester, NH & Leonise Caron Canada
LAWRENCE, Irene Olivette, Oct 9 1921 Sex:F Child# 2 William Lawrence Nashua, NH & Laura Burrelle Nashua, NH
LAWRENCE, Kathleen Ellen, Mar 17 1932 Sex:F Child# 5 Ed H Lawrence Framingham, MA & Barbara Thompson Providence, RI
LAWRENCE, Kerby Harris, Mar 12 1890 Sex:M Child# 1 Charles E Lawrence Pepperell, MA & Grace E Harris Harrisville
LAWRENCE, Louise Frances, Nov 3 1914 Sex:F Child# 3 Edmond T Lawrence Ayer, MA & Fannie Walton Nashua, NH
LAWRENCE, Marie Emma, Feb 5 1887 Sex:F Child# 5 Charls Lawrence Manchester & Eleonise Caron P Q
LAWRENCE, Narcisse G, Jun 25 1904 Sex:M Child# 3 Narcisse G Lawrence Manchester, NH & May E McGovern Methuen, MA
LAWRENCE, Olive, Jul 6 1891 Sex:F Child# 3 Alfred Lawrence Manchester, NH & Annie O'Hern Pepperell, MA
LAWRENCE, P Eaton, Mar 7 1917 Sex:M Child# 4 Edmund T Lawrence Ayer, MA & Fannie Walton Nashua, NH
LAWRENCE, Paul George, Jan 15 1912 Sex:M Child# 3 George Lawrence Manchester, NH & Wilhelmina Soucy Nashua, NH
LAWRENCE, Phyllis Saville, Nov 27 1923 Sex:F Child# 2 C Wallace Lawrence Lawrence, MA & Della Saville Weymouth, MA
LAWRENCE, Rachel Wilhelmine, Aug 1 1906 Sex:F Child# 3 George Lawrence Manchester, NH & Wilhelmine Soucy Nashua
LAWRENCE, Richard Normand, Dec 25 1930 Sex:M Child# 1 Andrien Lawrence Lowell, MA & Cecile Pontbriand Nashua, NH
LAWRENCE, Richard Walton, Aug 13 1909 Sex:M Child# 1 Edmund T Lawrence Ayer, MA & Fannie Walton Nashua, NH
LAWRENCE, Roger William, Jan 19 1920 Sex:M Child# 1 Wm Doras Lawrence Nashua, NH & Laura Burelle Nashua, NH
LAWRENCE, Roscoe E, Jul 31 1890 Sex:M Child# 1 Fred R Lawrence NH & Minnie J Cummings MA
LAWRENCE, Ruth Celia, Sep 17 1899 Sex:F Child# 4 Frank W Lawrence Mass & Mary R Hitchins Mass
LAWRENCE, Unknown, Oct 14 1910 Sex:M Child# 2 Edmund T Lawrence Ayer, MA & Fannie Walton Nashua, NH
LAWRENCE, Virginia Ann, Aug 6 1929 Sex:F Child# 4 Fred Lawrence Hollis, NH & Clara Johnson Nashua, NH
LAWSON, Harry P, Mar 15 1907 Sex:M Child# 1 Harry Lawson Fitchburg, MA & Margaret Courtney Ireland
LAWSON, Martin Francis, Jun 5 1908 Sex:M Child# 2 Harry C Lawson Somerville, MA & Margaret Courtney Ireland
LAWSON, Victor, Feb 8 1890 Sex:M Child# 10 Napoleon Lawson Canada & Melina Quintal Canada
LAWTON, Annberta Estelle, Aug 4 1919 Sex:F Child# 4 Benjamin E Lawton Boston, MA & Lula Ford Milford, NH
LAZOTT, Harlow Albert, Feb 2 1920 Sex:M Child# 2 Harlow Lazott Nashua, NH & Gertrude Taylor Salisbury, MA
LAZOTT, Leona May, Jul 2 1902 Sex:F Child# 5 Charles E Lazott Sciota, NY & Julia Mayo Altoona, NY
LAZOTT, Marguerite V, Aug 27 1897 Sex:F Child# 4 Charles E Lazott Sciota, NY & Julia J Mayo Alton, NY
LAZOTT, Marie Elinore, Feb 26 1922 Sex:F Child# 3 Harlow E A Lazott Nashua, NH & Gertrude Taylor Salisbury, MA
LAZOTT, Wesley Edward, Aug 19 1918 Sex:M Child# 1 Harlow E A Lazott Nashua, NH & Gertrude Taylor Salisbury, MA
LEABY, Timothy M, Aug 29 1890 Sex:M Child# 3 Timothy Leaby Ireland & Mary McSweeney Ireland
LEACH, Alfred Hermon, Jun 5 1912 Sex:M Child# 2 Maurice H Leach Litchfield, NH & May Greenleaf Hudson, MA
LEACH, Arthur David, Jr, Sep 10 1930 Sex:M Child# 4 Arthur D Leach Litchfield, NH & Clara B Hare Burke, NY
LEACH, Classon White, Mar 10 1922 Sex:M Child# 4 Ernest C Leach Litchfield, NH & Lizzie McQuesten Litchfield, NH
LEACH, Elizabeth, May 6 1921 Sex:F Child# 4 Maurice Leach Nashua, NH & May Greenleaf Hudson, MA
LEACH, Ellen Elaine, Dec 22 1917 Sex:F Child# 1 Harmon E Leach Litchfield, NH & Edith Stewart Moncton, NB
LEACH, Elton Kenneth, Apr 3 1915 Sex:M Child# 3 Maurice H Leach Litchfield, NH & May J Greenleaf Hudson, MA
LEACH, Joan Josephine, Dec 30 1933 Sex:F Child# 1 Alfred Leach Nashua, NH & Cora Morrissette Nashua, NH
LEACH, Richard Curtis, Aug 11 1916 Sex:M Child# 3 Clinton E Leach Litchfield, NH & Lizzie McQuesten Litchfield, NH
LEACH, Susan Helen, Aug 3 1934 Sex:F Child# 10 Ralph A Leach New Boston, NH & Helen Houghton New Boston, NH
LEAHY, Unknown, May 7 1899 Sex:M Child# 1 William C Leahy Hollis, NH & Nellie L Callahan Southboro, MA
LEANNEAUX, I S Blanche, Oct 19 1889 Sex:F Child# 2 George LeAnneaux Nashua, NH & Victorie Lesequie Canada
LEAOR, Harold Charles, Jul 29 1934 Sex:M Child# 1 Harry Leaor Nashua, NH & Marilda Fanfield Wilton, NH
LEAOR, Harry, Sep 12 1905 Sex:M Child# 2 Charles Leaor Sherbrook, PQ & Ethel Rich Munroe, ME
LEAOR, Mary Jane, Jan 14 1930 Sex:F Child# 1 Carl Leaor Meredith, NH & Lillian Martin New Bedford, MA
LEAOR, Mary Theresa Arleene, Dec 14 1934 Sex:F Child# 3 Carl Leaor NH & Lillian Martin Mass
LEAOR, Rachel Rita, Feb 26 1935 Sex:F Child# 2 Walter Leaor Nashua, NH & Rose Larouche Nashua, NH
LEAOR, Unknown, May 31 1889 Sex:M Child# 6 Ezra Leaor Canada & Maggie New York
LEAOR, Walter Gerard, Oct 31 1933 Sex:M Child# 1 Walter Leaor US & Rose Larouche Nashua, NH
LEAOR, Walter Howard, Jul 18 1900 Sex:M Child# 1 Charles Leaor NY & Ethel Riche Maine
LEAOSR, Joseph Carl, Jul 21 1933 Sex:M Child# 2 Carl Leaosr Meredith, NH & Lillian Martin New Bedford, MA
LEAR, Elizabeth Margaret, Jun 26 1923 Sex:F Child# 3 Charles L Lear W Chazy, NY & Esther Shenton Malden, MA
LEAR, Gladys Esther, Jul 30 1913 Sex:F Child# 1 Charles L Lear W Chazy, NY & Esther E Shenton Malden, MA
LEAR, Margery Elton, Apr 25 1918 Sex:F Child# 2 Charles L Lear W Chazy, NY & Esther Shenton Malden, MA
LEARD, Alice Leona, Feb 23 1913 Sex:F Child# 2 W A Leard Derry, NH & Helen Simonds Nashua, NH
LEARD, Camille Julia, Jul 29 1920 Sex:F Child# 1 Joseph Leard US & Julia Hudon Canada
LEARD, Claire Esther, Jun 7 1905 Sex:F Child# 1 John William H Leard Rockland, ME & Lillian A Rock Nashua, NH
LEARD, David Archie, Dec 29 1922 Sex:M Child# 7 Wallace Leard Nashua, NH & Helen Simonds Nashua, NH
LEARD, Florence Clarabel, Dec 1 1919 Sex:F Child# 6 Wallace Leard Derry, NH & Florence Simmonds Nashua, NH
LEARD, Frank Dayson, Mar 15 1907 Sex:M Child# 1 Dayson H Leard Derry, NH & Amanda Schofield Nova Scotia
LEARD, Frank Dayson, Oct 16 1929 Sex:M Child# 3 Frank Leard Nashua, NH & Gertrude Goodale Boston, MA

LEARD, Frank Dayson, Jr, Sep 19 1928 Sex:M Child# 2 F D Leard Nashua, NH & Gertrude Goodale Boston, MA
LEARD, Helen Priscilla, Feb 1 1932 Sex:F Child# Wallace Leard Derry, NH & Helen Symond Nashua, NH
LEARD, Kenneth Burton, Oct 1 1933 Sex:M Child# 4 Frank Leard Nashua, NH & G Goodearl Boston, MA
LEARD, Lucille Bernice, Jun 25 1927 Sex:F Child# 7 William Leard Nashua, NH & Helen Simons Nashua, NH
LEARD, Norma Elizabeth, Jul 3 1934 Sex:F Child# 4 Earl Leard S Acton, MA & Dorothy Dow Laconia, NH
LEARD, Percy William, Oct 15 1917 Sex:M Child# 4 Wallace Leard NH & Helen Colburn Nashua, NH
LEARD, Richard Edwin, Oct 9 1931 Sex:M Child# 7 Frank Leard Nashua, NH & Gertrude Goodearl Bath, ME
LEARD, Ruby, May 21 1908 Sex:F Child# 2 Dayson H Leard Derry, NH & Amanda Schofield Nova Scotia
LEARD, U Byrle, Apr 19 1914 Sex:F Child# 3 Wallace A Leard NH & Helen Colburn Nashua, NH
LEARY, Barbara Jean, Oct 26 1927 Sex:F Child# 1 Wilfrid Leary Pepperell, MA & Irene Salter Pepperell, MA
LEARY, Evelyn Irene, May 23 1930 Sex:F Child# 1 Henry Leary Pepperell, MA & Mildred Lund Hollis, NH
LEARY, James Francis, Dec 11 1933 Sex:M Child# 1 James F Leary Pepperell, MA & Helen Shepard Canada
LEARY, Janet Lucille, Apr 17 1932 Sex:F Child# 2 Wilfred E Leary Pepperell, MA & Irene Salter Pepperell, MA
LEARY, Maureen Jessie, Jun 11 1935 Sex:F Child# 3 Henry Leary E Pepperell, MA & Mildred Lund Hollis, NH
LEARY, Thomas Henry, Aug 2 1933 Sex:M Child# 2 Henry Leary Pepperell, MA & Mildred Lund Hollis, NH
LEAUDON, Unknown, Jul 23 1888 Sex:F Child# 3 James F Leaudon Canada & Mary R Bellett Canada
LEAVITT, George Alfred, Jan 4 1919 Sex:M Child# 1 Edward Leavitt Enfield, NH & Anna DeMontigny Nashua, NH
LEAVITT, Unknown, Sep 28 1914 Sex:M Child# 1 George C Leavitt Norway, ME & Blanche Rhodes Centralia, PA
LEAVITTE, Paul Eugene, Jan 30 1921 Sex:M Child# 2 Edward Leavitte Enfield, NH & Anna R DeMontigny Nashua, NH
LEAZOTT, Lucy Eleanor, Mar 11 1895 Sex:F Child# 2 Charles E Leazott Sciota, NY & Julia Mayo Altona, NY
LEAZOTT, Ralph W, Aug 16 1894 Sex:M Child# 1 Victor N Leazott Sciota, NY & Helen McSorley Woodstock, NB
LEAZOTTE, Bertha, Oct 2 1912 Sex:F Child# 7 Henry F Leazotte New York & Laura R Blain New York Stillborn
LEAZOTTE, Carroll Bertrand, Sep 6 1908 Sex:M Child# 1 Joseph E Leazotte Clinton Co, NY & Edna M Colburn Nashua, NH
LEAZOTTE, Charles W, Mar 12 1902 Sex:M Child# 3 Benn Leazotte NY & Lena Abare NY
LEAZOTTE, Eunice Elvira, Dec 21 1897 Sex:F Child# 2 Victor Leazotte NY & Lena Henry
LEAZOTTE, Eva May, Aug 31 1910 Sex:F Child# 4 Edmond Leazotte US & Edna M Colburn US
LEAZOTTE, Florence Ruth, Apr 28 1902 Sex:F Child# 1 E E Leazotte NY & Viola Keith Vermont
LEAZOTTE, Harlon E A, Sep 6 1893 Sex:M Child# 1 Charles Leazotte Sciota, NY & Julia J Mayo Sciota, NY
LEAZOTTE, Henry Frank, Jul 8 1906 Sex:M Child# 4 Henry F Leazotte US & Laura Blain US
LEAZOTTE, Irene Pearl, Feb 3 1904 Sex:F Child# 3 Henry F Leazotte US & Laura Blain Sciota, NY
LEAZOTTE, Joseph Demetrius, Aug 12 1898 Sex:M Child# 1 Alfred Leazotte Canada & Cemida Levesque Canada
LEAZOTTE, Joseph H L, Oct 15 1894 Sex:M Child# 7 William Leazotte Canada & Agnes Dionne Canada
LEAZOTTE, Joseph L A, Feb 27 1891 Sex:M Child# 5 William Leazotte Canada & Agnes Dionne Canada
LEAZOTTE, Laura Stella, Dec 24 1916 Sex:F Child# 9 Henry F Leazotte Sciota, NY & Laura Blain Sciota, NY
LEAZOTTE, Lemual Edward, Nov 14 1908 Sex:M Child# 5 Henry Leazotte US & Laura Blain US
LEAZOTTE, M Louise I, Sep 7 1892 Sex:F Child# 5 William Leazotte Canada & Agnes Dionne Canada
LEAZOTTE, Mary Yvonne, Oct 26 1906 Sex:F Child# 6 Charles E Leazotte Sciota, NY & Julia J Mayo Altoona, NY
LEAZOTTE, Mortimer Lorenzo, Mar 14 1910 Sex:M Child# 6 Henry Leazotte US & Laura Blain US
LEAZOTTE, Otis Henry, Dec 23 1898 Sex:M Child# 1 Henry Leazotte Sciota, NY & Laura Blain Sciota, NY
LEAZOTTE, Shirley Amelia, Nov 7 1913 Sex:F Child# 8 Henry P Leazotte Sciota, NY & Laura R Blain Sciota, NY
LEAZOTTE, Unknown, Sep 12 1888 Sex:M Child# 3 James F Leazotte New York & Luide S Clark New York
LEAZOTTE, Unknown, Sep 10 1895 Sex:M Child# 1 Bert Leazotte Sciota, NY & Sarah Charbonneau Sciota, NY
LEAZOTTE, Unknown, Nov 10 1907 Sex:M Child# 7 Charles E Leazotte Sciota, NY & Julia Mayo Sciota, NY Stillborn
LEBEDNICK, John Bruce, Nov 20 1933 Sex:M Child# 1 John A Labednick Nashua, NH & Erma Colby Rochester, NY Stillborn
LEBEDNIK, John, Sep 29 1908 Sex:M Child# 4 Andrew Lebednik Russia & Elan Mekriopute Russia
LEBEL, Euclide Roger, Oct 30 1933 Sex:M Child# 1 Euclide Lebel St Pascal, Quebec & Edna Soucy St Basil, NB
LEBEL, Gerard, Apr 14 1917 Sex:M Child# 8 Francois Lebel Canada & Praxede Levesque Canada
LEBEL, J Florian Lerard, Sep 25 1911 Sex:M Child# 7 Pierre Lebel Canada & Albrtn Bellefeuille Canada
LEBEL, Joseph Alfred, Feb 26 1893 Sex:M Child# 1 Joseph Lebel Canada & Marie Peltier Canada
LEBEL, Joseph Leo R, May 30 1905 Sex:M Child# 1 Francois Lebel Canada & Proxede Levesque Canada
LEBEL, Joseph Willie L, Jul 26 1909 Sex:M Child# 4 Francois Lebel Canada & Praxede Levesque Canada
LEBEL, Liliane, Jan 21 1910 Sex:F Child# 1 Joseph Lebel Canada & Marie Lafrance Canada
LEBEL, M Adele Lucienne, Jan 7 1912 Sex:F Child# 5 Francois Lebel Canada & Praxide Levesque Canada
LEBEL, M Claire Ita Simone, Sep 19 1913 Sex:F Child# 6 Francois Lebel Canada & Praxede Levesque Canada
LEBEL, M Jeanne Odile, Jan 10 1915 Sex:F Child# 7 Francois Lebel Canada & Proxede Levesque Canada
LEBEL, Marie Irma I, Jun 24 1910 Sex:F Child# 6 Pierre Lebel Canada & Albrtn Bellefeuille Canada
LEBEL, Marie Jeanne Bertha, May 24 1927 Sex:F Child# 1 Armand Lebel Canada & L LaRocque Lewiston, ME
LEBEL, Marie Rose A Y, Jan 5 1908 Sex:F Child# 3 Francois Lebel Canada & Praxede Levesque Canada
LEBEL, Roland, Apr 15 1911 Sex:M Child# 1 George Lebel Canada & Evangeline Marion Canada
LEBELLE, Jean Louis, Mar 6 1891 Sex:M Child# 5 Joseph Lebelle Canada & Josephine Gauthier Canada
LEBELLE, Nazaire Amedee, Mar 21 1893 Sex:M Child# 6 Joseph Lebelle Canada & Josephine Gauthier Canada
LEBELLE, Unknown, Aug 23 1890 Sex:M Child# 5 Edward Lebelle Canada & Emelie Dumour Canada Stillborn
LEBENDEUKE, William, Feb 14 1902 Sex:M Child# Andrew Lebendeuke Russia & Ellen Meplonptu Russia
LEBENNETT, Joseph, Apr 16 1920 Sex:M Child# 2 Peter Lebennett Lithuania Russia & Regina Blanchette Lowell, MA
LEBLANC, Albert Lionel, Aug 8 1920 Sex:M Child# 6 Arthur Leblanc US & Alice Morrisette US
LEBLANC, Albina, Dec 10 1889 Sex:F Child# 5 Leon M Leblanc Canada & Virginie Pepin Canada
LEBLANC, Alfred D, Nov 19 1887 Sex:M Child# Arthur Leblanc P Q & M DeMontigny Canada
LEBLANC, Almard Jean Philip, Feb 27 1925 Sex:M Child# 2 Philip Leblanc Canada & Ivon Bujold Canada
LEBLANC, Anna Diana, Apr 4 1893 Sex:F Child# 5 J B Leblanc Canada & Adeline Houde Canada
LEBLANC, Arthur Ernest, Aug 28 1898 Sex:M Child# 3 John Leblanc Canada & Emerentienne Tvon Canada
LEBLANC, Arthur Robert, Jan 18 1912 Sex:M Child# 1 Arthur Leblanc US & Alice Morisette US
LEBLANC, Arthur Wilfrid, Mar 11 1902 Sex:M Child# 7 J B Leblanc Canada & Aurelle Houde Canada
LEBLANC, Aurore, Sep 3 1890 Sex:F Child# 2 Arthur Leblanc Canada & Mary de Montigney Canada

LEBLANC, Aurore, Mar 3 1896 Sex:F Child# 5 Napoleon Leblanc Canada & Elise Dumont Canada
LEBLANC, Aurore Carmon, Apr 19 1925 Sex:F Child# 2 Albert Leblanc Canada & Corrine Marcoux Berlin, NH
LEBLANC, Aurore Emma, Mar 29 1893 Sex:F Child# 5 Arthur Leblanc Canada & Marie L Demontigny Canada
LEBLANC, Aurore Theresa, Apr 20 1929 Sex:F Child# 4 Albert Leblanc Canada & Asterie Marcoux Canada
LEBLANC, Beatrice Agnes, Jul 7 1909 Sex:F Child# 2 John Leblanc Nashua, NH & Regina Lefebvre Nashua, NH
LEBLANC, Beatrice Marie G, Aug 7 1918 Sex:F Child# 1 Dolard Leblanc Canada & Barbara Wurtelle Canada
LEBLANC, Blanche, Jul 15 1893 Sex:F Child# 1 Sylva Leblanc Canada & Caroline Belanger US
LEBLANC, Blanche Eva, Oct 29 1890 Sex:F Child# 3 J B Leblanc Canada & Adeline Houde Canada
LEBLANC, Blanche Jeannette, May 15 1922 Sex:F Child# 2 J B Leblanc Canada & Bertha Bellavance Canada
LEBLANC, Blanche Yvonne, Oct 15 1900 Sex:M Child# 4 John Leblanc Canada & Emerancienne Yvon Canada
LEBLANC, Camille Cecile, Apr 18 1921 Sex:F Child# 4 Antonio Leblanc Canada & Eva Gagnon Nashua, NH
LEBLANC, Cecilia Ironne, Aug 25 1894 Sex:F Child# 4 Napoleon Leblanc Canada & Elise Dumont Canada
LEBLANC, Claire Lillian, Sep 4 1921 Sex:F Child# 7 Arthur Leblanc Nashua, NH & Alice Morrissette Nashua, NH
LEBLANC, Clarence Edward, Mar 21 1920 Sex:M Child# 3 Edward A LeBlanc Warren, NY & B E Vandondoigne Peoria, IL
LEBLANC, Corade Honore, Sep 3 1917 Sex:M Child# 2 Amedee Leblanc NH & Corinne Plante NH
LEBLANC, Dorothy Irene, Nov 29 1932 Sex:F Child# 1 Robert Leblanc Nashua, NH & Eliz McNulty Hartford, CT
LEBLANC, Edgar John, Dec 11 1926 Sex:M Child# 3 John Leblanc Canada & Lea Plouffe Nashua, NH
LEBLANC, Edgar Romeo Girard, Dec 3 1925 Sex:M Child# 3 Louis H Leblanc Fair Haven, NY & Eva Bibeau Hollis, NH
LEBLANC, Edward S, Aug 26 1897 Sex:M Child# 2 John S Leblanc Farnham, PQ & Emerenciena Hiron Canada
LEBLANC, Ernest Arthur, Mar 6 1929 Sex:M Child# 1 Ernest A LeBlanc Nashua, NH & Helen Kashulines Nashua, NH
LEBLANC, Eva Edna, Jan 27 1913 Sex:F Child# 2 Arthur Leblanc US & Alice Morissette US
LEBLANC, Eva Louise, Jan 19 1908 Sex:F Child# 1 John Leblanc Nashua, NH & Regina Lefebvre Nashua, NH
LEBLANC, Felix Fortunat, Feb 21 1909 Sex:M Child# 2 Pierre Leblanc, Jr Nashua, NH & Clara St Onge Nashua, NH
LEBLANC, Florence Bertha, Nov 27 1925 Sex:F Child# 7 Antonio Leblanc Canada & Eva Gagnon Nashua, NH
LEBLANC, Florida Corona, Oct 9 1906 Sex:F Child# 1 Henri Leblanc Canada & Celanire Lavalle Canada
LEBLANC, Freddier Elector, Apr 1 1891 Sex:M Child# 1 Napoleon Leblanc Canada & Elise Dumont Canada
LEBLANC, Geneva Lorette, Feb 23 1933 Sex:F Child# Alfred Leblanc Canada & Althea Marcoux Canada
LEBLANC, George Ozias, Jul 22 1894 Sex:M Child# 6 Arthur Leblanc Canada & Mary D Montigny Canada
LEBLANC, Henrietta Bertha, Aug 19 1925 Sex:F Child# 5 Dolar LeBlanc Canada & Barbara Wartell Canada
LEBLANC, J Alphonse Wilfred, Mar 10 1913 Sex:M Child# 11 Joseph Leblanc Canada & Marie L Page Canada
LEBLANC, Jean Edmond, Dec 21 1919 Sex:M Child# 2 Adelard Leblanc Canada & Barbara Wartell Canada
LEBLANC, Jeanne, May 16 1924 Sex:F Child# 6 Antonio Leblanc Canada & Eva Gagnon Nashua, NH Stillborn
LEBLANC, Jeanne Lucille, Jan 26 1921 Sex:F Child# 3 Dollard Leblanc Canada & Barbarar Wartell Canada
LEBLANC, Jeanne Rita, Mar 28 1928 Sex:F Child# 8 Antoinia Leblanc Canada & Eva Gagnon Nashua, NH
LEBLANC, Jos Wilfrid Maurice, Sep 4 1928 Sex:M Child# 6 Jean B Leblanc Canada & Bertha Bellavance Canada
LEBLANC, Joseph Aime Roger, Feb 12 1924 Sex:M Child# 2 Henry Leblanc Canada & Eva Bebeau NH
LEBLANC, Joseph Alfred, May 16 1892 Sex:M Child# 2 Napoleon Leblanc Canada & Elise Dumont Canada
LEBLANC, Joseph Armand, Nov 2 1894 Sex:M Child# 2 Silva Leblanc Canada & Caroline Belanger Exeter, NH
LEBLANC, Joseph Arthur Wilfre, Feb 6 1925 Sex:M Child# 4 J B LeBlanc Canada & Bertha Bellavance Canada
LEBLANC, Joseph Avila, Jul 26 1895 Sex:M Child# 5 J B Leblanc Canada & Adeline Houde Canada
LEBLANC, Joseph Frederick A, May 10 1907 Sex:M Child# 1 Pierre Leblanc, Jr NH & Clara St Onge Canada
LEBLANC, Joseph G J B, Dec 5 1897 Sex:M Child# 5 Joseph Leblanc Canada & Mina Landry Canada
LEBLANC, Joseph Georges, Feb 22 1897 Sex:M Child# 6 J B Leblanc Canada & Adeline Houde Canada
LEBLANC, Joseph Henri, Jan 31 1898 Sex:M Child# 2 Francois Leblanc Canada & Clementine Mercier Canada
LEBLANC, Joseph Leo Armand, Jun 20 1922 Sex:M Child# 1 Henry Leblanc Canada & Eva Bibeau NH
LEBLANC, Joseph Omer Am'ee, Nov 6 1901 Sex:M Child# 6 Napoleon Leblanc Canada & Elsie Dumont Canada
LEBLANC, Joseph Paul William, Mar 7 1924 Sex:M Child# 1 Ovila Leblanc Nashua, NH & Irene Galipeau Nashua, NH
LEBLANC, Joseph Wilfred, Jan 10 1892 Sex:M Child# 4 Arthur Leblanc Canada & Mary Demontigny Canada
LEBLANC, Josephine Florette, Apr 27 1920 Sex:F Child# 1 Frederick Leblanc New York & Aurore Paul Nashua, NH
LEBLANC, Jules N H, Nov 18 1896 Sex:M Child# 7 Arthur Leblanc Canada & Marie Demontigny Canada
LEBLANC, Lea, Mar 9 1887 Sex:F Child# John Leblanc P Q & Vriginie Pepin P Q
LEBLANC, Lea Olivette, Jul 15 1910 Sex:F Child# 3 Pierre Leblanc Nashua, NH & Clara St Onge Nashua, NH
LEBLANC, Leopold Girard, Feb 19 1916 Sex:M Child# 3 Arthur Leblanc US & Alice Morissette US
LEBLANC, Lorraine Albina, Nov 23 1924 Sex:F Child# 1 Edward LeBlanc Nashua, NH & Albina Labrecque Nashua, NH
LEBLANC, Louis Honore, Apr 14 1892 Sex:M Child# 6 Jean M Leblanc Canada & Virginie Pepin Canada
LEBLANC, Lucien Julien, Jan 27 1918 Sex:M Child# 2 Antonio Leblanc Canada & Eva Gagnon Nashua, NH
LEBLANC, M R Blanche, Oct 6 1923 Sex:F Child# 3 J B Leblanc Canada & Bertha Bellavance Canada
LEBLANC, Maria Florida, May 11 1893 Sex:F Child# 1 Joseph Leblanc Canada & Delia Allard Canada
LEBLANC, Marie, Sep 8 1893 Sex:F Child# 1 William Leblanc Canada & M Louise Mercier Canada
LEBLANC, Marie, Jul 18 1914 Sex:F Child# 12 Joseph Leblanc Canada & Marie Luce Canada Stillborn
LEBLANC, Marie, Oct 31 1916 Sex:F Child# 1 Antonio Leblanc Canada & Eva Gagnon Nashua, NH Stillborn
LEBLANC, Marie Blanche C, May 10 1901 Sex:F Child# 7 Joseph Leblanc Canada & Lumina Landry Canada
LEBLANC, Marie Blanche Irene, Feb 12 1919 Sex:F Child# 2 Amedee Leblanc NH & Corinne Plante NH
LEBLANC, Marie Blanche M, Dec 12 1903 Sex:F Child# 5 John S Leblanc Canada & Emerencienne Yvon Canada
LEBLANC, Marie C A, Feb 26 1888 Sex:F Child# 3 Pierrie Leblanc P Q & Alphonsine Bienvena P Q
LEBLANC, Marie Cecile, Jan 9 1928 Sex:F Child# 1 Honore Leblanc Canada & Alice Theriault Nashua, NH
LEBLANC, Marie Elise, Jun 21 1893 Sex:F Child# 3 Napoleon Leblanc Canada & Elise Dumont Canada
LEBLANC, Marie Jeanne Irene, Apr 17 1929 Sex:F Child# 3 Philip Leblanc Canada & Yvonne Bujold Canada
LEBLANC, Marie Justine C, Apr 4 1906 Sex:F Child# 3 William Leblanc Newburyport, MA & Clarinda Fournier Canada
LEBLANC, Marie Lillienne Eva, Apr 19 1907 Sex:F Child# 6 John S Leblanc Canada & Emerencienne Yvon Canada
LEBLANC, Marie Rose Eva, Oct 21 1909 Sex:F Child# 10 Joseph LeBlanc Canada & Marie L Page Canada
LEBLANC, Marie Yvette Loretta, Feb 9 1929 Sex:F Child# 4 Louis H Leblanc Canada & Eva Bibeau Nashua, NH
LEBLANC, Marie Yvonne Dorothy, Jul 20 1924 Sex:F Child# 8 Arthur Leblanc US & Alice Morrissette US

LEBLANC, Mary Rose Flora, Apr 20 1896 Sex:F Child# 1 J S Leblanc Canada & Merentine Hivon Santon, Canada
LEBLANC, Norman Ephrem, Mar 8 1917 Sex:M Child# 4 Arthur Leblanc US & Alice Morrissette US
LEBLANC, Olena Lorraine, Apr 8 1919 Sex:F Child# 5 Arthur Leblanc US & Alice Morrissette US
LEBLANC, Olivette, Jun 28 1919 Sex:F Child# 3 Antonio Leblanc Canada & Eva Gagnon Nashua, NH
LEBLANC, Pauline, Dec 25 1935 Sex:F Child# 5 Louis H LeBlanc Canada & Eva Bibeau Nashua, NH
LEBLANC, Regina, Aug 8 1889 Sex:F Child# 2 Arthur Leblanc Canada & Mariede Montyguy Canada
LEBLANC, Regina Lea, Sep 15 1925 Sex:F Child# 4 Amedee Leblanc Nashua, NH & Corinne Plante Nashua, NH
LEBLANC, Robert George, Oct 28 1930 Sex:M Child# 3 John S Leblanc Canada & Lea Plouf Nashua, NH
LEBLANC, Robert Normand, Apr 11 1923 Sex:M Child# 5 Antonio Leblanc Canada & Eva Gagnon Nashua, NH
LEBLANC, Royal Raymond, Sep 3 1917 Sex:M Child# 1 Amedee Leblanc NH & Corinne Plante NH
LEBLANC, T Jeanne d'Arc, Mar 4 1921 Sex:F Child# 1 J B Leblanc Canada & Bertha Bellavance Canada
LEBLANC, Therese, Dec 17 1934 Sex:F Child# 3 Honore Leblanc Canada & Alice Theriault Nashua, NH
LEBLANC, Unknown, Apr 24 1887 Sex:F Child#  Herbert Leblanc P Q & Odile Logasse P Q Stillborn
LEBLANC, Unknown, Jun 5 1896 Sex:M Child# 1 Frank Leblanc Canada & Clementine Mercier Canada
LEBLANC, Unknown, Jun 5 1896 Sex:M Child# 1 Frank Leblanc Canada & Clementine Mercier Canada
LEBLOND, Jos Paul Emile, Feb 17 1926 Sex:M Child# 1 Emile Leblond Canada & Alice Belanger Canada
LEBLOND, Marie Cecile Elizabe, Nov 12 1928 Sex:F Child# 2 Emile Leblond Canada & Alice Belanger Canada
LEBLOND, Marie M Therese, Dec 30 1931 Sex:F Child# 3 Emile Leblond Ole D'Orleans, PQ & Alice Belanger Canada
LEBOEUF, Gerard, Jun 9 1925 Sex:M Child# 3 Louis LeBoeuf Tupper Lake, NY & Alma Dubois Nashua, NH
LEBOEUF, Rita, Jun 16 1920 Sex:F Child# 1 Louis LeBoeuf Tupper Lake, NY & Alma Dubois Nashua, NH
LEBOEUF, Theresa Imelda, Apr 14 1928 Sex:F Child# 2 Louis LeBoeuf New York & Alma Dubois Nashua, NH
LEBOEUF, Theresa Yvonne, Jan 2 1923 Sex:F Child# 1 Louis A LeBoeuf Hudson, NH & Alma Dubois Nashua, NH
LEBRACHE, Unknown, Mar 4 1890 Sex: Child# 1 Joseph Lebrache St John, NB & Lydia Horn Suncook, NH
LEBRANCHE, Jeanne Gratia, Apr 4 1906 Sex:F Child# 4 George Lebranche Canada & Anna Lavalle Canada
LEBRANCHE, Leopold, Jan 1 1932 Sex:M Child# 3 Honore Lebranche Canada & Alice Theriault Nashua, NH
LEBRECQUE, Marie, Oct 24 1893 Sex:F Child# 16 Albert Lebrecque Canada & Alvina Fontaine Canada
LEBRUN, Ferdinand Lucien, Jul 7 1916 Sex:M Child# 2 Louis Lebrun Canada & Lydia Jean Canada
LEBRUN, Francois G E, Jun 21 1890 Sex:M Child# 1 Francois H Lebrun Canada & Anna Goyett Canada
LEBRUN, Helena Camilia, Jul 19 1930 Sex:F Child# 7 Paul Lebrun Canada & Josephine Theriault Canada
LEBRUN, Jos J Bte Normand, Jul 1 1928 Sex:M Child# 2 Luke Lebrun Canada & R A Malenfant Canada
LEBRUN, Joseph, Jul 14 1917 Sex:M Child# 3 Louis Lebrun Canada & Lydia Jean Rockport, MA
LEBRUN, Joseph Gerard, May 14 1928 Sex:M Child# 4 Theophile Lebrun Canada & Delima Deschesnes Canada
LEBRUN, Joseph Louis Emile, Jan 10 1908 Sex:M Child# 1 Emile Lebrun Canada & Josephine Theriault Canada
LEBRUN, Lorette, Mar 24 1934 Sex:F Child# 8 Theophile Lebrun Canada & Delina Deschenes Canada
LEBRUN, Louisette, Mar 24 1934 Sex:F Child# 7 Theophile Lebrun Canada & Delina Deschenes Canada
LEBRUN, M An Jeanne d'Arc, Jan 2 1915 Sex:F Child# 1 Louis Lebrun Canada & Leda Jean Canada
LEBRUN, Maria Rita Fernande, Aug 25 1919 Sex:F Child# 4 Louis Lebrun Canada & Leda Jean Rockport, MA
LEBRUN, Marie Ange Lilianne, Aug 31 1920 Sex:F Child# 4 Louis Lebrun Canada & Leda Jean Rockport, MA
LEBRUN, Marie Martha Yolande, Aug 18 1923 Sex:F Child# 6 Louis LeBrun Canada & Leda Jean Rockport, MA
LEBRUN, Marie Regina Gilbert, Jan 30 1928 Sex:F Child# 6 Paul Lebrun Canada & Jose Theriault Canada
LECARE, Joseph, Oct 10 1893 Sex:M Child# 15 Teleshore Lecare Canada & Georgianna Beaudette Canada
LECERC, Amede Roland, Sep 16 1927 Sex:M Child# 5 Antoin Lecerc Canada & Dorilla Laroche Canada
LECHARTIER, Joseph, Dec 15 1909 Sex:M Child# 1 Adelard LeChartier Canada & Josephine Landry Canada Stillborn
LECLAIR, Alphonse, Mar 6 1927 Sex:M Child# 6 Frank Leclair Sherbrooke, Canada & Bessie Wheeler Nova Scotia
LECLAIR, Armand Osias, Jun 10 1907 Sex:M Child# 3 Epiphane Leclair Canada & Maria Lasalle Canada
LECLAIR, Conrad Romeo, Dec 31 1907 Sex:M Child# 11 Denis Leclair Canada & Clara Roy Canada
LECLAIR, Daniel Edward, Jun 5 1933 Sex:M Child# 3 (No Parents Listed)
LECLAIR, Edna I Beatrice, Feb 14 1922 Sex:F Child# 3 Theophile Leclair Canada & Lea Dumont Nashua, NH
LECLAIR, Francis A, Jul 2 1891 Sex:M Child# 4 Anseline Leclair Canada & Mathilda Lepage Canada
LECLAIR, George, May 11 1906 Sex:M Child# 2 Epiphane Leclair Canada & Maria Lasalle Canada
LECLAIR, Jos Edmond Maurice, May 4 1925 Sex:M Child# 4 Antonio Leclair Canada & Dorilla Laroche Canada
LECLAIR, Joseph Robert, Apr 17 1912 Sex:M Child# 6 Epiphane Leclair Canada & Maria Lasalle Canada
LECLAIR, Leo Ronald, Sep 3 1934 Sex:M Child# 8 Antonio Leclair Canada & Dorila Laroche Canada
LECLAIR, Lillian, Oct 24 1914 Sex:F Child# 5 Francis Leclair New York & Celina Grandmaison Nashua, NH
LECLAIR, Marie Alice, Dec 23 1900 Sex:F Child# 9 Ansemie Leclair Canada & M Lepage Canada
LECLAIR, Marie Cecile Laurett, Apr 19 1929 Sex:F Child# 1 William Leclair Nashua, NH & Albina Bechard Canada
LECLAIR, Marie Delina Rose, Sep 15 1918 Sex:F Child# 2 Joseph Leclair Nashua, NH & Delina Landry Nashua, NH
LECLAIR, Marie Irene, Feb 21 1901 Sex:F Child# 1 Georges Leclair Mass & Albina Gervais Canada
LECLAIR, Marie Lina J, Aug 10 1905 Sex:F Child# 5 Joseph Leclair Canada & Hermine Dube Canada
LECLAIR, Marie Madeline G, Oct 31 1933 Sex:F Child# 2 J W Leclair Nashua, NH & Albina Bechard St Pascal, PQ
LECLAIR, Mary Rita, Oct 30 1928 Sex:F Child# 8 Frank Leclair Canada & Bessie Whalen Nova Scotia
LECLAIR, Maud Etheline, Sep 10 1903 Sex:F Child# 15 Peter Leclair NY & Elizabeth Blair NY
LECLAIR, Oscar Simon, Jun 27 1929 Sex:M Child# 6 Antoine Leclair Canada & Dorilla Laroche Canada
LECLAIR, Raymond Ludger, Aug 3 1932 Sex:M Child# 1 Ludger Leclair Canada & Ida Martin Salem, MA
LECLAIR, Rita Colette, Jan 24 1919 Sex:F Child# 2 Jos Theo Leclair Canada & Lea Dumont Nashua, NH
LECLAIR, Unknown, Mar 11 1890 Sex:M Child# 1 Auguste Leclair Canada & Hermine Pouier Canada Stillborn
LECLAIR, Valarie Anne, Mar 22 1895 Sex:F Child# 6 Anselme Leclair Canada & Mathilde Lepage Canada
LECLAIR, Walter Willis, Apr 14 1935 Sex:M Child# 4 (No Parents Listed)
LECLAIRE, Adelard Ernest, Dec 31 1919 Sex:M Child# 10 Epiphane Leclaire Canada & Maria Lasalle Canada
LECLAIRE, Pauline, Dec 24 1906 Sex:F Child# 1 Paul B Leclaire Wilbraham, MA & Isabel Sargent Nashua, NH
LECLAIRE, Ruth Isabel, Jun 9 1908 Sex:F Child# 2 Paul LeClaire Wilbraham, MA & Isabel Sargent Nashua, NH
LECLAIRE, William, Apr 4 1897 Sex:M Child# 7 Anseline Leclaire Canada & Mathilda Lepage Canada
LECLERC, Adelard Leo, Jun 29 1917 Sex:M Child# 1 Joseph Leclerc Hudson, NH & Delima Landry Canada

LECLERC, Anne Anna, Sep 3 1902 Sex:F Child# 3 Joseph Leclerc Canada & Hermine Dube Canada
LECLERC, Annette Olivette, Mar 3 1924 Sex:F Child# 4 Theo Leclerc Canada & Lea Dumont Nashua, NH
LECLERC, Antoine Henri, Jul 16 1920 Sex:M Child# 1 Antoine Leclerc Canada &    Laroche Canada
LECLERC, Delvina Mathilda, Nov 30 1889 Sex:F Child# 3 Auselme Leclerc Canada & Mathilda Lepage Canada
LECLERC, Eva Alberta, Jun 24 1909 Sex:F Child# 1 Napoleon Leclerc Canada & Lea Levesque Canada
LECLERC, Gertrude Germain, Aug 14 1921 Sex:F Child# 2 Antoine Leclerc Canada & Dorila Laroche Canada
LECLERC, Gloria Rachel, Jun 30 1933 Sex:F Child# 7 Antoine Leclerc Canada & Dorilda Laroche Canada
LECLERC, Hermine Stella, Feb 16 1899 Sex:F Child# 2 Barthelemi Leclerc Canada & Hermine Dube Canada
LECLERC, Irene Florette, Mar 14 1920 Sex:F Child# 3 Joseph Leclerc Nashua, NH & Delima Landry Canada
LECLERC, Joseph Wilbrod R, Dec 21 1909 Sex:M Child# 2 Joseph Leclerc Canada & Alice Dionne Canada
LECLERC, Juliette Muriel, Sep 27 1923 Sex:F Child# 3 Antoine Leclerc Canada & Dorilda Laroche Canada
LECLERC, Laurette Rita, Aug 13 1927 Sex:F Child# 13 Ephirame Leclerc Canada & Maria Lasalle Canada
LECLERC, Lily Eva, Jan 15 1901 Sex:F Child# 2 Hermidas Leclerc Canada & Hermine Dube Canada
LECLERC, Lucille Aline, Sep 13 1913 Sex:F Child# 5 Joseph Leclerc Canada & Alice Dion Canada
LECLERC, M Therese Anita, Apr 6 1917 Sex:F Child# 9 Epiphane Leclerc Canada & Maria Lasalle Canada
LECLERC, Marcel Maurice, Aug 15 1927 Sex:M Child# 2 Delium Leclerc Canada & Rebecca Plante Nashua, NH
LECLERC, Marie Annette, Oct 5 1914 Sex:F Child# 1 Ludger Leclerc Canada & Eva Ouellette Canada Stillborn
LECLERC, Marie Cecile Annette, Jul 22 1912 Sex:F Child# 4 Joseph Leclerc Canada & Alice Dion Canada
LECLERC, Marie Jeannette, Feb 22 1922 Sex:F Child# 11 Epiphane Leclerc Canada & Marie Lasalle Canada
LECLERC, Marie Rose N R, Dec 17 1910 Sex:F Child# 3 Joseph Leclerc Canada & Alice Dion Canada
LECLERC, Paul Arthur, Sep 4 1925 Sex:M Child# 5 Theo Leclerc Canada & Lea Dumont Nashua, NH
LECLERC, Rose Anna, Sep 6 1902 Sex:F Child# 10 Anselme Leclerc Canada & Mathilda Lepage Canada
LECLERC, Unknown, Aug 14 1893 Sex:M Child# 4 Anseline Leclerc Canada & Georgine Lepage Canada
LECLERE, Jeanne D'Arc Lucille, Jan 3 1918 Sex:F Child# 1 J C Leclere Canada & Lea Dumont Nashua, NH
LECLERE, Leo Paul Edouard, Aug 19 1925 Sex:M Child# 12 Epiphane Leclere Canada & Marie Lasalle Canada
LECLERE, Marie Alice G, Nov 16 1907 Sex:F Child# 1 Joseph Leclere Canada & Alice Dion Canada
LECOMTE, Jeannine, Feb 6 1930 Sex:F Child# 1 Ernest Lecomte Canada & Rita Nadeau Canada
LECOURS, Joseph L E, May 28 1890 Sex:M Child# 3 Pierre Lecours Canada & Delphine Rousseau Canada
LEDEAU, Earl, Sep 5 1911 Sex:M Child# 1 E C Ledeau Nashua, NH & Mattie March Nashua, NH
LEDERE, Esdras, Dec 29 1887 Sex:M Child# 2 Anselme Ledere P Q & Mathilda Leprage Canada
LEDOUE, Joseph, Jul 22 1888 Sex:M Child# 4 Fred Ledoue St Albans, VT & Adill Gaulin Canada
LEDOUX, Agnes, May 3 1911 Sex:F Child# 5 Victor Ledoux Canada & Anna Desmarais New Hartford, CT
LEDOUX, Agnes Laura A, Jul 26 1892 Sex:F Child# 7 James Ledoux Vermont & Emma Canada
LEDOUX, Albert Raymond, Feb 5 1913 Sex:M Child# 1 John Ledoux Vermont & Eva Malenfant Canada
LEDOUX, Alice Marie, Dec 1 1913 Sex:F Child# 4 Regis W Ledoux Nashua, NH & Rose Trudeau Wisconsin
LEDOUX, Alida Eveline, Aug 2 1914 Sex:F Child# 6 Victor Ledoux Canada & Anna Desmarais New Hartford, CT
LEDOUX, Antoinette, Feb 14 1897 Sex:F Child# 9 Alfred Ledoux US & Odile Gaulin Canada
LEDOUX, Armand Wilfrid, May 18 1932 Sex:M Child# 4 George Ledoux Vermont & Blanche Masson Canada
LEDOUX, Arthur Homer, Jr, Dec 21 1935 Sex:M Child# 1 Arthur H Ledoux Nashua, NH & Ruth Bourdon Medford, MA
LEDOUX, Aurore, May 14 1891 Sex:F Child# 6 John Ledoux VT & Alice Danis VT
LEDOUX, Beatrice Marguerite, Sep 1 1908 Sex:F Child# 2 Samuel Ledoux US & Grace A Fosie US
LEDOUX, Beverly, Oct 10 1933 Sex:F Child# 3 Ernest E Ledoux Nashua, NH & Thelma Sherman Keene, NH
LEDOUX, Camille Edna, May 28 1906 Sex:F Child# 3 Victor Ledoux Canada & Anna Desmarais New Haven, CT
LEDOUX, Cecile Adrienne, Aug 17 1913 Sex:F Child# 5 Samuel Ledoux US & Agnes Foisie US
LEDOUX, Cecile Corinne, Aug 24 1927 Sex:F Child# 1 Emile Ledoux Nashua, NH & Rose Cote Canada
LEDOUX, Cecile Eveline, Nov 23 1922 Sex:F Child# 9 Victor Ledoux Canada & Anna Desmarais New Hartford, CT
LEDOUX, Cecile Laura, Oct 6 1919 Sex:F Child# 3 James M Ledoux St Albans, VT & M St Laurent Canada
LEDOUX, Corinne Jeannette, Mar 11 1893 Sex:F Child# 6 Fred Ledoux Vermont & Odille Gaulin Canada
LEDOUX, Delphine V, Nov 27 1900 Sex:F Child# 6 Lazard Ledoux Vermont & Victorine Cadoret Manchester, NH
LEDOUX, Doris, Jul 19 1927 Sex:F Child# 1 (No Parents Listed)
LEDOUX, Doris Rita, Jun 5 1928 Sex:F Child# 5 J M Ledoux Waterbury, VT & M St Laurent Canada
LEDOUX, Edmond T, Nov 28 1907 Sex:M Child# 2 Regis Ledoux Nashua, NH & Rosanna Trudeau Wisconsin
LEDOUX, Eloise Leocadie, Feb 17 1907 Sex:F Child# 1 Samuel Ledoux Canada & Grace Agnes Foisie US
LEDOUX, Elphege Jean, Feb 13 1893 Sex:M Child# 7 Toussaint Ledoux Vermont & Edmire Bourgeois Canada
LEDOUX, Emelie Adrienne, Jan 28 1904 Sex:F Child# 2 George Ledoux Nashua, NH & Bibienne Bonenfant Canada
LEDOUX, Ernest Arthur, Sep 6 1914 Sex:M Child# 2 John A Ledoux St Albans, VT & Eva Malenfant Canada
LEDOUX, Ernest Romeo, Jul 2 1917 Sex:M Child# 1 Alphonse Ledoux Canada & Lena Levesque Nashua, NH
LEDOUX, Eva Simone, Jun 28 1908 Sex:F Child# 2 Leopold Ledoux Canada & Zelida Beaulieu Canada
LEDOUX, Francis Ernest, Aug 21 1899 Sex:M Child# 1 George Ledoux Canada & Bibianne Bonenfant Canada
LEDOUX, Gabriel, Jul 27 1911 Sex:M Child# 3 Alfred Ledoux Canada & Victoria Manseau Canada
LEDOUX, Gaston Paul Emile, Mar 31 1922 Sex:M Child# 2 Emile Ledoux Nashua, NH & Octavie Boulon France
LEDOUX, George Emile Ber, Feb 22 1914 Sex:M Child# 4 Alfred Ledoux Nashua, NH & Victoria Manseau Canada
LEDOUX, Henri, Jul 23 1903 Sex:M Child# 1 Victor Ledoux Canada & Anna Desmarais New Hartford, CT
LEDOUX, Irene, Sep 19 1898 Sex:F Child# 10 Frederic Ledoux St Albans, VT & Odile Gaulin Canada
LEDOUX, Irene, Aug 26 1904 Sex:F Child# 6 Wilfrid Ledoux Canada & Elizabeth Boule Nashua, NH
LEDOUX, Irene Julia, Jan 6 1927 Sex:F Child# 2 Carl Ledoux St Albans, VT & Bertha Ducharme Lowell, MA
LEDOUX, J Arthur Homer, May 12 1911 Sex:M Child# 1 Joseph A Ledoux Nashua, NH & Blanche V Bogus Nashua, NH
LEDOUX, Jaclyn, Sep 30 1932 Sex:F Child# 1 Ernest E Ledoux Nashua, NH & Thelma Sherman Keene, NH
LEDOUX, Joseph, Jun 29 1914 Sex:M Child# 6 Samuel Ledoux US & Grace Foisie US
LEDOUX, Joseph Armand R, Sep 23 1908 Sex:M Child# 1 Henri A Ledoux Nashua, NH & Victoria Manseau Canada
LEDOUX, Joseph Arthur, Jun 30 1894 Sex:M Child# 7 Frederic Ledoux St Albans, VT & Odille Gaulin Canada
LEDOUX, Joseph C T, Mar 5 1890 Sex:M Child# 2 Lazard Ledoux St Albans, VT & Victorine Cadoret Manchester, NH
LEDOUX, Joseph Edward, May 25 1935 Sex:M Child# 1 Jos Ed Ledoux Nashua, NH & Yvonne Collier Litchfield, NH

LEDOUX, Joseph Frederic L, Apr 5 1910 Sex:M Child# 2 Alfred Ledoux Nashua, NH & Victoria Manseau Canada
LEDOUX, Joseph Henri A, Apr 26 1911 Sex:M Child# 3 Regis Ledoux Nashua, NH & Rosanna Trudeau Wisconsin
LEDOUX, Joseph Norbert B, Jun 2 1924 Sex:M Child# 3 George E Ledoux St Albans, VT & Blanche Mason Canada
LEDOUX, Josephat Edward, May 8 1912 Sex:M Child# 2 Josephat Ledoux Nashua, NH & Blanche Boggis Nashua, NH
LEDOUX, Lena Claire, Oct 9 1915 Sex:F Child# 2 James Ledoux St Albans, VT & Marianne St Laurent Canada
LEDOUX, Lena Geneva, Dec 12 1909 Sex:F Child# 4 Victor Ledoux Canada & Anna Desmarais New Hartford, CT
LEDOUX, Leo James, Mar 8 1914 Sex:M Child# 1 James Ledoux St Albans, VT & M A St Laurent Nashua, NH
LEDOUX, Lina Evangeline, Jul 23 1906 Sex:F Child# 1 Regis Ledoux Nashua, NH & Rosanna Trudeau Wisconsin
LEDOUX, Louis C E, Dec 14 1889 Sex:M Child# 1 Emery Ledoux St Albans, VT & Nellie Keenan Worcester, MA
LEDOUX, Lucien Germain, May 15 1909 Sex:M Child# 2 Edmond Ledoux Nashua, NH & Marie L St Onge Canada
LEDOUX, Luetta Eva, Nov 8 1909 Sex:F Child#  Leopold Ledoux Canada & Zalida Bariteau Canada
LEDOUX, M Vivian, Aug 24 1895 Sex:F Child# 8 Fred Ledoux St Albans, VT & Odile Gaulin Canada
LEDOUX, Marie, Oct 13 1888 Sex:F Child# 1 Ellazard Ledoux St Albans, VT & Sarah Cadout Manchester, NH
LEDOUX, Marie, Jul 27 1933 Sex:F Child# 1 Ralph Ledoux Lowell, MA & Louise Vien Canada
LEDOUX, Marie A, Sep 25 1893 Sex:F Child# 4 Lazard Ledoux St Albans, VT & Victorine Cadoret Manchester, NH
LEDOUX, Marie A C, Feb 3 1892 Sex:F Child# 2 Aime Ledoux St Albans, VT & Nellie Keenan Worcester, MA
LEDOUX, Marie A L, Dec 22 1898 Sex:F Child# 5 Lazard Ledoux St Albans, VT & Victorine Cadorette Manchester, NH
LEDOUX, Marie Blanche Doris, Oct 4 1921 Sex:F Child# 1 George S Ledoux St Albans, VT & Blanche Masson Canada
LEDOUX, Marie Jean Annette, Sep 17 1920 Sex:F Child# 5 Alphonse Ledoux Canada & Lina Levesque Nashua, NH
LEDOUX, Marie Josephine, Oct 20 1901 Sex:F Child# 5 Joseph W Ledoux Canada & Elizabeth Bouley Nashua, NH
LEDOUX, Marie Juliette, Mar 7 1895 Sex:F Child# 8 Jean Ledoux St Albans, VT & Alexina Danis Jericho, VT
LEDOUX, Marie Louise, Mar 15 1890 Sex:F Child# 5 Fred Ledoux VT & Odele Gauler Canada
LEDOUX, Marion G, Aug 12 1909 Sex:F Child# 2 Alfred Ledoux St Albans, VT & Elizabeth Moriarty Flushing, NY
LEDOUX, Mary Annette, Jan 11 1925 Sex:F Child# 4 James Ledoux Montpelier, VT & M A St Laurent Canada
LEDOUX, Mary Rose Y, Feb 8 1908 Sex:F Child# 7 Wilfrid Ledoux St Denis, Canada & Elisabeth Boulay Nashua, NH
LEDOUX, Normand, Jan 5 1918 Sex:M Child# 8 Victor Ledoux Canada & Anna Desmarais New Hartford, CT
LEDOUX, Osias Ernest, May 30 1905 Sex:M Child# 2 Victor Ledoux Canada & Anna Desmarais New Hartford, CT
LEDOUX, Paul Oscar Maurice, Feb 22 1916 Sex:M Child# 5 Alfred Ledoux Nashua, NH & Victoria Manseau Canada
LEDOUX, Rachel, Sep 25 1909 Sex:F Child# 3 Samuel Ledoux Canada & Grace A Foisy US
LEDOUX, Raoul, Apr 7 1915 Sex:M Child# 3 Alphonse Ledoux Canada & Lena Levesque Canada
LEDOUX, Raymond, Dec 28 1922 Sex:M Child# 1 Eddie Ledoux Pittsfield, NH & Mary Gadbois Canada
LEDOUX, Raymond Edouard, Dec 8 1912 Sex:M Child# 3 George Ledoux Canada & Bibianna Bonenfant Canada
LEDOUX, Raymond Gaston, Oct 22 1920 Sex:M Child# 1 Emile Ledoux Nashua, NH & Octavie Boulon Blois, France
LEDOUX, Raymond Irwin, Sep 8 1912 Sex:M Child# 2 Ernest Ledoux Nashua, NH & Mattie March Nashua, NH
LEDOUX, Regis W E, Nov 27 1887 Sex:M Child#  Toussaint Ledoux Richford, VT & Elmire Bourgois Canada
LEDOUX, Robert Paul, Nov 17 1915 Sex:M Child# 5 Regis W Ledoux Nashua, NH & Rosanna Trudeau Sturgeon Bay, WI
LEDOUX, Roger Antoino, Dec 18 1917 Sex:M Child# 4 Leopold Ledoux Canada & Zelida Bariteau NH
LEDOUX, Rose Anna, Jul 25 1903 Sex:F Child# 5 Wilfrid Ledoux Canada & Elizabeth Bouley Canada
LEDOUX, Shirley, Oct 10 1933 Sex:F Child# 2 Ernest E Ledoux Nashua, NH & Thelma Sherman Keene, NH
LEDOUX, Stella Josephine, May 20 1918 Sex:F Child# 1 Earl A Ledoux Pelham, NH & Bertha F Duchanes Lowell, MA
LEDOUX, Therese Eva, Dec 28 1915 Sex:F Child# 7 Victor Ledoux Canada & Anna Desmarais New Hartford, CT
LEDOUX, Unknown, Apr 11 1892 Sex:F Child# 6 Fred Ledoux Vermont & Odile Gaulin Canada Stillborn
LEDOUX, Unknown, Sep 7 1892 Sex: Child# 5 Louis Ledoux Canada & Georgiana Burel NY Stillborn
LEDOUX, Unknown, Mar 27 1902 Sex:F Child# 11 Alfred Ledoux Vermont & Odylle Golin Canada
LEDOUX, Unknown, Aug 19 1911 Sex:F Child# 4 Samuel Ledoux Canada & Grace Agnes Foisie US
LEDOUX, Unknown, Nov 28 1922 Sex:M Child# 2 George G Ledoux St Albans, VT & Blanche Maison Canada
LEDOUX, Winslos Albert, Apr 1 1907 Sex:M Child# 1 Edmond Ledoux NH & Marie L St Onge Canada
LEDOWE, Louis E C, Jul 5 1891 Sex:M Child# 3 Lezard Ledowe Canada & Victorine Cadoret Manchester, NH
LEDUKE, May Louisa, Mar 20 1893 Sex:F Child# 3 John Leduke Canada & Louisa Mandigo Canada
LEE, Adrian, Feb 14 1898 Sex:F Child# 6 James Lee Ireland & Bridget Gaffney Ireland
LEE, Agnes Mary, Dec 13 1921 Sex:F Child# 4 Joseph P Lee Nashua, NH & Rose A Cote Canada
LEE, Albert Joseph, Nov 1 1896 Sex:M Child# 5 James Lee Ireland & Bridget Gaffney Ireland
LEE, Ann Frances, Apr 5 1924 Sex:F Child# 4 John Lee Nashua, NH & Mary Shea Nashua, NH
LEE, Arthur Francis, Jun 7 1896 Sex:M Child# 2 John T Lee Nashua, NH & Ella F Coggen Pelham, NH
LEE, Barbara Ellwood, Jun 15 1917 Sex:F Child# 2 John Lee New York, NY & Clara Boston, MA
LEE, Bernard T, Feb 7 1892 Sex:M Child# 1 Miles Lee Ireland & Maggie Gilhooly Ireland
LEE, Dorothy Annette, Apr 6 1928 Sex:F Child# 4 Adelard Lee Canada & Delia Leconte Canada
LEE, Ellen, Mar 21 1887 Sex:F Child# 6 James Lee Ireland & Winifred Meglyn Ireland
LEE, Francis, Dec 2 1889 Sex:M Child# 5 Robert Lee Ireland & Bridget Morin Ireland
LEE, Francis Henry, Aug 12 1899 Sex:M Child# 3 John Lee Nashua, NH & Ella F Cogger Pelham, NH
LEE, George, Sep 27 1891 Sex:M Child# 5 John M Lee Ireland & Nora Lynch Ireland
LEE, Helen Sofia, May 13 1930 Sex:F Child# 1 Leo Robert Lee Nashua, NH & Josephine Kopka Nashua, NH
LEE, James Joseph, Sep 29 1893 Sex:M Child# 2 Myles Lee Ireland & Maggie Gilhooley Ireland
LEE, John William, Sep 21 1895 Sex:M Child# 4 James Lee Ireland & Bridget Gaffney Ireland
LEE, Joseph, May 2 1888 Sex:M Child# 4 Robert Lee Ireland & Bridget Winn Ireland
LEE, Joseph Alfred, Nov 5 1909 Sex:M Child# 1 Francis X Lee Pittsburgh, PA & Lizzie Bohan Ireland
LEE, Joseph Maurice, Nov 7 1924 Sex:M Child# 2 Adelard Lee Canada & Delia Lacomte Canada
LEE, Joseph Oscar Leo, Aug 30 1908 Sex:M Child# 1 Oscar Lee Canada & Elmire Levesque Canada
LEE, Kenneth Bernard, Jan 16 1931 Sex:M Child# 6 George Lee Nashua, NH & Octavie Maynard Nashua, NH
LEE, Leo Robert, Jr, Jul 22 1934 Sex:M Child# 2 Leo Robert Lee Nashua, NH & Josephine Kopka Nashua, NH
LEE, Marie Blanche Y, Aug 6 1911 Sex:F Child# 2 Oscar Lee Canada & Elmire Levesque Canada
LEE, Marie Doris Yvonne, Apr 30 1925 Sex:M Child# 5 Oscar Lee Canada & Elmire Levesque Canada
LEE, Marie Jeanne, Sep 6 1916 Sex:F Child# 4 Oscar Lee Canada & Elmire Levesque Canada

LEE, Marie Yvette Lena, Jan 13 1914 Sex:F Child# 3 Oscar Lee Canada & Elmire Levesque Canada
LEE, Marie Yvonne, Jun 9 1926 Sex:F Child# 3 Adelard Lee Canada & Delia Lacourte Canada
LEE, Martha Louise, May 11 1922 Sex:F Child# 3 John Lee Nashua, NH & Mary Shea Cambridge, MA
LEE, Mary Elizabeth, Aug 4 1920 Sex:F Child# 2 John Lee Nashua, NH & Mary Shea Mass
LEE, Mary Lucille, Dec 30 1917 Sex:F Child# 3 Joseph P Lee Nashua, NH & Rose A Cote Canada
LEE, Mary R, Aug 22 1902 Sex:F Child# 2 Myles Lee Ireland & Ann J Rock Nashua, NH
LEE, Mildred, Feb 16 1897 Sex:F Child# 2 Charles E Lee Waterbury, VT & Carrie Goodrich Northboro, MA
LEE, Mildred Bernadette, Jan 2 1925 Sex:F Child# 5 George Lee Nashua, NH & Octavie Maynard Nashua, NH
LEE, Mildred Marion, Nov 22 1899 Sex:F Child# 7 James Lee Ireland & Bridget Gaffney Ireland
LEE, Myles, Mar 31 1901 Sex:M Child# 1 Myles Lee Ireland & Ann Rock Nashua, NH
LEE, Napoleon George, Jan 16 1908 Sex:M Child# 4 Adelard Lee Canada & Lea Loiselle Chazy, NY
LEE, Normand, May 3 1926 Sex:M Child# 5 George Lee Nashua, NH & Octavie Maynard Nashua, NH
LEE, Raymond Frederick, Jan 4 1918 Sex:M Child# 1 George W Lee Nashua, NH & Octavie Maynard Nashua, NH
LEE, Robert Anthony, Sep 9 1927 Sex:M Child# 5 Joseph P Lee Nashua, NH & Rose Anna Cote Canada
LEE, Robert Francis, Apr 26 1913 Sex:M Child# 1 John Lee Nashua, NH & Mary Shea Mass
LEE, Roger William, Jun 25 1920 Sex:M Child# 2 George Lee Nashua, NH & Octavie Maynard Nashua, NH
LEE, Roland Maurice, Dec 13 1922 Sex:M Child# 3 George Lee Nashua, NH & Octavie Maynard Nashua, NH
LEE, Rose Barbara, Dec 19 1915 Sex:F Child# 2 Joseph P Lee Nashua, NH & Rose A Cote Canada
LEE, Rose Nancy, May 30 1931 Sex:F Child# 7 Joseph Lee Nashua, NH & Rose Cote Canada
LEE, Rosemun, Mar 3 1889 Sex:F Child# 3 John M Lee Ireland & Norah Lynch Ireland
LEE, Unknown, Sep 19 1895 Sex:F Child# 4 Wyles Lee Ireland & Maggie Gilhooley Ireland
LEE, Unknown, Sep 19 1895 Sex:F Child# 5 Wyles Lee Ireland & Maggie Gilhooley Ireland
LEE, Virginia Mary, Dec 12 1928 Sex:F Child# 6 Joseph P Lee Nashua, NH & Rose B Cote Canada
LEEDHAM, John Baxter, Jan 9 1922 Sex:M Child# 2 William Leedham Malden, MA & Alma Pare Medford, MA
LEFAIVRE, Armand, Jan 18 1898 Sex:M Child# 10 Hypolite Lefaivre Canada & M Anne Pauneton Canada
LEFAIVRE, Blanche, Sep 3 1896 Sex:F Child# 9 Hypolite Lefaivre Canada & Marie Anne Panneton Canada
LEFAVOR, Alice F, Apr 16 1893 Sex:F Child# 4 John Lefavor Litchfield, NH & Sarah Leyden NH
LEFAVOR, Charles, Jul 23 1887 Sex:M Child# 3 Charles A LeFavor Nashua, NH & Mary Fahey Ireland
LEFAVOR, Franklin Arthur, Dec 24 1911 Sex:M Child# 2 Arthur E Lefavor Milford, NH & Bertha May Tripp Portsmouth, NH
LEFAVOR, Mary, Nov 16 1889 Sex:F Child# 4 Charles A Lefavor Nashua, NH & Mary A Lefavor Ireland
LEFAVOR, Philip Edward, May 21 1917 Sex:M Child# 1 Philip Lefavor NH & Ida Potter Mass
LEFAVOR, Richard Thomas, Feb 17 1923 Sex:M Child# 2 Wm Thomas Lefavor Nashua, NH & Blanche Lizotte Nashua, NH
LEFAVOR, Robert Chester, Dec 30 1918 Sex:M Child# 2 Philip Lefavor Nashua, NH & Ida Potter Mass
LEFAVOR, Robert Paul, Jun 23 1924 Sex:M Child# 3 William Lefavor NH & Blanche Lizotte NH
LEFAVOR, Unknown, Dec 17 1921 Sex:M Child# 3 Philip J Lefavor Nashua, NH & Ida Potter Worcester, MA
LEFAVOR, William Charles, Jul 7 1920 Sex:M Child# 1 William T Lefavor Nashua, NH & Blanche E Lizotte Nashua, NH
LEFAVOR, William F, Sep 17 1894 Sex:M Child# Charles Lefavor Nashua, NH & Mary Fay Ireland
LEFEBVRE, Alice Eva, Feb 19 1927 Sex:F Child# 1 George Lefebvre Pepperell, MA & Valida Rioux Nashua, NH
LEFEBVRE, Anna Helene, Jan 11 1902 Sex:F Child# 13 Paul Lefebvre Canada & M A Panneton Canada
LEFEBVRE, Armande, Jan 31 1931 Sex:F Child# 5 Armand Lefebvre Nashua, NH & Gertrude Prevost Nashua, NH
LEFEBVRE, Beatrice Florilda, Jun 13 1917 Sex:F Child# 2 Victor Lefebvre Nashua, NH & Melina Pelletier Canada
LEFEBVRE, Beverly Jean, May 22 1928 Sex:F Child# 5 George Lefebvre Nashua, NH & Bertha Guptill Mexico, ME
LEFEBVRE, Come, Oct 18 1900 Sex:M Child# 12 H Lefebvre Canada & Maria Parmeton Canada
LEFEBVRE, Come Joram, Dec 21 1903 Sex:M Child# 3 Come Lefebvre Canada & Helena Lahale Canada
LEFEBVRE, Delia Yvonne, Feb 9 1906 Sex:F Child# 4 Come Lefebvre Canada & Helena Lahate Canada
LEFEBVRE, Dolores Gertrude, May 26 1934 Sex:F Child# 11 Donat Lefebvre Lowell, MA & Aurore Boisvert Canada
LEFEBVRE, Edmond Ernest, Jun 1 1904 Sex:M Child# 6 George Lefebvre Suncook, NH & Eva Lacourse Laconia, NH
LEFEBVRE, Edmond Ernest, Apr 28 1926 Sex:M Child# 1 Ernest Lefebvre Nashua, NH & Yvonne Rioux Nashua, NH
LEFEBVRE, Elizabeth Antoinette, Jan 10 1904 Sex:F Child# 6 Victor Lefebvre Nashua, NH & Amanda Proulx Canada
LEFEBVRE, Elizabeth Jennie, Apr 25 1925 Sex:F Child# 3 George Lefebvre Nashua, NH & Bertha G Guptill Mexico, ME
LEFEBVRE, Emile, Jun 24 1903 Sex:M Child# 14 Hypolite Lefebvre Canada & Marie A Panneton Canada
LEFEBVRE, Eva Jeannette, Jun 18 1930 Sex:F Child# 2 Joseph Lefebvre Brookline, NH & Mary Labombarde New York
LEFEBVRE, Georgianna L, Aug 9 1907 Sex:F Child# 5 Come Lefebvre Canada & Helena Lahaie Canada
LEFEBVRE, Irene, Feb 11 1921 Sex:F Child# 1 Wilfrid H Lefebvre Suncook, NH & Lillian Allison Manchester, NH
LEFEBVRE, Jos Roland Sylvia, Jul 4 1925 Sex:M Child# 1 Armand Lefebvre Nashua, NH & Gertrude Prevost Nashua, NH
LEFEBVRE, Joseph, Sep 4 1895 Sex:M Child# 2 Victor Lefebvre Nashua, NH & Amanda Proulx Canada
LEFEBVRE, Joseph Georges, Apr 19 1898 Sex:M Child# 12 Pierre Lefebvre Canada & Elise Desmarais Canada
LEFEBVRE, Joseph Wilfrid, May 5 1921 Sex:M Child# 4 Victor Lefebvre Nashua, NH & Melina Pelletier Canada
LEFEBVRE, Laura, Feb 22 1902 Sex:F Child# 5 George Lefebvre Suncook & Eva Lacourse Laconia
LEFEBVRE, Leeworth Lewis, Nov 10 1907 Sex:M Child# 1 Alphonse Lefebvre Lowell, MA & Lilian Tremblay Sciota, NY
LEFEBVRE, Leocadia, Jan 28 1899 Sex:F Child# 4 Victor Lefebvre Canada & Amanda Proulx Canada
LEFEBVRE, Lillian Mae, May 5 1934 Sex:F Child# 3 Joseph Lefebvre Brookline, NH & Mary Labombarde W Chazy, NY
LEFEBVRE, Lorette, May 12 1906 Sex:F Child# 15 Hypolite Lefebvre Canada & Marie A Panneton Canada
LEFEBVRE, Lorraine, Jul 3 1928 Sex:F Child# 3 Armand Lefebvre US & Gertrude Provost US
LEFEBVRE, Louis H A, Aug 28 1891 Sex:M Child# 3 Henri Lefebvre Canada & Eugenie Milette Canada
LEFEBVRE, M A Therese Rita, Aug 6 1930 Sex:F Child# 1 Joseph Lefebvre Nashua, NH & Rose Beland Canada
LEFEBVRE, Marcelle Marguerite, Jan 11 1930 Sex:F Child# 4 Armand Lefebvre Nashua, NH & Gertrude Prevost Nashua, NH
LEFEBVRE, Maria, Feb 23 1895 Sex:F Child# 8 Gedeon Lefebvre Canada & Maria Roy Canada
LEFEBVRE, Marie, Jun 2 1887 Sex:F Child# 7 Joseph Lefebvre P Q & Adelina Boisseau P Q
LEFEBVRE, Marie Amanda, Sep 1 1897 Sex:F Child# 3 Victor Lefebvre Nashua, NH & Amanda Proulx Canada
LEFEBVRE, Marie Helene, Feb 7 1892 Sex:F Child# 6 Hypolite Lefebvre Canada & Marie Parmeton Canada
LEFEBVRE, Marie Melina, Mar 2 1915 Sex:F Child# 1 Victor Lefebvre Nashua, NH & Melina Pelletier Canada
LEFEBVRE, Marie Theresa Lorett, Jan 19 1928 Sex:F Child# 2 Ernest Lefebvre Nashua, NH & Yvonne Rioux Nashua, NH

LEFEBVRE, Mary, Mar 14 1897 Sex:F Child# 4 Simeon Lefebvre Island Pond, VT & Belle Bailey Malone, NY
LEFEBVRE, Mary Alice, Dec 30 1907 Sex:F Child# 3 Napoleon Lefebvre Canada & Rose E Bissonnette Canada
LEFEBVRE, Mary Georgiana Rose, Feb 1 1926 Sex:F Child# 1 Joseph Levebvre Brookline, NH & Mary Labombard W Chazy, NY
LEFEBVRE, Maurice, Oct 30 1932 Sex:M Child# 10 D Lefebvre Lowell, MA & Aurore Boisvert Canada
LEFEBVRE, Nellie Ardina, Mar 9 1924 Sex:F Child# 2 George Lefebvre Nashua, NH & Bertha G Guptill Mexico, ME
LEFEBVRE, Pauline Bertha, Jan 10 1927 Sex:F Child# 4 George Lefebvre Nashua, NH & Bertha Guptill Mexico, ME
LEFEBVRE, Pierre Hector, Dec 20 1901 Sex:M Child# 5 Victor Lefebvre Nashua, NH & Amanda Proulx Canada
LEFEBVRE, Raymond, Aug 23 1909 Sex:M Child# 10 Simeon Lefebvre Three Rivers, VT & Della Hurlburt Lyon Mtn, NY
LEFEBVRE, Roland, Jun 25 1921 Sex:M Child# 1 (No Parents Listed)
LEFEBVRE, Roland Lake, May 28 1901 Sex:M Child# 1 Alfred P Lefebvre Nashua, NH & Emma Labounty New York
LEFEBVRE, Simeon Joseph, Mar 30 1907 Sex:M Child# 6 Simeon J Lefebvre Vermont & Delia Hurlburt New York
LEFEBVRE, Unknown, Dec 19 1892 Sex:M Child# 1 Simeon Lefebvre Island Pond, VT & Belle Bailey Plattsburg, NY
LEFEBVRE, Unknown, Aug 16 1894 Sex:M Child# 2 Simeon Lefebvre Island Pond, VT & Belle Bailey Plattsburg, NY
LEFEBVRE, Unknown, Aug 1 1895 Sex:M Child# 11 Pierre Lefebvre Canada & Elise Desmarais Canada
LEFEBVRE, Unknown, Mar 24 1902 Sex:M Child# 3 Simeon Lefebvre Island Pond, VT & Delia Copp Lion Mountain, NY
LEFEBVRE, Unknown, Sep 4 1905 Sex: Child# 4 Simeon Lefebvre US & Delia Hurlburt New York Stillborn
LEFEBVRE, Victor, Oct 7 1893 Sex:M Child# 1 Victor Lefebvre Nashua, NH & Amanda Proulx Canada
LEFEBVRE, Victor, Dec 24 1918 Sex:M Child# 3 Victor Lefebvre US & Melina Pelletier Canada
LEFEVBRE, Robert Geo Armand, Sep 7 1926 Sex:M Child# 2 Armand Lefevbre US & Gertrude Provost US
LEFEVRE, Helene, Jan 31 1893 Sex:F Child# 3 Polite Lefevre Canada & Marie A Pauthon Canada
LEFEVRE, Merwin L, Sep 9 1927 Sex:M Child# 3 George A Lefevre Nashua, NH & Rena N Tuttle Deerfield, NH
LEFEVRE, Philippe, Apr 8 1895 Sex:M Child# 8 Hypolite Lefevre Canada & Marie A Panneton Canada
LEFEVRE, Unknown, Jan 12 1890 Sex:M Child# 1 James Lefevre Canada & Marie Ouellet Canada
LEFLEUR, Marie Theresa, Nov 21 1928 Sex:F Child# 1 Gustave Lefleur Canada & Sylvia Ricard Nashua, NH
LEGALLEE, Frances Phebe, Mar 15 1934 Sex:F Child# 3 Howard S Legallee Somerville, MA & Phebe Tyler Contoocook, NH
LEGALLEE, Shirley Tyler, Sep 24 1921 Sex:F Child# 1 Howard S Legallee Somerville, MA & Phoebe Tyler Contoocook, NH
LEGARE, Francoise M Marie, Nov 16 1931 Sex:F Child# 2 Martin Legare Manchester, NH & Eva Boisvert Manchester, NH
LEGARE, Rachael Juliette, Jul 1 1928 Sex:F Child# 1 Martin Legare Manchester, NH & Eva Boisvert Manchester, NH
LEGASSE, Claire Doris Irene, Nov 5 1933 Sex:F Child# 1 Euclide Legasse Canada & Melvina Boyer Nashua, NH
LEGER, Alice Lucienne, Sep 28 1926 Sex:F Child# 1 Rock Leger Canada & Agnes Tessier Canada
LEGGIO, Unknown, Jan 8 1927 Sex:F Child# 2 Nicholas Leggio Greece & Christina Sconsas Greece
LEGOS, Gregory, Mar 27 1929 Sex:M Child# 4 John Legos Greece & A Clepopolous Greece
LEGRAND, Emma L, Nov 10 1902 Sex:F Child# Morris Legrand Canada & Mary Launguay New York
LEGRIS, Ernest Wallace, Jul 20 1924 Sex:M Child# 1 Wallace Legris Churubusco, NY & Ellen Gendron Shirley, MA
LEIGHTON, Momer Curtis, Nov 21 1928 Sex:M Child# 1 A T Leighton Maine & I R Hamel Nashua, NH
LEIGHTON, Norma Helen, Mar 7 1916 Sex:F Child# 2 Daniel Leighton Unionville, ME & Fabiola Poulin Webster, MA
LEIGHTON, Roger Kenneth, Jul 22 1912 Sex:M Child# 1 Daniel Leighton Unionville, ME & Fabiola Poulin Webster, MA
LEIGHTON, Royal Stanley, Jr, Dec 11 1934 Sex:M Child# 1 Royal S Leighton Chester, NH & Marion Campbell Hudson, NH
LEIGHTON, Unknown, Apr 11 1891 Sex:F Child# 1 Robert Leighton Portland, ME & Maria Moore Montreal, Canada
LEISHASH, Stanislaus, Feb 9 1909 Sex:M Child# 2 John Leishash Austria & Mary Tokash Austria
LEITH, Joseph John Alfred, Aug 5 1932 Sex:M Child# 3 David Leith Putnam, CT & Ida Nadeau Canada
LEITH, Marie Claire Germain, May 27 1923 Sex:F Child# 1 David Leith Conn & Ida Nadeau Canada
LEITH, Marie Jeannette, Sep 30 1920 Sex:F Child# 2 David Leith Conn & Ida Nadeau Canada
LEITH, Thelma, Feb 7 1919 Sex:F Child# 2 Joseph E Leith Lowell, MA & Marguerite Potter England
LELAND, Edgar Solon, Jr, Jan 4 1916 Sex:M Child# 1 Edgar Solon Leland Providence, RI & Tronell Gilkey Searsport, ME
LELAND, Jessie Lowese, Jul 4 1921 Sex:F Child# 2 John B Leland Mass & Myrtie Allard NH
LELMOND, Ralph Earle, Apr 7 1929 Sex:M Child# 1 Charles Lelmond Nashua, NH & Lottie Olive Whittle Nashua, NH
LEMAI, Mary Cora, Nov 14 1891 Sex:F Child# 2 Edmund Lemai Canada & Georgiana Lafreniere Maine
LEMAY, Adrien Eugene, Dec 27 1928 Sex:M Child# 1 Marjorie Lemay Manchester, NH & Susanna Gill Canada
LEMAY, Adrienne Lucille, Aug 22 1911 Sex:F Child# 3 Eugene Lemay Canada & Zephirine St Onge Canada
LEMAY, Agnes Theresa, Mar 20 1916 Sex:F Child# 2 Leo Paul Lemay Canada & Mary Donahoe Boston, MA
LEMAY, Alexander, Apr 2 1916 Sex:M Child# 5 Eugene Lemay Canada & Clementine Cloutier Canada
LEMAY, Anna A, Dec 29 1889 Sex:F Child# 15 Oliver Lemay Canada & Luee Quintal Canada
LEMAY, Arthur R, May 5 1910 Sex:M Child# 3 Eugene Lemay Canada & Zephirine St Onge Canada
LEMAY, Cecile, Nov 17 1928 Sex:F Child# 4 Homer Lemay Canada & Yvonne Dionne Canada
LEMAY, Cecile Pauline, Dec 4 1924 Sex:F Child# 3 Antonio Lemay Nashua, NH & Antoinette Dionne Nashua, NH
LEMAY, Emma, Nov 19 1897 Sex:F Child# 5 Edmond Lemay Canada & Georgianna L US
LEMAY, Eugene Robert, Nov 30 1917 Sex:M Child# 5 Eugene H Lemay Canada & Zephirine St Onge Canada
LEMAY, Eugenie Cecile, Jul 22 1903 Sex:F Child# 2 Pierre Lemay Canada & Eugenie Aubut Canada
LEMAY, Evangeline E C, Feb 11 1888 Sex:F Child# 14 Oliver Lemay Brompton, PQ & Luce Quintal P Q
LEMAY, Georgina E B, Sep 16 1891 Sex:F Child# 16 Olivier Lemay Canada & Luce Quintal Canada
LEMAY, Gerard, Sep 1 1927 Sex:M Child# 3 Omer Lemay Canada & Yvonne Drouin Canada
LEMAY, Henri, Oct 24 1898 Sex:M Child# 2 Joseph Lemay Canada & Delia Lachance Canada
LEMAY, Jeanne Louise, Aug 11 1934 Sex:F Child# 7 Omer Lemay Canada & Yvonne Dionne Canada
LEMAY, Joan Helen, Dec 5 1934 Sex:F Child# 1 Arthur R Lemay Nashua, NH & Helen Bennett Lyndeboro, NH
LEMAY, Joseph Edgar Henry, Oct 21 1920 Sex:M Child# 1 Jos Henry Lemay Nashua, NH & Alma Dambroise Nashua, NH
LEMAY, Joseph Edouard, Jun 23 1905 Sex:M Child# 1 Eugene Lemay Canada & Clementine Cloutier Canada
LEMAY, Joseph Eugene, Sep 23 1896 Sex:M Child# 1 Joseph Lemay Canada & Zelia Lachance Canada
LEMAY, Joseph Jacques Emile, Mar 30 1928 Sex:M Child# 1 Emile Lemay Canada & Marie Hamel Nashua, NH
LEMAY, Laura, Jan 10 1893 Sex:F Child# 3 Edw Lemay Canada & Georgiana Lafreniere Maine
LEMAY, Lionel Maurice, Feb 16 1921 Sex:M Child# 6 Eugene Lemay Nashua, NH & Zepherine St Onge Canada
LEMAY, Lucille Anna, Feb 1 1922 Sex:F Child# 2 Henri Lemay Nashua, NH & Alma Damboise Nashua, NH
LEMAY, Marie, Aug 29 1888 Sex:F Child# 3 Adelaide Lemay P Q & Thessile Christraud Chatauqua, NY

LEMAY, Marie Gertrude F, Oct 29 1932 Sex:F Child# 6 Omer Lemay Canada & Yvonne Dionne Canada
LEMAY, Marie Therese, Apr 19 1924 Sex:F Child# 3 Henri Lemay Nashua, NH & Alma D'Ambroise Nashua, NH
LEMAY, Marie Yvonne, Mar 22 1907 Sex:F Child# 2 Eugene Lemay Canada & Clementine Cloutier Canada
LEMAY, Mary Helen Olivette, Jan 18 1908 Sex:F Child# 1 Leopold J Lemay Canada & Mary A Donahue Boston, MA
LEMAY, Olivier E R, May 14 1907 Sex:M Child# 2 Eugene Lemay Canada & Zephirine St Onge Canada
LEMAY, Pierre Joseph A, Jun 6 1896 Sex:M Child# 1 Pierre Lemay Canada & Eugenie Aubut Canada
LEMAY, Rita Victoria, Dec 28 1924 Sex:F Child# 1 J Omer Lemay Canada & Yvonne Drouin Canada
LEMAY, Roger Marjoric, Dec 27 1928 Sex:M Child# 2 Marjoric Lemay Manchester, NH & Susanna Gill Canada
LEMAY, Roger Maurice, Jan 28 1922 Sex:M Child# 1 Antonio Lemay Nashua, NH & Antoinette Dionne Nashua, NH
LEMAY, Rosanna, Apr 18 1895 Sex:F Child# 4 Edmond Lemay Canada & Georgianna Lefrenier Westbrook, ME
LEMAY, Therese, Apr 3 1923 Sex:F Child# 2 Antonio Lemay Nashua, NH & Antoinette Dionne Nashua, NH
LEMAY, Unknown, Mar 19 1906 Sex:M Child# 1 Eugene Lemay Canada & Zephirine St Onge Canada Stillborn
LEMAY, Victor Andre, May 16 1926 Sex:M Child# 2 Omer Lemay Canada & Yvonne Dionne Canada
LEMELIN, Rita Lorraine, Mar 26 1930 Sex:F Child# 2 Philippe Lemelin Canada & Marie Bernier Canada
LEMELIN, Unknown, Oct 6 1896 Sex:M Child# 1 F X Lemelin Canada & Marie L Morneau Canada Stillborn
LEMERE, Unknown, Feb 22 1918 Sex:F Child# 1 Archie Lemere Nashua, NH & Vera Lucas Canada Stillborn
LEMERIS, Marie Adeline, Jun 5 1897 Sex:F Child# 1 Victor Lemeris Nashua, NH & Catherine Dupins Rouses Point, NY
LEMERIS, Rheaume Victor, Nov 15 1898 Sex:M Child# 2 Victor Lemeris Nashua, NH & Catherine Dupins Rouses Pt, NY
LEMERY, Albert, Nov 2 1921 Sex:M Child# 2 Edouard Lemery NH & Grace Trudeau Vermont Stillborn
LEMERY, Albina, Aug 25 1891 Sex:F Child# 5 Adelard Lemery Canada & Therrile Chartrand Ellensbury, NY
LEMERY, Alfred A, Jan 5 1887 Sex:M Child# 2 Adelard Lemery P Q & Thersile Ellenbury, NY
LEMERY, Alfred Randall, Oct 5 1926 Sex:M Child# 1 Alfred Lemery NH & Christina Fuller NH
LEMERY, Antoinette Theresa, May 12 1933 Sex:F Child# 5 Armand Lemery Nashua, NH & Anna Roy Mass
LEMERY, Beatrice Doris, Jun 10 1923 Sex:F Child# 1 Armand Lemery Nashua, NH & Marie Anna Roy Canada
LEMERY, Berusdette L, Nov 23 1893 Sex:F Child# 2 John Lemery Nashua, NH & Nellie A Sullivan Nashua, NH
LEMERY, Doris Adeline, Dec 11 1922 Sex:F Child# 3 Edward Lemery Nashua, NH & Grace Trudeau Vermont
LEMERY, Edmond N, Mar 20 1900 Sex:M Child# 3 Victor Lemery NH & Kate Dupuis NY
LEMERY, Edouard O, May 22 1901 Sex:M Child# 4 Victor Lemery Nashua, NH & Catherine Dupuis Rouses Point, NY
LEMERY, Elizabeth K, Jan 3 1896 Sex:F Child# 3 John Lemery Nashua, NH & Helen A Sullivan Nashua, NH
LEMERY, Ernestine P, Dec 21 1893 Sex:F Child# 6 Adelard Lemery Canada & Thersile Chartrande Ellensburg, NY
LEMERY, Eugene Arthur, Jun 17 1924 Sex:M Child# 1 Emile Lemery Nashua, NH & Eunice Riley Nashua, NH
LEMERY, Florence Priscilla, Dec 10 1929 Sex:F Child# 4 Armand Lemery Nashua, NH & Annie Roy Canada
LEMERY, Harvey E, Mar 31 1903 Sex:M Child# 10 Adelard Lemery Canada & Therese Chartrand Ellenburgh, NY
LEMERY, Irene Rita, Jun 11 1925 Sex:F Child# 2 Armand Lemery Nashua, NH & Marie A Roy Canada
LEMERY, Jane Elizabeth, May 29 1924 Sex:F Child# 1 John Lemery Nashua, NH & Juliette Tonelia Milford, NH
LEMERY, John William, Sep 15 1898 Sex:M Child# 4 John Lemery Fall River, MA & Nellie A Sullivan Nashua, NH
LEMERY, John William, Dec 1 1934 Sex:M Child# 2 John Lemery Nashua, NH & Juliette Tonella Milford, NH
LEMERY, Joseph A, Jan 19 1898 Sex:M Child# 8 Adelard Lemery Canada & Thersile Charland Ellenburg, NY
LEMERY, Joseph E Daniel, Apr 29 1931 Sex:M Child# 5 Armand Lemery Nashua, NH & Annie Roy Canada
LEMERY, Joseph Richard, Apr 18 1934 Sex:M Child# 4 Alfred Lemery Nashua, NH & Christine Fuller W Thornton, NH
LEMERY, Leonie, Nov 29 1889 Sex:F Child# 4 Adelard Lemery Canada & T Chartrand Ellenburg, NY
LEMERY, Lucille Lillian, Aug 2 1920 Sex:F Child# 1 Edward Lemery Nashua, NH & Grace Trudeau Middlebury, VT
LEMERY, Mary, Jun 8 1892 Sex:F Child# 1 Hermengilde Lemery Canada & Nellie Sullivan Nashua, NH
LEMERY, Mildred Catherine, Apr 6 1924 Sex:F Child# 3 Edward Lemery Nashua, NH & Grace Trudeau Middlebury, VT
LEMERY, Paul Alvin, May 22 1935 Sex:M Child# 2 Emile Lemery Nashua, NH & Eunice Riley Nashua, NH
LEMERY, Raymond Victor, Mar 3 1920 Sex:M Child# 1 Rheaume V Lemery Nashua, NH & Mable Holmes Mass
LEMERY, Robert B, May 11 1901 Sex:M Child# 5 John Lemery Nashua, NH & Nellie A Sullivan Nashua, NH
LEMERY, Robert Bartholomew, Nov 9 1929 Sex:M Child# 1 Robert Lemery Nashua, NH & Alta White Nashua, NH
LEMIANCE, Jean B A G, Jul 13 1893 Sex:M Child# 1 J B Lemiance Moors Fork, NY & Marie Dubois Moors Fork, NY
LEMIERE, Raymond, Apr 19 1922 Sex:M Child# 3 Aneas Lemiere Nashua, NH & Veronica Lucas Canada
LEMIEUX, Armand Alfred, Aug 17 1901 Sex:M Child# 1 Alfred Lemieux Moores, NY & Zelia Chagnon Nashua, NH
LEMIEUX, Claire Yvette, Dec 18 1910 Sex:F Child# 2 Pierre P Lemieux Canada & Emma Blanchette US
LEMIEUX, Florence Simone, Sep 20 1907 Sex:F Child# 1 Pierre Lemieux Canada & Emma Blanchette US
LEMIEUX, Jos Paul Arthur R, May 5 1925 Sex:M Child# 2 Arthur Lemieux Canada & Lucia Levesque Canada
LEMIEUX, Joseph Albert, May 26 1907 Sex:M Child# 3 Auguste Lemieux Canada & Diana Dube Canada
LEMIEUX, Joseph Hector, Apr 1 1906 Sex:M Child# 2 Auguste Lemieux Canada & Diana Dube Canada
LEMIEUX, Jules, Nov 25 1895 Sex:M Child# 11 Samuel Lemieux Canada & Clementine Belanger Canada
LEMIEUX, Louise C, Mar 13 1895 Sex:F Child# 2 John Lemieux Moores Forks, NY & Marie Dubois Moores Forks, NY
LEMIEUX, Lucia Gertrude, Dec 15 1904 Sex:F Child# 1 Auguste Lemieux Canada & Diana Dube Canada
LEMIEUX, M Evangeline, Apr 3 1895 Sex:F Child# 12 David Lemieux Canada & Marie Desanges Canada
LEMIEUX, Marguerite, Jan 3 1914 Sex:F Child# 3 P P Lemieux Canada & Alma Blanchette Indian Orchard, MA Stillborn
LEMIEUX, Marie A Argentil, Sep 1 1896 Sex:F Child# 2 Benjamin Lemieux Canada & Gentil Langlais Canada
LEMIEUX, Marie Alma, May 4 1894 Sex:F Child# 3 Frank Lemieux Canada & Adelina Guay Canada
LEMIEUX, Marie Gracia, Apr 29 1916 Sex:F Child# 13 Adelard Lemieux Canada & Georgiana Beaudoin Canada
LEMIEUX, Paul Roger, Jul 7 1927 Sex:M Child# 3 Armand Lemieux Nashua, NH & Annie Roy Canada
LEMIEUX, Romeo, May 19 1908 Sex:M Child# 1 Joseph Lemieux Canada & Helene Lemieux Canada
LEMIRANDE, Irene Isabelle, Nov 27 1932 Sex:F Child# 1 A Lemirande Canada & Jeanne Bechard Canada
LEMIRE, Achille Eneas, Dec 23 1895 Sex:M Child# 1 Octave Lemire Canada & Mathilde Novalle Canada
LEMIRE, Achille Francois, Mar 11 1901 Sex:M Child# 3 Eugene Lemire Canada & Delphine Lecours Canada
LEMIRE, Alfred, Sep 9 1899 Sex:M Child# 1 William Lemire NH & Regina Boisvert Canada
LEMIRE, Colette Jeannette, Aug 12 1925 Sex:F Child# 4 Archibald Lemire Nashua, NH & Veronica Lucas Canada
LEMIRE, Frances Eugenia, Nov 16 1926 Sex:F Child# 1 Edgar Lemire Nashua, NH & Lillian Moran Nashua, NH
LEMIRE, Joanne Virginia, Aug 30 1931 Sex:F Child# 1 Alfred W Lemire Nashua, NH & Thelma Ora Fifield Nashua, NH

LEMIRE, Joseph Henry Maurice, Feb 8 1927 Sex:M Child# 9 Albert Lemire Canada & Rose Dupreis Canada
LEMIRE, Loretta Regina, Sep 12 1915 Sex:F Child# 4 William Lemire Hooksett, NH & Regina Boisvert Canada
LEMIRE, M Therese Constance, Dec 13 1925 Sex:F Child# 8 Albert Lemire Canada & Rose Dupries Canada
LEMIRE, Marie Albina, Aug 9 1897 Sex:F Child# 1 Eugene Lemire Canada & Delphine Lecours Canada
LEMIRE, Marie B Irene, Mar 26 1899 Sex:F Child# 2 Octave Lemire Canada & Mathilde Naval Canada
LEMIRE, Marie L Blanche, May 25 1901 Sex:F Child# 3 Octave Lemire Canada & Mathilde Nauval Canada
LEMIRE, Marie Pauline, May 24 1928 Sex:F Child# 2 William J Lemire Lowell, MA & Laur'te Labranche Canada
LEMIRE, Normand, May 30 1919 Sex:M Child# 2 Aneas Lemire Nashua, NH & Veronica Lucas Nashua, NH
LEMIRE, Onesime Joseph, Aug 1 1899 Sex:M Child# 2 Eugene Lemire Canada & Delphine Lecours Canada
LEMIRE, Ralphe A, Aug 26 1907 Sex:M Child# 3 William Lemire Hooksett, NH & Regina Boisvert Canada
LEMIRE, William Alfred, May 26 1934 Sex:M Child# 2 Alfred Lemire Nashua, NH & Thelma Fifield Nashua, NH
LEMOINE, Joseph C E, May 15 1892 Sex:M Child# 6 Cleophas Lemoine Canada & Exilda Larive Canada
LEMOINE, Joseph G R A, Jul 2 1905 Sex:M Child# 8 Cleophas Lemoine Canada & Exilda Larivee St Albans, VT
LEMOINE, Joseph H R, Nov 23 1895 Sex:M Child# 7 Cleophas Lemoine Canada & Exilda Larive St Albans, VT
LEMOINE, Marie E A, Sep 5 1887 Sex:F Child# 4 Cleophas Lemoine P Q & Exilda Larive St Albans, VT
LEMOINE, Marie L, May 7 1890 Sex:F Child# 4 Cleopehas Lemoine Canada & Exilda Larive Vermont
LEMONT, Nedria, Aug 11 1909 Sex:F Child# 1 Horace Lemont France & Marjorie Barrows Yarmouth, NS
LEMONY, Joseph, Jan 8 1912 Sex:M Child# 2 Joseph Lemony Russia & Mary Tsipkous Russia
LEMPARKINTE, Joseph, May 4 1909 Sex:M Child# 1 Russia & Eva Lemparkinte Russia
LENATSAS, Unknown, Feb 14 1920 Sex:M Child# 2 Kostas Lenatsas Greece & Kalispa Dosa Greece
LENCOURT, Joseph, Aug 7 1888 Sex:M Child# 2 Alphonse Lencourt Canada & Yarie L Morin Canada
LENDRON, Joseph Victor J, Sep 1 1890 Sex:M Child# 4 Joseph Lendron Canada & Celina Patois Canada
LENIHAN, Unknown, Aug 16 1887 Sex:F Child# 1 John Lenihan Nashua, NH & Kate Sullivan Ireland
LENKOWICZ, Sophia, Dec 1 1918 Sex:F Child# 1 Bronislaw Lenkowicz Russia & Geneva Skipper Russia
LENNEUX, Joseph Alfred, May 23 1892 Sex:M Child# 11 David Lenneux Canada & Desange Roi Canada
LENNYRE, Joseph E E, Apr 20 1901 Sex:M Child# 2 William Lennyre Hooksett, NH & Regina Boisvert Canada
LEON, Marie, Mar 26 1888 Sex:F Child# 2 Joseph Leon Canada & Josephine Gagnon Canada
LEONARD, Marguerite, Jan 5 1921 Sex:F Child# 3 Thomas Leonard Lancaster, NH & Cecelia Cone Nashua, NH
LEONARD, Norman, Jr, Sep 18 1933 Sex:M Child# 1 Norman Leonard Milford, NH & Helen Kelpus Nashua, NH
LEONARD, Richard Wilson, Aug 6 1919 Sex:M Child# 2 Thomas Leonard NH & Cecelia Cone NH
LEONARD, Thomas James, May 18 1918 Sex:M Child# 1 Thomas Leonard NH & Cecila Cone NH
LEONARD, Unknown, Jan 26 1890 Sex:M Child# 2 Fred C Leonard Woolwich, ME & Mary E Newport, ME
LEONARDI, Howard Woodbury, Dec 29 1917 Sex:M Child# 3 Antonio P Leonardi Italy & Abbolina Cavichole Italy
LEONARDI, Joseph Michael, Jun 25 1910 Sex:M Child# 3 Michael Leonardi Italy & Emelinda Palovanchi Italy
LEONARDI, Mary Ann L, Mar 4 1903 Sex:F Child# 2 Antonio Leonardi Italy & Carvicole Ambolina Italy
LEOPAS, Unknown, Apr 11 1928 Sex:F Child# 3 Dem Leopas Greece & Anas Dramitinou Greece
LEOSANE, Joseph George, Jun 21 1894 Sex:M Child# 4 Henri Leosane Nashua, NH & Lea Godette Canada
LEPAGE, Alfred Joseph, Oct 19 1931 Sex:M Child# 7 Joseph Lepage Hillsborough, NH & Florence Provencher Weare, NH
LEPAGE, Colette Priscilla, May 10 1930 Sex:F Child# 8 Octave Lepage Canada & Alice Rousseau Canada
LEPAGE, David, Mar 19 1905 Sex:M Child# 5 J B Lepage Canada & Marie Malpin Altoona, NY
LEPAGE, George, Sep 8 1904 Sex:M Child# 4 Louis Lepage Canada & Amanda Poliquin Canada
LEPAGE, Hervey Gideon, Dec 28 1924 Sex:M Child# 5 Octave Lepage Canada & Alice Rousseau Canada
LEPAGE, Jos Camille Roland, Dec 4 1928 Sex:M Child# 2 Valmont Lepage Canada & Ernestine St Onge Canada
LEPAGE, Joseph Arnold Norman, Jan 23 1924 Sex:M Child# 4 Octave Lepage Canada & Alice Rousseau Canada
LEPAGE, Joseph Emile, Oct 5 1893 Sex:M Child# 1 Joseph Lepage Canada & Josephine Fournier Canada
LEPAGE, Joseph Marcel, Jun 7 1922 Sex:M Child# 3 Octave Lepage Canada & Alice Rousseau Canada
LEPAGE, Laura Antoinette, Aug 23 1921 Sex:F Child# 2 Octave Lepage Canada & Alice Rousseau Canada
LEPAGE, Laura Elmira, Jul 11 1903 Sex:F Child# 3 Louis Lepage Canada & Amanda Poliquin Canada
LEPAGE, Lorraine, Apr 21 1919 Sex:F Child# 1 Octave Lepage Canada & Alice Rousseau Canada
LEPAGE, Marcel Adelard, Apr 18 1913 Sex:M Child# 9 Louis Lepage Canada & Amanda Poliquin Canada
LEPAGE, Marie Bernadette, Mar 15 1899 Sex:F Child# 4 Joseph Lepage Canada & Josephine Lemerise Chicopee Falls, MA
LEPAGE, Marie Blanche, Sep 10 1890 Sex:F Child# 5 Joseph Lepage Canada & Alice Fournier Canada
LEPAGE, Mary Louise, Sep 30 1891 Sex:F Child# 6 Joseph Lepage Canada & Alice Fournier Canada
LEPAGE, Paul Maurice, May 19 1926 Sex:M Child# 6 Octave Lepage Canada & Alice Rousseau Canada
LEPAGE, Rachael Gilberte, Apr 10 1931 Sex:F Child# 9 Octave Lepage Canada & Alice Rousseau Canada
LEPAGE, Robert Adrian, Feb 12 1930 Sex:M Child# 6 Joseph Lepage Hillsboro, NH & Florence Provencher Weare, NH
LEPAGE, Unknown, Feb 12 1894 Sex:M Child# 3 James Lepage Canada & Celina Champagne Maine
LEPAZA, Genefo, Apr 23 1916 Sex:F Child# 2 Clement Lepaza Russia & Anna Hormats Russia
LEPEZA, Theodore, Apr 8 1914 Sex:M Child# 1 Clement Lepeza Russia & Anna Armata Russia
LEPIN, Julius, Feb 7 1921 Sex:M Child# 2 Justin Lepin Lithuania Russia & Marcella Antuchiz Lithuania Russia
LEPINE, Alphege, Nov 19 1906 Sex:M Child# 9 Alfred Lepine Canada & Agnes Boulet Canada
LEPINE, Armand Harve, Mar 15 1910 Sex:M Child# 10 Alfred Lepine Canada & Agnes Boulet Canada
LEPINE, Gerald Jos Louis, Jun 5 1928 Sex:M Child# 2 Donat Lepine Canada & Orise Collar Canada
LEPINE, Jeanne Yolande, Feb 28 1932 Sex:F Child# 3 Donat Lepine Canada & Orize Collard Canada
LEPINE, Joseph Albert, Sep 10 1904 Sex:M Child# 6 Mederic Lepine Canada & Marie Boulette Canada
LEPINE, Joseph Alfred, Dec 1 1898 Sex:M Child# 3 Alfred Lepine Canada & Agnes Boulette Canada
LEPINE, Joseph Amable O, Apr 27 1908 Sex:M Child# 8 Alfred Lepine Canada & Agnes Boulet Canada
LEPINE, Juliette Lillienne B, Mar 15 1910 Sex:F Child# 11 Alfred Lepine Canada & Agnes Boulet Canada
LEPINE, Loretta, Jan 13 1934 Sex:F Child# 4 Donat Lepine Canada & Aurise Callard Canada
LEPINE, Marie Annette A, Oct 18 1911 Sex:F Child# 12 Alfred Lepine Canada & Agnes Boulet Canada
LEPINE, Marie Yolande, Apr 20 1926 Sex:F Child# 1 Aime Lepine Canada & Alice Forcier Canada
LEPINE, Unknown, Sep 13 1897 Sex:M Child# 2 Alfred Lepine Canada & Agnes Boulette Canada Stillborn
LEPLANTE, Joseph Adolph Daniel, Jul 6 1918 Sex:M Child# 2 Adolphe Leplante Canada & Alida Masson Canada

LERKOVITCH, Stanislaus, May 7 1911 Sex:M Child# 2 Charles Lerkovitch Russia & Josephine Matskavitc Russia
LEROCQUE, Frances Marie, Dec 3 1925 Sex:F Child# 2 Hector Lerocque Canada & Alma Simard Nashua, NH
LESAGE, Albert, Dec 26 1892 Sex:M Child# John Lesage Ellenpond, VT & Rose Hood Presentation, PQ
LESAGE, Alfred Hornidas, May 26 1889 Sex:M Child# 6 Joseph Lesage Canada & Philomene Glande Champlain, VT
LESAGE, Charles F II, Jun 13 1887 Sex:M Child# Francois Lesage P Q & Suzanne Tremblay P Q
LESAGE, Claudette, Apr 29 1931 Sex:F Child# 3 Romeo Lesage Nashua, NH & Irene Vallee Nashua, NH
LESAGE, Elie Edgar, Nov 27 1909 Sex:M Child# 2 Oscar Lesage US & Augustine Lemoine US
LESAGE, George, May 15 1891 Sex:M Child# 7 Joseph Lesage Canada & Philomene Claude Canada
LESAGE, Gerald, Sep 21 1910 Sex:M Child# 5 John Lesage Nashua, NH & Delia Deschenes Canada
LESAGE, Henri, Oct 16 1892 Sex:M Child# 8 Joseph Lesage Canada & Philomene Slade Nashua, NH
LESAGE, Henri Theophile, Oct 29 1903 Sex:M Child# 2 John Lesage Nashua, NH & Emelie Deschanes Canada
LESAGE, Jeannette Edna, Mar 3 1917 Sex:F Child# 1 Albert Lesage Nashua, NH & Leda St Jean Quincy, MA
LESAGE, Juliette, Oct 8 1906 Sex:F Child# 3 John B Lesage Nashua, NH & Emelia Deschenes Canada
LESAGE, Leon Daniel, Sep 27 1908 Sex:M Child# 4 J B Lesage Nashua, NH & Amelia Deschenes Canada
LESAGE, Magloire, Apr 26 1895 Sex:M Child# 9 Joseph Lesage Canada & Philomene Claude Canada
LESAGE, Marie Bernadette, Mar 28 1895 Sex:F Child# 8 John Lesage Canada & Rose Houde Island Pond, VT
LESAGE, Marie gloria J, Sep 12 1924 Sex:F Child# 1 Romeo Lesage NH & Irene Vallie NH
LESAGE, Marie Irene, Dec 28 1904 Sex:F Child# 1 William Lesage Canada & Analie Adams Canada
LESAGE, Marie Jacqueline Luc, Sep 25 1927 Sex:F Child# 2 Romeo Lesage Nashua, NH & Irene Vallee Nashua, NH
LESAGE, Paul, Sep 1 1913 Sex:M Child# 6 Jean Bte Lesage Nashua, NH & Amelia Deschenes Canada
LESAGE, Pierre, Feb 4 1891 Sex:M Child# 6 John Lesage Canada & Rose Honde Canada
LESAGE, Roland Normand, Aug 8 1908 Sex:M Child# 1 Oscar Lesage US & Augustine Lemoine US
LESAGE, Romeo, Apr 29 1902 Sex:M Child# 1 John B Lesage Nashua, NH & Emelia Deschenes Canada
LESARD, Obeline, Jul 2 1891 Sex:F Child# 5 Pierre Lesard Canada & Zoe Bienvenue Canada
LESIEUR, Adeline Irene, Sep 14 1907 Sex:F Child# 5 Charles Lesieur Nashua, NH & Flora Morin Nashua, NH
LESIEUR, Cecile Dorilda, Mar 19 1914 Sex:F Child# 9 Charles Lesieur Nashua, NH & Flora Morin Nashua, NH
LESIEUR, Edouard Robert, Oct 19 1918 Sex:M Child# 10 Charles Lesieur Nashua, NH & Flora Morin Nashua, NH
LESIEUR, Elphege, Feb 25 1904 Sex:M Child# 3 Charles Lesieur Nashua, NH & Flora Morin Nashua, NH
LESIEUR, Eveline Camille, Sep 19 1921 Sex:F Child# 12 Charles Lesieur Nashua, NH & Flora Moria Nashua, NH
LESIEUR, Florina E M, Jun 16 1900 Sex:F Child# 4 Xavier Lesieur Canada & Alexina Boneau Canada
LESIEUR, Gertrude Livinia, Sep 26 1910 Sex:F Child# 7 Charles Lesieur Nashua, NH & Flora Morin Nashua, NH
LESIEUR, Jeannette Therese, Jun 13 1920 Sex:F Child# 10 Charles Lesieur Nashua, NH & Flora Morin Nashua, NH
LESIEUR, Joseph Henri, Oct 21 1901 Sex:M Child# 2 Joseph Lesieur Mass & Elmire Mailhotte NH
LESIEUR, Josephine Aldea, Apr 10 1899 Sex:F Child# 3 Xavier Lesieur Canada & Alexina Bonneau Canada
LESIEUR, Leo Raymond, Jul 30 1926 Sex:M Child# 1 Leo Lesieur Nashua, NH & J Maynard Nashua, NH
LESIEUR, Lillie Beatrice, Dec 29 1905 Sex:F Child# 4 Charles Lesieur Canada & Flora Morin Canada
LESIEUR, M Aurore, Jun 20 1895 Sex:F Child# 1 Xavier Lesieur Canada & Exina Bonneau Canada
LESIEUR, Madeline Joan, May 20 1935 Sex:F Child# 4 Leo Lesieur Nashua, NH & Jeannette Maynard Nashua, NH
LESIEUR, Marie Emelie, Sep 3 1900 Sex:F Child# 1 Joseph Lesieur Mass & Elmire Mallhoit NH
LESIEUR, Marie P A, Jun 30 1896 Sex:F Child# 2 Xavier Lesieur Canada & Exina Bonnaeu Canada
LESIEUR, Paul, Dec 26 1926 Sex:M Child# 1 Elphege Lesieur Nashua, NH & O Bilodeau Nashua, NH
LESIEUR, Raymond Roland, Apr 19 1912 Sex:M Child# 8 Charles Lesieur Nashua, NH & Flora Morin Nashua, NH
LESIEUR, Roland Maynard, Mar 13 1929 Sex:M Child# 2 Leo Lesieur Nashua, NH & Jeannette Maynard Nashua, NH
LESIEUR, Rose Yvonne I, Dec 9 1908 Sex:F Child# 6 Charles Lesieur Nashua, NH & Flora Morin Nashua, NH
LESIEUR, Unknown, Nov 19 1900 Sex:M Child# 1 Charles Lesieur Nashua, NH & Flora Morin Nashua, NH Stillborn
LESIEUR, Xavier Leon S, Jun 13 1902 Sex:M Child# 5 Xavier Lesieur Canada & Alexina Bonneau Canada
LESLIE, Martha Joan, Mar 2 1934 Sex:F Child# 1 Gordon Chas Leslie Hudson, NH & Barbara Bailey Nashua, NH
LESSARD, Albertine Lilian, Sep 1895 Sex:F Child# 11 John Lessard Canada & Philomene Gaudette Canada
LESSARD, Aldege George, Sep 30 1897 Sex:M Child# 2 Francis Lessard Littleton, MA & Claudia Fraser Canada
LESSARD, Ambrose Herman, Apr 8 1926 Sex:M Child# 3 Joseph Lessard Nashua, NH & Juliette Hudon Canada
LESSARD, Amedee Bernard, Jan 4 1929 Sex:M Child# 7 Elphege Lessard Nashua, NH & Florence Davis Fall River, MA
LESSARD, Angeline, Jul 19 1889 Sex:F Child# 4 Pierre Lessard Canada & Zoe Bienvenue Canada
LESSARD, Armand Ernest, Jan 21 1922 Sex:M Child# 2 Leo Lessard Nashua, NH & Mildred Bleau Nashua, NH
LESSARD, Arthur Eugene, Nov 29 1928 Sex:M Child# 4 Arthur Lessard Canada & D Parenteau Canada
LESSARD, Arthur Robert, Mar 7 1920 Sex:M Child# 2 Joseph Lessard Nashua, NH & Corana Boilard Nashua, NH
LESSARD, Arthur William, Dec 18 1923 Sex:M Child# 1 Aldege Lessard NH & Lydia Belanger NH
LESSARD, Conrad, Oct 21 1923 Sex:M Child# 2 Alphege Lessard Nashua, NH & Florence Davis Fall River, MA
LESSARD, Constance Jeanne, Jan 4 1933 Sex:F Child# 8 Elphege Lessard Nashua, NH & Florence Davis Fall River, MA
LESSARD, Edouard Roland, Jun 18 1921 Sex:M Child# 3 Joseph Lessard NH & Corana Boilard NH
LESSARD, Eliane, Jun 26 1902 Sex:F Child# 4 Francis Lessard Littleton, MA & Claudia Fraser Canada
LESSARD, Elphege, Sep 30 1898 Sex:M Child# 12 John Lessard Canada & Philomene Gaudette Canada
LESSARD, Eva Rose, Dec 18 1887 Sex:F Child# 6 John Lessard P Q & Philomene Gaudette Canada
LESSARD, Francis Norman, Sep 18 1930 Sex:M Child# 5 Aldege Lessard Nashua, NH & Lydia Belanger Nashua, NH
LESSARD, Genevieve Zoe, Jan 21 1918 Sex:F Child# 2 Henry L Lessard Nashua, NH & Louise Murray Winchendon, MA
LESSARD, Gertrude Mary Irene, Aug 8 1924 Sex:F Child# 2 Edward Lessard Manchester, NH & Irene Laflamme Manchester
LESSARD, Grace Josephine, May 29 1921 Sex:F Child# 3 O'Neil L Lessard Pepperell, MA & Mary E Duggan Nashua, NH
LESSARD, Henri, Aug 21 1891 Sex:M Child# 8 John Lessard Canada & Philomene Gaudette Canada
LESSARD, Irene Yvonne, Sep 28 1921 Sex:F Child# 3 Aldege Lessard NH & Lydia Belanger NH
LESSARD, J Leo Albert Adrien, Jun 16 1920 Sex:M Child# 1 Leo Lessard NH & Mildred Bleau NH
LESSARD, J Patrick Jerome, Mar 17 1922 Sex:M Child# 2 Joseph N Lessard US & Julia L Hudon Canada
LESSARD, Jean Victor, Jan 17 1925 Sex:M Child# 3 Elphage Lessard Nashua, NH & Florence Davis Fall River, MA
LESSARD, Jessie, Dec 15 1894 Sex:F Child# 8 Pierre Lessard Canada & Zoe Bieuvenue Canada
LESSARD, Joseph Adrien, Aug 5 1896 Sex:M Child# 1 Francis Lessard Littleton, MA & Claudia Fraser Canada

LESSARD, Joseph Geo Maurice, Sep 21 1918 Sex:M Child# 1 Joseph Lessard NH & Corona Boilard NH
LESSARD, Joseph Henry Sylvio, Jun 23 1926 Sex:M Child# 5 Joseph Lessard Nashua, NH & Coranna Boilard Nashua, NH
LESSARD, Joseph N L, Mar 11 1896 Sex:M Child# 5 Henri Lessard Nashua, NH & Lea Gaudette Canada
LESSARD, Leo, May 28 1899 Sex:M Child# 3 Francis Lessard Canada & Claudia Fraser Canada
LESSARD, Lil Pearl Rachelle, Mar 8 1920 Sex:F Child# 2 Aldege Lessard NH & Lydia Belanger NH
LESSARD, Louis Henri, Sep 10 1887 Sex:M Child# Pierre Lessard Canada & Zoe Bunvenue P Q
LESSARD, Louise Edith, Mar 26 1926 Sex:F Child# 4 Elphege Lessard Nashua, NH & Florence Davis Fall River, MA
LESSARD, Marcelle, Apr 11 1924 Sex:F Child# 3 Joseph N Lessard Nashua, NH & Julia Hudon Canada
LESSARD, Marie Gloria Carmeli, Jul 12 1923 Sex:F Child# 3 Leo Lessard Nashua, NH & Mildred Bleau Nashua, NH
LESSARD, Marie H, Dec 31 1897 Sex:F Child# 6 Henri Lessard Nashua, NH & Lea Gaudette Canada
LESSARD, Marie I L, Sep 14 1890 Sex:F Child# 1 Henri Lessard Nashua, NH & Lea Gaudet Canada
LESSARD, Marie L C, Dec 5 1889 Sex:F Child# 7 John Lessard Johnsbury, NH & Philomene Gaudet Canada
LESSARD, Mary Genevieve, Oct 23 1919 Sex:F Child# 2 O'Neil Lessard Pepperell, MA & Mary Duggan Nashua, NH
LESSARD, Melina Adeline, Nov 28 1892 Sex:F Child# 3 Henri Lessard Canada & Lea Gaudette Canada
LESSARD, Napoleon Noel, Dec 23 1892 Sex:M Child# John Lessard Canada & Philomene Gaudette Canada
LESSARD, Normand, Apr 5 1934 Sex:M Child# 9 Elphage Lessard Nashua, NH & Florence Davis Fall River, MA
LESSARD, Paul O'Neil, Sep 5 1918 Sex:M Child# 1 O'Neil I Lessard Pepperell, MA & Mary E Duggan Nashua, NH
LESSARD, Paul Richard Prudent, Apr 3 1928 Sex:M Child# 6 Joseph Lessard Nashua, NH & Corona Boilard Nashua, NH
LESSARD, Robert Adrien, Nov 29 1918 Sex:M Child# 1 Eldege G Lessard Nashua, NH & Lydia Belanger Nashua, NH
LESSARD, Robert Louis, May 7 1931 Sex:M Child# 7 Elphege Lessard Nashua, NH & Florence Davis Mass
LESSARD, Roger, Feb 13 1926 Sex:M Child# 1 Eddy Lessard Canada & Angeline Coulombe Canada
LESSARD, Rose A, Jun 27 1900 Sex:F Child# 13 John Lessard Canada & Philomine Gaudette Canada
LESSARD, Suzanne Amelia, Jul 3 1932 Sex:F Child# 5 Joseph Lessard Nashua, NH & Julia Hudon Canada
LESSARD, Sylvia Edith, Aug 2 1927 Sex:F Child# 5 Elphege Lessard US & Florence Davis US
LESSARD, Tharsile Philomene, Mar 30 1923 Sex:F Child# 1 Henry Lessard Canada & Georgianna Lessard US
LESSARD, Theodore Lambert, Oct 29 1923 Sex:M Child# 4 Joseph Lessard Canada & Corana Boilard Canada
LESSARD, Unknown, Sep 24 1927 Sex:M Child# 2 Edward Lessard Canada & A Coulombe Canada
LESSARD, Victor, Apr 1 1892 Sex:M Child# 2 Pierre Lessard Nashua, NH & Marie Roy Canada
LESSARD, Zoe Julienne, Oct 29 1892 Sex:F Child# 6 Pierre Lessard Canada & Julie Bienvenue Canada
LESSART, Joseph H, Sep 16 1891 Sex:M Child# 2 Henri Lessart Nashua, NH & Lea Gaudet Canada
LESSART, Joseph L, Jan 15 1899 Sex:M Child# 7 Henri Lessart Nashua, NH & Lea Gaudette Canada
LESSART, Marie G, Oct 14 1900 Sex:F Child# 8 Henri Lessart Nashua, NH & Lea Gaudette Canada
LESSIENAM, Laura, Apr 6 1914 Sex:F Child# 1 Pruno Lessienam Italy & Alice Bilodeau Nashua, NH Stillborn
LESSIEUR, Jeannette Lorraine, Apr 26 1932 Sex:F Child# 2 Elphege Lessieur Nashua, NH & Aurore Bilodeau Nashua, NH
LESSIEUR, Madeline Jacqueline, Feb 5 1931 Sex:F Child# 3 Leo Lessieur Nashua, NH & Jeannette Maynard Nashua, NH
LESTER, Nellie, Jan 31 1917 Sex:F Child# 3 Clements Lester Russia & Broni Mahuicka Russia
LETCHURTH, Unknown, Apr 18 1888 Sex:M Child# 1 Thomas Letchurth Mufensboro, IL & Nellie Scanlon Nashua, NH Stillbor
LETENDRE, Armand, Feb 14 1905 Sex:M Child# 4 John Letendre Manchester & Maria Theriault Canada
LETENDRE, Constance C Gertrude, Mar 19 1933 Sex:F Child# 3 Ernest Letendre Nashua, NH & Dora Bourgeignan Canada
LETENDRE, Eddie Ernest, Jan 6 1909 Sex:M Child# 6 John Letendre NH & Maria Theriault Canada
LETENDRE, Edouard Leo F, Sep 2 1899 Sex:M Child# 1 John Letendre Manchester, NH & Maria Theriault Canada
LETENDRE, Emile Robert, Jun 12 1903 Sex:M Child# 3 John Letendre Manchester, NH & Marie Theriault Canada
LETENDRE, Eva D R, Jun 26 1904 Sex:F Child# 9 Louis Letendre Canada & Georgiana Salvail Canada
LETENDRE, Gerard, Jun 30 1923 Sex:M Child# 2 Leo Letendre Nashua, NH & Olivine Laverdiere Canada
LETENDRE, Henri Alphonse, Aug 6 1911 Sex:M Child# 7 John Letendre Canada & Maria Therian Canada
LETENDRE, Jean G O, Aug 12 1901 Sex:M Child# 2 John Letendre Manchester, NH & Maria Theriault Canada
LETENDRE, John Edward, Feb 26 1896 Sex:M Child# 1 John Letendre Manchester & Cora White Boston, MA
LETENDRE, Jos Bernard Clement, Oct 31 1926 Sex:M Child# 2 Romuald Letendre Nashua, NH & Ellen R Moses Canada
LETENDRE, Joseph, Jun 10 1888 Sex:M Child# 2 Louis Letendre Canada & Georgeianna Salvail Canada
LETENDRE, Joseph E L, Apr 7 1892 Sex:M Child# 2 Pierre Letendre Manchester & Marie Dutilly Canada
LETENDRE, Joseph L D, Jun 6 1895 Sex:M Child# 3 George Letendre Manchester, NH & Marie Dutilly Canada
LETENDRE, Joseph M N, Jan 15 1892 Sex:M Child# 4 Louis Letendre Canada & Georgianna Salvail Canada
LETENDRE, Lil Jeannette Cecile, Oct 24 1914 Sex:F Child# 8 John Letendre Canada & Maria Theriault Canada
LETENDRE, Marie A I, Nov 29 1896 Sex:F Child# 4 George Letendre Manchester, NH & Marie Dutilly Canada
LETENDRE, Marie A R, Jun 18 1893 Sex:F Child# 5 Louis Letendre Canada & Georgiana Salvail Canada
LETENDRE, Marie C G, Mar 18 1897 Sex:F Child# 8 Louis Letendre Canada & Georgianna Salvail Canada
LETENDRE, Marie L, Apr 1 1898 Sex:F Child# 4 George Letendre Manchester, NH & Marie Dutilly Canada
LETENDRE, Marie P B, Feb 8 1896 Sex:F Child# 7 Louis Letendre Canada & Georgianna Salvail Canada
LETENDRE, Marie Rose Germaine, May 19 1928 Sex:F Child# 3 Romuald Letendre Nashua, NH & Marie St Laurent Canada
LETENDRE, Marie T, Dec 4 1894 Sex:F Child# 6 Louis Letendre Canada & Georgiana Salvail Canada
LETENDRE, Maurice H Leonard, Sep 29 1931 Sex:M Child# 2 Ernest Letendre Nashua, NH & Dora Bourguignon Canada
LETENDRE, Paul Louis, Dec 7 1922 Sex:M Child# 1 Rom P Letendre Nashua, NH & Marie A St Laurent Canada
LETENDRE, Pierre E T, Sep 4 1889 Sex:M Child# 3 Louis Letendre Canada & Georgianna Salvail Canada
LETENDRE, Sylvio C Daniel, Apr 18 1921 Sex:M Child# 1 Leo F Letendre NH & Olivine Laverdiere Mass
LETENDRE, Unknown, Jun 11 1930 Sex:M Child# 4 Romuald Letendre Nashua, NH & Marie A St Laurent Canada
LETENDRE, Veronique Agnes, Jun 7 1907 Sex:F Child# John Letendre Manchester, NH & Maria Theriault Canada
LETIVS, George, Aug 14 1912 Sex:M Child# 2 Michael Letives Russia & Anna Valasavitch Russia
LETOURNEURE, Josephine Alice, Nov 10 1894 Sex:F Child# 2 George Letourneure Nashua, NH & Josephine Emond Canada
LETOURNEUX, Eugene Napoleon, Nov 4 1893 Sex:M Child# 1 George Letourneux Nashua, NH & Josephine Emond Canada
LETOURNEUX, Lillian J, Mar 27 1903 Sex:F Child# 5 George Letourneux Nashua, NH & Josephine Emond Canada
LETOURNEUX, Marie Eva B, Jan 9 1900 Sex:F Child# 4 George Letourneux Nashua, NH & Josephine Emond Canada
LETRIS, John, May 18 1920 Sex:M Child# 4 Alexander Letris Russia & Agnes Molute Russia
LETTENEY, Donald Elmer, Sep 2 1906 Sex:M Child# 2 Frederick C Letteney Mass & Grace A Bagley Mass

LETTENEY, Paul Frederick, Aug 1 1905 Sex:M Child# 1 Frederick C Letteney Mass & Grace Bagley Boston, MA
LEVACK, Unknown, Jul 28 1890 Sex:M Child# 3 George Levack Scotland & Flora Jefts Manchester, NH
LEVAISSEUR, Unknown, Jun 9 1933 Sex:M Child# 1 Henry Lavaisseur Laconia, NH & Jeannette Garant Laconia, NH Stillbo
LEVANS, Joseph, Oct 13 1888 Sex:M Child# 2 Pierre Levans Canada & Delphine Boussia Canada
LEVEILLE, Alphonse, Sep 12 1905 Sex:M Child# 7 Alphonse Leveille Canada & Josephine Muller Canada
LEVEILLE, Edmond Eugene, Mar 28 1896 Sex:M Child# 4 Narcisse Leveille Canada & Lucie Bousquet Canada
LEVEILLE, Ernest Raymond, Apr 28 1921 Sex:M Child# 13 Alphonse Leveille Canada & Josephine Nickles Canada
LEVEILLE, George Albert, Nov 1 1909 Sex:M Child# 9 Alphonse Leveille Canada & Josephine Millaire Canada
LEVEILLE, Henri Wilfred, Nov 19 1911 Sex:M Child# 10 Alphonse Leveille Canada & Josephine Millaire Canada
LEVEILLE, Jos Roger Maurice, Oct 2 1923 Sex:M Child# 3 Frank Leveille NH & Yvonne Sylvain Canada
LEVEILLE, Leo Gerard, Jul 14 1929 Sex:M Child# 6 Frank Leveille Suncook, NH & Yvonne Sylvain Canada
LEVEILLE, Maria Josephine, Apr 19 1901 Sex:F Child# 4 Alphonse Leveille Canada & Josephine Miller Canada
LEVEILLE, Rachell Pauline, Nov 11 1931 Sex:F Child# 2 Alfred Leveille Nashua, NH & Irene Gauthier Nashua, NH
LEVEILLE, Sonia, Nov 18 1935 Sex:F Child# 1 Al Leveille, Jr Nashua, NH & Mild Richardson Manchester, NH
LEVEILLE, Unknown, May 12 1893 Sex:F Child# 4 Marcisse Leveille Canada & Lucie Bousquet Canada Stillborn
LEVEILLEE, Arthur Armand, Jan 15 1916 Sex:M Child# 11 Alphonse Leveillee Canada & Josephine Miller Canada
LEVEILLEE, Joseph Alfred, May 16 1904 Sex:M Child# 6 Alphonse Leveillee Canada & Josephine Miller Canada
LEVEILLEE, Joseph Jean Robert, Jan 12 1928 Sex:M Child# 5 Frank Leveillee Suncook, NH & Yvonne Sylvain Canada
LEVEILLEE, Roger, Jan 2 1934 Sex:M Child# 7 Frank Leveillee Suncook, NH & Yvonne Sylvain Canada
LEVEILLEE, Sylvia Yvonne, Feb 21 1908 Sex:F Child# 7 Alphonse Leveillee Canada & Josephine Miller Canada
LEVEILLES, Roger Maurice Philli, Jul 12 1935 Sex:M Child# 3 Alfred Leveilles Nashua, NH & Irene Gauthier Manchester
LEVENSON, Louis, Oct 3 1894 Sex:M Child# 1 Max Levenson Russia & Lina Lervis Russia
LEVEQUE, Albert S, Jan 28 1897 Sex:M Child# 1 Paul Leveque Canada & Georgiana Rocheleau Nashua, NH
LEVEQUE, Anna Rejina, Jan 8 1896 Sex:F Child# 13 Ferdinand Leveque Canada & Eseorie Boucher Canada
LEVEQUE, Bernadette, Jun 12 1896 Sex:F Child# 3 Fidime Leveque Canada & Angelina Gagne Canada
LEVEQUE, Edouard G, Oct 18 1887 Sex:M Child# Martial Leveque Canada & Marie Dufour Canada
LEVEQUE, Exora, Oct 1 1897 Sex:F Child# 14 Ferdinand Leveque Canada & Exora Boucher Canada Stillborn
LEVEQUE, Fidime P, Nov 24 1897 Sex:M Child# 4 Fidime Leveque Canada & Angeline Gagne Canada
LEVEQUE, Marie Aimee, Dec 6 1896 Sex:F Child# 3 Edmond Leveque Canada & Rosanna Dionne Canada
LEVEQUE, Victor Emile, Jul 31 1893 Sex:M Child# 1 Frederic Leveque Canada & Angeline Gague Canada
LEVEQUES, Anna Caroline, Jul 8 1892 Sex:F Child# 6 Ferdina Leveques Canada & Exorie Boucher Canada
LEVERDIERE, Oscar Roger, Dec 10 1927 Sex:M Child# 5 Joseph Leverdiere Canada & Emma Morin Canada
LEVESQUE, Adjutor, Aug 21 1909 Sex:M Child# 4 Deisre Levesque Canada & Delina Rheaume Canada
LEVESQUE, Adrienne J, Jun 12 1902 Sex:F Child# 6 Edmond Levesque Canada & Rosanna Dionne Canada
LEVESQUE, Albert, Jun 20 1906 Sex:M Child# 1 Charles Levesque Canada & Leontine Levesque Canada
LEVESQUE, Albert Armand, Aug 8 1924 Sex:M Child# 2 Prosper Levesque Mansfield, MA & Alex Pelletier Canada
LEVESQUE, Albert Sylvia, Jul 18 1907 Sex:M Child# 6 Treffle Levesque Canada & Eulalie Plourde Canada
LEVESQUE, Aldea Germaine, May 3 1910 Sex:F Child# 3 Donat Levesque Canada & Marie Boutin Canada
LEVESQUE, Alfred Adalbert, Mar 31 1898 Sex:M Child# 2 Alfred Levesque Canada & Antoinette Kerouac Canada
LEVESQUE, Alfred Eugene, Feb 1 1914 Sex:M Child# 1 Alfred Levesque Canada & Leontine Lizotte Canada
LEVESQUE, Alida, Jul 30 1908 Sex:F Child# 2 Joseph Levesque Canada & Lucia Lavoie Canada
LEVESQUE, Alphonse Lucien, Jan 22 1911 Sex:M Child# 6 Alphonse L Levesque Canada & Claudia Emond Canada
LEVESQUE, Alphonse Normand, Jun 26 1928 Sex:M Child# 1 Jos Levesque Uncasville, CT & B Levesque Nashua, NH
LEVESQUE, Andree Alfred Ronald, Oct 28 1933 Sex:M Child# 2 A Levesque Nashua, NH & Mabel Bishop Bay City, MI
LEVESQUE, Angelina, Aug 12 1901 Sex:F Child# 10 Treffe Levesque Canada & Angeline Lemieux Canada
LEVESQUE, Anice, May 28 1900 Sex:M Child# 1 Treffle Levesque Canada & Hulalie Plourde Canada
LEVESQUE, Ann Marie Hortense, Jul 26 1922 Sex:F Child# 1 Dem Levesque Canada & Aimee Cote Canada
LEVESQUE, Anne Marie G, Jul 26 1924 Sex:F Child# 2 Joseph Levesque Canada & Marie Lavoie Canada
LEVESQUE, Annette Rita, Mar 28 1926 Sex:F Child# 1 Albert Levesque Vermont & Angelina Levesque Canada
LEVESQUE, Anselm, Mar 6 1894 Sex:M Child# 4 A Levesque Canada & Victoria Pinnette Canada
LEVESQUE, Arthur, May 3 1906 Sex:M Child# 2 Jean Bte Levesque Canada & Marie Bois Canada
LEVESQUE, Audrey Margaret, Jun 4 1934 Sex:F Child# 1 Lionel Levesque Nashua, NH & Elizabeth Vaughan Troy, NY
LEVESQUE, Auguste, Jan 29 1935 Sex:M Child# 9 Jos H Levesque St Bruno, PQ & Marie L Levesque Mont Carmel, PQ
LEVESQUE, Aurele Gerard, Jun 14 1920 Sex:M Child# 8 George Levesque Canada & Lea Dube Canada
LEVESQUE, Beatrice Henrietta, Jun 23 1923 Sex:F Child# 1 Irence Levesque Nashua, NH & Ora Chartrain Manchester, NH
LEVESQUE, Blanche Dora, May 18 1907 Sex:F Child# 3 Desire Levesque Canada & Delina Rheaume Canada
LEVESQUE, Blanche Irene, Dec 23 1898 Sex:F Child# 2 Paul Levesque Canada & Georgiana Rocheleau Canada
LEVESQUE, Blanche Lucille, Nov 15 1911 Sex:F Child# 2 Thomas Levesque Canada & Margaret E Welitte Whitefield,
LEVESQUE, Cecile Antoinette, Feb 1 1917 Sex:F Child# 3 Joseph Levesque Canada & Eva Duhamel Nashua, NH
LEVESQUE, Cecile Georgianna, Nov 28 1934 Sex:F Child# 5 Joseph Levesque Norwich, CT & Bernadette Levesque Nashua
LEVESQUE, Celestine Beatrice, Nov 6 1915 Sex:F Child# 10 Jean Bte Levesque Canada & Marie Boris Canada
LEVESQUE, Charles Alphonse, Jul 12 1907 Sex:M Child# 3 Alphonse Levesque,Jr Canada & Claudia Hemond Canada
LEVESQUE, Charles Arthur, Oct 3 1922 Sex:M Child# 3 Pierre Levesque Canada & Louise Arel Canada
LEVESQUE, Charles Elmond, Aug 24 1903 Sex:M Child# 4 Joseph Levesque Canada & Alice Keroac Canada
LEVESQUE, Charles Eugene, Jul 31 1894 Sex:M Child# 1 George Levesque Canada & E Grandmaison Canada
LEVESQUE, Charles Leo, Jul 9 1911 Sex:M Child# 1 Charles Levesque Canada & Marie Dube Canada
LEVESQUE, Charles Leo, Nov 21 1906 Sex:M Child# 6 Paul Levesque Canada & Georgiana Rocheleau Nashua, NH
LEVESQUE, Cherry May, Mar 9 1930 Sex:F Child# 6 Eli Levesque Canada & Ruby Rosa Vermont
LEVESQUE, Claire, Sep 21 1935 Sex:F Child# 1 Horace Levesque Nashua, NH & Claudia Pelletier Nashua, NH
LEVESQUE, Cyprien Maxime, Nov 19 1914 Sex:M Child# 1 Cyprien Levesque Canada & Maria Chabot Canada
LEVESQUE, Daniel Joseph G, Aug 3 1930 Sex:M Child# 3 Ernest Levesque Canada & Rose Anna Levesque Canada
LEVESQUE, David Raoul, Nov 18 1913 Sex:M Child# 6 Desire Levesque Canada & Delina Rheaume Canada
LEVESQUE, Delina, Dec 8 1904 Sex:F Child# 1 Desire Levesque Canada & Delina Rheaume Canada

LEVESQUE, Dora Juliette, Aug 29 1924 Sex:F Child# 6 Joseph E Levesque Nashua, NH & Eva Duhamel Nashua, NH
LEVESQUE, Dorilda Madeleine, Jun 5 1914 Sex:F Child# 6 George Levesque Canada & Lea Dube Canada
LEVESQUE, Doris Elaine, Dec 13 1933 Sex:F Child# 1 Hilaire Levesque Nashua, NH & Helen St Germain Nashua, NH
LEVESQUE, Edmond Antoine, Jun 5 1917 Sex:M Child# 3 Cyprien Levesque Canada & Marie Chabot Canada
LEVESQUE, Elaine Ruby, May 7 1923 Sex:F Child# 5 Eli Levesque Canada & Ruby Cross Vermont
LEVESQUE, Elsie Anita, Jun 24 1925 Sex:F Child# 4 Joseph P Levesque Canada & Florence Nickerson US
LEVESQUE, Elzear Leo, Jan 31 1915 Sex:M Child# 3 Alphonse Levesque Canada & Marie L Levesque Canada
LEVESQUE, Emery John, May 16 1935 Sex:M Child# 4 Alfred Levesque Nashua, NH & Mabel Bishop Detroit, MI
LEVESQUE, Emile Armand, Aug 18 1913 Sex:M Child# 1 Joseph Levesque Canada & Eva Duhamel Nashua, NH
LEVESQUE, Emile Oswald, Aug 6 1916 Sex:M Child# 6 Marcel Levesque Canada & Alida Lord
LEVESQUE, Emma, Jun 5 1894 Sex:F Child# 12 Ferdinand Levesque Canada & Exoree Bouchard Canada
LEVESQUE, Ernest, May 15 1904 Sex:M Child# 1 J Baptiste Levesque Canada & Marie Bois Canada
LEVESQUE, Ernest Armand, Aug 25 1921 Sex:M Child# 5 Joseph Levesque Canada & Alexandrine Langlais Canada
LEVESQUE, Ernest Gerard, Apr 21 1923 Sex:M Child# 9 Alphonse Levesque Canada & Marie L Levesque Canada
LEVESQUE, Ernest Raoul, Mar 21 1930 Sex:M Child# 2 Raoul Levesque Canada & Lilliane Belanger Nashua, NH
LEVESQUE, Ernest Robert, Feb 27 1924 Sex:M Child# 3 E R Levesque Canada & Irene Manseau Canada
LEVESQUE, Ernestine Lena, May 8 1930 Sex:F Child# 11 Alphonse Levesque Canada & Claudia Emond Canada
LEVESQUE, Estelle Carmen, Apr 15 1931 Sex:F Child# 7 Joseph Levesque Canada & Marie Deschenes Canada
LEVESQUE, Estelle Rita, Mar 23 1925 Sex:F Child# 3 Treffle Levesque Nashua, NH & M Louise Brodeur Nashua, NH
LEVESQUE, Etienne Albert, Jun 11 1928 Sex:M Child# 1 Albert Levesque Canada & Rose Belanger Canada
LEVESQUE, Eugene, Jul 30 1925 Sex:M Child# 11 Alphonse Levesque Canada & Marie L Levesque Canada
LEVESQUE, Eva Blandina, Jan 23 1919 Sex:F Child# 2 Etienne Levesque Canada & Marie Louise Bibeau Canada
LEVESQUE, Eva Marie, Dec 29 1916 Sex:F Child# 3 Etienne Levesque Canada & Marie L Marquis Canada
LEVESQUE, Evelyn, Dec 12 1923 Sex:F Child# 3 Ernest Levesque Canada & Clara Evans Maine
LEVESQUE, Florence Lorraine, May 23 1928 Sex:F Child# 1 Sylvia Levesque Nashua, NH & Viola Lambert S Berwick, ME
LEVESQUE, Florent, Feb 2 1902 Sex:M Child# 1 Adelard Levesque Canada & Marie Levesque Canada
LEVESQUE, Florette Marguerite, Mar 1 1918 Sex:F Child# 3 Ralph Levesque Canada & Rachel Bizolle Canada
LEVESQUE, Francois, May 31 1908 Sex:M Child# 4 George Levesque Canada & Lea Dube Canada
LEVESQUE, George, Nov 13 1934 Sex:M Child# 1 George Levesque, Jr Nashua, NH & Albina Berube Nashua, NH
LEVESQUE, George Claude Lucien, Oct 25 1915 Sex:M Child# 10 Alphonse Levesque Canada & Claudia Emond Canada
LEVESQUE, George Sylvin, Jul 4 1895 Sex:M Child# 4 Joseph Levesque Canada & Clara Aprile Canada
LEVESQUE, George Treffle, Aug 3 1896 Sex:M Child# 5 James Levesque Canada & Clara April Canada
LEVESQUE, Gerald, Feb 28 1928 Sex:M Child# 1 David Levesque Nashua, NH & M A Michaud Canada
LEVESQUE, Gerard Leonard, Apr 23 1918 Sex:M Child# 11 J B Levesque Canada & Marie Bois Canada
LEVESQUE, Gertrude, Apr 2 1906 Sex:F Child# 5 Treffle Levesque Canada & Eulalie Plourde Canada
LEVESQUE, Gilberte Bertha, Aug 19 1904 Sex:F Child# 1 Marcel Levesque Canada & Alida Lard Canada
LEVESQUE, Harold Gayton, Jul 12 1935 Sex:M Child# 3 Edmond Levesque Nashua, NH & Ruth Gadbois Littleton, NH
LEVESQUE, Henry, May 24 1927 Sex:M Child# 10 A Levesque Canada & Marie L Levesque Canada
LEVESQUE, Horace, Aug 24 1913 Sex:M Child# 9 Treffle Levesque Canada & Eulalie Plourde Canada
LEVESQUE, Ida, Apr 16 1907 Sex:F Child# 3 Auguste Levesque Canada & Marie Lavoie Canada
LEVESQUE, Irene Lilliane, Sep 1 1915 Sex:F Child# 5 Donat Levesque Canada & Marie Boutin Canada
LEVESQUE, J Andre Albert, Oct 24 1912 Sex:M Child# 2 Charles Levesque Canada & Marie Dube Canada
LEVESQUE, J B Leonidas, Apr 10 1904 Sex:M Child# 1 Odias Levesque Canada & Vitaline Levesque Canada
LEVESQUE, J Edward Marcel, Jul 7 1922 Sex:M Child# 4 Joseph Levesque Canada & Florence Bujold Canada
LEVESQUE, J Jean B Emile, Dec 29 1911 Sex:M Child# 5 Damase Levesque Canada & Demerise Theriault Canada
LEVESQUE, J Philippe Lucien, Sep 18 1913 Sex:M Child# 2 Alphonse Levesque Canada & Marie L Levesque Canada
LEVESQUE, J Thomas Walter, Jul 29 1913 Sex:M Child# 6 Damase Levesque Canada & Demerise Theriault Canada
LEVESQUE, Jacqueline F, Mar 12 1920 Sex:F Child# 7 Marcel Levesque Canada & Aleda Lord Canada
LEVESQUE, Jean Andre, Aug 21 1935 Sex:M Child# 3 John Levesque Standish, NY & Laura Blair Nashua, NH
LEVESQUE, Jean Baptiste, Mar 22 1894 Sex:M Child# 1 Cyrille Levesque Canada & Apoline Thibeau Canada
LEVESQUE, Jean Baptiste, Apr 16 1896 Sex:M Child# 2 Louis Levesque Canada & Luce Canuel Canada
LEVESQUE, Jean Fernand, Nov 8 1932 Sex:M Child# 8 Jos T Levesque Canada & Marie Deschenes Canada Stillborn
LEVESQUE, Jeanne d'Arc, Dec 27 1920 Sex:F Child# 1 Ernest Levesque Canada & Rose Levesque Canada
LEVESQUE, Jeanne d'Arc Cecile, Apr 7 1919 Sex:F Child# 4 Cyprien Levesque Canada & Maria Chabot Canada
LEVESQUE, Jeannette, Aug 10 1921 Sex:F Child# 2 Etienne Levesque Canada & Cleandre Belanger Canada
LEVESQUE, John Francis, Mar 20 1927 Sex:M Child# 3 Charles Levesque Lowell, MA & Aileen Murphy Lowell, MA
LEVESQUE, Jos Antoine Maurice, May 5 1925 Sex:M Child# 3 Albert Levesque Canada & M Jeanie Carle Canada
LEVESQUE, Jos Dem't's L W, Jan 9 1902 Sex:M Child# 8 Joseph Levesque Canada & Clara April Canada
LEVESQUE, Jos Edward Roger, May 28 1926 Sex:M Child# 2 Arthur Levesque N Chelmsford, MA & Marie E Desclos Nashua
LEVESQUE, Jos Henry Donat, Oct 11 1927 Sex:M Child# 3 Arthur Levesque N Chelmsford, MA & Emma Desclos Newmarket, NH
LEVESQUE, Jos Irenee Conrad, Apr 20 1926 Sex:M Child# 2 Irenee Levesque Nashua, NH & Aurore Chartrain Manchester
LEVESQUE, Jos Placi Stanislaus, Jul 8 1918 Sex:M Child# 7 Stanislaus Levesque Canada & Claudia Lavoie Canada
LEVESQUE, Jos Prosper Marcel, May 7 1923 Sex:M Child# 1 Prosper Levesque Mansfield, MA & Alexina Pelletier Canada
LEVESQUE, Jos Prosper Maurice, Aug 27 1929 Sex:M Child# 2 Albert Levesque Fall River, MA & Marie Rose Belanger
LEVESQUE, Jos Robert Armand, May 10 1923 Sex:M Child# 2 Patrick Levesque Canada & Ida Raymond Canada
LEVESQUE, Jos Robert Charles, Dec 31 1927 Sex:M Child# 2 Etienne Levesque Canada & Rose A Charest Canada
LEVESQUE, Jos Rodolphe Normand, Apr 28 1918 Sex:M Child# 6 Marcel Levesque Canada & Alida Lord Canada
LEVESQUE, Jos Roger Romeo, May 30 1929 Sex:M Child# 2 Joseph Levesque Conn & Bernadette Levesque Nashua, NH
LEVESQUE, Joseph, Jul 1 1895 Sex:M Child# 17 Ambroise Levesque Canada & Olympe Dumais Canada
LEVESQUE, Joseph, May 31 1896 Sex:M Child# 1 Pierre Levesque Canada & Amanda Rioux Canada
LEVESQUE, Joseph, Dec 15 1911 Sex:M Child# 1 Ralph Levesque Canada & Rachel Bufold Canada
LEVESQUE, Joseph, Oct 6 1919 Sex:M Child# 13 J M Levesque Canada & Clara April Canada
LEVESQUE, Joseph, Sep 11 1923 Sex:M Child# 2 Albert Levesque Canada & Marie Jeanne Carle Canada Stillborn

```
LEVESQUE, Joseph, May 22 1925 Sex:M Child# 10 Gaudias Levesque Canada & Delvina Lizotte Canada Stillborn
LEVESQUE, Joseph, Aug 9 1929 Sex:M Child# 1 Thomas Levesque Nashua, NH & Geraldine Bernier Canada Stillborn
LEVESQUE, Joseph, Aug 17 1933 Sex:M Child# 8 J H Levesque Canada & Marie L Levesque Canada Stillborn
LEVESQUE, Joseph A, Jan 13 1897 Sex:M Child# 2 Thomas Levesque Canada & Florance Caissy Canada
LEVESQUE, Joseph A F, Dec 31 1896 Sex:M Child# 12 Francois Levesque Canada & Marie Martin Canada
LEVESQUE, Joseph Adrien, Nov 21 1905 Sex:M Child# 10 Joseph Levesque Canada & Clara April Canada
LEVESQUE, Joseph Albert, Jan 24 1896 Sex:M Child# 5 Euseberes Levesque Canada & Victoria Penette Canada
LEVESQUE, Joseph Albert L, Mar 10 1907 Sex:M Child# 4 J Bte Levesque Canada & Marie Bois Canada
LEVESQUE, Joseph Alfred, Jun 7 1893 Sex:M Child# 1 Louis Levesque Canada & Asilda Larouche Canada
LEVESQUE, Joseph Alfred D, Oct 12 1905 Sex:M Child# 2 Telephore Levesque Canada & Proxelle Gariepy Canada
LEVESQUE, Joseph Alfred J B, Jan 7 1914 Sex:M Child# 1 J Baptiste Levesque Canada & Agnes DeGrammont Canada
LEVESQUE, Joseph Alfred M, Oct 11 1900 Sex:M Child# 4 Lazare Levesque Canada & Clara Thibault Canada
LEVESQUE, Joseph Alfred Roger, Nov 17 1928 Sex:M Child# 6 Joseph Levesque Canada & M L Levesque Canada
LEVESQUE, Joseph Alphonse, Jun 22 1907 Sex:M Child# 9 Lazare Levesque Canada & Clara Thibault Canada
LEVESQUE, Joseph Alphonse Alb, Jul 16 1912 Sex:M Child# 1 Alphonse Levesque Canada & Marie Louise Levesque Canada
LEVESQUE, Joseph Armand Henri, May 11 1918 Sex:M Child# 1 Treffle G Levesque Nashua, NH & Marie L Brodeur Nashua
LEVESQUE, Joseph Art Albert, Mar 7 1915 Sex:M Child# 2 Joseph Levesque Canada & Malvina Bonvouloir Canada
LEVESQUE, Joseph Arthur, Jun 21 1911 Sex:M Child# 7 J B Levesque Canada & Marie Bois Canada
LEVESQUE, Joseph Arthur O, Jul 4 1901 Sex:M Child# 2 Pierre Levesque Canada & Marie Gauvin Canada
LEVESQUE, Joseph C E, Jun 5 1898 Sex:M Child# 6 Joseph Levesque Canada & Clara April Canada
LEVESQUE, Joseph Camile Raoul, Jun 23 1914 Sex:M Child# 6 Joseph Levesque Canada & Harmonia Soucy Canada
LEVESQUE, Joseph Claude E, Apr 4 1924 Sex:M Child# 14 Alph Levesque
LEVESQUE, Joseph Clovis, Mar 29 1917 Sex:M Child# 3 Augustus Levesque Canada & Justina Ouellette Canada
LEVESQUE, Joseph Cyprien, Jan 27 1898 Sex:M Child# 3 Louis Levesque Canada & Luce Canuel Canada
LEVESQUE, Joseph David Euclide, May 15 1904 Sex:M Child# 2 David Levesque Canada & Ferilda Ouillette Canada
LEVESQUE, Joseph Desire Roger, Mar 31 1918 Sex:M Child# 8 Desire Levesque Canada & Delina Rheaume Canada
LEVESQUE, Joseph Elisee, Dec 27 1906 Sex:M Child# 1 Joseph Levesque Canada & Alice Langlois Canada
LEVESQUE, Joseph Ernest T, Aug 8 1906 Sex:M Child# 1 Desire Levesque Canada & Maxzelia Grenier Canada
LEVESQUE, Joseph Etienne, May 30 1914 Sex:M Child# 1 Eitenne Levesque Canada & M Louise Marquis Canada
LEVESQUE, Joseph Etienne A, Oct 27 1909 Sex:F Child# 11 Lazare Levesque Canada & Clara Thibault Canada
LEVESQUE, Joseph Fortunat, Oct 28 1905 Sex:M Child# 1 Joseph Levesque Canada & Marie Soucy Canada
LEVESQUE, Joseph Francois, Feb 28 1891 Sex:M Child# 9 Francois Levesque Canada & Marie Martin Canada
LEVESQUE, Joseph George Albert, Aug 20 1912 Sex:M Child# 13 Lazare Levesque Canada & Clara Thibault Canada
LEVESQUE, Joseph George S, May 1 1903 Sex:M Child# 1 George Levesque Canada & Lea Dube Canada
LEVESQUE, Joseph Gerald, Apr 15 1924 Sex:M Child# 4 Pierre Levesque Canada & Loisa Arel Canada
LEVESQUE, Joseph Hector, Jul 27 1921 Sex:M Child# 8 Alphonse Levesque Canada & Marie Louise Levesqu Canada
LEVESQUE, Joseph Henri Romeo, May 24 1912 Sex:M Child# 1 Joseph Levesque Canada & Malvina Bonvouloir Canada
LEVESQUE, Joseph Iree, Jun 5 1892 Sex:M Child# 2 Joseph Levesque Canada & Clara Aprile Canada
LEVESQUE, Joseph Irenee, Dec 19 1893 Sex:M Child# 3 Joseph Levesque Canada & Clara Aprile Canada
LEVESQUE, Joseph Isidore, Dec 4 1927 Sex:M Child# 5 Joseph Levesque Canada & Florence Bujold Canada
LEVESQUE, Joseph Israel, Nov 6 1918 Sex:M Child# 1 Israel Levesque Canada & Anna Burque Mass
LEVESQUE, Joseph Israel, Oct 31 1922 Sex:M Child# 3 Israel Levesque Canada & Anna Burke Mass
LEVESQUE, Joseph Ivan, Oct 3 1906 Sex:M Child# 1 Donat Levesque Canada & Alma Boutin Canada
LEVESQUE, Joseph Jean Louis, Jan 8 1908 Sex:M Child# 3 Damase Levesque Canada & Demerise Theriault Canada
LEVESQUE, Joseph L, Apr 17 1900 Sex:M Child# 4 Louis Levesque Canada & Lucia Carvell Canada
LEVESQUE, Joseph L H, Jun 3 1899 Sex:M Child# 3 Lazarre Levesque Canada & Clara Thibault Canada
LEVESQUE, Joseph Leo, Jun 12 1916 Sex:M Child# 1 Benoit Levesque Canada & Antonia Roy Canada
LEVESQUE, Joseph Leo Henry, Sep 12 1898 Sex:M Child# 1 Antoine Levesque Canada & Philomene Ouellette Canada
LEVESQUE, Joseph Leo Roger, Feb 19 1922 Sex:M Child# 12 Jean B Levesque Canada & Marie Bois Canada
LEVESQUE, Joseph Leo W, Dec 31 1906 Sex:M Child# 2 Francois Levesque Canada & Eugenie Fortin Canada
LEVESQUE, Joseph Lionel D, Feb 15 1908 Sex:M Child# 2 Louis Levesque Canada & Wilhelmine Cote Canada
LEVESQUE, Joseph Louis R, Dec 27 1906 Sex:M Child# 2 Louis Levesque Canada & Amanda Dube Canada
LEVESQUE, Joseph Michel, Sep 29 1895 Sex:M Child# 2 Cyrille Levesque Canada & Pauline Thibault Canada
LEVESQUE, Joseph Pascal R, Apr 28 1905 Sex:M Child# 7 Lazare Levesque Canada & Clara Thibault Canada
LEVESQUE, Joseph Paul, Jun 26 1904 Sex:M Child# 5 Paul Levesque Canada & Georgiana Rocheleau Canada
LEVESQUE, Joseph Paul, Sep 14 1928 Sex:M Child# 14 Alph Levesque Canada & Marie L Levesque Canada
LEVESQUE, Joseph Pierre, Oct 17 1914 Sex:M Child# 9 Alphonse Levesque Canada & Claudia Emond Canada
LEVESQUE, Joseph Raymond, Sep 5 1925 Sex:M Child# 5 Pierre Levesque Canada & Louisa Arel Canada
LEVESQUE, Joseph Robert, Sep 12 1916 Sex:M Child# 3 Goudias Levesque Canada & Delvina Lissotte Canada
LEVESQUE, Joseph Roland, Jun 13 1921 Sex:M Child# 2 Pierre Levesque Canada & Louise Arel Canada
LEVESQUE, Joseph Roland, Jun 24 1930 Sex:M Child# 14 Alphonse Levesque Canada & Marie L Levesque Canada
LEVESQUE, Joseph Rolland, Apr 8 1915 Sex:M Child# 9 Joseph Levesque Mass & Marie Ouellette Canada
LEVESQUE, Joseph Sherman, Apr 27 1918 Sex:M Child# 3 Eli Levesque Canada & Rubie Ross Vermont
LEVESQUE, Joseph T Albert, Oct 13 1899 Sex:M Child# 9 Treffle Levesque Canada & Agnelina Lemieux Canada
LEVESQUE, Joseph Victor A, Jul 29 1895 Sex:M Child# 3 Achille Levesque Canada & Radagonde Duprey Canada
LEVESQUE, Joseph Wilfred P, Sep 15 1906 Sex:M Child# 2 Damase Levesque Canada & Demerise Theriault Canada
LEVESQUE, Joseph Wilfrid, Mar 1 1908 Sex:M Child# 5 J B Levesque Canada & Marie Bois Canada
LEVESQUE, Joseph Wilfrid, Feb 17 1910 Sex:M Child# 6 Joseph Levesque Canada & Marie Bois Canada
LEVESQUE, Joseph Z Cyprien, Sep 17 1899 Sex:M Child# 14 Anseme Levesque Canada & Odinasse Lavoie Canada
LEVESQUE, Juliette Anna, Apr 23 1925 Sex:F Child# Desire Levesque Canada & Delima Rheaume Canada
LEVESQUE, Laurent, Jun 23 1924 Sex:M Child# 1 George Levesque Nashua, NH & Marie St Laurent Canada
LEVESQUE, Leda Theodora, Nov 7 1910 Sex:F Child# 6 Joseph Levesque Mass & Marie Ouellette Canada
LEVESQUE, Leo Albert, Nov 26 1900 Sex:M Child# 5 Edm Levesque Canada & Rosanna Dionne Canada
```

LEVESQUE, Leo Claire, May 28 1910 Sex:F Child# 5 Frank Levesque Canada & Eugenie Voyer Canada
LEVESQUE, Leon Joseph, Jun 3 1933 Sex:M Child# 1 Ernest Levesque Nashua, NH & Simone Dionne Nashua, NH Stillborn
LEVESQUE, Leontine Lorette, Jun 20 1912 Sex:F Child# 7 Alphonse Levesque Canada & Marie Emond Canada
LEVESQUE, Leopold Etienne, Apr 12 1920 Sex:M Child# 3 Etienne Levesque Canada & Marie Louise Bibeau Canada
LEVESQUE, Leopoldine, Feb 25 1908 Sex:F Child# 3 Joseph Levesque Canada & Harmonia Soucy Canada
LEVESQUE, Lilian Beatrice, Mar 1 1900 Sex:F Child# 3 Paul Levesque Canada & Georgiana Rochilieu Nashua, NH
LEVESQUE, Lillian May A, Mar 30 1905 Sex:F Child# 1 Thomas Levesque Canada & Marguerite Willet Whitefield, NH
LEVESQUE, Lina Liliane, Aug 29 1907 Sex:F Child# 11 Joseph Levesque Canada & Clara April Canada
LEVESQUE, Lloyd Frances, Aug 15 1919 Sex:M Child# 1 Ernest Levesque Canada & Clara E Evans Alfred, ME
LEVESQUE, Loraine Rita, Jun 15 1922 Sex:F Child# 1 Albert Levesque Nashua, NH & Clara Marquis Nashua, NH
LEVESQUE, Lorette, Apr 13 1910 Sex:F Child# 3 Desire Levesque Canada & Mexzelia Grenier Canada
LEVESQUE, Louis, May 11 1902 Sex:M Child# Louis Levesque Canada & Marie Levesque Canada
LEVESQUE, Louis Hilaire, Apr 27 1932 Sex:M Child# 4 Sylvio Levesque Nashua, NH & Viola Lambert S Berwick, ME
LEVESQUE, Louis Irene, Jun 20 1906 Sex:F Child# 4 Demetrius Levesque Canada & Melie Anna Dube Canada
LEVESQUE, Louis Jos Raymond, Nov 11 1926 Sex:M Child# 4 Joseph Levesque Canada & Marie Deschesnes Canada
LEVESQUE, Louis Philippe, Mar 11 1900 Sex:M Child# 5 Fiderine Levesque Canada & Angelina Gagne Canada
LEVESQUE, Louis Roland, Nov 8 1906 Sex:M Child# 2 Joseph Levesque Canada & Armonia Soucy Canada
LEVESQUE, Louis Victor, Jan 31 1892 Sex:M Child# 4 Archille Levesque Canada & Radagonde Duperry Canada
LEVESQUE, Lucien Robert, Apr 8 1912 Sex:M Child# 4 Donat Levesque Canada & Alexina Boutin Canada
LEVESQUE, Ludger, Aug 31 1893 Sex:M Child# 15 Ambroise Levesque Canada & Olymphe Dumais Canada
LEVESQUE, Ludger Arthur, Aug 3 1917 Sex:M Child# 5 Alphonse Levesque Canada & Marie Louise Canada
LEVESQUE, M Aglae L Y, Feb 8 1909 Sex:F Child# 6 David Levesque Canada & Florida Ouellet Canada
LEVESQUE, M Aurore Claudia, Jan 15 1914 Sex:F Child# 6 Stanislaus Levesque Canada & Claudia Lavoie Canada
LEVESQUE, M Blanche L, Dec 2 1893 Sex:F Child# 5 Achille Levesque Canada & Radagonde Duperez Canada
LEVESQUE, M Germaine Sonia, Apr 26 1913 Sex:F Child# 3 Auguste Levesque Canada & Justine Ouellette Canada
LEVESQUE, M Germaine Yvonne, Nov 15 1922 Sex:F Child# 13 Alphonse Levesque Canada & Claudia Emond Canada
LEVESQUE, M Henriette Lillian, Nov 23 1920 Sex:F Child# 1 Albert Levesque Canada & Marie Jeanne Carle Canada
LEVESQUE, M Irene Evangeline, Mar 14 1915 Sex:F Child# 2 Godios Levesque Canada & Elvine Lizotte Canada
LEVESQUE, M Jeanne Cecile, Aug 1 1913 Sex:F Child# 8 Alphonse Levesque Canada & Claudia Emond Canada
LEVESQUE, M Juliette Ant, Aug 9 1921 Sex:F Child# 8 Stanislas Levesque Canada & Claudia Lavoie Canada
LEVESQUE, M Laura Jeanne D, Jun 15 1919 Sex:F Child# 9 Desire Levesque Canada & Delima Rheaume Canada
LEVESQUE, M Laurette Juliette, Aug 24 1911 Sex:F Child# 12 Lazare Levesque Canada & Clara Thibeault Canada
LEVESQUE, M Lucille Violette, Nov 7 1913 Sex:F Child# 1 Joseph Levesque Canada & Philomene Laplante Canada
LEVESQUE, M Philomene Simone, Jun 8 1917 Sex:F Child# 1 Joseph Levesque Canada & Florence Bugold Canada
LEVESQUE, M rose A Y, Sep 20 1908 Sex:F Child# 12 Joseph Levesque Canada & Clara Levesque Canada
LEVESQUE, M Simone Germaine, Jun 30 1914 Sex:F Child# 3 Charles Levesque Canada & Marie Dube Canada
LEVESQUE, M Yvonne L, Oct 11 1909 Sex:F Child# 5 Alphonse Levesque Canada & Claudia Hemond Canada
LEVESQUE, Margaret Valentine, Feb 14 1917 Sex:F Child# 2 Elie Levesque Canada & Ruby Ross Vermont
LEVESQUE, Maria, Oct 18 1908 Sex:F Child# 5 Alphonse Levesque Canada & Claudia Emond Canada
LEVESQUE, Maria Blanche Emma, Nov 3 1915 Sex:F Child# 7 Damase Levesque Canada & Demerise Theriault Canada
LEVESQUE, Maria Pelagie, Oct 2 1897 Sex:F Child# 11 Achille Levesque Canada & Elise Francoeur Canada
LEVESQUE, Maria Simone I, Jan 17 1903 Sex:F Child# 6 Francois Levesque Canada & Eugenie Fortin Canada
LEVESQUE, Marie, May 14 1916 Sex:F Child# 2 Joseph Levesque Canada & Philomene Laplante Canada Stillborn
LEVESQUE, Marie, Oct 22 1923 Sex:F Child# 9 Gaudias Levesque Canada & Delvinia Lizotte Canada Stillborn
LEVESQUE, Marie A Albina, Jun 7 1902 Sex:F Child# 5 Lazare Levesque Canada & Clara Thibeault Canada
LEVESQUE, Marie A Delores, Jan 11 1929 Sex:F Child# 4 Josephat Levesque Canada & Marie Lavoie Canada
LEVESQUE, Marie Albina, Feb 25 1900 Sex:F Child# 7 Joseph Levesque Canada & Clara April Canada
LEVESQUE, Marie Alice, May 29 1893 Sex:F Child# 10 Francois Levesque Canada & Marie Martin Canada
LEVESQUE, Marie Alice, Nov 1 1894 Sex:F Child# 11 Francois Levesque Canada & Marie Martin Canada
LEVESQUE, Marie Alice, Mar 9 1919 Sex:F Child# 5 Gaudias Levesque Canada & Delvina Lizotte Canada
LEVESQUE, Marie Alice A, Feb 25 1900 Sex:F Child# 1 Joseph Levesque Canada & Zoe Duval Canada
LEVESQUE, Marie Alice Cecile, Oct 6 1930 Sex:F Child# 7 Joseph H Levesque Canada & Marie L Levesque Canada
LEVESQUE, Marie Alice Rita, Oct 31 1909 Sex:F Child# 4 Damase Levesque Canada & Demerise Theriault Canada
LEVESQUE, Marie Alma, Jan 23 1899 Sex:F Child# 1 Pierre Levesque Canada & Marie Gauvin Canada
LEVESQUE, Marie Alma I, Apr 27 1906 Sex:F Child# 1 Louis Levesque Canada & Wilhelmine Cote Canada
LEVESQUE, Marie Angelina, Jul 8 1904 Sex:F Child# 6 Louis Levesque Canada & Luce Caluel Canada
LEVESQUE, Marie Anita, Jul 18 1908 Sex:F Child# 5 Joseph Levesque Canada & Marie Ouellette Canada
LEVESQUE, Marie Ann, Jul 19 1934 Sex:F Child# 5 Sylvio A Levesque Nashua, NH & Viola M Lambert S Berwick, ME
LEVESQUE, Marie Anna, Dec 14 1890 Sex:F Child# 1 Joseph Levesque Canada & Clara Aprile Canada
LEVESQUE, Marie Anna, Jun 6 1894 Sex:F Child# 1 Louis Levesque Canada & Luce Cannell Canada
LEVESQUE, Marie Anna B, May 1 1906 Sex:F Child# 8 Lazare Levesque Canada & Clara Thibault Canada
LEVESQUE, Marie Anna Olivette, Jul 15 1926 Sex:F Child# 4 J H Levesque Canada & Marie L Levesque Canada
LEVESQUE, Marie Anne Beatrice, Oct 15 1923 Sex:F Child# 2 Jos Henry Levesque Canada & Marie L Levesque Canada
LEVESQUE, Marie Anne Eva, Dec 15 1916 Sex:F Child# 1 Etienne Levesque, Jr Canada & Marie Louise Bibeau US
LEVESQUE, Marie Annette, Sep 8 1931 Sex:F Child# 16 Alphonse Levesque Canada & Marie L Levesque Canada
LEVESQUE, Marie Aurelie O, Feb 22 1898 Sex:F Child# 2 Lazarre Levesque Canada & Clara Thibault Canada
LEVESQUE, Marie Aurore C, Apr 11 1905 Sex:F Child# 1 Alphonse Levesque Canada & Claudia Emond Canada
LEVESQUE, Marie Beatrice, Apr 23 1916 Sex:F Child# 1 Pierre Levesque Canada & Laura Arel Canada
LEVESQUE, Marie Blance A, Mar 4 1906 Sex:F Child# 2 Desire Levesque Canada & Delina Rheaume Canada
LEVESQUE, Marie Blanche, Apr 15 1906 Sex:F Child# 3 George Levesque Canada & Lea Dube Canada
LEVESQUE, Marie Blanche E, Sep 2 1907 Sex:F Child# 7 Louis Levesque Canada & Luce Karmell Canada
LEVESQUE, Marie Blanche Y, Jan 31 1909 Sex:F Child# 1 Auguste Levesque Canada & Justine Ouellet Canada
LEVESQUE, Marie Bridget T, Nov 9 1930 Sex:F Child# 4 Ralph Levesque Canada & Rachel Bugold Canada

LEVESQUE, Marie Camile, Mar 25 1921 Sex:F Child# 1 Ernest Levesque Nashua, NH & Irene Manseau Canada
LEVESQUE, Marie Cecile, Sep 21 1918 Sex:F Child# 6 Alphonse Levesque Canada & Marie L Levesque Canada
LEVESQUE, Marie Cecile, Apr 24 1920 Sex:F Child# 1 Patrick Levesque Canada & Ida Raymond Canada
LEVESQUE, Marie Cecile, Mar 21 1922 Sex:F Child# 8 Gaudiose Levesque Canada & Delvina Lizotte Canada
LEVESQUE, Marie Cecilie Gertru, Aug 3 1925 Sex:F Child# 1 Etienne Levesque Canada & Rose A Charest Canada
LEVESQUE, Marie Clara, Feb 16 1896 Sex:F Child# 13 Arsene Levesque Canada & Odinas Lavoie Canada
LEVESQUE, Marie Clara Elise, Feb 13 1897 Sex:F Child# 1 Lazarre Levesque Canada & Clara Thibault Canada
LEVESQUE, Marie Clemence, Aug 22 1920 Sex:F Child# 3 Joseph Levesque Canada & Florance Bigeold Canada
LEVESQUE, Marie Delia B, Jul 25 1905 Sex:F Child# 1 Joseph Levesque Canada & Lucia Lavoie Canada
LEVESQUE, Marie Delmina, Aug 22 1897 Sex:F Child# 1 Maurice Levesque Canada & Delmina St Laurent Lawrence, MA
LEVESQUE, Marie Edith F, Mar 21 1903 Sex:F Child# 9 Joseph Levesque Canada & Clara April Canada
LEVESQUE, Marie Est Madeleine, Mar 7 1933 Sex:F Child# 9 E Levesque Mt Carmel, PQ & C Belanger St Andre, PQ
LEVESQUE, Marie Eugenie B, Oct 1 1905 Sex:F Child# 3 David Levesque Canada & Florida Ouellette Canada
LEVESQUE, Marie Eva, May 24 1906 Sex:F Child# 2 Alphonse Levesque Canada & Marie Emond Canada
LEVESQUE, Marie Eva E, Feb 22 1898 Sex:F Child# 7 Archille Levesque Canada & Rodogonde Landry Canada
LEVESQUE, Marie Eva Rose, Jul 9 1913 Sex:F Child# 1 Francois Levesque Canada & Marianne Levesque Nashua, NH
LEVESQUE, Marie Eva Y, Nov 18 1905 Sex:F Child# 3 Joseph Levesque Canada & Marie Ouellette Canada
LEVESQUE, Marie Florette, Aug 5 1909 Sex:F Child# 4 Joseph Levesque Canada & Harmonia Soucy Canada
LEVESQUE, Marie Florida J, Feb 2 1903 Sex:F Child# 1 David Levesque Canada & Florida Ouellette Canada
LEVESQUE, Marie Geraldine, Apr 9 1932 Sex:F Child# 1 Thomas Levesque Nashua, NH & Geraldine Bernier Canada
LEVESQUE, Marie Irene, Jul 1 1911 Sex:F Child# 8 Trefle Levesque Canada & Eulalie Plourde Canada
LEVESQUE, Marie Irene C, Dec 13 1930 Sex:F Child# 1 Thomas Levesque Canada & Anna Girard Canada
LEVESQUE, Marie Isabelle, Aug 28 1910 Sex:F Child# 7 David Levesque Canada & Dorilda Ouellette Canada
LEVESQUE, Marie Ivonne, Dec 23 1909 Sex:F Child# 1 Joseph Levesque Canada & Annie Labrie Canada
LEVESQUE, Marie Jannette, May 11 1916 Sex:F Child# 4 Alphonse Levesque Canada & Marie L Levesque Canada
LEVESQUE, Marie Jeanne, Jun 13 1923 Sex:F Child# 4 Octave Levesque Canada & Anna Emond Canada
LEVESQUE, Marie Jeannette, Jul 8 1914 Sex:F Child# 9 Louis Levesque Canada & Marie Hamel Canada
LEVESQUE, Marie Jeannette Rita, Jan 28 1928 Sex:F Child# 9 Stan Levesque Canada & Claudia Lavoie Canada
LEVESQUE, Marie Josephine, Mar 23 1897 Sex:F Child# 1 Alfred Levesque Canada & Antoinette Kerouac Canada
LEVESQUE, Marie Juliette, Nov 25 1912 Sex:F Child# 3 Joseph Levesque Canada & Rosanna Labelle Nashua, NH
LEVESQUE, Marie Juliette, Mar 7 1915 Sex:F Child# 7 Deisre Levesque Canada & Delima Rheaume Canada
LEVESQUE, Marie L Adelina, Oct 6 1901 Sex:F Child# 15 Arsene Levesque Canada & Odinasse Lavoie Canada
LEVESQUE, Marie L Yvette, Sep 9 1931 Sex:F Child# 4 Joseph Levesque Canada & Annie Labrie Canada
LEVESQUE, Marie Laura Cecile, Feb 12 1914 Sex:F Child# 8 Joseph Levesque Mass & Marie Ouellette Canada
LEVESQUE, Marie Laura E, Jan 21 1905 Sex:F Child# 1 Demase Levesque Canada & Demerise Theriault Canada
LEVESQUE, Marie Laure Dorothy, Dec 10 1932 Sex:F Child# 2 Wilfred Levesque Nashua, NH & G Bergeron Canada
LEVESQUE, Marie Lillian, Jan 21 1903 Sex:F Child# 3 Treffle Levesque Canada & Eulalie Plourde Canada
LEVESQUE, Marie Lorette S A, Jun 20 1905 Sex:F Child# 1 Louis Levesque Canada & Amanda Dube Canada
LEVESQUE, Marie Louise, May 21 1894 Sex:F Child# 1 Edward Levesque Canada & Rosanna Dionne Canada
LEVESQUE, Marie Louise C, Nov 25 1904 Sex:F Child# 2 Joseph Levesque Canada & Marie Ouellette Canada
LEVESQUE, Marie Marcella, Jan 2 1908 Sex:F Child# 2 Marcel Levesque Canada & Alida Lord Canada
LEVESQUE, Marie Margaret Doris, Jul 5 1932 Sex:F Child# 3 Jos Levesque Norwich, CT & B Levesque Nashua, NH
LEVESQUE, Marie Marguerite, Apr 15 1914 Sex:F Child# 4 Joseph Levesque Canada & Rose Anna Labelle Nashua, NH
LEVESQUE, Marie Muriel Yolande, Jul 5 1926 Sex:F Child# 3 Joseph Levesque Canada & Marie Lavoie Canada
LEVESQUE, Marie Olivette, Apr 10 1925 Sex:F Child# 1 Arthur Levesque N Chelmsford, MA & Emma Desclos Newmarket
LEVESQUE, Marie Rachel Rita, Mar 27 1926 Sex:F Child# 1 Joseph Levesque Canada & Marie L Gagne Canada
LEVESQUE, Marie Rachelle, Sep 24 1923 Sex:F Child# 2 Ernest Levesque Canada & Rose Anna Levesque Canada
LEVESQUE, Marie Rejeanne Lilli, Jun 12 1918 Sex:F Child# 3 Joseph Levesque Canada & Philomene Laplante Canada
LEVESQUE, Marie Rita Lillian, Apr 17 1928 Sex:F Child# 1 Leo Levesque Nashua, NH & M Blan Ausaint Nashua, NH
LEVESQUE, Marie Rose, Nov 29 1904 Sex:F Child# 4 Treffle Levesque Canada & Eulalie Plourde Canada
LEVESQUE, Marie Rose A, Feb 15 1909 Sex:F Child# 7 Treffle Levesque Canada & Eulalie Plourde Canada
LEVESQUE, Marie Rose A A, Apr 17 1900 Sex:F Child# 2 Maurice Levesque Canada & Delmina St Laurent Canada
LEVESQUE, Marie Rose Alma, May 6 1907 Sex:F Child# 4 Joseph Levesque Canada & Marie Ouellette Canada
LEVESQUE, Marie Rose Anna, Nov 21 1909 Sex:F Child# 5 Auguste Levesque Canada & Marie Lavoie Canada
LEVESQUE, Marie Rose D E, Jul 31 1903 Sex:F Child# 9 Telesphore Levesque Canada & Proxele Gariepy Canada
LEVESQUE, Marie Rose D J, Mar 25 1909 Sex:F Child# 2 Desire Levesque Canada & Mexzilda Grenier Canada
LEVESQUE, Marie T Jean d'Arc, Apr 7 1927 Sex:F Child# 11 Godias Levesque Canada & Delvina Lizotte Canada
LEVESQUE, Marie Theresa, Jun 14 1926 Sex:F Child# 2 Charles Levesque Canada & Leontine Levesque Canada
LEVESQUE, Marie Viola, Oct 5 1927 Sex:F Child# 6 Albert Levesque Nashua, NH & Cecile Guy Canada
LEVESQUE, Marie Virginie Jean, Nov 29 1933 Sex:F Child# 5 Joseph Levesque Norwich, CT & Bern Levesque Nashua, NH
LEVESQUE, Marie Yvonne, Dec 17 1919 Sex:F Child# 7 Alphonse Levesque Canada & Marie L Levesque Canada
LEVESQUE, Marie Yvonne, Jul 11 1926 Sex:F Child# 5 Albert Levesque Nashua, NH & Cecille Guy Canada
LEVESQUE, Marie Yvonne Ad S, Jul 23 1918 Sex:F Child# 11 Alphonse Levesque Canada & Claudia Emond Canada
LEVESQUE, Marie Zoe, Mar 13 1900 Sex:F Child# 2 Ernest Levesque Canada & Cloe Guerette Canada
LEVESQUE, Marriette Irene, Jul 20 1922 Sex:F Child# 2 Ernest Levesque Nashua, NH & Irene Manseau Canada
LEVESQUE, Maurice Donald, Jun 25 1929 Sex:M Child# 2 Sylvia Levesque Nashua, NH & Viola Lambert S Berwick, ME
LEVESQUE, Maurice Henri, Jan 1 1920 Sex:M Child# 4 Louis Levesque Canada & Wilhemine Cote Canada
LEVESQUE, Maurice Roger, Feb 14 1929 Sex:M Child# 1 Raoul Levesque Canada & Lillian Belanger Nashua, NH
LEVESQUE, Maurice Stanislas, May 6 1921 Sex:M Child# 5 Joseph Levesque Canada & Eva Duhamel Nashua, NH
LEVESQUE, Napoleon, Sep 18 1890 Sex:M Child# 7 Marcel Levesque Canada & Gracuise Carou Canada
LEVESQUE, Noel Joseph E, Dec 25 1924 Sex:M Child# 3 Joseph H Levesque Canada & Marie L Levesque Canada
LEVESQUE, Normand, Jan 31 1934 Sex:M Child# 3 Raoul Levesque Canada & Lillian Belanger Nashua, NH
LEVESQUE, Octave, Aug 6 1894 Sex:M Child# 2 Fidime Levesque Canada & Angelina Gagne Canada

LEVESQUE, Parfait, Nov 26 1904 Sex:m Child# 2 George Levesque Canada & Maria Dube Canada
LEVESQUE, Paul, Mar 7 1931 Sex:M Child# 5 Ernest Levesque Canada & Irene Manseau Canada
LEVESQUE, Paul, Dec 12 1931 Sex:M Child# 1 Parfait Levesque Nashua, NH & Rose Maynard Nashua, NH Stillborn
LEVESQUE, Paul Jean Andrew, Oct 19 1928 Sex:M Child# 2 John Levesque Standish, NY & Laura Blier Nashua, NH
LEVESQUE, Paul Normand G, Aug 22 1929 Sex:M Child# 1 Wilfrid O Levesque Nashua, NH & Germaine Bergeron Nashua, NH
LEVESQUE, Paul Roger, Oct 5 1912 Sex:M Child# 4 Marcel Levesque, Jr Canada & Alida Lord Canada
LEVESQUE, Paul Treffle, Apr 30 1928 Sex:M Child# 4 Treffle Levesque Nashua, NH & Louise Brodeur Nashua, NH
LEVESQUE, Pauline Constance, May 18 1935 Sex:F Child# 3 Parfait Levesque Nashua, NH & Rose Maynard Nashua, NH
LEVESQUE, Pauline Therese, Jan 27 1915 Sex:F Child# 3 Louis Levesque Canada & Wilhemine Cote Canada
LEVESQUE, Philippe Hubert, Aug 7 1918 Sex:M Child# 2 Joseph Levesque Canada & Florence Bejold Canada
LEVESQUE, Philomene Lucile, Oct 20 1914 Sex:F Child# 2 Ralph Levesque Canada & Rachel Bijold Canada
LEVESQUE, Pierre, Mar 12 1888 Sex:M Child# 2 Archele Levesque Canada & Radayonde Duperry Canada
LEVESQUE, Pierre Albert, Jan 24 1897 Sex:M Child# 8 Treffle Levesque Canada & Angelina Lemieux Canada
LEVESQUE, Pierre Edmond, Jun 21 1908 Sex:M Child# 4 Auguste Levesque Canada & Marie Lavoie Canada
LEVESQUE, Pierre Hector, Mar 26 1912 Sex:M Child# 8 David Levesque Canada & Florilda Ouellette Canada
LEVESQUE, Priscilla Theresa, May 20 1930 Sex:F Child# 1 Leo Levesque Epping, NH & Pearl White Canada
LEVESQUE, Rachel Fleurian, Mar 19 1910 Sex:F Child# 3 Marcel Levesque Canada & Alida Lord Canada
LEVESQUE, Rachel Jessie, Dec 12 1910 Sex:F Child# 5 Joseph Levesque Canada & Harmonia Soucy Canada
LEVESQUE, Rachel Therese, Feb 17 1931 Sex:F Child# 1 Roland Levesque Nashua, NH & Violet Charbonneau Nashua, NH
LEVESQUE, Raymond, Jul 11 1925 Sex:M Child# 4 Ernest Levesque Canada & Irene Manseau Canada
LEVESQUE, Raymond, Jun 13 1929 Sex:M Child# 2 David Levesque Nashua, NH & Marie A Michaud Canada
LEVESQUE, Raymond, Apr 30 1934 Sex:M Child# 2 Eustache Levesque Canada & Arline Paradise Fall River, MA
LEVESQUE, Raymond Ernest, Jan 31 1922 Sex:M Child# 2 Ernest Levesque Canada & Clara Evans Maine
LEVESQUE, Raymond G N, Oct 13 1927 Sex:M Child# 1 John Levesque Standish, NY & Laura Blier Nashua, NH
LEVESQUE, Raymond Wilfrid, Jun 30 1932 Sex:M Child# 2 Edmond Levesque Nashua, NH & Ruth Gadbois Littleton, NH
LEVESQUE, Richard Eli, Jan 7 1916 Sex:M Child# 2 Eli Levesque Canada & Ruby Ross Vermont
LEVESQUE, Rita, Aug 20 1930 Sex:F Child# 3 Joseph Levesque Conn & Bernadette Levesque Nashua, NH
LEVESQUE, Rita Olive, Oct 8 1924 Sex:F Child# 4 Polydore Levesque Canada & Odila Levesque Canada
LEVESQUE, Robert, Dec 7 1919 Sex:M Child# 1 Etienne Levesque Canada & Clarence Belanger Canada
LEVESQUE, Robert, Jan 24 1924 Sex:M Child# 4 Auguste Levesque Canada & Justine Ouellette Canada
LEVESQUE, Robert Armand, Sep 18 1926 Sex:M Child# 15 Alphonse Levesque Canada & Claudia Emond Canada
LEVESQUE, Robert Joseph, Nov 12 1933 Sex:M Child# 3 Robert Levesque Fall River, MA & Marie R Belanger Canada
LEVESQUE, Roger, Apr 5 1915 Sex:M Child# 10 Trefle Levesque Canada & Eulalie Plourde Canada
LEVESQUE, Roger Roland, May 22 1917 Sex:M Child# 7 George Levesque Canada & Marie Dube Canada
LEVESQUE, Roland, May 18 1917 Sex:M Child# 6 Donat Levesque Canada & Alma Boutin Canada
LEVESQUE, Roland Adrien, May 2 1927 Sex:M Child# 1 A Levesque Canada & Alice Berube Nashua, NH
LEVESQUE, Roland Albert, Jul 18 1929 Sex:M Child# 3 Albert Levesque Vermont & A Levesque Canada
LEVESQUE, Roland Edgar, May 14 1932 Sex:M Child# 2 Roland Levesque Nashua, NH & F Charbonneau US
LEVESQUE, Roland Emile, Feb 15 1929 Sex:M Child# 7 Albert Levesque Nashua, NH & Cecile Guy Canada
LEVESQUE, Roland Renee, Jul 31 1926 Sex:M Child# 3 Prospere Levesque Mansfield, MA & Alexina Pelletier Canada
LEVESQUE, Roland Roger, Jul 30 1931 Sex:M Child# 1 Eustache Levesque Canada & Arlene Paradis Fall River, MA
LEVESQUE, Romeo Armand, Jul 23 1905 Sex:M Child# 5 Joseph Levesque Canada & Alice Kerouac Canada
LEVESQUE, Ronald Leo, Jun 5 1932 Sex:M Child# 1 Leo A Levesque Nashua, NH & Juliet C Renault Nashua, NH
LEVESQUE, Ronald Leo, Oct 4 1935 Sex:M Child# 1 Louis Levesque Nashua, NH & Marie Boucher Nashua, NH
LEVESQUE, Rosalie Adrienne, Jan 16 1911 Sex:F Child# 5 Desire Levesque Canada & Delina Rheaume Canada
LEVESQUE, Rosanna, Apr 7 1910 Sex:F Child# 1 Joseph P Levesque Canada & Rosanna Labelle Nashua, NH
LEVESQUE, Rosanna, Sep 20 1913 Sex:F Child# 1 Gaudias Levesque Canada & Melvine Lizotte Canada
LEVESQUE, Rosanna Alma, Oct 6 1912 Sex:F Child# 2 Jean Bte Levesque Canada & Marie Bois Canada
LEVESQUE, Rose Eva, Feb 8 1921 Sex:F Child# 5 Cyprien Levesque Canada & Maria Chabot Canada
LEVESQUE, Rose Lilian, Feb 23 1912 Sex:F Child# 5 George Levesque Canada & Lea Dube Canada
LEVESQUE, Rose Yvonne, Sep 12 1905 Sex:F Child# 2 Auguste Levesque Canada & Marie Lavoie Canada
LEVESQUE, Salvia, Feb 9 1898 Sex:F Child# 4 Edmond Levesque Canada & Rosanna Dionne Canada
LEVESQUE, Simone Lorette, May 16 1915 Sex:F Child# 2 Etienne Levesque Canada & Marie L Marquis Canada
LEVESQUE, Sylvio Adelard, Nov 30 1920 Sex:M Child# 6 Gaudias Levesque Canada & Delvina Lizotte Canada
LEVESQUE, Sylvio Irence, Apr 16 1935 Sex:M Child# 1 Irence Levesque Nashua, NH & Eva Courcy Canada
LEVESQUE, Sylvio Joseph, Apr 25 1917 Sex:M Child# 3 Joseph Levesque Canada & Marie Anna Labrie Canada
LEVESQUE, Theodora, Jan 5 1915 Sex:F Child# 2 Joseph E Levesque Canada & Eva Duhamel US
LEVESQUE, Theresa Jeannine, Sep 29 1929 Sex:F Child# 5 Joseph Levesque Canada & Marie Deschenes Canada
LEVESQUE, Therese Lucienne, Apr 20 1924 Sex:F Child# 1 Albert Levesque Nashua, NH & Angelina Levesque Canada
LEVESQUE, Therese Lucille, Oct 20 1934 Sex:F Child# 1 Arthur Levesque Nashua, NH & Leopoldine Berube Canada
LEVESQUE, Therese Marie, Oct 22 1935 Sex:F Child# 8 Art J Levesque N Chelmsford, MA & Emma Desclos Newmarket, NH
LEVESQUE, Thomas Damase, Jul 10 1935 Sex:M Child# 1 Thomas Levesque Canada & Imelda Morin Canada
LEVESQUE, Thomas Roland, Nov 30 1920 Sex:M Child# 7 Gaudias Levesque Milton, NH & Elizabeth Donahue Nashua, NH
LEVESQUE, Unknown, Oct 2 1894 Sex:F Child# 16 Ambroise Levesque Canada & Olymphe Dumais Canada Stillborn
LEVESQUE, Unknown, Mar 6 1896 Sex:F Child# 3 Louis Levesque Canada & Marie Josephine Jean Canada Stillborn
LEVESQUE, Unknown, Oct 23 1900 Sex:M Child# 18 Ambroise Levesque Canada & Olympe Dumais Canada Stillborn
LEVESQUE, Unknown, Dec 16 1903 Sex:M Child# 1 Alphonse Levesque Canada & Claudia Emnd Canada
LEVESQUE, Unknown, Dec 28 1903 Sex:F Child# 6 Lazare Levesque Canada & Clara Thibault Canada
LEVESQUE, Unknown, Dec 28 1911 Sex:F Child# 10 Louis Levesque Canada & Marie Hamel Canada Stillborn
LEVESQUE, Unknown, Mar 25 1918 Sex:F Child# 4 Gaudias Levesque Canada & Delvina Lysotte Canada Stillborn
LEVESQUE, Unknown, Jan 5 1919 Sex:M Child# 1 Alfred Levesque Champlain, NY & Elise Levesque Canada
LEVESQUE, Unknown, Dec 24 1919 Sex:M Child# 4 Joseph Levesque Canada & Eva Duhamel Nashua, NH Stillborn
LEVESQUE, Unknown, May 13 1924 Sex:M Child# 10 Alphonse Levesque Canada & Marie L Levesque Canada Stillborn

LEVESQUE, Unknown, Aug 16 1924 Sex:M Child# 1 Joseph Levesque Canada & R A Bissonnette Nashua, NH Stillborn
LEVESQUE, Unknown, Jul 12 1927 Sex:M Child# 10 A Levesque Canada & Claudia Emond Canada Stillborn
LEVESQUE, Unknown, Sep 27 1927 Sex:M Child# 2 Omer Levesque Canada & A Paradis Epping, NH Stillborn
LEVESQUE, Unknown, Mar 21 1932 Sex:F Child# 7 Jos Levesque Canada & Eva Duhamel Nashua, NH Stillborn
LEVESQUE, Unknown, Oct 18 1934 Sex:F Child# 4 Albert Levesque Nashua, NH & Regina Levesque Canada
LEVESQUE, Virginia Belle, Jun 26 1928 Sex:F Child# 4 Eli Levesque Canada & Ruby Ross NH
LEVESQUE, Wilfred, Dec 28 1907 Sex:M Child# 7 Paul Levesque Canada & Georgiana Rocheleau Nashua, NH
LEVESQUE, Wilfrid Paul, Jan 16 1916 Sex:M Child# 2 Cyprien Levesque Canada & Maria Chabot Canada
LEVESQUE, William Ed, Jan 17 1902 Sex:M Child# 4 Paul Levesque Canada & G Rocheleau Nashua, NH
LEVESQUE, Willie, Feb 6 1897 Sex:M Child# 3 George Levesque Canada & E Grandmaison Canada
LEVESQUE, Yvonne, May 19 1914 Sex:F Child# 7 J Bte Levesque Canada & Marie Boris Canada
LEVESQUE, Yvonne Dora, Aug 17 1930 Sex:F Child# 3 Ernest Levesque Nashua, NH & Yvonne Rioux Nashua, NH
LEVESQUES, Joseph Louis, Nov 22 1892 Sex:M Child# 8 Telesphole Levesques Canada & Georgiana Terriault Canada
LEVIELLE, Alfred Jean, Feb 15 1929 Sex:M Child# 1 Alfred Levielle Nashua, NH & Irene Gauthier Taunton, MA
LEVILLE, Alida, Jun 3 1902 Sex:F Child# 4 Alphonse Leville Canada & Josephine Miller Canada
LEVILLE, Joseph, Apr 28 1917 Sex:M Child# 12 Alphonse Leville Canada & Josephine Miller Canada Stillborn
LEVILLE, Maurice Roger, Dec 17 1924 Sex:M Child# 4 Frank Leville Hooksett, NH & Yvonne Sylvain Canada
LEVINE, Elsie, Jul 7 1920 Sex:F Child# 2 Julius Levine Russia & Lena Mintz Russia
LEVINE, Ida, Feb 25 1921 Sex:F Child# 2 Joe Levine Russia & Rosa Fiman Russia
LEVINE, Lewis, Sep 11 1921 Sex:M Child# 3 Julius Levine Russia & Sara Mintz Russia Stillborn
LEVINE, Lillian, Jan 15 1919 Sex:F Child# 1 Julius Levine Russia & Lena Mintz Russia
LEVINE, Sam, Aug 18 1923 Sex:M Child# 4 Julius Levine Russia & Lena Mintz Russia
LEVINGSTON, Simon, Oct 23 1897 Sex:M Child# 2 Max Levingston Russia & Lina Lewis Russia
LEVKOWICZ, Bolaslov, Apr 25 1913 Sex:M Child# 3 Chris Levkowicz Russia & Josie Marzkawicz Russia
LEVOKWICZ, Agnes, May 27 1924 Sex:F Child# 2 B Levokwicz Poland & Geneva Skiper Poland
LEVSQUE, Joseph Gerard, Aug 29 1921 Sex:M Child# 2 Treffle G Levesque Nashua, NH & Marie Louise Brodeur Nashua, NH
LEWIS, Carroll Foster, Mar 2 1919 Sex:M Child# 1 Charles Lewis Bedford, NH & Bertha Lee Foster Merrimack, NH
LEWIS, Catherine Hill, May 29 1927 Sex:F Child# 2 Charles R Lewis Wales & Lorraine Baldwin Nashua, NH
LEWIS, Charles Baldwin, Aug 12 1925 Sex:M Child# 1 Charles R Lewis Wales & Lorraine Baldwin Nashua, NH
LEWIS, Frank T, Aug 4 1897 Sex:M Child# 2 Frank T Lewis Marlow & Ada S Scott Stoddard
LEWIS, George Kenneth, May 4 1902 Sex:M Child# 1 Leonard H Lewis Mumbles, S Wales & Josie D Boutelle Nashua, NH
LEWIS, Henry, Jun 17 1915 Sex:M Child# 1 Stuart Lewis Nova Scotia & Louise Hanrish Nova Scotia Stillborn
LEWIS, Isaac, Feb 11 1906 Sex:M Child# 5 Samuel Lewis Russia & Rachel Miller Russia
LEWIS, John, Oct 4 1935 Sex:M Child# 1 Henry Lewis Manchester, NH & Yvonne Cormier Lawrence, MA
LEWIS, Marion Crystal, Sep 1 1900 Sex:F Child# 1 W N Lewis Mass & Gertrude O McDonald NH
LEWIS, Marjorie Ann, Jun 4 1929 Sex:F Child# 3 Charles R Lewis Wales & Lorraine Baldwin Nashua, NH
LEWIS, Mildred, Jan 16 1917 Sex:F Child# 1 George Lewis Canada & Lois Harkust Canada
LEWIS, Phirna, Jun 6 1904 Sex:F Child# 3 Samuel Lewis Germany & Rachel Miller Germany
LEWIS, Priscilla, Sep 16 1912 Sex:F Child# 2 Robert E Lewis Milford, NH & Katherine Sexton Nashua, NH
LEWIS, Richard David, Aug 26 1909 Sex:M Child# 1 Robert E Lewis Milford, NH & Katherine B Sexton Nashua, NH
LEWIS, Richard Pennington, Jun 2 1918 Sex:M Child# 1 Richard B Lewis, Jr Nashua, NH & Lucille Pennington Dorcheste
LEWIS, Robert, Jun 23 1914 Sex:M Child# 1 Arthur Lewis Lowell, MA & Ruth McLoon Lowell, MA
LEWIS, Robert Colcord, Apr 29 1923 Sex:M Child# 6 Elbridge C Lewis Franklin, MA & Mary E Scasht Brooklyn, NY
LEWIS, Roberta Anne, Feb 27 1933 Sex:F Child# 2 Nicholas Lewis Boston, MA & Mary Ivan Derry, NH
LEWIS, Unknown, Sep 4 1887 Sex:F Child# 2 Edward A Lewis Milford, NH & Emma B Phelps Boston, MA Stillborn
LEWIS, Unknown, Nov 13 1888 Sex:M Child# 3 Edward A Lewis Medford & Ann R Phelps Boston
LEWIS, Unknown, Nov 6 1905 Sex:F Child# 1 Grover C Lewis Boothbay Harbor, ME & Nellie M Smith Stuben, ME
LEWIS, Unknown, Nov 10 1908 Sex:M Child# 6 Samuel Lewis Russia & Rachel Metana Russia Stillborn
LEWIS, William Garfield, May 29 1895 Sex:M Child# 3 Ed A Lewis Milford, NH & Anna R Phelps Boston, MA
LEZOTTE, Carl, Feb 9 1892 Sex:M Child# 5 James Lezotte NY & Linda Clark NH
LEZOTTE, Charles, Jan 30 1891 Sex:M Child# 4 James A Lezotte New York & Linda Clark New Hampshire
LEZOTTE, Marie R R, Nov 4 1889 Sex:F Child# 4 William Lezotte Canada & Agnes Dionne Canada
LHOMME, Lea Albina, Jan 17 1896 Sex:F Child# 2 John Lhomme Canada & Boe Dube Canada
LIACOPOULOS, George, Feb 24 1917 Sex:M Child# 4 John Liacopoulos Greece & Anna Liacopoulos Greece
LIAMOS, Unknown, Oct 8 1929 Sex:F Child# 2 Apostolos Liamos Greece & Evanthia Thormaides Greece
LIAMOS, Unknown, Jun 22 1930 Sex:M Child# 2 Sterios Liamos Greece & Polex Papanicolalou Greece
LIAMOS, Unknown, Oct 24 1932 Sex:M Child# 3 Sterios Liamos Greece & Anne Polepene Greece
LIAMOS, Unknown, Jun 30 1933 Sex:M Child# 4 Apostolos Liamos Greece & Evanthia Thoma Greece
LIAMOS, Unknown, Dec 10 1935 Sex:F Child# 1 Sterios Liamos Greece & Pol Papanicolaon Greece
LIANNOS, Unknown, Mar 20 1929 Sex:M Child# 1 Sterios Liannos Greece & P Papamicolrous Greece
LIBBEY, Alice Elizabeth, May 6 1928 Sex:F Child# 2 G Libbey Nashua, NH & Ethel M Clemons Andover, MA
LIBBEY, Clarence Daniel, May 16 1901 Sex:M Child# 1 Daniel C Libbey Cary, ME & Annie B Yates Warren, ME
LIBBEY, Frank Maxwell, May 5 1928 Sex:M Child# 1 Maxwell W Libbey Bangor, ME & Celia Holden Litchfield, NH
LIBBEY, Shirley Irene, Oct 10 1930 Sex:F Child# 2 Maxwell Libbey Bangor, ME & Celia Holden Litchfield, NH
LIBBY, Eleanor Dorothy, Apr 22 1910 Sex:F Child# 1 Mason A Libby Machias, ME & Dorothy Trickey Dover, NH
LICHCHICK, Unknown, May 20 1913 Sex:F Child# 1 (No Parents Listed)
LICOS, Unknown, Jun 4 1921 Sex:M Child# Athanssios Licos Greece & Zoe Konstontonou Greece
LIEDLEWICZ, Domicilla, Mar 3 1914 Sex:F Child# 6 Antony Liedlewicz Russia & Tofila Moncunzki Russia
LIEVENS, Elsie Marie, Oct 3 1930 Sex:F Child# 1 Edward Lievens Belgium & Alice Rundquist Dorchester, MA
LILLIS, Ernest George, Nov 4 1915 Sex:M Child# 1 Ernest T Lillis Hooksett, NH & Marjorie M Hill Hooksett, NH
LILLIS, William James, Oct 12 1920 Sex:M Child# 2 Ernest Theo Lillis Hooksett, NH & Marjorie M Hill Hooksett,
LINCOLN, Ortho Roland, Mar 9 1910 Sex:M Child# 2 Carroll I Lincoln St Albans, VT & Effie Blanchard W Chazy, NY
LINCOLN, Pearl Carroll, Oct 13 1907 Sex:F Child# 1 Carroll L Lincoln St Albans, VT & Effie M Blanchard W Chazy, NY

LIND, Unknown, Mar 15 1930 Sex:F Child# 1 David Lind Plattsburgh, NY & Mary Lavoie Nashua, NH
LINDQUIST, Edna Mary, Jun 21 1909 Sex:F Child# 1 Carl Lindquist Sweden & Eliza Maddox Nashua, NH
LINDSEY, Francis Ellsworth, Jan 7 1903 Sex:M Child# 1 William F Lindsey Woodsville, NH & Susan H Carkins Wilton, NH
LINDSEY, Marie Georgianna, Feb 24 1891 Sex:F Child# 1 Henri Lindsey Canada & Mathilda Gauthier Canada
LINDSEY, William F, Apr 11 1907 Sex:M Child# 2 William F Lindsey
LINGUIST, Unknown, Mar 19 1887 Sex:F Child# 4 John Linguist Sweden & Amanda Sweden
LINKIEWIEZ, John, Jun 13 1918 Sex:M Child# 1 boniface Linkiewiez Russia & Vincentina Saquawicz Russia
LINNA, Mary Ann, Nov 2 1935 Sex:F Child# 3 Wino Linna Finland & Tina Isasson Waheta, IL
LINNEHAN, John Patrick, Feb 8 1888 Sex:M Child# 2 Patrick Linnehan New York City & Margaret King Ireland
LINQUIST, John Henry, Nov 17 1908 Sex:M Child# 1 George Linquist Michigan & Ethel M Waters Nashua, NH
LINSCOTT, David Allen, Jan 5 1920 Sex:M Child# 1 Allen Linscott Gloucester, MA & May Clement Hudson, NH
LINSCOTT, Ruth, Aug 6 1922 Sex:F Child# 2 Allen Linscott Gloucester, MA & May Clement Hudson, NH
LINTHAS, Dominick, Jan 5 1911 Sex:M Child# 1 Lawrence Linthas Russia & Pertronila Nitilita Russia
LINTOT, Guy Herbert, Aug 30 1898 Sex:M Child# 2 Herbert C Lintot Canada & Sadie A Sargent E Weare
LINTOTT, Alice May, Jan 4 1904 Sex:F Child# 3 Herbert C Lintott Ditton, Quebec & Sadie Sargeant Weare, NH
LINTOTT, Arthur Lee, Aug 7 1907 Sex:M Child# 4 Herbert C Lintott Canada & Sadie A Sargent Weare, NH
LINTOTT, Bernice F, Apr 27 1903 Sex:F Child# 2 P A Lintott Canada & Fannie H Morris England
LINTOTT, Denice, Mar 9 1928 Sex:F Child# 4 Guy Lintott Nashua, NH & Genice McMaster Nashua, NH
LINTOTT, Genice, Mar 9 1928 Sex:F Child# 3 Guy Lintott Nashua, NH & Genice McMaster Nashua, NH
LINTOTT, Herbert Frank, Sep 16 1924 Sex:M Child# 1 Herbert Lintott Nashua, NH & Genice McMaster Nashua, NH
LINTOTT, Lucille, Jul 3 1926 Sex:F Child# 2 Guy Lintott Nashua, NH & Jenise MacMaster Nashua, NH
LINTOTT, Pearl Eva, May 9 1897 Sex:F Child# 1 John E Lintott Canada & Annie Morris London, Ont
LINTOTT, Unknown, Nov 19 1894 Sex:F Child# 1 Herbert C Lintott Canada & Sadie A Sargent E Weare, NH
LIOPA, Helene, Jan 1 1924 Sex:F Child# 2 Demetrius Liopa Greece & A Gramitinou Greece
LIOPAS, Unknown, Feb 10 1922 Sex:M Child# 1 James Liopas Greece & Anast Konstantinou Greece
LIOPAS, Unknown, Apr 24 1927 Sex:F Child# 4 Demetrius Liopas Greece & A Dramitinou Greece
LIOPOS, Angelike J, Aug 20 1925 Sex:F Child# 3 James Liopos Greece & A Gremmatinou Greece
LIPNISKY, Stephen, Apr 26 1914 Sex:M Child# 1 Antonie Lipnisky Russia & Josie Nason Russia
LISSKA, Edmund, Aug 25 1912 Sex:M Child# 3 Adelbert Lisska Austria & Franciska Wazwawick Austria
LISZKA, Eva, Aug 9 1911 Sex:F Child# 2 Jojieck Liszka Austria & Francizka Wachaick Austria
LITALIEN, Jos Lionel Lauriey, Feb 4 1928 Sex:M Child# 4 Isidore Litalien Canada & Eva Poirier Nashua, NH
LITALIEN, Maurice Dorien, May 1 1924 Sex:M Child# 3 Isidore Litalien Nashua, NH & Eva Poirier Nashua, NH
LITTLE, Arline Grace, Dec 15 1907 Sex:F Child# 2 Arthur W Little Concord, NH & Ethel A Martin Hudson, NH
LITTLE, Beatrice May, Mar 22 1897 Sex:F Child# 1 William M Little Concord, NH & Jennie Watkins England
LITTLE, Edna Elizabeth, Oct 25 1901 Sex:F Child# 1 Arthur W Little Concord & Ethel A Martin Hudson, NH
LITTLE, Ernestine, Dec 17 1919 Sex:F Child# 5 Arthur W Little Concord, NH & Ethel Martin Hudson, NH
LITTLE, Frank Webster, Apr 30 1893 Sex:M Child# 2 Jerome Little Chicago, IL & Fanny g Pine Plains, NY
LITTLE, Gladis Ellen, Dec 3 1899 Sex:F Child# 2 William M Little Concord, NH & Jennie Watkins England
LITTLE, Paul Hamblin, May 12 1930 Sex:M Child# 7 Philip Little Mass & Anna Brewer Maine
LITTLE, Stanley Willard, Nov 11 1925 Sex:M Child# 8 Joseph Little Easton, NH & Alice Chase Bath, NH
LITTLE, Unknown, May 8 1911 Sex:M Child# 3 Arthur W Little Concord, NH & Ethel Martin Hudson, NH
LITTLE, Unknown, Jun 16 1912 Sex:F Child# 4 Arthur Little Concord, NH & Ethel H Martin Hudson, NH
LITTLEFIELD, Ralph Franklin, Aug 30 1896 Sex:M Child# 2 Franklin Littlefield Gardner, ME & Maud Errington Boston
LITTLEFIELD, Unknown, Sep 19 1894 Sex:M Child# 2 George Littlefield Gardner, ME & Mary McGrath Pepperell, MA
LITWELV, Louis, Aug 25 1914 Sex:M Child# 5 Alvin Litwelv Austria & Fannie Sebalk Austria
LIVERMORE, Roger Lyman, Jul 22 1924 Sex:M Child# 4 William L Livermore W Townsend, VT & Mabel Batchelder Haverhill
LIVERNOIS, Albani, Oct 23 1890 Sex:M Child# 3 Joseph Livernois Canada & Zepherina Laydore Canada
LIVERNOIS, Evangeline, Jan 20 1893 Sex:F Child# 4 Joseph Livernois Canada & Zepherina Gagnon Canada
LIVESQUE, Perrie, Jul 5 1888 Sex:M Child# 6 Marcel Livesque Canada & Graciasue Carom Canada
LIVINGSTON, Carl Arthur R, Oct 31 1895 Sex:M Child# H A Livingston Greenville & Katie Mitchell Litchfield, NH
LIVINGSTON, Gordon Raymond, Apr 22 1926 Sex:M Child# 2 Carl Livingston Nashua, NH & Inabel Lund Dunstable, MA
LIVINGSTON, Robert Arthur, Mar 18 1921 Sex:M Child# 1 Carl Livingston Nashua, NH & Inabelle Lund Dunstable, MA
LIVINGSTON, Roy, Jun 29 1923 Sex:M Child# 1 Roy Livingston Nashua, NH & Ida Rollins Franklin, NH Stillborn
LIVINGSTON, Roy Eugene, Sep 26 1900 Sex:M Child# 2 H A Livingston NH & Katie A Mitchell NH
LIVINGSTON, Ruth, Dec 4 1893 Sex:F Child# 4 William L Livingston Nashua, NH & Mary Dana Nashua, NH
LIVINGSTON, Unknown, Jun 26 1889 Sex:F Child# 2 William H Livingston Nashua, NH & Mary E Nashua, NH
LIVINGSTON, Unknown, May 24 1891 Sex:F Child# 3 William Livingston Nashua, NH & Mary E Dane Nashua, NH
LIVINGSTONE, Edward, Mar 14 1902 Sex:M Child# 2 R Livingstone Worcester, MA & Mary McCann Worcester, MA
LIVINGSTONE, Unknown, Aug 14 1887 Sex:M Child# 1 W H Livingstone Nashua, NH & Mary E Dane Nashua, NH
LIZOTTE, Alma Ardath, Dec 1 1929 Sex:F Child# 3 Wilfred T Lizotte Nashua, NH & Phyllis R Lapointe Springfield
LIZOTTE, Charles Joseph, Feb 23 1920 Sex:M Child# 5 Charles A Lizotte Canada & Clerrina Ross Canada
LIZOTTE, Emelie, May 11 1907 Sex:F Child# 4 Joseph Lizotte Canada & Marie Lebrun Canada
LIZOTTE, Francis Kenneth, Jan 17 1931 Sex:M Child# 3 Wilfrid Lizotte Nashua, NH & Deborah Griffin N Weymouth, MA
LIZOTTE, Jeanette Irene, Mar 16 1925 Sex:F Child# 1 Francois Lizotte Canada & Helene Gaudette Canada
LIZOTTE, Joseph Bernard Marce, Aug 16 1927 Sex:M Child# 2 P Lizotte Canada & Mary Leclerc Greenville, NH
LIZOTTE, Joseph Metrius, May 15 1901 Sex:M Child# 3 Octave Lizotte Canada & Anna Bainville Canada
LIZOTTE, Joseph Octave, Aug 25 1904 Sex:M Child# 5 Octave Lizotte Canada & Anna Banville Canada
LIZOTTE, Joseph Paul, Jul 6 1906 Sex:M Child# 3 Joseph Lizotte Canada & Emma Lebrun Canada
LIZOTTE, Joseph Walter, Jul 22 1905 Sex:M Child# 2 Joseph Lizotte Canada & Emelia Lebrun Canada
LIZOTTE, Joseph Wilfrid, Jan 2 1902 Sex:M Child# 3 Charles Lizotte Canada & Clerina Ross Canada
LIZOTTE, Leo Arthur, Jul 1 1899 Sex:M Child# 2 Octave Lizotte Canada & Anna Bauville Canada
LIZOTTE, Leroy Edmond, Aug 25 1912 Sex:M Child# 3 Edmond Lizotte US & Edna M Colburn US
LIZOTTE, Loraine Claire, Mar 19 1927 Sex:F Child# 2 Francis Lizotte Canada & Helene Gaudette Canada

LIZOTTE, Lorraine Florence, Oct 16 1928 Sex:F Child# 1 Joseph Lizotte Nashua, NH & Laura Normando Vermont
LIZOTTE, M Anne Catherine, Nov 22 1912 Sex:F Child# 4 Joseph Lizotte Canada & Marie Lebrun Canada
LIZOTTE, Marie Annett Eva, May 5 1927 Sex:F Child# 1 Wilfrid Lizotte Canada & A Vaillancourt Canada
LIZOTTE, Marie Blanche E, Jan 21 1897 Sex:F Child# 1 Charles Lizotte Canada & Clerina Ross Canada
LIZOTTE, Marie Ivonne, Mar 19 1901 Sex:F Child# 2 Alfred Lizotte Canada & Cemida Levesque Canada
LIZOTTE, Marie Rose Leda, Dec 10 1923 Sex:F Child# 1 Albert Lizotte Canada & Yvonne Ouellette NH
LIZOTTE, Marie Valida, Feb 22 1899 Sex:F Child# 2 Charles Lizotte Canada & Clenina Ross Canada
LIZOTTE, Marie Yvonne, Apr 8 1904 Sex:F Child# 5 Charles Lizotte Canada & Clerina Ross Canada
LIZOTTE, Mary, May 8 1894 Sex:F Child# 6 James Lizotte US & Linda Clark US
LIZOTTE, Norma, Aug 13 1928 Sex:F Child# 3 W T Lizotte Nashua, NH & Phyllis Lapoint Springfield, VT
LIZOTTE, Normand Leo, Nov 2 1929 Sex:M Child# 2 Joseph Lizotte Nashua, NH & Normando Vermont
LIZOTTE, Olivette, Mar 16 1912 Sex:F Child# 3 Alfred Lizotte Canada & Celina Levesque Canada
LIZOTTE, Robert Conrad, Apr 10 1928 Sex:M Child# 2 Wilfrid Lizotte Nashua, NH & Deborah Griffin Mass
LIZOTTE, Roland, Sep 1 1905 Sex:M Child# 1 Joseph Lizotte Canada & Rose Dubois Worcester, MA
LIZOTTE, Roland Paul Joseph, May 29 1935 Sex:M Child# 1 Paul Lizotte Nashua, NH & Emil Thibodeau Augusta, ME
LIZOTTE, Ronald Normand, Apr 14 1927 Sex:M Child# 1 George Lizotte Canada & Rose A Gaudette Canada
LIZOTTE, Wilfred, Nov 13 1911 Sex:M Child# 1 Francois Lizotte Canada & Alphonsine Ouellette US Stillborn
LIZOTTE, Wilfred Joseph, Oct 7 1924 Sex:M Child# 1 Wilfred Lizotte Nashua, NH & Deborah Griffin N Weymouth, MA
LIZOTTE, Wilfrid Joseph, Sep 19 1897 Sex:M Child# 1 Octave Lizotte Canada & Anna Joubert Canada
LIZOTTE, Yvonne Joan, May 30 1931 Sex:F Child# 3 Francois Lizotte Canada & Helen Gaudette Canada
LIZZOTTE, Gerald Leonard, Jan 22 1934 Sex:M Child# 4 Frank Lizzotte Canada & Helen Gaudette Canada
LLOYD, Sydne Grace, May 16 1925 Sex:F Child# 1 Sidney Lloyd Kentville, NS & Pearl Booth Canada
LOCCK, Unknown, Jun 7 1924 Sex:F Child# 1 Walter Locck Poland & Josephine Krypa Poland Stillborn
LOCICCERO, Alan, Jun 13 1935 Sex:M Child# 1 Theo F Lociccero Milford, NH & Marguerite Wright Milford, NH
LOCICERO, Elivara, Sep 29 1926 Sex:F Child# 2 Anthony Locicero Italy & Antoinette Serio Milford, NH
LOCKE, Charles W, Apr 23 1921 Sex:M Child# 1 William A Locke Canada & Gladys Horne Morgan, VT
LOCKE, Elmer William, Oct 17 1935 Sex:M Child# 1 Percy Locke Nashua, NH & Ruth Knirsch Nashua, NH
LOCKE, Glenys Arlene, Jul 30 1919 Sex:F Child# 1 John E Locke Dover, NH & Blanche A Merrill Graniteville, MA
LOCKE, Greta Mildred, Sep 23 1930 Sex:F Child# 3 William Locke Canada & Gladys Horne Morgan, VT
LOCKE, Mildred Josephine, Nov 4 1906 Sex:F Child# 1 John H Locke Nova Scotia & Effie M McKay Nova Scotia
LOCKE, Richard, Aug 11 1910 Sex:M Child# 2 John H Locke Sherburn, NS & Effie McKay Sherburn, NS
LOCKHART, Charles C E, Jan 20 1895 Sex:M Child# 2 Charles W Lockhart Ketville, NS & Maud U Dorey Halifax, NS
LOCKHART, Dorothy Kimball, Aug 30 1921 Sex:F Child# 1 Everett Lockhart Nashua, NH & Helen Kimball Merrimack, NH
LOCKHART, Edwin R Wesley, Feb 23 1899 Sex:M Child# 4 Charles Wm Lockhart Newross R'd, NS & Maud N Dorey Halifax, NS
LOCKHART, Everett, Dec 3 1900 Sex:M Child# 5 C W Lockhart NS & Maud N Dorey NS
LOCKHART, Hilda Blanche, Apr 1 1904 Sex:F Child# 6 Charles W Lockhart Kentville, NS & Maude L Dorey Halifax, NS
LOCKHART, Lucille Miriam, Aug 30 1921 Sex:F Child# 2 Everett Lockhart Nashua, NH & Helen Kimball Merrimack, NH
LOCKHART, Maud Gertrude, Aug 13 1893 Sex:F Child# 1 Charles W Lockhart Nova Scotia & Maud Dorey Halifax, NS
LOCKHART, Stanley William, Jun 30 1897 Sex:M Child# 3 Charles W Lockhart Kentville, NS & Maud U Dorey Halifax, NS
LOCKWOOD, Jacqueline Anne, Sep 16 1931 Sex:F Child# 1 Charles W Lockwood New York & Gladys Nutbrown Nashua, NH
LOCKWOOD, Louis Philip, Feb 1 1933 Sex:M Child# 2 A L Lockwood Springfield, VT & J Jacques Nashua, NH
LOCKWOOD, Thelma Evelyn, Jun 23 1928 Sex:F Child# 2 Amos Lockwood Springfield, VT & Abbie Burke Springfield, VT
LOCKWOOD, Unknown, Jul 2 1931 Sex:F Child# 1 Amos Lockwood Vermont & Jeannette Jacques NH Stillborn
LOCUST, Vladia, Aug 1 1913 Sex:F Child# 1 Joseph Locust Russia & Amelia Porkus Russia
LODGE, Elizabeth Herexton, Nov 7 1923 Sex:F Child# 1 James A Lodge
LOETZIK, Edwiga, Aug 31 1912 Sex:F Child# 1 Peter Loetzik Russia & Annie Leistah Austria
LOGAN, Cynthia, Mar 22 1931 Sex:F Child# 2 James W Logan Lowell, MA & Alice M Walker Lowell, MA
LOGAN, Gladys Myrtle, Feb 21 1902 Sex:F Child# Archibald Logan St Johns, NB & Isabel Hooper St Johns, NB
LOGAN, Janet Melrose, Oct 17 1935 Sex:F Child# 3 James W Logan Lowell, MA & Alice M Walker Lowell, MA
LOGAN, Ralph Douglas, Jan 10 1932 Sex:M Child# 2 Doug Logan, Jr Glasgow, Scotland & Lois Bradley Nashua, NH
LOGAN, Virginia Lois, Feb 3 1931 Sex:F Child# 1 Douglas Logan Scotland & Lois Bradley Nashua, NH
LOJKA, Amelia, Dec 22 1924 Sex:F Child# 4 Peter Lojka Poland & Emelia Kozlowsko Poland
LOJKA, Anthony, Nov 1 1919 Sex:M Child# 2 Peter Lojka Russia & Amelia Koslowsko Russia
LOJKA, Helen, Jun 14 1916 Sex:F Child# 1 Peter Lojka Russia & Emelia Kozlowski Russia
LOJKA, Peter, Sep 30 1921 Sex:M Child# 3 Peter Lojka Poland & Emelia Koslowska Poland
LOKE, Bertram Leslie, Jul 25 1935 Sex:M Child# 1 Loren C Loke Hollis, NH & Bertha Burns Hollis, NH
LOMBARD, Phyllis Evelyn, Oct 11 1923 Sex:F Child# 1 Augustus L Lombard
LONDON, Archie B, Mar 7 1908 Sex:M Child# 3 Harry London Russia & Lena R Sharp Russia
LONDON, Hannah, Feb 1 1903 Sex:F Child# 2 Harry London Russia & Lena Sharp Russia
LONDON, Philip, Mar 15 1898 Sex:M Child# 1 Harry London Russia & Lina Sharp Russia
LONERGAN, William, Sep 19 1888 Sex:M Child# 7 Patrick Lonergan Ireland & Ellen Welch Boston, MA
LONES, Barbara Ann, May 18 1931 Sex:F Child# 4 Harry E Lones Tyngsboro, MA & Ruth J Dobens Nashua, NH
LONES, Ralph, May 27 1930 Sex:M Child# 3 Harry Lones Mass & Ruth Dobins NH
LONES, Richard, May 27 1930 Sex:M Child# 2 Harry Lones Mass & Ruth Dobins NH
LONES, Unknown, Feb 16 1903 Sex:F Child# 3 Thomas R Lones Nova Scotia & Susie Fairbanks Shelborn, MA
LONG, George Edward, May 26 1926 Sex:M Child# 1 Frank E Long St John, NB & Amy Kemp Stowe, VT
LONG, Katherine, Apr 24 1892 Sex:F Child# 3 William H Long Plymouth & Katherine Laconia
LONG, Louise Jennie, May 14 1929 Sex:F Child# 1 Walter Long St John, NB & Eva Emery Chelsea, MA
LONGSTAFF, Thomas Richmond Wm, Oct 9 1935 Sex:M Child# 2 William Longstaff England & Evelene H Hayes Boston, MA
LONGVAL, Joseph Robert Noel, Nov 13 1917 Sex:M Child# 2 Emile Longval Canada & Marie Turgeon Canada
LONGWAY, Charles Warren, Jul 23 1899 Sex:M Child# 4 Joseph Longway NY & Hermen Bresetes Canada
LONTINE, Eugenia Alberta M, May 20 1929 Sex:F Child# 4 Albert Lontine Newport, VT & Jennie Hill Newport, VT
LOOMIS, Barbara Ann, Nov 7 1932 Sex:F Child# 1 Clayton Loomis Bow, NH & Ruth Atwood Nashua, NH

LOOMIS, John Karl, Jr, Apr  5 1921 Sex:M Child# 1 J K Loomis, Sr Baraboo, WI & Ann I Shea Nashua, NH
LOOMIS, Robert Crawford, Aug 12 1922 Sex:M Child# 2 J Kenneth Loomis Baraboo, WI & Ann Irene Shea Nashua, NH
LOQUASK, Frank, Dec 5 1914 Sex:M Child# 3 Frank Loquask Russia & Louisa Sinkait Russia
LORAINE, Donald Ernest, Sep 15 1926 Sex:M Child# 2 Henry Loraine Nashua, NH & Jennie Karopy Nashua, NH
LORAINE, Florence Lucille, Apr 3 1923 Sex:F Child# 9 Louis Loraine New York & Addie Livernois New York
LORAINE, Henry Paul, Jr, May 21 1925 Sex:M Child# 1 Henry P Loraine Nashua, NH & Gertrude Pelletier Nashua, NH
LORAINE, Joseph Nap Alph, Dec 8 1902 Sex:M Child# 1 Benjamin Loraine Canada & Alphonsine Gaudreau Lowell, MA
LORAINE, M Delvina Jeannette, Sep 8 1916 Sex:F Child# 7 Louis Loraine New York & Addie Livernois New York
LORAINE, Marie Elizabeth, Jul 17 1918 Sex:F Child# 8 Louis Loraine New York & Addie Leveinois New York
LORAINE, Marie M M, Jun 9 1900 Sex:F Child# 3 Joseph Loraine Canada & Alphonsine Noel Canada
LORAINE, Robert Edward, Feb 9 1931 Sex:M Child# 4 Henry Loraine Nashua, NH & Gertrude Pelletier Nashua, NH
LORANDEAU, Alice, Jan 26 1893 Sex:F Child# 2 Euclide Lorandeau Canada & Mary Rouleau Canada
LORANDEAU, J O Alphonse, Aug 9 1894 Sex:M Child# 12 Joseph Lorandeau Canada & Delima Dube Canada
LORANDEAU, Joseph Armand H, Mar 4 1907 Sex:M Child# 2 Arthur Lorandeau Canada & Ida Lucas Canada
LORANDEAU, Marie Alice, Jun 24 1892 Sex:F Child# 10 Joseph Horandeau Canada & Delima Dube Canada
LORANDEAU, Marie Amanda, Aug 19 1891 Sex:F Child# 1 Euclide Lorandeau Canada & Marie Rouleau Canada
LORANDEAU, Marie Louise, Jun 24 1892 Sex:F Child# 9 Joseph Horandeau Canada & Delima Dube Canada
LORANGE, Marie Louise, Jun 14 1892 Sex:F Child# 10 Michel Lorange Canada & Rosalie Rock Canada
LORANGER, Armand Adrien, Jun 7 1923 Sex:M Child# 2 Eugene Loranger Canada & Lumina Thibault Nashua, NH
LORANGER, Cleophire, May 2 1892 Sex:F Child# 12 Joseph Loranger Canada & Cleophire Laporte Canada
LORANGER, Conrad Roland, Apr 30 1934 Sex:M Child# 4 Arthur Loranger Nashua, NH & Blanche Lefebvre Nashua, NH
LORANGER, Emma Jacqueline, Jul 23 1921 Sex:F Child# 1 Elphege Loranger Canada & Annette Trudel Nashua, NH
LORANGER, Emma M A, Dec 22 1890 Sex:F Child# 12 Joseph Loranger Canada & Clefire Laporte Canada
LORANGER, Hector Joseph, Aug 11 1927 Sex:M Child# 3 Arthur Loranger Canada & Alma R Simard Canada
LORANGER, John L, Dec 11 1887 Sex:M Child# 1 Antoine Loranger P Q & Mary Ireland
LORANGER, Jos Irenee Girard, Sep 24 1927 Sex:M Child# 9 Wilfrid Loranger Canada & Alice Bibeau Fisherville, MA
LORANGER, Leo Aldege, Apr 27 1916 Sex:M Child# 1 Aldege Loranger Canada & Ida Tremblay US
LORANGER, Louis A, Jan 25 1895 Sex:M Child# 14 Joseph Loranger Canada & Cleophire Laporte Canada
LORANGER, Lucille Rita Ida, Jul 19 1924 Sex:F Child# 2 Elphege Loranger Canada & Annette Trudel Nashua, NH
LORANGER, Marie Blanche A, Mar 17 1901 Sex:F Child# 12 Narcisse Loranger Canada & Cedulie Brodeur Canada
LORANGER, Marie E R, Nov 11 1889 Sex:F Child# 11 Joseph Loranger Canada & Cleophire Laporte Canada
LORANGER, Marie Pauline Theres, Apr 7 1926 Sex:F Child# 1 Wilfred Loranger Canada & Alice Bibeau Fisherville, MA
LORANGER, Maurice Roger, Feb 9 1925 Sex:M Child# 1 Arthur Loranger Nashua, NH & Blanche Lefebvre Nashua, NH
LORANGER, Ruth Goyette, Feb 9 1911 Sex:F Child# 1 Joseph Loranger Nashua, NH & May Legrand New York, NY
LORANGER, Theresa Annette, Feb 10 1929 Sex:F Child# 3 Arthur Loranger Nashua, NH & Blanche Lefebre Nashua, NH
LORD, Christina, Dec 15 1891 Sex:F Child#  John Lord Ireland & Ellen Cavanagh Ireland
LORD, Harry Chester, Jun 4 1918 Sex:M Child# 3 Henry C Lord Lynn, MA & Amy Veon Lynn, MA
LORD, Joseph E N, Jun 2 1891 Sex:M Child# 2 Amable Lord Canada & Arthemise Cote Canada
LORD, June Leora, Aug 31 1916 Sex:F Child# 1 Wilfrid H Lord Nashua, NH & Aurore E Tetreault Nashua, NH
LORD, Marie Rose, May 7 1890 Sex:F Child# 1 Joseph Lord Canada & Arthemise Cote Canada
LORD, Reginald George, Apr 10 1926 Sex:M Child# 1 Linwood H Lord Mass & Martha Burns Burlington, NS
LORD, Violet White, Mar 26 1904 Sex:F Child# 1 Levi W Lord Portsmouth, NH & Isabella White St George, NB
LOREINE, Richard, Jan 6 1928 Sex:M Child# 3 Henry Loreine Nashua, NH & Gertrude Pelletier Nashua, NH
LORING, Barbara, May 16 1927 Sex:F Child# 1 Norman R Loring Perry, ME & A E Barrett Eastport, ME
LORING, David Barrett, Jun 2 1935 Sex:M Child# 3 Norman R Loring Perry, ME & Augusta Barrett Eastport, ME
LORING, Melvin Linwood, Apr 5 1909 Sex:M Child# 1 Melvin L Loring Maine & Jennie Kimball Ossipee, NH
LORING, Norman Rockwood, Apr 18 1930 Sex:M Child# 2 Norman R Loring Perry, ME & Augusta Barrett Eastport, ME
LORRAINE, Unknown, Nov 15 1932 Sex:F Child# 5 H Lorraine Nashua, NH & Gertrude Pelletier Nashua, NH
LOSEK, Cheslow, Jul 20 1926 Sex:M Child# 2 Walter Losek Poland & Josie Krepa Poland
LOSOWSKY, Eva, Aug 3 1913 Sex:F Child# 8 John Losowsky Russia & Elizabeth Valotskous Russia
LOSRK, Wieuk, Nov 9 1931 Sex:M Child# 3 Walter Losrk Poland & Josepa Krypa Poland
LOSTOWKA, Stanislaus, May 12 1916 Sex:M Child# 1 Anthony Lostowka Russia & Bronia Petgonis Russia
LOTHIAN, Edith Evelyn, Aug 24 1915 Sex:F Child# 1 Walter Lothian Salem, MA & Evelyn Bal Everett, MA
LOTHROP, Frances, Oct 12 1927 Sex:F Child# 2 Arnold Lothrop Auburn, ME & Irene Bartlett Stoneham, MA
LOUGEE, Charles E, Oct 27 1892 Sex:M Child# 2 Fred A Lougee Bradford & Varrilla Bourke Mass
LOUGEE, Francis M, Nov 14 1916 Sex:M Child# 1 Frank A Lougee Springvale, ME & Alice G Meighan Hyde Park, MA
LOUGEE, Fred F, Nov 6 1890 Sex:M Child# 1 Fred A Lougee Bedford, NH & Vernelia Bank Massachusetts
LOUGEE, Kenneth Lawrence, Aug 19 1912 Sex:M Child# 3 Arthur L Lougee E Parsonsfield, ME & Celia McDonald Hyde Park
LOUGEE, Robert, May 4 1917 Sex:M Child# 4 Arthur Lougee E Parsonfield, ME & Celia McDonald Hyde Park, MA
LOUGEE, Unknown, Sep 20 1928 Sex:F Child# 1 Frank Lougee Springfield, ME & K Qualters Ashuelot, NH
LOUGHLIN, Charles Laurence, Dec 2 1897 Sex:M Child# 5 Charles L Loughlin Ireland & Katherine Gaffney Ireland
LOUKIDES, Charles, Jul 6 1924 Sex:M Child# 4 Theodore Loukides Greece & Annie Rakowskoi Poland
LOUKIDES, Unknown, Oct 31 1932 Sex:M Child# 10 Theo Loukides Greece & Annie Rakowska Poland
LOULAKIS, Unknown, Aug 29 1929 Sex:M Child# 6 Michael K Loulakis Greece & Sultana Pistolas Greece
LOULOKIS, Unknown, Aug 6 1924 Sex:M Child# 5 Michael Loulokis Greece & Sana Pistoles Greece
LOUTINE, Bernard Jeremiah E, Oct 21 1923 Sex:M Child# 2 Albert Loutine Newport, VT & Jennie Hill Newport, VT
LOUTINE, Oliver Z Francis, Aug 1 1921 Sex:M Child# 1 Albert Loutine Newport, VT & Jennie Hill Newport, VT
LOVAL, Donalda, Nov 11 1890 Sex:F Child# 2 Henry Loval Canada & Velleda Provencal Canada
LOVE, Ann, Mar 30 1931 Sex:F Child# 3 Joseph Love Webster, MA & Leona Kaans Hartford, CT
LOVEJOY, Artemus, Oct 11 1893 Sex:M Child# 4 Willis P Lovejoy Nashua, NH & Henrietta Downs Merrimack, NH
LOVEJOY, Carl Philip, Jan 20 1918 Sex:M Child# 2 Robert E Lovejoy Nashua, NH & Amelia Desmarais Nashua, NH
LOVEJOY, Eleanor Lorraine, Oct 22 1930 Sex:F Child# 2 Raymond F Lovejoy Hollis, NH & Emmaline Sargent Nashua, NH
LOVEJOY, Elwyn Raymond, Aug 7 1927 Sex:M Child# 1 R F Lovejoy Hollis, NH & Emmaline Sargent Nashua, NH

LOVEJOY, Evelyn Henrietta, Mar 8 1916 Sex:F Child# 2 Willis U Lovejoy Nashua, NH & Elizabeth Wilson Canada
LOVEJOY, George Dana, Nov 15 1929 Sex:M Child# 6 Robert L Lovejoy Nashua, NH & Marie Desmarais Nashua, NH
LOVEJOY, J Charles Edward, Aug 14 1922 Sex:M Child# 5 Robert E Lovejoy Nashua, NH & Amelia Desmarais Nashua, NH
LOVEJOY, Joseph Roger William, Nov 4 1920 Sex:M Child# 4 Robert E Lovejoy Nashua, NH & Amelia Desmarais Nashua, NH
LOVEJOY, Marie Yvonne M L, Sep 15 1919 Sex:F Child# 3 Robert Lovejoy Nashua, NH & Amelia Desmarais Nashua, NH
LOVEJOY, Mary Etta, Jan 8 1903 Sex:F Child# 5 Willis P Lovejoy Nashua, NH & Henrietta Downs Merrimack, NH
LOVEJOY, Mary S, Apr 21 1892 Sex:F Child# 3 Willis P Lovejoy Nashua, NH & Henrietta Downs Merrimack, NH
LOVEJOY, Robert E Jr, May 19 1916 Sex:M Child# 1 Robert E Lovejoy Nashua, NH & Amelia Desmarais Nashua, NH
LOVEJOY, Robert Earl, Jun 26 1895 Sex:M Child# 1 William H Lovejoy Nashua, NH & M Helen Woods NH
LOVEJOY, Ruth Elizabeth, Mar 2 1912 Sex:F Child# 1 Willis W Lovejoy Nashua, NH & Elizabeth M Wilson Aurora
LOVEJOY, Unknown, Mar 27 1899 Sex:F Child#  William H Lovejoy Nashua, NH & Nellie Woods Nashua, NH Stillborn
LOVEJOY, Willis W, Jan 22 1887 Sex:M Child# 2 Willis P Lovejoy Nashua, NH & Henrietta Merrimack
LOVELAND, Mary M, Jun 3 1896 Sex:F Child# 1 Charles E Loveland Mass & Clara M Curtis Mass
LOVELL, Carroll Montgomery, Feb 1 1925 Sex:M Child# 1 Henry Lovell Marblehead, MA & Helen Montgomery Marblehead
LOVELY, Charles, Jan 31 1916 Sex:M Child# 2 Charles Lovely New York & Violette Martin New York
LOVER, Unknown, Mar 23 1929 Sex:M Child# 4 Philip E Lover Milford, NH & Irene T Stickney Hollis, NH Stillborn
LOVERING, Unknown, May 6 1907 Sex:M Child#  Irving E Lovering Lowell, MA & Annie Lord Lowell, MA
LOVETT, Byron Nelson, Jun 1 1930 Sex:M Child# 2 Harry Lovett Lowell, MA & Eva Pollay Boston, MA
LOVETT, Hilliard Irwin, Feb 9 1926 Sex:M Child# 1 Harry L Lovett Lowell, MA & Eva Pollay Boston, MA
LOVETT, Marguerite Pearl, Nov 26 1918 Sex:F Child# 2 James Ervine Lovett E Lynn, MA & Velma Pearl Hill E Lynn, MA
LOW, Stanley Danna, Jul 14 1917 Sex:M Child# 1 Oscar F Low Sanford, ME & Elizabeth May Ordway Livermore Fls, ME
LOWE, John Henry, Aug 27 1894 Sex:M Child# 8 John Lowe Ireland & Ellen Cavenagh Ireland
LOWE, Julia Ann, Apr 8 1890 Sex:F Child# 3 John Lowe Ireland & Ellen Cavanagh Ireland
LOWE, Unknown, Mar 20 1887 Sex:M Child#  John Lowe Ireland & Helen Kavanah Ireland Stillborn
LOWE, Unknown, Apr 10 1892 Sex:F Child# 2 Arthur L Lowe Nashua, NH & Mabel A Kimball Nashua, NH
LOWE, William Patrick, Apr 23 1893 Sex:M Child# 6 John Lowe Ireland & Ellen Cavanagh Ireland
LOWELL, Stanley Parsons, Jan 8 1909 Sex:M Child# 4 Cordan A Lowell Greensboro, VT & Harriet M Moran Hopkinton, NH
LOWERY, Helen Elizabeth, Jul 10 1927 Sex:F Child# 1 William Lowery Canada & Alice Chapman Townsend, MA
LOZEAU, Albert Alphee, Nov 3 1918 Sex:M Child# 5 Eucharistes Lozeau Canada & Elphmeia Heroux Canada
LOZEAU, Albert Raymond, Mar 17 1917 Sex:M Child# 4 Euchariste Lozeau Canada & Pomelia Heroux Canada
LOZEAU, Armand, Nov 25 1908 Sex:M Child# 6 Marcel Lozeau Canada & Maria Paulus Canada
LOZEAU, Arzelia, Feb 9 1903 Sex:F Child# 6 Marcel Lozeau Canada & Marie Paul Canada
LOZEAU, Claude, Oct 30 1922 Sex:M Child# 8 Josephat Lozeau Canada & M A Aubuo Canada
LOZEAU, Flora Yvette, Dec 18 1913 Sex:F Child# 3 Joseph Lozeau Canada & Marie Anne Aubut Canada
LOZEAU, Jean, Jan 2 1916 Sex:M Child# 5 Josephat Lozeau Canada & Marianne Aubut Canada Stillborn
LOZEAU, Jeanne D'Arc Anita, Nov 11 1919 Sex:F Child# 7 Josephat Lozeau Canada & Marie A Aubut Canada
LOZEAU, Jos Louis Bertrand, Jul 9 1918 Sex:M Child# 6 Joseph Lozeau Canada & Marie Louise Aubut Canada
LOZEAU, Joseph Ernest, Oct 1 1924 Sex:M Child# 7 Euchariste Lozeau Canada & Ephemia Heroux Canada
LOZEAU, Joseph Pierre C L, Jun 15 1900 Sex:M Child# 4 M C Lozeau Canada & Maria Paulhus Canada
LOZEAU, Josephat, Feb 15 1915 Sex:M Child# 4 Josephat Lozeau Canada & Marie Anna Aubut Canada Stillborn
LOZEAU, Josephine, Apr 13 1906 Sex:F Child# 8 Marcel Lozeau Canada & Maria Paulus Canada
LOZEAU, Lillian Anita, Oct 25 1929 Sex:F Child# 9 Eucharriste Lozeau Canada & Elphema Heroux Canada
LOZEAU, Louise, Apr 13 1906 Sex:F Child# 9 Marcel Lozeau Canada & Maria Paulus Canada
LOZEAU, Marcel, Aug 19 1907 Sex:M Child# 9 Marcel Lozeau Canada & Maria Paulus Canada Stillborn
LOZEAU, Marie Cecilia, Jun 11 1899 Sex:F Child# 3 Marcel Lozeau Canada & Maria Paul Canada
LOZEAU, Melina, Jun 13 1905 Sex:F Child# 7 Marcel Lozeau Canada & Maria Paulus Canada Stillborn
LOZEAU, Raoul Raymond, Jul 3 1922 Sex:M Child# 6 Euchariste Lozeau Canada & Ephema Heroux Canada
LOZEAU, Robert, Mar 11 1932 Sex:M Child# 10 E Lozeau Canada & Alphema Heroux Canada
LOZEAU, Sylvio, May 4 1902 Sex:M Child# 5 Marcel Lozeau Canada & Maria Paul Canada
LOZEAU, Yvonne Rita, Apr 4 1927 Sex:F Child# 8 Euchariste Lozeau Canada & Alphena Heroux Canada
LOZY, Blanche Rose, Sep 9 1922 Sex:F Child# 3 Walter Lozy E Weare, NH & Emma Breintenfeld Jersey City, NJ
LUCAS, Charles A M, Jan 21 1889 Sex:M Child# 1 George A M Lucas Lowell, MA & Bertha L Ayer Jct, MA
LUCAS, Claire Lucille, Dec 27 1932 Sex:F Child# 2 Ferdinand Lucas Canada & L Pontbriand Nashua, NH
LUCAS, Joseph R Wilfrid, Feb 8 1899 Sex:M Child# 13 Ferdinand Lucas Canada & Marie Ouellette Canada
LUCAS, Marie, May 14 1888 Sex:F Child# 2 Joseph Lucas Canada & Marie Lagasse Canada
LUCAS, Marie A Ivonne, Mar 22 1896 Sex:F Child# 11 Ferdina Lucas Canada & Marie Ouellette Canada
LUCAS, Marie A R, Jun 18 1897 Sex:F Child# 12 Ferdina Lucas Canada & Mary Ouellette Canada
LUCAS, Paul Richard, Nov 29 1934 Sex:M Child# 1 Robert Lucas Canada & Irene Richard Nashua, NH
LUCAS, Unknown, Oct 22 1930 Sex:M Child# 1 Ferdinand Lucas Canada & Louisa Pontbriand Nashua, NH Stillborn
LUCAS, Vivian Lucie, Dec 13 1935 Sex:F Child# 2 Robert Lucas Canada & Irene Richard Nashua, NH
LUCE, Elizabeth Cochran, Dec 24 1917 Sex:F Child# 1 Charles Lyman Luce Manchester, NH & Edith Cochran New York
LUCE, Isabel Dunham, Apr 15 1925 Sex:F Child# 2 Charles L Luce Manchester, NH & Edith E Cochran New York, NY
LUCE, Unknown, Aug 11 1893 Sex:F Child# 4 Thomas D Luce Marthas Vineyard, MA & Lizzie N Nichols Merrimack, NH
LUCE, Unknown, May 31 1898 Sex:F Child# 5 T D Luce Marthas Vineyard, MA & L N Nichols Merrimack, NH
LUCEN, Joseph, Jan 22 1913 Sex:M Child# 4 Joseph Lucen Russia & Hedwig Szowich Russia
LUCHEN, John, Jan 13 1922 Sex:M Child# 13 Joseph Luchen Lithuania & Grace Sarkowicz Lithuania
LUCHUN, John, Dec 21 1907 Sex:M Child# 3 Joe Luchun Russia & Jadwick Luchun Russia
LUCIEN, Annie, Nov 15 1911 Sex:F Child# 5 Joseph Lucien Russia & Grace Sacorage Russia
LUCIEN, Frances, Feb 18 1935 Sex:F Child# 1 Joseph Lucien Nashua, NH & Marie Burke Lowell, MA
LUCIEN, Walter, Aug 9 1916 Sex:M Child# 8 Joseph Lucien Russia & Grace Sakavich Russia
LUCIER, Albert, Dec 27 1890 Sex:M Child# 2 Charles Lucier Nashua, NH & Mary Sweeney Nashua, NH
LUCIER, Alfred, Jul 7 1889 Sex:M Child# 1 Charles F Lucier Nashua, NH & Mary A Sweeney Nashua, NH
LUCIER, Alvin Augustus, Aug 7 1896 Sex:M Child# 1 A J Lucier Nashua, NH & Katherine A Doucet Merrimac, MA

LUCIER, Alvin Augustus, May 14 1931 Sex:M Child# 4 Alvin Lucier Nashua, NH & Catherine Lemery Nashua, NH
LUCIER, Andrew O, Oct 29 1912 Sex:M Child# 6 Paul Z Lucier Nashua, NH & Daisy Day Bellows Falls, VT
LUCIER, Beatrice Ruth, May 11 1894 Sex:F Child# 1 Olin P Lucier Nashua, NH & Alice L Sargent Nashua, NH
LUCIER, Bernard Paul, Jan 11 1932 Sex:M Child# 2 Zoel R Lucier Bellows Falls, VT & Doris L Schofield Nashua, NH
LUCIER, Camille Olivine E, Jan 5 1904 Sex:F Child# 2 Eben N Lucier Nashua, NH & Rose Anna Gagne Canada
LUCIER, Catherine, Oct 7 1896 Sex:F Child# 6 Charles F Lucier Nashua, NH & Mary Sweeney Nashua, NH
LUCIER, Catherine Constance, Apr 29 1924 Sex:F Child# 2 Alvin A Lucier Nashua, NH & Catherine Lemery Nashua, NH
LUCIER, Claire Denise, Aug 10 1909 Sex:F Child# 2 Edgar G Lucier Nashua, NH & Lillian M Labombarde Malone, NY
LUCIER, Daniel, Oct 25 1894 Sex:M Child# 5 Charles F Lucier Nashua, NH & Mary A Sweeney Nashua, NH
LUCIER, Donald Robert, Sep 22 1934 Sex:M Child# 2 Arthur J Lucier Lowell, MA & Nellie Irving Nashua, NH
LUCIER, Dustin S, Aug 5 1887 Sex:M Child# Dustin Lucier Nashua, NH & Mary Sullivan Lawrence, MA
LUCIER, Edward, Apr 21 1892 Sex:M Child# 3 Charles Lucier Nashua, NH & Mary Nashua, NH
LUCIER, Edward C, Jan 3 1887 Sex:M Child# Alfred Lucier Nashua, NH & Margaret O'Mara Ireland
LUCIER, Eleanor Grace, Jul 27 1911 Sex:F Child# 5 Ludger Lucier Nashua, NH & Grace Shipman New York
LUCIER, Eliane Genevieve, Aug 27 1913 Sex:F Child# 6 Ludger Lucier Nashua, NH & Grace Shipman Potsdam, NY
LUCIER, Eva, Sep 22 1911 Sex:F Child# 6 Narcisse Lucier Canada & Exilda Beaulieu Canada
LUCIER, Frank, Mar 8 1891 Sex:M Child# 3 Dustin E Lucier Nashua, NH & Mary Sullivan Lawrence, MA
LUCIER, Hasel Bernice, Jan 1 1896 Sex:F Child# 2 Olin P Lucier Nashua, NH & Alice Sargent Nashua, NH
LUCIER, Helen Agnes, Oct 2 1926 Sex:F Child# 3 Alvin A Lucier Nashua, NH & Catherine Lemery Nashua, NH
LUCIER, Helen Doucet, Jul 11 1905 Sex:F Child# 3 Alvin J Lucier Nashua, NH & Katherine Doucet Merrimac, MA
LUCIER, Heloise M, Sep 8 1911 Sex:F Child# 3 Edgar G Lucier Nashua, NH & Lillian M Labombarde Malone, NY
LUCIER, Irene, Sep 17 1908 Sex:F Child# 6 Henry Lucier Natick, RI & Lora Guill Waterloo, Canada
LUCIER, Irene Theresa, May 17 1898 Sex:F Child# 4 Olin P Lucier Nashua, NH & Alice Luella Sargent Nashua, NH
LUCIER, Joseph Albert, Jul 21 1914 Sex:M Child# 1 (No Parents Listed)
LUCIER, Leah, Jan 22 1906 Sex:F Child# 4 Henry Lucier Woonsocket, RI & Victoria Giel Canada
LUCIER, Leonore B S H, Nov 8 1894 Sex:F Child# 1 Elzear L Lucier Canada & Honorine Theriault Canada
LUCIER, Lorraine Marilyn, Oct 16 1930 Sex:F Child# 1 Arthur J Lucier Lowell, MA & Nellie D Irvine Nashua, NH
LUCIER, Louise Lemery, Apr 28 1922 Sex:F Child# 1 Alvin Lucier Nashua, NH & Catherine Lemery Nashua, NH
LUCIER, M Rachelle Clarisse, Feb 1 1919 Sex:F Child# 2 Henri Lucier New York & Marie F Salva Canada
LUCIER, Madeline Patricia, Nov 1 1931 Sex:F Child# 1 Ralph Joseph Lucier Nashua, NH & Hazel M Lowd Milford, NH
LUCIER, Margaret, Mar 4 1888 Sex:F Child# 2 Alfred H Lucier Nashua, NH & Margaret O Mara Ireland
LUCIER, Marie B L, May 13 1899 Sex:F Child# 2 Joseph D Lucier St Damase, PQ & Marie Guertin Nashua, NH
LUCIER, Marie Delia, May 20 1913 Sex:F Child# 9 Narcisse Lucier Canada & Exilda Bouleau Canada
LUCIER, Marie Elmira, Oct 14 1917 Sex:F Child# 2 Henri Lucier New York & Marie Salva Canada
LUCIER, Marie Irene J, Jan 22 1903 Sex:F Child# 1 Emile Lucier Nashua, NH & Eugenie Boilard Nashua, NH
LUCIER, Marie Jeanne, Jul 7 1897 Sex:F Child# 3 Joseph L Lucier Canada & Julie Laliberte Canada
LUCIER, Mary Anna, Aug 12 1897 Sex:F Child# 5 Georges A Lucier Nashua, NH & Julia Dillon Rutland, VT
LUCIER, Olina Elizabeth, Jan 16 1897 Sex:F Child# 3 Olin P Lucier Nashua, NH & Alice Luilla Sargent Nashua, NH
LUCIER, Olive, Jan 12 1890 Sex:F Child# 2 George A Lucier Nashua, NH & Juliet Dillon Rutland, VT
LUCIER, Paul Eben, Sep 18 1901 Sex:M Child# 1 Eben N Lucier Nashua, NH & Rosanna Gagne Canada
LUCIER, Paul Edmund, Nov 13 1892 Sex:M Child# 4 Dustin E Lucier Nashua, NH & Mary Sullivan Lawrence, MA
LUCIER, Paul Raymond, Jun 8 1904 Sex:M Child# 4 Joseph L Lucier Canada & Julie Laliberte Canada
LUCIER, Paul Richard, Aug 28 1910 Sex:M Child# 5 Zoel Lucier US & Daisy Roy US
LUCIER, Philip Edgar, Jan 19 1917 Sex:M Child# 5 Edgar G Lucier Nashua, NH & Lil M Labombarde Malone, NY
LUCIER, Regina Bertha, Dec 17 1915 Sex:F Child# 7 Zoel P Lucier US & Daisy Day US
LUCIER, Robert Walter, Aug 18 1909 Sex:M Child# 4 Ludger Lucier US & Grace Shipman US
LUCIER, Ruth Cecelia, Mar 11 1908 Sex:F Child# 4 Alvin J Lucier Nashua, NH & Katherine A Doucet Merrimac, MA
LUCIER, Sarah A, Apr 8 1894 Sex:F Child# 6 Peter A Lucier NH & M E Valcour Canada
LUCIER, Unknown, Jun 14 1898 Sex:F Child# 2 Alvin J Lucier Nashua, NH & Katherine A Doucet Merrimac, MA
LUCIER, Unknown, Apr 9 1916 Sex:M Child# 7 Nelson Lucier Canada & Xilda Beaulieu Canada
LUCIER, Ustelle Olivette, Nov 19 1895 Sex:F Child# 1 J D Lucier Canada & Mary Guertin Nashua, NH
LUCIER, Vivian A, Dec 15 1912 Sex:F Child# 4 Edgar G Lucier Nashua, NH & Lillian Labombarde Malone, NY
LUCIER, William Ernest, Sep 1 1893 Sex:M Child# 4 Charles Lucier Nashua, NH & Mary Sweeney Nashua, NH
LUCIER, Zoel Raymond, Jan 19 1930 Sex:M Child# 1 Zoel Raymond Lucier Vermont & Doris Schofield Nashua, NH
LUCKEIS, Frank, Jun 16 1904 Sex:M Child# 1 Bout Luckeis Russia & Adolphina Piptiski Russia
LUDDINGTON, Alice May, Jul 7 1895 Sex:F Child# 3 George Luddington Holyport, England & Annie M Bowers Henley, Eng
LUDDINGTON, Arthur Irving, Mar 6 1899 Sex:M Child# 5 George Luddington England & Annie Bowers England
LUDDINGTON, Inez M, Feb 22 1893 Sex:F Child# George Luddington England & Annie Bowers England
LUDDINGTON, Unknown, Oct 17 1897 Sex:F Child# 4 George Luddington England & Annie Bowers England Stillborn
LUISSIER, Marie Theresa Anita, Jun 9 1928 Sex:F Child# 1 William Luissier Lowell, MA & Lila Dauphinais Nashua, NH
LUKASAVICK, Antoinina, Mar 30 1914 Sex:F Child# 2 Cyprus Lukasavick Russia & Ant Sempercipute Russia
LUKASAVITCH, Eustina, Sep 14 1911 Sex:F Child# 1 Ciprien Lukasavitch Russia & Antonina Limpas Russia
LUKASAWICH, Albina, Apr 27 1919 Sex:F Child# 8 Cipr Lukasawich Russia & Antonia Lympatchsa Russia
LUKOSICIUS, Louise, Nov 21 1913 Sex:F Child# 2 Frank Lukosicius Russia & Louise Senders Russia
LUKSZAS, Staponas, Oct 10 1907 Sex:M Child# 2 Baltromy Lukszas Russia & Adolphina Guszeni Russia
LUKUS, Stanislaus, Jun 18 1913 Sex:M Child# 2 Lawrence Lukus Russia & Petronelia Watolatie Russia
LUNARCHE, Unknown, Oct 9 1890 Sex:M Child# 5 Joseph Lunarche Canada & Azalie Robichaud Canada Stillborn
LUNAZOS, Unknown, Dec 15 1913 Sex:M Child# 1 Costos Lunazos Greece & Drosula Kalzos Greece
LUND, Arthur Clarence, May 15 1906 Sex:M Child# 1 Clarence K Lund Nashua, NH & Flora A Cook Lubec, ME
LUND, Arthur Franklin, Jun 30 1900 Sex:M Child# 1 Clarence Kent Lund Nashua, NH & Grace I Loverin Colebrook, NH
LUND, Beatrice Winslow, Mar 28 1911 Sex:F Child# 1 Earl W Lund Nashua, NH & V Pearl Jones Nashua, NH
LUND, Beverly, Jul 1 1925 Sex:F Child# 5 Elmer T Lund Nashua, NH & Anne Grace Lund Dunstable, NH
LUND, Beverly Ann, Jun 13 1932 Sex:F Child# 2 F C Lund, Jr Nashua, NH & Gladys C White Cape Briton, NS

LUND, Dana Austin, Feb 6 1934 Sex:M Child# 7 Elmer Thomas Lund Nashua, NH & Annie Grace Lund Dunstable, MA
LUND, David Alan, Feb 6 1934 Sex:M Child# 6 Elmer Thomas Lund Nashua, NH & Annie Grace Lund Dunstable, MA
LUND, Dexter Earl, Jan 28 1918 Sex:M Child# 2 Earl W Lund Nashua, NH & Velma Pearl Jones Nashua, NH
LUND, Everett Marcus, Feb 19 1918 Sex:M Child# 2 Elmer Lund Nashua, NH & Annie Grace Lund Dunstable, MA
LUND, Francis W, Nov 25 1901 Sex:M Child# 2 Henry F Lund Hollis, NH & Helen M Wells Bethlehem
LUND, Frank William, May 26 1912 Sex:M Child# 2 Charles Henry Lund Hollis, NH & Nellie Olive Hayne Maynard, MA
LUND, Frederick, Jan 12 1905 Sex:M Child# 6 Frederick C Lund Milford, NH & Cora B Holt Windham, NH
LUND, George Marshall, Mar 10 1908 Sex:M Child# 2 Clarence K Lund Nashua, NH & Flora A Cook LaFete, NB
LUND, Harold White, Oct 27 1897 Sex:M Child# Fred C Lund Milford, NH & Cora B Holt Windham, NH
LUND, Harry Fred, Mar 11 1911 Sex:M Child# 3 Henry F Lund Hollis, NH & Helen M Wells Bethlehem
LUND, June Louise, Jun 29 1919 Sex:F Child# 1 Walter A Lund Hollis, NH & Ida L Wilkins Milford, NH
LUND, Lester Parker, Dec 30 1914 Sex:M Child# 1 Lester Parker Lund Nashua, NH & Bertha M Maker Worcester, MA
LUND, Margaret Vesta, Jun 1 1925 Sex:F Child# 2 Lester P Lund Nashua, NH & Bertha M Maher Worcester, MA
LUND, Mary Eliza, May 20 1891 Sex:F Child# 1 Marcus O Lund Nashua, NH & Fannie P Mitchell Nashua, NH
LUND, Paul George, Oct 28 1913 Sex:M Child# 3 Clarence K Lund Nashua, NH & Flora A Cook
LUND, Richard Kermit, Feb 9 1919 Sex:M Child# 3 Elmer T Lund Nashua, NH & Annie Lund Dunstable, MA
LUND, Shirley, Mar 26 1922 Sex:f Child# 4 Elmer T Lund Nashua, NH & Annie Lund Dunstable, MA
LUND, Shirley Mae, Dec 13 1929 Sex:F Child# 1 Frederick Lund Nashua, NH & Gladys White Cape Breton, NS
LUND, Unknown, Mar 14 1891 Sex:F Child# 1 Frederick C Lund Milford, NH & Cora B Holt Windham, NH
LUND, Unknown, Oct 12 1892 Sex:M Child# 2 Willis S Lund Milford, NH & Persis A Winslow Ascot, Canada
LUND, Unknown, Feb 19 1893 Sex:M Child# 2 Marcus O Lund Nashua, NH & Fannie P Mitchell Nashua, NH
LUND, Unknown, Jun 29 1918 Sex:M Child# 2 Lester Parker Lund Nashua, NH & Bertha M Maher Worcester, MA Stillborn
LUND, Virginia Ruth, Aug 4 1932 Sex:F Child# 1 Ralph F Lund Hollis, NH & Madeline Miner Pittsfield, VT
LUND, Winifred Ethel, Apr 25 1895 Sex:F Child# 1 Henry F Lund Hollis, NH & Helen N Wells Bethlehem
LUND, Wintrhop Elmer, Apr 9 1915 Sex:M Child# 1 Elmer T Lund Nashua, NH & Annie G Lund Dunstable, MA
LUONGO, Joseph Albert, Aug 11 1934 Sex:M Child# 6 Frank Luongo Italy & Mary Panlokas Italy
LUPIEN, Jos Edward Eare, Jul 13 1932 Sex:M Child# 1 Edw Lupien Manchester, NH & Marie Gingras Manchester, NH
LUPUTUZ, Unknown, May 10 1917 Sex:F Child# 4 Frank Luputuz Russia & Louise Sankas Russia
LUSCZYK, Anna, Sep 26 1924 Sex:F Child# 4 Simon Lusczyk Poland & Josephine Tulla Poland
LUSIGNAN, Blanche, Jan 15 1898 Sex:F Child# 2 Henry Lusignan US & Justine Dupre US
LUSIGNAN, Edouard, Jul 16 1900 Sex:M Child# 4 Henry Lusignan Mass & Justine Dupre NY
LUSIGNAN, Eileen Irene, Feb 9 1934 Sex:F Child# 2 Edward Lusignan Nashua, NH & Eva Munier Nashua, NH
LUSIGNAN, George Raymond, Oct 2 1922 Sex:M Child# 1 Henry G Lusignan Nashua, NH & Eva Larive Pepperell, MA
LUSIGNAN, Henry, Nov 10 1896 Sex:M Child# 1 Henry Lusignan US & Justine Dupre US
LUSIGNAN, Lillian Jeanette, Jan 14 1925 Sex:F Child# 3 Henry Lusignan Nashua, NH & Eva Larive Pepperell, MA
LUSIGNAN, Louise Estelle, Jun 18 1934 Sex:F Child# 4 Henry Lusignan Nashua, NH & Eva Larrivee Pepperell, MA
LUSIGNAN, Lucille Edna, Sep 10 1923 Sex:F Child# 2 Henry Lusignan Nashua, NH & Eva Larivee Pepperell, MA
LUSIGNAN, Theresa Lorraine, Jun 13 1928 Sex:F Child# 4 H Lusignan Nashua, NH & Eva Larive Pepperell, MA
LUSIGNAN, William, Jun 21 1899 Sex:M Child# 3 Henri Lusignan Douglass, MA & Scholastique Dupre Chazy, NY
LUSIGNANT, Raymond Jos Edward, Apr 15 1929 Sex:M Child# 1 Edward Lusignant Nashua, NH & Eva Munier Nashua, NH
LUSSIER, Alice Marcel Camille, Sep 9 1915 Sex:F Child# 3 Arthur Lussier Nashua, NH & Ernestine Jette Canada
LUSSIER, Anna Octavie, Aug 28 1921 Sex:F Child# 1 Octave Lussier Canada & Albertine Senecal Dracut, MA
LUSSIER, Cecile, Mar 5 1895 Sex:F Child# 11 Hypolite Lussier Canada & Denise Riendeau Canada
LUSSIER, Eugenie Lucille Adri, Mar 6 1918 Sex:F Child# 2 Eugen Lussier Canada & Cleo Anctil Canada
LUSSIER, Henri, Feb 29 1896 Sex:M Child# 1 Mizael Lussier Canada & Caliste Caron Canada
LUSSIER, Irene B, Aug 31 1891 Sex:F Child# 2 Joseph Lussier Canada & Julie Laliberte Canada
LUSSIER, J Eugene Armand R, Jun 6 1914 Sex:M Child# 1 Eugene Lussier Canada & Lea Anctil Canada
LUSSIER, Jennie Amelia, Jan 15 1888 Sex:F Child# 1 Ezard Lussier Canada & Eliza Jennatte Montreal
LUSSIER, Joseph A L N, Dec 8 1889 Sex:M Child# 1 Joseph Lussier Canada & Julie Laliberte Canada
LUSSIER, Joseph Henri Romeo, Jul 3 1912 Sex:M Child# 2 Octave Lussier Canada & Eugenie Poney Canada
LUSSIER, Joseph Octave T, Dec 23 1910 Sex:M Child# 1 Octave Lussier Canada & Eugenie Poney Canada
LUSSIER, Joseph Robert, Apr 6 1908 Sex:M Child# 1 Edgar G Lussier Nashua, NH & Lillian Labombarde New York
LUSSIER, Louis Camille, Nov 9 1889 Sex:M Child# 7 Victor Lussier Canada & Marie A Cardin Canada
LUSSIER, Louis Roland, Oct 15 1917 Sex:M Child# 2 Emery Lussier Canada & Rose Ledoux Canada
LUSSIER, M Bella Yvonne, Jul 6 1914 Sex:F Child# 3 Joseph Lussier Canada & Zelia Picard Canada
LUSSIER, M Jeannette Olivine, Sep 8 1921 Sex:F Child# 3 Henry Lussier New York & Marie Salva Canada
LUSSIER, Marie, Dec 31 1893 Sex:F Child# 1 Louis Lussier Canada & Cordelia Collerette US
LUSSIER, Marie E, Oct 22 1889 Sex:F Child# 3 Irisael Lussier Canada & Melvina Vadnais Canada
LUSSIER, Mary, Oct 13 1888 Sex:F Child# 1 George Lussier Nashua, NH & Julia Dillon Rutland, VT
LUSSIER, Mary L, Oct 18 1888 Sex:F Child# 2 Dustin E Lussier Nashua, NH & Mary Sullivan Lawrence, MA
LUSSIER, Olivier, Jan 24 1908 Sex:M Child# 4 Zoel Lussier US & Ethel Roy US
LUSSIER, Rosario, Mar 22 1897 Sex:M Child# 1 Canada & Undia Lussier Canada
LUSSIER, Unknown, Jan 11 1892 Sex:F Child# 2 Alfred Lussier Maine & Emelie Charron Mass Stillborn
LUSSIER, Unknown, Mar 19 1910 Sex:M Child# 1 Arthur Lussier Nashua, NH & Ernestine Jette Nashua, NH Stillborn
LUSSIER, Unknown, Sep 3 1912 Sex:M Child# 2 Arthur Lussier Nashua, NH & Ernestine Jette Canada Stillborn
LUSSIER, Victorine O, Feb 18 1887 Sex:F Child# 6 Victor Lussier P Q & Marieanne Cardin P Q
LUSTICKS, Veronica, Sep 25 1921 Sex:F Child# 2 Sam Lusticks Poland & Josie Turla Poland
LUSTIKAS, Agnes, Mar 7 1923 Sex:F Child# 3 Simon Lustikas Poland & Josie Turla Poland
LUSZOZYK, Fabian, Jul 22 1926 Sex:M Child# 5 Simon Luszozyk Poland & Josephine Turla Poland
LUSZYK, Joseph, Sep 14 1933 Sex:M Child# 6 Simon Luszyk Poland & Josephine Turio Poland
LUTHER, William Oscar, Mar 21 1917 Sex:M Child# 1 William Oscar Luther Mass & Rosanna F Murphy Mass
LUTZ, Mary Fay, May 17 1924 Sex:F Child# 1 William E Lutz New Bedford, MA & Mary Ellen Fay Salem, MA
LYCETTE, John J, Jr, Apr 16 1919 Sex:M Child# 3 John J Lycette Cambridge, MA & Delia V Coffey Nashua, NH

LYCETTE, Julia Helen, Aug 26 1911 Sex:F Child# 2 John J Lycette Cambridge, MA & Delia Coffey Nashua, NH
LYCETTE, Louise, Oct 14 1908 Sex:F Child# 1 John Lycette Cambridge, MA & Delia Coffey Nashua, NH
LYLE, Charles Arthur, Feb 16 1922 Sex:M Child# 4 Charles A Lyle Westford, MA & Mary Lee Pittsburgh, PA
LYLE, Dorothy, Oct 9 1919 Sex:F Child# 3 Arthur Lyle Lowell, MA & Mary Lee Pennsylvania
LYLE, Robert Keith, Jan 27 1916 Sex:M Child# 1 Charles Arthur Lyle Lowell, MA & Mary Lee Pittsburg, PA
LYMAN, Unknown, Apr 7 1888 Sex:F Child# 1 George E Lyman Alstead & Anna M Pike Isle Mot, VT
LYMAN, Unknown, Aug 1 1894 Sex:F Child# 5 George Lyman NH & Linnie Pike Vermont
LYNCH, Ann, May 28 1924 Sex:F Child# 3 Matthew Lynch Ireland & Annie Lynch Ireland
LYNCH, Barbara, Sep 21 1933 Sex:F Child# 1 John W Lynch Pepperell, MA & Char Preston Holden, MA
LYNCH, Bernard Joseph, Oct 18 1917 Sex:M Child# 1 Matthew Lynch Ireland & Annie Conlon Ireland
LYNCH, Donald Paul, Oct 27 1935 Sex:M Child# 3 Paul Lynch Barton, VT & Anna Seller Marrietta, NY
LYNCH, Harold Thomas, Jr, May 5 1930 Sex:M Child# 1 Harold T Lynch Pepperell, MA & Eleanor F Denahy Groton, MA
LYNCH, Hugh Daniel, Oct 10 1928 Sex:M Child# 1 Hugh Lynch New York & B Valcour Canada
LYNCH, John Francis, Jun 14 1930 Sex:M Child# 1 Francis Lynch Brookline, MA & Mary C Beaulieu Keene, NH
LYNCH, Joseph, Feb 9 1891 Sex:M Child# 4 Timothy Lynch New Hampshire & Kate Morgan Mass
LYNCH, Margaret May, Oct 9 1921 Sex:F Child# 2 Matthew Lynch Ireland & Annie Conlon Ireland
LYNCH, Martin Roland, Aug 14 1932 Sex:M Child# 3 Hugh Lynch NY & B Valcour Canada
LYNCH, Mary Elizabeth, Nov 10 1918 Sex:F Child# 1 John P Lynch S Berwick, ME & Christine C Ashe Brookfield, MA
LYNCH, Matthew Francis, Jan 20 1926 Sex:M Child# 4 Matthew Lynch Ireland & Annie Conlon Ireland
LYNCH, Robert Kenneth, Aug 4 1930 Sex:M Child# 2 Hugh Lynch New York & Bernadette Valcourt Canada
LYNCH, Theresa Ann, Apr 9 1930 Sex:F Child# 1 Edward Lynch Pepperell, MA & Ann Sullivan Ireland
LYNCH, Thomas Harold, Jul 29 1931 Sex:M Child# 2 Thomas H Lynch Peperell, MA & Eleanor Denahy Groton, MA
LYNN, Arthur E, Jun 12 1898 Sex:M Child# 5 William J Lynn Ireland & Sarah Charon Mass
LYNN, Charles Alfred, Jul 22 1910 Sex:M Child# 7 William J Lynn Ireland & Sarah Charron Townsend, MA
LYNN, Eleanor May, May 10 1920 Sex:F Child# 1 Arthur E Lynn Nashua, NH & Alma A Bradley Nashua, NH
LYNN, Ellen Veronica, Jul 21 1898 Sex:F Child# 3 James Lynn Ireland & Sarah McGuiness Ireland
LYNN, Francis Augustus, Mar 2 1897 Sex:M Child# 2 James Lynn Ireland & Sarah J McGinnis Ireland
LYNN, Francis Henry, Jul 15 1901 Sex:M Child# 6 William J Lynn Ireland & Sara J Charron Worcester, MA
LYNN, Genice Louise, Nov 11 1917 Sex:F Child# 4 George A Lynn Nashua, NH & Marion Duncklee Nashua, NH
LYNN, George A, Oct 6 1891 Sex:M Child# 2 William Lynn Ireland & Sarah Charron Mass
LYNN, Jacqueline Alva, Jan 12 1935 Sex:F Child# 2 Charles Lynn Nashua, NH & Doris Mason Nashua, NH
LYNN, Margaret Esther, Oct 18 1921 Sex:F Child# 2 Arthur Lynn Nashua, NH & Alma Bradley Nashua, NH
LYNN, Marjorie Lena, Nov 14 1915 Sex:F Child# 3 George Lynn Nashua, NH & Marion Duncklee Nashua, NH
LYNN, Mary Ellen, Dec 21 1893 Sex:F Child# 3 William J Lynn Ireland & Sarah J Wheeler Townsend, MA
LYNN, Raymond Arthur, Dec 4 1925 Sex:M Child# 5 Arthur E Lynn Mass & Alma A Bradley NH
LYNN, Sadie Jane, Mar 1 1902 Sex:F Child# 5 James Lynn Ireland & Sarah McGuiness Ireland
LYNN, Sarah I, Aug 30 1895 Sex:F Child# 4 William L Lynn Ireland & Sarah L Charron Townsend Center, MA
LYNN, Unknown, Oct 21 1907 Sex:M Child# 7 William Lynn Ireland & Sarah Wheeler Townsend, MA
LYNN, William Gregory, Jan 6 1901 Sex:M Child# 4 James Lynn Ireland & Sarah J McGinnes Ireland
LYON, Edward Stewart, Dec 28 1901 Sex:M Child# 2 John A Lyon Mass & Flora L Chase Nashua, NH
LYON, Ernest Whitney, Aug 30 1926 Sex:M Child# 1 Ernest Lyon Neponsett, MA & Jane Ford Nashua, NH
LYON, Everett William, Nov 3 1922 Sex:M Child# 5 Ernest Lyon Neponset, ME & Daisy Clement Hudson, NH
LYON, Jean Marian, Dec 17 1933 Sex:F Child# 2 Glen E Lyon Chelsea, VT & Adine Titus S Vershire
LYON, Mildred Anna, Aug 31 1898 Sex:F Child# 1 John A Lyon Pawtucket, RI & Flora L Chase Nashua, NH
LYON, Unknown, Dec 8 1903 Sex:F Child# 3 John A Lyon Pawtucket, RI & Flora L Chase Nashua, NH
LYON, Virginia Doris, Aug 2 1930 Sex:F Child# 2 Edward Lyon Nashua, NH & Doris Clement Hudson, NH
LYONS, Anita Leonora, Jul 12 1906 Sex:F Child# 1 George Lyons Nashua, NH & Mabel Blow Nashua, NH
LYONS, Burnadette Elizabeth, Aug 28 1906 Sex:F Child# 1 James F Lyons Nashua, NH & Carrie E Rushlow Alburgh, VT
LYONS, Elizabeth, Jul 6 1928 Sex:F Child# 1 Edward Lyons Nashua, NH & Doris Clement Hudson, NH Stillborn
LYONS, Gordon Joseph, Mar 28 1913 Sex:M Child# 2 Earl Brann Lyons Belgrade, ME & Anastasia Murphy Lynn, MA
LYONS, Isabella L, Jan 15 1911 Sex:F Child# 1 James F Lyons Milford, MA & Margaret Sullivan Ireland
LYONS, James, Jun 16 1897 Sex:M Child# 1 James Lyons Nashua, NH & Margaret Barrett Ireland
LYONS, James Francis, Jr, Feb 27 1917 Sex:M Child# 4 James F Lyons Nashua, NH & Carrie Rushlow Alb Spring, VT
LYONS, Patricia Antoinette, Sep 26 1910 Sex:F Child# 2 James F Lyons Nashua, NH & Carrie E Rushlow Alburgh Spr, VT
LYONS, Ruth Olive, Aug 5 1914 Sex:F Child# 2 James Lyons Milford, MA & Margaret Sullivan Ireland
LYONS, Thomas Oliver, Jun 16 1915 Sex:M Child# 3 James F Lyons Nashua, NH & Carrie Rushlow Alberg Springs, VT
LYONS, Unknown, Jan 7 1917 Sex:F Child# 3 Earl Bram Lyons Belgrade, ME & Anastatia Murphy Lynn, MA Stillborn
LYONS, Unknown, Jan 21 1923 Sex:F Child# 4 Earl B Lyons Belgrade, ME & Anastasia Murphy Lynn, MA Stillborn
LYSZCZAZ, Frank, May 31 1910 Sex:M Child# 3 John Lyszczaz Austria & Mary Tokash Austria
LYSZIAY, Helene, Aug 10 1911 Sex:F Child# 4 John Lysziay Poland & Mary Tokas Poland
LZWALOWICZ, Peter, Jun 19 1918 Sex:M Child# 3 Ronald Lzwalowicz Russia & Russia
M'CAUSLAND, Mildred Arlene, Aug 21 1917 Sex:F Child# 5 Phillip R M'Causland Pepperell, MA & Maude Greene Augus
MAAZ, Frances Moran, Jun 7 1918 Sex:F Child# 1 Francis H Maaz Austria & Annie T Moran Nashua, NH
MAAZ, John Irwin, Oct 17 1924 Sex:M Child# 2 Francis H Maaz Austria & Ann Moran Nashua, NH
MABREY, Erdine Lillian, Sep 4 1917 Sex:F Child# 1 Rexford C Mabrey Yarmouth, ME & Hazel L Smith Stuben, ME
MABRY, Dorothy E, Nov 6 1906 Sex:F Child# 2 R C Mabry Maine & Olive Wheeler Nashua, NH
MABRY, Eunice Evelyn, Dec 4 1919 Sex:F Child# 3 Roxford C Mabry Yarmouth, ME & Hazel L Smith Stuben, ME
MABRY, Florence E, Mar 21 1905 Sex:F Child# 1 R C Mabry Maine & Olive Wheeler
MABRY, Judson, May 9 1908 Sex:M Child# 3 Rexford C Mabry Maine & Olive M Wheeler Nashua, NH
MACADOO, Paul Francis, Sep 8 1921 Sex:M Child# 2 George Macadoo NH & Pauline Lucier NH
MACALISTER, Eleanor Frances, Mar 11 1922 Sex:F Child# 1 Hugh MacAlister Burnham, ME & Sadie Glendenning Gardner, ME
MACCANN, Donald James, Sep 19 1930 Sex:M Child# 1 George W MacCann Lowell, MA & Constance Thompson Hampton Fls
MACCANN, John Douglas, Mar 2 1934 Sex:M Child# 2 George F MacCann Lowell, MA & Constance C Thompson Hampton Fls

MACCLEMEN, Philip Carl, Jun 13 1929 Sex:M Child# 4 George F MacClemen Everett, MA & Marion Curtis Woburn, MA
MACDANIEL, Beverly Loraine, Jan 22 1933 Sex:F Child# 6 (No Parents Listed)
MACDANIEL, Mary Albina, Apr 7 1920 Sex:F Child# 4 (No Parents Listed)
MACDONALD, Alexander Gow, May 30 1919 Sex:M Child# 2 Alex G Macdonald Perth, Scotland & Hazel R Tandy Milford, NH
MACDONALD, Edward, Jr, Jun 8 1909 Sex:M Child# 1 Edward MacDonald Cambridge, MA & Lillien Frasier Boston, MA
MACDONALD, Glenn William, Apr 21 1925 Sex:M Child# 1 William MacDonald Greenwood, MA & Gladys Dudley Fiskdale, MA
MACDONALD, Grace Evelyn, Jul 27 1929 Sex:F Child# 2 William MacDonald Wakefield, MA & Gladys Dudley Fiskdale, MA
MACDONALD, Marjorie Ethel, May 11 1929 Sex:F Child# 3 Thomas MacDonald Barre, VT & Marguerite Adams Nashua, NH
MACDONOUGH, Sheila Ann, Aug 31 1933 Sex:F Child# 1 L MacDonough Waterbury, CT & Beatrice Bainey Lowell, MA
MACDUFFIE, Harriet Jean, Dec 29 1931 Sex:F Child# 2 Harry T MacDuffie Nashua, NH & Isabel Avard Nashua, NH
MACENNIS, Gordon Francis, Sep 13 1918 Sex:M Child# 2 Francis L MacEnnis Windsor, NS & Bessie Woods Hollis, NH
MACHAIS, Nicholas George, Dec 2 1917 Sex:M Child# 1 Nicholos Machais Greece & VssilikiGeorgeobolis Greece
MACHI, Attilio, Aug 27 1915 Sex:M Child# 1 Corrado Machi Italy & Lena Vince New York, NY
MACI, Agatha, Feb 9 1907 Sex:F Child# 1 Isidor Maci Russia & Anna Adomawic Russia
MACINK, Victoria, Mar 26 1922 Sex:F Child# 7 Harry Macink Poland & Mary Geurgol Poland
MACINTYRE, Donald Campbell, Aug 18 1926 Sex:M Child# 1 J MacIntyre E Fairfield, VT & Selma Campbell Nashua, NH
MACIZ, Charly, Jun 25 1912 Sex:M Child# 2 Jidori Maciz Russia & Anna Adomaci Russia
MACK, Beatrice Pauline, Feb 18 1922 Sex:F Child# 1 Matthew J Mack New York & Beatrice Reed Lowell, MA
MACK, Donald Alfred, Apr 15 1934 Sex:M Child# 1 Lloyd Mack Deerfield, NH & Emma Reynolds Epsom, NH
MACK, Ellen, Feb 13 1889 Sex:F Child# 6 John Mack Ireland & Ellen Ireland
MACKAY, Robert Swan, Dec 3 1934 Sex:M Child# 2 James MacKay Revere, MA & Mary Swan Boston, MA
MACKEWIECZ, Haronium, Apr 10 1909 Sex:M Child# 1 Haron Mackewiecz Poland & Pauline Urgwecz Poland
MACLAREN, Patricia Ann, Jan 15 1935 Sex:F Child# 3 Alfred MacLaren St Andrews, NB & Marjorie H Clock Candia, NH
MACLEAN, Helen Gertrude, Sep 9 1909 Sex:F Child# 3 John MacLean Nova Scotia & Agnes Anderson Scotland
MACOMBER, Clara E, Mar 28 1891 Sex:F Child# 1 Elmer A Macomber Maine & Etta M Harncy Nova Scotia
MACOMBER, George H, Nov 28 1896 Sex:M Child# 3 E A Macomber Maine & Etta F Harvey Nova Scotia
MACOMBER, Unknown, Sep 16 1894 Sex:F Child# 2 Elmer Macomber Maine & Ida Harvey Nova Scotia
MACOMBER, Unknown, Dec 29 1928 Sex:F Child# 1 George H Macomber Nashua, NH & Hazel Shippee Worcester, MA Stillborn
MACON, Unknown, May 19 1892 Sex:M Child#  John Macon Mass & M Legasse Mass
MACPHAIL, Edith Jessie, Jun 28 1914 Sex:F Child# 3 Alex MacPhail Bonbow, PEI & Andray Singleton Allston, PEI
MACPHEE, Ruth, May 5 1922 Sex:F Child# 3 John MacPhee Deerfield, NH & Mary K Marston Prince Edward Island
MACPHEE, Unknown, Sep 1 1926 Sex:F Child# 3 John MacPhee Deerfield, NH & Mary Marston Prince Edw Island
MACUNAS, Joseph, Sep 16 1926 Sex:M Child# 2 Joseph Macunas Lithuania & Gertrude Pelletier Lithuania
MACWHA, Gordon Walter, Oct 27 1921 Sex:M Child# 1 Hugh M MacWha Nashua, NH & Elizabeth Smith Orford, NH
MACWHA, Robert Winfred, Mar 22 1924 Sex:M Child# 2 Hugh M MacWha Nashua, NH & Elizabeth C Smith Orford, NH
MACZKAWCKA, Joseph, Dec 15 1916 Sex:M Child# 2 Joseph Maczkawcka Russia & Lena Pawlackwhs Russia
MADDOX, Charles Frederick, Sep 21 1899 Sex:M Child# 9 William Maddox England & Catherine Gaffney Ireland
MADDOX, Edward Paul, Nov 3 1918 Sex:M Child# 3 William Maddox, Jr Nashua, NH & Bessie Gaffney Nashua, NH
MADDOX, Gertrude, Aug 2 1895 Sex:F Child# 7 William Maddox England & Kate Gaffney Ireland
MADDOX, Kate Mabel, Nov 23 1891 Sex:F Child# 6 William Maddox England & Kate Gaffney Ireland
MADDOX, Mary, Jun 12 1908 Sex:F Child# 1 William F Maddox Nashua, NH & Elizabeth Gaffney Nashua, NH
MADDOX, Mary Emma, Nov 18 1889 Sex:F Child# 5 William Maddox England & Katie Gaffney England
MADDOX, Priscilla Beatrice, Aug 10 1897 Sex:F Child# 8 William Maddox Wales & Catherine Gaffney Ireland
MADDOX, Unknown, Sep 18 1893 Sex:F Child# 6 Wesley E Maddox Kennebunk, ME & Elizabeth Dolan Chicopee, MA
MADDOX, William Francis, Apr 23 1910 Sex:M Child# 2 William F Maddox Nashua, NH & Elizabeth Gaffney Nashua, NH
MADEAU, Anna R Hattie, May 12 1890 Sex:F Child# 2 Loeis Madeau Canada & Delvina Masse Canada
MADEN, Leslie, Feb 19 1928 Sex:M Child# 2 Charles Maden Waltham, MA & Georgianna Caron Nashua, NH
MADIGAN, Catherine Mary, Mar 31 1931 Sex:F Child# 4 Francis Madigan Ireland & Mary Gordon Ireland
MADIGAN, Edward Patrick, May 18 1934 Sex:M Child# 5 Francis Madigan Ireland & Mary Gordon Ireland
MADIGAN, Eileen Joan, Jul 29 1935 Sex:F Child# 6 Francis Madigan Ireland & Mary Gordon Ireland
MADIGAN, Francis James, Apr 23 1927 Sex:M Child# 1 James Madigan Ireland & Mary Gordon Ireland
MADIGAN, John Joseph, Jun 8 1929 Sex:M Child# 3 Francis J Madigan Ireland & Mary Gordon Ireland
MADIGAN, Robert William, May 2 1928 Sex:M Child# 2 Francis Madigan Ireland & Mary Gordon Ireland
MADRAYO, Unknown, May 31 1929 Sex:M Child# 1 Raymond Madrayo Spain & Alice Lafleur E Brookfield, MA Stillborn
MAGBY, Fanny May, May 13 1889 Sex:F Child# 3 Enoch Magby Belfast, ME & Mary Glasen Nashua, NH
MAGE, Louise, Oct 15 1919 Sex:F Child# 1 (No Parents Listed)
MAGEE, Unknown, Jul 20 1887 Sex:M Child# 5 Joseph M Magee Philadelphia & Hannah E Swatt Pt Pleasant, PA
MAGEE, Unknown,  Sex:M Child#  I W Magee Pennsylvania & Hannah E Pennsylvania
MAGERAN, M A Lumina, Jul 20 1894 Sex:F Child# 3 J A Mageran Canada & Regina Lagace Canada
MAGNAN, Joseph Arcade L, Oct 30 1902 Sex:M Child# 7 J F Magnan Canada & Regina Lagace Canada
MAGNAN, Joseph Octave A, Apr 20 1892 Sex:M Child# 1 Francois A Magnan Canada & Regina Lagace Canada
MAGNAN, Joseph Priaque, Jun 9 1907 Sex:M Child# 8 J F Magnan Canada & M Regina Lagace Canada
MAGNAN, M Eva Bertha A, Mar 20 1893 Sex:F Child# 2 F A Magnan Canada & Regina Lagace Canada
MAGNAN, Marie A L, Feb 22 1897 Sex:F Child# 5 J F Magnan Canada & Regina Lagace Canada
MAGNAN, Marie B T, Mar 12 1896 Sex:F Child# 4 J F Magnan Canada & Regina Lagace Canada
MAGNON, Adrien Joseph, Mar 18 1899 Sex:M Child# 6 J F Magnon Canada & Regina Lagace Canada
MAGNUSON, Donald Earl, Apr 17 1932 Sex:M Child# 2 H O Magnuson Nashua, NH & H M Burnett Nashua, NH
MAGNUSON, Shirley Edna, Oct 3 1929 Sex:F Child# 1 Harold O Magnuson Nashua, NH & Hazel May Burnett Nashua, NH
MAGOON, Gertrude Janet, Apr 1 1917 Sex:F Child# 11 Frank H Magoon Pike Hill, VT & Gertrude A Heald Carlisle, MA
MAGOON, Medeline May, Dec 26 1904 Sex:M Child# 2 Perley R Magoon Deerfield, NH & Julia C Donovan Epping, NH
MAGOON, Unknown, Dec 18 1892 Sex:F Child# 2 William Magoon Canada & Sadie H Wilson Cleveland, OH
MAGUIRE, Mary Elizabeth, Nov 10 1922 Sex:F Child# 1 Daniel Maguire Mass & Madeline Donlon Mass
MAGWOOD, Phyllis Ann, Feb 22 1935 Sex:F Child# 2 William W Magwood Salem, NH & Dorothy Reed Hudson, NH

MAHAR, Hazel Blanche, Apr 20 1902 Sex:F Child# 5 Patrick Mahar New Haven, CT & Mary Maynard St Albans, VT
MAHAR, Mary Pearl, May 27 1894 Sex:F Child# 1 Patrick Mahar Conn & Mary R Maynard Vermont
MAHAR, Patrick, Feb 8 1899 Sex:M Child# 4 Patrick Mahar New Haven, CT & Mary Maynard St Albans, VT
MAHER, Alice E, Oct 5 1895 Sex:F Child# 5 Patrick Maher Nashua, NH & Rose A Maynard St Albans, VT
MAHER, Cecile, Dec 14 1897 Sex:F Child# 3 Patrick Maher Nashua, NH & Rosealma Menard St Albans, VT
MAHER, Unknown, May 31 1906 Sex:F Child# 6 Patrick Maher Hartford, CT & Mary Maynard St Albans, VT Stillborn
MAHONEY, Eleanor Mary, Oct 1 1921 Sex:F Child# 3 William J Mahoney Ireland & Mary Egan Ireland
MAHONEY, Herman William, Oct 9 1935 Sex:M Child# 1 Herman Mahoney Virginia & Mildred Welton Pepperell, MA Stillborn
MAHONEY, Julien Morris, Aug 1 1915 Sex:M Child# 2 William Mahoney Ireland & Mary Egan Ireland
MAHONEY, Margaret Madeline, Jan 30 1917 Sex:F Child# 1 William T Mahoney Manchester, NH & Agnes Devine Manchester
MAHONEY, William Thomas, Sep 28 1913 Sex:M Child# 1 William J Mahoney Ireland & Mary K Egan Ireland
MAILHOT, Alfred Roland, May 17 1911 Sex:M Child# 1 Alfred Mailhot Canada & Bernadette Hysette Nashua, NH
MAILLARD, Denise Therese, Sep 4 1924 Sex:F Child# 1 Paul Maillard France & Berna St Amant Canada
MAILLOUX, Marie, Nov 3 1924 Sex:F Child# 15 Alcide Mailloux Canada & Caludia Plourde Canada Stillborn
MAILLOUX, Marie Blanche H, Dec 12 1901 Sex:F Child# 8 George Mailloux Canada & Marie Gregoire Canada
MAILLOUX, Marie Eva, Aug 4 1904 Sex:F Child# 10 George Mailloux Canada & Marie Gregoire Canada
MAILLOUX, Marie G, Dec 27 1906 Sex:F Child# 11 George Mailloux Montreal & Marie Gregoire Canada
MAILLOUX, Marie I B, Mar 3 1903 Sex:F Child# 9 George Mailloux Canada & Marie Gregoire Canada
MAIN, Donald R, Dec 25 1908 Sex:M Child# 1 Walter L Main Canada & Rose M Hodlin Milford, NH
MAIN, Doris Mary, Feb 14 1927 Sex:F Child# 3 George L Main Wilmington, Del & Delia Gaudette Lowell, MA
MAIN, Ellen H, Mar 22 1899 Sex:F Child# 6 George M Main Concord, NH & Nellie M Brattleboro, VT
MAIN, Elvin Emerson, Oct 6 1917 Sex:M Child# 1 Lyman Emerson Main Topsam, ME & Maude G Lockhart Nashua, NH
MAIN, Harland Irving, Nov 26 1918 Sex:M Child# 2 Lyman E Main Topsham, ME & Maud Lockhart Nashua, NH
MAIN, Jairetta Emily, Mar 31 1920 Sex:F Child# 3 Lyman Main Topsham, ME & Maude Lockhart Nashua, NH
MAIN, Robert Everett, Sep 4 1921 Sex:M Child# 4 Lyman E Main Topsham, ME & Maude G Lockhart Nashua, NH
MAINTAVES, Louis, Aug 24 1908 Sex:M Child# 1 John Maintaves Greece & Mary Segalon Greece
MAJDZIONAK, Unknown, Jul 1 1909 Sex:M Child# 5 Alex Majdzionak Russia & Michael Munshunska Russia Stillborn
MAJOIKA, Adam, Jan 25 1912 Sex:M Child# 1 Adam Majoika Russia & Albina Rounja Russia
MAJOR, Franklin Delano, Nov 8 1932 Sex:M Child# 5 Henry Major US & Mamie Bleau US
MAJOR, Frederick Alonzo, Nov 14 1896 Sex:M Child# 4 Frank A Major Swansville, ME & Juliet B Hoag Boscowen, NH
MAJOR, George Armand, Mar 5 1925 Sex:M Child# 4 Henry Major Nashua, NH & Mamie Blow Sciota, NY
MAJOR, Henry, May 10 1890 Sex:M Child# 3 Enoch R Major Belfast, ME & Mary Curran Nashua, NH
MAJOR, Jack Richard, Mar 14 1919 Sex:M Child# 2 E Henry Major Nashua, NH & Mamie Blow Sciota, NY
MAJOR, James Henry, Jul 28 1921 Sex:M Child# 3 Enoch H Major Nashua, NH & Mamie Blow Sciota, NY
MAJOR, Robert Henry, Sep 9 1917 Sex:M Child# 1 Enoch H Major, Jr Nashua, NH & Mamie Blow Sciota, NY
MAJOR, Unknown, May 15 1890 Sex:F Child# 2 Frank A Major Maine & Juliet E Hoagg NH
MAJOR, Unknown, Dec 24 1891 Sex:F Child# 3 Frank A Major Nashua, NH & Julia B Hoagg NH
MAJUKOSA, Nellie, Feb 5 1919 Sex:F Child# 4 Frank Majukosa Russia & Patronally Welch Russia
MAJURIAN, Mgurdich Hagbp, Jan 5 1925 Sex:M Child# 2 Jacob Majurian Armenia & Ant Dhamlyian Armenia
MAKA, Kerttie, May 9 1920 Sex:F Child# 1 Victor Maka Finland & Saimi Salmi Finland
MAKARAWICZ, Helena, Jun 6 1923 Sex:F Child# 3 Joseph Makarawicz Lithuania & Katherine Gedialis Lithuania
MAKARAWICZ, Josie, Sep 9 1916 Sex:F Child# 1 Victor Makarawicz Russia & Mik Melenkawicz Russia
MAKARAWICZ, Sophia, Oct 12 1921 Sex:F Child# 3 Victor Makarawicz Lithuania & Mechl Malinkawicz Poland
MAKARAWICZ, Victor, Aug 12 1925 Sex:M Child# 4 V Makarawicz Lithuania & M Malinkawicz Poland
MAKAREWIC, William, Feb 2 1918 Sex:M Child# 2 Victor Makarewic Russia & Mikalia Millinkevoic Russia
MAKAREWICH, Beni, Nov 28 1913 Sex:M Child# 4 Natens Makarewich Greece & Josephine Tatoronis Greece
MAKAREWICZ, Stanislaus, Jun 20 1916 Sex:M Child# 5 Mike Makarewicz Poland & Josia Poland
MAKARONITCH, Martin, Mar 23 1908 Sex:M Child# 1 Martin Makaronitch Poland & Josephine Tartarius Poland
MAKARSWICZ, Antos, Dec 5 1915 Sex:F Child# 2 Joseph Makarswicz Russia & Catherine Gedraluta Russia
MAKEPEACE, Earl George, Feb 5 1919 Sex:M Child# 3 George E Makepeace Nashua, NH & Minnie H Aubertine Nashua, NH
MAKEPEACE, Etha Gertrude, Jun 1 1906 Sex:F Child# 1 Fred A Makepeace Nashua, NH & Gertrude Grave Lawrence, MA
MAKEPEACE, Henry, Apr 1 1907 Sex:M Child# 2 Fred A Makepeace Nashua, NH & Gertrude Graves Florence, MA
MAKEPEACE, Minnie Evelyn, Oct 21 1916 Sex:F Child# 2 George E Makepeace Nashua, NH & Minnie H Aubertin Nashua, NH
MAKEPEACE, Unknown, Apr 14 1887 Sex:M Child# 1 E C Makepeace Nashua, NH & Isabella Stearns Nashua, NH
MAKEPEACE, Unknown, Jan 1 1889 Sex:M Child# 4 George E Makepeace Claremont & Ida Brown S Merrimack
MAKEPEACE, Unknown, Mar 14 1891 Sex:F Child# Eugene C Makepeace Nashua, NH & Isabelle Stearns Nashua, NH
MAKEPEACE, Unknown, Jul 20 1893 Sex:F Child# 6 George H Makepeace Concord & Ida M Brown S Merrimack, NH Stillborn
MAKER, Alice Louise, Feb 24 1909 Sex:F Child# 7 Elwin C Maker Cutler, ME & Margaret A Wilson Noyan, Canada
MAKER, Claud Maland, Jan 24 1894 Sex:M Child# 1 Elwyn C Maker Cutler, ME & Margarette A Wilson Canada
MAKER, Gladys Ella, Feb 25 1912 Sex:F Child# 8 Elwin C Maker Cutler, ME & Margaret A Wilson Noyan, PQ
MAKER, Ralph Elwin, Mar 3 1915 Sex:M Child# 9 Elwin C Maker Cutler, ME & Margaret A Wilson Canada
MAKER, Unknown, Aug 11 1901 Sex:M Child# 4 Edwin C Maker Cutler, ME & Margaret A Wilson Canada
MAKER, Unknown, Jan 16 1905 Sex:F Child# 5 Edwin C Maker Cutler, ME & Margaret Wilson Noyan, Canada
MAKER, Unknown, May 30 1906 Sex:F Child# 6 Elwin C Maker Cutler, ME & Margaret A Wilson Noyan, Canada
MAKER, Wilber Cushing, Apr 8 1922 Sex:M Child# 2 Claude M Maker Nashua, NH & Flora Eliz Cushing Rochester, NH
MAKOWSKI, Edmond, Feb 13 1918 Sex:M Child# 8 Joseph Makowski Russia & Josei Glygnock Austria
MAKOWSKI, Joseph, Nov 11 1911 Sex:M Child# 1 John Makowski Russia & Josei Glyacona Russia
MAKOWSKI, Ludwig, Aug 5 1916 Sex:M Child# 7 Joseph Makowski Russia & Josie Glyock Austria
MAKRES, George N, Jan 19 1919 Sex:M Child# 4 Nicolos Makres Greece & Fannie Makras Greece
MAKRIS, Helen Margaret, Aug 3 1927 Sex:F Child# 6 Nickolas Makris Greece & Fannie Dici Greece
MAKRIS, Kristina, Dec 23 1933 Sex:F Child# 8 Mitchell Makris Greece & Helen Zefirinon Greece
MAKRIS, Unknown, Dec 4 1913 Sex:F Child# 1 Mike Makris Greece & Helena Shairia Greece
MAKRIS, Unknown, Jun 20 1930 Sex:F Child# 8 Niclis Makris Greece & Fennie Tsintsira Greece

MAKYS, Peter, Dec 24 1925 Sex:M Child# 6 Nicholas Makys Greece & Fannie Chaugura Greece
MALATSAS, Catherine, Aug 12 1928 Sex:F Child# 3 Kostos Malatsas Greece & Lila Gilfallan Vermont
MALATZSKY, Stanislas, Jun 21 1908 Sex:M Child# 4 William Malatzsky Russia & Theresa Unikyta Russia
MALAVICH, Peter, Jun 29 1925 Sex:M Child# 2 Frank Malavich Poland & Ann Agnowski Lithuania
MALAWICZ, Adelka, Sep 28 1918 Sex:F Child# 3 Alex Malawicz Russia & Bronsilaw Sprayofska Russia
MALAWICZ, Bronislawa, Feb 21 1922 Sex:M Child# 4 Alex Malawicz Lithuania & Bronislawa Spagofska Lithuania
MALAWICZ, Josie, Jul 6 1917 Sex:F Child# 2 Alex Malawicz Poland Russia & B Sprovgovska Poland Russia
MALAWICZ, Mamie, Nov 16 1924 Sex:F Child# 5 Alex Malawicz Poland & B Sprogovska Poland
MALAWICZ, Peter, Jul 25 1915 Sex:M Child# 1 Alex Malawicz Russia & Braulney Spragofska Russia
MALAWICZ, William, Dec 10 1914 Sex:M Child# 1 Frank Malawicz Russia & Annie Adjalski Russia
MALAY, Henry Robert, Dec 2 1934 Sex:M Child# 2 Henry Malay Nashua, NH & Agnes Leukowicz Nashua, NH
MALAY, Joan, May 7 1935 Sex:F Child# 2 John H Malay Nashua, NH & Lucy Lucien Nashua, NH
MALAY, Lucy, Sep 7 1932 Sex:F Child# 1 John H Malay Nashua, NH & Lucy Lucien Nashua, NH
MALAY, Unknown, Aug 1 1930 Sex:M Child# 1 Henry Malay Nashua, NH & Agnes Lewkowicz Nashua, NH Stillborn
MALAY, William, Feb 9 1919 Sex:M Child# 7 John Malay Austria & Eva Gouinsky Austria
MALENFANT, Alphe Roger, Jun 9 1926 Sex:M Child# 1 Alphe Malenfant Nashua, NH & Lucia Paradis Canada
MALENFANT, Emmanuel Rodolphe, Dec 31 1927 Sex:M Child# 2 Alphee Malenfant Nashua, NH & Lucia Paradis Canada
MALENFANT, Henry, Dec 7 1899 Sex:M Child# 4 Napoleon Malenfant Canada & Marie Lafrance Canada
MALENFANT, Jean Ernest, Jun 17 1909 Sex:M Child# 13 Napoleon Malenfant Canada & Marie Lafrance Canada
MALENFANT, Joseph Alphe, Jan 21 1903 Sex:M Child# 12 Ovide Malenfant Canada & Elise Cote Canada
MALENFANT, Joseph Isidore A, Aug 27 1908 Sex:M Child# 1 Isidore Malenfant Canada & Ellen Gahouette Mass
MALENFANT, Joseph Louis N, Dec 29 1903 Sex:M Child# 11 Napoleon Malenfant Canada & Marie Lafrance Canada
MALENFANT, Joseph Rosario, Aug 23 1907 Sex:M Child# 12 Napoleon Malenfant Canada & Marie Lafrance Canada
MALENFANT, Marie A Jacqueline, Jun 13 1930 Sex:F Child# 1 Arthur Malenfant Canada & Marie A Lucas Canada
MALENFANT, Marie Isabella, Jun 10 1909 Sex:F Child# 2 Bruno Malenfant Canada & Charlotte Potvin Chateaugay, NY
MALENFANT, Marie Oliva, Nov 21 1901 Sex:F Child# 10 Joseph Nap Malenfant Canada & Marie Lafrance Canada
MALENFANT, Robert Donald, Sep 27 1931 Sex:M Child# 3 Alphe Malenfant Nashua, NH & Lucia Paradis Canada
MALENFAUT, Alphonse Henri, Oct 24 1898 Sex:M Child# 8 Napoleon Malenfaut Canada & Marie Lafrance Canada
MALENFAUT, Arlette R, Nov 10 1898 Sex:F Child#  J F Malenfaut Canada & Alma F Annis Hudson, NH
MALENFAUT, Marie A, Feb 3 1897 Sex:F Child# 7 N Malenfaut Canada & Marie Lafrance Canada
MALENFAUT, Marie Alice, Oct 15 1891 Sex:F Child# 9 Henri Malenfaut Canada & Lumina Gagnon Canada
MALENFAUT, Mary, Oct 19 1898 Sex:F Child#  Joseph Malenfaut Canada & Elize Cote Canada
MALETTE, Albert Joseph, Mar 19 1908 Sex:M Child# 12 Henri Malette Malone, NY & Victoria Malhiot Canada
MALETTE, Aldea Yvonne, Oct 19 1922 Sex:F Child# 3 Oscar Malette NH & Florida Leclerc Mass
MALETTE, Donald Robert, Apr 7 1934 Sex:M Child# 3 John Malette Nashua, NH & Isabelle Duval Wilton, NH
MALETTE, Doris Agnes, Oct 23 1928 Sex:F Child# 2 William Malette Nashua, NH & Alice Seguin Derry, NH
MALETTE, Henri F, Aug 9 1891 Sex:M Child# 1 Henri Malette Canada & Victoria Malhoit Canada
MALETTE, Joseph Alfred, Mar 16 1930 Sex:M Child# 7 Oscar Malette Nashua, NH & Flora LeClaire Fall River, MA
MALETTE, Joseph Edward, Mar 20 1924 Sex:M Child# 4 Oscar Malette NH & Florilda Leclerc NH
MALETTE, Joseph George R, Aug 11 1924 Sex:M Child# 2 Lionel Malette Canada & Rose Mathieu Canada
MALETTE, Leo Normand, Mar 26 1931 Sex:M Child# 3 William Malette Nashua, NH & Alice Seguin Derry, NH
MALETTE, Lillian Yvonne, Sep 24 1914 Sex:F Child# 15 Henri Malette Malone, NY & Victoria Mayotte Canada
MALETTE, Marie A, Jun 15 1903 Sex:F Child# 9 Henri Malette Malone, NY & Victoria Malhiot Canada
MALETTE, Marie E, Mar 28 1906 Sex:F Child# 11 Henry Malette Malone, NY & Victoria Malhiot Canada
MALETTE, Mary Joan P L, Jun 3 1930 Sex:F Child# 1 John Malette Nashua, NH & Isabelle Duval Wilton, NH
MALETTE, Oscar, Jun 9 1898 Sex:M Child# 6 Henri Malette Malone, NY & Victoria Malhiot Canada
MALETTE, Theresa, Apr 6 1925 Sex:F Child# 1 William Malette Nashua, NH & Alice Seynis Derry, NH
MALHIOT, Alfred, Mar 20 1893 Sex:M Child# 6 Joseph Malhiot Canada & Elmire Marquis Canada
MALHIOT, Henri Edmond, May 12 1897 Sex:M Child# 5 Paul Malhiot Canada & Zephirine Bellerose Canada
MALHIOT, Wilfrid, Jun 23 1890 Sex:m Child# 9 Joseph Malhiot Canada & Mary Fitzgerald Canada
MALHOIT, Alfred Emile, Oct 14 1928 Sex:M Child# 6 Irenee Malhoit Nashua, NH & Irene King Fall River, MA
MALHOIT, Alice, Nov 4 1904 Sex:F Child# 2 George Malhoit Nashua, NH & Marie Deschenes Canada
MALHOIT, Alida, Jul 30 1897 Sex:F Child# 7 Joseph Malhoit Canada & Elmire Marquis Canada
MALHOIT, Amedie, Mar 25 1902 Sex:F Child# 9 Joseph Malhoit Canada & Elmire Marquis Canada
MALHOIT, Beatrice Virginia, Mar 2 1923 Sex:F Child# 2 Rene E Malhoit Nashua, NH & Irene F Roy Three Rivers, MA
MALHOIT, Eugene Philip, Nov 7 1929 Sex:M Child# 7 Rene Malhoit Nashua, NH & Irene Roy Three Rivers, MA
MALHOIT, Irene Aubeline, Oct 8 1900 Sex:F Child# 1 George Malhoit Nashua, NH & Marie Deschesne Canada
MALHOIT, Jacqueline Louise, Aug 13 1926 Sex:F Child# 5 Irenee Malhoit Nashua, NH & Irene Roy Three Rivers, MA
MALHOIT, Joseph C, Jan 27 1891 Sex:M Child# 5 Joseph Malhoit Canada & Elmira Marquis Canada
MALHOIT, Lucille Irene, Mar 14 1924 Sex:F Child# 3 Irenee E Malhoit Nashua, NH & Irene F Roy Three Rivers, MA
MALHOIT, Marie, Apr 28 1888 Sex:F Child# 11 Joseph Malhoit P Q & Mary A Fitzgerald P Q
MALHOIT, Marie, Jun 26 1894 Sex:F Child# 3 Paul Malhoit Canada & Zepherine Bellerose Canada
MALHOIT, Paul H, Mar 2 1891 Sex:M Child# 2 Paul Malhoit Canada & Zepherine Bellerose Canada
MALHOIT, Paul Irenee Edward, Jun 12 1925 Sex:M Child# 4 Irenee E Malhoit Nashua, NH & Irene Roy Three Rivers, MA
MALHOIT, Pierre E, May 12 1889 Sex:M Child# 1 Paul Malhoit Canada & Zepherine Bellerose Canada
MALHOIT, Ray, Feb 5 1922 Sex:M Child# 1 Irenee Malhoit Nashua, NH & Irene Roy Three Rivers, MA
MALIAVICZIUS, John, Jun 13 1909 Sex:M Child# 1 Frank Maliaviczius Russia & Elena Alekciute Russia
MALIN, Malin, Jan 23 1888 Sex:F Child# 6 Richard Malin Warwick, England & Mary McCarty England Stillborn
MALINOWSKI, John, Jan 4 1914 Sex:M Child# 4 Stanslaws Malinowski Russia & Antonina Usdavinute Russia
MALITSOS, Margaret, Sep 28 1932 Sex:F Child# 1 Charles Malitsos Greece & Lila Gilfillan Vermont
MALLEN, Grace Marjorie, Mar 10 1918 Sex:F Child# 2 James P Mallen Nashua, NH & Grace Weeks Barrington, NH
MALLEN, James, Nov 17 1887 Sex:M Child# 4 James Mallen Ireland & Bridget Ireland
MALLEN, Nena, Jan 17 1892 Sex:F Child# 6 James Mallen Ireland & Bridget O'Hara Ireland

MALLETT, Arthur, Jun 6 1896 Sex:M Child# 5 Henri Mallett US & Victoria Malhoit Canada
MALLETT, Oscar, Jr, Sep 17 1925 Sex:M Child# 5 Oscar Mallett Nashua, NH & Florida Leclerc Fall River, MA
MALLETTE, Cora, Sep 18 1927 Sex:F Child# 6 Oscar Mallette Nashua, NH & Florilda Leclair Fall River, MA
MALLETTE, Eva, Mar 24 1902 Sex:F Child# 8 Henri Mallette Malone, NY & Victoria Malhoit Canada
MALLETTE, Ilene, Jun 1 1912 Sex:F Child# 14 Ira Mallette Malone, NY & Victoria Mayotte Canada
MALLETTE, John Leon, Dec 19 1932 Sex:M Child# 2 John Mallette Nashua, NH & Isabelle Duval Wilton, NH
MALLETTE, Joseph, Mar 31 1895 Sex:M Child# 4 Henri Mallette US & Victoria Malhoit Canada
MALLETTE, Joseph John, Sep 14 1904 Sex:M Child# 10 Henri Mallette Malone, NY & Vitaline Mailhoit Canada
MALLETTE, Marie Anne, Nov 26 1893 Sex:F Child# 3 Henri Mallette US & Victorine Malhiot Canada
MALLETTE, Marie C, Nov 8 1892 Sex:F Child# 2 Henri Mallette Malone, NY & Victoria Malhiot Canada
MALLETTE, Marie Florilda, May 12 1921 Sex:F Child# 2 Oscar Mallette NH & Florilda Leclerc Mass
MALLETTE, Raymond J, Jul 23 1933 Sex:M Child# 2 Raymond Mallette Nashua, NH & Mary Andrew Russia
MALLETTE, Rita Arlene, Jul 27 1934 Sex:F Child# 3 Raymond Mallette Nashua, NH & Mary Andrews Russia
MALLETTE, William E, May 10 1900 Sex:M Child# 7 Charles Mallette NY & Victoria Malhoit Canada
MALLETTE, William Normand, Nov 25 1931 Sex:M Child# 7 Oscar Mallette US & Flora Leclerc Mass
MALLEY, Unknown, Aug 28 1923 Sex:M Child# 2 Dennis Malley Pepperell, MA & Gertrude Pillsbury Milford, NH
MALLOY, John, May 31 1897 Sex:M Child# 5 William Malloy Ireland & Rose E Keeley England
MALLOY, Loretta Theresa, Aug 10 1928 Sex:F Child# 1 John Malloy Nashua, NH & Loretta Birchall Nashua, NH
MALLOY, William Edward, Jun 22 1890 Sex:M Child#  William Malloy Ireland & Rose Kelley Ireland
MALONSON, Harriet May, Oct 10 1916 Sex:F Child# 1 John L Malonson Nova Scotia & Myrtle Tufts Swampscott, MA
MALONTA, Vasilikie, May 1 1920 Sex:F Child# 1 Costas Malonta Greece & Helen Hagidamon Greece
MALONTAS, Unknown, Mar 12 1921 Sex:M Child# 2 Costas Malontas Greece & Helen Hagidamon Greece
MALOUIN, Barbara Joan, Feb 9 1932 Sex:F Child# 5 Leon F Malouin Canada & Barbara Gardiner NH
MALOUIN, John Alfred, Dec 5 1934 Sex:M Child# 6 Leon Malouin Canada & Barbara Gardiner Nashua, NH
MALOUIN, Justin R G, Oct 7 1927 Sex:F Child# 3 Leon F Malouin Canada & B M Gardiner Freemont, NH
MALOUIN, Leon, Jul 30 1930 Sex:M Child# 5 Leon Malouin Canada & Barbara Gardner Fremont, NH
MALOUIN, Leon Francis, Apr 15 1929 Sex:M Child# 4 Leon Malouin Canada & Barbara Gardner Fremont, NH
MALOUIN, Mary Natalie, Jun 29 1926 Sex:F Child# 2 Leon Malouin Canada & Barbara Gardner Fremont, NH
MALOUIN, Unknown, Jan 4 1925 Sex:F Child# 1 Leon F Malouin Canada & M Barb Gardner Fremont, NH Stillborn
MALOUTA, George Costas, Jun 24 1922 Sex:M Child# 3 Costas Malouta Greece & Helen Hagidamon Greece
MALOVITCH, Joseph, Feb 8 1911 Sex:M Child# 2 Frank Malovitch Russia & Lina Alexa Russia
MALOY, Forest Alvin, Apr 8 1916 Sex:M Child# 2 Austin W Maloy Brentwood, NH & Maude E Rock Mooers, NY
MALOY, Karl Williams, Mar 20 1912 Sex:M Child# 1 Austin William Maloy Brentwood, NH & Maude E Rock Mooers, NY
MAMOS, John D, Apr 24 1918 Sex:M Child# 5 Dimeter Mamos Greece & Banthia Miga Greece
MANAKIDIS, Michael, Feb 2 1913 Sex:M Child# 1 Theodore Manakidis Greece & Anastasia Manchou Greece
MANALAY, Unknown, May 6 1923 Sex:F Child# 3 Stalianon Manalay Greece & Christina Manalay Greece
MANAS, Rosa, Jun 19 1896 Sex:F Child# 3 Kapel Manas Russia & Harriet Portrie Russia
MANCEAU, Xavier, Aug 10 1904 Sex:M Child# 2 David Manceau Canada & Delia Paquin Canada
MANCHESTER, Unknown, Apr 11 1889 Sex:F Child# 1 Henry Manchester W Randolph, VT & Ella Manchester Vermont Stillborn
MANCHESTER, Unknown, Apr 24 1894 Sex:F Child# 3 Henry C Manchester W Randolph, VT & Ella J Jeannotte Sheldon, VT
MANCHEVITCH, Unknown, Jan 25 1916 Sex:F Child# 1 Holis Manchevitch Germany & Annie Ringaite Russia
MANCY, Dorothy G, Jan 13 1912 Sex:F Child# 1 William I Mancy Ayer, MA & Ida Bouchard Lynn, MA
MANDELSON, Allen David, Jun 22 1923 Sex:M Child# 2 Jacob C Mandelson Ontario, Canada & Etta Levine San Francisco
MANDELSON, Harriet Ruth, Apr 28 1920 Sex:F Child# 1 Jacob C Mandelson Ontario, Canada & Etta Levine San Francisco
MANDIGO, Catherine, Jan 13 1902 Sex:F Child# 4 John W Mandigo Swanton, VT & Ellen Nash Ireland
MANDIGO, Francis J, Apr 13 1896 Sex:M Child# 1 John W Mandigo Vermont & Ellen F Nash Ireland
MANDIGO, Henry, May 10 1895 Sex:M Child# 2 Richard Mandigo Canada & Mary Obin Plattsburg, NY
MANDIGO, Jessie H, Jul 7 1893 Sex:F Child# 1 Richard Mandigo Canada & Mary Obin NY
MANDIGO, John Joseph, Dec 8 1897 Sex:M Child# 2 John W Mandigo Squamscott, VT & Ellen Nash Ireland
MANDIGO, Mary Helen, Nov 16 1899 Sex:F Child# 3 John W Mandigo Vermont & Ellen Nash Ireland
MANDIGO, Unknown, Jun 27 1892 Sex:F Child# 3 Elmer M Mandigo Clarencville, CA & Ella F Quigley Francestown, NH
MANDRAVELIS, Aglaea, Oct 3 1934 Sex:F Child# 2 Michael Mandravelis Greece & Evangeline Xenetevme Greece
MANELAS, Unknown, Dec 25 1932 Sex:F Child# 3 Theo Manelas Greece & S Nicklesthomas Greece
MANEY, Lucile Alida, Jul 24 1913 Sex:F Child# 2 William Maney Ayer, MA & Alida Bouchard Lynn, MA
MANGENI, Louis, Aug 23 1900 Sex:M Child# 1 Michael Mangeni Italy & Emelda Padergani Italy
MANGINI, Annie, Jan 13 1903 Sex:F Child# 2 Michael Mangini Italy & Emile Pederzani Italy
MANGINI, Guy Pietro, Mar 4 1905 Sex:M Child# 3 Michael Mangini Italy & Emildi Paderzani Italy
MANIATES, Unknown, Jun 26 1923 Sex:F Child# 1 John Maniates Greece & Athena Dogopulo Greece
MANIJIAAN, Zabeal, Aug 19 1913 Sex:F Child# 3 Beadiras Manijiaan Turkey & Armonoubi Turkey
MANIJIAAN, Zarchi, Aug 19 1913 Sex:M Child# 2 Beadiras Manijiaan Turkey & Armonoubi Turkey
MANIUS, Grace, Aug 10 1928 Sex:F Child# 3 John Manius Lithuania & C Nephrinsky Lithuania
MANJIAVINOS, Unknown, Nov 22 1931 Sex:F Child# 2 Con Manjiavinos Greece & Marigoula Lalopoulos Greece
MANLEY, Florence Elizabeth, Sep 1 1910 Sex:F Child# 1 Otto Manley NH & Clara E Gagne Mass
MANLEY, Florence Veronica, Jan 29 1913 Sex:F Child# 4 William H Manley London, England & Mary Summerville Ireland
MANLEY, George Robert, Apr 5 1908 Sex:M Child# 2 William H Manley England & Minnie Somerville Ireland
MANLEY, George Robert, Jun 2 1935 Sex:M Child# 3 George R Manley NH & Bertha Robbins NH
MANLEY, Lillian Gladys, Aug 27 1932 Sex:F Child# 2 George Manley NH & Bertha Robbins NH
MANN, Raymond George, Nov 3 1920 Sex:M Child# 1 Howard Ralph Mann Deering, NH & Clara Ruth Miner Antrim, NH
MANNERING, William, Nov 13 1917 Sex:M Child# 2 Pat J Mannering Ireland & Mary A Harrington Ireland
MANNING, Barbara Jean, Jul 19 1923 Sex:F Child# 1 Thomas B Manning Francestown, NH & Marion Duffy Keene, NH
MANNING, Camille Loraine, Dec 27 1922 Sex:F Child# 2 Harry D Manning US & Leona Landry US
MANNING, Lena Mabel, Aug 31 1903 Sex:F Child# 5 Oscar H Manning NB & Mathilda Thompson Ireland
MANNING, Lloyd John, Aug 17 1925 Sex:M Child# 1 Lloyd Manning Milford, NH & Margaret Shea Wilton, NH

MANNING, Mary, Feb 13 1906 Sex:F Child# 1 Thomas Manning Ireland & Elisabeth Nash Nashua, NH
MANNING, Mary Agnes, Jul 28 1916 Sex:F Child# 1 Patrick J Manning Ireland & Mary Harrington Ireland
MANNING, Paul Mercer, Jun 22 1934 Sex:M Child# 1 Wendell P Manning Nova Scotia & Helen Irene Mercer Peterboro, NH
MANNING, Watt, Jun 19 1888 Sex:M Child# 3 Patrick Manning Ireland & Annie McLaughlin Ireland
MANOLEROS, Harviloupos, Sep 29 1921 Sex:M Child# 1 Stil Manoleros Greece & Christina Christese Greece
MANOLEY, Unknown, Jun 13 1925 Sex:M Child# 4 Steliano Manoley Greece & Chris Christaire Greece
MANONGIAN, Chak, Jun 5 1929 Sex:M Child# 3 Kirkor Manongian Turkey & Yagsa Saagziai Turkey
MANOTT, Unknown, Jul 22 1908 Sex:M Child# 7 Philip Manott Sciota, NY & Josephine Hiter Moore's, NY
MANSEAU, Alma Y, May 8 1893 Sex:F Child# 10 J B Manseau Canada & Agnes Fontaine Canada
MANSEAU, Blanche Irene, Oct 24 1891 Sex:F Child# 10 J B Manseau Canada & Agnes Fontaine Canada
MANSEAU, David Oscar, Oct 30 1896 Sex:M Child# 5 F X Manseau Canada & Edilda Ding Nashua, NH
MANSEAU, Edna Vera, May 25 1910 Sex:F Child# 2 John E Manseau Nashua, NH & Margaret McCarty Pepperell, MA
MANSEAU, Emma, Sep 25 1888 Sex:F Child# 4 Joseph Manseau Canada & Alesina Canada
MANSEAU, Exilda M A, Sep 8 1891 Sex:F Child# 2 F X Manseau Canada & Exilda Dean Nashua, NH
MANSEAU, Hector, Apr 30 1894 Sex:M Child# 4 Francis Manseau Canada & Exilda Dingo Nashua, NH
MANSEAU, Honovine D, Sep 24 1892 Sex:F Child# 3 Francois X Manseau Canada & Exilda Dean Nashua, NH
MANSEAU, John Henry, Jul 6 1890 Sex:M Child# 1 F E Manseau Canada & Exilda Dean Nashua, NH
MANSEAU, Joseph, Oct 30 1902 Sex:M Child# 7 Xavier Manseau Canada & Exilda Dean NH Stillborn
MANSEAU, Joseph Lorenzo, Jan 12 1892 Sex:M Child# 6 Joseph Manseau Canada & Alexina Canada
MANSEAU, Lucienne, Dec 22 1904 Sex:F Child# 8 F C Manseau Canada & Exilda Dean Nashua, NH
MANSEAU, Marie G H, May 28 1891 Sex:F Child# 1 Deus Manseau Canada & Georgianna Boisvert Nashua, NH
MANSEAU, Pearl Lilian, Jan 1 1900 Sex:F Child# 6 Xavier Manseau Canada & Ezilda Dean Nashua, NH
MANSER, Celena Clara, Sep 23 1908 Sex:F Child# 1 William H Manser England & Lillian E Deacon England
MANSFIELD, Alma Alena, May 25 1909 Sex:F Child# 2 Walter J Mansfield Windsor, VT & Lavina Jeannotte Nashua, NH
MANSFIELD, Elgridge Everett, Oct 4 1908 Sex:M Child# 1 Arthur L Mansfield S Chelmsford, MA & Susan E Guerin
MANSFIELD, Ellen Agnes, May 27 1891 Sex:F Child# 3 James A Mansfield Bondsville, MA & Ellen A Wills Nashua, NH
MANSFIELD, Frederick Walter, Jan 11 1908 Sex:M Child# 1 Walter J Mansfield Windsor, VT & Labina Jeannotte Nashua
MANSFIELD, George Henry, May 22 1919 Sex:M Child# 2 M W Mansfield New Boston, NH & Martha Lee Beverly, MA
MANSFIELD, James John, Dec 22 1894 Sex:M Child# 5 James Mansfield Bondsville, MA & Nellie Wills Nashua, NH
MANSFIELD, Mary, Jun 9 1888 Sex:F Child# 2 John F Mansfield Bronsonville, MS & Katie Carmody Bronsonville, MS
MANSFIELD, Mary Johanna, Aug 5 1889 Sex:F Child# 2 J A Mansfield Bonsville, MA & Ellen Willis Nashua, NH
MANSFIELD, Unknown, Aug 8 1887 Sex:F Child# 1 James A Mansfield Massachusetts & Nellie Nashua, NH
MANSFIELD, Wesley Brendon, Jun 16 1910 Sex:M Child# 2 Arthur L Mansfield Chelmsford, MA & Susan E Guerin Canada
MANSFIELD, Winfred Victor, Dec 21 1911 Sex:M Child# 3 Walter J Mansfield Windsor, VT & Lavina Jeanotte Nashua, NH
MANSUR, Charles Robert, Oct 24 1931 Sex:M Child# 2 Charles W Mansur Nashua, NH & Evelyn E Cote Lowell, MA
MANSUR, Charles William, May 4 1904 Sex:M Child# 1 Charles Mansur Groton, MA & Fannie Short Groton, MA
MANSUR, Florence, Dec 10 1907 Sex:F Child# 3 Charles Mansur Groton, MA & Fannie Short Groton, MA Stillborn
MANSUR, George William, Sep 12 1935 Sex:M Child# 3 Charles Mansur Nashua, NH & Evelyn Cote Lowell, MA
MANSUR, Jane Elizabeth, Sep 22 1928 Sex:F Child# 1 Kenneth Mansur Nashua, NH & Hazel Rockwell Troy, NY
MANSUR, Ruth, Aug 7 1929 Sex:F Child# 1 Charles Mansur, Jr Nashua, NH & Evelyn Cote Lowell, MA
MANTEL, Yolande Theresa, Mar 10 1928 Sex:F Child# 2 Ernest Mantel Canada & Lydia Deneault Nashua, NH
MANTSAVINOS, Triantafilos, Jun 30 1928 Sex:M Child# 1 K Mantsavinos Greece & M Lalopoulos Greece
MARAIS, Esther Jeanne, May 16 1904 Sex:F Child# 7 Auguste Marais Canada & Delphine Lachance Canada
MARAIS, Joseph Roland, Jun 3 1902 Sex:M Child# 3 Auguste Marais Canada & Delphine Lachance Canada
MARANDA, Agnes, Jun 18 1894 Sex:F Child# 6 Norbert Maranda Canada & Philomene Lapierre Canada
MARANDA, Alice, May 26 1893 Sex:F Child# 7 Norbert Maranda Canada & Philomene Lapierre Canada
MARANDA, Corinne, Oct 20 1895 Sex:F Child# 7 Norbert Maranda Canada & Philomene Lapierre Champlain, NY
MARANDA, Hermine Bertha, Dec 13 1891 Sex:F Child# 1 Leopold Maranda Canada & Hermine Caron Canada
MARANDA, Joseph Wilfred, Jun 22 1895 Sex:M Child# 2 Ovila Maranda Canada & Victoria Beland Canada
MARANDA, Louis, Sep 9 1890 Sex:M Child# 5 Norbert Maranda Canada & Philomene Sapilase Canada
MARANDA, Marie Hermine, Aug 30 1897 Sex:F Child# 8 Norbert Maranda Canada & Philomene Lapierre Champlain, NY
MARANDA, Ovila, Nov 6 1891 Sex:M Child# 4 Norbert Maranda Canada & Philomene Lapierre Canada
MARANDA, Ovila, Mar 27 1894 Sex:M Child# 1 James O Maranda Canada & Victoria Beland Nashua, NH
MARANDO, Celina, Jun 6 1888 Sex:F Child# 2 Norbert Marando Canada & Philomen Canada
MARANJIAN, Zadig George, Mar 13 1926 Sex:M Child# 2 David Maranjian Armenia & Mary Kazarosion Armenia
MARCEAU, Joseph Adelard, Feb 7 1898 Sex:M Child# 2 Xavier Marceau Canada & Rosanna Landry Canada
MARCH, Clara Hope, Jan 1 1924 Sex:F Child# 3 Howard M March Nashua, NH & Cecile Marois Nashua, NH
MARCH, Dorothy, Dec 12 1898 Sex:F Child# 1 Charles T March New Brunswick & Alberta Hanscom Portsmouth, NH
MARCH, Elmer Charles, Jun 13 1904 Sex:M Child# 4 Charles T March New Brunswick & Alberta Hanscom Portsmouth, NH
MARCH, Ethel May, Jun 2 1897 Sex:F Child# 1 Vine March Boston, MA & Hattie Gibson Nashua, NH
MARCH, Harry Stanley, Nov 27 1920 Sex:M Child# 1 Harry S March Canada & Rose Lemery Nashua, NH
MARCH, Helen Louise, May 10 1930 Sex:F Child# 2 Elwin March Nashua, NH & Norma Pierce Woburn, MA
MARCH, Howard Merle, Apr 18 1897 Sex:M Child# 6 James E March Boston, MA & Cassie F Malone St John, NB
MARCH, Leonard Earle, Nov 14 1911 Sex:M Child# 4 Vine F March Boston, MA & Hattie Gibson Nashua, NH
MARCH, Luther O, Feb 7 1901 Sex:M Child# 3 Vine F March Boston, MA & Hattie Gibson Nashua, NH
MARCH, Marjorie Claire, Nov 20 1924 Sex:F Child# 4 H M March Nashua, NH & Cecile Marois Nashua, NH
MARCH, Murray, Apr 22 1895 Sex:M Child# 5 James E March Boston, MA & Cassie Malone St John, NB
MARCH, Murray Edward, Apr 5 1907 Sex:M Child# 9 James E March Boston, MA & Cassie F Malone St Johns, NB
MARCH, Philip Elwin, Jul 13 1926 Sex:M Child# 1 Elwin A March Nashua, NH & Norma Pierce Woburn, MA
MARCH, Ruth Anne, Jan 2 1933 Sex:F Child# 1 L A March Nashua, NH & Caroline Grant Clifton, ME
MARCH, Unknown, Jun 11 1891 Sex:F Child# 2 James E March Boston, MA & Cassie F Malone St Johns, NB
MARCH, Unknown, Jun 30 1892 Sex:M Child# 3 James E March Boston, MA & Cassie Malone St John, NB
MARCH, Unknown, Mar 14 1894 Sex:F Child# 4 James E March Boston, MA & Cassie Malone St Johns, NB

MARCH, Unknown, Jun 16 1898 Sex:F Child# 7 James E March Mass & Cassie Malone New Brunswick
MARCH, Unknown, Jun 28 1898 Sex:M Child# 2 Vine March Boston, MA & Hattie Gibson Nashua, NH
MARCH, Unknown, Aug 12 1900 Sex:M Child#  Charles T March NB & Alberta Hanscome NY
MARCH, Unknown, Nov 21 1902 Sex:M Child# 3 Charles T March New Brunswick & Alberta Hanscom NH
MARCH, Walter A, Jan 1 1889 Sex:M Child# 1 James E March Boston, MA & Carrie Malone New Brunswick
MARCHA, Unknown, Mar 1 1892 Sex:M Child# 1 (No Parents Listed)
MARCHAND, Arthur George, Mar 1 1890 Sex:M Child# 3 George Marchand Canada & Emma Beauregard Nashua, NH
MARCHAND, Barbara Theresa, Feb 11 1929 Sex:F Child# 2 Salfrid Marchand Nashua, NH & Sylvia Lynch Orange, MA
MARCHAND, Ella M, Apr 4 1887 Sex:F Child#  George Marchand P Q & E Beauregard E Douglas, MA
MARCHAND, Gertrude, Jan 2 1905 Sex:F Child# 2 Joseph Marchand Canada & Marianne Demanche Canada
MARCHAND, Joseph, Oct 13 1912 Sex:M Child# 8 William B Marchand Canada & Lucinda Sawyer Canada
MARCHAND, Joseph Alderic, Oct 14 1907 Sex:M Child# 7 William B Marchand Canada & Lucinda Sawyer Canada
MARCHAND, Joseph Galfride A, Apr 29 1906 Sex:M Child# 6 William B Marchand Canada & Lucinda Sawyer Canada
MARCHAND, Joseph Henri, Jan 30 1903 Sex:M Child# 5 William Marchand Canada & Lucinda Sawyer Canada
MARCHAND, Joseph Louis A, Aug 29 1906 Sex:M Child# 3 Joseph Marchand Canada & Marie Demanche Canada
MARCHAND, Leo, Aug 22 1912 Sex:M Child# 6 Joseph Marchand Canada & Annie Demanche Canada
MARCHAND, Loretta, Oct 1 1907 Sex:F Child# 4 Joseph Marchand Canada & Marianne Demanche Canada
MARCHAND, Marie Lily, Jun 28 1910 Sex:F Child# 5 Joseph Marchand Canada & Anna Demanche Canada
MARCHAND, Nancy Florence, May 16 1933 Sex:F Child# 2 Henri Marchand Nashua, NH & M Gendron Nashua, NH
MARCHAND, Patricia Joan, Dec 29 1932 Sex:F Child# 3 S J Marchand Nashua, NH & Sylvia Lynch Orange, MA
MARCHENONIS, Robert Marston, Nov 17 1934 Sex:M Child# 2 Anthony Marchenonis
MARCLEY, Francis Leo, May 25 1919 Sex:M Child# 1 Frank J Marcley Rome, Italy & Helen R Kinville Douglas, NY
MARCORAVICA, Annie, Oct 8 1911 Sex:F Child# 3 Michael Marcoravica Russia & Josephine Tetariue Russia
MARCOTTE, Eugene Raymond, Jul 29 1931 Sex:M Child# 2 Omer Marcotte Derry, NH & Beatrice Parent S Ashburnham, MA
MARCOTTE, Gertrude Beatrice, Mar 26 1930 Sex:F Child# 1 Omer Marcotte Derry, NH & Beatrice Parent S Ashburnham, MA
MARCOTTE, Joan Beth, Sep 12 1928 Sex:F Child# 1 R H Marcotte Vermont & E L Mahon Elizabeth, NJ
MARCOTTE, Joseph, Feb 19 1928 Sex:M Child# 1 (No Parents Listed)
MARCOTTE, Mary Jane, Jul 31 1930 Sex:F Child# 2 Raymond Marcotte Winooski, VT & Elizabeth Mahon Jersey City, NJ
MARCOTTE, Raymond Henry, Sep 24 1935 Sex:M Child# 3 Raymond Marcotte Winooski, VT & Elizabeth Mahon Jersey City, NJ
MARCOUX, Celestine D, May 31 1900 Sex:F Child# 13 Alphonse Marcoux Canada & Cezarie Grondin Canada
MARCOUX, Conrad Ernest, May 18 1916 Sex:M Child# 3 Albert Marcoux Canada & Eva Lavoie Somersworth, NH
MARCOUX, Edmond Anatol, Sep 26 1914 Sex:M Child# 2 Albert Marcoux Canada & Eva Lavoie Somersworth, NH
MARCOUX, Edmond Gerard, Jul 19 1929 Sex:M Child# 5 Adelard Marcoux Canada & Reginas Demers Canada
MARCOUX, Ernest Noel, Dec 25 1923 Sex:M Child# 4 Alcide Marcoux Canada & Marie Levesque Nashua, NH
MARCOUX, Georgiana A, Mar 21 1902 Sex:F Child# 14 Alph Marcoux Canada & Cesaire Grondin Canada
MARCOUX, Heliodore, Jul 28 1910 Sex:M Child# 1 Joseph Marcoux Canada & Alexina Fournier Canada
MARCOUX, J B Napoleon, Apr 13 1902 Sex:M Child# 3 Elzear Marcoux Canada & Hermenie Bonneau Canada
MARCOUX, Jean B Lucien, Nov 5 1921 Sex:M Child# 3 Alcide Marcoux Canada & Marie Levesque Nashua, NH
MARCOUX, Jos Ernest Raymond, Jan 16 1919 Sex:M Child# 2 Ernest Marcoux Canada & Helen Clifford Mass
MARCOUX, Joseph Albert, Sep 11 1898 Sex:M Child# 1 Elzear Marcoux Canada & Hermine Bonneau Canada
MARCOUX, Joseph Lucien Raoul, Aug 9 1917 Sex:M Child# 1 Ernest Marcoux Canada & Helen Clifford Boston, MA
MARCOUX, Josephine Eva, Sep 5 1904 Sex:F Child# 15 Alphonse Marcoux Canada & Cezarie Groudin Canada
MARCOUX, Louis Henri, Jun 4 1917 Sex:M Child# 1 Alcide Marcoux Canada & Marie Levesque Nashua, NH
MARCOUX, Lucien Alcide, May 25 1919 Sex:M Child# 5 Albert Marcoux Canada & Eva Lavoie Canada
MARCOUX, Marie, May 11 1926 Sex:F Child# 11 Adelard Marcoux Canada & Regina Demers Canada
MARCOUX, Marie Antoinette Y, May 4 1920 Sex:F Child# 6 Albert Marcoux Canada & Eva Lavoie NH
MARCOUX, Marie Evangeline, Aug 25 1900 Sex:F Child# 2 Elzear Marcoux Canada & Hermine Bonneau Canada
MARCOUX, Marie Loretta, May 27 1917 Sex:F Child# 4 Albert Marcoux Canada & Eva Labounte Somersworth, NH
MARCOUX, Marie Lucille, Mar 11 1920 Sex:F Child# 2 Alcide Marcoux Canada & Mary Levesque Nashua, NH
MARCOUX, Marie Stella Graziel, Oct 27 1927 Sex:F Child# 11 Albert Marcoux Canada & Eva Lavoie NH
MARCOUX, Marie Therese Rita, Jan 22 1925 Sex:F Child# 3 Ernest Marcoux Canada & Helene Clifford Mass
MARCOUX, Paul Wilfred, Jun 4 1907 Sex:M Child# 17 Alphonse Marcoux Canada & Cezarie Grondin Canada
MARCOUX, Pauline Christine, Jun 21 1927 Sex:F Child# 5 Aleck Marcoux Canada & Marie Levesque Nashua, NH
MARCOUX, Romain Alphonse, Nov 13 1905 Sex:M Child# 16 Alphonse Marcoux Canada & Cezarie Constant Canada
MARCOUX, William Conrad, Jul 6 1921 Sex:M Child# 2 Joseph Marcoux Canada & Alexina Fournier Canada
MARCUS, Aaron Sumner, Oct 15 1926 Sex:M Child# 2 Bernard Marcus Russia & Martha Folsom Boston, MA
MARCUS, Celia, Mar 26 1914 Sex:F Child# 4 Frank N Marcus Russia & Annie B Sindalman Russia
MARCUS, Clara Rachel, Oct 29 1915 Sex:F Child# 5 Frank Marcus Russia & Annie Sindlemen Russia
MARGARITIS, Robert Milton, Feb 19 1934 Sex:M Child# 1 Milton Margaritis Greece & Florence April Nashua, NH
MARIARTY, Rose Christena, Dec 21 1903 Sex:F Child# 11 Richard Mariarty Ireland & Mary O'Brien London, England
MARIN, Ernest Edouard, May 13 1889 Sex:M Child# 11 Norbert Marin Canada & Zenalde Cazeau Canada
MARION, Albert, Aug 8 1889 Sex:M Child# 4 Avila Marion Canada & Elizabeth Bellerose Canada
MARION, Claire Lawrence, Jan 15 1921 Sex:F Child# 1 Jean Bap Marion Nashua, NH & Marie L Deschenes Canada
MARION, Donald Joseph, Jan 18 1911 Sex:M Child# 2 George P Marion Haverhill, MA & Margaret McMaster Dundee, PQ
MARION, Edmond E, Jul 16 1892 Sex:M Child# 5 Avila Marion Canada & Elizabeth Bellerose Canada
MARION, Ernestine, Oct 29 1890 Sex:F Child# 3 Raymond Marion Canada & Almeline Houde Canada
MARION, George Octave, May 18 1909 Sex:M Child# 1 George P Marion Haverhill, MA & Margaret McMaster Dundee, PQ
MARION, Jean Baptiste A I, Nov 15 1896 Sex:M Child# 7 Avila Marion Canada & Elizabeth Bellerose Canada
MARION, Leo Albert, Jr, Aug 17 1931 Sex:M Child# 3 Leo Albert Marion Dover, NH & Louise Cyr Benton, NH
MARION, Leopold Roger, Jan 2 1922 Sex:M Child# 1 Hormidas Marion Canada & Alice Marion Nashua, NH
MARION, Margaret Mary, Jan 14 1914 Sex:F Child# 3 George P Marion Haverhill, MA & Margaret McMaster Quebec
MARION, Marie O, Feb 17 1895 Sex:F Child# 9 Avila Marion Canada & Elizabeth Bellerose Canada
MARION, Renee Robert, Aug 28 1922 Sex:M Child# 2 John B Marion Nashua, NH & Mary L Deschenes Canada

MARION, Theresa, Feb 4 1928 Sex:F Child# 2 Leo Marion Dover, NH & Louise Cyr Bristol, NH
MARION, Unknown, Dec 30 1915 Sex:M Child# 7 George P Marion Haverhill, MA & Margaret McMaster Canada
MARKARAWICZ, Joseph, Nov 23 1924 Sex:M Child# 4 Joseph Markarawicz Lithuania & Katie Gediales Lithuania
MARKARIAN, Alice, Oct 1 1911 Sex:F Child# 9 George Markarian Armenia & Mary Aronian Armenia
MARKARIAN, Alice, Jun 10 1913 Sex:F Child# 11 George Markarian Armenia & Mary Kaurnaian Armenia
MARKARIAN, Alton, Sep 15 1907 Sex:F Child# 7 George Markarian Armenia & Mary Haronian Armenia
MARKARIAN, Araxis, Sep 25 1902 Sex:M Child# 3 George Markarian Turkey & Mary Hoirian Turkey
MARKARIAN, Beatrice, Oct 1 1911 Sex:F Child# 10 George Markarian Armenia & Mary Aronian Armenia
MARKARIAN, George Markar, Mar 2 1932 Sex:M Child# 1 M G Markarian Nashua, NH & Pearl E Hayward Nashua, NH
MARKARIAN, Martin, Apr 27 1905 Sex:M Child# 6 George Markarian Turkey & Mary Aronoin Turkey
MARKARIAN, Mary, Jul 22 1900 Sex:F Child# 2 George Markarian Russia & Mary Elrian Russia
MARKARIAN, Rachel, Aug 21 1915 Sex:F Child# 12 George Markarian Turkey & Mary Aronian Turkey
MARKARIAN, Somoim, Oct 6 1903 Sex:M Child# 4 George Markarian Turkey & Mary Aorien Turkey
MARKAVERICH, Adam, Sep 22 1920 Sex:M Child# 6 Mich Markaverich Lithuania & Josephine Ticerunis Lithuania
MARKEIUS, Unknown, Aug 30 1915 Sex:M Child# 2 Nicolas Markeius Greece & Fanny Gennevia Greece
MARKEVICH, Lillian Frances, Oct 9 1929 Sex:F Child# 2 Louis Markevich Poland & Helen Stuczymaka Cambridge, MA
MARKEWICH, Alexander, Dec 12 1915 Sex:M Child# 1 Branislaw Markewich Russia & Josepha Michalevick Russia
MARKEWICH, Paul Alexander, Feb 26 1935 Sex:M Child# 3 Louis Markewich Poland & Helen Stuczyaski Cambridge, MA
MARKEWICH, Unknown, Jun 29 1912 Sex:M Child# 1 Joseph Markewich Russia & Mikalina Markel Russia
MARKEWICZ, Bennie, Oct 25 1926 Sex:M Child# 1 John Markewicz Poland & J Stuczinski Poland
MARKEWICZ, Helen, Nov 2 1927 Sex:F Child# 1 Louis Markewicz Poland & Helen Stricziniski Cambridge, MA
MARKEWICZ, Walter, Jul 24 1928 Sex:M Child# 2 J Markewicz Poland & J Stuczynska Cambridge, MA
MARKIEL, Adolf, Oct 14 1923 Sex:M Child# 3 Walter Markiel Russia & Antonio Kisiel Russia
MARKLE, Yedviga, May 21 1910 Sex:M Child# 1 Ludwig Markle Russia & Antonetts Kissel Russia
MARKRIAN, Rosa, Jul 25 1901 Sex:F Child# 3 George Markrian Turkey & Mary Iranian Turkey
MARKROS, Unknown, Jun 6 1915 Sex:F Child# 2 Mike Markros Greece & Helen Zaphrios Greece
MARLOW, Unknown, Jul 4 1895 Sex:F Child# 13 Nelson Marlow Malone, NY & Mary Fectee Malone, NY Stillborn
MAROIS, Alice Lilian, May 29 1905 Sex:F Child# 4 Alphonse Marois Canada & Sourfranie Boilard Nashua, NH
MAROIS, Alphonse Harold, Oct 2 1908 Sex:M Child# 5 Alphonse Marois Canada & Sophronie Boilard Nashua, NH
MAROIS, Delia Josephine, Jul 8 1906 Sex:F Child# 7 Alfred Marois Canada & Josephine Ducheneau Canada
MAROIS, Jeannette, Jul 29 1922 Sex:F Child# 14 Alfred Marois Canada & Josephine Duchesneau Canada
MAROIS, Jos Adelard Lionel, Oct 20 1917 Sex:M Child# 13 Alfred Marois Canada & Josephine Duchesneau Canada
MAROIS, Joseph Emile, Jun 16 1909 Sex:M Child# 9 Alfred Marois Canada & Josephine Duchesneau Canada
MAROIS, Josephine H, Aug 9 1901 Sex:F Child# 4 Alfred Marois Canada & Josephine Duchesneau Canada
MAROIS, Marie Cecil V, Oct 24 1901 Sex:F Child# 3 Alphonse Marois Canada & Sophronie Boilard Nashua, NH
MAROIS, Marie Delia D, Nov 10 1899 Sex:F Child# 3 Alfred Marois Canada & Josephine Duchesneau Canada
MAROIS, Muriel Lena, Jul 26 1912 Sex:F Child# 11 Alfred Marois Canada & Josephine Duchesneau Canada
MAROIS, Napoleon, Sep 23 1902 Sex:M Child# 5 Alfred Marois Canada & Jos Ducheneau Canada
MAROIS, Unknown, Oct 23 1913 Sex:F Child# 12 Alfred Marois Canada & Josephine Duchesneau Canada Stillborn
MAROIS, Unknown, Aug 15 1922 Sex:M Child# 1 (No Parents Listed)
MAROIS, William Gerald, Nov 10 1912 Sex:M Child# 8 Alphonse Marois Canada & Sophronie Boilard Canada
MAROIS, Willie, Aug 23 1907 Sex:M Child# 8 Auguste Marois Canada & Jose Ducheneau Canada
MAROON, Hope, Sep 4 1931 Sex:F Child# 7 Richard Maroon Syria & Nemery Garem Syria
MAROON, Najella, Aug 15 1922 Sex:F Child# 3 Richard Maroon Syria & Membry Gamam Syria
MAROON, Odeeb, Apr 7 1927 Sex:M Child# 5 Richard Maroon Syria & Nemery Ganem Syria
MAROON, Unknown, Dec 11 1924 Sex:F Child# 4 Robert Maroon Syria & Membry Gansrau Syria
MAROTTE, Adelina, May 22 1910 Sex:F Child# 3 Edouard Marotte Sciota, NY & Victoria Garand Salem, MA
MAROTTE, Blanche, Jul 25 1896 Sex:F Child# 5 Phileas Marotte US & Josephine Dionne US
MAROTTE, Emma, Apr 4 1894 Sex:F Child#  Moses Marotte US & Melinda Duprey US
MAROTTE, George, Oct 28 1890 Sex:M Child#  Philias Marotte Moores Jct, NY & Josephine Dion Moores Jct, NY
MAROTTE, Isabelle, Jan 12 1909 Sex:F Child# 2 Edouard Marotte Sciota, NY & Victoria Garand Salem, MA
MAROTTE, Joseph Russul, Mar 24 1898 Sex:M Child# 6 Philias Marotte Sciota, NY & Josephine Iter Mooers, NY
MAROTTE, Marie, Mar 14 1889 Sex:F Child# 10 Noel Marotte Champlain, NY & Julia Boyer Plattsburg, NY
MAROTTE, Marie Melina, Apr 22 1902 Sex:F Child# 1 Willia Marotte New York & Florida Beaudoin Canada
MAROTTE, Mary, Oct 29 1891 Sex:F Child# 5 Moses Marotte New York & Milanda Marotte New York
MAROTTE, Unknown, May 2 1887 Sex:M Child#  Noel Marotte Champlain, NY & Julie Voyer Plattsburg, NY Stillborn
MAROTTE, Unknown, Dec 11 1894 Sex:F Child# 21 Noel Marotte US & Julie Boyer US
MAROTTE, Unknown, Oct 29 1897 Sex:M Child# 7 Moise Marotte NY & Lina Dupre NY Stillborn
MARQUIS, Adelard, Oct 22 1922 Sex:M Child# 1 Adelard Marquis Nashua, NH & Amanda Dimphonses Lowell, MA
MARQUIS, Adriane, Aug 8 1908 Sex:F Child# 2 Henry P Marquis Nashua, NH & Hermine Roy Canada
MARQUIS, Albert, Nov 24 1896 Sex:M Child# 2 Wilfrid Marquis Canada & Henrietta Gauthier Canada
MARQUIS, Albert Eugene, May 1 1914 Sex:M Child# 2 Alfred Marquis Canada & Julia Z Lessard Nashua, NH
MARQUIS, Albert Eugene, Jun 20 1920 Sex:M Child# 2 Ernest Marquis Nashua, NH & Marie Anne Arbour Canada
MARQUIS, Alphonse Donald, Mar 24 1934 Sex:M Child# 2 George Marquis Nashua, NH & Alphonsine Valliere Canada
MARQUIS, Armand, Feb 26 1911 Sex:M Child# 2 Emile Marquis Canada & Leonard Bastille Canada
MARQUIS, Armand Joseph Nap, Dec 10 1909 Sex:M Child# 7 John B Marquis Canada & Caroline Bouvouloir Canada
MARQUIS, Baptiste J P, Sep 21 1897 Sex:M Child# 1 Pierre Marquis Canada & Clara Pinault Canada
MARQUIS, Beatrice Marie G, Apr 3 1929 Sex:F Child# 8 Ernest Marquis Nashua, NH & Marianne Arbour Canada
MARQUIS, Blanche, May 15 1898 Sex:F Child# 1 Elie Marquis Canada & Ledivine Morin Canada
MARQUIS, Cecile Olivette, Jun 17 1913 Sex:F Child# 2 Arthur Marquis Canada & Marie Sirois Canada
MARQUIS, Cecille Jeannette, Feb 18 1909 Sex:F Child# 5 Albert Marquis Canada & Angele Levesque Canada
MARQUIS, Charles Albert, Dec 11 1909 Sex:M Child# 7 J A Marquis Canada & Marie Boucher Canada
MARQUIS, Charles Raymond, Oct 3 1919 Sex:M Child# 5 Hector Marquis Russia & Mary Valliska Russia

MARQUIS, Clara E A, Apr 1 1900 Sex:F Child# 4 Wilfrid Marquis Canada & Henrietta Gauthier Canada
MARQUIS, Clementine Rita, Jun 8 1927 Sex:F Child# 1 Albert Marquis Nashua, NH & Yvonne Lemay Nashua, NH
MARQUIS, Conrad Lambert, Sep 17 1933 Sex:M Child# 2 Ange Marquis Canada & Lucille Asselin Nashua, NH
MARQUIS, Corinne, Jun 16 1915 Sex:F Child# 3 Alfred Marquis Canada & Julia Lessard Nashua, NH
MARQUIS, David Joseph, Feb 16 1930 Sex:M Child# 2 Joseph Marquis Canada & Elizabeth Guyette Nashua, NH
MARQUIS, David Leopold, Sep 22 1911 Sex:M Child# 6 Oscar Marquis Canada & Marie Pelletier Canada
MARQUIS, Donald Roger, Jun 6 1935 Sex:M Child# 2 Hector Marquis Nashua, NH & Simonne Levesque Nashua, NH
MARQUIS, Doris May, Aug 18 1925 Sex:F Child# 1 Joseph Marquis Canada & Elizabeth Goyette Nashua, NH
MARQUIS, Elene Jacqueline, Dec 22 1930 Sex:F Child# 2 Leo Marquis Nashua, NH & Gracia Bibeau Canada
MARQUIS, Elisee, Jul 8 1906 Sex:F Child# 3 Oscar Marquis Canada & Marie Pelletier Canada
MARQUIS, Eva, Mar 22 1897 Sex:F Child# 12 George Marquis Canada & Adelaide Chasse Canada
MARQUIS, Flora May, Jun 18 1887 Sex:F Child# 1 Peter Marquis Nashua, NH & Regina Belanger Lowell, MA
MARQUIS, George Henry, Jul 20 1906 Sex:M Child# 1 Henry P Marquis, Jr Nashua, NH & Hermine Roy Canada
MARQUIS, Georgette, Nov 12 1931 Sex:F Child# 1 George Marquis US & Alphonsine Vallieres Canada
MARQUIS, Hector, Jul 9 1893 Sex:M Child# 1 Joseph Marquis Canada & Anna Caron Canada
MARQUIS, Henri, Jul 2 1900 Sex:M Child# 6 Omerilde Marquis Canada & Delima Pineault Canada
MARQUIS, Isidore Emile, Aug 19 1926 Sex:M Child# 10 Isidore Marquis Canada & Leda Pinette Canada
MARQUIS, J Leon Romeo, Sep 22 1911 Sex:M Child# 7 Oscar Marquis Canada & Marie Pelletier Canada
MARQUIS, Janet Mariange, Apr 20 1931 Sex:F Child# 1 Ange Marquis Canada & Lucille Asselin Nashua, NH
MARQUIS, Jean Baptiste, May 21 1900 Sex:M Child# 1 J B Marquis Canada & Caroline Bonvounoir Canada
MARQUIS, Jean Baptiste S, Dec 11 1902 Sex:M Child# 4 Joseph A Marquis Canada & Marie Boucher Canada
MARQUIS, Jean Bte Raymond, Mar 17 1915 Sex:M Child# 1 Theophile Marquis Canada & Aurore Gaudette US
MARQUIS, Jos Alfred Raymond, Jan 12 1921 Sex:M Child# 1 Jos Arthur Marquis Canada & Anna Boule Maine
MARQUIS, Jos Lambert Gray, Sep 15 1930 Sex:M Child# 1 Hector Marquis Nashua, NH & Simmone Levesque Nashua, NH
MARQUIS, Jos Norman Adrian, Dec 3 1934 Sex:M Child# 4 Adrian Marquis Canada & Eva Desrosiers Nashua, NH
MARQUIS, Joseph, Jan 19 1896 Sex:M Child# 3 Meril Marquis Canada & Adelima Pinault Canada
MARQUIS, Joseph, Oct 7 1897 Sex:M Child# 2 Joseph P Marquis Canada & Mary Proult Canada Stillborn
MARQUIS, Joseph, Jan 29 1906 Sex:M Child# 5 Pierre Marquis Canada & Clara Pinault Canada
MARQUIS, Joseph, Sep 1 1907 Sex:M Child# 6 Joseph A Marquis Canada & Marie Boucher Canada
MARQUIS, Joseph, Oct 1 1920 Sex:M Child# 1 (No Parents Listed)
MARQUIS, Joseph Adelard, Dec 11 1901 Sex:M Child# 3 Pierre Marquis Canada & Clara Pinault Canada
MARQUIS, Joseph Albert, Jun 10 1903 Sex:M Child# 1 Albert Marquis Canada & Angele Levesque Canada
MARQUIS, Joseph Andre Edgar, Feb 4 1916 Sex:M Child# 9 Joseph A Marquis Canada & Marie Boucher Canada
MARQUIS, Joseph Conrad Paul, Mar 27 1928 Sex:M Child# 1 Jean B Marquis Nashua, NH & Eva Soucy Nashua, NH
MARQUIS, Joseph D, Oct 28 1900 Sex:M Child# 3 Joseph Marquis Canada & Mary Boucher Canada
MARQUIS, Joseph Emile P, Jun 17 1908 Sex:M Child# 4 Oscar Marquis Canada & Marie Pelletier Canada
MARQUIS, Joseph G, Nov 27 1890 Sex:M Child# 4 Hamenegild Marquis Canada & Amelia Bissonette Canada
MARQUIS, Joseph H Armand, Apr 5 1931 Sex:M Child# 3 Albert Marquis Nashua, NH & Yvonne Lemay Nashua, NH
MARQUIS, Joseph H Norbert, Jun 25 1931 Sex:M Child# 1 Camille Marquis Canada & Rose Ouellette Canada
MARQUIS, Joseph Hector, Mar 16 1897 Sex:M Child# 4 Joseph O Marquis Canada & Anna Caron Canada
MARQUIS, Joseph Hector, Jun 17 1906 Sex:M Child# 5 John Marquis Canada & Caroline Bonvouloir Canada
MARQUIS, Joseph Henri, Oct 3 1907 Sex:M Child# 6 Jean B Marquis Canada & Caroline Bonvouloir Canada
MARQUIS, Joseph Jean B, Mar 4 1893 Sex:M Child# 1 Meril Marquis Canada & Delima Pinault Canada
MARQUIS, Joseph Louis, Aug 12 1906 Sex:M Child# 5 Joseph Marquis Canada & Marie Dionne Canada
MARQUIS, Joseph Roland, Sep 2 1911 Sex:M Child# 7 Pierre Marquis Canada & Clara Pineault Canada
MARQUIS, Joseph Roland Romeo, Dec 11 1912 Sex:M Child# 8 Oscar Marquis Canada & Marie Pelletier Canada
MARQUIS, Joseph Victor Roger, Oct 8 1916 Sex:M Child# 9 Pierre Marquis Canada & Flora Pinault Canada
MARQUIS, Joseph W T, Jan 14 1899 Sex:M Child# 3 Palicarpe Marquis Canada & Marie Proult Canada
MARQUIS, Joseph William, Mar 16 1899 Sex:M Child# 1 Joseph Marquis Canada & Desneige Ouellette Canada
MARQUIS, Joseph William, Apr 13 1902 Sex:M Child# 5 Wilfrid Marquis Canada & Henrietta Gauthier Canada
MARQUIS, Juliette, May 28 1907 Sex:F Child# 4 Albert Marquis Canada & Angele Levesque Canada
MARQUIS, Leo Armand, May 10 1905 Sex:M Child# 7 Wilfrid Marquis Canada & Henrietta Gauthier Canada
MARQUIS, Leo Ernest, Jan 4 1925 Sex:M Child# Ernest Marquis Nashua, NH & Marie A Arbour Canada
MARQUIS, Leo Louis Oscar, Jan 8 1905 Sex:M Child# 2 Oscar Marquis Canada & Marie Peltier Canada
MARQUIS, Leo Wm Jos D, Oct 20 1904 Sex:M Child# 4 Jean B Marquis Canada & Caroline Bonvouloir Canada
MARQUIS, Lillian Rita, Aug 26 1918 Sex:F Child# 1 Ernest Marquis Canada & M A Arlour Nashua, NH
MARQUIS, Louis O Wilbrode, Mar 7 1919 Sex:M Child# 11 Louis O Marquis Canada & Marie Pelletier Canada
MARQUIS, Lucien, Nov 27 1909 Sex:M Child# 11 David Marquis Canada & Arthemise Paradis Canada
MARQUIS, Lucienne, Nov 27 1909 Sex:F Child# 12 David Marquis Canada & Arthemise Paradis Canada
MARQUIS, M B Ivonne, Sep 27 1895 Sex:F Child# 3 Omerille Marquis Canada & Anna Caron Canada
MARQUIS, M Beatrice D Simone, Jul 19 1913 Sex:F Child# 8 Pierre Marquis Canada & Clara Pineault Canada
MARQUIS, M Bertha Germaine, May 11 1915 Sex:F Child# 9 Louis O Marquis Canada & Marie Pelletier Canada
MARQUIS, M Blanche Olivette, Jul 30 1913 Sex:F Child# 9 Jean Bte Marquis Canada & Caroline Bonvouloir Canada
MARQUIS, M Claire Elodie, May 18 1913 Sex:F Child# 4 Edouard Marquis Canada & Adele Rousseau Canada
MARQUIS, M Elise Florette, Nov 8 1913 Sex:F Child# 8 Joseph A Marquis Canada & Marie Boucher Canada
MARQUIS, M Irene Jeannette, Mar 24 1920 Sex:F Child# 12 Louis Oscar Marquis Canada & Marie Pelletier Canada
MARQUIS, M Irene Juliette, Nov 22 1911 Sex:F Child# 8 John Marquis Canada & Caroline Bonvouloir Canada
MARQUIS, M Lucille Olivette, Jan 4 1913 Sex:F Child# 1 Alfred Marquis Canada & Julia Lessard Nashua, NH
MARQUIS, M Rosalie Beatrice, Mar 1 1917 Sex:F Child# 10 Oscar Marquis Canada & Marie Pelletier Canada
MARQUIS, Marcel Napoleon, May 25 1906 Sex:M Child# 3 Albert Marquis Canada & Angele Levesque Canada
MARQUIS, Maria A, Aug 20 1889 Sex:F Child# 3 H Marquis Canada & A Bessonnette Canada
MARQUIS, Marie, Mar 25 1892 Sex:F Child# 5 Hermenegild Marquis Canada & Auselie Bissonnette Canada
MARQUIS, Marie A, Sep 4 1894 Sex:F Child# 2 Joseph Marquis Canada & Anna Caron Canada

MARQUIS, Marie A Clara, Sep 13 1899 Sex:F Child# 2 Pierre Marquis Canada & Clara Pinault Canada
MARQUIS, Marie Albina O, Dec 21 1903 Sex:F Child# 1 Louis Marquis Canada & Marie Peltier Canada
MARQUIS, Marie Alice, Apr 29 1905 Sex:F Child# 5 J A Marquis Canada & Marie Boucher Canada
MARQUIS, Marie Ange Beatrice, Feb 23 1933 Sex:F Child# 4 Philipe Marquis Canada & Marie Gautier Canada
MARQUIS, Marie Ange Lucille, Jan 16 1922 Sex:F Child# 3 Ernest Marquis Nashua, NH & M A Arbour Canada
MARQUIS, Marie Angela Annette, Oct 2 1928 Sex:F Child# 2 Albert Marquis Nashua, NH & Yvonne Lemay Nashua, NH
MARQUIS, Marie Angele Y, Jul 30 1909 Sex:F Child# 6 Pierre Marquis Canada & Clara Pinault Canada
MARQUIS, Marie Annette, Aug 2 1923 Sex:F Child# 8 Isidore Marquis Canada & Leda Pinette Canada
MARQUIS, Marie Blanche, Mar 23 1898 Sex:F Child# 5 Joseph Marquis Canada & Anna Caron Canada
MARQUIS, Marie C E, May 31 1898 Sex:F Child# 2 Joseph Marquis Canada & Marie Boucher Canada
MARQUIS, Marie Cecilie Annett, Oct 27 1933 Sex:F Child# 10 Ernest Marquis Nashua, NH & Blanche Arbour Canada
MARQUIS, Marie Delima E, Jan 25 1899 Sex:F Child# 5 Omerild Marquis Canada & Delima Pinault Canada
MARQUIS, Marie Eugenie, Aug 9 1894 Sex:F Child# 2 Meril Marquis Canada & Delima Pinault Canada
MARQUIS, Marie Eugenie L, Oct 4 1903 Sex:F Child# 2 Jean Bte Marquis Canada & Caroline Bonvouloir Canada
MARQUIS, Marie Florette, Apr 26 1910 Sex:F Child# 5 Oscar Marquis Canada & Marie Pelletier Canada
MARQUIS, Marie Gertrude Larei, Oct 22 1933 Sex:F Child# 2 Romeo Marquis Nashua, NH & J Levesque Nashua, NH
MARQUIS, Marie Jean Claire, Feb 17 1932 Sex:F Child# 1 Romeo Marquis Nashua, NH & J Levesque Nashua, NH
MARQUIS, Marie Jeanne Gloria, Dec 26 1929 Sex:F Child# 2 Adrien Marquis Canada & Eva Desrosier Nashua, NH
MARQUIS, Marie Louise Yvette, Jul 2 1926 Sex:F Child# 1 Leo Marquis Nashua, NH & Gracia Bibeau Canada
MARQUIS, Marie Paulette, May 25 1901 Sex:F Child# 4 Polycarpe Marquis Canada & Marie Proulx Canada
MARQUIS, Marie R Jacqueline, Feb 28 1931 Sex:F Child# 3 Adrien Marquis Canada & Eva Desrosiers Nashua, NH
MARQUIS, Marie Rita Lucienne, Mar 7 1928 Sex:F Child# 1 Lucien Marquis Canada & Marie L D'Amour Canada
MARQUIS, Marie Theresa, Nov 18 1927 Sex:F Child# 1 Adrien Marquis Canada & Eva Desrosiers Nashua, NH
MARQUIS, Marie Theresa Eva, Mar 22 1927 Sex:F Child# 7 Ernest Marquis Nashua, NH & Marianna Arbour Canada
MARQUIS, Marie Yvonne G, Nov 11 1901 Sex:F Child# 2 John Marquis Canada & Caroline Bonvonloir Canada
MARQUIS, Marietta, Sep 9 1932 Sex:f Child# 1 Emile Marquis US & Evelyn Paris Nashua, NH
MARQUIS, Mary, Feb 4 1901 Sex:F Child# 7 Merrill Marquis Canada & Anna Caron Canada Stillborn
MARQUIS, Mary Alice, Oct 8 1934 Sex:F Child# 2 Camille Marquis Canada & Rose Ouellette Canada
MARQUIS, Maurice, May 3 1928 Sex:M Child# 11 Isidore Marquis Canada & Leda Pinnette Canada
MARQUIS, Maurice, Nov 26 1930 Sex:M Child# 1 Elise Marquis Nashua, NH & Lucienne Ansant Canada
MARQUIS, Monette, Sep 2 1930 Sex:F Child# 12 Isidore Marquis Canada & Leda Pinette Canada
MARQUIS, Noela Geraldine, Dec 23 1930 Sex:F Child# 4 Philippe Marquis Canada & Maria Goulin Canada
MARQUIS, Normand, Aug 20 1924 Sex:M Child# 2 Theophile Marquis Canada & Flora Gaudette Nashua, NH
MARQUIS, Oscar Leo, Feb 18 1905 Sex:M Child# 4 Pierre Marquis Canada & Clara Pinault Canada
MARQUIS, Pauline M Blanche, Jul 12 1931 Sex:F Child# 9 Ernest Marquis Nashua, NH & Marie Anne Arbour Canada
MARQUIS, Pierre H, Jul 27 1887 Sex:M Child# 1 Hermene Marquis P Q & A Bissonnette P Q
MARQUIS, Raoul, Jul 30 1923 Sex:M Child# 4 Ernest Marquis Nashua, NH & Marie A Arbour Canada
MARQUIS, Raymond, Aug 13 1912 Sex:M Child# 7 Albert Marquis Canada & Angele Levesque Canada
MARQUIS, Raymond Normand, Jun 5 1924 Sex:M Child# 1 Wilfrid Marquis Oldtown, ME & Elmire Cassista Nashua, NH
MARQUIS, Richard Charles, Dec 14 1935 Sex:M Child# 2 Charles Marquis Nashua, NH & Dorothy Days Nashua, NH
MARQUIS, Richard Edward, Apr 2 1930 Sex:M Child# 2 Jean Baptiste Marqui Nashua, NH & Eva Soucy Nashua, NH
MARQUIS, Rita, Mar 21 1925 Sex:F Child# 9 Isidore Marquis Canada & Leda Pinette Canada
MARQUIS, Rita Marie Anne R, Jul 26 1929 Sex:F Child# 2 Philip Marquis Canada & Marie Gaulin Canada
MARQUIS, Robert Joseph Lionel, Nov 24 1914 Sex:M Child# 11 Jean Bapt Marquis Canada & Caroline Bonvouloir Canada
MARQUIS, Romeo, Apr 20 1906 Sex:M Child# 1 Alfred Marquis Canada & Marie Sirois Canada
MARQUIS, Romeo, Sep 22 1910 Sex:M Child# 6 Albert Marquis Canada & Angele Levesque Canada
MARQUIS, Rose Alma, Jan 12 1905 Sex:F Child# 2 Albert Marquis Canada & Angele Levesque Canada
MARQUIS, Stanley Gerard, Dec 21 1933 Sex:M Child# 1 Stan Marquis Canada & Alde Laroche Canada
MARQUIS, Sylvianne Jeanne, Aug 9 1931 Sex:F Child# 3 Jean Bapt Marquis Nashua, NH & Eva Soucy Nashua, NH
MARQUIS, Sylvio, Jan 10 1926 Sex:M Child# 6 Ernest Marquis Nashua, NH & Blanche Arbour Canada
MARQUIS, Theophile Napoleon, May 17 1904 Sex:M Child# 6 Wilfred Marquis Canada & Henrietta Gauthier Canada
MARQUIS, Therese Madeleine, Feb 16 1924 Sex:F Child# 6 Hector Marquis Canada & Eugenie Chouinard Canada
MARQUIS, Ulderic Ernest, Sep 13 1896 Sex:M Child# 1 Joseph Marquis Canada & Marie Boucher Canada
MARQUIS, Wilfrid Edmond, Oct 1895 Sex:M Child# 1 Wilfrid Marquis Canada & Henrietta Gauthier Canada
MARQUIS, Wilfrid Jos Onesime, Jun 29 1935 Sex:M Child# 1 Lucien Marquis Nashua, NH & Germ Bonenfant Nashua, NH
MARSAWICZ, Antonia, Dec 13 1915 Sex:F Child# 8 Adam Marsawicz Russia & Annie Koulick Russia
MARSH, Charles Elton, Jul 24 1906 Sex:M Child# 4 Charles H Marsh Haverhill, MA & Alice M Cross Albany, NY
MARSH, Esther, Jun 4 1905 Sex:F Child# 3 Charles A Marsh Haverhill & Alice Cross Albany, ME
MARSH, George Henry Clay, May 1 1900 Sex:M Child# 1 Fred C Marsh Nashua, NH & Lizzie A Clay Lowell, MA
MARSH, Helen A, Jan 23 1889 Sex:F Child# 2 Charles A Marsh Rhode Island & L A Moore Rhode Island
MARSH, Marion Elizabeth, Aug 31 1927 Sex:F Child# 1 G H C Marsh Nashua, NH & Mildrid Tibbetts Nashua, NH
MARSH, Ruth Elizabeth, Dec 2 1894 Sex:F Child# 1 Edward F Marsh Peabody, MA & H E M Buckham Nashua, NH
MARSHALL, Alan Edward, Sep 7 1927 Sex:M Child# 2 Edward Marshall Hudson, NH & Annie Flanders Nashua, NH
MARSHALL, Alfred, Feb 13 1910 Sex:M Child# 3 Harry Marshall England & Jeannie Bims England
MARSHALL, Alice Adelaide, Jul 29 1929 Sex:F Child# 5 George Marshall NH & Myrtie Lawrence NH
MARSHALL, Annie, Oct 27 1914 Sex:F Child# 3 Michael Marshall Russia & Annie Adamitz Russia
MARSHALL, Arlene, Jul 18 1923 Sex:F Child# 1 Harold H Marshall Hudson, NH & Eva Grace Morrill Worcester, MA
MARSHALL, Arlene Elizabeth, May 25 1928 Sex:F Child# 3 Charles H Marshall Hollis, NH & Marguerite Tatro Nashua, NH
MARSHALL, Beatrice Elsie, Sep 17 1909 Sex:F Child# 2 J Emery Marshall Nashua, NH & Elsie G Gustin Canada
MARSHALL, Byron Tewksbury, Sep 17 1909 Sex:M Child# 1 J Emery Marshall Nashua, NH & Elsie G Gustin Canada
MARSHALL, Caleb Russell, Mar 18 1913 Sex:M Child# 4 J Emery Marshall Nashua, NH & Elsie G Gustin Canada
MARSHALL, Carol Priscilla, Dec 20 1929 Sex:F Child# 7 Roy F Marshall Nashua, NH & Kittie Grover Cambridge, MA
MARSHALL, Charles Preston, Jr, Apr 9 1924 Sex:M Child# 4 Charles P Marshall Salem, MA & Doris Smith Boston, MA

MARSHALL, David Oscar, Mar 14 1928 Sex:M Child# 4 Harold Marshall Hudson, NH & Eva Morrill Worcester, MA
MARSHALL, Donald Edward, Feb 26 1932 Sex:M Child# 4 Charles H Marshall Hollis, NH & M Tetrault Nashua, NH
MARSHALL, Dorothy Ruth, Aug 24 1920 Sex:F Child# 2 George E Marshall Chelsea, MA & Myrtie Lawrence Hollis, NH
MARSHALL, Edward Francis, Jul 23 1910 Sex:M Child# 4 Harry I Marshall Nashua, NH & Emma W Smith Rangoon, Burma
MARSHALL, Edward Manuel, Nov 17 1935 Sex:M Child# 4 Joseph Marshall New Bedford, MA & Ethel Smith Pawtucket, RI
MARSHALL, Eleanor Agnes, Sep 25 1931 Sex:F Child# 8 Roy F Marshall Nashua, NH & Kittie Grover Cambridge, MA
MARSHALL, Elizabeth Eleanor, Jan 24 1931 Sex:F Child# 6 Harold Marshall Hudson, NH & Eva Morrill Worcester, MA
MARSHALL, Elmer E, Nov 21 1889 Sex:M Child# 2 Elmer H Marshall Nashua, NH & Nettie A Flagg Hollis, NH
MARSHALL, Evelyn Lucile, Aug 21 1897 Sex:F Child# 3 Elmer D Marshall Nashua, NH & Nettie Flagg Nashua, NH
MARSHALL, Frank Hadley, Oct 11 1926 Sex:M Child# 3 Harold Marshall Hudson, NH & Eva Morrill Worcester, MA
MARSHALL, George Earl, Jun 5 1914 Sex:M Child# 1 George E Marshall Chelsea, MA & Uyrtie E Lawrence Hollis, NH
MARSHALL, Gladys Shirley, Aug 8 1914 Sex:F Child# 1 Ray Flagg Marshall Nashua, NH & Kitte G Grover Boston, MA
MARSHALL, Harry Elwyn, Jul 24 1932 Sex:M Child# 6 George E Marshall Everett, MA & M Lawrence Hollis, NH
MARSHALL, Herbert Allen, Jan 17 1925 Sex:M Child# 2 Harold H Marshall Hudson, NH & Eva G Morrill Worcester, MA
MARSHALL, Hildah, Feb 4 1911 Sex:F Child# 3 J Emery Marshall Nashua, NH & Elsie G Gustin
MARSHALL, James Calvin, Mar 27 1928 Sex:M Child# 6 Roy F Marshall Nashua, NH & Kitty G Grover Cambridge, MA
MARSHALL, John Grover, Dec 16 1925 Sex:M Child# 5 Roy F Marshall Nashua, NH & Kittie G Grover Cambridge, MA
MARSHALL, Laurence Dudley, Mar 14 1923 Sex:M Child# 3 George Marshall Chelsea, MA & Myrtie Laurence Hollis, NH
MARSHALL, Louis Roy, Apr 14 1916 Sex:M Child# 2 Roy Flagg Marshall Nashua, NH & Kittie G Groves Boston, MA
MARSHALL, Myrtle May Elizabeth, May 17 1927 Sex:F Child# 4 G E Marshall Everett, MA & Myrtle Lawrence Hollis, NH
MARSHALL, Ray, Apr 15 1888 Sex:M Child# 1 Almond D Marshall Nashua, NH & Anna A Flagg Hollis
MARSHALL, Shirley Alice, May 30 1933 Sex:F Child# 5 Chris Marshall Hollis, NH & Marg Tetrault Nashua, NH
MARSHALL, Theodore Bacon, Nov 12 1918 Sex:M Child# 3 Roy Flagg Marshall Nashua, NH & Kittie Gladys Grover Cambridge
MARSHALL, Unknown, Oct 3 1892 Sex:M Child# 1 David O Marshall Hudson, NH & Gertrude H Smith Haverhill, MA
MARSHALL, Virginia, Apr 8 1924 Sex:F Child# 1 Edw G Marshall Hudson, NH & Annie L Flanders Nashua, NH
MARSHALL, Walter Armstrong, May 25 1929 Sex:M Child# 5 Harold H Marshall Hudson, NH & Eva G Morrill Worcester, MA
MARSHALL, William Arthur, Mar 2 1921 Sex:M Child# 4 Roy F Marshall Nashua, NH & Kittie Gladys Grover Cambridge, MA
MARSHOUK, John, Jun 24 1909 Sex:M Child# 1 Louis Marshouk Russia & Mary Valanitzki Russia
MARSTON, Edward, Dec 8 1927 Sex:M Child# 2 Walter Marston Poland & Antosa Swelka Poland
MARSTON, Grazia Alice, May 25 1901 Sex:F Child# 1 George H Marston Canada & Alice M Doyle Nashua, NH
MARTAIN, Irma Arlene, Jul 14 1909 Sex:F Child# 4 Merton M Martain Atkinson, NH & Hattie L Fortier Woodsville, NH
MARTEL, Andrea, Nov 12 1906 Sex:F Child# 1 Horace Martel Canada & Delima Brisson Canada
MARTEL, Arthur Arm, Jul 17 1902 Sex:M Child# 2 Henry Martel Canada & Alphonsine Legendre Canada
MARTEL, Francois Xavier, Feb 25 1890 Sex:M Child# 10 Auguste Martel Canada & Olivine Boullard Canada
MARTEL, G Marie B, Aug 6 1902 Sex:F Child# 4 Francis Martel Canada & Adeline Lavigne Canada
MARTEL, Harvey, Jr, May 24 1934 Sex:M Child# 2 Harvey Martel Hooksett, NH & Irene Ouelette Middlebury, VT
MARTEL, Horace Omer, Aug 28 1908 Sex:M Child# 2 Horace Martel US & Delima Brisson Canada
MARTEL, Isabelle O, Oct 31 1893 Sex:F Child# 1 Philibert Martel Canada & Rosanne Lemery Canada
MARTEL, Joseph H A, Apr 7 1898 Sex:M Child# 2 Francois Martel Canada & Adeline Lavigne Canada
MARTEL, Joseph P, Feb 27 1887 Sex:M Child# 12 Augustus Martel Canada & Olivine Roucilard Canada
MARTEL, Laurent Rosario, Dec 22 1900 Sex:M Child# 2 Desire Martel Canada & Valerie Boutin Canada
MARTEL, Marie E B A, Oct 16 1899 Sex:F Child# 3 Francois Martel Canada & Adeline Lavigne Canada
MARTEL, Marie Marguerite, Jul 17 1932 Sex:F Child# 3 O H Martel Nashua, NH & Blanche Binette Sanford, ME
MARTEL, Ovila, Jan 8 1894 Sex:F Child# 1 Francois Martel Canada & Adeline Lavicque Canada
MARTEL, Pauline, Jun 29 1933 Sex:F Child# 4 Omer Martel Nashua, NH & Blanche Binette Sanford, ME
MARTEL, Theade Raymond, Nov 28 1922 Sex:M Child# 2 Theade Martel NH & Florence Marshall NH
MARTELL, Cyril, Jan 30 1917 Sex:M Child# 7 Cyril Martell Montreal, Canada & Julia Bradley St Phillip, Canada
MARTELL, Florence Mae, Mar 12 1924 Sex:F Child# 3 Theade Martell Suncook, NH & Florence Marshall Hollis, NH
MARTIE, Alice Robertine, Aug 22 1891 Sex:F Child# 6 R Martie Canada & Eliza Mongeau Canada
MARTIN, Albert, Nov 10 1910 Sex:M Child# 1 Frank Martin
MARTIN, Albina, Mar 2 1892 Sex:F Child# 3 Elzear Martin Canada & Rosalie Dumond Canada
MARTIN, Alma, Apr 3 1911 Sex:F Child# 1 Ralph Martin Amesbury, MA & Celia Lynch Lowell, MA
MARTIN, Alphonse E, Sep 21 1894 Sex:M Child# 1 Antoine Martin Canada & Albina Leclair Canada
MARTIN, Andre Alve Paul, Jul 30 1913 Sex:M Child# 1 Wilfred Martin Canada & Marie Benoit Canada
MARTIN, Andrew Normand, Jan 23 1928 Sex:M Child# 1 Mederic Martin Canada & Rose Fortier Canada
MARTIN, Auguste J, Dec 27 1891 Sex:M Child# Godfroi Martin Canada & Onesime Lord Canada
MARTIN, Bessie Evelyn, Apr 10 1908 Sex:F Child# 3 Silas E Martin New Brunswick & Ethel Terrace New Brunswick
MARTIN, Betty Ann, Dec 16 1926 Sex:F Child# 5 Joseph Martin New Bedford, MA & Gladys Bouley Nashua, NH
MARTIN, Blanche, Nov 11 1914 Sex:F Child# 1 (No Parents Listed)
MARTIN, Blanche Yvonne, May 8 1916 Sex:F Child# 4 Napoleon Martin Canada & Celina Bouley Canada
MARTIN, Charles, Jul 1 1896 Sex:M Child# 2 Charles Martin Canada & Clara Ricard Greenville, NH
MARTIN, Charles Arthur, Mar 11 1900 Sex:M Child# 4 Thomas Martin Canada & M L Desmarais Canada
MARTIN, Charles Everett, Sep 18 1917 Sex:M Child# 6 Judson Martin New Brunswick & Mabel Cross Auburn, ME
MARTIN, Christine Adeline, Dec 23 1908 Sex:F Child# 2 Carlton W Martin White River Vlg, VT & Jennie E Cushman
MARTIN, Clara L, Sep 2 1926 Sex:F Child# 1 Felix E Martin Prince Edw Island & Edna B Barr Weymouth, NS
MARTIN, Cynthia Ann, May 6 1935 Sex:F Child# 1 Charles R Martin Sherbrooke, Quebec & Grace Gatcomb Nashua, NH
MARTIN, David Laurie, Aug 19 1905 Sex:M Child# 1 George Martin Scotland & Mary Laurie Scotland
MARTIN, Doris May, Nov 3 1906 Sex:F Child# 1 Charles H Martin
MARTIN, Doris May Wright, Feb 11 1924 Sex:F Child# 1 Arthur Martin Wilton, NH & Ethel Wright Wilton, NH
MARTIN, Elaine Marilyn, Jul 22 1933 Sex:F Child# 8 Joseph Martin New Bedford, MA & Gladys Bouley Nashua, NH
MARTIN, Elizabeth Ellen, Jan 27 1923 Sex:F Child# 1 George Martin Concord, NH & Elizabeth Adams Springfield, OH
MARTIN, Elzear, Jun 13 1894 Sex:M Child# 1 Thomas Martin Canada & M L Desmarais Canada
MARTIN, Emma, Feb 15 1891 Sex:F Child# 1 Hormidas Martin Canada & Corinne Caron Canada

MARTIN, Esther May, Sep 22 1906 Sex:F Child# 2 George Martin Scotland & Mary Laurie Scotland
MARTIN, Ethel Terris, Feb 19 1907 Sex:F Child# 2 Silas Martin Albert Mines, NB & Ethel Terris Hillsboro, NB
MARTIN, Eveline Leona, Jul 17 1901 Sex:F Child# 1 Charles Martin Canada & Eveline Desjardins Canada
MARTIN, Fernand Gaspa'd, Oct 28 1901 Sex:M Child# 2 C A Martin Canada & Aline Berube Canada
MARTIN, Francis, Feb 25 1914 Sex:M Child# 4 Robert C Martin Montgomery, VT & Fannie Kelton Montgomery, VT
MARTIN, George Rathborn, Dec 5 1924 Sex:M Child# 2 George R Martin Concord, NH & Elizabeth Adams Springfield, OH
MARTIN, Germaine Rita C, Dec 5 1930 Sex:F Child# 8 Moise Martin Canada & Maria Pelletier France
MARTIN, Gertrude Carmen, Mar 25 1929 Sex:F Child# 2 Mederic Martin Canada & Rose Fortier Canada
MARTIN, Gertrude M, Aug 11 1897 Sex:F Child# 1 F W Martin New Brunswick & Jessie Mayo Steuben, ME
MARTIN, Gladys Barbara, Nov 22 1930 Sex:F Child# 7 Joseph Martin, Jr New Bedford, MA & Gladys Bouley Nashua, NH
MARTIN, Gloria Genevieve, Dec 19 1928 Sex:F Child# 6 Joseph J Martin Mass & Gladys Bouley NH
MARTIN, Harry Joseph, Sep 26 1922 Sex:M Child# 2 Joseph J Martin New Bedford, MA & Gladys M Bouley Nashua, NH
MARTIN, Irene, Mar 15 1914 Sex:F Child# 1 Henry Martin Canada & Martha Nadeau Nashua, NH
MARTIN, Jane, Mar 24 1918 Sex:F Child# 1 William H Martin Hooksett, NH & Hazel D Bradley Nashua, NH
MARTIN, Janice Elizabeth, Oct 15 1922 Sex:F Child# 6 Arthur C Martin White River, VT & Elizabeth Mondy New York
MARTIN, Jeanette, Jan 5 1920 Sex:F Child# 2 John Martin Grovetown, NH & Maude Quimby Moultonboro, NH
MARTIN, Jeanne, Nov 4 1933 Sex:F Child# 1 Howard Martin Lansing, MI & Arlene Morgan Mass
MARTIN, Jos Edgar Robert, Jan 19 1922 Sex:M Child# 5 Henry Martin Rhode Island & Leopoldine Soucy Canada
MARTIN, Jos Louis Normand, Aug 28 1920 Sex:M Child# 4 Henri Martin Woonsocket, RI & Leopauldine Soucy Canada
MARTIN, Jos Roch Maurice, May 24 1925 Sex:M Child# 6 Henry Martin Rhode Island & Leopoldine Soucy Canada
MARTIN, Joseph, May 4 1913 Sex:M Child# 3 Henri Martin Canada & Malvina Poliquin Canada
MARTIN, Joseph, Feb 5 1928 Sex:F Child# 7 Moise Martin Canada & Marie Pelletier France
MARTIN, Joseph A A, Mar 7 1898 Sex:M Child# 1 Alphonse Martin Canada & Aline Berube Canada
MARTIN, Joseph Amede, Feb 11 1895 Sex:M Child# 6 Peter Martin Canada & Lea Gamarche Canada
MARTIN, Joseph Antoine, May 5 1901 Sex:M Child# 3 Antoine Martin Canada & Albina Leclerc Canada
MARTIN, Joseph Henri, Nov 13 1907 Sex:M Child# 1 Henri Martin Canada & Malvina Poliquin Canada
MARTIN, Joseph Henri Roger, Sep 3 1916 Sex:M Child# 2 Henri Martin Rhode Island & Leopoldine Soucy Canada
MARTIN, Joseph Jean, Sep 22 1895 Sex:M Child# 7 Godfroi Martin Canada & Anaise Lord Canada
MARTIN, Joseph Philippe, Nov 8 1906 Sex:M Child# 5 Antoine Martin Canada & Albina Leclerc Canada
MARTIN, Joseph Theodore, May 4 1908 Sex:M Child# 6 Antoine Martin Canada & Albina Leclerc Canada
MARTIN, Joseph Thomas, Apr 24 1897 Sex:M Child# 3 Thomas Martin Canada & Marie L Desmarais Canada
MARTIN, Lena, Mar 22 1908 Sex:F Child# 2 Judson Martin New Brunswick & Mabel Cross Auburn, ME
MARTIN, Lester Gilbert, Feb 1 1926 Sex:M Child# 3 George R Martin Concord, NH & Elizabeth Adams Springfield, OH
MARTIN, Lorraine Lucille, Jul 5 1933 Sex:F Child# 1 Arthur Martin Salem, MA & Yvonne Laroche Nashua, NH
MARTIN, Louisa, Jul 5 1888 Sex:F Child# 7 John Martin Canada & Delia Raymond Canada
MARTIN, Louise, Sep 14 1919 Sex:F Child# 7 Judson A Martin New Brunswick & Mabel Cross Auburn, ME
MARTIN, Lucille Jeannette, Jan 22 1920 Sex:F Child# 2 Wilfred Martin Canada & Emma Pelletier Canada
MARTIN, M Alida, Nov 2 1893 Sex:F Child# 10 John Martin Canada & Delia Raymond Canada
MARTIN, M Yvonne Olivette, Aug 21 1914 Sex:F Child# 1 Wilfrid Martin Canada & Emma Benoit Canada
MARTIN, Marie Ann Lorraine, Jan 27 1919 Sex:F Child# 3 Henri Martin NH & Leopoldine Soucy Canada
MARTIN, Marie Anne, Jan 27 1908 Sex:F Child# 3 Thomas Martin Mass & Delia Delucher Canada
MARTIN, Marie Evelyn, Feb 1 1916 Sex:F Child# 5 Henry Martin Nashua, NH & Malvina Poliquin Canada
MARTIN, Marie Florence, Jun 12 1918 Sex:F Child# 5 Napoleon Martin Canada & Celine Bresley Canada
MARTIN, Marie Florilda H, Apr 19 1911 Sex:F Child# 2 Henri Martin NH & Malvina Poliquin Canada
MARTIN, Marie Irene, Apr 4 1908 Sex:F Child# 2 Pierre Martin Canada & Marie Soucy Canada
MARTIN, Marie Leonore, Jun 7 1897 Sex:F Child# 11 Jean Martin Canada & Delia Raymond Canada
MARTIN, Marie Louise, Jan 13 1896 Sex:F Child# 2 Thomas Martin Canada & Marie L Desmarais Canada
MARTIN, Marie Louise, Feb 1 1897 Sex:F Child# 8 Godfroy Martin Canada & Anais Laure Canada
MARTIN, Marie Rose A, Dec 20 1910 Sex:F Child# 1 Henri Martin Rhode Island & Leopoldine Soucy Canada
MARTIN, Marie Virginie, May 25 1893 Sex:F Child#  Godfroi Martin Canada & Alavie Lord Canada
MARTIN, Mary Edna, Jul 7 1920 Sex:F Child# 6 Napoleon Martin Canada & Celina Bresby Canada
MARTIN, Mary Francis, Sep 16 1921 Sex:F Child# 2 William H Martin Hooksett, NH & Hazel D Bradley Nashua, NH
MARTIN, Mildred Martha, Oct 16 1921 Sex:F Child# 1 Joseph J Martin New Bedford, MA & Gladys M Bouley Nashua, NH
MARTIN, Napoleon, Feb 12 1908 Sex:M Child# 6 Jules Martin Canada & Jeanne Ducas Canada
MARTIN, Norma Norene, Jun 7 1927 Sex:F Child# 7 Arthur Martin White River Jct, VT & Elizabeth Monty New York
MARTIN, Patricia Carol, May 19 1935 Sex:F Child# 9 Joseph Martin New Bedford, MA & Gladys Bouley Nashua, NH
MARTIN, Paul Arthur, Jul 31 1892 Sex:M Child# 9 John Martin Canada & Delia Raymond Canada
MARTIN, Paul Stanislas, Jul 15 1922 Sex:M Child# 9 Arthur Martin Canada & Rose Martineau Canada
MARTIN, Rachel Dorothy, Jul 2 1925 Sex:F Child# 4 Jos J Martin, Jr New Bedford, MA & Gladys M Bouley Nashua, NH
MARTIN, Ralph Edward, Jan 25 1910 Sex:M Child# 3 Judson Martin Albert County, NB & Mabel H Cross Auburn, ME
MARTIN, Raoul, May 12 1917 Sex:M Child# 4 Arthur Martin Canada & Lucie Pelletier Canada
MARTIN, Richard Arthur, May 17 1921 Sex:M Child# 5 Arthur C Martin White River, VT & Elizabeth Monty Mooers, NY
MARTIN, Rosanna, Nov 12 1896 Sex:F Child# 2 Antoine Martin US & Albina Leclaire Canada
MARTIN, Ruby May, May 12 1897 Sex:F Child# 1 A Judson Martin New Brunswick & Grace Mott Sandy Hill, NY
MARTIN, Ruth, Jun 5 1913 Sex:F Child# 4 A Judson Martin New Brunswick & Mabel A Cross Auburn, ME
MARTIN, Theresa Doris, Feb 16 1928 Sex:F Child# 1 Arthur Martin Wilton, NH & Germaine Leclerc Nashua, NH
MARTIN, Therese, Oct 6 1932 Sex:F Child# 3 Henry Martin Plattsburgh, NY & Bertha Boissy Plattsburgh, NY
MARTIN, Therese Julia, May 8 1890 Sex:F Child# 8 John Martin Canada & Delia Raymond Canada
MARTIN, Unknown, Dec 28 1887 Sex:F Child# 3 Ezra A Martin Enfield, CT & Margaret J Clyde Dracut
MARTIN, Unknown, Oct 18 1895 Sex:F Child# 1 Charles W Martin Canada & Clara Ricard Greenville
MARTIN, Unknown, Jul 12 1897 Sex:F Child# 1 Carl W Martin White River Jct, VT & Jennie E Martin Suncook, NH
MARTIN, Unknown, Feb 19 1904 Sex:M Child# 1 Silas Edw Martin Hillsboro, NB & Ethel Terris Hillsboro, NB
MARTIN, Unknown, Jul 10 1905 Sex:M Child# 1 Judson Martin New Brunswick & Mabel Cross Auburn, ME

MARTIN, Unknown, Feb 25 1906 Sex:F Child# 2 Clayton G Martin Coventry, VT & Eva I Colby Sunapee, NH
MARTIN, Unknown, Dec 7 1914 Sex:M Child# 1 Henry Martin Nashua, NH & Maxina Poliquin Canada
MARTIN, Unknown, Sep 16 1915 Sex:F Child# 2 Arthur Martin England & Edith Reed Berlin
MARTIN, Unknown, Oct 22 1915 Sex:F Child# 5 Judson Martin NB & Mabel Cross Auburn, ME
MARTIN, Unknown, Oct 30 1922 Sex:M Child# 3 John R Martin Groveton, NH & Maude Quimby Moultonboro, NH
MARTIN, Wanita Shirley, Apr 4 1924 Sex:F Child# 3 Joseph J Martin New Bedford, MA & Gladys M Bouley Nashua, NH
MARTIN, William R, Oct 12 1902 Sex:M Child# 2 William W Martin Malone, NY & Margaret J Foran Chateauguay, NY
MARTIN, Yvonne Aurore C, Apr 25 1905 Sex:F Child# 4 Anthoine Martin Canada & Albina Leclerc Canada
MARTINAGE, Janet Eileen, Jul 21 1935 Sex:F Child# 2 Charles Martinage Salem, MA & Ridlon Macey S Groveton, MA
MARTOLOWSKY, Stanley, Sep 19 1918 Sex:M Child# 1 Adam Martolowsky Russia & Agnes Wirthal Austria
MARVELL, Janice Marilyn, Mar 10 1934 Sex:F Child# 1 James A Marvell Bridgewater, MA & Phyllis M Beverly Springfield
MARZUKA, Unknown, Nov 16 1921 Sex:F Child# 1 Adam Marzuka Poland & Josephine Bielapka Poland
MASIE, Raymond, Mar 29 1922 Sex:M Child# 2 Auguste Masie Canada & Eugenie Beaupre Arctic, RI
MASK, Shirley Ruth, May 20 1919 Sex:F Child# 1 George M Mask Greensboro, NC & June E Baker Nashua, NH
MASKON, Unknown, Jan 18 1917 Sex:F Child# 2 John D Maskon Greece & Frossym Paughrotides Greece
MASON, Agnes Teresa, Aug 18 1897 Sex:F Child# 3 Arthur Mason Ireland & Winnie Ford Ireland
MASON, Arline Muriel, Jul 16 1934 Sex:F Child# 2 Bernard A Mason S Lyndeboro, NH & Marion Venne Concord, NH
MASON, Emily Louise, Sep 11 1923 Sex:F Child# 1 Frank W Mason Franklin, VT & Susan Emily Lahate Belfast, France
MASON, Eunice Virginia, Jul 8 1927 Sex:F Child# 5 Samuel Mason Nashua, NH & Rose McDevit Ireland
MASON, Frank, Jul 13 1908 Sex:M Child# 1 Frank Mason Pennsylvania & Mary Murphy New York
MASON, George Edward, Mar 8 1935 Sex:M Child# 2 Walter Mason Nashua, NH & Rose Johansen Maine
MASON, Georgiana L, Dec 13 1910 Sex:F Child# 1 Walter B Mason Nashua, NH & Florence Long England
MASON, Joseph, Jun 17 1920 Sex:M Child# 3 Samuel F Mason Nashua, NH & Rose McDevitt Ireland
MASON, Joseph H Rolland, Feb 23 1915 Sex:M Child# 2 Gaspard Mason Canada & Donalda Belcourt NH
MASON, Marion Lucille, Feb 18 1911 Sex:F Child# 1 William Mason Scotland & Marion Learmouth Scotland
MASON, Mary Eileen, Sep 3 1932 Sex:F Child# 8 Samuel Mason Nashua, NH & Rose McDavitt Ireland
MASON, Mary Elizabeth, Oct 31 1895 Sex:F Child# 2 Arthur Mason Ireland & Minnie Ford Ireland
MASON, May, Jun 26 1896 Sex:F Child# 3 E J Mason Canada & May Noel Canada
MASON, Nellie Frances, Sep 14 1897 Sex:F Child# Gustavus Mason Nashua, NH & Hattie Bell Collins Manchester, NH
MASON, Norbert Leo Ros, Jan 28 1914 Sex:M Child# 1 Gaspard Mason Canada & Donalda Belcourt Manchester, NH
MASON, Otis James, Jan 16 1910 Sex:M Child# 2 Perley J Mason Milan, NH & Fannie E Moore Berwick, ME
MASON, Patricia, Apr 6 1925 Sex:F Child# 5 Samuel F Mason Nashua, NH & Rose McDevitt Ireland
MASON, Roland Horace, Nov 4 1908 Sex:M Child# 3 Harry E Mason Nashua, NH & Anna M Lathan Pontiac, RI
MASON, Rose, Jul 12 1921 Sex:F Child# 3 Samuel Mason Nashua, NH & Rose McDavitt Ireland
MASON, Samuel Francis, Sep 18 1894 Sex:M Child# 1 Arthur Mason Ireland & Winnie Ford Ireland
MASON, Theresa Catherine, Aug 7 1929 Sex:F Child# 7 Samuel Mason Nashua, NH & Rose McDavitt Ireland
MASON, Unknown, Oct 7 1891 Sex:M Child# 1 Charles Mason Maine & Lillie Webster NH
MASON, Unknown, Jul 26 1911 Sex:F Child# 3 Perley J Mason Milan, NH & Fanny Moore Berwick, ME
MASON, Unknown, Apr 16 1913 Sex:M Child# 4 Perley J Mason Milan, NH & Fannie E Moore Berwick, ME
MASON, Unknown, Jun 21 1915 Sex:M Child# 1 Alanson T Mason Groton, MA & Eva Edgerley S Framingham, MA
MASON, Unknown, Jun 17 1920 Sex:M Child# 2 Samuel F Mason Nashua, NH & Rose McDevitt Ireland Stillborn
MASON, Walter, May 13 1933 Sex:M Child# 1 Walter Mason Nashua, NH & Rose Johansen Scarsborough, ME
MASON, Walter Elmer, Jun 3 1913 Sex:M Child# 2 Walter B Mason Nashua, NH & Florence J Tong England
MASON, Wendall Roy, Aug 23 1924 Sex:M Child# 1 Benjamin Mason Acton Ctr, MA & Frances Hatch Canada
MASSE, Allie Corinne, Dec 21 1889 Sex:F Child# 1 Frank Masse Morris Jct & Celina Caron Canada
MASSE, Emma Jane, Jan 24 1894 Sex:F Child# 3 M A Masse Mass & Ella E Mansee NY
MASSE, Ferdinand Robert, May 5 1932 Sex:M Child# 8 Alfred Masse Canada & L Lamarche US
MASSE, George Alfred, Aug 31 1894 Sex:M Child# 3 Francois Masse NY & Celina Caron Canada
MASSE, J Leo Armand, Sep 10 1915 Sex:M Child# 1 Auguste Masse Canada & Eugenie Beaupre Canada
MASSE, Joseph, Jun 29 1888 Sex:M Child# 1 Joseph Masse Canada & Maria Cousmeau Canada
MASSE, Joseph, May 7 1892 Sex:M Child# 4 Joseph Masse Canada & Marie Cousineau Canada
MASSE, Madeline M Rose, Apr 25 1931 Sex:F Child# 7 Alfred Masse Canada & Lauvina Lamarche Vermont
MASSE, Marie Alice, Jan 3 1901 Sex:F Child# 2 Joseph Masse Canada & Marilda Desjardins Canada
MASSECK, Unknown, Jul 15 1888 Sex:F Child# 7 Herbert E Masseck New York & Mary Manning New York
MASSECK, Unknown, Jul 31 1893 Sex:M Child# 2 C Masseck Lowell, MA & May L Powell Spotsylvania, VA
MASSECOTTE, Blanche Rose Alva, May 1 1913 Sex:F Child# 3 Alfred Massecotte Canada & Marie Levesque Canada
MASSICOTTE, Alida Marie, Apr 25 1903 Sex:F Child# 1 Alfred Massicotte Canada & Marie Levesque Canada
MASSICOTTE, Marie Anne I, Jan 26 1905 Sex:F Child# 2 Alfred Massicotte Canada & Marie Levesque Canada
MASSIE, Roberta Elaine, Dec 4 1934 Sex:F Child# 2 Paul Robert Massie Barton, VT & Isabelle I Bonnette Hudson, NH
MASSIE, Sylvia Louise, Aug 17 1933 Sex:F Child# 1 Paul Massie Barton, VT & Isabelle Bonnette Hudson, NH
MASSON, Charles Emile, Aug 16 1902 Sex:M Child# 11 Norbert Masson Canada & D Sabourin Canada
MASSON, Joseph, Feb 5 1909 Sex:M Child# 13 Norbert Masson Canada & Domithilde Sabourin Canada Stillborn
MASSON, Marie Odinas F, Feb 19 1906 Sex:F Child# 12 Norbert Masson Canada & Domithilde Sabourin Canada
MASSON, Rita Estelle, Dec 31 1916 Sex:F Child# 2 Alanson Masson Groton, MA & Eva Edgerly S Framingham, MA
MASTEN, John, Sep 28 1921 Sex:M Child# 1 Walter Masten Poland & Antonia Swekla Poland
MASTERS, Gloria Rose, Mar 1 1922 Sex:F Child# 2 John H Masters Hurricane, MO & Phyllis R Lapointe Springfield
MASTERS, Iona Nevine, Jul 10 1923 Sex:F Child# 2 John H Masters Hurricane, MO & Phyllis R Lapoint Springfield
MASTIC, Unknown, Feb 18 1907 Sex:F Child# 1 Harley W Mastic New York & Mary F Archer Lowell, MA
MATBESS, Alfred George, Mar 6 1914 Sex:M Child# 2 Alfred G Matbess Keokuk, Iowa & Ruth C Roberts Keokuk, Iowa
MATHER, Helena, Dec 28 1891 Sex:F Child# 5 James Mather Ireland & Elizabeth O'Hara Ireland
MATHEWS, Unknown, Jan 21 1930 Sex:F Child# 1 William Mathews Boston, MA & Bertha Wells Dorset, VT
MATHIEN, Marie Amanda, Aug 13 1896 Sex:F Child# 2 Adelard Mathien Fitchburg, MA & Delina Roy Canada
MATHIEU, Leo Edward, Jan 16 1931 Sex:M Child# 2 Wilfrid Mathieu Biddeford, ME & Germaine Paquette Nashua, NH

MATHIEU, Madeleine Lorette, Jan 31 1935 Sex:F Child# 3 Wilfred Mathieu Maine & Germaine Paquette Nashua, NH
MATHIEU, Maggie, Jul 27 1895 Sex:F Child# 3 Wilber Mathieu US & Katie Coleman Ireland
MATHIEU, Paul Wilfred, Dec 29 1929 Sex:M Child# 1 Wilfrid Mathieu Maine & Germaine Paquette Nashua, NH
MATICH, Unknown, Feb 11 1920 Sex:M Child# 5 Harry Matich Russia & Mary Fourgan Russia
MATIOSKA, Joseph Banadas, Jun 30 1931 Sex:M Child# 1 Banadas Matioska Lithuania & Mary Tamulonis Nashua, NH
MATLESS, Alfred G, Jr, Jul 7 1911 Sex:M Child# 1 Alfred G Matless Keokuk, IA & Ruth C Roberts Keokuk, IA Stillborn
MATOIAN, Mary, Jun 17 1908 Sex:F Child# 1 Korkir Matoian Armenia & Markred Sahagian Armenia
MATOIAU, Christopher, Jul 16 1909 Sex:M Child# 2 Krickor Matoiau Turkey & Markrite Sahogian Turkey
MATOLOVITCH, Stanislawa, Mar 7 1912 Sex:F Child# 1 Alex Matolovitch Russia & Victoria Matoleftska Russia
MATOTT, Alva E, Feb 6 1897 Sex:M Child# 3 Alva A Matott Altona, NY & Zoe Duprey Sciota, NY
MATOTT, Ethel Elizabeth, Mar 7 1895 Sex:F Child# 2 Alvin D Matott New York & Zoe Duprey New York
MATOTT, May, May 11 1893 Sex:F Child# 1 Alva Matott Altona, NY & Zoa Duprey Sciota, NY
MATOTT, Stella, Sep 1 1899 Sex:F Child# Olva Matott NJ & Zoe Dripey Canada
MATOTT, Unknown, Nov 7 1900 Sex:M Child# Alvah Matott NY & Zoe Duprey NY Stillborn
MATOTT, Willard, Mar 6 1902 Sex:M Child# Alvah Matott NY & Lora Duplissee NY
MATSIS, Eleanor Louise, Aug 12 1928 Sex:F Child# 1 D N Matsis Greece & Mary Cramond Dundee, Scotland
MATSIS, Marjorie Elizabeth, Aug 7 1930 Sex:F Child# 2 Demetrius N Matsis Greece & Mary Cramond Scotland
MATSIS, Unknown, Jan 4 1918 Sex:M Child# 2 Michael Matsis Greece & Arzyro Boutsoulis Greece
MATSON, Theodore, Jun 6 1920 Sex:M Child# 3 Vine Matson Finland & Annie Ryder Finland
MATTE, Gerard Ambroise, Jan 30 1896 Sex:M Child# 9 Napoleon Matte Quebec, Dominion & Alice Bourque Montreal, PQ
MATTHEWS, Joseph, Jul 13 1899 Sex:M Child# 9 J W Matthews St Albans, VT & Zoe Hebert Sciota, NY Stillborn
MATTHEWS, Robert T, Mar 16 1910 Sex:M Child# 1 John Matthews Ireland & Florence Trufant Nashua, NH
MATTHEWSY, Vincente, Nov 25 1913 Sex:M Child# 4 John Matthewsy Russia & Annie Karatsaiute Russia
MATYASZKA, Beerey, Jul 11 1930 Sex:F Child# 2 William Matyaszka Lithuania & Petrie Stargis Lithuania
MATYASZKA, W Joseph, Feb 20 1919 Sex:M Child# 1 Wilhelm Matyaszka Russia & Pattie Stangis Russia
MAULEY, Ethel Elizabeth, Oct 10 1909 Sex:F Child# 3 William H Mauley England & Mary E Summerville Ireland
MAURAIS, Alfred, Nov 10 1896 Sex:M Child# 1 Alfred Maurais Canada & Josephine Duchsneau Canada
MAURAIS, Joseph Raymond, Jun 4 1906 Sex:M Child# 8 Auguste Maurais Canada & Delphine Lachance Canada
MAURAIS, Lina, Jun 30 1907 Sex:F Child# 2 Joseph Maurais Canada & Amanda Gagnon Canada
MAURAIS, Lionel Olivier, Mar 9 1905 Sex:M Child# 1 Joseph Maurais Canada & Amanda Gagnon Canada
MAURAIS, Marie Louise E, Apr 23 1907 Sex:F Child# 3 Auguste Maurais Canada & Delphine Lachance Canada
MAURAIS, Rose Delima Eva, Jul 3 1899 Sex:F Child# 5 Auguste Maurais Canada & Delphine Lachance Canada
MAURICE, Alfred Paul, Mar 11 1921 Sex:M Child# 1 Paul Maurice Nashua, NH & Gertrude Martel Manchester, NH
MAURICE, Arthur, Aug 19 1922 Sex:M Child# 3 Paul Maurice Nashua, NH & Gertrude Martel
MAURICE, David, Dec 12 1898 Sex:M Child# 12 Joseph Maurice Canada & Delima Croteau Canada
MAURICE, Joseph J Baptiste, Mar 19 1896 Sex:M Child# 10 Joseph Maurice Canada & Delima Croteau Canada
MAURICE, Marie R A, Mar 21 1889 Sex:F Child# 1 Evariste Maurice Canada & Rosanna Rolland Danielsonville, CT
MAURICE, Marie R A, Jul 16 1890 Sex:F Child# 2 Erariste Maurice Canada & Rosanna Rollard Danielsonville, CT
MAURICE, Marie Rose, Mar 19 1896 Sex:F Child# 9 Joseph Maurice Canada & Delima Croteau Canada
MAURICE, Paul, Jan 11 1895 Sex:M Child# 8 Joseph Maurice Canada & Delima Croteau Canada
MAURICE, Philomelin M, Sep 13 1889 Sex:F Child# 9 Duc Maurice Canada & Emma Duplesus Canada
MAURICE, Rosanna, Sep 30 1893 Sex:F Child# 7 Joseph Maurice Canada & Delima Croteau Canada
MAURICE, Unknown, Feb 2 1900 Sex:M Child# 13 Joseph Maurice Canada & Delima Croteau Canada
MAURIER, Unknown, May 12 1924 Sex:M Child# 3 Paul Maurier Nashua, NH & Gertrude Marcis Manchester, NH Stillborn
MAXHAM, Carol Rosina, Jul 8 1933 Sex:F Child# 3 C T Maxham S Pomfret, VT & Rosina M Blood Londonderry, NH
MAXHAM, David Lincoln, Feb 9 1927 Sex:M Child# 2 C T Maxham S Pomfret, VT & Rosina M Blood Londonderry, NH
MAY, Dana Franklin, Apr 14 1897 Sex:M Child# 4 William F May Peterboro, NH & Adeline I Shedd Merrimack, NH
MAYER, Unknown, Mar 1905 Sex:F Child# 11 Joseph Mayer Canada & Mary Menhin Canada
MAYNARD, Albert Ovila, Aug 1 1927 Sex:M Child# 2 Ovila Maynard Nashua, NH & Yvonne Marquis Nashua, NH
MAYNARD, Alice Germaine, Nov 13 1931 Sex:F Child# 2 Roland Maynard Nashua, NH & Lea Lapierre Canada
MAYNARD, Amedee, Feb 25 1892 Sex:M Child# 5 Napoleon Maynard Canada & Marie Landry Canada
MAYNARD, Blanche M, Jun 25 1903 Sex:F Child# 4 Alfred Maynard St Albans, VT & Cecilia Cognac Canada
MAYNARD, Clarence, Jan 13 1907 Sex:F Child# 5 Albert Maynard Canada & Lydia Rochette Canada
MAYNARD, Doris Muriel, Apr 27 1923 Sex:F Child# 3 Edward E Maynard Plattsburg, NY & Alice G Robbins Nashua, NH
MAYNARD, Earl Leo, Dec 9 1920 Sex:M Child# 2 Edward C Maynard Canada & Lea Ouellette Canada
MAYNARD, Edward Edgar, Mar 25 1919 Sex:M Child# 1 Edward E Maynard New York & Alice Robbins NH
MAYNARD, Ernest Albert, May 2 1925 Sex:M Child# 3 Albert Maynard Manchester, NH & Bertha Roy Manchester, NH
MAYNARD, Ernest George Mauric, Dec 8 1922 Sex:M Child# 3 Wilbrod Maynard Hooksett, NH & Antoinette Poulin Nashua
MAYNARD, Ernest Roland Archi, Dec 2 1913 Sex:M Child# 4 Emile Maynard Canada & Georgianna Salvail Nashua, NH
MAYNARD, Frank L, Sep 7 1893 Sex:M Child# 3 George E Maynard Vermont & Sarah McKean NH
MAYNARD, George E, Sep 14 1890 Sex:M Child# 2 George Maynard St Albans, VT & Sarah McKean Nashua, NH
MAYNARD, Henry, Jan 19 1929 Sex:M Child# 3 Joseph Maynard Canada & Leontine Dube Canada
MAYNARD, Irene Evelyn, Jun 16 1921 Sex:F Child# 2 Wilbrod Maynard Hooksett, NH & Antoinette Poulin Nashua, NH
MAYNARD, James Edward, Aug 19 1888 Sex:M Child# 1 George Maynard St Albans, VT & Sarah J McKean Nashua, NH
MAYNARD, Jane Lea, Jul 10 1927 Sex:F Child# 1 Ralph Maynard Ayer, MA & Florence Merrill Franklin, NH
MAYNARD, Jean Baptiste Conrad, Aug 6 1928 Sex:M Child# 3 Ovila Maynard Nashua, NH & Yvonne Marquis Nashua, NH
MAYNARD, Jeanne, Jul 3 1926 Sex:F Child# 1 Ovila Maynard Nashua, NH & Yvonne Marquis Nashua, NH
MAYNARD, Jeannette Adrienne, Oct 7 1904 Sex:F Child# 1 Emile Maynard Canada & Georgiana Salvail Nashua, NH
MAYNARD, Jos Adrien Maurice, Mar 10 1928 Sex:M Child# 7 Albert Maynard Canada & Eugenie Morissette Nashua, NH
MAYNARD, Jos Ovila Aldege, Aug 4 1922 Sex:M Child# 5 Albert Maynard Canada & Eugenie Morrissette Nashua, NH
MAYNARD, Joseph, May 12 1926 Sex:M Child# 4 Albert Maynard Manchester, NH & Bertha Roy Londonderry, NH Stillborn
MAYNARD, Joseph Adelard A, Nov 12 1905 Sex:M Child# 6 Adelard Maynard Canada & Marie Levesque Canada
MAYNARD, Joseph Arthur, Mar 5 1906 Sex:M Child# 1 Jean Maynard Canada & Marie Lavoie Canada

MAYNARD, Joseph Arthur Roger, Nov 22 1923 Sex:M Child# 6 Albert Maynard Canada & Eugenie Morrissette Nashua, NH
MAYNARD, Joseph Donald Gerard, Mar 17 1927 Sex:M Child# 1 Leo J Maynard Nashua, NH & Yvonne Nadeau Fort Kent, ME
MAYNARD, Joseph Omer A, Oct 13 1900 Sex:M Child# 1 Albert Maynard Canada & Lydia Rochette Canada
MAYNARD, Joseph Roland, Apr 13 1908 Sex:M Child# 1 Napoleon Maynard Canada & Dorilda Dube Canada
MAYNARD, Joseph Roland, Jun 5 1924 Sex:M Child# 2 Joseph Maynard Canada & Leontine Dube Nashua, NH
MAYNARD, Lovella, Jan 26 1895 Sex:F Child# 4 George E Maynard St Albans, VT & Sarah McKeon Nashua, NH
MAYNARD, Lucille Alma, Dec 20 1924 Sex:F Child# 4 W Maynard Nashua, NH & Antoinette Poulin Nashua, NH
MAYNARD, M Lucille Jeannette, Nov 3 1917 Sex:F Child# 1 W Maynard Nashua, NH & Antoinette Poulin Nashua, NH
MAYNARD, M Lucille Mildred, Mar 14 1917 Sex:F Child# 2 Albert P Maynard Canada & Eugenie Morrissette Nashua, NH
MAYNARD, M Olivette Germaine, Sep 29 1914 Sex:F Child# 1 Albert Maynard Canada & Eugenie Morrissette Nashua, NH
MAYNARD, M Rose Anna A, Jul 21 1908 Sex:F Child# 1 Jean Maynard Canada & Lea Jean Canada
MAYNARD, M Yvonne Jeannette, Mar 10 1920 Sex:F Child# 4 Albert P Maynard Canada & Eugenie Morrissette Nashua, NH
MAYNARD, Maria Edna, Apr 10 1920 Sex:F Child# 1 W Ernest Maynard Suncook, NH & Antoinette Poulin Nashua, NH
MAYNARD, Marie Bertha, Aug 5 1930 Sex:F Child# 1 Roland Maynard Nashua, NH & Lea Lapierre Canada
MAYNARD, Marie Cecil Rachael, Mar 11 1928 Sex:F Child# 1 Rodolph Maynard Nashua, NH & Alice Dube Nashua, NH
MAYNARD, Marie Delima, Jan 9 1900 Sex:F Child# 1 Adelard Maynard Canada & Marie Levesque Canada
MAYNARD, Marie Desneige, Mar 20 1902 Sex:F Child# 3 A Maynard Canada & Marie Levesque Canada
MAYNARD, Marie Doris, Jul 4 1928 Sex:F Child# 2 D J Maynard Nashua, NH & Yvonne Nadeau Fort Kent, ME
MAYNARD, Marie Irene, May 13 1909 Sex:F Child# 2 Napoleon Maynard Canada & Dorilla Dube Canada
MAYNARD, Marie Irene Bertha, Jan 24 1932 Sex:F Child# 9 Albert Maynard St Dominique, PQ & F Morrissette Nashua, NH
MAYNARD, Marie Lea Adrienne, Dec 9 1920 Sex:F Child# 2 Ovila Maynard Marlboro, MA & Alma D Jacques Lowell, MA
MAYNARD, Marie Loraine M, Jun 15 1908 Sex:F Child# 2 Emile Maynard Canada & Georgianna Salvail Nashua, NH
MAYNARD, Marie Louise, Jan 5 1901 Sex:F Child# 2 Adelard Maynard Canada & Marie Levesque Canada
MAYNARD, Marie Rose, May 6 1901 Sex:F Child# 1 Edmond Maynard Canada & Rosanna Lamothe Canada
MAYNARD, Maurice Robert, Mar 20 1931 Sex:M Child# 2 Rodolphe Maynard Nashua, NH & Alice Dube Nashua, NH
MAYNARD, Omer Roger, Sep 5 1913 Sex:M Child# 6 Albert Maynard Canada & Lydia Rochette Canada
MAYNARD, Ovila, Apr 5 1902 Sex:M Child# 2 Napoleon Maynard Canada & Lydia Rochette Canada
MAYNARD, Patricia Ann, Oct 12 1933 Sex:F Child# 1 Arthur Maynard Nashua, NH & Agnes Trott Manchester, NH
MAYNARD, Paul Emile, Jul 20 1927 Sex:M Child# 2 Arthur Maynard Canada & Pauline Charland Canada
MAYNARD, Paul Emile A, Jan 25 1910 Sex:M Child# 3 Emile Maynard Canada & Georgianna Salvail Nashua, NH
MAYNARD, Rachel Yvonne, Oct 9 1927 Sex:F Child# 5 Wilbrod Maynard Nashua, NH & A Poulin Nashua, NH
MAYNARD, Robert Francois, Jul 13 1931 Sex:M Child# 4 Ovila Maynard Nashua, NH & Yvonne Marquis Nashua, NH
MAYNARD, Roland Victor, Dec 14 1933 Sex:M Child# 3 Roland Maynard Nashua, NH & Lea Lapierre Nashua, NH
MAYNARD, Unknown, Jun 30 1921 Sex:M Child# 1 Joseph Maynard Canada &        Dube Canada
MAYNARD, Unknown, Jan 2 1929 Sex:M Child# 3 Arthur Maynard Canada & Pauline Charland Canada
MAYNARD, Victor Alfred, Jan 10 1916 Sex:M Child# 4 Jean Maynard Canada & Lea Jean Canada
MAYNOR, Augustus G, Dec 29 1892 Sex:M Child# 8 Christopher Maynor NY & Lucy Brouillette NY
MAYNOR, Frederick Roy, Sep 18 1895 Sex:M Child# 9 Christopher Maynor Peru, NY & Lucy Boyer Plattsburg, NY
MAYO, Beatrice Edith, May 27 1928 Sex:F Child# 2 Maylon Mayo Vermont & Edith Bellefleur NH
MAYO, Harold E, Nov 15 1896 Sex:M Child# 1 Bert Mayo New York & Agnes Pena Vermont
MAYO, Leo Eugene, May 21 1930 Sex:M Child# 3 Mylan Mayo Vermont & Edith Bellefleur NH
MAYO, Priscilla Elaine, Sep 20 1926 Sex:F Child# 1 Maylon Mayo Nashua, NH & Laura Richardson Milford, NH
MAYON, Albert Francis, Feb 17 1929 Sex:M Child# 1 Albert Mayon Northfield, VT & Velma Taylor Brookline, NH
MAYOTTE, Henry, Nov 4 1899 Sex:M Child# 8 Joseph Mayotte Canada & Elmire Marquis Canada
MAYOTTE, Joseph, Apr 27 1915 Sex:M Child# 1 Joseph Mayotte Nashua, NH & Gertrude Bossidy Richmond, MA
MAYOU, Joseph, Apr 17 1917 Sex:M Child# 1 (No Parents Listed)
MAYOU, Leonard Earl, Jan 20 1931 Sex:M Child# 2 Albert Mayou Montpelier, VT & Velma Taylor Brookline, NH
MAYOU, Thelma Irene, Apr 13 1931 Sex:F Child# 1 Edward Mayou Roxbury, VT & Lestina Parker Pepperell, MA
MAYROTE, Albertis, Nov 29 1889 Sex:M Child# 18 Noel Mayrote Champlain, NY & Julia Bouyer Plattsburg, NY
MAYROTT, Unknown, Oct 27 1897 Sex:F Child# 6 Howard Mayrott Pictou, NS & Magrot Baldarau Lancaster, England
MAYS, Joseph Gerald, Mar 2 1928 Sex:M Child# 1 Rheuben W Mays Georgia & Maria Nadeau Epping, NH
MAZEIKA, Bennie, Sep 20 1925 Sex:M Child# 2 Dan Mazeika Poland & Mary Makalawicz Poland
MAZEIKA, Stanislav, Dec 28 1920 Sex:M Child# 1 Daniel Mazeika Poland Russia & Mary Makalawicz Poland Russia
MAZINKEWICZ, Aurelia, May 28 1928 Sex:F Child# 11 S Mazinkewicz Poland & Mary Janusz Poland
MAZUKNA, Nellie, Jun 15 1917 Sex:F Child# 3 Frank Mazukna Russia & Petrola Welcha Russia
MCADOO, Allena Hazel, Jul 4 1933 Sex:F Child# 8 George McAdoo Nashua, NH & Pauline Lucier Nashua, NH
MCADOO, Andrea Elizabeth, Sep 9 1931 Sex:F Child# 7 George S McAdoo Nashua, NH & Pauline Lucier Nashua, NH
MCADOO, David Russell, Mar 18 1930 Sex:M Child# 6 George McAdoo Nashua, NH & Pauline Lucier Nashua, NH
MCADOO, Edwin, Oct 20 1925 Sex:M Child# 4 George McAdoo Nashua, NH & Pauline Lucier Nashua, NH
MCADOO, George, Feb 14 1896 Sex:M Child# 2 Samuel McAdoo Ireland & Mary A Clark Ireland
MCADOO, Jennie, Jun 13 1906 Sex:F Child# 5 Samuel McAdoo Ireland & Marion Clark Ireland
MCADOO, Jessie, Aug 19 1914 Sex:F Child# 1 Samuel McAdoo Ireland & Emma Matthews England
MCADOO, Korleen Beatrice, Sep 12 1934 Sex:F Child# 9 George McAdoo Nashua, NH & Pauline Lucier Nashua, NH
MCADOO, Marion Alice, Jul 30 1927 Sex:F Child# 5 George McAdoo Nashua, NH & Pauline Lucier Nashua, NH
MCADOO, Nellie Virginia, Dec 15 1915 Sex:F Child# 2 Samuel McAdoo Ireland & Emma Matthews England
MCADOO, Raymond Arthur, Aug 30 1923 Sex:M Child# 3 George McAdoo Nashua, NH & Pauline Lucier Nashua, NH
MCADOO, Robert, Dec 17 1897 Sex:M Child# 3 Samuel McAdoo Ireland & Mary A Clarke Ireland
MCADOO, Willieminea, Dec 18 1894 Sex:M Child# 1 Samuel McAdoo Ireland & Mary A Clark Ireland
MCAFEE, Barbara, Jan 14 1916 Sex:F Child# 4 Adam McAfee Bedford, NH & Mary Dufour Sable, MI
MCAFEE, Charles Dexter, Apr 2 1927 Sex:M Child# 7 Adam McAfee Grafton, MA & Mary Dufour Michigan
MCAFEE, Leon Howard, Aug 18 1896 Sex:M Child# 5 Thomas McAfee Bedford & Mary J Pate St John, NB
MCAFEE, Myrtis Mad May, Jan 11 1914 Sex:F Child# 3 Adam F McAfee Bedford, NH & Mary Dufour Sable, MI
MCAFEE, Norman Henry, May 29 1918 Sex:M Child# 5 Adam McAfee Biddeford, ME & May Dufour Michigan

MCAFEE, Paul, Dec 6 1912 Sex:M Child# 2 Adam McAfee US & Marie Dufour US
MCAFEE, Raymond, Sep 6 1911 Sex:M Child# 1 Adam McAfee US & Marie Dufour Canada
MCAFEE, Unknown, Aug 28 1887 Sex:M Child# 1 Thomas E McAfee Bedford & Mary A Pate St Johns, NB
MCAFEE, Unknown, Sep 22 1888 Sex:F Child# 2 Thomas E McAfee Bedford & Mary A Pate St Johns, NB
MCAFEE, Unknown, Aug 11 1891 Sex:F Child# 3 Thomas E McAfee Bedford & Mary A Pate St Johns, NB
MCAFEE, Unknown, Jan 28 1894 Sex:M Child# 4 Thomas E McAfee Bedford & Mary A Pate St Johns, NB
MCAFEE, Unknown, Jan 30 1922 Sex:M Child# 6 Adam McAfee Grafton, MA & May Doufour Sabel, MI
MCALISTER, Franklin H Jr, Feb 2 1926 Sex:M Child# 2 F H McAlister Enfield, NH & Julia L Dugas Sterling, MA
MCALISTER, Gerald Alan, May 1 1929 Sex:M Child# 3 Frank H McAlister Enfield, NH & Julie L Dugas Sterling, MA
MCALISTER, Grace Louise, Oct 5 1922 Sex:F Child# 1 Frank H McAlister Enfield, NH & Julia Dugas Sterling, MA
MCALLISTER, Francis Allen, Jun 15 1916 Sex:M Child# 1 Ral J McAllister Canaan, NH & Helen Cross Lebanon, NH
MCALPIN, Alice Mary, Jun 3 1908 Sex:F Child# 5 John McAlpin Calais, ME & Ann Jones Ireland
MCALPIN, Ann, May 17 1905 Sex:F Child# 3 John McAlpin Calais, ME & Ann Jones Ireland
MCALPIN, Evelyn Agnes, Mar 11 1907 Sex:F Child# 4 John McAlpin Calais, ME & Ann J Jones Ireland
MCALPIN, Grace Margaret, Jun 7 1903 Sex:F Child# 2 John McAlpin Calais, ME & Ann Jones Ireland
MCALPIN, Ruth Genevieve, Oct 25 1911 Sex:F Child# 7 John McAlpin Calais, ME & Annie Jones Ireland
MCALPINE, James, May 29 1910 Sex:M Child# 6 John McAlpine Calais, ME & Annie Jones Ireland
MCANNEY, Robert Hamilton, Jul 27 1933 Sex:M Child# 2 William McAnney Lowell, MA & Althea Haywood Nashua, NH
MCANNEY, William Howard, Sep 29 1930 Sex:M Child# 1 William H McAnney Lowell, MA & Althea Haywood Nashua, NH
MCARDLE, Unknown, Mar 12 1900 Sex:M Child# 1 (No Parents Listed)
MCARTHY, Jeremiah, Jan 22 1895 Sex:M Child# 4 William McArthy Ireland & Bridget Tracy Ireland
MCBEAN, John Alexander, Jan 28 1907 Sex:M Child# 2 John McBean Lewiston, ME & Katherine Mulqueen Ireland
MCBEAN, Viola Genevieve, Jan 28 1911 Sex:F Child# 3 John McBean Lewiston, ME & Katherine Mulqueen Ireland
MCBEIGH, John Edward, Nov 11 1890 Sex:M Child# 1 Daniel McBeigh Scotland & Jane Dunn Brooklyn, NY
MCBRIDE, Catherine, Jan 14 1923 Sex:F Child# 4 Bartholomew McBride Nashua, NH & Margaret Boyle New Castle, NB
MCBRIDE, Marion Aurelia, Sep 3 1920 Sex:F Child# 3 Bart McBride Nashua, NH & Margaret Boyle Newcastle, NB
MCBRIDE, Marjorie Jane, Dec 11 1910 Sex:F Child# 1 Frank McBride England & Minnie Ryan Nashua, NH
MCBRIDE, Mildred Naomi, Jan 14 1900 Sex:F Child# 1 Henry McBride Nashua, NH & L N Taylor Nashua, NH
MCBRIDE, Unknown, Jan 8 1895 Sex:M Child# 1 (No Parents Listed)
MCCABE, Edward, Apr 29 1908 Sex:M Child# 1 (No Parents Listed)
MCCABE, Harry B, Mar 19 1896 Sex:M Child# 9 William McCabe Malone, NY & Nellie Mullen Bangor, NY
MCCAFFREY, Eva Agnes, Jul 22 1903 Sex:F Child# 5 James McCaffrey Mass & Nellie A Fitzpatrick Mass
MCCAFFREY, Henry, Jun 4 1890 Sex:M Child# 1 Henry B McCaffrey Plattsburg, NY & Catherine Fuller Malone, NY
MCCAFFREY, Margaret Frances, Oct 14 1895 Sex:F Child# 4 James McCaffrey Winchendon, MA & Nellie Fitzpatrick Bo
MCCAIN, David Winthrop, Sep 11 1932 Sex:M Child# 4 F A McCain Nashua, NH & Irene T Lucier Nashua, NH
MCCAIN, Donald Robert, Jan 1 1924 Sex:M Child# 1 Elwell G McCain Lowell, MA & Vena L Wooley Springfield, MA
MCCAIN, Richard Ord, Jan 24 1928 Sex:F Child# 2 Francis McCain Nashua, NH & Irene Lucier Nashua, NH
MCCAIN, Robert Henry, Nov 23 1925 Sex:M Child# 1 Francis McCain Nashua, NH & Irene Lucier Nashua, NH
MCCAIN, Russell Francis, Jan 15 1931 Sex:M Child# 3 Francis A McCain Nashua, NH & Irene Lucier Nashua, NH
MCCAIN, Unknown, Nov 12 1902 Sex:M Child# 3 Albert G McCain England & Fannie Ord Canada
MCCANN, Arthur George, May 11 1902 Sex:M Child# 1 Thomas McCann NH & Laura Yvon Canada
MCCANN, Charles Joseph, Jun 14 1903 Sex:M Child# 3 Joseph McCann Worcester, MA & Margaret E Mahoney Ireland
MCCANN, Charles Joseph, Oct 14 1929 Sex:M Child# 2 Charles Jos McCann Nashua, NH & Helen A Zebrowski Maynard, MA
MCCANN, Hugh Robert, Mar 20 1931 Sex:M Child# 5 Henry J McCann Leominster, MA & Agnes E Crane Charlottetown, PA
MCCANN, Jos Albert Edouard, Jan 25 1926 Sex:M Child# 2 George McCann Nashua, NH & Zemilda Gagnon Nashua, NH
MCCANN, Leo Griffin, Jun 16 1916 Sex:M Child# 6 Michael H McCann Nashua, NH & Margaret M Griffin Ireland
MCCANN, Lillian Mary, Mar 25 1928 Sex:F Child# 1 Charles J McCann Nashua, NH & Hazel Zebrowski Maynard, MA
MCCANN, Mary, Jun 19 1888 Sex:F Child# 1 Pehelix McCann Ireland & Maggie McNamar Ireland Stillborn
MCCANN, Mary Cecelia, Nov 20 1913 Sex:F Child# 5 Michael H McCann Nashua, NH & Margaret M Griffin Ireland
MCCANN, Raymond Gerard, Dec 22 1927 Sex:M Child# 3 George McCann Nashua, NH & Zelinda Gagnon Nashua, NH
MCCANN, Thomas Roland, Jul 29 1922 Sex:M Child# 1 George A McCann Nashua, NH & Zelinda Gagnon Nashua, NH
MCCANN, Unknown, Jun 25 1892 Sex:M Child# 1 (No Parents Listed)
MCCANN, Unknown, Oct 26 1906 Sex:M Child# 4 Joseph C McCann Worcester, MA & Margaret E Mahoney Ireland Stillborn
MCCANN, Unknown, Jun 28 1909 Sex:M Child# 4 Michael H McCann Nashua, NH & Margaret Griffin Ireland
MCCANN, Unknown, Jul 4 1911 Sex:F Child# 2 George W McCann Lowell, MA & Alice Robinson New Brunswick
MCCANN, Walter Francis, Apr 16 1899 Sex:M Child# 1 Charles J McCann Nashua, NH & Margaret E Mahoney Ireland
MCCARN, Unknown, May 5 1901 Sex:F Child# 2 Joseph McCarn Nashua, NH & Margaret Mahony Ireland
MCCARTHY, Elaine Lucille, Jan 29 1928 Sex:F Child# 3 Corn McCarthy Vermont & Henrietta Gosselin Vermont
MCCARTHY, George, Aug 30 1892 Sex:M Child# 3 William McCarthy Ireland & Bridget Tracey Ireland
MCCARTHY, Harold, Dec 9 1901 Sex:M Child# 4 Eugene F McCarthy Milford, MA & Elizabeth Filypron Marlboro, MA
MCCARTHY, Henry Thomas, Feb 28 1921 Sex:M Child# 1 Henry S McCarthy NH & Helen Winn NH
MCCARTHY, Irene C A, Sep 23 1891 Sex:F Child# 1 William McCarthy Canada & Cora Riendeau Canada
MCCARTHY, John, Jul 14 1887 Sex:M Child# 1 William McCarthy Ireland & Bridget Tracey Ireland
MCCARTHY, John Farrell, Feb 26 1905 Sex:M Child# 4 Patrick McCarthy Ireland & Rose McCaffrey Ireland
MCCARTHY, Joseph Louis, Dec 9 1894 Sex:M Child# 2 William McCarthy Canada & Cora Riendeau NY
MCCARTHY, Joseph Olivier, Aug 22 1896 Sex:M Child# 3 William McCarthy Canada & Cora Riendeau Malone, NY
MCCARTHY, Katherine Mary, Dec 11 1930 Sex:F Child# 9 Michael J McCarthy Manchester, NH & Yvonne Pichette Manchester
MCCARTHY, Lucille Denise, Jan 2 1915 Sex:F Child# 2 Martin D McCarthy Boston, MA & Matilda E Morin Canada
MCCARTHY, Mary, Aug 5 1887 Sex:F Child# 1 Eugene McCarthy Ireland & Kate Ireland
MCCARTHY, Mary Catherine, Oct 6 1899 Sex:F Child# 3 E F McCarthy Mass & E F Fitzpatrick Mass
MCCARTHY, Mary Ellen, Mar 4 1900 Sex:F Child# 1 Pat McCarthy Ireland & Rose McCaffrey Ireland
MCCARTHY, Mary Josephine, Jan 22 1897 Sex:F Child# 5 William McCarthy Ireland & Bridget Tracy Ireland
MCCARTHY, Mary Madeline, Oct 5 1913 Sex:F Child# 1 Martin D McCarthy Boston, MA & Mathilda Morin Canada

MCCARTHY, Mary Margaret, Apr 23 1925 Sex:F Child# 5 Michael McCarthy Manchester, NH & Yvonne Pichette Manchester
MCCARTHY, Michael Joseph, Jr, Jul 16 1934 Sex:M Child# 10 Michael J McCarthy Manchester, NH & Yvonne Pichette
MCCARTHY, Patrick Leo, Jun 4 1903 Sex:M Child# 3 Patrick McCarthy Ireland & Rose McCaffrey Ireland
MCCARTHY, Patrick Stephen, Mar 15 1899 Sex:M Child# 6 William McCarthy Ireland & Bridget Tracey Ireland
MCCARTHY, Thomas Joseph, Oct 20 1901 Sex:M Child# 2 Patrick McCarthy Ireland & Rose McCaffrey Ireland
MCCARTHY, Unknown, Apr 28 1893 Sex:M Child# 2 William McCarthy Canada & Cordelia Riendeau Canada Stillborn
MCCARTHY, Unknown, Aug 17 1901 Sex:M Child#  William McCarthy Ireland & Bridget Tracey Ireland
MCCARTHY, Wilfrid Ovid, Jan 22 1908 Sex:M Child# 1 John J McCarthy Groton, MA & Justina Jauron Canada
MCCARTHY, William, Aug 25 1890 Sex:M Child# 2 William McCarthy Ireland & Bridget Tracey Ireland
MCCARTHY, William Dennis, Dec 17 1922 Sex:M Child# 3 Henry S McCarthy Nashua, NH & Helen Winn Nashua, NH
MCCARTY, Gladys, May 5 1899 Sex:F Child# 3 William F McCarty Wilton, NH & Lizzie E Peabody Middleton, MA
MCCARTY, Henry Sylvester, May 30 1895 Sex:M Child# 1 William F McCarty Wilton, NH & Lizzie E Peabody Middleton, MA
MCCARTY, Nellie Gertrude, Jun 12 1896 Sex:F Child# 2 William F McCarty Wilton, NH & Lizzie E Peabody Middleton, MA
MCCARVELL, Unknown, May 21 1917 Sex:  Child# 4 Celestin McCarvell Canada & Albina Cote Nashua, NH Stillborn
MCCARVILL, Avelyn Catherine, Jun 19 1916 Sex:F Child# 1 Bazil P McCarvill Nova Scotia & Eva Lampron US
MCCARVILL, Doris, Sep 3 1908 Sex:F Child# 2 James E McCarvill Canada & Georgiana Salvail Canada
MCCARVILL, Mary, Apr 8 1910 Sex:F Child# 3 James E McCarvill Canada & Georgianna Salva Canada
MCCARVILL, Oswald Harry, Feb 2 1913 Sex:M Child# 1 Celestine McCarvill Newfoundland & Albina Cote Nashua, NH
MCCARVILLE, Robert Emmett, Oct 22 1906 Sex:M Child# 1 James E McCarville Canada & Georgianna Shea Canada
MCCATCHEON, Marie Yvonne, Jan 31 1903 Sex:F Child# 7 James McCatcheon Mass & Alexina Monty Canada
MCCAUGHNEY, Albert James, May 31 1917 Sex:M Child# 5 John J McCaughney Ireland & Mary Bowen Ireland
MCCAUGHNEY, Andrew, May 19 1912 Sex:M Child# 2 John McCaughney Ireland & Mary Bowen Ireland
MCCAUGHNEY, George Francis, Dec 14 1915 Sex:M Child# 4 John J McCaughney Ireland & Mary M Bohan Ireland
MCCAUGHNEY, John Patrick, Feb 15 1914 Sex:M Child# 3 John McCaughney Ireland & Mary Bowen Ireland
MCCAUGNEY, Catherine Frances, Feb 26 1925 Sex:F Child# 8 John McCaugney Ireland & Margaret Bowen Ireland
MCCAUGNEY, Mary M, Jun 12 1910 Sex:F Child# 1 John McCaugney Ireland & Mary Bowen Ireland
MCCAUGNEY, Rose, Apr 15 1919 Sex:F Child# 6 John McCaugney Ireland & Mary Bowan Ireland
MCCAUGNEY, Unknown, Feb 22 1922 Sex:M Child# 7 John J McCaugney Ireland & Mary M Bohan Ireland Stillborn
MCCLEOD, Priscilla Gertrude, May 20 1922 Sex:F Child# 3 Nelson A McLeod Hollis, NH & Anna G Potter Rochester, NH
MCCLINTOCK, Unknown, Feb 22 1927 Sex:F Child# 1 J J McClintock Mass & Mabel Thompson Nashua, NH
MCCLOUD, Mary Ellen, Jun 14 1891 Sex:F Child# 1 John McCloud Nova Scotia & Melia Raymond Canada
MCCLURE, Emma Delia, Jun 12 1907 Sex:F Child# 4 Marvin McClure Highgate Sprgs, VT & Mary B Donahue St Albans, VT
MCCLURE, J Albert Armand, Jun 28 1914 Sex:M Child# 4 William McClure NH & Delima Dube Canada
MCCLURE, Joseph Frank Leo, Jan 16 1911 Sex:M Child# 2 William McClure NH & Delima Dube Canada
MCCLURE, Marie Loraine I, Jun 28 1906 Sex:F Child# 2 John McClure NH & Delima Dube
MCCLURE, Marie Wilda, Jul 22 1904 Sex:F Child# 1 William McClure NH & Delima Berube Canada
MCCOLLUM, Unknown, Dec 10 1890 Sex:F Child# 1 A M McCollum
MCCOMACK, Unknown, Sep 3 1896 Sex:M Child# 8 Patrick McComack Ireland & Mary Furey Ireland Stillborn
MCCONNELL, Bernard, Jul 31 1901 Sex:M Child# 4 Joseph McConnell Ireland & Margaret Winn Ireland
MCCORMACK, Annie Agnes, Sep 11 1897 Sex:F Child# 9 Patrick McCormack Ireland & Mary Furey Ireland
MCCORMACK, Doris Anne, Jan 26 1935 Sex:F Child# 1 D T McCormack Canada & Dorothy Rebidue Worcester, MA
MCCORMACK, Joseph, Jul 25 1892 Sex:M Child# 5 Patrick McCormack Ireland & Mary Flury Ireland
MCCORMACK, Lillian May, Mar 17 1894 Sex:F Child# 4 Patrick McCormack Ireland & Ireland
MCCORMACK, Mary Anne, Aug 3 1890 Sex:F Child# 3 Patrick McCormack Ireland & Mary Fury Ireland
MCCORMACK, Unknown, Sep 22 1891 Sex:M Child# 4 Patrick McCormack Ireland & Mary Fury Ireland Stillborn
MCCORMACK, Unknown, Aug 12 1895 Sex:M Child# 7 Patrick McCormack Ireland & Mary Furey Ireland Stillborn
MCCORMICK, Charles, Oct 10 1916 Sex:M Child# 4 William H McCormick Stoughton, MA & Elizabeth McLaughlin Randolph
MCCORMICK, John Thomas, Jun 1 1887 Sex:M Child# 1 Patrick McCormick Ireland & Mary Fury Ireland
MCCORRISON, Robert Keys, Jun 22 1931 Sex:M Child# 1 Carl E McCorrison Augusta, ME & Mildred Keys Bridgeport, CT
MCCORVILLE, Katherine, Aug 29 1898 Sex:F Child# 3 Joseph McCorville Ireland & Margaret Winn Ireland
MCCOURT, Viola Allen, Apr 22 1917 Sex:F Child# 1 William McCourt Boston, MA & Hattie A Allen Rockland, ME
MCCOY, Daniel Gregg, Mar 14 1910 Sex:M Child# 3 Daniel McCoy Hudson, NH & Bessie Rivers Enosburg, VT
MCCOY, Leon, Jul 7 1910 Sex:M Child# 1 Elgin L McCoy Hudson, NH & Flora B Weston Fremont, NH
MCCOY, Marguerette, Jan 17 1895 Sex:F Child# 4 John D McCoy Marblehead, MA & Mary E Foley Ireland
MCCOY, Raymond, Nov 17 1919 Sex:M Child# 7 Daniel G McCoy Hudson, NH & Bessie L Rivers Montgomery, VT
MCCURDY, Mary Elizabeth, Apr 11 1918 Sex:F Child# 1 William J McCurdy Maine & Margaret A Anderson Nashua, NH
MCCURDY, Nancy Helen, Oct 28 1932 Sex:F Child# 2 Guy V McCurdy Winthrop, ME & Mary M Kendall Nashua, NH
MCCURDY, Robert Kendall, Apr 17 1931 Sex:M Child# 1 Guy V McCurdy Winslow, ME & Mary M Kendall Nashua, NH
MCCUTCHEON, Alexina, Jul 10 1898 Sex:F Child# 6 John McCutcheon Fitchburg, MA & Alexina Monty Canada
MCCUTCHEON, Alfred, Dec 22 1909 Sex:M Child# 1 John McCutcheon Canada & Annie Burnham Ireland
MCCUTCHEON, Earl Paul Alfred, Jul 22 1918 Sex:M Child# 1 Alfred McCutcheon Canada & Lydia Pelletier NH
MCCUTCHEON, Helen Marie, Apr 6 1912 Sex:F Child# 1 James A McCutcheon St John, NB & Mabel A Willis Warren, NH
MCCUTCHEON, Henry Normand, Aug 15 1921 Sex:M Child# 2 Fred McCutcheon Canada & Lydia Pelletier Nashua, NH
MCCUTCHEON, Lucile, Dec 17 1911 Sex:F Child# 2 John A McCutcheon Montreal & Annie E Burnham Ireland
MCDEAMOTT, Charles, Jan 14 1890 Sex:M Child# 1 Charles McDeamott Lowell, MA & Elizabeth Finnigan Plattsburg, NY
MCDERMOTT, Catherine, Mar 1 1895 Sex:F Child# 3 John W McDermott Lawrence, MA & Catherine M Sullivan Nashua, NH
MCDERMOTT, Francis, Oct 10 1887 Sex:M Child# 6 Charles McDermott Nashua, NH & Lizzie Plattsburg, NY
MCDERMOTT, Helen, May 14 1894 Sex:F Child# 5 Thomas E McDermott Ireland & Alice L Burke Ireland
MCDERMOTT, Jennie, Jun 9 1891 Sex:F Child# 2 John W McDermott Lawrence, MA & Katherine M Sullivan Nashua, NH
MCDERMOTT, John, May 22 1914 Sex:M Child# 1 John L McDermott Franklin, NH & Eva McGloughlin Franklin, NH
MCDERMOTT, Margaret, Jun 11 1890 Sex:F Child# 3 Thomas McDermott Ireland & Alice Burke Ireland
MCDERMOTT, Margrett, Mar 14 1898 Sex:F Child#  Henry McDermott New York & Carrie McNamard New York
MCDERMOTT, Mary, Jun 26 1888 Sex:F Child# 2 Thomas McDermott Ireland & Alice Burke Ireland

MCDERMOTT, Rita, Apr 4 1915 Sex:F Child#  Edward McDermott Lowell, MA & Catherine Kelly England
MCDERMOTT, Unknown, Feb 13 1888 Sex:M Child# 2 Joseph P McDermott Nashua, NH & Kate O'Brien N Adams, MA
MCDERMOTT, Unknown, Apr 28 1892 Sex:F Child# 4 Thomas McDermott Ireland & Alice Burke Ireland
MCDERMOTT, Unknown, Aug 4 1892 Sex:M Child# 3 Joseph E McDermott Nashua, NH & Katie O'Brien N Adams, MA
MCDERMOTT, Walter Byron, Nov 11 1893 Sex:M Child# 3 Henry McDermott New York, NY & Sarah Bell Putnam, CT
MCDILLON, Unknown, Nov 7 1889 Sex:F Child# 2 Martin McDillon Ireland & Jane Ireland
MCDOFF, Rosa G, Oct 23 1887 Sex:F Child#  John McDoff Canada & Georgina Perreau Canada
MCDOLPHE, Arthur, Apr 15 1890 Sex:M Child# 5 John McDolphe Canada & Georgiana Perreault Canada
MCDONALD, Agnes Forrester, Apr 4 1912 Sex:F Child# 1 John M McDonald England & Christina Irwin Scotland Stillborn
MCDONALD, Douglas Halliday, Aug 28 1918 Sex:M Child# 2 Thomas H McDonald Barre, VT & Marguerite Adams Nashua, NH
MCDONALD, Ethel, Jun 21 1892 Sex:F Child# 1 William McDonald US & Katie US
MCDONALD, Francis A P, Mar 17 1910 Sex:M Child# 1 John McDonald Prince Edward Island & Kate Graves PEI
MCDONALD, George Alfred, Jul 15 1917 Sex:M Child# 1 James A McDonald Prince Edward Island & Theresa F Fernald
MCDONALD, Gordon Adams, May 20 1917 Sex:M Child# 1 Thomas H McDonald Barre, VT & Margaret Adams Nashua, NH
MCDONALD, Hazel May, Oct 19 1917 Sex:F Child# 4 John McDonald England & Christine Irvine Scotland
MCDONALD, Helen Anna, Sep 20 1911 Sex:F Child# 4 John McDonald Mooers Jct, NY & Kate Crowley Ireland
MCDONALD, John Edmund, Jan 12 1907 Sex:M Child# 2 John McDonald Mooers, NY & Kate Crowley Ireland
MCDONALD, John McKay, Apr 21 1913 Sex:M Child# 2 John M McDonald Sunderland, England & Christine Irvine Scotland
MCDONALD, Katherine H, Apr 7 1909 Sex:F Child# 3 John G McDonald Mooers, NY & Katherine Crowley Ireland
MCDONALD, Leonard Orvine, Feb 20 1915 Sex:M Child# 3 John M McDonald England & Christina Irvine Scotland
MCDONALD, Margaret Mary, May 2 1905 Sex:F Child# 1 John McDonald Moore's, NY & Katherine Crowley Ireland
MCDONALD, Richard Joseph, Apr 17 1922 Sex:M Child# 8 John McDonald Mooers, NY & Katherine Crowley Ireland
MCDONALD, Robert Francis, Apr 28 1918 Sex:M Child# 7 John G McDonald New York & Katherine Crowley Ireland
MCDONALD, Thomas, Jun 3 1913 Sex:M Child# 5 John McDonald Mooers, NY & Kate Crowley Ireland
MCDONALD, Timothy James, Jul 31 1915 Sex:M Child# 6 John McDonald Mooers, NY & Catherine Crowley Ireland
MCDONALD, Unknown, Apr 19 1889 Sex:M Child# 8 Alex McDonald Malone, NY & Abbie Nelligan Lowell, MA Stillborn
MCDONALD, Vera M, Mar 13 1892 Sex:F Child# 1 William J McDonald Burke, NY & Maud Severance Charlestown, MA
MCDONALD, Westley George, Dec 18 1908 Sex:M Child# 1 James McDonald
MCDOUGALD, John Allen, Mar 28 1909 Sex:M Child# 1 John A McDougald Nova Scotia & Helen A Crockett Merrimac, MA
MCDOUGALL, Dennis, Nov 15 1900 Sex:M Child# 5 John McDougall Nova Scotia & Rosanna Salva RI
MCDOUGALL, Marie Ruth, Sep 6 1906 Sex:F Child# 7 John McDougall Canada & Rosa Salva Canada
MCDOUGALL, Unknown, Oct 27 1898 Sex:F Child# 4 John A McDougall Nova Scotia & Rose Hilda Selvess Natic, RI
MCDUFFEE, Beatrice Eleanor, Feb 26 1910 Sex:F Child# 2 Leslie E McDuffee Bradford, VT & Nellie Rogers Strafford, VT
MCDUFFEY, William Edward, Jun 22 1934 Sex:M Child# 1 Wm Edward McDuffey Manchester, NH & Eleanore Lucier Nashua, NH
MCDUFFIE, Duane Philip, Feb 8 1913 Sex:M Child# 3 Lester E McDuffie Bradford, VT & Nellie Rogers Strafford, VT
MCDUFFIE, Ellis Rogers, May 5 1908 Sex:M Child# 1 Lester E McDuffie Bradford, VT & Nettie Rogers Strafford, VT
MCDUFFIE, Helen Grace, Oct 25 1915 Sex:F Child# 5 Lester E McDuffie Bradford, VT & Nellie Rogers Strafford, VT
MCDUFFIE, Hester Webster, Oct 25 1915 Sex:M Child# 4 Lester E McDuffie Bradford, VT & Nellie Rogers Strafford, VT
MCDUFFIE, Rachel Marie, Mar 8 1896 Sex:F Child# 1 Charles T McDuffie Rochester & Jennie M Clarke St Albans, VT
MCDUFFIE, Richard Thurston, Jul 11 1929 Sex:M Child# 1 Harry T McDuffie Nashua, NH & Isabelle Avard Nashua, NH
MCDUFFIE, Ruth Clarke, Apr 5 1897 Sex:F Child# 2 Charles T McDuffie Rochester & Jennie M Clarke St Albans, VT
MCDUFFIE, Unknown, Sep 6 1898 Sex:M Child# 3 Charles T McDuffie Rochester & Jennie M Clarke St Albans, VT
MCDUGAL, Anna Belle, May 17 1897 Sex:F Child# 3 John A McDugal Cape Breton, NS & Rose H Selvers Litchfield, NH
MCEVOY, Henry Albert, Dec 21 1933 Sex:M Child# 2 Alfred McEvoy Manchester, NH & Vitaline Tessier Nashua, NH
MCEVOY, Wilfred William, Feb 16 1932 Sex:M Child# 1 Alfred McEvoy Manchester, NH & Vitaline Tessier Nashua, NH
MCFARLAND, Katherine, Nov 20 1924 Sex:F Child# 2 M McFarland Ireland & Annie Kilkelley Ireland
MCFARLAND, Thomas Francis, Nov 16 1923 Sex:M Child# 1 Michael McFarland Ireland & Annie Kilkelly Ireland
MCGAFFEY, Mabel Caroline, Apr 18 1893 Sex:F Child# 2 Charles McGaffey Nashua, NH & Hattie Peters Greenville, NH
MCGAFFEY, Unknown, Dec 21 1890 Sex:M Child# 1 Charles H McGaffey Nashua, NH & Hattie G Peters Greenville, NH
MCGEE, Jewell, Jul 11 1917 Sex:F Child# 2 James H McGee Deerfield, IL & Theresa Emanuelson Sweden
MCGILVERY, Gladys Lilla, Apr 25 1901 Sex:F Child# 1 Murdock McGilvery NS & Carrie J Campbell NS
MCGIRLEY, Mary Florence, Jan 2 1911 Sex:F Child# 1 Philip A McGirley N Attleboro, MA & Katherine T Sullivan C
MCGIVNEY, Phillip Alexander, Apr 4 1917 Sex:M Child# 2 Phillip McGivney N Attleboro, MA & Catherine T Sullivan
MCGLOUGHLIN, Unknown, Dec 28 1895 Sex:M Child# 3 David McGloughlin Ireland & Mary Whalen Ireland
MCGLYNN, Frances Ed, Oct 19 1899 Sex:M Child# 4 John McGlynn Nashua, NH & Margaret Ryan Milford, NH
MCGLYNN, Helen Irene, Aug 15 1895 Sex:F Child# 2 John McGlynn Nashua, NH & Margaret Ryan Nashua, NH
MCGLYNN, John W, Nov 12 1889 Sex:M Child# 5 Patrick McGlynn Ireland & Bridget Winn Ireland
MCGLYNN, Kathleen Lorraine, Sep 12 1935 Sex:F Child# 2 Albert McGlynn Nashua, NH & Addie Asselin Scranton, PA
MCGLYNN, Leo James, Oct 18 1902 Sex:M Child# 6 John McGlynn Nashua, NH & Margaret Ryan Milford, NH
MCGLYNN, Margaret, Feb 17 1905 Sex:F Child# 7 John J McGlynn Nashua, NH & Margaret Ryan Milford, NH
MCGLYNN, Marlene Margaret, Aug 21 1934 Sex:F Child# 1 Albert McGlynn Nashua, NH & Addie Asselin Scranton, PA
MCGLYNN, Mary Agnes, Apr 26 1907 Sex:F Child# 8 John J McGlynn Nashua, NH & Margaret Ryan Milford, NH
MCGLYNN, Rose Hilda, Aug 20 1888 Sex:F Child# 1 Patrick McGlynn Ireland & Bridget Winn Ireland
MCGLYNN, Unknown, Nov 9 1897 Sex:M Child# 3 John McGlynn Nashua, NH & Margaret Ryan Milford, NH Stillborn
MCGLYNN, Unknown, Aug 5 1900 Sex:F Child# 1 Frank McGlynn Lowell, MA & Ada Taylor Nashua, NH
MCGLYNN, Unknown, Aug 5 1900 Sex:F Child# 2 Frank McGlynn Lowell, MA & Ada Taylor Nashua, NH
MCGLYNN, Unknown, Feb 25 1901 Sex:M Child# 5 John McGlynn Nashua, NH & Margaret Ryan Milford, NH
MCGLYNN, Unknown, Jan 11 1909 Sex:F Child# 9 John J McGlynn Nashua, NH & Margaret Ryan Milford, NH
MCGOWN, Roger Stillman, Jun 21 1898 Sex:M Child# 2 Admiran McGown Maine & Kate M Ober Maine
MCGRAIL, Joseph Vincent, Dec 26 1933 Sex:M Child# 1 Harold L McGrail
MCGRATH, Ann, Aug 4 1928 Sex:F Child# 1 Jos McGrath Pepperell, MA & Helen Lynch Pepperell, MA
MCGRATH, Francis, Apr 19 1928 Sex:M Child# 1 Francis McGrath Lowell, MA & Alice Gallagher Lowell, MA
MCGRATH, Margaret Agnes, Jun 30 1932 Sex:F Child# 2 Joseph McGrath Pepperell, MA & Helen Lynch Pepperell, MA

MCGRAW, Joseph A Normand, Mar 21 1931 Sex:M Child# 1 Joseph McGraw Maine & Germaine Bernetchez Canada
MCGRAW, Unknown, Jul 28 1920 Sex:F Child# 3 Charles McGraw McGraw, NY & Josephine Patrick Truxton, NY Stillborn
MCGRAW, Wilfrid Robert, Oct 28 1932 Sex:M Child# 2 Jos McGraw Maine & G Bernatchez Canada
MCGREENERY, Paul, May 3 1926 Sex:M Child# 2 Paul McGreenery Boston, MA & Agnes Boland Boston, MA
MCGUANE, Charles, Mar 8 1931 Sex:M Child# 1 John McGuane Ayer, MA & Margaret Attridge E Pepperell, MA
MCGUIGAN, Unknown, Oct 13 1910 Sex:F Child# 1 Terrance McGuigan Manchester, NH & Grace Weightman New York
MCGUIRE, Charles, Jun 7 1924 Sex:M Child# 2 Daniel McGuire S Boston, MA & Madeline Donlon Ayer, MA
MCGUIRE, John Andrew, Nov 17 1930 Sex:M Child# 1 John A McGuire, Jr Springfield, VT & Lucy Shea Nashua, NH
MCGUIRE, Lucy, Jun 6 1933 Sex:F Child# 3 John A McGuire Springfield, VT & Lucy Shea Nashua, NH
MCGUIRE, Mary Gloria, Jun 14 1931 Sex:F Child# 2 James McGuire Lancaster, NH & Alice Pelletier Nashua, NH
MCGUIRE, Robert, May 28 1935 Sex:M Child# 4 John A McGuire Springfield, VT & Lucy Shea Nashua, NH
MCGUIRE, Unknown, Jul 7 1892 Sex: Child# 1 John B McGuire Lowell, MA &  Ogdensburg, NY Stillborn
MCGUIRK, Francis Joseph, Feb 3 1901 Sex:M Child# 2 William McGuirk Lowell, MA & Mary Ann Sullivan Nashua, NH
MCGUIRK, William Patrick, Jul 3 1899 Sex:M Child# 1 William McGuirk Lowell, MA & Mary A Sullivan Nashua, NH
MCGURRAN, John Thomas, Mar 13 1892 Sex:M Child# 1 Andrew F McGurran Ireland & Bridget Moore Ireland
MCINNESS, Dorothy, Sep 23 1911 Sex:F Child# 5 Aubrey G McInness Russia & Pearl Green Russia
MCINNIS, Beatrice, Aug 21 1894 Sex:F Child# 6 Jacob McInnis Nova Scotia & Emma Moody Nova Scotia
MCINNIS, Effie M, Aug 31 1910 Sex:F Child# 3 Aubry G McInnis Nova Scotia & Pearl Green Kennebunk, ME Stillborn
MCINNIS, Minnie Viola, Dec 1 1908 Sex:F Child# 3 Aubry G McInnis Nova Scotia & Pearl E Greene Kennebunk, ME
MCINNIS, Shirley Arlene, Oct 6 1923 Sex:F Child# 3 James McInnis Prince Edw Island & Lizzie May Prince Edw Is
MCINTIRE, Joseph Franklin, Aug 27 1893 Sex:M Child# 3 David F McIntire Boston, MA & Kittie E Page Dunstable, MA
MCINTIRE, William Patrick, Aug 17 1896 Sex:M Child# 2 William McIntire Canada & Emma Grenier Canada
MCINTOSH, Alexander, Jun 4 1921 Sex:M Child# 4 William McIntosh Nashua, NH & Albina Cardin Canada
MCINTOSH, Anita Cecile, Jan 14 1915 Sex:F Child# 2 William McIntosh Nashua, NH & Albina Cardin Canada
MCINTOSH, Clarence Lewis, Aug 25 1917 Sex:M Child# 3 William McIntosh Nashua, NH & Albenia Cardin Canada
MCINTOSH, Guillaume, Nov 24 1889 Sex:M Child# 2 Louis McIntosh Canada & Georgina Marqus Maine
MCINTOSH, Lucile Rejane G, Jul 4 1912 Sex:F Child# 1 William McIntosh Nashua, NH & Albina Cardin Canada
MCINTOSH, Madeline Rita, Jul 15 1926 Sex:F Child# 6 William McIntosh Nashua, NH & Albina Cardin Canada
MCINTOSH, Pauline Ruth, Jun 8 1927 Sex:F Child# 2 George V McIntosh Nova Scotia & Ruth Lawrence Nashua, NH
MCINTOSH, Priscilla Fannie, Aug 19 1930 Sex:F Child# 3 George V McIntosh Nova Scotia & Ruth Lawrence Nashua, NH
MCINTOSH, Roy Lawrence, Feb 26 1921 Sex:M Child# 1 George V McIntosh Nova Scotia & Ruth Lawrence Nashua, NH
MCINTOSH, Unknown, Jan 19 1924 Sex:F Child#  William McIntosh Nashua, NH & Albina Cardin Canada Stillborn
MCINTYRE, Alma, May 13 1898 Sex:F Child# 3 William McIntyre Canada & Emma Lamare Canada
MCINTYRE, Joseph Henry, Sep 4 1901 Sex:M Child# 1 William McIntyre Nashua, NH & Alie Lussier Canada
MCINTYRE, Lilly, Mar 6 1895 Sex:F Child# 3 William McIntyre Norton Creek, Canada & Emma Lamoth St Phillips, Canada
MCINTYRE, Onaita Elaine, May 11 1929 Sex:F Child# 2 Jonathan D McIntyre Fairfield, VT & Velma Campbell Nashua, NH
MCINTYRE, Sylvia Bernice, Jan 16 1921 Sex:F Child# 1 Grover C McIntyre Dover, NH & Bernice Doying Nashua, NH
MCINTYRE, Thomas Solomon, Jul 27 1930 Sex:M Child# 4 William J McIntyre Canada & Yvonne Laforest Manchester, NH
MCKAY, Albert Thomas, Dec 18 1912 Sex:M Child# 3 Hamilton McKay New Brunswick,Canada & Mary A Daly Ireland
MCKAY, Cathel, Aug 16 1900 Sex:F Child#  O M McKay NS & Eliza Harris NS
MCKAY, Daniel, Dec 18 1896 Sex:M Child# 3 James D McKay Pembroke, ME & Elisabeth Ford Great Falls
MCKAY, David Alexander, Dec 23 1915 Sex:M Child# 4 Hamilton McKay Canada & Mary A Daly Ireland
MCKAY, Donald Erwin, May 4 1915 Sex:M Child# 1 Donald R McKay Nova Scotia & Angie F Niles Lynn, MA
MCKAY, Gerald Everett, Jan 18 1912 Sex:M Child# 1 Prince McGill McKay Nova Scotia & Celia M Clemons Ellenburg, NY
MCKAY, Gordon Bruce, Apr 28 1914 Sex:M Child# 2 Bruce M McKay Nova Scotia & Celia Climmons New York
MCKAY, Harold G, Oct 2 1904 Sex:M Child# 1 Thomas G McKay Shelburne, US & Cora J Dow Chelsea, MA
MCKAY, Jacqueline Lucille, Sep 22 1925 Sex:F Child# 1 Harold McKay Nashua, NH & Annaud Fraser Nashua, NH
MCKAY, James Cobham, Jr, May 7 1932 Sex:M Child# 1 James C McKay Boston, MA & Mary Swan Boston, MA
MCKAY, John Cameron, Apr 25 1900 Sex:M Child# 1 William J McKay Maine & Mary E Lucas Nashua, NH
MCKAY, Margaret Mary, Jul 12 1910 Sex:F Child# 1 Hamilton McKay New Brunswick & Mary A Daly Ireland
MCKAY, Mary Boyne, Sep 10 1902 Sex:F Child# 4 James D McKay Pembroke, ME & Elizabeth Ford Great Falls
MCKAY, May Florence, Apr 6 1930 Sex:F Child# 2 Harold McKay Nashua, NH & Armande Fraser Nashua, NH
MCKAY, Richard, Aug 18 1933 Sex:M Child# 2 Harold McKay Nashua, NH & Hermance Fraser Nashua, NH
MCKAY, Thomas Robert, Dec 6 1917 Sex:M Child# 3 P McGill McKay Shelburne, NS & Celia Clemons Ellenburg, NY
MCKAY, Unknown, Aug 13 1893 Sex:M Child# 2 Orin McKay Nova Scotia & Lizzie Harris Halifax, NS
MCKAY, Unknown, Jun 28 1895 Sex:M Child# 2 James D McKay Pembroke, ME & Lizzie Ford Great Falls
MCKAY, Unknown, Jun 16 1902 Sex:F Child# 2 William J McKay Pembroke, ME & Mary E DeLucas Nashua, NH
MCKAY, Unknown, Aug 27 1911 Sex:F Child# 2 Hamilton McKay New Brunswick & Mary A Daly Ireland
MCKAY, Walter Neil, Oct 12 1893 Sex:M Child# 1 James McKay Maine & Lizzie Lord Hillsboro, NH
MCKAY, William Lucas, Oct 1 1904 Sex:M Child# 3 William Joseph McKay Pembroke, ME & Eliza Lucas Nashua, NH
MCKEAN, Charles Perkins, Jun 25 1897 Sex:M Child# 3 Samuel P McKean Nashua, NH & Gertie Beaseley Rolla, VA
MCKEAN, James, Feb 13 1933 Sex:M Child# 2 James McKean Canada & Mary Whelton Nashua, NH
MCKEAN, Mary, Jun 19 1897 Sex:F Child# 3 Patrick McKean Ireland & Bridget Sullivan Ireland
MCKEAN, Norton, Jan 18 1891 Sex:M Child# 1 Albert J McKean Nashua, NH & Julia L Boston, MA
MCKENNA, Harold B, Mar 30 1908 Sex:M Child# 2 Frank McKenna Bethlehem, NH & Annie McKenna Livermore, NH
MCKENNA, Unknown, Mar 30 1908 Sex:F Child# 3 Frank McKenna Bethlehem, NH & Annie McKenna Livermore, NH Stillborn
MCKENNA, Unknown, Dec 23 1908 Sex:F Child# 1 Daniel F McKenna Mendon, MA & Mary E Justice Lawrence, MA
MCKENNEY, Henry, Oct 19 1928 Sex:M Child# 3 R B McKenney Pt Judith, RI & Teresa Cummings Nashua, NH
MCKEON, Elizabeth, May 8 1899 Sex:F Child# 4 Patrick McKeon Ireland & Bridget Sullivan Ireland
MCKEON, James, May 7 1894 Sex:M Child# 1 Patrick McKeon Ireland & Bridget Sullivan Ireland
MCKEON, Letitia, Dec 4 1895 Sex:F Child# 2 Patrick McKeon Ireland & Bridget Sullivan Ireland
MCKEON, Mary Louise, Sep 23 1931 Sex:F Child# 1 James KcKeon Nashua, NH & Mary Whelton Nashua, NH
MCKEOWN, Beverly, Aug 1 1931 Sex:F Child# 4 Fred D McKeown Attleboro, MA & Hazel M Maker Nashua, NH

MCKEOWN, Earle Wayne, Feb 16 1929 Sex:M Child# 3 Fred D McKeown Attleboro, MA & Hazel M Maker Nashua, NH
MCKEOWN, Fred D, Nov 23 1925 Sex:M Child# 1 Fred McKeown Middleboro, MA & Hazel Maker Moira, NY
MCKEOWN, Kenneth Lloyd, Apr 27 1927 Sex:M Child# 2 Fred McKeown Middleboro, MA & Hazel Maker Nashua, NH
MCKEOWN, Richard Loren, Oct 24 1932 Sex:M Child# 4 Fred McKeown Middleboro, MA & Hazel Maker Nashua, NH
MCKINLEY, Alice Laura, Mar 20 1934 Sex:F Child# 7 Ralph McKinley Caribou, ME & Grace Mae Burleigh Sanbornton, NH
MCKINLEY, Catherine Elizabeth, Apr 30 1927 Sex:F Child# 4 Ralph McKinley Maine & Grace Burleigh NH
MCKINLEY, Isabel Eliza, Feb 28 1925 Sex:F Child# 3 Ralph McKinley Caribou, ME & Grace Bevley Sanbornton, NH
MCKINLEY, John Edward, Apr 29 1932 Sex:M Child# 6 Ralph McKinley Maine & Grace Sanbern NH
MCKINLEY, Mary Goodhue, Aug 1 1933 Sex:F Child# 2 William McKinley
MCKINLEY, Merrill, Aug 23 1923 Sex:M Child# 3 Merrill McKinley Mooers, NY & Bessie Bell Chazy, NY
MCKINLEY, Unknown, Sep 17 1898 Sex:F Child# 2 Alonzo L McKinley Nova Scotia & Rose E Moulton Nashua, NH
MCKINLEY, Unknown, Jul 6 1900 Sex:M Child# 3 Alonzo L McKinley NS & Rose Moulton Nashua, NH
MCKINLEY, Unknown, Mar 22 1902 Sex:F Child# 4 Alonzo L McKinley Nova Scotia & Rose Moulton Nashua, NH
MCKINLEY, William Chester, Sep 19 1896 Sex:M Child# 1 Alonzo L McKinley Nova Scotia & Rose E Moulton Nashua, NH
MCKNIGHT, Robert Ernest, Aug 7 1930 Sex:M Child# 1 Freeman McKnight New Brunswick & Alice Bilodeau Canada
MCKNZIE, Sis, Jul 4 1903 Sex:F Child# 1 Donald McKnzie Canada & Bertha Woodward Francestown, NH
MCLAREN, Unknown, Apr 25 1920 Sex:F Child# 1 Samuel A McLaren Hampstead, NH & Ethel M Hill York, ME Stillborn
MCLARIN, Unknown, Aug 31 1888 Sex:M Child# 3 Frederic A McLarin Havelden, NY & Adaline Prouse Havelden, NY
MCLAUGHLIN, Bernard Philip, Jul 19 1899 Sex:M Child# 2 Bernard McLaughlin Ireland & Mary Gaffney Ireland
MCLAUGHLIN, Bernard Robert, Sep 14 1929 Sex:M Child# 1 Bernard McLaughlin Nashua, NH & Jennie McAdoo Nashua, NH
MCLAUGHLIN, Bernice Julia, May 15 1908 Sex:F Child# 3 Thomas McLaughlin Nashua, NH & Libbie Bolia Mooer's Fork, NY
MCLAUGHLIN, Catherine, Oct 23 1888 Sex:F Child# 1 Michael McLaughlin Ireland & Johanna Clancy Ireland
MCLAUGHLIN, Catherine Ann, May 24 1927 Sex:F Child# 7 P J McLaughlin Scotland & Lillian M Driscoll Nova Scotia
MCLAUGHLIN, Christopher D, Dec 20 1892 Sex:M Child# 1 Daniel McLaughlin Ireland & Minnie Whalen Ireland
MCLAUGHLIN, Edna Catherine, Sep 5 1926 Sex:F Child# 3 W McLaughlin Nashua, NH & Annie McNamara Fair Haven, VT
MCLAUGHLIN, Elenore, Apr 13 1904 Sex:F Child# 4 Philip McLaughlin Scotland & Delia J Moran Nashua, NH
MCLAUGHLIN, Frances Elizabeth, Apr 13 1904 Sex:F Child# 1 Thomas McLaughlin Nashua, NH & Libbie Bolia Moore's, NY
MCLAUGHLIN, Francis, Mar 26 1921 Sex:M Child# 4 Pat J McLaughlin Edenburgh, Scotland & Lillian M Driscoll NS
MCLAUGHLIN, John, Apr 29 1916 Sex:M Child# 1 Pat J McLaughlin Scotland & Lillian M Driscoll Nova Scotia
MCLAUGHLIN, Kenneth Francis, Sep 3 1928 Sex:M Child# 2 J W McLaughlin Nashua, NH & Alice G Martin Boston, MA
MCLAUGHLIN, Margaret Ann, May 26 1928 Sex:F Child# 4 W McLaughlin Nashua, NH & A McNamara Fairhaven, VT
MCLAUGHLIN, Margaret Hazel, Jan 18 1900 Sex:F Child# 2 Philip McLaughlin Scotland & Delia G Moran Nashua, NH
MCLAUGHLIN, Mary, Sep 15 1924 Sex:F Child# 2 W McLaughlin Nashua, NH & Anna McNamara Fairhaven, VT
MCLAUGHLIN, Mary Elizabeth, Apr 16 1894 Sex:F Child# 2 Daniel McLaughlin Ireland & Mary Whalen Ireland
MCLAUGHLIN, Mildred Mary, Oct 8 1905 Sex:F Child# 2 Thomas P McLaughlin Nashua, NH & Libbie Bolia Moore's, NY
MCLAUGHLIN, Octave Leo, Sep 21 1904 Sex:M Child# 3 John McLaughlin Canada & Eliza Dionne Canada
MCLAUGHLIN, Patricia Anne, Sep 29 1931 Sex:F Child# 2 Bernard McLaughlin Nashua, NH & Jennie M McAdoo Nashua, NH
MCLAUGHLIN, Patrick James, May 6 1923 Sex:M Child# 5 Patrick J McLaughlin Scotland & Lillian M Driscoll NS
MCLAUGHLIN, Paul, Jan 24 1919 Sex:M Child# 3 Pat J McLaughlin Scotland & Lillian M Driscoll Nova Scotia
MCLAUGHLIN, Paul Augustus, Jun 5 1922 Sex:M Child# 1 Christ McLaughlin Nashua, NH & Winnifred Cushing Concord, NH
MCLAUGHLIN, Philip, May 1 1890 Sex:M Child# 5 Patrick McLaughlin Ireland & Margaret Early Ireland
MCLAUGHLIN, Philip, Aug 23 1898 Sex:M Child# 1 Philip McLaughlin Edinboro, Scotland & Delia Moran Nashua, NH
MCLAUGHLIN, Philip, Nov 2 1917 Sex:M Child# 2 Patrick J McLaughlin Scotland & Lillian M Driscoll Nova Scotia
MCLAUGHLIN, Philip Joseph, Nov 26 1912 Sex:M Child# 5 Thomas P McLaughlin Nashua, NH & Libbie Bolice Mooers, NY
MCLAUGHLIN, Richard, Sep 7 1930 Sex:M Child# 5 Walter P McLaughlin Nashua, NH & Annie E McNamara Fairhaven, VT
MCLAUGHLIN, Robert, Mar 13 1906 Sex:M Child# 5 Philip H McLaughlin Scotland & Delia G Moran Nashua, NH
MCLAUGHLIN, Robert Martin, Apr 19 1934 Sex:M Child# 3 John Wm McLaughlin Nashua, NH & Alice G Martin W Roxbury, MA
MCLAUGHLIN, Thelma May, Sep 13 1904 Sex:F Child# 1 James McLaughlin Maynard, MA & Lucy Mansur Groton, MA
MCLAUGHLIN, Thomas, Dec 15 1892 Sex:M Child# 5 Thomas McLaughlin Ireland & Winifred Murray Ireland
MCLAUGHLIN, Unknown, Jan 17 1888 Sex: Child# 9 John McLaughlin Ireland & Ann Fallon Ireland Stillborn
MCLAUGHLIN, Unknown, Feb 8 1893 Sex:M Child# Patrick McLaughlin Ireland & Maggie Earley Ireland Stillborn
MCLAUGHLIN, Unknown, Jun 23 1899 Sex:M Child# 4 Daniel McLaughlin Ireland & Minnie Whalen Ireland Stillborn
MCLAUGHLIN, Walter, May 16 1894 Sex:M Child# 7 Patrick McLaughlin Ireland & Maggie Earley Ireland
MCLAUGHLIN, Walter, Aug 26 1922 Sex:M Child# 1 W P McLaughlin Nashua, NH & Ann McNamara Fair Haven, VT
MCLAUGHLIN, Winnefrid A, Oct 19 1902 Sex:F Child# 3 P McLaughlin Scotland & Delia Moran Nashua, NH
MCLAVEN, Unknown, Oct 30 1891 Sex:M Child# 4 Fred A McLaven Halviden, NY & Adaline Prouse Halviden, NY
MCLAVEY, Elmer Robert, Dec 5 1909 Sex:M Child# 1 John J McLavey Boston, MA & Cora M Goodwin N Pelham, NH
MCLAVEY, Geraldine Harriette, Aug 1 1931 Sex:F Child# 1 Edward McLavey Nashua, NH & Cora Jelley Nashua, NH
MCLAVEY, Virginia Louise, Apr 25 1933 Sex:F Child# 2 Ed McLavey US & Cora Jelly US
MCLEAN, Beverly Jeanne, May 28 1928 Sex:F Child# 1 Ernest L McLean Hardwick, VT & Lillian O'Neill Taunton, MA
MCLEAN, Robert, Nov 12 1932 Sex:M Child# 3 Ernest McLean Hardwick, VT & Lillian O'Neil Taunton, MA
MCLEE, Earl Leroy, Aug 15 1914 Sex:M Child# 1 James McLee Brookline, NH & Bernice M Myhaven Concord, NH
MCLELLAN, Donald Edward, Feb 19 1931 Sex:M Child# 1 Walter McLellan Boston, MA & Ruth Bradley Nashua, NH
MCLEOD, Arthur, Jul 8 1928 Sex:M Child# 4 Daniel McLeod Canada & F L Wright Canada
MCLEOD, Barbara, May 26 1916 Sex:F Child# 1 Arthur McLeod
MCLEOD, Bevery Grace, May 20 1922 Sex:F Child# 2 Nelson A McLeod Hollis, NH & Anna G Potter Rochester, NH
MCLEOD, Kenneth, Oct 28 1923 Sex:M Child# 4 Malcolm McLeod Prince Edw Island & Lillian Jones Boston, MA
MCLEOD, Kenneth A, Jun 17 1901 Sex:M Child# 1 Alexander McLeod Prince Edw Is & Marguerite McDonald Prince Edw Is
MCLEOD, Shirley May, Sep 19 1928 Sex:F Child# 5 Malcolm McLeod Prince Edw Island & Lillian Jones Charlestown, MA
MCLEOD, Wilbur Douglas, Jul 13 1931 Sex:M Child# 6 Malcolm McLeod Pr Edw Island & Lillian Jones Boston, MA
MCLINE, Marion Elizabeth, Sep 26 1920 Sex:F Child# 1 William F McLine London, England & M Elizabeth Jellerso
MCLOUD, Harold James, May 31 1926 Sex:M Child# 1 Harold McLoud Hollis, NH & Laura Fortin Nashua, NH
MCLOUD, Loraine Dorothy, Sep 11 1920 Sex:F Child# 2 Nelson A McLoud Hollis, NH & Anna G Potter Rochester, NH

MCLOUD, Roland Earl, May 16 1930 Sex:M Child# 2 Harold McLoud Hollis, NH & Laura Fortin Nashua, NH
MCLOUD, Shirley Elizabeth, Sep 10 1923 Sex:F Child# 4 Nelson A McLoud Hollis, NH & Anna G Potter Rochester, NH
MCLOUGHLIN, Catherine, Dec 29 1889 Sex:F Child# 4 T McLoughlin Ireland & Winnifred Ireland
MCLUCAS, John, Aug 16 1888 Sex:M Child# 3 Jacob McLucas N S & Emma M N S
MCMAHAR, Martin Frances, Nov 11 1898 Sex:M Child#  Martin McMahar Ireland & Bridget Neville Ireland
MCMAHON, Agnes Louise, Jan 3 1933 Sex:F Child# 4 Aug McMahon Nashua, NH & Helen McPeake Norwalk, CT
MCMAHON, Annie Agnes, Oct 4 1907 Sex:F Child# 1 (No Parents Listed)
MCMAHON, Augustus, Jun 27 1897 Sex:M Child# 8 John McMahon Ireland & Mary Murphy Ireland
MCMAHON, Barbara Elaine, Apr 22 1929 Sex:F Child# 1 John McMahon Nashua, NH & Edna Ratte Nashua, NH
MCMAHON, Christina, Nov 23 1900 Sex:F Child# 10 John McMahon Ireland & Mary Murphy Ireland
MCMAHON, Harry, Jan 12 1895 Sex:M Child# 6 John J McMahon Ireland & Mary Murphy Ireland
MCMAHON, John Augustus, Apr 13 1928 Sex:M Child# 1 Aug McMahon Nashua, NH & Helen McPeake Conn
MCMAHON, John Christopher, Dec 15 1896 Sex:M Child# 4 Martin McMahon Ireland & Bridget Mulqueen Ireland
MCMAHON, John Joseph, Jul 6 1893 Sex:M Child# 5 John J McMahon Ireland & Mary Murphy Ireland
MCMAHON, Julia anne, Apr 21 1931 Sex:F Child# 3 Augustus McMahon Nashua, NH & Helen McPeake Norwalk, CT
MCMAHON, Lucille Bertha, Sep 9 1925 Sex:F Child# 3 Martin McMahon Nashua, NH & Mary A Harvey Nashua, NH
MCMAHON, Mary, Apr 26 1922 Sex:F Child# 2 Martin McMahon Nashua, NH & Mary Harvey Nashua, NH
MCMAHON, Norman Martin, Dec 4 1919 Sex:M Child# 1 Martin F McMahon Nashua, NH & Mary H Harvey Nashua, NH
MCMAHON, Sarah Delia, Nov 22 1899 Sex:F Child# 9 John McMahon Ireland & Mary Murphy Ireland
MCMAHON, Unknown, Apr 9 1928 Sex:F Child# 4 Martin McMahon Nashua, NH & Mary Harvey Nashua, NH
MCMAHON, William Joseph, Aug 11 1929 Sex:M Child# 2 Augustus McMahon Nashua, NH & Helen McPeake S Norwalk, CT
MCMANN, Arthur, Apr 15 1896 Sex:M Child# 7 John McMann Ireland & Mary Murphy Ireland
MCMANN, Janet Norton, Jan 26 1931 Sex:F Child#  Edward N McMann Wakefield, MA & Mary F Connily Newfoundland
MCMASTER, Geneice, Aug 28 1899 Sex:F Child# 2 Frank McMaster Nashua, NH & Hattie E Armington Ludlow, VT
MCMASTER, Lucile, Jun 12 1895 Sex:F Child# 1 Frank A McMaster Nashua, NH & Hattie Armington Vermont
MCMERNY, John Dixon, Mar 19 1933 Sex:M Child# 1 John D McMerny Ayer, MA & Catherine O'Neil Gardner, MA
MCMILLIAN, Bruce S, Dec 25 1895 Sex:M Child# 2 Allan McMillian Nova Scotia & Mathilda Perry Nova Scotia
MCMURRAY, Harold Joseph, Jun 12 1925 Sex:M Child# 3 Homer McMurray Canada & Mary Galvin Fall River, MA
MCMURRAY, Robert, Feb 4 1928 Sex:M Child# 4 Homer McMurray Fall River, MA & Mary Galvin Fall River, MA
MCNABB, Frances Katherine, Aug 12 1905 Sex:F Child# 1 Frank J McNabb Lowell, MA & Ann E Barry Nashua, NH
MCNABB, John Joseph, Jul 16 1911 Sex:M Child# 6 Francis J McNabb Lowell, MA & Annie Barry Nashua, NH
MCNABB, Susan Irene, Feb 22 1914 Sex:F Child# 7 Frank J McNabb Lowell, MA & Amy Barry Nashua, NH
MCNABB, William Henry, Jun 14 1906 Sex:M Child# 2 Frank G McNabb Lowell, MA & Annie E Barry Nashua, NH
MCNALLY, Edward Harold, Apr 7 1931 Sex:M Child# 1 John E McNally New York & Lorraine Dufour Nashua, NH
MCNAMARA, Francis Joseph, Jan 1 1897 Sex:M Child# 2 Michael McNamara Ireland & Mary Gralton Ireland
MCNAMARA, Ida Ellen, Nov 9 1898 Sex:F Child# 3 Michael McNamara Ireland & Mary Gralton Ireland
MCNAMARA, Mary, Jul 3 1901 Sex:F Child# 4 Michael McNamara Ireland & Mary Gralton Ireland
MCNAMARA, Mary Lilian, Jul 9 1895 Sex:F Child# 1 Michael McNamara Ireland & Mary Gralton Ireland
MCNEILL, Irene, Aug 18 1902 Sex:F Child# 3 Ed L McNeill New York, NY & Gertrude A McWhorter Buffalo, NY
MCNERNY, Neil Thomas, May 16 1935 Sex:M Child# 2 John McNerny Ayer, MA & Katherine O'Neil Gardner, MA
MCNIFF, Elizabeth Ann, Apr 18 1933 Sex:F Child# 1 Henry McNiff Harvard, MA & M McLaughlin Nashua, NH
MCNIFF, Henry Francis II, Jan 19 1935 Sex:M Child# 2 Henry McNiff Harvard, MA & Marg McLaughlin Nashua, NH
MCNIFF, William, Mar 31 1889 Sex:M Child# 5 Peter McNiff Ireland & Maria Henry Ireland
MCNIFT, Patrick, Mar 11 1888 Sex:M Child# 3 Patrick McNift Ireland & Maria Henry Ireland
MCNULTY, Robert Edward, Apr 21 1923 Sex:M Child# 5 Harold McNulty Concord, NH & Helen A McGee Lancaster, MA
MCNULTY, Virginia Theresa, Sep 21 1927 Sex:F Child# 6 Harold McNulty Concord, NH & Helen McGee Lancaster, MA
MCPARTLAN, James Leo, Jan 18 1931 Sex:M Child# 2 Hugh McPartlan Scotland & Katherine Marshall Pepperell, MA
MCPARTLAN, Richard Norris, Aug 2 1932 Sex:M Child# 3 Hugh McPartlan Scotland & K Marshall Pepperell, MA
MCPARTLAN, Robert Francis, Jun 22 1935 Sex:M Child# 4 Hugh McPartlan Scotland & Cath Marshall Pepperell, MA
MCPARTLAND, Agnes Louise, Dec 11 1900 Sex:F Child# 4 Pat McPartland Ireland & Mary Winn Ireland
MCPARTLAND, Helen, Jun 29 1898 Sex:F Child# 3 Patrick McPartland Ireland & Mary Winn Ireland
MCPARTLAND, Katherine Ann, Jul 4 1896 Sex:F Child# 2 Patrick McPartland Ireland & Mary Winn Ireland
MCPARTLAND, Philip, Dec 25 1929 Sex:M Child# 1 Hugh McPartland Scotland & Katherine Marshall Groton, MA
MCPHAIL, Beillia Andery, Sep 8 1915 Sex:F Child# 3 Alexander McPhail Prince Edward Island & Isabella Andrey PEI
MCPHAIL, Leonard Ougilvy, Sep 23 1916 Sex:M Child# 5 Alexander McPhail Prince Edw Is & Isabel Andrey Prince Edw Is
MCPHEE, Ralph Marston, Dec 2 1920 Sex:M Child# 2 John McPhee Canada & Marie Raymond Canada
MCPHERSON, James, Jan 14 1893 Sex:M Child# 1 James McPherson Boston, MA & Lydia Quimby Boston, MA
MCQUADE, Bernard, Jun 19 1917 Sex:M Child# 2 John J McQuade Nashua, NH & Eva Bouley Middlebury, VT
MCQUADE, Helen, Apr 10 1921 Sex:F Child# 3 John J McQuade Nashua, NH & Eva Boulia Middlebury, VT
MCQUADE, John Joseph, Jan 27 1911 Sex:M Child# 1 John J McQuade Nashua, NH & Eva Bouley Middlebury, VT
MCQUESTEN, Barbara Nilda, Jul 10 1914 Sex:F Child# 2 Everett McQuesten Litchfield, NH & Anna W Holden Nashua, NH
MCQUESTEN, Bernice Scott, Dec 28 1909 Sex:F Child# 1 Everett S McQuesten Litchfield, NH & Anna H Holden Nashua, NH
MCQUESTEN, Eugene F, Jr, Apr 21 1892 Sex:M Child# 3 Eugene F McQuesten Litchfield, NH & Anna E Spalding Lawrence,MA
MCQUESTEN, Eugene Forest, Jul 25 1925 Sex:M Child# 1 Eugene McQuesten Nashua, NH & Marjorie Hunt Nashua, NH
MCQUESTEN, Josephine, Feb 7 1890 Sex:F Child# 2 Eugene F McQuesten Litchfield, NH & Anna Spalding Lawrence, MA
MCQUESTEN, Philip, Dec 27 1888 Sex:M Child# 1 Eugene F McQuesten Litchfield & Annie Spalding Lawrence, MA
MCQUESTEN, Ralph Luke, Oct 27 1893 Sex:M Child# 1 George B McQuesten Nashua, NH & Mabel Fiske Nashua, NH
MCQUESTEN, Ruth, Sep 3 1919 Sex:F Child# 3 Eu F McQuesten Litchfield, NH & Anna N Holden Nashua, NH
MCQUESTEN, Unknown, Feb 9 1892 Sex:M Child# 1 Francis H McQuesten Litchfield, NH & Catherine Frye Concord, NH
MCQUESTEN, Unknown, Dec 11 1896 Sex:M Child# 2 George B McQuesten Nashua, NH & Mabel J Fiske Nashua, NH
MCQUESTEN, Virginia, Jul 9 1927 Sex:F Child# 2 Eugene F McQuesten Nashua, NH & Marjorie R Hunt Nashua, NH
MCQUESTIN, Beverly Agnes, Jul 10 1935 Sex:F Child# 1 Fred McQuestin Litchfield, NH & Ena Denton Redford, NY
MCQUIRE, Augustus Shea, Jan 18 1932 Sex:M Child# 2 J A McQuire, Jr Springfield, VT & Lucy Shea Nashua, NH

MCRAY, Maurice M, Nov 12 1891 Sex:M Child# 1 Thoms McRay Nova Scotia & Elizabeth Harris Nova Scotia
MCSERLEY, Perley Earl, Jun 18 1898 Sex:M Child# Charles McSerley New Brunswick & Sarah Matotte Altona, NY
MCSHERRY, Fred, Apr 2 1898 Sex:M Child# 6 Frank McSherry Nashua, NH & Mary Carey Nashua, NH
MCSHERRY, Grace Mary, Feb 23 1889 Sex:F Child# 2 Frank McSherry Nashua, NH & Mary L Carry Nashua, NH
MCSHERRY, Nellie, Jul 27 1887 Sex:F Child# 1 Frank McSherry Nashua, NH & Mary L Carey Nashua, NH
MCSORLEY, Charles Boyd, Feb 20 1927 Sex:M Child# 2 Ernest McSorley Nashua, NH & Edna Boyd Boston, MA
MCSORLEY, Geraldine Janis, Dec 11 1924 Sex:F Child# 1 Ernest McSorley Nashua, NH & Edna Boyd Boston, MA
MCSORLEY, Royal R, Feb 10 1902 Sex:M Child# 5 Charles McSorley Maine & Sarah Matott New York
MCSWEENEY, Unknown, May 20 1920 Sex:M Child# 2 Bartho McSweeney Worcester, MA & Ella St Clair Stodda Nova Scotia
MCTIGHE, Paul, Feb 7 1906 Sex:M Child# 2 John T McTighe Boston, MA & Sarah E Flood Nashua, NH
MCTIGHE, Roger, Nov 12 1904 Sex:M Child# 1 John T McTighe Cambridge, MA & Sadie E Flood Nashua, NH
MCVEIGH, Clara, Jul 23 1913 Sex:F Child# 1 Thomas H McVeigh Nashua, NH & Jennie Gaffney Nashua, NH
MCVEIGH, Kate Josephine, Dec 23 1893 Sex:F Child# 2 John J McVeigh Ireland & Kate J Kelley Worcester, MA
MCVEIGH, Thomas Henry, Nov 22 1892 Sex:M Child# John McVeigh Ireland & Kate J Kelley Worcester, MA
MCVEIGH, Unknown, Mar 11 1915 Sex:F Child# 2 Thomas McVeigh Nashua, NH & Jennie Gaffney Nashua, NH Stillborn
MCWEENEY, Alice Frances, Dec 26 1907 Sex:F Child# 3 James McWeeney Nashua, NH & Nellie G McCarthy Burlington, MA
MCWEENEY, Annie, Jul 29 1899 Sex:F Child# 1 James McWeeney Nashua, NH & Nellie McCarthy Vermont
MCWEENEY, Charles John, Mar 3 1899 Sex:M Child# 1 Charles McWeeney Nashua, NH & Nellie Buckley Halifax, NS
MCWEENEY, James Douglass, Mar 1 1901 Sex:M Child# 2 James McWeeney Nashua, NH & Nellie McCarthy Burlington, MA
MCWEENEY, Loraine Blanch, Aug 9 1917 Sex:F Child# 2 Henry McWeeney Nashua, NH & Lea Francoeur Canada
MCWEENEY, Richard E M, Jan 8 1901 Sex:M Child# 2 Charles J McWeeney Nashua, NH & Nellie G Buckley Halifax, NS
MCWHA, Unknown, Dec 2 1895 Sex:M Child# 1 Harry E McWha St Stephen, NB & Helen (Adams) Gale Nashua, NH
MCWHA, Unknown, May 25 1897 Sex:F Child# 2 Harry E McWha St Stephens, NB & Helen M Adams Nashua, NH
MCWHA, Unknown, Nov 28 1898 Sex:F Child# 3 Harry E McWha St Stephens, NB & Helen M Adams Nashua, NH
MCWILLIAM, Donald, Aug 18 1890 Sex:M Child# 1 Allan McWilliam Nova Scotia & Mathilda Perry Nova Scotia
MEAD, Florence, Mar 31 1904 Sex:F Child# 8 Charles H Mead Plattsburg, NY & Etta C Marvin Plattsburg, NY
MEAD, Raymond F, Jul 7 1908 Sex:M Child# 1 Charles F Mead Nashua, NH & Sadie H Mead Hollis, NH
MEANEY, Arlene, Nov 1 1898 Sex:F Child# 1 John Meaney Ayer, MA & Anna Curran Nashua, NH
MEANEY, Louise, Dec 21 1901 Sex:F Child# 2 John E Meaney Ayer, MA & Anna Curran Nashua, NH
MEANY, Francis, Oct 2 1890 Sex:M Child# 6 Edward P Meany Ireland & Mary Hain Ireland
MEARS, Barbara Marie, Dec 11 1928 Sex:F Child# 4 Charles A Mears Hamilton, MA & Catherine Dolan Boston, MA
MEARS, Betty Ann, Jul 8 1931 Sex:F Child# 3 Herbert G Mears Hamilton, MA & Blanche Clifford Reeds Ferry, NH
MEARS, Catherine Phyllis, Oct 31 1920 Sex:F Child# 2 Charles A Mears Hamilton, MA & Catherine Dolan Boston, MA
MEARS, Elsie Frances, Jul 27 1918 Sex:F Child# 1 Charles A Mears Hamilton, MA & Catherine F Dolan Boston, MA
MEARS, Lillian Gray, Dec 29 1929 Sex:F Child# 2 Herbert Mears Hamilton, MA & Blanche Clifford Manchester, NH
MEARS, Loraine Etta, Jul 13 1933 Sex:F Child# 4 Herbert G Mears Hamilton, MA & Blanche Clifford Reeds Ferry, NH
MEARS, Pauline Florence, Nov 29 1927 Sex:F Child# 1 Herbert Mears Hamilton, MA & Blanche Clifford Reeds Ferry, NH
MEARS, Pauline Lucille, Sep 18 1923 Sex:F Child# 3 Charles Mears Hamilton, MA & Catherine Dolan Boston, MA
MEDELL, Anna Sophia, Sep 13 1910 Sex:F Child# 1 John Medell Lowell, MA & Bertha Lundgren Sweden
MEEBAU, Marie E, Jul 11 1891 Sex:F Child# 1 Joseph Meebau Ireland & Annie Donnahue Ireland
MEEBAU, William P, Jul 11 1891 Sex:M Child# 2 Joseph Meebau Ireland & Annie Donnahue Ireland
MEEHAN, Arlene Frances, Jun 14 1913 Sex:F Child# 2 H R Meehan Malone, NY & Nellie M Russell Manchester, NH
MEEHAN, Jeannette E, May 15 1911 Sex:F Child# 1 Herbert R Meehan Marlow, NH & Nellie M Russell Manchester, NH
MEEHAN, Teresa Mary, Jul 14 1922 Sex:F Child# 1 William Meehan Ireland & Alice Carrick NH
MEEHAN, Thomas Joseph, Sep 20 1925 Sex:M Child# 2 William Meehan Ireland & Alice Carrick Nashua, NH
MEHA, Unknown, Jan 30 1920 Sex:M Child# 3 Nicolovs Meha Greece & Lucia C Hatze Greece
MEINCKE, Nellie M, Aug 2 1892 Sex:F Child# 1 A M Meincke Brooklyn, NY & Blanche D Towne Somerville, MA
MEINCKE, Unknown, Feb 11 1894 Sex:M Child# 2 A M Meincke Brooklyn, NY & Blanche D Towne Somverville, MA
MEISTER, Unknown, May 13 1890 Sex:M Child# 2 William H Meister Nashua, NH & Minnie Fink Germany
MELAND, Joseph Alphonse, Sep 17 1911 Sex:M Child# 7 Louis Meland Canada & Marie Meunier Canada
MELAND, Marie Blanche Yvonne, Mar 4 1912 Sex:F Child# 5 Amede Meland Canada & Marianne Levesque Canada
MELANOVITCH, Victoria, Oct 4 1916 Sex:F Child# 4 Andrew Melanovitch Russia & Vinzula Zaryaukoska Russia
MELDUK, Victor, Sep 18 1917 Sex:M Child# 1 Mopolit Melduk Russia & Alice Koralska Russia
MELDZIAK, Francis, Dec 31 1918 Sex:M Child# 2 Napoleon Meldziak Russia & Heldia Koralska Russia
MELEA, Meaky, Nov 5 1908 Sex:M Child# 4 Andre Melea Austria & Eva Gourka Austria
MELENDY, Dorothy Ella, Feb 18 1918 Sex:F Child# 1 Fred E Melendy Nashua, NH & Lena A Kelley Conway, NH
MELENDY, Ella J, Jul 31 1891 Sex:F Child# 1 Albert C Melendy Nashua, NH & Cora M Smith Manchester, NH
MELENDY, George Lloyd, Apr 27 1918 Sex:M Child# 2 George E Melendy Melrose, MA & Katherine Smith Milford, NH
MELENDY, Janice Harriet, Sep 25 1925 Sex:F Child# 5 Fred E Melendy Nashua, NH & Lena Kelley Conway, NH
MELENDY, Kenneth Walter, Apr 16 1923 Sex:M Child# 4 Fred E Melendy Nashua, NH & Lena Kelley Nashua, NH
MELENDY, Leona Frances, Jul 24 1935 Sex:F Child# 1 Ernest Melendy Pepperell, MA & Yetive Pennimon Athol, MA
MELENDY, Pauline, Jul 14 1920 Sex:F Child# 2 George E Melendy Melrose, MA & Katherine Smith Milford, NH
MELENDY, Richard Albert, Dec 21 1918 Sex:M Child# 3 Fred C Melendy Nashua, NH & Lena A Kelley Conway, NH
MELENDY, Robert Arthur, Dec 21 1918 Sex:M Child# 2 Fred C Melendy Nashua, NH & Lena A Kelley Conway, NH
MELENDY, Unknown, Aug 30 1912 Sex:M Child# 1 Harlaw Melendy Wilton, NH & Susan Greene Sudbury, MA Stillborn
MELENSKI, Agnes, Jan 10 1902 Sex:F Child# 3 John Melenski Russia & Elizabeth Lebosfka Russia
MELLEN, Lena, Mar 29 1908 Sex:F Child# 3 John J Mellen Nashua, NH & Mary O'Connell Ireland
MELLEN, Lillian Julia, Jan 14 1914 Sex:F Child# 4 William Mellen Hudson, NH & Lillee Jones Nashua, NH
MELLEN, Mary, Dec 29 1909 Sex:F Child# 4 John Mellen Nashua, NH & Mary O'Connor Ireland
MELLEN, Ralph Fred, Jr, Mar 16 1926 Sex:M Child# 1 Ralph F Mellen Washington, NH & Lillian Hand Cambridge, MA
MELLEN, Teresa Mary, Aug 22 1909 Sex:F Child# 2 James Mellen Nahma, MI & Eva M Trombly Saratoga, NY
MELLEN, Unknown, Sep 5 1890 Sex:M Child# 4 Frank P Mellen Manchester, NH & Sarah A Clark Clarenceville, PQ
MELLIN, Dorothy Lucile, Jun 29 1913 Sex:F Child# 5 John J Mellin Nashua, NH & Mary O'Connor Ireland

MELLIS, Mary Millis, Dec 9 1905 Sex:F Child# 3 Joseph Mellis Russia & Mary Tenorewicz Austria
MELLON, Keith Hutton, Aug 19 1907 Sex:M Child# 1 James Mellon Wisconsin & Eva M Trombly Saratoga, NY
MELLON, Unknown, Aug 21 1912 Sex:F Child# 3 James Mellon Nahma, MI & Eva May Trombley Saratoga, NY
MELNECKY, Mecheslaw, Sep 28 1917 Sex:M Child# 1 Mech Melnecky Russia & Blanche Eikman Russia
MELOCHE, Isidore Olivier, Nov 2 1903 Sex:M Child# 1 Isidore Meloche Canada & Marie Migneault Canada
MELOCHE, Joseph Alfred A, Oct 17 1908 Sex:M Child# 2 Isidore Meloche Canada & Marie Mignault Canada
MELOCHE, Joseph Marcel, Oct 17 1908 Sex:M Child# 3 Isidore Meloche Canada & Marie Mignault Canada
MELOICH, Nellie, Jan 23 1918 Sex:F Child# 2 Frank Meloich Russia & Annie Escuti Russia
MELOS, Annie, Apr 15 1908 Sex:F Child# 4 Joe Melos Austria & Mary Tenorowics Austria
MELOSH, Josie, Jun 19 1921 Sex:M Child# 3 Joseph Melosh Poland & Amelia Walukwicz Poland
MELOWITCH, Stanley, Feb 12 1930 Sex:M Child# 7 Alexander Melowitch Poland &  Poland
MELVIN, Albert Starbird, Feb 4 1919 Sex:M Child# 2 Albert Melvin Lewiston, ME & Pauline Porter Nashua, NH
MELVIN, Alton Kenneth, Sep 17 1925 Sex:M Child# 7 Elmer C Melvin Manchester, NH & Dora Elliott Mason, NH
MELVIN, Ellsworth Barnett, May 27 1912 Sex:M Child# 1 Tolford D Melvin Hudson, NH & Sarah Maud Porter Nashua, NH
MELVIN, Mary M, May 11 1892 Sex:F Child# 4 George Melvin NY
MELVIN, Ruth Adel, Feb 10 1915 Sex:F Child# 3 (No Parents Listed)
MELVIN, Toeford J, Apr 9 1896 Sex:M Child# 1 Tolford D Melvin Hudson, NH & Mary E Fairbanks Nashua, NH
MELVIN, Unknown, Jun 25 1888 Sex:F Child# 4 Frank Melvin Merrimack & Mary Melvin Merrimack
MELVIN, Unknown, Aug 4 1890 Sex:M Child# 1 William R Melvin Hudson, NH & Nancy E Averill Portland, ME
MELVIN, Unknown, Sep 21 1922 Sex:M Child# 6 Albert Melvin Lunston, ME & Pauline Potter Nashua, NH Stillborn
MEMOS, Traiari, Jul 16 1911 Sex:M Child# 4 Demetrius Memos Greece & Vanitia Miga Greece
MEMOS, Unknown, Oct 24 1919 Sex:F Child# 10 Demetrios Memos Greece & Vantia Miza Greece
MEMOS, Unknown, Dec 24 1919 Sex:M Child# 1 Stergios Memos Greece & Leona Beltsios Greece Stillborn
MEMOS, Unknown, Oct 28 1932 Sex:M Child# 1 Peter Memos Greece & Alice Chamberlain Nashua, NH
MEMOS, Unknown, Oct 15 1934 Sex:F Child# 2 Peter Memos Greece & Alice Chamberlain Nashua, NH
MENARD, Albert Lionel, Nov 12 1913 Sex:M Child# 9 Adelard Menard Canada & Marie Levesque Canada
MENARD, Anita, Jul 3 1903 Sex:F Child# 3 Albert Menard Canada & Lydia Rochette Canada
MENARD, Blanche Eva, May 29 1900 Sex:F Child# 3 Damasse Menard Canada & Clodia Cote Canada
MENARD, Blanche Gertrude, Jul 3 1913 Sex:F Child# 3 Edmond Menard Canada & Rosanna Lamotte Canada
MENARD, Cecile M O, Sep 25 1899 Sex:F Child# 3 Alfred Menard St Albans, VT & Cecile Congnac Canada
MENARD, Diana, Oct 24 1904 Sex:F Child# 4 Albert Menard Canada & Lydia Rochette Canada
MENARD, Felix Joseph, Jan 14 1906 Sex:M Child# 7 Damase Menard Canada & Claudia Cote Canada
MENARD, Francois A, Dec 23 1896 Sex:M Child# 2 Alfred Menard St Albans, VT & Cecile Cognac Canada
MENARD, George, Jul 7 1903 Sex:M Child# 4 Adelard Menard Canada & Marie Levesque Lawrence, MA
MENARD, Gerard, May 19 1916 Sex:M Child# 7 Albert Menard Canada & Lydia Rochette Canada
MENARD, Henri Leo, Oct 10 1904 Sex:M Child# 2 Edmond Menard Canada & Rosanna Lamothe Canada
MENARD, Irene B B, Sep 4 1895 Sex:F Child# 1 Alfred Menard St Albans, VT & Cecile Cognac Canada
MENARD, Joseph Eduard, May 21 1905 Sex:M Child# 10 Albert Menard Canada & Exilda Houle Canada
MENARD, Joseph Ernest, Jan 1 1910 Sex:M Child# 1 Joseph Menard Mass & Aldea Carignan Canada
MENARD, Joseph Francois Leo, Apr 14 1899 Sex:M Child# 10 Christopher Menard Plattsburg, NY & Lucie Boyer Plattsburg
MENARD, Joseph Leo, Oct 11 1903 Sex:M Child# 6 Damasse Menard Canada & Claudia Cote Canada
MENARD, Joseph Norbert, Apr 27 1907 Sex:M Child# 7 Damase Menard Canada & Claudia Cote Canada
MENARD, Joseph Willibrod, Nov 30 1909 Sex:M Child# 2 Jean Menard Canada & Marie St Jean Canada
MENARD, Leo, Jul 7 1903 Sex:M Child# 5 Adelard Menard Canada & Marie Levesque Lawrence, MA
MENARD, Leona Noela Marie, Dec 28 1918 Sex:F Child# 1 Ovila Menard Canada & Lea Ouellette Canada
MENARD, Liliane, May 18 1911 Sex:F Child# 3 Jean Menard Canada & Lea Jean Canada
MENARD, Marie D B, Feb 10 1888 Sex:F Child# 9 Patrick Menard Canada & Sezaue Danseieau Canada
MENARD, Marie O, Jan 19 1895 Sex:F Child# 2 Jean B Menard Canada & Carmelite Brousseau Canada
MENARD, Marie Siliane, Nov 17 1918 Sex:F Child# 5 Jean Menard Canada & Lea Jean Canada
MENARD, Marie Wilda, Mar 11 1902 Sex:F Child# 5 Damasse Menard Canada & Clodia Cote Canada
MENARD, Mario O, Mar 12 1892 Sex:F Child# 4 Jean Bte Menard Canada & Carmelite Brousseau Canada
MENARD, Philibert Ovila, Sep 8 1910 Sex:M Child# 8 Adelard Menard Canada & Marie Levesque Lawrence, MA
MENARD, Rose Flora, Jul 20 1907 Sex:F Child# 7 Adelard Menard Canada & Marie Levesque Lawrence, MA
MENGINE, Unknown, Aug 14 1907 Sex:F Child# 1 Edie Mengine Russia & Plire Maejete Russia
MENIOS, Aritula, Sep 18 1923 Sex:F Child# 3 Demetrius Menios Greece & Evangeline Tegou Greece
MENNIER, Unknown, May 20 1900 Sex:F Child# 2 Joseph Mennier Canada & Josephine Dionne Canada
MENTER, Daniel C, Mar 16 1897 Sex:M Child# 6 George H Menter Londonderry, NH & Alice Brown Nova Scotia
MENTER, Ethel May, Jun 2 1895 Sex:F Child# 5 George H Menter NH & Alice Brown US
MERCER, Arlene May, Jul 19 1918 Sex:F Child# 1 Forest C Mercer Batesville, OH & Daisy Nyland S Natick, MA
MERCER, Barbara Anabel, Jan 25 1928 Sex:F Child# 1 Harold H Mercer Barnesville, OH & B Ger Webster Nashua, NH
MERCER, Edith Marie, Mar 3 1915 Sex:F Child# 1 Ross D Mercer Belmont, OH & Evan Aryell Nashua, NH
MERCER, Harold John, Jan 17 1926 Sex:M Child# 4 Rosa Mercer Delmont, OH & Eva Aryell Nashua, NH
MERCER, Paul Lowery, Apr 1 1926 Sex:M Child# 2 Ottis E Mercer Barnesville, OH & Sarah J Morgan Nashua, NH
MERCER, Paul Manning, Jan 4 1899 Sex:M Child# 2 William Mercer Plattsburgh, NY & Caroline F Cochrane Manchester, NH
MERCER, Phillip Webster, Dec 11 1934 Sex:M Child# 2 Harold Hubert Mercer Barnesville, OH & Beatrice Webster Nashua
MERCER, Richard Joseph, Apr 10 1919 Sex:M Child# 3 Ross Mercer Delmont, OH & Edith Aryell Nashua, NH
MERCER, Robert Sands, Feb 21 1925 Sex:M Child# 1 Ottis E Mercer Batesville, OH & Sarah J Morgan Nashua, NH
MERCER, Sandra Elaine, Nov 12 1935 Sex:F Child# 1 Boyd E Mercer Barnesville, OH & Alice French Hillsboro, NH
MERCER, Shirley Elizabeth, Sep 26 1924 Sex:F Child# 1 Kenneth Mercer Ohio & Lillian Bickford Berwick, ME
MERCER, Unknown, Sep 3 1916 Sex:F Child# 2 Ross D Mercer Ohio & Eva B Aryell Nashua, NH
MERCHAND, J David Clayton, Apr 4 1921 Sex:M Child# 9 Joseph Merchand Canada & Annie Demanche Canada
MERCHANT, Jeanne, Dec 9 1931 Sex:F Child# 2 Napoleon Merchant Canada & Yvonne Dube Nashua, NH
MERCHANT, Unknown, Jun 23 1921 Sex:M Child# 2 Harold R Merchant Penacook, NH & Bernice Boardman Orford, NH

MERCHANT, William Richard, Jun 23 1927 Sex:M Child# 1 Harold Merchant Concord, NH & Alice Bordeleau New Jersey
MERCIER, Albert, Jan 28 1915 Sex:M Child# 2 Henry Mercier Still River, MA & Rose Dutilly Salem, MA
MERCIER, Albert Roland, Aug 1 1932 Sex:M Child# 5 Albert Mercier Canada & M R Lafontaine Nashua, NH
MERCIER, Alfred Ernest, Dec 16 1932 Sex:M Child# 8 A N Mercier Peabody, MA & Irene Kerouac Nashua, NH
MERCIER, Beatrice Ann, Sep 1 1934 Sex:F Child# 6 Albert Mercier Canada & Marie R Lafontaine Canada
MERCIER, Beverly Jane, Dec 3 1929 Sex:F Child# 2 Kenneth L Mercier Barnsville, OH & Lillian Bickford Berwick, ME
MERCIER, Eva Therese, Aug 18 1922 Sex:F Child# 2 Arthur Mercier Mass & Irene Kerouac NH
MERCIER, Helen, Oct 16 1921 Sex:F Child# 1 Lawrence D Mercier Newport, VT & M Gertrude Kennedy Springfield, MA
MERCIER, Joseph Cyprien, Jul 13 1924 Sex:M Child# 3 Arthur Mercier Mass & Irene Kerouac NH
MERCIER, Joseph Emile A, May 14 1896 Sex:M Child# 2 William Mercier Canada & Marie Sirois Canada
MERCIER, Joseph Henry Robert, Jan 30 1921 Sex:M Child# 1 Arthur Mercier Peabody, MA & Irene Kerouac Nashua, NH
MERCIER, Leon Roger, Apr 17 1926 Sex:M Child# 4 Arthur Mercier Peabody, MA & Irene Kerouac Nashua, NH
MERCIER, Marguerite Fleurette, Mar 26 1929 Sex:F Child# 4 Albert Mercier Canada & M R Lafontaine Nashua, NH
MERCIER, Marie A Eugenie, May 18 1899 Sex:F Child# 4 William Mercier Canada & Marie Sirois Canada
MERCIER, Marie Rose Theresa, Jan 22 1928 Sex:F Child# 3 Albert Mercier Canada & M R Lafountaine Nashua, NH
MERCIER, Marie Yvonne A, May 24 1901 Sex:F Child# 5 William Mercier Canada & Marie Sirois Canada
MERCIER, Mary Louise, Jun 15 1921 Sex:F Child# 6 Joseph A Mercier Mass & Celina Caron Mass
MERCIER, Paul Walter, Jun 5 1931 Sex:M Child# 7 Arthur Mercier Peabody, MA & Irene Kerouac Nashua, NH
MERCIER, Pauline Hilda, Jan 8 1930 Sex:F Child# 6 Arthur Mercier Peabody, MA & Irene Kerouac Nashua, NH
MERCIER, Rita Amanda, Oct 3 1923 Sex:F Child# 1 Albert Mercier Canada & M R Lafontaine Nashua, NH
MERCIER, Rita Marie, Dec 15 1927 Sex:F Child# 5 Arthur Mercier Peabody, MA & Irene Kerouac Nashua, NH
MERCIER, Roland, Apr 29 1926 Sex:M Child# 2 Albert Mercier Canada & M R Lafontaine Nashua, NH
MERIN, Albert Romeo, May 15 1915 Sex:M Child# 6 Joseph Merin Canada & Ernestine Gauthier Canada
MERISKEY, Annie, Apr 13 1919 Sex:F Child# 5 Harry W Meriskey Russia & Mary corubloom Russia
MERRICK, Clarence Wilbur, Dec 30 1920 Sex:M Child# 1 Clarence A Merrick Sandown, NH & Eunice Hinckley Concord, NH
MERRICK, Lester Herbert, Mar 6 1922 Sex:M Child# 2 Clarence A Merrick Chelsea, MA & Arleen Duware E Pepperell, MA
MERRILL, Arthur Warren, May 18 1924 Sex:M Child# 1 Elmer W Merrill Deering, NH & Ethel Nylander Woodland, ME
MERRILL, Clair Golden, Dec 27 1911 Sex:F Child# 1 Herbert Merrill Lowell, MA & Ann Golden Plattsburg, NY
MERRILL, Esther, Nov 5 1919 Sex:F Child# 1 Archie Merrill Goffstown, NH & Ada E Gautier Merrimack, NH
MERRILL, Everett, Jan 26 1921 Sex:M Child# 3 Karl E Merrill Hudson, NH & Josephine Jeannotte Nashua, NH
MERRILL, Gertrude Elaine, Jun 5 1918 Sex:F Child# 2 Karl E Merrill Hudson, NH & Josei M Jeannotte Nashua, NH
MERRILL, Irene Retta, Feb 4 1911 Sex:F Child# 3 Edgar E Merrill Nashua, NH & Carrie Wood Canada
MERRILL, Justin Carter, Nov 30 1907 Sex:M Child# 1 Carl E Merrill Canada & H Evelyn Carter Lowell, MA
MERRILL, Katherine Joann, Apr 21 1918 Sex:F Child# 2 Cahrles W Merrill Franklin, NH & Delia Murphy Windsor, VT
MERRILL, Lorraine Margaret, Jan 30 1929 Sex:F Child# 2 Ernest W Merrill Maine & Gertrude Mayou Hollis, NH
MERRILL, Lucille, Aug 29 1912 Sex:F Child# 1 William C Merrill Fitch Bay, PQ & Hattie Hills Hudson, WI
MERRILL, Margaret Mary, May 6 1913 Sex:F Child# 1 Charles W Merrill Franklin, NH & Adelia M Murphy Windsor, VT
MERRILL, Marjorie Ruth, Nov 25 1921 Sex:F Child# 2 Archie Merrill Goffstown, NH & Ada Gauthier Merrimack, NH
MERRILL, Unknown, Jul 17 1916 Sex:F Child# 2 William C Merrill Fitch Bay, PQ & Hattie Hills Hudson, Wisconsin
MERRILL, Unknown, May 14 1922 Sex:M Child# 1 Leonard Merrill NH & Mary Burgoyne Peterboro, NH
MERRITT, Christina, Jul 14 1897 Sex:F Child# 5 John Merritt Ireland & Kate O'Donnell Ireland
MERRITT, Christopher, Oct 15 1922 Sex:M Child# 2 Christopher Merritt Nashua, NH & Nellie Keenan Wilton, NH
MERRITT, Edward, Oct 14 1891 Sex:M Child# 3 John M Merritt Ireland & Kate O'Donnell Ireland
MERRITT, Elizabeth, Nov 5 1888 Sex:F Child# 2 John Merritt Ireland & Kate O'Donnell Ireland
MERRITT, Robert, Aug 20 1921 Sex:M Child# 1 Christopher Merritt Nashua, NH & Nellie Keenan Wilton, NH
MERRUNE, Unknown, May 24 1889 Sex:M Child# 3 Narbert Merrune Canada & Rosanna Cognoe Canada Stillborn
MERRY, Jeannette June, Jun 18 1919 Sex:F Child# 1 Clarence Merry US & Rose Ricard US
MERRY, Unknown, Dec 9 1912 Sex: Child# 2 Oscar Merry Portland, ME & Delia Recard Nashua, NH Stillborn
MERTON, Charles, Oct 8 1901 Sex:M Child# 3 Charles G Merton Lowell, MA & Victoria Charron Manchester, NH
MESSENGER, Ann, Aug 3 1930 Sex:F Child# 1 George A Messenger Huntington, MA & Adelaide Walker Greenfield, MA
MESSER, Arthur Charles, Sep 1 1933 Sex:M Child# 3 Wendell Messer E Pepperell, MA & L Archambault E Pepperell, MA
MESSER, Barbara Arline, May 18 1926 Sex:F Child# 1 Wendell Messer E Pepperell, MA & L Archambault E Pepperell, MA
MESSER, Donald Wendell, Feb 23 1935 Sex:M Child# 4 Wendell Messer Pepperell, MA & Lil Archambault Pepperell, MA
MESSER, Eugene Paul, Apr 21 1929 Sex:M Child# 2 Wendell Messer Pepperell, MA & Lillian Archambault Pepperell, MA
MESSER, Harold, Oct 26 1908 Sex:M Child# 1 (No Parents Listed)
MESSER, Unknown, Aug 15 1898 Sex:F Child# 1 Adelbert Messer Hollis, NH & Clara Shaplin Concord, MA
MESSIC, Victoire I M J, Nov 18 1890 Sex:F Child# 1 Hounidas Messic Canada & Palmire Landry Canada
MESSIER, Adrien, Oct 16 1893 Sex:M Child# Francis Messier Canada & Amanda Lemoine Canada
MESSIER, Albertine, Nov 1 1889 Sex:F Child# 9 Francois Messier Canada & Rosanna Lemoine Canada
MESSIER, Anna Phebe, Feb 26 1891 Sex:F Child# 7 Adelard Messier Canada & Georgina Dumais Canada
MESSIER, Beatrice T, May 30 1920 Sex:F Child# 4 George H Messier Nashua, NH & Theresa E Gagnon Rindale, NH
MESSIER, Blanche Flora, Jun 12 1892 Sex:F Child# 10 Joseph Messier Canada & Athais Ouellette Canada
MESSIER, Cecile Lucie, May 6 1902 Sex:F Child# 2 Victor Messier Canada & Virginie Sarreau Canada
MESSIER, Charles Alfred, Aug 2 1930 Sex:M Child# 1 Thomas Messier Nashua, NH & Jennie Paro Nashua, NH
MESSIER, Donald Hector, Apr 1 1935 Sex:M Child# 4 Thomas Messier Nashua, NH & Eugenie Paro Nashua, NH
MESSIER, Earl Thomas, Sep 12 1935 Sex:M Child# 7 George Messier Nashua, NH & Theresa Gagnon Riverdale, NH
MESSIER, Flora L, Jun 7 1895 Sex:F Child# 2 Adelard Messier Canada & Malvina Langerin Brookfield, NY
MESSIER, Frederick, Sep 1 1888 Sex:M Child# 8 Francis Messier Canada & Roxanna Perroine Canada
MESSIER, George, Jr, Jul 18 1924 Sex:M Child# 3 George Messier Nashua, NH & Theresa Gagnon Riverdale, NH
MESSIER, Helene Phoebe, Feb 22 1899 Sex:F Child# 5 Hormisdas Messier Canada & Adele St Laurent Canada
MESSIER, Irene, Oct 19 1905 Sex:F Child# 3 Victor Messier Canada & Virginie Sareau Canada
MESSIER, Jacqueline Therese, Dec 2 1931 Sex:F Child# 2 Thomas Messier Nashua, NH & Jessie Paro Nashua, NH
MESSIER, Jean Baptiste A, Jun 24 1890 Sex:M Child# 1 Adelard Messier Canada & Melvina Langevin Brookfield, MA

MESSIER, Joan Maxine, Aug 17 1929 Sex:F Child# 5 Arthur Messier Newburyport, MA & Juliette Houle Hooksett, NH
MESSIER, Joseph, Sep 4 1889 Sex:M Child# 6 Adelord Messier Canada & G Dumas Canada
MESSIER, Joseph, Aug 6 1916 Sex:M Child# 1 George Messier Nashua, NH & Theresa Gagnon NH
MESSIER, Joseph Alphonse, Feb 27 1894 Sex:M Child# 9 Adelard Messier Canada & Georgiana Dumais Canada
MESSIER, Joseph Earnest, Jul 29 1897 Sex:M Child# 2 Joseph Messier Nashua, NH & Eliza Hebert Canada
MESSIER, Joseph R, Dec 5 1897 Sex:M Child# 4 Adelard Messier Canada & Malvina Langevin Brookfield, MA
MESSIER, Lillian Cecelia, Nov 4 1904 Sex:F Child# 1 Henry Messier Canada & Josephine Winn Nashua, NH
MESSIER, Louis Ernest, Apr 9 1888 Sex:M Child# 2 Joseph Messier Canada & Alice Lefebvre Nashua, NH
MESSIER, Lucienne Patricia, Nov 4 1926 Sex:F Child# 4 Arthur Messier Newburyport, MA & Juliette Houle Hooksett, NH
MESSIER, Marie Angelina, Nov 24 1892 Sex:F Child# 8 Adelard Messier Canada & Georgiana Dumais Canada
MESSIER, Marie Anne, Jul 6 1887 Sex:F Child# Hornisdas Messier P Q & Melina Gravel P Q
MESSIER, Marie E E, Jan 22 1887 Sex:F Child# 5 Adelard Messier P Q & G Dumais P Q
MESSIER, Marie Louise I, Apr 15 1887 Sex:F Child# Joachim Messier P Q & Anathalie Girard P Q
MESSIER, Marie Palmire, Jul 30 1892 Sex:F Child# 2 Hormidas Messier Canada & Palmire Landry Canada
MESSIER, Marie Virginia, Dec 9 1918 Sex:F Child# 3 George H Messier Nashua, NH & Theresa Gagnon Riverdale, NH
MESSIER, Marie Y L, Jul 2 1897 Sex:F Child# 1 Victor Messier Canada & Virginia Saro Canada
MESSIER, Martha Janet, May 9 1922 Sex:F Child# 1 Joseph Messier Fall River, MA & Elizabeth Flanigan Exeter, NH
MESSIER, Napoleon, Oct 1 1902 Sex:M Child# 3 Hormidas Messier Canada & Adele St Laurent Canada
MESSIER, Normand Alphonse, Jun 24 1929 Sex:M Child# 1 Ernest A Messier Newport, NH & Gracia M Messier Nashua, NH
MESSIER, Rachel Constance, Oct 26 1934 Sex:F Child# 1 Eli Messier Old Town, ME & Simonne Blouin Canada
MESSIER, Raymond Ernest, Feb 12 1932 Sex:M Child# 2 Ernest Messier Newburyport, MA & Gracia Messier Nashua, NH
MESSIER, Reine M, Jul 9 1902 Sex:F Child# 11 Adelard Messier Canada & Georgiana Dumais Canada
MESSIER, Richard Arthur, Jan 19 1920 Sex:M Child# 2 Arthur Messier Mass & Juliet Houle Nashua, NH
MESSIER, Rita Beth, Jul 17 1918 Sex:F Child# 1 Arthur Messier Mass & Juliet Houle NH
MESSIER, Robert Henry, Feb 24 1929 Sex:M Child# 6 George Messier Nashua, NH & Theresa Gagnon Riverdale, NH
MESSIER, Roger Rudolph Eli, Nov 5 1935 Sex:M Child# 2 Eli Messier Old Town, ME & Simonne Blouin Canada
MESSIER, Roland, Sep 10 1907 Sex:M Child# 4 Victor Messier Canada & Virginie Sarreau Canada
MESSIER, Rose Delima, Jun 27 1896 Sex:F Child# 1 Joseph Messier Lowell, MA & Elize Hebert Montreal, Canada
MESSIER, Thomas Henry, Jan 30 1907 Sex:M Child# 2 Henry Messier Canada & Josephine A Winn Nashua, NH
MESSIER, Unknown, Oct 22 1887 Sex:M Child# Francois Messier Canada & Rosanna Lemoine Canada Stillborn
MESSIER, Unknown, Aug 15 1917 Sex:M Child# 2 George H Messier Nashua, NH & Teresa Gagnon Riverdale, NH Stillborn
MESSIER, Unknown, Aug 25 1920 Sex:F Child# 5 Adrian Messier Nashua, NH & Beatrice Duclos Nashua, NH Stillborn
MESSIER, Unknown, Dec 14 1921 Sex:M Child# 3 Henry Messier Canada & Josephine A Winn Nashua, NH
MESZKAWSKI, Zokig, Dec 21 1914 Sex:F Child# 1 Joseph Meszkawski Russia & Elena Russia
METAYAR, Marie Oliva, Jan 16 1889 Sex:F Child# 2 Theophile Metayar Canada & Antonia D'Auteuil Canada
METAYER, Alphonse, Jun 11 1891 Sex:M Child# 3 Theophile Metayer Canada & Antonia Cote Canada
METAYER, Antoinette, May 1 1899 Sex:F Child# 6 Theophile Metayer Canada & Antonia D'Auteuil Canada
METAYER, Joseph A, May 11 1887 Sex:M Child# 1 Theophile Metayer Canada & A Dantenelle Canada
METAYER, Neolia, Jul 14 1893 Sex:F Child# 4 Theophile Metayer Canada & Antonia Cote Canada
METAYER, Raoul Valmore, Oct 27 1901 Sex:M Child# 7 Theophile Metayer Canada & Antonia Dauteuil Canada
METAYER, Thomas, Mar 13 1895 Sex:m Child# 5 Theophile Metayer Canada & Antonia D'Autereil Canada
METCALF, Helena Teresa, May 12 1926 Sex:F Child# 1 Leeda Metcalf Maine & Helena Murphy Carney, NJ
METCALF, Joseph Evan, Sep 5 1916 Sex:M Child# 1 Leeds Metcalf Maine & Alfida Levesque Canada
METCALF, M Louise Dorothy, Aug 7 1917 Sex:F Child# 2 Leeds Metcalf Maine & Alpheda Levesque Canada
MEUNIER, Dorothy Jean Gloria, Nov 20 1931 Sex:F Child# 2 Robert Meunier Nashua, NH & Lillian Dugel Canada
MEUNIER, Edouard Leo, Jul 8 1907 Sex:M Child# 3 Filosime Meunier Canada & Eliza Bonnette Canada
MEUNIER, Eugene Robert, Oct 28 1903 Sex:M Child# 1 Philoseme Meunier Canada & Eliza Bonnette Canada
MEUNIER, Joseph Arthur, Jun 30 1899 Sex:M Child# 1 Joseph Meunier Canada & Josephine Dionne Canada
MEUNIER, Joseph Leo, Mar 9 1911 Sex:M Child# 7 Joseph Meunier Canada & Josephine Dionne Canada
MEUNIER, Josephine Claire, Feb 20 1930 Sex:F Child# 1 Arthur Meunier Nashua, NH & Irene St Laurent Nashua, NH
MEUNIER, Leo Paul, Oct 29 1932 Sex:M Child# 2 A Meunier Nashua, NH & Irene St Laurent Nashua, NH
MEUNIER, M Rose Camille, Mar 20 1917 Sex:F Child# 8 Philosime Meunier Canada & Eliza Bonnette Canada
MEUNIER, M Yvonne Juliette, Jul 9 1914 Sex:F Child# 7 Joseph Meunier Canada & Josephine Dionne Canada
MEUNIER, Malvina, Jun 24 1909 Sex:F Child# 7 Joseph Meunier Canada & Marie Dionne Canada
MEUNIER, Marie Ida E, Dec 26 1903 Sex:F Child# 4 Joseph Meunier Canada & Josephine Dionne Canada
MEUNIER, Marie Lea Eva R, Jul 22 1901 Sex:F Child# 3 Joseph Meunier Canada & Josephine Dionne Canada
MEUNIER, Paul Edward Robert, Nov 8 1929 Sex:M Child# 1 Robert Meunier Nashua, NH & Lillian Dugal Canada
MEUNIER, Unknown, Jun 13 1908 Sex:F Child# 6 Joseph Meunier Canada & Josephine Dionne Canada Stillborn
MEUNIER, Valmore Laurent, Mar 25 1913 Sex:M Child# 6 Philosime Meunier Canada & Elisa Bonnette Canada
MEUNIER, Veronique Rita, Aug 5 1915 Sex:F Child# 7 Philosime Meunier Canada & Eliza Bonnette Canada
MEUNIER, Yvonne Cecile, Apr 7 1917 Sex:F Child# 10 Joseph Meunier Canada & Josephine Drouin Canada
MEUNIER, Yvonne Emelia L, Jan 26 1906 Sex:F Child# 2 Philosime Meunier Canada & Elise Bonnette Canada
MEWSKI, Joseph, Apr 26 1903 Sex:M Child# 4 John Mewski Russia & Liza Lavwsna Russia
MEYER, Donald Arthur, Feb 27 1927 Sex:M Child# 1 Howard A Meyer Nashua, NH & Mary A Ouillette Canada
MEYERS, Alban, May 23 1892 Sex:M Child# 9 Patrick Meyers Ireland & Margaret Hoey England
MEYERS, Carlton Edward, Jan 13 1935 Sex:M Child# 3 K Arthur Meyers Nashua, NH & Mary A Ouellette St Pacome, PQ
MEYERS, John, May 28 1889 Sex:M Child# 7 Patrick Meyers Ireland & Maggie Foley England
MEYERS, Mary, Mar 22 1891 Sex:F Child# 8 Patrick Meyers Ireland & Margaret Hoey England
MEYERS, Unknown, Aug 1 1887 Sex:M Child# 5 Patrick Meyers Ireland & Margaret Ireland
MEYROTT, Unknown, May 16 1891 Sex:M Child# 18 Noel Meyrott NY & Julia Bouger NY Stillborn
MICEK, Sophie, Aug 27 1905 Sex:F Child# 1 Stanislaus Micek Austria & Mary Stocek Austria
MICHAEL, Hrisula, Dec 28 1917 Sex:F Child# 1 Philip Michael Greece & Katie Kratson Greece
MICHAEL, Voychuk, Jun 2 1913 Sex:M Child# 2 Joseph Michael Russia & Agea Sergawicz Russia

MICHAELVIC, Ada, Jun 6 1914 Sex:F Child# 1 Peter Michaelvic Austria & Armata Johanna Austria
MICHAILIONIS, Waclowas, Nov 27 1911 Sex:M Child# 3 T Michailionis Russia & Agota Skluciute Russia
MICHALEWICZ, Meri, Dec 5 1911 Sex:M Child# 1 Jusef Michalewic Poland & Aga Sergewicz Poland
MICHALEWICZ, Unknown, Aug 28 1912 Sex:M Child# 3 Frank Michalewicz Russia & Adelia Czesryn Russia
MICHALWEICZ, William, May 22 1913 Sex:M Child# 4 Thomas Michalweicz Russia & Agnes Skiliante Russia
MICHAUD, Albert Leo, Nov 11 1914 Sex:M Child# 5 Arthur Michaud Canada & Mary Caron Canada
MICHAUD, Albert Victor, Jan 19 1890 Sex:M Child# 4 Joseph Michaud Canada & Elrine Morency Canada
MICHAUD, Alfred Wilfred, Jan 22 1933 Sex:M Child# 5 Wilfred Michaud Cacouna, PQ & Blanche Berube Hooksett, NH
MICHAUD, Alice Lucille, Feb 1 1919 Sex:F Child# 5 Philippe Michaud Canada & Emma Roy NH
MICHAUD, Arlene Marcella, Jun 23 1935 Sex:F Child# 2 Raoul Michaud Canada & Yvonne Roy Canada
MICHAUD, Armand, Apr 7 1903 Sex:M Child# 3 Louis Michaud Canada & Marie Meunier Canada
MICHAUD, Beatrice, Jun 12 1922 Sex:F Child# 1 Roland Michaud Nashua, NH & Sadie Fournier Mass
MICHAUD, Beatrice Fernande, Jun 16 1918 Sex:F Child# 1 Thomas Michaud Canada & Lydia Delisle Canada
MICHAUD, Charles A George, Sep 7 1901 Sex:M Child# 3 William Michaud Canada & Philomene Gagnon Canada
MICHAUD, Charles Edwin, Oct 25 1901 Sex:M Child# 1 Joseph Alp Michaud Canada & Mary Doherty Nashua, NH
MICHAUD, Charles Eugene, Jr, Aug 6 1931 Sex:M Child# 3 Charles E Michaud Nashua, NH & Marie Ange Bouchard Canada
MICHAUD, Claire Lucy, Sep 7 1935 Sex:F Child# 3 Edward Michaud Canada & Alice Thibault Canada
MICHAUD, Colette, Feb 1 1927 Sex:F Child# 2 Leo Michaud Burlington, VT & Alice Cote Nashua, NH
MICHAUD, Conrad Raymond, Nov 4 1906 Sex:M Child# 3 Alfred Michaud Canada & Marie Cote Canada
MICHAUD, Constance Theresa, Aug 28 1926 Sex:F Child# 1 Armand Michaud Nashua, NH & Hermina Simard Canada
MICHAUD, Donald, Jul 29 1931 Sex:M Child# 2 Roland Michaud Nashua, NH & Sadie Fournier Mass
MICHAUD, Dora Lillian, Dec 1 1914 Sex:F Child# 2 Theophile Michaud NH & Rose Ouellette NH
MICHAUD, Eva Rita Jeanine, Nov 15 1929 Sex:F Child# 4 Wilfrid Michaud Canada & Blanche Berube Hooksett, NH
MICHAUD, Fernando, Jan 15 1910 Sex:M Child# 5 Alphonse Michaud Canada & Domithilde Morin Canada
MICHAUD, Florence Anita, Jul 12 1924 Sex:F Child# 2 Wilfred Michaud Canada & Blanche Berube Hooksett, NH
MICHAUD, George Emile, Feb 22 1926 Sex:M Child# 3 Guillaume Michaud Canada & Albina Dupre Nashua, NH
MICHAUD, George Lionel, Mar 21 1935 Sex:M Child# 1 George Michaud Nashua, NH & Florence Cardin Nashua, NH
MICHAUD, Gerard Lionel, May 7 1913 Sex:M Child# 6 Amede Michaud Canada & Marie Levesque Canada
MICHAUD, Henri, Feb 23 1894 Sex:M Child# 2 John Michaud Canada & Victoria Belanger Canada
MICHAUD, J Alphonse Wilfrid, Jun 10 1919 Sex:M Child# 2 Guiillaume Michaud Canada & Albina Martin Canada
MICHAUD, J Wilfred Albert, Oct 15 1922 Sex:M Child# 1 Wilfred Michaud Canada & Blanche Berube Hooksett, NH
MICHAUD, Jean Muriel, Jul 5 1934 Sex:F Child# 1 Armand Michaud Nashua, NH & Rolande Durand Nashua, NH
MICHAUD, Jeanne D'Arc, Jun 17 1928 Sex:F Child# 16 Cyprien Michaud Canada & Claudia Lafrance Canada
MICHAUD, Jos Alfred Edgar, Aug 3 1934 Sex:M Child# 7 Wilfred J Michaud Canada & Blanche Berube Hooksett, NH
MICHAUD, Jos Guillaume Ray, Oct 17 1916 Sex:M Child# 1 Jos Gull Michaud Canada & Albina Martin Nashua, NH
MICHAUD, Jos Norman Henry, Apr 4 1929 Sex:M Child# 4 Guillaume Michaud Canada & Albina Martin Nashua, NH
MICHAUD, Jos Paul Emile, Jan 15 1921 Sex:M Child# 11 Arthur Michaud Canada & Marie Louise Caron Canada
MICHAUD, Joseph, Sep 8 1893 Sex:M Child# 4 Joseph Michaud Canada & Josephine Paradis Canada
MICHAUD, Joseph, Nov 7 1916 Sex:M Child# 6 Eloi Michaud Canada & Leopaldine Cote Canada Stillborn
MICHAUD, Joseph, Aug 21 1921 Sex:M Child# 1 Wilfred Michaud Canada & Blanche Berube Hooksett, NH
MICHAUD, Joseph A, Jul 25 1894 Sex:M Child# 7 Joseph Michaud Canada & Marie Lavoie Canada
MICHAUD, Joseph Adrien, Dec 15 1906 Sex:M Child# 3 Alphonse Michaud Canada & Domilde Morin Canada
MICHAUD, Joseph Albert, Oct 13 1904 Sex:M Child# 2 Amedee Michaud Canada & Marianne Levesque Canada
MICHAUD, Joseph Albert Roland, Feb 24 1924 Sex:M Child# 2 Edgar Michaud Canada & Blanche Michaud Nashua, NH
MICHAUD, Joseph Alcide Z, Dec 17 1906 Sex:M Child# 6 Alfred Michaud Canada & Celina St Laurent Canada
MICHAUD, Joseph Alfred L, Aug 12 1903 Sex:M Child# 1 Alfred Michaud Canada & Marie Cote Canada
MICHAUD, Joseph Alphonse L, Sep 21 1903 Sex:M Child# 4 William Michaud Canada & Philomene Gagnon Canada
MICHAUD, Joseph Arthur W, Dec 13 1905 Sex:M Child# 2 Alfred Michaud Canada & Marie Cote Canada
MICHAUD, Joseph Edmond A, Jan 15 1909 Sex:M Child# 1 Alfred Michaud Canada & Marie Therrien Potsdam, NY
MICHAUD, Joseph F Elzear, Jun 15 1893 Sex:M Child# 1 Elzear Michaud Canada & Philomene Berube Canada
MICHAUD, Joseph George A, May 5 1910 Sex:M Child# 5 Arthur Michaud Canada & Marie L Caron Canada
MICHAUD, Joseph Girard Desire, Mar 1 1926 Sex:M Child# 1 Lucien Michaud Canada & Adianna Roy Canada
MICHAUD, Joseph Harme Raymond, Apr 10 1927 Sex:M Child# 15 Cyprien Michaud Canada & Clotilda Lafrance Canada
MICHAUD, Joseph Leo, Oct 30 1906 Sex:M Child# 5 Louis Michaud Canada & Marie Meunier Canada
MICHAUD, Joseph Leo, Oct 23 1908 Sex:M Child# 6 Louis Michaud Canada & Marie Meunier Canada
MICHAUD, Joseph Leo R, Jul 6 1903 Sex:M Child# 3 Arthur Michaud Canada & Georgiana Belanger Canada
MICHAUD, Joseph Louis, Dec 30 1899 Sex:M Child# 1 Louis Michaud Canada & Marie Meunier Canada
MICHAUD, Joseph P, Dec 9 1890 Sex:M Child# 2 Pierre Michaud Canada & Adelaide Plourde Canada
MICHAUD, Joseph Raoul, Sep 4 1909 Sex:M Child# 2 Leon Michaud Canada & Alphonsine Cote Canada
MICHAUD, Joseph Roger, May 11 1924 Sex:M Child# 1 Joseph Michaud Lowell, MA & Ora Deshales Manchester, NH
MICHAUD, Joseph Roland O, May 29 1901 Sex:M Child# 2 Louis Michaud Canada & Marie Meunier Canada
MICHAUD, Joseph Roland S, Jan 26 1909 Sex:M Child# 2 Phillippe Michaud Canada & Emma Roy Nashua, NH
MICHAUD, Joseph Victor, Nov 7 1925 Sex:M Child# 14 Cyprien Michaud Canada & Claudia Lafrance Canada
MICHAUD, Joseph Wilfred A N, Dec 24 1904 Sex:M Child# 4 Louis Michaud Canada & Marie Meunier Canada
MICHAUD, Joseph Wm Edo L, Sep 16 1900 Sex:M Child# 2 William Michaud Canada & Philomene Gagnon Canada
MICHAUD, Josephine, May 24 1889 Sex:F Child# 2 Louis Michaud Canada & Josephine Peltier Canada
MICHAUD, L Joseph, Dec 31 1891 Sex:M Child# 2 Joseph Michaud Canada & Josephine Paradis Canada
MICHAUD, Leo Henri, Nov 8 1906 Sex:M Child# 1 Philippe Michaud Canada & Emma Roy US
MICHAUD, Louis Girard, Mar 2 1919 Sex:M Child# 10 Arthur Michaud Canada & Marie L Caron Canada
MICHAUD, Lucille, Dec 20 1917 Sex:F Child# 2 Albert Michaud Canada & Alberte Benoit Nashua, NH
MICHAUD, M Edwidge F, Jul 5 1911 Sex:F Child# 2 Alfred Michaud Canada & Clara Therrien New York
MICHAUD, M Julie A, Nov 8 1891 Sex:F Child# 8 Marcel Michaud Canada & Adele Beaulieu Canada
MICHAUD, Magella Yvonne, Jun 24 1930 Sex:F Child# 3 Lucien Michaud Canada & Diana Roy Canada

MICHAUD, Marie, Nov 29 1893 Sex:F Child# 4 Pierre Michaud Canada & Philomene Paul Canada
MICHAUD, Marie, Aug 4 1917 Sex:F Child# 1 Henri Michaud NH & Emme Dube Canada Stillborn
MICHAUD, Marie A, Oct 3 1889 Sex:F Child# 1 Pierre Michaud Canada & Adelaide Plourde Canada
MICHAUD, Marie A, May 2 1893 Sex:F Child# 9 Joseph Michaud Canada & Caroline Caron Canada
MICHAUD, Marie Alma, Feb 16 1891 Sex:F Child# 8 Joseph Michaud Canada & Caroline Caron Canada
MICHAUD, Marie Anne A, Oct 19 1903 Sex:F Child# 1 Amidie Michaud Canada & Marie A Levesque Canada
MICHAUD, Marie Aurore Lorrain, Apr 4 1928 Sex:F Child# 3 Wilfred Michaud Canada & Blanche Berube Hooksett, NH
MICHAUD, Marie B L, Sep 7 1902 Sex:F Child# 2 Arthur Michaud Canada & G Belanger Canada
MICHAUD, Marie Blanche E, Mar 16 1904 Sex:F Child# 1 Arthur Michaud Canada & Marie L Caron Canada
MICHAUD, Marie Enede, Jan 15 1911 Sex:F Child# 6 Alphonse Michaud Canada & Domitilde Morin Canada
MICHAUD, Marie Eva Rachel, Jul 15 1929 Sex:F Child# 2 Joseph Michaud Lowell, MA & Eva Roy Conn
MICHAUD, Marie Evelyn G, Jan 26 1916 Sex:F Child# 9 Arthur Michaud St Ann, PQ & M Louise Caron St Philip, PQ
MICHAUD, Marie Isabelle, Nov 10 1909 Sex:F Child# 4 Alfred Michaud Canada & Marie Cote Canada
MICHAUD, Marie Jeanne Loretta, Mar 16 1935 Sex:F Child# 1 Eugene Michaud Canada & Laura Duchesneau Nashua, NH
MICHAUD, Marie L B C, Sep 16 1900 Sex:F Child# 1 William Michaud Canada & Philomene Gagnon Canada
MICHAUD, Marie Liliane, Jan 16 1908 Sex:F Child# 4 Alfred Michaud Canada & Marie Cote Canada
MICHAUD, Marie Lilliane, Mar 11 1917 Sex:F Child# 9 Arthur Michaud Canada & Marie Louise Caron Canada
MICHAUD, Marie Linianne, Dec 20 1898 Sex:F Child# 3 Alfred Michaud Canada & Celina St Laurent Canada
MICHAUD, Marie Odelie Theresa, Jun 18 1928 Sex:F Child# 2 Lucien Michaud Canada & Odianna Roy Canada
MICHAUD, Marie Rita, Sep 13 1923 Sex:F Child# 12 Arthur Michaud Canada & Marie Louise Caron Canada
MICHAUD, Marie Rose, Jul 13 1907 Sex:F Child# 4 Arthur Michaud Canada & Marie Louise Caron Canada
MICHAUD, Marie Rose Anna, Oct 8 1899 Sex:F Child# 1 Arthur Michaud Canada & G Belanger Canada
MICHAUD, Marie Rose Beatrice, Sep 16 1912 Sex:F Child# 1 Theophile Michaud NH & Rose Delima Ouellett NH
MICHAUD, Marie Therese F, Jul 12 1930 Sex:F Child# 1 Arthur Michaud Lowell, MA & Hemedine Dumont Canada
MICHAUD, Marie Therese Germ, Jul 29 1918 Sex:F Child# 2 Henri Michaud NH & Emma Dube Canada
MICHAUD, Marie Yvonne, Jun 15 1905 Sex:F Child# 2 Arthur Michaud Canada & Emma Caron Canada
MICHAUD, Maurice Joseph Roger, Apr 12 1933 Sex:M Child# 1 Edgar Michaud Nashua, NH & Cora Fluet Manchester, NH
MICHAUD, Normand, Jan 8 1933 Sex:M Child# 1 Raoul Michaud Canada & Yvonne Roy Canada
MICHAUD, Oscar Louis Normand, Nov 24 1927 Sex:M Child# 1 Napoleon Michaud Canada & Simonne Dube Nashua, NH
MICHAUD, Oscar Robert, Oct 7 1925 Sex:M Child# 13 Arthur Michaud Canada & Marie L Caron Canada
MICHAUD, Paul Edouard, Jul 12 1923 Sex:M Child# 1 Leo L Michaud Burlington, VT & Alice Cote Nashua, NH
MICHAUD, Pauline, Jul 21 1933 Sex:F Child# 3 Leo Michaud Burlington, VT & Alice Cote Nashua, NH
MICHAUD, Pauline Louise Rache, Nov 2 1925 Sex:F Child# 2 Charles E Michaud Nashua, NH & M Ange Bouchard Black
MICHAUD, Rachel Gertrude, Nov 15 1919 Sex:F Child# 3 Albert Michaud Canada & Bertha Benoit Nashua, NH
MICHAUD, Rio Gilbert, May 8 1908 Sex:M Child# 4 Alphonse Michaud Canada & Domithilde Morin Canada
MICHAUD, Rita Juliette, Mar 4 1928 Sex:F Child# 1 Edouard Michaud Canada & Alice Thibault Canada
MICHAUD, Robert, Dec 22 1931 Sex:M Child# 2 Edouard Michaud Canada & Alice Thibault Canada
MICHAUD, Robert Edgar, May 26 1912 Sex:M Child# 3 Philip Michaud Canada & Emma Roy US
MICHAUD, Robert Edouard, Nov 26 1919 Sex:M Child# 4 Theophile Michaud NH & Rose Ouellette NH
MICHAUD, Roland Zenon, Aug 19 1927 Sex:M Child# 1 Joseph Michaud Lowell, MA & Eva Roy Willimantic, CT
MICHAUD, Theophile, Apr 12 1887 Sex:M Child#  Joseph Michaud P Q & Elvine Montrency P Q
MICHAUD, Theresa Mildred, Mar 29 1917 Sex:F Child# 3 Theophile Michaud NH & Rose Ouellette NH
MICHAUD, Unknown, Jun 23 1901 Sex:F Child# 4 Alfred Michaud Canada & Celina St Laurent Canada Stillborn
MICHAUD, Unknown, Oct 24 1920 Sex:M Child# 4 Albert Michaud Canada & Bertha Benoit Nashua, NH
MICHAUD, Unknown, Nov 28 1924 Sex:F Child# 1 Charles Michaud Nashua, NH & Marie A Bouchard Providence, RI
MICHAUD, Wilfred, Jan 15 1917 Sex:M Child# 1 Albert Michaud Canada & Bertha Benoit Nashua, NH
MICHENER, Barbara, Oct 11 1918 Sex:F Child# 3 Rudy Michener Pennsylvania & Madeline Force Illinois
MICHENER, Ruth, Feb 9 1916 Sex:F Child# 2 Rudy Michener Pennsylvania & Madelin Force Streeter, IL
MICHENIS, Unknown, Nov 29 1918 Sex:M Child# 4 Joseph Michenis Russia & Minnie Bukawicz Russia
MICHILIAONIS, Agee, Aug 7 1915 Sex:F Child# 5 Thomas Michiliaonis Russia & Agee Scklestuita Russia
MICHITSOS, Elen, Sep 22 1917 Sex:F Child# 4 George Michitsos Greece & Sophia Agorn Greece
MICHITSOS, Helene, Dec 28 1918 Sex:F Child# 2 George Michitsos Greece & Sophia Agonou Greece
MICHITSOS, Mary, Sep 4 1916 Sex:F Child# 2 George Michitsos Greece & Sophias Agorou Greece
MICHKINIS, Annie, Feb 2 1910 Sex:F Child# 1 Michael Michkinis Russia & Agae Yakavanuty Russia
MICHOLOPAS, Joseph, Aug 5 1915 Sex:M Child# 3 Michael Micholopas Russia & Aggie Lejoyska Russia
MICHOLOPAS, Stanley, Aug 5 1915 Sex:M Child# 2 Michael Micholopas Russia & Aggie Lejoyska Russia
MICKAILIONIS, Amelia, Jan 29 1910 Sex:F Child# 2 Thomas Mickailionis Russia & Aga Augevist Russia
MICLETTE, Albina, Jun 7 1888 Sex:F Child# 1 J B Miclette Canada & Perpetue Cota Canada
MICLETTE, Joseph A N, Dec 19 1889 Sex:M Child# 4 Joseph Miclette Canada & Virginia Chatel Holyoke, MA
MICLETTE, Joseph O, Dec 8 1887 Sex:M Child# 2 Joseph Miclette Canada & Virginie Chatel Holyoke, MA
MICLETTE, Marie Flavia, Aug 18 1891 Sex:F Child# 5 Joseph Miclette Canada & Virginnie Chatel Canada
MIEGINIS, Ciacialie, Jul 8 1909 Sex:F Child# 2 Edward Mieginis Russia & Pietre Miazilie Russia
MIGA, Unknown, Jun 22 1921 Sex:F Child# 8 Apostolos Miga Greece & Enthuna Agapoupulos Greece
MIGNAULT, Beatrice, Nov 18 1920 Sex:F Child# 6 Emile Mignault Canada & Adelia Rivard Canada
MIGNAULT, Joseph Charles Eug, Mar 2 1914 Sex:M Child# 12 Joseph Mignault Canada & Resina Dionne Canada
MIGNAULT, Joseph Donat, Jun 19 1901 Sex:M Child# 3 Joseph Mignault Canada & Resina Dionne Canada
MIGNAULT, Joseph Omer, Aug 4 1895 Sex:M Child# 13 Joseph Mignault Canada & Georgina Levesque Canada
MIGNAULT, Joseph Thomas, May 19 1909 Sex:M Child# 9 Joseph Mignault Canada & Resina Dionne Canada
MIGNAULT, Joseph Zephrina, Apr 29 1898 Sex:M Child# 15 Joseph Mignault Canada & Georgianna Levesque Canada
MIGNAULT, Leo Cyprien, Feb 14 1906 Sex:M Child# 5 Joseph Mignault Canada & Rosina Dionne Canada
MIGNAULT, Leona, Apr 11 1894 Sex:F Child# 12 Joseph Mignault Canada & Georgianna Levesque Canada
MIGNAULT, Marie A, Jul 24 1896 Sex:F Child# 14 Joseph Mignault Canada & Georgina Levesque Canada
MIGNAULT, Marie Anna, Aug 24 1898 Sex:F Child# 6 Evariste Mignault Canada & Marie Levesque Canada

MIGNAULT, Marie Dora Theresa, Nov 13 1928 Sex:F Child# 1 (No Parents Listed)
MIGNAULT, Marie Fernande, Nov 8 1923 Sex:F Child# 2 Zepherin Mignault Canada & Marie Langelier Canada
MIGNAULT, Marie Irene, Feb 15 1906 Sex:F Child# 6 Joseph Mignault Canada & Rosina Dionne Canada
MIGNAULT, Marie Lea A, Jul 22 1907 Sex:F Child# 8 Joseph Mignault Canada & Resina Dionne Canada
MIGNAULT, Marie Theresa, Jul 4 1917 Sex:F Child# 7 Emile Mignault Canada & Delia Rivard Canada
MIGNAULT, Marie Yvonne, Jun 16 1899 Sex:F Child# 2 Alfred Mignault Canada & Desina Dionne Canada
MIGNEAU, Joseph Frederick, Nov 5 1924 Sex:M Child# 1 Paul Migneau Canada & Exilda Normand US
MIGNEAULT, Alice Elizabeth, Jun 25 1925 Sex:F Child# 5 Maurice Migneault Canada & Helen Kinville New York
MIGNEAULT, Cecile, Jul 30 1923 Sex:F Child# 6 Emile Migneault Canada & Delia Rivard Canada
MIGNEAULT, Emile Normand Gerard, May 26 1912 Sex:M Child# 1 Emile Migneault Canada & Delia Rivard Canada
MIGNEAULT, Eugene Roger, May 6 1927 Sex:M Child# 4 E Migneault Canada & Florence Coulombe Canada
MIGNEAULT, Eva Germaine, Aug 1 1912 Sex:F Child# 11 Joseph Migneault Canada & Roseda Dionne Canada
MIGNEAULT, Gerard Alphonse, Apr 20 1931 Sex:M Child# 1 Alphonse Migneault Canada & Therese Jodouin Canada
MIGNEAULT, Girard, Jr, Nov 5 1932 Sex:M Child# 1 Girard Migneault Nashua, NH & Rachel Caron Nashua, NH
MIGNEAULT, Gisele Mary, Apr 20 1931 Sex:F Child# 2 Alphonse Migneault Canada & Therese Jodouin Canada
MIGNEAULT, J Alphonse Leonard, Nov 16 1913 Sex:M Child# 4 Emile Migneault Canada & Delia Rivard Canada
MIGNEAULT, Jos Edward Ernest, Jul 8 1932 Sex:M Child# 4 Thomas Migneault Canada & Denise Rivard Canada
MIGNEAULT, Lucile Eva, Apr 11 1919 Sex:F Child# 5 Julien J Migneault Nashua, NH & Helen Bernier Canada
MIGNEAULT, M Anne Lorraine, Feb 7 1915 Sex:F Child# 3 Emile Migneault Canada & Delia Rivard Canada
MIGNEAULT, Marguerite Rachel, Apr 1 1928 Sex:F Child# 10 Emile Migneault Canada & Delia Rivard Canada
MIGNEAULT, Marie, Jul 4 1918 Sex:F Child# 5 Emile Migneault Canada & Attelia Rivard Canada
MIGNEAULT, Marie Aurore, Nov 2 1903 Sex:F Child# 3 Joseph Migneault Canada & Rosima Dionne Canada
MIGNEAULT, Marie Blanche Cecile, Sep 29 1928 Sex:F Child# 5 Edouard Migneault Canada & F Coulombe Canada
MIGNEAULT, Marie Cecil, Apr 3 1931 Sex:F Child# 7 Edouard Migneault Canada & Florence Coulomb Canada
MIGNEAULT, Marie Roland A, Nov 30 1930 Sex:F Child# 3 Thomas Migneault Canada & Denise Rivard Canada
MIGNEAULT, Paul Emile, Jan 8 1926 Sex:M Child# 3 Zephirin Migneault Canada & Marie Langelier Canada
MIGNEAULT, Raymond Nazaire, May 22 1934 Sex:M Child# 9 Edward Migneault Canada & Florence Coulombe Canada
MIGNEAULT, Robert, May 30 1933 Sex:M Child# 8 Ed Migneault Canada & F Coulombe Canada
MIGNEAULT, Robert, May 5 1934 Sex:M Child# 2 Alphonse Migneault Canada & Theresa Jodoin Canada
MIGNEAULT, Roland, Oct 26 1925 Sex:M Child# 2 Paul Migneault Canada & Exilda Normand US
MIGNEAULT, Silvia Leonee, Dec 31 1925 Sex:F Child# 4 Oscar Migneault Nashua, NH & Bertha Bleau Altona, NY
MIGNEAULT, Simone Jeanine, Sep 26 1934 Sex:F Child# 1 Lucien Migneault Canada & Leda Bechard Canada
MIGNEAULT, Theresa, Jan 16 1928 Sex:F Child# 3 Paul Migneault Canada & Ezilda Normand Lawrence, MA
MIGNEAULT, Unknown, Jan 29 1935 Sex:F Child# 1 (No Parents Listed)
MIGNES, Zofija, Jul 30 1908 Sex:F Child# 1 Frank Mignes Russia & Isabella Bakanowski Russia
MIKALAWICZ, Philomena, Sep 11 1916 Sex:F Child# 3 Joseph Mikalawicz Russia & Agae Sergawicz Russia
MIKIAS, Unknown, Jan 15 1927 Sex:M Child# 4 Michael Mikias Greece & Helene Zafivini Greece
MIKIELONIS, Joseph, Oct 25 1908 Sex:M Child# 1 Thomasmus Mikielonis Russia & Agatha Schlistutie Russia
MIKOSKI, Andre, Nov 26 1914 Sex:M Child# 4 Joseph Mikoski Russia & Jose Russia
MIKOSKI, Chester, Aug 24 1919 Sex:M Child# 6 Joseph Mikoski Poland & Josei Mikosk Austria
MIKOSKI, Mary, Apr 1 1921 Sex:F Child# 10 Joseph Mikoski Poland & Josie Mikoski Poland Stillborn
MIKOSKI, Stanislaus, May 22 1913 Sex:M Child# 5 Joseph Mikoski Russia & Josephine Krenatz Russia
MIKOWSKI, Wonda, Nov 4 1923 Sex:F Child# 11 Joseph Mikowski Poland & Josie Mikowski Austria
MILAIRE, Joseph A, Jul 22 1900 Sex:M Child# 3 Edouard Milaire Canada & Emelie Lanrotte Mass
MILAIRE, Lydia Germaine, May 26 1931 Sex:F Child# 1 Emile Milaire Canada & Germaine Gilman New York
MILAISKI, Donald John, Mar 30 1935 Sex:M Child# 2 Joseph Milaiski Nashua, NH & Adrienne Gauthier Taunton, MA
MILAISKI, Robert Joseph, May 31 1932 Sex:M Child# 1 Joseph Milaiski Nashua, NH & Adrienne Gauthier Taunton, MA
MILAN, Clyde, Jun 2 1923 Sex:M Child# 1 Carroll Milan Pepperell, MA & Helen Whitcomb Pepperell, MA
MILAN, Robert, Jul 3 1908 Sex:M Child# 2 John Milan Pepperell, MA & Agnelina Dumaine Canada
MILAN, Ruth, Sep 5 1906 Sex:F Child# 1 John W Milan Pepperell, MA & Angelina Dumaine Canada
MILENAVICH, Antoinette, Jun 13 1921 Sex:F Child# 4 Andrew Milenavich Lithuania & Vincenta Lankoskas Lithuania
MILER, Peter, May 24 1904 Sex:M Child# 4 Andrew Miler Poland & Eva Gouz Poland
MILES, Howard Douglas, Nov 29 1932 Sex:M Child# 1 Clair Miles Amherst, Nova Scotia & Helen Lee Lowell, MA
MILES, Janet Claire, Sep 25 1934 Sex:F Child# 2 Clair Arthur Miles Nova Scotia & Helen Margaret Lee Lowell, MA
MILESKI, Malvina, May 3 1899 Sex:F Child# 3 Joseph Mileski Russia & Williamma Gajobi Russia
MILEWSKI, Mary, Aug 10 1896 Sex:F Child# 2 Joseph Milewski Russia & Icenti Giridis Russia
MILINOWICH, John, Mar 31 1915 Sex:M Child# 2 Andrew Milinowich Russia & Vensu Sacnechokous Russia
MILLER, Abraham, Jun 30 1914 Sex:M Child# 2 Sam Miller Russia & Annie Fagergson Russia
MILLER, Alice, Apr 2 1907 Sex:F Child# 6 Delphis Miller Canada & Marie Gagnon Canada
MILLER, Alida, Apr 30 1904 Sex:F Child# 4 Joseph Miller Canada & Marie Gagnon Canada
MILLER, Annie, Aug 7 1902 Sex:F Child# 6 Adam Miller Russia & Mary Poplobskey Russia
MILLER, Armand Wilfred, Aug 28 1924 Sex:M Child# 2 Wilfrid Miller Nashua, NH & Malvina Gagnon Nashua, NH
MILLER, Brenton Franklin, Dec 27 1906 Sex:M Child# 1 John F Miller Burlington, VT & Laura M Harris Nova Scotia
MILLER, David William, Dec 28 1934 Sex:M Child# 2 (No Parents Listed)
MILLER, Edward Charles, Jul 8 1914 Sex:M Child# 5 George J Miller Germany & Mary Springer Germany
MILLER, George Joseph, Dec 31 1910 Sex:M Child# 6 Delphis Miller Canada & Marie Gagnon Canada
MILLER, Harold, Jul 9 1900 Sex:M Child# 2 Oliver Miller NY & Maggie McGregor NJ
MILLER, Harold J, Aug 9 1918 Sex:M Child# 1 James O Miller Tyngsboro, MA & Minnie Rapson Shelton, CT
MILLER, Harold, Jr, Sep 8 1923 Sex:M Child# 1 Harold Miller NH & Grace Dutton NH
MILLER, Henry A, Jul 24 1898 Sex:M Child# 2 Frank H Miller White Village, VT & Josephine L Gregoire Maine
MILLER, Jean Baptiste P, Apr 6 1905 Sex:M Child# 5 Delphis Miller Canada & Marie Gagnon Canada
MILLER, John, Sep 11 1902 Sex:M Child# 3 Joseph Miller Russia & Domina Kroush Russia
MILLER, Jos Telesphore Ernes, Apr 12 1927 Sex:M Child# 1 Ernest Miller, Jr Canada & M V A Bilodeau Nashua, NH

MILLER, Joseph, Mar 28 1905 Sex:M Child# 7 Adam Miller Russia & Mary Poplousky Russia
MILLER, Joseph Adolphus, Oct 1 1909 Sex:M Child# 7 Adolphus Miller Canada & Mary Gagnon Canada
MILLER, Joseph Alphe, Apr 19 1934 Sex:M Child# 3 Ernest Miller Canada & Alma Bilodeau Nashua, NH
MILLER, Joseph Raymond, Apr 24 1929 Sex:M Child# 2 Ernest Miller, Jr Canada & Albina Bilodeau Nashua, NH
MILLER, Joseph Wilfrid, Apr 6 1901 Sex:M Child# 2 Delphis Miller Canada & Marie Gagnon Canada
MILLER, Joseph William, May 30 1935 Sex:M Child# 1 Joseph Miller Canada & Yvonne Provencher US
MILLER, Joseph, Jr, Jan 15 1931 Sex:M Child# 1 Joseph Miller Lithuania & Blanche Janis Lowell, MA
MILLER, Leonard, Aug 2 1903 Sex:M Child# 4 Alfred E Miller Richmond, PQ & Emelie Lamothe Worcester, MA
MILLER, Leonore Angeline, Mar 25 1911 Sex:F Child# 3 John F Miller Vermont & Laura M Harris Shellborne, NS
MILLER, Marie Alice, Nov 6 1902 Sex:F Child# 3 Delphis Miller Canada & Marie Gagnon Canada
MILLER, Marie Virgenie, Dec 8 1899 Sex:F Child# 1 Delphis Miller Canada & Marie Gagnon Canada
MILLER, Mary, Feb 3 1900 Sex:F Child# 1 Joseph Miller Poland & Domina Crouch Poland
MILLER, Maureen, Nov 28 1935 Sex:F Child# 1 Julian Miller Lithuania & Dorothy Ahearn Manchester, NH
MILLER, Michael, Mar 5 1901 Sex:M Child# 2 Joseph Miller Russia & Domina Krushe Russia
MILLER, Pauline Lucienne, Jul 29 1929 Sex:F Child# 4 Wilfrid Miller Nashua, NH & Malvina Gagnon Nashua, NH
MILLER, Pearl, May 12 1910 Sex:F Child# 1 Harry Miller Boston, MA & Minnie Weiner Boston, MA
MILLER, Peter, Oct 7 1904 Sex:M Child# 4 John Miller Russia & Domina Klush Russia
MILLER, Richard Joseph, Oct 17 1926 Sex:M Child# 1 William Miller New York & Adelina livernois New York
MILLER, Richard Oliver, Jun 26 1925 Sex:M Child# 2 Harold Miller Nashua, NH & Grace Dutton Hollis, NH
MILLER, Shirley Theresa, Feb 18 1928 Sex:F Child# 2 William Miller Plattsburg, NY & Delima Livernois New York
MILLER, Thomas, Jul 27 1890 Sex:M Child# 3 Thomas Miller Canada & Phebe Guertin Canada
MILLER, Thomas, May 25 1910 Sex:M Child# 1 Thomas Miller Canada & Amanda Laflamme Canada
MILLER, Unknown, Dec 13 1890 Sex:F Child# 1 Walter E Miller Burlington, VT & Edwina Lund Cleveland, OH
MILLER, Unknown, Jun 22 1892 Sex:M Child# 2 Walter E Miller Burlington, VT & Edwina Lund Cleveland, OH
MILLER, Unknown, Jun 11 1897 Sex:M Child# 1 Wilbert J Miller Moors, NY & Cora Mayo Manchester, NH
MILLER, Unknown, Aug 14 1898 Sex:F Child# 3 Walter E Miller Burlington, VT & Edwina Lund Cleveland, OH
MILLER, Virginia, Jan 4 1916 Sex:F Child# 6 George F Miller Germany & Mary Jarose Germany
MILLER, Walter, Oct 31 1933 Sex:M Child# 2 Joseph Miller Lithuania & Blanche Janis Lowell, MA
MILLETT, Eugene Rogers, Feb 25 1932 Sex:M Child# 1 R A Millett Readfield, ME & Eileen Spellman Nashua, NH
MILLETT, Herbert Allen, May 16 1910 Sex:M Child# 2 Eugene G Millett Washington & Pearl Griswold Nashua, NH
MILLETTE, Roy Raymond, Jan 30 1910 Sex:M Child# 13 Ira Millette Malone, NY & Victoria Mayhoit Canada
MILLETTE, Unknown, Jul 2 1888 Sex:F Child# 1 Charles Millette N Y & Clara Genette N Y
MILLEUR, Raymond Roland, Jan 20 1921 Sex:M Child# 1 Wilfrid Milleur NH & Malvina Gagnon NH
MILLIARD, Albert Gerard, Jul 8 1921 Sex:M Child# 10 Alfred Milliard Baltic, CT & Angeline Sirois Canada
MILLIARD, Florence Joanne, Jun 27 1935 Sex:F Child# 2 Joseph Milliard Grand Bay, Quebec & Hazel Sperry Amherst, NH
MILLIARD, Gerard Lionel, Feb 6 1914 Sex:M Child# 1 Vital Milliard Canada & M Louise Dube Nashua, NH
MILLIARD, Jos Donat Polidore, Apr 20 1923 Sex:M Child# 1 Alfred Milliard Baltic, CT & Angeline Sirois Canada
MILLIARD, Joseph Vital, Jun 13 1920 Sex:M Child# 9 Alfred Milliard Canada & Angeline Sirois Canada
MILLIES, Mary, May 17 1902 Sex:F Child# 2 Joseph Millies Poland & Mary Tamarovitz Poland
MILLIKEN, Almon Augustus, Aug 19 1920 Sex:M Child# 1 Wilbur G Milliken Portland, ME & Eleanor Hodge Lawrence, MA
MILLIKEN, Bertha May, Jun 27 1897 Sex:F Child# 3 E B Milliken Mechanic Falls, ME & Elsie M Warriner Munson, MA
MILLIKEN, James Roscoe, Oct 24 1895 Sex:M Child# 2 Edward B Milliken Mechanic Falls, ME & Elsie M Warrener Munson
MILLIKEN, Unknown, Dec 4 1893 Sex:F Child# 1 Edw B Milliken Mechanics Falls, ME & Elsie M Warrener Monson, MA
MILLIKEN, Wilbur, Jr, Mar 14 1922 Sex:M Child# 2 Wilbur Milliken Portland, ME & Eleanor Hodge Lawrence, MA
MILLINA, Antoinette, Apr 19 1926 Sex:F Child# 7 Felix Millina Lithuania & Styleana Stephana Lithuania
MILLINA, Unknown, Oct 5 1922 Sex:M Child# 6 Felix Millina Russia & Sefena Chakus Russia
MILLOON, Elizabeth Ann, Jul 15 1933 Sex:F Child# 1 Donald Milloon Lowell, MA & D M Stevens Lowell, MA
MILLS, Florence Ruth, Sep 30 1921 Sex:F Child# 4 Eugene Mills Saco, ME & Mary F Bartlett Lowell, MA
MILLS, Theodore, Apr 21 1913 Sex:M Child# 5 George Mills New York & Emma Willette New York Stillborn
MILLS, Unknown, Nov 22 1895 Sex:F Child# 1 Leon F Mills
MILLS, Unknown, Jun 3 1921 Sex:F Child# 3 Chester A Mills Somerville, MA & Florence E Bent Hyde Park, MA
MILNE, Dorothy, Jul 3 1905 Sex:F Child# 2 William Milne Ireland & Mary Connells US
MILNE, Lorraine Daphne, Jul 23 1929 Sex:F Child# 1 Alexander F Milne Aberdeen, Scotland & Ethel Wheeler Wilton, NH
MILOCZ, Stanley, Oct 2 1925 Sex:M Child# 4 Joe Milocz Poland & A Wahikiwicz Poland
MILOSH, John, Apr 27 1918 Sex:M Child# 6 Joseph Milosh Austria & Mary Tinarowitel Austria
MILROY, Henry Bruce, Jr, Jul 9 1934 Sex:M Child# 1 Henry Bruce Milroy Minnesota & Mildred McLaughlin Nashua, NH
MILTIMORE, Frances, Apr 8 1929 Sex:F Child# 1 Ralph I Miltimore Derry, NH & Marjorie Deacks Newton, MA
MILUR, John, Jan 7 1895 Sex:M Child# 1 Adam Milur Poland & Mary Poploski Poland
MINARD, Gladys, May 24 1891 Sex:F Child# 2 W O Minard Springfield & M J Page Maine
MINARD, Joseph Lucien Delph, Dec 18 1918 Sex:M Child# 3 Albert P Minard Canada & Eugenie Moussette Canada
MINARD, Unknown, Feb 2 1890 Sex:F Child# 1 Will O Minard NH & Minnie J Minard Maine
MINARELLI, Eras, Sep 15 1912 Sex:F Child# 4 Saverio Minarelli Italy & Alice Bordill Italy
MINER, Charles, Sep 27 1914 Sex:M Child# 10 Peter Miner Vermont & Minnie Cayquitue Canada
MINER, Edward Peter, Jan 21 1923 Sex:M Child# 4 Fred Miner Proctor, VT & Jennie Roberts Canada
MINER, Lillian, Oct 25 1913 Sex:F Child# 9 Peter Miner Winchendon, MA & Minnie Carpenter Canada
MINER, Marilyn Edith, Oct 15 1925 Sex:F Child# 1 Harold Miner Antrim, NH & Dora Wingate Leeds, England
MINER, Muriel Louise, Nov 28 1933 Sex:F Child# 3 William E Miner Highgate Spr, VT & Helen Davis NH
MINER, Nancy Ruth, Aug 10 1935 Sex:F Child# 4 William E Miner H G Springs, VT & Helen Davis Moultonboro, NH
MINER, Pauline Bernice, Aug 24 1927 Sex:F Child# 1 Harold Miner Leominster, MA & Beatrice L Levia Melrose, MA
MINER, Richard William, Feb 20 1935 Sex:M Child# 1 William Miner Troy, NH & Olivette Richard Nashua, NH
MINTZ, Sidney, Oct 14 1918 Sex:M Child# 9 Solomon Mintz Russia & Sarah Cohen Russia
MIQUETTE, Marie Rita Lilliene, Oct 9 1918 Sex:F Child# 3 Arthur Miquette Canada & Emelia Ricard Rhode Island
MIRAUCKAS, William, Aug 28 1913 Sex:M Child# 6 William Mirauckas Russia & Kartansia Bukewich Russia

MIRAULT, Joseph, Apr 24 1904 Sex:M Child# 8 Camile Mirault Canada & Justine Bourgois Canada
MIREAU, Marie Corinne, May 22 1905 Sex:F Child# 9 Camille Mireau Canada & Justine Bourgeois Canada
MIREAULT, Dorothy Elizabeth, Jul 1 1922 Sex:F Child# 1 Hector Mireault Canada & Margaret Hogan Newmarket, NH
MIREAULT, Lillian Patricia, Oct 3 1927 Sex:F Child# 4 Hector Mireault Canada & Margant Hogan Newmarket, NH
MIREAULT, Margaret Lucille, Nov 8 1923 Sex:F Child# 2 Hector Mireault Canada & Margaret Hogan Newmarket, NH
MIREAULT, Marie Rose Blanche, Aug 24 1916 Sex:F Child# 10 Camil Mireault Canada & Justine Bourgeois Canada
MIREAULT, Robert Howard, Nov 2 1925 Sex:M Child# 3 Hector Mireault Canada & Marg Hogan Newmarket, NH
MIRSKY, Beatrice, Jul 12 1918 Sex:F Child# 4 Aaron Mirsky Russia & Lela Canter Russia
MISCHINIS, Joseph, Jan 29 1917 Sex:M Child# 3 Mike Mischinis Russia Lithuania & Agae Yakamonita Russia Lithuania
MISHKINIS, Constantine, Jul 31 1911 Sex:F Child# 2 Mike Mishkinis Russia & Agae Yakavanuty Russia
MISIASZCK, John, Nov 8 1918 Sex:M Child# 3 Peter Misiaszck Poland & Joanne Armata Poland
MISIASZEK, Nellie, Aug 27 1923 Sex:F Child# 3 Albert Misiaszek Poland & Victoria Misiaszek Poland
MISISKI, Julia, Aug 24 1911 Sex:F Child# 2 John Misiski Austria & Henrietta Wes Austria
MISKAUSKIS, Frank, Dec 30 1923 Sex:M Child# 2 Joseph Miskauskis Russia & Helen Russia
MISKINIS, Michael, Sep 28 1906 Sex:M Child# 6 Samuel Miskinis Russia & Elize Lefebvre Nashua, NH
MISKINIS, Rose, Jun 14 1916 Sex:F Child# 4 Joseph Miskinis Russia & Minnie Bukarich Russia
MISZKESZNES, Julia Anna, Feb 23 1909 Sex:F Child# 7 Sam Miszkesznes Russia & Elise Lefebvre NH
MITCHELL, Basil, Mar 23 1896 Sex:M Child# 3 John Mitchell Mass & Bridget Donovan Ireland
MITCHELL, Emma G, Nov 17 1888 Sex:F Child# 2 James Mitchell Boston & Alice E Moore Burlington, VT
MITCHELL, Gilbert Everett, Jr, Jun 26 1921 Sex:M Child# 1 Gilbert E Mitchell Nashua, NH & Maude Pombrio Nashua, NH
MITCHELL, Janet, Mar 6 1909 Sex:F Child# 4 John W Mitchell Lancaster, MA & Mary J Clarke Nashua, NH
MITCHELL, John W, Sep 1 1889 Sex:M Child# 1 John W Mitchell Lancaster, MA & Mary J Clarke Nashua, NH
MITCHELL, Minnie Lucy, Apr 29 1910 Sex:F Child# 1 Rollins K Mitchell
MITCHELL, Muriel Marguerite, Jul 6 1930 Sex:F Child# 5 Joseph H Mitchell Philadelphia, PA & Eleanor Long Allp
MITCHELL, Ralph Warren, Mar 12 1923 Sex:M Child# 2 Gilbert Mitchell Nashua, NH & Maud Pontbriand Nashua, NH
MITCHELL, Rena L, Apr 10 1893 Sex:F Child# 1 John W Mitchell Mass & Bridget Donovan Ireland
MITCHELL, Unknown, Sep 20 1892 Sex:M Child# 1 Everett Mitchell Maine & Mary Kennedy New Brunswick
MITCHELL, Wilfred, Feb 17 1934 Sex:M Child# 4 Nicholas Mitchell NH & Pearl Damour New York Stillborn
MITCHELL, William Nicholas, Jul 25 1935 Sex:M Child# 5 Nicholas Mitchell Nashua, NH & Beatrice D'Amour Plattsburg
MITSIL, Unice, Aug 19 1923 Sex:M Child# 20 Peter Mitsil Greece & Panagrola Haintpylau Greece
MIZARA, Leon, Jan 4 1909 Sex:M Child# 4 Thomas Mizara Russia & Ona Weskintie Russia
MIZAROS, Alexandra, Sep 27 1910 Sex:F Child# 5 Tamosus Mizaros Russia & Ona Wieczkutie Russia
MIZER, Simon, Mar 9 1904 Sex:M Child# 1 Thomas Mizer Russia & Anna Weoskute Russia
MIZN, William, Mar 8 1916 Sex:M Child# 1 William Mizn Russia & Annie Timcantch Russia
MIZO, Charls, May 16 1902 Sex:M Child# 6 Carl M Mizo Vermont & Lilla Labounty Canada
MIZO, Fabian Carl, Jan 8 1904 Sex:M Child# 7 Carl Mizo Newport, VT & Dellie Labounty Eagen, VT
MIZO, Guy Clifton, Dec 28 1916 Sex:M Child# 1 Guy Mizo Newport, VT & Helen Smith Nashua, NH
MIZO, Mildred Winfred, Aug 28 1907 Sex:F Child# 9 Carl Mizo Vermont & Delia Labonte Vermont
MIZORIVE, Antony, Oct 20 1905 Sex:M Child# 2 Thomas Mizorive Russia & Anna Vetsckiz Russia
MIZOROCZ, Rosa, Apr 13 1907 Sex:F Child# 3 Jacobus Mizorocz Russia & Anna Weckis Russia
MLEA, Andrew, Apr 11 1907 Sex:M Child# 3 John Mlea Austria & Eva gounka Hungary
MLEY, Eva, Jun 1 1910 Sex:F Child# 4 Andro Mley Hungary & Eva Konko Hungary
MLEY, Joseph, May 5 1915 Sex:M Child# 10 Andro Mley Hungary & Eva Kouko Hungary
MOCAS, James Coleman, Jul 9 1922 Sex:M Child# 1 Demetrius P Mocas Greece & Flora May Coleman Vermont
MOCHLER, Honorie, Oct 1 1889 Sex:F Child# 2 James Mochler Ireland & Jennie Ryan Collinsville, CT
MOCHLER, Julia A, Oct 16 1887 Sex:F Child# 2 James Mochler Ireland & Jennie Southington, CT
MOEKAVITCH, John, Dec 15 1909 Sex:M Child# 2 Michael Moekavitch Russia & Josephine Tat Russia
MOHER, Margaret Loretta, Nov 11 1925 Sex:F Child# 5 Daniel Moher Ireland & Mary O'Neil Nashua, NH
MOIN, Agnes, Jul 10 1890 Sex:F Child# 3 Henry D Moin Londonderry, NH & Josephine Duchesneau Canada
MOISAN, Adolphe Elise, Jan 7 1895 Sex:M Child# 4 Ferd Moisan Canada & Adele Landry Canada
MOISAN, Joseph, Jan 15 1894 Sex:M Child# 3 Ferdinand Moisan Canada & Adele Landry Canada
MOISANT, Marie Elizabeth, Mar 1 1911 Sex:F Child# 10 Calixte Moisant Vermont & Lilia Labonte Vermont
MOISAU, Unknown, Dec 7 1891 Sex:M Child# 1 Ferd Moisau Canada & Delia Landry Canada Stillborn
MOISEAU, Unknown, Dec 12 1892 Sex:F Child# 2 Ferdinand Moiseau Canada & Adele Landry Canada
MOISON, Beatrice Grace, Jun 16 1900 Sex:F Child# 5 Calixte Moison Vermont & Lydia Labonte Vermont
MOKARAWICH, Mamie, Jul 1 1914 Sex:F Child# 1 Joseph Mokarawich Russia & Kate Gedialutia Russia
MOLEVIC, John, Jun 16 1914 Sex:M Child# 3 Anthony Molevic Russia & Anna Mirkate Russia
MOLEY, Eugenye, Sep 28 1917 Sex:F Child# 5 Antone Moley Russia & Anna Briksti Russia
MOLIR, Atanas, Jan 9 1916 Sex:M Child# 4 Atanas Molir Russia & Anan Brikat Russia
MOLIS, Minnie, Nov 5 1913 Sex:F Child# 1 Frank Molis Russia & Minnie Binepats Russia
MOLIWICZ, Alena, Nov 20 1911 Sex:F Child# 1 Antonas Moliwicz Russia & Anan Brikawicte Russia
MOLLOY, Agnes M, Jul 31 1911 Sex:F Child# 3 George W Molloy Lawrence, MA & Sarah Foran New York
MOLLOY, Anna, Jan 28 1899 Sex:F Child# 6 William Molloy Ireland & Rose Etta Keeley England
MOLLOY, Annie, Sep 18 1895 Sex:F Child# 10 John Molloy Ireland & Ellen W Gaffney Ireland
MOLLOY, Anthony J, Mar 18 1887 Sex:M Child# 1 William Molloy Ireland & Rose E Keely Ireland
MOLLOY, Anthony Robert, Aug 22 1920 Sex:M Child# 1 Anthony J Molloy Nashua, NH & Mary A Cullity Manchester, NH
MOLLOY, Eugene Patrick, Mar 17 1925 Sex:M Child# 3 Anthony Molloy Nashua, NH & Mary Cullity Manchester, NH
MOLLOY, James, Jul 11 1891 Sex:M Child# 8 John Molloy Ireland & Helen Gaffney Ireland
MOLLOY, John Edward, Nov 27 1921 Sex:M Child# 2 Anthony Molloy Nashua, NH & Mary Cullity Manchester, NH
MOLLOY, Marion Hazel, Jan 5 1909 Sex:F Child# 2 George W Molloy Lawrence, MA & Sarah M Foran Chateaugay, NY
MOLLOY, Mary Ann, Feb 8 1889 Sex:F Child# 2 William Molloy Ireland & Rose Molloy England
MOLLOY, Nellie Mary, Jun 1 1906 Sex:F Child# 1 George W Molloy Lawrence, MA & Sarah M Foran Chateaugay, NY
MOLTON, May Pauline, May 25 1917 Sex:F Child# 1 George Molton Lynn, MA & Adelaide M Austin Pepperell, MA

MONAHAN, Maria, Jan 15 1917 Sex:F Child# 1 Joseph Monahan
MONAHAN, Mary Margaret, Jun 20 1908 Sex:F Child# 2 Frank J Monahan Montreal, Canada & Mary E McGlynn Nashua, NH
MONAIE, Celine, Aug 4 1909 Sex:F Child# 1 Ernest Monaie France & Angelina Ledoux Canada Stillborn
MONARTY, Kenneth Philip, Apr 18 1925 Sex:M Child# 4 Dennis Monarty Nashua, NH & Amanda Caron Nashua, NH
MONAST, Jeanne Theresa, Feb 25 1927 Sex:F Child# 2 Antonio Monast Manchester, NH & Rose Allard Manchester, NH
MONAT, Marie B Eva, Jan 18 1896 Sex:F Child# 4 Joseph E Monat Canada & Marie A Gervais Colchester, CT
MONATY, Michael John, Aug 28 1889 Sex:M Child# 3 Piclant Monaty Ireland & Mary A O'Brien London
MONBLEAU, Jacqueline Mae, Aug 3 1933 Sex:F Child# 1 Wilfrid Monbleau Lowell, MA & Irene Russell Lowell, MA
MONBLEAU, John, Jul 4 1904 Sex:M Child# 8 Louis Monbleau Detroit, MI & Osanna Bedard Canada
MONBLEAU, Unknown, Dec 15 1887 Sex:F Child# 9 Narcisse Monbleau VT & Angeline Canada
MONCEAU, Joseph Louis E, Apr 5 1905 Sex:M Child# 1 Louis Monceau Vermont & Marie Theriault Canada
MONDOS, Roland Francis, Jul 7 1929 Sex:M Child# 1 Isadore Mondos Canada & Christine Moriarty Nashua, NH
MONDOUX, Alice, May 25 1917 Sex:F Child# 6 Alfred Mondoux Canada & Rose Anna Labonte Canada
MONDOUX, Blanche, Sep 16 1913 Sex:F Child# 5 Albert Mondoux Canada & Rose Anna Lebrun Canada
MONDOUX, Leo, Dec 10 1911 Sex:M Child# 4 Albert Mondoux Canada & Rosanna Labonte Canada
MONDOUX, Raymond Edgar, Apr 24 1932 Sex:M Child# 1 Edgar J Mondoux Suncook, NH & A Lacaillade W Bolton, VT
MONES, Frank, Apr 27 1926 Sex:M Child# 6 Dominic Mones Lithuania & Martha Mrozukena Lithuania
MONES, Mary, Mar 29 1928 Sex:F Child# 9 Dominic Mones Lithuania & Mar Marjoakna Lithuania
MONFILS, Cecile Rachel, Dec 28 1907 Sex:F Child# 3 George T Monfils Worcester, MA & Blanche Londreville Canada
MONFILS, Leonard, Aug 25 1904 Sex:M Child# 1 George Monfils Worcester, MA & Blanche Londreville Canada
MONFILS, Lorraine, Oct 1 1905 Sex:F Child# 2 George Monfils Worcester, MA & Blanche Londreville Canada
MONFILS, Oscar, Dec 4 1908 Sex:M Child# 4 George Monfils Worcester, MA & Blanche Londreville Canada
MONIER, Elizabeth, Jun 7 1893 Sex:F Child# 2 George Monier Canada & Elizabeth Avard Canada
MONIER, Frederic, Jun 6 1898 Sex:M Child# 6 George Monier Canada & Elizabeth Howard Canada
MONIER, George, Apr 12 1892 Sex:M Child# 2 George Monier Canada & Elizabeth Avard Canada
MONIER, Joseph Leo Olivier, Jul 18 1901 Sex:M Child# 1 Charles Monier Vermont & Anna Ouellette Canada
MONIER, Thomas, Jan 21 1895 Sex:M Child# 4 Georges Monier US & Elizabeth Avard Canada
MONIER, Unknown, May 12 1891 Sex:M Child# 1 George Monier Canada & Elizabeth Avard Canada Stillborn
MONIER, Uric, Jul 17 1900 Sex:M Child# 7 George Monier Canada & Elizabeth Howard Canada
MONIS, Felix John, Oct 27 1929 Sex:M Child# 4 John Monis Lithuania & Catherine Navithky Lithuania
MONIS, Julia, Jan 16 1922 Sex:F Child# 5 Dominik Monis Russia & Martha Mayokanitis Russia
MONIUS, Eleanor, Apr 5 1925 Sex:F Child# 2 John Monius Lithuania & Kath Naviskey Lithuania
MONIUS, Halic, Dec 17 1922 Sex:M Child# 1 John Monius Lithuania & Catherine Navidski Lithuania
MONKLEY, Joyce Susanne, Oct 7 1934 Sex:F Child# 2 William W Monkley Canada & Sue Cannon Canada
MONLAZIMES, Vasilike, Jan 12 1929 Sex:F Child# 2 Zaharias Monlazimes Greece & Rena Arkoleka Greece
MONNIER, Alida, Aug 17 1903 Sex:F Child# 2 Charles Monnier Vermont & Anna Ouellette Canada
MONREAU, Albina, Jul 14 1903 Sex:F Child# 3 Elzear Monreau Canada & Denise Girouard Nashua, NH
MONROE, Alfred, Jun 12 1897 Sex:M Child# 2 Jean Baptiste Monroe Canada & Anna Chenette Canada
MONROE, Maggie L, Oct 30 1893 Sex:F Child# 4 David Monroe NB & Eliza Robinson NB
MONRONTSIOS, Unknown, Aug 22 1919 Sex:F Child# 2 Chris Monrontsios Greece & Mary Spinanopoulos Greece
MONTELOZICH, Unknown, Apr 13 1913 Sex:M Child# 2 Alex Montelozich Russia & Victoria Senervais Russia
MONTGOMERY, Anna Mary, May 14 1892 Sex:F Child# 2 Thomas Montgomery NY & Mary Frankland Ireland
MONTGOMERY, Barbara, Oct 17 1921 Sex:F Child# 2 Frank Montgomery Nashua, NH & Obeline Bassett Hudson, NH
MONTGOMERY, Ruth M, Sep 17 1917 Sex:F Child# 1 Frank Montgomery Nashua, NH & Obeline Bassett Hudson, NH
MONTONNA, Carolyn Ryder, Nov 25 1931 Sex:F Child# 1 Oscar L Montonna Cape Vincent, NY & Helen Ryder Watertown, MA
MONTORMEY, Unknown, Sep 4 1888 Sex:F Child# 4 Frank Montormey Scotland & Alice Allen Scotland
MONTRONE, Nancy, Jun 14 1934 Sex:F Child# 4 John Montrone Italy & Mildred Rynn Nashua, NH
MONTRONE, Natalie, Jun 14 1934 Sex:F Child# 5 John Montrone Italy & Mildred Rynn Nashua, NH
MONTRONE, Patricia Margaret, Mar 15 1932 Sex:F Child# 3 John Montrone Italy & Mildred Rynn Canada
MONTROSE, Melinda A, Sep 29 1890 Sex:F Child# 1 Samuel P Montrose Mass & Lizzie A Morris Mass
MONTY, Claire Louise, Jun 13 1918 Sex:F Child# 2 Olier Monty Nashua, NH & Lea Plouff Nashua, NH
MONTY, Frank, Aug 5 1888 Sex:M Child# 1 Charles A Monty New York & Rose A Reynolds Maine
MONTY, George, May 17 1933 Sex:M Child# 1 Raymond Monty Nashua, NH & Alice Brault Nashua, NH
MONTY, Jeannette Corinne, Mar 3 1917 Sex:F Child# 1 Leo Monty Nashua, NH & Lea May Plouffe Nashua, NH
MONTY, Leo Francis, Oct 1 1905 Sex:M Child# 3 Louis Monty Canada & Emma Dutilly Canada
MONTY, Louis Alphonse, Mar 17 1891 Sex:M Child# 1 Louis Monty Canada & Emma Dutilly Canada
MONTY, Raymond L H, Apr 17 1903 Sex:M Child# 2 Louis Monty Canada & Emma Dutilly Canada
MONTY, Yolande, Nov 6 1934 Sex:F Child# 2 Raymond Monty Nashua, NH & Alice Brault Nashua, NH Stillborn
MOOAR, Willard Everett, Jan 25 1907 Sex:M Child# 2 Edmund Mooar Milford, NH & Rose Lefebvre Nashua, NH
MOODY, Gladys Penrose, Apr 30 1901 Sex:F Child# 1 William Moody NY & Burtha Nicholson Prince Edward Island
MOODY, James Augustus, Mar 28 1897 Sex:M Child# 1 James E Moody Claremont, NH & Minnie L Moody Claremont, NH
MOODY, June, Jun 21 1909 Sex:F Child# 2 John Moody Malden, MA & Mamie Walton Portland, ME
MOODY, Ralph Frederick, Apr 20 1904 Sex:M Child# 3 William Moody Loville, NY & Bertha Nicholson PEI
MOODY, Unknown, Jul 15 1891 Sex:M Child# 2 William H Moody Maine & Flora A Davis Maine
MOODY, Unknown, Apr 6 1901 Sex:M Child# 4 James W Moody S Carolina & Eliza Mullins S Carolina
MOODY, Unknown, Nov 29 1902 Sex:M Child# 2 William Moody Scoville & Bertha M Nicholson P E Island
MOODY, Unknown, Aug 27 1905 Sex:M Child# 4 William Moody New York & Bertha Nicholson Prince Edward Island
MOODY, William Joseph, Mar 4 1919 Sex:M Child# 1 Augustus W Moody Woburn, MA & Gertrude J Morahan Nashua, NH
MOON, Shirley May, Feb 15 1896 Sex:F Child# 3 H Moon Vermont & May Mackey Canada
MOONEY, Eugene Leroy, Dec 4 1935 Sex:M Child# 2 John Mooney St Johnsbury, VT & Pauline Feneff Littleton, NH
MOONEY, Frank Robert, Oct 15 1930 Sex:M Child# 2 Thomas Mooney Boston, MA & Libby Brault Nashua, NH
MOONEY, Gertrude, Jul 23 1891 Sex:F Child# 4 Charles E Mooney Canada & Mary J Looman Georgia, VT
MOONEY, Thomas William, Jun 13 1925 Sex:M Child# 1 Thomas Mooney Boston, MA & Libby C Breault Nashua, NH

MOORAD, Unknown, Feb 17 1898 Sex:F Child# 1 Paul Moorad Armenia & Christina Armenia
MOORADEAU, Manoog, Nov 7 1898 Sex:F Child# 4 Charles Mooradeau Armenia & Elmar Kabugian Armenia
MOORBY, Muriel Ellsworth, Mar 3 1919 Sex:F Child# 1 Benjamin Moorby England & Eva May Cole Bristol, RI
MOORBY, Robert Lawrence, Dec 15 1922 Sex:M Child# 1 Lawrence Moorby England & Jennie Coulthurst England
MOORE, Barbara, Jun 7 1925 Sex:F Child# 1 Lois E Moore Haverhill, MA & Jenette Grover Nashua, NH
MOORE, Brenda, Jun 7 1925 Sex:F Child# 2 Lois E Moore Haverhill, MA & Jenette Grover Nashua, NH
MOORE, Calvin Brock, Feb 17 1933 Sex:M Child# 2 Sidney W Moore Mass & Mildred Mason Mass
MOORE, Dora Madeline, Mar 19 1908 Sex:F Child# 3 James E Moore Madison, NH & Nellie M Heselton Conway, NH
MOORE, Doris Eileen, Aug 20 1906 Sex:F Child# 1 Winslow D Moore Ellsworth, ME & Sadie A Tebbetts Otis, ME
MOORE, Doris Ivy, Sep 4 1920 Sex:F Child# 3 Earle B Moore Hudson, NH & Vesta Harris Nashua, NH
MOORE, Dorothy June, Jun 10 1918 Sex:F Child# 4 George W Moore Warwick, MA & Lena June Hodgman Mason, NH
MOORE, Edgar F, Feb 7 1894 Sex:M Child# 2 Fred J Moore Canaan, ME & Ida A Packard Skowhegan, ME
MOORE, Eleanor Gladys, Apr 15 1929 Sex:F Child# 7 Earl B Moore Hudson, NH & Vesta Harris Nashua, NH
MOORE, Elsie Margaret, Feb 4 1908 Sex:F Child# 6 Aubrey W Moore S Limington, ME & Evelyn Ashton St John, NB
MOORE, Emily May, Jul 16 1924 Sex:F Child# 4 Chester W Moore Warwick, MA & Ethel Sloat New Brunswick
MOORE, Fred, Mar 12 1892 Sex:M Child# 1 Fred J Moore Pittsfield, ME & Ida Packard Skowhegan, ME
MOORE, George P, Sep 14 1919 Sex:M Child# 2 George P Moore Hollis, NH & Christine N Sargent Nashua, NH
MOORE, Gordon Arthur, Aug 18 1931 Sex:M Child# 8 Earl B Moore Hudson, NH & Vesta Harris Nashua, NH
MOORE, Harold Lester, Jun 14 1922 Sex:M Child# 4 Earle Moore Hudson, NH & Vesta Harris Nashua, NH
MOORE, Helen Frances, May 20 1916 Sex:F Child# 2 Chester W Moore Warwick, MA & Ethel P Sloat Queensburg, NS
MOORE, Irving Davis, Dec 3 1925 Sex:M Child# 1 Theodore Moore Canada & Mary Clough Canada
MOORE, Irwin F, Jul 29 1912 Sex:M Child# 8 Aubrey W Moore N Lemington & Evelyn Ashton
MOORE, John, Apr 18 1904 Sex:M Child# 1 Michael J Moore Ireland & Mary A Foley Worcester, MA
MOORE, John Edward, Nov 21 1905 Sex:M Child# 2 Michael Moore Ireland & Mary Foley Nashua, NH
MOORE, John Wright, Oct 28 1930 Sex:M Child# 2 John Jas Moore Ireland & Amy Wright Clinton, MA
MOORE, Kathleen Rose, Aug 22 1909 Sex:F Child# 7 Aubrey W Moore Maine & Evelyn Ashton New Brunsiwck
MOORE, Kenneth McKay, Aug 30 1923 Sex:M Child# 5 Earl B Moore Hudson, NH & Vesta Harris Nashua, NH
MOORE, Leonard Smith, Apr 28 1915 Sex:M Child# 3 George W Moore Warwick, MA & Lena J Hodgman Mason, NH
MOORE, Lois, Sep 9 1921 Sex:F Child# 3 Chester W Moore Warwick, MA & Ethel Sloat New Brunswick
MOORE, Marguerite Nellie, Jul 8 1918 Sex:F Child# 1 Howard C Moore Kittery Dep, ME & Marguerite D Wyeth Nashua, NH
MOORE, Marjorie Phyllis, Jan 7 1927 Sex:F Child# 6 Carle Moore Hudson, NH & Vesta Harris Nashua, NH
MOORE, Patricia Ann, Jul 24 1935 Sex:F Child# 6 Sidney Moore Cambridge, MA & Mildred Mason Cambridge, MA
MOORE, Richard Sargent, Apr 17 1929 Sex:M Child# 3 George Moore Hollis, NH & Christine Sargent Nashua, NH
MOORE, Robert Clyde, Oct 14 1929 Sex:M Child# 3 Clyde Moore Mass & Helen Gould Maine
MOORE, Robert Walter, Aug 17 1908 Sex:M Child# 1 John J Moore Ireland & Amy Wright Clinton, MA
MOORE, Shirley Evelyn, Jun 19 1922 Sex:F Child# 2 Clyde O Moore Everett, MA & Helen Trott Peak Isle, ME
MOORE, Sidney, Feb 17 1929 Sex:M Child# 1 Sidney Moore Cambridge, MA & Mildred Mason Cambridge, MA Stillborn
MOORE, Unknown, Nov 9 1899 Sex:M Child# 8 Fred J Moore Maine & Ida A Packard Maine
MOORE, Unknown, Jul 25 1927 Sex:F Child# 2 Theodore Moore Conway, NH & Marion Clough Haverhill, MA Stillborn
MOORE, Viola May, Oct 1 1921 Sex:F Child# 2 Howard C Moore Revere, MA & Marguerite Wyeth Nashua, NH
MOORE, Virginia, Sep 5 1917 Sex:F Child# 1 George P Moore Hollis, NH & Christine M Sargent Nashua, NH
MOORHOUSE, Ola, May 4 1933 Sex:F Child# 2 Henry Moorhouse Frediction NB, Can & Ola Boyer Manchester, NH
MOQUIN, Adelard Edward, Aug 24 1923 Sex:M Child# 1 Adelard Moquin Canada & Anne J Riley Nashua, NH
MORADIAN, Unknown, May 15 1900 Sex:F Child# 3 Charles Moradian Armenia & Almoth Boyajrian Armenia
MORAHAN, Unknown, Dec 25 1887 Sex:F Child# 4 Patrick Morahan Ireland & Julia Loomey Ireland
MORAIS, Joseph Auguste, Jul 23 1897 Sex:M Child# 3 Auguste Morais Canada & Delphine Lachance Canada
MORAIS, M Delphine B I, Jun 25 1895 Sex:F Child# 1 Auguste Morais Canada & Delphine Lachance Canada
MORAIS, Marie Anne, Jul 23 1896 Sex:F Child# 3 Alfred Morais Canada & Malvina Levesque Canada
MORAIS, Olivien Elise, Jun 2 1911 Sex:M Child# 3 Joseph Morais US & Amanda Gagnon Canada
MORAIS, Unknown, Mar 2 1896 Sex:M Child# 2 Auguste Morais Canada & Delphine Lachance Canada Stillborn
MORAN, Agnes Frances, Apr 18 1909 Sex:F Child# 3 Bernard G Moran Nashua, NH & Delia B Mulhern Fitchburg, MA
MORAN, Alice, Aug 31 1887 Sex:F Child# 8 Thomas Moran Ireland & Anna Lynch Ireland
MORAN, Alice, Jul 23 1923 Sex:F Child# 4 Frank Moran Nashua, NH & Catherine Howard Nashua, NH
MORAN, Alice Katherine, Nov 10 1922 Sex:F Child# 8 Bernard G Moran Nashua, NH & Della B Mulhern Fitchburg, MA
MORAN, Ann, Apr 18 1890 Sex:F Child# 12 John Moran Ireland & Ellen Ireland
MORAN, Ann Gertrude, Jan 15 1906 Sex:F Child# 1 Michael D Moran Ireland & Grace I Cutter Nashua, NH
MORAN, Ann Josephine, Sep 11 1901 Sex:F Child# 2 Thomas Moran Ireland & Ellen Courtney Ireland
MORAN, Barbara, Mar 14 1910 Sex:F Child# 4 Thomas F Moran Nashua, NH & Maude C Matthews Rouses Point, NY
MORAN, Bernard Joseph, Feb 23 1907 Sex:M Child# 1 Bernard G Moran Nashua, NH & Delia B Mulhern Fitchburg, MA
MORAN, Donald Paul, Oct 13 1935 Sex:M Child# 1 Paul R Moran Nashua, NH & Marjorie McNally Nashua, NH
MORAN, Doris, Dec 27 1908 Sex:F Child# 1 Gus Moran
MORAN, Dorothy, Aug 6 1907 Sex:F Child# 2 Thomas F Moran Nashua, NH & Maude C Matthews
MORAN, Edward, Jan 25 1934 Sex:M Child# 4 Michael Edward Moran Somersworth, NH & Helen Lynch Manchester, NH
MORAN, Edward P, Aug 19 1912 Sex:M Child# 5 Bernard G Moran Nashua, NH & Delia Mulhern Fitchburg, MA
MORAN, Elva, Nov 16 1901 Sex:F Child# 4 Charles Moran Nashua, NH & Elva Fuller Vermont
MORAN, Frank, May 12 1889 Sex:M Child# 9 Thomas Moran Ireland & Anna Lynch Ireland
MORAN, Frank, Apr 22 1897 Sex:M Child# 2 Frank J Moran Nashua, NH & Julia Humphrey Ireland
MORAN, Gilbert Francis, Aug 16 1918 Sex:M Child# 2 Frank J Moran Nashua, NH & Catherine E Howard Nashua, NH
MORAN, Hannah Teresa, Jan 25 1905 Sex:F Child# 4 Thomas J Moran Ireland & Helen Courtney Ireland
MORAN, Helen Ann, Jun 17 1917 Sex:F Child# 7 Bernard G Moran Nashua, NH & Delia B Mulhern Fitchburg, MA
MORAN, Helen Maria, Feb 21 1900 Sex:F Child# 1 Thomas J Moran Ireland & Ellen Courtney Ireland
MORAN, James Robert, Dec 25 1915 Sex:M Child# 6 Bernard G Moran Nashua, NH & Delia B Mulhern Fitchburg, MA
MORAN, Jennie E, Jan 24 1891 Sex:F Child# 1 James C Moran Mass & Emma E Martin Mass

MORAN, John Earle, Dec 11 1912 Sex:M Child# 1 John E Moran Nashua, NH & Annette L Morin Nashua, NH
MORAN, John McElroy, Nov 14 1931 Sex:M Child# 2 Kenneth M Moran Nashua, NH & Virginia McElroy Jamestown, ND
MORAN, John Patrick, Sep 1 1906 Sex:M Child# 5 Thomas J Moran Ireland & Ellen Courtney Ireland
MORAN, John Philip, Sep 5 1913 Sex:M Child# 3 Michael D Moran Ireland & Grace Cutter Nashua, NH
MORAN, John William, Mar 3 1908 Sex:M Child# 2 Bernard G Moran Nashua, NH & Delia Mulhern Fitchburg, MA
MORAN, Joseph Alfred, Oct 28 1900 Sex:M Child# 1 George Moran NH & Rosa Lefebvre NH
MORAN, Katherine, Jun 26 1903 Sex:F Child# 3 Thomas Moran Ireland & Helen Courtney Ireland
MORAN, Katherine Grace, Jul 2 1917 Sex:F Child# 5 Michael D Moran Ireland & Grace Cutter Nashua, NH
MORAN, Kenneth Matthews, Jul 7 1906 Sex:M Child# 1 Thomas F Moran Nashua, NH & Maude C Matthews Rouses Point, NY
MORAN, Kenneth McElroy, Sep 15 1930 Sex:M Child# 1 Kenneth M Moran Nashua, NH & Virginia McElroy Jamestown, ND
MORAN, Leo Edouard, Feb 9 1897 Sex:M Child# 1 Michael Moran Nashua, NH & Rose Courtemanche Nashua, NH
MORAN, Lillian Frances, May 8 1895 Sex:F Child# 1 Frank J Moran Nashua, NH & Julia Shea Ireland
MORAN, Lizzie Agnes, Nov 5 1891 Sex:F Child# 10 Thomas Moran Ireland & Anna Lynch Ireland
MORAN, Lorraine Rose, Sep 29 1928 Sex:F Child# 6 George Moran Nashua, NH & Mary A Petrain Canada
MORAN, Lucy, Jun 4 1897 Sex:F Child# 3 James H Moran Nashua, NH & Maud E Terrell Nashua, NH
MORAN, Madeline E, Sep 13 1908 Sex:F Child# 3 Thomas F Moran Nashua, NH & Maude C Matthews Rouses Point, NY
MORAN, Margaret Ann, Apr 9 1922 Sex:F Child# 3 Frank Moran Nashua, NH & Katherine Howard Nashua, NH
MORAN, Marguerite, Sep 9 1899 Sex:F Child# 3 James Moran NH & Maude Terrell NH
MORAN, Marie Rita Lucille, May 25 1925 Sex:F Child# 1 Henry Moran Canada & Yvonne Berube Nashua, NH
MORAN, Marjorie Elaine, Feb 20 1930 Sex:F Child# 1 Leo Moran Nashua, NH & Regina Poirier Nashua, NH
MORAN, Paul Anthony, Nov 22 1910 Sex:M Child# 4 Bernard G Moran Nashua, NH & Delia Mulhern Fitchburg, MA
MORAN, Paul Robert, Oct 25 1914 Sex:M Child# 4 Michael Moran Ireland & Grace Cutter Nashua, NH
MORAN, Pauline Andrea, Jun 29 1915 Sex:F Child# 2 John E Moran Nashua, NH & Annette L Morin Nashua, NH
MORAN, Philip B, Aug 15 1899 Sex:M Child# 1 Frank Moran Nashua, NH & Margaret Keon England
MORAN, Richard Henry, Aug 17 1918 Sex:M Child# 3 John E Moran Nashua, NH & Annette Leah Morin Nashua, NH
MORAN, Rita Mary, Dec 16 1923 Sex:F Child# 7 Michael Moran Ireland & Grace Cutter Nashua, NH
MORAN, Robert Edwin, Apr 10 1923 Sex:M Child# 4 John Moran Nashua, NH & Annette Morin Nashua, NH
MORAN, Therese Mabel, Jan 5 1931 Sex:F Child# 1 Joseph Moran Dunstable, MA & Obeline Goyait Nashua, NH
MORAN, Thomas Francis, Jan 17 1916 Sex:M Child# 5 Thomas F Moran Nashua, NH & Maude C Matthews Rouses Pt, NY
MORAN, Thomas Joseph, Mar 13 1912 Sex:M Child# 2 Michael D Moran Ireland & Grace Cutter Nashua, NH
MORAN, Unknown, Dec 15 1891 Sex:F Child# 1 Charles F Moran Nashua, NH & Elva Fuller Newark, VT
MORAN, Unknown, Jun 8 1892 Sex:M Child# John J Moran Ireland & Ellen Ireland Stillborn
MORAN, Unknown, Mar 28 1894 Sex:F Child# 1 James H Moran Nashua, NH & Maude Terrell Nashua, NH
MORAN, Unknown, Dec 23 1909 Sex:F Child# 4 James Moran Nashua, NH & Maude Tyrell
MORAN, Unknown, Jul 7 1912 Sex:M Child# 2 (No Parents Listed)
MORAN, Unknown, Dec 20 1915 Sex:M Child# 1 Frank J Moran Nashua, NH & Katherine H Howard Nashua, NH Stillborn
MORAN, Wilfred Joseph, Oct 8 1927 Sex:M Child# 1 Louis Moran Milford, NH & Alma Berry Pittsfield, NH Stillborn
MORAN, William, Dec 5 1888 Sex:M Child# 11 John Moran Ireland & Ellen Ireland
MORAN, William Frederick, May 5 1919 Sex:M Child# 6 Michael D Moran Ireland & Grace Cutter Nashua, NH
MORAN, William Henry, Feb 3 1896 Sex:M Child# 3 Burnard Moran Nashua, NH & Mary O'Brien Grandville
MORAN, William Herbert, Dec 9 1898 Sex:M Child# 3 Charles Moran Nashua, NH & Elra E Fuller Vermont
MORANDA, Celina A, May 5 1887 Sex:F Child# Norbert Moranda P Q & Philomene Lapierre Champlain, NY
MORAROS, Mary, Jul 31 1918 Sex:F Child# 1 Nicholas Moraros Greece & Helen Dezazos Greece
MORAZINES, Mary Diamantoula, Sep 8 1930 Sex:F Child# 1 John D Morazines Greece & Lascarina Raras Greece
MOREAU, Alice Eliane, Nov 30 1911 Sex:F Child# 11 Alfred Moreau Canada & Eugenie Roy Canada
MOREAU, Angela, Oct 16 1933 Sex:F Child# 15 Samuel Moreau Canada & A Tanguay Canada
MOREAU, Angelina, Nov 9 1901 Sex:F Child# 3 Alfred Moreau Canada & Eugenie Roy Canada
MOREAU, Anne Felicite, Mar 1 1922 Sex:F Child# 1 George Moreau Nashua, NH & Annie Bibeau Nashua, NH
MOREAU, Arthur Raymond, Jun 10 1923 Sex:M Child# 1 Arthur Jos Moreau Nashua, NH & Blanche Duquette Richford, VT
MOREAU, Cedric Louis, Oct 10 1924 Sex:M Child# 2 Arthur J Moreau Nashua, NH & Blanche Duquette Richford, VT
MOREAU, Charles Henri, Mar 29 1899 Sex:M Child# 7 Frederic Moreau Canada & Alphonsine Deschenes Canada
MOREAU, Conrad, Feb 8 1915 Sex:M Child# 13 Alfred Moreau Canada & Eugenie Roy Canada Stillborn
MOREAU, Delia, Feb 4 1902 Sex:F Child# 10 Frederic Moreau Canada & Alph Deschenes Canada Stillborn
MOREAU, Delima, Aug 14 1910 Sex:F Child# 15 Frederic Moreau Canada & Alphonsine Deschesne Canada
MOREAU, Edward Evariste, Mar 23 1933 Sex:M Child# 2 Evariste Moreau Nashua, NH & Aurore Boucher Nashua, NH
MOREAU, Estelle, May 22 1930 Sex:F Child# 13 Samuel Moreau Canada & Angelena Tanguay Canada
MOREAU, Eugenie Noella, Dec 26 1926 Sex:F Child# 10 Samuel Moreau Canada & Angelina Tanguay Canada
MOREAU, Ferdinand Aug, Dec 23 1902 Sex:M Child# 11 Norbert Moreau Canada & R A Cognac Canada
MOREAU, Fernande Juliette, Dec 11 1915 Sex:F Child# 15 Alfred Moreau Canada & Eugenie Roy Canada
MOREAU, Francis Romeo, May 25 1929 Sex:M Child# 12 Samuel Moreau Canada & Angelina Tanguay Canada
MOREAU, Germaine, Jan 1 1913 Sex:F Child# 10 Alfred Moreau Canada & Eugenie Roy Canada
MOREAU, Jeanne d'Arc Rita, Nov 4 1920 Sex:F Child# 19 Alfred Moreau Canada & Eugenie Roy Canada
MOREAU, Jos Armand Rolland, Mar 21 1933 Sex:M Child# 1 Romeo Moreau Nashua, NH & Jeanne Lavoie Canada
MOREAU, Jos Napoleon Norman, Nov 5 1933 Sex:M Child# 3 Norbert Moreau Canada & V Begnache Nashua, NH
MOREAU, Jos Roger Robert, Oct 20 1934 Sex:M Child# 4 Norbert Moreau Canada & Violet Begnache Nashua, NH
MOREAU, Joseph A H, Oct 14 1893 Sex:M Child# 6 Norbert Moreau Canada & Rosanna Cognac Canada
MOREAU, Joseph A R, Jan 3 1923 Sex:M Child# 3 Henry A Moreau Nashua, NH & Eugenie Thibodeau Manchester, NH
MOREAU, Joseph Leon, Sep 17 1904 Sex:M Child# 3 Edouard Moreau Canada & Arthemise Boucher Canada
MOREAU, Joseph Leon, Dec 23 1906 Sex:M Child# 4 Edouard Moreau Canada & Arthemise Boucher Canada
MOREAU, Joseph Louis Oscar, Mar 19 1927 Sex:M Child# 5 Henry Moreau Nashua, NH & E Thibodeau Manchester, NH
MOREAU, Joseph N Roland, Dec 5 1931 Sex:M Child# 2 Norbert Moreau Canada & Violet Begnache Nashua, NH
MOREAU, Joseph Norbert, Dec 7 1895 Sex:M Child# 5 Frederic Moreau Canada & Alphonsine Deschenes Canada
MOREAU, Joseph Norbert M, Jun 29 1929 Sex:M Child# 6 Henry Moreau Nashua, NH & Eugenie Thibodeau Manchester, NH

MOREAU, Joseph Victor, Oct 12 1908 Sex:M Child# 14 Frederic Moreau Canada & Alphonsine Deschesnes Canada
MOREAU, Jules Clement, Mar 14 1903 Sex:M Child# 11 Frederick Moreau Canada & Alphonsine Deschenes Nashua, NH
MOREAU, Julianne Marie, Jul 4 1931 Sex:F Child# 4 Arthur J Moreau Nashua, NH & Blanche Duquette Richford, VT
MOREAU, Juliene Fernande, Feb 19 1924 Sex:F Child# 8 Samuel Moreau Canada & Ang Tanguay Canada
MOREAU, Lea Eugenie, Jul 7 1904 Sex:F Child# 12 Frederic Moreau Canada & Alphonsine Deschesnes Canada
MOREAU, Leo Ovide, Apr 12 1905 Sex:M Child# 5 Alfred Moreau Canada & Eugenie Roy Canada
MOREAU, Lorenzo, Jan 10 1898 Sex:M Child# 9 Norbert Moreau Canada & Rosanna Coquac Canada
MOREAU, Lorette Marie Rita, Feb 2 1925 Sex:F Child# 4 Henry Moreau Nashua, NH & Eug Thibodeau Manchester, NH
MOREAU, Lorraine, May 28 1930 Sex:F Child# 1 Norbert Moreau Canada & Violette Begnache Nashua, NH
MOREAU, Louis Frederic, Jul 5 1900 Sex:M Child# 8 Frederic Moreau Canada & Alphonsine Deschene Canada
MOREAU, Louisa E, Aug 17 1897 Sex:F Child# 6 Frederic Moreau Canada & Alphonsine Deschene Canada
MOREAU, Ludivine, Nov 9 1903 Sex:F Child# 4 Alfred Moreau Canada & Eugenie Roy Canada
MOREAU, Marguerite Elizabeth, Aug 17 1916 Sex:F Child# 18 Frederic Moreau Canada & Alph Deschesnes Canada
MOREAU, Marie, Jul 11 1894 Sex:F Child# 5 Frederic Moreau Canada & Alphonsine Dechenes Canada
MOREAU, Marie A E, Jun 9 1890 Sex:F Child# 4 Norbert Moreau Canada & Rosanna Cognac Canada
MOREAU, Marie A I E A, Mar 22 1930 Sex:F Child# 2 George Moreau Nashua, NH & Annie Bibeau Nashua, NH
MOREAU, Marie A Presc'le, Nov 28 1901 Sex:F Child# 10 Norbert Moreau Canada & Rose Anna Cognac Canada
MOREAU, Marie Adele Melia, Jul 7 1912 Sex:F Child# 16 Fred Moreau Canada & Alphonsine Deschenes Canada
MOREAU, Marie Anna, Jun 3 1904 Sex:F Child# 14 Norbert Moreau Canada & Rosanna Cognac Canada
MOREAU, Marie Anna Ida, Jan 12 1900 Sex:F Child# 2 Alfred Moreau Canada & Eugenie Roy Canada
MOREAU, Marie Bernadette, Aug 18 1903 Sex:F Child# 2 Edouard Moreau Canada & Arthemise Boucher Canada
MOREAU, Marie L Albina, Dec 14 1898 Sex:F Child# 1 Ephrem Moreau Canada & Eugenie Roy Canada
MOREAU, Marie Louise Cecile, Aug 17 1916 Sex:F Child# 17 Frederic Moreau Canada & Alph Deschesnes Canada
MOREAU, Marie Lucienne Helen, Aug 15 1934 Sex:F Child# 8 Henry Alfred Moreau Nashua, NH & Eugenie Thibodeau MA
MOREAU, Marie R C, Jan 24 1887 Sex:F Child# 1 Norbert Moreau P Q & Rosanna Cognac P Q
MOREAU, Marie Rachael Paulin, Jun 2 1934 Sex:F Child# 3 Evariste Moreau Canada & Aurore Boucher Nashua, NH
MOREAU, Marie Yvonne Alice, Sep 14 1932 Sex:F Child# 7 Henry Moreau Nashua, NH & E Thibodeau Manchester, NH
MOREAU, Marilyn Genevieve, Jan 5 1928 Sex:F Child# 3 Arthur J Moreau Nashua, NH & Blanche Duquette Richford,
MOREAU, Mary, Jun 23 1888 Sex:F Child# 2 Robert Moreau Canada & Rosalinna Cognac Canada
MOREAU, Mary Lucille, May 28 1922 Sex:F Child# 3 Philip J Moreau Nashua, NH & Eva Lemere Hooksett, NH
MOREAU, Mary O C, Feb 3 1900 Sex:F Child# 10 Norbert Moreau Canada & Rosanna Cognac Canada
MOREAU, N Evariste, Jul 13 1891 Sex:M Child# 4 Norbert Moreau Canada & Rosanna Cognac Canada
MOREAU, Norbert Philip, Jul 16 1918 Sex:M Child# 1 Philip Moreau Nashua, NH & Eva Lemere Hooksett, NH
MOREAU, Oselina, Nov 2 1906 Sex:F Child# 6 Alfred Moreau Canada & Eugenie Roy Canada
MOREAU, Paul Frederic, Jul 12 1892 Sex:M Child# 5 Norbert Moreau Canada & Rosanna Cognac Canada
MOREAU, Raymond Alfred, Jul 3 1920 Sex:M Child# 2 Philip Moreau Nashua, NH & Eva Lemere Hooksett, NH
MOREAU, Regina Irene, Jan 4 1910 Sex:F Child# 8 Alfred Moreau Canada & Eugenie Roy Canada
MOREAU, Robert Donald, Feb 28 1932 Sex:M Child# 1 Alf Moreau, Jr Nashua, NH & Lumina Forcier Manchester, NH
MOREAU, Robert Raoul, Jul 29 1931 Sex:M Child# 14 Samuel Moreau Canada & Angelina Tanguay Canada
MOREAU, Roger Bernard, May 19 1928 Sex:M Child# 11 Samuel Moreau Canada & Angelina Tanguay Canada
MOREAU, Rosana Beatrice, Nov 2 1931 Sex:F Child# 1 Evoriste Moreau Canada & Aurore Boucher Nashua, NH
MOREAU, Sylvio, May 31 1908 Sex:M Child# 7 Alfred Moreau Canada & Eugenie Roy Canada
MOREAU, Theresa Florence, May 29 1925 Sex:F Child# 9 Samuel Moreau Canada & Ange Tanguay Canada
MOREAU, Unknown, Jul 5 1891 Sex:M Child# 3 Pierre Moreau Canada & Adeline Grichard Canada
MOREAU, Unknown, Jan 14 1922 Sex:M Child# 1 Henry Moreau Nashua, NH & M Eugenie Thibodeau Manchester, NH Stillborn
MOREAU, Unknown, Jan 14 1922 Sex:M Child# 2 Henry Moreau Nashua, NH & M Eugenie Thibodeau Manchester, NH
MOREAU, Yolande, Feb 8 1915 Sex:F Child# 14 Alfred Moreau Canada & Eugenie Roy Canada
MOREHOUSE, Margaret Anne, May 29 1930 Sex:F Child# 1 Horace C Morehouse Canada & Ola Boyer Manchester, NH
MOREL, Gertrude Rejeanne, Jun 12 1910 Sex:F Child# 1 Thomas Morel Canada & Adelina Richer Nashua, NH
MORENCY, Berthe A Lucienne, Oct 20 1896 Sex:F Child# 1 Alexandre Morency Canada & Alice Marie Canada
MORENCY, Elenore Dora, Jun 18 1898 Sex:F Child# 13 Leon Morency Canada & Philomene April Canada
MORENCY, Henri Albert, Dec 17 1915 Sex:M Child# 1 J B Morency Canada & Alphonsine Levesque Canada
MORENCY, Isidore, Jun 18 1893 Sex:M Child# 10 Leon Morency Canada & Philomene Aprile Canada
MORENCY, J Arthur Wilfred, Oct 15 1913 Sex:M Child# 4 Arthur Morency Canada & Emilia Hysette Nashua, NH
MORENCY, Jean Baptiste P, Apr 9 1905 Sex:M Child# 3 Donat Morency Canada & Albina Desautels Canada
MORENCY, Joseph D Alphonse, Jan 20 1902 Sex:M Child# 1 Donat Morency Canada & Albina Desautels Canada
MORENCY, Joseph Henri D, May 28 1908 Sex:M Child# 5 Donat Morency Canada & Albina Desautels Canada
MORENCY, Joseph Philippe, Oct 21 1896 Sex:M Child# 12 Leon Morency Canada & Philomene Lapril Canada
MORENCY, Joseph Pierre, Dec 20 1898 Sex:M Child# 2 Jean Morency Canada & Philomene Gagnon Canada
MORENCY, Louis Adrien, Jul 31 1906 Sex:M Child# 5 Jean Morency Canada & Philomene Gagnon Canada
MORENCY, Marie Andrea M, Nov 14 1906 Sex:F Child# 4 Donat Morency Canada & Albina Desautels Canada
MORENCY, Marie Blanche L, Aug 1 1900 Sex:F Child# 14 Leon Morency Canada & Philomene Lapril Canada
MORENCY, Marie Eleonore, Jun 23 1901 Sex:F Child# 4 Jean Morency Canada & Philomene Gagnon Canada
MORENCY, Marie Lea, May 21 1900 Sex:F Child# 3 Jean Morency Canada & Philomene Gagnon Canada
MORENCY, Marie Simonne, Sep 16 1923 Sex:F Child# 2 Ovide Morency Canada & Marie Lemieux Canada
MORENCY, Marie Yvonne, May 5 1921 Sex:F Child# 1 Ovide Morency Canada & Marie Lemieux Canada
MORENTCY, Marie Albina A, Aug 3 1903 Sex:F Child# 2 Donat Morentcy Canada & Albina Desautels Canada
MOREY, Jeannette, Apr 5 1918 Sex:F Child# 2 Edwin Morey Lexington, MA & Marion Buxton Nashua, NH
MOREY, Leonard Edwin, Apr 13 1916 Sex:M Child# 1 Edwin Morey Lexington, MA & Marion P Buxton Nashua, NH
MOREY, Unknown, Aug 12 1891 Sex:F Child# Hartson P Morey Wilmot & Ida R Knights Goshen
MOREY, Virginia, Jul 21 1921 Sex:F Child# 3 Edwin Morey Lexington, MA & Marion Buxton Nashua, NH
MORGAN, Allen Bryant, May 11 1927 Sex:M Child# 2 Bertha C Morgan Lemster, NH & Mary Reid Litchfield, NH
MORGAN, Charlotte Geraldine, May 19 1911 Sex:F Child# 1 George Morgan Palmer, MA & Fannie Richardson Clinton

MORGAN, Elizabeth Flora, Nov 24 1914 Sex:F Child# 1 Everett E Morgan W Springfield, NH & Jennie E Bills Pepperell
MORGAN, Ethelyn May, Jan 11 1925 Sex:F Child# 1 Benton C Morgan Unity, NH & May Reid Litchfield, NH
MORGAN, Grace, Jul 7 1889 Sex:F Child# 2 Nelson I Morgan NH & Nellie F Wilson NH
MORGAN, Jesse Johnson, Jr, Sep 20 1930 Sex:M Child# 1 Jesse J Morgan Sherman Mills, ME & Helen MacGowan Greenfield
MORGAN, Thomas P, Jan 13 1888 Sex:M Child# 1 Ernest Morgan Nashua, NH & Lizzie Sands Laconia
MORGAN, Unknown, Jan 6 1890 Sex:F Child# 3 E A Morgan Nashua, NH & Lizzie D Sands Laconia, NH
MORGAN, Unknown, Oct 17 1922 Sex:F Child# 3 Harold Morgan Mass & Vera Watts Nova Scotia
MORGAN, Velma Eunice, Jan 10 1919 Sex:F Child# 2 Everett E Morgan W Sprinfield, NH & Jennie E Bills Pepperell, MA
MORIARITY, Dennis, Sep 4 1899 Sex:M Child# 3 Dennis Moriarity Ireland & Mary Quinn Ireland
MORIARITY, John, Jun 18 1899 Sex:M Child# 5 John Moriarty Ireland & Delia Quinn Ireland
MORIARITY, Richard, Jun 14 1915 Sex:M Child# 1 Richard M Moriarity Nashua, NH & Mar J Fannergan Ireland
MORIARTY, Annie, Mar 31 1895 Sex:F Child# 1 Dennis Moriarty Ireland & Mary Quinn Ireland
MORIARTY, Bernard Leo, Oct 14 1898 Sex:M Child# 7 Richard Moriarty Ireland & Mary O'Brien London, England
MORIARTY, Catherine, Mar 13 1892 Sex:F Child# 3 John Moriarty Ireland & Delia Quinn Ireland
MORIARTY, Catherine, Jul 28 1901 Sex:F Child# 3 Dennis Moriarty Ireland & Mary Queny Ireland
MORIARTY, Christine, Dec 26 1908 Sex:F Child# 8 John Moriarty Ireland & Delia Quinn Ireland
MORIARTY, Daniel, Jan 23 1902 Sex:M Child# 3 Michael H Moriarty Ireland & Elizabeth F Shea Ireland
MORIARTY, Delia, Aug 28 1895 Sex:F Child# 4 John Moriarty Ireland & Delia Quinn Ireland
MORIARTY, Denise Madeline, Jul 19 1922 Sex:F Child# 3 Denis Moriarty Nashua, NH & Amanda Caron Nashua, NH
MORIARTY, Eileen Esther, Sep 21 1921 Sex:F Child# 4 Richard M Moriarty Nashua, NH & Margaret Finnegan Ireland
MORIARTY, Esther, Mar 11 1910 Sex:F Child# 7 Michael Moriarty Ireland & Elizabeth O'Shea Ireland
MORIARTY, Frances E, Jun 11 1908 Sex:F Child# 6 Michael Moriarty Ireland & Elizabeth O'Shea Ireland
MORIARTY, Francis, Dec 27 1906 Sex:M Child# 1 Richard Moriarty Ireland & Mary A O'Brien England
MORIARTY, Helen Madeline, Oct 13 1903 Sex:F Child# 6 John Moriarty Ireland & Delia Quinn Ireland
MORIARTY, James, Apr 29 1914 Sex:M Child# 1 Dennis Moriarty Ireland & Julia Dolly Ireland
MORIARTY, Joseph, Oct 20 1903 Sex:M Child# 4 Michael Moriarty Ireland & Elizabeth F Shea Ireland
MORIARTY, Louis, Nov 11 1900 Sex:M Child# 9 Richard Moriarty Ireland & Mary O'Brien England
MORIARTY, Maggie, Dec 6 1890 Sex:F Child# 2 John Moriarty Ireland & D Quinn Ireland
MORIARTY, Marguerite, Apr 7 1905 Sex:F Child# 5 Michael Moriarty Ireland & Elizabeth F Shea Ireland
MORIARTY, Martha, Jul 19 1900 Sex:F Child# 2 Michael H Moriarty Ireland & Elizabeth Shea Ireland
MORIARTY, Martha Mary, Nov 16 1917 Sex:F Child# 2 Richard M Moriarty Nashua, NH & Margaret Finnigan Ireland
MORIARTY, Mary, Nov 22 1897 Sex:F Child# 2 Dennis Moriarty Ireland & Mary Quin Ireland
MORIARTY, Mary, Nov 6 1898 Sex:F Child# 3 M H Moriarty Ireland & Elizabeth F O'Shea Ireland
MORIARTY, Mary Agnes, Dec 9 1901 Sex:F Child# 10 Richard Moriarty Ireland & Mary O'Brien England
MORIARTY, Mary Amande, Jan 30 1911 Sex:F Child# 1 Dennis Moriarty Nashua, NH & Armande Caron Nashua, NH
MORIARTY, Paul Richard, Apr 22 1923 Sex:M Child# 4 Richard M Moriarty Nashua, NH & Margaret Finnegan Ireland
MORIARTY, Rita Margaret, Nov 10 1916 Sex:F Child# 2 Richard Moriarty Nashua, NH & Margaret J Finnigan Ireland
MORIARTY, Rosalene, Nov 3 1904 Sex:F Child# 7 John Moriarty Ireland & Delia Quinn Ireland
MORIARTY, Sylvester, May 2 1893 Sex:M Child# 5 Richard Moriarty Ireland & Mary A O'Brien England
MORIARTY, Unknown, Oct 8 1887 Sex:M Child# 2 Richard Moriarty Ireland & Mary A O'Brien England
MORIARTY, Unknown, Oct 3 1891 Sex:M Child# 4 Richard Moriarty Ireland & Mary Ann O'Brien London, England
MORIARTY, Unknown, Dec 16 1913 Sex:M Child# 1 (No Parents Listed)
MORIL, Bertha May, Apr 25 1889 Sex:F Child# 2 George Moril Goshen, NH & Mary Bagley Nashua, NH
MORIN, Adelard, Apr 9 1887 Sex:M Child# 1 Henri Morin Londonderry, NH & Jose Duchesneau P Q
MORIN, Adrienne, Feb 15 1912 Sex:F Child# 2 Desire Morin Canada & Amelia Berube Canada
MORIN, Albert, Jan 9 1889 Sex:M Child# 2 Henry Morin Londonderry, NH & Josephine Duchesneau Canada
MORIN, Alberta, Jun 1 1899 Sex:F Child# 4 Cyrille Morin Canada & Alberta Francoeur Canada
MORIN, Albina, Sep 18 1898 Sex:F Child# 5 Charles Morin Canada & Marie Louise Havard Canada
MORIN, Alfred Albert, May 25 1914 Sex:M Child# 1 Oscar Morin Nashua, NH & Flora Saucier Canada
MORIN, Alfred Maurice, May 1 1928 Sex:M Child# 3 Joseph Morin Nashua, NH & Eva Gamache Nashua, NH
MORIN, Alice, Aug 20 1903 Sex:F Child# 4 Joseph Morin Canada & Arthemise Berube Canada
MORIN, Andrea, Dec 22 1908 Sex:F Child# 5 Alphonse Morin Canada & Alexina Sirois Canada
MORIN, Angelina, Apr 13 1896 Sex:F Child# 7 Joseph Morin Canada & Malvina Guichard Canada
MORIN, Anita Berthe, Nov 30 1905 Sex:F Child# 1 Ernest Morin Canada & Josephine Comeau Canada
MORIN, Anna Elmire, Jan 31 1905 Sex:F Child# 5 Joseph Morin Canada & Arthemise Berube Canada
MORIN, Annette, Sep 2 1904 Sex:F Child# 5 Adelard Morin Canada & Helene Martin Canada
MORIN, Annette Josephine, Nov 2 1918 Sex:F Child# 2 Odilon Morin Canada & Rosa Bouchard Nashua, NH
MORIN, Antoine, Dec 23 1894 Sex:M Child# 11 Antoine Morin Canada & Zoe Charron Canada
MORIN, Antoine, Dec 23 1894 Sex:M Child# 11 Antoine Morin Canada & Zoe Charron Canada
MORIN, Antonio Leo, Nov 29 1921 Sex:M Child# 5 Desire Morin Canada & Amelia Berube Canada
MORIN, Arthur, Mar 19 1889 Sex:M Child# 13 Michel Morin Canada & L Chamberland Canada
MORIN, Augustin, Jun 30 1890 Sex:M Child# Augustin Morin Canada & Virginie Trow Canada
MORIN, Aurelie F, Apr 5 1899 Sex:F Child# 12 Hermenegilde Morin Canada & Philomene Bellerose Canada
MORIN, Azaria Joseph, Jan 12 1895 Sex:M Child# 4 Michel Morin Canada & Josephine Descoteau Canada
MORIN, Beatrice, Mar 6 1908 Sex:F Child# 7 Adelard Morin Canada & Helene Martin Canada
MORIN, Berengere, Jan 8 1929 Sex:F Child# 3 Hormidas Morin Canada & Alma Ouillette Canada
MORIN, Blanche Albina, Dec 29 1926 Sex:F Child# 1 Narius Morin Canada & Armance Cote Canada
MORIN, Blanche Alice, Jun 9 1893 Sex:F Child# 6 Antoine Morin Canada & Olive Bienvenue Canada
MORIN, Cecile, Nov 1 1924 Sex:F Child# 7 Oscar Morin Nashua, NH & Clara Soucier Canada
MORIN, Cecile Adrienne, May 14 1916 Sex:F Child# 3 Oscar Morin Canada & Amelia Saucier Canada
MORIN, Charles, Jul 15 1897 Sex:M Child# 3 Charles Morin Canada & Marie L Havard Canada
MORIN, Claire Rita, May 28 1933 Sex:F Child# 3 Alexis Morin Graniteville, VT & Jeannette Martel Suncook, NH
MORIN, Claudia, Jun 7 1894 Sex:F Child# 16 Octave Morin Canada & Eliza Dube Canada

MORIN, Denise Jacqueline, Feb 9 1926 Sex:F Child# 1 Romeo Morin Canada & J Blanchett Nashua, NH
MORIN, Dorilda Estelle, May 3 1918 Sex:F Child# 3 Mayzano Morin Canada & Jeanne Lucier Canada
MORIN, Dorothy, Jun 29 1923 Sex:F Child# 4 Mark Morin Salem, MA & Lilly Michaud Canada
MORIN, Dorothy Jennie, Jul 4 1924 Sex:F Child# 1 George Morin Nashua, NH & Orise Petrin Canada
MORIN, Edgar, Oct 27 1904 Sex:M Child# 2 Jean B Morin Canada & Rosanna Laliberte Canada
MORIN, Edgar, Jan 3 1909 Sex:M Child# 1 Desire Morin Canada & Emelie Berube Canada
MORIN, Edmond, Aug 30 1900 Sex:M Child# 6 Michael Morin Canada & Josephine Descoteau Canada
MORIN, Edward W, Oct 15 1895 Sex:M Child# 10 Alphonse Morin Canada & Zoe Gaudet Canada
MORIN, Elaine Gloria, Mar 17 1934 Sex:F Child# 4 Oscar Morin Nashua, NH & Bertha Segouin Derry, NH
MORIN, Emily, Jan 13 1888 Sex:F Child# 9 Baptiste Morin Acton, PQ & Virginna Charon P Q
MORIN, Ernest, Nov 19 1922 Sex:M Child# 1 Henri Morin Canada & Emma Bellavance Canada
MORIN, Eugene, Jun 16 1888 Sex:M Child# 3 Augustine Morin Canada & Melina Trou Canada
MORIN, Eugene Henry, Jun 16 1915 Sex:M Child# 2 Oscar Morin Nashua, NH & Flora Saucier Canada
MORIN, Eva Rose, Dec 23 1891 Sex:F Child# 10 W Antoine Morin Canada & Zoe Charon Canada
MORIN, Eva Rose, Feb 27 1906 Sex:F Child# 1 Alphonse Morin Canada & Eva Blanchette Canada
MORIN, Evelina, May 28 1888 Sex:F Child# 5 Joseph Morin Canada & Hermine Daudelin Canada
MORIN, Florette Florence, Mar 22 1935 Sex:F Child# 1 Wilfred Morin Nashua, NH & Alice Theroux Nashua, NH
MORIN, Francis Anastase, Jun 29 1899 Sex:M Child# 12 Antoine Morin Canada & Zoe Charron Canada
MORIN, Gabrielle Antoinette, Jul 29 1929 Sex:F Child# 8 Oscar Morin Nashua, NH & Flora Saucier Canada
MORIN, Gedeon, Oct 8 1899 Sex:M Child# 6 Charles Morin Canada & M L Havard Canada
MORIN, Gerald Richard, Dec 20 1931 Sex:M Child# 4 Joseph Morin Nashua, NH & Eva Gamache Nashua, NH
MORIN, Gerard Armand, Aug 19 1930 Sex:M Child# 2 Sylvio Morin Canada & Annette Simard Nashua, NH
MORIN, Germaine Olivette, Nov 30 1921 Sex:F Child# 2 Armand Morin Nashua, NH & Alma Tardif Nashua, NH
MORIN, Gertrude, Aug 17 1915 Sex:F Child# 2 Mayzano Morin Canada & Jeanne Lucier Canada
MORIN, Gloria Vivienne, Oct 8 1931 Sex:F Child# 2 Louis Morin Canada & Rose Therriault Canada
MORIN, Hector E A, Jul 9 1892 Sex:M Child# 14 Misael Morin Canada & Emerise Desrocher Canada
MORIN, Henri I, Mar 22 1889 Sex:M Child# 4 Antoine Morin Canada & Olive Bienveau Canada
MORIN, Henrietta, May 14 1912 Sex:F Child# 3 Ernest Morin Canada & Josephine Corneau Canada
MORIN, Henry, Aug 25 1901 Sex:M Child# 2 Henry Morin Canada & Marie Gagne Canada Stillborn
MORIN, Henry Euclide, Jul 17 1891 Sex:M Child# 3 Amable Morin Canada & Margaret Guertin Canada
MORIN, Henry Joseph R, Oct 14 1929 Sex:M Child# 2 Henry Morin Canada & Yvonne Berube Nashua, NH
MORIN, Ina, Sep 9 1895 Sex:F Child# 6 Frank Morin Canada & Annie Brown Ireland
MORIN, Irene Andrienne, Dec 2 1913 Sex:F Child# 2 Elzear Morin Nashua, NH & Aime Lizotte Canada
MORIN, Irene Collette, Aug 5 1918 Sex:F Child# 1 Joseph Morin Nashua, NH & Eva Gamanche Nashua, NH
MORIN, Isabelle Annette, Dec 7 1926 Sex:F Child# 3 Armand Morin Nashua, NH & Anna Tardif Canada
MORIN, Jean Aime, Mar 16 1934 Sex:M Child# 2 Jean Morin Canada & Dora Cote Nashua, NH
MORIN, Jean Theodore, Apr 7 1905 Sex:M Child# 13 Hermenegilde Morin Canada & Philomene Bellerose Canada
MORIN, Jeanne Darc Lucille, Sep 28 1917 Sex:F Child# 4 Elzear Morin NH & Aime Leazotte Canada
MORIN, Jeanne Florence, May 26 1927 Sex:F Child# 4 Adelard Morin Canada & Juliette Levesque Canada
MORIN, Jeannette Eva, Sep 2 1921 Sex:F Child# 4 Mayzano Morin Canada & Jeanne Lussier Canada
MORIN, Joan Jeanine, Jan 19 1933 Sex:F Child# 1 Jean Morin St Herbert, PQ & Dora Cote Nashua, NH
MORIN, Jos Celestin Maurice, Jan 24 1933 Sex:M Child# 1 Celestin Morin Otter River, MA & Marie Theriault Nashua, NH
MORIN, Joseph, Dec 17 1928 Sex:M Child# 1 Sylvia Morin Canada & Annette Simard Nashua, NH
MORIN, Joseph A, Oct 9 1889 Sex:M Child# 1 Policarpe Morin Canada & C Grandmaison Canada
MORIN, Joseph A, Nov 10 1901 Sex:M Child# 2 Alphonse Morin Nashua, NH & Olevine Lefebvre Nashua, NH
MORIN, Joseph Albert, Apr 15 1904 Sex:M Child# 6 Cyrille Morin Canada & Edith Francoeur Canada
MORIN, Joseph Amable, Oct 25 1893 Sex:M Child# 3 Ovide Morin Canada & Eloise Deschenes Canada
MORIN, Joseph Arthur E, Feb 24 1898 Sex:M Child# 9 Amedee Morin Canada & Lucie Comtois Canada
MORIN, Joseph E, Mar 24 1887 Sex:M Child# 3 Joseph Morin P Q & Delvina Guichard P Q
MORIN, Joseph Elzear, Nov 19 1895 Sex:M Child# 17 Octave Morin Canada & Eliza Dube Canada
MORIN, Joseph Ernest, Dec 8 1895 Sex:M Child# 8 Amedee Morin Canada & Lucie Comtois Canada
MORIN, Joseph Escor, Oct 14 1897 Sex:M Child# 8 Joseph Morin Canada & Delvina Richard Canada
MORIN, Joseph Eusebe, Feb 12 1898 Sex:M Child# 1 Urbain Morin Canada & Dora Paradis Canada
MORIN, Joseph Exea, Jun 9 1902 Sex:M Child# 1 Charles Morin Canada & Cordelia Emond Canada
MORIN, Joseph George Irenee, Oct 2 1894 Sex:M Child# 1 Olivier Morin Canada & Blanzine Duperez Canada
MORIN, Joseph Hector, Dec 6 1892 Sex:M Child# 2 Ovide Morin Canada & Eloise Deschesne Canada
MORIN, Joseph Leonard, Aug 26 1920 Sex:M Child# 3 O Morin Nashua, NH & Rose Bouchard Nashua, NH
MORIN, Joseph Oscar Lucien, Jan 9 1914 Sex:M Child# 4 Will Morin Canada & Dorilda Girouard Canada
MORIN, Joseph Ovila, Sep 17 1896 Sex:M Child# 2 Cyrille Morin Canada & Edith Francoeur Canada
MORIN, Joseph P A, Jul 19 1891 Sex:M Child# 5 Antoine Morin Canada & Olive Bienvenue Canada
MORIN, Joseph Paul Ernest, Jan 25 1912 Sex:M Child# 3 William Morin Canada & Dorilda Girouard Canada
MORIN, Joseph Robert, Jul 26 1927 Sex:M Child# 1 Philip Morin Newport, VT & Eva Langlois Salem, MA
MORIN, Joseph Robert, Nov 12 1931 Sex:M Child# 4 Mezano Morin Riviere du Loup, PQ & Marie Jeanne Lucier Canada
MORIN, Joseph S Marcisse, Nov 7 1891 Sex:M Child# 1 Ovide Morin Canada & Eloise Deschene Canada
MORIN, Joseph Valmore, Aug 18 1917 Sex:M Child# 4 Oscar Morin Canada & Flora Saucier Canada
MORIN, Joseph W, Oct 15 1895 Sex:M Child# 11 Alphonse Morin Canada & Zoe Gaudet Canada
MORIN, Joseph Wilfred, Oct 19 1906 Sex:M Child# 1 David Morin Canada & Flora Genest Nashua, NH
MORIN, Josephine, Jun 5 1888 Sex:F Child# 1 Michael Morin Canada & Josephine Descoteau Canada
MORIN, Laura, Feb 11 1899 Sex:F Child# 2 Onesime Morin Canada & Laura Paradis Canada
MORIN, Lea, Oct 22 1890 Sex:F Child# 7 Alphonse Morin Canada & Zoe Gaudet Canada
MORIN, Leo Armand, Jun 22 1919 Sex:M Child# 1 Armand Morin Nashua, NH & Alma Tardy Nashua, NH
MORIN, Leo H, May 21 1892 Sex:M Child# 8 Alphonse Morin Canada & Zoe Gaudet Canada
MORIN, Liliane Berthe, Nov 26 1905 Sex:F Child# 3 J B Morin Canada & Rose A Laliberte Canada

MORIN, Lorette Lucille, Mar 22 1935 Sex:F Child# 2 Wilfred Morin Nashua, NH & Alice Theroux Nashua, NH
MORIN, Lorraine Blanche, Nov 30 1923 Sex:F Child# 3 Oscar Morin Nashua, NH & Bertha Seguin Derry, NH
MORIN, Louis Sylvio, Jul 20 1909 Sex:M Child# 4 Alphonse Morin Canada & Eva Blauchette Canada
MORIN, Louise Anna, Feb 7 1926 Sex:F Child# 1 Louis Morin Canada & Rose Therriault Canada
MORIN, Lucia Blanche, Mar 29 1900 Sex:F Child# 5 Ovide Morin Canada & Heloise Deschenes Canada
MORIN, Lucie Germaine, Mar 16 1910 Sex:F Child# 2 Ernest Morin Canada & Josephine Corneau Canada
MORIN, Lucille Olivette, Sep 30 1917 Sex:F Child# 1 Odilon Morin Canada & Rosa Bouchard Nashua, NH
MORIN, Lumina, Mar 28 1893 Sex:F Child# Octave Morin Canada & Eliza Dube Canada
MORIN, Lydia, Dec 31 1898 Sex:F Child# 2 Joseph Morin Canada & Arthemise Berube Canada Stillborn
MORIN, M Antoinette Flor, Jun 21 1919 Sex:F Child# 5 Oscar Morin Canada & Flora Saucier Canada
MORIN, M Antoinette Lucille, Aug 1 1921 Sex:F Child# 2 Augustin Morin Canada & M Antoinette Martin NH
MORIN, M Clarisse Lucile, Oct 10 1914 Sex:F Child# 1 Wilfrid Morin Nashua, NH & Lea Anctil Nashua, NH
MORIN, M Jeanne Lucille, Dec 10 1913 Sex:F Child# 11 Jean Bte Morin Canada & Eva Rioux Canada
MORIN, M Therese Beatrice, Jul 12 1913 Sex:F Child# 4 Desire Morin Canada & Emilia Berube Canada
MORIN, M Virginia Lucille, May 20 1922 Sex:F Child# 1 Eugene Morin Nashua, NH & Onida Thiffault Nashua, NH
MORIN, Marcel, Sep 3 1894 Sex:M Child# 3 Frank Morin Canada & Annie Brennan Ireland
MORIN, Marcel Camille, Dec 27 1930 Sex:M Child# 3 Amarius Morin Canada & Armance Cote Canada
MORIN, Maria C Adiana, Dec 14 1898 Sex:F Child# 4 Ovide Morin Canada & Elvise Deschenes Canada
MORIN, Marie, Dec 17 1928 Sex:F Child# 2 Sylvia Morin Canada & Annette Simard Nashua, NH
MORIN, Marie Alice, Oct 27 1897 Sex:F Child# 3 Cyrille Morin Canada & Edith Francoeur Canada
MORIN, Marie Alma, Feb 26 1903 Sex:F Child# 3 Henry Morin Canada & Domithilde Gagne Canada
MORIN, Marie Ann, Apr 30 1924 Sex:F Child# 2 Adelard Morin Canada & Juliette Levesque Canada
MORIN, Marie Annette D, Dec 5 1904 Sex:F Child# 4 Honore Morin Canada & Domithilde Gagne Canada
MORIN, Marie Aurelia A, Jun 24 1891 Sex:F Child# 2 Michel Morin Canada & Josephine Descateau Canada
MORIN, Marie Beatrice, May 17 1908 Sex:F Child# 1 William Morin Canada & Dorilda Girouard Canada
MORIN, Marie Blanche P, Aug 20 1934 Sex:F Child# 2 Celestin Morin Otter River, MA & Marie Theriault Nashua, NH
MORIN, Marie Cecile Rita, Jun 19 1932 Sex:F Child# 2 Alexis Morin Graniteville, VT & Jeanette Martel Suncook, NH
MORIN, Marie Celina, Feb 25 1892 Sex:F Child# 4 Damase Morin Canada & Caroline Caron Canada
MORIN, Marie D, Apr 27 1894 Sex:F Child# 6 Joseph Morin Canada & Delvina Guichard Canada
MORIN, Marie Darilla, Jul 29 1889 Sex:F Child# 9 Antoine Morin Canada & Zoe Charron Canada
MORIN, Marie Gabrielle S, May 29 1910 Sex:F Child# 2 William Morin Canada & Dorilda Girouard Canada
MORIN, Marie Lillian, May 9 1901 Sex:F Child# 9 Joseph Morin Canada & Devina Dichard Canada
MORIN, Marie Louise, Oct 13 1893 Sex:F Child# Charles Morin Canada & Marie L Avard Canada
MORIN, Marie R Claudia, Apr 23 1899 Sex:F Child# 1 Octave Morin Canada & Marie Poliguin Canada
MORIN, Marie Rosanna, Apr 25 1893 Sex:F Child# 10 Johnny Morin Canada & Eva Plourde Canada
MORIN, Marie Rosanna, Jul 16 1893 Sex:F Child# 16 Charles Morin Canada & Catherine St Aubin Canada
MORIN, Marie Rose, Nov 23 1891 Sex:F Child# 4 Henry Morin Nashua, NH & Josephine Duchesneau Canada
MORIN, Marie Rose Diana, Apr 10 1928 Sex:F Child# 2 Amerius Morin Canada & Armance Cote Canada
MORIN, Marie Theresa, Jul 4 1925 Sex:F Child# 3 Adelard Morin Canada & Juliette Levesque Canada
MORIN, Mary, Jan 26 1920 Sex:F Child# 6 Joseph Morin Canada & Laura Eva Ross Manchester, NH Stillborn
MORIN, Mary, May 31 1923 Sex:F Child# 2 Alfred Morin Lawrence, MA & Angeline Caron Canada Stillborn
MORIN, Mary C J A, Mar 3 1908 Sex:F Child# 1 Henry Morin St Henri, Canada & Adele Gagnon Canada
MORIN, Mary Claire, Sep 30 1933 Sex:F Child# 2 Henry Morin Canada & E Bellevance Canada
MORIN, Mary L A, Jul 5 1900 Sex:F Child# 1 Alphonse Morin ME & Alexina Sirois Canada
MORIN, Maurice Alphonse, Mar 6 1902 Sex:M Child# 5 Cyrille Morin Canada & Edith Francoeur Canada
MORIN, Maurice Raymond, Feb 20 1932 Sex:M Child# 3 Henri Morin Canada & Yvonne Berube Nashua, NH
MORIN, Morris Adrien Joe, Nov 28 1919 Sex:M Child# 5 Desire Morin Canada & Emelia Berube Canada
MORIN, Normand Gerald, Apr 28 1924 Sex:M Child# 2 Joseph A Morin Nashua, NH & Eva Gamache Nashua, NH
MORIN, Omer, Mar 18 1908 Sex:M Child# 3 Alphonse Morin Canada & Eva Blanchette Canada
MORIN, P E, Mar 9 1891 Sex:M Child# 5 Joseph Morin Canada & Delvina Grichard Canada
MORIN, Paul Roger, Apr 23 1923 Sex:M Child# 5 Mayzao Morin Canada & Jeanne Lucier Canada
MORIN, Polycarpe, Dec 6 1890 Sex:M Child# 2 Polycarpe Morin Canada & Caroline Grandmaison Canada
MORIN, Raoul, May 10 1906 Sex:M Child# 5 Adelard Morin Canada & Helene Martin Canada
MORIN, Raymond Roger, May 9 1935 Sex:M Child# 4 Alexie Morin Graniteville, VT & Jeannette Martel Suncook, NH
MORIN, Regina Rosanna, Apr 6 1901 Sex:F Child# 4 Joseph Morin Canada & Artemise Berube Canada
MORIN, Rita Etiennette, Nov 20 1919 Sex:F Child# 3 Edouard Morin Canada & Exilda Dube Canada
MORIN, Robert, Jul 21 1919 Sex:M Child# 1 Oscar Morin Nashua, NH & Bertha Seguin Derry, NH
MORIN, Robert Paul, Oct 18 1918 Sex:M Child# 3 Joseph H Morin St David, PQ & Corinne H Morse Nashua, NH
MORIN, Roger Adrien, Oct 1 1915 Sex:M Child# 3 Elzear Morin Nashua, NH & Aimee Lizotte Canada
MORIN, Roger Wilfrid, Dec 6 1921 Sex:M Child# 2 Wilfrid Morin Nashua, NH & Lea Anctil Nashua, NH
MORIN, Roland Fernande, Apr 29 1924 Sex:F Child# 4 Edmond Morin Newmarket, NH & Exilda Dube Canada
MORIN, Roland Gerard, Oct 20 1920 Sex:M Child# 2 Oscar Morin Nashua, NH & Bertha Seguin Derry, NH
MORIN, Romeo Eugene, Nov 18 1907 Sex:M Child# 4 J B Morin Canada & Rose Laliberte Canada
MORIN, Romeo Gerard, Nov 14 1916 Sex:M Child# 2 Edmond Morin Newmarket, NH & Ezilda Dube Canada
MORIN, Ronald, Feb 7 1935 Sex:M Child# 4 Sylvio Morin Canada & Annette Simard Nashua, NH
MORIN, Rosa Alma, Nov 24 1910 Sex:F Child# 5 Alphonse Morin Canada & Eva Blanchette Canada
MORIN, Rose Aimee Flora Mar, Jun 28 1912 Sex:F Child# 1 Elzear Morin Nashua, NH & Aimee Lizotte Canada
MORIN, Rose Alice, Jul 13 1903 Sex:F Child# 1 Jean Bte Morin Canada & Rossanna Laliberte Vermont
MORIN, Rose F, May 16 1894 Sex:F Child# 2 Alfred Morin Canada & Malvina Levesque Canada
MORIN, Rosemond Mary, May 3 1918 Sex:F Child# 1 Joseph Morin Canada & Josephine Hanson Canada
MORIN, Simone Loretta, Jun 26 1914 Sex:F Child# 11 Adelard Morin Canada & Helene Martin Canada
MORIN, Stanislas, Dec 5 1894 Sex:M Child# 2 Charles Morin Canada & Marie L Havard Canada
MORIN, Theresa Jeanne, Sep 20 1929 Sex:F Child# 1 Alexis Morin Graniteville, VT & Jeannette Martel Suncook, NH

MORIN, Unknown, Oct 22 1888 Sex:M Child# 1 Golycarpe Morin Canada & Caroline Trawdwins'n Canada
MORIN, Unknown, Dec 23 1889 Sex:M Child# 9 Pierre Morin Canada & Josephine Cornier Canada Stillborn
MORIN, Unknown, Sep 18 1898 Sex:M Child# 4 Charles Morin Canada & Marie Louise Havard Canada
MORIN, Unknown, Oct 14 1900 Sex:F Child# 1 Henri Morin Canada & Domitildie Gagne Canada
MORIN, Unknown, Jul 8 1910 Sex:M Child# 1 Leon Morin Canada & Carrie LaBrecque Nashua, NH
MORIN, Unknown, May 8 1911 Sex:F Child# 1 Joseph E Morin Canada & Corinne Morse Nashua, NH
MORIN, Unknown, Dec 27 1912 Sex:M Child# 1 Marzeno Morin Canada & Marie Jeanne Lucier Canada Stillborn
MORIN, Unknown, Sep 21 1913 Sex:F Child# 2 Joseph E Morin Canada & Corine Morse Canada Stillborn
MORIN, Unknown, Nov 18 1922 Sex:M Child# 1 Wilfred Morin Canada & Flora LaForest Nashua, NH Stillborn
MORIN, Unknown, Feb 4 1923 Sex:F Child# 6 Oscar Morin Nashua, NH & Bertha Sequin Canada
MORIN, Unknown, Aug 21 1928 Sex:F Child# 2 Wilfrid Morin Canada & Flora Laforest Nashua, NH
MORIN, Ursul Orila, Oct 21 1902 Sex:M Child# 1 Hermenigilde Morin Canada & P Bellerose Canada
MORIN, Victor, Nov 14 1887 Sex:M Child# 6 Alphonse Morin P Q & Zoe Gaudette P Q
MORIN, Victor J I, Aug 17 1887 Sex:M Child# 3 Antoine Morin P Q & Olive P Q
MORIN, Victor Rolland, Dec 24 1910 Sex:M Child# 1 Victor Morin NH & Ernestine Ouellette Canada
MORIN, Virginie, Mar 20 1887 Sex:F Child# Antoine Morin P Q & Zoe Charron P Q
MORIN, Wilfred, Mar 26 1892 Sex:M Child# 1 Joseph Morin Canada & Edith Francoeur Canada
MORIN, Wilfred J B, Jan 1 1900 Sex:M Child# 1 Charles Morin Canada & Euphremie Gagnon Canada
MORIN, Wilfred Jos Emile, Nov 17 1917 Sex:M Child# 7 Joseph T Morin Great Falls, NB & Enrestine Gauthier Canada
MORIN, William Roger, Jul 11 1915 Sex:M Child# 1 Arthur L Morin Nashua, NH & Ruth Parker Nashua, NH
MORIN, Zenon Raymond, Jan 24 1909 Sex:M Child# 12 Desire Morin Canada & Josephine Rousseau Canada
MORIS, Rachelle, Apr 21 1916 Sex:F Child# 1 Dominick Moris Russia & Martha Muzikute Russia
MORISERTE, Marie E C, Aug 21 1891 Sex:F Child# Joseph A Moriserte Canada & Dorila Aprille Canada
MORISETTE, Marie Alice, Jan 14 1890 Sex:F Child# 1 Archadries Morisette Canada & Dorila Anerille Canada
MORISSETTE, Albert Napoleon, Aug 28 1919 Sex:M Child# 1 Albert Morissette US & Marie Anne R Dube US
MORISSETTE, Arthur Louis E, Jan 27 1900 Sex:M Child# 3 Alphonse Morissette Canada & Marie L Paul New Hampshire
MORISSETTE, Claire Ann, Nov 4 1933 Sex:F Child# 2 L Morissette Nashua, NH & Shirley Erb Nashua, NH
MORISSETTE, Claire Irene, May 15 1927 Sex:F Child# 4 A G Morrissette Nashua, NH & Rose A Dube Milford, NH
MORISSETTE, Hermina Irene, Sep 18 1897 Sex:F Child# 1 Alphonse Morissette Canada & Marie Louise Paul Nashua, NH
MORISSETTE, Joseph Dana, Oct 5 1900 Sex:M Child# 9 J A Morissette Canada & Dorilda April Canada
MORISSETTE, Joseph George Albert, May 7 1898 Sex:M Child# 7 J A Morissette Canada & Dorilda Aprile Canada
MORISSETTE, Joseph Henri William, Jun 23 1908 Sex:M Child# 8 Alphonse Morissette Canada & M Louise Paul Nashua, NH
MORISSETTE, Joseph Wilfred, Oct 31 1892 Sex:M Child# 3 Joseph A Morissette Canada & Dorilda Aprile Canada
MORISSETTE, Marie B A, May 25 1899 Sex:F Child# 8 J A Morissette Canada & Dorilda April Canada
MORISSETTE, Marie Jennette, Nov 27 1898 Sex:F Child# 2 Alphonse Morissette Canada & Marie Louise Paul Nashua, NH
MORISSETTE, Marie Leona, Oct 12 1896 Sex:F Child# 6 Joseph A Morissette Canada & Dorilda Aprile Canada
MORISSETTE, Marie Yvonne, Nov 22 1904 Sex:F Child# 1 Joseph Morissette Canada & Alfrida Aprile Canada
MORISSETTE, Richard Albert, Sep 14 1932 Sex:M Child# 1 A Morissette Nashua, NH & Annette Cote Nashua, NH
MORISSETTE, Simone, Sep 8 1927 Sex:F Child# 1 Leo Morissette Canada & Aline Lessard Canada
MORISSEY, Charles Raymond, Apr 5 1914 Sex:M Child# 1 Charles Morissey US & Clarinda Mandeville US
MORIUS, Morta, Apr 20 1918 Sex:F Child# 3 Dominikas Morius Russia & Morta Mazuknaite Russia
MORLEY, Donald Patrick, Mar 21 1934 Sex:M Child# 1 Patrick Morley Manchester, NH & M Blanche Daigle Quebec
MORLOCK, Paul L, Feb 18 1919 Sex:M Child# 1 Herbert Morlock Winchendon, MA & Dorilda Levesque Canada
MORNE, Albert Rogers, Jul 1 1918 Sex:M Child# 6 Alphonse Morne Canada & Alescine Servois Nashua, NH
MORNEAU, Albert, Apr 14 1905 Sex:M Child# 4 Elzear Morneau Canada & Denise Girouard Nashua, NH
MORNEAU, Constance Therese, Oct 17 1934 Sex:F Child# 1 Arthur Morneau Greenville, NH & Arline Caron Greenville, NH
MORNEAU, Dorothy Laura, Aug 2 1930 Sex:F Child# 1 William Morneau Nashua, NH & Irene Morisette Lowell, MA
MORNEAU, Emile Harry, May 21 1914 Sex:M Child# 5 Henri Morneau NH & Georgiana Labonte NH
MORNEAU, Joseph, Jul 1 1905 Sex:M Child# 10 Louis Morneau Canada & Victoria Vincent Canada
MORNEAU, Joseph Aime A, Aug 1 1902 Sex:M Child# 8 Louis Morneau Canada & Victoria Vincent Canada
MORNEAU, Joseph Albert Alph, May 26 1901 Sex:M Child# 7 Louis Morneau Canada & Victoria Vincent Canada
MORNEAU, Joseph G Ed, Mar 20 1902 Sex:M Child# 1 Edouard Morneau Canada & Arthemise Boucher Canada
MORNEAU, Joseph L, Jan 22 1899 Sex:M Child# 1 Elzear Morneau Canada & Denise Girouard Nashua, NH
MORNEAU, Joseph Walter, Jul 17 1915 Sex:M Child# 7 Joseph Morneau Canada & Laura Blais Canada
MORNEAU, Leger, Sep 15 1900 Sex:M Child# 2 Elzear Morneau Canada & Denise Girouard Nashua, NH
MORNEAU, M Mildred Dorothy, Jan 8 1913 Sex:F Child# 1 Henri Morneau NH & Georgianna Labonte NH
MORNEAU, Marie Ange Lillian Y, Nov 29 1923 Sex:F Child# 4 Aurel Morneau Canada & Angelina Michaud Canada
MORNEAU, Marie Martha C, Dec 22 1930 Sex:F Child# 7 Edward Morneau Canada & Helena Pelletier Canada
MORNEAU, Marie Regina L, Sep 16 1903 Sex:F Child# 9 Louis Morneau Canada & Victoria Vincent Canada
MORNEAU, Pearl Beatrice, Aug 6 1910 Sex:F Child# 5 Elzear Morneau Canada & Denise Girouard US
MORNEAU, Unknown, Apr 23 1926 Sex:F Child# 1 Leo Morneau Nashua, NH & Sylvia Fugere Nashua, NH
MORNEAU, William, Jr, Jul 27 1933 Sex:M Child# 2 William Mourneau Lawrence, MA & Irene Morrissette Lowell, MA
MOROOKIAN, Hobanus, Nov 3 1926 Sex:M Child# 1 Bogos Morookian Armenia & Anais Caron Armenia
MOROS, Paul Eugene, Apr 7 1933 Sex:M Child# 1 Leon E Moros Schenectady, NY & Dolores Jenkins Forest, OH
MORRAN, Adeline, Mar 21 1887 Sex:F Child# 1 Pierre Morran Canada & Adeline Guichard Canada
MORREAU, Alfred, Mar 6 1891 Sex:M Child# 2 Alfred Morreau Canada & Alphonsine Deschene Canada
MORREAU, Arthur, Jun 6 1893 Sex:M Child# 4 Frederic Morreau Canada & Alphonsine Deschene Canada
MORREAU, Louis P, Oct 5 1895 Sex:M Child# 7 Norbert Morreau Canada & Rosanna Cognac Canada
MORREAU, Marie R, May 13 1887 Sex:F Child# 6 Edward Morreau Canada & Demesges Bossi Canada
MORREAU, Unknown, Apr 29 1892 Sex:M Child# 3 Frederic Morreau Canada & Alphonsine Deschene Canada Stillborn
MORRELL, Unknown, Aug 26 1892 Sex:M Child# 4 Charles H Morrell Nashua, NH & Harriet F Reed Nashua, NH
MORRELL, Unknown, Nov 8 1893 Sex:F Child# 5 Charles W Morrell Nashua, NH & Harriet F Reed Nashua, NH
MORRELL, Unknown, Dec 6 1899 Sex:F Child# 1 Byron F Morrell NH & Lillian M Hunt Canada

MORRELL, Unknown, Jun 15 1909 Sex:M Child# 5 Byron F Morrell Springfield, NH & Lily Hunt Bury, PQ
MORRIARTY, Mary A, Oct 20 1888 Sex:F Child# 1 John Morriarty Ireland & Bridget Quinn Ireland
MORRILL, Arthur Edward, Nov 21 1920 Sex:M Child# 1 Arthur L Morrill Short Falls, NH & Gertrude M Hill Hancock, NH
MORRILL, George J, Sep 13 1889 Sex:M Child# 3 George S Morrill Goshen, NH & Mary Bagley Nashua, NH
MORRILL, Grace Agnes, Feb 20 1907 Sex:F Child# 3 Byron Morrill Springfield & Lillie Hunt Canada
MORRILL, Harrietta, Apr 13 1888 Sex:F Child# 1 John P Morrill Nashua, NH & Addie S Downs Merrimack, NH
MORRILL, Helen Emeline, Mar 1 1902 Sex:F Child# 1 George J Morrill Nashua, NH & Susie M Parkhurst Wilton, NH
MORRILL, Henry, Aug 5 1889 Sex:M Child# 4 George S Morrill Goshen, NH & Mary Bagley Nashua, NH
MORRILL, Hester, Oct 2 1892 Sex:F Child# 3 Lester Morrill Manchester, England & Phoeba Londonderry, NH
MORRILL, Leslie Holt, Feb 10 1934 Sex:M Child# 3 Arthur E Morrill Merrimack, NH & Leona M Stone S Ashburnham, MA
MORRILL, Loren Edwin, Jun 23 1932 Sex:M Child# 2 Arthur E Morrill Merrimack, NH & Leona M Stone S Ashburnham, MA
MORRILL, Louis, Sep 17 1889 Sex:M Child# 1 George S Morrill Goshen, NH & Mary Bagley Nashua, NH
MORRILL, Marion Dimica, Oct 26 1890 Sex:F Child# 3 Charles W Morrill Nashua, NH & Harriet F Reed Nashua, NH
MORRILL, Robert Ellwyn, May 6 1922 Sex:M Child# 2 Arthur L Morrill Short Falls, NH & Gertrude Hill Hancock, NH
MORRILL, Roberta, Oct 13 1915 Sex:F Child# 1 Robert J Morrill
MORRILL, Unknown, Nov 24 1890 Sex:F Child# 3 John P Morrill Nashua, NH & Adelaide S Stevens Merrimack, NH
MORRILL, Unknown, Nov 9 1898 Sex:M Child# 4 Charles W Morrill Nashua, NH & Harriet F Read Nashua, NH
MORRILL, Unknown, Jul 24 1903 Sex: Child# 2 George J Morrill Nashua, NH & Susie M Parkhurst Wilton, NH
MORRILL, Unknown, Aug 25 1903 Sex:F Child# 2 Henry T Morrill Calais, ME & Ada E Armstrong Hudson, NH
MORRILL, Waldo Everett, Nov 22 1927 Sex:M Child# 3 Arthur L Morrill Short Falls, NH & Gertrude M Hill Hancock, NH
MORRIS, Alphonse, Oct 28 1888 Sex:M Child# 2 Joseph Morris Canada & Delina Croteau Canada
MORRIS, Anna, Feb 14 1917 Sex:F Child# 2 Dominikas Morris Russia & Martha Mazkanaite Russia
MORRIS, Anna Elizabeth, Jun 11 1922 Sex:F Child# 2 Philip Ed Morris Nashua, NH & Josephine McQuesten Nashua, NH
MORRIS, Bayard Eugene, Apr 7 1900 Sex:M Child# 1 Paul Morris NY & Henrietta Jimpson NY
MORRIS, Georges, Jul 7 1887 Sex:M Child# 2 Joseph Morris P Q & Delina Croteau P Q
MORRIS, John, Nov 21 1923 Sex:M Child# 4 Dominick Morris Lithuania & Martha Mazlurate Lithuania
MORRIS, Lina, Jun 10 1897 Sex:F Child# 11 Joseph Morris Canada & Delima Croteau
MORRIS, Margaret, Jun 27 1923 Sex:F Child# 3 Philip E Morris Nashua, NH & Josephine McQuesten Nashua, NH
MORRIS, Marie E, Dec 14 1889 Sex:F Child# 4 Joseph Morris Canada & Delina Croteau Canada
MORRIS, Philip, Oct 7 1887 Sex:M Child# 2 George R Morris Maine & Nellie A NH
MORRIS, Robert McQuesten, Sep 14 1920 Sex:M Child# 1 Philip Ed Morris Nashua, NH & Josephine McQuesten Nashua, NH
MORRIS, Roselle Elizabeth, Apr 20 1913 Sex:F Child# 1 James A Morris Pelham, NH & Jessie R Wheeler Nashua, NH
MORRIS, Ruth, Mar 23 1926 Sex:F Child# 4 Philip Morris Nashua, NH & J McQuesten Nashua, NH
MORRIS, Unknown, Feb 6 1920 Sex:M Child# 5 Thomas Morris Greece & Catherine Thavas Greece
MORRIS, Unknown, Apr 2 1925 Sex:M Child# 7 Dom Morris Lithuania & Mar Maraxinalb Lithuania Stillborn
MORRISETTE, Donat Leonel, Jan 6 1902 Sex:M Child# 4 Alph Morrisette Canada & Mary L Paul New Hampshire
MORRISETTE, George Leon, May 16 1923 Sex:M Child# 2 Jos Morrisette, Jr Nashua, NH & Aurore Lessard Nashua, NH
MORRISETTE, Jos Emile Antonio, Jan 12 1919 Sex:M Child# 14 Alphonse Morrisette Canada & Marie Louise NH
MORRISETTE, Joseph Romeo A, Mar 22 1895 Sex:M Child# 4 Joseph H Morrisette Canada & Dovilda Aprile Canada
MORRISETTE, Lucille Therese, Oct 31 1930 Sex:F Child# 1 Arthur Morrisette Nashua, NH & Lena Cote Nashua, NH
MORRISETTE, Marie Laura, Feb 11 1894 Sex:F Child# 4 Joseph A Morrisette Canada & Dorilda Aprile Canada
MORRISETTE, Yolande Regina, Dec 9 1935 Sex:F Child# 3 Leo Morrisette Canada & Aline Lessard Canada
MORRISON, Allan Chase, Sep 7 1935 Sex:M Child# 1 John J Morrison Cambridge, MA & Hazel Chase Lyndeboro, NH
MORRISON, Allan H, Sep 6 1897 Sex:M Child# 2 Charles A Morrison Milford, ME & Laura A Gordon Brewer, ME
MORRISON, Donald Richard, Mar 22 1928 Sex:M Child# 10 Charles H Morrison Concord, NH & Alice M Benjamin NS
MORRISON, Edna May, Oct 19 1902 Sex:F Child# 1 F E Morrison Nashua, NH & Edna Danley Nashua, NH
MORRISON, Frank Cerier, Dec 20 1924 Sex:M Child# 9 Charles Morrison Concord, NH & Alice Benjamin Nova Scotia
MORRISON, Gertrude Olive, Apr 24 1896 Sex:F Child# 1 E L Morrison Lynn & A O Smith Nashua, NH
MORRISON, James Wilson, Jun 12 1919 Sex:M Child# 7 Charles H Morrison Concord, NH & Alice Toucey Nova Scotia
MORRISON, John Leo, Nov 18 1905 Sex:M Child# 2 John L Morrison Pembroke, ME & J F Sullivan Canton, MA
MORRISON, Livernia M, Mar 4 1891 Sex:F Child# 1 Joseph H Morrison New York & Mary E Clark New York
MORRISON, Mary Eleanor, Apr 3 1902 Sex:F Child# 1 John L Morrison Pembroke, ME & Josephine T Sullivan Canton, MA
MORRISON, Philip Joseph, Apr 22 1910 Sex:M Child# 3 John L Morrison Pembroke, ME & Josephine Sullivan Canton, MA
MORRISON, Robert Edward, Jun 21 1921 Sex:M Child# 4 Charles H Morrison Concord, NH & Alice Benjamin Nova Scotia
MORRISON, Ruth Marion, Sep 21 1928 Sex:F Child# 1 Frank Morrison Belfast, ME & Mary Mongrain Canada
MORRISON, Sarah A, Nov 29 1890 Sex:F Child# 2 Samuel E Morrison VT & Allie S Baltch VT
MORRISON, Unknown, Jul 10 1905 Sex:M Child# 4 Charles A Morrison Bradley, ME & Laura A Gordon Brewer, ME
MORRISSETTE, George Albert, Feb 4 1923 Sex:M Child# 3 Geo E Morrissette Nashua, NH & Rose Dube Milford, NH
MORRISSETTE, Helene, Mar 3 1913 Sex:F Child# 10 Zenon Morrissette Canada & Marie L Banville Canada
MORRISSETTE, Howard Leslie, May 28 1931 Sex:M Child# 1 Lionel Morrissette Nashua, NH & Shirley Erb Nashua, NH
MORRISSETTE, Jean Baptiste H, May 10 1914 Sex:M Child# 11 Zenon Morrissette Canada & M Louise Banville Canada
MORRISSETTE, Jos Apl Rolland, Jun 26 1916 Sex:M Child# 2 Romeo Morrissette NH & Marie Rose Briand Canada
MORRISSETTE, Joseph Amedee, Apr 28 1906 Sex:M Child# 13 Joseph Morrissette Canada & Emma April Canada
MORRISSETTE, Joseph Arthur L, Jul 4 1903 Sex:M Child# 11 Joseph A Morrissette Canada & Dorilda April Canada
MORRISSETTE, Joseph Leo, May 23 1918 Sex:M Child# 3 Romeo Morrissette NH & Marie Rose Briand Canada
MORRISSETTE, Loraine Lena, May 21 1934 Sex:F Child# 2 Arthur Morrissette Nashua, NH & Lena Cote Nashua, NH
MORRISSETTE, M Alida L, Apr 22 1902 Sex:F Child# 10 J A Morrissette Canada & Dorilda April Canada
MORRISSETTE, M Lucille Olivette, May 4 1915 Sex:F Child# 1 Romeo Morrissette NH & Marie Rose Briand Canada
MORRISSETTE, M Marguerite Rac, Sep 26 1915 Sex:F Child# 12 Alphonse Morrissette Canada & M Louise Paul Nashua, NH
MORRISSETTE, Marie rose M, Jun 23 1903 Sex:F Child# 5 Alphonse Morrissette Canada & Marie Louise Paul NH
MORRISSETTE, Olivier Albert, Sep 4 1904 Sex:M Child# 6 Alphonse Morrissette Canada & Marie Louise Paul NH
MORRISSETTE, Paul Amedee, Aug 6 1906 Sex:M Child# 7 Alphonse Morrissette Canada & Marie Louise Paul NH
MORRISSETTE, Raymond Henri, Aug 5 1920 Sex:M Child# 2 Alb I Morrissette US & Rose Dube US

MORRISSETTE, Robert Raoul, Jan 12 1917 Sex:M Child# 13 Alp Morrissette Canada & Marie Louise Paul Nashua, NH
MORRISSETTE, Vincent Ronald, Jun 18 1935 Sex:M Child# 1 R Morrissette Nashua, NH & Rita Constant Nashua, NH
MORRISSEY, John Bartlett, Aug 30 1924 Sex:M Child# 2 J H Morrissey Ireland & Eliz G Reagan Boston, MA
MORRISSEY, Unknown, Dec 21 1922 Sex:M Child# 1 John H Morrissey Ireland & Elizabeth E Reagan Boston, MA Stillborn
MORROTTE, Ellen M, May 29 1887 Sex:F Child# 2 Philias Morrotte Sciota, NY & Josephine Dion Sciota, NY
MORSE, Allen Edward, Oct 2 1896 Sex:M Child# 1 Edward Morse Mass & Ellen M Norris Mass
MORSE, Betty Ann, Dec 10 1933 Sex:F Child# 9 George E Morse Nashua, NH & Gertrude Maddox Nashua, NH
MORSE, Betty Emma, Jun 18 1891 Sex:F Child# 1 John E Morse NH & Sarah E Karney NH
MORSE, Caleb H, Nov 20 1892 Sex:M Child# 2 George S Morse Lowell, MA & Etta O Perley Nashua, NH
MORSE, Catherine Etta, Jan 8 1891 Sex:F Child# 3 Rodney L Morse E Jaffrey, NH & Mary E Wills Nashua, NH
MORSE, Charles Maddox, Jun 12 1931 Sex:M Child# 8 George Morse Nashua, NH & Gertrude Maddox Nashua, NH
MORSE, Denise Elinor, Jul 22 1929 Sex:F Child# 10 Laurent Morse Lowell, MA & Agnes Girouard Nashua, NH
MORSE, Dorothy Lucille, Aug 5 1911 Sex:F Child# 3 Loren J Morse Lowell, MA & Agnes M Girouard Nashua, NH
MORSE, E J, Nov 20 1891 Sex:M Child# 2 Frank O Morse NY & Celina Caron NY
MORSE, Elaine Rita, Sep 27 1926 Sex:F Child# 6 George E Morse Nashua, NH & G A Maddox Nashua, NH
MORSE, Elmer R, Dec 2 1895 Sex:M Child# 6 H L Morse Newton, MA & Alice Christian Boston, MA
MORSE, Frank Clarence, Jul 8 1927 Sex:M Child# 1 Percy Morse S Merrimack, NH & Edith Buswell Bedford, NH
MORSE, Frank Devens, Oct 8 1922 Sex:F Child# 4 Walter R Morse Nashua, NH & Beatrice Devens E Jaffrey, NH
MORSE, George Henry, Jan 4 1896 Sex:M Child# 2 Enoch C Morse Massachusetts & Maria C Newton Massachusetts
MORSE, George William, Nov 22 1920 Sex:M Child# 3 George E Morse Nashua, NH & Gertrude A Maddox Nashua, NH
MORSE, Gertrude Mae, May 2 1921 Sex:F Child# 4 Ernest P Morse Truro, SD & Jennie E Arlin Ayer, MA
MORSE, Glenys Harriet, Sep 29 1922 Sex:F Child# 2 Elmer R Morse Nashua, NH & Madge B Bates Winthrop, MA
MORSE, Irene Barbara, Mar 6 1928 Sex:F Child# 7 Geo E Morse Nashua, NH & Gert A Maddox Nashua, NH
MORSE, James George, May 4 1899 Sex:M Child# 4 Rodney L Morse Fitzwilliam, NH & Mary E Wells Nashua, NH
MORSE, John Herbert, Sep 18 1920 Sex:M Child# 3 Walter R Morse Nashua, NH & Beatrice Devens E Jaffrey, NH
MORSE, Lorraine Etta, Feb 23 1913 Sex:F Child# 2 Loren F Morse Lowell, MA & Agnes M Girouard Nashua, NH
MORSE, Marion Gertrude, Jul 22 1918 Sex:F Child# 2 George E Morse Nashua, NH & Gertrude A Maddox Nashua, NH
MORSE, Mary Adrianne, Sep 18 1922 Sex:F Child# 6 Loren Morse Lowell, MA & Agnes Girouard Nashua, NH
MORSE, Mary Elizabeth, Sep 20 1925 Sex:F Child# 7 Loren Morse Lowell, MA & Agnes Girouard Nashua, NH
MORSE, Norine Mary, May 17 1925 Sex:F Child# 1 James Morse Nashua, NH & Agnes Sullivan Nashua, NH
MORSE, Paul Henry, Apr 19 1920 Sex:M Child# 5 Loren F Morse Lowell, MA & Agnes Girouard Nashua, NH
MORSE, Paul T, Oct 22 1922 Sex:M Child# 4 George E Morse Nashua, NH & Gertrude A Maddox Nashua, NH
MORSE, Philip Merrill, Aug 15 1902 Sex:M Child# Ira H Morse Chester & Lillian Little Manchester, NH
MORSE, Priscilla Christian, Jun 7 1925 Sex:F Child# 3 Elmer R Morse Nashua, NH & Madge B Bates Winthrop, ME
MORSE, Raymond Francis, Sep 4 1916 Sex:M Child# 1 George Morse Nashua, NH & Gertrude Maddox Nashua, NH
MORSE, Richard Emmott, Sep 9 1924 Sex:M Child# 5 George Morse Nashua, NH & Gertrude Maddox Nashua, NH
MORSE, Rodney James, Apr 10 1915 Sex:M Child# 3 Loren Morse Lowell, MA & Agnes Girouard Nashua, NH
MORSE, Roger Fessenden, Oct 31 1920 Sex:M Child# 1 Clarence A Morse Townsend, MA & Blanche E Fessenden
MORSE, Ruth Elba, Nov 15 1923 Sex:F Child# 5 Ernest Pierre Morse Truro, SD & Jennie Eva Arlen Ayer, MA
MORSE, Ruth Ellen, Mar 4 1892 Sex:F Child# 3 McClellan Morse Littleton & Mary Doyle Malone, NY
MORSE, Unknown, Mar 1 1888 Sex:F Child# 2 McClellen W Morse Littleton & Mamie E Doyle New York
MORSE, Unknown, Dec 11 1888 Sex:M Child# 4 Lewis H Morse Mass & Alice Christian Boston
MORSE, Unknown, Aug 29 1913 Sex:F Child# 1 Walter J Morse Rhode Island & Catherine Guerin Winchester, MA Stillborn
MORSE, Unknown, Sep 11 1926 Sex:M Child# 2 William E Morse Lowell, MA & Theresa Carrick Nashua, NH
MORSE, Walter Russell, Sep 22 1894 Sex:M Child# Lewis H Morse Mass & Alice C Boston, MA
MORSE, William Arthur, Dec 15 1917 Sex:M Child# 4 Loren F Morse Lowell, MA & Agnes Girouard Nashua, NH
MORSE, William Carrick, Sep 26 1920 Sex:M Child# 1 William Morse Lowell, MA & Theresa Carrick Nashua, NH
MORSEAU, Joseph Flavien, Dec 13 1905 Sex:M Child# 8 Calixte Morseau Derby, VT & Anastasia Labonte Derby, VT
MORTIN, Gerald Thomas, Apr 25 1903 Sex:M Child# 4 Charles G Mortin Lowell, MA & Victoria Charron Manchester, NH
MORTIS, Frank, Sep 9 1916 Sex:M Child# 2 Frank Mortis Russia & Petrona Guervtrich Russia
MORTLOCK, Beverly Loretta, Sep 29 1933 Sex:F Child# 2 H W Mortlock Hudson, NH & Jeanette Landry Nashua, NH
MORTLOCK, Edgar G, Apr 24 1892 Sex:M Child# 2 George A Mortlock London, England & L J Brown Nashua, NH
MORTLOCK, Edna Grace, Oct 20 1905 Sex:F Child# 7 George A Mortlock London, England & Louise J Brown Nashua, NH
MORTLOCK, Harry William, Aug 1 1929 Sex:M Child# 1 Harry Wm Mortlock Hudson, NH & Jeannette Landry Nashua, NH
MORTLOCK, Marion Louise, May 25 1896 Sex:F Child# 4 George A Mortlock London, England & Louise J Brown Nashua, NH
MORTLOCK, Robert Whitney, Feb 7 1898 Sex:M Child# 10 George Mortlock England & Nellie M Freeman Hinsdale, NH
MORTLOCK, Unknown, Aug 10 1894 Sex:F Child# 2 George Mortlock London, England & Nellie M Freeman Hinsdale, NH
MORTLOCK, Walter Edward, Aug 30 1894 Sex:M Child# 3 George A Mortlock England & Louise Brown NH
MORTON, Bernadette, Dec 14 1909 Sex:F Child# 9 Charles G Morton US & Victoria Charron US
MORTON, Blanche Euphemia, Oct 14 1908 Sex:F Child# 8 Charles G Morton US & Victoria Charron US
MORTON, Carlton Leo, Aug 26 1899 Sex:M Child# 1 Charles Morton Lowell, MA & Victoria Charron Manchester, NH
MORTON, Frances Theresa, Aug 24 1907 Sex:F Child# 7 Charles G Morton Lowell, MA & Victoria Charron Manchester, NH
MORTON, Frederick, Oct 14 1900 Sex:m Child# 2 Charles Morton Lowell, MA & Victoria Charron Manchester, NH
MORTON, Joseph, Mar 19 1898 Sex:M Child# 7 Edward W Morton Montreal, Canada & Annie M O'Hern Montreal, Canada
MORTON, Phyllis Eugenia, Feb 17 1931 Sex:F Child# 5 Stanley Morton Nashua, NH & Roberta Tetro Nashua, NH
MORTON, Regina Marie, Nov 19 1904 Sex:F Child# 5 Charles G Morton Lowell, MA & Victoria Charron Manchester, NH
MORTON, Ronald Francis, Jul 13 1932 Sex:M Child# 6 Stanley Morton Nashua, NH & Roberta Tatro Nashua, NH
MORTON, Stanislaus Joseph, Feb 10 1906 Sex:M Child# 6 Charles G Morton Lowell, MA & Victoria Charron Manchester, NH
MORTON, Stanislaus Joseph, Nov 7 1925 Sex:M Child# 1 Stanley Morton Nashua, NH & Roberta Tatro Nashua, NH
MORTON, Unknown, Aug 26 1898 Sex:M Child# 2 Lawrence E Morton Hudson, NH & Viola Stanley Pepperell, MA
MORTUZAS, Unknown, Feb 25 1918 Sex:F Child# 2 Constantine Mortuzas Russia & Armatolia Gudalis Russia
MOSES, Dorothy Ellen, May 23 1923 Sex:F Child# 2 Thomas L Moses New York & Elvira Hilliard NH
MOSES, Norman Nelson, Jun 29 1923 Sex:M Child# 3 Sylvanus B Moses Vermont & Rosa Gerow NH

MOSES, Roy Allen, Oct 31 1926 Sex:M Child# 4 Salvinus Moses Woodstock, VT & M A St Laurent Haverhill, MA
MOSES, William Samuel, Jul 7 1921 Sex:M Child# 1 Thomas L Moses New York & Elvira Hilliard NH
MOSS, Beatrice Lucile, Jul 31 1910 Sex:F Child# 2 Enrest C Moss Nashua, NH & Stella Recor W Chazy, NY
MOSS, Dorothy Elizabeth, May 1 1920 Sex:F Child# 1 Ernest C Moss Nashua, NH & Isabelle McDonald Canada
MOSS, Florence, Dec 6 1909 Sex:F Child# 3 Leon R Moss W Chazy, NY & Bertha F Smith Hollis, NH
MOSS, Harland Spalding, Jan 12 1906 Sex:M Child# 1 Leon R Moss W Chazy, NY & Bertha H Smith Hollis, NH
MOSS, Mary Agnes, Mar 13 1894 Sex:F Child# 1 Melvin Moss NY & Alice Munhall Wilton, NH
MOSS, Robert Henry, Sep 21 1910 Sex:M Child# 5 Melvin Moss New York & Alice Munhall Peterborough, NH
MOSS, Unknown, May 11 1891 Sex:M Child# 2 William H Moss New York & Rena J Lowell, MA
MOSS, Unknown, Jun 27 1895 Sex:F Child# 3 W H Moss NY & Rena Stearns Lowell, MA
MOSS, Unknown, Jun 14 1907 Sex:F Child# 2 Leon Roy Moss W Chazey, NY & Bertha H Smith Hollis, NH
MOSS, Unknown, Feb 23 1913 Sex:F Child# 3 Ernest C Moss Nashua, NH & Stella Recor W Chazy, NY
MOSS, Unknown, Sep 25 1913 Sex:M Child# 4 Enrest C Moss Nashua, NH & Stella Recor W Chazy, NY Stillborn
MOSS, Unknown, Nov 1 1915 Sex:F Child# 4 Ernest Moss Nashua, NH & Stella Recor W Chazy, NY Stillborn
MOSS, Unknown, Aug 13 1916 Sex:M Child# 6 Ernest C Moss Nashua, NH & Della Ricor W Chazy, NY
MOSS, Unknown, Nov 23 1930 Sex:M Child# 1 Donald H Moss Nashua, NH & Mary Paquin Lowell, MA Stillborn
MOTERS, Ursula, Dec 22 1914 Sex:F Child# 1 Frank Moters Russia & Patronel Gorezkawich Russia
MOTT, Earl Justin, Feb 26 1898 Sex:M Child# 1 Justin B Mott Sandy Hill, NY & Jennie S Stafford Ellenburg, NY
MOTUZAS, Helen, Apr 7 1922 Sex:F Child# 3 Costas Motuzas Russia & Anatalia Gudelis Russia
MOTUZOS, Stanislawa, Aug 11 1916 Sex:F Child# 1 Constant Motuzos Russia & Anatolia Gudelis Russia
MOULTON, Beatrice, Feb 7 1927 Sex:F Child# 1 William Moulton Nashua, NH & Helen Fairfield Nashua, NH
MOULTON, Beatrice Margaret, Jan 24 1933 Sex:F Child# 2 William Moulton Nashua, NH & Helen Fairfield Nashua, NH
MOULTON, Byron Kemp, May 25 1893 Sex:M Child# 1 Charles W Moulton Georgetown, MA & Ida L Thetford, VT
MOULTON, David Russell, Dec 18 1935 Sex:M Child# 1 Robert L Moulton Lynnfield Ctr, MA & Florence Kirker Taunton, MA
MOULTON, Everett Norman, Feb 13 1901 Sex:M Child# 2 Walter E Moulton York, ME & Maud B Whitlesey New Haven, CT
MOULTON, George Allen, Apr 1 1916 Sex:M Child# 1 Geo Allen Moulton Lewiston, ME & A Wil Schillenberge Germany
MOULTON, John Sherwood, Jan 31 1930 Sex:M Child# 1 Norman S Moulton Portsmouth, NH & Florence Horr Portland, ME
MOULTON, Karl James, Feb 2 1922 Sex:M Child# 2 George Moulton Lewiston, ME & Angie Schellenberg Germany
MOULTON, LaRoy K, Nov 6 1890 Sex:M Child# 3 William H Moulton Hooksett, NH & Linda F Warren, ME
MOULTON, Leroy Kendrick, May 31 1915 Sex:M Child# 4 Leroy Moulton Nashua, NH & Fida Cole Newport, VT
MOULTON, Lester, Mar 13 1902 Sex:M Child# 3 W E Moulton Maine & Maud B Whittlesy Conn
MOULTON, Lilla May, Sep 8 1906 Sex:F Child# 1 Edward S Moulton Andover, MA & Eva L Hutchins Burlington, VT
MOULTON, Marguerite Cole, Sep 15 1902 Sex:F Child# 1 Leroy K Moulton Nashua, NH & Fida Cole Newport, VT
MOULTON, Rosa F, Sep 11 1890 Sex:F Child# 2 William H Moulton Hooksett, NH & Linda F Warren, ME
MOULTON, Unknown, Sep 20 1909 Sex:F Child# 3 Leroy K Moulton Nashua, NH & Fida Cole Newport, VT Stillborn
MOULTON, Walter B, Mar 22 1900 Sex:M Child# 1 W E Moulton Boston, MA & M B Whittlesey Conn
MOULTON, William Carlos, May 9 1904 Sex:M Child# 2 Leroy K Moulton Nashua, NH & Fida Cole Newport, VT
MOULTON, William LeRoy, Aug 22 1929 Sex:M Child# 2 William C Moulton Nashua, NH & Helen Fairfield Nashua, NH
MOUNBLOW, William Amos, Jun 13 1909 Sex:M Child# 1 William Mounblow New York & Elsie Jelly St Albans, VT
MOURNEAU, Lionel, Feb 28 1925 Sex:M Child# 5 Aurele Mourneau Canada & Ange Michaud Canada
MOUSBAN, Arthur, Nov 8 1891 Sex:M Child# 3 Henry S Mousban Lowell, MA & Margaret Foley Nashua, NH
MOUSETTE, Claire Rhea, May 9 1932 Sex:F Child# 3 L A Mousette Nashua, NH & Anita E Caron Nashua, NH
MOUSETTE, George E, Jan 29 1903 Sex:M Child# 3 Joseph A Mousette Nashua, NH & Eva Desjardins Canada
MOUSSETTE, Doris Adrienne, Jan 20 1921 Sex:F Child# 1 Joseph A Moussette Nashua, NH & Aurore Tessier Nashua, NH
MOUSSETTE, Janet Irene, Sep 26 1930 Sex:F Child# 2 Louis A Moussette Nashua, NH & Eva Caron Nashua, NH
MOUSSETTE, Joseph A, Nov 22 1897 Sex:M Child# 2 Alfred Moussette Nashua, NH & Eva Desjardins Canada
MOUSSETTE, Louis Antoine, Feb 21 1908 Sex:M Child# 4 Joseph A Moussette Nashua, NH & Eva Desjardins Canada
MOUSSETTE, Madeleine Claudette, Apr 23 1934 Sex:F Child# 4 Louis A Moussette Nashua, NH & Anita E Caron Nashua, NH
MOUSSETTE, Marie E, Sep 9 1887 Sex:F Child# 3 Albert Moussette P Q & Emile P Q
MOUSSETTE, Marie E G, Jan 22 1896 Sex:F Child# 1 Joseph A Moussette Nashua, NH & Eva Desjardins Canada
MOUSSETTE, Maurice Louis, Dec 3 1928 Sex:M Child# 1 L Moussette Nashua, NH & Anita Caron Nashua, NH
MOVEAU, Joseph, Nov 9 1889 Sex:M Child# 1 F Moveau Canada & A Deschenes Canada
MUCHAVICH, Unknown, Sep 20 1920 Sex:M Child# 6 Michael Muchavich Romania & Josephine Letravonis Romania
MUCHAWICZ, Alphonsus, Oct 8 1922 Sex:m Child# 8 Mich Muchawicz Lithuania & Josephine Tetaronis Lithuania
MUCUNIS, Julia, Jun 9 1921 Sex:F Child# 5 Joseph Mucunis Russia & Jennie Mateeza Russia
MUDGETT, Unknown, May 17 1890 Sex:F Child# 3 George E Mudgett Laconia, NH & Rosetta Furnald Nashua, NH
MUIR, Alegra Cole, Sep 30 1935 Sex:F Child# 1 Walter J Muir Worcester, MA & Gladys P Cole Boston, MA
MUKRUS, Unknown, Feb 2 1917 Sex:F Child# 3 Nicolas Mukrus Greece & Fannie Zepolois Greece
MULAKA, Unknown, Mar 20 1906 Sex:F Child# 1 A Mulaka Russia & Veronica Ulan Russia
MULISKEE, Adam, Jul 12 1901 Sex:M Child# 2 Mick Muliskee Russia & Cophelia Zouty Russia
MULLEN, Bernard Stevens, Jan 13 1903 Sex:M Child# 2 Stevens Mullen NY & Clara Rivet NY
MULLEN, Edward James, Jun 7 1897 Sex:M Child# 12 Michael H Mullen Manchester, NH & Mary O'Brien England
MULLEN, Helen, Nov 3 1906 Sex:F Child# 2 Michael C Mullen Milford, NH & Jennie Burns Ireland
MULLEN, James Edward, Aug 10 1904 Sex:M Child# 1 Michael C Mullen Milford, NH & Jennie Burns Ireland
MULLEN, Lillian Pearl, Dec 8 1904 Sex:F Child# 2 Stephen Mullen NY & Laura Rivais NY
MULLEN, Madeleine Leona, Aug 7 1906 Sex:F Child# 4 Stevens B Mullen New York & Laura M Rivers New York
MULLEN, Margaret Ellen, Jun 28 1889 Sex:F Child# 5 James Mullen Ireland & Bridget O'Hearn Ireland
MULLEN, Mildred Marguerite, May 4 1914 Sex:F Child# 4 Steven B Mullen Malone, NY & Laura M Reeves Malone, NY
MULLEN, Unknown, Apr 18 1895 Sex:F Child# 3 Joseph Mullen Ireland & Kate Lane Ireland
MULLEN, Unknown, Mar 4 1896 Sex:M Child# 12 Michael H Mullen Ireland & Mary O'Brien England Stillborn
MULLER, Loretta Rita, Sep 5 1927 Sex:F Child# 3 Wilfrid Muller Nashua, NH & Malvina Gagnon Nashua, NH
MULLIGAN, William, May 10 1895 Sex:M Child# 1 William Mulligan Ireland & Mary Gilhooley Ireland
MULLIKIN, Lorraine Ann, Jul 6 1933 Sex:F Child# 1 Robert H Mullikin Manchester, NH & Evelyn Pelletier Nashua, NH

MULLIKIN, Robert Herman, Nov 16 1935 Sex:M Child# 2 R H Mullikin Manchester, NH & Evelyn Pelletier Nashua, NH
MULLIN, James, Apr 30 1887 Sex:M Child#  John Mullin Salem, MA & Mary Mitchell Lancaster, MA
MULLIN, Joseph, Jun 27 1935 Sex:M Child# 1 John Mullin New York, NY & Marg McConnell New York, NY Stillborn
MULLINS, Thomas Jefferson, May 20 1892 Sex:M Child# 3 Joseph Mullins Ireland & Katherine Lane Ireland
MULLINUSKI, Rita, Apr 26 1924 Sex:F Child# 4 S Mullinuski Russia & Antony Uzdavinis Russia
MULRANERTY, Ella, Jun 9 1892 Sex:F Child# 3 John Mulranerty Ireland & Kate Degnan Ireland
MULVANITY, Agnes, Sep 7 1894 Sex:F Child# 3 James Mulvanity Ireland & Kate Shea Ireland
MULVANITY, Augustus, Jan 16 1901 Sex:M Child# 1 Thomas F Mulvanity Nashua, NH & Adeline M Shea Nashua, NH
MULVANITY, Barbara Elizabeth, Jun 28 1918 Sex:F Child# 1 John J Mulvanity Nashua, NH & May A DuBray Adams, MA
MULVANITY, Catherine, Jan 31 1898 Sex:F Child# 4 James Mulvanity Ireland & Catherine T O'Shea Ireland
MULVANITY, Edward Donald, Jun 8 1913 Sex:M Child# 5 Thomas P Mulvanity Nashua, NH & Adeline Shea Nashua, NH
MULVANITY, Elizabeth, Aug 4 1894 Sex:F Child# 4 John Mulvanity Ireland & Kate Degnan Ireland
MULVANITY, Elizabeth A, Mar 11 1899 Sex:F Child# 11 James Mulvanity Ireland & Catherine T O'Shea Ireland
MULVANITY, Francis Creighton, Nov 18 1921 Sex:M Child# 2 John J Mulvanity Nashua, NH & Mae DuBray Adams, MA
MULVANITY, George Daniel, Oct 20 1902 Sex:M Child# 2 Thomas F Mulvanity Nashua, NH & Adeline M Shea Nashua, NH
MULVANITY, Gerald Thomas, Jan 30 1907 Sex:M Child# 4 Thomas F Mulvanity Nashua, NH & Adeline M Shea Nashua, NH
MULVANITY, Harold Francis, Aug 8 1905 Sex:M Child# 3 Thomas F Mulvanity Nashua, NH & Adeline M Shea Nashua, NH
MULVANITY, Jacqueline Jeanne, Jan 3 1924 Sex:F Child# 3 J J Mulvanity Nashua, NH & May Ann Dubray N Adams, MA
MULVANITY, James Francis, Jr, Oct 4 1911 Sex:M Child# 1 James F Mulvanity Nashua, NH & Nora Nute Nashua, NH
MULVANITY, John Doyle, May 23 1909 Sex:M Child# 4 John J Mulvanity Nashua, NH & Margaret White Ireland
MULVANITY, Joseph Edward, Mar 29 1893 Sex:M Child# 2 James Mulvanity Ireland & Katherine Shea Ireland
MULVANITY, Margaret Elizabeth, Jan 15 1915 Sex:F Child# 3 Michael Mulvanity Nashua, NH & Elizabeth Holland Milford
MULVANITY, Mary Lucille, Apr 12 1927 Sex:F Child# 1 A S Mulvanity Nashua, NH & Lucille Buckley Nashua, NH
MULVANITY, Paul, Apr 20 1903 Sex:M Child# 2 John Mulvanity Nashua, NH & Margaret White Ireland
MULVANITY, Robert, Aug 21 1904 Sex:M Child# 3 John J Mulvanity Nashua, NH & Margaret White Ireland
MULVANITY, Thomas Andrew, Dec 5 1891 Sex:M Child# 2 James Mulvanity Ireland & Kate Shea Ireland
MULVANITY, Unknown, Dec 12 1901 Sex:F Child# 1 John J Mulvanity Nashua, NH & Margaret M White Ireland Stillborn
MULVANITY, Unknown, Dec 27 1906 Sex:M Child# 1 Thomas W Mulvanity Nashua, NH & Minnie G Bradley Nashua, NH
MULVANITY, Unknown, Jul 20 1907 Sex:M Child# 1 M J Mulvanity Nashua, NH & Elizabeth Holland Milford, NH
MUNDE, Lizzie E, Apr 21 1893 Sex:F Child# 5 Charles Munde NB & Annie Robinson NB
MUNDY, Walter Arthur, Feb 2 1917 Sex:M Child# 1 Fred Mundy England & Francis Sailor Toledo, OH
MUNEZ, Lucia Elmore, Mar 19 1918 Sex:F Child# 1 Vasca E Munez Richmond, VA & Edith P Roberts Medford, MA
MUNHALL, Inez, Apr 18 1904 Sex:F Child# 2 John Munhall Peterboro, VT & Vida Gilman Tamworth, NH
MUNHALL, Mabel Frances, Sep 13 1900 Sex:F Child# 1 John F Munhall NH & Ada E Gilman NH
MUNIER, Irene Jacqueline, May 14 1934 Sex:F Child# 3 Arthur Joseph Munier Nashua, NH & Irene St Laurent Nashua, NH
MUNIER, Lucien Lionel, Apr 24 1909 Sex:M Child# 4 Philosime J Munier Canada & Eliza Bonnette Canada
MUNIER, Lucile, Apr 24 1909 Sex:F Child# 5 Philosime J Munier Canada & Eliza Bonnette Canada
MUNKOWICH, Unknown, Mar 25 1913 Sex:M Child# 2 Charles Munkowich Russia & Nellie Munkowich Russia
MUNRO, Alice, Jan 5 1896 Sex:F Child# 1 J B Munro Canada & Anna Chenette Nashua, NH
MUNRO, Clarence Harvey, Jul 23 1923 Sex:M Child# 2 David Harvey Munro New Brunswick & Louise Gilson NH
MUNROE, Charles Joseph, Nov 11 1914 Sex:M Child# 2 Walter D Munroe Mass & Florence Hazard Mass
MUNROE, James Clayton, Jul 30 1915 Sex:M Child# 1 David H Munroe Nova Scotia & Louise Gilson NH
MUNROE, James Hugh, Nov 24 1930 Sex:M Child# 1 Gordon Munroe Nova Scotia & Edith Reynolds Nova Scotia
MUNROE, Marie Elizabeth, Jan 22 1935 Sex:F Child# 2 Gordon Munroe Cole Harbor, NS & Edith Reynolds Dover, NS
MUNSON, Arthur W, Aug 24 1901 Sex:M Child# 1 Ernest W Munson Winthrop, NY & Melrose Hall Ogdensburg, NY
MUNSON, Earl Willis, Apr 2 1925 Sex:M Child# 1 Willis Munson Champlain, NY & Clara Gerow Woodstock, VT
MUNSON, Irene Rose, May 2 1934 Sex:F Child# 1 Leonard Munson Champlain, NY & Rose Chasseur Canada
MUNSON, James William, May 19 1896 Sex:M Child# 4 Byron Munson Carlisle, ME & Ada McCarvel Canada
MUNSON, Leonard Richard, Apr 12 1923 Sex:M Child# 1 Warren Munson Champlain, NY & Lillian Pontbriand Nashua, NH
MUNSON, Lorraine Blanche, Jul 1 1924 Sex:F Child# 2 Warren Munson Champlain, NY & Lillian Pontbriand Nashua, NH
MUNSON, Lucille Camille, Aug 21 1928 Sex:F Child# 3 Warren Munson Champlain, NY & L Pontbriand Nashua, NH
MUNSON, Rachel, May 23 1932 Sex:F Child# 5 Warren Munson Champlain, NY & Lillian Pontbriand Nashua, NH
MUNSON, Robert Warren, Feb 12 1930 Sex:M Child# 4 Warren Munson Champlain, NY & Lillian Pontbriand Nashua, NH
MUNTON, Alex Vincent Ant, Jan 18 1916 Sex:M Child# 2 Alexander Munton Northampton, England & Kathleen Crew England
MUNTON, Dorothy Pauline, Feb 15 1922 Sex:F Child# 3 Alexander Munton London, England & Kathleen Crewe England
MUNTON, Kathleen Mary Norah, May 17 1927 Sex:F Child# 4 Alex Munton London, England & Kathleen Crewe England
MURAUCKAS, Leonard, Nov 6 1910 Sex:M Child# 5 William Murauckas Russia & Kartancis Bukewic Russia
MURHE, Robert Townsend, Aug 13 1928 Sex:M Child# 1 Carroll R Murhe Readsboro, VT & D M Lavigne Burlington, VT
MURPHY, Arthur Leo, Jul 15 1893 Sex:M Child# 4 James H Murphy Boston, MA & Catherine McGrath Boston, MA
MURPHY, Bernard Almond, Jun 22 1915 Sex:M Child# 3 Morris H Murphy Ireland & Bridget O'Shea Ireland
MURPHY, Daniel Joseph, Jan 11 1915 Sex:M Child# 1 Michael Murphy Ireland & Bridget Bowen Ireland
MURPHY, David, Nov 7 1932 Sex:M Child# 2 Albert Murphy Louisville, KY & Lida Moulton S Nashua, NH
MURPHY, Dorothe Lillian, Nov 1 1933 Sex:F Child# 3 Albert Murphy Louisville, KY & Lilla Moulton Nashua, NH
MURPHY, Edith, Jun 1 1896 Sex:F Child# 1 John S Murphy Manchester & Edith M Greenwood Canada
MURPHY, Edward, Oct 22 1900 Sex:M Child# 6 Patrick J Murphy Ireland & Mary F Shea Nashua, NH
MURPHY, Edward James, Jul 7 1910 Sex:M Child# 2 Maurice J Murphy Ireland & Bridget M O'Shea Ireland
MURPHY, Eilene, Oct 25 1913 Sex:F Child# 1 John A Murphy Halifax, NS & Mary A Krieger Exeter, NH
MURPHY, Elizabeth Helene, Sep 27 1921 Sex:F Child# 2 Joseph F Murphy Lawrence, MA & Helen A Schreitirer Webster, MA
MURPHY, Estelle, Jul 26 1910 Sex:F Child# 1 Thomas Murphy Lawrence, MA & Molly Bradley Lawrence, MA
MURPHY, John Francis, Jun 12 1889 Sex:M Child# 1 Daniel B Murphy Goffstown, NH & Bridget O'Neil Concord, NH
MURPHY, John Joseph, Jr, Feb 9 1918 Sex:M Child# 4 John Thos Murphy Manchester, NH & Marguerite Tucker Rosend
MURPHY, Joseph, Feb 28 1904 Sex:M Child# 11 James H Murphy Portland, ME & Margaret Carsin Ireland
MURPHY, Josephine Allen, Jan 17 1920 Sex:F Child# 1 Joseph F Murphy Lawrence, MA & Helen A Schreiterir Webster, MA

MURPHY, Katharine, Nov 25 1890 Sex:F Child# 2 Patrick J Murphy Ireland & Mary F Shea Nashua, NH
MURPHY, Katherine, Dec 26 1920 Sex:F Child# 1 Maurice F Murphy Ireland & Josephine Kennedy Ireland
MURPHY, Kathleen, Apr 10 1935 Sex:F Child# 4 Albert Murphy Nashua, NH & Lilla Moulton Nashua, NH
MURPHY, Louis, Dec 15 1894 Sex:M Child# 4 Patrick J Murphy Ireland & Mary F Shea Nashua, NH
MURPHY, Louise Catherine, Oct 29 1927 Sex:F Child# 3 Joseph Murphy Lawrence, MA & Helen Schreiterer Webster, MA
MURPHY, Margaret, Apr 3 1916 Sex:F Child# 2 Michael Murphy Ireland & Bridget Bowen Ireland
MURPHY, Marjorie Alice, Aug 14 1920 Sex:F Child# 2 Edward J Murphy Canada & Alice Van Slett
MURPHY, Mary, Jun 17 1897 Sex:F Child# 5 Patrick J Murphy Ireland & Mary Shea Nashua, NH
MURPHY, Maurice Joseph, Dec 22 1908 Sex:M Child# 1 Maurice J Murphy Ireland & Bridget M O'Shea Ireland
MURPHY, Patricia Eleaine, Feb 20 1928 Sex:F Child# 1 Joseph Murphy Nashua, NH & Mildred Perreault Nashua, NH
MURPHY, Pauline, Dec 6 1891 Sex:F Child# 3 Patrick J Murphy Ireland & Mary F Shea Nashua, NH
MURPHY, Rita, Apr 9 1915 Sex:F Child# 2 John Murphy Halifax, NS & Mary Krieger Exeter, NH
MURPHY, Robert Joseph, Oct 18 1927 Sex:M Child# 3 Joseph Murphy Richmond, VA & Rose Arpin Manchester, NH
MURPHY, Unknown, May 6 1893 Sex:M Child# 1 Harry O Murphy Manchester, England & Maggie Clark Ireland
MURPHY, Unknown, May 8 1902 Sex:M Child# 10 James H Murphy Portland, ME & M Casseter Ireland
MURPHY, Unknown, Feb 28 1907 Sex:F Child# 1 Calvin Murphy Nova Scotia & May Stella Jewett New Brunswick
MURPHY, Veronica, Jun 10 1917 Sex:F Child# 3 John A Murphy Halifax, NS & Mary Krieger Exeter, NH
MURPHY, Walter H, Aug 27 1890 Sex:M Child# 3 Thomas H Murphy Ireland & Maggie E Early Ireland
MURPHY, Walter James, Nov 8 1929 Sex:M Child# 6 Moses Murphy Canada & Mary Carroll Barre, VT
MURRAY, Anna Margaret, Jul 1 1926 Sex:F Child# 2 William Murray Nashua, NH & Antoinette Laporte Nashua, NH
MURRAY, Blanchard M, Sep 21 1907 Sex:M Child# 1 Eben H Murray Plainfield, NS & Anna R Holdale Dawson, Minn
MURRAY, Delia Elizabeth, Dec 11 1930 Sex:F Child# 5 William Murray Nashua, NH & Antoinette Laporte Nashua, NH
MURRAY, Francis Patrick, Oct 29 1935 Sex:M Child# 9 William Murray Nashua, NH & Antoinette Laporte Nashua, NH
MURRAY, Gene Frances, May 14 1935 Sex:F Child# 2 Rob D Murray Fairfield, ME & Louise Campbell Beverly, MA
MURRAY, George Eldridge, Jan 20 1917 Sex:M Child# 2 Eld Stanley Murray Mass & Clara May Graham Mass
MURRAY, John, Oct 19 1890 Sex:M Child# 1 John Murray Vermont & Louisa Desmarais Vermont
MURRAY, Laura Jane, Mar 5 1932 Sex:F Child# 6 Wm H Murray Nashua, NH & A Laporte Nashua, NH
MURRAY, Matilda Jane, Jul 19 1898 Sex:F Child# 4 Matthew Murray Ireland & Sarah McPartland Ireland
MURRAY, Michael Joseph, May 30 1925 Sex:M Child# 3 William Murray Nashua, NH & Antoinette Laporte Nashua, NH
MURRAY, Phyllis, Dec 23 1922 Sex:F Child# 2 John Murray England & Mae Stevenson England
MURRAY, Raymond Elwin, Mar 24 1919 Sex:M Child# 3 E Stanley Murray Northboro, MA & Clara M Graham Walpole, MA
MURRAY, Theresa Mary, Mar 24 1934 Sex:F Child# 8 William Henry Murray Nashua, NH & Antoinette LaPorte Nashua, NH
MURRAY, Unknown, Feb 2 1887 Sex:M Child# 1 Thomas Murray Canada & Ella A Holmes West Concord
MURRAY, Unknown, Sep 24 1924 Sex:F Child# 4 John Sims Murray Washington, DC & Natalie Fippard Baltimore, MD
MURRAY, William Henry, Jul 3 1896 Sex:M Child# 2 Michael Murray England & Margaret Lane Ireland
MURRAY, William Henry, Jun 12 1933 Sex:M Child# 7 William H Murray Nashua, NH & Antoinette LaPorte Nashua, NH
MURTAUGH, James, Jan 25 1893 Sex:M Child# 6 James Murtaugh Ireland & Elizabeth O'Hear Ireland
MURTOUGH, Bridget, Aug 19 1888 Sex:F Child# 5 James Murtough Ireland & Elizabeth Oheiar Ireland
MUSEL, Bronislafs, Dec 29 1906 Sex:M Child# 4 Michael Musel Russia & Teofila Zenba Austria
MUSKAVITCH, Unknown, Nov 28 1911 Sex:M Child# 1  Russia & Annie Muskavitch Russia
MUSKAVITCH, Venedza, May 18 1910 Sex:F Child# 2 Heroim Muskavitch Russia & Paulina Urgilavitch Russia
MUSSER, Anna Mary, Jul 12 1923 Sex:F Child# 3 Karl B Musser Abilene, KS & Madge Rowley Kansas
MUZZEY, Marion Louise, Sep 19 1934 Sex:F Child# 2 Harland A Muzzey W Somerville, MA & Betay Leigh Howes Lebanon
MYCKO, Donald, Nov 30 1935 Sex:M Child# 2 Joseph Mycko Poland & Florence J King Berlin, NH
MYCKO, Dorothy, Feb 17 1933 Sex:F Child# 1 William Mycko Poland & Victoria Witkos Lowell, MA
MYCKO, Richard Joseph, May 5 1932 Sex:M Child# 1 Joseph Mycko Poland & Florence King Berlin, NH
MYCUE, Clara Grace, Jan 16 1927 Sex:F Child# 5 Earl M Mycue Ware, MA & Edith Trudeau Middlebury, VT
MYCUE, Earl Edward, Apr 15 1922 Sex:M Child# 2 Earl Mycue NH & Edith Trudeau Vermont
MYCUE, Frances Lillian, Sep 27 1920 Sex:F Child# 2 Earl Mycue Danbury, NH & Edith Trudeau Middlebury, VT
MYCUE, Roland Carl, Dec 29 1925 Sex:M Child# 5 Earl Mycue Danbury, NH & Edith Trudeau Middlebury, VT
MYCUE, Unknown, May 20 1919 Sex:F Child# 1 Earl Mycue Danbury, NH & Edith Trudeau Middlebury, VT
MYCUE, Unknown, Nov 5 1924 Sex:F Child# 4 Earl Mycue Danbury, NH & Edith Trudeau Vermont Stillborn
MYCUE, Viola Pauline, Sep 23 1923 Sex:F Child# 4 Earl Mycue Danbury, NH & Edith Trudeau Middlebury, VT
MYER, Charles Ed, Jul 8 1902 Sex:M Child# 2 Charles K Myer Sweden & Sadie Anderson Sweden
MYER, Konrad Arthur, Jun 29 1900 Sex:M Child# 1 Charles K Myer Sweden & Sadie Anderson Sweden
MYERS, Berton Elliott, Feb 5 1929 Sex:M Child# 2 Arthur Myers Nashua, NH & Mary Ouillette Canada
MYERS, Donald Irving, Oct 21 1934 Sex:M Child# 2 Ernest Charles Myers Saugerties, NY & Martha Kelley Nashua, NH
MYERS, James Ernest, Sep 28 1929 Sex:M Child# 1 Ernest Charles Myers Saugherties, NY & Martha Kelley Nashua, NH
MYERS, William, Dec 24 1908 Sex:M Child# 4 Max Myers Germany & Christine Luntz Germany
MYRAND, Alba, Aug 20 1905 Sex:F Child# 1 Philippe Myrand Canada & Alide Maranda Canada
MYSEN, Joseph, May 24 1913 Sex:M Child# 1 Isidore Mysen Russia & Eva Zenovski Russia
N, Jean Baptist E, Jul 18 1896 Sex:M Child# 1 Jean B N Canada & Marie Landry Canada
N, Marie Rose Obelina, Feb 16 1912 Sex:F Child# 5 Pierre N Canada & Marie Pelletier Canada
NACESKI, John, May 16 1930 Sex:M Child# 1 John Naceski Lithuania & Anna Marchenonis E Vandergrift, PA
NADEAU, Addie C, Dec 22 1895 Sex:F Child# 4 Louis Nadeau Moores Jct, NY & Velina Masse Moores Jct, NY
NADEAU, Adelard, Aug 15 1900 Sex:M Child# 8 Vital Nadeau Canada & Marie L Delaude Canada
NADEAU, Adele, Jul 6 1906 Sex:F Child# 4 Paul Nadeau Canada & Marie L Bonneville Canada
NADEAU, Albert, Jul 2 1903 Sex:M Child# 2 Paul Nadeau Canada & Mary L Bonneville Canada
NADEAU, Albert, Dec 11 1931 Sex:M Child# 4 Toussant Nadeau Canada & Adele Ouellette Canada
NADEAU, Albert Arthur, Jun 1 1925 Sex:M Child# 5 Amable Nadeau Canada & Laura Renaud Nashua, NH
NADEAU, Amelia, Aug 21 1888 Sex:F Child# 1 Louis Nadeau Moors, NY & Delvina Massi Moors Jct, NY
NADEAU, Arthur J, Jan 2 1900 Sex:M Child# 6 John Nadeau Canada & Clara Marquis Canada
NADEAU, Berthe Alphonsine, Jul 29 1899 Sex:F Child# 5 Charles Nadeau Canada & Amanda Gagnon Canada

NADEAU, Camil Marcel, Feb 16 1928 Sex:M Child# 6 Edmund Nadeau Maine & Bertha Fortier Canada
NADEAU, Carl Wilfred, Feb 26 1933 Sex:M Child# 1 Wilfred Nadeau Somersworth, NH & Edna Felton Nashua, NH
NADEAU, Cecile Isabelle, Apr 6 1923 Sex:F Child# 4 Aimable Nadeau Canada & Louise Renaud Nashua, NH
NADEAU, Charles Patrice, Nov 18 1893 Sex:M Child# 2 Charles Nadeau Canada & Amanda Gagnon Canada
NADEAU, Claire Lucille, Apr 3 1935 Sex:F Child# 1 Lewis G Nadeau Canada & Jeanette Shauvin Mass
NADEAU, Clara, Aug 11 1892 Sex:F Child# 1 Jean Nadeau Canada & Clara Marquis Canada
NADEAU, Clara, Sep 18 1893 Sex:F Child# 2 Vital Nadeau Canada & Meralie Deslandes Canada
NADEAU, Delia Julie, Apr 6 1894 Sex:F Child# 3 Joseph Nadeau NY & Marie Diny Michigan
NADEAU, Dima Levi, Feb 12 1892 Sex:M Child# 3 Louis Nadeau Canada & Delvina Masse Moore's Jct, NY
NADEAU, Donalda Florance, Oct 1 1917 Sex:F Child# 12 Paul Nadeau Canada & Georgiana Benoit Canada
NADEAU, Edmond Alphie, Oct 25 1926 Sex:M Child# 4 E E Nadeau Fort Kent, ME & Bertha Fortin Canada
NADEAU, Edouard Joseph, Oct 25 1926 Sex:M Child# 5 E E Nadeau Fort Kent, ME & Bertha Fortin Canada
NADEAU, Edouard Ray Joseph, Jul 7 1935 Sex:M Child# 3 Anatole Nadeau Canada & Gracia Lecompte Canada
NADEAU, Eugene John, Oct 2 1911 Sex:M Child# 2 George Nadeau Canada & Malvina Labbe Canada
NADEAU, Eugene Sifroi, Feb 3 1906 Sex:M Child# 8 Jean Nadeau Canada & Clara Marquis Canada
NADEAU, Exilia, Sep 4 1896 Sex:F Child# 4 Jean Nadeau Canada & Clara Marquis Canada
NADEAU, George, Jul 5 1890 Sex:M Child# 2 Thomas Nadeau Canada & Georgina Berube Canada
NADEAU, Georges, Jan 26 1896 Sex:M Child# 6 Vital Nadeau Canada & Merelise Delande Canada
NADEAU, Georgette Laurenne, Oct 23 1925 Sex:F Child# 3 Edmond C Nadeau Fort Kent, ME & Bertha Fortin Canada
NADEAU, Harve Irenee, Aug 23 1928 Sex:M Child# 14 Telesphore Nadeau Canada & Amanda Nadeau Canada
NADEAU, Ida, Aug 23 1918 Sex:F Child# 2 Amable Nadeau Canada & Louise Renaud Nashua, NH
NADEAU, Irene Naomi, Sep 13 1922 Sex:F Child# 2 Octave Nadeau Nashua, NH & Aimee Hoyt Canada
NADEAU, Irene Teresa, Apr 8 1921 Sex:F Child# 3 Amable Nadeau Canada & Louise Renaud Nashua, NH
NADEAU, J Louis Edmond, Apr 11 1915 Sex:M Child# 1 Theophile Nadeau Canada & Rose A Loranger Canada
NADEAU, Jean Baptiste Arthur, Feb 2 1913 Sex:M Child# 8 Paul Nadeau Canada & Marie L Borneville Canada
NADEAU, Jeannette, Dec 16 1915 Sex:F Child# 9 Paul Nadeau Canada & M Louise Banville Canada
NADEAU, Jos Gerard Edmond, Sep 16 1929 Sex:M Child# 2 Alcide Nadeau Maine & Beatrice Pelletier Mass
NADEAU, Jos Raymond Aime, Apr 25 1929 Sex:M Child# 6 Amable Nadeau Canada & Louise Renaud Nashua, NH
NADEAU, Joseph, Jun 14 1918 Sex:M Child# 10 Paul Nadeau St Azore, PQ & Marie L Bonneville Cornwall, Ont
NADEAU, Joseph A Aime, Jul 31 1897 Sex:M Child# 4 Charles Nadeau Canada & Amanda Gagnon Canada
NADEAU, Joseph Albert, Oct 1 1892 Sex:M Child# 3 Thomas Nadeau Canada & Georgianna Berube Canada
NADEAU, Joseph Armand, Jan 22 1920 Sex:M Child# 11 Paul Nadeau Canada & Marie L Bonneville Canada
NADEAU, Joseph Armand, May 31 1931 Sex:M Child# 1 Armand Nadeau Canada & Leona St Jean Canada
NADEAU, Joseph Auguste E, Dec 18 1908 Sex:M Child# 3 Leon Nadeau Canada & Eugenie Belanger Canada
NADEAU, Joseph C Roger, Jul 22 1926 Sex:M Child# 12 Telesphore Nadeau Canada & Amanda Nadeau Canada
NADEAU, Joseph Charles, Sep 5 1895 Sex:M Child# 4 Louis Nadeau Biddeford, ME & Olivine Dargie Canada
NADEAU, Joseph Edmond, Feb 28 1904 Sex:M Child# 9 Joseph Nadeau Canada & Exelia Bourassa Canada
NADEAU, Joseph Henri, Jun 2 1892 Sex:M Child# 2 Vital Nadeau Canada & Merelise Deslanges Canada
NADEAU, Joseph Hubert, Apr 17 1904 Sex:M Child# 1 Leon Nadeau Canada & Eugenie Belanger Canada
NADEAU, Joseph I D W, Mar 24 1894 Sex:M Child# 2 Damase Nadeau Canada & Rosanna Therowe Canada
NADEAU, Joseph J Bt, Feb 15 1898 Sex:M Child# 4 Thomas Nadeau Canada & Georgina Berube Canada
NADEAU, Joseph Leo, Aug 7 1906 Sex:M Child# 4 Auguste Nadeau Canada & Eugenie St Pierre Canada
NADEAU, Joseph Robert, Feb 28 1913 Sex:M Child# 6 Auguste Nadeau Canada & Marie St Pierre Canada
NADEAU, Joseph Roland, Mar 15 1912 Sex:M Child# 1 Aimable Nadeau Canada & Corinne Hysette Nashua, NH
NADEAU, Joseph Roland, Aug 30 1920 Sex:M Child# 1 Toussant Nadeau Canada & Adelia Ouellette Canada
NADEAU, Joseph T A, Aug 8 1887 Sex:M Child# 1 Thomas Nadeau P Q & Georgiana P Q
NADEAU, Joseph Theodore, Apr 1 1916 Sex:M Child# 2 Louis Nadeau Canada & Anna Lith Canada
NADEAU, Joseph W, Feb 10 1896 Sex:M Child# 3 Charles Nadeau Canada & Amanda Gagnon Canada
NADEAU, Joseph Wilfred, Dec 8 1924 Sex:M Child# 5 Theophile Nadeau Canada & Rose A Loranger US
NADEAU, Joseph Wilfrid, Nov 8 1919 Sex:M Child# 13 Paul Nadeau Canada & Georgiana Benoit Canada
NADEAU, Josephine, Oct 25 1904 Sex:F Child# 5 Jean Nadeau Canada & Rosanna Labbe Canada Stillborn
NADEAU, Josephine, Aug 7 1927 Sex:F Child# 13 B Amable Nadeau Canada & Amanda Nadeau Canada Stillborn
NADEAU, June Eva Alice, Jun 21 1934 Sex:F Child# 2 Armand Nadeau Nashua, NH & Leona St Jean Canada
NADEAU, Lea, Sep 30 1893 Sex:F Child# 2 Jean B Nadeau Canada & Clara Marquis Canada
NADEAU, Leo Paul, Feb 28 1932 Sex:M Child# 2 Anatole Nadeau Canada & Gracia Lecompte Canada
NADEAU, Louis, Feb 2 1893 Sex:M Child# 16 Damase Nadeau Canada & Philomene Canada
NADEAU, Louis N G, Mar 27 1897 Sex:M Child# 5 Louis Nadeau Biddeford & Alivine Dargie Canada
NADEAU, Louis Noel, Dec 28 1923 Sex:M Child# 13 Paul Nadeau Canada & Marie L Bonville Canada
NADEAU, Lucien Edwin, Jun 9 1925 Sex:M Child# 1 Alphe Nadeau Canada & Leona Bois Canada
NADEAU, Lucien U, Sep 5 1922 Sex:M Child# 5 Theophile Nadeau Canada & Rosalina Loranger Canada
NADEAU, Lucienne Annette, Oct 29 1933 Sex:F Child# 7 Theo Nadeau St Roberts, PQ & R A Laranger Biddeford, ME
NADEAU, Lucienne Lillian, Jun 3 1924 Sex:F Child# 5 Napoleon Nadeau Canada & Caroline Leblanc Canada
NADEAU, Lydia, Apr 24 1905 Sex:F Child# 3 Paul Nadeau Canada & Marie L Banoil Canada
NADEAU, M Amanda C, May 28 1892 Sex:F Child# 1 Charles Nadeau Canada & Amanda Gagnon Canada
NADEAU, M Helene Armande, Jan 26 1922 Sex:F Child# 14 Paul Nadeau Canada & Georgiana Benoit Canada
NADEAU, M Theresa Rosanna, May 29 1928 Sex:F Child# 1 Alside Nadeau Fort Kent, ME & Beatrice Pelletier Granite
NADEAU, Marianne Eva, Jul 21 1904 Sex:F Child# 3 Auguste Nadeau Canada & Marie St Pierre Canada
NADEAU, Marie, Jul 22 1896 Sex:F Child# 4 Moise Nadeau Canada & Marg'rte Larichliere Canada
NADEAU, Marie, Jun 12 1910 Sex:F Child# 6 Auguste Nadeau Canada & Eugenie St Pierre Canada
NADEAU, Marie, Jan 5 1915 Sex:F Child# 1 Louis Nadeau Canada & Anna Leath Canada
NADEAU, Marie, Jun 5 1923 Sex:F Child# 2 Paul Nadeau, Jr Canada & Lydia Lemieux Canada Stillborn
NADEAU, Marie A, Apr 13 1898 Sex:F Child# 5 Jean B Nadeau Canada & Clara Marquis Canada
NADEAU, Marie A D, Jan 6 1897 Sex:F Child# 1 Louis Nadeau Canada & Adelina Boutin Canada

NADEAU, Marie Anna, May 12 1908 Sex:F Child# 5 Auguste Nadeau Canada & Eugenie St Pierre Canada
NADEAU, Marie Anne, Nov 15 1894 Sex:F Child# 3 Vital Nadeau Canada & Marie L Delaude Canada
NADEAU, Marie B P, Apr 10 1892 Sex:F Child# 14 Damase Nadeau Canada & Philomene Canada
NADEAU, Marie D, Jun 22 1902 Sex:F Child# 1 Paul Nadeau Canada & M L Bauvil Canada
NADEAU, Marie Diana, Aug 24 1895 Sex:F Child# 3 Jean Nadeau Canada & Clara Marquis Canada
NADEAU, Marie E, Aug 11 1897 Sex:F Child# 2 Jean Baptiste Nadeau Canada & Marie Landry Canada
NADEAU, Marie Emelda, Feb 7 1917 Sex:F Child# 3 Louis Nadeau Canada & Anna Lith Canada
NADEAU, Marie Eugenie L, Oct 28 1901 Sex:F Child# 1 Auguste Nadeau Canada & Eugenie St Pierre Canada
NADEAU, Marie Helene E, Aug 28 1905 Sex:F Child# 2 Leon Nadeau Canada & Eugenie Belanger Canada
NADEAU, Marie I O, Apr 29 1901 Sex:F Child# 6 Charles Nadeau Canada & Amanda Gagnon Canada
NADEAU, Marie Irene Elmosa, Oct 17 1914 Sex:F Child# 13 Louis Nadeau Canada & Olive Lamothe Canada
NADEAU, Marie Josephine S, Mar 15 1930 Sex:F Child# 1 Anatole Nadeau Canada & Gracia Lecompte Canada
NADEAU, Marie Rolande, Sep 22 1924 Sex:F Child# 3 Paul Nadeau Canada & Lydia Lemieux Canada
NADEAU, Marie Therese Rita, May 5 1930 Sex:F Child# 15 Telesphore Nadeau New Brunswick & Amanda Nadeau NB
NADEAU, Mary Louise Lorraine, Jul 11 1935 Sex:F Child# 2 Albert Nadeau Nashua, NH & Emilda Demers Canada
NADEAU, Michel Arthur, Mar 10 1913 Sex:M Child# 3 George Nadeau Canada & Malvina Labbe Canada
NADEAU, Morris Jean, Feb 9 1924 Sex:M Child# 2 Edmond Nadeau Maine & Bertha Fortin Canada
NADEAU, Napoleon Wilfrid, Jan 5 1908 Sex:M Child# 6 Paul Nadeau Canada & Delima Bonneville Canada
NADEAU, Norman Alfred, Oct 26 1921 Sex:M Child# 1 Edmond Nadeau Fort Kent, ME & Bertha Fortin Granby, Canada
NADEAU, Octave, Jul 14 1893 Sex:M Child# 1 Octave Nadeau Canada & Georgiana Pinet Canada
NADEAU, Octave Albert, Feb 21 1900 Sex:M Child# 3 Louis Nadeau Canada & Adeline Boutin Canada
NADEAU, Paul Lawrence, Dec 30 1934 Sex:M Child# 2 Antonio W Nadeau Nashua, NH & Edna Louise Felton Nashua, NH
NADEAU, Paul Lucien, Oct 31 1921 Sex:M Child# 2 Toussaint Nadeau Canada & Adele Ouellette Canada
NADEAU, Philippe, Oct 30 1897 Sex:M Child# 7 Vital Nadeau Canada & Metalise Deslauges Canada
NADEAU, Philomene R, Mar 14 1894 Sex:F Child# 16 Damase Nadeau Canada & Philomene Nadeau Canada
NADEAU, Robert, Dec 11 1931 Sex:M Child# 3 Toussant Nadeau Canada & Adele Ouellette Canada
NADEAU, Ronald Charles, Oct 18 1928 Sex:M Child# 1 Clifford Nadeau Spencer, MA & Rose Cadieux Nashua, NH
NADEAU, Rosanna, Sep 27 1906 Sex:F Child# 6 Jean Nadeau Canada & Rosanna Labbe Canada
NADEAU, Rose Delima, Feb 2 1893 Sex:F Child# 15 Damase Nadeau Canada & Philomene Canada
NADEAU, Rose E, Oct 30 1916 Sex:F Child# 1 Amable Nadeau Canada & Louise Renaud Canada
NADEAU, Rosella, May 17 1902 Sex:F Child# 5 Jean Nadeau Canada & Clara Macken Canada
NADEAU, Rosie, Jun 11 1909 Sex:F Child# 6 Paul Nadeau Canada & Marie L Bauvil Canada
NADEAU, Thomas Joseph, Jan 21 1903 Sex:M Child# 2 Auguste Nadeau Canada & Julie St Pierre Canada
NADEAU, Unknown, Oct 10 1892 Sex:M Child# 5 Onesime Nadeau Canada & Philomene Canada
NADEAU, Unknown, Nov 10 1908 Sex:F Child# 1 Fred M Nadeau W Kennebunk, ME & May Belmont Wells Beach, ME
NADEAU, Unknown, Nov 11 1911 Sex:F Child# 2 Fred M Nadeau W Kennebunk, ME & Mary E Belmont Wells Beach, ME
NADEAU, Unknown, Feb 3 1913 Sex:M Child# 2 Aimable Nadeau Canada & Corinne Hysette Nashua, NH Stillborn
NADEAU, Unknown, Jun 23 1922 Sex:F Child# 12 Paul Nadeau Canada & Mary L Bonneville Canada Stillborn
NADEAU, Unknown, Mar 22 1928 Sex:M Child# 6 Theophile Nadeau Canada & Rose A Loranger US Stillborn
NADEAU, Yvon Lionel, May 2 1926 Sex:M Child# 2 Alphee Nadeau Maine & Leona Bois Canada
NADEN, Marjorie Roberta, Mar 8 1925 Sex:F Child# 1 Lester C Naden Waltham, MA & Georgina Caron Nashua, NH
NADOU, Maglva, Jul 21 1888 Sex:F Child# 2 James Nadou Centralville, MI & Mary Dean Sciota, NY
NADREAU, Beatrice Yvonne, Aug 2 1932 Sex:F Child# 2 Clifford Nadreau Mass & Rose Cadieux Nashua, NH
NADREAU, Harvey Leon, Mar 6 1930 Sex:M Child# 4 Armand Nadreau Mass & Vida Letendre Mass
NADZAIKA, John, May 27 1914 Sex:M Child# 1 Casimir J Nadzaika Russia & Annie Martinazute Russia
NADZEIKA, Edward, Dec 14 1934 Sex:M Child# 2 Stanley Madzeika Poland & Helen Sinekeo N Walpole, NH
NAGGLE, Delia, May 13 1890 Sex:F Child# 4 Ganet Naggle England & Maggie Culcair Ireland
NAGLE, George Edward, Aug 6 1891 Sex:M Child# 3 George Nagle Ireland & Bridget Ryan Ireland
NAGLE, Grace Helena, Sep 7 1893 Sex:F Child# 5 George Nagle Ireland & Bridget Ryan Ireland
NAGLE, Ida Selina, Jun 9 1897 Sex:F Child# 4 Garrett Nagle England & Margaret Coulkeen Ireland
NAGLE, Rose Isabelle, Jul 30 1897 Sex:F Child# 6 George Nagle Ireland & Bridget Ryan Ireland
NAGLE, Unknown, 1889 Sex:M Child# 4 Garrett Nagle Ireland & Maggie Culkey Ireland
NAGLE, William James, Nov 16 1895 Sex:M Child# 5 George Nagle Ireland & Bridget Ryan Ireland
NAGLIE, Helen, Oct 11 1922 Sex:F Child# 1 Harold Naglie Peterboro, NH & Helen Barry N Walpole, NH
NAGOIS, Unknown, Jul 12 1928 Sex:F Child# 1 Soterios Nagois Greece & Zaetsa Marinou Greece
NAHUN, Stanley, Mar 26 1917 Sex:M Child# 5 Anthony Nahun Russia & Elizabeth Sabolouski Russia
NAIDZIONAK, Wtadislow, Jun 27 1904 Sex:F Child# 2 Alex Naidzionak Russia & Michalina Monczuska Russia
NAJAKA, Julia, Sep 16 1921 Sex:F Child# 1 Stanislaus Najaka Poland & Helen Sweklo Bellows Falls, VT
NAJALIAN, Unknown, Nov 28 1903 Sex:M Child# 6 Elijah R Najalian Turkey & Rose Bohasian Turkey
NAJARIAN, Lizzie, Apr 28 1905 Sex:F Child# 7 Martin Najarian Asia & T Donaledian Asia
NAJARIAN, Margaret, Jun 22 1916 Sex:F Child# 2 Daniel Najarian
NAJARIAN, Varant Hagop, Nov 25 1922 Sex:M Child# 1 Jacob Najarian Armenia & Anteram Shamlyian Armenia
NAJDZIONAK, John, Jul 17 1908 Sex:M Child# 3 Alexander Najdzionak Russia & Mikalina Manchunski Russia
NAJZIONSK, Stanistaw, Dec 11 1902 Sex:M Child# 2 Alex Najzionsk Russia & M Naydzon Russia
NALETTE, Thomas, Nov 16 1924 Sex:M Child# 2 Amos B Nalette E Pepperell, MA & Catherine Sullivan E Pepperell, MA
NALIBON, Dorothy D, Jan 12 1917 Sex:F Child# 4 Samuel Nalibon Russia & Tillie Lavene Russia
NANNIS, Ida, May 30 1907 Sex:F Child# 1 Myer Nannis Russia & Lillian Rosenbloom Russia
NANNIS, Pearl, Jan 19 1917 Sex:F Child# 3 Myer Nannis Russia & Lillian Rosenbloom Russia
NANTELLE, Richard Edward, May 7 1922 Sex:M Child# 1 Charles Nantelle Mass & Lillian Davidson Concord, NH
NARANJIAN, Goolegart Rose, Jan 11 1924 Sex:F Child# 1 David Naranjian Turkey & Mary Kazarosian Turkey
NARCKICWISZ, Antonia, Sep 2 1898 Sex:F Child# 4 John Narckicwisz Wilno, Russia & Anna Musia Austria
NARDAIDKA, Jadwiga, Oct 9 1912 Sex:F Child# 1 William Nardaidka Russia & Mikalina Skalawich Russia
NARGAGIAN, Louisa, Dec 7 1912 Sex:F Child# 4 Garabed Nargagian Armenia & Nayle Stepanian Armenia

NARGOSSIAN, Vartan Jurayre, Sep 3 1907 Sex:M Child# 1 Garabed Nargossian Armenia & Zelia Estephen Armenia
NARINKAVITCH, John, Jan 23 1906 Sex:M Child# 4 John Narinkavitch Russia & Annie Mousha Austria
NARKIS, Donald Paul, Oct 5 1935 Sex:M Child# 2 Joseph Narkis Nashua, NH & Stef Kamenecki Poland
NARKIS, Robert Joseph, May 23 1934 Sex:M Child# 1 Joseph Narkis Nashua, NH & Stephanie Kamencki Poland
NARKPVITCH, Wanda, Oct 23 1914 Sex:F Child# 1 Zenon Narkpvitch Russia & Stephania Swabowich Russia
NARKUN, Andrew, Oct 24 1922 Sex:M Child# 7 Ant Narkun Russia & Lucy Sebalouska Russia
NARKUN, Anna, Dec 21 1913 Sex:F Child# 4 Anthony Narkun Russia & Lizzie Sabaliuskute Russia
NARKUN, Julionas, Sep 6 1919 Sex:M Child# 6 Anthony Narkun Russia & Levernora Subaloski Russia
NARKUN, Unknown, Aug 31 1911 Sex:M Child# 2 Anthony Narkun Russia & S Sabaliukutie Russia
NARKUNAS, Joseph, Sep 1 1912 Sex:M Child# 3 Anthony Narkunas Russia & Louisa Sabolanzkiuti Russia
NARKUNAS, Vytantos, Jan 25 1932 Sex:M Child# 8 Anthony Narkunas Lithuania & L Saboleraska Lithuania
NARO, Abraham Norman, Oct 17 1921 Sex:M Child# 5 Abraham Naro Sciota, NY & Alice Stone Nashua, NH
NARO, Alice May, May 21 1918 Sex:F Child# 3 Abraham Naro Sciota, NY & Alice L Stone Nashua, NH
NARO, Harold Herbert, Mar 3 1925 Sex:M Child# 7 Abraham Naro Sciota, NY & Alice L Stone Nashua, NH
NARO, Jos Leo Raymond, Jan 4 1928 Sex:M Child# 5 Henry Naro Sciota, NY & Angeline Gendron Canada
NARO, Joseph Adelard, Jun 2 1924 Sex:M Child# 1 Levi Naro Altona, NY & Clara Picard Nashua, NH
NARO, Joseph Albert, Apr 27 1924 Sex:M Child# 3 Henry Naro Scotia, NY & Angelina Gendron St Francis, Canada
NARO, Joseph Ernest Wilfri, May 13 1923 Sex:M Child# 6 Abraham Naro Sciota, NY & Alice Stone Nashua, NH
NARO, Joseph Gerard Roland, Feb 25 1923 Sex:M Child# 2 Henry Naro New York & Angeline Gendron Canada
NARO, Joseph Henry Robert, Jul 27 1932 Sex:M Child# 7 Henry Naro New York & A Gendron Canada
NARO, Joseph Levi Henry, Sep 26 1935 Sex:M Child# 8 Henry Naro Sciota, NY & Angelina Gendron Canada
NARO, Joseph Roger Maurice, Nov 13 1925 Sex:M Child# 4 Henry Naro Sciota, NY & Angeline Gendron Canada
NARO, Levi George, Apr 21 1916 Sex:M Child# 2 Abraham Naro New York & Alice Stone Nashua, NH
NARO, Marie Anita Y, Aug 31 1930 Sex:F Child# 6 Henry Naro Sciota, NY & Angeline Gendron Canada
NARO, Mary Alice Albina, Nov 28 1921 Sex:F Child# 1 Henry Naro Canada & Angene Gendron Canada
NAROIZ, Levi Henry, Jun 30 1920 Sex:M Child# 4 Abraham Naroiz Sciota, NY & Alice Stone Nashua, NH
NARRIS, Simon, Mar 31 1898 Sex:M Child# 7 Simon C Narris Russia & Fannie Annie Cohen Russia
NARTOF, Charley, Apr 22 1897 Sex:M Child# 1 Moyk Nartof Russia & A Huravizouvna Russia
NARTOFF, Frank, Sep 6 1911 Sex:M Child# 8 Mike Nartoff Russia & Alexandra Urage Russia
NARTOFF, Juanita Elizabeth, Oct 16 1931 Sex:F Child# 2 Robert Nartoff Nashua, NH & Rose Chesnulevich Nashua, NH
NARTOFF, Robert Joseph, Jr, Mar 17 1930 Sex:M Child# 1 Robert J Nartoff Nashua, NH & Rose Chesnelevich Nashua, NH
NARTOFF, Sophia, May 12 1902 Sex:F Child# 5 Maciey Nartoff Russia & Al'x'da Zuv'yer'wrin Russia
NARTOL, Wekton, Jul 17 1898 Sex:M Child# 2 Frank Nartol Europe & Alexandra Rer'towna Europe
NASELOBSKY, Sophia, May 28 1914 Sex:F Child# 2 William Naselobsky Russia & Annie Bawolevish Russia
NASH, Allen Russell, Jul 15 1932 Sex:M Child# 1 John Russell Nash Nashua, NH & Lucille Burque Nashua, NH
NASH, David, Nov 15 1897 Sex:M Child# 4 David J Nash Ireland & Nellie M Greene Ireland
NASH, Delia, Jan 17 1891 Sex:F Child# 2 James Nash Ireland & Hannorah M Sullivan Ireland
NASH, Dennis E, Jan 11 1894 Sex:M Child# 4 Dennis Nash Ireland & Maggie Conroy Ireland
NASH, Dorothy Lucille, May 14 1927 Sex:F Child# 2 Myron Nash Cutler, ME & Eula Hogan Virginia
NASH, Everett Leo, Dec 14 1911 Sex:M Child# 1 Dennis Nash US & Eda Burnham US
NASH, Frances, Jun 1 1897 Sex:F Child# 6 Dennis Nash Ireland & Margaret Conroy Ireland
NASH, George, Dec 1 1901 Sex:M Child# 6 David Nash Ireland & Nellie Green Ireland
NASH, Gerald Quentin, Oct 6 1923 Sex:M Child# 5 Ralph W E Nash Berwick, ME & Lillian R Class Millers Falls, MA
NASH, Irene, Jul 15 1922 Sex:F Child# 4 Dennis J Nash Nashua, NH & Bertha F Chase Nashua, NH
NASH, Jason Philip, Sep 28 1920 Sex:M Child# 4 Ralph W E Nash Berwick, ME & Lillian R Class Millers Falls, MA
NASH, John, Dec 4 1889 Sex:M Child# 1 James Nash Ireland & Nora Sullivan Ireland
NASH, John, Apr 2 1899 Sex:M Child# 5 David Nash Ireland & Nellie M Greene Ireland
NASH, John Patrick, Dec 17 1889 Sex:M Child# 1 Dennis Nash Ireland & Maggie Conroy Ireland
NASH, John Russell, Aug 24 1910 Sex:M Child# 1 Jeremiah Nash Ireland & Anna Sullivan Ireland
NASH, Lawrence Monroe, Sep 2 1917 Sex:M Child# 2 Ralph W E Nash Berwick, ME & Lillian R Class Montague, MA
NASH, Leo, Jun 2 1904 Sex:M Child# 10 Dennis H Nash Ireland & Margaret Conroy Ireland
NASH, Lillian, Apr 18 1906 Sex:F Child# 11 Dennis H Nash Ireland & Margaret Conroy Ireland
NASH, Madeline Irene, Jan 30 1914 Sex:F Child# 2 Dennis Nash Nashua, NH & Bertha Chase Nashua, NH
NASH, Margaret, Nov 11 1891 Sex:F Child# 7 John Nash Ireland & Nellie Sullivan Ireland
NASH, Margaret, Jun 16 1892 Sex:F Child# 3 Dennis H Nash Ireland & Margaret Courcy Ireland
NASH, Margaret, Jan 30 1896 Sex:F Child# 3 David Nash Ireland & Nellie Greene Ireland
NASH, Marie Georgianna, Dec 21 1918 Sex:F Child# 3 Ralph W E Nash Berwick, ME & Lillian R Class Millers Falls, MA
NASH, Mary, Mar 15 1891 Sex:F Child# 2 Dennis Nash Ireland & Maggie Coursy Ireland
NASH, Mary Ellen, Jul 6 1892 Sex:F Child# 1 David Nash Ireland & Nellie M Greene Ireland
NASH, Mary Pearl, Mar 31 1915 Sex:F Child# 3 Dennis Nash Nashua, NH & Bertha Chase Nashua, NH
NASH, Muriel Bertha, May 22 1912 Sex:F Child# 1 Dennis J Nash Nashua, NH & Bertha F Chase Nashua, NH
NASH, Olive Gertrude, Apr 16 1908 Sex:F Child# 2 John Nash Nashua, NH & Mabel Kehoe Lowell, MA
NASH, Peter, Feb 2 1899 Sex:M Child# 7 Dennis H Nash Ireland & Margaret Conroy Ireland
NASH, Ralph Class, Mar 17 1916 Sex:M Child# 1 Ralph W E Nash Berwick, ME & Lillian R Class Millers Falls, MA
NASH, Roger Benjamin, Mar 13 1926 Sex:M Child# 6 Ralph W E Nash Berwick, ME & Lillian R Class Millers Falls, MA
NASH, Unknown, Jul 24 1888 Sex:F Child# 1 Dennis A Nash Ireland & Mary Ireland
NASH, Unknown, Feb 23 1892 Sex:M Child# 1 L F Nash Addison, ME & L M Maker Cutler, ME
NASH, Unknown, Jun 25 1902 Sex:M Child# 9 Dennis Nash Ireland & Maggie Conroy Ireland
NASH, Unknown, Jan 23 1907 Sex:F Child# 1 John F Nash Nashua, NH & Mabel Prentis Albany, NY
NASH, Unknown, Apr 19 1919 Sex:M Child# 2 Dennis Nash Nashua, NH & Edith Burnham Nashua, NH
NASH, Walter, Sep 2 1900 Sex:M Child# 8 Dennis H Nash Ireland & Margaret Conroy Ireland
NASON, Freda Phyllis, Nov 7 1934 Sex:F Child# 3 (No Parents Listed)
NASON, Leroy E, Aug 29 1902 Sex:M Child# 2 Clinton L Nason Dover, NH & Sarah R Fogg Enfield, NH

NASON, Pauline Julia, Feb 6 1919 Sex:F Child# 5 Perley Nason Vermont & Louise Spencer Vermont
NASON, Richard Clark, Dec 16 1931 Sex:M Child# 1 (No Parents Listed)
NASON, Unknown, Mar 24 1899 Sex:F Child# 1 Truman A Nason Tracy, NB & Mable R Butterfield Chester
NASON, Unknown, Sep 20 1900 Sex:F Child# 2 T A Nason Canada & Mabel Butterfield NH
NASON, Virginia Caroline, Nov 15 1907 Sex:F Child# 1 George H Nason Woburn, MA & Caroline Black Montreal, Canada
NASTON, Teofilio, Dec 20 1920 Sex:F Child# 5 Martin Naston Russia & Mary Chimavitch Russia
NATALE, Joseph G, Apr 28 1894 Sex:M Child# Joseph E Natale Boston, MA & Addie Fay Ireland
NATHAN, Wallace, Jr, Sep 23 1920 Sex:M Child# 3 Wallace Nathan Maine & Elizabeth Cummings Mass
NATROFF, Boliesloff, Dec 13 1903 Sex: Child# 5 Michael Natroff Russia & Alexanda Russia
NATSIKAS, Unknown, Jan 16 1917 Sex:F Child# 10 Evangelos Natsikas Greece & Ariti Yota Greece Stillborn
NAULT, Albert theodore, Feb 12 1906 Sex:M Child# 5 Frank Nault Canada & Clara Duvarney Canada
NAULT, Blanche Delia, Jul 28 1908 Sex:F Child# 2 Olivier Nault Vermont & Sophie Dupre Fall River, MA
NAULT, Cecile Clara, Jan 5 1920 Sex:F Child# 4 Olivier Nault Vermont & Sophie Dupre Fall River, MA
NAULT, Clara M A, Aug 14 1894 Sex:F Child# 1 Frank Nault Manchester & Clara Duverney Canada
NAULT, Ephrem L, Jun 8 1901 Sex:M Child# 1 Frank Nault Barton, VT & Eugenie Gauthier Canada
NAULT, Joseph Olivier Alber, Jul 19 1918 Sex:M Child# 3 Olivier Nault Vermont & Sophie Dufie Mass
NAUNCZYK, Antoni Stephan, Apr 30 1925 Sex:M Child# 1 Stephan Naunczyk Poland & Anna Kirpluk Poland
NAUSS, Nancy Elizabeth, Jun 11 1928 Sex:F Child# 2 Earl F Nauss New Cumberland & Minta E Skinner Huntington
NAVICKAS, Jonas Feliks, Aug 30 1921 Sex:M Child# 1 Vincus Navickas Lithuania & Malvina Vaskeliavicu Lithuania
NAWIK, Peter, May 1 1914 Sex:M Child# 2 James Nawik Russia & Annie Siluck Russia
NAY, Carl Ferson, Sep 7 1898 Sex:M Child# 5 William Franklin Nay Peterborough, NH & Adeline I Shedd Merrimack, NH
NEEDHAM, Marie A B Y, Mar 31 1905 Sex:F Child# 5 Francois Needham Springfield, MA & Josephine Soucy Canada
NEEDHAM, Unknown, Dec 27 1889 Sex:M Child# 3 Charles Needham Chicago, IL & Mary Currier Henniker, NH
NEFF, Alonzo E, May 6 1893 Sex:M Child# 1 Edward W Neff Nashua, NH & Mary Dennis New York
NEFF, Mary Bell, Oct 16 1894 Sex:F Child# 2 Edward W Neff NH & Mary Dennis Vermont
NEFF, Unknown, Aug 6 1888 Sex:M Child# 1 Manifred E Neff Nashua, NH & Ella Ladd Iowa City, IA
NEFF, William Frank, Dec 25 1896 Sex:M Child# 3 Edward Neff Nashua, NH & Mary Dennis New York
NEFT, Unknown, Aug 27 1900 Sex:M Child# 4 Edward Neft NH & Mary Dennis NY
NEIDZORICKI, Chester, Jan 12 1928 Sex:M Child# 5 John Neidzoricki Poland & Helen Saplock Poland
NELLIGNAN, William John, Sep 30 1925 Sex:M Child# 2 John Nellignan Bangor, ME & Gertrude Frenette Port Kent, ME
NELSON, Beryl Lucile, Aug 13 1912 Sex:F Child# 1 Oscar B Nelson Amherst, NH & Lillian M Frennette Nashua, NH
NELSON, Carl Williams, Jun 26 1935 Sex:M Child# 1 Carl Eric Nelson New York, NY & Elsa Oja Milford, NH
NELSON, Christine, Aug 24 1899 Sex:F Child# 1 William A Nelson Iowa & Mary E Cummings Nashua, NH
NELSON, Donald Cummings, Sep 6 1904 Sex:M Child# 2 William A Nelson Waterloo, Iowa & Mary E Cummings Nashua, NH
NELSON, Donna, Aug 2 1934 Sex:F Child# 1 Guy Herbert Nelson Amherst, NH & Marion Shepard Milford, NH
NELSON, Lucretia, Feb 19 1912 Sex:F Child# 2 Warren B Nelson Nashua, NH & Mabelle Griswold Nashua, NH
NELSON, Rober Myles, Mar 24 1934 Sex:M Child# 1 Myles R Nelson Vermont & Louise Holton Hudson, NH
NELSON, Ruth, Jul 29 1906 Sex:F Child# 3 William A Nelson Iowa & Mary E Cummings Nashua, NH
NELSON, Ruth J, Aug 22 1891 Sex:F Child# 6 Nels Nelson Sweden & Mary Nelson Sweden
NELSON, Samuel Cotton, Feb 27 1928 Sex:M Child# 2 Carl W Nelson Sweden & Eugenie Florentine Clinton, MA Stillborn
NELSON, Unknown, Jan 16 1888 Sex:F Child# 4 N Nelson Sweden & Mary Halequest Sweden
NELSON, Unknown, Jan 4 1890 Sex:F Child# 3 Nels Nelson Sweden & Mary Halquist Sweden
NELSON, Unknown, May 2 1920 Sex:F Child# 4 Walter B Nelson Basted, Sweden & Marie Olson Mora, Sweden
NELSON, Warren Campbell, Sep 25 1908 Sex:M Child# 1 Warren B Nelson Nashua, NH & Mabel L Griswold Nashua, NH
NELSON, William Raymond, Jul 24 1922 Sex:M Child# 2 Wm Farrar Nelson England & Nellie Jeffrey England
NELVILLE, Louis Gregg, Jr, Jul 20 1900 Sex:M Child# 2 Louis G Nelville NH & Pearl Richardson NH
NENOS, Lefkothea J, Jul 23 1925 Sex:F Child# 2 John Nenos Greece & Elizabeth Koliadesi Greece
NENOS, Unknown, Dec 21 1923 Sex:F Child# 1 John Nenos Greece & Elftheria Nicoliades Greece
NEPREU, Marie Emelina, Jan 1 1909 Sex:F Child# 4 Alfred Nepreu Canada & Angelina Bachaud Canada
NEPVEN, Mary Emaline L, Feb 24 1906 Sex:F Child# 2 Alfred Nepven Canada & Angeline Buchand Canada
NEPVEU, Norman Conrad, May 3 1933 Sex:M Child# 1 Armand Nepveu Nashua, NH & Velma M Berube Lebanon, NH
NERBONNE, Olita Alfreda, Sep 23 1921 Sex:F Child# 1 Alfred R Nerbonne Manchester, NH & Olita Vivian DuBray Pho
NEVEA, Blanche Claire, Feb 19 1905 Sex:F Child# 1 Charles E Nevea Canada & Blandine Kerouac Canada
NEVEN, George Rogers, Oct 19 1917 Sex:M Child# 7 Charles E Neven Canada & Blandine Kerouac Canada
NEVEN, Jos Sylvio Romeo, May 31 1927 Sex:M Child# 9 Evangeliste Neven Canada & E Rochette Canada
NEVEN, Mervin Ralph, May 5 1926 Sex:M Child# 2 Cleomene Neven Canada & Andrea Bonneau Nashua, NH
NEVEN, Ovide Lionel, Oct 4 1918 Sex:M Child# 3 Evangeliste Neven Canada & Ernestine Rochette Canada
NEVERETT, Joseph, Nov 22 1932 Sex:M Child# 2 Joseph Neverett New York & Victoria Gelinas Nashua, NH
NEVERETT, Mary, Dec 8 1933 Sex:F Child# 6 Joseph Neverett Sciota, NY & Victoria Gelinas Nashua, NH Stillborn
NEVERETT, Ronald Joseph, Dec 27 1931 Sex:M Child# 4 Joseph Neverett Sciota, NY & Victoria Gelinas Nashua, NH
NEVERETTE, Marie Melva Ida, Dec 20 1930 Sex:F Child# 2 Joseph Neverette Sciota, NY & Victoria Gelinas Nashua, NH
NEVERETTE, Unknown, May 20 1929 Sex:M Child# 1 Joseph Neverette Sciota, NY & Victorine Gelinas Nashua, NH
NEVERS, Unknown, Oct 12 1923 Sex:F Child# 5 Leon C Nevers Lancaster, NH & Rose A Chappell Lowell, MA
NEVEU, Armand, Jan 3 1907 Sex:M Child# 2 Charles E Neveu Canada & Blandine Kerouac Canada
NEVEU, Aurore Juliette, Jul 30 1908 Sex:F Child# 3 Charles E Neveu Canada & Pauline Kerouac Canada
NEVEU, Cecile Delia, Apr 21 1916 Sex:F Child# 1 Evangeliste Neveu Canada & Ernestine Rochette Canada
NEVEU, Cecile Hermine, Apr 17 1912 Sex:F Child# 4 Charles E Neveu Canada & Blandine Kerouac Canada
NEVEU, Charles Edouard, Apr 28 1901 Sex:M Child# 11 Onesime Neveu Canada & Elma Lampron Canada
NEVEU, Donat Romeo, Oct 17 1913 Sex:M Child# 8 Alfred Neveu Canada & Angelina Bachand Canada
NEVEU, Henri Armace, Jan 4 1908 Sex:M Child# 3 Alfred Neveu Canada & Angelina Bachand Canada
NEVEU, J Edward Sylvio, Sep 20 1915 Sex:M Child# 6 Charles E Neveu Canada & Blandine Kerouac Canada
NEVEU, Jacqueline Muriel, Aug 9 1925 Sex:F Child# 1 Oscar Neveu Canada & Carona Casavant Canada
NEVEU, Louis Theodore, Aug 21 1911 Sex:M Child# 6 Alfred Neveu Canada & Angelina Bachand Canada

NEVEU, Marie Estelle Doris, Jun 5 1929 Sex:F Child# 10 Evangeliste Neveu Canada & Ernestine Rochette Canada
NEVEU, Marie Laura O, Jun 7 1910 Sex:F Child# 6 Alfred Neveu Canada & Angelina Bachaud Canada
NEVEU, Marie Rita Irene, Apr 10 1920 Sex:F Child# 4 Evangeliste Neveu Canada & Ernestine Rochette Canada
NEVEU, Marie Veronique, Jan 2 1915 Sex:F Child# 10 Alfred Neveu Canada & Angelina Bacland Canada
NEVEU, Maurice Cleon, Feb 3 1929 Sex:M Child# 2 Oscar Neveu Canada & Corona Casavant Canada
NEVEU, Roger Roland, Feb 20 1924 Sex:M Child# 7 Evangeliste Neveu Canada & Ernestine Rochette Canada
NEVEU, Rose Leonie Marie, Jun 29 1913 Sex:F Child# 5 Charles Ed Neveu Canada & Blandine Kerouac Canada
NEVEU, Theresa Odelva, Nov 6 1925 Sex:F Child# 8 Evangeliste Neveu Canada & Ernestine Rochette Canada
NEVEUX, J Jeanne d'Arc, Apr 15 1921 Sex:F Child# 5 Evangeliste Neveux Canada & Ernestine Rochette Canada
NEVEUX, Joseph Ed Wilfrid, Jul 3 1922 Sex:M Child# 6 Evangeliste Neveux Canada & Ernestine Rochette Canada
NEVEUX, Yvonne Gertrude, Sep 3 1917 Sex:F Child# 2 Evangeliste Neveux Canada & Ernestine Rochette Canada
NEVILLE, Christine, Nov 13 1900 Sex:F Child# 5 Dennis Neville Ireland & Bridget Griffin Ireland
NEVILLE, Isabelle Norina, Aug 17 1903 Sex:F Child# 2 John Neville Ireland & Mary Sheedy Ireland
NEVILLE, James, Apr 11 1897 Sex:M Child# 4 Dennis Neville Ireland & Bridget Griffin Ireland
NEVILLE, James Robert, Dec 8 1931 Sex:M Child# 3 James Neville Nashua, NH & Catherine Driscoll E Pepperell, MA
NEVILLE, Mary Dorothy, Apr 14 1921 Sex:F Child# 8 Robert J Neville Canada & Augusta Hackett Mass
NEVILLE, Mary Madeleine, Oct 6 1904 Sex:F Child# 3 John Neville England & Mary Sheedy England
NEVILLE, Mary Phyllis, Mar 10 1930 Sex:F Child# 2 James Neville Nashua, NH & Catherine Driscoll Pepperell, MA
NEVILLE, Mary Rose, Oct 29 1890 Sex:F Child# 1 Dennis Neville Ireland & Bridget Griffin Ireland
NEVILLE, Natalie, Feb 1 1898 Sex:F Child# 1 Louis Gregg Neville Wilton, NH & Pearl Richardson Keene, NH
NEVILLE, Nellie Josephine, Oct 23 1892 Sex:F Child# 3 James Neville Ireland & Bridget Mulgreen Ireland
NEVILLE, Unknown, Jan 18 1896 Sex:M Child# 3 Dennis Neville Ireland & Bridget Griffin Ireland Stillborn
NEVILLE, Unknown, Dec 23 1926 Sex:M Child# 1 James Neville Nashua, NH & Katherine Driscoll Pepperell, MA Stillborn
NEVILLE, William Henry, May 17 1893 Sex:M Child# 2 Dennis Neville Ireland & Bridget Griffin Ireland
NEWELL, Anne, Dec 2 1934 Sex:F Child# 1 Benjamin C Newell Derry, NH & Barbara Benson Derry, NH
NEWMAN, Annie S, Mar 24 1914 Sex:F Child# 2 Israel Newman Russia & Sarah Weisberg Russia
NEWMAN, Bertha Priscilla, Mar 6 1921 Sex:F Child# 2 Alvah Newman Tremont, ME & Clara Eaton Hudson, NH
NEWMAN, Fannie, May 8 1916 Sex:F Child# 3 Israel Newman Russia & Sarah Tiezburg Russia
NEWMAN, Gloria Esther, Jan 19 1935 Sex:F Child# 1 Rob A Newman Waltham, MA & Bessie Shattuck Nashua, NH
NEWMAN, Gwendolyn Pearl, Apr 13 1910 Sex:F Child# 1 John D Newman Mansfield, MA & May E Nihan Attleboro, MA
NEWMAN, Joseph, Nov 21 1916 Sex:M Child# 4 Louis Newman Russia & Rosie Sheiff Russia
NEWMAN, Leo, Dec 31 1918 Sex:M Child# 3 Louis Newman Russia & Rose Sheff Russia
NEWMAN, Morise, Jul 13 1918 Sex:M Child# 4 Israel Newman Russia & Sarah Weisberg Russia
NEWMAN, Philip, Jan 1 1914 Sex:M Child# 3 Louis Newman Russia & Rose Shif Russia
NEWMAN, Unknown, Jul 22 1921 Sex:M Child# 5 Israel Newman Russia & Slavia Vaisborg Russia
NEWTON, Catherine Christian, Aug 29 1908 Sex:F Child# 2 George W Newton Winchendon, MA & Christina Thrower N D
NEWTON, Charles Gilbert, Sep 10 1907 Sex:M Child# 2 W F H Newton New Britain, CT & Rachel T Sanborn Franklin
NICHOLAS, Unknown, Aug 16 1913 Sex:F Child# 1 John Nicholas Greece & Sophia Posi Greece
NICHOLS, Arthur Edward, Jr, Dec 2 1917 Sex:M Child# 4 Arthue E Nichols Nashua, NH & Etta B York Fremont, NH
NICHOLS, Barbara Lorraine, Dec 31 1920 Sex:F Child# 5 Arthur E Nichols Nashua, NH & Etta B York Fremont, NH
NICHOLS, Bernice Marion, Dec 7 1924 Sex:M Child# 7 Arthur E Nichols Nashua, NH & Etta B York Fremont, NH
NICHOLS, Beverly Jane, Apr 7 1923 Sex:F Child# 3 William Nichols Manchester, NH & Mary Charron Ayer Jct, MA
NICHOLS, Claude Earle, Dec 1 1914 Sex:M Child# 2 Grovenor D Nichols Manchester, NH & Annie Floyd Shelbourne, MA
NICHOLS, Clayton Lester, Jun 22 1917 Sex:M Child# 1 William Bert Nichols Mass Lake, NH & Mary Jane Charron Ayer
NICHOLS, Dula, Jan 16 1896 Sex:F Child# 4 Franck C Nichols Nashua, NH & Frank Smith Nashua, NH
NICHOLS, Ella Irene, Sep 29 1916 Sex:F Child# 3 Grosvenor D Nichols Manchester, NH & Annie Floyd Shelbourne, MA
NICHOLS, Ernest Gilbert, Jun 5 1933 Sex:M Child# 5 Ernest Nichols St Johnsbury, VT & Bertha Mooney St Johnsbury
NICHOLS, Florence Alice, Feb 4 1925 Sex:F Child# 2 John Nichols Lyndeboro, NH & Cecile Berwick Burlington, VT
NICHOLS, Howard Willoby, Apr 4 1894 Sex:M Child# 1 John W Nichols Hudson, NH & Mary C Nye Nashua, NH
NICHOLS, John, Jan 23 1924 Sex:M Child# 1 John Nichols Lyndeborough, NH & Cecil Berwick Brownington, VT Stillborn
NICHOLS, Julia, Sep 12 1893 Sex:F Child# 5 Frank C Nichols Nashua, NH & Clara B Smith Fryeburg, ME
NICHOLS, Lillian Ruby, Nov 12 1913 Sex:F Child# 2 Arthur E Nichols Nashua, NH & Etta Belle York Freemont, NH
NICHOLS, Norma Constance, Jun 13 1932 Sex:F Child# 4 Ernest Nichols St Johnsbury, VT & Bertha Mooney St Johnsbury
NICHOLS, Normand Conrad, Jun 13 1932 Sex:M Child# 3 Ernest Nichols St Johnsbury, VT & Bertha Mooney St Johnsbury
NICHOLS, Phylis Virginia, May 15 1919 Sex:F Child# 2 William B Nichols Manchester, NH & Mary Jane Charron Ayer
NICHOLS, Richard Thomas, Aug 25 1935 Sex:M Child# 3 George Nichols Pepperell, MA & Eleanor Rice Townsend, MA
NICHOLS, Robert Eugene, May 9 1931 Sex:M Child# 2 Wesley E Nichols Mt Vernon, NH & Myrtle S Webster Milford, NH
NICHOLS, Robert Lester, Jul 6 1923 Sex:M Child# 6 Arthur E Nichols Nashua, NH & Etta B York Fremont, NH
NICHOLS, Ruth Ardelia, May 12 1911 Sex:F Child# 1 Arthur E Nichols Nashua, NH & Etta Belle York Fremont, NH
NICHOLS, Unknown, Jan 17 1888 Sex: Child# 1 Frank C Nichols Nashua, NH & Clara B Smith Bangor, ME Stillborn
NICHOLS, Unknown, Oct 16 1889 Sex:M Child# 1 John M Nichols Hudson & Mary C Nashua, NH
NICHOLS, Unknown, May 30 1891 Sex:M Child# 1 Grovernor D Nichols Nashua, NH & Emma Godfrey Brunswick, NS Stillborn
NICHOLS, Unknown, Jul 3 1893 Sex:F Child# 5 Willie S Nichols Nashua, NH & Ida W Taylor Lynn, MA
NICHOLS, Unknown, Aug 8 1894 Sex:F Child# 10 Jesse Nichols Windham, NH & Ida Newport, NH
NICHOLS, Unknown, Feb 6 1896 Sex:F Child# 3 John W Nichols Hudson, NH & Mary C Nye Nashua, NH
NICHOLS, Unknown, Sep 2 1926 Sex:F Child# 2 John W Nichols Vermont & Cecilia Berwick Vermont Stillborn
NICHOLS, Wesley Eugene, Feb 16 1930 Sex:M Child# 1 Wesley E Nichols Mt Vernon, NH & Myrtle Webster Milford, NH
NICHOLS, William Bert, Nov 16 1924 Sex:M Child# 4 William Nichols Manchester, NH & Mary Charron Ayer, MA
NICHOLS, William Eugene, Jr, May 1 1924 Sex:M Child# 7 William E Nichols
NICHOLS, William Malcombe, Aug 20 1910 Sex:M Child# 1 William F Nichols Newburyport, MA & Mary Haselton Haverhill
NICHOLSON, Barbara J Inman, Dec 26 1931 Sex:F Child# 3 (No Parents Listed)
NICKERSON, Lucille, Sep 14 1908 Sex:F Child# 4 Harry A Nickerson Wilton, NH & Nellie Hardy Milford, NH
NICKLES, Harold Everard, Mar 14 1891 Sex: Child#  Charles Nickles Hudson, NH & Alice M Chase Cambridge, MA

NICKOLS, Robert Frances, May 11 1931 Sex:M Child# 2 George Nickols Pepperell, MA & Elinor Rice Townsend, MA
NIDZOWEISKI, Edward, Jan 27 1926 Sex:M Child# 4 John Nidzoweiski Poland & Helen Sablock Poland
NIDZOWEISKI, Florence, Jan 27 1926 Sex:F Child# 3 John Nidzoweiski Poland & Helen Sablock Poland
NIEDZWICKI, John, Jan 8 1927 Sex:M Child# 1 Felix Niedzwicki Poland Russia & Malvina Kanges Poland Russia
NILASZAWSK, Albert, Mar 24 1915 Sex:M Child# 2 William Nilaszawsk Russia & Aurelia Uskauskti Russia
NILES, Evelyn P, Nov 26 1894 Sex:F Child# Charles Niles Mass & Henrietta Parkhurst NH
NILES, George Sanders, Nov 17 1908 Sex:M Child# 3 William P Niles Warehouse Pt, CT & Serena G Sanders Cambridge, MA
NILES, Lucy Alden, Jun 30 1935 Sex:F Child# 2 George S Niles Nashua, NH & Elizabeth Meader Rochester, NH
NILES, Margaret Sidney, Aug 25 1932 Sex:F Child# 1 George Niles Nashua, NH & Eliz Meader Rochester, NH
NILES, Serena Olmstead, Jan 16 1904 Sex:F Child# 1 William P Niles Warehouse Pt, CT & Serena G Sanders Cambridge
NIMES, Stanley, Jan 22 1916 Sex:M Child# 2 Alex Nimes Chicopee, MA & Josie Wappa Austria
NIQUE, Marie Laura, May 8 1917 Sex:F Child# 2 Arthur Nique Canada & Emelia Ricard Rhode Island
NIQUETTE, Gaston Origene, Sep 24 1927 Sex:M Child# 2 Alphonse Niquette Adams, MA & Valida Berthiaume Taftville, CT
NIQUETTE, Lea Florilda, Jun 18 1905 Sex:F Child# 1 Theophile Niquette Canada & M L Lamontagne Canada
NIQUETTE, M Claire Lillian, May 6 1922 Sex:F Child# 3 Oscar Niquette Canada & Rose Morrissette Canada
NIQUETTE, M Rosa Emilia Ger, Apr 13 1916 Sex:F Child# 1 Arthur Niquette Canada & Emelia Record NH
NIQUETTE, Marie Cecile Fleuret, Jul 30 1925 Sex:F Child# 4 Arthur Niquette Canada & Amelia Ricard Rhode Island
NIQUETTE, Marie Cecile Gilbert, Oct 6 1928 Sex:F Child# 10 Alphonse Niquette Adams, MA & V Berthiaume Taftville, CT
NIQUETTE, Marie Irene, Jun 28 1932 Sex:F Child# 11 A Niquette Adams, MA & V Berthiaume Taftville, CT
NIQUETTE, Marie Jeanne Yvette, Jan 6 1924 Sex:F Child# 4 Oscar Niquette Canada & Rosa Morrissette Canada
NIQUETTE, Marie R Constance, Aug 26 1932 Sex:F Child# 6 Oscar Niquette Canada & Rose Morrissette Canada
NIQUETTE, Marie Yvette Lucille, Nov 20 1925 Sex:F Child# 5 Oscar Niquette Canada & Rose Morrissette Canada
NIQUETTE, Roger Albert, May 15 1928 Sex:M Child# 1 Albert Niquette Canada & Donalda Bernier Canada
NIZORAS, Thomas, Jan 26 1914 Sex:M Child# 7 Thomas Nizoras Russia & Anna Vickis Russia
NIZZAS, Unknown, Feb 28 1918 Sex:M Child# 1 Michael Nizzas Greece & Marie Floros Greece
NODDING, Mary Elizabeth, May 22 1889 Sex:F Child# 1 Charles A Nodding
NOEL, Albert, Feb 24 1903 Sex:M Child# 4 Alphonse Noel Canada & Beatrice Martel Canada
NOEL, Aldege Adrien, Sep 16 1903 Sex:M Child# 6 Stanislas Noel Canada & Elise Michaud Canada
NOEL, Alfred Armand, Jul 13 1923 Sex:M Child# 3 Wilfred Noel Nashua, NH & Maria Belanger Nashua, NH
NOEL, Alfred Elise, May 25 1910 Sex:M Child# 4 Pierre Noel Canada & Marie Pelletier Canada
NOEL, Annette Camille, Dec 15 1924 Sex:F Child# 5 Emery Noel Nashua, NH & Rose Belanger Nashua, NH
NOEL, Antonio, Aug 25 1899 Sex:M Child# 4 Francis Noel Canada & Adeline Chabot Canada
NOEL, Antonio, Dec 21 1909 Sex:M Child# 9 Alphonse Noel Canada & Beatrice Martel Canada
NOEL, Arthur, Jun 10 1902 Sex:M Child# 5 Stanislas Noel Canada & Elise Michaud Canada
NOEL, Arthur Leo, Aug 8 1912 Sex:M Child# 2 Arthur Noel Canada & Louise Decelles Canada
NOEL, Blanche Evangeline, Feb 17 1901 Sex:F Child# 3 Alphonse Noel Canada & Beatrice Martel Canada
NOEL, Cecile Gertrude, Dec 4 1915 Sex:F Child# 9 Louis Noel Canada & Melina Rousseau Canada
NOEL, Charles Eugene, Jul 30 1907 Sex:M Child# 8 Stanislas Noel Canada & Elise Michaud Canada
NOEL, Charles Eugene, Nov 2 1909 Sex:M Child# 9 Stanislas Noel Canada & Elise Michaud Canada
NOEL, Claire Gabrielle, Jun 7 1918 Sex:F Child# 10 Louis Noel St Helen, PQ & Melina Rousseau St E de B, PQ
NOEL, Clovis Normand, Feb 1 1927 Sex:M Child# 7 Emery Noel Nashua, NH & Rose Belanger Nashua, NH
NOEL, Conrad Raymond, Mar 30 1905 Sex:M Child# 7 Stanislas Noel Canada & Elise Michaud Canada
NOEL, Daura, Nov 9 1890 Sex:F Child# 5 Napoleon Noel Canada & Rosilda Morin Canada
NOEL, Edgar Gerald, May 11 1920 Sex:M Child# 6 Arthur Noel Canada & Louise Decelle Canada
NOEL, Edward, Aug 20 1918 Sex:M Child# 4 Alfred Noel US & Alma Boutin Canada
NOEL, Emery V J Alex, Sep 8 1898 Sex:M Child# 2 Stanislas Noel Canada & Elise Michaud Canada
NOEL, Emma Viola, Jun 1 1914 Sex:F Child# 3 Arthur Noel Canada & Louise Decelle Canada
NOEL, Etta Maryland, Aug 3 1893 Sex:F Child# 3 James R Noel Ireland & Mary Rivers Ogdensburg, NY
NOEL, Eva Angelina, Jun 6 1908 Sex:F Child# 5 Louis Noel Canada & Melina Rousseau Canada
NOEL, Francois X Maurice, May 28 1914 Sex:M Child# 8 Louis Noel Canada & Melina Rousseau Canada
NOEL, Frederic Pierre, Sep 5 1904 Sex:M Child# 1 Pierre Noel Canada & Marie Peltier Canada Stillborn
NOEL, Gabrielle Pauline, May 8 1931 Sex:F Child# 9 Emery Noel Nashua, NH & Rose Belanger Nashua, NH
NOEL, Gerard Donald, Dec 23 1935 Sex:M Child# 7 Wilfred Noel Nashua, NH & Marie Belanger Nashua, NH
NOEL, Gerard Edmond, Jul 29 1910 Sex:M Child# 1 Arthur Noel Lowell, MA & Emelia Fortin Nashua, NH
NOEL, Gerard Fernando, Jul 31 1916 Sex:M Child# 12 Stanislas Noel Canada & Elise Michaud Canada
NOEL, Germaine, Feb 12 1911 Sex:F Child# 10 Alphonse Noel Canada & Beatrice Martel Canada
NOEL, Hector Robert, Apr 20 1920 Sex:M Child# 1 Emery Noel Nashua, NH & Rose Alma Belanger Nashua, NH
NOEL, Hector Vincent N, Apr 5 1904 Sex:M Child# 2 Alphonse Noel Canada & Beatrice Martel Canada
NOEL, J Emile, Sep 4 1898 Sex:M Child# 2 Alphonse Noel Canada & Beatrice Martel Canada
NOEL, J Lionel Desire, Jul 23 1911 Sex:M Child# 4 Ovide Noel Canada & Marie Berube Canada
NOEL, Jean Conrad, Aug 15 1929 Sex:M Child# 8 Emery Noel Nashua, NH & Rose Belanger Nashua, NH
NOEL, Jeannette Irene S, Jun 27 1906 Sex:F Child# 4 Louis Noel Canada & Melina Rousseau Canada
NOEL, Jos Wilfred Robert, Apr 6 1918 Sex:M Child# 1 Wilfred Noel Nashua, NH & Marie Belanger Nashua, NH
NOEL, Joseph, Oct 22 1895 Sex:M Child# 5 Napoleon Noel Canada & Rosilda Morin Canada
NOEL, Joseph Archille, Feb 13 1901 Sex:M Child# 3 Napoleon Noel Canada & Philomene Boutot Canada
NOEL, Joseph Bernard, May 21 1916 Sex:M Child# 5 Arthur Noel Lowell, MA & Amelia Fortin Nashua, NH
NOEL, Joseph Leo, Mar 3 1905 Sex:M Child# 3 Louis Noel Canada & Emerilda Rousseau Canada
NOEL, Joseph Wilfrid, Nov 10 1897 Sex:M Child# 1 Napoleon Noel Canada & P Thiboutte Canada
NOEL, Laurent Arthur, May 25 1928 Sex:M Child# 7 Arthur J Noel Lowell, MA & Emelia Fortin Nashua, NH
NOEL, Leo, Jul 27 1907 Sex:M Child# 3 Pierre Noel Canada & Marie Pelletier Canada
NOEL, Leo Alfred, Apr 16 1915 Sex:M Child# 2 Alfred Noel Nashua, NH & Emma Boutin Canada
NOEL, Lilian Annette, Apr 4 1907 Sex:F Child# 7 Alphonse Noel Canada & Beatrice Martel Canada
NOEL, Lillian Rita, Nov 3 1913 Sex:F Child# 1 Alfred Noel Canada & Alma Boutin Canada

NOEL, Lionel Maurice, Aug 23 1914 Sex:M Child# 4 Arthur Noel Lowell, MA & Emilia Fortin Nashua, NH
NOEL, Lorraine Jeanne, Aug 30 1923 Sex:F Child# 4 Emery Noel Nashua, NH & Rose Belanger Nashua, NH
NOEL, Louis Albert, Dec 20 1915 Sex:M Child# 4 Arthur Noel Canada & Louisa Decelle Canada
NOEL, Louis Alfred, Nov 12 1911 Sex:M Child# 7 Louis Noel Canada & Melina Rousseau Canada
NOEL, Lucille Edna, May 18 1922 Sex:F Child# 3 Emery Noel Nashua, NH & Rose Belanger Nashua, NH
NOEL, M Camille Dolores, Apr 4 1913 Sex:F Child# 3 Arthur Noel Lowell, MA & Emilia Fortin Nashua, NH
NOEL, M Rachel E, Nov 29 1911 Sex:F Child# 2 Arthur Noel Canada & Emilia Fortin Canada
NOEL, Madeleine Blanche, Jun 23 1915 Sex:F Child# 1 Wilfred Noel Canada & Emma Collette Sciota, NY
NOEL, Marie A, Nov 23 1900 Sex:F Child# 1 Alphonse Noel Canada & Nellie Jean Canada
NOEL, Marie Alberta A, Dec 28 1903 Sex:F Child# 4 Napoleon Noel Chateauguay, NY & Philomene Theboutot Canada
NOEL, Marie Cordelia, Jul 10 1902 Sex:F Child# 1 Louis Noel Canada & Melina rousseau Canada
NOEL, Marie Delia, May 23 1898 Sex:F Child# 2 Napoleon Noel Canada & Marie Lemoine Otter River, MA
NOEL, Marie Etitia, Jan 22 1904 Sex:F Child# 2 Louis Noel Canada & Melina Rousseau Canada
NOEL, Marie Irena, Dec 15 1906 Sex:F Child# 2 Ovide Noel Canada & Marie Berube Canada
NOEL, Marie Malvina, Oct 14 1910 Sex:F Child# 6 Louis S Noel Canada & Hermina Rousseau Canada
NOEL, Marie Marguerite, Mar 25 1901 Sex:F Child# 4 Stanislas Noel Canada & Elise Michaud Canada
NOEL, Marie Philomene, May 3 1899 Sex:F Child# 2 Napoleon Noel Canada & Philomene Thiboutote Canada
NOEL, Marie R Yvonne, Sep 8 1899 Sex:F Child# 3 Stanislas Noel Canada & Elise Michaud Canada
NOEL, Marie Regina, Apr 26 1901 Sex:F Child# 4 Napoleon Noel, Jr Canada & Marie Lemoine Mass
NOEL, Marie Rose D, Apr 15 1896 Sex:F Child# 1 Napoleon Noel Canada & Marie Lemoine Otter River, MA
NOEL, Norman Albert, Apr 18 1925 Sex:M Child# 5 Alfred Noel Canada & Alma Boutin Canada
NOEL, Ozelia, Oct 3 1894 Sex:F Child# 11 Louis Noel Canada & Alphonsine Petit Canada
NOEL, Paul Ralph, Nov 2 1926 Sex:M Child# 5 Wilfred Noel Nashua, NH & Maria Belanger Nashua, NH
NOEL, Paul Robert, Dec 31 1917 Sex:M Child# 6 Arthur Noel Lowell, MA & Amelia Fortin Nashua, NH
NOEL, Pauline Constance, Jan 25 1935 Sex:F Child# 1 Maurice Noel Nashua, NH & Olivette Turcotte Nashua, NH
NOEL, Pauline Juliette, Aug 16 1932 Sex:F Child# 1 L A Noel Nashua, NH & Mary M L Dube Nashua, NH
NOEL, Philippe, Dec 24 1905 Sex:M Child# 5 Alphonse Noel Nashua, NH & Beatrice Martel Canada
NOEL, Raymond Albert, Aug 26 1928 Sex:M Child# 3 Edwin Noel Springdale, ME & Lena Maurice Nashua, NH
NOEL, Renie Raymond, Oct 1 1919 Sex:M Child# 2 Wilfred Noel Nashua, NH & Marie Belanger Nashua, NH
NOEL, Robert Louis, Mar 18 1917 Sex:M Child# 3 Alfred Noel US & Alma Boutin Canada
NOEL, Roger Maurice, Jun 6 1925 Sex:M Child# 4 Wilfred Noel Nashua, NH & Marie Belanger Nashua, NH
NOEL, Roland, May 30 1919 Sex:M Child# 5 Arthur Noel Canada & Louise Decelle Canada
NOEL, Roland Eugene, Apr 14 1934 Sex:M Child# 11 Emery Noel Nashua, NH & Rose Belanger Nashua, NH
NOEL, Rosilda, Dec 3 1899 Sex:F Child# 3 Napoleon Noel Canada & Mary La Moine Mass
NOEL, Simone Therese, Apr 17 1921 Sex:F Child# 2 Emery Noel Nashua, NH & Rose Anna Belanger Nashua, NH
NOEL, Stanislaus Richard, Feb 1 1927 Sex:M Child# 6 Emery Noel Nashua, NH & Rose Belanger Nashua, NH
NOEL, Theresa Rita, Dec 11 1929 Sex:F Child# 6 Wilfrid Noel Canada & Marie Belanger Nashua, NH
NOEL, Therese Cecile, Nov 22 1919 Sex:F Child# 13 Stanislas Noel Canada & Elise Michaud Canada
NOEL, Therese Lucienne, Oct 13 1912 Sex:F Child# 10 Stanislaus Noel Canada & Elise Michaud Canada
NOEL, Unknown, Jul 7 1888 Sex: Child# 4 Napoleon Noel Canada & Esallia Morin Canada Stillborn
NOEL, Unknown, May 26 1904 Sex:M Child# 1 Ovide Noel Canada & Marie Berube Canada Stillborn
NOEL, Wilfred, Jun 30 1897 Sex:M Child# 1 Stanislas Noel Canada & Elise Michaud Canada
NOEL, Wilfrid Arthur, Dec 31 1910 Sex:M Child# 1 Arthur Noel Canada & Louise Decelles Canada
NOEL, Yvette, Jan 3 1933 Sex:F Child# 10 Emery Noel Nashua, NH & Rose Belanger Nashua, NH
NOEL, Yvonne, Feb 22 1906 Sex:F Child# 2 Pierre Noel Canada & Marie Pelletier Canada
NOLAN, Edward Joseph, Jan 27 1923 Sex:M Child# 3 Edward J Nolan Nashua, NH & Florence MacDonnell Judique, CB,
NOLAN, John Edward, May 1 1926 Sex:M Child# 2 John Nolan Winchendon, MA & Florida Bernier Nashua, NH
NOLAN, Joseph Irving, Jul 1 1913 Sex:M Child# 1 Joseph B Nolan Nashua, NH & Alberta Sanborn Pelican Rapids, MN
NOLAN, Kittie May, Jul 17 1891 Sex:F Child# 2 Owen F Nolan Lawrence, MA & Hannah Murphy Dover, NH
NOLAN, Mary Lucille Rita, Mar 15 1925 Sex:F Child# 1 John Nolan Winchendon, MA & Florida Bernier Nashua, NH
NOLAN, Robert Harold, Jul 18 1935 Sex:M Child# 1 Kenneth Nolan Kittery, ME & Vera Flagg Wellesley Hills, MA
NOLAN, Unknown, Feb 8 1917 Sex:M Child# 2 Joseph B Nolan Nashua, NH & Alberta Sanborn Pel Rap, Minn Stillborn
NOMER, Bertha, Oct 16 1896 Sex:F Child# 5 George S Nomer US & Elizabeth Avard Canada
NOONAN, Alice Louise, Jun 23 1899 Sex:F Child# 1 Winslow Noonan Maine & Delia Richard NH
NOONAN, Arthur Carlton, Nov 17 1919 Sex:M Child# 2 Carlton Noonan Brockton, MA & Ella Hunt Nova Scotia
NOONAN, Catherine, Oct 19 1896 Sex:F Child# 2 Dennis Noonan Nashua, NH & Ellen M Harrington Cambridge, MA
NOONAN, Dennis, Nov 24 1901 Sex:M Child# 5 Dennis Noonan Canada & Allen Harrington Canada
NOONAN, George, Sep 20 1905 Sex:M Child# 7 Dennis Noonan NH & Ellen Harrington Mass
NOONAN, John, Jan 2 1900 Sex:M Child# 4 Dennis P Noonan Nashua, NH & Ellen Harrington Cambridge, MA
NOONAN, Joseph, Aug 28 1907 Sex:M Child# 8 Dennis Noonan NH & Ellen Harrington Mass
NOONAN, Marguerite, May 2 1903 Sex:F Child# 6 Dennis Noonan Mass & Ellen Harrington Mass
NOONAN, Mary, Jul 28 1898 Sex:F Child# 3 Dennis Noonan Nashua, NH & Helen Harrington Cambridge, MA
NOONAN, Paul J, Aug 3 1895 Sex:M Child# 4 John D Noonan E Boston, MA & A Gooding Portland, ME
NOONAN, Unknown, Sep 22 1895 Sex:F Child# 1 Dennis Noonan Nashua, NH & Ellen M Harrington Cambridge, MA Stillborn
NOONAN, William G, Dec 5 1897 Sex:M Child#  John D Noonan Boston, MA & Agnes Gooding Portland, ME
NORAL, Lucie, May 20 1888 Sex:F Child# 7 Joseph Noral Canada & Sarah Dubseuil Canada
NORCROSS, Nelson Alva, Mar 14 1903 Sex:M Child# 3 Charles H Norcross Chesterfield & Gertrude A Crouch Marlow
NORCROSS, Unknown, Dec 20 1889 Sex:F Child# 1 Charles H Norcross Nashua, NH & Gertrude A Couch Nashua, NH
NORCROSS, Unknown, Jun 16 1895 Sex:M Child# 1 Homer O Norcross Templeton, MA & Julia M Bow Woburn, MA
NORDOFF, Unknown, Aug 8 1899 Sex:F Child# 3 Mike Nordoff Russia & Alexnadria Uravich Russia
NOREIKIS, Anna, Sep 15 1911 Sex:F Child# 4 Kastis Noreikis Russia & Lucia Tekor Russia
NOREIKIS, Antonas, May 14 1907 Sex:M Child# 1 Nastantin Noreikis Russia & Lucie Tekocarti Russia
NOREIKIS, Leon, May 6 1910 Sex:M Child# 1 Leon Noreikis Russia & Kotrina Stanewievitz Russia

NOREJKIS, Mary, Sep 8 1912 Sex:F Child# 4 Kostant Norejkis Poland & Lucia Tekor Poland
NOREYKIS, Mary, Dec 10 1908 Sex:F Child# 2 Constantin Noreykis Russia & Lucya Tekorius Russia
NORGOSIAN, Vartan G, Jun 14 1909 Sex:M Child# 2 Garabed Norgosian Armenia & Nazlez Stephonion Armenia
NORGRIS, Josephas, Jun 23 1910 Sex:M Child# 3 Constant Norgris Russia & Lucya Tekorajtie Russia
NORICK, Stanislaus, Sep 10 1918 Sex:M Child# 2 Michael Norick Russia & Felicen Senci Russia
NORMAN, Frank Edouard, Feb 18 1896 Sex:M Child# 4 Paul Norman Canada & Josephine Dumoulin Canada
NORMAN, Harold, May 1 1903 Sex:M Child# 2 Thomas Norman Glasgow, Scotland & Emma Fisher Canada
NORMAN, Joseph, Sep 18 1902 Sex:M Child# 7 Paul Norman Canada & Josephine Mesmoulins US
NORMAN, Lillian V, May 13 1898 Sex:F Child# 5 Paul Norman Canada & Josephine Dumoulin Canada
NORMAND, Henry, Nov 17 1894 Sex:M Child# 3 Paul Normand Canada & Josephine Dumonlin Canada
NORMAND, Joseph Achille, Sep 22 1905 Sex:M Child# 5 John Normand Canada & Angelina Goulet Canada
NORMAND, Joseph Alphonse, Sep 22 1905 Sex:M Child# 6 John Normand Canada & Angelina Goulet Canada
NORMAND, Joseph Raymond, Feb 19 1907 Sex:M Child# 8 John Normand Canada & Angelina Goulet Canada
NORMAND, Louise M C, Aug 20 1889 Sex:F Child# 14 Louis Normand Canada & A Archambault Canada
NORMAND, Marie Angelina, Jan 23 1904 Sex:F Child# 5 John Normand Canada & Angelina Goulet Canada
NORMAND, Paul Wilfred, May 14 1892 Sex:M Child# 1 Paul Normand Canada & Josephine Dumoulin S Vill, VT
NORMAND, Pierre A, Aug 31 1887 Sex:M Child# 10 Louis Normand P Q & Alphonsine Cohoes, NY
NORMANDIN, Edouard Robert, Oct 30 1904 Sex:M Child# 3 Pierre Normandin US & Julienne Pontbriand US
NORMANDIN, Ernest, Oct 22 1922 Sex:M Child# 8 Philip Normandin Canada & Eva Milette NH
NORMANDIN, Gladys, Jul 14 1902 Sex:F Child# 2 Peter Normandin Plattsburg, NY & J Pontbriand Sciota, NY
NORMANDIN, Marguerite G, Mar 15 1908 Sex:F Child# 4 Emile Normandin Canada & Maria Routhier Canada
NORMANDIN, Urene M, Dec 31 1898 Sex:F Child# 1 Petre Normandin US & Julienne Roubriand US
NORMANDINE, Unknown, Dec 13 1928 Sex:F Child# 1 R Normandine Canada & Loretta Frenette Lowell, MA Stillborn
NOROSKIE, Helena, Aug 11 1915 Sex:F Child# 4 Hados Noroskie Russia & Katherine Stacek Russia
NORRIS, Unknown, Jan 8 1930 Sex:M Child# 4 Nicholas Norris Greece & Katherine Kasaraky Nashua, NH
NORTHRUP, Sidney Kenneth, Jan 2 1912 Sex:M Child# 3 Fenwick E Northrup Kingstown, NB & Ellen Frances Clough T
NORTON, Alfred M, May 18 1904 Sex:M Child# 1 Walter F Norton E Boston, MA & Mabel G Stevens Salmon Falls, NH
NORTON, Clinton Paul, May 17 1935 Sex:M Child# 3 Omer A Norton Merrimack, NH & Clara Burgess Candia, NH
NORTON, Elizabeth Ann, Aug 21 1932 Sex:F Child# 4 Jas A Norton Nashua, NH & Mary Sullivan Nashua, NH
NORTON, Hazel Marion, Feb 10 1897 Sex:F Child# 1 Laurence E Norton Hudson, MA & Viola Stanley Pepperell, MA
NORTON, James Norris, Jul 24 1918 Sex:M Child# 1 James Norton Nashua, NH & Mary Sullivan Nashua, NH
NORTON, Omer, Nov 19 1894 Sex:M Child# 3 Lewis A Norton Middletown, CT & Mary Petipaw Halifax, NS
NORTON, Otis Kenneth, Jul 16 1929 Sex:M Child# 2 Omer Norton Merrimack, NH & Clara Burgess Candia, NH
NORTON, Richard, Aug 16 1921 Sex:M Child# 3 James Norton Nashua, NH & Mary Sullivan Nashua, NH
NORTON, Richard Lewis, Aug 8 1925 Sex:M Child# 1 Omer Norton Nashua, NH & Clara Burgess Canada
NORTON, Robert Sullivan, Apr 16 1920 Sex:M Child# 2 James Norton Nashua, NH & Mary Sullivan Nashua, NH
NORTON, Unknown, Nov 2 1890 Sex:M Child# 3 Jesse O Norton Elizabeth, NY & Minnie Mignault Saranac, NY
NORTON, Unknown, Feb 24 1900 Sex:M Child# 2 Ernest Norton Mass & Lillian Childs Newfoundland
NORWICH, James, Sep 4 1915 Sex:M Child# 2 James Norwich Russia & Anna Cerliuk Russia
NORWISH, Melvina Grey, Jun 18 1901 Sex:F Child# 1 Jesley Grey Norwish Russia & Lizzie Barnsata Russia
NOUKAKIS, Rosa, Aug 23 1915 Sex:F Child# 5 Gust Noukakis Russia & Lucy Takouis Russia
NOVESKI, Unknown, Apr 21 1921 Sex:F Child# 1 Walter Noveski Lithuania & Tofela Sarachek Lithuania Stillborn
NOVICK, Wesley John, Sep 16 1934 Sex:M Child# 1 Wesley Novick Prussia & Arline Malette Nashua, NH
NOVIK, Genefa, Jul 28 1916 Sex:F Child# 1 Mike Novik Russia & Filixia Castola Russia
NOWALK, Gladson Joseph, Mar 25 1935 Sex:M Child# 7 Michael Nowalk Palmer, MA & Mary Robichaud NH
NOYES, Beatrice Ellen, Jul 1 1903 Sex:F Child# 3 Charles H Noyes Atkinson & Caroline B Noyes Willoughby Lake, VT
NOYES, Hermon Bemis, Mar 18 1899 Sex:M Child# 1 Charles Hermon Noyes Atkinson & Caroline R Bemis Willowby Lake, VT
NOYES, Janice May, Oct 30 1925 Sex:F Child# 4 William T Noyes Haverhill, MA & Mae J Burno Johnson, VT
NOYES, Jessie Winona, Aug 1 1926 Sex:F Child# 7 Harrison H Noyes Lowell, MA & Iola M Stevens Rumney, NH
NOYES, Roland Modglin, Nov 25 1932 Sex:M Child# 8 Harry H Noyes Lowell, MA & Iola Stevens Rumney, NH
NOYES, Unknown, Jul 15 1901 Sex:F Child# 2 Charles H Noyes Atkinson & Caroline R Bemis Willouby Lake, VT
NUGENT, George, Mar 3 1891 Sex:M Child#  George P Nugent Fairfield, VT & Delia Powers Liverpool, England
NUGENT, George, Sep 10 1895 Sex:M Child#  George P Nugent Fairfield, VT & Delia Powers Liverpool, England
NUGENT, John Leo, Mar 28 1897 Sex:M Child# 9 George P Nugent Fairfield, VT & Delhia B Powers Liverpool, England
NUGENT, Unknown, Jun 15 1892 Sex:M Child# 6 George P Nugent Fairfield, VT & Delia Powers Liverpool, England
NUGENT, Unknown, Apr 16 1894 Sex:M Child# 7 George P Nugent St Albans, VT & Delia Powers Liverpool, England
NULMIS, Anthony, Jul 23 1910 Sex:M Child# 1 Anthony Nulmis Russia & Lizzie Sibelluski Russia
NUNEZ, John Bristol, Jul 29 1922 Sex:M Child# 2 Vasco Nunez Richmond, VA & Edith Roberts Medford, MA
NUSENOFF, Ella, Aug 1 1915 Sex:F Child# 4 Sam Nusenoff Russia & Bessie Cohen Russia  Stillborn
NUSENOFF, Esther Marion, Feb 24 1918 Sex:F Child#  Samuel Nusenoff Russia & Bessie Cohen Russia
NUSENOFF, Leo Aleck, Jul 11 1916 Sex:M Child# 5 Sam Nusenoff Russia & Bessie Cohen Russia
NUTBROWN, Aubrey Stevens, Feb 22 1930 Sex:M Child# 1 Aubrey Nutbrown Manchester, NH & Olive Lockwood Matamoras
NUTBROWN, Gladys Maude, Aug 31 1908 Sex:F Child# 2 Stephen R Nutbrown Canada & Margaret Ring St Johns, NB
NUTBROWN, Ronald Charles, Aug 14 1931 Sex:M Child# 2 Aubrey Nutbrown Manchester, NH & Olive Lockwood Matamoros
NUTBROWN, Unknown, Jan 9 1889 Sex:F Child# 1 Thomas Nutbrown Canada & Emily Daniels England
NUTE, Alice Ann, Sep 10 1919 Sex:F Child# 3 Robert H Nute Nashua, NH & Mary E Graves England
NUTE, Alice Gordon, Sep 26 1925 Sex:F Child# 3 John Nute Nashua, NH & Agnes Gardner Dunstable, MA
NUTE, Allen Gardner, Sep 26 1925 Sex:M Child# 4 John Nute Nashua, NH & Agnes Gardner Dunstable, MA
NUTE, Charles Francis, Sep 9 1923 Sex:M Child# 5 Robert Nute Nashua, NH & Mary E Greaves England
NUTE, Edna Evelyn, Apr 17 1927 Sex:F Child# 5 John H Nute Nashua, NH & Agnes C Gardner Dunstable, MA
NUTE, Edward William, May 10 1922 Sex:M Child# 4 Robert Nute Nashua, NH & Mary E Greaves Lancashire, England
NUTE, Margaret Jane, Jul 26 1916 Sex:F Child# 2 Robert Nute Nashua, NH & Mary Greaves Oldham, England
NUTE, Marion Agnes, May 29 1932 Sex:F Child# 5 John H Nute Nashua, NH & Agnes C Gardner Dunstable, MA

NUTE, Raymond, Mar 28 1924 Sex:M Child# 1 Ray S Nute Nashua, NH & Lillian Nute Nashua, NH Stillborn
NUTE, Robert Emmett, Feb 15 1915 Sex:M Child# 1 Robert H Nute Nashua, NH & Mary Ellen Greaves England
NUTE, Unknown, Aug 31 1891 Sex: Child# 5 Charles H Nute Nashua, NH & Maggie Hough Ireland
NUTE, Unknown, Oct 8 1897 Sex:M Child# 1 George Nute Nashua, NH & Flora E Woodward Dunstable, MA Stillborn
NUTE, Unknown, Jun 25 1923 Sex:F Child# 2 John Nute Nashua, NH & Agnes Gardner Dunstable, MA Stillborn
NUTE, Unknown, Apr 25 1930 Sex:M Child# 7 John Nute Nashua, NH & Agnes Gardner Dunstable, MA Stillborn
NUTTER, Unknown, Sep 21 1890 Sex:F Child# 4 George J P Nutter Pittsfield, NH & Effie V Wallace Reeds Ferry, NH
NUTTING, Charles E, Aug 5 1887 Sex:M Child# 3 Charles F Nutting Pepperell & Anna Manchester, VT
NUTTING, Doris May, Oct 1 1920 Sex:F Child# 1 (No Parents Listed)
NUTTING, Ernestine Rose, Jul 27 1934 Sex:F Child# 1 (No Parents Listed)
NUTTING, Frank Allen, Oct 11 1915 Sex:M Child# 1 Frank Nutting Nashua, NH & Bernice B Tipping Brockville
NUTTING, George H Sleeper, Nov 20 1899 Sex:M Child# 2 George F Nutting NH & Mary O'Brien Ireland
NUTTING, Howard Ellsworth, Oct 10 1919 Sex:M Child# 2 Frank A Nutting Nashua, NH & Bernice B Tipping Brockville
NUTTING, Roger Norman, Jan 3 1930 Sex:M Child# 7 Harry R Nutting Greenville, NH & Annie E Ashe Roslindale, MA
NUTTING, Unknown, Oct 11 1889 Sex:F Child# 5 Charles Nutting Pepperell, MA & Ann Woodard Nashua, NH
NUTTING, Unknown, Aug 11 1891 Sex:M Child# 3 Charles F Nutting Pepperell, MA & Anna Woodward Nashua, NH Stillborn
NYE, Harold Morey, Jan 1 1912 Sex:M Child# 1 Harry E Nye Nashua, NH & Blanche S Morey Nashua, NH
NYE, Prentiss Carlton, Jr, Jul 29 1926 Sex:M Child# 1 Prentiss C Nye Chesham, NH & Helen Warren Lyndeboro, NH
NYLAND, Henry Joseph, Jr, May 30 1921 Sex:M Child# 1 Henry J Nyland S Natick, MA & Madeline Curran Concord, NH
NZDAVIN, Josephine, May 18 1903 Sex:F Child# 2 John Nzdavin Russia & Eva Nzdavin Russia
O'BLENIS, Jane Frances, Mar 25 1930 Sex:F Child# 1 Oscar O'Blenis Nova Scotia & Dorothy Nadeau Nashua, NH
O'BRIEN, Agnes Maria, Aug 1 1914 Sex:F Child# 2 Edward W O'Brien Gardner, MA & Margaret Flynn New York, NY
O'BRIEN, Alice, Jun 9 1908 Sex:F Child# 4 Thomas E O'Brien Nashua, NH & Mary Ryan Ireland
O'BRIEN, Ann, Jun 12 1896 Sex:F Child# 7 Thomas O'Brien Ireland & Katherine Fahy Ireland
O'BRIEN, Annie, Nov 7 1894 Sex:F Child# 8 John Birchell Ireland & Mary O'Brien Ireland
O'BRIEN, Clara, Apr 28 1921 Sex:F Child# 1 George O'Brien New York & Victoria Proulx Mass
O'BRIEN, Constance, Sep 23 1916 Sex:F Child# 2 John F O'Brien Ayer, MA & May Melanson Pepperell, MA
O'BRIEN, Doris Anne, Mar 23 1913 Sex:F Child# 1 Patrick J O'Brien Ireland & Margaret Callahan Boston, MA
O'BRIEN, Elizabeth Mary, May 26 1923 Sex:F Child# 1 Maurice O'Brien E Pepperell, MA & Agnes Warren Nashua, NH
O'BRIEN, Francis, Apr 9 1910 Sex:M Child# 1 Francis E O'Brien Nashua, NH & Katherine Walsh England
O'BRIEN, Frederick Ignatius, Jan 29 1892 Sex:M Child# 7 James O'Brien NY & Lucy Flemming Canada
O'BRIEN, Gloria Muriel, Dec 13 1925 Sex:F Child# 2 S John O'Brien Lowell, MA & G E Ackles England
O'BRIEN, Harold, May 13 1911 Sex:M Child# 1 Harry O'Brien
O'BRIEN, Harold Joseph, Jun 6 1896 Sex:M Child# 1 James O'Brien Ireland & M J McLaughlin Ireland
O'BRIEN, Helen, Jul 13 1912 Sex:F Child# 2 Frank E O'Brien Nashua, NH & Katherine Walsh Lowell, MA
O'BRIEN, Helena Marie, Mar 21 1915 Sex:F Child# 2 Patrick O'Brien Ireland & Margaret Winn Boston, MA
O'BRIEN, Homer Ernest, Aug 21 1902 Sex:M Child# 8 John O'Brien Manchester, England & Julia Sheehan Ireland
O'BRIEN, Ilene, Mar 11 1907 Sex:F Child# 3 Thomas F O'Brien Nashua, NH & Mary E Ryan Ireland
O'BRIEN, James Conrad, Jul 2 1930 Sex:M Child# 1 Francis O'Brien Monson, MA & Agnes Fitzgerald Monson, MA
O'BRIEN, James Henry, Aug 21 1887 Sex:M Child# 5 James O'Brien Troy, NY & Jos Flemming P Q
O'BRIEN, Jane, Mar 3 1923 Sex:F Child# 3 John O'Brien Ayer, MA & Mae Melonson Pepperell, MA
O'BRIEN, John Charles, Jun 24 1893 Sex:M Child# 8 James O'Brien Waterford, NY & Lucy Flemming Hemingford, PQ
O'BRIEN, John F, Jr, Nov 9 1912 Sex:M Child# 1 John F O'Brien Ayer, MA & Mary Melanson Pepperell, MA
O'BRIEN, John Francis, Mar 7 1895 Sex:M Child# 3 John O'Brien Manchester, England & Julia Sheehan Ireland
O'BRIEN, John Francis, Oct 3 1924 Sex:M Child# 4 J F O'Brien Ayer, MA & May Melanson Pepperell, MA
O'BRIEN, Joseph, Nov 19 1916 Sex:M Child# 1 Martin O'Brien NH & Hattie Lafleur New York
O'BRIEN, Joseph, Jul 25 1920 Sex:M Child# 1 Joseph O'Brien Lawrence, MA & Adolphe Bergeron Rochester, NH
O'BRIEN, Julia Lillian, Jan 25 1898 Sex:F Child# 5 John O'Brien England & Julia Sheean Ireland
O'BRIEN, Mabel Katherine, Apr 12 1905 Sex:F Child# 1 Thomas F O'Brien Lewiston, ME & Genevieve A Marnes NY
O'BRIEN, Margaret, Sep 12 1917 Sex:F Child# 3 Patrick O'Brien Ireland & Margaret Callahan Boston, MA
O'BRIEN, Margaret Mary, May 16 1898 Sex:F Child# 2 James O'Brien Ireland & Margaret McLaughlin Ireland
O'BRIEN, Marion Gay, Mar 12 1920 Sex:F Child# 1 Dennis O'Brien Newburg, NY & Jennie Ackerman Richfield, NJ
O'BRIEN, Marion Lucy, Aug 27 1923 Sex:F Child# 1 Frederick L O'Brien Nashua, NH & Marion Bugbee Nashua, NH
O'BRIEN, Mary Ellen, Sep 21 1894 Sex:F Child# 6 Thomas J O'Brien Ireland & Katherine Fahey Ireland
O'BRIEN, May, Sep 16 1930 Sex:F Child# 8 Patrick J O'Brien Ireland & Margaret Callahan Roxbury, MA
O'BRIEN, Rita, Nov 1 1924 Sex:F Child# 6 Patrick O'Brien Ireland & Margaret Callahan Roxbury, MA
O'BRIEN, Robert Jay, Aug 29 1917 Sex:M Child# 1 Robert F O'Brien Townsend, MA & Jeanne Cournoyer Greenville, NH
O'BRIEN, Sarah Agnes, Sep 19 1911 Sex:F Child# 2 Thomas F O'Brien Lewiston, ME & Genevieve Marnes Beekmantown, NY
O'BRIEN, Sarah Elizabeth, Aug 19 1907 Sex:F Child# 1 Peter O'Brien Ireland & Mary Curtin Scotland
O'BRIEN, Theresa, Nov 15 1927 Sex:F Child# 7 Patrick O'Brien Ireland & Margaret Callahan Roxbury, MA
O'BRIEN, Thomas, Sep 15 1893 Sex:M Child# 5 Thomas J O'Brien Ireland & Kate Fahey Ireland
O'BRIEN, Thomas Aut, Dec 27 1902 Sex:M Child# 1 Thomas O'Brien Nashua, NH & Mary Ryan Ireland
O'BRIEN, Thomas Edward, Feb 26 1931 Sex:M Child# 1 Thomas A O'Brien Nashua, NH & Mary C Amirault Nova Scotia
O'BRIEN, Thomas Patrick, Apr 9 1923 Sex:M Child# 5 Patrick O'Brien Ireland & Margaret Callahan Roxbury, MA
O'BRIEN, Unknown, Mar 10 1905 Sex:M Child# 2 Thomas E O'Brien Nashua, NH & Mary Ryan Ireland
O'BRIEN, Unknown, Jul 12 1912 Sex:M Child# 6 Thomas E O'Brien Nashua, NH & Mary Ryan Ireland Stillborn
O'BRIEN, Unknown, Apr 3 1920 Sex:M Child# 2 Patrick O'Brien Amesbury, MA & Harriet Maxfield Rochester, NH
O'BRIEN, Unknown, Jan 2 1924 Sex:F Child# 3 George O'Brien Lowell, MA & Mary Auberton Lowell, MA Stillborn
O'BRIEN, William, Oct 27 1910 Sex:M Child# 5 Thomas E O'Brien Nashua, NH & Mary Ryan Ireland
O'CLAIR, Jeanne Miriam, May 11 1926 Sex:F Child# 2 Edward O'Clair Franklin, NH & Mary Matherson Danvers, MA
O'CLAIR, Robert Matherson, Feb 28 1923 Sex:M Child# 1 Edward O'Clair Franklin, NH & Danvers, MA
O'CONNELL, Anna B, Jun 26 1902 Sex:F Child# 3 Timothy A O'Connell Nashua, NH & A M Lally Nashua, NH
O'CONNELL, Catherine Jennie, Apr 9 1898 Sex:F Child# 4 Daniel O'Connell Berwick, ME & Jennie Burns Nashua, NH

O'CONNELL, Dale Gilbert, Nov 28 1918 Sex:M Child# 1 Wm H O'Connell Nashua, NH & Irene Pontbriand Nashua, NH
O'CONNELL, Daniel F, Jan 18 1892 Sex:M Child# 2 Daniel O'Connell Berwick, ME & E Jennie Burns Nashua, NH
O'CONNELL, Hilda Katherine, Dec 18 1909 Sex:F Child# 7 Timothy O'Connell Nashua, NH & Annie Lally Nashua, NH
O'CONNELL, Joseph Peter, Jan 23 1914 Sex:M Child# 1 Peter O'Connell Springfield, MA & Mary O'Connor Springfield
O'CONNELL, Margaret G, Nov 12 1905 Sex:F Child# 4 Timothy O'Connell Nashua, NH & Annie M Lally Nashua, NH
O'CONNELL, Mary Christina, Dec 9 1900 Sex:F Child# 2 Timothy O'Connell Nashua, NH & Ann Lally Nashua, NH
O'CONNELL, Paul Leander, Nov 9 1912 Sex:M Child# 8 Timothy A O'Connell Nashua, NH & Annie Lally Nashua, NH
O'CONNELL, Robert Daniel, Aug 30 1908 Sex:M Child# 6 Timothy A O'Connell Nashua, NH & Annie M Lally Nashua, NH
O'CONNELL, Unknown, Aug 2 1887 Sex:F Child# 4 Jeremiah O'Connell Salmon Falls, NH & Mary Glinn Lawrence, MA
O'CONNELL, Unknown, Jul 18 1890 Sex:F Child# 1 Daniel O'Connell Berwick, ME & E J Burns Nashua, NH
O'CONNELL, Unknown, Nov 30 1899 Sex:M Child# 1 Timothy O'Connell Nashua, NH & Annie Lally Nashua, NH
O'CONNELL, William John, Jan 30 1907 Sex:M Child# 5 Tim A O'Connell Nashua, NH & Ann M Lally Nashua, NH
O'CONNOR, Bernard John, Sep 17 1911 Sex:M Child# 1 Cornelius B O'Connor Ticonderoga, NY & Katherine F Geary Le
O'CONNOR, Charles Gerald, Jul 26 1921 Sex:M Child# 1 Charles G O'Connor Boston, MA & Florence Hitchinson Digby
O'CONNOR, John P, Feb 27 1888 Sex:M Child# 2 John J O'Connor N S & Rose Fallon Ireland
O'CONNOR, Unknown, Oct 14 1895 Sex:F Child# 7 John O'Connor St Johns, NB & Rose Fallon Ireland Stillborn
O'CONNOR, Unknown, Jan 11 1897 Sex:M Child# 8 John O'Connor St John, NB & Rose Fallon Ireland Stillborn
O'DONNELL, Annie, Aug 22 1914 Sex:F Child# 3 Patrick O'Donnell Ireland & Annie Welch Ireland
O'DONNELL, Donalda Edith, Feb 22 1918 Sex:F Child# 2 Edward J O'Donnell Coaticook, Quebec & Mary Cashon Lancaster
O'DUYER, Leo, Jan 2 1901 Sex:M Child# 11 John O'Duyer Ireland & Mary Hamahan Ireland
O'DWYER, Arline Bertha, Mar 22 1899 Sex:F Child# 10 John O'Dwyer Ireland & Mary Hannahan Ireland
O'DWYER, Caran Brandon, Apr 19 1896 Sex:M Child# 8 John O'Dwyer Ireland & Mary Hanrahan Ireland
O'DWYER, Gertrude Ann, Feb 18 1898 Sex:F Child# 9 John O'Dwyer Ireland & Mary Hanrahan Ireland
O'DWYER, Robert M, Jan 1 1904 Sex:M Child# 13 John O'Dwyer Ireland & Mary Hanrahan Ireland
O'DWYER, Teresa Agnes, Sep 28 1916 Sex:F Child# 1 Joseph O'Dwyer Nashua, NH & Christina Cote Chicago, IL
O'DWYER, Walter Henry, Aug 21 1894 Sex:M Child# 7 John O'Dwyer Ireland & Mary Hanrahan Ireland
O'GILVIE, Guy, Sep 3 1916 Sex:M Child# 3 J O'Gilvie S Dummerston, VT & Belle White Hudson, NH Stillborn
O'GRADY, John A, Jun 21 1894 Sex:M Child# 2 John J O'Grady England & Annie J Kelley Worcester, MA
O'HARE, Harold Patrick, Jan 1 1911 Sex:M Child# 2 John C O'Hare Lowell, MA & Nellie Griffen Ireland
O'HARE, James Francis, Feb 9 1910 Sex:M Child# 2 John C O'Hare Lowell, MA & Nellie Griffin Ireland
O'HARE, John Cornelius, May 13, 1907 Sex:M Child# 1 John C O'Hare Lowell, MA & Nellie Griffin Ireland
O'HARE, Martin, Feb 10 1914 Sex:M Child# 5 John C O'Hare Lowell, MA & Nellie Griffin Ireland
O'HARE, Mary Agnes, Mar 28 1899 Sex:F Child# 1 John F O'Hare Ireland & Minnie Toomey Lowell, MA
O'HARE, Mary Mildred, Apr 17 1912 Sex:F Child# 4 John C O'Hare Lowell, MA & Nellie Griffin Ireland
O'LEARY, James Cornelius, Jan 23 1929 Sex:M Child# 1 Robert O'Leary Milford, NH & Elizabeth McCarthy Manchester, NH
O'LEARY, Mary, Dec 8 1913 Sex:F Child# 1 Eugene J O'Leary Winchendon, MA & Lena Ryan Nashua, NH
O'LEARY, Robert Leonard, Oct 26 1931 Sex:M Child# 2 Robert O'Leary Milford, NH & Elizabeth McCarthy Manchester, NH
O'LEARY, Ruth, Dec 3 1916 Sex:F Child# 2 Eugene J O'Leary Winchendon, MA & Helena Ryan Nashua, NH
O'LIGNY, Willis A, Dec 17 1892 Sex:M Child# 5 Wilber O'ligny Chazy, NY & Rose Goyet Chazy, NY
O'MALLEY, Harold Richard, Oct 30 1922 Sex:M Child# 1 John O'Malley Eastport, ME & Elizabeth Cross Mass
O'MARA, Teresa Margaret, Nov 28 1898 Sex:F Child# 1 Philip O'Mara Clinton Co, NY & Delia Gralton Ireland
O'MARA, Theresa, Nov 17 1904 Sex:F Child# 3 Philip O'Mara NY & Delia Graeton Ireland
O'MEARA, Frances Gonzage, Nov 5 1900 Sex:F Child# 2 Philip O'Meara NY & Delia Gralton Ireland
O'MEARA, Roger Raymond, May 21 1906 Sex:M Child# 4 Philip O'Meara New York & Delia Gratton Ireland
O'NEAL, Nellie Josephine, Jan 7 1891 Sex:F Child# 2 Dennis O'Neal Nashua, NH & Eliza Edwards Manchester, NH
O'NEAL, Patrick William, Apr 1 1890 Sex:M Child# 1 Jerry O'Neal Ireland & Julia Sullivan Ireland
O'NEAL, Unknown, Sep 10 1891 Sex:M Child# 1 Michael H O'Neal Ohio & Mary E Galvan Dublin, Ireland
O'NEIL, Abbie Sybil, Apr 12 1901 Sex:F Child# 6 Patrick O'Neil Ireland & Bessie Breman Ireland
O'NEIL, Agnes, Oct 5 1912 Sex:F Child# 12 Jeremiah O'Neil Ireland & Julia Sullivan Ireland
O'NEIL, Albert J, Apr 18 1891 Sex:M Child# 4 William O'Neil New York & Mary Burns Nashua, NH
O'NEIL, Albert James, Apr 23 1924 Sex:M Child# 1 Ralph F O'Neil Nashua, NH & Mad Thompson Nashua, NH
O'NEIL, Alfred Patrick, Sep 1 1914 Sex:M Child# 1 Patrick O'Neil Ireland & Josephine Sullivan Ireland
O'NEIL, Alice, Nov 15 1895 Sex:F Child# 3 Dennis O'Neil Nashua, NH & Mary A O'Shea Ireland
O'NEIL, Alice, Jul 29 1906 Sex:F Child# 9 Jeremiah O'Neil Ireland & Julia Sullivan Ireland
O'NEIL, Alice Mary, Jul 24 1916 Sex:F Child# 1 Charles H O'Neil Nashua, NH & Sarah A McLaughlin Bridgeport, CT
O'NEIL, Allen Thomas, May 3 1934 Sex:M Child# 1 Thomas F O'Neil, Jr Milford, NH & Elizabeth White Milford, NH
O'NEIL, Ann Elizabeth, Jun 19 1923 Sex:F Child# 4 Charles O'Neil Nashua, NH & Sarah A McLaughlin Bridgeport, CT
O'NEIL, Anna Julia, Jun 10 1914 Sex:F Child# 1 Eugene O'Neil Ireland & Mary Molloy Nashua, NH
O'NEIL, Arthur Galvin, Apr 24 1896 Sex:M Child# 3 Michael H O'Neil E St Louis, IL & Mary E Galvin Dublin, Ireland
O'NEIL, Catherine Theresa, Feb 25 1894 Sex:F Child# 2 Dennis O'Neil Nashua, NH & Mary A O'Shea Ireland
O'NEIL, Celia, Apr 11 1905 Sex:F Child# 12 Jeremiah O'Neil Manchester, NH & Lucy Buckley Boston, MA
O'NEIL, Charles Henry, Nov 21 1917 Sex:M Child# 2 Charles H O'Neil Nashua, NH & Sarah A McLaughlin Bridgeport, CT
O'NEIL, Charlotte May, Apr 25 1926 Sex:F Child# 1 Walter O'Neil E Pepperell, MA & Eva Shepardson Mansfield, MA
O'NEIL, Daniel Alfred, May 16 1890 Sex:M Child# 1 Patrick O'Neil Ireland & Bessie Brennan Ireland
O'NEIL, Edward, Sep 13 1892 Sex:M Child# 3 Patrick O'Neil Ireland & Bessie Brennan Ireland
O'NEIL, Edwin Campbell, Apr 16 1894 Sex:M Child# 1 James O'Neil Cleveland, OH & Minnie C O'Neil Nova Scotia
O'NEIL, Elizabeth, Sep 8 1901 Sex:F Child# 4 James O'Neil Cleveland, OH & Mary Campbell Nova Scotia
O'NEIL, Elizabeth, Feb 27 1905 Sex:F Child# 7 Patrick O'Neil Ireland & Elizabeth Brennan Ireland
O'NEIL, Esther, Jul 21 1908 Sex:F Child# 6 James O'Neil Cleveland, OH & Minnie Campbell Nova Scotia
O'NEIL, George, Jun 30 1895 Sex:M Child# Jeremiah O'Neil Ireland & Julia Sullivan Ireland
O'NEIL, George Andrew, Dec 9 1898 Sex:M Child# 5 Dennis O'Neil Nashua, NH & Mary Ann Shea Ireland
O'NEIL, Gloria Schoolcraft, Feb 25 1932 Sex:F Child# 2 (No Parents Listed)
O'NEIL, Grace, Mar 28 1902 Sex:F Child# 7 Jeremiah O'Neil Ireland & Julia Sullivan Ireland

O'NEIL, Helene, Aug 18 1901 Sex:F Child# 10 Jeremiah O'Neil Manchester, NH & Lucie Buckley Boston, MA
O'NEIL, Herbert, Oct 15 1904 Sex:M Child# 8 Jeremiah O'Neil Ireland & Julia Sullivan Ireland
O'NEIL, Irene, May 27 1921 Sex:F Child# 1 George O'Neil Nashua, NH & Mary Gray Nashua, NH
O'NEIL, James, Jun 6 1906 Sex:M Child# 5 James O'Neil Cleveland, OH & Minnie Campbell Nova Scotia
O'NEIL, James, Aug 1 1924 Sex:M Child# 3 Edwin O'Neil Nashua, NH & Helen Burns Nashua, NH
O'NEIL, James Arthur, Jun 4 1922 Sex:M Child# 2 John Arthur O'Neil Nashua, NH & Helen Greenleaf Merrimack, NH
O'NEIL, James Henry, Jun 10 1892 Sex:M Child# 1 Dennis O'Neil Nashua, NH & Mary A Shea Ireland
O'NEIL, James William, Dec 30 1926 Sex:M Child# 2 Frank O'Neil Milford, NH & Loretta Fahey Nashua, NH
O'NEIL, Jane Mary, May 17 1930 Sex:F Child# 3 Ralph F O'Neil Nashua, NH & Madeline A Thompson Nashua, NH
O'NEIL, Jeremiah, Jul 14 1899 Sex:M Child# 8 J J O'Neil Manchester, NH & Lucy Buckley Boston, MA
O'NEIL, Jeremiah F, Apr 14 1898 Sex:M Child# 5 Jeremiah O'Neil Ireland & Julia Sullivan Ireland
O'NEIL, John, Jul 9 1891 Sex:M Child# 2 Patrick O'Neil Ireland & Bessie Brennan Ireland
O'NEIL, John A, Nov 22 1897 Sex:M Child# 4 Dennis O'Neil Nashua, NH & Mary A Shea Ireland
O'NEIL, John Joseph, Feb 3 1904 Sex:M Child# 2 John O'Neil Ireland & Bridget Coyne Ireland
O'NEIL, Josephine, Jul 14 1899 Sex:F Child# 9 J J O'Neil Manchester, NH & Lucy Buckley Boston, MA
O'NEIL, Josia Elina, Jan 6 1889 Sex:F Child# 2 John O'Neil NY & Mary Hocke Ireland
O'NEIL, Kate, Dec 8 1893 Sex:F Child# 3 Jeremiah O'Neil Ireland & Julia Sullivan Ireland
O'NEIL, Kate I, Dec 12 1889 Sex:F Child# 1 Dennis O'Neil Nashua, NH & Lizzie F Edwards Manchester, NH
O'NEIL, Katherine M, May 9 1902 Sex:F Child# 1 John O'Neil Ireland & Bridget Coyne Ireland
O'NEIL, Lillian Teresa, Nov 15 1920 Sex:F Child# 1 George A O'Neil Nashua, NH & Florence T Harvey Lebanon, NH
O'NEIL, Lucille, Mar 7 1911 Sex:F Child# 11 Jeremiah O'Neil Ireland & Julia Sullivan Ireland
O'NEIL, Margaret Elizabeth, Mar 31 1894 Sex:F Child# 4 Patrick O'Neil Ireland & Bessie Brennan Ireland
O'NEIL, Margaret Flora, Mar 11 1889 Sex:F Child# 1 John O'Neil Ireland & Mary Malone Ireland
O'NEIL, Marion, Apr 26 1926 Sex:F Child# 3 L Arthur O'Neil Nashua, NH & Helen Greenleaf Merrimack, NH
O'NEIL, Mary, Jul 7 1895 Sex:F Child# 5 Patrick O'Neil Ireland & Bessie Brennan Ireland
O'NEIL, Mary Agnes, Feb 17 1905 Sex:F Child# 1 Frank J O'Neil Cornwall, Ont & Elizabeth B O'Brien St Albans, VT
O'NEIL, Mary Cataline, Mar 17 1893 Sex:F Child# 2 Michael H O'Neil E St Louis, IL & Mary E Galvin Dublin, Ireland
O'NEIL, Mary Elizabeth, Sep 8 1890 Sex:F Child# 2 John O'Neil Ireland & Mary Malone Ireland
O'NEIL, Mary Elizabeth, Nov 24 1922 Sex:F Child# 2 Edwin O'Neil Nashua, NH & Helen L Burns Nashua, NH
O'NEIL, Mary Lorreta, Oct 12 1897 Sex:F Child# 3 James O'Neil Cleveland, OH & Minnie L Campbell Nova Scotia
O'NEIL, Mildred, Dec 23 1908 Sex:F Child# 10 Jeremiah O'Neil Ireland & Julia Sullivan Ireland
O'NEIL, Paul, Oct 17 1926 Sex:M Child# 5 Frank O'Neil Nashua, NH & Mary Noonan Nashua, NH
O'NEIL, Philip, Jul 16 1891 Sex:M Child# 2 Jeremiah O'Neil Ireland & Julia Sullivan Ireland
O'NEIL, Ralph, Jul 7 1899 Sex:M Child# 7 W M O'Neil New York & M A O'Neil Nashua, NH
O'NEIL, Richard, Apr 6 1923 Sex:M Child# 4 Jerry F O'Neil Nashua, NH & Mary Noonan Nashua, NH
O'NEIL, Richard Francis, Mar 20 1922 Sex:M Child# 3 Francis O'Neil Nashua, NH & Mary Noonan Nashua, NH
O'NEIL, Robert, May 22 1901 Sex:M Child# 6 Jeremiah O'Neil Ireland & Julia Sullivan Lawrence, MA
O'NEIL, Robert, Jul 12 1918 Sex:M Child# 1 Frank J O'Neil Nashua, NH & Mary Moran Nashua, NH
O'NEIL, Robert, Oct 19 1921 Sex:M Child# 3 Charles H O'Neil Nashua, NH & Sarah A McLaughlin Bridgeport, CT
O'NEIL, Robert, Oct 8 1933 Sex:M Child# 1 Paul O'Neil Beverly, MA & Bernice Cressum Nashua, NH
O'NEIL, Russell Henry, Apr 23 1924 Sex:M Child# 2 Ralph F O'Neil Nashua, NH & Mad Thompson Nashua, NH
O'NEIL, Thomas Almon, May 31 1910 Sex:M Child# 7 James O'Neil Cleveland, OH & Minnie Campbell Nova Scotia
O'NEIL, Thomas Eugene, Dec 6 1916 Sex:M Child# 2 Eugene O'Neil Ireland & Mary Molloy Nashua, NH
O'NEIL, Thomas Galvin, May 10 1929 Sex:M Child# 5 Charles O'Neil Nashua, NH & Sarah McLaughlin Bridgeport, CT
O'NEIL, Unknown, Oct 22 1888 Sex:M Child# 3 William O'Neil New York & Mary Bowens Nashua, NH
O'NEIL, Unknown, Jul 7 1898 Sex:M Child# 7 Jeremiah O'Neil Manchester, NH & Lucy Buckley Peterborough, NH
O'NEIL, Unknown, Dec 5 1901 Sex:M Child# 4 Michael H O'Neil E St Louis, IL & Mary E Galvan Dublin, Ireland
O'NEIL, Unknown, Jan 27 1902 Sex:M Child# 8 William M O'Neil NY & Mary Burns Nashua, NH
O'NEIL, Unknown, Dec 11 1919 Sex:F Child# 1 John Art O'Neil Nashua, NH & Helen Greenleaf Merrimack, NH Stillborn
O'NEIL, Unknown, Jul 15 1920 Sex:F Child# 2 Francis O'Neil Nashua, NH & Mary Noonan Nashua, NH
O'NEIL, Unknown, Jul 10 1921 Sex:F Child# 1 Robert E O'Neil Nashua, NH & Mary Gillhooley Nashua, NH Stillborn
O'NEIL, Walter Wesley, Jr, Dec 17 1928 Sex:M Child# 2 W W O'Neil E Pepperell, MA & Eva Shepardson Mansfield, MA
O'NEILL, Harry M, Aug 6 1893 Sex:M Child# 5 Martin O'Neill Hollis, NH & Mary Burns Nashua, NH
O'NEILL, James William, Apr 25 1892 Sex:M Child# 3 John O'Neill Ireland & Maria Malone Ireland
O'SULLIVAN, Mary Kate, Feb 27 1893 Sex:F Child# 3 John O'Sullivan Ireland & Mary Flynn Ireland
OBAN, Clayton Clyde, Oct 23 1919 Sex:M Child# 1 Nathan C Oban Lebanon, NH & Geraldine R Elkin Nashua, NH
OBAN, Lorretta Catherine, Oct 23 1919 Sex:F Child# 2 Nathan C Oban Lebanon, NH & Geraldine R Elkin Nashua, NH
OBAN, Marie Lillian, Dec 19 1922 Sex:F Child# 4 Nathan Oban Lebanon, NH & Geraldine Elkins Nashua, NH
OBAN, Marjorie Lucille, Oct 28 1925 Sex:F Child# 3 Raymond Oban Lebanon, NH & Marg Anderson Lowell, MA
OBAN, Miriam Ruth, Dec 19 1927 Sex:F Child# 5 Nathan Oban Lebanon, NH & Geraldine Elkins Nashua, NH
OBAN, Raymond Paul, Oct 14 1918 Sex:M Child# 1 Raymond Oban W Lebanon, NH & Marguerite Anderson Lowell, MA
OBAN, Unknown, Jun 19 1924 Sex:M Child# 3 Nathan Oban Lebanon, NH & Geraldine Elkins Nashua, NH Stillborn
OBAN, William Nathan, Mar 5 1920 Sex:M Child# 2 Raymond H Oban Lebanon, NH & Marguerite Anderson Lowell, MA
OBEA, George Henry, Apr 18 1927 Sex:M Child# 1 George Obea Pepperell, MA & Olive Smith Pepperell, MA
OBEA, Unknown, Jun 15 1926 Sex:M Child# 1 Frank Obea Pepperell, MA & Alice Toomey Pepperell, MA
OBEN, Gladys May, Oct 28 1906 Sex:F Child# 7 Henry J Oben Canada & Lillian Martin Hartford, CT
OBER, Donald Francis, Oct 25 1894 Sex:M Child# Frank Ober NH & Sarah Jenkins NH
OBER, Mabel Almira, Jan 10 1890 Sex:F Child# 1 H J Ober Chazy, NY & Mabel B Long Burlington, VT
OBIN, Albina Beatrice, Mar 21 1923 Sex:F Child# 8 Edward Obin Plattsburg, NY & Georgianna Marquis Nashua, NH
OBIN, George Louis, Apr 9 1921 Sex:M Child# Edward Obin Plattsburg, NY & Georgianna Marquis Nashua, NH
OBIN, Georgianna Christine, Nov 9 1919 Sex:F Child# 6 Edward Obin New York & Georgianna Marquis Nashua, NH
OBIN, J Edouard Augusta, Jul 12 1914 Sex:M Child# 4 Edouard Obin New York & Georgiana Marquis Nashua, NH
OBIN, Mabel, Oct 31 1897 Sex:F Child# Lewis Obin Canada & Mary Lature NY

OBIN, Marie Eveline D, Oct 29 1910 Sex:F Child# 2 Joseph Obin New York & Marie Gendron Canada
OBIN, Marie Pearl Louise, Jun 17 1912 Sex:F Child# 3 Edouard Obin New York & Georgianna Marquis Canada
OBIN, Marie Rose Cecile, Apr 15 1918 Sex:F Child# 4 Joseph Obin Plattsburg, NY & Mary Gendron Quaticoke, PQ
OBIN, Mary Irene, Jun 8 1911 Sex:F Child# 2 J Edward Obin Plattsburg, NY & Georgianna Marquis Nashua, NH
OBLICKENSKI, Alphonse, May 29 1930 Sex:M Child# 6 Joseph Oblickenski Poland & Frances Ukenawich Poland
OCKSHOM, John, May 11 1916 Sex:M Child# 2 Denis Ockshom Russia & Mackolo Russia
ODESSE, Rose Eva, Sep 3 1924 Sex:F Child# 1 Emery Odesse Canada & Marie Turgeon Canada
ODOMAITIS, Marianna, Jun 26 1913 Sex:F Child# 3 John Odomaitis Russia & Anna Monkewicouta Russia
OFFSONK, Edwina, May 18 1916 Sex:F Child# 1 Joseph Offsonk Russia & Christina Stanofka Russia
OFSONK, Binnie, Jul 27 1921 Sex:M Child# 6 Joseph Ofsonk Poland & Christina Stanank Poland
OFSONK, Joseph, Apr 23 1917 Sex:M Child# 2 Joseph Ofsonk Russia & Christina Stanova Russia
OFSONK, Yanina, May 24 1918 Sex:F Child# 3 Joseph Ofsonk Russia & Christine Stanofka Russia
OFSOUK, Vladislav, May 23 1920 Sex:M Child# 5 Joseph Ofsouk Poland Russia & Christina Stanauk Poland Russia
OFSOUK, Vlarine, May 27 1920 Sex:F Child# 4 Joseph Ofsouk Poland Russia & Christina Stanauk Poland Russia
OGAGE, Martha, Jul 29 1909 Sex:F Child# 1 Stanislas Ogage Russia & Annie Urbanovitch Russia
OGILVIE, Joan Olive, Dec 17 1932 Sex:F Child# 1 Clayton Ogilvie Brattleboro, VT & Mildred Rich N Andover, MA
OGILVIE, Mildred Arlene, Aug 26 1909 Sex:F Child# 2 Arthur A Ogilvie Vermont & Bertha Underhill Hudson, NH
OGILVIE, Shirley Ann, Oct 8 1934 Sex:F Child# 2 Clayton Ogilvie Brattleboro, VT & Mildred Rich N Andover, MA
OHANNASIAN, Hernanie, Jan 26 1915 Sex:F Child# 3 Kerkor Ohannasian Armenia & Astig Ohannasian Armenia
OKALOWICZ, John, Jul 27 1913 Sex:M Child# 1 William Okalowicz Russia & Teklo Berciute Russia
OKLOWICH, Julius, Dec 17 1920 Sex:M Child# 3 William Oklowich Lithuania & Thecla Bartis Lithuania
OKLOWY, Wilolas, Nov 28 1916 Sex:M Child# 2 William Oklowy Russia & Teklo Batise Russia
OKMAN, John, Sep 21 1895 Sex:M Child# 2 Peter Okman Poland & Katie Zalin Poland
OKMAN, Mary Monica, Feb 18 1897 Sex:F Child# 2 Peter Okman Russia & Katie Zalomes Russia
OKOLOVICH, Robert John, Jul 7 1935 Sex:M Child# 1 John Okolovich Nashua, NH & Helen Twadarsky Portage, PA
OLDFIELD, Unknown, Jun 19 1899 Sex:M Child# 5 Harry Oldfield Canada & Annie Laaura Warden Canada
OLECHNOWICZ, Leonidi, Apr 22 1917 Sex:M Child# 2 Vincente Olechnowicz Russia & Mary Janowski Russia
OLENA, Arthur Raymond, Sep 13 1918 Sex:M Child# 2 William J Olena Sciota, NY & Ida Santerre Ayer Jct, MA
OLENA, Irene Rosella, Jun 30 1923 Sex:F Child# 1 Willis A Olena Nashua, NH & Antoinette Murauckas Germany
OLIGNEY, Elmire I, Sep 13 1894 Sex:F Child# 6 Wilbur Oligney NY & Rose Goyette NY
OLIGNY, Cybille, Apr 2 1903 Sex:F Child# 8 Wilber Oligny Chazy, NY & Rosalie Goyette Sciota, NY
OLIGNY, Joseph E, Oct 13 1897 Sex:M Child# 7 Wilbur Oligny Chasey, NY & Rose Goyette Chazy, NY
OLINSKI, Philip Richard, Sep 29 1904 Sex:M Child# 1 Philip M Olinski Canada & Louise Jordan Mass
OLIVER, Audrey Althea, Jun 16 1933 Sex:F Child# 5 Carl Oliver Athal, MA & Beaulah Chapman Westfield, MA
OLIVIER, Lillian A, May 23 1901 Sex:F Child# 1 Nactair Olivier Manchester, NH & Regina Boule Nashua, NH
OLSEN, Harold Bailey, Nov 19 1928 Sex:M Child# 1 H B Olsen Lexington, MA & Dorrice Bradish Perkinsville, VT
OLSEN, Henry Arthur, Nov 24 1896 Sex:M Child# 5 Charles Emil Olsen Sweden & Emma Rosendel Sweden
OLSEN, Janet, Jul 17 1930 Sex:F Child# 2 Harold Olsen Lexington, MA & Dorice Bradish Perkinsville, VT
OLSEN, Ruth, Apr 28 1894 Sex:F Child# 2 Charles Olsen Sweden & A E Rosendal Sweden
OLSON, Bernard, Jul 22 1915 Sex:M Child# 2 George Olson Sweden & M Louise Fraser Canada
OLSON, Doris Estelle, Apr 21 1914 Sex:F Child# 2 George Olson Sweden & M Louise Fraser Canada
OLSON, Marie Clara Rina, Mar 1 1924 Sex:F Child# 1 Henry Olson NH & Albertine Dube Canada
OLSON, Richard Elmer, Sep 5 1912 Sex:M Child# 1 George Olson Sweden & Marie Louis Fraser Canada
OLSON, Robert Louis Joseph, May 20 1918 Sex:M Child# 4 George Olson Sweden & Marie Louise Fraser Canada
OLSON, Venan, Jun 1 1928 Sex:M Child# 7 Joseph Olson Poland & C Stanowska Poland
OLZANSKA, Zofia, Aug 24 1914 Sex:F Child# 5 Joseph Olzanska Russia & Apolinio Azekay Russia
OMARA, Philip Robert, Apr 8 1909 Sex:M Child# 5 Philip Omara Ireland & Delia Gratton Ireland
ONOROSKI, Boleslof, May 29 1910 Sex:m Child# 2 Wladyslaw Onoroski Russia & Katarzyna Slosek Austria
ONOROSKI, Florentyna, Nov 14 1921 Sex:F Child# 7 Vladyshr Onoroski Poland & Katyrzyna Slosek Poland
ONOROSKI, Frank, Nov 2 1911 Sex:M Child# 2 William Onoroski Russia & Kate Stuski Austria
ONOROSKI, John, Aug 27 1913 Sex:M Child# 4 Vladislaw Onoroski Russia & Karitzyna Slosek Austria
ONOROSKI, Unknown, Sep 6 1920 Sex:F Child# 6 Wadyslaw Onoroski Poland & Katarzyne Slouk Poland
ONOROSKI, Unknown, Aug 20 1929 Sex:M Child# 11 Vladyslaw Onoroski Poland & Katzyna Szlosek Poland
ONOWSKI, Joany, Feb 8 1927 Sex:M Child# 7 W Onowski Poland & Katyrzena Slocek Poland
ONOWSKI, Stanislaus, Apr 3 1923 Sex:M Child# 9 Vladyslaw Onowski Poland & Katheryna Slosek Poland
OPICCI, Mary Rosa Lutia, Aug 14 1898 Sex:F Child#  Ferdinando Opicci Palma, Italy & Santa Blondi Palma, Italy
OPIE, Frederick Romani, Sep 27 1929 Sex:M Child# 1 Frederick James Opie Quincy, MA & Rita Romani Milford, NH
OPOWICH, John, Jul 19 1909 Sex:M Child# 1 Frank Opowich Russia & Antoinette Galanoski Russia
OPPICI, Rosie Anna, Aug 30 1904 Sex:F Child# 4 Ferdinand Oppici Italy & Santa Blondi Italy
OPPIEI, Louisa, Mar 14 1902 Sex:F Child# 2 Ernesto Oppiei Italy & Bertina Amarilli Italy
ORASTE, Christophas, Aug 19 1911 Sex:M Child# 1 William Oraste
ORBON, Frank, Nov 8 1913 Sex:M Child# 1 John Orbon Russia & Arshula Yaxt Russia
ORDE, Alan Locke, Jr, Mar 7 1932 Sex:M Child# 2 Alan Orde Lynn, MA & Beryl Reed Webster, NH
ORDE, David Melvin, Jun 26 1929 Sex:M Child# 1 Alan Orde Lynn, MA & Bearl Reed Berlin, NH
ORDWAY, Arthur Wallace, Feb 27 1911 Sex:M Child# 1 Carl W Ordway Merrimack, NH & Mable Hills Nashua, NH
ORDWAY, George Clayton, Mar 27 1913 Sex:M Child# 2 Carl Ordway Merrimack, NH & Mabel Hills Nashua, NH
ORENS, Prescott Raymond, Jan 17 1928 Sex:M Child# 1 Percy George Orens Brookfield, MA & Hor' Blackenberg Nashua, NH
ORESTIS, Mary, Mar 28 1916 Sex:F Child# 3 Vasilios Orestis Greece & Katherine Pappas Greece
ORLOWSKI, John B, Jan 13 1913 Sex:M Child# 3 John Orlowski Russia & Mary Stancik Russia
ORRIS, Ari William, Oct 15 1915 Sex:M Child# 1 Sam Orris Russia & Rebecca Pressman Russia
ORZECHOWSKI, Mary Kate, Feb 25 1897 Sex:F Child# 1 W Orzechowski Poland & Kejoty Orzechowski Poland
OSBORN, Charles R, Sep 8 1893 Sex:M Child# 4 George O Osborn Nashua, NH & Ellen Bowers Maine
OSGOOD, Charles George, Sep 9 1931 Sex:M Child# 3 Robert F Osgood Nashua, NH & Emily Wright Newport, NH

OSGOOD, Dexter Trow, Feb 3 1907 Sex:M Child# 1 Horace E Osgood Canada & Ethel H Trow Nashua, NH
OSGOOD, Dorothy, Mar 5 1909 Sex:F Child#  Horace E Osgood Canada & Ethel Trow Nashua, NH
OSGOOD, Dorothy, Feb 6 1919 Sex:F Child# 1 Herman A Osgood Hyde Park, MA & Annie Davenport England
OSGOOD, Earl Abbott, Apr 20 1904 Sex:M Child# 1 Herman A Osgood Lowell, MA & Nellie Barclay Hyde Park, MA
OSGOOD, Elizabeth Louise, Jun 25 1933 Sex:F Child# 4 Robert F Osgood Nashua, NH & Emily Wright Newport, NH
OSGOOD, Fred, Feb 15 1897 Sex:M Child# 2 Fred J Osgood Canada & Grace Nutter N Weare, NH
OSGOOD, Gladys Mathilda, Jul 12 1903 Sex:F Child# 3 Benjamin B E Osgood Canada & Mary J Suitor Canada
OSGOOD, Howard, Feb 6 1897 Sex:M Child# 1 Edward Osgood Canada & Nellie E Gorham Canada
OSGOOD, Mildred Leda, Aug 24 1931 Sex:F Child# 2 Frederick Osgood Nashua, NH & Mildred Bradley Nashua, NH
OSGOOD, Robert, Jun 26 1906 Sex:M Child# 3 Benjamin G E Osgood Canada & Mary Jane Suitor Victory, VT
OSGOOD, Robert Fellows, Jr, Aug 3 1927 Sex:M Child# 1 R F Osgood Nashua, NH & Emily E Wright Newport, NH
OSGOOD, Roger Hale, Nov 2 1912 Sex:M Child# 4 Horace E Osgood Canada & Ethel Hale Trow Nashua, NH
OSGOOD, Ruth, Jan 21 1911 Sex:F Child# 2 Horace Osgood Canada & Ethel Trow Nashua, NH
OSGOOD, Shirley Helen, Nov 23 1925 Sex:F Child# 1 Frederick Osgood Nashua, NH & Mildred Bradley Nashua, NH
OSGOOD, William Edward, Mar 24 1926 Sex:M Child# 5 Horace Osgood Canada & Ethel H Trow Nashua, NH
OSINER, Emmabelle June, Oct 7 1928 Sex:F Child# 5 F James Osiner Bridgewater, VT & Olivine Marois Canada
OSMER, Frances Olivene, Jan 22 1922 Sex:F Child# 2 Frank J Osmer Taftsville, VT & Olivine Marois Canada
OSMER, Harriet Maria, Sep 21 1923 Sex:F Child# 2 Frank J Osmer Taftsville, VT & Olivene Marois Canada
OSMER, Lester Earl, Sep 18 1930 Sex:M Child# 6 Frank J Osmer Bridgewater, VT & Olivene Marois Canada
OSMER, Rita May Ruth, Jun 10 1927 Sex:F Child# 4 Frank J Osmer Bridgewater, VT & Olivine Marois Canada
OSTBURG, Richard Smith, Feb 6 1922 Sex:M Child# 1 Ralph A Ostburg, Jr Boston, MA & Dorothy Smith Holidaysburg
OSTERIOS, Maria, Aug 11 1915 Sex:F Child# 2 George Osterios Greece & Trigona Demetris Greece
OSTRANDA, Clara Eva, Jan 14 1896 Sex:F Child# 1 Charles E Ostranda Sweden & Elvina P Samelson Sweden
OSTRANDER, Lillian May, May 13 1906 Sex:F Child# 1 Sumner Ostrander Hoosic Falls, NY & Abbie A Green Billerica
OSTRANDER, William Arthur, May 30 1909 Sex:M Child# 2 Sumner A Ostrander Williamston, MA & Alice A Green Bille
OTIS, Roland Eugene, Aug 8 1933 Sex:M Child# 1 (No Parents Listed)
OTIS, Unknown, Jul 14 1892 Sex:F Child# 5 Andrew M Otis Nashua, NH & Etta Taylor Merrimack, NH
OUCHDAVINIS, Joseph, Jan 30 1913 Sex:M Child# 6 John Ouchdavinis Russia & Eva Sustavikos Russia
OUCHDAVINUS, Theophila, Jun 25 1915 Sex:F Child# 5 Stanley Ouchdavinus Russia & Ant Ouchdavinus Russia
OUELLETTE, Ernestine Josephine, May 3 1905 Sex:F Child# 6 Arthur Ouelette Canada & Josephine Belanger Canada
OUELETTE, Georges, Jun 28 1896 Sex:M Child# 1 George Ouelette Canada & Celina Belanger Canada
OUELLETTE, Joseph E, Jun 29 1889 Sex:M Child# 2 Joseph Ouelette Canada & Marie Marchand Canada
OUELLETTE, Joseph H, Jan 12 1900 Sex:M Child# 5 Alfred Ouelette Nashua, NH & Denise Caissy Canada
OUELETTE, Odias, Jan 17 1894 Sex:M Child# 5 Alphonse Ouelette Canada & Hermine Gagnon Canada
OUELLETTE, Raymond Nelson, Jun 11 1935 Sex:M Child# 2 Nelson Ouelette Nashua, NH & Dorothy Lamb Nashua, NH
OUELLET, Marie Clarie A, Oct 29 1910 Sex:F Child# 5 France Ouellet Canada & Osilia Levesque Canada
OUELLETTE, Adelard, Jan 20 1897 Sex:M Child# 8 Thomas Ouellette Canada & Philomene Godin Canada
OUELLETTE, Adelard Joseph, Jan 5 1917 Sex:M Child# 2 Adelard Ouellette Vermont & Philomene Morency Vermont
OUELLETTE, Albert, Jul 20 1890 Sex:M Child# 4 Octave Ouellette Canada & Marie Pinette Canada
OUELLETTE, Albert, Apr 5 1892 Sex:M Child# 1 Henry Ouellette NY & Delphine Marotte NY
OUELLETTE, Albert, Apr 5 1904 Sex:M Child# 5 Arthur Ouellette Canada & Josephine Belanger Canada
OUELLETTE, Albert Arthur, Apr 3 1908 Sex:M Child# 8 Alexis Ouellette Canada & Victoria Levesque Canada
OUELLETTE, Albert Joseph, Sep 11 1930 Sex:M Child# 3 Alfred Ouellette Mass & Bernadette Hickey Lowell, MA
OUELLETTE, Anna, Feb 3 1898 Sex:F Child# 9 Thomas Ouellette Canada & Philomene Godin Canada
OUELLETTE, Antoine, Apr 26 1907 Sex:M Child# 7 Alexis Ouellette Canada & Victoria Levesque Canada
OUELLETTE, Antonia Alice, Jan 5 1893 Sex:F Child# 2 Alcide Ouellette Canada & Victoria Levesque Canada
OUELLETTE, Armine, Dec 2 1900 Sex:F Child# 5 Joseph Ouellette Canada & Armine Gagnon Canada
OUELLETTE, Arsene William, Sep 13 1913 Sex:M Child# 6 Arthur Ouellette Canada & Marie L Ouellette Canada
OUELLETTE, Arthur, Mar 9 1898 Sex:M Child# 2 Fortunat Ouellette Canada & Rosalie Levesque Canada
OUELLETTE, Arthur, May 26 1899 Sex:M Child# 1 Arthur Ouellette Canada & Donuthilde Ladry Canada
OUELLETTE, Arthur, Feb 26 1909 Sex:M Child# 3 Francis Ouellette Canada & Oselia Levesque Canada
OUELLETTE, Arthur Albert, Oct 18 1910 Sex:M Child# 10 Alexis Ouellette Canada & Victoria Levesque Canada
OUELLETTE, Arthur Andre A, Dec 8 1910 Sex:M Child# 4 Arthur Ouellette Canada & Marie L Ouellette Canada
OUELLETTE, Arthur Trefle, Dec 12 1911 Sex:M Child# 11 Alexis Ouellette Canada & Victoria Levesque Canada
OUELLETTE, Aurore Celina E, Sep 11 1908 Sex:F Child# 2 Arthur Ouellette St Pacome, PQ & Marie L Ouellette Canada
OUELLETTE, Beatrice, Aug 5 1924 Sex:F Child# 4 Arthur Ouellette Nashua, NH & Anna Meretta Nashua, NH
OUELLETTE, Blanche Germaine, Apr 24 1909 Sex:F Child# 9 Alexis Ouellette Canada & Victoria Levesque Canada
OUELLETTE, Camille Joseph E, Nov 11 1906 Sex:M Child# 2 Camille Ouellette Canada & Georgiana April Canada
OUELLETTE, Carmen Beatrice, Mar 13 1920 Sex:F Child# 2 Cyprien Ouellette Nashua, NH & Marianne Jean Nashua, NH
OUELLETTE, Cecile Andrea, Feb 17 1905 Sex:F Child# 5 Wilfrid Ouellette Canada & Cordelia Lucas Canada
OUELLETTE, Cecile Pauline, Sep 7 1934 Sex:F Child# 1 Adrien Ouellette Nashua, NH & Cecile Dornellier Lowell, MA
OUELLETTE, Cecile Simonne, Oct 2 1921 Sex:F Child# 2 William Ouellette Chazy, NY & Wilhelmine Ouellette Canada
OUELLETTE, Charles N, Mar 29 1887 Sex:M Child# 1 Adolphe Ouellette P Q & Anna Michaud P Q
OUELLETTE, Charles Philippe, Jul 31 1907 Sex:M Child# 6 Joseph Ouellette Canada & Zoe Sirois Canada
OUELLETTE, Claire, Oct 16 1934 Sex:F Child# 4 David Ouellette Canada & Alice Levesque Nashua, NH
OUELLETTE, Claire Joan, Jan 31 1932 Sex:F Child# 3 Odios Ouellette US & Florida Dechenes Canada
OUELLETTE, Claire Viola, Sep 10 1919 Sex:F Child# 3 Sylvio Ouellette Canada & Delisia Lesage Nashua, NH
OUELLETTE, David Alfred, Dec 2 1909 Sex:M Child# 3 Arthur Ouellette Canada & Marie E Ouelette Canada
OUELLETTE, Demetrius Rene, Jul 4 1909 Sex:M Child# 2 Omer Ouellette Bay City, MI & Marie L Dube Canada
OUELLETTE, Dora Denise, Feb 7 1913 Sex:F Child# 4 Joseph Ouellette Canada & Anna Berube Canada
OUELLETTE, Earl Odrose, Sep 23 1922 Sex:M Child# 3 Odrose Ouellette Nashua, NH & Florida Duchesneau Nashua, NH
OUELLETTE, Edouard Albert, Oct 13 1909 Sex:M Child# 7 Joseph Ouellette Canada & Zoe Sirois Canada
OUELLETTE, Edourdina, Jan 30 1892 Sex:F Child# 3 Joseph Ouellette Canada & Thenais Marchand Canada

OUELLETTE, Ernest, Jan 6 1903 Sex:M Child# 2 Eddy Ouellette Chazy, NY & Lillie Duchesneau Nashua, NH
OUELLETTE, Ernest, Mar 25 1904 Sex:M Child# 3 Ernest Ouellette Canada & Hectorine Boisvert Canada
OUELLETTE, Ernest Joseph Thomas, Feb 10 1924 Sex:M Child# 1 Ernest Ouellette Old Town, ME & Bertha Guerrette NH
OUELLETTE, Eugene G, Nov 17 1897 Sex:M Child# 3 Joseph Ouellette Canada & Marie L Lemire Canada
OUELLETTE, Eva, Mar 5 1900 Sex:F Child# 2 Germain Ouellette Canada & Parmelia Thibault Canada
OUELLETTE, Eva, Apr 23 1901 Sex:F Child# 8 Damas Ouellette Canada & Ephemie Cote Canada
OUELLETTE, Eva Eugenie, Jan 1 1903 Sex:F Child# 1 Alfred Ouellette Canada & Marie L Dube Canada
OUELLETTE, Ferdinand, May 30 1906 Sex:M Child# 6 Wilfrid Ouellette Canada & Cordelie Lucas Canada Stillborn
OUELLETTE, Frederic J O, Nov 12 1898 Sex:M Child# 4 Joseph Ouellette Canada & Marie Lemire Canada
OUELLETTE, George Vital, Aug 15 1904 Sex:M Child# 1 George Ouellette Canada & Georgiana Drouin Canada
OUELLETTE, Gerard, Jan 9 1916 Sex:M Child# 1 Adelard Ouellette Barre, VT & Philomene Morency Morgan Center, VT
OUELLETTE, Gerard Sylvio, Oct 8 1930 Sex:M Child# 2 Sylvio Ouellette Epping, NH & Aurore Desmarais Nashua, NH
OUELLETTE, Gerard, Jr, May 14 1933 Sex:M Child# 1 Gerard Ouellette Canada & Gabrielle Ledoux Nashua, NH
OUELLETTE, Germaine Beatrice, Aug 6 1907 Sex:F Child# 7 Wilfrid Ouellette Canada & Cordelia Lucas Canada
OUELLETTE, Gertie, Dec 31 1893 Sex:F Child# 11 Marcel Ouellette US & Marie Marotte US
OUELLETTE, Gloria Catherine, Apr 17 1933 Sex:F Child# 2 Romeo Ouellette Lawrence, MA & Kathleen Dunn Scotland
OUELLETTE, Grace, May 12 1904 Sex:F Child# 1 Fred Ouellette Canada & Eva Woodward Nashua, NH
OUELLETTE, Helene Martha, Feb 27 1911 Sex:F Child# 3 Omer Ouellette Bay City, MI & Marie Louise Dube Canada
OUELLETTE, Henry, Jun 24 1902 Sex:M Child# 11 Thomas Ouellette Canada & P Gaudin Canada
OUELLETTE, Henry Patrick, Aug 31 1910 Sex:M Child# 1 Joseph Ouellette US & Anna Dufour US
OUELLETTE, Irene Estelle, May 6 1917 Sex:F Child# 2 Arthur Ouellette Nashua, NH & Annie Marrott Nashua, NH
OUELLETTE, J Adrien Alphonse, Mar 25 1922 Sex:M Child# 4 Adelard Ouellette Vermont & Philomene Morency Vermont
OUELLETTE, J B Augustin, Jul 25 1900 Sex:M Child# 2 Joseph Ouellette Canada & Anna Berube Canada
OUELLETTE, J Normand Henry, Jun 1 1922 Sex:M Child# 2 Albert Ouellette NH & Marguerite Downey Mass
OUELLETTE, Jean Baptiste, Aug 31 1896 Sex:M Child# 12 William Ouellette Canada & Josephine Gagnon Canada
OUELLETTE, Jean Baptiste, Sep 27 1897 Sex:M Child# 4 Joseph Ouellette Canada & Zoe Sirois Canada
OUELLETTE, Jean Raymond, May 23 1921 Sex:M Child# 3 Cyprien Ouellette Nashua, NH & M A Jean Nashua, NH
OUELLETTE, Jos Albert Octave, Dec 7 1920 Sex:M Child# 1 Albert Ouellette NH & M L Yvonne Sylvain Canada
OUELLETTE, Jos Andres Robert, Aug 17 1934 Sex:M Child# 7 Leo Ouellette Canada & Eva Dupont Canada
OUELLETTE, Jos Walter Eugene, Jun 6 1917 Sex:M Child# 6 Omar Ouellette Michigan & Marie Louise Dube Canada
OUELLETTE, Joseph, Jul 28 1889 Sex:M Child# 6 Charles Ouellette Canada & Emilie Peltier Canada
OUELLETTE, Joseph, Aug 15 1896 Sex:M Child# 3 Alfred Ouellette Canada & Denise Caissy Canada
OUELLETTE, Joseph, Aug 15 1908 Sex:M Child# 8 Wilfrid Ouellette Canada & Cordelia Lucas Canada Stillborn
OUELLETTE, Joseph, Feb 5 1909 Sex:M Child# 5 Eddie Ouellette New York & Lillienne Duchesneau NH
OUELLETTE, Joseph A, Mar 14 1890 Sex:M Child# 3 Adolphe Ouellette Canada & Anna Michard Canada
OUELLETTE, Joseph A Cyprien, Nov 8 1899 Sex:M Child# Arthur Ouellette Canada & Josephine Belanger Canada
OUELLETTE, Joseph A E, Jul 25 1912 Sex:M Child# 4 Joseph Ouellette Canada & Margaret DeRoche PEI
OUELLETTE, Joseph A Maurice, Sep 5 1931 Sex:M Child# 6 Arthur Ouellette Canada & Eva Marois Cambridge, MA
OUELLETTE, Joseph Adelard, Oct 5 1895 Sex:M Child# 1 Joseph Ouellette Canada & Mary Lemire Canada
OUELLETTE, Joseph Adrien, Nov 8 1914 Sex:M Child# 5 Omer Ouellette Bay City, MI & Marie L Dube Canada
OUELLETTE, Joseph Albert, May 31 1900 Sex:M Child# 1 Joseph Ouellette Canada & Cedelia Beaulieu Canada
OUELLETTE, Joseph Alexis, Jan 18 1901 Sex:M Child# 2 Alexis Ouellette Canada & Victoria Levesque Canada
OUELLETTE, Joseph Alexis A, Jun 23 1903 Sex:M Child# 4 Alexis Ouellette Canada & Victoria Levesque Canada
OUELLETTE, Joseph Alexis A, Sep 19 1905 Sex:M Child# 6 Alexis Ouellette Canada & Victoria Levesque Canada
OUELLETTE, Joseph Alfred, Nov 11 1902 Sex:M Child# 2 Alfred Ouellette Canada & Joseph Boisvert Canada
OUELLETTE, Joseph Alphonse W, May 31 1908 Sex:M Child# 1 Joseph Ouellette Canada & Margaret Roche PEI
OUELLETTE, Joseph E, Sep 6 1895 Sex:M Child# 4 Joseph Ouellette Canada & Marie Marchand Canada
OUELLETTE, Joseph E Armand, Oct 23 1896 Sex:M Child# 1 Alexis Ouellette Canada & Josephine Nadeau Canada
OUELLETTE, Joseph Ed A, Jan 7 1902 Sex:M Child# 3 Joseph Ouellette Canada & Anna Berube Canada
OUELLETTE, Joseph G, Feb 16 1894 Sex:M Child# 5 Adolphe Ouellette Canada & Anna Michaud Canada
OUELLETTE, Joseph Louis Emile, Jun 11 1912 Sex:M Child# 5 Arthur Ouellette Canada & Marie Louise Ouellet Canada
OUELLETTE, Joseph Marcellin, Jul 26 1896 Sex:M Child# 1 Fortunat Ouellette Canada & Rosalie Leveque Canada
OUELLETTE, Joseph N, Jan 9 1895 Sex:M Child# 2 Alfred Ouellette Canada & Denis Caissey Canada
OUELLETTE, Joseph Paul Gerard, Sep 14 1923 Sex:M Child# 1 Napoleon Ouellette Canada & Marie Anna Corbin Canada
OUELLETTE, Joseph Raymond, Jun 6 1904 Sex:M Child# 5 Luc Ouellette Canada & Eugenie Peltier Canada
OUELLETTE, Joseph Romeo, Feb 19 1899 Sex:M Child# 3 Luc Ouellette Canada & Eugenie Peltier Canada
OUELLETTE, Joseph Theodore, Apr 12 1911 Sex:M Child# 3 Joseph Ouellette Canada & Margaret Derocher PEI
OUELLETTE, Joseph Wilfrid, Nov 27 1899 Sex:M Child# 5 Joseph Ouellette Canada & Mary Lemire Canada
OUELLETTE, Julia Mary, Feb 8 1919 Sex:F Child# 2 Alexis Ouellette Canada & Georgiana Boucher Canada
OUELLETTE, Juliette Beatrice, Sep 24 1905 Sex:F Child# 2 George Ouellette Canada & Georgiana Drouin Canada
OUELLETTE, Leare Fleurette, Mar 13 1930 Sex:F Child# 4 Wilfred Ouellette Nashua, NH & Raymonde Laroche Nashua, NH
OUELLETTE, Leo, Dec 26 1903 Sex:M Child# 4 Wilfred Ouellette Canada & Cordelia Lucas Canada
OUELLETTE, Leonard, Jun 14 1893 Sex:M Child# 2 Henry Ouellette US & Delphine Marotte US
OUELLETTE, Lilian, Sep 1 1896 Sex:F Child# 7 Octave Ouellette Canada & Marie Pinnette Canada
OUELLETTE, Lillian Doris, May 31 1920 Sex:F Child# 1 Alfred Ouellette E Douglas, MA & Bernice Hickey Lowell, MA
OUELLETTE, Lionel Albert, Sep 29 1921 Sex:M Child# 1 Andrew Ouellette Canada & Clothilde Fredette Canada
OUELLETTE, Lionel Octave, Dec 13 1921 Sex:M Child# 2 Arthur Ouellette Canada & Eva Marois Mass
OUELLETTE, Louis Achille, Sep 21 1902 Sex:M Child# 5 Joseph Ouellette Canada & Zoe Sirois Canada
OUELLETTE, Louis Edouard, Mar 8 1902 Sex:M Child# 3 Alexis Ouellette Canada & Victoria Levesque Canada
OUELLETTE, Louise Philip, Oct 6 1909 Sex:F Child# 2 Joseph Ouellette Canada & Marguerite Deroche PEI
OUELLETTE, Lucile Amelia, Dec 17 1913 Sex:F Child# 1 Edouard J Ouellette Canada & Amelia Beauregard US
OUELLETTE, Lucille, Sep 15 1920 Sex:F Child# 1 Ozias Ouellette Nashua, NH & Florida Duchesneau Nashua, NH
OUELLETTE, M Celina Dorina, Nov 26 1912 Sex:F Child# 2 David Ouellette Canada & Leona Pelletier NH

OUELLETTE, M E Estelle Yvette, Jul 21 1915 Sex:F Child# 2 Sylvio Ouellette Canada & Denisca Lesage NH
OUELLETTE, M Gertrude C J A, Jun 20 1919 Sex:F Child# 7 Omer Ouellette Bay City, MI & Mary Louise Dube Canada
OUELLETTE, M Regina Camille, Apr 30 1922 Sex:F Child# 2 Andrew Ouellette Nashua, NH & Irene Pelletier Canada
OUELLETTE, Mable Mary, May 25 1905 Sex:F Child# 8 John H Ouellette New York & Hattie V Porter New York
OUELLETTE, Marguerite Simonne, May 24 1920 Sex:F Child# 1 Arthur Ouellette Canada & Eva Marois Concord, MA
OUELLETTE, Marie, Jul 6 1921 Sex:F Child# 2 Odias Ouellette Nashua, NH & Florida Duchneau Canada
OUELLETTE, Marie, Mar 17 1933 Sex:F Child# 1 Omer Ouellette Canada & Rose Gendron Nashua, NH
OUELLETTE, Marie A, Dec 21 1891 Sex:F Child# 4 Adolphe Ouellette Canada & Anna Michaud Canada
OUELLETTE, Marie A D, May 18 1898 Sex:F Child# 1 Joseph Ouellette Canada & Anna Berube Canada
OUELLETTE, Marie Alice, Feb 16 1898 Sex:F Child# 2 Joseph Ouellette Canada & Marie Fournier Canada
OUELLETTE, Marie Alma, Feb 19 1899 Sex:F Child# 1 Germain Ouellette Canada & Parmela Thibault Canada
OUELLETTE, Marie Alma I, Jul 12 1907 Sex:F Child# 1 Arthur Ouellette Canada & M Louise Ouellette Canada
OUELLETTE, Marie Anne L, Oct 31 1907 Sex:F Child# 2 Francis Ouellette Canada & Ozelia Levesque Canada
OUELLETTE, Marie Aurore, Jan 16 1892 Sex:F Child# 4 Alphonse Ouellette Canada & Armine Gagnon Canada
OUELLETTE, Marie Beatrice, Aug 17 1894 Sex:F Child# 5 Octave Ouellette Canada & Marie Pinette Canada
OUELLETTE, Marie C G, Feb 25 1902 Sex:F Child# 3 Joseph Ouellette Canada & Marie Fournier Canada
OUELLETTE, Marie D, Jul 9 1895 Sex:F Child# 1 Luc Ouellette Canada & Eugenia Peltier Canada
OUELLETTE, Marie D, Feb 12 1898 Sex:F Child# Alfred Ouellette Canada & Denis Caissy Canada
OUELLETTE, Marie Delvina, Dec 20 1891 Sex:F Child# 2 Pierre Ouellette Canada & Amanda Marsevault Canada
OUELLETTE, Marie Doris Javine, Oct 8 1930 Sex:F Child# 6 Leo Ouellette Canada & Eva Dupont Canada
OUELLETTE, Marie E E, Nov 11 1896 Sex:F Child# 2 Joseph Ouellette Canada & Mary Lemire Canada
OUELLETTE, Marie Emma, Nov 25 1892 Sex:F Child# 2 Joseph Ouellette Canada & Zoe Sirois Canada
OUELLETTE, Marie Eva, Sep 4 1895 Sex:F Child# 1 Joseph Ouellette Canada & Marie Fournier Canada
OUELLETTE, Marie Eva, Mar 25 1897 Sex:F Child# 2 Luc Ouellette Canada & Eugenie Peltier Canada
OUELLETTE, Marie Eva, Dec 6 1900 Sex:F Child# 1 Ernest Ouellette Canada & H Boisvert Canada
OUELLETTE, Marie Eva Alice, Aug 16 1904 Sex:F Child# 4 Alexis Ouellette Canada & Victoria Levesque Canada
OUELLETTE, Marie Eva R, Apr 27 1901 Sex:F Child# 2 Wilfrid Ouellette Canada & Cordelia Lucas Canada
OUELLETTE, Marie G, Dec 18 1891 Sex:F Child# 3 Cyril Ouellette Canada & Mary C Desroche Canada
OUELLETTE, Marie Helene A, Jan 30 1900 Sex:F Child# 14 William Ouellette Canada & Josephine Gagnon Canada
OUELLETTE, Marie Ireine Yvonne, Jan 26 1913 Sex:F Child# 12 Alexis Ouellette Canada & Victoria Levesque Canada
OUELLETTE, Marie Irene D, Aug 26 1904 Sex:F Child# 3 Edward Ouellette New York & Lillian Duchesneau NH
OUELLETTE, Marie Louise Ida, Jan 29 1913 Sex:F Child# 6 Francois Ouellette Canada & Ozellia Levesque Canada
OUELLETTE, Marie Marguerite, Dec 8 1892 Sex:F Child# 1 Joseph Ouellette Canada & Marie Leclair Canada
OUELLETTE, Marie Rene Mae, May 21 1933 Sex:F Child# 6 Leo Ouellette Canada & Eva Dupont Canada
OUELLETTE, Marie Rose, Jan 2 1903 Sex:F Child# 4 Arthur Ouellette Canada & Josephine Belanger Canada
OUELLETTE, Marie Teresa B, May 1 1924 Sex:F Child# 1 Joseph P Ouellette Nashua, NH & B Duhamel Canada
OUELLETTE, Marie Victoria, Dec 15 1899 Sex:F Child# 1 Alexis Ouellette Canada & Victoria Levesque Canada
OUELLETTE, Marie Yvonne, May 22 1924 Sex:F Child# 1 Arthur Ouellette Canada & Elizabeth LeBelle Canada
OUELLETTE, Marie Zelia, Jan 28 1891 Sex:F Child# 1 Joseph Ouellette Canada & Zoe Sirois Canada
OUELLETTE, Marthe Yolande, Mar 16 1930 Sex:F Child# 1 Arthur J Ouellette Nashua, NH & Gabrielle Beaulieu Canada
OUELLETTE, Mary, Oct 2 1910 Sex:F Child# 3 Alfred Ouellette Canada & Mary Collins US
OUELLETTE, Mary, Sep 7 1931 Sex:F Child# 3 Walter Ouellette Bay City, MI & Elsie Marquis Canada Stillborn
OUELLETTE, Mary Alice, May 9 1910 Sex:F Child# 1 Arthur Ouellette Nashua, NH & Annie Marotte Nashua, NH
OUELLETTE, Mary Gabriel Rita, Jan 28 1921 Sex:F Child# 8 Omer Ouellette Bay City, MI & Mary L Dube Canada
OUELLETTE, Mary Helen Denise, Jan 18 1925 Sex:F Child# 1 Nelson Ouellette Nashua, NH & Dorothy Lamb Nashua, NH
OUELLETTE, Mary L Diane, Aug 31 1931 Sex:F Child# 3 Ernest Ouellette Maine & Bertha Guerette Nashua, NH
OUELLETTE, Mary Lillian, Aug 23 1921 Sex:F Child# 1 Rene Ouellette Canada & Evelyn Soucy Canada
OUELLETTE, Mary Louise, Nov 14 1935 Sex:F Child# 2 Adrian Ouellette Nashua, NH & Cecille Cornelier Mass
OUELLETTE, Mary Olivine, Sep 27 1891 Sex:F Child# 10 Jean Ouellette Canada & Adele Levesque Canada
OUELLETTE, Mary Regina, Mar 15 1920 Sex:F Child# 1 Andrew J Ouellette Lawrence, MA & Irene Pelletier Canada
OUELLETTE, Melina, Oct 26 1898 Sex:F Child# 8 Octave Ouellette Canada & Marie Pinette Canada
OUELLETTE, Nelson, May 20 1922 Sex:M Child# 2 Alfred Ouellette E Douglas, MA & Bernice Hickey Lowell, MA
OUELLETTE, Noela Carmen, Dec 25 1911 Sex:F Child# 8 Joseph Ouellette Canada & Zoe Sirois Canada
OUELLETTE, Normande Mildred, Apr 25 1930 Sex:F Child# 1 Emile Ouellette Canada & Mildred Belanger Mass
OUELLETTE, Paul Girard, Jul 17 1933 Sex:M Child# 3 Joseph Ouellette Canada & B Duhamel Canada
OUELLETTE, Philomene, Aug 10 1887 Sex:F Child# 1 Thomas Ouellette P Q & Philomene Godin P Q
OUELLETTE, R Sylvio Normand, Jan 7 1914 Sex:M Child# 1 Sylvio Ouellette Canada & Delisca Lesage Nashua, NH
OUELLETTE, Raymond, Jun 29 1933 Sex:M Child# 2 Arthur Ouellette Nashua, NH & Gabrielle Beaulieu Canada
OUELLETTE, Rita Corinne, Nov 29 1920 Sex:F Child# 4 Sylvio Ouellette Canada & Delissa Lesage Nashua, NH
OUELLETTE, Rita Marie, May 20 1919 Sex:F Child# 3 Adelard Ouellette Barre, VT & Philomene Morency Morganso, VT
OUELLETTE, Robert Andre, Feb 29 1924 Sex:M Child# 3 Albert Ouellette Nashua, NH & Margaret Downey Salem, NH
OUELLETTE, Robert Normand, Sep 14 1932 Sex:M Child# 2 Emile Ouellette Canada & Mildred Belanger US
OUELLETTE, Robert Paul, Dec 17 1931 Sex:M Child# 3 Henri Ouellette Nashua, NH & Agnes Dobens Nashua, NH
OUELLETTE, Roland Edgar, Feb 3 1922 Sex:M Child# 1 David Ouellette Canada & Alice Levesque Nashua, NH
OUELLETTE, Romeo, Aug 25 1917 Sex:M Child# 1 Alexis Ouellette Canada & Georgiana Boucher Canada
OUELLETTE, Rose Yvonne, Aug 15 1906 Sex:F Child# 1 Francis Ouellette Canada & Oselia Levesque Canada
OUELLETTE, Ruth Edna Artimise, Sep 7 1919 Sex:F Child# 2 Walter Ouellette Bay City, MI & Elise Marquis Canada
OUELLETTE, Sylvia, Jul 17 1932 Sex:F Child# 3 Sylvio Ouellette NH & A Desmarais NH
OUELLETTE, Sylvia Jeannine, Nov 18 1933 Sex:F Child# 1 Napoleon Ouellette Canada & Rose Eva Asselin Nashua, NH
OUELLETTE, Sylvio, Aug 11 1910 Sex:M Child# 13 Pierre Ouellette Canada & Amanda Marceau Canada
OUELLETTE, Thomas, Mar 20 1900 Sex:M Child# 10 Thomas Ouellette Canada & Philomene Gaudin Canada
OUELLETTE, Unknown, May 11 1887 Sex:M Child# Marcel Ouellette NY & Marie Marotte Champlain Stillborn
OUELLETTE, Unknown, May 11 1887 Sex:M Child# Marcelle Ouellette Canada & Mary Canada Stillborn

OUELLETTE, Unknown, Sep 2 1887 Sex:M Child# 1 Joseph Ouellette P Q & Marie P Q Stillborn
OUELLETTE, Unknown, May 27 1892 Sex:F Child# 10 Marcel Ouellette NY & Mary Marotte NY Stillborn
OUELLETTE, Unknown, Jun 19 1894 Sex:M Child# 3 Joseph Ouellette Canada & Zoe Sirois Canada
OUELLETTE, Unknown, Aug 27 1900 Sex:M Child# 6 Joseph Ouellette Canada & Mary Lemire Canada Stillborn
OUELLETTE, Unknown, Aug 27 1900 Sex:M Child# 7 Joseph Ouellette Canada & Mary Lemire Canada
OUELLETTE, Unknown, Aug 22 1903 Sex:M Child# 6 Alfred Ouellette Canada & Denise Quessy Canada
OUELLETTE, Unknown, Oct 12 1912 Sex:M Child# 4 Omer Ouellette Bay City, MI & Marie Louise Dube Canada
OUELLETTE, Unknown, Feb 5 1924 Sex:M Child# 4 Sylvio Ouellette Nashua, NH & Delesca Lesage Nashua, NH
OUELLETTE, Unknown, May 2 1930 Sex:F Child# 6 Napoleon Ouellette Canada & Blanche Marquis Canada
OUELLETTE, Viviane Murielle, Feb 8 1919 Sex:F Child# 1 Cyprien Ouellette Nashua, NH & M A Jean Nashua, NH
OUELLETTE, Wilfred, Apr 18 1900 Sex:M Child# 1 Wilfred Ouellette Canada & Cordelia Ducas Canada
OUELLETTE, Wilfred Ludger, Jun 5 1908 Sex:M Child# 1 Omer Ouellette Bay City, MI & Marie Louise Dube Canada
OUILETTE, Alfred Raymond, Sep 10 1925 Sex:M Child# 3 Arthur Ouilette Canada & Eva Marois US
OUILETTE, Florence Gertrude, May 22 1925 Sex:F Child# Albert Ouilette Nashua, NH & Marg Downey Mass
OUILETTE, Jos Albert Andrew, Jun 5 1925 Sex:M Child# 1 A E Ouilette Nashua, NH & Blanche Chaput Nashua, NH
OUILETTE, Lorraine, May 23 1925 Sex:F Child# 2 Emile Ouilette Lawrence, MA & Lena Drouin NH
OUILETTE, Lucille Pearl, Aug 22 1925 Sex:F Child# 4 Cyprien Ouilette Nashua, NH & M Anne Jean Nashua, NH
OUILETTE, Marie, Feb 3 1888 Sex:F Child# 2 Alphonse Ouilette Canada & Arminel Gagnon Canada
OUILETTE, Marie Antoinette L, Jun 4 1925 Sex:F Child# 2 Arthur Ouilette Canada & Isabelle Lebelle Canada
OUILETTE, Rita Irene, Mar 6 1926 Sex:F Child# 2 Henry Ouilette Nashua, NH & Agnes M Dobens Nashua, NH
OUILETTE, Theresa Lucie, Oct 1 1925 Sex:F Child# 7 Joseph A Ouilette Canada & Rose Landry Canada
OUILETTE, Yvette Rita, Jan 2 1927 Sex:F Child# 2 Ernest Ouilette Oldtown, ME & Bertha Guerette Nashua, NH
OUILLETTE, Adrien Vincent, Jul 19 1926 Sex:M Child# 1 C H Ouillette Canada & Blanche Bernier Canada
OUILLETTE, Agnes Louise, Jan 25 1925 Sex:F Child# 1 Adelard Ouillette Brookline, NH & Jessie Farnsworth Brookline
OUILLETTE, Alice Yvonne, Jul 19 1929 Sex:F Child# 5 David Ouillette Canada & Alice Levesque Nashua, NH
OUILLETTE, Annette, Apr 21 1928 Sex:F Child# 4 Arthur Ouillette Canada & Eva Marois Nashua, NH
OUILLETTE, Arthur Richard, Dec 28 1923 Sex:M Child# 3 Rene Ouillette Canada & Evelyn Soucy Canada
OUILLETTE, Charles Henry, Oct 29 1926 Sex:M Child# Leo Ouillette Canada & Eva Dupont Canada
OUILLETTE, Claire Theresa, Jan 15 1927 Sex:F Child# 2 David Ouillette Canada & Alice Levesque Nashua, NH
OUILLETTE, Flora Loretta, Aug 16 1928 Sex:F Child# 3 Wilfred Ouillette Manchester, NH & R Laroche Nashua, NH
OUILLETTE, Jean Rene, Dec 8 1929 Sex:M Child# 2 J B Ouillette Canada & Henrietta Desbiens Canada
OUILLETTE, Jeannette, Nov 2 1926 Sex:F Child# 4 Rene Ouillette Canada & Evelyn Soucy Canada
OUILLETTE, Jeannette, Apr 21 1928 Sex:F Child# 5 Arthur Ouillette Canada & Eva Marois Nashua, NH
OUILLETTE, Louise Marie, Aug 17 1929 Sex:F Child# 1 Sylvio Ouillette Epping, NH & Aurore Desmarais Nashua, NH
OUILLETTE, Marie, Sep 8 1888 Sex:F Child# 2 Adolphe Ouillette Canada & Anna Michard Canada
OUILLETTE, Marie B Lorraine, Feb 5 1929 Sex:F Child# 2 Albert Ouillette Nashua, NH & Blanche Chaput Nashua, NH
OUILLETTE, Marie Marguerite, Aug 2 1928 Sex:F Child# 2 Jos Ouillette Nashua, NH & B Duhamel Canada
OUILLETTE, Marie Stella Aurore, Sep 15 1927 Sex:F Child# 1 Jean B Ouillette Canada & H Desbiens Canada
OUILLETTE, Marie Theresa Alice, Jun 2 1928 Sex:F Child# 1 Oscar Ouillette Fall River, MA & Clara Girard Canada
OUILLETTE, Marie Theresa E Oliv, Mar 9 1927 Sex:F Child# 2 Wilfrid Ouillette Manchester, NH & R Laroche Nashua, NH
OUILLETTE, Mary Frances, Jun 16 1927 Sex:F Child# 2 A J Ouillette Nashua, NH & Jessie Farnsworth Brookline, NH
OUILLETTE, Theresa Emma, Jul 8 1926 Sex:F Child# 6 Jos A Oillette Vermont & Phoebe Morency Morgan Center, VT
OUILLETTE, Theresa Lorraine, Sep 28 1927 Sex:F Child# 2 Napoleon Ouillette Canada & Marie A Corbin Canada
OUIMETTE, Alice Yvonne, Jun 9 1907 Sex:F Child# 1 Athanase Ouimette Canada & Albina Demers Canada
OUIMETTE, Omer Leo, Dec 12 1908 Sex:M Child# 2 Athanase Ouimette Canada & Albina Demers Canada
OUIMETTE, Omer Louis, Sep 29 1911 Sex:M Child# 3 Joseph A Ouimette Canada & Albina Demers Canada
OUIMETTE, Rene, May 28 1908 Sex:M Child# 1 Arthur Ouimette Canada & Emelie Demers Canada
OVAGUMIAND, Bearch, Nov 6 1906 Sex:M Child# 1 Misag Ovaguimiand Armenia & Kahoohly Bokoscian Armenia
OVDE, Mary Ellen, Mar 14 1934 Sex:F Child# 4 Alan L Ovde Lynn, MA & Beryl Reed Berlin, NH
OVERKA, John, May 31 1911 Sex:M Child# 1 John Overka Russia & A Waszkeliavicute Russia
OVERKO, John, Apr 9 1915 Sex:M Child# 1 James Overko Russia & Marcella Salacuta Russia
OVERLACK, Gordon Burns, Nov 7 1902 Sex:M Child# 1 Martin Overlack Maine & Edith M Burns Milford, NH
OWEN, Joseph, Mar 30 1893 Sex:M Child# 5 John Owen England & Mary A Roach England
OWENS, Mary A, Feb 28 1889 Sex:F Child# 5 John Owens England & Mary Ann Roach England
PACE, Jane Achsah, Jul 4 1921 Sex:F Child# 1 Edward Pace Grants Pass, OR & Hazel Storer Nashua, NH
PACEL, Marie O Gabrielle, Oct 21 1924 Sex:F Child# 3 Joseph Pacel, Jr NH & Leda Laquerre Canada
PACKOR, Mary, Jul 21 1922 Sex:F Child# 7 William Packor Lithuania & Petrolina Bartis Lithuania
PACZAPOWICH, Alfons, Jun 21 1910 Sex:M Child# 1 Alfons Paczapowich Russia & Leosia Gentwayanna Russia
PADDLEFORD, Albert Clifton, Dec 23 1895 Sex:M Child# 4 Seth E Paddleford Littleton & Sarah Dustin Hill
PADIOS, Cleopatra, Aug 2 1911 Sex:F Child# 2 John Padios Greece & Jule Dova Greece
PADIOS, Eleftherios, Jan 25 1919 Sex:M Child# 5 Tissis Padios Greece & Zioulou Z Padios Greece
PADIOS, Kasios, Jun 30 1916 Sex:M Child# 6 John Padios Greece & Rosie Dovas Greece
PAGE, Alice Florence, Oct 9 1925 Sex:F Child# 1 Arthur Page Canada & Bertha Perron Nashua, NH
PAGE, Andrew Leslie, Feb 25 1897 Sex:M Child# 2 Andrew H Page Bedford, MA & Effie M Marshall Thornton's Ferry, NH
PAGE, Anna Loraine, Nov 28 1923 Sex:F Child# 3 Wilfred Page Ausable Chasm, NY & Nettie Smith Derry, NH
PAGE, Bertha Elizabeth, Mar 18 1891 Sex:F Child# 2 William H Page
PAGE, Catherine Gertrude, Aug 29 1893 Sex:F Child# 1 Bartholemew Page Ireland & Mary Diggins Ireland
PAGE, Dorothy Eleanor, Jul 2 1925 Sex:F Child# 2 Warren Page Nashua, NH & Alice Guest Hollis, NH
PAGE, Evelyn Ruth, Sep 18 1912 Sex:F Child# 1 Howard F Page N Woburn, MA & Emma Parker Granby, Quebec
PAGE, Fred Warren, Mar 15 1902 Sex:M Child# 2 Warren Page Nashua, NH & Celina Grandmaison Nashua, NH
PAGE, George Sidney, Jr, Oct 25 1900 Sex:M Child# G S Page New York & Lavilla Annis NH
PAGE, George William, Feb 23 1893 Sex:M Child# 3 W H Page Nashua, NH & Rosanna Caron Canada
PAGE, James, Aug 27 1930 Sex:M Child# 1 James Page Los Angeles, CA & Jane Gamble Manchester, NH

PAGE, Joseph, Aug 26 1901 Sex:M Child#  Will Page NY & Lina Caron Canada
PAGE, Joseph Louis O'Neil, Sep 26 1926 Sex:M Child# 2 Felix Page Canada & Bertha Perron NH
PAGE, Lemuel Whitney, Apr 8 1907 Sex:M Child# 1 Harry E Page Ausable Chasm, NY & Hattie I Shaw Sebatus, ME
PAGE, Louise Ermina, Oct 19 1911 Sex:F Child# 1 Fred R Page Washington, NH & G M Barnhardt Nashua, NH
PAGE, Marjorie, Aug 22 1911 Sex:F Child# 3 Harry E Page Ausable, NY & Hattie Shaw Sebatus, ME
PAGE, Mary, Oct 19 1909 Sex:F Child# 1 (No Parents Listed)
PAGE, Norman, Feb 18 1909 Sex:M Child# 2 Harry E Page Ausable, NY & Hattie I Shaw Sabbatis, ME
PAGE, Pearl Hannah, Sep 27 1889 Sex:F Child# 1 William Page Manchester, NH & Hannah Carson Canada
PAGE, Robert, Jul 22 1933 Sex:M Child# 4 Felix Page Canada & Bertha Perron Nashua, NH
PAGE, Robert Shaw, Jan 13 1917 Sex:M Child# 4 Harry E Page Ausable, NY & Hattie I Shaw Sabatus, ME
PAGE, Shirley Frances, Oct 2 1921 Sex:F Child# 2 Wilfred H Page Ausable Chasm, NY & Nettie F Smith Derry, NH
PAGE, Unknown, May 31 1894 Sex:F Child# 1 Eugene H Page Hygate, NY & Mary J Garrish Sharon
PAGE, Unknown, Jul 9 1899 Sex:M Child# 5 William Henry Page Manchester, NH & Lonore A Caron Canada
PAGE, Unknown, Dec 9 1900 Sex:F Child# 1 E W Page New York & Lulu Hodgman Nashua, NH
PAGE, Unknown, Jan 3 1903 Sex:M Child# 6 William Page Manchester, NH & Lena A Coran Quebec, Canada
PAGE, Unknown, May 29 1928 Sex:F Child# 4 Warren Page NH & Alice Guest Hollis, NH
PAGE, Warren Henry, May 16 1895 Sex:M Child# 4 William H Page Manchester, NH & Lana Caron Canada
PAGE, Warren Henry, Jr, May 27 1927 Sex:M Child# 3 Warren H Page Nashua, NH & Alice C Guest Nashua, NH
PAIGE, Bert Lewis, Oct 20 1897 Sex:M Child# 2 Eugene H Paige Ryegate, VT & Mary J Gerrish Sharon
PAIGE, Elaine Louilla, Mar 20 1933 Sex:F Child# 1 George S Paige Nashua, NH & Helen Burns Nashua, NH
PAIGE, Harold P, Feb 25 1893 Sex:M Child#  James H Paige NH & Flora Putnam NH
PAIGE, Mabel, Feb 11 1908 Sex:F Child# 8 William H Paige Manchester, NH & Leona Charron Canada
PAIGE, Pearl Jeanine June, Jun 3 1934 Sex:F Child# 4 Alfred W Paige Nashua, NH & Eva Demarais Nashua, NH
PAIGE, Theresa Ann, Jul 23 1926 Sex:F Child# 2 Alfred W Paige Mass & Eva Desmarais NH
PAINE, Alan Davis, May 13 1933 Sex:M Child# 4 Franklin Paine Rhode Island & Mildred Davis NH
PAINE, Franklin Thomas, Jr, Mar 15 1926 Sex:M Child# 2 Franklin T Paine Barrington, RI & Mildred L Davis Nashua, NH
PAINE, Kenneth Jeremiah, Feb 25 1927 Sex:M Child# 4 Willard Paine Marblehead, MA & Josephine Cronin Nashua, NH
PAINE, Robert Paul, May 9 1917 Sex:M Child# 1 Willard Paine Marblehead, MA & Josephine Cronin Nashua, NH
PAINE, Wesley John, Mar 15 1926 Sex:M Child# 3 Franklin T Paine Barrington, RI & Mildred L Davis Nashua, NH
PAINE, Willard Charles, Apr 3 1928 Sex:M Child# 5 Willard Paul Paine Marblehead, MA & Josephine Cronin Nashua, NH
PALARDY, Marie Agnes, Aug 4 1922 Sex:F Child# 5 Louis E Palardy Canada & Anna McComb Canada
PALARDY, Marie Rose Blanche, Jul 24 1917 Sex:F Child# 4 Damase Palardy Canada & Marie Morency Sydney, ME
PALIQUIN, George, Dec 23 1901 Sex:M Child# 2 John Paliquin Canada & Elmina L'Abbe Canada
PALIQUIN, Joseph, Nov 5 1900 Sex:M Child# 1 Jean Paliquin Canada & Almina Label Canada
PALIQUIN, Joseph Charles, Mar 19 1894 Sex:M Child# 1 Joseph Paliquin Canada & Marceline Guilmette Canada
PALIQUIN, Lucille Adrienne, Sep 19 1918 Sex:F Child# 9 George Paliquin Canada & Rose Anna Desmarais Nashua, NH
PALKINS, Norma Pearl, Oct 9 1933 Sex:F Child# 1 Lewis Palkins Lithuania & Mary Cowile Harris, RI Stillborn
PALM, Lempi, Dec 27 1917 Sex:F Child# 3 John Palm Finland & Jennie Ware Finland
PALMER, Barbara, Apr 17 1924 Sex:F Child# 1 Donald Palmer New Haven, CT & Clara Stevens Stannard, VT
PALMER, Dana Leavitt, Jan 5 1934 Sex:M Child# 3 Ralph Daniels Palmer Nashua, NH & Mabel Bickford Windham, NH
PALMER, David George, Jul 19 1925 Sex:M Child# 2 Donald Palmer New Haven, VT & Clara Stevens Stanstead, VT
PALMER, David Lee, May 17 1930 Sex:M Child# 1 Rufus Palmer Pepperell, MA & Bertha McMahon Groton, MA
PALMER, Dorothy Elizabeth, Oct 29 1931 Sex:F Child# 2 Ralph Palmer Nashua, NH & Mabelle Bickford Windham, NH
PALMER, Frank Bailey, Jr, Feb 9 1917 Sex:M Child# 3 Frank B Palmer S Hampton, NH & Bessie M Winslow S Hampton, NH
PALMER, George Raymond, Sep 4 1930 Sex:M Child# 1 Ralph Palmer Nashua, NH & Mabel Bickford Windham, NH
PALMER, Graham Painsfard, Aug 22 1927 Sex:M Child# 1 G F Palmer Stattvile, NY & Alma Dalrymple Boston, MA
PALMER, Mary Cynthia, Nov 24 1898 Sex:F Child# 1 Raymond F Palmer Pelham, NH & Iva S Daniels Litchfield, NH
PALMER, Robert Charles, Aug 12 1925 Sex:M Child# 5 George Palmer Manchester, NH & Harriet Keniston Auburn, NH
PALMER, Ruth Evelyn, Feb 18 1906 Sex:F Child# 3 Raymond F Palmer Pelham, NH & Iva S Daniels Litchfield, NH
PALMER, Unknown, Sep 19 1900 Sex:M Child# 2 R F Palmer NH & Eva Daniels NH
PALMER, Unknown, Apr 18 1904 Sex:F Child# 3 R Frank Palmer Pelham, NH & Eva S Daniels Litchfield, NH
PALMER, Unknown, Sep 4 1905 Sex:F Child# 1 (No Parents Listed)
PALMER, Unknown, Feb 8 1914 Sex:F Child# 1 Perley R Palmer Lynn, MA & Nellie Keith Essex Jct, VT
PALMER, Vivian, Mar 11 1909 Sex:F Child# 1 Joseph C Palmer
PALSER, Unknown, May 17 1891 Sex:F Child# 3 A W Palser Nova Scotia & Mary E Brown Nova Scotia
PANAGOLIS, Peter, Sep 12 1908 Sex:M Child# 2 George Panagolis Greece & Elen Panagolis Greece
PANAGOULAS, Unknown, Feb 26 1917 Sex:F Child# 6 Peter Panagoulas Greece & Vasilo Econonopolas Greece
PANAGOULIS, Bangelis, Sep 3 1916 Sex:M Child# 1 Loue Panagoulis Athens, Greece & Constina Carousi Greece
PANAGULIS, Unknown, Jun 23 1918 Sex:F Child# 5 Peter Panagulias Greece & Agnes Stown Greece
PANANVILLIE, Anastasia, Jun 1 1913 Sex:F Child# 1 Lodon Pananvillie Greece & Irene Stamelos Greece
PANEGULUS, James, Jan 5 1915 Sex:M Child# 4 James Panegulus Greece & Wangelia Candus Greece
PANETHON, Marie L O, Mar 14 1893 Sex:F Child# 3 Gedeon Panethon Canada & Odile Marquis Canada
PANETON, Arthur I, Jan 3 1892 Sex:M Child# 2 Gedeon Paneton Canada & Odile Marquis Canada
PANGOLIA, Pano, Aug 10 1910 Sex:M Child# 1 Theodore Pangolia Greece & Irini Stamelo Greece
PANIMIAN, Zavan, Jun 20 1914 Sex:M Child# 3 K Panimian Armenia & Ckarian Voker Armenia
PANNETON, Marie Ernestine, Feb 17 1899 Sex:F Child# 9 Alfred Panneton Canada & Josephine Duplessis Canada
PANNETON, Unknown, Jun 2 1904 Sex:M Child# 1 Gedeon Panneton Canada & Clarilda Belanger Canada
PANOS, Unknown, Oct 29 1921 Sex:F Child# 1 George Panos Greece & Konstantines Sinopou Greece
PANTON, Marie A E, Nov 7 1890 Sex:F Child# 1 Gideon Panton Canada & Odele Marquis Canada
PAPACHRISTO, George, Feb 25 1916 Sex:M Child# 2 Arthur Papachristo Greece & Amanda Poliquin Nashua, NH
PAPACONSTANTINO, Unknown, Nov 2 1921 Sex:F Child# 2 S Papaconstantinou Greece & Kyriacoula Doron Greece
PAPADAPOULOS, Unknown, Feb 7 1920 Sex:M Child# 2 George Papadapoulos Greece & Helen Photion Greece
PAPADEMUS, Unknown, Jun 19 1922 Sex:M Child# 2 George Papademus Greece & Athena Souflesis Greece

PAPAGEORGE, Unknown, Sep 3 1933 Sex:M Child# 1 A Papageorge Greece & Cleo Padios Nashua, NH
PAPAHARISIS, Mary I, Aug 11 1923 Sex:F Child# 6 John Papaharisis Greece & Diamondie Qteriu Greece
PAPAJOHN, George S, Apr 23 1924 Sex:M Child# 1 Spisos Papajohn Greece & S Gouldasis Greece
PAPATHENASIA, Unknown, Dec 25 1919 Sex:F Child# 5 A Papathenasia Greece & Alexandre K Philipou Greece
PAPAYIAN, Paran, Apr 7 1909 Sex:F Child# 3 Marsuppe Papayian Armenia & Altoiri Bogosian Armenia
PAPCHARISSON, Unknown, Nov 16 1919 Sex:F Child# 4 John Papcharisson Macedonia & Diawanda Sterion Macedonia
PAPDEMIS, Unknown, May 20 1918 Sex:F Child# 1 James Papdemis Greece & Koula Kohener Greece
PAPELIS, Peter, Jan 31 1925 Sex:M Child# 3 Mateush Papelis Lithuania & Julia Mishkouckas Lithuania
PAPILLON, Ezerald, Jul 20 1897 Sex:m Child# 2 Thomas Papillon Canada & Genievre Rose Canada
PAPILLON, Joseph George Albert, May 9 1896 Sex:M Child# 1 J Thomas Papillon Canada & Genivievre Ross Canada
PAPILLON, Joseph Napoleon, Oct 22 1899 Sex:M Child# 4 Thomas Papillon Canada & Juliette Ross Canada
PAPILLON, Marie R D, Sep 20 1898 Sex:F Child# 2 Thomas Papillon Canada & Genevieve Ross Canada
PAPLOUSKI, Eulia, Oct 27 1909 Sex:F Child# 1 William Paplouski Russia & Barbara Darskaty Russia
PAPLOWSKA, Ennie, Aug 31 1909 Sex:F Child# 4 Mike Paplowska Russia & Marcialia Nazariute Russia
PAPLOWSKI, Josie, Jan 19 1913 Sex:F Child# 2 Anton Paplowski Russia & Medje Balchikow Russia
PAPPACHRISTO, Adrienne, May 31 1919 Sex:F Child# 3 Art Pappachristo Greece & Hermina Poliquin Nashua, NH
PAPPACHRISTOU, Madeline, Jul 31 1921 Sex:F Child# 1 Art Pappachristou Greece & Mary Gaffney Nashua, NH
PAPPADEMAS, Unknown, Jun 9 1933 Sex:M Child# 6 Jas Pappademas Greece & Koula Greece
PAPPADIMOS, George D, Oct 12 1919 Sex:M Child# 2 Dem Pappadimos Greece & Koula Capanois Greece
PAPPAGIANOPOULO, Unknown, Jun 4 1933 Sex:M Child# 1 C Pappagianopoulos Greece & Olga Tsamis Greece
PAPPAJOHN, Unknown, May 7 1927 Sex:F Child# 2 Spiros Pappajohn Greece & S Gioldasi Greece
PAPPAS, Christos, Jul 30 1912 Sex:M Child# 6 Louis Pappas Greece & Lizzie Pappas Greece
PAPPAS, Drago, Jan 21 1919 Sex:F Child# 1 Thomas N Pappas Greece & Fazon K Apunskalou Greece
PAPPAS, George, Oct 9 1910 Sex:M Child# 1 James Pappas Greece & Evangela Ckonga Greece
PAPPAS, Houla, Jul 4 1908 Sex:F Child# 1 Nicholas Pappas Greece & Helen Karla Greece
PAPPAS, James, Nov 28 1918 Sex:M Child# 9 Michael Pappas Greece & Vesalicki Hispawo Greece
PAPPAS, Stephano, Jan 7 1917 Sex:m Child# 4 Louis Pappas Greece & Theodora Mike Greece
PAPPAS, Unknown, Dec 12 1911 Sex:F Child# 1 Peter Pappas Greece & Ravela Econom Greece
PAPPAS, Unknown, Jun 30 1915 Sex:M Child# 3 Peter Pappas Greece & Alice Econopopulos Greece
PAPPAS, Unknown, Feb 27 1916 Sex:F Child# 4 James Pappas Greece & Vagilia Condus Greece
PAPPAS, Unknown, Mar 15 1917 Sex:M Child# 3 Nicholas Pappas Greece & Helena Pappchentis Greece Stillborn
PAPPAS, Unknown, Apr 3 1917 Sex:M Child# 7 Mike Pappas Macedonia & Alice Spanios Macedonia
PAPPAS, Unknown, Nov 10 1917 Sex:M Child# 5 James Pappas Greece & Evangelia Condus Greece
PAPPAS, Unknown, Dec 2 1919 Sex:M Child# 7 Louis Pappas Greece & Theodora Nicholos Greece
PAPPAS, Unknown, Mar 14 1923 Sex:M Child# 4 Thomas Pappas Greece & Euphemia Cortes Greece
PAPPAS, Unknown, Jun 13 1923 Sex:M Child# 7 James Pappas Greece & Evangele Scontsas Greece
PAPPS, Mildred E, Feb 16 1904 Sex:F Child# 1 Theodore B Papps Claremont, NH & Ella C Beau Woodstock, VT
PAQUEREAU, Pauline Gertrude, May 13 1928 Sex:F Child# 1 Henry Paquereau Pepperell, MA & Marion Jalbert Lowell, MA
PAQUET, Albert M, Nov 17 1896 Sex:M Child# 12 Michael Paquet Canada & Olive Migneault Canada
PAQUET, Emilie G, Apr 16 1891 Sex:F Child# 7 Michel Paquet Canada & Olive Migneault Canada
PAQUET, Emma V C, Aug 31 1894 Sex:F Child# 11 Michel Paquet Canada & Olive Migneault Canada
PAQUET, Eugene R, Feb 2 1891 Sex:M Child# 10 August Paquet Canada & Delphine Guerin Canada
PAQUET, Henri A, Jun 6 1887 Sex:M Child# 8 Auguste Paquet P Q & Delphine Guren P Q
PAQUET, Iris Marlene, Feb 18 1935 Sex:F Child# 1 Alfred Paquet Derry, NH & Alice Grover Green, ME
PAQUET, Louis W, Jul 6 1889 Sex:M Child# 8 Michel Paquet Canada & Olive Migneault Canada
PAQUET, Marie I, Jul 1 1899 Sex:F Child# 14 Michel Paquet Canada & Olive Migneault Canada
PAQUET, Marie Laura, Sep 5 1895 Sex:F Child# 10 Achille Paquet Canada & Louise Demers Canada
PAQUET, Moise P, Jan 31 1893 Sex:M Child# 8 Michel Paquet Canada & Olive Migneault Canada
PAQUET, Unknown, Nov 28 1900 Sex:F Child# 15 Michel Paquet Canada & Olive Migneault Canada Stillborn
PAQUET, William A, Mar 29 1897 Sex:M Child# 1 Alfred Paquet Sandown & Addie Bull Altona, NY
PAQUETTE, Albert, May 1 1919 Sex:M Child# 1 J B Paquette Canada & Maria Bilodeau Canada
PAQUETTE, Albert Irenee, Nov 16 1904 Sex:M Child# 3 Isidore Paquette Canada & Leonide April Canada
PAQUETTE, Albert Raymond, Apr 26 1920 Sex:M Child# 4 Onesime Paquette Canada & Florilda Roy Canada
PAQUETTE, Alfred Roland, Jun 5 1908 Sex:M Child# 5 Isidore Paquette Canada & Leonide April Canada
PAQUETTE, Alice, May 21 1902 Sex:F Child# 9 Charles Paquette Canada & Leocadie Pelletier Bay City, MI
PAQUETTE, Andrew Conrad, Jul 19 1922 Sex:M Child# 5 Louis Paquette Canada & Eva Rose Lessard US
PAQUETTE, Bertie, Jun 2 1899 Sex:M Child# Charles Paquette Canada & Loquadie Pelletier Bay City, MI
PAQUETTE, Blanche Yolande, Sep 24 1920 Sex:F Child# 4 Louis W Paquette US & Eva Rose Lessard US
PAQUETTE, Cecile Lucille, Feb 8 1916 Sex:F Child# 2 Louis W Paquette US & Eva Rose Lessard US
PAQUETTE, Doris Albertine, Feb 22 1934 Sex:F Child# 7 J B Paquette Canada & Marie Bilodeau Canada
PAQUETTE, Doris Theresa, Oct 20 1926 Sex:F Child# 1 Everiste Paquette New York & Magelia Floyd Nashua, NH
PAQUETTE, Ernest, Jul 25 1888 Sex:M Child# 9 Augustus Paquette Canada & Delphine Guerin Canada
PAQUETTE, Ernest, Apr 7 1906 Sex:M Child# 11 Charles Paquette Canada & Carrie Pelletier Bay City, MI
PAQUETTE, Ethel, Jun 25 1902 Sex:F Child# 2 Alfred Paquette Hooksett, NH & Ida Bull Altoona, NY
PAQUETTE, Evelyn Rachel, Dec 31 1927 Sex:F Child# 7 Louis Paquette Nashua, NH & Eva Lessard Nashua, NH
PAQUETTE, Florence Gertrude, Dec 12 1909 Sex:F Child# 6 Isidore Paquette Canada & Leonide April Canada
PAQUETTE, Gertrude Laurette, Jul 21 1906 Sex:F Child# 4 Isidore Paquette Canada & Leonide April Canada
PAQUETTE, Henri, Dec 8 1889 Sex:M Child# 13 Alfred Paquette Canada & Catherine Belanger Canada
PAQUETTE, Henriette Christine, Jan 27 1921 Sex:F Child# 1 Alexander Paquette Canada & Henriette Jasmin France
PAQUETTE, Irene Exilda, Jun 26 1903 Sex:F Child# 2 Isidore Paquette Canada & Leonide April Canada
PAQUETTE, Jeanne Irene, Sep 28 1925 Sex:F Child# 4 J B Paquette Canada & Marie Bellodeau Canada
PAQUETTE, Jeanne Madeleine, Aug 8 1935 Sex:F Child# 7 Louis Paquette Nashua, NH & Eva Rose Lessard Nashua, NH
PAQUETTE, Jos Edouard Isidore, Dec 15 1917 Sex:M Child# 3 L W P Paquette US & Eva Rose Lessard US

PAQUETTE, Joseph, Jan 6 1888 Sex:M Child# 7 Michael Paquette P Q & Olive Jenvault Canada
PAQUETTE, Joseph, Jun 10 1909 Sex:M Child# 2 John Paquette NH & Evelyn Leclerc Canada
PAQUETTE, Joseph, Sep 28 1934 Sex:M Child# 3 Joseph F Paquette Nashua, NH & Pauline Stratton Vermont
PAQUETTE, Joseph A H, Jun 16 1896 Sex:M Child# 6 Charles Paquette Canada & Leocadie Pelletier Bay City, MI
PAQUETTE, Joseph Armand F, Mar 24 1906 Sex:M Child# 9 H Paquette Canada & Marie G Michaud Canada
PAQUETTE, Joseph Paul Ralph, Sep 21 1915 Sex:M Child# 4 Jean Bte Paquette NH & Evelyn A Leclerc Canada
PAQUETTE, Lawrence E, Dec 20 1912 Sex:M Child# 4 Napoleon T Paquette Manchester, NH & Agnes Gendron New Brunswick
PAQUETTE, Leo Thomas, Nov 26 1931 Sex:M Child# 3 Moses Paquette Nashua, NH & Gertrude Graham S Boston, MA
PAQUETTE, Louis Roger, Jul 6 1913 Sex:M Child# 1 Louis W Paquette US & Eva Rose Lessard US
PAQUETTE, Marie, Jun 14 1915 Sex:F Child# 2 Jean Bte Paquette Canada & Marie O Gagne Canada Stillborn
PAQUETTE, Marie Adrienne G, Oct 10 1905 Sex:F Child# 2 Thomas Paquette NH & Corona Brouillard NH
PAQUETTE, Marie Gillette Doret, Mar 29 1912 Sex:F Child# 3 Thomas Paquette NH & Corona Brouillard NH
PAQUETTE, Marie Rose Ida, Mar 21 1899 Sex:F Child# 11 Achille Paquette Canada & Marie Louise Demers Canada
PAQUETTE, Mary Amanda, Jul 22 1932 Sex:F Child# 1 F Paquette Nashua, NH & Amanda Odesse Manchester, NH
PAQUETTE, Mary Rose Colette, Aug 9 1933 Sex:F Child# 2 Joseph Paquette Nashua, NH & Pauline Stratton Vermont
PAQUETTE, Maurice, Mar 26 1914 Sex:M Child# 2 Onesime Paquette Canada & Florilda Roy Canada
PAQUETTE, Norine Agnes, Mar 17 1935 Sex:F Child# 1 Leonard Paquette Manchester, NH & Yvonne Cote Lowell, MA
PAQUETTE, Normand Irenee, May 26 1927 Sex:M Child# 2 E Paquette Nashua, NH & Alma Lefebvre Nashua, NH
PAQUETTE, Olive Mary, May 29 1925 Sex:F Child# 3 Moses Paquette Nashua, NH & Gertrude Wall Mineville, NY
PAQUETTE, Olivette Bernadette, Jan 15 1923 Sex:F Child# 3 J B Paquette Canada & Marie Bilodeau Canada
PAQUETTE, Olivine Lorette, May 1 1931 Sex:F Child# 5 J B Paquette Canada & Maria Bilodeau Canada
PAQUETTE, Philias L, May 31 1898 Sex:M Child# 13 Michael Paquette Canada & Olive Migneault Canada
PAQUETTE, Robert Ernest, Jul 7 1919 Sex:M Child# 2 Moise A Paquette Nashua, NH & Gertrude Wall Minerville, NY
PAQUETTE, Robert Pantaleon, Nov 19 1920 Sex:M Child# 2 J B Paquette Canada & Maria Bilodeau Canada
PAQUETTE, Rodolphe Aime, May 14 1925 Sex:M Child# 1 Fernando Paquette Nashua, NH & R A Lefebvre Nashua, NH
PAQUETTE, Sarto Leo, Nov 24 1903 Sex:M Child# 1 Thomas Paquette Sandown & Corona Brouillard Nashua, NH
PAQUETTE, Stella Delima, Sep 2 1897 Sex:F Child# 7 Charles Paquette Canada & Leocadee Pelletier Bay City, MI
PAQUETTE, Sylvio, Sep 6 1909 Sex:M Child# 12 Charles Paquette Canada & Leocadie Pelletier Bay City, MI
PAQUETTE, Therese Lucienne, Aug 25 1932 Sex:F Child# 6 J B Paquette Canada & M Bilodeau Canada
PAQUETTE, Unknown, Jan 21 1889 Sex:F Child# 8 Alfred Paquette Canada & Catherine Belanger Canada Stillborn
PAQUETTE, Unknown, Jun 29 1913 Sex:F Child# 1 John Paquette
PAQUETTE, Violet Adeline, Feb 4 1920 Sex:F Child# 1 Louise Paquette Canada & Evelyn LeFleur E Chazy, NY
PAQUETTE, Violetta Geraldine, Sep 30 1916 Sex:F Child# 2 Ernest Paquette Canada & Florilda Roy Canada
PAQUETTE, Yvonne Andrea, May 31 1902 Sex:F Child# 1 Isidore Paquette Canada & Leonide April Canada
PAQUETTE, Yvonne Elisa, Jul 9 1903 Sex:F Child# 10 Charles Paquette Canada & Leocadie Pelttier Bay City, MI
PAQUIN, Ernest, Jul 30 1893 Sex:M Child# 9 Felix Paquin Canada & Elodie St Pierre Canada
PAQUIN, Frank Edward, May 16 1898 Sex:M Child# 1 Charles Ed Paquin Salem & Grace Barrett Athol, MA
PAQUIN, George, Dec 17 1896 Sex:M Child# 11 Felix Paquin Canada & Elovie St Pierre Canada
PAQUIN, Joseph Edward, Mar 31 1889 Sex:M Child# 8 Felix Paquin Canada & M St Pierre Canada
PAQUIN, Marie A, Mar 22 1887 Sex:F Child# 2 Damase Paquin Canada & Delphine Lefevre Canada
PAQUIN, Marie A, Jan 3 1895 Sex:F Child# 3 Liboire Paquin Lawrence, MA & Eleonore Vaillancour Canada
PAQUIN, Marie R, Sep 17 1893 Sex:F Child# 2 Liboire Paquin Lawrence, MA & Eleonore Vaillancour Canada
PARADIS, Achille Emile, Mar 28 1907 Sex:M Child# 2 Joseph Paradis Canada & Josephine Sirois Canada
PARADIS, Alonzo, Feb 25 1898 Sex:M Child# 6 Luc Paradis Canada & Marie Morel Canada
PARADIS, Amedee, Apr 26 1907 Sex:M Child# 10 Louis Paradis Canada & Celina Lavoie Canada
PARADIS, Antoine, Jun 19 1905 Sex:M Child# 2 Joseph Paradis Canada & Emma Moreau Canada
PARADIS, Armand, Nov 29 1928 Sex:M Child# 1 Victory Paradis Nashua, NH & Alice Mailloux Canada
PARADIS, Arthur Hector, Nov 15 1909 Sex:M Child# 4 Joseph Paradis Canada & Josephine Sirois Canada
PARADIS, Arthur Xavier, Oct 21 1927 Sex:M Child# 1 Joseph Paradis Canada & Alice Prudhomme Canada
PARADIS, Bertha, Aug 27 1918 Sex:F Child# 11 Adelard Paradis Canada & Marie Beaulieu Canada
PARADIS, Bertrand, Jan 10 1925 Sex:M Child# 3 Alphonse Paradis Exeter, NH & Rose Cormier Canada
PARADIS, Claire Jean, Mar 23 1926 Sex:F Child# 3 Alphonse Paradis Exeter, NH & Rose Cormier Canada
PARADIS, Emmeline Marie Rose, May 1 1918 Sex:F Child# 5 Paul Paradis Canada & Grace Bishop Maine
PARADIS, Eustache Thomas, Dec 26 1914 Sex:M Child# 5 Ephrem Paradis Canada & E Dionne Canada
PARADIS, Eva, Jan 12 1917 Sex:F Child# 5 Louis Paradis Canada & Laura Levesque Canada
PARADIS, Florence Marguerite, Aug 6 1921 Sex:F Child# 3 Ernest Paradis Canada & A Dube Canada
PARADIS, Florence Pauline, Jan 9 1933 Sex:F Child# 1 Albert Paradis Greenville, NH & Yvonne Bouley Greenville, NH
PARADIS, Geralda Noela, May 12 1931 Sex:F Child# 3 Victor Paradis Nashua, NH & Alice Mailloux Canada
PARADIS, Helene Marianne, Jan 23 1933 Sex:F Child# 4 Victor Paradis Nashua, NH & Alice Mailloux Canada
PARADIS, Herve Roger, Apr 16 1913 Sex:M Child# 1 Joseph Paradis Canada & Elise Laplante Nashua, NH
PARADIS, Irene Juliette, Jul 4 1911 Sex:F Child# 2 Louis Paradis Canada & Laura Levesque Canada
PARADIS, Ita Violet, Feb 21 1928 Sex:F Child# 4 Alphonse Paradis Canada & Rose Cormier Canada
PARADIS, J Alphonse Ernest, Mar 3 1921 Sex:M Child# 4 Alphonse Paradis Canada & Rose Dube Canada
PARADIS, J Louis Armand, Mar 16 1913 Sex:M Child# 3 Louis Paradis, Jr Canada & Laura Levesque Canada
PARADIS, Jean Louis Joseph, Jul 22 1905 Sex:M Child# 1 Jean Paradis Canada & Aurore Plourde Canada
PARADIS, Jean Paul, Mar 26 1915 Sex:M Child# 2 Joseph Paradis Canada & Elise Laplante Nashua, NH
PARADIS, Jos Alfred Valmar, Oct 26 1923 Sex:M Child# 6 Alphonse Paradis Canada & Rose Dube Canada
PARADIS, Jos Camille Romeo, Dec 11 1934 Sex:M Child# 5 Victor Paradis Nashua, NH & Alice Mailloux Canada
PARADIS, Joseph, Aug 10 1893 Sex:M Child# 5 Louis Paradis Canada & Celina Lavoie Canada
PARADIS, Joseph, Apr 26 1922 Sex:M Child# 13 Adelard Paradis Canada & Marie Beaulieu Canada Stillborn
PARADIS, Joseph Albert, Sep 5 1901 Sex:M Child# 8 Luc Paradis Canada & Marie Morel Canada
PARADIS, Joseph Albert, May 5 1930 Sex:M Child# 2 Victor Jos Paradis Nashua, NH & Alice Mailloux Canada
PARADIS, Joseph Alvida, Jul 21 1894 Sex:M Child# 4 Luc Paradis Canada & Marie Morelle Canada

PARADIS, Joseph Carl, Aug 9 1914 Sex:M Child# 4 Louis Paradis Canada & Laure Levesque Canada
PARADIS, Joseph Edouard, Sep 9 1916 Sex:M Child# 4 Paul Paradis Canada & Graciuse Levesque Maine
PARADIS, Joseph Edward, Jan 4 1904 Sex:M Child# 9 Louis Paradis Canada & Celina Lavoie Canada
PARADIS, Joseph Ovilla, Dec 4 1891 Sex:M Child# 2 Charles Paradis Canada & Edmire Sinard Canada
PARADIS, Joseph Paul Ernest, Feb 8 1915 Sex:M Child# 1 Ernest Paradis Canada & Regina Dube Canada
PARADIS, Joseph Raoul, Jun 27 1900 Sex:M Child# 7 Luc Paradis Canada & Marie Morel Canada
PARADIS, Juliette, Apr 9 1896 Sex:F Child# 5 Luc Paradis Canada & Marie Morel Canada
PARADIS, Leo, Mar 4 1904 Sex:M Child# 1 Joseph Paradis Canada & Emma Moreau Canada
PARADIS, Leo E, Jun 6 1901 Sex:M Child# 1 Thomas Paradis Canada & Marie Dionne Canada
PARADIS, Leo Peter, May 19 1929 Sex:M Child# 6 Louis Paradis Canada & L Levesque Canada
PARADIS, Leon, Aug 7 1890 Sex:M Child# 1 Charles Paradis Canada & Elmire Simard Canada
PARADIS, Lorette Frances, Nov 23 1921 Sex:F Child# 3 Joseph Paradis Canada & Elise Laplante Nashua, NH
PARADIS, Louise Alvina, Dec 24 1892 Sex:F Child# 3 Charles Paradis Canada & Elmire Simard Canada
PARADIS, M Antoinette Aline, Jun 17 1919 Sex:F Child# 3 Alphonse Paradis Canada & Rose Dube Canada
PARADIS, M Jeanne Gabrielle, Feb 2 1922 Sex:F Child# 1 Thomas Paradis Canada & Alpheda Gagne Canada
PARADIS, Marie, Aug 29 1892 Sex:F Child# 3 Luc Paradis Canada & Marie Morel Canada
PARADIS, Marie Alice, May 26 1916 Sex:F Child# 2 Ernest Paradis Canada & Regina Dube Canada
PARADIS, Marie Cecile Pauline, Oct 26 1934 Sex:F Child# 3 Joseph A Paradis Canada & Marie E C Mailloux Canada
PARADIS, Marie Eulalia Jean, Feb 12 1918 Sex:F Child# 1 Louis Paradis N D Bois, PQ & Jeannette Pelletier Canada
PARADIS, Marie Graziella, Oct 23 1923 Sex:F Child# 4 Joseph Paradis Mass & Marie Plourde Canada
PARADIS, Marie Liliane, Jan 28 1910 Sex:F Child# 1 Louis Paradis Canada & Laura Levesque Canada
PARADIS, Marie Rose, Sep 19 1892 Sex:F Child# 3 Alcide Paradis Canada & Arthemise Roussel Canada
PARADIS, Marie Sara, Nov 23 1892 Sex:F Child# 1 Joseph Paradis Canada & Lea St Jean Lewiston, ME
PARADIS, Mary Marguerite, Dec 3 1934 Sex:F Child# 2 Flavius Paradis Canada & Beatrice St Laurent Haverhill, MA
PARADIS, Maurice Gerald, Feb 19 1926 Sex:M Child# 6 Louis Paradis Canada & Laura Levesque Canada
PARADIS, Palma Theresa, Aug 9 1926 Sex:F Child# 4 Joseph Paradis Canada & Elise LaPlante Nashua, NH
PARADIS, Paul Normand, May 21 1923 Sex:M Child# 6 Ephrem Paradis Canada & Leocadie Rousseau Canada
PARADIS, Rachel J T, Jan 15 1926 Sex:F Child# 2 Romeo Paradis Canada & Evelyn Lee Bangor, ME
PARADIS, Robert Raymond, Aug 14 1922 Sex:M Child# 5 Alphonse Paradis Canada & Rose Dube Canada
PARADIS, Romeo George, Jr, Apr 21 1923 Sex:M Child# 1 Romeo Paradis Warwick, Canada & Evelyn Spellman Bangor, ME
PARADIS, Sue, Oct 24 1890 Sex:F Child# 2 Luc Paradis Canada & Marie Morel Canada
PARADIS, Unknown, Dec 9 1922 Sex:F Child# 1 Alphonse Paradis Exeter, NH & Rose Cormier Canada
PARADIS, Unknown, Dec 9 1922 Sex:F Child# 2 Alphonse Paradis Exeter, NH & Rose Cormier Canada
PARADIS, Unknown, Jan 4 1924 Sex:F Child# 3 Alphonse Paradis Exeter, NH & Martha Cormier Canada
PARADIS, Unknown, Mar 28 1930 Sex:F Child# 1 Paul Paradis Canada & Olivette Grandmaison Nashua, NH
PARADISE, Annita Lucile, Apr 12 1906 Sex:F Child# 1 Henry M Paradise Redford, NY & Eva M Goyette Sciota, NY
PARADISE, Jos Louis Oliver, Apr 15 1920 Sex:M Child# 2 Louis Paradise Canada & Jeannette Pelletier Canada
PARADISE, Joseph Alphe Girard, Dec 14 1931 Sex:M Child# 2 Alfred Paradise Canada & Cecille M Mayou Canada
PARADISE, Joseph G Ernest, Jan 23 1931 Sex:M Child# 3 Joseph Paradise Canada & Alice Prudhomme Canada
PARADISE, Louise Lillian, Mar 20 1900 Sex:F Child# 1 H M Paradise NJ & Minnie Sweeney Nashua, NH
PARADISE, Marie Carmel Theresa, Jul 6 1926 Sex:F Child# 7 Alphonse Paradise Canada & Rose Dube Canada
PARADISE, Marie Jeanne d'Arc, Nov 14 1920 Sex:F Child# 12 Adelard Paradise Canada & Marie Beaulieu Canada
PARADISE, Mary Carmelle R, Jul 3 1930 Sex:F Child# 1 Alfred Paradise Canada & Cecile Mailloux Canada
PARADISE, Oliver Joseph, Aug 26 1920 Sex:M Child# 5 Oliver Paradise Canada & Elvina Blair Francestown, NH
PARADISE, Phyllis Eva, Dec 23 1933 Sex:F Child# 1 Claude Paradise Derry, NH & Verna English Baring, ME
PARADISE, Roland Edouard, Feb 2 1916 Sex:M Child# 2 Alphonse Paradise Canada & Rose Dube Canada
PARAGOUL, Mary, Jan 12 1911 Sex:F Child# 4 George Paragoul Greece & Nellie State Greece
PARDIN, Alma, Jun 19 1890 Sex:F Child# 2 Pierre Pardin Canada & Anna Gereau Canada
PARE, Daniel, Jan 10 1926 Sex:M Child# 10 Wilfrid Pare Canada & Anastasie Bernard Mass
PARE, Gerald, Apr 19 1910 Sex:M Child# 1 Gerald Pare Biddeford, ME & Rose A Forcier Canada
PARE, Gerald Robert, Jan 2 1928 Sex:M Child# 12 Ferdinand Pare Canada & Philomene Gaumont Canada
PARE, Gertrude, Jun 17 1926 Sex:F Child# 11 Ferdinand Pare Canada & Philosine Gaumont Canada
PARE, J Urbain Hormidas, Mar 12 1912 Sex:M Child# 2 Gerald Pare Maine & Rose Alba Forcier Canada
PARE, Marie Violette Luc, Dec 20 1914 Sex:F Child# 3 Gerald Pare Maine & Rose Alba Forcier Canada
PARENT, Adelina Elise, Apr 10 1903 Sex:F Child# 8 Antoine Parent W Chazy, NY & Josephine Simard Canada
PARENT, Agnes, Jul 18 1913 Sex:F Child# 13 Antoine Parent US & Josephine Simard Canada
PARENT, Andrea Gertrude, Jan 22 1926 Sex:F Child# 2 Leo Parent Nashua, NH & Andrea Rodier Nashua, NH
PARENT, Anna Josephine, Dec 14 1906 Sex:F Child# 10 Antoine Parent US & Josephine Simard Canada
PARENT, Anna Rochelle, Jan 23 1905 Sex:F Child# 2 Henry E Parent Canada & Alma Laurendeau Canada
PARENT, Annette, May 3 1926 Sex:F Child# 1 Leo Parent Nashua, NH & Olida Pelletier Canada
PARENT, Beatrice Irma Marie, Mar 12 1927 Sex:F Child# 1 Alphonse Parent Nashua, NH & A Grandmaison Nashua, NH
PARENT, Charles Amedee, Apr 26 1898 Sex:M Child# 4 Amedee Parent Canada & Maria Landry Canada
PARENT, Dellia Corinna, May 14 1889 Sex:F Child# 3 Deseire Parent Canada & Severance Bernier Canada
PARENT, Edmund Thomas, Dec 17 1934 Sex:M Child# 4 Edward Parent W Chazy, NY & Bertha Rock Burke, NY
PARENT, Eileen Ann, Oct 27 1930 Sex:F Child# 2 Edward Parent W Chazy, NY & Bertha Rock Burke, NY
PARENT, Elias, May 16 1907 Sex:M Child# 1 Etienne Parent Canada & Adelia Michaud Canada
PARENT, Ernest, Jun 8 1891 Sex:M Child# 4 Desire Parent Canada & Emerance Bernier Canada
PARENT, Eva Yvonne, Sep 26 1907 Sex:F Child# 2 Prudent Parent Canada & Eva Tessier Canada
PARENT, Everett Edward, Dec 21 1928 Sex:M Child# 2 Edward Parent W Chazy, NY & Bertha Rock Burke, NY
PARENT, Florence Georgette, Dec 10 1933 Sex:F Child# 4 Doria Parent Canada & Marie Millette Canada
PARENT, G Joseph Stanislas, Nov 9 1917 Sex:M Child# 1 Prudent Parent Canada & Lea Duchesneau Canada
PARENT, Gerard Roger, Sep 29 1920 Sex:M Child# Joseph Parent Canada & Rose Levesque Canada
PARENT, Germaine Y S, Sep 11 1908 Sex:F Child# 3 Joseph Parent US & Rosanna Levesque Canada

PARENT, Henri William, Oct 11 1913 Sex:M Child# 3 Joseph H Parent Canada & Alma Laurendeau Canada
PARENT, Henry Louis, Feb 3 1904 Sex:M Child# 7 Amedee Parent Canada & Maria Landry Canada
PARENT, Ida, Jan 12 1904 Sex:F Child# 2 George Parent Canada & Emerance Doyon Canada
PARENT, Isabelle Evelina, Mar 2 1908 Sex:F Child# 11 Albert J Parent Canada & Marie A Boisvert Canada
PARENT, James Henry, May 31 1912 Sex:M Child# 12 Antoine Parent US & Josephine Simard Canada
PARENT, Joseph, Apr 21 1912 Sex:M Child# 1 (No Parents Listed)
PARENT, Joseph Alphonse, Oct 15 1899 Sex:M Child# 5 Amede Parent Canada & Maria Landry Canada
PARENT, Joseph Doria Henry, Mar 30 1928 Sex:M Child# 3 Doria Parent Canada & Marie Millette Canada
PARENT, Joseph S L, Jun 11 1906 Sex:M Child# 1 Prudent Parent Canada & Eva Tessier Canada
PARENT, Leda Nora, May 16 1901 Sex:F Child# 6 Antoine Parent W Chazy, NY & Josephine Simard Canada
PARENT, Lenore, Mar 18 1898 Sex:F Child# 4 Antoine Parent US & Josephine Simard Canada
PARENT, Leon, Oct 24 1910 Sex:M Child# 11 Antoine Parent US & Josephine Simard Canada
PARENT, Leopold, Oct 22 1900 Sex:M Child# 6 Amedie Parent Canada & Marie Landry Canada
PARENT, Lilian Jeannette, Apr 15 1910 Sex:F Child# 4 Joseph Parent Canada & Rosanna Levesque Canada
PARENT, Lina, May 19 1905 Sex:F Child# 9 Antoine Parent Canada & Josephine Simard Canada
PARENT, Louise Beatrice, Apr 10 1903 Sex:F Child# 7 Antoine Parent W Chazy, NY & Josephine Simard Canada
PARENT, M A Adelia, Nov 3 1894 Sex:F Child#  Amedee Parent Canada & Marie Landry Canada
PARENT, M Anne, Jun 29 1895 Sex:F Child# 2 Antoine Parent US & Josephine Simard Canada
PARENT, Malvina, Aug 9 1896 Sex:F Child# 3 Antoine Parent US & Josephine Simard Canada
PARENT, Marie Agnes, Oct 16 1916 Sex:F Child# 1 Paul Parent Canada & Agnes Henry Nashua, NH
PARENT, Marie Angeline Delci, Jan 10 1927 Sex:F Child# 2 Doria Parent Canada & Marie Millette Canada
PARENT, Marie Blanche Gertr, Sep 26 1923 Sex:F Child# 1 Doria Parent Canada & Marie Millette Canada
PARENT, Marie Jean Teresa, Nov 28 1930 Sex:F Child# 4 Doria Parent Canada & Marie Millett Canada
PARENT, Marie Lucienne Cecil, Feb 13 1935 Sex:F Child# 5 Leo Parent Nashua, NH & Alida Pelletier Canada
PARENT, Marie Lydia J, Sep 2 1899 Sex:F Child# 5 Antoine Parent NY & Josephine Simard Canada
PARENT, Marie Rosalda, Jan 25 1895 Sex:F Child# 5 Desire Parent Canada & Severance Bernier Canada
PARENT, Marie Rosanna, Nov 11 1893 Sex:F Child# 4 Amedee Parent Canada & Marie Landry Canada
PARENT, Marie Rose, Apr 14 1890 Sex:F Child# 1 Joseph Parent Canada & Isabel Thibodeaux Canada
PARENT, Marie Rose, Feb 25 1896 Sex:F Child# 3 Amedee Parent Canada & Marie Landry Canada
PARENT, Mary Joan, May 12 1933 Sex:F Child# 3 Edward Parent W Chazy, NY & Bertha Rock Burke, NY
PARENT, Nazaire, Dec 21 1915 Sex:M Child# 14 Antoine Parent US & Josephine Simard Canada
PARENT, Normand, Sep 6 1928 Sex:M Child# 3 Leo Parent Nashua, NH & Olida Pelletier Canada
PARENT, Olivier Armand, Apr 12 1903 Sex:M Child# 1 Henri Parent Canada & Alma Lorandeau Canada
PARENT, Paul, Dec 3 1917 Sex:M Child# 2 Paul Parent Lowell, MA & Agnes Henry Nashua, NH Stillborn
PARENT, Paul John, Mar 25 1919 Sex:M Child# 3 Paul Nap Parent Canada & Agnes Mary Henry Nashua, NH
PARENT, Philippe Romeo, Sep 9 1906 Sex:M Child# 10 Albert J Parent Canada & Marie A Boisvert Canada
PARENT, Raymond Leo, Jun 24 1930 Sex:M Child# 2 Alphonse Parent Nashua, NH & Alida Grandmaison Canada
PARENT, Roger, Dec 7 1924 Sex:M Child# 1 Leo Parent Nashua, NH & Andrea Rodier Nashua, NH
PARENT, Rose Lorette, Apr 10 1914 Sex:F Child# 6 Joseph Parent Canada & Rose Levesque Canada
PARENT, Unknown, Mar 10 1913 Sex:M Child# 5 Joseph Parent Canada & Rosanna Levesque Canada Stillborn
PARENT, Wilda, Aug 15 1901 Sex:F Child# 6 Eugene Parent Canada & Josephine Grenier Canada
PARENT, Wilfred, Mar 30 1909 Sex:M Child# 1 Regis Parent Van Buren, ME & Elsire Paradis Canada
PARFITT, John William, Jr, May 18 1913 Sex:M Child# 4 John W Parfitt Otto, Iowa & Bertha Conrad Washington, IA
PARFITT, Peter Conrad, Jul 27 1914 Sex:M Child# 5 John W Parfitt Iowa & Anna B Conrad Iowa
PARIAS, Dimetra, Jul 28 1917 Sex:F Child# 8 John Parias Greece & Haidow Dova Greece
PARIDIS, Joseph, Jun 29 1889 Sex:M Child# 1 Joseph Paridis Canada & Marie Morel Canada Stillborn
PARIS, Antonio G, Feb 4 1901 Sex:M Child# 3 Alphonse Paris Canada & Cesena Girard Canada
PARIS, Donat H, Jun 30 1903 Sex:M Child# 5 Alphonse Paris Canada & Clarina Girard Canada
PARIS, Edouard Armand, Jun 22 1897 Sex:M Child# 3 Louis Paris NY & Amanda St Onge Canada
PARIS, Emile, Nov 27 1898 Sex:M Child# 7 Leo Paris NY & Amanda St Onge Canada
PARIS, Ernest A, Jul 14 1902 Sex:M Child# 4 Alphonse Paris Canada & Clarina Girard Canada
PARIS, Jeanne d'Arc, Jun 19 1925 Sex:F Child# 10 Ferdinand Paris Canada & Felonise Gamache Canada
PARIS, Jos Arthur Gerard, Jun 18 1919 Sex:M Child# 2 Arthur Paris Canada & Rose Abour Nashua, NH
PARIS, Joseph A, Jun 17 1898 Sex:M Child# 1 Alphonse Paris Canada & Clarina Girard Canada
PARIS, Joseph Leo Albert, Jan 16 1896 Sex:F Child# 3 Leo Paris NY & Amanda St Onge Canada
PARIS, Joseph O, Jun 4 1887 Sex:M Child# 7 Louis Paris P Q & Elenore Mousette P Q
PARIS, Joseph Wilbrod, Jun 9 1923 Sex:M Child# 3 Arthur Paris Nashua, NH & Mary Rose Arbour Nashua, NH
PARIS, Marie, Aug 25 1899 Sex:F Child# 2 Alphonse Paris Canada & Clarina Girard Canada
PARIS, Marie Mabel, Mar 6 1892 Sex:F Child# 3 Leo Paris Glens Falls, NY & Amanda St Onge Canada
PARIS, R Dl Lucile Avelin, Apr 12 1916 Sex:F Child# 2 Arthur Paris Canada & Dalima Abour Nashua, NH
PARIS, Unknown, Feb 12 1891 Sex:F Child# 2 Leo Paris Glens Falls, NY & Amanda St Onge Canada Stillborn
PARISEAU, George Francis, Sep 9 1913 Sex:M Child# 4 Joseph F Pariseau Canada & Marie L Prunier Canada
PARISEAU, Vita Theresa Yvonne, Nov 1 1927 Sex:F Child# 1 Eugene Pariseau Holyoke, MA & Germaine Leclere Canada
PARIZEAU, Gertrude Rose, May 3 1907 Sex:F Child# 1 Joseph Parizeau Lowell, MA & Louisa Prunier Holyoke, MA
PARIZEAU, Joseph F, Jul 23 1908 Sex:M Child# 2 Joseph Parizeau Canada & Louisa Prunier Canada
PARK, Everett William, Sep 9 1922 Sex:M Child# 1 Frank M Park Syracuse, NY & Gladys M Thompson Nashua, NH
PARKER, Barbara Ann, Apr 14 1929 Sex:F Child# 1 Lambert Parker Pepperell, MA & Ruth Burnham Winchester, MA
PARKER, Benjamin Dodge, Nov 4 1918 Sex:M Child# 2 Frank Laton Parker Litchfield, NH & Agnes Casey Ireland
PARKER, Charles Melendy, Oct 17 1927 Sex:M Child# 1 Gerry F Parker Litchfield, NH & Helen R Melendy Temple, NH
PARKER, Charles Norris, May 23 1892 Sex:M Child# 1 Charles D Parker Nashua, NH & Jennie A Norris Springfield, MA
PARKER, Edward M, Nov 1 1895 Sex:M Child# 1 James E Parker Vermont & Susan H Marshall Hudson, NH
PARKER, Eldora, Feb 6 1917 Sex:F Child# 1 Frank Laton Parker Litchfield, NH & Agnes Casey Ireland
PARKER, Elizabeth Katherine, Oct 10 1926 Sex:F Child# 1 Ralph Parker Milford, NH & Florence Baker Woburn, MA

PARKER, Elmer Williams, Nov 27 1889 Sex:M Child# 1 William C Parker New York & Maggie Griffin Troy, NY
PARKER, Ernest Edmund, Jan 12 1913 Sex:M Child# 1 Clarence C Parker Hudson, NH & Mary E Beron Montgomery, VT
PARKER, Florence Lettie, Oct 5 1891 Sex:F Child# 1 Seth C Parker New Hampshire & Orrie Brown Epsom
PARKER, Florence Louisa, Mar 5 1897 Sex:F Child# 1 Clarence C Parker Hudson, NH & Hattie L Robinson Hudson, NH
PARKER, Francis Laton, Jul 11 1921 Sex:M Child# 3 Frank L Parker Litchfield, NH & Agnes Casey Ireland
PARKER, Fred W, Sep 30 1910 Sex:M Child# 4 Fred Parker Plattsburg, NY & Macia Abernatha Pennsylvania
PARKER, Frederic Cecil, Mar 18 1933 Sex:M Child# 1 Malcolm S Parker Sherman Mills, ME & Sara Mazza Oakfield, NY
PARKER, Frederick James, Mar 31 1908 Sex:M Child# 2 James E Parker Fairlee, VT & Susan H Marshall Hudson, NH
PARKER, George Thomas, Jan 14 1931 Sex:M Child# 2 Lambert Parker Pepperell, MA & Ruth Burnham Winchendon, MA
PARKER, Gertrude Emelie, Apr 7 1903 Sex:F Child# 2 Pheneas A Parker Mass & Lillian Durocher NY
PARKER, Glenn Ray, Feb 21 1929 Sex:M Child# 4 Glenn R Parker Pepperell, MA & Dorothy Holt Nashua, NH
PARKER, Harry Lee, Oct 12 1898 Sex:M Child# 2 Frederick Parker Plattsburg, NY & Macy Abernetha Williamsport, PA
PARKER, Hattie Mabel, Jul 18 1921 Sex:F Child# 1 Lawrence J Parker Roxbury, NH & Doris Wilson Bennington, NH
PARKER, John Bachelder, Jul 15 1932 Sex:M Child# 2 Ralph M Parker Milford, NH & Flor K Baker Woburn, MA
PARKER, June Adeline, Nov 23 1919 Sex:F Child# 5 Harold Parker Keene, NH & Bessie Irwin Sheldon, VT
PARKER, Leonard Baldwin, Apr 13 1935 Sex:M Child# 2 Leonard Parker Bedford, MA & Claire Devereux Roxbury, MA
PARKER, Lucille, Jan 19 1908 Sex:F Child# 1 Charles H Parker Candia, NH & Edna D McGregor Nashua, NH
PARKER, Marilyn, Oct 24 1928 Sex:F Child# 4 Leslie W Parker Pepperell, MA & Mary L Butler Derry, NH
PARKER, Marion Etta, Mar 2 1934 Sex:F Child# 1 Leonard B Parker Bedford, MA & Claire Devereux Roxbury, MA
PARKER, Marion Josephine, Nov 4 1900 Sex:F Child# 1 P A Parker Mass & Lillian M Desrocher NY
PARKER, Marjorie Blanche, Feb 13 1927 Sex:F Child# 6 Charles R Parker Amherst, NH & Susane Patterson Merrimack, NH
PARKER, Mildred Magdalene, Dec 20 1913 Sex:F Child# 4 John A Parker Lyon Mt, NY & Florence Carrone Peru, NY
PARKER, Nina Holt, Mar 3 1927 Sex:F Child# 3 Glenn Parker Pepperell, MA & Dorothy Holt Nashua, NH
PARKER, Norma Lorraine, Sep 26 1924 Sex:F Child# 2 Glenn Ray Parker Pepperell, MA & Dorothy Holt Nashua, NH
PARKER, Patricia Joan, Aug 13 1934 Sex:F Child# 4 Lambert Parker Pepperell, MA & Ruth Burnham Winchendon, MA
PARKER, Pauline Florence, May 28 1923 Sex:F Child# 1 Lambert A Parker Pepperell, MA & Doris Shattuck Pepperell, MA
PARKER, Peter Alland, Jan 9 1935 Sex:M Child# 5 Glenn R Parker Pepperell, MA & Dorothy Holt Nashua, NH
PARKER, Philip George, Feb 4 1927 Sex:M Child# 2 Roland E Parker Wilton, NH & Lucy I Farrell Wilton, NH
PARKER, Phyllis Elaine, Jun 19 1923 Sex:F Child# 1 Glenn Parker Pepperell, MA & Dorothy Holt Nashua, NH
PARKER, Ralph Leonard, Nov 1 1916 Sex:M Child# 5 John H Parker Lyon Mt, NY & Florence Carrowe Peru, NY
PARKER, Raymond Earl, Oct 24 1931 Sex:M Child# 1 (No Parents Listed)
PARKER, Richard, Feb 11 1933 Sex:M Child# 3 Lambert Parker Peterboro, NH & Ruth Burnham Winchendon, MA
PARKER, Richard Allen, May 12 1913 Sex:M Child# 2 Thomas O Parker Pepperell, MA & Lucy Woodward Conway, MA
PARKER, Richard Edward, Jul 16 1927 Sex:M Child# 2 Walter Parker Peterboro, NH & Ruth Moran Nashua, NH
PARKER, Robert Guy, Apr 27 1930 Sex:M Child# 4 Walter M Parker Peterboro, NH & Ruth Moran Nashua, NH
PARKER, Robert McAllister, Apr 7 1928 Sex:M Child# 3 Roland Parker Wilton, NH & Lucy Farrell Wilton, NH
PARKER, Roland Clyde, Apr 27 1930 Sex:M Child# 3 Walter M Parker Peterboro, NH & Ruth Moran Nashua, NH
PARKER, Roland Elmer, Jul 8 1922 Sex:M Child# 1 Roland E Parker Wilton, NH & Lucy Farrell Wilton, NH
PARKER, Rowen C, Jul 10 1887 Sex:M Child# 1 Henry C Parker Westfield, VT & Clara H Stetson Nashua, NH
PARKER, Steven, Aug 23 1916 Sex:M Child# 1 (No Parents Listed)
PARKER, Unknown, Jun 22 1887 Sex: Child# 2 George H Parker New Hampshire & Jennie New Hampshire Stillborn
PARKER, Unknown, Jun 22 1887 Sex:F Child# 3 George H Parker New Hampshire & Jennie New Hampshire
PARKER, Unknown, Sep 12 1888 Sex:F Child# 4 John F Parker Amherst & Sadie A Smith Nashua, NH Stillborn
PARKER, Unknown, Jan 15 1890 Sex:F Child# 2 Charles A Parker Nashua, NH & Della M Abbot Hudson, NH
PARKER, Unknown, Mar 27 1890 Sex:F Child# 3 George H Parker Warren, NH & Jennie E Lisbon, NH
PARKER, Unknown, Jun 20 1891 Sex:M Child# 2 William C Parker Glen Harbor, MI & Maggie Griffin Troy, NY
PARKER, Unknown, Sep 17 1891 Sex:F Child# 5 George H Parker Warren & Jennie E Lisbon
PARKER, Unknown, Oct 20 1893 Sex: Child# 2 William C Parker Glen Falls, MI & Maggie Griffin Cohoes, NY
PARKER, Unknown, Aug 7 1895 Sex:F Child# 1 Fred Parker New York & Mary Ebernethy Pennsylvania
PARKER, Unknown, Dec 23 1895 Sex:M Child# 5 Benjamin Parker Ashby, MA & Martha Smith Groton, MA Stillborn
PARKER, Unknown, Sep 23 1912 Sex:M Child# 3 John A Parker Lyon Mt, NY & Florence Carrone Peru, NY
PARKER, Unknown, Sep 18 1918 Sex:M Child# 4 Charles R Parker Amherst, NH & Susan B Patterson Merrimack, NH
PARKER, Unknown, Oct 10 1923 Sex:M Child# 1 Edward Parker Hudson, NH & Grace Pillips Hudson, NH Stillborn
PARKER, Unknown, Apr 30 1931 Sex:F Child# 1 Lunnie H Parker Manchester, NH & Florence Richardson Milford, NH
PARKER, Virginia Louise, Apr 16 1925 Sex:F Child# 2 Leslie W Parker Pepperell, MA & Mary Butler Derry, NH
PARKER, Walter Munroe, Aug 18 1922 Sex:M Child# 1 Walter M Parker Peterboro, NH & Ruth B Moran Nashua, NH
PARKHURST, Elizabeth Maud, Apr 6 1895 Sex:F Child# 1 Almon Parkhurst NH & Nina M Moore NH
PARKHURST, Ellessifean Frances, Jan 13 1908 Sex:F Child# 1 George Parkhurst Wilton, NH & Marietta Pease Boston, MA
PARKHURST, Unknown, Dec 26 1909 Sex:F Child# 2 George Parkhurst Wilton, NH & Marietta Pease Boston, MA
PARKINSON, Alfred R, Sep 22 1927 Sex:M Child# 4 A W Parkinson Ireland & K Sullivan Ireland
PARKINSON, Elizabeth Teresa, May 8 1919 Sex:F Child# 2 Alfred Parkinson Ireland & Katherine Sullivan Ireland
PARKINSON, Louise May, May 16 1917 Sex:F Child# 1 Alfred W Parkinson Ireland & Catherine Sullivan Ireland
PARKINSON, Virginia Helen, May 6 1923 Sex:F Child# 3 Alfred Parkinson Ireland & Catherine Sullivan Ireland
PARMENTER, Grace, Oct 30 1889 Sex:F Child# 4 Albert Parmenter Sudbury, MA & Emma Pendle Canada
PARMENTER, Unknown, Feb 3 1891 Sex:M Child# 2 A E Parmenter New York & Nova Scotia Stillborn
PARMETON, Raymond A, Apr 25 1907 Sex:M Child# 2 Gideon Parmeton Canada & Claudia Belanger Canada
PARMIGIN, Mary Anne, Mar 1 1894 Sex:F Child# 3 Joseph Parmigin Italy & Marie Petit Canada
PARNELL, Jean Frances, May 17 1922 Sex:F Child# 4 William B Parnell Nova Scotia & Alice E Rowell Nashua, NH
PARNELL, Robert Gordon, Sep 19 1918 Sex:M Child# 3 William B Parnell Nova Scotia & Alice E Rowell Nashua, NH
PARNELL, Ruth Ellen, Jun 24 1911 Sex:F Child# 2 William B Parnell Nova Scotia & Alice E Rowell Nashua, NH
PARO, Frank Arthur, Apr 26 1902 Sex:M Child# 1 Frank A Paro Malone, NY & Jennie Cook Torrington, CT
PARO, George Amedose, May 5 1896 Sex:M Child# 10 Alfred Paro
PARO, Jacqueline Nellie, Aug 20 1931 Sex:F Child# 2 Alfred Paro Nashua, NH & Josephine Butler Oxford, MA

PARO, Joseph Victor, Apr 3 1894 Sex:M Child# 9 Alfred M Paro Champlain, NY & Delia Fountain Savoy, MA
PARO, Pauline Theresa, Sep 9 1929 Sex:F Child# 1 Lionel Paro Nashua, NH & Lucille Levesque Graniteville, VT
PARRETT, Emily, Feb 8 1902 Sex:F Child# 1 Charles P Parrett England & Mary F Crowley Ireland
PARRISH, Eleanor Dorothy, Mar 30 1926 Sex:F Child# 1 Malcolm F Parrish Tyngsboro, MA & Esther C Ohison Lowell, MA
PARRISH, Frank Taylor, Feb 28 1906 Sex:M Child# 1 Fred A Parrish Salem, NH & Edith L Taylor Springfield, MA
PARROTT, Frank William, Mar 14 1905 Sex:M Child# 2 Charles Parrott England & Mary Crowley Ireland
PARSKUS, Anton, Jan 29 1907 Sex:M Child# 4 Anton Parskus Russia & Marcelle Ezdinta Russia
PARSONS, Louis Leonard, Nov 24 1927 Sex:M Child# 1 L L Parsons Chelsea, MA & Kathleen Parsons St Albans, VT Stillbo
PARSYCH, Casimir, Oct 7 1931 Sex:M Child# 9 Frank Parsych Poland & Leona Bodeges Poland
PARTTEY, Michael, Apr 17 1888 Sex:M Child# 1 Michael Parttey Ireland & Mary Sterrit Ireland
PASHKIEWIEZ, Joseph Cyprus, Jul 24 1918 Sex:M Child# 4 Cyprus Pashkiewiez Russia & Michalina Overka Russia
PASHUVICZ, Michael, May 8 1915 Sex:M Child# 2 Cyprus Pashuvicz Russia & Mikalina Owurka Russia
PASKALEY, Aristotle, Nov 27 1928 Sex:M Child# 1 George G Paskaley Greece & M A Kasapi Turkey
PASKALEY, Catherine, Dec 26 1929 Sex:F Child# 2 George Paskaley Greece & Magdalene Kasapi Turkey
PASKALY, Unknown, May 10 1920 Sex:F Child# 2 Antonis Paskaly Greece & Atanasia Dimaritz Greece
PASKAWICZ, Stanislaus, Sep 19 1908 Sex:M Child# 1 Felix Paskawicz Russia & Mary Karyshutie Russia
PASKEVICH, Adam, Oct 21 1929 Sex:M Child# 4 Cyprien Paskevich Lithuania & Michalina Overka Lithuania Stillborn
PASKEVICH, Joan Michalina, Oct 21 1929 Sex:F Child# 5 Cyprien Paskevich Lithuania & Michalina Overka Lithuania
PASKIAWICIUZ, Nellie, May 15 1911 Sex:F Child# 2 F Paskiawiciuz Russia & Mary Kianszute Russia
PASSIAS, Nicholas, Jun 13 1928 Sex:M Child# 1 Spiros Passias Greece & S Apostolopoulos Greece
PASSIAS, Unknown, Dec 26 1929 Sex:F Child# 2 Spiros Passias Greece & Sophia Apostolopoulo Greece
PASTOI, Jackson, Dec 14 1915 Sex:M Child# 2 Harry Partoi Russia & Eva B Gordon Russia
PASTOR, Bernard, Mar 12 1922 Sex:M Child# 4 Harry Pastor Russia & Eva Gordon Russia
PASTOR, Charles Ruben, Aug 30 1930 Sex:M Child# 6 Harry Pastor Russia & Eva Gordon Russia
PASTOR, Irving, Dec 24 1923 Sex:M Child# 5 Harry Pastor European Russia & Eva Gordon European Russia
PASTOR, Sylvia Annette, Jul 22 1920 Sex:F Child# 3 Harry Pastor Russia & Eva Gordon Russia
PATCH, Fletcher, Aug 13 1927 Sex:M Child# 2 Philip F Patch Francestown, NH & Bernice C Hayes Manchester, NH
PATENANDE, Joseph Louis, Dec 12 1896 Sex:M Child# 3 Julien Patenande Canada & Georgianna Thibault Canada
PATENAUD, Moses, Nov 19 1917 Sex:M Child# 4 Moses Patenaud Bedford, NY & Eva Alpha Hamlin Burlington, VT
PATENAUDE, Corade, Aug 21 1892 Sex:M Child# 10 Theophile Patenaude Canada & Celina Gaudet Canada
PATENAUDE, Eva B, Apr 16 1890 Sex:F Child# 9 Theophile Patenaude Canada & Celina Gaudet Canada
PATENAUDE, George, Jun 17 1899 Sex:M Child# 14 Theophile Patenaude Canada & Celina Gaudette Canada
PATENAUDE, Jean B E, Mar 18 1889 Sex:M Child# 1 Jean B Patenaude Canada & Delia Gaudett Canada
PATENAUDE, Orlando, Oct 17 1916 Sex:M Child# 3 Moise A Patenaude Redford, NY & Eva Hamlin Burlington, VT
PATENAUDE, Renee Archie, Dec 5 1920 Sex:F Child# 1 Lionel Patenaude Canada & Emma Bourgoine Canada
PATENAUDE, William, Apr 12 1889 Sex:M Child# 12 Jean Patenaude Canada & Marianne Dumaine Canada
PATENEAUDE, Georgianna, Sep 19 1887 Sex:F Child# 7 Theo Pateneaude P Q & Celina Gaudet P Q
PATENEAUDE, Henry L, Mar 18 1892 Sex:M Child# 3 Jean Bte Pateneaude Canada & Delia Gaudet Canada
PATENEAUDE, Wilfred E, Jan 3 1891 Sex:M Child# 2 Bt Pateneaude Canada & Delia Gaudet Canada
PATIAS, Cleopatra, Sep 18 1912 Sex:F Child# 4 John Patias Greece & Rose Pacas Greece
PATINZKIE, Anieta, Feb 27 1909 Sex:F Child# 3 Michael Patinzkie Russia & Domicelia Stanioniz Russia
PATKUS, Dorothy Grace, Oct 5 1926 Sex:F Child# 4 Felix Patkus Russia & Ida Wood Mass
PATKUS, Felix Gordon, Jun 11 1928 Sex:M Child# 5 Felix Patkus Germany & Ida Wood Fall River, MA
PATKUS, Loraine Patkus, Apr 5 1923 Sex:F Child# 3 Felix Patkus Lithuania & Ida Wood Fall River, MA
PATNAUD, Beatrice Evelyn, Nov 18 1917 Sex:F Child# 3 Arthur G Patnaud Artic Center, RI & Georgie E Thompson Or
PATNAUDE, Gilbert Jerome, Sep 14 1933 Sex:M Child# 2 R Patnaude Coopersville, NY & Noella Patnaude Lowell, MA
PATNEAUDE, Blanche Tessier, Apr 4 1894 Sex:F Child# 11 Theophile Patneaude Canada & Celina Canada
PATON, Francis William, Aug 12 1933 Sex:M Child# 2 Francis A Paton Salem, NH & Josephine Hough Nashua, NH
PATON, Katherine Anne, Aug 1 1935 Sex:F Child# 3 Francis A Paton NH & Josephine Hough Nashua, NH
PATOUROS, George, Jan 19 1916 Sex:M Child# 1 Costos Patouros Greece & Sultana Zardavas Greece
PATR, Mary, Jul 2 1919 Sex:F Child# 2 John Patr Russia & Branisclawa Belda Russia
PATRICK, Lewis, Feb 7 1902 Sex:M Child# 3 Samuel Patrick Windsor, VT & Susan L Applin Marlboro
PATRICK, Loraine, Feb 7 1902 Sex:F Child# 4 Samuel Patrick Windsor, VT & Susan L Applin Marlboro
PATRY, Edward, Mar 12 1909 Sex:M Child# 5 Harry Patry US & Josephine Tremblay US
PATSIS, Andreas, Oct 10 1916 Sex:M Child# 3 Dinos Patsis Greece & Karicloci Trianta Greece
PATTEN, Dorothy Lyman, Feb 22 1901 Sex:F Child# 1 William H Patten Westmoreland, NH & Mary D Lyman Braintree, MA
PATTEN, Lizzie L, Jan 8 1889 Sex:F Child# 6 George F Patten Skowhegan, ME & Nellie Hadley Laconia, NH
PATTEN, Marjorie, Jun 27 1891 Sex:F Child# 2 William H Patten Westmoreland, NH & Mary R Rugg NH
PATTEN, Theresa Eva, Apr 7 1923 Sex:F Child# 2 Clarence Patten Alexandria, NH & Nettie Nutting Kennebunk, ME
PATTEN, Unknown, Aug 17 1889 Sex:M Child# 4 Wilbur L Patten Maine & Mabel Powers Worcester, MA
PATTEN, Unknown, Jan 8 1889 Sex:F Child# 5 George F Patten Skowhegan, ME & Nellie Hadley Laconia, NH Stillborn
PATTEN, Victor Roger, Sep 19 1929 Sex:M Child# 6 Clarence E Patten Alexandria, NH & Nettie A Nutting Kennebunk
PATTEN, William Lyman, May 20 1900 Sex:M Child# 1 Charles T Patten NH & L R Lyman Vermont
PATTERSON, Barbara, Dec 7 1934 Sex:F Child# 8 Horace P Patterson S Merrimack, NH & Annie Linscott Manchester, NH
PATTERSON, Charles Amos, Jun 8 1919 Sex:M Child# 1 Harold Patterson Pawtucket, RI & Grace Bonasera Sicily
PATTERSON, Dana Alan, Jun 3 1933 Sex:M Child# 7 H P Patterson S Merrimack, NH & Annie Linscott Manchester, NH
PATTERSON, Hazel Pearl, Jul 14 1926 Sex:F Child# 3 Horace Patterson S Merrimack, NH & Annie Linscott Manchester, NH
PATTERSON, Helen Louise, Feb 4 1930 Sex:F Child# 5 Horace P Patterson S Merrimack, NH & Annie E Linscott Mancheste
PATTERSON, Horace Putnam, Apr 26 1928 Sex:M Child# 4 H P Patterson S Merrimack, NH & Annie Linscott Manchester, NH
PATTERSON, James Robert, Oct 16 1931 Sex:M Child# 6 Horace Patterson S Merrimack, NH & Annie Linscott Manchester
PATTERSON, Margaret Alice, Feb 24 1910 Sex:F Child# 1 Thomas Patterson England & Mary O'Brien Ireland
PATTERSON, Mildred Grace, Nov 9 1922 Sex:F Child# 3 Harold A Patterson Pawtucket, RI & Grace Bonasera Italy
PATTERSON, Ruth Anna, Jan 17 1923 Sex:F Child# 1 Horace P Patterson S Merrimack, NH & Annie E Linscott Manchester

PATTERSON, Unknown, Jun 12 1891 Sex:M Child# 6 James Patterson
PATTERSON, Unknown, Sep 3 1892 Sex:F Child# 6 James Patterson Ireland & Mary B Jordan Goysboro, NS
PATTI, Anthony Battola, Sep 13 1930 Sex:M Child# 1 Antonio Patti Italy & Mary Marino Cambridge, MA
PATTI, Richard Lawrence, Mar 16 1932 Sex:M Child# 2 Anthony Patti Italy & Mary Marino Lyndonville, VT
PATURAS, George Henry, May 25 1921 Sex:M Child# 1 George Paturas Greece & Grace Tuting New York, NY
PATVICH, Helen, Oct 31 1901 Sex:F Child# 9 Joseph Patvich Russia & Anna Romszoewich Russia
PATVICH, John, Mar 8 1903 Sex:M Child# 10 Joseph Patvich Russia & Anna Rouswicz Russia
PATVICH, Sophia, Aug 23 1899 Sex:M Child# 8 Joseph Patvich Russia & Anna Romszevicz Russia
PAUK, Shirley Mary, Jun 18 1935 Sex:F Child# 1 Edward Pauk Lawrence, MA & Blanche Rioux Nashua, NH
PAUL, Amede, Jan 6 1892 Sex:M Child# 9 Joseph Paul Canada & Philomene Monty Canada
PAUL, Antoine, Oct 5 1902 Sex:M Child#  A Paul Canada & Josephine Burelle Nashua, NH
PAUL, Armand, Aug 18 1892 Sex:M Child# 1 Euclide Paul Canada & Marie Paradis Canada
PAUL, Armand, Jul 19 1897 Sex:M Child# 6 Amable Paul Canada & Josephine Burrell Nashua, NH
PAUL, Aurore, Mar 11 1893 Sex:F Child# 4 Amable Paul Canada & Josephine Burel Nashua, NH
PAUL, Clare Constance, Aug 31 1927 Sex:F Child# 1 Louis Paul Webster, MA & B Villeneuve Haverhill, MA
PAUL, Dorothy Berle, May 5 1923 Sex:F Child# 2 Albert Paul Nashua, NH & Lillian Russell Nashua, NH
PAUL, Edouard R, Nov 15 1897 Sex:M Child# 3 Euclide Paul Canada & Marie Paradis Canada
PAUL, Florence Anita, May 21 1924 Sex:F Child# 2 Armand Paul Nashua, NH & Eva Jacques Lowell, MA
PAUL, Georgianna, Jan 28 1891 Sex:F Child# 3 Amable Paul Canada & Josephine Burel Nashua, NH
PAUL, Henry J B, Jun 24 1889 Sex:M Child# 2 Amable Paul Canada & Josephine Bird Nashua, NH
PAUL, Janet Louise, Aug 18 1920 Sex:F Child# 1 Amedee Paul Nashua, NH & Ruth Rochelle Concord, NH
PAUL, Jessie, Dec 24 1898 Sex:F Child#  James R Paul Scotland & Jessie Harlin Scotland
PAUL, Joseph Adolphe, Feb 23 1895 Sex:M Child# 5 Amable Paul Canada & Josephine Burrell Nashua, NH
PAUL, Joseph Amedee, Jul 19 1897 Sex:M Child# 7 Amable Paul Canada & Josephine Burrell Nashua, NH
PAUL, Joseph Dorilda, Jul 26 1901 Sex:M Child# 9 Amable Paul Canada & Josephine Burelle NH
PAUL, Joseph Maurice Henry, Jan 16 1925 Sex:M Child# 4 Henry Paul Nashua, NH & Madeline Pelletier Nashua, NH
PAUL, Julia, Nov 11 1899 Sex:F Child# 8 Abel Paul Canada & Josephine Burrell Nashua, NH
PAUL, Juliette, Jun 13 1904 Sex:F Child# 5 Euclide Paul Canada & Marie Paradis Canada
PAUL, Lucille Germain, Jan 20 1922 Sex:F Child# 1 Armand Paul Nashua, NH & Eva Jacques Lowell, MA
PAUL, M Louise Rachelle, Jul 14 1920 Sex:F Child# 2 Joseph Paul NH & Leda Laquerre Canada
PAUL, Maria, Nov 13 1887 Sex:F Child#  Amable Paul Canada & Josephine Burelle Nashua, NH
PAUL, Marie, Jun 14 1911 Sex:F Child# 1 Joseph Paul Canada & Ida Laquerre Canada
PAUL, Marie A Sylvia, Dec 1 1898 Sex:F Child# 4 Euclide Paul Nashua, NH & Marie Paradis Canada
PAUL, Marie Ange J, Jun 25 1908 Sex:F Child# 6 Euclide Paul Nashua, NH & Marie Paradis Canada
PAUL, Mary Rachel, Nov 23 1920 Sex:F Child# 2 Henry J Paul Nashua, NH & Madeline Pelletier Nashua, NH
PAUL, Normand Maurice, May 22 1925 Sex:M Child# 3 Armand Paul Nashua, NH & Eva Jacques Lowell, MA
PAUL, Philip Edward, Sep 20 1928 Sex:M Child# 2 Amedee Paul Nashua, NH & Ruth Rochelle Concord, NH
PAUL, Russell C, Feb 26 1922 Sex:M Child# 1 Albert J Paul Nashua, NH & Lillian Russell Nashua, NH
PAUL, Unknown, Jan 13 1895 Sex:F Child# 2 Euclide Paul Canada & Marie Paradis Canada  Stillborn
PAUL, Victor Leo, Sep 6 1923 Sex:M Child# 3 Henry J Paul Nashua, NH & Madeline Pelletier Nashua, NH
PAULHUS, Marie Georgiana Rita, Aug 9 1925 Sex:F Child# 5 Arthur Paulhus Canada & Geo Millette Canada
PAULIN, Marie Lorette, Sep 16 1904 Sex:F Child# 1 Remi Paulin Canada & Leopoldine Parent Canada
PAULKUS, J Arthur Doria, Nov 5 1922 Sex:M Child# 4 Arthur Paulkus Canada & Georgianna Milette Canada
PAULOS, Unknown, Apr 29 1923 Sex:M Child# 4 Nicholas Paulos Greece & Alexandra Amaropopol Greece
PAULOWSKI, Unknown, May 30 1918 Sex:M Child# 1 Anthony Paulowski Russia & Evan Kikulas Russia Stillborn
PAUNATON, Lucen, Aug 22 1897 Sex:M Child# 5 Gideon Paunaton Canada & Andel Marquis Canada
PAUNPOULIS, Costaducos, Dec 29 1911 Sex:M Child# 2 James Paunpoulis Greece & Evangela John Greece
PAUQUETTE, Anclon, Dec 14 1892 Sex:F Child# 2 William Pauquette Vermont & Delphine Nadeau Malone, NY
PAVLOWSKI, Anthony Joseph, Jul 9 1918 Sex:M Child# 5 Anton Pavlowski Russia & Nastia Belchikoo Russia
PAVLOWSKI, John, Aug 10 1916 Sex:M Child# 4 Anton Pavlowski Russia & Nadina Balchikow Russia
PAVLOWSKY, Gregory, Oct 27 1914 Sex:M Child# 3 Anton Pavlowsky Russia & Nadia Balchiko Russia
PAVLOWSKY, Mania, Mar 24 1920 Sex:F Child# 6 Anton Pavlowsky Russia & Nastia Balchiko Russia
PAWLOUSKI, Kazimira, Feb 22 1920 Sex:F Child# 2 Antonas Pawlouski Russia & Eva Kikilate Russia
PAWLOWSKI, William, Jun 4 1906 Sex:M Child# 3 Michael Pawlowski Russia & Marcialie Mizara Russia
PAWLUKEWICEZ, Bolieslow, Feb 2 1918 Sex:M Child# 1 Ant'y Pawlukewicez Russia & Wincenta Folkowski Russia
PAWLUKIEWICZ, Leodia, Nov 12 1919 Sex:F Child# 2 Antoin Pawlukiewicz Russia & Vincenta Falkouska Russia
PAWLUKIEWUCZ, Felica, Jul 27 1922 Sex:F Child# 1 Antoni Pawlukiewucz Lithuania & Wincenta Talkuski Lithuania
PAXVIN, Joseph Emile, Dec 15 1894 Sex:M Child# 10 Felix Paxvin Canada & Elodie St Pierre Canada
PAYIER, Marie S A, May 11 1893 Sex:F Child# 1 Arthur Payier Canada & Leontine Laquene Canada
PAYNE, Dorothy, Jun 18 1928 Sex:F Child# 2 Edmund Payne E Lyme, CT & Ruth Winslow Nashua, NH
PAYNE, Ruth, Apr 17 1918 Sex:F Child#  Harry James Payne Coventry, England & Annie Philbrook Shelburne
PAYNE, Winslow Cummings, Jul 24 1921 Sex:M Child# 1 Edmond F Payne E Lyme, CT & Ruth Winslow Nashua, NH
PAYSON, Myrtle, Dec 11 1924 Sex:F Child# 1 Ernest W Payson Saugus, MA & Pauline Fendell Boston, MA
PAZNIOKAS, Frank, May 20 1916 Sex:M Child# 1 Adam Pazniokas Russia & Helen Lenkawicz Russia
PEABODY, Charles William, Jan 16 1919 Sex:M Child# 1 Art H Peabody Pelham, NH & Mabel Ruth Guild Methuen, MA
PEABODY, Nellie, May 13 1933 Sex:F Child# 1 Wilbur Peabody Lynn, MA & Dorothy Martin Nashua, NH
PEACE, Arthur Wilbur, Jun 11 1895 Sex:M Child# 6 James W Peace Sheffield, England & Hannah M Jubb Sheffield, Eng
PEAKOR, Thomas, Oct 10 1907 Sex:M Child# 1 William Peakor Russia & Pietry Bortis Russia
PEARSON, Charles, Jun 18 1888 Sex:M Child# 1 G B Pearson Nashua, NH & Jennie E Wadleigh Nashua, NH
PEARSON, Floyd Lester, Jul 8 1916 Sex:M Child# 2 William W Pearson Charlotte, NC & Cora Abbott Unity, NH
PEARSON, Leonard S, Aug 27 1891 Sex:M Child# 1 E W Pearson Epping, NH & M G Snow Nashua, NH
PEARSON, Leonard W, Aug 27 1890 Sex:M Child# 1 E W Pearson Epping, NH & M G Snow Nashua, NH
PEARSON, Marie, Nov 21 1906 Sex:F Child# 1 Ludger Pearson Canada & Eva Morency Canada

PEARSON, William Walter, Nov 8 1914 Sex:M Child# 1 William W Pearson Charlotte, NC & Cora B Abbott Unity, NH
PEARSONS, Alford, Jul 14 1893 Sex:M Child# 1 Alphonse Pearsons Hingham, ME & Charlotte M Concord
PEASE, Dorothy, Nov 3 1896 Sex:F Child# 4 Bertis A Pease Wilton, ME & Lena B Flagg Lowell, MA
PEASE, Eileen Elizabeth, Jul 30 1911 Sex:F Child# 1 William S Pease Nashua, NH & Winifred G Croft W Enosburg, VT
PEASE, Eleanore, Apr 16 1891 Sex:F Child# 1 Bertis A Pease Wilton, ME & Linna B Flagg Lowell, MA
PEASE, Emery Edmond, Oct 3 1918 Sex:M Child# 2 Emery E Pease Vasselboro, ME & Doris L Oliver Anapolis, NS
PEASE, Hazel E Boutelle, Dec 14 1898 Sex:F Child#  Arthur L Pease Western, VT & Annie L Boutelle Amherst, NH
PEASE, Robert A, Nov 21 1893 Sex:M Child# 2 Bertis A Pease Wilton, ME & Linna B Flagg Lowell, MA
PEASE, Roger, Jun 26 1892 Sex:M Child# 1 Edwin Pease Hudson, MA & Catherine Hudson, NH
PEASE, Ruth, May 13 1898 Sex:F Child# 5 Bertis A Pease Wilton, ME & Linna B Flagg Lowell, MA
PEASE, Unknown, Sep 12 1887 Sex:M Child# 5 C R Pease Maine & Mary F NH
PEASE, Unknown, May 4 1889 Sex:M Child# 5 C R Pease Maine & Mary F Flagg New Hampshire
PEASELEY, Unknown, Jul 1 1890 Sex:F Child# 10 Frank Peaseley Nashua, NH & Ella M Brown Nashua, NH
PEASLEY, Unknown, May 1 1887 Sex:F Child# 6 Frank Peasley Nashua, NH & Ella M Brown Windsor
PEASLEY, Unknown, Oct 17 1888 Sex:M Child# 9 Frank Peasley Nashua, NH & Elle M Brown Windsor
PEAVY, Walter H, Jun 18 1905 Sex:M Child# 2 Walter A Peavy NH & A E Gorman England
PECKER, Unknown, Aug 28 1900 Sex:F Child# 5 George L Pecker NH & Susan Hutchinson NH
PECKHAM, Unknown, Oct 19 1892 Sex:F Child# 1 Fred E Peckham Salem, MA & Clara Thompson Nashua, NH
PEDARZANI, Elene May, Jan 23 1910 Sex:F Child# 1 Guy Pedarzani Italy & Elizabeth Phelan Ireland
PEDERZANI, Albert Paul, Apr 10 1907 Sex:M Child# 2 Raphael Pederzani Italy & Louise Antolini New York
PEDERZANI, Doris Augusta, Jan 4 1916 Sex:F Child# 3 Rafael Pederzani Italy & Louise Antolini New York, NY
PEDERZANI, Guy Anthony, Mar 12 1914 Sex:M Child# 2 Guy Pederzani Italy & Elizabeth Phelan Ireland
PEDERZANI, Louis Gregory, Dec 27 1920 Sex:M Child# 3 Guy Pederzani Italy & Elizabeth Phelan Ireland
PEDERZANI, Mary Eva, Oct 29 1905 Sex:F Child# 1 Rafael Pederzani Italy & Louise Antolini New York
PEDERZANI, Nathalie Eugenie, Feb 11 1923 Sex:F Child# 4 Guy Pederzani Italy & Elizabeth Phelan Limerick, Ireland
PEDNEAU, Emilienne Olivette, Feb 2 1910 Sex:F Child# 6 Elzear Pedneau Canada & Blanche David Canada
PEDRO, James, Aug 8 1914 Sex:M Child# 8 Mike Pedro Italy & Elizabeth Salvidor Italy
PEIVARUNAS, Unknown, Dec 3 1929 Sex:F Child# 5 Martin Peivarunas Lithuania & Marcella Salyet Lithuania Stillborn
PEJPACHRISTO, Isidore, Jun 2 1914 Sex:M Child# 1 Athos Pejpachristo Greece & Amanda Poliquin Canada
PELKEY, Lillian Irene, Oct 1 1923 Sex:F Child# 1 Anthony Pelkey Vermont & Lillian Marrois Nashua, NH
PELKEY, Marie Ivonne, Jan 16 1906 Sex:F Child# 6 Joseph Pelkey Canada & Helen Frasier Canada
PELKEY, Marion Alice, Nov 16 1927 Sex:F Child# 3 Charles Pelkey Orange, VT & Laura Duprey New York
PELKEY, Mary Ann, Jul 27 1911 Sex:F Child# 14 Joseph Pelkey Canada & Zoe M Michaud Canada Stillborn
PELKEY, Palmyre E I, Jun 12 1909 Sex:F Child# 1 Marcel Pelkey Canada & Palmyre Pelkey Canada
PELKEY, Pauline Rose, Jul 5 1926 Sex:F Child# 2 Charles Pelkey Orange, VT & Laura Duprey New York
PELKEY, Raymond Arthur, Jun 4 1922 Sex:M Child# 1 Charles Pelkey Orange, VT & Laura Dupre Chazy, NY
PELKEY, Susie A, Jan 29 1889 Sex:F Child# 2 Winter E Pelkey Champlain, NY & Alice Pearle Champlain, NY
PELKEY, Unknown, Jan 11 1890 Sex:M Child# 3 Dexter E Pelkey Champlain, NY & Alice O Pearl Champlain, NY
PELKEY, Unknown, Aug 23 1907 Sex:F Child# 2 Joseph Pelkey Milford, NH & Margaret Varley Wilton, NH
PELKIS, Stanislas, Mar 30 1902 Sex:M Child# 2 Antoine Pelkis Russia & Mora Klatka Austria
PELKY, Marie Emelinda, Aug 22 1896 Sex:F Child# 11 W E Pelky NY & Elizabeth St Michel NY
PELKY, Robert Lloyd, Jul 12 1912 Sex:M Child# 1 William H Pelky Allenburg, NY & Minnie B Adams Tilton, NH
PELLERIN, Alexandrina, Jun 13 1892 Sex:F Child# 5 August Pellerin Canada & Philomene Bernier Canada
PELLERIN, Dorothy, Mar 18 1926 Sex:F Child# 2 Ulderic Pellerin Canada & Adeline Pellerine Canada
PELLERIN, Jos Donah Raoul, Aug 12 1920 Sex:M Child# 1 George Pellerin Canada & Eugenie Gagne Canada
PELLERIN, Joseph Amable, Feb 12 1895 Sex:M Child# 1 Amable Pellerin Canada & Eugene Bouchard Canada
PELLERIN, Marie Elmire, Mar 20 1890 Sex:F Child# 4 Auguste Pellerin Canada & Philomene Bernice Canada
PELLERIN, Marie Louise, Sep 29 1895 Sex:F Child# 1 Amable Pellerin Canada & Marie R Caron Canada
PELLERIN, Robert Camillo, Jul 15 1930 Sex:M Child# 1 Camille Pellerin Canada & Elise Mailloux Canada
PELLETIER, Albert, Jun 29 1909 Sex:M Child# 3 George Pelletier Canada & Marie St Jean Canada
PELLETIER, Albert, Jan 19 1928 Sex:M Child# 7 Amedee Pelletier Boscawen, NH & Nelida Hebert Canada
PELLETIER, Alberta Rachel, Jul 2 1908 Sex:F Child# 9 Onesime Pelletier Canada & Emma Levesque Canada
PELLETIER, Alexina Jeannette, Mar 12 1916 Sex:F Child# 8 Eustache Pelletier Canada & Alexina Gagnon Canada
PELLETIER, Alfred, May 30 1902 Sex:M Child#  Joseph Pelletier Canada & Rose Mansfield Canada
PELLETIER, Alfred, Jan 19 1928 Sex:M Child# 6 Amedee Pelletier Boscawen, NH & Nelida Hebert Canada
PELLETIER, Alice, May 10 1933 Sex:F Child# 4 Joseph E Pelletier Canada & B A Corbierre Nashua, NH Stillborn
PELLETIER, Alice Irene, Oct 29 1923 Sex:F Child# 2 Joseph E Pelletier Canada & Adrienne Corbiere Nashua, NH
PELLETIER, Alice Leona, Nov 15 1923 Sex:F Child# 1 Napoleon Pelletier Nashua, NH & Mary Rock Malone, NY
PELLETIER, Alice Theresa Isabel, Dec 4 1926 Sex:F Child# 2 Edouard Pelletier Bayview, MA & Anna Rivard Nashua, NH
PELLETIER, Alice Yvonne, Aug 27 1912 Sex:F Child# 2 Martial Pelletier Canada & Palmire Pelletier Canada
PELLETIER, Amelia Jeannette, Jun 6 1910 Sex:F Child# 4 George Pelletier Canada & Marie Anctil Canada
PELLETIER, Andrew, Oct 24 1924 Sex:M Child# 2 Anthony Pelletier Lyndonville, VT & Lillian Marois Nashua, NH
PELLETIER, Anita Olivette, Aug 1 1915 Sex:F Child# 2 Omer Pelletier Nashua, NH & Marguerite Theroux Nashua, NH
PELLETIER, Anna, May 18 1912 Sex:F Child# 1 Amedee Pelletier Canada & Clerida Hebert Canada
PELLETIER, Antonio, Apr 6 1906 Sex:M Child# 7 Onesime Pelletier Canada & Emma Levesque Canada
PELLETIER, Armand T, May 24 1902 Sex:M Child# 3 Damase Pelletier Canada & Virginie Pellerin Canada
PELLETIER, Arsene Sylvio, Dec 5 1915 Sex:M Child# 4 Bernard Pelletier Canada & Claudia Gagnon NH
PELLETIER, Arthur, Dec 28 1905 Sex:M Child# 1 Jean Pelletier Canada & Amelia Thiboutot Nashua, NH
PELLETIER, Arthur Richard, Feb 9 1929 Sex:M Child# 2 Irving Pelletier Nashua, NH & Aline Richard Canada
PELLETIER, Arthur Roger, Jan 3 1923 Sex:M Child# 5 Adelard Pelletier Nashua, NH & Arzelia Delude Canada
PELLETIER, Beatrice Agnes, Jan 15 1917 Sex:F Child# 3 Omer Pelletier NH & Marguerite Theroux NH
PELLETIER, Blanche Martha, Feb 17 1931 Sex:F Child# 2 Francois Pelletier Nashua, NH & Blanche Girouard Nashua, NH
PELLETIER, Celina, Nov 2 1915 Sex:F Child# 3 Martial Pelletier Canada & Palmire Pelletier Canada

PELLETIER, Charles Eugene, Oct 30 1896 Sex:M Child# 2 Joseph Pelletier Canada & Helene Fraser Canada
PELLETIER, Claire Louise, Feb 6 1932 Sex:F Child# 1 Paul Pelletier Nashua, NH & L Provencher Canada
PELLETIER, Claire Louise, Sep 20 1935 Sex:F Child# 4 Louis Pelletier Nashua, NH & S Sinkervitch Nashua, NH
PELLETIER, Conrad Arvelia, Oct 5 1926 Sex:M Child# 1 Alphonse Pelletier Canada & Anene Morin Canada
PELLETIER, Conrad Francis, Feb 25 1927 Sex:M Child# 5 Francis Pelletier Nashua, NH & Blanche Girouard Hudson, NH
PELLETIER, Dorothy Ann, Feb 16 1935 Sex:F Child# 3 Ernest Pelletier Canada & Catherine McCann Roxbury, MA
PELLETIER, Dorothy Corinne, Mar 7 1925 Sex:F Child# 1 Alphonse Pelletier Canada & Corinne Merchant Willimantic, CT
PELLETIER, Dosity A Joseph, Mar 9 1899 Sex:M Child# 1 Damase Pelletier Canada & Virginie Pelerin Canada
PELLETIER, Eileen Rose, Nov 21 1931 Sex:F Child# 6 Victor S Pelletier Boscawen, NH & Margaret Baker Nashua, NH
PELLETIER, Elaine Stella, Jun 19 1927 Sex:F Child# 1 Louis Pelletier Nashua, NH & Stella Suirewitch Nashua, NH
PELLETIER, Estelle Yvonne, Jul 22 1935 Sex:F Child# 4 Irving Pelletier Nashua, NH & Aline Richard Canada
PELLETIER, Fernand, Jan 29 1927 Sex:M Child# 3 Joseph Pelletier Canada & Florence Bechard Nashua, NH
PELLETIER, Florence Evelyn Gene, Dec 18 1935 Sex:F Child# 1 Sylvio Pelletier Nashua, NH & Geneva Ledoux Nashua
PELLETIER, Gabrielle Anne, Jan 2 1931 Sex:F Child# 2 Leo Pelletier Nashua, NH & Rosalina Blouin Canada
PELLETIER, Gabrielle Marguerite, Apr 12 1929 Sex:F Child# 3 Roland Pelletier Nashua, NH & Monique Laroche Nashua
PELLETIER, George Edgar, Apr 30 1925 Sex:M Child# 1 Alphie Pelletier S Berwick, ME & Rose Ouillette Canada
PELLETIER, George Gerard, Jul 9 1922 Sex:M Child# 1 Telesphore Pelletier Maine & Aline Bouley Nashua, NH
PELLETIER, George Maurice, Jun 22 1923 Sex:M Child# 7 Omer Pelletier Nashua, NH & Marguerite Theros Nashua, NH
PELLETIER, George Renee, Oct 22 1932 Sex:M Child# 4 Geo R Pelletier Nashua, NH & Alice Perron Suncook, NH
PELLETIER, George W A, Feb 22 1897 Sex:M Child# 3 Louis Pelletier Canada & Ida Gagnon
PELLETIER, Gerald, Dec 18 1927 Sex:M Child# 5 Anthony Pelletier Vermont & Lillian Marois Nashua, NH
PELLETIER, Gerald Antoine, Mar 25 1928 Sex:M Child# 2 Roland Pelletier Nashua, NH & Monica Laroche Nashua, NH
PELLETIER, Gerard Edgar, Oct 26 1907 Sex:M Child# 1 J O V Pelletier Canada & Alice Dube Canada
PELLETIER, Gertrude Evelyne, Jun 1 1905 Sex:F Child# 1 John Pelletier Coopersville, NY & Mary Ellen Dupee NY
PELLETIER, Guillaume, Jan 13 1913 Sex:M Child# 7 Eustache Pelletier Canada & Marie Gagnon Canada
PELLETIER, Helena Liliane, Dec 8 1899 Sex:F Child# 4 Joseph Pelletier Canada & Helene Fraser Canada
PELLETIER, Henry Maurice, Nov 12 1931 Sex:M Child# 2 Sylvio Pelletier Nashua, NH & Gracia Larochette Canada
PELLETIER, Hermance E, May 3 1907 Sex:F Child# 2 John Pelletier Canada & Emilia Thiboutot Canada
PELLETIER, Irene Alice, Dec 11 1924 Sex:F Child# 5 Amedee Pelletier Boscawen, NH & Melina Hebert Canada
PELLETIER, Irenee M, Feb 26 1925 Sex:M Child# 7 Omer Pelletier Canada & Marg Theroux Nashua, NH
PELLETIER, Isabelle, Jun 25 1908 Sex:F Child# 3 J B Pelletier Canada & Emilia Thiboutat Canada
PELLETIER, J Lucien Marcel, Aug 29 1921 Sex:M Child# 1 Joseph Pelletier Canada & Florentine Bechard Nashua, NH
PELLETIER, J Phedime Robert, Nov 20 1911 Sex:M Child# 3 Phedime Pelletier Canada & Exilda Morin Canada
PELLETIER, J Raymond Ernest, Mar 22 1913 Sex:M Child# 2 Alfred Pelletier Canada & Amanda Lafrance Canada
PELLETIER, Jane, Feb 11 1934 Sex:F Child# 3 Louis Pelletier Nashua, NH & Stella Simkiewicz Nashua, NH
PELLETIER, Jean Baptiste, Aug 12 1912 Sex:M Child# 4 Jean Pelletier Canada & Emilia Thiboutot Canada
PELLETIER, Jeanne Mabel, Nov 13 1929 Sex:F Child# 3 Napoleon Pelletier Canada & Albina Larocque Nashua, NH
PELLETIER, John Ernest, Feb 1 1908 Sex:M Child# 2 John Pelletier New York & Mary Ellen Dupee Beekmantown, NY
PELLETIER, Jos Alphonse Robert, Jun 30 1920 Sex:M Child# 2 Alphonse Pelletier Canada & Florida Lucier Mass
PELLETIER, Jos Amedee Oliver J, Mar 4 1923 Sex:M Child# 4 Amedee Pelletier Nashua, NH & Melida Hebert Canada
PELLETIER, Jos G D Armand, Jun 16 1934 Sex:M Child# 1 Armand Pelletier St Damase, PQ & Irene Couture Nashua, NH
PELLETIER, Jos Henri Girard, Nov 12 1920 Sex:M Child# 5 Bernard Pelletier Canada & Claudia Gagnon NH
PELLETIER, Jos Henry Aurel, Jan 22 1921 Sex:M Child# 4 Hormidas Pelletier Canada & Celina Vallie Maine
PELLETIER, Jos Roger Remi, May 25 1929 Sex:M Child# 1 Albert A Pelletier Nashua, NH & Mary L Aubut Nashua, NH
PELLETIER, Jos Romeo Conrad, Feb 3 1926 Sex:M Child# 2 Philip Pelletier Nashua, NH & Lydia Briand Canada
PELLETIER, Jos Wil Rolland, Mar 16 1919 Sex:M Child# 6 Simeon Pelletier Canada & Alice Deschesnes NH
PELLETIER, Jos Woodrow Alfred, Nov 26 1917 Sex:M Child# 3 Max A Pelletier Boscawen, NH & Melida Hebert Montreal
PELLETIER, Joseph, Apr 18 1907 Sex:M Child# 11 Alphonse Pelletier Canada & Celina Ratte Canada
PELLETIER, Joseph, May 13 1909 Sex:M Child# 12 Joseph Pelletier Canada & Zoe Michaud Canada Stillborn
PELLETIER, Joseph, Aug 4 1910 Sex:F Child# 3 Arsene Pelletier Canada & Stella Leyden Brattleboro, VT Stillborn
PELLETIER, Joseph Albert, Aug 15 1895 Sex:M Child# 1 Joseph Pelletier Canada & Helene Fraser Canada
PELLETIER, Joseph Albert, Oct 30 1922 Sex:M Child# 2 Renee Pelletier NH & Alice Perron NH
PELLETIER, Joseph Alfred, Mar 27 1910 Sex:M Child# 13 Joseph Pelletier Canada & Zoe Michaud Canada
PELLETIER, Joseph Arthur, Sep 5 1896 Sex:M Child# 12 Louis Pelletier Canada & Delima Dube Canada
PELLETIER, Joseph Augure N, Feb 22 1904 Sex:M Child# 8 Thomas Pelletier Canada & Arthemise Gagnon Canada
PELLETIER, Joseph Charles, Sep 12 1923 Sex:M Child# 2 Napoleon Pelletier Milford, NH & Rose Gagnon Nashua, NH
PELLETIER, Joseph Edouard, Oct 5 1921 Sex:M Child# 1 Edouard Pelletier Bayview, MA & Anna Rivard Nashua, NH
PELLETIER, Joseph Ernest L, Aug 7 1905 Sex:M Child# 10 Alphonse Pelletier Canada & Celina Ratte Canada
PELLETIER, Joseph Ernest Rene, Sep 22 1921 Sex:M Child# 1 Rene Pelletier NH & Alice Perron NH
PELLETIER, Joseph George A R, Nov 7 1919 Sex:M Child# 2 George Pelletier Canada & Leonie Turcotte Canada
PELLETIER, Joseph H A, Jun 21 1896 Sex:M Child# 12 Cleophas Pelletier Canada & Phemie Senechal Canada
PELLETIER, Joseph Kerney M, Nov 2 1905 Sex:M Child# 2 Joseph Pelletier Canada & Hermance Berube Canada
PELLETIER, Joseph L S, Oct 6 1905 Sex:M Child# 3 Eustache Pelletier Canada & Alexina Gagnon Canada
PELLETIER, Joseph Leo N, Dec 12 1908 Sex:M Child# 1 (No Parents Listed)
PELLETIER, Joseph Lionel, Sep 4 1909 Sex:M Child# 1 Leon Pelletier Nashua, NH & B Paquette Canada
PELLETIER, Joseph Louis H, Mar 31 1906 Sex:M Child# 2 Louis Pelletier Canada & Lumina Roy Canada
PELLETIER, Joseph Maurice, May 24 1918 Sex:M Child# 3 Hormidas Pelletier Canada & Celina Vallee Maine
PELLETIER, Joseph Maurice A, Feb 2 1924 Sex:M Child# 2 Joseph Pelletier Canada & Florence Bechard Nashua, NH
PELLETIER, Joseph Octave Vital, Nov 21 1917 Sex:M Child# 4 Jos O V Pelletier Canada & Alice Dube Canada
PELLETIER, Joseph Oscar, Oct 6 1893 Sex:M Child# 4 Georges Pelletier Canada & Virginie Gagnon Canada
PELLETIER, Joseph Pierre, Mar 2 1899 Sex:M Child# 13 Cleophas Pelletier Canada & Euphemie St Jean Canada
PELLETIER, Joseph Raoul, Nov 29 1923 Sex:M Child# 1 Joseph Pelletier Tyngsboro, MA & Sylvia Gagnon Canada
PELLETIER, Joseph Raymond, Feb 10 1918 Sex:M Child# 5 Semicon Pelletier Canada & Alice Deschesne NH

PELLETIER, Joseph Rene Paul, May 31 1932 Sex:M Child# 2 Nap Pelletier Canada & Victoria Levesque Fall River, MA
PELLETIER, Joseph Victor Sylvio, May 27 1914 Sex:M Child# 2 Simeon Pelletier Canada & Alice Deschenes Canada
PELLETIER, June, Feb 6 1932 Sex:F Child# 2 Wilfrid Pelletier Nashua, NH & A Hammond Sudbury, VT
PELLETIER, Leo, Jul 21 1905 Sex:M Child# 9 Thomas Pelletier Canada & Arthemise Gagnon Canada
PELLETIER, Leonard, Dec 2 1923 Sex:M Child# 1 Philippe Pelletier Nashua, NH & Lydia Briand Canada
PELLETIER, Leonide Alberta, Oct 2 1921 Sex:F Child# 5 Omer Pelletier Nashua, NH & Margaret Theroux Nashua, NH
PELLETIER, Lerard, Nov 19 1911 Sex:M Child# 6 Eustache Pelletier Canada & Eina Gagnon Canada
PELLETIER, Loretta Madeline, Aug 10 1927 Sex:F Child# 2 Napoleon Pelletier Canada & Albina Levesque Nashua, NH
PELLETIER, Lorette, Apr 10 1931 Sex:F Child# 3 Irving Pelletier Nashua, NH & Aline Richard Canada
PELLETIER, Loria, Apr 5 1918 Sex:F Child# 6 Louis Pelletier Canada & Lumina Roy Canada
PELLETIER, Lorraine, Apr 26 1925 Sex:F Child# 1 Wilfred Pelletier Nashua, NH & Leona Bonnette Nashua, NH
PELLETIER, Lorraine, Oct 12 1927 Sex:F Child# 3 Jos E Pelletier Canada & A Corbiere Nashua, NH
PELLETIER, Lorraine Jeannette, Jan 26 1922 Sex:F Child# 2 Frank Pelletier Nashua, NH & Blanche Girouard Hudson, NH
PELLETIER, Lorraine Juliette, Mar 1 1928 Sex:F Child# 3 Edouard Pelletier Bayview, MA & Anna Rivard Nashua, NH
PELLETIER, Louis Philippe, Apr 17 1902 Sex:M Child# 5 Aurelie Pelletier Canada & Adelina Chasseur Canada
PELLETIER, Louis Romeo, Mar 6 1909 Sex:M Child# 2 Joseph O V Pelletier Canada & Alice M Dube Canada
PELLETIER, Lucienne Elizabeth, Dec 27 1930 Sex:F Child# 2 Alphee Pelletier S Berwick, ME & Rose Ouellette Canada
PELLETIER, Lucile Simonne, Jan 8 1916 Sex:F Child# 5 Louis Pelletier Canada & Lumina Roy Canada
PELLETIER, Lucille Jeanne d'Arc, May 1 1919 Sex:F Child# 4 Omer Pelletier Nashua, NH & Margaret Theroux Nashua, NH
PELLETIER, Lucille Loraine M, Oct 11 1918 Sex:F Child# 5 Fitzime Pelletier Canada & Exilda Morin Canada
PELLETIER, Lucille Nancy, Sep 17 1932 Sex:F Child# 1 Alfred Pelletier Nashua, NH & Marie Dionne Canada
PELLETIER, M Alexandra, Jun 12 1894 Sex:F Child# 3 Elzear Pelletier Canada & Flavie Pellerin Canada
PELLETIER, M Alexandrine Ger, Jan 24 1914 Sex:F Child# 2 Hormidas Pelletier Canada & Celina Vallee Maine
PELLETIER, M Alice, Aug 7 1895 Sex:F Child# 2 Louis Pelletier Canada & Ida Gagnon Canada
PELLETIER, M Amanda Cecile, Dec 19 1915 Sex:F Child# 4 Alfred Pelletier Canada & Amanda Lafrance Canada
PELLETIER, M Anita Antoinette, Jun 29 1913 Sex:F Child# 4 Leon Pelletier Nashua, NH & Marianne Paquette Canada
PELLETIER, M B Alexandrine, Jul 10 1913 Sex:F Child# 2 Bernard Pelletier Canada & Claudia Gagnon Nashua, NH
PELLETIER, M Delima Olivette, Oct 15 1914 Sex:F Child# 5 Leon Pelletier Nashua, NH & Marie A Paquette Canada
PELLETIER, M Eliz Anabelle, Jun 29 1917 Sex:F Child# 6 Leon Pelletier Nashua, NH & Marie Anne Paquette Canada
PELLETIER, M J Dorothy, Jan 8 1922 Sex:F Child# 8 Leon Pelletier Nashua, NH & Marienne Paquette Canada
PELLETIER, M L Christiana, Nov 7 1902 Sex:F Child# 6 Onesime Pelletier Canada & Emma Levesque Canada
PELLETIER, M Lucille Arthmise, Feb 23 1915 Sex:F Child# 2 Amedee Pelletier Canada & Nelida Hebert Canada
PELLETIER, M Marg Leonore, Nov 10 1914 Sex:F Child# 3 Alfred Pelletier Canada & Amanda Lafrance Canada
PELLETIER, M R Delima Florence, Feb 23 1913 Sex:F Child# 3 Joseph O V Pelletier Canada & Alice Dube Canada
PELLETIER, M Rose Alice, Jul 11 1908 Sex:F Child# 1 George Pelletier Canada & M Anna Anctil Canada
PELLETIER, M Rose Isabelle, May 29 1913 Sex:F Child# 1 Simeon Pelletier Canada & Alice Deschesne NH
PELLETIER, Marcella Florence, Apr 23 1932 Sex:F Child# 10 Omer Pelletier Nashua, NH & Margaret Theroux Nashua, NH
PELLETIER, Margaret Elizabeth, Feb 25 1927 Sex:F Child# 4 Francis Pelletier Nashua, NH & Blanche Girouard Hudson
PELLETIER, Marguerite Iolande, Jul 13 1911 Sex:F Child# 1 Demetrius Pelletier Canada & Desanges Pelletier Canada
PELLETIER, Marguerite Pauline, Apr 12 1913 Sex:F Child# 10 Aurele Pelletier Canada & Adeline Chasseur Canada
PELLETIER, Marianne Alice, Dec 27 1929 Sex:F Child# 3 Alphonse Pelletier Canada & Anesie Morin Canada
PELLETIER, Marie, Jan 23 1914 Sex:F Child# 2 Phidime Pelletier Canada & Exilda Morin Canada
PELLETIER, Marie, Mar 27 1915 Sex:F Child# 3 Simeon Pelletier Canada & Alice Deschenes Nashua, NH
PELLETIER, Marie, Oct 17 1921 Sex:F Child# 1 Napoleon Pelletier Milford, NH & Rose Gagnon Nashua, NH
PELLETIER, Marie Alice Juliette, Aug 25 1911 Sex:F Child# 1 Hormidas Pelletier Canada & Celina Vallee Maine
PELLETIER, Marie Angelina, Aug 27 1898 Sex:F Child# 14 Louis Pelletier Canada & Delima Dube Canada
PELLETIER, Marie Ann Georgette, Jan 12 1929 Sex:F Child# 1 Napoleon Pelletier Canada & Victoria Levesque Fall
PELLETIER, Marie Anne, Apr 17 1894 Sex:F Child# 11 Cleophas Pelletier Canada & Euphemie St Charles Canada
PELLETIER, Marie Anne, Jul 1 1903 Sex:F Child# 2 Eustache Pelletier Canada & Alexina Gagnon Canada
PELLETIER, Marie Annita, Apr 8 1911 Sex:F Child# 3 Pantalim Pelletier Nashua, NH & Marianne Paquette Canada
PELLETIER, Marie Beatrice, Mar 7 1912 Sex:F Child# 4 Arsene Pelletier Canada & Stella Laedun Canada
PELLETIER, Marie Beatrice Irene, Mar 29 1920 Sex:F Child# 5 Alfred Pelletier Canada & Amanda Lafrance Canada
PELLETIER, Marie Blanche, Mar 18 1897 Sex:F Child# 10 Henri Pelletier Canada & Celanire Plourde Canada
PELLETIER, Marie Blanche, Jul 6 1898 Sex:F Child# 10 Henri Pelletier Canada & Celanire Plourde Canada
PELLETIER, Marie Blanche, Mar 24 1921 Sex:F Child# 3 George Pelletier Canada & Leonie Turcott Canada
PELLETIER, Marie Blanche Jean, Sep 21 1917 Sex:F Child# 1 Onesime Pelletier Canada & Celina Roy Canada
PELLETIER, Marie Cecile, Dec 30 1915 Sex:F Child# 1 George Pelletier Canada & Leonie Turcotte Canada
PELLETIER, Marie Cecile Irene, Jun 21 1919 Sex:F Child# 1 Alphonse Pelletier Canada & Florilda Lucier Mass
PELLETIER, Marie Cecile Irene, Dec 29 1926 Sex:F Child# 1 T Pelletier Canada & Irene Lavoie Canada
PELLETIER, Marie Claudia Delima, Aug 18 1912 Sex:F Child# 1 Bernard Pelletier Canada & Claudia Gagnon NH
PELLETIER, Marie D P, Apr 9 1897 Sex:F Child# 3 Onesime Pelletier Canada & Emma Levesque Canada
PELLETIER, Marie Emma Bern, Jan 19 1916 Sex:F Child# 6 Frank Pelletier Vermnt & Angile Cyr Vermont
PELLETIER, Marie Eva, Feb 1 1908 Sex:F Child# 3 Joseph Pelletier Canada & Hermance Berube Canada
PELLETIER, Marie Gabrielle T, Mar 16 1924 Sex:F Child# 3 F K Pelletier NH & B Girouard NH
PELLETIER, Marie Ida, Aug 27 1898 Sex:F Child# 13 Louis Pelletier Canada & Delima Dube Canada
PELLETIER, Marie Ivonne, Aug 25 1902 Sex:F Child# 7 Thomas Pelletier Canada & Arthemise Gagnon Canada
PELLETIER, Marie Jeannette Ber, Dec 13 1919 Sex:F Child# 7 Leon Pelletier Nashua, NH & Marie Anne Paquette Canada
PELLETIER, Marie L F, Sep 12 1891 Sex:F Child# 1 Elzear Pelletier Canada & Flavie Pellerin Canada
PELLETIER, Marie Laura, Jul 18 1897 Sex:F Child# Thomas Pelletier Canada & Arthemise Gagnon Canada
PELLETIER, Marie Leda, Mar 13 1896 Sex:F Child# 4 Elzear Pelletier Canada & Flavie Pelerin Canada
PELLETIER, Marie Marguerite E, Jun 28 1932 Sex:F Child# 3 Albert Pelletier Nashua, NH & M L Aubut Nashua, NH
PELLETIER, Marie Olivette, Sep 10 1926 Sex:F Child# 2 Joseph Pelletier Tyngsboro, MA & Sylvia Gagnon Tyngsboro, MA
PELLETIER, Marie Rita, Sep 12 1923 Sex:F Child# 3 Napoleon Pelletier Milford, NH & Rose Gagnon Nashua, NH

PELLETIER, Marie Rita Cecile, Jan 8 1927 Sex:F Child# 4 Irving Pelletier Nashua, NH & Aline Richard Canada
PELLETIER, Marie Rita Edna, May 1 1928 Sex:F Child# 6 Joseph Pelletier Nashua, NH & Marie A Landry Canada
PELLETIER, Marie Rosalie, Mar 28 1898 Sex:F Child# 3 Joseph Pelletier Canada & Helene Fraser Canada
PELLETIER, Marie Rose Irene, May 30 1911 Sex:F Child# 1 (No Parents Listed)
PELLETIER, Marie Rose L, Dec 3 1908 Sex:F Child# 1 (No Parents Listed)
PELLETIER, Marie Stella, May 29 1907 Sex:F Child# 1 Arsene Pelletier Canada & Stella Leedow Brattleboro, VT
PELLETIER, Marie Theresa Bertha, Oct 29 1926 Sex:F Child# 3 Irenee Pelletier Nashua, NH & Alice Perron Suncook, NH
PELLETIER, Marie Therese, May 31 1923 Sex:F Child# 4 Phedime Pelletier Canada & Exilda Morin Canada
PELLETIER, Marie Therese, Oct 13 1925 Sex:F Child# 1 Zephyres Pelletier Canada & Ernestine Poitras Canada
PELLETIER, Marion Jean D'Arc C, May 25 1933 Sex:F Child# 1 Jean B Pelletier Nashua, NH & A Boissonault Nashua, NH
PELLETIER, Mary, Feb 13 1920 Sex:F Child# 2 Victor S Pelletier Boscawen, NH & Margaret Baker Nashua, NH
PELLETIER, Mary, Oct 24 1924 Sex:F Child# 3 Anthony Pelletier Lyndonville, VT & Lillian Marois Nashua, NH
PELLETIER, Maurice Bertrand, Dec 28 1927 Sex:M Child# 2 Alphonse Pelletier Canada & Anesie Morin Canada
PELLETIER, Muriel Germaine, Apr 9 1926 Sex:F Child# 1 Napoleon Pelletier Canada & Albina Levesque Nashua, NH
PELLETIER, Muriel Madeleine, Aug 11 1930 Sex:F Child# 8 Amedee Pelletier Boscawen, NH & Melida Hebert Montreal
PELLETIER, Norman Anthony, Oct 25 1925 Sex:M Child# 4 Anthony Pelletier Vermont & Lillian Marois Nashua, NH
PELLETIER, Normon Alphonse, Jan 24 1927 Sex:M Child# 8 Homer Pelletier Nashua, NH & Mar Theroux Nashua, NH
PELLETIER, Octave Alcide, Sep 14 1910 Sex:M Child# 4 Louis Pelletier Canada & Lumina Roy Canada
PELLETIER, Oliver Amedee, Jun 3 1931 Sex:M Child# 7 Anthony Pelletier Vermont & Lillian Marois Nashua, NH
PELLETIER, Palmyra Rita, Dec 9 1923 Sex:F Child# 4 Romuald Pelletier Nashua, NH & Albertine Pellerin Canada
PELLETIER, Palmyre, Jun 11 1906 Sex:F Child# 18 Albini Pelletier Canada & Laura Lamare Canada
PELLETIER, Paul, Jul 13 1901 Sex:M Child# 5 Onesime Pelletier Canada & Emma Levesque Canada
PELLETIER, Paul Ernest, Apr 13 1927 Sex:M Child# 1 J H Pelletier Canada & Marie B McClure Nashua, NH
PELLETIER, Paul Maurice Silvia, Nov 8 1918 Sex:M Child# 2 Adelard Pelletier Nashua, NH & Eva Paquette Ausable, NY
PELLETIER, Paul Rene, Jan 20 1927 Sex:M Child# 2 Telesphore Pelletier Winn, ME & Aline Bouley Nashua, NH
PELLETIER, Paul Richard, Mar 22 1917 Sex:M Child# 11 Auvelle Pelletier Canada & Adeline Lechasseur Canada
PELLETIER, Pauline Helen, Apr 17 1923 Sex:F Child# 2 Alphonse Pelletier Greenville, NH & Helen Perrault Concord, NH
PELLETIER, Pearl Irene, Aug 6 1911 Sex:F Child# 3 Adelard Pelletier Nashua, NH & Arzelia Delude Canada
PELLETIER, Phyllis Theresa, Mar 15 1931 Sex:F Child# 2 Louis Pelletier Nashua, NH & Stella Sinkawich Nashua, NH
PELLETIER, Pierre, Jun 29 1909 Sex:M Child# 2 George Pelletier Canada & Marie St Jean Canada
PELLETIER, Rachael Claire, Nov 29 1932 Sex:F Child# 3 Leo Pelletier Nashua, NH & Rose A Blouin Canada
PELLETIER, Rachel Eveline, Aug 21 1921 Sex:F Child# 1 Joseph Pelletier Canada & A G Corbiere Nashua, NH
PELLETIER, Rachel Irene, Sep 25 1929 Sex:F Child# 7 Romuald Pelletier Nashua, NH & Albertine Pellerin Canada
PELLETIER, Raoul, Aug 6 1905 Sex:M Child# 4 Alfred Pelletier Canada & Josephine Chasse Canada
PELLETIER, Raymond, Dec 3 1895 Sex:M Child# 3 Solomon Pelletier US & Martha Ryan US
PELLETIER, Raymond Gerard, Mar 18 1931 Sex:M Child# 4 Edouard Pelletier Bayview, MA & Anna Rivard Nashua, NH
PELLETIER, Raymond Normand, Aug 17 1919 Sex:M Child# 4 Adelard Pelletier Nashua, NH & Arzelia Delude Canada
PELLETIER, Richard Theodore, Apr 16 1930 Sex:M Child# 6 Anthony Pelletier US & Lillian Marois NH
PELLETIER, Robert Duane, Nov 28 1924 Sex:M Child# 2 Leo Pelletier Tyngsboro, MA & Vivian Holt Nashua, NH
PELLETIER, Robert Maurice, Nov 27 1919 Sex:M Child# 1 Francois Pelletier Canada & Blanche Girouard Nashua, NH
PELLETIER, Roger Norman P, Jun 21 1924 Sex:M Child# 3 Adelard Pelletier Nashua, NH & Eva Paquette Ausable, MI
PELLETIER, Romeo Roland, May 29 1927 Sex:M Child# 1 Roland Pelletier Nashua, NH & Monica Laroche Nashua, NH
PELLETIER, Romuald Gerard, Dec 10 1924 Sex:M Child# 5 Romuald Pelletier Canada & Albertine Pellerin Canada
PELLETIER, Rose, Dec 2 1907 Sex:F Child# 6 Damase Pelletier Canada & Virginie Pellerin Canada
PELLETIER, Rudolph Napoleon, Dec 11 1927 Sex:M Child# 2 Napoleon Pelletier Nashua, NH & Mary Rock Malone, NY
PELLETIER, Sylvio, May 15 1906 Sex:M Child# 2 Adelard Pelletier Nashua, NH & Arselie Delude Canada
PELLETIER, Sylvio Robert, May 23 1921 Sex:M Child# 7 Simeon Pelletier Canada & Alice Deschesnes NH
PELLETIER, Theresa, Jan 31 1929 Sex:F Child# 1 Leo Pelletier Nashua, NH & R A Blouin Canada
PELLETIER, Theresa Blanche, Nov 11 1926 Sex:F Child# 5 Joseph Pelletier NH & Marie A Landry Canada
PELLETIER, Theresa Cecelia, Sep 9 1929 Sex:F Child# 9 Homer Pelletier Nashua, NH & Margaret Theroux Nashua, NH
PELLETIER, Theresa Sylvia, Nov 14 1927 Sex:F Child# 1 Sylvio Pelletier Nashua, NH & G Rochette Canada
PELLETIER, Therese Evelyn, Jan 4 1930 Sex:F Child# 5 Victor S Pelletier Boscawen, NH & Margaret Baker Nashua, NH
PELLETIER, Therese Rachel Yvonn, Jan 14 1934 Sex:F Child# 5 Edouard Pelletier Bayview, MA & Anna Rivard Nashua, NH
PELLETIER, Thomas Ambrose, Dec 10 1924 Sex:M Child# 4 Victor Pelletier Boscawen, NH & Margaret Baker Nashua, NH
PELLETIER, Unknown, May 27 1892 Sex:F Child# 1 Joseph Pelletier Canada & Desina Bernier Canada Stillborn
PELLETIER, Unknown, Feb 18 1912 Sex:F Child# 1 Alfred Pelletier Acton, PQ & Amanda Lafrance Notre Dame, PQ St
PELLETIER, Unknown, Nov 6 1914 Sex:F Child# 3 Bernard Pelletier Canada & Claudia Gagnon Nashua, NH Stillborn
PELLETIER, Unknown, Jan 3 1920 Sex:M Child# 10 Eustache Pelletier Canada & Alexian Gagnon Canada Stillborn
PELLETIER, Unknown, Aug 29 1921 Sex:M Child# 1 Romeo P Pelletier Lawrence, MA & Yvonne Pluard Nashua, NH Stillborn
PELLETIER, Unknown, Jan 23 1924 Sex:M Child# 1 Eustache Pelletier Canada & Alex Gagnon Canada Stillborn
PELLETIER, Unknown, Mar 4 1933 Sex: Child# Leon Pelletier Canada & Irene Boucher Nashua, NH
PELLETIER, Victor, Jun 2 1901 Sex:M Child# 5 Joseph Pelletier Canada & Helene Fraser Canada
PELLETIER, Victor Albert, Apr 30 1931 Sex:M Child# 2 Albert A Pelletier Nashua, NH & Mary Louise Aubut Nashua, NH
PELLETIER, Wilfred, Aug 3 1913 Sex:M Child# 1 Adelard J Pelletier Nashua, NH & Eva Paquette Oskoda, Michigan
PELLETIER, Wilfred Aurel, Aug 12 1935 Sex:M Child# 3 Wilfred Pelletier Nashua, NH & Alberta Hammond Sudbury, VT
PELLETIER, Wilfrid Simeon, Apr 11 1916 Sex:M Child# 4 Simeon Pelletier Canada & Alice Deschenes Nashua, NH
PELLETIER, William, Jul 23 1907 Sex:M Child# 4 Eustache Pelletier Canada & Alexina Gagnon Canada
PELLETIER, William, Dec 6 1915 Sex:M Child# 1 Victor S Pelletier Boscawan, NH & Margaret B Baker Nashua, NH
PELLETIER, Xavier Auguste, Jul 4 1928 Sex:M Child# 1 Dosithe Pelletier Canada & B Lamontagne Canada
PELLETIER, Yvonne, Oct 15 1909 Sex:F Child# 4 Joseph Pelletier Canada & Hermance Berube Canada
PELLETIER, Yvonne Alberta, Apr 23 1914 Sex:F Child# 1 Omer Pelletier Nashua, NH & Marguerite Theroux Nashua, NH
PELLETIER, Yvonne Edith, Oct 5 1907 Sex:F Child# 4 Louis T Pelletier Canada & Delvinia Pelletier Canada
PELLIGIAN, Alice, Mar 21 1906 Sex:F Child# 3 Harry Pelligian Armenia & Osanna Mananian Armenia

PELOQUIN, Joseph Leo Raoul, Jun 18 1904 Sex:M Child# 4 Pierre Peloquin Canada & Marie L Bernier Canada
PELTAH, John, Mar 13 1895 Sex:M Child# 2 Frank Peltah Austria & Keda Barthevez Austria
PELTAK, Uadislawa, Jan 2 1905 Sex:M Child# 4 Ludwik Peltak Russia & Bromistawa Stiepsin Russia
PELTHIER, Eva Rose, Feb 28 1893 Sex:F Child# 6 Hilaire Pelthier Canada & Eugenia Potras Canada
PELTHIER, Francois P, Sep 18 1887 Sex:M Child# 11 Francois Pelthier Canada & Margarite Pineau Canada
PELTHIER, Frederic, Jan 9 1893 Sex:M Child# 10 Cleophas Pelthier Canada & Euphemie Senechal Canada
PELTHIER, Mary, Jun 8 1891 Sex:F Child# 5 Luc Pelthier Canada & Louise Delaire Canada
PELTHIER, Mary Anna, May 1 1892 Sex:F Child# 9 Israel Pelthier Canada & Elconard Chaumard Canada
PELTHIER, Unknown, Jul 1 1891 Sex:F Child# 1 (No Parents Listed)
PELTHIER, Unknown, Sep 1 1891 Sex:F Child# 4 George Pelthier Canada & Virginnie Gagnon Canada Stillborn
PELTIER, Adelard, Oct 7 1887 Sex:M Child# Helaide Peltier Canada & Eugenie Poitras Canada
PELTIER, Albina, Mar 1 1896 Sex:F Child# 2 Elzeard Peltier Canada & Clerina Peltier Canada
PELTIER, Alfred, Oct 24 1894 Sex:M Child# 2 Solomon Peltier US & Mary Ryne US
PELTIER, Alfred, Oct 23 1900 Sex:M Child# 2 Alfred Peltier Canada & Josephine Chasse Canada
PELTIER, Alfred, May 27 1905 Sex:M Child# 7 Orelle Peltier Canada & Adeline Canada
PELTIER, Andrea Lucille, Feb 5 1908 Sex:F Child# 9 Orel Peltier Canada & Adeline Chasseur Canada
PELTIER, Auguste Conrad, Nov 9 1903 Sex:M Child# 6 Aurelle Peltier Canada & Adelina Chasseur Canada
PELTIER, Berthe Loraine, Sep 21 1900 Sex:F Child# 4 Aurele Peltier Canada & Adeline Chasseur Canada
PELTIER, Edith Doris, Aug 4 1911 Sex:F Child# 1 Clifford Peltier US & Alice Sirois Canada
PELTIER, Elanie, Dec 31 1891 Sex:F Child# 5 Helaire Peltier Canada & Eugene Portras Canada
PELTIER, Elizabeth, Nov 8 1892 Sex:F Child# 10 W E Peltier Canada & Elizabeth St Michel Canada
PELTIER, Emma Adelina, Jan 15 1894 Sex:F Child# 1 Orelle Peltier Canada & Adeline Chasseur Canada
PELTIER, Irving, Dec 2 1904 Sex:M Child# 1 Adelard Peltier Nashua, NH & Arzelia Delude Canada
PELTIER, James Francis Xavier, Jan 19 1918 Sex:M Child# 10 Eustache Peltier Canada & Alexina Gagnon Canada Stillbor
PELTIER, Jeannette Edna, Feb 18 1907 Sex:F Child# 8 Orel Peltier Canada & Adeline Lechasseur Canada
PELTIER, Joseph A F, Sep 3 1892 Sex:M Child# 9 Francois Peltier Canada & Celina Jalbert Canada
PELTIER, Joseph Damase L, Sep 21 1902 Sex:M Child# 5 Jos Lazare Peltier Canada & Genevieve Gagne Canada
PELTIER, Joseph Hormidas A, Jan 17 1904 Sex:M Child# 4 Damase Peltier Canada & Virginie Pellerin Canada
PELTIER, Joseph Louis, Oct 5 1903 Sex:M Child# 9 Alphonse Peltier Canada & Celina Ratte Canada
PELTIER, Joseph Napoleon, Mar 18 1890 Sex:M Child# 1 Israel Peltier Canada & Emma Aprille Canada
PELTIER, Joseph O, Jun 17 1887 Sex:M Child# 2 Joseph Peltier P Q & Rose Maxfield P Q
PELTIER, Joseph Roland, Nov 23 1903 Sex:M Child# 10 Joseph Peltier Canada & Rosie Maxfield Canada
PELTIER, Joseph Romnald A, Nov 11 1900 Sex:M Child# 2 Donase Peltier Canada & Virgenie Pellerin Canada
PELTIER, Josephine, Mar 20 1891 Sex:F Child# 9 W E Peltier Plattsburg, NY & Eliz St Michel Plattsburg, NY
PELTIER, Josephine A, Jul 25 1902 Sex:F Child# 3 Alfred Peltier Canada & Josephine Peltier Canada
PELTIER, Lea Delima, May 8 1904 Sex:F Child# 1 Louis Theo Peltier Canada & Delvina Peltier Canada
PELTIER, Loretta Therese, Jan 26 1907 Sex:F Child# 1 John Peltier Canada & Adelina Lemay Canada
PELTIER, M Delia B, Dec 17 1891 Sex:F Child# 1 George Peltier Canada & Elise Beaulieu Canada
PELTIER, M Magdeleine, Sex:F Child# 4 Thomas Peltier Canada & Arthemise Gagnon Canada
PELTIER, Margarit M, Sep 13 1887 Sex:F Child# W E Peltier Plattsburg & Eliza St Michel Plattsburg
PELTIER, Marie, Oct 21 1900 Sex:F Child# Alfred Peltier Canada & Celina Ouellette Canada
PELTIER, Marie A, Oct 18 1891 Sex:F Child# 9 Cleophas Peltier Canada & Phemie Seneschal Canada
PELTIER, Marie A Laura, Jan 10 1893 Sex:F Child# 2 George Peltier Canada & Elise Beaulieu Canada
PELTIER, Marie Amelia, Jun 4 1904 Sex:F Child# 1 Joseph Peltier Canada & Hermence Berube Canada
PELTIER, Marie Aurore, Mar 24 1900 Sex:F Child# 1 Joseph Peltier Canada & Ernestine Tremblay Canada
PELTIER, Marie B D B, Apr 29 1892 Sex:F Child# 1 Wilfred Peltier Canada & Marie Benjamin Canada
PELTIER, Marie Blanche, Dec 20 1900 Sex:F Child# 4 Alfred Peltier Canada & Julia Peltier Canada
PELTIER, Marie Delhia, Feb 9 1889 Sex:F Child# 3 Joseph Peltier Canada & Rosa Maxfield Canada
PELTIER, Marie Juliette, Nov 25 1903 Sex:F Child# 6 Alfred Peltier Mass & Eliza Robichaud Canada
PELTIER, Marie L M, Sep 21 1889 Sex:F Child# 3 Alphonse Peltier Canada & Celina Ratte Canada
PELTIER, Marie Louise, Dec 7 1893 Sex:F Child# 5 Albany Peltier Canada & Laura Lamare Canada
PELTIER, Marie Louise, Oct 19 1904 Sex:F Child# 5 Jean B Peltier Canada & Mary L Peltier Canada
PELTIER, Marie Lumina E, May 11 1904 Sex:F Child# 1 Louis Peltier Canada & Lumina Roy Canada
PELTIER, Marie Zoe, Jul 8 1908 Sex:F Child# 11 Joseph Peltier Canada & Zoe Michaud Canada
PELTIER, Matilda, Dec 19 1890 Sex:F Child# 8 Francois Peltier Canada & Celina Talbert Canada
PELTIER, Napoleon, Jul 2 1900 Sex:M Child# 8 Alphonse Peltier Canada & Celina Ratte Canada
PELTIER, Regina, Jun 10 1890 Sex:F Child# 4 Hilare Peltier Canada & Eugenie Poitras Canada
PELTIER, Renie, Sep 10 1899 Sex:M Child# 6 Thomas Peltier Canada & Arthemise Gagnon Canada
PELTIER, Rose Aimee, Apr 11 1908 Sex:F Child# 1 Leon Peltier US & Marie Anne Paquette Canada
PELTIER, Rose Emma, Jul 18 1899 Sex:F Child# 4 Onesime Peltier Canada & Emma Levesque Canada
PELTIER, Rose Eva, Mar 27 1895 Sex:F Child# 2 Orelle Peltier Canada & Adeline Chasseur Canada
PELTIER, Wilfrid A, Jan 13 1897 Sex:M Child# 3 Aurelle Peltier Canada & Adeline Chasseur Canada
PENDLETON, Dorothy Jane, Apr 14 1927 Sex:F Child# 3 R A Pendleton Brewer, ME & Florence Emery Boston, MA
PENEAN, Marie Delina, Jul 6 1889 Sex:F Child# 4 Thomas Penean Canada & Demerise Russell Canada
PENEAU, Mary, Mar 23 1890 Sex:F Child# 3 George Peneau Canada & Annie McCarthy Ireland
PENEAULT, Joseph, Mar 19 1896 Sex:M Child# 1 Alfred Peneault Cambridge, MA & Delia Jeanbarre Nashua, NH
PENET, Gena, Jul 6 1890 Sex:F Child# 3 Theophile Penet France & Marie Colliers Ireland
PENET, Pierre, Jun 27 1888 Sex:M Child# 1 Pierre Penet Canada & Clephire Lefebvre Canada
PENETTE, Emile, Jan 22 1889 Sex:M Child# 7 Ontime Penette Canada & J Muquet Canada
PENKOFSKI, Unknown, Apr 4 1919 Sex:M Child# 2 James Penkofski Russia & Fells Medzonski Russia
PENNETON, Marie Rose, May 11 1894 Sex:F Child# 4 Gedeon Panneton Canada & Odile Marquis Canada
PENNINGTON, Jeannette, Aug 29 1920 Sex:F Child# 1 Clifford Pennington Salem, NJ & Anna Lavoie Nashua, NH
PENNY, Unknown, Dec 3 1900 Sex:M Child# 2 Charles Penny New York & Grace W Bignall Nashua, NH

PENO, Elizabeth Mary, Mar 28 1924 Sex:F Child# 5 George A Peno Nashua, NH & Laura Galipeau Nashua, NH
PENO, Frank, Jr, Jun 4 1932 Sex:M Child# 2 Frank Peno Nashua, NH & Mary Aubut Nashua, NH
PENO, Letitia Della B Mary, Feb 1 1918 Sex:F Child# 3 George A Peno Nashua, NH & Laura P Gallipeau Nashua, NH
PENO, Marie Cecile, Aug 27 1915 Sex:F Child# 2 Henry Peno Nashua, NH & Laura Morrissette Nashua, NH
PENO, Mary Bertha, Jan 17 1935 Sex:F Child# 3 Frank Peno Nashua, NH & Mary Aubut Nashua, NH
PENO, Normand Conrad, Apr 14 1935 Sex:M Child# 1 Armand Peno Nashua, NH & Rita Fleury Nashua, NH
PENO, Richard Paul, Apr 12 1931 Sex:M Child# 1 Frank Peno Nashua, NH & Mary Aubut Nashua, NH
PENO, Unknown, Mar 18 1888 Sex:M Child# 2 George Peno Canada & Amerlia Carter Ireland
PENSKOFSKI, Sophia, Oct 2 1916 Sex:F Child# 1 John Penskofski Russia & Helen Klaukopki Russia Stillborn
PENTLAND, Thomas Edward, Jan 6 1929 Sex:M Child# 1 Louis Pentland Concord, NH & Marion Peckard N Tonawanda, NY
PEOROSKY, Mary, Sep 30 1912 Sex:F Child# 4 Martin Peorosky Russia & Sohpia Kurturg Russia
PEPERIZA, Unknown, Dec 11 1916 Sex:F Child# 1 Nicholas Peperiza Greece & Sophia Greece Stillborn
PEPIER, Marie Lucienne, May 23 1902 Sex:F Child# 8 John B Pepier Canada & Leda Rochette Canada
PEPIN, Anna Lilliane, Mar 29 1931 Sex:F Child# 3 Camille Pepin NH & Beatrice Soucy Nashua, NH
PEPIN, Arthur, Jun 26 1904 Sex:M Child# 1 Joseph Pepin Canada & T Lamontaque Canada
PEPIN, Camille Normand, May 3 1932 Sex:M Child# 4 Camille Pepin US & Beatrice Soucy Nashua, NH
PEPIN, Edna Elizabeth, Mar 3 1909 Sex:F Child# 7 Zorab Pepin Canada & Bertha M Beaulieu US
PEPIN, Helena, Sep 6 1898 Sex:F Child# 4 Serob Pepin Canada & Bertha Beaulieu New York
PEPIN, Honore Saul, Jul 17 1897 Sex:M Child# 2 Theodore Pepin Canada & Dinas Laliberte Canada
PEPIN, Joseph, Apr 26 1889 Sex:M Child# 3 Arrene Pepin Canada & Delina Hiendeun Canada
PEPIN, Joseph, Jun 5 1901 Sex:M Child# 3 Theophitus Pepin Canada & Dina Laliberte Canada Stillborn
PEPIN, Joseph, Oct 6 1923 Sex:M Child# 1 Elie Pepin Canada & Elmire Marchand Canada Stillborn
PEPIN, Joseph Edouard, Jan 27 1895 Sex:M Child# 1 Zorab Pepin Canada & Bertha Beaulieu NY
PEPIN, Leo, Dec 29 1906 Sex:M Child# 3 Didier Pepin Canada & Maria Fournier Canada
PEPIN, Loretta Madeleine, May 9 1930 Sex:F Child# 2 Camille Pepin US & Beatrice Soucy Nashua, NH
PEPIN, Louis Arthur, Nov 10 1903 Sex:M Child# 1 Dedier Pepin Canada & Maria Fournier Canada
PEPIN, Louis Gonzague, May 2 1920 Sex:M Child# 1 Louis Pepin Canada & Delina Parent Nashua, NH
PEPIN, Lucille, Dec 12 1928 Sex:F Child# 1 Camile Pepin Hooksett, NH & Beatrice Soucy Nashua, NH
PEPIN, M Augustine, Jul 22 1895 Sex:F Child# 3 Antoine Pepin Canada & Marie Levesque Canada
PEPIN, Maria, Oct 31 1906 Sex:F Child# 2 Joseph J Pepin Canada & Perpetue Lamontagne Canada
PEPIN, Marie Hermine, Feb 13 1896 Sex:F Child# 2 Zorah Pepin Canada & Bertha Beaulieu Sciota, NY
PEPIN, Marie Irene Theresa, Jun 27 1929 Sex:F Child# 1 Elzear Pepin Canada & Cedulie Boulanger Canada
PEPIN, Paul Ludger, Jan 18 1934 Sex:M Child# 5 Camille Pepin Nashua, NH & Beatrice Soucy Nashua, NH
PEPIN, Roland Sylvio, Jan 20 1905 Sex:M Child# 2 Didier Pepin Canada & Maria Fournier Canada
PEPIN, Theophitus N T, Nov 1 1894 Sex:M Child# 1 Theophitus Pepin Canada & M L D Laliberte Canada
PEPIN, Unknown, Jan 18 1891 Sex:F Child# 2 Arsene Pepin Canada & Delina Reindeau Canada Stillborn
PEPIN, Unknown, Sep 11 1897 Sex:F Child# 3 Zorab Pepin Canada & Bertha Beaulieu Sciota, NY Stillborn
PEPIN, Unknown, May 12 1900 Sex:M Child# 2 Alfred Pepin Canada & Maria Lefebvre Canada
PEPPERAS, Unknown, Oct 7 1921 Sex:M Child# 1 Nicholas Pepperas Greece & Vasilike Kitsak Greece
PEPPERS, Unknown, Aug 27 1887 Sex:M Child# 1 Frank Peppers Portland & Kate Tanzy N S
PEPPIN, Irene, Oct 17 1900 Sex:F Child# L Peppin Ireland & Bertha Ireland
PEPSINGOS, Stephanos, Jul 4 1924 Sex:M Child# 3 Nickolis Pepsingos Greece & S Chrysopoulon Greece
PERASKI, Robert Stanley, Mar 30 1925 Sex:M Child# 1 Stanley Peraski Nashua, NH & Marguerite Evans Nashua, NH
PERAULT, Unknown, Jul 1 1889 Sex:M Child# 6 E D Perault Canada & Elvira Ledeau Vermont Stillborn
PERDUE, Richard, May 7 1935 Sex:M Child# 1 W L Perdue Manchester, NH & Shirley L Parson Manchester, NH
PEREAU, Unknown, Aug 30 1890 Sex:F Child# 3 Joseph Pereau VT & Mary NH
PEREAULT, Louis Philipe, Nov 6 1888 Sex:M Child# 5 Eugene D Pereault Canada & Eleanor St Albans, VT
PERKINS, Alice, Nov 14 1931 Sex:F Child# 1 (No Parents Listed)
PERKINS, Celestia Chase, Oct 1 1907 Sex:F Child# 1 Henry A Perkins Madison, NH & Ida May Grover Wardsboro, VT
PERKINS, Doris Emma, Sep 25 1921 Sex:F Child# 1 Herbert S Perkins Conway, NH & May E Sherburn Canaan, NH
PERKINS, Eddie Edward, Apr 22 1932 Sex:M Child# 7 Fred Perkins Meredith, NH & Rose Nadeau Nashua, NH
PERKINS, Ethel Delia, May 4 1924 Sex:F Child# 6 Fred C Perkins Claremont, NH & Ethel M Cobbett Wilton, NH
PERKINS, Everett M, Jun 30 1910 Sex:M Child# 1 Herbert H Perkins Somerville, MA & Helen K Shallies Hallowell, ME
PERKINS, Fred P, Jr, Oct 20 1918 Sex:M Child# 3 Fred C Perkins Claremont, NH & Ethel Corbbett Wilton, NH
PERKINS, Geneva, Jun 30 1914 Sex:F Child# 1 John H Perkins Cambridge, MA & M Hazel Sanders Nashua, NH
PERKINS, James Albert, Jul 21 1910 Sex:M Child# 1 Archie D Perkins Antrim, NH & Mary Leona Harris Antrim, NH
PERKINS, John Paul Arthur, May 7 1925 Sex:M Child# 1 Frederick Perkins Meredith, NH & Rose Nadeau Nashua, NH
PERKINS, Leslie Roy, Feb 9 1923 Sex:M Child# 5 Fred C Perkins Claremont, NH & Ethel Cobbett Wilton, NH
PERKINS, Mary Jane, Apr 13 1935 Sex:F Child# 4 Herbert Perkins Milford, NH & Frances Osgood Suncook, NH
PERKINS, Richard, Feb 1 1930 Sex:M Child# 9 Fred C Perkins NH & Ethel Cobbitt NH
PERKINS, Roland Frederick, Aug 6 1927 Sex:M Child# 2 Frederick Perkins Nashua, NH & Rose Nadeau Nashua, NH
PERKINS, Ruth, Jan 6 1900 Sex:F Child# 1 O M Perkins Providence, RI & G E Osborne Canada
PERKINS, Unknown, Apr 23 1920 Sex:M Child# 4 Fred C Perkins Claremont, NH & Ethel Cobbett Wilton, NH
PERMENDINE, Marie Exina, Sep 25 1892 Sex:F Child# 2 Joseph Permendine Canada & Marie Peltier Canada
PERO, Fannie Sawyer, Jan 6 1894 Sex:F Child# 7 Leander Pero Keysville, NY & Anne Leazotte Plattsburg, NY
PERO, Floyd Leon, Feb 17 1912 Sex:M Child# 1 Lewis Elwin Pero Nashua, NH & Delina E Derosa Nashua, NH
PERO, Gerard Henry, Sep 25 1926 Sex:M Child# 4 Wendell L Pero Canada & Delvina Beaulieu Canada
PERO, Ina E, Oct 27 1890 Sex:F Child# 3 Leander Pero Roysville, NY & Amy Leazott Plattsburg, NY
PERO, Unknown, Apr 8 1899 Sex:M Child# 5 Leardu Pero Keesville, NY & Annie Leazotte Chazy, NY
PERRAULT, Alexis, Jan 18 1901 Sex:M Child# 3 Philippe Perrault Canada & Lucie Ross Canada
PERRAULT, Aurele Wilfrid, Sep 3 1901 Sex:M Child# 6 Arsene Perrault Canada & Palmire Gregoire N Yarmouth, ME
PERRAULT, Cecilia Edmee, Jun 6 1890 Sex:F Child# 6 E D Perrault Canada & Eleonore Ledoux VT
PERRAULT, Ernest Patrick, Mar 17 1909 Sex:M Child# 5 John H Perrault Canada & Exilda Girouard NH

PERRAULT, Eugene, Jan 28 1903 Sex:M Child# 5 Eugene D Perrault Canada & Azilda Bonneau Canada
PERRAULT, Eugene G D, Nov 21 1896 Sex:M Child# 9 E Damase Perrault Canada & Eleonore Ledoux St Albans, VT
PERRAULT, Exilia Philomene, Oct 1 1906 Sex:F Child# 2 John H Perrault Canada & Exilia Girouard NH
PERRAULT, Jacqueline Patricia, Mar 17 1925 Sex:F Child# 6 Alex Perrault Canada & Alice Lajoie US
PERRAULT, Joseph Alphonse, Apr 22 1899 Sex:M Child# 5 Joseph Perrault Canada & Eugenie Therien Canada
PERRAULT, Joseph Henri, Mar 31 1901 Sex:M Child#  John Perrault Canada & Exelia Girouard NH
PERRAULT, Joseph Louis H, Oct 5 1902 Sex:M Child# 1 Joseph Perrault Canada & Louise Obin Canada
PERRAULT, Leopoldine Evelina, Sep 23 1906 Sex:F Child# 1 Felix M Perrault Canada & Leopoldine Poney Canada
PERRAULT, Lucille Jeannette, Mar 14 1932 Sex:F Child# 2 Lionel Perrault Nashua, NH & Lucille Levesque Canada
PERRAULT, Rodolphe Achille, Jun 28 1906 Sex:M Child# 2 Alexandre Perrault Canada & Alice Lajoie US
PERREAULT, Adele Simone, Mar 12 1909 Sex:F Child# 6 Alfred Perreault Canada & Clarinde Bernier Canada
PERREAULT, Annette Lucille, Sep 3 1927 Sex:F Child# 1 J S Perreault Canada & C A Bourgoin Canada
PERREAULT, Arthur, Jul 27 1900 Sex:M Child# 3 Alfred Perreault Canada & Clarento Bernier Canada
PERREAULT, Benjamin, Mar 12 1909 Sex:M Child# 7 Alfred Perreault Canada & Clarinde Bernier Canada
PERREAULT, Benjamin N, May 18 1910 Sex:M Child# 8 Alfred Perreault Canada & Clarinte Bernier Canada
PERREAULT, Cecile Anita, Jun 22 1915 Sex:F Child# 10 Alfred Perreault US & Clarinthe Bernier Canada
PERREAULT, Cecille, Apr 28 1892 Sex:F Child# 7 E D Perreault Canada & Eleanore Ledoux Vermont
PERREAULT, Claire Antoinette, Dec 2 1919 Sex:F Child# 5 Alexander Perreault Canada & Elice Lajoie US
PERREAULT, Cnrad A, Apr 1 1905 Sex:M Child# 1 Alexandre Perreault Canada & Alice Lajoie Nashua, NH
PERREAULT, Constance, Dec 30 1935 Sex:F Child# 2 Conrad Perreault Nashua, NH & Alicia Enright Nashua, NH
PERREAULT, Delia I, Mar 5 1897 Sex:F Child# 2 Alfred Perreault Cambridge, MA & Delia Jeanbarre Nashua, NH
PERREAULT, Denis Clarinda, Oct 25 1904 Sex:F Child# 4 Alfred Perreault Canada & Clarinda Bernier Canada
PERREAULT, Donald Rodolphe, Dec 19 1929 Sex:M Child# 1 Rodolphe Perreault Nashua, NH & Ruth Cutter Nashua, NH
PERREAULT, Dora Irene, Oct 16 1905 Sex:F Child# 3 Alfred Perreault Canada & Julia Lucier Canada
PERREAULT, Dorothy Anna, Aug 10 1909 Sex:F Child#  Joseph F Perreault Canada & Louise Obin Plattsburgh, NY
PERREAULT, Dorothy Jessie, Jul 12 1910 Sex:F Child# 4 Joseph P Perreault Canada & Louise Obin Plattsburgh, NY
PERREAULT, Ellen Pauline, Oct 15 1905 Sex:F Child# 2 Louis Perreault Canada & Philomene Larouche Canada
PERREAULT, Emma Evelyn, Jun 15 1907 Sex:F Child# 3 Louis Perreault Canada & Philomene Larouche Canada
PERREAULT, Felix Joseph Henri, Jul 7 1911 Sex:M Child# 2 Felix Perreault Canada & Leopoldine Poney Canada
PERREAULT, Frederick J, Oct 14 1909 Sex:M Child# 5 Louis Perreault Canada & Phoebe Larouche Canada
PERREAULT, Georgette Therese, Sep 8 1910 Sex:F Child# 2 Joseph Perreault Nashua, NH & Emma Laneville Canada
PERREAULT, Gerard Marie Robert, May 25 1912 Sex:M Child# 3 Eugene D Perreault Canada & Annie Fugere Canada
PERREAULT, Herminie Odile, Nov 4 1913 Sex:F Child# 3 Joseph Perreault Nashua, NH & Emma Lanneville Canada
PERREAULT, Joseph Augustin, Jan 30 1905 Sex:M Child# 2 Joseph Perreault Canada & Louisa O Aubin NY
PERREAULT, Joseph Charles, Jul 26 1895 Sex:M Child# 12 Benjamin Perreault Canada & Sophie Leblanc Canada
PERREAULT, Joseph Eugene R, Sep 11 1910 Sex:M Child# 2 E Damase Perreault Canada & Emelie A Fugere Canada
PERREAULT, Joseph Henri A, May 7 1897 Sex:M Child# 1 Alfred Perreault Nashua, NH & Clorinthe Bernier Canada
PERREAULT, Joseph Pierre, Apr 23 1899 Sex:M Child# 2 Joseph Perreault Canada & Aurore Rousselle Canada
PERREAULT, Josephine, Nov 29 1898 Sex:F Child# 10 E Damase Perreault Canada & Eleonore Ledoux St Albans, VT Stillbo
PERREAULT, Leona, Jul 15 1890 Sex:F Child# 1 Arthur Perreault St Albans, VT & Valerie Lam Canada
PERREAULT, Lionel Hector, Apr 1 1908 Sex:M Child# 4 Alfred Perreault Adams, MA & Julia Lucier Canada
PERREAULT, Louis Felix, Feb 8 1904 Sex:M Child# 1 Louis Perreault Canada & Philomene Larouche Canada
PERREAULT, Lucille Gabriel, Oct 24 1912 Sex:F Child# 9 Alfred Perreault Canada & Clorinde Bernier Canada
PERREAULT, Ludovic, Oct 30 1917 Sex:M Child# 4 Joseph Perreault Nashua, NH & Emma Lanneville Canada Stillborn
PERREAULT, Malvina Eugenie, Jul 20 1904 Sex:F Child# 2 Alfred Perreault Adams, MA & Julia Lucier Canada
PERREAULT, Marie A Andrea, Dec 2 1898 Sex:F Child# 2 Alfred Perreault Nashua, NH & Clorinthe Bernier Canada
PERREAULT, Marie Donalda, Feb 9 1904 Sex:F Child# 6 George Perreault Canada & Rosalie Levesque Canada
PERREAULT, Maurice Marcel, Jun 6 1918 Sex:M Child# 11 Alfred Perreault Nashua, NH & Clarinda Bernier Canada
PERREAULT, Napoleon Oscar, Apr 29 1893 Sex:M Child# 9 E D Perreault Canada & Eleonore Ledoux Vermont
PERREAULT, Paul Noel, Dec 25 1912 Sex:M Child# 4 Alex Perreault US & Alice Lajoie US
PERREAULT, Sandra, Dec 30 1935 Sex:F Child# 1 Conrad Perreault Nashua, NH & Alicia Enright Nashua, NH
PERREAULT, Therese Olivette, Feb 1 1908 Sex:F Child# 3 Alex Perreault Canada & Alice Lajoie Nashua, NH
PERREAULT, Unknown, Aug 26 1909 Sex:M Child# 1 Joseph Perreault Nashua, NH & Emma Laneville Canada
PERREAULT, Vitaline Florence, Apr 26 1907 Sex:F Child# 5 Alfred Perreault NH & Clorinthe Bernier Canada
PERREAULT, William, Jul 3 1903 Sex:M Child# 1 Alfred Perreault Adams, MA & Julia Lucier Canada
PERRET, Augustine, Aug 14 1894 Sex:F Child# 6 William Perret France & Mary Collier Ireland
PERRET, Joseph, Nov 24 1888 Sex:M Child# 2 Theoplite Perret France & Mary Collins Ireland
PERRET, Mare A L, Aug 17 1887 Sex:F Child# 1 Theophile Perret France & Mary Collins Ireland
PERRETTE, Nellie May, May 17 1893 Sex:F Child# 5 Theop Perrette Canada & Mary Colliers Ireland
PERRON, Albert, May 23 1910 Sex:M Child# 12 Ernest Perron Canada & Malvina Cloutier Canada
PERRON, Amedee Henri, Jul 29 1914 Sex:M Child# 13 Ernest Perron Canada & Malvina Cloutier Canada
PERRON, Edmond, Dec 2 1911 Sex:M Child# 12 Ernest Perron Canada & Malvina Cloutier Canada
PERRON, Emelienne, Sep 27 1907 Sex:F Child# 10 Ernest Perron Canada & Malvina Cloutier Canada Stillborn
PERRON, Joseph, Nov 4 1907 Sex:M Child# 11 Ernest Perron Canada & Malvina Cloutier Canada Stillborn
PERRON, Joseph Emilien L, Mar 14 1906 Sex:M Child# 9 Ernest Perron Canada & Albina Cloutier Canada
PERRON, Joseph Irene Robert, Nov 15 1919 Sex:M Child# 16 Ernest Perron Canada & Alvina Cloutier Canada
PERRON, Lucienne Yvette, Feb 9 1916 Sex:F Child# 15 Ernest Perron Canada & Malvina Cloutier Canada
PERRON, Marie Rose A, Feb 8 1909 Sex:M Child# 10 Ernest Perron Canada & Alvina Cloutier Canada
PERRON, William Raymond, Feb 11 1913 Sex:M Child# 13 Ernest Perron Canada & Malvina Cloutier Canada
PERRY, Arlene Helen, Feb 26 1920 Sex:F Child# 2 Harold W Perry Cambridge, MA & Pearl Seabury Newburg, ME
PERRY, Arlene Pearl, May 8 1916 Sex:F Child#  Harold W Perry Cambridge, MA & Pearl Seabury Newbury, ME Stillborn
PERRY, Dorothy Laura, Feb 28 1920 Sex:F Child# 3 Lloyd M Perry Windsorville, CT & Laura Holden Nashua, NH
PERRY, Elizabeth Huldah, Nov 5 1910 Sex:F Child# 4 W G Perry Campton, NH & Flora J Barnard E Weare, NH

PERRY, Fred Clark, Jan 4 1918 Sex:M Child# 2 Lloyd M Perry Windsorville, CT & Laura L Holden Nashua, NH
PERRY, John, Jr, Jan 2 1932 Sex:M Child# 1 John Perry Canada & Mary Reagan County Cork, Ireland
PERRY, Lawrence Boone, Jr, Apr 28 1924 Sex:M Child# 1 Lawrence B Perry Lake Boom, MA & Eva Robinson Pepperell, MA
PERRY, Lawrence Hazard, Aug 27 1921 Sex:M Child# 4 Lloyd Perry Windsorville, CT & Laura S Holden Nashua, NH
PERRY, Lloyd Holden, Mar 8 1916 Sex:M Child# 1 Lloyd M Perry Rhode Island & Laura Holden Nashua, NH
PERRY, Mary Eleanor, Nov 8 1920 Sex:F Child# 2 Anthony Perry Prince Edward Island & Violet Chamberlain NH
PERRY, Richard Charles, Jan 17 1934 Sex:M Child# 6 Lloyd M Perry Windsorville, CT & Laura Holden Nashua, NH
PERRY, Robert Merriam, Jun 6 1931 Sex:M Child# 5 Floyd Perry Conn & Laura Holden Nashua, NH
PERRY, Unknown, Jul 2 1891 Sex:F Child# 4 Daniel W Perry Dublin & Emma A Cook Nashua, NH
PERRY, Unknown, Aug 17 1902 Sex:F Child# 4 John J Perry Strafford & Grace Bell Athens, VT
PERRY, Unknown, Aug 7 1933 Sex:M Child# 1 Gerald Perry Cabot, VT & Ila Uric St Albans, VT Stillborn
PETARYS, Unknown, Jan 13 1917 Sex:F Child# 1 George Petarys Greece & Pan Nicolas Greece
PETATIS, Unknown, Dec 28 1913 Sex:M Child# 5 Charles Petatis Russia & Mary gudaitis Russia Stillborn
PETAZZI, Leona Louise, Jun 12 1908 Sex:F Child# 1 Edward Petazzi Italy & Prezhansco Carolina Italy
PETEE, Bertha Lorraine, Dec 2 1887 Sex:F Child# 1 A Wilfred Petee Canada & Anna R Chagnon Canada
PETERS, Barbara June, Jun 18 1923 Sex:F Child# 5 Otto Peters St John, NB & Rena Byers St John, NB
PETERS, Clinton Francis, Oct 22 1902 Sex:M Child# 1 Clinton R Peters Lexington, MA & A McCarville Somerset
PETERS, Doris Alfreda, Apr 6 1915 Sex:F Child# 1 Otto Peters St John, NB & Rena Byers St John, NB
PETERS, Dwight Leonard, Dec 1 1926 Sex:M Child# 2 Howard Peters St John, NB & Gladys Oben Nashua, NH
PETERS, Frederick, Jul 16 1916 Sex:M Child# 2 Otto Peters St John, NB & Rena Vyers St John, NB
PETERS, Gloria Alice, Sep 4 1920 Sex:F Child# 1 Wayne Peters Maria, NS & Gertrude Currier Adams, MA
PETERS, Gloria Louise, Nov 5 1932 Sex:F Child# 3 Howard Peters Canada & Gladys Oban NH
PETERS, Hazel Maud, Jan 11 1894 Sex:F Child# 1 Levi E Peters Greenville, NH & Ella M Tufts Mansfield, MA
PETERS, Howard Henry, May 4 1924 Sex:M Child# 1 Howard Peters Canada & Gladys Oban Nashua, NH
PETERS, Jerome, Mar 4 1892 Sex:M Child# 1 John Peters Canada & Mary J Manchester, NH
PETERS, John, Jan 10 1911 Sex:M Child# 3 John Peters Russia & Marccia Rondonuite Russia
PETERS, Joseph, Apr 3 1915 Sex:M Child# 2 George Peters Russia & Lipneska Armelia Russia
PETERS, Madlyn Jean, Mar 8 1925 Sex:F Child# 6 Otto Peters New Brunswick & Rena Byers St John, NB
PETERS, Marion Pearl, Mar 22 1919 Sex:F Child# 3 Otto Peters St John, NB & Rena Beers St John, NB
PETERS, Pauline Esther, Aug 17 1935 Sex:F Child# 2 Fred Peters Fairfield, ME & Hazel Grasale Burlington, VT
PETERS, Rena Mae, May 12 1921 Sex:F Child# 4 Otto Peters St John, NB & Rena Bryers St John, NB
PETERS, Richard Alden, Sep 9 1935 Sex:M Child# 2 Burton Peters St Johns, NB & Harriet Gibbons St Johns, NB
PETERS, Robert Ralph, Aug 13 1929 Sex:M Child# 1 Wm Arthur S Peters St John, NB & Eidth J McCutcheon Wilsford,
PETERS, Virginia Rosemond, Mar 7 1926 Sex:F Child# 1 Clarence Peters St John, NB & Jean Gibbons St John, NB
PETERS, Wayne Richard, Apr 21 1935 Sex:M Child# 7 Otto Peters St John, NB & Rena Byers St John, NB
PETERSON, Alga Florence, Aug 18 1896 Sex:F Child# 12 Samuel Peterson Sweden & Louisa Johnson Sweden
PETERSON, David E, Aug 14 1897 Sex:M Child# 3 Gustave Peterson Sweden & Bessie Anderson Sweden
PETERSON, Emma A, Aug 8 1894 Sex:F Child# 3 August C Peterson Vermont & Lucinda O Mays Vermont
PETERSON, Esther Johanna, Sep 5 1894 Sex:F Child# Gustavus Peterson Sweden & Bessie Anderson Sweden
PETERSON, John David, Dec 9 1924 Sex:M Child# 2 W R Peterson Bedford, MA & Helen L Reed E Dracut, VT
PETERSON, Julia O, Oct 1 1895 Sex:F Child# 2 Gusty Peterston Sweden & Bessie Anderson Sweden
PETERSON, Mildred, Jul 19 1905 Sex:F Child# 2 John Peterson S Boston, MA & Anna Butterfield Vermont
PETERSON, Nancy, Jul 11 1926 Sex:F Child# 1 David Peterson Nashua, NH & Andrea Cadwell Nashua, NH
PETERSON, Walter Rutherford, Jr, Sep 19 1922 Sex:M Child# 1 W R Peterson, Sr Bedford, MA & Helen L Reed E Dorse
PETIPACE, Harry Louis, Nov 28 1892 Sex:M Child# 1 Patrick Petipace Canada & Canada
PETIT, Beatrice G, Jan 15 1898 Sex:F Child# 5 Charles H Petit Canada & Delvina Lucier Canada
PETIT, Bernadette, Aug 2 1892 Sex:F Child# 1 Charles H Petit Canada & Delvina Lucier Canada
PETIT, Charles E Ludger, Nov 1 1903 Sex:M Child# 7 Charles H Petit Canada & Delvina Lucier Canada
PETIT, Henriette, Jan 19 1896 Sex:F Child# 1 Charles H Petit Canada & Delvina Lucier Canada
PETIT, I Richer, Mar 4 1900 Sex:M Child# 6 Charles H Petit Canada & Delvina Lucier Canada
PETIT, Marie Andrea, Feb 16 1889 Sex:F Child# 2 A Wilfred Petit Canada & Anna R Chagnon Canada
PETIT, Unknown, Jan 5 1895 Sex:F Child# 3 Charles S Petit Canada & Delvina Lucier Canada Stillborn
PETIT, Unknown, Dec 28 1900 Sex:F Child# 5 Napoleon Petit Canada & Marie E Hudon Canada
PETITGROW, Joseph David, Jan 1 1889 Sex:M Child# 1 Ernest Petitgrow Canada & Malvina Cote Canada
PETRAIN, Clarice, Sep 30 1934 Sex:F Child# 3 Astrid Petrain Canada & Adele Rivard Nashua, NH
PETRAIN, Joseph Roland, Oct 28 1927 Sex:M Child# 3 H Petrain Canada & Ida Hudon Nashua, NH
PETRAIN, Marie Estelle Jean, Aug 24 1933 Sex:F Child# 2 Astride Petrain Canada & Odille Rivard Nashua, NH
PETRALIS, John, Jul 24 1913 Sex:M Child# 4 John Petralis Russia & Martzella Petralina Russia
PETRAUSKAS, Stanley, May 12 1918 Sex:M Child# 4 William Petrauskas Russia & Josie Bartis Russia
PETRAYIS, Ludvica, Sep 19 1906 Sex:F Child# 1 John Petryis Russia & Rodognis Martella Russia
PETRIN, Cecile Lillian, May 9 1934 Sex:F Child# 3 Wilfred Petrin Canada & Lillian Marchand Nashua, NH
PETRIN, Emile, Apr 4 1909 Sex:M Child# 12 Ovide Petrin Canada & Rosanna Brouillard Canada
PETRIN, Jos Wilfrid Robert, Jun 30 1932 Sex:M Child# 2 Wilfred Petrin Canada & L Marchand Nashua, NH
PETRIN, Joseph Roger, May 24 1931 Sex:M Child# 1 Astride Petrin Canada & Adila Rivard Nashua, NH
PETRIN, M Fabiola Olivette, Sep 18 1914 Sex:F Child# 1 Ovide Petrin Canada & Olivine Rochette Canada
PETRIN, Marie Terese J D, Nov 11 1930 Sex:F Child# 1 Wilfred Petrin Canada & Lillian Marchand Nashua, NH
PETRIN, Normand William, Aug 30 1926 Sex:M Child# 2 H Petrin Canada & Alida Hudon Nashua, NH
PETRITIS, Adele, Jan 2 1913 Sex:F Child# 4 Charles Petritis Russia & Mary Gudaytis Russia
PETRO, James A, Jan 31 1893 Sex:M Child# 1 Lewis L Petro NH & Mary M Lambert NH
PETROPOULOU, Jenny, Apr 2 1925 Sex:F Child# 1 Jas Petropoulou Greece & Christina Leinake Greece
PETROPOULOU, Unknown, Aug 7 1933 Sex:F Child# 3 G Petropoulou Greece & Christina Demaki Greece
PETROS, Unknown, Nov 2 1934 Sex:M Child# 3 Andrew Petros Greece & Alexandra Demakis Greece
PETROSIS, Kostos, Aug 9 1913 Sex:M Child# 2 Nicholas Petrosis Greece & Helene Papachristos Greece

PETROU, Stamaton, May 21 1904 Sex:F Child# 1 Taxiarches Petrou Greece & Angelica Hingos Greece
PETRY, Arthur Fernard, Jun 7 1931 Sex:M Child# 3 Fernard Petry Long Island & Priscilla Wallace Nashua, NH
PETRY, Douglas Arthur, Nov 14 1928 Sex:M Child# 2 Fernand Petry Farmingdale, NY & P Wallace Nashua, NH
PETRY, Ronald Carlton, Nov 20 1926 Sex:M Child# 1 Bernard M Petry
PETRY, Rudge, Jul 6 1934 Sex:M Child# 4 Fernard Petry Hixsfield, LI, NY & Priscilla Wallace Nashua, NH
PETSIKONAS, Jennie Helen, Aug 20 1925 Sex:F Child# 2 W Petsikonas Lithuania & Helen Ganistch Lithuania
PETSIKORRES, Unknown, Apr 28 1927 Sex:M Child# 9 W Petsikorres
PETSIKOUES, Brunsla, Dec 13 1919 Sex:F Child# 1 Wilh Petsikoues Lithuania Russia & Helena Geniewicz Lithuania
PETTIER, Eleanore, Aug 25 1888 Sex:F Child# 10 Joseph Pettier Canada & Eleanor Caron Canada
PETTIER, Marie Rose, Jan 18 1888 Sex:F Child# 1 Francois H Pettier St Luce, PQ & Ida April P Q
PETTIER, Mary Clara, Nov 8 1888 Sex:F Child# 3 Heloise Pettier Canada & Eugene Podras Canada
PETTIER, Melendy, Jul 11 1889 Sex:F Child# 8 W E Pettier Plattsburg, NY & Elizabeth St Michael Plattsburg, NY
PETTIGREW, Unknown, Sep 3 1909 Sex:F Child# 6 William M Pettigrew W Newton, MA & Jennie L Smith Andover, NH
PETTINGILL, Ned Harrison, Jan 8 1922 Sex:M Child# 3 Henry H Pettingill NH & Grace N Simonds Texas
PETUK, Josephine, Mar 19 1918 Sex:F Child# 2 George Petuk Russia & Amelia Lapineski Russia
PETULIS, Peter, Oct 5 1909 Sex:M Child# 1 Charles Petulis Russia & Mary Gudajtis Russia
PETUTIS, Annie, Oct 22 1914 Sex:F Child# 6 Charley Petutis Russia & Mary Gouditis Russia
PETUTIS, Anthony, Nov 26 1920 Sex:M Child# 8 Charley Petutis Lithuania Russia & Mary Gonditis Lithuania Russia
PETUTIS, Anthony, Nov 26 1920 Sex:M Child# 8 Charley Petutis Poland, Russia & Veronica Matelowska Poland Russia
PETUTIS, Eva, Aug 20 1916 Sex:F Child# 1 Joseph Petutis Russia & Cleopha Voletka Russia
PETUTIS, John, Jan 15 1917 Sex:M Child# 7 Charley Petutis Russia - Lithuania & Mary Gouditis Russia - Lithuania
PETUTIS, Joseph, Oct 14 1911 Sex:M Child# 3 Charles Petutis Russia & Gesotoi Gudentys Russia
PETUTIS, Mary, Sep 15 1910 Sex:F Child# 2 Charles Petutis Russia & Mary Gudajcus Russia
PETUTYS, Nellie, Oct 10 1920 Sex:F Child# 2 Joseph Petutys Russia & Kliaroajai Russia
PEVARUNIS, Bernice, Oct 12 1917 Sex:F Child# 3 Martin Pevarunis Russia & Mary Schulaite Russia
PEVIET, Elmina, Apr 17 1891 Sex:F Child# 9 Antoine Peviet Canada & Georgina Marquis Canada
PEYER, Joseph Arthur, May 8 1897 Sex:M Child# 3 Arthur Peyer Canada & Leontine Laquerre Canada
PEYER, Joseph Georges, Apr 11 1895 Sex:M Child# 2 Arthur Peyer Canada & Leontine Laguerre Canada
PEYER, Joseph Victor, Oct 18 1894 Sex:M Child# 1 Victor Peyer Canada & Flavie Gagnon Canada
PEYER, M Eva, Aug 10 1895 Sex:F Child# 2 Edmond Peyer Canada & Flora Garceau Canada
PEZZULA, Joseph Archie, Aug 13 1924 Sex:M Child# 1 Anthony Pezzula Italy & Pauline Carpenter Milford, NH
PHALEN, Francis Valentine, Sep 3 1901 Sex:M Child# 2 Patrick Phalen Ireland & Nellie E Lane Ireland
PHALEN, Inez, Jan 6 1904 Sex:F Child# 2 Thomas A Phalen Ireland & Isabelle Foley Nashua, NH
PHALEN, William J, Mar 24 1897 Sex:M Child# 2 John Phalen Ireland & Elizabeth McGlynn Ireland
PHANEUF, Alberta A, Nov 7 1902 Sex:F Child# 7 J B Phaneuf Canada & Parmelie Chartrand Canada
PHANEUF, Albertine Parmelie, Aug 20 1921 Sex:F Child# 1 Albert G Phaneuf NH & Marie F Stanton NH
PHANEUF, Albina, May 15 1901 Sex:F Child# 6 J B Phaneuf Canada & Parmelie Chartrand Canada
PHANEUF, Alice Albina, Jul 18 1902 Sex:F Child# 4 Ang Phaneuf Canada & Adeline Avard Vergennes, VT
PHANEUF, Auguste Elphege, Apr 4 1894 Sex:M Child# 1 Auguste Phaneuf Canada & Adeline Havard Vergennes, VT
PHANEUF, Benjamin, Jun 6 1897 Sex:M Child# 8 Horace C Phaneuf Canada & Cordelia Petit Canada
PHANEUF, Charles Frederic, Dec 2 1891 Sex:M Child# 6 Antoine Phaneuf Moore's Fork, NY & Melinda Linton Moores, NY
PHANEUF, Claire Guilberte, Feb 11 1923 Sex:F Child# 12 Albert Phaneuf NH & Lorraine Stanton NH
PHANEUF, Constance Antonia, Apr 13 1924 Sex:F Child# 3 Albert G Phaneuf NH & Lorraine Stanton NH
PHANEUF, Delima, Feb 20 1894 Sex:F Child# 3 Michel Phaneuf Canada & Delia Lussier Canada
PHANEUF, Edith Eva, Apr 12 1890 Sex:F Child# 5 St P Phaneuf Canada & Cordelia Petit Canada
PHANEUF, Eleanor Zelfrid, Nov 14 1929 Sex:F Child# 6 Albert Phaneuf Manchester, NH & Lorraine Stanton Nashua, NH
PHANEUF, Gracie, Jul 9 1888 Sex:F Child# 4 H C Phaneuf Canada & Cordelia Petit Canada
PHANEUF, Jean Baptiste, May 29 1899 Sex:M Child# 5 Jean Bapt Phaneuf Canada & Parmalie Chartrand Manchester, NH
PHANEUF, John Baptiste, May 16 1934 Sex:M Child# 3 Arthur Phaneuf Nashua, NH & Lillian Vassar Nashua, NH
PHANEUF, Joseph Armand, Apr 30 1898 Sex:M Child# 4 Baptiste Phaneuf Canada & Parmelie Chartrand Manchester, NH
PHANEUF, Joseph Arthur O, Mar 7 1905 Sex:M Child# 8 Jean B Phaneuf Canada & Parmelie Chartrand NH
PHANEUF, Joseph Leo, Jun 24 1922 Sex:M Child# 2 Philip Phaneuf Voluntown, CT & Yvonne Belanger Canada
PHANEUF, Marie Alice T, Jun 19 1909 Sex:F Child# 2 Auguste Phaneuf Canada & Delima Messier Canada
PHANEUF, Marie Annette E, Feb 3 1909 Sex:F Child# 10 J B Phaneuf Canada & Parmelie Chartrand NH
PHANEUF, Marie Delima, Dec 29 1907 Sex:F Child# 1 Augusta Phaneuf Canada & Delima Messier Canada
PHANEUF, Marie Jacqueline, May 2 1916 Sex:F Child# 2 Horace H Phaneuf NH & Lucienne Turcotte Mass
PHANEUF, Marie Julie, Feb 22 1904 Sex:F Child# 5 Auguste Phaneuf Canada & Adeline Avard Vergennes, VT
PHANEUF, Marie Rose A, Jun 25 1907 Sex:F Child# 9 Jean Bte Phaneuf Canada & Parmelie Chartrand NH
PHANEUF, Marie Rosianna, Nov 1 1898 Sex:F Child# 1 Joseph Phaneuf Canada & Marie L Lawrence Canada
PHANEUF, Mary Gloria Yolande, Mar 8 1926 Sex:F Child# 1 Arthur Phaneuf Nashua, NH & Lillian Vassar Nashua, NH
PHANEUF, Maurice, Jun 12 1894 Sex:M Child# 7 H C Phaneuf Canada & Cordelia Petit Canada
PHANEUF, Oscar Amedie, Aug 1 1899 Sex:M Child# 3 Auguste Phaneuf Canada & Adeline Havard Nashua, NH
PHANEUF, Patricia Jane, Apr 8 1930 Sex:F Child# 2 Arthur Phaneuf NH & Lillian Vassar NH
PHANEUF, Paul Hubert, Apr 17 1914 Sex:M Child# 1 Horace Phaneuf Nashua, NH & Lucienne Turcotte Mass
PHANEUF, Philias Wilfred, Jun 4 1896 Sex:M Child# 2 August Phaneuf Canada & Adeline Havard Canada
PHANEUF, Rita Louise, Jul 27 1926 Sex:F Child# 1 Wilfrid Phaneuf Nashua, NH & Annie Bacigolupos Berlin, NH
PHANEUF, Roger Maurice, Jun 6 1925 Sex:M Child# 2 Wilfred Phaneuf Nashua, NH & Rose Guilemette Nashua, NH
PHANEUF, Unknown, Jul 9 1893 Sex:F Child# 6 H C Phaneuf Canada & Cordelia Petit Canada Stillborn
PHANEUF, Unknown, Feb 26 1926 Sex:M Child# 3 Philip Phaneuf Valentine, CT & Yvonne Belanger Canada Stillborn
PHANEUF, Victor, Jul 21 1898 Sex:M Child# 9 Horace C Phaneuf Canada & Cordelia Petit Canada
PHANEUF, Wilfrid Auguste, Apr 9 1921 Sex:M Child# 1 Wilfrid P Phaneuf Nashua, NH & Rose Guilmette Nashua, NH
PHELAN, Anthony Valentine, Jul 3 1908 Sex:M Child# 5 Thomas A Phelan Ireland & Isabella C Foley Nashua, NH
PHELAN, Charles L J, Sep 28 1912 Sex:M Child# 7 Thomas Phelan Ireland & Isabella Foley Nashua, NH

PHELAN, Jos Richard, Nov 29 1929 Sex:M Child# 1 Francis Phelan Nashua, NH & Eva Hebert Nashua, NH
PHELAN, Joseph, May 27 1902 Sex:M Child# 1 Thomas A Phelan Ireland & Isabella C Foley Nashua, NH
PHELAN, Joyce Louise, May 22 1933 Sex:F Child# 3 Anthony Phelan Nashua, NH & Rose Lindsay Rhode Island
PHELAN, Mary, Oct 23 1906 Sex:F Child# 4 Thomas A Phelan Ireland & Isabella C Foley Nashua, NH
PHELAN, Patricia Ann, Jul 26 1930 Sex:F Child# 1 Joseph Phelan Nashua, NH & Lillian Lewis Nashua, NH
PHELAN, Patrick, Nov 2 1904 Sex:M Child# 4 John Phelan Ireland & Elizabeth Glynn Ireland
PHELAN, Paul Eugene, Feb 22 1915 Sex:M Child# 8 Thomas A Phelan Ireland & Isabella Galey Nashua, NH
PHELAN, Rose Maureen, May 1 1931 Sex:F Child# 2 Anthony Phelan Nashua, NH & Rose Lindsey Providence, RI
PHELAN, Ruth May, Jul 15 1935 Sex:F Child# 4 Anthony Phelan Nashua, NH & Rose Lindsey Nashua, NH
PHELAN, Thomas F, Jan 17 1905 Sex:M Child# 3 Thomas A Phelan Ireland & Isabella Foley Nashua, NH
PHELAN, Unknown, Feb 6 1896 Sex:F Child# 1 John T Phelan Ireland & Lizzie McGlynn Ireland
PHELAN, Vincent Desmond, Apr 6 1910 Sex:M Child# 6 Thomas Phelan Ireland & Isabelle Foley Nashua, NH
PHELAN, William, May 11 1930 Sex:M Child# 1 Anthony Phelan Nashua, NH & Rose Lindsay Providence, RI
PHELPS, Charlotte Grace, Feb 7 1917 Sex:F Child# 1 Merle Phelps Nashua, NH & Hazel Cote Nashua, NH
PHELPS, Esta Elizabeth, Oct 6 1906 Sex:F Child# 3 Edward V Phelps Winchester, MA & Grace M Garland Nashua, NH
PHELPS, George O, Mar 8 1896 Sex:M Child# 2 Arthur W Phelps Worcester, MA & Emma G Osborn Nashua, NH
PHELPS, Hazel, Jan 14 1907 Sex:F Child# 1 Brooks N Phelps NH & Daisy Dean NH
PHELPS, Joseph John, Jul 8 1901 Sex:M Child# 1 John Phelps Pittsfield, MA & May G Kelley Ashuelot
PHELPS, Lester G, May 3 1894 Sex:M Child#  E V Phelps Mass & Grace Garland Nashua, NH
PHELPS, Lucy M, Dec 14 1887 Sex:F Child# 1 Sidney W Phelps New Hampshire & Clara L Nashua, NH
PHELPS, Myrle, Jun 12 1893 Sex:F Child# 2 Sidney Phelps NH & Carrie L Bailey Nashua, NH
PHELPS, Unknown, Apr 5 1893 Sex:F Child# 1 Arthur W Phelps Worcester, MA & Emma G Osborn Nashua, NH
PHELPS, Unknown, Aug 15 1893 Sex:M Child# 2 Albert E Phelps Bolton Centre, PQ & Annie Belforde Potton, PQ
PHELPS, Unknown, Sep 20 1918 Sex:F Child# 3 John W Phelps Pittsfield, MA & May G Kelley Ashuelot
PHELPS, Unknown, Sep 3 1927 Sex:M Child# 3 Wallace Phelps Nashua, NH & Alice Holt Nashua, NH Stillborn
PHELPS, Wallace Edw, Jul 25 1899 Sex:M Child# 2 Edward V Phelps Mass & Grace M Garland Nashua, NH
PHILBRICK, Doris Mae, Sep 30 1922 Sex:F Child# 2 Edward Philbrick W Springfield, NH & Gertrude Messer Sunapee, NH
PHILBRICK, Eleanor Gertrude, Sep 28 1932 Sex:F Child# 4 Ed C Philbrick Springfield, NH & Gert E Messer Sunapee, NH
PHILBRICK, Mariam Evelyn, Mar 13 1930 Sex:F Child# 3 Edward Philbrick Springfield, NH & Gertrude Messer Sunapee, NH
PHILBRICK, Ruth Elizabeth, Nov 15 1927 Sex:F Child# 3 E H Philbrick Springfield, NH & Mary Fowell Lebanon, NH
PHILBRICK, Sumner Esmon, Oct 17 1919 Sex:M Child# 1 Sum E Philbrick Springfield, NH & Edna H Bertrand Nashua, NH
PHILBRICK, Wesley Alfred, Nov 26 1920 Sex:M Child# 2 Ed Hrrson Philbrick Springfield, NH & Mary Culver Truell
PHILIP, Cecile Muriel, Jul 25 1934 Sex:F Child# 7 Mathias Philip Canada & Phoebe Melanson Vermont
PHILIPALOPOULAS, Papie Frosini, Apr 17 1908 Sex:M Child# 1 A Philipalopoulas Greece & Ana Papos Greece
PHILIPS, Unknown, Dec 2 1902 Sex:F Child# 2 Erwin H Philips Bethlehem & Grace Blood Groton, MA
PHILIPS, Unknown, Apr 9 1912 Sex:M Child# 1 Clarence C Philips Sandown, NH & Marguerite O'Neil Nashua, NH Stillborn
PHILLIPS, Barbara Joan, Apr 2 1935 Sex:F Child# 1 Edward Phillips Worcester, MA & Alice Glidden Greenville, NH
PHILLIPS, Cynthia A, Feb 24 1931 Sex:F Child# 3 Robert T Phillips Boston, MA & Elizabeth Kittredge Milford, NH
PHILLIPS, Harry Johns, Nov 7 1893 Sex:M Child# 2 William J Phillips Hooksett, NH & Sarah Johns Pittsfield, NH
PHILLIPS, Ray Warren, May 8 1901 Sex:M Child# 1 Irving H Phillips Bethlehem & Grace H Blood Groton, MA
PHIPPARD, Albert William, Oct 4 1896 Sex:M Child# 8 William J Phippard Newfoundland & Lizzie M Welch Newfoundland
PHIPPARD, Carol Elizabeth, Nov 2 1935 Sex:F Child# 2 H W Phippard Nashua, NH & Isabel Roche Nashua, NH
PHIPPARD, David William, Jun 25 1896 Sex:M Child# 3 Frank Phippard Newfoundland & Anna M Wills Nashua, NH
PHIPPARD, Eileen Ann, Jun 8 1934 Sex:F Child# 1 George Phippard Nashua, NH & Eileen Sullivan Nashua, NH
PHIPPARD, Elizabeth, Jul 24 1898 Sex:F Child# 9 William J Phippard Newfoundland & Elizabeth Welch Newfoundland
PHIPPARD, Emma Louise, Oct 1 1904 Sex:F Child# 4 James B Phippard Newfoundland & Nellie Mooney Newfoundland
PHIPPARD, George Francis, Jun 15 1935 Sex:M Child# 2 George Phippard Nashua, NH & Eileen Sullivan Nashua, NH
PHIPPARD, Helene, May 20 1913 Sex:F Child# 16 William Phippard Newfoundland & Elizabeth Walsh Newfoundland
PHIPPARD, Henry, Oct 20 1903 Sex:M Child# 12 William J Phippard Newfoundland & Elizabeth Walsh
PHIPPARD, James, Mar 6 1922 Sex:M Child# 5 John N Phippard Newfoundland & Nellie Mooney Newfoundland Stillborn
PHIPPARD, John, Jun 22 1907 Sex:M Child# 14 William J Phippard Newfoundland & Elizabeth Walch Newfoundland
PHIPPARD, Margaret, Feb 25 1898 Sex:F Child# 4 Frank Phippard Newfoundland & Annie M Wills Nashua, NH
PHIPPARD, Mary Elizabeth, Oct 15 1912 Sex:F Child# 1 James Phippard Newfoundland & Nellie Mooney Newfoundland
PHIPPARD, Miriam, Jan 19 1911 Sex:F Child# 15 William Phippard Newfoundland & Elizabeth Walsh Newfoundland
PHIPPARD, Paul Maurice, Jan 9 1906 Sex:M Child# 13 William G Phippard Newfoundland & Elizabeth M Walsh Newfoundland
PHIPPARD, Roland J, Dec 21 1893 Sex:M Child# 6 William Phippard Newfoundland & Lizzie Welch Newfoundland
PHIPPARD, Rose Eleanor, Oct 1 1915 Sex:F Child# 3 James Phippard Newfoundland & Nellie Mooney Newfoundland
PHIPPARD, Stanislas, Feb 5 1900 Sex:M Child# 10 William Phippard Newfoundland & Elizabeth Walsh Newfoundland
PHIPPARD, Stanley Elbert, Feb 22 1918 Sex:M Child# 1 Stanley Phippard Nashua, NH & Grace Emily Smith Nashua, NH
PHIPPARD, Unknown, Jan 1 1900 Sex:M Child# 1 R Phippard Newfoundland & A Kelley Boston, MA
PHIPPARD, William John, Nov 3 1913 Sex:M Child# 2 James R Phippard Newfoundland & Nellie Mooney Newfoundland
PHIPPERD, George, Jan 26 1902 Sex:M Child# 11 William J Phipperd Newfoundland & Elizabeth Walsh Newfoundland
PIAKOUS, Joseph, Sep 24 1913 Sex:M Child# 5 William Piakous Russia & Gertrude Burges Russia
PIALTOS, Constantinos, Jan 30 1920 Sex:M Child# 2 James Pialtos Greece & Fanny Yakos Greece
PIALTOUS, Constantine George, Aug 9 1921 Sex:M Child# 1 George Pialtous Greece & Virginia J Pappas Greece
PICARD, Aimie Conrad Lionel, May 27 1933 Sex:M Child# 1 Jos C Picard Canada & Louisa Bibeau Canada
PICARD, Delia Florence, Oct 6 1922 Sex:F Child# 4 Joseph A Picard Lowell, MA & Della Rousseau Nashua, NH
PICARD, Elizabeth Irene, Mar 28 1924 Sex:F Child# 1 Lionel Picard Canada & Eliza Tremblay Plattsburgh, NY
PICARD, Joseph Alfred Eugene, Mar 31 1918 Sex:M Child# 2 Pierre Picard Canada & Angelina Gaureau Canada
PICARD, Joseph C Robert, Jul 23 1931 Sex:M Child# 5 Oscar Picard Canada & Clara Lavoie Nashua, NH
PICARD, Joseph Ernest, Apr 20 1918 Sex:M Child# 1 Oscar Picard Canada & Clara Lavoie Nashua, NH
PICARD, Joseph Lawrence, Oct 6 1922 Sex:M Child# 3 Joseph A Picard Lowell, MA & Della Rousseau Nashua, NH
PICARD, Joseph Normand R, Jun 4 1924 Sex:M Child# 3 Oscar Picard Canada & Clara Lavoie NH

PICARD, Marie Clara, Mar 15 1899 Sex:F Child# 13 Anselme Picard Canada & Elmire Deberge Canada
PICARD, Marie Rita, Apr 3 1921 Sex:F Child# 2 Oscar Picard Canada & Clara Lavoie NH
PICARD, Marie Theresa Doroth, Mar 10 1926 Sex:F Child# 4 Oscar Picard Canada & Clara Lavoie NH
PICARD, Paul Joseph Roger, Aug 4 1931 Sex:M Child# 4 Wilfred Picard Canada & Aurore Soucy Canada
PICARD, Roland J Abbe, Aug 13 1921 Sex:M Child# 2 Abbe Picard Lowell, MA & Delia Rousseau Nashua, NH
PICARD, Unknown, Mar 27 1901 Sex:F Child# 5 Charles Picard Vermont & Marie Quintal Vermont
PICARD, Victorine Lea, Jul 4 1902 Sex:F Child# 2 Louis Picard Canada & Elvine West Ware, MA
PICHE, Mary Eva Alice, May 12 1891 Sex:F Child# 3 Ludger Piche Canada & Albina Cote Canada
PICHER, Elizabeth Louise, Sep 24 1914 Sex:M Child# 1 Carl Picher Milford, NH & Mary Hooper Mass
PICHETTE, Marie Florilda, Aug 14 1897 Sex:F Child# 2 Joseph Pichette Canada & Agnes Adams Canada
PICIKONIS, Anna, Dec 29 1917 Sex:F Child# 4 John Picikonis Russia Lithuania & Wiklorya Wilcynska Russia Lithuania
PICKERING, David Earle, Jul 27 1926 Sex:M Child# 5 Samuel Pickering Manchester, NH & Elise Bixby Manchester, NH
PICKERING, Nancy Mary, Mar 14 1924 Sex:F Child# 4 Samuel Pickering Manchester, NH & Elsie Bixby Manchester, NH
PICKETT, Unknown, Apr 23 1900 Sex:M Child# 10 Scott Pickett NC & Lena Seabrook NC
PICKETT, Unknown, Apr 23 1900 Sex:M Child# 9 Scott Pickett NC & Lena Seabrook NC
PIDGEON, Joseph, Jan 11 1900 Sex:M Child# 6 Henry Pidgeon Vermont & Virginie M Frenette Nashua, NH Stillborn
PIECEWICZ, Unknown, Mar 31 1919 Sex:M Child# 2 Tieofil Piecewicz Russia & Amelia Mrkr Russia
PIECIWICZ, Charles, Dec 6 1917 Sex:M Child# 1 Tofilio Pieciwicz Russia & Amelia Maker Russia
PIERCE, Barbara, Jul 17 1926 Sex:F Child# 1 Everett Pierce New York & Elizabeth Marsh Worcester, MA
PIERCE, Beverly Ann, Jul 11 1934 Sex:F Child# 3 Theodore Pierce Nashua, NH & Emma Martin Manchester, NH
PIERCE, Charles R, Apr 20 1894 Sex:M Child# 1 Arthur M Pierce Mass & May A Holbrook NH
PIERCE, Hester Elizabeth, Jun 27 1903 Sex:F Child# 1 John W Pierce St John, NB & Jessie M Wood Nashua, NH
PIERCE, Norris Henry, Jun 14 1896 Sex:M Child# 2 Arthur E Pierce NH & Beatrice E Everett Mass
PIERCE, Paul Horace, Oct 12 1925 Sex:M Child# 4 Joseph F Pierce Irving, MA & Grace Linton Nashville, TN
PIERCE, Robert, Mar 19 1932 Sex:M Child# 1 Theodore Pierce Nashua, NH & Emma Martin Mt Vernon, NH
PIERCE, Theodore Wood, Jan 10 1905 Sex:M Child# 2 John W Pierce Norton, NB & Jessie M Wood Nashua, NH
PIERCE, Theodore, Jr, Jul 12 1933 Sex:M Child# 2 Theodore Pierce Nashua, NH & Emma Isabelle Manchester, NH
PIERCE, Unknown, Apr 27 1887 Sex:F Child# 2 George R Pierce Nashua, NH & T L New Jersey
PIERCE, Unknown, Apr 23 1889 Sex:F Child# 3 George R Pierce Nashua, NH & Lilly N Pierce New Jersey
PIERCE, Unknown, May 21 1890 Sex:F Child#  Henry Pierce Goffstown, NH & Ida B Whitcomb S Stafford, VT
PIERCY, Anne Therese, Sep 29 1935 Sex:F Child# 4 John Piercy NH & Mary Nangle NH
PIERRE, Francis, Jun 25 1921 Sex:M Child# 2 Clarence Pierre Fairlee, VT & Ruth Carr Andover, NH
PIETHKIWICZ, Louise, Oct 16 1923 Sex:F Child# 1 Joseph Piethkiwicz Poland & Mary Buleikia Poland
PIETKEWAH, Boleslaw, Mar 6 1897 Sex:M Child# 1 Alphonse Pietkewah Russia & Michalina Mazel Russia
PIETKICIVICZ, Edward, Nov 21 1899 Sex:M Child# 2 Alp Pietkicivicz Poland & Micheline Mazel Poland
PIETUCH, Dominic, Aug 4 1922 Sex:M Child# 2 John Pietuch Poland & Bronislawa Baryea Poland
PIETUCH, Joseph, Aug 29 1915 Sex:M Child# 1 Frank Pietuch Russia & Bronie Borilla Russia
PIETUCK, Gunefa, Jun 29 1925 Sex:F Child# 4 John Pietuck Poland & Bruislava Baryla Poland
PIGEON, Agnes Emelie, Jan 12 1901 Sex:F Child# 7 Andre Pigeon Vermont & Virginie Pigeon Nashua, NH
PIGEON, Alfred H, Oct 21 1891 Sex:M Child# 1 Andre Pigeon Vermont & Virginia Frenette Nashua, NH
PIGEON, Anna V, Jun 18 1893 Sex:F Child# 2 Andre Pigeon Vermont & Virginie Frenette Nashua, NH
PIGEON, Carrie M, Apr 8 1897 Sex:F Child# 4 Andre Pigeon Vermont & Virginie Frenette Nashua, NH
PIGEON, G A, Jan 25 1899 Sex:M Child# 5 Andre Pigeon Bridgeport, VT & Virginie Frenette Nashua, NH Stillborn
PIGEON, Marie O A, Jun 8 1895 Sex:F Child# 3 Andre Pigeon Vermont & Virginie Frenette Nashua, NH
PIKE, Dolores Rita, Feb 2 1932 Sex:F Child# 1 Percy Pike Halifax, VT & Eleanor Marquis Canada
PIKE, Geraldine Mae, Jun 8 1931 Sex:F Child# 3 Oren Pike Manchester, NH & Doris May Brown Nashua, NH
PIKE, Margaret Irene, Nov 23 1929 Sex:F Child# 2 Oren Newell Pike Gardner, MA & Doris Brown Portland, ME
PIKE, Marjorie Louise, Aug 10 1924 Sex:F Child# 1 Lewis Robert Pike Nashua, NH & Sadie Kelley Nashua, NH
PIKE, Nancy Elinor, May 6 1933 Sex:F Child# 2 Percy Pike Nashua, NH & Elinor Marquis Canada
PIKE, Unknown, Aug 16 1887 Sex:M Child# 2 Samuel B Pike Epping & Flora M Jenness Portsmouth
PILIGIAN, Rosie, Sep 5 1909 Sex:F Child# 4 Harry Piligian Armenia & Osanna Mananian Armenia
PILIGRIAN, Paul Harry, Jun 22 1929 Sex:M Child# 1 Paul Piligrian Nashua, NH & Araxie Barsanian Worcester, MA
PILLIGIAN, Ashgain, Feb 24 1905 Sex:F Child# 4 Harry Pilligian Turkey & Onsana Manan Turkey
PILLIGIAN, Harry, Dec 2 1903 Sex:M Child# 3 Harry Pilligian Armenia &  Armenia
PILLSBURY, Ann, Mar 19 1930 Sex:F Child# 2 Harold Pillsbury Pelham, NH & Joanna Colbert Pepperell, MA
PILLSBURY, Bernadette, Dec 30 1933 Sex:F Child# 1 Irving Pillsbury Pepperell, MA & Marion Riley Pepperell, MA
PILLSBURY, Betty Helene, Sep 22 1923 Sex:F Child# 1 Irving Pillsbury Pepperell, MA & Mary H Lillis Pepperell, MA
PILLSBURY, Marion Catherine, Feb 5 1924 Sex:F Child# 4 Leo Pillsbury Mt Vernon, NH & Catherine McGrath E Pepperell
PILLSBURY, Mary Jane, Jan 19 1925 Sex:F Child# 2 Irving Pillsbury Pepperell, MA & Mary H Lillis Pepperell, MA
PILLSBURY, Mildred Cecilia, Sep 17 1926 Sex:F Child# 5 Leo Pillsbury Mont Vernon, NH & Catherine McGrath Pepperell
PILLSBURY, Paul Walter, Oct 31 1934 Sex:M Child# 1 Walter Pillsbury Derry, NH & Ruth LeClair Nashua, NH
PILLSBURY, Russell E, Jul 15 1929 Sex:M Child# 1 Russell E Pillsbury E Pepperell, MA & Marion Wildes S Groveland
PINARD, Amanda Theresie, Jan 31 1925 Sex:F Child# 1 Ernest Pinard US & Elizabeth Lefebvre US
PINARD, Bertha, Mar 19 1906 Sex:F Child# 5 Theodore Pinard US & Angelina Gendron US
PINARD, Henri, Nov 9 1908 Sex:M Child# 7 Theodore Pinard Canada & Angelina Gendron US
PINARD, J Norbert Dollard, Jun 6 1914 Sex:M Child# 11 Adolph T Pinard St Johnsbury, VT & Angelina Gendron Nashua
PINARD, Joseph, Apr 29 1919 Sex:M Child# 1 (No Parents Listed)
PINARD, Jovite Moise, Oct 9 1909 Sex:M Child# 8 Theodore Pinard Canada & Angelina Gendron US
PINARD, Laura Evelena, Sep 30 1916 Sex:F Child# 12 Theodore Pinard St Johnsbury, VT & Angelina Gendron Canada
PINARD, Lillian Jeanne, Jan 22 1919 Sex:F Child# 13 Theodore Pinard Canada & Angelina Gendron US
PINARD, Louis Paul Emile, Aug 24 1912 Sex:M Child# 10 Theodore Pinard US & Angelina Gendron US
PINARD, Olena Agnes, Feb 10 1902 Sex:F Child# 2 Adolphe T Pinard Canada & A Gendron Nashua, NH
PINARD, Paul Alfred, Nov 20 1929 Sex:M Child# 1 Jovide Pinard Nashua, NH & Florine Michaud Nashua, NH

PINARD, Raymond Ernest, Aug 17 1903 Sex:M Child# 3 Caliste Pinard Canada & Angelina Gendron NS
PINARD, Raymond Ernest, May 18 1929 Sex:M Child# 2 Ernest Pinard Nashua, NH & Elizabeth Lefebvre Nashua, NH
PINARD, Rosalie Althea, Aug 27 1907 Sex:F Child# 6 Theodore Pinard Canada & Angelina Gendron US
PINARD, Therese Albea, Apr 7 1911 Sex:F Child# 9 Theodore Pinard Canada & Angelina Gendron US
PINARD, Yvonne Lea, Jan 2 1905 Sex:F Child# 4 Theodore Pinard Canada & Angelina Gendron Canada
PINAULT, Edgar, Jan 31 1901 Sex:M Child# 6 Alexandre Pinault Canada & Celanire Anctil Canada
PINAULT, Eugenie, Mar 10 1894 Sex:F Child# 15 Hubert Pinault Canada & Marie Bonville Canada
PINAULT, Francois Joseph, Aug 29 1904 Sex:M Child# 14 Thomas Pinault Canada & Demerise Roussel Canada
PINAULT, Joseph, Jan 27 1901 Sex:M Child# 11 Thomas Pinault Canada & Demerise Roussel Canada Stillborn
PINAULT, Joseph Andre, Oct 26 1896 Sex:M Child# 1 Andre Pinault Canada & Clodia Deschesne Canada
PINAULT, Joseph Louis A, Nov 18 1900 Sex:M Child# 4 Andre Pinault Canada & Claudia Deschesne Canada
PINAULT, Joseph Luc E, Apr 1 1899 Sex:M Child# 3 Andre Pinault Canada & Clodia Deschesne Canada
PINAULT, Joseph Theo A, Aug 28 1902 Sex:M Child# 12 Thomas Pinault Canada & Demerise Roussel Canada
PINAULT, M Aimee, Dec 25 1895 Sex:F Child# 8 Thomas Pinault Canada & Demerise rousselle Canada
PINAULT, Marie Demerise, Jan 22 1898 Sex:F Child# 11 Thomas Pinault Canada & Demerise Rouessel Canada
PINAULT, Marie Doris Grace, Aug 15 1932 Sex:F Child# 3 Charles Pinault Canada & Blanche Santerre Canada
PINAULT, Marie Fannie R, Nov 12 1899 Sex:F Child# 10 Thomas Pinault Canada & Demerise Roussel Canada
PINAULT, Marie L Cecile, Nov 30 1897 Sex:F Child# 2 Andre Pinault Canada & Claudia Deschesne Canada
PINAULT, Marie Louise, Apr 29 1892 Sex:F Child# 14 Hubert Pinault Canada & Marie Mandeville Canada
PINAULT, Marie Malvina, Dec 9 1894 Sex:F Child# 7 Thomas Pinault Canada & Demerise Roussell Canada
PINAULT, Sylvio Theodore, Feb 28 1927 Sex:M Child# 1 Theodore Pinault Nashua, NH & Orra Bergeron Lowell, MA
PINCINCE, Richard Ulric, Jul 31 1934 Sex:M Child# 1 Ulric Pincince Canada & Cecile Desroche Suncook, NH
PINEAU, Clara Regina, Feb 13 1893 Sex:F Child# 6 Thomas Pineau Canada & Desmerise Roussel Canada
PINEAU, Ellen, Jan 19 1892 Sex:F Child# 4 George Pineau Canada & Annie McCarthy Ireland
PINEAU, Joseph A, Apr 21 1887 Sex:M Child# 1 Alex Pineau Canada & Celanie St Jean Canada
PINEAU, Marie D R, Apr 5 1887 Sex:F Child# 4 William Pineau P Q & Philomene Fontaine P Q
PINEAU, Mary D, Nov 9 1887 Sex:F Child# 3 Thomas Pineau Canada & Des Rousselle Canada
PINEAU, Michel, Jan 3 1892 Sex:M Child# 1 Joseph Pineau Canada & Leontine Dube Canada
PINEAU, Robert George, Oct 3 1911 Sex:M Child# 1 George E Pineau US & Laura Galipeau US
PINEAU, Rochelle, May 15 1922 Sex:F Child# 4 George Pineau Nashua, NH & Laura Galipeau Nashua, NH
PINEAULT, Dora Loretta, Jul 9 1910 Sex:F Child# 5 Alexandre Pineault Mass & Dora Gagnon Mass
PINEAULT, Francois George, Nov 13 1913 Sex:M Child# 2 George Pineault US & Laura Galipeau US
PINEAULT, Joseph Armand W, Mar 30 1911 Sex:M Child# 16 Thomas Pineault Canada & Demerise Roussel Canada
PINEAULT, Marie Diana, Nov 17 1913 Sex:F Child# 1 Henri Pineault NH & Laura Morrissette NH
PINEAULT, Marie Rose D, May 9 1896 Sex:F Child# 16 Hubert Pineault Canada & Marie Banville Canada
PINEAULT, Paula Mariette, Sep 10 1927 Sex:F Child# 2 Charles Pineault Canada & Blanche Santerre Canada
PINEAULT, Raymond Roland, Aug 30 1926 Sex:M Child# 1 Charles Pineault Canada & Blanche Santerre Canada
PINET, Armand, Aug 11 1894 Sex:M Child# 12 Antime Pinet Canada & Georgina Marquis Canada
PINET, Joseph, Dec 5 1889 Sex:M Child# 8 Antoine Pinet Canada & Georgina Marquis Canada
PINET, Joseph Horace C, Mar 30 1930 Sex:M Child# 2 Leo Pinet Canada & Andrea R Gagnon Nashua, NH
PINET, Lionel Alfred, Feb 1 1914 Sex:M Child# 3 David Pinet Nashua, NH & Edourdina Bourgoin Canada
PINET, Paul David, Jun 26 1908 Sex:M Child# 1 David Pinet Nashua, NH & Edouardina Bourgoin Nicolet, PQ
PINET, Robert Joseph, Jun 6 1911 Sex:M Child# 2 David Pinet Nashua, NH & Edouardina Bourgoin Canada
PINETAS, Unknown, Sep 26 1922 Sex:F Child# 2 George Pinetas Greece & Aspasia Malitses Greece
PINETAS, Zisis, Jul 23 1929 Sex:M Child# 4 Georges Pinetas Greece & Aspafiz Malitsos Greece
PINETTE, Albert, Jan 29 1919 Sex:M Child# 1 Jos Aime Pinette Canada & Beatrice Ouellette Nashua, NH
PINETTE, Alfred Girourd, May 24 1933 Sex:M Child# 2 Alfred Pinette Canada & Marjorie Landry Mass
PINETTE, Alfreda Dora, Nov 11 1931 Sex:F Child# 1 Alphe Pinette Canada & Marjorie Landry Nashua, NH
PINETTE, Elmire, Jun 13 1893 Sex:F Child# 11 Antrine Pinette Canada & Georgiana Marquis Canada
PINETTE, Georgianna, Feb 28 1907 Sex:F Child# 1 Anthime Pinette NH & Anna Morneau Canada
PINETTE, Gertrude Estelle, Oct 9 1929 Sex:F Child# 1 J B Pinette Canada & Bernadette Raymond Canada
PINETTE, Gilbert Raymond, Dec 26 1921 Sex:M Child# 1 Pierre E Pinette Nashua, NH & Marie Kerouac Canada
PINETTE, Joseph, Apr 10 1892 Sex:M Child# 10 Antoine Pinette Canada & Georgiana Marquis Canada
PINETTE, Joseph, Aug 29 1896 Sex:M Child# 13 Arethime Pinette Canada & Georgianna Marquis Canada
PINETTE, Joseph Arthur, Jan 11 1890 Sex:M Child# 2 Pierre Pinette Canada & Clafle Lefevre Canada
PINETTE, Joseph Girard, Apr 7 1920 Sex:M Child# 14 Alex Pinette Nashua, NH & Derilda Sirois Canada
PINETTE, Joseph Henri Roland, May 29 1912 Sex:M Child# 4 Jos Anthime Pinette Nashua, NH & Anna Morneau Canada
PINETTE, Joseph Maurice, Apr 15 1923 Sex:M Child# 15 Wm Albani Pinette NH & Dorilda Sirois Canada
PINETTE, Joseph Raoul, Jan 10 1918 Sex:M Child# 6 Joseph Pinette Nashua, NH & Anna Morneau Canada
PINETTE, Marie Bertha G, Jan 18 1910 Sex:F Child# 3 Joseph A Pinette Nashua, NH & Anna Morneau Canada
PINETTE, Marie Germaine G, Oct 5 1908 Sex:F Child# 2 Anthime Pinette, Jr NH & Anna Morneau Canada
PINETTE, Pierre Lucien, Jun 26 1923 Sex:M Child# 2 Pierre Pinette, Jr NH & Marie Kerouac Canada
PINETTE, Rachel Ida, Nov 22 1934 Sex:F Child# 1 Victor Pinette Canada & Anita Plante Nashua, NH
PINKHAM, Donald, Jan 21 1917 Sex:M Child# 1 Charles Pinkham Brockton, MA & Jennie Lewis Digby, NS
PINKHAM, Harold Newton, Jan 24 1907 Sex:M Child# 4 Fred Pinkham Wilton, NH & Mabel Brooks New Boston, NH
PINKHAM, Winton Linwood, May 25 1920 Sex:M Child# 1 Philip R Pinkham Detroit, MI & Clara Morrison Lee, NH
PINNETT, Roger Lionel, Jun 4 1924 Sex:M Child# 1 Cleophas Pinnett Canada & Yvonne Pelletier Canada
PINNETTE, David Donat, Sep 26 1934 Sex:M Child# 3 Alfred Pinnette Canada & Marjorie Landry Somerville, MA
PINNETTE, Lucille Lota Marie, Dec 22 1925 Sex:F Child# 3 Cleophis Pinnette Canada & Yvonne Pelletier Canada
PINNETTE, Philippe, Mar 16 1888 Sex:M Child# Napolean Pinnette Canada & Sarah Bouequest Canada
PINOS, Irene, Aug 1 1907 Sex:F Child# 1 John Pinos Greece & Angelica Slimonda Greece
PINOWASKI, Charles, Apr 21 1919 Sex:M Child# 13 Urban Pinowaski Austria & Carolina Polaska Austria
PINSONEAULT, Gloria Anita, Mar 23 1925 Sex:F Child# 1 L Pinsoneault Chicago, IL & Leora Blood Pepperell, MA

PINSONNEAULT, Gerald Allan, Jul 24 1929 Sex:M Child# 3 Louis Pinsonneault Chicago, IL & Lena Blood Pepperell, MA
PINSONNEAULT, Robert Edward, Feb 14 1927 Sex:M Child# 2 D Pinsonneault Chicago, IL & Leora Blood Pepperell, MA
PIPIRINGOS, George N, Jan 8 1918 Sex:M Child# 1 Mickolaos Pipiringos Greece & Sophia Greece
PIPIRINGOS, Unknown, Mar 20 1927 Sex:M Child# 6 N Pipiringos Greece & S Chrysopoulos Greece
PIPLAR, Richard Alvin, Sep 2 1921 Sex:M Child# 1 Clarence L Piplar Nashua, NH & Edith A Mygatt Franklin, NH
PIPLAR, Unknown, Feb 2 1893 Sex:M Child#  George W Piplar Nashua, NH & Laura Lewis Nova Scotia
PIRCIEWICZ, Alphonse, Sep 14 1925 Sex:M Child# 3 Teofil Pirciewicz Poland & Amelia Maks Poland
PIRCUKONIS, Mary, Jan 9 1914 Sex:F Child# 2 John Pircukonis Russia & Victoria Welezilskei Russia
PIROWASKI, Alexandra, May 29 1908 Sex:F Child# 5 Urban Pirowaski Austria & Karolina Polaszki Austria
PIROWASKI, Bolesof, Sep 15 1910 Sex:M Child# 7 Urber Pirowaski Austria & Carolina Palascky Austria
PIROWASKI, Carold, Jun 18 1912 Sex:M Child# 8 Urban Pirowaski Austria & Carolina Polascek Austria
PIROWASKI, Frank, Aug 27 1908 Sex:M Child# 1 Henry Pirowaski Russia & Suzanna Shliva Russia
PIROWASKI, Mary, Apr 20 1912 Sex:F Child# 3 Andre Pirowaski Austria & Suzanna Shliva Austria
PIROWASKY, Stanislav, Aug 13 1910 Sex:M Child# 2 Frank Pirowasky Austria & Victoria Krupsky Austria
PISARCIK, Annie, Jan 3 1917 Sex:F Child# 1 Anthony Pisarcik Russia & Marie Krosouskas Russia
PISCOPO, Richard Benjamin, Apr 3 1932 Sex:M Child# 1 Benjamin J Piscopo Boston, MA & Lorraine Webster Nashua, NH
PISCOPO, Robert Edward, Nov 24 1935 Sex:M Child# 2 Benjamin J Piscopo Boston, MA & Lorraine Webster Nashua, NH
PITANIS, Unknown, Sep 4 1935 Sex:F Child# 2 James Pitanis Greece & Bessie Dimtsios Nashua, NH
PITARSK, Mary, Feb 26 1921 Sex:F Child# 3 Joseph Pitarsk Lithuania & Sophie Aldonia Lithuania Stillborn
PITARYS, Demetrios, Aug 19 1935 Sex:M Child# 1 Christo Pitarys Greece & Anna Tassios Lowell, MA
PITARYS, Unknown, Aug 31 1922 Sex:F Child# 8 James Pitarys Greece & Catherine Manta Greece
PITARYS, Unknown, Oct 8 1924 Sex:M Child# 8 James Pitarys Greece & Catherine Manta Greece
PITARYS, Unknown, Sep 4 1926 Sex:F Child# 8 James Pitarys Greece & A Mantha Greece
PITARYS, Unknown, Nov 3 1929 Sex:M Child# 3 James Pitarys Greece & Catharna Mantta Greece
PITENIS, Unknown, May 8 1934 Sex:M Child# 1 James Pitenis Greece & Bessie Dimtsios Nashua, NH
PITINES, Panolope M, Jun 29 1928 Sex:M Child# 1 Mitza Pitines Greece & Vasilike Gooda Greece
PITKIVIZ, Sophia, Jan 14 1902 Sex:F Child# 3 Alphonse Pitkiviz Poland & Mickelina Marzil Poland
PITOSIS, John, Oct 9 1915 Sex:M Child# 2 Nicolas R Pitosis Greece & El N Papchristos Greece
PIVARUM, Bronislaw, Sep 1 1912 Sex:M Child# 1 Peter Pivarum Russia & Amelia Gurska Russia
PIVOVARSKI, Peter, Jun 25 1909 Sex:M Child# 3 Urban Pivovarski Austria & Karolina Polasick Austria
PIVOVARSKI, Genofefa, Jan 6 1916 Sex:F Child# 10 Urban Pivowarski Poland & Caloldina Polasizk Poland
PIWARON, Jennie, Dec 18 1924 Sex:F Child# 4 Peter Piwaron Lithuania & Helen Baronski Poland
PIWOWARSKI, Eugene Donald, Jul 13 1932 Sex:M Child# 1 B Piwowarski Nashua, NH & Agnes Badar Poland
PIWOWARSKI, Richard Joseph, Mar 12 1934 Sex:M Child# 2 Bolek Piwowarski Nashua, NH & Agnes Badar Poland
PLACE, Irene, Nov 25 1914 Sex:F Child# 1 John Place Scotland & Minnie Locke England
PLACE, John, May 21 1918 Sex:M Child# 2 John Place Scotland & Minnie Locke England
PLACETTE, Adrienne Irene, Jul 7 1925 Sex:F Child# 4 Willia Placette Canada & Laura Lavoie Salem, MA
PLAITE, Walter Edward, Jan 9 1918 Sex:M Child# 4 Lawrence B Plaite St Louis, MO & Bertha I Willette Nashua, NH
PLAMONDON, Emile, May 17 1900 Sex:M Child# 2 Louis Plamondon Canada & Louise Arseneault Canada
PLAMONDON, Joseph Alphonse, Mar 22 1892 Sex:M Child# 3 Theophile Plamondon Canada & Louise Desmarais St Albans, VT
PLAMONDON, Joseph Arthur, May 16 1894 Sex:M Child# 3 Theophile Plamondon Canada & Louise Demarais St Albans, VT
PLAMONDON, Joseph Georges, Mar 10 1896 Sex:M Child# 4 Theophile Plamondon Canada & Louisa Desmarais St Albans, VT
PLAMONDON, Louise, Sep 21 1921 Sex:F Child# 1 George Plamondon Nashua, NH & Marie Richard Nashua, NH
PLANKEY, Unknown, Aug 6 1927 Sex:F Child# 1 G J Plankey Lowell, MA & Loretta Cristofono Fitchburg, MA
PLANTE, Adlina, Jan 26 1898 Sex:F Child# 1 (No Parents Listed)
PLANTE, Alcide Girard Joseph, Nov 23 1927 Sex:M Child# 1 Ovila Plante Canada & Emma Cloutier Canada
PLANTE, Armand George, Oct 1 1930 Sex:M Child# 3 Ovila Plante Canada & Emma Cloutier Canada
PLANTE, Cecilia Anita, Mar 14 1910 Sex:F Child# 2 Hormidas Plante NH & Phebeanna Lagesse Mass
PLANTE, Cordelia, Apr 12 1889 Sex:F Child# 3 Magloire Plante Canada & Hermene Lefebvre Canada Stillborn
PLANTE, Corina, Apr 19 1890 Sex:F Child# 2 W M Plante Canada & Exelie Jette Canada
PLANTE, Denise Rebecca, Apr 3 1907 Sex:F Child# 11 Simeon Plante Canada & Elmire Fleury Canada
PLANTE, Emelie Collette M, Jun 2 1927 Sex:F Child# 8 Eugene Plante Canada & Alma Pelletier Canada
PLANTE, Emile, Mar 24 1906 Sex:M Child# 10 Simeon Plante Canada & Elmire Fleury Canada
PLANTE, Gabrielle, Sep 16 1916 Sex:F Child# 1 Eugene Plante Canada & Alma Pelletier Canada
PLANTE, Georgette Rebecca, Feb 26 1923 Sex:F Child# 2 Willie Plante Canada & Laura Laine Canada
PLANTE, Gerard Simeon, Oct 2 1921 Sex:M Child# 1 William Plante Canada & Laura Larne Salem, MA
PLANTE, Jean B E S, Oct 17 1924 Sex:M Child# 7 Eugene Plante Canada & Alma Pelletier Canada
PLANTE, Jeannette Dolores, May 9 1919 Sex:F Child# 3 Eugene Plante Canada & Alma Pelletier Canada
PLANTE, Jos Charles Eugene, Apr 25 1928 Sex:M Child# 8 Simeon Plante Canada & Rosanna Richard Canada
PLANTE, Joseph Fernand, Nov 13 1921 Sex:M Child# 1 Ovila Plante Canada & Rose Robidoux Canada
PLANTE, Loretta Febianna, Nov 23 1904 Sex:F Child# 1 Hormidas Plante NH & Febianna Lagesse Mass
PLANTE, Louisa Adela, Aug 17 1917 Sex:F Child# 4 Hormidas Plante Nashua, NH & Phebeanna Lagasse Athol, MA
PLANTE, Magloise, Dec 11 1890 Sex:F Child# 4 Magloire Canada & Armine Lefevre Nashua, NH
PLANTE, Marguerite Rita, Aug 29 1920 Sex:F Child# 4 Eugene Plante Canada & Alma Pelletier Canada
PLANTE, Marie Aurore R, Jan 14 1897 Sex:F Child# 7 Magloire Plante Canada & Hermine Lefebvre Nashua, NH
PLANTE, Marie Beatrice C Ani, Mar 16 1927 Sex:F Child# 7 Simeon Plante Canada & Rosanna Richard Canada
PLANTE, Marie Elmire Alexina, Feb 15 1912 Sex:F Child# 1 Simeon Plante Canada & Alexina Labonte Canada
PLANTE, Marie Juliette C, Jul 4 1929 Sex:F Child# 9 Simeon Plante Canada & Rosanna Richard Canada
PLANTE, Marie Laurette, Jan 9 1923 Sex:F Child# 2 Ovila Plante Canada & Rose Robidoux Canada
PLANTE, Marie Olivette Noela, Dec 30 1928 Sex:F Child# 2 Ovila Plante Canada & Emma Cloutier Canada
PLANTE, Marie Rose Agnes, Jan 20 1923 Sex:F Child# 6 Eugene Plante Canada & Alma Pelletier Canada
PLANTE, Noel Eugene, Dec 21 1921 Sex:M Child# 5 Eugene Plante Canada & Alma Pelletier Canada
PLANTE, Pambe Camille, Jan 30 1918 Sex:F Child# 2 Eugene Plante Canada & Alma Pelletier Canada

PLANTE, Robert Ovid, Jan 28 1916 Sex:M Child# 3 Hormidas Plante NH & Fabianna Lagesse Mass
PLANTE, Therese Emile, Feb 7 1924 Sex:F Child# 3 William Plante Canada & Laura Larne Canada
PLANTE, Yvonne Adrienne, Dec 8 1909 Sex:F Child# 12 Simeon Plante Canada & Hermine Fleury Canada
PLANTIER, Eusebe Henri, Jan 16 1902 Sex:M Child# 4 Henri Plantier Canada & Josephine Bonnette Canada
PLANTIER, George Francis M, Jan 4 1932 Sex:M Child# 10 Gerald A Plantier Nashua, NH & Blanche Shepard Putnam, CT
PLANTIER, Joseph A G, Jun 17 1898 Sex:M Child# 2 Henri Plantier Canada & Josephine Bouette Canada
PLANTIER, Joseph E Leon, Oct 26 1896 Sex:M Child# 1 Henri Plantier Holyoke, MA & Josephine Bouette Canada
PLANTIER, Richard Terrence, Mar 27 1934 Sex:M Child# 11 Gerald A Plantier Nashua, NH & Blanche Shepard, Putnam, CT
PLANTIER, Rodolphe F Romeo, Apr 19 1904 Sex:M Child# 5 Henri Plantier Canada & Josephine Bonnette Canada
PLATE, Beatrice Irene, Dec 17 1920 Sex:F Child# 5 Lawrence Plate St Louis, MO & Bertha I Willette Nashua, NH
PLATE, Ella Naomi, Dec 3 1913 Sex:F Child# 2 Lawrence Plate St Louis, MO & Bertha Willette Nashua, NH
PLATE, Lawrence Irving, Jul 20 1916 Sex:M Child# 3 Lawrence Plate NH & Bertha Ouellette Nashua, NH
PLATE, Melvin Porter, May 30 1911 Sex:M Child# 1 Lawrence Plate St Louis, MO & Bertha Willett Nashua, NH
PLATTE, Bertha, Jun 29 1933 Sex:F Child# 1 Melvin P Platte Nashua, NH & Josephine Powlowsky Nashua, NH
PLATTE, Harriet, Jun 29 1933 Sex:F Child# 2 Melvin P Platte Nashua, NH & Josephine Powlowsky Nashua, NH
PLATTE, Nancy Virginia, Jun 16 1935 Sex:F Child# 3 Melvin P Platte Nashua, NH & Jos Pawlawski Nashua, NH
PLEAN, Unknown, Jan 21 1887 Sex:M Child#  Liloire Plean Canada & Adelaide Charette P Q Stillborn
PLEAU, Aimee, Nov 17 1899 Sex:M Child# 3 Joseph Pleau Canada & Malvina Gagnon Canada
PLEAU, Albertine, May 27 1893 Sex:F Child# 1 Treffle Pleau Canada & Arline Hamelin Canada
PLEAU, Alfred, Mar 11 1888 Sex:M Child# 5 Libore Pleau Canada & Adlaide Chorell Canada
PLEAU, Louis E, Sep 3 1897 Sex:M Child# 2 Joseph Pleau Canada & Philomene Gagnon Canada
PLEAU, Marie Anne, Jul 17 1891 Sex:F Child# 2 Henry Pleau Nashua, NH & Ida Jeannotte New York
PLEAU, Marie Blanche, Sep 21 1892 Sex:F Child# 4 Henry Pleau Nashua, NH & Ida Jeannotte NY
PLEAU, Marie Daura, Jul 17 1891 Sex:F Child# 3 Henry Pleau Nashua, NH & Ida Jeannotte New York
PLEAU, Remi Arthur, Nov 16 1895 Sex:M Child# 1 Joseph Pleau Canada & O Gagnon Canada
PLEAU, Unknown, Jun 24 1890 Sex:F Child# 1 Henry Pleau Nashua, NH & Lida Jeannotte NY Stillborn
PLEAU, Unknown, Feb 14 1894 Sex:M Child# 1 Joseph Pleau Canada & Philomene Gagnon Canada Stillborn
PLEDZAVITCH, Mary, Nov 22 1908 Sex:F Child# 7 Michael Pledzavitch Russia & Julia Ourbanovitch Russia
PLEDZAVITCH, Zophia, Sep 16 1910 Sex:F Child# 6 Michael Pledzavitch Russia & Drula Urbanovitch Russia
PLETTE, Lucien Maurice, Aug 13 1918 Sex:M Child# 2 Rolland Plette Mass & Rose Bourbault Canada
PLETTE, Lucy Dora, Aug 7 1919 Sex:F Child# 3 Roland Plette Mass & Aurore Bourbeau Canada
PLETTE, M Auriel Dolores, Mar 5 1921 Sex:F Child# 4 Roland Plette Gardner, MA & Aurore Bourbeau Canada
PLONDE, Joseph, Mar 3 1900 Sex:M Child# 7 Charles Plonde Canada & Claudia Peltier Canada
PLONDE, Marie, Mar 3 1900 Sex:F Child# 8 Charles Plonde Canada & Claudia Peltier Canada
PLOUDRE, Omer, Sep 22 1899 Sex:M Child# 1 Ludger Ploudre Canada & Lea Levesque Canada
PLOUF, Donald Melburne, Oct 14 1923 Sex:M Child# 8 Henry Plouf Mass & Susie Jackson Nashua, NH
PLOUF, Frank Arthur, Sep 17 1912 Sex:M Child# 3 Henry J Plouf Holyoke, MA & Susan M Jackson Nashua, NH
PLOUF, John, Jan 24 1921 Sex:M Child# 7 Henry Plouf Holyoke, MA & Susan Jackson Nashua, NH
PLOUF, Margaret, Jan 10 1918 Sex:F Child# 5 Edwin J Plouf Holyoke, MA & Susie M Jackson Nashua, NH
PLOUF, Unknown, Jan 5 1920 Sex:F Child# 6 Henry J Plouf Holyoke, MA & Susie Jackson Nashua, NH Stillborn
PLOUFF, Marie, Jul 31 1887 Sex:F Child# 7 Clement Plouff P Q & Cordelia Mesion P Q
PLOUFFE, Blanche Jackson, Apr 27 1916 Sex:F Child# 3 Henry Plouffe Holyoke, MA & Susie Jackson Nashua, NH
PLOUFFE, Ida Louise, Jun 6 1903 Sex:F Child# 5 Francois Plouffe Canada & Lea Fortier NH
PLOUFFE, Joseph Georges, Mar 7 1897 Sex:M Child# 4 Francois Plouffe Canada & Lea Fortier Derry, NH
PLOUFFE, Joseph William, Jun 12 1917 Sex:M Child# 1 George Plouffe Nashua, NH & Anna Gaudette Prince Edward Is
PLOUFFE, Lea May, Jan 3 1894 Sex:F Child# 3 Francois Plouffe Canada & Julie Fortier NH
PLOUFFE, Marie Leda, Jan 28 1896 Sex:F Child# 4 Samuel Plouffe Canada & Ephenie Bernier Canada
PLOUFFE, Unknown, Sep 9 1896 Sex:M Child# 4 Samuel Plouffe Canada & Phemie Bernier Canada Stillborn
PLOUFFE, Unknown, Jul 16 1897 Sex:M Child# 9 Samuel Plouffe Canada & Euphemie Bernier Canada Stillborn
PLOURDE, Annette Gilbert, Jul 24 1924 Sex:F Child# 3 Joseph Plourde Canada & Yvonne Gauvin Canada
PLOURDE, Cecile Catherine, Mar 21 1920 Sex:F Child# 1 Joseph Plourde Canada & Yvonne Gauvin Canada
PLOURDE, Gerard, May 5 1916 Sex:M Child# 1 Thomas Plourde Canada & Marie F Ferland Canada
PLOURDE, Gerard Normand, Aug 29 1922 Sex:M Child# 1 Amedee Plourde Nashua, NH & Juliette Gagnon Nashua, NH
PLOURDE, Jos Paul Raymond, Sep 30 1927 Sex:M Child# 1 Eucide Plourde Canada & G Nadeau Canada
PLOURDE, Joseph Honore, Mar 7 1909 Sex:M Child# 1 Honore Plourde Canada & Delia Pelletier Nashua, NH
PLOURDE, Joseph Omer, Mar 12 1900 Sex:M Child# 2 Elzear Plourde Canada & Philomene Lavoie Canada
PLOURDE, M Blanche Cecile, Nov 21 1913 Sex:F Child# 12 Joseph Plourde Canada & Lea Levesque Canada
PLOURDE, M Priscilla Venise, Oct 21 1922 Sex:F Child# 2 Horace Plourde NH & Blanche Caron Maine
PLOURDE, M Rose Annette, Aug 14 1922 Sex:F Child# 2 Joseph Plourde Canada & Yvonne Gauvin Canada
PLOURDE, Marianne Yvonne, Oct 11 1933 Sex:F Child# 5 Joseph Plourde Canada & Yvonne Gauvin Canada
PLOURDE, Marie Anna, Nov 20 1896 Sex:F Child# 2 Joseph Plourde Canada & Anna Dupere Canada
PLOURDE, Marie Eva, Feb 5 1909 Sex:F Child# 2 Ludger Plourde Canada & Emma Levesque Canada
PLOURDE, Marie Gertrude Medor, Feb 1 1924 Sex:F Child# 3 Horace Plourde NH & Blanche Caron Maine
PLOURDE, Marie Jeanne d'Arc, Oct 8 1920 Sex:F Child# 1 Horace Plourde NH & Blanche Caron Maine
PLOURDE, Marie Laura, Nov 1 1907 Sex:F Child# 1 Ludger Plourde Canada & Emme Levesque Canada
PLOURDE, Marie Zelia, Mar 26 1901 Sex:F Child# 14 Octave Plourde Canada & Sara Anctil Canada
PLOURDE, Philip Leon, Feb 8 1926 Sex:M Child# 4 Joseph Plourde Canada & Yvonne Gauvin Canada
PLOURDE, Zebedie, Jul 10 1893 Sex:F Child# 11 Joseph Plourde Canada & Georgiana Levesque Canada
PLUMMER, Belle, Jul 17 1888 Sex:F Child# 1 Elberu W Plummer Londonderry & Nellie Coughlin Ayer, MA
PLUMMER, Carolyn Mae, Jun 19 1935 Sex:F Child# 1 Bernard Plummer Londonderry, NH & Mabel Nugent Londonderry, NH
PLUMMER, Dora, Feb 28 1891 Sex:F Child# 1 Winfield S Plummer Bedford & Alice Waterhouse Albany, ME
PLUMMER, Ellen Louise, Aug 22 1921 Sex:F Child# 1 Fred D Plummer Laconia, NH & Marie Louise Busiel Laconia, NH
PLUMMER, Unknown, Jun 10 1888 Sex:M Child# 3 Charles M Plummer Bradford & Priscilla Johnson Portland, ME

POBEDESK, Zona, Jul 12 1910 Sex:F Child# 2 Stan Pobedesk Russia & Anna Rallak Russia
POFF, Bertha Thompson, Apr 6 1894 Sex:F Child# 2 Robert Poff Hudson, NH & Lizzie Thompson Ireland
POFF, Charles Henry, Feb 5 1890 Sex:M Child# 1 Robert N Poff Hudson, NH & Lizzie J Thompson Ireland
POFF, Dorothy Blanche, Apr 16 1935 Sex:F Child# 2 Sylvester Poff Nashua, NH & Cecile Trombley Nashua, NH
POFF, Frank Lester, Jan 1 1897 Sex:M Child# 1 Francis H Poff Hudson, NH & Mary J Luman Georgia, VT
POFF, Irene Marguerite, Mar 23 1891 Sex:F Child# 2 George E Poff Hudson, NH & Mary Connor Ireland
POFF, Norman Frank, Jan 19 1933 Sex:M Child# 1 Sylvester Poff NH & Cecile Trombley NH
POFF, Pracy J, Aug 31 1889 Sex:M Child# 3 John Poff New Hampshire & Isabella M Pierce New Hampshire
POFF, Sylvester Augustus, Aug 10 1906 Sex:M Child# 6 Frank L Poff Hudson, NH & Jane Luman Georgia, VT
POFF, Unknown, Dec 19 1887 Sex:F Child# 1 George E Poff Hudson & Mary Connors Ireland
POFF, Unknown, Apr 23 1897 Sex:M Child# 3 John Poff Hudson, NH & I M Sterling Maine Stillborn
POINIER, Marie, Aug 27 1888 Sex:F Child# 3 Pierre Poinier Canada & Elmira Peltier Canada
POIRIER, A, Feb 2 1897 Sex:M Child# 2 Joseph Poirier Canada & Amanda Castonguay Canada Stillborn
POIRIER, Adrienne, Jan 17 1907 Sex:F Child# 5 Paul Poirier Canada & Augustine Ouellette Canada
POIRIER, Alfred Normand, Nov 30 1921 Sex:M Child# 5 Samuel J Poirier Canada & Alice M Messier Nashua, NH
POIRIER, Amedee, May 22 1896 Sex:M Child# 1 Joseph Poirier Canada & Amanda Castonguay Canada
POIRIER, Dorothy, Apr 11 1925 Sex:F Child# 1 Ludovie Poirier Canada & Jeanne Daston Canada
POIRIER, Ephrem, Dec 2 1906 Sex:M Child# 1 Ephrem Poirier Canada & Laura Langlois Canada
POIRIER, Estelle Virginie Ali, Jan 4 1913 Sex:F Child# 3 Samuel J Poirier Canada & Alice M Messier Nashua, NH
POIRIER, Fleur Ange H, Mar 3 1907 Sex:F Child# 1 Samuel Poirier Canada & Alice Messier Nashua, NH
POIRIER, Gerard France, Jul 10 1918 Sex:M Child# 4 Samuel Poirier Roxt Falls, PQ & Alice Messier Nashua, NH
POIRIER, Herbert, Jan 26 1920 Sex:M Child# 4 Wilfrid Poirier Canada & Rose Poulin Lowell, MA
POIRIER, Irene Lorelie, Apr 18 1921 Sex:F Child# 6 Wilfrid Poirier Canada & Rose Anna Boule Lowell, MA
POIRIER, Isabelle, May 29 1908 Sex:F Child# 6 Paul Poirier Canada & Augustine Ouellette Canada
POIRIER, J Ovila Alfred, Mar 28 1922 Sex:M Child# 4 Oliva Poirier Hinsdale, NH &  Canada
POIRIER, Jos George Edouard, May 5 1928 Sex:M Child# 8 Oliva Poirier Hinsdale, NH & Elizabeth Lagace Canada
POIRIER, Jos Lionel Edmond, Jun 17 1917 Sex:M Child# 1 Edmond Poirier US & Rosanna Cote Canada
POIRIER, Jos Raymond A, Feb 22 1920 Sex:M Child# 3 Edmond Poirier NH & Rose Alma Cote Canada
POIRIER, Joseph, May 15 1888 Sex:M Child# 6 Lewis Poirier Canada & Celina Bossi Canada
POIRIER, Joseph, Dec 3 1923 Sex:M Child# 1 Ludovic Poirier Canada & Marie A J D'Astour Canada Stillborn
POIRIER, Joseph E, Oct 23 1895 Sex:M Child# 6 Pierre Poirier Canada & Elmire Peltier Canada
POIRIER, Joseph Edmond, Jun 11 1894 Sex:M Child# 2 Elie Poirier Canada & Arth Ouellette Canada
POIRIER, Joseph Isidore, Nov 26 1901 Sex:M Child# 2 Paul Poirier Canada & Augustine Ouellette Canada
POIRIER, Joseph Roland, Nov 16 1917 Sex:M Child# 1 Oliver Poirier Hinsdale, NH & Elizabeth Lagasse Canada
POIRIER, Joseph Roland M, Mar 10 1924 Sex:M Child# 1 Paul Poirier NH & Elise Bernier NH
POIRIER, Joseph Romeo, Dec 30 1914 Sex:M Child# 1 Wilfrid Poirier Canada & Rose Boule Lowell, MA
POIRIER, Juliette, Jan 23 1932 Sex:F Child# 10 Ovila Poirier Hinsdale, NH & Elizabeth Lagasse Canada Stillborn
POIRIER, Lionel, Mar 27 1917 Sex:M Child# 2 Wilfrid Poirier Nashua, NH & Marie Boule
POIRIER, Loretta Pearl, Aug 3 1929 Sex:F Child# 3 Paul Poirier Canada & Eline Bernier Nashua, NH
POIRIER, Lynwood Alvin, Jun 11 1928 Sex:FM Child# 2 Alvin Poirier Fremont, NH & Mabel King Grafton, NH
POIRIER, M Elizabeth Cecile, Jan 5 1919 Sex:F Child# 2 Oliva Poirier NH & Elizabeth Lagasse Canada
POIRIER, Marie, Jun 24 1923 Sex:F Child# 5 Oliva Poirier NH & Elizabeth Lagasse Canada
POIRIER, Marie Antoinette Ali, Nov 9 1924 Sex:F Child# 6 Samuel J Poirier Canada & Alice M Poirier Nashua, NH
POIRIER, Marie Beatrice Cecil, Aug 3 1920 Sex:F Child# 3 Oliva Poirier NH & Elizabeth Lagace Canada
POIRIER, Marie E, May 15 1892 Sex:F Child# 1 Pierre Poirier Canada & Hermins Letendre Canada
POIRIER, Marie Irene, Sep 16 1904 Sex:F Child# 4 Paul Poirier Canada & Augustine Ouellette Canada
POIRIER, Marie Ivonne, Oct 24 1896 Sex:F Child# 3 Henri Poirier Canada & Eusepie Montbleau Detroit, MI
POIRIER, Marie Olivette, May 7 1925 Sex:F Child# 6 Olive Poirier NH & Elizabeth Legace Canada
POIRIER, Marie Regina, Aug 1 1903 Sex:F Child# 3 Paul Poirier Canada & Augustine Ouellette Canada
POIRIER, Marie Rose Alma, May 4 1899 Sex:F Child# 1 Paul Poirier Canada & Augustine Ouellette Canada
POIRIER, Marie Rose Lorr El, Aug 23 1918 Sex:F Child# 2 Edmond Poirier NH & Rose Anna Cote Canada
POIRIER, Marie Theresa Anna, May 5 1928 Sex:F Child# 7 Oliva Poirier Hinsdale, NH & Elizabeth Lagace Canada
POIRIER, Mary Irene F, Sep 2 1930 Sex:F Child# 9 Oliver Poirier Hinsdale, NH & Elizabeth Lagasse Montreal, Canada
POIRIER, Mignon Jeannette, Dec 31 1909 Sex:F Child# 1 Damase Poirier Canada & Ernestine Bergeron Canada
POIRIER, Noel Roger, Dec 25 1910 Sex:M Child# 2 Samuel Poirier Canada & Alice Messier US
POIRIER, Olivette, Oct 11 1918 Sex:F Child# 3 Wilfred Poirier Bedford, PQ & Irene Bouley Lowell, MA
POIRIER, Paul, Jun 26 1897 Sex:M Child# 3 Elie Poirier Canada & Arthemise Ouellette Canada
POIRIER, Reginald Edmund, Oct 11 1927 Sex:M Child# 2 Paul Poirier Nashua, NH & Elise Bernier Nashua, NH
POIRIER, Rita, Jan 12 1908 Sex:F Child# 5 Henri Poirier Canada & Emelie Montbleau US
POISSON, Omer, Nov 27 1919 Sex:M Child# 1 Omer Poisson Canada & Adele Gagnier Canada
POITRAS, Adelard, Jan 22 1896 Sex:M Child# 1 Will Poitras Canada & Clerina Prince Canada
POITRAS, Alberta, Jun 8 1894 Sex:F Child# 3 Thomas Poitras Canada & Emma Peltier Canada
POITRAS, Alice, Dec 25 1899 Sex:F Child# 3 Willie Poitras Canada & Clarina Prince Canada
POITRAS, Arthur Joseph, Dec 5 1896 Sex:M Child# 4 Thomas Poitras Canada & Emme Pelletier Canada
POITRAS, Charles Eugene, Oct 14 1889 Sex:M Child# 1 Thomas Poitras Canada & Euna Peltier Canada
POITRAS, Clarina, Dec 24 1897 Sex:F Child# 2 Willie Poitras Canada & Clarina Prince Canada
POITRAS, David, Feb 8 1909 Sex:M Child# 1 Ernest Poitras Canada & Marie April Canada
POITRAS, Dora, Feb 15 1902 Sex:F Child# 4 William Poitras Canada & Clarina Prince Canada
POITRAS, Eugenie Marguerite F, Aug 13 1925 Sex:F Child# 2 H Paul Poitras Lawrence, MA & Rose Dionne Lowell, MA
POITRAS, George, Mar 30 1909 Sex:M Child# 2 Ernest Poitras Canada & Marie April Canada
POITRAS, George Joseph, Jun 30 1909 Sex:M Child# 2 Ernest Poitras Canada & Marie April Canada Stillborn
POITRAS, Jos Omer Romeo, Jun 7 1916 Sex:M Child# 1 Napoleon Poitras Canada & Rose Anna Fournier NH
POITRAS, Leda Pauline, Aug 16 1910 Sex:F Child# 1 Thomas Poitras Canada & Leda Pelletier Canada Stillborn

POITRAS, M Ange Ernestine, Mar 23 1921 Sex:F Child# 5 Napoleon Poitras Canada & Rose Anna Fournier NH
POITRAS, Marie A P, Jan 15 1892 Sex:F Child# 2 Thomas Poitras Canada & Emma Peltier Canada
POITRAS, Marie Alice Germaine, Aug 27 1918 Sex:F Child# 3 Napoleon Poitras Canada & Rose Anna Fournier NH
POITRAS, Marie Anne Theresa, Jul 23 1924 Sex:F Child# 2 H Poitras Lawrence, MA & Rose Dion Lowell, MA
POITRAS, Marie Elise, Feb 12 1909 Sex:F Child# 2 Thomas Poitras Canada & Elise Laplante Canada
POITRAS, Marie Rose A J, Jun 16 1908 Sex:F Child# 6 William Poitras Canada & Clarina Prince Canada
POITRAS, Marie Rose Rita, Nov 1 1919 Sex:F Child# 4 Napoleon Poitras Canada & Rose Anna Fournier NH
POITRAS, Yvonne, Mar 29 1904 Sex:F Child# 5 William Poitras Canada & Clarina Prince Canada
POJELOJETE, Unknown, Dec 1 1913 Sex:M Child# 2 Stomat Pojelojete Greece & Georgia Micopolo Greece
POKSTA, Frania, Dec 3 1915 Sex:F Child# 4 George Poksta Russia & Mary Schmikezer Russia
POKSTA, Julius, Jul 7 1917 Sex:M Child# 5 George Poksta Russia & Mary Smariga Russia
POKUSTA, Felix, Jun 20 1912 Sex:M Child# 2 George Pokusta Russia & Mary Smarego Russia
POLACK, June, Apr 2 1935 Sex:F Child# 1 Andrew Polack
POLAK, Fred, Mar 5 1920 Sex:M Child# 4 Simon Polak Austria & Theodora Pasec Austria
POLAK, Geniveve, Sep 16 1916 Sex:F Child# 3 Simon Polak Austria & Theodora Passak Austria
POLANSKE, Broneslawa, Oct 31 1920 Sex:F Child# 3 Leo Polanske Russia & Age Radzienuka Russia
POLANSKI, Sophia, Jul 2 1922 Sex:F Child# 2 Henry Polanski Russia & Carolina Validska Austria
POLARDS, Isadore, Dec 20 1888 Sex:F Child# 8 Isadore Polards Canada & Louise Larruel Canada
POLASKA, Andrew, May 20 1920 Sex:M Child# 1 Andrew Polaska Russia & Carolina Boilika Austria
POLASKI, John Walter, Dec 13 1933 Sex:M Child# 3 William Polaski Nashua, NH & Melvina Klimas Nashua, NH
POLASKI, Pauline Rose, Jul 3 1931 Sex:F Child# 2 William Polaski Nashua, NH & Melvina Climas Nashua, NH
POLE, Annie Louise, Feb 12 1931 Sex:F Child# 4 Andrew Pole Russia & Caroline Baliska Austria
POLETTI, Jeanne Rita, Jan 13 1933 Sex:F Child# 1 Elio Poletti Italy & Rita Brunelle NH
POLI, Helen Stella, Feb 22 1928 Sex:F Child# 3 Andrew Poli Russia & Caroline Balick Russia
POLIQUIN, Albert, Jun 22 1904 Sex:M Child# 3 Jean Poliquin Canada & Lumina Labbe Canada
POLIQUIN, Albert J Raymond, Dec 17 1931 Sex:M Child# 1 Albert Poliquin Nashua, NH & Alice Martin Nashua, NH
POLIQUIN, Annette Rita, May 7 1924 Sex:F Child# 3 Pierre Poliquin Canada & Lea Jean Canada
POLIQUIN, Arthur Henri, Nov 5 1906 Sex:M Child# 7 Adelard Poliquin Canada & Josephine Nadeau Canada
POLIQUIN, Beverley Ann, Sep 4 1930 Sex:F Child# 1 Ernest Poliquin Nashua, NH & Ruth Young NH
POLIQUIN, Clara Lucile, Jan 31 1916 Sex:F Child# 12 Adelard Poliquin Canada & Josephine Nadeau Canada
POLIQUIN, Corinne Theresa, Apr 3 1927 Sex:F Child# 2 Adelard Poliquin Nashua, NH & Irene Galipeau Nashua, NH
POLIQUIN, Ernest Edgar, Oct 31 1910 Sex:M Child# 7 George Poliquin Canada & Rose Desmarais St Albans, VT
POLIQUIN, Felix Normand, Jul 8 1929 Sex:M Child# 1 Alfred Poliquin Nashua, NH & Simone Ledoux Nashua, NH
POLIQUIN, George Albert, Mar 22 1903 Sex:M Child# 1 George Poliquin Canada & Rosanna Desmarais Nashua, NH
POLIQUIN, Gerald, Oct 3 1925 Sex:M Child# 11 George Poliquin Canada & A Desmarais Nashua, NH
POLIQUIN, Helen Dora, Sep 29 1922 Sex:F Child# 2 Pierre Poliquin Canada & Lena Jean Canada
POLIQUIN, Henri Edouard, Aug 14 1906 Sex:M Child# 5 George Poliquin Canada & Rosanna Desmarais Nashua, NH
POLIQUIN, J Moise Robert, May 19 1915 Sex:M Child# 8 George Poliquin Canada & Rose Anna Desmarais Canada
POLIQUIN, Jos Gerard Edward, Mar 18 1933 Sex:M Child# 1 Arthur Poliquin Nashua, NH & Corrine Bouchard Canada
POLIQUIN, Joseph, Apr 10 1906 Sex:M Child# 4 Jean Poliquin Canada & Elmina Labbe Canada
POLIQUIN, Joseph A, Jul 7 1902 Sex:M Child# 5 Adelard Poliquin Canada & Josephine Nadeau Canada
POLIQUIN, Joseph Arthur I, Nov 15 1910 Sex:M Child# 9 Adelard Poliquin Canada & Josephine Nadeau Canada
POLIQUIN, Joseph Eugene, Nov 28 1903 Sex:M Child# 4 Joseph Poliquin Canada & Marceline Guillemet Canada
POLIQUIN, Joseph Pierre, Jun 19 1914 Sex:M Child# 1 Pierre Poliquin Canada & Odelie Carbonneau Canada
POLIQUIN, Juliette C, Feb 23 1909 Sex:F Child# 5 George Poliquin Canada & Rosanna Desmarais Nashua, NH
POLIQUIN, Leo Robert, Sep 2 1920 Sex:M Child# 1 Joseph Poliquin Nashua, NH & Marie Rose Belanger Canada
POLIQUIN, Lionel Albert, Feb 11 1927 Sex:M Child# 4 Pierre Poliquin Canada & Lea Jean Canada
POLIQUIN, Lucienne Beatrice, May 30 1913 Sex:F Child# 7 George Poliquin Canada & Rosanna Desmarais Nashua, NH
POLIQUIN, M Wilhelmine L, Dec 3 1911 Sex:F Child# 1 Pierre Poliquin Canada & Delvina Beriault Canada
POLIQUIN, Marcedes Rose, Feb 4 1919 Sex:F Child# 13 Adelard Poliquin Canada & Josephine Nadeau Canada
POLIQUIN, Marie, Jul 17 1896 Sex:F Child# 2 Joseph Poliquin Canada & Marie Guilmette Canada
POLIQUIN, Marie Alma Rita, Mar 30 1930 Sex:F Child# 3 Adelard Poliquin Nashua, NH & Irene Galipeault Nashua, NH
POLIQUIN, Marie Irene, Nov 15 1910 Sex:F Child# 8 Adelard Poliquin Canada & Josephine Nadeau Canada
POLIQUIN, Marie Loraine, Oct 17 1934 Sex:F Child# 3 Alfred Poliquin Nashua, NH & Simone Ledoux Nashua, NH
POLIQUIN, Marie Rose, Feb 8 1913 Sex:F Child# 10 Adelard Poliquin Canada & Josephine Nadeau Canada
POLIQUIN, Marie Rose Beatrice, Sep 27 1912 Sex:F Child# 6 Joseph Poliquin Canada & Marceline Guilmette Canada
POLIQUIN, Mildred Hazel, Dec 29 1932 Sex:F Child# 2 Ernest Poliquin Nashua, NH & Ruth Young Merrimack, NH
POLIQUIN, Napoleon, Jan 29 1905 Sex:M Child# 3 George Poliquin Canada & Rosanna Desmarais Canada
POLIQUIN, Paul Romeo, Sep 24 1914 Sex:M Child# 3 Irene Poliquin Canada & Delvina Benault Nashua, NH
POLIQUIN, Rachelle Juliette, Dec 7 1915 Sex:F Child# 4 Irence Poliquin Canada & Delvina Bariault Nashua, NH
POLIQUIN, Roger Leopold, Dec 9 1921 Sex:M Child# 10 George Poliquin Canada & Rose Anna Nashua, NH
POLIQUIN, Stella Olivine, Apr 14 1921 Sex:F Child# 1 Pierre Poliquin Canada & Lea Jean Canada
POLIQUIN, Unknown, Feb 8 1913 Sex:F Child# 3 Pierre Poliquin Canada & Delima Beriault Nashua, NH
POLIQUIN, Unknown, Dec 29 1914 Sex:M Child# 11 Adelard Poliquin Canada & Josephine Nadeau Canada
POLIQUIN, Unknown, Jul 11 1931 Sex:M Child# 2 Alfred Poliquin Nashua, NH & Simone Ledox Nashua, NH
POLIQUIN, Yvonne, Aug 16 1923 Sex:F Child# 1 Leo Poliquin Nashua, NH & Alma Prince Nashua, NH
POLIQUIN, Yvonne Irene, Mar 5 1904 Sex:F Child# 2 George Poliquin Canada & Rose Desmarais Nashua, NH
POLIZON, Unknown, Mar 31 1928 Sex:F Child# 2 William Polizon Greece & Mary Manules Greece
POLLARD, Frederick Cleveland, Jun 7 1928 Sex:M Child# 1 Fred C Pollard Shrewsbury, MA & Gertrude Holt Nashua, NH
POLOFSKI, Unknown, Nov 19 1911 Sex:F Child# 1 Anthony Polofski Russia & Nadjer Belchakoff Russia
POLOJSKI, William, Mar 4 1918 Sex:M Child# 3 Leo Polojski Russia & Agator Mikota Russia
POLOQUIN, Joseph Alphonse, Apr 12 1903 Sex:M Child# 6 Pierre Poloquin Canada & Marie L Bernier Canada
POLOSKAS, Feleoka, Feb 21 1905 Sex:F Child# 1 Mikal Poloskas Russia & Marcelia Mizeruti Russia

POLOSKI, Constansilas, Dec 11 1912 Sex:M Child# 4 Constansilas Poloski Russia & Annie Kobaski Russia
POLOSKI, William, May 21 1929 Sex:M Child# 1 William Poloski Nashua, NH & Melvina Klimas Nashua, NH
POMBRIA, Richard William, Sep 3 1918 Sex:M Child# 4 Ardle Pombria Sciota, NY & Edith Mousseau Sciota, NY
POMBRIAND, Alfred, Aug 17 1897 Sex:M Child# 5 Simeon Pombriand US & Marie Joulin Canada
POMBRIAND, Eliza, Jul 13 1890 Sex:F Child# 3 Charles Pombriand NY & Josephine Phaneuf Nashua, NH
POMBRIAND, Emma Ida, Mar 12 1892 Sex:F Child# 4 Charles Pombriand Nashua, NH & Josephine Phaneuf NY
POMBRIAND, Hector Girouard, Mar 30 1929 Sex:M Child# 5 Hector Pombriand Worcester, MA & Vivian Moison Vermont
POMBRIAND, Joseph J B L, May 20 1924 Sex:M Child# 1 Leo Pombriand Nashua, NH & Adrienne Landry Nashua, NH
POMBRIANT, M Louise, Feb 19 1894 Sex:F Child# 3 Simeon H Pombriant Springfield, MA & Mary Jolin Canada
POMBRIANT, Marie Lillian, Jan 26 1896 Sex:F Child#  Simeon H Pombriant Springfield, MA & Mary John Canada
POMBRIO, Alfred Allard, Aug 29 1935 Sex:M Child# 4 Leon Pombrio Lowell, MA & Julia Duffy Nashua, NH
POMBRIO, Arthur J, Oct 20 1922 Sex:M Child# 1 Leory Pombrio New York & Eva Columbe Nashua, NH
POMBRIO, Aurore Jeannette, Dec 22 1921 Sex:F Child# 1 Floyd Pombrio Vermont & Beatrice Mayotte Plattsburg, NY
POMBRIO, Barbara, Jul 17 1913 Sex:F Child# 1 Edward Pombrio Nashua, NH & Florence Mansur Groton, MA
POMBRIO, Beatrice May, Mar 17 1913 Sex:F Child# 2 Joseph Pombrio Nashua, NH & Sadie Bouley Nashua, NH
POMBRIO, Dorothy Marie, Sep 25 1927 Sex:F Child# 2 Leroy Pombrio Sciota, NY & Eva Columb Nashua, NH
POMBRIO, Gerard Arthur, Jul 23 1918 Sex:M Child# 3 John Henry Pombrio Nashua, NH & Sadie Bouley Nashua, NH
POMBRIO, Richard Gerald, Nov 1 1933 Sex:M Child# 2 Max Pombrio Nashua, NH & Anna L Soucy Canada
POMBRIO, Robert David, Jul 7 1932 Sex:M Child# 1 M Pombrio Barre, VT & Anne Soucy New Brunswick
POMBRIO, Theresa Veneta, Oct 3 1928 Sex:F Child# 1 Leon Pombrio Sciota, NY & Julia Duffy Nashua, NH
POMERLEAU, Blanche Clare, Sep 29 1929 Sex:F Child# 2 Alfred Pomerleau Canada & Helene Levesque Nashua, NH
POMERLEAU, Paul Irence, May 17 1923 Sex:M Child# 1 Alphonse Pomerleau Nashua, NH & Helene Levesque Nashua, NH
POMERLEAU, Unknown, Feb 28 1932 Sex:F Child#  Doria Pomerleau Canada & Anne Marie Poulin Canada
POMEROY, Mary Rita, Dec 11 1919 Sex:F Child# 1 Neal Pomeroy Canada & Amanda Ricard Nashua, NH
POND, Elsie Margaret, Aug 14 1931 Sex:F Child# 1 Alvin L Pond Milford, NH & Marjorie Crowell Milford, NH
POND, Lucy Martha, Jun 17 1920 Sex:F Child# 5 Charles Pond Nashua, NH & Mary Summerville Ireland
POND, Marie Alice, Jul 21 1890 Sex:F Child# 1 Walter Pond Sherry Village, MA & Emilina Jacques
POND, Marie L Anna, Jan 16 1893 Sex:F Child# 2 Walter Pond Nashua, NH & Melina Jacques Canada
PONDRETTE, Rita Lucille, Aug 23 1920 Sex:F Child# 1 Edouard Pondrette Canada & Laura Roy Manchester, NH
PONDRIO, Unknown, Dec 4 1911 Sex:F Child# 1 Joseph Pondrio Nashua, NH & Sadie Bouley Nashua, NH Stillborn
PONEY, Adrien Joseph Lionel, May 10 1918 Sex:M Child# 3 Joseph Poney St George, PQ & Adele Bonenfant Nashua, NH
PONEY, Alexis Alfred, Apr 6 1902 Sex:M Child# 12 Pierre Poney Canada & Albina Ouellette Canada
PONEY, Doris Theresa, Oct 12 1928 Sex:F Child# 1 Felix Poney Nashua, NH & Alma Gagnon Nashua, NH
PONEY, J B Felix Armand, Aug 9 1917 Sex:M Child# 8 Jean Baptiste Poney Canada & Leopoldine Proulx Canada
PONEY, Joseph, Jan 25 1909 Sex:M Child# 4 J B Poney Canada & Leopoldine Proulx Canada
PONEY, Joseph Edward H, Nov 29 1906 Sex:M Child# 2 Jean B Poney Canada & Leopoldine Proulx Canada
PONEY, Joseph Jean B R, Nov 10 1919 Sex:M Child# 4 Joseph Poney Canada & Adele Bonenfant Nashua, NH
PONEY, Lucille Irene, Sep 18 1930 Sex:F Child# 2 Felix Poney Nashua, NH & Alma Gagnon Nashua, NH
PONEY, Marie Marguerite I, Feb 13 1908 Sex:F Child# 3 Jean B Poney Canada & Leopoldine Proulx Canada
PONEY, Rita Annette Gloria, Jun 24 1925 Sex:F Child# 6 Joseph Poney Canada & Adelle Bonenfant Nashua, NH
PONEY, Robert Gerald Joseph, Nov 11 1914 Sex:M Child# 1 Joseph Poney Canada & Adele Bonenfant Nashua, NH
PONEY, Roland Ernest Joseph, Jan 30 1924 Sex:M Child# 5 Joseph Poney Canada & Adele Bonenfant Nashua, NH
PONEY, Wilber Paul Joseph, May 25 1917 Sex:M Child# 2 Joseph Poney Canada & Adelle Bonenfant Nashua, NH
PONOJEFSKI, Mary, May 11 1913 Sex:F Child# 1 Frank Ponojefski Russia & Mary Martin Russia
PONT BRIAND, Alice, Oct 27 1899 Sex:F Child# 6 S Pont Briand Vermont & Marie Jolin Canada
PONT BRIAND, Georgiana, Oct 24 1887 Sex:F Child#  Chas Pont Briand Nashua, NH & Josie Phaneuf Champlain
PONT BRIAND, Irene Anna, Mar 8 1900 Sex:F Child# 7 Charles Pont Briand Canada & Josephine Phaneuf New York
PONT BRIAND, Joseph Lawrence, Jan 14 1900 Sex:M Child# 1 Antoine Pont Briand New York & Emilie Milette New York
PONT BRIAND, Leo, Aug 14 1897 Sex:M Child# 5 Maxime Pont Briand Sciota, NY & Exeline Monty Canada
PONT BRIAND, Marie, Feb 7 1896 Sex:F Child# 5 Francis Pont Briand Canada & Rose Monty Canada
PONT BRIAND, Omer, Jan 21 1899 Sex:M Child# 6 Alphon Pont Briand Sciota, NY & Exceline Monty Canada
PONT BRIAND, Therise, Jan 20 1896 Sex:F Child# 6 Charles Pont Briand Canada & Josephine Phaneuf Canada
PONT BRIAND, William, Jun 29 1890 Sex:M Child# 4 Francis Pont Briand Canada & Rosanna Monty Canada
PONT BUAND, Edward, Mar 13 1888 Sex:M Child# 1 Francois Pont Buand Canada & Rosline Monty Canada
PONTBRIAND, Agnes Cecile, Mar 9 1904 Sex:F Child# 7 Simeon Pontbriand Canada & Marie Jolin Canada
PONTBRIAND, Albert, Jul 30 1894 Sex:M Child# 4 Maxime Pontbriand Canada & Exelime Monty Canada
PONTBRIAND, Alexander Marcel, Jun 1 1917 Sex:M Child# 4 Joseph Pontbriand US & Angeline Bourque Canada
PONTBRIAND, Andre Robert, Feb 21 1911 Sex:M Child# 1 Joseph Pontbriand Canada & Angelina Bourque Canada
PONTBRIAND, Annette Lucienne, Apr 16 1913 Sex:F Child# 2 Jean Pontbriand US & Angeline Bourque Canada
PONTBRIAND, Claire, Jul 10 1925 Sex:F Child# 2 H D Pontbriand Worcester, MA & Vivian Moisan Vermont
PONTBRIAND, Henri, Jan 12 1894 Sex:M Child# 5 Charles Pontbriand Canada & Josephine Phaneuf Canada
PONTBRIAND, Henri Hormidas, Jul 30 1904 Sex:M Child# 1 Jean Pontbriand Canada & Hortense Gauthier Canada
PONTBRIAND, Hormidas, Feb 23 1915 Sex:M Child# 3 Joseph Pontbriand Canada & Angeline Bourque Canada
PONTBRIAND, Joseph Ernest, Aug 11 1908 Sex:M Child# 8 Simeon Pontbriand US & Marie Jaulin Canada
PONTBRIAND, Louis, Jun 4 1890 Sex:M Child# 1 Mascime Pontbriand Chazy, NY & Execline Monty Canada
PONTBRIAND, Mary Geraldine, Sep 6 1918 Sex:F Child# 1 Albert Pontbriand Nashua, NH & Ada Labombard Orange, MA
PONTBRIAND, Olida, May 8 1892 Sex:F Child# 2 Simeon Pontbriand Sciota, NY & Marie Jolin Canada
PONTBRIAND, Olivier, Oct 12 1891 Sex:M Child#  Mascime Pontbriand Canada & Exeline Monty Canada
PONTBRIAND, Olivine Beatrice, Oct 19 1905 Sex:F Child# 7 Maximo Pontbriand Sciota, NY & Exeline Monty Canada
PONTBRIAND, Romeo, Apr 22 1893 Sex:M Child# 3 Marciene Pontbriand Canada & Exelina Monty Canada
PONTBRIANT, Leonie Anita, Nov 7 1920 Sex:F Child# 1 Leo Pontbriant Nashua, NH & Amanda Godin Nashua, NH
PONTIS, Josie, Sep 24 1917 Sex:F Child# 3 Mike Pontis Lithuania Russia & Mary Gesukawicz Lithuania Russia
PONY, Joseph, Aug 3 1919 Sex:M Child# 3 John G Pony Canada & Leopoldine Proulx Canada Stillborn

POOLE, Gertrude, Jan 30 1918 Sex:F Child# 4 A D Poole Prince Edward Island & Gertrude Becker England
POPE, Bertha, May 30 1892 Sex:F Child# 1 Eugene J Pope Canada & Cora E McMannis Canada
POPE, Naomi Muriel, Jul 23 1901 Sex:F Child# 2 Eugene J Pope Canada & Cora E McManus Canada
POPE, Ruth, Mar 2 1902 Sex:F Child# 1 Eaton H Pope Canada & Delia Lafay Vermont
POPLOWSKI, Anton, Mar 23 1911 Sex:M Child# 1 Antony Poplowski Russia & Mary Lutchinski Russia
POPLOWSKI, Mary, Dec 5 1912 Sex:F Child# 2 Anton Poplowski Russia & Mary Lutshinski Russia
PORKUS, Zophia, Nov 29 1909 Sex:F Child# 2 Benedict Porkus Russia & Stephania Stulpinas Russia
PORSHKUS, Vladislas, May 1 1908 Sex:M Child# 1 Benedict Porshkus Russia & Stourpinas Stephania Russia
PORTER, Arlene Dorothy, Apr 17 1924 Sex:F Child# 2 Philip Porter Russia & Hattie Horlink Lowell, MA
PORTER, Cora Bell, Aug 14 1889 Sex:F Child# 3 Lovit Porter Canada & Henriette Mabell Marion, NY
PORTER, Greta Alene, Jun 25 1921 Sex:F Child# 1 Alvin Porter Fremont, NH & Mabel King Grafton, NH
PORTER, James, Aug 16 1904 Sex:M Child# 4 Albert Porter NH & Annie Chambers Ireland
PORTER, Jean Gerald, Mar 6 1926 Sex:M Child# 1 David Porter Brookline, NH & Cora Bourgeois Hooksett, NH
PORTER, Lewis E, Dec 10 1889 Sex:M Child#  Louis N Porter Canada & Henriette M Russell Lawrence, MA
PORTER, Merritt F, Dec 26 1888 Sex:M Child# 1 B F Porter Nashua, NH & Adiell C Hill Isle La Mott, VT
PORTER, Paul Wilson, Jan 9 1930 Sex:M Child# 2 Ralph Porter Brookline, NH & Bessie Wheeler Brookline, NH
PORTER, Roy Homer, Dec 24 1896 Sex:M Child# 6 Arthur D Porter New Haven, CT & Clara Walker Ashfield, MA
PORTER, Sylvia Freda, Sep 22 1919 Sex:F Child# 1 Philip Porter Russia & Hattie Horlink Lowell, MA
PORTER, Unknown, Dec 13 1887 Sex:M Child# 4 A D Porter Middlebury, VT & Clara E Walker Ashfield, MA Stillborn
PORTER, Unknown, Jun 18 1889 Sex:F Child# 4 Arthur D Porter New Haven, VT & Clara E Walker Ashfield, MA
PORTER, Unknown, Mar 18 1891 Sex:F Child# 2 Peter F Porter Canada & Adelle Hill Vermont
PORTER, Unknown, Jun 27 1893 Sex:M Child# 4 Peter F Porter Canada & Adell C Hill Isle La Mott, VT Stillborn
PORTER, Unknown, Feb 6 1900 Sex:F Child# 2 Albert Porter New Hampshire & Annie James Ireland
PORTER, Unknown, Dec 20 1901 Sex:F Child# 3 Albert Porter NH & Annie Chamber Ireland
PORTER, William Everett, Feb 5 1926 Sex:M Child# 2 William E Porter St Stevens, NB & Mabel Mercer Belmont, OH
PORTRAIS, Paul Andre, Nov 18 1931 Sex:M Child# 3 Paul Portrais US & Rose Dionne Lowell, MA
PORUSTA, Unknown, May 31 1911 Sex:F Child# 1 George Porusta Russia & Mary Smilega Russia
POSEVOTONSKI, Florentine, Oct 17 1902 Sex:F Child# 2 Charles Posevotonski Russia & Frances Celukosiska Russia
POSKIAVCUS, Julia, Jan 9 1914 Sex:F Child# 1 Cyprinas Poskiavcus Russia & Michaline Ovierko Russia
POSKIWICH, Jose, May 7 1916 Sex:F Child# 3 Sypris Poskiwich Russia & Mikaline Oweska Russia
POSNER, Virginia Elaine, Sep 20 1935 Sex:F Child# 2 Eli Posner Providence, RI & Minnie Jacobson Portland, ME
POTRY, Henry Antoine, Oct 20 1905 Sex:M Child# 2 Henry Potry New York & Josephine Tremblay New York
POTRY, Jane Josephine, May 20 1932 Sex:F Child# 2 Harry Potry Nashua, NH & Andrea Guenette Nashua, NH
POTRY, John, Apr 6 1894 Sex:M Child# 1 Henry Potry Coopersville, NY & Amelia Collette Champlain, NY
POTRY, Joseph C Ernest, Jul 14 1926 Sex:M Child# 2 Alfred Potry NH & Eva Bouchard Nashua, NH
POTRY, Joseph Fred, Oct 25 1900 Sex:M Child# 3 Henry Potry New York & Amelia Collins New York
POTRY, Joseph Rodolph, Mar 9 1922 Sex:M Child# 1 Alfred Potry Nashua, NH & Eva Bouchard Nashua, NH
POTRY, May Ruth, Jan 5 1897 Sex:F Child# 2 Henry Potry NY & Amelia Collins NY
POTRY, Natalie Gloria, Oct 22 1930 Sex:F Child# 1 Harry Potry, Jr Nashua, NH & Andrea Guenette Nashua, NH Stillborn
POTRY, Raphael, Dec 14 1907 Sex:M Child# 4 Harry Potry Coopersville, NY & Josephine Tremblay Altoona, NY
POTRY, Viola May, Apr 17 1904 Sex:F Child# 1 Harry Potry Cooperville, NY & Josie Trombly Altona, NY
POTTER, Bertha, Feb 16 1903 Sex:F Child# Clarence F Potter Clinton, MA & Nellie B Norwood Worcester, MA
POTTER, Beryl Elizabeth, Dec 8 1929 Sex:F Child# 5 Geo Henry Potter Worcester, MA & Mary McAfee Merrimack, NH
POTTER, Clarence Edward, May 10 1919 Sex:M Child# 2 George H Potter Worcester, MA & Mary McAfee Merrimack, NH
POTTER, Ethel May, Nov 8 1889 Sex:F Child# 2 Harry V Potter England & Kate M Murphy Ireland
POTTER, George Henry, Jr, Jul 5 1926 Sex:M Child# 3 George H Potter Worcester, MA & Mary McAfee Merrimack, NH
POTTER, Glenda May, Feb 2 1933 Sex:F Child# 3 H H Potter Mass & Florence M Cross NH
POTTER, Henry Clayton, Dec 1 1915 Sex:M Child# 1 George H Potter Worcester, MA & Mary E McAfee Merrimack, NH
POTTER, Howard Herbert, Oct 13 1926 Sex:M Child# 1 Howard Potter Northboro, MA & Florence Cross Franklin, NH
POTTER, Lawrence E, Mar 10 1916 Sex:M Child# 1 Charles E Potter Ayer, MA & Alice M Jones Nashua, NH
POTTER, Nathalie, Jul 28 1923 Sex:F Child# 2 Charles E Potter Ayer, MA & Alice Jones Nashua, NH
POTTER, Norman Kenneth, Apr 26 1928 Sex:M Child# 4 George H Potter Worcester, MA & Mary McAfee Merrimack, NH
POTTER, Shirley Elaine, Jun 9 1931 Sex:F Child# 2 Howard H Potter Northboro, MA & Florence M Cross Franklin, NH
POTTER, William Henry, Aug 26 1887 Sex:M Child#  Henry V Potter England & Mary Murphy Ireland
POTVIN, Arthur E J, Aug 18 1902 Sex:M Child# 1 Joseph A Potvin Canada & Nancy Goyette Nashua, NH
POTVIN, Blanche Noela, Dec 25 1907 Sex:F Child# 3 Joseph A Potvin Canada & Nancy Goyette Nashua, NH
POTVIN, Gertrude Beatrice, May 30 1904 Sex:F Child# 2 Joseph A Potvin Canada & Nancy Goyette Canada
POTVIN, Leo Albert Francois, Aug 11 1912 Sex:M Child# 2 Jean Potvin Vermont & Marie Lachance NH
POTVIN, Marie Therese, Apr 1 1910 Sex:F Child# 4 Joseph A Potvin Canada & Nancy Goyette Nashua, NH
POTVIN, Paul, May 25 1912 Sex:M Child# 1 Stanislaus Potvin Canada & Rosalba Morin Canada
POUDRETT, M Louise Doris, Dec 16 1921 Sex:F Child# 2 Edward Poudrett Canada & Laura Roy Manchester, NH
POUDRETTE, Mary Laura Theresa, May 3 1923 Sex:F Child# 3 Edward Poudrette Canada & Laura Roy NH
POUKSTA, Annie, Jan 10 1923 Sex:F Child# 7 George Pouksta Poland & Mary Smaeger Poland
POUKSTA, Edwiga, Aug 31 1913 Sex:F Child# 3 George Pouksta Russia & Mary Smaryga Russia
POULAS, Mary, Oct 16 1923 Sex:F Child# 4 Thomas Poulas Greece & Anna Hebert Nashua, NH
POULIN, Albert Cyrille, Apr 21 1896 Sex:M Child# 4 Alfred Poulin Canada & Parmelie Dumarais Canada
POULIN, Albert Hector Joseph, Jun 9 1934 Sex:M Child# 1 Hector Poulin Nashua, NH & Juliette Berube Hooksett, NH
POULIN, Alfred Eugene, Feb 8 1898 Sex:M Child# 8 Joseph Poulin Canada & Salama Avard Canada
POULIN, Alfred O, Dec 21 1893 Sex:M Child# 2 Alfred Poulin Canada & Parmelia Desmarais Canada
POULIN, Alfred, Jr, Sep 25 1927 Sex:M Child# 1 Alfred Poulin Nashua, NH & Mae T Milliken Ayer, MA
POULIN, Alida Alice, Oct 16 1895 Sex:F Child# 7 Joseph Poulin Canada & Salema Havard Canada
POULIN, Annette Gloria, Jun 4 1925 Sex:F Child# 1 Louis Poulin Nashua, NH & Corinne Mallett Nashua, NH
POULIN, Armand Joseph Robert, Jul 2 1933 Sex:M Child# 2 Armand Poulin Nashua, NH & Irene Poliquin Nashua, NH

POULIN, Augustine Louis, Feb 24 1892 Sex:M Child# 5 Joseph Poulin Canada & Salome Avard Canada
POULIN, Berthe Eva, Jun 15 1899 Sex:F Child# 6 Alfred Poulin Canada & Parmelie Desmarais Canada
POULIN, Charles Georges E, Mar 18 1895 Sex:M Child# 3 Alfred Poulin Canada & Parmelie Desmarais Canada
POULIN, Collette, Jul 22 1924 Sex:F Child# 4 Wilfred Poulin Canada & Melanie Lessard Canada
POULIN, Constance Lucille, Oct 9 1928 Sex:F Child# 2 A L Poulin Nashua, NH & Celia Aryell Nashua, NH
POULIN, Daniel Christopher, Sep 14 1903 Sex:M Child# 1 Arthur Poulin Nashua, NH & Alma Morin Canada
POULIN, Edna, Aug 28 1921 Sex:F Child# 2 George Poulin Nashua, NH & Alma Gaudette Nashua, NH
POULIN, Evelina, May 27 1890 Sex:F Child# 5 Alphonse Poulin Canada & Cordelia Beaudry Canada
POULIN, Florence Priscilla, Sep 11 1917 Sex:F Child# 1 George Poulin Nashua, NH & Alma Gaudette Nashua, NH
POULIN, Francois Xavier, Apr 30 1890 Sex:M Child# 4 Joseph Poulin Canada & Celina Havard Canada
POULIN, George, Dec 18 1916 Sex:M Child# 1 Thomas Poulin Greece & Anna Hebert NH
POULIN, Hector Gilbert, Apr 22 1932 Sex:M Child# 6 Edward Poulin Suncook, NH & Clara Budro Nashua, NH
POULIN, Henri Leon, Sep 1 1897 Sex:M Child# 5 Alfred Poulin Canada & Parmelie Desmarais Canada
POULIN, Jeannette Alma, Jul 10 1901 Sex:F Child# 7 Alfred Poulin Canada & Parmelie Desmarais Canada
POULIN, Jeannette Lucille, Nov 13 1917 Sex:F Child# 1 Edmond E Poulin US & Yvonne Lussier US
POULIN, Joseph A H, Oct 30 1898 Sex:M Child# 3 Hilaire Poulin Canada & Georgianna Kerouac Canada
POULIN, Joseph E, Apr 11 1887 Sex:M Child# 4 Alphonse Poulin P Q & Cordelia Beaudry P Q
POULIN, Joseph E A, Dec 4 1894 Sex:M Child# 7 Alphonse Poulin Canada & Cordelia Beaudry Canada
POULIN, Joseph E E, Jul 30 1896 Sex:M Child# 8 Alphonse Poulin Canada & Cordelia Beaudry Nashua, NH
POULIN, Joseph Louis A, Mar 2 1901 Sex:M Child# 10 Alphonse Poulin Canada & Cordelia Beaudry Canada
POULIN, Joseph Robert, Aug 4 1930 Sex:M Child# 3 Fred Poulin Nashua, NH & Celia Aryell Nashua, NH
POULIN, Joseph Victor A, Jul 26 1908 Sex:M Child# 7 Joseph Poulin Canada & Marie Drouin Canada
POULIN, Leo Albert, Aug 12 1903 Sex:M Child# 10 Joseph Poulin Canada & Solema Avard Canada
POULIN, Leonard Raymond, Jul 20 1935 Sex:M Child# 2 Hector Poulin Nashua, NH & Juliette Berube Hooksett, NH
POULIN, Lucille Annette, Jul 29 1916 Sex:F Child# 1 Walter Poulin Webster, MA & Alice Ledoux Nashua, NH
POULIN, M Annett Germaine, Jun 7 1917 Sex:F Child# 1 William N Poulin Suncook, NH & Marie G Plourde Nashua, NH
POULIN, M B Isabelle, Oct 12 1905 Sex:F Child# 2 Arthur Poulin Nashua, NH & Alma Morin Canada
POULIN, M Louise, Mar 6 1901 Sex:F Child# 6 Geroges Poulin Canada & Amelia Tremblay Canada
POULIN, Marie, Aug 23 1921 Sex:F Child# 2 Edmond Poulin US & Yvonne Pineau US
POULIN, Marie, Nov 27 1926 Sex:F Child# 4 Raoul Poulin Webster, MA & Juliette Poulin Nashua, NH Stillborn
POULIN, Marie A A, Sep 9 1892 Sex:F Child# 1 Alfred Poulin Canada & Parmelie Desmarais Canada
POULIN, Marie Alma, Apr 30 1898 Sex:F Child# 9 Alphonse Poulin Canada & Cordelia Beaudry Canada
POULIN, Marie B J, Jul 10 1896 Sex:F Child# 2 Hilaire Poulin Canada & Georgianna Kerouac Canada
POULIN, Marie Rose, Oct 6 1893 Sex:F Child# 6 Joseph Poulin Canada & Salema Havard Canada
POULIN, Marie Rose Yvonne, Oct 26 1931 Sex:F Child# 1 Armand Poulin Nashua, NH & Irene Poliquin Nashua, NH
POULIN, Muriel Lorraine, Nov 4 1928 Sex:F Child# 1 Walter Poulin Nashua, NH & Muriel Gamache Nashua, NH
POULIN, Pauline June, Nov 3 1931 Sex:F Child# 2 Walter Poulin Nashua, NH & Muriel Gamache Nashua, NH
POULIN, Peter Edmond, Jul 28 1923 Sex:M Child# 3 Valmour Poulin Nashua, NH & Grace O'Neil Mass
POULIN, Raymond L A, Apr 4 1897 Sex:M Child# 7 Cyrille Poulin Canada & Leontine Grenier Canada
POULIN, Rene Ernest, Oct 4 1892 Sex:M Child# 6 Alphonse Poulin Canada & Cordelia Beaudry Canada
POULIN, Robert Joseph, Oct 26 1929 Sex:M Child# 2 Alfred Poulin Nashua, NH & Mae Miliken Ayer, MA
POULIN, Rosalie Pearl, Jul 26 1924 Sex:F Child# 3 Edward Poulin Suncook, NH & Clara Budro Nashua, NH
POULIN, Shirley Ann, Apr 30 1935 Sex:F Child# 4 Alfred Poulin Nashua, NH & Celia Ariel Nashua, NH
POULIN, Sybel Eleanor, Dec 1 1916 Sex:F Child# 1 Edward Poulin Suncook, NH & Clara Budro Nashua, NH
POULIN, Thelma, Feb 24 1919 Sex:F Child# 2 Edward Poulin Suncook, NH & Clara Budro Nashua, NH
POULIN, Unknown, Jul 25 1926 Sex:F Child# 4 Valmor Poulin Nashua, NH & Grace O'Neil Holyoke, MA Stillborn
POULIN, Valmore, Jr, Apr 15 1921 Sex:M Child# 3 Valmore Poulin Nashua, NH & Grace O'Neil Mass
POULIN, Victor Charles, Jan 11 1918 Sex:M Child# 1 Valmor Poulin Nashua, NH & Grace O'Neil Mass
POULIN, Walter Noel, Dec 25 1928 Sex:M Child# 5 Ed Poulin Suncook, NH & Clara Rose Budro Nashua, NH
POULIN, Walter Phileas, Feb 26 1900 Sex:M Child# 9 J H Poulin Canada & Salome Avard Canada
POULIN, Yvonne, Apr 2 1895 Sex:F Child# 1 Hiliare Poulin Canada & Georgianna Sirois Canada
POULIOT, Fortuna, Aug 9 1895 Sex:F Child# 2 Dominique Pouliot Canada & Marie Caron Canada
POULIOT, Jean Baptiste, Jul 1 1903 Sex:M Child# 1 Francois Pouliot Canada & Leda St Jean Nashua, NH
POULIOT, Wilfrid, Sep 13 1896 Sex:M Child# 2 Charles Pouliot Canada & Marie Ouellette Canada
POULOS, Mary, Nov 11 1912 Sex:F Child# 1 Nicholas Poulos Greece & Mary Ambroulie Greece
POULOS, Unknown, Apr 14 1916 Sex:F Child# 2 James Poulos Greece & Theodora Greece
POULOUSKY, Louise, Apr 20 1915 Sex:F Child# 5 Mike Poulousky Russia & Minie Marcisca Russia
POURIER, Unknown, May 5 1891 Sex:F Child# 10 Napoleon Pourier Canada & Camelia Croteau Canada
POURIKAS, Andizone, Mar 11 1916 Sex:F Child# 2 George Pourikas Greece & Helen Halios Greece
POURIKAS, Satereos, Mar 12 1917 Sex:M Child# 3 George Pourikas Greece & Helen Hallis Greece
POUTRE, Laurent Louis, Apr 1 1914 Sex:M Child# 1 Omer Poutre Canada & Maria Halde Canada
POVEY, Bertha Manilla, Jun 18 1898 Sex:F Child#  William Povey England & Bertha McCommic Canada
POVEY, Leonard James, Feb 8 1904 Sex:M Child# 3 William N Povey England & Bertha McCormick Canada
POVEY, Rita Geraldine, Mar 29 1896 Sex:F Child# 1 William Povey England & Bertha McCarmick Canada
POVILIAN, Annie, Jul 26 1916 Sex:F Child# 1 Carol Povilian Russia & Genaefa Zeienkwicz Russia
POWELKER, John, May 15 1919 Sex:M Child# 6 George Powelker Poland Russia & Mary Smartygot Poland Russia
POWELL, Albert Cranston, Jr, Dec 25 1932 Sex:M Child# 3 A C Powell Townsend, MA & Blanche Wyman Townsend, MA
POWELL, Alice Frances, Jan 12 1911 Sex:F Child# 1 Charles F Powell Townsend, MA & Georgianna Corkum Nova Scotia
POWELL, Donald Wayne, Mar 8 1913 Sex:M Child# 1 Charles H Powell Townsend, MA & Estelle F Frinell Plattsburg, NY
POWELL, Estella Frances, Aug 22 1922 Sex:F Child# 4 Charles W Powell Townsend, MA & Estella F Finell Altona, NY
POWELL, Jessie Finnell, Oct 15 1918 Sex:F Child# 3 Charles W Powell Townsend, MA & Stella F Finnell New York
POWELL, Mary Ellen, Dec 30 1915 Sex:F Child# 2 Charles H Powell Townsend, MA & Stella Fuinell Plattsburgh, NY
POWELL, Mildred Eva, Jan 7 1918 Sex:F Child# 3 William E Powell England & Lillian Greene Lunenburg, MA

POWELL, Theresa Elizabeth, Nov 13 1916 Sex:F Child# 1 Perley O Powell Townsend, MA & Lillian Grimes Charlestown
POWELL, Unknown, Nov 16 1916 Sex:M Child# 2 William E Powell England & Lillian Bolton Troy, NY
POWERS, Alfred L, Apr 6 1892 Sex:M Child# 1 James A Powers Mass & Mary L Eastman Mass
POWERS, Alice Bertha, Jun 22 1921 Sex:F Child# 3 Percy Powers Bethlehem, NH & Alice Innis Lawrence, MA
POWERS, Alice Gertrude, Jun 4 1891 Sex:F Child# 2 Daniel E Powers Ireland & Maggie O'Brien Ireland
POWERS, Anna Elizabeth, Jul 16 1930 Sex:F Child# 5 Henry Powers E Pepperell, MA & Delia Gordon Ireland
POWERS, Bernard Michael, Mar 22 1927 Sex:M Child# 3 Henry P Powers E Pepperell, MA & Delia Gordon Ireland
POWERS, Doris Helen, Feb 10 1929 Sex:F Child# 4 Henry P Powers Pepperell, MA & Delia Gordon Ireland
POWERS, Florence, Jun 3 1894 Sex:F Child# 2 James H Powers Nashua, NH & Frances E Connor Milford, NH
POWERS, George Merrill, Jun 19 1916 Sex:M Child# 1 Pery M Powers Bethlehem, NH & Mary A Innis Lawrence, MA
POWERS, Henry Patrick, Feb 6 1926 Sex:M Child# 2 Henry P Powers E Pepperell, MA & Delia J Gordon Ireland
POWERS, Irene Gertrude, Dec 8 1909 Sex:F Child# 4 Edward Powers Worcester, MA & Katherine Egan Somerville, MA
POWERS, Madeline, Apr 19 1918 Sex:F Child# 1 Maurice Powers Lawrence, MA & Merilla Landry Systan, Canada
POWERS, Mary J, Apr 3 1890 Sex:F Child# 1 Daniel E Powers Ireland & Maggie O'Brien Ireland
POWERS, Mary Katherine, Nov 5 1924 Sex:F Child# 1 Henry Powers Pepperell, MA & Delia Gordon Ireland
POWERS, Nathalie M, Sep 6 1909 Sex:F Child# 1 John Powers New York, NY & Annie Monty Boston, MA
POWERS, Phyllis Gertrude, Aug 17 1910 Sex:F Child# 1 William W Powers Milford, NH & Gertrude E Rolfe Canada
POWERS, Unknown, Jun 21 1899 Sex:M Child# 1 Thomas Powers Beckertown, NY & Lily Labelle W Chazy, NY
POWERS, William Maysant, Jul 20 1918 Sex:M Child# 2 Percy Merrill Powers Bethlehem & Mary A Innis Lawrence, MA
POWILAN, Gadwiga, Mar 4 1918 Sex:F Child# 2 Charlie Powilan Russia & Genofa Zailinikawocz Russia
POWLOWSKIS, Anthony, Apr 3 1922 Sex:M Child# 2 Antonas Powlowskis Russia & Eva Russia
PRACKER, Peter, Aug 6 1912 Sex:M Child# 4 William Pracker Russia & Pietrone Biweas Russia
PRANAUSKAS, Joseph, Mar 28 1920 Sex:M Child# 1 Frank Pranauskas Lithuania Russia & Domith Dempsh Hartshorn, OH
PRANIK, Joseph, Jun 5 1912 Sex:M Child# 1 Stephen Pranik Russia & Fannie Pictkicwicz Russia Stillborn
PRANIK, Richard Cheslaw, Jul 26 1913 Sex:M Child# 1 Stephen Pranik Russia & Wanda Pietkiewicz Russia
PRATT, Howard Merton, Aug 14 1904 Sex:M Child# 1 Henry H Pratt Essex, CT & Minnie Mills Springfield, MA
PRATT, Robert Bawley, May 27 1931 Sex:M Child# 1 Robert M Pratt Bering, ME & Ruth Bawley Sanford, ME
PRATT, Unknown, Oct 8 1887 Sex:F Child# 1 Julius J Pratt Waterville, VT & Mary J Suitor Victory, VT
PRATT, Unknown, Oct 13 1900 Sex:M Child# 11 Joseph Pratt Canada & Melina Chicoine RI
PRATTE, Hector, Jul 10 1899 Sex:M Child# 8 Joseph Pratte Canada & Melina Chicoine Canada
PRATTE, Henri, Nov 2 1897 Sex:M Child# 8 Joseph Pratte Canada & Melina Chicoine Canada
PRECOURT, Joseph Jules Richard, Jan 8 1932 Sex:M Child# 3 Richard Precourt Canada & A D Laflamme Lowell, MA
PRECOURT, Marie Claire J, Aug 20 1930 Sex:F Child# 2 Richard Precourt Canada & Denise A LaFlamme Lowell, MA
PRECOURT, Marie Theresa J, Jul 8 1929 Sex:F Child# 1 Richard Precourt Canada & A D Laflamme Lowell, MA
PRESAS, Amelia, Jan 3 1917 Sex:F Child# 1 Spiros Prezas Kertezy & Vasilo Kolotraki Sirbani
PRESCOTT, Carl Oliver, Aug 15 1896 Sex:M Child# 4 Clifford H Prescott Westford, MA & Augusta E Downing Dunstable
PRESCOTT, Carl William, Apr 20 1921 Sex:M Child# 2 Carl G Prescott Meredith, NH & Jennie M Nickerson Wilton, NH
PRESCOTT, Marvis Jane, Aug 15 1918 Sex:F Child# 1 Carl G Prescott Meridith, NH & Jennie M Nickerson Wilton, NH
PRESTIFINO, Josephine Olive, Jan 15 1929 Sex:F Child# 1 Antony Prestifino Italy & Virginia Patte Italy
PRESTON, Eugene Julius, Sep 1 1915 Sex:M Child# 4 John Preston Randolph, VT & Grace E Stafford Hancock, VT
PRESTON, Frank, Aug 17 1892 Sex:M Child# 1 Henry J Preston Dunstable, MA & Elvira Hudson, NY
PRESTON, Leon, Oct 2 1911 Sex:M Child# 1 Fred Preston Rutland, VT & Ethel Hain Burlington, VT
PREVOST, Albertine G, Dec 19 1905 Sex:F Child# 2 Arthur Prevost Canada & Amanda Bariteau Canada
PREVOST, Antoine Sylvio, Jul 25 1903 Sex:M Child# 1 Arthur Prevost Canada & Amanda Bariteau Canada
PREVOST, Conrad, Jul 16 1917 Sex:M Child# 4 Frank Prevost New York & Cordelia Lemieux New York
PREVOST, David, Apr 12 1895 Sex:M Child# 6 Joseph Prevost Canada & Mathilde Laplante Canada
PREVOST, Sylvio Aurel, Dec 1 1935 Sex:M Child# 1 Sylvio Prevost Nashua, NH & Aurore Boisvert Canada
PREW, Charles M, Feb 24 1887 Sex:M Child# 2 Charles Prew Boston & Hattie NH
PREW, Dorothy Helen, Jun 22 1910 Sex:F Child# 1 Peter Prew NH & Theresa Healy NH
PREW, Robert Hugh, Sep 24 1911 Sex:M Child# 2 Peter Prew Wilton, NH & Theresa Healy Wilton, NH
PRIEST, Chester A, Dec 2 1892 Sex:M Child# 2 Fred K Priest Nashua, NH & Mary A Costello NY
PRIMEAU, Barbara Ann, Jan 17 1933 Sex:F Child# 2 Edward Primeau New York & Agnes Ohearn N Walpole, NH
PRIMEAU, Edward John, Sep 24 1929 Sex:M Child# 1 Edward Primeau Malone, NY & Agnes Ahearn Bellows Falls, NY
PRIMROSE, Louise Mary, Nov 3 1924 Sex:F Child# 1 N E Primrose Groveland, MA & Flor R Woodcock Georgetown, MA
PRIMROSE, Norma Florence, Oct 18 1927 Sex:F Child# 2 Norman Primrose Groveland, MA & F Woodcock Georgetown, MA
PRIMROSE, Richard Earle, May 16 1929 Sex:M Child# 3 Norman Primrose Bradford, MA & Florence Woodcock Georgetown, MA
PRINCE, Alice, Jul 1 1907 Sex:F Child# 5 Adelard Prince Canada & Marie Larouche Canada
PRINCE, Arlene Eva, Oct 11 1935 Sex:F Child# 17 Henry Prince Nashua, NH & Clara Lafleche Southbridge, MA
PRINCE, Arthur Romeo, Jun 25 1920 Sex:M Child# 6 Henri Prince Nashua, NH & Clara Lafleche Southbridge, MA
PRINCE, Aurore, May 4 1894 Sex:F Child# 6 Exila Prince Canada & Louise Houle Canada
PRINCE, Blanche Germaine, Feb 7 1906 Sex:F Child# 2 Joseph Prince Canada & Eugenie Martel Canada
PRINCE, Calixte A, Jul 31 1902 Sex:M Child# 3 Adelard Prince Canada & Marie Larouche Canada
PRINCE, Cecile Stella, Jun 1 1929 Sex:F Child# 9 Joseph A E Prince Manchester, NH & Delima Bernaquez Lawrence, MA
PRINCE, Celina, Oct 22 1895 Sex:F Child# 6 W Prince Canada & Marie Grandmaison Canada
PRINCE, Elaine Cecile, Apr 1 1934 Sex:F Child# 16 Henry Prince Nashua, NH & Clara Lafleche Southbridge, MA
PRINCE, Elise, May 2 1900 Sex:F Child# 1 Joseph Prince Canada & Marie Levesque Canada
PRINCE, Florence Rachelle, Oct 13 1914 Sex:F Child# 2 Henry Prince Nashua, NH & Clara Lafleche Southbridge, MA
PRINCE, George Pable, Dec 18 1926 Sex:M Child# 8 A E Prince Manchester, NH & Delima Bernaquez Lawrence, MA
PRINCE, Henry Edgar, Apr 1 1929 Sex:M Child# 13 Henry Prince Nashua, NH & Clara LaFlache Mass
PRINCE, Joseph, Aug 19 1889 Sex:M Child# 2 William Prince Canada & M L Grandmaison Canada
PRINCE, Joseph Arthur, Nov 28 1898 Sex:M Child# 1 Adelard Prince Canada & Marie Larouche Canada
PRINCE, Joseph Arthur, Jun 6 1901 Sex:M Child# 2 Joseph Prince Canada & Marie Levesque Canada
PRINCE, Joseph Arthur, Aug 8 1906 Sex:M Child# 6 Joseph Prince Canada & Marie Levesque Canada

PRINCE, Joseph C, Apr 20 1891 Sex:M Child# 3 William Prince Canada & Marie Grandmaison Canada
PRINCE, Joseph Henri, May 13 1905 Sex:M Child#  Joseph Prince Canada & Marie Levesque Canada
PRINCE, Joseph Rudolphe, Jan 5 1893 Sex:M Child# 1 Joseph Prince Canada & Alma Faucher Canada
PRINCE, Joseph V, Sep 17 1887 Sex:M Child# 1 William Prince P Q & Marie P Q
PRINCE, Marie Alma, Jun 20 1903 Sex:F Child# 4 Joseph A Prince Canada & Marie Levesque Canada
PRINCE, Marie Beatrice, Jul 18 1904 Sex:F Child# 1 Joseph Prince Canada & Eugenie Martel Canada
PRINCE, Marie Carmel Lorrain, Apr 8 1934 Sex:F Child# 11 Eugene Prince Manchester, NH & Delima Bernaquez Lawrence
PRINCE, Marie Louise, Jun 14 1902 Sex:F Child# 3 Joseph Prince Canada & Marie Levesque Canada
PRINCE, Marie Philomene, Sep 8 1904 Sex:F Child# 4 Adelard Prince Canada & Marie Larouche Canada
PRINCE, Maurice Lawrence, Jan 12 1932 Sex:M Child# 9 Eugene A Prince Manchester, NH & Delima Bernaquez Lawrence, MA
PRINCE, Pierre Norman, Feb 21 1933 Sex:M Child# 10 Albert E Prince Manchester, NH & D Bernachez Lawrence, MA
PRINCE, Robert Eugene, Aug 2 1930 Sex:M Child# 8 Eugene Prince Manchester, NH & Delima Bernagey Lawrence, MA
PRINCE, Rose, Apr 11 1900 Sex:F Child# 3 Odorore Prince Canada & Marie Larouche Canada
PRINCE, Theresa Lorraine, Mar 23 1932 Sex:F Child# 15 Henry H Prince Nashua, NH & Clara LaFlache Southbridge, MA
PRINCE, Unknown, Jun 26 1893 Sex:F Child# 3 Exilia Prince Canada & Louise Houle Canada Stillborn
PRINCE, Unknown, Sep 20 1895 Sex:M Child# 6 Exilia Prince Canada & Louise Houle Canada Stillborn
PRINCE, Unknown, Sep 5 1897 Sex:M Child# 8 Exilia Prince Canada & Louise Houle Canada Stillborn
PRINCE, Unknown, Dec 14 1898 Sex:M Child# 9 Exilia Prince Canada & Louise Houle Canada
PRINCE, Unknown, Mar 9 1900 Sex:M Child# 7 William Prince Canada & Marie Grandmaison Canada Stillborn
PRINCE, Unknown, Apr 22 1925 Sex:F Child# 10 Henry Prince Canada & Clara Lafleche Canada
PRINCE, Wilfred, Oct 20 1893 Sex:M Child# 5 William Prince Canada & Marie Grandmaison Canada
PRISKE, Vivian Mae, May 18 1934 Sex:F Child# 1 John M Priske Penzance, England & Mae Harris Calumet, MI
PROCTER, Norman Patterson, Mar 14 1932 Sex:M Child#  George E Procter Wrentham, MA & Lola S Patterson US
PROCTOR, Arleen, Nov 25 1905 Sex:F Child# 1 Richard H Proctor Nashua, NH & Jessie Clement Hudson, NH
PROCTOR, Clayton Billings, Jr, Sep 24 1916 Sex:M Child# 2 Clayton B Proctor Hollis, NH & Alice May Garland Eng
PROCTOR, Joan, Jun 22 1915 Sex:F Child# 1 Clayton Proctor Hollis, NH & Alice May Garland England
PROCTOR, Nathalie, Aug 31 1918 Sex:F Child# 3 Clayton B Proctor Hollis, NH & Alice M Garland England
PROCTOR, Patricia, Jul 14 1920 Sex:F Child# 4 Clayton B Proctor Hollis, NH & Alice M Garland England
PROCTOR, Unknown, Jan 11 1887 Sex:F Child# 4 Nathaniel Proctor Hollis & Lizzie Billings Acton, MA
PRODROMAN, Panagiota, Sep 27 1915 Sex:F Child# 2 John Prodroman Greece & Sultana Tseazron Greece
PROSSER, Pauline, Oct 15 1926 Sex:F Child# 2 Ernest Prosser Mass & Lena Maynard New York
PROTROSKI, Malvina, Mar 1 1914 Sex:F Child# 3 William Protroski Russia & Agata Barcikona Russia
PROUDE, Charles H, Sep 12 1889 Sex:M Child# 1 Jim Proude Canada & Victorie Larrynon Douglas, MA
PROULE, Arthur, Dec 11 1898 Sex:M Child# 1 Arthur Proule Canada & Olina Demoulia Dunstable, MA Stillborn
PROULX, Adrienne, Feb 9 1909 Sex:F Child# 2 Michel Proulx Canada & Elizabeth Morency Canada
PROULX, Albert Gerard, Jun 21 1932 Sex:M Child# 2 Albert Proulx Epping, NH & Beatrice Theriault Nashua, NH
PROULX, Cecile, Nov 20 1904 Sex:F Child# 1 Michel Proulx Canada & Elizabeth Morency Canada
PROULX, Mary Jane, Apr 21 1931 Sex:F Child# 1 Albert Proulx Epping, NH & Beatrice Theriault Nashua, NH
PROULX, Mary Marceline Joan, May 12 1934 Sex:F Child# 1 Alfred Proulx NH & Mary Dube Canada
PROULX, Unknown, Apr 20 1892 Sex:F Child# 1 Zotique Proulx Canada & Jennie Joyal Canada Stillborn
PROULX, Unknown, Jun 29 1893 Sex:F Child# 3 Aurele Proulx Canada & Adele Mercier Canada Stillborn
PROULX, Unknown, Aug 27 1918 Sex:M Child# 2 Arthur Proulx Canada & Zoe Richard Canada Stillborn
PROVANCHER, Joseph Edgar, May 2 1897 Sex:M Child# 1 Alex Provancher Canada & Anna Audet Canada
PROVASALI, Joan Mildred, Nov 17 1930 Sex:F Child# 1 Tullio P Provasali Barre, VT & Mildred J Heaps Lawrence, MA
PROVENCAL, Charles E, Mar 15 1890 Sex:M Child# 1 Chrismus Provencal Canada & Mary Richards Canada
PROVENCAL, Elzear, Aug 26 1894 Sex:M Child# 4 Noel Provencal Canada & Corinne Larichadiere Canada
PROVENCAL, Eva Evangeline, May 20 1912 Sex:F Child# 4 Alex Provencal Canada & Marie Gagnon Canada
PROVENCAL, Joseph, Mar 15 1890 Sex:M Child#  Noel Provencal Canada & Corinne Laucheliere Canada
PROVENCAL, Joseph E N, Oct 20 1891 Sex:M Child# 2 Noel Provencal Canada & C Larichalliere Canada
PROVENCAL, Joseph P G, Dec 3 1889 Sex:M Child# 2 N Provencal Canada & Leona Pepin Canada
PROVENCAL, Louis Gonzague, Mar 31 1909 Sex:M Child# 2 Alexandre Provencal Canada & Marie Gagnon Canada
PROVENCAL, M Anne Alice, May 19 1913 Sex:F Child# 5 Alexandre Provencal Canada & Marie Gagnon Canada
PROVENCAL, M Rose Delima, Jul 31 1909 Sex:F Child# 7 Joseph Provencal Canada & Delima Gagne Canada
PROVENCAL, Marie A E, Jul 10 1896 Sex:F Child# 5 Noel Provencal Canada & A Laricheliere Canada
PROVENCAL, Noel I P, Feb 17 1893 Sex:M Child# 3 Noel Provencal Canada & Corinne Laricheliere Canada
PROVENCAL, Reginald Elzear, Jul 13 1929 Sex:M Child# 1 Elzear Provencal Nashua, NH & Regina Berube Nashua, NH
PROVENCAL, Robert Roland, Oct 18 1920 Sex:M Child# 1 George J Provencal Canada & Mary B Lusignan Nashua, NH
PROVENCHER, Alphonse, Jul 21 1918 Sex:M Child# 4 Bruno Provencher Nicolette, PQ & Elmire Pellerin Nashua, NH
PROVENCHER, Amede, Nov 30 1926 Sex:M Child# 8 Bruno Provencher Canada & Elmire Pellerin Nashua, NH
PROVENCHER, Armand Rolland, Oct 2 1915 Sex:M Child# 2 Bruno Provencher Canada & Elmire Pelerin Nashua, NH
PROVENCHER, Beatrice V, May 15 1893 Sex:F Child# 7 Damase Provencher Canada & Vitaline Crepeau Canada
PROVENCHER, Cecile Anita, Mar 25 1921 Sex:F Child# 2 Pierre Provencher Nashua, NH & Antoinette Morin Nashua, NH
PROVENCHER, J Louis Bruno, Mar 20 1913 Sex:M Child# 1 Bruno Provencher Canada & Elmire Pellerin Nashua, NH
PROVENCHER, James R, Nov 22 1896 Sex:M Child# 9 D Provencher Canada & Vitaline Crepeau Canada
PROVENCHER, Jeannette, Feb 17 1917 Sex:F Child# 1 Pierre Provencher Nashua, NH & Antoinette Morin Nashua, NH
PROVENCHER, Joseph, Nov 5 1920 Sex:M Child# 5 Bruno Provencher Canada & Elmire Pellerin Canada
PROVENCHER, Joseph Avila A, Nov 15 1905 Sex:M Child# 7 Avila Provencher Canada & Clara Noel Canada
PROVENCHER, Marie A E, Apr 12 1892 Sex:F Child# 6 Damase Provencher Canada & Vitaline Crepeau Canada
PROVENCHER, Marie A I, Jan 10 1900 Sex:F Child# 11 Damase Provencher Canada & Vitaline Crepeau Canada
PROVENCHER, Marie Aurore Y, May 12 1904 Sex:F Child# 6 Ovila Provencher Canada & Sarah Noel Canada
PROVENCHER, Marie C A, Nov 26 1902 Sex:F Child# 12 D Provencher Canada & Victaline Crepeau Canada
PROVENCHER, Marie Dora A, Jun 30 1902 Sex:F Child# 4 A Provencher Canada & Anna Audette Canada
PROVENCHER, Marie E, Oct 24 1898 Sex:F Child# 10 Damase Provencher Canada & Vitaline Crepeau Canada

PROVENCHER, Marie Emelida, Feb 8 1899 Sex:F Child# 2 Alexander Provencher Canada & Anna Audette Canada
PROVENCHER, Marie Emerilda, Oct 7 1900 Sex:F Child# 3 Alexandre Provencher Canada & Anna Audette Canada
PROVENCHER, Marie Exilia E, Mar 4 1905 Sex:F Child# 6 Joseph P Provencher Canada & Delima Gagne Canada
PROVENCHER, Marie Therese, Jul 5 1922 Sex:F Child# 3 Pierre Provencher Canada & Antoinette Morin Nashua, NH
PROVENCHER, Napoleon Girard, Feb 5 1923 Sex:M Child# 6 Bruno Provencher Canada & Elmire Pellerin Nashua, NH
PROVENCHER, Omer P, Jul 9 1894 Sex:M Child# 8 Damase Provencher Canada & Vitaline Crepeau Canada
PROVENCHER, Ovila Leo Eugene, Dec 29 1910 Sex:M Child# 3 Alexandre Provencher Canada & Marie Gagnon Canada
PROVENCHER, Paul, Oct 25 1921 Sex:M Child# 6 Bruno Provencher Canada & Elmire Pellerin Nashua, NH
PROVENCHER, Unknown, Nov 21 1916 Sex:M Child# 3 Bruno Provencher Canada & Elmire Pelletier Nashua, NH Stillborn
PROVENCIER, Joseph, Jun 28 1888 Sex:M Child# 1 Udjore Provencier Canada & Lena Peppin Canada
PROVOST, Celina Albina, Dec 10 1894 Sex:F Child# 11 Toussant Provost Canada & Maria Masta Canada
PROVOST, J Lucien Alcide, Sep 3 1912 Sex:M Child# 7 Ludger Provost Canada & Rosina Archambault Canada
PROVOST, Joseph Auguste H, Mar 11 1909 Sex:M Child# 5 Ludger Provost Canada & Rose A Archambault Canada
PROVOST, Julia, Oct 29 1891 Sex:F Child# 3 Joseph S Provost Canada & Emilie Lincoln Canada
PROVOST, Marie Aurore V, Feb 26 1911 Sex:F Child# 6 Ludger Provost Canada & Rosina Archambault Canada
PROVOST, Marie Rose Albertine, Aug 14 1907 Sex:F Child# 4 Ludger Provost Canada & Regina Archambault Canada
PROVOST, Melina, Apr 14 1891 Sex:F Child# 8 Toussaint Provost Canada & Marie Masta Canada
PROVOST, Rose, Jun 13 1896 Sex:F Child# 12 Toussaint Provost Canada & Marie Masta Canada
PROVOST, Unknown, Nov 28 1895 Sex:M Child# 12 Francois A Provost Canada & Thersile Mercier Canada Stillborn
PRUDHONE, Unknown, Oct 19 1935 Sex:M Child# 1 Art Prudhone Adams, MA & Cora Towle New York, NY Stillborn
PRUETTE, Yolande Doris, Jan 22 1931 Sex:F Child# 3 Joseph Pruette Canada & Bernadette Raymond Nashua, NH
PRUITIS, Mary, Apr 27 1915 Sex:F Child# 1 Michael Pruitis Russia & Mary Josichawicz Russia
PRUNEAU, Bertha Theresa, Sep 2 1926 Sex:F Child# 3 Alfred Pruneau Warren, RI & Emilia Mateau Canada
PRUNIER, Aurore Jeannette, Oct 31 1910 Sex:F Child# 2 Fred Prunier Holyoke, MA & Aurore Riendeau Nashua, NH
PRUNIER, Frederick Paul, Nov 9 1909 Sex:M Child# 1 Frederick Prunier Holyoke, MA & Aurore Riendieu Nashua, NH
PRUNIER, Maurice Albert, Oct 17 1915 Sex:M Child# 3 Fred P Prunier Holyoke, MA & Aurore Riendeau Nashua, NH
PRUNSKI, Alphonse, Jul 3 1925 Sex:M Child# 2 James Prunski Lithuania & Nellie Gregas Lithuania
PRUSAK, Gynia, Apr 23 1915 Sex:M Child# 3 John Prusak Russia & Nellie Markaska Russia
PRUSAK, Leocardia, Jul 27 1912 Sex:F Child# 2 John Prusak Russia & Nellie Markoffsky Russia
PRUSAK, Unknown, Jul 12 1911 Sex:M Child# 1 John Prusak Russia & Nellie Markoska Russia
PRUTSALIS, Andrew Arthur, May 25 1930 Sex:M Child# 1 Arthur Prutsalis Greece & Polixene Pernanes Greece
PRUTSALIS, Unknown, Dec 24 1929 Sex:F Child# 1 Thomas J Prutsalis Greece & Aglia M Katsoupis Marlboro, MA
PRUTSALIS, Unknown, Jun 17 1931 Sex:F Child# 2 Thomas Prutsalis Greece & Aglaia Katsoupis Marlboro, MA
PRUTSALIS, Unknown, Mar 27 1934 Sex:M Child# 3 Thomas J Prutsalis Greece & Agala Katsoupis Marlboro, MA
PRZEWOZNIK, Joseph, Dec 21 1905 Sex:M Child# 1 Andrew Przewoznik Russia & Anna Obara Russia
PSILOPOULOS, Unknown, Dec 31 1934 Sex:M Child# 1 Lewis Psilopoulos Nashua, NH & Katina Adams Nashua, NH
PTESKA, Unknown, Jul 17 1915 Sex:M Child# 1 Joseph Pteska Russia & Josie Aldanis Russia Stillborn
PUCKETT, Glena Vivian, Feb 1 1921 Sex:F Child# 5 Lawrence Puckett South Carolina & Lottie M Holden Nashua, NH
PUCKETT, Glendon Fenelon, Apr 23 1922 Sex:M Child# 6 Laurence Puckett S Carolina & Lottie M Holden Nashua, NH
PUCKETT, Serdena Arlene, Jan 1 1929 Sex:F Child# 8 Laurence G Puckett S Carolina & Lottie M Hodlin Nashua, NH
PUCKETT, Theodore Pauline, Oct 13 1925 Sex:M Child# 7 Law G Puckett S Carolina & Lottie M Holden Nashua, NH
PUFFER, Richard Gardner, Aug 21 1932 Sex:M Child# 1 R G Puffer Boston, MA & Ruth Moores Boston, MA
PUKNOSKY, Frank, Mar 21 1907 Sex:M Child# 2 Urban Puknosky Austria & Karoline Polasak Austria
PULOS, Nickles, Apr 4 1915 Sex:M Child# 1 Gus Pulos Greece & Mary Kawsarskas Greece
PULSIFER, Janice, Nov 13 1932 Sex:F Child# 1 Nerval Pulsifer
PUPOLIS, Melvina, Jul 5 1916 Sex:F Child# 2 Motrkis Pupolis Russia & Julia Meskovsky Russia
PURCELL, Unknown, Nov 10 1901 Sex:M Child# 1 Michael Purcell Cambridge, MA & Mary E Sullivan Lawrence, MA
PURDY, Maitland Arthur, Jan 15 1925 Sex:M Child# 5 Edmond M Purdy Nova Scotia & Lena Andrews Claremont, NH
PURDY, Unknown, May 7 1920 Sex:F Child# 4 John Bernard Purdy Brockton, MA & Louise G Carr St John, NB
PURICAS, Elethrias, Dec 29 1914 Sex:M Child# 1 George Puricas Greece & Eleny Holis Greece
PURWINIS, Stanislas, Jan 26 1922 Sex:M Child# 2 Mike Purwinis Lithuania & Annie Matachinska Lithuania
PUSHEE, Richmond L, Aug 28 1902 Sex:M Child# 1 George F Pushee Nashua, NH & Grace M Tinker New Britain, CT
PUTALIS, Felix, Jun 12 1915 Sex:M Child# 3 Joseph Putalis Russia & Eustria Nakite Russia
PUTALIS, Joseph, Jun 12 1915 Sex:M Child# 2 Joseph Putalis Russia & Eustria Nakite Russia
PUTELL, Julius, Feb 2 1913 Sex:F Child# 1 Joseph Putell Russia & Justine Narkiest Russia
PUTIS, Anna, Mar 1 1920 Sex:F Child# 4 Michael Putis Russia & Mary Josakantch Russia
PUTIS, John, Feb 9 1924 Sex:M Child# 6 Michael Putis Lithuania & Mary Josecevitch Lithuania
PUTIS, Julia, Jun 3 1921 Sex:F Child# 5 Mike Putis Lithuania & Mary Gesuhavicz Lithuania
PUTNAM, Annie May, May 17 1887 Sex:F Child# 4 Charles B Putnam Nashua, NH & Ellen A Lowell
PUTNAM, Charles Vincent, Mar 24 1914 Sex:M Child# 2 Fred N Putnam Nashua, NH & Elsie E Regan Bondsville, MA
PUTNAM, Cornelius Henry, Jun 5 1901 Sex:M Child# 1 Walter N Putnam Vermont & Flora Woodward Dunstable, MA
PUTNAM, Earl, Apr 26 1915 Sex:M Child# 1 (No Parents Listed)
PUTNAM, George, Nov 13 1903 Sex:M Child# 4 Mark P Putnam Milford & Laura A Pond
PUTNAM, Guy Cornelius, Mar 13 1930 Sex:M Child# 3 Warren Putnam Nashua, NH & Almida Doucette Boston, MA
PUTNAM, Helen Flora, May 3 1911 Sex:F Child# 5 Walter H Putnam Mass & Carrie Page Vermont
PUTNAM, Helen Mariette, Apr 19 1908 Sex:F Child# 2 Algernon W Putnam S Lyndeboro, NH & Lucy A Daniels London,
PUTNAM, Jeanne, Nov 22 1927 Sex:F Child# 2 Howard Putnam Nashua, NH & Almada Doucette Boston, MA
PUTNAM, John Cornelius, Oct 20 1933 Sex:M Child# 2 Guy C Putnam Jamaica, VT & Elizabeth Pierce Hollis, NH
PUTNAM, Laura, May 15 1902 Sex:F Child# 3 Mark P Putnam Milford, NH & Laura A Pond Shirley, MA
PUTNAM, Lester Herbert, Jun 18 1931 Sex:M Child# 1 Guy C Putnam West Jamaica, VT & Elizabeth Pineo Hollis, NH
PUTNAM, Marion, Jun 24 1906 Sex:F Child# 1 Herbert L Putnam Nashua, NH & Ethel M Burtt Bennington, NH
PUTNAM, Neil Frederick, Nov 20 1911 Sex:M Child# 1 Fred N Putnam Nashua, NH & Elsie N Regan Bondsville, MA
PUTNAM, Therese Lorraine, Mar 9 1934 Sex:F Child# 4 W Howard Putnam Nashua, NH & Almada Doucet Boston, MA

PUTNAM, Unknown, Mar 13 1887 Sex:F Child# 4 John B Putnam Boston & Aurilla Pelham
PUTNAM, Unknown, Nov 29 1893 Sex:F Child# 1 Walter A Putnam Vermont & Hattie M Proctor NH Stillborn
PUTNAM, Unknown, Dec 26 1894 Sex:F Child# 1 Mark Putnam Milford & Laura A Pond Shirley
PUTNAM, Unknown, Jan 17 1899 Sex:F Child# 2 Mark P Putnam Milford, NH & Laura Pond Nashua, NH
PUTNAM, Warren Howard, Aug 6 1905 Sex:M Child# 3 Walter H Putnam Vermont & Carrie Page Charlestown, MA
PUTNAM, Warren Howard, Oct 25 1926 Sex:M Child# 1 Howard Putnam Nashua, NH & Almada Doucette Boston, MA
PUTNEY, Albion, Sep 18 1911 Sex:M Child# 5 Charles Putney Somerville, MA & Ella Maclaren Danville, NH
PUTNEY, Orlando, May 15 1889 Sex:M Child# 3 Eldridge Putney Canada & Malvina Tracy Manchester
PUTNEY, Samuel N, Mar 20 1889 Sex:M Child# 2 Arthur K Putney Newbury, MA & Jane E Clarke Cambridge, MA
PUVOISKI, Anthony, Nov 9 1935 Sex:M Child# 7 John Puvoiski Poland & Mollie Henry Ireland
PUVOISKI, John, Nov 9 1935 Sex:M Child# 6 John Puvoiski Poland & Mollie Henry Ireland
PUWARUNAS, Anthony, Dec 8 1915 Sex:M Child# 2 Martin Puwarunas Russia & Mary Szaulaite Russia
PWEKOWSKI, Joseph, Jan 31 1921 Sex:M Child# 2 And Pwekowski Russia & Ellen Japonski Russia
PYE, Dorothy Viola, Aug 17 1931 Sex:F Child# 1 John H Pye Hillsboro, NH & Bertha V Jones Methuen, MA
QUEEN, Louis, Aug 25 1888 Sex:F Child# 1 Harris Queen Russia & Sarah Melanarsky Russia
QUERN, Simon, Jan 27 1892 Sex:M Child# 8 Louis Quern Russia & Sarah Melansky Russia
QUIGLEY, Edward Terrance, Feb 9 1922 Sex:M Child# 1 James Quigley Nashua, NH & Elsie Pelkey Sciota, NY
QUIGLEY, George Francis, Feb 21 1897 Sex:M Child# 3 Terrence Quigley Ireland & Hannah Twomey Ireland
QUIGLEY, James Daniel, Jul 17 1894 Sex:M Child# Terrence Quigley Ireland & Hannah Toomey Ireland
QUIGLEY, James Donald, Feb 3 1927 Sex:M Child# 4 James Quigley Nashua, NH & Elsie Pelkey New York
QUIGLEY, Jane Evelyn, Sep 9 1928 Sex:F Child# 5 James Quigley Nashua, NH & Elsie Pelkey Sciota, NY
QUIGLEY, John Patrick, Dec 5 1931 Sex:M Child# 6 James Quigley Nashua, NH & Elsie Pelkey New York
QUIGLEY, Lucille Mary, Sep 16 1924 Sex:F Child# 3 James Quigley Nashua, NH & Elsie Pelkey Sciota, NY
QUIGLEY, Nora Elizabeth, Sep 6 1923 Sex:F Child# 2 James D Quigley Nashua, NH & Elsie M Pelkey Sciota, NY
QUIMBY, Susan, Sep 27 1892 Sex:F Child# 1 Alexander Quimby Henniker, NH & Susan Nashua, NH
QUINN, Charles P, Jul 11 1891 Sex:M Child# 2 Charles P Quinn Dover, NH & Lizzie Earley Manchester, NH
QUINN, Gertrude, Mar 13 1893 Sex:F Child# 3 Charles P Quinn Dover, NH & Lizzie Earley Manchester, NH
QUINN, Mabel M, Jul 19 1897 Sex:F Child# 3 James J Quinn Worcester, MA & Mary E Collins Cohoes, NY
QUINN, Marion A, Sep 23 1892 Sex:F Child# 1 Joseph J Quinn Cincinnati, OH & Bessie Mumford W Rutland, VT
QUINN, Mary Ann, Oct 14 1889 Sex:F Child# 1 Charles P Quinn Dover, NH & Lizzie Earley Manchester, NH
QUINT, Alice Louise, Jun 23 1928 Sex:F Child# Roger B Quint Peabody, MA & Fannie Goding Nashua, NH
QUINT, Doris Mae, Mar 21 1926 Sex:F Child# 2 Roger Quint Quincy, MA & Fanny Godang Nashua, NH
QUINT, Gloria Lillian, May 19 1933 Sex:F Child# 7 Roger B Quint Peabody, MA & Fannie Goding Nashua, NH
QUINT, Helen Grace, Jan 11 1932 Sex:F Child# 6 Roger B Quint Peabody, MA & Fannie E Goding Nashua, NH
QUINT, Roger William, May 26 1924 Sex:M Child# 1 Roger Quint Peabody, MA & Fannie Golding Nashua, NH
QUINT, Shirley Ann, Sep 17 1930 Sex:F Child# 5 Roger B Quint Peabody, MA & Fannie E Goding Nashua, NH
QUINT, Virginia Lorena, Oct 18 1929 Sex:F Child# 4 Roger B Quint Quincy, MA & Fannie E Goding Nashua, NH
QUINTAL, Charles Prudent, Dec 13 1895 Sex:M Child# 7 Cyrille Quintal Canada & Virginie Maston Canada
QUINTAL, Edmound, Jul 21 1888 Sex:M Child# 3 Cyrille Quintal Canada & Virginia Marston Canada
QUINTAL, Joseph Henri T, Jul 17 1890 Sex:M Child# 5 Cyrille Quintal Canada & Virginie Masta Canada
QUINTAL, M Virgine A, Jul 12 1892 Sex:F Child# 2 Guillaume Quintal Canada & Virginie Tiepanier Canada
QUINTAL, Marie Eva, Dec 15 1890 Sex:F Child# 1 Cyrille Quintal Canada & Virginie Trepanier Canada
RABADEAU, Elizabeth Jane, Jun 3 1931 Sex:F Child# 3 Roger J Rabadeau Milford, NH & Luella Scribner Portland, ME
RABADEAU, Phyllis Rose, Aug 12 1920 Sex:F Child# 1 Roger Rabadeau Milford, NH & Luella Scribner Portland, ME
RABOIN, Arthur, Jul 31 1907 Sex:M Child# 6 Arthur Raboin Canada & Arzelina Richer Canada
RABOUIN, Louis Alfred, Mar 19 1899 Sex:M Child# 2 Alfred Rabouin Canada & Octavie Rousseau Canada
RABY, Adelard Henry, Mar 2 1910 Sex:M Child# 4 Adelard Raby Canada & Leonide Maynard Canada
RABY, Beatrice Ella, Jun 14 1908 Sex:F Child# 6 Berth Raby New York & Lilly Ouellette New York
RABY, Bernice H, Feb 28 1905 Sex:F Child# 2 Pliny Raby New York & Lilian Budro New York
RABY, Claude Alfred Narcis, Jan 29 1927 Sex:M Child# 1 Claude Raby Nashua, NH & Mary J Salvail Nashua, NH
RABY, Doris Geneve, Mar 28 1911 Sex:F Child# 7 Burtt Raby New York & Lilly Ouellette New York
RABY, Doris Loretta, Oct 28 1933 Sex:F Child# 6 Herbert Raby Nashua, NH & Melvina Lorraine Nashua, NH
RABY, Edith May, Jul 3 1895 Sex:F Child# 1 Burt Raby Clinton, NY & Lila Ouellette Clinton, NY
RABY, Eleanor Lillian, Jun 13 1914 Sex:F Child# 4 O R Raby W Chazy, NY & Lillian Budro W Chazy, NY
RABY, Eugene Lloyd, Mar 26 1904 Sex:M Child# 2 Edwin L Raby US & Leda Mayo US
RABY, Hattie May, Feb 13 1905 Sex:F Child# 5 Charles Raby New York & Amanda Levesque Canada
RABY, Herbert E, Dec 2 1897 Sex:M Child# 2 Herbert J Raby Plattsburg, NY & Lily Alice Oulette W Chazy, NY
RABY, Irene Anita, Jun 10 1908 Sex:F Child# 3 Pliny Raby New York & Lillian Budro Nashua, NH
RABY, Jos Ernest Conrad, Mar 12 1917 Sex:M Child# 1 Joseph Raby Canada & Georgianna Laflotte Canada
RABY, Joseph Edouard, Jul 22 1906 Sex:M Child# 3 William Raby Canada & Alice Morin Canada
RABY, Joseph William, Oct 13 1904 Sex:M Child# 1 William Raby Canada & Alice Morin Canada
RABY, Leonide Lea, Nov 4 1902 Sex:F Child# 1 Adelard Raby Canada & Leonide Menard Canada
RABY, Lester Leo, Aug 25 1904 Sex:M Child# 5 Bert Raby New York & Lillian Ouellette New York
RABY, Louise Leda Pearl, Oct 27 1921 Sex:F Child# 6 Adelard Raby Canada & A Maynard Canada
RABY, Lucille, Jun 18 1921 Sex:F Child# 1 Herbert Raby Nashua, NH & Malvina Loraine Nashua, NH
RABY, Lucy Mabel, Feb 24 1920 Sex:F Child# 5 Pliney Raby W Chazy, NY & L Budro W Chazy, NY
RABY, Mabel J, Jul 4 1898 Sex:F Child# 1 Pleney Raby Chazy, NY & Lillian Beaudreau Chazy, NY
RABY, Marie Rose Rita, Sep 10 1920 Sex:F Child# 1 Arthur Raby Canada & Rose Drouin NH
RABY, Mary Lucy, Jul 2 1899 Sex:F Child# 3 Bert Raby Plattsburgh, NY & Lillie Willette Chazy, NY
RABY, Maurice Gerard, Dec 23 1928 Sex:M Child# 4 Herbert Raby Nashua, NH & Malvina Lareine Nashua, NH
RABY, Normand Romeo, Aug 28 1925 Sex:M Child# 3 Herbert Raby Nashua, NH & Malvina Laravie Nashua, NH
RABY, Patricia Jane, Mar 25 1928 Sex:F Child# 2 Claude Raby Nashua, NH & Mary J Salvail Nashua, NH
RABY, Paul Gordon, Jan 19 1915 Sex:M Child# 1 Hilbur F Raby Nashua, NH & Etta M Cobb Townsend, VT

RABY, Priscilla Theresa, Dec 4 1931 Sex:F Child# 3 Herbert Raby Nashua, NH & Melvina Lorraine Nashua, NH
RABY, Rachelle, May 12 1919 Sex:F Child# 5 Adelard Raby Canada & Leonnie Maynard Canada
RABY, Rebecca, Apr 26 1889 Sex:F Child# 2 Robert Raby Plattsburg & Rebecca Valparaiso, IN
RABY, Richard Arthur, Nov 14 1932 Sex:M Child# 1 (No Parents Listed)
RABY, Robert, May 6 1887 Sex:M Child# 1 Robert Raby Plattsburg, NY & Rebecca Beaulieu Indiana
RABY, Robert, Jun 23 1894 Sex:M Child# 1 Charles Raby NY & Marie Levesque Canada
RABY, Rosa Angeline, May 26 1896 Sex:F Child# 3 Charles Raby Plattsburg, NY & Amanda Levesque Canada
RABY, Royal, Mar 28 1902 Sex:M Child# 4 Bert Raby New York & Lillie Ouellette New York
RABY, Ruth, Dec 3 1892 Sex:F Child# 1 Charles Raby NY & Amanda Levesques Canada
RABY, Sylvia, Dec 18 1907 Sex:F Child# 4 William Raby Canada & Alice Morin Canada
RACETTE, Joseph Henri A, Aug 20 1902 Sex:M Child# 2 Walter Racette Canada & Marie Chasse Canada
RACETTE, Joseph Henri W, Mar 22 1904 Sex:M Child# 3 Walter Racette Canada & Marie Chasse Canada
RACETTE, Walter Alfred, Feb 6 1906 Sex:M Child# 4 Walter Racette Canada & Marie Chasse Canada
RACHETTE, Joseph Wilfred O, Nov 14 1900 Sex:M Child# 5 Charles Rachette Canada & Alphon'e Provencher Canada
RACICOT, Hazel Doris, May 10 1926 Sex:F Child# 10 Amedee Racicot Manchester, NH & Annie Kirk Bangor, ME
RACICOT, Lucille Dolores, Jun 14 1924 Sex:F Child# 1 Mederic Racicot Canada & Alice Terrien Canada
RACINE, Blanche, Nov 8 1926 Sex:F Child# 9 Joseph Racine Canada & Emerilda Berube Hooksett, NH
RACINE, Constance Lucille, May 12 1928 Sex:F Child# 3 Joseph Racine Canada & Emerilda Berube Hooksett, NH
RACINE, Joseph Paul Archile, Nov 26 1924 Sex:M Child# 1 Joseph Racine Canada & Emerelda Berube NH
RACINE, Ruth Elizabeth, Sep 28 1922 Sex:F Child# 2 Elroy Racine Hartford, CT & Elizabeth Lucier Nashua, NH
RACINE, Unknown, Oct 15 1921 Sex:F Child# 1 Elroy D Racine Concord, NH & Elizabeth C Lucier Nashua, NH Stillborn
RADFORD, Marion Jean, Oct 23 1920 Sex:F Child# 3 Edward P Radford Oshkosh, WI & Irene McBride New Albany, IN
RADIEWICZ, Michael, Jul 25 1924 Sex:M Child# 1 Adam Radiewicz Poland & A Shouborelka Poland
RADZOKAWICZ, John, May 26 1918 Sex:M Child# 2 Adam Radzokawicz Russia & Frania Grushwka Russia
RAFFERTY, Nora Agnes, Jun 23 1892 Sex:F Child# 4 Michael J Rafferty Ireland & Mary A Skerrit Ireland
RAFFERTY, Norah Agnes, Jul 13 1893 Sex:F Child# 3 Michael Rafferty Ireland & Mary Sperritt Ireland
RAFFERTY, Unknown, Jan 2 1890 Sex:M Child# 2 Michael Rafferty Ireland & Mary Skerrit Ireland
RAGDONOWICH, Stanislas John, May 8 1903 Sex:M Child# 1 John Ragdonowich Russia & Agatha Stanapedis Russia
RAGULES, Elviga, Sep 12 1915 Sex:F Child# 1 Anthony Ragules Russia & Elizabeth Algon Russia
RAICHE, Benjamin Louis, Mar 24 1912 Sex:M Child# 1 Charles Raiche Brighton, MA & Sophie Hanks E Granby, CT
RAICHE, Jos Russell Henry, Mar 14 1933 Sex:M Child# 5 Henry Raiche Canada & Alda Beaulieu Canada
RAINVILLE, Jean Eugene R, Mar 28 1901 Sex:M Child# 3 Jean Rainville Canada & Marie Blanchette NH
RAINVILLE, Marie Eugene, Aug 7 1898 Sex:F Child# 1 Jonny Rainville Nashua, NH & Marie Blanchet Edmondston, NB
RAISKIN, Alice, Jan 16 1904 Sex:F Child# 2 William Raiskin Russia & Helen Kochinsky Russia
RAISKIN, William, Jan 16 1904 Sex:M Child# 1 William Raiskin Russia & Helen Kochinsky Russia
RAJADSKIS, Bronislava, Dec 25 1910 Sex:F Child# 1 Petrus Rajadskis Russia & Petroneli Slolpinate Russia
RAJOTTE, Annie Alice, Sep 13 1933 Sex:F Child# 3 Henri Rajotte Canada & Rose Morin Canada
RAJOTTE, Marie Rose Ida, Jul 28 1928 Sex:F Child# 2 Herve Rajotte Canada & Roseanna Morin Canada
RAJOTTE, Marie Theresa L, Jul 25 1929 Sex:F Child# 2 Hervi Rajotte Canada & Rose Thibault Canada
RALSTON, Herbert Winton, Mar 28 1927 Sex:M Child# 4 Herbert Ralston Boston, MA & Vera Pillsbury Londonderry, NH
RALSTON, John Dix, Apr 5 1921 Sex:M Child# 1 Herbert W Ralston Boston, MA & Vera D Pillsbury Londonderry, NH
RAMANOWSKI, Clement, Nov 2 1924 Sex:M Child# 3 C Ramanowski Poland & L Ramanowski Poland
RAMBT, Woclaw, Mar 31 1915 Sex:M Child# 1 Alexander Rambt Russia & Mary Ojop Russia
RAMEIKA, Julius, Sep 18 1918 Sex:M Child# 1 William Rameika Russia & Rosa Akstin Russia
RAMMER, Harry, Oct 21 1897 Sex:M Child# 1 Isaac Rammer Russia & Ada Goodman Russia
RAMSDELL, Alice Scott, Dec 5 1907 Sex:F Child# 2 Arthur D Ramsdell Peterboro, NH & Alice L McQuesten Litchfield, NH
RAMSDELL, George Allen, Nov 10 1902 Sex:M Child# 1 Arthur D Ramsdell Peterboro, NH & Alice McQuesten Litchfield, NH
RAMSEY, Bettie, Oct 7 1928 Sex:F Child# 1 Harry Ramsey Littleton, NH & Leah Ryan Southington, CT
RAMSTRON, Gertrude Anna, Dec 9 1927 Sex:F Child# 4 Carl Ramstron Sudbury, MA & Grace Smith Nashua, NH
RANAN, James, Nov 2 1889 Sex:M Child# 4 Patrick Ranan Ireland & Magy Kavanaugh Ireland
RANCOUR, Alfred, Oct 27 1897 Sex:M Child# 5 Georges Rancour US & Marie Poulin Canada
RANCOUR, Alfred, Sep 19 1906 Sex:M Child# 1 Amede Rancour Canada & Laudiana Beaulieu Canada
RANCOUR, Frank D C, May 3 1911 Sex:M Child# 4 Frank Rancour Fairfield, ME & Emma Largess Canada
RANCOUR, Joseph Adrien, Jul 28 1907 Sex:M Child# 2 Amedee Rancour Canada & Laudina Beaulieu Canada
RANCOUR, Violina, May 31 1902 Sex:F Child# 3 Frank Rancour Canada & Emma Lagesse Canada
RANCOURT, Alphonse Amedee, Oct 19 1909 Sex:M Child# 4 Amedee Rancourt Canada & Laudiana Beaulieu Canada
RANCOURT, Joseph Albert J B, Dec 22 1910 Sex:M Child# 5 Amedee Rancourt Canada & Laudiana Beaulieu Canada
RANDALL, Albert William, Jun 8 1925 Sex:M Child# 2 Justin Randall Maine & Olive Sprague Maine
RANDALL, Betty Jane, Aug 25 1921 Sex:F Child# 8 Harold M Randall Chester, VT & Edith Hopkins Hudson, NH
RANDALL, Charles Howard, Jan 29 1910 Sex:M Child# 1 Harold M Randall Chester, VT & Edith L Hopkins Hudson, NH
RANDALL, Dorothy Holmes, Jul 27 1932 Sex:F Child# 1 L Alton Randall Nashua, NH & Mary Edna Erb Nashua, NH
RANDALL, Gordon Arthur, Aug 11 1918 Sex:M Child# 6 Harold M Randall Chester, VT & Edith L Hopkins Hudson, NH
RANDALL, Justin H, Nov 11 1923 Sex:M Child# 1 Justin H Randall Milbridge, ME & Olive Sprague Milbridge, ME
RANDALL, Leroy Alton, Jun 22 1902 Sex:M Child# 4 Alton W Randall Harrington, ME & Grace M Farnsworth Columbia
RANDALL, Norma, May 28 1908 Sex:F Child# 6 Alton W Randall Harrington, ME & Grace M Farnsworth Milbridge, ME
RANDALL, Percy L, Jan 14 1891 Sex:M Child# 3 M L Randall NH & Ida Day VT
RANDALL, Phyllis Elaine, Feb 22 1913 Sex:F Child# 3 Harold M Randall Chester, VT & Edith L Hopkins Hudson, NH
RANDALL, Richard Stuart, Apr 20 1920 Sex:M Child# 7 Harold M Randall Chester, VT & Edith L Hopkins Hudson, NH
RANDALL, Unknown, Aug 14 1903 Sex:M Child# 5 Alton W Randall Harrington, ME & Grace Farnsworth Milbridge, ME
RANDANIE, Mary, Apr 23 1904 Sex:F Child# 1 Felix Randanie Russia & Walerka Kasrecutic Russia
RANDELL, Dorothy Abbie, Aug 22 1911 Sex:F Child# 7 A W Randell Maine & Grace Farnsworth Maine
RANNEY, Unknown, Jul 7 1895 Sex:F Child# 1 H K Ranney
RAPCES, Henry, Nov 3 1920 Sex:M Child# 5 Stanley Rapces Poland Russia & Karolinor Austria

RAPSES, Stanley Charles, Aug 1 1914 Sex:M Child# 2 Stanley Rapses Russia & Jennie Szlastas Russia
RAPSESS, Bronka, Dec 1 1911 Sex:F Child# 1 Stanley Rapsess Russia & Jennie Szlashta Russia
RAPSIS, Alec John, Jun 26 1916 Sex:M Child# 3 Stanley Rapsis Russia & Jennie Szlasta Russia
RASH, Marie Rose B, Feb 26 1907 Sex:F Child# 1 Nelson Rash Vermont & Rose A Labonne Conn
RASINAWICZ, Joseph, Mar 31 1917 Sex:M Child# 1 Antonio Rasinawicz Russia & Julia Vaskilawiczte Russia
RASKIEWICZ, Edward, Sep 24 1932 Sex:M Child# 2 Z Raskiewicz Fall River, MA & W Barnatowick Poland
RASKIEWICZ, Ruth, Jan 30 1935 Sex:F Child# 3 Zygm Raskiewicz Fall River, MA & W Barnatowich Lithuania
RASKIEWICZ, Zygmunt, Aug 20 1930 Sex:M Child# 1 Zygmunt Raskiewicz Fall River, MA & Wilmena Barnatowich Europe
RASMISLAWICZ, Stanislaw, Jul 5 1918 Sex:M Child# 2 Adam Rasmislawicz Russia & Keda Gourka Austria
RASMOVICH, Peter Paul, Jan 24 1927 Sex:M Child# 5 A Rasmovich Lithuania & Julia Wescalavich Lithuania
RASMOWICH, Anthony Peter, Apr 21 1918 Sex:M Child# 2 Anthony Rasmowich Russia & Julia Waskilowich Russia
RASMUSSEN, Charles Albert, Mar 15 1921 Sex:M Child# 7 Charles Rasmussen Denmark & Effie B Wright Rhode Island
RASZYMOVICH, John Stanley, Mar 8 1920 Sex:M Child# 3 Anthony Raszymovich Lithuania & Julia Wiscylavic Lithuania
RATHAWICZ, Sophia, Oct 22 1916 Sex:F Child# 1 Joseph Rathawicz Russia & Helena Varsotska Russia
RATHENBERG, Elizabeth, May 19 1919 Sex:F Child# 2 Jacob J Rathenberg Worcester, MA & Dora Simon Amsterdam, NY
RATKEVITCH, Unknown, Apr 3 1908 Sex:F Child# 1 Simon Ratkevitch Russia & Alberta Yakzzis Russia
RATKEVITCH, Unknown, Jun 29 1910 Sex:M Child# 2 Simon Ratkevitch Russia & Alberta Yakzzie Russia
RATKEWICZ, John, Apr 7 1912 Sex:M Child# 3 Simon Ratkewicz Russia & Alberta Jakzie Russia
RATKIEWICZ, Joseph, Sep 11 1921 Sex:M Child# 4 Joseph Ratkiewicz Poland & Helen Varsotska Poland
RATKIEWICZ, Vanda, Dec 18 1917 Sex:F Child# 2 Jos Ratkiewicz Russia & Helen Varvowski Russia
RATKIEWICZ, Zenona, Nov 27 1929 Sex:M Child# 9 Joseph Ratkiewicz Poland & Helen Varsotska Poland
RATOF, John M, Jun 5 1926 Sex:M Child# 12 Joseph Ratof Russia & J Standivich Lithuania
RATOF, Robert, Jul 12 1924 Sex:M Child# 11 John Ratof Poland & Jose Stenerits Poland
RATOFF, Annie, Dec 19 1920 Sex:F Child# 7 John Ratoff Poland & Josephine Stanewicz Poland
RATOFF, Felix, Apr 13 1915 Sex:M Child# 4 John Ratoff Russia & Zosia Ratoff Russia
RATOFF, Josie, Oct 9 1919 Sex:F Child# 9 Thomas Ratoff Poland & Josie Ratoff Poland
RATOUT, Agnes, Jan 7 1917 Sex:F Child# 7 John Ratout Russia & Josephine Stanawich Russia
RATTE, Alma, Oct 21 1894 Sex:F Child# 4 Henri Ratte Canada & Josephine Pellerin Canada
RATTE, Edna, Feb 17 1902 Sex:F Child# 3 Peter Ratte Canada & Nellie D Holden Lowell, MA
RATTE, Joseph Henri, May 3 1896 Sex:M Child# 5 Henri Ratte Canada & Josephine Pelerin Canada
RATTEY, Ernest Henry Albert, Jan 13 1916 Sex:M Child# 2 Henry Joseph Rattey Nashua, NH & Annie Reardon Nashua, NH
RATZBURG, Gladys Irene, Oct 28 1909 Sex:F Child# 3 Victor Ratzburg Texas & Victoria Davis N Dakota
RATZBURG, Lucille Arldeen, Feb 2 1907 Sex:F Child# 1 Victor P Ratzburg Dallas, TX & Victoria Davis Fargo, ND
RATZBURG, Paul Davis, Mar 6 1908 Sex:M Child# 2 Victor Ratzburg Texas & Victoria Davis North Dakota
RAUDONIS, Agnes, Nov 22 1920 Sex:F Child# 12 William Raudonis Lithuania Russia & Agnes Romacatie Lithuania Russia
RAUDONIS, William, Apr 1 1914 Sex:M Child# 8 William Raudonis Russia & Margaret Pamekatis Russia
RAUSKOLB, Ilse Joyce, Mar 27 1932 Sex:F Child# 1 F W Rauskolb Somerville, MA & Mildred G Clarke Somerville, MA
RAUSKOLB, Linda Isabelle, Jan 28 1934 Sex:F Child# 2 Fred W Rauskolb Somerville, MA & Mildred Clarke Somerville, MA
RAVENELL, Ravul, Feb 13 1892 Sex:M Child# 4 Irenee Ravenell Canada & Adelaide Richard Canada
RAVENELLE, Albert Leo, Dec 21 1924 Sex:M Child# 2 Irene D Ravenelle Nashua, NH & Antoinette Burque Nashua, NH
RAVENELLE, Alice Gicette, May 26 1906 Sex:F Child# 4 Theodore Ravenelle Canada & Leonie Beauregard Canada
RAVENELLE, Armand Horace, Aug 14 1908 Sex:M Child# 5 T O Ravenelle Canada & Theodosie Beauregard Canada
RAVENELLE, Clair Gloria, Jun 6 1924 Sex:F Child# 2 Raoul Ravenelle Nashua, NH & Rachael Leblanc Manchester, NH
RAVENELLE, Cornelie Theresa, Oct 6 1900 Sex:F Child# 1 T O Ravenelle Canada & T Beauregard Canada
RAVENELLE, Cozette Adele, Mar 5 1925 Sex:F Child# 3 George E Ravenelle Nashua, NH & Win C Gauthier Newport, VT
RAVENELLE, Denise Adelaide, Apr 11 1922 Sex:F Child# 2 George E Ravenelle Nashua, NH & Winnifred C Gauthier Newport
RAVENELLE, Eloise Adelle, Aug 5 1926 Sex:F Child# 1 Norbert Ravenelle Nashua, NH & Phoebe Messier Nashua, NH
RAVENELLE, George Emile, Feb 22 1897 Sex:M Child# 1 Irene Ravenelle Canada & Adelaide Richard Canada
RAVENELLE, Irence D, Sep 19 1887 Sex:M Child#  Irence Ravenelle Canada & Adelaide Richard P Q
RAVENELLE, Irene Blanche, Sep 11 1922 Sex:F Child# 1 Luc Ravenelle US & Blanche Boisvert US
RAVENELLE, Jean B L, Aug 18 1895 Sex:M Child# 6 Irence Ravenelle Canada & Adelaide Richard Canada
RAVENELLE, Jeanne Rebecca, Nov 25 1900 Sex:F Child# 9 Irence Ravenelle Canada & Adelaide Richard Canada
RAVENELLE, L M C, Dec 21 1922 Sex:F Child# 1 Irenee D Ravenelle Nashua, NH & Antoinette M Burque Nashua, NH
RAVENELLE, Laura Emma, Oct 14 1889 Sex:F Child# 3 Irence Ravenelle Canada & Adelaide Richard Canada
RAVENELLE, Leo Theodore, Apr 4 1893 Sex:M Child# 5 Irence Ravenelle Canada & Adelaide Richard Canada
RAVENELLE, Lucille Juliette, Jun 4 1922 Sex:F Child# 1 Raoul Ravenelle Nashua, NH & Rachael Leblanc Manchester, NH
RAVENELLE, Luke Paul, May 18 1924 Sex:M Child# 2 Luke Ravenelle Nashua, NH & Blanche Boisvert Nashua, NH
RAVENELLE, Marie Theresa, Jun 25 1926 Sex:F Child# 3 Luke Ravenelle Nashua, NH & Blanche Boisvert Nashua, NH
RAVENELLE, Maurice Edgar, May 27 1931 Sex:M Child# 5 Luc Ravenelle Nashua, NH & Blanche Boisvert Nashua, NH
RAVENELLE, Norbert Antonio, Jun 12 1902 Sex:M Child# 2 Theodore Ravenelle Canada & L Beauregard Canada
RAVENELLE, Paul Hector, Jul 11 1898 Sex:M Child# 8 Irenee Ravenelle Canada & Adelaide Richard Canada
RAVENELLE, Paula Rachelle, Aug 10 1902 Sex:F Child# 10 Irene Ravenelle Canada & Adelaide Richard Canada
RAVENELLE, Paula Solange, Aug 9 1913 Sex:F Child# 6 Theodore Ravenelle Canada & Theodosie Beauregard Canada
RAVENELLE, Richard Wilfred, Jan 27 1930 Sex:M Child# 4 Luc Ravenelle Nashua, NH & Blanche Boisvert Nashua, NH
RAVENELLE, Rita Annette, Apr 1 1930 Sex:F Child# 4 George E Ravenelle Nashua, NH & Winnifred C Gauthier Newport
RAVENELLE, Roland Girard, Apr 3 1926 Sex:M Child# 3 D D Ravenelle Nashua, NH & Marie A Burque Nashua, NH
RAVENELLE, Toussaint R, Apr 21 1904 Sex:M Child# 3 J Theo Ravenelle Canada & Theod'sie Beauregard Canada
RAVENELLE, Unknown, Mar 27 1921 Sex:F Child# 1 George E Ravenelle Nashua, NH & Winnifred C Gauthier Newport, VT
RAVENELLE, Unknown, Oct 19 1928 Sex:M Child# 3 Raoul Ravenelle Nashua, NH & Rachel Leblanc Manchester, NH Stillborn
RAWILSON, Geraldine Dorothy, Mar 19 1921 Sex:F Child# 1 Herbert M Rawilson Hudson, NH & Margaret T O'Brien Nashua
RAY, Frederic, Sep 11 1918 Sex:M Child# 8 Seward W Ray Hyde Park, MA & Cora Knapp W Fitchburg, MA
RAYMOND, Antoine Camile, Aug 9 1927 Sex:M Child# 2 Antoine Raymond Canada & Irene Pinette Canada
RAYMOND, Arthur, Oct 28 1928 Sex:M Child# 3 A Raymond Canada & Irene Pinette Canada

RAYMOND, Arthur Gerard, Mar 26 1933 Sex:M Child# 7 A Raymond Canada & Irene Pinette Canada
RAYMOND, Charles Marcel Frank, Jan 8 1934 Sex:M Child# 8 Joseph A Raymond Canada & Alphonsine Tanguay Canada
RAYMOND, Colette Muriel, Aug 2 1934 Sex:F Child# 1 Honore Raymond Salem, MA & Lillian Allie Nashua, NH
RAYMOND, Ernest Morris, Sep 22 1934 Sex:M Child# 2 Morris Raymond Barre, VT & Florence Bernier Manchester, NH
RAYMOND, Ernest Wilfred, Aug 21 1932 Sex:M Child# 6 Tracey Raymond Goffstown, NH & Hilda French Amherst, NH
RAYMOND, Eva May, Oct 18 1927 Sex:F Child# 2 Tracy Raymond Goffstown, NH & Hilda French Amherst, NH
RAYMOND, Francis Xavier, Aug 11 1926 Sex:M Child# 1 Lucien Raymond Canada & Maria Duperre Canada
RAYMOND, George Francis, Feb 28 1916 Sex:M Child# 3 Elmer Raymond NH & Mabel Butterick Wilton, NH
RAYMOND, Gertrude Rita, Mar 18 1931 Sex:F Child# 5 Antoine Raymond Canada & Irene Pinette Canada
RAYMOND, Glenton Alice, Sep 15 1924 Sex:M Child# 3 John G Raymond Winchester, NH & Judith Wildes Nelson, NH
RAYMOND, Gordon Francis, Apr 10 1914 Sex:M Child# 1 John G Raymond NH & Julia F Wildes NH
RAYMOND, Guy Tracy, Oct 22 1926 Sex:M Child# 1 Tracy Raymond Goffstown, NH & Hilda French Amherst, NH
RAYMOND, Irene Florence, Aug 14 1926 Sex:F Child# 1 Antoine Raymond Canada & Irene Pinette Canada
RAYMOND, Jos Fernard A, Jan 8 1930 Sex:M Child# 4 Antoine Raymond Canada & Irene Pinette Canada
RAYMOND, Jos Leo Eustache, Oct 30 1920 Sex:M Child# 1 Eustache Raymond Canada & Leda Dionne NH
RAYMOND, Jos Roland Raymond, Aug 23 1932 Sex:M Child# 7 Alph Raymond Canada & A Tanguay Canada
RAYMOND, Joseph Amand, Apr 2 1925 Sex:M Child# 1 Cyric Raymond Canada & Rose Rioux Nashua, NH
RAYMOND, Joseph Arm L, Jul 2 1905 Sex:M Child# 2 Joseph Raymond Canada & Alma Brunelle Canada
RAYMOND, Kathleen Jean, Jan 4 1932 Sex:F Child# 1 E M Raymond Barre, VT & F May Bernier Manchester, NH
RAYMOND, Lewis Irving, Sep 1 1928 Sex:M Child# 3 Tracy Raymond Goffstown, NH & Hilda French Amherst, NH
RAYMOND, Louis Philip Francis, Aug 22 1925 Sex:M Child# 1 Louis J Raymond Canada & Aurore Tardiff Canada
RAYMOND, Lucille, Mar 27 1918 Sex:F Child# 1 Alphonse Raymond Canada & Alphonsene Tanguay Canada
RAYMOND, Lucille Pauline, Sep 19 1934 Sex:F Child# 7 Antoine Raymond Canada & Irene Pinette Canada
RAYMOND, M Cecile Leda, Nov 8 1921 Sex:F Child# 2 Eustache Raymond Canada & Lena Dionne NH
RAYMOND, M Dora Alice, Oct 4 1914 Sex:F Child# 7 Joseph G Raymond Canada & Rose Pelletier Canada
RAYMOND, Marcel, Jun 15 1925 Sex:M Child# 2 Paul Raymond Canada & Amanda Raymond Canada
RAYMOND, Marie Irene, Mar 5 1923 Sex:F Child# 6 Isidore Raymond Canada & Marguerite Van Ness Mass
RAYMOND, Marie M J'Arc, May 29 1930 Sex:F Child# 2 Lucien Raymond Canada & Marie D Dupere Canada
RAYMOND, Marie M P, Mar 16 1930 Sex:F Child# 2 Louis Raymond Canada & Aurore Tardif Canada
RAYMOND, Marie Rose Elmire, Feb 9 1919 Sex:F Child# 2 Pierre Raymond Canada & Mat Archambeault Canada
RAYMOND, Marjorie Florence, Aug 7 1921 Sex:F Child# 2 John G Raymond Winchester, NH & Julia Wildes Nelson, NH
RAYMOND, Maurice Etienne, Dec 3 1925 Sex:M Child# 1 Joseph Raymond Canada & Marie L Lavoie Canada
RAYMOND, Pauline Elizabeth, Nov 28 1932 Sex:F Child# 2 Walter Raymond Lawrence, MA & Eliz Ermolovitch Nashua, NH
RAYMOND, Peary Elmer, May 12 1911 Sex:M Child# 1 Elmer Raymond NH & Mabel Buttrick NH
RAYMOND, Roland, Oct 4 1931 Sex:F Child# 5 Alphonse Raymond Canada & Alphonsine Tanguay Nashua, NH
RAYMOND, Unknown, Jan 26 1921 Sex:F Child# 2 Joseph A Raymond Canada & Alphonsine Tanguay Canada
RAYMOND, Unknown, Sep 2 1923 Sex:M Child# 3 Alphonse Raymond Canada & Alphonsine Tanguay Canada
RAYMOND, Unknown, Dec 13 1929 Sex:M Child# 4 Tracy I Raymond Goffstown, NH & Hilda French Amherst, NH
RAYMOND, Unknown, Jul 11 1930 Sex:M Child# 5 Alphonse Raymond Canada & Alphonsine Tanguay Canada
RAYNOLDS, Henry Ernest, Aug 10 1889 Sex:M Child# 5 William Raynolds Manchester, NH & Anna Lamb Canada
RAYOTTE, Alice, Dec 9 1896 Sex:F Child# 6 Pierre Rayotte Canada & Marie Cardin Canada
RAYOTTE, Arthue E, Jul 22 1904 Sex:M Child# 9 Pierre Rayotte Canada & Marie Cardin Canada Stillborn
RAYOTTE, Eva, Dec 9 1896 Sex:F Child# 6 Pierre Rayotte Canada & Marie Cardin Canada
RAZEKIEWICZ, John, Apr 11 1920 Sex:M Child# 2 Joe Razekiewicz Russia & Christina Trapelioz Russia
RAZKIENWICZ, Seraphina, Aug 9 1917 Sex:F Child# 1 Jos Razkienwicz Russia & Christina Psapeliez Russia
RAZOVITCH, Theophilus, Oct 10 1907 Sex:M Child# 1 Nicoden Razovitch Russia & Antonia Grantuski Russia
RAZZAVITCH, Joseph Rogers, Jun 27 1914 Sex:M Child# 2 Michael Razzavitch Russia & Antonia Bolavitch Russia
READ, Anna Gardner, Sep 21 1901 Sex:M Child# 7 Sheridan P Read Paril, IL & Anna G Noyes Clinton, Iowa
READ, Barbara Ann, Feb 25 1934 Sex:F Child# 1 Clayton Alfred Read Reeds Ferry, NH & Priscilla Clyde Hudson, NH
READ, Edward Ernest Joseph, Jul 8 1932 Sex:M Child# 3 A E Read Merrimack, NH & Rosilda Lefebvre Nashua, NH
READ, Georgete Ida, Sep 13 1928 Sex:F Child# 1 Albert E Read Merrimack, NH & Rosilva Lefebvre Nashua, NH
READ, Lewis Franklin, Mar 14 1906 Sex:M Child# 1 Clayton F Read Reeds Ferry, NH & Annie N Porter Plattsburg, NY
READ, Margaret Holyoke, May 31 1930 Sex:F Child# 1 George H Read Malden, MA & Marion Brigham St Albans, VT
READ, Unknown, Jan 16 1893 Sex:M Child# 2 A W Read England & Annie McKay Scotland
READ, Unknown, Dec 30 1894 Sex:F Child# 1 Stanley Read Russia & Mary Young Germany
READ, Walter Albert, Feb 22 1930 Sex:M Child# 2 Albert E Read Merrimack, NH & Rosilda Lefebvre Nashua, NH
REAGER, Gordon Nathan, Jan 12 1908 Sex:M Child# 3 Nathan J Reager New York, NY & Sadie J Coote Wilbraham, MA
REARDON, Albert Joseph, Mar 31 1905 Sex:M Child# 6 Timothy Reardon Ireland & Josephine Diggins Ireland
REARDON, Albert Raymond J, Nov 22 1924 Sex:M Child# 1 Albert Reardon Nashua, NH & Alice Gamache Nashua, NH
REARDON, Dan Francis, Feb 16 1901 Sex:M Child# 4 Timothy Reardon Ireland & Johanna Diggins Ireland
REARDON, Daniel Joseph, May 28 1906 Sex:M Child# 3 Daniel Reardon Ireland & Margaret Diggins Ireland
REARDON, Esther, Aug 28 1899 Sex:F Child# 3 Tim Reardon Ireland & Johannah Higgins Ireland
REARDON, Jeanette Theresa, Jun 20 1931 Sex:F Child# 5 Albert Reardon Nashua, NH & Alice Gamache Nashua, NH
REARDON, John Paul, Sep 10 1909 Sex:M Child# 4 Daniel D Reardon Ireland & Margaret Diggins Ireland
REARDON, Margaret Lillian, Apr 10 1903 Sex:F Child# 2 Daniel Reardon Ireland & Margaret Diggins Ireland
REARDON, Margaret M, Mar 3 1907 Sex:F Child# 7 Timothy Reardon Ireland & Josephine Diggins Ireland
REARDON, Marjorie, Aug 24 1925 Sex:F Child# 1 Daniel Reardon Nashua, NH & Yvonne Mailloux Newport, VT
REARDON, Mary A, Apr 24 1913 Sex:F Child# 6 Daniel Reardon Ireland & Margaret Diggins Ireland
REARDON, Phyllis Yvonne, Nov 21 1926 Sex:F Child# 2 Daniel Reardon Nashua, NH & Yvonne Mailloux Newport, VT
REARDON, Thelma Marguerite, Sep 26 1928 Sex:F Child# 2 Albert Reardon Nashua, NH & Alice Gamache Nashua, NH
REARDON, Thomas Francis, Aug 12 1906 Sex:M Child# 2 Daniel Reardon Ireland & Margaret Diggins Ireland
REARDON, Thomas Robert, May 24 1933 Sex:M Child# 2 Thomas Reardon Nashua, NH & Anita Pelletier Canada
RECARD, Paul Ernest, Sep 13 1926 Sex:M Child# 2 Adelard Recard

RECARD, Unknown, Feb 15 1930 Sex:M Child# 6 Ralph Recard Nashua, NH & Madeleine Lafont France Stillborn
RECOR, Velma, Sep 26 1914 Sex:F Child# 1 Joseph C Recor Chazy, NY & Lucy M Haskins Nashua, NH Stillborn
RECORD, Constance, Sep 9 1931 Sex:F Child# Edgar Record Nashua, NH & June Flanagan Lowell, MA
RECORD, Estelle, Sep 30 1929 Sex:F Child# 8 Edgar Record Nashua, NH & Jane Flanagan Lowell, MA
RECORD, Judith, Jun 10 1934 Sex:F Child# 1 Louis Record Antrim, NH & Eva Wakely Lisbon Falls, ME
RECORD, June, Nov 10 1924 Sex:F Child# 5 Edgar J Record Hudson, NH & Jane Flanagan Lowell, MA
RECORD, Patricia, Aug 1 1928 Sex:F Child# 7 Edgar Record Nashua, NH & Jane Flanagan Lowell, MA
RECORD, Yolande Estelle Anna, Jan 5 1925 Sex:F Child# 4 Ralph Record Nashua, NH & Madeline Lapoint France
REDMOND, Almon John, Mar 6 1919 Sex:M Child# 2 Thomas H Redmond Jersey City, NJ & Alice Cross Westfield, VT
REDMOND, Harry Andrew, Jan 27 1918 Sex:M Child# 1 Thomas H Redmond Jersey City, NJ & Alice Cross Westfield, VT
REDMOND, William, Apr 19 1895 Sex:M Child# 2 John Redmond Poland & Aimee Pelletier Nashua, NH
REDMUND, Alfred Leroy, Oct 12 1889 Sex:M Child# 1 William S Redmund Maine & Mary Jane West Brooklyn, NY
REDMUND, Marie, Feb 27 1894 Sex:F Child# 1 John Redmund Europe & Aimee Pelletier NY
REED, Birnice Patria, Dec 5 1916 Sex:F Child# 1 George Reed Wilton, NH & Chloe Maloney Saranac Lake, NY
REED, Charles Edward, Nov 3 1894 Sex:M Child# 1 Ora J Reed Claremont, NH & Maggie Black Winooski, VT
REED, Charline Pearl, Oct 5 1921 Sex:F Child# 2 Charles A Reed Mason, NH & Pearl Sanders Canaan, NH
REED, Charlotte Mary, Feb 24 1892 Sex:F Child# 3 Charles F Reed Alton, NH & Dora Manning Franklin Falls, NH
REED, Donald, Apr 7 1890 Sex:M Child# 1 E R Reed Canada & Mary Stalker Canada
REED, Fred, Dec 4 1891 Sex:M Child# 1 A W Reed England & Annie McRay Mass
REED, Gertrude Lillian, Oct 31 1916 Sex:F Child# 1 Charles A Reed Mason, NH & Pearl A Saunders W Canaan, NH
REED, Grace, Apr 1 1916 Sex:F Child# 2 Wilfrid Reed Canada & Anna Walker Scotland
REED, Harold Ernest, Sep 23 1914 Sex:M Child# 1 Fred L Reed Nashua, NH & Bertha Lawrence E Pepperell, MA
REED, Harriet Lila S, Oct 30 1900 Sex:F Child# 1 D S Reed Thorntons Ferry, NH & Caroline Stevens Vermont
REED, Helen, May 5 1901 Sex:f Child# 4 Stanley Reed NB & Lena Houitt NB
REED, Helen Eldora, Feb 27 1916 Sex:F Child# 1 George Dustin Reed Nashua, NH & Stella Irene King Hudson Falls,
REED, John Augustus, Mar 31 1929 Sex:M Child# 1 Mendall A Reed Tyngsboro, MA & Mary Delia Bradley Pond, NY
REED, Louis Franklin, Jr, Sep 20 1925 Sex:M Child# 1 Louis F Reed Nashua, NH & Mildred Forrence Nashua, NH
REED, Lurietta, Aug 12 1910 Sex:F Child# 1 Edward Reed Providence, RI & Cora Newman NH
REED, Lydia Rebecca, Sep 11 1916 Sex:F Child# 2 Fred L Reed Nashua, NH & Bertha Lawrence E Pepperell, MA
REED, Margaret Mary, Oct 7 1918 Sex:F Child# 1 Arthur G Reed Nashua, NH & Ellen M Fitzgerald Manchester, NH
REED, Morton, Mar 6 1915 Sex:M Child# 1 Norton H Reed Somerville, MA & Beryl T Turner Quincy, MA
REED, Robert Arthur, Dec 5 1927 Sex:M Child# 2 Lewis F Reed Nashua, NH & M I Forrence Nashua, NH
REED, Ruth Elizabeth, Oct 5 1919 Sex:F Child# 5 Ernest A Reed Reeds Ferry, NH & Grace Lindsay Hancock, NH
REED, Unknown, Feb 22 1888 Sex:F Child# 1 John R Reed Mass & Lizzie Reed Mass
REED, Unknown, Oct 24 1893 Sex:F Child# 2 Burton I Reed Portsmouth, NH & Alice Thurston Dexter, ME
REED, Unknown, Mar 11 1916 Sex:M Child# 2 Morton Hol Reed Somerville, MA & B Thelma Turner Quincy, MA
REEF, Lester Edward, Aug 28 1920 Sex:M Child# 7 Fred H Reef Germany & Anna Walter Philadelphia, PA
REES, Raymond William, Jul 6 1909 Sex:M Child# 3 Lucian W Rees Liverpool, NS & Catherine Nicholson PEI
REES, Unknown, Nov 15 1910 Sex:M Child# 4 Lucian Rees Liverpool, NS & Catherine Nicholson Prince Edward Island
REES, Unknown, Oct 26 1912 Sex:F Child# 1 John Robert Rees Liverpool, NS & Nira Bethana Davis Nashua, NH
REES, Velma Catherine, Sep 19 1912 Sex:F Child# 5 Lucien W Rees Nova Scotia & Catherine Nicholson PEI
REESE, Thelma, Sep 30 1902 Sex:F Child# W L Reese Nova Scotia & Cath Nicholson Prince Edward Island
REGIS, David, Nov 2 1893 Sex:M Child# 2 Joseph Regis Canada & Josephine Goyette Canada
REGIS, Marie Laura, Apr 5 1895 Sex:F Child# 3 Joseph Regis Canada & Josephine Goyet Nashua, NH
REICH, Arlene, Sep 6 1925 Sex:F Child# 2 William Reich New York, NY & June Markey Lawrence, MA
REICHARD, Claire Flavia, Jun 26 1933 Sex:F Child# 1 John M Reichard Allentown, PA & Lillian Reardon Nashua, NH
REICHARD, John Mohr, Nov 28 1934 Sex:M Child# 2 John M Reichard Allentown, PA & Lillian Reardon Nashua, NH
REID, Patricia, Jul 1 1923 Sex:F Child# 1 Sylvester A Reid Litchfield, NH & Dorothy Barlow Manchester, NH
REID, Unknown, Apr 19 1901 Sex:F Child# 1 Elijah N Reid Nova Scotia & Lornid Leopold Nova Scotia
REIHER, Carolina, Oct 7 1921 Sex:F Child# 1 Laurence Reiher Boston, MA & Emily Stewart Suncook, NH
REILLEY, Richard, Oct 24 1906 Sex:M Child# 10 Peter L Reilley Nashua, NH & Mary E Coffey Nashua, NH
REILLY, John, Apr 27 1892 Sex:M Child# 10 John Reilly Ireland & Margaret Degnan Ireland
REILLY, Joseph, Apr 27 1892 Sex:M Child# 9 John Reilly Ireland & Margaret Degnan Ireland
REILLY, Peter Leo, Jan 21 1892 Sex:M Child# 3 Peter Reilly Nashua, NH & Mary Coffey Nashua, NH
REILLY, Philip McClellan, Oct 6 1922 Sex:M Child# 3 Charles E Reilly
REINDEAU, Alfred, Mar 2 1891 Sex:M Child# 1 Alfred Reindeau Nashua, NH & Cordelia Richard Nashua, NH
REISE, Unknown, May 13 1897 Sex:M Child# John Reise Russia & Ausuilla Qatsclie Russia Stillborn
RELATION, Everett Louis, Aug 6 1918 Sex:M Child# 7 Francis E Relation New York & Cora Pelkey New York
RELATION, Francis Earl, Mar 24 1905 Sex:M Child# 2 Francis Relation New York & Cora Peltier New York
RELATION, William Harold, Aug 31 1903 Sex:M Child# 1 Francis Relation New York & Cora D Pelkey New York
RELLAS, Christos D, Mar 18 1922 Sex:M Child# 1 James Rellas Greece & Athena Menda Greece
RELLAS, Shirmo, Feb 6 1923 Sex:F Child# 2 James Rellas Greece & Athena Minton Greece
REMILLARD, Eileen Marie, Aug 30 1922 Sex:F Child# 3 Ernest Remillard St Albans, VT & Helen Hughes Vermont
REMILLARD, Ernest Joseph, Apr 29 1921 Sex:M Child# 2 Ernest Remillard Vermont & Helen Hughes Vermont
REMILLARD, Lorraine May, Jul 11 1928 Sex:F Child# 4 J W Remillard Vermont & Delia Canton Canada
REMILLARD, Roland Ovilla, Aug 6 1929 Sex:M Child# 5 Joseph Remillard Vermont & Delia Canton Canada
RENAND, Joseph, Jan 22 1896 Sex:M Child# 5 Jean Bte Renand
RENARD, Theresa M Yvonne, Apr 23 1931 Sex:F Child# 1 (No Parents Listed)
RENAUD, Albert, Aug 21 1890 Sex:M Child# 8 Joseph Renaud Canada & Delia Marion Canada
RENAUD, Arthur Ralph R, Feb 6 1907 Sex:M Child# 2 George Renaud Canada & Delia Jette Canada
RENAUD, Bernadette Marie R, Aug 28 1928 Sex:F Child# 4 Edward Renaud Canada & R Chouinard Canada
RENAUD, Clara Germaine J, Mar 20 1909 Sex:F Child# 4 George Renaud Canada & Delia Jette Canada
RENAUD, Hormidas T, Mar 1 1894 Sex:M Child# 11 Joseph Renaud Canada & Delia Marion Canada

RENAUD, Lena Marie, Nov 5 1902 Sex:F Child# 3 Joseph Renaud Canada & Adele Cote Canada
RENAUD, Leo, Mar 30 1901 Sex:M Child# 2 Joseph Renaud Canada & Adele Cote Canada
RENAUD, Lorraine Ellen, May 9 1924 Sex:F Child# 1 Arthur Renaud Nashua, NH & Ruth Patridge Manchester, NH
RENAUD, Lucile Irene Leona, Jul 14 1914 Sex:F Child# 6 Georges Renaud Canada & Delia Jette Canada
RENAUD, Marie, Feb 1 1908 Sex:F Child# 3 George Renaud Canada & Delia Jette Canada
RENAUD, Marie Camille, Feb 2 1918 Sex:F Child# 8 George Renaud Canada & Delia Jette Canada Stillborn
RENAUD, Marie Emma, Mar 7 1893 Sex:F Child# 4 Jean B Renaud Canada & Marguerite Chartier Canada
RENAUD, Maurice Ernest, Mar 21 1916 Sex:M Child# 7 Joseph Renaud Canada & Delia Jette Canada
RENAUD, Robert Raymond, Jul 31 1911 Sex:M Child# 5 George Renaud Canada & Delia Jette Canada
RENAUD, Romeo, Aug 29 1905 Sex:M Child# 1 George Renaud Canada & Delia Jette Canada
RENAUD, Violet Marg Aurore, Nov 7 1919 Sex:F Child# 1 Henry Renaud Lawrence, MA & Emma Renaud Nashua, NH
RENEAUD, Eugenie, Nov 17 1891 Sex:F Child# 9 Joseph Reneaud Canada & Delia Marion Canada
RENEAUD, Joseph, Jun 18 1887 Sex:M Child# 6 Joseph Reneaud P Q & Delia Marion P Q
RENEAUD, Joseph, Jan 31 1893 Sex:M Child# 10 Joseph Reneaud Canada & Delia Marion Canada
RENEAUD, Pierre, Jul 22 1889 Sex:M Child# 7 Joseph Reneaud Canada & Delia Marion Canada
RENEAUD, Raymond, Jun 9 1895 Sex:M Child# 12 Joseph Reneaud Canada & Delia Marion Canada
RENKER, Elsie Dorothy, Sep 14 1931 Sex:F Child# 2 Jacob Renker Frankfort, Germany & Dora Busch Frankfort, Germany
RENNIE, Gretchen J, Oct 14 1929 Sex:F Child# 5 Grandison L Rennie Mass & Isabelle DesRochers Canada
RENO, Moise, Apr 28 1893 Sex:M Child# 7 Magloire Reno Nashua, NH & Marie Bouchard Canada
RENO, Ruby Leah, Sep 7 1887 Sex:F Child# 4 Peter Reno Canada & Emma Stiles Greenfield
RENOUD, Willie, Jun 2 1899 Sex:M Child# 1 Joseph Renoud Canada & Adele Cote Canada
RENSHAW, Blanche May, Dec 24 1931 Sex:F Child# 1 Alvah Renshaw Somerville, MA & Meriam Gilman Rehoboth, MA
RENSHAW, David Arthur R, Dec 17 1924 Sex:M Child# 1 Alvah G Renshaw Somerville, MA & Helen M Wallace Hanover, NH
RENSHAW, Nancy Virginia, Mar 29 1929 Sex:F Child# 3 Alvah G Renshaw Somerville, MA & Helen M Wallace Hanover, NH
RENSHAW, Robert Stuart, Jun 23 1926 Sex:M Child# 2 Alvah Renshaw Mass & Helen Wallace Hanover, NH
RENTOUNIS, Christina, Dec 30 1916 Sex:F Child# 1 Michael Rentounis Greece & Mary Karvela Greece
RENTOUNIS, Unknown, Dec 1 1917 Sex:F Child# 2 Michael Rentounis Greece & Mary J Karvella Greece
REPESKA, Jules, Apr 27 1904 Sex:M Child# 1 John Repeska Poland & Helena Borotck Poland
REUTOUMI, Christina, Dec 22 1916 Sex:F Child# 2 Dimitris Reutoumi Greece & Mary Karbela Greece
REVERE, Priscilla Marie, Jan 24 1930 Sex:F Child# 1 Paul Revere NH & Beatrice Berube Lyndonville, VT
REVOIR, Albert Edgar, Jul 24 1904 Sex:M Child# 1 Charles Revoir Vermont & Sophia Minor Vermont
REVOIR, Charles Albert, May 12 1906 Sex:M Child# 2 Charles Revoir Vermont & Sophia Minor Vermont
REYNOLDS, Arthur Benjamin, Dec 4 1896 Sex:M Child# 7 William Reynolds Manchester, NH & Annie Lamb Canada
REYNOLDS, Arthur Patrick, Sep 16 1925 Sex:M Child# 1 Benjamin Reynolds Nashua, NH & Anna Hagerty Nashua, NH
REYNOLDS, Bernice, Jul 30 1928 Sex:F Child# 3 Wm W Reynolds Nashua, NH & Emma Hudon Nashua, NH
REYNOLDS, Carrie, Sep 5 1892 Sex:F Child# 2 Timothy Reynolds Newburgh, NY & Jane Fishkill, NY
REYNOLDS, Charles Atkins, Feb 7 1907 Sex:M Child# 3 William B Reynolds Orange, MA & Clara L Bailey Nashua, NH
REYNOLDS, Charles Elrade, Dec 11 1895 Sex:M Child# 1 George E Reynolds Nashua, NH & Lena Henry St George, NB
REYNOLDS, Chester Raymond, Oct 27 1901 Sex:M Child# 9 William Reynolds Manchester, NH  & Anna Lamb Canada
REYNOLDS, Dorothy Elizabeth, Feb 7 1923 Sex:F Child# 1 Carl G Reynolds Washington, NH & Laura M Wright NS
REYNOLDS, Ellen, Jan 31 1916 Sex:F Child# 2 Edward P Reynolds Bedford, NH & Mary Burnham Ireland
REYNOLDS, Emma Gertrude, Feb 10 1918 Sex:F Child# 1 Wilfred Reynolds Nashua, NH & Emma Desrosier Vermont
REYNOLDS, Grover Cleveland, Mar 15 1889 Sex:M Child# 3 George C Reynolds New York City & Berne J Ray Mass
REYNOLDS, Harold Bernard, Aug 22 1920 Sex:M Child# 1 Har B J Reynolds Nashua, NH & Blanche Jean Nashua, NH
REYNOLDS, Harold Kenneth, Nov 7 1923 Sex:M Child# 4 Wilfred J Reynolds Nashua, NH & Emma S Derosier Richford, VT
REYNOLDS, Harry, Dec 24 1898 Sec:M Child# 8 William Reynolds Manchester, NH & Anna Lamb Canada
REYNOLDS, Harry Carr, Feb 16 1921 Sex:M Child# 1 Herbert R Reynolds Nashua, NH & Ruby Bartlett Raymond, NH
REYNOLDS, James, Feb 25 1933 Sex:M Child# 2 G E Reynolds Lowell, MA & Mary McKay Nashua, NH
REYNOLDS, Jean, Oct 4 1931 Sex:F Child# 1 George B Reynolds Lowell, MA & Mary McKay Nashua, NH
REYNOLDS, Jean Therese, Mar 18 1930 Sex:F Child# 1 Raymond Reynolds Nashua, NH & Rose Anna Dumont Canada
REYNOLDS, Joan Patricia, Mar 18 1930 Sex:F Child# 2 Raymond Reynolds Nashua, NH & Rose Anna Dumont Canada
REYNOLDS, Leo, May 6 1893 Sex:M Child# 3 John Reynolds Nashua, NH & Nellie A Boston, MA
REYNOLDS, Lester J, Nov 8 1898 Sex:M Child# 4 John P Reynolds Nashua, NH & Nellie A Reynolds Boston, MA
REYNOLDS, Marion Irene, Feb 20 1920 Sex:F Child# 2 Wilfred J Reynolds Nashua, NH & Emma S Derosier Richford, VT
REYNOLDS, Marjorie Frances, Aug 22 1922 Sex:F Child# 2 Harold Reynolds Nashua, NH & Blanche Jean Nashua, NH
REYNOLDS, Mary Elizabeth, Jan 23 1935 Sex:F Child# 3 Geo B Reynolds Lowell, MA & Mary McKay Nashua, NH
REYNOLDS, Paul Kenneth, Sep 12 1928 Sex:M Child# 2 Benjamin Reynolds Nashua, NH & Anna Hagerty Nashua, NH
REYNOLDS, Phyllis Mae, Apr 9 1922 Sex:F Child# 3 Wilfred J Reynolds Nashua, NH & Emma S Dero Richford, VT
REYNOLDS, Rita Eva, Sep 24 1918 Sex:F Child# 2 William W Reynolds Nashua, NH & Emma Hudon Nashua, NH
REYNOLDS, Ruth Anne, Dec 16 1911 Sex:F Child# 1 Edward F Reynolds Bedford, NH & Mary Burnham Ireland
REYNOLDS, Theodore Carl, Aug 23 1924 Sex:M Child# 2 Carl G Reynolds Washington, NH & Laura M Wright Nova Scotia
REYNOLDS, Unknown, Mar 26 1889 Sex:F Child# 2 John Reynolds Nashua, NH & Nellie A Reynolds Boston, MA
REYNOLDS, Unknown, Dec 3 1894 Sex:M Child# 3 William B Reynolds Mass & Clara L Bailey Nashua, NH
REYNOLDS, Unknown, Feb 6 1915 Sex:F Child# 1 William W Reynolds Nashua, NH & Emma Hudon Nashua, NH
RHEAUME, David, Jun 20 1907 Sex:M Child# 2 Joseph Rheaume Canada & Rosalie Pelletier Canada
RHEAUME, Joseph Hormidas, Nov 13 1922 Sex:M Child# 11 Joseph G Rheaume Canada & Rosalie Pelletier Canada
RHEAUME, Joseph Wilfred D, Aug 8 1908 Sex:M Child# 3 Lindsey Rheaume Canada & Rosalie Pelletier Canada
RHEAUME, M Germaine Delina, Aug 18 1916 Sex:F Child# 8 Joseph G Rheaume Canada & Rose Pelletier Canada
RHEAUME, M Laura Delima, Jan 21 1913 Sex:F Child# 6 Joseph Rheaume Canada & Rosalie Pelletier Canada
RHEAUME, Marie Adrienne A, Oct 1 1909 Sex:F Child# 4 Joseph Rheaume Canada & Rosalie Pelletier Canada
RHEAUME, Marie Olivette Beatr, Mar 17 1912 Sex:F Child# 5 Joseph Rheaume Canada & Rosalie Pelletier Canada
RHEAUME, Marie Rita Margaret, May 19 1925 Sex:F Child# 12 Joseph Rheaume Canada & Rosalee Pelletier Canada
RHEAUME, Mary Irene Rita A, Dec 10 1927 Sex:F Child# 1 David Rheaume Nashua, NH & Irene Bonenfant Nashua, NH

RHEAUME, Mary Jane Lucille, Jul 25 1921 Sex:F Child# 10 Joseph Rheaume Canada & Rosalie Pelletier Canada
RHEAUME, Normand Arthur, Jan 4 1929 Sex:M Child# 1 Wilfred Rheaume Nashua, NH & Stella Bissonnette Nashua, NH
RHEAUME, Robert Joseph, Jul 8 1920 Sex:M Child# 9 Joseph Rheaume Canada & Rosallie Pelletier Canada
RHEAUME, Rose Eva, Jul 11 1906 Sex:F Child# 1 Joseph Rheaume Canada & Rosalie Pelletier Canada
RHODES, Hazel Gladias, Sep 17 1896 Sex:F Child# 2 Fred Rhodes Mooers, NY & Sarah McDonald Mooers, NY
RHODES, Pearl Francena, Oct 18 1896 Sex:F Child# 3 Printis S Rhodes NY & Kate F Wills Nashua, NH
RHODES, Unknown, Jul 26 1895 Sex:F Child# 1 Fred Rhodes Mooers, NY & Sarah McDonald Mooers, NY
RIBAULT, Joseph Edouard, Mar 21 1897 Sex:M Child# 2 Aime Bibault Canada & Marie L Salvail Nashua, NH
RICARD, Agnes Lillian, Nov 16 1923 Sex:F Child# 4 Leo Ricard Nashua, NH & Bernadette Boucher Canada
RICARD, Arthur, Jun 7 1932 Sex:M Child# 5 Donat Ricard Canada & Aurore Levesque Nashua, NH
RICARD, Beatrice Edith, Nov 15 1914 Sex:F Child# 1 Irenee L Ricard NH & Bernadette Boucher Canada
RICARD, Beattise, May 16 1891 Sex:F Child# 6 Arthur Ricard Canada & Rosilda Lagace Canada
RICARD, Cecile, Oct 3 1907 Sex:F Child# 6 Adelard Ricard Canada & Heloise Levesque Canada
RICARD, Cecile Lillian, Dec 14 1928 Sex:F Child# 6 John B Ricard Rhode Island & Eveline Houle Pepperell, MA
RICARD, Charlotte Jacqueline, May 23 1929 Sex:F Child# 2 Leo Ricard Nashua, NH & Modeste Sirois Canada Stillborn
RICARD, Claudia, Dec 27 1892 Sex:F Child# 6 Dolphis Ricard
RICARD, Clovis Raymond, Jun 8 1908 Sex:M Child# 1 Alphonse Ricard US & Delvina Guertin US
RICARD, Cyriac, Feb 3 1898 Sex:M Child# 10 Arthur Ricard Canada & Rosilda Lagasse Canada
RICARD, D Alphonse, Oct 16 1891 Sex:M Child# 2 Alphonse Ricard Canada & Elise Ranoie Canada
RICARD, Doris Lucille, Dec 16 1931 Sex:F Child# 6 Leo Ricard Nashua, NH & Bernadette Boucher Canada
RICARD, Dorothy, Jun 11 1931 Sex:F Child# 3 Wilfred Ricard Nashua, NH & Estelle Blazoa Lowell, MA
RICARD, Elizabeth Annette, Jul 15 1932 Sex:F Child# 4 Leo Ricard Nashua, NH & Modeste Sirois Canada
RICARD, Elizabeth Lucille, Mar 3 1925 Sex:F Child# 3 Leon Ricard Nashua, NH & Marie A Caron Canada
RICARD, Elize, Mar 1 1890 Sex:F Child# 1 Alphonse Ricard Canada & Elise Rioux Nashua, NH
RICARD, Ernest Maurice, Jul 7 1923 Sex:M Child# 4 Delphis Ricard Nashua, NH & Rosanna Lavoie Nashua, NH
RICARD, Ernest Roland, Jan 21 1920 Sex:M Child# 2 Leo Ricard Nashua, NH & Bernadette Boucher Canada
RICARD, Eugene Euclide, May 21 1934 Sex:M Child# 1 Eugene E Ricard Greenville, NH & Adrienne Vielleux Canada
RICARD, Florida, Oct 6 1899 Sex:F Child# 9 Delphis Ricard Canada & G Pelletier Canada
RICARD, Frederic, Feb 26 1899 Sex:M Child# 11 Arthur Ricard Canada & Rosilda  Lagasse Canada Stillborn
RICARD, Guy Raymond, Sep 9 1921 Sex:M Child# 2 Ralph Ricard Nashua, NH & Madeleine Lafont France
RICARD, Herve Charles Eugene, Mar 26 1927 Sex:M Child# 5 Ralph Ricard Nashua, NH & Madeline Lafont France
RICARD, Huguette Vivian, Nov 19 1922 Sex:F Child# 3 Ralph Ricard Nashua, NH & Madeleine Lafont France
RICARD, Irene, Sep 7 1914 Sex:F Child# 1 Delphis Ricard US & Rose Anna Lavoie US
RICARD, Irene Leona, Feb 19 1925 Sex:F Child# 5 Leo Ricard Nashua, NH & Bern Boucher Canada
RICARD, Jean Baptiste, Jul 4 1901 Sex:M Child# 10 Delphis Ricard Canada & Georgiana Pelletier Canada
RICARD, Jean Baptiste Albert, Apr 10 1916 Sex:M Child# 1 Jean Baptiste Ricard Rhode Island & Eveline Houle MA
RICARD, John Edward, Jr, Sep 21 1933 Sex:M Child# 2 John E Ricard Nashua, NH & Germaine Gagnon Nashua, NH
RICARD, Jos Albert Adrien, Jun 16 1919 Sex:M Child# 8 Wilfred Ricard Canada & Alexina Anthaya Canada
RICARD, Jos Amedee Arthur, Sep 30 1920 Sex:M Child# 3 Jean Bap Ricard Rhode Island & Eveline Houle Mass
RICARD, Jos Ernest Harold, Aug 1 1923 Sex:M Child# 4 J Bte Ricard Rhode Island & Evelyn Houle Mass
RICARD, Jos Oscar Rolland, Jun 29 1919 Sex:M Child# 3 Delphis Ricard NH & Rose Anna Lavoie NH
RICARD, Joseph, May 30 1888 Sex:M Child# 3 Dolphis Ricard Etna, RI & Georganna Peltier Canada
RICARD, Joseph, Sep 24 1889 Sex:M Child# 9 Olivier Ricard Canada & Almina Dion Canada
RICARD, Joseph, Mar 17 1902 Sex:M Child# 3 Narcisse Ricard Mass & Cesaire Charrette Maine
RICARD, Joseph Adrian Irenee, Apr 10 1923 Sex:M Child# 2 Leon Ricard Nashua, NH & Marie Ange Caron Canada
RICARD, Joseph George, Jan 8 1899 Sex:M Child# 1 Narcisse Ricard Worcester, MA & Sarah Charette Oldtown, ME
RICARD, Joseph H, Apr 23 1892 Sex:M Child# 9 Oliver Ricard Canada & Hermine Dion Canada
RICARD, Joseph Leo, Jan 8 1903 Sex:M Child# 6 Alphonse Ricard Canada & Elsie Rioux Canada
RICARD, Joseph Leo Donald, Nov 14 1934 Sex:M Child# 5 Leo Ricard Nashua, NH & Modese Sirois Canada
RICARD, Joseph Ulderic, May 23 1891 Sex:M Child# 6 Ulderic Ricard Canada & Merance Charet Canada
RICARD, Leandre Irenee, Feb 19 1894 Sex:M Child# 8 Arthur Ricard Canada & Rosilda Lagasse Canada
RICARD, Leo Ernest, Mar 25 1929 Sex:M Child# 3 Jos Donat Ricard Canada & Aurore Levesque Nashua, NH
RICARD, Leo Henri, Apr 10 1905 Sex:M Child# 12 Arthur Ricard Canada & Rosilda Lagasse Canada
RICARD, Leo Raymond, Jul 7 1923 Sex:M Child# 5 Delphis Ricard Nashua, NH & Rosanna Lavoie Nashua, NH
RICARD, Leon, Oct 24 1895 Sex:M Child# 2 Georges Ricard Canada & Marie Rioux Canada
RICARD, Loraine, Nov 28 1923 Sex:F Child# 1 John E Ricard Nashua, NH & Germaine Gagnon Nashua, NH
RICARD, Louis Paul, Jun 27 1916 Sex:M Child# 2 Dolphis Ricard US & Rose Anna Lavoie US
RICARD, Louise Alphonse, Jun 14 1893 Sex:M Child# 1 George Ricard Canada & Marie Rioux Canada
RICARD, M Anita Emilia, Mar 5 1915 Sex:F Child# 5 Wilfred Ricard Canada & Alexina Antaya Canada
RICARD, M Blanche Olivette, Jun 27 1917 Sex:F Child# 6 Wilfred Ricard Canada & Alexine Anthaya Canada
RICARD, M Blanche Pauline, Mar 21 1921 Sex:F Child# 9 Wilfred Ricard Canada & Alexina Anthaya Canada
RICARD, M Cel Adrienne, Jun 16 1919 Sex:F Child# 7 Wilfred Ricard Canada & Alexina Anthaya Canada
RICARD, M Gilberta Yvonne, Dec 1 1929 Sex:F Child# 2 Albert Ricard Mass & Alice Dube Canada
RICARD, Marie, Jul 15 1909 Sex:F Child# 2 Wilfrid Ricard Canada & Regina Anthaya Canada
RICARD, Marie A A, Apr 8 1891 Sex:F Child# 5 Dolphis Ricard Mass & Georgina Peltier Canada
RICARD, Marie Aurore Rita, Dec 9 1926 Sex:F Child# 1 Donat Ricard Canada & Aurore Levesque Nashua, NH
RICARD, Marie Blanche Y, Apr 22 1906 Sex:F Child# 5 Adelard Ricard Canada & Eloise Levesque Canada
RICARD, Marie C G, Aug 31 1889 Sex:F Child# 4 Delphis Ricard RI & Virginia Peltier Canada
RICARD, Marie Clara, Sep 2 1900 Sex:F Child# 2 Narcisse Ricard Mass & Sarah Charette Maine
RICARD, Marie Clea, Sep 6 1912 Sex:F Child# 4 Wilfred Ricard Canada & Alexina Anthaya Canada
RICARD, Marie Collette Lorai, Nov 25 1927 Sex:F Child# 5 Jean B Ricard Natick, RI & Evelyn Houle Pepperell, MA
RICARD, Marie Irene Emelia, Feb 10 1918 Sex:F Child# 2 Jean Baptiste Ricard Rhode Island & Evelyn Houle Mass
RICARD, Marie Lena, Dec 19 1910 Sex:F Child# 3 Wilfrid Ricard Canada & Alexina Anthaya Canada

RICARD, Marie Rose, Feb 1 1888 Sex:F Child# 4 Arthur Ricard Canada & Rasilda Lagassi Canada
RICARD, Marie Rose, Sep 1 1899 Sex:F Child# 5 Alphonse Ricard Canada & Elise Rioux Canada
RICARD, May Florence, Oct 7 1922 Sex:F Child# 3 Leo Ricard Nashua, NH & Bernadette Boucher Canada
RICARD, Muriel Linette, Jun 17 1928 Sex:F Child# 4 Leon Ricard Nashua, NH & Marie Anne Caron Canada
RICARD, Muriel Ruth, Dec 14 1925 Sex:F Child# 1 Joseph L Ricard Nashua, NH & Philomene Sirois Canada
RICARD, Normand, May 21 1931 Sex:M Child# 4 Donat Ricard Canada & Aurore Levesque Nashua, NH
RICARD, Pauline Mary, Jul 10 1925 Sex:F Child# 1 Wilfred Ricard Nashua, NH & Eselie Blozon Lowell, MA
RICARD, Raymond Kenneth, Aug 25 1924 Sex:M Child# 1 Adelard Ricard Centerville, RI & Yvonne Boucher Nashua, NH
RICARD, Rochel, Nov 7 1930 Sex:M Child# 5 Leon Ricard Nashua, NH & Marie A Caron Canada
RICARD, Sylvia, Aug 23 1905 Sex:F Child# 12 Delphis Ricard Canada & Georgiana Peltier Canada
RICARD, Toussaint, Nov 1 1892 Sex:M Child# 7 Arthur Ricard Canada & Rosilda Lagace Canada
RICARD, Unknown, Mar 13 1928 Sex:F Child# 1 Wilfrid Ricard Greenville, NH & Adrienne Cadieux Nashua, NH Stillborn
RICARD, Victor Raoul, Mar 6 1896 Sex:M Child# 9 Arthur Ricard Canada & Rosa Lajasse Canada
RICARD, Wilfred, Sep 3 1903 Sex:M Child# 11 Delphis Ricard Canada & Georgiana Peltier Canada
RICARD, Wilfred, Dec 21 1925 Sex:M Child# 4 Armand Ricard Canada & Diana Fortin Warren, RI
RICARD, William Alfred, Dec 29 1891 Sex:M Child# 4 William Richard Canada & Albertine Gendron Canada
RICARD, Yvonne Irene, Mar 20 1928 Sex:F Child# 2 Joseph Ricard Canada & Aurore Levesque Nashua, NH
RICE, Dorothy J, Aug 12 1902 Sex:F Child# 2 Herbert E Rice Webster & Josephine Nelson Dalton
RICE, Earl Albert, Jun 27 1902 Sex:M Child# 2 E A Rice Northfield, VT & Hattie A Dole Northfield, VT
RICE, Hazel Velma, Jul 11 1893 Sex:F Child# 1 Edwin A Rice Northfield, VT & Hattie A Dole Northfield, VT
RICE, Marilyn Nichols, Mar 16 1932 Sex:F Child# 2 Joseph Rice Twillingate, Canada & Hazel Nichols Hollis, NH
RICE, Nancy Claire, Oct 21 1931 Sex:F Child# 1 Earl Rice Nashua, NH & Marion Leonardi Nashua, NH
RICE, Unknown, Jun 14 1895 Sex:M Child# 1 Frank E Rice Northfield, VT & Ruthvene A Senter Litchfield, NH
RICE, Unknown, Aug 3 1900 Sex:F Child# 1 H E Rice NH & Josephine Nelson NH
RICE, William Everett, Sep 7 1919 Sex:M Child# 2 William E Rice Medford, MA & Jennie L Holmes Pepperell, MA
RICH, Catherine Lucile, Aug 29 1911 Sex:F Child# 1 Joseph Rich Brockton, MA & Mary S O'Brien Nashua, NH
RICH, Elizabeth Ann, Feb 5 1933 Sex:F Child# 1 Harry E Rich Salem, NH & Marion Elliott Elmwood, NH
RICH, Marion Ruth, Aug 26 1920 Sex:F Child# 1 Louis Rich Manchester, NH & Golda Friedman Buchanan, VA
RICH, Nancy, Nov 3 1935 Sex:F Child# 1 Charles Rich Swanton, VT & Mona Conner Exeter, NH
RICH, Nancy Ruth, May 11 1934 Sex:F Child# 2 Harry Rich Salem, NH & Marion Elliott Hancock, NH
RICH, Raymond H, Jan 30 1909 Sex:M Child# 1 Harry F Rich New Bedford, MA & Emma Scott Calais, ME
RICH, Unknown, Jul 28 1934 Sex:M Child# 1 John P Rich, Jr Swanton, VT & Olive Hussey Nashua, NH
RICHAL, Joseph Napoleon, Apr 28 1889 Sex:M Child# 7 Joseph Richal Canada & Aurelia Semard Plattsburg, NY
RICHARD, Adrienne Cecile, Feb 13 1924 Sex:F Child# 2 Alphonse Richard Canada & Marie Larivee Michigan
RICHARD, Albert, Mar 7 1896 Sex:M Child# 1 Joseph Richard Canada & Albina Richer Canada
RICHARD, Albert, Jul 5 1904 Sex:M Child# 1 Francois Richard Canada & Celestine Bonin Canada
RICHARD, Albert Ernest, Mar 28 1923 Sex:M Child# 1 Albert Richard Nashua, NH & A Landry Lowell, MA
RICHARD, Albert Harold, Apr 12 1925 Sex:M Child# 2 Albert Richard Nashua, NH & Marie A Landry Lowell, MA
RICHARD, Albert Leo, Oct 28 1898 Sex:M Child# 3 A M Richard Canada & Alida Guertin Nashua, NH
RICHARD, Alfred, Dec 12 1890 Sex:M Child# 4 Alphonse Richard Canada & Oryphena Guichard Canada
RICHARD, Alfred Albert, May 8 1911 Sex:M Child# 7 Demetrius Richard Canada & Melina Dube Canada
RICHARD, Alfred Jos Jean Chas, Jan 17 1925 Sex:M Child# 7 Charles Richard Canada & Marilda Belanger Canada
RICHARD, Alice, Sep 13 1900 Sex:F Child# 4 Joseph Richard Canada & Albina Richer Canada
RICHARD, Alma Lorette, Mar 11 1893 Sex:F Child# 1 Arthur M Richard Canada & Alida Guertin Nashua, NH
RICHARD, Alphonse, Sep 9 1894 Sex:M Child# 7 Alphonse Richard Canada & Orphena Guichard Canada
RICHARD, Alphonse, Jul 10 1907 Sex:M Child# 8 Arthur M Richard Canada & Alma Guertin Nashua, NH
RICHARD, Alphonse A, Feb 27 1902 Sex:M Child# 5 A M Richard Canada & Alida Guertin Nashua, NH
RICHARD, Amanda, Jan 1 1896 Sex:F Child# 10 Joseph Richard Canada & Amelia Simard Canada
RICHARD, Amedie, Jan 31 1899 Sex:M Child# 8 Alphonse Richard Canada & Orphena Guichard Canada
RICHARD, Andrea, Mar 1 1900 Sex:F Child# 9 Alphonse Richard Canada & Orphena Guichard Canada
RICHARD, Angele, Feb 3 1888 Sex:F Child# 5 Livenor Pont Richard Springfield, MA & Delhia Leblanc Canada
RICHARD, Angelina, Aug 31 1896 Sex:F Child# 6 Alphonse Richard Canada & Orpheno Guichard Canada
RICHARD, Anita, Oct 17 1909 Sex:F Child# 6 Demetrius Richard Canada & Melina Dube Canada
RICHARD, Auguste, Dec 16 1907 Sex:M Child# 5 Demetrius Richard Canada & Marie Dube Canada
RICHARD, Beatrice Sylvia, Feb 15 1906 Sex:F Child# 12 Alphonse Richard US & Orphena Guichard Canada
RICHARD, Charles, Apr 28 1902 Sex:M Child# 5 Joseph Richard Canada & Albina Richer Canada
RICHARD, Charles Wilfrid, Jul 22 1900 Sex:M Child# 4 A M Richard Canada & Alida Guertin Nashua, NH
RICHARD, Claire Edna, Jun 13 1927 Sex:F Child# 3 Albert Richard Nashua, NH & Marie A Landry Nashua, NH
RICHARD, Claire Marie, Mar 19 1931 Sex:F Child# 1 George A Richard Nashua, NH & Lucy A Beaudet Canada
RICHARD, Cordila, Mar 31 1888 Sex:F Child# 4 Alphonso Richard Canada & Ophena Guichard Canada
RICHARD, Doris Elaine, Jan 6 1935 Sex:F Child# 7 Albert Richard Nashua, NH & Marie A Landry Nashua, NH
RICHARD, Eva, Dec 11 1904 Sex:F Child# 6 Joseph Richard Canada & Albina Richer Canada
RICHARD, Eva Rose, Sep 8 1897 Sex:F Child# 10 Joseph Richard Canada & Aurelee Simard Canada
RICHARD, Fernande, Sep 23 1909 Sex:F Child# 10 A M Richard Canada & Aida Guertin Nashua, NH
RICHARD, Francois X O, Mar 18 1900 Sex:M Child# 3 Alfred Richard NH & Josephine Veseau NH
RICHARD, Frs Philias, Nov 17 1904 Sex:M Child# 3 Demetrius Richard Canada & Emeliana Dube Canada
RICHARD, George Arthur, Nov 2 1896 Sex:M Child# 2 Arthur Richard Canada & Alida Guertin Nashua, NH
RICHARD, George Herbert, Sep 6 1925 Sex:M Child# 1 Philipe Richard Lawrence, MA & Lillian Green Nashua, NH
RICHARD, Helen Elizabeth, Oct 13 1922 Sex:F Child# 3 Howard C Richard Saco, ME & Dorothy Witham Malden, MA
RICHARD, Henri, Sep 21 1911 Sex:M Child# 9 Arthur Richard Canada & Alida Guertin Nashua, NH
RICHARD, Henry, Dec 2 1890 Sex:M Child# 12 Moise Richard Canada & Tie Cote Canada
RICHARD, Henry, Mar 4 1905 Sex:M Child# 11 Alphonse Richard Nashua, NH & Orphina Guichard Canada
RICHARD, Herold Essera, May 26 1912 Sex:M Child# 2 Noe Joseph Richard NH & Dora A Adams Mass

RICHARD, Irene Beatrice, Nov 4 1913 Sex:F Child# 1 Louis Richard Canada & Albina Paris Legony, MI
RICHARD, Isaac, Jan 26 1890 Sex:M Child# 5 Arthur Richard Canada & Rosilda Lagassa Canada
RICHARD, J Alphonse P A, Dec 28 1911 Sex:M Child# 3 Alphonse Richard Canada & Mary Lamy Michigan
RICHARD, Jean Baptiste, Nov 18 1901 Sex:M Child# 1 Jean Bpt Richard Canada & Alice Dube Canada
RICHARD, Joseph, Jul 10 1897 Sex:M Child# 1 Mederic Richard Nashua, NH & Alice Beland Canada
RICHARD, Joseph, May 26 1910 Sex:M Child# 2 Alphonse Richard Canada & Mary Lamie Michigan
RICHARD, Joseph A Henri, Nov 7 1897 Sex:M Child# 1 Alfred Richard Nashua, NH & Josephine Veseau Nashua, NH
RICHARD, Joseph Adelard, Feb 13 1897 Sex:M Child# 2 Joseph Richard Canada & Euphemie Landry Canada
RICHARD, Joseph Albert, Mar 11 1914 Sex:M Child# 8 Demetrius Richard Canada & Melina Dube Canada
RICHARD, Joseph Charles Eug, Jul 24 1900 Sex:M Child# 5 Joseph Richard Canada & Fenice Landry Canada
RICHARD, Joseph Dewey O, Mar 18 1900 Sex:M Child# 2 Alfred Richard NH & Josephine Veseau NH
RICHARD, Joseph Paul, Nov 5 1934 Sex:M Child# 12 Charles Richard Canada & Emilda Belanger Canada
RICHARD, Joseph Paul Edmund, Apr 1 1927 Sex:M Child# 1 Adrien Richard Nashua, NH & Y Morrissette Nashua, NH
RICHARD, Leo Emile, Apr 5 1903 Sex:M Child# 6 Arthur M Richard Canada & Alida Guertin Nashua, NH
RICHARD, Leo Hermon, Sep 12 1920 Sex:M Child# 4 Philias J Richard Nashua, NH & Catherine McCaffrey Ireland
RICHARD, Leo L, Dec 8 1897 Sex:M Child# 2 Alfred Richard Canada & Nattie Dufresne Nashua, NH
RICHARD, Leo Thomas, Jan 8 1919 Sex:M Child# 1 Alp Richard, Jr US & Celina Ouellette US
RICHARD, Lorraine, May 22 1928 Sex:F Child# 4 Albert Richard Nashua, NH & Marianna Landry Nashua, NH
RICHARD, Louis Adrien, Jan 18 1904 Sex:M Child# 1 Napoleon Richard Canada & Delia Desmarais Nashua, NH
RICHARD, Louis Antoine, Jul 15 1913 Sex:M Child# 11 Arthur M Richard Canada & Alida Guertin Nashua, NH
RICHARD, Lucile Marguerite, Apr 17 1917 Sex:F Child# 2 Louis Richard Canada & Albina Paris Canada
RICHARD, Lucile Gertrude, Feb 27 1922 Sex:F Child# 3 Francis Richard Canada & Celestine Bois Canada
RICHARD, Lucille Sylvia, Feb 5 1916 Sex:F Child# 3 Noe Richard Nashua, NH & Hermance Boucher Canada
RICHARD, M Albina Cordelia, Mar 3 1917 Sex:F Child# 2 Philias Richard NH & Catherine McCaffrey Ireland
RICHARD, M Blanche Rachelle, Oct 19 1915 Sex:F Child# 1 Philip Richard NH & Catherine McCaffrey Ireland
RICHARD, M Leonie I Annette, May 8 1914 Sex:F Child# 4 Alphonse Richard Canada & Mary Laurie Michigan
RICHARD, Marcel Willie, Aug 3 1926 Sex:M Child# 8 Charles Richard Canada & Emerie Belanger Canada
RICHARD, Maria D Victoria, Dec 20 1898 Sex:F Child# 1 Charles Richard Canada & Delia Causineau Canada
RICHARD, Marie, Sep 19 1897 Sex:F Child# 2 Philip Richard Canada & Lizzie Blanchard Canada
RICHARD, Marie, Jul 5 1904 Sex:F Child# 1 Jean B Richard Canada & Alice Dube Canada
RICHARD, Marie Alice J, Jan 6 1903 Sex:F Child# 12 Jean B Richard Canada & Alice Dube Canada
RICHARD, Marie Ange Ida, Nov 22 1928 Sex:F Child# 9 Charles Richard Canada & E Belanger Canada
RICHARD, Marie Blanche, Jan 13 1897 Sex:F Child# 3 Joseph Richard Canada & Euphemie Landry Canada
RICHARD, Marie Blanche E, Oct 15 1907 Sex:F Child# 1 Alphonse Richard Canada & Marie Lamy Centerville, MI
RICHARD, Marie Cecile Simone, Jan 30 1924 Sex:F Child# 6 Charles Richard Canada & Merilda Belanger Canada
RICHARD, Marie Emelia, Dec 2 1901 Sex:F Child# 6 Joseph Richard Canada & Euphemie Landry Canada
RICHARD, Marie Fernand R, Aug 3 1930 Sex:F Child# 10 Charles E Richard Canada & Emeralda Belanger Canada
RICHARD, Marie Louise, Mar 30 1897 Sex:F Child# 4 Alphonse Richard Canada & Elise Rioux Canada
RICHARD, Marie Rose, Sep 9 1905 Sex:F Child# 4 J Bte Richard Canada & Alice Dube Canada
RICHARD, Mary Rose Alma, Jun 18 1899 Sex:F Child# 4 Joseph Richard Canada & Euphemie Landry Canada
RICHARD, Octave, Nov 18 1889 Sex:F Child# 1 Octave Richard Nashua, NH & Marie Alix CT
RICHARD, Oscar Ernest, Nov 7 1895 Sex:M Child# 1 Alfred Richard Canada & Nettie Dufresne Nashua, NH
RICHARD, Philias, Aug 17 1892 Sex:M Child# 6 Alphonse Richard Canada & Arphena Guichard Canada
RICHARD, Raoul Remi, Mar 17 1905 Sex:M Child# 7 Arthur M Richard Canada & Alida Guertin Nashua, NH
RICHARD, Rheaume, Jan 28 1899 Sex:M Child# 2 Joseph Richard Canada & Albina Richer Canada
RICHARD, Rita Yvonne, Feb 19 1921 Sex:F Child# 2 Francois Richard Canada & Celestine Bois Canada
RICHARD, Roger, Nov 12 1931 Sex:M Child# 5 Albert Richard Nashua, NH & Marianna Landry Lowell, MA
RICHARD, Roland Joseph Oscar, Nov 17 1918 Sex:M Child# 3 Philippe Richard Nashua, NH & Katherine McCaffery Ireland
RICHARD, Romeo Edmond, Jun 29 1922 Sex:M Child# 2 Albert Richard Nashua, NH & Yvonne Tellier Nashua, NH
RICHARD, Rosanna, Jun 22 1903 Sex:F Child# 2 Demetrius Richard Canada & Melina Dube Canada
RICHARD, Unknown, Nov 9 1891 Sex:M Child# 8 Joseph Richard Canada & Aurelia Simard Canada Stillborn
RICHARD, Unknown, Feb 22 1898 Sex:F Child# 2 Joseph Richard Canada & Albina Richie Lancaster, MA
RICHARD, Unknown, Feb 9 1902 Sex:M Child# 4 Alfred Richard NH & Josephine Veseau NH
RICHARD, Unknown, Mar 21 1911 Sex:M Child# 1 Noe Richard Nashua, NH & Hermance Boucher Iberville, PQ
RICHARD, Unknown, Dec 2 1912 Sex:M Child# 4 Alphonse Richard Canada & Marie Lamie Michigan Stillborn
RICHARD, Unknown, Apr 2 1922 Sex:M Child# 1 Arthur Richard Nashua, NH & Ezilia Dragon Milford, NH Stillborn
RICHARD, William, Apr 16 1902 Sex:M Child# 1 Demetrius Richard Canada & Meliana Dube Canada
RICHARDS, Carmen, Apr 6 1918 Sex:F Child# 2 Henry Richards Nashua, NH & Anna Morin St Louis, PQ
RICHARDS, Claire Florence, Oct 23 1918 Sex:F Child# 4 Noe Richards Nashua, NH & Hermanie Boucher Canada
RICHARDS, Doris May, Jan 3 1909 Sex:F Child# 3 Isaac F Richards Appleton, ME & Sadie M Borneman Waldoboro, ME
RICHARDS, George A, May 18 1914 Sex:M Child# 2 Noe Richards Nashua, NH & Hermence Boucher Canada
RICHARDS, John P Reynolds, Jun 19 1931 Sex:M Child# 1 Horace W S Richards
RICHARDS, Lawrence Everett, Jul 14 1930 Sex:M Child# 1 Ellsworth Richardson Salem, MA & Rachel Chapman Pepperell
RICHARDS, Mary Ann Alice, Nov 27 1916 Sex:F Child# 9 Demintuis Richards Canada & Mayleana Dube Canada
RICHARDS, Raymond Paul, Feb 5 1934 Sex:M Child# 1 Albert Paul Richards Nashua, NH & Esther Clyde Hudson, NH
RICHARDS, Susanne Putnam, Oct 1 1933 Sex:F Child# 3 L Richards S Lyndeboro, NH & Helen Mitchell Freeport, ME
RICHARDS, Unknown, Mar 23 1916 Sex:F Child# 1 Henry J Richards Nashua, NH & Anna Morin Canada
RICHARDSON, Barbara, Jun 5 1920 Sex:F Child# 6 Arthur C Richardson Milford, NH & Lizzie McKay Amherst, NH
RICHARDSON, Chester Leon, Sep 10 1910 Sex:M Child# 2 Victor Richardson Vermont & Jennie Alison Vermont
RICHARDSON, David Charles, Nov 4 1922 Sex:M Child# 7 A C Richardson Milford, NH & Lizzie B McKay Ponema, NH
RICHARDSON, Donald, Jun 20 1918 Sex:M Child# 2 Howard Richardson Wattsfield, VT & Marion Crosby Philadelphia, PA
RICHARDSON, Dorothy Dalton, Jul 14 1919 Sex:F Child# 1 Charles Richardson Plaistown, NH & Alice Dalton Calais, ME
RICHARDSON, Dorothy Elizabeth, Jun 14 1920 Sex:F Child# 3 Howard Richardson Wattsfield, VT & E Marion Crosby PA

RICHARDSON, Elizabeth Hansen, Jun 5 1932 Sex:F Child# 2 R A Richardson Lynn, MA & Jennie G Hanson Concord, NH
RICHARDSON, Esther F, Apr 1 1906 Sex:F Child# 1 James A Richardson Lempster, NH & Esther S Campbell Windham, NH
RICHARDSON, Ethel Laura, Jan 30 1903 Sex:F Child# Ira A Richardson Nashua, NH & Mary Ellen Morrison Nashua, NH
RICHARDSON, Frank Perry, Jun 7 1921 Sex:M Child# 1 Ralph Richardson Providence, RI & Virgie Crokett Merrimac, MA
RICHARDSON, Fred Waldo, Oct 20 1932 Sex:M Child# W Richardson Nashua, NH & Lillian Urvin Pomfret, VT
RICHARDSON, Harriet Edith, Nov 16 1924 Sex:F Child# 5 H P Richardson Milford, NH & M Flor Harper Canada
RICHARDSON, Joyce K, Jan 16 1909 Sex:F Child# 1 Howard L Richardson Waitsfield, VT & E Marion Crosby Philadelphia
RICHARDSON, Lee Milton, Oct 8 1934 Sex:M Child# 2 Ellsworth Richardson Salem, MA & Rachel Chapman Pepperell, MA
RICHARDSON, Oscar Billings, Nov 17 1914 Sex:M Child# 1 Benj B Richardson Midgie, NB & Elizabeth Stock Ayer Cli
RICHARDSON, Robert Alerson, May 21 1935 Sex:M Child# 3 R A Richardson Lynn, MA & Jennie Hansen Concord, MA
RICHARDSON, Robert Bancroft, Mar 5 1932 Sex:M Child# 3 R B Richardson Lowell, MA & Anna M Lee Lowell, MA
RICHARDSON, Stanley Harper, Feb 22 1921 Sex:M Child# 2 Harry P Richardson Milford, NH & Margaret Harper Montreal
RICHARDSON, Unknown, Oct 24 1888 Sex:M Child# 3 Herbert C Richardson Winchendon, MA & Mercy R Thomas Hanson, MA
RICHARDSON, Unknown, Oct 14 1902 Sex:M Child# 5 Fred R Richardson Vermont & Delia Fontaine Mass
RICHER, Alice Adrienne, Sep 10 1910 Sex:F Child# 1 Albert Richer Nashua, NH & Helene Malenfant Canada
RICHER, Aurore Cecile, Apr 17 1893 Sex:F Child# 4 Joseph Richer Manchester, NH & Leona Laroude Canada
RICHER, Claude Raymond, Oct 14 1918 Sex:M Child# 1 Napoleon Richer Nashua, NH & Exilda Girouard Nashua, NH
RICHER, Doris Isabell, Oct 27 1916 Sex:F Child# 2 Moise Richer Nashua, NH & Mary Dalton Dundee, Scotland
RICHER, Grace Isabelle, May 27 1915 Sex:F Child# 1 Moses Richer Nashua, NH & Mary Dalton Scotland
RICHER, Irene Olivette, Dec 1 1932 Sex:F Child# 4 Napoleon Richer NH & Exilda Girouard NH
RICHER, Jesse, Jan 21 1890 Sex:F Child# 9 Isaac Richer Canada & Emelie Lefebore Canada
RICHER, Joseph Albert, Dec 30 1914 Sex:M Child# 1 Albert Richer Nashua, NH & Marie Levesque Canada Stillborn
RICHER, Joseph H H, Dec 22 1893 Sex:M Child# 10 Isaac Richer Canada & Emelie Lefebvre Canada
RICHER, Lucille Rita, Dec 19 1919 Sex:F Child# 2 Napoleon Richer Nashua, NH & Exilia Girouard Nashua, NH
RICHER, Marie C, Mar 31 1887 Sex:F Child# 7 Isaac Richer P Q & Emelie Lefebvre P Q
RICHER, Napoleon, Dec 14 1896 Sex:M Child# 11 Isaac Richer Canada & Emelie Lefebvre Canada
RICHER, Roland Leo, May 18 1928 Sex:M Child# 3 Napoleon Richer Nashua, NH & Exilda Girouard Nashua, NH
RICHIE, Pearl Ernestine, Oct 27 1891 Sex:F Child# 3 F A Richie NH & Estella V Prescott Fitchburg, MA
RICHMOND, George Arnold, Mar 22 1892 Sex:M Child# 3 William S Richmond Winthrop, ME & Mary J West Brooklyn, NY
RICHMOND, George P, Nov 16 1890 Sex:M Child# 1 Moses P Richmond Canada & Nellie A Moore Mass
RICHMOND, Lucille Belle R, Sep 16 1913 Sex:F Child# 4 Lawrence Richmond Springfield, MA & May Caplejohn Jackson
RICHMOND, Ruth W, Jun 4 1902 Sex:F Child# 4 Will Richmond Maine & Mary West
RICHMOND, Ruth Weston, Mar 22 1892 Sex:F Child# 2 William S Richmond Winthrop, ME & Mary J West Brooklyn, NY
RICHMOND, Winthrop Edson, Apr 19 1916 Sex:M Child# 1 George A Richmond Nashua, NH & Ardell E Edson Nashua, NH
RICORD, Alfred, Mar 24 1895 Sex:M Child# 3 Alphonse Ricord Canada & Elise Lavoie Canada
RICORD, J Fernand Leon, Apr 5 1921 Sex:M Child# 1 Leon Ricord NH & M A Antoinette Caron Canada
RICORD, Joseph Roger, Aug 26 1926 Sex:M Child# 2 Wilfred Ricord Nashua, NH & Estelle Blazon Lowell, MA
RIDDLE, Wallace Grafton, Oct 17 1927 Sex:M Child# 1 Wallace G Riddle Milford, NH & Lillian Rimmi Websterville, MA
RIDEOUT, Camille A P, Jan 22 1903 Sex:F Child# 3 Lewis Rideout Hollis, NH & Angeline Robichaud Nashua, NH
RIDEOUT, Hazel I, Apr 24 1894 Sex:F Child# 1 Frank P Rideout Wilton, NH & Ida L Donahue Freeport, ME
RIDEOUT, Mary E, Aug 26 1894 Sex:F Child# 1 Lewis Rideout Hollis, NH & Angelina Robichaud Nashua, NH
RIDGE, John French, Jun 10 1908 Sex:M Child# 2 John Ridge St Petersburg,Russia & Sadie French Concord, NH
RIEDLE, Maude Amanda, Jul 20 1923 Sex:F Child# 3 Joan Riedle Roxbury, MA & Maude E Lamour Lowell, MA
RIEITER, Helen, Nov 10 1924 Sex:F Child# 4 Miles Rieiter Manchester, NH & Helen Sweeney Manchester, NH
RIEL, Cecile, Aug 3 1898 Sex:F Child# 5 Joseph Riel Mooers, NY & Phoebe Laporte Mooers, NY
RIEL, Eva, Apr 3 1895 Sex:F Child# 4 Joseph Riel Moores, NY & Phoebe Laporte Moores, NY
RIEL, Irene, Aug 7 1903 Sex:F Child# 6 Joseph Riel Canada & Phoebe Laporte Canada
RIEL, Irene, Oct 29 1907 Sex:F Child# 9 Joseph Riel US & Phoebe Laporte US
RIEL, Marie, Aug 12 1901 Sex:F Child# 6 Joseph Riel Canada & Phoebee Laporte Moores Jct, NY
RIELEY, Bernard Joseph, Jun 4 1889 Sex:M Child# 10 John M Rieley Ireland & Maggie Degan Ireland
RIELLY, Unknown, Dec 3 1902 Sex:F Child# 8 Peter Rielly Nashua, NH & Mary Coffey Nashua, NH
RIELLY, William J, Sep 21 1888 Sex:M Child# 1 Peter Rielly New York & Mary Cofly Nashua, NH
RIENDEAU, Aldea, Jan 14 1890 Sex:F Child# 7 Narcisse Riendeau Vermont & Sophie Salvail Canada
RIENDEAU, Alfred, Sep 13 1888 Sex:F Child# 14 Alfred Riendeau Canada & Theotise Geblanc Canada
RIENDEAU, Alice Theresa Marie, Feb 10 1926 Sex:F Child# 2 Louis Riendeau Lowell, MA & Almanda Poliquin Somersworth
RIENDEAU, Anna, Aug 18 1919 Sex:F Child# 1 Frederick Riendeau Nashua, NH & Anna Sirois Nashua, NH Stillborn
RIENDEAU, Attala, May 15 1896 Sex:F Child# 4 Noe Riendeau US & Melendy Belair US
RIENDEAU, Blanche Marianna, Jul 11 1913 Sex:F Child# 2 John Riendeau Nashua, NH & Marie Anctil Canada
RIENDEAU, Charles L Joseph, Jul 1 1931 Sex:M Child# 3 Louie M Riendeau Lowell, MA & Viola M Poliquin Somersworth
RIENDEAU, Cora, Feb 23 1911 Sex:F Child# 1 John B Riendeau Nashua, NH & Marie Louise Anctil Canada
RIENDEAU, Eva, Jul 7 1894 Sex:F Child# 3 Noe Riendeau US & Melinda Belais US
RIENDEAU, Henrietta, Jan 11 1892 Sex:F Child# 8 Narcisse Riendeau Canada & Sophie Salvail Canada
RIENDEAU, Irane, Sep 11 1893 Sex:F Child# 9 Narcisse Riendeau Vermont & Sophie Salvail Canada
RIENDEAU, Joseph William, Jan 25 1896 Sex:M Child# 6 Joseph Riendeau Canada & Marie Sylvestre Canada
RIENDEAU, Lorette Rachel, Feb 2 1921 Sex:F Child# 3 Frederick Riendeau Nashua, NH & Anne Sirois Nashua, NH
RIENDEAU, Louis Lionel, Jul 4 1921 Sex:M Child# 1 Louis Riendeau US & Viola Poliquin Nashua, NH
RIENDEAU, Marie, Aug 18 1919 Sex:F Child# 2 Frederick Riendeau Nashua, NH & Anna Sirois Nashua, NH Stillborn
RIENDEAU, Marie A, Feb 15 1887 Sex:F Child# 6 Narcisse Riendeau Vermont, N S & Sophie Salvail P Q
RIENDEAU, Marie A C, Jun 16 1887 Sex:F Child# 4 Joseph Riendeau P Q & Marie Sylvestre P Q
RIENDEAU, Marie I A, Jul 27 1890 Sex:F Child# 5 Joseph Riendeau Canada & Marie Sylvestie Canada
RIENDEAU, Narcisse E, Feb 20 1887 Sex:M Child# 12 Alfred Riendeau Canada & Theotise Leblanc Canada
RIETAS, Constadenia, Feb 11 1918 Sex:F Child# 2 George Rietas Greece & Mary Bucos Greece
RIGAS, Christina, Sep 30 1920 Sex:F Child# 1 James Rigas Greece & Fortina Rotscus Greece

RIGAS, George, Apr 19 1922 Sex:M Child# 2 John Dimos Rigas Greece & Fortina Rotsius Greece
RIGG, Arthur Roland, Oct 1 1927 Sex:M Child# 2 William Rigg England & Ruby Morneau Lawrence, MA
RIGG, Kenneth, Sep 4 1933 Sex:M Child# 3 William Rigg England & Ruby Morneau Lawrence, MA
RIGGS, Elwin Augustus, Sep 16 1910 Sex:M Child# 2 Frank L Riggs Buckton, NY & Minnie Merrill Woburn, MA
RIGGS, Harlan Fremont, Feb 22 1907 Sex:M Child# 1 Frank Lelan Riggs Stockholm, NY & Minnie I Merrill Woburn, MA
RIGGS, Vincent William, Nov 10 1922 Sex:M Child# 1 William Riggs England & Ruby Morneau Lawrence, MA
RIGNEY, Charles Raymond, Mar 16 1912 Sex:M Child# 2 Charles B Rigney Nashua, NH & Rose Morin Nashua, NH
RIGNEY, Dora Gertrude, Mar 28 1894 Sex:F Child# 2 Charles E Rigney Malone, NY & Dora J Healey Boston, MA
RIGNEY, Helen, Jul 1 1888 Sex:F Child# 1 John W Rigney Malone & Mary Ellen Rigney Nashua, NH
RIGNEY, James LeRoy, Jan 20 1893 Sex:M Child# 1 Charles E Rigney Malone, NY & Dora J Healey Boston, MA
RIGNEY, Leroy Paul, Apr 6 1921 Sex:M Child# 4 Charles B Rigney Nashua, NH & Rose A Morin Nashua, NH
RIGNEY, Mary Catherine, May 9 1897 Sex:F Child# 3 Charles E Rigney Malone, NY & Dora J Healy Boston, MA
RIGNEY, Robert William, Jun 26 1889 Sex:M Child# 2 John W Rigney Nashua, NH & Mary E Nashua, NH
RIGNEY, Unknown, Jan 2 1893 Sex:M Child# 1 Frank Rigney NY & Mary Keenan Lowell, MA
RIGNEY, Unknown, Dec 17 1913 Sex:M Child# 3 Charles E Rigney Nashua, NH & Rose A Morin Nashua, NH
RIGNON, Henry, Oct 19 1890 Sex:M Child# 1 Henry Rignon New York & Etta Reynolds Nashua, NH
RILEY, Catherine, Sep 8 1898 Sex:F Child# 7 Henry P Riley Malone, NY & Annie Lynch Ireland
RILEY, Charles, Jun 25 1894 Sex:M Child# 5 H P Riley Malone, NY & Annie Lynch Ireland
RILEY, Charles E, Sep 5 1887 Sex:M Child# 9 John M Riley Ireland & Margaret Degnan Ireland
RILEY, Charles Richard, Nov 30 1918 Sex:M Child# 1 Charles E Riley New York & Grace E Connor Nashua, NH
RILEY, Edward, May 29 1892 Sex:M Child# 4 Henry P Riley New York & Annie Lynch Ireland
RILEY, George Francis, Mar 15 1890 Sex:M Child# 3 Henry Riley NY & Anna Lynch Ireland
RILEY, Grace May, Mar 24 1907 Sex:F Child# 1 Webster C Riley Calais, ME & Florence E Budrow Franklin, NH
RILEY, Harry, Jun 4 1896 Sex:M Child# 5 Peter Riley Nashua, NH & Mary Coffee Ireland
RILEY, John Frances, Dec 3 1897 Sex:M Child# 2 Thomas J Riley Nashua, NH & Ellen N T Moran England
RILEY, Joseph Herbert, Dec 22 1908 Sex:M Child# 5 Webster Riley Maine & Maud Frost Maine
RILEY, Lawrence, Oct 20 1896 Sex:M Child# 6 Henry P Riley Burke, NY & Annie Lynch Ireland
RILEY, Mary E, May 26 1893 Sex:F Child# 4 John Riley Ireland & Maggie Degnan Ireland
RILEY, Owen, Sep 19 1896 Sex:M Child#  Owen Riley New York & Ella M Hobart Nashua, NH
RILEY, Pauline, Jul 6 1920 Sex:F Child# 2 Charles E Riley New York & Grace Connor Nashua, NH
RILEY, Rebecca, Jan 26 1905 Sex:F Child# 9 Peter L Riley Nashua, NH & Mary E Coffey Nashua, NH
RILEY, Richard Doliver, Nov 3 1930 Sex:M Child# 1 Melville S Riley Gloucester, MA & Helen A Doliver Adams, MA
RILEY, Rose M, May 4 1887 Sex:F Child# 1 Henry P Riley Malone, NY & Annie Lynch Ireland
RILEY, Ruth, Oct 27 1898 Sex:F Child# 6 Peter L Riley Nashua, NH & Mary Coffee Nashua, NH
RILEY, Thomas H, May 8 1887 Sex:M Child# 3 Julius Riley Ireland & Margaret Ireland
RILEY, Thomas Joseph, Jul 5 1896 Sex:M Child# 1 Thomas J Riley Nashua, NH & Ellen Moran England
RILEY, Unknown, Jan 19 1896 Sex:F Child# 14 John M Riley Ireland & Maggie Dagnan Ireland Stillborn
RILEY, Unknown, Feb 22 1897 Sex:M Child# 16 John Riley Ireland & Margaret Degnan Ireland Stillborn
RILEY, Unknown, May 26 1912 Sex:M Child# 1 James Riley Malden, MA & Corinne Deschamps Nashua, NH
RILEY, Unknown, Sep 20 1926 Sex:F Child# 1 William Riley Nashua, NH & Catherine Owens Newmarket, NH Stillborn
RILEY, Unknown, Jun 17 1929 Sex:F Child# 2 William Riley Nashua, NH & Catherine Owens Newmarket, NH
RILEY, William Henry, Dec 12 1888 Sex:M Child# 2 Henry Riley N Y & Ann Lynch Ireland
RILEY, William John, Dec 23 1930 Sex:M Child# 3 William H Riley Nashua, NH & Katherine Owens Newmarket, NH
RILLAS, Unknown, Jul 14 1929 Sex:M Child# 5 Peter Rillas Greece & Varvara Sirigon Greece
RINEY, Frances, Dec 26 1890 Sex:F Child# 4 John Riney Ireland & Maggie Shea Boston, MA
RINEY, John, Aug 16 1888 Sex:M Child# 3 John Riney Ireland & Maggie Riney Cambridge, MA
RINEY, John, Dec 25 1893 Sex:M Child# 5 John Riney Ireland & Maggie Shed Boston, MA
RINEY, Robert, Dec 19 1889 Sex:M Child# 10 Patrick Riney Ireland & E Fittspatrick Ireland
RINEY, Unknown, Jun 20 1888 Sex:F Child# 5 Dan P Riney Ireland & Annie Ireland
RING, Adelbert E Clark, Dec 4 1919 Sex:M Child# 3 Forrest W C Ring Barnstead, NH & Dora Barber Three Rivers, MA
RING, Frances Elizabeth, Jan 23 1915 Sex:F Child# 2 Robert G Ring Wilton, NH & Olive Livermore Wilton, NH
RING, Helen Livermore, Oct 25 1916 Sex:F Child# 3 Robert G Ring Wilton, NH & Olive Livermore Wilton, NH
RINQUETTE, Joseph Roger R, Feb 4 1924 Sex:M Child#  Albert Rinquette Canada & Olivine A Couture Gonic, NH
RIORDAN, Hannah Maria, Jan 8 1898 Sex:F Child# 2 Timothy Riordan Ireland & Josei Diggins Ireland
RIORDAN, Kate A, Jan 8 1896 Sex:F Child# 1 Timothy Riordan Ireland & Johanna Diggins Ireland
RIOUX, Albina, Jun 1 1894 Sex:F Child# 4 Dieudonna Rioux Canada & Amanda Ouellette Canada
RIOUX, Albina Rita, Apr 30 1925 Sex:F Child# 2 Clement Rioux Nashua, NH & Mode St Laurent Nashua, NH
RIOUX, Alice Celia, Jul 23 1906 Sex:F Child# 5 Alphonse Rioux Canada & Delima Ouellette Canada
RIOUX, Alphonse, Jr, Oct 18 1935 Sex:M Child# 3 Alphonse Rioux Canada & Marie E Casista Nashua, NH
RIOUX, Andrea D, May 21 1900 Sex:F Child# 8 Dieudonne Rioux Canada & Amanda Ouellette Canada
RIOUX, Arthur, May 5 1897 Sex:M Child# 1 Arthur Rioux Canada & Marie Cayouette Canada
RIOUX, Arthur, Mar 31 1903 Sex:M Child# 9 Dieudonne Rioux Canada & Amanda Ouellette Canada
RIOUX, Arthur, Feb 24 1908 Sex:M Child# 2 Alfred Rioux Canada & Helene Cote Canada
RIOUX, Clement, Jan 12 1899 Sex:M Child# 7 Dieudonne Rioux Canada & Amanda Ouellette Canada
RIOUX, Desire Normand, Jun 26 1922 Sex:M Child# 1 Clement Rioux Nashua, NH & Modeste St Laurent Nashua, NH
RIOUX, Emelia, Jun 3 1907 Sex:F Child# 5 George Rioux Canada & Lea Meunier Canada
RIOUX, Eugenie, Jan 8 1908 Sex:F Child# 11 Dieudonne Rioux Canada & Amanda Ouellette Canada
RIOUX, Eva Rose Valida, Apr 30 1900 Sex:F Child# 2 Alphonse Rioux Canada & Delima Ouellette Canada
RIOUX, Francois Xavier, Feb 12 1900 Sex:M Child# 1 Philias Rioux Canada & Marie April Canada
RIOUX, George, Apr 19 1902 Sex:M Child# 1 George Rioux Canada & Lea Meunier Canada
RIOUX, George Aldege M, Aug 6 1902 Sex:M Child# 3 Arthur Rioux Canada & Marie Cailloutte Canada
RIOUX, Georgina, Aug 4 1891 Sex:F Child# 12 Octave Rioux Canada & Georgina Chasse Canada
RIOUX, Gloria, Feb 8 1932 Sex:F Child# 2 Leo Rioux Nashua, NH & Josephine Marois Nashua, NH

RIOUX, Hector, Sep 25 1920 Sex:M Child# 1 Alphonse Rioux Canada & Melina Desjardins Canada
RIOUX, Henri, Oct 24 1892 Sex:M Child# 1 Dieudonne Rioux Canada & Amanda Ouellet Canada
RIOUX, Irene Josephine, Nov 8 1926 Sex:F Child# 2 Wilfred Rioux Nashua, NH & Melina Marois Nashua, NH
RIOUX, Irene Mary, Sep 23 1915 Sex:F Child# 12 George Rioux Canada & Lea Meunier Canada
RIOUX, Isabelle Lorraine, Sep 23 1915 Sex:F Child# 11 George Rioux Canada & Lea Meunier Canada
RIOUX, Jean B Raymond, Jun 13 1920 Sex:M Child# 4 Joseph Rioux Canada & Marie A Vaillancourt Nashua, NH
RIOUX, Joseph, Oct 25 1904 Sex:M Child# 10 Dieudonne Rioux Canada & Amanda Ouellette Canada
RIOUX, Joseph, Mar 25 1924 Sex:M Child# 3 Wilfred Rioux Canada & Alice Cormier Maine Stillborn
RIOUX, Joseph Edouard, Apr 12 1897 Sex:M Child# 6 Dieudonne Rioux Canada & Amanda Ouellette Canada
RIOUX, Joseph Eugene, Jan 22 1899 Sex:M Child# 1 Arsene Rioux Canada & Desauges Rioux Canada
RIOUX, Joseph Geo Leonide, Oct 1 1902 Sex:M Child# 3 Timothe Rioux Canada & Marie Ouellette Canada
RIOUX, Joseph Girard, Dec 18 1924 Sex:M Child# 1 Wilfred Rioux Nashua, NH & Malina Marois Nashua, NH
RIOUX, Joseph Henri Lucien, May 20 1912 Sex:M Child# 1 Joseph Rioux Canada & Marianna Vaillancourt Nashua, NH
RIOUX, Joseph Israel, Apr 16 1904 Sex:M Child# 3 George Rioux Canada & Lea Meunier Canada
RIOUX, Joseph Louis, Mar 28 1902 Sex:M Child# 3 Arsene Rioux Canada & Desange Rioux Canada
RIOUX, Joseph Normand, Jan 2 1926 Sex:M Child# 1 David Rioux Canada & Regina Thibault NH
RIOUX, Joseph Paul Charles, Apr 25 1916 Sex:M Child# 2 Joseph Rioux Canada & M Anna Vaillancourt Nashua, NH
RIOUX, Joseph Roland Irenee, Oct 31 1927 Sex:M Child# 1 Willie Rioux Canada & Emma Plante Manchester, NH
RIOUX, Joseph Simon, Mar 19 1914 Sex:M Child# 10 George Rioux Canada & Leah Merier Canada
RIOUX, Joseph Wilfrid, Apr 14 1901 Sex:M Child# 2 Timothy Rioux Canada & Marie Ouellette Canada
RIOUX, Josephine Atala, Aug 18 1908 Sex:F Child# 4 Philias Rioux Canada & Marie April Canada
RIOUX, Lea, Aug 2 1895 Sex:F Child# 5 Dieudonne Rioux Canada & Amanda Ouellette Canada
RIOUX, Lena Juliette, Feb 19 1935 Sex:F Child# 1 Lucien Rioux Nashua, NH & Olivette Desautels Nashua, NH
RIOUX, Leo Arthur, Dec 17 1920 Sex:M Child# 16 George Rioux Canada & Lea Maunier Canada
RIOUX, Leo Conrad, Aug 15 1929 Sex:M Child# 1 Leo Rioux Nashua, NH & Josephine Marois Nashua, NH
RIOUX, Leon, Jan 7 1900 Sex:M Child# 2 Arsene Rioux Canada & Desange Rioux Canada
RIOUX, Leona Rita, Dec 18 1920 Sex:F Child# 17 George J Rioux Canada & Lea Maunier Canada
RIOUX, Lillian Blanche, Oct 9 1909 Sex:F Child# 7 George Rioux Canada & Lea Meunier Canada
RIOUX, Lina, Aug 10 1901 Sex:F Child# 3 Thomas Rioux Canada & Delvina Ross Canada
RIOUX, M Bertha Lorraine, Mar 25 1919 Sex:F Child# 15 George Rioux Canada & Lea Meunier Canada
RIOUX, M Georgianna, Dec 7 1891 Sex:F Child# 13 Paul Rioux Canada & Marie Lavoie Canada
RIOUX, M Susienne Laurette, Jul 12 1917 Sex:F Child# 3 Joseph Rioux Canada & Marie A Vaillancourt Nashua, NH
RIOUX, Margaret Rita, Oct 16 1922 Sex:F Child# 1 Delphus Rioux Canada & Nora Morin Waterville, ME
RIOUX, Marie, Sep 26 1926 Sex:F Child# 2 David Rioux Canada & Regina Thibault NH  Stillborn
RIOUX, Marie Celina B, Oct 4 1921 Sex:F Child# 3 Pilip Rioux Canada & Roseanna Bellavance Canada
RIOUX, Marie E Delia, Dec 17 1898 Sex:F Child# 1 Alphonse Rioux Canada & Delima Ouellette Canada
RIOUX, Marie E R J, Mar 27 1903 Sex:F Child# 2 George Rioux Canada & Lea Meunier Canada
RIOUX, Marie Elisa L, Jun 23 1908 Sex:F Child# 6 George Rioux Canada & Lea Meunier Canada
RIOUX, Marie Lorraine There, Feb 25 1934 Sex:F Child# 2 Nazaire Rioux Canada & Lumina Morin Nashua, NH
RIOUX, Marie Louise Eugenie, Dec 22 1917 Sex:F Child# 1 Philippe Rioux Canada & Rose Anna Bellavance Canada
RIOUX, Marie Rose Alma, May 17 1903 Sex:F Child# 2 Philias Rioux Canada & Marie April Canada
RIOUX, Napoleon Alfred, Apr 14 1903 Sex:M Child# 3 Alphonse Rioux Canada & Delima Ouellette Canada
RIOUX, Pauline Laura, Aug 4 1932 Sex:F Child# 2 Alphonse Rioux Canada & Marie A Casista Nashua, NH
RIOUX, Pearl Marie, Mar 16 1933 Sex:F Child# 1 Nazaire O Rioux Canada & Lumina M Morin Nashua, NH
RIOUX, Philip Arthur, Jun 28 1926 Sex:M Child# 4 Philip Rioux Canada & R Bellavance Canada
RIOUX, Phyllis Joan, May 26 1932 Sex:F Child# 1 Philip Rioux Worcester, MA & Rose Marchenonis E Vandergrift, PA
RIOUX, Raymond, Mar 20 1917 Sex:M Child# 13 George Rioux Canada & Lea Meunier Canada
RIOUX, Robert, Mar 20 1917 Sex:M Child# 14 George Rioux Canada & Lea Meunier Canada
RIOUX, Robert Ovila, Feb 1 1934 Sex:M Child# 1 Ovila Rioux Sherbrooke, Quebec & Rachel Ackerman Newark, NJ
RIOUX, Roland, Dec 23 1927 Sex:M Child# 3 Wilfrid Rioux Nashua, NH & Melina Marois Nashua, NH
RIOUX, Rolande Priscilla, Oct 26 1928 Sex:F Child# 2 Willie Rioux Canada & Emma Plante Salem, MA
RIOUX, Sylvio Roger Paul, Jul 15 1929 Sex:M Child# 1 Octave Rioux Canada & Edna Lavoie Nashua, NH
RIOUX, Theresa Lareine, Apr 29 1927 Sex:F Child# 3 Clement Rioux Nashua, NH & M St Laurent Nashua, NH
RIOUX, Ulric Paul, Dec 12 1935 Sex:M Child# 5 Philippe Rioux Canada & Rose A Bellavance Canada
RIOUX, Wilfred Herald, Mar 20 1925 Sex:M Child# 3 Wilfred Rioux Canada & Alice Cormier Van Buren, ME
RIOUX, Yvonne Hugette, Sep 1 1904 Sex:F Child# 6 Alphonse Rioux Canada & Delima Ouelette Canada
RIOUX, Yvonne Maria, Mar 11 1906 Sex:F Child# 4 George Rioux Canada & Lea Meunier Canada
RIPLEY, Joseph Adolph, Feb 5 1897 Sex:M Child# 2 Joseph D Ripley Canada & Mary Roi Canada
RIPLEY, Unknown, Nov 25 1889 Sex:F Child# 4 Allen M Ripley Londonderry, NH & Belle Fellows Derry, NH
RITCHIE, Frank Eugene, Dec 16 1895 Sex:M Child# 4 Fred A Ritchie NH & Estella Prescott
RITCHIE, Gladys, Apr 7 1888 Sex:F Child# 2 Fred A Ritchie Groveton, MA & Estella Prescott Fitchburg, MA
RITKWICZ, Anthony, Jun 17 1917 Sex:M Child# 5 Simon Ritkwicz Russia & Beatrice Yakezuta Russia
RITSON, Daniel Dickerson, Dec 19 1933 Sex:M Child# 1 Daniel D Ritson Brooklyn, NY & M L Campbell Hudson, NH
RITTENBERG, George Henry, Mar 20 1909 Sex:M Child# 1 Otto Rittenberg Detroit, MI & Lillian Fortier Northampton
RIVAIS, Emile Napoleon, Jun 30 1904 Sex:M Child# 5 Napoleon Rivais NH & Anna Faubert Canada
RIVAIS, Marie Gertrude, Sep 1 1905 Sex:F Child# 6 Napoleon Rivais NH & Anna Faubert Canada
RIVAIS, Marie Laure, Apr 22 1903 Sex:F Child# 4 Napoleon Rivais NH & Anna Faubert Canada
RIVARD, Albert Armand L, Dec 21 1908 Sex:M Child# 4 Napoleon Rivard Canada & Celina Langlais Canada
RIVARD, Albert Auguste, Oct 14 1901 Sex:M Child# 3 Auguste Rivard Canada & Cordelia Pelletier Canada
RIVARD, Alice Bertha, Mar 16 1908 Sex:F Child# 1 Pierre Rivard Canada & Bertha Briere Canada
RIVARD, Anna Delvina, Jan 13 1902 Sex:F Child# 8 Joseph Rivard Canada & Delvina Pelletier Canada
RIVARD, Auguste, Jan 18 1913 Sex:M Child# 15 Joseph Rivard Canada & Josephine Pelletier Canada
RIVARD, Edouard, Jul 16 1893 Sex:M Child# 2 Joseph Rivard Canada & Delvina Peltier Canada

RIVARD, Ernest Norman, Dec 28 1934 Sex:M Child# 1 (No Parents Listed)
RIVARD, Eugene Auguste, Mar 9 1910 Sex:M Child# 13 Joseph Rivard Canada & Delvina Pelletier Canada
RIVARD, Eugenie, Aug 21 1898 Sex:F Child#  Thomas Rivard Canada & Eugenie Mignault Canada Stillborn
RIVARD, Henri Aime, May 13 1914 Sex:M Child# 10 Joseph Rivard Canada & Delvina Pelletier Canada
RIVARD, Henry, Apr 5 1903 Sex:M Child# 8 Joseph Rivard Canada & Delvina Peltier Canada
RIVARD, J B Sylvio, Feb 14 1907 Sex:M Child# 10 Joseph Rivard Canada & Delvina Pelletier Canada
RIVARD, Jos Edouard Roland, Dec 10 1916 Sex:M Child# 3 Napoleon Rivard Canada & Marie Lagace Canada
RIVARD, Jos Ernest Edw, Nov 27 1930 Sex:M Child# 11 Napoleon Rivard Canada & Marie Lagasse Canada
RIVARD, Jos Geo Edouard, Feb 22 1927 Sex:M Child# 9 Napoleon Rivard Canada & Marie Lagace Canada
RIVARD, Joseph, Jan 16 1895 Sex:M Child# 3 Joseph Rivard Canada & Delvina Peltier Canada
RIVARD, Joseph, Mar 17 1901 Sex:M Child# 12 Thomas Rivard Canada & Eugenie Mignon Canada Stillborn
RIVARD, Joseph A, Nov 8 1887 Sex:M Child#  Eusebe Rivard Canada & Georgina Caron Canada
RIVARD, Joseph A, Mar 20 1892 Sex:M Child# 1 Joseph Rivard Canada & Amanda Decoteau Canada
RIVARD, Joseph E Robert, Feb 20 1929 Sex:M Child# 10 Napoleon Rivard Canada & Marie Lagasse Canada
RIVARD, Joseph Gagne, Oct 22 1929 Sex:M Child# 3 (No Parents Listed)
RIVARD, Joseph Raoul, Mar 2 1924 Sex:M Child# 7 Napoleon Rivard Canada & Marie Lagasse Canada
RIVARD, Laurette Mea, Mar 17 1908 Sex:F Child# 11 Joseph Rivard Canada & Delvina Pelletier Canada
RIVARD, Leo, May 28 1902 Sex:M Child# 3 Michel Rivard Canada & Clara Bernier Canada
RIVARD, M A Josephine, Sep 5 1893 Sex:F Child# 3 Eusebe Rivard Canada & Georgiana Caron Canada
RIVARD, M elizabeth Elise, Jul 5 1914 Sex:F Child# 1 Napoleon Rivard Canada & Marie Lagasse Canada
RIVARD, M J d'Arc Gabrielle, Jul 23 1921 Sex:F Child# 6 Napoleon Rivard Canada & Marie Lagace Canada
RIVARD, Marie, Oct 24 1927 Sex:F Child# 8 Thomas Rivard Canada & Rose A Despres Canada
RIVARD, Marie Alice, Apr 19 1898 Sex:F Child# 5 Joseph Rivard Canada & Delvina Pelletier Canada
RIVARD, Marie Anna Jeannette, Apr 8 1925 Sex:F Child# 8 Napoleon Rivard Canada & Muriel Lagace Canada
RIVARD, Marie Anne, Nov 6 1915 Sex:F Child# 2 Napoleon Rivard Canada & Marie Lagace Canada
RIVARD, Marie B Irene, Mar 8 1920 Sex:F Child# 5 Napoleon Rivard Canada & Marie Lagasse Canada
RIVARD, Marie Elise, Jun 26 1902 Sex:F Child# 1 Omer Rivard Canada & Alexina Berube Canada
RIVARD, Marie G J L, Jun 1 1907 Sex:F Child# 3 Napoleon Rivard Canada & Celina Langlais Canada
RIVARD, Marie Laure A, Dec 8 1897 Sex:F Child# 7 Peter Rivard Canada & Eugenie Mignault Canada
RIVARD, Marie Rosa, Jan 15 1900 Sex:F Child# 6 Joseph Rivard Canada & Delvina Pelletier Canada
RIVARD, Marie rose, Dec 6 1903 Sex:F Child# 2 Omer Rivard Canada & Alexina Berube Canada
RIVARD, Marie Rose de L, Mar 14 1901 Sex:F Child# 2 Michel Rivard Canada & Clara Bernier Canada
RIVARD, Marie Therese Stella, Aug 7 1932 Sex:F Child# 12 Nap Rivard St Pascal, PQ & Marie Lagasse Montreal, PQ
RIVARD, Odile Celina, Aug 6 1911 Sex:F Child# 14 Joseph Rivard Canada & Delvina Pelletier Canada
RIVARD, Olivette Eugenie, Aug 31 1926 Sex:F Child# 1 Ernest Rivard Canada & Irene Jeannotte Nashua, NH
RIVARD, Onesime, Dec 22 1896 Sex:M Child# 4 Joseph Rivard Canada & Delphina Pelletier Canada
RIVARD, Paul, Oct 24 1921 Sex:M Child# 1 Gerard Rivard Canada & Anna Gervais Westford, MA
RIVARD, Robert, Apr 30 1924 Sex:M Child# 5 Etienne D Rivard Canada & Louise St Jules Canada
RIVARD, Thomas, Sep 17 1900 Sex:M Child# 11 Thomas Rivard Canada & Eugenie Ulignon Canada Stillborn
RIVARD, Yvonne Alberta, Jul 19 1904 Sex:F Child# 11 Thomas Rivard Canada & Eugenie Mignon Canada
RIVARD, Yvonne Celina, Mar 29 1900 Sex:F Child# 2 Auguste Rivard Canada & Cordelia Pelletier Canada
RIVARD, Yvonne Eva, Dec 26 1904 Sex:F Child# 9 Joseph Rivard Canada & Delvina Peltier Canada
RIVER, Leon Napoleon, Dec 24 1895 Sex:M Child# 3 Joseph River Salem, MA & Elizabeth Gallagher Ireland
RIVERE, Priscilla Claire, Apr 24 1921 Sex:F Child# 8 Alex Rivere Canada & Zelia Lemieux Canada
RIVERNIDER, Francis Braton, Dec 21 1913 Sex:M Child# 1 Francis Rivernider Fall River, MA & Crete I Tilliatt Wo
RIVERS, Fred, Apr 25 1888 Sex:M Child# 3 John A Rivers New York & Mary Glode New York
RIVERS, Joseph Robert, Apr 15 1894 Sex:M Child# 2 Joseph P Rivers Salem, MA & Lizzie Gallagher Ireland
RIVERS, Paul Denis, Apr 1 1892 Sex:M Child# 1 Joseph P Rivers Salem, MA & Elizabeth Gallagher Ireland
RIVERS, Sylvia May, Sep 27 1916 Sex:F Child# 3 Frank Eugene Rivers Montgomery, VT & Della May Case Milville, NY
RIVET, Edwin, Nov 18 1901 Sex:M Child# 3 Napoleon Rivet Nashua, NH & Anna Faubert Canada
RIVET, M Priscilla Albertin, Aug 26 1928 Sex:F Child# 1 Rosario Rivet Canada & Marie Asselin Burke, Idaho
RIVET, Marie Elizabeth, Jan 10 1898 Sex:F Child# 4 Joseph Rivet Salem, MA & Elizabeth Gallagher Ireland
RIVET, Marie Joan Doris, May 22 1934 Sex:F Child# 2 Rosario Rivet Canada & Mary Asselin Idaho
RIVET, Pierre Paul, Oct 24 1898 Sex:M Child# 1 Napoleon Rivet Nashua, NH & Anna Fanbert Canada
RIVET, Vivianne Adelia, Dec 7 1906 Sex:F Child# 7 Napoleon Rivet US & Anna Faubert Canada
RIVET, Wilfrid, Sep 2 1900 Sex:M Child# 2 Napoleon Rivet Nashua, NH & Anna Faubert Canada
RIVIER, Gerald Normand, Aug 16 1932 Sex:M Child# 3 Raymond Rivier Nashua, NH & Ger Blanchette Canada
RIVIER, Jos Raymond Paul, Dec 4 1929 Sex:M Child# 1 Raymond Rivier Nashua, NH & Gertrude Blanchette Nashua, NH
RIVIERE, Alphonse Roland, Sep 9 1912 Sex:M Child# 5 Alex Riviere Canada & Zelia Lemieux Canada
RIVIERE, Anna Lawrence, Apr 9 1905 Sex:F Child# 2 Alexandre Riviere Canada & Zelia Lemieux Canada
RIVIERE, Donald, May 10 1931 Sex:M Child# 2 Raymond Riviere Nashua, NH & Gertrude Blanchette Nashua, NH
RIVIERE, Leonard Edmond, Aug 20 1934 Sex:M Child# 4 Raymond Riviere Nashua, NH & Gertrude Blanchett Canada
RIVIERE, Marie Anne A, Jun 10 1903 Sex:F Child# 1 Alexis Riviere Canada & Zelia Lemieux Canada
RIVIERE, Maurice, Oct 23 1910 Sex:M Child# 4 Alexis Riviere Canada & Zelia Lemieux Canada
RIVIERE, Raymond Paul, Dec 2 1908 Sex:M Child# 3 Alexis Riviere Canada & Zelia Lemieux Canada
RIVIERE, Sirnone Corinne, Jun 2 1918 Sex:F Child# 7 Hescandre Riviere Canada & Zelia Lemieux Nashua, NH
RIVIERE, Theresa, Feb 14 1916 Sex:F Child# 6 Alexis Riviere Canada & Angelia Lemieux US
RIX, Hazel Mae, Aug 16 1899 Sex:F Child# 1 John J Rix Rutland, VT & Nathe Cummings NH
ROACHE, Irene Elisabeth, Jan 26 1910 Sex:F Child# 3 James H Roache Ireland & Lizzie Summerville Ireland
ROACHE, Lillian Mary, Mar 28 1912 Sex:F Child# 4 James H Roache Ireland & Lizzie Summerville Ireland
ROBBINS, Beatrice Elizabeth, Oct 3 1921 Sex:F Child# 1 Orin Robbins NH & Lillia Kelly NH
ROBBINS, Bertha Victoria, Apr 22 1912 Sex:F Child# 2 Carl Ed Robbins Nashua, NH & Bertha Blanchard Nashua, NH
ROBBINS, Carl Edward, May 19 1917 Sex:M Child# 3 Carl Edward Robbins Mass & Bertha Blanchard Nashua, NH

ROBBINS, Charles Calvin, Oct 21 1923 Sex:M Child# 2 Roger Robbins Pepperell, MA & Lydia Waite Wilder, VT
ROBBINS, Charles Henry, Aug 13 1895 Sex:M Child# 1 Charles Robbins Dunstable, MA & Julia H Woodward Fitchburg, MA
ROBBINS, Clara Abie, Jun 2 1897 Sex:F Child# 2 E A Robbins Nelson & Jessie Strong N Hartland, VT
ROBBINS, Dane, Sep 23 1902 Sex:M Child# 3 Charles Robbins Nashua, NH & Julia Woodward Nashua, NH
ROBBINS, David Freeman, Dec 2 1924 Sex:M Child# 3 Roger S Robbins Pepperell, MA & Lydia Waite Wilder, VT
ROBBINS, Elaine, Nov 18 1932 Sex:F Child# 2 D F Robbins Pepperell, MA & Mary Parker Pepperell, MA
ROBBINS, Flora Etta, Oct 31 1904 Sex:F Child# 4 Charles Robbins Nashua, NH & Julia Woodward Nashua, NH
ROBBINS, Gladys Isabelle, Oct 3 1909 Sex:F Child# 1 Carl E Robbins Nashua, NH & Bertha M Blanchard Nashua, NH
ROBBINS, Harriett N, May 19 1915 Sex:F Child# 2 Luther Robbins Nashua, NH & Ethel H Dunyou Portsmouth, NH
ROBBINS, Helen, Apr 1 1922 Sex:F Child# 1 Carl Robbins Nashua, NH & Rose Bockis Newbury, NY
ROBBINS, Henry Orlando, Jul 12 1914 Sex:M Child# 8 Charles J Robbins Nashua, NH & Julia Woodward Ashly, NH
ROBBINS, Irene May, Mar 17 1928 Sex:F Child# 1 Dana C Robbins Nashua, NH & Agnes Nauceder Gilsum, NH
ROBBINS, Isabelle Henrietta, Aug 8 1924 Sex:F Child# 6 Samuel Robbins Nashua, NH & M L Vaillancourt Nashua, NH
ROBBINS, Jane, Feb 16 1933 Sex:F Child# 5 Carl Robbins Nashua, NH & Rose Backis Newburg, NY
ROBBINS, Janet Adele, Mar 5 1934 Sex:F Child# 3 Lyman Robbins Pepperell, MA & Mary Parker Pepperell, MA
ROBBINS, Joan Blanche, Aug 13 1932 Sex:F Child# 2 Oren Robbins W Windham, NH & L Beatrice Kelley Sandown, NH
ROBBINS, John, Jul 30 1916 Sex:M Child#  Charles J Robbins Nashua, NH & Julia Woodward Ashby, MA Stillborn
ROBBINS, John Paul, Aug 21 1934 Sex:M Child# 3 Oren Robbins Windham, NH & Lillie Kelley Sandown, NH
ROBBINS, Josiath Thayer, Jun 4 1925 Sex:M Child# 5 Carl E Robbins Nashua, NH & Maud Fairbrother Vermont
ROBBINS, Kenneth Reed, Feb 16 1904 Sex:M Child# 3 Fred F Robbins Albany, VT & Lucy M Davis Wayland, MA
ROBBINS, Lester L, Apr 6 1897 Sex:M Child# 2 George W Robbins Auburn, ME & Blanche M Butler Hudson, NH
ROBBINS, Normand Oswald, Nov 10 1920 Sex:M Child# 4 Charles Robbins Nashua, NH & M L Vaillancourt Nashua, NH
ROBBINS, Patricia May, Mar 21 1925 Sex:F Child# 1 Dana C Robbins Nashua, NH & Hilda M Bell W Chazy, NY Stillborn
ROBBINS, Paul Dana, Jul 9 1931 Sex:M Child# 3 Dana Robbins Nashua, NH & Agnes Nauceder Gilsum, NH
ROBBINS, Rachell Jeannette I, Dec 21 1918 Sex:F Child# 3 Charles H Robbins NH & M L Spillancourt NH
ROBBINS, Ralph Chester, Oct 10 1927 Sex:M Child# 7 Samuel Robbins Nashua, NH & Mary Val Nashua, NH
ROBBINS, Raymond Lorenzo, Oct 25 1911 Sex:M Child# 7 Charles J Robbins Nashua, NH & Julia Woodward Ashby, MA
ROBBINS, Reuel James, Jan 9 1895 Sex:M Child# 1 George W Robbins Auburn, ME & Blanche M Butler Hudson, NH
ROBBINS, Robert, Jul 16 1925 Sex:M Child# 3 Carl Robbins Nashua, NH & Rose Bokis Newburg, NY
ROBBINS, Ruth Elizabeth, Aug 23 1914 Sex:F Child# 1 Francis W Robbins Fitchburg, MA & Helen M Robbins Fitchburg, MA
ROBBINS, Samuel Josiah, Nov 1 1922 Sex:M Child# 5 Charles Robbins Nashua, NH & Marie L Vaillancourt Nashua, NH
ROBBINS, Silvia, Mar 31 1917 Sex:F Child# 2 Charles H Robbins,Jr Nashua, NH & Marie L Vaillancourt Nashua, NH
ROBBINS, Susie Ada, Jan 11 1930 Sex:F Child# 6 Carl E Robbins Nashua, NH & Maud Fairbrothers Westminster, VT
ROBBINS, Unknown, Mar 8 1916 Sex:M Child# 1 Charles H Robbins Nashua, NH & M L Vaillancourt Nashua, NH
ROBBINS, Unknown, Jan 23 1927 Sex:F Child# 4 Carl Robbins Nashua, NH & Rose Bockis New York Stillborn
ROBBINS, Wallace Alfred, Oct 11 1894 Sex:M Child# 1 E A Robbins Vermont & Jessie Strong Nelson, NH
ROBBINS, Wilfred, Apr 17 1910 Sex:M Child# 6 Charles Robbins Nashua, NH & Julia Woodward Ashby, MA
ROBBINS, William Goodwin, Mar 27 1924 Sex:M Child# 2 Carl Robbins Nashua, NH & Rose Bockis Newburg, NY
ROBERGE, Bertha Lucille, Sep 4 1927 Sex:F Child# 3 Amedee Roberge Salmon Falls, NH & Marie Chouinard Canada
ROBERGE, Gerard Norman, Aug 12 1935 Sex:M Child# 1 Joseph Roberge Salmon Falls, NH & Rosanna Levesque Nashua, NH
ROBERGE, Gertrude Florence M, Aug 27 1929 Sex:F Child# 4 Amede Roberge Salmon Falls, NH & Marie Chouinard Canada
ROBERGE, Godefroi, Oct 15 1921 Sex:M Child# 3 Ernest Roberge Canada & Albertine Dumas Canada
ROBERGE, Lorraine Theresa, Jun 29 1925 Sex:F Child# 2 Amedee J Roberge Salmon Falls, NH & Marie U Choinard Canada
ROBERGE, Margaret, May 7 1923 Sex:F Child# 1 Napoleon Roberge Canada & Mary M Soucy Nashua, NH
ROBERGE, Marie, Jun 20 1915 Sex:F Child# 11 Eugene Roberge Canada & Albertine Dumais Canada
ROBERT, Arthur, Mar 28 1922 Sex:M Child# 6 Joseph Robert Canada & Marie Bilodeau Canada
ROBERTS, Charles Henry, Oct 20 1911 Sex:M Child# 3 William Roberts Canada & Emma L Moore Palmer, MA
ROBERTS, Charles Oscar, May 13 1930 Sex:M Child# 4 Harold F Roberts Concord, NH & Viola Gallop New Brunswick
ROBERTS, Cora Belle, Jan 22 1910 Sex:F Child# 2 William Roberts Canada & Emma L Moore Farmer, MA
ROBERTS, George S, Jr, Apr 30 1908 Sex:M Child# 5 Geo S Roberts, Sr Durham, ME & Margaret McPherson Manchester, NH
ROBERTS, Helen Marie, Jan 27 1925 Sex:F Child# 10 Charles Roberts Southbridge, MA & Naomee Roberts Southbridge, MA
ROBERTS, Joseph Fred, Aug 23 1922 Sex:M Child# 2 William Roberts Canada & Celestine Dionne Somersworth, NH
ROBERTS, Joseph Rosario Wm, Oct 6 1920 Sex:M Child# 1 William Roberts Canada & Celestine Dionne Somersworth, NH
ROBERTS, Lauretta, Jun 26 1911 Sex:F Child# 7 George S Roberts Durham, ME & Margaret McPherson Manchester, NH
ROBERTS, Margaret, Mar 10 1910 Sex:F Child# 6 Goerge S Roberts Durham, ME & Margaret McPherson Manchester, NH
ROBERTS, Marion Alice, Sep 12 1895 Sex:F Child# 2 George M Roberts Plattsburg, NY & Nellie A McAlvon Beckmantown,NY
ROBERTS, Rosamond, Jul 15 1924 Sex:F Child# 3 William Roberts Canada & Celestine Dion Somersworth, NH
ROBERTS, Roy Roland, Mar 3 1912 Sex:M Child# 1 James J Roberts Passaic, NJ & Janet MacMurray Belfast, Ireland
ROBERTS, Ruth Esther, Jun 28 1915 Sex:F Child# 4 William Roberts Canada & Emma Moore Palmer, MA
ROBERTS, Unknown, Jul 10 1894 Sex:F Child# 1 Louis G Roberts Sheffield & Alta L Gay Shelburn, MA
ROBERTS, Unknown, Jun 29 1898 Sex:M Child# 3 George M Roberts Plattsburg, NY & Nellie A McAloon Beakmantown, NY
ROBERTS, Unknown, Oct 31 1899 Sex:M Child# 4 George N Roberts NY & Nellie A McAloon NY
ROBERTS, Unknown, Dec 25 1901 Sex:F Child# 5 George M Roberts Plattsburg, NY & Nellie McLoon Beckmantown, NY
ROBERTS, Wenona Laura, Mar 14 1903 Sex:F Child# 6 George M Roberts Plattsburg, NY & Mellie A McAlorn Beckmantown,NY
ROBICHAUD, Amidee, Feb 26 1900 Sex:M Child# 5 Ludger Robichaud Canada & Mathilde Levesque Canada
ROBICHAUD, Arthur, Feb 16 1935 Sex:M Child# 2 (No Parents Listed)
ROBICHAUD, Frederick, Jan 2 1892 Sex:M Child# 1 John Robichaud Canada & Fanyette Canada
ROBICHAUD, Irene Alma, Oct 12 1915 Sex:F Child# 5 Joseph Robichaud Canada & Maria Picard Canada
ROBICHAUD, J Alfred, Oct 20 1902 Sex:M Child# 6 Ludger Robichaud Canada & Mathilde Levesque Canada
ROBICHAUD, J Alfred Romeo, May 13 1911 Sex:M Child# 2 Joseph Robichaud Canada & Maria Picard Fall River, MA
ROBICHAUD, J Sylvio Adelard, Sep 23 1914 Sex:M Child# 4 Joseph Robichaud Canada & Marie Picard Fall River, MA
ROBICHAUD, Jean Baptiste E, Dec 22 1896 Sex:M Child# 3 Ludger Robichaud Canada & Mathilde Levesque Canada
ROBICHAUD, Jean Baptiste Leon, Oct 6 1911 Sex:M Child# 4 Leon Robichaud NH & Bessie Nutter NH

ROBICHAUD, Joseph A S, Dec 8 1905 Sex:M Child# 7 Ludger Robichaud Canada & Mathilda Levesque Canada
ROBICHAUD, Joseph Arsene E, May 19 1910 Sex:M Child# 1 Joseph Robichaud Canada & Maria Picard Canada
ROBICHAUD, Joseph Ludger, Jul 4 1894 Sex:M Child# 1 Ludger Robichaud Canada & Mathilde Levesque Canada
ROBICHAUD, Leon, Oct 27 1904 Sex:M Child# 1 Leon F Robichaud Hollis, NH & Bessie M Nutter Nashua, NH
ROBICHAUD, Lucille Marie L, Aug 24 1907 Sex:F Child# 2 Leon Robichaud Mass & Bessie M Nutter NH
ROBICHAUD, M Corinne L, Nov 5 1902 Sex:F Child# 2 George Robichaud Canada & Ernestine Lizotte Canada
ROBICHAUD, M Juliette Lillian, May 3 1913 Sex:F Child# 3 Joseph Robichaud Canada & Maria Picard Fall River, MA
ROBICHAUD, Madeline Ruth, Sep 26 1908 Sex:F Child# 3 Leon Robichaud Mass & Bessie M Nutter NH
ROBICHAUD, Marie, Dec 17 1919 Sex:F Child# 4 Philippe Robichaud Canada & Oliva Lavoie Canada
ROBICHAUD, Marie A C C, Feb 25 1887 Sex:F Child# 9 Jean Bte Robichaud P Q & Candide Cote P Q
ROBICHAUD, Marie Anne G, Oct 31 1908 Sex:F Child# 7 Ludger Robichaud Canada & Mathilde Levesque Canada
ROBICHAUD, Marie Blanche, Jan 12 1896 Sex:F Child# 2 Ludger Robichaud Canada & Mathilde Levesque Canada
ROBICHAUD, Marie Blanche M, Jan 29 1900 Sex:F Child# 1 George Robichaud Nashua, NH & Ernestine Lizotte Canada
ROBICHAUD, Marie Louise Irene, Dec 1 1917 Sex:F Child# 3 Philippe Robichaud Canada & Oliva Lavoie Canada
ROBICHAUD, Marie Yvette Oliva, Jun 17 1914 Sex:F Child# 1 Philippe Robichaud Canada & Oliva Lavoie Canada
ROBICHAUD, Mariel Mathilda, Aug 5 1898 Sex:F Child# 4 Ludger Robichaud Canada & Mathilde Levesque Canada
ROBICHAUD, Maud, Sep 20 1902 Sex:F Child# 2 William A Robichaud Nashua, NH & Maud Burzean Milbury, VT Stillborn
ROBICHAUD, Otis Joseph, Apr 7 1915 Sex:M Child# 1 Otis Robichaud E Jaffrey, NH & Della Bourginon Peterborough, NH
ROBICHAUD, Raymond Eugene, Aug 28 1930 Sex:M Child# 2 Raymond Robichaud Canada & Rolande Langlois Nashua, NH
ROBICHAUD, Rita Ann, Jul 26 1931 Sex:F Child# 2 (No Parents Listed)
ROBICHAUD, Robert, Jan 14 1927 Sex:M Child# 3 Joseph Robichaud Canada & Anna St Pierre Greenville, NH
ROBICHAUD, Roger Eugene, Apr 29 1916 Sex:M Child# 4 Willie Robichaud Canada & Oliva Lavoie Canada
ROBICHAUD, Roland, Jun 29 1921 Sex:M Child# 4 Philip Robichaud Canada & Olive Lavoie Canada
ROBICHAUD, Unknown, Jan 25 1888 Sex:F Child# 4 Evangelite Robichaud St Simond, Canada & Marie Robichaud Canada
ROBICHAUD, Unknown, Feb 6 1892 Sex:F Child# 6 Jean E Robichaud St Rosalie, Canada & Mary L Asselin Camada
ROBICHAUD, Unknown, May 29 1928 Sex:M Child# 1 R Robichaud Canada & Rolande Langlois Nashua, NH Stillborn
ROBICHAUD, Unknown, Jul 21 1929 Sex:M Child# 1 Emile Robichaud Nashua, NH & Anne Doyle Nashua, NH Stillborn
ROBIDAS, Marie Claire Lucille, Sep 21 1934 Sex:F Child# 6 Alphonse Robidas Canada & Ernestine Lapointe Canada
ROBIDOUX, Alfred, Jul 21 1900 Sex:M Child# 1 Alfred Robidoux NY & Mary Huto NY
ROBIE, Everett Warwick, Mar 6 1934 Sex:M Child# 1 Harrison A Robie Londonderry, NH & Florence Snow Nashua, NH
ROBILLARD, Bernardette, Apr 11 1889 Sex:F Child# 6 Remi Robillard Canada & Marie Couter Canada
ROBILLARD, Charles, Nov 24 1890 Sex:M Child# 2 Charles Robillard Canada & Emerilda Canada
ROBILLARD, Charles E Camille, Dec 2 1898 Sex:M Child# 2 J A L Robillard Canada & Eugenie Archambault Nashua, NH
ROBILLARD, Emile, Sep 20 1893 Sex:M Child# 2 Adelard Robillard Canada & Antonia Desjardins Canada
ROBILLARD, Ernest Clovis L, Nov 7 1899 Sex:M Child# 3 J A L Robillard Canada & Eugenie Archambault Nashua, NH
ROBILLARD, M Blanche A, Aug 10 1895 Sex:M Child# 1 Charles Robillard Canada & Merilda Dube Canada
ROBILLARD, M Louise Antonia, May 22 1892 Sex:F Child# 1 Adelard Robillard Canada & Antonia Desjardins Canada
ROBILLARD, Marguerite A, Apr 16 1895 Sex:F Child# 1 Ligore Robillard Canada & Eugenie Archambeau Nashua, NH
ROBILLARD, Marie A H, Sep 23 1887 Sex:F Child# 1 Henry Robillard P Q & Henriette P Q
ROBILLARD, Marie B, Oct 21 1889 Sex:F Child# 1 Charles Robillard Canada & Marie Dube Canada
ROBILLARD, Marie Louise, Jun 22 1893 Sex:F Child# 3 Charles Robillard Canada & Merilda Dube Canada
ROBILLARD, Ovila, Feb 26 1895 Sex:M Child# 4 Joseph Robillard Canada & Josephine Vincent Canada
ROBIN, Joseph P A, Aug 27 1895 Sex:M Child# 10 Charles Robin Canada & Hermine Quintal Canada
ROBINSON, Alice May, Jul 31 1889 Sex:F Child# 2 W F Robinson NY & Mary Hogan Northfield, VT
ROBINSON, Anna Loretta, Mar 27 1891 Sex:F Child# 3 Willard F Robinson New York & Mary Hogan Northfield, VT
ROBINSON, Austin Henry, Apr 25 1893 Sex:M Child# 4 Millard F Robinson Plattsburg, NY & Mary E Hogan Northfield, VT
ROBINSON, Bessie, Nov 18 1887 Sex:F Child# 1 W F Robinson NY & Mary Hogan Northfield, VT
ROBINSON, Cynthia Marion, Dec 12 1933 Sex:F Child# 2 Glenn Robinson Nashua, NH & Gloria Hopkins Lincoln, MA
ROBINSON, David Glenn, Jun 27 1931 Sex:M Child# 1 Glenn D Robinson Nashua, NH & Gloria Hopkins Francestown, NH
ROBINSON, Dorothy Louise, Jan 27 1924 Sex:F Child# 4 Roger Robinson Boston, MA & Bertha Rowell Salem, MA
ROBINSON, Dorothy May, Dec 26 1919 Sex:F Child# 3 William Robinson Maine & Julia Christian Montreal, Canada
ROBINSON, Earl Edward, Sep 20 1909 Sex:M Child# 5 H S Robinson St Albans, VT & Florence Rood Lowell, MA
ROBINSON, Elizabeth Frances, Oct 15 1923 Sex:F Child# 1 William Robinson Nashua, NH & Enola Brown Nashua, NH
ROBINSON, Eugene F, Nov 23 1889 Sex:M Child# 3 John H Robinson Cornish & Isabel Chamberlain Plymouth
ROBINSON, Fanney, Oct 3 1899 Sex:F Child# 3 A Robinson Russia & Jennie Fagenson Russia
ROBINSON, Glenn Darius, Mar 7 1910 Sex:M Child# 1 Darius Robinson Nashua, NH & Agnes M Grannels Vergennes, VT
ROBINSON, Granville Hill, Jan 8 1910 Sex:M Child# 1 Frank Robinson Nashua, NH & Mary L Hill Hudson, NH
ROBINSON, Gregory G, Jan 20 1917 Sex:M Child# 2 Darius E Robinson Boston, MA & Agnes M Grannels Vergennes, VT
ROBINSON, Henry John, May 29 1910 Sex:M Child# 2 Clinton J Robinson Hudson, NH & Emma Boilard Nashua, NH
ROBINSON, James Clemon, Jun 25 1908 Sex:M Child# 1 Clinton Robinson NH & Rose A Boilard NH
ROBINSON, Lena M, Jul 17 1891 Sex:F Child# 1 William F Robinson Nashua, NH & Ida M Pierce Massachusetts
ROBINSON, Robinson, Jun 16 1890 Sex:M Child# 3 George Robinson
ROBINSON, Sarah, Feb 15 1903 Sex:F Child# 4 Abraham Robinson Russia & Jennie Fagenson Russia
ROBINSON, Unknown, Oct 20 1887 Sex:M Child# 1 W H Robinson NY & Mary Foley Ireland
ROBINSON, Unknown, Apr 17 1888 Sex:M Child# 1 Charles Robinson Clifton, NY & Beatrice M Chappel NY
ROBINSON, Unknown, Mar 10 1889 Sex:M Child# 2 William H Robinson Keene, NH & Mary Ireland
ROBINSON, Unknown, Feb 20 1891 Sex:M Child# John Robinson
ROBINSON, Unknown, Aug 12 1893 Sex:F Child# 2 William F Robinson NH & Ida M Pierce Mass
ROBINSON, Unknown, Sep 2 1899 Sex:F Child# 4 William F Robinson Nashua, NH & Ida M Pierce Cambridge, MA
ROBINSON, Unknown, Jul 8 1910 Sex:F Child# 1 Fred J Robinson England & Elsie Marcel Worcester, MA
ROBINSON, Virginia, Feb 9 1921 Sex:F Child# 2 Roger Robinson Boston, MA & Bertha Rowell Salem, NH
ROBINSON, Walter Frederick, Feb 11 1913 Sex:M Child# 2 Frederick J Robinson England & Elsie Marcelle Worcester, MA
ROBINSON, Walter W, Nov 8 1888 Sex:M Child# 6 David Robinson Sutton & S Emma Bailey Cornish

ROBITA, Yolanda Albertine, Feb 23 1925 Sex:F Child# 4 Frank Robita Italy & Florida Lucier Mass
ROBITAILLE, Joseph, Mar 25 1925 Sex:M Child# 4 Anthony Robitaille New Bedford, MA & Palmyra Lemos Azores Island
ROBITAILLE, Palmyra, Feb 4 1924 Sex:F Child# 3 A P Robitaille New Bedford, MA & Palmyra Lemos Azores Islands
ROBITO, Frank Romeo, Nov 11 1928 Sex:M Child# 6 Frank Robito Italy & Florida Lucier Lowell, MA
ROBY, Charles, Feb 16 1901 Sex:M Child# 4 Charles Roby New York & Amanda Levesque Canada
ROBY, Edward Arthur, Oct 18 1930 Sex:M Child# 3 Claude Roby Nashua, NH & Mary Jane Salvail Nashua, NH
ROBY, Louise, Apr 9 1924 Sex:F Child# 1 Gerald Roby Sutton, NH & Alice Moody Sutton, NH
ROBY, Luther A, Nov 11 1894 Sex:M Child# 3 Charles A Roby Nashua, NH & Kate Lowell, MA
ROBY, Marie Rose I, Mar 20 1906 Sex:F Child# 2 Adelard Roby Canada & Leonide Maynard Canada
ROBY, Marie Yvonne, Aug 19 1905 Sex:F Child# 2 William Roby Canada & Alice Morin Canada
ROBY, Unknown, Feb 1891 Sex:F Child# 2 Charles A Roby Nashua, NH & Katie A Lowell, MA
ROCH, Marie Liliane, Mar 3 1906 Sex:F Child# 3 Joseph Roch Canada & Marie Leblanc Canada
ROCH, Unknown, Aug 27 1913 Sex:F Child# 7 Joseph Roch Canada & Marie Leblanc Canada Stillborn
ROCHE, Edward, Jan 10 1901 Sex:M Child# 1 Ed Roche England & Mary Griffin Shirley, MA
ROCHE, Isabelle Catherine, Oct 9 1908 Sex:F Child# 2 James H Roche Ireland & Lizzie Summerville Ireland
ROCHE, James Sherry, Mar 29 1918 Sex:M Child# 5 James H Roche Ireland & Elizabeth Comiwell Ireland
ROCHE, Rose Helen, Aug 14 1907 Sex:F Child# 1 James H Roche Ireland & Eliz Summerville Ireland
ROCHELEAU, Jean Baptiste, May 4 1910 Sex:M Child# 2 Nelson Rocheleau US & Rosanna Norbonne Canada
ROCHELLE, Virginia Elizabeth, Sep 8 1924 Sex:F Child# 1 F Rochelle Concord, NH & Lizzie Dudley Nashua, NH
ROCHETTE, Cecile Gertrude, Jun 3 1915 Sex:F Child# 1 Omer Rochette Canada & Mederise Fortin US
ROCHETTE, Jos Alcide Edgar, Aug 24 1923 Sex:M Child# 1 I E Albert Rochette Mass & Yvonne Cote Canada
ROCHETTE, Jos Raymond Omer, Nov 2 1928 Sex:M Child# 5 Omer Rochette Canada & Mederise Fortin Canada
ROCHETTE, Joseph E Edouard, Jan 31 1898 Sex:M Child# 14 Alcide Rochette Canada & Marie Patri Canada
ROCHETTE, Joseph E G, Jul 30 1894 Sex:M Child# 12 Alcide Rochette Canada & Marie Patrie Canada
ROCHETTE, Joseph Hilaire, Jun 23 1897 Sex:M Child# 3 Charles Rochette Canada & A Provencher Canada
ROCHETTE, Joseph Marcel Alcide, Feb 6 1925 Sex:M Child# 4 Omer Rochette Canada & Mederise Fortin Canada
ROCHETTE, Joseph Maurice Leo, Oct 12 1926 Sex:M Child# 3 Albert Rochette Nashua, NH & Yvonne Cote Canada
ROCHETTE, Joseph Patrick, Mar 6 1896 Sex:M Child# 2 Charles Rochette Canada & Alphonsine Provan'r Canada
ROCHETTE, Juliette Elmire, Apr 25 1928 Sex:F Child# 2 William Rochette Concord, NH & M Anne Pepin Canada
ROCHETTE, Lydia Donalda, Jul 25 1899 Sex:F Child# 4 Charles Rochette Canada & Alphonsine Provenchr Canada
ROCHETTE, Malvina Olivine, Feb 4 1933 Sex:F Child# 2 W Rochette Canada & Malvina Lafrance Canada
ROCHETTE, Marie Laure, Nov 25 1896 Sex:F Child# 14 Alcide Rochette Canada & Marie Patri Canada
ROCHETTE, Marie Theresa, Mar 15 1929 Sex:F Child# 4 Albert Rochette Nashua, NH & Yvonne Cote Canada
ROCHETTE, Normand Leonard, Apr 20 1921 Sex:M Child# 3 Omer Rochette Canada & Mederise Fortin Mass
ROCHETTE, Paul Romeo, Jun 20 1926 Sex:M Child# 6 William Rochette Concord, NH & M A Pepin Canada
ROCHETTE, Roland, Aug 27 1932 Sex:M Child# 3 William Rochette Concord, NH & Marianne Pepin Canada
ROCHETTE, Sylvio Lionel, Mar 25 1919 Sex:M Child# 2 Omer Rochette Canada & Midirise Fortin US
ROCHETTE, Wilfred Robert, Sep 7 1925 Sex:M Child# 1 Wilfred Rochette Canada & Margaret Lafrance Canada
ROCK, Albert Louis, Apr 22 1924 Sex:M Child# 6 Herbert P Rock Nashua, NH & Cecile Antaya Nashua, NH
ROCK, Alfred, May 13 1896 Sex:M Child# 1 Magloire Rock Canada & Celinia Michaud Canada
ROCK, Alice, Jul 9 1890 Sex:F Child# 8 William Rock Ireland & Celia Gaffney Ireland
ROCK, Catherine M Agnes, Mar 20 1918 Sex:F Child# 3 Herbert Rock Nashua, NH & Cecile Antaya Nashua, NH
ROCK, Catherine Rice, Dec 30 1907 Sex:F Child# 1 Willard A Rock Rouses Pt, NY & Emma C Rice Wilmington, Del
ROCK, Donald Clarence, Oct 21 1931 Sex:M Child# 4 Clarence M Rock Malone, NY & Yvonne F Courcy Nashua, NH
ROCK, Eleanor, Dec 16 1918 Sex:F Child# 2 Timothy F Rock Nashua, NH & Elizabeth Hough Nashua, NH
ROCK, Frances, Jun 6 1907 Sex:F Child# 4 Timothy J Rock Nashua, NH & May Mellen St Albans, VT
ROCK, Francis Augustus, Sep 5 1928 Sex:M Child# 6 Hubert Rock Nashua, NH & Cecile Antaya Nashua, NH
ROCK, Grace H, Feb 21 1895 Sex:F Child# Lewis Rock New York & Annie White New York
ROCK, Herbert Patrick, Jul 1 1894 Sex:M Child# 1 Michael Rock Ireland & Margaret Toomey Ireland
ROCK, Hubert Joseph Wilber, Oct 9 1913 Sex:M Child# 1 Hubert Rock Nashua, NH & Celia Antaya Nashua, NH
ROCK, Jos Theresa Emile, Jun 18 1925 Sex:M Child# 1 Clarence Rock New York & Yvonne Courcy Nashua, NH
ROCK, Joseph Emery, Jul 4 1899 Sex:M Child# 3 Magloire Rock Canada & Celina Michaud Canada
ROCK, Joseph Leo Robert, Apr 30 1922 Sex:M Child# 4 Joseph Rock Canada & Marie Leblanc Canada
ROCK, Katherine J, Aug 12 1896 Sex:F Child# 2 Michael Rock Ireland & Margaret J Toomey Ireland
ROCK, Loretta Mary, Jul 2 1921 Sex:F Child# 3 Timothy F Rock Nashua, NH & Elizabeth Haugh Nashua, NH
ROCK, Lucy Cecile, Jan 4 1923 Sex:F Child# 1 Emery Rock Nashua, NH & Laura Pelletier Canada
ROCK, Madaline Claire, Aug 12 1904 Sex:F Child# 2 Timothy J Rock Nashua, NH & Mary Mellen St Albans, VT
ROCK, Marie Blanche L, Sep 11 1900 Sex:F Child# 2 Joseph Rock Canada & Cedulie Dufour Canada
ROCK, Marie Doris P, Jan 18 1930 Sex:F Child# 7 Hubert Rock Nashua, NH & Cecile Antaya Nashua, NH
ROCK, Marie Ivonne, Jun 27 1898 Sex:F Child# 2 Magloire Rock Canada & Celina Michaud Canada
ROCK, Mary Julia Dorothy, Nov 24 1927 Sex:F Child# 2 Clarence H Rock Constable, NY & Yvonne Courcy Nashua, NH
ROCK, Normand Emile, Nov 25 1926 Sex:M Child# 2 Emery Rock Nashua, NH & Laura Pelletier Canada
ROCK, Paul Mellen, May 17 1902 Sex:M Child# 1 Timothy J Rock Nashua, NH & Mary A Mellen St Albans, VT
ROCK, Ralph Eugene, Feb 13 1900 Sex:M Child# 1 Herbert L Rock New York & Lilly Clement New Hampshire
ROCK, Richard Warren, Dec 20 1926 Sex:M Child# 2 Ralph Rock Nashua, NH & Mildred Small Somerville, MA
ROCK, Robert John, Jan 25 1932 Sex:M Child# 1 John Rock Nashua, NH & Marcella St Onge Nashua, NH
ROCK, Robert Joseph, May 25 1922 Sex:M Child# 3 Herbert Rock Nashua, NH & Celia Antaya Nashua, NH
ROCK, Shirley Elizabeth, Mar 10 1923 Sex:F Child# 1 Ralph E Rock Nashua, NH & Mildred Small Somerville, MA
ROCK, Timothy Joseph, Mar 7 1906 Sex:M Child# 3 Timothy J Rock Nashua, NH & May Mellon St Albans, VT
ROCK, Unice Margaret, May 23 1926 Sex:F Child# 7 Hubert Rock Nashua, NH & Celia Antaya Nashua, NH
ROCK, Unknown, Jun 9 1887 Sex:M Child# 7 William Rock Ireland & Celia Ireland
ROCK, Unknown, Oct 2 1889 Sex:F Child# 1 Wesley Rock New York & Bridget Rock New York
ROCK, Unknown, Aug 23 1889 Sex:F Child# 6 John Rock Ireland & Ireland

ROCK, Willard Eugene, Jul 9 1930 Sex:M Child# 3 Clarence M Rock Malone, NY & Yvonne Courcy Nashua, NH
ROCK, William, Jun 23 1916 Sex:M Child# 1 Timothy Rock Nashua, NH & Elizabeth Haugh Nashua, NH
ROCK, Yvette Marcella, Jan 30 1928 Sex:F Child# 1 Alfred Rock Nashua, NH & Lea Trottier Nashua, NH
ROCKFORD, Unknown, Oct 24 1921 Sex:F Child# 1 David Rockford Springfield, MA & Doris Wilder Boston, MA
ROCKWAY, Sidney Herman, Mar 21 1893 Sex:M Child# 1 Frank Rockway NH & Elizabeth Holbrook NH
ROCKWELL, Lydia ann, Mar 5 1929 Sex:F Child# 4 Leslie Rockwell Whitewater, WI & Dorothea Hand Brookline, NH
ROCKWOOD, Dorothy May, Dec 2 1930 Sex:F Child# 7 George E Rockwood Boston, MA & Helen Chapin NH
RODAK, Bolestaw, Mar 15 1917 Sex:M Child# 1 Pawett Rodak Russia & Amelia Krypich Russia
RODGERS, Alice M, May 25 1897 Sex:F Child# 9 Henry H Rodgers Stratford, VT & Chastina D Patterson Washington,
RODGERS, Andrew F S, Jun 22 1930 Sex:M Child# 2 Andrew F Rodgers Nashua, NH & Elsie D Hall Canada
RODGERS, Norma Shirley, Sep 2 1927 Sex:F Child# 1 A F Rodgers NH & Elsie D Hall Canada
RODIER, Alice, Mar 22 1902 Sex:F Child# 5 Albert Rodier Nashua, NH & Delima Ouellette Canada
RODIER, Amelia, Jan 22 1905 Sex:F Child# 7 Albert Rodier Nashua, NH & Delima Ouelette Canada
RODIER, Andrea Vitaline, Dec 28 1907 Sex:F Child# 4 Louis Rodier Canada & Eugenie Demanche Canada
RODIER, Armand, Jul 4 1921 Sex:M Child# 1 Henry Rodier Nashua, NH & Rosanna Deschamp Nashua, NH
RODIER, Arthur, Aug 27 1902 Sex:M Child# 2 Louis Rodier Canada & Eugenie Demanche Canada
RODIER, Arthur Wilfrid, Oct 26 1908 Sex:M Child# 2 J B Rodier H S, ME & Omerise Gagnon Canada
RODIER, Blanche Andrea, Dec 2 1906 Sex:F Child# 9 Albert Rodier Nashua, NH & Delima Ouellette Canada
RODIER, Camille, Aug 4 1914 Sex:F Child# 5 Hormidas Rodier Biddeford, ME & Marie Brisson Canada
RODIER, Cecile, Sep 11 1919 Sex:F Child# 4 John B Rodier Biddeford, ME & Omerine Gagnon Canada
RODIER, Delphis, Mar 15 1899 Sex:M Child# 2 Hormidas Rodier Canada & Marie Brisson Canada
RODIER, Ernest J A A, Jun 12 1897 Sex:M Child# 1 Albert Rodier Nashua, NH & Delima Ouellette Canada
RODIER, Eugenie O M, Nov 10 1898 Sex:F Child# 1 Louis Rodier Canada & Eugneie Demauche Canada
RODIER, Evangeline, Feb 15 1908 Sex:F Child# 10 Albert Rodier Nashua, NH & Delima Ouellette Canada
RODIER, Francois Albert, Jan 12 1901 Sex:M Child# 4 Albert Rodier New Hampshire & Delima Ouellette Canada
RODIER, George, Aug 20 1916 Sex:M Child# 1 (No Parents Listed)
RODIER, George Alfred, Oct 1 1912 Sex:M Child# 12 Albert Rodier Nashua, NH & Delia Ouellette Canada
RODIER, Henri, Nov 19 1897 Sex:M Child# 1 Hormisdas Rodier Canada & Marie Brisson Canada
RODIER, Henri Albert, Aug 8 1906 Sex:M Child# 1 Dean Rodier Biddeford, ME & Armerine Gagnon Canada
RODIER, Hormidas Damase, Oct 19 1923 Sex:M Child# 2 Henry Rodier Nashua, NH & Rose Deschamps Biddeford, ME
RODIER, Jean Baptiste E, Oct 7 1898 Sex:M Child# 2 Albert Rodier Nashua, NH & Delima Ouellette Canada
RODIER, Jeannette, Jun 10 1904 Sex:F Child# 3 Louis Rodier Canada & Eugenie Demanche Canada
RODIER, Jos Albert Emile, Sep 20 1929 Sex:M Child# 1 Emile Rodier Nashua, NH & Lillian Dancause Nashua, NH
RODIER, Joseph Arthur L, Aug 4 1903 Sex:M Child# 6 Albert Rodier Nashua, NH & Marie Ouellette Canada
RODIER, Joseph Napoleon, Apr 20 1901 Sex:M Child# 3 Hormidas Rodier Biddeford & Mary Brisson Canada
RODIER, Lorette, Jul 8 1925 Sex:F Child# 3 Henry Rodier Nashua, NH & R A Deschamps Nashua, NH
RODIER, Louis A, Sep 6 1887 Sex:M Child# Jean Bte Rodier Canada & Josepte Bouly Canada
RODIER, Lucille Agnes H, Mar 31 1911 Sex:F Child# 11 Albert Rodier Nashua, NH & Delia Ouellette Canada
RODIER, Marie Lea, Jun 12 1909 Sex:F Child# 10 Albert Rodier Nashua, NH & Malvina Ouellette Canada
RODIER, Miliane, Sep 29 1906 Sex:F Child# 4 Hormidas Rodier Biddeford, ME & Marie Brisson Canada
RODIER, Pauline, Mar 24 1931 Sex:F Child# 1 (No Parents Listed)
RODIER, Rachel Rita, Feb 13 1931 Sex:F Child# 6 Henri Rodier Nashua, NH & Rose Anna Deschamp Nashua, NH
RODIER, Rita Lucille, Mar 21 1927 Sex:F Child# 1 Ernest Rodier Nashua, NH & Eva Levesque Nashua, NH
RODIER, Rita Violet, Apr 16 1922 Sex:F Child# 1 Napoleon Rodier Nashua, NH & Irene Bernier Canada
RODIER, Roland Joseph, Feb 16 1930 Sex:M Child# 5 Henri Rodier Nashua, NH & Rose Anna Deschamp Nashua, NH
RODIER, Stella Liliane, Apr 16 1905 Sex:F Child# 1 Napoleon Rodier Biddeford, ME & Leopoldine Rossignol Canada
RODIER, Theresa, Nov 23 1926 Sex:F Child# 4 Henry Rodier Nashua, NH & R A Deschamps Nashua, NH
RODIER, Theresa Lillian, Jul 6 1928 Sex:F Child# 2 Ernest Rodier Nashua, NH & Eva Levesque Nashua, NH
RODIER, Thomas Arthur Joseph, Aug 25 1935 Sex:M Child# 4 Arthur Rodier Canada & Ann Wilette Oldtown, ME
RODIER, Yvonne Irene, Oct 31 1899 Sex:F Child# 3 Albert Rodier Nashua, NH & Delima Ouellette Canada
RODIS, Nicolaos Ch, Jan 24 1924 Sex:M Child# 1 Christos Rodis Greece & Helenia Haris Greece
RODONIUS, Unknown, Apr 24 1911 Sex:M Child# 2 William Rodonius Russia & Mary Angius Russia
RODONNIS, Agnes, Jan 29 1917 Sex:F Child# 10 William Rodonnis Russia & Agnes Racmacka Russia
RODRIGUE, Eleanor Jean, Aug 2 1934 Sex:F Child# 2 John Rodrigue Puerto Rico & Hazel Crowell Dover, NH
ROGAZZI, Iris, Mar 1 1909 Sex:F Child# 4 Antonio Rogazzi Italy & Delia Cremonini Italy
ROGERS, Andrew Francis, Sep 6 1907 Sex:M Child# Henry F Rogers England & Susan Summerville England
ROGERS, Carl Brown, Aug 31 1893 Sex:M Child# 1 Ned E Rogers NH & Lizzie Harvey NH
ROGERS, Doris Natalie, Mar 5 1910 Sex:F Child# 2 Albert Rogers Canada & Mabel E Sawyer Pepperell, MA
ROGERS, Edmond Victor, Jun 5 1909 Sex:M Child# 3 Edmond Rogers Vermont & Lina Martin Nashua, NH
ROGERS, Edward Hobson, May 1 1922 Sex:M Child# 1 Norman H Rogers Nashua, NH & Erma Clark Dunstable, MA
ROGERS, Edward Leonard, Jun 11 1905 Sex:M Child# 4 John Rogers N Adams, MA & Bessie Murphy Fall River, MA
ROGERS, Florence Lovejoy, Dec 4 1919 Sex:F Child# 3 Willis L Rogers Stockbridge, VT & Lizzie Lovejoy Nashua, NH
ROGERS, Francis Gertrude, Mar 25 1915 Sex:F Child# 2 Willis L Rogers Stockbridge, VT & Lizzie Lovejoy Nashua, NH
ROGERS, George E, Jul 29 1916 Sex:M Child# 5 Albert H Rogers Toronto, Canada & Mabel E Sawyer E Pepperell, MA
ROGERS, George H, Oct 23 1903 Sex:M Child# 2 Henry Rogers England & Susan Somerville Ireland
ROGERS, George Philip Arthur, Aug 25 1928 Sex:M Child# 1 George Rogers Nashua, NH & Ella Landry New Brunswick
ROGERS, Granville A, Jul 19 1887 Sex:M Child# 1 Frank A Rogers Vermont & Anna B Gorham, ME
ROGERS, Hazel Marion, May 29 1889 Sex:F Child# 1 Leon V Rogers Altona, NY & Hattie Stearns Ashburnham, MA
ROGERS, Hazel May, May 23 1895 Sex:F Child# 2 Ned E Rogers NH & Lizzie Harvey Derry, NH
ROGERS, Helene, Mar 20 1908 Sex:F Child# 2 Edward Rogers Jericho, VT & Lina Martin Nashua, NH
ROGERS, Irving Gilman, Jan 1 1912 Sex:M Child# 3 Albert Rogers Toronto, Canada & Mabel E Sawyer Pepperell, MA
ROGERS, John Everett, Mar 27 1906 Sex:M Child# 3 John H Rogers New Brunswick & Rose Etta Teller Westboro, MA
ROGERS, John Gerard, Jul 10 1907 Sex:M Child# 5 John J Rogers N Adams, MA & Bessie Murphy Fall River, MA

ROGERS, Joseph, Oct 30 1917 Sex:M Child# 9 Michael Rogers Greece & Katharine Greibis Greece
ROGERS, Luella Anna, Oct 11 1920 Sex:F Child# 5 William Rogers Canterbury, NH & Anna McCue Danbury, NH
ROGERS, Margaret Loney, May 6 1908 Sex:F Child# 1 Willis L Rogers Pittsfield, VT & Lizzie Lovejoy Nashua, NH
ROGERS, Marie Lina F, Jan 28 1905 Sex:F Child# 1 Edouard Rogers Vermont & Lina Martin Nashua, NH
ROGERS, Mary Ellen, Mar 24 1905 Sex:F Child# 3 Francis H Rogers England & Susan Summerville Ireland
ROGERS, Michael, Oct 30 1917 Sex:M Child# 8 Michael Rogers Greece & Katharine Greibis Greece
ROGERS, Norman Harvey, Jul 24 1897 Sex:M Child# Ned E Rogers Henniker, NH & Lizzie Harvey Derry, NH
ROGERS, Robert Maurice, Jul 11 1922 Sex:M Child# 1 Robert Rogers Mass & Elizabeth Couillard NH
ROGERS, Roscoe Albertine, Apr 21 1907 Sex:F Child# 4 Albert H Rogers Toronto, Canada & Mabel E Sawyer Pepperell, MA
ROGERS, Ruth Geneva, Aug 16 1919 Sex:F Child# 1 Earle Rogers Nashua, NH & Bernice Hunt Nova Scotia
ROGERS, Susanna, Jul 24 1911 Sex:F Child# 5 Henry F Rogers Ireland & Susanna Summerville Ireland
ROGERS, Unknown, Feb 7 1889 Sex:M Child# 1 Mellen Rogers Warren, NH & Mary L Andrews Hudson, NH
ROGERS, Unknown, Apr 22 1890 Sex:M Child# 1 Elbridge Rogers
ROGERS, Unknown, May 11 1895 Sex:M Child# 1 Carroll Rogers Manchester & Mary Valancour Canada
ROGERS, Unknown, Feb 16 1901 Sex:M Child# 5 George Rogers Rochester & Mary F Heloron Boston, MA
ROGERS, Unknown, Dec 10 1923 Sex:F Child# 2 Norman H Rogers Nashua, NH & Erma Clark Dunstable, MA Stillborn
ROGERS, Walter Haywood, Sep 18 1908 Sex:M Child# 4 John Rogers New Brunswick & Rose E Teller Westboro, MA
ROGERS, William Allen, Dec 11 1924 Sex:M Child# 3 Norman H Rogers Nashua, NH & Erma G Clark Dunstable, MA
ROGERS, Willis Artemus, Jun 21 1928 Sex:M Child# 4 Willis L Rogers Vermont & Lizzie Lovejoy Nashua, NH
ROHAN, Mary, Dec 1 1913 Sex:F Child# 1 Peter Rohan Russia & Lillian Miskowska Russia Stillborn
ROI, Marie L A, Jul 1 1900 Sex:F Child# 1 John Roi Canada & Marie Louise Benoit Canada
ROLF, Herbert Warner, Jul 3 1916 Sex:M Child# 3 Dwight Rolf Canada & Minnie M Wilkuis New York
ROLFE, Donald Emery, Feb 23 1914 Sex:M Child# 2 Hiram Rolfe Canada & Hodga Hanson Nashua, NH
ROLFE, Dwight Joshua, Jr, Nov 30 1926 Sex:M Child# 4 Dwight J Rolfe Canada & Minnie Wilkins Black Brook, NY
ROLFE, Gerald Samuel, May 19 1910 Sex:M Child# 2 Dwight Rolfe Canada & Minnie Wilkins New York
ROLFE, Gerald Samuel, Dec 1 1932 Sex:M Child# 1 Gerald Rolfe Nashua, NH & Hazel Wood Weare, NH
ROLFE, L Allen, Feb 4 1920 Sex:M Child# 3 Hiram F Rolfe Canada & Haiga Hanson Nashua, NH
ROLFE, Leon Carlton, Apr 8 1907 Sex:M Child# 1 Leon A Rolfe Lowell, MA & Myrtle White Deering, NH
ROLFE, Merton Alden, Oct 5 1930 Sex:M Child# 4 Hiram F Rolfe Canada & Holga Hanson Nashua, NH
ROLFE, Thelma Lucile, Apr 24 1911 Sex:F Child# 1 Hiram F Rolfe Canada & Halga Hanson Nashua, NH
ROLFE, Verna Mae, Nov 22 1933 Sex:F Child# 2 Gerald S Rolfe Nashua, NH & Hazel Wood Weare, NH
ROLHON, Unknown, Mar 30 1917 Sex:M Child# 1 Christo Rolhon Macedonia & Pagona Palimedo Macedonia
ROLLAND, Anne Lea, Dec 6 1934 Sex:F Child# 5 Harry Rolland St Albans, VT & Leona Bergeron Winooski, VT
ROLLAND, Harry Francis, Dec 26 1927 Sex:M Child# 3 Harry Rolland St Albans, VT & Leona Bergeron Winooski, VT
ROLLAND, Irma, Nov 3 1925 Sex:F Child# 2 Harry Rolland St Albans, VT & Leona Bergeron Winooski, VT
ROLLAND, Mary Leona, Jan 30 1932 Sex:F Child# 4 Harry Rolland St Albans, VT & Leona Bergeron Winooski, VT
ROLLINS, Albert James, Feb 22 1898 Sex:M Child# 3 Frank H Rollins Manchester, NH & Maggie Conlahan Nashua, NH
ROLLINS, Alice Idelia, Aug 16 1921 Sex:F Child# 2 Charles A Rollins Hudson, NH & Mildred Eastman Nashua, NH
ROLLINS, Charles A, Jul 23 1895 Sex:M Child# 2 George Rollins Manchester & Idelia Daniels Vermont
ROLLINS, Clayton Wallace, Jan 19 1925 Sex:M Child# 7 Irvine A Rollins Nashua, NH & Edith N Laflamme Nashua, NH
ROLLINS, Edith May, May 12 1896 Sex:F Child# 4 David M Rollins Vermont & Lizzie B Smith NH
ROLLINS, Edna Elizabeth, Jun 26 1925 Sex:F Child# 2 Auger Rollins Londonderry, NH & Blanche Morin Canada
ROLLINS, Ellsworth Adams, Apr 1 1924 Sex:M Child# 2 Perley Rollins Salem, MA & Ada Adam Kennebunkport, ME
ROLLINS, Elwyn Justin, Jun 24 1896 Sex:M Child# 4 Irvin A Rollins Pelham, NH & Minnie E Shattuck Nashua, NH
ROLLINS, Eunice Geneva, Mar 27 1923 Sex:F Child# 2 Wesley Rollins Nashua, NH & Corinne Sirois Canada
ROLLINS, Fred S, Nov 20 1897 Sex:M Child# George Rollins Mass & Lucy Mayo Michigan
ROLLINS, George Eastman, Sep 29 1922 Sex:M Child# 3 Charles Rollins Hudson, NH & Mildred Eastman Nashua, NH
ROLLINS, Gerald Martin, Sep 19 1926 Sex:M Child# 8 Irvine A Rollins Nashua, NH & Edith Laflamme Nashua, NH
ROLLINS, Gilbert Carl, Sep 24 1922 Sex:M Child# 2 Justin Rollins Nashua, NH & Corine Dube Fall River, MA
ROLLINS, Gloria Carmen, Feb 12 1921 Sex:F Child# 1 Justin Rollins Nashua, NH & Corine Dube Fall River, MA
ROLLINS, Irvin Alfred, Mar 16 1913 Sex:M Child# 2 Irvin Alfred Rollins Nashua, NH & Edith Laflamme Nashua, NH
ROLLINS, Janet Ruth, Oct 2 1935 Sex:F Child# 1 Irvine Rollins, Jr Nashua, NH & Ruth Ford Nashua, NH
ROLLINS, John Colby, Oct 17 1892 Sex:M Child# 1 James H Rollins Francestown, NH & Fanny Sargent Antrim, NH
ROLLINS, Kenneth Himgeford, Jun 14 1917 Sex:m Child# 4 Irvin A Rollins Nashua, NH & Edith Laflamme Nashua, NH
ROLLINS, Maude L, Mar 9 1887 Sex:F Child# 3 David M Rollins Greenboro & Lizzie B Francestown
ROLLINS, Naomi Anita, Oct 31 1919 Sex:F Child# 5 Irvine Rollins Nashua, NH & Edith Laflamme Nashua, NH
ROLLINS, Natalie Lorraine, Mar 20 1927 Sex:F Child# 2 Raymond Rollins Nashua, NH & Leona Lazott Nashua, NH
ROLLINS, Olla May, Aug 23 1911 Sex:F Child# 1 Irving A Rollins Nashua, NH & Edith M Laflamme Nashua, NH
ROLLINS, Perley Earle, Feb 21 1919 Sex:M Child# 1 Wesley E Rollins Nashua, NH & Corine Sirois Canada
ROLLINS, Ralph Henry, Aug 29 1923 Sex:M Child# 1 Rugar Rollins Londonderry, NH & Blanche Morin Canada
ROLLINS, Raymond H, Apr 19 1897 Sex:M Child# 3 George H Rollins Manchester, NH & Adelia Daniels Georgia, VT
ROLLINS, Richard Geo, Sep 12 1926 Sex:M Child# 3 Rugar Rollins Londonderry, NH & Blanche Morin Canada
ROLLINS, Robert Harrison, Jun 12 1923 Sex:M Child# 1 Raymond Rollins Nashua, NH & Leona Lazott Nashua, NH
ROLLINS, Shirley Madeleine, Jan 27 1920 Sex:F Child# 1 Perley E Rollins Salem, MA & Ada Adams Kennebunk, ME
ROLLINS, Thelma, Aug 31 1914 Sex:F Child# 3 Irving A Rollins Nashua, NH & Edith Laflamme Nashua, NH
ROLLINS, Unknown, Aug 7 1891 Sex:F Child# 1 Irvin A Rollins Pelham, NH & Minnie E Shattuck Nashua, NH Stillborn
ROLLINS, Unknown, Jul 24 1892 Sex:M Child# 2 Irvin A Rollins Pelham, NH & Minnie E Shattuck Nashua, NH
ROLLINS, Unknown, Dec 7 1893 Sex:M Child# 1 George H Rollins Manchester & Idelia L Daniels Georgia, VT
ROLLINS, Unknown, Jun 18 1894 Sex:M Child# 1 Frank H Rollins Manchester, NH & Maggie Coulahan Nashua, NH
ROLLINS, Unknown, Oct 16 1896 Sex:F Child# 2 Frank H Rollins Manchester, NH & Margaret Callahan Nashua, NH Stillbor
ROLLINS, Warren Earlfred, Jul 26 1922 Sex:M Child# 6 Irvine A Rollins Nashua, NH & Edith M Laflamme Nashua, NH
ROLLINS, Westly E, Jan 25 1898 Sex:M Child# 5 Irving A Rollins Pelham, NH & Minnie E Shattuck Nashua, NH
ROLO, Arthur Firmer, Jul 15 1925 Sex:M Child# 4 Firmer Rolo Nashua, NH & Florence Simmons Boscawen, NH

ROLO, Emile Charles, Oct 4 1891 Sex:M Child# 4 John Rolo Nashua, NH & Georgie Wright Nashua, NH
ROLO, Everett Oliver, Jul 29 1910 Sex:M Child# 4 Henry F Rolo Nashua, NH & Gertrude Stockwell New York
ROLO, Kenneth, Jan 29 1914 Sex:M Child# 8 John Rolo Nashua, NH & Georgiana Wright Nashua, NH Stillborn
ROLO, Madeline Gertrude, May 25 1912 Sex:F Child# 5 Henry F Rolo Nashua, NH & Gertruck Stockwell New York
ROLO, Marilia Emma, Aug 6 1903 Sex:F Child# 3 Henry Rolo Nashua, NH & Gertrude Stockwell Moore's, NY
ROLO, Merton Frederick, Jun 30 1920 Sex:M Child# 1 Firmand Rolo Nashua, NH & Florence Simmons Boscawen, NH
ROLO, Richard, Feb 7 1923 Sex:M Child# 3 Firmen Rolo Nashua, NH & Florence Simmons Boscawen, NH
ROLO, Unknown, Jan 9 1901 Sex:F Child# 2 Stockwell Rolo Nashua, NH & Gertrude Stockwell Moore's, NY
ROLO, Virginia May, May 13 1921 Sex:F Child# 2 Firmin Rolo Nashua, NH & Florence Simmons Boscawen, NH
ROLSIOS, Unknown, Apr 26 1916 Sex:F Child# 7 Makis Rolsios Greece & Vasilia Gubas Greece
ROMANI, Cynthia, May 4 1931 Sex:F Child# 2 Henry A Romani Milford, NH & Hazel Pettengill Amherst, NH
ROMANIS, Franka, Dec 2 1915 Sex:M Child# 2 Hylary Romanis Russia & Victoria Chemonis Russia
ROMANOWICK, Gonefa, Oct 22 1915 Sex:F Child# 1 Clemens Romanowick Russia & Makalowic Locaidina Russia
ROMANOWSKI, Frances, Oct 5 1923 Sex:F Child# 2 Clement Romanowski Poland & Desconda Michelowitc Poland
ROMEL, Frank, Aug 17 1929 Sex:M Child# 1 Julien Romel Poland & Agnes Jackob Poland
ROMEL, Waliero, May 3 1914 Sex:M Child# 1 Giliori Romel Russia & Victoria Sumonis Russia
ROMEO, Raoul, Sep 12 1908 Sex:M Child# 2 Donat Romeo Canada & Alma Boutin Canada
ROMER, Richard William, Feb 25 1913 Sex:M Child# 2 George Benj Romer Cincinnati, OH & Aurelia Marshall Detroit, MI
ROMER, Unknown, Sep 29 1914 Sex:F Child# 3 George B Romer Cincinnati, OH & Aurelia Marshall Detroit, MI
RONDEAU, Blanche Yvonne, Jul 27 1906 Sex:F Child# 2 Alphonse Rondeau Canada & Adeline Vanasse Canada
RONDEAU, Germaine Alice, Jan 13 1930 Sex:F Child# 1 Adrian Rondeau Lawrence, MA & Emily Hardy Bangor, ME
RONDEAU, Inez Margaret, Mar 29 1934 Sex:F Child# 1 Adrian Rondeau Lawrence, MA & Mary Hardy Nashua, NH
RONDEAU, Jacqueline Lorraine, Mar 17 1934 Sex:F Child# 2 Adrian Rondeau Lawrence, MA & Emily Hardy Bangor, ME
RONDEAU, Joseph, Nov 23 1909 Sex:M Child# 5 Alphonse Rondeau Canada & Adeline Vanasse Canada Stillborn
RONDEAU, Joseph Arthur, Nov 5 1915 Sex:M Child# 13 Joseph Rondeau Canada & Alice Emmon Canada
RONDEAU, Marie Antoinette A, Aug 2 1904 Sex:F Child# 1 Alphonse Rondeau Canada & Adeline Vanasse Canada
RONDEAU, Marie Rose, Jun 7 1918 Sex:F Child# 14 Joseph Rondeau Canada & Alice Amond Canada
RONDEAU, Marie Yvette Elaine, Mar 2 1934 Sex:F Child# 2 Albert Rondeau Canada & Lucienne Dumas Canada
RONDEAU, Rita Carmen, Oct 4 1931 Sex:F Child# 1 Albert Rondeau Canada & Lucienne Dumas Canada
RONDONIS, Annie, Nov 3 1905 Sex:F Child# 2 Alex Rondonis Poland & Walka Hazzata Poland
RONIS, Malvina, Nov 18 1915 Sex:F Child# 1 Anthony Ronis Russia & Mathil Chesnolawicz Russia
ROOD, Adele, Oct 13 1913 Sex:F Child# 1 (No Parents Listed)
ROOD, Arnold Herman, Aug 5 1915 Sex:M Child# 1 Herman Rood Vermont & Bertha Hebert NH
ROOD, Claire Bertha, Mar 28 1935 Sex:F Child# 7 Herman Rood Swanton, VT & Bertha Herbert Montreal, PQ
ROOD, David W Herbert, Nov 3 1921 Sex:M Child# 3 Herman Rood Swanton, VT & Bertha Herbert Canada
ROOD, Herman Joseph, May 19 1932 Sex:M Child# 6 Herman J Rood Swanton, VT & Bertha Herbert Montreal, Canada
ROOD, Pearl Edna, Nov 25 1923 Sex:F Child# 4 Hermon Rood Scranton, PA & Bertha Herbert Canada
ROOD, Richard Francis, Jan 23 1931 Sex:M Child# 3 William A Rood Wilton, NH & Beatrice Martel Wilton, NH
ROOD, Vernice Harold R, Feb 20 1920 Sex:F Child# 2 Herman J Rood Swanton, VT & Berth Herbert Canada
ROODE, Natalie Lewis, Sep 9 1913 Sex:F Child# 1 Harold N Roode Haverhill, MA & Norma Lewis Chicago, IL
ROONEY, Donald Joseph, Mar 27 1922 Sex:M Child# 1 Joseph H Rooney Waltham, MA & Julien E Shea Cambridge, MA
ROOT, Unknown, Mar 5 1903 Sex:M Child# 2 Bert Clifton Root Westbrook, ME & Caro A Goff Auburn, ME
ROQUE, Merena, Jun 7 1887 Sex:F Child# Magloire Roque P Q & Clarisee Delude P Q
ROQUE, Wilfred, Jan 4 1899 Sex:M Child# 1 Joseph Roque Canada & Marie Leblanc Canada
ROSACK, Peter, Aug 3 1907 Sex:M Child# 3 Wala Rosack Poland & Josie Corosa Poland
ROSE, Bertram Charles, Jun 26 1902 Sex:M Child# 3 Bertram Rose NB & Mary Chestnut NB
ROSE, Chester, Oct 29 1910 Sex:M Child# 2 Clarence E Rose Lowell, MA & Clare Dole Lowell, MA
ROSE, Edna Ruth, Jan 20 1933 Sex:F Child# 2 H F Rose Carlisle, MA & B Thompson Lowell, MA
ROSE, Harold Paul, Jul 30 1922 Sex:M Child# 1 William Rose Brookfield, MA & Marie Louise Boney France
ROSE, Helen M, Oct 21 1900 Sex:F Child# Bertram Rose NY & Mary Chestnut NB
ROSE, Lena, Feb 26 1897 Sex:F Child# 3 Samuel Rose Russia & Annie Zebr Austria
ROSE, Myrtle Ann, Jul 17 1934 Sex:F Child# 3 Herbert F Rose Carlisle, MA & Blanche Thompson Lowell, MA
ROSE, Sam, Dec 14 1895 Sex:M Child# 2 Sam Rose Russia & Annie Zimba Austria
ROSE, Unknown, Jun 30 1893 Sex:F Child# 1 Sim Rose Russia & Anna Russia Stillborn
ROSEDOF, Rena Pauline, Jul 27 1928 Sex:F Child# 1 Theo Rosedof Nashua, NH & Loretta Charron Nashua, NH
ROSETTE, Marie Anne, Jan 8 1901 Sex:F Child# 1 Walter Rosette Canada & Marie Chasse Canada
ROSI, James Edward, Sep 27 1919 Sex:M Child# 1 James Edw Rosi Quincy, MA & Agnes Gallagher Charlestown, MA
ROSINOVICK, Virginia Julia, Oct 2 1924 Sex:F Child# 4 A Rosinovick Lithuania & J Machelowick Lithuania
ROSNLISIWICZ, Jennie, Sep 16 1916 Sex:F Child# 1 Adam Rosnlisiwicz Russia & Kate Gorka Russia
ROSS, Eddie, May 22 1899 Sex:M Child# 6 Sam Ross Russia & Annie Zember Austria
ROSS, Eva, Apr 9 1903 Sex:F Child# 1 Jean B Ross Canada & Marie Tanguay Canada
ROSS, Flore Annette B, Feb 3 1903 Sex:F Child# 4 Solomon Ross Canada & Laura Jolie Canada
ROSS, George Henry, Jun 17 1889 Sex:M Child# 4 harles H Ross Manchester & Emma Merchant Montreal, Canada
ROSS, Gilbert Raymond, Jun 3 1905 Sex:M Child# 5 Solomon Ross Canada & Laura Joly Canada
ROSS, Harold David, Mar 13 1912 Sex:M Child# 2 George J Ross Springfield, MA & Rosalie K Zehetmayer Austria
ROSS, Jean Baptiste, Nov 24 1893 Sex:M Child# 1 Odilon Ross Canada & Amanda Michaud Canada
ROSS, Joseph Emile, Nov 1 1895 Sex:M Child# 2 Odilion Ross Canada & Amanda Michaud Canada
ROSS, Joseph J Baptiste, Sep 14 1898 Sex:M Child# 3 J B Ross Canada & Clara Narceau Canada
ROSS, Joseph L Normand, Sep 29 1931 Sex:M Child# 4 Jean Baptiste Ross Nashua, NH & Fabiola Cote St Eloie, PQ
ROSS, Joseph Leo, Jul 30 1905 Sex:M Child# 2 Jean B Ross Canada & Marie Sirois Canada
ROSS, Joseph Ned Bertrand, Apr 30 1922 Sex:M Child# 3 Jean B Ross Nashua, NH & Fabiola Cote Canada
ROSS, Joseph Rob Lester, Aug 25 1933 Sex:M Child# 5 Jean B J Ross Nashua, NH & Fabrola Cote Canada
ROSS, Julien Roger, Jul 4 1917 Sex:M Child# 2 J B Ross Canada & Fabiola Cote Canada

ROSS, Laurette Cecile, Mar 13 1907 Sex:F Child# 6 Solomon Ross Canada & Laura Joly Albany, NY
ROSS, M Sylvia Juliette, Oct 3 1911 Sex:F Child# 7 Solomon Ross Canada & Laura Joly Canada
ROSS, Marie A D, Sep 22 1902 Sex:F Child# 1 J Baptiste Ross Canada & Emma Sirois Canada
ROSS, Marie L D, Aug 5 1896 Sex:F Child# 2 Solomon Ross Canada & Laura Joly Albany, NY
ROSS, Marie Pearl Vivianne, Jun 8 1923 Sex:F Child# 2 Emile Ross Nashua, NH & Amanda Bernier Canada
ROSS, Martha Marie, Apr 22 1903 Sex:F Child# 2 (No Parents Listed)
ROSS, Mary, Jun 20 1897 Sex:F Child# 1 William Ross Nova Scotia & Maggie McCabe Ireland
ROSS, Raymond Odilon, Sep 6 1934 Sex:M Child# 1 Odilon Ross Canada & Marie Beaulieu Canada
ROSS, Rudolph Wilhelm, Aug 7 1926 Sex:M Child# 2 Rudolph W Ross Finland & Amanda Erickson Finland Stillborn
ROSS, Russell Ronald, Oct 19 1935 Sex:M Child# 1 Louis Ross Canada & Marcella Levesque Nashua, NH
ROSS, S J Baptiste, Nov 1 1897 Sex:M Child# 3 Solomon Ross Canada & Laura Joly Albany, NY
ROSS, Unknown, Nov 11 1887 Sex:M Child# 3 Charles H Ross Manchester & Emma M Montreal
ROSS, Unknown, Oct 19 1889 Sex:M Child# 1 Charles Ross England & Annie Fayakerly England
ROSS, Unknown, Apr 28 1894 Sex:M Child#  Samuel Ross Australia & Hannah Australia
ROSS, William, Feb 24 1898 Sex:M Child# 4 Sim Ross
ROSSE, Francois Achilles, Jan 20 1890 Sex:M Child# 6 Francois Rosse Canada & Hermenie Ferland Canada
ROSSI, Agnes Ellen, Dec 30 1929 Sex:F Child# 6 Ernest Rossi Quincy, MA & Agnes Gallagher Charlestown, MA
ROSSI, Ernest Francis, Feb 3 1927 Sex:M Child# 5 Ernest Rossi Milford, NH & Agnes Gallagher Charlestown, MA
ROSSI, Rita Marie, Sep 5 1922 Sex:F Child# 3 Ernest Rossi Quincy, MA & Agnes Gallagher Charlestown, MA
ROSSI, Virginia Frances, Nov 1 1920 Sex:F Child# 2 Ernest F Rossi Quincy, MA & Agnes E Gallagher Charlestown, MA
ROSSIGNAL, M Josephine, Dec 31 1895 Sex:F Child# 2 Alfred Rossignal Canada & Dorilda St Pierre Canada
ROSSIGNAL, Marie Clara, Dec 5 1894 Sex:F Child# 1 Alfred Rossignal Canada & Dorilda St Pierre Canada
ROSSIGNOL, Joseph Wilfred, Jun 18 1934 Sex:M Child# 3 Joseph Rossignol Canada & Marie Michaud Canada
ROSSIGNOL, Marie, Oct 10 1913 Sex:F Child# 13 Horace Rossignol Canada & Azilda Proulx Canada Stillborn
ROSSIGNOL, Normand Lucien, Apr 12 1926 Sex:M Child# 1 Joseph Rossignol Canada & Marie Michaud Canada
ROSSISTER, Laurence, Jun 24 1923 Sex:M Child# 7 John Rossiter Ireland & Mary Burroughs Ctr Barnstead, NH
ROSSITER, Irene, Dec 25 1924 Sex:F Child# 2 Martin Rossiter Milford, NH & Rose Keeley Fall River, MA
ROSTOWSKY, Peter, Jan 3 1905 Sex:M Child# 1 John Rostowsky Russia & Anna Traygilsa Russia
ROSYTINO, Virginia, Jul 25 1928 Sex:F Child# 3 Joseph Rosytino Lithuania & Agatha Galantinas Lithuania
ROTHENBERG, David, Sep 3 1930 Sex:M Child# 6 Jacob Rothenberg Worcester, MA & Dora Simon Amsterdam, NY
ROTHENBERG, Eve, Apr 27 1924 Sex:F Child# 4 Jacob Rothenberg Worcester, MA & Dora Simon Amsterdam, NY
ROTHENBERG, Jean, Feb 26 1922 Sex:F Child# 3 Jacob Rothenberg Worcester, MA & Dora Simon Amsterdam, NY
ROTHENBERG, Joan, May 10 1928 Sex:F Child# 5 Jacob Rothenberg Worcester, MA & Dora Simon Amsterdam, NY
ROTHENBERG, Ruth Helen, Oct 31 1917 Sex:F Child# 1 Jacob Rothenberg Worcester, MA & Doris Simon Amsterdam, NY
ROTHEWICZ, Unknown, Oct 18 1919 Sex:F Child# 3 Joseph Rothewicz Poland & Helen Wersocki Poland
ROTKIEWICZ, Czeslawa, Jun 19 1926 Sex:F Child# 1 Joseph Rotkiewicz Poland & Helen Varsotski Poland
ROTKIEWICZ, Marguerite, Nov 2 1934 Sex:F Child# 1 (No Parents Listed)
ROTKIEWICZ, Mary, Oct 20 1921 Sex:F Child# 6 Joseph Rotkiewicz Poland & Helen Versotika Poland
ROTKIEWICZ, Vital, Apr 7 1923 Sex:M Child# 5 Joseph Rotkiewicz Poland & Helen Varsotski Poland
ROUDONIS, Alphonse, Oct 17 1917 Sex:M Child# 4 Felix Roudonis Lithuania & Valeria Kashstute Lithuania
ROUDONIS, John, Jan 9 1912 Sex:M Child# 3 Felix Roudonis Russia & Waterina Kasecutie Russia
ROUGHAM, Eileen, Jan 25 1914 Sex:F Child# 2 John Rougham Nashua, NH & Julia Griffin Ireland
ROUGHAM, John, Jul 22 1911 Sex:M Child# 1 Thomas Rougham Nashua, NH & Mabel McKeowen Mass
ROUGHAN, Catherine, Apr 19 1912 Sex:F Child# 1 John Roughan Nashua, NH & Julia F Griffin Ireland
ROUGHAN, Frances, May 2 1916 Sex:F Child# 3 John Roughan Nashua, NH & Julia Griffin Ireland
ROUGHAN, Frederick James, Apr 16 1916 Sex:M Child# 5 Thomas Roughan Nashua, NH & Mabel McKeown Arlington, MA
ROUGHAN, Gertrude, Aug 3 1913 Sex:F Child# 3 Thomas J Roughan Nashua, NH & Mabel G McKeown Arlington, MA
ROUGHAN, James, Aug 14 1890 Sex:M Child# 5 James Roughan Ireland & Mary Owens Ireland
ROUGHAN, Mary Elizabeth, Dec 9 1914 Sex:F Child# 4 Thomas Roughan Nashua, NH & Mabel McKeown Arlington, MA
ROUGHAN, Thomas, Jul 2 1912 Sex:M Child# 2 Thomas Roughan Nashua, NH & Mabel G McKeown Arlington, MA
ROUGHAN, William Joseph, Oct 21 1917 Sex:M Child# 6 Thomas Roughan Nashua, NH & Mabel McKeon Arlington, MA
ROULE, Marguerite May, May 25 1901 Sex:F Child#  Frank M Roule Plattsburg, NY & Emma M Lear Altona, NY
ROULEAU, Anna Lucile, Nov 24 1904 Sex:F Child# 6 Telesphore Rouleau Canada & Antoin'e Simonneau Canada
ROULEAU, Dora, Jan 30 1898 Sex:F Child# 1 (No Parents Listed)
ROULEAU, Joseph Alfred Roland, Aug 16 1932 Sex:M Child# 2 Ernest Rouleau Canada & Irene Proulx Epping, NH
ROULEAU, Joseph Desire, Jun 23 1893 Sex:M Child# 2 Gregoire Rouleau Canada & Delima Theriault Canada
ROULEAU, Loraine R, Mar 8 1909 Sex:F Child# 3 David A Rouleau Fall River, MA & Mary Riley Chalam, NY
ROULEAU, Marie A A, Sep 18 1903 Sex:F Child# 5 Telesphore Rouleau Canada & Antoinette Simoneau Canada
ROULEAU, Marie Diana, Mar 15 1901 Sex:F Child# 3 Telesphore Rouleau Canada & Antoine's Simonneau Canada
ROULEAU, Marie Louise, Feb 6 1895 Sex:F Child# 3 Gregoire Rouleau Canada & Delima Theriault Canada
ROULEAU, Marie Madeline L, Oct 10 1924 Sex:F Child# 1 R A Rouleau Haverhill, MA & Beatrice Kerouac Nashua, NH
ROULEAU, Marie Sara Ida, Dec 31 1898 Sex:F Child# 1 Telesphore Rouleau Canada & Antoinette Simoneau Canada
ROULEAU, Marie Yvonne, Apr 20 1902 Sex:F Child# 3 Telesphore Rouleau Canada & A Simonneau Canada
ROULEAU, Mary Elmire, May 27 1892 Sex:F Child# 1 Gregoire Rouleau Canada & Delima Teriault Canada
ROULEAU, Narcisse, Apr 14 1894 Sex:M Child# 1 Narcisse Rouleau Salem, MA & Marie guertin Nashua, NH
ROULEAU, Robert John, Jul 25 1934 Sex:M Child# 3 Ernest Rouleau Canada & Irene Proulx Epping, NH
ROULUSKENICIAN, Alphonse, Jun 29 1926 Sex:M Child# 3 W Rouluskenician Lithuania & Mikalice Svenalis Lithuania
ROULX, Richard Wilfrid, Feb 25 1927 Sex:M Child# 1 Wilfred Roulx Canada & Hazel Bennett Manchester, NH
ROUNDY, Marian T, May 5 1892 Sex:F Child# 1 Elmer E Roundy Holliston, MA & Minnie L Taylor Nashua, NH
ROUNDY, Unknown, Jun 20 1898 Sex:F Child# 2 Elmer Roundy Holliston, MA & Minnie L Taylor Nashua, NH
ROUSA, Eva, Jun 3 1924 Sex:F Child#  Vasil Rousa Greece & Horiclea Memor Greece
ROUSELL, Marie L Germaine, Sep 21 1931 Sex:F Child# 5 Simon Rousell Canada & Yvonne Michaud Canada
ROUSELLE, Alfred Ronald, Mar 15 1932 Sex:M Child# 1 A Rouselle Canada & Yvonne Levesque Canada

ROUSSA, Unknown, May 20 1930 Sex:M Child# 2 Vanilios Roussa Greece & Hariclea Memos Greece
ROUSSEAU, Adelard, Mar 14 1893 Sex:M Child# 5 Aime Rousseau Canada & Marie Pleau Canada
ROUSSEAU, Amelia, May 28 1895 Sex:F Child# 6 Amie Rousseau Canada & Marie Pleau Canada
ROUSSEAU, Anna Yvonne, Aug 31 1902 Sex:F Child# 2 Ludger Rousseau Canada & Lea Roy Canada
ROUSSEAU, Arthur, Nov 19 1897 Sex:M Child# 6 Alphonse Rousseau Canada & Celina Dube Canada
ROUSSEAU, Arthur Moise, Jan 29 1904 Sex:M Child# 4 Eusebe Rousseau Canada & Emma Bazinet Canada
ROUSSEAU, Blanche Irene, Apr 21 1906 Sex:F Child# 5 Eusebe Rousseau Canada & Emma Bazinet Canada
ROUSSEAU, Charles Normand, Mar 22 1932 Sex:M Child# 5 Joseph Rousseau Canada & Rose Gendron Nashua, NH
ROUSSEAU, Delia, Jun 15 1899 Sex:F Child# 7 Aime Rousseau Canada & Marie Pleau Canada
ROUSSEAU, Emile, Mar 5 1902 Sex:F Child# 6 Napoleon Rousseau Canada & Marie Berube Canada
ROUSSEAU, Emmanuel, Jan 17 1897 Sex:M Child# 10 Joseph Rousseau Canada & Melina Lessard Canada
ROUSSEAU, Ernest T, Feb 24 1891 Sex:M Child# 8 Edward Rousseau Canada & Christine Riowe Canada
ROUSSEAU, Florida, May 17 1889 Sex:F Child# 3 Aime Rousseau Canada & Mary Pleau Canada
ROUSSEAU, George Antonio, Aug 26 1900 Sex:M Child# 2 Edouard Rousseau Canada & Aure Guilban Canada
ROUSSEAU, Honore, Dec 4 1929 Sex:M Child# 4 Joseph Rousseau Canada & Rose Gendron Nashua, NH
ROUSSEAU, Irene, Dec 21 1920 Sex:F Child# 3 Joseph Rousseau Canada & Rose Gendron Nashua, NH
ROUSSEAU, Jean Paul Lionel, Feb 13 1920 Sex:M Child# 2 Aime Rousseau Canada & Marie Anne Caron Canada
ROUSSEAU, Joseph, Nov 5 1901 Sex:M Child# 4 Hypolite Rousseau Canada & Philomene Malenfant Canada
ROUSSEAU, Joseph, Jul 3 1927 Sex:M Child# 2 Antonio Rousseau Canada & Lumina Boule Canada Stillborn
ROUSSEAU, Joseph Alexandre, Jan 11 1905 Sex:M Child# 10 Aime Rousseau Canada & Marie Pleau Canada
ROUSSEAU, Joseph Alphonse, Feb 27 1894 Sex:M Child# 5 Alphonse Rousseau Canada & Celina Dube Canada
ROUSSEAU, Joseph Henri A, Mar 14 1903 Sex:M Child# 4 Edouard Rousseau Canada & Amee Guilbault Nashua, NH
ROUSSEAU, Joseph Hubert, May 26 1892 Sex:M Child# 5 Hubert Rousseau Canada & Odile Perrault Canada
ROUSSEAU, Joseph J Hubert, Sep 8 1890 Sex:M Child# 4 Hubert Rousseau Canada & Odile Perreault Canada
ROUSSEAU, Joseph L R, Jan 19 1902 Sex:M Child# 6 Ferdinand Rousseau Canada & Clara Rousseau Canada
ROUSSEAU, Joseph Leo Paul, Jul 27 1922 Sex:M Child# 2 Alfred Rousseau Canada & Claudia Beland NH
ROUSSEAU, Joseph Louis Aime, Sep 25 1904 Sex:M Child# 1 Aime Rousseau Canada & Marie Ann Caron Canada
ROUSSEAU, Laurendo, Sep 25 1906 Sex:M Child# 11 Aime Rousseau Canada & Marie Pleau Canada
ROUSSEAU, Lillian May, Jul 18 1916 Sex:F Child# 1 Adelard Rousseau Nashua, NH & Rose Towns Francestown, NH
ROUSSEAU, Lorette, Apr 22 1914 Sex:F Child# 1 Joseph Rousseau Canada & R Anna Gendron Nashua, NH
ROUSSEAU, Marguerite Beatrice, Jan 6 1909 Sex:F Child# 6 Eusebe Rousseau Canada & Emma Basinet Canada
ROUSSEAU, Marie A E, Mar 23 1893 Sex:F Child# 1 Ferdinand Rousseau Canada & Clara Rousseau Canada
ROUSSEAU, Marie Anne Georgette, Aug 5 1924 Sex:F Child# 1 Louis Rousseau Nashua, NH & Blanche Perron Allenstown, NH
ROUSSEAU, Marie Anne H, Jun 20 1901 Sex:F Child# 1 Ludger Rousseau Canada & Lea Roy Canada
ROUSSEAU, Marie B O, Dec 24 1890 Sex:F Child# 3 Alphonse Rousseau Canada & Celina Dube Canada
ROUSSEAU, Marie Emelia E, Nov 25 1903 Sex:F Child# 7 Napoleon Rousseau Canada & Marie Berube Canada
ROUSSEAU, Marie Helen Rita, Jun 21 1921 Sex:F Child# 1 Alfred Rousseau Canada & Claudia Beland NH
ROUSSEAU, Marie L A, Oct 1 1902 Sex:F Child# 9 Aime Rousseau Canada & Marie Pleau Canada
ROUSSEAU, Marie Olina, Jan 11 1892 Sex:F Child# 4 Alphonse Rousseau Canada & Celina Dube Canada
ROUSSEAU, Mathilda, Aug 7 1904 Sex:F Child# 3 Hypolite Rousseau Canada & Marie Malenfaut Canada
ROUSSEAU, Noemie E, May 19 1898 Sex:F Child# 10 Joseph L Rousseau Canada & Melina Lessard Canada
ROUSSEAU, Olive Rita, Mar 21 1915 Sex:F Child# 2 Joseph Rousseau Canada & Rose Gendron Nashua, NH
ROUSSEAU, Pabiola, Jul 28 1891 Sex:F Child# 4 Aime Rousseau Canada & Marie Pleau Canada
ROUSSEAU, Philippe, Nov 18 1907 Sex:M Child# 1 Philbert Rousseau Canada & Lida Laroche Canada
ROUSSEAU, Rose A, Sep 6 1887 Sex:F Child# 3 Hubert Rousseau Canada & Odile Perreault Canada
ROUSSEAU, Theodore, Nov 28 1933 Sex:M Child# 6 Joseph H Rousseau Canada & Rose Gendron Nashua, NH Stillborn
ROUSSEAU, Unknown, Feb 25 1935 Sex:F Child# 3 J A Rousseau Canada & Lumina Boule Canada Stillborn
ROUSSEAU, Valeda Rosalda, May 4 1901 Sex:F Child# 8 Aime Rousseau Canada & Marie Pleau Canada
ROUSSEAU, Virginie, Nov 6 1887 Sex:F Child#  Alphonse Rousseau P Q & Celina Dube P Q
ROUSSEAU, Yvonne Lea, Oct 7 1902 Sex:F Child# 5 Hypolite Rousseau Canada & P Malenfant Canada
ROUSSEL, Charles Henri, Nov 2 1895 Sex:M Child# 3 Pierre Roussel Canada & Delphine Fugere Canada
ROUSSEL, Donalda Lorette, Jul 4 1918 Sex:F Child# 1 Edgar Roussel Nashua, NH & Donalda Provenchal Conticook, Canada
ROUSSEL, Joseph, Nov 20 1903 Sex:M Child# 1 Henry Roussel Canada & Leda Fournier Canada
ROUSSEL, Joseph, Mar 8 1927 Sex:M Child# 1 Simon Roussel Canada & Yvonne Michaud Canada Stillborn
ROUSSEL, Joseph Adelard A, Jan 8 1903 Sex:M Child# 7 Ludger Roussel Canada & Adeline Fugere Canada
ROUSSEL, Joseph Duc, Sep 28 1890 Sex:M Child# 2 Joseph Roussel Canada & Eliza Paradis Canada
ROUSSEL, Joseph Elzear, Aug 25 1892 Sex:M Child# 1 Ludger Roussel Canada & Delphine Champagne Canada
ROUSSEL, Joseph Emile W, Oct 12 1906 Sex:M Child# 9 Ludger Roussel Canada & Delphine Fugere Canada
ROUSSEL, Joseph Thomas F, Aug 3 1907 Sex:M Child# 2 Thomas Roussel Canada & Caroline Provost Canada
ROUSSEL, Louis J, Dec 20 1895 Sex:M Child# 4 Alphonse Roussel Canada & Lea Ouellette Canada
ROUSSEL, Ludger Emile, Jan 19 1894 Sex:M Child# 2 Ludger Roussel Canada & Delphine Champagne Canada
ROUSSEL, Marie Albina D, Apr 22 1901 Sex:F Child# 6 Ludger Roussel Canada & Delphine Fugere Canada
ROUSSEL, Marie Arthemise, Apr 21 1899 Sex:F Child# 5 Ludger Roussel Canada & Delphine Fugere Canada
ROUSSEL, Marie Pearl Lina, Jan 19 1907 Sex:F Child# 1 Ernest Roussel Canada & Albina Delude Canada
ROUSSEL, Marie Theresa, May 17 1929 Sex:F Child# 3 Louis Roussel Canada & Hermance Rossignol Fall River, MA
ROUSSEL, Marie Yvonne Ann, Jul 19 1911 Sex:F Child# 3 Leon Roussel Canada & Alphonsine Corbin Canada
ROUSSEL, Simone Lucille, Nov 18 1928 Sex:F Child# 3 Simon Roussel Canada & Yvonne Michaud Canada
ROUSSEL, Unknown, Jun 23 1889 Sex:M Child# 3 Louis Roussel Canada & A Dionne Canada  Stillborn
ROUSSEL, Unknown, Nov 19 1933 Sex:M Child#  Adrienne Roussel Nashua, NH & Mary Rowbothain Lowell, MA
ROUSSELL, Cecil Marie, Aug 24 1924 Sex:F Child# 2 Agenord Roussell Canada & Yvonne Gagnon Canada
ROUSSELL, Irene Rita, Jan 26 1926 Sex:F Child# 3 Angela Roussell Canada & Yvonne Gagnon US
ROUSSELL, Joseph, Dec 27 1927 Sex:M Child# 2 Simon Roussell Canada & Yvonne Michaud Canada Stillborn
ROUSSELL, Marie Laurianne, Sep 30 1923 Sex:F Child# 3 Alphonse Roussell Canada & Anna Plourde Canada

ROUSSELL, Unknown, Aug 24 1921 Sex:F Child# 1 Charles Roussell Nashua, NH & Elizabeth Turner Canada
ROUSSELLE, Almosa Gabrielle, Feb 28 1925 Sex:F Child# 6 Edgar Rousselle Canada & Donalda Provencal Canada
ROUSSELLE, Armand, Sep 20 1924 Sex:M Child# 1 Arthur Rousselle Nashua, NH & Julia Lavoie Canada
ROUSSELLE, Arthur, Jan 3 1910 Sex:M Child# 2 Thomas Rousselle Canada & Corinne Prevost Canada
ROUSSELLE, Bibiane Rita, Jan 23 1933 Sex:F Child# 6 S Rousselle Canada & Yvonne Michaud Canada
ROUSSELLE, Charles L, Aug 7 1931 Sex:M Child# 3 Pierre Rousselle Canada & Diana St Pierre Canada
ROUSSELLE, Claire Annette, Nov 21 1922 Sex:F Child# 2 Charles Rousselle Nashua, NH & Elizabeth Turner Canada
ROUSSELLE, Cyrille Normand, May 16 1930 Sex:M Child# 4 Simon Rousselle Canada & Yvonne Michaud Canada
ROUSSELLE, Dorothy, Jul 23 1928 Sex:F Child# 2 Leo Rousselle Lowell, MA & Y Malenfant Canada
ROUSSELLE, Henri Gerard, Mar 20 1912 Sex:M Child# 12 Ludger Rousselle Canada & Clarine Fugere Canada
ROUSSELLE, Henry Arthur, Nov 19 1922 Sex:M Child# 4 Edgar Rousselle Nashua, NH & Donalda Provencal Canada
ROUSSELLE, Irene, Aug 30 1904 Sex:F Child# 8 Ludger Rousselle Canada & Marie Fugere Canada
ROUSSELLE, Jeanne d'Arc Antoin, Dec 10 1922 Sex:F Child# 1 Adgenord Rousselle Nashua, NH & Yvonne Gagnon Manchester
ROUSSELLE, Jeannette, Nov 7 1917 Sex:F Child# 1 Louis Rousselle Canada & Armance Rossignol Fall River, MA
ROUSSELLE, Jos Alphonse Ritchie, Oct 27 1926 Sex:M Child# 5 Alphonse Rousselle Canada & Anna Plourde Canada
ROUSSELLE, Joseph, May 9 1889 Sex:M Child# 1 Joseph Rousselle Canada & Eliza Paradis Canada
ROUSSELLE, Joseph Alfred, Aug 5 1908 Sex:M Child# 10 Ludger Rousselle Canada & Delphine Fugere Canada
ROUSSELLE, Joseph Armand, Apr 6 1921 Sex:M Child# 2 Louis Rousselle Canada & Hermance Rossignol Fall River, MA
ROUSSELLE, Joseph Ernest, Oct 7 1910 Sex:M Child# 11 Ludger Rousselle Canada & M Fugere Canada
ROUSSELLE, Joseph Ludger, Feb 2 1920 Sex:M Child# 2 Edgar Rousselle Nashua, NH & Donalda Provencal Canada
ROUSSELLE, Joseph Paul, May 1 1931 Sex:M Child# 4 Louis Rousselle Canada & Hermance Rossignol Nashua, NH
ROUSSELLE, Joseph Robert Earl, Dec 27 1933 Sex:M Child# 3 Leo Rousselle Nashua, NH & Yvonne Malenfant Canada
ROUSSELLE, Leo Raymond, Mar 26 1921 Sex:M Child# 3 Edgar Rousselle Nashua, NH & Donalda Provencal Canada
ROUSSELLE, Leo Richard, Dec 10 1926 Sex:M Child# 1 Leo Rousselle Lowell, MA & Yvonne Malenfant Canada
ROUSSELLE, Louis George, Apr 30 1926 Sex:M Child# 7 Edgar Rousselle Canada & Donalda Provencal Canada
ROUSSELLE, M Louise Anna D, Aug 20 1925 Sex:F Child# 3 Pierre Rousselle Canada & Diana Rousselle Canada
ROUSSELLE, Marie Louise, Sep 8 1913 Sex:F Child# 3 Thomas Rousselle Canada & Corinne Prevost Canada
ROUSSELLE, Marie Madeline, May 5 1933 Sex:F Child# 5 Louis Rousselle Canada & H Rosignol Canada
ROUSSELLE, Normand, Sep 20 1924 Sex:M Child# 2 Arthur Rousselle Nashua, NH & Julia Lavoie Canada
ROUSSELLE, Pierre Honore, Nov 7 1904 Sex:M Child# 2 Pierre Rousselle Canada & Marie Fournier Canada
ROUSSELLE, Pierre Joseph, May 28 1897 Sex:M Child# 4 Ludger Rousselle Canada & Delphine Champagne Canada
ROUSSELLE, Pierre Sylvia, Nov 21 1920 Sex:F Child# 1 Pierre Rousselle Canada & Diana St Pierre Canada
ROUSSELLE, Robert Fernald, Jan 29 1924 Sex:M Child# 5 Edgar Rousselle Nashua, NH & D Provencal Canada
ROUSSELLE, Unknown, Sep 27 1919 Sex:M Child# 17 Ludger Rousselle Canada & Malvina Fugere Canada
ROUSSELLE, Unknown, Jan 29 1934 Sex:M Child# 7 Simon Rousselle Canada & Yvonne Michaud Canada Stillborn
ROUSSELLE, Wilfred Romeo, May 19 1915 Sex:M Child# 4 Thomas Rousselle Canada & Corinne Prevost Canada
ROUSSLAU, Cordelia, Apr 28 1887 Sex:F Child# Aimie Rousslau P Q & Marie Pleau P Q
ROUX, Helene Rita, Jul 7 1920 Sex:F Child# 1 Oscar Roux Canada & Eva Roy NH
ROUXAL, Exilda, Dec 7 1889 Sex:F Child# 2 Jean B Rouxal Canada & Exilda Migneau Canada
ROWAN, Anna, Sex:F Child# 2 Thomas Rowan Ireland & Ann Birchall Ireland
ROWE, Joyce Ann, Jul 28 1934 Sex:F Child# 1 Ethan Rowe Burlington, VT & Albertine Beauchemin Nashua, NH
ROWE, Philip Tilton, Jun 17 1931 Sex:M Child# 3 Francis Robert Rowe Brentwood, NH & Dora Baraby Nashua, NH
ROWE, Robert Francis, Aug 17 1929 Sex:M Child# 2 Francis Robert Rowe Portsmouth, NH & Dora Baraby Nashua, NH
ROWE, Unknown, Apr 14 1888 Sex:M Child# 2 C C Rowe New Hampton & Lielu Paine Vergennes, VT
ROWE, Unknown, Jun 9 1929 Sex:M Child# 5 Roland Rowe Boston, MA & Clara McMahon Ayer, MA
ROWELL, Barbara Mae, Jan 23 1935 Sex:F Child# 2 Clarence Rowell Hudson, NH & Elsie M Giroux Paris, ME
ROWELL, Byron, Jun 2 1891 Sex:M Child# 1 Clinton M Rowell US & Gettie Mamley England
ROWELL, Clifton Harold, Sep 3 1924 Sex:M Child# 1 H C Rowell Nashua, NH & Zoula I Feryall Hudson, NH
ROWELL, Darwin, Apr 11 1902 Sex:M Child# 4 Clinton M Rowell Bedford & G G Mansley Bristol, England
ROWELL, Fred Winston, Feb 22 1931 Sex:M Child# 3 Harold Rowell Nashua, NH & Zoula Ferryall Hudson, NH
ROWELL, Joan Elsie, Jan 27 1933 Sex:F Child# 1 C Rowell Hudson, NH & Elsie Giroux Paris, ME
ROWELL, Louis Edwin, Nov 30 1931 Sex:M Child# 2 Edwin E Rowell Litchfield, NH & Winnibel Merrill W Buxton, ME
ROWELL, Mazell Louise, Dec 30 1929 Sex:F Child# 2 Harold Rowell Nashua, NH & Zoula Feryall Hudson, NH
ROWELL, Unknown, Mar 26 1895 Sex:M Child# 3 Clinton M Rowell Bedford & Gertrude A Manseau Bristol, England
ROWELL, Unknown, Sep 3 1904 Sex:M Child# 5 Clinton M Rowell Bedford, NH & Gertrude A Mansley Bristol, England
ROWEN, Unknown, Jun 16 1888 Sex:F Child# 4 John Rowen Ireland & Mary Owens Ireland
ROWLAND, Edward, Dec 21 1893 Sex:M Child# 5 Lynde W Rowland Branford, CT & Edna Johnson Branford, CT
ROY, Adrienne, Oct 20 1908 Sex:F Child# 4 Alfred Roy Canada & Anaise Morency Canada
ROY, Albert, Mar 31 1902 Sex:M Child# 2 Alfred Roy Canada & Celanire Blanchette Canada
ROY, Albert, Apr 28 1907 Sex:M Child# 4 Joseph Roy Canada & Rosa Bisson Canada
ROY, Alice, Mar 8 1891 Sex:F Child# 8 Leon Roy Canada & Sara LeSieur Canada
ROY, Alma, May 4 1897 Sex:F Child# 11 Leon Roy Canada & Sarah Lesieur Canada
ROY, Amanda, Jul 7 1908 Sex:F Child# 4 Joseph Roy Canada & Rose Bisson Canada
ROY, Amanda Stella, Jul 26 1922 Sex:F Child# 1 Adjutor Roy Canada & Albia Terrien Warren, RI
ROY, Andre Franklin, Mar 6 1933 Sex:M Child# 7 Joseph Roy Canada & Cecile Dube US
ROY, Andre Germain, Aug 8 1905 Sex:M Child# 2 Emile Roy Canada & Leda Legendre Canada
ROY, Anna S, Sep 23 1897 Sex:F Child# 2 Philippe Roy Canada & Corrinne Lavigne Canada
ROY, Antoine, Apr 24 1902 Sex:M Child# 1 P H Roy Nashua, NH & Rosanna Lesieur Nashua, NH
ROY, Armand J Ernest, May 24 1911 Sex:M Child# 6 Donat Roy Canada & Azilda Bilodeau Canada
ROY, Arthur, May 29 1906 Sex:M Child# 3 Alfred Roy Canada & Anais Morency Canada
ROY, Arthur A A, Sep 4 1896 Sex:M Child# 12 Pierre Roy Canada & Honorine Boisseau Canada
ROY, Arthur Oscar, Jan 24 1925 Sex:M Child# 5 Arthur Roy Canada & Rose Drouin Nashua, NH
ROY, Aurele Mayton, Sep 21 1926 Sex:M Child# 1 Octave Roy Newport, VT & Edith Bellefleur Portsmouth, NH

ROY, Aurore, Jul 2 1893 Sex:F Child# 9 Leon Roy Canada & Sara Lesieur Canada
ROY, Aurore, Dec 18 1902 Sex:F Child# 6 Philippe Roy Canada & Corinne Lavigne Canada
ROY, Aurore Clarina, Oct 12 1910 Sex:F Child# 6 Joseph Roy Canada & Rose Bisson Canada
ROY, Cecile Eva, Sep 30 1916 Sex:F Child# 3 Joseph Roy Canada & Cecile Pelletier Mass
ROY, Cecile Zephirine, Mar 14 1907 Sex:F Child# 9 Philippe Roy Canada & Corinne Levigne Canada
ROY, Conrad Wilfred, Jan 11 1932 Sex:M Child# 4 Joseph Roy Nashua, NH & Eliza Migneault Canada
ROY, Donat Joseph, Oct 22 1908 Sex:M Child# 4 Donat Roy Canada & Azilda Billodeau Canada
ROY, Edith A, Sep 11 1894 Sex:F Child# 11 Pierre Roy Canada & Honorine Boisseau Canada
ROY, Edith Arline, Apr 4 1916 Sex:F Child# 1 James L Roy Maine & May Jones Vermont
ROY, Edna Beatrice, Jun 21 1903 Sex:F Child# 5 Frank E Roy Saranac, NY & Phoebe Emmott New York
ROY, Edouard, Apr 4 1914 Sex:M Child# 6 Francois Roy Canada & Roseanna Lauzon Canada
ROY, Eleanor Mildred, Jul 19 1935 Sex:F Child# 1 Raymond F Roy Nashua, NH & Eleanor Spring Nashua, NH
ROY, Emile, Apr 7 1900 Sex:M Child# 12 Leon Roy Canada & Sarah Lesieur Canada
ROY, Emile, Jun 15 1906 Sex:M Child# 2 Joseph Roy US & Regina Roy US
ROY, Ernest, Dec 7 1889 Sex:M Child# 1 Georges A Roy Canada & Alfeda Lancier Canada
ROY, Ernest, Mar 7 1907 Sex:M Child# 1 J B Roy Canada & Josephine Lizotte Canada
ROY, Eugene, Oct 25 1904 Sex:M Child# 3 George Roy St Albans, VT & Emma Rousseau Canada
ROY, Eugene Paul, Sep 16 1923 Sex:M Child# 1 Hector Roy Canada & Regina Fortin Canada
ROY, Eunice, Jan 1 1921 Sex:F Child# 4 George A Roy Canada & Irene Rood Stafford S, CT
ROY, Eva Aglae, Jun 6 1909 Sex:F Child# 5 Hormidas Roy Mass & Clara Vanasse Canada
ROY, Eva Alice, Jul 15 1906 Sex:F Child# 3 Philibert Roy Canada & Rosie Levesque Canada
ROY, George, Jr, Sep 21 1916 Sex:M Child# 1 George Roy Canada & Irene Rood Stafford Sp, CT
ROY, Gerard Alphonse, Jun 6 1932 Sex:M Child# 2 Leo Roy Canada & Loretta Levesque Nashua, NH
ROY, Gerard Lionel, Oct 17 1918 Sex:M Child# 2 Joseph Roy NH & Eliza Mignault Canada
ROY, Gerard Roger, Apr 30 1921 Sex:M Child# 1 Joseph Roy Canada & Louisa Leblanc Nashua, NH
ROY, Gloria Anne, Oct 19 1935 Sex:F Child# 5 Joseph Roy Nashua, NH & Eliza Migneault Canada
ROY, Henri, May 23 1901 Sex:M Child# 5 Philippe Roy Canada & Corinne Lavigne Canada
ROY, Henry Eugene, Jun 20 1921 Sex:M Child# 1 Antoine Roy Canada & Ernestine Therien Canada
ROY, Irene, Jan 13 1931 Sex:F Child# 7 George Roy Canada & Irene Rood Conn
ROY, Irene Aurore D, Dec 12 1911 Sex:F Child# 5 George Roy Vermont & Emma Rousseau Canada
ROY, Irene Detima, Jul 18 1918 Sex:F Child# 4 Joseph Roy Canada & Cecile Dube US
ROY, Isabelle, Jan 8 1909 Sex:F Child# 10 Philippe Roy Canada & Corinne Lavigne Canada
ROY, Isabelle Andrea, Jun 26 1897 Sex:F Child# 1 J Oscar Roy Canada & Aimee Gladu Canada
ROY, J William Romeo, Dec 12 1913 Sex:M Child# 1 Joseph Roy Canada & Cecile Dube Fall River, MA
ROY, Jean Denis, Jul 30 1933 Sex:M Child# 1 Herve Roy Canada & G Laliberte Canada
ROY, Jean Lucille, Jan 30 1917 Sex:F Child# 1 Joseph Roy US & Eliza Migneau Canada
ROY, Jeanette Lucille P, Aug 4 1925 Sex:F Child# 2 Octave Roy Canada & Eliza Dionne Canada
ROY, Jeanne Rita, Jan 25 1929 Sex:F Child# 4 Adjutor Roy Canada & Albea Therrien Warren, RI
ROY, Jeannette, Feb 20 1910 Sex:F Child# 5 Donat Roy Canada & Azilda Bilodeau Canada
ROY, Jos Albert Almont, Jul 12 1918 Sex:M Child# 5 Isidore Roy St Angele, PQ & Rosanna Lee St Pier M, PQ
ROY, Jos Ephrem Roger, Oct 1 1920 Sex:M Child# 5 Elphege Roy Canada & M Louise Cloutier Canada
ROY, Jos Geo Albert, Sep 8 1926 Sex:M Child# 1 Alfred Roy Nashua, NH & Angelina Cadorette Nashua, NH
ROY, Joseph A, Apr 24 1894 Sex:M Child# 13 Andre Roy Canada & Adele Lavoie Canada
ROY, Joseph Adelard, Jan 22 1897 Sex:M Child# 1 William Roy Burlington, VT & Virginie Couture Levy, PQ
ROY, Joseph Alfred, Aug 12 1905 Sex:M Child# 4 Joseph Roy Canada & Marie Veilleux Canada
ROY, Joseph Alfred, Nov 4 1915 Sex:M Child# 2 Joseph Roy Canada & Cecile Dube Fall River, MA
ROY, Joseph Alfred A, Aug 27 1905 Sex:M Child# 4 Hormidas Roy Mass & Clara Vanasse Canada
ROY, Joseph Alfred E, Dec 18 1905 Sex:M Child# 6 Simeon Roy Canada & Marie A Lampron Canada
ROY, Joseph Armand, Dec 3 1925 Sex:M Child# 1 Arcidas Roy Canada & Adeline Soucy Canada
ROY, Joseph Cyrille, Mar 18 1905 Sex:M Child# 8 Philippe Roy Canada & Corinne Lavigne Canada
ROY, Joseph Dominique, Dec 1 1895 Sex:M Child# 1 Dominique Roy Canada & Valeria Boutin Canada
ROY, Joseph Eugene A, Apr 18 1895 Sex:M Child# 16 Joseph Roy Canada & Leontine Gagnon Canada
ROY, Joseph Henri, Aug 27 1901 Sex:M Child# 1 Joseph Roy Canada & Aglaie Therrien Canada
ROY, Joseph Henri, Oct 19 1901 Sex:M Child# 2 Hormidas Roy Mass & Clara Vanasse Canada
ROY, Joseph Hormidas R, Oct 18 1903 Sex:M Child# 3 Hormidas Roy Mass & Clara Vanasse Canada
ROY, Joseph Louis, Mar 30 1896 Sex:M Child# 2 Joseph Roy Canada & Eugenie Michaud Canada
ROY, Joseph Louis Viateur, Nov 9 1918 Sex:M Child# 4 Elphege Roy Canada & Marie L Cloutier Canada
ROY, Joseph Merille E, Aug 31 1899 Sex:M Child# 3 William Roy Mass & Virginie Couture Canada
ROY, Joseph Napoleon, Feb 27 1893 Sex:M Child# 11 Jean Roy Canada & Josephine Lamontagne Canada
ROY, Joseph Napoleon Alb, May 22 1904 Sex:M Child# 5 Simeon Roy NH & Marie A Lampron Canada
ROY, Joseph Oscar, Oct 14 1919 Sex:M Child# 6 Isidore Roy Canada & Marie Lee Canada
ROY, Joseph Oscar S, Oct 12 1902 Sex:M Child# 4 Simeon Roy NH & Marie A Lampron Canada
ROY, Joseph Oscor, Sep 11 1897 Sex:M Child# 3 Joseph Roy Canada & Eugenie Michaud Canada
ROY, Joseph Raymond, Mar 5 1916 Sex:M Child# 2 Elphege Roy Canada & M Louise Cloutier Canada
ROY, Joseph Robert A, Jul 17 1911 Sex:M Child# 6 Hormidas Roy Mass & Clara Vanasse Canada
ROY, Joseph Roland, Jul 16 1913 Sex:M Child# 7 Donat Roy Canada & Azilda Bilodeau Canada
ROY, Joseph Thomas, Oct 16 1921 Sex:M Child# 6 Joseph Roy Canada & Cecile Dube Fall River, MA
ROY, Joseph Vital, Jan 8 1895 Sex:M Child# 12 Elzear Roy Canada & Delvina Bolduc Canada
ROY, Joseph Wilfrid, Mar 28 1910 Sex:M Child# 4 Philibert Roy Canada & Rosanna Levesque Canada
ROY, Lawrence, Mar 2 1934 Sex:M Child# 12 Theophile Roy Canada & Alvine Poulin Canada
ROY, Leo, Feb 26 1932 Sex:M Child# 3 Alfred Roy Nashua, NH & A Cadorette Nashua, NH
ROY, Leo David, Oct 12 1914 Sex:M Child# 2 Hilaire Roy Canada & Marie Levesque Canada
ROY, Leonard Telesphore, Jul 7 1909 Sex:M Child# 1 Joseph N Roy Canada & Amanda Laquerre Canada

ROY, Liliane, Feb 5 1917 Sex:F Child# 2 Joseph Napoleon Roy Canada & Amanda Laquerre Canada
ROY, Lina Beatrice, Jul 28 1904 Sex:F Child# 1 Joseph Roy Canada & Regina Roy Nashua, NH
ROY, Lorette Irene, Aug 3 1924 Sex:F Child# 2 Joseph Roy Canada & Louise Lachance Nashua, NH
ROY, Lorraine Theresa, Apr 3 1928 Sex:F Child# 5 George Roy Gardiner, ME & Fedora Mandor Biddeford, ME
ROY, Louis Paul, Sep 9 1928 Sex:M Child# 2 Alferd Roy Nashua, NH & A Cadorette Nashua, NH
ROY, Louis Philippe, Oct 12 1898 Sex:M Child# 3 Philippe Roy Canada & Corinne Lavigne Canada
ROY, Lucien, Nov 9 1907 Sex:M Child# 3 Donat Roy Canada & Exilda Bilodeau Canada
ROY, Lucien Robert, Jun 6 1928 Sex:M Child# 1 Joseph Roy Canada & Adeline Deneault Nashua, NH
ROY, Luciennia Sylviana, Dec 29 1914 Sex:F Child# 6 Georges Roy Vermont & Emma Rousseau Canada
ROY, M Doretha Anita, Aug 31 1920 Sex:F Child# 4 William Roy Canada & Alfreda Cadieux Canada
ROY, M Elmire, Jun 12 1895 Sex:F Child# 1 Simeon Roy Nashua, NH & Marie A Lampron Canada
ROY, M Helene Olivette, May 25 1919 Sex:F Child# 8 Hormidas Roy Mass & Clara Vanasse Canada
ROY, M Jeanne, Jun 24 1913 Sex:F Child# 2 Hilaire Roy Canada & Marie Levesque Canada
ROY, M L Clara Imelda, Nov 27 1913 Sex:F Child# 7 Hormidas Roy Mass & Clara Vanasse Canada
ROY, M Louise, Dec 28 1895 Sex:F Child# 14 Andre Roy Canada & Adele Lavoie Canada
ROY, M Louise O Z, Jul 13 1893 Sex:F Child# 10 Pierre Roy Canada & Honorine Boisseau Canada
ROY, M Rose Anna, Apr 10 1908 Sex:F Child# 6 J B Roy Canada & Philomene St Pierre Canada
ROY, Marie Alice, Dec 18 1905 Sex:F Child# 3 Joseph Roy Canada & Alice Bisson Canada
ROY, Marie Aurore, Dec 20 1898 Sex:F Child# 4 Joseph Roy Canada & Eugenie Michaud Canada
ROY, Marie E M, Jul 18 1900 Sex:F Child# 1 George Roy VT & Emma Rousseau Canada
ROY, Marie Eva, Dec 3 1893 Sex:F Child# 14 Joseph Roy Canada & Leontine Gagnon Canada
ROY, Marie Eva Carmel, Jun 6 1933 Sex:F Child# 4 Arsidas Roy Canada & Adelina Soucy Nashua, NH
ROY, Marie Jeanne Lucille, Apr 11 1931 Sex:F Child# 1 Amie Roy Canada & Rose Beloveau Canada
ROY, Marie Lena, Jul 1 1903 Sex:F Child# 4 William Roy Burlington, VT & Virginie Couture Canada
ROY, Marie Louise Irene, Jan 3 1911 Sex:F Child# 8 Amedee Roy Canada & Marie Gagne Canada
ROY, Marie Mathilda, Aug 18 1900 Sex:F Child# 3 Simeon Roy NH & Marie Amre Lampron Canada
ROY, Marie Muriel Theresa, Oct 16 1928 Sex:F Child# 2 Gonzague Roy Canada & M A Levesque Canada
ROY, Marie O G, Oct 24 1891 Sex:F Child# 9 Pierre Roy Canada & Honorine Boisseau Canada
ROY, Marie Olivette Cecil, Jan 14 1917 Sex:F Child# 4 Isidore Roy Canada & Rosanna Lee Canada
ROY, Marie R, Aug 23 1889 Sex:F Child# 8 Pierre Roy Canada & Honorine Boisseau Canada
ROY, Marie R Regina, Nov 11 1899 Sex:F Child# 4 Philippe Roy Canada & Corinne Lavigne Canada
ROY, Marie Regina, Apr 13 1892 Sex:F Child# 10 Francois Roy Canada & Marie Bronseau Canada
ROY, Marie Roland L, Jul 24 1929 Sex:F Child# 3 Areidas Roy Canada & Adelina Soucy Nashua, NH
ROY, Marie Rose, Aug 4 1903 Sex:F Child# 2 P H Roy Nashua, NH & Rosanna Lesieur Nashua, NH
ROY, Marie Rose A, May 17 1900 Sex:F Child# 3 Joseph Roy Canada & Marie Veilleux Canada
ROY, Marie Rose Anna, Jul 27 1903 Sex:F Child# 1 Joseph Roy Canada & Rose Bisson Canada
ROY, Marie T Isabelle, Sep 26 1917 Sex:F Child# 3 Alphege Roy Canada & Marie Louise Cloutie Canada
ROY, Marie Teresa Colombe, Oct 11 1927 Sex:F Child# 2 Arsedas Roy Canada & Delia Soucy Nashua, NH
ROY, Marvis, Jun 26 1922 Sex:F Child# 5 George J Roy Canada & Irene Rood Stafford S, CT
ROY, Mary, Oct 17 1904 Sex:F Child# 1 (No Parents Listed)
ROY, Mary Jane Annette, Aug 23 1926 Sex:F Child# 6 Arthur Roy Canada & Mary Rose Drouin NH
ROY, Maurice A Gladu, Jun 30 1899 Sex:M Child# 2 J O Roy Canada & Aimee Gladu Canada
ROY, Maurice Emile, May 1 1929 Sex:M Child# 1 Emile Roy Nashua, NH & Andrea Lozeau Shirley, MA
ROY, Mederic Albert, Dec 21 1923 Sex:M Child# 2 Adjutor Roy Canada & Albea Terrien Warren, RI
ROY, Mildred Lillian, May 28 1912 Sex:F Child# 2 Frank Roy Nashua, NH & Mintie R Knott Nashua, NH
ROY, Moise, Jun 29 1887 Sex:M Child# 8 Francois Roy P Q & Marie Brousseau P Q
ROY, Normand Alfred O, Jul 9 1930 Sex:M Child# 1 Donat Roy Canada & Clarinda Perreault Nashua, NH
ROY, Olivette Florette, Jul 23 1916 Sex:F Child# 1 Wilfrid Roy Nashua, NH & Lea Trottier Nashua, NH
ROY, Paul Emile F, May 21 1904 Sex:M Child# 1 Emile Roy Canada & Leda Legendre Canada
ROY, Pauline, May 22 1931 Sex:F Child# 1 Leo Roy Canada & Laurette Levesque Nashua, NH
ROY, Pearl Sarah, Jun 21 1922 Sex:F Child# 3 Joseph Roy NH & Elise Migneault Canada
ROY, Philbert Leo, Sep 30 1907 Sex:M Child# 3 Philbert Roy Canada & Rosanna Levesque Canada
ROY, Philibert Avila, Nov 12 1912 Sex:M Child# 6 Philibert Roy Canada & Roseanna Levesque Canada
ROY, Philibert Omer, Jul 25 1916 Sex:M Child# 7 Philibert Roy Canada & Rose Levesque Canada
ROY, Philibert T W, May 21 1905 Sex:M Child# 1 Philibert Roy Canada & Rosanna Levesque Canada
ROY, Priscilla, Mar 18 1918 Sex:F Child# 2 George J Roy Canada & Irene Rood Stafford Sprgs, CT
ROY, Rachel Therese, Jun 24 1930 Sex:F Child# 10 Theophile Roy Canada & Alvine Poulin Canada
ROY, Raoul Alfred, Aug 2 1902 Sex:M Child# 2 George Roy Montgomery, VT & Emma Rousseau Canada
ROY, Raymond Frank, Jul 24 1909 Sex:M Child# 1 Frank Roy Nashua, NH & Mintie R Knott Nashua, NH
ROY, Regina, May 11 1893 Sex:F Child# 4 Philippe Roy Canada & Camille Boucher Canada
ROY, Rene Louis Joseph, Mar 15 1927 Sex:M Child# 1 Gonzague Roy Canada & Marie Levesque Canada
ROY, Rita Mathilda, Dec 27 1930 Sex:F Child# 2 Joseph Roy US & Evelina Deneault Nashua, NH
ROY, Robert Charles, May 17 1923 Sex:M Child# 1 Victor Roy Nashua, NH & Catherine Colan Worcester, MA
ROY, Robert Henry, Aug 4 1930 Sex:M Child# 7 Arthur Roy Canada & Rose Daniels Canada
ROY, Robert Lucien, Jan 4 1935 Sex:M Child# 3 Leo Roy Canada & Lorette Levesque Nashua, NH
ROY, Robert Normand, Jun 5 1934 Sex:M Child# 3 Joseph Roy Canada & Adeline Deneault Nashua, NH
ROY, Roger, Feb 23 1927 Sex:M Child# 7 Joseph Roy Canada & Cecile Dube Fall River, MA
ROY, Roger Alfred, Jul 22 1935 Sex:M Child# 1 Phillip Roy Canada & Antoinette Ledoux Nashua, NH
ROY, Romeo Philibert, Jun 9 1922 Sex:M Child# 7 Philibert Roy Canada & Rose Levesque Canada
ROY, Ronald, Sep 30 1934 Sex:M Child# 2 Emile Roy Nashua, NH & Andrea Lozeau Shirley, MA
ROY, Rosanna, Jul 24 1890 Sex:F Child# Joseph Roy Canada & Amelie Theberge Canada
ROY, Rose Alma, Feb 14 1905 Sex:F Child# 2 Alfred Roy Canada & Anais Morency Canada
ROY, Rose Therese, May 25 1924 Sex:F Child# 1 Octave Roy Canada & Eliza Dionne Canada

ROY, Theresa Rejeanne, Jan 18 1926 Sex:F Child# 3 Adjutor Roy Canada & Albea Terrien Warren, RI
ROY, Unknown, Oct 16 1890 Sex:M Child# 3 George Roy Canada & Virginia Pagnon Canada Stillborn
ROY, Unknown, Dec 3 1895 Sex:M Child# 3 Philippe Roy Canada & Corinne Lavique Canada
ROY, Unknown, Oct 8 1899 Sex:M Child# 1 Ovide Roy Canada & Emma Morin NH Stillborn
ROY, Unknown, May 12 1903 Sex:M Child# 1 Alfred Roy Canada & Eloise Morentcy Canada
ROY, Unknown, May 18 1904 Sex:M Child# 1 Philibert Roy Canada & Rose Levesque Canada
ROY, Unknown, Dec 8 1914 Sex:M Child# 1 Joseph Roy Canada & Eva Desmarais Canada Stillborn
ROY, Unknown, Aug 6 1919 Sex:M Child# 5 Joseph Roy Canada & Cecile Dube Canada Stillborn
ROY, Unknown, Aug 24 1919 Sex:F Child# 2 George Roy
ROY, Victor J, Jul 15 1898 Sex:M Child# 4 Frank Roy New York & Phoebe Hamlot New York
ROY, Victor J, Jan 1 1925 Sex:M Child# 2 Victor J Roy Nashua, NH & Catherine Dolan Worcester, MA
ROY, Victoria F A, Jul 28 1893 Sex:F Child# 1 Achille Roy Canada & Victoria Caron Canada
ROY, Virginia, Aug 19 1931 Sex:F Child# 1 (No Parents Listed)
ROY, Wilfrid, Aug 26 1895 Sex:M Child# 10 Leon Roy Canada & Sara Lesieur Canada
ROY, Willie Wilfrid, Jun 18 1900 Sex:M Child# 1 Thomas Roy Canada & Rosanna Good Canada
ROY, Yolande, Oct 11 1931 Sex:F Child# 3 Gonzague Roy Canada & Marie A Levesque Canada
ROY, Yvonne Flora, Dec 17 1904 Sex:F Child# 3 P H Roy Nashua, NH & Rose Lesieur Nashua, NH
ROYAJIAN, Mary, Apr 17 1898 Sex:F Child# 2 John Royajian Armenia & Anna guscana Armenia
ROZANES, Adolphe, Dec 14 1914 Sex:M Child# 1 Adolphe Rozanes Russia & Dominica Stangis Russia
RUBIN, Sarah Elizabeth, Aug 6 1923 Sex:F Child# 1 Joseph Rubin Russia & Jennie Kagan Russia
RUBITA, Marie Theresa Gloria, Oct 28 1927 Sex:F Child# 5 Frank Rubita Italy & Florida Lucier Mass
RUBITO, Bianco, Jan 20 1930 Sex:M Child# 7 Frank Rubito Italy & Florida Lucier Mass
RUBITO, Rita Rachelle, Sep 26 1923 Sex:F Child# 1 Frank Rubito Italy & Florida Lucier Mass
RUCZ, Joe, Apr 20 1916 Sex:M Child# 1 Stanley Rucz Russia & Mary Adomouis Russia Stillborn
RUCZ, Tophila, Oct 14 1917 Sex:F Child# 2 Stanislas Rucz Poland Russia & Martha Poland Russia
RUDAK, Anna, Nov 23 1921 Sex:F Child# 4 Pawel Rudak Nashua, NH & Anmelia Rupo Poland
RUDAK, Anthony, Mar 13 1919 Sex:M Child# 2 Pawel Rudak Russia & Nellie Krypa Russia
RUDAK, Sophia, Jul 18 1920 Sex:F Child# 3 Powel Rudak Poland & Amelia Rudak Poland
RUDEATES, Eva, May 17 1923 Sex:F Child# 5 Anthony Rudeates Lithuania & Eva Armolsock Lithuania
RUDNICK, Joseph Harry, Jan 3 1921 Sex:M Child# 2 Louis Rudnick Russia & Bertha Singer Russia
RUDNICK, Lillian Esther, Dec 4 1917 Sex:F Child# 1 Louis Rudnick Russia & Bertha Singer Russia
RUDZ, Bronica, Dec 30 1920 Sex:F Child# 3 Stanley Rudz Russia & Martha Adamowicz Russia
RUEST, Georges A C, Mar 8 1887 Sex:M Child# 2 Archille Ruest P Q & Olympe Ouellette P Q
RUEST, Joseph, Jul 23 1888 Sex:M Child# 3 Archille Ruest Canada & Olymps Oaillette Canada
RUEST, Marie B Yvomre, Feb 20 1898 Sex:F Child# 8 Achille Ruest Canada & Olympe Ouellette Canada
RUEST, Marie I D, Nov 3 1899 Sex:F Child# 2 Ernest Ruest Canada & Alphonsine Verrette Canada
RUET, Joseph Argee, Aug 13 1896 Sex:M Child# 7 Achille Ruet Canada & Olympe Ouellette Canada
RUET, Marie Eva, Jun 1 1895 Sex:F Child# 6 Achille Ruet Canada & Olympe Ouellette Canada
RUF, Elizabeth Esther, Apr 8 1911 Sex:F Child# 3 Frederick H Ruf Germany & Annie Marie Walter Philadelphia, PA
RUF, Frederick Henry, Mar 6 1912 Sex:M Child# 4 Frederick Henry Ruf, Germany & Annie Marie Walter Philadelphia, PA
RUF, Louisa Lillian, Dec 29 1914 Sex:F Child# 4 Fred Ruf Germany & Anna Walter Philadelphia, PA
RUF, Walter Leslie, Oct 10 1918 Sex:M Child# 6 Fred H Ruf Germany & Anna Walter Philadelphia, PA
RUFFLE, Evelyn May, Dec 8 1910 Sex:F Child# 1 Pearl Garfld Ruffle Shirley, MA & Katherine Williamson Canada
RUFFLE, George R, Oct 19 1922 Sex:M Child# 1 George R Ruffle Stoddard, NH & Agnes Manyon Ireland
RUGZISS, Marie, Nov 23 1888 Sex:F Child# 1 David Rugziss Canada & Azilda Varlept Canada
RUITER, Esther, Mar 27 1932 Sex:F Child# 3 Miles L Ruiter Manchester, NH & Helen Sweeney Manchester, NH
RUITER, Miles Leon, Feb 21 1933 Sex:M Child# 7 Miles L Ruiter Manchester, NH & H V Sweeney Manchester, NH
RULE, Joseph Henry, Apr 20 1899 Sex:M Child# 1 George Rule New York & Marie St Jean Canada
RUNNELLS, Dorothy May, May 11 1910 Sex:F Child# 2 Ernest A Runnells Hanover, NH & Ina M Baxter Antrim, NH
RUONALA, Joan Ruth, Dec 26 1929 Sex:F Child# 1 Eli Ruonala Lanesville, MA & Ruth Darling Boston, MA
RUONALA, John Edward, Mar 7 1934 Sex:M Child# 1 Edward Oscar Ruonala Gloucester, MA & Philomene Galletly MA
RUSH, Freida Bernice, Nov 5 1919 Sex:F Child# 1 Robert Rush Mattawamkeag, ME & Iva Kirkland Lagrange, ME
RUSH, Harland Fay, Sep 8 1925 Sex:M Child# 3 Robert Hueda Rush Matwamkeag, ME & Iva Kirkland LaGrange, MA
RUSH, Robert, Mar 23 1922 Sex:M Child# 2 Robert Rush Mattawamkeag, ME & Iva Kirkland Oldtown, ME
RUSSEAU, Joseph Esdras, Jun 22 1894 Sex:M Child# 2 Ferdinand Russeau Canada & Clara Canada
RUSSEAU, Marie Eliane, Jun 22 1898 Sex:F Child# 1 Edouard Russeau Canada & Aura Guilbault Canada
RUSSELL, Arthur Daniel, Apr 28 1918 Sex:M Child# 2 Arthur D Russell Nashua, NH & Annie Cunningham Ireland
RUSSELL, Barbara Helen, Jan 22 1926 Sex:F Child# 1 Herbert E Russell Bath, ME & Mildred K Smith Nashua, NH
RUSSELL, Dean Preston, Jan 13 1920 Sex:M Child# 3 Perley Russell Greenfield, NH & Angie Conn Antrim, NH
RUSSELL, Emma May, Dec 17 1919 Sex:F Child# 5 Charles Russell Mason, NH & Esther Croquette Newton, NH
RUSSELL, Esther Frances, Jan 9 1914 Sex:F Child# 3 Charles F Russell Mason, NH & Esther F Crockett Newton, NH
RUSSELL, Florence Anna, Nov 19 1923 Sex:F Child# 1 John Russell New York & Gertrude Porter Nashua, NH
RUSSELL, Frank H, Jun 16 1916 Sex:M Child# 3 Charles Russell Mason, NH & Ester Crockett Newton, NH
RUSSELL, Gladys Evelyn, May 14 1918 Sex:F Child# 4 Charles Russell Mason, NH & Esther Crockett Newton
RUSSELL, Harry Linwood, Oct 10 1902 Sex:M Child#  Ernest L Russell NH & Bessie M Robertson Vermont
RUSSELL, Johanna, Feb 27 1926 Sex:F Child# 6 Daniel Russell Nashua, NH & Anna Cunningham Ireland
RUSSELL, John Francis, Jan 22 1921 Sex:M Child# 4 Daniel Russell Nashua, NH & Annie Cunningham Ireland
RUSSELL, John Walter, Nov 4 1935 Sex:M Child# 1 George F Russell Peterboro, NH & Evelyn Converse Hollis, NH
RUSSELL, Joseph Euclide L, Jan 2 1925 Sex:M Child# 4 Alphonse Russell Canada & Anna Plourde Canada
RUSSELL, Lillian Lorette, Jun 14 1910 Sex:F Child# 1 William E Russell Lebanon & May Duchesneau Canada
RUSSELL, Lillian Theresa, Feb 19 1917 Sex:F Child# 1 Daniel A Russell Nashua, NH & Annie Cunningham Ireland
RUSSELL, Lucille Mary, Sep 15 1919 Sex:F Child# 3 Daniel Russell Nashua, NH & Annie Cunningham Ireland
RUSSELL, Maria, May 3 1898 Sex:F Child# 1 Emile Russell Canada & Adelle Dion Canada

RUSSELL, Marion Laura, Feb 7 1912 Sex:F Child# 1 Charles F Russell Mason, NH & Esther F Crokett Newton, NH
RUSSELL, Mary Ruth, Jun 20 1908 Sex:F Child# 1 Harry G Russell Nashua, NH & June McCoy Portland, ME
RUSSELL, Richard Allen, May 1 1921 Sex:M Child# 7 Charles Russell Mason, NH & Esther Crocket Newton, NH
RUSSELL, Robert Charles, May 1 1921 Sex:M Child# 6 Charles Russell Mason, NH & Esther Crocket Newton, NH
RUSSELL, Ruth Helen, May 1 1921 Sex:F Child# 8 Charles Russell Mason, NH & Esther Crocket Newton, NH
RUSSELL, Unknown, Apr 13 1887 Sex:M Child# 1 S B Russell Canada & Fanny F Maine
RUSSELL, Unknown, May 3 1888 Sex:F Child# 2 A B Russell Canada & Cora Voter Farmington, ME
RUSSELL, Unknown, Apr 3 1891 Sex:M Child# 2 Herbert A Russell Mass & Etta E Osgood Canada
RUSSELL, William Lewis, Sep 8 1917 Sex:M Child# 2 William Russell Nashua, NH & Addie Duchesneau Nashua, NH
RUSSELL, William Moore, Aug 13 1920 Sex:M Child# 2 George Russell Lafayette, IN & Teresa J Martin Nashua, NH
RUSSELL, William Tolles, Jun 5 1915 Sex:M Child# 1 John F Russell
RUSSEN, Catherine Josephine, Nov 10 1922 Sex:F Child# 5 Daniel Russen Nashua, NH & Anna Cunningham Ireland
RUTLAND, Unknown, Jun 19 1888 Sex:M Child# 1 Unknown Nashua, NH & Fanny Rutland Mass
RUTOUB, Stanley, Apr 8 1918 Sex:M Child# 6 John Rutoub Russia & Josephine Stannock Russia
RYAN, Agnes Theresa, Apr 16 1909 Sex:F Child# 5 Michael Ryan Ireland & Bridget Barrett Ireland
RYAN, Albert Leo, Dec 14 1894 Sex:M Child# 13 James Ryan Ireland & Kate McSherry Ireland
RYAN, Alene, Jan 14 1919 Sex:F Child# 3 Michael H Ryan Hudson, NY & Josephine Driscoll Chelsea, MA
RYAN, Ann, Aug 9 1902 Sex:F Child# 5 Richard Ryan Ireland & Mary Barrett Ireland
RYAN, Ann, Apr 21 1906 Sex:F Child# 3 Michael Ryan Ireland & Mary Winn Ireland
RYAN, Arthur, Mar 1 1896 Sex:M Child# 14 James Ryan Ireland & Kate McSherry Ireland
RYAN, Barbara Ann, Jul 27 1929 Sex:F Child# 4 Arthur Ryan Nashua, NH & Agnes Lee Pittsburgh, PA
RYAN, Beverly Ann, Feb 20 1928 Sex:F Child# 4 William H Ryan Nashua, NH & Eva Roy Nashua, NH
RYAN, Cynthia Marie, Oct 16 1934 Sex:F Child# 1 William Ryan Pepperell, MA & Edna Rivers Fitchburg, MA
RYAN, Eliza, Jul 26 1888 Sex:F Child# 5 Mike Ryan Plattsburg, NY & Mary Riley N Y
RYAN, Elizabeth, Dec 6 1888 Sex:F Child# 8 James Ryan Ireland & Catherine McSherry Ireland
RYAN, Ellen, Dec 8 1889 Sex:F Child# 6 Michael Ryan Plattsburg, NY & Mary Reilly Chatauguay, NY
RYAN, Eva Mary, Jun 15 1890 Sex:F Child# 9 James Ryan Ireland & Kate McSherry Ireland
RYAN, Evelyn Evangela, Sep 18 1899 Sex:F Child# 14 James Ryan Ireland & Catherine McSherry Ireland
RYAN, Frances Virginia, Jun 5 1932 Sex:F Child# 6 William H Ryan Nashua, NH & Eva Roy Nashua, NH
RYAN, George Augustus, Aug 19 1891 Sex:M Child# 11 James Ryan Ireland & Catherine McSherry Ireland
RYAN, Gloria Mary, Jun 12 1923 Sex:F Child# 1 William H Ryan Nashua, NH & Eva D Roy Nashua, NH
RYAN, Ida May, Nov 12 1906 Sex:F Child# 5 Michael Ryan Ireland & Bridget Barrett Ireland
RYAN, James, Sep 10 1918 Sex:M Child# 1 James Ryan Manchester, NH & Margaret Fallon Nashua, NH
RYAN, James Leo, Dec 8 1922 Sex:M Child# 1 Arthur M Ryan Nashua, NH & Agnes Lee Pittsburgh, PA
RYAN, John Patrick, Jul 14 1901 Sex:M Child# 2 Michael Ryan Ireland & Bridget Barrett Ireland
RYAN, John Winn, Nov 15 1927 Sex:M Child# 3 Arthur Ryan Nashua, NH & Agnes Lee Pittsburgh, PA
RYAN, Joseph Francis, Sep 21 1894 Sex:M Child# 1 Richard Ryan Ireland & Mary Barrett Ireland
RYAN, Katie A, Aug 5 1893 Sex:F Child# 12 James Ryan Ireland & Kate McSherry Ireland
RYAN, Lucy Ann, Jan 4 1928 Sex:F Child# 1 William T Ryan Lowell, MA & Mary Donovan Lowell, MA
RYAN, Margaret, Apr 5 1887 Sex:F Child# 4 Michael H Ryan Plattsburg & Mary N Y
RYAN, Margaret C, Dec 18 1896 Sex:F Child# 2 Richard Ryan Ireland & Mary Barrett Ireland
RYAN, Marie K, Aug 18 1891 Sex:F Child# 1 Richard A Ryan Ireland & Kate Leddy Ireland
RYAN, Mary A, Aug 6 1888 Sex:F Child# 3 Patrick Ryan Ireland & Maggie Leveny Ireland
RYAN, Mary A, May 15 1896 Sex:F Child# Dennis F Ryan Lawrence, MA & Mary Nashua, NH
RYAN, Mary Delia, May 30 1898 Sex:F Child# 3 Daniel Ryan Lawrence, MA & Mary Ann Bligh Nashua, NH
RYAN, Mary Gertrude, Aug 15 1898 Sex:F Child# 3 Richard Ryan Ireland & Mary Barrett Ireland
RYAN, Mary Jane, Mar 1 1935 Sex:F Child# 1 Frank Ryan Nashua, NH & Anna Bagley Peterborough, NH
RYAN, Nellie Cristena, Jan 10 1897 Sex:F Child# 3 Frank Ryan Jay, VT & Jennie Sargent Pattin, PQ
RYAN, Oliver S, Jan 13 1896 Sex:M Child# 2 Frank Ryan
RYAN, Richard Ed, Nov 13 1902 Sex:M Child# 1 John J Ryan Milford, NH & M Gertrude Dobbens Nashua, NH
RYAN, Richard Robert, Nov 27 1926 Sex:M Child# 2 Arthur Ryan Nashua, NH & Agnes Lee Pittsburgh, PA
RYAN, Rita Norma, Aug 28 1926 Sex:F Child# 3 William H Ryan Nashua, NH & Eva Roy Nashua, NH
RYAN, Robert Henry, Jun 16 1904 Sex:M Child# 3 Michael Ryan Ireland & Bridget Barrett Ireland
RYAN, Robert Richard, Aug 23 1929 Sex:M Child# 5 William H Ryan Nashua, NH & Eva Roy Nashua, NH
RYAN, Ryan, Sep 11 1891 Sex:M Child# 3 John H Ryan Uxbridge, MA & Katie Modeler Ireland
RYAN, Sadie May, Jun 17 1906 Sex:F Child# 6 Richard Ryan Ireland & Mary Barrett Ireland
RYAN, Thomas M, May 10 1892 Sex:M Child# 7 Michael H Ryan Plattsburg, NY & Mary Reilly Chatauguay, NY
RYAN, Unknown, Jun 11 1887 Sex:F Child# 7 James Ryan Ireland & Kate McSherry Ireland
RYAN, Unknown, Sep 6 1893 Sex:M Child# 7 Michael H Ryan Plattsburg, NY & Mary Riley Chautauqua, NY Stillborn
RYAN, Unknown, Jun 9 1895 Sex:M Child# 1 Frank Ryan Jay, VT & Jennie Sargent Canada
RYAN, Unknown, Oct 6 1900 Sex:M Child# 4 Richard Ryan Ireland & Mary Barrett Ireland
RYAN, Unknown, Sep 17 1920 Sex:M Child# 4 Frank Ryan Nashua, NH & Dora Haselton Hudson, NH
RYAN, Vivian May, Aug 12 1890 Sex:F Child# 2 Dennis J Ryan Canada & Amela Yettan Ellensburg, NY
RYAN, William Edward, Aug 28 1899 Sex:M Child# 1 Michael Ryan Ireland & Bridget Barrett Ireland
RYAN, William Henry, Jr, Nov 2 1924 Sex:M Child# 2 William H Ryan Nashua, NH & Eva D Roy Nashua, NH
RYDER, Unknown, Mar 18 1898 Sex:F Child# 5 John C Ryder Clinton, MA & Emma J Henry Halifax, NS
RYNN, Harry, Nov 11 1897 Sex:M Child# 8 Patrick Rynn Ireland & Margaret Kevany Ireland
RYNN, Henry, Nov 18 1892 Sex:M Child# 6 Patrick Rynn Ireland & Maggie Kaveny Ireland
RYNN, John, Nov 30 1890 Sex:M Child# 5 Patrick Rynn Ireland & Maggie Kaveny Ireland
RYNN, Leo, May 15 1899 Sex:M Child# 9 Patrick Rynn Ireland & Margaret Kareney Ireland
RYNN, Mildred, Mar 19 1903 Sex:F Child# 10 Patrick Rynn Ireland & Margaret Raveny Ireland
RZEZNIKIENWICH, John, Oct 24 1908 Sex:M Child# 1 John Rzeznikienwich Austria & Rosa Shutan Austria
SABALASKA, Amelia, Apr 10 1914 Sex:F Child# 1 Anthony Sabalaska Russia & Amelia Iaksuka Russia

SABALENSKI, Juze, May 8 1907 Sex:M Child# 1 Anthony Sabalenski Russia & Mary Galaniute Russia
SABALIOUSKI, Ellen, Jan 12 1916 Sex:F Child# 6 Anthony Sabaliouski Russia & Mary Doremg Russia
SABELMAN, Annie, Jan 2 1910 Sex:F Child# 1 Max Sabelman Russia & Fannie Kline Austria
SABER, Phene, Jul 15 1897 Sex:F Child# 5 Samuel Saber Russia & Dora Ticktin Russia
SABER, Unknown, Sep 8 1900 Sex:F Child# 6 Samuel Saber Russia & Dora Ticktin Russia
SABETTE, Pierre, Dec 23 1889 Sex:M Child# 4 Joseph Sabette Canada & Josephine Gauthier Canada
SABLUSKI, Joseph, Feb 4 1911 Sex:M Child# 5 Anthony Sabluski Russia & Mary Darling Russia
SABR, Eva, Mar 1 1894 Sex:F Child# 3 Sem Sabr Russia & Dora Fictin Russia
SACOULAS, Constantinos, Apr 1 1915 Sex:M Child# 1 Lewis Sacoulas Greece & Penelope Scorda Greece
SADAWSKI, Mary, Sep 14 1916 Sex:F Child# 4 Peter Sadawski Russia & Mary Davy Russia
SADD, Sumner Harry, Jul 28 1905 Sex:M Child# 3 George G Sadd Ellington, CT & Lillian I Wheeler Nashua, NH
SADD, Unknown, Feb 25 1898 Sex:F Child# 1 George G Sadd Ellington, Canada & Lillian L Wheeler Nashua, NH
SADD, Unknown, Oct 15 1900 Sex:F Child# 2 George G Sadd Conn & L I Wheeler Nashua, NH
SADLER, Geo Joseph Thomas, Aug 2 1929 Sex:M Child# 2 Paul Sadler Nashua, NH & Ruth Jacobs Flather Dorchester, MA
SADLER, Paul, Sep 9 1901 Sex:M Child# 1 George L Sadler Windsor Locks, CT & Nellie F Mongovan Nashua, NH
SADLER, Paul, Jr, Aug 7 1926 Sex:M Child# 1 Paul Sadler Nashua, NH & Ruth Flather Dorchester, MA
SAGENE, Joseph Ernest, Oct 20 1898 Sex:M Child# 6 Francois Sagene Canada & Georgianna Bernier Canada
SAGER, Clark Day, Mar 3 1902 Sex:M Child# 4 Luther Sager Vermont & Mamie McCulla Vermont
SAGER, Eleanor Ruth, Jun 5 1917 Sex:F Child# 1 Charles S Sager Jericho, VT & Mabel Batchelder Haverill, MA
SAGER, Harold Edmond, Nov 9 1909 Sex:M Child# 1 Luther N Sager Colchester, VT & Ella McCutcheon St John, NB
SAGER, Unknown, Nov 13 1898 Sex:F Child#  Luther M Sager Colchester, VT & Mary McCuen Colchester, VT
SAGERE, Joseph Romuald, Mar 2 1895 Sex:M Child# 3 Francois Sagere Canada & Georgianna Bernier Canada
SAGERIE, Joseph, Aug 23 1896 Sex:M Child# 4 Francois S Sagerie Canada & Georgiana Bernier Canada
SAGERS, Charlotte Annie, Mar 20 1891 Sex:F Child# 2 John L Sagers Londonderry & Beatrice R Burns Canada
SAHAGIAN, Aiznev, Jul 9 1922 Sex:F Child# 1 Kachdoor Sahagian Armenia & Eliza Shpzian Turkey
SAHAJIAN, Daajkian, Jun 26 1907 Sex:M Child# 8 Avedis Sahajian Armenia & Onam Sarkisian Armenia
SAIDON, Marie L, Jul 21 1889 Sex:F Child# 1 Alfred Saindon Canada & Rosalie Lavique Nashua, NH
SAILER, Clara Lucille, Sep 21 1911 Sex:F Child# 2 Charles E Sailer Reigilsville, NJ & Florence H Gendron Nashua, NH
SAILER, Clara Melba, Dec 23 1903 Sex:F Child# 6 Sherman T Sailer Holland, NJ & Clara Tinsman Rigelsville, NJ
SAILER, Helen Emma, Apr 26 1918 Sex:F Child# 3 Charles E Sailer Reigelsville, NJ & Florence H Gendron Nashua, NH
SAINDON, Jos R Ludg Ernest, Jan 17 1917 Sex:M Child# 2 Eugene Saindon Maine & Alba Tetro Canada
SAKAIL, Richard Paul, Jun 2 1929 Sex:M Child# 2 Emile Harry Sakail Nashua, NH & Sylviana Bellavance Nashua, NH
SAKAUSKI, Unknown, Jan 6 1925 Sex:F Child# 5 Michael Sakauski Lithuania & Rachael Stangeck Lithuania Stillborn
SAKAWECUS, Aliasia, Jan 18 1909 Sex:F Child# 2 Adamas Sakawecus Russia & Kazi Walentukicutie Russia
SAKAWICZ, Antony, Oct 23 1910 Sex:M Child# 3 Adam Sakawicz Russia & Kazimerka Walentuke Russia
SAKELAROPOWLAS, Dimitra, Aug 29 1916 Sex:F Child# 3 Peter Sakelaropowlas Greece & Tasia Andrianopo Greece
SAKOWICZ, Alix, May 12 1907 Sex:F Child# 1 Adam Sakowicz Russia & Kazine Wolentkiwicz Russia
SAKOWICZ, Mary, Feb 2 1912 Sex:F Child# 1 William Sakowicz Russia & Antonette Antalwick Russia
SAKOWICZ, Walter, May 10 1916 Sex:M Child# 4 William Sakowicz Russia & Antonina Antolawicz Russia
SAKOWICZ, Zofai, Feb 9 1915 Sex:F Child# 3 William Sakowicz Russia & Antosa Antolowicz Russia
SAKVEA, Albert, Sep 18 1916 Sex:M Child# 1 Peter Sakvea Russia & Viola Mizoris Russia
SALCS, Julia, Sep 17 1917 Sex:F Child# 1 Charles Salcs Russia & Cary Avjon Russia
SALISBURG, Norman William, Aug 7 1934 Sex:M Child# 3 William Salisburg Putnam, CT & Arlene Sears Nashua, NH
SALISBURY, Evelyn Mae, Jun 22 1931 Sex:F Child# 1 William Salisbury Putnam, CT & Arline Sears Nashua, NH
SALISBURY, Glenn Harrison, Dec 12 1935 Sex:M Child# 4 Wm P Salisbury Putnam, CT & Arline Sears Nashua, NH
SALISBURY, Loretta Jean, Jul 5 1932 Sex:F Child# 2 W P Salisbury Putnam, CT & Arline M Sears Nashua, NH
SALMAN, Unknown, Nov 20 1932 Sex:M Child# 1 F Salman US & Blanche Nuronoff US
SALUTA, Agatha, May 15 1906 Sex:F Child# 3 William Saluta Russia & Mary Russia
SALVA, George Albert, Jul 24 1904 Sex:M Child# 1 David Salva Canada & Marie Boucher Canada
SALVA, Joseph O, Dec 23 1890 Sex:M Child# 8 Olivier Salva Canada & Marie Lavigne Canada
SALVA, Marie I, Feb 18 1889 Sex:F Child# 6 Oliver Salva Canada & Marie Gourgne Canada
SALVAIL, Aldea Marie A, Feb 24 1898 Sex:F Child# 3 Pierre Salvail Canada & Adele Laforest Canada
SALVAIL, Alice R, Apr 1 1887 Sex:F Child#  Joseph Salvail P Q & Amie Dube P Q
SALVAIL, Anna A, Oct 23 1888 Sex:F Child# 3 Joseph Salvail Canada & Amie Dube Canada
SALVAIL, Aurore, Feb 5 1893 Sex: Child# 1 Pierre Salvail Canada & Adele Laforest Canada
SALVAIL, Clara, Feb 21 1887 Sex:F Child# 3 Narcisse Salvail Canada & Mary Cote Canada
SALVAIL, Claudia, Feb 21 1887 Sex:F Child# 2 Narcisse Salvail Canada & Mary Cote Canada
SALVAIL, Elaine Barbara, Nov 17 1931 Sex:F Child# 1 Peter Salvail Nashua, NH & Rose Babourbeau Canada
SALVAIL, Euclide, Nov 27 1891 Sex:M Child# 6 Nazaire Salvail Canada & Clarissse Dube Canada
SALVAIL, Flora, Oct 27 1894 Sex:F Child# 2 Pierre Salvail Canada & Adele Laforest Canada
SALVAIL, George Silvia, Dec 26 1891 Sex:M Child# 4 Joseph Salvail Canada & Aime Dube Canada
SALVAIL, Gerard Jos Raymond, Aug 8 1923 Sex:M Child# 3 Hormidas Salvail Canada & Aldea Forcier Canada
SALVAIL, Izama Anita, Mar 20 1899 Sex:F Child# 3 Oswald P Salvail Fall River, MA & Rose Boberly Greenville, NH
SALVAIL, James, Oct 21 1891 Sex:M Child# 7 Pierre Salvail Canada & Louise Dean Canada
SALVAIL, Joseph Ed Rolland, Oct 29 1900 Sex:M Child# 11 Narcisse H Salvail Canada & Marie Cote Canada
SALVAIL, Joseph Emile, Jul 7 1897 Sex:M Child# 9 Narcisse Salvail Canada & Marie Cote Canada
SALVAIL, Joseph G A, Sep 21 1901 Sex:M Child# 2 Pierre C Salvail NH & Glorida L Heureux Canada
SALVAIL, Joseph Henri, Nov 8 1895 Sex:M Child# 8 Narcisse Salvail Canada & Marie Cote Canada
SALVAIL, Juliette, Jan 1 1894 Sex:F Child# 7 Narcisse Salvail Canada & Velarie Cote Canada
SALVAIL, Leo, Oct 17 1915 Sex:M Child# 2 Hormidas Salvail Canada & Aldea Forcier Canada
SALVAIL, Liliane Juliette, Jan 3 1912 Sex:F Child# 1 Joseph Salvail Canada & Marie Lepine Canada
SALVAIL, Lucille Mary, Jul 4 1924 Sex:F Child# 1 Henry J Salvail Nashua, NH & Eudoxie Gauthier Taunton, MA
SALVAIL, M Rose Jeanne, Jun 15 1913 Sex:F Child# 2 Joseph Salvail Canada & Marie Lepine Canada

SALVAIL, Madeline Therese, Apr 17 1932 Sex:F Child# 1 Roland Salvail Nashua, NH & Yvonne Lizotte Nashua, NH
SALVAIL, Marie A G, Jun 30 1904 Sex:F Child# 1 Albert Salvail Nashua, NH & Marie Tessier Canada
SALVAIL, Marie Anne, Mar 28 1890 Sex:F Child# 5 Narcisse Salvail Canada & Marie Cote Canada
SALVAIL, Marie C Aurore, Oct 22 1896 Sex:F Child# 7 Nazaire Salvail Canada & Claris Dube Canada
SALVAIL, Marie Emma I, Feb 4 1903 Sex:F Child# 12 Narcisse N Salvail Canada & Marie Cote Canada
SALVAIL, Marie Genevieve, Jan 2 1913 Sex:F Child# 3 Telesphore Salvail NH & Elisabeth Chartrand Vermont
SALVAIL, Marie Jeanne, Mar 3 1899 Sex:F Child# 10 Narcisse Salvail Canada & Marie Cote Canada
SALVAIL, Marie Leona L, Jan 19 1906 Sex:F Child# 14 Narcisse Salvail Canada & Marie Cote Canada
SALVAIL, Marie Yvonne Rachel, Sep 12 1912 Sex:F Child# 1 Hormidas Salvail Canada & Aldea Forcier Canada
SALVAIL, Obeline, Oct 23 1897 Sex:F Child# 3 Peter Salvail Nashua, NH & Augusta Dallieu Nashua, NH
SALVAIL, Oscar, Oct 4 1891 Sex:M Child# 6 Narcisse Salvail Canada & Marie Cote Canada
SALVAIL, Pierre Cyrille H, Jul 22 1900 Sex:M Child# 1 P C Salvail NH & Glorida H Henreaux Canada
SALVAIL, Robert Arthur, Jul 24 1926 Sex:M Child# 1 Emile Salvail Nashua, NH & S Bellavance Nashua, NH
SALVAIL, Romeo, Jul 15 1894 Sex:M Child# 2 Pierre Salvail Canada & Augusta Dallaire Canada
SALVAIL, Ronald, Aug 24 1934 Sex:M Child# 3 Harry Salvail Nashua, NH & Sylvia Bellavance Nashua, NH
SALVAIL, Unknown, May 11 1893 Sex:F Child# 1 Pierre Salvail Nashua, NH & Augusta Dallaire Nashua, NH
SALVAIL, Unknown, Dec 5 1893 Sex:F Child# 5 Joseph Salvail Canada & Aime Dube Canada Stillborn
SALVAIL, Unknown, Mar 27 1895 Sex:F Child# 6 Joseph Salvail Canada & Aimee Dube Canada Stillborn
SALVAIL, Unknown, Sep 7 1896 Sex:F Child# 7 Pierre Salvail Canada & Louise Ding Michigan Stillborn
SALVAIL, Yolande, Aug 7 1912 Sex:F Child# 14 Narcisse Salvail Canada & Marie Cote Canada
SALVER, Maurice, Jul 2 1892 Sex:M Child# 4 Barney Salver Russia & Rebecca Shooper Russia
SAMARIS, Unknown, Dec 22 1920 Sex:M Child# 3 John Samaris Greece & Eva Statis Greece
SAMKOFSKI, Joseph, May 15 1915 Sex:M Child# 3 Charles Samkofski Russia & Catherine Zurafski Russia
SAMPSON, Charles Phillip, Feb 28 1904 Sex:M Child# 5 Edward Sampson Rhode Island & Mary Lessor Maine
SAMPSON, Ernest Henry, Oct 13 1913 Sex:M Child# 7 William Sampson New York & Mary Davis North Carolina Colored
SAMPSON, Eva Isabell, Feb 28 1904 Sex:F Child# 6 Edward Sampson Rhode Island & Mary Lessor Maine
SAMPSON, Florence E, Mar 14 1902 Sex:F Child# 4 Ed D Sampson Conn & Mary Lessor Maine
SAMPSON, George Richard, May 1 1906 Sex:M Child# 7 Edward Sampson Conn & Mary Lessard Maine
SAMPSON, Lewis Henry, Oct 4 1894 Sex:M Child# 1 Edward Sampson Willimantic, CT & Mary M Lessor Skowhegan, ME
SAMPSON, Mabel L, Jun 17 1911 Sex:F Child# 5 William Sampson New York & Mary Davis Oxford, NC Colored
SAMPSON, Medora, Feb 23 1898 Sex:F Child# 3 Joseph Sampson Canada & Luce Paquette Canada
SAMPSON, Perley, Jul 27 1916 Sex:M Child# 9 William Sampson Deposit, NY & Mary Davis Oxford, NC Colored
SAMPSON, Robert George, Sep 28 1932 Sex:M Child# 1 Geo H Sampson E Boston, MA & Edna Davis Dover, NH
SAMPSON, Roy Edward, Dec 28 1900 Sex:M Child# 3 Edward D Sampson Conn & Mary Lessor Maine
SAMPSON, Viola Belle, May 2 1915 Sex:F Child# 8 William Sampson Deposit, NY & Mary Davis Oxford, NC Colored
SAMUELSON, Amelia M, Oct 2 1887 Sex:F Child# 2 O Samuelson Sweden & Mary McCarthy Wilton, NH
SAMUELSON, Henry F, Oct 6 1890 Sex:M Child# 3 A Samuelson Sweden & Mary McCarthy Wilton, NH
SANBORN, Harry E, Aug 19 1893 Sex:M Child# 2 E H Sanborn Concord, NH & Helen J Shaw Pittsfield, NH
SANBORN, Henry Eaton, May 11 1904 Sex:M Child# 1 Charles C Sanborn Concord, NH & Helen Eaton Nashua, NH
SANBORN, John C, Aug 28 1892 Sex:M Child# 5 Frank L Sanborn Pittsfield & Ellen G Groton, MA
SANBORN, Unknown, Dec 20 1887 Sex:M Child# 1 Warren A Sanborn E Andover & Jennie J Hoit N Weare, NH
SANBORN, Unknown, Sep 13 1932 Sex:M Child# 1 Harold Sanborn Lowell, MA & Mary Hodge Lowell, MA  Stillborn
SANBORN, William, Jul 1 1888 Sex:M Child# 5 Fred Sanborn Concord & Jennie Sanborn Haverhill
SANBROWN, John Andrew, Apr 17 1901 Sex:M Child# 4 Thomas M Sanbrown Mass & Inez Smith Mass
SANCHEZ, Ralph Edgar, Apr 15 1928 Sex:M Child# 2 Edward Sanchez E Boston, MA & Jane McNally New York
SANDBEND, Unknown, Sep 18 1893 Sex:F Child# 1 Carl Sandbend
SANDBLOW, Annato, Oct 22 1894 Sex:F Child# 7 Alfred Sandblow Sweden & Charlotte Carlson Sweden
SANDBORN, Judith Selina, Aug 4 1892 Sex:F Child# 6 Alfred J Sandborn Sweden & Charlotte K Castor Sweden
SANDERS, Allen Wesley, Aug 19 1913 Sex:M Child# 3 Leon A Sanders Nashua, NH & Katherine G Simmons W Windham, NH
SANDERS, Bernice Kimball, Mar 23 1897 Sex:F Child# 1 Philip S Sanders Nashua, NH & Maud I Kimball Nashua, NH
SANDERS, Harry D, Jun 28 1901 Sex:M Child# 3 A L Sanders Vermont & Emma M Bernard Hudson, NH
SANDERS, James, Jan 27 1890 Sex:M Child# 3 James Sanders Nashua, NH & Emma J Hosmer Nashua, NH
SANDERS, Muriel P, Apr 25 1911 Sex:F Child# 2 Philip Sanders Washington, VT & Maud Kimball Nashua, NH
SANDERS, Robert Louis, Jul 30 1910 Sex:M Child# 1 Louis H Sanders Nashua, NH & Mary Conlon Lynn, MA
SANDERS, Ruby M, Jun 3 1887 Sex:F Child# 2 James A Sanders Nashua, NH & Emma J Hosmer Nashua, NH
SANDERS, Unknown, Jun 29 1890 Sex:M Child# 2 Charles F Sanders Nashua, NH & Ora B Shattuck Hollis, NH
SANDERS, Unknown, Aug 31 1891 Sex:M Child# 4 James Sanders Nashua, NH & Emma J Hosmer Nashua, NH
SANDERS, Unknown, Dec 8 1902 Sex:F Child# 1 Louis Sanders Nashua, NH & Mary Jones Nashua, NH
SANDERS, Unknown, Jan 12 1916 Sex:M Child# 4 Leon A Sanders Nashua, NH & Catherine G Simmons W Windham, NH
SANDLAND, Carl Seth, Dec 14 1902 Sex:M Child# 4 Carl L Sandland Sweden & Emma Olson Sweden
SANDLUM, Unknown, Apr 5 1899 Sex:M Child#  C L Sandlum Sweden & Emma Olson Sweden Stillborn
SANDLUND, Eva Albertina, Oct 1 1900 Sex:F Child# 4 Carl S Sandlund Sweden & Emma S Olson Sweden
SANDLUND, John Arthur, Feb 10 1896 Sex:M Child# 2 Charles L Sandlund Sweden & Emmee O Sandlund Sweden
SANFORD, Lena D, Jan 27 1907 Sex:F Child# 1 Albert F Sanford Royalston, MA & Eva Stewart Vermont
SANFORD, Lorraine, Jan 3 1930 Sex:F Child# 2 Loran Sanford Laconia, NH & Helen Hartwell Pepperell, MA
SANGSTER, Arlene Rachel, Apr 9 1926 Sex:F Child# 1 James Sangster Milford, NH & Blanche Kalderara Barre, VT
SANITSKY, Helena, Feb 17 1920 Sex:F Child# 1 Walter Sanitsky Russia & Ludwiga Boroska Russia
SANKOPSKI, Unknown, Aug 19 1920 Sex:M Child# 9 Charles Sankopski Poland & Katie Zerofski Poland
SANSTERRE, Hormidas, Apr 15 1897 Sex:M Child# 1 Adelard Sansterre Canada & Adeline Brisson Canada
SANSTERRE, Marie Alice, Jun 30 1898 Sex:F Child# 2 Adelard Sansterre Canada & Adeline Brisson Canada
SANTERRE, Arthur, Oct 4 1933 Sex:M Child# 1 Arthur Santerre Nashua, NH & Cecile Beauleau New Brunswick
SANTERRE, Elmer Andre, Nov 6 1934 Sex:M Child# 7 Hormidas Santerre Nashua, NH & Mildred Lavoie Nashua, NH
SANTERRE, Joseph, Jul 6 1923 Sex:M Child# 1 Hormidas Santerre Nashua, NH & Mildred Lavoie Nashua, NH Stillborn

SANTERRE, Joseph Girard Adrien, Aug 5 1928 Sex:M Child# 5 H G Santerre Nashua, NH & Mildred Lavoie Nashua, NH
SANTERRE, Leo Benedictor, Sep 27 1909 Sex:M Child# 1 Olivier Santerre Canada & Catherine Cavanaugh Canada
SANTERRE, Leo Normand, Oct 11 1933 Sex:M Child# 7 A Santerre Nashua, NH & Mildred Lavoie Nashua, NH
SANTERRE, Lucien Guy Albert, Jun 27 1932 Sex:M Child# 6 H J Santerre Nashua, NH & Mildred Lavoie Nashua, NH
SANTERRE, Marie Anna Olivette, Dec 8 1926 Sex:F Child# 2 Adelard Santerre Canada & Anna Plourde Canada
SANTERRE, Marie Therese Anna, Jul 10 1924 Sex:F Child# 2 Hormidas Santerre Nashua, NH & Mildred Lavoie Nashua, NH
SANTERRE, Mary Rita Theresa, Jun 20 1930 Sex:F Child# 3 Adelard Santerre Canada & Anna Plourde Nashua, NH
SANTERRE, Paul Roger, Mar 2 1921 Sex:M Child# 1 Arthur Santerre Nashua, NH & Donalda Deneault Nashua, NH
SANTERRE, Reginald Roger, Dec 12 1926 Sex:M Child# 4 Hormidas Santerre Nashua, NH & Mildred Lavoie Nashua, NH
SANTERRE, Robert Jos Uldoric, Sep 9 1925 Sex:M Child# 3 H G Santerre Nashua, NH & Mildred Lavoie Nashua, NH
SAPARITA, Unknown, Apr 20 1911 Sex:M Child# 4 Lingi Saparita Italy & Almenia Milano Italy
SAPITOWICZ, Maria, Mar 22 1913 Sex:F Child# 2 Stanislaw Sapitowicz Russia & Catherine Zinkawicz Russia
SAPOS, Mary, Jan 9 1918 Sex:F Child# 1 Spiro Z Sapos Greece & Stella Gazape Greece
SARAGHAN, Unknown, Nov 29 1914 Sex:F Child# 3 Edw J Saraghan Ireland & Carrie B Morse Amherst, NH Stillborn
SARAH, Joseph Emile, Dec 23 1898 Sex:M Child# 4 Joseph Sarah Canada & Eveline Grandmaison Canada
SARCOLA, Julia, Sep 3 1919 Sex:F Child# 3 Peter Sarcola Russia & Viola Miserut Russia
SARDENIS, Aristave, May 1 1917 Sex:M Child# 11 George Sardenis Greece & Mary Lantyons Greece
SARDENIS, Athenia, Mar 28 1916 Sex:F Child# 9 George Sardenis Greece & Maria Lauzeau Greece
SARDENIS, Tosia, May 1 1917 Sex:F Child# 10 George Sardenis Greece & Mary Lantyons Greece
SARDOUNIS, Vasilis, Oct 20 1916 Sex:M Child# 2 Louis Sardounis Greece & Antriana Macrona Greece
SARGENT, Arlene, Mar 12 1924 Sex:F Child# 4 James A Sargent Windham, NH & Bertha Lund Dunstable, MA
SARGENT, Carl H, Apr 25 1892 Sex:M Child# 2 Charles H Sargent NH & Mattie A Clark NH
SARGENT, Catherine Frances, Jan 13 1912 Sex:F Child# 9 Avacles Sargent Armenia & Mary Tassayian Armenia
SARGENT, Chester Dana, Nov 25 1918 Sex:M Child# 2 James A Sargent Windham, NH & Bertha Lund Dunstable, MA
SARGENT, Constance Dorothy, Mar 11 1935 Sex:F Child# 6 Conrad Sargent Dunstable, MA & Claire Bell Lowell, MA
SARGENT, Earl Milton, Jun 4 1909 Sex:M Child# 1 Morey W Sargent Campello, MA & Nellie F Richardson E Weare, NH
SARGENT, Elizabeth, Feb 15 1900 Sex:F Child# 3 Avadis Sargent Turkey & Osuma Guvosian Turkey
SARGENT, Elizabeth, Jul 23 1907 Sex:F Child# 2 Harold M Sargent Nashua, NH & Lizzie M Tuft Mass
SARGENT, Ethel C, Mar 25 1902 Sex:F Child# 1 Harold M Sargent Nashua, NH & Lizzie M Tufts Westboro, MA
SARGENT, Ethel S, Jun 22 1895 Sex:F Child# 3 Charles Sargent Milford, NH & Mattie Clark Milford, NH
SARGENT, Eunise, May 11 1896 Sex:F Child# 12 W Frank Sargent Hudson, NH & Minnie Cullum Ireland
SARGENT, Frank Frederick, Apr 16 1924 Sex:M Child# 1 Conrad Sargent Dunstable, MA & Claire Bell Lowell, MA
SARGENT, Harrison Allen, May 28 1927 Sex:M Child# 2 H F Sargent Bradford, VT & Ada Allen Epping, NH
SARGENT, Herbert Adelbert, Dec 14 1927 Sex:M Child# 3 Conrad F Sargent Dunstable, MA & Claire Bell Lowell, MA
SARGENT, Howard Bernard, Sep 26 1910 Sex:M Child# 1 John Sargent Manchester, NH & Edith Stevens Manchester, NH
SARGENT, Jack F, Jr, Feb 12 1918 Sex:M Child# 2 Jack F Sargent Portland, ME & Gertrude Clara Mace Kittery, ME
SARGENT, John Bradford, Dec 2 1929 Sex:M Child# 4 Conrad F Sargent Dunstable, MA & Clara Bell Lowell, MA
SARGENT, Juanita Ethel, Jul 25 1925 Sex:F Child# 2 Conrad F Sargent Dunstable, MA & Claire Bell Lowell, MA
SARGENT, Marguerite, Jun 20 1890 Sex:F Child# 3 Fayette S Sargent Piermont, NH & H Frances Hall Revere, MA
SARGENT, Marion Alice, May 25 1921 Sex:F Child# 3 James A Sargent W Windham, NH & Bertha E Lund Dunstable, MA
SARGENT, Muriel Alice, Nov 23 1931 Sex:F Child# 5 Conrad Sargent Dunstable, MA & Claire Bell Lowell, MA
SARGENT, Raymond Walter, Jun 30 1901 Sex:M Child# 3 Walter J Sargent Washington & Mary J Simonds Orange, W VA
SARGENT, Rosa, Sep 16 1910 Sex:F Child# 8 Avaches Sargent Armenia & Mary Tazsayiari Armenia
SARGENT, Sargent, Mar 23 1889 Sex:F Child# 1 Charles H Sargent Milford, NH & Mattie A Clark Milford, NH
SARGENT, Unknown, Jul 10 1888 Sex:M Child# 1 Fayette S Sargent Vermont & F Franca Hall Revere, MA
SARGENT, Unknown, Nov 3 1889 Sex: Child# 3 John Sargent Penacook, NH & Carrie Jewett Laconia, NH
SARGENT, Unknown, Apr 7 1894 Sex:F Child# 11 William F Sargent Hudson, NH & Bridget Cullen Ireland
SARGENT, Unknown, Jan 19 1899 Sex:F Child# 1 Walter S Sargent Lebanon & Bertha Smith Windham
SARGENT, Unknown, Apr 18 1932 Sex:M Child#   James A Sargent W Windham, NH & Bertha E Lund Dunstable, MA
SARGENT, Warren Lund, Aug 26 1927 Sex:M Child# 4 J A Sargent W Windham, NH & Bertha E Lund Dunstable, MA
SARGENT, Wesley Alvin, Jun 10 1917 Sex:M Child# 1 James A Sargent Windham, NH & Bertha Lund Dunstable, MA
SARKARLASKI, Mary, Jul 12 1915 Sex:F Child# 4 Joseph Sarkarlaski Russia & Patronilla Vasolefsk Russia
SAROUIT, Rita Gertrude, Feb 24 1925 Sex:F Child# 2 Henry Sarouit Manchange, RI & Gertrude Garry Woonsocket, RI
SARTORELLI, Ugo Joseph, Jul 25 1925 Sex:M Child# 1 C Sartorelli Italy & Josephine Sassi Italy
SARTORELLI, Unknown, Jun 13 1929 Sex:F Child# 2 Cherabeno Sartorelli Italy & Josephine Sassy Italy
SARTWELL, Evelyn May, Mar 15 1900 Sex:F Child# 7 Burdick Sartwell NY & Nettie Matott NY
SASALKA, Stanley, May 8 1917 Sex:M Child# 3 John Sasalka Russia & Amelia Paelchesk Russia
SASSE, Agnes Blanche, Jun 15 1906 Sex:F Child# 1 Frederic Sasse London, England & Marie L Delude Canada
SASSE, Lena Pearl, Jun 1 1910 Sex:F Child# 2 Fred Sasse England & Marie L Delude Canada
SASSE, Olivia Theresa, Mar 26 1921 Sex:F Child# 3 George Sasse Italy & Angelina Rossi Italy
SATKOWSKI, Annie, Feb 18 1918 Sex:F Child# 3 Mike Satkowski Russia & Rosa Stanchick Russia
SATSAR, Jean Baptist, Apr 18 1889 Sex:M Child# 2 Simon Satsar Canada & Victorie Gaforest Canada
SATT, Stanley, Oct 24 1914 Sex:M Child# 3 Charles Satt Russia & Antonina Sylowich Russia
SAUDWELL, Lorne William, Jun 6 1919 Sex:M Child# 5 John W Saudwell Manchester, NH & Clara E Brown Gilmanton, NH
SAUNDERS, Arthur T, Nov 27 1896 Sex:M Child# 3 W E Saunders Nashua, NH & Sarah Sumner England
SAUNDERS, Barbara Mae, Feb 22 1921 Sex:F Child# 1 James A Saunders Worcester, MA & Mae Mober Manchester, NH
SAUNDERS, Charles Edward, Jul 4 1924 Sex:M Child# 1 Frank Saunders Newfoundland & Angela Marigan Newfoundland
SAUNDERS, Charles Frederick, Jul 27 1911 Sex:M Child# 2 Leon A Saunders Nashua, NH & Grace Bean W Windham, NH
SAUNDERS, Constance Louise, Jan 26 1931 Sex:F Child# 4 Theodore Saunders Pepperell, MA & Ella Rowell Salem, MA
SAUNDERS, Doris Isabel, Sep 19 1927 Sex:F Child# 5 Charles E Saunders Newfoundland & Eleanor Johnson Sweden
SAUNDERS, Elsie Irene, Oct 28 1928 Sex:F Child# 6 Charles E Saunders Newfoundland & Elinor Johnson Sweden
SAUNDERS, Ernest Vernon, Dec 13 1929 Sex:M Child# 1 Leon A Saunders Nashua, NH & Beatrice L Chisholm Somerville, MA
SAUNDERS, Ethel Summers, Feb 19 1894 Sex:F Child# 2 William E Saunders Nashua, NH & Sarah M Summers England

SAUNDERS, Harry A, Sep 2 1889 Sex:M Child# 1 B P Saunders Nashua, NH & Jenny Colburn Nashua, NH
SAUNDERS, Helen Margaret, Jan 9 1926 Sex:F Child# 4 Charles Saunders Newfoundland & Eleanor Johnson Sweden
SAUNDERS, Henry Eugene E, Sep 16 1895 Sex:M Child# 1 George Saunders Kinsley Falls & Albina Lamarche Nashua, NH
SAUNDERS, Lorraine, May 26 1934 Sex:F Child# 1 Theodore Saunders Clinton, MA & Helen Stone Orange, MA
SAUNDERS, Mary Eugenia, May 23 1924 Sex:F Child# 2 Theo Saunders Pepperell, MA & Ella May Salem, MA
SAUNDERS, Mary Louise, Jun 25 1922 Sex:F Child# 3 Charles E Saunders Carbonear, Newfndlnd & Eleanor Johnson Sweden
SAUNDERS, Mildred, Jan 18 1913 Sex:F Child# 1 John Saunders Canada & Marie Dube Canada
SAUNDERS, Mildred Mary, Sep 27 1917 Sex:F Child# 7 Leon A Saunders Nashua, NH & Grace Timmons W Windham, NH
SAUNDERS, Ralph Edward, Mar 4 1929 Sex:F Child# 3 Theodore Saunders Pepperell, MA & Ella Rowell Salem, MA
SAUNDERS, Ralph Henry, Mar 1 1926 Sex:M Child# 2 Frank Saunders Newfoundland & Angela Madigan Newfoundland
SAUNDERS, Richard Wilbur, Mar 15 1934 Sex:M Child# 5 Theodore Saunders Pepperell, MA & Ella Rowell Salem, NH
SAUNDERS, Roger Irving, Aug 13 1932 Sex:M Child# 1 A B Saunders Everett, MA & Kath Thomas Kansas
SAUNDERS, Roland Henry, Mar 26 1909 Sex:M Child# 1 Harry S Saunders Holston, MA & Lulu M Austin Wilton, NH
SAUNDERS, Theodore Prescott, Oct 10 1922 Sex:M Child# 1 Theodore P Saunders Lunenburg, MA & Ella M Rowell Salem, NH
SAUNDERS, Unknown, Sep 21 1888 Sex:M Child# 1 Charles F Saunders Nashua, NH & Ora B Shattuck Nashua, NH
SAUNDERS, Unknown, Sep 5 1910 Sex:F Child# 2 Fred Saunders Canada & Alma Agnew N Chelmsford, MA Stillborn
SAUSTERRE, Joseph, Jun 16 1893 Sex:M Child# 1 Octave Sausterre Canada & Marie Caron Canada
SAUSTERRE, Joseph Emile, Feb 26 1900 Sex:M Child# 3 Adelard Sausterre Canada & Adeline Brisson Canada
SAUSTERRE, Joseph Evangeliste, Mar 12 1895 Sex:M Child# 2 Octave Sausterre Canada & Marie Caron Canada
SAUSTERRE, Ovila, Aug 18 1895 Sex:M Child# 9 Francois Sausterre Canada & Clarisse Boivin St Albans, VT
SAUVE, Marie Ozanie, Jun 9 1897 Sex:F Child# 2 David Sauve Canada & Marie Daucause Canada
SAVAGE, Albert H, Apr 12 1887 Sex:M Child# 2 Albert H Savage Champlain, NY & Mary Allard Perry Mills, NY
SAVAGE, Albert Walter, Mar 1 1928 Sex:M Child# 2 Carl Savage Keene, NH & Ellen W Lee Nashua, NH
SAVAGE, Alice Christine, Dec 28 1896 Sex:F Child# 6 John D Savage Greenwich, CT & Mary A Gill Ireland
SAVAGE, Andrea Lee, Feb 20 1925 Sex:F Child# 1 Carl Savage Keene, NH & Ellen W Lee Nashua, NH
SAVAGE, Anna M, Oct 12 1921 Sex:F Child# 2 Charles Savage Nashua, NH & Mary Conry New Jersey
SAVAGE, Charles H, Aug 4 1896 Sex:M Child# 2 Ed L Savage Vermont & Mary F Butterfield Litchfield, NH
SAVAGE, Charles Rufus, Aug 25 1920 Sex:M Child# 1 Charles Savage Nashua, NH & Mary Conty Freehold, NJ
SAVAGE, Edward Thomas, Nov 22 1923 Sex:M Child# 4 Charles Savage Nashua, NH & Mary Conry Freehold, NJ
SAVAGE, Elizabeth Mary, Jan 10 1923 Sex:F Child# 3 Charles H Savage Nashua, NH & Mary Conry New Jersey
SAVAGE, Helen, Jan 3 1899 Sex:F Child# 7 John D Savage Greenwich, CT & Mary Gill Ireland
SAVAGE, Joseph Henry, Sep 11 1925 Sex:M Child# 5 Charles Savage Nashua, NH & Mary Conry Freehold, NJ
SAVAGE, Mildred, Aug 24 1901 Sex:F Child#  Charles Savage Bangor, ME & Maude L Southard Hudson Village, ME
SAVAGE, Unknown, Mar 22 1887 Sex: Child# 3 John D Savage Greenwich, CT & Mary A Gill Ireland
SAVAGE, Unknown, Sep 28 1889 Sex:M Child# 4 John D Savage Greenwich, CT & Mary A Gill Ireland
SAVAGE, Unknown, Dec 9 1929 Sex:F Child# 3 George Savage Lowell, MA & Lea Venette Athol, MA Stillborn
SAVAGE, William, Sep 21 1893 Sex:M Child# 5 John D Savage Greenwich, CT & Mary A Gill Ireland
SAVARD, David Arthur, Nov 12 1931 Sex:M Child# 2 Arthur F Savard Lowell, MA & Lee Mary Dube Milford, NH
SAVARD, Donald Raymond, Oct 7 1935 Sex:M Child# 3 Art Jos Savard Lowell, MA & Leah Dube Milford, NH
SAVIKI, William Joseph, Feb 18 1935 Sex:M Child# 1 Wm Jos Saviki Poland & Mary Grohosky Nashua, NH
SAVOIE, Beatrice Helen, Sep 9 1927 Sex:F Child# 3 George R Savoie N Bedford, MA & Alice Noonan Nashua, NH
SAVOIE, Florida, Apr 7 1895 Sex:F Child# 1 Joseph Savoie Canada & Marie Languerand Canada
SAVON, Joseph, Jun 9 1919 Sex:M Child# 10 Joseph Savon Canada & Claudia Levesque Canada
SAVSEIKAS, John, Jul 9 1906 Sex:M Child# 1 Auguste Savseikas Russia & Agata Alieswliscutie Russia
SAWTELL, Ernest Wilfred, Jun 29 1917 Sex:M Child# 4 William Sawtell Mass & Emma Gates New York
SAWTELL, Henry Eugene, Jan 12 1914 Sex:M Child# 5 William Sawtell Mass & Emma Gates New York
SAWTELL, Jean, Oct 18 1926 Sex:F Child# 1 Edgar Sawtell Nashua, NH & Clara Tiernan Nashua, NH
SAWTELLE, Edgar A, May 31 1895 Sex:M Child# 3 Fred H Sawtelle Maine & H McCall
SAWTELLE, Frederick Erwin, Jul 29 1915 Sex:M Child# 3 William E Sawtelle Shirley, MA & Emma Gates Mooers, NY
SAWTELLE, Marguerite L, Mar 22 1893 Sex:F Child# 2 Fred H Sawtelle Maine & Henrietta McCall California
SAWTELLE, Pauline H, Dec 6 1896 Sex:F Child# 4 Fred H Sawtelle Newburgh & Henrietta W McCall San Francisco, CA
SAWYER, Elizabeth, Apr 20 1895 Sex:F Child# 7 Henry Sawyer New York & Zoe Desmarais Canada
SAWYER, George Moore, Nov 1 1932 Sex:M Child# 1 Geo C Sawyer Weare, NH & Eva M Moore Calais, ME
SAWYER, Sarah Wilkins, Oct 5 1932 Sex:F Child# 3 D F Sawyer Milford, NH & Alice Oliver Lisbon, NH
SAWYER, Shirley, Mar 19 1923 Sex:F Child# 1 Fred Sawyer NH & Eva Greeley Londonderry, NH
SAWYER, Unknown, May 31 1888 Sex:F Child# 4 George A Sawyer NH & Helen T Sawyer NH
SAWYER, Unknown, Aug 10 1889 Sex:M Child# 1 Frank Sawyer Derry, NH & Kate Sree Pepperell, MA
SAWYER, Unknown, Feb 2 1893 Sex:F Child# 6 Henry Sawyer Canada & Zoe Desmarias Canada
SAWYER, Unknown, Apr 13 1896 Sex:M Child# 1 Chandler Sawyer Coopersville, NY & Emma Adams Manchester, NH Stillborn
SAWYER, Unknown, Jul 30 1913 Sex:M Child# 1 James Sawyer New York & Mary Smith Vermont
SAXBY, Roger Earl, Dec 20 1920 Sex:M Child# 1 Earl J Saxby Burke, VT & Marion D Leonard Washington, VT
SAYER, Dorothy Helen, Sep 23 1926 Sex:F Child# 3 Jos Emile Sayer Canada & Myrtie Kelley Jonesport, ME
SAYMACK, Adelia, Mar 2 1921 Sex:F Child# 1 Joseph Saymack Russia & Helena Markel Russia
SCANLAN, Francis, Aug 6 1889 Sex:F Child# 6 John Scanlan Nashua, NH & Nellie O'Brien Boston, MA
SCARR, Grace Isabella, Jan 30 1904 Sex:F Child# 4 John F Scarr England & Margrite A Puddick Ireland
SCHALLENGER, Joan May, Aug 26 1933 Sex:F Child# 2 (No Parents Listed)
SCHASNY, Mary, Mar 23 1909 Sex:F Child# 1 Theodore Schasny Russia & Darrier Lecetsza Russia
SCHELL, Maud, Apr 24 1893 Sex:F Child# 1 Franz J Schell Boston, MA & Hattie C Parsons Concord, NH
SCHELL, Paul Joseph, Jun 11 1898 Sex:M Child# 3 Franz Schell Boston, MA & Hattie Parsons Concord, NH
SCHELL, Ruth, Jul 11 1895 Sex:F Child# 2 Franz J Schell Boston, MA & Hattie J Parsons Concord, NH
SCHIER, Richard Arthur, Dec 9 1924 Sex:M Child# 4 John Schier Mass & Margaret Cronin Ireland
SCHLATTER, Unknown, Aug 8 1906 Sex:F Child# 4 Jacob Schlatter Austria & Anna Schutter Austria
SCHLENSKY, Stanley, Oct 8 1911 Sex:M Child# 2 Alex Schlensky Russia & Leonarda Kosolowecz Russia

SCHLINK, Marjorie Arlene, Dec 30 1915 Sex:F Child# 2 Harry E Schlink Hoboken, NJ & Gladys Bailey Manchester, NH
SCHLINK, Roger Albert, Mar 20 1914 Sex:M Child# 1 Harry E Schlink Hoboken, NJ & Gladys Bailey Manchester, NH
SCHLONGUS, Charles, Apr 20 1916 Sex:M Child# 2 Charles Schlongus Russia & Eva Margotis Russia
SCHMIDT, Antonina, Dec 31 1910 Sex:F Child# 1 Peter Schmidt Russia & Helen Silakitcha Russia
SCHMIDT, Gertrude Mary, Jun 5 1924 Sex:F Child# 1 Halbest Schmidt Germany & Gertrude Kahier Germany
SCHMIEDTGAN, Philipp Heronaun, Jan 16 1918 Sex:M Child# 1 Rufolf Schmiedtgan Germany & Amy F Williamson Framingham
SCHMIEDTGEN, Elizabeth, Feb 4 1920 Sex:F Child# 2 Rudolph Schmiedtgen Germany & Amy Williamson Framingham, MA
SCHNECK, Francis Mor Chase, Oct 30 1918 Sex:M Child# 1 Henry Paul Schneck Connecticut & Alice Chase Pepperell, MA
SCHNEIDER, Edwina E, Jun 11 1892 Sex:F Child# 3 Walter W Schneider Bedford & Lizzie M Coombs Pittsfield
SCHOFIELD, Alice Theresa, Jul 26 1911 Sex:F Child# 2 Augustus E Schofield Nova Scotia & Margaret O'Brien Ireland
SCHOFIELD, Arline Berle, Apr 8 1919 Sex:F Child# 2 Stewart Schofield Woffile, NS & Ida Charron Ayer, MA
SCHOFIELD, Bertrand Arnold, Aug 12 1922 Sex:M Child# 7 Warren Schofield Nova Scotia & Lilly Leard Derry, NH
SCHOFIELD, Bessie May, May 1 1914 Sex:F Child# 1 Steward Schofield Nova Scotia & Ida Charron Ayer, MA
SCHOFIELD, Cecile Eva, Dec 28 1919 Sex:F Child# 2 Clifford Schofield
SCHOFIELD, Cleophas, Oct 18 1918 Sex:M Child# 1 Clifford Schofield Scotland & Marie Dube Nashua, NH
SCHOFIELD, Constance Jean, Feb 14 1935 Sex:F Child# 1 Wallace Schofield Nashua, NH & Helen Kopka Nashua, NH
SCHOFIELD, Donald Kenneth, Oct 9 1926 Sex:M Child# 9 Warren Schofield NH & Lillian Leard NH
SCHOFIELD, Doris, May 25 1906 Sex:F Child# 1 Warren E Schofield Nova Scotia & Matilda Leard Nova Scotia
SCHOFIELD, Earl Leroy, Dec 6 1906 Sex:M Child# 8 Harris Schofield Nova Scotia & Delia Dorman Nova Scotia
SCHOFIELD, Earl Leroy, Sep 1 1928 Sex:M Child# 1 E L Schofield Nashua, NH & Helen Loud Amherst, NH
SCHOFIELD, Lawrence, Jul 31 1915 Sex:M Child# 4 Warren Schofield Nova Scotia & Lillie Leard Derry, NH
SCHOFIELD, Lewis Henry, Dec 15 1921 Sex:M Child# 3 Clifford Schofield Canada & Marie Dube Nashua, NH
SCHOFIELD, Muriel Helen, Apr 23 1930 Sex:F Child# 2 Earl L Schofield Nashua, NH & Helen Lowd Amherst, NH
SCHOFIELD, Ray Wilson, Oct 20 1928 Sex:M Child# 5 W E Schofield Milton, MA & Lillie A Leard Derry, NH
SCHOFIELD, Ruby, Oct 15 1913 Sex:F Child# 3 Warren Schofield Mass & Lilly Leard NH
SCHOFIELD, Sylvia, Jul 26 1924 Sex:F Child# 8 Warren Schofield Littleton, NH & Lillian Leard Derry, NH
SCHOFIELD, Vernon Everett, Aug 12 1920 Sex:M Child# 6 Warren Schofield Marlboro, MA & Tillie Leard Derry, NH
SCHOFIELD, Victor Lincoln, Feb 18 1921 Sex:M Child# 3 Steward W Schofield Nova Scotia & Ida Sharron Ayer, MA
SCHOFIELD, Viola Leonna, Jul 23 1910 Sex:F Child# 1 Warren Schofield Nashua, NH & Lilia Leard Derry, NH
SCHOFIELD, Walter Elmer, Aug 15 1912 Sex:M Child# 2 Warren E Schofield Milton, MA & Lilly A Leard Derry, NH
SCHOFIELD, Warren Leslie, Apr 26 1918 Sex:M Child# 5 Warren Schofield Milton, MA & Lillie Leard Derry, NH
SCHOFIELD, William Joseph, Dec 3 1892 Sex:M Child# 1 William Schofield Franklin, VT & Mary Greenwood Mansonville
SCHOLAS, Phylis, Aug 15 1927 Sex:F Child# 7 Peter Scholas Poland & Neriereco Mizars Lithuania
SCHRACISK, Unknown, Jun 29 1916 Sex:F Child# 6 Henry Schracisk Russia & Josephine Charis Russia
SCHREITERER, Carl, Jr, May 26 1926 Sex:M Child# 1 Carl Schreiterer Webster, MA & Hazel Bosworth Mass
SCHREITERER, Robert, Sep 27 1927 Sex:M Child# 2 Carl Schreiterer Webster, MA & Hazel Bosworth Mass
SCHRICHICK, William, Feb 7 1913 Sex:M Child# 4 Andrew Schrichick Russia & Josephine Chirius Russia
SCHRIER, Fannie, Aug 2 1906 Sex:F Child# 3 Byman Schrier Russia & Sadie Vaisbord Russia
SCHULTZ, Anne, Oct 18 1929 Sex:F Child# 3 Francis Schultz Somerville, MA & Josephine Wilson Watertown, MA
SCHVAICK, Unknown, Feb 19 1914 Sex:M Child# 5 Andrew Schvaick Russia & Josephine Chirwick Russia
SCILLER, John, Oct 26 1910 Sex:M Child# 5 Joseph Sciller Poland & Matine Welquache Poland
SCKAWICZ, Florence, Jun 13 1920 Sex:F Child# 3 Alex Sckawicz Lithuania Russia & Josephine Yakolin Lithuania Russia
SCKIMKOWSI, Peter, Jun 29 1910 Sex:M Child# 4 Frank Sckimkowsi Russia & Stuslore Parmsktese Russia
SCONSAS, Unknown, Oct 6 1921 Sex:F Child# 5 George Sconsas Greece & Tephin Rudeler Greece
SCONTSAS, Archibald, Oct 23 1927 Sex:M Child# 7 George Scontsas Greece & Zafiro Pappas Greece
SCONTSAS, Ethel, Jan 4 1925 Sex:F Child# 6 George Scontsas Greece & Zaphiro Pappas Greece
SCONTSAS, Unknown, Apr 25 1920 Sex:M Child# 4 George Scontsas Greece & Dephpis ruckles Greece
SCONTSAS, Unknown, Apr 10 1930 Sex:M Child# 8 George Scontsas Greece & Zeplus Christopapas Greece
SCONTZAS, Unknown, Jun 2 1913 Sex:M Child# 1 Leo Scontzas Greece & Sophie Pappas Greece
SCOTT, Barbara Ann, Jul 25 1932 Sex:F Child# 4 Bernard Scott Pepperell, MA & Helen Frazer Liverpool, England
SCOTT, Beverly Lourene, Mar 27 1929 Sex:F Child# 2 Harold Scott Derry, NH & Edith Coombs Windham, NH
SCOTT, Charlotte Mellisa, Mar 17 1925 Sex:F Child# 1 Everett Scott Groton, MA & Charlotte Brown Hanover, NH
SCOTT, Effie Elizabeth, Jul 2 1929 Sex:F Child# 2 John Laurence Scott Minersville, PA & Agnes Simister William
SCOTT, Unknown, Jun 3 1890 Sex:M Child# 1 James Scott Scotland & Lillian Salvas RI
SCOTT, Wattles Felix, Jul 30 1913 Sex:M Child# 2 Charles Scott Russia & Antona Suslawicz Russia
SCOTTON, Unknown, Aug 31 1890 Sex:M Child# 3 John Scotton Waterbury, CT & Georgie Dallison Philadelphia, PA
SCOUSA, Christos, Nov 17 1915 Sex:M Child# 3 George Scousa Greece & Sophia Pacla Greece
SCOVEY, Mabel Reardon, Dec 4 1911 Sex:F Child# 2 Herbert Scovey Lowell, MA & Nellie Reardon Lowell, MA
SCULLY, Charlotte Elizabeth, Nov 6 1932 Sex:F Child# 1 Charles Scully Lincoln, NH & O E Hendrickson Wilton, NH
SCULLY, Patricia Annette, Sep 11 1931 Sex:F Child# 1 Patrick Scully Lincoln, NH & Annette Gardner Bradley, ME
SCULLY, Unknown, May 18 1933 Sex:F Child# 1 Robert Scully Lincoln, NH & Alma Trembly Nashua, NH
SCUTA, Marie, Nov 17 1904 Sex:F Child# 3 John Scuta Russia & Stanistowa Zieba Russia
SCZIESMULIEW, John, Oct 29 1903 Sex:M Child# 2 M Scziesmuliew Russia & Anna Kluszutee Russia
SDISKA, Anna, Mar 1 1918 Sex:F Child# 11 Peter Sdiska Russia & Mary Davie Russia
SEAMAN, Agnes Jeannette N, Dec 23 1926 Sex:F Child# 4 Ambrose Seaman Nashua, NH & B Bonenfant Nashua, NH
SEAMAN, Ambrose W, Oct 7 1893 Sex:M Child# 3 William R Seaman Ireland & E A O'K England
SEAMAN, Elinor Aurita, Dec 17 1921 Sex:F Child# 1 Ambrose W Seaman Nashua, NH & Blanche Bonenfant Nashua, NH
SEAMAN, Ernest Robert, Jr, Jan 8 1923 Sex:M Child# 2 Ernest Robert Seaman Nashua, NH & Lena Leola Danforth Ne
SEAMAN, Exilia Mildred, Mar 27 1923 Sex:F Child# 2 Ambrose Wm Seaman Nashua, NH & Blanche Bonenfant Nashua, NH
SEAMAN, Gertrude, Aug 9 1908 Sex:F Child# 4 Henry E Seaman Manchester, NH & Elizabeth Varnum Manchester, NH
SEAMAN, Harold Clifton, Jul 27 1918 Sex:M Child# 3 Clarence Seaman Nashua, NH & Beatrice Willette St Johnsbury, VT
SEAMAN, James Joseph, Aug 6 1929 Sex:M Child# 5 Ernest Seaman Nashua, NH & Lena Danforth New Bedford, MA
SEAMAN, Kenneth Leonard, Nov 21 1924 Sex:M Child# 3 Robert Seaman Nashua, NH & Lena Danforth New Bedford, MA

SEAMAN, Leroy Ambrose, Apr 26 1926 Sex:M Child# 4 Ernest Seaman Nashua, NH & Lena Danforth New Bedford, MA
SEAMAN, Norman Eugene, Jan 22 1905 Sex:M Child# 3 Henry E Seaman Manchester, NH & Elizabeth Varnum Manchester, NH
SEAMAN, Paul William, Mar 25 1921 Sex:M Child# 1 Ernest Seaman Nashua, NH & Lena Danforth New Bedford, MA
SEAMAN, Pauline Frances, Mar 20 1913 Sex:F Child# 4 Harry E Seaman Manchester, NH & Elizabeth P Varnum Manchester
SEAMAN, Unknown, Dec 24 1891 Sex:F Child# 2 William R Seaman London, England & Elliner E O'Hare Ireland
SEAMAN, Unknown, May 6 1912 Sex:F Child# 1 Clarence H Seaman Nashua, NH & Beatrice E Willette St Johnsbury, VT
SEAMAN, William R, Jan 30 1890 Sex:M Child# 1 William R Seaman England & Elenor O'Hare Ireland
SEAMAN, William Robert, Oct 30 1924 Sex:M Child# 3 Ambrose Seaman Nashua, NH & Blanche Bonenfant Nashua, NH
SEARLES, Beatrice May, Feb 9 1921 Sex:F Child# 3 Ellsworth Searles Pelham, NH & Grace Christy Nashua, NH
SEARLES, Dorothy Grace, Apr 29 1912 Sex:F Child# 1 Robert Searles Pelham, NH & Grace Christy Nashua, NH
SEARLES, Edwin A, Jr, Feb 9 1932 Sex:M Child# 3 Edwin A Searles Pelham, NH & Beatrice Patnaude Derry, NH
SEARLES, Evelyn Katherine, Mar 24 1922 Sex:F Child# 4 Ellsworth Searles Pelham, NH & Grace Christie Nashua, NH
SEARLES, Josephine Elianor, Nov 11 1925 Sex:F Child# 6 Elsw R Searles NH & Grace Christie Nashua, NH
SEARLES, Lena Adaline, Jun 5 1893 Sex:F Child# 9 Charles W Searles Merrimack, NH & Helen M Marvell Mont Vernon, NH
SEARLES, Louise, Feb 15 1924 Sex:F Child# 5 Ellsworth Searles Pelham, NH & Grace Christy Nashua, NH Stillborn
SEARLES, Robert Ellsworth, Aug 11 1919 Sex:M Child# 2 Ellsworth Searles Pelham, NH & Grace Christy Nashua, NH
SEARLES, Unknown, Mar 3 1890 Sex:M Child# 8 Charles U Searles Merrimack, NH & Helen M Maud Mt Vernon, NH
SEARLES, Unknown, Oct 3 1891 Sex:M Child# 3 Charles W Searles,Jr Merrimack & Helen M Mont Vernon, NH
SEARLES, Unknown, Apr 25 1899 Sex:F Child# 2 Walter E Searles Townsend, MA & Susie Mann Edgcomb Woburn, MA
SEARLES, Unknown, Aug 8 1920 Sex:M Child# 1 Arthur Searles
SEARLS, Cora, Oct 9 1888 Sex:F Child# 7 Charles M Searls Merrimack & Helen M Marble Mt Vernon, NH
SEARS, Roland, Nov 13 1915 Sex:M Child# 2 George R Sears Milford, NH & Blanche M Clark Winter Park, FL
SEARS, Winston Clark, Jul 30 1920 Sex:M Child# 3 George R Sears Milford, NH & Blanch Clark Winter Park, FL
SEAVEY, Betty Jane, Jan 22 1934 Sex:F Child# 1 Lawrence Seavey Rye, NH & Evelyn Remick Portsmouth, NH
SEAVEY, Kenneth Earl, Jun 29 1925 Sex:M Child# 2 Earl Seavey Merrimack, NH & Lena Pinard Nashua, NH
SEAVEY, Lillian Emma, Aug 17 1890 Sex:F Child# 3 Charles R Seavey NH & Emma L Merrill NH
SEBALOWSKI, John B, Nov 1 1915 Sex:M Child# 1 John Sebalowski Russia & Albina Tamalonis Russia
SEBALUSKI, Joseph, Dec 8 1913 Sex:M Child# 1 Joseph Sebaluski Russia & Advalga Vilcachuta Russia
SECORD, Donald Lester, Nov 16 1900 Sex:M Child# 6 E S Secord NB & Maggie J Irvin NB
SECORD, Edna Lillian, Nov 13 1893 Sex:F Child# 2 Edwin S Secord NB & Maggie J Irwine NB
SECORD, Frank Everett, Oct 22 1896 Sex:M Child# 4 Edwin S Secord New Brunswick & Maggie J Irvine Nova Scotia
SECORD, Frank H, Dec 2 1892 Sex:M Child# 1 Edwin S Secord NB & Maggie J Irvine NS
SECORD, Grace Eratta, Aug 28 1899 Sex:F Child# 3 Daniel Secord NB & Jessie Monroe Mass
SECORD, Lawrence Odber, Feb 27 1903 Sex:M Child# 7 Edwin S Secord New Brunswick & Margaret J Irvin New Brunswick
SECORD, Ruth Marion, Jun 10 1899 Sex:F Child# 5 Edwin S Secord NB & Margaret G Irving NB
SECORD, Unknown, Jun 15 1895 Sex:F Child# 3 Edwin S Secord New Brunswick & Maggie J Irving Nova Scotia
SECORD, Unknown, Feb 15 1898 Sex:F Child# 2 Dan Secord NB & Jessie Monroe NS
SECORD, William, Jan 12 1897 Sex:M Child# 1 Daniel B Secord New Brunswick & Jessie Monroe Nova Scotia
SECOURS, Joseph F, Oct 20 1891 Sex:M Child# 4 Pierre Secours Canada & Delphine Brousseau Canada
SEDACH, Marjorie Jean, Sep 25 1935 Sex:F Child# 1 Joseph Sedach Westford, MA & Laurette Bonnette Nashua, NH
SEDER, Leonard Avern, Jul 18 1915 Sex:M Child# 1 Jack Seder Mass & Helen Rich New York
SEDLEVITCH, Annie, Mar 31 1916 Sex:F Child# 9 Jacob Sedlevitch Russia & Tikla Urantch Russia
SEDLEWETCH, John, Sep 27 1901 Sex:M Child# 1 Jacob Sedlewetch Russia & Takly Yuronitch Russia
SEDLEWICZ, Eugene, Aug 26 1929 Sex:M Child# 3 Peter Sedlewicz Russia & Agnes Swist Russia
SEDLEWICZ, Josepha, Oct 1 1904 Sex:F Child# 1 Joseph Sedlewicz Russia & Marcella Watkowicz Russia
SEDLEWICZ, Lenora, Mar 9 1926 Sex:F Child# 2 Della Sedlewicz Lithuania & Agnes Smith Poland
SEDLEWICZ, Lucille, Oct 27 1932 Sex:F Child# 1 Horton Sedlewicz Hollis, NH & Lucille Milaisky Nashua, NH
SEDLEWICZ, Marianne, Oct 27 1929 Sex:F Child# 1 J J Sedlewicz Nashua, NH & Mary Michaelewicz Nashua, NH
SEDLEWICZ, Unknown, Nov 1 1917 Sex:M Child# 10 Jacob Sedlewicz Russia & Hulda Uranich Russia Stillborn
SEELEY, Ethel May, Nov 6 1892 Sex:F Child# Edwin F Seeley Glens Falls, NY & Mary L Winters Manchester, NH
SEELEY, Henry F, Nov 17 1891 Sex:M Child# 1 Edwin Seeley Glens Falls, NY & Mary L Winters Manchester, NY
SEELEY, Ralph Harris, Sep 24 1910 Sex:M Child# 1 Dow H Seeley Waterville, NH & Roxanna West Chester, VT
SEGOUIN, Alma Dianne, Jan 28 1907 Sex:F Child# 7 George Segouin Canada & Dina Levesque Canada
SEGOUIN, Cyrille William, Nov 17 1903 Sex:M Child# 6 George Segouin Canada & Dina Levesque Canada
SEGOUIN, Joseph Roland Irenee, Mar 28 1918 Sex:M Child# 1 Joseph Segouin Nashua, NH & Marie Lou St Pierre St L
SEGOUIN, Marie Florida Juliet, Mar 5 1927 Sex:F Child# 3 Silvio Segouin Nashua, NH & Rose A Beaupre Canada
SEGOUIN, Marie Sylvie Florenc, Jan 17 1925 Sex:F Child# 1 Sylvia Segouin Nashua, NH & Rose A Beaupre Canada
SEGOUIN, Marie T R, Jan 12 1926 Sex:F Child# 2 Sylvia Segouin Nashua, NH & Rose A Beaupre Canada
SEGOUIN, Wilfrid Leger, Jan 2 1902 Sex:M Child# 5 George Segouin Canada & Dina Levesque Canada
SEGUIN, Doria Armand Edgar, Jul 1 1912 Sex:M Child# 1 Joseph Seguin Canada & Cecelia Soucy Canada
SEGUIN, Joseph Alphonse, Jul 21 1918 Sex:M Child# 3 Joseph Seguin St Jean, PQ & Cecila Soucy St Antorois, PQ
SEGUIN, Louis, Jr, Apr 17 1932 Sex:M Child# 1 Louis Seguin Canada & Margaret Kennedy Canada
SEGUIN, Phyllis, Mar 31 1926 Sex:F Child# 4 Louis Seguin Canada & Mary Donovan London, England
SEGUIN, Robert Normand, Nov 18 1931 Sex:M Child# 1 Leo Seguin Derry, NH & Agnes Letendre Nashua, NH
SEIDLEWICTZ, Lucile, Apr 4 1915 Sex:F Child# 6 Anthony Seidlewictz Russia & Thophilia Moncunrie Russia
SEIFERT, Kathryn Agnes, Oct 23 1927 Sex:F Child# 1 Waldo Seifert Manchester, NH & Hazel Donovan Pelham, NH
SEIGAL, Lawrence Leonard, May 9 1929 Sex:M Child# 1 Alexander Seigal Russia & Anna R Nusenoff Lynn, MA
SEILER, Barbara Lois, Jul 27 1908 Sex:F Child# 1 Charles E Seiler Riedilsville, NY & Florence H Gandoon Nashua, NH
SEISICKI, Raymond, Jun 13 1923 Sex:M Child# 2 Peter Seisicki Poland & Helen Chapalys Poland
SELIARS, Mary Letitia, Mar 6 1891 Sex:F Child# 1 Thomas Seliars New York & Mary Meaney Ireland
SELINSKIE, Unknown, Nov 27 1912 Sex:F Child# 4 Mike Selinskie Russia & Lavina Kortalorich Russia
SELLARS, John Francis, Dec 15 1892 Sex:M Child# 2 Thomas Sellars NY & Mary Meaney Ireland
SELLERS, Catherine Helena, Apr 6 1895 Sex:F Child# Thomas Sellers NY & Mary Meaney Ireland

SELLGA, Unknown, Nov 3 1891 Sex:M Child# 9 John P Sellga Sweden & Louisa Johnson Sweden
SELVIS, Arthur Roland, May 3 1906 Sex:M Child# 2 David Selvis NH & Mary Busley Canada
SELVIS, Eleanor Madeline, Sep 22 1929 Sex:F Child# 2 Roland Selvis Nashua, NH & Irene LaFontaine Nashua, NH
SELVIS, Joseph David, Jul 4 1908 Sex:M Child# 3 David Selvis Litchfield, NH & Mary Boucher Canada
SELVIS, Roland Donald Joseph, Aug 19 1928 Sex:M Child# 1 Roland Selvis Nashua, NH & Irene LaFontaine Nashua, NH
SELVIS, Rudolphe Joseph, Sep 27 1909 Sex:M Child# 4 David Selvis NH & Mary Bushy Canada
SELVIS, Theodore, Sep 27 1909 Sex:M Child# 5 David Selvis NH & Mary Bushy Canada
SEMMIES, Tepance, May 8 1918 Sex:F Child# 2 Stanislaw Semmies Russia & Franciska Todwekae Russia
SENACAL, Andrew Richard, Oct 21 1932 Sex:M Child# 6 Hector Senacal Mass & Angelina Turcotte Canada
SENATE, George Augustus, Aug 31 1891 Sex:M Child# 2 William Senate Glens Falls, NY & Agnes L Hamilton Morse's
SENECAL, Aline Pirrman, Apr 24 1890 Sex:F Child# 2 Felise Senecal Canada & Josephine Boulay Canada
SENECAL, Catherine May, Apr 3 1915 Sex:F Child# 1 George Senecal Lewiston, ME & Ethel Wright Pepperell, MA
SENECAL, Hector, Nov 2 1894 Sex:M Child# 2 Joseph Senecal US & Lumina Bleau US
SENECAL, Hector, Feb 16 1920 Sex:M Child# 1 Hector Senecal Lowell, MA & Angeline Turcotte Canada
SENECAL, Henri, Jan 18 1894 Sex:M Child# 8 Narcisse Senecal Canada & Delia Monette Canada
SENECAL, J O Armil Gideon, Oct 22 1917 Sex:M Child# 3 Oscar Senecal NH & Rosilda Drouin NH
SENECAL, Joseph, Mar 8 1920 Sex:M Child# 5 Oscar Senecal Nashua, NH & Rose Drouin Nashua, NH
SENECAL, Joseph Alfred, Mar 27 1916 Sex:M Child# 2 Oscar Senecal NH & Rosilda Drouin NH
SENECAL, Joseph Raymond, Dec 22 1918 Sex:M Child# 4 Oscar Senecal NH & Rose Drouin NH
SENECAL, Louis Joseph Maurice, Dec 1 1933 Sex:M Child# 4 Albert Senecal Canada & Yvonne Gignac Canada
SENECAL, Marguerite Rosilda, Jul 21 1922 Sex:F Child# 2 Hector Senecal Nashua, NH & Angeline Turcotte Canada
SENECAL, Marie, Oct 12 1898 Sex:F Child# 4 Joseph Senecal Plattsburg, NY & Lumina Blow Sciota, NY
SENECAL, Marie, Oct 9 1902 Sex:F Child# 1 Narcisse Senecal New York & Marie Morency Canada
SENECAL, Marie, Aug 3 1926 Sex:F Child# 10 Oscar R Senecal Nashua, NH & Rosilda Drouin Nashua, NH
SENECAL, Marie E, Aug 1 1891 Sex:F Child# 7 Marcisse Senecal Moore's, NY & Delia Monette Moore's, NY
SENECAL, Marie E A, Feb 5 1895 Sex:F Child# 3 Louis Senecal Canada & Orise Thibodeau Canada
SENECAL, Marie V G, Mar 23 1896 Sex:F Child# 4 Louis Senecal Canada & Aurise Thibodeau Canada
SENECAL, Mary Rita Olivette, Jun 26 1922 Sex:F Child# 6 Oscar R Senecal Nashua, NH & Rosilda Drouin Nashua, NH
SENECAL, Oscar, Dec 11 1896 Sex:M Child# 3 Joseph Senecal US & Lumina Bleau US
SENECAL, Reine F D, Mar 19 1889 Sex:F Child# 1 Philippe Senecal Canada & Josephine Boulay Hudson, MA
SENECAL, Unknown, Feb 13 1921 Sex:F Child# 1 Henry Senecal Maine & Nellie Boutwell Peterboro, NH
SENECAL, Unknown, Jul 6 1923 Sex:M Child# 7 Oscar Senecal Nashua, NH & Rose H Drouin Nashua, NH
SENECAL, Unknown, Mar 27 1924 Sex:M Child# 4 Hector Senecal Lowell, MA & Ang Turcotte
SENECAL, Yolande, Nov 4 1925 Sex:F Child# 5 Hector Senecal Nashua, NH & Angelina Turcotte Canada
SENECHAL, Alphonse Albert, Jan 19 1903 Sex:M Child# 1 Charles Senechal Canada & Beatrice Lizotte Canada
SENECHAL, Felix Raymond, Jan 24 1927 Sex:M Child# 1 Auguste Senechal Nashua, NH & Antoinette Plante Canada
SENECHAL, Joseph, Sep 13 1933 Sex:M Child# 2 August Senechal Nashua, NH & Antoinette Plante Canada
SENECHAL, Pierre Eugene, Apr 9 1899 Sex:M Child# 5 Charles Senechal Canada & Beatrice Lizotte Canada
SENGUERAND, Joseph Prospere, Apr 21 1890 Sex:M Child# 2 Remi Senguerand Canada & Olymphe Levesque Canada
SENICE, Adam, Nov 22 1915 Sex:M Child# 1 Adam Senice Russia & Gussie Awijenaite Russia
SENNOTT, Ruth Elizabeth, Jan 14 1921 Sex:F Child# 1 Ernest C Sennott S Portland, ME & Lillian F Baker Concord, NH
SENTER, Blanche, May 14 1891 Sex:F Child# 3 William T Senter Hudson, NH & Sevilla Barrett Mason, NH
SENTER, William, Apr 14 1890 Sex:M Child# 2 William T Senter Hudson, NH & Savilla Barrett Mason, NH
SENTERRE, Olivette Lydia, Mar 10 1923 Sex:F Child# 2 Arthur Senterre Nashua, NH & Donalda Deneault Nashua, NH
SENVILLE, Fred Ricard, Jul 11 1897 Sex:M Child# 1 Fred A Senville
SEOTA, Anna, Oct 16 1900 Sex:F Child# 1 John Seota Poland & Stanislas Zimba Poland
SEPERIK, Unknown, Sep 19 1915 Sex:F Child# 2 William Seperik Russia & Stella Courtkorvick Russia
SERCICZIK, James, Apr 1 1911 Sex:M Child# 3 Andrew Serciczik Russia & Josie Tehenuty Russia
SERECHARLES, Rosanna, Jul 21 1891 Sex:F Child# Charles Serecharles Canada & Beatrice Leazott Canada
SEREICZIK, John, Aug 9 1920 Sex:M Child# 5 Michael Sereiczik Russia & Tophilia Exepcik Russia
SEREICZIK, Joseph, May 6 1910 Sex:M Child# 2 Andrew Sereiczik Russia & Josie Cherus Russia
SEREICZIK, Stanley, Jul 1 1915 Sex:M Child# 1 Stevens Sereiczik Russia & Antosia Gaydronta Russia
SERENCZYK, Michael, May 10 1914 Sex:M Child# 1 Michael Serenczyk Russia & Tophilia Baucha Russia
SERGAWICZ, John, Oct 20 1923 Sex:M Child# 1 Louis Sergawicz Poland & Leocadie Migalawicz Poland
SERGAY, Theophila, Feb 24 1909 Sex:F Child# 1 Andrew Sergay Russia & Josie Cherouty Russia
SERGERIE, Marie Bernier, Aug 18 1897 Sex:F Child# 5 Francois Sergerie Canada & Georgina Bernier Canada Stillborn
SERGIEWICZ, Leonora Helen, Feb 28 1927 Sex:F Child# 2 Louis Sergiewicz Poland & L Mechiewicz Poland
SERVALAWICZ, Maria, May 24 1912 Sex:F Child# 2 Roland Servalawicz Russia & Agae Greguita Russia
SERVANT, Marie Therese B, Jun 2 1935 Sex:F Child# 1 John Servant Fall River, MA & Beatrice Poliquin Nashua, NH
SERYCHIK, John, Jan 15 1908 Sex:M Child# 2 August Serychik Russia & Agata Chesnas Russia
SETEGESIK, Peter, Aug 1 1915 Sex:M Child# 2 Michael Seregesik Russia & Tophilia Ecepsek Russia
SETENDE, Joseph E, Jun 1 1890 Sex:M Child# 1 George Setende Manchester, NH & Marie Dutilly Canada
SEVAIL, Laura, Jul 14 1888 Sex:F Child# 4 Narcisse Sevail Canada & Marie Cote Canada
SEVERENSE, Mary Elizabeth, Jun 12 1934 Sex:F Child# 2 Albert Severense Vermont & Mary Moriarty Worcester, MA
SEVIGNY, Joseph Hector, Apr 23 1922 Sex:M Child# 4 Theophile P Sevigny Canada & Rosanna Routhier Berlin, NH
SEVIGNY, Wm Joseph Armand, Apr 14 1923 Sex:M Child# 5 Pierre T Sevigny Canada & Rose Anna Routhier NH
SEVILL, Sevill, May 31 1889 Sex:M Child# 1 Charles S Sevill Portsmouth, NH & Anna S Reed Nashua, NH
SEWERCHUKY, William, Oct 12 1915 Sex:M Child# 2 Adam Sewerchuky Russia & Anna Eckasilla Russia
SEXTON, John Field, Aug 21 1918 Sex:M Child# 1 Ralph E Sexton Nashua, NH & Mary Field Nashua, NH
SEXTON, Richard, Dec 21 1919 Sex:M Child# 2 Ralph E Sexton Nashua, NH & Mary Field Nashua, NH
SEXTON, Unknown, Nov 4 1915 Sex:M Child# 2 Neil L Sexton Treon, NY & Bernice Callahan Winchendon, MA
SEXTON, Unknown, Aug 16 1929 Sex:F Child# 4 John Sexton Ireland & Hannah Donnelly N Andover, MA
SEYER, Jos Emile Roland, Nov 18 1930 Sex:M Child# 2 Ernest E R Seyer Canada & Albertine Thibodeau Canada

SEYER, Marie Therese Irene, Sep 5 1934 Sex:F Child# 3 Ernest Thomas Seyer St Nazaire, PQ & Albertine Thibodeau
SEYMOUR, Bert Arthur, Aug 29 1905 Sex:M Child# 6 Thomas E Seymour Canada & Maud R Eaton Lowell, MA
SEYMOUR, Constance Rose, Apr 3 1921 Sex:F Child# 1 Nelson Seymour Nashua, NH & Gertrude Gendron Nashua, NH
SEYMOUR, Gertrude Lucinda, Aug 7 1906 Sex:F Child# 7 Thomas Seymour Canada & Maude Eaton Lowell, MA
SEYMOUR, Henry Edward, Feb 14 1922 Sex:M Child# 3 Emile J Seymour Canada & Flora Robbins Nashua, NH
SEYMOUR, Raymond Wilfred, May 30 1923 Sex:M Child# 3 Nelson Seymour Nashua, NH & Gertrude Gendron Nashua, NH
SEYMOUR, Richard Sylvio, Jul 31 1929 Sex:M Child# 4 Nelson Seymour Nashua, NH & Gertrude Gendron Nashua, NH
SEYMOUR, Robert Walter, Jul 1 1922 Sex:M Child# 2 Nelson Seymour Nashua, NH & Gertrude Gendron Nashua, NH
SEYMOUR, Ruth Claire, Jul 29 1931 Sex:F Child# 5 Nelson Seymour Nashua, NH & Gertrude Gendron Nashua, NH
SHABER, Ima, Mar 5 1896 Sex:M Child# 4 Samuel Shaber Russia & Dore Ticktin Russia
SHADECK, Joseph, Mar 3 1906 Sex:M Child# 1 Amede Shadeck Belgique & Celina Jeannotte Canada
SHAER, Myrna Ann, Mar 7 1933 Sex:F Child# 1 D L Shaer Lynn, MA & Roseland Blake Newburyport, MA
SHAFIDAS, Helen, Sep 27 1926 Sex:F Child# 1 John Shafidas Greece & Mary Papachristou Greece
SHAHALA, Anthony, Feb 10 1926 Sex:M Child# 6 Peter Shahala Russia & Valaco Miser Russia
SHAHALA, Peter, Feb 10 1926 Sex:M Child# 5 Peter Shahala Russia & Valaco Miser Russia
SHALETIS, Mary, Jan 18 1927 Sex:F Child# 3 Charles Shaletis Lithuania & Carolina Augomas Lithuania
SHALORACUS, Joseph, Jul 31 1914 Sex:M Child# 1 Joseph Shaloracus Russia & Ant Waizgesdruki Russia
SHAMLIAN, Annie, Jan 13 1908 Sex:F Child# 1 Aram Shamlian Armenia & Madza Alexanian Armenia
SHAMLIAN, Unknown, Aug 16 1901 Sex:M Child# 1 Aram Shamlian Turkey & Mariasa Aliseanian Turkey Stillborn
SHAMLIAN, Unknown, Apr 17 1902 Sex:F Child# 2 Avam Shamlian Turkey & M Maritza Turkey Stillborn
SHAMLIAN, Zudra, Aug 22 1904 Sex:M Child# 1 Harry Shamlian Armenia & Aznu Badigan Armenia
SHANAHAN, Marguerite Barbara, Nov 26 1927 Sex:F Child# 3 R D Shanahan Nashua, NH & Lily M Shackford Bow, NH
SHANAHAN, Mildred, May 3 1926 Sex:F Child# 2 Roland Shanahan Nashua, NH & Lily M Stackford Hooksett, NH
SHANAHAN, Roland David, Feb 28 1932 Sex:M Child# 4 R D Shanahan Nashua, NH & Lilley Shackford Bow, NH
SHANAHAN, Ronand, Jan 28 1903 Sex:M Child# 1 David Shanahan Nashua, NH & Eva Brickey Nashua, NH
SHANAHAN, Thomas Edward, Dec 30 1935 Sex:M Child# 5 Roland Shanahan Nashua, NH & Lily M Shackford Bow, NH
SHANAKAS, Unknown, Aug 4 1922 Sex:M Child# 9 Nicholas Shanakas Greece & Anastasia Maroras Greece
SHAPERO, Frances, Nov 13 1922 Sex:F Child# 1 Abraham Shapero England & Edith Fagerson Poland
SHAPIRO, Alice, Dec 19 1916 Sex:F Child# 6 Sam Shapiro New York, NY & Beacke Yevian New York, NY
SHAPIRO, Arline, Mar 9 1927 Sex:F Child# 3 Alfred Shapiro London, England & Edith Fagerson Poland
SHAPIRO, Leonard Paul, Aug 1 1929 Sex:M Child# 2 Maurice D Shapiro Russia & Hannah G Goodman Nashua, NH
SHAPIRO, Milton, Sep 9 1902 Sex:M Child# 1 Harry Shapiro Russia & Hattie Simmons
SHAPIRO, Rosalie, Dec 18 1925 Sex:F Child# 2 Alfred Shapiro Nashua, NH & Edith Fagerson Nashua, NH
SHAPIRO, Sumner, Jan 13 1926 Sex:M Child# 1 Maurice Shapiro Russia & Hannah Goodman Nashua, NH
SHARBONEAU, John Frederick, Dec 20 1894 Sex:M Child# 3 John F Sharboneau Altona, NY & Olive Carter N Haverhill
SHARBONEAU, Unknown, Mar 14 1895 Sex:M Child# 12 Frank Sharboneau Canada & Margaret Lafayette Chazy, NY
SHARON, Lida, May 11 1888 Sex:F Child# 1 Francois Sharon Canada & Delia Benoit Canada
SHARP, Gerald Marshall, Jun 20 1927 Sex:M Child# 3 M N Sharp New Brunswick & Mary Young N Gloucester, ME
SHARP, Joseph, Oct 19 1892 Sex:M Child# 12 Simon Sharp Russia & Jennie Russia
SHARP, Thelma Mary, Aug 17 1929 Sex:F Child# 4 Marshall N Sharp New Brunswick & Mary Young New Gloucester, ME
SHARP, Unknown, Oct 20 1892 Sex:F Child# 12 Simon Sharp Russia & Russia
SHARPE, Arnold Morton, Apr 25 1918 Sex:M Child# 4 Hymen Sharpe Russia & Fanny Udelovitch Russia
SHARPE, Bernard, Jul 10 1909 Sex:M Child# 2 Hymen J Sharpe Russia & Fannie S Udelovitch Russia
SHARPE, Max, Mar 3 1912 Sex:M Child# 3 Hyman J Sharpe Russia & Fannis S Lovett Russia
SHARPE, Myron Nelson, Aug 11 1923 Sex:M Child# 5 Hymen Sharpe Russia & Fannie Russia
SHARPE, Unknown, Feb 27 1921 Sex:F Child# 1 Claude Sharpe New York & Mary Bernier Canada
SHATTUCK, Barbara Adelaide, Oct 5 1927 Sex:F Child# 2 Forrest Shattuck Pepperell, MA & Marion Osborne Quincy, MA
SHATTUCK, Barbara Frances, Nov 8 1914 Sex:F Child# 2 Frank J Shattuck Nashua, NH & Rena Messer Lynn, MA
SHATTUCK, Bessie Aldenia, Jun 9 1910 Sex:F Child# 2 Edward Z Shattuck Nashua, NH & Alice B Jones Nashua, NH
SHATTUCK, Doris, Jan 9 1921 Sex:F Child# 1 Roger Shattuck Pepperell, MA & Dorothy Blood Pepperell, MA
SHATTUCK, Emma Thayer, Feb 7 1892 Sex:F Child# 4 Elbert P Shattuck Flushing, NJ & Nancy Elkins Canaan, NH
SHATTUCK, Frank Joel, Jr, May 3 1917 Sex:M Child# 3 Frank J Shattuck Nashua, NH & Rena Messer Lynn, MA
SHATTUCK, George Messer, Jul 10 1911 Sex:M Child# 3 Frank J Shattuck Nashua, NH & Rena Messer Lynn, MA
SHATTUCK, Leland, May 25 1888 Sex:M Child# 2 Edward L Shattuck Brookline & Elyse M Knight Nashua, NH
SHATTUCK, Leon Richard, Jul 10 1925 Sex:M Child# 3 W L Shattuck Pepperell, MA & A L Andrews Fitchburg, MA
SHATTUCK, Lydia Ann, Jan 10 1896 Sex:F Child# 7 Frank L Shattuck Pepperell, MA & Mary Campbell Nashua, NH
SHATTUCK, Patricia Elizabeth, Jan 6 1923 Sex:F Child# 1 Howard E Shattuck Pepperell, MA & Bernice Eliz Colby
SHATTUCK, Patricia May, Aug 6 1925 Sex:F Child# 1 Forrest Shattuck Pepperell, MA & Marion Osborne Quincy, MA
SHATTUCK, Phyllis Mae, Jul 12 1924 Sex:F Child# 2 Roger Shattuck Pepperell, MA & Dorothy Blood Pepperell, MA
SHATTUCK, Susan M, Aug 17 1890 Sex:F Child# 1 William Shattuck Brookline, NH & Susan A Wood Medford, MA
SHATTUCK, Unknown, Aug 16 1887 Sex:M Child# 4 Frank L Shattuck Pepperell & M A Campbell Nashua, NH
SHATTUCK, Unknown, Aug 21 1890 Sex:M Child# 3 Edwin L Shattuck Brookline, NH & Elouise Knights Nashua, NH
SHATTUCK, Unknown, Oct 15 1892 Sex:M Child# 5 Frank S Shattuck Pepperell, MA & Mary Campbell Nashua, NH Stillborn
SHATTUCK, Unknown, Jun 9 1893 Sex:M Child# 6 Frank L Shattuck Pepperell, MA & Mary L Campbell Nashua, NH
SHATTUCK, Unknown, Oct 24 1894 Sex:M Child# 7 Frank L Shattuck Pepperell, MA & Mary L Campbell Nashua, NH
SHATTUCK, Unknown, May 21 1907 Sex:F Child# 1 Alfred Shattuck Nashua, NH & Grace Chamberlain Nashua, NH
SHATTUCK, Wilfrid Sylvio, Jun 8 1916 Sex:M Child# 1 Wm Lewis Shattuck Nashua, NH & Delvina Landry Nashua, NH
SHATTUCK, William Edward, Apr 5 1912 Sex:M Child# 3 Edward Z Shattuck Nashua, NH & Alice Bertha Jones Nashua, NH
SHAUNNESSY, Elizabeth, Aug 30 1889 Sex:F Child# 4 George W Shaunnessy Manchester, NH & Bridget Doyle Salem, MA
SHAW, Doris Mellie, May 9 1910 Sex:F Child# 2 Harry E Shaw Lisbon, ME & Bertha L Dunlap Nashua, NH
SHAW, Ethel Leona, Jun 7 1910 Sex:F Child# 2 Harry D Shaw Victoria, NB & Dora L Hill Nashua, NH
SHAW, Frederic Elijah, Feb 3 1914 Sex:M Child# 1 E Ray Shaw Lisbon, ME & Louise E Tolles Nashua, NH
SHAW, Harry Dow, Jun 19 1907 Sex:M Child# 1 Harry D Shaw Victory, NB & Dora Leona Hill Nashua, NH

SHAW, Irma Grace, Jul 27 1903 Sex:F Child# 1 Harry E Shaw Lisbon, ME & Bertha L Dunlap Nashua, NH
SHAW, June Louise, Aug 14 1932 Sex:F Child# 1 H D Shaw, Jr Nashua, NH & Evelyn Paige Cleveland, OH
SHAW, Perley, Apr 12 1914 Sex:M Child# 3 Harry D Shaw New Brunswick & Leola Hill Nashua, NH
SHAW, Roger Tolles, Nov 26 1919 Sex:M Child# 2 Elijha R Shaw Lisbon, ME & Louise E Tolles Nashua, NH
SHAW, Sanford K, May 27 1902 Sex:M Child# 5 Renal W Shaw NB & Mertie Bonnell NB
SHEA, Albert, Jun 17 1890 Sex:M Child# 2 John F Shea Nashua, NH & Nellie McManners Aurora, IL
SHEA, Alphonse G, May 13 1894 Sex:M Child# 2 John Shea Nashua, NH & Alida Jodoin Canada
SHEA, Angela Ward, Sep 15 1895 Sex:F Child# 4 James Shea Nashua, NH & Rosie Smith Ireland
SHEA, Bartholemew, Sep 17 1898 Sex:M Child# 4 Bartholomew Shea Ireland & Mary Diggins Ireland
SHEA, Bartholemew G, Mar 3 1897 Sex:M Child# 1 John J Shea Ireland & Mary E Diggins Ireland
SHEA, Bridget A, Oct 17 1887 Sex:F Child# 1 James Shea Nashua, NH & Rosa Smith England
SHEA, Catherine, Jul 13 1899 Sex:F Child# 4 Dennis Shea Ireland & Kate Murphy Ireland
SHEA, Daniel, Feb 27 1921 Sex:M Child# 4 Daniel Shea New Bedford, MA & Marguerite Upham
SHEA, Daniel Francis, Jun 1 1922 Sex:M Child# 1 Daniel F Shea Nashua, NH & Margaret E Owens Newmarket, NH
SHEA, Doris Agnes, Jun 12 1912 Sex:F Child# 9 John Shea Ireland & Mary Diggins Ireland
SHEA, Dorothy May, Jan 8 1927 Sex:F Child# 6 William E Shea Gordon, PA & Dorilda Lucas Canada
SHEA, Edvert Lane, Nov 4 1892 Sex:M Child# 3 James Shea Nashua, NH & Rose Smith Ireland
SHEA, Edw Francis, Apr 29 1896 Sex:M Child# 3 Bartholemew Shea Ireland & Mary Diggins Ireland
SHEA, Edward, May 5 1892 Sex:M Child# 1 Daniel J Shea Cambridge, MA & Addie B Launier Plattsburg, NY
SHEA, Edward A, Jul 29 1934 Sex:M Child# 4 Edward A Shea Nashua, NH & Germaine Lavoie Nashua, NH
SHEA, Edward Aug, Jun 28 1902 Sex:M Child# 4 John Shea Ireland & Mary Diggins Ireland
SHEA, Eleanor Mary, Sep 4 1924 Sex:F Child# 1 Jeremiah Shea Wilton, NH & Doris Wilson Dover, NH
SHEA, Eva Lucille, Aug 16 1917 Sex:F Child# 2 W E Shea Gordon, PA & Dorilda Lucas Canada
SHEA, Frank, Sep 7 1892 Sex:M Child# 3 John F Shea Nashua, NH & Nellie McManus Aurora, IL
SHEA, Frank, Nov 3 1892 Sex:M Child# 2 John H Shea Boston, MA & Mary Halpine Milford, NH
SHEA, Hannah, Sep 16 1893 Sex:F Child# 2 Dennis Shea Ireland & Kate M Murphy Ireland
SHEA, Isabel Louise, Jan 6 1928 Sex:F Child# 2 Alfred Shea Nashua, NH & Lillian Larivee Nashua, NH
SHEA, Jeanne Alice A, Nov 24 1930 Sex:F Child# 2 George A Shea Nashua, NH & Emma Levesque New York
SHEA, John, Dec 9 1888 Sex:M Child# 1 John Shea Nashua, NH & Nellie Aurora, IL
SHEA, John A, Nov 28 1896 Sex:M Child# 4 John Shea Nashua, NH & Alida Jodoin Canada
SHEA, John Francis, Sep 28 1894 Sex:M Child# 2 Bartholemew Shea Ireland & Mary Diggins Ireland
SHEA, John Robert, Aug 5 1898 Sex:M Child# 2 John Shea Ireland & Mary Diggins Ireland
SHEA, Joseph, Oct 27 1894 Sex:M Child# 3 Dennis Shea Ireland & Kate M Murphy Ireland
SHEA, Joseph Gilmore, Oct 27 1918 Sex:M Child# 1 Joseph L Shea Nashua, NH & Mary Gilmore Rhode Island
SHEA, Katherine, Jan 16 1898 Sex:F Child# 5 James Shea Nashua, NH & Rose Smith Ireland
SHEA, Katherine Mary, Sep 24 1925 Sex:F Child# 3 Daniel F Shea Nashua, NH & Marg E Owens Newmarket, NH
SHEA, Katheryn, Jul 7 1903 Sex:F Child# 1 Augustus W Shea Nashua, NH & Lucy E Kelley Newburyport, MA
SHEA, Lea Charette, Jul 6 1898 Sex:F Child# 1 Edward F Shea Lowell, MA & Mary E Robinson England
SHEA, Leo Alfred, Aug 25 1926 Sex:M Child# 1 Alfred Shea Nashua, NH & Lillian Larivee Nashua, NH
SHEA, Leo Andre, Dec 19 1907 Sex:M Child# 6 John Shea Nashua, NH & Alida Jodoin Canada
SHEA, Lucy, Jul 29 1904 Sex:F Child# 2 Augustus W Shea Nashua, NH & Lucy E Kelly Newburyport, MA
SHEA, Lucy, Jan 9 1927 Sex:f Child# 4 Daniel F Shea Nashua, NH & Clarissa Lavoie Nashua, NH
SHEA, Marcil Therrese Evel, Feb 7 1923 Sex:F Child# 4 William E Shea Ashland, PA & Dorilda Lucas Canada
SHEA, Margaret Frances, Jan 17 1924 Sex:F Child# 2 Daniel F Shea Nashua, NH & Margaret Owens Newmarket, NH
SHEA, Marguerite Lillian, Oct 24 1915 Sex:F Child# 1 W E Shea Pottsville, PA & Dorilda Lucas Canada
SHEA, Marie Rose Florence, Jun 25 1920 Sex:F Child# 3 W E Shea Iceland, PA & Dorilda Lucas Canada
SHEA, Mary, Aug 7 1906 Sex:F Child# 6 John B Shea Ireland & Mary Diggins Ireland
SHEA, Mary Agnes, Sep 23 1918 Sex:F Child# 1 John J Shea Ireland & Eva Sullivan Ireland
SHEA, Mary Alice, Feb 12 1898 Sex:F Child# 5 John E Shea Nashua, NH & Ida Jodoin Canada
SHEA, Patrick Francis, Jun 29 1890 Sex:M Child# 1 John Shea Ireland & Mary Sullivan Ireland
SHEA, Pauline Mary, Dec 19 1928 Sex:F Child# 2 Edward Shea Nashua, NH & Germaine Lavoie Nashua, NH
SHEA, Peter Elwell, Jun 17 1929 Sex:M Child# 2 Omer James Shea Wilton, NH & Frances Elwell Milford, MA
SHEA, Ralph Leonard, Jul 9 1908 Sex:M Child# 7 John B Shea Ireland & Mary A Diggins Ireland
SHEA, Rita, Mar 6 1930 Sex:F Child# 3 Edward Shea Nashua, NH & Germaine Lavoie Nashua, NH Stillborn
SHEA, Rita Mary, Aug 8 1922 Sex:F Child# 2 Joseph L Shea Nashua, NH & Marie R Gilmore Westerly, RI
SHEA, Rose, Aug 20 1890 Sex:F Child# 2 James Shea Nashua, NH & Rose Smith Ireland
SHEA, Teresa, Jun 5 1901 Sex:F Child# 6 James Shea Nashua, NH & Rose Smith Ireland
SHEA, Theresa Lillian, Jun 25 1924 Sex:F Child# 1 George A Shea Nashua, NH & Emma Levesque Altona, NY
SHEA, Thomas, Apr 2 1899 Sex:M Child# 5 John F Shea Nashua, NH & Nellie McMannus Aurore, IL
SHEA, Thomas Richard, Jun 6 1904 Sex:M Child# 5 John Shea Ireland & Mary Diggins Ireland
SHEA, Unknown, Jun 8 1892 Sex:F Child# 1 Dennis Shea Ireland & Kate Murphy Ireland  Stillborn
SHEA, Unknown, Jan 3 1895 Sex:M Child# 2 Daniel J Shea Cambridge, MA & Addie Launiere Plattsburg, NY
SHEA, Unknown, May 8 1895 Sex:M Child# 3 John Shea Nashua, NH & Alida Jodoin Canada  Stillborn
SHEA, Unknown, Jun 29 1895 Sex:F Child# 4 John F Shea Nashua, NH & Nellie McManus Aurora, IL
SHEA, Unknown, Oct 9 1912 Sex:M Child# 2 John Shea Ireland & Jenny Sullivan Hudson, NH Stillborn
SHEA, William Edward, Jan 13 1927 Sex:M Child# 1 Edward Shea Nashua, NH & Germaine Lavoie Nashua, NH
SHEAFE, Muriel Gould, Sep 22 1908 Sex:F Child# 4 Wayland H Sheafe Amesbury, MA & Nellie M Hurst Rockport, MA
SHECKUS, Annie, Dec 14 1905 Sex:F Child# 2 Vithold Sheckus Russia & Sophia Stenulonis Russia
SHECKUS, Vitold, Feb 4 1905 Sex:M Child# 1 Vitold Sheckus Russia & Zoffej Stanulionis Russia
SHEDD, Joseph Ellsworth, Sep 3 1894 Sex:M Child# 1 Elmer E Shedd Merrimack, NH & Annie Bell March St Johns, NB
SHEDD, Ladd, Mar 1 1888 Sex:M Child# 1 George A Shedd Nashua, NH & Florence C Whitcomb Townsend, MA
SHEDD, Marjorie March, Jul 15 1897 Sex:F Child# 2 Elmer E Shedd NH & Annie B March New Brunswick
SHEDD, Nellie M, Nov 7 1890 Sex:F Child# 1 Elmer E Shedd Merrimack, NH & Nellie M Jones Northfield, VT

SHEDD, Unknown, Nov 21 1887 Sex:M Child# 2 Nathaniel W Shedd Roxbury, MA & Elizabeth J Hubbard Manchester
SHEDLOWSKI, Julia, Jan 21 1926 Sex:F Child# 4 John Shedlowski Poland & Albina Tamolawicz Lithuania
SHEEHAN, Catherine, Oct 30 1895 Sex:F Child# 1 Jeremiah Sheehan Ireland & Anne Madigan Ireland
SHEEHAN, Paul Bernard, Jul 2 1922 Sex:M Child# 2 Michael Sheehan Canada & Susan Falls Canada
SHEEHAN, Unknown, Feb 20 1902 Sex:M Child# 4 Jeremiah Sheehan Ireland & Annie Madigan Ireland
SHEEHAN, Vincent, Jul 8 1920 Sex:M Child# 1 Michael Sheehan Canada & Susan Falls Canada
SHEEHAN, William Thomas, Jan 8 1898 Sex:M Child# 2 Jeremiah Sheehan England & Annie Madigan Ireland
SHEFFIELD, Norman Lewis, Feb 16 1915 Sex:M Child# 2 Edward M Sheffield Ironstone, MA & Grace C Johnson Uxbridge, MA
SHEFFIELD, Robert Newton, Nov 10 1916 Sex:M Child# 3 Ed Newton Sheffield Uxbridge, MA & Grace Johnson Uxbridge, MA
SHEFFIELD, William Johnson, May 9 1919 Sex:M Child# 4 Ed N Sheffield Uxbridge, MA & Grace Johnson Uxbridge, MA
SHELDON, Ernest Bradbury, Sep 1 1927 Sex:M Child# 3 George Sheldon Salem, MA & Viola Bradbury Cambridge, MA
SHELDON, June, Jun 2 1930 Sex:F Child# 1 Stacy H Sheldon Windham, NH & Freida L Low Windham, NH
SHELDON, Warren Edmund, May 19 1920 Sex:M Child# 1 Stacy Herbert Sheldon Windham, NH & Nellie G Fosher Bedford
SHENTON, Enoch, Nov 30 1914 Sex:M Child#  Charles M Shenton Durham, NH & Rosella M Saunders Worcester, MA
SHENTON, Ethel Margaret, Dec 25 1911 Sex:F Child# 1 James H Shenton Malden, MA & Almeda Armstrong Mooers, NY
SHENTON, Ruth Elizabeth, Aug 10 1908 Sex:F Child# 1 Charles M Shenton Durham, NH & Ethel V Cotton Nashua, NH
SHEPARD, Evelyn, Aug 6 1929 Sex:F Child# 4 Clarence Shepard Brunswick, ME & Alice Warren Peabody, MA
SHEPARD, Maurice John, Mar 7 1896 Sex:M Child#  Ralph Shepard New York & Jennie Shelly New York
SHEPARD, Norma, Jun 6 1920 Sex:F Child# 2 Basil W Shepard Hudson, NH & Ethel Merrill Hudson, NH
SHEPARD, Unknown, Nov 24 1916 Sex:F Child# 2 Roy Shepard Nashua, NH & Mamie Peno Nashua, NH
SHEPARD, William Chipman, Jan 23 1917 Sex:M Child# 1 Wilbur S Shepard Waddington, NY & Marion L Bassett Madrid
SHEPARD, William Merrill, Mar 9 1935 Sex:M Child# 6 Basil Shepard Hudson, NH & Ethel Merrill Hudson, NH
SHEPHERD, Lena Marion, Sep 9 1920 Sex:F Child# 6 Alfred H Shepherd Litchfield, NH & Ada E Armstrong Hudson, NH
SHEPHERD, Pansy Mae, Feb 25 1926 Sex:F Child# 1 Henry Shepherd Litchfield, NH & Esther Shepherd Salem, NH
SHEPHERD, Paul Roy Octave, Feb 16 1918 Sex:M Child# 2 Morris J Shepherd Nashua, NH & Alexina Poney Canada
SHEPHERD, Unknown, Dec 14 1894 Sex:M Child# 2 Ralph Shepherd
SHEPPARD, Harry Shelly, Feb 7 1916 Sex:M Child# 1 Roy Sheppard Nashua, NH & Mamie Peno Nashua, NH
SHEPPARD, Joseph Rob Maurice, Feb 13 1916 Sex:M Child# 1 Maurice Sheppard Nashua, NH & Alice A Poney Nashua, NH
SHEPPARD, Walter Pierce, Jan 20 1931 Sex:M Child# 1 Walter Sheppard Chelsea, MA & Helen Pierce Somerville, MA
SHERIDAN, Francis Richard, Nov 11 1908 Sex:M Child# 2 Edwin H Sheridan Dover, NH & Julia E Goodale Derry, VT
SHERIDAN, Phyllis Anne, May 11 1934 Sex:F Child# 1 Edwin Sheridan Nashua, NH & Evelyn Duane Maine
SHERIDAN, Unknown, May 26 1907 Sex:M Child# 1 Edwin H Sheridan Dover, NH & Julia Emma Goodais Barre, VT
SHERIDAN, Unknown, Apr 3 1911 Sex:M Child# 3 Edwin H Sheridan Dover, NH & Julia E Goodale Derry, VT
SHERLOCK, James Edmond, Aug 9 1923 Sex:M Child# 3 James A Sherlock Manchester, NH & Marie L Beaubien Canada
SHERLOCK, Louise Clara, Aug 12 1922 Sex:F Child# 2 James Sherlock NH & Marie Beaulieu Canada
SHERLOCK, Theresa, Jan 30 1928 Sex:F Child# 4 James Sherlock Manchester, NH & Marie Beaulieu Canada
SHERMAN, Beverly Rose, Feb 11 1931 Sex:F Child# 2 Stephen R Sherman Somerset, MA & Mary E Sherman Fall River, MA
SHERMAN, Dorothy Helen, Apr 4 1911 Sex:F Child# 1 Reuben L Sherman Vermont & Bessie H Haskins Vermont
SHERMAN, Eleanor Ruth, Feb 10 1927 Sex:F Child# 2 Howard Sherman Nashua, NH & Florena Lewis Leominster, MA
SHERMAN, Howard K B, Jun 6 1900 Sex:M Child# 1 E R Sherman Mass & Loraine M Beverley NH
SHERMAN, Lawrence K, May 2 1897 Sex:M Child# 1 Olin F Sherman Vermont & Chloe Lawrence Connecticut
SHERMAN, Louise, Jun 30 1934 Sex:F Child# 1 Harold W Sherman Roxbury, MA & Ethel Miller Woburn, MA
SHERMAN, Malcolm W, Sep 20 1935 Sex:M Child# 2 H W Sherman Roxbury, MA & Ethel Miller Woburn, MA
SHERMAN, Mattie Emma, Dec 7 1891 Sex:F Child# 1 Arthur B Sherman Mass & Minnie E Scott Mass
SHERMAN, Sophia, Jul 8 1910 Sex:F Child# 1 Sam Sherman Russia & Polly Berger Russia
SHERWIN, Dorothy Etta, Jul 18 1919 Sex:F Child# 3 Fred H Sherwin Nashua, NH & Bertha E Pillsbury Biddeford, ME
SHERWIN, Lillian Pillsbery, Aug 19 1909 Sex:F Child# 1 Fred H Sherwin Nashua, NH & Bertha E Pillsbery Maine
SHERWIN, Phillip Harrison, Jun 5 1917 Sex:M Child# 2 Fred H Sherwin Nashua, NH & Bertha E Pillsbury Biddeford, ME
SHESKA, Paul George, Jul 12 1927 Sex:M Child# 1 Stephen Sheska Austria & Eva Beauregard Nashua, NH
SHILOSKI, Jennie, Nov 12 1926 Sex:F Child# 5 Jacob Shiloski Poland & Mary ginglo Poland
SHINKAWICH, Nellie, Jun 22 1909 Sex:F Child# 1 Joe Shinkawich Austria & Ludwig Linkowska Austria
SHINKONIS, Frank, Mar 16 1926 Sex:M Child# 4 Anthony Shinkonis Lithuania & C Alenseavicz Lithuania
SHINKOWICH, Annie, Sep 4 1916 Sex:F Child# 1 Tony Shinkowich Russia & Zetzello Alexantch Russia
SHIRKEY, Albert Vincent, Dec 3 1932 Sex:M Child# 3 Joseph Shirkey Boston, MA & Anna Gerna Lithuania
SHLASEK, Peter, Jun 29 1915 Sex:M Child# 5 Wollen Shlasek Austria & Annie Starchak Austria
SHLIVA, John, Jan 8 1910 Sex:M Child# 3 Urban Shliva Austria & Keida Koagek Austria
SHLIVA, Mary, Aug 31 1908 Sex:F Child# 2 Urban Shliva Austria & Quaida Knaszak Austria
SHLIVA, Vladislav, Aug 8 1911 Sex:M Child# 4 Urban Shliva Austria & Kaida Kakargicz Austria
SHLUTS, Unknown, Aug 6 1905 Sex:M Child# 1 John Shluts Russia & Mary Kozdr Russia
SHOEN, William Rogers, Dec 17 1923 Sex:M Child# 3 William Earl Shoen Stockholm, NY & Eldora Williams Montreal
SHORES, Jennie S, May 31 1887 Sex:F Child# 3 (No Parents Listed)
SHOREY, Sumner B, May 30 1901 Sex:M Child# 1 Clarence Shorey New Castle, ME & Margaret Faucett Ashton, England
SHORT, Nattie, Jul 30 1896 Sex:F Child# 12 George Short Nashua, NH & Rose Gerow Hudson, ME
SHORTELL, J Aloysius Fugero, Oct 1 1921 Sex:M Child# 1 James J Shortell Ansonia, CT & Rose Alba Fugero Nashua, NH
SHRER, Ida, Mar 23 1904 Sex:F Child# 1 Hymen Shrer Russia & Sadie Vaisbord Russia
SHRER, Unknown, Jul 2 1905 Sex:F Child# 2 Hyman Shrer Russia & Sadie Vaisbord Russia Stillborn
SHUMSKY, Aniella, Mar 8 1910 Sex:F Child# 2 William Shumsky Russia & Katagena Wilkovski Russia
SHUMSKY, Sigismond, Aug 14 1918 Sex:M Child# 4 William Shumsky Russia & Kate Vilkowsky Russia
SHUMSKY, Wanda, Aug 30 1915 Sex:F Child# 4 William Shumsky Russia & Kaida Wilkoska Russia
SHUNSKY, Vatsiof, Jul 29 1911 Sex:M Child# 2 William Shunsky Russia & Kate Wilkovsky Russia
SHURKUS, Peter, Oct 2 1921 Sex:M Child# 3 Antonas Shurkus Russia & Kazenna Kuduz Russia
SHURKUS, Stepunig, May 13 1923 Sex:F Child# 4 Anthony Shurkus Russia & Kazi Kydys Russia
SHUSTA, Lillian, Aug 7 1920 Sex:F Child# 1 William Shusta Russia & Sarah Zimberg Nashua, NH

SHUSTER, Jackson Lee, Nov 21 1933 Sex:M Child# 4 William Shuster Russia & Sarah Zimberg Nashua, NH
SHUSZE, Waleria, Jan 4 1915 Sex:F Child# 2 Thomas Shusze Russia & Anna Kikilite Russia
SHUTA, Camillo, Sep 17 1910 Sex:M Child# 3 Salvatore Shuta Italy & Camille Belea Italy
SHVIRAGO, Alexander, Mar 10 1911 Sex:M Child# 2 Michael Shvirago Russia & Amelia Mikanovitch Russia
SHVIRAGO, Stanislaw, Apr 8 1913 Sex:M Child# 3 Mike Shvirago Russia & Emelia Mikanaita Russia
SIBOLUCKY, John, Sep 6 1916 Sex:M Child# 2 Anthony Sibolucky Russia & Amilk Jakezoct Russia
SIDDALL, Ruth, Dec 2 1921 Sex:F Child# 8 Ernest Siddall Manchester, NH & Annie Schreiber Austria
SIDEBOTHAM, Gordon Lionel, Sep 25 1912 Sex:M Child# 1 Melvin H Sidebotham Biddeford, ME & Elizabeth Nimno Some
SIDLEWIER, Marie, Jun 21 1893 Sex:F Child# 1 Andrew Sidlewier Russia & Marie Pelletier US
SIEGEL, Unknown, May 13 1933 Sex:M Child# 2 Alex Siegel Russia & Anna Nusenoff Lynn, MA
SIERGIEWICZ, Annie, Oct 12 1929 Sex:F Child# 3 Ludwick Siergiewicz Poland & Lookadia Michalevicz Poland
SIESICK, Fredrich Peter, Aug 10 1933 Sex:M Child# 4 Peter Siesick Poland & Helen Chanalis Poland
SIESICKI, David, Aug 24 1927 Sex:M Child# 3 Peter Siesicki Poland & Helen Chapanis Poland
SIGORIEN, Alice Eva, Nov 29 1890 Sex:F Child# 1 George Sigorien Canada & Dina Levesque Canada
SIGOUIN, Georges Edouard, Jan 25 1893 Sex:M Child# 2 Georges Sigouin Canada & Dina Leveque Canada
SIGOUIN, Gerard J Silvio, Oct 20 1931 Sex:M Child# 4 Sylvio Sigouin Nashua, NH & Rose A Beaupre Canada
SIGOUIN, Joseph Elzear, Dec 26 1893 Sex:M Child# 3 George Sigouin NY & Dina Levesque Canada
SIGOUIN, Joseph Sylvio, Jan 9 1898 Sex:M Child# 4 George Sigouin Canada & Dina Levesque Canada
SIGOUIN, Marie Anne Emelia, May 26 1918 Sex:F Child# 1 George Sigouin Nashua, NH & Emelia St Pierre St Louise,
SIGUIN, J Conrad Jerome, Apr 8 1915 Sex:M Child# 2 Joseph Siguin Canada & Cecilia Soucy Canada
SIKOWICH, Mary, May 10 1912 Sex:F Child# 1 John Sikowich Russia & Annie Awiznica Russia
SILLA, Mary, Jun 14 1907 Sex:F Child# 2 Joseph Silla Poland & Martha Valcois Poland
SILLERS, James Donald, Oct 9 1921 Sex:M Child# 3 James W Sillers Canada & Alice Wheeler Hollis, NH
SILLEY, Antonia, Aug 26 1905 Sex:F Child# 1 Andrew Silley Russia & Tofulya Menczimska Russia
SILLGA, Sillga, Jun 10 1889 Sex:M Child# 8 John P Sillga Sweden & Louisa Johnson Sweden
SILONEYUS, Stanislaus, Apr 26 1914 Sex:M Child# 1 Charles Siloneyus Russia & Eva Margartin Russia
SILVA, Beatrice Ann, Jan 25 1933 Sex:F Child# 1 Joseph Silva Spain & Dorothy Morrill Milford, NH
SILVER, Joseph Arthur, Jun 14 1931 Sex:M Child# 6 Edmond Silver Littleton, NH & Lucy Cyr St David, ME
SILVER, Joseph Peter Girard, Aug 23 1929 Sex:M Child# 5 Joseph E Silver Littleton, NH & Lucy Cyr St David, ME
SILVER, Lucy, Oct 24 1926 Sex:F Child# 3 J Edward Silver NH & Lucy Cyr Maine
SILVER, Unknown, Mar 10 1887 Sex:F Child# 2 George D Silver Craftsbury, VT & Lulu Hannon Nashua, NH
SILVERMAN, Dorothy Ruth, Aug 12 1912 Sex:F Child# 1 Morris Silverman Russia & Ida F Goodman Russia
SILVIO, Marie, Dec 14 1916 Sex:F Child# 2 Antonio Silvio Spain & Emelia Meniet Spain
SIMAKINKA, Felomine, Feb 9 1917 Sex:F Child# 4 Joseph Simakinka Poland & Ludvika Oleckaska Poland
SIMANOVITCH, Constantin, Aug 19 1911 Sex:M Child# 3 Constant Simanovitch Russia & Josepha Glenska Russia
SIMARD, Albert Alphonse, Jan 18 1913 Sex:M Child# 1 Joseph Simard Canada & Alexina Gagnon Canada
SIMARD, Alfred Paul, Dec 13 1931 Sex:M Child# 2 Alfred Simard Nashua, NH & Leona Blow Nashua, NH
SIMARD, Alma, Apr 28 1914 Sex:F Child# 2 Joseph Simard Canada & Alexina Gagnon Canada Stillborn
SIMARD, Alphonse Donald, Sep 7 1929 Sex:M Child# 5 Alphonse Simard Canada & Alphonsine Gagnon Canada
SIMARD, Anne Cecile, Feb 5 1925 Sex:F Child# 9 Joseph Simard Canada & Alexana Gagnon Canada
SIMARD, Beatrice, Feb 27 1923 Sex:F Child# 3 Jean Simard Canada & Alma Simard Canada
SIMARD, Beatrice Gabrielle, Nov 7 1922 Sex:F Child# 1 Edouard Simard Canada & Eugenie Dionne Canada
SIMARD, Conrad Lionel, Oct 20 1919 Sex:M Child# 6 Joseph Simard Canada & Alexina Gagnon Canada
SIMARD, Edgar Raymond, Sep 7 1929 Sex:M Child# 11 Joseph Simard Canada & Alefina Gagnon Canada
SIMARD, Elise, Feb 3 1896 Sex:F Child# 2 Phineas Simard Canada & Marie Simard Canada
SIMARD, Ernest Gerard, May 26 1918 Sex:M Child# 5 Joseph Simard Canada & Alexina Gagnon Canada
SIMARD, Ernest Norbert, Jan 31 1926 Sex:M Child# 1 Ludger E Simard Salem, MA & Gloria G Gamache Nashua, NH
SIMARD, Frederic Lionel, Jan 12 1901 Sex:M Child# 10 Henri Simard Canada & Malvina Scott Canada
SIMARD, Ida Yvonne, Dec 5 1901 Sex:F Child# 1 Auguste Simard Canada & Albertine Beaulieu Canada
SIMARD, Jos H D Raymond, Feb 9 1932 Sex:M Child# 2 Hector J Simard Nashua, NH & Azilda Thibault Canada
SIMARD, Joseph, Mar 17 1926 Sex:M Child# 2 Michael Simard Canada & Rose Emery Nashua, NH Stillborn
SIMARD, Joseph, Aug 23 1931 Sex:M Child# 3 Napoleon Simard Canada & Leonie Pelletier Canada Stillborn
SIMARD, Joseph A H, Mar 9 1905 Sex:M Child# 1 Alphonse Simard Canada & Marie A Beaulieu Canada
SIMARD, Joseph A Roland, Sep 13 1897 Sex:M Child# 1 Emile Simard Canada & Marie Anne Brien Canada
SIMARD, Joseph Alfred, Dec 8 1910 Sex:M Child# 2 Alfred Simard Canada & Amanda Dube Canada
SIMARD, Joseph Alphonse E, May 10 1903 Sex:M Child# 2 Auguste Simard Canada & Albertine Beaulieu Canada
SIMARD, Joseph Cleophas H, Aug 27 1908 Sex:M Child# 1 Wilfrid Simard Canada & Amanda Dube Canada
SIMARD, Joseph Henri, May 26 1896 Sex:M Child# 2 Joseph Simard Canada & Alexandrina Gendron Canada
SIMARD, Joseph Leo Paul, Sep 11 1906 Sex:M Child# 8 Nazaire Simard Canada & Leda Ouellette Canada
SIMARD, Joseph Lucien A, Nov 28 1902 Sex:M Child# 14 Michel Simard Canada & Leonard Grondin Canada
SIMARD, Juliette Germaine, Sep 9 1904 Sex:F Child# 3 Auguste Simard Canada & Albertine Beaulieu Canada
SIMARD, Laurette Irene, Mar 13 1917 Sex:F Child# 4 Joseph Simard Canada & Alexina Gagnon Canada
SIMARD, Leo Daniel, Jan 1 1935 Sex:M Child# 4 Napoleon Simard Canada & Leonie Pelletier Canada
SIMARD, Leonard Ludger, Mar 1 1927 Sex:M Child# 2 Ludger E Simard Salem, MA & G G Gamache Nashua, NH
SIMARD, Loretta Theresa, Aug 12 1932 Sex:F Child# 2 Emile Simard Nashua, NH & Amanda Godin Nashua, NH
SIMARD, Malvina, Aug 21 1895 Sex:M Child# 11 Napoleon Simard Canada & Catherine Simard Canada
SIMARD, Marie, Apr 17 1894 Sex:F Child# Philias Simard Canada & Marthe Canada
SIMARD, Marie Aldea, Mar 19 1912 Sex:F Child# 3 Alfred Simard Canada & Amanda Dube Canada
SIMARD, Marie Alice Alma, Mar 13 1901 Sex:F Child# 3 Philippe Simard Canada & Ludivine Gareau Canada
SIMARD, Marie Blanche A, Aug 30 1909 Sex:F Child# 10 Nazaire Simard Canada & Leda Ouelette Canada
SIMARD, Marie E Rosalia, Jan 15 1899 Sex:F Child# 6 Henri Simard Canada & Malvina Scott Canada
SIMARD, Marie Elise, Jan 10 1897 Sex:F Child# 4 Elzear Simard Canada & Marie Marcoux Canada
SIMARD, Marie Evelina, Jan 10 1901 Sex:F Child# 4 Narcisse Simard Canada & Leda Ouellette Canada

SIMARD, Marie Josephine Dora, Mar 16 1902 Sex:F Child# 5 Nazaire Simard Canada & Leda Ouellette Canada
SIMARD, Marie N D Y, Jan 28 1930 Sex:F Child# 1 Hectorian Simard Nashua, NH & Azilda Thibeault Canada
SIMARD, Maurice Napoleon, Jun 17 1927 Sex:M Child# 2 Napoleon Simard Canada & Leonie Pelletier Canada
SIMARD, Nazaire, Dec 26 1894 Sex:M Child# 1 Joseph Simard Canada & Alexandrina Gendron Canada
SIMARD, Nazaire, Jan 15 1897 Sex:M Child# 1 Nazaire Simard Canada & Leda Ouellette Canada
SIMARD, Osias, Jun 9 1907 Sex:M Child# 5 Alphonse Simard Canada & Elise Simard Canada
SIMARD, Paul Armand, Mar 14 1926 Sex:M Child# 1 Napoleon Simard Canada & Leonie Pelletier Canada
SIMARD, Pauline Joan, Dec 24 1928 Sex:F Child# 1 Alfred Simard Canada & Leona Bleau Nashua, NH
SIMARD, Raymond, Jan 10 1914 Sex:M Child# 4 Alfred Simard Canada & Amanda Dube Canada
SIMARD, Raymond Emile, Sep 14 1933 Sex:M Child# 2 Emile Simard US & Mabel Godin Nashua, NH
SIMARD, Remi, Sep 8 1896 Sex:M Child# Henri Simard Canada & Malvina Scott Canada
SIMARD, Richard Harvey, Aug 20 1935 Sex:M Child# 13 Joseph Simard Canada & Alexina Gagnon Canada
SIMARD, Rita Jeanne, Dec 20 1923 Sex:F Child# 8 Joseph Simard Canada & Alexina Gagnon Canada
SIMARD, Robert, May 12 1915 Sex:M Child# 3 Joseph Simard Canada & Alexina Gagnon Canada
SIMARD, Roger Gerard, Sep 8 1918 Sex:M Child# 6 Alfred Simard Nashua, NH & Amanda Dube Canada
SIMARD, Roger Normand, Dec 16 1926 Sex:M Child# 10 Joseph Simard Canada & Alexina Gagnon Canada
SIMARD, Rosario Armand, Aug 29 1921 Sex:M Child# 7 Joseph Simard Canada & Alexina Gagnon Canada
SIMARD, Rose Anna, Aug 25 1895 Sex:F Child# 7 Henri Simard Canada & Malvina Scott Canada
SIMARD, Theresa Mary, Aug 2 1931 Sex:F Child# 1 Edward Simard Nashua, NH & Marie R Levesque Nashua, NH
SIMARD, Therese Madeline, Nov 27 1920 Sex:F Child# 1 Michel E Simard Hancock, NH & Minnie Magoon Greenfield, NH
SIMARD, Thomas, Apr 5 1890 Sex:M Child# 5 Napoleon Simard Canada & Catherine Canada
SIMARD, Wilfred Laurent, Apr 12 1933 Sex:M Child# 12 Joseph Simard Canada & Alexina Gagnon Canada
SIMARD, Yvonne, Feb 16 1911 Sex:F Child# 12 Joseph Simard Canada & Rosanna Simard Canada
SIMBERG, Anna, Sep 14 1903 Sex:F Child# 9 Louis Simberg Russia & Fanny Tirkosh Russia
SIMBERG, Annette Ray, Nov 20 1923 Sex:F Child# 1 Nathan Simberg Germany & Sarah E Chirarg Germany
SIMBERG, Jack, Aug 28 1901 Sex:M Child# 8 L Simberg Russia & Fannie Roskosky Russia
SIMBERG, Marie Annette Rita, Sep 23 1926 Sex:F Child# 2 Nathan Simberg Canada & Bernadette Blais Canada
SIMBERG, Moses, Jun 19 1900 Sex:M Child# 7 Lewis Simberg Russia & Fannie Hartskopski Russia
SIMBERG, Sera, May 1 1897 Sex:F Child# 4 Lewis Simberg Russia & Fene Rachckvosky Russia
SIMKONIS, Unknown, Nov 25 1922 Sex:M Child# 4 Ant Simkonis Lithuania & Cecelia Aleksawicz Lithuania
SIMKOSKI, Euzebe, Jul 17 1897 Sex:M Child# 1 Dominique Simkoski Russia & Annie Bergyloi Russia
SIMKOWSKI, Frank, Aug 24 1905 Sex:M Child# 3 Frank Simkowski Russia & Stanislow Jorinkski Russia
SIMKUS, Wadislaus, Jun 26 1903 Sex:M Child# Frank Simkus Russia & Stase Porinkorot Russia
SIMMONS, Joseph, Mar 26 1921 Sex:M Child# 1 Roy Simmons New Brunswick & Eugenie Sirois Canada Stillborn
SIMMONS, Martha Loraine, Jan 10 1923 Sex:F Child# 2 Roy Simmons New Brunswick & Jennie Sirois Canada
SIMMONS, Unknown, Feb 28 1902 Sex:M Child# Frank Simmons Mass & Ethel L Haynes NY
SIMMONS, Unknown, Nov 20 1906 Sex:F Child# 3 Frank Simmons Boston, MA & Ethel L Haines New York
SIMO, John, Sep 4 1932 Sex:M Child# 2 Nicholas Simo Greece & Cornelia Kazana Turkey
SIMON, Evalina, Jul 31 1894 Sex:F Child# 6 E Simon Poland & Mary Davis Poland
SIMON, H Robert Shaddock, Jul 10 1920 Sex:M Child# 1 Joseph Simon Lowell, MA & Dora Shaddock Russia
SIMONDS, Betty, Nov 30 1929 Sex:F Child# 1 Irving Simonds Winchester, MA & Alice Burton England
SIMONDS, Charles, Dec 30 1889 Sex:M Child# 3 Frederick Simonds Georgia & Mary C Neil Nashua, NH
SIMONDS, Esther Vera, Jul 3 1928 Sex:F Child# 4 L M Simonds Billerica, MA & Vera L Baldwin Nashua, NH
SIMONDS, Herbert Warren, Dec 12 1920 Sex:M Child# 3 Lester Simonds Mass & Vera Baldwin Nashua, NH
SIMONDS, Howard Merton, Feb 4 1918 Sex:M Child# 1 Lester M Simonds Mass & Vera Baldwin Nashua, NH
SIMONDS, Jean Carolyn, Jul 18 1927 Sex:F Child# 1 Lee Simonds Lyme, NH & Doris Crenner Somerville, MA
SIMONDS, Milton Robert, Apr 2 1930 Sex:M Child# 2 Harold M Simonds Mass & Effie Burke Canada
SIMONDS, Phyllis Ann, Apr 14 1932 Sex:F Child# 2 Irving R Simonds Winchester, MA & Alice M Burton England
SIMONDS, Raymond, Aug 28 1919 Sex:M Child# 2 Lester M Simonds Mass & Vera Ella Baldwin Nashua, NH
SIMONDS, Unknown, Apr 25 1894 Sex:F Child# 1 Frank P Simonds
SIMONEAU, Alex Louis Norman, Jun 21 1935 Sex:M Child# 2 Alex Simoneau Canada & Delia Parent Nashua, NH
SIMONEAU, Armelle Celine, Aug 4 1932 Sex:F Child# 1 Alex Simoneau Plessisville, PQ & Lydia Parent Nashua, NH
SIMONEAU, Edgar Louis Joseph, Oct 18 1924 Sex:M Child# 1 D Simoneau Graniteville, VT & Leda Soucy Canada
SIMONEAU, Emile Lucien, May 8 1903 Sex:M Child# 2 Thomas Simoneau Canada & Josephine Doyen Canada
SIMONEAU, Gerard Arthur, Jul 19 1929 Sex:M Child# 4 Leo Simoneau Lewiston, ME & Alice Girard Nashua, NH
SIMONEAU, Jeannette Rolande, Nov 14 1930 Sex:F Child# 4 Leo Simoneau Lewiston, ME & Alice Girard Nashua, NH
SIMONEAU, Jos Maurice Denis, Aug 8 1929 Sex:M Child# 9 Armand Simoneau Canada & Leda Mercier Canada
SIMONEAU, Jos Noel B Gabriel, Dec 25 1922 Sex:M Child# 5 Armand Simoneau Canada & Leda Mercier Canada
SIMONEAU, Joseph Gilbert Conra, Aug 18 1914 Sex:M Child# 2 Armand Simoneau Canada & Leda Mercier Canada
SIMONEAU, Joseph Marcel Romeo, Mar 11 1934 Sex:M Child# 1 Armand Simoneau Canada & Leda Mercier Canada
SIMONEAU, Joseph Paul Aurele, Oct 4 1926 Sex:M Child# 1 J W Simoneau Barre, VT & Reina Pellerin Lawrence, MA
SIMONEAU, Joseph Raymond, Dec 3 1930 Sex:M Child# 5 Delphis Simoneau US & Leda Soucy Canada
SIMONEAU, Lionel Dolar Adrien, Jan 17 1913 Sex:M Child# 1 Armand Simoneau Canada & Leda Mercier Canada
SIMONEAU, M L C Gilbert, Oct 10 1921 Sex:M Child# 4 Armand Simoneau Canada & Leda Mercier Canada
SIMONEAU, Marcelle Rita, Nov 6 1929 Sex:F Child# 2 Joseph Simoneau Webster, Vt & Reina Pelerin Lawrence, MA
SIMONEAU, Marie Colette Isabel, Jan 5 1926 Sex:F Child# 7 Armand Simoneau Canada & Leda Mercier Canada
SIMONEAU, Marie Rose C Rita, Mar 3 1926 Sex:F Child# 2 Delphis Simoneau
SIMONEAU, Maurice Roger, May 2 1924 Sex:M Child# 2 Leo Simoneau Lewiston, ME & Alice Girard Nashua, NH
SIMONEAU, Normand Roger, Jun 15 1931 Sex:M Child# 2 Joseph Simoneau Websterville, VT & Rena Pellerin Lawrence, MA
SIMONEAU, Paul Emile Armand, May 23 1931 Sex:M Child# 10 Armand Simoneau Canada & Leda Mercier Canada
SIMONEAU, Rene Joseph, May 19 1934 Sex:M Child# 4 Joseph Simoneau Websterville, VT & Rena Pellerin Lawrence, MA
SIMONEAU, Rene L Melchior, Jan 14 1917 Sex:M Child# 3 Armand Simoneau Canada & Leda Mercier Canada
SIMONEAU, Robert Conrad, Dec 16 1929 Sex:M Child# 4 Delphis Simoneau Canada & Leda Soucy Canada

SIMONEAU, Rock Laurent, Aug 9 1924 Sex:M Child# 6 Armand Simoneau Canada & Leda Mercier Canada
SIMONEAU, Ronald Norman, Nov 16 1935 Sex:M Child# 1 Alfred Simoneau Nashua, NH & Germaine Moreau Nashua, NH
SIMONEAU, Theresa, Jul 8 1928 Sex:F Child# 3 D Simmoneau Graniteville, VT & Leda Soucy Canada
SIMONNEAU, Lucien, Aug 7 1904 Sex:M Child# 3 Thomas Simonneau Canada & Josephine Doyon Canada
SIMONOVITCH, Joseph, Oct 6 1908 Sex:M Child# 1 Castan Simonovitch Poland & Josephine Glyska Poland
SIMONOWICZ, Constantina, Apr 20 1913 Sex:F Child# 6 Constantin Simonowic Russia & Eusepa Gluska Russia
SIMOULIS, Unknown, Sep 10 1919 Sex:F Child# 1 Monolis Simoulis Greece & Thanasia Stathopolon Greece
SIMOULIS, Unknown, Sep 2 1927 Sex:M Child# 4 Emanuel Simoulis Greece & A Stathias Greece
SIMPSON, Ray, Jul 25 1906 Sex:M Child# 2 H A Simpson Vermont & Emma Taylor Leominster, MA
SIMSES, John Peter, Feb 3 1913 Sex:M Child# 1 Peter Simses Russia & Alice Strempak Austria
SIMSES, Richard, Apr 14 1924 Sex:M Child# 2 Peter Simses Lithuania & Alice Strimpek Poland
SIMSON, Unknown, Oct 27 1900 Sex:F Child# 3 C M Simson NH & A M Donohue New York
SINILEUS, Julia, Apr 1 1917 Sex:F Child# 5 Peter Sinileus Russia & Ellen Schlake Russia
SINKAVITCH, Josie, Aug 19 1910 Sex:F Child# 4 Michael Sinkavitch Russia & Marcelina Tregnovitc Russia
SINKEWICZ, Anna, Aug 3 1904 Sex:F Child# 1 Michael Sinkewicz Russia & Marcela Trewoicz Russia
SINKEWICZ, Mary, Apr 13 1912 Sex:F Child# 2 Joseph Sinkewicz Russia & Ludwiga Olekouski Austria
SINKEWITCH, Romalda, Mar 5 1920 Sex:M Child# 35 Joseph Sinkewitch Russia & Ludwkes Wlybouska Austria
SINKEZICZ, Malvina, Nov 20 1908 Sex:F Child# 3 Michael Sinkezicz Russia & Marcelina Treinwicz Russia
SINKIEWICZ, Albert, Mar 27 1920 Sex:M Child# 5 Frank Sinkiewicz Lithuania Russia & Annie Virchovsky Lithuania
SINKIEWICZ, Ganefa, Sep 1 1926 Sex:F Child# 4 Chris Sinkiewicz Poland & Asbieta Iremitch Poland
SINKIEWICZ, Joseph, Jul 27 1921 Sex:M Child# 3 Boniface Sinkiewicz Russia & Vincenta Stakawicz Russia
SINKIEWICZ, Peter, Sep 6 1919 Sex:M Child# 2 Bon Sinkiewicz Poland Russia & Vincento Stakawicz Poland Russia
SINTA, Stanislas, Sep 13 1902 Sex:M Child# 2 John Sinta Russia & Stanistowa Zeba Russia
SIRDENIS, Angelos, Sep 3 1913 Sex:M Child# 6 George Sirdenis Greece & Mary Tago Greece
SIRDENIS, Apostolas, Sep 3 1913 Sex:M Child# 5 George Sirdenis Greece & Mary Tago Greece
SIRDENIS, Apostolos, Sep 3 1913 Sex:M Child# 7 George Sirdenis Greece & Mary Tago Greece
SIRDINI, Charles, Jan 26 1912 Sex:M Child# 2 George Sirdini Greece & Mary Loudon Greece
SIRDINI, Katherine, Jan 26 1912 Sex:F Child# 3 George Sirdini Greece & Mary Loudon Greece
SIREKA, Watslaf, Mar 13 1916 Sex:M Child# 2 Michael Sireka Russia & Anna Clemasihka Russia
SIRMALAWICZ, Lena, Jun 15 1915 Sex:F Child# 3 Rolla Sirmalawicz Russia & Agae Greginta Russia
SIRMINTIS, Zophia, Aug 4 1914 Sex:F Child# 1 Stanislaw Sirmintis Russia & Franciska Ferboty Russia
SIROIS, Achile Joseph, Jan 27 1891 Sex:M Child# 1 Sirias Sirois Canada & Antonia Dischene Canada
SIROIS, Alice, Feb 1 1896 Sex:F Child# 5 Joseph Sirois Canada & Marie Rioux Canada
SIROIS, Alice Marie, Oct 29 1909 Sex:F Child# 1 Hormidas Sirois Canada & Alice Dufour Canada
SIROIS, Alma Gertrude, Apr 19 1900 Sex:F Child# 2 Joseph Sirois Canada & Hermin St Onge Canada
SIROIS, Bernard, Feb 7 1929 Sex:M Child# 8 John L Sirois Nashua, NH & Beatrice Demers Canada
SIROIS, Bertha Antoinette, Jun 17 1904 Sex:F Child# 3 Joseph Sirois Canada & Hermine St Onge Canada
SIROIS, Charles Eugene, Dec 22 1903 Sex:M Child# 3 Philippe Sirois Canada & Desneiges Parent Canada
SIROIS, Conrad Arthur Andre, Apr 28 1926 Sex:M Child# 6 John Sirois Nashua, NH & Beatrice Demers Canada
SIROIS, Cyprien, Jan 21 1894 Sex:M Child#  Louis Sirois Canada & Geraldine Morency Canada
SIROIS, Dalila Juliette, Aug 13 1897 Sex:F Child# 4 Paul Sirois Canada & Dalila Larne Canada
SIROIS, Dorothy, Feb 14 1931 Sex:F Child# 2 Leo Sirois Canada & Yvonne Paradis Canada
SIROIS, Dorothy Constance, Jul 10 1923 Sex:F Child# 2 Amedee Sirois Canada & Lea Goyette Nashua, NH
SIROIS, Emile Arthur, May 15 1891 Sex:M Child# 9 Elzear Sirois Canada & Marguerite Marquis Canada
SIROIS, Estelle Anne, Mar 16 1921 Sex:F Child# 2 John Sirois Nashua, NH & Beatrice Demers Canada
SIROIS, Eugene Conrad, Jun 6 1927 Sex:M Child# 7 John L Sirois Nashua, NH & Beatrice Demers Canada
SIROIS, Florilda, Nov 10 1896 Sex:F Child# 3 Zephirin Sirois Canada & Marie Guerette Canada
SIROIS, Henri, Apr 30 1896 Sex:M Child# 11 Elzeard Sirois Canada & Marguerite Marquis Canada
SIROIS, J B Alexandre, Aug 20 1909 Sex:M Child# 9 Alfred Sirois Canada & Hermine Chasse Canada
SIROIS, Jacqueline, Aug 22 1931 Sex:F Child# 2 Henry James Sirois Nashua, NH & Anna Finnigan Nashua, NH
SIROIS, Jean Baptiste, Jun 19 1902 Sex:M Child# 2 Philippe Sirois Canada & Desanges Parent Canada
SIROIS, Jean Baptiste A, Apr 19 1907 Sex:M Child# 8 Alfred Sirois Canada & Hermine Chasse Canada
SIROIS, Jean Ludger, Dec 20 1890 Sex:M Child# 2 John Sirois Canada & Prascede Michaud Canada
SIROIS, John Ludger, Feb 8 1920 Sex:M Child# 1 John Ludger Sirois Nashua, NH & Beatrice Demers Canada
SIROIS, Jos Angemille Phelix, Apr 22 1918 Sex:M Child# 2 Edward Sirois Newmarket, NH & Louisa McMurray Canada
SIROIS, Jos George Aime, Apr 10 1927 Sex:M Child# 3 George Sirois Canada & Aurore Gagnon Canada
SIROIS, Jos Roland Alph, Sep 19 1919 Sex:M Child# 3 Edward Sirois Somersworth, NH & Louisa McMurray Canada
SIROIS, Joseph A Dewey, Mar 27 1899 Sex:M Child# 1 Joseph Sirois Canada & Hermine St Onge Canada
SIROIS, Joseph Arthur, Jan 26 1899 Sex:M Child# 5 Paul Sirois Canada & Delia Larue Canada
SIROIS, Joseph Charles, May 4 1892 Sex:M Child# 1 Joseph Sirois Canada & Marie Rheaume Canada
SIROIS, Joseph Corade, Jul 13 1914 Sex:M Child# 7 Joseph Sirois Canada & Malvina Lavoie Canada
SIROIS, Joseph David, Nov 29 1893 Sex:M Child# 2 Paul Sirois Canada & Delia Laure Canada
SIROIS, Joseph David, Oct 8 1895 Sex:M Child# 3 Paul Sirois Canada & Delia Larue Canada
SIROIS, Joseph Desire, Mar 29 1905 Sex:M Child# 14 Simon S Sirois Canada & Eugenie Chenard Canada
SIROIS, Joseph Felix, Apr 25 1898 Sex:M Child# 4 Cyrias Sirois Canada & Antonia Deschenes Canada
SIROIS, Joseph H, Nov 3 1894 Sex:M Child# 2 Zepherin Sirois Canada & Marie Guerrette Canada
SIROIS, Joseph Henri T, Aug 15 1907 Sex:M Child# 2 Joseph Sirois Canada & Malvina Lavoie Canada
SIROIS, Joseph Leo Alphe, Nov 8 1915 Sex:M Child# 8 Joseph Sirois Canada & Malvina Lavoie Canada
SIROIS, Joseph Leon, Sep 4 1924 Sex:M Child# 5 John L Sirois Nashua, NH & Beatrice Demers Magog, Canada
SIROIS, Joseph Maurice Ralph, Aug 7 1918 Sex:M Child# 2 Joseph Sirois Canada & Alma Paradise Canada
SIROIS, Joseph Nap Edgar, Dec 26 1905 Sex:M Child# 1 Joseph Sirois Canada & Marie Alice Dion Nashua, NH
SIROIS, Joseph Odillon, Apr 6 1892 Sex:M Child# 6 Lazare Sirois Canada & Diana Lavoie Canada
SIROIS, Joseph Oscar E, Apr 11 1906 Sex:M Child# 1 Joseph Sirois Canada & Malvina Lavoie Canada

SIROIS, Joseph Paul, Sep 14 1923 Sex:M Child# 4 John L Sirois Nashua, NH & Beatrice Demers Magog, RI
SIROIS, Joseph T E, Jul 11 1903 Sex:M Child# 2 Thomas Sirois Canada & Eugenie Deschamps Canada
SIROIS, Joseph Thomas, Mar 22 1908 Sex:M Child# 5 Thomas Sirois Canada & Eugenie Deschamps Canada
SIROIS, Joseph W I, Oct 3 1892 Sex:M Child# 1 Napoleon Sirois Canada & Delia Larue Canada
SIROIS, Liliane, Sep 22 1908 Sex:F Child# 3 Joseph Sirois Canada & Malvina Lavoie Canada
SIROIS, Louis J, May 4 1898 Sex:M Child# 6 Joseph Sirois Canada & Marie Rheaume Canada
SIROIS, Lucille Madeline, Aug 16 1917 Sex:F Child# 1 Med Sirois Canada & Leah Goyett Nashua, NH
SIROIS, Ludger, Dec 4 1892 Sex:M Child# 10 Elzeard Sirois Canada & Marguerite Mescier Canada
SIROIS, M Blanche Lucille, Feb 15 1922 Sex:F Child# 3 John L Sirois Nashua, NH & Beatrice Demers Canada
SIROIS, M Blanche Yvonne, Jun 29 1921 Sex:F Child# 3 Hormidas Sirois Canada & Elise Raymond Canada
SIROIS, Marie Alice, Aug 13 1903 Sex:F Child# 3 Jean Bte Sirois Canada & Philomene St Pierre Canada
SIROIS, Marie Alice, Feb 10 1905 Sex:F Child# 7 Alfred Sirois Canada & Hermine Chasse Canada
SIROIS, Marie Alice, Jul 13 1916 Sex:F Child# 4 Hormidas Sirois Canada & Elise Raymond Canada
SIROIS, Marie Alice E, Apr 8 1908 Sex:F Child# 2 Joseph Sirois Canada & Alice Dion Nashua, NH
SIROIS, Marie Armantine Dori, Aug 8 1912 Sex:F Child# 6 Joseph Sirois Canada & Malvina Lavoie Canada
SIROIS, Marie D Ida, Aug 29 1903 Sex:F Child# 6 Alfred Sirois Canada & Hermine Chasse Canada
SIROIS, Marie Eugenie, Mar 28 1909 Sex:F Child# 6 Thomas Sirois Canada & Eugenie Deschamps Canada
SIROIS, Marie Exilia E, Jun 18 1906 Sex:F Child# 4 Thomas Sirois Canada & Eugenie Deschamps Canada
SIROIS, Marie H Virginie, Jan 31 1898 Sex:F Child# 1 Michel Sirois Canada & Helene Courcy Canada
SIROIS, Marie Irene, Feb 12 1910 Sex:F Child# 4 Joseph Sirois Canada & Malvina Lavoie Canada
SIROIS, Marie Jeanne I, Oct 14 1928 Sex:F Child# 1 Joseph Sirois Lawrence, MA & Isabelle Plante New Bedford, MA
SIROIS, Marie R S, Aug 4 1892 Sex:F Child# 1 Zepherin Sirois Canada & Marie Guerette Canada
SIROIS, Marie Rose Jeanne, Mar 13 1911 Sex:F Child# 5 Joseph Sirois Canada & Malvina Lavoie Canada
SIROIS, Mary Janice, Apr 24 1932 Sex:F Child# 2 William Sirois Grand Falls, NB & Rose Fox Pawtucket, RI
SIROIS, Muriel Jeannine, Mar 28 1930 Sex:F Child# 1 Leo Paul Sirois Canada & Yvonne Paradis Canada
SIROIS, Napoleon, Sep 6 1890 Sex:M Child# 10 Louis Sirois Canada & Geraldine Morency Canada
SIROIS, Octave, Mar 19 1894 Sex:M Child# 7 Lazare Sirois Canada & Dina Lavoie Canada
SIROIS, Philippe, Mar 7 1901 Sex:M Child# 1 Philippe Sirois Canada & Denise Parent Canada
SIROIS, Pierre, Dec 16 1892 Sex:M Child# 2 Sirias Sirois Canada & Antonia Deschenes Canada
SIROIS, Pierre, Jun 29 1894 Sex:M Child# 4 Joseph Sirois Canada & Marie Rheaume Canada
SIROIS, Thomas, Aug 1 1906 Sex:M Child# 5 J Bte Sirois Canada & Marie St Pierre Canada
SIROIS, Unknown, Jun 12 1893 Sex:M Child# 2 Joseph Sirois Canada & Marie Rheaume Canada
SIROIS, Unknown, Jun 12 1893 Sex:M Child# 3 Joseph Sirois Canada & Marie Rheaume Canada
SIROIS, Unknown, Apr 29 1900 Sex:M Child# 3 Thomas Sirois Canada & Eugenie Deschamps Canada Stillborn
SIROIS, Unknown, Nov 28 1916 Sex:M Child#  Joseph A Sirois Canada & Alma Paradis Canada
SIROIS, Unknown, Jul 19 1923 Sex:M Child# 2 George Sirois Canada & Aurore Gagnon Canada Stillborn
SIROIS, Unknown, Jan 4 1930 Sex:F Child# 1 Henri Sirois Nashua, NH & Anna Finnigan Nashua, NH Stillborn
SIRUSES, Edward Walter, Jan 27 1931 Sex:M Child# 3 Peter Siruses Lithuania & Alice Strempak Poland
SISKO, Joseph J, Mar 24 1913 Sex:M Child# 1 Stanley Sisko Russia & Helen Boukawich Russia
SIWTEWICZ, John, Aug 18 1906 Sex:M Child# 2 Antony Siwtewicz Russia & Tosita Menczunsks Russia
SKAFIDAS, Gregorios Spiros, Aug 31 1928 Sex:M Child# 2 John Skafidas Greece & M Pappachristo Greece
SKAFIDAS, Konstantinos Apos, Jan 25 1935 Sex:M Child# 3 John Skafidas Greece & Mary Panachristou Greece
SKAL, Casimir, Jul 7 1911 Sex:M Child# 3 Adam Skal Russia & Edwiga Jutofth Russia
SKAL, Gewidga, Sep 6 1909 Sex:F Child# 2 Adam Skal Russia & Gerwidga Gottoff Russia
SKELTON, Edward Charles, Mar 29 1920 Sex:M Child# 1 John C Skelton London, England & Lillian Houghton Dorchester,MA
SKIBALE, Annie, Sep 3 1911 Sex:F Child# 1 Jacob Skibale Russia & Antenina Raudemiute Russia
SKILLINGS, Everett Sinnett, Jr, May 28 1911 Sex:M Child# 1 Everett S Skillings Maine & Hattie E Stevens Manchester
SKILLINGS, Hattie E, Aug 25 1913 Sex:F Child# 2 Everett S Skillings Portland, ME & Hattie Stevens Manchester, NH
SKILLMAN, Harold Arthur, Apr 30 1923 Sex:M Child# 3 Bernard Skillman Christian Sta, VA & Winnie Bailey Nashua, NH
SKINNER, Elmer Chester, Nov 22 1899 Sex:M Child# 2 Edson M Skinner Canada & Clara B Newton S Lyndeborough, NH
SKINNER, Unknown, Sep 18 1897 Sex:M Child# 1 Edson M Skinner Newport, VT & Clara B Newton S Lyndeboro, NH Stillborn
SKINNER, Unknown, Jun 8 1907 Sex:M Child# 4 Edson M Skinner Quebec & Clara B Newton S Lyndeboro, NH
SKIOTAS, Marie, Aug 22 1910 Sex:F Child# 2 Thomas Skiotas Russia & Rasia Akasamivitzka Russia
SKIRKEY, John, Mar 28 1924 Sex:M Child# 1 Joseph Skirkey S Boston, MA & Anna Geina Lithuania
SKIRSKEY, Joseph, Mar 6 1926 Sex:M Child# 2 Joseph Skirskey S Boston, MA & Anna Geena Nashua, NH
SKLUT, Anthony, Jun 18 1913 Sex:M Child# 2 John Sklut Russia & Rosie Arasinowich Russia
SKLUT, John, Jun 18 1913 Sex:M Child# 3 John Sklut Russia & Rosie Arasinowich Russia
SKORB, Jane Doris, Mar 12 1935 Sex:F Child# 2 William Skorb Nashua, NH & Anna Ashey Hartland, VT
SKORB, Joan Claire, May 5 1933 Sex:F Child# 1 William Skorb Nashua, NH & Anna Ashley Vermont
SKORB, Patricia Doris, Dec 15 1933 Sex:F Child# 1 Stanley Skorb Nashua, NH & Juliette Forcier Hooksett, NH
SKORL, Antoni, Apr 13 1912 Sex:M Child# 5 Wojeick Skorl Russia & Anna Latives Russia
SKORL, Stanley, Jan 17 1911 Sex:M Child# 4 William Skorl Russia & Annie Latives Russia
SKORT, Julian, Dec 8 1917 Sex:M Child# 8 Wozciech Skort Russia & Annie Latwich Russia
SKROBLES, Marjorie Evangeline, Aug 18 1921 Sex:F Child# 1 John Skrobles Scranton, PA & Florence Marshall Hollis, NH
SKUITAS, Olga, Apr 25 1916 Sex:F Child# 5 John Skuitas Russia & Rosia Asazinovitch Russia
SLACK, Barbara Priscilla, Oct 8 1922 Sex:F Child# 1 John Slack Nebraska & Gertrude M Black Boston, MA
SLAMIN, Myron, May 21 1896 Sex:M Child# 2 Thomas H Slamin Natick, MA & Clara Holdbrook Concord
SLASEK, Ed Robert, Feb 22 1931 Sex:M Child# 9 Frank Slasek Poland & Sophia Kogut Poland
SLASEK, Teddy, Aug 6 1930 Sex:M Child# 7 Jacob Slasek Poland & Mary Gingle Poland
SLASK, Wanda, Feb 13 1914 Sex:F Child# 4 Frank Slask Austria & Sophia Kognt Austria
SLATE, Anna P, Jun 7 1890 Sex:F Child# 6 Clarence Slate NH & Anna P Pendergast NH
SLATE, Annie F, Aug 10 1888 Sex:F Child# 5 Clarence A Slate Londonderry & Annie Pendergast New Market, NH
SLATE, Dorothy A, Mar 23 1912 Sex:F Child# 1 Charles H Slate Londonderry, NH & Anna T McKean Dorchester, MA

SLATONIS, Nellie, Mar 1 1928 Sex:F Child# 4 William Slatonis Russia & Nellie Kibirstis Russia
SLATTERY, James Raymond, May 6 1924 Sex:M Child# 2 James Slattery Nashua, NH & Dora Ouellette Nashua, NH
SLATTERY, John Patrick, Nov 8 1902 Sex:M Child# 3 Joseph Slattery Nashua, NH & Ann O'Neil Ireland
SLATTERY, Joseph Eugene, Sep 17 1900 Sex:M Child# 2 Joseph T Slattery Nashua, NH & Ann O'Neil Ireland
SLATTERY, Marguerite J, Mar 23 1905 Sex:F Child# 4 Joseph T Slattery Nashua, NH & Ann O'Neil Ireland
SLATTERY, Marie Bessie Dora, Jan 9 1921 Sex:F Child# 1 James Slattery Groton, MA & Dora Ouillette Nashua, NH
SLATTERY, Unknown, Aug 21 1899 Sex:M Child# 1 Joseph Slattery Nashua, NH & Annie O'Neil Ireland Stillborn
SLATUNAS, Stanley, Apr 4 1916 Sex:M Child# 1 William Slatunas Russia & Nellie Slatunas Russia
SLATUNIS, Julius, Jul 1 1918 Sex:M Child# 2 William Slatunis Russia & Nellie Kebuskis Russia
SLAVASH, Edward, Oct 13 1915 Sex:M Child# 4 Frank Slavash Austria & Mary Pitkka Austria
SLAVE, Unknown, May 12 1907 Sex:M Child# 2 Urban Slave Russia & Katazina Kuchazek Russia
SLAVIN, Frances Margaret, Feb 4 1907 Sex:F Child# 1 John J Slavin St Louis, MO & Margaret Moran Nashua, NH
SLAVIN, Robert Thomas, Sep 30 1911 Sex:M Child# 2 John J Slavin St Louis, MO & Margaret Moran Nashua, NH
SLAVOSKY, Julius A, Feb 10 1909 Sex:M Child# 3 Abraham B Slavosky Russia & Sarah Sharp Russia
SLAWSBY, Abraham, Nov 16 1922 Sex:M Child# 2 Harry Slawsby Russia & Rose Belinsky Russia Stillborn
SLAWSBY, Eunice, Jan 11 1912 Sex:F Child# 4 Abraham B Slawsby Russia & Sarah Sharp Russia
SLAWSBY, Leona Pearl, Oct 18 1915 Sex:F Child# 5 Abraham B Slawsby Russia & Sarah E Sharp Russia
SLAWSBY, Unknown, Feb 26 1907 Sex:M Child# 2 Abraham B Slawsby Russia & Sarah E Sharp Russia
SLAWSKY, Bert, Jun 1 1905 Sex:M Child# 1 Abraham Slawsky Russia & Sarah Sharpe Russia
SLAYTON, Nancy, Nov 29 1934 Sex:F Child# 2 Howard Slayton Manchester, NH & Marion Marshall Milford, NH
SLEEPER, Mabel Florette, Nov 4 1917 Sex:F Child# 7 Frank W Sleeper Pelham, NH & Mary Salvas Nashua, NH
SLEVEK, Rudolph Adam, Nov 26 1927 Sex:M Child# 6 Jacob Slevek Poland & Mary Gingle Poland
SLINEY, Walter Joseph, Oct 6 1920 Sex:M Child# 4 John Sliney E Pepperell, MA & Mary Cleary Groton, MA
SLIVA, Julia, Aug 8 1913 Sex:F Child# 5 Urbin Sliva Austria & Kate Kuliazyk Austria
SLOAN, Barbara, May 18 1916 Sex:F Child# 2 William L Sloan Amherst, NH & Elen E Nelson Goffstown, NH
SLOAN, Lois Estelle, Nov 10 1932 Sex:F Child# 1 Frank Sloan Amherst, NH & Sarah Goddard England
SLOCEK, Edward Peter, Jan 6 1910 Sex:M Child# 4 Stanislaus Slocek Austria & Annie Luper Austria
SLOCOMB, Mildred Alice, Nov 8 1933 Sex:F Child# 2 Clayton Slocomb Hollis, NH & Lois Messer Merrimack, NH
SLOCUMB, Clayton Wright, Aug 21 1931 Sex:M Child# 1 Clayton W Slocumb Hollis, NH & Louise Messer Merrimack, NH
SLONAUSKY, Nathan, Apr 21 1891 Sex:M Child# 1 Morris Slonausky Russia & Mary Brozufsky Russia
SLOSCEK, Bolasof Joseph, Jun 10 1911 Sex:M Child# 5 Stanislaus Sloscek Austria & Ann Lupas Austria
SLOSEK, Felicia, Mar 25 1927 Sex:F Child# 6 Frank Slosek Poland & Sophia Kagut Poland
SLOSEK, Genieve, Mar 5 1916 Sex:F Child# 5 Frank Slosek Austria & Sophia Kogut Austria
SLOSEK, Lily, Aug 21 1923 Sex:F Child# 3 Joseph Slosek Austria & Ann Hamufa Poland
SLOSEK, Mary, Nov 18 1905 Sex:F Child# 2 Stanislaus Slosek Austria & Ann Lupor Austria
SLOSEK, Mary, Oct 18 1923 Sex:F Child# 8 Frank Slosek Poland & Sophia Kogut Poland
SLOSIK, Fred, Nov 21 1921 Sex:M Child# 2 Joseph Slosik Poland & Anna Slosik Poland
SMALL, Asbury Warren, Nov 1 1915 Sex:M Child# 1 Asbury Small Charlestown, MA & Elizabeth Brown Nashua, NH
SMALL, Asbury, Jr, Jul 18 1919 Sex:M Child# 2 Asbury Small Charlestown, MA & Elizabeth Brown Nashua, NH
SMALL, Blanche Marv'tte, Oct 13 1901 Sex:F Child#  James Small Maine & Lillian M Blackstone Maine
SMALL, Harry Waldo, Mar 19 1917 Sex:M Child# 2 Asbury Small Charlestown, MA & Elizabeth Brown Nashua, NH
SMALL, Helen, Jul 15 1899 Sex:F Child# 9 William C Small Maine & Katie G Clifford Maine
SMALL, John Albert, Jul 31 1906 Sex:M Child# 5 John A Small Limington, ME & Lillian M Warren Somersworth, NH
SMALL, Oramandel Albert, Apr 4 1930 Sex:M Child# 1 Ormandel A Small Maine & Delia Keenan Nashua, NH
SMALL, Unknown, Jun 29 1903 Sex: Child# 10 William C Small Stockton, ME & Kate G Clifford Searsport, ME
SMALLEY, Goldie Etta May, Jan 17 1892 Sex:F Child# 1 Sheridan P Smalley Maine & Estella M Rock New York
SMARDEN, Mary, Dec 1 1892 Sex:F Child# 6 James Smarden Canada & Regina Brette Canada
SMARDON, Unknown, Jan 23 1891 Sex:M Child# 5 James F Smardon Canada & Angelina Bilette Canada
SMART, Leslie Harold, Jun 19 1923 Sex:M Child# 1 Harold B Smart Davisville, NH & Ruth M Hood Hopkinton, NH
SMEITAMI, Adolfena, Mar 23 1918 Sex:F Child# 1 Frank Smeitami Austria & Victoria Klus Austria
SMELGAVITCH, Annie, Jan 29 1908 Sex:F Child# 2 George Smelgavitch Russia & Patronella Tanonkate Russia
SMELGAVITCH, Stanislawa, Dec 28 1909 Sex:F Child# 3 George Smelgavitch Russia & Petronelle Denokity Russia
SMIETANA, Bolislaw, Aug 5 1921 Sex:M Child# 3 Frank Smietana Poland & Victoria Klus Poland
SMILES, Unknown, Jun 30 1912 Sex:M Child# 1 Samuel Smiles
SMITH, Abigail G, Apr 21 1891 Sex:F Child# 1 George F Smith Nashua, NH & Hattie M Greenleaf Nashua, NH
SMITH, Albert Eaton, Jan 16 1919 Sex:M Child# 2 Albert E Smith Hudson, NH & Florence Small Stockton, ME
SMITH, Albert John, Jun 3 1892 Sex:M Child# 3 Albert Smith Nashua, NH & Mary A Houston Nashua, NH
SMITH, Alfred Edward, Nov 9 1900 Sex:M Child# 5 Thomas Smith Ireland & Ann Delaurey Ireland
SMITH, Annie E, Jan 13 1890 Sex:F Child# 2 Walter J Smith New Jersey & Mary Fornier New Brunswick
SMITH, Arthur Morris, Apr 2 1911 Sex:M Child# 4 Arthur H Smith Halifax, NS & Elsie G Robinson Somerville, MA
SMITH, Barbara Ann, Jul 21 1930 Sex:F Child# 5 Shirley R Smith Canton, ME & Helen K Bartlett Stoneham, MA
SMITH, Barbara Ann, Dec 13 1932 Sex:F Child# 9 H D Smith Hudson, NH & Blanche Greeley Londonderry, NH
SMITH, Barbara May, May 12 1910 Sex:F Child# 4 William F Smith Dennora, NY & Julia Callahan Ireland
SMITH, Beatrice Elizabeth, Oct 24 1917 Sex:F Child# 1 Samuel E Smith Amherst, NH & Bertha M Wilkins Bedford, NH
SMITH, Beatrice Hosford, Nov 21 1896 Sex:F Child# 9 James A Smith Nashua, NH & Emme J Cummings Plaistow, NH
SMITH, Beatrice M, Sep 22 1891 Sex:F Child# 1 Freeman Smith New Hampshire & Minnie Greer Nashua, NH
SMITH, Bernice Margaret, Jan 26 1897 Sex:F Child# 4 Walter J Smith Elizabeth, NJ & Mary Fournier Woodstock, NB
SMITH, Betty Elaine, Aug 28 1930 Sex:F Child# 8 Herbert Smith Hudson, NH & Blanche Greeley Londonderry, NH
SMITH, Carl Henry, Aug 28 1918 Sex:M Child# 4 Wilber Smith Strafford, NH & Adelia Shanley Keene, NH
SMITH, Catherine Elizabeth, May 22 1919 Sex:F Child# 1 Frank Smith Mass & Elizabeth Hunt Mass
SMITH, Catherine Marcella, Nov 26 1917 Sex:F Child# 1 Albert E Smith Hudson, NH & Florence H Small Stockton, ME
SMITH, Charles F, Apr 26 1895 Sex:M Child# 2 Charles E Smith Chili & Lizzie A Flanders Weare
SMITH, Charles Norman, Mar 6 1935 Sex:M Child# 2 Stanley N Smith Hill, NH & Elsie Lequin Lowell, MA

SMITH, Clara Malvina, Oct 29 1906 Sex:F Child# 1 George S Smith Middlesex, MA & Etta M Stewart Hudson, NH
SMITH, Clarence L, Jan 6 1894 Sex:M Child#  Edgar Smith Hudson, NH & Addie Austin Canada
SMITH, Clifford Franklin, Apr 23 1926 Sex:M Child# 2 Lorenzo D Smith Bennington, NH & Carrie Jones Nashua, NH
SMITH, Clyde Francis, Oct 12 1933 Sex:M Child# 2 Raymond Smith Exeter, NH & Mary McLean Sidney, NS
SMITH, Cora Lillian, Feb 26 1908 Sex:F Child# 1 Wilber F Smith Strafford, NH & Adelia Stanley Keene, NH
SMITH, David Randolph, Feb 15 1932 Sex:M Child# 2 S R Smith Reading, PA & Grace Wagner Bethel, PA
SMITH, Dolores Ann, Nov 27 1931 Sex:F Child# 1 Raymond Smith Exeter, NH & Mary McLean Nova Scotia
SMITH, Donald, Feb 14 1891 Sex:M Child# 3 George A Smith Nashua, NH & Fannie Green Ireland
SMITH, Donald Lee, Apr 28 1910 Sex:M Child# 2 Lee S Smith Burke, NY & Rose Bellen Nashua, NH
SMITH, Donald Richard, Jun 3 1929 Sex:M Child# 2 William R Smith Bridgeport, CT & Arline Munson E Pepperell, MA
SMITH, Donald Robert, Sep 24 1931 Sex:M Child# 1 Stanley Smith Hill, NH & Elsie Luquin Lowell, MA
SMITH, Donna Elvira, Sep 3 1927 Sex:F Child# 7 Herbert D Smith Hudson, NH & Blanche Greeley Londonderry, NH
SMITH, Dora May, Jul 9 1903 Sex:F Child# 1 Edward J Smith Nashua, NH & Edith Bell Porter Hudson, NH
SMITH, Doris Lillian, Jun 20 1910 Sex:F Child# 1 Don Smith Nashua, NH & Emme F Philbrick Thorntons Ferry, NH
SMITH, Doris Williams, Apr 21 1912 Sex:F Child# 2 Arthur W Smith Nashua, NH & Ethylin A Batchelder Haverhill
SMITH, Douglas Alexander, Apr 25 1929 Sex:M Child# 1 John Smith England & Jean Jackson Scotland
SMITH, Dwight Walter, Jul 17 1928 Sex:M Child# 1 Dwight Smith Springfield, VT & Marian Oban Lebanon, NH
SMITH, Earl Jewell, Feb 22 1920 Sex:M Child# 5 Wilber Smith Stafford, NH & Addie Stanley Keene, NH
SMITH, Edna Muriel, Nov 4 1909 Sex:F Child# 2 Wilbur F Smith Strafford, NH & Adelia E Shanley Keene, NH
SMITH, Edward D, Nov 7 1887 Sex:M Child# 3 Edward D Smith Conn & Emma A Melvin Conn
SMITH, Edward George, Dec 10 1919 Sex:M Child# 5 George H Smith Milford, NH & Elizabeth Brennan Wilton, NH
SMITH, Edward H, Sep 21 1890 Sex:M Child# 2 Peter Smith Smithville, VA & Ellen Scott Richmond, VA
SMITH, Edward Harvey, Jun 18 1897 Sex:M Child# 3 George F Smith Nashua, NH & Hattie M Greenleaf Nashua, NH
SMITH, Edwin Leo, Apr 27 1898 Sex:M Child# 5 Albert Smith Nashua, NH & Mary Eostice Nashua, NH
SMITH, Eileen Bernadette, Oct 23 1934 Sex:F Child# 10 Harry Smith Grand Rapids, WI & Cecile Beauregard St Albe
SMITH, Elbridge Alvah, Aug 15 1919 Sex:M Child# 1 Ellis Alvah Smith Newport, VT & Marguerite McInnis Portsmouth, NH
SMITH, Elizabeth Deering, Feb 20 1922 Sex:F Child# 2 Deering G Smith Hudson, NH & M Stevens Hamblett Nashua, NH
SMITH, Ellen Mae, Jul 15 1931 Sex:F Child# 1 David K Smith Milford, NH & Mary E Powers Vermont
SMITH, Emma, Nov 7 1896 Sex:F Child# 4 John Smith Canada & Lea Guy Canada
SMITH, Ernest Edward, May 15 1914 Sex:M Child# 5 Harry L Smith Natick, MA & Bernice Cutler Nashua, NH
SMITH, Ernestine Annette, Jun 22 1919 Sex:F Child# 1 Ernest E A Smith Canada & Anna V Bushey Andover, MA
SMITH, Evelyn, May 4 1933 Sex:F Child# 1 William Smith Lyon Mt, NY & Evelyn Mellor Waterbury, CT
SMITH, Forest Wallace, Aug 22 1900 Sex:M Child#  George H Smith
SMITH, Frances Amelia, Dec 20 1926 Sex:F Child# 5 Eugene Smith Philips, ME & Edna Campbell Mexico, ME
SMITH, Frank Charles, Feb 10 1930 Sex:M Child# 1 Frank E Smith Ossining, NY & Glendolin Mocasen Canada
SMITH, Frederick Thomas, Sep 8 1933 Sex:M Child# 1 Fred T Smith Lexington, VA & Mamie Forst Milford, NH
SMITH, George Raymond, Jan 1 1911 Sex:M Child# 8 Albert J Smith Nashua, NH & Mary A Eustace Nashua, NH
SMITH, George Waldo, Oct 19 1908 Sex:M Child# 2 Harry L Smith Milford, MA & Bernice Cutler Nashua, NH
SMITH, Gladys Blaylock, Jun 12 1920 Sex:F Child# 5 Harry J Smith Lowell, MA & Rose Watson Nashua, NH
SMITH, Gladys Mary, Apr 15 1923 Sex:F Child# 4 Eugene M Smith Philips, ME & Alua Campbell Mexico, ME
SMITH, Greta, Aug 20 1894 Sex:F Child# 3 Walter J Smith
SMITH, Guy E, Oct 21 1901 Sex:M Child# 4 Harry Smith Amherst, NH & Kate M Bills Amherst, NH
SMITH, Harold Dustin, May 25 1925 Sex:M Child# 6 Herbert D Smith Hudson, NH & Blanche Greeley Londonderry, NH
SMITH, Harold Joseph, Oct 19 1906 Sex:M Child# 7 Albert G Smith Nashua, NH & Mary A Eustace Nashua, NH
SMITH, Harry Edward, Jr, Dec 20 1897 Sex:M Child# 2 Harry E Smith Amherst & Kate Mabel Bills Amherst
SMITH, Harry Edward, Jr, Sep 14 1927 Sex:M Child# 1 Harry E Smith Nashua, NH & M Rosedosky Chelsea, MA
SMITH, Harry Edwin, Jul 15 1910 Sex:M Child# 1 George Smith Salem, NH & Lizzie Hemphill Bow, NH
SMITH, Harry Lester, Jr, May 6 1911 Sex:M Child# 3 Harry L Smith Natick, MA & Bernice Cutter Nashua, NH
SMITH, Hazel Amanda, Jan 30 1906 Sex:F Child# 1 Guy Atwell Smith Nashua, NH & Amanda M Clark Milbridge, ME
SMITH, Helen, Jan 18 1899 Sex:F Child# 7 Thomas Smith Ireland & Ann Gilhooley Ireland
SMITH, Helen, Apr 28 1914 Sex:F Child# 4 Frederick Smith Pepperell, MA & Mary Dwyer Boston, MA
SMITH, Henri, Mar 14 1893 Sex:M Child# 2 John Smith Canada & Lea Guy Canada
SMITH, Henry F, May 1 1927 Sex:M Child# 1 Henry Smith Somerville, MA & Evelyn Lorraine Nashua, NH
SMITH, James Earl, Aug 20 1909 Sex:M Child# 2 James Smith Gloucester, MA & Mae Perry Gloucester, MA
SMITH, James H, Feb 10 1889 Sex:M Child# 1 Thomas Smith Ireland & Annie Smith Ireland
SMITH, James Morrison, Jan 28 1925 Sex:M Child# 5 Eugene Smith Phillips, ME & Elma Campbell Mexico, ME
SMITH, James William, Feb 17 1934 Sex:M Child# 6 Rupert Smith Lyndeboro, NH & Annie Balmforth Oldham, England
SMITH, Jane Emma, Jun 14 1889 Sex:F Child# 2 James E Smith Mass & Mary J Stevens Mass
SMITH, Jean Frances, Aug 6 1910 Sex:F Child# 2 Ernest O Smith Hopkinton, MA & Hope M Roberts Boston, MA
SMITH, Jeanette Eva, Sep 18 1910 Sex:F Child# 1 Charles E Smith England & Jennie Baker Nashua, NH
SMITH, Jeffrey Richard, Nov 6 1928 Sex:M Child# 1 Jeffrey Smith W Roxbury, MA & Mary Jackson Boston, MA
SMITH, Jessie Elizabeth, Jun 7 1912 Sex:F Child# 4 Harry Lester Smith Natick, MA & Bernice Cutter Nashua, NH
SMITH, Joan Ann, Jan 2 1935 Sex:F Child# 1 George R Smith Nashua, NH & Anna Batura Nashua, NH
SMITH, John Clark, Nov 4 1910 Sex:M Child# 3 Guy A Smith Nashua, NH & Amanda Clark Millbridge, ME
SMITH, John Richard, Feb 21 1932 Sex:M Child# 4 Ellis Smith Newport, VT & Margaret McInnis Portsmouth, NH
SMITH, Katherine Helen, Jul 31 1934 Sex:F Child# 4 Harry E Smith Nashua, NH & Amonica Rosedosky Chelsea, MA
SMITH, Kenneth, Dec 23 1926 Sex:M Child# 3 John J Smith California & Lilly Fillmany Germany
SMITH, Kenneth Gerry, Jul 30 1908 Sex:M Child# 1 Leon S Smith Burke, NY & Rose Bellan Nashua, NH
SMITH, Lea Blanche, Dec 4 1894 Sex:F Child# 3 John Smith Canada & Lea Gay Canada
SMITH, Leona Ruth, Apr 11 1905 Sex:F Child# 2 William T Smith NY & Julia Callahan Ireland
SMITH, Levi A, Jul 27 1889 Sex:M Child# 2 Levi A Smith Nashua, NH & Johanna Ryan Ireland
SMITH, Lillian Marguerite, Mar 24 1910 Sex:F Child# 1 Harry Smith St John, NB & Elizabeth Johnson St John, NB
SMITH, Llewellyn D, Apr 18 1898 Sex:M Child# 3 Herbert L Smith Hudson, NH & Lottie S DeWolfe Charlestown, MA

SMITH, Louis Hormiodas, Dec 18 1891 Sex:M Child# 1 John Smith Canada & Lea Guey Canada
SMITH, Lucille, Jul 3 1909 Sex:F Child# 1 Guy A Smith Burke, NY & Lelia B Hanks Lincoln, VT
SMITH, Lucille, Feb 11 1924 Sex:F Child# 1 Lorenzo Smith Antrim, NH & Carrie Jones Nashua, NH
SMITH, Mabel, Dec 31 1890 Sex:F Child# 2 Albert Smith Nashua, NH & Mary Housten Nashua, NH
SMITH, Mabel Gertrude, Nov 14 1903 Sex:F Child# 5 Harry E Smith Amherst & Kate M Bills Amherst
SMITH, Marcella Mary, Dec 2 1935 Sex:F Child# 1 Joseph Smith Poland & Patric Baranauski Nashua, NH
SMITH, Marguerite, Feb 11 1921 Sex:F Child# 1 Girard Smith Canada & Marie St Laurent Canada
SMITH, Marguerite Winifred, Jan 25 1930 Sex:F Child# 3 Lorenzo D Smith Antrim, NH & Carrie H Jones Nashua, NH
SMITH, Maria, Mar 2 1889 Sex:F Child# 2 Frank E Smith Nashua, NH & Mary Carry Ireland
SMITH, Marion Gladys, Feb 29 1892 Sex:F Child# 2 Walter J Smith Elizabethport, NJ & Mary Fournier Woodstock, NH
SMITH, Marion Hinckley, Oct 20 1919 Sex:F Child# 1 Alfred W Smith Dorchester, MA & Mabel A Rossister
SMITH, Marion Louisa, Feb 3 1900 Sex:F Child# 4 H L Smith Hudson, NH & Lottie DeWolfe Charlestown, MA
SMITH, Marion Plathe, Jul 16 1918 Sex:F Child# 1 John Claude Smith North Carolina & Marguerite Haskins Aldrich
SMITH, Marion W, Feb 28 1922 Sex:F Child# 1 Robert Smith Gardner, MA & Sliney Borey Maldenville, MA
SMITH, Marjorie Ada, Jan 5 1926 Sex:F Child# 2 Edwin W Smith Nashua, NH & Mina C Woods Greenfield, NH
SMITH, Marjorie Joyce, Aug 4 1935 Sex:F Child# 10 Herb D Smith Hudson, NH & Blanche Greeley Londonderry, NH
SMITH, Mark Irving, Mar 11 1912 Sex:M Child# 2 Harry T Smith Nashua, NH & Rene Irma Watson Nashua, NH
SMITH, Mary, Nov 2 1911 Sex:F Child# 1 John Smith Austria & Veronica Pippa Austria
SMITH, Mary, May 19 1934 Sex:F Child# 1 George Francis Smith Andover, VT & Alice Leonard Rutland, VT
SMITH, Mary Ethel, Jun 5 1891 Sex:F Child# 3 Frank E Smith Nashua, NH & Mary Carey Ireland
SMITH, Mildred Genevieve, Aug 26 1907 Sex:F Child# 3 William Smith Plattsburg, NY & Julia Callahan Ireland
SMITH, Minnie Myrtle, Dec 6 1899 Sex:F Child# 2 Marion W Smith Ind & Adelle Fulton Fletcher, VT
SMITH, Myrtle Beverly, Nov 28 1927 Sex:F Child# 4 John J Smith California & Lilly Fellmann Germany
SMITH, Nedra Isabel, Oct 23 1907 Sex:F Child# 1 Lester Smith Milford, MA & Bernice Cutter Nashua, NH
SMITH, Nellie, Apr 15 1906 Sex:F Child# 4 Fred Smith Woburn, MA & Lizzie Coy Manchester, NH
SMITH, Patricia Frances, Dec 11 1925 Sex:F Child# 3 Elias S Smith Newport, VT & Marg McGeinvis Portsmouth, NH
SMITH, Patrick, Jun 18 1890 Sex:M Child# 2 Thomas Smith Ireland & Ann Gillooby Ireland
SMITH, Perley, Sep 27 1893 Sex:M Child# 4 George A Smith Peterboro & Fannie Greene Ireland
SMITH, Raymond Fowler, Jun 16 1913 Sex:M Child# 1 Fred R Smith New Boston, NB & Jennie Fowler Smithtown, NB
SMITH, Richard Payne, Jul 26 1922 Sex:M Child# 4 Albert E Smith Hudson, NH & Florence H Small Stockton, ME
SMITH, Robert, Sep 19 1927 Sex:M Child# 4 Shirley Smith Bath, ME & Helen Bartlett Stoneham, MA
SMITH, Robert Curtis, Sep 30 1922 Sex:M Child# 1 Samuel D Smith Amherst, NH & Ruth E Curtis Greenwood, MA
SMITH, Robert Edward, Jan 11 1924 Sex:M Child# 2 Ellis A Smith Newport, VT & Margaret McGinnis Portsmouth, NH
SMITH, Robert Edward, Nov 27 1928 Sex:M Child# 2 Henry Smith Somerville, MA & Eveline Lorraine Nashua, NH
SMITH, Robert Greeley, Feb 20 1922 Sex:M Child# 1 Deering G Smith Hudson, NH & M Stevens Hamblett Nashua, NH
SMITH, Robert Homer, Jul 15 1909 Sex:M Child# 1 Walter E Smith Lawrence, MA & Esther F Harrington Hancock, NH
SMITH, Robert William, Jan 11 1924 Sex:M Child# 3 Eric Lewis Smith Germany & Elizabeth Colburn Kingston, NY
SMITH, Roland Bartlett, Jul 29 1935 Sex:M Child# 6 Shirley R Smith Canton, ME & Helen Bartlett E Stoneham, ME
SMITH, Rose Ann, Mar 27 1889 Sex:F Child# 1 Albert Smith Nashua, NH & Mary A Houston Nashua, NH
SMITH, Ruth, Nov 17 1891 Sex:F Child# 1 Albin M Smith Nashua, NH & Effie D A Elkins N Troy, VT
SMITH, Ruth Harriet, Jan 28 1915 Sex:F Child# 3 Wilbur F Smith Stafford, NH & Adelia Shanley Keene, NH
SMITH, Ruth Lillian, Apr 14 1903 Sex:F Child# 6 Albert J Smith NH & Mary A Eustace NH
SMITH, Shirley, Aug 27 1926 Sex:F Child# 3 Guy A Smith Burke, NY & Lelia Hanks Lincoln, VT
SMITH, Shirley, Aug 8 1931 Sex:F Child# 2 Jeffrey P Smith W Roxbury, MA & Mary Jackson W Roxbury, MA
SMITH, Tena Margaret, Aug 5 1922 Sex:F Child# 1 Edwin W Smith NH & Vina C Woods NH
SMITH, Thelma Muriel, Mar 17 1914 Sex:F Child# 4 Harry J Smith Lowell, MA & Rose I Watson Nashua, NH
SMITH, Thomas George, Jul 4 1891 Sex:M Child# 3 Thomas J Smith Ireland & Annie Gilhooley Ireland
SMITH, Unknown, Jan 6 1887 Sex:M Child# 1 Frank E Smith Nashua, NH & Mary H Ireland
SMITH, Unknown, Jul 20 1888 Sex:F Child# 5 William F Smith Nashua, NH & Ada M Bells Hollis, NH
SMITH, Unknown, Jun 14 1890 Sex:M Child# 2 Malcomb W Smith Canada & Eva M Whitman Canada
SMITH, Unknown, Apr 1 1892 Sex:F Child# 1 Henry B Smith Springfield, MA & Hattie M Wright Nashua, NH
SMITH, Unknown, Dec 5 1892 Sex:M Child# 4 Frank Smith Nashua, NH & Mary Carey Ireland
SMITH, Unknown, Jan 11 1893 Sex: Child# 3 Peter Smith Virginia & Ellen Richmond, VA
SMITH, Unknown, Mar 5 1893 Sex:M Child# 2 George F Smith Nashua, NH & Hattie M Greenleaf Nashua, NH
SMITH, Unknown, May 14 1893 Sex:M Child# 1 Everett U Smith Swans Isle, ME & Lizzie M Case Nashua, NH
SMITH, Unknown, Oct 18 1893 Sex:F Child# 1 Samuel P Smith Bingam, ME & Alice Sherbert Skowhegan, ME
SMITH, Unknown, Jan 24 1894 Sex:F Child# 8 Elbridge G Smith Burke, NY & Amy Babcock Alburgh, NY
SMITH, Unknown, Jun 27 1894 Sex:F Child# 2 Henry B Smith Springfield, MA & Hattie M Wright Nashua, NH
SMITH, Unknown, Jul 30 1894 Sex:M Child# 4 Peter Smith Richmond, VA & Ellen VA Colored
SMITH, Unknown, Aug 31 1894 Sex:F Child# 3 Herbert Smith Royalston, VT & Maria Buzzell Dayton, ME
SMITH, Unknown, Apr 2 1895 Sex:F Child# 5 F X Smith Nashua, NH & Mary Carry Ireland Stillborn
SMITH, Unknown, Jun 9 1895 Sex:F Child# 2 Malcolm W Smith Canada & Minnie Lynn Sweden
SMITH, Unknown, Aug 20 1897 Sex:F Child# 4 Herbert E Smith Royalton, VT & Maria J Busiel Dayton, ME
SMITH, Unknown, Jul 22 1898 Sex:M Child# 1 Alfred G Smith Bingham, ME & Edith J Bradeen Charlestown, MA
SMITH, Unknown, Feb 18 1899 Sex:M Child# 9 Elbridge G Smith Burke, NY & Amy Babcock Albany, VT
SMITH, Unknown, Oct 30 1899 Sex:F Child# 1 Murton Smith NY & Ada Eaton Nashua, NH
SMITH, Unknown, Nov 16 1899 Sex:M Child# 3 Harry E Smith NH & Kate M Bills NH
SMITH, Unknown, Oct 1 1900 Sex:F Child# 2 Merton E Smith Nashua, NH & Ada Eaton Nashua, NH
SMITH, Unknown, Feb 3 1902 Sex:M Child# 2 Merton Smith Burke, NY & Ada C Eaton Nashua, NH Stillborn
SMITH, Unknown, Jul 19 1902 Sex:M Child# 5 Levi A Smith Nashua, NH & Johanna Ryan Ireland Stillborn
SMITH, Unknown, Oct 4 1905 Sex:M Child# 6 Harry Edward Smith Amherst, NH & Kate M Bills Amherst, NH
SMITH, Unknown, Jan 12 1907 Sex:F Child# 7 Harry Edw Smith Amherst, NH & Mabel Kate Bills Amherst, NH
SMITH, Unknown, Oct 9 1910 Sex:M Child# 9 Harry E Smith Amherst, NH & Catherine M Bills Amherst, NH

SMITH, Unknown, Apr 20 1911 Sex:F Child# 1 John Smith Russia & Mary Asmanskutie Russia
SMITH, Unknown, Dec 18 1912 Sex:F Child# 5 William T Smith Danvora, NY & Julia Callahan Ireland
SMITH, Unknown, May 4 1916 Sex:M Child# 1 Irvin A Smith Hudson, NH & Bertha Shatury Hudson, NH
SMITH, Unknown, Jun 23 1919 Sex:M Child# 1 (No Parents Listed)
SMITH, Unknown, Nov 4 1920 Sex:M Child# 3 Albert E Smith Hudson, NH & Florence H Small Stockton Sp, ME
SMITH, Vernon Charles, Oct 29 1925 Sex:M Child# 2 John J Smith California & Lily Fillman Germany
SMITH, Vinnie Ivan, Nov 11 1935 Sex:M Child# 3 Albert E Smith Fort Kent, ME & Violet Burgin Belfast, ME
SMITH, Walter C, Dec 27 1894 Sex:M Child# 4 Levi A Smith Nashua, NH & Johannah Ryan Ireland
SMITH, Wilfred Austin, Apr 21 1911 Sex:M Child# 2 Guy Smith Burke, NY & Lela Hanks Lincoln, VT
SMITH, William Newton, Aug 2 1928 Sex:M Child# 1 Newton W Smith Londonderry, NH & Christine Doherty Pelham, NH
SMITH, William Reginald, Jan 30 1917 Sex:M Child# 6 William T Smith Dannamora, NY & Julia Callahan Ireland
SMITH, Winnifred May, Jul 17 1924 Sex:F Child# 1 Edgar Smith
SMOLAK, Anna Jane, Oct 4 1929 Sex:F Child# 3 George Smolak New York, NY & Frances J Harris Kearsarge, MI
SMOLAK, George Robert, Aug 26 1928 Sex:M Child# 2 George Smolak New York, NY & Frances J Harris Kearsarge, MI
SMULKIS, Peter, Apr 30 1912 Sex:M Child# 2 Peter Smulkis Russia & Helen Silekite Russia
SMULKIS, Petrona, Aug 11 1914 Sex:F Child# 3 Peter Smulkis Russia & Helen Shelerka Russia
SMYENIOS, Unknown, Oct 5 1922 Sex:F Child# 1 Christos Smyenios Greece & Evangele Kortzis Greece
SMYRNIAS, Constantine, Apr 11 1931 Sex:M Child# 2 Louis Smyrnias Greece & Christine Koltaidas Greece
SMYRNIOS, Unknown, Oct 2 1926 Sex:F Child# 2 Christos Smyrnios Greece & Evangeline Kortzis Greece
SNEY, Unknown, Sep 22 1891 Sex:F Child# 1 Joseph Sney Nashua, NH & Florentine Morisette Canada
SNOW, Albert William, Nov 22 1929 Sex:M Child# 1 Nathan Snow Harbor Grace, NF & Isabel Harwood Newfoundland
SNOW, Barbara Elaine, Jun 1 1927 Sex:F Child# 3 W A D Snow Halifax, NS & E Chamberlain Nashua, NH
SNOW, Bernice Ruth, Sep 25 1920 Sex:F Child# 9 Warwick Snow England & Edith E Evans England
SNOW, Charles Richard, Aug 2 1924 Sex:M Child# 2 Lloyd H Snow Lowell, MA & Bertha Horne N Glascow, NH
SNOW, Dorothy Irene, May 27 1906 Sex:F Child# 1 Harry B Snow Kankakee, IL & Olive Bowles Windham, NH
SNOW, Dorothy Mae, Dec 11 1935 Sex:F Child# 3 Nathaniel Snow Harbor Grace, NF & Isabel Harwood Newfoundland
SNOW, Edith Bessie, Oct 12 1908 Sex:F Child# 3 William Snow England & Edith Evans England
SNOW, Florence Alma, Apr 14 1910 Sex:F Child# 4 William Snow England & Edith Evans England
SNOW, Fred Donald, Oct 18 1904 Sex:M Child# 2 Fred M Snow Nashua, NH & Grace V Holt Nashua, NH
SNOW, Herbert William, Aug 21 1911 Sex:M Child# 5 William Snow England & Edith Evans England
SNOW, Isabelle Louise, Feb 15 1933 Sex:F Child# 2 Nathaniel Snow Newfoundland & Isabelle Harwood Newfoundland
SNOW, Janet, Jan 22 1928 Sex:F Child# 1 H Parsons Snow Harbor Grace, NF & Laura E Dean New London, NH
SNOW, Jean Audry, Jun 25 1922 Sex:F Child# 3 Andrew L Snow
SNOW, Jeannette Ethel, Dec 1 1906 Sex:F Child# 2 Warwick Snow England & Edith Evans England
SNOW, Joan Marjorie, Mar 24 1930 Sex:F Child# 4 Andrew Snow Rhode Island & Hazel Gleave Lawrence, MA
SNOW, John, Jun 25 1926 Sex:M Child# 2 William A Snow Halifax, NS & E Chamberlain Nashua, NH
SNOW, June, Mar 3 1917 Sex:F Child# 7 Warwick Snow Devonshire, England & Edith Hester Evans Suffolk, England
SNOW, Kenneth Lawrence, Sep 11 1934 Sex:M Child# 1 Roy E Snow Nashua, NH & Mae Strait Lanett, AL
SNOW, Margaret Lillian, May 8 1915 Sex:F Child# 6 William Snow England & Edith Edmunds England
SNOW, Percy Louis, Sep 15 1918 Sex:M Child# 8 Warwick Snow England & Edith Evans England
SNOW, Phyllia Arline, Dec 1 1928 Sex:F Child# 4 William D Snow Nova Scotia & E M Chamberlain Nashua, NH
SNOW, Phyllis, Oct 13 1900 Sex:F Child# 1 Fred M Snow Nashua, NH & Grace B Holt Nashua, NH
SNOW, Robert Arthur, Oct 20 1926 Sex:M Child# 3 Lloyd H Snow Lowell, MA & Bertha E Horne Glasgow, NS
SNOW, Roy Evans, Sep 27 1905 Sex:M Child# 1 Warwick Snow England & Edith Evans England
SNUILKIZ, Elena, Aug 2 1913 Sex:F Child# 3 Peter Snuilkiz Russia & Elena Sileikite Russia
SNYDER, Leon, Dec 13 1919 Sex:M Child# 3 Leon J Snyder Burlington, VT & Ruby Pearl Holbrook Nashua, NH
SOBOLMICH, Unknown, Apr 10 1914 Sex:M Child# 1 Anthony Sobolmich Russia & Amelia Gassutis Russia Stillborn
SOLOMAN, Louise K, Jun 17 1912 Sex:F Child# 1 George S Soloman Manchester, NH & Marie N Featherstone Nashua, NH
SOMERVILLE, George, May 14 1898 Sex:M Child# 1 John Somerville Ireland & Mary Earley Ireland
SOMERVILLE, Unknown, Jan 1 1912 Sex:M Child# 9 John Somerville Ireland & Mary Earley Ireland
SOMES, Marjorie Mabel, Dec 4 1929 Sex:F Child# 1 Elmer Somes Edgecomb, ME & Mildred Robbins Pepperell, MA
SOMKOSEKA, Unknown, Mar 15 1902 Sex:F Child# 1 Frank Somkoseka Poland & Carrie Paskofse Poland
SONBELA, Peter, Jun 14 1913 Sex:M Child# 2 Joseph Sonbela Russia & Aniella Kourta Russia
SONYENIOS, Unknown, Feb 19 1924 Sex:F Child# 2 Christos Sonyenios Greece & Evangele Kerzes Greece
SORAJIAN, Unknown, Jul 1 1901 Sex:F Child# 4 Audis Sorajian Harpoot & Owsenda Tevsosian Casaria Stillborn
SOREAULT, Joseph George H, Aug 10 1905 Sex:M Child# 10 Joseph Soreault Canada & Hermine Grenier Canada
SORKES, Antones, Jun 13 1916 Sex:M Child# 1 Antones Sorkes Russia & Karze Koiclis Russia
SOUCI, Joseph Albert, Mar 25 1903 Sex:M Child# 5 Joseph Souci Canada & Sophie Anctil Canada
SOUCI, Joseph Wilfred, Mar 2 1893 Sex:M Child# 6 Joseph Souci Canada & Elise Loranger Canada
SOUCY, Albert, Nov 2 1920 Sex:M Child# 9 Andre Soucy Canada & Anne Mignault Canada
SOUCY, Albert Ernest, May 3 1931 Sex:M Child# 5 Arthur Joseph Soucy Nashua, NH & Rose M Boucher Fall River, MA
SOUCY, Alexander Omer, Aug 1 1916 Sex:M Child# 15 Didier Soucy Canada & Delvina Paradis Canada
SOUCY, Alfred, May 24 1909 Sex:M Child# 3 Joseph Soucy Canada & Alexina Simard Canada
SOUCY, Alfred Roger, Mar 13 1913 Sex:M Child# 1 George Soucy Canada & Cecilia Ouellette Canada
SOUCY, Alfred Romeo, May 1 1907 Sex:M Child# 2 Joseph Soucy Canada & Alexina Simard Canada
SOUCY, Alma Beatrice, Nov 24 1905 Sex:F Child# 8 Didier Soucy Canada & Delvina Paradis Canada
SOUCY, Anita Lucille, Apr 5 1915 Sex:F Child# 14 Didier Soucy Canada & Delvina Paradis Canada
SOUCY, Anita Rachel, Mar 22 1923 Sex:F Child# 11 Andrew Soucy Canada & Anne Migneault Canada
SOUCY, Ann Evelyn, Aug 28 1932 Sex:F Child# 1 Henry A Soucy Nashua, NH & Cecilia Cleary Nashua, NH
SOUCY, Anne Marie Rita, Jan 1 1919 Sex:F Child# 3 Charles Soucy Canada & Elmire Parent Canada
SOUCY, Armand Henry, Oct 8 1904 Sex:M Child# 1 Joseph Soucy Canada & Alexina Simard Canada
SOUCY, Armand Roger, Jun 15 1918 Sex:M Child# 7 Andre Soucy Canada & Marie A Mignault Canada
SOUCY, Arthur Albert, Dec 7 1910 Sex:M Child# 2 Xavier Soucy Canada & Laura Soucy Canada

SOUCY, Arthur Ronald, Jan 4 1928 Sex:M Child# 2 Arthur Soucy Canada & Viola Gaudette Hudson, MA
SOUCY, Beatrice Bertina, Dec 30 1902 Sex:F Child# 6 Didire Soucy Canada & Delphine Paradis Canada
SOUCY, Bernadette, Apr 3 1910 Sex:F Child# 11 Didier Soucy Canada & Delvina Paradis Canada
SOUCY, Blanche Alberta, Dec 26 1927 Sex:F Child# 9 Auguste Soucy Canada & Rose A Hudon Canada
SOUCY, Blanche Annette, May 31 1918 Sex:F Child# 3 Thomas Soucy Canada & Elise Lepage Canada
SOUCY, Blanche R, Feb 8 1909 Sex:F Child# 1 Andre Soucy Canada & Marianne Mignault Canada
SOUCY, Camille Euclide, Apr 24 1924 Sex:M Child# 5 Pierre Soucy Nashua, NH & Alvine Landry Canada
SOUCY, Cecile Marie Louise, Nov 23 1918 Sex:F Child# 4 Joseph Soucy Canada & Alexina Simard Canada
SOUCY, Charles Adelard, May 30 1913 Sex:M Child# 3 F X Soucy Canada & Laura Raby Cambridge, MA
SOUCY, Claire Florence, Nov 6 1933 Sex:F Child# 7 Arthur J Soucy Nashua, NH & Rose Boucher Fall River, MA
SOUCY, Della Yvonne, Jun 10 1935 Sex:F Child# 8 Arthur J Soucy Nashua, NH & Rose M Boucher Fall River, MA
SOUCY, Diana Lucille, Aug 19 1920 Sex:F Child# 3 Pierre Soucy Nashua, NH & Alvine Landry Canada
SOUCY, Donald Arthur, Jun 1 1933 Sex:M Child# 1 John D Soucy Wilton, NH & Bertha Pelletier Greenville, NH
SOUCY, Dorothy, Sep 25 1923 Sex:F Child# 6 Thomas Soucy Canada & M A Berube Canada
SOUCY, Edward Emile, Oct 4 1923 Sex:M Child# 4 Emile Soucy Canada & Blanche Bedard Nashua, NH
SOUCY, Ella Adeline, Feb 14 1927 Sex:F Child# 4 Arthur J Soucy Nashua, NH & Marie R Boucher Fall River, MA
SOUCY, Emelie Anna, Nov 21 1898 Sex:F Child# 3 Andre Soucy Canada & Emelie Arsenault Canada
SOUCY, Emile, Nov 4 1892 Sex:M Child# 1 Joseph Soucy Canada & Sophie Anctil Canada
SOUCY, Euzebe L, Sep 21 1899 Sex:M Child# 4 Dedie Soucy Canada & Delvina Paradis Canada
SOUCY, Eva Laura, Mar 20 1922 Sex:F Child# 10 Andrew Soucy Canada & M A Migneault Canada
SOUCY, Gerard, Aug 13 1918 Sex:M Child# 2 Pierre Soucy Nashua, NH & Alvine Landry Canada
SOUCY, Germaine Cecile, Apr 26 1913 Sex:F Child# 2 Auguste Soucy Canada & Rosanna Hudon Canada
SOUCY, Gertrude, Jul 28 1907 Sex:F Child# 8 Didier Soucy Canada & Delvina Paradis Canada
SOUCY, Henri David, Jul 15 1901 Sex:M Child# 13 Alphonse Soucy Canada & Odelie Caron Canada
SOUCY, Henry Raymond, Sep 18 1922 Sex:M Child# 4 Pierre Soucy Nashua, NH & Alvine Landry Canada
SOUCY, J Alfred Nor Alphege, Sep 26 1915 Sex:M Child# 2 Thomas Soucy Canada & M Anna Berube Canada
SOUCY, J Alfred Romeo, Oct 10 1914 Sex:M Child# 4 Francois X Soucy Canada & Laura Raby Boston, MA
SOUCY, J Romeo Lionel, Dec 26 1913 Sex:M Child# 2 Joseph Soucy Canada & Annie Viel Canada
SOUCY, Janine Viola, Jun 26 1931 Sex:F Child# 1 Ralph Soucy Nashua, NH & Jeanne Mailloux Canada
SOUCY, Jeanne d'Arc, Jan 22 1916 Sex:F Child# 5 Andre Soucy Canada & Anne Mignault Canada
SOUCY, Jeanne D'Arc Cecile, Aug 28 1920 Sex:F Child# 4 Thomas Soucy Canada & Elise Lepage Canada
SOUCY, Jeannette, Apr 20 1922 Sex:F Child# 3 Joseph C Soucy Canada & Clara Blain Nashua, NH
SOUCY, Joan Barbara, Sep 11 1933 Sex:F Child# 1 Henry Soucy Boston, MA & Anna Brady Nashua, NH
SOUCY, Jos Benj Raymond, Nov 19 1917 Sex:M Child# 16 Didier Soucy Canada & Delvina Paradis Canada
SOUCY, Jos Ronald Raoul, Feb 8 1933 Sex:M Child# 2 Raoul Soucy Nashua, NH & Jean Mayou Canada
SOUCY, Joseph, Oct 26 1903 Sex:M Child# 7 Andre Soucy Canada & Amelie Arseneau Canada
SOUCY, Joseph Adelard, Dec 5 1893 Sex:M Child# 1 Joseph Soucy Canada & Amanda Dufour Canada
SOUCY, Joseph Andre, Jr, Dec 11 1926 Sex:M Child# 14 Andre Soucy Canada & Anna Migneault Canada
SOUCY, Joseph Charles Rob, Apr 18 1916 Sex:M Child# 2 George Soucy Canada & Cecelia Ouellette Canada
SOUCY, Joseph E, Jan 15 1896 Sex:M Child# 2 Andre Soucy Canada & Emelie Arseneau Canada
SOUCY, Joseph E, Nov 4 1900 Sex:M Child# 5 Dedie Soucy Canada & Delvina Paradis Canada
SOUCY, Joseph Francis, Mar 9 1892 Sex:M Child# 2 Dominique Soucy Canada & Palmyre Bourgouin Canada
SOUCY, Joseph Gerard, Sep 29 1915 Sex:M Child# 4 Ernest Soucy Canada & Virginie Bilodeau Canada
SOUCY, Joseph Jean Henri, Oct 29 1900 Sex:M Child# 1 Jean Soucy Canada & Clara Levesque Canada
SOUCY, Joseph L, Aug 23 1896 Sex:M Child# 2 Dedier Soucy Canada & Delvina Paradis Canada
SOUCY, Joseph Leo, Jun 6 1911 Sex:M Child# 2 Ernest Soucy Canada & Virginie Bilodeau Canada
SOUCY, Joseph Leo A, Sep 28 1903 Sex:M Child# 2 Demetrius Soucy Canada & Clorilda Chouinard Canada
SOUCY, Joseph Lionel, Sep 17 1916 Sex:M Child# 2 Thomas Soucy Canada & Elise Lepage Canada
SOUCY, Joseph Paul L, Mar 6 1919 Sex:M Child# 2 Arthur Soucy Canada & Alice Pigeon Canada
SOUCY, Joseph Raoul, Mar 5 1912 Sex:M Child# 3 Andre Soucy Canada & Anne Migneault Canada
SOUCY, Joseph Robert Xavier, May 5 1917 Sex:M Child# 3 Thomas Soucy Canada & Marie Anna Berube Canada
SOUCY, Joseph Roger, Feb 12 1913 Sex:M Child# 2 J C Soucy Canada & Clara Blain Nashua, NH
SOUCY, Laurier, Feb 17 1917 Sex:M Child# 6 Andre Soucy Canada & M Migneault Canada
SOUCY, Leon, Feb 27 1902 Sex:M Child# 3 Arthur Soucy Canada & Adele Bastille Canada
SOUCY, Leon, Mar 23 1917 Sex:M Child# 1 Pierre Soucy Nashua, NH & Alvine Landry Canada
SOUCY, Loretta Clara, May 7 1911 Sex:F Child# 1 Joseph C Soucy Canada & Clara Blain Nashua, NH
SOUCY, Louis Ernest, Oct 26 1920 Sex:M Child# 4 Thomas E Soucy Canada & Marie Anna Burreby Canada
SOUCY, Louis Helmeric, Nov 5 1906 Sex:M Child# 9 Andre Soucy Canada & Emelie Arseneau Canada
SOUCY, Lucille, Feb 8 1917 Sex:F Child# 2 Charles Soucy Canada & Elmire Parent Canada
SOUCY, Luck Bertrand, Nov 14 1925 Sex:M Child# 1 Luck Soucy Canada & Josephine Beaulieu Canada
SOUCY, M Jeanne Madeline, May 5 1913 Sex:F Child# 13 Didier Soucy Canada & Delvina Paradis Canada
SOUCY, M Louise Alice, Oct 30 1893 Sex:F Child# 3 Dominigue Soucy Canada & Palmyre Bourgouin Canada
SOUCY, M Odelie Germaine, Jul 17 1913 Sex:F Child# 3 Ernest Soucy Nashua, NH & Virginie Bilodeau Canada
SOUCY, M Rose Rachelle, Oct 4 1914 Sex:F Child# 1 Thomas Soucy Canada & Marie Anna Berube Canada
SOUCY, Marguerite Lucille, Nov 14 1912 Sex:F Child# 1 Joseph Soucy Canada & Anna Viel Canada
SOUCY, Marie, Sep 5 1919 Sex:F Child# 1 Arthur Soucy Nashua, NH & Rose Boucher Fall River, MA
SOUCY, Marie, Jan 5 1920 Sex:F Child# 1 Arthur Soucy Canada & Regina Beaulieu Canada Stillborn
SOUCY, Marie, Sep 19 1927 Sex:F Child# 5 Arthur Soucy Canada & Alice R Pigeon Canada
SOUCY, Marie A, May 1 1895 Sex:F Child# 1 Dedier Soucy Canada & Delvina Paradis Canada
SOUCY, Marie A, Oct 12 1897 Sex:F Child# 3 Dedie Soucy Canada & Delvina Paradis Canada
SOUCY, Marie A B, Sep 1 1902 Sex:F Child# 2 Jean Soucy Canada & Clara Levesque Canada
SOUCY, Marie Alice, Jun 29 1895 Sex:F Child# 2 Joseph Soucy Canada & Sophie Auctil Canada
SOUCY, Marie Alice, May 1 1902 Sex:F Child# 1 Charles Soucy Canada & Florida Chouinard Canada

SOUCY, Marie Annie, Jan 4 1897 Sex:F Child# 1 Ludger Soucy Canada & Alexina Bourgouin Canada
SOUCY, Marie Carmel, Sep 4 1919 Sex:F Child# 8 Andre Soucy Canada & M A Mignault Canada
SOUCY, Marie D, May 25 1900 Sex:F Child# 4 Andre Soucy Canada & Emelie Arseneault Canada
SOUCY, Marie Eva, Mar 14 1905 Sex:F Child# 3 Jean Soucy Canada & Clara Levesque Canada
SOUCY, Marie Germaine A, Sep 30 1908 Sex:F Child# 1 Didier Soucy Canada & Delvina Paradis Canada
SOUCY, Marie Jeanne Alice, Jan 3 1911 Sex:F Child# 1 August Soucy Canada & Rose A Hudon Canada
SOUCY, Marie Jeanne Alice, Jan 3 1912 Sex:F Child# 1 Auguste Soucy Canada & Rose Anna Hudon Canada
SOUCY, Marie Lorette, Jun 17 1916 Sex:F Child# 1 Charles Soucy Canada & Elmire Parent Canada
SOUCY, Marie Julietta A, Sep 2 1906 Sex:F Child# 4 Jean Soucy Canada & Clara Levesque Canada
SOUCY, Marie M Y, Aug 23 1900 Sex:F Child# 2 Arthur Soucy Canada & Adele Bastille Canada
SOUCY, Marie R Iva Rita, Oct 14 1920 Sex:F Child# 3 George L Soucy Canada & Cecilia Ouellette Canada
SOUCY, Marie Rose Beatrice, Jan 10 1919 Sex:F Child# 6 Auguste Soucy Canada & Rose Anna Hudon Canada
SOUCY, Marie Therese, Oct 25 1925 Sex:F Child# 13 Andrew Soucy Canada & M A Vigneault Canada
SOUCY, Martha Cecelia, Aug 31 1926 Sex:F Child# 4 Arthur Soucy Canada & Alice Pigeon Canada
SOUCY, Mary, Jul 19 1935 Sex:F Child# 2 Paul Soucy Nashua, NH & Mary St Pierre St Anne, NB
SOUCY, Mary Ann Sylvia, Jul 9 1935 Sex:F Child# 1 Roger Soucy Nashua, NH & Jeannette LaRose Canada
SOUCY, Mary Lorraine Virgin, May 19 1934 Sex:F Child# 1 Leo Soucy Nashua, NH & Germaine Cloutier Canada
SOUCY, Monica, Dec 11 1927 Sex:F Child# 4 Charles Soucy Canada & Elmire Parent Canada
SOUCY, Noella Leda, Dec 24 1926 Sex:F Child# 2 Luke Soucy Canada & Josephine Beaulieu Canada
SOUCY, Normand, Mar 24 1924 Sex:M Child# 12 Andre Soucy Canada & M Anna Mignault Canada
SOUCY, Paul Emile, Feb 21 1910 Sex:M Child# 1 Ernest Soucy Canada & Eugenie Bilodeau Canada
SOUCY, Paul Raymond, Mar 6 1922 Sex:M Child# 5 Thomas Soucy Sandown, NH & Eunice Hinckley Concord, NH
SOUCY, Paul Roger, Aug 4 1935 Sex:M Child# 1 (No Parents Listed)
SOUCY, Pierre, May 18 1894 Sex:M Child# 1 Andre Soucy Canada & Emilie Arseneault Canada
SOUCY, Pierre Albert, Dec 1 1930 Sex:M Child# 7 Thomas Soucy Canada & Anna Berube Canada
SOUCY, Roger Ernest, May 16 1934 Sex:M Child# 1 Paul Soucy Nashua, NH & Mary St Pierre St Anne, NB
SOUCY, Roland, Jan 1 1911 Sex:M Child# 2 Andre Soucy Canada & Anne Mignault Canada
SOUCY, Roland Edmund, May 3 1932 Sex:M Child# 4 Arthur J Soucy Nashua, NH & Rose Boucher Fall River, MA
SOUCY, Rose Alice Gertrude, Oct 2 1921 Sex:F Child# 3 Arthur Soucy Canada & Alice Pigeon Canada
SOUCY, Sylvio, Apr 2 1902 Sex:M Child# 5 Andee Soucy Canada & Emelie Arseneau Canada
SOUCY, Therese Emilda, Jul 24 1914 Sex:F Child# 3 Auguste Soucy Canada & Rosanna Hudon Canada
SOUCY, Ulderic Romeo, Mar 8 1904 Sex:M Child# 7 Didier Soucy Canada & Delima Paradis Canada
SOUCY, Unknown, Mar 28 1893 Sex:M Child# 1 Andre Soucy Canada & Emelie Arseneau Canada Stillborn
SOUCY, Unknown, Dec 27 1911 Sex:M Child# 12 Didier Soucy Canada & Marie Paradis Canada Stillborn
SOUCY, Unknown, Aug 1 1922 Sex:F Child# 2 Arthur Soucy Canada & Angelina Beaulieu Canada Stillborn
SOUCY, Unknown, Aug 3 1926 Sex:M Child# 1 Sylvio Soucy Nashua, NH & Marion Lavoie Canada Stillborn
SOUCY, Victor, Oct 8 1904 Sex:M Child# 8 Andre Soucy Canada & Emelie Arseneau Canada
SOUCY, Wilfred, Jun 7 1909 Sex:M Child# 3 Demetrius Soucy Canada & Clara Chouinard Canada
SOUCY, Wilfrid Gerard, Jan 8 1916 Sex:M Child# 1 Arthur Soucy Canada & Alice Canada
SOUCY, Yolande Fedora, Mar 7 1926 Sex:F Child# 6 Pierre Soucy Nashua, NH & Alvin Landry Canada
SOULAKIS, Unknown, Jul 13 1922 Sex:M Child# 4 Nichol Soulakis Greece & Lena Pistovela Greece
SOUNSANE, Unknown, Aug 15 1912 Sex:M Child# 6 James Sounsane Greece & Stasula Demitros Greece
SOUSANIS, Ellen, Jul 12 1905 Sex:F Child# 2 James Sousanis Greece & Slavroulan James Greece
SOUSANIS, George D, Nov 3 1909 Sex:M Child# 4 Dervas Sousanis Greece & Slavroula Demetre Greece
SOUTHER, Unknown, Nov 14 1921 Sex:M Child# 2 William B Souther Seabrook, NH & Lillian Farnum Manchester, NH Stillbo
SOWCHICKA, Unknown, Jan 13 1917 Sex:M Child# 4 Michael Sowchicka Russia & Tophelia Aksinas Russia Stillborn
SOWELLIS, John, Sep 9 1904 Sex:M Child# 1 Nekles Sowellis Greece & Paraxchive Narhaw Greece
SOWSAN, Unknown, Aug 22 1916 Sex:M Child# 7 James Sowsan Greece & Stansola Andrianpz Greece
SOZILALIS, John, Jun 16 1913 Sex:M Child# 2 A Sozilalis Russia & B Rodonute Russia
SPACHAYS, Georgia, Feb 6 1912 Sex:F Child# 3 Henry Spachays Russia & Amelia Pivarun Russia
SPALDING, Carolyn, May 1 1927 Sex:F Child# 1 Willis A Spalding Hollis, NH & Hannah Burton England
SPALDING, Cecil Otis, Jul 2 1903 Sex:M Child# 3 Frank C Spalding Milford, NH & Mary E Storer Lebanon, ME
SPALDING, Edwin F, Feb 27 1891 Sex:M Child# 1 E G Spalding NH & M J Flanders Mass
SPALDING, Hugh Donald, Dec 6 1917 Sex:M Child# 2 Louis L Spalding Nashua, NH & Ada Nutbrown Nashua, NH
SPALDING, Mary Dorothea, Aug 27 1929 Sex:F Child# 1 George D Spalding Nashua, NH & Mary Perkins Boston, MA
SPALDING, Mary E, Sep 12 1887 Sex:F Child# 1 Charles H Spalding Pelham & Anna Lovejoy Hollis, NH
SPALDING, Rupert M, Oct 2 1904 Sex:M Child# 2 Frank C Spalding Milford, NH & Mary E Storer Lebanon, ME
SPALDING, Unknown, Aug 22 1890 Sex:M Child# 2 Charles Spalding NH & Anna Lovejoy Hollis, NH
SPALDING, Unknown, Jan 2 1894 Sex:M Child# 3 Charles Spalding Pelham, NH & Anna Lovejoy Hollis, NH
SPANOF, James, Apr 10 1916 Sex:M Child# 2 Nickles Spanof Greece & A Papadrisamon Greece
SPAULDING, Albert F, Oct 28 1890 Sex:M Child# 3 C F Spaulding W Windsor, VT & Ida M Strong Hartford, VT
SPAULDING, Carleton Philip, Jun 13 1915 Sex:M Child# 1 William J Spaulding Fremont, NH & Cora F Buzzell Haverhill
SPAULDING, Carroll Sumner, Mar 26 1930 Sex:M Child# 2 Willis A Spaulding Hollis, NH & Hannah Burton England
SPAULDING, Charles A, Mar 11 1893 Sex:M Child# 2 Charles C Spaulding Nashua, NH & Nellie B Fuller Hudson, NH
SPAULDING, Dorotha A, Feb 28 1897 Sex:F Child# 1 Louis P Spaulding Milford, NH & Lillie Anderson Nashua, NH
SPAULDING, Flossie M, Jan 14 1893 Sex:F Child# 2 Charles F Spaulding Vermont & Ida M Strong Vermont
SPAULDING, John Frederick, Apr 8 1920 Sex:M Child# 3 Louis L Spaulding Nashua, NH & Ada Nutbrown Nashua, NH
SPAULDING, Mary, Jul 23 1891 Sex:F Child# 1 Charles E Spaulding Nashua, NH & Nellie B Fuller Hudson, NH
SPAULDING, Ruth Edna, Feb 25 1908 Sex:F Child# 4 Louis F Spaulding Milford, NH & Lillian J Anderson Nashua, NH
SPAULDING, Sally, Apr 5 1933 Sex:F Child# 2 M C Spaulding Peterboro, NH & F Walker Melrose, MA
SPAULDING, Unknown, Jul 20 1889 Sex:M Child# 2 Charles L Spaulding Nashua, NH & Sarah B Hudson, NH
SPAULDING, Unknown, May 4 1892 Sex:M Child# 1 Hollen C Spaulding Janesville, WI & Lucile Brisbine Plattsburg, NY
SPAULDING, Walter Lund, Jan 7 1912 Sex:M Child# 2 Charles C Spaulding Nashua, NH & Myrtie Lund Hollis, NH

SPDAN, Nazival, Jan 14 1921 Sex:F Child# 3 Kabil Spdan Syria & Rita Thaia Syria
SPEAR, Fred W, Aug 9 1894 Sex:M Child# 2 William W Spear Nashua, NH & Ella O Spencer Maine
SPEAR, Henry T, Oct 7 1897 Sex:M Child# 2 Harry G Spear Nashua, NH & Mary A Fairfield New Boston, NH
SPEAR, Philip, Aug 26 1895 Sex:M Child# 1 Harry G Spear Nashua, NH & Mary A Fairfield New Boston, NH
SPEAR, Ralph D, Jun 18 1897 Sex:M Child# 3 William W Spear Nashua, NH & E O Spencer Maine
SPEAR, Unknown, Aug 12 1899 Sex:M Child# 3 H G Spear Nashua, NH & Mary Fairfield New Boston, NH
SPECTUOS, Stanislawa, Mar 24 1909 Sex:F Child# 1 Henry Spectuos Russia & Amelia Pevaronus Russia
SPELLMAN, Alice C, Sep 26 1899 Sex:F Child# 3 H W Spellman Nashua, NH & Alice A Sweeney Milford, NH
SPELLMAN, Anna, Feb 17 1907 Sex:F Child# 7 William Spellman Nashua, NH & Anna Doyle Nashua, NH
SPELLMAN, Anna May, May 31 1894 Sex:F Child# 1 Henry W Spellman Nashua, NH & Alice A Sweeney Milford, NH
SPELLMAN, Frank Harold, Dec 15 1896 Sex:M Child# 2 William Spellman Canada & Annie Doyle Nashua, NH
SPELLMAN, Louise Rita, Oct 25 1912 Sex:F Child# 8 William Spellman Canada & Annie Doyle Nashua, NH
SPELLMAN, Mary Helen, Mar 13 1898 Sex:F Child# 3 William Spellman Canada & Annie Doyle Nashua, NH
SPELLMAN, Robert Edward, Feb 7 1906 Sex:M Child# 6 William R Spellman Nashua, NH & Annie Doyle Nashua, NH
SPELLMAN, Roland Henry, Nov 5 1903 Sex:M Child# 5 William R Spellman Nashua, NH & Annie Doyle Nashua, NH
SPELLMAN, Sarah, Dec 27 1895 Sex:F Child# 2 Frank Spellman Nashua, NH & Margaret M Hallisey Ireland
SPELLMAN, William N, Aug 15 1901 Sex:M Child# 4 William R Spellman Nashua, NH & Anna Doyle Nashua, NH
SPELLMAN, William R, Jun 21 1908 Sex:M Child# 1 William R Spellman Lowell, MA & Anna Maynard Plattsburg, NY
SPELLMAN, William Robert, Jul 5 1923 Sex:M Child# 1 William Jos Spellman Nashua, NH & Marigold Hall Rochester, NH
SPENCE, Anabelle, Apr 10 1922 Sex:F Child# 3 Samuel A T Spence Nashua, NH & Marion Shattuck Amherst, NH
SPENCE, Anna Isabel, Aug 21 1899 Sex:F Child# 2 David T Spence Nashua, NH & Mary A Stanton Somersworth, NH
SPENCE, Bertha McDonald, Jul 18 1892 Sex:F Child# 13 David Spence Scotland & Margaret Taylor Scotland
SPENCE, David, Dec 27 1897 Sex:M Child# 1 David T Spence Nashua, NH & Mary A Stanton Somersworth, NH
SPENCE, Dorothy, May 5 1897 Sex:F Child# 4 Samuel Spence Ireland & Josie Frazer Nova Scotia
SPENCE, Elizabeth Margaret, Mar 6 1924 Sex:F Child# 3 Joseph K Spence Nashua, NH & Violet Peters St Johns, NB
SPENCE, Harold David, Jun 8 1921 Sex:M Child# 2 Joseph K Spence Nashua, NH & Violet Peters St John, NB
SPENCE, J Donald, Jul 22 1919 Sex:M Child# 1 Joseph K Spence Nashua, NH & Violet Peters St John, NB
SPENCE, John Taylor, Apr 16 1906 Sex:M Child# 3 David Spence, Jr Nashua, NH & Mary A Stanton Somersworth, NH
SPENCE, Margaret, Jun 6 1896 Sex:F Child# 19 David Spence Glasgow, Scotland & Margaret Taylor Glasgow, Scotland
SPENCE, Olive R, Jun 27 1895 Sex:F Child# 3 Samuel Spence Ireland & Jessie Frazer Nova Scotia
SPENCE, Patricia Ann, Jan 26 1935 Sex:F Child# 4 Joseph K Spence Nashua, NH & Violet Peters St John, NB
SPENCE, Robert Caldwell, Apr 19 1919 Sex:M Child# 2 Sam A T Spence Nashua, NH & Marion A Shattuck Amherst, NH
SPENCE, Samuel A, Sep 4 1889 Sex:M Child# 12 Dora Spence
SPENCE, Samuel Shattuck, Jun 10 1917 Sex:M Child# 1 Samuel A T Spence Nashua, NH & Marion A Shattuck Amherst, NH
SPENCE, Unknown, Nov 16 1887 Sex:F Child# 11 David Spence Scotland & Margaret Taylor Scotland
SPENCE, William Alexander, Nov 16 1892 Sex:M Child# 14 David Spence Glasgow, Scotland & Margaret Taylor Glasgow
SPENCER, Clifford S, Feb 23 1922 Sex:M Child# 1 Clifford S Spencer Bloomfield, VT & Cecil A Normando Bloomfield
SPENCER, Kenneth Edward, Oct 27 1928 Sex:M Child# 2 Clifford Spencer Bloomfield, VT & Cecile Normando Bloomfield
SPIATOUS, Romuald, Nov 2 1910 Sex:M Child# 2 Hendrick Spiatous Russia & Amelia Pivarounos Russia
SPILIOPOULOS, Unknown, Oct 5 1922 Sex:F Child# 4 Vsilios Spiliopoulos Greece & Penagoula Cadopoulou Greece
SPILLANE, Dennis P, Nov 28 1893 Sex:M Child# 1 Dennis P Spillane Nashua, NH & Mary Gilhooley Ireland
SPILLANE, George, Jun 2 1934 Sex:M Child# 5 John Spillane Nashua, NH & Mary Kelly Manchester, NH
SPILLANE, Helen, Feb 16 1900 Sex:F Child# 4 Dennis Spillane Nashua, NH & Mary Gilhooley Ireland
SPILLANE, John Leonard, Jun 6 1928 Sex:M Child# 1 J L Spillane Nashua, NH & Mary V Kelley Manchester, NH
SPILLANE, Leonard Joseph, Dec 14 1931 Sex:M Child# 2 John L Spillane Nashua, NH & Mary Kelley Manchester, NH
SPILOPLOS, Alice, May 3 1916 Sex:F Child# 2 Vagely Spiloplos Greece & Philipoopoo Greece
SPINNEY, Spinney, May 3 1889 Sex:M Child# 2 Leander E Spinney Kittery, ME & Minnie S Fellows Nashua, NH
SPINNEY, Unknown, Mar 23 1888 Sex:M Child# 1 Leander E Spinney Kittery, ME & Minnie S Fellows Nashua, NH
SPIRACOS, Unknown, Jul 22 1919 Sex:M Child# 1 John H Spiracos Haverhill, MA & Anna K Bredenberg Sweden
SPLAN, Ann Madeline, Jun 7 1897 Sex:F Child# 3 Dennis Splan Nashua, NH & Mary Gilhooley Ireland
SPLAN, John, Apr 19 1895 Sex:M Child# 2 Dennis Splan Nashua, NH & Mary Gilhooley Ireland
SPLAN, Margaret Etta, Apr 27 1902 Sex:F Child# 5 Dennis Splan Nashua, NH & Mary Gilhooly Ireland
SPOFFORD, Unknown, Apr 3 1904 Sex: Child# 5 Herbert L Spofford Westboro, MA & Lillian E Colier Holbrook, MA
SPOILAS, Dorothy, Mar 10 1920 Sex:F Child# 2 William Spoilas Greece & Lillian Lados Greece
SPRAGUE, Glenn Richard, Jun 8 1934 Sex:M Child# 3 Frederick Sprague Mass & Gladys Byrd Amherst, NH
SPRAGUE, Marion Leone, Dec 23 1896 Sex:F Child# 1 Oscar F Sprague Norwell, MA & Mary F Temple Nashua, NH
SPRAGUE, Unknown, Jun 14 1920 Sex:M Child# 3 Harris Sprague Grand L S, ME & Mary Louise Fagga Burlington, VT
SPRAGUE, Walter, Jun 14 1892 Sex:M Child# 3 Hutchins Sprague Lawrence, MA & Annie Wells Litchfield, NH
SPRIGNIGS, Pearl, Jul 19 1916 Sex:F Child# 1 Henry E Sprignigs Waterville, CT & Ellen Buddell Eustis, PQ Stillborn
SPRING, Eunice Eleanor, Sep 24 1913 Sex:F Child# 3 John R Spring Lebanon, NH & Eunice D Denison Royalton, VT
SPRING, Richard Dudley, Jun 24 1915 Sex:M Child# 4 John R Spring Lebanon, NH & Eunice D Ennison Royalton, VT
SPRINGER, Unknown, Jun 21 1909 Sex:F Child# 3 Sanford R Springer Ellsworth, ME & Edith Horsman Bradford, England
SPRINGMAN, Pauline Josephine, Jul 19 1925 Sex:F Child# 9 Harry Springman New York & Georgia Marquis Nashua, NH
SPRINGUE, Alice Lillian, Sep 29 1919 Sex:F Child# 2 Walter C Springue Marlboro, MA & Florence M Hosking Wharton
SPYLIOS, Mary, May 30 1918 Sex:F Child# 1 William Spylios Greece & Lillian Ladeos Greece
SQUIRES, Henry O, May 17 1891 Sex:M Child# 1 George W Squires Nashua, NH & Nellie Nealley Springfield, MA
SRECIK, Julia, Sep 3 1918 Sex:F Child# 2 Constantine Srecik Russia & Victoria Walsivoich Russia
SREYEZIK, Joseph, Jun 12 1918 Sex:M Child# 4 Michael Sreyezik Russia & Tophilia Ezepak Russia
SRULETANA, Genowefor, Sep 16 1914 Sex:F Child# 1 Frank Sruletana Austria & Anella Tokarezek Austria
ST AMAND, Joseph Lucien, Dec 26 1929 Sex:M Child# 9 Arthur St Amand Canada & Cecelia Fafard Canada
ST AMAND, Marie J A V, Jul 19 1896 Sex:F Child# 2 George St Amand Canada & Amanda Belanger Canada
ST AMANT, Albert Paul, May 29 1933 Sex:M Child# 3 H St Amant Canada & Diana Lambert Canada
ST AMANT, Leo Armase, Feb 3 1931 Sex:M Child# 10 Arthur St Amant Canada & Arselia Fafard Canada

ST AMANT, Odelie Lillian, Jul 5 1928 Sex:F Child# 7 A St Amant Canada & Arselia Fafard Canada
ST AMANT, Philippe Arthur, Mar 27 1933 Sex:M Child# 11 A St Amant Canada & Asselia Faford Canada
ST ARMOND, Lauretta Collette, Feb 1 1922 Sex:F Child# 1 Armase St Armond Canada & Julianna Lambert Natick, RI
ST ARNANT, Theresa Gertrude, Nov 2 1923 Sex:F Child# 2 Hermase St Arnant Canada & Julianna Lambert Wales, MA
ST CHARLES, Marie Anne, Oct 25 1893 Sex:F Child# 2 Charles St Charles Canada & Beatrice Lizotte Canada
ST CHARLES, Narcisse, Jul 23 1896 Sex:M Child# 4 Charles St Charles Canada & Beatrice Lizotte Canada
ST CYR, Frederick, Jul 11 1901 Sex:M Child# 1 Peter St Cyr Canada & Abbie Brennan Ireland
ST CYR, Unknown, Jul 20 1902 Sex:M Child# 2 Peter St Cyr Canada & Abbie Bruneau Ireland
ST DENIS, Joseph, Apr 30 1927 Sex:M Child# 8 Joseph St Denis Wisconsin &
ST DENIS, Marie Alice Laura, Sep 16 1924 Sex:F Child# 7 Joseph St Denis Wisconsin & Agnes Lavallee NH
ST DENNIS, Unknown, Mar 5 1897 Sex:F Child# 7 Andrew St Dennis Canada & Jennie Woodbey Suckertown, NY
ST FRANCIS, Joseph, Mar 10 1907 Sex:M Child# 1 E A St Francis Nashua, NH & Eugenie Simoneau Canada Stillborn
ST FRANCIS, Unknown, Oct 28 1924 Sex:F Child# 4 Henry St Francis Canada & Marie L Emond Canada
ST FRANCOIS, Allison, Mar 17 1934 Sex:F Child# 1 Cleo St Francois Nashua, NH & Hazel Cummings East Haven, VT
ST FRANCOIS, Arthur Telesphore, Mar 10 1910 Sex:M Child# 2 Philias St Francois Canada & Claudia Lessard Nashua, NH
ST FRANCOIS, Cleo Lord, May 27 1910 Sex:M Child# 2 Elzear St Francois Canada & Rose Lord Canada
ST FRANCOIS, Ernest Arthur, Jan 2 1909 Sex:M Child# 3 Henry St Francois Canada & Joanna L Baldwin RI
ST FRANCOIS, Jos Roland Theodore, May 5 1917 Sex:M Child# 1 Henri St Francois Canada & Marie Louise Emond Canada
ST FRANCOIS, Louis Henri, Dec 11 1902 Sex:M Child# 1 Henri St Francois St Albans, VT & Johanna L Baldwin New York
ST FRANCOIS, Lucille Rita, Oct 31 1921 Sex:F Child# 2 Henry L St Francois St Albans, VT & Marie Louise Emon Canada
ST FRANCOIS, Mary June Gloria, Jul 20 1924 Sex:F Child# 1 George St Francois Canada & Lillian Pelletier Nashua, NH
ST FRANCOIS, Normand, Feb 22 1920 Sex:M Child# 2 Henri L St Francois St Albans, VT & M L Emond Canada
ST FRANCOIS, Robert Gerald, Nov 2 1908 Sex:M Child# 1 Elzear St Francois Canada & Rose Lord Canada
ST FRANCOIS, Veronique, Jan 8 1906 Sex:F Child# 2 Henry St Francois St Albans, VT & Johanna Baldwin Rhode Island
ST GEORGE, Unknown, Jun 22 1893 Sex:M Child# 2 Theodore St George
ST GEORGE, William, Jul 12 1894 Sex:M Child# 3 Theo St George Rutland, VT & Susan Bennett Worcester, MA
ST GERMAIN, Helene Therese E, Apr 2 1902 Sex:F Child# 3 S St Germain Canada & Helene Cote Vermont
ST GERMAIN, John Joseph Norman, Nov 14 1932 Sex:M Child# 2 J St Germain Canada & Marie A Boucher Canada
ST GERMAIN, Joseph, Mar 23 1891 Sex:M Child# 10 Joseph St Germain Canada & Melvina Larose Canada
ST GERMAIN, Joseph Solomon, Apr 10 1904 Sex:M Child# 4 Solomon St Germain Canada & Nellie Cote Vermont
ST GERMAIN, Leon Odine, Feb 3 1900 Sex:M Child# 2 Solomon St Germain Canada & Nellie Cote Vermont
ST GERMAIN, Remi Romeo, Aug 27 1907 Sex:M Child# 1 Remi St Germain Canada & Exilda Girouard Canada
ST GERMAIN, Unknown, Aug 2 1896 Sex:F Child# Joseph St Germain Canada & Malvina Larose Canada Stillborn
ST GERMAIN, William, Mar 4 1888 Sex:M Child# 8 Antonie St Germain Canada & Gacia St Arunger Canada
ST GERMAINE, Edgar David, Jr, Sep 5 1928 Sex:M Child# 2 E D St Germaine Canada & Clementine Martin Sanford, ME
ST GERMAINE, Marie Yvonne, Feb 20 1931 Sex:F Child# 1 John St Germaine Canada & Marie A Boucher Canada
ST GERMAINE, Rita, Jan 1 1926 Sex:F Child# 1 Ed St Germaine Canada & Clementine Martin Sanford, ME
ST JACQUES, Alarie, Oct 18 1911 Sex:M Child# 5 Hector St Jacques US & Florida Dupont Canada
ST JACQUES, Dolores Lucille, Sep 10 1907 Sex:F Child# 2 Hector St Jacques US & Florida Dupont Canada
ST JACQUES, Fedora, Jan 31 1913 Sex:M Child# 6 Hector St Jacques US & Florida Dupont Canada
ST JACQUES, Germaine Florida, Apr 7 1906 Sex:F Child# 1 Hector St Jacques US & Florida Dupont Canada
ST JACQUES, Heobienne, Sep 25 1908 Sex:F Child# 3 Hector St Jacques US & Florida Dupont Canada
ST JACQUES, Joseph Gerald, Oct 31 1916 Sex:M Child# 8 Hector St Jacques Manchester, NH & Florida Dupont Canada
ST JACQUES, Leo Gerard, Dec 12 1934 Sex:M Child# 1 Emile St Jacques Nashua, NH & Irene Laquerre Nashua, NH
ST JACQUES, Blanche Camil, Apr 30 1918 Sex:F Child# 9 Hector St Jacques Manchester, NH & Florida Dupont Canada
ST JACQUES, Marie Sophronie, Dec 26 1909 Sex:F Child# 4 Hector St Jacques NH & Florida Dupont Canada
ST JACQUES, Paul Lionel, Dec 29 1914 Sex:M Child# 7 Hector St Jacques US & Florida Dupont Canada
ST JACQUES, Robert Richard, Oct 26 1932 Sex:M Child# 1 (No Parents Listed)
ST JEAN, Alice, Aug 30 1891 Sex:F Child# 6 Auguste St Jean Canada & Cesarie Dumais Canada
ST JEAN, Amedee, Nov 2 1899 Sex:M Child# 11 Joseph St Jean Canada & Eugenie Couillard Canada
ST JEAN, Camille Edgar, Jan 31 1890 Sex:M Child# 1 Theophile St Jean Canada & Ernestine Leblanc Canada
ST JEAN, Cecelia Pauline, Dec 27 1924 Sex:F Child# 6 Pearl St Jean Canada & Cecelia Perrault Canada
ST JEAN, Doris Yvette, Sep 9 1920 Sex:F Child# 1 Donat St Jean Canada & Irene Dane Nashua, NH
ST JEAN, Dorothy Clare, Jan 20 1926 Sex:F Child# 1 Louis St Jean Canada & Mary Moriarty Nashua, NH
ST JEAN, Florame, Jun 1 1904 Sex:F Child# 15 Joseph St Jean Canada & Florame Hudon Canada
ST JEAN, Florence Juliette, Aug 10 1907 Sex:F Child# 4 Paul St Jean Canada & Amanda Marquis Canada
ST JEAN, Harvey Armand, Nov 19 1929 Sex:M Child# 1 Leon St Jean Canada & Elizabeth Trembly Altona, NY
ST JEAN, Jos Herve Maurice, Sep 29 1920 Sex:M Child# 3 Paul St Jean Canada & Cecile Perreault Canada
ST JEAN, Jos Laurian Raymond, May 28 1932 Sex:M Child# 5 Donat St Jean St Francoise, PQ & Irene Dube Nashua, NH
ST JEAN, Joseph A, Jan 10 1894 Sex:M Child# 10 Nazaire St Jean Canada & Philomene Levesque Canada
ST JEAN, Joseph A G, Jan 15 1892 Sex:M Child# 9 Nazaire St Jean Canada & Philomene Levesque Canada
ST JEAN, Joseph A Henri, Oct 31 1896 Sex:M Child# 10 Arsene St Jean Canada & Caroline Ouellette Canada
ST JEAN, Joseph Alvarez, Jun 5 1922 Sex:M Child# 5 Raymond St Jean Central Falls, RI & Florida Chagnon Canada
ST JEAN, Joseph Emile T, Apr 27 1901 Sex:M Child# 5 Theophile St Jean Canada & Marie Lavoie Canada
ST JEAN, Joseph Pierre N, Jul 20 1894 Sex:M Child# 5 Arsene St Jean Canada & Emelie St Jean Canada
ST JEAN, Joseph S, Jun 25 1890 Sex:M Child# 4 Joseph St Jean Canada & Philomene Levesque Canada
ST JEAN, Joseph T, Nov 3 1887 Sex:M Child# 4 Joseph St Jean P Q & Angelina P Q
ST JEAN, Lorette, Mar 4 1904 Sex:F Child# 2 Paul St Jean Canada & Amanda Marquis Canada
ST JEAN, Louis, Jun 3 1888 Sex:M Child# 1 Arsine St Jean Canada & Emillie Deschanis Canada
ST JEAN, Maria Laura, Apr 6 1904 Sex:F Child# 4 Joseph St Jean Canada & Marie Levesque Canada
ST JEAN, Marie Alice, Sep 11 1902 Sex:F Child# 1 Paul St Jean Canada & Amanda Marquis Canada
ST JEAN, Marie Anne, Oct 4 1907 Sex:F Child# 12 Noel St Jean Canada & Marie Beaulieu Canada
ST JEAN, Marie Clodia, Feb 20 1896 Sex:F Child# 2 Theophile St Jean Canada & Marie Lavoie Canada

ST JEAN, Marie Eugenie, Jun 26 1900 Sex:F Child# 14 Joseph St Jean Canada & Florina Hudon Canada
ST JEAN, Marie Florette D, Oct 29 1921 Sex:F Child# 2 Donah St Jean Canada & Irene Dube NH
ST JEAN, Marie Lea, Jul 7 1897 Sex:F Child# 13 Joseph St Jean Canada & Eugenie Couillard Canada
ST JEAN, Marie Simone G, Aug 11 1924 Sex:F Child# 3 Donat St Jean Canada & Irene Dube NH
ST JEAN, Noel Robert, Jun 24 1930 Sex:M Child# 1 Noel St Jean Canada & Juliette Marquis Nashua, NH
ST JEAN, Unknown, Jul 12 1891 Sex:M Child# 2 Theophile St Jean Canada & Ernestine Leblanc Canada Stillborn
ST JOHN, Joseph Arthur, Apr 22 1898 Sex:M Child# 1 Joseph St John Canada & Mary Levesque Canada
ST JOHN, Robert, Jan 8 1918 Sex:M Child# 4 Raymond St John Center Falls, RI & Floridia Chagnon Canada
ST LAURENT, Adelard Romeo, Oct 1 1903 Sex:M Child# 5 Charles St Laurent Canada & Parmelia St Laurent Canada
ST LAURENT, Agnes, Dec 5 1903 Sex:F Child# 2 Joseph St Laurent Canada & Delia Lessard Canada
ST LAURENT, Alfred Lidowa, Jun 21 1906 Sex:M Child# 8 Desire St Laurent Canada & Emma Sirois Canada
ST LAURENT, Alfred Sylvio, Jul 31 1907 Sex:M Child# 5 Philippe St Laurent Canada & Marie Beaulieu Canada
ST LAURENT, Alger Sylvio, Oct 5 1908 Sex:M Child# 7 Charles St Laurent Canada & Cornelia St Laurent Canada
ST LAURENT, Alice Agnes, May 17 1903 Sex:F Child# 1 Philippe St Laurent Canada & Marie Beaulieu Canada
ST LAURENT, Annette Pauline, Jul 1 1927 Sex:F Child# 1 G St Laurent Nashua, NH & Lucille Boucher Nashua, NH
ST LAURENT, Antoine, Feb 7 1927 Sex:F Child# 2 Simon St Laurent Nashua, NH & Rosa Labrie Canada
ST LAURENT, Antonio, May 16 1904 Sex:M Child# 2 Philippe St Laurent Canada & Marie Beaulieu Canada
ST LAURENT, Beatrice Loretta, Nov 1 1923 Sex:F Child# 5 Albert St Laurent Nashua, NH & Melina Ouillette Nashua, NH
ST LAURENT, Celina Irene, Sep 17 1907 Sex:F Child# 9 Desire St Laurent Canada & Emma Sirois Canada
ST LAURENT, Charles Arthur, Feb 5 1901 Sex:M Child# 3 Charles St Laurent Canada & Carmelia St Laurent Canada
ST LAURENT, Charles Eugene, Apr 29 1897 Sex:M Child# 2 Theophile St Laurent Canada & Adele Bisson Canada
ST LAURENT, Clare Geneva, May 23 1926 Sex:F Child# 6 Albert St Laurent Nashua, NH & Melina Ouellette Nashua, NH
ST LAURENT, Conrad, Feb 19 1921 Sex:M Child# 3 Albert St Laurent Nashua, NH & Melina Ouellette Nashua, NH
ST LAURENT, Desire Phileas, Aug 26 1899 Sex:M Child# 3 Desire St Laurent Canada & Emma Sirois Canada
ST LAURENT, Dori Guilbert, Apr 30 1909 Sex:M Child# 2 Arthur St Laurent Canada & Anna Lemieux Canada
ST LAURENT, Emma P Carmel, Apr 24 1931 Sex:F Child# 4 Simon St Laurent Nashua, NH & Rosa Labrie Canada
ST LAURENT, Gerard Jeanel, Feb 9 1929 Sex:M Child# 3 Simon St Laurent Nashua, NH & Rosa Labrie Canada
ST LAURENT, Germaine Olivette, Sep 3 1918 Sex:F Child# 15 Desire St Laurent Canada & Emma Sirois Canada
ST LAURENT, Gertrude Yvonne, Sep 5 1912 Sex:F Child# 12 Desire St Laurent Canada & Emma Sirois Canada
ST LAURENT, Henri, Nov 20 1920 Sex:M Child# 1 Adelard St Laurent Canada & Yvonne Ricard Greenville, NH
ST LAURENT, Henry Rudolph, Nov 21 1927 Sex:M Child# 3 J E St Laurent Canada & Mary Jean Nashua, NH
ST LAURENT, Jean, Mar 13 1932 Sex:F Child# 4 G D St Laurent Nashua, NH & Lucille F Boucher US
ST LAURENT, Jean Desire, Apr 15 1926 Sex:M Child# 1 Simon St Laurent Nashua, NH & Rose Labrie Canada
ST LAURENT, Jean Marie George, May 7 1923 Sex:F Child# 17 Desire St Laurent Canada & Emma Sirois Canada
ST LAURENT, Joseph A A, Mar 5 1897 Sex:M Child# 3 Auguste St Laurent Canada & Ernestine DeBoisbr'n Canada
ST LAURENT, Joseph Arthur G, May 1 1902 Sex:M Child# 1 Joseph St Laurent Canada & Delia Lessard Canada
ST LAURENT, Joseph Charles Gerard, Aug 4 1933 Sex:M Child# 5 A St Laurent Canada & Yvonne Ricard Greenville, NH
ST LAURENT, Jos Emile Henry, Sep 26 1928 Sex:M Child# 2 Charles St Laurent Nashua, NH & Juliette Lacroix Nashua, NH
ST LAURENT, Joseph Felix R, Sep 25 1906 Sex:M Child# 16 Francois St Laurent Canada & Lazarie Martel Canada
ST LAURENT, Joseph N Albert, Apr 19 1898 Sex:M Child# 2 Desire St Laurent Canada & Emma Sirois Canada
ST LAURENT, Joseph Roger Leo, Oct 29 1927 Sex:M Child# 1 Zenon St Laurent Canada & Sadie Roy Conn
ST LAURENT, Joseph T H, Oct 7 1903 Sex:M Child# 6 Desire St Laurent Canada & Emma Sirois Canada
ST LAURENT, Leda Fleurette, May 1 1911 Sex:F Child# 11 Desire St Laurent Canada & Emma Sirois Canada
ST LAURENT, Louis Philippe, Jun 28 1899 Sex:M Child# 2 Charles St Laurent Canada & Carmelia St Laurent Canada
ST LAURENT, Malvina M, Oct 27 1902 Sex:F Child# 10 Octave St Laurent Canada & M Boilard Canada
ST LAURENT, Marie Alice, Aug 17 1900 Sex:F Child# 4 Desire St Laurent Canada & Emma Sirois Canada
ST LAURENT, Marie Anne M, Dec 24 1901 Sex:F Child# 5 Desire St Laurent Canada & Emma Sirois Canada
ST LAURENT, Marie Annette, Aug 18 1907 Sex:F Child# 1 Arthur St Laurent Canada & Anna Lemieux Canada
ST LAURENT, Marie E Albina, Sep 26 1896 Sex:F Child# 1 Desire St Laurent Canada & Emma Sirois Canada
ST LAURENT, Marie Juliette Alice, Jan 9 1914 Sex:F Child# 13 Desire St Laurent Canada & Emma Sirois Canada
ST LAURENT, Marie Louise, Jun 9 1897 Sex:F Child# 1 Charles St Laurent Canada & Carmelia St Laurent Canada Stillbor
ST LAURENT, Marion Lucille, Mar 8 1923 Sex:F Child# 2 Joseph St Laurent Canada & Marie Jean Nashua, NH
ST LAURENT, Mary Irene Theresa, Jan 3 1928 Sex:F Child# 4 Adelard St Laurent Canada & Yvonne Ricard Greenville, NH
ST LAURENT, Mary Jeannette, Aug 6 1924 Sex:F Child# 3 A St Laurent Canada & Yvonne Ricard Greenville, NH
ST LAURENT, Maurice, May 9 1915 Sex:M Child# 14 Desire St Laurent Canada & Emma Sirois Canada
ST LAURENT, Maurice Rosario, Sep 16 1930 Sex:M Child# 3 Charles St Laurent Nashua, NH & Juliette Lacroix Canada
ST LAURENT, Nap Ellsworth, Jan 6 1930 Sex:M Child# 8 Albert St Laurent Nashua, NH & Melina Ouellette Nashua, NH
ST LAURENT, Noel Raymond, Dec 26 1919 Sex:M Child# 2 Albert St Laurent Nashua, NH & Albina Ouellette Nashua, NH
ST LAURENT, Odilon Desire, Feb 6 1919 Sex:M Child# 1 Albert St Laurent Nashua, NH & Albina Ouellette Nashua, NH
ST LAURENT, Orel Aquilas, Apr 3 1910 Sex:M Child# 8 Charles St Laurent Canada & Cornelia St Laurent Canada
ST LAURENT, Paul, Mar 11 1928 Sex:M Child# 7 Albert St Laurent Nashua, NH & Melina Ouillette Nashua, NH
ST LAURENT, Paul Richard, Apr 11 1932 Sex:M Child# 9 A St Laurent Nashua, NH & Melina Ouellette Nashua, NH
ST LAURENT, Philippe, Sep 14 1906 Sex:M Child# 4 Philippe St Laurent Canada & Marie Beaulieu Canada
ST LAURENT, Robert Gerald, Oct 2 1933 Sex:M Child# 10 A St Laurent Nashua, NH & Melina Ouellette Nashua, NH
ST LAURENT, Robert Joseph, Jun 14 1917 Sex:M Child# 1 Jos E St Laurent Canada & Marie F Jean Nashua, NH
ST LAURENT, Robert Maxime, Nov 10 1929 Sex:M Child# 2 Maxime St Laurent Canada & Mary B Gelinas NH
ST LAURENT, Roland Aquilas, May 28 1924 Sex:M Child# 1 C A St Laurent Nashua, NH & Juliette Lacroix Canada
ST LAURENT, Romeo, Jul 21 1906 Sex:M Child# 3 Joseph St Laurent Canada & Delia Lessard Canada
ST LAURENT, Simon Emile, Jun 14 1907 Sex:M Child# 6 Charles St Laurent Canada & Cornelia St Laurent Canada
ST LAURENT, Simon Narcisse, Jan 3 1905 Sex:M Child# 7 Desire St Laurent Canada & Emme Sirois Canada
ST LAURENT, Ula Alberta, Sep 7 1922 Sex:F Child# 4 Albert St Laurent Nashua, NH & Melina Ouellette Nashua, NH
ST LAURENT, Unknown, Mar 4 1931 Sex:M Child# 2 Gilbert St Laurent Nashua, NH & Lucille Boucher Nashua, NH Stillborn
ST LAURENT, Unknown, Mar 4 1931 Sex:M Child# 3 Gilbert St Laurent Nashua, NH & Lucille Boucher Nashua, NH Stillborn

ST LAURENT, Wilfrid A, Jul 26 1902 Sex:M Child# 4 Charles St Laurent Canada & P St Laurent Canada
ST LAURENT, Yvonne, Apr 27 1905 Sex:F Child# 3 Philippe St Laurent Canada & Marie Beaulieu Canada
ST LAURENT, Yvonne Jeanne d'Arc, Jun 30 1920 Sex:F Child# 16 Desire St Laurent Canada & Emma Sirois Canada
ST MARTIN, Irene Alberta, Dec 11 1907 Sex:F Child# 1 Albert St Martin Canada & Oliva Winner Canada
ST MARTIN, Jean Baptiste, Nov 15 1916 Sex:M Child# 6 James St Martin Fall River, MA & Claudia Guay Canada Stillborn
ST MARTIN, Joseph Irlande Aime, Aug 6 1912 Sex:M Child# 4 Jacques St Martin Mass & Claudia Guay Canada
ST MARTIN, Joseph James, Jan 30 1920 Sex:M Child# 5 John St Martin Fall River, MA & Claudia Guay Canada
ST MARTIN, Marie Ida, Aug 12 1915 Sex:F Child# 5 Jacques St Martin US & Claudia Guay Canada
ST MARTIN, Ralphsale Joseph, Dec 15 1905 Sex:M Child# 2 James St Martin Canada & Claudia Guay Canada
ST MICHEL, Henry Elzear, Feb 5 1897 Sex:M Child# 2 Theodore St Michel NY & Zoe Ouellette Caribou, ME
ST MICHELS, Joseph Isaac, Jan 13 1896 Sex:M Child# 1 Isaac M St Michels NY & Zoe Ouellette Caribou, ME
ST ONGE, Agnes E D, Feb 5 1892 Sex:F Child# 6 Victor St Onge Canada & Clara Boule Canada
ST ONGE, Alberta Olivette, Jan 5 1914 Sex:F Child# 8 Albert St Onge Clinton, Iowa & Rebecca Beauchesne Mass
ST ONGE, Alphonse A, Aug 27 1889 Sex:M Child# 4 Victor St Onge Canada & Clara Boule Canada
ST ONGE, Annette A B, Dec 18 1895 Sex:F Child# 9 Victor St Onge Canada & Clara Boule Canada
ST ONGE, Camile Aurelie, Sep 19 1911 Sex:F Child# 1 Wilfred St Onge Canada & Christine Lemay Nashua, NH
ST ONGE, Camille Juliette, May 18 1919 Sex:F Child# 3 George St Onge Canada & Albertine Bernier Canada
ST ONGE, Charles A B, Jul 17 1910 Sex:M Child# 7 J B St Onge Canada & Marie Brodeur Canada
ST ONGE, Claire Rachel, Jan 5 1926 Sex:F Child# 5 Geo E St Onge Canada & Albertine Bernier Canada
ST ONGE, Claude W B, Oct 3 1890 Sex:M Child# 5 Victor St Onge Canada & Clara Boule Canada
ST ONGE, Doraine Frances, May 4 1932 Sex:F Child# 3 Alfred St Onge Canada & Ella A Ackerman Nashua, NH
ST ONGE, Estelle Solange, Jul 11 1918 Sex:F Child# 3 Wilfred St Onge Province Quebec & Christine Lemay Nashua, NH
ST ONGE, Eva, Nov 5 1894 Sex:F Child# 8 Victor St Onge Canada & Clara Boule Canada
ST ONGE, Eva C A, Apr 25 1909 Sex:F Child# 6 Jean B St Onge Nashua, NH & Marie Brodeur Canada
ST ONGE, Florence Beatrice, May 11 1922 Sex:F Child# 4 George E St Onge Canada & Albertine Bernier Canada
ST ONGE, George V R, May 22 1898 Sex:M Child# 1 George St Onge Canada & Emma Lafleur Ashburnham, MA
ST ONGE, Hector, May 24 1888 Sex:M Child# 3 Victor St Onge Canada & Claria Boule Canada
ST ONGE, J Ovila Rolland, Jul 8 1915 Sex:M Child# 2 Joseph St Onge Canada & Albertine Levesque Canada
ST ONGE, Jean Baptiste P R, Jul 6 1903 Sex:M Child# 3 Jean Bte St Onge Nashua, NH & Marie E Brodeur Canada
ST ONGE, Jeanette Fernande, Aug 14 1924 Sex:F Child# 2 Ovila St Onge Canada & Emilda Plourde Canada
ST ONGE, Joseph, Aug 3 1930 Sex:M Child# 1 Dominique St Onge Canada & Adelaide Beland Canada
ST ONGE, Joseph Leonard Romeo, Sep 6 1926 Sex:M Child# 3 Ovila St Onge Canada & Imelda Plourde Canada
ST ONGE, Joseph Lucien Rollan, Mar 27 1916 Sex:M Child# 9 Albert St Onge Clinton, Iowa & Rebecca Beauchene Canada
ST ONGE, Josysha Zephir, Oct 8 1899 Sex:M Child# 2 George St Onge Canada & Emma Lafleur Mass
ST ONGE, Lea M P, Jul 1 1901 Sex:F Child# 2 J Bte St Onge Nashua, NH & Marie E Brodeur Canada
ST ONGE, Lucille C M, Nov 25 1905 Sex:F Child# 4 Jean B St Onge Nashua, NH & Marie C Brodeur St Hyacinthe, PQ
ST ONGE, M Adrienne Marg, Apr 21 1913 Sex:F Child# 2 Wilfred St Onge Canada & Christine Lemay Nashua, NH
ST ONGE, M Albertine Yvonne, Oct 4 1916 Sex:F Child# 3 Joseph St Onge Canada & Albertine Levesque Canada
ST ONGE, M C Mar Georgette, Nov 23 1917 Sex:F Child# 2 George St Onge Canada & Albertine Bernier Canada
ST ONGE, M Marg Therese, Dec 1 1915 Sex:F Child# 1 George St Onge Canada & Albertine Bernier Canada
ST ONGE, Marguerite B I, Jun 13 1907 Sex:F Child# 5 Jean Bte St Onge Nashua, NH & Marie Brodeur St Hyacinthe, PQ
ST ONGE, Marie Alice Cecile, Apr 18 1914 Sex:F Child# 1 Joseph St Onge Canada & Albertine Levesque Canada
ST ONGE, Marie Delienne Beat, Jul 12 1918 Sex:F Child# 4 Joseph St Onge St Pactome, PQ & Albertine Levesque Pa
ST ONGE, Marie E, Mar 14 1898 Sex:F Child# 1 Jean B St Onge Nashua, NH & Marie E Brodeur Canada
ST ONGE, Marie Estella C, Jul 5 1929 Sex:F Child# 2 Alfred St Onge Canada & Ella L Eckerman Nashua, NH
ST ONGE, Olina, Jan 1 1893 Sex:F Child# 7 Victor St Onge Canada & Clara Boule Canada
ST ONGE, Rachelle Yvette M, Jun 16 1927 Sex:F Child# 2 Alphedas St Onge Canada & Marie Laverdiere Nashua, NH
ST ONGE, Raymond Arthur, Jun 15 1915 Sex:M Child# 1 Arthur A St Onge Nashua, NH & Clara Bouley Canada
ST ONGE, Rene Roland, Jun 2 1934 Sex:M Child# 3 Ovila St Onge Canada & Emelda Plourde Canada
ST ONGE, Roger Wilfred Maurice, Apr 25 1926 Sex:M Child#  Wilfred St Onge Canada & Christine Lemay Nashua, NH
ST ONGE, Simone, Dec 31 1928 Sex:F Child# 4 Ovila St Onge Canada & Imelda Plourde Canada
ST ONGE, Theodore Lucien, Mar 4 1925 Sex:M Child# 1 Alfidas St Onge Canada & Marie Laverdiere Canada
ONGE, Willie Real, Jun 4 1923 Sex:M Child# 1 Ovila St Onge Canada & Imelda Plourde Canada
ST PETER, Donald LeRoy, Apr 28 1933 Sex:M Child# 1 Donald St Peter S Burlington, VT & Wilma Blair Burlington, VT
ST PETER, Unknown, Jun 10 1930 Sex:F Child# 2 Donald St Peter Burlington, VT & Wilma Blair Burlington, VT Stillborn
ST PIERRE, Albert Victor, Feb 7 1902 Sex:M Child# 3 Pierre St Pierre Canada & Henriette Caron Canada
ST PIERRE, Alfred, Nov 6 1900 Sex:M Child# 4 Horner St Pierre Canada & Clemence Levesque Maine
ST PIERRE, Charles Eugene, Feb 6 1908 Sex:M Child# 3 Thomas St Pierre Canada & Marie Ouellette Canada
ST PIERRE, Dorothy M Jeannette, Jun 8 1927 Sex:F Child# 3 A St Pierre Canada & Alexina Arquin Canada
ST PIERRE, Emile Alphonse R, Apr 5 1924 Sex:M Child# 1 Alphonse St Pierre Canada & Alexina Arguin Canada
ST PIERRE, Eugenia Lydia, Apr 2 1909 Sex:F Child# 9 Louis St Pierre Canada & Eugenie Archambault Canada
ST PIERRE, Florette Marie J G, Nov 15 1925 Sex:F Child# 2 Alph St Pierre Canada & Alexina Arguin Canada
ST PIERRE, Genine, Nov 23 1934 Sex:F Child# 2 Louis St Pierre St Paul, Canada & Martha Soucy St Basil, NB
ST PIERRE, Irene, Mar 15 1926 Sex:F Child# 2 Joseph St Pierre Canada & M Boggis Nashua, NH
ST PIERRE, Jos Alfred Adelard, Jan 6 1921 Sex:M Child# 4 Amedee St Pierre Canada & Caroline Talbot Canada
ST PIERRE, Jos Edward Arthur, Mar 18 1918 Sex:M Child# 2 Amedee St Pierre Canada & Caroline Talbot Canada
ST PIERRE, Jos Gerard Alphonse, May 5 1928 Sex:M Child# 2 David St Pierre Canada & Irene Boulanger Nashua, NH
ST PIERRE, Joseph, Aug 25 1892 Sex:M Child# 1 Joseph St Pierre Canada & Hermine Rouleau Canada
ST PIERRE, Joseph Albert David, Sep 21 1920 Sex:M Child# 1 David St Pierre Canada & Irene Boulanger Nashua, NH
ST PIERRE, Joseph Arsene, Jul 12 1893 Sex:M Child# 4 Napoleon St Pierre Canada & Anaise St Onge Canada
ST PIERRE, Joseph Edouard, Dec 27 1900 Sex:M Child# 4 Adolphe St Pierre Canada & Marie Brouillard Canada
ST PIERRE, Joseph Emile, Nov 14 1907 Sex:M Child# 8 Louis St Pierre Canada & Albina Archambault Canada
ST PIERRE, Joseph Fernando, Oct 31 1919 Sex:M Child# 3 Amedee St Pierre Canada & Caroline Talbot Canada

ST PIERRE, Joseph Jean Paul, Mar 31 1930 Sex:M Child# 4 Joseph St Pierre Canada & Marguerite Boggis Nashua, NH
ST PIERRE, Joseph Leo, Nov 2 1919 Sex:M Child# 5 Aurelin St Pierre Canada & Eugenie Caron Canada
ST PIERRE, Joseph Louis, May 11 1910 Sex:M Child# 10 Louis St Pierre Canada & Malvina Archambault Canada
ST PIERRE, Joseph Ovila, Feb 22 1901 Sex:M Child# 2 Joseph St Pierre Canada & Georgiana Sirois Canada
ST PIERRE, Joseph Robert, Jul 27 1927 Sex:M Child# 3 Joseph St Pierre Canada & Marguerite Boggis Nashua, NH
ST PIERRE, Joseph Romeo, Jan 17 1918 Sex:M Child# 4 Aurelin St Pierre St Louise, PQ & Eugenie Caron Canada
ST PIERRE, Josephine R A, Oct 17 1898 Sex:F Child# 2 Ephrem St Pierre Canada & Claudia Gagnon Canada
ST PIERRE, Marie A P, Aug 15 1891 Sex:F Child# 4 Joseph St Pierre Canada & Hermene Blanchet Canada
ST PIERRE, Marie Alexandra M, Nov 22 1899 Sex:F Child# 3 Henri St Pierre Canada & Marie Proulx Canada
ST PIERRE, Marie Alice, Dec 2 1900 Sex:F Child# 2 Pierre St Pierre Canada & Henrietta Caron Canada
ST PIERRE, Marie Alma, Oct 2 1897 Sex:F Child# 2 Henri St Pierre Canada & Marie Proulx Canada
ST PIERRE, Marie Anne, Jan 31 1900 Sex:F Child# 1 Joseph St Pierre Canada & Georgina Sirois Canada
ST PIERRE, Marie Eva Lea, Jun 20 1903 Sex:F Child# 4 Pierre St Pierre Canada & Henriette Caron Canada
ST PIERRE, Marie Florence, Feb 29 1904 Sex:F Child# 1 Thomas St Pierre Canada & Marie Ouellette Canada
ST PIERRE, Marie Rose A, Oct 4 1905 Sex:F Child# 2 Thomas St Pierre Canada & Marie Ouellette Canada
ST PIERRE, Melanie, Jan 2 1896 Sex:F Child# 1 Ephrem St Pierre Canada & Claudia Gagnon Canada
ST PIERRE, Pauline Loraine, Aug 31 1930 Sex:F Child# 2 Joseph St Pierre Canada & Cora Pepin Hooksett, NH
ST PIERRE, Reginald, Aug 18 1932 Sex:M Child# 1 L St Pierre Canada & Martha Soucy Canada
ST PIERRE, Rita Mildred, Jul 17 1929 Sex:F Child# 1 Joseph St Pierre Canada & Cora Pepin NH
ST PIERRE, Robert, Apr 1 1925 Sex:M Child# 1 Joseph St Pierre Canada & Margaret Boggis US
ST PIERRE, Sophie Mathilde, Nov 9 1893 Sex:F Child# 2 Olivier St Pierre Canada & Hermine Rouleau Canada
ST PIERRE, Theresa Juliette M, May 20 1925 Sex:F Child# 1 Henry St Pierre
ST PIERRE, Thomas Leo, May 16 1903 Sex:M Child# 4 Joseph St Pierre Canada & Georgiana Sirois Canada
STACHOWSKI, Annie, Jun 13 1913 Sex:F Child# 3 John Stachowski Russia & Mary Alukonas Russia
STACKLIN, Robert George, Nov 3 1931 Sex:M Child# 3 Stephen J Stacklin Nashua, NH & Daisy E Hubbard Annapolis, MD
STACKPOLE, Charles Thomas, Jun 1 1929 Sex:M Child# 5 Charles T Stackpole Portsmouth, NH & Ethel Sinclair Canada
STACKPOLE, Ruth, Jun 7 1903 Sex:F Child# 1 William E Stackpole Blue Hill, ME & Anna F Colby Bennington, NH
STAKENUNIS, Dory, Jan 5 1905 Sex:F Child# 3 James Stakenunis Russia & Mary Mouchonska Russia
STAKNIS, Eva, Apr 30 1916 Sex:F Child# 3 Mike Staknis Russia & Mary Stantchic Russia
STAKNIS, William, Sep 28 1918 Sex:M Child# 4 Mike Staknis Russia & Mary Stanchick Russia
STAKORIS, Unknown, Aug 10 1923 Sex:F Child# 5 Mike Stakoris Russia & Mary Statgic Russia Stillborn
STALKUS, Antoine, Jan 10 1907 Sex:M Child# 1 Frank Stalkus Russia & Anna Komontshot Russia
STAMOULI, Unknown, Jan 24 1917 Sex:M Child# 4 (No Parents Listed)
STANAPIEDIS, Sophia, Aug 15 1918 Sex:F Child# 1 Mike Stanapiedis Russia & Sophia Petrovska Russia
STANAWICZ, Antony, Aug 5 1915 Sex:M Child# 1 Felix Stanawicz Russia & Annie Kermela Russia
STANCOMBE, Doris Lovedy, Jul 14 1930 Sex:F Child# 3 William Stancombe Dunstable, MA & Inez Bentley England
STANCOMBE, Herbert Wayne, Dec 21 1932 Sex:M Child# 4 W A Stancombe Dunstable, MA & Inez Bertley England
STANCOMBE, Maurice James, May 7 1920 Sex:M Child# 1 Andrew Stancombe Dunstable, MA & Inez Bentley England
STANCOMBE, William Ernest, Oct 6 1925 Sex:M Child# 2 W A Stancombe Dunstable, MA & Inez Bentley, Yorkshire England
STANGUS, Frank, Mar 8 1910 Sex:M Child# 1 Alexander Stangus Russia & Sarah Balokvitch Russia
STANIELS, Joseph, Mar 13 1927 Sex:M Child# 2 Joseph Staniels Lithuania & Apolonia Kupchun Lithuania
STANIUM, Virginia Anne, Sep 13 1932 Sex:F Child# 3 W Stanium Russia & J Walkowski Russia
STANLEY, Helen, Jul 18 1933 Sex:F Child# 6 George Stanley St Louis, MO & Mary Marks St Louis, MO
STANTON, Alfred, Mar 2 1910 Sex:M Child# 2 Ernest Stanton Canada & Alice Gendron Canada
STANTON, Annie, Aug 13 1891 Sex:F Child# 10 Joseph T Stanton Canada & Zelfride Despardin Canada
STANTON, Claire, Aug 8 1921 Sex:F Child# 6 William L Stanton Wilton, NH & Julia Brennan Wilton, NH
STANTON, Edmund, Jul 4 1917 Sex:M Child# 4 William Stanton Wilton, NH & Julie Brennan Wilton, NH
STANTON, Gilbert Haynes, Mar 16 1911 Sex:M Child# 7 Edwin M Stanton Saranac, NY & Nellie L Ward Saranac, NY
STANTON, Henry Walter, Dec 16 1897 Sex:M Child# 8 J T Stanton Canada & Celfride Desjardins Canada
STANTON, Lucy Nina, Dec 16 1906 Sex:F Child# 1 Thomas B Stanton Yarmouth & Lucy I Stanley Norwich, ME
STANTON, Mary, Jul 12 1927 Sex:F Child# 7 William Stanton Lyndeboro, NH & Julie Brennan Wilton, NH
STANTON, Mary Virginia, Dec 2 1923 Sex:F Child# 1 John F Stanton Somersworth, NH & Margaret M Benson Nashua, NH
STANTON, Unknown, Dec 30 1888 Sex:M Child# 5 Andrew A Stanton Northfield, VT & Lucia Cushin Westmoreland, NH
STANULIS, Mary Ann, Jul 30 1930 Sex:F Child# 3 Joseph Stanulis Lithuania & Apollonia Kupchun Lithuania
STANULIS, Sophie, Jun 18 1918 Sex:F Child# 1 Joseph Stanulis Russia & Apolonia Kuptunas Russia
STANUM, Anastasia Sabina, Feb 3 1915 Sex:F Child# 1 Walter Stanum Russia & Edoga Vlokowska Russia
STANUN, Freda Helen, Apr 29 1917 Sex:F Child# 3 Walter Stanun Russia & Edwidga Walkowska Russia
STANUN, Mamerta Waclaw, May 12 1916 Sex:M Child# 2 Walter Stanun Russia & Edwiza Wolkouska Russia
STANYAN, Joseph, Nov 23 1896 Sex:M Child# 3 Michael Stanyan Russia & Michilini Rundoma'k Russia
STAPANIN, Julianna, Jun 18 1909 Sex:F Child# 1 Michael Stapanin Russia & Martha Statkus Russia
STAPANION, Joseph, Oct 7 1914 Sex:M Child# 6 Hipolit Stapanion Russia & Domiceli Porkas Russia
STAPLES, Donald Frederick, Dec 12 1924 Sex:M Child# 1 Ernest Staples Lawrence, MA & Mildred G Wizelt Plymouth, MA
STAPLES, Wilbur Arnold, May 9 1925 Sex:M Child# 2 George A Staples Esmond RI & Isabel Grierson Scotland
STAPONYAN, Mikolai, Apr 27 1908 Sex:M Child# 1 Hypolit Staponyan Russia & Domycela Poskus Russia
STARK, Abbie, Jun 11 1888 Sex:F Child# 1 Frank B Stark Charlestown & Minnie Doyle Ireland
STARK, Ruth Mildred, May 22 1898 Sex:F Child# 1 Walter E Stark Nashua, NH & Lottie S Henry Iron Mt, NY
STARKIE, Rita, Jun 30 1920 Sex:F Child# 2 Robert W Starkie Ireland & Margaret Gorman Lowell, MA
STARKIE, Robert Edward, Oct 29 1918 Sex:M Child# 1 Robert W Starkie Ireland & Margaret Gorman Lowell, MA
STARKIS, Mary Frances, Aug 12 1923 Sex:F Child# 3 Robert Starkis Ireland & Margaret Gorman Lowell, MA
STARR, Cynthia Mary, Oct 8 1934 Sex:F Child# 2 Uno Starr Maynard, MA & Elvie Williams Maynard, MA
STARR, David Crandall, Oct 30 1932 Sex:M Child# 1 Uno H Starr Maynard, MA & Elvie Williams Maynard, MA
STARR, Donald, Dec 8 1903 Sex:M Child# 1 William F Starr White River Jct, VT & Edna A Calhoun Canada
STARR, Lloyd Calhoun, Apr 30 1909 Sex:M Child# 2 William F Starr White River Jct, VT & Edna A Calhoun Canada

STARRATT, Matilda J, Sep 27 1906 Sex:F Child# 3 William H Starratt Nova Scotia & Effie Davis Nova Scotia
STARZKAWSKIS, Petroneli, Jun 29 1907 Sex:F Child# 4 John Starzkawskis Russia & Petroneli Beleckati Russia
STASAUSKAS, Peter, Apr 6 1919 Sex:M Child# 5 Joseph Stasauskas Russia & Mary Almkouinte Russia
STASZKAWOKIS, Stanislaus, Sep 19 1905 Sex:M Child# 3 John Staszkawokis Russia & Petronili Beleckati Russia
STASZKAWSHITS, John, May 29 1903 Sex:M Child# 2 John Staszkawshits Russia & Petroneli Beleckati Russia
STASZKICKEI, Zope, Feb 23 1910 Sex:M Child# 5 John Staszkickei Russia & Petroneli Seleckatti Russia
STATHIAS, Helen Catherine, Oct 21 1925 Sex:F Child# 1 George Stathias Greece & Edna Hill Pepperell, MA
STATOUS, Johanna, Oct 9 1907 Sex:F Child# 1 Anton Statous Russia & Barb Barzonavitch Russia
STATUNIS, William, May 18 1925 Sex:M Child# 3 William Statunis Russia & Nellie Kibuski Russia
STAVACH, Frank, Sep 2 1923 Sex:M Child# 7 Franz Stavach Poland & Mary Petko Poland
STAVASH, Alexander, Aug 25 1913 Sex:F Child# 3 Frank Stavash Austria & Mary Pitkam Austria
STAVASH, Anton, Sep 24 1910 Sex:M Child# 2 Frank Stavash Austria & Mary Pithka Austria
STAVASH, Brunislava, Jun 2 1921 Sex:F Child# 7 Frank Stavash Poland & Mary Pitka Poland
STAVASH, Victoria, Mar 31 1912 Sex:F Child# 2 Frank Stavash Austria & Mary Pitcka Austria
STAVELEY, Annie Louise, Oct 20 1897 Sex:F Child# 1 Robert Staveley England & Barbara E Buchanan Littleton, MA
STAVELEY, Unknown, Oct 6 1900 Sex:M Child# 2 Robert Staveley England & Barbara E Buchanan Mass Stillborn
STAVELEY, Unknown, Aug 20 1902 Sex:F Child# 3 Robert Staveley England & B E Buchanan Littleton, MA
STAVELY, Unknown, Feb 9 1904 Sex:F Child# 4 Robert Stavely England & Barbara E Buchanan Littleton, MA Stillborn
STAVRICOS, George, Oct 8 1908 Sex:M Child# 1 Peter Stavricos Greece & Pota Adams Greece
STAW, Hazel G, Mar 1 1899 Sex:F Child# 2 Cecil Staw Brookline & Lizzie Crowler Groton, MA
STAWEZ, John, Aug 13 1913 Sex:M Child# 4 John Leo Stawez Russia & Katie Basiaskas Russia
STEARNS, Anna, Dec 9 1889 Sex:F Child# 1 Henry Stearns Lexington, MA & Jessie Tileston Barton
STEARNS, Frank A, Apr 26 1901 Sex:M Child# 1 Frank A Stearns Hollis, NH & Hattie Allen Coventry, VT
STEARNS, Howard K, Jan 28 1892 Sex:M Child# 1 C K Stearns Milford, NH & N A Whidden Londonderry, NH
STEARNS, Howard K, Jan 25 1898 Sex:M Child# 4 Charles C Stearns Milford, NH & N A Whidden Londonderry, NH
STEARNS, Janet Louise, Apr 8 1927 Sex:F Child# 1 Glenn A Stearns Winchester, NH & Mildred Chaplin Nashua, NH
STEARNS, Kenneth Downing, Nov 2 1930 Sex:M Child# 2 Ralph A Stearns Bath, ME & Prudence P Downing Truro, NS
STEARNS, Robert Franklin, Apr 9 1934 Sex:M Child# 3 Ralph Stearns Maine & Prudence Downing Conn
STEARNS, Russell Glenn, Jan 18 1926 Sex:M Child# 2 Walter Stearns Hudson, NH & Jennie Saunders Gloucester, MA
STEARNS, Ruth L, Mar 19 1893 Sex:F Child# 2 Charles K Stearns Milford, NH & N A Whidden Londonderry, NH
STEARNS, Unknown, Jan 24 1890 Sex:M Child# 3 Willie D Stearns Lowell, MA & Louisa V Stark Sciota, NY
STEARNS, Unknown, Aug 28 1895 Sex:F Child# 3 Charles K Stearns Milford, NH & N A Whidden Londonderry, NH
STEARNS, Unknown, Mar 4 1896 Sex:M Child# 1 Otis Stearns Nashua, NH & Laura E Leazotte Plattsburg, NY Stillborn
STEARNS, Unknown, May 24 1909 Sex:F Child# 2 Frank A Stearns Hollis, NH & Hattie Allen Coventry, VT
STEARNS, Walter Herbert, Dec 23 1923 Sex:M Child# 1 Walter Stearns Hudson, NH & Jennie Saunders Gloucester, MA
STEARSHESKI, Joseph, May 13 1909 Sex:M Child# 1 Joseph Stearsheski Russia & Mary Lukonute Russia
STECKEVICZ, Joan Eleanor, Sep 12 1934 Sex:F Child# 5 Alphonse Steckevicz Poland & Eleanor Wolensevicz Poland
STECKWICZ, Charles, May 9 1914 Sex:M Child# 3 Paul Steckwicz Russia & Bessie Ganuazweska Russia
STECKWICZ, John, May 9 1914 Sex:M Child# 2 Paul Steckwicz Russia & Bessie Ganuazweska Russia
STEED, Eva Alice, Feb 5 1894 Sex:F Child# 1 Thomas Steed
STEEL, Barbara Frances, Feb 23 1927 Sex:F Child# 1 Ralph H Steel Hudson, NH & Frances Goodwin Rowley, MA
STEEL, Unknown, Jun 22 1919 Sex:M Child# 3 Charles Steel Hudson, NH & Mina A Boyd Rockland, NS
STEELE, Alice Bell, Jul 27 1895 Sex:F Child# 1 George S Steele Hudson, NH & Edith F Colburn Hudson, NH
STEELE, Charlene E, Sep 14 1909 Sex:F Child# 1 Fred G Steele Goshen, NH & Addie B Moody Lancaster, NH
STEELE, Charles Edward, Dec 23 1907 Sex:M Child# 2 Charles E Steele Milford, NH & May L Felch Francestown, NH
STEELE, Freda May, Sep 1 1906 Sex:F Child# 1 Charles E Steele Peterboro, NH & May L Felch Francestown, NH
STEELE, Richard Duane, Aug 20 1931 Sex:M Child# 2 Ralph Steele Hudson, NH & Frances Goodwin Rowley, MA
STEELE, Unknown, Apr 14 1889 Sex:F Child# 1 Charles A Steele Hudson & Ida F Gray Nashua, NH
STEELE, Unknown, Jul 4 1910 Sex:M Child# 3 Charles E Steele Milford, NH & Mary L Felch Francestown, NH Stillborn
STEEPE, Unknown, Jan 23 1900 Sex:F Child# 3 John Steepe Russia & Tophelia Miller Russia
STEFANOWICZ, Edward, Oct 16 1927 Sex:M Child# 1 Emile Stefanowicz Russia & F Sedlewicz Nashua, NH
STEGER, Paul, Aug 16 1918 Sex:M Child# 1 Watson Steger Russia & Sophia Ruthowska Russia
STEGER, Pauline Phyllis, Feb 28 1923 Sex:F Child# 2 Watson Steger Russia & Sophia Rutkowski Russia
STELLA, Mary, Mar 26 1907 Sex:F Child# 4 John Stella Russia & Mary Monchowsky Russia
STELLOS, Unknown, Dec 8 1931 Sex:M Child# 1 Kleanthis Stellos Greece & Anna Loukides Greece
STELLOS, Unknown, May 4 1933 Sex:M Child# 2 C Stellos Greece & Anna Loukides Turkey
STEP, Ursula, May 16 1897 Sex:F Child# 1 John Step Russia & Theophilia Millers Russia
STEPANIA, Josie, Aug 16 1913 Sex:F Child# 5 Hippolite Stepania Russia & Domitilda Poskus Russia
STEPANIONIS, Domithilda, Jan 30 1918 Sex:F Child# 5 Hyppolite Stepanioni Russia & Domithilda Porsh Russia
STEPANIONIS, Edward, Aug 31 1921 Sex:M Child# 10 H Stepanionis Poland & Domithilde Porskus Lithuania
STEPANIONIS, Mary, Jan 13 1916 Sex:F Child# 7 Hypolite Stepanionis Russia & Domithilda Porskus Russia
STEPANOVITCH, Helena, Jun 29 1909 Sex:F Child# 2 Hyppol Stepanovitch Russia & Domithilda Porskus Russia
STEPANOVITCH, Theodorus, Dec 27 1910 Sex:M Child# 3 Hipolyte Stepanovitc Russia & Domitilda Porskus Russia
STEPANOWICZ, Alex, Aug 9 1912 Sex:M Child# 4 Hppolite Stepanowicz Russia & Domitilda Porskus Russia
STEPANYON, Bernard, Aug 13 1919 Sex:M Child# 9 Hyp Stepanyon Lithuania Russia & Domith Parshkus Lithuania Russia
STEPHENS, Alice Helen, Jan 5 1903 Sex:F Child# 1 Frank V Stephens Smithville, ME & Adexren Beaudry Malone, NY
STEPHESON, Arnold Burns, Jul 11 1902 Sex:M Child# 1 H I Stepheson NS & Elizabeth Burns NB
STERGION, Andreas P, Feb 28 1917 Sex:M Child# 1 Peter Stergion Greece & Athina Lafagany Greece
STERGION, Soterios P, Jul 19 1924 Sex:M Child# 3 Peter Stergion Greece & Athena Lafazan Greece
STERGION, Unknown, Apr 1 1923 Sex:F Child# 3 Peter Stergion Greece & Athen Lafazan Greece Stillborn
STERGION, Unknown, Apr 14 1923 Sex:M Child# 2 George Stergion Greece & Lambrin Kantonine Greece
STERGIOS, Unknown, Sep 9 1935 Sex:F Child# 7 George Stergios Greece & A Makris Greece
STERGIS, Unknown, Aug 9 1916 Sex:M Child# 1 George Stergis Greece & Masulia Kojoca Greece

STERN, Annie, Dec 24 1908 Sex:F Child# 5 Samuel S Stern Russia & Goldie Grodzensky Russia
STERNS, Esther, Jul 23 1902 Sex:F Child# 2 Samuel Sterns Russia & Gertie Grodsensky Russia
STERNS, Leo Harold, Jan 28 1907 Sex:M Child# 5 Samuel Sterns Russia & Goldie Grodzensky Russia
STEVENS, Alan Douglas, Aug 17 1926 Sex:M Child# 3 David P Stevens Nashua, NH & Ruth Ackley Pepperell, MA
STEVENS, Alice Louise, Jun 12 1915 Sex:F Child# 1 Harold W Stevens Nashua, NH & Tirzah Ring Richford, VT
STEVENS, Arthur Franklin, Nov 22 1920 Sex:M Child# 4 Arthur Stevens Brooklyn, NY & Frank M Buchanan Bath, NH
STEVENS, Barbara, Feb 28 1928 Sex:F Child# 2 L B Stevens Nashua, NH & Alice E Shields Ferndale, WA
STEVENS, Barbara Jane, Aug 11 1930 Sex:F Child# 2 Mervin E Stevens Stanford, CT & Evelyn M Haskell Nashua, NH
STEVENS, David, Jul 9 1908 Sex:M Child# 1 George Stevens Vermont & Phoebe Blanchette Canada
STEVENS, David, Sep 13 1922 Sex:M Child# 1 Raymond S Stevens Nashua, NH & Katherine Andrews Nashua, NH
STEVENS, David Allen, Nov 28 1933 Sex:M Child# 3 Mervin Stevens Conn & Evelyn Haskell Nashua, NH
STEVENS, David Edgar, Jan 14 1918 Sex:M Child# 4 David M Stevens Smithfield, ME & Effie Brown Nashua, NH
STEVENS, Dorothy Carolyn, Dec 12 1909 Sex:F Child# 4 I Frank Stevens Waterville, ME & Mabel Ellis Augusta, ME
STEVENS, Dorothy May, Apr 29 1913 Sex:F Child# 4 David M Stevens Belgrade, ME & Effie L Cutter Nashua, NH
STEVENS, Edward, Mar 22 1913 Sex:M Child# 4 Edward A Stevens Woodsville, NH & Mary Jane Hatfield England
STEVENS, Edwin Bradley, Jul 8 1928 Sex:M Child# 2 P E Stevens Nashua, NH & Marion Bradley Wellsville, NY
STEVENS, Frances Ann, Jan 28 1929 Sex:F Child# 4 David P Stevens Nashua, NH & Ruth D Ackley E Pepperell, MA
STEVENS, George Isaac, Feb 26 1908 Sex:M Child# 2 Edwin A Stevens Woodsville, NH & Mary Jane Hatfield Sheffield
STEVENS, Grace Sarah, Dec 27 1911 Sex:F Child# 3 Edwin A Stevens Woodsville, NH & Mary Jane Hatfield Sheffield
STEVENS, Harold Oliver, Sep 1 1904 Sex:M Child# 2 Frank V Stevens Smithfield, ME & Dexerine Beaudry Malone, NY
STEVENS, Helen Irene, Aug 27 1910 Sex:F Child# 3 David M Stevens Maine & Effie Cutter Nashua, NH
STEVENS, Helen Lois, Aug 20 1902 Sex:F Child# 4 David Stevens, Jr Nashua, NH & Nettie L Knowles Wilton, ME
STEVENS, Henry Bouton, Feb 22 1935 Sex:M Child# 4 Merv E Stevens Stamford, CT & Evelyn Haskell Nashua, NH
STEVENS, Isaac Blaine, Mar 12 1896 Sex:M Child#  Isaac Frank Stevens Waterville, ME & Mabel Ellis Augusta, ME
STEVENS, James, Aug 27 1934 Sex:M Child# 1 Frederick B Stevens Hillsboro, NH & Ruth Mitchell Leominster, MA
STEVENS, John Bartlett, Apr 16 1916 Sex:M Child# 6 L Frank Stevens Waterville, ME & Mabel Ellis Augusta, ME
STEVENS, Lawrence Nye, Apr 9 1915 Sex:M Child# 5 Frank Stevens Waterville, ME & Mabel Ellis Augusta, ME
STEVENS, Leroy Ellsworth, Sep 30 1921 Sex:M Child# 4 Leroy Ells Stevens Paris, ME & Mary Jane Hatfield Nashua, NH
STEVENS, Lester D, May 8 1894 Sex:M Child# 1 H I Stevens Westport, NY & Nellie F Davis Dunstable, MA
STEVENS, Lizzie May, Feb 21 1889 Sex:F Child# 1 Frank W Stevens Lake Village & Alice Duffy Nashua, NH
STEVENS, Marjorie, Oct 31 1923 Sex:F Child# 2 George Stevens Everett, MA & Catherine Mallon Nashua, NH
STEVENS, Mary Mildred, Nov 19 1925 Sex:F Child# 3 George Stevens Everett, MA & Catherine Mallen Nashua, NH
STEVENS, Mervin Eugene, Jr, Dec 21 1928 Sex:M Child# 1 M E Stevens Stamford, CT & E M Haskell Nashua, NH
STEVENS, Norman Dennison, Mar 4 1932 Sex:M Child# 5 David P Stevens Nashua, NH & Ruth Ackley E Pepperell, MA
STEVENS, Patricia, Apr 4 1930 Sex:F Child# 3 Isaac B Stevens Nashua, NH & Alice E Shields Ferndale, WA
STEVENS, Pauline Lowell, May 5 1915 Sex:F Child# 2 Clark D Stevens Lina, Wisconsin & Rose M Hemmines Bargon,
STEVENS, Philip Ellis, May 20 1899 Sex:M Child# 2 L Frank Stevens Waterville, ME & Mabel Ellis Augusta, ME
STEVENS, Philip Ellis, Jr, Apr 5 1927 Sex:M Child# 1 Philip E Stevens Nashua, NH & Marian S Bradley Wellsville, NY
STEVENS, Priscilla, Aug 9 1923 Sex:F Child# 2 David P Stevens Nashua, NH & Ruth Ackley Pepperell, MA
STEVENS, Ralph D, May 21 1891 Sex:M Child# 1 David Stevens Nashua, NH & Nettie Knowles Wilton, ME
STEVENS, Raymond S, Apr 15 1894 Sex:M Child#  David Stevens Nashua, NH & Nellie Knowles Maine
STEVENS, Robert David, Aug 11 1921 Sex:M Child# 1 David P Stevens Nashua, NH & Ruth Ackley Pepperell, MA
STEVENS, Sarah Marian, Nov 27 1931 Sex:F Child# 3 Philip Ellis Stevens Nashua, NH & Marion S Bradley Wellsville, NY
STEVENS, Unknown, Jan 18 1888 Sex:F Child# 2 William D Stevens Lowell & Louise Stark Sciota, NY
STEVENS, Unknown, Jan 15 1890 Sex:M Child# 7 Almor Stevens Greenfield, NH & Hannah J Ross New London, CT
STEVENS, Unknown, Jul 7 1892 Sex:M Child# 2 Aylmer L Stevens Peterboro & Hannah J Rose St Albans, VT
STEVENS, Unknown, Oct 11 1892 Sex: Child# 2 David P Stevens Nashua, NH & Nellie Knowles Wilton, ME
STEVENS, Unknown, Dec 10 1903 Sex:M Child# 3 Samuel Stevens Russia & Gertie Grodonski Russia
STEVENS, Unknown, Apr 10 1907 Sex:F Child# 1 Edwin A Stevens Lyndonville, VT & Mary J Hatfield Sheffield, England
STEVENS, Unknown, Oct 18 1915 Sex:F Child# 5 David M Stevens Smitheld, ME & Effie Cutter Nashua, NH
STEVENS, Unknown, Feb 14 1927 Sex:F Child# 1 (No Parents Listed)
STEVENS, William Henry, Aug 12 1916 Sex:M Child# 2 Frank J Stevens Suncook, NH & Catherine M Foley Ireland
STEWART, Charles C W, Aug 22 1901 Sex:M Child# 2 Charles C Stewart New York & Martha Kennedy New York
STEWART, Constance Emily, Apr 26 1929 Sex:F Child# 1 Peter Stewart Bellows Falls, VT & C Yanuszewski Nashua, NH
STEWART, George Franklin, Sep 15 1918 Sex:M Child# 1 George F Stewart Maine & Isabelle Richards Strafford, NH
STEWART, John, Aug 1 1934 Sex:M Child# 2 John Stewart Ohio & Mary Williamson Portland, OR
STEWART, Margaret, Dec 31 1915 Sex:F Child# 4 Robin Stewart
STICKEY, Helen Elvina, Jul  1901 Sex:F Child# 2 Fred S Stickey Plainfield & Alice L Stevens Springfield, NH
STICKNEY, Elmer James, Jan 3 1905 Sex:M Child# 3 Fred S Stickney Plainfield, NH & Alice L Flanders Springfield, NH
STICKNEY, Jean Lillian, Jun 18 1928 Sex:F Child# 2 Jas E Stickney Nashua, NH & M Sullivan Denver, CO
STICKNEY, Jeannette Marion, Jun 18 1928 Sex:F Child# 1 Jas E Stickney Nashua, NH & M Sullivan Denver, CO
STICKNEY, Pauline Elsie, Sep 14 1929 Sex:F Child# 3 James Stickney Nashua, NH & Margaret Sullivan Denver, CO
STICKNEY, Priscilla, Mar 30 1920 Sex:F Child# 3 Ernest M Stickney Wilton, NH & Florence Lease New Boston, NH
STICKNEY, Unknown, Jun 20 1889 Sex:M Child# 1 Walter A Stickney
STICKNEY, Unknown, Jan 20 1891 Sex:F Child# 1 Fred S Stickney Plainfield, NH & Alice N Flanders Springfield, NH
STIELLMAN, Unknown, Jul 30 1910 Sex:F Child# 2 Pooly Stiellman Russia & Mary Saluta Russia
STIERNA, Edmund, Jan 4 1921 Sex:M Child# 2 Stanley Stierna Lithuania Russia & Elizabeth Ukimawicz Lithuania
STILES, Kenneth Royal, Sep 19 1911 Sex:M Child# 2 Roy W Stiles Elgin, NB & Anne G Tighe Milford, NH
STILLINGS, Mildred Verona, Sep 28 1920 Sex:F Child# 1 Adolph Stillings Bartlett, NH & Mildred Croft E Fairfield, VT
STILLINGS, Oakley Read, Jul 27 1922 Sex:F Child# 2 Adolph Stillings Barlett, NH & Mildred Croft E Fairfield, VT
STILLMAN, Martha, Oct 19 1926 Sex:F Child# 3 Harold Stillman Rochester, NY & Anita Gregory Columbia, SA
STILLMAN, Sylvai, Aug 11 1920 Sex:F Child# 1 Harold D Stillman Rochester, NY & Anita B Gregory Colombia, So America
STIMSON, Lloyd Kit, Feb 14 1935 Sex:M Child# 1 Lloyd Stimson Milford, NH & Isabel Smith Scotland

STINSON, Donald Chester, Feb 22 1926 Sex:M Child# 1 Eugene Stinson Hollis, NH & Mabel Smith Milford, NH
STITHAM, Allan, Apr 25 1926 Sex:M Child# 3 Harry Stitham Brunswick, ME & Lillian Conway Manchester, NH
STITHAM, Marion Elizabeth, Jun 24 1931 Sex:F Child# 4 Harry Stitham Canada & Elizabeth Connelly Manchester, NH
STITHAN, Wallace Lester, May 22 1924 Sex:M Child# 2 Harry Stithan Canada & Lillian Conley Manchester, NH
STOCKLEY, Elizabeth Ann, Jul 17 1935 Sex:F Child# 1 Charles Stockley Rome, NY & Helen Puvoiarska Nashua, NH
STOCKRER, Barbara Ida, Aug 2 1924 Sex:F Child# 2 Robert Stockrer Lawrence, MA & Ida Herald Lawrence, MA
STOCKREY, Robert Frank, Jr, May 1 1926 Sex:M Child# 3 Robert F Stockrey Lawrence, MA & Ida Herold Lawrence, MA
STOCKWELL, Christina Alice, Dec 28 1920 Sex:F Child# 1 Ray D Stockwell Swanton, VT & Sarah K Thompson Scotland
STOCKWELL, Roy Delmond, Jr, Aug 1 1927 Sex:M Child# 2 R D Stockwell Swansett, VT & Sarah Thompson Scotland
STODDARD, George Rodney, Oct 6 1909 Sex:M Child# 1 George R Stoddard Colebrook, NH & Delia F Lovejoy Medford, MA
STODDARD, Unknown, Mar 15 1909 Sex:F Child# 2 William A Stoddard Stratford, NH & Winona B Tyler Lunenburg, VT
STOEHRER, Barbara Ann, Dec 11 1932 Sex:F Child# 4 R F Stoehrer Lawrence, MA & L A Herold Lawrence, MA
STOKES, Wilfred Frederick, Dec 9 1930 Sex:M Child# 3 John R Stokes Woburn, MA & Dorothy E Simons Stoneham, MA
STOLOSKI, Rosie, May 28 1892 Sex:F Child# 7 Jacob Stoloski Polish, Russia & Dovi Cajunci Polish, Russia
STOMIUM, Mary, Jan 3 1911 Sex:F Child# 3 Stanislaus Stomium Russia & Sophia Alexbetter Russia
STONE, Ella, Jan 26 1933 Sex:F Child# 9 George Stone Worcester, MA & Ella Ferry Manchester, NH Stillborn
STONE, Hiram Perley, Mar 15 1892 Sex:M Child# 2 Hiram J Stone Bridgewater, CT & Betty Crane Bow Mills
STONE, Joseph Leo, Aug 4 1902 Sex:M Child# 2 Henry W Stone NY & Sophronie Chalifoux NY
STONE, Marie Irene B, Aug 6 1907 Sex:F Child# 3 Henry Stone New York & Sophonie Chalifoux New York
STONE, Norman Ernest, Feb 25 1934 Sex:M Child# 1 Ernest George Stone Manchester, NH & Arlene Sargent Hooksett, NH
STONE, Walter John, Jul 24 1918 Sex:M Child# 4 George Ed Stone Worcester, MA & Ella Ferry Manchester, NH
STORER, Achsah, Sep 11 1904 Sex:F Child# 5 Cecil Storer Brookline, NH & Lizzie Cramley Groton, MA
STORER, Ella Martha, Dec 10 1905 Sex:F Child# 5 Cecil Storer Brookline, NH & Elizabeth Crowley Groton, MA
STORER, Sebyl E, Aug 9 1897 Sex:F Child# 1 Cecil Storer Brookline & Lizzie Crowley Groton, MA
STORM, Eleanor, Jan 31 1924 Sex:F Child# 4 Stephen Storm NH & Katherine Barns NH
STORM, Richard Barnes, Jul 19 1922 Sex:M Child# 3 Stephen Storm Nashua, NH & Katherine Barnes Nashua, NH
STORM, Shirley, Jul 14 1919 Sex:F Child# 1 Stephen G W Storm Nashua, NH & M Katherine Barnes Nashua, NH
STORM, Stephen George, Dec 8 1890 Sex:M Child# 2 Stephen J Storm St John, NB & Julia E Works E Constable, NY
STOTOWOSKY, Julia, Jul 27 1894 Sex:F Child# 8 Jacob Stotowosky Poland & Dora Abrams Poland
STOWELL, Elizabeth Mary, Nov 30 1924 Sex:F Child# 3 Charles Stowell Bedford, NH & Bertha Foster Reeds Ferry, NH
STOWELL, John Freeman, Jul 25 1921 Sex:M Child# 2 Charles L Stowell Bedford, NH & Bertha Lee Foster Merrimack, NH
STOWOSZ, Matilda Stawaz, Mar 30 1918 Sex:F Child# 5 Frank Stowosz Austria & Victoria Patkor Austria
STRADOSKI, Stanislas, Mar 27 1908 Sex:M Child# 3 Adam Stradoski Russia & Martian Martull Russia
STRASDOWSKI, Alsbiata, Apr 9 1910 Sex:F Child# 4 Hardom Strasdowski Russia & Martiona Harlowskait Russia
STRATTON, Carl Parker, Mar 11 1913 Sex:M Child# 2 Jerome B Stratton Brookfield, VT & Grace Parker Lyndeboro, NH
STRATTON, Harold Herbert, Jul 13 1901 Sex:M Child# 3 Herbert E Stratton W Chazy, NY & Mary E O'Neil W Chazy, NY
STRATTON, Mildred G, Feb 13 1906 Sex:F Child# 1 Jerome B Stratton Brookfield, VT & Grace E Parker Lyndeboro, NH
STRATTON, Unknown, Nov 9 1893 Sex:F Child# 2 Frank Wm Stratton Northfield, MA & Edna R Hutchins Hudson, NH
STRAUT, John, Sep 23 1935 Sex:M Child# 4 John Straut Latvia & Emma Osling Latvia
STREET, Lionel Alexander, Jan 13 1935 Sex:M Child# 1 Lionel Street Revere, MA & Arlene Murphy Quincy, MA
STREETER, Unknown, Jun 17 1887 Sex:M Child# 2 A H Streeter N Townsend & Mabel Stevens Lake Village
STRNA, Stanislaus, May 16 1919 Sex:M Child# 1 Stanislaus Strna Lithuania Russia & Elizabeth Ucavich Lithuania
STROMB, Rita Helen, Aug 16 1921 Sex:F Child# 1 Elic G K Stromb Eksjos, Sweden & Ellen Maria Johnson Sweden
STRONG, May, Nov 16 1893 Sex:F Child# 1 Clifford Strong US & Emma Ouellette US
STRONG, May, Sep 6 1896 Sex:F Child# 2 Clifford Strong US & Emma Ouellette US
STUART, Unknown, Aug 20 1902 Sex:M Child# 3 Chauncey Stuart New York & Martha Kennedy New York
STULKUS, Frank, Mar 29 1909 Sex:M Child# 2 Frank Stulkus Russia & Annie Komontchol Russia
STYLIANOS, Demetrios P, Jul 2 1922 Sex:M Child# 7 Peter Stylianos Greece & Zoe Nicholason Greece
STYLIANOS, Polixeni P, Feb 8 1920 Sex:F Child# 5 Peter Stylianos Greece & Zoe Nicclaon Greece
STYLIANOS, Unknown, Sep 14 1915 Sex: Child# 5 James Stylianos Greece & Sultana Granan Greece Stillborn
STYLIANOS, Unknown, Sep 21 1916 Sex:F Child# 5 Peter Stylianos Greece & Zote Meolass Greece
STYLIANOS, Unknown, Jan 23 1919 Sex:M Child# 4 Peter Stylianos Greece & Zoe Nicolas Greece
STYLIANOS, Unknown, May 29 1921 Sex:F Child# 9 Peter Stylianos Greece & Zoe Zakec Greece
STYLIANOS, Unknown, Jul 2 1925 Sex:M Child# 9 Peter Stylianos Greece & Jeravis Nicholas Greece Stillborn
STYLUA, Joseph, Jun 26 1916 Sex:M Child# 1 Stany Stylua Russia & Eliz Guckinewicz Russia
SUBELMAN, Unknown, Dec 18 1903 Sex:M Child# 4 Israel Subelman Russia & Minnie Weinberg Russia
SUBLUSKIE, Eva, Feb 21 1920 Sex:F Child# 7 Anthony Subluskie Russia & Mary Darling Russia
SUGHAM, Unknown, Feb 22 1889 Sex:M Child# 4 Thomas Sugham Ireland & Mary Shea Ireland
SUGHRUE, Agnes, Mar 17 1906 Sex:F Child# 3 Timothy I Sughrue Ireland & Nellie M Murphy Ireland
SUGHRUE, Barbara, Feb 25 1922 Sex:F Child# 4 Timothy A Sughrue Nashua, NH & Mary Moran Nashua, NH
SUGHRUE, Daniel Gerald, Oct 13 1908 Sex:M Child# 1 Daniel Sughrue Ireland & Katherine Sullivan Ireland
SUGHRUE, Ellen, May 2 1915 Sex:F Child# 2 Dennis Sughrue Ireland & Catherine Moody Lowell, MA
SUGHRUE, Esther, Apr 26 1897 Sex:F Child# 8 Thomas Sughrue Ireland & Mary Shea Ireland
SUGHRUE, Hazel Elizabeth, Feb 4 1911 Sex:F Child# 5 Timothy Sughrue Ireland & Nellie Murphy Ireland
SUGHRUE, Jean, Nov 6 1919 Sex:F Child# 2 Timothy G Sughrue Nashua, NH & Mary Moran Nashua, NH
SUGHRUE, Maurice Francis, Oct 7 1904 Sex:M Child# 2 Timothy Sughrue Ireland & Nellie Murphy Ireland
SUGHRUE, May, May 4 1893 Sex:F Child# 3 Thomas Sughrue Ireland & Mary Shea Ireland
SUGHRUE, Richard, Jan 27 1921 Sex:M Child# 3 Timothy G Sughrue Nashua, NH & Mary F Moran Nashua, NH
SUGHRUE, Rita Marie, Oct 13 1921 Sex:F Child# 3 Dennis Sughrue Ireland & Catharine F Moody Lowell, MA
SUGHRUE, Ruth S, Apr 7 1903 Sex:F Child# 10 Thomas Sughrue Ireland & Mary Shea Ireland
SUGHRUE, Theresa, Mar 25 1908 Sex:F Child# 4 Timothy Sughrue Ireland & Nellie Murphy Ireland
SUGHRUE, Thomas Alfred, Feb 14 1901 Sex:M Child# 9 Thomas Sughrue Ireland & Mary Shea Ireland
SUGHRUE, Thomas Henry, Jul 6 1903 Sex:M Child# 1 Timothy Sughrue Ireland & Nellie M Murphy Ireland

SUGHRUE, Timothy G, Mar 22 1918 Sex:M Child# 1 Timothy Sughrue Nashua, NH & Mary F Moran Nashua, NH
SUGRUE, Agnes, Feb 7 1891 Sex:F Child# 5 Thomas Sugrue Ireland & Mary Shea Ireland
SUKOSIUS, Unknown, Jul 24 1918 Sex:F Child# 4 Frank Sukosius Russia & Louisa Lenkus Russia
SULLIVAN, Agatha, Nov 9 1920 Sex:F Child# 5 John Sullivan Cambridge, MA & Ellen Healey E Cambridge, MA
SULLIVAN, Agnes, Jan 9 1898 Sex:F Child# 5 Dand Sullivan Ireland & Mary White Ireland
SULLIVAN, Agnes, May 24 1902 Sex:F Child# 7 Jeremiah J Sullivan Ireland & Mary A Sughrue Ireland
SULLIVAN, Agnes Patricia, Jul 1 1918 Sex:F Child# 1 Matthew Sullivan Ireland & Agnes Moran Nashua, NH
SULLIVAN, Agnes Patricia, Jan 21 1932 Sex:F Child# 8 Dennis Sullivan Nashua, NH & Mary Conlon Ireland
SULLIVAN, Agnes T, May 10 1900 Sex:F Child# 6 Daniel J Sullivan Ireland & Nora Shea Ireland
SULLIVAN, Albert Arthur, Sep 15 1930 Sex:M Child# 2 Napoleon J Sullivan Fall River, MA & Genev'e Courtemanche
SULLIVAN, Alexander, Feb 6 1890 Sex:M Child# 4 Alexander Sullivan Nashua, NH & Johanna Ireland
SULLIVAN, Alice, Sep 9 1895 Sex:F Child# 5 John L Sullivan Ireland & Mary Flynn Ireland
SULLIVAN, Ann May, Aug 15 1910 Sex:F Child# 2 David Sullivan Ireland & Margaret Horgan Ireland
SULLIVAN, Anna Madeline, Nov 14 1917 Sex:F Child# 5 Dennis J Sullivan Ireland & Hannah Clifford Ireland
SULLIVAN, Anna May, Mar 9 1908 Sex:F Child# 2 Daniel Sullivan Ireland & Winifred Fox Ireland
SULLIVAN, Anna Theresa, Mar 8 1913 Sex:F Child# 2 John P Sullivan Weymouth, MA & Anne M Sullivan Ireland
SULLIVAN, Anne, Nov 14 1891 Sex:F Child# 5 John F Sullivan E Weymouth, MA & Rose McSherry Nashua, NH
SULLIVAN, Annie Marie, May 9 1902 Sex:F Child# 7 Daniel J Sullivan Ireland & Nora Shea Ireland
SULLIVAN, Arthur, Apr 13 1898 Sex:M Child# 6 John F Sullivan E Weymouth, MA & Rose McSherry Nashua, NH
SULLIVAN, Arthur Emile, Feb 28 1932 Sex:M Child# 3 Nap J Sullivan Fall River, MA & G Courtemanche Nashua, NH
SULLIVAN, Brendon Robert, Nov 23 1918 Sex:M Child# 2 John P Sullivan Ireland & Honora Sullivan Nashua, NH
SULLIVAN, Catherine, Aug 1 1898 Sex:F Child# 2 John D Sullivan Ireland & Catherine McBride Nashua, NH
SULLIVAN, Catherine, Jul 13 1908 Sex:F Child# 4 Patrick J Sullivan Nashua, NH & Johanna White Ireland
SULLIVAN, Catherine, May 28 1909 Sex:F Child# 2 John J Sullivan Nashua, NH & Nora O'Conner Ireland
SULLIVAN, Catherine Anna, Jan 9 1914 Sex:F Child# 3 Dennis J Sullivan Ireland & Hannah Clifford Ireland
SULLIVAN, Catherine Louise, Jul 29 1910 Sex:F Child# 1 William F Sullivan Lowell, MA & Mary E Thomas Lowell, MA
SULLIVAN, Cecilia, Oct 24 1904 Sex:F Child# 5 John L Sullivan Ireland & Bridget Sullivan Ireland
SULLIVAN, Clair Sylvia, Oct 15 1912 Sex:F Child# 3 John L Sullivan Nashua, NH & Clair Laplante Nashua, NH
SULLIVAN, Claire Marie, Apr 15 1917 Sex:F Child# 1 John P Sullivan Ireland & Lenora Sullivan Nashua, NH
SULLIVAN, Daniel, Feb 3 1890 Sex:M Child# 1 John Sullivan Ireland & Mary J Flynn Ireland
SULLIVAN, Daniel, Jan 8 1900 Sex:M Child# 2 John D Sullivan Nashua, NH & Catherine McBride Nashua, NH
SULLIVAN, Daniel J, Jul 30 1892 Sex:M Child# 2 Jerry J Sullivan Ireland & Mary Sughrue Ireland
SULLIVAN, Daniel J, Dec 2 1892 Sex:M Child# 2 Daniel J Sullivan Ireland & Hannorah Shea Ireland
SULLIVAN, Daniel Richard, Aug 18 1926 Sex:M Child# 6 Denis Sullivan Nashua, NH & Mary Conlon Ireland
SULLIVAN, David Augustus, Feb 23 1893 Sex:M Child# 10 Matthew Sullivan Ireland & Mary Fitzgerald Ireland
SULLIVAN, David Michael, Sep 3 1895 Sex:M Child# 4 David Sullivan Ireland & Mary White Ireland
SULLIVAN, Delia, Aug 9 1891 Sex:F Child# 4 John P Sullivan Nashua, NH & Delia Bresnahan Ireland
SULLIVAN, Dennis Jeremiah, Jun 13 1919 Sex:M Child# 2 Dennis F Sullivan Nashua, NH & Mary Coulon Ireland
SULLIVAN, Dennis Joseph, May 16 1915 Sex:M Child# 4 Dennis J Sullivan Ireland & Hannah Clifford Ireland
SULLIVAN, Dolores Lillian, Jul 7 1933 Sex:F Child# 1 Murch Sullivan Eastport, ME & E Demontigny Nashua, NH
SULLIVAN, Dorothy Jean, Apr 10 1921 Sex:F Child# 1 William Sullivan Nashua, NH & Mildred Jean Nashua, NH
SULLIVAN, Eileen, May 30 1914 Sex:F Child# 1 John E Sullivan Worcester, MA & Alice V Waugh Nashua, NH
SULLIVAN, Elizabeth, Aug 17 1889 Sex:F Child# 11 Jerry D Sullivan Ireland & Mary Shea Ireland
SULLIVAN, Elizabeth Mary, Feb 9 1924 Sex:F Child# 4 John Sullivan Ireland & Kath McCarthy Ireland
SULLIVAN, Elnora Blanche, Dec 24 1934 Sex:F Child# 1 John Louis Sullivan Peterborough, NH & Blanche Gagne Hudson,NH
SULLIVAN, Evelyn Mary, Feb 24 1895 Sex:F Child# 1 Jeremiah D Sullivan Ireland & Catherine Shea Ireland
SULLIVAN, Frances Royle, Jun 4 1912 Sex:F Child# 2 William F Sullivan Lowell, MA & Mary E Thomas Lowell, MA
SULLIVAN, Francis, Dec 3 1888 Sex:M Child# 10 Dennis H Sullivan Nashua, NH & Mary Shea Ireland
SULLIVAN, Frank, Oct 18 1889 Sex:M Child# 4 John A Sullivan E Weymouth & Rose McSherry Nashua, NH
SULLIVAN, Frederick, Jan 10 1926 Sex:M Child# 6 John Sullivan Nashua, NH & Claire Laplante Nashua, NH
SULLIVAN, Genevieve Myrtle, Oct 23 1918 Sex:F Child# 5 John Sullivan Nashua, NH & Irene Gerard Peterborough, NH
SULLIVAN, George, Jan 12 1902 Sex:M Child# 6 David Sullivan Ireland & Mary A White Ireland
SULLIVAN, George Edward, Jan 26 1894 Sex:M Child# 3 D J Sullivan Ireland & Nora Shea Ireland
SULLIVAN, George Edward, Oct 7 1918 Sex:M Child# 2 Daniel J Sullivan,Jr Nashua, NH & Elizabeth Trombley New York
SULLIVAN, George Henry, Jan 17 1892 Sex:M Child# 2 John Sullivan Ireland & Mary Flynn Ireland
SULLIVAN, Gerald Martin, Jun 18 1898 Sex:M Child# 2 Jeremiah Sullivan Ireland & Katherine Shea Ireland
SULLIVAN, Gertrude, Feb 26 1891 Sex:F Child# 5 Alexander Sullivan Nashua, NH & Johanna Sullivan Ireland
SULLIVAN, Grace May, May 1 1898 Sex:F Child# 5 Daniel J Sullivan Ireland & Nora Shea Ireland
SULLIVAN, Helen, Jun 6 1898 Sex:F Child# 2 John E Sullivan Hollis, NH & Margaret F Siske Nashua, NH
SULLIVAN, Helen Catherine, Jan 26 1931 Sex:F Child# 1 William Sullivan Troy, NY & Mary Ellen Abare Troy, NY
SULLIVAN, Helen Maria, Dec 16 1900 Sex:F Child# 4 John D Sullivan Nashua, NH & Katie McBride Nashua, NH
SULLIVAN, Ilene, Jan 30 1901 Sex:F Child# 3 John Sullivan Ireland & Bridget Sullivan Ireland
SULLIVAN, Irving Raymond, Mar 20 1922 Sex:M Child# 1 Murch Sullivan Eastport, ME & Mabel Lund Dunstable, MA
SULLIVAN, James, Jul 22 1905 Sex:M Child# 3 John J Sullivan Ireland & Rose F Scanlan Nashua, NH
SULLIVAN, James, Sep 4 1916 Sex:M Child# 4 John Sullivan Nashua, NH & Irene Girard Mass
SULLIVAN, Jeremiah, Nov 23 1896 Sex:F Child# 5 Jeremiah Sullivan Ireland & Mary Lugrie Ireland
SULLIVAN, Jeremiah F, Jun 2 1910 Sex:M Child# 3 John J Sullivan Nashua, NH & Norah O'Connell Ireland
SULLIVAN, Jeremiah J, Dec 21 1889 Sex:M Child# 4 John L Sullivan Lowell, MA & Margaret Sullivan Nashua, NH
SULLIVAN, Joan Patricia, Oct 23 1932 Sex:F Child# 2 Lawrence Sullivan Newton, MA & Lillian Russell Lawrence, MA
SULLIVAN, John, Dec 16 1888 Sex:M Child# 3 John F Sullivan Weymouth, MA & Rose McSherry Nashua, NH
SULLIVAN, John, Sep 23 1904 Sex:M Child# 7 John Sullivan E Weymouth, MA & Rose McSherry Nashua, NH
SULLIVAN, John, Sep 11 1907 Sex:M Child# 6 John L Sullivan Ireland & Bridget Sullivan Ireland
SULLIVAN, John, Aug 5 1915 Sex:M Child# 3 John A Sullivan Nashua, NH & Irene Girard Ayer, MA

SULLIVAN, John, Oct 28 1916 Sex:M Child# 2 John A Sullivan Ireland & Catherine McCarthy Ireland
SULLIVAN, John, Apr 6 1923 Sex:M Child# 4 Denis F Sullivan Nashua, NH & Mary Conlon Ireland
SULLIVAN, John A, Jan 8 1892 Sex:M Child# 1 Daniel J Sullivan Ireland & Nora A Shea Ireland
SULLIVAN, John Arthur, Mar 2 1894 Sex:M Child# 3 Jeremiah J Sullivan Ireland & Mary Sughrue Ireland
SULLIVAN, John Arthur, Jul 25 1924 Sex:M Child# 5 John L Sullivan Nashua, NH & Claire Laplante Nashua, NH
SULLIVAN, John E, Jul 11 1895 Sex:M Child# 1 John E Sullivan Hollis, NH & Maggie Siske Nashua, NH
SULLIVAN, John Edward, Jun 28 1892 Sex:M Child# 1 David Sullivan Ireland & Mary A White Ireland
SULLIVAN, John Edward, Apr 12 1894 Sex:M Child# 4 John Sullivan Ireland & Mary Flynn Ireland
SULLIVAN, John Edward, Oct 20 1897 Sex:M Child# 2 Michael P Sullivan Ireland & Bridget Callahan Ireland
SULLIVAN, John Everett, Sep 26 1932 Sex:M Child# 5 Wm J Sullivan Nashua, NH & Mildred Jean Nashua, NH
SULLIVAN, John Francis, Nov 18 1909 Sex:M Child# 1 Thomas Sullivan Nashua, NH & Mary Houlihan Milford, NH
SULLIVAN, John Joseph, Oct 12 1898 Sex:M Child# 7 John Sullivan Ireland & Mary Flinn Ireland
SULLIVAN, John Patrick, Mar 13 1905 Sex:M Child# 2 Patrick J Sullivan Nashua, NH & Johanna White Ireland
SULLIVAN, John Robert, May 7 1903 Sex:M Child# 2 John Sullivan Ireland & Rose Scanlan Nashua, NH
SULLIVAN, John, Jr, May 12 1920 Sex:M Child# 3 John P Sullivan E Weymouth, MA & Anna M Sullivan Ireland
SULLIVAN, Joseph, Mar 21 1931 Sex:M Child# 3 William Sullivan Pepperell, MA & Mary Fallon N Chelmsford, MA
SULLIVAN, Joseph Cornelius, Dec 17 1892 Sex:M Child# 7 John J Sullivan Ireland & Alsie Fallon Ireland
SULLIVAN, Joseph David, Aug 31 1909 Sex:M Child# 1 John L Sullivan Nashua, NH & Clair Laplant Nashua, NH
SULLIVAN, Josephine, Apr 15 1910 Sex:F Child# 5 Patrick J Sullivan Nashua, NH & Johanna White Ireland
SULLIVAN, Julia, Oct 30 1895 Sex:F Child# John F Sullivan Lowell, MA & Maggie Nashua, NH
SULLIVAN, Julia Edna, Oct 28 1910 Sex:F Child# 2 John L Sullivan Nashua, NH & Clair Laplante Nashua, NH
SULLIVAN, Kate, Nov 6 1889 Sex:F Child# 5 John J Sullivan Ireland & Bridget Sullivan Ireland
SULLIVAN, Katherine, Aug 2 1905 Sex:F Child# 1 Michael Sullivan Ireland & Delia Shea Nashua, NH
SULLIVAN, Katherine, Aug 17 1924 Sex:F Child# 5 John P Sullivan E Weymouth, MA & Anna Sullivan Ireland
SULLIVAN, Katherine Mary, Jan 23 1914 Sex:F Child# 2 John A Sullivan Ireland & Katherine McCarthy Ireland
SULLIVAN, Leo Paul, Jan 8 1916 Sex:M Child# 4 John L Sullivan Nashua, NH & Claire Laplante Nashua, NH
SULLIVAN, Lettiea V, Feb 19 1901 Sex:F Child# 2 Jeremiah Sullivan Ireland & Minnie McHenry Ireland
SULLIVAN, Lizzie, Jun 14 1888 Sex:F Child# 8 John D Sullivan Ireland & Mary Courtney Nashua, NH
SULLIVAN, Madeline Gertrude, Feb 23 1910 Sex:F Child# 1 Cornelius Sullivan Nashua, NH & Mary Bywater Groton, MA
SULLIVAN, Madge, Jun 2 1890 Sex:F Child# 3 Michael Sullivan Ireland & Bridget Cavenagh Ireland
SULLIVAN, Marcella, Apr 11 1903 Sex:F Child# 4 John L Sullivan Ireland & Bridget Sullivan Ireland
SULLIVAN, Margaret, Jul 17 1888 Sex:F Child# 3 Alexandrie Sullivan Nashua, NH & Johanna Sullivan Ireland
SULLIVAN, Margaret, Apr 25 1894 Sex:F Child# 5 John Sullivan Nashua, NH & Delia Bresnahan Ireland
SULLIVAN, Margaret, May 26 1898 Sex:F Child# 6 Jeremiah J Sullivan Ireland & Mary A Sughrue Ireland
SULLIVAN, Margaret, Oct 5 1899 Sex:F Child# 2 J L Sullivan Ireland & Bridget Sullivan Ireland
SULLIVAN, Margaret, Oct 5 1906 Sex:F Child# 3 Patrick J Sullivan Nashua, NH & Johanna White Ireland
SULLIVAN, Margaret Gertrude, Jun 27 1912 Sex:F Child# 2 Dennis J Sullivan Ireland & Hannah Clifford Ireland
SULLIVAN, Margaret M, Aug 4 1900 Sex:F Child# 1 John Sullivan Ireland & Rose Frances S Nashua, NH
SULLIVAN, Margaret Mary, Dec 29 1911 Sex:F Child# 1 John P Sullivan Weymouth, MA & Annie M Sullivan Ireland
SULLIVAN, Margaret Mary, Feb 25 1923 Sex:F Child# 2 William J Sullivan Nashua, NH & Mildred Jean Nashua, NH
SULLIVAN, Mark, Mar 27 1917 Sex:M Child# 2 Philip J Sullivan Ireland & Florence M Riley Pepperell, MA
SULLIVAN, Mary, Feb 2 1907 Sex:F Child# 3 Jere M Sullivan Ireland & Minnie McHenry Ireland
SULLIVAN, Mary, May 2 1927 Sex:F Child# 2 William Sullivan Pepperell, MA & Mary Fallon N Chelmsford, MA
SULLIVAN, Mary Agnes, May 23 1891 Sex:F Child# 12 I D Sullivan Ireland & Mary Shea Ireland
SULLIVAN, Mary Ann, Sep 5 1889 Sex:F Child# 1 Eugene Sullivan Ireland & Catherina A Willard Nashua, NH
SULLIVAN, Mary Catherine, Apr 15 1892 Sex:F Child# 4 Michael Sullivan Ireland & Bridget Cavanagh Ireland
SULLIVAN, Mary Ellen, Jan 22 1896 Sex:F Child# 4 Daniel J Sullivan Ireland & Nora Shea Ireland
SULLIVAN, Mary Evelyn, Aug 21 1896 Sex:F Child# 1 John M Sullivan Ireland & Bridget A Sullivan Ireland
SULLIVAN, Mary Frances, Aug 12 1891 Sex:F Child# 1 J J Sullivan Ireland & Mary Sughrue Ireland
SULLIVAN, Mary Frances, Aug 9 1893 Sex:F Child# 2 David Sullivan Ireland & Mary A White Ireland
SULLIVAN, Mary H, Ap 5 1911 Sex:F Child# 1 Dennis Sullivan Ireland & Hannah Clifford Ireland
SULLIVAN, Mary Jane, Feb 5 1904 Sex:F Child# 1 Patrick Sullivan Nashua, NH & Hannah White Ireland
SULLIVAN, Mary Theresa, Apr 25 1928 Sex:F Child# 7 Denis Sullivan Nashua, NH & Mary Conlon Ireland
SULLIVAN, Micahel, Sep 13 1888 Sex:M Child# 2 Michael Sullivan Ireland & Bridget Cavanaugh Ireland
SULLIVAN, Mildred Theresa, Sep 3 1911 Sex:F Child# 2 Thomas Sullivan Nashua, NH & Mary Holohan Milford, NH
SULLIVAN, Nancy, Nov 28 1889 Sex:F Child# John D Sullivan Ireland & Mary Ireland
SULLIVAN, Nora, Aug 20 1890 Sex:F Child# 8 Matthew Sullivan Ireland & Mary Fitzgerald Ireland
SULLIVAN, Norman Henry, Mar 21 1911 Sex:M Child# 6 John E Sullivan Hollis, NH & Margaret F Siske Nashua, NH
SULLIVAN, Patricia Mary, Mar 13 1929 Sex:F Child# 1 Geo Edward Sullivan Nashua, NH & Isabel Lucier Nashua, NH
SULLIVAN, Patrick, Oct 3 1888 Sex:M Child# 7 Matthew Sullivan Ireland & Mary Fitzgerald Ireland
SULLIVAN, Patrick Francis, Jan 17 1909 Sex:M Child# 1 David P Sullivan Ireland & Margaret Horgan Ireland
SULLIVAN, Patrick Henry, Jul 24 1899 Sex:M Child# 1 Jeremiah Sullivan Ireland & Minnie McHenry England
SULLIVAN, Paul C, Dec 23 1900 Sex:M Child# 3 John E Sullivan NH & Margaret F Siske Nashua, NH
SULLIVAN, Paul Davis, Nov 23 1902 Sex:M Child# 2 Timothy F Sullivan Nashua, NH & Matie Davis Westfield, MA
SULLIVAN, Pauline Helen, Jan 27 1928 Sex:F Child# 4 William Sullivan Nashua, NH & Mildred Jean Nashua, NH
SULLIVAN, Philip, Jun 17 1904 Sex:M Child# 4 John E Sullivan Hollis, NH & Margaret F Siske Nashua, NH
SULLIVAN, Raymond C, Dec 25 1896 Sex:M Child# 6 Alexander Sullivan Nashua, NH & Johanna Sullivan Ireland
SULLIVAN, Richard James, Aug 15 1903 Sex:M Child# 8 Daniel Sullivan Ireland & Mora Shea Ireland
SULLIVAN, Richard Lionel, May 30 1933 Sex:M Child# 4 N J Sullivan Fall River, MA & G Courtemanche Nashua, NH
SULLIVAN, Richard T, Aug 24 1915 Sex:M Child# 4 William F Sullivan Lowell, MA & Mary Thomas Lowell, MA
SULLIVAN, Robert, Feb 8 1889 Sex:M Child# 8 Jeremiah C Sullivan Ireland & Mary L Sullivan Ireland
SULLIVAN, Robert, Sep 26 1916 Sex:M Child# 6 William F Sullivan Lowell, MA & Mary Thomas Lowell, MA
SULLIVAN, Robert Leo, Oct 17 1899 Sex:M Child# 8 J L Sullivan Ireland & Mary Flynn Ireland

SULLIVAN, Robert Leonard, Sep 24 1924 Sex:M Child# 1 Frank Sullivan Nashua, NH & Emma Terrien N Adams, MA
SULLIVAN, Robert Louis, May 17 1929 Sex:M Child# 1 Napoleon J Sullivan Fall River, MA & G Courtemanche Nashua, NH
SULLIVAN, Roger Francis, Jun 21 1917 Sex:M Child# 1 Dennis F Sullivan Nashua, NH & Mary Conlon Ireland
SULLIVAN, Roger T, Mar 24 1908 Sex:M Child# 7 John E Sullivan Hollis, NH & Margaret F Siske Nashua, NH
SULLIVAN, Rose, Aug 10 1896 Sex:F Child# 6 John Sullivan Ireland & Mary Flynn Ireland
SULLIVAN, Rose Ann, Feb 17 1902 Sex:F Child# 10 John Sullivan Ireland & Mary Flynn Ireland
SULLIVAN, Sara Elizabeth, Sep 13 1898 Sex:F Child# 2 Timothy F Sullivan Nashua, NH & Julia A Shea Portsmouth, NH
SULLIVAN, Shirley Elizabeth, Nov 11 1922 Sex:F Child# 1 George Sullivan Veazie, ME & Elizabeth O'Neil Nashua, NH
SULLIVAN, Teressa, Nov 27 1887 Sex:F Child# 3 John F Sullivan Nashua, NH & Maggie T Nashua, NH
SULLIVAN, Theresa, Dec 7 1891 Sex:F Child# 4 Dennis Sullivan Nashua, NH & Mary Sullivan Ireland
SULLIVAN, Theresa Mary, Apr 27 1923 Sex:F Child# 2 Matthew Sullivan Ireland & Agnes Moran Nashua, NH
SULLIVAN, Thomas, Dec 19 1887 Sex:M Child# 7 Jeremiah Sullivan Ireland & Mary Nashua, NH
SULLIVAN, Thomas, Jan 12 1902 Sex:M Child# 7 David Sullivan Ireland & Mary A White Ireland
SULLIVAN, Thomas A, Nov 18 1896 Sex:M Child# 5 Dennis Sullivan Nashua, NH & Mary Sullivan Ireland
SULLIVAN, Thomas Edouard, Nov 9 1924 Sex:M Child# 5 Dennis Sullivan Ireland & Mary Coulin Ireland
SULLIVAN, Thomas Edward, Nov 30 1900 Sex:M Child# 4 John Sullivan Ireland & Mary Flint Ireland
SULLIVAN, Thomas Joseph, Sep 4 1913 Sex:M Child# 3 Thomas Sullivan Nashua, NH & Mary Hallorhan Milford, NH
SULLIVAN, Thomas Rmnd, May 31 1927 Sex:M Child# 1 Thomas Sullivan E Pepperell, MA & Margaret Connolly Dunstable, MA
SULLIVAN, Timothy, May 16 1892 Sex:M Child# 1 Michael P Sullivan Ireland & Bridget Callahan Ireland
SULLIVAN, Timothy Joseph, Dec 22 1922 Sex:M Child# 4 John P Sullivan E Weymouth, MA & Anna Sullivan Ireland
SULLIVAN, Unknown, Jan 4 1887 Sex:M Child# 2 John Sullivan Nashua, NH & Delia Sullivan Ireland
SULLIVAN, Unknown, Mar 30 1887 Sex:M Child# 2 Alex Sullivan Nashua, NH & Johanna Ireland
SULLIVAN, Unknown, Mar 2 1888 Sex:F Child# 9 Jerry D Sullivan Ireland & Mary Shea Ireland
SULLIVAN, Unknown, Jul 13 1888 Sex:F Child# 6 John Sullivan Ireland & Bridget Fallen Ireland Stillborn
SULLIVAN, Unknown, Mar 7 1889 Sex: Child# 3 John P Sullivan Nashua, NH & Dula B Sullivan Ireland
SULLIVAN, Unknown, Jul 15 1890 Sex:F Child# 3 James E Sullivan Ireland & Maggie F Driscoll Ireland
SULLIVAN, Unknown, Jun 20 1891 Sex:F Child# 5 John F Sullivan Lowell, MA & Maggie Huntington Nashua, NH
SULLIVAN, Unknown, Sep 16 1893 Sex:M Child# 14 Jeremiah D Sullivan Ireland & Mary A Shea Ireland Stillborn
SULLIVAN, Unknown, Oct 7 1893 Sex:M Child#  John F Sullivan Lowell, MA & Maggie Nashua, NH
SULLIVAN, Unknown, Oct 2 1894 Sex:F Child# 3 David M Sullivan Ireland & Mary A White Ireland
SULLIVAN, Unknown, Jun 4 1895 Sex:F Child# 1 Timothy F Sullivan Nashua, NH & Julia Ann Portsmouth, NH
SULLIVAN, Unknown, Jul 9 1898 Sex:M Child# 8 John T Sullivan Lowell, MA & Margaret Nashua, NH
SULLIVAN, Unknown, Nov 26 1900 Sex:F Child# 1 T F Sullivan Nashua, NH & Matie F Davis Mass
SULLIVAN, Unknown, Apr 11 1908 Sex:M Child# 1 James D Sullivan Ireland & Katherine O'Neil Ireland Stillborn
SULLIVAN, Unknown, Jan 21 1913 Sex:M Child# 1 John A Sullivan Ireland & Katherine McCarthy Ireland Stillborn
SULLIVAN, Unknown, Apr 9 1915 Sex:M Child# 1 Phillip J Sullivan Ireland & Florence M Riley Pepperell, MA
SULLIVAN, Unknown, Nov 1 1931 Sex:M Child# 2 William J Sullivan Troy, NH & Mary Ellen Abare Troy, NH
SULLIVAN, Walter, Sep 16 1906 Sex:M Child# 1 Daniel E Sullivan Ireland & Winnifred Fox Ireland
SULLIVAN, Walter Andrew, Nov 11 1906 Sex:M Child# 9 Daniel Sullivan Ireland & Nora Shea Ireland
SULLIVAN, William, Feb 7 1921 Sex:M Child# 3 Dennis F Sullivan Nashua, NH & Mary Conlon Ireland
SULLIVAN, William, Mar 15 1924 Sex:M Child# 3 William Sullivan Nashua, NH & Mildred Jean Nashua, NH
SULLIVAN, William Edward, Jun 3 1889 Sex:M Child# 1 John E Sullivan Nashua, NH & Rose Early Nashua, NH
SULLIVAN, William Edward, Jr, Mar 10 1923 Sex:M Child# 1 Wm Edward Sullivan Nashua, NH & Bessie Dionne Nashua, NH
SULLIVAN, William Francis, May 29 1925 Sex:M Child# 1 William Sullivan Pepperell, MA & Mary Fallon N Chelmsford, MA
SULLIVAN, William Francis, Jr, Oct 8 1913 Sex:M Child# 3 William F Sullivan Lowell, MA & Mary E Thomas Lowell, MA
SULLIVAN, William J, Mar 18 1895 Sex:M Child# 4 Jeremiah J Sullivan Ireland & Mary Sughran Ireland
SULLO, Mary, Apr 7 1923 Sex:F Child# 2 Ludovic Sullo Milford, MA & Sella Stanio New York, NY
SUMMERVILLE, Andrew, Sep 16 1906 Sex:M Child# 6 John Summerville England & Mary Early England
SUMMERVILLE, Andrew Stevens, Sep 28 1909 Sex:M Child# 8 John Summerville Ireland & Mary Earley Ireland
SUMMERVILLE, Irene Elizabeth, Jul 26 1905 Sex:F Child# 5 John Summerville Ireland & Mary Ann Earley Ireland
SUMMERVILLE, Irene Marguerite, Sep 12 1907 Sex:F Child# 7 John Summerville Ireland & Mary Earley Ireland
SUMMERVILLE, Mary Christena, Nov 27 1903 Sex:F Child#4 John Summerville Ireland & Mary Earley Ireland
SUMMERVILLE, Rose Annie, Jan 24 1900 Sex:F Child# 2 John Summerville Ireland & Mary Annie Early Ireland
SUMNER, Earl, Jr, Sep 1 1926 Sex:M Child# 1 Earl Sumner Peterboro, NH & Mary Sullivan Ireland
SUMNER, Walter W, Jun 18 1918 Sex:M Child# 1 Walter W Sumner Boston, MA & Ina Alexandra Peterboro, NH
SUMPTER, Harold Aloysius, Dec 13 1901 Sex:M Child# 2 Joseph A Sumpter Holyoke, MA & Margaret M Sullivan Ireland
SUMPTER, Robert J, Jun 15 1900 Sex:M Child# 1 Joseph Sumpter Mass & Margaret Sullivan Ireland
SUNAKIEWK, Wtordzslaw, Jul 31 1914 Sex:M Child# 3 Joseph Sunakiewk Poland & Ludwka Olechowska Poland
SUNARD, Joseph Arthur, Feb 20 1898 Sex:M Child# 3 Joseph Sunard Canada & Alexandrina Gendron Canada
SUNDELL, Dora, Sep 7 1900 Sex:F Child# 8 William Sundell Russia & Flora Viner Russia
SUNDSTROM, Unknown, May 11 1924 Sex:M Child# 2 Gustaf Sundstrom Worcester, MA & B Laflamme Lewiston, ME Stillborn
SUNKOVSKI, Joseph Daniel, Dec 15 1921 Sex:M Child# 7 Charles Sunkovski Poland & Casa Zoravski Poland
SUNNEILLE, John Francis, Jan 12 1902 Sex:M Child# 3 John Sunneille Ireland & Marie Early Ireland
SUPPLE, Helen Mez, Jul 24 1918 Sex:F Child# 1 John J Supple Pepperell, MA & Mez M Damon Kennebunk, ME
SUPRY, Joseph Maurice M, Sep 10 1908 Sex:M Child# 1 William F Supry Concord, NH & Leona Landry Nashua, NH
SUPRY, Maurice Milton, Mar 22 1929 Sex:M Child# 1 Maurice Supry Nashua, NH & Antoinette Dumaine Nashua, NH
SUPRY, William Francis, Mar 3 1932 Sex:M Child# 2 Maurice Supry Nashua, NH & A Dumaine Nashua, NH
SUSAULKA, Sophia, May 1 1913 Sex:F Child# 1 John Susaulka Russia & Amelia Polchelski Russia
SUSENES, John James, Jul 17 1907 Sex:M Child# 3 James Susenen Greece & Stanroche Susanes Greece
SVEKOLA, Antoysa, Aug 6 1910 Sex:F Child# 3 Florian Svekola Russia & Ludwiss Becker Russia
SVEMALIS, Marie Anne, Aug 20 1915 Sex:F Child# 1 Julius Svemalis Russia & Edwiga Salazuita Russia
SVINAWICZ, John, May 19 1914 Sex:M Child# 5 Constantin Svinawicz Russia & Josie Glensky Russia
SVIRSKAS, Joseph, Mar 10 1926 Sex:M Child# 1 Peter Svirskas Lithuania & Nellie Knisute Lithuania

SVOIDERSKI, Antosa, Mar 1 1914 Sex:M Child# 1 Amd Svoiderski Russia & Anni J Krossoia Russia
SWADAS, Eva, Aug 31 1912 Sex:F Child# 2 John Swadas Russia & Mary Ashmacy Russia
SWAIN, Aurora, Aug 8 1901 Sex:F Child# 6 Frederick Swain Conn & Bridget Humphrey Ireland
SWAIN, Charles Andrews, May 28 1900 Sex:M Child# 1 George L Swain NH & Kate B Andrews Ohio
SWAIN, Earl John, May 19 1898 Sex:M Child# 4 Fred Swain Canada & B Mary Humphrey Ireland
SWAIN, Edith May, Jul 31 1899 Sex:F Child# 5 Frederick Swain Conn & Bridget Humphries Ireland
SWAIN, Ella A, Jul 12 1890 Sex:F Child# 1 Fred D Swain New Britain, CT & B Mary Humphrey Ireland
SWAIN, Ethel Grace S, Feb 15 1903 Sex:F Child# 7 Frederick Swain Conn & Bridget Humphries Ireland
SWAIN, Katherine, May 27 1908 Sex:F Child# 8 Frederick W Swain New Britain, CT & Bridget Humphrey Ireland
SWAIN, Unknown, Dec 28 1902 Sex:M Child# 2 George L Swain Nashua, NH & Kate Andrews Galipolis, OH
SWAIN, William F, Sep 1 1894 Sex:M Child# 2 Frederick W Swain Glastonbury, CT & Bridget Humphrey Ireland
SWALLOW, Clara, Jan 26 1897 Sex:F Child# 1 Herbert J Swallow Peterboro, NH & Florence Austin Dunstable, MA
SWALOWIC, Sophia, Jul 15 1916 Sex:F Child# 2 Jeromy Swalowic Russia & Stanislava Narkawicz Russia
SWAN, Unknown, Nov 16 1889 Sex:F Child# 4 James Swan Canada & A Bellette Canada
SWANSON, Ralph Edward, Jan 17 1920 Sex:M Child# 1 Ralph B Swanson Titusville, PA & Ethel M Hutchinson Excelsior
SWART, Elizabeth, Mar 31 1892 Sex:F Child# 1 William D Swart NY & Elizabeth Roby Nashua, NH
SWART, William R, Jan 7 1894 Sex:M Child# 2 William D Swart NY & Elizabeth Roby Nashua, NH
SWEDERSKY, Unknown, Feb 28 1914 Sex:M Child# 2 Antony Swedersky Russia & Mary Kaushaulaus Russia Stillborn
SWEENEY, Bartholemew, Jan 26 1887 Sex:M Child# 2 Miles J Sweeney Ireland & Ellen Cowen Quebec
SWEENEY, Cora Frances, Feb 16 1895 Sex:F Child# 3 William Sweeney Norwalk, CT & Bridget Considine Limerick, Ireland
SWEENEY, Daniel, Jun 25 1906 Sex:M Child# 2 John Sweeney Ireland & Mary Connor Ireland
SWEENEY, Daniel Joseph, Dec 11 1903 Sex:M Child# 3 Daniel Sweeney Ireland & Elizabeth Connell Ireland
SWEENEY, Dennis Francis, Oct 17 1897 Sex:M Child# 5 George F Sweeney Nashua, NH & Margaret A Cohen Nashua, NH
SWEENEY, Edward, Jun 11 1890 Sex:M Child# 1 William Sweeney Norwalk, CT & Bridget Constanine Ireland
SWEENEY, Edward Patrick, Jul 1 1904 Sex:M Child# 1 John Sweeney Ireland & Mary Connor Ireland
SWEENEY, Elizabeth, Aug 6 1928 Sex:F Child# 2 James Sweeney Nashua, NH & Catherine Coggins New Haven, CT
SWEENEY, Ella Belle, Dec 26 1898 Sex:F Child# 6 George F Sweeney Nashua, NH & Margaret A Cohen Nashua, NH
SWEENEY, Ellen, Feb 15 1892 Sex:F Child# 7 Peter Sweeney Ireland & Mary Killkelley Ireland
SWEENEY, Ellen Veronica, Dec 8 1918 Sex:F Child# 8 Daniel Sweeney Ireland & Elizabeth O'Connell Ireland
SWEENEY, George, Nov 4 1891 Sex:M Child# 1 George F Sweeney Nashua, NH & Margaret Cohen Nashua, NH
SWEENEY, George Francois, Jul 13 1918 Sex:M Child# 1 Dennis Sweeney US & Marie Dube US
SWEENEY, James Augustus, Aug 29 1895 Sex:M Child# 4 George F Sweeney Nashua, NH & Margaret A Cohen Nashua, NH
SWEENEY, James Augustus, Jan 11 1926 Sex:M Child# 1 James Sweeney Nashua, NH & Catherine Coggins New Haven, CT
SWEENEY, Jean Norman, Nov 13 1919 Sex:M Child# 2 Dennis Sweeney Nashua, NH & Marie Dube Nashua, NH
SWEENEY, John Leonard, Aug 16 1907 Sex:M Child# 1 John P Sweeney Ireland & Mary Connor Ireland
SWEENEY, John Patrick, Nov 16 1901 Sex:M Child# 2 Daniel Sweeney Ireland & Elizabeth Connell Ireland
SWEENEY, Leo Anthony, Jul 10 1912 Sex:M Child# 7 Daniel Sweeney Ireland & Elizabeth Conell Ireland
SWEENEY, Margaret E, Aug 29 1892 Sex:F Child# 2 George F Sweeney Nashua, NH & Margaret A Cohen Nashua, NH
SWEENEY, Mary Agnes, Feb 20 1900 Sex:F Child# 1 Daniel Sweeney Ireland & Elizabeth O'Connell Ireland
SWEENEY, Mary Margaret, Nov 2 1892 Sex:F Child# 2 William Sweeney Norwalk, CT & Bridget Constadine Ireland
SWEENEY, Peter, Dec 27 1889 Sex:M Child# 6 Peter Sweeney Ireland & Mary Killkelley Ireland
SWEENEY, Unknown, May 17 1887 Sex:F Child# 3 Peter Sweeney Ireland & Mary Ireland
SWEENEY, Unknown, Oct 25 1888 Sex:M Child# 1 Peter Sweeney Ireland & Mary Ireland Stillborn
SWEENEY, Unknown, Oct 15 1905 Sex:M Child# 4 Daniel Sweeney Ireland & Elizabeth Connell Ireland
SWEENEY, William, Sep 25 1894 Sex:M Child# 8 Peter Sweeney Ireland & Mary Kilkelly Ireland
SWEET, Benjamin, Jul 26 1915 Sex:M Child# 2 Anthony Sweet Russia & Mary Karsonius Russia
SWEET, Edgar, Jul 31 1888 Sex:M Child# 1 A J M Sweet New York & Alice Warren Maine
SWEETLAND, Agnes F, Feb 23 1901 Sex:F Child# 1 Frank Sweetland Marblehead, MA & Sylvia P Dane Nashua, NH
SWEKLA, Alphonse, May 17 1926 Sex:M Child# 2 Ambrose Swekla Poland & H Marchenovicz Vandergrift, PA
SWEKLA, Joseph, Sep 28 1924 Sex:M Child# 1 Ambrose Swekla Poland & L Marchenawick E Vandergift, PA
SWEKLO, Marian, May 3 1935 Sex:F Child# 1 Adam Sweklo Pittsburgh, PA & Anna Narkunas Nashua, NH
SWETT, Alan Milton, Mar 26 1917 Sex:M Child# 1 Archie Milton Swett Antrim, NH & Helen Cathrine Hills Antrim, NH
SWETT, Robert Cummings, Jun 1 1920 Sex:M Child# 2 Archie M Swett Antrim, NH & Helen C Hills Antrim, NH
SWICLER, Mary, Oct 24 1907 Sex:F Child# 2 Flourn Swicler Russia & Ludreis Backus Russia
SWICTEK, Frederick, Nov 22 1918 Sex:M Child# 1 Michael Swictek Poland & Nellie Misiaszek Poland
SWIFT, Duane Francis, Oct 15 1925 Sex:M Child# 4 Clyde H Swift Crown Point, NY & Lillian Lewis Londonderry, NH
SWIFT, Floyd Warren, Nov 21 1923 Sex:M Child# 3 Clyde H Swift Crown Point, NY & Lillian F Lewis Londonderry, NH
SWIFT, Guilford Addison, Dec 3 1927 Sex:M Child# 5 Clyde H Swift Crown Pt, NY & Lillian Lewis Londonderry, NH
SWIFT, Helen May, Jul 13 1921 Sex:F Child# 2 Clyde H Swift Crown Pt, NY & Jillian F Lewis Londonderry, NH
SWIFT, Kay Almeda, Aug 13 1935 Sex:F Child# 7 Clyde Swift Crown Point, NY & Lillian Lewis Londonderry, NH
SWIFT, Ralph Clyde, Aug 10 1919 Sex:M Child# 1 Clyde N Swift Crown Pt, NY & Lillian Lewis Londonderry, NH
SWIFT, Ruth Nancy, May 17 1930 Sex:F Child# 6 Clyde H Swift New York & Lillian Lewis NH
SWIFT, Sadie Gladys, Feb 7 1904 Sex:F Child# 1 Clyde H Swift Crown Pt, NY & Louisa Labonte Greenfield, NH
SWIKLA, Elena, Oct 19 1905 Sex:F Child# 1 Flioress Swikla Russia & L Bakaroucka Russia
SWINDELL, Eva Maria, Oct 21 1911 Sex:F Child# 5 Caswell Swindell Stonewall, NC & Sadie C Boyd Newberg, NC Colored
SWOKLA, Joseph, Sep 22 1912 Sex:M Child# 4 Pliorian Swokla Russia & Lindwisa Bakanoski Russia
SYER, Jos Ernest Robert, Mar 29 1920 Sex:M Child# 1 Ernest Syer Canada & Albertine Thibodeau Canada
SYLOSEK, Stanislaus, May 5 1904 Sex:M Child# 1 Stanislaus Sylosek Poland & Anna Lupa Poland
SYLVAIN, Albert Horace Jos, Apr 29 1920 Sex:M Child# 2 Horace Sylvain Canada & Angelina Bilodeau Canada
SYLVAIN, Jos Robert Leonard, Mar 26 1929 Sex:M Child# 6 Honore Sylvain Canada & Angelina Bilodeau Canada
SYLVAIN, Leo Amil J, Dec 13 1921 Sex:M Child# 3 Horace Sylvain Canada & Agneline Billadieu Canada
SYLVAIN, Marie Jeannette B, Apr 13 1919 Sex:F Child# 1 Horace Sylvain Canada & Angelina Bilodeau Canada
SYLVAIN, Mary Gertrude, Jul 8 1925 Sex:F Child# 4 Horace Sylvain Canada & A Bilodeau Canada

SYLVAIN, Philidor Romeo, Sep 8 1921 Sex:M Child# 2 Ludger Sylvain Canada & Eugenie Bilodeau Canada
SYLVAIN, Roger, Sep 28 1920 Sex:M Child# 1 Ludger Sylvain Canada & Eugenie Bilodeau Canada
SYLVAIN, Roger, Sep 5 1926 Sex:M Child# 5 Horace Sylvain Canada & Angelina Bilodeau Canada
SYLVESTER, Benjamin Edward, Oct 8 1917 Sex:M Child# 1 John D C Sylvester N Shapleigh, ME & Emma H Gibson Nashua, NH
SYLVESTER, Frederick Ralph, Jul 4 1903 Sex:M Child# Fred Sylvester Canada & Jane Sanschagrin Cooper's Ville,
SYLVESTER, Frederick Romeo, Sep 21 1907 Sex:M Child# 4 Frederick Sylvester Nashua, NH & Any Sawyer Rouses Pt, NY
SYLVESTER, George F, Jr, Aug 5 1913 Sex:M Child# 1 George F Sylvester Boston, MA & Alice M Smith Boston, MA
SYLVESTER, Jane, Apr 17 1924 Sex:F Child# 2 George A Sylvester Nashua, NH & Bertha Dufault Canada
SYLVESTER, Katherine, Jan 11 1905 Sex:F Child# 2 Fredrk H Sylvester Nashua, NH & Amy Sawyer Coohenville, NY
SYLVESTER, Lucille Adele, Dec 29 1918 Sex:F Child# 1 Frank Sylvester Littleton, NH & Yvonne Soucy Nashua, NH
SYLVESTER, Mary Jane, Aug 3 1932 Sex:F Child# 1 F R Sylvester Nashua, NH & Emilda Bellavance Nashua, NH
SYLVESTRE, Azilda, Jan 29 1912 Sex:F Child# 4 Armand Sylvestre Canada & Azilda Tetreau US
SYLVESTRE, Conrad, Jun 1 1907 Sex:M Child# 2 Armand Sylvestre Canada & Azilda Tetreau US
SYLVESTRE, Emerilda, Feb 11 1906 Sex:F Child# 4 Romeo Sylvestre Canada & Aglae Lampron Canada
SYLVESTRE, Eva Therese, Oct 1 1901 Sex:F Child# 2 Romeo Sylvestre Canada & Aglae Lampron Nashua, NH
SYLVESTRE, Florence, Feb 7 1903 Sex:F Child# 3 Romeo Sylvestre Canada & Aglae Lampron Nashua, NH
SYLVESTRE, Gabrielle, Dec 6 1909 Sex:F Child# 3 Armand Sylvestre Canada & Azilda Tetreault US
SYLVESTRE, Hector Raymond, Jul 19 1907 Sex:M Child# 2 Antonio N Sylvestre Nashua, NH & Susan B Foster New York
SYLVESTRE, Joseph, Jun 27 1907 Sex:M Child# 5 Romuald Sylvestre Canada & Aglae Lampron US
SYLVESTRE, Joseph Ralph A, Apr 2 1905 Sex:M Child# 1 Antonio N Sylvestre Canada & Susan F Foster New York
SYLVESTRE, Lillian J, Feb 24 1902 Sex:F Child# 1 Frederick Sylvestre Nashua, NH & A J Sanschagrin US
SYLVESTRE, Orelle, May 24 1905 Sex:M Child# 1 Armand Sylvestre Canada & Azilda Tetreau St Albans, VT
SYLVESTRE, Raoul Armand, Sep 1 1909 Sex:M Child# 6 Romeo Sylvestre Canada & Aglae Lampron Nashua, NH
SYLVESTRE, Roland Robert, Apr 15 1917 Sex:M Child# 5 Armand Sylvestre Canada & Azilda Tetreault US Stillborn
SYLVESTRE, Ronald Leon, Nov 21 1899 Sex:M Child# 1 Ronald Sylvestre Canada & Aglae Lampron Nashua, NH
SYMANOURCZ, Stanley, Jan 13 1921 Sex:M Child# 7 Wasyl Symanourcz Russia & Tafelia Teresewicz Russia
SYMMES, Deborah, Feb 7 1931 Sex:F Child# 3 Russell Symmes Winchester, MA & Elizabeth Hawkes Charlemont, MA
SYMMES, Virginia, Jul 20 1929 Sex:F Child# 2 Russell Symmes Winchester, MA & Elizabeth Hawkes Charlemont, MA
SYMONAITIS, Peter, Jul 30 1903 Sex:M Child# 3 John Symonaitis Russia & Kata Russia
SYMONAITYS, Unknown, May 4 1902 Sex:M Child# 2 John Symonaitys Russia & R Katanzyna Russia
SYNCKONOWITCH, Alda, Oct 23 1922 Sex:F Child# 6 J Synckonowitch Poland & Josephn Synckonowitc Poland
SYRENE, Wilfred, Jr, Feb 20 1926 Sex:M Child# 2 Wilfred Syrene Tilton, NH & Mary rondonis Nashua, NH
SYSALKA, Jennie, Apr 22 1923 Sex:F Child# 1 Frank Sysalka Poland & Helen Yakubowicz Poland
SYSALKA, Wanda, Jul 7 1926 Sex:F Child# 2 Frank Sysalka Poland & Helen Jacob Poland
SZAKOLA, Peter, Sep 1 1917 Sex:M Child# 2 Peter Szakola Russia & Viola Miscer Russia
SZAKOLA, William, Nov 26 1922 Sex:M Child# 4 Peter Szakola Poland & Walerko Marjzar Lithuania
SZARAMETA, Mary, Jul 17 1927 Sex:F Child# 1 Joseph Szarameta Lithuania & D Ubemitie Lithuania
SZLOSECK, Amela, Jul 13 1907 Sex:F Child# 3 Stanislaw Szloseck Russia & Anna Lupa Russia
SZLOSEK, Theodora Sophia, Apr 4 1920 Sex:F Child# 1 Joseph M Szlosek Austria & Anna Hunra Austria
SZLOSIK, Mary, Feb 18 1918 Sex:F Child# 8 Frank Szlosik Austria & Sofia Kogat Austria
SZNETOWSKI, Vickel, Jun 10 1918 Sex:M Child# 1 Adam Sznetowski Russia & Suzanna Dogan Russia
SZORKES, Karze, Oct 16 1917 Sex:F Child# 2 Antones Szorkes Russia & Karze Koidis Russia
SZUKIEWICZ, Stefania, Oct 31 1925 Sex:F Child# 4 John Szukiewicz Poland & Lud Zowesiah Poland
SZUSZE, Kasimir, Dec 7 1913 Sex:M Child# 1 Leona Szusze Russia & Anna Kikilate Russia
SZUSZHIEWICZ, Irene, Jun 28 1929 Sex:F Child# 5 John Szuszhiewicz Poland & Ludwicka Zaweslak Poland
SZUSZKIEWICZ, Phyllis, Nov 2 1923 Sex:F Child# 3 John Szuszkiewicz Poland & Ludwiga Zawysiak Poland
SZWANKOS, Frank, May 12 1915 Sex:M Child# 2 Frank Szwankos Russia & Kate Kristotide Russia
SZYDLOWSKY, Annie, Feb 22 1918 Sex:F Child# 2 John Szydlowsky Russia & Albina Tamolaviez Russia
SZYDLOWSKY, Anthony, Jan 26 1923 Sex:M Child# 3 John Szydlowsky Poland & Albina Tamolowicz Lithuania
SZYMAK, John, Feb 8 1923 Sex:M Child# 2 Joseph Szymak Poland & Helen Markel Poland
TABER, Julia Teahan, May 25 1918 Sex:F Child# George W Taber Fitchburg, MA & Julia T Teahan Vail, Iowa
TABOR, Barbara Ann, Oct 14 1935 Sex:F Child# 1 Herbert C Tabor Crossville, TN & Cath T Bouchea Nashua, NH
TABOR, Reginald Forrest, Oct 15 1919 Sex:M Child# 1 Forrest H Tabor Hampstead, NH & Kate A Ladd Freemont, NH
TACKOWSKI, Edwina, Sep 13 1916 Sex:F Child# 1 Edward Tackowski Russia & Josie Kospatchoue Russia
TACY, Alice Burke, Dec 29 1932 Sex:F Child# 2 Oscar Tacy S Hadley Falls & H McDermott Nashua, NH
TACY, Helen Virginia, Jul 1 1928 Sex:F Child# 1 Oscar Tacy Mass & Helen McDermott Nashua, NH
TAFE, Charles Henry, May 27 1921 Sex:M Child# 4 Charles Tafe NH & Mary Sweeney Mass
TAFE, Elizabeth, Jul 21 1916 Sex:F Child# 1 Charles Tafe Nashua, NH & Mary Sweeney Mass
TAFE, Eugene, Sep 15 1918 Sex:M Child# 2 Charles Tafe NH & Mary C Sweeney Mass
TAFE, Frank Edward, Dec 4 1922 Sex:M Child# 2 Frank Edward Tafe Nashua, NH & Delia E Lefavor Nashua, NH
TAFE, Helen Lucile, Jul 23 1920 Sex:F Child# 1 Frank Tafe Nashua, NH & Delia Lefavor Nashua, NH
TAFE, Henry, Apr 20 1891 Sex:M Child# 6 Thomas H Tafe Nashua, NH & Mary Hovan Ireland
TAFE, Mary, Jul 21 1916 Sex:F Child# 2 Charles Tafe Nashua, NH & Mary Sweeney Mass
TAFE, Thomas, Apr 18 1898 Sex:M Child# 10 Thomas Tafe Nashua, NH & Mary Horan Ireland
TAGGART, Bryant Alden, Jul 15 1935 Sex:M Child# 1 Richard Taggart Wilton, NH & Elizabeth Bryant Nashua, NH
TAGGART, Unknown, May 28 1887 Sex:M Child# 2 Fred E Taggart Litchfield & Emma Nashua, NH
TAGGART, William James, Jun 16 1914 Sex:M Child# 3 Harold W Taggart Nashua, NH & Eva M Richardson Wilton, NH
TAISTO, Martti, Nov 1 1909 Sex:M Child# 2 Heikki Taisto Finland & Anna Tamier Finland
TAIT, Horace Allen, Sep 21 1913 Sex:M Child# 2 Robert Ellery Tait Gloucester, MA & Helen F Priest Fairfield, ME
TAIT, Roberta Frances, Mar 25 1912 Sex:F Child# 2 Robert E Tait Gloucester, MA & Helen Priest Shawmut, ME
TAKAS, George, Jan 19 1918 Sex:M Child# 2 Christos K Takas Greece & Ellen G Karagunis Greece
TALBOT, Athala, May 12 1896 Sex:F Child# 2 F K Talbot Canada & M Louise Samson Canada
TALBOT, Margaret Gertrude, Feb 19 1935 Sex:F Child# 1 Romeo Talbot Lawrence, MA & Marie A Levesque Nashua, NH

TALBOT, Marie Anna Doris, Aug 10 1922 Sex:F Child# 2 Wilfrid Talbot Canada & Alice Marcoux Canada
TALBOT, Ola Mae, Mar 13 1921 Sex:F Child# 1 Leon W Talbot Georgeville, Quebec & Jennie Foss Norway, VT
TALBOT, Unknown, Jan 17 1934 Sex:M Child# 1 (No Parents Listed)
TALLIER, Magdalene, Jun  1901 Sex:F Child# 1 Joseph Tallier Poland & Ann Hovofsky Poland
TALUSKY, Kate, Jul 18 1890 Sex:F Child# 6 Jacob Talusky Poland & Dora Abraham Poland
TAMALONIS, Beruta, Oct 9 1918 Sex:F Child# 1 Peter Tamalonis Russia & Agae Krusius Russia
TAMANA, Stanislaws, Aug 22 1914 Sex:M Child# 2 Stanislaws Tamana Russia & Mary Zchempack Austria
TAMAULONIS, Frank, Feb 12 1916 Sex:M Child# 1 Jim Tamaulonis Russia & Justa Gilmsrkail Russia
TAMBLIN, Dorathy, May 8 1897 Sex:F Child# 4 Myron C Tamblin NY & Ida E Clark NY
TAMBLIN, Myra E, Apr 1 1903 Sex:F Child# 6 Myron C Tamblin Stockholm, NY & Ida E Clark Brasher, NY
TAMBLIN, Unknown, Feb 21 1900 Sex:M Child# 5 Myron C Tamblin New York & Ida Clark New York
TAMBLING, Clark D, Sep 15 1893 Sex:M Child# 3 Myron C Tambling Stockholm, NY & Ida E Clark Brasher, NY
TAMLIEWICZ, Edward, Jun 26 1907 Sex:M Child# 8 William Tamliewicz Russia & Victoria Maczinis Russia
TAMLIS, Wladza, Jun 20 1908 Sex:F Child# 2 Anthony Tamlis Russia & Alena Karpicus Russia
TAMLONAS, Lend, Dec 27 1912 Sex:M Child# 5 John Tamlonas Russia & Alena Aidukunte Russia
TAMOLAVITCH, Joseph, Jul 17 1909 Sex:M Child# 4 James Tamolavitch Russia & Judwisa Arckstin Russia
TAMOLAVITCLE, Watsias, Jan 26 1909 Sex:M Child# 9 William Tamolavitcle Russia & Victoria Mishkynis Russia
TAMOLONIS, Joseph, Jul 21 1913 Sex:M Child# 1 Peter Tamolonis Russia & Antonina Putkouskos Russia
TAMOLONIS, Josie, Aug 2 1914 Sex:F Child# 4 Jim Tamolonis Russia & Eva Volongawicz Russia
TAMOLONIS, Peter, Aug 4 1912 Sex:M Child# 2 John Tamolonis Russia & Mamie Ketawicz Russia
TAMOLONVICZ, Julia, Jul 28 1916 Sex:F Child# 14 William Tamolonvicz Russia & Antona Michkinis Russia
TAMPOSI, Nicholas, Feb 18 1918 Sex:M Child# 1 Nasi M Tamposi Romania & Aspasia Gapatolica Romania
TAMUKEWICH, Leonard, May 16 1918 Sex:M Child# 15 William Tamukewich Russia & Victoria Urleskmute Russia
TAMULESICUS, Aldona, Mar 21 1921 Sex:F Child# 2 Peter Tamulesicus Lithuania Russia & Agnes Krusis Lithuania Russia
TAMULEWICH, Stanis, Apr 8 1907 Sex:M Child# 2 Didila Tamulewich Russia & Augustina Weraniz Russia
TAMULEWICS, Francisna, Mar 14 1912 Sex:F Child# 11 William Tamulewics Russia & Victoria Miszkute Russia
TAMULEWICZ, Lucia, May 8 1907 Sex:F Child# 2 Ignac Tamulewicz Russia & Eva Walangiewicz Russia
TAMULEWICZIUS, Bronce, Aug 21 1907 Sex:F Child# 3 Z Tamulewiczius Russia & L Akseyuntie Russia
TAMULEWIES, Casimer, Apr 26 1904 Sex:M Child# 5 William Tamulewies Russia & Victoria Miezkinis Russia
TAMULEWITCH, Mary, Jan 4 1910 Sex:F Child# 2 Peter Tamulewitch Russia & Salomy Makerovitch Russia
TAMULIAWICKZIRS, Mary, Jun 5 1909 Sex:F Child# 3 John Tamuliawickzirs Russia & Alena Aidukeniute Russia
TAMULIAWICZ, John, Apr 7 1907 Sex:M Child# 1 John Tamuliawicz Russia & Alena Aldukeniute Russia
TAMULIAWICZ, Josie, Jun 17 1905 Sex:F Child# 1 A Tamuliawicz Russia & Kazilina Mazgialis Russia
TAMULIEUZCY, John, May 27 1904 Sex:M Child# 1 Zlywoit Tamulieuzcy Russia & Liza Aksen Russia
TAMULISK, Bronzi, Aug 21 1907 Sex:M Child# 3 James Tamulisk Russia & Julia Youblitie Russia
TAMULOMIS, Katherine, Jan 27 1915 Sex:F Child# 13 William Tamulomis Russia & Victoria Mieskinis Russia
TAMULONIS, Josie, May 17 1915 Sex:F Child# 5 John Tamulonis Russia & Helen Adonkonat Russia
TAMULONIS, Lillian Julia, Sep 17 1932 Sex:F Child# 3 John Tamulonis Lithuania & Isabella Chaplick Lithuania
TAMULONIS, Unknown, Jun 28 1923 Sex:F Child# 3 Vanna Tamulonis Lithuania & Usta Vitunskas Lithuania Stillborn
TAMULOWICH, Joseph, May 28 1918 Sex:M Child# 1 Bolesius Tamulowich Russia & Vincenta Ocstimte Russia
TANANA, Alice, Aug 17 1911 Sex:F Child# 1 Stanislav Tanana Russia & Mary Schimpa Austria
TANANA, Brunisleva, Jun 28 1917 Sex:F Child# 3 Stanislaw Tanana Russia & Mary Tcheonpuck Austria
TANANA, Edwin, May 29 1920 Sex:M Child# 5 Stanislav Tanana Poland Russia & Mary Shempeck Austria
TANGUAY, Constance Beatrice, Apr 18 1935 Sex:F Child# 1 Aime Tanguay Canada & Delia Laforest Nashua, NH
TANGUAY, Edouard Emile, Nov 15 1928 Sex:M Child# 3 Alphonse Tanguay Nashua, NH & Philomene Berube Canada
TANGUAY, Ermond Edouard, Jun 25 1914 Sex:M Child# 1 Edouard Tanguay Kingsbridge, NY & Edith Shirley Montreal
TANGUAY, Florence, Jan 9 1923 Sex:F Child# 1 Ernest Tanguay Canada & Aldea Malette NH
TANGUAY, Gabrielle, Aug 26 1922 Sex:F Child# 3 Arthur A Tanguay Canada & Annie Provencher Canada
TANGUAY, Girard Didier, May 2 1920 Sex:M Child# 1 Philippe Tanguay Canada & Anna Soucy Nashua, NH
TANGUAY, Jos Maurice Ludger, Nov 7 1934 Sex:M Child# 4 Julian Tanguay Canada & Ida Boucher Lawrence, MA
TANGUAY, Jos Romeo Leo, Oct 8 1928 Sex:M Child# 6 A T Tanguay Canada & Yvonne Brunette Canada
TANGUAY, Jos Samuel Henri, Aug 20 1935 Sex:M Child# 5 Jos J Tanguay Canada & Marianne Boucher Lawrence, MA
TANGUAY, Joseph Adrien E, Apr 21 1930 Sex:M Child# 7 Arthur T Tanguay Canada & Yvonne Brunette Canada
TANGUAY, Joseph Alfred E, Feb 12 1908 Sex:M Child# 2 Alfred Tanguay Canada & Elise Breton Canada
TANGUAY, Joseph Ernest Andrew, Sep 30 1927 Sex:M Child# 5 Arthur Tanguay Canada & Yvonne Brunette Canada
TANGUAY, Joseph Marcel, Jul 22 1928 Sex:M Child# 1 Julien Tanguay Canada & A Boucher Lawrence, MA
TANGUAY, Loretta Camille, Jun 14 1919 Sex:F Child# 1 Joseph Tanguay Canada & Leonie Fredette Canada
TANGUAY, Lucille, Aug 26 1922 Sex:F Child# 4 Arthur A Tanguay Canada & Annie Provencher Canada
TANGUAY, M Antoinette Therese, Nov 23 1921 Sex:F Child# 3 Wilfrid Tanguay Canada & Marie R Morrissette Canada
TANGUAY, Marianne Irene, Mar 9 1930 Sex:F Child# 3 Julien Tanguay Canada & Ida Boucher Lawrence, MA
TANGUAY, Marie Claire, Feb 9 1921 Sex:F Child# 1 Alphonse Tanguay Canada & Philomene Berube Canada
TANGUAY, Marie Irene B, Nov 20 1910 Sex:F Child# 6 Jean B Tanguay Canada & Delvina Ross Canada
TANGUAY, Marie Louise Yvette, May 12 1933 Sex:F Child# 1 Ulric Tanguay Canada & Yvonne Roberts Canada
TANGUAY, Marie Rita, Jan 27 1920 Sex:F Child# 3 Eustache Tanguay Canada & Marie Poitras Canada
TANGUAY, Marie Rose Eva, Dec 25 1903 Sex:F Child# 5 Jean Bte Tanguay Canada & Delvina Ross Canada
TANGUAY, Marie Theresa, Mar 28 1919 Sex:F Child# 1 Arthur Tanguay Canada & Anna Provencher Canada
TANGUAY, Marie Yolande Claire, May 15 1923 Sex:F Child# 1 Paul Tanguay Canada & Rose Chabot Canada
TANGUAY, Mary Louise May, May 3 1925 Sex:F Child# 2 Ernest Tanguay Canaan, NH & Aldia Mallette Nashua, NH
TANGUAY, Pauline, Sep 11 1934 Sex:F Child# 2 Ulric Tanguay Canada & Yvonne Robert Canada
TANGUAY, Robert, Apr 22 1932 Sex:M Child# 3 Julien Tanguay Canada & Ida Boucher Lawrence, MA
TANGUAY, Robert Rodolphe, Sep 22 1920 Sex:M Child# 2 Arthur Tanguay Canada & Eva Provencher Canada
TANGUAY, Rose Irene, Mar 17 1922 Sex:F Child# 2 Alphonse Tanguay Canada & Philomene Berube Canada
TANGUAY, Shirley, Dec 15 1915 Sex:F Child# 2 Edward Tanguay Brooklyn, NY & Edith McCord Canada

TANGUAY, Theresa Cecil, Oct 15 1926 Sex:F Child# 4 Arthur Tanguay Canada & Yvonne Breault Canada
TANRULWICKAS, Julius, Aug 30 1905 Sex:M Child# 2 James Tanrulwickas Russia & Ludwig Ackson Russia
TAPLEY, Cara E, Jun 8 1893 Sex:F Child# 5 Horace Tapley NB & Cora E Reynolds NB
TAPLEY, Horace M, Jan 12 1889 Sex:M Child# 4 Horace Tapley New Brunswick & Cora A Reynolds New Brunswick
TARACMEZ, John, Jul 30 1916 Sex:M Child# 1 Michael Taracmez Russia & Mary Letices Russia
TARANICWICZ, Mary, May 22 1917 Sex:F Child# 1 John Taranicwicz Russia & Ant Melankawitch Russia
TARANTINO, Richard Louis, May 24 1932 Sex:M Child# 2 S A Tarantino Plymouth, MA & Laura Bourgeois N Providence, RI
TARDIE, Unknown, Mar 2 1911 Sex:M Child# 4 Frank Tardie Vermont & Fedora Berube Vermont
TARDIF, Alfred Armase, Jan 18 1923 Sex:M Child# 3 J Aime Tardif Canada & Alice Poitras Canada
TARDIF, Alice P Rolande, Jun 5 1926 Sex:F Child# 2 Henry Tardif Canada & Dorothy Quickley New York
TARDIF, Aurele Raoul, Apr 27 1921 Sex:M Child# 5 Paul Tardif Canada & Angelina Valcour Canada
TARDIF, Joseph Sylvio, Apr 28 1901 Sex:M Child# 2 Sylvio Tardif Canada & Alphonsine Brisson Canada
TARDIF, M Josephine Y, Apr 6 1902 Sex:F Child# 3 Sylvio Tardif Canada & Josephine Brisson Canada
TARDIF, Marcella Gloria Ther, Jun 5 1927 Sex:F Child# 6 Paul Tardif Canada & Angelina Valcour Canada
TARDIF, Roland I L H, Jul 5 1923 Sex:M Child# 1 Henry Tardif Canada & Dorothy Quigley New York, NY
TARDIFF, Romeo Joseph, May 24 1903 Sex:M Child# 5 Sylvio Tardiff Canada & Josephine Brisson Canada
TARDIFF, Unknown, Sep 14 1913 Sex:F Child# 1 Frank X Tardiff Canada & Clara Palardy Nashua, NH
TARDY, Adelard, Jul 20 1899 Sex:M Child# 2 Sylvio Tardy Canada & Alphonsine Brisson Canada
TARIBECZ, Stephen, Dec 26 1917 Sex:M Child# 2 Stanley Taribecz Russia & Scholia Kursewicz Russia
TARLTON, John William, Apr 27 1923 Sex:M Child# 9 Arthur S Tarlton Chester, NH & Janette Johnson Epping, NH
TARTALIS, Robert Michael, Aug 21 1931 Sex:M Child# 1 Michael Tartalis Nashua, NH & Emily Desmarais Derry, NH
TARTARCZUK, Robert Chester, May 8 1918 Sex:M Child# 1 Anthony Tartarczuk Poland & Anna Pietkiewicz Wareham, MA
TARTILIER, Michael, Apr 14 1911 Sex:M Child# 1 Michael Tartilier Russia & Antoria Ermatainy Russia
TARULEVICH, Peter, Jul 19 1920 Sex:M Child# 7 Ant Tarulevich Russia & Helen Karpachute Russia
TARULEWICZ, Unknown, Jul 26 1913 Sex:M Child# 4 Anthony Tarulewicz Russia & Lena Karpicz Russia
TARULVEIZE, Adele, Sep 16 1914 Sex:F Child# 5 Anthony Tarulveize Russia & Alena Karpicz Russia
TASCHEREAU, Conrad Leonard Jos, Dec 27 1929 Sex:M Child# 3 Morris Taschereau Maine & Beatrice Chouinard Canada
TASCHEREAU, M Annette Beatrice, Aug 28 1928 Sex:F Child# 2 M C Taschereau Biddeford, ME & B Chouinard Canada
TASCHEREAU, Romeo Roland, Aug 12 1931 Sex:M Child# 4 Maurice Taschereau Maine & Beatrice Chourard Canada
TASSANARI, Raymond, Jan 18 1910 Sex:M Child# 2 Fred Tassanari Italy & Alice Trombly New York
TASSANARI, Raymond, Dec 28 1921 Sex:M Child# 3 Primo Tassanari Italy & Elsie Bilodeau Nashua, NH
TASSAUARI, Albert Joseph, Oct 5 1919 Sex:M Child# 3 Primo Tassauari Italy & Elsie Bilodeau Nashua, NH
TATARCUK, Titus Albert, Nov 24 1934 Sex:M Child# 1 Titus Tatarcuk US & Mary Stancik US
TATARIZUK, Edward Albert, Sep 4 1919 Sex:M Child# 2 Ant Tatarizuk Poland Russia & Anna Pietkiewicz Wareham, MA
TATE, Francis, Jul 21 1893 Sex:M Child# 9 Thomas Tate
TATE, Gordon Blakely, Sep 4 1930 Sex:M Child# 5 Rupert Tate Vermont & Rose Moulton NH
TATENAROSIS, Stanilaus, Jul 4 1908 Sex:M Child# 2 Mike Tatenarosis Russia & Anna Gumbraige Russia
TATERNINIS, Josie, Jan 9 1919 Sex:F Child# 1 Mike Taterninis Lithuania & Agie Suska Lithuania
TATRO, Alberta Evelyn, Jul 18 1929 Sex:F Child# 2 Roland Tatro Nashua, NH & Nettie Hanscomb Hudson, NH
TATRO, Betty Mae, Mar 9 1931 Sex:F Child# 3 Roland Henry Tatro Nashua, NH & Nettie Hanscomb Hudson, NH
TATRO, George R, Nov 26 1900 Sex:M Child# 1 Charles Tatro Vermont & Elizabeth Howes Mass Stillborn
TATRO, Marguerite, Feb 21 1903 Sex:F Child# 2 Charles E Tatro Burlington, VT & Elizabeth S Howes Lawrence, MA
TATRO, Marion, Apr 4 1923 Sex:F Child# 1 (No Parents Listed)
TATRO, Oliver H, Aug 16 1904 Sex:M Child# 3 Charles E Tatro Burlington, VT & Elizabeth S Howes Lawrence, MA
TATRO, Pearl, Dec 5 1909 Sex:F Child# 4 Charles E Tatro Burlington, VT & Elizabeth Howes Lawrence, MA
TATRO, Roland Henry, Jr, Aug 6 1925 Sex:M Child# 1 Roland H Tatro Nashua, NH & Nettie Hanscomb Hudson, NH
TATRO, Ruberita, Sep 4 1906 Sex:F Child# 4 Charles E Tatro Burlington, VT & Elizabeth Howes Lawrence, MA
TATSAWICH, Paul, Feb 21 1920 Sex:M Child# 1 Paul Tatsawich Russia & Amelia Yuktwich Russia
TAUMASIAN, Unknown, Sep 21 1930 Sex:M Child# 3 Memas Taumasion Armenia & Veronica Daporian Armenia
TAYLOR, Albert, Mar 10 1913 Sex:M Child# 11 George Taylor Forest, NY & Katherine Ryan Milford, NH
TAYLOR, Ethel, Oct 3 1890 Sex:F Child# 2 Robert H Taylor Ravenswood, NY & Theresa McCarthy Boston, MA
TAYLOR, Fred W, Aug 8 1910 Sex:M Child# 3 William Taylor Nova Scotia & Minne E Watson Nashua, NH
TAYLOR, Grace Adelaide, Apr 9 1889 Sex:F Child# 1 Robert Taylor New York & Theresa McCarthy Boston, MA
TAYLOR, Helen Etta, Jun 19 1904 Sex:F Child# 1 William B Taylor Nova Scotia & Minnie E Watson Nashua, NH
TAYLOR, Howard Henry, May 28 1920 Sex:M Child# 1 Howard Taylor Ashton, RI & Josephine Walden Nashua, NH
TAYLOR, James Andrew, Apr 25 1897 Sex:M Child# 1 Moses Taylor Forest, NY & Lizzie Taylor New Brunswick
TAYLOR, John Robert, Jul 10 1914 Sex:M Child# 12 George Taylor Forrest, NY & Katherine Ryan Milford, NH
TAYLOR, John Ryan, May 6 1932 Sex:M Child# 1 George E Taylor Amherst, NH & Edna L Garrett Nashua, NH
TAYLOR, Joseph, Mar 10 1913 Sex:M Child# 9 George Taylor Forest, NY & Katherine Ryan Milford, NH
TAYLOR, Lois, Feb 24 1934 Sex:F Child# 3 John Taylor Lowell, MA & Mildred Northrup Lowell, MA
TAYLOR, Madeline M, Jul 30 1895 Sex:F Child# 1 Stephen Taylor Vermont & Alice O'Brien Vermont
TAYLOR, Raymond Bradley, Oct 15 1929 Sex:M Child# 3 Robert Taylor Brookline, NH & Ethel Musgrave Sidney, NS
TAYLOR, Richard, Mar 8 1917 Sex:M Child# 13 George Taylor Forest, NY & Catherine Ryan Milford, NH
TAYLOR, Richard David, May 20 1935 Sex:M Child# 1 George Taylor Milford, NH & Germaine Soucy Nashua, NH
TAYLOR, Robert, Mar 10 1913 Sex:M Child# 10 George Taylor Forest, NY & Katherine Ryan Milford, NH
TAYLOR, Shirley Edna, Aug 29 1929 Sex:F Child# 1 Francis Taylor Altona, NY & Edna Pelletier Nashua, NH
TEBBETTS, Foster, Sep 28 1889 Sex:M Child# 7 Hanson Tebbetts Sherbrooke, Canada & Louise Blake Lowell, MA
TEBBETTS, Louise, Aug 20 1891 Sex:F Child# 8 Hanson E Tebbetts Sherbrooke, Canada & Louise Blake Lowell, MA
TEBBETTS, Mildred L, Jan 14 1904 Sex:F Child# 1 Fred Tebbetts Manchester, NH & Marion Campbell England
TEDASCA, Paul Herbert, Dec 28 1928 Sex:M Child# 3 S Tedasca Italy & Ruth Weaver Waltham, MA
TEFFT, Eleanor Mary, Jun 30 1931 Sex:F Child# 2 Howard M Tefft Westerly, RI & Frances White Flint, MI
TELFER, James Stuart, Jun 27 1932 Sex:M Child# 2 Robert S Telfer Evansville, IN & Walcot S Telfer Lafayette, IN
TELFER, Robert Stockdale, Jr, Jul 12 1934 Sex:M Child# 3 Robert S Telfer Evansville, IN & Sophie W Stewart Lafayett

TELLIER, Ernest Leo, Aug 13 1896 Sex:M Child# 5 Napoleon Tellier NY & Apolline Charron Canada
TELLIER, Georges E, May 21 1895 Sex:M Child# 4 Napoleon Tellier Canada & Paulina Caron Canada
TELLIER, Irene Beatrice, Apr 17 1901 Sex:F Child# 6 Napoleon Tellier Sciota, NY & Paulina Charron Canada
TELLIER, Joseph Gerard Roger, Jul 26 1924 Sex:M Child# 1 Herman Tellier Canada & Rose Turcott Canada
TELLIER, Laura Amanda, Feb 28 1893 Sex:F Child# Napoleon Tellier Canada & Paulina Charron Canada
TELLIER, Leo Ernest, Nov 18 1916 Sex:M Child# 1 Leo Ernest Tellier Nashua, NH & Celia Poney Canada Stillborn
TELLIER, Magloire Alfred, Jul 1 1890 Sex:M Child# 2 Napoleon Tellier Sciota, NY & Apalina Charron Canada
TELLIER, Marie L Rolande, Mar 3 1926 Sex:F Child# 3 Gideon Tellier Canada & Louise Carrier NH
TELLIER, Marie Violet Alma, Oct 2 1924 Sex:F Child# 2 Gedeon Tellier Canada & M L V Carvier Canada
TELLIER, Mary Helen Irene, Jul 1 1934 Sex:F Child# 2 Alpheri Tellier Providence, RI & Mary Descheneau Canada
TELLIER, Paul Emile, Oct 25 1926 Sex:M Child# 5 Honore Tellier Canada & Justine St Gelais NH
TELLIER, Theodore Peckett, Mar 6 1896 Sex:M Child# 4 Theodore Tellier Sangate, VT & Marcia J Peckett Burlington,VT
TELLIER, Unknown, Mar 13 1892 Sex:F Child# 1 Theodore Tellier Vermont & Marcia Peckett Burlington, VT
TELSINSKI, Paul, Feb 19 1922 Sex:M Child# 3 Frank Telsinski Lithuania & Eva Staskowska Lithuania
TEMPLE, Ann, Oct 21 1897 Sex:F Child# 4 John P Temple Ireland & Elizabeth J Sweeney Frontier, NY
TEMPLE, Anthony, Feb 5 1901 Sex:M Child# 6 John P Temple Ireland & Elizabeth Sweeney Frontier, NY
TEMPLE, Benedict, Jan 12 1896 Sex:M Child# 3 John P Temple Ireland & Elizabeth J Sweeney New York
TEMPLE, Edward Patrick, Apr 5 1908 Sex:M Child# 9 John P Temple Ireland & Elizabeth J Sweeney Frontier, NY
TEMPLE, Elizabeth Jane, Apr 8 1932 Sex:F Child# 1 Joseph Temple Nashua, NH & Algenia Robinson Columbia Valley, NH
TEMPLE, Joan Frances, May 5 1933 Sex:F Child# 2 Jos F Temple Nashua, NH & Algenia Burrill Columbia Valley, NH
TEMPLE, John, May 25 1903 Sex:M Child# 7 John P Temple Ireland & Elizabeth J Sweeney Frontier, NY
TEMPLE, John Albert, Aug 13 1935 Sex:M Child# 4 Joseph Temple Nashua, NH & Algenia Burrill Nashua, NH
TEMPLE, Joseph Francis, Dec 7 1893 Sex:M Child# 1 John P Temple Ireland & Elizabeth J Sweeney Frontier, NY
TEMPLE, Keran, Jul 25 1899 Sex:M Child# 5 John P Temple Ireland & Lizzie J Sweeney Frontier, NY
TEMPLE, Margaret C, Dec 21 1894 Sex:F Child# John P Temple Ireland & Eliza J Sweeney Ireland
TEMPLE, Mary, Oct 18 1905 Sex:F Child# 8 John P Temple Ireland & Elizabeth J Sweeney Frontier, NY
TEMSPOUNOS, Unknown, Jul 31 1919 Sex:M Child# 2 Thomas Temspounos Greece & Helen Papachristo Greece
TEMULEWICH, Unknown, Jan 2 1920 Sex:M Child# 2 Peter Temulewich Lithuania & Alice Semontis Lithuania
TEMULIAWICZUS, Annie, Apr 29 1911 Sex:F Child# 2 Bolesus Temuliawiczu Russia & Acenta Akucinte Russia
TENERAWICH, Giansel, Dec 2 1909 Sex:F Child# 4 Mike Tenerawich Austria & Bridget Vetzarwich Austria
TENEROWICZ, Stefania, Feb 5 1911 Sex:F Child# 5 Marcy Tenerowicz Poland & Bronistawa Woictowic Poland
TENGUERAND, Olymph R D, Jul 25 1891 Sex:F Child# 3 Reney Tenguerand Canada & Olymphe Levesque Canada
TENNANT, Unknown, May 22 1891 Sex:F Child# 8 Charles H Tennant Merrimack, NH & Clara Gardner Merrimack, NH
TENOROWICZ, Adam, Aug 5 1913 Sex:M Child# 7 Mike Tenorowicz Russia & Bridget Vetzawich Russia
TENOROWITCH, Marie, Sep 11 1917 Sex:F Child# 9 Mike Tenorowitch Poland Russia & Bridget Austria
TENORWICH, Matalia, Aug 24 1909 Sex:F Child# 3 Henry Tenorwich Russia & Alice Kopitska Russia
TENOVOWICZ, Toodeus, Jun 6 1905 Sex:F Child# 1 Mike Tenovowicz Austria & Bronislaiva Austria
TERBINOS, Mary, Dec 20 1916 Sex:F Child# 1 Anastasias Terbinos Greece & Annie Pappas Greece
TEREICWITCH, Anna, Jul 26 1910 Sex:F Child# 7 Jasper Tereicwitch Russia & Lichvitia Perzwaduti Russia
TERENOWICH, Stanis, Jan 13 1908 Sex:M Child# 3 Mike Terenowich Austria & Bridget Vetzawich Austria
TERESAWICZ, Unknown, Feb 10 1925 Sex:M Child# 2 Chris Teresawicz Poland & Amelia Shedlowska Poland
TERRASSAWICH, Anna, Aug 3 1908 Sex:F Child# 1 Dom Terrassawich Russia & Carolina Chashun Russia
TERRELL, Albert Wilmarth, Feb 6 1924 Sex:M Child# 1 John Caleb Terrell Nashua, NH & Mary A Cadorette Nashua, NH
TERRIEN, Albert Paul, Jr, Jul 7 1925 Sex:M Child# 3 Albert Terrien Littleton, NH & Desneiges Dufour Anaconda,
TERRIEN, Anne, Feb 16 1929 Sex:F Child# 4 Albert Terrien Littleton, NH & Desneiges Dufour Anaconda, Mont
TERRIEN, Florence, Oct 21 1911 Sex:F Child# 7 Joseph Terrien US & Elizabeth Annis US
TERRIEN, George, Mar 8 1923 Sex:M Child# 2 Albert Terrien Littleton, NH & Desneiges Dufour Anaconda, Mont
TERRIEN, John, Mar 23 1921 Sex:M Child# 1 Albert Terrien NH & Desneiges Dufour Anaconda, Mont
TERRIEN, Lillie Irene, Oct 13 1905 Sex:F Child# 5 Isaac Terrien Canada & Arthemise Masse Canada
TERRIEN, Marie Oliva, Dec 4 1897 Sex:F Child# 5 Joseph Terrien Canada & Elmire Champagne Canada
TERRIEN, Wilfred Joseph, Jan 28 1901 Sex:M Child# 3 Joseph Terrien Canada & Jennie Larouche Nashua, NH
TERRILL, Adaline Grace, Nov 5 1913 Sex:F Child# Albert W Terrill Nashua, NH & Ida May Bowers Pepperell, MA
TERRILL, Cullen James, Nov 25 1926 Sex:M Child# 1 John C Terrill Milford, NH & Alma Cote Nashua, NH
TERRIS, George Everett, Nov 3 1916 Sex:M Child# 2 James M Terris Hillsboro, NB & Hattie R Hancock Black River, NB
TERRIS, Ira Austin, Sep 3 1915 Sex:M Child# 1 James M Terris Hillsboro, NH & Hattie R Hancock Black River, NB
TERRIS, James Murray, Jr, Mar 30 1921 Sex:M Child# 4 James M Terris New Brunswick & Hattie Hancock Nova Scotia
TERRIS, Julia Elizabeth, Nov 22 1918 Sex:F Child# 3 James M Terris Ayer, MA & Hattie R Hancock Nova Scotia
TERRIS, Lillian Vesta, Sep 26 1902 Sex:F Child# 4 George E Terris NB & Lilla M McGilvery Nova Scotia
TERZIS, John, Jun 21 1916 Sex:M Child# 2 Christis Terzis Greece & Sophia Nouzouka Greece
TESSANARI, Eveline L, Jul 9 1908 Sex:F Child# 1 A Fred Tessanari Italy & Alice Trombly New York
TESSIANAN, Joseph, Sep 1 1915 Sex:M Child# 2 Pedro Tessianan Italy & Elize Bilodeau Nashua, NH
TESSIER, Alfred Amedee, Apr 11 1898 Sex:M Child# 1 Alfred Tessier Canada & Elise Gagnon Canada
TESSIER, Alfred Andrew York, Jun 29 1918 Sex:M Child# 1 Alexander Tessier Nashua, NH & Lizzie York Fremont, NH
TESSIER, Anne A Rolande, Jul 27 1931 Sex:F Child# 2 Roland F Tessier Nashua, NH & Lena Lamoureux Nashua, NH
TESSIER, Arthur Edward, May 18 1927 Sex:M Child# 2 Alfred Tessier Nashua, NH & Josephine Latour Nashua, NH
TESSIER, Arthur Ernest, Aug 18 1909 Sex:M Child# 9 Alfred Tessier Canada & Elise Gagnon Canada
TESSIER, Arthur Robert Henry, Nov 7 1923 Sex:M Child# 8 Eugene Tessier Canada & Dorilla L Tessier Canada
TESSIER, Charlotte Elsie, Mar 6 1925 Sex:F Child# 1 Alexander Tessier Nashua, NH & Rose Beaupre Canada
TESSIER, Cora Irene, Jan 28 1922 Sex:F Child# 7 Eugene Tessier Canada & Dorella Tessier Canada
TESSIER, Delphis, Jun 16 1913 Sex:M Child# 2 Joseph Tessier Canada & Ezilia Picard Canada
TESSIER, Diana Lumina, Mar 19 1908 Sex:F Child# 8 Alfred Tessier Canada & Elise Gagnon Canada
TESSIER, Elise Yvonne Marie, Dec 12 1917 Sex:F Child# 5 Eugene Tessier Canada & Dorilla Canada
TESSIER, Elizabeth, Jul 22 1901 Sex:F Child# 1 Henry E Tessier Nashua, NH & Mary McDermott Nashua,

TESSIER, Elodie Pearl, May 14 1906 Sex:F Child# 7 Alfred Tessier Canada & Elise Gagnon Canada
TESSIER, Emma Joanne, Jul 26 1902 Sex:F Child# 3 Ernest Tessier Nashua, NH & Albina Leclair Nashua, NH
TESSIER, Ernest, Mar 27 1907 Sex:M Child# 8 Ernest Tessier Nashua, NH & Albina Leclair Nashua, NH Stillborn
TESSIER, Ernest F R, May 28 1900 Sex:M Child# 1 E F Tessier Nashua, NH & Albina V Leclair Nashua, NH
TESSIER, Eugene, Jan 8 1909 Sex:M Child# 2 Eugene Tessier Canada & Dorila Tessier Canada Stillborn
TESSIER, Eugene Arthur O, Mar 7 1903 Sex:M Child# 5 George O Tessier Nashua, NH & Lumina Lagace Canada
TESSIER, Eva Clara, Jul 6 1915 Sex:F Child# 4 Joseph Tessier Canada & Exilia Picard Canada
TESSIER, Frederick A, Oct 1 1901 Sex:M Child# 2 Ernest Tessier Nashua, NH & Albina Leclair Nashua, NH
TESSIER, George F Raoul, Dec 29 1899 Sex:M Child# 3 George O Tessier Nashua, NH & M L Lagace Canada
TESSIER, George Napoleon Jas, Apr 13 1904 Sex:M Child# 1 Napoleon Tessier Canada & Bernice Whittemore Pepperell, MA
TESSIER, Georgiana Clara, Mar 23 1910 Sex:F Child# 3 Eugene Tessier Canada & Dorila Tessier Canada
TESSIER, Gertrude Edna, May 10 1909 Sex:F Child# 2 Napoleon Tessier Canada & Bernice Whittemore Pepperell, MA
TESSIER, Girard, Jan 2 1916 Sex:M Child# 17 Ernest F Tessier Nashua, NH & Albina Leclaire Nashua, NH
TESSIER, Henri Alphonse E, Dec 28 1906 Sex:M Child# 7 George O Tessier Nashua, NH & M Lumina Lagasse Canada
TESSIER, J Albert, Mar 8 1911 Sex:M Child# 12 Ernest Tessier Nashua, NH & Albina Leclair Nashua, NH Stillborn
TESSIER, J Jean Paul Vincent, Dec 10 1914 Sex:M Child# 10 George O Tessier Nashua, NH & Lumina Lagace Canada
TESSIER, Jannette Marie, Aug 7 1903 Sex:F Child# 2 Henry Tessier Nashua, NH & Marie McDermott Nashua, NH
TESSIER, Joseph, Apr 9 1917 Sex:M Child# 1 Henri Tessier Canada & Marie Anna Gelinas Canada
TESSIER, Joseph A Samuel, Nov 17 1899 Sex:M Child# 2 Alfred Tessier Canada & Elise Gagnon Canada
TESSIER, Joseph E, Sep 24 1901 Sex:M Child# 12 Alfred Tessier Canada & Adeline Gagnon Canada
TESSIER, Joseph Gerald, Apr 14 1922 Sex:M Child# 1 Joseph Tessier Canada & Marion Pelletier Nashua, NH
TESSIER, Joseph Gerard, Dec 27 1915 Sex:M Child# 17 Ernest Tessier Nashua, NH & Albina Leclair Nashua, NH
TESSIER, Joseph Roger S, Jan 19 1905 Sex:M Child# 6 George O Tessier Nashua, NH & Lumina Lagasse Canada
TESSIER, Juliette Claire, Apr 12 1934 Sex:F Child# 1 Gerard Tessier Manchester, NH & Lucienne Robert Rosaire
TESSIER, Leon Conrad, Jul 28 1889 Sex:M Child# 13 Joseph Tessier Canada & Zoe Jeannotte Montreal
TESSIER, Lionel, Mar 6 1912 Sex:M Child# 1 Joseph Tessier Canada & Exilia Picard Canada
TESSIER, Louisa, Feb 20 1891 Sex:F Child# 1 Frank Tessier New York & Alphonsine Levesque Canada
TESSIER, Lumina G, Nov 20 1898 Sex:F Child# 2 G O Tessier Nashua, NH & Lumina Lagace Canada
TESSIER, M Blanche Jean, Mar 17 1919 Sex:F Child# 6 Joseph Tessier Canada & Exilda Picard Canada
TESSIER, M Cecile Alberta, Apr 23 1920 Sex:F Child# 1 Eugene Tessier Canada & Dora Tessier Canada
TESSIER, M Claire F Jeanne d', Jul 18 1912 Sex:F Child# 9 G O Tessier Nashua, NH & Lumina Lagace Canada
TESSIER, Margaret Cecile, Jun 14 1926 Sex:F Child# 2 Alexander Tessier Nashua, NH & Rose Beaupre Canada
TESSIER, Marie, Oct 31 1914 Sex:F Child# 16 Ernest F Tessier Nashua, NH & Albina Leclerc Nashua, NH
TESSIER, Marie A A, Jul 20 1899 Sex:F Child# 1 Joseph Tessier Canada & Lea Malenfant Canada
TESSIER, Marie A S J, Jul 18 1897 Sex:F Child# 1 Georges Tessier Nashua, NH & Lumina Lagace Canada
TESSIER, Marie Adeline V, May 21 1906 Sex:F Child# 1 Eugene Tessier Canada & Dorilla Tessier Canada
TESSIER, Marie Anna Juliette, Oct 30 1912 Sex:F Child# 13 Ernest Tessier Nashua, NH & Albina Leclair Nashua, NH
TESSIER, Marie Ernestine, Dec 21 1911 Sex:F Child# 13 Ernest Tessier Nashua, NH & Albina Leclair Nashua, NH
TESSIER, Marie Eugenie, Sep 27 1902 Sex:F Child# 4 Alfred Tessier Nashua, NH & Elise Gagnon Canada
TESSIER, Marie Juliette M S, Feb 21 1908 Sex:F Child# 8 George O Tessier Nashua, NH & Marie Lumina Lagace Canada
TESSIER, Marie M I, Jun 15 1901 Sex:F Child# 4 George O Tessier Nashua, NH & M Lumina Lagace Nashua, NH
TESSIER, Marie Paule, Aug 15 1935 Sex:F Child# 5 Roland Tessier Nashua, NH & Lena Lamoureux Nashua, NH
TESSIER, Mariette Leonie, Sep 17 1932 Sex:F Child# 3 Roland Tessier Nashua, NH & Lena Lamoureux Nashua, NH
TESSIER, Marion May, Aug 11 1909 Sex:F Child# 1 Napoleon L Tessier Nashua, NH & Sarah Scully Nashua, NH
TESSIER, Mary Rita, Sep 25 1923 Sex:F Child# 2 Joseph Tessier Canada & Marion Pelletier Nashua, NH
TESSIER, Mary T Juliette, Mar 13 1931 Sex:F Child# 3 Alexander Tessier Nashua, NH & Rose Beaupre Canada
TESSIER, Noel, Dec 25 1903 Sex:M Child# 5 Alfred Tessier Canada & Elise Gagnon Canada
TESSIER, Normand Ludger, May 5 1926 Sex:M Child# 2 Ernest Tessier Nashua, NH & Alphonse Lavoie Canada
TESSIER, Pauline Edna, Mar 4 1899 Sex:F Child# 2 Charles A Tessier Nashua, NH & Alice A Danley Nashua, NH
TESSIER, Raphael V G, Jan 19 1887 Sex:M Child# 10 Frederic Tessier P Q & Anna Olivier P Q
TESSIER, Roland Homer, Mar 7 1923 Sex:M Child# 1 Ernest Tessier Nashua, NH & Alphonsine Lavoie Canada
TESSIER, Romuald A, Jan 23 1901 Sex:M Child# 3 Alfred Tessier Canada & Elise Gagnon Canada
TESSIER, Rosanna Andrea, Jan 19 1905 Sex:F Child# 6 Alfred Tessier Canada & Elise Gagnon Canada
TESSIER, Theresa Anna Irene, Jul 13 1928 Sex:F Child# 3 Alf A Tessier Nashua, NH & Josephine Latour Nashua, NH
TESSIER, Unknown, Apr 4 1894 Sex:F Child# 2 Frank Tessier NY & Alphonsine Levesque Canada
TESSIER, Unknown, Sep 8 1895 Sex:F Child# 11 Alfred Tessier Canada & Elise Gagnon Canada
TESSIER, Unknown, May 12 1898 Sex:F Child# 1 Charles A Tessier Nashua, NH & Alice A Danley Nashua, NH Stillborn
TESSIER, Unknown, May 16 1900 Sex: Child# 3 Charles A Tessier Nashua, NH & Alice A Danley Nashua, NH Stillborn
TESSIER, Unknown, Oct 2 1903 Sex:F Child# 4 Ernest F Tessier Nashua, NH & Albina Leclair Nashua, NH Stillborn
TESSIER, Unknown, Nov 6 1904 Sex:M Child# 5 Ernest Tessier Nashua, NH & Albina Leclair Nashua, NH Stillborn
TESSIER, Unknown, Oct 4 1905 Sex:M Child# 6 Ernest F Tessier Nashua, NH & Albina Leclerc Nashua, NH Stillborn
TESSIER, Unknown, Jun 28 1906 Sex:M Child# 7 Ernest F Tessier Nashua, NH & Albina Leclair Nashua, NH Stillborn
TESSIER, Unknown, Apr 5 1908 Sex:F Child# 9 Ernest F Tessier Nashua, NH & Albina Leclerc Nashua, NH
TESSIER, Unknown, Apr 3 1909 Sex:F Child# 10 Ernest F Tessier Nashua, NH & Albina Leclerc Nashua, NH Stillborn
TESSIER, Unknown, Aug 12 1913 Sex:F Child# 15 Ernest F Tessier Nashua, NH & Albina Leclair Nashua, NH Stillborn
TESSIER, Veronica Louise V, Jan 24 1930 Sex:F Child# 1 Roland Tessier Nashua, NH & Lena Lamoureux Nashua, NH
TESSIER, Wayne Paul, Dec 28 1933 Sex:M Child# 1 Roland Tessier Nashua, NH & Mildred LaPonsie Lowell, MA
TESSIER, Wilfrid Avila, Jun 1 1917 Sex:M Child# 5 Joseph Tessier Canada & Exilia Picard Canada
TESTA, John, Aug 24 1914 Sex:M Child# 1 Enbaldo E Testa Italy & Anna Calabro Waterbury, CT
TETERANS, Annie, Jun 4 1910 Sex:F Child# 3 Mike Teterans Russia & Annie Gumbrage Russia
TETLER, George William, Sep 25 1929 Sex:M Child# 1 Geo William Tetler Lawrence, MA & Irene Willette Nashua, NH
TETRAULT, Francois Xavier, Sep 8 1895 Sex:M Child# 2 Frank Tetrault Vermont & Marie L Lagace Canada
TETRAULT, Joseph Henry, Jul 8 1905 Sex:M Child# 2 Wilfrid Tetrault Canada & Georgiana Houle Canada

TETRAULT, Leo Joseph, Feb 5 1921 Sex:M Child# 5 John F Tetrault Jewett City, CT & Elesa Roux Canada
TETRAULT, Marie Rosanna, Apr 10 1917 Sex:F Child# 3 John Tetrault Connecticut & Elsie Rioux Canada
TETREAU, Arthur Avila, Oct 21 1896 Sex:M Child# 4 Arthur Tetreau St Albans, VT & Valerie Lampron Canada
TETREAU, Eva, Jun 13 1893 Sex:F Child# 3 Arthur Tetreau Canada & Velerie Lampron Canada
TETREAU, Eveline Clara, Nov 4 1891 Sex:F Child# 2 Arthur Tetreau Canada & Valeria Lampson Canada
TETREAU, M Clara Yvonne, Sep 8 1922 Sex:F Child# 6 John Tetreau Jewett City, CT & Elise Rioux Canada
TETREAU, Marie, Dec 31 1915 Sex:F Child#  John Tetreau Jewett City, CT & Elise Rioux Canada Stillborn
TETREAU, Roland, Jul 14 1898 Sex:M Child# 5 Arthur Tetreau Canada & Valerie Lampron Canada
TETREAULT, Albert Delphis, Aug 2 1919 Sex:M Child# 4 J B Tetreault Jewett City, CT & Elise Rioux Canada
TETREAULT, Elmer Francis, Nov 17 1911 Sex:M Child# 4 Henry J Tetreault Canada & Delia D Girard Putnam, CT
TETREAULT, Henri Philippe, Oct 14 1917 Sex:M Child# 2 Marcel Tetreault Canada & Laura Descoteaux Canada
TETREAULT, J M Philip Roland, May 30 1914 Sex:M Child# 1 Marcel H Tetreault Canada & Laura Descoteaux Canada
TETREAULT, Julia Gertrude, Nov 1 1910 Sex:F Child# 5 John Tetreault Canada & Cesarie Breault Canada
TETREAULT, Marie Celina, Dec 31 1915 Sex:F Child# 2 Jean Bte Tetreault Canada & Elise Rioux Canada
TETREAULT, Raymond Edward, Aug 21 1910 Sex:M Child# 5 Henry J Tetreault Canada & Delia Girard Putnam, CT
TETREAULT, Victor Lafayette, Sep 14 1917 Sex:M Child# 5 Aime Tetreault US & Marie L Descoteaux Canada
TEVEQUE, L Omer Adelaide, Nov 16 1889 Sex:M Child# 3 Achille Teveque Canada & B Depew Canada
THANOS, Unknown, Nov 25 1917 Sex:F Child# 2 Alexander Thanos Greece & Athena Korvella Greece
THAYER, Florette Lillian, Jun 22 1908 Sex:F Child# 3 Frank F Thayer Mason, NH & Milia M Desmarais Nashua, NH
THAYER, Forest, Oct 21 1905 Sex:M Child# 1 Frank F Thayer Mason & Marie Desmarais Nashua, NH
THAYER, Unknown, Jun 6 1891 Sex:M Child# 2 Charles Thayer
THEALL, Melvina Richard, Feb 26 1926 Sex:F Child# 1 Melvin Theall
THEFORUST, Mary A Eva, Oct 9 1889 Sex:F Child# 2 Joseph Theforust Canada & Claude Germain Canada
THEIAU, William, Jan 25 1888 Sex:M Child#  Michael Theiau Canada & Marie Levesque Canada
THEODOEPOULOS, Penelope, Nov 5 1914 Sex:F Child# 5 Alex Theodoepoulos Greece & Atha Mehalopoulos Greece
THEODORE, Marie Anna, Sep 24 1898 Sex:F Child# 4 Jean Theodore Plattsburg, NY & Nellie Barrette Canada
THEODORE, Marie Dora Eva, Nov 17 1900 Sex:F Child# 5 Jean Theodore NY & Emelie Barette Canada
THEODORE, Unknown, Mar 15 1918 Sex:F Child# 1 Louis Theodore Grecce & Gramaton Sardenia Greece
THEOHARIS, Anastasias, Mar 10 1925 Sex:M Child# 2 Jos D Theoharis Greece & Masie Nashopoulos Greece
THEOHARIS, Unknown, Nov 19 1921 Sex:F Child# 1 Demetrios Theoharis Greece & Marie Kaziopordon Greece
THEOS, Pauline, May 21 1921 Sex:M Child# 7 John Theos Greece & Olebia Thanus Greece
THEOTHOROU, Unknown, Sep 5 1919 Sex:M Child# 2 Louis Theothorou Greece & Grmato Sardenis Greece
THERAULT, Timothy, Jan 17 1927 Sex:M Child# 6 Henry Therault NH & Lena Desautels NH
THEREAU, Marie Louise, Jun 24 1893 Sex:F Child# 6 Michel Thereau Canada & Marie Deveque Canada
THEREAU, William, Apr 1 1889 Sex:M Child# 3 Michel Thereau Canada & Marie Levesque Canada
THEREAULT, Mary Lena, Apr 24 1932 Sex:F Child# 9 Henry Thereault NH & Ora Derau't NH
THEREOUX, Joseph P V, Oct 13 1890 Sex:M Child# 2 Joseph Thereoux Canada & Rosanna Boisseau Canada
THERIAN, Arthur, Jul 11 1897 Sex:M Child# 9 Michael Therian Canada & Marie Leveque Canada
THERIAN, Christine, Dec 28 1899 Sex:F Child# 5 Adolphe Therian Canada & Hermine Plourde Canada Stillborn
THERIAN, Ernest, Jun 12 1896 Sex:M Child# 8 Michel Therian Canada & Marie Leveque Canada
THERIAN, Henri I, Jul 15 1898 Sex:M Child# 1 Joseph Therian Canada & Leopoldine Beaulieu Canada
THERIAN, Odelie, Dec 28 1899 Sex:F Child# 4 Adolphe Therian Canada & Hermine Plourde Canada Stillborn
THERIAU, Claudia, Apr 22 1891 Sex:F Child# 3 Israel Theriau Canada & Marie Gagnon Canada
THERIAU, Ludger, Jun 30 1889 Sex:M Child# 2 Israel Theriau Canada & Marie Gagnon Canada
THERIAU, Napoleon, Dec 1 1887 Sex:M Child# 1 Israel Theriau Canada & Marie Gagnon Canada
THERIAU, Rosanna, Mar 24 1887 Sex:F Child#  Henri Theriau P Q & Maria Belanger P Q
THERIAU, Rose Alma, Sep 28 1894 Sex:F Child#  Michel Theriau Canada & Marie Dube Canada
THERIAULT, Adrien Alfred, Feb 6 1915 Sex:M Child# 8 Joseph Theriault Canada & Adelina Doucette Nashua, NH
THERIAULT, Albert Marcel, Dec 17 1912 Sex:M Child# 3 Marcel Theriault Brunswick, Canada & Anita Jodoin Nashua, NH
THERIAULT, Alfred Joseph, Jul 10 1912 Sex:M Child# 9 Desire Theriault Canada & Donalda St Pierre Canada
THERIAULT, Alfred Leopold, Apr 25 1910 Sex:M Child# 8 Joseph Theriault Canada & Leopoldine Beaulieu Canada
THERIAULT, Alfred Roland, Nov 2 1906 Sex:M Child# 6 Joseph Theriault Canada & Leopoldine Beaulieu Canada
THERIAULT, Andrea Rosilda, Oct 21 1899 Sex:F Child# 2 Joseph Theriault Canada & Leopoldine Beaulieu Canada
THERIAULT, Antoine Leo G, Apr 19 1930 Sex:M Child# 1 Antoine Theriault New Brunswick & Eva Levesque New Brunswick
THERIAULT, Antoinette, Dec 17 1915 Sex:F Child# 1 Alfred Theriault Nashua, NH & Albina Theriault Canada
THERIAULT, Armand Adrien, Apr 25 1910 Sex:M Child# 6 J P Theriault Canada & Mathilda Ouellette Canada
THERIAULT, Arthur Alfred F, Oct 3 1906 Sex:M Child# 7 Desire Theriault Canada & Donalda St Pierre Canada
THERIAULT, Auguste, Sep 4 1924 Sex:M Child# 15 Joseph Theriault Canada & Leopoldine Beaulieu Canada
THERIAULT, Beatrice, Apr 12 1908 Sex:F Child# 8 Desire Theriault Canada & Donalda St Pierre Canada
THERIAULT, Beatrice, Mar 15 1909 Sex:F Child# 1 William Theriault Nashua, NH & Mathilde Dugas Canada Stillborn
THERIAULT, Bertha A, Sep 30 1900 Sex:F Child# 2 George Theriault Canada & Zelma Deschamps Nashua, NH
THERIAULT, Camille, Feb 11 1935 Sex:M Child# 4 Charles Theriault Canada & August Philippe Canada
THERIAULT, Camille Emelienne, May 29 1910 Sex:F Child# 1 Joseph Theriault Canada & Elise Morin Canada
THERIAULT, Charles Honore, May 18 1930 Sex:M Child# 2 Charles E Theriault Canada & Augustine Philippe Canada
THERIAULT, Charles Romeo, Sep 4 1910 Sex:M Child# 2 William Theriault Nashua, NH & Mathilde Dugas Canada
THERIAULT, Clara Louise, May 19 1921 Sex:F Child# 1 Arthur Theriault Nashua, NH & Elizabeth Levesque New York
THERIAULT, Doris Beatrice, Mar 19 1927 Sex:F Child# 1 Emile Theriault Nashua, NH & Claire Trempe Canada
THERIAULT, Edward Roland Roger, Dec 31 1923 Sex:M Child# 2 Arthur Theriault NH & Elizabeth Levesque New York
THERIAULT, Emile Joseph, Apr 29 1903 Sex:M Child# 11 Jean B Theriault Canada & Albais Marquis Canada
THERIAULT, Eva, Mar 3 1902 Sex:F Child# 10 Michael Theriault Canada & Marie Levesque Canada
THERIAULT, Felix John, Jun 25 1933 Sex:M Child# 3 Henri Theriault Nashua, NH & Eva Neverette Nashua, NH
THERIAULT, Flora Elmire, Aug 24 1905 Sex:F Child# 6 Desire Theriault Canada & Donalda St Pierre Canada
THERIAULT, Florence Elizabeth, Feb 21 1920 Sex:F Child# 2 Henri Theriault Nashua, NH & Aurore Desautels Nashua, NH

THERIAULT, Gerard, Sep 6 1926 Sex:M Child# 2 Joseph Theriault Canada & M A Migneault Canada
THERIAULT, Gerard Lucien, Apr 7 1915 Sex:M Child# 4 Jean Theriault Canada & Philomene Beaulieu Canada
THERIAULT, Harry Marcel, May 13 1909 Sex:M Child# 1 Marcel Theriault St George, NB & Anita Jodoin Nashua, NH
THERIAULT, Hermione Olivette, Sep 2 1913 Sex:F Child# 3 Joseph Theriault Canada & Elise Morin Nashua, NH
THERIAULT, J Napoleon Lionel, Mar 26 1914 Sex:M Child# 3 Alfred Theriault Canada & Anna Beaudoin Vermont
THERIAULT, J Simeon Regne, Sep 13 1913 Sex:M Child# 10 Joseph Theriault Canada & Leopoldine Beaulieu Canada
THERIAULT, Jacqueline Annette, Sep 25 1930 Sex:F Child# 2 Charles E Theriault Nashua, NH & Claire I Trempe Canada
THERIAULT, Jean Baptiste Elie, May 12 1916 Sex:M Child# 6 Jean Theriault Canada & Philomene Beaulieu Canada
THERIAULT, Jean Bte Henrie, Jun 13 1903 Sex:M Child# 9 Henri Theriault Canada & Marie Belanger Canada
THERIAULT, Jean Jos Rodolph, Jun 12 1929 Sex:M Child# 1 Jean Theriault Nashua, NH & Eve Sylvain Canada
THERIAULT, Jos M Normand, Apr 12 1931 Sex:M Child# 5 Joseph Theriault Canada & Marianna Migneault Canada
THERIAULT, Jos Ovila Gedeon, Oct 2 1919 Sex:M Child# 13 Joseph Theriault Canada & Leopoldine Beaulieu Canada
THERIAULT, Jos Paul Roland, May 18 1929 Sex:M Child# 1 Joseph Theriault Nashua, NH & Yvonne Fournier Salem, MA
THERIAULT, Jos Robert Alphege, May 19 1917 Sex:M Child# 12 Joseph Theriault Canada & Leopoldine Beaulieu Canada
THERIAULT, Joseph, Jul 22 1893 Sex:M Child# 1 Joseph Theriault Canada & Caroline St Pierre Canada
THERIAULT, Joseph, Jan 8 1904 Sex:M Child# 1 Joseph Theriault Canada & Adelina Doucette NH
THERIAULT, Joseph Albert, Dec 19 1898 Sex:M Child# 1 Desire Theriault Canada & Donalda St Pierre Canada
THERIAULT, Joseph Alfred, Sep 2 1906 Sex:M Child# 10 Henry Theriault Canada & Maria Belanger Canada
THERIAULT, Joseph Alfred Ernest, Feb 9 1932 Sex:M Child# 2 Jean Theriault Nashua, NH & Eva Sylvain Canada
THERIAULT, Joseph Alphe, Feb 16 1896 Sex:M Child# 1 Policarpe Theriault Canada & Marie Proulx Canada
THERIAULT, Joseph Armand Roger, Aug 1 1912 Sex:M Child# 3 Jean Theriault Canada & Philomene Beaulieu Canada
THERIAULT, Joseph D S, Jan 31 1912 Sex:M Child# 6 Joseph Theriault Canada & Adeline Doucet Nashua, NH
THERIAULT, Joseph Emile, Jan 23 1901 Sex:M Child# 6 J Bte Theriault Canada & Emelie Cyr Canada
THERIAULT, Joseph Ernest, Mar 11 1894 Sex:M Child# 4 Henri Theriault Canada & Marie Belanger Canada
THERIAULT, Joseph Henri, Oct 30 1896 Sex:M Child# 1 Eugene Theriault Canada & Arthemise Gagne Canada
THERIAULT, Joseph J B A, Jun 24 1902 Sex:M Child# 4 Pierre Theriault Canada & Apolline Chasse Canada
THERIAULT, Joseph Leo Paul, Jun 20 1919 Sex:M Child# 2 Napoleon Theriault Nashua, NH & Emma Dionne Canada
THERIAULT, Joseph Lougee, Dec 23 1906 Sex:M Child# 11 Michael Theriault Rimouski, Quebec & Mary Bishop Cacounn
THERIAULT, Joseph Paul, Sep 25 1900 Sex:M Child# 2 Desire Theriault Canada & Donalda St Pierre Canada
THERIAULT, Joseph Phillip S, May 24 1910 Sex:M Child# 5 Joseph Theriault Canada & Adeline Doucet Nashua, NH
THERIAULT, Joseph Polycarpe, Oct 8 1903 Sex:M Child# 1 Polycarpe Theriault Canada & Mathilda Ouellette Canada
THERIAULT, Joseph Rodolphe, May 11 1933 Sex:M Child# 1 (No Parents Listed)
THERIAULT, Joseph S F J B, Sep 4 1906 Sex:M Child# 3 Joseph Theriault Canada & Adelina Doucette Nashua, NH
THERIAULT, Juliette, May 16 1908 Sex:F Child# 7 Joseph Theriault Canada & Leopoldine Beaulieu Canada
THERIAULT, Juliette, Oct 4 1911 Sex:F Child# 2 Joseph Theriault Canada & Stephanie Morin Nashua, NH
THERIAULT, Laurette Marguerite, Mar 12 1913 Sex:F Child# 2 Alfred Theriault Canada & Anna Beaudoin St Johnsbury, VT
THERIAULT, Leo George, Feb 9 1907 Sex:M Child# 3 P S Theriault Canada & Mathilda Ouellette Canada
THERIAULT, Loraine Mary, Mar 24 1922 Sex:F Child# 3 Henry Theriault NH & Ora Desautel Nashua, NH
THERIAULT, Loretta Corinne, Dec 30 1922 Sex:F Child# 5 Joseph Theriault Canada & Elise Morin Nashua, NH
THERIAULT, Lorette Adrienne, Jan 27 1911 Sex:F Child# 2 Jean Theriault Canada & Philomene Beaulieu Canada
THERIAULT, Louis C E, Nov 20 1903 Sex:M Child# 3 George Theriault Canada & Alma Deschamps Nashua, NH
THERIAULT, Louis Edgar, Aug 5 1915 Sex:M Child# 11 Joseph Theriault Canada & Leopoldine Beaulieu Canada
THERIAULT, Louisa Andria, Feb 22 1913 Sex:F Child# 7 Joseph Theriault Canada & Adeline Doucette Nashua, NH
THERIAULT, Lucille Juliette, Jul 11 1933 Sex:F Child# 2 Antoine Theriault Canada & E Levesque Canada
THERIAULT, Ludger, Dec 2 1911 Sex:M Child# 3 Willie Theriault Nashua, NH & Mathilde Dugas Canada
THERIAULT, M Antoinette Jean, Mar 13 1914 Sex:F Child# 1 (No Parents Listed)
THERIAULT, M Cecile Alberte, Jun 13 1921 Sex:F Child# 14 J C Theriault Canada & Leopoldine Beaulieu Canada
THERIAULT, M Corrinne Eveline, Sep 19 1915 Sex:F Child# 4 William Theriault Nashua, NH & Matilde Dugas Nashua, NH
THERIAULT, M Deneige Juliette, Jan 11 1914 Sex:F Child# 4 William Theriault Nashua, NH & Mathilde Dugas Canada
THERIAULT, Marie, Dec 8 1907 Sex:F Child# 4 Polycarpe Theriault Canada & Mathilda Ouellette Canada Stillborn
THERIAULT, Marie A C, Nov 22 1898 Sex:F Child# 2 Eugene Theriault Canada & Arthemise Gagnon Canada
THERIAULT, Marie A Elmire, Jul 30 1899 Sex:F Child# 5 J B Theriault Canada & Emelie Cyr Canada
THERIAULT, Marie Alice, Dec 20 1899 Sex:F Child# 3 Eugene Theriault Canada & Arthemise Gagne Canada
THERIAULT, Marie Almina I, Apr 20 1904 Sex:F Child# 5 Desire Theriault Canada & Donalda St Pierre Canada
THERIAULT, Marie Ange Jeanne, Dec 11 1917 Sex:F Child# 1 Leopold Theriault Nashua, NH & Anna Dionne Canada
THERIAULT, Marie Anna, Feb 4 1892 Sex:F Child# 4 Henry Theriault Canada & Marie Belanger Canada
THERIAULT, Marie Anne, Oct 28 1895 Sex:F Child# 3 Charles Theriault Canada & Anna Desjardins Canada
THERIAULT, Marie Artemise, May 20 1896 Sex:F Child# 6 Henri Theriault Canada &  Canada
THERIAULT, Marie Celina, Apr 3 1902 Sex:F Child# 4 Eugene Theriault Canada & Arthesime Gagne Canada
THERIAULT, Marie Denise A, Jun 6 1905 Sex:F Child# 2 Joseph Theriault Canada & Adelina Doucet Nashua, NH
THERIAULT, Marie Donalda, Jan 7 1903 Sex:F Child# 4 Desire Theriault Canada & Donalda St Pierre Canada
THERIAULT, Marie Eva, Aug 29 1916 Sex:F Child# 2 Ernest Theriault Nashua, NH & Rose Cardin Nashua, NH
THERIAULT, Marie Eva Pearl, Dec 8 1897 Sex:F Child# 7 Henri Theriault Canada & Maria Belanger Canada
THERIAULT, Marie Irene, Jan 17 1913 Sex:F Child# 1 (No Parents Listed)
THERIAULT, Marie Irene L, Aug 6 1905 Sex:F Child# 5 Eugene Theriault Canada & Arthemise Gagne Canada
THERIAULT, Marie Jeanne Cecile, Mar 27 1916 Sex:F Child# 9 Joseph Theriault Canada & Adelina Doucette Nashua, NH
THERIAULT, Marie R Albina, Jul 29 1900 Sex:F Child# 8 Henri Theriault Canada & Marie Belanger Canada
THERIAULT, Marie Rose, Jun 20 1927 Sex:F Child# 1 Joseph Theriault Chicopee, MA & Alvina Francoeur Nashua, NH
THERIAULT, Marie Rose Bernadett, Feb 19 1918 Sex:F Child# 10 Joseph Theriault St Flavie, PQ & Adelina Doucette
THERIAULT, Marie Therese R, Mar 12 1930 Sex:F Child# 5 Joseph Theriault Canada & Marie A Migneault Canada
THERIAULT, Maurice Rodolphe, Mar 14 1931 Sex:M Child# 2 Antoine Theriault Canada & Evangeline Levesque Canada
THERIAULT, Muriel Gloria E, Oct 6 1929 Sex:F Child# 1 Arthur Theriault Nashua, NH & Josephine Marquis Canada
THERIAULT, Omer Alcide, Aug 29 1910 Sex:M Child# 12 Henry Theriault Canada & Maria Belanger Canada

THERIAULT, Paul Edmond, Jan 15 1925 Sex:M Child# 1 Jean Theriault Nashua, NH & A Bourgnignon Canada
THERIAULT, Paul Gerard, Nov 29 1916 Sex:M Child# 10 L P Theriault Canada & Mathilda Ouellette Canada
THERIAULT, Paul Robert, Dec 7 1913 Sex:M Child# 4 Jean Theriault Canada & Philomene Beaulieu Canada
THERIAULT, Pearl B, Oct 12 1897 Sex:F Child# 1 George Theriault Quebec & Minnie Deschamps Nashua, NH
THERIAULT, Pierre, Sep 4 1888 Sex:M Child# 14 Alphonse Theriault Canada & Honorine Chank Canada
THERIAULT, Rachel Isabel A, Aug 9 1930 Sex:F Child# 8 Henry J Theriault Nashua, NH & Ora Desautels NH
THERIAULT, Ralph Sylvio, Apr 13 1927 Sex:M Child# 4 J A Theriault Canada & B Blanchette Canada
THERIAULT, Raoul Albert, Dec 2 1908 Sex:M Child# 5 J P Theriault Canada & Mathilda Ouellette Canada
THERIAULT, Raymond, Feb 3 1906 Sex:M Child# 2 J P Theriault Canada & Mathilda Ouellette Canada
THERIAULT, Rita Lelia, Jul 24 1923 Sex:F Child# 4 Henry Theriault NH & Ora Desautels NH
THERIAULT, Rita Marie A, Jun 17 1925 Sex:F Child# 1 Joseph Theriault Canada & Marie A Mignault Canada
THERIAULT, Robert, Dec 5 1934 Sex:M Child# 1 Alfred Theriault Nashua, NH & Maria Paradis Canada
THERIAULT, Rochelle Florette, Jul 8 1918 Sex:F Child# 4 Joseph Theriault Nashua, NH & Eline A Morin Montreal
THERIAULT, Romeo, Feb 24 1901 Sex:M Child# 3 Joseph Theriault Canada & Leopoline Beaulieu Canada
THERIAULT, Ronald Louis, May 22 1935 Sex:M Child# 1 Louis Theriault Nashua, NH & Ida Cournoyer Montreal, Canada
THERIAULT, Rosanna, Aug 1 1915 Sex:F Child# 1 Ernest Theriault Nashua, NH & Rose Anna Cardin Nashua, NH
THERIAULT, Rose Alma, Jan 12 1905 Sex:F Child# 5 Joseph Theriault Canada & Leopoldine Beaulieu Canada
THERIAULT, Sylvia, Aug 12 1913 Sex:F Child# 10 Deisre Theriault Canada & Donalda St Pierre Canada
THERIAULT, Thelma Albina, Jan 26 1918 Sex:F Child# 4 Alfred Theriault Canada & Anna Blaudoin Nova Scotia
THERIAULT, Therese Jacqueline, Mar 21 1934 Sex:F Child# 10 Henri Theriault Nashua, NH & Aurore Desautels Nashua, NH
THERIAULT, Unknown, Jan 25 1891 Sex:F Child# 15 Alphonse Theriault Canada & Anoime Chink Canada Stillborn
THERIAULT, Unknown, Jan 26 1891 Sex:F Child# 3 Henri Theriault Canada & Marie Belanger Canada
THERIAULT, Unknown, Apr 8 1901 Sex:M Child# 2 Alexis Theriault Vermont & Aglaide Fournier Canada
THERIAULT, Unknown, Sep 25 1908 Sex:M Child# 4 Joseph Theriault Ste Falvie, PQ & Adelina Doucet Nashua, NH
THERIAULT, Unknown, Apr 19 1911 Sex:M Child# 2 Marcel Theriault St George, NB & Anita Jodoin Nashua, NH
THERIAULT, Unknown, Mar 21 1927 Sex:M Child# 1 Henry Theriault Nashua, NH & Eva Neverett Sciota, NY Stillborn
THERIAULT, V Rochelle Aline, May 29 1932 Sex:F Child# 3 Romeo Theriault Nashua, NH & Gracia Bibeau St Germain
THERIAULT, Wilfred Almond Henry, Jun 14 1925 Sex:M Child# 5 Henry Theriault Nashua, NH & Ora Desautils Nashua, NH
THERIAULT, Yvonne Edna, Mar 13 1911 Sex:F Child# 7 Polycarpe Theriault Canada & Mathilda Ouellette Canada
THERIAULT, Yvonne Isabelle, Feb 1 1903 Sex:F Child# 4 Joseph Theriault Canada & Leopoldine Beaulieu Canada
THERIEN, David, Jan 21 1887 Sex:M Child# Thomas Therien Canada & E Montrency P Q
THERIEN, Gerard Adrien, Jan 30 1912 Sex:M Child# 9 Joseph Therien Canada & Leopoldine Beaulieu Canada
THERIEN, Ida, Nov 28 1907 Sex:F Child# 1 Joseph Therien Canada & Eugenie Larouche Nashua, NH
THERIEN, Marie, Nov 28 1899 Sex:F Child# 3 Adolph Therien Canada & Hermine Plourde Canada Stillborn
THERIEN, Marie E, Jan 13 1890 Sex:F Child# 2 Joseph Therien Canada & Elmire Champagne Canada
THERIEN, Rosanna, Feb 17 1893 Sex:F Child# 8 Xavier Therien Canada & Henriette Poirier St Albans, VT
THERIEN, Silvio Henri, Feb 15 1908 Sex:M Child# 2 Clement Therien Canada & Celina Brochu Canada
THERIEN, Unknown, Feb 18 1893 Sex:F Child# 9 Xavier Therien Canada & Henriette Poirier St Albans, VT Stillborn
THEROUER, Gertrude A, Apr 10 1896 Sex:F Child# 5 Joseph Therouer Canada & Rosanna Boisseau Canada
THEROUSE, Ivonne C, Jul 13 1900 Sex:F Child# 7 Joseph Therouse Canada & Rosanna Boisseau Canada
THEROUX, Alexander O, Oct 7 1895 Sex:M Child# 4 Irence Theroux Canada & Emelie Girard Canada
THEROUX, Alice Beatrice, Feb 23 1906 Sex:F Child# 9 Joseph Theroux Canada & Rosanna Boisseau Canada
THEROUX, Camille Gloria, Feb 2 1931 Sex:F Child# 2 Walter Theroux Nashua, NH & Stella Pelletier Nashua, NH
THEROUX, Charles Emile Joseph, May 23 1915 Sex:M Child# 3 Valmore Theroux Nashua, NH & Angelina Masson Canada
THEROUX, Clementine L, May 16 1892 Sex:F Child# 3 Joseph Theroux Canada & Rosanna Boisseau Canada
THEROUX, Domitilde Lilian, Apr 7 1912 Sex:F Child# 2 Valmore Theroux US & Angelina Masson Canada
THEROUX, Doris Rita, Dec 10 1925 Sex:F Child# 1 Joseph P Theroux Nashua, NH & Flora Boislais Manchester, NH
THEROUX, Eliana A, Jun 29 1898 Sex:F Child# 6 Joseph Theroux Canada & Rosanna Boisseau Canada
THEROUX, Emelien Roland, Oct 3 1909 Sex:M Child# 12 Joseph Theroux Canada & Rosanna Boisseau Canada
THEROUX, Ernest R, Jul 21 1909 Sex:M Child# 2 Dorilla Theroux Canada & A Lavoie Malone, NY
THEROUX, Estelle Ada, Dec 21 1927 Sex:F Child# 1 Albert Theroux Nashua, NH & Rose Poulin Nashua, NH
THEROUX, Eudore H, Jan 24 1894 Sex:M Child# 4 Joseph Theroux Canada & Rosanna Boisseau Canada
THEROUX, Germaine, Jun 25 1920 Sex:F Child# 1 George Theroux Nashua, NH & Stella Beaulieu Canada
THEROUX, Helene Leonie, Aug 15 1902 Sex:F Child# 2 Louis Theroux Canada & Virginie Douillet Canada
THEROUX, Horace, Oct 12 1891 Sex:M Child# 3 Irenee Theroux Canada & Emilie Girard Canada
THEROUX, Irene Gertrude, Aug 22 1907 Sex:F Child# 1 Doria Theroux Canada & Rosa Lavoie Malone, NY
THEROUX, Irene Gladys, Aug 26 1907 Sex:F Child# 10 Joseph Theroux Canada & Rosanna Boisseau Canada
THEROUX, J Herbert Romeo, Nov 16 1921 Sex:M Child# 2 Joseph G Theroux NH & Stella Beaulieu Canada
THEROUX, J Irene, Nov 28 1888 Sex:F Child# 1 Irenie Theroux Canada & Emilie Girard Canada
THEROUX, Jeannette Beatrice, Jul 19 1913 Sex:F Child# 4 Dorila Theroux Canada & Rose Lavoie Malone, NY
THEROUX, Joseph A U, Sep 30 1889 Sex:M Child# 1 Joseph Theroux Canada & Rose D Boisseau Canada
THEROUX, Joseph Andree, Mar 19 1898 Sex:M Child# 2 Alexandre Theroux Canada & Audelie Lacourse Canada
THEROUX, Joseph George, Apr 2 1904 Sex:M Child# 2 Louis Theroux Canada & Virginie Goyette Canada
THEROUX, Joseph Georges, Mar 9 1897 Sex:M Child# 1 Alexandre Theroux Canada & Andelie Lacourse Canada
THEROUX, Joseph Paul Leo, Sep 13 1926 Sex:M Child# 2 Joseph P Theroux Nashua, NH & Flora Boisclaire Manchester, NH
THEROUX, Joseph Pierre Willie, Aug 22 1900 Sex:M Child# 3 Alexandre Theroux Canada & Audelia Lacourse Canada
THEROUX, Joseph Walter E, Mar 23 1906 Sex:M Child# 5 Alexandre Theroux Canada & Aurelie Lacourse Canada
THEROUX, Louis Philippe A, Feb 20 1911 Sex:M Child# 1 Louis Theroux Canada & Exilda Pepin Nashua, NH
THEROUX, M Anne Gilberte, Nov 25 1913 Sex:F Child# 7 Alexandre Theroux Canada & Adelie Lacourse Canada
THEROUX, Marie, Feb 4 1910 Sex:F Child# 1 Joseph Theroux Canada & Amelia Pepin Canada
THEROUX, Marie Germaine, May 25 1917 Sex:F Child# 4 Valmore Theroux Nashua, NH & Angelina Mason Canada
THEROUX, Marie Juliette, Oct 30 1911 Sex:F Child# 6 Alex Theroux Canada & Adelie Laporte Canada
THEROUX, Mercia Therese, May 19 1902 Sex:F Child# 8 Joseph Theroux Canada & Rosanna Boisseau Canada

THEROUX, Normand, Nov 10 1929 Sex:M Child# 1 Walter Theroux Nashua, NH & Stella Pelletier Nashua, NH
THEROUX, Paul Adrien, Jan 3 1904 Sex:M Child# 4 Alex Theroux Canada & Odelie Lacourse Canada
THEROUX, Philias I, Sep 1 1890 Sex:M Child# 2 Irenie Theroux Canada & Emelie Girard Canada
THEROUX, Rachael Lena, Feb 28 1929 Sex:F Child# 3 Joseph Theroux Nashua, NH & Flora Boisclaire Manchester, NH
THEROUX, Rose Anna A A, May 14 1911 Sex:F Child# 1 Valmore Theroux Canada & Angeline Mason Canada
THEROUX, Virginie, Oct 7 1901 Sex:F Child# 1 Louis Theroux Canada & Virgine Doullet Canada
THEROUX, Yvonne Stella, Apr 26 1911 Sex:F Child# 3 Doria Theroux Canada & Rosa Lavoie Malone, NY
THERRIAULT, Aurore Delphine, Sep 13 1918 Sex:F Child# 1 Henri Therriault NH & Aurore Desautel NH
THERRIAULT, Conrad Joseph, Feb 20 1935 Sex:M Child# 1 Simeon Therriault Nashua, NH & Jeannette Theroux Nashua, NH
THERRIAULT, Dorothy Blanche, Sep 13 1924 Sex:F Child# 3 Joseph A Therriault Canada & Blanche Blanchette Canada
THERRIAULT, Jules, Mar 6 1928 Sex:M Child# 3 Nap Therriault Nashua, NH & Anna Dionne Canada Stillborn
THERRIAULT, Juliette Amelia, Oct 15 1921 Sex:F Child# 2 Joseph A Therriault Canada & Blanche Beaudette Canada
THERRIAULT, Leonie Annette, Mar 29 1928 Sex:F Child# 3 Jos Therriault Canada & Marie Migneault Canada
THERRIAULT, Jeannette, Aug 27 1935 Sex:F Child# 10 Joseph Therriault Canada & Marian Migneault Canada Stillborn
THERRIAULT, Maurice Real, Sep 2 1932 Sex:M Child# 3 Charles Therriault Canada & Aug Philippe Canada
THERRIAULT, Ovill Edgar, Nov 10 1928 Sex:M Child# 7 Henry Therriault Nashua, NH & Ora Desautels Nashua, NH
THERRIAULT, Robert Joseph, Jan 17 1929 Sex:M Child# 2 John Therriault Nashua, NH & Alice Bourguignon Canada
THERRIAULT, Therese Wilda, Mar 20 1918 Sex:F Child# 1 J A Therriault Canada & Blanche Blanchette Canada
THERRIEN, Alfred Maurice, Mar 31 1932 Sex:M Child# Alfred Therrien Canada & Emeliene US
THERRIEN, Arthur Louis Hector, May 26 1918 Sex:M Child# 2 Euclid Therrien Manchester, NH & Marie Ann Harpin Canada
THERRIEN, Barbara Ann, Oct 22 1935 Sex:F Child# 1 George Therrien Chazy, NY & Frances Askham Nashua, NH
THERRIEN, Elizabeth Marie A, Oct 9 1929 Sex:F Child# 3 Andrew Therrien Berlin, NH & Aurore Laviolette Barre, VT
THERRIEN, Jean, Dec 7 1919 Sex:F Child# 3 Euclid Therrien Manchester, NH & Mary Ann Harpin Canada
THERRIEN, Joseph, Jan 31 1909 Sex:F Child# 2 Joseph Therrien Canada & Eugenie Larouche Nashua, NH
THERRIEN, Marie Agnes I, Nov 1 1906 Sex:F Child# 6 Isaac Therrien Canada & Arthemise Masse Canada
THERRIEN, Marie Philomene, Apr 16 1913 Sex:F Child# 5 Joseph Therrien Canada & Eugenie Larouche Nashua, NH
THERRIEN, Marie Rita, Nov 20 1919 Sex:F Child# 7 Joseph Therrien Canada & Eugenie Larouche Nashua, NH
THERRIEN, Raymond Wilfred, May 20 1933 Sex:M Child# 4 Andrew Therrien Berlin, NH & Aurora Laviolette Greece
THERRIEN, Wilfred Eldege, Jan 22 1912 Sex:M Child# 4 Joseph Therrien Canada & Eugenie Larouche Nashua, NH
THIBAUDEAU, Roland Ronald, Feb 18 1932 Sex:M Child# 1 R Thibaudeau Nashua, NH & Yvette Pare Canada
THIBAULT, Alice Albertide, Dec 25 1902 Sex:F Child# 3 F X Thibault Canada & Odelie Levesque Canada
THIBAULT, Alice Anita, Sep 15 1923 Sex:F Child# 4 Charles Thibault Canada & Florida Thibault Canada
THIBAULT, Aline, Oct 9 1933 Sex:F Child# 9 Henri Thibault Canada & V Laverdure Worcester, MA
THIBAULT, Anita Eva, Dec 28 1918 Sex:F Child# 3 Charles Thibault Canada & Forida Canada
THIBAULT, Anna Leona, Apr 21 1906 Sex:F Child# 5 F X Thibault Canada & Odelie Levesque Canada
THIBAULT, Anne Albina, Jan 3 1908 Sex:F Child# 8 Joseph Thibault Canada & Marie Belanger Canada
THIBAULT, Annette, Apr 22 1927 Sex:F Child# 6 Henry Thibault Canada & V Laverdiere Worcester, MA
THIBAULT, Antonio, May 30 1908 Sex:M Child# 1 J C Thibault Canada & M L Casista Canada
THIBAULT, Armand, Mar 26 1924 Sex:M Child# 5 Henri Thibault Canada & Vir Laverdiere Worcester, MA
THIBAULT, Auguste Euclide, Mar 1 1897 Sex:M Child# 1 Joseph Thibault Canada & Arthemise Dube Canada
THIBAULT, Camille, Apr 26 1929 Sex:M Child# 7 Henry Thibault Canada & Virginie Laverdi Worcester, MA
THIBAULT, Cecilia, Aug 1 1920 Sex:F Child# 3 Henri Thibault Canada & Virginie Laverdiere Worcester, MA
THIBAULT, Conrad, Oct 4 1927 Sex:M Child# 1 Wilfrid Thibault Nashua, NH & Estelle Francoeur Nashua, NH
THIBAULT, Hilaire George, Aug 10 1901 Sex:M Child# 2 F Thibault Canada & Audelie Levesque Canada
THIBAULT, Jean Bte, Jun 2 1894 Sex:M Child# 1 Paul Thibault Canada & Anais Theriault Canada
THIBAULT, Jos Henri, May 13 1931 Sex:M Child# 8 Henri Thibault Canada & Virginie Laverdiere Worcester, MA
THIBAULT, Joseph, Jul 16 1918 Sex:M Child# 5 Charles Thibault Canada & Marie Louise Cosista Canada Stillborn
THIBAULT, Joseph E Arnold, Jan 21 1898 Sex:M Child# 1 Paul Thibault Canada & Josephine Levesque Canada
THIBAULT, Joseph Jean B D, Jun 24 1906 Sex:M Child# 5 Joseph Thibault Canada & Marie Belanger Canada
THIBAULT, Joseph Louis, Aug 21 1899 Sex:M Child# 2 Paul Thibault Canada & Josephine Levesque Canada
THIBAULT, Joseph Wilfrid, Sep 21 1900 Sex:M Child# 3 Joseph Thibault Canada & Marie Belanger Canada
THIBAULT, Laura Regina, Aug 9 1899 Sex:F Child# 2 Joseph Thibault Canada & Arthemise Dube Canada
THIBAULT, Laura Yvonne, Apr 6 1904 Sex:F Child# 3 F A Thibault Canada & Odelie Levesque Canada
THIBAULT, Lillian Marie, Apr 8 1922 Sex:F Child# 4 Henry Thibault Canada & Virginia Laverdiere
THIBAULT, Louis Philippe, Jun 7 1920 Sex:M Child# 7 Charles Thibault Canada & M L Casista Canada
THIBAULT, Madeleine L, Aug 26 1910 Sex:F Child# 2 Charles Thibault Canada & Marie L Casista Canada
THIBAULT, Marguerite Rita, Apr 14 1919 Sex:F Child# 2 Henri Thibault Canada & Virginie Laverdure Worcester, MA
THIBAULT, Marie Louise L, Mar 26 1899 Sex:F Child# 1 Joseph Thibault Canada & Marie Belanger Canada
THIBAULT, Marie Regina, Nov 25 1901 Sex:F Child# 3 Joseph Thibault Canada & Marie Belanger Canada
THIBAULT, Melanie, Nov 6 1896 Sex:F Child# 2 H Thibault Canada & Cordelia Dubrenil Canada
THIBAULT, Raymond Wilfrid, Apr 21 1930 Sex:M Child# 2 Wilfrid Thibault Nashua, NH & Estelle Francoeur Nashua, NH
THIBAULT, Robert Leo, Feb 22 1917 Sex:M Child# 2 Charles Thibault Canada & Florida Canada
THIBAULT, Roland Albert, Feb 28 1908 Sex:M Child# 1 Jean Thibault Canada & Philomene Beaulieu Canada
THIBAULT, Roland Albert Roger, Aug 8 1927 Sex:M Child# 1 Emile Thibault Greenville, NH & Beatrice Paradis
THIBAULT, Simon Raymond, Jul 11 1917 Sex:M Child# 4 Charles Thibault Canada & M L Cassista Canada
THIBAULT, Sylvio, Mar 23 1918 Sex:M Child# 1 Louis Thibault Canada & Roxanna Morin Canada
THIBAULT, Victor, Feb 17 1894 Sex:M Child# 5 Francis Thibault Canada & Josephine Faubert Canada
THIBAULT, Vivian, Aug 15 1934 Sex:F Child# 1 Antonio Thibault Nashua, NH & Antoinette Pelletier Nashua, NH
THIBEAU, Albina, Jul 2 1901 Sex:F Child# 7 Francis Thibeau Canada & Josephine Faubert Canada
THIBEAU, Attala, Jul 2 1901 Sex:F Child# 8 Francis Thibeau Canada & Josephine Faubert Canada
THIBEAU, Jeanne, May 31 1899 Sex:F Child# 6 Francis Thibeau Ireland & Josephine Faubert Ireland
THIBEAU, Unknown, Jan 12 1895 Sex:M Child# 5 Adelard Thibeau Canada & Marie Dufresne Canada Stillborn
THIBEAULT, George, Apr 19 1917 Sex:M Child# 1 Henri Thibeault Canada & Virginia Laverdiere Canada

THIBEAULT, Joseph, Feb 10 1913 Sex:M Child# 10 John Thibeault Canada & Alice Briand Canada
THIBEAULT, Lorette Marie, Oct 4 1914 Sex:F Child# 1 Charles Thibeault Canada & Florida Michaud Canada
THIBEAULT, Marie, May 9 1892 Sex:F Child# 4 Adelard Thibeault Canada & Marie Dufrenes Rouse's Point, NY
THIBEAULT, Marie Claudia Roland, Aug 21 1923 Sex:F Child# 3 Francis Thibeault Canada & Delima Bonenfant Canada
THIBEAULT, Marie L, Jun 26 1892 Sex:F Child# 4 Francis Thibeault Canada & Josephine Faubert Canada
THIBEAULT, Marie O, Apr 30 1900 Sex:F Child# 1 Francois Thibeault Canada & Odelie Levesque Canada
THIBEAULT, Robert Joseph M, Dec 3 1914 Sex:M Child# 3 Charles Thibeault Canada & M L Cassista Canada
THIBEAULT, Wilfred, Dec 20 1903 Sex:M Child# 9 Francis Thibeault Canada & Josephine Faubert Canada
THIBEAUTOL, Joseph, Jul 17 1895 Sex:M Child# 7 Arthur Thibeautol Canada & Celina Morel Canada
THIBODEAU, Alexina Elizabeth, May 1 1921 Sex:F Child# 5 Clifford Thibodeau Richford, VT & Mabel Cross Broom
THIBODEAU, Ernest Napoleon, Jan 27 1893 Sex:M Child# 2 Jules Thibodeau Canada & Emelie Ploude Canada
THIBODEAU, Henry E Oliver, Apr 27 1922 Sex:M Child# 1 H E O Thibodeau Richford, VT & Agnes LaCross Providence, RI
THIBODEAU, J B Leon, Apr 2 1900 Sex:M Child# 6 Jules Thibodeau Canada & Emelie Plourde Canada
THIBODEAU, J Remi Aldemar, Jun 16 1914 Sex:M Child# 5 Louis Thibodeau Canada & Rose Cyr Canada
THIBODEAU, J Theophile Rene, Sep 25 1915 Sex:M Child# 6 Octave Thibodeau Canada & Eugenie Belanger Canada
THIBODEAU, Jos Octave Wallace, Oct 16 1918 Sex:M Child# 7 Octave Thibodeau Canada & Jennie Belanger Canada
THIBODEAU, Joseph, Apr 19 1918 Sex:M Child# 1 Theophile Thibodeau Canada & Georgianna Drouin Canada Stillborn
THIBODEAU, Joseph E E, Jul 11 1892 Sex:M Child# 3 Ephreme Thibodeau Canada & Lea Dufault Canada
THIBODEAU, Joseph E O, Aug 21 1894 Sex:M Child# 3 Jules Thibodeau Canada & Emelie Plourde Canada
THIBODEAU, Joseph H C, May 3 1897 Sex:M Child# 6 Ephreme Thibodeau Canada & Lea Dufault Canada
THIBODEAU, Joseph W L, Jul 25 1896 Sex:M Child# 4 Jules Thibodeau Canada & Emelie Plourde Canada
THIBODEAU, Julien A, Sep 1 1891 Sex:M Child# 1 Jules Thibodeau Canada & Emilie Plonde Canada
THIBODEAU, June, Jun 23 1933 Sex:F Child# 2 Romeo Thibodeau Canada & Yvette Pare Canada
THIBODEAU, Louis P, May 11 1894 Sex:M Child# 4 Ephreme Thibodeau Canada & Lea Dufault Canada
THIBODEAU, M Adrienne Eva, May 9 1917 Sex:F Child# 8 Policarpe Thibodeau Canada & Celina Boucher Canada
THIBODEAU, M Olivette Jeannette, May 23 1921 Sex:F Child# 8 Marcel Thibodeau Canada & Malvina Boucher Canada
THIBODEAU, Marianne, Jul 8 1898 Sex:F Child# 5 Jules Thibodeau Canada & Emeline Plourde Canada
THIBODEAU, Marie, Jan 31 1909 Sex:F Child# 11 Ephrem Thibodeau Canada & Lea Dufaulx Canada
THIBODEAU, Marie Andrea, Sep 29 1901 Sex:F Child# 8 Ephrem Thibodeau Canada & Lea Dufault Canada
THIBODEAU, marie Cecile Y, Aug 15 1930 Sex:F Child# 1 Alfred Thibodeau Canada & Dora Morin Lowell, MA
THIBODEAU, Marie Malvina Alma, Aug 31 1918 Sex:F Child# 7 Marcel Thibodeau Canada & Malvina Boucher Canada
THIBODEAU, Marie R E, Dec 27 1890 Sex:F Child# 2 Ephreme Thibodeau Canada & Lea Dufault Canada
THIBODEAU, Marie Violette, Jul 20 1912 Sex:F Child# 4 Louis Thibodeau Canada & Rose Cyr Canada
THIBODEAU, Marie Vitaline, Jan 10 1914 Sex:F Child# 5 Octave Thibodeau Canada & Eugenie Belanger NH
THIBODEAU, Martin, Oct 6 1890 Sex:M Child# 3 Adelard Thibodeau Canada & Marie Dufresne Canada
THIBODEAU, Roland, Nov 6 1916 Sex:M Child# 7 Louis Thibodeau Maine & Rose Cyr Maine
THIBODEAU, Therese Joan, Dec 7 1931 Sex:F Child# 1 Davidas Thibodeau Canada & Sylvia Claveau Nashua, NH
THIBODEAU, Unknown, Sep 30 1895 Sex:M Child# 5 Ephrem Thibodeau Canada & Lea Dufault Canada Stillborn
THIBODEAU, Unknown, May 3 1921 Sex:F Child# Octave Thibodeau Canada & Eugenie Belanger Canada Stillborn
THIBODEURE, Marie Aurise D, Jan 20 1890 Sex:F Child# 1 Euph'e M Thibodeure Canada & Lea Derfault Canada
THIBOUTOT, Arthur Cleophas, May 24 1909 Sex:M Child# 2 Arthur Thiboutot Canada & Antonia Pelletier Canada
THIBOUTOT, Florencetia, May 22 1924 Sex:F Child# 5 H L Thiboutot Nashua, NH & Mary Laforest Canada
THIBOUTOT, Irene Laurette, Sep 25 1911 Sex:F Child# 4 Arthur Thiboutot Canada & Antonia Pelletier Canada
THIBOUTOT, Jean B Robert, May 3 1922 Sex:M Child# 4 Omer Thiboutot Nashua, NH & Marie Laforest Canada
THIBOUTOT, Joseph, Dec 21 1929 Sex:M Child# 7 Omer Thiboutot Nashua, NH & Marie Laforest Canada Stillborn
THIBOUTOT, Joseph D Achille, Apr 19 1899 Sex:M Child# 1 Achille Thiboutot Canada & Diana Ouellette Canada
THIBOUTOT, Joseph Hector, Jan 14 1890 Sex:M Child# 4 Arthur Thiboutot Canada & Celina Morel Canada
THIBOUTOT, Louis, Dec 24 1890 Sex:M Child# 5 Arthur Thiboutot Canada & Celina Moxelle Canada
THIBOUTOT, Louis Dolard, Oct 15 1910 Sex:M Child# 3 Arthur Thiboutot Canada & Antonia Pelletier Canada
THIBOUTOT, Louis Jos Thos Al, Nov 3 1918 Sex:M Child# 1 Louis Thiboutot Canada & Eldora Desjaidais Canada
THIBOUTOT, Marie A, Aug 7 1925 Sex:F Child# Omer Thiboutot Nashua, NH & Marie A Laforest Canada Stillborn
THIBOUTOT, Marie Juliette A, Dec 13 1907 Sex:F Child# 1 Arthur Thiboutot Canada & Antonia Pelletier Canada
THIBOUTOT, Rose Alma, Apr 21 1898 Sex:F Child# 9 Arthur Thiboutot Canada & Celina Morel Canada
THIBOUTOT, Unknown, Dec 24 1896 Sex:M Child# 8 Arthur Thiboutot Canada & Celina Morel Canada
THIBOUTOT, Unknown, May 25 1923 Sex:M Child# 1 Andrew Thiboutot Nashua, NH & Yvonne Deschamps Nashua, NH
THIFAULT, M Odina A, Jun 19 1892 Sex:F Child# 3 Zotique Thifault Canada & Belanie Germain Canada
THIFAUT, Arsene Elisee, Jan 10 1894 Sex:M Child# 5 Jotique Thifaut Canada & Belanie Germain Canada
THIFFAULT, Adiana Philipine, Aug 23 1898 Sex:F Child# 7 Zotique Thiffault Canada & Celanire Germain Canada
THIFFAULT, Stephanie, Aug 23 1902 Sex:F Child# 8 Zotique Thiffault Canada & C St Germain Canada
THIVIERGE, Dorothy Lillian, Jun 4 1917 Sex:F Child# 4 Louis Thivierge Canada & Lillian McCabe Malone, NY
THIVIERGE, Irene Beatrice, Dec 16 1909 Sex:F Child# 2 Louis Thivierge Quebec & Lillian McCabe New York
THIVIERGE, Mildred, Dec 21 1907 Sex:F Child# 1 Louis Thivierge Canada & Lillian McCabe Malone, NY
THOMAS, Benjamin, Jun 24 1910 Sex:M Child# 2 Benjamin Thomas England & Lucille Brown Mass
THOMAS, Earle William, Sep 24 1906 Sex:M Child# 1 Henry C Thomas England & Emma W Thomas New York
THOMAS, Fay Lucille, Mar 13 1934 Sex:F Child# 5 Ernest Thomas Chester, VT & Doris Whitten Chester, VT
THOMAS, Fred Leroy, Jr, Jul 28 1911 Sex:M Child# 2 Fred Leroy Thomas Brownville, ME & Nettie Louise Manchester, NH
THOMAS, James Leo, Sep 21 1928 Sex:M Child# 2 Donald Thomas Wolfeboro, NH & Ruth Rockwell Troy, VT
THOMAS, Jean, Feb 15 1923 Sex:F Child# 2 Norman Thomas Chelsea, MA & Florence Light Chelsea, MA
THOMAS, John Francis, May 25 1933 Sex:M Child# 1 John J Thomas Peterboro, NH & Frances K Shea Wilton, NH
THOMAS, Kathryn Layson, Feb 26 1907 Sex:F Child# 1 Benjamin Thomas England & Lucile I Brown Mass
THOMAS, Kenneth Adney, Apr 14 1918 Sex:M Child# 6 Frank A Thomas Brownsville, ME & Ida A Sawyer Hillsborough, NH
THOMAS, Lillian Sawyer, Dec 31 1913 Sex:F Child# 4 Frank A Thomas Brownville, ME & Ida Sawyer Wolfeboro, NH
THOMAS, Marie, May 8 1919 Sex:F Child# 1 Robert Thomas Bayonne, NJ & Marie Hanrahan Nashua, NH

434

THOMAS, Norman Taylor, Jr, Jun 11 1918 Sex:M Child# 1 Norman T Thomas Chelsea, MA & Florence Light Chelsea, MA
THOMAS, Robert, May 8 1919 Sex:M Child# 2 Robert Thomas Bayonne, NJ & Marie Hanrahan Nashua, NH
THOMAS, Unknown, Nov 3 1910 Sex:F Child# 2 Frank A Thomas Brownville, MA & Ida A Sawyer Hillsborough, NH
THOMAS, Veronica Katherine, May 27 1929 Sex:F Child# 1 Henry Thomas US & Katherine Galvin US
THOMAS, Zatae, Apr 30 1933 Sex:F Child# 3 W E Thomas Nashua, NH & Alice Lintott Nashua, NH
THOMASIAN, Unknown, Dec 5 1929 Sex:M Child# 2 Memos Thomasian Armenia & Veronica Sabastian Armenia Stillborn
THOMPSON, Alice, Sep 30 1910 Sex:F Child# 4 James Thompson England & Catherine Gallagher Ireland
THOMPSON, Almira M, Apr 9 1905 Sex:F Child# 1 Henry H Thompson Boston, MA & Jennie Wellman Nashua, NH
THOMPSON, Anne Elizabeth, Jan 21 1931 Sex:F Child# 1 William Thompson Nashua, NH & Ruth Martin Sherbrooke, Quebec
THOMPSON, Arlene Belmont, May 10 1913 Sex:F Child# 3 Henry Hill Thompson Boston, MA & Jennie Wellman Nashua, NH
THOMPSON, Carole Ann, Mar 14 1935 Sex:F Child# 2 Arch Thompson Wilton, NH & Hester Enright Nashua, NH
THOMPSON, Catharine Mabel, Jul 10 1903 Sex:F Child# 2 John H Thompson New York & Catharine F Meihert
THOMPSON, Edna Elaine, Aug 28 1933 Sex:F Child# 2 George Thompson
THOMPSON, Ernest Dewey, May 19 1898 Sex:M Child# 2 Irving A Thompson Lee & Anna Townes Kerwinsville, PA
THOMPSON, Florence Anabell, Feb 6 1917 Sex:F Child# 4 Henry H Thompson Boston, MA & Jennie Wellman Nashua, NH
THOMPSON, Francis Earl, May 27 1924 Sex:M Child# 8 Earl Thompson Milford, NY & Ber Stanbridge Hunter, NY
THOMPSON, George Clifford, Aug 30 1904 Sex:M Child# 2 George F Thompson Londonderry, NH & Henrietta C Small Stockto
THOMPSON, Gladys H, Sep 3 1896 Sex:F Child# 1 W L Thompson Epping, NH & E C Hodgin Calais, ME
THOMPSON, Gladys M, Dec 28 1894 Sex:F Child# 1 Everett Thompson Nashua, NH & Mary Durgan E Boston, MA
THOMPSON, Hattie, Jul 25 1895 Sex:F Child# 3 George A Thompson Manchester, MA & Sadie McClain Cape B
THOMPSON, Hazel, Jun 22 1891 Sex:F Child# 1 John H Thompson Ashland, NH & Cora E Fellows Concord, NH
THOMPSON, Helen, Jul 29 1924 Sex:F Child# 1 Carl T Thompson Leominster, MA & Marion G Vincent Boston, MA
THOMPSON, Helen Margurite, Feb 19 1900 Sex:F Child# 1 Earl Thompson Unity, ME & Nora Sullivan Nashua, NH
THOMPSON, Joyce Martha, Nov 29 1928 Sex:F Child# 1 A Thompson, Jr Wilton, NH & Hester Enright Nashua, NH
THOMPSON, Lois Edna, Dec 28 1907 Sex:F Child# 1 James Thompson, Jr Andover, MA & Edna Canfield Ashley Falls, MA
THOMPSON, Louis Arthur, Mar 27 1934 Sex:M Child# 1 (No Parents Listed)
THOMPSON, Mary Irene, Dec 17 1927 Sex:F Child# 9 Earl Thompson Milford, NY & Bertha Stanbridge Hunter, NY
THOMPSON, Minnie, Jul 14 1892 Sex:F Child# 2 George R Thompson Haverill, MA & Sadie McLane Cape Breton
THOMPSON, Phillip C, May 28 1903 Sex:M Child# 1 George F Thompson Londonderry, NH & Henrietta C Small Stockton
THOMPSON, Raymond Lee, Jun 26 1895 Sex:M Child# 1 E A Thompson Lee & Anna Townes Pennsylvania
THOMPSON, Ruth E, Nov 11 1906 Sex:F Child# 3 George F Thompson Londonderry, NH & Henrietta C Small Stockton Sp
THOMPSON, Sheila Ann, Jul 6 1935 Sex:F Child# 1 Fitzroy Thompson Bethlehem, NH & Marjorie A Lewis Sanbornton, NH
THOMPSON, Unknown, Jun 23 1890 Sex:M Child# 3 M E R Thompson Saco, ME & Mary Howell New Brunswick
THOMPSON, Unknown, Dec 11 1890 Sex:F Child# 2 Charles H Thompson Nashua, NH & Mary Dion Canada Stillborn
THOMPSON, Unknown, Nov 19 1891 Sex:F Child# 1 M L Thomspon Maine & Lena P Philbrick NH
THOMPSON, Unknown, Dec 5 1894 Sex:F Child# 3 M S Thompson Wilton, ME & Lena Philbrick Mount Vernon, ME
THOMPSON, Unknown, Jul 25 1895 Sex:F Child# 2 John H Thompson NH & Cora E Fellows NH Stillborn
THOMPSON, Unknown, Apr 18 1899 Sex:F Child# 1 Clifford A Thompson Winthrop, ME &
THOMPSON, Unknown, Mar 27 1900 Sex: Child#  Irving Thompson
THOMPSON, Unknown, Nov 1 1901 Sex:M Child# 1 Eben P Thompson Crownpoint, NY & Nellie Spaulding Nashua, NH
THOMPSON, Unknown, Jun 2 1917 Sex:M Child# 1 Murray Thompson Sanbornton, NH & Josephine Curtis Lakeport, NH
THOMPSON, Unknown, Mar 29 1919 Sex:F Child# 1 Charles A Thompson Lee, NH & Mary A Durgin Amesbury, MA Stillborn
THOMPSON, Vinnie, Dec 26 1897 Sex:F Child# 1 A M Thompson Effingham Falls & Alice A Davis Effingham
THOMPSON, Westley Francis, Jan 12 1905 Sex:M Child# 1 M V B Thompson Biddeford, ME & Maggie Maloney Ireland
THOMPSON, William, Nov 28 1903 Sex:M Child# 2 William L Thompson Epping & Ella C Hodgins Calais, ME
THOMPSON, William Richard, Feb 25 1935 Sex:M Child# 2 William Thompson Nashua, NH & Ruth Martin Sherbrooke, PQ
THORNTON, John Courtney, May 14 1922 Sex:M Child# 1 Alex Thornton St Louis, MO & Esther Oliver Surry, ME
THORNTON, Randall Gray, Mar 10 1930 Sex:M Child# 1 Randall Thornton Dorchester, MA & Mae Van Lenten Garfield, MA
THORPE, Paul, Jun 7 1916 Sex:M Child# 2 Harry Thorpe Pittsfield, NH & Mary Jaseman Fall River, MA
THRASHER, Alden Bowler, Dec 1 1923 Sex:M Child# 2 Carlton Thrasher Plainfield, NJ & Florence Bowler Barre, VT
THRASHER, Nancy Elizabeth, Sep 7 1920 Sex:F Child# 1 Carlton W Thrasher Plainfield, NJ & Florence E Bowler Barre
THUNBERG, Jon Carl, Aug 4 1934 Sex:M Child# 1 Carl A Thunberg Cambridge, MA & Leona D Snow Orange, MA
THURBER, Constance, Nov 9 1920 Sex:F Child# 1 George F Thurber Nashua, NH & Muriel Davis Nashua, NH
THURBER, Dorothy, Apr 23 1892 Sex:F Child# 2 Lester F Thurber Vermont & Lizzie E Little New York
THURBER, George F, Feb 5 1888 Sex:M Child# 1 Lester F Thurber Vermont & Lizzie E Little Newport
THURBER, George Freeman, Sep 6 1923 Sex:M Child# 2 George F Thurber Nashua, NH & Muriel Davis Nashua, NH
THURSTON, Anna Etta, Sep 26 1900 Sex:F Child# 6 John A Thurston NH & Alice Gregoire Maine
THURSTON, Marie, Oct 16 1893 Sex:F Child# 1 John Thurston US & Alice Gregoire US
TIATRANSKI, Peter, Oct 18 1908 Sex:M Child# 1 William Tiatranski Russia & Agie Siernsie Russia
TIBBETS, Albert A, Dec 18 1888 Sex:M Child# 7 Simeon J Tibbets P Q & Sarah F Blake Lawrence, MA
TIBBETTS, Alice Mary, May 29 1925 Sex:F Child# 2 George E Tibbetts Nashua, NH & Nellie Moore Manchester, NH
TIBBETTS, Catherine Mary, Dec 21 1913 Sex:F Child# 3 Charles Tibbetts NH & Elizabeth Ryan Nashua, NH
TIBBETTS, Daniel Sullivan, Nov 10 1921 Sex:M Child# 2 Cecil B Tibbetts Marshfield, VT & Florence Nichols Hudson, NH
TIBBETTS, Edna Louise, Apr 9 1895 Sex:F Child# 1 Frank E Tibbetts Manchester, NH & F Belle Danley Nashua, NH
TIBBETTS, Eleanor Janet, Apr 2 1917 Sex:F Child# 1 Grover C Tibbetts Nashua, NH & Ella M Winslow Nashua, NH
TIBBETTS, Fred H, Aug 24 1896 Sex:M Child# 2 Frank E Tibbetts Manchester, NH & Francis Belle Danley Nashua, NH
TIBBETTS, George Emmet, Sep 15 1896 Sex:M Child# 1 George J Tibbetts Manchester, NH & Alice Wills Nashua, NH
TIBBETTS, George Emmett, Jr, Oct 30 1926 Sex:M Child# 3 George E Tibbetts Nashua, NH & Nellie Moore Manchester
TIBBETTS, Helene Barbara, Mar 13 1923 Sex:F Child# 3 George E Tibbetts Nashua, NH & Nellie Moore Manchester, NH
TIBBETTS, Manly Grant, Apr 15 1912 Sex:M Child# 2 Elmer E Tibbetts Maine & Lewie Burrett Vermont
TIBBETTS, Marjorie, Feb 10 1911 Sex:F Child# 2 Fred H Tibbetts Manchester, NH & Marion Campbell Liverpool, England
TIBBETTS, Marshall Atwood, Nov 28 1921 Sex:M Child# 3 Leon Tibbetts Dover, NH & Elizabeth Atwood Orange, MA
TIBBETTS, Milton Baron, Sep 29 1913 Sex:M Child# 1 Milton Tibbetts Campbello, MA & Pearl Sandee Dorchester, MA

TIBBETTS, Nada Miriam, Apr 18 1921 Sex:F Child# 3 Grover Tibbetts Nashua, NH & Ella M Winslow Nashua, NH
TIBBETTS, Natali Margaret, Apr 18 1921 Sex:F Child# 2 Grover Tibbetts Nashua, NH & Ella M Winslow Nashua, NH
TIBBETTS, Paul Edison, Oct 27 1914 Sex:M Child# 4 Elmer E Tibbetts Maine & Luvia R Burnett Vermont
TIBBETTS, Raymond, May 26 1923 Sex:M Child# 3 Cecil B Tibbetts Marshfield, VT & Florence Nichols Hudson, NH
TIBBETTS, Samuel H, May 3 1887 Sex:M Child# 6 Hanson E Tibbetts Canada & Louisa J Lowell, MA
TIBBETTS, Stanley Morrell, Apr 13 1913 Sex:M Child# 3 Elmer E Tibbetts Maine & Lubie Burnett Vermont
TIBBETTS, Unknown, Sep 4 1893 Sex:M Child# 8 Simeon J Tibbetts Canada & Sarah Blake Lowell, MA
TIBBETTS, Unknown, Jul 3 1898 Sex:F Child# 3 Frank E Tibbetts Manchester, NH & F Belle Danley Nashua, NH
TIBBETTS, Unknown, Oct 27 1933 Sex:M Child# 2 Cecil Tibbetts Marshfield, VT & Julia Lucey Boston, MA
TIBBETTS, Unknown, Sep 25 1935 Sex:M Child# 3 Cecil Tibbetts Marshfield, VT & Julia Lucey Boston, MA
TIBBITTS, Arnold Elsworth, Feb 8 1911 Sex:M Child# 1 Elmer Tibbitts Maine & Lucy Burnett Vermont
TIBBITTS, Unknown, Aug 19 1892 Sex:F Child# 1 Arthur H Tibbitts Salem, MA & Etta M Stanley Canaan, NH
TIBEAULT, Albert, Sep 27 1890 Sex:M Child# 3 Francois Tibeault Canada & Josephine Feaubert Canada
TIERNAN, Charles Martin, Jan 31 1904 Sex:M Child# 4 Martin P Tiernan Milford, MA & Mary J Dumas Burlington, VT
TIERNAN, Martin Charles, Dec 9 1927 Sex:M Child# 1 Charles Tiernan Nashua, NH & Yvonne Parent Nashua, NH
TIERNEY, James Francis, Jul 24 1890 Sex:M Child# 4 Martin H Tierney Lowell, MA & Sarah E Gallagher Lowell, MA
TIERNEY, Robert Henry, Jul 22 1888 Sex:M Child# 3 Martin Tierney Lowell & Sarah E Jallaber Lowell, MA
TIERNEY, Thomas Joseph, Jr, Jul 3 1932 Sex:M Child# 1 Thomas J Tierney E Pepperell, MA & Sophie Cutler W Groton, MA
TIERRIEN, Martin O, Jun 28 1899 Sex:M Child# 3 Martin Tierrien Ireland & Josephene Dumas Canada
TIFFAND, Marie Clara, Jan 3 1895 Sex:F Child# 5 Zotique Tiffand Canada & Celanire Germain Canada
TIGHE, Elizabeth Ellen, Sep 3 1919 Sex:F Child# 1 James J Tighe Meridan, CT & Mary E Birchall Nashua, NH
TIGHE, Helen V, Jan 6 1900 Sex:F Child# 5 Lawrence B Tighe Lowell, MA & Mary A Connor NY
TIGHE, James A, Aug 8 1921 Sex:M Child# 2 James J Tighe Meriden, CT & Marie E Birchall Nashua, NH
TIGHE, Lawrence Albert, Dec 6 1934 Sex:M Child# 1 Lawrence Tighe Wilton, NH & Ruth Burns Nashua, NH
TIGHE, Lawrence B, Oct 13 1897 Sex:M Child# 4 Lawrence W Tighe Lowell, MA & Mary Connor NY
TIGHE, Margaret Celestia, Oct 13 1890 Sex:F Child# 3 Lawrence U Tighe Lowell, MA & Mary Connor NY
TIKAS, Unknown, Nov 20 1918 Sex:F Child# 1 John Tikas Greece & Obugas Gimontria Greece
TILDEN, Unknown, Aug 12 1887 Sex:M Child# 2 Rosha M Tilden Stockholm, NY & Eva I Stockholm, NY
TILDEN, Unknown, Nov 7 1909 Sex:M Child# 1 Charles R Tilden Nashua, NH & Jessie M Collins New Mexico
TILLINGHAST, Millie Lepha, Feb 22 1925 Sex:F Child# 1 George Tillinghast Hanson, MA & Bessie L Rollins Windham, NH
TILLOTSON, David, Nov 7 1905 Sex:M Child# 3 John B Tillotson Vermont & Catherine Spence Yarmouth, NS
TILLOTSON, David, Jr, Oct 9 1928 Sex:M Child# 1 David Tillotson Nashua, NH & Etta Leona Shaw Nashua, NH
TILLOTSON, Douglass, Jan 8 1904 Sex:M Child# 2 John B Tillotson Orford, NH & Catherine Spence Yarmouth, NS
TILTON, Hannah M, Mar 18 1888 Sex:F Child# 1 Osmun Tilton Nashua, NH & A Shattuck Pepperell, MA
TILTON, Meader, Mar 19 1888 Sex:F Child# 1 Osman B Tilton Great Falls & Alice S Shattuck Pepperell, MA
TIMALONIS, Mulvin, Feb 10 1920 Sex:F Child# 6 John Timalonis Russia & Alma Aidukeniute Russia
TIMON, Irene Margaret, Mar 19 1916 Sex:F Child# 1 Andrew Timon Claremont, NH & Leona Gagnon Nashua, NH
TIMON, Philip Leo, Apr 11 1918 Sex:M Child# 2 Andrew Timon NH & Leona Gagnon NH
TINKER, Alva Glidden, Oct 1 1913 Sex:M Child# 1 Charles L Tinker Nashua, NH & Sophronia E Tuttle Nova Scotia
TINKER, Charlotte, Aug 26 1908 Sex:F Child# 1 Willis Tinker Nashua, NH & Charlotte M Rock Altona, NY
TINKER, Duncan Forbes, Nov 27 1929 Sex:M Child# 2 Herbert Tinker Savannah, GA & Lyla Forbes Nashua, NH
TINKER, Janet Ellen, Oct 7 1911 Sex:F Child# 3 Willis H Tinker Nashua, NH & Charlotte M Rock Altona, NY
TINKER, John, Oct 12 1909 Sex:M Child# 2 Willis H Tinker Nashua, NH & Charlotte M Rock Altona, NY
TINKER, Joseph William, Jan 29 1916 Sex:M Child# 5 Willis H Tinker Nashua, NH & Charlotte Rock Altona, NY
TINKER, Patricia, May 21 1924 Sex:F Child# 1 Herbert Tinker Savannah, GA & Lyler Forbes Nashua, NH
TINKER, Rebecca, Oct 16 1913 Sex:F Child# 3 Willis Tinker Nashua, NH & Charlotte Rock Altoona, NY
TINKER, Robert Luther, Aug 4 1918 Sex:M Child# 6 William Tinker Nashua, NH & Charlotte Rock Altona, NY
TINKER, Threasa, Jan 22 1888 Sex:F Child# 6 Ezekell Tinker Leominster & Abbie A Richmond Canada
TINKLE, Seamon, Feb 26 1916 Sex:F Child# 2 Morris Tinkle Russia & Esther Springer Russia
TINNIGAN, Annie, Feb 26 1897 Sex:F Child# 2 John Tinnigan Boston, MA & Alice McWeeney Nashua, NH
TIPPARD, Anna M, Mar 22 1893 Sex:F Child# 1 Frank Tippard Newfoundland & Anna M Wells Nashua, NH
TIPPING, Allen Barker, Nov 10 1916 Sex:M Child# 3 Hobart Tipping Canada & Edna Barker Nashua, NH
TIPPING, Hobart Eugene, Feb 14 1915 Sex:M Child# 2 Hobart E Tipping Canada & Edna Barker Nashua, NH
TIPPING, Lois Evelyn, Aug 22 1922 Sex:F Child# 4 Hobart Tipping Canada & Edna Barker Nashua, NH
TIPPING, Ruth Elizabeth, Feb 14 1913 Sex:F Child# 1 Hobart E Tipping Canada & Edna Barker Nashua, NH
TIPTON, Frances Marie, May 28 1909 Sex:F Child# 1 Wallace Tipton Canada & Jeannie Galoppe Vermont
TIRIALS, Marcota Nosta, Nov 11 1908 Sex:F Child# 1 George Tirials Russia & Agnes Nosta Russia
TIRRELL, Beverly Nanette, Sep 23 1928 Sex:F Child# 3 Fred D Tirrell Quincy, MA & E L Woodward York, ME
TITCOMB, Unknown, Jun 14 1889 Sex:M Child# 1 Albert Titcomb Hudson & Annie Ferryall Sciota, NY
TITCOMB, Unknown, Jan 29 1891 Sex:F Child# 2 Albert O Titcomb, Jr Hudson, NH & Annie Ferryall Sciota, NY
TITCOMB, Unknown, Nov 7 1895 Sex:M Child# 3 Albert O Titcomb
TITUS, Barbara Louise, Dec 4 1934 Sex:F Child# 1 George Titus Manchester, NH & Elizabeth Burns Manchester, NH
TITUS, Dorothy Mae, Dec 12 1930 Sex:F Child# 1 Harold A Titus Canada & Esther Bullard Nashua, NH
TIVNAN, Joseph Byron Jr, Aug 23 1903 Sex:M Child# 2 Joseph B Tivnan Boston, MA & Margaret F Sullivan Nashua, NH
TIVNAN, Margaret Olive, Apr 9 1902 Sex:F Child# 1 Joseph B Tivnan Boston, MA & M F Sullivan Nashua, NH
TLKENICZ, Joseph, Mar 8 1917 Sex:M Child# 6 Frank Tlkenicz Russia & Rose Mischenis Russia
TOBLE, Unknown, Mar 23 1889 Sex:M Child# 1 George W Toble Wilton, NH & Minnie Toble Maine
TOICEREWITCZ, Frances, Jan 21 1923 Sex:F Child# 2 Paul Toicerewitcz Poland & Amelia Toicerewitcz Poland
TOIVE, Leon Alfred, Apr 19 1916 Sex:M Child# 3 Laurence Toive Italy & Hattie Brown Richford, VT
TOLD, Dorothy Lucille, Oct 2 1927 Sex:F Child# 1 Charles L Told Winchendon, MA & Beatrice Davis Lyndonville, VT
TOLEY, Helen May, Jun 7 1897 Sex:F Child# 1 John T Toley Pepperell, MA & Mary E Burns Nashua, NH
TOLKACZ, Alvin, May 11 1920 Sex:M Child# 2 Joseph Tolkacz Poland & Domiciala Wasilwska Russia
TOLLES, Elizabeth, May 11 1905 Sex:F Child# 1 James U Tolles Dunstable, MA & Josie Hobson Barnes Nashua, NH

TOLLES, Frederick Barnes, Apr 18 1915 Sex:M Child# 2 James U Tolles Dunstable, MA & Josie H Barnes Nashua, NH
TOLLES, Unknown, Aug 3 1888 Sex:F Child# 1 Willard C Tolles Nashua, NH & Ellen F Kendall Dunstable, MA
TOLSKACZ, John, Dec 31 1922 Sex:M Child# 3 Joseph Tolskacz Russia & Annie Waislewska Russia
TOLVE, Ralph Arthur, Feb 5 1911 Sex:M Child# 2 Lawrence Tolve Italy & Hattie E Brown Vermont
TOMALAVITCH, John, May 24 1906 Sex:M Child# 7 William Tomalavitch Russia & Victoria Mishkmis Russia
TOMALEWCZUS, Mary, Jun 5 1905 Sex:F Child# 1 A Tomalewczus Russia & Eva Walenow Russia
TOMALIEWICZ, Witsenses, Sep 14 1913 Sex:F Child# 12 William Tomaliewicz Russia & Victoria Mizkiutie Russia
TOMALONIS, Lena, Jul 22 1910 Sex:F Child# 3 Jim Tomalonis Russia & Eva Volangavitch Russia
TOMALONIS, Peter, May 9 1924 Sex:M Child# 2 Peter Tomalonis Lithuania & Antoria Tomalonis Lithuania
TOMALONIS, Unknown, Jan 24 1917 Sex:M Child# 2 Tan Tomalonis Russia & Ustena Vetueski Russia
TOMALONIS, Unknown, Jun 6 1921 Sex:F Child# 1 John Tomalonis Lithuania & Isabella Chaplik Lithuania
TOMASIAN, Vahsag, Jun 1 1908 Sex:M Child# 3 Vartan Tomasian Armenia & Orsan Boyhosian Russia
TOMASIAN, Vartan Warren, Jun 13 1935 Sex:M Child# 1 Arch Tomasian Nashua, NH & Steph Sinkervitch Nashua, NH
TOMKAVIT, Joseph, Mar 31 1895 Sex:M Child# 1 Juska Tomkavit Poland & Mary Kozot Poland
TOMKIN, Unknown, Oct 14 1891 Sex:F Child# 1 P W Tomkin Canada & A E Keating Canada
TOMLEWIG, Julia, Apr 19 1914 Sex:F Child# 7 Zigmon C Tomlewig Russia & Lucodia Huckston Russia
TOMLIEWICZ, Frank, May 6 1905 Sex:M Child# 6 William Tomliewicz Russia & Victoria Mieszkivoz Russia
TOMLIEWZC, Pietras, Aug 3 1910 Sex:M Child# 10 William Tomliewzc Russia & Wictoria Mieszuinis Russia
TOMOISIAN, Unknown, Nov 12 1928 Sex:M Child# 1 Menas Tomoisian Turkey & V Depoian Harput, Turkey Stillborn
TOMOU, Anastasia, Aug 19 1932 Sex:F Child# 2 Nicholas Tomou Greece & Agnes T Dokou Greece
TOMULAWICUS, Atanas, Aug 12 1906 Sex:M Child# 2 Atanas Tomulawicus Russia & Kasimirka Mazgialis Russia
TONELLA, Carol Amelia, May 5 1930 Sex:F Child# 1 Stephen M Tonella Milford, NH & Hazel Grader Marblehead, MA
TONG, Alice Louise, Apr 13 1921 Sex:F Child# 3 Percy J Tong England & Mary Wood England
TONG, Archibald Henry, Dec 6 1907 Sex:M Child# 1 John A Tong England & Mary Duncan England
TONG, Arthur James, Feb 7 1925 Sex:M Child# 4 Percy James Tong England & May Wood England
TONG, George Henry, Jun 11 1913 Sex:M Child# 3 George H Tong England & Delia Flynn Ireland
TONG, Henry Arthur, Jul 20 1913 Sex:M Child# 2 Percy James Tong England & May Wood England
TONG, Kenneth Roland, May 24 1934 Sex:M Child# 2 Roland Tong Nashua, NH & Marjorie Frank Boston, MA
TONG, Louise Matilda, Dec 20 1910 Sex:F Child# 2 George A Tong England & Bridget Flynn Ireland
TONG, Margaret, Jul 6 1923 Sex:F Child# 4 George Tong England & Delia Flynn Ireland
TONG, Mary Catherine, Jan 7 1917 Sex:F Child# 4 George Tong England & Delia Flynn Ireland
TONG, Roland Percival, Sep 29 1911 Sex:M Child# 1 Percy J Tong England & May Wood England
TONG, Teresa, Jun 24 1908 Sex:F Child# 1 George A Tong England & Delia Flynn Ireland
TONG, Unknown, Dec 28 1932 Sex:F Child# 1 Roland Tong Nashua, NH & Marjorie Frank Boston, MA Stillborn
TONGAS, Marjory Elizabeth, Jun 22 1917 Sex:F Child# 2 Elie Tongas Canada & Beatrice Nearer Lowell, MA
TOOTHAKER, Janice Cady, May 16 1932 Sex:F Child# 1 C C Toothaker Berlin, NH & Beatrice S Currull Portland, ME
TORNASIAN, Bojos, Nov 25 1911 Sex:M Child# 4 Vactan Tornasian Turkey & Osanna Bojosian Turkey
TORREY, Charlotte Marion, Nov 24 1920 Sex:F Child# 1 Lester Torrey Boston, MA & Marion Dow Hollis, NH
TORREY, Franklin Richard, Nov 23 1926 Sex:M Child# 4 Lester Torrey Boston, MA & Marion Dow Hollis, NH
TORREY, Martha Josephine, Dec 9 1931 Sex:F Child# 6 Lester W Torrey Boston, MA & Marion Dow Hollis, NH
TORREY, Nancy Putnam, Apr 21 1930 Sex:F Child# 5 Lester W Torrey Boston, MA & Marion Dow Hollis, NH
TOTALER, Mike, Feb 1 1909 Sex:M Child# 2 Adam Totaler Russia & Marionica Katkowich Russia
TOTKACY, Joseph John, May 6 1915 Sex:M Child# 1 Joseph Totkacy Russia & Domicelle Vaselevske Russia
TOUBINIS, John, Nov 23 1902 Sex:M Child# 1 John Toubinis Russia & Mary Graqutia Russia
TOULATICZ, Charles, Oct 5 1915 Sex:M Child# 1 Charles Toulaticz Russia & Mary Karolictz Russia
TOULIOT, Joseph Leon, Oct 12 1902 Sex:M Child# 2 Joseph Touliot Canada & Marie A Ouellette Canada
TOULIOT, Marie Emma, May 30 1904 Sex:F Child# 3 Joseph Touliot Canada & Marianna Ouellette Canada
TOULOUSE, Lorraine Rita, Oct 2 1919 Sex:F Child# 1 Jos R Toulouse Lewiston, ME & Yvonne Lussier Gloucester, MA
TOURNAN, Ruth Janet, Jan 10 1934 Sex:F Child# 3 Charles M Tournan Nashua, NH & Yvonne E Parent Nashua, NH
TOUTANT, Joseph Emery O, Jun 10 1911 Sex:M Child# 3 Oscar Toutant Canada & Anna Houle Canada
TOUTANT, Marie Anna R E, Feb 3 1910 Sex:F Child# 2 Oscar Toutant Canada & Anora Houle Canada
TOWER, Janet, Sep 11 1922 Sex:F Child# 1 Sidney Tower Pepperell, MA & Clare Linscott Troy, ME
TOWER, Ramona, Dec 5 1923 Sex:F Child# 2 Sidney Tower Pepperell, MA & Clare Linscott Troy, ME
TOWLE, Donald Sumner, May 9 1912 Sex:M Child# 1 William S Towle Chichester, NH & Emma L Woodcock Lawrence, MA
TOWMIER, Marie Rita Therese, Dec 16 1924 Sex:F Child# 1 Wilfred Towmier Greenville, NH & Edith Lacroix Greenville
TOWNE, Janet Elsie, Aug 13 1932 Sex:F Child# 2 Warren Towne Cambridge, MA & Elsie Scott Haverhill, MA
TOWNE, Kenneth Warren, Jul 8 1929 Sex:M Child# 1 Warren H Towne Cambridge, MA & Elsie Osborn Scott Haverhill, MA
TOWNE, Louis Allen, Aug 6 1895 Sex:M Child# 1 Fred D Towne Milford, NH & Emma J Allen Johnstown, PA
TOWNE, Ray Colburn, Jan 7 1900 Sex:M Child# 3 Fred D Towne Milford, NH & Emma J Allen Johnstown, PA
TOWNE, Vera, Mar 2 1898 Sex:F Child# 2 Fred D Towne Milford, NH & Emma J Allen Johnstown, PA
TOWNER, Unknown, Jan 7 1891 Sex:F Child# 3 W S Towner NY & Eliza Belcher NY
TOWNLEY, Doris, Mar 12 1909 Sex:F Child# 2 Arthur H Townley
TOWNSHEND, Bruce Douglas, Jr, Jan 15 1934 Sex:M Child# 1 Bruce D Townshend Canada & Natalie Blake Nashua, NH
TRACEY, Frances Cecelia, Jul 16 1925 Sex:F Child# 2 Earl Tracey Ellenburg, NY & Anna Davine W Rutland, VT
TRACY, Florence Mildred, Feb 4 1922 Sex:F Child# 4 George Tracy Nashua, NH & Ida Jarest Wilton, NH
TRACY, Mary E, Apr 10 1889 Sex:F Child# 4 William Tracy Adams, MA & S Fittspatrick Groton, MA
TRACY, Milton George, May 23 1907 Sex:M Child# 1 George G Tracy Nashua, NH & Ida Jarest Wilton, NH
TRACY, Paul Joseph, Oct 15 1909 Sex:M Child# 2 George G Tracy Nashua, NH & Ida Jarest Wilton, NH
TRACY, Robert Edward, Feb 6 1912 Sex:M Child# 3 George G Tracy Nashua, NH & Ida Jarest Wilton, NH
TRAHAN, Henry Addison, Jul 25 1923 Sex:M Child# 1 Wilfred Trahan Laconia, NH & Irene Gendron Bardwell, MA
TRAHAN, Raymond, Jun 30 1921 Sex:M Child# 1 Emelia Trahan NH & Olivine Lefavor Canada
TRAKEM, Helen, May 4 1919 Sex:F Child# 1 Anthony Trakem Lithuania Russia & Helen Ukenawetcha Lithuania Russia
TRAMOWICZ, William, Aug 4 1914 Sex:M Child# 9 Jasper Tramowicz Russia & Louise Pasnachutz Russia

TRANIAVIUS, Alphonse, May 8 1920 Sex:M Child# 3 John Traniavius Russia & Christina Kumpa Russia
TRANOWICH, Virginia T, Sep 11 1921 Sex:F Child# 1 Andrew Tranowich Russia & Annie Grigerte Russia
TRANOWICK, Veleia, Aug 2 1923 Sex:F Child# 2 Andrew Tranowick Russia & Annie Gregos Russia
TRAVER, Daisy, Nov 12 1906 Sex:F Child# 2 L A Traver Canada & Bertha Miller New York
TRAVER, Walter J, Apr 12 1908 Sex:M Child# 3 L A Traver Canada & Bertha Miller New York
TRAVERS, Alva Catherine, Oct 17 1914 Sex:F Child# 4 Peter F Travers Cambridge, MA & Catherine E Murphy Boston, MA
TRAVERS, Evelyne Marie, Dec 9 1923 Sex:F Child# 8 Peter Travers Cambridge, MA & Catherine Murphy Boston, MA
TRAVERS, Paul Edward, Feb 7 1919 Sex:M Child# 6 Peter F Travers Cambridge, MA & Katherine F Murphy Boston, MA
TRAVERS, Peter Francis, Jr, Apr 18 1916 Sex:M Child# 5 Peter Travers Boston, MA & Katherine Murphy Boston, MA
TRAVERS, Unknown, Sep 6 1894 Sex:F Child# 1 George W Travers Richford, VT & Helen McDonald Calais, ME
TRAVERS, Unknown, Nov 28 1908 Sex:M Child# 2 Peter Travers Boston, MA & Catherine Murphy Boston, MA Stillborn
TRAXLER, Marjorie Jean, Sep 16 1933 Sex:F Child# 7 Paul Traxler Bennington, NH & Dorothy Collins Keene, NH
TRAYES, Shirley Frances, Jul 29 1920 Sex:F Child# 2 Asa W Trayes Malden, MA & Marguerite Brodley Nashua, NH
TREDTIN, Harold Charles, Mar 27 1924 Sex:M Child# 1 Harold Tredtin Canada & Agnes Marine Plattsburgh, NY
TREGNOWICZ, Annie, Mar 20 1913 Sex:F Child# 1 John Tregnowicz Russia & Christina Kumpiuta Russia
TREGNOWICZ, John, May 16 1913 Sex:M Child# 1 Antony Tregnowicz Russia & Isabella Ackstein Russia
TREGNOWICZ, Malwidga, Jun 20 1912 Sex:F Child# 3 Leonard Tregnowicz Russia & Antonina Svekola Russia
TREINOWICZ, John, Sep 4 1918 Sex:M Child# 2 John Treinowicz Russia & Christina Klemens Russia
TREMBLAY, Aldege W Clovis, Apr 15 1921 Sex:M Child# 6 Ulysse Tremblay Canada & Alma Guichard Canada
TREMBLAY, Alfred, May 23 1897 Sex:M Child# 5 Israel Tremblay Canada & Philomene Joubert Canada
TREMBLAY, Alfred Edgar, Nov 4 1910 Sex:M Child# 4 Adelard Tremblay Canada & Marie Roy Canada
TREMBLAY, Antoine Lawrence, Sep 2 1917 Sex:M Child# 9 Edouard Tremblay Altona, NY & Claudia Caron Canada
TREMBLAY, Antoinette Lucienne, Nov 24 1923 Sex:F Child# 4 Cleophas Tremblay New York & Emme Desautels Nashua, NH
TREMBLAY, Armand Laval, Apr 15 1921 Sex:M Child# 5 Ulysse Tremblay Canada & Alma Guichard Canada
TREMBLAY, Aurele Normand, Jan 29 1927 Sex:M Child# 3 Edouard Tremblay Sciota, NY & Lydia Delisle Canada
TREMBLAY, Aurore A, May 29 1901 Sex:F Child# 3 Wilbur Tremblay Altona, NY & Regina Lavigne Canada
TREMBLAY, Avila, Apr 11 1896 Sex:M Child# 1 Wilbur Tremblay Canada & Regina Lavique Canada
TREMBLAY, Beatrice, Mar 20 1933 Sex:F Child# 2 Louis Tremblay Nashua, NH & Grace Coulombe Canada
TREMBLAY, Cecile Eva, Nov 24 1909 Sex:F Child# 4 Edouard Tremblay New York & Caludia Caron Canada
TREMBLAY, Claire Lorraine, Sep 3 1935 Sex:F Child# 7 Edward Tremblay New York & Lydia Delisle Canada
TREMBLAY, Constance, Feb 8 1924 Sex:F Child# 3 Arthur Tremblay Canada & Laura Aubut Nashua, NH
TREMBLAY, Delia, Jul 23 1894 Sex:F Child# 1 Arthur Tremblay Champlain, NY & Marie Beaulieu Fall River, MA
TREMBLAY, Devina, Sep 4 1895 Sex:F Child# 4 Olivier Tremblay Canada & Flavia Ross Canada
TREMBLAY, Donald Robert, Jul 29 1930 Sex:M Child# 2 J Francis A Tremblay Hooksett, NH & Wilda Fortin Nashua, NH
TREMBLAY, Dorilda, Mar 16 1907 Sex:F Child# 12 Israel Tremblay Canada & Philomene Joubert Canada
TREMBLAY, Doris Ina, Jul 15 1932 Sex:F Child# 2 Royal Tremblay Lawrence, MA & Lillian Lessard Nashua, NH
TREMBLAY, Edmour Leonard, May 27 1920 Sex:M Child# 1 Edouard Tremblay NH & Elianne Archambault Maine
TREMBLAY, Edouard Albert, May 3 1914 Sex:M Child# 2 Ulysse Tremblay Canada & Alma Guichard Canada
TREMBLAY, Elie Gerald, Oct 4 1922 Sex:M Child# 2 Arthur A Tremblay Canada & Laura Aubut Nashua, NH
TREMBLAY, Emilia, Apr 28 1896 Sex:F Child#  Pierre Tremblay Canada & Marie Gagnon Canada
TREMBLAY, Emma Evelyn, Oct 10 1900 Sex:F Child# 2 A C Tremblay NY & Emma A Perreault Canada
TREMBLAY, Ernest, Feb 6 1923 Sex:M Child# 1 Leo Tremblay Nashua, NH & Louise Bissonnette Nashua, NH
TREMBLAY, Ernest Antonio, Feb 15 1902 Sex:M Child# 6 Adelard Tremblay Canada & Lea Caron Canada
TREMBLAY, Ernest Cyprien Lotie, Sep 10 1912 Sex:M Child# 5 Edouard Tremblay Sciota, NY & Claudia Caron Canada
TREMBLAY, Esther Lilian, Aug 12 1900 Sex:F Child# 1 Aime Tremblay Nashua, NH & Philonise Dion Vermont
TREMBLAY, Eva, Sep 29 1898 Sex:F Child# 1 Israel Tremblay Canada & Philomene Janbert Canada
TREMBLAY, Eva Elodia, Jan 4 1893 Sex:F Child# 5 David Tremblay Canada & Rosanna Leblanc Canada
TREMBLAY, Excie Muriel, Jun 11 1932 Sex:F Child# 5 Ed Tremblay Sciota, NY & Lydia Delisle Canada
TREMBLAY, Florence, Feb 1 1923 Sex:F Child# 1 Edouard Tremblay Altona, NY & Lydia Delisle Canada
TREMBLAY, Fredeline Rita, May 5 1922 Sex:F Child# 3 Clifford Tremblay US & Emma Desautels Nashua, NH
TREMBLAY, Gabrielle Florette, Nov 21 1910 Sex:F Child# 2 William Tremblay NH & Marie Menard NH
TREMBLAY, George Henri, Mar 18 1916 Sex:M Child# 6 Thomas Tremblay Canada & Julie Livernois New York
TREMBLAY, Harriet Marie, Feb 14 1909 Sex:F Child# 1 (No Parents Listed)
TREMBLAY, Harvey Wilfred, Jun 1 1924 Sex:M Child# 2 Leo Tremblay Plattsburg, NY & Louise Bissonnette Nashua, NH
TREMBLAY, Hector, Jun 9 1897 Sex:M Child# 11 Napoleon Tremblay US & Josephine Nadeau US
TREMBLAY, Hormidas, Apr 5 1895 Sex:M Child# 3 Israel Tremblay Canada & Philomene Joubert Canada
TREMBLAY, Jacqueline Rosemond, Mar 24 1926 Sex:F Child# 4 Arthur Tremblay Canada & Laura Aubut Nashua, NH
TREMBLAY, Jos Francis Albert, May 29 1929 Sex:M Child# 1 Francis Tremblay Hooksett, NH & Wilda Fortin Nashua, NH
TREMBLAY, Jos Isaac Alphonse, Oct 15 1916 Sex:M Child# 1 Clifford Tremblay New York & Emma Desautel Nashua, NH
TREMBLAY, Jos Richard Edward, Oct 16 1920 Sex:M Child# 2 Cleophas J Tremblay Sciota, NY & Emma Desautels Nashua, NH
TREMBLAY, Joseph, Nov 10 1895 Sex:M Child# 2 Arthur Tremblay Canada & Marie Beaulieu Canada
TREMBLAY, Joseph, Jun 19 1929 Sex:M Child# 4 Edouard Tremblay Altona, NY & Lydia Delisle Canada
TREMBLAY, Joseph Adelard, Sep 7 1896 Sex:M Child# 2 Adelard Tremblay Canada & Lea Caron Canada
TREMBLAY, Joseph Arthur, May 11 1914 Sex:M Child# 5 Thomas Tremblay Canada & Julie Livernois New York
TREMBLAY, Joseph Clarence, Sep 2 1917 Sex:M Child# 8 Edouard Tremblay Altona, NY & Claudia Caron Canada
TREMBLAY, Joseph Ernest, May 2 1914 Sex:M Child# 1 Norris A Tremblay Canada & Anna Malette US Stillborn
TREMBLAY, Joseph G A, Jul 11 1892 Sex:M Child# 3 George Tremblay Canada & Louise Monette Canada
TREMBLAY, Joseph Raymond, Jul 11 1907 Sex:M Child# 1 Napoleon Tremblay New York & Philomene Paradis NH
TREMBLAY, Joseph Raymond W, Oct 9 1911 Sex:M Child# 5 Michel Tremblay Canada & Josephine Dube Canada
TREMBLAY, Joseph Theodore, Jul 23 1905 Sex:M Child# 1 Edward Tremblay Sciota, NY & Claudia Caron Canada
TREMBLAY, Laval Paul Dollard, Jun 30 1921 Sex:M Child# 2 Arthur A Tremblay Canada & Laura Aubut Nashua, NH
TREMBLAY, Leo, Sep 3 1901 Sex:M Child# 1 Frank Tremblay NY & Delima Tremblay NY
TREMBLAY, Leo, Aug 17 1906 Sex:M Child# 2 Edouard Tremblay Sciota, NY & Claudia Caron Canada

TREMBLAY, Lillian M, Mar 18 1898 Sex:F Child# 1 Alfred Tremblay Sciota, NY & Emma Perreault Canada
TREMBLAY, Loraine Anita, May 8 1934 Sex:F Child# 3 Louis Tremblay Nashua, NH & Grace Coulombe Canada
TREMBLAY, Lucienne A Lilianne, Aug 29 1916 Sex:F Child# 3 Ulysse Tremblay Canada & Alma Guichard Canada
TREMBLAY, Lucille Annette, Jan 27 1935 Sex:F Child# 4 Leo Tremblay Dannemore, NY & Louise Bissonette Nashua, NH
TREMBLAY, Lucille Virginie, Feb 5 1915 Sex:F Child# 5 Adelard Tremblay Canada & Marie Roy Canada
TREMBLAY, M Corrinne Lillian, Dec 12 1913 Sex:F Child# 2 Francois R Tremblay New York & Emelia Plante Mass
TREMBLAY, M Florence Cecile, Mar 9 1915 Sex:F Child# 1 Napoleon Tremblay New York & Delia Paradis NH
TREMBLAY, M Florida, Aug 19 1895 Sex:F Child# 1 Johnny Tremblay Canada & Lea Caron Canada
TREMBLAY, M Irene Bertha, Apr 26 1908 Sex:F Child# 5 Wilber Tremblay Sciota, NY & Regina Lavigne Canada
TREMBLAY, M R Alma Irene, Apr 9 1913 Sex:F Child# 1 Ulysse Tremblay Canada & Alma Guichard Canada
TREMBLAY, Marie, Sep 21 1911 Sex:F Child# 4 Thomas Tremblay Canada & Julie Livernois New York
TREMBLAY, Marie, May 8 1912 Sex:F Child# 3 Napoleon Tremblay New York & Philomene Paradis NH Stillborn
TREMBLAY, Marie A Adeline, Feb 1 1899 Sex:F Child# 4 Adelarde Tremblay Canada & Lea Caron Canada
TREMBLAY, Marie Aurore, Mar 22 1900 Sex:F Child# 7 Israel Tremblay Canada & Philomene Joubert Canada
TREMBLAY, Marie B Pauline, Aug 20 1905 Sex:F Child# 4 Wilbur Tremblay New York & Regina Lavigne Canada
TREMBLAY, Marie Blanche, Dec 31 1905 Sex:F Child# 9 Napoleon Tremblay New York & Josephine Nadeau New York
TREMBLAY, Marie Blanche A, Feb 16 1899 Sex:F Child# 2 Wilber Tremblay Altona, NY & Regina Lavigne Canada
TREMBLAY, Marie Blanche F, Apr 26 1900 Sex:F Child# 5 Adelard Tremblay Canada & Lea Caron Canada
TREMBLAY, Marie Elizabeth, Jul 10 1903 Sex:F Child# 7 Adelard Tremblay Canada & Lea Caron Canada
TREMBLAY, Marie Emma, Mar 8 1894 Sex:F Child# 2 Israel Tremblay Canada & Philomene Joubert Canada
TREMBLAY, Marie Estelle A, Feb 25 1910 Sex:F Child# 2 Napoleon Tremblay New York & Philomene Paradis NH
TREMBLAY, Marie Eva, Dec 26 1897 Sex:F Child# 3 Adelard Tremblay Canada & Lea Caron Canada
TREMBLAY, Marie Fleurette R, Dec 18 1923 Sex:F Child# 1 Francis Tremblay Canada & Lorette Plourde Canada
TREMBLAY, Marie Laura, Aug 18 1901 Sex:F Child# 8 Israel Tremblay Canada & Philomene Joubert Canada
TREMBLAY, Marie Malvina I, Jan 10 1908 Sex:F Child# 1 William Tremblay NH & Marie Menard NH
TREMBLAY, Maurice, Nov 5 1931 Sex:M Child# 2 Louis Tremblay Nashua, NH & Grace Coulombe Canada
TREMBLAY, May Lorraine, Jul 8 1919 Sex:F Child# 3 Norris A Tremblay Canada & Anna Malette Nashua, NH
TREMBLAY, Napoleon Ernest, Oct 31 1905 Sex:M Child# 11 Israel Tremblay Canada & Philomene Joubert Canada
TREMBLAY, Rachel Lorette, May 20 1935 Sex:F Child# 4 Louis Tremblay Nashua, NH & Grace Coulombe Canada
TREMBLAY, Raymond Maurice, Jan 9 1925 Sex:M Child# 2 Edward Tremblay Sciota, NY & Lydia Delille Canada
TREMBLAY, Reginald, Jun 2 1916 Sex:M Child# 1 Norris Tremblay Canada & Anna Malette Nashua, NH
TREMBLAY, Roland Patrick A, Mar 17 1918 Sex:M Child# 2 Norris Tremblay St Agnes, Canada & Anna Malette Nashua
TREMBLAY, Rosalina Marie, May 6 1903 Sex:F Child# 9 Israel Tremblay Canada & Philomene Joubert Canada
TREMBLAY, Rosilia, Jun 26 1895 Sex:F Child# 6 Napoleon Tremblay US & Josephine Nadeau US
TREMBLAY, Theresa Joan C, Jul 28 1930 Sex:F Child# 1 Royal Tremblay Graniteville, VT & Lillian Lessard Nashua, NH
TREMBLAY, Viateur Ernest, Apr 26 1914 Sex:M Child# 6 Edouard Tremblay Sciota, NY & Claudia Caron Canada
TREMBLAY, Victor Henri, Nov 18 1907 Sex:M Child# 3 Edouard Tremblay Sciota, NY & Claudia Caron Canada
TREMBLAY, William, Dec 6 1887 Sex:M Child# 7 Charles Tremblay Plattsburg, NY & Leda St Michel Plattsburg, NY
TREMBLEY, Doris Marie Therese, Feb 7 1924 Sex:F Child# 8 Dennis Trembley Highgate, VT & Bertha Trembley Mooers, NY
TREMBLEY, Ernest Albert L, Apr 29 1905 Sex:M Child# 8 Adelard Trembley Canada & Lea Caron Canada
TREMBLEY, Fred Napoleon, Feb 19 1904 Sex:M Child# 3 Alfred Trembley NY & Emma Perreault Canada
TREMBLEY, Jos Alb Ulysse Arth, Jan 4 1918 Sex:M Child# 4 Ulyse Trembley Canada & Alma Guichard Canada
TREMBLEY, Marie Jeanne, Jun 13 1904 Sex:F Child# 10 Israel Trembley Canada & Philomene Joubert Canada
TREMBLEY, Robert Arthur, Aug 7 1925 Sex:M Child# 3 Leo Trembley New York & M L Bissonnette Nashua, NH
TREMPE, Jean Baptiste, Jul 24 1902 Sex:M Child# 2 John Trempe Canada & Marie L Benoit Canada
TREMPE, Jeanne Yolande, May 15 1930 Sex:F Child# 2 Amedee Trempe Nashua, NH & Jeanne Claveau Nashua, NH
TREMPE, Loretta Aurore, Jul 19 1928 Sex:F Child# 1 Amedee Trempe Nashua, NH & M J Claveau Nashua, NH
TRENHOLM, Unknown, May 10 1891 Sex:F Child# 1 Tweedy F Trenholm Port Elgin, NB & Nettie H Tinker
TRENOWIC, Dominikas, Jul 8 1906 Sex:M Child# 4 Gasper Trenowic Russia & Linoluisia Pozniakni Russia
TRENOWICZ, Algirdas, May 7 1921 Sex:M Child# 3 Andrew Trenowicz Lithuania & Vinea Tamolawicz Lithuania
TRENOWICZ, Stanislaw, May 17 1920 Sex:M Child# 1 Sigmond Trenowicz Lithuania Russia & Frusina Petruczunas Lithuania
TRENOWITCH, Isabelle, Dec 25 1916 Sex:F Child# 4 Leonard Trenowitch Russia & Antolka Swaklonta Russia
TREYNOVICZ, William, Mar 12 1908 Sex:M Child# 2 Leonard Treynovicz Lithuania & Anolks Swioklute Lithuania
TREYNOVITCH, Malvina, Jan 17 1904 Sex:F Child# 2 Jasper Treynovitch Russia & Ludivica Paznerknite Russia
TREYNSWICH, Joan, Jul 12 1931 Sex:F Child# 1 William Treynswich Nashua, NH & Eva Mae Mellon Nashua, NH
TREYNVOC, Mary, Feb 2 1903 Sex:F Child# 1 Lenord Treynvoc Poland & Antonia Svoiokluti Poland
TREZEVITCH, Bolaslov, Jun 5 1911 Sex:M Child# 4 Chrs Trezevitch Russia & Michelina Chernicesk Russia
TRIBOUTOT, Jean Baptiste, Dec 19 1892 Sex:M Child# 6 Arthur Triboutot Canada & Celina Morelle Canada
TRINGOSON, Paul Leo, Sep 18 1930 Sex:M Child# 1 Charles Tringoson Bulgaria & Eva Messier Nashua, NH
TRINOVITCH, Leonard, Nov 6 1911 Sex:M Child# 8 Jasper Trinovitch Russia & Ludivica Perznakatz Russia
TRITES, Howard Patrick, Dec 2 1934 Sex:M Child# 1 Howard Trites Chelmsford, MA & Yvette Ouellette Oldtown, ME
TROBEZ, John, Apr 18 1916 Sex:M Child# 1 Stanilaus Trobes Poland & Skola Poland Stillborn
TROKIAN, Veronica, Mar 16 1926 Sex:F Child# 3 Anthony Trokian Lithuania & Helen Ukanawicz Lithuania
TROMBLEY, Cora, May 7 1893 Sex:F Child# 5 Nazaire Trombley New York & Josephine Nadeau New York
TROMBLEY, Francis R, Jul 14 1906 Sex:M Child# 1 Francis R Trombley New York & Emily Plante Mass
TROMBLEY, Julia Bertha, Jul 3 1921 Sex:F Child# 4 Dennis Trombley Vermont & Bertha Trombley New York
TROMBLEY, Unknown, Sep 27 1891 Sex:F Child# 7 Oscar Trombley New York & Jennie Rock New York
TROMBLEY, Unknown, Jun 1 1898 Sex:M Child# 6 David Trombley Plattsburgh, NY & Rose Anna Leblanc Canada Stillborn
TROMBLY, Arthur, Aug 13 1897 Sex:M Child# 3 Arthur Trombly New York & Mary Beaulieu Fall River, MA
TROMBLY, Doris Marie Theresa, Mar 2 1934 Sex:F Child# 1 Francis Trombly Nashua, NH & Germaine Lavoie Nashua, NH
TROMBLY, Edmond Alderd, Aug 29 1916 Sex:M Child# 7 Edward Trombly New York & Claudia Caron Canada
TROMBLY, Henry James, Jun 12 1897 Sex:M Child# 1 William Trombly Coopersville, NY & Jennie Blow Sciota, NY
TROMBLY, Lorraine Marie, Mar 26 1931 Sex:F Child# 7 Frederick W Trombly Springfield, VT & Bertha Couture Canada

TROMBLY, Louis, Jun 18 1889 Sex:M Child# 5 Napoleon Trombly New York & Josephine Nadeau New York
TROMBLY, Mary, Mar 25 1896 Sex:F Child# 11 Victor Trombly Canada & Regina Trudelle Canada
TROMBLY, Pearl Edith, Oct 31 1906 Sex:F Child# 3 George H Trombly Green Bay, WI & Frances W Davis Mooers, NY
TROMBLY, Richard Allen, Nov 13 1912 Sex:M Child# 4 George Trombly Green Bay, WI & Frances Davis Mooers, NY
TROMBLY, Rosana, Jan 28 1889 Sex:F Child# 3 David Trombly Canada & Rosana Lebanc Canada
TRONAWICH, Frank, Oct 21 1913 Sex:M Child# 1 Ezeido Tronawich Russia & Katie Guida Russia
TROOBOOCH, Fuice, Nov 2 1894 Sex:M Child# 6 Solomon Troobooch Russia & Sarah Rapron Russia
TROTTIER, Adrien Alphe, Mar 12 1933 Sex:M Child# 4 Alphe Trottier US & Mattie Loraine US
TROTTIER, Armand E, May 21 1922 Sex:M Child# 1 Alphee Trottier Nashua, NH & Martha Lorraine Nashua, NH
TROTTIER, Conrad Armand, Jun 25 1895 Sex:M Child# 2 Joseph Trottier Canada & Alphonsine Gariepy Canada
TROTTIER, Eloise, Dec 27 1904 Sex:F Child# 1 Albert J Trottier Canada & Mary E Shanahan Nashua, NH
TROTTIER, Ernest A, Oct 10 1899 Sex:M Child# 3 Louis Trottier Vermont & Albertine Lucas Canada
TROTTIER, George Noel, Dec 25 1923 Sex:M Child# 2 Alphe Trottier Nashua, NH & Martha Loraine Nashua, NH
TROTTIER, Georgette, Jun 8 1897 Sex:F Child# 3 Joseph Trottier Canada & Alphonsine Garipey Canada
TROTTIER, Hector Leon, Aug 5 1923 Sex:M Child# 2 Lusic Trottier Canada & Irene Masse Canada
TROTTIER, Joseph, Jan 1 1897 Sex:M Child# 1 Louis Trottier St Albans, VT & Albertine Lucas Canada
TROTTIER, Joseph A, Apr 6 1894 Sex:M Child# 1 Joseph Trottier Canada & Alphonsine Gariepy Canada
TROTTIER, Joseph Leopold B, Mar 3 1901 Sex:M Child# 3 Wilfrid Trottier Canada & Delia Cloutier RI
TROTTIER, Joseph Romeo, Feb 6 1898 Sex:M Child# 1 Wilfrid Trottier Canada & Delia Cloutier Woonsocket, RI
TROTTIER, Marie Gabriel Eliza, Jan 22 1921 Sex:F Child# 1 Lusip Trottier Canada & Irene Masse Canada
TROTTIER, Marie L B, Jan 23 1898 Sex:F Child# 2 Louis Trottier St Albans, VT & Albertine Lucas Canada
TROTTIER, Mary Celice R Anna, Apr 21 1926 Sex:F Child# 3 Lusik Trottier Canada & Irene Messe Canada
TROTTIER, Maurice Alfred, Jul 26 1927 Sex:M Child# 3 Alphee Trottier Nashua, NH & Martha Lorraine Nashua, NH
TROTTIER, Oscar, Oct 31 1905 Sex:M Child# 12 Xavier Trottier Canada & Adelaide Morasse Canada
TROUP, James Bruce, Aug 8 1921 Sex:M Child# 1 James B Troup Scotland & Mary J Bruce Scotland
TROVER, Myra Grace, Jan 1 1900 Sex:F Child# 2 George W Trover Richford, VT & Helen V McDonald Calais, ME
TROW, Charles Allen, Dec 15 1935 Sex:M Child# 3 Earl M Trow Mt Vernon, NH & Margaret Eaton Fitchburg, MA
TROW, Dorothy May, Feb 5 1923 Sex:F Child# 3 Theron Trow Nashua, NH & Bessie Stevens New Boston, NH
TROW, Gertrude Olive, Apr 3 1917 Sex:F Child# 1 Theron A Trow Nashua, NH & Bessie Stevens N Lyndeboro, NH
TROW, Kenneth George, Jan 31 1926 Sex:M Child# 4 Theron Trow Nashua, NH & Bessie Stevens S Lyndeboro, NH
TROW, Mildred, Feb 11 1905 Sex:F Child# 1 Harry W Trow Nashua, NH & Emma J McAfee Bedford, MA
TROW, Myrtle, May 17 1906 Sex:F Child# 2 William Trow Mt Vernon, NH & Florence McDonald Nashua, NH
TROW, Theron A, Jr, Apr 30 1921 Sex:M Child# 2 Theron A Trow Nashua, NH & Bessie Stevens New Boston, NH
TROW, Unknown, Oct 1 1888 Sex:M Child# 4 Freeman B Trow Goshen, NH & Mary Molms Londonderry, NH
TROW, William, Oct 1 1903 Sex:M Child# 1 Elmer F Trow Mt Vernon, NH & Flora G McDonald Nashua, NH
TRUAX, Beatrice Jean, Sep 20 1925 Sex:F Child# 3 James F Truax Malaga, OH & Hazel Mercer Batesville, OH
TRUAX, Lois Marjorie, Mar 22 1922 Sex:F Child# 2 James A Truax Melaga, OH & Hazel Ferne Mercer Atlas, OH
TRUAX, Unknown, Oct 26 1918 Sex:F Child# 1 James Truax Ohio & Hazel Mercier Ohio Stillborn
TRUBACZ, Anthony, Jun 1 1932 Sex:M Child# 6 Stanley Trubacz Poland & S Kursewicz Poland
TRUBACZ, Felixia, Feb 1 1926 Sex:F Child# 3 Stanios Trubacz Russia & Scholia Kursewicz Russia
TRUBACZ, Marion, Aug 15 1927 Sex:F Child# 4 Stanley Trubacz Poland & Schola Kursewicz Poland
TRUBASZ, Peter, Apr 29 1931 Sex:M Child# 5 Stanislau Trubasz Poland & Scholsiasta Kursawic Poland
TRUCHEWICZ, Yadvenia, Jul 11 1912 Sex:F Child# 5 Charles Truchewicz Russia & Mikalina Chernoski Russia
TRUDA, Marion Alice, Oct 16 1891 Sex:F Child# 1 Vincent Truda Italy & Mary J Boston, MA
TRUDEAU, Albert Edgar, Jul 7 1920 Sex:M Child# 8 Henry T Trudeau Sturgeon Bay, WI & Agnes Ouellette Nashua, NH
TRUDEAU, Albina Pearl, Jan 15 1919 Sex:F Child# 6 Henry Trudeau Sturgeon Bay, WI & Agnes Ouellette Nashua, NH
TRUDEAU, Alice Lauretta, May 19 1917 Sex:F Child# 5 Henry Trudeau Sturgeon Bay, WI & Agnes Ouellette Nashua, NH
TRUDEAU, Claire, Dec 18 1921 Sex:F Child# 9 Eugene Trudeau Canada & Delia Bolduc Lawrence, MA
TRUDEAU, Edith Beatrice, Dec 14 1907 Sex:F Child# 3 Henry Trudeau Bay City, MI & Agnes Ouellette Nashua, NH
TRUDEAU, Edwidge Cecilia, May 7 1903 Sex:F Child# 2 Elzear Trudeau Sturgeon Bay, WI & Leontine Morin Canada
TRUDEAU, Emile, Oct 14 1909 Sex:M Child# 5 Henry Trudeau Sturgeon Bay, WI & Agnes Ouellette Nashua, NH
TRUDEAU, Lilian Irene, Mar 12 1905 Sex:F Child# 2 Henry Trudeau Sturgeon Bay, WI & Agnes Ouelette Nashua, NH
TRUDEAU, Marie B Yvonne, Apr 16 1922 Sex:F Child# 1 Stanley Trudeau Vermont & Regina Cloutier NH
TRUDEAU, Marie Theresa, Sep 30 1925 Sex:M Child# 8 Henry Trudeau Sturgeon Bay, WI & Agnes Ouilette Nashua, NH
TRUDEAU, Mary Irene Beatrice, Jun 30 1925 Sex:F Child# 4 Stanley Trudeau Middlebury, VT & Regina Cloutier Nashua,NH
TRUDEAU, Robert Ronald, Jun 29 1935 Sex:M Child# 2 Walter Trudeau Vermont & Adrienne Cadieux Nashua, NH
TRUDEAU, Theobald, Aug 20 1903 Sex:M Child# 1 Henry Trudeau Sturgeon Bay, WI & Agnes Ouellette Nashua, NH
TRUDEAU, Ulric Olivia, Mar 23 1902 Sex:M Child# 1 Elzear Trudeau Medford, WI & Leontine Morin Canada
TRUDEL, Adeline Helene, Oct 20 1910 Sex:F Child# 12 Hector Trudel Canada & Emma Desmarais St Albans, VT
TRUDEL, Alma A A, Apr 26 1899 Sex:F Child# 3 Hector Trudel Canada & Emma Desmarais St Albans, VT
TRUDEL, Arthur Edward, Aug 12 1931 Sex:M Child# 4 Theodore Trudel Nashua, NH & Lena Edwards Nashua, NH
TRUDEL, Barbara Ann, Dec 10 1934 Sex:F Child# 5 Theodore Trudel Nashua, NH & Lena Edwards Nashua, NH
TRUDEL, Bernard Philippe, May 22 1908 Sex:M Child# 10 Hector Trudel Canada & Emma Desmarais St Albans, VT
TRUDEL, Doris May, Feb 9 1926 Sex:F Child# 1 T H D Trudel Nashua, NH & H A Edwards Nashua, NH
TRUDEL, Emela Exilda, Mar 12 1898 Sex:F Child# 4 Edouard Trudel Canada & Exilda Trudel Canada
TRUDEL, Eva, Feb 24 1906 Sex:F Child# 8 Hector Trudel Canada & Emma Desmarais St Albans, VT
TRUDEL, Germaine, Feb 1 1912 Sex:F Child# 13 Hector Trudel Canada & Emma Desmarais St Albans, VT
TRUDEL, Gertrude M, Jul 6 1907 Sex:F Child# 9 Hector Trudel Canada & Emma Desmarais Vermont
TRUDEL, Hercule H L, Dec 29 1901 Sex:M Child# 5 Hecter Trudel Canada & Emma Desmarais Canada
TRUDEL, Leona Olive J, Dec 4 1918 Sex:F Child# 15 Hector Trudel Canada & Emma Desmarais Vermont
TRUDEL, Lillian Olivine, Apr 7 1904 Sex:F Child# 4 Hector Trudel Canada & Emma Desmarais St Albans, VT
TRUDEL, Louis Eugene, Apr 8 1914 Sex:M Child# 14 Hector Trudel Canada & Emma Desmarais St Albans, VT
TRUDEL, Marie A E, Jun 24 1896 Sex:F Child# 1 Hector Trudel Canada & Emma Desmarais St Albans, VT

TRUDEL, Marie Adelina, Dec 7 1905 Sex:F Child# 1 Edmond Trudel Canada & Adelina Demers Canada
TRUDEL, Marie E Q, Oct 12 1897 Sex:F Child# 2 Hector Trudel Canada & Emma Desmarais St Albans, VT
TRUDEL, Marjorie Theodora, May 23 1928 Sex:F Child# 2 Theo H Trudel Nashua, NH & Lena Edwards Nashua, NH
TRUDEL, Rose Claudia A, Oct 1 1909 Sex:F Child# 11 Hector Trudel Canada & Emma Desmarais St Albans, VT
TRUDEL, Theodore Daniel, Jan 27 1903 Sex:M Child# 6 Hector Trudel Canada & Emma Desmarais St Albans, VT
TRUDEL, Theodore H, Sep 6 1929 Sex:M Child# 3 Theodore Trudel Nashua, NH & Lena Edwards Nashua, NH
TRUDEL, Unknown, Dec 29 1930 Sex:M Child# 6 Arthur Trudel Worcester, MA & Dorothy Parent Burlington, VT
TRUDELLE, Alice E A, Oct 3 1900 Sex:F Child# 4 Hector Trudelle Canada & Emma Desmarais Vermont
TRUE, Unknown, Oct 16 1889 Sex:M Child# 2 Phelix True Wilton, NH & Adele Meriur Canada
TRUEBLOOD, Hartley Winslow, Sep 2 1929 Sex:M Child# 1 Roscoe Trueblood Mt Pleasant, Iowa & Pauline Pemberton
TRUELL, Nancy Gail, Oct 21 1933 Sex:F Child# 1 Harry Truell Enfield, NH & Hazel Wheeler Nashua, NH
TRUFANT, Arthur, Apr 11 1897 Sex:M Child# 4 John M Trufant Harpswell, ME & Flora E Turner Levant, ME
TRUFANT, Bertha Adelie, Dec 10 1922 Sex:F Child# 2 Ralph S Trufant Brunswick, ME & Anna J McDonald Prince Edw Islan
TRUFANT, Elizabeth Ann, Oct 30 1917 Sex:F Child# 2 Frank A Trufant Nashua, NH & Marion E Chase Nashua, NH
TRUFANT, Ernest, Mar 16 1893 Sex:M Child# 3 John M Trufant Harpswell, ME & Flora E Turner Lavant, ME
TRUFANT, Esther Louise, Aug 24 1919 Sex:F Child# 3 Frank A Trufant Nashua, NH & Marian E Chase Nashua, NH
TRUFANT, Mary Elizabeth, Aug 10 1921 Sex:F Child# 1 Ralph S Trufant Brunswick, ME & Anna MacDonald Prince Edw Islan
TRUFANT, Ralph Sam, Jr, Feb 21 1924 Sex:M Child# 3 Ralph Trufant Brunswick, ME & Anna MacDonald Prince Edw Island
TRUFANT, Richard Frank, Jan 5 1922 Sex:M Child# 4 Frank A Trufant Nashua, NH & Marion Ethel Chase Nashua, NH
TRUFANT, Unknown, Jan 18 1890 Sex:M Child#  John M Trufant Harpswell, ME & Flora E Turner Levant, ME
TRUFAUT, Flossie May, Aug 12 1891 Sex:F Child# 2 John M Trufaut Harpswell, ME & Flora E Turner Levant, ME
TRULL, Clara, Nov 3 1895 Sex:F Child# 1 Edward C Trull NH & Minnie E Lake New York
TRULL, Meredith Ann, Jul 31 1934 Sex:F Child# 1 B Franklin Trull N Tewksbury, MA & Bernice McQuesten Nashua, NH
TRULL, Unknown, Aug 13 1899 Sex:F Child# 2 Edward C Trull NH & Mary E Lake NY
TRUMBLAY, Marie Daura, Jul 11 1891 Sex:F Child# 4 Napoleon Trumblay New York & Josephine Nadeau New York
TRUMBLE, Alfred Randolph, Jan 7 1903 Sex:M Child# 1 Frank Trumble Wayland, MA & Gertrude Donohoe Montpelier, VT
TRUMBLE, Helen Anna, Feb 28 1913 Sex:F Child# 2 Charles F Trumble Scituate, MA & Gertrude Donohoe Montpelier, VT
TRUMBLE, Willard Irwin, Jun 23 1904 Sex:M Child# 2 Charles F Trumble Cochituate, MA & G G Donohue Montpelier, VT
TRUMBULL, Shirley Mae, Aug 7 1929 Sex:F Child# 2 Willard I Trumbull Nashua, NH & Alice Adams E Candia, NH
TRUMBULL, Unknown, Dec 20 1890 Sex:F Child# 1 Allie F Trumbull NH & Neffie A Largill NH
TRUMBULL, Unknown, Sep 18 1927 Sex:M Child# 1 W L Trumbull Nashua, NH & Alice R Adams Candia, NH
TSAGROS, Unknown, Apr 21 1914 Sex:F Child# 2 Christos Tsagros Greece & Aftehea Sconga Greece
TSAMTSIS, Jacqueline, Dec 16 1935 Sex:F Child# 1 Chris Tsamtsis Greece & Amelia Badaris Nashua, NH
TSATSA, Andrew, Jan 17 1914 Sex:M Child# 2 Peter Tsatsa Greece & Mary Aguran Greece
TSATSA, Unknown, Jun 10 1933 Sex:F Child# 3 John Tsatsa Greece & Kleanthe Lokedas Greece
TSATSG, Thomas, May 24 1916 Sex:M Child# 4 Peter Tsatsg Greece & Mary Agwion Greece
TSATSONES, Unknown, Jul 30 1916 Sex:F Child# 1 Theodore Tsatsones Greece & Panageota Bouroume Greece
TSENTSIAS, Unknown, Nov 17 1923 Sex:F Child#  Demetrius Tsentsias Greece & Mary Arahovites Greece
TSIARAS, John, Oct 11 1914 Sex:M Child# 2 James Tsiaras Greece & Arete Litsa Greece
TSIATSOS, Unknown, Jul 15 1930 Sex:M Child# 2 Zeses Tsiatsos Greece & Kleanthe Loukides Asia Minor
TSIBINLIARAS, Coslas, May 4 1916 Sex:M Child# 5 Athos Tsibinliaras Greece & Tasig Butsig Greece
TSINICA, Unknown, Nov 22 1911 Sex:M Child# 2 Nicles Tsinica Greece & Nitsi Nicles Greece
TSITSO, John, Jul 8 1910 Sex:M Child# 1 Peter Tsitso Greece & Kate B Gondoma Greece
TSITSO, Vesali, Oct 5 1913 Sex:M Child# 2 Peter Tsitso Greece & Catherine Gogero Greece
TUBEINE, Zioege, Jan 15 1911 Sex:F Child# 2 Simon Tubeine Russia & Louisa Angrulionis Russia
TUBENIS, Mary, Sep 13 1908 Sex:F Child# 1 Simon Tubenis Russia & Leonora Anchulonis Russia
TUBENUS, Alphonse, Jan 4 1910 Sex:M Child# 6 John Tubenus Russia & Mary Gregutie Russia
TUBINIS, Mary, Jan 19 1915 Sex:F Child# 4 Andrew Tubinis Russia & Mary Koflofski Russia
TUCKER, Annie, Apr 18 1895 Sex:F Child#  Horace Tucker Nova Scotia & Katie Shea New Foundland
TUCKER, Elizabeth, Feb 13 1908 Sex:F Child# 2 Howard I Tucker Lyon Mtn, NY & Ethel Duncan Faversham, England
TUCKER, Grace Inez, Aug 3 1925 Sex:F Child# 2 Allen J Tucker Akron, OH & Inez Smith Pelham, NH
TUCKER, Phoebe May, May 9 1905 Sex:F Child# 1 Howard I Tucker Lyon Mtn, NY & Ethel Duncan England
TUCOCWICZ, Frank, Sep 19 1906 Sex:M Child# 1 Mark Tucocwicz Austria & Bronistwa Wuclswick Austria
TUFTS, Harry, Dec 29 1924 Sex:M Child# 3 Harry Tufts Springfield, MA & Shirley Cummings Pembroke, NH Stillborn
TUFTS, Jane Milliken, Mar 21 1917 Sex:F Child# 1 William Tufts Boston, MA & Jane Peare Milliken Palmer, MA
TUFTS, Palma Estina, Jul 3 1931 Sex:F Child# 1 Harry Warren Tufts Springfield, MA & Shirley Cummings Pembroke, NH
TULLOCH, Unknown, Apr 11 1910 Sex:M Child# 4 William A Tulloch Nashua, NH & Edith Taylor England
TULLY, Michael, Mar 31 1898 Sex:M Child# 1 Michael Tully Lowell, MA & Mary Connors Arthen Rye, Ireland
TUMBLAY, Francois David, Nov 3 1890 Sex:M Child# 4 David Tumblay Sciota, NY & Rosanna Leblanc Canada
TUMELLE, Robert Louis, May 28 1933 Sex:M Child# 11 David Tumelle Rhode Island & Octavia Rodier Nashua, NH
TUPPER, Anna Bertha, Oct 28 1897 Sex:F Child# 3 Horace E Tupper Nova Scotia & Catharine Shea Newfoundland
TUPPER, Delia, Aug 26 1900 Sex:F Child# 2 Joseph H Tupper NH & Mary McAsh Ireland
TUPPER, Dorothy, May 28 1908 Sex:F Child# 3 Joseph H Tupper Plymouth, NH & Mary McCue Ireland
TUPPER, Eva Jennie, Feb 5 1900 Sex:F Child# 5 H E Tupper Nova Scotia & Kate Shea Newfoundland
TUPPER, Jessilce Ida, Aug 30 1899 Sex:F Child# 1 James C Tupper NS & Mabel E Holt NH
TUPPER, Lois Margaret, Jul 12 1906 Sex:F Child# 2 Ansel Tupper Jonesborough, ME & Clara E Cowan Linwick, Quebec
TUPPER, Nancy Hancock, Jun 25 1925 Sex:F Child# 2 Harold Tupper Nashua, NH & Dor W Daggart Concord, NH
TUPPER, Pamelia Wing, Dec 3 1922 Sex:F Child# 1 Harold F Tupper Nashua, NH & Dorothy Wing Daggett Concord, NH
TUPPER, Unknown, Mar 19 1898 Sex:F Child# 1 Joseph H Tupper Holderness & Mary McCue Ireland
TUPPER, Unknown, Jan 21 1899 Sex:M Child# 1 Ansel Tupper Maine & Clara E Cowan Lingwick, CA
TUPPER, William, Sep 20 1896 Sex:M Child#  Horace E Tupper Nova Scotia & Kate Shea Newfoundland
TURCHI, Armanda, Oct 6 1922 Sex:F Child# 2 A Turchi Italy & Tresa Tonella Concord, NH
TURCHI, Bruno, Nov 22 1924 Sex:M Child# 3 Armendo Turchi Italy & Teresa Tonella Concord, NH

TURCHI, Leo Guilu, Jun 25 1918 Sex:M Child# 1 Armanda Turchi Italy & Teresa Tonella Concord, NH
TURCOTT, David Ronald, Apr 27 1935 Sex:M Child# 4 O'Neil Turcott Maine & Elizabeth Pierce Nashua, NH
TURCOTT, Rosanna, Jan 13 1892 Sex:F Child# 13 Napoleon Turcott Canada & Azilda Dumont Canada
TURCOTTE, Charlotte L Florence, Mar 5 1920 Sex:F Child# 1 Ernest Turcotte Canada & Marian Marquis Canada
TURCOTTE, Claire Gloria, Aug 14 1925 Sex:F Child# 2 Joseph Turcotte Canada & Louise Douville Nashua, NH
TURCOTTE, Claire Rita, Nov 6 1924 Sex:F Child# 4 C Turcotte Canada & Yvonne Hamel Canada
TURCOTTE, H P Gerald Rodolph, Dec 8 1922 Sex:M Child# 4 Adelard Turcotte Canada & Helene Antaya Nashua, NH
TURCOTTE, J Alfred Emile, Jun 13 1911 Sex:M Child# 1 Omer Turcotte Canada & Delia Pelltier Canada
TURCOTTE, J Fidele Rosaire, Apr 24 1913 Sex:M Child# 4 Philemon Turcotte Canada & Angelina Girouard Nashua, NH
TURCOTTE, Jacques A, Dec 13 1894 Sex:M Child# 16 Napoleon Turcotte Canada & Azilda Dumont Canada
TURCOTTE, Jeanne Marguerite, Feb 2 1920 Sex:F Child# 3 Adelard Turcotte Canada & Helene Antaya Nashua, NH
TURCOTTE, Joseph Girard, May 11 1918 Sex:M Child# 5 Philemon Turcotte Canada & Angelina Girouard Nashua, NH
TURCOTTE, Joseph Norman Ulric, Jan 23 1932 Sex:M Child# 6 Adelard Turcotte Canada & Ellen Antaya Nashua, NH
TURCOTTE, Louis P, Jan 27 1897 Sex:M Child# 18 Napoleon Turcotte Canada & Azilda Dumont Canada
TURCOTTE, Lucille, Mar 2 1913 Sex:F Child# 1 Joseph Turcotte Canada & Louise Douville Nashua, NH
TURCOTTE, M Alienne Lorette, Aug 4 1917 Sex:F Child# 1 Louis P Turcotte Canada & Dora Berube Canada
TURCOTTE, Marcel Roger, Feb 28 1922 Sex:M Child# 6 Philemon Turcotte Canada & Angelina Girouard Nashua, NH
TURCOTTE, Maria A, Jan 24 1894 Sex:F Child# 15 Napoleon Turcotte Canada & Ozilda Dumont Canada
TURCOTTE, Marie A, Mar 15 1893 Sex:F Child# 14 Napoleon Turcotte Canada & Azilda Dumont Canada
TURCOTTE, Marie Andrea, Mar 18 1907 Sex:F Child# 1 Philemon Turcotte Canada & Angelina Girouard Canada
TURCOTTE, Marie Anne Ther Isa, Oct 8 1918 Sex:F Child# Adelard Turcotte Canada & Helen Atayan Nashua, NH
TURCOTTE, Marie Estelle May, Apr 25 1928 Sex:F Child# 1 Adelard Turcotte Canada & Helene Antaya Nashua, NH
TURCOTTE, Marie Olivette, Apr 9 1915 Sex:F Child# 1 Adelard Turcotte Canada & Helene Antaya Nashua, NH
TURCOTTE, Marie Rose C, Mar 31 1909 Sex:F Child# 3 Philemore Turcotte Canada & Angelina Girouard Canada
TURCOTTE, Pierre A, Oct 5 1890 Sex:M Child# 12 Napoleon Turcotte Canada & Azilda Dumont Canada
TURCOTTE, Pierre A, Nov 29 1895 Sex:M Child# 17 Napoleon Turcotte Canada & Ozilda Dumont Canada
TURCOTTE, Raymond George, Feb 22 1921 Sex:M Child# 3 Calixte Turcotte Canada & Yvonne Hamel Canada
TURCOTTE, Richard Pascal, Jun 18 1932 Sex:M Child# 3 O'Neil Turcotte Berwick, ME & Hester Eliz Pierce Nashua, NH
TURCOTTE, Roger Earl, Mar 24 1928 Sex:M Child# 5 Calixte Turcotte Canada & Yvonne Hamel Canada
TURCOTTE, Romeo, Mar 6 1911 Sex:M Child# 3 Philemon Turcotte Canada & Angelina Girouard Canada
TURELL, Unknown, Oct 28 1888 Sex:F Child# 4 Uriah H Truell Greenwood, ME & Emma Sands Livingston, C E
TUREWICZ, Bolestan, Sep 2 1904 Sex:M Child# 4 Kazimicz Turewicz Russia & Domicela Monczunza Russia
TURGEON, Delvina Alice, Dec 25 1902 Sex:F Child# 1 Ludger Turgeon Canada & Delvina Berube Canada
TURGEON, Edouard, Oct 9 1904 Sex:M Child# 2 Ludger Turgeon Canada & Delina Berube Canada
TURGEON, Florette Sylvia, Jan 25 1910 Sex:F Child# 3 Ludger Turgeon Canada & Delvina Berube Canada
TURGEON, Joseph Fernand, Aug 8 1923 Sex:M Child# 5 Octave Turgeon Canada & Alice Alaire Canada
TURGEON, Loraine Eva, Jun 2 1932 Sex:F Child# 9 Octave Turgeon Canada & Alice Allaire Canada
TURGEON, Lucien Wilfrid, Jul 2 1927 Sex:M Child# 7 Octave Turgeon Canada & Alice Allaire Canada
TURGEON, Octave Gerald, Apr 28 1925 Sex:M Child# 6 Octave Turgeon Canada & Alice Allaire Canada
TURGEON, Therese Alice, May 17 1930 Sex:F Child# 8 Octave Turgeon Canada & Alice Allaire Canada
TURGIS, George, Jun 12 1917 Sex:M Child# 3 Christos Turgis Greece & Sophie Vizouka Greece
TURLA, Jennette Virginia, May 22 1926 Sex:F Child# 6 Adolph Turla Poland & V Chotkevitch Poland
TURMEL, Marie Jeannette, Jul 28 1920 Sex:F Child# 3 David Turmel Rhode Island & Octavia Rodier Nashua, NH
TURMELL, Joseph Leo Edgar, Jul 7 1926 Sex:M Child# 6 David Turmell Central Falls, RI & Octavie Rodier Nashua, NH
TURMELLA, Maurice David, Mar 3 1929 Sex:M Child# 8 David Turmella Rhode Island & Octavia Rodier Nashua, NH
TURMELLE, Cecile, Mar 25 1923 Sex:F Child# 4 David Turmelle Rhode Island & Octavia Rodier Nashua, NH
TURMELLE, Rejane, Nov 1 1918 Sex:F Child# 2 David Turmelle Central Falls, RI & Octavie Rodier Nashua, NH
TURMELLE, Rita, Oct 5 1927 Sex:F Child# 7 David Turmelle Rhode Island & Octavie Rodier Nashua, NH
TURMELLE, Theresa Dorothy, Jun 5 1930 Sex:F Child# 9 David Turmelle Rhode Island & Octavia Rodier Nashua, NH
TURNER, Alice, Nov 13 1917 Sex:F Child# 2 David Turner Rhode Island & Octavia Rodier Nashua, NH Stillborn
TURNER, Chester Damon, Jul 12 1920 Sex:M Child# 2 Chester D Turner Rockland, MA & Nellie Montgomery Nashua, NH
TURNER, Daniel Oliver, Oct 31 1893 Sex:M Child# 5 Winfield S Turner Augusta, ME & Mary J Hazleton Fitchburg, MA
TURNER, Dorothy Ann, Oct 29 1919 Sex:F Child# 2 Walter F Turner Warren, NH & Eliza Ann Brown Manchester, NH
TURNER, Dorothy Margaret, Apr 28 1908 Sex:F Child# 2 Josiah W Turner Abington, MA & M C Kingsbury Holliston, MA
TURNER, Eleanor, Aug 27 1904 Sex:F Child# 1 Edward Turner E Charscon, VT & Maude Pierce Barton, VT
TURNER, Hubert George, Jul 12 1926 Sex:M Child# 2 Wilfred Turner Nashua, NH & Anna Scouvnac France
TURNER, Jean Ardrian, Sep 23 1931 Sex:F Child# 2 Mancy Turner Bronsville, TN & Mary Turner Maryville Colored
TURNER, Richard William, Jul 9 1930 Sex:M Child# 1 Joseph Turner Mexico & Pauline Heddeman Manchester, NH
TURNER, Robert Donald, May 26 1922 Sex:M Child# 1 Winford Turner Nashua, NH & Anna Scornica France
TURNER, Roger, Mar 13 1927 Sex:M Child# 1 Carl W Turner Nebraska & Catherine Cassidy Milford, NH
TURNER, Rosina Sara, Oct 15 1900 Sex:F Child# 2 Daniel H Turner ME & Gertrude Penfield VT
TURNER, Unknown, Oct 18 1888 Sex:M Child# 1 George W Turner N Y & Emma J Stark Ellenburg, NH
TURNER, Unknown, Aug 15 1892 Sex:M Child# 2 George W Turner Saranac, NY & Emma Starks Ellenburg, NY
TURNER, Unknown, Feb 21 1898 Sex:F Child# 1 Daniel H Turner Augusta, ME & Gertrude E Penfield Holland, VT
TURNER, Unknown, Apr 8 1898 Sex:M Child# 3 George W Turner Saranac, NY & Emma Stark Ellenburg, NY
TUTTLE, Alice Ada, Mar 12 1926 Sex:F Child# 2 Weare Tuttle Bernardsville, NJ & Gladys Holt Pembroke, NH
TUTTLE, David Ernest, Aug 8 1927 Sex:M Child# 7 W H Tuttle Newfields, NH & J E Witherill Portsmouth, NH
TUTTLE, Joan Helen, Jul 9 1923 Sex:F Child# 3 George Tuttle Henniker, NH & Rubie Wilkins Nashua, NH
TUTTLE, Joanne Stella, Apr 4 1933 Sex:F Child# 1 Fred E Tuttle Wilton, NH & Stella Fournier Gardner, MA
TUTTLE, June Eva, Jul 13 1934 Sex:F Child# 2 Fred Tuttle Wilton, NH & Stella Fournier Gardner, MA
TUTTLE, Ray, Jun 29 1890 Sex:M Child# 1 George Tuttle Alstead, NH & Alice Cate Allenstown, NH
TUTTLE, Raymond Clair, Nov 13 1924 Sex:F Child# 1 Weare Tuttle New Jersey & Gladys Holt Pembroke, NH
TUTTLE, Richard Roscoe, Jr, Sep 10 1928 Sex:M Child# 1 R R Tuttle Wilton, NH & B A Pettingill S Lyndeboro, NH

TUTTLE, Unknown, Dec 26 1887 Sex:M Child# 5 Charles S Tuttle Barnstead & Ella M Hale Waltham, MA
TUTTLE, Unknown, Oct 12 1892 Sex:M Child# 2 George W Tuttle Alstead, NH & Alice Cate Allenstown, NH
TWARDOSKY, Betty Rose, Feb 18 1934 Sex:F Child# 4 Joseph Twardosky Pennsylvania & Josephine Porst Utica, NY
TWARDOSKY, Eleanor Anna, Nov 12 1931 Sex:F Child# 2 Morton Twardosky Portage, PA & Mary Stockley New York
TWARDOSKY, Helen Theresa, Jan 16 1930 Sex:F Child# 2 Joseph Twardosky USA & Josephine Porst USA
TWARDOSKY, Joseph Stanley, Jr, Mar 29 1932 Sex:M Child# 3 Joseph Twardosky Portage, PA & Josephine Porst Utica, NY
TWARDOSKY, Marion Edward, Oct 24 1929 Sex:M Child# 1 Marion Twardosky PA & Mary Stockley Rome, NY
TWARDOSKY, Phyllis L, May 20 1928 Sex:F Child# 1 Jos Twardosky Poland & Josephine Porst New York
TWEED, Ruth Helen, Aug 15 1920 Sex:F Child# 2 Harrie C Tweed Sandwich, NH & Lida A Bradshaw Gardner, MA
TWICHELL, Unknown, Apr 13 1895 Sex:M Child# 7 Charles N Twichell
TWISS, Erma Lucy, Jul 27 1919 Sex:F Child# 1 Walter F Twiss Boston, MA & Ethel May Wheeler Nashua, NH
TWISS, Pearl Evelyn, Feb 28 1915 Sex:F Child# 2 Howard A Twiss Springfield, MA & Jennie Antrim Amherst, NH
TWITCHELL, Lester Chase T, Jun 25 1901 Sex:M Child# 1 Henry A Twitchell Williamsburg & Helen L Chase Nashua, NH
TWITCHELL, Unknown, Apr 13 1905 Sex:F Child# 2 Henry A Twitchell Williamsburg, MA & Helen L Chase Nashua, NH
TYERIEN, Napoleon Conrad, Nov 25 1914 Sex:M Child# 6 Joseph Tyerien Canada & Eugenie Larouche Nashua, NH
TYLER, Donald Albert, Dec 15 1927 Sex:M Child# 1 Albert Tyler England & M Desmarais Milford, NH
TYLER, Earl Paul, Mar 18 1931 Sex:M Child# 3 Albert Tyler England & Marguerite Desmarais Milford, NH
TYLER, Ernest Ralph, Aug 16 1929 Sex:M Child# 2 Albert Tyler England & Marguerite Demers Milford, NH
TYLER, Robert Richard, Apr 30 1933 Sex:M Child# 4 Albert Tyler England & M Desmarais Milford, NH
UATON, Florence, Apr 2 1917 Sex:F Child# 8 Jozef Uaton Russia & Julia Kotowiz Austria
UDITSKI, Mary, Jan 9 1911 Sex:F Child# 3 William Uditski Russia & Therasa Unekiuta Russia
UDITZKI, Annie, Nov 9 1914 Sex:F Child# 4 William Uditzki Russia & Theresa Yunekinta Russia
UDITZKI, Frank, Sep 30 1909 Sex:M Child# 2 William Uditzki Russia & Teresa Unikiute Russia
UDOT, Basil, Mar 4 1933 Sex:M Child# 3 Alex Udot Poland & Annie Kapitska Russia
UDOT, Mary, Mar 4 1917 Sex:F Child# 1 Alexander Udot Russia & Anna Kapacce Russia
UDOT, Michael, Nov 24 1928 Sex:M Child# 2 Alex Udot Poland & Emma Kapiczka Poland
UKALAWITCH, Stanley, Jan 5 1917 Sex:M Child# 1 Joseph Ukalawitch Russia - Lithuania & Antoni Kosaulis Russia
UKANAWICZ, Anthony, Jan 8 1928 Sex:M Child# 4 Jos Ukanawicz Lithuania & Annie Kessell Lithuania
UKANAWICZ, Joseph, Mar 30 1926 Sex:M Child# 4 Joseph Ukanawicz Lithuania & A Kashulines Lithuania
UKRAN, Frank, Jun 11 1914 Sex:M Child# 2 John Ukran Russia & Domitilda Akoutcka Russia Stillborn
UKRIM, Unknown, Dec 28 1926 Sex:M Child# 5 John Ukrim Lithuania & D Akuckavicz Lithuania
UKRIN, John, Jr, Apr 26 1913 Sex:M Child# 1 John Ukrin Russia & Domitelda Akoritka Russia
UKRYN, Josephine, Apr 14 1922 Sex:F Child# 4 John Ukryn Russia & Domicely Akuckaity Russia
UKRYN, Stasia, Nov 21 1917 Sex:F Child# 3 John Ukryn Russia & Domitsel Akicka Russia
ULBIN, Anne, Apr 21 1919 Sex:F Child# 2 John Ulbin Russia & Elenore Zekawicz Russia
ULBIN, Daniel, Jan 13 1925 Sex:M Child# 6 John Ulbin Poland & Eleanor Diskiewicz Poland
ULBIN, Joseph, Nov 27 1917 Sex:M Child# 1 John Ulbin Russia & Leonora Zekovicz Russia
ULBIN, Leohadja, Feb 14 1926 Sex:M Child# 7 John Ulbin Poland & E Dzikewicz Poland
ULBIN, Mary, Sep 12 1923 Sex:F Child# 5 John Ulbin Poland & Eleanore Dikiewicz Poland
ULCICKAS, Simon Joseph, Sep 18 1932 Sex:M Child# 1 Simon Ulcickas Nashua, NH & M Legataviciute Lithuania
ULCZICKES, Mamie, Apr 19 1909 Sex:F Child# 3 George Ulczickes Russia & Paulina Bakowanska Russia
ULVIN, Wanda, Aug 29 1922 Sex:F Child# 4 John Ulvin Russia & Lenora Dzikewicz Russia
UNDERHILL, Denyse, Nov 28 1933 Sex:F Child# 1 George Underhill Nashua, NH & Dorothy Carrier Amesbury, MA
UNDERHILL, George Winthrop, Sep 20 1892 Sex:M Child# 2 George A Underhill Nashua, NH & Helen Bell Nashua, NH
UNDERHILL, Jean Helen, Jan 14 1928 Sex:F Child# 1 K Bell Underhill Nashua, NH & Helen H Chase Nashua, NH
UNDERHILL, Karl Bell, Mar 14 1889 Sex:F Child# 1 George A Underhill Nashua, NH & Helen M Bell Nashua, NH
UNDERHILL, Sandra, Apr 3 1935 Sex:F Child# 2 George Underhill Nashua, NH & Dorothy Carrier Amesbury, MA
UNNAS, Julia, Oct 5 1912 Sex:F Child# 1 Jacob Unnas Austria & Mary Os Austria
UPHAM, Charles Willis, Jul 3 1922 Sex:M Child# 2 Harlan W Upham Nashua, NH & Grace E Copp Merrimack, NH
UPHAM, Donald Bart, May 21 1932 Sex:M Child# 10 Henry Upham NH & Alberta Dionne Canada
UPHAM, Harlan Willie, Mar 4 1892 Sex:M Child# 1 Charles H Upham Amherst & E H Woodward Amherst, NH
UPHAM, Marjorie Ida, Jan 12 1903 Sex:F Child# 6 Charles H Upham Amherst, NH & H Isabel Woodward Amherst, NH
UPHAM, Unknown, Feb 11 1935 Sex:F Child# 11 Henry Upham NH & Alberta Dionne Canada
UPSTONE, Eunice Lea, Apr 24 1922 Sex:F Child# 1 Lee Sanborn Upstone Nashua, NH & Dorothy L Page Londonderry, NH
UPSTONE, Ray Reuben, Feb 11 1906 Sex:M Child# 3 James E Upstone Canada & Lynlia M Sanborn Canada
UPSTONE, Unknown, May 25 1898 Sex:M Child# 2 James E Upstone Broome, Quebec & Lynlia M Sanborne Broome, Quebec
URBALWICAZ, Powlina, Jun 22 1919 Sex:F Child# 2 Peter Urbalwicaz Russia & Annie Ougen Russia
URBAN, Annie, Apr 14 1915 Sex:F Child# 2 John Urban Russia & Ursulia Yoksta Russia
URBANAVICUS, John, Jan 12 1922 Sex:M Child# 2 Cipras Urbanavicus Russia & Antonia Savlowicutis Russia
URBANAVICZ, Anielka, Jan 19 1914 Sex:F Child# 3 John Urbanavicz Russia & Rosa Mizzonia Russia
URBANAVICZIUS, William, Dec 5 1911 Sex:M Child# 2 Joseph Urbanavicziius Russia & Rosa Mizoma Russia
URBANAVIENS, Charles Robert, Dec 19 1925 Sex:M Child# 3 C Urbanaviens Lithuania & A Lantavicusts Lithuania
URBANAWICZ, Vittaros, Aug 11 1914 Sex:M Child# 2 Andrew Urbanawicz Russia & Mary Swaboyitch Russia
URBANOS, Aurelia, Jan 19 1921 Sex:F Child# 1 Cipras Urbanos Russia & Antoina Sawlavicus Russia
URBANOVITCH, Joseph, Aug 17 1909 Sex:M Child# 1 Kazalis Urbanovitch Russia & Anna Mezarietie Russia
URBONA, Elizabieta, May 3 1907 Sex:F Child# 1 Franciskus Urbona Russia & Barbara Ragonskati Russia
URBONAS, Ludwiga, Feb 7 1912 Sex:F Child# 3 Bernard Urbonas Russia & Karalina Jankauskas Russia
URQUEHART, Unknown, Nov 5 1889 Sex:F Child# 7 Louis Urquehart Nova Scotia & Emma E Vermont
URQUHART, Burton Wilson, Feb 16 1919 Sex:M Child# 2 Cla S Urquhart Nashua, NH & Ruby Pearl Jones Moncton, NB
URQUHART, Daisy May, Jul 9 1922 Sex:F Child# 3 Clarence Urquhart Nashua, NH & Pearl Jones New Brunswick
URQUHART, Unknown, May 1 1887 Sex:M Child# 6 Louis Urquhart British America & Emma Vermont
URQUHART, William Forrest, Mar 3 1915 Sex:M Child# 1 Clarence S Urquhart Nashua, NH & R Pearl Jones NB
USTIN, Brontia, Sep 4 1919 Sex:F Child# 1 Lapin Ustin Lithuania Russia & Matiella Antousk Lithuania Russia

UTKA, Florence Theresa, Jan 1 1931 Sex:F Child# 5 Anthony Utka Lithuania & Anna Kupchunas Lithuania
UTKA, Gineefa, Aug 8 1913 Sex:F Child# 1 Antony Utka Russia & Annie Kupeguhen Russia
UTKA, Joseph Michael, Jan 1 1931 Sex:M Child# 6 Anthony Utka Lithuania & Anna Kupchunas Lithuania
UTKA, Josephine, Jun 1 1916 Sex:F Child# 3 Anthony Utka Russia & Annie Capture Russia
UTKA, Sophia, Jun 17 1922 Sex:F Child# 4 Anthony Utka Lithuania & Annie Kuptic Lithuania
UZDANYN, Unknown, Mar 2 1917 Sex:M Child# 8 John Uzdanyn Russia & Eva Shesteuska Russia Stillborn
UZDAREN, Johnny, Jul 28 1907 Sex:M Child# 3 John Uzdaren Russia & Eva Sartavitch Russia
UZDARMIN, Unknown, Aug 10 1918 Sex:F Child# 4 Joseph Uzdarmin Russia & Helena Dobrwouski Russia
UZDAVINIS, Amelia, Dec 5 1915 Sex:F Child# 2 Stanley Uzdavinis Russia & Annie Puvlowski Russia
UZDAWIN, Rachela, Aug 16 1901 Sex:F Child# 3 Joseph Uzdawin Russia & Eva Czarniavoska Russia
UZDAWIN, William, Jul 7 1910 Sex:M Child# 2 Joseph Uzdawin Poland & Helena Dobrawolski Poland
UZDAWINES, Unknown, Sep 18 1898 Sex:F Child# 1 Joseph Uzdawines Russia & Eva Czerneske Russia
UZDOWIN, Unknown, Jun 27 1904 Sex:F Child# 2 John Uzdowin Russia & Eva Szastawicka Russia Stillborn
VACCA, Eleanor Jean, Sep 8 1931 Sex:F Child# 6 Dominico Vacca Italy & Madeline Matrocola Italy
VACCA, Maurice, Dec 8 1933 Sex:M Child# 1 Dominic Vacca Italy & M Mastricola Italy Stillborn
VACCA, Pauline Madeline, Mar 16 1927 Sex:F Child# 4 Dominick Vacca Italy & M Mastricola Italy
VACCO, Dorothy Isabelle, Aug 20 1929 Sex:F Child# 5 Dominic Vacco Italy & Madeline Mastricola Italy
VACCO, Yolande, May 21 1925 Sex:F Child# 3 Domenico Vacco Italy & Mad Mastricola Italy
VACHNAIS, Emile, Feb 9 1889 Sex:M Child# 2 Arthur Vachnais Canada & D Grandmaison Canada
VACHON, Emelie, Apr 5 1894 Sex:F Child# 7 Adolphe Vachon Canada & Edeste Deroscher Canada
VACHON, Rachael Jeannette, Nov 25 1932 Sex:F Child# 1 Gustave Vachon Canada & Eugenie Bousay Canada
VADCHONCOEUR, Wilfrid Jean Edouard, Aug 24 1923 Sex:M Child# 6 Wilfrid Vadchoncoeur Canada & Estelle Topping C
VADMAIS, Aime Sylvio, Jun 9 1899 Sex:M Child# 1 Adolphe Vadmais Canada & Adelina Melancon Lawrence, MA
VADNAIS, Arthur Rene, Feb 14 1933 Sex:M Child# 5 Albert Vadnais Ireland & Annie McLean Ireland
VADNAIS, Charles Adolphe, Sep 2 1902 Sex:M Child# 2 Adolphe Vadnais Canada & Adelina Melancon Lawrence, MA
VADNAIS, Leo Gaston, Jan 3 1934 Sex:M Child# 7 Albert R Vadnais Canada & Anna McLean Ireland
VAGGE, Alvin Arthur, Feb 28 1929 Sex:M Child# 3 John Vagge Italy & Alice Biathrow Nashua, NH
VAGGE, Donald James, Apr 21 1930 Sex:M Child# 4 John Vagge Italy & Alice Biathrow Nashua, NH
VAGGE, John L, Jr, Nov 17 1925 Sex:M Child# 1 John L Vagge Italy & Alice Biathrow Nashua, NH
VAGGE, Unknown, Aug 23 1927 Sex:F Child# 2 John L Vagge Genoa, Italy & Alice Biathrow Nashua, NH
VAICUNIS, Mary, May 3 1927 Sex:F Child# 2 Ignotos Vaicunis Russia & Rose Volickuta Russia
VAILLAINCOURT, Joseph C, Dec 4 1895 Sex:M Child# 14 Firmine Vaillaincour Canada & Euphemie Bousay Canada
VAILLANCOURT, Adrienne L, Feb 4 1902 Sex:F Child# 1 Josep't Vaillancourt Canada & Clara Levesque Canada
VAILLANCOURT, Alphonse Clement, Mar 21 1918 Sex:M Child# 8 Joseph Vaillancourt Canada & Marie Soucy Nashua, NH
VAILLANCOURT, Antoinette Doris, Nov 4 1928 Sex:F Child# 1 A Vaillancourt Canada & Anna Henry Canada
VAILLANCOURT, Arlene Joan, Mar 18 1935 Sex:F Child# 3 H Vaillancourt Lewiston, ME & Alma Noel Nashua, NH
VAILLANCOURT, Augustin Romeo, Dec 15 1916 Sex:M Child# 7 Joseph Vaillancourt Canada & Marie Soucy Nashua, NH
VAILLANCOURT, Cecile Yvette, Jul 23 1923 Sex:F Child# 6 Chas E Vaillancourt Nashua, NH & Beatrice Ricard Nashua, NH
VAILLANCOURT, Dorothy Arline, Feb 20 1932 Sex:F Child# 2 H Vaillancourt Nashua, NH & Eva Trudeau Middlebury, VT
VAILLANCOURT, Eleanor Rita, Aug 2 1924 Sex:F Child# 11 Joseph Vaillancourt Canada & Marie Soucy Nashua, NH
VAILLANCOURT, Enrest Raymond, Jan 17 1917 Sex:M Child# 2 John B Vaillancourt Nashua, NH & Celia Boucher Nashua, NH
VAILLANCOURT, Euphemie M L, Apr 2 1894 Sex:F Child# 13 Firmin Vaillancourt Canada & Euphemie Bonsens Canada
VAILLANCOURT, Ferdinand Adrien, Feb 12 1912 Sex:M Child# 4 Joseph Vaillancourt Canada & Marie Soucy Nashua, NH
VAILLANCOURT, Florence Edna S, Jul 12 1921 Sex:F Child# 10 Joseph Vaillancourt Canada & Marie Soucy Nashua, NH
VAILLANCOURT, George Edouard, Oct 23 1913 Sex:M Child# 5 Joseph Vaillancourt Canada & Marie Soucy Nashua, NH
VAILLANCOURT, Gertrude B L, Jul 10 1930 Sex:F Child# 1 Henry Vaillancourt Nashua, NH & Eva Trudeau Middlebury, VT
VAILLANCOURT, Gertrude Pauline, Jul 7 1923 Sex:F Child# 2 Henry Vaillancourt Milford, NH & Rosamona LaReine NH
VAILLANCOURT, Gilberte Dolores, Aug 7 1933 Sex:F Child# 3 A Vaillancourt Canada & Eva Henry Canada
VAILLANCOURT, Harvey Ovila, Feb 16 1928 Sex:M Child# 5 A C Vaillancourt Lewiston, ME & Eva Dichard Nashua, NH
VAILLANCOURT, Henri Armand, Dec 9 1908 Sex:M Child# 2 Joseph Vaillancourt Canada & Marie E Soucy Nashua, NH
VAILLANCOURT, J Roland Henry, Nov 16 1921 Sex:M Child# 1 Henry Vaillancourt Milford, NH & Rosanna Lareine Nashua,NH
VAILLANCOURT, Jean Bte, Aug 23 1894 Sex:M Child# 6 Adolphe Vaillancourt Canada & Emelie Boneufaut Canada
VAILLANCOURT, Jean Bte Adolphe, Jun 6 1915 Sex:M Child# 1 John B Vaillancourt Nashua, NH & Cecile Boucher Nashua,NH
VAILLANCOURT, Jeannette, Jul 15 1930 Sex:F Child# 2 Antoine Vaillancourt Canada & Eva Henry Canada
VAILLANCOURT, Jos Alfred Leo, Sep 25 1921 Sex:M Child# 1 Arthur Vaillancourt Lewiston, ME & Marie Anne Houde Canada
VAILLANCOURT, Jos Leo Adelard, Jul 6 1920 Sex:M Child# 3 Alf C Vaillancourt Lewiston, ME & Eva Dichard Nashua, NH
VAILLANCOURT, Joseph, Jun 7 1888 Sex:M Child# 2 Adolphe Vaillancourt Canada & Emelia Bonepart Canada
VAILLANCOURT, Joseph, Sep 6 1895 Sex:M Child# 9 Louis Vaillancourt Canada & Marie Roy Canada
VAILLANCOURT, Joseph, Feb 5 1900 Sex:M Child# 4 Pierre Vaillancourt Canada & Diana Rouleau Canada
VAILLANCOURT, Joseph Leo A, Jan 11 1898 Sex:M Child# 2 Pierre Vaillancourt Canada & Diana Rouleau Canada
VAILLANCOURT, Joseph Zephyrin, Apr 17 1896 Sex:M Child# 2 George Vaillancourt Canada & Lucie Jodoin Canada
VAILLANCOURT, Leo Roger, Sep 6 1926 Sex:M Child# 1 Henry Vaillancourt Lewiston, ME & Alma Noel Nashua, NH
VAILLANCOURT, Leopold, Oct 4 1926 Sex:M Child# 1 W Vaillancourt Salmon Falls, NH & Alice Caron Canada
VAILLANCOURT, Lorraine Nancy, Oct 11 1932 Sex:F Child# 2 H Vaillancourt Maine & Alma Noel Nashua, NH
VAILLANCOURT, Louis Albert, Jul 14 1914 Sex:M Child# 4 Wilfrid Vaillancourt Canada & M Louise Fortier Canada
VAILLANCOURT, Lucille Rita, Mar 19 1931 Sex:F Child# 2 Wilfrid Vaillancourt Salmon Falls, NH & Alice Caron Canada
VAILLANCOURT, M Louise Alice Ida, May 15 1913 Sex:F Child# 3 J W Vaillancourt Canada & M Louise Fortier Canada
VAILLANCOURT, Maria Beatrice, Mar 17 1906 Sex:F Child# 1 Joseph Vaillancourt Canada & Marie Soucy Nashua, NH
VAILLANCOURT, Marie Ann Rita, Nov 22 1927 Sex:F Child# 8 C E Vaillancourt Nashua, NH & Beatrice Ricard Nashua, NH
VAILLANCOURT, Marie B, Sep 5 1889 Sex:F Child# 11 Firmin Vaillancourt Canada & Euphemie Bonsens Canada
VAILLANCOURT, Marie Delima, Sep 10 1901 Sex:F Child# 5 Pierre Vaillancourt Canada & Diana Rouleau Canada
VAILLANCOURT, Marie Ivonne, Oct 10 1900 Sex:F Child# 3 Joseph Vaillancourt Canada & Clara Levesque Canada
VAILLANCOURT, Marie Madeline, Aug 12 1917 Sex:F Child# 1 Alfred C Vaillancour Maine & Eva Dichard NH

VAILLANCOURT, Marie Sara Ida, Jan 28 1897 Sex:F Child# 1 Pierre Vaillancourt Canada & Diana Rouleau Canada
VAILLANCOURT, Marie Therese Cecile, Aug 26 1925 Sex:F Child# 12 Joseph Vaillancourt Canada & Marie Soucy Nashua
VAILLANCOURT, Maurice Armand, Jul 16 1930 Sex:M Child# 9 Chas E Vaillancourt Nashua, NH & Beatrice Ricard Nashua
VAILLANCOURT, Paul Gerard, Dec 22 1924 Sex:M Child# 7 Charles Vaillancourt Nashua, NH & Beatrice Ricard Nashua
VAILLANCOURT, Paul H, Sep 14 1890 Sex:M Child# 12 Firmin Vaillancourt Canada & Euphamie Bousend Canada
VAILLANCOURT, Rachael Theresa, Sep 25 1921 Sex:F Child# 5 Charles Vaillancourt Nashua, NH & Beatrice Ricard Nashua
VAILLANCOURT, Rachel Jeanne, Aug 31 1919 Sex:F Child# 9 Joseph Vaillancourt Canada & Marie Soucy Nashua, NH
VAILLANCOURT, Robert Armand, May 27 1918 Sex:M Child# 3 Geo B Vaillancourt Nashua, NH & Cecil Boucher Nashua, NH
VAILLANCOURT, Robert Eugene, Mar 9 1920 Sex:M Child# 4 Charles Vaillancourt Nashua, NH & Beatrice Ricard Nashua
VAILLANCOURT, Rosario Arthur, Mar 6 1919 Sex:M Child# 2 Alf C Vaillancourt Lewiston, ME & Eva Guichard Nashua, NH
VAILLANCOURT, Rosilda Annette, Apr 16 1915 Sex:F Child# 1 Charles Vaillancourt Nashua, NH & Beatrice Ricard Nashua
VAILLANCOURT, Stanislas Lucien, Jan 1 1915 Sex:M Child# 6 Joseph Vaillancourt Canada & Marie Soucy Nashua, NH
VAILLANCOURT, Theodorine, Apr 14 1893 Sex:F Child# 5 Adolphe Vaillancourt Canada & Emelie Bonenfaut Canada
VAILLANCOURT, Theresa Lorraine, Apr 17 1926 Sex:F Child# 3 Henry Vaillancourt Milford, NH & Rose Anna Loreine
VAILLANCOURT, Therese, Oct 26 1932 Sex:F Child# 1 L Vaillancourt Lewiston, ME & Lea Dazon Nashua, NH
VAILLANCOURT, Unknown, Apr 17 1899 Sex:F Child# 3 Pierre Vaillancourt Canada & Diana Rouleau Canada Stillborn
VAILLANCOURT, Unknown, Aug 3 1916 Sex:M Child# 2 Charles Vaillancourt Nashua, NH & Beatrice Ricard Nashua, NH
VAILLANCOURT, Unknown, Mar 30 1920 Sex:M Child# 4 John B Vaillancourt Nashua, NH & Cecilia Boucher Nashua, NH
VAILLANCOURT, Wilfred Euclide, Sep 10 1923 Sex:M Child# 4 Alfred Vaillancourt Lewiston, ME & Eva Dichard Nashua, NH
VAILLENCOURT, Joseph Wilfred Roger, Jun 9 1918 Sex:M Chtd# 3 Charles Vaillencourt Nashua, NH & Beatrice Ricard
VAISBORD, Annie, Jun 30 1901 Sex:F Child# 4 Louis Vaisbord Russia & Ida Rhea Russia
VAISBORD, Eva, Dec 29 1905 Sex:F Child# 6 Louis Vaisbord Russia & Ida Rearra Russia
VAISBORD, Max Simon, Aug 15 1913 Sex:M Child# 7 Louis Vaisbord Russia & Ida Rier Russia
VALADAS, Annie, Aug 4 1914 Sex:F Child# 1 John Valadas Russia & Annie Tartela Russia
VALADE, Constance Lorraine, May 7 1933 Sex:F Child# 1 (No Parents Listed)
VALADE, Joseph Hector, Oct 14 1914 Sex:M Child# 2 Joseph T Valade Canada & Clara Pelkey Nashua, NH
VALCOUR, Cecile, Jul 14 1903 Sex:F Child# 4 Leon Valcour Canada & Joseph Deboisbrien Canada
VALCOUR, Germaine Olivine, Feb 8 1900 Sex:F Child# 2 Leon Valcour Canada & Jse'e Deboisbrillant Canada
VALCOUR, Horace Adrien, Oct 27 1906 Sex:M Child# 5 Leon Valcour Canada & Josephine Deboisbrie Canada
VALCOUR, Joseph, Jul 28 1908 Sex:M Child# 9 Etienne Valcour Canada & Maude Isle Canada
VALCOUR, Romeo, Jul 20 1908 Sex:M Child# 6 Leon Valcour Canada & Josphn Deboisbriant Canada
VALCOURT, Jos Leonard Norman, Dec 26 1925 Sex:M Child# 1 Leon Valcourt Canada & Lida Levesque Vermont
VALCOURT, Lionel Wilfred, Aug 26 1897 Sex:M Child# 1 Leon Valcourt Canada & Josephine Brien Canada
VALCOURT, Mahlon Roger, Jun 9 1929 Sex:M Child# 3 Leon Valcourt Canada & Leda Levesque Graniteville, VT
VALCOURT, Marie Luella Theresa, Dec 24 1926 Sex:F Child# 2 Leon Valcourt Canada & Leda Levesque Vermont
VALENTINE, Nancy Elizabeth, Nov 21 1935 Sex:F Child# 1 Rodger Valentine Nashua, NH & Antonia Koadolas Nashua, NH
VALENTINE, Roger Brown V, Apr 22 1910 Sex:M Child# 1 Goulding Valentine Champlain, NY & Jennie E Brown Waltham, MA
VALERIE, Marie Laura J, Jun 7 1900 Sex:F Child# 3 Gilbert Valerie Canada & Angele Brisson Canada
VALEY, Eva Rose, Sep 28 1917 Sex:F Child# 4 Louie Valey Old Towne, ME & Lilly Demanche Canada
VALINKAVITCH, Stanislav, Aug 24 1911 Sex:M Child# 1 Alex Valinkavitch Russia & Annie Chebluk Austria
VALISTKA, Mary, Apr 1 1910 Sex:F Child# 3 George Valistka Russia & Benigna Sbaklutia Russia
VALKOBSKI, Annie, Mar 7 1921 Sex:F Child# 8 Anthony Valkobski Russia & Mary Valecheski Russia
VALLANCOURT, Marie A, Mar 27 1890 Sex:F Child# 3 Adolphe Vallancourt Canada & Emelie Bonenfant Canada
VALLE, Fred, Nov 23 1892 Sex:M Child# 1 Odul Valle Canada & Angeline Cote Canada
VALLE, Irene Sylvia, Sep 11 1922 Sex:F Child# 5 Louis Valle Oldtown, ME & Lilly Demanche Canada
VALLE, Unknown, Mar 31 1893 Sex:F Child# 3 Joseph Valle Canada & Delphine Gagnon Canada Stillborn
VALLEE, Irene Lorette, Oct 27 1904 Sex:F Child# 1 (No Parents Listed)
VALLEE, Joseph Alfred, Oct 10 1896 Sex:M Child# 5 James Vallee Canada & Delphine Gagnon Canada
VALLEE, Joseph Willie, Jun 28 1895 Sex:M Child# 4 Joseph Vallee Canada & Delphine Gagnon Canada
VALLEE, Marie, Nov 10 1893 Sex:F Child# Theodule Vallee Canada & Angeline Cote Canada
VALLEE, Marie Alida, May 16 1898 Sex:F Child# 4 Joseph Vallee Canada & Delphine Gagnon Canada
VALLEE, Marie Georgiana, Mar 17 1894 Sex:F Child# 3 Joseph Vallee Canada & Delphine Gagnon Canada
VALLEE, Marie Jeannette, Dec 30 1910 Sex:F Child# 1 Louis Vallee Maine & Lilly Demanche Canada
VALLEE, Marie Philomene, Feb 21 1892 Sex:F Child# 1 Joseph Vallee Canada & Delphine Gagnon Canada
VALLEE, Rose Anna, Jun 5 1895 Sex:F Child# 3 Odule Vallee Canada & Angeline Cote Canada
VALLEE, Unknown, Mar 12 1900 Sex:F Child# 7 Joseph Vallee Canada & Delphine Gagnon Canada Stillborn
VALLEE, Yvonne Beatrice, Aug 5 1913 Sex:F Child# 2 Louis Vallee Mass & Lillian Demanche Canada
VALLENCOUR, Maria B, Apr 4 1888 Sex:F Child# 10 Firmin Vallencour Canada & Euphenne Bonseams Canada
VALLEY, Charles Edward, Sep 30 1910 Sex:M Child# 2 Cahrles E Valley Canada & Minerva Crocker Springfield, MA
VALLEY, Joseph Arthur, Apr 27 1915 Sex:M Child# 3 Louis A Valley Old Town, ME & Lillie Demanche Canada
VALLEY, Philemon Joseph, Jul 13 1916 Sex:M Child# 9 Philemon Valley Canada & Ledia Andros Georgetown, MA
VALLIERE, Evelyn Winifred, Apr 4 1935 Sex:F Child# 1 Leo Valliere Lawrence, MA & Winifred Felton Milford, NH
VALLY, Marie C, Sep 23 1900 Sex:F Child# 9 Alex Vally Canada & Bernadette Gra'dm'n Canada
VALRAN, Henri, Nov 28 1893 Sex:M Child# 11 Norbert Valran Canada & Emelie Veinlette Canada
VALUAITAVICH, Unknown, Aug 19 1914 Sex:F Child# 5 Anthony Valuaitavich Russia & Agres Chalenwich Russia
VALVOUR, Napoleon Charles, Jul 27 1901 Sex:M Child# 3 Leon Valvour Canada & Josephine Sirois Canada
VALZ, Donald Joseph, Sep 10 1933 Sex:M Child# 2 Dino Valz Italy & Irma Trentini Milford, NH
VAMPSON, William Hiram, Aug 11 1912 Sex:M Child# 6 William D Vampson Deposit, NY & Mary Davis Oxford, NC Colored
VAN SHRYS, Unknown, Feb 28 1914 Sex:M Child# 1 Adolph Van Shrys Holland & Catherine Welch Nashua, NH Stillborn
VAN SLUYS, Gerard, Aug 18 1916 Sex:M Child# 2 Adolph Van Sluys Holland & Catherine Welch Nashua, NH
VANAKAROS, Unknown, Jul 9 1921 Sex:F Child# 2 Christos Vanakaros Greece & Martina Stamation Greece
VANASSE, Joseph W, Feb 15 1894 Sex:M Child# 3 Louis Vanasse Canada & Olivine D'Orge Canada
VANASSE, Louis I, Apr 4 1892 Sex:M Child# 2 Louis Vanasse Canada & Olivine D'orge Canada

VANASSE, Marie L, Mar 13 1898 Sex:F Child# 5 Louis Vanasse Canada & Marie D'Orge Canada
VANASSE, Marie M, Oct 8 1890 Sex:F Child# 1 Louis Vanasse Canada & Malvina Dodge Canada
VANASSE, Normand P B, Dec 3 1902 Sex:M Child# 7 Louis Vanasse Canada & Olivine Dodge Canada
VANASSE, Oscar, Jan 5 1896 Sex:M Child# 4 Louis Vanasse Canada & Olivine D'orge Canada
VANASSE, Unknown, May 15 1900 Sex:M Child# 6 Louis Vanasse Canada & Olivine Dodge Canada Stillborn
VANDER VOEL, Ethel Barbara, May 16 1919 Sex:F Child# 1 Dirk Vander Voel Holland & Martha A Jones Lawrence, MA
VANDEWASKI, Helen, Mar 7 1915 Sex:F Child# 6 Anthony Vandewaski Russia & Katherine Wolander Russia
VANDOLOSKI, Agnes Evelyn, Feb 16 1932 Sex:F Child# 1 Steve Vandoloski Nashua, NH & Agnes Lasik Nashua, NH
VANDONIS, Unknown, Feb 15 1910 Sex:M Child# 2 Frank Vandonis Russia & Christina Greguta Russia
VANESSE, Ernest Louis E, Sep 24 1920 Sex:M Child# 3 Oscar Vanesse US & Elizabeth Stone Canada
VANGOS, Bassil, May 6 1917 Sex:M Child# 1 Alexander Vangos Greece & Aspasia Papilis Greece
VANIER, Richard Paul, Apr 12 1932 Sex:M Child# 4 Alfred Vanier Suncook, NH & Irene Mercier Newport, VT
VANTINE, Donald E, Jan 5 1893 Sex:M Child# 1 George E Vantine Lowell, MA & Annie R Morrison Chelsea, Ont
VANTINE, Donald Robert, Oct 4 1925 Sex:M Child# 3 Donald E Vantine Nashua, NH & Vivian McNamara Vermont
VANTINE, Flora Mae, Oct 22 1913 Sex:F Child# 1 Donald E Vantine Nashua, NH & Alice Willey Colebrook, NH
VANTINE, Robert Urquhart, Jun 7 1895 Sex:M Child# 2 George E Vantine Lowell, MA & Annie R Morrison Chelsea, Ont
VANTINE, Unknown, Oct 7 1916 Sex:F Child# 1 Donald Vantine Nashua, NH & Vivian McNamara Westmore, VT
VANTINE, Virginia Mary, Sep 2 1917 Sex:F Child# 1 James Jos Vantine Lawrence, MA & Elizabeth M Carney Melrose, MA
VARELLA, Milfred, Apr 16 1920 Sex:F Child# 8 Joseph Varella Portugal & Bessie Smith Rhode Island Colored
VARELLA, Tiburcio, Aug 11 1921 Sex:M Child# 9 Joseph Varella Portugal & Bessie Smith Providence, RI Colored
VARETSKA, Joseph, May 2 1912 Sex:M Child# 4 Constantin Varetska Russia & Dorothy Gregiuta Russia
VARETSKAS, Peter, Jun 5 1910 Sex:M Child# 3 Constant Varetskas Russia & Dorotha Gregiuta Russia
VARITSKA, Kasimir, Oct 26 1916 Sex:M Child# 2 John Varitska Russia & Polonia Stavash Austria
VARNEY, Unknown, Mar 26 1889 Sex:F Child# 1 John H Varney NH & Nellie G NH
VASELUCK, Martsy, Feb 24 1911 Sex:M Child# 1 Mike Vaseluck Russia & Michalina Gydecoynis Russia
VASHIET, Stanislawa, Aug 8 1913 Sex:F Child# 1 Mike Vashiet Russia & Stefana Galawich Russia
VASIAS, Alestedes, Mar 5 1916 Sex:M Child# 2 John Vasias Greece & Rosa Koltidos Greece
VASIAS, Mary, Mar 27 1912 Sex:F Child# 1 John Vasias Greece & Rosa Deintre Turkey
VASILIAS, Louis Theodore, Feb 11 1920 Sex:M Child# 5 Arestas Vasilias Greece & Catherine Papas Greece
VASILIER, Helen Ageligiei, Jul 2 1924 Sex:F Child# 3 Nicolas Vasilier Greece & M Dramatinos Greece
VASILOFSKY, Charles, Sep 7 1915 Sex:M Child# 3 William Vasilofsky Russia & Anne Petrenofsky Russia
VASSAR, Helen Agnes, Aug 27 1931 Sex:F Child# 4 Royal Vassar Barre, VT & Angeline Nartoff Nashua, NH
VASSAR, Herold Alexander, Mar 5 1901 Sex:M Child# 2 George Vassar New York & Jennie Dowling NH
VASSAR, June Rena, Jun 5 1931 Sex:F Child# 3 Richard Vassar US & Evelyn Abood US
VASSAR, Lawrence Earle Roger, Jan 13 1933 Sex:M Child# 1 Earle Vassar Plattsburgh, NY & Anna Krugla Berlin, NH
VASSAR, Marie Elyse Gladeus, Jan 18 1908 Sex:F Child# 3 George Vassar New York & Jennie Dowling NH
VASSAR, Marie Lillienne E, Apr 23 1905 Sex:F Child# 2 George Vassar New York & Jennie Dowling NH
VASSAR, Randall J, Jul 15 1925 Sex:M Child# 2 Royal E Vassar Barre, VT & Angeline Martoff Nashua, NH
VASSAR, Regina Mary, May 31 1924 Sex:F Child# 1 Royal Vassar Vermont & Agneline Nartoff Nashua, NH
VASSAR, Reginald Charles, Sep 29 1901 Sex:M Child# 4 Robert E Vassar NY & Lilly Tremblay NY
VASSAR, Ruth Agnes, Jul 26 1907 Sex:F Child# 5 Robert E Vassar NY & Lillienne Tremblay NY
VASSAR, Virginia Theresa, Jun 5 1930 Sex:F Child# 3 Royal Vassar Barre, VT & Angeline Nartoff Nashua, NH
VASSEUR, Veronica Ruby, Aug 18 1929 Sex:F Child# 1 Reginald Vasseur Nashua, NH & Beatrice Richard Nashua, NH
VAUGHAN, Robert Cecil, Aug 1 1921 Sex:M Child# 1 Arthur C Vaughan Wales & Margaret Donovan Peterboro, NH
VAUGHN, Estelle Alma, Jul 30 1927 Sex:F Child# 1 J A Vaughn Texas & Lillian J Lavoie Nashua, NH
VAUGHN, Unknown, Aug 9 1887 Sex:F Child# 2 Edwin Vaughn Raynham, MA & Annie Jobert Malone, NY
VAVELA, Unknown, May 1 1919 Sex:M Child# 4 Joseph Vavela C Verde, Santiago & Bessie Semedo Providence, RI Colored
VAVELA, Unknown, May 1 1919 Sex:F Child# 4 Joseph Vavela C Verde, Santiago & Bessie Semedo Providence, RI Colored
VAZZANA, Lucrezia Antoinette, Apr 8 1926 Sex:F Child# 3 Salvatore Vazzana Italy & Lily Vence New York, NY
VEILLETTE, Joseph Louis A, Jul 17 1901 Sex:M Child# 1 Joseph Veillette Canada & Marie Berube Canada
VEILLETTE, Joseph Thomas A, Jul 30 1902 Sex:M Child# 2 Joseph Veillette Canada & Marie Berube Canada
VEILLEUX, Joseph Lionel, Jul 30 1910 Sex:M Child# 5 Peter Veilleux Canada & Mary Veilleux Canada
VEILLEUX, Lillian, Jun 25 1924 Sex:F Child# 2 Napoleon Veilleux Canada & Yvonne Desrosier Canada
VEILLIEUX, Loraine, Mar 3 1926 Sex:F Child# 3 Napoleon Veillieux Canada & Yvonne Desrosier Canada
VEK, Charles, Aug 10 1912 Sex:M Child# 1 Charls Vek Russia & Annie Sylorizi Russia
VENNE, Carmelle, Apr 17 1929 Sex:F Child# 10 Charles Venne Lawrence, MA & Georgianna Lemay Canada
VERANIS, William, Jr, Sep 8 1927 Sex:M Child# 1 William Veranis Lithuania & Phyllis Powlowski Nashua, NH
VERMETTE, G Wilfred Joseph, Feb 2 1921 Sex:M Child# 1 Wilfred Vermette S Berwick, ME & Alma Vaillancourt Salmon Fl
VERMETTE, J Wilfred Noel, Dec 24 1922 Sex:M Child# 2 Wilfred Vermette Salmon Falls, NH & Alma Vaillancourt Salmon
VERMETTE, Jos Emile Ernest, Nov 18 1930 Sex:M Child# 1 Albert Vermette Canada & Ida Bernard Canada
VERMETTE, Joseph Conrad Leon, Sep 21 1925 Sex:M Child# 4 Wilfred Vermette Salmon Falls, NH & Alma Vaillancourt
VERMETTE, Marie Yvonne, May 26 1924 Sex:F Child# 3 Wilfred Vermette Salmon Falls, NH & Alma Vaillancourt Salmon Fl
VERNEZ, Alphonse, Apr 25 1926 Sex:M Child# 2 Frank Vernez Poland & Amelia Drengil Poland
VERZANA, Mamie, Jan 17 1918 Sex:F Child# 2 Charles Verzana Italy & Lily Vinci New York, NY
VESTON, Brunislav, Oct 13 1920 Sex:M Child# 1 William Veston Lithuania Russia & Adele Gerour Lithuania Russia
VEZINA, Richard George, Nov 4 1935 Sex:M Child# 3 Girard Vezina Canada & Simone Tessier Nashua, NH
VEZZANA, Nicholas, Nov 16 1915 Sex:M Child# 1 Charles Vezzana Italy & Lillian Vinci New York, NY
VIAN, Louis, Aug 21 1900 Sex:M Child# 2 Athanase Vian Canada & Alma Noel Canada
VIAU, Emile Elenore, Jun 24 1898 Sex:M Child# 1 Athanase Viau Canada & Rose Alma Noel Canada
VICIAU, Blanche, Jan 5 1897 Sex:F Child# 7 Eusebe Viciau Canada & Caroline Harvey Canada
VICTOR, Ralph Paul, Oct 8 1916 Sex:M Child# 3 Charles Victor Lowell, MA & Florence Trudeau Middlebury, VT
VIECSKIS, Phyllis, Mar 3 1926 Sex:F Child# 3 Leon Viecskis Russia & Minnie Mizer Russia
VIEL, Adelard R, Mar 23 1903 Sex:M Child# 3 Francois Viel Canada & Josephine Dufour Canada

VIEL, Albert Wilbrod, Jun 19 1904 Sex:M Child# 4 Francois Viel Canada & Josephine Dufour Nashua, NH
VIEL, Joseph Paul E A, Aug 30 1900 Sex:M Child# 1 Francois Viel Canada & Josephine Dufour Canada
VIEL, Marie Marguerite L, Feb 22 1911 Sex:F Child# 3 Joseph Viel Canada & Eulalie Lavoie Canada
VIEL, Romeo Achille, Feb 25 1902 Sex:M Child# 2 Francois Viel Canada & Josephine Dufour Canada
VIENS, Adrian Harvey, Apr 6 1926 Sex:M Child# 4 Harvey Viens Nashua, NH & Mary Jellison Nashua, NH
VIENS, Adrien, May 12 1894 Sex:M Child# 3 Toussaint Viens Canada & Josephine Gagnar Canada
VIENS, Carey, Jun 23 1891 Sex: Child# 3 Louis Viens Burlington, VT & Regina Laglace Canada
VIENS, Catherine Irene, Jan 31 1925 Sex:F Child# 3 Harvey Viens Nashua, NH & Mary F Jellison Nashua, NH
VIENS, Joseph, May 22 1890 Sex:M Child# 2 Toutsaint Viens Canada & Josephine Gagnon Canada
VIENS, Joseph Alva, Apr 13 1899 Sex:M Child# 4 Toussaint Viens Canada & Josephine Gagnon Canada
VIENS, Louis, Mar 15 1932 Sex:M Child# 2 (No Parents Listed)
VIENS, Marie A C, Jul 22 1887 Sex:F Child# 1 Tousssaint Viens P Q & Josephine Gagnon P Q
VIENS, Mary Frances, Jan 9 1921 Sex:F Child# 2 Harvey Viens NH & Mary Frnces Jellison NH
VIGNAULT, David Amedee, Nov 25 1894 Sex:M Child# 6 John J Vignault Canada & Emma Pelletier Canada
VIGNAULT, Emile George Lucien, Feb 7 1916 Sex:M Child# 4 Jos Julien Vignault Nashua, NH & Helene Bernier Canada
VIGNAULT, Joseph Conrad S, Dec 22 1909 Sex:M Child# 1 Julien J Vignault Nashua, NH & Helene Bernier Fraserville
VIGNEAULT, Delia Bertha, May 26 1935 Sex:F Child# 1 Lucien Vigneault Lowell, MA & Rachel Vigneault Nashua, NH
VIGNEAULT, Emma Ida, Dec 22 1890 Sex:F Child# 5 Joseph Vigneault VT & Emma Peltier Canada
VIGNEAULT, George Remi Jean, Jun 3 1916 Sex:M Child# 2 Oscar Vigneault Nashua, NH & Bertha Bleau Sciota, NY
VIGNEAULT, Gerard Maurice, Feb 4 1933 Sex:M Child# 2 S Vigneault Nashua, NH & Aldea Tanguay Nashua, NH
VIGNEAULT, John Victor Clayton, Sep 27 1923 Sex:M Child# 3 Oscar Vigneault Nashua, NH & Bertha Bleau Sciota, NY
VIGNEAULT, Marguerite Rachel, May 29 1911 Sex:F Child# 2 Joseph Vigneault Nashua, NH & Helen Bernier
VIGNEAULT, Marie E E, Mar 10 1889 Sex:F Child# 4 Joseph Vigneault Haverhill, MA & Emma Peltier Canada
VIGNEAULT, Paul Sylvio, May 26 1930 Sex:M Child# 1 Sylvio Vigneault Nashua, NH & Ardelia Tanguay Canada
VIGNEAULT, Rachelle, May 15 1914 Sex:F Child# 1 Oscar Vigneault Nashua, NH & Bertha Bleau Sciota, NY
VIGNEAULT, Therese Leonie, Sep 30 1913 Sex:F Child# 3 Julien J Vigneault Nashua, NH & Helen Bernier Canada
VIGNOLA, Normand, Aug 4 1928 Sex:M Child# 7 Jos Vignola Canada & Elmiria Normand Lowell, MA
VILAS, Nickles, May 20 1916 Sex:M Child# 1 John Vilas Greece & A Lekopooloo Greece
VILLANCOURT, Charles E, Oct 25 1891 Sex:M Child# 4 Adolphe Villancourt Canada & Emelie Bonenfaut Canada
VILLANCOURT, Joseph Arthur, Jul 12 1891 Sex:M Child# 1 A Villancourt Canada & Melida Bissonnette Canada
VILLENEUVE, Louise Irene, Aug 22 1926 Sex:F Child# 4 Armand Villeneuve Haverhill, MA & L Vadeboncoeur Haverhill, MA
VILLENEUVE, Marie Clare C, Oct 13 1924 Sex:F Child# 3 Arm Villeneuve Haverhill, MA & I Vadeboncoeur Haverhill, MA
VILLINCON, Unknown, Sep 11 1922 Sex:M Child# 2 Armand Villincon Haverhill, MA & Irene Vadeboncoeur Haverhill, MA
VILLNTCH, Helena, Aug 28 1917 Sex:F Child# 2 Brounslaw Villntch Russia & Josephine Crtosku Russia
VINCAKENIS, Joseph, Dec 5 1918 Sex:M Child# 1 Joseph Vincakenis Russia & Ora Malawicz Russia
VINCENT, Eliona, Jul 10 1901 Sex:F Child# 2 George Vincent Canada & Angelique Guerette Canada
VINCENT, Frances, Mar 22 1925 Sex:F Child# 3 Arthur J Vincent Somersworth, NH & Olivene Poulin Barrington, NH
VINCENT, Gladys, Jun 30 1894 Sex:F Child# 1 Stanford W Vincent Brockton, MA & Marcia A Armes Canterbury
VINCENT, Marie Florida, Jun 15 1899 Sex:F Child# 1 George Vincent Mass & Angelique Guerette Canada
VINCENT, Myron Stanford, Jul 17 1897 Sex:M Child# 2 Stanford W Vincent Taunton, MA & Marcia A Armes NH
VINCENT, Shelley D, Jr, Aug 10 1911 Sex:M Child# 1 Shelley D Vincent Barre, VT & Julia Glenton Nashua, NH
VIRCHOW, Catherine Ann, Apr 23 1930 Sex:F Child# 3 Hugo A Virchow Germany & Catherine Warren Nashua, NH
VIRCHOW, Warren Edgar, Mar 8 1922 Sex:M Child# 2 Hugo Virchow Germany & Catherine Warner Mass
VISKEN, Zima, Nov 2 1915 Sex:F Child# 1 Alex Visken Russia & Anna Gutor Russia
VIVELAMOUR, Florence, Feb 15 1897 Sex:F Child# Joseph Vivelamour US & Marceline Belair US
VIVIER, Joseph P Romeo, Jan 26 1904 Sex:M Child# 6 Joseph Vivier Canada & Marie Edesse Cote Canada
VOIDENN, Unknown, Nov 28 1914 Sex:M Child# 5 John Voidenn Austria & Annie Godoivatch Austria Stillborn
VOISINE, Irene, Dec 11 1935 Sex:F Child# 1 Ronald Voisine St Basil, NB & Ida Dionne Riv du Loup, PQ
VOLCOLCUS, Mary, Oct 27 1923 Sex:F Child# 10 Anthony Volcolcus Russia & Mary Velichka Russia Stillborn
VOLKAVITCH, Anthony, Jan 19 1910 Sex:M Child# 2 John Volkavitch Russia & Anna Udanis Russia
VOLKAVITCH, Stan, Dec 5 1909 Sex:M Child# 4 Stanislas Volkavitch Russia & Zophia Maiofsky Russia
VOLKOFSKY, Agnes, Dec 25 1913 Sex:F Child# 2 John Volkofski Russia & Eva Jovgild Russia
VOLKOFSKY, Unknown, Nov 21 1912 Sex:F Child# 1 John Volkofsky Russia & Eva Yargin Russia Stillborn
VOLKORSKY, John, Feb 4 1919 Sex:M Child# 5 John Volkorsky Russia & Eva Javean Russia
VOLONTOKAWICZ, Isabelle, Aug 15 1917 Sex:F Child# 2 John Volontokawicz Russia & Eva Sekawicz Russia
VOLONTOKOWICZ, Peter, Jun 28 1915 Sex:M Child# 3 Gaspar Volontokowicz Russia & Nellie Artkumnuta Russia
VOLTCHUCK, John, Jul 10 1917 Sex:M Child# 1 Peter Voltchuck Poland Russia & Mary Vilbick Poland Russia
VONDALOSKA, Zofee Katherine, Aug 15 1930 Sex:F Child# 2 Alex Vondaloska Nashua, NH & Katrinka Kuchalska Lowell, MA
VONDALOSKI, Anthony, Jul 22 1908 Sex:M Child# 3 Anthony Vondaloski Poland & Katherine Aulinder Poland
VONDELL, Arthur Henry, Oct 19 1912 Sex:M Child# 1 Julius F Vondell Woodstock, VT & Eva Flagg Fitzwilliam, NH
VONDELL, Helen Mabel, Jun 15 1914 Sex:F Child# 2 Julius Vondell Woodstock, VT & Eva Flagg Fitzwilliam, NH
VOSOTAS, James, Aug 3 1928 Sex:M Child# 3 D Vosotas Greece & V Dimskis Greece
VOTER, Maud Hazel, Aug 17 1892 Sex:F Child# 1 Charles A Voter Farmington, ME & Lulie M Sherman Northboro, MA
VOTER, Pauline, Feb 5 1897 Sex:F Child# 2 Charles Voter Farmington, ME & Lulu Sherman Northboro, MA
VOUZVOULAKIS, Marie, Oct 16 1922 Sex:F Child# 1 Dem Vouzvoulakis Greece & Anastasia Marines Greece
VOYEFSKA, John, Oct 23 1915 Sex:M Child# 1 John Voyefska Russia & Josephine Amon Russia
VOYER, Marie Gabrielle, Apr 28 1922 Sex:F Child# 12 Ludger Voyer Canada & Marcella Veilleux Canada
VYETTE, Henri, Jul 13 1893 Sex:M Child# 2 J B Vyette Canada & Sophie Grandmaison Canada
WACTANIK, Boleotow, Mar 5 1908 Sex:M Child# 1 Austria & Franciszka Wactanik Austria
WADE, Wade, Aug 4 1889 Sex:F Child# 1 William R Wade Stanstead, C E & Mary D Howard Birmingham, NY
WADLEG, Ruth Elizabeth, Apr 14 1923 Sex:F Child# 1 Clarence B Wadleg Kingston, NH & Cornelia E French Nashua, NH
WADLEIGH, Ralph Stuart, Jan 17 1935 Sex:M Child# 4 Clar B Wadleigh Kingston, NH & Cornelia French Nashua, NH
WAICGUNAS, Tofilia, Jul 23 1914 Sex:F Child# 1 James Waicgunas Russia & Regina Welickute Russia

WAIGHT, Alfred Henry, Jul 22 1901 Sex:M Child# 1 Alfred E Waight England & Elizabeth Jones Canada
WAILT, Barbara, Jun 8 1924 Sex:F Child# 2 Ralph Wailt Boston, MA & Mary Dodge Brookline, NH
WAINSUYS, Peter, Dec 23 1913 Sex:M Child# 3 Louis Wainsuys Russia & Aliana Molute Russia
WAISWILAS, Ann Shirley, Jul 9 1935 Sex:F Child# 3 Anth Waiswilas Lithuania & Ruth Brockelbank Newburyport, MA
WAISWILAS, Anthony Andrew, Jr, Jan 7 1933 Sex:M Child# 2 A A Waiswilas Lithuania & R Brockelbank Newburyport, MA
WAISWILOS, Albina, Feb 23 1933 Sex:F Child# 2 Jos Waiswilos Lithuania & A Szidlewski Lithuania
WAISWILOS, Ruth Catherine, Sep 30 1931 Sex:F Child# 1 Anthony Waiswilos Lithuania & Ruth Brockelbank Newburyport,MA
WAITE, Marguerite Eleanor, Feb 15 1911 Sex:F Child# 1 Ira Merrill Waite Dunbarton, NH & Mary E Tucker Hopkinton, NH
WAIZNIS, Maclas, Mar 6 1912 Sex:M Child# 2 Ludwikas Waiznis Russia & Alana Malute Russia
WALANCZUS, Helen, Jun 20 1906 Sex:F Child# 1 August Walanczus Russia & Antonia Russia
WALCH, James Harold, Apr 25 1932 Sex:M Child# 1 Myron S Walch Hollis, NH & T M Taggart Limerick, ME
WALCH, Joseph, Apr 2 1899 Sex:M Child# 2 Joseph Walch England & Jane Whitehead England
WALCH, Myron David, Oct 31 1933 Sex:M Child# 2 Myron S Walch Hollis, NH & Thelma Taggart Limerick, ME
WALCH, Unknown, Dec 13 1893 Sex:F Child# 2 James A Walch Litchfield, NH & Clara S Swallow Cincinnati, OH
WALCH, Unknown, Mar 17 1923 Sex:M Child# 1 Preston B Welch Clinton, MA & Jeannette R Tessier Nashua, NH
WALCOWSKI, Eloza, Jul 19 1920 Sex:F Child# 6 John Walcowski Russia & Eva Yvgel Russia
WALDRON, Harold Percy, Jul 15 1896 Sex:M Child# 2 William W Waldron Elizabeth, NJ & Edna M Gray Boston, MA
WALDRON, Unknown, Jul 10 1910 Sex:M Child# 2 Arthur Waldron Surry, NH & Lillian McIntosh Stoddard, NH
WALDRON, Unknown, Jul 27 1919 Sex:M Child# 3 Leslie M Waldron Antrim, NH & Gertrude Sweatt Jaffrey, NH
WALDRON, Unknown, Mar 12 1921 Sex:M Child# 4 Leslie M Waldron Antrim, NH & Gertrude Sweat E Jaffrey, NH
WALEN, Rosa, Aug 1 1899 Sex:F Child# 3 John Walen Russia & Rosa Guertin Nashua, NH
WALENCRUS, Andrew, Aug 23 1907 Sex:M Child# 2 Augustin Walencrus Russia & Antonina Wilis Russia
WALENCRUS, Andrew, Aug 23 1907 Sex:M Child# 3 Augustin Walencrus Russia & Antonina Wilis Russia
WALENTENSKRESIC, Julia, Jul 4 1914 Sex:F Child# 1 Wm Walentenskresic Russia & Bane Grig Russia
WALENTUHIAWICIU, William, Aug 12 1908 Sex:M Child# 1 A Walentuhiawicius Russia & Agie Ciasnulawicutie Russia
WALENTUKEWICZ, Peter, Aug 6 1911 Sex:M Child# 1 John Walentukewicz Russia & Eva Szakawiciute Russia
WALKER, Altha Elsie, Jun 27 1900 Sex:F Child# 1 F R Walker Mass & Lilia B Smith NH
WALKER, Bessie, Aug 8 1892 Sex:F Child# 1 Henry Walker Vermont & Carrie Monroe Mass
WALKER, Elizabeth Proctor, Nov 20 1929 Sex:F Child# 2 Clarence R Walker Warren, ME & Mildred Proctor Tilton, NH
WALKER, Herbert Leroy, Mar 14 1891 Sex:M Child# 1 Judson M Walker Nashua, NH & Sophronia Lawrence Manchester, NH
WALKER, James Lomer, Nov 12 1926 Sex:M Child# 2 Reginald Walker Ossipee, NH & Edree Gouin Wolfeboro, NH
WALKER, John Ames, Mar 16 1929 Sex:M Child# 3 Reginald Walker NH & Edrie Edin Gowin NH
WALKER, Joseph, Jan 17 1893 Sex:M Child# 3 Joseph Walker England & Georgiana Sirois Canada
WALKER, Joseph, Dec 21 1895 Sex:M Child# 1 Joseph Walker Nashua, NH & Rosanna Girouard Canada
WALKER, Logan Lewis, Apr 25 1896 Sex:M Child# George L Walker England & Mary E Brooks Brookline, NH
WALKER, Marie Eugenie, Mar 9 1898 Sex:F Child# Joseph Walker London, England & Georgianna Sirois Canada
WALKER, Nina Alvarez, Feb 11 1897 Sex:F Child# 3 Ed W Walker Nashua, NH & Mary E Symonds Milford, NH
WALKER, Reginald Guy, Dec 5 1924 Sex:M Child# 1 R G Walker Ossipee, NH & Edrie E Gouin Wolfeboro, NH
WALKER, Rhelda Hattie, Apr 18 1901 Sex:F Child# 1 John T Walker Florence, MA & Lida J Beasley Raleigh, W VA
WALKER, Unknown, Jan 6 1887 Sex:M Child# 2 W H Walker Natick, MA & Nellie Hudson
WALKER, Unknown, Jul 15 1888 Sex:M Child# 1 Joseph Walker England & Giorganna Servia Canada
WALKER, Unknown, Nov 19 1889 Sex:F Child# 1 Edward W Walker Nashua, NH & Mary E Simonds Milford, NH
WALKER, Unknown, Jul 18 1891 Sex:F Child# 2 Edward W Walker Nashua, NH & Mary E Simonds Milford, NH
WALKER, Unknown, Apr 18 1894 Sex:F Child# W A Walker Mass & Lillia E Searles NH
WALKER, Willard, Feb 27 1913 Sex:M Child# 1 John Walker Nashua, NH & Helen Banfield Nashua, NH
WALL, Elizabeth May, Aug 16 1920 Sex:F Child# 2 Michael P Wall Ireland & Annie Kelley Ireland
WALL, James Campbell, Mar 5 1919 Sex:M Child# 3 John Edward Wall Northfield, MA & Lucy A Campbell Northfield, MA
WALL, Thomas Michaud, Jun 15 1919 Sex:M Child# 1 Michael P Wall Ireland & Annie M Kelly Ireland
WALLACE, Arthur Herman, Feb 10 1915 Sex:M Child# 1 Herman J Wallace Nashua, NH & Alice Soucy Canada
WALLACE, Doris Carrick, Apr 29 1907 Sex:F Child# 7 Jewell Wallace Cava Hill, NB & Minnie G Dane Nashua, NH
WALLACE, Elmer Leroy, Mar 14 1911 Sex:M Child# 6 Frank K Wallace Nashua, NH & Olive B Banks Boston, MA
WALLACE, Elmer Leroy, Jr, Nov 2 1933 Sex:M Child# 1 Elmer L Wallace Nashua, NH & Dorothy Young Nashua, NH
WALLACE, Frank Irving, Jan 6 1907 Sex:M Child# 3 Frank K Wallace Nashua, NH & Olive Bertha Banks Boston, MA
WALLACE, Glen Lewis, Mar 18 1922 Sex:M Child# 2 Robert G Wallace Ohio & Hannah M Alexander Windham, NH
WALLACE, Herbert Leighton, Dec 23 1907 Sex:M Child# 4 Frank K Wallace Nashua, NH & Olive B Banks Boston, MA
WALLACE, Herman Jewell, Aug 27 1896 Sex:M Child# 4 Jewell Wallace Caver Hill, NB & Minnie G Dane Nashua, NH
WALLACE, Ina, Jan 21 1890 Sex:F Child# 4 Alonzo S Wallace Bristol, ME & Mary F Maynard Lowell, MA  Stillborn
WALLACE, John Edward Richard, Jan 13 1931 Sex:M Child# 2 Herman Wallace Nashua, NH & Marie T Deschamp Nashua, NH
WALLACE, Judith Ann, Sep 5 1935 Sex:F Child# 3 Maynard Wallace Hanover, NH & Phoebe George Florence, AL
WALLACE, Louise Bell, Oct 24 1909 Sex:F Child# 5 Frank K Wallace Nashua, NH & Olive B Banks Boston, MA
WALLACE, Margaret, Jun 20 1909 Sex:F Child# 1 William H Wallace Philadelphia, PA & Margaret McInness Nova Scotia
WALLACE, Mariam, Feb 27 1906 Sex:F Child# 3 Arthur L Wallace Lowell, MA & Dorotha Goss St Johnsbury, VT
WALLACE, Paul Robert, Oct 8 1928 Sex:M Child# 1 Herman Wallace Nashua, NH & Marie Deschamps Nashua, NH
WALLACE, Phoebe Joan, Sep 25 1930 Sex:F Child# 1 Maynard Wallace Hanover, NH & Phoebe George Florence, AL
WALLACE, Raymond Dane, Jul 31 1893 Sex:M Child# 2 Jewell Wallace Caver Hill, NB & Minnie Dane Nashua, NH
WALLACE, Rotha Matilda, Jun 1 1892 Sex:F Child# 1 Jewell Wallace Haverhill, NB & Minnie Dane Nashua, NH
WALLACE, Ruth, Feb 27 1906 Sex:F Child# 4 Arthur L Wallace Lowell, MA & Dorotha Goss St Johnsbury, VT
WALLACE, Unknown, Jun 5 1891 Sex:M Child# 1 Charles M Wallace Jackson, ME & Mary J Simmons Knox, ME
WALLACE, Unknown, Nov 22 1894 Sex:M Child# 7 James Wallace Ireland & Ireland Stillborn
WALLACE, Unknown, Dec 14 1894 Sex:F Child# 3 Jewell Wallace Caver Hill, NB & Minnie G Dane Nashua, NH
WALLACE, Unknown, Mar 1 1898 Sex:F Child# 5 Jewell Wallace Caver Hill, NB & Minnie Dane Nashua, NH
WALLACE, Unknown, Aug 25 1899 Sex:F Child# 6 Jewell Wallace NB & Minnie Dane Nashua, NH
WALLAN, Michael, Apr 17 1917 Sex:M Child# 1 Michael Wallan Russia & Mary Karith Russia

WALLING, Louis, Mar 9 1922 Sex:M Child# 5 Edwain Walling Rhode Island & Mabel Auberchout Mass
WALLING, Mabel, Aug 31 1925 Sex:F Child# 8 Edward Walling Rhode Island & Mabel Auberchout Mass
WALLING, Mabel Esther, Aug 14 1923 Sex:F Child# 6 Eddie Walling Rhode Island & Mabel Aubichon Mass
WALLING, Mary Anna, Jun 28 1924 Sex:F Child# 6 Edward Walling Rhode Island & Mabel Aubuchon Mass
WALLING, Vital John, Apr 28 1927 Sex:M Child# 3 A Walling Lithuania & Helen Geaniatch Lithuania
WALSH, James Francis, Apr 9 1931 Sex:M Child# 3 James Walsh Arlington, MA & Eileen Dwyer Nashua, NH
WALSH, James Francis, Jun 28 1933 Sex:M Child# 4 James F Walsh Arlington, MA & Eileen Dwyer Nashua, NH
WALSH, Preston Thomas, Feb 2 1925 Sex:M Child# 2 Preston T Walsh Clinton, MA & Jeanette Tessier Nashua, NH
WALSH, Walsh, Mar 24 1889 Sex:F Child# 1 James A Walsh Litchfield, NH & Clara Swallow Kansas
WALTERS, Beverly Elizabeth, Aug 15 1923 Sex:F Child# 3 Frank C Walters Nashua, NH & Hazel Croft E Fairfield, VT
WALTERS, Elmer James, Apr 12 1895 Sex:M Child# 2 Frank J Walters Lynn, MA & Sadie E Ryan S Lee, NH
WALTERS, Francis, Feb 1894 Sex:M Child# 5 Charles Walters England & Emma J O'Brien England
WALTERS, Frank C, Jul 5 1892 Sex:M Child# 1 Frank J Walters Lynn, MA & Sarah E Ryan South Lee, NH
WALTERS, John, Sep 23 1892 Sex:M Child# 7 Charles Walters England & Emma Brien England
WALTERS, Unknown, Nov 15 1889 Sex:F Child# 6 Charles Walters England & Emma J O'Brien England
WALTERS, Unknown, Oct 15 1928 Sex:M Child# 5 Frank C Walters Nashua, NH & Hazel Croft Fairfield, VT
WALTERS, Wayland F, Oct 30 1918 Sex:M Child# 1 Frank C Walters Nashua, NH & Hazel J Croft E Fairfield, VT
WALTERS, Y Croft, Mar 27 1921 Sex:M Child# 2 F Clifton Walters Nashua, NH & Hazel J Croft E Fairfield, VT
WALTON, Joseph Paul, Oct 31 1923 Sex:M Child# 12 Henry A Walton Boston, MA & Louise Weston Nashua, NH
WALTON, Madeline, Mar 2 1913 Sex:F Child# 2 Harry I Walton Nashua, NH & May G Russell Nashua, NH
WALTON, Martha Elizabeth, Oct 31 1923 Sex:F Child# 10 Henry A Walton Boston, MA & Louise Weston Nashua, NH
WALTON, Paul, Jun 4 1911 Sex:M Child# 1 Harry M Walton Nashua, NH & Grace Ella Brown Nashua, NH Stillborn
WALTON, Thomas Mark, Oct 31 1923 Sex:M Child# 11 Henry A Walton Boston, MA & Louise Weston Nashua, NH
WALTON, Unknown, Jun 15 1909 Sex:F Child# 1 Carl J Walton Nashua, NH & Mary O Lucier Nashua, NH
WANCAWICZ, Wanda, Dec 5 1912 Sex:F Child# 1 Wiktoe Wancawicz Russia & Julia Bogdonowicz Russia
WAOINSKI, Bertha, Jan 3 1917 Sex:F Child# 1 Stanley Waoinski Russia & Anna Krucszos Russia
WARASZKA, Lorna Ann, Mar 15 1935 Sex:F Child# 1 John Waraszka Nashua, NH & Virginia Degasis Nashua, NH
WARD, Barbara Louise, Jul 15 1928 Sex:F Child# 1 W F Ward Wilton, NH & M L McCalvey E Weare, NH
WARD, Carl Theodore, Mar 30 1909 Sex:M Child# 2 Charles Ward Falmouth, MA & Mabel Wilson Lynn, MA
WARD, Elgee Leonard, May 16 1921 Sex:M Child# 3 John E Ward Canada & Bertha Harvey Claremont, NH
WARD, John Ernest, Jr, Jul 30 1918 Sex:M Child# 2 John E Ward Cableton, Canada & Bertha Harvey Claremont, NH
WARD, Marjorie, May 30 1908 Sex:F Child# 2 Wallace Ward Woburn, MA & Olive Garby Walpole, MA
WARD, Paul S, Dec 23 1892 Sex:M Child# 3 B L Ward NH & Ida M Smith Maine
WARD, Pauline Frances, Nov 3 1929 Sex:F Child# 2 Donald Francis Ward Wilton, NH & Mira L McCalvey E Weare, NH
WARD, Robert Valentine, Jul 8 1930 Sex:M Child# 2 Roy Valentine Ward New Brunswick & Constance Nye Sandown, NH
WARD, Unknown, Aug 1 1895 Sex:M Child# 2 P S Ward Rutland, VT & Katie J Wallace Philadelphia, PA
WARDEN, Unknown, Oct 1 1898 Sex:M Child# 2 John B Warden Ellenburg, NY & Ella Wyman Chelsea, MA
WARDER, Marie, Aug 13 1894 Sex:F Child# 1 Andrew Warder Poland & Katie Merritt Poland
WARDNER, Barbara June, Jun 22 1913 Sex:F Child# 1 Frederick Wardner Woodstock, VT & Mildred Otis Nashua, NH
WARDNER, Frederick Alton, Apr 11 1915 Sex:M Child# 2 Frederick A Wardner Woodstock, VT & Mildred Otis Nashua,
WARDNER, George Calvin, Sep 10 1923 Sex:M Child# 6 Frederick Wardner Woodstock, VT & Mildred Otis Nashua, NH
WARDNER, Norma, Feb 4 1921 Sex:F Child# 5 Fred H Wardner Woodstock, NH & Mildred Otis Nashua, NH
WARDNER, Otis Fletcher, May 16 1916 Sex:M Child# 3 Frederick A Wardner Woodstock, VT & Mildrid T Otis Nashua, NH
WARDNER, Robert Edward, Nov 12 1918 Sex:M Child# 4 Frederick A Wardner Woodstock, VT & Mildred Otis Nashua, NH
WARE, Fred Albert, Jr, May 14 1921 Sex:M Child# 3 Fred A Ware Hancock, NH & Bertha Clark Hancock, NH
WARE, John Glover, Jr, Nov 28 1930 Sex:M Child# 2 John G Ware Marblehead, MA & Pauline M Wright Milford, NH
WARE, Marjorie Betty, Aug 5 1924 Sex:F Child# 3 George C Ware Wrentham, MA & Lula Brander Providence, RI
WARFLEY, Joseph, Jul 12 1889 Sex:M Child# 1 Patrick J Warfley Ireland & Mary F Shea Nashua, NH
WARLEY, Chester William, Aug 19 1931 Sex:M Child# 1 Reginald Warley Tyngsboro, MA & Beatrice Drew Dunstable, MA
WARREN, Addie M, Sep 17 1854 Sex:F Child# 2 John Q A Warren Winthrop, ME & Maria J Windsor, VT
WARREN, Agnes, Oct 6 1893 Sex:F Child# 9 Michael F Warren Newburyport, MA & Liza J Moran Lowell, MA
WARREN, Burtt E, Jr, Jul 8 1911 Sex:M Child# 2 Burtt E Warren Lowell, MA & Effie L West Canada
WARREN, Esther Margaret, Dec 17 1895 Sex:F Child# 10 Michael Warren Newburyport, MA & Eliza Moran Lowell, MA
WARREN, Helen, Dec 18 1896 Sex:F Child# 3 Cornelius Warren Lowell, MA & Mary Lavin Amherst, NH
WARREN, Helen E, Nov 4 1887 Sex:F Child# 6 Michael Warren Newburyport, MA & Eliza Moran Lowell, MA
WARREN, Henry E, Aug 3 1889 Sex:M Child# 9 Michael Warren Newburyport, MA & Lizzie Moran Lowell, MA
WARREN, Jessie May, May 12 1920 Sex:F Child# 1 John Warren Boston, MA & Lydia C Gelinas Nashua, NH
WARREN, John, Sep 15 1904 Sex:M Child# 1 John W Warren Nashua, NH & Mary Brennan Nashua, NH Stillborn
WARREN, John D, May 29 1893 Sex:M Child# 2 Cornelius H Warren Lowell, MA & Mary E Lavin Amherst, NH
WARREN, Joseph Arthur, May 22 1919 Sex:M Child# 4 Jos Arthur Warren Leominster, MA & Andena Guilbert Canada
WARREN, Mary Ann, Sep 14 1889 Sex:F Child# 1 John H Warren Hudson & Annie Poulin Montreal
WARREN, Mary F, Oct 6 1891 Sex:F Child# 8 Michel Warren Mass & Eliza Moran Lowell, MA
WARREN, Miriam N, Oct 28 1902 Sex:F Child# 1 Burtt E Warren Lowell, MA & Effie Somers Canada
WARREN, Unknown, Aug 1 1889 Sex:M Child# 2 John Warren Ireland & Maggie Woran Ireland Stillborn
WARREN, Unknown, Aug 2 1890 Sex:M Child# 1 Peter R Warren England & Mary Davis England
WARREN, Unknown, Jul 1 1891 Sex:M Child# 1 Cornelius H Warren Lowell, MA & Mary E Lavin Amherst, NH Stillborn
WARREN, William M, Sep 18 1852 Sex:M Child# 1 John Q A Warren Winthrop, ME & Maria J Windsor, VT
WARRINGTON, Charles Leslie, Jan 13 1918 Sex:M Child# 2 Leslie Warrington Nashua, NH & Mary Sullivan Ireland
WARRINGTON, John Edgar, Oct 25 1931 Sex:M Child# 7 Leslie Warrington New Brunswick & Mary Sullivan Ireland
WARRINGTON, Mary, May 7 1926 Sex:F Child# 5 Leslie Warrington New Brunswick & Mary Sullivan Ireland
WARRINGTON, Paul William, Jul 29 1927 Sex:M Child# 6 Leslie Warrington New Brunswick & Mary Sullivan Ireland
WARRINGTON, Rita Mary, May 14 1919 Sex:F Child# 3 L L Warrington New Brunswick & Mary Sullivan Ireland
WARRINGTON, Unknown, Sep 9 1916 Sex:M Child# 1 Leslie L Warrington New Brunswick & Mary Sullivan Cork, Ireland

WARSOWICZ, Dominic, Nov 9 1925 Sex:M Child# 4 A Warsowicz Poland & Julia Oleham Poland
WASHBURN, Irene, Jul 28 1903 Sex:F Child# 1 Bert Washburn Maple Grove, NY & Maria Lamb Chateauguay, NY
WASKAVITCH, Anna, Jun 26 1910 Sex:F Child# 1 Josephus Waskavitch Russia & Pietra Kucminte Russia Stillborn
WASLANK, Unknown, Jun 4 1916 Sex:M Child# 2 Michael Wasland Russia & Stefenia Halmanski Russia
WASLUK, Patrick, Mar 17 1923 Sex:M Child# 3 Mike Wasluk Vilma, Russia & Sefania Wasluk Vilma, Russia
WASOVICH, Unknown, Oct 17 1922 Sex:M Child# 3 Andrew Wasovich Russia & Julia Worklete Russia
WATERHOUSE, Gary Edward, Jun 24 1932 Sex:M Child# 2 T Waterhouse, Jr N Billerica, MA & Ethel Greeley Londonderry,NH
WATERHOUSE, Thomas Jr, Mar 22 1927 Sex:M Child# 1 T J Waterhouse Lowell, MA & Ethel Greeley Londonderry, NH
WATERS, Unknown, Apr 2 1888 Sex:M Child# 6 Charles Waters London, England & Emma Waters London, England
WATKINS, Barbara, Jul 18 1925 Sex:F Child# 3 Herman Watkins Weare, NH & Mildred Cadwell Fitchburg, MA
WATKINS, Doris Christina, Nov 16 1912 Sex:F Child# 2 Guy V Watkins Weare, NH & Marguerite Lang Germany
WATKINS, Dorothy May, Apr 28 1920 Sex:F Child# 1 Herman C Watkins Weare, NH & Mildred Caldwell Fitchburg, MA
WATKINS, Ethel Violet, Oct 12 1921 Sex:F Child# 2 Herman Watkins Weare, NH & Mildred Caldwell Fitchburg, MA
WATKINS, Marion Ella, Jun 29 1929 Sex:F Child# 4 Herman Watkins Weare, NH & Mildred Caldwell Fitchburg, MA
WATKINS, Unknown, Oct 23 1911 Sex:F Child# 1 Guy B Watkins Weare, NH & Margaret Lenz Germany
WATKINS, William Joseph, Jun 17 1896 Sex:M Child# 1 Joseph W Watkins England & Abbie B Parnell Nova Scotia
WATSON, Catharine, Jul 31 1921 Sex:F Child# 1 Ray H Watson Nashua, NH & Rose McGinnis Ireland
WATSON, Eileen May, May 12 1921 Sex:F Child# 1 Chester L Watson Worcester, MA & Mary E White Canada
WATSON, Everett William, May 27 1928 Sex:M Child# 3 Harold Watson Nashua, NH & Rose McGinnis Ireland
WATSON, Frederick Edward, Apr 5 1913 Sex:M Child# 2 Roland H Watson Nashua, NH & Blanche Lund Nashua, NH
WATSON, Frederick Lund, Mar 5 1912 Sex:M Child# 1 Roland Watson Nashua, NH & Blanche Lund Nashua, NH
WATSON, George Alex, Nov 22 1895 Sex:M Child# 10 James Watson Scotland & Agnes Spence Scotland
WATSON, Harold Webster, Apr 27 1923 Sex:M Child# 2 Harold Rex Watson Nashua, NH & Rose McGinnis Ireland
WATSON, John, Jun 5 1924 Sex:M Child# 3 Chester Watson Worcester, MA & Emily White Prince Edw Island
WATSON, Madeline Estelle, Jun 20 1926 Sex:F Child# 4 Chester Watson Worcester, MA & Emily White Prince Edw Island
WATSON, Nellie Gertrude, Nov 26 1896 Sex:F Child# 1 Garret Watson, Jr Richmond, VA & Annie Wendenburg Richmond, VA
WATSON, Robert Conal, Aug 3 1922 Sex:M Child# 2 Chester Watson Mass & Emily White Canada
WATSON, Robert, Jr, Sep 23 1934 Sex:M Child# 2 Robert Watson Maine & Anna Stewart Boston, MA
WATSON, Unknown, Jan 13 1887 Sex:M Child# 2 Mark E Watson Canada & Nannie Pelmira, ME
WATSON, Unknown, Apr 30 1888 Sex:M Child# 3 James F Watson Derby, VT & Julia Batchelder Hudson, NH
WATSON, Unknown, Jan 18 1889 Sex:M Child# 3 Mark E Watson Canada & Mamie Hubbard Canada
WATT, Unknown, Dec 11 1889 Sex:F Child# 6 Duane F Watt Weston, VT & Edith Woodard Hanover, NH
WATT, Unknown, Dec 14 1913 Sex:F Child# 3 John V Watt England & Lucretia George Illinois Stillborn
WATT, Vida Adeline, Jan 18 1906 Sex:F Child# 2 John Watt England & Lucretia George Illinois
WATTS, Doris Viola, Jun 11 1904 Sex:F Child# 1 John Vass Watts England & Lucretia V George Illinois
WATTS, Mary Alice, Sep 7 1912 Sex:F Child# 1 Herbert Watts England & Alice Hutchinson England
WATTS, Phyllis Nellie, May 6 1925 Sex:F Child# 6 Neil Watts Londonderry, NH & Fauny Roby Londonderry, NH
WATTS, Ralph, Oct 11 1923 Sex:M Child# 5 Neil Watts Londonderry, NH & Fanny L Robie Londonderry, NH
WATTS, Sherley Lavinia, Apr 12 1927 Sex:F Child# 7 Neil Watts Londonderry, NH & Fannie Robie Londonderry, NH
WATTS, Thelma Claudia, Jul 11 1911 Sex:F Child# 5 Roland G Watts Mooers, NY & Anna C Walker Ellenburg, NY
WATTS, Unknown, Jun 2 1899 Sex:F Child# 3 Robert Watts Mooers, NY & Anna Walker Ellenburg Ctr, NY Stillborn
WAUGH, Helen, Jan 28 1893 Sex:F Child# 4 William Waugh Ireland & Maria McIverny Ireland
WAUGH, John Joseph, Jan 20 1902 Sex:M Child# 5 William Waugh Ireland & Maria McInerney Ireland
WAYE, Madeline Joan, Dec 17 1932 Sex:F Child# 1 Charles H Waye Vermont & Irene Dubuque Nashua, NH
WAYMAN, Mary Anne, Apr 5 1890 Sex:F Child# 2 Charles W Wayman England & Honovah Meeban Ireland
WEBB, George Raymond, Jun 19 1923 Sex:M Child# 1 John Raymond Webb Highgate, VT & Bertrude Cullen Orange, MA
WEBBER, Forrest Ralph, Jun 1 1928 Sex:M Child# 2 Carroll Webber Windham, NH & P Hannemann Germany
WEBBER, Philip Frederick, Sep 24 1912 Sex:M Child# 1 Frederick B Webber Portland, ME & Christie P Holt Pembroke. NH
WEBBER, Thelma, May 16 1927 Sex:F Child# 1 Carroll O Webber Windham, NH & P K Hannemann Germany Stillborn
WEBER, Albert, Jun 6 1912 Sex:M Child# 2 Albert Weber US & Clara Desmarais Nashua, NH
WEBSTER, Blanche, Aug 10 1907 Sex:F Child# 3 Leroy M Webster Nashua, NH & Mary Jelly Nashua, NH
WEBSTER, Blanche Powers, Jun 15 1903 Sex:F Child# 1 Edgar C Webster
WEBSTER, Donald Earle, Jul 22 1929 Sex:M Child# 2 John Alden Webster Nashua, NH & Lois Thompson Nashua, NH
WEBSTER, Dora Frances, Jul 21 1897 Sex:F Child# 1 Charles H Webster Nashua, NH & Cora O Prescott Nashua, NH
WEBSTER, Fred D, Jan 7 1897 Sex:M Child# 3 George A Webster Boscawen, NH & Alice Brown Nashua, NH
WEBSTER, Fritz Malcolm, Dec 1 1892 Sex:M Child# 1 Herbert F Webster Nashua, NH & Lizzie Howe Canada
WEBSTER, Gladys May, Apr 21 1910 Sex:F Child# 1 Charles Webster Vermont & Kathleen B Shores Thornton, NH
WEBSTER, gloria Alden, May 27 1928 Sex:F Child# 1 John A Webster Nashua, NH & Lois E Thompson Nashua, NH
WEBSTER, Helen B, Feb 24 1892 Sex:F Child# 4 Fred R Webster NS & NS
WEBSTER, Henry Willard, Mar 8 1904 Sex:M Child# 2 Leory H Webster Nashua, NH & Mary L Jelley Nashua, NH
WEBSTER, J Alden, May 20 1905 Sex:M Child# 2 Edgar C Webster Maine & Marion Rowell Nashua, NH
WEBSTER, Lafe Irene, Mar 12 1896 Sex:F Child# 4 George F Webster New York & Mary H Smith New York
WEBSTER, Marion Edith, Feb 7 1905 Sex:F Child# 2 Sumner D Webster Nashua, NH & Edith H Knott Dracut, MA
WEBSTER, Sumner Stevens, Oct 7 1911 Sex:M Child# 3 E C Webster Fryeburg, NY & Marion S Powell Nashua, NH
WEBSTER, Tulussie H, Feb 14 1891 Sex:F Child# 2 George H Webster New York & Mary H Smith New York
WEBSTER, Unknown, Apr 30 1888 Sex:F Child# 3 Jonathan P Webster Manchester & Eanonette Gaskell Ausable, NY
WEBSTER, Unknown, Aug 18 1889 Sex:M Child# 1 George H Webster Moores, NY & Mary H Smith Moores, NY
WEBSTER, Unknown, Jun 15 1890 Sex:F Child# 4 Fred R Webster New York & Minnie N Wood New York
WEBSTER, Unknown, Jul 11 1892 Sex:M Child# 2 Solon W Webster Irasburg, VT & Hannah C Patterson Sanbornton, NH
WEBSTER, Unknown, May 29 1896 Sex:M Child# 1 Fred G Webster Alstead, NH & Minnie Flanders Litchfield, NH Stillborn
WEBSTER, Unknown, Jan 29 1902 Sex:M Child# 1 Sumner D Webster Nashua, NH & Edith H Knott Dracut, MA
WEBSTER, Unknown, Dec 14 1902 Sex:M Child# 1 Leroy H Webster Nashua, NH & Mary L Jelly Nashua, NH
WEBSTER, Unknown, Oct 31 1910 Sex:F Child# 3 Sumner D Webster Nashua, NH & Edith H Knott Dracut, MA

WEBSTER, Wallace Rowell, Apr 22 1913 Sex:M Child# 4 E C Webster Fryeburg, ME & Marion Rowell Nashua, NH
WEBSTER, Webster, May 12 1889 Sex:M Child# 1 Solon W Webster Johnsbury, VT & Henrietta Patterson Sanbornton, NH
WEBSTER, Wilbur Parady, Oct 22 1930 Sex:M Child# 7 George J Webster Mars Hill, ME & Ada Parady Kingman, ME
WECOJA, Unknown, Sep 10 1923 Sex:M Child# 1 S Janson Wecoja Russia & Emma Weikldain Finland
WEEKS, Francis William, Aug 15 1913 Sex:M Child# 2 Charles A Weeks New Brunswick & Catherine McKinnon PEI
WEEKS, Robert, Mar 26 1916 Sex:M Child# 3 Charles A Weeks Canada & Catherine McKinnon Canada
WEIDENE, Unknown, Sep 16 1915 Sex:M Child# 3 Walter Weidene Mecansil, NY & Agatha Hackett Pepperell, MA
WEIGHTMAN, Unknown, Jan 24 1890 Sex:F Child# 1 Minor Weightman NY & Mary Matoll NY
WEILER, Gertrude Sophie, Sep 18 1908 Sex:F Child# 2 Nicholas M Weiler Boston, MA & Rachel O'Brien Warren, RI
WEISBERG, Solomon, Jan 16 1898 Sex:M Child# 3 Louis Weisberg Russia & Ida Lata Russia
WEITZEKIENAS, Vitold, Oct 23 1920 Sex:M Child# 2 Jos Weitzekienas Lithuania Russia & Annie Malawicz Lithuania
WEJRIK, John, Jul 15 1915 Sex:M Child# 2 Mike Wejrik Austria & Fanny Woyrik Austria
WELCH, Alma Louise, Aug 31 1919 Sex:F Child# 3 Vernon Welch Kennebunk, ME & Elmire Damboise Nashua, NH
WELCH, Catherine, Mar 2 1889 Sex:F Child# 2 William Welch Ireland & Mary McBride Ireland
WELCH, Catherine Ellen, Apr 8 1934 Sex:F Child# 3 Thomas J Welch Nashua, NH & Margaret Sullivan Nashua, NH
WELCH, Chester Irving, Oct 14 1927 Sex:M Child# 5 Vernon Welch Kennebunkport, ME & E Dambroise Nashua, NH
WELCH, Dorothy Beatrice, Aug 14 1922 Sex:F Child# 5 Vernon Welch Maine & Elmire Damboise NH
WELCH, Edna Helen, Oct 22 1916 Sex:F Child# 2 Vermon Welch Kennebunk, ME & Elmire Damboise Nashua, NH
WELCH, John, Aug 18 1891 Sex:M Child# 3 William H Welch Ireland & Mary E McBride Ireland
WELCH, John H, Mar 16 1896 Sex:M Child#  Morris Welch Ireland & M Lee Lowell, MA
WELCH, Joseph, Oct 11 1896 Sex:M Child# 5 William H Welch Ireland & Mary E McBride Ireland
WELCH, Madeline, Aug 31 1928 Sex:F Child# 1 Richard Welch Nashua, NH & Esther Sughrue Nashua, NH
WELCH, Margaret Olive, Jul 31 1897 Sex:F Child# 6 Morris Welch Ireland & Margaret Lee Lowell, MA
WELCH, Margaret Rose, May 3 1931 Sex:F Child# 2 Thomas J Welch Nashua, NH & Margaret Sullivan Nashua, NH
WELCH, Mary, Dec 20 1899 Sex:F Child# 7 Maurice Welch Ireland & Margaret Lee Lowell, MA
WELCH, Mary Gertrude, Jun 15 1899 Sex:F Child# 6 William H Welch Ireland & Mary E McBride Ireland
WELCH, Richard, Jan 16 1887 Sex:M Child# 1 William H Welch Ireland & Mary McBride Ireland
WELCH, Richard, Jun 26 1890 Sex:M Child# 4 Maurice Welch Ireland & Margaret A Lee Lowell, MA
WELCH, Richard, Oct 25 1896 Sex:M Child# 2 John Welch Ireland & Catharine T Foley Nashua, NH
WELCH, Richard Allen, Nov 28 1920 Sex:M Child# 4 Vernon Welch Russia & Mary G Karailute Russia
WELCH, Richard Francis, Jr, Jul 28 1932 Sex:M Child# 2 Richard Welch Nashua, NH & Esther Sughrue Nashua, NH
WELCH, Thomas, Jul 1 1898 Sex:M Child# 3 John Welch Ireland & Catherine T Foley Nashua, NH
WELCH, Unknown, Mar 18 1888 Sex:F Child# 1 Morris Welch Ireland & Maggie Lee Pelham, NH
WELCH, Unknown, Jan 12 1901 Sex:M Child# 1 Emery E Welch Pitston, ME & Hattie E Reynolds Bath, ME
WELCH, Unknown, Dec 30 1929 Sex:F Child# 1 Thomas Welch Nashua, NH & Margaret Sullivan Nashua, NH
WELCH, Unknown, Aug 31 1933 Sex:M Child# 1 William Welch Lyndeboro, NH & B Richardson Lyndeboro, NH Stillborn
WELCHAUS, Unknown, Jul 11 1912 Sex:F Child# 2 Edward Welchaus Lancaster, PA & Eva May Averill Burlington, VT
WELCKIS, Anthony, Jul 5 1911 Sex:M Child# 2 Thomas Welckis Russia & M Rushcachinona Russia
WELCOME, Frank, Dec 27 1914 Sex:M Child# 1 Frank Welcome
WELCOME, Helen, Mar 8 1892 Sex:F Child# 1 Samuel J Welcome Montreal, Canada & Frances Montreal, Canada
WELCOME, Unknown, Feb 16 1919 Sex:F Child# 2 Phillip Welcome Canada & Lucy Devasky Russia
WELCZKA, Joseph Willez, Sep 1 1915 Sex:M Child# 2 William Welczka Russia & Miholina Borkofsky Russia
WELDON, Thomas Francis, Sep 27 1891 Sex:M Child# 1 Dennis Weldon Lowell, MA & Mary Gilhooly Ireland
WELICKA, John, Dec 3 1913 Sex:M Child# 4 George Welicka Russia & Benigara Snigolas Russia
WELLDON, Paul Astwood, May 10 1916 Sex:M Child# 1 Paul A Welldon St John, NB & Tena Burke Nashua, NH
WELLER, Marjorie, Aug 10 1915 Sex:F Child# 3 Nicholas M Weller Boston, MA & Rachel O'Brien Warren, RI
WELLMAN, Clayton Irwin, Mar 16 1913 Sex:M Child# 1 Irwin T Wellman Nashua, NH & Edith Rogers Strafford, VT
WELLMAN, Donald F, Jun 16 1919 Sex:M Child# 4 Irvin J P Wellman Nashua, NH & Edith Roger Stratford, VT
WELLMAN, Edward Winfield, Aug 26 1914 Sex:M Child# 2 Irving T Wellman Nashua, NH & Edith J Rogers Norwich, VT
WELLMAN, Grace, Oct 13 1929 Sex:F Child# 1 Harold B Wellman Nashua, NH & Lillian Harrigan Nashua, NH
WELLMAN, Harold Arthur, May 19 1916 Sex:M Child# 3 Irvin Wellman Nashua, NH & Edith Rogers Hanover, NH
WELLMAN, Mary Ann, May 20 1931 Sex:F Child# 2 Harold Wellman Nashua, NH & Lillian Harrigan Nashua, NH
WELLMAN, Unknown, Mar 18 1892 Sex:M Child#  William B Wellman Mont Vernon, NH &  Brookline, NH
WELLMAN, Unknown, Nov 20 1900 Sex:F Child# 6 W B Wellman NH & A Colburn NH
WELLMAN, Unknown, Aug 26 1919 Sex:F Child# 1 Harold Wellman Nashua, NH & Dora Merrill Brownsville, ME Stillborn
WELLS, Augustus S, Jun 21 1893 Sex:M Child# 3 William H Wells Nashua, NH & Mary A Harrington Nashua, NH
WELLS, Calvin James, Dec 16 1933 Sex:M Child# 1 Huntington Wells Westford, MA & Lydia Goodwin Pelham, NH
WELLS, Carolyn Louise, Aug 12 1932 Sex:F Child# 2 Harry W Wells Nashua, NH & P E Batchelder Haverhill, MA
WELLS, David Lincoln, Aug 17 1927 Sex:M Child# 1 H W Wells Nashua, NH & Pearl Batchelder Haverhill, MA
WELLS, Esther I, Sep 6 1905 Sex:F Child# 3 George L Wells New York & N M Butler Hudson, NH
WELLS, Flora, Sep 30 1902 Sex:F Child#  Gordon Wells Plymouth & Mary Ash Boston, MA
WELLS, Francis Leo, Jul 24 1896 Sex:M Child# 2 George E Wells Grafton, NY & Mary A O'Connell Ireland
WELLS, Fred Richardson, Feb 23 1897 Sex:M Child# 5 Gordon Wells Plymouth & Mary Ash Boston, MA
WELLS, George E, Nov 9 1892 Sex:M Child#  George E Wells Ireland & Mary A Cornell NH
WELLS, Harry W, Apr 16 1896 Sex:M Child# 2 George L Wells NY & N M Butler Hudson, NH
WELLS, Henry William, Jun 14 1904 Sex:M Child# 5 George E Wells New Jersey & M A Connell Ireland
WELLS, Herman E B, Aug 20 1901 Sex:M Child# 1 Edwin C Wells Maine & Bessie Delaney Canada
WELLS, James Edward, Jul 18 1900 Sex:M Child# 8 William H Wells Nashua, NH & Mary Harrington Ireland
WELLS, Joseph Pearl, Aug 9 1899 Sex:M Child# 3 George E Wells NJ & Mary Ann O'Connor Ireland
WELLS, Mary Anne, Jun 21 1893 Sex:F Child# 1 William H Wells Nashua, NH & Mary A Harrington Nashua, NH
WELLS, Ruth L, Jan 26 1895 Sex:F Child# 1 G L Wells New York & N M Butler Hudson, NH
WELLS, Sydney P, May 11 1923 Sex:M Child# 2 Arthur Wells Hudson, NH & Mildred Patterson Wardsboro, VT
WELLS, Unknown, Sep 19 1888 Sex:M Child# 1 Gorden Wells Plymouth & Mary A Ash Boston

WELLS, Unknown, Apr 26 1889 Sex:M Child# 13 Frank Wells E Cambridge & Annie Brady Jersey City Stillborn
WELLS, Unknown, Nov 12 1889 Sex: Child# 2 Gordon Wells Plymouth & Mary Ash Boston, MA
WELLS, Unknown, Nov 15 1889 Sex:M Child# 1 Joseph E Wells NH & Ada A NH
WELLS, Unknown, Oct 25 1894 Sex:M Child# 3 Gordon Wells Plymouth, NH & Mary Ash Boston, MA
WELLS, Unknown, Dec 6 1900 Sex:M Child# 4 George E Wells NH & Mary A O'Connor Ireland
WELLS, Unknown, Dec 14 1923 Sex:F Child# 2 Leo Wells Nashua, NH & Hazel Cote Nashua, NH
WELLS, Virginia Elizabeth, Nov 14 1921 Sex:F Child# 1 Arthur Wells Hudson, NH & Mildred I Patterson Wardsboro,
WELLS, William Davis, Jun 21 1893 Sex:M Child# 2 William H Wells Nashua, NH & Mary A Harrington Nashua, NH
WELSH, William Henry, Jun 21 1894 Sex:M Child# 4 William Welsh Ireland & Mary E McBride Ireland
WELTON, Evelyn, Dec 19 1919 Sex:F Child# 8 Henry A Welton Boston, MA & Louisa R Weston Nashua, NH
WELTON, George, Dec 11 1893 Sex:M Child# 2 Dennis M Welton Lowell, MA & Mary A Gilhooley Ireland
WELTON, James Leo, Feb 12 1898 Sex:M Child# 4 Dennis Welton Lowell, MA & Mary Gilhooly Ireland
WELTON, Mary Ann, Jun 20 1921 Sex:F Child# 8 Henry Welton Boston, MA & Louisa Weston Nashua, NH
WENCIUS, John, Apr 27 1908 Sex:M Child# 1 Joseph Wencius Russia & Annick Barthiawich Russia Stillborn
WENCIUS, Mary, Apr 27 1908 Sex:F Child# 2 Joseph Wencius Russia & Annick Barthiawich Russia
WENCIUS, Mary, Aug 1 1909 Sex:F Child# 2 Joseph Wencius Russia & Nellie Parlkewich Russia
WENSLAW, Unknown, Feb 25 1895 Sex:F Child# 1 Ovid F Wenslaw Ascot, PQ & Flora Cummings Nashua, NH
WENTWORTH, Gertrude May, Nov 2 1922 Sex:F Child# 3 Shir A Wentworth Jackson, NH & Persis F Cleveland Hyde Park, MA
WENTWORTH, June Silvia, Nov 30 1917 Sex:F Child# 1 Lawrence Wentworth Remford, ME & Esther Perkins W Kennebunk, ME
WENTWORTH, Laurence Arnold, Jr, Dec 10 1919 Sex:M Child# 2 Laurence Wentworth Rumford, ME & Esther M Perkins ME
WENTWORTH, Norma Wright, Mar 13 1927 Sex:M Child# 1 E Wentworth Hollis, NH & Gladys Wright Hartford, CT
WENTWORTH, Norman Arthur, May 25 1903 Sex:M Child# 2 A G Wentworth Worcester, MA & Blanche G Horne Wakefield, MA
WERSOWISH, Felina, Feb 7 1921 Sex:F Child# 2 Andrew Wersowish Poland Russia & Julia Oleclmo Poland Russia
WESSELL, Charles, Apr 25 1909 Sex:M Child# 1 Charles Wessell New York, NY & Bertha Wendell Somerville, MA
WESSON, Dexter, Aug 8 1914 Sex:M Child# 1 Harold L Wesson Nashua, NH & Sylvina Wells Adams, MA
WESSON, Donald Adams, Oct 7 1922 Sex:M Child# 4 Ernest W Wesson Nashua, NH & Katherine Murtaugh Nashua, NH
WESSON, Earle F, Jun 4 1911 Sex:M Child# 1 Ernest F Wesson Nashua, NH & Kate Mutangle Nashua, NH
WESSON, Ray Ernest, Dec 12 1913 Sex:M Child# 2 Ernest F Wesson Nashua, NH & Kate Murtaugh Nashua, NH
WESSON, Richard James, May 27 1920 Sex:M Child# 3 Ernest F Wesson Nashua, NH & Catherine Murtaugh Nashua, NH
WEST, Frederick Leo, Jr, Apr 3 1926 Sex:M Child# 1 Frederick West Mass & Alice Sughrue Nashua, NH
WEST, Robert Sughrue, Apr 17 1930 Sex:M Child# 3 Frederick West Pepperell, MA & Alice Sughrue Nashua, NH
WEST, Unknown, Feb 28 1887 Sex:M Child# 1 Joseph L West New York, NY & Theodat N S
WEST, Unknown, May 22 1890 Sex:F Child# 2 Joseph L West Nashua, NH & Theodake Haliday NS
WEST, Unknown, Jan 18 1929 Sex:F Child# 2 Leo West Nashua, NH & Alice Sughrue Nashua, NH
WESTERHOFF, John Lambert, Jr, Jun 2 1928 Sex:M Child# 4 J L Westerhoff Emden, Germany & Lila Takles Malden, MA
WESTERHOFF, Phillis Lorraine, Mar 3 1924 Sex:F Child# 3 J L Westerhoff Germany & Lila Takles Malden, MA
WESTERN, George Lee, May 13 1898 Sex:M Child# John H Western Nashua, NH & Elsie L Howard Winchendon, MA
WESTMARTNI, Patrick, Jan 10 1911 Sex:M Child# 2 Thomas Westmartni Nova Scotia & Mary Plummer E Boston, MA
WESTON, Andrew Norman, Sep 1 1926 Sex:M Child# 5 William H Weston Windsor, VT & Jennie M Boyd Stamford, CT
WESTON, Carol Ann, Apr 16 1935 Sex:F Child# 2 Eugene Weston Waterville, MA & Irene B Ethier Winchendon, MA
WESTON, Martha Elizabeth, Apr 8 1925 Sex:F Child# 4 William H Weston Windsor, VT & Jennie M Boyd Stamford, CT
WESTON, Natalie Ann, Sep 19 1930 Sex:F Child# 5 Richard Wm Weston Amherst, NH & Sevie Towne Wilton, NH
WESTON, Nellie, Feb 25 1890 Sex:F Child# 5 Edward E Weston Nashua, NH & Christiana Woodward Lyndeboro, NH
WESTON, Paul Alfred, Jun 17 1932 Sex:M Child# 1 Raymond Weston Fitzwilliam, NH & Cora Raymond Merrimack, NH
WESTON, Roberta Ellen, Sep 26 1927 Sex:F Child# 4 R W Weston Amherst, NH & Cevie Towne Wilton, NH
WESTON, Ruth Eleanora, Jan 9 1909 Sex:F Child# 2 Valentine B Weston Waterville, VT & Nellie Dufeney Berkshire
WESTON, Unknown, Nov 11 1891 Sex:F Child# 1 Edwin G Weston Winchendon, MA & Sadie McKean Nashua, NH
WESTON, William Boyd, Sep 17 1920 Sex:M Child# 3 William H Weston Vermont & Jennie M Boyd Stamford, CT
WETHERBEE, Unknown, Apr 10 1932 Sex:M Child# 1 H K Wetherbee Lakeport, NH & Elva M Clements Watertown, MA
WETMORE, Myrtle Pearl, May 12 1907 Sex:F Child# 1 Louis Wetmore Nova Scotia & Myrtle O'Neil Salem, MA
WETMORE, Robert Allen, Jul 22 1922 Sex:M Child# 2 Albert C Wetmore New Brunswick & Mary Ellen Colburn Hollis, NH
WETMORE, Ruth Ellen, Jan 30 1921 Sex:F Child# 1 Albert E Wetmore New Brunswick & Mary E Colburn Hollis, NH
WETMORE, Stanley Gordon, May 23 1908 Sex:M Child# 2 Louis Wetmore New Brunswick & Myrtle O'Neil Salem, MA
WEYMOUTH, Alice Heath, Mar 26 1912 Sex:F Child# 3 Russell E Weymouth China, ME & Delia E Heath Hallowell, ME
WEYMOUTH, Charles William, Feb 18 1929 Sex:M Child# 1 Charles Wm Weymouth Augusta, ME & Rachael Smith Stoddard, NH
WEYMOUTH, Delia Alta, Nov 7 1933 Sex:F Child# 2 C W Weymouth Augusta, ME & Rachel Smith Stoddard, NH
WEYMOUTH, Herbert MacWhinnie, Dec 15 1913 Sex:M Child# 4 Russell E Weymouth China, ME & Delia Heath Hallowell, ME
WEYMOUTH, Julia Mary, Jul 16 1916 Sex:F Child# 5 Russell E Weymouth China, ME & Delia Ethel Heath Hallowell, ME
WEYMOUTH, Russel Eaton, Aug 2 1918 Sex:M Child# 6 Russel E Weymouth China, ME & Delia Heath Hallowell, ME
WEZBICKI, Helen, Sep 23 1925 Sex:F Child# 4 Adolf Wezbicki Poland & Mary Volanin Poland
WHALEY, Donald, Jun 26 1923 Sex:M Child# 9 Ernest Whaley Nashua, NH & Agnes Mahoney Dorchester, MA
WHEELER, Burton McNeil, Mar 22 1913 Sex:M Child# 5 Jerrie W Wheeler Nashua, NH & Elizabeth MacNeil St Johns, NB
WHEELER, Calvin Dana, Jul 22 1918 Sex:M Child# 1 Harold Lee Wheeler Nashua, NH & Mar D MacPherson Concord, NH
WHEELER, Carolyn Mae, Jan 27 1932 Sex:F Child# 3 Orin Wheeler Milford, NH & Evelyn McEwen Dixville, Quebec
WHEELER, Charles McEwen, Apr 6 1930 Sex:M Child# 2 Oran A Wheeler Milford, NH & Evelyn McEwen Canada
WHEELER, Clifton M, Aug 29 1904 Sex:M Child# 2 Jerry W Wheeler Nashua, NH & Elizabeth MacNeil St John, NB
WHEELER, Clinton Erwin, Jul 1 1910 Sex:M Child# 2 Walter E Wheeler Hooksett, NH & Mabel E Connor Manchester, NH
WHEELER, Donna Myrle, Dec 30 1934 Sex:F Child# 1 Ernest Fred Wheeler Nashua, NH & Dorothea Cummings Saugus, MA
WHEELER, Edward Franklin, Mar 21 1906 Sex:M Child# 3 Charles E Wheeler Stowe, MA & Nettie A Wheeler Hollis, NH
WHEELER, Ernest, Oct 31 1906 Sex:M Child# 6 Courtland Wheeler Islelamotte, VT & Olive A Swinerton Somersworth, NH
WHEELER, Ernest R, Jun 5 1890 Sex:M Child# 8 J Frank Wheeler Gardner, MA & Mary E Kimball Wilton, NH
WHEELER, Evelyn Viola, Aug 25 1904 Sex:F Child# 2 Charles E Wheeler Stowe, MA & Nettie A Wheeler Hollis, NH
WHEELER, Floyd, Aug 4 1908 Sex:M Child# 7 Courtland Wheeler Alberg, VT & Olive Sivimington Somersworth, NH

WHEELER, George E, Aug 2 1900 Sex:M Child#  E J Wheeler NH & Beatrice Crusoe NH
WHEELER, Gussey, May 10 1892 Sex:F Child# 2 Charles Wheeler Loudon & May Rochester
WHEELER, Harold L, Mar 5 1889 Sex:M Child# 3 Calvin P Wheeler Nashua, NH & Laura M Clement Nashua, NH
WHEELER, Hazel, Sep 20 1904 Sex:F Child# 5 Courtland Wheeler Isle LaMotte & Oline A Swinerton Somersworth, NH
WHEELER, Jessie R, Jan 15 1887 Sex:F Child# 2 Calvin P Wheeler Nashua, NH & Lura Clement Nashua, NH
WHEELER, John Richard, Jul 23 1924 Sex:M Child# 8 Norman Wheeler Farmington, NH & Ethel Smith Nashua, NH
WHEELER, Laurice Gertrude, Dec 19 1914 Sex:F Child# 5 Charles E Wheeler Stowe, MA & Nettie Wheeler Hollis, NH
WHEELER, Lillian M, Dec 12 1890 Sex:F Child# 1 C A Wheeler Mass & L M Jandren Mass
WHEELER, Loraine, Jun 18 1909 Sex:F Child# 4 Jerrie W Wheeler Nashua, NH & Elizabeth MacNeil St John, NB
WHEELER, Lucy Ann, May 16 1902 Sex:F Child# 3 George Wheeler Nashua, NH &  Lynn, MA
WHEELER, Margaret Elinor, Oct 7 1933 Sex:F Child# 4 Oren Wheeler Milford, NH & Evelyn McEwen Barreford, Quebec
WHEELER, Margery Elizabeth, Jan 30 1919 Sex:F Child# 4 Norman E Wheeler Farmington, NH & Ethel Smith Nashua, NH
WHEELER, Marjorie E, Aug 24 1917 Sex:F Child# 2 Milton E Wheeler Lawrence, MA & Elmina F Leavitt Fitchburg, MA
WHEELER, Mary M, May 12 1915 Sex:F Child# 2 Norman C Wheeler Farmington, NH & Ethel M Smith Nashua, NH Stillborn
WHEELER, Mildred, Mar 9 1904 Sex:F Child# 1 Jefferson M Wheeler Hollis, NH & Hattie Tracy Amity, ME
WHEELER, Mildred Mary, Feb 20 1920 Sex:F Child# 4 Norman C Wheeler Farmington, NH & Ethe Smith Nashua, NH
WHEELER, Murry Star, Jul 25 1909 Sex:M Child# 1 Frank W Wheeler Hollis, NH & Clara E Wheeler Hollis, NH
WHEELER, Nathalie E, Nov 8 1902 Sex:F Child# 1 Jerry W Wheeler New Brunswick & Elizabeth McNeill New Brunswick
WHEELER, Norman Kirkland, Nov 4 1921 Sex:M Child# 7 Norman K Wheeler Farmington, NH & Ethel M Smith Nashua, NH
WHEELER, Oline Annie, May 14 1911 Sex:F Child# 8 Courtland Wheeler Alburg, VT & Oline A Swinerton Somersworth, NH
WHEELER, Oren Shelden, Nov 19 1928 Sex:M Child# 1 Oren A Wheeler Milford, NH & Evelyn McEwen Canada
WHEELER, Paul, May 31 1915 Sex:M Child# 9 Cutland Wheeler Alburg, VT & Olive Swinerton Somersworth, NH
WHEELER, Paul Norman, Jun 2 1914 Sex:M Child# 1 Norman Wheeler Farmington, NH & Ethel Smith Nashua, NH Stillborn
WHEELER, Raymond Milton, Mar 30 1916 Sex:M Child# 1 Milton E Wheeler Lawrence, MA & Elmina F Leavitt Fitchburg, MA
WHEELER, Raymond P, Jun 4 1916 Sex:M Child# 3 Norman C Wheeler Farmington, NH & Ethel M Smith Nashua, NH
WHEELER, Reginald Milton, Jul 23 1907 Sex:M Child# 2 Jefferson Wheeler Hollis, NH & Hattie Tracy Amity, ME
WHEELER, Unknown, Nov 2 1889 Sex:F Child# 2 Curtice Wheeler Isle Mott, VT & Agatha Reed Isle Mott, VT
WHEELER, Unknown, Jun 8 1891 Sex:M Child# 3 Curtis Wheeler Islamont, VT & Agatha Reed Islamont, VT
WHEELER, Unknown, Jun 6 1892 Sex:M Child# 1 Nelson A Wheeler Mass & Effie Sleeper Mass
WHEELER, Unknown, Feb 4 1895 Sex:F Child# 1 Arthur A Wheeler Nashua, NH & Kate McKay Pembroke, ME
WHEELER, Unknown, Sep 30 1895 Sex:F Child# 3 George A Wheeler Nashua, NH & Edith M Taylor Lynn, MA
WHEELER, Unknown, Feb 28 1901 Sex:M Child# 4 George A Wheeler Nashua, NH & Edith M Taylor Lynn, MA
WHEELER, Unknown, Mar 31 1903 Sex:M Child# 2 Elmer J Wheeler Hooksett, NH & Beatrice Cruson Hollis, NH
WHEELER, Unknown, Sep 6 1905 Sex:F Child# 1 Sylvester Wheeler Vernon, VT & Edna C Butler Hinsdale, NH Stillborn
WHEELER, Unknown, Jun 25 1907 Sex:F Child# 3 Jerry Wheeler Nashua, NH & Elizabeth McNeil New Brunswick
WHEELER, Unknown, Feb 7 1909 Sex:M Child# 3 Jefferson M Wheeler Hollis, NH & Hattie P Tracy Amity, ME
WHEELER, Unknown, Jan 23 1911 Sex:M Child# 3 Charles F Wheeler Stowe, MA & Nettie A Wheeler Hollis, NH
WHEELER, Unknown, Feb 11 1921 Sex:M Child# 11 Albert F Wheeler E Jaffrey, NH & Imogene Perry Dublin, NH
WHEELER, Vida Ellen, Apr 1 1893 Sex:F Child# 4 Curtis Wheeler Isle La Motte, VT & Agatha Reed Isle La Motte, VT
WHEELER, Walter E, Dec 19 1907 Sex:M Child# 1 Walter E Wheeler
WHEELER, Wilfred, Dec 8 1934 Sex:M Child# 1 (No Parents Listed)
WHELTON, Barbara Ann, Aug 18 1933 Sex:F Child# 5 G B Whelton Nashua, NH & Eileene Flanagan Lowell, MA
WHELTON, George Bernard, Sep 16 1929 Sex:M Child# 3 Geo B Whelton Nashua, NH & Eileen Flanagan Lowell, MA
WHELTON, Joseph, Oct 11 1931 Sex:M Child# 4 George B Whelton Nashua, NH & Eileen Flanagan Lowell, MA
WHELTON, Kathaleen, Jul 4 1926 Sex:F Child# 2 George Whelton Nashua, NH & Eileen Flanagan Lowell, MA
WHIDDEN, Duane Alberto, Jul 21 1910 Sex:M Child# 1 Frank A Whidden Auburn, NH & Birdie Rhodes Nashua, NH
WHIDDEN, Glenn Howard, Mar 27 1928 Sex:M Child# 2 M H Whidden Nashua, NH & Hazel Harwood Nashua, NH
WHIDDEN, Hazel Belle, Mar 15 1897 Sex:F Child# 3 Frank A Whidden Nashua, NH & Hattie Ward Maine
WHIDDEN, Muriel Loraine, Nov 12 1911 Sex:F Child# 2 Frank A Whidden Auburn, NH & Birdie Rhodes Nashua, NH
WHIDDEN, Norris H, Aug 23 1894 Sex:M Child# 1 Frank Whidden NH & Hattie Ward US
WHIDDEN, Phyllis Elaine, Sep 4 1920 Sex:F Child# 1 Maurice H Whidden Nashua, NH & Hazel Harwood Nashua, NH
WHIDDEN, Unknown, Mar 12 1896 Sex:M Child# 2 Frank Whidden Nashua, NH & Hattie Ward Maine Stillborn
WHIPPLE, Daniel Bickford, Aug 7 1895 Sex:M Child# 4 Henry J Whipple Canada & C M White N Andover, MA
WHIPPLE, Donald, Sep 14 1934 Sex:M Child# 3 Winthrop Whipple Burlington, VT & Simonne Lemieux Nashua, NH
WHIPPLE, Martha, Mar 22 1915 Sex:F Child# 3 Walter Whipple Salem, MA & Alice L Reeves Salem, MA
WHIPPLE, Stephen Walter, Sep 19 1930 Sex:M Child# 1 Wintrhop Whipple Burlington, VT & Simonne Lemieux Nashua, NH
WHIPPLE, Winthrop, Nov 1 1931 Sex:M Child# 2 Winthrop Whipple Burlington, VT & Simonne Lemieux Nashua, NH
WHIRTWART, Stanislav, Aug 12 1910 Sex:M Child# 3 Alvin Whirtwart Austria & Fannie Sebuck Austria
WHITCOMB, Eddie Ward, Mar 12 1928 Sex:M Child# 3 H J Whitcomb Brookline, NH & Jane Ward Canada
WHITCOMB, Edward, Jun 24 1892 Sex:M Child# 3 Edward Whitcomb Brattleboro, VT & Carrie White River Jct, VT
WHITCOMB, Evelyn Jane, Feb 16 1927 Sex:F Child# 2 Harlan Whitcomb Brookline, NH & Jane Ward Canada
WHITE, Barbara Ann, May 2 1932 Sex:F Child# 1 Francis White Lowell, MA & Esther Halmon Lowell, MA
WHITE, Benjamin, Jun 24 1905 Sex:M Child# 3 Samuel H White S Boston, MA & Bessie E Brown Raymond, NH
WHITE, Brooks Spaulding, Apr 12 1922 Sex:M Child# 1 Alpheus B White Peterboro, NH & Charlotte Spaulding Peterboro
WHITE, Carroll Butler, Dec 4 1895 Sex:M Child#  Charles W White Wilton, NH & Lu Abbie Butler Greenfield, NH
WHITE, Carroll David, Jun 28 1917 Sex:M Child# 1 Charles David White Antrim, NH & Carolyn May Myers Nashua, NH
WHITE, Carroll Wiley, Feb 23 1931 Sex:M Child# 1 Carroll Butler White Nashua, NH & Ferne Wiley Nashua, NH
WHITE, Catherine Anna, Feb 8 1921 Sex:F Child# 1 William R White Amherst, NH & Anna M McGillicuddy S Boston, MA
WHITE, Charles, Feb 8 1934 Sex:M Child# 5 William White Boston, MA & Elsie Austin Swanton, VT
WHITE, Clarence Henry, May 8 1911 Sex:M Child# 1 Clarence Henry White Nova Scotia & Mary L Dehlman Nashua, NH
WHITE, Clarissa Dodge, Sep 21 1898 Sex:F Child# 4 Charles L White Nashua, NH & Marguerite D Dodge Hampton Falls
WHITE, Doris Isabel, May 6 1911 Sex:F Child# 6 Samuel White S Boston, MA & Bessie Brown Raymond, NH
WHITE, Edward Joseph, May 18 1921 Sex:M Child#  Edward White Baltimore, MD & Grace McLean Presque Isle, ME

WHITE, Ellsworth Morse, Aug 21 1914 Sex:M Child# 2 John M White Southville, NS & Lillie M Doucette Tidvill, NS
WHITE, Irving C, Apr 30 1894 Sex:M Child# 2 Obed J White Missouri & Cora J Jenning NJ
WHITE, John Humphrey, Dec 20 1892 Sex:M Child# 2 John P White Ireland & Catherine Shea Ireland
WHITE, John Thomas, Jul 3 1896 Sex:M Child# 4 William J White New York & Mary A Corridy Nashua, NH
WHITE, John William, Jan 20 1892 Sex:M Child# 2 William J White New York, NY & Mary A Cassidy Worcester, MA
WHITE, Joseph P, Jan 29 1895 Sex:M Child# 3 John P White Ireland & Catherine Shea Ireland
WHITE, Katherine Dodge, Mar 15 1896 Sex:F Child# 3 Charles L White Nashua, NH & Margurette D Dodge Hampton Falls
WHITE, Leighton Edward, Nov 28 1909 Sex:M Child# 2 Edward T White Weymouth, MA & Myrtie E Eaton Nashua, NH
WHITE, Lester, Oct 14 1897 Sex:M Child# 3 Charles W White Wilton, NH & Lu A Butler Greenfield, NH
WHITE, Lionel Norman, Apr 19 1932 Sex:M Child# 1 Leo White Meredith, NH & Irma LaRochelle Somersworth, NH
WHITE, Mary, Jul 28 1890 Sex:F Child# 1 John P White Ireland & Catherine Shea Ireland
WHITE, Mary Weston, Nov 17 1894 Sex:F Child# 1 Charles W White Wilton, NH & Lu A Butler Greenfield, NH
WHITE, Norman Dexter, Sep 16 1933 Sex:M Child# 3 Carroll White Nashua, NH & Ferne Wiley Nashua, NH
WHITE, Phyllis Irene, Dec 26 1930 Sex:F Child# 3 Webster W White Jonesport, ME & Lottie Pace Pontiac, RI
WHITE, Russell, May 21 1890 Sex:M Child# 1 Obed J White Palmyra, MO & Cora Jersey City, NJ
WHITE, Sadie C, Jun 7 1892 Sex:F Child# 1 John C White Keene & Henrietta Marlow
WHITE, Samuel Woodrow, Mar 30 1914 Sex:M Child# 6 Samuel H White S Boston, MA & Bessie E Brown Raymond, NH
WHITE, Thomas, Sep 10 1898 Sex:M Child# 5 William White New York, NY & Mary A Cassidy Worcester, MA
WHITE, Thomas Francis, May 7 1912 Sex:M Child# 1 Thomas F White Nashua, NH & Anna Gallagher Worcester, MA
WHITE, Unknown, May 22 1888 Sex:M Child# 2 William White Scotland & Celina White Westford, MA
WHITE, Unknown, Apr 14 1890 Sex:M Child# 1 Charles H White Lyndeboro, NH & Clara Emerson Londonderry, NH
WHITE, Unknown, Nov 15 1894 Sex:M Child# 5 William J White New York, NY & Mary A Cassidy Worcester, MA
WHITE, Unknown, Nov 22 1906 Sex:F Child# 4 Samuel H White S Boston, MA & Bessie E Brown Raymond, NH
WHITE, Unknown, Aug 9 1909 Sex:F Child# 5 Samuel H White S Boston, MA & Bessie E Brown Raymond, NH
WHITE, Unknown, Jul 7 1910 Sex:M Child#  J M White
WHITE, Unknown, Dec 12 1933 Sex:F Child# 2 Fred White Mineville, NY & Laura Paul Francestown, NH Stillborn
WHITE, Vera M, May 25 1906 Sex:F Child# 1 Edward T White Weymouth & Myrtie Eaton Nashua, NH
WHITEHOUSE, Marie Alma, Aug 20 1921 Sex:F Child# 1 Merrill Whitehouse Rochester, NH & Eva Furnell Rochester, NH
WHITELY, Kenneth William, Dec 15 1935 Sex:M Child# 1 Kenneth Whitely Haverhill, MA & Gertrude Maney Nashua, NH
WHITMAN, George Warren, Aug 11 1898 Sex:M Child# 1 Fred E Whitman Nova Scotia & Gertrude F Gilson Marlboro
WHITMAN, Pauline Almeda, Dec 8 1931 Sex:F Child# 4 Keith Whitman Nova Scotia & Alice Benjamin Auburn, ME
WHITNEY, Alfred, Jan 22 1899 Sex:M Child# 2 Charles H Whitney Nashua, NH & Zepherine Plante Canada
WHITNEY, Clarence Eugene, Dec 30 1893 Sex:M Child# 1 Eugene P Whitney Nashua, NH & Myra B White Nashua, NH
WHITNEY, Doris Elizabeth, Jul 15 1905 Sex:F Child# 3 Eugene P Whitney Nashua, NH & Myra B White Nashua, NH
WHITNEY, Dorothy Allura, Aug 14 1897 Sex:F Child# 1 J Odell Whitney Salem, ME & Harriett Ingham Bristol, England
WHITNEY, Earle Leonard, May 11 1928 Sex:M Child# 5 Earle H Whitney Lancaster, NH & Cora E Flanders Warren, NH
WHITNEY, Elvira, Feb 16 1908 Sex:F Child# 1 Darrold Whitney Vermont & Lucy Lombard Vermont
WHITNEY, Everett Anderson, Apr 10 1906 Sex:M Child# 1 William E Whitney Nashua, NH & Anna Anderson Sweden
WHITNEY, Fannie Katharine, Mar 10 1890 Sex:F Child# 2 Charles H Whitney Nashua, NH & Annie Fisher Nashua, NH
WHITNEY, Glen Earl, Apr 19 1926 Sex:M Child# 4 Earl Whitney NH & Cora Flanders NH
WHITNEY, Gloria Marie, Jul 29 1932 Sex:F Child# 5 E W Whitney Vermont & Edith Burnham Milford, NH
WHITNEY, Henry, Jun 12 1888 Sex:M Child# 1 Charles H Whitney Nashua, NH & Annie F Fisher Nashua, NH
WHITNEY, James M, Jun 1 1899 Sex:M Child# 2 James F Whitney Nashua, NH & Anna Marshall Nashua, NH
WHITNEY, John Henry, Jan 13 1908 Sex:M Child# 2 Pearl E Whitney Mass & Elfreda Erenst Nova Scotia
WHITNEY, June Elaine, Jun 21 1927 Sex:F Child# 3 Edgar Whitney Vermont & Edith Burnham Milford, NH
WHITNEY, Lelwellyn Burton, Jan 27 1930 Sex:M Child# 6 Earl Whitney Lancaster, NH & Cora Flanders Warren, NH
WHITNEY, Marilyn Patricia, Mar 3 1932 Sex:F Child# 7 Earl Whitney Lancaster, NH & Cora Ellen Warren, NH
WHITNEY, Marshall, Jul 9 1904 Sex:M Child# 3 James F Whitney Nashua, NH & Anna Marshall Nashua, NH
WHITNEY, Mary Electa, Feb 26 1930 Sex:F Child# 4 Edgar W Whitney Westford, VT & Edith Burnham Milford, NH
WHITNEY, Norma Edith, Feb 18 1925 Sex:F Child# 3 Edward Whitney Westford, VT & Edith Burnham Milford, NH
WHITNEY, Philip Russell, Jul 7 1897 Sex:M Child# 2 Eugene P Whitney Nashua, NH & Myra B White Nashua, NH
WHITNEY, Phillip Richard, Mar 18 1933 Sex:M Child# 8 Earl Whitney NH & Cora Flanders NH
WHITNEY, Ralph Elbert, May 6 1908 Sex:M Child# 4 Ira L Whitney Vermont & Edna Burdick Vermont
WHITNEY, Richard Duane, Aug 10 1933 Sex:M Child# 2 S J Whitney Hillsboro, NH & Eva Durant Litchfield, NH
WHITNEY, Sandra Ann, Mar 1 1934 Sex:F Child# 1 Everett Whitney Nashua, NH & Louise Wingate E Framingham, MA
WHITNEY, Unknown, Jul 31 1891 Sex:M Child# 1 Samuel Whitney Salem, ME & Carrie A Hardy Lempster
WHITNEY, Unknown, Dec 19 1895 Sex:F Child# 1 James F Whitney Nashua, NH & Anna M Marshall Nashua, NH
WHITNEY, Unknown, Oct 2 1898 Sex:M Child# 2 J Odell Whitney Salem, ME & Harriette Ingham England
WHITNEY, Ward Parker, Sep 30 1906 Sex:M Child# 4 James F Whitney Nashua, NH & Anna Marshall Nashua, NH
WHITTEMORE, Alice Madeline, Jan 6 1899 Sex:F Child# 6 Fred Whittemore Nashua, NH & Alice E Gay Pepperell, MA
WHITTEMORE, Barbara Avis, May 22 1926 Sex:F Child# 8 Charles Whittemore Nashua, NH & Margaret Bowen Manitoba
WHITTEMORE, Betty Ann, Mar 6 1929 Sex:F Child# 3 George Whittemore Cuba & Jessie Green Nashua, NH
WHITTEMORE, Charles Reginald, Mar 27 1914 Sex:M Child# 5 Charles P Whittemore Nashua, NH & Margaret Bowen Manitoba
WHITTEMORE, Chester Moses, Jul 19 1907 Sex:M Child# 4 Charles Whittemore Nashua, NH & Margaret Bowen Manitoba
WHITTEMORE, Elizabeth, Feb 15 1909 Sex:F Child# 1 Edward S Whittemore Nashua, NH & Emma C Reutlinge Philadelphia
WHITTEMORE, Fannie Elizabeth, Aug 10 1901 Sex:F Child# 2 Charles Whittemore Nashua, NH & Margaret Bowen Manitoba
WHITTEMORE, Franklin Henry, Feb 10 1899 Sex:M Child# 1 Charles P Whittemore Nashua, NH & Margaret C Bowen Manitoba
WHITTEMORE, Fred Leon, Oct 31 1890 Sex:M Child# 4 Fred Whittemore Nashua, NH & Alice E Gay Pepperell, MA
WHITTEMORE, George Edward, Aug 29 1926 Sex:M Child# 1 G Whittemore Cuba & Jessie Green Nashua, NH
WHITTEMORE, Hazel Thelma, Aug 30 1910 Sex:F Child# 4 Leory Whittemore Mass & Eva Rideout NH
WHITTEMORE, Lenore Joyce, Jan 12 1934 Sex:F Child# 5 George Whittemore Garden City, Cuba & Jessie Green Nashua, NH
WHITTEMORE, Richard, Nov 18 1889 Sex:M Child# 3 Fred Whittemore Nashua, NH & Alice E Gay Pepperell, MA
WHITTEMORE, Roy Lionel, Feb 4 1919 Sex:M Child# 7 Charles Whittemore Nashua, NH & Marguerite Bowen Brandon, MA

WHITTEMORE, Ruth Marian, Sep 28 1913 Sex:F Child# 3 Edward Whittemore Nashua, NH & Emma C Reutlinger Philadelphia
WHITTEMORE, Unknown, Oct 20 1887 Sex:M Child# 2 Fred Whittemore Nashua, NH & Alice Gay Pepperell, MA
WHITTEMORE, Unknown, Mar 17 1892 Sex:F Child# 1 Chas P Whittemore Nashua, NH & Lucinda Bowen Nova Scotia
WHITTEMORE, Wesley Arthur, Oct 18 1916 Sex:M Child# 6 Charles Whittemore Nashua, NH & Margaret Bowen Manitoba
WHITTEN, Barbara Christine, Jan 12 1925 Sex:F Child# 1 Chester Whitten Vermont & Mabel Thompson Wilton, NH
WHITTEN, Jay Robert, Dec 1 1929 Sex:M Child# 2 Harold Whitten Chester, VT & Lillian Champagne Greenville, NH
WHITTEN, June Marie, May 20 1928 Sex:F Child# 1 Harold Whitten Chester, VT & Lillian Champagne Greenville, NH
WHITTEN, Shirley Ellen, May 2 1930 Sex:F Child# 1 Clarence E Whitten Nashua, NH & Estella I Read Milford, NH
WHITTLE, Dick, Aug 8 1889 Sex:M Child# 2 Henry F Whittle Nashua, NH & Josie H Hall Nashua, NH
WHITTLE, Donna A, Feb 20 1896 Sex:F Child# 5 Harry Whittle Nashua, NH & Josei H Hale Nashua, NH
WHITTLE, Ethel Hale, Apr 25 1887 Sex:F Child# 1 Harry F Whittle Nashua, NH & Josie Hale Hollis, NH
WHITTLE, Frank Hale, Apr 19 1897 Sex:M Child# 6 Harry Whittle Nashua, NH & Josie Hale Hollis, NH
WHITTLE, Gertrude K, Mar 31 1894 Sex:F Child# 4 Harry F Whittle Nashua, NH & Josie H Hale Nashua, NH
WHITTLE, Lottie Olive, Dec 24 1903 Sex:F Child# 7 Harry F Whittle Nashua, NH & Jessie Hale Hollis, NH
WHITTLE, Scott Lovering, Jun 6 1892 Sex:M Child# 3 Harry F Whittle Nashua, NH & Josie H Hale Nashua, NH
WHITWORTH, Francis Thomas, Feb 9 1900 Sex:M Child# 2 Thomas Whitworth England & Mary Lefebvre England
WHITWORTH, Gertrude, Jan 10 1894 Sex:F Child# 1 Thomas Whitworth England & Mary Lefevre England
WHYTE, Esther Gertrude, Mar 29 1902 Sex:F Child# 7 William J Whyte New York, NY & Marie A Cassidy Worcester, MA
WIDENER, Cynthia Ann, Dec 29 1935 Sex:F Child# 1 Albert Widener Worcester, MA & Helena Baranowski Nashua, NH
WIECKIS, Monica, Mar 19 1913 Sex:F Child# 2 Leon Wieckis Russia & Monica Meganute Russia
WIECZKIS, Mary, Dec 13 1910 Sex:F Child# 1 Leon Wieczkis Russia & Monika Wieczkine Russia
WIECZKUTE, Julia, Nov 5 1915 Sex:F Child# 3 Leonos Wieczkute Russia & Monica Mizarute Russia
WIEZFFISKI, Henry, Nov 20 1915 Sex:M Child# 1 Adolf Wiezffiski Russia & Mary Wolanin Austria
WIGGIN, Gladys Henrietta, Mar 2 1918 Sex:F Child# 4 Charles Wiggin Medway, MA & May Elliott N Woburn, MA
WIGGIN, Norma Eleanor, Jul 23 1923 Sex:F Child# 3 Enod Wiggin Vermont & Rose Lintott Nashua, NH
WIGGIN, Paul Lintott, Jun 29 1915 Sex:M Child# 2 Ellon Wiggin Corinth, VT & Rose Lintott Nashua, NH
WIGGIN, Virginie Lucille, Jun 20 1914 Sex:F Child# 1 Ellon Wiggin Cornish, VT & Rose Luitoll Nashua, NH
WIGGINTON, Esther, Oct 10 1903 Sex:F Child# 1 W T Wigginton Medford, MA & Edith Belle Blood Nashua, NH
WIGGINTON, Unknown, Apr 7 1898 Sex:F Child# 1 George F Wigginton Taunton, MA & Ella M Coffin Martinez, CA
WILBUR, Blanche Eva, Sep 9 1924 Sex:F Child# 4 Percy Wilbur Mass & Eva Jameson NH
WILBUR, Marion Louise, Jun 29 1926 Sex:F Child# 4 Percy Wilbur Framingham, MA & Eva Jameson Hooksett, NH
WILCOTT, Esther Josephine, Jan 18 1891 Sex:F Child# 1 Charly Wilcott Marlboro, MA & Sophie Demers Coaticook
WILCOX, Alice Luella, Feb 14 1913 Sex:F Child# 6 Charles Wilcox Nashua, NH & Alice Earley Manchester, NH
WILCOX, Aurelia, Apr 19 1903 Sex:F Child# 1 Charles N Wilcox Manchester, NH & Alice E Earley Nashua, NH
WILCOX, Donald James, Aug 22 1925 Sex:M Child# 4 Raymond J Wilcox Nashua, NH & Irene Fifield Nashua, NH
WILCOX, Doris Mabel, Nov 7 1908 Sex:F Child# 2 George P Wilcox Westford, VT & Anna B Whitney Fletcher, VT
WILCOX, Eva A A, Jan 22 1892 Sex:F Child# 2 Charles Wilcox Marlboro, MA & Sophie Dumais Canada
WILCOX, Georgiana Pearl, Jul 4 1916 Sex:F Child# 3 George P Wilcox Westford, VT & Anna B Whitney Fletcher, VT
WILCOX, John Dennison, Mar 24 1905 Sex:M Child# 2 Charles N Wilcox Nashua, NH & Alice E Earley Manchester, NH
WILCOX, John Franklin, Jul 24 1932 Sex:M Child# 4 William Wilcox Nashua, NH & Dorothy Haskins Concord, MA
WILCOX, Lester George, Oct 20 1901 Sex:M Child# 1 George P Wilcox Westford, VT & Anna Whitney Fletcher, VT
WILCOX, Marilyn Kathryn, May 26 1929 Sex:F Child# 2 William Wilcox Nashua, NH & Dorothy Haskins Concord, MA
WILCOX, Marjorie Bernice, May 25 1930 Sex:F Child# 4 Raymond J Wilcox Nashua, NH & Irene Fifield Nashua, NH
WILCOX, Mildred Elizabeth, Aug 19 1927 Sex:F Child# 3 Raymond G Wilcox NH & Irene Fifield NH
WILCOX, Peter Charles, Sep 23 1933 Sex:M Child# 5 William J Wilcox Nashua, NH & Dorothy Haskins Concord, MA
WILCOX, Ruth, Jul 27 1911 Sex:F Child# 5 Charles N Wilcox Nashua, NH & Alice Earley Manchester, NH
WILCOX, Ruth Marguerite, Jan 26 1923 Sex:F Child# 1 Raymond G Wilcox Nashua, NH & Irene Fifield Nashua, NH
WILCOX, Unknown, Aug 21 1909 Sex:F Child# 4 Charles N Wilcox Nashua, NH & Alice Early Manchester, NH
WILCOX, William Joseph, Mar 8 1907 Sex:M Child# 3 Charles N Wilcox Nashua, NH & Alice E Earley Manchester, NH
WILCOX, William Joseph, Mar 30 1931 Sex:M Child# 3 William Wilcox Nashua, NH & Dorothy Haskins Concord, MA
WILDER, Alice Leona, Mar 8 1900 Sex:F Child# 3 W E Wilder Mass & Martha E Wyeth Mass
WILDES, Ann Mary, Jan 13 1928 Sex:F Child# 1 Lyman Wildes Mass & Eleanor Curtis Mass
WILDES, Barbara Louise, Nov 15 1913 Sex:F Child# 1 Kenneth N Wildes Melrose, MA & Mildred L Aldrich Melrose, MA
WILEJTO, Henry, Jan 4 1917 Sex:M Child# 1 Alexander Wilejto Russia & Genowefa Michomenis Russia
WILENKRIKENIE, Nellie, Apr 19 1919 Sex:F Child# 2 W Wilenkrikenie Russia & Benginac Russia
WILENS, Gerald Lionel, Oct 30 1910 Sex:M Child# 1 Joseph S Wilens Poland & Sarah A Winograd Poland
WILEY, Bernice Margritte, Dec 23 1893 Sex:F Child# 1 Archibald L Wiley Rouses Point, NY & Lena J Trull Greenwood
WILEY, George Lyndhurst, Nov 7 1896 Sex:M Child# 2 Archie L Wiley Rouses Point, NY & Gertrude L Trull Paris, ME
WILEY, John, Jun 19 1912 Sex:M Child# 6 Andro Wiley Hungary & Eva Konko Hungary
WILEY, Unknown, Mar 25 1891 Sex:F Child# 1 John H Wiley Fryeburg & Maud M Wright Richmond, PQ
WILEY, Unknown, Feb 19 1898 Sex:F Child# 1 George Henry Wiley Champlain, NY & Ida Rebecca Davis Nashua, NH
WILEY, Unknown, Aug 13 1898 Sex:F Child# 3 Archie L Wiley Rouses Pt, NY & Gertrude L Truell Paris, ME
WILFRID, Joseph H Palicarpe, Sep 12 1898 Sex:M Child# 3 Marquis Wilfrid Canada & Henrietta Gauthier Canada
WILKAITES, Jacqueline Antoinett, Jan 16 1934 Sex:F Child# 1 Anthony Wilkaites Nashua, NH & Lillian Rodier Nashua,NH
WILKANSKAS, Joseph, Oct 14 1917 Sex:M Child# 6 Ant Wilkanskas Lithuania Russia & Mary Wiliska Lithuania Russia
WILKAS, Mary, May 9 1913 Sex:F Child# 3 Adam Wilkas Russia & Mikaline Mareshuwich Russia
WILKASKA, Julionas, Oct 3 1919 Sex:M Child# 7 Anthony Wilkaska Canada & Eufemie Choinard Canada
WILKASKAS, John Anthony, Sep 20 1922 Sex:M Child# 9 Ant Wilkaskas Russia & Mary Walitska Russia
WILKIALIS, Amelia, Jun 16 1914 Sex:F Child# 5 Adam Wilkialis Russia & Mical Naruskevicz Russia
WILKIATES, Unknown, Apr 20 1919 Sex:F Child# 6 Adam Wilkiates Russia & Helena Naraskowich Russia
WILKINS, Alice J, Apr 22 1892 Sex:F Child# 3 E E Wilkins New Hampshire & Ruth E Martin Vermont
WILKINS, Charles, May 25 1900 Sex:M Child# 10 George R Wilkins NH & Mary Bowman Vermont
WILKINS, Chester, May 25 1900 Sex:M Child# 11 George R Wilkins NH & Mary Bowman Vermont

WILKINS, Edward George, Apr 5 1920 Sex:M Child# 2 Fred Wilkins Nashua, NH & Elma Boucher Nashua, NH
WILKINS, Elenor Agnes, Mar 26 1919 Sex:F Child# 1 Fred E Wilkins Nashua, NH & Alma E Boucher Nashua, NH
WILKINS, Fred J Ernest, Mar 31 1896 Sex:M Child# 7 George R Wilkins Milford, NH & Mary Bowman Bradbury, VT
WILKINS, George H D, May 12 1898 Sex:M Child# 8 George Wilkins Milford, NH & Mary E Bowman Brattleboro, VT
WILKINS, Gladys, May 30 1888 Sex:F Child# 1 E E Wilkins N H & R E Martin Vermont
WILKINS, Harold A Jr, Jul 29 1919 Sex:M Child# 1 Harold A Wilkins Townsend, MA & Frances A Little Boston, MA
WILKINS, Ina May, Oct 1 1910 Sex:F Child# 1 Ernest Wilkins Nashua, NH & Loula M Abbot Andover, MA
WILKINS, Inez May, Oct 29 1890 Sex:F Child# 5 George R Wilkins Milford, NH & Mary Peters Brattleboro, VT
WILKINS, Kathrine, Mar 5 1890 Sex:F Child# 2 George T Wilkins Bradford, NH & Jennie H Blaisdell Lowell, MA
WILKINS, Phyllis Frances, Dec 23 1930 Sex:F Child# 1 Clarence E Wilkins Mt Vernon, NH & Inez C Payne Canton
WILKINS, Ralph E, Oct 22 1890 Sex:M Child# 2 E E Wilkins New Hampshire & R E Martin Vermont
WILKINS, Rosie E, Aug 25 1890 Sex:F Child# 1 C S Wilkins Merrimack, NH & N H Bassford NY
WILKOUSKOS, William, Oct 21 1915 Sex:M Child# 5 Toney Wilkouskos Russia & Mary Velickute Russia
WILLARD, Chester Sanderson, Jan 28 1896 Sex:M Child# 7 Herbert E Willard Harvard, MA & Mary Sanderson Sterling, MA
WILLARD, Unknown, Mar 26 1895 Sex:M Child# 1 Frank E Willard Moriah, NY & Jane Campbell Keeseville, NY
WILLCOT, Roxana, Jan 27 1893 Sex:F Child# 3 Charles Willcot Marlboro, MA & Sophie Dumais Canada
WILLENS, Sumner Harold, Aug 9 1916 Sex:M Child# 2 Joseph Willens Russia & Sarah Winograd Russia
WILLERMET, David, Dec 16 1928 Sex:M Child# 1 P Willermet France & Catherine Beach Rockland, ME
WILLET, Francis T, Dec 23 1894 Sex:M Child# 5 Thomas Willet Canada & Phebe Gordon Canada
WILLET, Paul, Jan 16 1896 Sex:M Child# 7 Thomas Willet Canada & Phoeby Gordon Canada
WILLETT, Anna Geneva, Apr 6 1901 Sex:F Child# 6 John Willett Chazy, NY & Hattie Porter Chazy, NY
WILLETT, Anthony Alfred, Apr 16 1913 Sex:M Child# 4 Alfred Willett Canada & Breeda Mary Collins Warren, MA
WILLETT, Bertha Jane, Nov 13 1894 Sex:F Child# 5 John H Willett Chazy, NY & Hattie Portier Cottage, St Lawrence
WILLETT, Elizabeth Emily, Nov 3 1910 Sex:F Child# 1 Wilmer A Willett New York & Eva L Taylor Burlington, MA
WILLETT, Gertrude Ruth, Nov 12 1896 Sex:F Child# 6 John H Willett Sciota, NY & Hattie V Porter Chazy, NY
WILLETT, Melvin, Mar 12 1893 Sex:M Child# 4 John H Willett Chazy, NY & Hattie N Porter Chazy, NY
WILLETT, Unknown, Oct 5 1893 Sex:M Child# 5 Thomas Willett Canada & Phebe Gordon Canada Stillborn
WILLETT, Unknown, Oct 29 1900 Sex:M Child#   Edw Willett New York & L Duchesneau Nashua, NH
WILLETT, Wilmer Dexter, May 23 1913 Sex:M Child# 2 Wilmer Willett US & Eva Taylor US
WILLETTE, Alfred Ellis, Jun 18 1917 Sex:M Child# 4 Wilmer Willette New York & Eva Taylor Mass
WILLETTE, Alvin John, Dec 6 1923 Sex:M Child# 1 Alvin Willette NH & Jeanne Berube Canada
WILLETTE, Beatrice Marguerite, Jul 22 1931 Sex:F Child# 6 Chas O Willette Lewiston, ME & Frances Whittemore Nashua
WILLETTE, Charles Joseph, May 8 1921 Sex:M Child# 2 Charles O Willette Lewiston, ME & Frances E Whittemore Nashua
WILLETTE, Donald, Sep 20 1935 Sex:M Child# 2 Homer Willette Canada & Rose Gendron Nashua, NH
WILLETTE, Donald Clifton, Jan 14 1929 Sex:M Child# 5 Charles Willette Lewiston, ME & Frances Whittemore Nashua, NH
WILLETTE, Doris Gertrude, Aug 20 1920 Sex:F Child# 1 Melvin Willette Nashua, NH & Gladys Stone S Ashburnham, MA
WILLETTE, Ferdinand Ed Raymond, Dec 9 1920 Sex:M Child# 2 Walter Willette Plattsburgh, NY & Alice G Robbins NY
WILLETTE, Franke Ambrozy, Apr 4 1922 Sex:M Child# 3 Paul Willette Poland & Fannie Kaslowska Poland
WILLETTE, Harry Vincent, May 26 1924 Sex:M Child# 3 Charles Willette Maine & Frances Whitmore NH
WILLETTE, Helena, Dec 4 1918 Sex:F Child# 2 Paul Willette Russia & Fannie Kaslova Russia
WILLETTE, Jennie, Jul 26 1915 Sex:F Child# 3 Wilmer Willette New York & Eva Taylor US
WILLETTE, Joseph Gilbert, May 9 1892 Sex:M Child# 4 Thomas Willette Canada & Phoebe Gordon Canada
WILLETTE, Joseph W, Oct 12 1888 Sex:M Child# 2 Thomas Willette Canada & Phebe Gordon Canada
WILLETTE, Mable Bertha, Apr 25 1933 Sex:F Child# 6 Alvin Willette Lion Mt, NY & Victorine Lovely Nashua, NH
WILLETTE, Marie Claire Lucille, Mar 14 1925 Sex:F Child# 2 Ernest Willette Nashua, NH & Annie Marquis Canada
WILLETTE, Mary Roselda, Sep 19 1923 Sex:F Child# 5 Leo J Willette Morgan Center, VT & Phoebe Morency Morgan
WILLETTE, Norma Therese, Apr 13 1919 Sex:F Child# 1 Charles O Willette Lewiston, ME & Frances Whittemore Nashua, NH
WILLETTE, Rita Annette, Sep 30 1923 Sex:F Child# 1 Enrest Willette Nashua, NH & Amy Marquis Canada
WILLETTE, Robert Francis, Jul 20 1933 Sex:M Child# 7 Charles Willette Lewiston, ME & F Whittemore Nashua, NH
WILLETTE, Ruth Rose, Apr 25 1933 Sex:F Child# 7 Alvin Willette Lion Mt, NY & Victorine Lovely Nashua, NH Stillborn
WILLETTE, Thelma Lucille, Feb 27 1912 Sex:F Child# 1 William Willette Chazy, NY & Wilhelm Ouellette Canada
WILLETTE, Unknown, Oct 10 1924 Sex:M Child# 1 (No Parents Listed)
WILLIAM, Richard Kemp, Aug 30 1926 Sex:M Child# 3 Leslie William Pepperell, MA & Mary L Butler Derry, NH
WILLIAMS, David James, Oct 5 1932 Sex:M Child# 1 F J Williams Tyngsboro, MA & Helena Mallon Nashua, NH
WILLIAMS, Doris Genevieve, Jan 7 1932 Sex:F Child# 5 E F Williams Littleton, NH & Eliz E Cushing Littleton, NH
WILLIAMS, Earl Franklin, Feb 28 1923 Sex:M Child# 4 Earl F Williams Littleton, NH & Elizabeth Cushing Littleton, NH
WILLIAMS, Earle Herbert, Mar 8 1929 Sex:M Child# 2 Earle Williams S Lyndeboro, NH & Dorothy Rice Nashua, NH
WILLIAMS, Edward Everett, Jun 22 1912 Sex:M Child# 1 (No Parents Listed)
WILLIAMS, Eileen, Aug 11 1915 Sex:F Child# 1 Forrest Williams The Fork, ME & Bertha Bates Norridgewalk, ME
WILLIAMS, Gordon Edmund, Nov 8 1935 Sex:M Child# 1 Edmund H Williams Taunton, MA & Doris Smith Nashua, NH
WILLIAMS, Irving Manton, Jul 31 1910 Sex:M Child# 1 Irving M Williams Providence, RI & Ethel Smith Central Fls, RI
WILLIAMS, James Thomas, Oct 30 1934 Sex:M Child# 2 Earle Williams S Lyndeboro, NH & Dorothy Rice Nashua, NH
WILLIAMS, Jane Rice, Sep 17 1935 Sex:F Child# 4 Earle L Williams S Lyndeboro, NH & Dorothy Rice Nashua, NH
WILLIAMS, Jno W, Jun 11 1904 Sex:M Child# 4 John W Williams Wilmington, NC & Emma Holland Baltimore, MD Colored
WILLIAMS, Leonard Clark, Sep 27 1933 Sex:M Child# 7 Earl Williams Littleton, NH & E Cushing Littleton, NH
WILLIAMS, Lucille, Oct 21 1922 Sex:F Child# 2 Arthur Williams Plymouth, PA & Mary Maynard Nashua, NH
WILLIAMS, Mary, Jun 20 1897 Sex:F Child# 1 Joseph Williams Greece & Mamie Carlin Greece
WILLIAMS, Pearl Myria, Dec 17 1926 Sex:F Child# 5 Carl F Williams NH & Elizabeth Cushing NH
WILLIAMS, Randall Augustus, Jul 4 1900 Sex:M Child# 2 R M Williams Florida & Florence Myers Vermont
WILLIAMS, Russell George, Aug 28 1934 Sex:M Child# 1 Russell Williams Pepperell, MA & Florence Swett Leominster, MA
WILLIAMS, Unknown, May 14 1888 Sex:M Child# 7 O S Williams Derham, ME & Sylvian E M Brooks Lewiston, ME
WILLIAMS, Unknown, May 28 1899 Sex:F Child# 1 John W Williams Wilmington, NC & Emma Holland Baltimore, MD Colored
WILLIAMS, Unknown, May 10 1902 Sex:F Child# 3 John W Williams Wilmington, NC & Emma Holland Baltimore, MD Colored

WILLIAMS, William Franklin, Jr, May 21 1928 Sex:M Child# 3 William F Williams New York & Mary A Byrne Newfoundland
WILLIAMSON, Alice May, May 11 1926 Sex:F Child# 4 A Williamson Edinburgh, Scotland & Mabel Rice Newport, VT
WILLIAMSON, Archibald, Oct 8 1922 Sex:M Child# 2 Ar Williamson Edinburg, Scotland & Maybelle Rice Newport, VT
WILLIAMSON, Arleen Ruth, May 20 1934 Sex:F Child# 9 Archibald Williamson Scotland & Maybelle Rice Newport, VT
WILLIAMSON, Calvin Russell, Dec 7 1932 Sex:M Child# 8 A Williamson Scotland & Maybelle Rice Newport, VT
WILLIAMSON, Dorothy Maybelle, Mar 10 1930 Sex:F Child# 6 Archibald Williamson Scotland & Maybelle Rice Newport, VT
WILLIAMSON, Elizabeth Mary, Apr 12 1928 Sex:F Child# 5 Arch Williamson Scotland & Maybelle Rice Newport, VT
WILLIAMSON, Helen Edna, Nov 2 1920 Sex:F Child# 1 Archibald Williamson Scotland & Maybelle Rice Newport, VT
WILLIAMSON, James Douglas, Jun 7 1918 Sex:M Child# 9 John R Williamson England & Bertha C Anderson Sweden
WILLIAMSON, Patricia Constance, Sep 18 1931 Sex:F Child# 7 A Williamson Scotland & Mabel Rice Newport, VT
WILLIAMSON, Thomas Calvin, May 27 1924 Sex:M Child# 3 A Williamson Edinburgh, Scotland & Mabel Rice Newport, VT
WILLKINS, Earle Winston, Dec 4 1917 Sex:M Child# 3 Leon W Willkins Milford, NH & Belle E Shattuck E Bridgewater, MA
WILLOUGHBY, Unknown, Dec 27 1888 Sex:M Child# 6 James Willoughby Boston & Jennie L Howare Chelmsford, MA
WILLOUGHBY, Unknown, Dec 15 1891 Sex:F Child# 7 James H Willoughby Boston, MA & Jennie L Howard Chelmsford, MA
WILLS, David A, Jan 4 1898 Sex:M Child# 6 William H Wills Nashua, NH & Mary Harrington Ireland
WILLS, John Francis, Mar 21 1896 Sex:M Child# 5 William H Wills Nashua, NH & Mary A Harrington Ireland
WILLS, Unknown, Apr 2 1899 Sex:F Child# 7 William Wills Nashua, NH & Mary Harrington Ireland Stillborn
WILLS, William Thomas, Nov 7 1894 Sex:M Child# 4 William H Wills Nashua, NH & Mary E Harrington Ireland
WILMOT, Anna Lillian, Jun 1 1933 Sex:F Child# 4 Clarence Wilmot Concord, NH & Zelma Bears W Harwich, MA
WILMOT, Augustus C, Mar 10 1888 Sex:M Child# 1 William C Wilmot Dwight, IL & Lillian Russell Lineus, ME
WILMOT, Eugene F, Jun 29 1935 Sex:M Child# 5 Clarence Wilmot US & Zelena Bearse US
WILMOT, Fay Gloria, Mar 15 1927 Sex:F Child# 1 C J Wilmot Concord, NH & Zelma A Bearse W Norwich, MA
WILMOT, Norma Lois, Jan 8 1931 Sex:F Child# 3 Clarence T Wilmot Concord, NH & Zelma A Bearse W Norwich, MA
WILMOT, Unknown, Dec 1 1889 Sex:M Child# 2 William Wilmot
WILMOT, Wade Alvin, Dec 19 1935 Sex:M Child# 1 Herb L Wilmot Concord, NH & Rita Guyette W Chazy, NY
WILSON, Adelbert Colby, Jul 11 1907 Sex:M Child# 1 Frank A Wilson Hudson, NH & Nettie O Colby Nashua, NH
WILSON, Alice Olive, May 13 1905 Sex:F Child# 1 Eugene R Wilson S Lyndeboro, NH & Aurelia Paquette Sandown, NH
WILSON, Annie, Jul 28 1920 Sex:F Child# 4 Frank L Wilson Lawrence, MA & Ethel Hardy Manchester, NH
WILSON, Arthur Frank, Jul 4 1908 Sex:M Child# 2 Frank A Wilson Hudson, NH & Nettie Colby Nashua, NH
WILSON, Byron Henry, Nov 9 1916 Sex:M Child# 2 Arthur L Wilson Nerory, ME & Annie Lizzie Cate Nashua, NH
WILSON, Charles Harold, Feb 10 1918 Sex:M Child# 2 George H Wilson Nashua, NH & Florence Weldon Groton, MA
WILSON, Doris Ella Bailey, Jan 4 1921 Sex:F Child# 2 Gordon Wilson Sherbrooke, Quebec & Winnie Bailey Nashua, NH
WILSON, Dorothy May, Nov 26 1921 Sex:F Child# 1 Elmer Wilson Maine & Gladys Gilson NH
WILSON, Edward Winthrop, Apr 20 1932 Sex:M Child#  Edw W Wilson Winthrop, MA & R D Beiermeister Boston, MA
WILSON, Elizabeth Eva, Mar 10 1918 Sex:F Child# 3 Arthur Wilson Newry, ME & Annie L Cate Nashua, NH
WILSON, Frank Edward, Dec 2 1926 Sex:M Child# 2 Frank Wilson Italy & Mary Macchi Milford, NH
WILSON, Frederick R, Aug 22 1898 Sex:M Child# 2 H M Wilson Nashua, NH & Louisa Anthony Providence, RI
WILSON, George, Apr 30 1913 Sex:M Child# 1 Harvey Wilson St John, NB & Angelina H Bouffard Nashua, NH
WILSON, George Harold, Oct 2 1893 Sex:M Child# 1 Willis H Wilson S Lyndeboro & Ella D Holman Lowell, MA
WILSON, Harold E, Sep 17 1899 Sex:M Child# 2 Arthur T Wilson NY & Lillian B Smith Nashua, NH
WILSON, Harriet Marguerite, Feb 5 1915 Sex:F Child# 2 Harvey Wilson Woodstock, NB & Angelina Bouffard Nashua, NH
WILSON, Helen Anna, Jun 15 1909 Sex:F Child# 1 Arthur R Wilson Newry, ME & Lizzie Cate Nashua, NH
WILSON, Helen Frances, Apr 7 1924 Sex:F Child# 1 Donald Wilson Newport, VT & Dora R Hackett New York
WILSON, Janet Inez, Mar 20 1924 Sex:F Child# 2 Harold Wilson Portland, ME & Inez Lizotte Nashua, NH
WILSON, John, May 20 1934 Sex:M Child# 2 John Elliott Wilson New York & Jane Inness Nova Scotia
WILSON, Joseph, Jul 25 1919 Sex:M Child# 1 Harold Wilson Peterboro, NH & Rosie Saucier Greenville, NH Stillborn
WILSON, Josephine Christine, Dec 21 1924 Sex:F Child# 1 Frank Wilson Italy & Mary T Macochi Milford, NH
WILSON, Kenneth Merton, Jul 6 1928 Sex:M Child# 4 W M Wilson Bakersfield, VT & Mildred L Irving Boston, MA
WILSON, Latitia Emily, Mar 22 1922 Sex:F Child# 5 Frank L Wilson Lawrence, MA & Ethel Hardy Manchester, NH
WILSON, Mary Lucille, Nov 14 1927 Sex:F Child# 2 Cyrus Wilson Litchfield, NH & Mary McQuesten Litchfield, NH
WILSON, Mary Marguerite, Feb 9 1912 Sex:F Child# 1 Eddie Wilson New York, NY & Blanche Messier Nashua, NH
WILSON, Mildred Nilla, Aug 31 1921 Sex:F Child# 7 John Wilson Prince Edward Island & Gertrude Dunbar Manchester, NH
WILSON, Nira A, Feb 14 1896 Sex:F Child# 1 Frank M Wilson Benton & Frankie M Dexter Lisbon
WILSON, Norman M, Aug 29 1909 Sex:M Child# 1 Robert G Wilson N Carolina & Julia A Nichols Statesville, NC
WILSON, Orpha Myrtle, Apr 20 1910 Sex:F Child# 2 William E Wilson Altona, NY & Mary E Newcombe Salem, NH
WILSON, Paul William, Apr 18 1926 Sex:M Child# 2 William Wilson New York & Harriet Ballou NH
WILSON, Phyllis Eveline, Oct 6 1924 Sex:F Child# 1 Cyrus Wilson Litchfield, NH & Mary McQuesten Litchfield, NH
WILSON, Priscilla Marjorie, Feb 10 1935 Sex:F Child# 2 Charles E Wilson Boston, MA & Marjorie L Howe Malden, MA
WILSON, Richard A, Apr 26 1901 Sex:M Child# 3 H M Wilson Nashua, NH & Louisa Anthony Providence, RI
WILSON, Robert Elmer, Oct 24 1925 Sex:M Child# 2 Walter E Wilson Francestown, NH & Mary J Knowles Bennington, VT
WILSON, Robert Jay Whitney, Jan 14 1926 Sex:M Child# 1 Robert Wilson Worcester, MA & Etta Whitney Providence, RI
WILSON, Rosalyn Elaine, Jul 24 1929 Sex:F Child# 3 Cyrus Wilson Litchfield, NH & Mary McQuesten Litchfield, NH
WILSON, Ruth, Aug 11 1914 Sex:F Child# 1 George S Wilson S Lyndeboro, NH & Edna A Gangloff S Lyndeboro, NH
WILSON, Thomas, May 23 1897 Sex:M Child# 1 Arthur T Wilson Niagara Falls, NY & Lillian B Smith Nashua, NH
WILSON, Unknown, Apr 3 1888 Sex:M Child# 4 Charles H Wilson
WILSON, Unknown, Apr 2 1890 Sex:M Child# 1 H M Wilson Nashua, NH & Louisa Anthony Providence, RI
WILSON, Unknown, Nov 29 1914 Sex:M Child# 11 Arthur C Wilson Waterville, ME & Lila Stitham New Brunswick Stillborn
WILSON, Unknown, Oct 5 1930 Sex:M Child# 4 Cyrus Wilson Litchfield, NH & Mary McQuesten Litchfield, NH
WILSON, Willis Adelbert, Dec 24 1916 Sex:M Child# 1 George H Wilson Nashua, NH & Florence Welden Groton, MA
WILSON, Wilson, May 17 1889 Sex:M Child# 1 Arthur Wilson Nashua, NH & Sarah Stewart Sandown, NH
WILTON, Katherine, Mar 14 1897 Sex:F Child# 10 Frederick Wilton England & Emma J O'Brien England
WILTON, Mary A, Feb 8 1895 Sex:F Child# 3 Dennis F Wilton Lowell, MA & Mary A Gilhooley Ireland
WINDRICK, Lottie Ruth, Jun 27 1893 Sex:F Child# 2 Herman F Windrick Germany & Anna O Taubert Germany

WINER, Anna, Dec 30 1924 Sex:F Child# 2 Harry Winer Russia & Eva Simon Nashua, NH
WINER, Judith Rose, Dec 6 1929 Sex:F Child# 4 Harry Winer Russia & Eva Simon Nashua, NH
WINER, Ruth, Sep 1 1927 Sex:F Child# 3 Harry Winer Russia & Eva Simon Nashua, NH
WINER, Samuel Robert, Mar 5 1920 Sex:M Child# 1 Harry Winer Russia & Eva Simon Nashua, NH
WINGATE, Dearborn, Jun 29 1927 Sex:M Child# 1 Homer Wingate Sanford, ME & K Dearborn Nashua, NH
WINN, Albert Dresser, Aug 27 1929 Sex:M Child# 2 John Winn Lynn, MA & Myrtle Gardner Nashua, NH
WINN, Ann Louise, Aug 13 1919 Sex:F Child# 3 Charles Winn Nashua, NH & Marie O'Hearne Taunton, MA
WINN, Celia, Jun 23 1895 Sex:F Child# 4 John Winn Ireland & Celia Degnan Ireland
WINN, Celia, Apr 24 1907 Sex:F Child# 9 John Winn Ireland & Celia Degnan Ireland
WINN, Charles, Nov 6 1902 Sex:M Child# 3 John W Winn Canada & Celia Degnan Canada
WINN, Charles Francis, Jr, Jan 1 1933 Sex:M Child# 2 Charles Leo Winn Nashua, NH & Mary H Culhane Brooklyn, NY
WINN, Charles Stephen, Sep 13 1917 Sex:M Child# 3 Charles A Winn Nashua, NH & Marie O'Hearn Taunton, MA
WINN, Charline, Jan 8 1899 Sex:F Child# 1 Leon E Winn Hudson, NH & Alice Mortlock Nashua, NH
WINN, Dorothy Mary, May 31 1931 Sex:F Child# 1 Charles Winn Nashua, NH & Mary Culhane Brooklyn, NY
WINN, Elizabeth Mary, Jul 27 1904 Sex:F Child# 3 James Winn Ireland & Annie Kareney Ireland
WINN, Elizabeth Rose, Jan 8 1923 Sex:F Child# 5 Charles A Winn Nashua, NH & Marie O'Hearne Taunton, MA
WINN, Helen Elizabeth, Nov 21 1907 Sex:F Child# 1 John H Winn Nashua, NH & Mary E Mullen Milford, NH
WINN, James, Mar 28 1903 Sex:M Child# 9 Michael Winn England & Jennie Keating Holyoke, MA
WINN, James Joseph, Mar 20 1906 Sex:M Child# 4 James Winn Ireland & Ann Kaveny Ireland
WINN, Joan Claire, May 4 1934 Sex:F Child# 2 Edmund J Winn Nashua, NH & Irene Cote Lowell, MA
WINN, John, Jun 23 1895 Sex:M Child# 5 John Winn Ireland & Celia Degnan Ireland
WINN, John Edward, Dec 16 1907 Sex:M Child# 5 James Winn Ireland & Ann Kaveney Ireland
WINN, John Thomas, Mar 21 1927 Sex:M Child# 6 Charles A Winn Nashua, NH & Marie O'Hearne Taunton, MA
WINN, John, Jr, Oct 28 1896 Sex:M Child# 6 John Winn Ireland & Celia Degnan Ireland
WINN, Katherine Denis, Aug 18 1912 Sex:F Child# 3 John Winn Nashua, NH & Mary Mullen Greenville, NH
WINN, Kathryn Virginia, Sep 7 1934 Sex:F Child# 2 Thomas D Winn Ireland & Kathryn Wilcox Nashua, NH
WINN, Lillian Emma, Nov 15 1917 Sex:F Child# 1 Frank A Winn Pelham, NH & Effie Mae Wyeth Nashua, NH
WINN, Margaret, Jul 13 1893 Sex:F Child# 1 Michael Winn Ireland & Marie Moran Ireland
WINN, Marguerite Marie, Jan 13 1916 Sex:F Child# 1 Charles A Winn Nashua, NH & Marie O'Hern Taunton, MA
WINN, Mary, Nov 5 1892 Sex:F Child# 2 John Winn Ireland & Celia Degnan Ireland
WINN, Mary Elizabeth, Apr 24 1921 Sex:F Child# 4 John H Winn Nashua, NH & Mary Mullen Greenville, NH
WINN, P James Greenwood, Jul 20 1920 Sex:M Child# 1 Patrick James Winn Nashua, NH & Eleanor Greenwood Valley
WINN, Patrick James, Dec 19 1893 Sex:M Child# 3 John Winn Ireland & Celia Degnan Ireland
WINN, Robert Joseph, Jun 2 1921 Sex:M Child# 4 Charles Winn Nashua, NH & Marie O'Hearn Taunton, MA
WINN, Susanne Alice, May 16 1933 Sex:F Child# 1 Thomas Winn Ireland & Katherine Wilcox Nashua, NH
WINN, Thomas Dominic, Sep 7 1934 Sex:M Child# 3 Thomas D Winn Ireland & Kathryn Wilcox Nashua, NH
WINN, Unknown, Aug 11 1889 Sex:F Child# 12 Thomas Winn Ireland & Bridget Flynn Ireland
WINN, Unknown, Oct 19 1891 Sex:F Child# 1 John Winn Ireland & Celia Deglon Ireland
WINN, Unknown, Apr 16 1901 Sex:F Child#  John Winn Ireland & Celia Degnan Ireland Stillborn
WINNER, Eugene, Aug 8 1901 Sex:M Child# 11 Amable Winner Canada & Rosilda Duquette Canada
WINNER, Marie Jeanne, Jun 30 1897 Sex:F Child# 9 Amable Winner Canada & Azilda Duquette Canada
WINNER, Marie Rose L, Dec 19 1903 Sex:F Child# 12 Amable Winner Canada & Rosilda Duquette Canada
WINNER, Marie Rosilda, Feb 21 1899 Sex:F Child# 10 Amable Winner Canada & Rosilda Duquette Canada
WINOGRAD, Leila, Sep 4 1931 Sex:F Child# 1 Charles I Winograd Fall River, MA & Evelyn Rosenfeld Lowell, MA
WINSLOW, Ada, May 21 1896 Sex:F Child# 7 Nelson H Winslow Andover, MA & Minnie P Russell Linneus, ME
WINSLOW, Bertha M, Aug 1 1887 Sex:F Child# 4 Nelson H Winslow Maine & Minnie Maine
WINSLOW, Clara Belle, Jul 28 1892 Sex:F Child# 4 John Winslow Maine & Clara Malley Mass
WINSLOW, Gerald Ralph, Aug 27 1928 Sex:M Child# 2 Minton A Winslow Nashua, NH & Violet Jane Estes Nashua, NH
WINSLOW, Joseph R Donald, Mar 21 1931 Sex:M Child# 1 George Winslow Hudson, NH & Lena Noel Canada
WINSLOW, Marian Louise, Nov 7 1921 Sex:F Child# 1 Rupert A Winslow Nashua, NH & Edna D Hunt Nashua, NH
WINSLOW, Mary Elaine, Oct 17 1934 Sex:F Child# 2 George Winslow Hudson, NH & Lena Noel Canada
WINSLOW, Minnie H, Mar 24 1894 Sex:F Child# 6 Nelson H Winslow Andover, ME & Minnie P Russell Linneus, ME
WINSLOW, Minton Alviron, Jun 26 1895 Sex:M Child# 5 Horace F Winslow Ascot, Canada & Emma F Boyd Londonderry, NH
WINSLOW, Muriel Ella, Oct 29 1920 Sex:F Child# 1 Minton Winslow Nashua, NH & Violet Estes Nashua, NH
WINSLOW, Nelson B, Aug 13 1890 Sex:M Child# 5 Nelson H Winslow Maine & Minnie Russell Maine
WINSLOW, Phyllis Mae, Nov 27 1924 Sex:F Child# 2 Rupert A Winslow Nashua, NH & Edna D Hunt Nashua, NH
WINSLOW, Ralph Tolles, May 4 1890 Sex:M Child# 3 Horace F Winslow Canada & Emma F Boyd Londonderry, NH
WINSLOW, Richard Boyd, Dec 4 1929 Sex:M Child# 3 Rupert A Winslow Nashua, NH & Edna D Hunt Nashua, NH
WINSLOW, Rupert Ambrose, Sep 20 1897 Sex:M Child# 6 Horace F Winslow Ascot, PQ & Emma F Boyd Londonderry, NH
WINSLOW, Unknown, Jun 19 1887 Sex:M Child# 2 Horace F Winslow Canada & Emma F Boyd Londonderry, NH
WINSLOW, Unknown, Aug 8 1890 Sex:M Child# 3 John R Winslow Maine & Clara Healey Massachusetts
WINSLOW, Vera, Mar 6 1894 Sex:F Child# 4 Horace F Winslow Ascot, Canada & Emma F Boyd Londonderry, NH
WINTERBOTTOM, Robert Henry, Feb 22 1921 Sex:M Child# 1 Henry Winterbottom England & Bertha McAdoo Nashua, NH
WINTERS, Kennett Asa, Mar 7 1908 Sex:M Child# 2 Asa J Winters Woods Falls, NY & Alice Wilson S Lyndeboro, NH
WINTERS, Ralph W, May 24 1909 Sex:M Child# 3 Asa J Winters Woods Falls, NY & Alice M Wilson Lyndeboro, NH
WINTERS, Russell, Aug 28 1906 Sex:M Child# 1 Asa J Winters Woods Falls, NY & Alice M Wilson Lyndeboro, NH
WINTERS, Vera E, Jan 14 1893 Sex:F Child# 1 Lot R Winters NY & Mary McFarland Maine
WINTHROP, Unknown, Sep 3 1931 Sex:F Child#  Leroy Winthrop Bath, ME & Genevieve Bradford E Lansing, MI
WIREN, Alice Florence, Apr 20 1916 Sex:F Child# 1 Ralph A Wiren Caribou, ME & Florence B Crawford Blaine, ME
WIREN, Allen Ralph, Apr 23 1918 Sex:M Child# 2 Ralph A Wiren Caribou, ME & Florence B Crawford Blaine, ME
WIRRICK, Frank, Oct 7 1916 Sex:M Child# 1 Brunislaw Wirrick Russia & Josephine Shuntowska Russia
WIRTANEN, Howard Irving, Sep 15 1934 Sex:M Child# 3 Waino Wirtanen Maynard, MA & Dorothea Fessenden Brookline, NH
WIRTANEN, Theodore Eugene, Jul 28 1928 Sex:M Child# 1 Waine Wirtanen Maynard, MA & D Fessenden Brookline, NH

WIRWICZ, Bolaslow, Oct 15 1918 Sex:M Child# 1 Frank Wirwicz Russia & Aurelia Dougil Russia
WISCHESS, Peter, Aug 1 1913 Sex:M Child# 5 John Wischess Austria & Mary Tockus Austria
WISE, Albertine Hazel, Oct 13 1918 Sex:F Child# 1 Albert B Wise Portland, ME & Pauline Harris Nashua, NH
WISE, Blanche Agnes, Sep 21 1935 Sex:F Child# 1 Earl Wise Reeds Ferry, NH & Joseph Langvine Bedford, NH
WISEMAN, Anna, Aug 21 1915 Sex:F Child# 6 Morus Wiseman Russia & Rosie Brown Russia
WISEMAN, Celia, Nov 5 1913 Sex:F Child# 4 Morris Wiseman Russia & Rosie Brown Russia
WISEMAN, Douglas Carl, Feb 28 1935 Sex:M Child# 1 Howard Wiseman Belville, Ont & Ruth Aiken Lowell, MA
WISEMAN, Gilbert, Feb 11 1921 Sex:M Child# 8 Morris Wiseman Russia & Rose Brown Russia
WISEMAN, Harry, Jun 19 1910 Sex:M Child# 2 Maurice Wiseman Russia & Rosie Brown Russia
WISEMAN, Harry, Mar 11 1921 Sex:M Child# 6 Joe Wiseman Russia & Esther Russell Nashua, NH
WISEMAN, Hattie, Apr 17 1908 Sex:F Child# 1 Morris Wiseman Russia & Rosie Brown Russia
WISEMAN, Ida, Jan 13 1912 Sex:F Child# 3 Morris Wiseman Russia & Rosie Brown Russia
WISEMAN, Mary, Jan 12 1909 Sex:F Child# 3 Joseph Wiseman Russia & Etta Russell Russia
WISEMAN, Max, Dec 17 1916 Sex:M Child# 7 Morris Wiseman Russia & Bessie Brown Russia
WISEMAN, Phillip, Sep 22 1906 Sex:M Child# 1 Joe Wiseman Russia & Etta Russell Russia
WISEMAN, Samuel, Aug 21 1915 Sex:M Child# 5 Morus Wiseman Russia & Rosie Brown Russia
WITHINS, Mary Alma, Feb 1 1924 Sex:F Child# 1 Samuel W Withins Halifax, NS & Ida M Pugle Burnside, NH
WITIJTA, Goneffa, Aug 18 1915 Sex:F Child# 1 Paul Witijta Russia & Felinsa Kaglanki Russia
WITKOWSKI, Unknown, Apr 6 1931 Sex:M Child# 1 John Witkowski Lithuania & Mary Bleviuete Lithuania
WLEZISZKI, Unknown, Nov 19 1907 Sex:M Child# 2 George Wleziszki Russia & Powia Bakanowski Russia
WNJCIK, Nellie, May 12 1914 Sex:F Child# 1 Mike Wnjcik Austria & Fannie Kostak Austria
WODYKA, Maryjanna, Sep 17 1906 Sex:F Child# 1 Eddy Wodyka Poland & Bronistowa Nismise Poland
WOEDEYA, Unknown, May 19 1910 Sex:M Child# 6 John Woedeya Austria & Annie Gdowersz Austria
WOJDJIA, Stanislaus, Mar 28 1921 Sex:M Child# 12 John Wojdjia Austria & Annie Godwycz Austria
WOLCZEK, Sophie, Mar 16 1922 Sex:F Child# 2 Peter Wolczek Poland & Mary Webek Poland
WOLEN, Beruta Nellie, Nov 3 1920 Sex:F Child# 2 James Wolen Lithuania Russia & Elizabeth Sovoika Lithuania Russia
WOLEN, John Henry, May 17 1896 Sex:M Child# 1 John Wolen Russia & Rosa Guertin Nashua, NH
WOLEN, M Rose Josephine, Mar 8 1915 Sex:F Child# 1 (No Parents Listed)
WOLEN, Mary, Jun 17 1913 Sex:F Child# 2 James Wolen Russia & Elizabeth Sowolich Russia
WOLEN, Rosa Louisa, Mar 8 1898 Sex:F Child# 2 John Wolen Russia & Rosa Guertin Nashua, NH
WOLEZYK, Peter, Jan 11 1924 Sex:M Child# 3 Peter Wolezyk Poland & Mary Webek Poland
WOLFEMAN, Unknown, Jul 19 1888 Sex:M Child# 3 Julius Wolfeman Russia & Minnie Prussia
WOLFMAN, Simeon, Jun 9 1889 Sex:M Child# 5 Julius Wolfman Poland & Minnie Poland
WOLFMAN, Unknown, Jun 17 1893 Sex:F Child# 7 Julius Wolfman Russia & Emelia Harris Russia
WOLFSOHN, Ester, Sep 8 1909 Sex:F Child# 5 Jacob Wolfsohn Russia & Ida Sadafski Russia
WOLFSON, Celia, Mar 24 1912 Sex:F Child# 8 Jacob Wolfson Russia & Ida Sidowsky Russia
WOLFSON, Dora, Feb 10 1917 Sex:F Child# 1 Abraham Wolfson Europe & Jennie Wolfson Europe
WOLFSON, Harry, May 11 1914 Sex:M Child# 8 J Wolfson
WOLFSON, Mary, Nov 14 1907 Sex:F Child# 6 Jacob Wolfson Russia & Ida Sidousky Russia
WOLFSON, Unknown, Apr 27 1916 Sex:M Child# 9 Jacob Wolfson Russia & Ida Sederski Russia  Stillborn
WOLKOVITCH, Alexandra, Oct 21 1908 Sex:F Child# 3 Stanislas Wolkovitch Russia & Zophia Mojaska Russia
WOLKOWSKI, Stanley Peter, Jan 29 1918 Sex:M Child# 3 John Wolkowski Russia & Eva Yovgon Russia
WOLKOWSKI, Tony John, May 24 1916 Sex:M Child# 3 John Wolkowski Russia & Eva Javgel Russia
WOLLEN, John, Nov 23 1917 Sex:M Child# 1 Ben Wollen Russia & Galtrousia Yakavooni Russia
WOLLEN, Marie Beatrice Simon, Jun 21 1923 Sex:F Child# 2 John wollen NH & Evelin Sarault Canada
WOLLEN, Marie Therese Rita, Nov 5 1921 Sex:F Child# 1 John Wollen Nashua, NH & Eveline Sarault Canada
WOLLEN, Virginia, Aug 1 1925 Sex:F Child# 3 James Wollen Russia & Elizabeth Swiokla Russia
WOLOSKA, Philomene, Dec 14 1920 Sex:F Child# 2 Raymond Woloska Russia & Wesonika Suita Austria
WONDOTOWSKI, Bolestaw, Sep 1 1906 Sex:M Child# 2 Anthony Wondotowski Russia & Katherine Luwezen Russia
WOOD, Anna Pauline, Mar 27 1895 Sex:F Child# 1 Egbert L Wood Mass & Anna Thomas Pennsylvania
WOOD, Donald Roger, Nov 24 1926 Sex:M Child# 4 Ralph M Wood New Brunswick & Lillian May Leaf E Weare, NH
WOOD, Evelyn Emma, Dec 26 1925 Sex:F Child# 1 Edward G Wood Newport, RI & Evelyn Relishaw Somerville, MA
WOOD, George Otis, Aug 24 1905 Sex:M Child# 2 Otis A R Wood Nashua, NH & Millie Bugbee Windham, NH
WOOD, Graham Wayne, Jun 16 1930 Sex:M Child# 1 Francis J Wood England & Thelma Locke Hollis, NH
WOOD, Howard Percival, Apr 7 1912 Sex:M Child# 7 Victor Leon Wood Liverpool, NS & Bertha J Forsyth Sheffield
WOOD, Joseph George, Jun 21 1901 Sex:M Child# 1 (No Parents Listed)
WOOD, Leland Roy, Dec 7 1931 Sex:M Child# 2 Francis John Wood England & Thelma Locke Hollis, NH
WOOD, Mabel G, Apr 9 1889 Sex:F Child# 2 William G Wood Maine & Lizzie Mahoney Ireland
WOOD, Mildred Esther, May 20 1920 Sex:F Child# 3 Ralph M Wood New Brunswick & Lillian May Leaf W Weare, NH
WOOD, Millie Bugbee W, Apr 10 1901 Sex:F Child# 1 Otis A R Wood Nashua, NH & Millie Bugbee Windham Ctr, NH
WOOD, Pauline Hazel, Jan 22 1918 Sex:F Child# 4 Charles J Wood Saginaw, MI & Eva M Racene Canada
WOOD, Raymond Victor, Dec 11 1908 Sex:M Child# 6 Victor L Wood Nova Scotia & Bertha Forsyth Nova Scotia
WOOD, Robert Clark, Nov 12 1920 Sex:M Child# 2 Benjamin O Wood, Jr Atkinson, NH & Ethel M Whittemore Worcester, MA
WOOD, Ruth, Dec 15 1918 Sex:F Child# 5 Harry Orlando Wood Hartland, VT & Anna Pierce Fry Woodstock, VT
WOOD, Unknown, Nov 8 1889 Sex:M Child# 5 George B Wood Troy, NY & Lizzie Sawyer Nashua, NH
WOOD, Unknown, Nov 8 1889 Sex:M Child# 4 George B Wood Troy, NY & Lizzie Sawyer Nashua, NH
WOOD, Unknown, Aug 28 1917 Sex: Child# 1 Eugene Wood Moosup, CT & Rose Noel Willimantic, CT  Stillborn
WOOD, Viola Sarah, Sep 2 1912 Sex:F Child# 2 Joseph Wood Canada & Emma Porter Fisherville, MA
WOODARD, George H, Jun 21 1905 Sex:M Child# 1 William Woodard Vermont & Ida Snow Northboro, MA
WOODBILL, Yanina, May 22 1912 Sex:F Child# 1 Andrew Woodbill Russia & Mary Swaboitch Russia
WOODBURY, Arthur, Jul 23 1916 Sex:M Child# 1 Clar E Woodbury Nashua, NH & Gladys Hodgdon Berlin, NH
WOODBURY, Conrad, Mar 4 1925 Sex:M Child# 1 Thomas Woodbury Briston, CT & Mary Peiltas Bristol, CT
WOODBURY, Daisy Velma, Nov 16 1901 Sex:F Child# 4 S B Woodbury Westbrook, ME & Hattie Teague Portland, ME

WOODBURY, Dorothy Emma, Jun 21 1908 Sex:F Child# 1 Leroy Woodbury Nashua, NH & Mary Sanders Nashua, NH
WOODBURY, Eddie Evelyn, Feb 28 1906 Sex:F Child# 2 Thurlow F Woodbury Portland, ME & Jennie Kenter Nashua, NH
WOODBURY, Edgar Albert, Dec 21 1932 Sex:M Child# 1 N E Woodbury Nashua, NH & Hattie Dary Maine  Stillborn
WOODBURY, Frank Henry, Aug 1 1904 Sex:M Child# 2 Thurlow F Woodbury Maine & Jennie Menter Nashua, NH
WOODBURY, Gladys, Feb 28 1922 Sex:F Child# 1 McLean Woodbury Bedford, NH & Christine Moffie Boston, MA
WOODBURY, Harriett, Aug 31 1903 Sex:F Child# 10 Edgar W Woodbury Londonderry, NH & Eva J Wheeler Nashua, NH
WOODBURY, Ines May, Aug 12 1923 Sex:F Child# 1 Lester B Woodbury Ipswich, MA & Lydia Rosanna Carkin Greenland, MA
WOODBURY, John C, Mar 3 1909 Sex:M Child# 11 Charles E Woodbury Londonderry, NH & Eva Wheeler Nashua, NH
WOODBURY, LeRoy, Jun 15 1887 Sex:M Child# 2 Charles E Woodbury Londonderry & Eva J Wheeler Nashua, NH
WOODBURY, Lois Annette, Aug 2 1904 Sex:F Child# 1 William L Woodbury Nashua, NH & Mary Ingalls Hooksett, NH
WOODBURY, Luke A, Mar 25 1893 Sex:M Child#  Edgar Woodbury NH & Eva Wheeler NH
WOODBURY, Malcolm Leroy, Aug 7 1910 Sex:M Child# 2 B Leroy Woodbury Nashua, NH & Mary L Sanders Nashua, NH
WOODBURY, Paul Samuel, Jan 1 1918 Sex:M Child# 2 Clarice A Woodbury Nashua, NH & Gladys Hodgdon Berlin, NH
WOODBURY, Ruth, Mar 13 1895 Sex:F Child# 6 Edgar Woodbury Londonderry, NH & Eva Wheeler Nashua, NH
WOODBURY, Unknown, Sep 10 1888 Sex:M Child# 3 Charles E Woodbury Londonderry & Eva J Wheeler Nashua, NH
WOODBURY, Unknown, Jan 19 1891 Sex:M Child# 4 E C Woodbury NH & E J Wheeler Nashua, NH  Stillborn
WOODBURY, Unknown, Sep 15 1923 Sex:M Child# 4 Clarence A Woodbury Nashua, NH & Gladys Hodgon Berlin, NH Stillborn
WOODBURY, William Harvey, Jan 1 1918 Sex:M Child# 3 Clarice A Woodbury Nashua, NH & Gladys Hodgdon Berlin, NH
WOODCOCK, Unknown, Jul 5 1888 Sex:M Child# 6 John Woodcock N H & Victoria Hoyt Newport, VT  Stillborn
WOODGER, George Edward, Jan 5 1915 Sex:M Child# 1 Percy W Woodger England & Eva Damboise Nashua, NH
WOODMAN, Carolyn, Aug 20 1909 Sex:F Child# 2 Ernest Woodman White Plains, NY & Carolyn Graves Marblehead, MA
WOODMAN, Lucille, Oct 10 1920 Sex:F Child# 2 Rodney Woodman Medford, MA & Mildred Kimball Milford, NH
WOODMAN, Patricia, Aug 11 1931 Sex:F Child# 1  Auburn, NH & Gertrude Woodman Windham, NH
WOODMAN, Richard Tolford, Sep 11 1928 Sex:M Child# 1 Ralph Woodman W Medford, MA & Elizabeth Tolford Wilton, NH
WOODMAN, Rodney Canfield, Dec 27 1924 Sex:M Child# 3 R C Woodman Medford, MA & Mildred Kimball Milford, NH
WOODMAN, Sylvia, Oct 10 1920 Sex:F Child# 1 Rodney Woodman Medford, MA & Mildred Kimball Milford, NH
WOODMAN, Unknown, Mar 30 1916 Sex:M Child# 2 Charles W Woodman Amesbury, MA & Elsie H Feruald Haverhill, MA
WOODS, Adelbert Nelson, Nov 18 1906 Sex:M Child# 2 Sever Woods Nashua, NH & Bulah Blanchard Rhode Island
WOODS, Charles Everett, Jr, Aug 17 1931 Sex:M Child# 1 Charles E Woods Ayer, MA & Blanche Hunter Tyngsboro, MA
WOODS, Clarence Elmer, Sep 22 1897 Sex:M Child# 4 Frank Woods Canada & Mary Ann Flynn Canada
WOODS, Clifford S, Jul 1 1893 Sex:M Child# 1 John V Woods Hollis, NH & Eliza M Clifford Warren, NH
WOODS, Dorothy Evon, Sep 9 1916 Sex:F Child# 3 Charles J Woods Saginaw, MI & Eva M Racine Canada
WOODS, Eloise Elizabeth, Mar 16 1914 Sex:F Child# 2 Ernest S Woods Nashua, NH & Lillian Hacker Worcester, MA
WOODS, Evelyn Rita, May 28 1922 Sex:F Child# 3 Charles J Woods Saginaw, MI & Eva M Racine Canada
WOODS, Irena Winona, Nov 24 1905 Sex:F Child# 1 Ernest S Woods Nashua, NH & Lilly H Hacker Worcester, MA Stillborn
WOODS, Marion Jane, Apr 5 1924 Sex:F Child# 6 Charles J Woods Saginaw, MI & Eva M Racine Canada
WOODS, Mildred Isabel, Jul 27 1896 Sex:F Child# 3 John V Woods Hollis, NH & Eliza M Clifford Warren, NH
WOODS, Natalie Swanton, Jan 2 1929 Sex:F Child# 1 George W Woods Dunstable, MA & Inez D Sullivan New Bedford, MA
WOODS, Olive May, Mar 18 1892 Sex:F Child# 2 W G Woods Vermont & Eliza Green Ireland
WOODS, Robert Clifton, Nov 18 1917 Sex:M Child# 1 George H Woods Rochester, NH & Esther Edgerly Rochester, NH
WOODS, Unknown, Nov 5 1894 Sex:M Child# 2 John V Woods NH & Eliza M Clifford NH
WOODS, Unknown, Mar 6 1899 Sex:M Child# 4 George F Woods Goffstown, NH & Lena Wakefield Westboro, MA
WOODS, Unknown, Jul 2 1909 Sex:F Child# 3 Sever R Woods Nashua, NH & Tena Blanchard Pawtucket, RI
WOODS, Unknown, Feb 9 1911 Sex:M Child# 4 Sever R Woods Nashua, NH & Tena Blanchard Pawtucket, RI
WOODS, Unknown, Jul 22 1917 Sex:M Child# 3 Edward Woods Nashua, NH & Ella May McMan Malden, MA
WOODS, William Leo, Nov 30 1894 Sex:M Child# 3 Frank L Woods Canada & Mary A Flynn Canada
WOODWARD, Alice May, Oct 28 1907 Sex:F Child# 3 Leon O Woodward Nashua, NH & Mary Cummings Hudson, NH
WOODWARD, Bryant Orville, Jul 4 1903 Sex:M Child# 1 Leon O Woodward Nashua, NH & Mary E Cummings Hudson, NH
WOODWARD, Charles M, Jul 2 1889 Sex:M Child# 1 George A Woodward Warren, NH & K H Woodmul Prussia
WOODWARD, Emile Ray, Nov 22 1909 Sex:M Child# 1 Ray Woodward Mass & Delia M Nagle NH
WOODWARD, Florence, Sep 19 1892 Sex:F Child#  Frank A Woodward New Hampshire & Carrie S Fellows New Hampshire
WOODWARD, George, Oct 14 1892 Sex:M Child# 3 George A Woodward Warner, NH & Catherine Cook Germany
WOODWARD, John Kendall, Dec 30 1916 Sex:M Child# 3 Ray Woodward Townsend, MA & Delia Nagle Nashua, NH
WOODWARD, Marietia Ella, Jan 31 1911 Sex:F Child# 2 Clarence E Woodward Lyndeboro, NH & Grace E Matthews Tyngs
WOODWARD, Mildred Frances, Aug 14 1912 Sex:F Child# 2 Ray B Woodward Townsend, MA & Delia M Nagle Nashua, NH
WOODWARD, Preston Earle, Feb 17 1910 Sex:M Child# 1 Clarence E Woodward Lyndeboro, NH & Grace E Matthews Tyngs
WOODWARD, Raymond C, Jun 8 1905 Sex:M Child# 2 Leon O Woodward Nashua, NH & Mary E Cummings Hudson, NH
WOODWARD, Unknown, Oct 1 1887 Sex:F Child# 2 Frank A Woodward Warner, NH & Carrie S Fellows Newbury, NH
WOODWARD, Unknown, Nov 24 1888 Sex: Child# 1 Edward Woodward Manchester & Nellie Nashua, NH
WOODWARD, Unknown, Jun 21 1890 Sex:M Child# 2 George A Woodward Warner & Jennie Cook Germany
WOODWARD, Unknown, Aug 16 1890 Sex:F Child# 3 Frank A Woodward Warner, NH & Carrie S Fellows Newbury, NH
WOODWARD, Unknown, Apr 23 1895 Sex:M Child# 5 Frank A Woodward Warner, NH & Carrie S Fellows Newbury, NH
WOODWARD, Unknown, Nov 4 1897 Sex:M Child# 6 Frank A Woodward Warner, NH & Carrie S Fellows Newbury, NH
WOODWARD, Unknown, Apr 24 1899 Sex:F Child# 7 Frank A Woodward Warner, NH & Carrie S Fellows Newbury, NH
WOODWARD, Walter Clarence, Dec 14 1893 Sex:M Child# 4 George A Woodward Warner & Catherine H Cook Germany
WOOLEN, Marie Rita, Apr 30 1926 Sex:F Child# 3 John Woolen Nashua, NH & Eveline Sarault Canada
WOOLEN, Peter, Oct 24 1901 Sex:M Child# 4 John Woolen Russia & Rose Guertin Nashua, NH
WOOLEN, Unknown, Dec 3 1906 Sex:M Child# 6 Joe Woolen Russia & Maglena Antonovitch Russia  Stillborn
WOOLEN, Unknown, Aug 15 1907 Sex:F Child# 8 Joe Woolen Russia & Magde Antonovitch Russia  Stillborn
WOOLEY, Eleanor Mary, Sep 1 1930 Sex:F Child# 2 Melvin E Wooley Springfield, MA & Alice Thompson Nashua, NH
WOOLEY, Natalie Ruth, Mar 15 1924 Sex:F Child# 1 George W Wooley Springfield, MA & Violet Bixby Newton Jct, NH
WOOLEY, Unknown, Nov 9 1916 Sex:F Child# 5 John C Wooley Waterloo, Canada & Jane Amelia Neil Grandy, Canada
WOOLLEY, Milton Eugene, May 2 1925 Sex:M Child# 1 Melvin Woolley Springfield, MA & Alice Thompson Nashua, NH

WORCESTER, Ada Melvina, Jan 20 1911 Sex:F Child# 3 Wilber D Worcester Mason, NH & Lena McEwan Chelmsford, MA
WORCESTER, Mary, Mar 2 1926 Sex:F Child# 2 W W Worcester Cambridge, MA & Lou Mae Dutton Montpelier, VT
WORDEN, Ethel May, Aug 12 1895 Sex:F Child# John B Worden New York & Etta A Wyman Mass
WORDOLOSKI, Stanley Wondolski, Feb 17 1918 Sex:M Child# 5 Anthony Wordoloski Russia & Catherine Olender Russia
WORKMAN, Warren Allen, Jul 6 1926 Sex:M Child# 2 A Workman Maine & Lena Joy Maine
WOROUSKA, John, Apr 7 1912 Sex:M Child# 1 John Worouska Russia & Apolina Stowocz Russia
WORRAD, David William, Sep 11 1927 Sex:M Child# 6 Joseph V Worrad England & Eva Brousseau Manchester, NH
WORRAD, Madeline Virginia, Mar 22 1925 Sex:F Child# 5 Joseph Worrad England & Eva Brousseau Manchester, NH
WORRAD, Shirley Winifred, Aug 20 1922 Sex:F Child# 4 Joseph Worrad Leicester, England & Eva Brousseau Manchester,NH
WORRINGTON, Clara Frances, Aug 19 1920 Sex:F Child# 4 Leslie L Worrington New Brunswick & Mary Sullivan Ireland
WORSOVICH, Mary, Jul 23 1919 Sex:F Child# 1 Andrew Worsovich Russia & Julia Olechna Russia
WORTHEN, John Adams 3rd, May 17 1928 Sex:M Child# 1 J A Worthen, Jr Nashua, NH & Mary Singleton Westfield, MA
WORTHERN, John Adams, Jan 21 1906 Sex:M Child# 4 John A Worthern Melrose, MA & Hattie Collins Manchester, NH
WOYSZUISZ, Maryanna, Mar 20 1910 Sex:F Child# 1 Ludwik Woyszuisz Russia & Heliemo Molionko Russia
WRAY, Edward A, Jul 6 1893 Sex:M Child# 1 Robert Wray Moors, NY & Laura Matott Champlain, NY
WRAY, Unknown, Nov 7 1894 Sex:M Child# 2 Robert Wray Mooers Forks, NY & Laura Matott Champlain, NY
WRENN, June Marie, Jun 17 1928 Sex:F Child# 1 Leo J Wrenn Nashua, NH & Angelina Morin Nashua, NH
WRENN, Norman Edward, Dec 17 1933 Sex:M Child# 3 Leo J Wrenn Nashua, NH & Angeline Morin Nashua, NH
WRENN, Robert Maurice, May 17 1931 Sex:M Child# 3 Leo J Wrenn Nashua, NH & Angelina M Morin Nashua, NH
WRENN, Unknown, Jun 13 1929 Sex:M Child# 2 Leo Wrenn Nashua, NH & Angelina Morin Nashua, NH  Stillborn
WRENN, Unknown, Jun 13 1929 Sex:M Child# 3 Leo Wrenn Nashua, NH & Angelina Morin Nashua, NH  Stillborn
WRIGHT, Alice L, Jun 30 1887 Sex:F Child# 1 Edward Wright Nashua, NH & Alfretta Bulo Nashua, NH
WRIGHT, Alice May, May 15 1897 Sex:F Child# 1 Charles F Wright Wilton, NH & Alice G Burgess Harvard, MA
WRIGHT, Arthur H, Sep 26 1893 Sex:M Child# 1 W B Wright Pepperell, MA & N E Gates Hollis, NH
WRIGHT, Bertha, Jun 23 1888 Sex:F Child# 1 Abraham Wright Manchester, NH & Gertie R Duncklee Greenfield, NH
WRIGHT, Charles H, Sep 25 1901 Sex:M Child# 1 Charles H Wright Hoosic Falls, NY & Mary A Spellman Nashua, NH
WRIGHT, Clarence Roy, Sep 14 1893 Sex:M Child# 5 Edward Wright Nashua, NH & Alfaretta Bowers Nashua, NH
WRIGHT, David George, May 22 1932 Sex:M Child# 3 H E J Wright Nashua, NH & Nellie M Patinsky Nashua, NH
WRIGHT, Dexter Charles, Jun 26 1914 Sex:M Child# 1 Arthur D Wright Nashua, NH & Ruth Hardy Nashua, NH
WRIGHT, Earl H, Mar 13 1902 Sex:M Child# 2 Harry E Wright Nashua, NH & Effie Harrington RI
WRIGHT, Edward, Sep 8 1888 Sex:M Child# 2 Edward Wright Nashua, NH & Alfredda Bowers Nashua, NH
WRIGHT, Edward Thomas, Nov 28 1932 Sex:M Child# 1 Edw J Wright Spokane, WA & Louise E Jenkins Londonderry, NH
WRIGHT, Elizabeth Adelaide, Mar 26 1923 Sex:F Child# 4 Clarence H Wright Brookline, NH & Avis Caroline Darv Di
WRIGHT, Ernest James, May 31 1934 Sex:M Child# 2 Edw J Wright Spokane, WA & Louise Jenkins Londonderry, NH
WRIGHT, Flossie Maria, Feb 10 1891 Sex:F Child# 4 Edward Wright Nashua, NH & Alfretta Bowers Nashua, NH
WRIGHT, Frances Almira, Aug 15 1934 Sex:F Child# 2 Albert E Wright Dedham, MA & Melva Reed Tyngsboro, MA
WRIGHT, Glen Edward, Nov 28 1921 Sex:M Child# 1 Chester D Wright Nashua, NH & Lottie B Parmenter Attleboro, MA
WRIGHT, Harold, Sep 10 1899 Sex:M Child# 8 Edward Wright Nashua, NH & Alfretta Bowers Nashua, NH
WRIGHT, Henry E, Oct 21 1900 Sex:M Child# 1 Harry Wright Nashua, NH & Effie Blanchard RI
WRIGHT, Herbert Arnold, Oct 29 1932 Sex:M Child# 1 Albert E Wright Dedham, MA & Melva Reed Tyngsboro, MA
WRIGHT, Lemuel Dary, Mar 1 1913 Sex:M Child# 1 Clarence H Wright Brookline, NH & Avis Caroline Dary Dighton, MA
WRIGHT, Marjorie May, Mar 26 1908 Sex:F Child# 4 Harry W Wright Nashua, NH & Effie D Blanchard Pawtucket, RI
WRIGHT, Nancy Elizabeth, Jan 22 1926 Sex:F Child# 1 Charles A Wright Pepperell, MA & Dorothy Seymour Providence, RI
WRIGHT, Paul Albert, Jun 15 1920 Sex:M Child# 3 Clarence H Wright Brookline, NH & Avis C Darv Dighton, MA
WRIGHT, Philip Lincoln, Jul 9 1914 Sex:M Child# 2 Clarence Wright Brookline, NH & Avis C Dary Dighton, MA
WRIGHT, Ralph Roland, Dec 8 1935 Sex:M Child# 4 Harry E Wright Nashua, NH & Nellie Patinsky Nashua, NH
WRIGHT, Reva Ann, Mar 11 1927 Sex:F Child# 2 Chester D Wright Nashua, NH & Lottie Parmenter Attleboro, MA
WRIGHT, Richard Theodore, Feb 17 1906 Sex:M Child# 3 Harry Wright Nashua, NH & Effie Blanchard Rhode Island
WRIGHT, Robert, Sep 3 1928 Sex:M Child# 2 H E J Wright Nashua, NH & Nellie Patinsky Nashua, NH
WRIGHT, William Frederick, Dec 4 1935 Sex:M Child# 3 Edward Wright Spokane, WA & Louise Jenkins Londonderry, NH
WRIGHT, William Kenneth, Aug 17 1910 Sex:M Child# 5 Harry W Wright Nashua, NH & Effie D Blanchard Rhode Island
WROBEL, Anna, Sep 26 1903 Sex:F Child# 1 John Wrobel Russia & Andre Keidy Russia
WROBEL, John, Jan 29 1906 Sex:M Child# 3 Paivel Wrobel Russia & Jatmiza Wrobel Russia
WROBEL, Mary, Aug 8 1909 Sex:F Child# 5 John Wrobel Austria & Jadwega Wytwical Austria
WROBEL, Peter, Nov 17 1904 Sex:M Child# 2 John Wrobel Russia & Gadwiga Wystswat Russia
WROBEL, Sophia, Dec 17 1907 Sex:F Child# 3 John Wrobel Russia & Ladwiga Wgawort Russia
WRUTEL, Michael, Mar 22 1912 Sex:M Child# 7 John Wrutel Russia & Ludwia Wytwot Russia
WURANCKAS, Paul Peter, Aug 17 1915 Sex:M Child# 7 William Wuranckas Russia & Kastorup Bakae Russia
WURDEMAN, Unknown, Dec 9 1935 Sex:F Child# 1 Bruce Wurdeman Chicago, IL & Emma Smith Worcester, MA
WYETH, Herbert Joseph, Mar 1 1895 Sex:M Child# 2 George H Wyeth Townsend, MA & Jennie Sullivan Hollis, NH
WYETH, Perley A, Dec 30 1887 Sex:M Child# 2 Williard B Wyeth Townsend & Maggie Altoona, NY
WYETH, Sarah Leila, Aug 12 1896 Sex:F Child# 3 George H Wyeth Townsend, MA & Jane F Sullivan Hollis, NH
WYETH, Unknown, Sep 9 1893 Sex:M Child# 1 George H Wyeth Townsend, MA & Jennie Sullivan Hollis, NH
WYETH, Unknown, Sep 17 1893 Sex:M Child# Willard Wyeth Mass & Maggie McClennan NY
WYMAN, Albert Aaron, Apr 7 1909 Sex:M Child# 2 George A Wyman Ayer, MA & Evelyn Leclair Canada
WYMAN, George Louis, Jan 11 1931 Sex:M Child# 2 William W Wyman Yarmouth, NS & Mary Ellen Hart Goffstown, NH
WYMAN, George William, Jun 7 1935 Sex:M Child# 1 Horace Wyman Staten Island, NY & Jona Farrow Tyngsboro, MA
WYMAN, Virginia Helen, Mar 17 1925 Sex:F Child# 1 William Wyman Yarmouth, NS & Goffstown, NH
WYMAN, William Wentworth, Aug 9 1934 Sex:M Child# 3 William N Wyman Yarmouth, NS & Mary Ellen Hart Goffstown, NH
WYNICZ, Alphonse, Jul 30 1918 Sex:M Child# 4 Bronislaw Wynicz Russia & Josephine Chempofska Russia
WYNN, Anna Marguerite, Jun 17 1909 Sex:F Child# 6 James Wynn Ireland & Ann Kaveny Ireland
WYNN, Charles Leo, Apr 13 1900 Sex:M Child# 2 James Wynn Ireland & Ann Kaveney Ireland
WYNN, Michael Francis, Jun 7 1900 Sex:M Child# 1 James Wynn Ireland & Ann Kareney Ireland

WYNOTT, Lawrence, Jan 27 1935 Sex:M Child# 3 Lawrence R Wynott Watertown, MA & Lillian Leard S Acton, MA
WYNOTT, Raymond Wallace, Dec 15 1928 Sex:M Child# 1 L R Wynott Watertown, MA & Lillian Leard S Acton, MA
WYNOTT, Sylvia Lorraine, Feb 13 1933 Sex:F Child# 2 Lawrence Wynott Concord, NH & Lillie Leard Mass
XABASENCHE, William, Aug 6 1907 Sex:M Child# 2 Alex Xabasenche Russia & Zofe Alexa Russia
XENETIMENOS, Cianula, Oct 30 1917 Sex:F Child# 3 Adamos Xenetimenos Greece & Agalaista Tamanakis Greece
XENETIMENOS, George, Oct 30 1917 Sex:M Child# 2 Adamos Xenetimenos Greece & Agalaista Tamanakis Greece
YAFFA, Joseph, Mar 30 1911 Sex:M Child# 5 Abraham Yaffa Russia & Eva Affsa Russia
YAGIELLOWICZ, Bronislaw, Sep 5 1924 Sex:M Child# 1 D Yagiellowicz Poland & P Staviewicz Poland
YAGIELLOWICZ, Edward, May 21 1929 Sex:M Child# 3 Brnslas Yagiellowicz Russia & Petroncia Stanewicz Russia
YAGIELLOWICZ, Geneva, Jun 29 1926 Sex:F Child# 2 B Yagiellowicz Poland & Patronella Poland
YAGIELLOWICZ, Wanda, Dec 12 1931 Sex:F Child# 4 Bronis Yagiellowicz Russia & Patricia Staniewicz Russia
YAKAICZ, Peter, Apr 13 1911 Sex:M Child# 1 Peter Yakaicz Russia & Casimira Doukintat Russia
YAKIACIS, John, Sep 8 1907 Sex:M Child# 1 Julius Yakiacis Russia & Annie Garancikutie Russia
YANIKEWICZ, Helen Rita, Mar 29 1930 Sex:F Child# 5 Joseph Yanikewicz Russia & Helen Legatavicute Russia
YANISKEWICH, Stanisclaus, Dec 21 1924 Sex:M Child# 3 Jos Yaniskewich Lithuania & Julia Segatancute Lithuania
YANUSKEWICUIRS, Wituatas, Feb 11 1920 Sex:M Child# 2 Jos Yanuskewicuirs Russia & Ulena Legataveuk Russia
YAPLE, Wellington, Jul 17 1918 Sex:M Child# 1 George Skilu Yaple Virginia, IL & Emily B Platt Chicago, IL
YARMALAWICZ, Stephania, Feb 27 1920 Sex:M Child# 1 Louis Yarmalawicz Poland Russia & Josie Petka Poland Russia
YARMOLOVICH, Unknown, Aug 8 1931 Sex:F Child# 6 Louis Yarmolovich Russia & Josie Pitko Poland
YARSKAUSKI, Mary Ann, Dec 27 1922 Sex:F Child# 1 Joseph Yarskauski Lithuania & Mary Ann Vaisivilute Lithuania
YASOLAVITCH, Annie, Feb 17 1907 Sex:F Child# 1 Joseph Yasolavitch Russia & Anton Crabonavitch Russia
YATES, Edward Warren, Nov 15 1904 Sex:M Child# 2 Edward Yates Warren, ME & Maud Dandley Nashua, NH
YEATON, Bernadette, Jul 9 1922 Sex:F Child# 1 Conrad D Yeaton Pittsfield, NH & Agnes Lally Boston, MA
YEATON, Frederick White, Sep 24 1933 Sex:M Child# 4 Fred W Yeaton Maine & Ella Bowers Nashua, NH
YECHNIEWICH, Alphonse, Jan 9 1912 Sex:M Child# 2 Joe Yechniewich Russia & Malvena Allesbetta Russia
YELOSKI, Joan E, Apr 15 1933 Sex:F Child# 1 Henry Yeloski Nashua, NH & G Cloutier Nashua, NH
YEOKOBOSH, Elizabeth, Aug 9 1912 Sex:F Child# 4 Joseph Yeokobosh Russia & Annie Yeokobosh Russia
YEUTTER, Evelyn Ann, Nov 26 1930 Sex:F Child# 1 Robert Yeutter Germany & Gertrude Kuhn Germany
YEUTTER, Robert Frederick, Jul 12 1934 Sex:M Child# 2 Robert Yeutter Germany & Gertrude Kuhn Germany
YIKAWIC, Frank, Sep 27 1907 Sex:M Child# 1 Frank Yikawic Russia & Roose Mieskniutie Russia
YOMAS, Albert, Apr 16 1914 Sex:M Child# 2 Jacob Yomas Austria & Mary Lao Austria
YONAKEA, Peter, Aug 13 1916 Sex:M Child# 2 Leo Yonakea Russia & Orsula Barkawich Russia Stillborn
YONKOUSKI, Frank, Dec 20 1912 Sex:M Child# 3 John Yonkouski Russia & Eva Zuniewicz Russia
YONKOVICZ, Agnes, Nov 26 1920 Sex:F Child# 2 Stanislaw Yonkovicz Nashua, NH & Jessie L Cole Salem, MA
YONKOWSKI, Stanislas, May 25 1910 Sex:M Child# 1 Joseph Yonkowski Russia & Eva Zunavitch Russia
YONKOWSKY, Joseph, Jan 27 1912 Sex:M Child# 2 Joseph Yonkowsky Russia & Eva Zinevitch Russia
YORK, Alwyn Stafford, Jun 3 1911 Sex:M Child# 2 Walter Henry York Bangor, ME & Maybel L Stafford Bangor, ME
YORK, Andrew Jackson, Jul 19 1924 Sex:M Child# 3 Jesse A York Fremont, NH & Harriet Dudley Hollis, NH
YORK, Beatrice Alida, Jan 3 1923 Sex:F Child# 4 Carroll L York Fremont, NH & Nellie Clement Fremont, NH
YORK, Doris Helen, Jun 13 1911 Sex:F Child# 1 Walter A York Vermont & Winnie Dustin Nashua, NH
YORK, Eleanor May, Sep 26 1928 Sex:F Child# 6 Jesse York Fremont, NH & Harriet Dudley Hollis, NH
YORK, Jesse Andrew, Jr, Feb 9 1926 Sex:M Child# 4 Jesse A York Fremont, NH & Harriet J Dudley Hollis, NH
YORK, Jessie Viola, Jul 11 1915 Sex:F Child# 2 Walter E York Brentwood & Winnifred L Dustin Nashua, NH
YORK, Louise Frances, May 3 1923 Sex:F Child# 2 Jesse A York Fremont, NH & Harriet Dudley Hollis, NH
YORK, Richard Maurice, Nov 7 1921 Sex:M Child# 1 Jesse York Fremont, NH & Harriet Dudley Hollis, NH
YORK, Roland Willis, Oct 16 1934 Sex:M Child# 10 Jesse York NH & Harriet Dudley Hollis, NH
YORK, Ruth Elizabeth, Aug 25 1931 Sex:F Child# 7 Jesse York Fremont, NH & Harriette Dudley Hollis, NH
YORK, Shirley, Jun 30 1930 Sex:F Child# 7 Jesse York Fremont, NH & Harriet Dudley Hollis, NH
YORK, Unknown, Sep 11 1927 Sex:M Child# 5 Jesse York Fremont, NH & Harriet Dudley Hollis, NH
YORKES, John, Nov 18 1900 Sex:M Child# 8 Frank Yorkes Russia & Sarah Herbert Russia
YOUKOWIEZ, Vladislaw, Sep 5 1918 Sex:M Child# 1 Stanislaw Youkowiez Russia & Veronica Matslewska Russia
YOUNAS, John, Jun 19 1916 Sex:M Child# 3 Jacob Younas Austria & Mary Wus Austria
YOUNG, Albert William, Apr 5 1933 Sex:M Child# 3 F A Young Mass & E Chater NH
YOUNG, Alfred James, May 18 1934 Sex:M Child# 4 Francis Albert Young Mass & Esmeralda Chase NH
YOUNG, Arthur Gilbert, Apr 9 1916 Sex:M Child# 1 William A Young W Auburn, MA & Lina Matson Finland-Russia
YOUNG, Arthur Roland, Dec 8 1925 Sex:M Child# 1 Ralph C Young Greenville, PA & Ruth A Pape Nashua, NH
YOUNG, Barbara Mae, Aug 2 1929 Sex:F Child# 1 Francis A Young Everett, MA & Esmeralda Chates Laconia, NH
YOUNG, Bernice A, Nov 23 1894 Sex:F Child# 1 Walter H Young Methuen, MA & Rubie A Gray Nashua, NH
YOUNG, Carl Haven, Jun 21 1897 Sex:M Child# 2 Walter H Young Methuen, MA & Rubie A Gray Nashua, NH
YOUNG, Donald, Nov 13 1897 Sex:M Child# Aaron Young Worcester, MA & Mary A McDonald Rochester, NH
YOUNG, Doris May, Nov 30 1919 Sex:F Child# 5 Harry J Young Patterson, NJ & Edith Dow Lee, NH
YOUNG, Dorothy Nora, May 14 1916 Sex:F Child# 6 Philippe Young NH & Exilda Bouleau NH
YOUNG, Edward Vincent, Apr 4 1933 Sex:M Child# 2 Ed V Young Everett, MA & Rose E Davy Laconia, NH
YOUNG, Elaine Marion, Mar 26 1935 Sex:F Child# 1 Andrew Young Scotland & Marion Merrill Milford, NH
YOUNG, Elaine Rose, Jul 1 1931 Sex:F Child# 1 Edward Young Mass & Rose Davy NH
YOUNG, Ella Jeanette, Aug 9 1909 Sex:F Child# 3 Orin J Young Mass & Mary Phaneuf New York
YOUNG, Ernest Theodore, Sep 3 1902 Sex:M Child# 1 William E Young Manchester, NH & Ada E Colby Francestown, NH
YOUNG, Helen Margaret, Aug 20 1935 Sex:F Child# 5 Francis A Young Mass & Esmeralda Chase NH
YOUNG, Jean Doris, Sep 5 1906 Sex:M Child# 4 John Young Mass & Mary Phaneuf New York
YOUNG, Joseph, Jul 24 1895 Sex:M Child# 1 O D Young Lawrence, MA & Mary A McDonald Rochester, NH
YOUNG, Leon Colby, May 12 1904 Sex:M Child# 2 William E Young Manchester, NH & Ada E Colby Francestown, NH
YOUNG, Marie Agnes A, Mar 19 1903 Sex:F Child# 3 Philippe Young NH & Exilda Rouleau NH
YOUNG, Marie Beatrice Flor, Feb 18 1918 Sex:F Child# 7 Philippe Young NH & Exilda Rouleau NH

YOUNG, Marie Lillienne, Aug 6 1910 Sex:F Child# 5 Philippe Young NH & Exilda Rouleau NH
YOUNG, Mildred Ruth, Feb 16 1931 Sex:F Child# 2 Francis A Young Everett, MA & Esmerelda Chase Lakeport, NH
YOUNG, Nancy Lucille, May 11 1933 Sex:F Child# 1 Ernest Young Nashua, NH & Katherine Young S Randolph, VT
YOUNG, Orren, Dec 12 1904 Sex:M Child# 3 Orren J Young Methuen, MA & Mary J Phaneuf Champlain, NY
YOUNG, Virginia Margaret, Apr 18 1919 Sex:F Child# 3 Charles H Young Tuftonboro, NH & Florence Caulfield Boston, MA
YOZUKWICZUS, John, Apr 7 1908 Sex:M Child# 3 Jonos Yozukwiczus Russia & Karola Gringinte Russia
YUCKNEWICK, Anidienie, Jul 30 1920 Sex:F Child# 2 Joseph Yucknewick Russia & Antainia Kasiulis Russia
YUDICKY, Helen, Mar 29 1926 Sex:F Child# 4 William Yudicky Poland & Theresa Yudicky Poland
YUKNEWICZ, Peter, Nov 28 1916 Sex:M Child# 1 Peter Yuknewicz Russia & Stepan Werkew Russia
YUKOREWICZ, Stella, Jun 22 1919 Sex:F Child# 2 Joseph Yukorewicz Russia & Antonia Kesulie Russia
YUONAUSKA, Annie, Oct 27 1915 Sex:F Child# 1 Gabris Yuonauska Russia & Marcelia Trincite Russia
YUREICHA, Stasie, Sep 27 1902 Sex:F Child# 3 Charles Yureicha Russia & D Monchiouske Russia
YVON, Antoinette, Jul 29 1907 Sex:F Child# 2 Arthur Yvon Canada & Rose A Desmarais Nashua, NH
YVON, Edouard Armand, Feb 24 1908 Sex:M Child# 3 Adelard Yvon Canada & Emma Boucher Canada
ZABINAS, Unknown, Apr 11 1928 Sex:M Child# 6 A Zabinas Greece & N Poppalopous Greece
ZABUKAS, Nellie, May 9 1919 Sex:F Child# 1 John Zabukas Lithuania Russia & Mary Bursqis Lithuania Russia
ZAIKOWICZ, Josephine, Sep 27 1917 Sex:F Child# 2 Stanley Zaikowicz Russia & Antonia Mickawicz Russia
ZAKURVICZ, Stanley, Feb 28 1919 Sex:M Child# 4 Stanley Zakurvicz Russia & Antosia Mickiewiz Russia
ZAKWEZICH, Mary, May 3 1916 Sex:F Child# 1 Stan Zakwezich Russia & Antonie Melchekeaz Russia
ZALANKAS, Staponas, Oct 27 1912 Sex:M Child# 1 Klemencas Zalankas Russia & Morta Deimatoit Russia
ZALANSKAS, Walerijonas, Jan 2 1916 Sex:M Child# 2 Clement Zalanskas Russia & Morta Damoutas Russia
ZALANSKY, Lena, Apr 28 1903 Sex:F Child# 1 John Zalansky Russia & Agnes Hualki Russia
ZANKOUSKI, Stanislaus, Sep 2 1912 Sex:M Child# 1 Stanislaus Zankouski Russia & Louise Spakanski Russia
ZANTER, Antanas, Apr 12 1915 Sex:M Child# 1 Antanas Zanter Russia & Tuulka Akscinuite Russia
ZAPENAS, Adam, May 16 1911 Sex:M Child# 9 George Zapenas Russia & Annie Lativis Russia
ZAPENAS, Alphonse, Aug 16 1918 Sex:M Child# 1 Sylvester Zapenas Russia & Leonora Boslowich Russia
ZAPENAS, Analka, Nov 27 1914 Sex:F Child# 4 Joseph Zapenas Russia & Analka Barisoshuite Russia
ZAPENAS, George, May 16 1911 Sex:M Child# 8 George Zapenas Russia & Annie Lativis Russia
ZAPENAS, Pauline Annie, Sep 4 1930 Sex:F Child# 1 Anthony Zapenas Lithuania & Constance Ulcickas Nashua, NH
ZAPENAS, Stanislaus, Oct 20 1913 Sex:M Child# 1 Stanley Zapenas Russia & Julia Kewckauska Russia
ZAPENAS, Tolespore, Apr 3 1917 Sex:M Child# 7 Sylvester Zapenas Russia & Lanora Radowich Russia
ZAPENIS, Marie, Dec 21 1906 Sex:F Child# 4 Soubaster Zapenis Russia & Laura Buslwisz Russia
ZAPIANIS, Levenora Annie, Aug 18 1910 Sex:F Child# 6 Sylvester Zapianis Russia & Levenora Bouslavitch Russia
ZARCKAS, Rita, Aug 15 1917 Sex:F Child# 1 Sylvester Zarckas Russia & Ursula Russia
ZARMARKUGSIS, Andrew, Sep 11 1926 Sex:M Child# 4 P Zarmarkugsis Greece & Mary Benn England
ZEALER, John Raymond, Jul 6 1902 Sex:M Child# 1 Clarence Zealer Havre de Grace, MD & M E Martin Nashua, NH
ZEALON, Kenneth Robert, Sep 17 1910 Sex:M Child# 6 Clarence J Zealon Maryland & Mary Martin Nashua, NH
ZEALOR, Barbara Frances, Feb 11 1931 Sex:F Child# 1 Winfred C Zealor Nashua, NH & Evelyn Bishop St Johnsbury, VT
ZEALOR, Clarence Galaway, Feb 21 1913 Sex:M Child# 7 Clarence Zealor Havre de Grace, MD & Mary E Martin Nashua, NH
ZEALOR, Genevieve Louise, Apr 29 1914 Sex:F Child# 9 Clarence Zealor Havre de Grace, MD & Mary E Martin Nashua, NH
ZEALOR, Mary Ellen, Jan 4 1908 Sex:F Child# 4 Clarence J Zealor Havre de Grace, MD & Mary Ellen Martin Nashua, NH
ZEALOR, Patrick B, Apr 29 1914 Sex:M Child# 10 Clarence Zealor Havre de Grace, MD & Mary E Martin Nashua, NH
ZEALOR, Virginia Frances, Jul 10 1905 Sex:F Child# 2 Clarence Zealor Havre de Grace, MD & Mary E Martin Nashua, NH
ZEALOR, William Martin, Oct 17 1909 Sex:M Child# 5 Clarence J Zealor Havre de Grace, MD & Mary E Martin Nashua, NH
ZEALOR, Winifred Clayton, Sep 30 1906 Sex:M Child# 3 Clarence J Zealor Maryland & Mary E Martin Nashua, NH
ZEARLIS, Peter, Aug 18 1911 Sex:M Child# 3 William Zearils Russia & Amelia Nevichis Russia
ZEBOLIS, Albert, Jul 21 1916 Sex:M Child# 1 John Zebolis Russia & Urshule Margaite Russia
ZEDALIS, Adolph Joseph, Dec 5 1917 Sex:M Child# 5 Adolphe Zedalis Russia & Rosa Tereiczik Russia
ZEDALIS, John, May 6 1913 Sex:M Child# 4 William Zedalis Russia & Amelia Navitzki Russia
ZEDALIS, Joseph, May 3 1917 Sex:M Child# 6 William Zedalis Russia & Amelia Wavisky Russia
ZEDALIS, Josie, Dec 20 1910 Sex:F Child# 1 Adolphe Zedalis Russia & Rosa Siaretshikuta Russia
ZEDALIS, Josie, Jul 9 1916 Sex:F Child# 2 Joseph Zedalis Russia & Mar Volontokawicz Russia
ZEDALIS, Julius, Feb 13 1921 Sex:M Child# 6 Adolphe Zedalis Lithuania Russia & Rosa Sereizick Lithuania Russia
ZEDALIS, Mary, Nov 11 1912 Sex:F Child# 2 Stan Zedalis Russia & Emma Zobretkinta Russia
ZEDEALIS, Unknown, Dec 16 1907 Sex:M Child# 2 Peter Zedealis Russia & Mattie Simonajtis Russia
ZEDELL, Alphonse, Sep 10 1914 Sex:M Child# 5 William Zedell Russia & Amelia Navitch Russia
ZEDIALIS, Joseph, Jan 30 1915 Sex:M Child# 1 Joseph Zedialis Russia & Mar Volontokawicz Russia
ZEGEKEVITCH, Adolpha, May 2 1920 Sex:M Child# 11 Joyn Zegekevitch Russia & Caroline Grigas Russia
ZELICHOUSKI, Wanda, Apr 30 1905 Sex:F Child# 5 Andrew Zelichouski Russia & Katryna Ozaroska Russia
ZELICHOWSKI, Frank, Dec 3 1906 Sex:M Child# 6 Andrew Zelichowski Russia & Kadi Ogarofska Russia
ZELINSKY, Julia, Mar 24 1909 Sex:F Child# 2 Martin Zelinsky Russia & Helen Baranowsky Russia
ZELONIS, Annie, Mar 28 1909 Sex:M Child# 1 Peter Zelonis Russia & Theo Larinkovitch Russia
ZELONIS, Gactana, Jan 20 1908 Sex:F Child# 2 Peter Zelonis Russia & Theo Narinkavitch Russia
ZELOSKI, Frank Allen, May 22 1933 Sex:M Child# 1 F X Zeloski Nashua, NH & Rita M Owens Baring, ME
ZELOWSKI, Helen, Nov 11 1908 Sex:F Child# 7 Andre Zelowski Russia & Katharina Ogerofska Russia
ZELOWSKI, Julia, Nov 17 1910 Sex:F Child# 8 Andrew Zelowski Russia & Catherine Ogarofski Russia
ZELSQEE, Maria Amelia, Jul 22 1896 Sex:F Child# 3 William Zelsqee Poland & Amerlia Milouvna Poland
ZENKIEWICH, Stanislawa, Aug 18 1910 Sex:F Child# 1 Frank Zenkiewich Russia & Annie Werszki Russia
ZEPALICK, Goneuf, Jun 21 1916 Sex:F Child# 2 Andrew Zepalick Russia & Helena Michalowicz Russia
ZEPANAS, Nancy Mary, Sep 18 1932 Sex:F Child# 2 Anthony Zepanas Lithuania & Con Ulicicokas Nashua, NH
ZEPANES, Peter, Feb 22 1907 Sex:M Child# 2 Joseph Zepanes Russia & Anelka Zepanes Russia
ZEPANIS, Hendrick, Nov 29 1908 Sex:M Child# 5 Sylvester Zepanis Russia & Leonora Buslavitch Russia
ZERBA, Anthony Stanley, Jul 4 1933 Sex:M Child# 1 Anthony Zerba Poland & C Pivowarski Nashua, NH

ZERBA, Caroline Elizabeth, Dec 25 1935 Sex:F Child# 3 Anthony Zerba Poland & Carol Pivowarski Nashua, NH
ZERBA, Joseph Walter, Jul 20 1934 Sex:M Child# 2 Anthony Zerba Poland & Caroline Piwowarski Nashua, NH
ZERBINOS, Andrew, Nov 13 1924 Sex:M Child# 4 A Zerbinos Greece & N Papadopoulou Greece
ZERBINOS, Jean, Jul 19 1921 Sex:M Child# 2 Paul Zerbinos Greece & Laurenze Damiozon France
ZERBINOS, Nickolaos, Jun 14 1923 Sex:M Child# 3 Paul Zerbinos Greece & Lauraine Damigon France
ZEUSSMANN, Harry, Mar 14 1916 Sex:M Child# 2 Jacob Zeussmann Russia & Sadie Shapiro Russia
ZEWONKUS, Anthony, Jun 6 1910 Sex:M Child# 1 Frank Zewonkus Russia & Christine Christos Russia
ZEZUKOWICH, Unknown, Jul 13 1918 Sex:F Child# 11 John Zezukowich Russia & Caroline Gregates Russia
ZIBLATT, Daniel Abbot, Feb 18 1935 Sex:M Child# 2 Maurice Ziblatt New York & Rose Filler Russia
ZIBOLIS, George, Feb 22 1932 Sex:M Child# 4 John Zibolis Lithuania & Ursula Margaite Lithuania
ZIBOLIS, John Vitold, Nov 22 1927 Sex:M Child# 3 John Zibolis Lithuania & Ursula Margaite Lithuania
ZIEDELIS, Daniel, Oct 4 1926 Sex:M Child# 1 Michael Ziedelis Europe & Marion Barsetes Europe
ZIEDIALIS, Albert, Aug 7 1909 Sex:M Child# 3 Peter Ziedialis Russia & Martha Ciminati Russia
ZILONES, Charles, Nov 21 1899 Sex:M Child# 2 George Zilones Russia & Pleuvena Clapsima Russia
ZILONES, Marie, Feb 20 1902 Sex:F Child# 3 George Zilones Russia & Josephine Shlebirer Austria
ZILONES, Yuliana, Jun 2 1898 Sex:F Child# 1 George Zilones Europe & Pauline Chlobicirona Europe
ZIMBERG, Ella, Jan 25 1896 Sex:F Child# 5 Lewis Zimberg Russia & Fannie Koski Russia
ZIMBERK, Joseph, Jun 1 1894 Sex:M Child# 4 Lewis Zimberk Russia & Fannie Rakisk Russia
ZIMMERMAN, Aurore I, Mar 8 1897 Sex:F Child# 1 J C Zimmerman Syracuse, NY & Aurore Girouard Nashua, NH
ZIMMERMAN, Carl E, Jul 30 1898 Sex:M Child# 2 Julius Zimmerman Syracuse, NY & Aurore Girouard Nashua, NH
ZIMMERMAN, Joseph E E, Jan 5 1900 Sex:M Child# 3 Julius Zimmerman NY & Aurore Girouard Nashua, NH
ZINDEHE, John, Feb 24 1903 Sex:M Child# 1 John Zindehe Russia & Rose Wevighice Russia
ZINKAWICZ, John, Oct 11 1911 Sex:M Child# 2 Frank Zinkawicz Russia & Annie Weskuscz Russia
ZINTA, Unknown, May 8 1907 Sex:M Child# 2 Felix Zinta
ZIPENAS, Mabel, Sep 9 1915 Sex:F Child# 2 Stanley Zipenas Russia & Julia Karkauska Russia
ZITSENKI, Unknown, Apr 3 1913 Sex:F Child# 2 Joseph Zitsenki Russia & Ferzina Pietruzinari Russia Stillborn
ZIUKI, Annie, Jun 14 1916 Sex:F Child# 4 Frank Ziuki Russia & Annie Wewkskhowski Russia
ZIUS, Elaine Myrtle, Oct 23 1933 Sex:F Child# 1 Eugene Zius Haverhill, MA & Iola Bills Amherst, NH
ZOATSKI, Brunislav, Aug 7 1910 Sex:F Child# 2 Joseph Zoatski Russia & Annie Repsite Russia
ZOGARFO, Unknown, Feb 15 1917 Sex:M Child# 1 Antonio Zogarfo Greece & Stella Greece
ZOGRAFOS, Unknown, Dec 19 1918 Sex:F Child# 1 Antozus Zografos Greece & Steale Zografos Greece
ZOTIQUE, Blanche M, Jun 21 1896 Sex:F Child# 6 Thiffault Zotique Canada & Germaine Celainre Canada
ZUBICK, Betty Ann, May 5 1933 Sex:F Child# 1 Miles Zubick New York, NY & Rhoda Sperberg Boston, MA
ZUK, Mary Amelia, Jun 9 1916 Sex:F Child# 1 Antoine Zuk Poland-Russia & Amelia Bogden Poland-Russia
ZUKAWAWICH, William, Mar 14 1918 Sex:M Child# 2 peter Zukawawich Russia & Stella Veskania Russia
ZUKOSKY, Sophia, Apr 2 1919 Sex:F Child# 3 Edouard Zukosky Poland Russia & Josephine Kosprez Poland Russia
ZULANSKI, Martin, Sep 21 1906 Sex:M Child# 1 Martin Zulanski Russia & Lena Barenarski Russia
ZURALIS, Nicholas, Jan 24 1917 Sex:M Child# 2 James Zuralis Greece & Panane George Greece
ZUREK, Robert Charles, May 8 1933 Sex:M Child# 1 Charles Zurek Manchester, NH & C Michelck Poland
ZURLER, Tachveza, Jul 31 1906 Sex:F Child# 2 William Zurler Russia & Malwina Oleknoecez Russia
ZURLIS, Louis, Dec 26 1904 Sex:M Child# 1 William Zurlis Russia & Malvina Ohknowicz Russia
ZURLIS, Ludvic, Jan 1 1914 Sex:M Child# 1 Ludvic Zurlis Russia & Josephine Akstin Russia
ZURLIS, Ludvik, Jan 4 1914 Sex:M Child# 1 Ludvik Zurlis Russia & Josephine Akstin Russia
ZURLIS, Paulema, May 2 1919 Sex:F Child# 2 Ludwig Zurlis Russia & Josephine Axtin Russia
ZURWELL, Virginia, Jun 22 1914 Sex:F Child# 4 Joseph Zurwell Russia & Adeline Bakawiske Russia
ZUSMAN, Esther, Apr 17 1918 Sex:F Child# 4 Jacob Zusman Russia & Sadie Shapiro Russia
ZUSSMAN, Agnes, Dec 14 1920 Sex:F Child# 5 Jake Zussman Russia & Sarah Shapers Russia
ZWICZILA, Michal, Sep 19 1913 Sex:M Child# 2 Paul Zwiczila Russia & Anna Wolukewich Russia